Educators
Resource
Directory

2013/14

Tenth Edition

Educators
Resource
Directory

- *Race to the Top* Summary
- Associations & Organizations
- Professional Development
- Consultants
- Financial Resources
- Conferences & Trade Shows
- Opportunities Abroad
- National & State Statistics

**SCHOOL OF EDUCATION
CURRICULUM LABORATORY
UM-DEARBORN**

A SEDGWICK PRESS Book

Grey House
Publishing

PUBLISHER: Leslie Mackenzie
EDITOR: Richard Gottlieb
EDITORIAL DIRECTOR: Laura Mars

PRODUCTION MANAGER: Kristen Thatcher
PRODUCTION ASSISTANTS: Kevin Bierfeldt, Janet Kurland, Brittany O'Brien

MARKETING DIRECTOR: Jessica Moody

Grey House Publishing, Inc.
4919 Route 22
Amenia, NY 12501
518.789.8700
FAX 518.789.0545
www.greyhouse.com
e-mail: books@greyhouse.com

First edition published 1994
Tenth edition published 2013
Printed in Canada

ISBN: 978-1-61925-113-7 softcover
ISSN: 1549-7224

Table of Contents

SECTION ONE: Resources

1.   **Associations & Organizations**

2.   **Conferences & Trade Shows**

3.   **Consultants** 63

4.   **Teaching Opportunities Abroad**

5.   **Financial Resources**

Introduction

This tenth edition of *Educators Resource Directory* is a comprehensive resource designed to provide educators, administrators, and other education professionals with immediate access to a unique combination of 6,268 educational resources and 195 charts of educational statistics and rankings.

Praise for previous edition:

"... an important reference source overflowing with information educators may use for their own improvement or as an aid for winning a ... Race to the Top grant. ... The glossary is handy and the indexes are accurate. All school, public and academic libraries need an up to date education directory ... and this is a worthy choice."

American Reference Books Annual

"... This handy tool, appropriate for larger public and academic libraries as well as school districts, will be highly valuable to those writing education grants ... "

Library Journal

Race to the Top

Listings in *Educators Resource Directory* include associations, publications, trade shows, workshops and training programs designed not only to help educators advance professionally, but also to give them the resources they need to help their students, their schools, and their state win President Obama's *Race to the Top*. This competitive grant program, now in its third year, is designed to encourage and reward states that 1. create conditions for education innovations and reform, 2. achieve significant improvement in student outcomes, and 3. implement ambitious plans in core education reform areas. Following this introduction is a comprehensive *Race to the Top* Executive Summary, followed by details about those states that have continued to progress in the second year of the program.

This important reference provides tools for classroom and career management, and resources that truly make a difference in job, school, and student performance. Listings in this comprehensive volume are thoughtfully organized in 13 chapters and 76 subchapters, making information significantly easier to access than the unfocused data available online or scattered in dozens of different sources. Statistics and rankings are designed to help states, school districts, and individual educators better understand their educational environment, crucial to making informed decisions on careers, curriculum and funding.

SECTION ONE: RESOURCES

Educators Resource Directory includes 6,268 listings in **Section One,** with current contact information, including 6,656 key contact names, 4,307 fax numbers, 3,124 e-mail addresses, and 4,299 web sites. This section includes the following categories:

Associations & Organizations disseminate information, host seminars, provide educational literature and promote study councils. This chapter organizes 743 associations into 16 distinct categories from *Administration* to *Technology*.

The chapter on **Conferences & Trade Shows** lists everything from large conventions of classroom resources and equipment suppliers to small, specialized conferences that target rural education and specific teaching challenges. Events are listed regionally.

Consultants gives information on educational consulting services, including curriculum-building guidance, school district organizations, and facility format.

Teaching Opportunities Abroad includes not only U.S. government schools, but also American schools overseas. The chapter is organized geographically by region, and provides contact information, grade level and enrollment numbers on 1,215 schools.

Details on 626 grants, foundations and scholarships can be found in **Financial Resources**. Learn how to obtain funds for individual professional advancement, schools, programs, students, and education districts and communities.

The 455 **Professional Development** listings include *Associations, Awards, Conferences* and *Training Materials.*

Publications lists 973 directories, magazines and journals, divided into 16 subjects. Find where to publish research findings, which testing materials best suit your needs, how to incorporate technology into your classroom, and where to find innovative classroom supplies.

Publishers includes 349 educational publishers of textbooks, testing resources and specific curriculums.

Research results on general learning and training issues, and data on specific subjects, like *Gifted & Talented, Educational Media* and *Scientific Learning,* is easy to find from the nearly 80 **Research Centers** profiled in this edition.

The chapter on **School Supplies** focuses on the latest in *Classroom Technology, Scientific Equipment, Furniture* and *Sports & Playground Equipment.*

Software, Hardware & Internet Resources includes 16 subchapters from *Administration* to *Technology in Education* that provide easy access to everything from educational computer programs to web sites with information on classroom resources for every level and subject.

Testing Resources includes resources for written materials and web sites in six categories: *Elementary Education, Language Arts, Mathematics, Music & Art, Reading* and *Secondary Education.*

SECTION TWO: STATISTICS, RANKINGS & GLOSSARY

Section Two includes 195 charts in 8 main categories and 18 subcategories. From elementary to post secondary levels, these statistics and rankings include data not only on the American educational system, but also on Canadian and international education.

The main categories are *Educational Attainment *Elementary & Secondary Education *Federal Programs *International Comparisons *Libraries & Educational Technology *Outcomes of Education *Post-secondary Education *Canadian Education. Specific topics include degrees, enrollment, completions, dropouts, faculty, revenues, expenditures, and student behavior. Many tables offer state-by-state rankings.

Using the most current data available, this section helps to complete the picture for educators making career development decisions, for school administrators interested in comparing fiscal health and educational scores, and for anyone doing educational research.

Following the statistics and rankings is a **Glossary** with over 100 education terms from Accountability to Vocational.

SECTION THREE: INDEXES

Entry & Publisher Name Index – alphabetical list of both entry names and the companies that publish the listed material. Publishers and parent organizations are boldfaced.

Geographic Index – state-by-state listing of all entries.

Subject Index – organized by core subjects plus Special Education, Technology, and No Child Left Behind (NCLB) related listings.

Educators Resource Directory 2013/14 is also available for subscription via Grey House OnLine Database. Subscribers can do customized searches that instantly locate needed information. Visit http://gold.greyhouse.com or call 800-562-2139 to set up a free trial.

RACE TO THE TOP – DISTRICT

EXECUTIVE SUMMARY

U.S. DEPARTMENT OF EDUCATION
WASHINGTON, D.C. 20202

AUGUST 2012

BACKGROUND

Race to the Top is authorized under sections 14005 and 14006 of the American Recovery and Reinvestment Act (ARRA). The Race to the Top State competitions provided incentives to States to adopt bold and comprehensive reforms in elementary and secondary education and laid the foundation for unprecedented innovation. A total of 46 States and the District of Columbia put together plans to implement college- and career-ready standards, use data systems to guide learning and teaching, evaluate and support teachers and school leaders, and turn around their lowest-performing schools. The purpose of the Race to the Top – District competition is to build on the lessons learned from the State competitions conducted under the Race to the Top program and to support bold, locally directed improvements in learning and teaching that will directly improve student achievement and educator effectiveness.

The Race to the Top – District competition invites applicants to demonstrate how they can personalize education for all students in their schools. The Race to the Top – District competition is aimed squarely at classrooms and the all-important relationship between educators and students. An LEA or consortium of LEAs receiving an award under this competition will build on the lessons learned from and the progress of States and districts in implementing reforms in the four core educational assurance areas through Race to the Top and other key programs. A successful applicant will provide teachers the information, tools, and supports that enable them to meet the needs of each student and substantially accelerate and deepen each student's learning. These LEAs will have the policies, systems, infrastructure, capacity, and culture to enable teachers, teacher teams, and school leaders to continuously focus on improving individual student achievement and closing achievement gaps. These LEAs will also make equity and access a priority and aim to prepare each student to master the content and skills required for college- and career-readiness, provide each student the opportunity to pursue a rigorous course of study, and accelerate and deepen students' learning through attention to their individual needs. As important, they will create opportunities for students to identify and pursue areas of personal academic interest – all while ensuring that each student masters critical areas identified in college- and career-ready standards or college- and career-ready high school graduation requirements.

KEY DATES

- Technical Assistance Webinars:
  - Overview of the Race to the Top - District Competition: August 16 or 21, 2012
- Intent to Apply Due: August 30, 2012
- Application Due: October 30, 2012
- Grant Award Announcement: December 2012

OVERVIEW OF PROGRAM AND POINTS

Selection Criteria
A. Vision (40 total points)
(A)(1) Articulating a comprehensive and coherent reform vision *(10 points)*
(A)(2) Applicant's approach to implementation *(10 points)*
(A)(3) LEA-wide reform & change *(10 points)*
(A)(4) LEA-wide goals for improved student outcomes *(10 points)*
B. Prior Record of Success and Conditions for Reform (45 total points)
(B)(1) Demonstrating a clear track record of success *(15 points)*
(B)(2) Increasing transparency in LEA processes, practices, and investments *(5 points)*
(B)(3) State context for implementation (*10 points*)
(B)(4) Stakeholder engagement and support *(10 points)*
(B)(5) Analysis of needs and gaps (*5 points*)
C. Preparing Students for College and Careers (40 total points)
(C)(1) Learning *(20 points)*
(C)(2) Teaching and Leading *(20 points)*
D. LEA Policy and Infrastructure (25 total points)
(D)(1) LEA practices, policies, rules *(15 points)*
(D)(2) LEA and school infrastructure *(10 points)*
E. Continuous Improvement (30 total points)
(E)(1) Continuous improvement process *(15 points)*
(E)(2) Ongoing communication and engagement *(5 points)*
(E)(3) Performance measures *(5 points)*
(E)(4) Evaluating effectiveness of investments *(5 points)*
F. Budget and Sustainability (20 total points)
(F)(1) Budget for the project *(10 points)*
(F)(2) Sustainability of project goals *(10 points)*
Competitive Preference Priority (10 total points)
Optional Budget Supplement (Scored separately - 15 total points)

ABSOLUTE PRIORITIES

Absolute Priority 1: Personalized Learning Environments.
Absolute Priority 2: Non-Rural LEAs in Race to the Top States.
Absolute Priority 3: Rural LEAs in Race to the Top States.
Absolute Priority 4: Non-Rural LEAs in non-Race to the Top States.
Absolute Priority 5: Rural LEAs in non-Race to the Top States.

Race to the Top States are those that received Phase 1, 2, or 3 Race to the Top grants: Arizona, Colorado, Delaware, the District of Columbia, Florida, Georgia, Hawaii, Illinois, Kentucky, Louisiana, Maryland, Massachusetts, New Jersey, New York, North Carolina, Ohio, Pennsylvania, Rhode Island, and Tennessee. LEAs in States that received only a Race to the Top Early Learning Challenge grant must indicate Absolute Priority 4 or 5.

ELIGIBILITY REQUIREMENTS

To be eligible for a grant under this competition:

(a) An applicant must be an individual LEA (as defined in the notice) or a consortium of LEAs from the 50 States, the District of Columbia, and the Commonwealth of Puerto Rico.

(i) LEAs may apply for all or a portion of their schools, for specific grades, or for subject-area bands (e.g., lowest-performing schools, secondary schools, schools connected by a feeder pattern, middle school math, or preschool through third grade).

(ii) Consortia may include LEAs from multiple States.

(iii) Each LEA may participate in only one Race to the Top – District application.

(b) An applicant must serve a minimum of 2,000 participating students (as defined in the notice) or may serve fewer than 2,000 participating students (as defined in the notice) provided those students are served by a consortium of at least 10 LEAs and at least 75 percent of the students served by each LEA are participating students (as defined in the notice).

(c) At least 40 percent of participating students (as defined in the notice) across all participating schools (as defined in the notice) must be students from low-income families, based on eligibility for free or reduced-price lunch subsidies under the Richard B. Russell National School Lunch Act, or other poverty measures that LEAs use to make awards under section 1113(a) of the ESEA. If an applicant has not identified all participating schools (as defined in the notice) at the time of application, it must provide an assurance that within 100 days of the grant award it will meet this requirement.

(d) An applicant must demonstrate its commitment to the core educational assurance areas (as defined in the notice), including, for each LEA included in an application, an assurance signed by the LEA's superintendent or CEO that—

(i) The LEA, at a minimum, will implement no later than the 2014-2015 school year—

(A) A teacher evaluation system (as defined in the notice);

(B) A principal evaluation system (as defined in the notice); and

(C) A superintendent evaluation (as defined in the notice);

(ii) The LEA is committed to preparing all students for college or career, as demonstrated by—

(A) Being located in a State that has adopted college- and career-ready standards (as defined in the notice); or

(B) Measuring all student progress and performance against college- and career-ready graduation requirements (as defined in the notice);

(iii) The LEA has a robust data system that has, at a minimum—

(A) An individual teacher identifier with a teacher-student match; and

(B) The capability to provide timely data back to educators and their supervisors on student growth (as defined in the notice);

(iv) The LEA has the capability to receive or match student level preschool through 12th grade and higher education data; and

(v) The LEA ensures that any disclosure of or access to personally identifiable information in students' education records complies with FERPA.

(e) Required signatures for the LEA or lead LEA in a consortium are those of the superintendent or CEO, local school board president, and local teacher union or association president (where applicable).

BUDGET REQUIREMENTS:

An applicant's budget request for all years of its project must fall within the applicable budget range as follows:

Number of participating students	Award range
2,000-5,000 or Fewer than 2,000, provided those students are served by a consortium of at least 10 LEAs and at least 75 percent of the students served by each LEA are participating students (as defined in the notice)	$5-10 million
5,001-10,000	$10-20 million
10,001-25,000	$20-30 million
25,001+	$30-40 million

The Department will not consider an application that requests a budget outside the applicable range of awards, not including any optional budget supplements included in the application.

ABSOLUTE PRIORITIES

Absolute Priority 1: Personalized Learning Environments. To meet this priority, an applicant must coherently and comprehensively address how it will build on the core educational assurance areas (as defined in the notice) to create learning environments that are designed to significantly improve learning and teaching through the personalization of strategies, tools, and supports for students and educators that are aligned with college- and career-ready standards (as defined in the notice) or college- and career-ready graduation requirements (as defined in the notice); accelerate student achievement and deepen student learning by meeting the academic needs of each student; increase the effectiveness of educators; expand student access to the most effective educators; decrease achievement gaps across student groups; and increase the rates at which students graduate from high school prepared for college and careers.

Absolute Priority 2: Non-Rural LEAs in Race to the Top States. To meet this priority, an applicant must be an LEA or a consortium of LEAs in which more than 50 percent of participating students (as defined in the notice) are in non-rural LEAs in States that received awards under the Race to the Top Phase 1, Phase 2, or Phase 3 competition.

Absolute Priority 3: Rural LEAs in Race to the Top States. To meet this priority, an applicant must be an LEA or a consortium of LEAs in which more than 50 percent of participating students (as defined in the notice) are in rural LEAs (as defined in the notice) in States that received awards under the Race to the Top Phase 1, Phase 2, or Phase 3 competition.

Absolute Priority 4: Non-Rural LEAs in non-Race to the Top States. To meet this priority, an applicant must be an LEA or a consortium of LEAs in which more than 50 percent of participating students (as defined in the notice) are in non-rural LEAs in States that did not receive awards under the Race to the Top Phase 1, Phase 2, or Phase 3 competition.

Absolute Priority 5: Rural LEAs in non-Race to the Top States. To meet this priority, an applicant must be an LEA or a consortium of LEAs in which more than 50 percent of participating students (as defined in the notice) are in rural LEAs (as defined in the notice) in States that did not receive awards under the Race to the Top Phase 1, Phase 2, or Phase 3 competition.

SELECTION CRITERIA

A. Vision (40 total points)

(A)(1) <u>Articulating a comprehensive and coherent reform vision</u> *(10 points)*

The extent to which the applicant has set forth a comprehensive and coherent reform vision that builds on its work in four core educational assurance areas (as defined in the notice) and articulates a clear and credible approach to the goals of accelerating student achievement, deepening student learning, and increasing equity through personalized student support grounded in common and individual tasks that are based on student academic interests.

(A)(2) <u>Applicant's approach to implementation</u> *(10 points)*

The extent to which the applicant's approach to implementing its reform proposal (e.g., schools, grade bands, or subject areas) will support high-quality LEA-level and school-level implementation of that proposal, including—

> (a) A description of the process that the applicant used or will use to select schools to participate. The process must ensure that the participating schools (as defined in the notice) collectively meet the competition's eligibility requirements;
> (b) A list of the schools that will participate in grant activities (as available); and
> (c) The total number of participating students (as defined in the notice), participating students (as defined in the notice) from low-income families, participating students (as defined in the notice) who are high-need students (as defined in the notice), and participating educators (as defined in the notice). If participating schools (as defined in the notice) have yet to be selected, the applicant may provide approximate numbers.

(A)(3) <u>LEA-wide reform & change</u> *(10 points)*

The extent to which the application includes a high-quality plan describing how the reform proposal will be scaled up and translated into meaningful reform to support district-wide change beyond the participating schools (as defined in the notice), and will help the applicant reach its outcome goals (e.g., the applicant's logic model or theory of change of how its plan will improve student learning outcomes for all students who would be served by the applicant).

(A)(4) <u>LEA-wide goals for improved student outcomes</u> *(10 points)*

The extent to which the applicant's vision is likely to result in improved student learning and performance and increased equity as demonstrated by ambitious yet achievable annual goals that are equal to or exceed State ESEA targets for the LEA(s), overall and by student subgroup (as defined in the notice), for each participating LEA in the following areas:

> (a) Performance on summative assessments (proficiency status and growth).
> (b) Decreasing achievement gaps (as defined in the notice).
> (c) Graduation rates (as defined in the notice).
> (d) College enrollment (as defined in the notice) rates.

Optional: The extent to which the applicant's vision is likely to result in improved student learning and performance and increased equity as demonstrated by ambitious yet achievable annual goals for each participating LEA in the following area:

> (e) Postsecondary degree attainment.

B. Prior Record of Success and Conditions for Reform (45 total points)

(B)(1) <u>Demonstrating a clear track record of success</u> *(15 points)*

The extent to which each LEA has demonstrated evidence of—

 A clear record of success in the past four years in advancing student learning and achievement and increasing equity in learning and teaching, including a description, charts or graphs, raw student data, and other evidence that demonstrates the applicant's ability to—

(a) Improve student learning outcomes and close achievement gaps (as defined in the notice), including by raising student achievement, high school graduation rates (as defined in the notice), and college enrollment (as defined in the notice) rates;

(b) Achieve ambitious and significant reforms in its persistently lowest-achieving schools (as defined in the notice) or in its low-performing schools (as defined in the notice); and

(c) Make student performance data (as defined in the notice) available to students, educators (as defined in the notice), and parents in ways that inform and improve participation, instruction, and services.

(B)(2) Increasing transparency in LEA processes, practices, and investments *(5 points)*
The extent to which each LEA has demonstrated evidence of—
A high level of transparency in LEA processes, practices, and investments, including by making public, by school, actual school-level expenditures for regular K-12 instruction, instructional support, pupil support, and school administration. At a minimum, this information must include a description of the extent to which the applicant already makes available the following four categories of school-level expenditures from State and local funds:

(a) Actual personnel salaries at the school level for all school-level instructional and support staff, based on the U.S. Census Bureau's classification used in the F-33 survey of local government finances (information on the survey can be found at http://nces.ed.gov/ccd/f33agency.asp);

(b) Actual personnel salaries at the school level for instructional staff only;

(c) Actual personnel salaries at the school level for teachers only; and

(d) Actual non-personnel expenditures at the school level (if available).

(B)(3) State context for implementation (*10 points*)
The extent to which each LEA has demonstrated evidence of—
Successful conditions and sufficient autonomy under State legal, statutory, and regulatory requirements to implement the personalized learning environments described in the applicant's proposal.

(B)(4) Stakeholder engagement and support *(10 points)*
The extent to which each LEA has demonstrated evidence of—
Meaningful stakeholder engagement in the development of the proposal and meaningful stakeholder support for the proposal, including—

(a) A description of how students, families, teachers, and principals in participating schools (as defined in the notice) were engaged in the development of the proposal and, as appropriate, how the proposal was revised based on their engagement and feedback, including—

(i) For LEAs with collective bargaining representation, evidence of direct engagement and support for the proposals from teachers in participating schools (as defined in the notice); or

(ii) For LEAs without collective bargaining representation, at a minimum, evidence that at least 70 percent of teachers from participating schools (as defined in the notice) support the proposal; and

(b) Letters of support from such key stakeholders as parents and parent organizations, student organizations, early learning programs, tribes, the business community, civil rights organizations, advocacy groups, local civic and community-based organizations, and institutions of higher education.

(B)(5) Analysis of needs and gaps (*5 points*)
The extent to which each LEA has demonstrated evidence of—
A high-quality plan for an analysis of the applicant's current status in implementing personalized learning

environments and the logic behind the reform proposal contained within the applicant's proposal, including identified needs and gaps that the plan will address.

C. Preparing Students for College and Careers (40 total points)

(C)(1) <u>Learning</u> *(20 points)*

The extent to which the applicant has a high-quality plan for improving learning and teaching by personalizing the learning environment in order to provide all students the support to graduate college- and career-ready. This plan must include an approach to implementing instructional strategies for all participating students (as defined in the notice) that enable participating students to pursue a rigorous course of study aligned to college- and career-ready standards (as defined in the notice) and college- and career-ready graduation requirements (as defined in the notice) and accelerate his or her learning through support of his or her needs. The quality of the plan will be assessed based on the extent to which the applicant proposes an approach that includes the following:

Learning: An approach to learning that engages and empowers all learners, in particular high-need students, in an age-appropriate manner such that:

    (a) With the support of parents and educators, all students—

        (i) Understand that what they are learning is key to their success in accomplishing their goals;

        (ii) Identify and pursue learning and development goals linked to college- and career-ready standards (as defined in the notice) or college- and career-ready graduation requirements (as defined in the notice), understand how to structure their learning to achieve their goals, and measure progress toward those goals;

        (iii) Are able to be involved in deep learning experiences in areas of academic interest;

        (iv) Have access and exposure to diverse cultures, contexts, and perspectives that motivate and deepen individual student learning; and

        (v) Master critical academic content and develop skills and traits such as goal-setting, teamwork, perseverance, critical thinking, communication, creativity, and problem-solving;

    (b) With the support of parents and educators, there is a strategy to ensure that each student has access to—

        (i) A personalized sequence of instructional content and skill development designed to enable the student to achieve his or her individual learning goals and ensure he or she can graduate on time and college- and career-ready;

        (ii) A variety of high-quality instructional approaches and environments;

        (iii) High-quality content, including digital learning content (as defined in the notice) as appropriate, aligned with college- and career-ready standards (as defined in the notice) or college- and career-ready graduation requirements (as defined in the notice);

        (iv) Ongoing and regular feedback, including, at a minimum—

            (A) Frequently updated individual student data that can be used to determine progress toward mastery of college- and career-ready standards (as defined in the notice), or college- and career-ready graduation requirements; and

            (B) Personalized learning recommendations based on the student's current knowledge and skills, college- and career-ready standards (as defined in the notice) or college- and career-ready graduation requirements (as defined in the notice), and available content, instructional approaches, and supports; and

        (v) Accommodations and high-quality strategies for high-need students (as defined in the notice) to help ensure that they are on track toward meeting college- and career-ready standards (as defined in the notice) or college- and career-ready graduation requirements (as defined in the notice); and

    (c) Mechanisms are in place to provide training and support to students that will ensure that they understand how to use the tools and resources provided to them in order to track and manage their learning.

(C)(2) <u>Teaching and Leading</u> (*20 points*)

The extent to which the applicant has a high-quality plan for improving learning and teaching by personalizing the learning environment in order to provide all students the support to graduate college- and career-ready. This plan must include an approach to implementing instructional strategies for all participating students (as defined in the notice) that enable participating students to pursue a rigorous course of study aligned to college- and career-ready standards (as defined in the notice) and college- and career-ready graduation requirements (as defined in the notice) and accelerate his or her learning through support of his or her needs. The quality of the plan will be assessed based on the extent to which the applicant proposes an approach that includes the following:

Teaching and Leading: An approach to teaching and leading that helps educators (as defined in the notice) to improve instruction and increase their capacity to support student progress toward meeting college- and career-ready standards (as defined in the notice) or college- and career-ready graduation requirements (as defined in the notice) by enabling the full implementation of personalized learning and teaching for all students such that:

    (a) All participating educators (as defined in the notice) engage in training, and in professional teams or communities, that supports their individual and collective capacity to—

        (i) Support the effective implementation of personalized learning environments and strategies that meet each student's academic needs and help ensure all students can graduate on time and college- and career-ready;

        (ii) Adapt content and instruction, providing opportunities for students to engage in common and individual tasks, in response to their academic needs, academic interests, and optimal learning approaches (e.g., discussion and collaborative work, project-based learning, videos, audio, manipulatives);

        (iii) Frequently measure student progress toward meeting college- and career-ready standards (as defined in the notice), or college- and career-ready graduation requirements (as defined in the notice) and use data to inform both the acceleration of student progress and the improvement of the individual and collective practice of educators; and

        (iv) Improve teachers' and principals' practice and effectiveness by using feedback provided by the LEA's teacher and principal evaluation systems (as defined in the notice), including frequent feedback on individual and collective effectiveness, as well as by providing recommendations, supports, and interventions as needed for improvement.

    (b) All participating educators (as defined in the notice) have access to, and know how to use, tools, data, and resources to accelerate student progress toward meeting college- and career-ready graduation requirements (as defined in the notice). Those resources must include—

        (i) Actionable information that helps educators (as defined in the notice) identify optimal learning approaches that respond to individual student academic needs and interests;

        (ii) High-quality learning resources (e.g., instructional content and assessments), including digital resources, as appropriate, that are aligned with college- and career-ready standards (as defined in the notice) or college- and career-ready graduation requirements (as defined in the notice), and the tools to create and share new resources; and

        (iii) Processes and tools to match student needs (see Selection Criterion (C)(2)(b)(i)) with specific resources and approaches (see Selection Criterion (C)(2)(b)(ii)) to provide continuously improving feedback about the effectiveness of the resources in meeting student needs.

    (c) All participating school leaders and school leadership teams (as defined in the notice) have training, policies, tools, data, and resources that enable them to structure an effective learning environment that meets individual student academic needs and accelerates student progress through common and individual tasks toward meeting college- and career-ready standards (as defined in the notice) or college- and career-ready graduation requirements (as defined in the notice). The training, policies, tools, data, and resources must include:

(i) Information, from such sources as the district's teacher evaluation system (as defined in the notice), that helps school leaders and school leadership teams (as defined in the notice) assess, and take steps to improve, individual and collective educator effectiveness and school culture and climate, for the purpose of continuous school improvement; and

(ii) Training, systems, and practices to continuously improve school progress toward the goals of increasing student performance and closing achievement gaps (as defined in the notice).

(d) The applicant has a high-quality plan for increasing the number of students who receive instruction from effective and highly effective teachers and principals (as defined in the notice), including in hard-to-staff schools, subjects (such as mathematics and science), and specialty areas (such as special education).

D. LEA Policy and Infrastructure (25 total points)
The extent to which the applicant has a high-quality plan to support project implementation through comprehensive policies and infrastructure that provide every student, educator (as defined in the notice), and level of the education system (classroom, school, and LEA) with the support and resources they need, when and where they are needed. The quality of the plan will be determined based on the extent to which--

(D)(1) LEA practices, policies, rules *(15 points)*
The applicant has practices, policies, and rules that facilitate personalized learning by—

(a) Organizing the LEA central office, or the consortium governance structure (as defined in the notice), to provide support and services to all participating schools (as defined in the notice);

(b) Providing school leadership teams in participating schools (as defined in the notice) with sufficient flexibility and autonomy over factors such as school schedules and calendars, school personnel decisions and staffing models, roles and responsibilities for educators and noneducators, and school-level budgets;

(c) Giving students the opportunity to progress and earn credit based on demonstrated mastery, not the amount of time spent on a topic;

(d) Giving students the opportunity to demonstrate mastery of standards at multiple times and in multiple comparable ways; and

(e) Providing learning resources and instructional practices that are adaptable and fully accessible to all students, including students with disabilities and English learners; and

(D)(2) LEA and school infrastructure *(10 points)*
The LEA and school infrastructure supports personalized learning by—

(a) Ensuring that all participating students (as defined in the notice), parents, educators (as defined in the notice), and other stakeholders (as appropriate and relevant to student learning), regardless of income, have access to necessary content, tools, and other learning resources both in and out of school to support the implementation of the applicant's proposal;

(b) Ensuring that students, parents, educators, and other stakeholders (as appropriate and relevant to student learning) have appropriate levels of technical support, which may be provided through a range of strategies (e.g., peer support, online support, or local support);

(c) Using information technology systems that allow parents and students to export their information in an open data format (as defined in the notice) and to use the data in other electronic learning systems (e.g., electronic tutors, tools that make recommendations for additional learning supports, or software that securely stores personal records); and

(d) Ensuring that LEAs and schools use interoperable data systems (as defined in the notice) (e.g., systems that include human resources data, student information data, budget data, and instructional improvement system data).

E. Continuous Improvement (30 total points)

Because the applicant's high-quality plan represents the best thinking at a point in time, and may require adjustments and revisions during implementation, it is vital that the applicant have a clear and high-quality approach to continuously improve its plan. This will be determined by the extent to which the applicant has—

(E)(1) <u>Continuous improvement process</u> *(15 points)*

A strategy for implementing a rigorous continuous improvement process that provides timely and regular feedback on progress toward project goals and opportunities for ongoing corrections and improvements during and after the term of the grant. The strategy must address how the applicant will monitor, measure, and publicly share information on the quality of its investments funded by Race to the Top – District, such as investments in professional development, technology, and staff;

(E)(2) <u>Ongoing communication and engagement</u> *(5 points)*

Strategies for ongoing communication and engagement with internal and external stakeholders; and

(E)(3) <u>Performance measures</u> *(5 points)*

Ambitious yet achievable performance measures, overall and by subgroup, with annual targets for required and applicant-proposed performance measures. For each applicant-proposed measure, the applicant must describe—

    (a) Its rationale for selecting that measure;

    (b) How the measure will provide rigorous, timely, and formative leading information tailored to its proposed plan and theory of action regarding the applicant's implementation success or areas of concern; and

    (c) How it will review and improve the measure over time if it is insufficient to gauge implementation progress.

The applicant must have a total of approximately 12 to 14 performance measures.

The chart below outlines the required and applicant-proposed performance measures based on an applicant's applicable population.

Applicable Population	Performance Measure
All	a) The number and percentage of participating students, by subgroup (as defined in the notice), whose teacher of record (as defined in the notice) and principal are a highly effective teacher (as defined in the notice) and a highly effective principal (as defined in the notice); and b) The number and percentage of participating students, by subgroup (as defined in the notice), whose teacher of record (as defined in the notice) and principal are an effective teacher (as defined in the notice) and an effective principal (as defined in the notice).
PreK-3	a) Applicant must propose at least one age-appropriate measure of students' academic growth (e.g., language and literacy development or cognition and general learning, including early mathematics and early scientific development); and b) Applicant must propose at least one age-appropriate non-cognitive indicator of growth (e.g., physical well-being and motor development, or social-emotional development).
4-8	a) The number and percentage of participating students, by subgroup, who are on

	track to college- and career-readiness based on the applicant's on-track indicator (as defined in the notice); b) Applicant must propose at least one grade-appropriate academic leading indicator of successful implementation of its plan; and c) Applicant must propose at least one grade-appropriate health or social-emotional leading indicator of successful implementation of its plan.
9-12	a) The number and percentage of participating students who complete and submit the Free Application for Federal Student Aid (FAFSA) form; b) The number and percentage of participating students, by subgroup, who are on track to college- and career-readiness based on the applicant's on-track indicator (as defined in the notice); c) Applicant must propose at least one measure of career-readiness in order to assess the number and percentage of participating students who are or are on track to being career-ready; d) Applicant must propose at least one grade-appropriate academic leading indicator of successful implementation of its plan; and e) Applicant must propose at least one grade-appropriate health or social-emotional leading indicator of successful implementation of its plan.

(E)(4) Evaluating effectiveness of investments *(5 points)*

Plans to evaluate the effectiveness of Race to the Top – District funded activities, such as professional development and activities that employ technology, and to more productively use time, staff, money, or other resources in order to improve results, through such strategies as improved use of technology, working with community partners, compensation reform, and modification of school schedules and structures (e.g., service delivery, school leadership teams (as defined in the notice), and decision-making structures).

F. Budget and Sustainability *(20 total points)*

The extent to which—

(F)(1) Budget for the project *(10 points)*

The applicant's budget, including the budget narrative and tables—

    (a) Identifies all funds that will support the project (e.g., Race to the Top – District grant; external foundation support; LEA, State, and other Federal funds); and

    (b) Is reasonable and sufficient to support the development and implementation of the applicant's proposal; and

    (c) Clearly provides a thoughtful rationale for investments and priorities, including--

        (i) A description of all of the funds (e.g., Race to the Top – District grant; external foundation support; LEA, State, and other Federal funds) that the applicant will use to support the implementation of the proposal, including total revenue from these sources; and

        (ii) Identification of the funds that will be used for one-time investments versus those that will be used for ongoing operational costs that will be incurred during and after the grant period, as described in the proposed budget and budget narrative, with a focus on strategies that will ensure the long-term sustainability of the personalized learning environments; and

(F)(2) Sustainability of project goals *(10 points)*

The applicant has a high-quality plan for sustainability of the project's goals after the term of the grant. The plan should include support from State and local government leaders and financial support. Such a plan may include a budget for the three years after the term of the grant that includes budget assumptions, potential sources, and uses of funds.

Competitive Preference Priority *(10 total points)*
Competitive Preference Priority: Results, Resource Alignment, and Integrated Services. The Department will give priority to an applicant based on the extent to which the applicant proposes to integrate public or private resources in a partnership designed to augment the schools' resources by providing additional student and family supports to schools that address the social, emotional, or behavioral needs of the participating students (as defined in the notice), giving highest priority to students in participating schools with high-need students (as defined in the notice). To meet this priority, an applicant's proposal does not need to be comprehensive and may provide student and family supports that focus on a subset of these needs.

To meet this priority, an applicant must—

(1) Provide a description of the coherent and sustainable partnership that it has formed with public or private organizations, such as public health, before-school, after-school, and social service providers; integrated student service providers; businesses, philanthropies, civic groups, and other community-based organizations; early learning programs; and postsecondary institutions to support the plan described in Absolute Priority 1;

(2) Identify not more than 10 population-level desired results for students in the LEA or consortium of LEAs that align with and support the applicant's broader Race to the Top – District proposal. These results must include both educational results and other education outcomes (e.g., children enter kindergarten prepared to succeed in school, children exit third grade reading at grade level, and students graduate from high school college- and career-ready) and family and community supports (as defined in the notice) results;

(3) Describe how the partnership would –

(a) Track the selected indicators that measure each result at the aggregate level for all children within the LEA or consortium and at the student level for the participating students (as defined in the notice);

(b) Use the data to target its resources in order to improve results for participating students (as defined in the notice), with special emphasis on students facing significant challenges, such as students with disabilities, English learners, and students affected by poverty (including highly mobile students), family instability, or other child welfare issues;

(c) Develop a strategy to scale the model beyond the participating students (as defined in the notice) to at least other high-need students (as defined in the notice) and communities in the LEA or consortium over time; and

(d) Improve results over time;

(4) Describe how the partnership would, within participating schools (as defined in the notice), integrate education and other services (e.g., services that address social-emotional, and behavioral needs, acculturation for immigrants and refugees) for participating students (as defined in the notice);

(5) Describe how the partnership and LEA or consortium would build the capacity of staff in participating schools (as defined in the notice) by providing them with tools and supports to –

(a) Assess the needs and assets of participating students (as defined in the notice) that are aligned with the partnership's goals for improving the education and family and community supports (as defined in the notice) identified by the partnership;

(b) Identify and inventory the needs and assets of the school and community that are aligned with those goals for improving the education and family and community supports (as defined in the notice) identified by the applicant;

(c) Create a decision-making process and infrastructure to select, implement, and evaluate supports that address the individual needs of participating students (as defined in the notice) and support improved results;

(d) Engage parents and families of participating students (as defined in the notice) in both decision-making about solutions to improve results over time and in addressing student, family, and school needs; and

(e) Routinely assess the applicant's progress in implementing its plan to maximize impact and resolve challenges and problems; and

(6) Identify its annual ambitious yet achievable performance measures for the proposed population-level and describe desired results for students.

Optional Budget Supplement

An eligible applicant may apply for additional funding (beyond the applicable maximum level provided) up to a maximum of $2 million for each optional budget supplement to address a specific area that is supplemental to the plan for addressing Absolute Priority 1. The request for additional funding must be designed as a separate project that, if not funded, will not adversely affect the applicant's ability to implement its proposal and meet Absolute Priority 1. Applications for this funding will be judged on the extent to which the applicant has a clear, discrete, and innovative solution that can be replicated in schools across the Nation. In determining the extent to which the request for an optional budget supplement meets this standard, the Department will consider—

(1) The rationale for the specific area or population that the applicant will address (e.g., strategies to assess hard to measure skills and traits such as perseverance, critical thinking, and communication; strategies for increasing diversity across schools and LEAs and within schools and classrooms; data systems; predictive algorithms; content-tagging schemes; new curriculum and online supports for students re-entering school from the juvenile justice system; or a credit recovery program design to support English learners newly entering into secondary school and the quality and feasibility of the proposal for addressing that area);

(2) A high-quality plan for how the applicant would carry out activities that would be co-developed and implemented across two or more LEAs (either participating in the full Race to the Top – District application, or not participating in the full Race to the Top – District application); and

(3) The proposed budget (up to $2 million) for each budget supplement, and the extent to which the proposed budget will be adequate to support the development and implementation of activities that meet the requirements of this notice, including the reasonableness of the costs in relation to the objectives, design, and significance of the proposed project activities and the number of students to be served.

Note, an optional budget supplement may include a proposal to utilize, across two or more districts, robust measures of student status and growth that assess hard to measure skills and traits such as goal-setting, teamwork, perseverance, critical thinking, communication, creativity, and problem-solving across multiple academic domains and enable evaluation of group and individual learning experiences. The Department believes that utilizing these measures will contribute to the continuous improvement of personalized learning experiences and the tools and resources that support their implementation.

APPLICATION REQUIREMENTS

The application requirements are:

(1) State comment period. Each LEA included in an application must provide its State at least 10 business days to comment on the LEA's application and submit as part of its application package--

    (a) The State's comments or, if the State declined to comment, evidence that the LEA offered the State 10 business days to comment; and

    (b) The LEA's response to the State's comments (optional).

(2) Mayor (or city or town administrator) comment period. Each LEA included in an application must provide its mayor or other comparable official at least 10 business days to comment on the LEA's application and submit as part of its application package --

    (a) The mayor or city or town administrator's comments or, if that individual declines to comment, evidence that the LEA offered such official 10 business days to comment; and

    (b) The LEA's response to the mayor or city or town administrator comments (optional).

(3) Consortium. For LEAs applying as a consortium, the application must--

    (a) Indicate, consistent with 34 CFR 75.128, whether—

        (i) One member of the consortium is applying for a grant on behalf of the consortium; or

        (ii) The consortium has established itself as a separate, eligible legal entity and is applying for a grant on its own behalf;

    (b) Be signed by--

        (i) If one member of the consortium is applying for a grant on behalf of the consortium, the superintendent or chief executive officer (CEO), local school board president, and local teacher union or association president (where applicable) of that LEA; or

        (ii) If the consortium has established itself as a separate eligible legal entity and is applying for a grant on its own behalf, a legal representative of the consortium; and

    (c) Include, consistent with 34 CFR 75.128, for each LEA in the consortium, copies of all memoranda of understanding or other binding agreements related to the consortium. These binding agreements must —

        (i) Detail the activities that each member of the consortium plans to perform;

        (ii) Describe the consortium governance structure (as defined in the notice);

        (iii) Bind each member of the consortium to every statement and assurance made in the application; and

        (iv) Include an assurance signed by the LEA's superintendent or CEO that—

            (A) The LEA, at a minimum, will implement no later than the 2014-2015 school year—

                (1) A teacher evaluation system (as defined in the notice);

                (2) A principal evaluation system (as defined in the notice); and

                (3) A superintendent evaluation (as defined in the notice);

            (B) The LEA is committed to preparing students for college or career, as demonstrated by—

                (1) Being located in a State that has adopted college- and career-ready standards (as defined in the notice); or

                (2) Measuring all student progress and performance against college- and career-ready graduation requirements (as defined in the notice);

            (C) The LEA has a robust data system that has, at a minimum—

                (1) An individual teacher identifier with a teacher-student match; and

                (2) The capability to provide timely data back to educators and their supervisors on student growth (as defined in the notice);

(D) The LEA has the capability to receive or match student-level preschool through 12th grade and higher education data; and

(E) The LEA ensures that any disclosure of or access to personally identifiable information in students' education records complies with the Family Educational Rights and Privacy Act (FERPA); and

(v) Be signed by the superintendent or CEO, local school board president, and local teacher union or association president (where applicable).

DEFINITIONS

Achievement gap means the difference in the performance between each subgroup (as defined in the notice) within a participating LEA or school and the statewide average performance of the LEA's or State's highest-achieving subgroups in reading or language arts and in mathematics as measured by the assessments required under the Elementary and Secondary Education Act of 1965 (ESEA), as amended.

College- and career-ready graduation requirements means minimum high school graduation expectations (e.g., completion of a minimum course of study, content mastery, proficiency on college- and career-ready assessments) that are aligned with a rigorous, robust, and well-rounded curriculum and that cover a wide range of academic and technical knowledge and skills to ensure that by the time students graduate high school, they satisfy requirements for admission into credit-bearing courses commonly required by the State's public four-year degree-granting institutions.

College- and career-ready standards means content standards for kindergarten through 12th grade that build towards college- and career-ready graduation requirements (as defined in the notice). A State's college- and career-ready standards must be either (1) standards that are common to a significant number of States; or (2) standards that are approved by a State network of institutions of higher education, which must certify that students who meet the standards will not need remedial course work at the postsecondary level.

College enrollment means the enrollment of students who graduate from high school consistent with 34 CFR 200.19(b)(1)(i) and who enroll in a public institution of higher education in the State (as defined in section 101(a) of the Higher Education Act of 1965, as amended, 20 U.S.C. 1001) within 16 months of graduation.

Consortium governance structure means the consortium's structure for carrying out its operations, including--

(1) The organizational structure of the consortium and the differentiated roles that a member LEA may hold (e.g., lead LEA, member LEA);

(2) For each differentiated role, the associated rights and responsibilities, including rights and responsibilities for adopting and implementing the consortium's proposal for a grant;

(3) The consortium's method and process (e.g., consensus, majority) for making different types of decisions (e.g., policy, operational);

(4) The protocols by which the consortium will operate, including the protocols for member LEAs to change roles or leave the consortium;

(5) The consortium's procedures for managing funds received under this grant;

(6) The terms and conditions of the memorandum of understanding or other binding agreement executed by each member LEA; and

(7) The consortium's procurement process, and evidence of each member LEA's commitment to that process.

Core educational assurance areas means the four key areas originally identified in the American Reinvestment and Recovery Act (ARRA) to support comprehensive education reform: (1) adopting standards and assessments that prepare students to succeed in college and the workplace and to compete in the global economy; (2) building data systems that measure student growth and success, and inform teachers and principals with data about how they can improve instruction; (3) recruiting, developing, rewarding, and retaining effective teachers and principals, especially where they are needed most; and (4) turning around lowest-achieving schools.

Digital learning content means learning materials and resources that can be displayed on an electronic device and shared electronically with other users. Digital learning content includes both open source and commercial content. In order to comply with the requirements of the Americans with Disabilities Act of 1990 and Section 504 of the Rehabilitation Act of 1973, as amended, any digital learning content used by grantees must be accessible to individuals with disabilities, including individuals who use screen readers. For additional information regarding the application of these laws to technology, please refer to www.ed.gov/ocr/letters/colleague-201105-ese.pdf and www.ed.gov/ocr/docs/dcl-ebook-faq-201105.pdf.

Discipline means any disciplinary measure collected by the 2009-2010 or 2011-2012 Civil Rights Data Collection (see http://ocrdata.ed.gov).

Educators means all education professionals and education paraprofessionals working in participating schools (as defined in the notice), including principals or other heads of a school, teachers, other professional instructional staff (e.g., staff involved in curriculum development, staff development, bilingual/English as a Second Language (ESL) specialists, or instructional staff who operate library, media, and computer centers), pupil support services staff (e.g., guidance counselors, nurses, speech pathologists), other administrators (e.g., assistant principals, discipline specialists), and education paraprofessionals (e.g., assistant teachers, bilingual/ESL instructional aides).

Effective principal means a principal whose students, overall and for each subgroup, achieve acceptable rates (e.g., at least one grade level in an academic year) of student growth (as defined in the notice) as defined in the LEA's principal evaluation system (as defined in the notice).

Effective teacher means a teacher whose students achieve acceptable rates (e.g., at least one grade level in an academic year) of student growth (as defined in the notice) as defined in the LEA's teacher evaluation system (as defined in the notice).

Family and community supports means—
(1) Child and youth health programs, such as physical, mental, behavioral, and emotional health programs (e.g., home visiting programs; Head Start; Early Head Start; programs to improve nutrition and fitness, reduce childhood obesity, and create healthier communities);
(2) Safety programs, such as programs in school and out of school to prevent, control, and reduce crime, violence, drug and alcohol use and gang activity; programs that address classroom and school-wide behavior and conduct; programs to prevent child abuse and neglect; programs to prevent truancy and reduce and prevent bullying and harassment; and programs to improve the physical and emotional security of the school setting as perceived, experienced, and created by students, staff, and families;
(3) Community stability programs, such as programs that: (a) provide adult education and employment opportunities and training to improve educational levels, job skills, and readiness in order to decrease unemployment, with a goal of increasing family stability; (b) improve families' awareness of, access to, and use of a range of social services, if possible at a single location; (c) provide unbiased, outcome-focused, and comprehensive financial education, inside and outside the classroom and at every life stage; (d) increase access to traditional financial institutions (e.g., banks and credit unions) rather than alternative financial institutions (e.g., check cashers and payday lenders); (e) help families increase their financial literacy, financial assets, and savings; and (f) help families access transportation to education and employment opportunities; (g) provides supports and services to students who are homeless, in foster care, migrant, or highly mobile; and
(4) Family and community engagement programs that are systemic, integrated, sustainable, and continue through a student's transition from K–12 schooling to college and career. These programs may include family literacy programs and programs that provide adult education and training and opportunities for family members and other members of the community to support student learning and establish high expectations for student educational achievement; mentorship programs that create positive relationships

between children and adults; programs that provide for the use of such community resources as libraries, museums, television and radio stations, and local businesses to support improved student educational outcomes; programs that support the engagement of families in early learning programs and services; programs that provide guidance on how to navigate through a complex school system and how to advocate for more and improved learning opportunities; and programs that promote collaboration with educators and community organizations to improve opportunities for healthy development and learning.

Four intervention models means the turnaround model, restart model, school closure, and transformational model as defined by the final requirements for the School Improvement Grant (SIG) program, published in the Federal Register on October 28, 2010 (75 FR 66363).

Graduation rate means the four-year or extended-year adjusted cohort graduation rate as defined by 34 CFR 200.19(b)(1).

High-need students means students at risk of educational failure or otherwise in need of special assistance and support, such as students who are living in poverty, who attend high-minority schools (as defined in the notice), who are far below grade level, who have left school before receiving a regular high school diploma, who are at risk of not graduating with a diploma on time, who are homeless, who are in foster care, who have been incarcerated, who have disabilities, or who are English learners.

High-minority school is defined by the LEA in a manner consistent with its State's Teacher Equity Plan, as required by section 1111(b)(8)(C) of the ESEA. The LEA must provide, in its Race to the Top – District application, the definition used.

Highly effective principal means a principal whose students, overall and for each subgroup, achieve high rates (e.g., one and one-half grade levels in an academic year) of student growth (as defined in the notice) as defined under the LEAs principal evaluation system (as defined in the notice).

Highly effective teacher means a teacher whose students achieve high rates (e.g., one and one-half grade levels in an academic year) of student growth (as defined in the notice) as defined under the LEAs teacher evaluation system (as defined in the notice).

Interoperable data system means a system that uses a common, established structure such that data can easily flow from one system to another and in which data are in a non-proprietary, open format.

Local educational agency is an entity as defined in section 9101(26) of the ESEA, except that an entity described under section 9101(26)(D) must be recognized under applicable State law as a local educational agency.

Low-performing school means a school that is in the bottom 10 percent of performance in the State, or that has significant achievement gaps, based on student academic performance in reading/language arts and mathematics on the assessments required under the ESEA, or that has a graduation rate (as defined in the notice) below 60 percent.

Metadata means information about digital learning content such as the grade or age for which it is intended, the topic or standard to which it is aligned, or the type of resource it is (e.g., video, image).

On-track indicator means a measure, available at a time sufficiently early to allow for intervention, of a single student characteristic (e.g., number of days absent, number of discipline referrals, number of credits earned), or a composite of multiple characteristics, that is both predictive of student success (e.g., students demonstrating the measure graduate at an 80 percent rate) and comprehensive of students who succeed (e.g., of all graduates, 90 percent demonstrated the indicator). Using multiple indicators that are collectively comprehensive but vary by student characteristics may be an appropriate alternative to a single indicator that applies to all students.

Open data format means data that are available in a non-proprietary, machine-readable format (e.g., Extensible Markup Language (XML) and JavaScript Object Notation (JSON)) such that they can be understood by a computer. Digital formats that require extraction, data translation such as optical character recognition, or other manipulation in order to be used in electronic systems are not machine-readable formats.

Open-standard registry means a digital platform, such as the Learning Registry, that facilitates the exchange of information about digital learning content (as defined in the notice), including (1) alignment of content with college- and career-ready standards (as defined in the notice) and (2) usage information about learning content used by educators (as defined in the notice). This digital platform must have the capability to share content information with other LEAs and with State educational agencies.

Participating school means a school that is identified by the applicant and chooses to work with the applicant to implement the plan under Absolute Priority 1, either in one or more specific grade spans or subject areas or throughout the entire school and affecting a significant number of its students.

Participating student means a student enrolled in a participating school (as defined in the notice) and who is directly served by an applicant's plan under Absolute Priority 1.

Persistently lowest-achieving school means, as determined by the State, consistent with the requirements of the SIG program authorized by section 1003(g) of the ESEA,[1] (1) any Title I school in improvement, corrective action, or restructuring that (a) is among the lowest-achieving five percent of Title I schools in improvement, corrective action, or restructuring or the lowest-achieving five Title I schools in improvement, corrective action, or restructuring in the State, whichever number of schools is greater; or (b) is a high school that has had a graduation rate as defined in 34 CFR 200.19(b) that is less than 60 percent over a number of years; and (2) any secondary school that is eligible for, but does not receive, Title I funds that (a) is among the lowest-achieving five percent of secondary schools or the lowest-achieving five secondary schools in the State that are eligible for, but do not receive, Title I funds, whichever number of schools is greater; or (b) is a high school that has had a graduation rate as defined in 34 CFR 200.19(b) that is less than 60 percent over a number of years.

To identify the lowest-achieving schools, a State must take into account both (1) the academic achievement of the "all students" group in a school in terms of proficiency on the State's assessments under section 1111(b)(3) of the ESEA in reading or language arts and in mathematics combined; and (2) the school's lack of progress on those assessments over a number of years in the "all students" group.

Principal evaluation system means a system that: (1) is used for continual improvement of instructional leadership; (2) meaningfully differentiates performance using at least three performance levels; (3) uses multiple valid measures in determining performance levels, including, as a significant factor, data on student growth (as defined in the notice) for all students (including English learners and students with disabilities), as well as other measures of professional practice (which may be gathered through multiple formats and sources, such as observations based on rigorous leadership performance

---

[1] The Department considers schools that are identified as Tier I or Tier II schools under the School Improvement Grants Program (see 75 FR 66363) as part of a State's approved FY 2009 or FY 2010 applications to be persistently lowest-achieving schools. A list of these Tier I and Tier II schools can be found on the Department's Web site at http://www2.ed.gov/programs/sif/index.html

standards, teacher evaluation data, and student and parent surveys); (4) evaluates principals on a regular basis; (5) provides clear, timely, and useful feedback, including feedback that identifies and guides professional development needs; and (6) is used to inform personnel decisions.

Rural local educational agency means an LEA, at the time of the application, that is eligible under the Small Rural School Achievement (SRSA) program or the Rural and Low-Income School (RLIS) program authorized under Title VI, Part B of the ESEA. Eligible applicants may determine whether a particular LEA is eligible for these programs by referring to information on the Department's Web site at http://www2.ed.gov/programs/reapsrsa/eligible12/index.html.

School leadership team means a team that leads the implementation of improvement and other initiatives at the school and is composed of the principal or other head of a school, teachers, and other educators (as defined in the notice), and, as applicable, other school employees, parents, students, and other community members. In cases where statute or local policy, including collective bargaining agreements, establishes a school leadership team, that body shall serve as the school leadership team for the purpose of this program.

Student growth means the change in student achievement for an individual student between two or more points in time, defined as—
(1) For grades and subjects in which assessments are required under ESEA section 1111(b)(3): (a) a student's score on such assessments; and (b) may include other measures of student learning, such as those described in (2) below, provided they are rigorous and comparable across schools within an LEA.
(2) For grades and subjects in which assessments are not required under ESEA section 1111(b)(3): alternative measures of student learning and performance, such as student results on pre-tests, end-of-course tests, and objective performance-based assessments; performance against student learning objectives; student performance on English language proficiency assessments; and other measures of student achievement that are rigorous and comparable across schools within an LEA.

Student-level data means demographic, performance, and other information that pertains to a single student.

Student performance data means information about the academic progress of a single student, such as formative and summative assessment data, information on completion of coursework, instructor observations, information about student engagement and time on task, and similar information.

Subgroup means each category of students identified under section 1111(b)(2)(C)(v)(II) of the ESEA, as well as any combined subgroup used in the State accountability system and approved by the Department in a State's request for ESEA flexibility.

Superintendent evaluation means a rigorous, transparent, and fair annual evaluation of an LEA superintendent that provides an assessment of performance and encourages professional growth. This evaluation must reflect: (1) the feedback of many stakeholders, including but not limited to educators, principals, and parents; and (2) student outcomes.

Teacher evaluation system means a system that: (1) is used for continual improvement of instruction; (2) meaningfully differentiates performance using at least three performance levels; (3) uses multiple valid measures in determining performance levels, including, as a significant factor, data on student growth (as defined in the notice) for all students (including English learners and students with disabilities), as well as other measures of professional practice (which may be gathered through multiple formats and sources, such as observations based on rigorous teacher performance standards, teacher portfolios, and student and parent surveys); (4) evaluates teachers on a regular basis; (5) provides clear, timely, and useful feedback, including feedback that identifies and guides professional development needs; and (6) is used to inform personnel decisions.

Teacher of record means an individual (or individuals in a co-teaching assignment) who has been assigned the lead responsibility for a student's learning in a subject or course.

Source: www2ed.gov/programs/racetothetop.../2012-executive-summary.pdf

States Continue Progress During Second Year of Race to the Top

FEBRUARY 1, 2013 – Today the U.S. Department of Education released state-specific reports for 12 Race to the Top grantees, detailing their progress on transforming education at the local level. The reports highlight the second-year work and accomplishments of states awarded funding through the first two phases of Race to the Top: Delaware, the District of Columbia, Florida, Georgia, Hawaii, Maryland, Massachusetts, New York, North Carolina, Ohio, Rhode Island and Tennessee.

"Race to the Top has sparked dramatic changes, and in only the second year of the program we're seeing those results reach the classroom," said U.S. Secretary of Education Arne Duncan. "Most states have made tremendous strides and met aggressive timelines on work that has the potential to transform public education for years to come. Comprehensive education reform isn't easy, and a few states have faced major challenges in implementing their plans. As we reach the halfway point, we need to see every state show results."

The 12 reports provide detailed, transparent summaries of each state's accomplishments and challenges in year two, which covered the 2011-12 school year, as well as the milestones they have ahead for year three. Each state's work is measured against its own plan and progress in year two of its Race to the Top grant.

States reached a number of benchmarks in year two, as they implemented unique plans built around Race to the Top's four assurance areas: implementing college- and career-ready standards and assessments, building robust data systems to improve instruction, supporting great teachers and school leaders, and turning around persistently low-performing schools. Some states made strategic investments to develop tools and resources for educators, students and parents; launch state-level support networks; or develop additional science, technology, engineering and math (STEM) schools or programs. Others launched new pipelines for teachers and leaders, supported key efforts to turn around low-performing schools, or implemented teacher and principal evaluations to better support educators and inform continuous improvement.

The Department's Implementation and Support Unit (ISU) has partnered with states to track progress and provide feedback as they implement large-scale reform. Where states encountered delays and challenges, the ISU worked with them on adjustments to help move the work forward, while holding states accountable to their commitments. ISU officials will continue to provide annual updates about states' progress under Race to the Top.

In addition to the year two state reports, today the Department posted Annual Performance Report (APR) data from states that received Race to the Top funding in phases one, two and three. This data helped to inform the year two reports, which were also developed with information from site visits, communications with state staff, and other performance reports. The APR helps to advance the Department's efforts to provide transparent information and allow the public to follow grantees' progress in implementing reform plans and meeting ambitious goals for student outcomes, including performance measures, student growth and closing achievement gaps.

The Race to the Top program, which made its first awards in 2010, has provided 24 states and D.C. with about $5 billion through three phases of the flagship competition and two rounds of the Race to the Top-Early Learning Challenge. Last year, the Department launched the first Race to the Top-District program, which will fund 16 applicants – representing 55 school districts across 11 states and D.C. – with close to $400 million to support locally developed plans that will prepare every student to succeed in college and their careers. The Department's fiscal year 2013 budget requested an additional $850 million for the Race to the Top program to address the unmet demand of states and districts that have demonstrated a commitment to aggressive and comprehensive education reform.

For more information about the Race to the Top program, and to review the 12 state-specific year two reports and APR data, visit: http://www2.ed.gov/programs/racetothetop/index.html. Or contact Press Office (202) 401-1576, press@ed.gov.

General

1 ASPIRA Association
1444 I Street NW
Suite 800
Washington, DC 20005-6543
202-835-3600
Fax: 202-835-3613
E-mail: info@aspira.org
http://www.aspira.org
Founded in 1961 the ASPIRA Association promotes the empowerment of the Puerto Rican and Latino community by developing and nurturing the leadership, intellectual, and cultural potential of its youth so that they may contribute their skills and dedication to the fullest development of the Puerto Rican and Latino community everywhere.

Ronald Blackburn-Moreno, President/CEO
John Villamil-Casanova, Executive Vice President

2 Advance Program for Young Scholars
ADVANCE Program
NSU Box 5671
Natchitoches, LA 71497
318-357-4500
Fax: 318-357-4547
E-mail: palmerh@nsula.edu
http://http://advance.nsula.edu
From chemistry to history, from foreign languages to ecology, the program offers a broad spectrum of academic opportunities to the qualified 12-17 year old student.

David Wood PhD, Director
Harriette Palmer, Assistant Director

3 Alliance for Parental Involvement in Education
PO Box 59
East Chatham, NY 12060-59
518-392-6900
E-mail: allpie@taconic.net
http://www.allpie.org
Seeks to nurture parents' natural teaching abilities and offer tools and resources, public, private and home in becoming active participants in the education of their children.

Katharine Houk, Executive Director

4 American Academy of Pediatrics
141 NW Point Boulevard
Elk Grove Village, IL 60007-1098
847-434-4000
800-433-9016
Fax: 847-434-8000
E-mail: kidsdoc@aap.org
http://www.aap.org
Committed to the attainment of optimal physical, mental and social health for all infants, children, adolescents and young adults.

Thomas K. McInerny, MD, FAAP, President
Errol R Alden, MD, Executive Director

5 American Association for Vocational Instructional Materials (AAVIM)
220 Smithonia Road
Winterville, GA 30683-1418
706-742-5355
800-228-4689
Fax: 706-742-7005
E-mail: sales@aavim.com
http://www.aavim.com
Develops, produces and distributes quality instructional materials for career education instructors, students, and administrators.

Gary Farmer, Director
Vicki J Eaton, Art Director/Production Coordinator

6 American Council for Drug Education
50 Jay Street
Brooklyn, NY 11201
718-222-6641
800-378-4435
Fax: 212-595-2553
E-mail: acde@phoenixhouse.org
http://www.phoenixhouse.org
Distributes packaged information about drugs and the consequences of their use and identifies effective community programs to address the drug problem in the country.

Founded: 1977

William F Current, Executive Director

7 American Council of Trustees and Alumni
1726 M Street NW
Suite 802
Washington, DC 20036
202-467-6787
E-mail: info@goacta.org
http://www.goacta.org
An independent, non-profit organization committed to academic freedom, excellence, and accountability at America's colleges and universities. Works with alumni, donors, trustees, and education leaders across the United States to support liberal arts education, uphold high academic standards, safeguard the free exchange of ideas on campus, and ensure that the next generation receives a philosophically rich, high-quality college education at an affordable price.

Founded: 1995

8 American Council on Education (ACE)
1 Dupont Circle NW
Washington, DC 20036
202-939-9300
Fax: 202-833-4730
E-mail: comments@ace.nche.edu
http://www.acenet.edu
Represents accredited degree-granting colleges and universities directly and through national and regional higher education associations. Seeks to advance education and serves as an advocate for adult education.

Molly Corbett Broad, President
Tully R Cornick, Executive Director

9 American Council on Rural Special Education (ACRES)
West Virginia University
509 Allen Hall
PO Box 6122
Morgantown, WV 26506-6122
304-293-3450
888-866-3822
E-mail: acres-sped@mail.wvu.edu
http://acres-sped.org
The organization is comprised of special educators, general educators, related service providers, administrators, teacher trainers, researchers, and parents committed to the enhancement of services to students and individuals living in rural America.

Todd Sundeen, Chair
Buddy Hooper, Chair Elect

10 American Driver and Traffic Safety Education Association (ADTSEA)
Highway Safety Services
1434 Trim Tree Road
Indiana, PA 15701
724-801-8246
877-485-7172
Fax: 724-349-5042
E-mail: office@adtsea.org
http://www.adtsea.org

The purpose of the American Driver and Traffic Safety Education Association is to promote quality traffic safety education by publishing policies and guidelines. ADTSEA conducts conferences, workshops, seminars and consultative services and educational materials.

Connie Sessoms, Jr., President
Brett Robinson, Executive Director

11 American Federation of Teachers
555 New Jersey Avenue NW
Washington, DC 20001
202-879-4400
Fax: 202-879-4556
E-mail: online@aft.org
http://www.aft.org
The AFT is a union of professionals that champions fairness, democracy, economic opportunity and high quality public education, healthcare and public services for our students, their families and our communities. The AFT is committed to advancing these principles through the work that their members do.

Randi Weingarten, President
Lorreta Johnson, Executive VP

12 American Montessori Society
116 East 16th Street
New York, NY 10003
212-358-1250
Fax: 212-358-1256
E-mail: ams@amshq.org
http://www.amshq.org
Provides the leadership and inspiration to make Montessori a significant voice in education. The Society advocates quality Montessori education, strengthens members through its services, and champions Montessori principles to the greater community.

Marilyn E Stewart, President
Kathy Roemer, Vice President

13 American School Health Association
4340 East West Highway
Suite 403
Bethesda, MD 20814
301-652-8072
Fax: 301-652-8077
E-mail: info@ashaweb.org
http://www.ashaweb.org
A nonprofit organization founded to protect and improve the health and well-being of children and youth by supporting comprehensive, preschool-12 school health programs.

Linda Morse, RN, MA, CHES, President
Holly Hunt, MA, President-Elect

14 American Society for Engineering Education
1818 N Street NW
Suite 600
Washington, DC 20036-2479
202-331-3500
Fax: 202-265-8504
E-mail: aseeexec@asee.org
http://www.asee.org
A nonprofit organization of individuals and institutions committed to furthering education in engineering and engineering technology.

Founded: 1893

Norman Fortenberry, Executive Director

15 Association For Childhood Education International
1101 16th St NW
Suite 300
Washington, DC 20036
202-372-9986
800-423-3563

1

Fax: 202-372-9989
http://www.acei.org
To promote and support in the global community the optimal education, development, and well-being of children, from birth through early adolescence, and to influence the professional growth of educators and the efforts of others who are committed to the needs of children in a changing society.

Debora Wisneski, President

16   Association for Business Communication (ABC)
Virginia Tech
335 Shanks Hall
Blacksburg, VA 24061
540-231-8460
E-mail:
abcoffice@businesscommunication.org
http://www.businesscommunication.org
Committed to fostering excellence in business communication scholarship, research, education, and practice.

Jim Dubinsky, Executive Director
Marilyn Buerkens, Office Manager

17   Association for Community-Based Education
1806 Vernon Street NW
Washington, DC 20009-1217
202-462-6333
Offers technical assistance on planning, management and program development for community-based education. Further education through discussion groups, forums, panel lectures, as well, study and research.

Christofer Zachariadis, Executive Director

18   Association for Disabled Students
University of Oklahoma
Disability Resource Center
620 Elm Avenue, Suite 166
Norman, OK 73019-2093
405-325-3852
Fax: 405-325-4491
E-mail: drc@ou.edu
http://drc.ou.edu
Also known as ADS, this student organization provides a forum for support, regular meetings, and social and recreational activities. ADS sponsors Disability Awareness Week each October and Disability Arts Week the first week of April. ADS also sponsors a wheelchair basketball team, affiliated with the Intercollegiate Wheelchair Division of the National Wheelchair Basketball Association. The team competes nationally.

Suzette Dyer, Director

19   Association for Environmental and Outdoor Education (AEOE)
PO Box 187
Angelus Oaks, CA 92305
714-838-8990
714-474-1377
E-mail: TraciFesko@cusd.com
http://www.aeoe.org
The Association for Environmental and Outdoor Education supports and inspires educators in their quest for the knowledge, skills, and attitudes essential to help all learners understand, appreciate and care for their environment.

Reed Schneider, President
Helen M De La Maza, Membership Chair

20   Association for Gender Equity Leadership in Education
317 S. Division St., PM #54
Ann Arbor, MI 48104
734-769-2456
Fax: 734-769-2456
E-mail: businessmgr@agele.org
http://www.agele.org
A national organization for gender equity specialists and educators. Individuals and organizations committed to reducing sex role stereotyping for females and males. Services include an annual national training conference, a quarterly newsletter and a membership directory. Members may join task forces dealing with equity related topics such as computer/technology issues, early childhood, male issues, sexual harassment prevention, sexual orientation and vocational issues.

Marta Larson, Business Manager
Keith Eccarius, Communications Manager

21   Association for Integrative Studies
School of Interdisciplinary Studies
Miami University
501 E. High Street
Oxford, OH 45056-3653
513-529-2213
Fax: 513-529-5849
E-mail: newellwh@miamioh.edu
http://www.units.muohio.edu/aisorg
The Association for Integrative Studies is an interdisciplinary professional organization founded in 1979 to promote the interchange of ideas among scholars and administrators in all of the arts and sciences on intellectual and organizational issues related to furthering integrative studies. Incorporated as a non-profit educational association in the State of Ohio, it has an international membership.

Bill Newell, Executive Director
Rick Szostak, President

22   Association for Middle Level Education
4151 Executive Parkway
Suite 300
Westerville, OH 43081
614-895-4730
800-528-6672
Fax: 614-895-4750
E-mail: info@amle.org
http://www.amle.org
AMLEhas been a voice for those committed to the educational and developmental needs of young adolescents. AMLE is the only national education association dedicated exclusively to those in middle level grades.

Jeff La Roux, President
Mike Muir, President-Elect

23   Association for Play Therapy
3198 Willow Avenue
Suite 110
Clovis, CA 93612
559-294-2128
Fax: 559-294-2129
E-mail: info@a4pt.org
http://www.a4pt.org
Founded in 1982 APT promotes the value of play, play therapy and credentialed play therapists by advancing the psychosocial development and mental health of all people and sponsoring and supporting those programs, services and related activities that promote public understanding of play therapy.

Kathryn Lebby, Chief Operating Officer
Bill Burns, President/CEO

24   Association for Supervision & Curriculum Development (ASCD)
1703 N Beauregard Street
Alexandria, VA 22311-1714
703-578-9600
800-933-2723
Fax: 703-575-5400
E-mail: member@ascd.org
http://www.ascd.org
A membership organization that develops programs, products, and services essential to the way educators learn, teach, and lead.

Founded: 1943

Sara Magana Shubel, President
Kathy Clayton, Executive Director

25   Association of American Educators
27405 Puerta Real
Suite 230
Mission Viejo, CA 92691
949-595-7979
800-704-7799
Fax: 949-595-7970
http://www.aaeteachers.org
Provides professional benefits and services to educators, including liability insurance, scholarships and grants, and professional resources.

Gary Beckner, Executive Director

26   Association of Boarding Schools
1 North Pack Square
Suite 301
Asheville, NC 28801
828-258-5354
Fax: 828-258-6428
E-mail: tabs@schools.com
http://www.schools.com
A marketing consortium founded in 1975 of 300 boarding schools that seeks to increase the applicant pool of member schools by increasing public awareness of benefits and advantages of boarding school education. TABS is a resource for educators seeking training, research, guidance and support on all issues pertaining to the residential school experience.

Founded: 1975

Steve Banks, Director of Operations
Peter Upham, Executive Director

27   Association of Educators in Private Practice
1839 Batten Hollow Road
Vienna, VA 22182
709-938-2429
800-252-3280
Fax: 703-242-1479
E-mail: spines@educationindustry.org
http://www.educationindustry.org
To promote increased public support for the education industry in order to improve educational opportunities and outcomes for all students.

Steven Pines, Executive Director
Jim Giovannini, Board President

28   Association of Teacher Educators
PO Box 793
Manassas, VA 20113
703-934-6018
Fax: 703-591-3049
E-mail: info@ate1.org
http://www.ate1.org
The mission of the Association of Teacher Educators is to improve the effectiveness of teacher education through leadership in the development of quality programs to prepare teachers, by analyzing issues and practices relating to professional development, and by providing opportunities for the personal and professional growth of Association members.

Founded: 1920

Jim Alouf, President-Elect
Terrell Peace, President

29   Attention Deficit Disorder Association
PO Box 7557
Wilmington, DE 19803-9997

800-939-1019
Fax: 800-939-1019
E-mail: info@add.org
http://www.add.org
ADDA, provides information, resources and networking opportunities to help adults with Attention Deficit/Hyperactivity Disorder (AD/HD) lead better lives.

Evelyn P Green, MS.Ed, President
Linda Roggli, PCC, VP

30 Awards and Recognition Association
4700 W Lake Avenue
Glenview, IL 60025
847-375-4800
800-344-2148
Fax: 888-374-7257
E-mail: info@ara.org
http://www.ara.org
The purpose of ARA is to advance the capabilities and growth of businesses whose primary focus is the manufacture, distribution or sales of awards and recognition goods and services. ARA is the essential component for success in the awards and recognition business.

B J Bailey Jr, President
Guy Barone, President-Elect

31 Better Chance
240 W 35th Street
Floor 6
New York, NY 10001-2506
646-346-1310
800-562-7865
Fax: 646-346-1311
http://www.abetterchance.org
Our mission is to substantially increase the number of well-educated young people of color who are capable of assuming positions of responsibility and leadership in American society.
Founded: 1963

Sandra E Timmons, President
Chantal Stevens, Director

32 CHADD: Children & Adults with Attention Deficit/Hyperactivity Disorder
8181 Professional Place
Suite 150
Landover, MD 20785
301-306-7070
800-233-4050
Fax: 301-306-7090
E-mail: conference@chadd.org
http://www.chadd.org
National nonprofit organization which offers advocacy, information and support for patients and parents of children with attention deficit disorders. Maintains support groups, provides a forum for continuing education about ADHD, and maintains a national resource center for information about ADD.

Russell L Shipley, Chief Development Officer
Ruth Hughes, PhD, CEO

33 Cable in the Classroom
25 Massachusetts Avenue NW
Suite 100
Washington, DC 20001
202-222-2335
Fax: 202-222-2336
E-mail: help@ciconline.org
http://www.ciconline.org
Promotes visionary, sensible, responsible and effective use of cable's broadband technology and services and content in learning and teaching. Represents the cable industry's

commitment to education by showcasing a variety if cable initiatives in education.

Frank Gallagher, Executive Director
Helen Dimsdale, Deputy Executive Director

34 Center for Civic Education
21600 Oxnard Street
Suite 500
Woodland Hills, CA 91367
818-591-9321
800-350-4223
Fax: 818-591-9330
E-mail: cce@civiced.org
http://www.civiced.org
Non-profit, nonpartisan educational corporation dedicated to fostering the development of informed, responsible participation in civic life by citizens committed to values and principles fundamental to American constitutional democracy.

Charles Quigley, Executive Director
Margaret Branson, Associate Director

35 Center for Lifelong Learning
American Council on Education
One Dupont Circle NW
Washington, DC 20036-1193
202-939-9300
E-mail: lifelong_learning@acenet.edu
http://www.acenet.edu
ACE's Center for Lifelong Learning (CLLL) has led the national movement to recognize and promote adult learner programs in higher education.

Susan Porter Robinson, Vice President
Mary Beth Lakin, Associate Director

36 Center on Education Policy
2140 Pennsylvania Ave. NW
Room 103
Washington, DC 20037
202-994-9050
Fax: 202-994-8859
E-mail: cep-dc@cep-dc.org
http://www.cep-dc.org
Understand the role of public education in a democracy and the need to improve the academic quality of public schools. Help citizens make sense of the conflicting make sense of conflicting perceptions about publilic education and create the conditions that will lead to better public schools.

Jack Jennings, President/CEO
Arturo Pacheco PhD, Director

37 Center on Human Policy
805 S Crouse Avenue
101 Hoople Building
Syracuse, NY 13244-2280
315-443-3851
800-894-0826
Fax: 315-443-4338
E-mail: staylo01@syr.edu
http://disabilitystudies.syr.edu
Promotes its mission of inclusion by developing and sponsoring academic programs and courses, conferences and publications, research and training programs, and public education and advocacy efforts on behalf of, and with, people with disabilities.
Founded: 1971

Steven J Taylor, Co-Director
Arlene S Kanter, Co-Director

38 Citizens for Educational Freedom
498 Woods Mill Road
Manchester, MO 63011-4144
636-686-7101
Fax: 636-686-7173
E-mail: citedfree@educational-freedom.org
http://www.educational-freedom.org
Secures legal recognition for the right of parents to direct and control the education of

their children; secures freedom of choice in education of their children, including an alternative to the government-established school system.
Founded: 1959

Mae Duggan, President/CEF
Herman Kriegshauser, Executive Director

39 Civic Practices Network
Brandeis University
60 Turner Street
Waltham, MA 02154
617-736-4890
Fax: 617-736-4891
E-mail: cpn@cpn.org
http://www.cpn.org
Collaborative and nonpartisan project dedicated to bring practical tools for public problem solving into communities and institutional settings across America.

Carmen Sirianni, Co-Editor
Lewis Friedland, Co-Editor

40 Constitutional Rights Foundation
601 S Kingsley Drive
Los Angeles, CA 90005
213-487-5590
Fax: 213-386-0459
E-mail: crf@crf-usa.org
http://www.crf-usa.org
Seeks to instill in our nation's youth a deeper understanding of citizenship through values expressed in our Constitution and its Bill of Rights, and educate them to become active and responsible participants in our society. Dedicated to assuring our country's future by investing in our youth today.

Jonathan Estrin, President
John L. Plaxco, Development Director

41 Council for Advancement & Support of Education
1307 New York Avenue NW
Suite 1000
Washington, DC 20005-4701
202-328-2273
Fax: 202-387-4973
E-mail: memberservicecenter@case.org
http://www.case.org
An international membership association that advances and supports educational institutions by providing knowledge, standards, advocacy and training designed to strengthen the combined efforts of alumni relations, communications, fundraising, marketing and allied professionals. CASE helps members raise funds for campus projects, produce recruitment materials, market their institutions to prospective students, diversify the profession and foster public support of education.

John Lippincott, President
Cassie McVeety, Chair

42 Council for Christian Colleges and Universities
321 Eighth Street NE
Washington, DC 20002
202-546-8713
http://www.cccu.org
To advance the cause of Christ-centered higher education and to help our institutions transform lives by faithfully relating scholarship and service to biblical truth.
Founded: 1976

43 Council for Exceptional Children
2900 Crystal Drive
Suite 1000
Arlington, VA 22202-3557
703-620-3660
888-232-7733
Fax: 703-264-9494

E-mail: service@cec.sped.org
http://www.cec.sped.org
The Council for Exceptional Children works to improve the educational success of individuals with disabilities and/or gifts and talents.

Marilyn Friend, President
Bruce Ramirez, Executive Director

44   Council for the Accreditation of Educator Preparation
2010 Massachusetts Avenue NW
Suite 500
Washington, DC 20036
202-223-0077
Fax: 202-296-6620
E-mail: caep@CAEPnet.org
http://www.CAEPnet.org
Professional accrediting organization for schools, colleges and departments of education and alternative educator preparation providers in the United States.

James G. Cibulka, President
Deborah Eldridge, Sr. VP Accreditation

45   Council of Graduate Schools
1 Dupont Circle NW
Suite 230
Washington, DC 20036-1173
202-223-3791
Fax: 202-331-7157
E-mail: pmcallister@cgs.nche.edu
http://www.cgsnet.org
CGS has been the national voice for the graduate dean community. The only national organization in the United States that is dedicated solely to the advancement of graduate education and research. This is accomplished through advocacy in policy, innovative research and the development and dissemination of the best practices.

Patricia McAllister, VP Government Relations
Leontyne Goodwin, Manager External Affairs

46   Council of Independent Colleges
One Dupont Circle NW
Suite 320
Washington, DC 20036-1142
202-466-7230
Fax: 202-466-7238
E-mail: cic@cic.nche.edu
http://www.cic.edu
The major national organization that focuses on providing services to leaders of independent colleges and universities as well as conferences, seminars, and other programs that help institutions to improve the quality of education, administrative and financial performance, and institutional visibility.

Founded: 1956

47   Council on Postsecondary Accreditation
1 Dupont Circle NW
Suite 230
Washington, DC 20036-1173
202-223-3791
Fax: 202-331-7157
E-mail: general_inquiries@cgs.nche.edu
http://www.cgsnet.org
Has been the national voice for the graduate dean community. The only national organization in the United States that is dedicated solely to the advancement of graduate education and research.

Patricia McAllister, VP Government Relations
Belle Woods, Manager External Affairs

48   Crittenton Women's Union
Crittenton Women's Union
One Washington Mall
2nd Floor
Boston, MA 02108
617-259-2900
Fax: 617-247-8826
E-mail: info@liveworkthrive.org
http://www.liveworkthrive.org
Crittenton Women's Union transforms the course of low-income women's lives so that they can attain economic independence and create better futures for themselves and their families.

Elisabeth Babcock, MCRP, Ph.D, President/CEO
Charles Carter, Jr., Ph.D, LICSW, Vice President/COO

49   Disability Rights Education & Defense Fund
3075 Adeline Street
Suite 210
Berkeley, CA 94703
510-644-2555
800-348-4232
Fax: 510-841-8645
E-mail: info@dredf.org
http://www.dredf.org
The mission of the Disability Rights Education and Defense Fund is to advance the civil and human rights of people with disabilities through legal advocacy, training, education, and public policy and legislative development.

Jenny Kern, Esq., President
Claudia Center, Esq., Treasurer

50   Drug Information & Strategy Clearinghouse
3109 Lubbock Ave
Fort Worth, TX 76109
800-955-2232
Provides housing officials, residents and community leaders with information and assistance on drug abuse prevention and trafficking control techniques.

Nancy Kay, Director

51   EF Educational Tours
1 Education Street
Cambridge, MA 02141-1883
800-637-8222
Fax: 617-619-1803
http://www.eftours.com
EF Educational Tours helps educators like you enrich what you teach in the classroom with international group travel. Your students actually learn it by living it by experiencing the world's very best historic, cultural and natural sights.

Founded: 1965

Martha H Doyle, President
Amy Connolly, Director of Customer Service

52   ERIC - Education Resources Information Center
655 15th Street NW
Suite 500
Washington, DC 20005
800-538-3742
http://www.eric.ed.gov/
The ERIC mission is to provide a comprehensive, easy-to-use, searchable, Internet-based bibliographic and full-text database of education research and information that also meets the requirements of

the Education Sciences Reform Act of 2002.

Arthuree Wright, Interim Library Director
Alvin Walker, Jr, Product Development Manager

53   ERIC Clearinghouse on Assessment & Evaluation
University of Maryland
1129 Shriver Laboratory
College Park, MD 20742-5701
301-405-7449
800-464-3742
Fax: 301-405-8134
E-mail: feedback3@ericae.net
http://www.ericae.net
Disseminates education information on topics pertaining to tests and other measurement devices, research design and methodology.

Lawrence M Rudner, Director
Carol Boston, Associate Director

54   ERIC Clearinghouse on Rural Education & Small Schools
Edvantia
PO Box 1348
Charleston, WV 25325-1348
304-347-0400
800-624-9120
Fax: 304-347-0487
E-mail: info@edvantia.org
http://www.edvantia.org
Works in partnership with clients to provide workable solutions to issues facing education today. Services grounded in research and best practices and delivered by social scientists, former teachers, administrators and state evaluation leaders.

Doris Redfield, Ph.d, President

55   Easter Seals Communications
Easter Seals
233 South Wacker Drive
Suite 2400
Chicago, IL 60606
312-726-6200
800-221-6827
Fax: 312-726-1494
E-mail: info@easter-seals.org
http://www.easterseals.com
Easter Seals provides exceptional services, education, outreach, and advocacy so that people living with autism and other disabilities can live, learn, work and play in our communities.

Stephen F. Rossman, Chairman
Richard F. Vincent, Treasurer

56   Education Commission of the States
700 Broadway
#810
Denver, CO 80203-3442
303-299-3600
Fax: 303-296-8332
E-mail: ecs@ecs.org
http://www.ecs.org
To help states develop effective policy and practice for public education by providing data, research, analysis and leadership; and by facilitating collaboration, the exchange of ideas among the states and long-range strategic thinking

Jeremy Anderson, President
John Hickenlooper, Chairman

57   Education Development Center
43 Foundry Avenue
Waltham, MA 02453-8313
617-969-7100
Fax: 617-969-5979
E-mail: contact@edc.org
http://www.edc.org
EDC designs, delivers and evaluates programs addressing some of the world's challenges in education, health and economic opportunity. working with the public-sector and private partners, EDC

uses the power of people and systems to improve education, health promotion and care, workforce preparation, communications technologies and civic engagement. Services include research, training, educational materials and strategy.

Founded: 1958

Luther Luedtke, President
Steve Anzalone, Vice President

58   Education Extension
Oklahoma State University-Stillwater
327 Willard
Stillwater, OK 74078-4034
405-744-6254
800-765-8933
Fax: 405-744-7713
E-mail: education.outreach@okstate.edu
http://education.okstate.edu
The school counseling specialization prepares students to work as school counselors in public schools, serving students, teachers, and parents.

Dr Pamela Fry, Dean
Dr C Robert Davis, Associate Dean

59   Education, Training and Research Associates
4 Carbonero Way
Scotts Valley, CA 95066
831-438-4060
Fax: 831-438-4284
http://www.etr.org
To maximize the physical, social and emotional health of all individuals, families and communities by advancing the work of health, education and social service providers through high-quality research, publications, information resources and programs.

Dan McCormick, MHA, BS, CEO
Dave Kitchen, MBA, COO

60   Educational Equity Concepts
Educational Equity Center at FHI 360
71 5th Avenue
6th Floor
New York, NY 10003
212-243-1110
Fax: 212-627-0407
E-mail: eec@fhi360.org
http://www.edequity.org
EEC develops programs and materials that promote bias-free learning in school and after school. We provide professional development, consulting services and community partnerships. Our goal is to eliminate inequities based on gender, race/ethnicity, disability and level of family income.

Merle Froschl, Co-Founder/Co-Director
Linda Coln, Program Manager

61   Educational Register
Vincent-Curtis
PO Box 724
Falmouth, MA 02541-0724
508-457-6473
Fax: 508-457-6499
E-mail: register@vincentcurtis.com
http://www.theeducationalregister.com
Hundreds of illustrated announcements describing a variety of private boarding schools and resident summer programs in the United States, Canada and Europe, together with articles by school heads and camp directors of interest to parents of students 10-18.

Stanford B Vincent, Editor

62   Equity Clearinghouse
Mid-Continent Regional Educational Laboratory
4601 DTC Boulevard
Suite 500
Denver, CO 80237-2596
303-337-0990
Fax: 303-337-3005
http://www.mcrel.org
Researchers and education consultants work together to provide educators with research-based, practical guidance on the issues and challenges facing k-16 education. Data analyses, scientific studies, field-tested products and services and reports, articles, books and tools are all crated and delivered to help with challenges facing education today.

Timothy Waters, President/CEO
Judy Richards, Chair

63   Excelencia in Education
1717 N Street NW
2nd Floor
Washington, DC 20036
202-785-7350
Fax: 202-785-7351
http://www.edexcelencia.org
Aims to accelerate higher education success for Latino students by providing data-driven analysis of the educational status of Latino students and by promoting education policies and institutional practices that support their academic achievement.

64   FHI 360
2224 E NC Highway 54
Durham, NC 27713
919-544-7040
Fax: 919-544-7261
E-mail: web@aed.org
http://www.aed.org
Assists schools, colleges and other educational institutions of developing countries in researching, planning, designing, implementing and evaluating development programs. In the US, manages the Center for Youth Development and Policy Research (disadvantaged youth), Disabilities Studies and Services Center (clearinghouse on special education and children with disabilities), National Institute for Work and Learning (school-to-work transition), and schools and Community Services Department.

Founded: 1961

Albert J. Siemens, PhD, CEO
Robert Murphy, MBA, CFO

65   Facing History & Ourselves
16 Hurd Road
Brookline, MA 02445-6919
617-232-1595
800-856-9039
Fax: 617-232-0281
E-mail: info@facing.org
http://www.facinghistory.org
Facing History is an international nonprofit that helps teachers and students link the past to moral choices they face today.

Founded: 1976

Margot Strom, President

66   Family Centered Learning Alternatives (FCLA)
Context Institute
PO Box 946
Langley, WA 98260
360-221-6044
Fax: 360-221-6045
http://www.context.org
Supports parents' right to choose the educational environment best suited for their children's needs and to promote homeschooling as a legal nationwide learning alternative.

Eric Stewart, Founder/Director
Debra Stewart, Founder/Director

67   Foundation for Student Communication
Princeton University
48 University Place
Princeton, NJ 8544
609-258-1111
Fax: 609-258-1222
http://www.businesstoday.org
Student subscribers and conference participants who promote communication among students and business persons.

Founded: 1968

Sloan Rudberg, President
Andrea Wolberg, Director of Finance

68   Friends Council on Education
1507 Cherry Street
Philadelphia, PA 19102
215-241-7245
Fax: 215-241-7299
E-mail: Info@friendscouncil.org
http://www.friendscouncil.org
A national organization of Friends schools, which assists teachers, students and families by providing publications and programs supporting Friends values in the classroom and in the life of the school community.

Founded: 1931

Irene McHenry, Executive Director
Amy Brimmer, Outreach/Development

69   Gifted Child Society
190 Rock Road
Glen Rock, NJ 07452-1736
201-444-6530
Fax: 201-444-9099
E-mail: admin@gifted.org
http://www.giftedchildsociety.com
Educational enrichment and support services specifically designed for gifted children. Assistance to parents in raising gifted children to full and productive adulthood. Professional training to encourage educators to meet the special needs of those children and a greater effort to win public recognition and acceptance of these special needs.

Founded: 1957

Gina G Riggs, Executive Director

70   Girls Incorporated
120 Wall Street
New York, NY 10005-3902
212-509-2000
Fax: 212-509-8708
E-mail: communications@girlsinc.org
http://www.girlsinc.org
A national nonprofit youth organization dedicated to inspiring all girls to be strong, smart, and bold. Informal education programs encorage girls to master physical, intellectual and emotional challenges.

Founded: 1864

Judy Vredenburgh, President/CEO
Ellen Stafford-Sigg, Chairman

71   Global Exploration for Educators Organization
2945 Morris Rd
Ardmore, PA 19003
877-600-0105
http://www.geeo.org
A non-profit organization dedicated to encouraging and assisting as many teachers as possible to travel abroad and then share their experiences with their students upon their return to the classroom.

Jesse Weisz, Founder/Executive Director

72 HEATH Resource Center at the National Youth Transitions Center
George Washington University
HEATH Resource Center
2134 G Street N.W.
Washington, DC 20052-0001
202-973-0904
800-544-3284
Fax: 202-994-3365
E-mail: askheath@gwu.edu
http://www.HEATH.gwu.edu
The HEATH Resource Center has served as a national clearinghouse on postsecondary education for individuals with disabilities, managed by the George Washington University Graduate School of Education and Human Development. Now the HSC Foundation has partnered with the George Washington University to expand the content of this resource and to designate it as the official site of The HSC Foundation's National Youth Transitions Center.

Founded: 2000

Dr Lynda West, Principal Investigator
Dr Joel Gomez, Co-Principal Investigator

73 Independent Schools Association of the Southwest (ISAS)
Energy Square
505 N Big Spring Street
Suite 406
Midland, TX 79701
432-684-9550
800-688-5007
Fax: 432-684-9401
E-mail: rdurham@isasw.org
http://www.isasw.org
Independent Schools Association of the Southwest (ISAS) is a voluntary membership association of private schools. The membership of ISAS consists of 84 schools located in Arizona, Kansas, Louisiana, Mexico, New Mexico, Oklahoma and Texas enrolling over 38,000 students. A central purpose of ISAS is to encourage, support and develop the highest standard for independent schools of the region and to recognize by formal accreditation those schools in which these standards are maintained.

Founded: 1955

Rhonda Durham, Executive Director
Jananne McLaughlin, Accreditation Director

74 Institute for Educational Leadership
4455 Connecticut Avenue NW
Suite 310
Washington, DC 20008
202-822-8405
Fax: 202-872-4050
E-mail: iel@IEL.ORG
http://www.iel.org
To build the capacity of individuals and communities to work together - across policies, programs and sectors, to prepare all children and youth for post-secondary education, careers and citizenship

Martin J Blank, President/CEO

75 InterAction - American Council for Voluntary International Action
1400 16th Street, NW
Suite 210
Washington, DC 20036
202-667-8227
Fax: 202-667-8236
E-mail: ia@interaction.org
http://www.interaction.org/
Using its collective voice Interaction hopes to shape important policy decisions on relief and long term development issues

including foreign assistance, the environment, women, health, education and agriculture.

Sam Worthington, President/CEO

76 International Association of Educators for World Peace
2013 Orba Drive NE
Huntsville, AL 35811-2414
256-534-5501
Fax: 256-536-1018
E-mail: info@iaewp.org
http://www.iaewp.org
To contribute to the improvement of man's ability to live at peace, to educate world citizens for peaceful co-existence and cooperation so that all people may have free access to the achievement of science and civilization. Belief that international understanding and world peace can be attained through education.

Dr Charles Mercieca, President
Dr Surya Nath Prasad, Executive Vice President

77 International Society for Technology in Education
1710 Rhode Island Avenue NW
Suite 900
Washington, DC 20036
202-861-7777
866-654-4777
Fax: 202-861-0888
http://www.iste.org
Providing leadership and service to improve teaching and learning by advancing the effective use of technology in education.

Brian Lewis, MA, CAE, CEO
Craig Thibaudeau, Chief External Affairs

78 Jewish Education Council
Jewish Federation Greater Seattle
2031 Third Avenue
Seattle, WA 98121-2412
206-443-5400
Fax: 206-443-0303
E-mail: info@jewishinseattle.org
http://www.jewishinseattle.org
Works to ensure a vibrant Jewish cimmunity that is connected locally, in Israel and worldwide.

Liat Zaidenberg, Education Director

79 Jewish Education Service of North America
JESNA
318 W 39th Street
5th Floor
New York, NY 10018
212-284-6950
Fax: 212-284-6951
E-mail: info@jesna.org
http://www.jesna.org
Ensure that Jewish education is the best that it can be in all of its variety. JESNA's role is to strengthen communities and their educational offerings by providing tested solutions, leveraging partnerships, promoting synergies, and building the connections that strengthen us all.

David Steirman, President
Mandell L Berman, Honorary Chair

80 Jewish Educators Assembly
Broadway and Locust Avenue
PO Box 413
Cedarhurst, NY 11516
516-569-2537
Fax: 516-295-9039
E-mail:
jewisheducators@jewisheducators.org
http://www.jewisheducators.org

Promotes excellence among educators committed to Conservative Jewish education by advancing professionalism, encouraging leadership, pursuing lifelong learning and building community. Serve educators in their efforts to strengthen the Conservative Movement and inspire greater Jewish learning. JEA will be the leading advocate for the welfare of the Jewish educator and for the best practices in Jewish education.

Fred Nathan, President
Edward Edelstein, Executive Director

81 John Dewey Society for the Study of Education & Culture
1801 NW 11th Road
Gainesville, FL 32605-5323
352-378-7365
http://www.johndeweysociety.org
Founded in 1935, John Dewey's commitment to the use of critical and reflective intelligence in the search for solutions to crucial problems in education and culture.

Deron Boyles, President
Kyle Greenwalt, Secretary/Treasurer

82 Learning Disabilities Association of America (LDA)
Learning Disabilities Association of America
4156 Library Road
Pittsburgh, PA 15234-1349
412-341-1515
888-300-6710
Fax: 412-344-0224
E-mail: info@ldaamerica.org
http://www.ldanatl.org
(LDA) is a national network, with 14, 00 national state and local members individuals with learning disabilities, their families and the professionals who work with them. LDA is dedicated to identifying causes and promoting prevention of learning disabilities and to enhancing the quality of life for all individuals with learning disabilities and their families by encouraging effectiveidentification, interventions, fostering research and protecting their rights under the law.

Founded: 1963

Patricia Latham, President
B J Wiemer, VP

83 Lutheran Education Association
7400 Augusta Street
River Forest, IL 60305
708-209-3343
Fax: 708-209-3458
E-mail: lea@lea.org
http://www.lea.org
Seeks to spark ideas, thoughts and practices among Lutherans. The Lutheran Education Association links, equips and affirms educators and workers in ministry for the purpose of building up the body of Christ.

Dr Jonathan Laabs, Executive Director
Kathy Slupik, Executive Assistant

84 MATRIX: A Parent Network and Resource Center
94 Galli Drive
Suite C
Novato, CA 94949
415-884-3535
800-578-2592
Fax: 415-884-3555
E-mail: info@matrixparnets.org
http://www.matrixparents.org
Matrix provides training and information to parents of children of any age with all disabilities-physical, cognitive, emotional and learning. The Matrix network consists of parent training and info centers, family empowerment centers and family resource centers.

Nora Thompson, Executive Director
Deborah Daniels-Smith, Technical Assistance Coord.

85 National Academy of Education
500 5th Street, NW
Washington, DC 20001-9580
202-334-2341
Fax: 202-334-2350
E-mail: info@naeducation.org
http://www.naeducation.org
Advances quality education research and its use in policy formation and practice. Offers professional development fellowship programs as well.

Susan Fuhrman, President
Edward Haertel, VP

86 National Alliance for Safe Schools
PO Box 335
Slanesville, WV 25444-0335
304-496-8100
888-510-6500
Fax: 304-496-8105
E-mail: nass@frontiernet.net
http://www.safeschools.org
Founded in 1977 NASS a non-profit corporation, ascribes to the belief that schools need to take back control and identify what the local issues are that may be causing fear and anxiety on the part of the students and staff. Once local issues have been identified, school administrators, working with students, teachers, parents and support staff, are able to effect change.

Peter D Blauvelt, CEO/President

87 National Association For Gifted Children
1331 H St NW
Suite 1001
Washington, DC 20005
202-785-4268
Fax: 202-785-4248
E-mail: nagc@nagc.org
http://www.nagc.org
Organization of parents, teachers, educators, other professionals, and community leaders who unite to address the unique needs of children and youth with demonstrated gifts and talents as well as those children who may be able to develop their talent potential with appropriate educational experiences.

Nancy Green, Executive Director
Paula Olszewski-Kubilius, President

88 National Association for Asian and Pacific American Education
PO Box 3471
Palos Verdes Peninsula, CA 90274
818-677-6853
Fax: 818-366-2714
E-mail: naapae@naapae.net
http://www.naapae.net
Objectives are to enhance awareness of multicultural studies in the United States as well as to promote the inclusion of Asian and Pacific American culture and history into the school curriculum. In addition to these, NAAPAE looks to maintain a network of educators and community members to share information and resources, support research on Asian and Pacific American educational needs and encourage Asian and Pacific Americans to aim for leadership roles.
Founded: 1977

John N Tsuchida, President
Betty Jeung, Vice President

89 National Association for Developmental Education (NADE)
500 N Estrella Parkway
Suite B2 PMB 412
Goodyear, AZ 85338
877-233-9455
Fax: 623-792-5747
E-mail: office@nade.net
http://www.nade.net

Seeks to improve the theory and practice of developmental educational all levels of the educational spectrum, the professional capabilities of developmental educators and the design of programs to prepare developmental educators. "Helping underprepared students prepare, prepared students advance, and advanced students excel"

Rebecca Goosen, M.S., Ed.S., Ed.D, President
Patti Levine-Brown, MPA, Ed.S., Vice President

90 National Association for Legal Support of Alternative Schools (NALSAS)
PO Box 2823
Santa Fe, NM 87504-2823
505-474-0300
E-mail: nalsas@msn.com
http://www.nalsas.org/
It was originally designed to help interested persons/organizations locate/evaluate/create viable alternatives to traditional schooling approaches including home study.
Founded: 1973

Ed Nagel, CEO

91 National Association for Year-Round Education
PO Box 711386
San Diego, CA 92171-1386
619-276-5296
Fax: 858-571-5754
E-mail: info@nayre.org
http://www.NAYRE.org
Founded in 1972 NAYRE fosters and disseminates information about year-round education as a way to improve educational programs.

Richard Coleman, President
Sam Pepper, Executive Director

92 National Association of Catholic School Teachers
1700 Sansom Street
Suite 903
Philadelphia, PA 19103
215-665-0993
800-996-2278
Fax: 215-568-8270
E-mail: Rita@NACST.com
http://www.nacst.com
Unifies, advises and assists Catholic school teachers in matters of collective bargaining.

Rita C Schwartz, President
William Blumstein, Executive Vice President

93 National Association of Federally Impacted Schools
Hall of the States
444 N Capitol Street NW
Suite 419
Washington, DC 20001-1512
202-624-5455
Fax: 202-624-5468
E-mail: johnfork@nafisdc.org
http://www.nafisdc.org
NAFIS is a corporation of school districts through the country organized primarily to educate Congress on Impact Aid. The association works to ensure that the needs of federally connected children are met with adequate federal funds.

John Forkenbrock, Executive Director
Rick Carson, President

94 National Association of Secondary School Principals
1904 Association Drive
Reston, VA 20191-1537

703-860-0200
866-647-7253
Fax: 703-476-5432
E-mail: nhs@nassp.org
http://www.nassp.org
NASSP promotes excellence in middle level and high school leadership through research based professional development, resources, and advocacy so that every student can be prepared for postsecondary learning opportunities and be workforce ready.

JoAnn Bartoletti, Executive Director
Denise Greene-Wilkinson, President

95 National Association of Special Education Teachers
1250 Connecticut Avenue NW
Suite 200
Washington, DC 20036
800-754-4421
E-mail: contactus@naset.org
http://www.naset.org
Dedicated to rendering all possible support and assistance to professionals who teach children with special needs.

Roger Pierangelo, Executive Director
George Giuliani, Executive Director

96 National Association of State Boards of Education
2121 Crystal Drive
Suite 350
Arlington, VA 22202
703-684-4000
800-368-5023
Fax: 703-836-2313
E-mail: boards@nasbe.org
http://www.nasbe.org
NASBE works to strengthen state leadership in educational policymaking, promote excellence in the education of all students, advocate equality of access to educational opportunity, and assure continued citizen support for public education.

Jim Kohlmoos, CEO
Bradley Hall, Deputy Director

97 National Association of Student Councils (NASC)
1904 Association Drive
Reston, VA 20191
703-860-0200
866-647-7253
Fax: 703-476-5432
E-mail: nasc@nasc.us
http://www.nasc.us
Promote student participation within school and its community, encourage development of new student councils, assist in student councils becoming more effective, assist state associations of student councils, provide leadership training for council members and advisors, encourage and support healthy living for young poeple.

Scott D Thompson, Executive Officer

98 National Association of Trade & Industrial Instructors
Canadian Valley Vo Tech
6505 East Highway 66
El Reno, OK 73036-579
405-262-2629
Fax: 405-422-2354
Founded in 1965 the National Association of Trade and Industrial Instructors seeks to improve communication among members and to support the needs of classroom teachers.

Carol McNish, President
Greg Winters, Superintendent

99 National Board for Professional Teaching Standards
11827 Tech Com
Suite 200
San Antonio, TX 78233
888-780-7805
Fax: 888-811-3514
http://www.nbpts.org
Formed to advance the quality of teaching and learning by developing professional standards for accomplished teaching, creating a voluntary system to certify teachers who meet those standards and integration certified teachers into educational reform efforts.
Founded: 1987

100 National Catholic Educational Association
1005 N Glebe Rd
Suite 525
Arlington, VA 22201
800-711-6232
Fax: 703-243-0025
E-mail: nceaadmin@ncea.org
http://www.ncea.org
Rooted in the Gospel of Jesus Christ, the National Catholic Educational Association (NCEA) is a professional membership organization that provides leadership, direction and service to fulfill the evangelizing, catechizing and teaching mission of the Church.
Karen M Ristau, President
Wilton Gregory, Chairman

101 National Center For School Engagement
450 Lincoln St
Suite 100
Denver, CO 80203
303-837-8466
E-mail: info@schoolengagement.org
http://www.schoolengagement.org
Provides training and technical assistance, research and evaluation to school districts, law enforcement agencies, courts, as well as state and federal agencies.
Ken Seeley, Founder/CEO

102 National Center for Learning Disabilities
381 Park Avenue S
Suite 1401
New York, NY 10016
212-545-7510
888-575-7373
Fax: 212-545-9665
E-mail: ncld@ncld.org
http://www.ncld.org
The National Center for Learning Disabilities (NCLD) works to ensure that the nation's 15 million children, adolescents and adults with learning disabilities have every opportunity to succeed in school, work and life.
Frederic M Poses, Chairman of the Board
James H Wendorf, Executive Director

103 National Coalition for Parent Involvement in Education (NCPIE)
1400 L Street NW
Suite 300
Washington, DC 20005
202-289-6790
Fax: 202-289-6791
E-mail: ferguson@ncpie.org
http://www.ncpie.org/
National Coalition for Parent Involvement in Education (NCPIE) advocates the involvement of parents and families in their children's education, and to foster relationships between home, school, and commu-

nity to enhance the education of all our nation's young people.
Sue Ferguson, Chairperson
Hilda Crespo, Vice President

104 National Coalition of Alternative Community Schools
1129 Gault Drive
Ypsilanti, MI 48198
734-483-7040
888-771-9171
Fax: 734-482-7436
E-mail: ncacs2@earthlink.net
http://www.ncacs.org
Our mission is to unite and organize a grassroots movement of learners and learning communities dedicated to participant control, liberation from all forms of oppression, and the pursuit of freedom.
Terri Wheeler, Treasurer

105 National Coalition of Independent Scholars
PO Box 19302
Jonesboro, AR 72403
E-mail: Info@NCIS.org
http://www.ncis.org
Provide information for the creation of local organizations of independent scholars
Founded: 1989
Lisa Purry, President
Jolanta Wrobel Best, Vice President

106 National Commission for Cooperative Education
WACE
Suite 125
600 Suffolk Street
Lowell, MA 01854
Fax: 978-934-4084
E-mail: ncce@co-op.edu
http://www.co-op.edu
Organization linking higher institutions, employers and public authorities through research, programs, and services designed to advance learning where education and work experience are linked.
Founded: 1962
Dr Paul J Stonely, CEO
Marty Ford, Director

107 National Consortium for Academics and Sports
University of Central Florida
PO Box 161400
Orlando, FL 32816-1400
407-823-4770
Fax: 407-823-3542
E-mail: rlapchick@bus.ucf.edu
http://www.ncasports.org
To create a better society by focusing on educational attainment and using the power and appeal of sport to positively affect social change.
Founded: 1985
Dr Richard Lapchick, President/CEO
Keith L Lee, VP

108 National Council for Black Studies
National Council for Black Studies
University of Cincinnati
Africana Studies Department, Box 210370
Cincinnati, OH 45221-0370
513-556-0785
E-mail: info@ncbsonline.org
http://www.ncbsonline.org
Promote academic excellence and social responsibility in the discipline of Africana/Black Studies through the production and dissemination of knowledge,

professional development and training, and advocacy for social change and social justice.
Sundiata Cha-Jua, President
Amilcar Shabazz, Secretary

109 National Council for Science and the Environment
1101 17th Street NW
Suite 250
Washington, DC 20036
202-530-5810
Fax: 202-628-4311
E-mail: ncse@ncseonline.org
http://www.ncseonline.org
Improve the scientific basis of environmental decision making through an accurate understanding of the underlying science, its meaning and limitations, and the potential consequences of their action or inaction.
Founded: 1990
David Blockstein, Ph.D., Senior Scientist
Peter Saundry, Executive Director

110 National Council of Higher Education
National Education Association (NEA)
1201 16th Street NW
Room 410
Washington, DC 20036-3290
202-833-4000
Fax: 202-822-7974
E-mail: nche@nea.org
http://www.nea.org
Our mission is to advocate for education professionals and to unite our members and the nation to fulfill the promise of public education to prepare every student to succeed in a diverse and interdependent world
Dennis Van Roekel, President
Lily Eskelsen, VP

111 National Council of Urban Education Associations
National Education Association (NEA)
1201 16th Street NW
Washington, DC 20036-3290
202-833-4000
Fax: 202-822-7974
E-mail: ncuea@nea.org
http://www.nea.org
NCUEA is a caucus of local affiliates of the National Education Association (NEA), which is dedicated to strengthening member advocacy and making the NEA more responsive to member needs. Promote and advance high quality Public Education is urban schools by empowering and supporting local associations, leaders and members.
Dennis Van Roekel, President
Lily Eskelsen, VP

112 National Council on Measurement in Education
2424 American Lane
Suite 3800
Madison, WI 53704
608-443-2487
Fax: 608-443-2474
E-mail: plovelace@ncme.org
http://www.ncme.org
NCME is a professional organization for individuals involved in assessment, evaluation, testing, and other aspects of educational measurement
Plumer Lovelace III, Executive Director
Jane Shepard, Administrative Officer

113 National Council on Rehabilitation Education (NCRE)
1099 E. Champlain Drive
Suite A, PMB #137
Fresno, CA 90720
559-906-0787
Fax: 559-412-2550

E-mail: info@ncre.org
http://www.ncre.org
A professional organization of educators dedicated to quality services for persons with disabilities through education and research.
Jared C. Schultz, PhD, CRC, LVRC, President
Maureen McGuire-Kuletz, EdD, CRC, Vice-President

114   National Council on Student Development (NCSD)
PO Box 3948
Parker, CO 80134
866-972-0717
Fax: 303-755-7363
E-mail: ncsd@ncsdonline.org
http://www.ncsdonline.org
NCSD is to promote knowledge, expertise and professional development opportunities; support decision-making based on empirical and ethical principles, and demonstrate a commitment to the personal and professional advancement of student development professionals through advocacy and education.
Nicole Singleton, Executive Director
Daniel Herbst, President

115   National Dissemination Center for Children with Disabilities
1825 Connecticut Ave NW
Suite 700
Washington, DC 20009
202-884-8200
800-695-0285
Fax: 202-884-8441
E-mail: nichcy@fhi360.org
http://www.nichcy.org
The center that provides information to the nation on disabilities in children and youth; programs and services for infants, children, and youth with disabilities; IDEA, the nation's special education law; No Child Left Behind, the nation's general education law; and research-based information on effective practices for children with disabilities.
Lisa Savard, Sales/Marketing Director
Suzanne Ripley, Project Director

116   National Education Association
1201 16th Street NW
Washington, DC 20036-3290
202-833-4000
Fax: 202-822-7974
E-mail: ncuea@nea.org
http://www.nea.org
Advocate for education professionals in the effort to prepare every student to succeed in a diverse world.
Dennis Van Roekel, President
Lily Eskelsen, VP

117   National Education Association Student Program
National Education Association (NEA)
1201 16th Street NW
Washington, DC 20036-3290
202-833-4000
Fax: 202-822-7974
E-mail: ncuea@nea.org
http://www.nea.org
Strive to promote community partnerships; foster leadership through pre-professional opportunities and peer mentoring; promote membership among diverse populations, provide networking support; supplement formal teacher-education training, promote the national accreditation of teacher-education training; recruit and retain pre-professional members and maintain a presence at all NEA conferences.
Dennis Van Roekel, President
Lily Eskelsen, VP

118   National Education Association-Retired
National Education Association (NEA)
1201 16th Street NW
Washington, DC 20036-3290
202-833-4000
Fax: 202-822-7974
http://www.nea.org/retired
NEA-Retired exists to meet the needs of retired education employees.
Barbara Matteson, President
Tom Curran, Vice President

119   National Education Policy Institute
National Alliance of Black School Educators
310 Pennsylvania Avenue
Washington, DC 20003
202-608-6310
800-221-2654
Fax: 202-608-6319
E-mail: info@nabse.org
http://www.nabse.org
NABSE is the nation's premiere non-profit organization devoted to furthering the academic success for the nation's children - particularly children of African descent. NABSE is dedicated to improving both the educational experiences and accomplishments of African American youth through the development and use of instructional and motivational methods that increase levels of inspiration, attendance and overall achievement.
Bernard Hamilton, Ed.D., President
Quentin Lawson, Executive Director

120   National Lekotek Center
2001 N Clybourn
Chicago, IL 60614
773-528-5766
800-366-7529
Fax: 773-537-2992
E-mail: lekotek@lekotek.org
http://www.lekotek.org
Therapeutic toy lending library and play education for children ages 0-8 with disabilities. Lekotek uses interactive play experiences and the learning that results to promote the inclusion of children with special needs into family and community life.
Deidre Pate Omahen, Director of Programs
Macy Welch, Executive Director

121   National Organization on Disability
77 Water Street
Suite 204
New York, NY 10005
646-505-1191
Fax: 646-505-1184
E-mail: info@nod.org
http://www.nod.org
Expands the participation and contribution of America's 54 million men, women and children with disabilities in all aspects of life. By raising disability awareness through programs and information, together we can work toward closing the participation gaps.
Carol Glazer, President
Governor Tom Ridge, Chairman

122   National Rural Education Association
Purdue University
Beering Hall of Liberal Arts & Ed
100 N University St
W Lafayette, IN 47907
765-494-0086
Fax: 765-496-1228
E-mail: jehill@purdue.edu
http://www.nrea.net
Organization of rural school administrators, teachers, board members, regional service agency personnel, researchers, business and industry representatives and others interested in maintaining the vitality of rural school systems across the country.
Founded: 1907
Dr. John Hill, Executive Director
Phil Gerik, President

123   National School Boards Association
1680 Duke Street
Alexandria, VA 22314-3455
703-838-6722
Fax: 703-683-7590
E-mail: info@nsba.org
http://www.nsba.org
Not-for-profit Federation of state associations of school boards across the United States. Its mission is to foster excellence and equity in public education through school board leadership.
Thomas Gentzel, Executive Director
Marie Bilik, CEO

124   National School Public Relations Association
15948 Derwood Road
Rockville, MD 20855
301-519-0496
Fax: 301-519-0494
E-mail: nspra@nspra.org
http://www.nspra.org
Advance education through responsible public relations and communication that leads to success for all students. This can be accomplished by developing and providing a variety of diverse projects, services and professional development ideas to our members as well as to other education leaders interested in improving their communication efforts.
Rich Bagin, APR, Executive Director
Karen H. Kleinz, APR, Associate Director

125   National Society for Experiential Education
19 Mantua Road
Mt. Royal, NJ 08061
856-423-3427
Fax: 856-423-3420
E-mail: nsee.@talley.com
http://www.nsee.org
National Society for Experiential Education (NSEE) is a nonprofit membership association of educators, businesses, and community leaders. NSEE also serves as a national resource center for the development and improvement of experiential education programs nationwide.
Founded: 1971
Ron Kovach, President
Jim Colbert, VP

126   National Society for the Study of Education (NSSE)
University of Illinois at Chicago
525 W 120th Street
New York, NY 10027
312-996-4529
773-702-7748
Fax: 773-702-9756
E-mail: nsse@uic.edu
http://www.nsse-chicago.org/
The National Society for the Study of Education (NSSE) is an organization of education scholars, professional educators, and policy makers dedicated to the improvement of education research, policy, and practice. NSSE's mission is to advance the study and practice of education by providing accessible scholarship and promoting informed discourse about

the challenges and opportunities of education in a democratic society.

Founded: 2008

David Hansen, Board of Directors
Deborah Loewenberg Ball, Board of Directors

127   National Student Exchange

4656 W Jefferson Boulevard
Suite 140
Fort Wayne, IN 46804
260-436-2634
Fax: 260-436-5676
E-mail: bworley@nse2.org
http://www.nse.org
The National Student Exchange (NSE) is a program for undergraduate exchange within the United States and Canada. Instead of crossing oceans, NSE students cross state, regional, provincial, and cultural borders. NSE students gain insight into the historical and cultural makeup of different regions, improve their communication skills with individuals from different backgrounds and prepare themselves to live and work in a culturally diverse society.

Founded: 1968

Bette Worley, President
Wendel Wickland, Vice President

128   National Telemedia Council

517 N Segoe Rd
Suite 210
Madison, WI 53703
608-274-3107
Fax: 608-257-7714
E-mail: ntc@danenet.wicip.org
http://www.danenet.org
Offers on-site technical support, technical training and technical planning and consulting services. DANEnet is dedicated to helping Dane County non-profits find and use quality information technology that efficiently serves their mission.

Eric Howland, Director
John Jordan, Community Outreach

129   National Women's Student Coalition (NWSC)

United States Student Association
1211 Connecticut Avenue NW
Suite 406
Washington, DC 20036
202-640-6570
Fax: 202-223-4005
E-mail: ussa@usstudents.org
http://www.usstudents.org
National Women's Student Coalition (NWSC), an affiliate of the United States Student Association, provides a space for women of different economic backgrounds, races, sexual orientations, religions and abilities to come together and strategize ways to increase campus safety, diversity, fight against bias related violence and build women's leadership.

Tiffany Dena Loftin, President
Sophia Zaman, VP

130   National Women's Studies Association

National Women's Studies Association
11 E. Mount Royal Avenue
Suite 110
Baltimore, MD 21202
410-528-0355
Fax: 410-528-0357
E-mail: nwsaoffice@nwsa.org
http://www.nwsa.org
The National Women's Studies Association shows the ways in which women's studies are vital to education; demonstrate

the contributions of feminist scholarship; and to promote relationships between scholarship, teaching and civic engagement in understandings of culture and society.

Founded: 1977

Allison Kimmich, Executive Director
Bonnie Thornton Dill, President

131   Native American Homeschool Association

474 Brush Creek Road
Fries, VA 24330
540-636-1020
Fax: 540-636-1464
http://www.expage.com/page/nahomeschool2
Association of Native American homeschoolers.

Misty Dawn Thomas Ruff, Tribal Chairwoman

132   New England School Development Council

28 Lord Rd
#210
Marlborough, MA 01752
508-481-9444
Fax: 508-481-5655
http://www.nesdec.org
Helps schools achieve and maintain high performing status through education management tools.

133   North American Association for Environmental Education (NAAEE)

2000 P Street NW
Suite 540
Washington, DC 20036
202-419-0412
Fax: 202-419-0415
E-mail: info@naaee.net
http://www.naaee.net
Teaches children and adults how to learn about and investigate their environment and to make intelligent, informed decisions about how they can take care of it.

October

Judy Braus, Executive Director
Christiane Maertens, Deputy Director

134   North American Association of Educational Negotiators

PO Box 1068
Salem, OR 97308
503-588-2800
Fax: 503-588-2813
E-mail: execdir@naen.org
http://www.naen.org
Improves the knowledge and performance of K-12 school district, community college, and university, management negotiators by advancing their professional status, providing a forum for effective communication, and encourage information exchanges among educational negotiators.

Linda Goers, President
Lisa Freiley, President-Elect

135   North American Students of Cooperation

PO Box 180048
Chicago, IL 60618-7715
773-404-2667
Fax: 773-404-2668
E-mail: info@nasco.coop
http://www.nasco.coop
Organizes and educates affordable group equity co-ops and their members for the

purpose of promoting a community oriented co-operative movement.

Tom Pierson, Executive Director
Jim Jones, Sr Director of Development

136   Northwest Commission on Colleges and Universities

1910 University Drive
Boise, ID 83725
208-426-1000
Fax: 208-334-3228
E-mail: sclemens@boisestate.edu
http://www.boisestate.edu
Assure educational quality, enhance institutional effectiveness, and foster continuous improvement of colleges and universities in the Northwest region through analytical institutional self-assessment and critical peer review based upon evaluation criteria that are objectively and equitably applied to institutions with diverse missions, characteristics and cultures.

Bob Kustra, President
Sona Andrews, Vice President for Academic

137   Odyssey of the Mind

Creative Competitions, Inc.
406 Ganttown Road
Sewell, NJ 08080
856-256-2797
Fax: 856-256-2798
E-mail: info@odysseyofthemind.com
http://www.odysseyofthemind.com
An international educational program that provides creative problem-solving opportunities for students from kindergarten through college. With creativity and imaginative paths to problem solving, students learn skills that will provide them with the ability to solve problems for a lifetime.

Samuel Micklus, Founder

138   PACER Center

8161 Normandale Boulevard
Bloomington, MN 55437
952-838-9000
888-248-0822
Fax: 952-838-0199
E-mail: pacer@pacer.org
http://www.pacer.org
Founded in 1976 PACER a coalition of organizations founded on the concept of Parents Helping Parents. PACER strives to improve and expand opportunities that enhance the quality of life for children and young adults with disabilities and their families. Helps parents become informed and effective representatives for their children in early childhood, school-age and vocational settings through agencies and appropriate service.

Paula F Goldberg, Executive Director
Mary Schrock, CEO

139   Parents, Let's Unite for Kids

516 N 32nd Street
Billings, MT 59101-6003
406-255-0540
800-222-7585
Fax: 406-255-0523
E-mail: info@pluk.org
http://www.pluk.org
Parent's Let's Unite for Kids unites parents, professionals, families and friends of children with special needs to support one another, and share information for the benefit of their children.

Founded: 1984

William J O'Connor II, President
Dave Rye, Vice President

140   Peace & Justice Studies Association

220 Grove Avenue
Prescott, AZ 86301
928-350-2008
E-mail: randall@peacejusticestudies.org
http://www.peacejusticestudies.org

Bring together academics, K-12 teachers and grassroots activists to explore alternatives to violence and share visions and strategies for peacebuilding, social justice and social change. PJSA also serves as a professional association for scholars in the filed of peace and conflict resolution studies and is the North-American affiliate of the International Peace Research Association.

Founded: 2001

Randall Amster, Executive Director
Cris Toffolo, Board Co-Chair

141 Public Relations Student Society of America
33 Maiden Lane
11th Floor
New York, NY 10038-5150
212-460-1474
Fax: 212-995-0757
E-mail: prssa@prsa.org
http://www.prssa.org
The PRSSA is the foremost organization for students interested in public relations and communications. We seek to advance the public relations profession by nurturing generations of future professionals. We advocate rigorous academic standards for public relations education, the highest ethical principles and diversity in the profession.

Lauren Gray, National President
Jeneen Garcia, VP

142 Religious Education Association (REA)
PO Box 200392
Evans, CO 80620-0392
765-225-8836
Fax: 970-351-1269
E-mail: reaapprre@msn.com
http://www.religiouseducation.net
Creates opportunities for exploring and advancing the interconnected practices of scholarship, research, teaching, and leadership in faith communities, academic institutions, and the wider world community.

Dr Lucinda Huffaker, REA Executive Secretary
Yolanda Smith, President

143 STEM Education Coalition
700 North One Lafayette Center
1120 20th Street NW
Washington, DC 20036
202-223-1187
Fax: 202-973-8211
http://www.stemedcoalition.org
Works to raise awareness in congress, the administration, and other organizations about the critical role that STEM education plays in enabling the U.S to remain the economic and technological leader of the global marketplace of the 21st century.

James Brown, Executive Director

144 Sexuality Information & Education Council of the US
90 John Street
Suite 704
New York, NY 10038
212-819-9770
Fax: 212-819-9776
E-mail: mrodriguez@siecus.org
http://www.siecus.org
SIECUS promotes sexuality education for people of all ages, protect sexual rights, and expand access to sexual health services. SIECUS trains educators, advocates for the sound public policies related to sexuality, and provides information and resources on a host of sexuality topics.

Monica Rodriguez, President/CEO
Jason Osher, COO

145 Society for the Advancement of Excellence in Education (SAEE)
1889 Springfield Road
Suite 225
Kelowna, BC V1Y-5V5
250-717-1163
Fax: 250-717-1134
E-mail: info@saee.ca
http://www.saee.ca/
Provides non-partisan education research and information to policy-makers, education partners and the public. Our purpose is to encourage higher performance throughout Canada's public education system.

Founded: 1996

Elizabeth Bredberg, Research Director
Mame McCrea Silva, General Manager

146 Solution Tree
555 North Morton Street
Bloomington, IN 47404
812-336-7700
800-733-6786
Fax: 812-336-7790
E-mail: info@solution-tree.com
http://www.nes.org
Strive to be the premier provider of books, videos, multimedia resources, and professional development opportunities designed to help educators throughout the United States and Canada realize continuous school improvement and connect with youth at risk.

Founded: 1987

Karen Bailey, Representative
Deb McDonald, Representative

147 Southeastern Library Association
PO Box 950
Rex, GA 30273
678-466-4334
Fax: 678-466-4349
E-mail: gordonbaker@clayton.edu
http://selaonline.org
A unifying force strong enough to influence legislation and to attract foundation and federal funds for regional library projects. This has resulted in two regional library surveys, the adoption of school library standards, the establishment of state library agencies and the position state school library supervisor; the founding of library schools; the sponsoring of a variety of informative workshops and the publication of significant regional research.

Michael Seigler, President
Gordon Baker, Vice President

148 Summit Vision
5640 Lynx Drive
Westerville, OH 43081
614-403-3891
Fax: 614-895-8326
E-mail: tmcbane@wideopenwest.com
http://www.summit-vision.com
Summit Vision believes that through the use of adventure and experiential learning tools, people have the opportunity to reach their full potential—both individually and as part of a larger team.

Trey McBane, President
Larissa Kopestonsky, VP

149 Teach Plus
374 Congress St
Suite 502
Boston, MA 02210
617-428-0700
E-mail: info@teachplus.org
http://www.teachplus.org
To improve the outcomes for urban children by ensuring that a greater proportion of students have access to effective, experienced teachers.

150 Utah Library Association (ULA)
PO Box 708155
Sandy, UT 84070-8155
801-200-3129
E-mail: anna.neatrour@gmail.com
http://ula.org
The mission of the Utah Library Association is to serve the professional development and educational needs of its members and to provide leadership and direction in developing and improving library and information services in the state. The Association also initiates and supports legislation promoting library development and monitors legislation that might threaten Utah libraries and librarians.

Andy Spackman, President
Anna Neatrour, Executive Director

151 Wilderness Education Association
2150 N 107th St.
Suite 205
Seattle, WA 98133
206-367-8704
800-572-3015
Fax: 206-367-8777
E-mail: nationaloffice@weainfo.org
http://www.weainfo.org
The Wilderness Education Association is a not-for-profit organization whose purpose is to educate the general public and outdoor leaders in the appropriate use of wildlands and protected areas by developing and implementing educational curricula, programs and by forming strategic alliances with federal land management agencies, conservation groups and all organizations that benefit from wildlands and feel that the existence of wildlands is important to the quality of life

Ricky Haro, VP
Mike McGowan, President

152 World Trade Centers Association
420 Lexington Avenue
Suite 518
New York, NY 10170
212-432-2626
800-937-8886
E-mail: wtcawtca.org
http://wtcaonline.com
Fosters a global Trade Center Network that enhances the brand and promotes prosperity through trade and investment.

Ghazi Abu Nahl, Chairman
Bella Heule, President

General

153 Music Teachers National Association
441 Vine Street
Suite 3100
Cincinnati, OH 45202-3004
513-421-1420
888-512-5278
Fax: 513-421-2503
E-mail: mtnanet@mtna.org
http://www.mtna.org
Advance the value of music study and music making to society while supporting the careers and professionalism of teachers of music. MTNA provides a collective voice for teachers worldwide and powerful alliance for music teaching professionals.

Gary Ingle, Executive Director
Benjamin D. Caton, President

Administration

154 American Association of Collegiate Registrars & Admissions Officers
1 Dupont Circle NW
Suite 520
Washington, DC 20036
202-293-9161
Fax: 202-872-8857
E-mail: reillym@aacrao.org
http://www.aacrao.org
Promotes higher education and furthers the professional development of members working in admissions, enrollment management, financial aid, institutional research, records and registration.

Michael Reilly, Executive Director
Martha Henebry,
Membership/Publications Dir

155 American Association of School Administrators
1615 Duke Street
Alexandria, VA 22314
703-528-0700
Fax: 703-841-1543
E-mail: Info@aasa.org
http://www.aasa.org
The mission of the American Association of School Administrators is to support and develop effective school system leaders who are dedicated to the highest quality public education for all children

Daniel A Domenech, Executive Director
Chuck Woodruff, Associate Executive Director

156 American Education Finance Association (AEFA)
258 Norman Hall
PO Box 117049
Gainesville, FL 32611-7049
352-392-2391
Fax: 303-670-8986
E-mail: AEFA@coe.ufl.edu
http://www.afajof.org
Promotes understanding of means by which resources are generated, distributed and used to enhance human learning.

Founded: 1976

Sheridan Titman, President
Robert Stambaugh, President-Elect

157 Association of School Business Officials International
ASBO International Annual Meetings and Exhibits
11401 N Shore Drive
Reston, VA 20190-4200
703-478-0405
866-682-2729
Fax: 703-708-7060
E-mail: jmusso@asbointl.org
http://www.asbointl.org
Provide programs and services to promote the highest standards of school business management practices, professional growth, and the effective use of educational resources.

Founded: 1910

John D Musso, Executive Director
Charles E Linderman, President

158 Council of Chief State School Officers
1 Massachusetts Avenue NW
Suite 700
Washington, DC 20001-1431
202-336-7000
Fax: 202-408-8072

E-mail: info@ccsso.org
http://www.ccsso.org
Envision a system of schooling in each state that ensures high standards of performance and prepares each child to succeed as a productive member of a democratic society.

Mitchell Chester, President
Terry Holiday, President Elect

159 Independent Schools Association of the Central States
1165 N Clark Street
Suite 311
Chicago, IL 60610
312-255-1244
Fax: 312-255-1278
E-mail: info@isacs.org
http://www.isacs.org
The purpose of ISACS is to promote the development of strong learning communities characterized by high achievements, social responsibility, and independence of governance, programs and policies.

1165 pages

Keith Shahan, President
Amanda Brown, Program Manager

160 NASPA - Student Affairs Administrators in Higher Education
111 K Street, NE
10th Floor
Washington, DC 20002
202-265-7500
Fax: 202-898-5737
E-mail: office@naspa.org
http://www.naspa.org
NASPA is the leading voice for student affairs administration, policy, and practice, and affirms the commitment of the student affairs profession to educating the whole student and integrating student life and learning. With more than 12,000 members at 1,400 campuses, and representing 29 countries, NASPA is the foremost professional association for student affairs administrators, faculty, and graduate and undergraduate students.

Kevin Kruger, President

161 National Association for Supervision and Curriculum Development (ASCD)
1703 N Beauregard Street
Alexandria, VA 22311-1714
703-578-9600
800-933-2723
Fax: 703-575-5400
E-mail: member@ascd.org
http://www.ascd.org
A membership organization that develops programs, products, and services essential to the way educators learn, teach, and lead.

Kathy Clayton, Executive Director
Debra Hill, President

162 National Association of Elementary School Principals
1615 Duke Street
Alexandria, VA 22314-3483
703-684-3345
800-386-2377
Fax: 703-549-5568
E-mail: naesp@naesp.org
http://www.naesp.org
Advocate for support principals need to achieve the highest results for children, families and communities.

Gail Connelly, Executive Director
Ernie Mannino, CEO

163 National Association of Principals of Schools for Girls (NAPSG)
23490 Caraway Lakes Drive
Bonita Springs, FL 34135-8441
239-947-6196
Fax: 239-390-3245
E-mail: napsg@mac.com
http://www.napsg.org
Provides forum for school leaders to learn from each other in the interest of the education of girls and young women.

Bruce W Galbraith, Executive Director
Bessie Speers, President

164 National Association of Private Schools for Exceptional Children
1522 K Street NW
Washington, DC 20005
202-408-3338
Fax: 202-408-3340
E-mail: napsec@aol.com
http://www.napsec.org
Provides funding for educational, research and charitable activities, and special projects for NAPSEC and/or other related and similar organizations.

Founded: 1971

Sherry Kolbe, Executive Director

165 National Association of Secondary School Principals
1904 Association Drive
Reston, VA 20191-1537
703-860-0200
800-253-7746
Fax: 703-476-5432
E-mail: nhs@nassp.org
http://www.nassp.org
To promote excellence in school leadership and to provide members with a wide variety of programs and services to assist them in administration, supervision, curriculum planning, and effective staff development.

JoAnn D. Bartoletti, Executive Director
Denise Greene-Wilkinson, President

166 National Association of State Directors of Special Education
225 Reinekers Lane
Suite 420
Alexandria, VA 22314
703-519-3800
Fax: 703-519-3808
E-mail: nasdse@nasdse.org
http://www.nasdse.org
A nonprofit corporation that promotes and supports education programs for students with disabilities in the United States and outlying areas.

Colleen Riley, President
Bill East, Executive Director

167 National Association of Student Financial Aid Administrators
1101 Connecticut Avenue NW
Suite 1100
Washington, DC 20036-4303
202-785-0453
Fax: 202-785-1487
E-mail: Web@NASFAA.org
http://www.nasfaa.org
A nonprofit corporation of postsecondary institutions, individuals, agencies and students interested in promoting the effective administration of student financial aid in the United States.

Justin Draeger, President/CEO
Ron Day, National Chair

168 National Council of State Directors of Adult Education
444 N Capitol Street, NW
Suite 422
Washington, DC 20001

202-624-5250
Fax: 202-624-1497
E-mail: dc2@ncsdae.org
http://www.ncsdae.org
to attend to legislative needs and concerns, to work with other adult education organizations, to exchange ideas and solve common problems, and to establish and maintain a nationwide communication network regarding national policy and legislative issues.
Founded: 1967

Reecie Stagnolia, Chairman
Dr Lennox McLendon, Executive Director

169 National Data Bank for Disabled Student Services
University of Maryland
Room 0126, Shoemaker Building
College Park, MD 20742
301-314-7682
301-314-7682
Fax: 301-405-0813
http://www.inform.umd.edu
Provides assessment of statistics related to services, staff, budget and other components of disabled student services programs across the country.

Vivian S Boyd, Director
Jo Ann Hutchinson, Assistant Director, DSS

170 National Institute for School and Workplace Safety
257 Plaza Drive
Suite B
Oviedo, FL 32765-6457
407-366-4878
Fax: 407-977-1210
http://www.nisws.com
Believes that every school and workplace must implement school and workplace safety standards. Committed to enhance school and workplace safety and to increase awareness of school and workplace safety issues.

Steven Burhoe, CEO

171 National School Safety Center
141 Duesenberg Drive
Suite 7B
Westlake Village, CA 91362-3815
805-373-9977
Fax: 805-373-9277
E-mail: info@schoolsafety.us
http://www.schoolsafety.us
Serves as an advocate for safe, secure and peaceful schools worldwide and as a catalyst for the prevention of school crime and violence.
Founded: 1984

Ronald D Stephens, Executive Director
June Lane Arnette, Associate Director

172 Psychological Corporation
19500 Bulverde Road
San Antonio, TX 78259
210-339-8190
800-627-7271
Fax: 800-232-1223
http://www.pearsonassess.com
Our mission is to improve teaching and learning. We help student, families, educators, and professionals use assessment, research, and innovative technologies to promote learning and personal development, advance academic achievement, and transform educational communities.

Doug Kubash, President/CEO
Karamjeet Singh, SVP/Chief Technology Officer

Early Childhood Education

173 Building Blocks For Literacy
183 Talcott Rd
Suite 101
Williston, VT 05495-9209
802-878-2332
http://www.buildingblocksforliteracy.org
Promotes early literacy skills for children in child care and preschool environments.
Founded: 1997

174 Child Care Information Exchange
Exchange Press, Inc.
17725 NE 65th Street
B-275
Redmond, WA 98052
425-883-9394
800-221-2864
Fax: 425-861-9386
E-mail: infor@ChildCareExchange.com
http://www.ccie.com
Exchange has promoted the exchange of ideas among leaders in early childhood programs worldwide through its magazine, books, training products, training seminars, and international conferences.

Bonnie Neugebauer, Editor in Chief
Debra Hartzell, Advertising

175 Dimensions of Early Childhood
Southern Early Childhood Association
PO Box 55930
Little Rock, AR 72215-5930
501-221-1648
800-305-7322
Fax: 501-227-5297
E-mail: info@southernearlychildhood.org
http://www.southernearlychildhood.org
Southern Early Childhood Association has brought together preschool, kindergarten, and primary teachers and administrators, caregivers, program directors, and individuals working with and for families, to promote quality care and education for young children.

Nancy Jane Chesire, President
Kathy Attaway, President-Elect

176 Division for Early Childhood
The Council for Exceptional Children
27 Fort Missoula Road
Suite 2
Missoula, MT 59804
406-543-0872
Fax: 406-543-0887
E-mail: dec@dec-sped.org
http://www.dec-sped.org
The Division for Early Childhood promotes policies and advances evidence-based practices that support families and enhance the optimal development of young children who have or are at risk for developmental delays and disabilities.

Sarah Mulligan, Executive Director
Cynthia Wood, Associate Executive Director

177 Education Advisory Group
6239 Woodlawn Avenue North
Seattle, WA 98810
206-323-1838
Fax: 206-267-1325
http://www.eagstrategies.com
Specializes in matching children with learning environments. Helps families identify concerns and establish priorities about their child's education.

178 National Early Childhood Technical Assistance Center
ECTA Center
517 S Greensboro Street
Carrboro, NC 27510
919-962-2001
919-843-3269
Fax: 919-966-7463
E-mail: ectacenter@unc.edu
http://www.nectac.org
NECTAC is the national early childhood technical assistance center supported by the U.S. Department of Education's Office of Special Education Programs.

Lynne Kahn, Director
Joan Danaher, Associate Director

179 National Educational Systems (NES)
6333 De Zavala
Suite 106
San Antonio, TX 78249
800-231-4380
Fax: 210-699-4674
E-mail: info@shopnes.com
http://www.shopnes.com
NES is committed to providing quality materials to its customers and prides itself on the friendly customer service that is readily available.

Lupe Garza, Owner
Diana Garza, Owner

180 National Head Start Association
1651 Prince Street
Alexandria, VA 22314
703-739-0875
866-677-8724
Fax: 703-739-0878
http://www.nhsa.org
The National Head Start Association is a private not-for-profit membership organization dedicated exclusively to meeting the needs of Head Start children and their families.

Ron Herndon, Chairman
Linda Broyles, Vice-Chairperson

181 National Institute for Early Education Research
73 Easton Avenue
New Brunswick, NJ 08901-1879
848-932-4350
http://www.nieer.org
Conducts and communicates research to support high-quality, effective early childhood education for all young children.

Jen Fitzgerald, Public Information Officer

Elementary Education

182 Center for Play Therapy
University of North Texas
1400 Highland Street
Room 14
Denton, TX 76203-0829
940-565-3864
Fax: 940-565-4461
E-mail: cpt@unt.edu
http://www.centerforplaytherapy.com
Encourages the unique development and emotional growth of children through the process of play therapy, a dynamic interpersonal relationship between a child and a therapist trained in play therapy procedures. Provides training, research, publications, counseling services and acts as a clearinghouse for literature in the field.

Sue Bratton, Director
Garry Landreth, Founder

183 Clearinghouse on Early Education and Parenting (CEEP)
University of Illinois at
Urbana-Champaign
51 Gerty Drive
Champaign, IL 61820-7469
217-333-1386
877-275-3227
Fax: 212-244-7732
E-mail: ecap@illinois.edu
http://ecap.crc.illinois.edu
The Clearinghouse on Early Education and Parenting (CEEP) is part of the Early Childhood and Parenting (ECAP) Collaborative at the University of Illinois at Urbana-Champaign. CEEP provides publications and information to the worldwide early childhood and parenting communities on topics relating to the physiological, psychological and cultural development of children from birth through early adolescence.

Lilian G Katz Ph.D, Co-Director
Bernard Cesarone, Assitant Director Pub &Tech

184 National Association for the Education of Young Children
1313 L Street, NW
Suite 500
Washington, DC 20005-4101
202-232-8777
800-424-2460
Fax: 202-328-1846
E-mail: naeyc@naeyc.org
http://www.naeyc.org
Supports those interested in serving and acting on behalf of the needs and rights of the education of young children.

Jarlean Daniel, Executive Director
Adele B Robinson, Deputy Executive Director

185 Tribeca Learning Center-PS 150
334 Greenwich Street
New York, NY 10013
212-732-4392
Fax: 212-766-5895
E-mail: Info@ps150.net
http://www.ps150.net
Tribeca Learning Center, PS 150 opened in 1987 as a public school that encourages student-centered learning and family involvement fostering the optimal development and learning of every child and reaffirming the pivotal role of the elementary school. The school offers specialized classes in art, music, dance, technology and library as well as daily classroom activities which encourage the integration of a child's academic development, emotional-social growth, and the arts.

Brian Fingeret, President
Laura Cohen, Coordinator

186 Voyager Expanded Learning
Cambium Learning Group
17855 Dallas Parkway
Suite 400
Dallas, TX 75287
214-932-3213
888-899-1995
Fax: 888-589-0085
E-mail:
jnowakowski@voyagerlearning.com
http://www.voyagerlearning.com
Voyager Expanded Learning is a leading provider of in-school core reading programs, reading and math intervention programs, and professional development programs for school districts throughout the United States
Founded: 1994

David Cappellucci, President
Ron Klausner, CEO

Employment

187 English Language Fellow Program
Center for Intercultural Development Center
3300 Whitehaven Street
Suite 1000
Washington, DC 20007
202-687-2608
Fax: 202-687-2555
E-mail: elf@georgetown.edu
http://www.elfellowprogram.org
The English Language Fellow Program provides American professional expertise in teaching English as a foreign language by sending American experts on ten-month fellowships to overseas academic institutions to improve foreign teachers' and students' access to diverse perspectives on a broad variety of issues, giving foreign teachers and students information enabling them to better understand and convey concepts about American values, democratic representative government, and free enterprise.

Magdalena Potocka, Director
Katherine Alisa Mustter, Program Officer

188 Graphic Arts Education & Research Foundation
1899 Preston White Drive
Reston, VA 20191
703-264-7200
866-381-9839
Fax: 703-620-3165
E-mail: gaerf@npes.org
http://www.gaerf.org
To advance knowledge and education in the field of graphic communications by supporting programs that prepare the workforce of the future. 1

James H. Mayes, Chairman
Ralph J. Nappi, President

189 Graphic Arts Technical Foundation
200 Deer Run Road
Sewickley, PA 15143
412-741-6860
800-910-4283
Fax: 412-741-2311
E-mail: printing@printing.org
http://www.gain.net
Deliver products and services that enhance the growth, efficiency, and profitability of its members and the industry through: Advocacy, Education, Research, and Technical information

Denna Hower, Marketing Coordinator
Mary Garnett, Executive Vice President

190 Health Occupations Students of America
6021 Morriss Road
Suite 111
Flower Mound, TX 75028
972-874-0062
800-321-4672
Fax: 972-874-0063
E-mail: hosa@hosa.org
http://www.hosa.org
Provides health occupations educators with a student organization used to recruit and develop a competent and motivated work force for the health care field.

David Kelly, National President
Jim Koeninger, Executive Director

191 Mountain Pacific Association of Colleges and Employers
16 Santa Ana Place
Walnut Creek, CA 94598
925-934-3877
Fax: 925-906-0922
E-mail: info@mpace.org
http://www.mpace.org
The Mountain-Pacific Association of Colleges and Employers, Inc. is committed to attaining a pluralistic, diverse membership, and providing access to all programs and resources to individuals regardless of race, color, national origin, religion, gender, age, sexual orientation, veteran status, disability, or appearance

Deborah Dobbs, Executive Director
Patty Bishop, President

192 NPES: Association for Suppliers of Printing, Publishing & Converting Technologies
1899 Preston White Drive
Reston, VA 20191
703-264-7200
Fax: 703-620-0994
E-mail: npes@npes.org
http://www.npes.org
A US trade association representing more than 400 companies that manufacture and distribute equipment, software and supplies used across the workflow of nearly every printing, publishing and converting process.

Ralph J Nappi, President
William K Smythe Jr, Vice President

193 National Business Education Association
1914 Association Drive
Reston, VA 20191-1596
703-860-8300
Fax: 703-620-4483
E-mail: nbea@nbea.org
http://www.nbea.org
NBEA is committed to the advancement of the professional interest and competence of its members and provides programs and services that enhance members' professional growth and development.

Ramona Schoenrock, President
Janet M. Treichel, Executive Director

194 Windsor Mountain International
One World Way
Windsor, NH 03244
603-478-3066
800-862-7760
Fax: 603-478-5260
E-mail: mail@WindsorMountain.org
http://www.windsormountain.org/
Windsor Mountain International was founded in 1961, as Interlocken International Camp, hosting young people from more than 60 countries through international youth travel programs where students learn by doing, thereby enriching their lives with lasting friendships, new skills, self discovery, and increased environmental and cross-cultural awareness.

Kerry Labovitz, Director
Jake Labovitz, Owner/Director

195 Women's International League for Peace & Freedom
U.S. Section
11 Arlington Street
Boston, MA 02116
617-266-0999
Fax: 617-266-1688
http://www.wilpf.org

Works to create an environment of political, economic, social and psychological freedom for all members of the human community, so that true peace can be enjoyed by all.

Tanya Henderson, National Director
Laura Roskos, President

Guidance & Counseling

196 **American Association of Sex Educators, Counselors & Therapists (AASECT)**
1444 I Street NW
Suite 700
Washington, DC 20005
202-449-1099
Fax: 202-216-9646
E-mail: info@aasect.org
http://www.aasect.org
Interest in promoting understanding of human sexuality and healthy sexual behavior.

Founded: 1967

Dee Ann Walker, Executive Director
Dr Patricia Schiller, Founder

197 **American Counseling Association**
5999 Stevenson Avenue
Alexandria, VA 22304-3302
800-347-6647
Fax: 800-473-2329
E-mail: membership@counseling.org
http://www.counseling.org
A not-for-profit, professional and educational organization that is dedicated to the growth and enhancement of the counseling profession.

Brad Erford, ACA President

198 **American School Counselor Association**
1101 King Street
Suite 625
Alexandria, VA 22314
703-683-2722
800-306-4722
Fax: 703-683-1619
E-mail: asca@schoolcounselor.org
http://www.schoolcounselor.org
Supports school counselors' efforts to help students focus on academic, personal/social and career development so they achieve success in school and are prepared to lead fulfilling lives as responsible members of society.

Richard Wong, Executive Director
Jill Cook, Assistant Director

199 **Association for Addicted Professionals**
1521 Hillary Street
New Orleans, LA 70118-4007
504-286-5000
Sustains an information network of substance abuse/chemical dependency training programs in higher education.

Thomas Lief, Director

200 **Association of Educational Therapists**
7044 S. 13th Street
Oak Creek, WI 53154
414-908-4949
Fax: 414-768-8001
E-mail: aet@aetonline.org
http://www.aetonline.org
Founded in 1979 the Association of Educational Therapists establishes professional standards and defines roles, responsibilities and ethics of educational therapists; studies techniques, technologies, philosophies and research related to educational therapy; represents/defines educational therapy to the community, school and professional group; provides opportunities for continued professional growth.

Jeanette Rivera, President
Alice Pulliam, President-Elect

201 **ERIC/CASS Virtual Libraries: Online Resources for Parents, Teachers, and Counselors**
Computer Sciences Corporation
655 15th Street SW
Suite 500
Washington, DC 20005
800-538-3742
http://www.eric.ed.gov
Collects and disseminates information on counseling, guidance and student services. (ERIC/CASS) serves counseling and student professionals as well as parents who have an interest in personal and social factors that affect learning and development. ERIC/CASS has developed virtual libraries to provide online access to full-text documents on topics within its scope.

Robert Boruch, Chairman
John Collins, ERIC Steering Committee

202 **International Association of Counseling Services**
101 S Whiting Street
Suite 211
Alexandria, VA 22304-3415
703-823-9840
Fax: 703-823-9843
E-mail: iacsinc@earthlink.net
http://www.iacsinc.org
IACS is committed to furthering the visibility of the counseling profession and improving its quality. IACS has evolved standards that define professional quality and has established criteria for accreditation which reflect these standards.

Nancy E Roncketti, Executive Officer
Rattana Thanagosol, Administrative Assistant

203 **National Association of School Psychologists**
4340 E West Highway
Suite 402
Bethesda, MD 20814
301-657-0270
866-331-6277
Fax: 301-657-0275
E-mail: center@naspweb.org
http://www.nasponline.org
Founded in 1977 the National Association of School Psychologists is a professional association representing over 22,000 school psychologists and related professionals.

Laura Benson, COO
Susan Gorin, Executive Director

International

204 **Academic Travel Abroad**
1920 N Street NW
Suite 200
Washington, DC 20036
202-785-9000
800-556-7896
Fax: 202-342-0317
E-mail: epawlowski@academic-travel.com
http://www.academic-travel.com
Create unparalleled, educational travel programs to satisfy curious travelers.

Founded: 1950

David Parry, Chairman
Kate Simpson, President

205 **Alberta Association of Recreation Facility Personnel**
Box 100
Cochrane, AB T4C-1A4
403-851-7626
888-253-7544
Fax: 403-851-9181
E-mail: office@aarfp.com
http://www.aarfp.com
A provincial organization dedicated to providing excellence in training and professional development for individuals involved in the operation of recreation facilities.

Founded: 1978

Aaron Singh, President
Kim Snell, Executive Director

206 **Alberta Council on Admissions and Transfer**
10155-102 Street
11th Floor
Edmonton, AB T5J-4L5
780-422-9021
800-232-7215
Fax: 780-422-3688
E-mail: acat@gov.ab.ca
http://www.acat.gov.ab.ca
Responsible for developing policies, guidelines and procedures designed to facilitate transfer agreements among post-secondary programs.

Founded: 1974

Ron Woodward, Chairman
Marg Leathem, Director

207 **American Friends Service Committee**
Human Resources
1501 Cherry Street
Philadelphia, PA 19102-1429
215-241-7000
Fax: 215-241-7275
E-mail: afscinfo@afsc.org
http://www.afsc.org
The American Friends Service Committee carries out service, development, social justice, and peace programs throughout the world. Founded by Quakers in 1917 to provide conscientious objectors with an opportunity to aid civilian war victims, AFSC's work attracts the support and partnership of people of many races, religions, and cultures.

Arlene Kelly, Presiding Clerk
Phil Lord, Assistant Clerk

208 **American Schools Association of Central America, Columbia-Caribbean and Mexico**
1209 San Dario Ave
Suite 92-96
Laredo, TX 78040
011 52 81 83384454
E-mail: skeller@tri-association.org
http://www.tri-association.org
Works with over 60 schools to improve the quality of teaching and learning, provide avenue for communication between schools, facilitate cooperation with national, state, local and non-governmental and more in the field of international education.

Sonia Keller, Executive Director
Paul Williams, President

209 **Aprovecho Research Center**
80574 Hazelton Rd.
PO Box 1175
Cottage Grove, OR 97424
541-942-8198
E-mail: aprovecho.mail@gmail.com
http://www.aprovecho.org
A non-profit organization whose purpose is To research, develop, and disseminate technological solutions for meeting the basic hu-

man needs of low income and impoverished people and communities in third world countries, in order to help relieve their suffering, improve their health, enhance their safety, and reduce their adverse impacts on their environment.

Jeremy Roth, Director
Rosemary Kirincic, Outreach Coordinator

210 Associated Schools Project Network
UNESCO
7 Place de Fontenoy
Paris, France 75352
33(0)1 45 68 10 00
Fax: 331-43067925
E-mail: aspnet@unesco.org
http://www.unesco.org
Network of committed schools engaged in fostering and delivering quality education, in pursuit of peace, liberty, justice and human development, in order to meet the pressing educational needs of children and young people throughout the world.

Livia Saldari, International Coordinator
Fouzia Belhami, Program Specialist

211 Association Of International Education Administrators
2204 Erwin Rd
Box 90404
Durham, NC 27708-0402
919-668-1928
Fax: 919-684-8749
http://www.aieaworld.org
To provide an effective voice on significant issues within international education at all levels, to improve and promote international education programming and administration within institutions of higher education, to establish and maintain a professional network among international education institutional leaders, and to cooperate in appropriate ways with other national and international groups having similar interests.
Founded: 1982

212 Association for Asian Studies
Association For Asian Studies, Inc.
825 Victors Way
Suite 310
Ann Arbor, MI 48108
734-665-2490
Fax: 734-665-3801
E-mail: mpaschal@asian-studies.org
http://www.asian-studies.org
Founded in 1941 the Association for Asian Studies seeks through publications, meetings, and seminars to facilitate contact and an exchange of information among scholars to increase their understanding of East, South, and Southeast Asia.

Michael Paschal, Executive Director
Bob Snow, Director of Development

213 Association for Canadian Education Resources
Unit 44, Flamewood Drive
Mississauga, ON L4Y-3P5
905-275-7685
Fax: 905-275-9420
E-mail: acerinfo@rogers.com
http://www.acer-acre.org
Initiate and facilitate development, production and promotion of Canadian materials to meet the needs of today's learners especially those monitoring changes in forest biodiversity.

Alice Casselman, President
Irene Katkov, Chairman

214 Association for Canadian Studies in the US
1740 Massachusetts Ave NW
Nitze 516
Washington, DC 20036
202-775-9007
Fax: 202-775-0061
E-mail: info@acsus.org
http://www.acsus.org
Committed to raising awareness and understanding of Canada and the bilateral relationship.

Myrna Delson-Karan, President
Nadine Fabbi, Secretary

215 Association of American International Colleges & Universities
PO Box 21021
Pylea, Thessaloniki
Greece 555-10
33-4-42-23-39-35
Fax: 33-4-42-21-11-38
E-mail: rjackson@act.edu
http://www.aaicu.org
Encourages collaboration and the sharing of information and resources among schools which share many issues in common.
Founded: 1971

Panos Vlachos, President

216 Association of American Schools of Brazil
Conjunto E, Lotes 34/37
SGAS 605
Brasilia, DF, Brazil 70200-650
55 (61) 3442 9700
Fax: 55 (61) 3442 9729
E-mail: cjohnson@eabdf.br
http://www.eabdf.br
Provides a US accredited, pre-K through grade 12 program based on a comprehensive college preparatory curriculum taught in English to students of all nationalities.

Elizabeth Lopez, Principal
Michael Ellis, Board President

217 Association of American Schools of Central America
American School of Tequciqalpa
c/o United States Embassy
Tequciqalpa, M.D.C., Honduras
504-239-3333
Fax: 504-239-6162
E-mail: ccorrales@amschool.org
http://www.aascaonline.net
Provides opportunities for school communities to participate in activities to develop their full potential, social responsibility and global citizenship.

Linda Niehaus, President
Maria Motz, President (Principal's)

218 Association of American Schools of South America
1911 NW 150 Ave
Suite 101
Pembroke Pines, FL 33028
954-436-4034
Fax: 954-436-4092
E-mail: ppoore@aassa.com
http://www.aassa.com
Provide and promote programs and services to member schools to enhance the quality of American International Education. As an organization, AASSA values service leadership, quality and effectiveness.

Paul Joslin, President
Paul Poore, Executive Director

219 Association of British Schools in Spain
c/o Urbanizacion Los Pinos
S-N 18690, Almunecar, Granada
Spain
34-958-639-003
Fax: 34-958-639-003
E-mail: info@nabss.org
http://www.nabss.org
Defends members' interests, maintain the quality of British education in Spain, and support school development.

Donat Morgan, President
Roger Deign, VP

220 Association of Christian Schools International
731 Chapel Hills Drive
PO Box 65130
Colorado Springs, CO 80920-5130
719-528-6906
800-367-0798
Fax: 719-531-0631
E-mail: membership@acsi.org
http://www.acsi.org
Promotes Christian education and provides training and resources to Christian schools and educators. Strengthen Christian school and equip educators worldwide as they prepare students academically, spiritually and culturally.

Brian S Simmons, President

221 Association of International Educators (NAFSA)
1307 New York Avenue NW
8th Floor
Washington, DC 20005-4701
202-737-3699
Fax: 202-737-3657
E-mail: inbox@nafsa.org
http://www.nafsa.org
Serves international educators and their institutions and organizations by setting standards of good practice, providing training and professional development opportunities, providing networking opportunities, and advocating for international education.

Marlene Johnson, Executive Director/CEO
Victor C Johnson, Senior Advisor Public Policy

222 Association of International Schools in Africa
Peponi Road
P O Box 14103, Nairobi
Kenya 00800
254 (20) 2697442
Fax: 254 (20) 418 0596
E-mail: info@aisa.or.ke
http://www.aisa.or.ke
Facilitates communications, cooperation, and professional growth among member schools. Promotes intercultural understanding and friendships as well as facilitating collaboration between its members, host country schools, and other regional and professional groups.

Peter Bateman, Executive Director
John Roberts, Chairperson

223 Atlantic Provinces Special Education Authority
5940 S Street
Halifax, Nova Scotia
Canada B3H-1S6
902-424-8500
Fax: 902-424-0543
E-mail: apsea@apsea.ca
http://www.apsea.ca
Provide quality services and supports, in collaboration with our partners, to meet the educational needs of children and youth from birth to 21 who are blind/visually impaired(BVI) and/or deaf/hard of hearing(DHH).

Bertram Tulk, Superintendent

224 British American Educational Foundation
520 Summit Avenue
Oradell, NJ 07649
201-261-4438
http://www.baef.org
Founded by a group of American alumni of British schools, the BAEF is a non-profit charitable foundation governed by a Board of Directors, comprised primarily of alumni, and a President.

Laurel Zimmermann, Executive Director
Denise Bryan, Founder

225 CARE
151 Ellis Street NE
Atlanta, GA 30303-2400
404-681-2552
800-422-7385
Fax: 404-589-2651
E-mail: managemyaccount@care.org
http://www.care.org
CARE is a leading humanitarian organization fighting global poverty

Founded: 1945

Helene D Gayle, President/CEO
W Bowman Cutter, Chair

226 Canadian Association of Communicators in Education
2900 Don Reid Drive
Ottawa, ON K1H-1E1
E-mail: khamilton@qesba.qc.ca
http://www.cace-acace.org
Promote and contribute to the development of professional communication services in the Canadian education sector.

Founded: 1984

Kim Hamilton, President
Maxeen Jolin, VP

227 Canadian Association of Independent Schools
2 Ridley Road
PO Box 3013
St. Cathatines, ON L2R-7C3
905-684-5658
Fax: 905-684-5057
E-mail: execasst@cesi.edu
http://cais.ca
Explore and pursue exemplary leadership, training, research and international standards of educational excellence.

Anne-Marie Kee, Executive Director

228 Canadian Council for the Advancement of Education
4 Cataraqui Street
Suite 310
Kingston, ON K7K-1Z7
613-531-9213
Fax: 613-531-0626
E-mail: admin@ccaecanada.org
http://www.ccaecanada.org
The Canadian Council for the Advancement of Education (CCAE) fosters excellence in Canadian education by providing bilingual programs and services to professionals in institutional advancement.

Melana Soroka, President
Mark Hazlett, Executive Director

229 Canadian Memorial Chiropractic College
6100 Leslie Street
Toronto, ON M2H-3J1
416-482-2340
800-463-2923
Fax: 416-646-1114
E-mail: communications@cmcc.ca
http://www.cmcc.ca
CMCC is a registered organization in chiropractic education and research dedicated to delivering world class chiropractic education, research and patient care.

Founded: 1945

Jean A Moss, President

230 Canadian Society for the Study of Education
260 Dalhousie Street
Suite 204 Ottawa, Ontario
Canada K1N-7E4
613-241-0018
Fax: 613-241-0019
E-mail: csse-scee@csse.ca
http://www.csse-scee.ca
To promote the advancement of Canadian research and scholarship in education. In order to fulfill its mandate

Founded: 1972

Fernand Gervais, President
Marc-Andre Ethier, VP

231 Catholic Medical Mission Board
10 W 17th Street
New York, NY 10011-5765
212-242-7757
800-678-5659
Fax: 212-645-1485
E-mail: info@cmmb.org
http://www.cmmb.org
To provide quality healthcare programs and services, without discrimination, to people in need around the world.

Founded: 1912

Bruce Wilkinson, President/CEO
Michael Doring Connelly, Chairman

232 Central and Eastern European Schools Association
American International School of Zagreb
Vocarska 106
Zagreb 10000
Croatia
+385-1-460-9935
Fax: +385-1-460-9936
E-mail: office@ceesa.org
http://www.ceesa.org
A collaborative community of international schools which enhances school effectiveness and inspires student learning and development.

Kathey Stetson, Executive Director
David Ottaviano, Chmn, Executive Committee

233 Commonwealth of Learning
1055 W Hastings Street
Suite 1200
Vancouver, BC V6E-2E9
604-775-8200
Fax: 604-775-8210
E-mail: info@col.org
http://www.col.org
An intergovernmental organization created by Commonwealth Heads of Government to encourage the development and sharing of open learning/distance education knowledge, resources and technologies.

Founded: 2001

Asha S. Kanwar, President/CEO
Vis Naidoo, VP

234 Communicating for America
112 E Lincoln Avenue
PO Box 677
Fergus Falls, MN 56537
218-739-3241
800-432-3276
Fax: 218-739-3832
E-mail: memberbenefits@cain.org
http://www.communicatingforamerica.org
Promotes agriculture, protects business and farmland ownership and creates education
opportunities with international exchange programs.

Wayne Nelson, President
Milt Smedsrud, Chairman/CEO

235 Concern-America Volunteers
2015 N Broadway Avenue
PO Box 1790
Santa Ana, CA 92706-1790
714-953-8575
800-266-2376
Fax: 714-953-1242
E-mail: concamerinc@earthlink.net
http://www.concernamerica.org
Train local populations in health, education, agriculture and/or environmental health enabling them to build local, functional and social systems meeting basic needs

Founded: 1972

John Straw, Executive Director
Denis Garvey, Director of Development

236 Cordell Hull Foundation for International Education
501 Fifth Avenue
Third Floor
New York, NY 10017
212-300-2138
Fax: 646-349-3455
E-mail: cordellhull@aol.com
http://www.cordellhull.org
Offers programs to improve relations between the United States and other countries, primarily through educational and cultural exchange.

Marianne Mason, Executive Director

237 Council of British International Schools
St. Mary's University College
Strawberry Hill
Twickenham, UK TW1-4SX
44(0) 208 240 4142
Fax: 44(0) 208 240 4255
E-mail: executive.director@cobis.org.uk
http://www.cobis.org.uk
COBIS is a Membership Association of British Schools of quality and is a member of the Independent Schools Council (ISC) of the United Kingdom.

Trevor Rowell, Chairman
Colin Bell, Executive Director

238 Council of Education Facility Planners-International
11445 E. Via Linda
Suite 2-440
Scottsdale, AZ 85259
480-391-0840
Fax: 480-391-0940
E-mail: contact@cefpi.org
http://www.cefpi.org
Advocacy and education of general public; resource for planning effective educational facilities; research/information showing link between students success and educational facility/design—- improving the places where children learn.

Irene Nigaglioni, Chairman
David M. Waggoner, Vice-Chair

239 Council of Ministers of Education, Canada
95 St Clair Avenue W
Suite 1106
Toronto, Ontario, Canada M4V-1N6
416-962-8100
Fax: 416-962-2800
E-mail: information@cmec.ca
http://www.cmec.ca
CMEC provides leadership in education at the pan-Canadian and international levels and contributes to the fulfillment of the con-

stitutional responsibility for education conferred on provinces and territories.

Jean-Gilles Pelletier, Administration Director
Andrew Parkin, Director General

240 Council on Foreign Relations
The Harold Pratt House
58 E 68th Street
New York, NY 10065
212-434-9400
Fax: 212-434-9800
http://www.cfr.org
Resource for its members, government officials, business executives, journalists, educators and students, civic and religious leaders, and other interested citizens to help them better understand the world and foreign policy choices facing the United States and other countries.

Richard Haass, President
Jeffrey Reinke, Chief of Staff

241 Council on Hemispheric Affairs
1250 Connecticut Avenue NW
Suite 1C
Washington, DC 20036
202-223-4975
888-922-9261
Fax: 202-223-4979
E-mail: coha@coha.org
http://www.coha.org
Promotes the common interests of the hemisphere, raise the visibility of regional affairs and increase the importance of the inter-American relationship, as well as encourage the formulation of rational and constructive US policies towards Latin America.

Founded: 1975

Larry Birns, Director

242 Council on International Educational Exchange (CIEE)
300 Fore Street
Portland, ME 04101
207-553-4000
800-407-8839
Fax: 207-553-4299
E-mail: contact@ciee.org
http://www.ciee.org
CIEE is a United States non-governmental international education organization. CIEE creates and administers programs that allow high school and university students and educators to study and teach abroad.

Robert E. Fallon, President/CEO

243 Council on Islamic Education
10055 Slater Avenue
Suite 250
Fountain Valley, CA 92708
714-839-2929
Fax: 714-839-2714
E-mail: info@cie.org
http://www.cie.org
CIE is formally comprised of Muslim academic scholars of religion, history, political science, cultural studies, communications, education, and other fields, along with a full-time professional staff with expertise on matters related to U.S. education, civics, politics, the media, faith communities and other components of American society and the institutional system.

Founded: 1990

Shabbir Mansuri, Founding Director
Munir A Shaikh, Executive Director

244 Cultural Vistas
440 Park Avenue S
2nd Floor
New York, NY 10016
212-497-3500
Fax: 212-497-3535
E-mail: info@culturalvistas.org
http://www.culturalvistas.org
Cultural Vistas is committed to its mission to enrich minds, advance global skills, build careers and connect lives through international exchange.

Robert Fenstermacher, President & CEO
Linda Boughton, CFO & Senior VP

245 East Asia Regional Council of Overseas Schools
Barangay Mamplasan
Binan, Laguna
Philippines 4024
+63 (02) 697-9170
Fax: +63 (49) 511-4694
E-mail: info@earcos.org
http://www.earcos.org
Inspires adult and student learning through its leadership and service and fosters intercultural understanding, global citizenship and exceptional educational practices within our learning community,

Tim Carr, President
Dick Krajczar, Executive Director

246 Global Learning
22 Mary Ann Drive
Brick, NJ 08723
732-281-8929
Fax: 723-528-1027
E-mail: globallearningnj@comcast.net
http://www.globallearningnj.org/
A non-profit educational organization that translates the world's growing interdependence into educational activities for teachers, students, librarians, and educational systems, from elementary school through college and in community settings

Jeffrey L Brown, Executive Director
Paula Gotsch, Associate Director

247 Institute of Cultural Affairs
4750 N Sheridan Road
Chicago, IL 60640
773-769-6363
800-742-4032
Fax: 773-944-1582
E-mail: Chicago@ica-usa.org
http://www.ica-usa.org/
Releasing the capacity for positive, sustainable futures.

Founded: 1962

Terry Bergda, CEO

248 Institute of International Education
809 United Nations Plaza
New York, NY 10017-3580
212-883-8200
Fax: 212-984-5452
http://www.iie.org
Advance international education and access to education worldwide. Manages scholarship, training, exchange & leadership programs.

Allan Goodman, President/CEO
Rajika Bhandari, VP Research & Evaluation

249 International Association Of Medical Science Educators
3327B US Route 60 E
Huntington, WV 25705
304-522-1270
Fax: 304-523-9701
http://www.iamse.org

To advance medical education through faculty development and to ensure that the teaching and learning of medicine continues t o be firmly grounded in science.

Founded: 1988

250 International Association for Continuing Education & Training
1760 Old Meadow Road
Suite 500
McLean, VA 22102
703-506-3275
Fax: 703-506-3266
E-mail: info@iacet.org
http://www.iacet.org
Promote and enhance quality in continuing education and training through research, education and the development and continuous improvement of criteria, principles and standards.

Michael Todd Shinholster, President
Kristopher Newbauer, President-Elect

251 International Association for the Exchange of Students for Technical Experience
440 Park Avenue South
2nd Floor
New York, NY 10016-3519
212-497-3530
Fax: 212-997-3584
E-mail: iaeste@culturalvistas.org
http://www.iaesteunitedstates.org
Operate a practical training exchange program between members in order to enhance technical and professional development. Promote international understanding and goodwill amongst students, academic institutions, employers and the wider community.

Gina Del Tito, Associate Program Manager
Katerina Holubova, Senior Program Director

252 International Association of Students in Economics & Business Management (AIESC)
11 Hanover Square
Suite 1700
New York, NY 10005
212-757-3774
Fax: 212-757-4062
E-mail: info@aiesecus.org
http://www.aiesecus.org/
Agency offering international internships, experience leadership and participate in a global learning environment. Offers young people the opportunity to be global citizens, to change the world and get experience and skills that matter today.

Founded: 1956

Cole Wirpels, President
Lucia Trochez, VP Communications

253 International Baccalaureate American Global Centre
7501 Wisconsin Ave
Suite 200 W
Bethesda, MD 20814
301-202-3000
Fax: 301-202-3033
E-mail: ibid@ibo.org
http://www.ibo.org
Aims to develop inquiring, knowledgeable and caring young people who help to create a better and more peaceful world through intercultural understanding and respect.

Carol Bellamy, Chair
Jeffrey Beard, Director General

254 International Baccalaureate Organization
Route des Morillons 15
Grand-Saconnex, Geneve
Switzerland CH-1218

+41 22 309 2540
Fax: +44 22 791 0277
E-mail: ibhq@ibo.org
http://www.ibo.org
The International Baccalaureate (IB) aims to develop inquiring, knowledgeable and caring young people who help create a better and more peaceful world through intercultural understanding and respect.

Jeffrey Beard, Director General
Carol Bellamy, Chair

255 International Graphic Arts Education Association (IGAEA)
1899 Preston White Drive
Reston, VA 26191
http://www.igaea.org
The International Graphic Arts Education Association (IGAEA) is an association of educators in partnership with industry, dedicated to sharing theories, principles, techniques and processes relating to graphic communications and imaging technology.

Tom Carrig, President
Monika Zarzycka, President-Elect

256 International Physicians for the Prevention of Nuclear War
66-70 Union Square
#204
Somerville, MA 02143-1024
617-440-1733
Fax: 617-440-1734
E-mail: ippnwbos@ippnw.org
http://www.ippnw.org
Federation of national medical organizations in 62 countries representing doctors, medical students, health workers and concerned citizens whose goal is creating a more peaceful and secure world freed from the threat of nuclear annihilation.

Michael Christ, Executive Director
Douglas Kline, Director of Administration

257 International Research and Exchanges Board (IREX)
IREX
2121 K Street NW
Suite 700
Washington, DC 20037
202-628-8188
Fax: 202-628-8189
E-mail: irex@irex.org
http://www.irex.org
Promotes positive lasting change globally. Enable local individuals and institutions to build key elements of a vibrant society: quality education; independent media; and strong communities.

W Robert Pearson, President
Joyce Warner, VP/ Chief of Staff

258 International Schools Services
15 Roszel Road
PO Box 5910
Princeton, NJ 08543
609-452-0990
Fax: 609-452-2690
E-mail: iss@iss.edu
http://www.iss.edu
Advance the quality of international education for children across the globe by providing comprehensive, world-class services and solutions for learning communities and corporations throughout the world.

Roger Hove, President
Kristin Evins, CFO

259 International Society For Technology In Education
1710 Rhode Island Ave NW
Suite 900
Washington, DC 20036

866-654-4777
Fax: 202-861-0888
http://www.iste.org
Improving learning and teaching by advancing the effective use of technology in PK-12 and teacher education.

260 International Society for Business Education
US Chapter
1914 Association Drive
Reston, VA 20191-1596
703-860-8300
Fax: 703-620-4483
E-mail: mrbsherry@comcast.net
http://www.isbeusa.org
Form an interactive exchange among individuals at national and international levels to assist with the development of the globalization process as it applies to Business Education.

Marilyn Sherry, President
Lee Kantin, President-Elect

261 International Studies Association (ISA)
University of Arizona
324 Social Sciences
Tucson, AZ 85721
520-621-7715
Fax: 520-621-5780
E-mail: isa@isanet.org
http://www.isanet.org
Promote research and education in international affairs and to give American scholars and practitioners interested in international studies a regional base for developing and sharing research.
Founded: 1959

Thomas J Volgy, Executive Director
Lyn Brabant, Director of Administration

262 Mediterranean Association of International Schools (MAIS)
Apartado 80
Madrid
Spain 28080
34-91-740-1900
Fax: 34-91-357-2678
E-mail: info@amerschmad.org
http://www.mais-web.org
Improve quality of education in member schools: promote professional development of faculty, administrators and school board members, effect communication and interchange and create international understanding.
Founded: 1981

Sister Anne M Hill, President
Saara Tatem, VP

263 National Registration Center for Study Abroad
PO Box 1393
Milwaukee, WI 53201-1393
414-278-0631
Fax: 414-271-8884
E-mail: study@nrcsa.com
http://www.nrcsa.com
Improve international understanding through educational exchanges. NRCSA welcomes participants of all ages, nationalities, and occupations.
Founded: 1968

Mike Wittig, General Manager

264 Near East-South Asia Council of Overseas Schools (NESA)
Gravias 6 Aghia Paraskevi
Athens, Greece 15342
+30 210 600-9821
Fax: +30 210 600-9928
E-mail: nesa@nesacenter.org
http://www.nesacenter.org

Maximize student learning by facilitating sustainable and systemic school improvement based on the best practices of American and international education.

David J Chojnacki, Executive Director
Kevin Schafer, President

265 Ontario Business Education Partnership
170 Louisa Steert
Kitchener, ON N2H 5
519-208-5966
888-672-7996
Fax: 519-208-5919
E-mail: sherryl@obep.on.ca
http://www.obep.ca
Facilitate a network among government-supported and private sector partners enabling informed relationships between industry and educators, effective communication of government programs and shaping of new policy and well-supported experiential learning opportunities in Ontario communities.
Founded: 1999

Sherryl Petricevic, Executive Director
Jeremy Hill, Co-Chair

266 Ontario Operative Education Association
35 Reynar Drive
Quispamsis, NB E2G-1J9
Fax: 506-849-8375
E-mail: OCEA@Rogers.com
http://www.ocea.on.ca
Promote the development of Cooperative Education, Work Experience, School-Work Transition and OYAP Programs and to assist in the professional growth of members.

Donna Thomson, President
Donna Flasza, VP

267 Operation Crossroads Africa
PO Box 5570
New York, NY 10027
212-289-1949
Fax: 212-289-2526
E-mail: oca@igc.org
http://www.operationcrossroadsafrica.org
Promote understanding of Africa and the African Diaspora based on the belief that one can truly enter another culture only by living and working in it. Operation Crossroads Africa is a cross cultural exchange program.
Founded: 1958

James Robinson Ph.D, Founder
Willis Logan, President

268 Opportunities Industrialization Centers International (OIC)
1500 Walnut St
Suite 1304
Philadelphia, PA 19102-3295
215-842-0220
Fax: 215-842-2276
E-mail: info@oici.org
http://www.oici.org
OIC International provides individuals with the education, skills and confidence they need to help themselves, their households and their communities.

Crispian Kirk, President/CEO
Edmund D Cooke Jr, Chair of the Board

269 People to People International
911 Main Street
Suite 2110
Kansas City, MO 64105
816-531-4701
Fax: 816-561-7502
E-mail: ptpi@ptpi.org
http://www.ptpi.org
Enhance international understanding and friendship through educational, cultural and

humanitarian activities involving the exchange of ideas and experiences directly among peoples of different countries and diverse cultures.

Mary Eisenhower, President/CEO
Mark Stansberry, Chairman

270 Phi Delta Kappa International
320 W. Eighth Street
Suite 216
Bloomington, IN 47404
812-339-1156
800-766-1156
Fax: 812-339-0018
E-mail: memberservices@pdkintl.org
http://www.pdkintl.org
One of largest education associations in the world with members dedicated to improving education. Hundreds of chapters give members the opportunity to network with like-minded educators.

Kathleen Andreson, President
William J Bushaw, Executive Director

271 School Milk Foundation of New Foundland and Labrador
27 Sagona Avenue
Mount Pearl
Canada, NL A1N-4P8
709-364-2776
Fax: 709-364-8364
E-mail: info@schoolmilkfdn.nf.net
http://www.schoolmilk.nl.ca
Foundation promoting consumption of milk amongst school aged children—- part of giving children a healthy active lifestyle.
Founded: 1991

272 Teach Overseas
International Schools Services
15 Roszel Road
PO Box 5910
Princeton, NJ 8543
609-452-0990
Fax: 609-452-2690
E-mail: iss@iss.edu
http://www.iss.edu/
Placed over 17,000 K-12 teachers and administrators in overseas schools since 1955. Most candidates attend US-based International Recruitment Centers where ISS candidates interview with overseas school heads seeking new staff.

Kristin Evins, CFO
Roger Hove, President

273 Teachers of English to Speakers of Other Languages
1925 Ballenger Ave
Suite 550
Alexandria, VA 22314-6820
703-836-0774
888-547-3369
Fax: 703-836-7864
E-mail: info@tesol.org
http://www.tesol.org
TESOL is an international professional organization whose mission is to ensure excellence in English language to speakers of other languages.

Suzanne Panferov, President
Deena Boraie, President-Elect

274 United Nations Development Program
One United Nations Plaza
New York, NY 10017-3515
212-906-5000
Fax: 212-906-5001
E-mail: ohr.recruitment.hq@undp.org
http://www.undp.org
Help countries rebuild and share solutions to achieve poverty reduction, democratic governance, crisis prevention and recovery, environment and energy for sustainable development. Help developing countries attract and use aid effectively.

Helen Clark, Administrator
Rebecca Grynspan, Associate Administrator

275 Visions in Action
2710 Ontario Road NW
Washington, DC 20009-2154
301-944-3370
Fax: 202-588-9344
E-mail: visions@visionsinaction.org
http://www.visionsinaction.org
Visions in Action is committed to achieving social and economic justice in the developing world through grassroots programs and communities of self-reliant volunteers

Shaun Skelton PhD, Director
Samuel Bong, Int'l Exchange Prog. Mgr.

276 World Association of Publishers, Manufacturers & Distributors
Worlddidac
Bollwerk 21, PO Box 8866 CH-3001
Bern
Switzerland
+41 31 311 76 82
Fax: +41 31 312 17 44
E-mail: info@worlddidac.org
http://www.worlddidac.org
Global trade association for companies providing products for education and training at all levels.

Beat Jost, Director General
Kateryna Schuetz, Project Manager

277 World Learning
1 Kipling Rd
PO Box 676
Brattleboro, VT 05302
800-257-7751
Fax: 802-258-3508
E-mail: info@worldlearning.org
http://www.worldlearning.org
A non-profit organization that empowers people and strengthens institutions through education, exchange, and development programs.

Language Arts

278 American Association of Teachers of French
Southern Illinois University
Mailcode 4510
Carbondale, IL 62901-4510
618-453-5731
Fax: 618-453-5733
E-mail: abrate@siu.edu
http://www.frenchteachers.org
Founded in 1927, AATF is the largest national association of French teachers in the world with nearly 10,000 members.

Jayne Abrate, Executive Director
Mary Helen Kashuba, President

279 American Council on Education in Journalism and Mass Communication (ACEJMC)
University of Kansas
Stauffer Flint Hall
1435 Jayhawk Blvd
Lawrence, KS 66045-7575
785-864-3973
Fax: 785-864-5225
E-mail: sshaw@ku.edu
http://www2.ku.edu/~acejmc
The Accrediting Council on Education in Journalism and Mass Communications, or ACEJMC, is responsible for the evaluation of professional journalism and mass communications programs in colleges and universities. These programs offer education to prepare students for careers in advertising, newspaper or magazine journalism, photo journalism, public relations, radio and television broadcasting and related fields.

Susanne Shaw, Executive Director
Peter Bhatia, President

280 American Council on the Teaching of Foreign Languages
1001 N Fairfax Street
Suite 200
Alexandria, VA 22314
703-894-2900
Fax: 703-894-2905
E-mail: headquarters@actfl.org
http://www.actfl.org
National organization dedicated to the improvement and expansion of the teaching and learning of all languages at all levels of instruction.

Toni Theisen, President
Mary Lynn Redmond, President-Elect

281 American Speech-Language-Hearing Association
2200 Research Boulevard
Rockville, MD 20852-3289
301-296-5700
800-498-2071
Fax: 301-296-8580
E-mail: actioncenter@asha.org
http://www.asha.org
Support speech-language pathologists, audiologists and speech, language and hearing scientists. Advocate for persons with communication and related disorders, advancing communication science, promote effective human communication.

Patricia A. Prelock, President
Elizabeth S. McCrea, President Elect

282 Association of Schools of Journalism and Mass Communication (ASJMC)
234 Outlet Pointe Boulevard
Columbia, SC 29210-5667
803-798-0271
Fax: 803-772-3509
E-mail: aejmchq@aol.com
http://www.asjmc.org
ASJMC works to support the purposes of schools of journalism and mass communication in order to encourage high standards in administration, raise professional standards and promote public understanding.

Jennifer McGill, Executive Director
Peggy Kuhr, President

283 Center for Applied Linguistics (CAL)
4646 40th Street NW
Washington, DC 20016-1859
202-362-0700
Fax: 202-362-3740
E-mail: info@cal.org
http://www.cal.org
Working to improve communication through better understanding of language and culture. CAL's staff of researchers and educators conduct research, design and develop instructional materials and language tests, provide technical assistance and professional development, conduct needs assessments and program evaluations, and disseminate information and resources related to language and culture.

Joy Kreeft Peyton, Senoir Fellow
Deborah Kennedy, Adult Eng. Language VP

284 ERIC Clearinghouse on Languages and Linguistics
Eric Program c/o CSC
655 15th Street NW
Suite 500
Washington, DC 20005
202-362-0700
800-538-3742
Fax: 202-362-3740
E-mail: ericpub@csc.com
http://www.eric.ed.gov
Promotes and improves the teaching and learning of languages, Identifies and solves problems related to language and culture.

John Collins, Steering Committee
Mark Constas, Steering Committee

285 International Dyslexia Association (IDA)
40 York Road
4th Floor
Baltimore, MD 21204-2044
410-296-0232
800-222-3123
Fax: 410-321-5069
E-mail: info@interdys.org
http://www.interdys.org/
The International Dyslexia Association (IDA) is a scientific and educational organization dedicated to the study and treatment of the learning disability dyslexia as well as related language based differences.

Lee Grossman, Executive Director
Eric Q Tridas, President

286 Journalism Education Association
Kansas State University
103 Kedzie Hall
Manhattan, KS 66506-1505
785-532-5532
866-532-5532
Fax: 785-532-5563
E-mail: jea@spub.ksu.edu
http://www.jea.org
Among JEA's 2,100 members are journalism teachers and publications advisers, media professionals, press associations, adviser organizations, libraries, yearbook companies, newspapers, radio stations and departments of journalism.

Mark Newton, President
Sarah Nichols, Vice President

287 National Association for Bilingual Education
NABE Marketplace
8701 Georgia Ave
Suite 700
Silver Spring, MD 20910
240-450-3700
Fax: 240-450-3799
E-mail: nabe@nabe.org
http://www.nabe.org
Advocate for our nation's Bilingual and English Language Learners and families and to cultivate a multilingual multicultural society by supporting and promoting policy, programs, pedagogy, research and professional development that yield academic success, value native language, lead to English proficiency and respect cultural and linguistic diversity.

Eudes Budhi, President
Santiago V. Wood, Ed.D, National Executive Director

288 National Council of Teachers of English
1111 W Kenyon Road
Urbana, IL 61801-1096
217-328-3870
877-369-6283
Fax: 217-328-9645

E-mail: public_info@ncte.org
http://www.ncte.org
Promotes the development of literacy, the use of language to construct personal and public worlds and to achieve full participation in society, through the learning and teaching of English and the related arts and sciences of language.

Sandy Hayes, President
Ernest Morrell, President-Elect

289 National Federation of Modern Language Teachers Association (NFMLTA)
c/o University of Wisconsin-Madison
460 Pierce Street
Monterey, CA 93940
831-647-6510
Fax: 831-647-6514
E-mail: mlj@miis.edu
http://mlj.miis.edu//nfmlta.htm
The purposes of the National Federation of Modern Language Teachers Associations (NFMLTA) are the expansion, promotion, and improvement of the teaching of languages, literatures, and cultures throughout the United States, by a variety of activities including but not limited to the publication of The Modern Language Journal.

Carol Klee, President
Aleidine Moeller, VP

290 National Network for Early Language Learning (NELL)
PO Box 75003
Oklahoma City, OK 73147
405-604-0041
Fax: 405-604-0491
E-mail: nnell@wfu.edu
http://www.nnell.org
Provide leadership to advocate for and support successful early language learning and teaching.

Nadine Jacobsen-McLean, Vice President
Rita Oleksak, President

291 National Research Center on English Learning and Achievement
School of Education
University of Albany
1400 Washington Avenue
Albany, NY 12222-100
518-442-4985
Fax: 518-442-4953
E-mail: educationdean@uamail.albany.edu
http://www.albany.edu
Conduct research dedicated to gaining knowledge to improve students' English and literacy achievement.

Janet I Angelis, Associate Director
Judith A. Langer, Co-Director

292 Sigma Tau Delta
Northern Illinois University
Department of English
Northern Illinois University
DeKalb, IL 60115-2867
815-981-9974
E-mail: sigmatd@niu.edu
http://www.english.org
Main purpose is to confer distinction upon students of the English language and literature in undergraduate, graduate and professional studies. Sigma Tau Delta also recognizes the accomplishments of professional writers who have contributed to the fields of language and literature.

Gloria Hochstein, President-Elect
Sarah Dangelantonio, President

293 Teachers & Writers Collaborative
520 Eighth Avenue
Suite 2020
New York, NY 10018-3306
212-691-6590
888-266-5789
Fax: 212-675-0171
E-mail: info@twc.org
http://www.twc.org
Educate the imagination by offering innovative creative writing programs for students and teachers and by providing a variety of publications and resources to support learning through the literary arts.

Amy Swauger, Director
Jade Triton, Director of Operations

Library Services

294 American Library Association (ALA)
50 E Huron
Chicago, IL 60611-2795
312-944-6780
800-545-2433
Fax: 312-440-9374
E-mail: ala@ala.org
http://www.ala.org
Created to provide leadership for the development, promotion and improvement of library and information services and the profession of librarianship in order to enhance learning and ensure access for all.

Molly Raphael, President-Elect
James G Neal, Treasurer

295 Asian American Curriculum Project (AACP)
529 E Third Avenue
San Mateo, CA 94401
650-375-8286
800-874-2242
Fax: 650-375-8797
E-mail: aacpinc@asianamericanbooks.com
http://www.asianamericanbooks.com
Educate the public about the great diversity of the Asian American experience, through the books we distribute; fostering cultural awareness and to educate Asian Americans about their own heritage, instilling a sense of pride. AACP believes that the knowledge which comes from the use of appropriate materials can accomplish these goals.

Florence M Hongo, President
Shizue Yoshina, Vice President

296 Association for Library & Information Science Education
65 E Wacker Place
Suite 1900
Chicago, IL 60601-7246
312-795-0996
Fax: 312-419-8950
E-mail: contact@alise.org
http://www.alise.org
Promotes innovation and excellence in research, teaching and service for educators and scholars in Library and Information Science and cognate disciplines internationally through leadership, collaboration, advocacy and dissemination of research.

January

Melissa Gross, President
Kathleen Combs, Executive Director

297 Council on Library Technical Assistants (COLT)
900 University Avenue
Riverside, CA 92521

951-872-1012
E-mail: lowen@ucr.edu
http://colt.ucr.edu
An international organization which works to address the issues and concerns of library support staff personnel. The issues cover areas such as technical education, continuing education, certification, job description uniformity and goals of gaining recognition and respect for the professional work done.

Founded: 1967

Jackie Hite, President
Chris Egan, VP

298   International Association of School Librarianship
65 E. Wasker Place
Suite 1900
Chicago, IL 60601-7246
Fax: 312-419-8950
E-mail: iasl@mlahq.org
http://www.iasl-online.org
Provides an international forum for those people interested in promoting effective school library media programs as viable instruments in the educational process. Also provides guidance and advice for the development of school library programs and the school library profession.

Dr Diljit Singh, President
Lorense Das, VP: Association Operations

299   Literary Research Association
7044 S 13th St
Oak Creek, WI 53154
414-908-4924
Fax: 414-768-8001
http://www.literaryresearchassociation.org
A community of scholars dedicated to promoting research that enriches the knowledge, understanding, and development of lifespan literacies in a multicultural and multilingual world.

Founded: 1950

Robert Jimenez, President
Betsy Purcell, Association Manager

300   Pro LiBRA Associates Inc.
436 Springfield Avenue
Summit, NJ 07901-2618
908-918-0077
800-262-0070
Fax: 908-918-0977
E-mail: staffing@prolibra.com
http://www.prolibra.com
PRO LiBRA Associates Inc., is a library service company providing experienced personnel who are specialists in all facets of library service and maintenance to corporations, public entities and individuals. Pro LiBRA has been actively involved staffing libraries and information centers.

Margaret Bennett, Owner/President

Mathematics

301   Eisenhower National Clearinghouse for Mathematics and Science Education
1275 Kinnear Road
Columbus, OH 43212
614-378-4567
800-471-1045
Fax: 614-523-0883
E-mail: info@goENC.com
http://www.goenc.org
Provides excellent resources for professional development programs and for district curriculum coordinators. We can help

by providing carefully selected online resources to support effective teaching and learning in K-12 math and science.

Len Simutis, President

302   Mathematical Association of America (MAA)
1529 18th Street NW
Washington, DC 20036-1358
202-387-5200
800-741-9415
Fax: 202-265-2384
E-mail: maahq@maa.org
http://www.maa.org
Advance the mathematical science, especially at the collegiate level by encouraging effective curriculum and teaching, supporting research, foster scholarship, professional growth and cooperation among professional and students and promote general understanding of mathematics.

Paul Zorn, President
Bob Devaney, President-Elect

303   National Council of Teachers of Mathematics
1906 Association Drive
Reston, VA 20191-1502
703-620-9840
800-235-7566
Fax: 703-476-2970
E-mail: nctm@nctm.org
http://www.nctm.org
The National Council of Teachers of Mathematics is a public voice of mathematics education, providing vision, leadership and professional development to support teachers in ensuring equitable mathematics learning of the highest quality for all students.

Linda M. Gojak, President
Kichoon Yang, Executive Director

Music & Art

304   American Art Therapy Association, Inc.
National Office American Art Therapy Association
4875 Eisenhower Avenue
Suite 240
Alexandria, VA 22304
700-548-5860
888-290-0878
Fax: 703-783-8468
E-mail: info@arttherapy.org
http://www.arttherapy.org
Organization of professional dedicated to the belief that making art is healing and life enhancing.

Mercedes ter Maat, Ph.D, President
Susan Corrigan, Executive Director

305   American Dance Therapy Association
10632 Little Patuxent Parkway
Suite 108
Columbia, MD 21044-3273
410-997-4040
Fax: 410-997-4048
E-mail: info@adta.org
http://www.adta.org
Establish, maintain and support the highest standards of professional identity and competence among dance/movement therapists by promoting education, training, practice and research. Provides avenues of communication among dance/movement therapists and those working in related fields

and increases public awareness of dance/movement therapy.

Sharon Goodill, President
Judy Wager, VP

306   American Musicological Society
6010 College Station
Brunswick, ME 04011-8451
207-798-4243
877-679-7648
Fax: 207-798-4254
E-mail: ams@ams-net.org
http://www.ams-net.org
A non-profit organization to advance research in the various fields of music as a branch of learning and scholarship.

Robert Judd, Executive Director
Al Hipkins, Office Manager

307   Arts Education Partnership
One Massachusetts Avenue NW
Suite 700
Washington, DC 20001-1431
202-326-8693
http://www.aep-arts.org
Dedicated to securing a high-quality arts education for every young person in America.

Founded: 1995

Sandra Ruppert, Director

308   Future Music Oregon
School of Music
1225 University of Oregon
Eugene, OR 97403-1225
541-346-5652
Fax: 541-346-0723
E-mail: stolet@uoregon.edu
http://pages.uoregon.edu/fmo/home
Educational Institute dedicated to the exploration of sound and its creation, and to new forms of musical and new media performance and to the innovative use of computers and other recent technologies to create expressive music and media composition.

Jeffrey Stolet, Director
Brad Foley, Dean, School of Music/Dance

309   International Technology and Engineering Educators Association (ITEEA)
1914 Association Drive
Suite 201
Reston, VA 20191
703-860-2100
Fax: 703-860-0353
E-mail: iteea@iteea.org
http://www.iteea.org
Advance technological capabilities for all people and to nurture and promote the professionalism of those engaged in these pursuits. Meet professional needs and interests of its members as well as improve public understanding of technology, innovation, design and engineering.

William F. Bertrand, President
Steven A. Barbato, Executive Director

310   International Thespian Society
Educational Theatre Association
2343 Auburn Avenue
Cincinnati, OH 45219-2815
513-421-3900
Fax: 513-421-7077
E-mail: info@schooltheatre.org
http://www.schooltheatre.org
Shaping lives through theatre education- honoring student achievement, supporting educators and influencing public opinion. Thespian troupes serve students in grades nine through twelve, and Junior Thespian troupes serve students in grades six through eight.

Founded: 1929

Julie Woffington, Executive Director
Jim Flanagan, Director of Operations

312 Kennedy Center Alliance for Arts Education
John F Kennedy Center for the Performing Arts
PO Box 101510
Arlington, VA 22210
202-416-8817
800-444-1324
Fax: 202-416-8802
E-mail: kcaaen@kennedy-center.org
http://www.kennedy-center.org/education/kcaaen
Advance the quality of education through the inclusion of the arts in K-12 curriculum. The Kennedy Center supports the growth and development of the network and the efforts of participating State Alliances through staff consultation, professional development and other resources.
Nancy Welch w/Andrea Greene, Author
Michael Kaiser, President
David M Rubenstein, Chairman

313 National Art Education Association
1806 Robert Fulton Drive
Suite 300
Reston, VA 20191-1590
703-860-8000
800-299-8321
Fax: 703-860-2960
E-mail: info@arteducators.org
http://www.arteducators.org
Advance visual arts education to fulfill human potential and promote global understanding.
Founded: 1947
Deborah B. Reeve, Ed.D, Executive Director
Dr Robert Sabol, President

314 National Association for Music Education
1806 Robert Fulton Drive
Reston, VA 20191
703-860-4000
800-336-3768
Fax: 703-860-1531
E-mail: mbrserv@menc.org
http://www.nafme.org
The MENC serves millions of students through activities from pre-school and up and works to ensure every student has access to comprehensive, well-balanced, and high quality music instruction taught by qualified teachers.
72 pages
ISSN: 0027-4321
Michael Butera, Executive Director/CEO
Mike Blakeslee, Deputy Exec Dir/COO

315 National Association of Schools of Music (NASM)
11250 Roger Bacon Drive
Suite 21
Reston, VA 20190-5248
703-437-0700
Fax: 703-437-6312
E-mail: info@arts-accredit.org
http://nasm.arts-accredit.org/
NASM is an organization of schools, conservatories, colleges and universities, with approximately 638 accredited members. It establishes national standards for undergraduate and graduate degrees and other credentials.
Founded: 1924
Samual Hope, Executive Director
Karen P. Moynahan, Associate Director

316 National Dance Education Organization
8609 Second Ave
Suite 203 B
Silver Spring, MD 20910
301-585-2880
Fax: 301-585-2888
http://www.ndeo.org
Affords every citizen equal access and opportunity to quality dance arts education regardless of gender, age, race or culture, socio-economic status, ability or interest.
Founded: 1998

317 National Endowment For The Arts
1100 Pennsylvania Ave
Washington, DC 20506
202-682-5400
http://www.nea.gov
To advance artistic excellence, creativity, and innovation for the benefit of individuals and communities.
Joan Shigekawa, Acting Chairman

318 National Guild of Community Schools of the Arts
National Guild for Community Arts Education
520 8th Avenue
Suite 302
New York, NY 10018
212-268-3337
Fax: 212-268-3995
E-mail: jonathanherman@nationalguild.org
http://www.nationalguild.org
Supports and advances access to lifelong learning opportunities in the arts. Foster the creation and development of community arts education organizations by providing research and information resources, professional development networking opportunities and funding and by advocating on behalf of the field.
Jonathan Herman, Executive Director
Kenneth Cole, Associate Director

319 National Institute of Art and Disabilities
551 23rd Street
Richmond, CA 94804-1626
510-620-0290
Fax: 510-620-0326
E-mail: gallery@niadart.org
http://www.niadart.org
NIAD is an innovative visual arts center assisting adults with developmental and other physical disabilities.
Deborah Dyer, Executive Director
Brian Stechshshulte, Gallery Director

Physical Education

320 American Alliance for Health, Physical Education, Recreation and Dance(AAHPERD)
1900 Association Drive
Reston, VA 20191-1598
703-476-3400
800-213-7193
Fax: 703-476-9527
E-mail: info@aahperd.org
http://www.aahperd.org
Promote and support leadership, research, education and best practices in the professions that support creative, healthy and active lifestyles.
E Paul Roetert, CEO
Irene Cucina, President

321 International Council for Health, Physical Education and Recreation
1900 Association Drive
Reston, VA 20191-1598
703-476-3462
Fax: 703-476-9527
E-mail: ichper@aahperd.org
http://www.ichpersd.org
ICHPERSD is committed to fostering the essence of education in HPERSD fields through international understanding and goodwill, safeguarding peace, freedom, and respect for human dignity. ICHPERSD is committed to promoting quality HPERSD programs, professional standards, scholarly pursuits, research, and exchanges of knowledge among its constituent members, as well as other concerned professionals and institutions.
Dr Adel M. Elnashar, President
Dr Magda Al-Shazly, Secretary General

322 National Association for Girls and Women in Sports
1900 Association Drive
Reston, VA 20191-1598
703-476-3453
800-213-7193
Fax: 703-476-4566
E-mail: nagws@aahperd.org
http://www.aahperd.org/nagws
Develop and deliver equitable and quality sport opportunities for all girls and women through relevant research, advocacy, leadership development, educational strategies and programming in a manner that promotes social justice and change.
Lynda Ransdell, President
Heidi Parker, VP

323 National Association of Academic Advisors for Athletics
240 Jeter Drive
300 Case Academic Center
Raleigh, NC 27695-9007
919-513-1007
Fax: 919-513-0541
E-mail: info@nfoura.org
http://www.nfoura.org
Aim is to promote academic achievement and personal development among student athletes.
Bart Byrd, President
Jim Pignataro, President-Elect

324 National Association of Sport and Physical Education
1900 Association Dr
Reston, VA 20191
703-476-3410
800-213-7193
Fax: 703-476-8316
E-mail: naspe@aahperd.org
http://www.aahperd.org/naspe
To enhance knowledge, improve professional practice, and increase support for high quality physical education, sport, and physical activity programs.
Mary Jo Sariscsany, President
Steve Mitchell, President Elect

325 National Athletic Trainers' Association
2952 Stemmons Freeway
Suite 200
Dallas, TX 75247-6196
214-637-6282
Fax: 214-637-2206
E-mail: webmaster@nata.org
http://www.nata.org

Enhance the quality of health care provided by certified athletic trainers and to advance the athletic training profession.

Jim Thornton, President
Eve Becker-Doyle, Executive Director

326 President's Council on Fitness, Sports & Nutrition
President's Council on Fitness, Sports & Nutrition
Tower Bldg
1101 Wootton Pkwy, Suite 560
Rockville, MD 20852
202-276-9567
Fax: 202-276-9860
E-mail: fitness@hhs.gov
http://www.fitness.gov
Promotes programs motivating people to make healthy lifestyle choices including good nutrition and regular physical activity in order to lead active, healthy lives.

Shellie Pfohl, Executive Director
Shannon Foster, Communications/Public Aff

327 Sporting Goods Manufacturers Association
8505 Fenton Street
Suite 211
Silver Spring, MD 20910
301-495-6321
Fax: 301-495-6322
E-mail: mmay@sgma.com
Boosts amateur sports and physical education at all levels.

Mike May, Executive Director

Reading

328 Clearinghouse on Reading, English & Communication
ERIC Program
c/o CSC 655 15th St NW
Suite 500
Washington, DC 20005
202-362-0700
800-538-3742
Fax: 202-362-3740
E-mail: ericpub@csc.com
http://www.eric.ed.gov
Provide a comprehensive, easy to use, searchable, internet based bibliographic and full text database of education research and information that also meets the requirements of the Education Sciences Reform Act of 2002.

John Collins
Mark Constas

329 International Reading Association
International Reading Association
800 Barksdale Road
PO Box 8139
Newark, DE 19714-8139
302-731-1600
800-336-7323
Fax: 302-731-1057
E-mail: customerservice@reading.org
http://www.reading.org
Promote reading by continuously advancing the quality of literacy instruction and research worldwide.

Carrice C. Cummins, President
Marcie Craig, Executive Director

330 National Center for ESL Literacy Education
CAELA Newtwork
c/o Center for Applied Linguistics
4646 40th Street NW, Suite 200
Washington, DC 20016-1859

202-362-0700
Fax: 202-363-7204
E-mail: caelntwork@cal.org
http://www.cal.org/
Improve communication through better understanding of language and culture by promoting the teaching & learning of languages, solving problems related to language and culture, resource for information about language and conducting research on issues related to language and culture.

Donna Christian, President
Joy Kreeft Peyton, Vice President

331 National Contact Hotline
Contact Center, Inc.
PO Box 81826
Lincoln, NE 68501-1826
800-228-8813
A 25-year-old information and referral agency, to help individuals with literacy problems. Maintains a database of over 7,000 literacy programs across the country and the 7-day hotline.

332 ProLiteracy Worldwide
104 Marcellus Street
Syracuse, NY 13204
315-422-9121
888-528-2224
Fax: 315-422-6369
E-mail: info@proliteracy.org
http://www.proliteracy.org
ProLiteracy champions the power of literacy to improve the lives of adults and their families creating a world where everyone can read, write and use technology to lead healthy, productive and fulfilling lives.

Kevin Morgan, Interim President/CEO
Nikki Zollar, Secretary

333 Reading Recovery Council of North America
500 W Wilson Bridge Road
Suite 250
Worthington, OH 43085-5218
614-310-7323
Fax: 614-310-7345
E-mail: jjohnson@readingrecovery.org
http://www.readingrecovery.org
We prevent literacy failure by supporting specialized and continuous professional development that results in strong teaching to improve student achievement.

Jady Johnson, Executive Director
Linda Wilson, Executive Assistant

Secondary Education

334 American Driver & Traffic Safety Education Association (ADTSEA)
National Education Association (NEA)
Indiana University of Pennsylvania
1434 Trim Tree Road
Indiana, PA 15701
724-801-8246
877-485-7172
Fax: 724-349-5042
E-mail: office@adtsea.org
http://www.adtsea.org
Develop and promote a level of excellence among driver education professionals in the delivery of instruction to the novice driver; thus equipping the novice driver with skills for driving in today's challenging highway transportation system.

Connie Sessoms, Jr., President
Stan Henderson, President-Elect

335 Association for Institutional Research
Association for Institutional Research
1435 E Piedmont Drive
Suite 211
Tallahassee, FL 32308
850-385-4155
Fax: 850-385-5180
E-mail: air@airweb.org
http://www.airweb.org
Provides educational resources, best practices and professional development opportunities for more than 4,000 members.

Randy Swing, Ph.D., Executive Director
Donna Carlsen, Membership Coordinator

336 Association for Middle Level Education
4151 Executive Parkway
Suite 300
Westerville, OH 43081
614-895-4730
800-528-6672
Fax: 614-895-4750
E-mail: info@amle.org
http://www.amle.org
AMLE has been a voice for those committed to the educational and developmental needs of young adolescents. AMLE is the only national education association dedicated exclusively to those in the middle level grades.

Jeff La Roux, President
William D. Waidelich, Ed.D., Executive Director

337 Close-Up Foundation
1330 Braddock Place
Suite 400
Alexandria, VA 22314
703-706-3300
800-336-5479
Fax: 703-706-0001
E-mail: info@closeup.org
http://www.closeup.org
Informs, inspires and empowers young people to exercise their rights and accept the responsibilities of citizens in a democracy.

Joel Jankowsky, Chairman, Board of Directors
Timothy S Davis, President/CEO

338 College Board
The College Board National Office
45 Columbus Avenue
New York, NY 10023-6917
212-713-8000
Fax: 212-713-8282
E-mail: store.help@collegeboard.org
http://www.collegeboard.com
The College Board seeks to ensure all students are prepared to succeeed in college, helps students connect with and complete a college education and is a leading advocate and resource for excellence and equity in education.

David Coleman, President
Herb Elish, COO

339 National Business Education Association
1914 Association Drive
Reston, VA 20191-1596
703-860-8300
Fax: 703-620-4483
E-mail: nbea@nbea.org
http://www.nbea.org
NBEA is committed to the advancement of the professional interest and competence of its members and provides programs and services that enhance members' professional growth and development.

Ramona Schoenrock, President
Marlene T. Stout, President-Elect

Science

340 Academy of Applied Science
24 Warren Street
Concord, NH 03301
603-228-4530
Fax: 603-228-4730
E-mail: admin@aas-world.org
http://www.aas-world.org
Promotes interest of youth in the applied science, disseminate results of scientific research and studies. Nationally recognized resource center offering enrichment programs for children and professional development for teachers and administrators.

Sheldon Apsell, Chairman
Joanne Hayes-Rines, Vice-President

341 American Association of Physics Teachers
One Physics Ellipse
College Park, MD 20740-3845
301-209-3311
Fax: 301-209-0845
http://www.aapt.org
To enhance the understanding and appreciation of physics through teaching.

Founded: 1930

Beth Cunningham, Executive Officer

342 Association for Advancement of Computing in Education (AACE)
PO Box 1545
Chesapeake, VA 23327-1545
757-366-5606
Fax: 703-997-8760
E-mail: info@aace.org
http://www.aace.org
An international, not-for-profit educational organization advancing information technology in education and e-learning research, development, learning and its practical application.

Gary H Marks Ph.D, Executive Director

343 Association for Science Teacher Education
9324 27th Avenue
Eau Claire, WI 54703
715-838-0893
Fax: 715-838-0893
E-mail: ExecutiveDirector@TheASTE.org
http://theaste.org
Promotes leadership and support for professionals involved in the education and development of teachers of science at all levels. ASTE advances practice and policy through scholarship, collaboration and innovation in science teacher education across the world.

John Tillotson, President
Robert Hollon, Executive Director

344 Association of Science-Technology Centers
1025 Vermont Avenue NW
Suite 500
Washington, DC 20005-6310
202-783-7200
Fax: 202-783-7207
E-mail: info@astc.org
http://www.astc.org
The Association of Science-Technology Centers (ASTC) is an organization of science centers and museums dedicated to furthering the public understanding of science among increasingly diverse audiences. ASTC encourages excellence and innovation in informal science learning by serving and linking its members worldwide and advancing their common goals.

Bryce Seidl, President
Nohora Hoyos, Executive Director

345 California Biomedical Research Association
PO Box 19340
Sacramento, CA 95819-0340
916-558-1515
Fax: 916-558-1523
E-mail: info@ca-biomed.org
http://www.ca-biomed.org
To promote and protect the continued advancement of human and animal health through biomedical research, teaching, and testing

Michael B. Ballinger, Chair
Boris Predovich, President and CEO

346 Energy Education Group(Educators for the Environment)
The California Study, Inc.
664 Hilary Drive
Tiburon, CA 94920
415-435-4574
Fax: 415-435-7737
E-mail: energyforkeeps@aol.com
http://www.energyforkeeps.org
Provides information about where our electricity comes from and how energy choices affect our lives, our environment and future generations.

Marilyn Nemzer, Executive Director
Deborah Page, Lead Writer

347 Geothermal Education Office
664 Hilary Drive
Tiburon, CA 94920
Fax: 415-435-7737
E-mail: 24hrcleanpower@gmail.com
http://www.geothermal.marin.org
To promote public understanding about geothermal resources and its importance in providing clean sustainable energy while protecting our environment.

Marliyn L Nemzer, Executive Director

348 History of Science Society
University of Notre Dame
440 Geddes Hall
Notre Dame, IN 46556
574-631-1194
Fax: 574-631-1533
E-mail: Info@hssonline.org
http://www.hssonline.org
Foster interest in the history of science and its social and cultural relations.

Founded: 1924

Robert J Malone, Executive Director
Greg Macklem, Society Coordinator

349 Institute for Earth Education
Cedar Cove
PO Box 115
Greenville, WV 24945
304-832-6404
Fax: 304-832-6077
E-mail: info@ieetree.org
http://www.eartheducation.org
An international network of individuals and organizations committed tot developing a serious educational response to the environmental problems of the earth.

Steve Van Matre, Chairman
David Dodson, Office Coordinator

350 National Association for Research in Science Teaching (NARST)
12100 Sunset Hills Road
Suite 130
Reston, VA 20190-3221
703-234-4138
Fax: 703-435-4390
E-mail: info@narst.org
http://www.narst.org
NARST is a worldwide organization of professionals committed to the improvement of science teaching and learning through research. NARST promotes research in science education and the communication of knowledge generated by the research. The ultimate goal of NARST is to help all learners achieve science literacy.

William C Kyle JR, Executive Director
Sharon Lynch, President

351 National Association of Biology Teachers
1313 Dolley Madison Boulevard
Suite 402
McLean, VA 22101
703-264-9696
888-501-6227
Fax: 703-790-2672
E-mail: office@nabt.org
http://www.nabt.org
Empowers educators to provide the best possible biology and life science education for all students.

Mark Little, President
Jaclyn Reeves-Pepin, Executive Director

352 National Association of Geoscience Teachers
200 Division St
Suite 210
Northfield, MN 55057
507-222-5634
Fax: 507-222-5175
http://www.nagt.org
Works to foster improvement in the teaching of the earth sciences at all levels of formal and informal instruction, to emphasize the cultural significance of the earth sciences and to disseminate knowledge in this field to the general public..

Cathryn Manduca, Executive Director

353 National Center for Science Education
420 40th Street
Suite 2
Oakland, CA 94609-2688
510-601-7203
800-290-6006
Fax: 510-601-7204
E-mail: info@ncse.com
http://www.ncse.com
Provides information and resources for schools, parents and concerned citizens working to keep evolution and climate science in public school education. We educate the press and the public about the scientific and educational aspects of controversies surrounding the teaching of evolution and climate change and supply needed information and advice to defend good science education at local, state and national levels.

ISSN: 1064-2358

Eugenie C Scott, Executive Director

354 National Earth Science Teachers Association
PO Box 20854
Boulder, CO 80308-3854
http://www.nestanet.org
To facilitate and advance excellence in Earth and space science education.

Founded: 1983

Missy Holzer, President
Roberta Johnson, Executive Director

355 National Institute for Science Education
1025 W Johnson Street
Suite 753
Madison, WI 53706-1706
608-263-4200
E-mail: uw-wcer@education.wis.edu
http://www.wcer.wisc.edu/nise

A partnership of the University of Wisconsin-Madison and the National Center for Improving Science Education, Washington, DC, with funding from the National Science Foundation. Strives to strengthen the nation's science enterprise by helping to extend science, mathematics, engineering and technology literacy to all students.

Andrew C Porter, Director
Norman Webb, Associate Director

356 National Science Teachers Association
1840 Wilson Boulevard
Arlington, VA 22201-3000
703-243-7100
800-782-6782
Fax: 703-243-7177
E-mail: pubinfo@nsta.org
http://www.nsta.org
A member-driven organization that publish books and journals for science teachers from kindergarten through college. Provide ways for science teachers to connect with one another, inform congress and the public on questions affecting science literacy and a well educated work force.

Dr. Karen L. Ostlund, President
Bill Badders, President-Elect

357 School Science and Mathematics Association
245 Willard
Stillwater, OK 74078
405-744-8018
http://www.ssma.org
Promotes research, scholarship, and practice that improves school science and mathematics and advances the integration of science and mathematics.

Founded: 1901

358 Science Service
1719 N Street NW
Washington, DC 20036-2888
202-785-2255
Fax: 202-785-1243
E-mail: webmaster@societyforscience.org
http://www.societyforscience.org
Society for Science & the Public (SSP) is a nonprofit 501(c) (3) organization dedicated to the public engagement in scientific research and education. Promote the understanding and appreciation of science and the vital role it plays in human advancement: to inform, educate, inspire.

Elizabeth Marincola, President/Publisher
H Robert Horvitz, Chair

Social Studies

359 African-American Institute
42nd Floor Chanin Building
380 Lexington Avenue
New York, NY 10168-4298
212-949-5666
Fax: 212-682-6174
E-mail: aainy@aaionline.org
http://www.aaionline.org
Promote enlightened engagement between Africa and America through education, training and dialogue.

Amini Kajunju, President/CEO
Kofi A Appenteng, Co-Founder/Chair

360 Association Of American Geographers
1710 16th St NW
Washington, DC 20009-3198
202-234-1450
Fax: 202-234-2744
E-mail: gaia@aag.org
http://www.aag.org
A non-profit scientific and educational society that contributes to the advancement of geography.

Founded: 1904

361 Center for Education Studies
American Textbook Council
1150 Park Ave
12th Floor
New York, NY 10128-599
212-289-5177
http://www.historytextbooks.org
The council reviews history textbooks and other educational materials. It is dedicated to improving the social studies curriculum and civic education in the nation's elementary and high schools.

Founded: 1989

Gilbert T Sewall, Director
Stapley W Emberling, Assistant Director

362 Council for Indian Education
1240 Burlington Avenue
Billings, MT 59102-4224
406-248-3465
Fax: 406-248-1297
E-mail: cie@cie-mt.org
http://www.cie-mt.org
A non-profit corporation that publishes books sold to elementary schools. The council only publishes material that accurately interprets Native American life, culture and ideals to educate Native American readers on their background and history, and to help other readers gain a better understanding of Native Americans.

Hap Gilliland, President/Editor

363 ERIC Clearinghouse for Social Studies Education
Indiana University, Social Studies Dev. Center
2805 E Tenth Street
Suite 140
Bloomington, IN 47408-2698
812-855-3838
800-266-3815
Fax: 812-855-0455
E-mail: ericso@indian.edu
http://www.servicelearning.org
The primary mission of the CSSIE is to improve education in the social studies (history, geography, economics, civics, anthropology, and the social sciences) in elementary and secondary schools. A secondary mission of the CSSIE is to meet professional development needs of the international community of educators through in-service training, content seminars, and curriculum workshops in all curriculum areas.

Dr Terrance Mason, Director
Jane E Henson, Associate Director

364 National Council for Geographic Education
1145 17th St NW
Room 7620
Washington, DC 20036
202-862-8683
E-mail: ncge@ncge.org
http://www.ncge.org
To enhance the status and quality of geography teaching and learning.

Founded: 1915

365 National Council for the Social Studies
8555 Sixteenth Street
Suite 500
Silver Spring, MD 20910
301-588-1800
800-683-0812
Fax: 301-588-2049
E-mail: sgriffin@ncss.org
http://www.socialstudies.org
Social studies educators teach students the content knowledge, intellectual skills, and civic values they need for college, career and civic life. The National Council for the Social Studies provides leadership, service and support for all social studies educators.

Founded: 1921

Susan Griffin, Executive Director
Michael Simpson, Publications Director

366 New England History Teachers Association
Bentley University
Waltham, MA 02452-4705
617-646-0557
E-mail: info@nehta.org
http://www.nehta.org
NEHTA provides teachers, students and academics opportunities to engage in meaningful conversations about the teaching and learning of history and its related disciplines.

Founded: 1897

Edward Dorgan, President
Stephen Armstrong, Vice President

367 North American Association for Environmental Education
2000 P Street NW
Suite 540
Washington, DC 20036
202-419-0412
Fax: 202-419-0415
E-mail: communicator@naaee.org
http://www.naaee.org
Advances environmental education and supports environmental educators in Canada, the United States and Mexico.

October

Michael A. Marzolla, President

368 Society for History Education
PO Box 1578
Borrego Springs, CA 92004
760-767-5938
562-985-8703
Fax: 760-767-5938
E-mail: conniegeorge@thehistoryteacher,org
http://www.csulb.edu/~histeach/ AND
www.thehistoryteacher.org/
Serves as a network for those interested in history and its importance in the classroom.

Connie George, General Manager
Troy Johnson, Board of Directors President

369 Western History Association
University of Alaska Fairbanks
Department of History
605 Gruening
Fairbanks, AK 99775-6460
907-474-6508
E-mail: westernhistoryassociation@gmail.com
http://www.westernhistoryassociation.wildapricot.org
The Western History Association promotes the study and teaching of the North American West as both a frontier and a region.

Founded: 1961

Donald Worster, President
Margaret Connel-Szasz, President-Elect

Technology in Education

370   Agency for Instructional Technology
1800 N StoneLake Drive
Bloomington, IN 47404
812-339-2203
800-457-4509
Fax: 812-333-4218
E-mail: info@ait.net
http://www.ait.net
Provides services and products to enhance student learning. AIT is one of the largest providers of instructional TV programs and other educational media in North America.

Founded: 1962

Robert E. Yocum Jr., President/CEO
Ruth Blankenbaker, Vice Chair

371   Alliance for Technology Access Conference
Alliance for Technology Access
1119 Old Hunboldt Road
Jackson, TN 38301
731-554-5282
Fax: 731-554-5283
E-mail: ATAinfo@ATAccess.org
http://www.ataccess.org
Increases the use of technology by children and adults with disabilities and functional limitations. Encourages and facilitates the empowerment of people with disabilities to participate fully in their communities through public education, information and referral, capacity building in community organizations and advocacy/policy efforts.

James Allison, President
Bob Van der Linde, VP

372   Association for Career and Technical Education
1410 King Street
Alexandria, VA 22314
703-683-3111
800-826-9972
Fax: 703-683-7424
E-mail: acte@acteonline.org
http://www.acteonline.org
The Association for Career and Technical Education is dedicated to the advancement of education that prepares youth and adults for careers.

Founded: 1926

Karen Mason, President
Doug Major, President-Elect

373   Association for Educational Communications & Technology
PO Box 2447
1800 Stonelake Drive
Bloomington, IN 47402-2447
812-335-7675
877-677-2328
Fax: 812-335-7678
E-mail: aect@aect.org
http://www.aect.org
Provides leadership in educational communications and technology by linking a wide range of professionals holding a common interest in the use of educational technology and its application learning process.

Mark Childress, President
Dr. Phillip Harris, Executive Director

374   Center for Educational Technologies
316 Washington Avenue
Wheeling, WV 26003-6243
304-243-2388
800-624-6992
Fax: 304-243-2497
E-mail: webmaster@cet.edu
http://www.cet.edu

The Center for Educational Technologies is an internationally recognized education facility that houses cutting edge educational technology such as rooms wired for distance learning, videoconferencing, multimedia development for the web and much more.

Charles Wood, Executive Director
Laurie Ruberg, Associate Director

375   Computer Using Educators, Inc (CUE)
877 Ygnacio Valley Road
Suite 200
Walnut Creek, CA 94596
925-478-3460
Fax: 925-934-6799
E-mail: cueinc@cue.org
http://www.cue.org
Provides leadership and support to advance student achievement in the educational technology community.

Mike Lawrence, Executive Director
Marisol Valles, Director of Operations

376   Consortium for School Networking
1025 Vermont Avenue NW
Suite 1010
Washington, DC 20005-3007
202-861-2676
866-267-8747
Fax: 202-393-2011
E-mail: info@cosn.org
http://www.cosn.org
CoSN is committed to providing the leadership, community and advocacy tools essential for the success of school district technology leaders. CoSN empowers educational leaders to leverage technology to realize engaging learning environments.

Keith Krueger, CEO
Irene Spero, COO

377   EDUCAUSE
282 Century Place
Suite 5000
Louisville, CO 80027
303-449-4430
Fax: 303-440-0461
E-mail: info@educause.edu
http://www.educause.edu
A nonprofit association whose mission is to advance higher education by promoting the intelligent use of information technology.

Malcolm Brown, Director
Diana G Oblinger, President and CEO

378   Educational Technology Center
360 Huntington Avenue
215 Snell Library
Boston, MA 02115
617-373-2350
Fax: 617-373-3768
E-mail: teaching@neu.edu
http://www.edtech.neu.edu
The exploration, development and dissemination of technology to enhance teaching, learning and research goals. The Center is also an agent of change, helping to formulate policy on technology-supported teaching and learning

Dr. Laurie Poklop, Associate Director
Audrey Aduama, Assistant Director

379   International Society for Technology in Education
1710 Rhode Island Ave NW
Suite 900
Washington, DC 20036
202-861-7777
866-654-4777
Fax: 202-861-0888
E-mail: iste@iste.org
http://www.iste.org

Providing leadership and service to improve teaching and learning by advancing the effective use of technology in PK-12 and teacher education.

Kecia Ray, Ed.D., President-Elect
Holly Jobe, President

380   MarcoPolo
WorldCom Foundation
One Verizon Way
Basking Ridge, NJ 07920
509-374-1951
800-360-7955
Fax: 908-630-2660
E-mail: oposewa@edumedia.com
http://www.marcopolo-education.org
A non-profit consortium of premier national and international education organizations and the MCI Foundation dedicated to providing high quality internet and professional development to teachers and students throughout the United States.

Oksana Posewa, Project Manager
Della Cronin, Prog Officer Communications

381   National Association of Media and Technology Centers
PO Box 9844
Cedar Rapids, IA 52409
319-654-0608
Fax: 319-654-0609
http://www.namtc.org
Committed to promoting leadership among its membership through networking, advocacy, and support activities that will enhance the equitable access to media, technology, and information services to educational communities.

Denise Grasso, President
Slly Lindtren, President-Elect

382   National Institute on Disability and Rehabilitation Research
U.S. Department of Education
400 Maryland Avenue SW
Washington, DC 20202-2572
202-245-7640
800-872-5327
Fax: 202-245-7323
E-mail: nidrr-mailbox@ed.gov
http://www.ed.gov/about/offices/list/osers/nidrr
Generates new knowledge and promotes its effective use to improve the abilities of people with disabilities to perform activities of their choice in the community, and also to expand society's capacity to provide full opportunities and accommodations for its citizens.

Founded: 1978

Arne Duncan, Secretary of Education
Leonard L Haynes III, Executive Director

383   Technology & Media Division
The Council for Exceptional Children
2900 Crystal Drive
Suite 1000
Arlington, VA 22202-3557
703-620-3660
888-232-7733
Fax: 703-264-9494
E-mail: contactus@tamcec.org
http://www.tamcec.org
The purpose of TAM is to support educational participation and improved results for individuals with disabilities and diverse learning needs through the selection, acquisition, and use of technology.

Joel Mittler, President

384   Technology Student Association
1914 Association Drive
Reston, VA 20191-1540

703-860-9000
888-860-9010
Fax: 703-758-4852
E-mail: general@tsaweb.org
http://www.tsaweb.org
Leadership and opportunities in technology, innovation, design and engineering. Members apply STEM concepts through co-curricular programs.

Kevin Terronez, President
Matthew Strinden, President-Elect

385 Technology and Children
International Technology Education Association
1914 Association Drive
Suite 201
Reston, VA 20191-1539
703-860-2100
Fax: 703-860-0353
E-mail: iteea@iteea.org
http://www.iteea.org
To advance technological capabilities for all people and to nurture and promote the professionalism of those engaged in these pursuits. ITEA seeks to meet the professional needs and interests of members as well as to improve public understanding of technology, innovation, design, and engineering education and its contributions.

Steven A. Barbato, Executive Director
William F. Bertrand, President

386 Telemetrics
6 Leighton Place
Mahwah, NJ 07430-3198
201-848-9818
Fax: 201-848-9819
E-mail: info@telemetricsinc.com
http://www.telemetricsinc.com
offers a comprehensive line of camera robotics and control systems for broadcast, industrial, educational and military applications.
Founded: 1950

Anthony C Cuomo, President
Jim Wolfe, Sales Manager

387 Twenty First Century Teachers Network: The McGuffey Project
888 17th Street NW
12th Floor
Washington, DC 20006
202-429-0572
Fax: 202-296-2962
E-mail: info@mcguffey.org
http://www.21ct.org/
A nationwide, non-profit initiative of the McGuffey Project, dedicated to assisting K-2 teachers learn, use and effectively integrate technology in the curriculum for improved student learning.

Wade D Sayer, Project Director, Director Program Development

388 V-LINC
V-LINC
2301 Argonne Drive
Baltimore, MD 21218
410-554-9134
800-772-7372
Fax: 410-261-2907
E-mail: info@linc.org
http://www.v-linc.org
V-LINC was created out of a merger between Learning Independence through computers and Volunteers for Medical Engineering. V-LINC's focus is on improving the independence and quality of life for individuals with disabilities. Provides innovative technology solutions and training

that assist individuals in their home, community and workplace.
Founded: 2010

Theo Pinette, Executive Director
John Walker, Project Coordinator

Alabama

389 Alabama Business Education Association
A&M University
School of Business
PO Box 429
Normal, AL 35762
256-372-4799
Fax: 256-851-5568
E-mail: karzetta@bellsouth.net
http://www.alabamabusinessed.org
A professional association for business and marketing educators at the secondary and post-secondary levels.

Karzetta Bester, President
Emma Fault, President-Elect

390 Alabama Commission on Higher Education
PO Box 302000
Montgomery, AL 36130-2000
334-242-1998
800-960-7773
Fax: 334-242-0268
E-mail:
deborah.nettles@ache.alabama.gov
http://www.ache.alabama.gov
Provides information on the state's education programs, college and universities, financial aid assistance programs, grants, scholarships, continuing education programs, and career opportunities.

391 Alabama Education Association
422 Dexter Avenue
Montgomery, AL 36104-3743
334-834-9790
800-392-5839
Fax: 334-262-8377
E-mail: myaea@alaedu.org
http://www.myaea.org
Serves as an advocate for Alabama teachers and leads in the advancement of equitable and quality public education.

Dorothy Strickland, President
Dr. Henry Mabry, Executive Secretary

392 Alabama Library Association
9154 Eastchase Parkway
Suite 418
Montgomery, AL 36117
334-414-0113
877-563-5146
Fax: 334-265-1281
E-mail: admin@allanet.org
http://www.allanet.org
Non-profit corporation formed to encourage and promote the welfare of libraries and professional interests of librarians in Alabama. Provides leadership for the development, advocacy and improvement of library and information services and to promote the profession of librarianship, in order to enhance learning and ensure access to information for all.

Emily Tish, President
Jeff Simpson, President-Elect

393 Alabama Public Library Service
6030 Monticello Dr
Montgomery, AL 36130
334-213-3900
800-723-8459
Fax: 334-213-3993

E-mail: vcarr@apls.state.al.us
http://www.statelibrary.alabama.gov

394 Alabama State Council on the Arts
201 Monroe St
Suite 110
Montgomery, AL 36104
334-240-4076
800-548-2546
Fax: 334-240-3269
E-mail: staff@arts.alabama.gov
http://www.arts.state.al.us
Promotes high-quality education in the arts.

395 Alabama State Education for Homeless Children and Youth
Gordon Persons Building, Room 5348
PO Box 302101
Montgomery, AL 36130-3901
334-242-8199
888-725-9321
Fax: 334-242-0496
E-mail: bthompson@alsde.edu
http://www.alsde.edu/html/home.asp
Ensures that all homeless children and youth have equal access to the same free, appropriate public education.

Alaska

396 Alaska Association of School Librarians
PO Box 101085
Anchorage, AK 99510-1085
907-269-6569
800-776-6566
Fax: 907-269-6580
E-mail: association@akasl.org
http://www.akasl.org
Advances a high standard for the school librarian profession and the library information program in the schools of Alaska.

Nicole Roohi, President
Wendy Stout, President-Elect

397 Alaska Commission on Postsecondary Education
PO Box 110505
Juneau, AK 99811-0505
907-465-2962
800-441-2962
Fax: 907-465-5316
E-mail: customer_service@acpe.state.ak.us
http://www.acpe.alaska.gov
Provides information on the state's education programs, colleges and universities, financial aid assistance programs, grants, scholarships, continuing education programs, and career opportunities.

398 Alaska Library Association
PO Box 81084
Fairbanks, AK 99708
907-459-1020
Fax: 907-459-1024
E-mail: webdeveloper@akla.org
http://www.akla.org
Provides leadership and advocacy for the educational and political concerns of the library community in Alaska. Encourages cooperation among libraries and related groups, safeguards intellectual freedom, and promotes access to information for all Alaskans.

Linda Wynne, President
Stacey Glaser, President-Elect

399 Alaska State Council on the Arts
411 West Fourth Ave
Suite 1E
Anchorage, AK 99501-2343
907-269-6610
888-278-7424
Fax: 907-269-6601

E-mail: gina.brown@alaska.gov
http://www.eed.state.ak.us/aksca
Promotes high-quality education in the arts.

400 Alaska State Education for Homeless Children and Youth
801 West 10th St, Suite 200
PO Box 110500
Juneau, AK 99811-0500
907-465-3826
877-854-5437
Fax: 907-465-2989
E-mail: eed.webmaster@alaska.gov
http://www.eed.state.ak.us/tls/titleX/home.s
html
Ensures that all homeless children and youth have equal access to the same free, appropriate public education.

Arizona

401 Arizona Commission for Postsecondary Education
2020 North Central Ave
Suite 650
Phoenix, AZ 85004-4503
602-258-2435
Fax: 602-258-2483
E-mail: acpe@highered.gov
http://www.azhighered.gov
Provides information on the state's education programs, colleges and universities, financial aid assistance programs, grants, scholarships, continuing education programs, and career opportunities.

402 Arizona Commission on the Arts
471 West Roosevelt St
Phoenix, AZ 85003-1326
602-771-6501
Fax: 602-256-0282
E-mail: info@azarts.gov
http://www.azarts.gov
Promotes high-quality education in the arts.

403 Arizona Library Association
1030 E Baseline Road
Suite 105-1025
Tempe, AZ 85283
480-609-3999
Fax: 480-609-3939
E-mail: admin@azla.org
http://www.azla.org
Promotes library service and librarianship in libraries of all types in the state of Arizona.

Debbie Hanson, Executive Director

404 Arizona School Boards Association
2100 N Central Avenue
Suite 200
Phoenix, AZ 85004-1441
602-254-1100
800-238-4701
Fax: 602-254-1177
http://www.azsba.org
Promotes community volunteer governance of public education and continuous improvement of student success by providing training, leadership and assistance to public school governing boards.

Randy Schiller, President
Dr. Timothy Ogle, Executive Director

405 Arizona State Education for Homeless Children and Youth
1535 West Jefferson St
Bin 14
Phoenix, AZ 85007
602-542-4963
800-352-4558
Fax: 602-542-5175
E-mail: frank.migali@azed.gov

http://www.azed.gov/schooleffectiveness/sp
ecialpops/homeless
Ensures that all homeless children and youth have equal access to the same free, appropriate public education.

406 Arizona State Library, Archives, and Public Records
1700 West Washington
Suite 200
Phoenix, AZ 85007
602-926-4035
800-228-4710
Fax: 602-256-7983
E-mail: services@lib.az.us
http://www.lib.az.us

Arkansas

407 Arkansas Arts Council
323 Center St
1500 Tower Building
Little Rock, AR 72201-2606
501-324-9766
Fax: 501-324-9207
E-mail: info@arkansasarts.com
http://www.arkansasarts.com
Promotes high-quality education in the arts.

408 Arkansas Business Education Association
Bryant Junior High School
201 Sullivan
Bryant, AR 72022
501-847-5620
Fax: 501-847-5627
E-mail: keliason@nettleschools.net
http://www.abea.us
A professional association comprised of business and marketing educators involved at the secondary and post-secondary levels. Promotes quality education in all phases of business and to encourage professional growth and cooperative interaction among all individuals involved in this sector of education.

Michael Lentz, President
Tammy Ward, President-Elect

409 Arkansas Department of Higher Education
114 East Capitol
Little Rock, AR 72201-3818
501-371-2000
Fax: 501-371-2001
E-mail: rickj@adhe.edu
http://www.adhe.edu
Provides information on the state's education programs, colleges and universities, financial aid assistance programs, grants, scholarships, continuing education programs, and career opportunities.

410 Arkansas Education Association
1500 W 4th Street
Little Rock, AR 72201
501-375-4611
800-632-0624
Fax: 501-375-4620
E-mail: ldimond@nea.org
http://www.aeaonline.org
Advocates for education professionals and unites members and the state to fulfill the promise of public education to prepare every student to succeed in a diverse and interdependent world.

Donna Morey, President
Brenda Robinson, VP

411 Arkansas Library Association
PO Box 958
Benton, AR 72018-0958

501-860-7585
Fax: 501-778-4014
E-mail: arlib2@sbcglobal.net
http://www.arlib.org
Furthers the professional development of all library staff members, fosters communication and cooperation among librarians, trustees and friends of libraries; increases the visibility of libraries among the general public and funding agencies; to serve as an advocate for librarians and libraries.

Founded: 1911

Lynda Hampel, Executive Administrator
Patricia Miller, President

412 Arkansas State Education for Homeless Children and Youth
Four Capitol Mall, Arch Ford Bldg
Room 305-B
Little Rock, AR 72201-1071
501-682-4847
Fax: 501-682-3372
E-mail: cindy.hogue@arkansas.gov
http://www.askansased.org
Ensures that all homeless children and youth have equal acces to the same free, appropriate public education.

California

413 California Arts Council
1300 I St
Suite 930
Sacramento, CA 95814
916-322-6555
800-201-6201
Fax: 916-322-6575
E-mail: dgolling@cac.ca.gov
http://www.cac.ca.gov
Promotes high-quality education in the arts.

414 California Association for Bilingual Education
16033 E San Bernardino Rd
Covina, CA 91722-3900
626-814-4441
Fax: 626-814-4640
http://www.bilingualeducation.org

415 California Business Education Association
PO Box 2591
Walnut Creek, CA 94595
925-295-1104
Fax: 925-295-1104
E-mail: cbeaquestions@cbeaonline.org
http://www.cbeaonline.org
The prime mission of CBEA is to recognize, encourage, and promote excellence in business disciplines. Also, it is to collaborate with other disciplines and other groups dedicated to this mission.

Irina Weisblat, President
Lisa Natwick, Secretary

416 California Classical Association-Northern Section
San Francisco State University
Department of Classics
San Francisco, CA 94132
415-253-2267
Fax: 415-338-2514
E-mail: ccanorth@yahoo.com
http://www.ccanorth.org
Funds support programs to enrich and promote Classical Studies.

Founded: 1969

Mary McCarty, President
Holly Coty, VP

417 California Foundation for Agriculture in the Classroom
2300 River Plaza Drive
Sacramento, CA 95833
916-561-5625
800-700-2482
Fax: 916-561-5697
E-mail: info@learnaboutag.org
http://www.LearnAboutAg.org
Our mission is to increase awareness and understanding of agriculture among California's educators and students. Our vision is an appreciation of agriculture by all.
Judy Culbertson, Executive Director
Mindy DeRohan, Communications Coordinator

418 California Library Association
2471 Flores St
San Mateo, CA 94403
650-376-0886
Fax: 650-539-2341
E-mail: info@cla-net.org
http://www.cla-net.org
Provides leadership for the development, promotion, and improvement of library services, librarianship, and the library community. A resource for learning about new ideas and technology.
Derek Wolfgram, President
Rosario Garza, Executive Director

419 California Reading Association
638 Camino De Los Mares
Suite H130/476
San Clemente, CA 92673
714-435-1983
Fax: 714-435-0269
E-mail: kathy@californiareads.org
http://www.californiareads.org
CRA is an independent, self-governing organization dedicated to increasing literacy in California.
Kathy Belanger, Administrative Director
Lynn Gurnee, President

420 California School Library Association
6444 E. Spring Street
#237
Long Beach, CA 90815-1553
888-655-8480
Fax: 888-655-8480
E-mail: info@csla.net
http://www.csla.net
Advocates, educates and collaborates to ensure the all California students and educators are effective users of ideas and information.
Jane Lofton, President

421 California State Homeless Education
1430 N St
Suite 4401
Sacramento, CA 95814
916-319-0383
866-856-8214
Fax: 916-319-0126
E-mail: lwheeler@cde.ca.gov
http://www.cde.ca.gov/sp/hs
Ensures that all homeless children and youth have equal access to the same free, appropriate public education.

422 California Student Aid Commission
PO Box 419027
Rancho Cordova, CA 95741-9027
916-526-7590
888-224-7268
Fax: 916-526-8004
E-mail: studentsupport@csac.ca.gov
http://www.csac.ca.gov

Provides information on the state's education programs, college and universities, financial aid assistance programs, grants, scholarships, continuing education programs, and career opportunities.

423 California Teachers Association
1705 Murchison Drive
Burlingame, CA 94010
650-697-1400
Fax: 650-552-5002
E-mail: webmaster@cta.org
http://www.cta.org
Protects and promotes the well-being of California teachers by improving the conditions of teaching and learning and advancing the cause of universal education.
Dean E. Vogel, President
Eric Heins, Vice President

424 Northern California Comprehensive Assistance Center
730 Harrison Street
San Francisco, CA 94107
415-565-3000
877-493-7833
Fax: 415-565-3012
E-mail: plloyd@wested.com
http://www.wested.org
WestEd's Assessment and Standards Development Services program has helped shape effective statewide assessment and accountability systems nationwide. Works with education and other communities to promote excellence, achieve equity, and improve learning for children, youth and adults.
Sri Ananda, Chief Program Officer
Glen Harvey, Chief Executive Officer

425 WestEd
730 Harrison Street
San Francisco, CA 94107-1242
415-565-3000
877-493-7833
Fax: 415-565-3012
E-mail: dtorres@wested.org
http://www.WestEd.org
A research, development and service agency, works with education and other communities to promote excellence, achieve equity, and improve learning for children, youth and adults. WestEd has offices in Georgia, Arizona, Vermont, Illinois and Washington DC as well.
Danny Torres, Publications Manager
Glen H. Harvey, CEO

Colorado

426 Colorado Association of Libraries
3030 W 81st Ave
Westminster, CO 80031
303-463-6400
Fax: 303-458-0002
E-mail: cal@cal-webs.org
http://www.cal-webs.org
The Colorado Association of Libraries (CAL) is the common bond, voice, and power for the library community. Advocate for quality library services, support access to information and foster the professional development.
Stephen Sweeney, President
Kari May, VP/President-Elect

427 Colorado Business Educators
Prairie High School
300 Thomas
Box 82
New Rayemr, CO 80742

970-437-5386
Fax: 970-437-5732
E-mail: jean.sykes@mcclave.k12.co.us
http://www.cbeweb.org
Supports business educators in Colorado with curriculum material and career networking.
Lucinda Carpenter, President
Rebecca Diggs, Secretary

428 Colorado Community College & Occupational Education System
9101 E Lowry Boulevard
Denver, CO 80230-6011
303-620-4000
Fax: 303-620-4030
E-mail: marybeth.noble@cccs.edu
http://www.cccs.edu
The Colorado Community College System comprises the state's largest system of higher education serving more than 117,000 students annually. Provides an accessible, responsive learning environment that facilitates the achievement of educational, professional and personal goals.
Nancy McCallin, President
Claire Kuhns, Executive Asst to President

429 Colorado Council on the Arts
1625 Broadway
Suite 2700
Denver, CO 80202
303-892-3802
Fax: 303-892-3848
E-mail: jeanette.albert@state.co.us
http://www.coloarts.org
Promotes high-quality education in the arts.

430 Colorado Department of Higher Education
1560 Broadway
Suite 1600
Denver, CO 80202
303-866-2723
Fax: 303-866-4266
E-mail: executivedirector@dhe.state.co.us
http://www.highered.colorado.gov
Provides information on the state's education programs, colleges and universities, financial aid assistance programs, grants, scholarships, continuing education programs, and career opportunities.

431 Colorado Education Association
1500 Grant Street
Denver, CO 80203-1800
303-837-1500
800-332-5939
Fax: 303-837-9006
http://www.coloradoea.org
The Colorado Education Association is a voluntary membership organization of 38,000 K-12 teachers and education support professionals; higher education faculty and support professionals; retired educators; and students preparing to become teachers.
Kerrie Dallman, President
Amie Baca-Oehlert, Vice President

432 Colorado State Education for Homeless Children and Youth
201 East Colfax Ave
Room 306 E
Denver, CO 80203-1799
303-866-6930
Fax: 303-866-6785
E-mail: scott_d@cde.state.co.us
http://www.cde.state.co.us/cdeprevention/homeless_index.htm
Ensures that all homeless children and youth have equal opportunity to the same free, appropriate public education.

Connecticut

433 **Connecticut Business & Industry Association (CBIA)**
350 Church Street
Hartford, CT 06103-1126
860-244-1900
Fax: 860-278-8562
E-mail: bellj@cbia.com
http://www.cbia.com
Serves as an advocate for the general business and industry community in Connecticut. Promotes a business climate that is globally competitive, encourages communication and cooperation among businesses, government, the private sector and general public.

Jim Bell, Business Consulting Director
Joe Budd, Media/Public Relations

434 **Connecticut Commission on Culture and Tourism**
1 Constitution Plaza
Hartford, CT 06103
860-256-2800
Fax: 860-256-2811
E-mail: leigh.johnson@ct.gov
http://www.cultureandtourism.org/cct/site/default.asp
Promotes high-quality education in the arts.

435 **Connecticut Department of Higher Education**
61 Woodland St
Hartford, CT 06105-2326
860-947-1800
Fax: 860-947-1310
E-mail: lnegro@ctdhe.org
http://www.ctdhe.org
Provides information on the state's education programs, colleges and universities, financial aid assistance programs, grants, scholarships, continuing education programs, and career opportunities.

436 **Connecticut Education Association (CEA)**
Capitol Place
21 Oak Street
Suite 500
Hartford, CT 06106-8001
860-525-5641
800-842-4316
Fax: 860-725-6323
E-mail: johny@cea.org
http://www.cea.org
CEA advocates for teachers and public education, lobbying legislators for the resources public schools need and campaigning for high standards for teachers and students.

Mark Waxenberg, Executive Director
Linette Branham, Dir. Policy/Pro. Practice

437 **Connecticut Educational Media Association**
21 Oak Street
Suite 500
Hartford, CT 06106
860-525-5641
800-842-4316
Fax: 860-725-6323
http://www.cea.org
Professional association of Connecticut school library media specialist.

Shelia Cohen, President
Jeff Leake, Vice President

438 **Connecticut State Education for Homeless Children and Youth**
25 Industrial Park Rd
Middletown, CT 06457
860-807-2058
Fax: 860-807-2127
E-mail: louis.tallarita@ct.gov
http://www.sde.ct.gov
Ensures that all homeless children and youth have equal access to the same free, appropriate public education.

Delaware

439 **Delaware Business Education Association**
Delcastle High School
140 Brennen Drive
Newark, DE 19713
302-454-2164
E-mail: rhuddj@christina.k12.de.us
Fosters business education in the state of Delaware.

Jennifer Rhudd, President
Lisa Stoner, Membership Director

440 **Delaware Division of Libraries**
121 Duke Of York St
Dover, DE 19901
302-739-4748
800-282-8696
Fax: 302-739-8436
E-mail: sonja.brown@state.de.us
http://www.state.lib.de.us

441 **Delaware Division of the Arts**
820 North French St
Wilmington, DE 19801
302-577-8278
302-577-6561
E-mail: delarts@state.de.us
http://www.artsdel.org
Promotes high-quality education in the arts.

442 **Delaware Higher Education Commission**
820 North French St
Wilmington, DE 19801
302-577-5240
800-292-7935
Fax: 302-577-6765
E-mail: dhec@doe.k12.de.us
http://www.doe.k12.de.us/dehc
Provides information on the state's education programs, colleges and universities, financial aid assistance programs, grants, scholarships, continuing education programs, and career opportunities.

443 **Delaware Library Association**
PO Box 816
Dover, DE 19903-816
816-531-2468
Fax: 302-831-1631
E-mail: danbradbury@gossagesager.com
http://www2.lib.udel.edu/dla
Promotes the profession of librarianship and provides library information and media services to the people of Delaware through a unified library community.

Terri Jones, President
Christine Payne, VP/Conference Planning Chair

444 **Delaware State Education Association**
136 East Water Street
Dover, DE 19901-3630
302-734-5834
866-734-5834
Fax: 392-674-8499
E-mail: pamela.nichols@dsea.org
http://www.dsea.org/
The Delaware State Education Association is a union of public school employees that advocates for the rights and interests of its members and outstanding public education for all students.

Frederika Jenner, President
Mike Hoffman, VP

445 **Delaware State Education for Homeless Children and Youth**
401 Federal St
Suite 2
Dover, DE 19901
302-735-4273
Fax: 301-739-4483
Ensures that all homeless children and youth have equal access to the same free, appropriate public education.

District of Columbia

446 **American Council on Education Library & Information Service**
American Council on Education
1 Dupont Circle NW
Suite 1B-20
Washington, DC 20036-1193
202-939-9300
Fax: 202-833-4730
E-mail: comments@ace.nche.edu
http://www.acenet.edu
The council seeks to provide leadership and a unifying voice on key higher education issues and to influence public policy through advocacy, research, and program initiatives.

Jospeh Aoun, Chair
Diana Natalicio, Vice Chair/Chair-elect

447 **Associates for Renewal in Education (ARE)**
Brenda Strong Nixon Community Complex
45 P Street NW
Brenda Strong Nixon Community Complex
Washington, DC 20001-1133
202-483-9424
Fax: 202-667-5299
E-mail: info@areinc.org
http://www.areinc.org
A multi project agency working to improve the quality of life and education of the young people of the District of Columbia, with an emphasis on youth-at risk and under served populations.

Dayna Nokes, President/CEO
Evie Saunders Davis, Deputy Finance/HR

448 **District Of Columbia Commission on the Arts and Humanities**
1371 Harvard St NW
Washington, DC 20009
202-724-5613
Fax: 202-724-4493
E-mail: carolyn.parker@dc.gov
http://www.dcarts.dc.gov
Promotes high-quality education in the arts.

449 **District of Columbia Library Association**
Benjamin Franklin Station
PO Box 14177
Washington, DC 20044
202-872-1112
E-mail: April.King@dc.gov
http://www.dcla.org
Provides library services to the residents of D.C. and represents the region at the Council of the American Library Association, promoting general and joint enterprises with the American Library Association and other library groups.

Jacqueline Protka, President
Amanda Wilson, VP/President-Elect

450 District of Columbia Office of the State Superintendent of Education
441 Fourth St NW
Suite 350 North
Washington, DC 20001
202-727-6436
877-485-6751
Fax: 202-727-2834
E-mail: osse@dc.gov
http://www.osse.dc.gov
Provides information on the state's education programs, colleges and universities, financial aid assistance programs, grants, scholarships, continuing education programs, and career opportunities.

Florida

451 Florida Arts
500 South Bronough St
Tallahassee, FL 32399-0250
850-245-6470
Fax: 850-245-6497
E-mail: info@florida-arts.org
http://www.florida-arts.org
Promotes high-quality education in the arts.

452 Florida Association for Media in Education
16350 Bruce B. Downs Blvd
#46545
Tampa, FL 33647
813-380-5673
Fax: 850-531-8344
E-mail: www.floriaeducators@gmail.com
http://www.floridamedia.org
FAME advocates for every student in Florida to be involved in and have open access to a quality school library media program administered by a highly competent, certified library media specialist. FAME is a collaborative, responsive, dynamic network for Florida library media professionals.

Cora P. Dunkley, Ph.D, President
Lou Greco, VP

453 Florida Business Technology Education Association
c/o Palm Beach County School District
3310 Forest Hill Boulevard
C-225
West Palm Beach, FL 33406
561-434-7395
E-mail: sslarsen@bellsouth.net
http://www.fbtea.org
Fosters business education in the state of Florida.

Connie Myrick, President
Sue Larsen, Treasurer

454 Florida Education Association
213 South Adams Street
Tallahassee, FL 32301
850-201-2800
888-807-8007
Fax: 850-222-1840
http://www.feaweb.org
Advocates the right to a free, quality public education for all. Advances professional growth, development and status of all who serve the students in Florida's public schools. Engages members and communities to ensure that all students learn and succeed in a diverse world.

Andy Ford, President
Joanne McCall, Vice President

455 Florida Library Association (FLA)
164 NW Madison Street
Suite 104
Lake City, FL
386-438-5795
850-322-5005
Fax: 386-438-5796
E-mail: fla.admin@comcast.net
http://www.flalib.org
The Florida Library Association (FLA) develops programs and undertakes activities to earn it a leadership position for all areas of librarianship. FLA provides opportunities for librarians and support staff in Florida to advance their skills so that they can maintain their effectiveness in the new information age.

Faye C Roberts, Executive Director
Ruth O'Donnell, Conference Manager

456 Florida State Office Of Student Financial Assistance
1940 North Monroe St
Suite 70
Tallahassee, FL 32303-4759
850-410-5180
888-827-2004
Fax: 850-487-1809
E-mail: theresa.antworth@fldoe.org
http://www.floridastudentfinancialaid.org
Provides information on the state's education programs, colleges and universities, financial aid assistance programs, grants, scholarships, continuing education programs, and career opportunities.

Georgia

457 Georgia Association of Educators
100 Crescent Center Parkway
Suite 500
Tucker, GA 30084
678-837-1118
800-282-7142
Fax: 678-837-1100
http://www.gae2.org
The Georgia Association of Educators is a professional organization for public education professionals.

Christopher Turner, Executive Director
Sid Chapman, VP

458 Georgia Business Education Association (GBEA)
Perry High School
1307 N Avenue
Perry, VA 31069
478-988-6315
E-mail: lary.debra@newton.k12.ga.us
http://www.georgiagbea.org
Serves individuals and groups involved in instruction, administration, research and dissemination of information for/about business at all instructional levels.

Dwionne Freeman, President
Renee Waters, President Elect

459 Georgia Council for the Arts
260 14th St NW
Suite 401
Atlanta, GA 30318-5360
404-685-2787
Fax: 404-685-2788
E-mail: gaarts@gaarts.org
http://www.gaarts.org
Promotes high-quality education in the arts.

460 Georgia Library Association
PO Box 793
Rex, GA 30273

678-466-4334
800-999-8558
Fax: 678-466-4349
E-mail: karamullen@clayton.edu
http://gla.georgialibraries.org
Provides support and encouragement for libraries to advance the educational, cultural, and economic life of the state.

Diana Very, President
Susan Morris, VP

461 Georgia Parents & Teachers Association
114 Baker Street NE
Atlanta, GA 30308-3366
404-659-0214
800-782-8632
Fax: 404-525-0210
E-mail: gapta@bellsouth.net
http://www.georgiapta.org
A powerful voice for children, families and communities advocating for the education, engagement and empowerment of every child in the state of Georgia.

Donna Kosicki, President
Rita Erves, President Elect

462 Georgia Public Library Service
1800 Century Plaza
Suite 150
Atlanta, GA 30345-4304
404-235-7200
Fax: 404-235-7201
http://www.georgialibraries.org

463 Georgia State Education for Homeless Children and Youth
205 Jesse Hill Jr Drive SE
1866 Twin Towers East
Atlanta, GA 30334
404-656-2004
Fax: 404-657-1534
E-mail: jjohnson@doe.k12.ga.us
Ensures that all homeless children and youth have equal access to the same free, appropriate public education.

464 Georgia Student Finance Commission
2082 East Exchange Place
Tucker, GA 30084
770-724-9000
800-505-4732
Fax: 770-724-9089
E-mail: gsfcinfo@gsfc.org
http://www.gsfc.org
Provides information on the state's education programs, colleges and universities, financial aid assistance programs, grants, scholarships, continuing education programs, and career opportunities.

465 Southeastern Library Association
PO Box 950
Rex, GA 30273
678-466-4334
Fax: 678-466-4349
E-mail: karamullen@clayton.edu
http://selaonline.org
A unifying force strong enough to influence legislation and to attract foundation and federal funds for regional library projects.

Michael Seigler, President
Gordon N. Baker, President-Elect

Hawaii

466 Hawaii Business Education Association
Leeward Community College
Normadeene Musick
96-045 Ala Ike
Pearl City, HI 96782-3393
808-455-0206
Fax: 808-453-6735

E-mail: president@hbea.org
http://www.hbea.org
HBEA is devoted exclusively to serving individuals and groups engaged in instruction, administration, research, and dissemination of information for and about business and technology. Hosts conferences and other professional improvement opportunities.

Jean Hara, President
Angeline Nelson, VP

467 Hawaii Education Association (HEA)
1953 S. Beretania St.
Suite 5C
Honolulu, HI 96826
808-949-6657
866-653-9372
Fax: 808-944-2032
E-mail: hea.office@heaed.com
http://www.heaed.com
Strengthens and supports quality education for all through the enrichment and growth of future, current and retired educators as well as through acknowledgment of their contribution to the community.

June Motokawa, President
Ron Toma, VP

468 Hawaii Library Association
PO Box 4441
Honolulu, HI 96812-4441
808-292-2068
Fax: 808-956-5968
E-mail:
hawaii.library.association@gmail.com
http://www.hlaweb.org
Promotes library service and librarianship in Hawaii in cooperation and affiliation with the American Library Association and other groups having allied objectives.

Christine Pawliuk, President
Christina Abelardo, VP/President-Elect

469 Hawaii State Education for Homeless Children and Youth
595 Pepeekeo St
Building H Room 1
Honolulu, HI 96825
808-394-1384
866-927-9095
Fax: 808-394-1388
http://www.doe.k12.hi.us/programs/index.htm
Ensures that all homeless children and youth have equal access to the same free, appropriate public education.

470 Hawaii State Foundation on Culture and the Arts
250 South Hotel St
Honolulu, HI 96813
808-586-0300
Fax: 808-586-0308
http://www.hawaii.gov/sfca
Promotes high-quality education in the arts.

471 Hawaii State Postsecondary Education Commission
2444 Dole St
Room 209
Honolulu, HI 96822-2302
808-956-8213
Fax: 808-956-5158
E-mail: bor@hawaii.edu
http://www.hawaii.edu/offices/bor
Provides information on the state's education programs, colleges and universities, financial aid assistance programs, grants, scholarships, continuing education programs, and career opportunities.

472 Hawaii State Teachers Association (HSTA)
1200 Ala Kapuna Street
Honolulu, HI 96819
808-833-2711
Fax: 808-839-7106
E-mail: info@hsta.org
http://www.hsta.org
Supports the professional roles of teachers, advocates for teachers' interests, and assures quality education for Hawaii's youth.

Wil Okabe, President
Alvin Nagasako, Executive Director

Idaho

473 Idaho Commission for Libraries
325 West State St
Boise, ID 83702
208-334-2150
800-458-3271
Fax: 208-334-4016
http://www.libraries.idaho.gov

474 Idaho Commission on the Arts
2410 N Old Penitentiary Rd
PO Box 83720
Boise, ID 83720-0008
208-334-2119
800-278-3863
Fax: 208-334-2488
E-mail: info@arts.idaho.gov
http://www.arts.idaho.gov
Promotes high-quality education in the arts.

475 Idaho Education Association
620 N 6th Street
PO Box 2638
Boise, ID 83701
208-344-1341
800-727-9922
Fax: 208-336-6967
E-mail: info@idahoea.org
http://www.idahoea.org
Advocates the professional and personal well-being of its members and the vision of excellence in public education.

Rick Jones, VP
Penni Cyr, President

476 Idaho Library Association
PO Box 8533
Moscow, ID 83843-1033
208-334-2150
Fax: 208-334-4016
http://www.idaholibraries.org
Supports the library community in Idaho and encourages both students and professionals to engage with the services that libraries offer.

Gena Marker, President
Karen Yother, VP/President-Elect

477 Idaho State Homeless Education Program Office
650 West State
PO Box 83720
Boise, ID 83720-0027
208-332-6978
800-432-4601
Fax: 208-334-2228
http://www.sde.state.id.us/homeless/default.asp
Ensures that all homeless children and youth have equal access to the same free, appropriate public education.

Illinois

478 Illinois Affiliation of Private Schools for Exceptional Children
Lawrence Hall Youth Services
4833 N Francisco Avenue
Chicago, IL 60625-3640
773-769-3500
http://www.iapsec.org
A non-profit organization consisting of private schools serving Illinois children with exceptional needs and works to maintain the quality of special education made available to special needs students.

Ken Carwell, President
Sol Rappaport, Secretary

479 Illinois Art Council
100 W Randolph St
Chicago, IL 60601
312-814-6750
800-237-6994
Fax: 312-814-1471
E-mail: iac.info@illinois.gov
http://www.state.il.us/agency/iac
Promotes high-quality education in the arts.

480 Illinois Association of School Administrators
2648 Beechler Court
Springfield, IL 62703-7305
217-753-2213
Fax: 217-753-2240
http://www.iasaedu.org

481 Illinois Association of School Business Officials
Northern Illinois University
108 Carroll Avenue
DeKalb, IL 60115
815-753-1276
Fax: 815-516-0184
E-mail: grizaffigi@vvsd.org
http://www.iasbo.org
Provides its members and stakeholders a comprehensive range of professional development activities and services through networking and participation.

Mark E. Staehlin, President
Michael A Jacoby, Executive Director

482 Illinois Business Education Association (IBEA)
8536 E Jackson Street
Du Quoin, IL 62832-4078
Fax: 618-542-5528
E-mail: president@ibea.org
http://www.ibea.org
Promoting the profession and providing the environment and encouragement to improve professional endeavors

Ethel Holladay, Executive Director
Jodee Werkheiser, President

483 Illinois Citizens' Education Council
100 East Edwards Street
Springfield, IL 62704-1999
217-544-0706
Fax: 217-333-2736
Association of 120,000 members composed of Illinois elementary and secondary teachers, higher education faculty and staff, educational support professionals, retired educators, and college students preparing to become teachers.

Anne Davis, President
Ken Swanson, Vice President

484 Illinois Education Association
100 E Edwards Street
Springfield, IL 62704-1999

217-544-0706
800-252-8076
Fax: 217-544-7383
http://www.ieanea.org
Represents public, academic, and special libraries as well as librarians, library assistants, trustees, students and library vendors. Promotes excellence and equity in public education and acts as the advocacy organization for all public education employees.

Cinda Klickna, President
Kathi Griffen, Vice President

485 Illinois Homeless Education Program
100 N First St
Springfield, IL 62777-0001
217-557-7323
800-215-6379
http://www.isbe.state.il.us/homeless/default.htm
Ensures that all homeless children and youth have equal access to the same free, appropriate public education.

486 Illinois Library Association
33 W Grand Avenue
Suite 401
Chicago, IL 60654-6799
312-644-1896
Fax: 312-644-1899
E-mail: ila@ila.org
http://www.ila.org
The Illinois Library Association is the voice for Illinois libraries and the millions who depend on them. Provides leadership for the development, promotion and improvement of library services in Illinois and for the library community in order to enhance learning and ensure access to information for all.

Pamela Van Kirk, President
Stu Erickson, Executive Director

487 Illinois School Library Media Association
PO Box 598
Canton, IL 61520
309-649-0911
Fax: 309-649-0916
E-mail: islma@islma.org
http://www.islma.org
Promotes student interaction, and continuing education of school library media specialists, and collaboration among parents, community members, teachers and administrators as they prepare students for life-long learning.

Christine Graves, President
Debra Turner, President-Elect

488 Illinois Student Assistance Commission
1755 Lake Cook Rd
Deerfield, IL 60015-5209
847-948-8500
800-899-4722
Fax: 847-831-8549
E-mail: collegezone@isac.org
http://www.collegezone.com
Provides information on the state's education programs, colleges and universities, financial aid assistance programs, grants, scholarships, continuing education programs, and career opportunities.

Indiana

489 Indiana Arts Commission
150 W Market St
Indianapolis, IN 46204-2211

317-232-1268
Fax: 317-232-5595
E-mail: indianaartscommission@iac.in.gov
http://www.in.gov/arts
Promotes high-quality education in the arts.

490 Indiana Association of School Business Officials
1 N Capital Avenue
Suite 1215
Indianapolis, IN 46204-2095
765-639-3586
Fax: 317-639-4360
E-mail: dcosterison@indiana-asbo.org
http://www.indiana-asbo.org
The Indiana Association of School Business Officials is a professional organization which strives for the promotion and union of those individuals involved in school business affairs such as finance, accounting, purchasing, maintenance and operations, human resources, facilities and grounds, food service, technology, and transportation.

Lynn Kwilasz, President
Steve Sonntag, VP

491 Indiana Business Education Association
8103 E. Highway 36
Box 180
Avon, IN 46123
765-653-3149
Fax: 317-232-9121
E-mail: gvalenti@usi.edu
http://ind-ibea.org
Promotes business education as a central component to essential life skills, career and workplace preparation and life-long learning.

John Dawson, President
Scott Truelove, VP

492 Indiana Commission for Higher Education
101 W Ohio St
Suite 550
Indianapolis, IN 46204-1984
317-464-4400
Fax: 317-464-4410
http://www.che.in.gov
Provides information on the state's education programs, colleges and universities, financial aid assistance programs, grants, scholarships, continuing education programs, and career opportunities.

493 Indiana Library Federation
941 E 86th Street
Suite 260
Indianapolis, IN 46240
317-257-2040
Fax: 317-257-1389
E-mail: askus@ilfonline.org
http://www.ilfonline.org
Fosters the professional growth of its members and promotes all libraries in Indiana.

Robin Crumrin, President
Marcia Au, President-Elect

494 Indiana State Teachers Association
150 W Market Street
Suite 900
Indianapolis, IN 46204
317-263-3400
800-382-4037
Fax: 317-655-3700
http://www.ista-in.org
Provides the resources necessary to enable local affiliates to effectively advocate for

members, children and for public education.

Nathan Schnellenberger, President
Teresa Meredith, Vice President

Iowa

495 Iowa Arts Council
600 E Locust
Des Moines, IA 50319-0290
515-281-5773
Fax: 515-242-6498
http://www.iowaartscouncil.org
Promotes high-quality education in the arts.

496 Iowa Business Education Association
Highway 150 S
PO Box 400
Calmar, IA 52132-400
515-471-8005
Fax: 563-562-4363
E-mail: rselwood@mchsi.com
http://www.ibeaonline.org
Works to discover and serve the needs of business education in Iowa.

Patrick Geer, President
Crystal Combs, President-Elect

497 Iowa College Student Aid Commission
200 10th St
4th Floor
Des Moines, IA 50309
515-725-3400
800-383-4222
Fax: 515-725-3401
E-mail: info@iowacollegeaid.org
http://www.iowacollegaid.org
Provides information on the state's education programs, colleges and universities, financial aid assistance programs, grants, scholarships, continuing education programs, and career opportunities.

498 Iowa Library Association
525 SW 5th Street
Suite A
Des Moines, IA 50309
515-282-8192
800-452-5507
Fax: 515-282-9117
http://www.iowalibraryassociation.org
The Iowa Library Association advocates for quality library services for all Iowans and provides leadership, education and support for members.

Lorraine Borowski, President
Mary Heinzman, VP/President-Elect

499 Iowa State Education Association
777 Third Street
Des Moines, IA 50309
515-471-8000
800-445-9358
E-mail: ISEAnews@isea.org
http://www.isea.org
Designed to promote and support quality education.

Tammy Wawro, President
Mary Jane Cobb, Executive Director

500 Iowa State Education for Homeless Children and Youth
400 E 14th St
Des Moines, IA 50319-0146
515-281-3999
Fax: 515-242-6025
http://www.iowa.gov/educate
Ensures that all homeless children and youth have equal access to the same free, appropriate public education.

Kansas

501 Educating Homeless Children and Youth
120 SE 10th Ave
Topeka, KS 66612-1182
785-296-6714
Fax: 785-296-5867
http://www.ksde.org
Ensures that all homeless children and youth have equal access to the same free, appropriate public education.

502 Kansas Arts Commission
700 SW Jackson
Suite 1004
Topeka, KS 66603-3774
785-296-3335
866-433-0688
Fax: 785-296-4989
E-mail: kac@arts.ks.gov
http://www.arts.state.ks.us

503 Kansas Association of School Librarians
8517 W Nothridge
Wichita, KS 67205
http://kasl.typepad.com/kasl
Association of school librarians in the state of Kansas.

Judy Eller, Executive Secretary
Cindy Pfeiffer, President

504 Kansas Board of Regents
1000 SW Jackson St
Suite 520
Topeka, KS 66612-1368
785-296-3421
Fax: 785-296-0983
http://www.kansasregents.org

505 Kansas Business Education Association
Fory Hays State University
600 Park Street
Hays, KS 67601
785-628-4019
Fax: 785-628-5398
http://www.ksbea.org
Fosters business education in the state of Kansas.

Founded: 1949

Jean Anna Sellers, Contact
Gina Stanley, President

506 Kansas Education Association
715 SW 10th Avenue
Topeka, KS 66612-1686
785-232-8271
Fax: 785-232-6012
E-mail: KNEAnews@knea.org
http://www.knea.org
Empowers its members to promote quality public schools, strengthen the teaching profession, and improve the well-being of members.

Founded: 1862

Blake West, President
Sherri Yourdon, Vice President

507 Kansas Library Association
1020 SW Washburn
Topeka, KS 66604
785-580-4518
Fax: 785-580-4595
E-mail: kansaslibraryassociation@yahoo.com
http://www.kansaslibraryassociation.org
KLA develops a legislative push card, tracks legislation and keeps association members and the library community at large informed on the status of bills related to library issues

Laura Loveless, President
Denise Smith, First Vice President

Kentucky

508 Kentucky Arts Council
500 Mero St
21st Floor, Capital Plaza Tower
Frankfort, KY 40601-1987
502-564-3757
888-833-2787
Fax: 502-564-2839
E-mail: kyarts@ky.gov
http://www.artscouncil.ky.gov
The Kentucky Arts Council is the state government agency responsible for developing and promoting support for the arts in Kentucky. The agency creates opportunities for people to find value in the arts, participate in the arts and benefit from the arts through programs, grants and services.

Lori Meadows, Executive Director
Chris Cathers, Program Branch Manager

509 Kentucky Department for Libraries and Archives
300 Coffee Tree Rd
Frankfort, KY 40601
502-564-8300
800-928-7000
Fax: 502-564-5773
http://www.kdla.ky.gov

510 Kentucky Education for Homeless Children and Youth
500 Mero St
Frankfort, KY 40601
502-564-3141
Fax: 502-564-8149
http://www.education.ky.gov/kde/default.htm

511 Kentucky Higher Education Assistance Authority
PO Box 798
Frankfort, KY 40602-0798
502-696-7200
800-928-8926
Fax: 502-696-7496
E-mail: inquiries@kheaa.com
http://www.kheaa.com

512 Kentucky Library Association
1501 Twilight Trail
Frankfort, KY 40601
502-223-5322
Fax: 502-223-4937
E-mail: info@kylibasn.org
http://www.kylibasn.org
Holds a conference in October and publishes a journal.

Kim Goff, Associate Director
John Underwood, Executive Secretary

513 Kentucky School Media Association
Scott County School
1080 Cardinal Drive
Georgtown, KY 40324
E-mail: mroberts@scott.k12.ky.us
http://www.kysma.org
Promotes the use of media in schools.

Tara Griffith, President
Fred Tilsley, Secretary

514 Mountain-Plains Business Education Association(M-PBEA)
Newcastle High School
4771 West Scott Road
Beatrice, NE 68310
307-746-2713
E-mail: tlandenb@gmail.com
http://www.mpbea.org
The Mountain-Plains Business Education Association (M-PBEA) is an affiliate of the National Business Education Association (NBEA), a professional organization serving individuals and groups engaged in instruction, administration, research, and dissemination of information for and about business. M-PBEA is comprised of the following states and provinces: Colorado, Kansas, Manitoba, Nebraska, New Mexico, North Dakota, Oklahoma, Saskatchewan, South Dakota, Texas, and Wyoming.

Sheryl Piening Keller, President
Connie Lindell, Kansas State Representative

Louisiana

515 Louisiana Association of Business Educators
Alfred M Barbe High School
2200 W McNeese Street
Lake Charles, LA 70615
337-478-3628
Fax: 337-474-6782
E-mail: spiening@southeast.edu
http://www.laabe.org
Foster business education in the state of Louisiana.

Marilyn Gastineau, President
Joseph Lane Jr, Vice President

516 Louisiana Association of Educators
8322 One Calais Avenue
Baton Rouge, LA 70821
225-343-9243
800-256-4523
Fax: 225-343-9272
E-mail: joyce.haynes@lae
http://www.lae.org
Dedicated to improving the education profession and the quality of education. Affiliated with National Education Association.

Joyce Haynes, President
Bruce Hunt, Executive Director

517 Louisiana Association of School Business Officials (LASBO)
PO Box 1029
Gonzales, LA 70707-1029
225-644-0619
Fax: 225-644-0122
E-mail: cctripp@eatel.net
http://www.lasbo.org/
To promote excellence and professional ethical standards in the practice of public school business finance by educating and training our membership in the most efficient and economic methods of conducting our business affairs

Founded: 1993

Tami Austin, President-elect
Juanita Duke, President

518 Louisiana Division of the Arts
1051 N Third St
PO Box 44247
Baton Rouge, LA 70804-4247
225-342-8180
Fax: 225-342-8173
http://www.crt.state.la.us/arts

519 Louisiana Education for Homeless Children and Youth
PO Box 94064
Baton Rouge, LA 70804
225-342-3031
877-453-2721

http://www.doe.state.la.us/lde/eia/1315.html

520   Louisiana Library Association
8550 United Plaza Boulevard
Suite 1001
Baton Rouge, LA 70809
225-922-4642
877-550-7890
Fax: 225-408-4422
E-mail: office@llaonline.org
http://www.llaonline.org
Holds a conference in March and publishes a journal.
Founded: 1925

Beth Paskoff, Registration
Melissa Elrod, Chair

521   Louisiana Office of Student Financial Assistance
PO Box 91202
Baton Rouge, LA 70821-9202
225-922-1012
800-259-5626
Fax: 225-922-0790
E-mail: custserv@osfa.la.gov
http://www.osfa.la.gov

Maine

522   Education for Homeless Children and Youth
State House Station #23
Augusta, ME 04333-0023
207-624-6637
Fax: 207-624-6624
http://www.state.me.us/education/tdae

523   Maine Arts Commission
State House Station #25
Augusta, ME 04333-0025
207-287-2724
Fax: 207-287-2725
E-mail: mainearts.info@maine.gov
http://www.mainearts.maine.gov

524   Maine Association of School Libraries
PO Box 634
Augusta, ME 04333
207-287-5620
Fax: 207-287-5624
E-mail: MASL@gwi.net
http://www.maslibraries.org
Dedicated to total involvement between Library Media Specialists, support staff and students.

Eileen Broderick, President
Joyce Lucas, Secretary

525   Maine Library Association
PO Box 634
Augusta, ME 04332-634
207-623-8428
Fax: 207-626-5947
E-mail: MASL@gwi.net
http://mainelibraries.org/home.php
is to promote and enhance the value of libraries and librarianship, to foster cooperation among those who work in and for libraries, and to provide leadership in ensuring that information is accessible to all citizens via their libraries

Eileen Broderick, President
Joan Kiszely, Executive Secretary

Maryland

526   Division of Library Development and Services
200 W Baltimore St
Baltimore, MD 21201-2595
410-767-0435
Fax: 410-333-2507

527   Maryland Educational Media Organization
PO Box 21127
Baltimore, MD 21228
http://www.tcps.md.us
Brings students and information regarding educational media together.

Dorothy D'Ascanio, President
Patricia Goff, Secretary

528   Maryland Higher Education Commission
839 Bestgate Rd
Annapolis, MS 21401-3013
410-260-4500
800-974-0203
Fax: 410-260-3200
http://www.mhec.state.md.us

529   Maryland Library Association
1401 Hollins Street
Baltimore, MD 21223
410-947-5090
Fax: 410-947-5089
E-mail: mla@mdlib.org
http://www.mdlib.org
Maryland Library Association provides leadership for those who are committed to libraries by providing opportunities for professional development and communication and by advocating principles and issues related to librarianship and library service.

Margaret Carty, Executive Director
Kate Monagan, Executive Assistant

530   Maryland State Arts Council
175 W Ostend
Baltimore, MD 21230
410-767-6555
Fax: 410-333-1062
http://www.msac.org

531   Maryland State Teachers Association
140 Main Street
Annapolis, MD 21401-2003
410-263-6600
800-448-6782
Fax: 410-263-3605
E-mail: feedback@mseanea.org
http://www.mstanea.org/
Organization representing 60,000 Maryland teachers, support professionals, retired educators, school administers, higher education faculty, and future educators.

Clara B Floyd, President
Betty Weller, VP

Massachusetts

532   Board of Library Commissioners
98 N Washington St
Suite 401
Boston, MA 02114
617-725-1860
800-952-7403
Fax: 617-725-0140
http://www.mblc.state.ma.us

533   Massachusetts Business Educators Association
Amherst Regional High School
21 Mattoon Street
Amherst, MA 01002
413-549-9700
Fax: 413-549-9704
E-mail: www.ma-mbea.org
Fosters business education in the state of Massachusetts.

Mary Ann Shea, Contact

534   Massachusetts Cultural Council
10 St James Ave
Boston, MA 02116-3803
617-727-3668
800-232-0960
Fax: 617-727-0044
E-mail: mcc@art.state.ma.us
http://www.massculturalcouncil.org

535   Massachusetts Department of Higher Education
One Ashburton Place
Boston, MA 02108-1696
617-994-6950
Fax: 617-727-6397
http://www.mass.edu

536   Massachusetts Library Association
PO Box 535
Bedford, MA 01730
781-275-7729
Fax: 781-998-0393
E-mail: mlaoffice@masslib.org
http://www.masslib.org
The mission of the Government Relations Advisory Board is to represent the interests of all libraries to the state legislature on behalf of the citizens of the Commonwealth

Elizabeth Hacala, VP/President elect
Dinah O'Brien, President

537   Massachusetts Teachers Association
20 Ashburton Place
Boston, MA 02108-2727
617-878-8000
800-392-6175
Fax: 617-742-7046
E-mail: awass@massteacher.org
http://www.massteacher.org
The MTA is a union, dedicated to improving the workplace and the quality of life for all education employees and to protecting their hard-won rights. MTA and local affiliates are highly democratic organizations in which members' views and concerns are vital to the development of policies and programs.

Anne Wass, President
Paul Toner, Vice President

538   New England Library Association
55 North Main Street
Unit 49
Belchertown, MA 01007
413-813-5254
E-mail: rscheier@gmail.com
http://www.nelib.org
Provides educational and leadership opportunities for library staff in support of improved library services for the people of New England.

Deborah Kelsey, President
Deb Hoadley, Vice President

539   Office for the Education of Homeless Children and Youth
75 Pleasant St
Malden, MA 02148-4906
781-338-6330
Fax: 781-338-3090
http://www.doe.mass.edu

Michigan

540 Education for Homeless Children and Youth
608 W Allegan St
PO Box 30008
Lansing, MI 48909
517-241-1162
Fax: 517-241-0247
http://www.michigan.gov/homeless

541 Michigan Association for Media in Education
1407 Rensen Street
Suite 3
Lansing, MI 48910
517-394-2808
Fax: 517-394-2096
E-mail: mame@mame.gen.mi.us
http://www.mame.gen.mi.us
Michigan Association for Media in Education is an independent, professional association of library media specialists dedicated to educational, literary and technological excellence in library / media services in Michigan's schools.

Roger Ashley, Executive Director
Diane Nye, Media Spectrum

542 Michigan Association of School Administrators
1001 Centennial Way
Suite 300
Lansing, MI 48917-9279
517-327-5910
Fax: 517-327-0779
E-mail: jscofield@gomasa.org
http://www.gomasa.org/
Professional organization serving superintendents and their first line of assistants.

Dan Pappas, Associate Executive Director
Jon Tomlanovich, Associate Executive Director

543 Michigan Council for Arts and Cultural Affairs
702 W Kalamazoo St
PO Box 30705
Lansing, MI 48909-8205
517-241-4011
Fax: 517-241-3979
E-mail: artsinfo@michigan.gov
http://www.michigan.gov/arts

544 Michigan Education Association
1216 Kendale Boulevard
PO Box 2573
East Lansing, MI 48826-2573
517-332-6551
800-292-1934
Fax: 517-337-5598
E-mail: webmaster@mea.org
http://www.mea.org/
A self-governing education association, representing more than 157,000 teaches, faculty, and education support staff throughout the state.

Iris Salters, President
Steven Cook, Vice President

545 Michigan Elementary & Middle School Principals Association
1980 N College Road
Mason, MI 48854
517-694-8955
800-227-0824
Fax: 517-694-8945
E-mail: bob@memspa.org
http://www.memspa.org
Professional organization serving elementary and middle level principals as they deliver quality educational experiences to the students of Michigan by providing leadership, legislative advocacy, professional development and guidance.

Paul Liabenow, Executive Director
Rob Kauffman, President

546 Michigan Library Association
1407 Rensen Street
Suite 2
Lansing, MI 48910
517-394-2774
Fax: 517-394-2675
E-mail: mla@mlcnet.org
http://www.mla.lib.mi.us
The Michigan Library Association is a professional organization dedicated to the support of its members, to the advancement of librarianship, and to the promotion of quality library service for all Michigan citizens.

Kathy Irwin, President
Larry Neal, President-Elect

547 Student Financial Services Bureau
430 W Allegan
PO Box 30047
Lansing, MI 48909-7547
800-642-5626
Fax: 571-241-0155
http://www.michigan.gov/studentaid

Minnesota

548 Education Minnesota
41 Sherburne Avenue
St. Paul, MN 55103-2196
651-227-9541
800-652-9073
Fax: 651-292-4802
http://www.educationminnesota.org
Education Minnesota is the largest advocate for public education in the state. Our 70,000 members work at all levels from pre-kindergarten through post-secondary, at public schools, state residential schools and college campuses.

Thomas A Dooher, President
Paul Mueller, Vice President

549 Minnesota Business Educators
2620 Eleventh Avenue NW
Rochester, MN 55901-7722
507-282-7079
Fax: 507-282-4925
E-mail: rhmeyer@rconnect.com
http://www.mbei-online.org
To keep abreast with the state legislature and with issues related to business education

Mary Flesberg, Past President
Cindy Drahos, President

550 Minnesota Congress of Parents, Teachers & Students/Minnesota PTA
1667 Snelling Avenue
N Suite 111
Saint Paul, MN 55108
651-999-7320
800-672-0993
Fax: 651-999-7321
E-mail: mnptaofc@mnpta.org
http://www.mnpta.org
Minnesota PTA, an affiliate of the National PTA, extends the concept of a volunteer organization engaged in educating parents and teachers on issues affecting children and youth. It supports public education and the welfare of children.
Founded: 1922

Rosie Loeffler Kemp, President
Bonnie Beery, Secretary

551 Minnesota Library Association
1821 University Avenue West
Suite S256
Saint Paul, MN 55104
651-999-5343
877-867-0982
Fax: 651-917-1835
E-mail:
mlaoffice@mnlibraryassociation.org
http://www.mnlibraryassociation.org
MLA meets the interests of its members by facilitating educational opportunities, supporting strong ethical standards, and fostering connections between the library community and various constituencies. MLA organizes an annual multi-day fall conference that features approximately 70 programs planned and sponsored by divisions, sections, round tables and committees.
Founded: 1891

Anna Hulseberg, Treasurer
Carla Urban, President

552 Minnesota School Boards Association
1900 W Jefferson Avenue
Saint Peter, MN 56082-3015
507-934-2450
800-324-4459
Fax: 507-931-1515
E-mail: gabbott@mnmsba.org
http://www.mnmsba.org
The purpose of the Association is to support, promote and enhance the work of public school boards.

Walter Hautala, President
Greg Abbott, MSBA Dir. of Communications

553 Office of Higher Education
1450 Energy Park Dr
Suite 350
St Paul, MN 55108-5227
651-259-3901
800-657-3866
Fax: 651-642-0597
http://www.ohe.state.mn.us

554 State Arts Board
400 Sibley St
Suite 200
Saint Paul, MN 55101-1928
651-215-1600
800-866-2787
Fax: 651-215-1602
http://www.arts.state.mn.us

Mississippi

555 Education for Homeless Children and Youth
359 North West St
PO Box 771
Jackson, MS 39205-0771
601-359-3499
Fax: 601-359-2587
http://www.mde.k12.ms.us/acad/is/homeles
s.htm

556 Mississippi Advocate for Education
775 N State Street
Jackson, MS 39202-3086
601-354-4463
800-530-7998
Fax: 601-352-7054
E-mail: mmarks@nea.org
http://www.maetoday.nea.org
The Mississippi Association of Educators advocates great public schools for every child by empowering members, providing services

and promoting parental/community
environment.

Kevin F Gilbert, President
Seyed Darbandi, Vice President

557 Mississippi Arts Commission
501 North West St
Suite 1101A
Jackson, MS 39201
601-359-6030
Fax: 601-359-6008
http://www.arts.state.ms.us

**558 Mississippi Business Education
Association**
Itawamba Community College
2176 S Eason Boulevard
Tupelo, MS 38801
662-620-5001
Fax: 601-982-5801
E-mail: acbrown@nmsd.k12.ms.us
http://www.ms-mbea.org
To establish and maintain active state lead-
ership in promotion of all types of business
and technology education

Aimee Brown, President
Judith Hurtt, President-Elect

**559 Mississippi Institutions of Higher
Learning**
3825 Ridgewood Rd
Jackson, MS 39211-6453
601-432-6623
800-327-2980
Fax: 601-432-6972
http://www.ihl.state.ms.us

560 Mississippi Library Association
PO Box 13687
Jackson, MS 39236-3687
601-981-4586
Fax: 601-981-4501
E-mail: info@misslib.org
http://www.misslib.org
Provides professional leadership for the
development, promotion, and the improvement of library and information services
and the profession of librarianship in order
to enhance learning and ensure access to
information for all.

Stephen Cunetto, President
Lynn F. Shurden, Vice-President

561 Mississippi Library Commission
3881 Eastwood Dr
Jackson, MS 39211
601-432-4111
800-647-7542
Fax: 601-432-4478
E-mail: mslib@mlc.lib.ms.us
http://www.mlc.lib.ms.us

Missouri

**562 Education for Homeless Children
and Youth**
PO Box 480
Jefferson City, MO 65102
573-526-3232
Fax: 573-526-6698

563 Missouri Arts Council
815 Olive St
Suite 16
Saint Louis, MO 63101-1503
314-340-6845
866-407-4752
Fax: 314-340-7215
E-mail: moarts@ded.mo.gov
http://www.missouriartscouncil.org

**564 Missouri Association of
Elementary School Principals**
3550 Amazonas Drive
Jefferson City, MO 65109
573-638-2692
Fax: 573-556-6270
E-mail: maesp@mcsa.org
http://www.mcsa.org
MAESP is a statewide professional association that has grown to include over 1,000
school administrators. The services provided by MAESP to its membership have
also increased as members have identified
and approved long-range plans incorporating key services.

Matthew Martz, President
Connie Browning, President-Elect

**565 Missouri Association of Secondary
School Principals**
2409 W Ash Street
Columbia, MO 65203-45
573-445-5071
Fax: 573-445-6416
E-mail: massp@moassp.org
http://www.moassp.org
The mission of the Missouri Association of
Secondary School Principals is to improve
secondary education through positive leadership and the enhancement of student performance. In pursuing the mission of
MASSP, the Association shall be involved
in providing information and leadership;
encouraging research and service; promoting high educational standards; focusing
attention on state educational issues; providing for the general welfare of
principals; and working with other
organizations.

Ron Helms, President
Jenny Swanson, Secretary

**566 Missouri Congress of Parents &
Teachers/Missouri PTA**
2101 Burlington Street
Columbia, MO 65203
573-445-4161
800-328-7330
Fax: 573-445-4163
E-mail: kimw@mopta.org
http://www.mopta.org
A powerful voice for all children, a relevant resource for all families and communities and a strong advocate for the
education and well-being of every child.

Mary Oyler, President
Kim Weber, Vice President and Director

**567 Missouri Department of Higher
Education**
3515 Amazonas Dr
Jefferson City, MO 65109
573-751-2361
800-473-6757
Fax: 573-751-6635
E-mail: info@dhe.mo.gov
http://www.dhe.mo.gov

568 Missouri Library Association
3212-A Lemone Industrial Boulevard
Columbia, MO 65201-45
573-449-4627
Fax: 573-449-4655
E-mail: mla001@more.net
http://www.molib.org
A non-profit, educational organization operating to promote library service, the profession of librarianship, and cooperation
among all types of libraries and organiza-

tions concerned with library service in Missouri.
Founded: 1900

Kimberlee Ried, President
Margaret Booker, Executive Director

569 Missouri National Education Association
1810 E Elm Street
Jefferson City, MO 65101-4174
573-634-3202
Fax: 573-634-5646
http://www.mnea.org
The Missouri National Education Association is
an advocate for public schools, public school students and public school employees
November annual
1,500 attendees

Ben Simmons, Executive Director
Chris Guinther, President

570 Missouri State Teachers Association
PO Box 458
407 S Sixth Street
Columbia, MO 65205-4201
573-442-3127
800-392-0532
Fax: 573-443-5079
E-mail: membercare@msta.org
http://www.msta.org
A grassroots organization made up of local community teachers associations in each school
district.

Tami Pasley, Board of Directors
Russell Smithson, Vice President

**571 North Central Business Education
Association (NCBEA)**
Mineral Area College
803 Rambling Brook Circle
Elgin, IL 60124
573-243-9513
Fax: 573-243-9524
E-mail: satbfl@aol.com
http://www.ncbea.org
The objectives of this Association are to improve
the relationship in business education at the state,
regional, and national levels; to promote the professional growth of those in business education;
to promote better business education through
whatever means seem desirable; and to offer assistance and service to state associations within
the region.

Kim Schultz, President
Susan Elwood, Secretary

Montana

**572 Education for Homeless Children and
Youth**
1300 11th Ave
PO Box 202501
Helena, MT 59620-2501
406-444-2036
Fax: 406-444-3924
http://www.opi.state.mt.us/homeless

573 Montana Arts Council
830 N Warren St
PO Box 202201
Helena, MT 59620-2201
406-444-6430
800-282-3092
Fax: 406-444-6548
http://www.art.mt.gov

**574 Montana Association of County School
Superintendents**
1134 Butte Avenue
Helena, MT 59601
406-442-2510
http://www.sammt.org/macss

Organization of school superintendents.

Darrell Rud, Executive Director
Julia Sykes, Associate Director

575 Montana Association of School Librarians (MASL)
PO Box 2107
Jefferson City, MO 65109
573-893-4155
Fax: 573-635-2858
E-mail: masl_org@earthlink.net
http://www.maslonline.org/
Montana Association of School Librarians/MASL is a professional organization for library media specialists who work in Missouri schools.

Linda Weatherspoon, President
Sandy Roth, Treasurer

576 Montana Library Association
PO Box 1352
Belgrade, MT 59714-3126
406-579-3121
Fax: 406-243-2060
http://www.mtlib.org
Holds a conference in April and publishes a journal.

Debra Kramer, Executive
Della Dubbe, President

577 Western Business and Information Technology Educators (WBITE)
Hardin High School
720 N Terry
Hardin, MT 59034
406-665-6300
Fax: 406-665-1909
E-mail: odellj@hardin.k12.mt.us
http://www.nbea.org/aboutrda.html
Western Business and Information Technology Educators, an affiliate of the National Business Education Association seeks to share educational experiences preparing individuals to excel as consumers, workers, and citizens in our economic systems. WBITE is comprised of Alaska, Alberta, American Samoa, Arizona, British Columbia, California, Guam, Hawaii, Idaho, Montana, Nevada, Northern Marianas Islands, Northwest Territories, Oregon, Utah, Yukon and Washington.

Julie O'Dell, President
Roy Kamida, Treasurer

Nebraska

578 Education for Homeless Children and Youth
301 Centennial Mall S
PO Box 94987
Lincoln, NE 68509
402-471-2968
Fax: 402-471-0117
http://www.nde.state.ne.us

579 Nebraska Arts Council
1004 Farnam St
Omaha, NE 68102
402-595-2122
800-341-4067
Fax: 402-595-2334
http://www.nebraskaartscouncil.org

580 Nebraska Library Association
1402 N Jackson
Lexington, NE 68850
402-826-2636
Fax: 402-471-6244
E-mail: nebraskalibraries@gmail.com
http://www.nebraskalibraries.org

The Nebraska Library Association supports and promotes all libraries, library media centers and library services in the state.

Pam Bohmfalk, President
Scott Childers, Vice President

581 Nebraska Library Commission
1200 N Street
Suite 120
Lincoln, NE 68508-2023
402-471-2045
800-307-2665
Fax: 402-471-2083
http://www.nlc.nebraska.gov

582 Nebraska State Business Education Association
Wayne State College
1111 Main Street-Gardner Hall 206F
Wayne, NE 68787
402-375-7255
E-mail: paarnes1@wsc.edu
http://www.nsbea.org
Foster business education in the state of Nebraska.

Patricia Arneson, Contact
Janelle Stansberry, President

583 Nebraska State Education Association
605 S 14th Street
Suite 200
Lincoln, NE 68508
402-475-7611
800-742-0047
Fax: 402-475-2630
http://www.nsea.org
NSEA is a member-directed union of professional educators and education support professionals dedicated to providing quality public education for the students of Nebraska.

Mark Shively, Director
Leann Widhalm, Director

Nevada

584 Education for Homeless Children and Youth
700 E Fifth St
Carson City, NV 89701-5096
775-687-9235
Fax: 775-687-9250
http://www.nde.doe.nv.gov/si.htm

585 Nevada Arts Council
716 N Carson St
Suite A
Carson City, NV 89701
775-687-6680
Fax: 775-687-6688
http://www.nevadaculture.org

586 Nevada Library Association
West Charleston Library
Clark County Library District
Las Vegas, NV 89030
702-507-3941
Fax: 702-649-2576
E-mail: rjdebuff@hotmail.com
http://www.nevadalibraries.org
The purpose of NLA shall be to promote library service of the highest quality for all present and potential users of libraries in Nevada.

Founded: 1946

Jeanette Hammons, President
Robbie DeBuff, Executive Secretary

587 Nevada State Education Association
1890 Donald Street
Reno, NV 89502
775-828-6732
800-232-6732
Fax: 775-828-6745
http://www.nsea-nv.org
Advocate the professional rights and economic security of its members, while also serving as the prominent voice for excellence in public education in Nevada.

Terry Hickman, Executive Director
Lynn Warne, President

New Hampshire

588 Education for Homeless Children and Youth
101 Pleasant St
Concord, NH 03301-3860
603-271-3840
Fax: 603-271-2760

589 New Hampshire Business Education Association
Newfound Regional High School
2500 N River Road
Manchester, NH 3106
603-926-3395
Fax: 603-926-5418
E-mail: mmatarazzo@rivier.edu
http://www.nhbea.org
Fosters business education in the state of New Hampshire.

Karen Hvizda, President
Maria Matarazzo, Business Administration Dir

590 New Hampshire Education Association
60 Connolly Parkway
Suite 103
Concord, NH 00654-2425
603-224-7751
866-556-3264
Fax: 603-224-2648
http://www.neanh.org
To strengthen and support public education and to serve our members' professional, political, economic and advocacy needs.

Rhonda Wesolowski, President
Jim Sweeny, Executive Director

591 New Hampshire Library Association
LGC, PO Box 617
Concord, NH 03302-617
603-641-4123
Fax: 603-641-4124
E-mail: annie.donahue@unh.edu
http://www.nhlibrarians.org
advance the interests of its members through advocacy on library issues and increasing public awareness of library service; to support the professional development of its members; to foster communication and encourage the exchange of ideas among its members; and to promote participation in the association and its sections.

Annie Donahue, Conference Committee
Steven Butzel, President

592 New Hampshire Postsecondary Education Commission
3 Barrell Court
Suite 300
Concord, NH 03301-8543
603-271-2555
Fax: 603-271-2696
http://www.state.nh.us/postsecondary

593 State Council of the Arts
Two 1/2 Beacon St
Suite 225
Concord, NH 03301
603-271-2789
Fax: 603-271-3584
http://www.nh.gov/nharts

New Jersey

594 Education for Homeless Children and Youth
PO Box 500
Trenton, NJ 08625-0500
609-984-4974
Fax: 609-292-1211
http://www.state.nj.us/education

595 Educational Media Association of New Jersey
PO Box 610
Trenton, NJ 08607
609-394-8032
Fax: 609-394-8164
http://www.emanj.org
Promotes the use of media in education.

Sue Henis, President

596 Higher Education Student Assistance Authority
4 Quakerbridge Plaza
PO Box 540
Trenton, NJ 08625-0540
609-588-3226
800-792-8670
Fax: 609-588-7389
http://www.hesaa.org

597 New Jersey Education Association (NJEA)
180 W State Street
Trenton, NJ 08607-1211
609-599-4561
800-359-6049
Fax: 609-392-6321
E-mail: lmaher@njea.org
http://www.njea.org
The mission of the New Jersey Education Association is to advance and protect the rights, benefits, and interests of members, and promote a quality system of public education for all students.

Joyce Powell, President
Stephen K Wollmer, Director of Communications

598 New Jersey Library Association
PO Box 1534
Trenton, NJ 08607
609-394-8032
Fax: 609-394-8164
E-mail: ptumulty@njla.org
http://www.njla.org
Advocates for advancement of library services for the residents of New Jersey; provides continuing education and networking opportunities for librarians; supports principles of intellectual freedom and promotes access to library materials for all.

Patricia A Tumulty, Executive Director
Susan Rice, Office Manager

599 New Jersey School-Age Care Coalition
231 North Avenue West
Westfield, NJ 07090
908-789-0259
Fax: 908-789-4237
http://www.njsacc.org

600 New Jersey State Council on the Arts
225 W State St
Trenton, NJ 08625-0306
609-292-6130
Fax: 609-989-1440
http://www.njartscouncil.org

601 New Jersey State Department of Education Resource Center
PO Box 500
Trenton, NJ 08625-500
609-292-4469
http://www.state.nj.us/education
Provide leadership to prepare all students for their role as citizens and for the career opportunities of the 21st century.

Josephine Hernandez, President
Arcelio Aponte, Vice President

New Mexico

602 Mountain Plains Business Education Association(M-PBEA)
c/o Newcastle High School
4771 West Scott Road
Beatrice, NE 68310
307-746-2713
E-mail: tlandenb@gmail.com
http://www.mpbea.org
The Mountain-Plains Business Education Association (M-PBEA), an affiliate of the National Business Education Association (NBEA), is a professional organization serving individuals and groups engaged in instruction, administration, research, and dissemination of information for and about business. M-PBEA is comprised of the following states and provinces: Colorado, Kansas, Manitoba, Nebraska, New Mexico, North Dakota, Oklahoma, Saskatchewan, South Dakota, Texas, and Wyoming.

Sheryl Piening Keller, President
DeLayne Havlovic, M-PBEA Treasurer

603 National Education Association of New Mexico
2007 Botulph
Santa Fe, NM 87505
505-982-1916
Fax: 505-982-6719
http://www.nea-nm.org
The NEA-NM and its affiliates will be the recognized advocate for students, public education, and public education employees in New Mexico.

Eduardo Holgun, Political Affairs Specialist
Sharon Morgan, President

604 New Mexico Arts
PO Box 1450
Santa Fe, NM 87504-1450
505-827-6490
800-879-4278
Fax: 505-827-6043
http://www.nmarts.org

605 New Mexico Higher Education Department
1068 Cerrillos Rd
Santa Fe, NM 87505-1650
505-476-8400
800-279-9777
Fax: 505-476-8453
http://www.hed.state.nm.us

606 New Mexico Library Association (NMLA)
PO Box 26074
Albuquerque, NM 87125
505-400-7309
Fax: 505-891-5171
E-mail: admin@nmla.org
http://www.nmla.org
The New Mexico Library Association is a non-profit organization dedicated to the support and promotion of libraries and the development of library personnel through education and the exchange of ideas to enrich the lives of all New Mexicans.

Cassandra Osterloh, President
Lorie Christian, Administrator

New York

607 Business Teachers Association of New York State
5260 Rogers Road
Apt A-5
Hamburg, NY 14075
315-369-6133
Fax: 315-369-6216
E-mail: President@btanys.org
http://www.btanys.org
The Business Teachers Association of New York State provides networking, support, and professional growth opportunities for its members to effectively educate today's students for tomorrow's global economy.

Sharon L Keller, Secretary/Awards Director
Susan Hall, President

608 Education for Homeless Children and Youth
151 W 30th Street
New York, NY 10001
800-388-2014
Fax: 212-807-6872
http://www.nysteachs.org

609 New York Library Association (NYLA)
6021 State Farm Road
Albany, NY 12210-1802
518-432-6952
800-252-6952
Fax: 518-427-1697
E-mail: info@nyla.org
http://www.nyla.org/
The Association was the first state-wide organization of librarians in the United States.

Michael J Borges, Executive Director
Johanna Geiger, Deputy Director

610 New York State Council on the Arts
175 Varick St
New York, NY 10014
212-627-4455
Fax: 212-620-5911
http://www.nysca.org

611 New York State Higher Education Services Corporation
99 Washington Ave
Albany, NY 12255
518-473-1574
888-697-4371
Fax: 518-474-2839
http://www.hesc.org

612 New York State United Teachers (NYSUT)
800 Troy-Schenectady Road
Latham, NY 12210-2455
518-213-6000
800-342-9810
Fax: 518-213-6409
E-mail: mediarel@nysutmail.org

http://www.nysut.org/cps/rde/xchg/nysut/hs .xsl/index.htm
Through a representative democratic structure, New York State United Teachers improves the professional, economic and personal lives of our members and their families, strengthens the institutions in which they work, and furthers the cause of social justice through the trade union movement.

Richard C Iannuzzi, President
Linda Stanczik, Regional Staff Director

North Carolina

613 Homeless Education Program
PO Box 5367
Greensboro, NC 27435
336-315-7491
Fax: 336-315-7457
http://www.serve.org/hepnc

614 North Carolina Arts Council
109 E Jones St
Paleigh, NC 27601
919-807-6502
Fax: 919-807-6532
http://www.ncarts.org

615 North Carolina Association for Career and Technical Education
PO Box G
Catawba, NC 28609-5159
828-241-3910
Fax: 919-782-8096
E-mail: tony.bello@gmail.com
http://www.actenc.org
Act as a central agency in keeping the people of the state informed of the mission, scope, needs, quality, importance, and contributions of career and technical education .

Paul Heiderpiem, Author
Scot Whitfield, President
Tom H Jones, Executive Director

616 North Carolina Association of Educators (NCAE)
700 S Salisbury Street
Raleigh, NC 27601
919-832-3000
800-662-7924
Fax: 919-829-1626
E-mail: colleen.borst@ncae.org
http://www.ncae.org
NCAE's mission is to advocate for members and students, to enhance the education profession, and to advance public education.

Colleen Borst, Executive Director
Kevin Spragley, Associate Executive Director

617 North Carolina Business Education Association(NCBEA)
King's College
700 E Stonewall Street
Suite 400
Charlotte, NC 28202
980-343-2738
Fax: 704-348-2029
E-mail: bpetersen@kingscollegecharlotte.edu
http://www.ncbea.org
NCBEA seeks to promote and improve the quality of business education at all levels through membership activities and meetings and through cooperation with public and private educational agencies and institutions with related professional organizations and with business and industry.

Becky Petersen, Executive Director
Cindi Sweeney, President Elect

618 North Carolina Department of Public Instruction (DPI)
301 N Wilmington Street
Education Building, Suite 5540
Raleigh, NC 27601
919-807-3952
Fax: 919-807-3826
E-mail: information@dpi.state.nc.us
http://www.ncpublicschools.org
The North Carolina Department of Public Instruction (DPI) is the agency charged with implementing the State's public school laws and the State Board of Education's policies and procedures governing pre-kindergarten through 12th grade public education. DPI develops the Standard Course of Study which describes the subjects and course content that should be taught in North Carolina public schools and develops the assessments and accountability model used to evaluate school and district success.

Melissa E Bartlett, Executive Director
Peter Asmar, Chief Information Officer

619 North Carolina Library Association (NCLA)
1841 Capital Blvd
Raleigh, NC 27604
919-839-6252
Fax: 919-839-6253
E-mail: nclaonline@ibiblio.org
http://www.nclaonline.org
An affiliate of the American Library Association and the Southeastern Library Association, the North Carolina Library Association (NCLA) is a statewide organization concerned with the total library community in North Carolina. NCLA's purpose is to promote libraries, library and information services, librarianship, intellectual freedom and literacy. Holds conferences in September and October and publishes a journal.

Sherwin Rice, VP/President elect
Wanda Brown, President

620 North Carolina State Education Assistance Authority
PO Box 13663
Research Triangle Park, NC 27709-3663
919-549-8614
866-866-2362
Fax: 919-549-8481
http://www.cfnc.org

North Dakota

621 Education for Homeless Children and Youth
600 E Boulevard Ave
Bismarck, ND 58505-0440
701-328-4646
888-605-1951
Fax: 701-328-4770

622 North Dakota Council on the Arts
1600 E Century Ave
Bismarck, ND 58503-0649
701-328-7590
Fax: 701-328-7595
http://www.nd.gov/arts

623 North Dakota Education Association (NDEA)
301 N 4th Street
Bismarck, ND 58501-5005
701-223-0450
Fax: 701-224-8535
E-mail: Dakota.draper@ndea.org
http://nd.nea.org/
Since 1887, the North Dakota Education Association has been advocating on behalf of North Dakota students and their teachers.

NDEA's mission is to improve the political climate and economic conditions for public education and the status of teaching professionals and educational employees, in addition to promoting educational excellence, innovation, and equal opportunity in working toward the elimination of all forms of discrimination.

Dakota Draper, President
Mark Berntson, Vice President

624 North Dakota Library Association
604 East Boulevard Avenue
Bismarck, ND 58502-1595
701-328-3495
Fax: 701-231-7138
E-mail: alpeterson@nd.gov
http://www.ndla.info
The North Dakota Library Association is concerned with the needs and rights of all citizens of North Dakota to have free access to library collections of sufficient scope and quality to provide the means for fruitful inquiry.
ISSN: 0882-4746
150 attendees and 25 exhibits

Cathy Langemo, Executive Secretary
Phyllis Ann K Bratton, President

Ohio

625 Education for Homeless Children and Youth
25 S Front St
Mail Stop 404
Columbus, OH 43215
614-466-4161
877-644-6338
Fax: 514-752-1622

626 Ohio Arts Council
727 E Main St
Columbus, OH 43205-1796
614-466-2613
888-243-8622
Fax: 614-466-4479
http://www.oac.state.oh.us

627 Ohio Association of School Business Officials
8050 North High Street
Suite 170
Columbus, OH 43235
614-431-9116
800-64 -2726
Fax: 614-431-9137
http://www.oasbo-ohio.org
The Ohio Association of School Business Officials is a not-for-profit educational management organization dedicated to learning, utilizing and sharing the best methods and technology of school business administration.

David A Varda, Executive Director
Mark Pepera, Treasurer

628 Ohio Association of Secondary School Administrators
8050 N High Street
Suite 180
Columbus, OH 43235-6484
614-430-8311
Fax: 614-430-8315
http://www.oassa.org
The Ohio Association of Secondary School Administrators is dedicated to the adnocacy and welfare of its members. Our mission is to provide high standards of leadership through professional development, political astuteness, legislative influence, positive public re-

lations and collaboration with related organization.

Craig S Kupferberg, President
James J Harbuck, Executive Director

629 Ohio Library Council
1105 Schrock Road
Suite 440
Columbus, OH 43229-1174
614-410-8092
Fax: 614-410-8098
E-mail: olc@olc.org
http://www.olc.org
The Ohio Library Council is the State wide professional association which represents the interests of Ohio's public libraries as well as their trustess, friends and staff. The OLC is governed by a Board of Directors composed of three library employees with an MLIS degree, three library trustees currently serving on library boards, and seven a-l arge members.

Margaret Danziger, President
Douglas Evans, Executive Director

630 Ohio Technology Education Association (OTEA)
c/o State Supervisor
25 South Front Street
Room 509
Edison, OH 43320
419-946-2071
Fax: 614-995-5568
E-mail: william_s@treca.org
http://www.otea.info/
The mission of the Ohio Technology Education Association (OTEA) is to promote technological literacy for all Ohio students; provide leadership in curriculum and professional development; inform governmental and educational decision makers on technological literacy issues; advocate society wide the understanding of technological literacy and why it is vital; and form and maintain alliances with the business and industrial community.

Richard A Dieffenderfer Ph.D, State Supervisor
Timothy N Tryon, Executive Director

Oklahoma

631 Education for Homeless Children and Youth
2500 N Lincoln Blvd
Oklahoma City, OK 73105
405-521-2846
Fax: 405-521-2998
http://www.sde.ok.us

632 Oklahoma Arts Council
PO Box 52001-2001
Oklahoma City, OK 73152-2001
405-521-2931
Fax: 405-521-6418
http://www.arts.ok.gov

633 Oklahoma Department of Libraries
200 NE 18th St
Oklahoma City, OK 73105
405-521-2502
800-522-8116
Fax: 405-525-7804
http://www.odl.state.ok.us

634 Oklahoma Education Association (OEA)
323 East Madison Avenue
PO 18485
Oklahoma City, OK 73154

402-528-7785
800-522-8091
Fax: 405-524-0350
E-mail: lodom@okea.org
http://www.okea.org
The Oklahoma Education Association (OEA) supports public education as the cornerstone of a democratic society in that education employees, parents, community leaders and elected officials should work together to promote quality education. OEA has 40,000 members, comprised of public school teachers, coaches, counselors, and administrators; nurses, librarians, custodians, cafeteria workers, bus drivers, secretaries; retired teachers; and education majors at Oklahoma colleges and universities.

Roy Bishop, President
Lela Odom, Executive Director

635 Oklahoma Library Association (OLA)
P.O. Box 6550
Edmond, OK 73013
405-525-5100
Fax: 405-525-5103
E-mail: kboies@sbcglobal.net
http://www.oklibs.org
The Oklahoma Library Association works to strengthen the quality of libraries, library services and librarianship in Oklahoma. Members of OLA work in public, school, academic and special libraries of all sizes. Members include professional, paraprofessional and clerical library staff, library trustees, Friends, students, volunteers, vendors of library products and services and many others. Holds a conference in April and publishes a journal.

Sarah Robbins, President
Leslie Langley, Marketing/Communications

Oregon

636 AFT-Oregon (American Federation of Teachers-Oregon)
7035 SW Hampton Street
Tigard, OR 97223-8313
503-595-3880
Fax: 503-595-3887
E-mail: AFTOregon@aft-oregon.org
http://or.aft.org/
Charted in 1952, AFT-Oregon, a state affiliate of the American Federation of Teachers, AFL-CIO, is a non-profit organization representing some 11,000 Oregon workers in K-12, community college and higher education in faculty and classified positions; and child care workers, in both public and private sectors. AFT-Oregon, in coalition with other unions and community groups, advocates for quality education and health care for all Oregonians, and gives working people a voice in our state's capitol.

Mark Schwebke, President
Richard Schwarz, Executive VP

637 Homeless Education Program
255 Capitol St NE
Salem, OR 97310-0203
503-947-5781
Fax: 503-378-5156
http://www.ode.state.or.us/go/homelessed

638 Oregon Arts Commission
775 Summer St NE
Salem, OR 97301-1284
503-986-0082
Fax: 503-986-0082
http://www.oregonartcommission.org

639 Oregon Association of Student Councils (OASC)
707 13th Street SE
Suite 100
Salem, OR 97301-4035
503-480-7206
Fax: 503-581-9840
E-mail: sara@oasc.org
http://www.oasc.org
The Oregon Association of Student Councils (OASC) is a non-profit member association, serving middle and high schools throughout the state. It provides leadership development to both students and advisors and is sponsored by the Confederation of Oregon School Administrators.

Sara S Nilles, Program Director

640 Oregon Education Association (OEA)
6900 SW Atlanta Street
Portland, OR 97223
503-684-3300
800-858-5505
Fax: 503-684-8063
E-mail: larry.wolf@oregoned.org
http://www.oregoned.org
The mission of the Oregon Education Association (OEA) is to assure quality public education for every student in Oregon by providing a strong, positive voice for school employees. OEA's school funding priority, established in December 2002, seeks to restore stable and adequate funding for Oregon's schools and community colleges so that all Oregon students have access to a quality public education.

Larry Wolf, President
Jerry Caruthers, Executive Director

641 Oregon Educational Media Association
PO Box 277
Terrebonne, OR 97760
503-625-7820
E-mail: j23hayden@aol.com
http://www.oema.net
To provide progressive leadership to ensure that Oregon students and educators are effective users of ideas and information, and to pursue excellence in school library media programs by advocating information literacy for all student, supporting reading instruction and enjoyment of literature, supporting the highest levels of library media services in schools, strengthening member professionalism through communications and educational opportunities and promoting visibility in education, governme

Jim Hayden, Executive Director
Merrie Olson, President

642 Oregon Library Association (OLA)
P.O. Box 3067
La Grande, OR 97850-2042
503-370-7019
Fax: 503-587-8063
E-mail: ola@olaweb.org
http://www.olaweb.org
The mission of the Oregon Library Association is to promote and advance library service through public and professional education and cooperation. Holds a conference in March and publishes two journals.

Mary Ginnane, President
Connie A Cohoon, Vice President

643 Oregon Student Assistance Commission
1500 Valley River Dr
Suite 100
Eugene, OR 97401
541-687-7400
800-452-8807
Fax: 541-687-7414
http://www.osac.state.or.us

Pennsylvania

644 Office of Postsecondary Higher Education
333 Market St
Harrisburg, PA 17126-0333
717-787-5041
Fax: 717-772-3622
http://www.pdehighered.state.pa.us/higher/site/default.asp

645 Pennsylvania Council on the Arts
215 Finance Building
Harrisburg, PA 17120
717-787-6883
Fax: 717-783-2538
http://www.pacouncilonthearts.org

646 Pennsylvania Library Association (PaLA)
220 Cumberland Parkway
Suite 10
Mechanicsburg, PA 17055
717-766-7663
800-622-3308
Fax: 717-766-5440
E-mail: glenn@palibraries.org
http://www.palibraries.org
The Pennsylvania Library Association (PaLA) is a professional non-profit organization with strong volunteer leadership, dedicated to the support of its members, to the advancement of librarianship, and to the improvement and promotion of quality library service for citizens of the Commonwealth.

Glenn Miller, Executive Director
Mary O Garm, President

647 Pennsylvania School Librarians Association
9 Saint James Avenue
Somerville, MA 02144
617-628-4451
http://www.psla.org
Provides school librarians/media specialists with educational opportunities and current information through publications, workshops, seminars and conferences

Marg Foster, Secretary
Nancy S Latanision, President

648 Pennsylvania State Education Association (PSEA)
400 N 3rd Street
PO Box 1724
Harrisburg, PA 17105-1724
717-255-7000
800-944-7732
Fax: 717-255-7124
E-mail: cdumaresq@psea.org
http://www.psea.org
PSEA's mission is to advocate for quality public education and our members through collective action. PSEA is a member-driven organization, headed by elected officers, an executive director and a board of directors.

James P Testerman, President
John F Springer, Executive Director

Rhode Island

649 Higher Education Assistance Authority
560 Jefferson Blvd
Suite 100
Warwick, RI 02886-1304
401-736-1100
800-922-9855
Fax: 401-732-3541
http://www.riheaa.org

650 National Education Association Rhode Island (NEARI)
99 Bald Hill Road
Cranston, RI 02920
401-463-9630
Fax: 401-463-5337
E-mail: RWalsh@nea.org
http://www.neari.org/matriarch/default.asp
The NEA Rhode Island is both a union and a professional organization.

Robert A Walsh Jr, Executive Director
Vincent P Santaniello, Deputy Executive Director

651 Rhode Island Association of School Business Officials
600 Mount Pleasant Avenue
Building #16, RIC
Providence, RI 02908
401-272-9811
Fax: 401-272-9834
http://www.riasp.org
Is an umbrella association serving elementary, middle level, and high school leaders from all across Rhode Island. Affiliated with both the National Association of Elementary School Principals (NAESP) and the National Association of Secondary School Principals (NASSP)

Norma Cole, President
Arlene Miguel, Secretary

652 Rhode Island Educational Media Association
6946 Camp Avenue
Suite 402
North Kingstown, RI 02852
401-398-7500
Fax: 401-886-0855
E-mail: www@ride.ri.net
http://www.ri.net
RINET provides complete Internet solutions for organizations that serve children, such as schools, libraries, municipalities, as well as high quality technology programs and services in support of K-12 teaching, learning and administration
Founded: 1999

Mike Mello, Membership Chairman
Sharon Hussey, Executive Director

653 Rhode Island Library Association
PO Box 6765
Providence, RI 02940
401-943-9080
Fax: 401-946-5079
E-mail: book_n@yahoo.com
http://www.rilibraryassoc.org
The Rhode Island Library Association is a profesional association of Librarians, Library Staff, Trustees, and library supporters whose purpose is to promote the profession of librarianship and to improve the visibility, accessibility, responsiveness and effectiveness of library and information services throughout Rhode Island.

Christopher Laroux, President
Laura Marlane, Vice President

654 State Council on the Arts
One Capitol Hill
Providence, RI 02908
401-222-3880
Fax: 401-222-3018
http://www.arts.ri.gov

South Carolina

655 Education for Homeless Children and Youth
1429 Senate St
Suite 1114-E
Columbia, SC 29201
803-734-3215
Fax: 803-734-3043
http://www.ed.sc.gov/

656 South Carolina Arts Commission
1800 Gervais St
Columbia, SC 29201
803-734-8696
Fax: 803-734-8526
http://www.state.sc.us/arts

657 South Carolina Commission on Higher Education
1333 Main St
Suite 200
Columbia, SC 29201
803-737-2260
877-349-7183
Fax: 803-737-2297
http://www.che.sc.gov

658 South Carolina Education Association (SCEA)
421 Zimalcrest Drive
Columbia, SC 29210
803-772-6553
800-422-7232
Fax: 803-772-0922
E-mail: help@thescea.org
http://www.thescea.org/
Professional association for educators in South Carolina.

Aaron Wallace, Executive Director
Carolyn Randolph, Assistant Executive Director

659 South Carolina Library Association
PO Box 1763
Columbia, SC 29202
803-252-1087
Fax: 803-252-0589
E-mail: scla@capconsc.com
http://www.scla.org
Informs members of issues and to provide training and networking opportunities.

Libby Young, President
Rayburne Turner, Vice President

South Dakota

660 Education for Homeless Children and Youth
700 Governors Dr
Pierre, SD 57501
605-773-6400
Fax: 605-773-3782

661 Mountain Plains Library Association (MPLA)
14293 West Center Drive
Lakewood, CO 80228
303-985-7795
E-mail: mpla_execsecretary@operamail.com
http://www.mpla.us
The Mountain Plains Library Association (MPLA) is a twelve state association of librarians, library paraprofessionals and friends of libraries in Arizona, Colorado, Kansas, Montana, Nebraska, Nevada, New Mexico, North Dakota, Oklahoma, South Dakota, Utah and Wyoming. Its purpose is to promote the development of librarians and li-

braries by providing significant educational and networking opportunities. Holds conferences in September, October and November. Also publishes a newsletter.

Judy Zelenski, Interim Executive Secretary
Dan Chaney, MPLA Webmaster

662 South Dakota Arts Council
711 E Wells Ave
Pierre, SD 57501-3369
605-773-3301
800-952-3625
Fax: 605-773-5657
http://www.artscouncil.sd.gov

663 South Dakota Education Association (SDEA)
441 E Capitol Avenue
Pierre, SD 57501
605-224-9263
800-529-0090
Fax: 605-224-5810
E-mail: Bryce.Healy@sdea.org
http://www.sdea.org/
The South Dakota Education Association/SDEA advocates new directions for public education, providing professional services that benefit students, schools and the public.

Bryce Healy, Executive Director
Paul McCorkle, CFO/CIO

664 South Dakota Library Association
28363 472nd Ave
Worthing, SD 57707
605-343-3750
E-mail: bkstand@rap.midco.net
http://www.sdlibraryassociation.org
The SD Library Association strives to promote library service of the highest quality for present and potential SD library users; to provide opportunities for professional involvement of all persons engaged in any phase of librarianship within the state; and to further the professional development of SD librarians, trustees, and library employees.

Jan Brue Enright, President
Laura Olson, Secretary/Treasurer

Tennessee

665 Education for Homeless Children and Youth
710 James Robertson Parkway
Nashville, TN 37243-0379
615-532-6309
Fax: 615-253-5706

666 Tennessee Arts Commission
401 Charlotte Ave
Nasville, TN 37243-0780
615-532-5934
Fax: 615-741-8559
http://www.arts.state.tn.us

667 Tennessee Association of Secondary School Principals (TASSP)
2671 Bebe Branch Lane
Knoxville, TN 37928
423-309-6187
866-737-2777
Fax: 865-687-2341
E-mail: tassp@bellsouth.net

The mission of the Tennessee Association of Secondary School Principals is: to promote professional standards of practice for secondary school administrators; provide

high quality professional development experiences for rural, urban, and suburban administrators, statewide, based on their common and unique professional development needs; and advocate on behalf of secondary administrators in their efforts to provide high quality education for all students.

Dana Finch, President
Tommy Everette, Executive Director

668 Tennessee Higher Education Commission
404 James Robertson Parkway
Suite 1900
Nashville, TN 37243-0830
615-741-3605
Fax: 615-741-6230
http://www.state.tn.us/thec

669 Tennessee Library Association
PO Box 241074
Memphis, TN 38124-1074
901-485-6952
Fax: 615-269-1807
E-mail: arhuggins1@comcast.net
http://www.tnla.org
Promote the establishment, maintenance, and support of adequate library services for all people of the state.

Annelle R Huggins, Executive Director
Dinah Harris, President

670 Tennessee School Boards Association
525 Brick Church Park Drive
Nashville, TN 37207
615-815-3900
800-448-6465
Fax: 615-815-3911
E-mail: webadmin@tsba.net
http://www.tsba.net
The mission of the Tennessee School Boards Association is to assist school boards in effectively governing school districts.

Founded: 1953

Tammy Grissom, Executive Director
David Pickler, President

Texas

671 Texas Association of Secondary School Principals (TASSP)
1833 S IH-35
Austin, TX 78741
512-443-2100
Fax: 512-442-3343
E-mail: aarguello@tassp.org
UELLO@TASSP.ORG
HTTP://WWW.TASSP.ORG/
TASSP provides proactive leadership to systemically change schools into learning communities in which all students and other participants achieve their full potential as life long learners in a diverse and changing society.

Bob Alvey, President
Tom Leyden, Associate Executive Director

672 Texas Commission on the Arts
PO Box 13406
Austin, TX 78711-3406
512-463-5535
800-252-9415
Fax: 512-475-2699
http://www.arts.state.tx.us

673 Texas Higher Education Coordinating Board
PO Box 12788
Austin, TX 78711-2788
512-427-6101
800-242-3062
Fax: 512-427-6127
http://www.thecb.state.tx.us

674 Texas Homeless Education Office
2901 N IH35
Austin, TX 78722
512-475-8765
800-446-3142
Fax: 512-471-6193

675 Texas Library Association (TLA)
3355 Bee Cave Road
Suite 401
Austin, TX 78746-6763
512-328-1518
800-580-2852
Fax: 512-328-8852
E-mail: tla@txla.org
http://www.txla.org
The Texas Library Association is a professional organization that promotes librarianship and library service in Texas. Through legislative advocacy, continuing education events, and networking channels, TLA offers members opportunities for service to the profession as well as for personal growth.

Patricia H Smith, Executive Director
Gloria Meraz, Communications Director

Utah

676 Education for Homeless Children and Youth
250 East 500 S
PO Box 144200
Salt Lake City, UT 84114-4200
801-538-7975
Fax: 801-538-7991
http://www.schools.utah.gov

677 Utah Arts Council
617 East South Temple
Salt Lake City, UT 84102
801-320-9794
Fax: 801-533-3210
http://www.arts.utah.gov

678 Utah Education Association (UEA)
875 E 5180 S
Murray, UT 84107-5299
801-266-4461
800-594-8996
Fax: 801-265-2249
E-mail: mark.mickelsen@utea.org
http://www.utea.org
The mission of the Utah Education Association (UEA) is to advance the cause of public education in partnership with others: strengthen the teaching profession, promote quality schools for Utah's children, and advocate the well-being of members.

Kim Campbell, President
Mark Mickelsen, Executive Director

679 Utah State Library Division
250 North 1950 W
Suite A
Salt Lake City, UT 84116-7901
801-715-6777
800-433-1479
Fax: 801-715-6767
http://www.library.utah.gov

680 Utah System of Higher Education
60 South 400 W
Salt Lake City, UT 84101-1284

801-321-7103
Fax: 801-321-7156
http://www.utahsbr.edu

Vermont

681 Education for Homeless Children and Youth
120 State St
Montpelier, VT 05620-2501
802-828-5148
Fax: 802-828-0573
http://www.education.vermont.gov/new/html/pgm_homeless.html

682 Vermont Arts Council
136 State St
Montpelier, VT 05633-6001
802-828-3778
Fax: 802-828-3363
http://www.vermontartscouncil.org

683 Vermont Department of Libraries
109 State St
Montpelier, VT 05609-0601
802-828-3261
Fax: 802-828-2199
http://www.libraries.vermont.gov

684 Vermont Library Association
PO Box 803
Burlington, VT 05402
802-388-3845
Fax: 802-388-4367
E-mail: vlaorg@sover.net
http://www.vermontlibraries.org
The Vermont Library Association is an educational Organization working to develop, promote, and improve library and information services and librarianship in the state of Vermont.

Judah S Hamer, President
David Clark, Chapter Councilor

685 Vermont National Education Association (VTNEA)
10 Wheelock Street
Montpelier, VT 05602-3737
802-223-6375
800-649-6375
Fax: 802-223-1253
E-mail: vtnea@together.net
http://www.vtnea.org/
The Vermont National Education Association is a voluntary organization of 11,000 Vermont teachers and education support professionals, their purpose being to make sure that members have a satisfying work environment where they are acknowledged for the work they perform and where the work they perform helps students do their best.

Joel D Cook, Executive Director
Darren M Allen, Communications Director

686 Vermont Student Assistance Corporation
10 East Allen St
PO Box 2000
Winooski, VT 05404-2601
http://www.vsac.org

687 Volunteers for Peace
7 Kilburn Street
Suite 316
Burlington, VT 05401
802-540-3060
E-mail: vfp@vfp.org
http://www.vfp.org
Volunteers for Peace promotes intercultural education, service learning and community

development, so that people from diverse backgrounds can work together.

Megan Brook, Executive Director
Scott Simpson, President

Virginia

688 Action Alliance for Virginia's Children and Youth
701 E Franklin Street
Suite 807
Richmond, VA 23219
804-649-0184
Fax: 804-649-0161
E-mail: info@vakids.org
http://www.vakids.org
Nonprofit and non-partisan, Voices for Virginia's Children is a persistent voice of reason in advocating for better lives and futures for children. The Commonwealth's only statewide multi-issue organization advocating for children and youth, Voices promotes sound, far-reaching program and policy solutions, focusing on early care and education, health care, family economic success, and foster care and adoption.

James V Duty, Chairman
John R Morgan, Executive Director

689 Division of Student Leadership Services
701 East Franklin Street
Richmond, VA 23288-0001
804-285-2829
Fax: 804-285-1379
http://www.vaprincipals.org
Organization that sponsors the Virginia Student Councils Association; the Virginia Association of Honor Societies; and the Virginia Association of Student Activity Advisers.

Dr. Randy Barrack, President

690 Eastern Business Education Association (EBEA)
1914 Association Drive
Reston, VA 20191-1596
703-860-8300
Fax: 703-620-4483
E-mail: nbea@nbea.org
http://www.nbea.org
NBEA is committed to the advancement of the professional interest and competence of its members and provides programs and services that enhance members' professional growth and development.

Sharon Fisher-Larson, President
Janet M Treichel, Executive Director

691 Education for Homeless Children and Youth
PO Box 8795
Williamsburg, VA 23187-8795
757-221-4002
877-455-3412
Fax: 757-221-5300
http://www.wm.edu/hope

692 Organization of Virginia Homeschoolers
PO Box 5131
Charlottesville, VA 22905
866-513-6173
Fax: 804-946-2263
E-mail: info@vahomeschoolers.org
http://www.vahomeschoolers.org
The Organization of Virginia Homeschoolers' most effective action is screening legislation for potential impact on homeschoolers. We pay attention to a large list of topics: home instruction statute, tutor

provision, religious exemption provision, driver training, truancy, curfews, tax credits, and more.

Parrish Mort, President
Kenneth L Payne, Executive Director

693 Southern Association of Colleges & Schools
Virginia Secondary & Middle School Committee
PO Box 7007
Radford, VA 24142-7007
540-831-5399
Fax: 540-831-6309
E-mail: mdalderm@runet.edu
http://www.sacs.org
Public and private school accreditation organization. 12,000 member schools in 11 southern state regions. 430 middle and secondary SACS member schools in Virginia.

Dr. Emmett Sufflebarger, President
Lanny Holsinger, President-Elect

694 State Council of Higher Education for Virginia
101 North 14th St
Richmond, VA 23219
804-225-2600
Fax: 804-225-2604
http://www.schev.edu

695 Virginia Alliance for Arts Education
PO Box 70232
Richmond, VA 23255-0232
804-740-7865
Fax: 804-828-2335
http://www.socialarchive.iath.virginia.edu
To promote aesthetic and creative art education for the development of the individual at all levels in the commonwealth of Virginia. To assist teachers in improving the quality of art education. To organize and conduct panels, forums, lectures, and tours for art educators and the general public on art and art instruction. To keep the public informed of the arts through whatever means are available.

Founded: 1974

Margaret Edwards, Division Director

696 Virginia Association for Health, Physical Education, Recreation & Dance
817 W Franklin Street
Box 842037
Richmond, VA 23284-2037
800-918-9899
Fax: 800-918-9899
http://www.vahperd.org
VAHPERD is a professional association of educators that advocate quality programs in health, physical education, recreation, dance and sport. The association seeks to facilitate the professional growth and educational practices and legislation that will impact the profession.

Judith Clark, President

697 Virginia Association for Supervision and Curriculum Development
33074 Clay Street
Hopewell, VA 23860
804-458-9554
E-mail: vascd1@verizon.net
http://www.vaascd.org/
VASCD is an organization committed to excellence in education by providing programs and services that promote quality instruction for lifelong learning.

Linda Hyslop, Executive Director
Judy Lam, Administrative Coordinator

698 Virginia Association for the Education ofthe Gifted
PO Box 26212
Richmond, VA 23260-6212
804-355-5945
Fax: 804-355-5137
E-mail: vagifted@comcast.net
http://www.vagifted.org
The Virginia Association for the Gifted supports research in gifted education and advocates specialized preparation for educators of the gifted. The association disseminates information, maintains a statewide network of communication, and cooperates with organizations and agencies to improve the quality of education in the Commonwealth of Virginia.

Liz Nelson, Executive Director

699 Virginia Association of Elementary School Principals
1805 Chantilly Street
Richmond, VA 23230
804-355-6791
Fax: 804-355-1196
E-mail: info@vaesp.org
http://www.vaesp.org
Nonprofit professional association advocating for public education and equal educational opportunities. Promotes leadership of school administrators, principals as educational leaders, and provides professional development opportunities.

Thomas L Shortt, Executive Director
Jeanne Grady, Operations Director

700 Virginia Association of Independent Specialized Education Facilities
6802 Paragon Place
Suite 525
Richmond, VA 23230
804-282-3592
Fax: 804-282-3596
E-mail: info@vais.org
http://www.vais.org
The Virginia Association of Independent Schools is a service organization that promotes educational, ethical and professional excellence. Through its school evaluation/accreditation program, attention to professional development and insistence on integrity, the Association safeguards the interests of its member schools.

Kimberly E Failon, Director Professional Develo
Sally K Boese, Executive Director

701 Virginia Association of Independent Schools
6802 Paragon Place
Suite 525
Richmond, VA 23230
804-282-3592
Fax: 804-282-3596
E-mail: info@vais.org
http://www.vais.org
The Virginia Association of Independent Schools is a service organization that promotes educational, ethical and professional excellence. Through its school evaluation/accreditation program, attention to professional development and insistence on integrity, the Association safeguards the interests of its member schools.

Kimberly E Failon, Director Professional Develo
Sally K Boese, Executive Director

702 Virginia Association of School Superintendents
1805 Chantilly Street
PO Box 400265
Richmond, VA 2323-4265
804- 5-2
Fax: 434-982-2942
http://vass.edschool.virginia.edu/
The Virginia Association of School Superintendents (VASS) is a professional organization dedicated to the mission of providing leadership and advocacy for public school education throughout the Commonwealth of Virginia.

J Andrew Stamp, Associate Executive Director
Alfred R Butler IV, Executive Director

703 Virginia Association of School Business Officials
Williamsburg-James City County Public Schools
PO Box 8783
Williamsburg, VA 23187-8783
757-253-6748
Fax: 757-253-0173
http://www.vasbo.org/
The mission of the Virginia Association of School Business Officials is to promote the highest standards of school business practices for its membership through professional development, continuing education, networking, and legislative impact.

David C Papenfuse, Division Director

704 Virginia Association of School Personnel Administrators
800 E City Hall Avenue
Norfolk, VA 23510-2723
757-340-1217
Fax: 757-340-1889
E-mail: president@vaspa.org
http://www.vaspa.org/
The Virginia Association of School Personnel Administrators helps personnel/human resources professionals improve their administrative skills and grow extensively in their profession.

Eddid P Antoine II, Division Director
Barbara Warren Jones, President

705 Virginia Commission for the Arts
223 Governor St
Richmond, VA 23219-2010
804-225-3132
Fax: 804-225-4327
http://www.arts.virigina.gov

706 Virginia Congress of Parents & Teachers
1027 Wilmer Avenue
Richmond, VA 23227-2419
804-264-1234
866-482-497
Fax: 804-264-4014
E-mail: info@vapta.org
http://www.vapta.org
The Virginia Congress of Parents and Teachers, better known as the Virginia PTA is a volunteer child advocacy association working for ALL children and youth in the Commonwealth of Virginia.

Melissa S Nehrbass, President
Eugene A Goldberg, Executive Director

707 Virginia Consortium of Administrators for Education of the Gifted
RR 5 Box 680
Farmville, VA 23901-9011

804-225-2884
Fax: 814-692-3163
http://www.vagifted.org
Catherine Cottrell, Division Director

708 Virginia Council for Private Education
1901 Huguenot Road
Suite 301
Richmond, VA 23235
804-423-6435
Fax: 804-423-6436
E-mail: jwebster@vcpe.org
http://www.vcpe.org
The Virginia Council for Private Education (VCPE) oversees accreditation of nonpublic preschool, elementary and secondary schools in the Commonwealth.

George McVey, President
Joanne L Webster, Vice President

709 Virginia Council of Administrators of Special Education
Franklin County Public Schools
25 Bernard Road
Rocky Mount, VA 24151
703-493-0280
Fax: 540-483-5806
E-mail: kkirst@k12albemarle.org
http://www.vcase.org
The Virginia Council of Administrators of Special Education is a professional organization that promotes professional leadership through the provision of collegial support and current information on recommended instructional practices as well as local, state and national trends in Special Education for professionals who serve students with disabilities in order to improve the quality and delivery of special education services in Virginia's public Schools

Dr. Sheila Bailey, President
Wyllys VanDerwerker, President-Elect

710 Virginia Council of Teachers of Mathematics
1033 Backwoods Road
Virginia Beach, VA 23455-6617
757-671-7316
E-mail: gnelson@vctm.org.
http://www.vctm.org/
The purpose of the Virginia Council of Teachers of Mathematics is to stimulate an active interest in mathematics, to provide an interchange of ideas in the teaching of mathematics, to promote the improvement of mathematics education in Virginia, to provide leadership in the professional development of teachers, to provide resources for teachers and to facilitate cooperation among mathematics organizations at the local, state and national levels

Ellen Smith Hook, Division Director
Ian Shenk, President

711 Virginia Council on Economic Education
301 W Main Street
Box 844000
Richmond, VA 23284-4000
804-828-1627
Fax: 804-828-7215
E-mail: shfinley@vcu.edu
http://www.vcee.org
Goal is for students to understand our economy and develop the life-long decision-making skills they need to be effective, informed citizens, consumers, savers, investors, producers and employees.

Yvonne Toms Allmond, Senior Vice President
Sallie Garrett, Contact

712 Virginia Education Association
116 S 3rd Street
Richmond, VA 23219
804-648-5801
800-552-9554
Fax: 804-775-8379

E-mail: kboitnott@veanea.org
http://www.veanea.org/
VEA is a statewide community of more than 60,000 teachers and school support professionals working for the betterment of public education in the Commonwealth. First organized in 1863, VEA has consistently advocated for quality instruction and curriculum, adequate funding, and excellent working conditions for Virginia public employees.

Robert Whitehead, Executive Director
Kitty Boitnott, President

713 Virginia Educational Media Association
PO Box 2743
Fairfax, VA 22031-2743
703-764-0719
Fax: 703-272-3643
E-mail: jremler@pen.k12.va.us
http://www.vema.gan.va.us
Aim is to promote literacy, information access and evaluation, love of literature, effective use of technology, collaboration in the teaching and learning process, intellectual freedom, professional growth, instructional leadership and lifelong learning.

Jean Remler, Executive Director
Terri Britt, President

714 Virginia Educational Research Association
3354 Taleen Court
Annandale, VA 22003-1161
703-698-1325
Fax: 703-698-0587
E-mail: mpowell@ctb.com
http://www.va-edresearch.org
The mission of the Educational Research Service is to improve the education of children and youth by providing educators and the public with timely and reliable research and information.

Dr. Edith Carter, Assistant Professor
Michaeline M Powell, President

715 Virginia High School League
1642 State Farm Boulevard
Charlottesville, VA 22911-8609
434-977-8475
Fax: 434-977-5943
E-mail: ktillry@vhsl.org
http://www.vhsl.org
The Virginia High School League is an alliance of Virginia's public high schools that promotes education, leadership, sportsmanship, character and citizenship for students by establishing and maintaining high standards for school activities and competitions.

Craig Barbrow, President
Susan Bechtol, Chairman

716 Virginia Library Association
PO Box 56312
Virginia Beach, VA 23503-0277
757-583-0041
Fax: 757-583-5041
E-mail: lhahne@coastalnet.com
http://www.vla.org
The Virginia Library Association is a statewide organization whose purpose is to develop, promote, and improve library and information services and the profession of librarianship in order to advance literacy and learning and to ensure access to information in the Commonwealth of Virginia.

Linda Hahne, Executive Director

717 Virginia Middle School Association
11138 Marsh Road
Bealeton, VA 22712-9360

703-439-3207
Fax: 540-439-2051
http://www.vmsa.org/
Lisa Norris, President
Virginia Jones, President Elect

718 Virginia School Boards Association
200 Hansen Road
Charlottesville, VA 22911
434-295-8722
800-446-8722
Fax: 434-295-8785
http://www.vsba.org
The Virginia School Boards Association is a voluntary, nonpartisan association whose primary mission is the advancement of education through the unique American tradition of local citizen control of, and accountability for, the Commonwealth's public schools.

Gina Patterson, Assistant Executive Director
Frank E Barham, Executive Director

719 Virginia Student Councils Association
4909 Cutshaw Avenue
Richmond, VA 23230
804-355-2777
Fax: 804-285-1379
E-mail: rbarrack@vassp.org
http://www.vassp.org/vsca.html
Assist school principals and assistant principals in providing leadership to their schools and communities for the purpose of improving the education of Virginia's youth.

Randy D Barrack, Executive Director
Lawrence W Lenz, President

720 Virginia Vocational Association
10259 Lakeridge Square Court
Suite G
Ashland, VA 23005-8159
804-365-4556

Jean Holbrook, President
Kathy Williams, Executive Director

Washington

721 Education for Homeless Children and Youth
600 Washington St SE
PO Boc 47200
Olympia, WA 98504-7200
360-725-6050
Fax: 360-664-3575
http://www.k12.wa.us/homelessed/default.aspx

722 Washington Education Association
32032 Weyerhaeuser Way S
PO Box 9100
Federal Way, WA 98063-9100
253-941-6700
Fax: 253-946-4735
http://www.washingtonea.org
The mission of the Washington Education Association is to advance the professional interests of its members in order to make public education the best it can be for students, staff and communities

Mary Lindquist, President
Mike Ragan, VP

723 Washington Library Association
23607 Highway 99
Suite 2-C
Edmonds, WA 98026
425-967-0739
Fax: 425-771-9588
E-mail: info@wla.org
http://http://wla.org/

Washington's citizens rely upon libraries to further their education, enhance their skills in the work place, fully function in today's global society, and enrich and enjoy their daily lives. The Washington Library Association, with a membership of over 1300 individuals and 39 institutions, provides the leadership needed to develop, improve, and promote library services to all Washington residents

ISSN: 8756-4173

Becky Shaddox, Executive Director
Kristin Crowe, Executive Director

724 Washington State Arts Commission
PO Box 42675
Olympia, WA 98504-2675
360-753-3860
Fax: 360-586-5351
http://www.arts.wa.gov

725 Washington State Higher Education Coordinating Board
917 Lakeridge Way
PO Box 43430
Olympia, WA 98504-3430
360-753-7800
Fax: 360-753-7808
http://www.hecb.wa.gov

West Virginia

726 Commission of the Arts
199 Kanawha Blvd E
Charleston, WV 25305-0300
604-558-0240
Fax: 304-558-3560
http://www.wvculture.org

727 Education for Homeless Children and Youth
1900 Kanawha Blvd E
Charleston, WV 25305-0330
304-558-8833
Fax: 304-558-5042
http://www.wvde.state.wv.us/institutional

728 Edvantia
1031 Quarrier Street
PO Box 1348
Charleston, WV 25325-1348
304-347-0400
800-624-9120
Fax: 304-347-0487
E-mail: info@edvantia.org
http://www.edvantia.org
Edvantia is a nonprofit corporation committed to helping client-partners improve education and meet federal and state mandates. Schools, districts, and state education agencies-as well as publishers and service providers-rely on Edvantia's core capabilities in research, evaluation, professional development, and technical assistance to help them succeed.

Nancy Balow, Author
Patricia Hammer, Director of Communications
Carolyn Luzader, Communications Specialist

729 West Virginia Education Association
1558 Quarrier Street
Charleston, WV 25311-2497
304-346-5315
800-642-8261
Fax: 304-346-4325
http://www.wvea.org
We are education employees like you who care deeply about children and public educa-

tion. We help employees throughout the state face the demands of their profession

Dale Lee, President
Wayne Spangler, Vice President

730 West Virginia Higher Education Policy Commission
1018 Kanawha Blvd E
Suite 700
Charleston, WV 25301
304-558-0699
Fax: 304-558-1011
http://www.hepc.wvnet.edu

731 West Virginia Library Association
PO Box 5221
Charleston, WV 25361
304-558-2045
Fax: 304-558-2044
E-mail: webmaster@wvla.org
http://www.wvla.org
The West Virginia Library Association (WVLA) was established in 1914 to promote library service and librarianship in West Virginia. Since then, WVLA has offered leadership in the development and expansion of library services of all types

Myra Ziegler, President
Olivia L Bravo, Chairperson

732 West Virginia Library Commission
1900 Kanawha Blvd E
Charleston, WV 25305-0620
304-558-2041
800-642-9021
Fax: 304-558-2044
http://www.librarycommission.lib.wv.us

Wisconsin

733 Division for Libraries, Technology, and Community Learning
125 S Webster St
PO Box 7841
Madison, WI 53707-7841
608-266-2205
800-441-4563
Fax: 608-266-8770
http://www.dpi.wi.gov/dltcl

734 Education for Homeless Children and Youth Program
125 S Webster St
PO Box 7841
Madison, WI 53707-7841
608-261-6322
800-441-4563
Fax: 607-267-0364
http://www.dpi.wi.gov/homeless

735 Wisconsin Arts Board
101 E Wilson St
Madison, WI 53702

608-266-0190
Fax: 608-267-0380
http://www.artsboard.wisconsin.gov

736 Wisconsin Education Association Council
33 Nob Hill Drive
PO Box 8003
Madison, WI 53708-8003
608-276-7711
800-362-8034
Fax: 608-276-8203
E-mail: AskOnWEAC@weac.org.
http://www.weac.org
To fulfill the promise of a democratic society, the mission of the Wisconsin Education Association Council is to promote respect and support for quality public education and to provide for the professional and personal growth and economic welfare of members.

Mary Bell, President
Dan Burkhalter, Executive Director

737 Wisconsin Educational Media Association
PO Box 206
Boscobel, WI 53809
608-375-6020
E-mail: wemtamanager@hughes.net
http://www.wemaonline.org
Providing programs and services that enhance the professional growth of all members

Courtney Rounds, Association Manager
Jo Ann Carr, President

738 Wisconsin Higher Educational Aids Board
131 W Wilson St
Suite 902
Madison, WI 53703
608-267-2206
Fax: 607-267-2808
http://www.heab.state.wi.us

739 Wisconsin Library Association
4610 South Biltmore Lane
Suite A1
Madison, WI 53718-8345
608-245-3640
Fax: 608-245-3646
E-mail: wla@scls.lib.wi.us
http://www.wla.lib.wi.us/
WLA brings together and supports people from all types of libraries to advocate and work for the improvement and development of library and information services for all of Wisconsin

Pat Chevis, President
Lisa Strand, Executive Director

Wyoming

740 Education for Homeless Children and Youth
2300 Capitol Ave
Cheyenne, WY 82002-0050
307-777-5315
Fax: 307-777-7633
http://www.k12.wy.us/fp.asp

741 Wyoming Arts Council
2320 Capitol Ave
Cheyenne, WY 82002
307-777-7742
Fax: 307-777-5499
http://www.wyoarts.state.wy.us

742 Wyoming Education Association
115 E 22nd Street
Suite 1
Cheyenne, WY 82001-3795
307-634-7991
Fax: 800-778-8161
E-mail: mkruse@nea.org
http://www.wyoea.org
Advance public education at all levels by creating equitable educational opportunity for all learners, promoting the highest quality standards for the profession, and expanding the rights and furthering the interests of educational personnel.

Kathryn Valido, President
Craig Williams, Vice President

743 Wyoming Library Association
PO Box 1387
Cheyenne, WY 82003-1387
307-632-7622
Fax: 307-638-3469
E-mail: grottski@aol.com
http://www.wyla.org
Promotes library service and profession of librarianship in Wyoming.

Cynthia Twing, President
Laura Grott, Executive Secretary

744 Wyoming School Boards Association
2323 Pioneer Avenue
Cheyenne, WY 82001-3274
307-634-1112
Fax: 307-634-1114
E-mail: wsba@wsba-wy.org
http://www.wsba-wy.org
The official voice of local school boards.

Gregg Blikre, President
Mike Eathorne, President-Elect

International

745 ACSI Teachers' Convention
Assocation of Christian Schools
International
731 Chapel Hills Drive
PO Box 65130
Colorado Springs, CO 80920
719-528-6906
800-367-0798
Fax: 791-531-0716
E-mail: exhibitors@acsi.org
http://www.acsi.org
Educational convention for administrators,
school board members, and early childhood
educators that encourages staff and volunteer
development throughout the year.

50000 attendees

Brian S. Simmons, President
Janet Stump, Public Relations

**746 AISA School Leaders' Retreat and
Educators Conference**
Association of International Schools in
Africa
Peponi Road
PO Box 14103, Nairobi
Kenya 00800
254-20-2697442
Fax: 254-20-4183272
E-mail: info@aisa.or.ke
http://www.aisa.or.ke
Facilitates communications, cooperation,
and professional growth among member
schools. Promotes intercultural understand-
ing and friendships as well as facilitating col-
laboration between its members, host country
schools, and other regional and professional
groups.

Annual/October

Peter Bateman, Executive Director

**747 Association for Childhood Education
International Bi-Annual Conference**
Assn for Childhood Educational
International
1101 16th St. N.W.
Suite 300
Washington, DC 20036
202-372-9986
800-423-3563
Fax: 202-372-9989
E-mail: headquarters@acei.org
http://www.acei.org
Symposium focusing on education for bi-lin-
gual and culturally diverse children, interna-
tional issues and offers over 200 workshops.

April
50 booths with 1000 attendees

Debora Wisneski, President
Carrie Whaley, President Elect

**748 Association for Experiential
Education Annual Conference**
3775 Iris Avenue
Suite 4
Boulder, CO 80301-2043
303-440-8844
866-522-8337
Fax: 303-440-9581
E-mail: membership@aee.org
http://www.aee.org
Annual international and regional conference dedicated to promoting, defining, developing, and applying the theories and
practices of experiential education.

November
1,200 attendees

Mary Breunig, President
Leslie Stevens, Office Manager

749 CIEE Annual Conference
Council on International Educational
Exchange
300 Fore Street
Portland, ME 04101
207-553-7600
800-407-8839
Fax: 207-553-7699
E-mail: conference@ciee.org
http://www.ciee.org
Open to study-abroad advisors, administrators, faculty and other international education professionals. The conference is an
opportunity to share ideas, keep up with developments in the field, and meet with colleagues from around the world.

November

**750 Center for Critical Thinking and
Moral Critique Annual International**
Po Box196
Tomales, CA 94971
707-878-9100
800-833-3645
Fax: 707-878-9111
E-mail: cct@criticalthinking.org
http://www.criticalthinking.org
Over 1,200 educators participate to discuss
critical thinking and educational change.

March, July

Dr Linda Elder, President

**751 Council for Advancement and
Support of Education**
1307 New York Avenue NW
Suite 1000
Washington, DC 20005-4701
202-328-2273
Fax: 202-387-4973
E-mail: conferences@case.org
http://www.case.org
Offers numerous opportunities in the United
States, Canada, Mexico, mainland Europe,
and the United Kingdom to network with
colleagues.

Fall/Winter

John Lippincott, President
Richard Salatiello, Sr Conference Program
Coord.

**752 Council for Learning Disabilities
International Conference**
1184 Antioch Road
Box 405
Overland Park, KS 66210
913-491-1011
Fax: 913-491-1012
E-mail: cldinfo@cldinternational.org
http://www.cldinternational.org
Intensive interaction with and among professional educators and top LD researchers.
Concise, informative and interesting forums
on topics from effective instruction to
self-reliance are presented by well-known
professionals from across the country and
around the world.

October
35 booths with 800 attendees

Diane Bryant, Conference Contact
Judy Voress, Conference Contact

**753 Council of British Independent
Schools in the European
Communities Annual Conference**
St. Mary's University Palace
Strawberry Hill
Twickenham, UK TW1-4SX
44(0) 208 240 4142
Fax: 44(0) 208 240 4255
E-mail: excecutive.director@cobis.org.uk
http://www.cobis.org.uk

Conference for members of senior management educational teams.

May
75 attendees and 20 exhibits

Colin Bell, Executive Director
Suzanne Howarth, Membership

**754 European Council of International
Schools**
146 Buckingham Palace Road
Fourth Floor
London, UK SW1W-9TR
+44 0 20 7824 7040
Fax: +44 0 20 7824 7041
E-mail: ecis@ecis.org
http://www.ecis.org
Support professional development, curriculum and instruction, leadership and good
governance in international schools located
in Europe and around the world.

April, November

Michelle Clue, Conference Coordinator
Jean Vahey, Executive Director

**755 Hort School: Conference of the
Association of American Schools**
International School of Panama
P.O. Box 0819-02588
Panama City
507-293-3000
Fax: 507-266-7808
E-mail: isp@isp.edu.pa
http://www.isp.edu.pa
Educates and inspires our students to reach
their full potential and contribute to the world
by providing an exemplary English language
education enriched by our multicultural
community.

October
600 attendees and 35 exhibits

Rajiv Bhat, Director
Terry McCoy, President

**756 International Association of Teachers
of English as a Foreign Language**
Darwin College
University of Kent
Canterbury, Kent, UK CT2-7NY
44-1227-824430
Fax: 44-1227-824431
E-mail: generalenquires@iatefl.org
http://www.iatefl.org
Plenary sessions by eminent practitioners, a
large number of workshops, talks and round
tables given by other speakers, an ELT Re-
sources Exhibition and Pre-Conference
Events organized by Special Interest Groups.

April
80 booths with 1500 attendees

Alison Medland, Conference Organizer
Glenda Smart, Executive Director

757 International Awards Market
Awards and Recognition Association
4700 W Lake Avenue
Glenview, IL 60025
847-375-4800
800-344-2148
Fax: 888-374-7257
E-mail: info@ara.org
http://www.ara.org
Providing outstanding business and educational opportunities for both retailers and
suppliers. Retailers can view the latest industry products, take advantage of special show
offers and benefit from a full educational
program.

Feb, March, Nov
200 booths with 6,000 attendees

Lori Warren, President

758 International Conference
World Association for Symphonic Bands
& Ensembles
1037 Mill Street
San Luis Obispo, CA 93401
805-541-8000
Fax: 805-543-9498
E-mail: admin@wasbe2005.com
http://www.wasbe.org
WASBE is a nonprofit, international association open to individuals, institutions,
and industries interested in symphonic
bands and wind ensembles. Dedicated to
enhancing the quality of the wind band
throughout the world and exposing its
members to new worlds of repertoire, musical culture, people and places.

Every 2 years
Bert Aalders, President

**759 International Congress for School
Effectiveness & Improvement**
International Congress Secretariat
86 Ellison Road
Springwood
Australia NSW-2777
61 2 4751 7974
Fax: 61 2 4751 7974
E-mail: admin@icsei.net
http://www.icsei.net
The purpose of building and using an expanded base for advancing research, practice and policy in the area of school
effectiveness and improvement. The Congress offers the opportunity to exchange
information and networking for the
educational community.

January
500 attendees

Dr. Lorna Earl, President
Dr. Alma Harris, President Elect

**760 International Dyslexia Association
Annual Conference**
40 York Road
4th Floor
Baltimore, MD 21204-2044
410-296-0232
800-ABC-D123
Fax: 410-321-5069
E-mail: info@interdys.org
http://www.interdys.org
Provide the most comprehensive range of
information and services that address the
full scope of dyslexia and related difficulties in learning to read and write.

November
3000 attendees

Darnella Parks, Conference Manager
Kristen Penczek, Conference Director

761 International Exhibit
National Institute for Staff &
Organizational Dev.
University of Texas
1912 Speedway, Stop D5600
Austin, TX 78712-1607
512-471-7545
Fax: 512-471-9426
E-mail: membership@nisod.oeg
http://www.nisod.org
The largest international conference to fo-
cus specifically on the celebration of teach-
ing, learning, and leadership excellence.

May
1500 attendees

Sheryl Powell, Conference Director

**762 International Listening Association
Annual Convention**
International Listening Association
Box 164
Belle Plaine, MN 56011

952-594-5697
Convention topics cover broad spectrum of
listening practice and research. Papers,
panels, courses, practice and workshops
can be found at the convention in effort to
network, spread research and new practices in effetcive listening training,

June
Dr. Nanette Johnson-Curiskis, Executive
Director
Debra Worthington, Convention Planner

**763 International Multicultural
Institute (IMCI) Annual
Conference**
International Multicultural Institute
595 6th Street
Brooklyn, NY 11215
718-832-8625
http://www.imciglobal.org
Brings together practitioners from across
the country and around the world to explore diversity and multiculturalism in
both personal and professional contexts.
Leaders from academia, business, and government present the latest thinking and action on diversity issues to conference
participants.

June
Nancy J. Di Dia, Executive Director
Margaret Regan, President

**764 International Reading Association
Annual Convention**
800 Barksdale Road
PO Box 8139
Newark, DE 19714-8139
302-731-1600
800-336-7323
Fax: 302-731-1057
E-mail: customerservice@reading.org
http://www.reading.org
Contains exhibitors involved in various
lectures and workshops dealing with illiteracy, literature and some library science
courses.

May
800 booths with 13M attendees

Carrice C. Cummins, President
Marcie Craig Post, Executive Director

**765 International Technology
Education Association Conference**
1914 Association Drive
Suite 201
Reston, VA 20191-1539
703-860-2100
Fax: 703-860-0353
E-mail: iteea@iteea.org
http://www.iteea.org
Provides teachers with new and exciting
ideas for educating students of all grade
levels. The conference gives educators an
opportunity for better understanding of the
constant changes that take place in technology education.

varies
150 booths with 2,200+ attendees

Ken Starkman, Program Chair
Christine Maggio, Exhibit Opportunities

766 International Trombone Festival
International Trombone Association
PO Box 441
Coppell, TX 75019
888-684-2361
Fax: 888-684-2362
E-mail: jon@trombonefestival.net
http://www.trombone.net
Annual festival giving trombonists the op-
portunity to meet and share with other

trombonists for performances, lectures, exhibits,
competitions and more.

June
John Drew, President
Jon Bohls, Festivals Director

**767 Learning Disabilities Association of
America International Conference**
4156 Library Road
Pittsburgh, PA 15234-1349
412-341-1515
Fax: 412-344-0224
E-mail: info@ldaamerica.org
http://www.ldanatl.org
The largest meeting on learning disabilities (LD)
in the world. Disabled, parents, various educators
and administrators. The conference follows a general theme set by LDAA.

Febuary
95 booths with 2600 attendees and 300 exhibits

Mary Clare Reynolds, Executive Director

National

768 AAUW National Convention
American Association of University Women
1111 16th Street NW
Washington, DC 20036
202-785-7700
800-326-2289
Fax: 202-872-1425
E-mail: convention@aauw.org
http://www.aauw.org
The nation's leading voice promoting education
and equity for women and girls. Speakers, panels
and workshops allow for networking with other
AAUW members and explore opportunities to
further empower women.

Katie Broendel, Media/PR Manager
Christy Jones, Membership Director

**769 ASCD Annual Conference & Exhibit
Show**
1703 N Beauregard Street
Alexandria, VA 22311-1714
703-578-9600
800-933-2723
Fax: 703-575-5400
E-mail: member@ascd.org
http://www.ascd.org
Explore the big ideas in education today, or examine new developments in your content area or
grade level. Stretch your professional development learning into new areas, or pick an issue you
care about most and examine it in depth.

March
12000 attendees

Barbara Gleason, Public Information Director
Christy Guilfoyle, Public Relations Specialist

770 AZLA Conference
Arizona Library Association
1030 E Baseline Road
Suite 105-1025
Tempe, AZ 85283
480-609-3999
Fax: 480-998-7838
E-mail: admin@azla.org
http://www.azla.org
Advance the education advantages of the state
through libraries, and to promote general interest
in library extension (traveling libraries). Sometimes conference is a joint venture between two li-
braries(2014 held by AZLA and MPLA libraries).

November
90+ booths with 2,000 attendees

Rene Tanner, Conference Planning

771 AdvancED
National Study of School Evaluation
9115 Westside Parkway
Alpharetta, GA 30009-4958
678-392-2285
888-413-3669
Fax: 847-995-9088
E-mail: contactus@advanc-ed.org
http://www.advanc-ed.org
Annual international summit held in Washington, DC. Share research on best educational practices, research based products. Research helps shape educational policy and strengthen learning practices worldwide.

November

Dr. Mark A Elgart, President/CEO

772 American Association for Employment in Education Annual Conference
American Association for Employment in Education
947 E. Johnstown Rd.
#170
Gahanna, OH 43230
614-485-1111
800-678-6010
Fax: 360-244-7802
E-mail: aaee@osu.edu
http://www.aaee.org
Disseminate information on the educational marketplace, and job search process. Promote ethical standards and practices in the employment process. Promote dialogue and cooperation among institutions which prepare educators and institutions which provide employment opportunities.

November
20 booths with 150-200 attendees

Doug Peden, Executive Director
Diana Sanchez, Nat'l Conference Prog. Chair

773 American Association of Colleges for Teacher Ed Annual Meeting and Exhibits
1307 New York Avenue NW
Suite 300
Washington, DC 20005-4701
202-293-2450
Fax: 202-457-8095
E-mail: aacte@aacte.org
http://www.aacte.org
Learning event for educator preparation professionals. Oppportunities for networking, advancing understanding of new concepts and theories, hear new research and discover innovative practices and programs.

Feb
75 booths with 2400 attendees

Sharon P Robinson, President/CEO
Gail M. Bozeman, VP Meetings and Events

774 American Association of French Teachers Conference
American Association of French Teachers
Mailcode 4510
Southern Illinois University
Carbondale, IL 62901-4510
618-453-5731
Fax: 618-453-5733
E-mail: aatf@frenchteachers.org
http://www.frenchteachers.org/convention
Conventions regularly occur in French-speaking areas. Representing the French language in North America and to encourage the dissemination, both in the schools and in the general public, of knowledge concerning all aspects of the culture and

civilization of France and the French-speaking world.

July
1100 attendees

Dr Jayne Abrate, Executive Director

775 American Association of Physics Teachers National Meeting
One Physics Ellipse
College Park, MD 20740-3311
301-209-3311
Fax: 301-209-0845
E-mail: aapt-meet@aapt.org
http://www.aapt.org
Gives members the opportunity to network, discuss innovations in teaching methods and share the results of research about teaching and learning.

summer & winter

Tiffany Hayes, Director of Conferences
Cerena Cantrell, Associate Program Director

776 American Association of School Administrators National Conference on Education
1615 Duke Street
Alexandria, VA 22314
703-528-0700
Fax: 703-841-1543
E-mail: info@aasa.org
http://www.aasa.org
For school administrators to hear education leaders, exhibits, vendors for public education and network with others sharing practices and learning new ways in education. Support and develop effective school system leaders dedicated to the highest quality public education for all children.

Daniel Domenech, Executive Director
Christopher Daw, Director of Conferences

777 American Association of School Librarians National Conference
American Library Association
50 E Huron Street
Chicago, IL 60611
312-280-4382
800-545-2433
Fax: 312-280-5276
E-mail: aasl@ala.org
http://www.ala.org/aasl
An open conference holding seminars, workshops and tours of local libraries and facilities.

October
3,000 attendees

Julie Walker, Executive Director
Melissa Jacobsen, Professional Development Mgr

778 American Association of Sexuality Educators, Counselors & Therapists Conference
1444 I Street NW
Suite 700
Washington, DC 20005-1960
202-449-1099
Fax: 202-216-9646
E-mail: aasect@aasect.org
http://www.aasect.org
Facilitate productive discussions about identity and human sexuality; encourage interdisciplinary, intergenerational and cross-cultural collaboration and networking of current sexual health topics; provide opportunities for developing and refining skills

in sexuality education, therapy, counseling and research

06/20-06/24
50 booths with 400-500 attendees

Dee Ann Walker, Executive Director
Carey Roth Bayer, Conference Co Chair

779 American Camp Association National Conference
American Camp Association
5000 State Road 67 N
Martinsville, IN 46151-7902
765-342-8456
800-428-2267
Fax: 765-342-2065
E-mail: conference@ACAcamps.org
http://www.acacamps.org
Largest national camp conference hosted in the United States. Focuses on professional development, networking and commerce.

February
175 booths with 1500 attendees

Peg Smith, CEO
Kim Bruno, Marketing Manager

780 American Council on Education Annual Meeting
American Council on Education
1 Dupont Circle NW
Washington, DC 20036-1110
202-939-9300
Fax: 202-833-4760
E-mail: annualmeeting@ace.nche.edu
http://www.acenet.edu
Brings together higher education leaders form all sectors. The ACE Annual Meeting is seen as the go-to event to network with colleagues, hear about emerging trends from national thought leaders and learn about new approaches to campus challenges.

March
74 booths

Stephanie Marshall, Meeting Services Director
Wendy Bresler, Program Planning

781 American Council on the Teaching of Foreign Languages Annual Conference
101 N Fairfax Street
Suite 200
Alexandria, VA 22314
703-894-2900
Fax: 703-894-2905
E-mail: morehouse@actfl.org
http://www.actfl.org
More than 600 professional development opportunities, including pre and post convention workshops and sessions focused on all aspects of teachiing and learning languages and cultures.

November
250 booths with 6,000+ attendees

Julia Richardson, Convention Coordinator
Marty Abbott, Executive Director

782 American Counseling Association Annual Conference & Expo
American Counseling Association
5999 Stevenson Avenue
Alexandria, VA 22304-3302
703-823-9800
800-347-6647
Fax: 703-823-0252
E-mail: rhayes@counseling.org
http://www.counseling.org
Education sessions, speakers, mental health training and time and space for networking

with other professionals in the mental health field.

March
4000 attendees
Robin Hayes, Convention & Meeting Contact
Theresa Holmes, Convention & Meeting Contact

783 American Educational Research Association Annual Meeting
1430 K Street
Suite 1200
Washington, DC 20005-3078
202-238-3200
Fax: 202-238-3250
E-mail: annualmtg@aera.net
http://www.aera.net
Talks, courses, papers submissions related to the meeting theme and education research as a whole.

April
120 booths with 12M attendees
Felice J Levine, Executive Director
Laurie Cipriano, CMO, Director

784 American Indian Science & Engineering Society Annual Conference
AISES
PO Box 9828
Albuquerque, NM 87119-9828
505-765-1052
Fax: 505-765-5608
E-mail: info@aises.org
http://www.aises.org
Provides an opportunity for networking, educational workshops, a career fair, showcase academic research and study and how to bridge the waysbewtween tradition and STEM.

November
3000 attendees
Chris Echohawk, Vice Chair
Dr. Mary Jo Ondrechen, Chair

785 American Library Association (ALA) Annual Conference
American Library Association
50 E Huron
Chicago, IL 60611
312-944-6780
800-545-2433
Fax: 312-440-9374
E-mail: ala@ala.org
http://www.ala.org
Programs, updates, conversations about key issues like digital content, e-books, technology in libraries, books, leadership, literacy advocacy, community engagement and library marketing. Also a great way to network with other librarians and libraries.

June/January
20000+ attendees
Alicia Babcock, Conference Services
Keith Fiels, Executive Director

786 American Mathematical Society
American Mathematical Society
201 Charles Street
Providence, RI 02904-2294
401-455-4000
800-321-4267
Fax: 401-331-3842
E-mail: meet@ams.org
http://www.ams.org
Advance mathematical achievement, encouraging research and provide communication necessary to progress in the field. Preserve, supplement and utilize the re-

sults of the research of mathematicians throughout the world.

January
Dr. Donald McClure, Executive Director
Penny Pina, Director
Meetings/Conference

787 American Montessori Society Conference
116 East 16th St
New York, NY 10003
212-358-1250
Fax: 212-358-1256
E-mail: ams@amshq.org
http://www.amshq.org
Promotes quality Montessori education for all children from birth to 18 years of age. Conference participants share knowledge and research and strengthen bonds while creating new networks.

May
75 booths with 1000 attendees
Kathy Roemer, President
Joyce S. Pickering, Vice President

788 American Psychological Association Annual Conference
750 1st Street NE
Washington, DC 20002-4242
202-336-5500
800-374-2721
Fax: 202-336-6123
E-mail: convention@apa.org
http://www.apa.org
A national conference attended by psychologists from around the world. The conference has workshops, lectures, discussions, roundtables and symposiums.

August

13,000 attendees
Donald N Bersoff, Ph.D, JD, President

789 American Public Health Association Annual Meeting
American Public Health Association
800 I Street NW
Washington, DC 20001-3710
202-777-2742
Fax: 202-777-2534
E-mail: anna.keller@apha.org
http://www.apha.org
The premier platform to share successes and failures, discover exceptional best practices and learn from expert colleagues and the latest research in the field.

November
650 booths with 13000 attendees
Georges C. Benjamin, Executive Director
James E. Dale, CoA Chair

790 American School Health Association's National School Conference
4340 East West Highway
Suite 403
Bethesda, MD 20814-5960
301-652-8072
Fax: 301-652-8077
E-mail: info@ashaweb.org
http://www.ashaweb.org
Attendees include school nurses, health educators, health counselors, physicians and students. During the five-day conference, presentations are made by ASHA members, government officials and health education professionals.

October
40 booths with 700 attendees
Linda Morse, President
Julie Greenfield, Mkting/Conferences Director

791 American Speech-Language-Hearing Association Annual Convention
ASHA
2200 Research Blvd.
Rockville, MD 20850-3289
301-296-5700
800-638-8255
Fax: 301-296-8580
E-mail: convention@asha.org
http://www.asha.org
A scientific and professional conference of speech-language pathology, audiology and other professionals. Opportunity to learn about latest evidence based research , enhance clinical skills, improve technique and gain new tools and resources to advance career.

Annual
November
400 booths with 12,000 attendees
Arlene A Pietranton, CEO
Patricia A. Prelock, President

792 American Technical Education Association Annual Conference
American Technical Education Association
Dunwoody College of Technology
818 Dunwoody Blvd.
Minneapolis, MN 55403
612-381-3315
E-mail: info@ateaonline.org
http://www.ateaonline.org
Administrators/directors and faculty of various technical institutes, junior colleges, universities and colleges. Topics cover all aspects of computer assisted instruction, distance education and technical education. Professional development opportunity for all involved in postsecondary technical education.

March
35 booths with 700 attendees and 75 exhibits
Dr. Sandra Krebsbach, Executive Director
DeeAnn Bilben, Administrative Assistant

793 Annual Effective Schools Conference
7227 North 16th Street
Suite 190
Phoenix, AZ 85020
866-626-7556
Fax: 888-756-7628
E-mail: now@4aplus.com
http://www.effectiveschoolsconference2013.com
Latest research and methods for creating successful educational environments where all students can reach their academic potential. Gain valuable hands-on experience, learn proven implementation strategies and hear from some of the greatest minds in the field.

March

Amber Countiss
Annie Hanks

794 Annual NCEA Convention & Exposition
National Catholic Educational Association
1005 North Glebe Road
Suite 525
Arlington, VA 22201-3852
571-257-0010
800-711-6232
Fax: 703-243-0025
E-mail: nceaadmin@ncea.org
http://www.ncea.org
Attendees represent all aspects of Catholic and faith based education from pre-school to universities, to local parishes and more. Provides development sessions, departmental meetings, special events in order to gain knowledge and network with fellow colleagues.

Annually
April
Regina M. Haney, Executive Director
Amy Durkin, Convention/Events

795 Association for Behavior Analysis Annual Convention
Association for Behavior Analysis
550 W. Centre Ave.
Portage, MI 49024-5364
269-492-9310
Fax: 269-492-9316
E-mail: convention@abainternational.org
http://www.abainternational.org
Psychologists, psychology faculty and students, counselors and social workers are among the attendees of this conference offering over 25 exhibitors. The conference is research and education oriented.

43 booths

Maria E Malott, PhD, CEO

796 Association for Behavioral and Cognitive Therapies Annual Convention
305 7th Avenue
16th Floor
New York, NY 10001-6008
212-647-1890
Fax: 212-647-1865
E-mail: mebrown@abct.org
http://www.abct.org
Provide participants with clinical knowledge of specific issues or new research in the field, networking possibilities, clinical roundtable, panel discussions on training and symposia of the presentation of data or research.

November
2,000 attendees

Mary Ellen Brown, Education/Mtg Services Dir.
Mary Jane Eimer, Executive Director

797 Association for Education Finance and Policy
6703 Madison Creek
Columbia, MO 65203
573-814-9878
Fax: 314-256-2831
E-mail: info@aefpweb.org
http://www.aefpweb.org
The conference theme changes yearly; this year the focus is education renewal and reform and the fact that domestic policy and global economic competition challenge our education system. The conference will present, discuss and evaluate the latest research on education topics and current reforms and policy directions.

March
3000 attendees

Deborah Cunningham, President
Angela M. Hull, Executive Director

798 Association for Education in Journalism and Mass Communication Convention
AEJMC
234 Outlet Pointe Boulevard
Suite A
Columbia, SC 29210-5667
803-798-0271
Fax: 803-772-3509
http://www.aejmc.org
Featuring the latest in technology as well as special sessions on teaching, research and public service in the various components of journalism and mass communication — from advertising and public relations to radio and television journalism to media management and newspapers.

August
1,500 attendees

Fred Williams, Convention Manager
Jennifer McGill, Executive Director

799 Association for Persons with Severe Handicaps Annual Conference
1001 Connecticut Ave NW
Suite 235
Washington, DC 20036
202-540-9020
Fax: 202-540-9019
E-mail: info@tash.org
http://www.tash.org
Provides a forum for individuals with disabilities, families, researchers, educators, scholars, and others to create dialogue around creating action for social and systems reform.

December
2,500 attendees

Barbara Trader, Executive Director

800 Association for Play Therapy Conference
Association for Play Therapy
3198 Willow Avenue
Suite 110
Clovis, CA 93612
559-294-2128
Fax: 559-294-2129
E-mail: info@a4pt.org
http://www.a4pt.org
Major interdisciplinary event for mental health professionals wishing to earn continuing education credit for licensure or credentialing, network with popular authors, speakers and vendors and enjoy extra curricular activities with peers.

October
1000 attendees

Kathryn Lebby, Events Coordinator
Bill Burns, Executive Director

801 Association for Science Teacher Education Annual Meeting
The Association For Science Teacher Education
5040 Haley Center
Auburn, AL 36849
972-690-2496
E-mail: executivedirector@theaste.org
http://www.theaste.com
Offers programs in science, mathematics and environmental education with a wide variety of teachers and professors attending.

January

Kathy Cabe Trundle, President
Bob Hollon, Executive Director

802 Association for the Advancement of International Education
Nova Southeastern University
11501 N. Military Trail
Palm Beach Gardens, FL 33418
561-805-2193
Fax: 561-805-2187
E-mail: g.nicoll@nove.edu
http://www.aaie.org
Provides the organizational leadership to initiate and promote an understanding of the need for and the support of American/International education.

February
70 booths with 550 attendees

Elleana Austin, Administrative Assistant
Elsa Lamb, Executive Director

803 Association for the Education of Gifted Underachieving Students Conference
6 Wildwood Street
Burlington, MA 01803
651-962-5385
E-mail: aegusquestions@gmail.com
http://www.aegus1.org
Attended by teachers, professors, administrators and social workers, this conference deals with cultural awareness and education of the disabled and gifted students.

April

Lois Baldwin, President
Terry Neu, Vice President

804 Association for the Study of Higher Education Annual Meeting
University Of Nevada
4505 S. Maryland Parkway
453068
Las Vegas, NV 89154-3068
702-895-2737
Fax: 702-895-4269
E-mail: ashe@unlv.edu
http://www.ashe.ws
Promotes collaboration among its members and others engaged in the study of higher education; as a community of scholarly practice and as practicing scholars and educators.

November

Kim Nehls, Executive Director
Christal Allen, Conference Coordinator

805 Association of American Colleges & Universities Annual Meeting
Association of American Colleges & Universities
1818 R Street NW
Washington, DC 20009-1604
202-387-3760
Fax: 202-265-9532
http://www.aacu.org
Bringing together college educators from across institutional types, disciplines, and departments. Providing participants with innovative ideas and practices, and shaping the direction of their educational reform efforts.

January
1,200 attendees

Carol Geary, President

806 Association of Community College Trustees Conference
1233 20th Street NW
Suite 301
Washington, DC 20036-2907
202-775-4667
Fax: 202-223-1297
E-mail: acctinfo@acct.org
http://www.acct.org
Exists to develop effective lay governing board leadership to strengthen the capacity of community colleges to achieve their missions on behalf of their communities.

1500+ attendees

J. Noah Brown, President/CEO
Lila Farmer, Conference Logistics Coord.

807 Association of Science-Technology Centers Incorporated Conference
Association of Science-Technology Centers Incorp.
1025 Vermont Avenue NW
Suite 500
Washington, DC 20005-3516
202-783-7200
Fax: 202-783-7207
E-mail: conference@astc.org
http://www.astc.org
An organization of science centers and museums dedicated to furthering the public understanding of science. ASTC encourages excellence and innovation in informal science learning by serving and linking its members worldwide and advancing the common goals.

October
165 booths with 1600 attendees

David Corson, Mgr. Conference/Exhibit Hall
Nina Humes, Meetings/Conference Coord.

808 CHADD: Children & Adults with Attention Deficit/Hyperactivity Disorder
CHADD
8181 Professional Place
Suite 150
Landover, MD 20785
301-306-7070
800-233-4050
Fax: 301-306-7090
http://www.chadd.org
National non-profit organization which offers advocacy, information and support for patients and parents of children with attention deficit disorders. Maintains support groups, provides a forum for continuing education about ADHD, and maintains a national resource center for information about ADD.

October
60 booths with 1,500 attendees

Marsha Bokman, Mtgs/Events Director

809 Center for Appalachian Studies Annual Conference
Appalachian Studies Center
One John Marshall Drive
Huntington, WV 25755-0918
304-696-2904
E-mail: mthomas@marshall.edu
http://www.appalachianstudies.org
Central theme each year about some facet of Appalachia- communities, landscapes, evoulution of their work together-history, etc.

March

Katherine Ledford, Conference Chair
Mary Thomas, Executive Director

810 Center on Disabilities Conference
Students with Disabilities Resources
1811 Nordhoff
Bayramian Hall 110
Northridge, CA 91330-8264
818-677-1200
E-mail: conference@csun.edu
http://www.csun.edu/cod
Provides a setting for researchers, practitioners, exhibitors, end users, speakers and participants to share knowledge and best practices in the field of assistive technology.

March
130 booths with 4800 attendees

Wayne Fernades, Mktg/Events Manager
Sandy Plotin, Managing Director

811 Choristers Guild's National Festival & Directors' Conference
Choristers Guild
12404 Park Central Drive
Suite 100
Dallas, TX 75251-1802
469-398-3606
800-246-7478
Fax: 469-398-3611
E-mail: conferences@mailcg.org
http://www.choristersguild.org
Enables leaders to nurture the spiritual and musical growth of children and youth.

June

Jim Rindelaub, Director
Eve Hehn, Conferences

812 Closing the Gap
526 Main Street
PO Box 68
Henderson, MN 56044-0068
507-248-3294
Fax: 507-248-3810
E-mail: info@closingthegap.com
http://www.closingthegap.com

Conference themes change yearly. Always focus on technology and how it changes—primarily with assistive technology.

October
150+ booths with 2400 attendees

Jan Latzke, Conference Registration
Connie Kneip, VP/General Manager

813 Conference for Advancement of Mathematics Teaching
Texas Education Agency
PO Box 200669
Austin, TX 78720-0669
512-335-2268
Fax: 512-335-8517
E-mail: camt@camtonline.org
http://www.camtonline.org
Exhibits educational materials useful to mathematics teachers; education of the use of technology on the classroom and effective use of manipulative materials in the classroom.

July
175 booths with 7.5M-8M attendees

Joyce Polanco, Program Chair

814 Council for Exceptional Children Annual Convention
The Council for Exceptional Children
2900 Crystal Drive
Suite 1000
Arlington, VA 22202-3557
703-620-3660
888-232-7733
Fax: 703-264-1637
E-mail: service@cec.sped.org
http://www.cec.sped.org
Largest professional organization dedicated to improving educational results of individuals with disabilities and the gifted. 50,000 members. Educational sessions, endless opportunities to network with others working with children and learn about new and pending legislation and explore cutting edge products and services.

April
437 booths with 7000 attendees and 299 exhibits

Christy A. Chambers, President
Mikki Garcia, Executive Director

815 EDUCAUSE Anuual Convention
282 Century Place
Suite 5000
Louisville, KY 80027
303-449-4430
Fax: 303-440-0461
E-mail: info@educause.edu
http://www.educause.edu
Provides opportunity for educators to network with colleagues and learn form each other by sharing experience, ideas and information through presentations and sessions.

October
4,000+ attendees and 180 exhibits

Diana Oblinger, President
Beverly Williams, Conference Director

816 Educational Publishing Summit
Association of Educational Publishers
300 Martin Luther King Blvd.
Suite 200
Wilmington, DE 19801
302-295-8350
Fax: 302-656-2918
E-mail: mail@aepweb.org
http://www.aepweb.org
Presents a range of informative and practical sessions that address all issues relating

to the development and distribution of high-quality learning resources.

June

Charlene F Gaynor, CEO
JoAnn McDevitt, VP Sales/Mrktg/Business Dev.

817 Educational Theatre Association Conference
Educational Theatre Association
2343 Auburn Avenue
Cincinnati, OH 45219-2815
513-421-3900
Fax: 513-421-7077
E-mail: mpeitz@edta.org
http://www.edta.org
Supports the association's mission by supporting educators through networking opportunities, educational workshops, speakers and resources that can enrich students' educational experience.

September
2,400 attendees

Julie Woffington, Executive Director
Gloria McIntyre, President

818 Foundation for Critical Thinking Regional Workshop & Conference
Foundation for Critical Thinking
PO Box 196
Tomales, CA 94971
707-878-9100
800-833-3645
Fax: 707-878-9111
E-mail: cct@criticalthinking.org
http://www.criticalthinking.org
Investigates and reports on the value and use of analytical thinking programs and curriculum in the classroom.

July

Dr Linda Elder, President

819 Gifted Child Society Conference
190 Rock Road
Glen Rock, NJ 07452-1736
201-444-6530
Fax: 201-444-9099
E-mail: admin@gifted.org
http://www.gifted.org
Provides educational enrichment and support for gifted children through national advocacy and various programs.

September
250 attendees

Janet L Chen, Executive Director

820 INFOCOMM Tradeshow
InfoComm International
11242 Waples Mill Road
Suite 200
Fairfax, VA 22030
703-273-7200
800-659-7469
Fax: 703-273-5924
E-mail: inief@chiefmfg.com
http://www.infocommshow.org
Designed for professionals in the audiovisual, information communications and system integration industries. Attendees can explore audiovisual products and services from the industry's leading manufacturers, and there are educational seminars, workshops and labs taught with a focus on technology, trends and the best practices in the country.

June

David Labuskes, Executive Director
Jason McGraw, Sr. VP Expositions

821 Independent Education Consultants Association Conference
3251 Old Lee Highway
Suite 510
Fairfax, VA 22030-1504
703-591-4850
800-888-4322
Fax: 703-591-4860
E-mail: info@IECAonline.com
http://www.IECAonline.com
Attended by consultants, school, college and program admissions officers, administrators and staff and related service companies. Workshops and discussions led by leaders in their fields including specialists in educational trends, college admissions and boarding school issues, adolescent development, learning differences and emotional disorders and treatments.
Spring & Fall
400 booths with 800 attendees

Mark H Sklarow, Executive Director
Rachel King, Conference Manager

822 International Performance Improvement Conference
International Society for Performance
PO Box 13035
Silver Spring, MD 20910
301-587-8570
Fax: 301-587-8573
E-mail: info@ispi.org
http://www.ispi.org
Provides educational opportunities with sessions in multiple formats across multiple tracks, keynote presentations, networking opportunities with other performance minded professionals across the spectrum of performance improvement disciplines.
April
60 booths with 1500 attendees

Ellen Kaplan, Conference Manager

823 Iteachk
Staff Development for Educators
10 Sharon Road
PO Box 577
Peterborough, NH 03458
603-924-9621
800-462-1478
Fax: 800-337-9929
http://www.sde.com
Explore new technology engaging teachers and students, new games and tools for students, meet and learn from nation's top kindergarten experts, use strategies right away and network with others.

Jim Grant, Executive Director/Founder
Terra Tarango, President

824 Journalism Education Association
Kansas State University
103 Kedzie Hall
Manhattan, KS 66506-1505
785-532-5532
866-532-5532
Fax: 785-532-5563
E-mail: lindarp@ksu.edu
http://www.jea.org/
An organization of about 2,300 journalism teachers and advisers, offers two national teacher-student conventions a year, quarterly newsletter and magazines, bookstore and national certification program. This association serves as a leader in scholastic press freedom and media curriculum.

Mark Newton, President
Sarah Nichols, Vice President

825 Lutheran Education Association National Administrators Conference
Lutheran Education Association
7400 Augusta Street
River Forest, IL 60305
708-209-3343
Fax: 708-209-3458
E-mail: lea@lea.org
http://www.lea.org
Presentations devoted to positive partnerships—parish partnerships, public/government, community, international— that will serve will in the future.

Cheryl Ehlers, Conference Chair
Jonathan C Laabs, Executive Director

826 MEMSPA Annual State Conference
Michigan Elementary & Middle School Principals
Association
1980 N. College Road
Mason, MI 48854
517-694-8955
800-227-0824
Fax: 517-694-8945
E-mail: bob@memspa.org
http://www.memspa.org
Professional association for elementary & middle level principals.
Annual/December

Paul Liabenow, Executive Director
Rob Kauffman, President

827 Modern Language Association Annual Conference
26 Broadway
3rd Floor
New York, NY 10004-1789
646-576-5000
Fax: 646-458-0030
E-mail: convention@mla.org
http://www.mla.org
Opportunity for memberes to share scholarly findings and teaching experience and discuss trends in the academy.
January
2000+ attendees

Rosemary G. Feal, Executive Director

828 Music Teachers Association National Conference
Music Teachers National Association
441 Vine Street
Suite 3100
Cincinnati, OH 45202-3004
513-421-1420
888-512-5278
Fax: 513-421-2503
E-mail: mtnanet@mtna.org
http://www.mtna.org
Supports and supplies music teachers with information on development and training.
March
160 booths with 2000 attendees

Brian Shepard, Deputy Executive Director
Gary L. Ingle, Executive Director/CEO

829 NAAEE Annual Conference
North American Assoc for Environmental Education
2000 P Street NW
Suite 540
Washington, DC 20036
202-419-0412
Fax: 212-419-0415
E-mail: info@naaee.net
http://www.naaee.net

Promotes environmental education in the classroom and public, shares the latest research and information.
October
1000+ attendees

Judy Braus, Executive Director
Lori Mann, Conference Manager

830 NAFSA: National Association of International Educators
1307 New York Ave. NW
8th Floor
Washington, DC 20005-4701
202-737-3699
800-836-4994
Fax: 202-737-3657
E-mail: inbox@nafsa.org
http://www. nafsa.org
Annual meeting of professionals in the field of international education, for training workshops, educational sessions, networking opportunities and special events.
May
150 booths with 8,500 attendees

Marlene M. Johnson, Executive Director/CEO
Chris Seamens, Conference Program, Coord.

831 NASDSE National Conference
National Association of State Directors of Special
Education
225 Reinekers Lane, Suite 420
Alexandria, VA 22314
703-519-3800
Fax: 703-519-3808
E-mail: nasdse@nasdse.org
http://www.nasdse.org
Multiple presentations, Annual business meeting for state directors and networking opportunities.

Colleen Riley, President
Bill East, Executive Director

832 NASPA Annual Conference
NASPA-Student Affairs Administrators in Higher
Education
111 K Street NE, 10th Floor
Washington, DC 20002
202-265-7500
Fax: 202-898-5737
E-mail: office@naspa.org
http://www.naspa.org
Exchange ideas with peers, earn continuing education credits, build new partnerships with vendors, gain tools and ideas and remain current on issues.
Annual/March
5000 attendees

Kevin Kruger, President
Arlene Kidwell, Sr. Director of Meetings

833 NELA Annual Conference
New England Library Association
55 North Main Street
Unit 49
Belchertown, MA 01007
413-813-5254
Fax: 603-654-3526
E-mail: rscheier@gmail.com
http://www.nelib.org
Bringing together librarians from New England in a forum to educate and network about moving libraries into the 21st century.
600 attendees

Robert Scheier, Association Administrator
Mary Ann Rupert, Conference Manager

834 NJLA Spring Conference
New Jersey Library Association
PO Box 1534
Trenton, NJ 08607
609-394-8032
Fax: 609-394-8164
E-mail: ptumulty@njla.org
http://www.njla.org
1139 attendees
Patricia A Tumulty, Executive Director
Susan Rice, Office Manager

835 NSTA Annual Conference
National Science Teachers Association
1840 Wilson Boulevard
Arlington, VA 22201-3000
703-243-7100
888-400-6782
Fax: 703-243-7177
E-mail: conferences@nsta.org
http://www.nsta.org
To promote excellence and innovation in science teaching and learning for all. Discover strategies for improving science teaching and learning, engage in professional discussions, receive the latest information of science education and network with colleagues from across the country and the globe.
April
Dr. Karen L. Ostlund, President
Dr. Gerald F. Wheeler, Interim Executive Director

836 National Academy Foundation NEXT
National Academy Foundation
218 West 40th Street
5th Floor
New York, NY 10018
212-635-2400
Fax: 212-635-2409
http://www.naf.org
Formerly the Institute for Staff Development, NEXT is a professional learning experience that will ignite innovation and spread effective practices across
July
JD Hoye, President
David Moore, Sr. VP Programs

837 National Alliance of Black School Educators Conference
310 Pennsylvania Avenue SE
Washington, DC 20003-3819
202-608-6310
800-221-2654
Fax: 202-608-6319
E-mail: info@nabse.org
http://www.nabse.org
Teachers, principals, specialists, superintendents, school board members and higher education personnel. Educational workshops, plenary sessions, informative presentations, public forums, networking and fellowship.
November
300 booths with 6,000 attendees
Quentin R Lawson, Executive Director
Ed Potillo, Conference Director

838 National Art Education Association Annual Convention
National Art Education Association
1806 Robert Fulton Drive
Suite 300
Reston, VA 20191-1590
703-860-8000
Fax: 703-860-2960
E-mail: info@arteducators.org
http://www.arteducators.org
Provides substantive professional development services that include the advance-

ment of knowledge in all sessions, events and activities for the purpose of improving visual arts instruction in American schools.
March
171 booths with 5,000 attendees
Kathy Duse, Conference Manager
Deborah B. Reeve, Executive Director

839 National Association for Bilingual Education
8701 Georgia Avenue
Suite 700
Silver Spring, MD 20910-4018
240-450-3700
Fax: 240-450-3799
E-mail: nabe@nabe.org
http://www.nabe.org
Contains publishers and Fortune 500 companies displaying educational materials and multi-media products. Educational materials, products and services for use in linguistically and culturally diverse learning environments.
March
350 booths with 2,000+ attendees
Dr. Santiago Wood, Executive Director
Nilda Aguirre, Conference Coordinator

840 National Association for College Admission Counseling Conference
Nat'l Association for College Admission Counseling
1050 N Highland Street
Suite 400
Arlington, VA 22201-2818
703-836-2222
800-822-6285
Fax: 703-243-9375
E-mail: info@nacacnet.org
http://www.nacacnet.org
Membership association offering information to counselors and guidance professionals working in the college admissions office.
September
142 booths with 4,000 attendees
Joyce E. Smith, CEO
Bethany Blue Chirico, Director of Conference/Mtgs

841 National Association for Girls and Women in Sports Yearly Conference
1900 Association Drive
Reston, VA 20191-1598
703-476-3543
800-213-7193
Fax: 703-476-4566
E-mail: nagws@aahperd.org
http://www.aahperd.org/nagws
An association providing information for girls and women in sports.
March/April
280 booths with 6,000 attendees
Lynda Ransdell, President
Sandra K. Sims, VP of Programs/Convention

842 National Association for Multicultural Education
NAME National Office
2100 M Street
Suite 170-245
Washington, DC 20037
202-628-6263
Fax: 202-628-6264
E-mail: name@nameorg.org
http://www.nameorg.org
Opportunity to build networks, confront challenges and renews sense of possibility and hope in making schools and societies a

better place through community advocacy and multicultural education.
Bette Tate Beaver, Executive Director

843 National Association of Biology Teachers Conference
1313 Dolley Madison Blvd.
Suite 402
McLean, VA 22101
703-264-9696
888-501-6228
Fax: 703-790-2672
E-mail: office@nabt.org
http://www.nabt.org
Speakers, hands-on workshops, informative sessions teaching biology in the 21st century.
November
140 booths with 1,700 attendees
Jaclyn Reeves-Pepin, Executive Director
Matthew D. Wells, Conference Committee

844 National Association of Elementary School Principals Conference
1615 Duke Street
Alexandria, VA 22314-3406
703-684-3345
800-386-2377
Fax: 703-549-5568
E-mail: naesp@naesp.org
http://www.naesp.org
Products and services in the educational market shopping area. Industry leaders offer solutions on areas such as teacher recruitment and retention, integration of the new common core standards, leading school change and improving student learning and running the best possible building- from the cafeteria to the parking lot.
April
300 booths
Gail Connelly, Executive Director
Deborah Young, Director, Convention/Mtgs.

845 National Association of Independent Schools Conference
National Association of Independent Schools
1129 20th Street NW
Suite 800
Washington, DC 20036-3425
202-973-9700
Fax: 888-316-3862
E-mail: annualconference@nais.org
http://www.nais.org
New ways to cultivate leadership in independent schools- for administrators, faculty and students- with workshops and speakers.
February/March
166 booths with 4000 attendees
Patrick Bassett, President
Amy Ahart, Director Annual Conference

846 National Association of Private Schools for Exceptional Children Conference
1522 K Street NW
Suite 1032
Washington, DC 20005-1211
202-408-3338
Fax: 202-408-3340
E-mail: napsec@aol.com
http://www.napsec.com
This in an annual conference that is held for administrators/directors/principals and private school educators.
January
300 attendees and 8 exhibits
Sherry L. Kolbe, Executive Director/CEO

847 National Association of School Psychologists Annual Convention
4340 EW Highway
Suite 402
Bethesda, MD 20814

301-657-0270
866-331-6277
Fax: 301-657-0275
E-mail: convention@naspweb.org
http://www.nasponline.org
Gathering of school psychologists and related professionals, offering workshops, seminars, symposia, papers, presentations and exhibits on topics from solutions for individual children to answers to your most difficult professional challenges and find ways to be a more efficient and effective practitioner.

April
100 booths with 4000 attendees

Susan Gorin, Executive Director
Marcia Harvey, Manager, Conventions

848 National Association of State Directors of Teacher Education and Certification Conference
1629 K Street NW
Suite 300
Washington, DC 20006
202-204-2208
Fax: 202-204-2210
E-mail: nasdtec@attbi.com
NASDTEC is the National Association of State Directors of Teacher Education and Certification. It is the organization that represents professional standards boards and commissions and state departments of education in all 50 states.

June

Phillip S. Rogers, Executive Director

849 National Association of Student Financial Aid Administrators
1101 Connecticut Avenue NW
Suite 1100
Washington, DC 20036-4303
202-785-0453
Fax: 202-785-1487
http://www.nasfaa.org
Provides valuable, up-to-date information on the student aid programs from financial aid veterans. Unique training and professional development opportunity that will equip student aid professionals with the tools to better serve students and families. Also receive individual guidance from the U.S. Department of Education and learn about product and software innovations.

July
July
105 booths with 3,000 attendees

Barbara Kay Gordon, Conference Contact
Justin Draeger, President

850 National Black Child Development Institute Annual Conference
1313 L Street NW
Suite 110
Washington, DC 20005-4110
202-833-2220
800-556-2234
Fax: 202-833-8222
E-mail: moreinfo@ndcdi.orh
http://www.nbcdi.org
Educators and professionals in early care and education; elementary and secondary education and administration; child welfare and youth development; research; and local, state and federal policy convene to gain knowledge and acquire skills needed to ensure a quality future for all children and youth.

October

Felicia DeHaney, Pd.D, President/CEO
Keami Harris, Director of Programs

851 National Coalition of Alternative Community Schools
PO Box 1451
Ann Arbor, MI 48106
505-474-4312
888-771-9171
E-mail: office@ncacs.org
http://www.ncacs.org
Students, parents and teachers come together to learn how to teach and learn from one another. Workshops, networking

April

Kristin Lamoureux, Contact

852 National Coalition of ESEA Title 1 Parents
310 Pennsylvania Ave. SE
3rd Floor
Washington, DC 20003
205-923-7955
Fax: 205-925-5403
E-mail: ethomas@nctic1p.org
http://www.nctic1p.org
Annual In-Service Professional Development conference on current education laws, legislation and educational issues with the assistance of the Department of Education.

October

Ernestine Thomas, President

853 National Conference on Student Services
Magna Publications
2718 Dryden Drive
Madison, WI 53704
608-246-3590
800-206-4805
Fax: 608-246-3597
E-mail: carriej@magnapubs.com
http://www.magnapubs.com
Build strong foundation as a student leader, secure leadership skills and experience a possibly life-changing event.

April
35 booths with 500 attendees

Susan Liimata, Conference Manager
Catherine Stover, Managing Editor

854 National Congress on Aviation and Space Education
Omni Rosen Hotel
Orlando, FL
334-953-5095
E-mail: bspick@cap.af.mil
http://www.cap.af.mil
Provides educators with the tools that make classroom learning fun.

April

855 National Council of Higher Education
National Education Association (NEA)
1201 16th Street NW
Washington, DC 20036-3207
202-822-7162
Fax: 202-822-7974
E-mail: nche@nea.org
http://www.nea.org
Assessing a 20 year journey of the academy.

February, March
400 attendees

Rachel Hendrickson, Coordinator

856 National Council on Alcoholism & Drug Abuse
8790 Manchester Road
Brentwood, MO 63144
314-962-3456
Fax: 314-968-7394
E-mail: ncada@ncada-stl.org
http://www.ncada-stl.org

A not-for-profit community health agency serving the metropolitan St. Louis area, provides educational materials on substance abuse and addiction, information and referral services, prevention and intervention.

Harriet Kopolow, Director Prevention

857 National Dropout Prevention Center/Network Conference
205 Martin Street
Clemson, SC 29631-1555
864-656-2599
800-443-6392
Fax: 864-656-0136
E-mail: ndpc@clemson.edu
http://www.dropoutprevention.com
Concentrating on programs and services for educators and counselors who deal with at-risk students.

October
100 booths with 1000 attendees

Jay Smink, Executive Director
John Peters, Network Coordinator

858 National Education Association-Retired
National Education Association (NEA)
1201 16th Street NW
Washington, DC 20036-3207
202-822-7125
Fax: 202-822-7974
http://www.nea.org/retired
Serves as a resource in the maintenance of quality public education, promotes improved services and legislation for seniors, provides training for members and serves as a vehicle for local input to the National Education Association.

150 attendees

Deborah C Jackson, Manager
Todd Crenshaw, Coordinator

859 National Guild of Community Schools of the Arts Conference
520 8th Avenue
Suite 302, 3rd Floor
New York, NY 10018
212-268-3337
Fax: 212-268-3995
E-mail: info@natguild.org
http://www.nationalguild.org
The National Guild of Community Schools of the Arts fosters and promotes the creation and growth of high-quality arts education in communities across the country. The Guild provides community arts organizations with multiple levels of support, including training, advocacy, information resources, and high-profile leadership in arts education.

November
15 booths with 300 attendees and 15 exhibits

Noah Xifr, Director Membership/Oper.

860 National Head Start Association Annual Conference
1651 Prince Street
Alexandria, VA 22314-2818
703-739-0875
Fax: 703-739-0878
http://www.nhsa.org
Seeks to advance program development, policy and promote training of the Head Start program professionals.

May

A Renee Battle, CMP, Conference Contact
Ruby Lewis-Riar, Conference Assistant

861 National In-Service Conference
National Association for Music Education (NAFME)
1806 Robert Fulton Drive
Reston, VA 20191-4348

703-860-4000
800-336-3768
Fax: 703-860-1531
http://www.musiced.nafme.org
Opportunities to network with peers from across the United States, professional development sessions giving tools and techniques for use in classrooms, receptions and keynote speakers.

April

Michael A. Butera, Executive Director/CEO

862   National Institute for School and Workplace Safety Conference
160 International Parkway
Suite 250
Heathrow, FL 32746
407-804-8310
Fax: 407-804-8306
http://www.nisws.com/
Believes that every school and workplace must implement school and workplace safety standards.

April
80 attendees

Wolfgang Halbig, CEO/Manager

863   National Parent-Teacher Association Annual Convention & Exhibition
1787 Agate Street
Eugene, OR 97403-1923
503-346-4414
Addresses parent-teacher involvement in education. Includes lectures, workshops and seminars for parents and professionals.

June

864   National Reading Styles Institute Conference
PO Box 737
Syosset, NY 11791-3933
512-224-4555
800-331-3117
Fax: 516-921-5591
http://www.nrsi.com
This conference addresses reading instruction and the problems of illiteracy.

July

Juliet Carbo, Conference Contact

865   National Rural Education Annual Convention
National Rural Education Association
230 Education
Colorado State University
Fort Collins, CO 80523-0001
970-491-1101
Fax: 970-491-1317
Exchanges ideas, practices and better ways to enhance rural educational school systems.

October
30 booths with 400 attendees

Joseph T Newlin, PhD, Conference Contact

866   National Rural Education Association Annual Convention
National Rural Education Association
820 Van Vleet Oval
Room 227
Norman, OK 73019
Fax: 405-325-7959
E-mail: bmooney@ou.edu
http://www.nrea.net
The NREA will be the leading national organization providing services which enhance educational opportunities for rural schools and their communities.

October
35 booths with 400 attendees

Bob Mooneyham, Executive Director

867   National School Boards Annual Conference
1680 Duke Street
Alexandria, VA 22314-3493
703-838-6722
Fax: 703-683-7590
http:// ww.nsba.org/itte
The nation's largest policy and training conference for local education officials on national and federal issues affecting public schools in the U.S.

March
7,000 attendees and 300 exhibits

Sandra Folks, Conference/Meetings Coord.
Karen Miller, Exhibit Services Manager

868   National School Conference Institute
11202 N 24th Street
Suite 103
Phoenix, AZ 85029
602-371-8655
888-399-8745
Fax: 602-371-8790
http://www.nscinet.com
Our purpose is to increase every student's opportunity for academic success.

869   National School Supply & Equipment Association
NSSEA Essentials
8380 Colesville Road
Silver Spring, MD 20910
301-495-0240
800-395-5550
Fax: 301-495-3330
E-mail: awatts@nssea.org
http://www.nessa.org
Lists 1,500 member dealers and manufacturers representatives for school supplies, equipment and instructional materials.

March
1200 booths with 5,000 attendees and 700 exhibits

Adrienne Dayton, VP of Marketing/Communicatio
DeShuna Spencer, Editor/Communications Manage

870   National Society for Experiential Education Conference
National Society for Experiential Education
3509 Haworth Drive
Suite 207
Raleigh, NC 27609-7235
919-787-3263
Fax: 919-787-3381
E-mail: info@nsee.org
http://www.nsee.org
To foster the effective use of experience as an integral part of education, in order to empower learners and promote the common good.

October
600-700 attendees

871   National Student Assistance Conference
1270 Rakin Drive
Suite F
Troy, MI 48033-2843
800-453-7733
Fax: 800-499-5718
Learn to maintain and improve safe, drug free schools, student assistance programs.

Develop skills to implement the Principles of Effectiveness. Choose from workshops and skill building sessions.

872   National Women's History Project Annual Conference
3440 Airway Drive
Suite F
Santa Rosa, CA 95403-8518
707-636-2888
Fax: 707-636-2909
E-mail: nwhp@aol.commailto:nwhp@nwhp.org
http://www.nwhp.org
Posters, reference books, curriculum materials and biographies of American women in all subjects for grades K-12.

July
72 attendees

Molly Murphy MacGregor, Conference Manager

873   Natural Learning Institute Seminar
54385 Pine Crest Ave
Idyllwild, CA 92549
951-691-0139
Fax: 951-659-0242
http://www.naturallearninginstitute.org

Linda Hargan, President

874   Neag Center for Gifted Education and Talent Development Conference
University of Connecticut
2131 Hillside Road
Unit 3007
Storrs, CT 06269-3007
860-486-4826
Fax: 860-486-2900
http://www.gifted.uconn.edu
Provides educators with research based practical strategies for engagement and enrichment learning for all students, as well as meeting the needs of gifted and talented students.

Annual

JoAnn Easton, Confratute

875   New Learning Technologies
Society for Applied Learning Technology
50 Culpeper Street
Warrenton, VA 20186
540-347-0055
800-457-6812
Fax: 540-349-3169
E-mail: info@lti.org
http://www.salt.org
To provide a comprehensive overview of the latest in research, design, and development in order to furnish attendees information on systems that are applicable to their organizations.

876   New Learning Technologies Conference
Society for Applied Learning Technology
50 Culpeper Street
Warrenton, VA 20186
540-347-0055
800-457-6812
Fax: 540-349-3169
E-mail: info@lti.org
http://www.salt.org
For over 30 years the Society has sponsored conferences which are educational in nature and bring together senior professionals from government, industry, academia and the military to present the latest developments in the field of learning and training technologies.

August
20 booths with 400 attendees

Raymond G Fox, President

877   North American Montessori Teachers' Association
13693 Butternut Road
Burton, OH 44021

440-834-4011
Fax: 440-834-4016
E-mail: staff@montessori-namta.org
http://www.montessori-namta.org/
Professional organization for Montessori teachers and administrators. Services include The NAMTA Journal and other publications, videos and slide shows. Conferences in January and March.

David J Kahn, Executive Director

878 Parents as Teachers National Center Conference
2228 Ball Drive
Saint Louis, MO 63146
314-432-4330
Fax: 314-432-8963
E-mail: patnc@patnc.org
http://www.patnc.org
An international early childhood parent education and family support program designed to enhance child development and school achievement through parent education accessible to all families. Serves families throughout pregnancy and until their child enters kindergarten, usually age 5.

April-May
40 booths with 1400+ attendees

Susan S Stepleton, President/CEO
Cheryl Dyle-Palmer, Director Operations

879 Retention in Education Today for All Indigenous Nations
National Conference Logistics Center
University of Oklahoma
1639 Cross Center Drive, Suite 101
Norman, OK 73019-7820
405-325-3760
800-203-5494
Fax: 405-325-7075
E-mail: tmonnard@ou.edu
http://www.conferencepros.com
National conference designed to discuss and share retention strategies for indigenous students.

Theresa Monnard, Program Coordinator

880 SERVE Conference
SERVE
5900 Summit Avenue, #201
Browns Summit, NC 27214
336-315-7400
800-755-3277
Fax: 336-315-7457
E-mail: jsanders@serve.org
http://www.serve.org
The Regional Educational Laboratories are educational research and development organizations supported by contracts with the US Education Department, National Institute for Education Sciences. Specialty area: Expanded Learning Opportunities.

October-November

Jack Sanders, Executive Director

881 STEMtech Conference
League for Innovation in the Community College
4505 East Chandler Boulevard
Suite 250
Phoenix, AZ 85048
480-705-8200
Fax: 480-705-8201
E-mail: harris@league.org
http://www.league.org
Emphasizes student success in science, technology, engineering and mathematics (STEM) at all levels.

October
3,000 attendees

Robin Piccilliri, Meeting Planner

882 School Equipment Show
830 Colesville Road
Suite 250
Silver Spring, MD 20910-3297
301-495-0240
800-395-5550
Fax: 301-495-3330
E-mail: customerservice@nnsea.org
http://www.nnsea.org
Annual show featuring exhibits from manufacturers of school equipment such as bleachers, classroom furniture, lockers, playground and athletic equipment, computer hardware, software, etc.

February

Elizabeth Bradley, Conference Contact

883 Sexual Assault and Harassment on Campus Conference
c/o Sexual Conference
PO Box 1338
Holmes Beach, FL 34218-1338
800-537-4903
http://www.ed.mtu.edu
Topics include gender based hate crime, sexual assault investigators, generational legacy of rape, innovations in the military, sexual harassment in K-12, updates on date-rape drugs and many more. Hosted by the Hyatt Orlando Hotel in Kissimmee, Florida.

Karen McLaughlin, Conference Co-Chair
Alan McEvoy, Conference Co-Chair

884 Society for Research in Child Development Conference
5720 S Woodlawn Avenue
Chicago, IL 60637-1603
773-702-7700
Fax: 773-702-9756
Working to further research in the area of child development and education.

March/April
40 booths

Barbara Kahn, Conference Contact

885 Teacher Link: An Interactive National Teleconference
Center for the Study of Small/Rural Schools
555 E Constitution Street
Room 138
Norman, OK 73072-7820
405-325-1450
Fax: 405-325-7075
E-mail: jcsimmons@ou.edu
http://cssrs.ou.edu
Prevention Series

Spring
5 booths with 100 attendees

Jan C Simmons, Director

886 Teachers of English to Speakers of Other Languages Convention and Exhibit
1925 Ballenger Avenue
Suite 550
Alexandria, VA 22314
703-836-0774
888-547-3369
Fax: 703-836-6447
http://www.tesol.org
Leading worldwide professional development opportunity. Simulating program of presentations sponsored by nineteen interest sections, a half-dozen caucus groups and TESOL's advocacy division as well as sessions invited especially for their relevance to our work and our students.

March
245 booths with 8000 attendees

Bart Ecker, Manager
Rosa Aronson, Executive Director

887 Teaching for Intelligence Conference
SkyLight
2626 S Clearbrook Drive
Arlington Heights, IL 60005
847-290-6600
800-348-4474
Fax: 877-260-2530
E-mail: info@irisskylight.com
http://www.iriskylight.com
Focuses on student achievement, brain-based learning and multiple intelligences.

April

888 Technology & Learning Schooltech Exposition & Conference
212-615-6030
http://www.SchoolTechExpo.com
Over 150 targeted sessions specifically designed for all education professionals: technology directors, teachers, principals, superintendents and district administrators.

889 Technology Student Conference
Technology Student Association
1914 Association Drive
Reston, VA 20191-1538
703-860-9000
Fax: 703-758-4852
http://www.tsawww.org
Devoted to the needs of technology education students and supported by educators, parents, and business leaders who believe in the need for a technologically literate society.

June
2,500 attendees

Rosanne White, Conference Manager

890 Technology in 21st Century Schools
National School Conference Institute
PO Box 37527
Phoenix, AZ 85069-7527
602-371-8655
Fax: 602-371-8790
http://www.nscinet.com
Conference will cover managing the Internet, literacy skills, Web Site designs, short and long term planning, creating curriculum, and staff development. Being held at the Boston Park Plaza Hotel in Boston, Massachusetts.

July

Alan November

891 Technology, Reading & Learning Difficulties Conference
International Reading Association
19 Calvert Court
Piedmont, CA 94611
510-594-1249
888-594-1249
Fax: 510-594-1838
http://www.trld.com
Focuses on ways to use technology for reading, learning difficulties, staff development, adult literacy, and more.

January

892 Training of Trainers Seminar
Active Parenting Publishers
1955 Vaughn Road NW
Suite 108
Kennesaw, GA 30144-8943
770-429-0565
800-825-0060
Fax: 770-429-0334
E-mail: cservice@activeparenting.com
http://www.activeparenting.com
Delivers quality education programs for parents, children and teachers to schools, hospitals, social services organizations, churches and the corporate market.

Dana McKie, Training Coordinator

893 U.S. Conference on Adult Literacy (USCAL)
Proliteracy
104 Marcellus Street
Syracuse, NY 13204
315-422-9121
888-528-2224
Fax: 315-422-6369
E-mail: infor@proliteracy.org
http://www.proliteracy.org
Bring together adult literacy advocates and educators to share new ideas, learn from leading thinkers and inspire one another.

November
50 booths with 1,000 attendees

Robyn Smith, Conference/Events Coord.
David Harvey, President

894 USC Summer Superintendents' Conference
University of Southern California, School of Ed.
Waite Room 901
Los Angeles, CA 90089-0001
213-740-2182
Fax: 213-749-2707
E-mail: lpicus@bcf.usc.edu
A select group of educational leaders nationwide engaged in reform practices offer discussions with nationally renowned speakers; tour innovative schools; and network with colleagues from the United States, Great Britain and Australia.

Lawrence O Picus, Conference Director
Carolyn Bryant, Conference Coordinator

Northeast

895 Clonlara School Annual Conference Home Educators
Clonlara Home Based Education Programs
1289 Jewett Street
Ann Arbor, MI 48104-6201
734-769-4511
Fax: 734-769-9629
E-mail: info@clonlara.org
http://www.clonlara.org
Clonlara School is committed to illuminating educational rights and freedoms through our actions and deep dedication to human rights and dignity.

June
300 attendees

Terri Wheeler, Associate Director

896 Connecticut Library Association
PO Box 85
Williamantic, CT 06226-0085
860-465-5006
Fax: 860-465-5004
E-mail: kmcnulty@avon.lib.ct.us
Holds a conference in April and publishes a journal.

April
1000 attendees and 100 exhibits

Karen McNulty, President
Mary Rupert, Manager

897 Hoosier Science Teachers Association Annual Meeting
5007 W 14th Street
Indianapolis, IN 46224-6503
317-244-7238
Fax: 317-486-4838
Papers, workshops, demonstrations and presentations in each area of science.

February
78 booths

Edward Frazer, Conference Contact

898 Illinois Library Association Conference
Illinois Library Association
33 W Grand Avenue
Suite 301
Chicago, IL 60654-4306
312-644-1896
Fax: 312-644-1899
E-mail: ila@ila.org
http://www.ila.org
More than 70 program sessions, exploring nearly every facet of library services, from building projects and professional recruitment to storytelling and the latest revisions of AACR2.

September
2,400+ attendees

Cyndi Robinson, Conference Manager
Bob Doyle, Executive Director

899 Illinois Vocational Association Conference
230 Broadway
Suite 150
Springfield, IL 62701-1138
217-585-9430
Fax: 217-544-0208
E-mail: iva@eosinc.com
Equipment and supplies, publications, teaching aids, computers and food services.

February
75 booths with 600 attendees

Karen Riddle, Conference Contact

900 National Association of Student Financial Aid Administrators
1101 Connecticut Avenue NW
Suite 1100
Washington, DC 20036-3453
202-785-0453
Fax: 202-785-1487
http://www.nasfaa.org
Exists to promote the professional preparation, effectiveness, and mutual support of persons involved in student financial aid administration.

May
40 booths

Suzy Allen, President

901 New Jersey School Boards Association Annual Meeting
413 W State Street
PO Box 909
Trenton, NJ 08605-0909
609-695-7600
888-886-5722
Fax: 609-695-0413
http://www.njsba.org
School/office supplies, furniture, equipment, counseling services and more.

October
630 booths with 9,000 attendees

Wendy L. Wilson, Conference Contact

902 New York State Council of Student Superintendents Forum
111 Washington Avenue
Suite 104
Albany, NY 12210-2210
518-449-1063
Fax: 518-426-2229
Offers educational products and related services.

February
12 booths

Dr. Claire Brown, Conference Contact

903 Northeast Regional Christian Schools International Association
845 Silver Spring Plaza
Suite B
Lancaster, PA 17601-1183
717-285-3022
Fax: 717-285-2128
http://www.acsi.org
40 booths.

November

Alan Graustein, Conference Contact

904 Ohio Library Council Trade Show
35 E Gay Street
Suite 305
Columbus, OH 43215-3138
614-221-9057
Fax: 614-221-6234
Exhibits will offer products and services for library administrators and professionals.

May

Lori Hensley, Exhibits Manager

905 Ohio School Boards Association Capital Conference & Trade Show
700 Brooksedge Boulevard
Westerville, OH 43081-2820
614-891-6466
Provides school officials from Ohio an opportunity to gain information about products, equipment, materials and services.

November
425 booths

Richard Lewis, Conference Contact

906 Satellites and Education Conference
189 Schmucker Science Center
W Chester University
West Chester, PA 19383
610-436-1000
Fax: 610-436-2790
http://www.sated.org/eceos
The Satellite Educators Association was established in 1988 as a professional society to promote the innovative use of satellite technology in education and disseminate information nationally to all members.

March
15 booths with 200 attendees

Nancy McIntyre, Director

907 UNI Overseas Recruiting Fair
University of Northern Iowa
102 Gilchrist Hall
Cedar Falls, IA 50614-0390
319-273-2083
Fax: 319-273-6998
E-mail: overseas.placement@uni.edu
http://www.uni.edu/placement/overseas
About 160 recruiters from 120 schools in 80 countries recruit at this fair for certified K-12 educators.

February

Tracy Roling, Coordinator

908 Wisconsin Vocational Association Conference
44 E Mifflin Street
Suite 104
Madison, WI 53703-2800
608-283-2595
Fax: 608-283-2589
Trade and industry vendor equipment and book publishers.

April
50 booths

Linda Stemper, Conference Contact

Northwest

909 Montana High School Association Conference
1 S Dakota Street
Helena, MT 59601-5111
406-442-6010
School athletic merchandise.
January
15 booths
Dan Freund, Conference Contact

910 Nebraska School Boards Association Annual Conference
140 S 16th Street
Lincoln, NE 68508-1805
402-475-4951
Fax: 402-475-4961
60 booths exhibiting products and services directed at the public school market.
November
60 booths
Burma Kroger, Conference Contact

911 North Dakota Vocational Educational Planning Conference
State Capitol
600 East Boulevard Avenue, Dept. 270
Bismarck, ND 58505
701-328-3180
Fax: 701-328-1255
E-mail: cte@nd.gov
http://www.nd.gov/cte/
August
30 booths
Ernest Breznay, Conference Contact

912 Pacific Northwest Library Association
Boise Public Library
715 Capitol Boulevard
Boise, ID 83702
208-384-4026
Fax: 208-384-4156
E-mail: sprice@pobox.ci.boise.id.us
Oldest regional library association in the United States and the only binational association in North America.
Heidi Chittim, President
Kelsey Keyes, First VP/President-Elect

913 WA-ACTE Career and Technical Exhibition for Career and Technical Education
Washington Association for Career & Tech Education
PO Box 315
Olympia, WA 98507-0315
360-786-9286
Fax: 360-357-1491
E-mail: kal@wa-acte.org
http://www.wa-acte.org
August
40 booths with 1,000 attendees
Tim Knue, Executive Director

Southeast

914 Association for Continuing Higher Education Conference
Trident Technical College
PO Box 118067
Charleston, SC 29423-8067
843-722-5546
Fax: 843-574-6470

15 tabletops.
October
Dr. Wayne Whelan, Executive VP

915 Center for Play Therapy Summer Institute
University of North Texas
PO Box 311337
Denton, TX 76203
940-565-3864
Fax: 940-565-4461
E-mail: cpt@coefs.coe.unt.edu
http://www.centerforplaytherapy.com
Encourage the unique development and emotional growth of children through the process of play therapy, a dynamic interpersonal relationship between a child and a therapist trained in play therapy procedures. The therapist provides the child with selected play materials and facilitates a safe relationship to express feelings, thoughts, experiences and behaviors through play, the child's natural medium of communication.
July
500 attendees
Garry Landreth PhD, Director

916 Missouri Library Association Conference
1306 Business 63 S
Suite B
Columbia, MO 65201
573-449-4627
Fax: 573-449-4655
E-mail: jmccartn@mail.more.net
http://www.mlnc.com/~mla/
The mission of the Missouri Library Network Corporation (MLNC) is to organize and deliver to its member libraries and other contracting entities OCLC-based information services, related electronic services and content, and training in the management and use of information.
October
75 booths with 400 attendees
Margaret Conroy, President
Jean Ann McCartney, Executive Director

917 National Youth-At-Risk Conference
Georgia Southern University
PO Box 8124
Statesboro, GA 30460
912-681-5555
Fax: 912-681-0306
http://http://ceps.georgiasouthern.edu/conted/nationalyouthatrisk.h
Stresses education and development for professionals working with at-risk students.
February
Sybil Fickle, Conference Contact

918 Technology and Learning Conference
National School Boards Association
1680 Duke Street
Alexandria, VA 22314
703-838-6722
Fax: 703-683-7590
E-mail: info@nsba.org
http://www.nsba.org
This conference offers programs, equipment, services, and ideas. It will be held at the Dallas Convention Center.

Southwest

919 CBEA State Conference
Westin Hotel
400 West Broadway
San Diego, CA 92109

925-295-1104
E-mail: cbeaquestions@cbeaonline.org
http://www.cbeaonline.org
Annual conference featuring computer workshops, information sessions, speakers, exhibitions, tours and more.
11/15-11/17 2013
200 attendees
Susan White, Office Manager

920 Children's Literature Festival
Department of Library Science
Sam Houston State University
PO Box 2236
Huntsville, TX 77341-2236
936-294-1614
Fax: 936-294-3780
This annual event is sponsored by the Department of Library Science at Sam Houston State University.

921 Colorado Library Association Conference
3030 W 81st Avenue
Westminister, CO 80031
303-463-6400
Fax: 303-458-0002
E-mail: executivedirector@cal-web.org
http://www.cal-webs.org
October
60 booths with 450 attendees
Terri Switzer, President
Linda Conway, Vice President

922 Phoenix Learning Resources Conference
12 W 31st Street
New York, NY 10001-4415
212-629-3887
800-221-1274
Fax: 212-629-5648
Supplemental and remedial reading and language arts programs for early childhood, K-12, and adult literacy programs.
Alexander Burke, President
John Rothermich, Executive VP

923 Southwest Association College and University Housing Officers
Sam Houston State University
PO Box 2416
Huntsville, TX 77341-2416
936-294-1812
Fax: 936-294-1920
Products and services for college and university housing.
Febuary/March
45 booths
E Thayne King, Conference Contact

924 Texas Classroom Teachers Association Conference
PO Box 1489
Austin, TX 78767-1489
512-477-9415
Fax: 512-469-9527
http://www.tcta.org
Educational materials, fundraising and jewelry.
February
150 booths
Jan Lanfear, Conference Contact

925 Texas Library Association Conference
3355 Bee Cave Road
Suite 401
Austin, TX 78746-6763
512-328-1518
800-580-2852
Fax: 512-328-8852

E-mail: pats@txla.org
http://www.txla.org
Established in 1902 to promote and improve library services in Texas.

March
750 booths with 6,000 attendees

Herman L Totten, President
Kathy Pustyovsky, Meetings Manager

926 Texas Vocational Home Economics Teachers Association Conference

3737 Executive Center Drive
Suite 210
Austin, TX 78731-1633
512-794-8370

July/August

Terry Green, Conference Contact

927 Western History Association Annual Meeting

University of New Mexico
Mesa Room 1080
Albuquerque, NM 87131-0001
505-277-5234
Fax: 505-277-6023
Exhibits by book sellers.

October
45 booths

Paul Hutton, Conference Contact

General

928 Accuracy Temporary Services Incorporated
1431 E 12 Mile Road
Madison Heights, MI 48071-2653
248-399-0220
Educational consultant for public and private schools.

Howard Weaver, President

929 Add Vantage Learning Incorporated
6805 Route 202
New Hope, PA 18938
800-230-2213
Fax: 215-579-8391
http://http://www.vantagelearning.com/
Management and educational consultant for the general public.

Jim Pepitone, Chairman

930 Advance Infant Development Program
2232 D Street
Suite 203
LaVerne, CA 91750-5409
909-593-3935
Fax: 909-593-7969
Business and educational consultant for general trade.

Diane Hinds, President
Jeanine Coleman, Executive Director

931 Aguirre International Incorporated
555 Airport Boulevard
Suite 400
Burlingame, CA 94010-3349
650-373-4900
Fax: 650-348-0260
E-mail: aguirre@aiweb.com
http://http://aguirre-1.interliant.com/aiweb/home.nsf/Home?OpenPage
Educational, data, market analysis, statistical and research consultants for US Government Agencies.

Edward Aguirre, President
Ronald Rodgers, Senior VP Operations

932 American International Schools
2203 Franklin Road SW
Roanoak, VA 24014-1109
852-233-3812
Fax: 852-233-5276
E-mail: asisadmin@ais.edu.hk
American International School is pledged to preparing students to contribute to an increasingly international and interdependent world. AIS strives to provide an atmosphere conducive to building interpersonal relationships and global awareness. AIS is committed to working closely with students and families to attain academic excellence and to inspire the growth of well-rounded individuals.

Andrew Hurst, President
Lewis C Smith Jr, Executive VP

933 Area Cooperative Educational Services
350 State Street
North Haven, CT 06473
203-498-6881
Fax: 203-498-6817
http://http://www.aces.org
ACES is the regional educational service center for twenty-five school districts in south central Connecticut.

Robert D Parker, Marketing Specialist
Craig W Edmondson, Executive Director

934 Aspira of Penna
2726 N 6th Street
Philadelphia, PA 19133-2714
215-229-1226
Educational consultant for educational institutions.

Oscar Cardona, President

935 Association for Refining Cross-Cultured International
Japanese American Cultural Center
244 S San Pedro Street
Suite 505
Los Angeles, CA 90012
213-620-0696
Fax: 213-620-0930
E-mail: support@eryugaku.org
http://www.arcint.com
Educational consultants for international studies.

Chiey Nomura, Director

936 Association of Christian Schools International
PO Box 69103
Colorado Springs, CO 80962-3509
719-528-6906
Fax: 719-531-0631
E-mail: webmaster@acsi.org
http://www.acsi.org
Educational consultant for Christian Schools.

Brian S Simmons, President

937 Auerbach Central Agency for Jewish Education Incorporated
7607 Old York Road
Melrose Park, PA 19027-3010
215-635-8940
Fax: 215-635-8946
E-mail: lbalaban@acaje-jop.org
http://www.acaje.org
Educational consultants.

Lynne Balaban, Director

938 Basics Plus
921 Aris Avenue
Suite C
Metairie, LA 70005-2200
504-832-5111
Fax: 504-832-5110
Educational consultants.

Scott Green, President

939 Beacon Education Management
112 Turnpike Road
Suite 107
Westborough, MA 01581
508-836-4461
800-789-1258
Fax: 508-836-2604
http://www.beaconedu.com
A K-12, education services company that offers contracted management services to public schools and charter school boards. Currently operating 27 charter schools in Massachusetts, Michigan, Missouri and North Carolina.

940 Beverly Celotta
13517 Haddonfield Lane
Gaitherburg, MD 20878
301-330-8803
E-mail: drbev@comcast.net
http://www.celotta.net
Provides psychological and educational services to organizations that serve children and parents.

941 Bluegrass Regional Recycling Corporation
360 Thompson Road
Lexington, KY 40508-2045

859-233-7300
Fax: 859-233-7787
Consultants for educational, training, and services for governments and school systems.

Douglas Castle, Chairman

942 CPM Educational Program
1233 Noonan Drive
Sacramento, CA 95822-2569
916-446-9936
Fax: 916-444-5263
http://www.cpm.org
Educational and training consultants for school districts.

Gthomas Sallee, President Human Resource Dir
Carol Cho, Regional Coordinator

943 Caldwell Flores Winters
2187 Newcastle Avenue
Suite 201
Cardiff, CA 92007-1848
760-634-4239
800-273-4239
Fax: 760-436-7357
E-mail: cfw@cfwinc.com
http://http://www.cfwinc.com/index.html
Offers educational counsel to school districts.

Ernesto Flores, President
Scott Gaudineer, AIA, Program Executive

944 Career Evaluation Systems
1024 N Oakley Boulevard
Suite 4
Chicago, IL 60622-3586
773-772-9595
800-448-7552
Fax: 773-772-5010
Testing instruments for vocational evaluation.

945 Carnegie Foundation for the Advancement of Teaching
51 Vista Lane
Stanford, CA 94305
650-566-5100
Fax: 650-326-0278
E-mail: publications@carnegiefoundation.org
http://http://www.carnegiefoundation.org/
Educational consultant for the educational field.

Anthony S Bryk, President

946 Carney Sandoe & Associates
44 Bromfield Street
Boston, MA 02108-4608
617-542-0260
Fax: 617-542-9400
http://www.carneysandoe.com/
Educational consultant for private schools.

James H Carney, Chairman/President

947 Carter/Tardola Associates
419 Pleasant Street
Suite 307
Beloit, WI 53511
608-365-3163
Fax: 608-365-5961
E-mail: tardola@tucm.net
http://http://www.carter-tardola.com/
Evaluates program, administration, staff, resource and time organization, and utilization of resources. Proposal development, language skills development, diversity training.

Betty Tardola, Educational Consultant

948 Center for Educational Innovation
28 W 44th Street
Suite 300
New York, NY 10036-6600

212-302-8800
Fax: 212-302-0088
E-mail: vchabrier@cei-pea.org
http://www.cei-pea.org/
Educational consultant for private and commercial accounts.

Vivian Chabrier, Director

949 Center for Professional Development & Services
408 N Union Street
Po Box 7888
Bloomington, IN 47407-0789
812-339-1156
800-766-1156
Fax: 812-339-0018
E-mail: information@pdkintl.org
http://www.pdkintl.org
Examines school district curriculum management system. Determines how effectively a school district designs and delivers its curriculum.

Sandra Crowther, Ed D, President
Kathleen Andreson, President-Elect

950 Center for Resource Management
200 International Drive
Suite 201
Portsmouth, NH 03801
603-427-0206
Fax: 603-427-6983
E-mail: info@crminc.com
Employment, human resources, educational, development, training, computer software, organizational and management consultants for Human Service Agencies and Educational Institutions/ Schools.

Mary Ann Lachat, Chairman/President
Martha Anderson, Vice President

951 Child Like Consulting Limited
700 E Rambling Drive
Wellington, FL 33414-5010
561-798-5847
800-487-6725
Fax: 866-468-4555
Training in literacy, music, classroom and learning center management.

952 Children's Educational Opportunity Foundation
901 McClain Road
Suite 802
Bentonville, AR 72712-9242
479-273-6957
Fax: 479-273-9362
Educational consultant for institutions.

Fritz Steiger, President

953 Childs Consulting Associates
514 Lakeside Drive
Mackinaw City, MI 49701
231-436-4099
Fax: 231-436-4101
E-mail: info@childs.com
http://www.childs.com
Educational, schools and technology consultants for schools, banking and automotive industries.

John W Childs, Chief Executive Officer
Jack Keck, Vice President

954 Classroom
245 5th Avenue
Room 1901
New York, NY 10016-8728
212-545-8400
800-258-0640
Fax: 212-481-7178
http://www.classroominc.org

Technology based curriculum and teacher professional development for middle school and high school use.

George Demarco, VP
Jane Canner, President

955 Coalition of Essential Schools
1814 Franklin Street
Suite 700
Oakland, CA 94612
510-433-1451
Fax: 510-433-1455
The Coalition of Essential Schools (CES) is a leading comprehensive school reform organization, fundamentally changing the way people think about teaching and learning and transforming American education.

Hudi Podolsky, Executive Director

956 College Bound
17316 Edwards Road
Suite 180
Cerritos, CA 90703
562-860-2127
Fax: 562-860-1957
E-mail: info@collegeboundca.org
http://www.collegeboundca.org
Educational consultants.

Johnnie Savoy, President
Cynthia Moore, Executive Assistant

957 College Entrance Examination Board
45 Columbus Avenue
New York, NY 10023-6917
212-713-8000
E-mail: emonts@umich.edu
http://www.collegeboard.com
Educational, research, testing and financial consultant for learning institutions and students.

Gaston Caperton, President
Lester P Monts, Chair

958 Community Connections
1695 Old West Broad Street
Athens, GA 30606
706-353-1313
800-924-5085
Fax: 706-353-1375
E-mail: jmeehan@communityconnection211.org
http://www.communityconnection211.org
Educational consultant for the general public.

Julie Meehan, Director

959 Community Foundation for Jewish Education
618 S Michigan Avenue
10th Floor
Chicago, IL 60605-1901
312-913-1818
Fax: 312-913-1763
Educational consultant for the general public and schools.

Howard Swibel, President

960 Connecting Link
387 Coopers Pond Drive
Suite 1
Lawrenceville, GA 30044-5231
770-979-5804
Fax: 770-931-6831
Business and educational consultants for teachers.

Dr. Bernard F Cleveland, President

961 Conover Company
4 Brookwood Court
Appleton, WI 54914-8618
920-231-4667
800-933-1933

Fax: 800-933-1943
E-mail: sales@conovercompany.com
http://www.conovercompany.com
Training and setting up workplace literacy programs; emotional intelligence assessment and skill enhancement; functional literacy software, career exploration and assessment software

Rebecca Schmitz, Member

962 Consortium on Reading Excellence
2560 Ninth Street
Suite 220
Berkley, CA 94710-1923
888-249-6165
Fax: 888-460-4520
E-mail: info@corelearn.com
http://www.corelearn.com
Educational consultant for public and private schools.

Bill Honing, President
Linda Diamond, CEO

963 Continuous Learning Group Limited Liability Company
500 Cherrington Corporate Center
Site 350
Pittsburgh, PA 15108
412-269-7240
Fax: 412-269-7247
E-mail: info@clg.com
http://www.clg.com
Educational consultants.

Hillary Potts, President, CEO

964 Corporate Design Foundation
20 Park Plaza
Suite 400
Boston, MA 02116-4303
617-566-7676
E-mail: admin@cdf.org
Educational consultant for universities and colleges.

Peter G Lawrence, Chairman

965 Corporate University Enterprise
7600 Leesburg Pike West Building
Suite 202
Falls Church, VA 22043
703-848-0070
866-848-1675
Fax: 703-848-0071
E-mail: info@cuenterprise.com
Corporate University Enterprise, Inc. is and educational consulting firm designed to bring a strategic approach to workforce education in both private and public organizations. The company was incorporated in 1998 and has since served clients throughout the United States, Europe, and Asia.

John H. Wells, Senior Advisor
Karen Barley, President

966 Council for Aid to Education
215 Lexington Avenue
21st floor
New York, NY 10016-1599
212-661-5800
Fax: 212-661-9766
http://www.cae.org
Non-profit educational consultant for government and commercial concerns.

Roger Benjamin, President
Michael Rich, Vice President

967 Council on Occupational Education
41 Perimeter Center E
#640
Atlanta, GA 30346-1903
770-396-3898
800-917-2081
Fax: 770-396-3790
E-mail: bowmanh@council.org
http://www.council.org

Managerial and educational consultant for post secondary technical education institutions.

Dr. Harry Bowman, President
Gary Puckett, CEO

968 Creative Learning Consultants
1990 Market Road
Marion, IL 62959-1906
800-729-5137
Fax: 800-844-0455
E-mail: info@piecesoflearning.com
http://www.piecesoflearning.com
Educational consulting for school districts, teachers, book stores and parents.

Stanley Balsamo, Secretary/Treasurer
Kathy Balsamo, President

969 Creative Learning Systems
2065 S Escondido Blvd
Suite 108
Escondido, CA 92025
800-458-2880
Fax: 858-592-7055
E-mail: info@creativelearningsystems.com
http://www.creativelearningsystems.com
Educational consulting firm.

Matt Dickstein, Chief Executive Officer

970 Dawson Education Cooperative
711 Clinton Street
Suite 201
Arkadelphia, AR 71923-5921
870-246-3077
Fax: 870-246-5892
E-mail: rds@dawson.dsc.k12.ar.us
http://www.dawson.dsc.k12.ar.us
Educational consulting group.

Nathan Gills, President

971 Dawson Education Service Cooperative
711 Clinton Street
Suite 201
Arkadelphia, AR 71923-5921
870-246-3077
Fax: 870-246-5892
http://www.dawson.dsc.k12.ar.us
Educational and organizational consultants for school districts

Becky Jester, Director

972 Designs for Learning
2233 University Ave W
Suite 450
St. Paul, MN 55114-1634
651-645-0200
Fax: 651-645-0240
E-mail: dalley@designlearn.net
http://www.designlearn.net
Educational consultants for primary schools and the private sector.

David Alley, President
Andrew Adelmann, Project Coordinator

973 Direct Instructional Support Systems
535 Lakeview Plaza Blvd.
Suite B
Worthington, OH 43085-4146
614-846-8946
Fax: 614-846-1794
Educational consultant for public and private agencies.

Gary Moore, President

974 Dr. Anthony A Cacossa
4300 N Charles Street
Apartment 9B
Baltimore, MD 21218-1052
410-889-1806
Fax: 410-889-1806
Assists schools in marketing academic programs that offer internship opportunities.

975 EPIE Institute: Educational Products Information Exchange Institute
103 West Montauk Highway
PO Box 590
Hampton Bays, NY 11946-4006
631-728-9100
E-mail: kkomoski@epie.org
http://www.epie.org
Curriculum development, training and evaluation of education products.

976 EPPA Consulting
1116 Comanche Trail
Georgetown, KY 40324-1071
502-863-6053
Fax: 502-867-0157
E-mail: eppa@juno.com
Strategic and operational planning.

Theo R Leverenz, PhD, Contact, Owner

977 East Bay Educational Collaborative
317 Market Street
Warren, RI 02885
401-245-4998
Fax: 401-253-6547
http://www.ebecri.org
Business and educational consultant for member school districts.

Gerald Kowalczyk, Executive Director

978 East Central Educational Service Center
1601 Indiana Avenue
Connersville, IN 47331
765-825-1247
Fax: 765-825-2532
E-mail: harrison@ecesc.k12.in.us
http://www.ecesc.k12.in.us
Educational services for school districts in East Central Indiana.

William J Harrison, Executive Director

979 Edge Learning Institute
2515 South Hood Street
Tacoma, WA 98402-3320
253-272-3103
800-858-1484
Fax: 253-572-2668
E-mail: cihrig@edgelearning.com
http://www.edgelearning.com
Educational consultants for the general public, commercial concerns, government agencies and school districts.

Chris Ihrig, CEO
Anita Paige, Vice President

980 Edison Schools
485 Lexington Avenue
2nd Floor
New York, NY 10017
212-419-1600
Fax: 212-419-1746
E-mail: information@edisonlearning.com
http://www.edisonschools.com
The country's largest private manager of public schools. Implemented its design in 79 public schools, including 36 charter schools, which it operates under management contracts with local school districts and charter school boards.

Jeff Wahl, President, CEO

981 Education Concepts
9861 Strausser Street
Canal Fulton, OH 44614
330-497-1055
Fax: 330-966-8000
E-mail: info@ed-concepts.com
http://www.ed-concepts.com
Professional development programs for early childhood educators.

982 Education Data
1305 E Waterman
Witchata, KS 67211
800-248-4135
Expertise in organizational needs assessments.

983 Education Development Center
55 Chapel Street
Newton, MA 02158
617-969-7100
Fax: 617-969-5979
http://www.edc.org
Developing programs in science, mathematics, reading, writing, health and special education.

984 Education Management Consulting LLC
49 Coryell Street
Lambertville, NJ 08530
609-397-8989
800-291-0199
Fax: 609-397-1999
E-mail: edragan@edmgt.com
http://www.edmgt.com
Consultation for schools on special education and administration consultation for lawyers working on education and school related issues.

Dr. Edward F Dragan, President

985 Educational Consultants of Oxford
10431 Highway 51 S
Courtland, MS 38620
601-563-8954
All areas of educational information services, tutoring, scholarship information, and non-traditional and overseas training.

986 Educational Credential Evaluators
260 East Highland Avenue
PO Box 514070
Milwaukee, WI 53202
414-289-3400
Fax: 414-289-3411
E-mail: eval@ece.org
http://www.ece.org
Evaluates foreign educational credentials.

James Frey, President
Margit Schatzman, VP

987 Educational Data Service
236 Midland Avenue
Saddle Brook, NJ 07663-4604
973-340-8800
Fax: 973-340-0078
http://www.ed-data.com
Educational and school consulting for Boards of Education.

Gil Wohl, President
Alan Wohl, Chairman

988 Educational Information & Resource Center
900 Hollydell Drive
Sewell, NJ 08080
856-582-7000
Fax: 856-582-4206
E-mail: info@eirc.org
http://www.eirc.org
Programs and consulting services for schools, on many topics from teaching techniques to technical assistance.

989 Educational Resources
8910 W 62nd Terrace
Shawnee Mission, KS 66202-2814
913-362-4600
Fax: 913-362-4627
Educational consulting for colleges.

Michael Frost, President
Karen Harrison, VP

990 Educational Services Company
3535 East 96th Street
Suite 126
Indianapolis, IN 46240-1754
317-818-3535
888-351-3535
Fax: 317-818-3533
http://www.educationalservicesco.com
Educational and management consulting for primary and secondary schools.

Douglas Cassman, President
William McMaster, Secretary

991 Educational Specialties
9923 S Wood Street
Chicago, IL 60643-1809
773-445-1000
Fax: 773-445-5574
http://www.educationalspecialties.com
Educational consultant for schools.

Elois W Steward, President

992 Educational Systems for the Future
14650 Viburnum Drive
Dayton, MD 21036
410-531-3737
Fax: 410-531-3939
E-mail: info@esf-protainer.com
http://www.esf-protainer,com
Development of teaching skills, training needs analysis, and training management.

993 Educational Technology Design Consultants
100 Allentown Parkway
Suite 110
Allen, TX 75002
972-727-1234
Fax: 972-727-1491
http://www.etdc.com/html/about_us.html
Developing system design for virtual campus control and support.

994 Educational Testing Service
Rosedale Road
Princeton, NJ 08541-0001
609-921-9000
Fax: 609-734-5410
http://www.ets.org
Educational and professional consulting for schools.

Kurt M. Landgraf, President
Sharon Robison, COO, Senior VP

995 Edusystems Export
820 Wisconsin Street
Walworth, WI 53184-9765
262-275-5761
Fax: 262-275-2009
E-mail: sales@edusystems.com;admin@edusystems.com
Expertise in educational systems.

996 Effective Schools Products
2199 Jolly Road
Suite 160
Okemos, MI 48864-5983
517-349-8841
800-827-8041
Fax: 517-349-8852
http://www.effectiveschools.com
Publishing consultants for schools, teachers, directors of planning and others in this field.

Ruth Lezotte, PhD, President

997 Effective Training Solutions
103 Linden Street
Oakland, CA 94607-1447
510-834-1901
800-949-5035
Fax: 510-834-1905
E-mail: boris@trainingsuccess.com
http://www.trainingsuccess.com
Design and implementation of training strategies. Proficiency training-performance improvement training.

Ingrid Gudenas, CEO

998 Efficacy Institute
182 Felton Street
Waltham, MA 02453-4134
781-547-6060
Fax: 781-547-6077
E-mail: info@efficacy.org
http://www.efficacy.org
Non-profit, educational consultants for educational and community service institutions.

Jeff P Howard, President
Mike Hyter, Treasurer

999 Emerging Technology Consultants
216 Heritage Lane
New Brighton, MN 55112
651-639-3973
Fax: 651-639-3973
Serves as a connection between technology producers and the education and training industries.

Richard Pollak, Chief Executive Officer
Rubyanna Pollak, President

1000 Epistemological Engineering
5269 Miles Avenue
Oakland, CA 94618-1044
510-653-3377
866-341-3377
Fax: 866-879-7797
E-mail: publications@eeps.com
http://www.eeps.com
Educational consultants.

Tim Erickson, President

1001 Examiner Corporation
600 Marshall Avenue
Suite 100
St. Paul, MN 55102-1723
651-451-7360
800-395-6840
Fax: 651-451-6563
E-mail: examine@xmn.com
Educational and certification evaluation instruments.

Gary C Brown, President
Michelle Smith, Sales and Marketing

1002 Excell Education Centers
3807 Wilshire Boulevard
Los Angeles, CA 90010-3101
213-386-1953
Educational and planning consultants.

Raymond Hahl, Owner

1003 FPMI Communications
707 Fiber Street NW
Huntsville, AL 35801-5833
256-539-1850
Fax: 256-539-0911
http://www.fmpi.com
Educational management consulting.

1004 First District Resa
201 West Lee Street
P.O. Box 780
Brooklet, GA 30415
912-842-5000
Fax: 912-842-5161
http://www.fdresa.org
Educational consultants for the general public and commercial concerns.

Shelly Smith, Executive Director

1005 Foundation for Educational Innovation
401 M Street SW
2nd Floor, Suite 1
Washington, DC 20024-2610
202-554-7400
Fax: 202-554-7401
Educational consultant for educational/school systems.

Archie Prioleau, President

1006 George Dehne & Associates
3331 Cotton Field Drive
Mt. Pleasant, SC 29466-3836
843-971-9088
800-942-7427
Fax: 843-971-7759
http://www.dehne.com
Educational and business consultants for commercial concerns and colleges.

George Dehne, President

1007 Health Outreach Project
825 Cascade Avenue
Atlanta, GA 30331-8362
404-755-6700
Educational consultants.

Sandra McDonald, President

1008 Higher Education Consortium
2233 University Avenue W
Suite 210
St. Paul, MN 55104-1205
651-646-8831
Fax: 651-659-9421
Educational consultants.

Jenny Keyser, Executive Director

1009 Highlands Program
PO Box 76168
Atlanta, GA 30358-3915
404-497-0835
Educational consultants for educational institutions, corporations and consumers.

Don Hutcheson, President

1010 Howard Greene Associates
60 Post Road W
Westport, CT 06880-4208
203-226-4257
Fax: 203-226-5595
E-mail: counseling@howardgreeneassociates.com
http://www.greenesguides.com
Educational consultants for school systems and individuals.

Howard Greene, President

1011 Huntley Pascoe
19125 N Creek Parkway
Bothel, WA 98011-8035
425-485-0900
Fax: 425-487-1825
Educational consultant for architects, utility companies, computer facilities, school districts and hospitals.

Roger Huntley, President

1012 Ingraham Dancu Associates
1265 Lakevue Drive
Butler, VA 16002
724-586-8761
Fax: 724-586-6638
E-mail: dedance@msn.com
Development planning for educational and industrial clients.

Dr. Daniel Dancu, Contact

1013 Innovative Learning Group
10261 Canteberry Street
Westchester, IL 60154-1780
708-865-7752

Educational consultants for schools and the general public.

Joseph Elliott, President

1014 Innovative Programming Systems
9001poplar Bridge Road
Bloomington, MN 55437
612-835-1290
Development of instructional and training programs.

1015 Insight
12 S 6th Street
Suite 510
Minneapolis, MN 55402-1510
612-338-5777
Educational consultants for commercial concerns.

Mark Kovatch, President

1016 Institute for Academic Excellence
901 Deming Way
Suite 301
Madison, WI 53717-1964
608-664-0965
Fax: 608-664-382
Educational consultants for K-12 schools.

John Hickey, Chairman

1017 Institute for Development of Educational Activities
259 Regency Ridge
Dayton, OH 45459
937-434-6969
Fax: 937-434-5203
E-mail: ideadayton@aol.com
http://www.idea.com
Assistance for administrators and teachers of elementary and secondary schools.

1018 Institute for Global Ethics
91 Camden Street
Suite 403
Rockland, ME 04843-1703
207-594-6658
800-729-2615
Fax: 207-594-6648
E-mail: ethics@globalethics.org
http://www.globalethics.org
Educational consultants for the general public, corporations and educators.

Rushworth Kidder, President

1019 Interface Network
321 SW 4th Avenue
Suite 502
Portland, OR 97204-2323
503-222-2702
Fax: 503-222-7503
E-mail: www.daggettt.com
http://info@leaderEd.com
Educational consultant for the United States Department of Education, businesses, school districts and other governmental agencies.

1020 International Center for Leadership in Education
1587 Route 146
Rexford, NY 12148
518-399-2776
Fax: 518-399-7607
E-mail: info@leadered.com
http://www.leadered.com
Educational consultants for educational institutions, governments and commercial concerns.

Willard R Daggett, President

1021 International Schools Association
3, Chemin des Tulipiers
CH-1208, Geneva
Switzerland
39-011-645-967
Fax: 39-011-643-298

E-mail: info@isaschools.org
http://www.isaschools.org
Provides advisory and consultative services to its international and internationally minded member schools, as well as to other organizations in the field of education, such as UNESCO. The Association promotes innovations in international education, conducts conferences and workshops and publishes various educational materials.

Katherine Kastoryano, Executive Director

1022 J&Kalb Associates
300 Pelham Road
Suite 5K
New Rochelle, NY 10805
914-636-6154
Consulting experience to school districts.

1023 JCB/Early Childhood Education Consultant Service
813 Woodchuck Place
Bear, DE 19701
302-836-8505
Program design and cross-cultural staff development through seminars.

1024 JJ Jones Consultants
1206 Harrison Avenue
Oxford, MS 38655-3904
662-234-6755
Educational consultant for high school and college students.

JJ Jones, Owner

1025 JP Associates Incorporated
131 Foster Avenue
Valley Stream, NY 11580-4726
516-561-7803
Fax: 516-561-4066
Educational consultant for schools.

Jane Dinapoli, President

1026 Janet Hart Heinicke
1302 W Boston Avenue
Indianola, IA 50125
515-961-8933
Fax: 515-961-8903
E-mail: heinicke@simpson.edu
Development of new programs and maintenance strategies.

1027 Jobs for California Graduates
2525 O Street
Merced, CA 95340-3634
209-385-8466
Educational consultants for high school students.

Obie Obrien, Director

1028 John McLaughlin Company
1524 S Summit Avenue
Sioux Falls, SD 57105
605-332-4900
Fax: 605-339-1662
http://www.mclaughlincompany.com
Advises companies regarding private-sector activities in K-12 and higher education.

John Laughlin, Owner

1029 Johnson & Johnson Associates
3970 Chain Bridge Road
Fairfax, VA 22030-3316
703-359-5969
800-899-6363
Fax: 703-359-5971
E-mail: info@jjaconsultants.com
http://www.jjaconsultants.com
Educational consultants for governmental agencies and commercial concerns.

Dr. Johnson Edosomwan, President/CEO

1030 Joseph & Edna Josephson Institute
9841 Airport Blvd.
Suite 300
Los Angeles, CA 90045-6621
310-846-4800
800-711-2670
Fax: 310-846-4858
http://charactercounts.org
Educational consultant for organizations, government, businesses and the general public.

Michael Josephson, President

1031 Kaludis Consulting Group
1050 Conn Avenue NW
Suite 10
Washington, DC 20036
202-772-3120
Fax: 202-331-1428
E-mail: info@kaludisconsulting.com
http://www.kaludisconsulting.com
Educational consultants for colleges and universities.

George Kaludis, President/Chairman
Barry M Cohen, Senior Vice President

1032 Kentucky Association of School Administrators
152 Consumer Lane
Suite 154
Frankfort, KY 40601-8489
502-875-3411
800-928-kasa
Fax: 502-875-4634
E-mail: webmaster@kasa.com
Educational consultant for school administrators.

V Wayne Young, Director

1033 Kleiner & Associates
8636 SE 75th Place
Mercer Island, WA 98040-5235
206-236-0608
Educational consultants for public and private institutions.

Charles Kleiner, Owner

1034 Lawrence A Heller Associates
324 Freeport Road
Pittsburgh, PA 15238-3422
412-820-0670
Fax: 412-820-0669
Development and implementation of educational programs.

1035 Leona Group
4660 S Hagadorn Road
Suite 500
East Lansing, MI 48823-5353
517-333-9030
Fax: 517-333-4559
http://www.leonagroup.com
Currently manages more than 40 school sites in Michigan, Arizona, Ohio and Indiana

Dr. Bill Coats, CEO

1036 Linkage
200 Wheeler Road
Burlington, MA 01803-7305
781-402-5400
Fax: 781-402-5556
E-mail: info@linkage-inc.com
http://www.linkageinc.com
Linkage, Inc. is a global organizational development company that specializes in leadership development.

Philip Harkins, President

1037 Logical Systems
605 E 1st Street
Suite 101
Rome, GA 30161-3109

706-234-9896
Fax: 706-290-0998
http://www.logsysinc.com
Educational consultants for school districts.

Francis Ranwez, President

1038 Los Angeles Educational Alliance for Restructuring Now
445 S Figueroa Street
Los Angeles, CA 90071
323-255-3276
Fax: 213-626-5830
E-mail: asant@ccf-la.org
Educational consulting for school systems.

Mary Chambers, Vice President
Michael Roos, President

1039 Louisiana Children's Research Center for Development & Learning
1 Galleria Blvd.
Suite 903
Metairie, LA 70001-3036
504-840-9786
Fax: 504-840-9968
http://www.cdl.org
Educational consultants for the general public.

Alice P Thomas, President, CEO

1040 MK & Company
132 Bronte Street
San Francisco, CA 94110
415-826-5923
Program development and project management for educational products, services and organizations.

1041 MPR Associates
2150 Shattuck Avenue
Suite 800
Berkeley, CA 94704-1321
510-849-4942
Fax: 510-849-0794
E-mail: info@mprinc.com
http://www.mprinc.com
Educational consultants for governmental, educational and commercial concerns including law firms.

Gary Hoachlander, President

1042 Magi Educational Services Incorporated
7-11 Broadway
Suite 402
White Plains, NY 10601-3546
914-682-1861
Fax: 914-682-1760
E-mail: info@westchesterinst.com
http://www.westchesterinst.org
Educational consultant for educational institutions.

Dr. Ronald Szczypkowski, President

1043 Management Concepts
8230 Leesburg Pike
Suite 800
Vienna, VA 22182-2639
703-790-9595
800-506-4450
Fax: 703-790-1371
E-mail: csmith@managementconcepts.com
http://www.managementconcepts.com
Educational consultants for commercial and governmental concerns.

Thomas F. Dungan lll, CEO

1044 Management Simulations
540 W Frontage Road
Suite 3270
Winnetka, IL 60093-1250

877-477-8787
E-mail: welcome@capsim.com
http://www.capsim.com
Educational consultants for commercial concerns and universities.

Daniel Smith, President

1045 Marketing Education Resource Center
1375 King Avenue
PO Box 12279
Columbus, OH 43212-2220
614-486-6708
800-448-0398
Fax: 614-486-1819
http://www.mbaresearch.org
Educational, development and curriculum consulting for high schools and post secondary schools.

James R Gleason Ph.D., President, CEO

1046 Maryland Educational Opportunity Center
2700 Gwynns Falls
Baltimore, MD 21216
410-728-3400
888-245-2774
Fax: 410-523-6340
E-mail: edhoward@meoconline.com
http://www.meoconline.com
Consultant services for educational institutions.

Ellen Howard, Executive Director

1047 Maryland Elco Incorporated Educational Funding Company
4740 Chevy Chase Drive
Chevy Chase, MD 20815-6461
301-654-8677
Fax: 301-654-7750
http://www.efconline.com
Educational, accounting and billing consultants for service and vocational schools and businesses.

Nicholas Cokinos, Chairman

1048 Mason Associates
142 N Mountain Avenue
Montclair, NJ 07042
201-744-9143
Educational services for independent secondary schools, colleges and universities.

1049 Matrix Media Distribution
28310 Roadside Drive
Suite 237
Agoura, CA 91301-4951
818-865-3470
Educational consultant for the educational market.

Paul Luttrell, President

1050 McKenzie Group
1100 17th Street NW
Suite 1100
Washington, DC 20036-4638
202-466-1111
Fax: 202-466-3363
Educational consultant for commercial concerns and government.

Floretta D McKenzie, President

1051 Measurement
423 Morris Street
Durham, NC 27701-2128
919-683-2413
Fax: 919-425-7726
http://www.measurementinc.com
Educational, research, testing and printing consultant for schools, state governments and private businesses.

Henry H Scherich, President/CEO

1052 Measurement Learning Consultants
80920 Highway 10
Tolovana Park, OR 97145
503-436-1464
Business, educational, testing and development consultants for the general public and commercial concerns such as schools.

Albert G Bennyworth, Partner

1053 Merrimack Education Center
101 Mill Road
Chelmsford, MA 01824-4844
978-256-3985
Fax: 978-937-5585
http://www.mec.edu
Educational consultant for educational facilities.

John Barranco, Executive Director

1054 Michigan Education Council
40440 Palmer Road
Canton, MI 48188-2034
734-729-1000
Fax: 734-729-1004
Educational consultant for individuals.

Dawud Tauhidi, Director

1055 Midas Consulting Group
4600 S Syracuse Street
Suite 900
Denver, CO 80237
303-256-6500
Fax: 866-790-9500
E-mail: info@midasconsultinggroup.com
http://www.midasconsultinggroup.com
Educational consultant for schools, universities, training centers and government agencies.

Michael Blimes, Executive Consultant

1056 Miller, Cook & Associates
1606 Bellview Avenue
Suite 1
Roanoke, VA 24014-4923
540-345-4393
800-591-1141
Fax: 239-394-2656
E-mail: info@millercook.com
http://www.millercook.com
Educational consultants for colleges and universities.

William B Miller, President

1057 Model Classroom
4095 173rd Place SW
Bellvue, WA 98008-5929
425-746-0331
Educational consultant for school districts, commercial concerns and the Department of Education.

Cheryl Avena, Owner

1058 Modern Educational Systems
15 Limestone Terrace
Ridgefield, CT 06877-2621
203-431-4144
Educational consultant for schools.

Edward T McCormick, President

1059 Modern Red Schoolhouse Institute
1901 21st Avenue
South Nashville, TN 37212-1502
615-320-8804
888-275-6774
Fax: 615-320-5366
E-mail: info@mrsh.com
http://www.mrsh.com
Educational consultant for school districts.

Sally B Kilgore, President

1060 Montana School Boards Association
863 Great Northern Blvd.
Suite 301
Helena, MT 59601-5156

406-442-2180
Fax: 406-442-2194
E-mail: cwilson@mtsba.org
http://www.mtsba.org
Training, educational and school districts consultant for school boards.

Charles Wilson, President

1061 Montgomery Intermediate Unit 23

1605 W Main Street
Suite B
Norristown, PA 19403-3268
610-539-8550
Fax: 610-539-5073
http://www.mciu.org
Educational consultants for professional associations, groups and student organizations.

Marc Lieberson, President

1062 Moore Express

865 Pancheri Drive
Idaho Falls, ID 83402
208-523-6276
Educational consultant for public school districts, state and local governments and commercial concerns.

Lawry Wilde, President

1063 Mosaica Education

42 Broadway
Suite 1039
New York, NY 10004
212-292-0305
Fax: 212-232-0309
http://www.mosaicaeducation.com
Manages public schools either under contract with local school districts or funded directly by states under charter school laws that permit private management.

Gene Eidelman, President

1064 Multicorp

1912 Avenue K
Suite 210
Plano, TX 75074-5960
972-551-8899
Computer and educational consultant.

Fred Sammet, Chairman

1065 National Center on Education & the Economy

2000 Pennsylvania Avenue NW
Suite 5300
Washington, DC 20006-4507
202-379-1800
Fax: 202-293-1560
E-mail: info@ncee.org
http://www.ncee.org
Educational consultant for schools.

Marc S Tucker, President

1066 National Evaluation Systems

30 Gatehouse Road
PO Box 226
Amherst, MA 01004
Fax: 413-256-8221
Educational testing, test development, and assessment for education agencies.

1067 National Heritage Academies

3850 Broadmoor Avenue SE
Suite 201
Grand Rapids, MI 49512
877-223-6402
Fax: 616-575-6801
E-mail: info@heritageacademies.com
http://www.heritageacademies.com
Manages 22 charter academies (K-8) in Michigan and North Carolina.

2007, Author
Jeff Clark, President, CEO

1068 National Reading Styles Institute

179 Lafayette Drive
Syosset, NY 11791
516-921-5500
800-331-3117
Fax: 516-921-5591
E-mail: readingstyle@nrsi.com
http://www.nrsi.com
Educational consultants for schools and educators.

Marie Carbo, Executive Director

1069 National School Safety and Security Services

PO Box 110123
Cleveland, OH 44111
216-251-3067
E-mail: kentrump@aol.com
http://www.schoolsecurity.org
National consulting firm specializing in school security and crisis preparedness training, security assessments, and related safety consulting for K-12 schools, law enforcement, and other youth safety providers.

Kenneth S Trump, President/CEO

1070 Noel/Levitz Centers

2350 Oakdale Blvd.
Coralville, IA 52241-9581
319-626-8380
800-876-1117
Fax: 319-626-8388
http://www.noellevitz.com
Educational consultant for colleges and universities.

Tom Williams, President/CEO

1071 Ome Resa

2023 Sunset Boulevard
Steubenville, OH 43952-1349
740-283-2050
Fax: 740-283-1500
E-mail: angie.underwood@omeresa.net
http://www.omeresa.net
Educational consultants for school districts.

Angela Underwood, Executive Director

1072 Oosting & Associates

200 Seaboard Lane
Franklin, TN 37067-8237
615-771-7706
Fax: 615-771-7810
Educational consultants for colleges and universities.

Dr. Kenneth Oosting, President

1073 Pamela Joy

1049 Whipple Avenue
Suite A
Redwood City, CA 94062-1414
650-368-9968
Fax: 650-368-2794
Educational consultants for schools.

Pamela Joy, Owner

1074 Parsifal Systems

155 N Craig Street
Pittsburgh, PA 15213
412-682-8080
Fax: 412-682-6291
Educational consultants for commercial concerns and schools.

Marcia Morton, President

1075 Paul H Rosendahl, PHD

240 Mohouli Street
Hilo, HI 96720-2445
808-935-5233
Fax: 808-961-6998
Science, archaeology, historical, resources and management consultant for developers, government agencies, educational institutions, groups and individuals.

Paul H Rosendahl, Owner

1076 Perfect PC Technologies

15012 Red Hill Avenue
Tustin, CA 92780-6524
714-258-0800
Computer consultants for commercial concerns, schools and institutions.

Neil Lin, President

1077 Performa

124 N Broadway
De Pere, WI 54115
920-336-9929
Fax: 920-336-2899
E-mail: jeffk@performaic.com
http://www.performainc.com
Planning and facility consultants for higher education, manufacturing and government agencies.

Jeff Kanzelberger, CEO
Doug Page, Chief Operating Officer

1078 Poetry Alive!

70 Woodfin Place
Suite WW4C
Asheville, NC 28801
828-255-7636
800-476-8172
Fax: 828-232-1045
E-mail: poetry@poetryalive.com
http://www.poetryalive.com
Educational consultants for commercial concerns and school systems.

Bob Falls, President

1079 Post Secondary Educational Assistance

1210 20th Street S
Suite 200
Birmingham, AL 35205-3814
205-930-4930
Fax: 205-930-4905
E-mail: clientservices@peaccorp.com
http://www.peaccorp.com
Educational consultant for commercial concerns.

Kenneth Horne, President

1080 Prevention Service

7614 Morningstar Avenue
Harrisburg, PA 17112-4226
717-651-9510
Educational consultant for corporations, private health clubs, school districts and other organizations.

Mark Everest, President

1081 Princeton Review

2315 Broadway
2nd Floor
New York, NY 10024-4332
212-874-8282
Fax: 212-874-0775
Educational consultants for commercial concerns.

John Katzman, President

1082 Priority Computer Services

4001 Technology Drive
South Bend, IN 46628
574-236-5979
866-661-9049
E-mail: priority@pcserv-inc.com
http://www.prioritycomputer.biz
Computer consultant for commercial education.

Ben Hahaj, President

1083 Prism Computer Corporation
2 Park Plaza
Suite 1060
Irvine, CA 92614-8520
800-774-7622
Fax: 949-553-6559
Educational consultant for manufacturers, government agencies and colleges.

Micheal A Ellis, President

1084 Professional Computer Systems
849 E Greenville Avenue
Winchester, IN 47394-8441
765-584-2288
Fax: 765-584-1283
Computer consultants for businesses, schools and municipalities.

Steve Barnes, President

1085 Professional Development Institute
280 S County Road
Suite 427
Longwood, FL 32750-5468
407-834-5224
Educational consultants for US Department of Transportation and commercial concerns.

Elsom Eldridge, Jr, President

1086 Profiles
507 Highland Avenue
Iowa City, IA 52240-4516
319-354-7600
Fax: 319-354-6813
Educational consultants for school districts and commercial concerns.

Douglas Paul, President

1087 Pyramid Educational Consultants
13 Garfield Way
Newark, DE 19713
302-368-2515
800-732-7462
Fax: 302-368-2516
E-mail: pyramid@pecs.com
http://www.pecsusa.com
Educational consultant for general trade, historical commissions and other public bodies.

Andrew Bondy, President
Lori Frost, Vice President

1088 Quality Education Development
41 Central Park West
New York, NY 10023
212-724-3335
800-724-2215
Fax: 212-724-4913
E-mail: info@qedconsulting.com
Structures courses that promote knowledge and understanding through interactive learning, and communication programs.

1089 Quantum Performance Group
5050 Rushmore Road
Palmyra, NY 14522-9414
315-986-9200
Educational consultant for commercial concerns, including schools.

Dr. Mark Blazey, President

1090 Rebus
4111 Jackson Road
Ann Arbor, MI 48103-1827
734-668-4870
Fax: 734-913-4750
Educational consultant for schools and school districts.

Linda Borgsdorf, President

1091 Records Consultants
10826 Gulfdale Street
San Antonio, TX 78216-3607
210-366-4127
Fax: 210-366-0776
Educational consultant for school districts and municipalities.

Lang Glotfelty, President

1092 Regional Learning Service of Central New York
770 James Street Office
Syracuse, NY 13203-1644
315-446-0500
Fax: 315-446-5869
Educational consultants for commercial concerns.

Rebecca Livengood, Executive Director

1093 Reinventing Your School Board
Aspen Group International,Inc
PO Box 260301
Highlands Ranch, CO 80163-0301
303-478-0125
Fax: 208-248-6084

Linda Dawson, Contact
Dr. Randy Quinn, Contact

1094 Relearning by Design
447 Forcina Hall
PO Box 7718
Ewing, NJ 08628-0718
609-771-2921
Fax: 609-637-5130
E-mail: info@relearning.org
http://www.relearning.org

Grant Wiggins, Author/Editor
Jacquelyn Nance, Chair

1095 Research Assessment Management
816 Camarillo Springs Road
Camarillo, CA 93012-9441
805-987-5538
Fax: 805-987-2868
Educational consultants for governmental agencies and commercial concerns.

Adrienne McCollum, PhD, President

1096 Robert E Nelson Associates
120 Oak Brook Center
Suite 208
Oak Brook, IL 60523
630-954-5585
Fax: 630-954-5606
Consulting for private colleges, universities and secondary schools.

1097 Rookey Associates
1740 Little York Xing
Little York, NY 13087
607-749-2325
Educational consultant for school districts, public utility companies and the government.

Ernest J Rookey, President

1098 Root Learning
810 W S Boundary Street
Perrysburg, OH 43551-5200
419-874-0077
Fax: 419-874-4801
Business, educational, employment consultant for commercial concerns.

Randall Root, Chairman/CEO

1099 School Management Study Group
1649 Lone Peoh Drive
Salt Lake City, UT 84117
801-277-3725
Fax: 801-277-4547

Organization seeking to promote improvement of schools and to involve educators in critical school problems.

Donald Thomas, President
Dale Holden, Associate

1100 SchoolMatch by Public Priority Systems
110 Mohawk Trail
Wayne, NJ 07470
973-831-1757
An educational consultant for private and public schools.

John Pinto, President

1101 Sensa of New Jersey
110 Mohawk Trail
Wayne, NJ 07470-5030
973-831-1757
An educational consultant for private and public schools.

John Pinto, President

1102 Shirley Handy
19860 Bloss Avenue
Hilmar, CA 95324-8308
209-668-4142
Fax: 209-668-1855
http://www.n-e-n.com
Educational consultants for school districts and teachers.

Shirley Handy, Owner

1103 Sidney Kreppel
704 E Benita Boulevard
Vestal, NY 13850-2629
607-754-6870
Educational consultants.

Sidney Kreppel, Owner

1104 Solutions Skills
565 E Tennessee Street
Tallahassee, FL 32308-4981
850-681-6543
Fax: 850-681-6543
http://www.solutionskills.com
Business and educational consultants for state and governments, educational, medical and legal publishing companies.

Randall Vickers, President

1105 Special Education Service Agency
3501 Denali Street
Suite 101
Anchorage, AK 99503-1068
907-562-7372
Fax: 907-561-7383
E-mail: sesa@sesa.org
http://www.sesa.org
Educational consultant for school districts.

Nancy Nagarkar, Executive Director

1106 Sports Management Group
918 Parker Street
Suite A-13
Berkeley, CA 94710
510-849-3090
Fax: 510-849-3094
E-mail: tsmq@sportsmqmt.com
http://www.sportsmgnt.com
Educational consulting for universities.

Lauren Livingston, President

1107 Stewart Howe Alumni Service of New York
3109 N Triphammer Road
Lansing, NY 14882
607-533-9200
E-mail: programs@stewarthowe.com
http://www.stewarthowe.com
Educational consultants for college organizations.

Peter McChesney, Director

1108 Strategies for Educational Change
11 Whitby Court
Mount Holly, NJ 08060
609-261-1702
E-mail: barbd@prodigy.net
Development of programs for youths at risk.

1109 Success for All Foundation
200 W Towsontown Boulevard
Baltimore, MD 21204-5200
410-616-2300
800-548-4998
Fax: 410-324-4444
E-mail: sfainfo@successforall.net
http://www.successforall.net
A not-for-profit organization dedicated to the development, evaluation and dissemination of proven reform models for preschool, elementary and middle schools.

Nancy Madden, Ph.D., CEO

1110 Teachers Curriculum Institute
244 W El Cam
Mountain View, CA 94040-4234
650-856-0565
800-497-6138
Fax: 800-343-6828
E-mail: infor@teachtci.com
http://www.teachtci.com
Educational consultant for schools and teachers.

Bert Bower, President

1111 Teachers Service Association
1107 E Lincoln Avenue
Orange, CA 92865-1939
714-282-6342
Educational consultants for schools and teachers.

Richard Ghysels, Secretary Treasurer

1112 Tech Ed Services
One World Trade Center
8th Floor
Long Beach, CA 90831
562-869-1913
800-832-4411
Fax: 562-869-5673

E-mail: info@techedservices.com
http://techedservices.com
Computer, planning and training consultant for k-12 educators and adult educators.

Patricia K Sanford, President
Brenna Terrones, Corporate Specialists

1113 Technical Education Research Centers
2067 Massachusetts Avenue
Cambridge, MA 02140-1340
617-873-9600
Fax: 617-873-9601
E-mail: communications@terc.edu
http://www.terc.edu
Educational consultant for the National Science Foundation and the Department of Education.

Arthur Nelson, Chairman

1114 Tesseract Group
4111 E. Ray Road
Suite 2
Phoenix, AZ 85044
480-706-2500
Fax: 480-759-0160
http://www.tesseractgroup.org
An integrated education management company, serving private and public charter elementary, middle and high schools in six states.

Michael Lynch, CEO

1115 Timothy Anderson Dovetail Consulting
936 Nantasket Avenue
Hull, MA 02045-1453
781-925-3078
Fax: 781-925-9830
Educational consultant for businesses.

Eric Anderson, Owner

1116 University Research
7200 Wisconsin Avenue
Suite 600
Bethesda, MD 20814-4811
301-654-8338
Fax: 301-941-8427

Educational consultants for the federal government along with other government and private sectors.

Barbara M. Turner, President

1117 University of Georgia-Instructional Technology
630 Aderhold Hall
Athens, GA 30602
706-542-4110
Fax: 706-542-4240
E-mail: coeinfo@uga.edu
http://www.coe.uga.edu
Instructional design and development.

Aurthur M. Horne, Dean
Pedro R Portes, Professor

1118 Uplinc
48 Capital Drive
West Springfield, MA 01089
413-693-0700
E-mail: sales@uplinc.com
http://www.uplinc.com
Computer consultants for commercial, general public and educational concerns.

Ron Marino, President

1119 William A Ewing & Company
505 S Main Street
Suite 700
Orange, CA 92868
714-245-1850
Fax: 714-456-1755
E-mail: ewingo@aol.com
http://www.members.aol.com/ewingo
Expertise in compensation and classification.

1120 Wisconsin Technical College System Foundation
1 Foundation Circle
Waunakee, WI 53597-8914
608-849-2424
Fax: 608-849-2468
Educational consultant for educational institutions and businesses.

Loren Brumm, Executive Director

Africa

1121 Alexandra House School
King George V Avenue
Floreal
Mauritius
230-696-4108
Fax: 230-696-4108
E-mail:
admin@alexandrahouseschool.com
http://www.alexandrahouseschool.com
A private English Primary day school in Mauritius for boys and girls between 4 and 11 years of age. Cater for approximately 100 children and provide a British curriculum with a strong international flavour.

M Wrenn-Beejadhur, Principal

1122 American International School-Dhaka
United Nations Road Baridhara
Dhaka
Bangladesh
880-2-882-2414
Fax: 880-2-883-3175
E-mail: info@ais-dhaka.net
http://www.ais-dhaka.net
Provides a program based on American educational principles to students from an international community, creates an academic and social environment that challenges students to achieve their potential, become life-long learners and contribute to changing global society.

Kyra Buchko, President
Diane Lindsey, Vice President

1123 American International School-Johannesburg
Private Bag X 4
Bryanston 2021
Republic of South Africa
011 464 1505
Fax: 27-11-464-1327
E-mail: info@aisj-jhb.com
http://www.aisj-jhb.com
Serves a diverse community of students from around the world and provides a challenging education emphasizing academic excellence through a collaborative partnership with families and staff. Our program inspires and prepares the students to become responsible world citizens with a passion for life long learning.

Andy Page-Smith, Director
Ellinor Parkes, Admissions Coordinator

1124 American International School-Zambia
PO Box 31617
Lusaka
Zambia
260-211-260509 (10
Fax: 260-211-260-538
E-mail: SpecialPerson@aislusaka.org
http://www.aislusaka.org
Committed to being a leading IB World School, offering a balanced, academically rigorous and internationally recognized college preparatory education and seeks to enable its students to become successful, lifelong learners, as well as humane, self-directed, confident and well-rounded individuals.

Chris Mulind, Director
Jim Anderson, Secondary Principal

1125 American School of Kinshasa
Unit 31550
APO AE
09828

243-884-6619
Fax: 243-884-1161
E-mail: irene.epp@gmail.com
http://www.tasok.cd
rawing on the strengths of a committed and culturally diverse community, The American School of Kinshasa aims to provide a high quality American primary and secondary education for English speaking students living in the Democratic Republic of Congo

Irene Epp, Superintendent
Fiona M Merali, Business Manager

1126 American School-Tangier
Rue Christophe Colomb
Tangier 9000
Morocco
212-39 93 98 27/28
Fax: 212-39 94 75 35
E-mail: ast@tangeroise.net.ma
http://http://www.theamericanschooloftangier.com/
An independent, coeducational day and boarding school which offers an educational program from prekindergarten through grade 12 for students of all nationalities.

Brian Horvath, Head of School

1127 American School-Yaounde
BP 7475
Yaounde
Cameroon
237-2223-0421
Fax: 237-2223-6011
E-mail: school@asoy.org
http://asoy.org
Ensures that all students achieve high academic success, demonstrate critical thinking skills, and become responsible and compassionate, global citizens prepared for their next stage in life; as gained through an enriched, American curriculum and offered in a challenging, secure, and diverse environment.

Paul Sheppard, School Director

1128 Arundel School
28 Arundel School Road
PO Box MP 91 Mount Pleasant
Harere, Zimbabwe
263-4-335654/7
Fax: 263 4 335671 / 304
E-mail: head@arundel.ac.zw
http://http://www.arundel.ac.zw/
Gives all students the opportunity to reach their full potential, both in and out of the classroom. This is achieved through an active educational program, which encompasses the search for excellence in the fields of academic endeavour, culture, sports and personal development.

G Alcock, Principal

1129 Arusha International School
PO Box 733
Moshi, Kilimanjaro
Tanzania
255-27-275-5004
Fax: 255-27-275-2877
E-mail: director@ismoshi.net
http://www.ismoshi.org
Offers a fully accredited, academically rigorous international education for students of ages three to nineteen years old.

Barry Sutherland, CEO
Bob Woods, Director

1130 Asmara International Community School
117-19 Street, #6
PO Box 4941, Asmara
Eritrea

291-1-161-705
Fax: 291-1-161-705
E-mail: johnston@gmail.com
http://www.aicsasmara.com
Grade levels pre K-12.

Paul Johnston, Director

1131 Banda School
PO Box 24722
Nairobi
Kenya 00502
254-20-8891220/260
Fax: 254-20-8890004
E-mail: bandaschool@swiftkenya.com
http://www.bandaschool.com
Meet the educational needs of children living in and around Nairobi whose parents required a Preparatory School education for their children but who did not wish them to go to boarding school overseas.

Michael D Dickson, Headmaster
W Rutter, Deputy Head

1132 Bishop Mackenzie International Schools
PO Box 102
Lilongwe
Malawi
265-1-756-364
Fax: 265-1-751-374
E-mail: info@bmismw.com
http://bmis.ecis.org
The mission of the school is to prepare students to become responsible, self-reliant, contributing and productive citizens of our ever-changing world.

Peter Todd, Director
Janette Johnson, Primary Head Teacher

1133 Braeburn High School
Kisongo Campus
Gitanga Road
PO Box 45112 GPO Nairobi
Kenya 00100
254-20-5018000
Fax: 254-20-3872310
E-mail: andy.hill@braeburn.ac.ke
http://www.braeburn.com
This is a co-educational international boarding school following the British National Curriculum (University of Cambridge International General Certificate of Secondary Education Examinations IGCSE), with boarding options.

R E Diaper, Principal
Mr. Terry L. K. Childs, CEO

1134 Braeburn School
Gitanga Road
PO Box 45112 GPO Nairobi
Kenya 00100
254-722 68557
Fax: 254-2-572310
E-mail: scott.webber@braeburn.ac.ke
http://www.braeburn.com
This school caters to close to 600 children from 61 different countries.

R E Diaper, Principal
Mr. Terry L. K. Childs, CEO

1135 British International School Cairo
km 38, Cairo-Alex Desert Road
Beverly Hills, 6th of October
Egypt, EG
202-3859-2000
Fax: 202-3859-1720
E-mail: info@bisc.edu.eg
http://www.bisc.edu.eg
The School was established in 1976 to provide a balanced and challenging education based on British principles and curricula to meet the needs of the children of the expatriate British and Anglo-Egyptian communities; children from the Commonwealth and other countries with educational systems based upon British standards; children of the English-speaking Egyptian

community and other nationalities tied to British-type schooling.

Simon O'Grady, Assistant
Ahmed Ezz, Principal

1136 British School-Lom
BP 20050
Lome
Togo
228-222-606
Fax: 228-222-498
E-mail: admin@bsl.tg
http://www.bsl.tg
We value not only academic success but encourage talent of all kinds, whether in academic studies, art, drama, music or games; and that we take the position that the pupil who is kind and helpful, who has a positive attitude to school life and fellow pupils, is considered every bit as worthwhile as the brilliant scholar, artist or athlete.

1137 British School-Lom
BP 20050
Lome
Togo
228-226-46-06
Fax: 228-226-49-89
E-mail: bsl@cafe.tg
http://www.bsl.tg
This school offers an English based curriculum for 120 day students and 95 boarding students (110 boys; 105 girls), ages 4-18. The school is an independent, co-educational day and boarding school. External exams from the University of London and Cambridge-UK plus International Baccalaureate (IB) is offered. Applications needed to teach include science, pre-school, French, math, social sciences, administration, Spanish, reading, German, English and physical education.

1138 British Yeoward School
Parque Taoro
Tenerife
Spain, ES 38400
00-34-922-384685
Fax: 00-34-922-37-35-65
E-mail: office@yeowardschool.org
http://www.yeowardschool.org
The International British Yeoward School provides a high quality British education for children of all ages in an open, multi-cultural environment; allowing each child to achieve their full potential in a positive learning community

Karen Hernndez, Head of Primary Grades
Alan Halstead, Head of School

1139 Broadhurst Primary School
Private Bag BR 114 Broadhurst
Garborone
Botswana, BW
267-3971-221
Fax: 267-307987
E-mail: broadhurst@info.bw
http://www.info.bw
To create, together with the family, a caring environment of learning and experience, in which children may develop their potential to the full, may acquire the knowledge and skills to equip them for living, may experience the best that the human spirit has achieved, may develop respect for themselves, for other people and the world around them and have the courage to make a difference to future

Rehana Khan, Head Teacher
Michael Eisen, Deputy Headteacher

1140 Brookhouse Preparatory School
PO Box 24987- 00502
Nairobi
Kenya

254-20-2430260
Fax: 254-20-891641
E-mail: info@brookhouse.ac.ke
http://http://www.brookhouse.ac.ke/index.asp
Provides education in general computer literacy.

Eric Mulind, School Coordinator

1141 Cairo American College
PO Box 39
Maadi 11431
Cairo, EG 11431
20-2-755-5505
Fax: 20-2-2519-6584
E-mail: support@cacegypt.org
http://www.cacegypt.org
Cairo American College is a world class learning environment that affirms the voice, passions and talents of students and inspires them to use their hearts and minds as global citizens.

Nivine Captan-Amr, Board Chair
Elizabeth Bredin, Secretary

1142 Casablanca American School
Route de la Mecque,Lotissement Ougo
Casablanca, Morocco 20150
212-22-214-115
Fax: 212-22-212-488
E-mail: cas@cas.ac.ma
http://www.cas.ac.ma
To offer the best possible U.S. and international university preparatory education program, curriculum and instruction for its students.

Simohamed Erroussafi, President
Karima Abisourour, Vice President

1143 Cavina School
PO Box 43090
Nairobi
Kenya
254-2-3866011
Fax: 254-2-3866676
E-mail: cavina@iconnect.co.ke
http://www.cavina.ac.ke
Cavina aims to develop many qualities in the children who come through her gates - academic excellence, an inquiring mind, a sense of moral and social responsibility, and most of all a recognition of their relationship with their Creator who has revealed Himself through His son Jesus.

Massie Bloofield, Headmaster/Managing Director

1144 Dakar Academy
BP 3189 Route des Peres Maristes
Dakar, Senegal
West Africa
221-33-832-06-82
Fax: 221-33-832-17-21
E-mail: office@dakar-academy.org
http://www.dakar-academy.org
Dakar Academy exists to partner in the advancement of the Kingdom of God through serving missionary families by providing education services for their children

Charlie Campbell, Chairman
Joseph Rosa, Director

1145 Greensteds School
Private Bag
Nakuru
Kenya
254 50 50770
Fax: 254 50 50775
E-mail: office@greenstedsschool.com
http://http://www.greenstedsschool.com/
An international school for boys and girls.

MP Bentley, Headmaster

1146 Harare International School
66 Pendennis Road
Mount Pleasant
Harare, Zimbabwe
(263 4) 870514/5
Fax: 263-4-883-371
E-mail: his@his.ac.zw
http://www.his-zim.com
Grade levels prekindergarten through twelfth, with enrollment of 376.

Marcel Gerrmann, Board Chair
Shannon Brauchli, Vice Chair

1147 Hillcrest Secondary School
PO Box 24819
Nairobi
Kenya 00502
254-20-882-222
Fax: 254-20-882-350
E-mail: admin@hillcrest.ac.ke
http://http://www.hillcrest.ac.ke/secondary/
Mixed boarding school.

Christopher Drew, Head Teacher

1148 International Community School-Addis Ababa
PO Box 70282
Addis Adaba
Ethiopia
251-11-3-711-544
Fax: 251-11-371-0722
E-mail: info@icsaddis.edu.et
http://http://www.icsaddis.edu.et/
An independent, coeducational day school which offers an educational program from prekindergarten through grade 12 for students of all nationalities.

Jim Laney, Director

1149 International School-Kenya
PO Box 14103
Nairobi
Kenya 00800
254-20-418-3622
Fax: 254-20-418-3272
E-mail: info@isk.ac.ke
http://www.isk.ac.ke
Students from many backgrounds go to this school, which prepares them for successful transitions to other schools and universities around the world, offering both a North American Hogh School Diploma as well as the International Baccalaureate Diploma to its graduates.

John Roberts, Director
Jodi Lake, Curriculum Coordinator

1150 International School-Moshi
PO Box 733
Moshi, Kilimanjaro
Tanzania
255-27-275-5004
Fax: 255-27-275-2877
E-mail: school@ismoshi.org
http://www.ismoshi.org
The school inspires individuals to be lifelong learners in a global community.

Bob Woods, Director of ISM
Keiron White, Head, Moshi Campus

1151 International School-Tanganyika
United Nations Road
PO Box 2651, Dar es Salaam
Tanzania
255-22-2151817/8
Fax: 255-22-2152077
E-mail: ist@raha.com
http://www.istafrica.com
IST aspires to provide an outstanding international education. We value and respect cultural diversity and embrace the people and natural environment of Tanzania. Within this safe, secure and caring community students

reach their full potential as citizens of the world.

David Shawver, Director
Nazir Thawer, General Manager

1152 John F Kennedy International School
CH-3792 Saanen
Switzerland
41-033-744-1372
Fax: 41- 033-744-8982
E-mail: lovell@jfk.ch
http://www.jfk.ch
Boarding day school for boys and girls aged 5-14 years.

William Lovell, Co-Director
Sandra Lovell, Co-Director

1153 Kabira International School
PO Box 34249
Kampala
Uganda
256-0414-530-472
Fax: 256-0414-543-444
E-mail: office@kisu.com
http://www.kabiraschool.com
Grade levels Pre-K through 8, school year - September - July

Emma Whitney, Admissions
Elaine Whelen, Principal

1154 Kestrel Manor School
Ring Road Westlands
PO Box 14489, Nairobi
Kenya 00200
254-20-3740-311
E-mail: info@kestrelmanorschool.com
http://www.kestrelmanorschool.com
Coeducational school for children Kindergarten through secondary schooling.

1155 Khartoum American School
PO Box 699
Khartoum
Sudan
249-15-577-0105
Fax: 249-183-512044
E-mail: kas@krtams.org
http://www.krtams.org
An independent, coeducational day school which offers an educational program from prekindergarten through grade 12 for students of all nationalities.

Gregory Hughes, Superintendent
Brad Waugh, Principal

1156 Kigali International School
Caisse Sociale Estates, Gaculiro
BP 6558
Kigali, Rwanda
250-0783307282
Fax: 250-72128
E-mail: office.kics@gmail.com
http://www.kicsrw.org
Non-profit, co-educational day school

Bryan Hixson, Chairman
Mark Thiessen, Vice Chairman

1157 Kingsgate English Medium Primary School
Box 169
Mafeteng, 900 Lesotho
Africa
Kingsgate is the only non-denominational primary school in the district. The curriculum is English-based offered to a total of 460 day students (240 boys; 220 girls), PreK-7. Overseas teachers are welcome with the length of stay being one year, with housing provided. Applications needed to teach include pre-school and reading.

M Makhothe, Principal

1158 Kisumu International School
PO Box 1276
Kisumu
Kenya
254-35-21678
E-mail: admin@kis.co.ke
http://www.kisumu.braeburn.com
This school is located on the shores of Lake Victoria and offers a unique education to students of all nationalities and cultural backgrounds. The total enrollment of the school is 35 day students, in grades K-7. The school does participate in the teacher exchange programs, with the length of stay being two years with housing provided by the school. Applications needed to teach include science, preschool, math, social sciences, English and physical education.

Neena Sharma, Principal

1159 Lincoln Community School
American Embassy Accra
N126/21 Dedeibaa Street
Abelemkpe, Accra
Ghana, West Africa
233 30 277 4018
Fax: 233 302 78 09 85
E-mail: headofschool@lincoln.edu.gh
http://www.lincoln.edu.gh
is committed to inspiring students to achieve the highest standards of intellectual and personal development through a stimulating and comprehensive program.

Dennis Larkin, Head of School
Sanjay Rughani Tanzanian, President

1160 Lincoln International School of Uganda
PO Box 4200
Kampala
Uganda
256-41-4200374/8/9
Fax: 256-41-200303
E-mail: dtodd@isumail.ac.ug
http://www.lincoln.ac.ug
Grade levels Pre-K through 12, school year August - June

Daniel Todd, Dean of Studied/Admission
Jim Campbell, Chairman

1161 Maru A Pula School
Plot 4725
Maruapula Way
Botswana 00045
267-391-2953
Fax: 267-397-3338
E-mail: principal.map@gmail.com
http://www.maruapula.org/
Maru-a-Pula is a dynamic, world-class school rooted in Botswana. We offer a rigorous curriculum that prepares students for entry to highly selective universities and to pursue challenging careers. Through programmes emphasizing self-discipline and community service, each student learns personal and social responsibility.

Andrew S Taylor, Principal

1162 Mombasa Academy
PO Box 86487
Mombasa
Kenya, KE
254-11-471629
Fax: 254-11-221484
E-mail:
msaacademy@swiftmombasa.com
http://www.msaacademy.com
Our aim is to help our pupils to reach their true potential. Within the academic and extra-curricular frameworks, staff offer pupils considerable personal support; warm and productive working relations are a distinguishing feature of our community and are instrumental in helping each girl and boy on the road towards maturity and self-fulfillment

Kishor Joshi, Headmaster
FJ Bentley, Founder

1163 Northside Primary School
PO Box 897
Gaborone
Botswana
267-395-2440
Fax: 267-395-3573
E-mail: administration@northsideschool.net
http://www.northsideschool.net
In Gaborone, Botswana, Northside Primary School provides education in English and serves the needs of primary school children of all nationalities.

Mandy Watson, Headteacher

1164 Nsansa School
PO Box 70322
Ndola
Zambia
26-2-611753
Fax: 26-2-618465
This school offers an English curriculum to 185 day students (96 boys; 124 girls), in grades K-7. Length of stay for overseas teachers is one year with housing provided. Student/teacher ratio is 20:1.

Nel Mather, Principal

1165 Peterhouse
Private Bag 3741
Marondera
Zimbabwe
263 (0)279 - 22200
Fax: 263 (0)279 - 24200
E-mail: peterhouse@peterhouse.co.zw
http://www.peterhouse.org
This Anglican school offers an English based curriculum for 19 day students and 790 boarding students (535 boys; 255 girls), in Form I-Form VI. The school is willing to participate in a teacher exchange program with the length of stay being one year, with housing provided. Applications needed to teach include science, math, and physical education.

JB Calderwood, Rector

1166 Rabat American School
1 Bis Rue Emir Ibn Abdelkade
Agdal, Rabat
Morocco 10000
212-537-671-476
Fax: 212-537-670
Fax: 212-537-670-963
E-mail: info@ras.ma
http://www.ras.ma
We provide our students with a breadth of experiences which encourage them to realize their full potential and allow them to acquire the knowledge, skills, character, and confidence to contribute positively and responsibly to an ever-changing, interconnected world.

Paul W Johnson, Director

1167 Rift Valley Academy
PO Box 80
Kijabe, 00220
Kenya
254-20-3246-249
Fax: 254-20-3246-111
E-mail: rva@rva.org
http://www.rva.org
RVA is a Christian boarding school located in central Kenya. The academy, a branch of Africa Inland Mission International, exists to provide a quality education in a nurturing environment for the children of missionaries serving in Africa.

Roy E Entwistle, Principal
Tim Cook, Superintendent

1168 Rosslyn Academy
PO Box 14146
Nairobi
Kenya 00800
254-20-263-5294
Fax: 254-20-263-5281
E-mail: info@rosslynacademy.com
http://www.rosslynacademy.com
The purpose of Rosslyn Academy is to provide a K-12 North American and Christian-oriented educational program for children of missionaries. Rosslyn also welcomes children from privately sponsored families who are in sympathy with the philosophy of the school.

Phil Dow, Superintendent
Don McGavran, Director of Operations

1169 Sandford English Community School
PO Box 30056 MA
Addis Ababa
Ethiopia
251-11-123-38-92
Fax: 251-11-123-3728
E-mail: admission@sandfordschool.org
http://www.sandfordschool.org
A co-educational, non-boarding, nursery to pre University institution. Its committed to providing a standard of education that is accepted within Ethiopia and by the international community.

Jon D P Lane, Head of Primary School
Tsegaye Kassa, Senior Manager

1170 Schutz American School
51 Schutz Street
PO Box 1000
Alexandria, Egypt 21111
(20) (3) 576-2205
Fax: (20) (3) 576-0229
E-mail: jlujan@schutzschool.org.eg
http://www.schutzschool.org.eg
A single campus houses PreK-3 through grade twelve in two main classroom buildings and an auditorium/ classroom complex, as well as the administrative center, dining room, resident staff housing, clinic, art room, computer labs, libraries and snack bar. Sports facilities on the campus include basketball, volleyball, tennis and football courts, a half-size grass soccer pitch, and a swimming pool and weight training room.

Dr Joyce Lujan, Head of School
Nathan Walker, Upper School Principal

1171 Sifundzani School
PO Box A286, Swazi Plaza
Mbabane
Swaziland
268-404-2465
Fax: 268-404-0320
E-mail: sifundzani@realnet.co.sz
A coeducational day school which offers an educational program from grades 1 through 10 for students of all nationalities.

Ella Magongo, Principal

1172 Sir Harry Johnston Primary School
Kalimbuka Road
Zomba PO Box 52
Malawi
265-1525280
Fax: 265 888202374
E-mail: admin@shjzomba.com
http://www.shjzomba.com

Una Barras-Hargan, Headteacher

1173 St. Barnabas College
34 Langeberg Avenue Bostmont Johann
PO Box 88188 Newclare
South Africa 02112
011-27-474-2055
Fax: 011-27-474-2249

E-mail: theronn@stbarnabas.co.za
http://www.stbarnabas.co.za
St Barnabas College is a co-educational secondary school in Johannesburg. It is well known as a centre of excellence. The school's mission is to provide quality secondary education to young people, the main criterion for admission being intellectual potential and the motivation to succeed.

Glynn Blignaut, Headmaster
Faizel Panker, Deputy Headmaster

1174 St. Mary's School
Rhapta Road, PO Box 40580- 00100
Nairobi
Kenya
254-020-4444569
Fax: 254-020-4446191
E-mail: info@stmarys.ac.ke
http://www.stmarys.ac.ke
We are a Catholic Private School committed to our international character in the provision of a spiritual, intellectual and physical education. We aim at developing the gifts of the young in an atmosphere which encourages the ethos of self-expression and mutual respect with a view to their facing the future responsibly, with confidence and courage.

John Awiti, Head of School
Rosemary Abuodha Omogo, Deputy Principal

1175 St. Paul's College
St. Paul's United Theological College
Po Private Bag
Limuru
Kenya 00217
254 - 20 - 2020505
Fax: 254-66-73033
E-mail:
assistantregistrar@stpaulslimuru.ac.ke
http://www.stpaulslimuru.ac.ke/
The school prepares men and women for ministry in the Christian Church and present day society.

Samuel Kobia, Chancellor
Joseph Galgalo, Vice Chancellor

1176 Tigoni Girls Academy
Box 10
Limuru
Kenya
This Academy is a small, closely knit community of individuals from different cultures in which physical, emotional, creative and intellectual development is fortified in all aspects of daily life. Total enrollment is 40 boarding students, ages 11-16. Applications from overseas include science, math, social sciences, French, Spanish and English. Length of stay for overseas teachers is 2 years with housing provided. The Academy is affiliated with the Church of England.

Duncan Kelly, Principal

1177 Waterford-Kamhlaba United World College
PO Box 52
Mbabane
Swaziland
011-268-422-0866
Fax: 011-268-422-0088
E-mail: admissions@waterford.sz
http://www.waterford.sz/index.php
This school offers a curriculum based in English for 181 day students and 295 boarding (251 boys; 226 girls), in grades 6-12. Overseas teachers length of stay is three years with housing provided. Applications needed to teach include math, English, and physical education.

Laurence Nodder, Principal
Bruce Wells, Deputy Principal

1178 Westwood International School
PO Box 2446
Gabarone
Botswana
011-267-390-6736
Fax: 011-267-390-6734
E-mail: westwood-admissions@info.bw
http://www.westwoodis.com
Westwood International School shall provide students with a quality international education that shall effectively prepare them for access to tertiary study and the world of work, and enable them to confidently meet future challenges as life long learners

Phyllis Hildebrandt, Principal
Michael Francis, Director

1179 Windhoek International School
Private Bag
Windhoek
Namibia 16007
264-61-241-783
Fax: 264-61-243-127
E-mail: k.jarman@wis.edu.na
http://www.wis.edu.na
The Windhoek International School prepares its students to be inquiring, knowledgeable and caring participants in the global arena through an international curriculum of the highest standard. WIS embraces the diversity of its students from the international community and Namibia, in an atmosphere of mutual respect, tolerance and educational enrichment for all

Catherine O'Connor-Smith, Secretary
Neville Field, Chairperson

Asia, Pacific Rim & Australia

1180 Aiyura International Primary School
PO Box 407
Ukarumpa Papua
New Guinea

Perry Bradford, Principal

1181 Ake Panya International School
158/1 Moo 3 Hangdong-Samoeng Road
Banpong, Hangdong, Chiang Mai 50230
Thailand
66-53-36-5303
Fax: 66-53-365-304
E-mail: akepanya@cm.ksc.co.th
http://www.akepanya.co.th
Grade levels 1-12, school year August - June

Barry Sutherland, Headmaster
Holly Shaw, Director of Studies

1182 Alotau International Primary School
PO Box 154
Alotau, Milne Bay Province
Papua New Guinea
675-641-1078
Fax: 675-641-1627
E-mail: alotauis@iea.ac.pg
http://www.iea.ac.pg

Lucy Kula, Principal

1183 Amelia Earhart Intermediate School
Unit 5166
APO AP 96368
Okinawa
011-81-611-734-132
Fax: 011-81-611-734-720
E-mail: aeis_okinawa@pac.dodea.edu
http://www.earhart-is.pac.dodea.edu
Success in Education is a Partnership in Responsibility characterized by the opportunities and the guidance necessary to motivate learners, the desire and ability to be successful in human interactions, to access and pro-

cess information, and to accept personal responsibility for all decisions made throughout one's lifetime.

Deborah Carlson, Principal

1184 American International School-Dhaka

P.O. Box: 6106
Gulshan, Dhaka 1212
Bangladesh
880-2-882-2452
Fax: 880-2-882-3175
E-mail: info@ais-dhaka.net
http://www.ais-dhaka.net
Provides a program based on American educational principles to students from an international community, creates an academic and social environment that challenges students to achieve their potential, become life-long learners and contribute to changing global society.

Richard Boerner, Superintendent
Kyra Buchko, President

1185 American International School-Guangzhou

No 3 Yan Yu Street S
Ersha Island, Yuexiu District
Guangzhou PR China 51010
86-20-8735-3392
Fax: 86-20-8735-3339
E-mail: admissions@aisgz.org
http://http://www.aisgz.org/
Prepares students for entrance into the very best universities in the world is enhanced by being in the cultural center of Guangzhou and Southern China.

Joseph Stucker, Director
Katherine Farrell, Chair

1186 American School-Bombay

SF 2 G Block
Bandra Kurla Complex
Mumbai 400 0
91 22 6772 7272
Fax: 91 22 6252 6666
E-mail: admissions@asbindia.org
http://www.asbindia.org
ASB delivers a dynamic educational program that encourages each student to achieve her or his highest potential. While ASB is a U.S. style school, the Indian setting and multi-national community, representing over 51 countries, brings children who have varied experiences together to learn in a rich and unique environment

Paul M Fochtman, Superintendent

1187 American School-Guangzhou (China)

Number 3 Yan Yu Street S
Ersha Island, Yuexiu District
Guangzhou, China 51010
8620-8735-3393
Fax: 8620-8735-3339
E-mail: admissions@aisgz.org
http://http://www.aisgz.org/
An independent, coeducational day school which offers an educational program from kindergarten through grade 12

Joseph Stucker, Director
Paul Wood, Principal

1188 American School-Japan

1-1 Nomizu 1
Chofu-shi, Tokyo
Japan 182-0
0422-34-5300
Fax: 0422-34-5303
E-mail: info@asij.ac.jp
http://www.asij.ac.jp
The American School in Japan is a private, coeducational day school which offers an educational program from nursery through grade 12 for students of all nationalities, but it primarily serves the American community living in the Tokyo area. The school was founded in 1902. The school year comprises 2 semesters extending from September to January and January to June.

Ed Ladd, Headmaster

1189 Aoba International School

2-10-34 Aobadai
Meguro-Ku, Tokyo
Japan 153-0-42
03-3461-1442
Fax: 81-3-3463-9873
E-mail: meguro@aobajapan.jp
http://www.aobaonline.jp
A co-educational school located on campuses in Meguro and Suginami. Over 550 students are enrolled in classes from pre-kindergarten to grade nine.

Neal Dilk, Head of School
Chiharu Uemura, VP

1190 Ashgabat International School

Berzengi, Ata Turk Street
Ashgabat
Turkmenistan
386-12-007870
Fax: 386-12-007871
E-mail: ashgabat@qsi.org
http://tkm.qsi.org
Offers high quality education in the English language for elementary students from three years through thirteen years of age.

Brad Goth, Director

1191 Bali International School

PO Box 3259
Denpasar
Bali, Indonesia
62-361-288-770
Fax: 62-361-285-103
E-mail: admin@baliis.net
http://www.baliinternationalschool.com
Provides educational excellence in a supportive, secure environment, preparing students to thrive and succeed as responsible citizens in a changing world. Offers the three IB Programs (PYP, MYP and DP) and is accredited by WASC.

Chris Akin, Director
Russell McGrath, PS-12 Assistant Principal

1192 Bandung Alliance International School

Jalan Bujanggamanik Kav 2
Kota Baru Parahyangan
Bandung, Indonesia 40553
62-22-8681-3949
Fax: 62-22-8681-3953
E-mail: info@baisedu.org
http://www.baisedu.org
BAIS operates as a private non-profit school to serve the international community. BAIS provides quality education in the traditions of classic, conservative ethics and values.

Pete Simano, Director
Charity Lamertha, Elementary Principal

1193 Bandung International School

Jl Suria Sumantri No 61
Bandung
West Java, Indonesia 40164
62-22-201-4995
Fax: 62-22-201-2688
E-mail: bisadmin@poboxes.com
http://www.bisdragons.com
At Bandung International Scholl, it is our vision to be a preeminent school providing world class secular education in the English language to the children of expatriates and others while maintaining strong links with the Indonesian community

Henri Behelmans, Head of School
Mark Holland, Chair

1194 Bangalore International School

Geddalahalli, Hennur Bagalur Road
Kothanur Post
Bangalore, India 560 0
91-802-846-5060
Fax: 91-802-846-5059
E-mail: info@bisedu.co.in
http://www.bangaloreinternationalschool.com
Provides internationally recognized standards of education with an India ethos and enable students to fulfill their potential in a culturally rich atmosphere.

Anuradha Monga, Principal

1195 Bangkok Patana School

643 Lasalle road Sukhumvit 105 Bang
Bangkok, Thailand 10260
6602-398-0200
Fax: 6602-399-3179
E-mail: reception@patana.ac.th
http://www.patana.ac.th
We are an academically directed school, focussed on our commitment to offer all of our students the best intellectual and physical preparation for higher education.

Tej Bunnag, Chairman
Kulvadee Siribhadra, Director

1196 Beijing BISS International School

No 17, Area 4 An Zhen Xi Li
Chaoyang District, Beijing
China 10002
86-10-6443-3151
Fax: 86-10-6443-3156
E-mail: Admissions@biss.com.cn
http://www.biss.com.cn
To educate and empower our students to attain personal excellence and positively impact the world.

Chan Ching Oi, CEO
Ettie Zilber, Head of School

1197 Bob Hope Primary School

Unit 5166
APO AP 96368-5166
Okinawa, Japan 96368-5166
11-81-611-734-0093
Fax: 11-81-98-934-6806
E-mail: bhps.okinawa@pac.dodea.edu
http://www.bob-hope-ps.pac.dodea.edu
The Bob Hope Primary School community is committed to teaching basic skills using developmentally appropriate strategies.

Jim Journey, Principal
Luldes Giraud, Vice Principal

1198 Bogor Expatriate School

PO Box 258
Jalan Papandayan 7, Bogor 16151
Indonesia
62-251-324360
Fax: 62-251-328512
Mission is to provide opportunities to foster positive attitudes towards learning.

Chris Rawlins, Head of School
Lance Kelly, Principal

1199 Bontang International School

15 Roszel Road
Po Box 5910
Princeton, NJ 08543
62-548551176
E-mail: iss@iss.edu
An international school with an English/Japanese based curriculum for twenty day students (6 boys; 14 girls), grades PreK-8. Student/teacher ration 5:1.

Roger Hove, Executive Vice President

1200 Brent International School-Manila
Brentville Subdivision
Mamplasan, Bian, Laguna
Philippines 04024
63 (049) 511-4330
Fax: 632-633-8420
E-mail: webmaster@brent.edu.ph
http://www.brent.edu.ph
Brent Schools, in a Christian ecumenical environment in the Philippines, are committed to develop individual students as responsible global citizens and leaders in their respective communities, with a multicultural and international perspective, and equipped for entry to colleges and universities throughout the world.

Dick B Robbins, Headmaster
Jeffrey W Hammett, Deputy Headmaster

1201 Brent School
Brent Road
PO Box 35, Baguio City
Philippines 02600
63 (074) 442-3628
Fax: 63 (074) 442-2260
E-mail: webmaster@brent.edu.ph
http://www.brentschoolbaguio.com
Brent Schools, in a Christian ecumenical environment in the Philippines, are committed to develop individual students as responsible global citizens and leaders in their respective communities, with a multicultural and international perspective, and equipped for entry to colleges and universities throughout the world.

Dick B Robbins, Headmaster
Ursula Banga-an Daoey, Deputy Head

1202 British International School
Bintayo Jaya Sektor IX JI
Raya Jomabang Ciledug Pondok Aren
Jakarta, ID 15227
62-21-745-1670
Fax: 62-21-745-1671
E-mail: enquiries@bis.or.id
http://www.bis.or.id
The new premises and facilities enable the school to excel further in the range of opportunities and experiences that can be offered to its students.

Christian Barkei, Principal
Brian Dallamore, Chairman

1203 British School Manila
36th Street University Park Forth B
Fort Bonifacio Global City
Taguig, PH
63 2 860 4800
Fax: 63 2 860 4900
E-mail:
admissions@britishschoolmanila.org
http://www.britishschoolmanila.org
The British School Manila will deliver the highest standard of education in the Philippines for British children and for English speaking children of other nationalities The British School Manila provides outstanding education for English speaking children of all nationalities aged 3-18, based on an adapted form of the National Curriculum of England, and the I.B. Diploma

Chris Mantz, Head of School
Glenn Hardy, Head of Primary School

1204 British School-Muscat
PO Box 1907
Ruwi
Oman 00112
0096824600842
Fax: 00968 24601062
E-mail: admin@britishschoolmuscat.com
http://www.britishschoolmuscat.com
The Vision of the British School-Muscat is to offer the highest quality British education to children of wide ranging abilities and nationalities. It values cultural diversity and provides a caring, innovative and stimulating environment, realizing the full potential and celebrating the success of every student. The School's curriculum will also develop the child as a whole person, provide them with learning-to-learn skills and will prepare them to lead a successful life in an inter-cultural wor

Kai Vacher, Principal
Deirdre Selway, Registrar

1205 Calcutta International School Society
18 Lee Road
Calcutta 700 020
India
http://www.calcuttais.edu.in
This school offers an English-based curriculum to 480 day students (230 boys; 250 girls), grades Nursery-12. CIS follows GCE London Curriculum. The cultures represented by the student body include expatriates, NRIs, local children. The student body is mainly Indians. Highly qualified individuals offering excellent results. The school is willing to participate in a teacher exchange program with the length of stay being 1-2 years, with no housing provided.

N Chatterjee, Principal
L Chaturvedi, Faculty Head

1206 Caltex American School
CPI Rumbal
Pekanbaru, Sumatra Riau
Indonesia
62-765-995-501
Fax: 62-765-996-321
Grade level preK through 8.

Daniel Hovde, Superintendent

1207 Camberwell Grammar School
55 Mout Albert Road
Canterbury 3126, Victoria
Australia
61 3 9835 1777
Fax: 61 3 9836 0752
E-mail: registrar@cgs.vic.edu.au
http://http://www.cgs.vic.edu.au/index.asp
Independent boys school.

CF Black, Principal

1208 Canadian Academy
4-1 Koyo Cho Naka
Higashinada-Ku, Kobe
Japan 658-0-32
81-78-857-0100
Fax: 81-78-857-3250
E-mail: hdmstr@canacad.ac.jp
http://www.canacad.ac.jp/canacad/welcome.html
Canadian Academy inspires students to inquire, reflect, and choose to compassionately impact the world throughout their lives.

Fred Wesson, Headmaster
Charles Kite, Assistant Headmaster

1209 Canadian School-India
14/1 Kodigehalli Main Road
Sahakar Nagar, Bangalore 560 092
India
91-80-343-8414
Fax: 91-80-343-6488
E-mail: csib@vsnl.com
http://www.canschoolindia.org
Grade levels K-13, school year August - June

T Alf Mallin, Principal

1210 Canberra Grammar School
40 Monaro Crescent
Red Hill
Australia ACT 2
02-6260-9700
Fax: 02-6260-9701
E-mail: headmaster@cgs.act.edu.au
http://www.cgs.act.edu.au
To develop a cultured man, ready for today's world and the future, balanced in intellectual, spiritual, emotional and physical aspects, with a love of learning and a willingness to serve fellow students and the wider community

Justin Garrick, Headmaster
Alan Ball, Head of Senior School

1211 Carmel School-Hong Kong
10 Borrett Road
Mid-Levels
Hong Kong
852-2964-1600
Fax: 852-2813-4121
E-mail: admin@carmel.edu.hk
http://www.carmel.edu.hk
Carmel School is committed to providing children living in Hong Kong with the highest international standard of secular and Jewish education. Through small classes and individual attention, the school offers a supportive environment that develops students' confidence, imagination and skills, in both academic and social spheres.

Edwin Epstein, Head of School
Kaisha Chow, Operations Director

1212 Casa Montessori Internationale
17 Palm Avenue Forbes Park Makati
Etro Manila D-3117
Philippines
Pre-nursery, nursery and kindergarten classes.

Carina Lebron, Principal

1213 Cebu International School
Banilad Road
PO Box 735, Cebu City 6000
Philippines
(63 32)401-1900
Fax: (63 32) 401-1904
E-mail: deidref@cis.edu.ph
http://http://www.cis.edu.ph/main.aspx
The primary aim of Cebu International School is to develop well-balanced global citizens who are intelligent, dynamic, respectful of universal moral values within a multicultural environment, and able to cope responsibly in an ever-changing interdependent world.

Deidre Fischer, Superintendent
Jenny Basa, Dean of Student Services

1214 Central Java Inter-Mission School
Jl Nakula Sadewa Raya Number 55
Salatiga, Jateng
Indonesia 50722
62-298-311673
Fax: 62-298-321609
E-mail: office@mountainviewics.org
http://www.mountainviewics.org
Primary intent of the school is that all students be thoroughly exposed to Scripture and that they find and sustain a vital relationship to Jesus Christ through Holy Spirit.

Wllliam J Webb III, Superintendent
Kirk Thornton, Assistant Superintendent

1215 Central Primary School
Winston Churchill Avenue
Port Vila
Republic of Vanuatu
678-23122
Fax: 678-22526
E-mail: central@vanuatu.com.vu
http://www.central.herts.sch.uk
Meet the needs of children from most countries and to provide an equivalent level of ed-

ucation for local children in an 'English as a First Language' context.

John Path, Chairman
John Lee Solomon, PEO

1216 Chiang Mai International School

PO Box 38
13 Chetupon Road
Thailand, TH 50000
665-324-2027
Fax: 665-324-2455
E-mail: info@cmis.ac.th
http://www.cmis.ac.th
Encourage the development of students' abilities in critical, analytical, and independent thinking, demonstrated in fluent oral and written communication.

Lance Potter, Principal
Sinturong Pannavalee, Director

1217 Chinese International School

1 Hau Yuen Path
Braemar Hill, Hong Kong
China
852-2510-7288
Fax: 852-2510-7488
E-mail: cis_info@cis.edu.hk
http://www.cis.edu.hk
Committed to the achievement of academic excellence and is characterized and enriched by its dual-language program in Chinese and English.

Theodore S Faunce, Headmaster
Li Bin, Deputy Head of School

1218 Chittagong Grammar School

Sarson Valley, 448/B Joynagar,
Chiottagong
Bangladesh
88-031-632900
E-mail: cgslower@hotmail.com
http://www.chittagonggrammarschool.com
Dedicated to the total growth and development of each student. Provides the students a broad, challenging and sound education to enable children to achieve the highest standards of which they are capable.

Afran Sanchita, Teacher
Akther Sharmin, Teacher

1219 Colombo International School

28, Gregory's Road
Colombo 7
Sri Lanka
94-11-269-7587
Fax: 94-11-269-9592
E-mail: management@cis.lk
http://www.cis.lk
English medium co-educational day school with separate Infant, Junior and Secondary sections.

M.J. Chappell, Principal
Armyne Wirasinha, Chairman

1220 Concordia International School-Shanghai

999 Mingyue Road, Jinqiao, Pudong
Shanghai
201206, China
86-21-5899-0380
Fax: 86-21-5899-1685
E-mail: admissions@ciss.com.cn
http://www.ciss.com.cn
Concordia's vision to offer academic excellence in a faith-based, caring community finds its roots in the 150-year educational tradition of the Lutheran Church-Missouri Synod.

James Koerschen, Head of School
Carol Ann Tonn-Bourg, Director of Admissions

1221 Cummings Elementary School

Unit 5039
APO AP
Japan 96319-5039
81-3117-66-2226
Fax: 81-3117-62-5110
E-mail: pcumming@pac.dodea.edu
http://www.cummings-es.pac.dodea.edu
We, the community of Cummings Elementary School, are committed to guiding our students to become successful learners and responsible citizens in an ever-changing world

Scott Sterry, Principal

1222 Dalat School

11200 Penang
Tanjung Bunga
Malaysia
60-4-899-2105
Fax: 60-4-890-2141
E-mail: info@dalat.org
http://www.dalat.org
The mission of Dalat International School is to prepare young people to live fully for God in a rapidly changing world by enabling them to understand, evaluate, and reconcile that world with the foundation of God's unchanging values.

Karl Steinkamp, Director
Fred Colburn, High School Principal

1223 Dover Court Prep School

Dover Road
Singapore, 139644
Singapore
65-67757664
Fax: 65-67774165
E-mail: admin@dover.edu.sg
http://www.dovercourt.org
To teach goals of the learning process, which is facilitated through encouraging pupils to pose and solve problems, take risks, demonstrate responsible attitudes and behaviour, adopt a critical and self-evaluative approach to their work.

Maureen Roach, Director
Catherine Alliott, Chief Executive Officer

1224 Ela Beach International School

PO Box 1137
Boroko
Papua New Guinea
675-325-2183
Fax: 675-325-7925
E-mail: bmackinlay@temis.iea.ac.pg
This school consists of 262 boys and 222 girl day students in PreK-Grade 6. The length of stay for overseas teachers is three years with housing provided. School enrollment is made up of 260 PNG children, 224 non PNG children, overseas and PNG staff team teaching in mixed age group classrooms.

Bruce E Mackinlay, Principal

1225 Elsternwick Campus-Wesley College

577 Street Kilda Road
Melbourne
Australia 03004
61-3-8102-6100
Fax: 61 3 8102 6054
E-mail: stkildaroad@wesleycollege.net
http://www.wesleycollege.net
Wesley College is a coeducational school of the Uniting Church which has enriched the lives of thousands of young people, since it opened on 18 January 1866 as a boy's boarding school. In its 140 year history, it has experienced the influence of 14 principals, each of whom has in turn, enriched the life of the College.

Jack Moshakis, Executive Director
Helen Drennen, Principal

1226 Faisalabad Grammar School

Kohinoor Nagar
Faisalabad 728593
Pakistan
http://www.fgschools.edu.pk
This Islamic school offers a curriculum taught in both English and Urdu to 2,000 day students (1,000 boys; 1,000 girls), in Junior Nursery up to eighteen years of age. The school runs 50% of classes in Matriculation Streams Local, and 50% in 'O' and 'A' level University of Cambridge UK examinations. Applications needed to teach include science, math, English and computers, with the length of stay for overseas teachers being one year.

RY Saigol Sarfraz, Principal
N Akhtar, VP

1227 Faith Academy

MCPO Box 2016
Makati City
Philippines 00706
11-632-248-5000
Fax: 63-2-658-0026
E-mail: vanguard@faith.edu.ph
http://www.faith.edu.ph
Faith Academy envisions expanding children's educational delivery options to meet the needs of the missions enterprise throughout Asia.

Tom Hardeman, Superintendent
Mike Hause, Deputy Superindentent

1228 French International School

165 Blue Pool
Happy Valley, SAR, Hong Kong
China
852-257-76217
Fax: 852-257-79658
E-mail: lfi@lfis.edu.hk
http://www.fis.edu.hk
To provide, together with families, a nurturing, culturally diverse community that inspires our young people to realize their true potential as confident, independent learners and responsible global citizens with moral values and integrity.

Francis Cauet, Headmaster
Samuel Hureau, Administrator

1229 Fukuoka International School

3-18-50 Momochi
Sawara-ku, Fukuoka
Japan 00814-6
81-92-841-7601
Fax: 81-92-841-7602
E-mail: adminfis@fka.att.ne.jp
http://www.fis.ed.jp
To create a dynamic learning environment in which students can be educated in high international academic standards. We strive to be a model of unity in diversity in which the individual is respected in each student is challenged at his/her own level.

Linda Gush, Head of School
Daniel Habel, Dean of Students

1230 Garden International School

16 Jalan Kiara 3, Off Jalan Bukit K
Kuala Lumpur
Malaysia 50480
011-60-3-6209-6888
Fax: 011-60-3-6201-2468
E-mail: admissions@gardenschool.edu.my
http://www.gardenschool.edu.my
Grade levels Pre-K through eleventh.

Simon Mann, Principal
Dato' Loy Teik Ngan, Chairman

1231 Geelong Grammar School-Glamorgan
14 Douglas Street
Toorak, Victoria
Australia 03142
011-61-3-9829-1444
Fax: 011-61-3-9826-2829
E-mail: toorakcampus@ggs.vic.edu.au
http://www.ggs.vic.edu.au
Geelong Grammar School offers an exceptional Australian education. Our students are girls and boys who see the richness of the world through confident eyes.

Lisa Marchetti, Fundraising Coordinator
Stephen Meek, Principal

1232 German Swiss International School
11 Guildford Road, The Peak
Hong Kong
China
011-852-2849-6216
Fax: 011-852-2849-6347
E-mail: gsis@gsis.edu.hk
http://www.gsis.edu.hk
Encourage and foster the talents of our students - as well-rounded individuals, responsible team members and open-minded citizens of the 21st century.

Hans PeterNaef, COO
Jens-Peter Green, Principal

1233 Glenunga International High School
99 L'Estrange Street
Glenuga
South Australia 05064
011-61-8-8379-5629
Fax: 011-61-8-8338-2518
E-mail: glenunga@gihs.sa.edu.au
http://www.gihs.sa.edu.au
Grade levels 8-12.

Wendy Johnson, Principal
Jeremy Cogan, Deputy Principal

1234 Good Hope School-Kowloon
303 Clear Water Bay Road
Kowloon
Hong Kong
011-852- 2321-0250
Fax: 011-852- 2324-8242
E-mail: goodhope@ghs.edu.hk
http://www.ghs.edu.hk
Provides equal opportunities to develop their moral, intellectual, physical, social, emotional and artistic aspects of life.

Pauline Yuen, Supervisor
Paul Chow, Principal

1235 Goroka International School
PO Box 845
Goroka EHP
Papua New Guinea
011-675-732-1452
Fax: 011-675-732-2146
E-mail: gorokais@online.net.pg
http://www.iea.ac.pg
Provide education of a high academic standard from early childhood to grade 12.

James M Masa, Principal

1236 Hebron School-Lushington Hall
Lushington Hall, Ootacamund
Tamil Nadu
India 64300
11-91-42-3244-2372
Fax: 11-91-42-3244-1295
E-mail: admin@hebronooty.org
http://www.hebronooty.org
Independent, international Christian school.

Mark Noonan, Principal

1237 Hillcrest International School
PO Box 249
Sentani 99352
Papua, Indonesia
011-62-967-591460
Fax: 011-62-967-592673
E-mail: director@hismk.org
http://www.hismk.org
HIS is a Christian international school. Teachers must raise their own support, normally with a mission. Enrollment consists of 97 day students and 24 boarding (53 boys; 68 girls), in grades K-12.

Margaret Hartzler, Director
Ryan Kennedy, Director

1238 Hiroshima International School
3-49-1 Kurakake
Asakita-Ku
Hiroshima, Japan 739-1
011-81-82-843-4111
Fax: 011-81-82-843-6399
E-mail: info@hiroshima-is.ac.jp
http://www.hiroshima-is.ac.jp
The Hiroshima International School is an independent, coeducational day school which offers educational programs from preschool through grade 12. The school year comprises 2 semesters extending from early September to mid-June.

Peter MacKenzie, Principal

1239 Hokkaido International School
1-55, 5-Jo, 19-Chome
Hirahishi, Toyohira-Ku
Sapporo, Japan 062-0
011-81-11-816-5000
Fax: 011-81-11-816-2500
E-mail: his@his.ac.jp
http://www.his.ac.jp
A private, coeducational day and boarding school which offers an America-style education from preschool through grade 12.

Michael Branson, Headmaster
Eri Kashiwabara, Business Manager

1240 Hong Kong International School
1 Red Hill Road
Tai Tam, Hong Kong
Republic of China
011-852-3149-7000
Fax: 011-852-2813-8740
E-mail: Advancement@hkis.edu.hk
http://www.hkis.edu.hk
The Hong Kong International School is a private, Christian, coeducational day school which offers an educational program from pre-primary through grade 12 for students of all nationalities and religious backgrounds. The school year comprises 2 semesters extending approximately from August 19 to January 16 and from January 19 to June 12.

Doug Werth, Chair
David Condon, Head of School

1241 Ikego Elementary School
PSC 474 Box 300
FPO, AP
Japan 96351-300
011-81-46-806-8320
Fax: 011-81-46-806-8324
E-mail: principal_ikegoes@pac.dodea.edu
http://www.ikego-es.pac.dodea.edu
Provides developmentally-appropriate learning experiences that teaches, problem solving, critical thinking, make responsible choices.

Scott Finlay, Principal

1242 International Christian School
1 On Muk Lane
Shek Mun
N.T. Hong Kong

011-852-3920 0010
Fax: 011-852-2336-6114
E-mail: ics@ics.edu.hk
http://www.ics.edu.hk
International Christian School is an exceptional school for a number of reasons. Every ICS graduate has enrolled in a college or university somewhere in the world.

Jack Young, Board Chair
Noel Chu, Executive Assistant

1243 International Community School
1225 The Parkland Road
Khwaeng Bangna, Khet Bangna Bangkok
Thailand 10260
011-66-2-338-0777
Fax: 011-66-2-338-0778
E-mail: info@icsbangkok.com
http://www.icsbangkok.com
Based on the Bible, in partnership with parents, we teach the whole student to know and apply wisdom for the good of our world and the glory of God.

Darren Gentry, Headmaster
Gary Opfer, High School Principal

1244 International School Manila
University Parkway
Fort Bonifacio Global City, Taguig
Philippines 01634
011-63-2-840-8400
Fax: 011-63-2-840-8405
E-mail: superintendent@ismanila.com
http://www.ismanila.com
International School Manila is an independent international school whose structure, traditions and style emanate from the United States and whose curriculum and methodology reflect the best in worldwide educational research and practice. Our school is diverse and dynamic, and our students have the highest aspirations for their education and future lives.

William Brown, High School Principal
David Toze, Superintendent

1245 International School of the Sacred Heart
4-3-1 Hiroo, Shibuya-ku
Tokyo
Japan 150-0
011-81-3-3400-3951
Fax: 011-81-3-3400-3496
E-mail: info@issh.ac.jp
http://www.issh.ac.jp
ISSH is a multicultural Catholic school that warmly welcomes students and families from many faiths. The Pre-Kindergarten and Kindergarten classes for 3, 4 and 5 year olds are for boys and girls, while grades 1-12 are for girls only.

Yvonne Hayes, Headmistress
Charmaine Young, High School Principal

1246 International School-Bangkok
39/7 Soi Nichada Thani,Samakee Road
Nonthaburi
Thailand 11120
011-66-2-963-5800
Fax: 011-66-2-583-5432
E-mail: daladk@isb.ac.th
http://www.isb.ac.th
Our Vision states that our students will make extraordinary academic progress. They become smart about their own learning processes, understanding what does and does not work for them as learners.

Dr Bill Gerritz, Head of School
Dr Ugo Costessi, Deputy Head of School/CFO

1247 International School-Beijing
10 An Hua Street
Shunyi District,,Beijing
China 10131
86-10-8046-2345
Fax: 86-10-8046-2001
E-mail: isb-info@isb.bj.edu.cn
http://www.isb.bj.edu.cn
Educate and inspire students to reach their unique potential and contribute positively to society by providing a world class education enriched by diversity and the Chinese culture.

Thomas Hawkins, Head of School
Rodney Fagg, High School Principal

1248 International School-Eastern Seaboard
PO Box 6
Banglamung, Chonburi
Thailand 20150
(6638) 372 591
Fax: (6638) 372 950
E-mail: ise@ise.ac.th
http://www.ise.ac.th
Prepare an international student population for higher education and lifelong learning by emphasizing higher level thinking skills, effective communication, global responsibilities, and personal wellness within a cooperative and supportive school community.

Robert Brewitt, Superintendent
Heather Naro, Elementary Principal

1249 International School-Fiji
PO Box 10828
Laucala Beach Estate, Suva
Fiji Islands
11-679-3393-560
Fax: 11-679-3340-017
E-mail: info@international.school.fj
http://www.international.school.fj
An independent co-educational day school offering pre-school, primary and secondary education and offers excellent education and a caring and nurturing environment for young people. The curriculum includes International Baccalaureate (Primary Years Programme, Middle Years Programme, Diploma Programme), University of Cambridge - International General Certificate of Secondary Education and the Australian Capital Territory Year 12 Certificate and University Admissions Index (UAI).

Dianne Korare, Principal
Sera Brown, Registrar

1250 International School-Ho Chi Minh City
16 Vo Truong Toan St
An Phu Ward, District 2, Ho Ci Minh City
Vietnam
84-8-898-9100
Fax: 84 (8) 3 519-4110
E-mail: admissions@ishcmc.edu.vn
http://www.ishcmc.com
The school provides and teaches the students about intellectual, emotional, social, creative, linguistic, cultural, moral, aesthetic and physical needs of each students. The school seeks to involve parents in the education of their children through regular communication.

Sean O'Maonaigh, Headmaster
Chris Byrne, Admissions/Marketing

1251 International School-Kuala Lumpur
PO Box 12645
Kuala Lumpur
Malaysia 50784

603-4259-5600
Fax: 603-4257-9044
E-mail: iskl@iskl.edu.my
http://www.iskl.edu.my
Offers its students a superior education to prepare them to be responsible world citizens who think creatively, reason critically, communicate effectively and learn enthusiastically throughout life.

Paul Chmelik, Headmaster
Amina O'Kane, Admissions Director

1252 International School-Lae
PO Box 2130
Lae, Morobe
Papua New Guinea 00411
011-675-479-1425
Fax: 011-675-472-3485
E-mail: mail@tisol.iea.ac.pg
http://www.tisol.ac.pg
Offers high quality education, from ages 18 months to grade 8. The curriculum prepares students for national and international success.

Neal Mather, Principal

1253 International School-Manila
Univeristy Parkway
Fort Bonifacio, Taguig City
Philippines 01634
632-840-8488
Fax: 632-840-8489
E-mail: superintendent@ismanila.com
http://http://www.ismanila.org/portal/alias__/lang__en/tabID__1/Des
An independent international school whose structure, traditions and style emanate from the United States. It aims to build a community of reflective learners who are passionate, caring and responsible contributors to the world in which we live.

Ray Dempsey, President
David Toze, Superintendent

1254 International School-Penang-Uplands
Jalan Sungai Satu
Batu Feringgi, Penang
Malaysia 11100
011-604-8819-777
Fax: 011-604-8819-778
E-mail: info@uplands.org
http://www.uplands.org
Uplands aims to provide excellent international education for students of all nationalities in a challenging multi-cultural environment. It favours methods of teaching which foster the joys of learning, discovery and enquiry, aiming to nurture students into thinking, learning, caring and striving to meet the needs of a better world.

John Horsfall, Acting Principal
M R Chandran, Chair

1255 International School-Phnom Penh, Cambodia
146 Norodom Boulevard
PO Box 138, Phnom Penh
Cambodia
855-23-213-103
Fax: 855-23-213-104
E-mail: ispp@ispp.edu.kh
http://www.ispp.edu.kh
ISPP empowers students, in a caring international environment, to achieve their potential by pursuing personal and academic excellence, and to grow as responsible global citizens who celebrate diversity.

Barry Sutherland, Director
Laura Watson, Chairperson

1256 International School-Phnom Penh-Cambodia
146 Norodom Boulevard
PO Box 138, Phnom Penh
Cambodia
855-23-213-103
Fax: 855-23-361-002
E-mail: ispp@ispp.edu.kh
http://www.ispp.edu.kh
ISPP empowers students, in a caring international environment, to achieve their potential by pursuing personal and academic excellence, and to grow as responsible global citizens who celebrate diversity.

Barry Sutherland, Director
Laura Watson, Chairperson

1257 International School-Pusan
798 Nae-ri, Gijang-eup
Gijang-gun, Busan 619-902
South Korea
82 51 742-3332
Fax: 82 51 742 3375
E-mail: enquiries@bifskorea.org
http://www.isbusan.org
The school possess a caring, family-like ethos, giving the children a high level of self-confidence and esteem, and teaching them tolerance and respect for other cultures.

Stephen Palmer, Principal
Thomas Walker, Chairman

1258 International School-Singapore
25 Paterson Road
Singapore 23851
(65) 6235 5844
Fax: (65) 6732 5701
E-mail: admissions@iss.edu.sg
http://www.iss.edu.sg
ISS mission is to provide a multicultural educational environment for our students in which they achieve academic success, personal growth and become socially responsible and active global citizens with an appreciation of learning as a life-long process.

Mak Lai Ying, Principal
Anthony Race, Headmaster

1259 International School-Ulaanbaatar
Four Seasons Garden, Khan-Uul Distr
1st Khoroo, PO Box 36/10
Ulaanbaatar, Mongolia 17032
976-70160010
Fax: 976-70160012
E-mail: administration@isumongolia.edu.mn
http://www.isumongolia.edu.mn
The International School of Ulaanbaatar seeks to offer the best educational system possible, based on an international curriculum.

Gregory Rayl, Director
Tuul Arildii, Deputy Director

1260 Island School
20 Borrett Road
Mid Levels
Hong Kong
852-2524-7135
Fax: 852-2840-1673
E-mail: school@mail.island.edu.hk
http://www.island.edu.hk
An international, co-educational, comprehensive school, providing secondary education for children of all nations who can benefit from an education through the medium of English.

Pinder Wong, Council Chairman
Chris Binge, Principal

1261 Ivanhoe Grammar School
PO Box 91
The Ridgeway, Ivanhoe, Victoria
Australia 03079
61 3 9490 1877
Fax: 61 3 9497 4060

E-mail: info@ivanhoe.com.au
http://www.igs.vic.edu.au
Our mission is to be a community of learning that develops in students the skills and values that will prepare them for the challenges and responsibilities of adult citizenship.

Roderick D Fraser, Principal
Andrew Sloane, Head of School

1262 JN Darby Elementary School
PSC 485 Box 99
FPO, AP
Japan 96321
011-81-956-50-8800
Fax: 011-81-956-50-8804
E-mail: Darby_ES@pac.dodea.edu
http://http://www.darby-es.pac.dodea.edu/
The Darby Community promotes academic and social excellence so all students can become positive contributors to society.

Joy Jaramillo, Principal

1263 Jakarta International School
PO Box 1078/JKS
Jakarta 12010
Indonesia
(62-21) 750-3644
Fax: 62-21-765-7852
E-mail: parentnet@jisedu.org
http://www.jisedu.org
JIS is a place where people from almost 60 countries come together to share ideas, experiences and values.

Tim Carr, Head of School

1264 Japan International School
7-5-1 Hikarigaoka
Shibuya-Ku, Tokyo 168-0081
Japan
81-3-3335-6620
Fax: 81-3-3332-6930
E-mail: hikarigaoka@aobajapan.jp
http://http://www.aobaonline.jp/
Student of all nationalities, and religions are welcome.

Charles S Barton, Headmaster

1265 John McGlashan College
2 Pilkington Street
Maori Hill, Dunedin
New Zealand
03-467-6620
Fax: 03-467-6622
http://www.mcglashan.school.nz
ohn McGlashan College is an integrated, Year 7-13, secondary school for boys. The roll comprises approximately 380 dayboys from Dunedin city and its surrounds and 110 boarders, most of whom come from rural Otago and Southland. In addition, up to 20 international students are enrolled each year

K Michael Corkery, Principal
Neil Garry, Deputy Principal

1266 Kansai Christian School
282-2 Oaza Misato, Heguri-cho, Ikom
Nara Ken 636-0904
Japan
0745-45-6422
Fax: 011-81-745-45-6422
E-mail: office@kansaichristianschool.com
http://www.kansaichristianschool.com
Kansai Christian School was established in 1970 to provide a general education in a Christian environment for children of the evangelical missionary community

Albert Greeff, Principal

1267 Kaohsiung American School
35 Sheng Li Road
Tzuo-Ying District (813)
Taiwan
886-7-583-0112
Fax: 886-7-582-4536

E-mail: dchang@kas.kh.edu.tw
http://www.kas.kh.edu.tw
Kaohsiung American School (KAS) is a private, non-profit Pre-K - 12 institution with 330 students offering college preparatory programs leading to a U.S. high school diploma. It is located in Kaohsiung, a city of 1.5 million in southwestern Taiwan.

Tom Farrell, Superintendent
Deborah Taylor, Assistant Director

1268 Kellett School
2 Wah Lok Path
Wah Fu, Pokfulam
Hong Kong
852-2551-8234
Fax: 852-2875-0262
E-mail: admissions@kellettschool.com
http://www.kellettschool.com
Kellett School is an independent non-for-profit school catering to the English-speaking children living in Hong Kong. The school is operated by Kellett School Association Limited through a Board of Governors; seven of whom are parents, elected by the Association, and the remaining three are ex-officio members. All parents become members of the Association.

Ann McDonald, Principal

1269 Kilmore International School
40 White Street
Kilmore, Victoria
Australia 03764
61-357-822-211
Fax: 61-357-822-525
E-mail: info@kilmore.vic.edu.au
http://www.kilmore.vic.edu.au
The Kilmore International School is an independent, non-denominational, co-educational boarding and day school for academically motivated students undertaking their secondary education (Years 7-12 inclusive).

John Settle, Principal

1270 Kinabalu International School
PO Box 12080
88822 Kota Kinabalu, Sabah
Malaysia
608-822-4526
Fax: 608-824-4203
E-mail: kismy@streamyx.com
http://www.kis.edu.my
This school offers an English-based curriculum for 100 day students (50 boys; 50 girls), ages 3-13 years.

1973 pages

Stuart McLay, Principal
Elis Ho, Office Manager

1271 King George V School
2 Tin Kwong Road
Homantin, Kowloon
Hong Kong
852-2711-3029
Fax: 852-2760-7116
E-mail: office@kgv.edu.hk
http://www.kgv.edu.hk
Non selective secondary school which provides a broad.

Ed Wickins, Principal
Richard Bradford, Vice Principal

1272 Kitakyushu International School
Yahata Higashi-ku, Takami 2,
Shinnittetsu, Shijo, Kitakyushu
Japan
81-93-652-0682
This school offers an English based curriculum for 8 day students (2 boys; 6 girls), in kindergarten through elementary. The school is always looking for dedicated and qualified teachers to teach children and adults in

school and preschool (especially female teachers). Applications needed include preschool and English.

Ann Ratnayake, Principal

1273 Kodaikanal International School
Seven Roads Junction, PO Box 25
Kodaikanal, Tamil Nadu
India 624 1-0101
91-4542-247-500
Fax: 91-4542-241-109
E-mail: contact@Kis.in
http://www.kis.in
Kodaikanal Internationa lSchool is an autonomous residential school with a broad college-oriented curriculum, serving young people from a wide diversity of cultures. The School's academic program is intentionally set within a community life based on the life and teaching of Jesus Christ and devoted to service in India and the whole human community.

Geoffrey Fisher, Principal
Gregg Faddegon, Vice Principal

1274 Kooralbyn International School
Shop 1, 29 Wellington Bundock Drive
Kooralbyn QLD 4285
Australia
61-7-5544-6111
Fax: 61-7-5544-6702
E-mail: info@kooralbyn.com
http://www.tkis.qld.edu.au
Aims to provide students with a broad liberal education.

Geoff Mills, Principal

1275 Kowloon Junior School
20 Perth Street
Ho Man Tin, Kowloon
Hong Kong
852-2714-5279
Fax: 852 2760 4438
E-mail: office@kjs.edu.hk
http://www.kjs.edu.hk
Primary students learn English, math, science, technology, history, geography, art, music and physical education.

Mark Cripps, Principal
Deborah Graham, ESF Representative

1276 Kyoto International School
Kitatawara-cho,Nakadachiuri-sagaru
Yoshiyamachi-Dori, Kamigyo-ku, Kyoto
Japan 00602-8247
81-75-451-1022
Fax: 81-75-451-1023
E-mail: kis@kyotointernationalschool.org
http://www.kyoto-is.org
Independent day school, offering education from Preschool level through to Middle School

Annette Levy, Head of School
Amanda Gillis-Furutaku, Board Chair

1277 Lahore American School
American Consulate General Lahore
15 Upper Mall, Canal Bank
Lahore
Pakistan 54000
92-42-576-2406
Fax: 92-42-571-1901
E-mail: las@las.edu.pk
http://www.las.edu.pk
An independent, coeducational day school which offers an educational program from nursery through grade 12 for students of all nationalities.

Kathryn Cochran, Superintendent
Imran Aslam, Board Chair

1278 Lanna International School Thailand
300 Grandview Moo 10
Chiang-Mai to Hang Dong, T Mae-hea,
A. M
Thailand 50100
66-53-806-231
Fax: 66-53-271-159
E-mail: head@lannaist.ac.th
http://www.lannaist.ac.th
t is the goal of Lanna International School
to prepare its students to be responsible
world citizens who demonstrate a commitment to life-long learning and the application of that learning to the improvement of
self, and local and global communities.

Roy Lewis, Head of School
Ajarn Kannika, School Director

1279 Lincoln School
PO Box 2673
Rabi Bhawan, Kathmandu
Nepal
977-1-4270482
Fax: 977-142-7268
Fax: 977-1-4272685
E-mail: info@lsnepal.com.np
http://www.lsnepal.com
is an independent, international school in
Kathmandu, Nepal with an American Curriculum

Allan Bredy, Director
Craig Baker, Principal

1280 Malacca Expatriate School
2443-C Jalan Batang Tiga
Tanjung Kling, Melaka
Malaysia 76400
011-60-6-315-4970
Fax: 011-60-6-315-4970
E-mail: sossb@pd.jaring.my
http://www.meschool.virtualave.net
Mission is provide a high standard of learning. The students benefit from a high level
of individual attention because of their low
student to teacher ratio.

Susheila Samuel, Principal

1281 Marist Brothers International School
1-2-1 Chimori-cho
Suma-ku, Kobe
Japan 654-0
011-81-787-326266
Fax: 011-81-787-326268
E-mail: enquiries@marist.ac.jp
http://www.marist.ac.jp
The philosophy of MBIS is designed to
awaken students to the realities of life and
to prepare them for the future. school aims
to give to each student a well-rounded education incorporating the academic, moral,
social and physical aspects of life.

Ed Fitzgerald, Principal
Geraldo de Couto, Vice Principal

1282 Matthew C Perry Elementary School
PSC 561 Box 1874
FPO Iwakuni 96310 0019
Japan
011-81-827-79-3447
Fax: 011-81-827-79-6490
E-mail: principal.perryes@pac.dodea.edu
http://www.perry-es.pac.dodea.edu/
Committed to promoting student achievement in a positive safe environment. It provides a quality education for every student
based on the needs of each child.

Shelia Cary, Principal
Christopher Racek, Asst. Principal

1283 Matthew C Perry Middle & High School
PSC 561 Box 1874
FPO Iwakuni 96310 1874
Japan
011-81-827-79-5449
Fax: 011-81-827-79-4600
E-mail: principal.perryhs@pac.dodea.edu
http://www.perry-es.pac.dodea.edu/

Morgan Nugent, Principal
Robert Funk, Assistant Principal

1284 Mentone Boys Grammar School
63 Venice Street
Mentone, Victoria
Australia 03194
011-61-3-9584-4211
Fax: 011-61-3-9581-3290
E-mail: enquiry@mentonegrammar.net
http://www.mentonegrammar.net
We are a school for boys and girls providing a flexible and sensitive approach which
considers what boys and girls need at various stages of their development.

Mal Cater, Principal
Simon Appel, Chairman

1285 Mercedes College
540 Fullarton Road
Springfield 5062
South Australia
011-61-8-8372-3200
Fax: 011-61-8-8379-9540
E-mail:
info@mercedes.adl.catholic.edu.au
http://www.mercedes.adl.catholic.edu.au/
index.cfm
Mercedes College, in Adelaide, South Australia, is a Reception to Year 12 Catholic
co-educational school in the Mercy tradition.

Peter Daw, Principal
Steve Bowley, Business Manager

1286 Methodist Ladies College
207 Barkers Road Kew
Victoria 3101
Australia
011-61-3-9274-6333
Fax: 011-61-3-9819-2345
E-mail: college@mlc.vic.edu.au
http://www.mlc.vic.edu.au
This college prepares its students for the
world of tomorrow by liberating their talents through challenge, enrichment, and
opportunity in a supportive Christian environment. Committed to technology and to
student initiated learning so each girl from
year five onward works with her personal
computer to understand the present and
shape the future. Total enrollment: 2,135
day students; 105 boarding. Grade range
K-12. The school is willing to participate
in a teacher exchange program.

Rosa Swtorelli, Principal
Louise Adler, Chairperson

1287 Minsk International School
DOS/Administrative Officer
7010 Minsk Place
Washington, DC 20521-7010
375-172-343-035
Fax: 375-172-343-035
E-mail: mis@open.by
http://www.minsk.qsischool.org
An independent, coeducational day school
which offers an educational program from
kindergarten through grade 8 for students
of all nationalities. Enrollment 11.

Stanley Harrison Orr, Director

1288 Moreguina International Primary School
PO Box 438
Konedobu Papua
New Guinea

Wayne Coleman, Principal

1289 Morrison Christian Academy
136-1 Shui Nan Road
Taichung 40679
Taiwan, TW 40679
11-886-4-2297-3927
Fax: 11-886-4-2292-1174
E-mail: mcgillt@mca.org.tw
http://www.mca.org.tw
Morrison Academy exists to meet the educational
needs of the children of missionaries throughout
Taiwan, helping fulfill Christ's commission to go
into all the world. Morrison seeks to provide a
Christ-centered school culture where all students,
from missionary and non-missionary families, experience a Biblically-integrated quality education. Therefore, Morrison structures learning so
that students may develop the knowledge, discernment, and ability to dynamically impact their
world as Christian

Tim McGill, Superintendent
Matt Strange, Director of Curriculum

1290 Mount Hagen International School
PO Box 945
Mount Hagen
Papua New Guinea
675-542-1964
Fax: 675-542-1840
E-mail: mhis@online.net.pg
http://www.iea.ac.pg
It is envisaged that students enrolled at the Mount
Hagen International School will always remain
encouraged by their schooling. They will earn an
education of International standard, their learning
will be contextualized within Papua New Guinea
culture, and they will learn how to become productive members of their community

Bruce Imatana, Principal

1291 Mt Zaagham International School
PT Freeport
Tembagapura W Papua
Indonesia
62 901 407876
Fax: 62 901 403170
E-mail: joecuthbertson@efmi.com
http://mzis.org
Grade levels Pre-K through 98, school year September - June. Two campuses Tembagapura and
Kuala Kencana

Barney Latham, Superintendent
Richard Ledger, Principal

1292 Murray International School
PO Box 1137
Boroko
Papua New Guinea
675-325-2183
Fax: 675-325-7925
E-mail: ssavage@temis.iea.ac.pg
http://www.elamurray.ac.pg
Non-profit, private, co-educational day school
that provides quality international standard education for the expatriate and local community in
Port Moresby.

Suzanne Savage, Principal
Marlene Filippi, Deputy Principal

1293 Murree Christian School
Jhika Gali, Murree Hills
Punjab
Pakistan 47180
0092-513-410321
Fax: 0092-513-411668
E-mail: mcs@mcs.org.pk
http://www.mcs.org.pk

This school offers an English-based curriculum for 20 day students and 140 boarding students (75 boys; 85 girls), in grades K-12. Murree Christian School educates the children of missionaries from 14 different countries working in Pakistan and the region. Living allowances rather than salaries are awarded. Overseas teacher stay is two years with housing provided by the school.

Phil Billing, Director
Linda Fisher, HS Faculty Head

1294 Mussoorie International School

Srinagar Estate, Mussoorie 248179
Uttarakhand
India
91-135-2632007
Fax: 91-135-2631160
E-mail: misadmission@gmail.com
http://www.misindia.net
One of the leading residential educational institutions for girls and is recognized for its progressive education with a definite account on India culture and traditions.

HK Rawal, Principal
A. Ghosh, Headmaster

1295 Nagoya International School

2686 Minamihara, Nakashidami
Moriyama-ku, Nagoya, 463-0002
Japan
81-52-736-2025
Fax: 81-52-736-3883
E-mail: info@nis.ac.jp
http://www.nagoyais.jp
Envisions a school community devoted to developing the skills, attitudes, and values that allow students to realize their full potential, lead lives of purpose, and become responsible, global citizens.

Rob Risch, Headmaster

1296 Narrabundah College

Jerrabomberra Avenue
Narrabundah, ACT 2604
Australia
61-2-6205-6999
Fax: 61-2-6205-6969
E-mail: laura.beacroft@cbit.net.au
http://www.narrabundahc.act.edu.au
This college is a government college for years 11 and 12 students - the final two years of secondary education. It offers a challenging curriculum in a caring environment and meets the needs of an international community.

Steve Kyburz, Head of School
Laura Beacroft, Board Chair

1297 New International School of Thailand

36 Sukhumvit Soi 15
Bangkok, TH 10110
66-2651-2065
Fax: 66-2253-3800
E-mail: nist@nist.ac.th
http://www.nist.ac.th
Co-educational, day school, IBO World School

Simon Leslie, Headmaster
Adrian Watts, Deputy Head

1298 Nile C Kinnick High School

PSC 473 Box 95
FPO, AP
96349-95
011-81-46816-7392
Fax: 011-81-46-816-7278
E-mail: Kinnick_Principal@pac.dodea.edu
http://www.kinnick-hs.pac.dodea.edu
The mission of Nile C. Kinnick High School is to challenge students to maximize potential in order to prepare them to be responsible and productive citizens in an ever-changing world.

Lorenzo Brown, Principal

1299 Nishimachi International School

2-14-7 Moto Azabu
Minato-ku Tokyo
Japan 106-0-46
81-3-3451-5520
Fax: 81-3-3456-0197
E-mail: info@nishimachi.org
http://www.nishimachi.ac.jp
Offers a dual-language, multicultural program ro 430 student k-9.

Terence Christian, Headmaster

1300 Okinawa Christian School International

1835 Zakimi, Yomitan-son
Okinawa 904-0301
Japan
81-098-958-3000
800-446-6423
Fax: 81-098-958-6279
E-mail: info@ocsi.org
http://www.ocsi.org
Provides a major educational support base for the international community living on Okinawa.

Rich Barnett, Contact
Randel J Hadley, Superintendent

1301 Osaka International School

4-4-16 Onohara Nishi
Mino-shi, Osaka, 562-0032
Japan
81-72-727-5050
Fax: 81-72-727-5055
E-mail: addmissions@senri.ed.jp
http://www.senri.ed.jp
OIS is an English-language-based, preK-12 grade coeducational college-preparatory school.

John Searle, Head of School

1302 Osaka YMCA International High School

6-7-34 Benten Minato-ku
Osaka 552-0007
Japan
06-4395-1002
Fax: 06-4395-1004
E-mail: general-inquiry@oyis.org
http://www.oyis.org
OYIS strives to be a leading provider of international education for the citizens and residents of Osaka and its environs.

John Murphy, Principal

1303 Osan American High School

Unit 2037
APO AP 96278-0005
Korea
011-82-31-661-9076
Fax: 011-82-31-661-9121
E-mail:
PRINCIPAL.OSANHS@pac.dodea.edu
http://www.osan-hs.pac.dodea.edu
Provides student with successful, productive and rewarding educational experiences.

Timothy Erickson, Principal
Truly Schramm, Assistant Principal

1304 Osan Elementary School

Unit 2037
APO, AP 96278-2037
Korea
011-82-31-661-6912
Fax: 011-82-31-661-5733
E-mail: david.petree.pac.dodea.edu
http://www.osan-es.pac.dodea.edu
Provides quality and challenging educational opportunities for all students to become critical thinkers, life-long learners, and productive citizens in a global society.

Mia Plourde, Secretary
David Petree, Principal

1305 Overseas Children's School

PO Box 9, Pelawatte
Battaramulla
Sri Lanka
94 11 2784920-2
Fax: 94-11-2784999
E-mail: admin@osc.lk
http://www.osc.lk
OSC develops the whole person as a responsible learner striving for personal excellence within a culturally diverse school

Areta Williams, Head of School
Jerry Huxtable, Chair

1306 Overseas Family School

25 F Paterson Road
Singapore 23851
65-6738-0211
Fax: 65-6733-8825
E-mail: executive_director@ofs.edu.sg
http://www.ofs.edu.sg
To focus on the individual needs of every student and to provide a supportive atmosphere designed to help students achieve personal academic goals.

David Perry, Chairman
Irene Wong, Executive Director

1307 Overseas School of Colombo

Pelawatte
PO Box 9, Battaranmulla
Sri Lanka
94 11 2784920-2
Fax: 94 11 2784999
E-mail: admin@osc.lk
http://www.osc.lk
OSC develops the whole person as a responsible learner striving for personal excellence within a culturally diverse school.

Areta Williams, Head of School
Jerry Huxtable, Chair

1308 Pacific Harbour International School

PO Box 50
Pacific Harbour, Deuba
Fiji Islands
679-450-0005
Fax: 679-450-566
http://www.isbi.com

Janet Tuni, Principal

1309 Pasir Ridge International

Unocal-po Box 3-tampines S
Balikpapan 9152
Singapore
62-542-543-474
Fax: 62-542-767-126
E-mail: prschool@bpp.mega.net.id
http://pasirridgeinternationalschool.com
Grade levels preK through 8.

Kathryn Carter-Golden PhD, Principal

1310 Peak School

20 Plunketts Road
The Peak
Hong Kong
852-2849 7211
Fax: 852-2849 7151
E-mail: office@peakschool.net
http://www.ps.edu.hk
Helping promote a better understanding of Americans on the part of the peoples served

Annette Ainsworth, Principal/Secretary
Bill Garnett, Vice Principal

1311 Phuket International Preparatory School
115/15 Moo 7 Thepkasattri Road
Thepkasattri, Thalang, Phuket 83110
Thailand
66 (0)76 336 000
Fax: 66 (0)76 336 081
E-mail:
info@phuketinternationalacademy.com
http://http://www.phuketinternationalaca
demy.com

Agnes Hebler, Principal

1312 Popondetta International School
PO Box 10
Popondetta, Papua
New Guinea

Michael Whitting, Principal

1313 Prahram Campus-Wesley College
577 St Kilda Road-Prahran
Melbourne
Australia
61 3 8102 6100
Fax: 61 3 8102 6054
E-mail: stkildaroad@wesleycollege.net
http://http://www.wesleycollege.net

AB Conabere, Principal

1314 Pusan American School
Do DOS
Pusan 96259
South Korea
82-51-801-7528
Fax: 82-51-803-1729
E-mail: pas@pac.odedodea.edu

Alexia Venglek, Principal

1315 Pusan Elementary & High School
Unit 15625
APO AP 96259-0005, Pusan
Korea
82-52-801-7528
Fax: 82-51-803-1729

1316 QSI International School-Phuket
Box 432 A Muang
Phuket 83000
Thailand
66-076-354-077
Fax: 66-76-354077
E-mail: phuket@qsi.org
http://www.qsi.org
To keep this urge to learn alive in every
child in QSI schools. Our schools are established to provide in the English language a
quality education for students in the cities
we serve.

Khun Janrita Hnobnorb, Administrative
Coordinator
Alan Siporin, Director

1317 QSI International School-Zhuhai
No. 168 Anning Road
Xianzhou District
Zuhai, China 51900
86-756-815-6134
Fax: 86-756-8189021
E-mail: zhuhai@qsi.org
http://http://www.qsi.org/zhu_home/cont
act.htm
To keep this urge to learn alive in every
child in QSI schools. Our schools are established to provide in the English language a
quality education for students in the cities
we serve.

Matthew Farwell, Director

1318 Quarry Bay School
6 Hau Yuen Path Braemar Hill
North Point, Hong Kong
China

852 2566 4242
Fax: 852 2887 9849
E-mail: debra.gardiner@qbs.edu.hk
http://www.qbs.edu.hk
Our aim is to encourage in our children the
enjoyment of learning by providing activities both in and outside the classroom
which help to develop confident, happy
and successful individuals.

Mina Dunstan, Principal

1319 Rabaul International School
PO Box 855
Rabaul Enbp, Papua
New Guinea
675-982-8770
Fax: 675-982-8770
http://www.iea.ac.pg

Ian Smith, Principal

1320 Richard E Byrd Elementary School
PSC 472 Box 12
FPO
Japan, AP 96348-12
011-81-45-281-4815
Fax: 011-81-45-281-4870
http://www.byrd-es.pac.dodea.edu
Richard E. . Byrd envisions a school un-
bound by traditional school concepts of
time, location and age requirements. Byrd
Elementary School will provide all students with vast opportunities for learning
and civic involvement

Gwen Baxter-Oakley, Principal

1321 Robert D Edgren High School
Unit 5040
APO
Japan, AP 96319-5040
011-81-176-77-4377
Fax: 011-81-176-77-4959
E-mail:
principal_*edgren_hs@pac.dodea.edu
http://www.edgren-hs.pac.dodea.edu
Committed to helping students develop ac-
ademically, socially, physically and emo-
tionally in a global community.

Gerogia Watters, Principal

1322 Ruamrudee International School
6 Ramkamhaeng 184 Road
Minburi, Bangkok
Thailand 10510
66-2-518-0320
Fax: 66-2-518-0334
E-mail: info@rism.ac.th
http://www.rism.ac.th/risweb
Grade levels K-12, school year August -
June

Fr. Leo Travis, Director
Dave Parsons HS Principal

1323 Saigon South International School
Tan Phong Ward
Ho Chi Minh City
Vietnam
(84-8) 5413-0901
Fax: (84-8) 5413-0902
E-mail: info@ssis.edu.vn
http://www.ssischool.org
Saigon South International School is a college preparatory school committed to the
intellectual and personal development of
each student in preparation for a purposeful life as a global citizen.

Robert Crowther, Headmaster
Charles Barton, Head of School

1324 Sancta Maria International School
41 Karasawa Minami-ku
Yokohama
Japan

Sr Mary Elizabeth Doll, Principal

1325 School at Tembagapura
PO Box 616 Cairns
Queensland 4870
Australia

Bruce Goforth, Principal

1326 Scots PGC College
60 Oxenham Street
Warwick, QLD
Australia 04370
61 7 4666 9811
Fax: 61 7 4666 9812
E-mail: postbox@scotspgc.qld.edu.au
http://www.scotspgc.qld.edu.au
Our philosophy of schooling rests squarely on the
belief that a true education encourages young people to question and explore, to develop a strong
sense of personal identity, to strive to achieve
one's best, and to value the act of serving without
losing one's desire to lead.

Michael Harding, Principal
Nigel Grant, Director of Learning

1327 Seisen International School
12-15 Yoga 1-chome
Setagaya-Ku, Tokyo
Japan 158-0-97
03-3704-2661
Fax: 033701-1033
E-mail: sisinfo@seisen.com
http://www.seisen.com
Seisen International School seeks to provide a
happy, stable and secure environment in which
students are prepared through teaching and example, to live in a world of tremendous challenge and
rapid change.

Concesa Martin, Headmistress

1328 Semarang International School
Asad Ave-Mohammedpur
Semarang, Central Java
Indonesia 50254
62-24-8311-424
Fax: 62-24-8311-994
E-mail: info@semarangis.or.id
http://www.semarangis.or.id
Offer Semarang 's international community high
quality and affordable education based on the International Baccalaureate Organization's Primary
Years Programme, (PYP) philosophy. Provide an
educational and motivational base from which
each pupil may take his or her place with confidence in any school in any country in the medium
of English.

Barry Burns, Principal

1329 Seoul Academy
988-5, Daechi-dong
Kangamku Seoul
Korea 135-2
82-02-554-1690
Fax: 82-2-562-0451
E-mail: sais5541690@hanmail.net
http://http://www.seoulacademy.net/
Grade levels pre-K through eighth.

Thomas O'Connor, Director

1330 Seoul British School
55 Yonhi Dong Sudaemun Ku
Seoul
Korea
822-330-3100
http://www.seoulforeign.org

Richard Schlueter, Principal

1331 Seoul Elementary School
Unit 15549
APO, AP
Korea 96205-5549
011-82-2-7916-4613
Fax: 011-82-2-793-6925
E-mail: principal.seoules@pac.dodea.edu
http://www.seoul-es.pac.dodea.edu
Provides standards based instruction in a safe learning environment which fosters independent thinking and respects cultural diversity through collaboration among staff, students, parents and community

Catherine Yurica, Principal

1332 Seoul Foreign School
55 Yonhi-Dong Sodaemun-Gu
Seoul
Korea 120-8-113
82-2-330-3100
Fax: 82-2-335-1857
E-mail: sfsoffice@seoulforeign.org
http://www.sfs.or.kr
As has been true throughout our history, Seoul Foreign School is committed to academic excellence. Our rigorous college preparatory curriculum - which includes the International Baccalaureate diploma program - and our dynamic learning environment challenge students to achieve their full intellectual potential. Equally, we cherish Christian values which encourage our students to develop strong character, live and work with integrity, and accept responsibility for themselves and others.

John Engstrom, Head of School
Barry Benger, Director Human Resources

1333 Seoul High School
Unit 15549
APO, AP
South Korea 96205-5549
011+82-2-7918-5261
Fax: 011+82-2-7918-8822
http://www.seoul-hs.pac.dodea.edu
Seoul American High School is located on Yongsan Army Base in the center of Seoul, Korea. The school complex is comprised of eight buildings containing over 60 classrooms and special purpose rooms.

Richard Schlueter, Principal

1334 Shanghai American School
258 Jin Feng Lu
Huacao Town, Minhang Dist. Shanghai
China 20110
86-21-6221-1445
Fax: 86-21-6221-1269
E-mail: admission@saschina.org
http://www.saschina.org
Shanghai American School, in partnership with parents, fosters the development of each student's personal potential through a balance of the academic, physical, social, emotional and ethical aspects of life. SAS provides a challenging American core curriculum with an international perspective that inspires a passion for learning and intellectual vitality.

Kerry Jacobson, Superintendent
Andrew Torris, Deputy Superintendent

1335 Shatin College
3 Lai Wo Lane
Sha Tin
Hong Kong
852 26991811
Fax: 852 26950592
E-mail: info@shatincollege.edu.hk
http://www.shatincollege.edu.hk

Independent, coeducational, secondary school within the English Schools Foundation

David Cottam, Principal
Grahame Carder, Chairman

1336 Shatin Junior College
3A Lai Wo Lane
Fo Tan, New Terreteries
Hong Kong
852 2692 2721
Fax: 852 2602 5572
E-mail: info@sjs.esf.edu.hk
http://http://www.sjs.edu.hk/
At Sha Tin Junior School we aim to provide a secure and happy environment in which a child can develop their academic, social and physical potential to the full.

Perry Tunesi, Principal

1337 Shirley Lanham Elementary School
PSC 477 Box 38
FPO AP
Japan 96306-5
011-81-467-63-3664
Fax: 011-81-467-63-4476
E-mail: Principal.lanhames@pac.dodea.edu
http://www.lanham-es.pac.dodea.edu
We are preparing all students to be responsible, positive contributors within a diverse, global community.

Dave Russell, Principal

1338 Singapore American School
40 Woodlands Street 41
Singapore 73854
65-6363-3403
Fax: 65-6363-3408
E-mail: communications@sas.edu.sg
http://www.sas.edu.sg
The Singapore American School is committed to providing each student an exemplary American educational experience with an international perspective.

Brent Mutsch, Superintendent

1339 Sollars Elementary School
Unit 5041
APO, AP
Japan 96319-5041
011-81-176-77-3933
Fax: 011-81-176-77-3873
E-mail:
PRINCIPAL.SOLLARSES@pac.dodea.edu
http://www.sollars-es.pac.dodea.edu

Dana Chandler, Principal

1340 South Island School
50 Nam Fung Road
Aberdeen
Hong Kong
852-255- 931
Fax: 852-255- 881
E-mail: sis@mail.sis.edu.hk
http://www.sis.edu.hk
School Aims to develop students' confidence, self-esteem and a range of positive values and personal qualities and to produce enthusiastic, active, independent and lifelong learners.

Graham Silverthorne, Principal
Roberta Kam, Admission

1341 St. Andrews International School-Bangkok
Pridi Banomyong 20/1
Sukhumvit Soi 71, Prakanong, Bangkok
Thailand 10110
(+66) 23 81 23 87-
Fax: (+66) 23 91 52 27
E-mail: info@standrews.ac.th
http://http://www.standrews.ac.th/

Our mission is to provide an inclusive, international education in a happy, supportive and stimulating environment, where all the needs of the individual learner are met and students are inspired to achieve their full potential enabling them to become responsible global citizens

Paul Schofield, Head of School
Jamsai Anuvongchareon, Director

1342 St. Christopher's School
10 Nunn Road
Penang
Malaysia 10350
604-226-3589
Fax: 604-226-4340
E-mail: principal@scips.org.my
http://www.scips.org.my
St. Christopher's International Primary School of Penang, caters for expatriates' and also Malaysian children. It is located in one of the most sought after residential areas on the island of Penang Malaysia.

John G Jones, Principal

1343 St. John's International School
Ladprao
Bangkok
Thailand 10900
662-513-8575
Fax: +66 2 513 5273
E-mail: sjiadmin@stjohn.ac.th
http://www.international.stjohn.ac.th
A holistic British style school preparing students of all nationalities to become life long learners and effective communicators in the global community.

Chainarong Monthienvic, Principal

1344 St. Joseph International School
5-16-10 Shibamata, Katsushika-ku
Tokyo
Japan 125-0
035-694-4550
E-mail: schray@stjoseph-k.org
http://www.stjoseph-k.org
Coeducational day/boarding school, preschool through grade 12.

James Mueller, Principal
Thomas Schray, Head Teacher

1345 St. Joseph's International Primary School
177 Currie Street
Nambour
New Guinea
54 -19 -22
http://www.stjosephsnambour.qld.edu.au

Barbara D'Arbon, Principal

1346 St. Mark's College
46 Pennington Terrace
North Adelaide
Australia, SA 05006
08-8334-5600
Fax: 08-8267-4694
E-mail: stmarks@stmarkscollege.com.au
http://www.stmarkscollege.com.au
Grade levels Pre-K through 12, school year March - December

Rose Alwyn, Headmaster
James Raw, Dean

1347 St. Mary's International School
1-6-19 Seta Setagaya-ku
Tokyo
Japan 158-8
813-370- 341
Fax: 813-370- 195
E-mail: michelj@smis.ac.jp
http://www.smis.ac.jp
St. Mary's is committed to educating boys to be lifelong learners of good character who

demonstrate academic, physical, artistic, and moral excellence, respect for religious and cultural beliefs, and responsibility as international citizens.

Michel Jutras, Headmaster
Br Lawrence G Lambert, Elementary
School Principal

1348 St. Maur International School

83 Yamate-cho Naka-ku
Yokahama
Japan 231-8
81-45-641-5751
Fax: 81-45-641-6688
E-mail: office@stmaur.ac.jp
http://www.stmaur.ac.jp
he basic objective of Saint Maur International School is to provide a Pre-school, Elementary and Secondary education for international students residing in Japan, by using the English language as the primary medium of instruction. An international student is defined as a student whose life experiences span more than one cultural dimension. From this basic goal stem specific objectives which fall into three conceptual categories: spiritual, cultural, and academic.

Jeanette K Thomas, Head of School
Richard B Rucci, Coordinating Principal

1349 St. Michael's International School

17-2 Nakayamate-dori 3-chome
Chuo-ku, Kobe-shi 650-0004
Japan
81-78-231-8885
Fax: 81-78-231-8899
E-mail: head@smis.org
http://www.smis.org
Provides a distinctive Primary education within a positive culture of academic excellence and caring family community.

Aileen Pardon, Principal
Paul Grisewood, Head of School

1350 St. Stephen's International School

998 Viphavadi Rangsit Road
Lad Yao, Chatuchak, Bangkok
Thailand 10900
66-2-5130270
Fax: 66-2-9303307
E-mail: info@sis.edu
http://www.sis.edu
To encourage all students in their studies, personal life and in all their interactions to strive for excellence on their journey to becoming effective and compassionate citizens and leaders. Our goal is to nurture a culture and a community of learners creating a unique East meets West environment.

Richard A Ralphs, School Director
Gary Rodbard, Principal

1351 St. Xavier's Greenherald School

Asad Ave-Mohammedpur
Dhaka 1207
Bangladesh

Mary Imelda, Principal

1352 Stearley Heights Elementary School

Unit 5166
APO Kadena 96368 5166
Okinawa 36368
001-81-611-694-452
Fax: 001-81- 98-934-681
E-mail:
Stearley-Heights.Principal@pac.dodea.edu
http://http://www.stearley-es.pac.dodea.edu

Thomas Godbold, Principal

1353 Sullivans Elementary School

PSC 473, Box 96
Yokosuka 96349 0096
Japan
011-81-468-16-7336
Fax: 011-81-468-16-7865
E-mail:
principal_*sullivan_es@pac.dodea.edu
http://www.sullivans-es.pac.dodea.edu

Walter Wilhoit, Principal

1354 Surabaya International School

CitraRaya International Village
Citra Raya, Lakarsantri
Tromol Pos 2/SBDK, Surabaya
Indonesia 60225
62-31-741-4300
Fax: 62-31-741-4334
E-mail: sisadmin@sisedu.net
http://www.sisedu.net
The Surabaya International School Community is committed to developing the social, emotional, physical, creative, and intellectual abilities necessary for its students to become reasoning, responsible, contributing, successful members of our global community.

Larry Jones, Superintendent
Christopher Burke, Chairperson

1355 TEDA International School-Tianjin

Number 72 Third Avenue Teda
Tianjin, CN 30045
86 -2 6-2261
Fax: 86 -2 6-0018
E-mail:
Principal@tedainternationalschool.net
http://www.tedainternationalschool.net
provide outstanding education to the students of all nationalities.

Nick Bowley, Director
Joseph Azmeh, Headmaster

1356 Tabubil International School

PO Box 408 Tabubil
Tabubil
Papua New Guinea
675-548-9233
Fax: 675-542-9641
E-mail: tabis@online.net.pg
http://www.tis.ac.pg
To provides a high quality international school education catering to the varied needs of Tabubil's multicultural mining community. The school employs a well motivated and productive staff, with good working conditions and a high degree of community involvement

SE Walker, Principal

1357 Taegu Elementary & High School

Unit 15623
APO Taegu 96218 0005
Korea

Leon Rivers, Principal

1358 Taipei American School

800 Chung Shan N Road Section 6
Taipei
Taiwan 11152
886-2-287-39900
Fax: 886-2-287-31641
E-mail: admissions@tas.edu.tw
http://www.tas.edu.tw
Our mission is to inspire each student to be a confident, creative, caring and moral individual prepared to adapt and succeed anywhere in a rapidly changing world. We provide an American-based education with a global perspective that results in a love of

learning, academic excellence, a balanced life, and service to others.

Sharon D Hennessy, Superintendent
Ira B Weislow, Business Manager

1359 Tanglin Trust Schools

95 Portsdown Road
Singapore 13929
65-67780711
Fax: 65-67775862
E-mail: admissions@tts.edu.sg
http://www.tts.edu.sg
Our vision is to be the premier school, providing the highest quality learning experiences for 3 to 18 year olds, and cultivating strong relationships in an environment where the individual is important. Our students enjoy a rich and stimulating all-round education which prepares them thoroughly for life in a rapidly-changing and competitive world.

Ronald Stones, Head of School
Peter Derby-Crook, CEO

1360 Thai-Chinese International School

101/177 Moo 7 Soi Mooban Bangpleeni
Prasertsin Road Bangplee Yai
Samutprakarn, TH 10540
66-2-260-8202
E-mail: tcis@schoolmail.com
http://www.tcis.ac.th
provide an education which allows each student to develop his/her full being in all areas of human development, academic, physical, emotional, spiritual and social, to interact as critical and compassionate thinkers, and to become a responsible member of our global society.

1361 Timbertop Campus

Timbertop PB-Mansfield
Victoria 3722
Australia
61 3 5733 6777
Fax: 61 3 5777 5772
E-mail: timbertop@ggs.vic.edu.au
http://http://www.ggs.vic.edu.au/Contact.aspx

Stephen Meek, Principal

1362 Traill Preparatory School

34-36 S01
18 Ramkhamheng Road, Huamark Bangkok
Thailand
660-271- 877
Fax: 660-271- 854
http://www.traillschool.ac.th

AM Traill, Principal

1363 Ukarumpa High School

PO Box 406
Ukarumpa Via Lae, Papua
New Guinea
675-737-4498
Fax: 675-737-4618
http://www.ukarumpainternationalschool.org

Steve Walker, Principal

1364 United Nations International School-Hanoi

Phu Thuong Ward Lac Long Quan Road
Tay Ho District
Veitnam, VN
(84 4) 3758 1551
Fax: (84 4) 3758 1542
E-mail: info@unishanoi.org
http://www.unishanoi.org
A private, nonprofit, English language, coeducational day school which offers an educational program from prekindergarten through grade 12 for the expatriate community of Hanoi.

Chip Barder, Head of School

1365 United World College-SE Asia
1207 Dover Road
PO Box 15, Singapore 9111
Singapore 13965
65 6775 5344
Fax: 65 6778 5846
E-mail: info@uwcsea.edu.sg
http://www.uwcsea.edu.sg
The United World College Movement makes education a force to unite people, nations and cultures for peace and a sustainable future. We educate individuals to take responsibility for shaping a better world
Julian Whiteley, Head of College
Geraint Jones, Assistant Head of College

1366 University Vacancies in Australia
Australian Vice-Chancellors' Committee
GPO Box 1142
Canberra City
Australia
61-02-6285-8200
Fax: 60-02-6285-8211
E-mail: contact@universitiesaustralia.edu.au
Universities Australia was established on 22 May 2007 as the industry peak body representing the university sector.
G Withers, Chief Executive Officer
P Rodely, Committee Executive Officer

1367 Vientiane International School
PO Box 3180
Phonesavanh Road, Saphanthong Tai Villag
Lao PDR
856 21 486001
Fax: 856 21 486009
E-mail: contact@vislao.com
http://www.vislao.com/
Vientiane International School (VIS) is an independent, non-profit day school offering a quality international-standard curriculum from Preschool (3 year olds) through Grade 12 (18 year olds).
Greg Smith, Director

1368 Wellesley College
PO Box 41037
Eastbourne, Lower Hutt 5047, Wellington
New Zealand
64 -56 -03
Fax: 64 -56 -28
E-mail: office@wellesley.school.nz
http://www.wellesley.school.nz
Wellesley is a full independent primary day school for boys from Year 0 (aged five) to Year 8.
Warren Owen, Principal
Charlotte Gendall, Board member

1369 Wesley International School
Kotak Pos 275
Malang, East Java
Indonesia 65101
62-341-586410
Fax: 62-341-586413
E-mail: wesley@wesleyinterschool.org
http://www.wesleyinterschool.org
Our mission at Wesley International School is to provide students with a Christ-centered education: one that inspires them to live a Godly life, that instills a biblical worldview, and produces academic excellence-an education that will prepare our students to impact and bless their world with knowledge, insight, action and love
Paul Richardson, HS Principal
Jonathan Heath, Director

1370 Western Academy of Beijing
PO Box 8547
10 Lai Guang Ying dong Lu, Beijing 10010
China
86-10-8456-4155
Fax: 86 10 6433-3974
E-mail: wabinfo@wab.edu
http://www.wab.edu
The Western Academy of Beijing offers a challenging and caring, community based educational environment in which students are active participants in the learning process
Robert Landau, Director
Karen O'Connell, Deputy Chair

1371 Wewak International Primary School
PO Box 354
Wewak Esp, Papua
New Guinea
Darian Sullavan, Principal

1372 Woodstock School
Mussoorie
Uttarakhand
India 24817
91-135-632-610
Fax: 91-135-632-885
E-mail: mail@woodstock.ac.in
http://www.woodstock.ac.in
Woodstock aims to develop responsible global citizens and leaders by providing a world-class international education, rooted in its Christian heritage and values, for a diverse group of students, especially from families in Christian or public service, in an Indian Himalayan environment
David Laurenson, Principal
Thomas Chandy, President

1373 Xiamen International School
262 Xingbei San Lu, Xinglin
Jimei, Xiamen, Fujian
China
86-592-625-6581
Fax: 86-592-625-6584
E-mail: askxis@xischina.com
http://www.xischina.com
Develops confident, knowledgeable students who enjoy life-long learning, demonstrate global awareness and contribute compassionately to the world around them.
Paul Raschke, Headmaster
Yuan Yuan Deng, Vice Chairman

1374 Yew Chung Shanghai International School
18 W Rong Hua Road, Gubei New Area
Shanghai
China 20110
(8621) 6219 5910
Fax: (8621) 6219 0675
E-mail: enquiry@ycef.com
http://www.ycis-sh.com
Provide an all-round education that nurtures the whole person - spiritual, academic, physical, social and emotional that includes relationships with others.
Andrew Mellor, Co-Principal
Julie Zheng, Co-Principal

1375 Yogyakarta International School
P.O. Box 1175
Yogyakarta 55011, Jalan Cendrawasih No.1
Indonesia
62-274-625965
Fax: 62-274-625966
E-mail: board@ yis-edu.org
http://http://www.yis-edu.org/
Operates as a not for profit social foundation and is overseen by a School Board made up of both parents and non-parents.
Chris Scott, Principal

1376 Yokohama International School
258 Yamate-cho Naka-ku
Yokohama
Japan 231-0
81-45-622-0084
Fax: 81-45-621-0379
E-mail: yis@yis.ac.jp
http://www.yis.ac.jp
Provides the highest-quality, balanced education to internationally minded students in an inquiring and supportive environment.
Simon Taylor, Headmaster
John Inge, Chairman

1377 Yokota East Elementary School
DoDDS P J YE Unit 5072
APO, Yokota 96328 5072
Japan 96328
81-3117-55-5503
Fax: 81-3117-55-5502
E-mail: principal.mendel@pac.dodea.edu
http://http://www.mendel-es.pac.dodea.edu
Yokota East Elementary School is located on Yokota Air Force Base near Tokyo, Japan. There are approximately 900 students grades K-6.
Hattie Phipps, Principal

1378 Yokota High School
DoDDS P J YH Unit 5072
APO AP
Japan 96328-5072
011-81-3117-55-701
Fax: 011-81-3117-55-722
E-mail: principal_*yokotahs@pac.dodea.edu
http://www.yokota-hs.pac.dodea.edu
Yokota High School, working in partnership with the family and local community, provides a safe, academically-inspiring environment in which all students will develop to their maximum potential as life-long learners and responsible participants in an ever-changing global society.
Darrell Mood, Principal

1379 Yokota West Elementary School
DoDDS P J YW Unit 5072
APO AP
Japan 96328-5072
011-81-3117-55-761
Fax: 011-81-3117-55-573
E-mail: principal_*yokota_west_es@pac.dodea.edu
http://www.ywes.pac.dodea.edu
Sharon Carter, Principal

1380 Yonggwang Foreign School
Ceii Site Office
PO Box 9, Yonggwang-Kun 513-880
Korea
Eleanor Jones, Principal

1381 Zama Junior High & High School
USA Garrison, Camp Zama
APO, Honshu 96343 0005
Japan
Samuel Menniti, Principal

1382 Zukeran Elementary School
Unit 35017
FPO AP
Japan 96379-5017
011-81-611-7452576
Fax: 011-81-098-892-795
E-mail: Zukeran.Principal@pac.dodea.edu
http://www.zukeran-es.pac.dodea.edu
Zukeran Elementary School shares the vision of creating a community of learners actively engaged in the pursuit of the knowledge, skills and experiences necessary to empower

all children to meet the challenges of the 21st century.

Cindy Templeton, Principal
Roger Reade, Assistant Principal

Central & South America

1383 Academia Cotopaxi American International School

De las Higuerillas y Alondras
Quito
Ecuador
593-2-246-7411
Fax: 593-2-244-5195
E-mail: info@cotopaxi.k12.ec
http://www.cotopaxi.k12.ec
Premier English-language school from early childhood through secondary school.

Kurt Kywi, President
Robert Moss, Vice President

1384 American Cooperative School

Lawton 20
Paramaribo
Suriname
597-49-9461
Fax: 597-498-853
E-mail: acs_suriname@sil.org
http://www.acslp.org
A private, coeducational day school which offers an educational program from prekindergarten through grade 12 for students of all nationalities.

Frank Martens, Administrator

1385 American Elementary & High School

Caixa Postal 7432
01064-970, Sao Paulo
Brazil
55-11-3842-2499
Fax: 55-11-3842-9358
E-mail: graded@eagle.aegsp.br
A private, coeducational day school which offers a full college-preparatory educational program from preschool through grade 12 for students of all nationalities.

Dr Gunther Brandt, Principal

1386 American International School-Bolivia

Casilla 5309
Cochabamba
Bolivia
591-4-428-8577
Fax: 591-4-428-8576
E-mail: administracion@aisb.edu.bo
http://www.aisb.edu.bo
The American International School of Bolivia was founded in 1993 as an international, non-governmental, co-educational day school. The AIS/B educational system covers from Early Childhood education up to the IB program in grades 11 and 12 for students representing all nationalities and socio-economical levels.

Dr Silke Marina Scholer, Director General
Tatiana Jimenez BA, Chief Administrator

1387 American International School-Lincoln Buenos Aires

Andres Ferreyra 4073
B1637 AOS La Lucila, Buenos Aires
Argentina
(54)(11) 4851-1700
Fax: 54-11-479-02117
E-mail: pacha_c@lincoln.edu.ar
http://www.lincoln.edu.ar
Provides education based on United States accredited curriculum in an environment of academic excellence that develops ethical, responsible and globally conscious world citizens.

Phil T Joslin, Superintendent

1388 American School

PO Box (01) 35
El Salvador
503-26-38-330
Fax: 503-26-38-385
E-mail: recruiting@amschool.edu.sv
http://www.amschool.edu.sv
Founded in 1946 and is an independent, international, coeducational, college-preparatory institution

Yolanda de Lopez, Director of Admissions

1389 American School Foundation AC

Bondojito 215
Colonia Las Americas
Mexico City, Mexico 01120
52-55-5227-4900
Fax: 52-55-5273-4357
E-mail: asf@asf.edu.mx
http://www.asf.edu.mx
is an academically rigorous, international, university preparatory school, which offers students from diverse backgrounds the best of American independent education

Julie Hellmund, Director

1390 American School Foundation-Guadalajara

Colomos 2100, Coronel Providencia
Guadalajara, Jalisco
Mexico 44640
52 (33) 3648-0299
Fax: 52-33-3817-3356
E-mail: asfg@asfg.mx
http://www.asfg.mx
Educating students in a bilingual, bicultural and secular environment to be purposeful learners, critical and creative thinkers, effective communicators and community contributors, based on a foundation of honor, freedom and commitment

David McGrath, Principal
Jabet Heinze, Superintendent

1391 American School Foundation-Monterrey

Ave. Ignacio Morones Prieto No. 150
Col. San Isidro, Santa Catarina, N.L.
Nuevo Leon, Mexico 66190
(52)-81-5000-4400
Fax: (52)-81-5000-4428
E-mail: jeff.keller@asfm.edu.mx
http://www.asfm.edu.mx
A private, nonprofit, coeducational day school which offers an educational program from nursery through grade 12 for students of all nationalities.

Dr. Jeffrey Keller, Superintendent

1392 American School-Belo Horizonte

Avenida Deputado Cristovan Chiaradia 120
Caixa Postal 1701
Bairro Buritis, Belo Horizonte
30575-440
Brazil
55-31-378-6700
Fax: 55-31-378-6878
E-mail: eabh@eabh.com.br
http://www.eabh.com.
A coeducational, private day school which offers an educational program from prekindergarten through grade 12 for students of all nationalities.

Sid Stewart, Principal

1393 American School-Brasilia

SGAS 605
Bloco E, Lotes 34/37
Brasilia,DF,Brazil 70200-650
55 (61) 3442-9700
Fax: 55 (61) 3442-9729
E-mail: kpuzic@eabdf.br
http://www.eabdf.br
A private, coeducational day school which offers an educational program from prekindergarten through grade 12 for students of all nationalities

Barry Dequanne, Headmaster
Beth Lopez, Lower School Principal

1394 American School-Campinas

Rua Cajamar, 35 - Jardim Alto da Ba
Campinas- SP
Brazil 13090
55 19 2102-1000
Fax: 55 19 2102-1016
http://http://www.escolaamericanadecampinas.com.br/?contact

Steve Herrara, Superintendent

1395 American School-Durango

Francisw Sarabia #416 Pte
Durango 34000
Mexico
(618) 813-36-36
Fax: (618) 811-28-39
E-mail: colegio_americano@cadurango.edu.mx
http://http://www.cadurango.edu.mx

Dr Jorge O Nelson, Principal

1396 American School-Guatemala

11 Calle 1579 Zona 15 Vista Hermosa
Guatemala
Guatemala
502-690-
Fax: 502-698-
E-mail: director@cag.edu.gt
http://www.cag.edu.gt
is to educate independent, critical-thinking, responsible, bilingual individuals prepared to meet the challenges of the future

Robert Gronniger, General Director
Edward Langlais, High School Principal

1397 American School-Guayaquil

PO Box 3304
Guayaquill
Ecuador
593-4-255-503
Fax: 593-4-250-453
E-mail: dir_asg@gye.satnet.net
http://www.americanschool.edu.ec
Grade levels K-12, school year April - January

Francisco Andrade, Interim General Director
Patricia Ayala de Coronel, HS Principal

1398 American School-Laguna Verde

Veracruz, Mexico

Maurice H Blum, Principal

1399 American School-Lima

Apartado 18-0977
Lima 18
Peru
51-14-35-0890
Fax: 51 1 619-9301
E-mail: fdr@amersol.edu.pe
http://www.amersol.edu.pe/fdr/
is to empower our students to pursue their passion for learning, lead lives of integrity and create socially responsible solutions.

Caron Kluznik, Superintendent

1400 American School-Pachuca

Valle de Anahuac S/N Valle de San J
ZC: 42083 Pachuca de Soto Hidalgo
Mexico
01-771 713 9608
Fax: 52-771-85077

E-mail: admisiones@americana.edu.mx
http://http://www.americana.edu.mx/
Grade levels prekindergarten through ninth.

Nicforo Ramirez, General Director

1401 American School-Puebla

Apartado 665
Puebla
Mexico
http://http://www.cap.edu.mx/english/

Dr Arthur W Chaffee, Principal

1402 American School-Puerto Vallarta

PO Box 2-280
Puerto Vallarta, Jalisco 48300
Mexico
52 322-221-1525
Fax: (52) 322-226-7677
E-mail: Info@aspv.edu.mx
http://http://www.aspv.edu.mx

Gerald Selitzer, Director

1403 American School-Recife

408 S e Souza Street
Boa Viagem
Brazil 51030-60
55 81 3341.4716
Fax: 55-81-341-0142
E-mail: info@ear.com.br
http://www.ear.com.br
A private, coeducational day school which
offers an instructional program from
prekindergarten through grade 12 for students of all nationalities.

George Takacks, Superintendent

1404 American School-Tampico

Hidalgo # 100
Tancol, Tampico
Mexico
52-12-272-081
Fax: 52-12-280-080
E-mail: racevedo@ats.edu.mx
http://www.ats.edu.mx
Grade levels N through tenth.

Emma deSalazar, Headmaster

1405 American School-Torreon

Paseo del Algodn y Boulevard Carlo
Fracc Los Viedos Torren, Coahuila
Mexico 27019
871222 51 00 TO 0
Fax: 871 733 26 68
E-mail: cat@cat.mx
http://www.cat.mx
A prestigious center of academic excellence
dedicated to creating life-long learners and
ethical leaders in a global and changing
world.

Makhlouf Ouyed, Director General
Martha Martinez, Business Manager

1406 Anglo American School

PO Box 3188-1000
San Jose
Costa Rica
506-279-2626
Fax: 506-279-7894
E-mail: angloam@racsa.co.cr
http://www.aas.ru
Grade levels Pre-K through 6, school year
February - November

Virginia Hine Barrantes, Principal

1407 Anglo Colombian School

Apaptado Aereo 253393
Bogota
Colombia
http://www.anglocolombiano.edu.co

David Toze, Principal

1408 Anglo-American School

Calle 37
Avenida Central, 1000 San Jose
Costa Rica
495-231-447
E-mail: angloam@sd.racsa.co.cr
http://www.aas.ru

Virginia Hine, Principal

1409 Antofagasta International School

Avda. Jaime Guzman Errazurz #04300
Antofagasta
Chile
56 - 55 - 694900
Fax: 56 - 55 - 694912
E-mail: ais@ais.cl
http://www.ais.cl
A Pre-Kindergarten through 12th grade educational institution that is dedicated to offering a challenging, English-based curriculum
to its students.

Carlos Ignacio Figueroa Ahumada,
Principal
Carlos Arturo Calussen Calvo, Chairman

1410 Asociacion Colegio Granadino

AA 2138
Manizales, Caldas
Colombia
57-68-745-774
Fax: 57-68-746-066
E-mail: granadino@emtelsa.multi.net.co
http://www.granadino.edu.co
Grade levels Pre-K through 12, school year
August - June

Gonzalo Arango, General Director

1411 Asociacion Escuelas Lincoln

Andres Ferreyra 4073
B1636 AOS La Lucila, Buenos Aires
Argentina
(54)(11) 4851-1700
Fax: 54-11-4790-2117
E-mail: joslin_p@lincoln.edu.ar
http://www.lincoln.edu.ar
Provide an education based on United States
accredited curriculum

Phil Joslin, Superintendent
Claudia Pacha, Admissions

1412 Balboa Elementary School

Unit 9025
APO Balboa 34002
Panama
818-241-1801
http://www.gusd.net

Susan Beattie, Principal

1413 Balboa High School

Unit 9025
APO Balboa 34002
Panama
818-241-1801
http://www.gusd.net

Ernest Holland, Principal

1414 Barker College

91 Pacific Highway
Hornsby
NSW, Australia 02077
612-984- 83
Fax: 02 -4 6-3
E-mail: reception@barker.nsw.edu.au
http://www.barker.nsw.edu.au
That Barker College be, and be recognized as,
a leading Australian Christian independent
school, which provides a broadly-based education and encourages young people to strive
to fulfil their potential, and which is acknowledged as a centre of excellence in pastoral care and in teaching and learning

Jimmy Cappanera, Principal
Roderic Kefford, Headmaster

1415 Belgrano Day School

Juramento 3035
Ciudad de Buenos Aires
Argentina c1428
54 -1 -81
Fax: 54 -1 -786
E-mail: rrpp@bdsnet.com.ar
http://www.bds.edu.ar
We cooperate with the family to offer bilingual education quality for the training of future leaders and citizens of the world
committed to the common good, free, responsible, creative and respectful of diversity and
dissent.

Maria Matilde V Green, President
Carol Halle, Faculty Head

1416 Bilingue School Isaac Newton

Chihuahua, Mexico

Lauya Gonzalez Valenzula, Principal

1417 British American School

AA 4368
Barranquilla
Colombia 28277
704-341-3236
http://britishschoolofcharlotte.org

Rafael Ortegon Rocha, Principal

1418 British School-Costa Rica

PO Box 8184-1000
San Jose
Costa Rica 02232-7833
50 - 2 -0 0
Fax: 50 - 2 -2 7
E-mail: britsch@racsa.co.cr
http://http://www.thebritishschoolofcostaric
a.com/

David John Lloyd, Principal

1419 British School-Rio de Janeiro

R Real Grandeza 99
Botafogo, Rio de Janeiro
Brazil, BR 22281-30
55(21) 2539-2717
Fax: 55(21) 2244-5591
E-mail: edu@britishschool.g12.br
http://www.britishschool.g12.br
The British School aims to develop responsible, well-informed, open-minded, confident
and caring individuals by providing an educational community within which all pupils
are motivated to realize their full potential
through a challenging British-based education in a non-discriminatory and bi-cultural
environment

Paul Wiseman, Director
Adam Reid, Chairman

1420 British School-Venezuela

Sector 8 and Sector 12
Panchkula
India 13410
91-172-5028556
E-mail: tbs@thebritishschool.org
http://www.thebritishschool.org
aims to provide education with global standards. This will not only make students
studying in the school eligible for higher education in the institutions across the world but
also give NRI's settled abroad, an opportunity to send their children to such schools to
have a better idea of the social system back
home.

TBS Panchkula, Principal
U Sethi, Board Member

1421 Buenos Aires International Christian Academy

Red de Escuelas Mundiales Cristiana
Av Libertador General San Mart-n 2170
Buenos Aires, AR 01646

5411 4549 1300
Fax: 5411 4549 1300
E-mail: info@baica.com
http://www.baica.com
Our school is unique in that we are home to both Argentineans and the expat community.

Andy Simon, Principal
Robert Newman, Director

1422 Caribbean International School
Box 1594
Cristobal Colon
Panama
507-445-0933
http://cis.edu.pa

Anderson, Principal

1423 Centro Cultural Brazil-Elementary School
Rua Jorge Tibirica 5
11100 Santos, Sao Paulo
Brazil

Newton Antonio Martin, Principal

1424 Cochabamba Cooperative School
Casilla 1395
Cochabamba
Bolivia 01395
591-42-987-61
Fax: 591-42-329-06
E-mail: Cwieburg@ccs.edu.bo
http://www.ccs.edu.bo
President

Provide attendees

Carl Wieburg, Director
Jos Leonis, Manager

1425 Colegio Abraham Lincoln
Calle 170, # 51A-81
SedePrimaria Avenue Calle 170 #65-31
Columbia
571-676-7360
http://www.abrahamlincoln.edu.co
Promoting human development within a humanistic philosophy and pruricultural.

Amparo Rueda, Director

1426 Colegio Alberto Einstein
PO Box 5018
Av. Diego Vsquez de Cepeda N77-157
Quito, Ecuador
(593-2)2477-901
Fax: 2470-144
E-mail: einstein@einstein.k12.ec
http://http://www.einstein.k12.ec/home-e.html

Benjamin Tobar, Principal
Raquel Katzkowicz, General Director

1427 Colegio Americano De Guayaquil
Juan Tanca Marengo Avenue PO Box 33
Guayaquil
Ecuador
593-4-255-03
Fax: 593-4-250-453
E-mail: info@colegioamericano.edu.ec
http://www.colegioamericano.edu.ec
Provide an education with the highest standards of quality, thus contributing to the improvement of our society.

Stanley Whitman, Principal
Francisco Andrade, Association President

1428 Colegio Anglo Colombiano
Avenida 19 # 152A-48
Bogota
, DC
571-259-5700
E-mail:
admissions@anglocolombiano.edu.co
http://www.anglocolombiano.edu.co

Our purpose is to educate human beings with open minds, real social awareness and the power of critical thinking.

David Toze, Principal
Catherine Cushnan, Admission

1429 Colegio Bilingue Juan Enrigue
Pestalozzi AC
Veracruz
Mexico

Michael S Garber, Principal

1430 Colegio Bolivar
Calle 5 Number 122-21 V-a Pance
Cali
Colombia
(57-2) 684 8600
Fax: 57-2-555-2041
E-mail: cbinfo@colegiobolivar.edu.co
http://www.colegiobolivar.edu.co
Colegio Bolivar is an educational community whose mission is to educate its students in a bilingual, democratic environment to be autonomous, and to demonstrate a spirit of inquiry and collaboration, a commitment to excellence, and the highest aspirations for the welfare of both the individual and society.

Joseph Nagy, Director
Richard Martin, Dean of Students

1431 Colegio Columbo Britanico
Apartado Aereo 5774
Cali
Colombia
http://www.colombobritanico.edu.co

Ian Watson, Principal

1432 Colegio Gran Bretana
Carrera 51 #215-20
Bogota
Colombia
57-1-676-0391
Fax: 57-1-676-0426
E-mail: admissions@cgb.edu.co
http://http://www.cgb.edu.co/
Grade levels N-10, school year August-June

Daryl Barker, Director
David Simpson, Deputy Director

1433 Colegio Granadino
AA 2138 Manizales
Colombia
57-6-874-57-74
Fax: 57-6-874-60-66
E-mail:
granadino@emtelsa.multi.net.com
http://www.granadino.edu.co
Early Childhood, Elementary, Middle School and High School

Gonzalo Arango, Principal
Robert Sims, Director

1434 Colegio Interamericano de la Montana
Boulevard La Montana
Finca El Socorro, Zona 16
Guatemala, GT 01016
502 2200.2990
Fax: 502-3-641-779
http://www.interamericano.edu.gt
The mission of Colegio Interamericano is to prepare its students for life and for studies anywhere in the world, by orienting them towards being responsible members of society.

Dr Michael Farr, General Director
Griselda de Amezquita, Head of Human Resources

1435 Colegio Jorge Washington
Zona Norte, Anillo Vial Km.12
Cartagena
Colombia, CO
57-5-673 5505
Fax: 57-5-665-6447
E-mail: director@cojowa.edu.co
http://cojowa.edu.co
The mission of the George Washington School is to form bilingual and bicultural citizens who possess high ethical values and commitment to the search for academic excellence and success in life.

Pete Nonnenkamp, Director
Maritza Garcia, Assistant Director

1436 Colegio Karl C Parrish
Kilometer 2 Antigua Via a Puerto Co
Barranquilla
Colombia, CO 52962
57-5-359-8929
Fax: 57-5-359-8828
E-mail: mail@kcparrish.edu.co
http://www.kcparrish.edu.co
strives to provide an environment that results in students displaying personal integrity and character in their relationships both within and outside the school.

Laura Horbal Rebolledo, Director
Hectalina Donado, Elementary School Principal

1437 Colegio Montelibano
AA 6823 Cerromatoso
Montelibano, Bogota
Colombia

Francisco Cajiao, Principal

1438 Colegio Nueva Granada
Carrera 2 Este Number 70-20
Bogota
Colombia, CO
57-1-2123511
Fax: 57-1-211-3720
E-mail: sngrana@COL1.telecom.com.co
http://www.cng.edu
Prepare tomorrow's leaders by educating the mind, nurturing the spirit, and strengthening the body.

Barry McCombs PhD, Director
Michael Adams, Deputy Director

1439 Colegio Peterson SC
Apartado Postal 10-900
DF 11000
Mexico
52-5-81-30-11-4
Fax: 52-5-81-31-38-5
E-mail: kapm@mail.internet.com.mx
http://www.peterson.edu

Marvin Peterson, Principal

1440 Colegio San Marcus
61 Ourense
Buenas Aires
Argentina 32004
988-247-4
Fax: 988- 39-5
E-mail: csmarcos@csmarcos.com
http://www.csmarcos.com
Collegio San Marcos was established in 1988, when it began its first year of dentures, being recognized by the Galician regional government, as accredited Vocational Training Second Grade, under the Order of May 20 1.988 of the Department of Education and University (DOG num.110 June 1988).

Susana Raffo, Principal

1441 Colegio Ward
Hector Coucheiro 599
1706 DF Sarmiento, Ramos Mejia
Buenos Aires, Argentina

541- 46-8 03
E-mail: info@ward.edu.ar
http://www.ward.edu.ar
Ruben Carlos Urcola, Principal
Daniel Campagna, Director

1442 Costa Rica Academy
Apartado Postal 4941
San Jose 1000
Costa Rica
506-239-03-76
Fax: 506-239-06-25
A private, coeducational school which offers an educational program from prekindergarten through grade 12 for students of all nationalities.

William D Rose, BS, Med, Principal

1443 Cotopaxi Academy
PO Box 17-11-6510
Quito
Ecuador
593-2-246-7411
Fax: 593-2-244-5195
E-mail: info@cotopaxi.k12.ec
http://www.cotopaxi.k12.ec
Premier English-language early childhood through secondary school in Ecuador. The internationally recognized program is aggressively sought out by all National and International parents who truly want to join a partnership to provide the very best education possible for their children.

Eddie Wexler, Principal
Kurt Kywi, President

1444 Country Day School
Apartado 1139 - 1250
Escazu
Costa Rica
(506) 2289 - 0919
Fax: (506) 2228 - 2076
E-mail: gloria_doll@cds.ed.cr
http://www.cds.ed.cr
CDS is an American School serving an international population. Accredited by the Middle States Association of Colleges and Schools in the United States, and by the Costa Rican Ministry of Education

Gloria Doll, Director
Maria Fernanda Cardona, Admissions Coordinator

1445 Crandon Institute
Casilla Correo 445
Montevideo
Uruguay
248- 33-5
http://www.crandon.edu.uy
This school offers a curriculum taught in Spanish for 2,000 day students (700 boys; 1,300 girls), in high school through junior college level (home economics, commercial). The school, affiliated with the Methodist church, employs 300 teachers.

Marcos Rocchietti, Principal

1446 Curundu Elementary School
Unit 0925
APO Curundu 34002 0005
Panama

Clifford Drexler, Principal

1447 Curundu Junior High School
Unit 0925
APO Curundu 34002 0005
Panama

Charles Renno, Principal

1448 Edron Academy-Calz Al Desierto
Desierto de los Leones 5578
Mexico City 01740
Mexico

5-585-30-49
Fax: 5-585-28-46
http://www.edron.edu.
Richard Gilby Travers, Principal

1449 El Abra School
Phelps Dodge Corporation
Calama
Chile
56-55-313-600
Fax: 56-55-315-182
E-mail: elabraschool@hotmail.com
Grade levels K-11, school year August - June

Margaret Maclean, Head of School

1450 English School
AA 51284
Bogota
Colombia

Leonard Mabe, Principal

1451 Escola Americana do Rio de Janeiro
Estrada Da Gavea 132
Rio de Janeiro
Brazil 22451-263
(916) 458-5932
Fax: 55-21-259-4722
E-mail: americanrio@ax.apc.org
http://www.earj.com.br
Escola Americana motivates engaged learners to become independent critical thinkers in a multicultural community.

Dr Dennis Klumpp, Principal
Caren Addis, Director of Admissions

1452 Escola Maria Imaculada
Rua Vigrio Joao de Pontes, 537, Ch
Sao Paulo
Brazil 04748
551- 2-01 7
Fax: 551- 55-1 77
http://http://www.chapelschool.com/
Gerald Gates, Principal

1453 Escuela Anaco
Avenue Jose Antonio Anzoategui, KM
Anaco
Venezuela
58 -82 -22 2
E-mail: director@ESCUELAANACO.COM
http://princeton.iss.edu
Offers a United States High School Diploma with a full schooling program from Day Care through Grade 12. Also have on-line courses to enhance our program. Uses the best of the educational standards of the states of California, New York, and Virginia.

Francene Conte, Principal
Bill Kralovec, Director

1454 Escuela Bilingue Santa Barbara
Apartado 342-El Marchito
San Pedro Sila
Honduras
504-659-3053
Fax: 504-659-3059
E-mail: mochitoschool@breakwater.hn
http://princeton.iss.edu
Grade levels preK through 8.

John P Leddy, Principal

1455 Escuela Bilingue Valle De Sula
Apartado 735
San Pedro Sula
Honduras

Carole A Black, Principal

1456 Escuela International Sampedrana
Col Gracias A Dios 500 mts W Hospit
San Pedro Sula
Honduras
504-566-2722
Fax: 504-566-1458

E-mail: eperez@seishn.com
http://www.seishn.org
EIS seeks to be the premier school in the city of San Pedro Sula, the country of Honduras and region of Central America through the use of best teaching practices with the goal of reaching all of its students.

Gregorg E Werner, Principal
Ronald Vair, Superintendent

1457 Escuela Las Palmas
Apartdo 6-2637
Panama
797-530-
http://www.cmpuentealto.cl
Aleida Molina, Principal

1458 Foreign Students School
Avenue Station B
#6617-6615 Esquina 70
Miramar Havana City, Cuba

Gillian P Greenwood, Principal

1459 Fort Clayton Elementary School
2000 Park Place Avenue
APO, Fort Clayton 34004 0005
Panama, TX
817-814-5400
http://www.lilybclayton.org

Barbara Seni, Principal

1460 Fort Kobbe Elementary School
Unit 0714
APO, Fort Kobbe 34001 0005
Panama

Dr Vinita Swenty, Principal

1461 Fundacion Colegio Americano de Quito
Manuel Benigno Cueva N80 - 190 Urba
PO Box 17-01-157, Carcel,n, Quito
Ecuador, DC
(593) 2 3976 300
Fax: 593-2-472-972
E-mail: dirgeneral@fcaq.k12.ec
http://www.fcaq.k12.ec
Grade levels Pre-K through 12, school year September - June.

Susan Barbara, Director General

1462 George Washington School
Apartado Aereo 2899
Cartagena
Colombia
57-5-665-3396
Fax: 57-5-665-6447
A private, coeducational day school which offers and educational program from prekindergarten through grade 12 for students of all nationalities.

Steven Fields, Principal

1463 Grange School
Casilla 218
Correo 12, Santiago
Chile
(56) 2- 5981500?
Fax: 56-2-227-1204
E-mail: admissions@grange.cl
http://www.grange.cl
Places great importance on the idea of 'fair play', a concept with connotations of sportsmanship, rule obedience, and honesty

Mike Freeman, Headmaster
Carolina Varela, Deputy Headmaster

1464 Greengates School
Avenue Circumbalacion Pte 102
Baliones De San Mateo, Naucalpah
Edo de Mexico, Mexico 53200
52-55-5373-0088
Fax: 52-55-5373-0765

E-mail: sarav@greengates.edu.mx
http://www.greengates.edu.mx
Grade levels prekindergarten through twelfth.
Susan E Mayer, Principal

1465 Howard Elementary School

805 Long Hollow Pike
Gallatin
Panama, TN 37066
615-452-3025
http://www.hes.sumnerschools.org
Jean Lamb, Principal

1466 Inst Tecnologico De Estudios

Apartado Postal 28B
Chihuahua
Mexico
528- 83-8 20
http://www.itesm.edu
Hector Chavrez Barron, Principal

1467 International Preparatory School

PO Box 20015-LC
Santiago
Chile
56-2-321-5800
Fax: 56-2-321-5821
E-mail: info@tipschool.com
http://www.internationalpreparatoryschool.com
Grade levels Pre-K through 12, school year March - December
Lesley Easton-Allen, Headmistress
Pamela Thomson, Curriculum Coordinator

1468 International School Nido de Aguilas

Avenida El Rodeo 14200
Santiago
Chile
(562) 339-8105
Fax: 56-2-216-7603
E-mail: abattistoni@nido.cl
http://www.nido.cl
The International School Nido de Aguilas is committed to offering each student excellence in the pursuit of academic achievement in preparation for attendance at a US, Chilean or other international university, all within the framework of a challenging US-based, English-language curriculum. We encourage open-mindedness, global diversity, environmental awareness, community service and the development of leadership skills, including integrity, responsibility and self-discipline.
Dr Don Bergman, Headmaster
Jared Harris, HS Principal

1469 International School-Curitiba

Av Dr Eug^nio Bertolli
3900 Santa Felicidade, Curitiba, Paran
Brazil 18241
413-525-7400
Fax: 413-525-7499
E-mail: isc@iscbrazil.com~
http://www.iscbrazil.com
It is a private, nonprofit, self-governed school that serves students and families from our local and international community; offers a U.S. based curriculum in English with American, Brazilian and International Baccalaureate diplomas; commits to academic and personal excellence and prepares students for universities around the world.
Elizabeth Mello, Principal 1-12
Bill Pearson, Superintendent

1470 International School-La Paz

CC1075870 Villa Dolores
La Paz, Cordoba
Argentina
LH Sullivan, Principal

1471 International School-Panama

PO Box 0819-02588
El Dorado
Panama
(507) 293-3000
Fax: 507-266-7808
E-mail: isp@isp.edu.pa
http://www.isp.edu.pa
A private, coeducational day school which offers an educational program from prekindergarten through grade 12 for students of all nationalities.
Rajiv Bhatt, Director
Jania Jacob, Business Manager

1472 Karl C Parrish School

Km 2 Antigua via a Puerto
Barranquilla
Colombia
(57-5) 3598929
Fax: 57-5-3598828
E-mail: mail@kcparrish.edu.co
http://www.kcparrish.edu.co
Karl C. Parrish is a private, non-sectarian, non-profit elementary and secondary school that is open to children of all nationalities.
Laura H Rebolledo, Director

1473 Liceo Pino Verde

Vereda Los Planes kilometro 5
Va Cerritos Entrada 16, El Tigre
Colombia
963-379368
E-mail: info@liceopinoverde.edu.co
http://www.liceopinoverde.edu.co
This school teaches English as a second language; builds strong human values; develops logical thinking skills and prepares students for the world of technology and communication. Enrollment consists of 110 day students (57 boys; 53 girls, in grades PK-12. Overseas teachers are welcome to apply with the length of stay being two years, with housing provided. Applications needed to teach include science, math and English.
Luz Stella Rios Patino, Principal

1474 Limon School

P.O. Box 249
847 F Avenue
Limon, CO 80828
719-775-2350
Fax: 719-775-9052
http://limonbadgers.com
strive to provide a safe environment and develop responsible and productive citizens who have the knowledge and skills to seize their chosen opportunities
Chris Selle, Principal

1475 Lincoln International Academy

PO Box 52-7444
Miami, FL 33152
1 (305) 395-4825
E-mail: lincoln@lincoln.edu.ni
http://www.lincoln.edu.ni
instilling in them solid Christian and human virtues as taught by the Catholic faith, challenging them to reach their full intellectual capacity and achieve a high integral academic excellence in order to face the challenges of today's world. providing

them with English instruction while preserving our Hispanic-Nicaraguan culture.
Henningston Hammond, Operation Manager
Adolfo Gonzalez, General Director

1476 Mackay School

Vicuna Mackenna 700
Renaca
Chile
563-223- 660
Fax: 563-223- 667
http://www.mackay.cl
Nigel William Blackbur, Principal

1477 Marian Baker School

Apartado 4269
San Jose
Costa Rica 01000
560-273-3426
Fax: 506-273-4609
E-mail: mbschool@sol.racsa.co.cr
http://www.mbs.ed.cr/
Marian Baker School (MBS) is an International English speaking school educating preschool through high school students.
Linda Niehaus, Director
Bonnie Heigold, Business Manager

1478 Marymount School

1026 Fifth Avenue
Barranquilla
Colombia, NY 10028
212-744-4486
Fax: 212-744-0163
http://www.marymountnyc.org
Dr. Kathleen Cunniffe, Principal

1479 Metropolitan School

7281 Sarah Avenue
Maplewood, MO 63143
314-644-0850
E-mail: nsmith@metroschool.org
The School is dedicated to providing a highly individualized educational experience for middle and senior high school students whose potential has not been recognized and/or meaningfully challenged in traditional school settings.
Judi Thomas, Head of School

1480 Modern American School

Cerro del Hombre 18
Col. Romero de Terreros
Mexico
565-476-
http://www.modernamerican.edu.mx
To provide our students with the educational elements which will promote the optimum development of the intellect, instill social awareness and emotional sensitivity, encourage artistic creativity, and emphasize physical well-being, aiming for excellence toward future success

1481 Northlands Day School

Roma 1210
1636 Olivos, Buenos Aires
Argentina
541-147-1 84
Fax: 541- 47-1 84
http://www.northlands.org.ar/
This bilingual day school for girls offers modern facilities, sports, etc. on a spacious campus. Languages spoken include English and Spanish and total enrollment is 1,100 students, ranging in grade from K1-12. Overseas teachers are accepted, with the length of stay being 2-6 years with housing provided.
Susan Brooke Jackson, MA, Principal

1482 Our Lady of Mercy School

Rua Visconde de Caravelas
48, Botafogo, Rio de Janeiro
Brazil
336-722-7204
http://www.ourladyofmercyschool.org

Our Lady of Mercy School is an American Catholic English speaking school whose main purpose is to educate the whole student towards global understanding.

Charles Lyndaker, Superintendent

1483 Pan American Christian Academy

1730 Link Road
04829-310 Sao Paulo
Brazil
480.471.5339
Fax: 55-11-59289591
E-mail: info@paca.com.br
http://www.paca.com.br
American international school located in the city of Sao Paulo, working with 350 students from different parts of the world with an American-style pre-school through high school education. Since 1960, we've served the local and international community of Sao Paulo.

Micheal Epp, Superintendent

1484 Pan American School-Bahia

Caixa Postal 231
Salvador
Brazil, SA 40901-970
55-71-3368-8400
Fax: 55-71-3368-8441
E-mail: info@escolapanamericana.com
http://www.escolapanamericana.com
A private, coeducational day school which offers a program from preschool through grade 12 for students of all nationalities.

Mary Jo Heatherington, PhD,
Superintendent

1485 Pan American School-Costa Rica

Apartado 474
Monterrey
Costa Rica, NL 64000
(81) 83-42-07-78
Fax: (81) 83-40-27-49
E-mail: dadmission@pas.edu.mx
http://www.pas.edu.mx
Offer excellent educational programs in English that foster the integral development of students.

Robert Arpee, Director

1486 Pan American School-Monterrey

Hidalgo 656 Pte
Apartado Postal 474, Monterrey 64000
Mexico
(81) 83-42-07-78
http://www.pas.edu.mx
This school offers an English curriculum for 1,393 day students and 100 boarding students (709 boys; 684 girls), grades preschool through nine. The school is willing to participate in a teacher exchange program with the length of stay being one year. Applications needed to teach include science, preschool, math, reading, English, and physical education.

Tobert L Arpee, Principal
Lenor Arpee, Faculty Head

1487 Pan American School-Porto Alegre

Rua Joao Paetzel 440
91 330 Porto Alegre
Brazil
555- 33-4 58
http://www.panamerican.com.br

Jennifer Sughrue, Principal

1488 Panama Canal College

Unit 0925
APO Balboa 34002 0005
Panama
http://www.educationusapanama.wetpaint.com

1489 Prescott Anglo American School

PO Box 1036
Arequipa
Peru
http://www.prescott.edu.pe
This school offers a Spanish/English curriculum for 1,050 day students (450 boys; 600 girls) in grades K-12. Students are taught English three hours a day, so they can reach an intermediate level in grade 9, and high intermediate in grades 11-12.

Jorge Pachecot, Principal

1490 Redland School

272 Military Road
Cremorne
Chile, NS 02090
612-990- 313
Fax: 612-990- 322
http://www.redlands.nsw.edu.au
This school offers an English/Spanish curriculum to 820 day students (420 boys; 400 girls), in grades PreK-12. The student body is mostly Chilean and 90% of the teachers are Chilean. However, overseas teachers are welcome, with the applications being pre-school and English.

Richard Collingwood-Selby, Principal

1491 Reydon School for Girls

5178 Cruz Chica
Sierras de Cordoba, Cordoba
Argentina

NJ Milman, Principal

1492 Saint George's School

Carrera 92 No 156-88, Suba
Bogota
Colombia
057-168- 917
E-mail: sanjorge@sgs.edu.co
http://www.sgs.edu.co

Mary De Acosta, Principal

1493 Santa Cruz Cooperative School

Barrio Las Palmas Calle Barcelona #
Casilla 753 Santa Cruz
Bolivia
(591) (3) 353-0808
Fax: (591) (3) 352-6993
E-mail: william.j.mckelligott@gmail.com
http://www.sccs.edu.bo
College preparatory school equipping students with the necessary skills and values to be citizens and leaders for the 21st century. Preparing students to become productive citizens, leaders and life-long learners.

William J McKelligott, Director General
Hugo Paz, Board Director

1494 Santa Margarita School

22062 Antonio ParkwayRancho Santa
Surco, Lima
Peru, CA 92688
949-766-6000
http://www.smhs.org

Guillermo Descalzi, Principal

1495 St. Albans College

110 Clearwater Road
Lynnwood Glen Pretoria
South Africa
271-234- 122
Fax: 271-236- 191
E-mail: robertr@stalbanscollege.com
http://www.stalbanscollege.com
St Alban's College is a learning community of boys, staff and parents. We are forward looking, committed to quality and service, and we pursue innovative strategies and encourage personal responsibility in the inter-

est of all-round development of the boy as he journeys towards manhood.

Tom Hamilton, Headmaster
Carlos Palermo, Faculty Director

1496 St. Andrew's Scots School

Rosales 2809
Olivos
Argentina 01636
54-114-799-8318
Fax: 54-114-799-8318
E-mail: admissions@sanandres.esc.edu.ar
http://www.sanandres.esc.edu.ar
St. Andrew's Scots School aims to graduate responsible citizens committed to serving Argentina and contributing to its equitable development through a well-balanced, bilingual education which meets high international standards and fosters a joy for learning.

Gabriel Rshaid, Headmaster
Ana Repila, Admissions Director

1497 St. Catherine's School

Carbajal 3250
1426 Capital Federal, Buenos Aires
Argentina
54-114-552-4353
Fax: 54-114-554-4113
E-mail: stcath@ciudad.com.ar
http://www.redeseducacion.com.ar
Pre-K through 12, school year March-December

Mabel Manzitti, Principal

1498 St. George's College

Guido 800 CP
Quilmes, Buenos Aires
Argentina 01878
(5411) 4254-8237
Fax: 54-11-425-30030
E-mail: info@stgeorge.com.ar
http://www.stgeorge.com.ar
Our mission is to provide students of varying abilities and backgrounds between the ages of 3 - 18 with a bilingual, fully integrated education of the highest calibre in order that they may develop their potential to the full in an appropriately resourced co-educational environment which nurtures individual development, independent thinking and the highest moral standards.

Derek Pringle, Headmaster
Peter Ashton, Deputy Headmaster

1499 St. Hilda's College

Cowley Place Oxford
OX4 1DY
England
44-1865-276884
Fax: 44-1865-276816
E-mail: college.office@st-hildas.ox.ac.uk
http://www.st-hildas.ox.ac.uk
To promote the education of women within Oxford University and the tradition of excellence in women's education which it pioneered.

Sheila Forbes, Principal
Lucia Nixon, Senior Tutor

1500 St. John School

Casilla 284
Concepcion
Chile
http://www.sjs.org
St. John School is a bilingual school that caters to children from PK through grade twelve. The student body includes 1,170 day students (580 boys and 590 girls). The school does participate in teacher exchange programs with the length of stay for teachers being two years. The languages spoken include

Spanish and English and the student/teacher ratio is 10:1.

Chris Pugh, Principal

1501 St. Margaret's British School-Girls
Calle Saint Margaret
150 Lomas de Montemar
Chile
451-00 -
E-mail: admissions@stmargarets.cl
http://www.stmargarets.cl
St. Margarets objective is to protect in its pupil its motto: Recte Fac Nec Time (Do Right , Fear not) This implies assigning value to great ideals, acting fairly and courteously, having sound judgement, enriched understanding, a discipline manner and making responsible use of their freedom.

Margery Byrne, Principal
Avril Cooper, Headmistress

1502 St. Paul's School
325 Pleasant Street
Concord, NH 03301-2591
603-229-4600
http://www.sps.edu
St. Paul's School is a fully residential academic community that pursues the highest ideals of scholarship. We strive to challenge our students intellectually and morally - to nurture a love for learning and a commitment to engage as servant leaders in a complex world.

Richardo Pons, Principal
William R Matthews, Jr, Rector

1503 St. Pauls School
1600 St Paul's Drive
Clearwater, FL 33764
727-536-2756
Fax: 727-531-2276
http://www.st.pauls.edu
To educate and inspire young minds in a challenging and nurturing community of learning.

AH Thurn, Principal
Angel W Kytle, Head of the School

1504 St. Peter's School
Pacheco 715
1640 Martinez, Buenos Aires
Argentina
http://www.st.peterspanchgani.org

Joy Headland, Principal

1505 Teaching Opportunities in Latin America for US Citizens
Organization of American States
17th & Constitution Avenue NW
Washington, DC 20036
202-458-3000
Fax: 202-458-3967
http://www.st.peterspanchgani.org
Supports teaching abroad opportunities.

1506 The American School Foundation of Monterrey
Ave. Ignacio Morones Prieto No. 150
Santa Catarina, N.L., C.P.
Mexico, MX 66190
(52)-81-5000-4400
Fax: (52)-81-5000-4428
E-mail:
jeff.keller@missouri.asfm.edu.mx
http://www.asfm.edu.mx
providing the type of learning environment which will prepare its students to successfully assume their role in the international community during the current millennium.

Jeff Keller, Superintendent
Jeff Farrington, Principal

1507 Uruguayan American School
Av Saldon de Rodriguez
Montevideo
Uruguay 11500-3360
598-2-600-7681
Fax: 598-2-606-1935
E-mail: MSchramm@uas.edu.uy
http://www.uas.edu.uy
Uruguayan American School is to provide, together with the family, a balanced college preparatory education. UAS integrates a US style curriculum with Uruguayan studies to equip our national and international students to be successful in a diverse, ever changing world

Mike Schramm, Director
Cecilia Burgueo, UP Coordinator

1508 William T Sampson
Elementary & High School
PSC 1005 Box 49
FPO, Guantanamo Bay 09593 0005
Cuba

Eastern Europe

1509 American Academy Larnaca
Gregory Afxentious Avenue
PO Box 40112, Larnaca
Cyprus 06301
357-248-5400
Fax: 357-246-1046
E-mail: info@academy.ac.cy
http://www.academy.ac.cy
Non-profit making school that is supported by an active multi-functional operation to achieve its core purpose: pre-school to University entrance education of the highest standard. It is a private, selective, co-educational, independent school, registered under the Private Schools' Law, 1971, of the Republic of Cyprus and uniquely, is run by its own graduates.

Doros Neocleous, Principal
Tom Widdows, Director

1510 American College-Sofia
PO Box 873
Sofia
Bulgaria 01000
(359-2) 434 10 08
Fax: (359-2) 434 10 09
E-mail: acs@acs.bg
http://www.acs.bg
The primary mission is to educate Bulgarian youth, it embraces qualified students of all nationalities, races and faiths in the belief that a wide variety of students will enrich educational opportunities for all.

Paul Johnson, President
Maria Angelova, Deputy Director

1511 American International School-Bucharest
Sos Pipera-Tunari 196
Voluntari Jud Ilfov 077190
Romania
40-21-2044300
Fax: 40-21-2044306
E-mail: office@aisb.ro
http://www.aisb.ro
The American International School of Bucharest is a multicultural and international learning community, located in Romania. English is the principal language of instruction.

David Ottaviano Ed D, Director
Tamara Shreve, Elementary Principal

1512 American International School-Budapest
PO Box 53
Budapest
Hungary 01525
36 26 556 000
Fax: 36 26 556 003
E-mail: admissions@nk.aisb.hu
http://www.aisb.hu
The American International School of Budapest (AISB) is a private and independent co-educational day school governed by a Board of Directors elected and appointed from the parent community. Established in 1973 by the United States Embassy to serve United States Government employees' dependents, AISB currently serves the needs of a rapidly expanding international population, including children of the local and expatriate business and diplomatic communities.

Ray Holliday Bersegeay, School Director
Larry Kinde, Chairman

1513 American International School-Cyprus
PO Box 23847, 11 Kassos Street
1086 Nisocia
Cyprus
357-22-316345
Fax: 357-22-316549
E-mail: aisc@aisc.ac.cy
http://www.aisc.ac.cy
Founded in 1987, a private, coeducational, college preparatory day school providing a first class American and international university preparatory education within the Cyprus local community that incorporates a Greek as a First Language program for our Cypriot students.

Michelle Kleiss, Director
Terry Wolfson, Principal

1514 American International School-Krakow
Lusina ul. sw. Floriana 57
30-698 Krakw
Poland
48 12 270-1409
Fax: 48 12 270-1409
E-mail: director@iskonline.org
http://www.aisk.kompit.com.pl
Affiliated with the American School of Warsaw, AISK is an independent, coeducational day school which offers an educational program from preschool through grade 8 for students of all nationalities.

Ellen Deitsch Stern, Director

1515 American International School-Vienna
Salmannsdorfer Strasse 47
A-1190 Vienna
Austria
43-1-40-132-0
Fax: 43-1-40-132-5
E-mail: info@ais.at
http://www.ais.at
Provide a culture of educational excellence, a nurturing environment, and an atmosphere of open communication and aims to prepare a diverse student body for higher education; to inspire the youth to realize their potential; to foster life-long learning, tolerance, personal integrity, and democratic values; and to prepare students to become responsible adults, with respect for different cultures and beliefs.

Carol Kluznik, Director
Gail McMillan, HS Principal

1516 American School of Bucharest
Sos Pipera-Tunari 196
Voluntari Jud Ilfov
Romania 07719
40-21-2044300
Fax: 40-21-2044306
E-mail: office@aisb.ro
http://www.aisb.ro
An independent, international, coeducational day school which offers an educational program from

prekindergarten through grade 12 for students of all nationalities.

David Ottaviano, Director
Jeri Guthrie Corn, Chair

1517 Asuncion Christian Academy
Avenida Santisimo Sacramento
1181 Casilla 1562
Asuncion, Paraguay-1209
011-595-21-607-378
Fax: 011-595-21-604-855
E-mail: aca@aca.edu.py
http://http://www.acaknights.org/
Asuncion Christian Academy believes that the best education to prepare a student for adult life is an education based upon the truth of God's Word and having a growing and personal relationship with Jesus Christ.

Bethany Abreu, Director

1518 Falcon School
PO Box 23640
Nicosia
Cyprus 01685
357 22 424781
Fax: 357 22 313764
E-mail: falconschool@cytanet.com.cy
http://http://www.falconschool.ac.cy/default.asp?id=261

Nikolas Michael Ieride, Principal

1519 Gimnazija Bezigrad
Periceva ulica 4
PO Box 2504
Ljubljana 01001-1001
Fax: 010-044-
E-mail: info@gimb.org
http://www.gimb.org
Assistance to parents in raising gifted children to full and productive adulthood

Cyril Dominko, Principal
Janez Sustersic, Director

1520 International Elementary School-Estonia
Juhkentali 18
Tallinn
Estonia 10132
372-666-4380
Fax: 372-666-4383
E-mail: office@ise.edu.ee
http://www.ise.edu.ee
Provide high-quality, international education; maximize personal potential; develop life-long learners who appreciate diversity; foster active, compassionate world citizens

Don Fitzmahan, Director
Terje Akke, PYP Coordinator

1521 International School-Belgrade
Temisvarska 19
Belgrade
Serbia 11040
381 11 206-9999
Fax: 381 11 206-9940
E-mail: isb@isb.rs
http://http://www.isb.rs/main/?pgid=263
An independent, coeducational day school which offers an educational program from kindergarten through grade 8 for students of all nationalities.

Dr. Eric Sands, Director
Sanja Ilic, Admissions Director

1522 International School-Budapest
P.O. Box 53
Budapest
Hungary 01525
36 26 556 000
Fax: 36 26 556 003
E-mail: admissions@aisb.hu
http://http://www.aisb.hu/DOCS/1/contact.html

Grade levels N-8, school year August - June
Ray Holliday-Bersegeay, Director

1523 International School-Estonia
Juhkentali 18
Tallinn
Estonia 10132
372-666-4380
Fax: 372-666-4383
E-mail: office@ise.edu.ee
http://www.ise.edu.ee
Provides high-quality, international education, maximize personal potential, develop life-long learners who appreciate diversity and foster active, compassionate world citizens.

Don Fitzmahan, Terje
Akke PYP Coordinator

1524 International School-Latvia
Viestura iela 6a
Jurmala
Latvia LV 20
(+371) 6775 5146
Fax: (+371) 6775 5009
E-mail: merliha@isl.edu.lv
http://www.isl.edu.lv
Offers English-language, academically challenging programmes designed to develop life-long learners who are critical, creative and open-minded thinkers prepared and motivated to meet the diverse challenges of an ever-changing environment; act with integrity and responsibility locally and globally to transform their world in positive ways and appreciate and respect human diversity.

Larry Molacek, Director
Kevin Reimer, Deputy Director

1525 International School-Paphos
100 Aristotelous Savva Avenue
PO Box 62018, Paphos
Cyprus 08025
26 821700
Fax: 26 942541
E-mail: info@isop-ed.org
http://www.isop-ed.org
The school caters for the needs of children from Kindergarten to Year 13. Its mission is to serve each and every one of the pupils as part of our school family and as an individual.

Litsa Olympiou, Headmistress

1526 International School-Prague
Nebusicka 700
164 00 Prague 6
Czech Republic
420 2 2038 4111
Fax: 420-2-2038-4555
E-mail: ispmail@isp.cz
http://www.isp.cz
Educates students to be responsible, productive, ethical and healthy citizens with the ability to think creatively, reason critically, and communicate effectively through a variety of educational philosophies and methods, combining the best methodology and practices from a variety of national systems with an international perspective.

Rajiv Bhatt, Director
Barry Freckmann, Business Manager

1527 International Teachers Service
47 Papakyriazi Street
Larissa, Greece
41-253856
Fax: 41-251022
A recruitment service for teachers of English in Greece. Must have a BA/BS in education preferably English and/or EFL training or past experience in EFL and be a native speaker of English.

Fani Karatzou

1528 Kiev International School
3A Svyatoshinsky Provuluk
Kyiv
Ukraine 03115
380-44-452-2792
Fax: 380-44-452-2998
E-mail: kiev@qsi.org
http://www.qsi.org
Kyiv International School, a private non-profit institution

Scott D'Alterio, Director
David Pera, Director Instruction

1529 Limassol Grammar-Junior School
10 Manoli Kalomiri & Theklas Lisiot
PO Box 51340
Limassol, Cyprus 03504
357-257-7933
Fax: 357-257-7818
E-mail: junior@grammarschool.com.cy
http://www.grammarschool.com.cy/services.htm
The primary goal of the Grammar School is to provide its students with a solidly grounded liberal education. Thus, it seeks to encourage the intellectual, spiritual, and physical development of its students.

EWP Foley, Principal
Demetris Gregoriou, Director

1530 Logos School of English Education
33-35 Yialousa Street
PO Box 51075 Limassol
Cyprus 03501
357-25336061
Fax: 357-25335578
E-mail: Principal@Logos.ac.cy
http://www.logos.ac.cy

Gary Love, Principal

1531 Magyar British International School
H-1519 Budapest
PO Box 219, Budapest
Hungary
361-466-9794
http://www.bisb.hu

Mary E Pazsit, Principal

1532 Melkonian Educational Institute
PO Box 1907
Nicosia
Cyprus
http://www.englishschool.ac.cy/?link=contact.php
An Armenian boarding school with high academic standards.

S Bedikan, Principal

1533 Private English Junior School
P.O Box 23575
Nicosia
Cyprus 01684
357-22 -9930
Fax: 357-22 -9930
E-mail: info@englishschool.ac.cy
http://www.englishschool.ac.cy/?link=contact.php

Vassos Hajierou, BA, Principal

1534 QSI International School-Bratislava
Karloveska 64
Bratislava
Slovak Republic 842-2
421-2-6542-2844
Fax: 421-2-6541-1646
E-mail: bratislava@qsi.org
http://www.qsi.org
To keep this urge to learn alive in every child in QSI schools. Our schools are established to provide in the English language a quality education for students in the cities we serve.

Britt Brantley, Director

1535 QSI International School-Ljubljana
Dolgi most 6A
1000 Ljubljana
Solvenia
386-1-2441750
Fax: 386-1-2441754
E-mail: ljubljana@qsi.org
http://www.qsi.org
To keep this urge to learn alive in every child in QSI schools. Our schools are established to provide in the English language a quality education for students in the cities we serve.

Jay Loftin, Director

1536 QSI International School-Tbilisi
Village Zurgovani
Tbilisi
Republic of Georgia
995-32-53767
Fax: 995-32-322607
E-mail: tbilisi@qsi.org
http://www.qsi.org
To keep this urge to learn alive in every child in QSI schools. Our schools are established to provide in the English language a quality education for students in the cities we serve.

James Rehberg, Director

1537 QSI International School-Yerevan
PO Box 82, Ashtarok Highway
Yerevan
Republic of Armenia 37501
374-10-349130
Fax: 374-10-397599
http://www.qsi.org/arm_home
To keep this urge to learn alive in every child in QSI schools. Our schools are established to provide in the English language a quality education for students in the cities we serve.

Douglas Shippert, Director

Middle East

1538 ACI & SEV Elementary School
Inonu Caddesi No 476
Goztepe, Izmir
Turkey 35290
90-232-285-3401
Fax: 90-232-246-1674
E-mail: channa@aci.k12.tr
http://www.aci.k12.tr
Contribute to the growth of individuals who combine self-confidence with a firm sense of personal, social, and environmental responsibility. Enable students to be strong bilinguals in English and Turkish, well-educated adults, lifelong learners, and efficient communicators, who have developed skills, accountability, and attitudes for leading a fulfilling life and for serving their country and humanity.

Charles C Hanna, Director
Anet Gomel, Turkish First Vice Principal

1539 Abdul Hamid Sharaf School
PO Box 6008
Amman
Jordan 11118
962-615-2418
Fax: 962-651-2462
E-mail: ahss@go.com.jo
http://www.ahss.edu.jo
A private, coeducational, K-12 day school serving the needs of a diverse group of students, international and local. Languages

of instruction for the basic subjects are Arabic and English.

Sue Dahdah, Director

1540 Abquaiq Academy
PO Box 31677
Al-Khobar
Saudi Arabia 31952
966-3 5-6 04
Fax: 966-3 5-6 23
E-mail: abqaiq@isgdh.org
The sole purpose of the school is for serving the educational needs of children from expatriate families.

Vineeta Dambal, Administrator/Principal

1541 Al Ain English Speaking School
PO Box 17939
Al Ain
United Arab Emirates
00971-3-7678636
Fax: 00971-3-767-1973
E-mail: school@aaess.sch.ae
http://www.aaess.com
Al Ain English Speaking School is a member of the Association of British Schools in the Middle East and the Incorporated Association of Preparatory Schools (UK). The basic curriculum is that of the National Curriculum of England.

Peter Hodge, Principal

1542 Al Bayan Bilingual School
PO Box 24472
Safat 13105
Kuwait
965 2227 - 5000
Fax: 965 2227 - 5002
E-mail: bbsjadm@bbs.edu.kw
http://www.bbs.edu.kw
A non-profit Arabic-English university preparatory educational institution, which fosters an environment for students to develop the intellectual qualities, ethical values, and positive attitudes required for effective participation and leadership in the overall development of Kuwait and the rapidly changing world.

Brian L McCauley, Director

1543 Al Khubairat Community School
PO Box 4001
Abu Dhabi
United Arab Emirates
971-244- 228
Fax: 971-244-6819
E-mail: principal@britishschool.sch.ae
http://www.britishschool.sch.ae
British curriculum school for children aged 3 to 18. It is a non-profit school administered by a Board consisting of parent representatives and nominees of the British Ambassador.

Paul Coackley, Principal

1544 Al Rabeeh School
PO Box 41807
Abu Dhabi
United Arab Emirates
971 2 4482856
Fax: 971 2 4482854
http://http://www.alrabeeh.sch.ae/

HJ Kadri, Principal

1545 Al-Nouri English School
PO Box 46901
Fahaheel
Kuwait

PD Oldfield, Principal

1546 Al-Worood School
PO Box 46673
Abu Dhabi
United Arab Emirates
971-2-444-7655
Fax: 971-2-444-9732
E-mail: alworood@emirates.net.ae
http://http://www.alworood.sch.ae/alworood/StaticContentDetails.asp
Grade levels N-12, school year September - June

Ahmed Osman, Academic Principal
Abdulla Al Nuwais, President

1547 American Collegiate Institute
Inonu Caddesi #476 Goztepe
Izmir
Turkey 35290
90-232-285-3401
Fax: 90-232-246-4128
E-mail: channa@aci.k12.tr
http://www.aci.k12.tr
Offers a 1 + 4 year academic program. Students enter the school based upon a competitive national high-school entrance exam needing to improve their English language skills go into the intensive English one-year preparatory program before entering the school's rigorous four-year educational program.

Charles C Hanna, Director
Anet Gomel, First Vice Principal

1548 American Community School
Rue de Paris, Jel El Bahr
PO Box 11-8129, Riad El Solh
Beirut, Lebanon 01107-2260
961-1-374-370
Fax: 961-1-366-050
E-mail: gdamon@acs.edu.lb
http://www.acs.edu.lb
Founded in 1905, an independent, non-profit, non-sectarian, pre-K-12 coeducational day school.

George Damon, Headmaster
David Warren, Deputy Headmaster

1549 American Community School-Abu Dhabi
PO Box 42114
Abu Dhabi
United Arab Emirates
971-2-681-5115
Fax: 971-2-681-6006
E-mail: acs@acs.sch.ae
http://www.acs.sch.ae
The mission is to empower and inspire all students to define and shape their futures, pursue their dreams and contribute to society.

Dr George Robinson, Superintendent
Waheeda Al Tamimi, Administrative Assistant

1550 American Community School-Beirut
Rue de Paris, Jel El Bahr
PO Box 11-8129, Riad El Solh
Beirut, Lebanon 01107-2260
961-1-374-370
Fax: 961-1-366-050
E-mail: gdamon@acs.edu.lb
http://www.acs.edu.lb
Founded in 1905, an independent, non-profit, non-sectarian, pre-K-12 coeducational day school. It draws students from both the Lebanese and international communities in Lebanon and embraces diversity in race, gender, religion, national origin and economic background.

Dr George Robinson, Superintendent
David Warren, Deputy Headmaster

1551 American International School
PO Box 22090
Doha
Qatar
974-445-0150
Fax: 974-445-0157

E-mail: info@asd.edu.qa
http://http://www.asd.edu.qa/
The American School of Doha is an independent, U.S. accredited, college preparatory school, committed to provide the highest standard of educational excellence, through an enriched American curriculum.

Deborah Welch, Director
Michael Shahen, High School Principal

1552 American International School-Abu Dhabi
PO Box 5992
Abu Dhabi
United Arab Emirates
971-2-444-4333
Fax: 971-2-444-4005
E-mail: admissions@aisa.sch.ae
http://www.aisa.sch.ae
Founded in 1995 to serve the needs of the local and expatriate residents of Abu Dhabi who want their children to pursue both American and International Baccalaureate curricula in an international setting.

Gareth Jones, Director
Abdulla Al-Hashly, Chairman

1553 American International School-Israel
PO Box 484, 65 Hashomron St
Even Yehuda
Israel 40500
972-9-890-1000
Fax: 972-9-890-1001
E-mail: aisrael@wbais.org
http://http://www.wbais.org/~joomla/index.php?option=com_frontpage&
An independent, coeducational day school which offers an educational program from kindergarten through grade 12 for students of all nationalities.

Richard Detwiler, Principal

1554 American International School-Kuwait
PO Box 3267
Salmiya
Kuwait 22033
(965) 22255155
Fax: (965) 22255156
E-mail: director@aiskuwait.org
http://www.aiskuwait.org
Grade levels kindergarten through twelfth.

Samera Al Rayes, Owner/Director
Noreen Hawley, Superintendent

1555 American International School-Muscat
PO Box 584
Azaiba Postal Code 130
Sultanate of Oman
968 24 595 180
Fax: 968 24 503 815
E-mail: taism@omantel.net.com
http://www.taism.com
Pursues academic excellence for students in the international community through an American-based education that develops ethical, responsible, and globally conscious life-long learners.

Kevin Schafer, Director
Keith Boniface, High School Principal

1556 American International School-Riyadh
PO Box 990
Riyadh
Saudi Arabia 11421

966-1-491-4270
Fax: 966-1-491-7101
E-mail: registration@ais-r.edu.sa
http://aisr.org
As a school committed to excellence, we will educate and inspire our students to be responsible, productive and ethical world citizens with the skills and passion to think creatively, reason critically, communicate effectively and learn continuously. We will accomplish this in an American educational environment characterized by high measurable standards and a clearly defined, appropriately interrelated college preparatory curriculum, implemented by a superior staff in partnership with parents a

Dr. Dennis Larkin, Superintendent

1557 American School-Doha
PO Box 22090
Doha
Qatar
974-4459-1500
Fax: 974-4459-1570
E-mail: dwelch@asd.edu.ga
http://www.asd.edu.qa/pages/sitepage.cfm?page=32659
is an independent, U.S. accredited, college preparatory school, committed to provide the highest standard of educational excellence, through an enriched American curriculum

Deborah Welch, Director
Colin Boudreau, High School Principal

1558 American School-Kuwait
PO Box 6735
Hawalli
Kuwait 32040
965-266-4341
Fax: 965-265-0438
E-mail: ask@ask.edu.kw
http://www.ask.edu.kw
It is a privately owned, independent coeducational day school which offers a general academic curriculum for students of all nationalities

Bernard Mitchell, Superintendent
Fawsi Hasan, Arabic Studies Principal

1559 American-British Academy
PO Box 372
Medinat Al Sultan Qaboos
Sultanate of Oman PC 11
968-24603646
Fax: 968-24603544
E-mail: admin@abaoman.edu.om
http://www.abaoman.edu.om
Provides an international education of the highest quality to enable students to be confident, responsible, caring life-long learners.

Mona Nashman-Smith, Superintendent
Rod Harding, Director of Operations

1560 Amman Baccalaureate School
PO Box 441
Sweileh Amman
Jordan 11910
962-6-541-1191/7
Fax: 962-6-541-2603
E-mail: info@abs.edu.jo
http://www.abs.edu.jo
A coeducational and non-profit school which caters to students aged 3-18 years that offers an academically rigorous programme, enriched by extensive co-curricular activities, that culminates in the International Baccalaureate Diploma or Certificates.

Stuart Bryan, Principal
Robert Jones, Vice-Principal

1561 Anglican International School-Jerusalem
82 Rechov Haneviim
PO Box 191 Jerusalem
Israel 91001
972-2-567-7200
Fax: 972-2-538-474
E-mail: hoskino@aisj.co.il
http://www.aisj.co.il
An internationally accredited, pre-Kindergarten to Grade 12 [ages 3-18] school. It creates student-focused academic and educational environment which aspires to achieve excellence.

Owen Hoskin, Director
Matthew Dufty, Deputy Principal

1562 Ankara Elementary & High School
PSC 89 Unit 7010
APO, Ankara 09822 7010
Turkey
011-90-312-287-253
Fax: 011-90-312-285-179
E-mail:
AnkaraEHS.Principal@eu.dodea.edu
http://http://www.anka-ehs.eu.dodea.edu/
Kathleen Reiss, Principal
Rosie Uluer, Assistant Principal

1563 Arab Unity School
PO Box 10563
Rashidiya, Dubai
United Arab Emirates
971-4-886-226
Fax: 971 4 2886321
E-mail: auschool@amirates.net.ae
http://www.arabunityschool.com/aus/home.htm
Provide an equal opportunity, to all students, to develop their intellectual faculties and to awaken their latent, creative talents, irrespective of their ethnic background.

Zainab A Taher, Founder Director

1564 Baghdad International School
PO Box 571
Baghdad
Iraq
Amen A Rihani, Principal

1565 Bahrain Bayan School
PO Box 32411
Isa Town
Bahrain
973-682-227
Fax: 973-780-019
E-mail: bayanschool@bayan.edu.bh
http://www.bayanschool.edu.bh
A bilingual, coeducational, college preparatory school with an international curriculum and faculty. It aims to preserve the tenets of Arabic /Islamic values, to assist students to a depth of cross-cultural knowledge and to promote the global perspective necessary for future world citizens.

Dr Nakhle Wehbe, Director General
Gilbert Daoura, Operations Manager

1566 Bahrain Elementary & High School
Psc 451 Box 690
FPO Bahrain
Bahrain 09834-5200
973 1772-7828
Fax: 973 1772-8583
http://http://www.bahr-ehs.eu.dodea.edu/
Grade levels K-12.

Gail Anderson, Principal

1567 Bahrain School
PO Box 934
Juffair
Bahrain

973 1772-7828
Fax: 973 1772-8583
E-mail:
BahrainEHS.Principal@eu.dodea.edu
http://http://www.bahr-ehs.eu.dodea.edu/
To provide a safe environment in which our students are challenged to their maximum potential as responsible members of a multi-cultural society.

Gail Anderson, Principal
Laura Bleck, Assistant Principal

1568 Bilkent University Preparatory School-Bilkent International School

East Campus
Bilkent Ankara
Turkey 06800
90 312 290 53 61
Fax: 90 312 266 49 63
E-mail: school@bups.bilkent.edu.tr
http://www.bupsbis.bilkent.edu.tr
BUPS serves the educational needs of selected Turkish students while BIS serves the needs of selected international students in the Ankara area.

James Swetz, Director
Dan Keller, Associate Director

1569 Bishop's School

PO Box 2001
Amman
Jordan
962-6-653668
This Episcopal boy's school, founded in 1936, teaches both the Jordanian Curricula and the London University General Certification of Education Curriculum. Total enrollment is 855 day students in grades 1-12. Length of stay for teachers is one year with no housing provided. Languages spoken are English and Arabic.

Najib F Elfarr, Principal
Jamil Ismair, Faculty Head

1570 British Aircraft Corp School

PO Box 3843
Riyadh
Saudi Arabia
MR Pound, Principal

1571 British Embassy Study Group

Sehit Ersan Caddesi 46A, 06680
Cankaya Ankara
Turkey 06680
90 (312) 468 6563
Fax: 90 (312) 468 6239
E-mail: admin@besg.org
http://www.besg.org
BESG is a co-educational primary school with 135 children aged between 3 and 11, representing nearly 26 countries. We are known as a friendly and caring British school, which values a holistic approach to education

Dawn Akyurek, Head Teacher
Katie Vincent, Deputy Head Teacher

1572 British International School-Istanbul

Dilhayat Sokak No:18 Etiler
Istanbul
Turkey, TR
90 (0) 212 257 51
Fax: 90-0-212-257 53 33
E-mail: registrar2@bis.k12.tr
http://www.bis.k12.tr
The British International School Istanbul (BISI) provides a wide range of educational choices for international families. We are a private, coeducational school providing British-style international educa-

tion for 520 students of 40 nationalities between the ages of 2r and 18.

Graham Pheby, Principal
Roger Short, Governor of the School

1573 Cairo American College

PO Box 39
Maadi 11431
Cairo, EG 11431
(20-2) 2755-5507
Fax: 20-2-519-6584
E-mail: support@cacegypt.org
http://www.cacegypt.org
Cairo American College is a world class learning environment that affirms the voice, passions and talents of students and inspires them to use their hearts and minds as global citizens.

Nivine Captan-Amr, Board Chair
Elizabeth Bredin, Secretary

1574 Cambridge High School

PO Box 60835
Dubai
United Arab Emirates
971 - 4 282 4646
Fax: 971 - 4 282 4109
E-mail: cambridge@cis-dxb.ae
http://www.gemscis-garhoud.com

David Mcaughlin, Principal
Nigel Cropley, Vice Principal

1575 Continental School (Sais British)

PO Box 6453
Jeddah 21442
Saudi Arabia
966-269-9001
Fax: 966-269-9194
E-mail: conti@conti.sch.sa
http://www.continentalschool.com
Inspire in students a love of learning using a child centered, British style of education. Strive for excellence, recognizing, celebrating and encouraging a spirit of internationalism.

Bruce Gamwell, Director
Marina Alibhai, Registrar

1576 Dhahran Academy International School Group

PO Box 31677
Al Khobar 31952
Saudi Arabia 31952
966-3-330-0555
Fax: 966-3-330-2450
E-mail: info@isgdh.org
http://www.isgdh.org
Grades preSchool-11, enrollment 994.

Norma Hudson, Superintendent

1577 Dhahran Central School

PO Box 31677
Dhahran 31311
Saudi Arabia 31952
966-3-330-0555
Fax: 966-3-330-2450
E-mail: info@isgdh.org
http://www.isgdh.org

Norma Hudson, Principal

1578 Dhahran Hills School

PO Box 31677
Dhahran 31311
Saudi Arabia 31952
966-3-330-0555
Fax: 966-3-330-2450
E-mail: info@isgdh.org
http://www.isgdh.org

Norma Hudson, Principal

1579 Doha College-English Speaking

PO Box 7660
Doha Qatar
Arabian Gulf
974-806-770
Fax: 974-806-311
E-mail: dess@dess.org
http://www.dess.org
An independent, coeducational day school which offers an educational program from children of all nationalities from kindergarten through grade12.

E Goodwin, Principal
Emad Turkman, Chairman

1580 Doha English Speaking School

PO Box 7660
Doha
Qatar
(974) 44592750
Fax: (974) 44592761
E-mail: dess@dess.org
http://www.dess.org
Create a happy, secure, stimulating and supportive learning environment

Emad Turkman, Chairman
Eddie Liptrot, Head Teacher

1581 Doha Independent School

PO Box 5404
Doha Qatar
Arabian Gulf
http://www.dohaacademy.net

SJ Williams, Principal

1582 Emirates International School

PO Box 6446
Dubai
United Arab Emirates
971-4-348-9804
Fax: 971-4-348-2813
E-mail: mail@eischools.ae
http://www.eischools.ae
We offer a broad international education, in English, designed for local and expatriate students, that promotes excellence in all academic activities. It is our mission to enhance the educational, social and physical development of our students encouraging them to think analytically and creatively in preparation for the next stage of their education.

Daryle Russell, EdD, Headmaster
Jason Kirwin, HS Principal

1583 English School-Fahaheel

PO Box 7209
Fahaheel
Kuwait 64003
096-023-1010
Fax: 096-023-1054
E-mail: esf@skee.com
http://www.skee.com
The English School Fahaheel recognizes the need for all students to be made aware of the demands placed upon them for Further Education and the world of work.

Ibrahim J Shuhaiber, Chairman
John J MacGregor, Principal

1584 English School-Kuwait

PO Box 379
Safat
Kuwait 13004
965-256-7205
Fax: 965-256-7147
http://www.tes.edu.kw
The English School was founded in 1953 under the auspices of the British Embassy and is the longest established school in Kuwait catering for the expatriate community. The School operates as a not-for-profit independent co-educational establishment providing the highest standards in edu-

cation for children of Pre-Preparatory and Preparatory School age.

William James Strath, Principal
Richard Davis, Chair

1585 English Speaking School

PO Box 2002
Dubai
United Arab Emirates
974-445- 275
Fax: 974-445- 276
E-mail: dess@dessdubai.com
http://www.dessdxb.com
The school opened in 1963 in the upstairs room of a villa where expatriate workers were housed. There was one class which was taught by parents and a British Officer called Flight Lieutenant F. Loughman.

Bernadette McCarty, Principal
David Hammond, Headteacher

1586 Enka Okullari-Enka Schools

Sadi Gulcelik Spor Sitesi
Istinye, Istanbul
Turkey 34460
90-212-276-05-4547
Fax: 90-212-286-59-3035
E-mail: mailbox@enkaschools.com
http://www.princeton.iss.edu
Enka Schools provide an international education for our students. We have a well qualified and passionate group of teachers from Turkey and overseas. Most of our students are Turkish while some of them have international backgrounds.

Darlene Fisher, Director
Ayten Yilmaz, Preschool Principal

1587 Gulf English School

PO Box 2440
Doha
Qatar
974-445-8 77
Fax: 974-448-1 25
E-mail: info@gulfenglishschool.com
http://www.gulfenglishschool.com
Provide a positive and stimulating environment which facilitates individual learning, encourages experimentation, and develops critical thinking and problem solving skills. We must enable each student to achieve his or her best in the pursuit of academic excellence, and give them the confidence to be independent thinkers, able to assume responsibility and leadership and to take their place in the wider world

Paul Andrews, Principal
Tim Brosnan, Faculty Head

1588 Habara School

PO Box 26510
Bahrain
973-172- 173
http://www.ameinfo.com

PM Wrench, Principal

1589 IBN Khuldoon National School

Po Box 20511
Manama
Bahrain
973-16-687-073
Fax: 973-17-689-028
E-mail: info@ikns.edu.bh
http://www.ikns.edu.bh
This IBN school is a private, fee paying, non-profit, coeducational, accredited middle states school. The curriculum offered to the 1,210 day students (630 boys and 580 girls) in grades K-12, is English/Arabic. The school is willing to participate in a teacher exchange program with the applications

needed being science, math, social sciences, pre-school and English.

Kamal Abdel-Nour, President
Ghada R Bou Zeineddine, Principal

1590 Incirlik Elementary School

Unit 7180 Box 270
APO AE 09824
Turkey
011-90-322-316-310
Fax: 011-90-322-332-757
E-mail:
IncirlikEHS.Principal@eu.dodea.edu
http://http://www.inci-ehs.eu.dodea.edu/

Mary Davis, Principal

1591 Incirlik High School

Unit 7180 Box 270
APO AE 09824
Turkey
011-90-322-316-310
Fax: 011-90-322-332-757
E-mail:
IncirlikEHS.Principal@eu.dodea.edu
http://http://www.inci-ehs.eu.dodea.edu/

Dr. Donald Torrey, Principal

1592 Infant School-House #45

Khalil Kando Gardens Road, 5651
Manama
Bahrain

Maria Stiles, Principal

1593 International Community School

PO Box 2002
Amman
Jordan 11181
962-6 5-2 10
Fax: 962-6 5-2 71
E-mail: office@ics-amman.edu.jo
http://www.ics-amman.edu.jo
Ours is a school where people matter. ~We want good results for each student, according to his or her own abilities in the classroom, in sport , music, drama or art.

John Light, Principal
Sue Hill, Primary Head

1594 International School of Choueifat

PO Box 7212
Abu Dhabi
United Arab Emirates
971-2-446-1444
Fax: 971-2-446-1048
E-mail: iscad@sabis.net
http://www.iscad-sabis.net
Over the last 27 years hundreds of students have graduated from The International Schools of Choueifat in the region and then graduated from top universities in the world. In the UK, these universities include Oxford, Cambridge, LSE, Bristol, Edinburgh, Bath, Birmingham, Liverpool, The Imperial College of Science and Technology and all other Colleges of London University.

Marilyn Abu-Esber, Director

1595 Istanbul International Community School

Karaagac Mahallesi, G 72 Sokak No:1
Buyukcekmece , Istanbul
Turkey 34866
90-212-857-8264
Fax: 90-212-857-8270
E-mail: jlewis@iics.k12.tr
http://www.iics.k12.tr
Through its challenging curriculum and strong staff-student relationships, IICS provides a caring environment that inspires each student to excel and to be inquisitive, cre-

ative, compassionate, balanced and internationally-minded.

Peter Welch, Headmaster
Sean Murphy, Primary Principal

1596 Izmir Elementary & High School

PSC 88
APO, Izmir 09821 0005
Turkey

Terry Emerson, Principal

1597 Jeddah Preparatory School

British Consulate, Box 6316
Jeddah 21442 Saudi Arabia
265-235-
Fax: 065-183-
E-mail: registrar@jpgs.org
http://http://www.jpgs.org/

John GF Parsons, Principal

1598 Jubail British Academy

PO Box 10059 Madinat Al Jubail
Jubail 31961
Saudi Arabia
966.3.341.7550
Fax: 966.3.341.6990
E-mail: mmcdougall@isgdh.org
http://http://www.isg-jubail.org/

Norman Edwards, Principal

1599 Jumeirah English Speaking School

PO Box 24942, Dubai
United Arab Emirates
971-4-394-5515
Fax: 971-4-394-3531
E-mail: jess@jess.sch.ae
http://http://www.jess.sch.ae/Home.aspx

CA Branson, Headmaster
RD Stokoe, Director

1600 King Faisal School

PO Box 94558, Riyadh 11614
Saudia Arabia
966-1-482-0802
Fax: 966-1-482-1521
E-mail: kfs@kfs.sch.sa
http://www.kfs.sch.sa/English/adefault.aspx
Grade levels preK-12, enrollment 600.

Mohammed Al-Humood, Director General

1601 Koc School

PK 60-Tuzla
Istanbul
Turkey 34941
(90)216 585 6200
Fax: 90-216-304-1048
E-mail: info@kocschool.k12.tr
http://www.kocschool.k12.tr
The goal of KoO School is to be respected nationally and internationally as a model K-12 school, offering an educational program of the highest academic and ethical standards.

Suna Kirac, Chairman

1602 Kuwait English School

PO Box 8640
Salmiya 22057
Kuwait
256-552-
Fax: 256-293-
E-mail: keschool@kes.edu.kw
http://http://www.kes.edu.kw/?page_id=69

Craig Halsall, Principal

1603 Mohammed Ali Othman School

PO Box 5713
Taiz Yeman
Arab Republic
967-422-3671
Fax: 967-4 2-1495
http://www.maoschoolyemen.com.ye
Mohammed Ali Othman School is a well established school which has been running for

over thirty years. At present it has around a thousand students from the Foundation Stage through to Year 12

Abdulla Ahmad, Principal
Fowzia Abdo Saeed, Deputy Head

1604 Nadeen Nursery & Infant School

PO Box 26367
Adliya
Bahrain
973-177- 888
Fax: 973-177- 888
E-mail: info@nadeenschool.com
http://www.nadeenschool.info/
Nadeen School is dedicated to providing a caring, nurturing, and stimulating environment in which all children can learn and thrive. All of our students are treated with respect, care, and with the utmost sensitivity to their individual needs and requirements.

Pauline Puri, Principal

1605 New English School

PO Box 6156
Hawalli
Kuwait, KW 32036
[00965] 25318060
Fax: [00965] 25319924
E-mail: admin@neskt.com
http://www.neskt.com
Private, co-educational day-school to offer a British style curriculum from Kindergarten to 'A' level.

Tareq S Rajab, Founder

1606 Pakistan International School-Peshawar

23 Sahibzada Abdual Qayyum Road
University Town
Peshawar
92-441-4428
Fax: 92-441-7272
http://www.isbi.com
An independent, coeducaional day school which offers an educational program from prekindergarten through grade 8 and supervised correspondence study for the high school grades for all expatriate nationalities.

Angela Coleridge, Principal

1607 Rahmaniah-Taif-Acad International School

American Consulate General, Dhahran District Saudi Arabia
03 -30 -555
Fax: 03 -30 -450
http://www.isgdh.org
Dean May, Principal

1608 Ras Al Khaimah English Speaking School

PO Box 975
Ras Al Khaimah
United Arab Emirates
971-7-362-441
Fax: 971-7-362-445
http://www.rakess.net
Roy Burrows, Principal

1609 Ras Tanura School

PO Box 6140
Ras Tanura
Saudi Arabia 31311
067-367-
E-mail: david.weston@aramco.com
http://www.saudiaramco.com
David Weston, Principal

1610 Sanaa International School

PO Box 2002
Sanaa
Yemen
967-1-370192
Fax: 967-1-370-193
E-mail: qsi-sanaa@qsi.org
http://www.qsi.org/yem_home/yem_home.htm
Sanaa International School, a non-profit institution that opened in September 1971 offers a high quality education in the English language for pre-school, elementary, and secondary students. The Campus is located on 34 acres on the outskirts of Sanaa constructed and entered in September 1978.

Mr. Philip Weirich, Director

1611 Saudi Arabian International British School

PO Box 85769
Riyadh
Saudi Arabia 11612
966- 12-8 23
Fax: 966- 12-8 23
E-mail: principal@britishschoolriyadh.com
http://www.britishschoolriyadh.com
Improve standards of teaching, learning and citizenship within a safe and secure environment. Our Mission Statement and School Improvement Plan provide the direction for the future development of our pupils and the continuous improvement of our school.

Peter Wiles, Acting Principal
Terry Sayce, Chairman

1612 Saudi Arabian International School-Dhahran

SAIS-DD, Box 677
Dhahran International Airport
Dhahran 31932, Saudi Arabia
996-3-330-0555
Fax: 966-3-330-0555
E-mail: brent_mutsch%sais@macexpress.org
http://http://www.isgdh.org/
Dr. Leo Ruberto, Principal

1613 Saudi Arabian International School-Riyadh

PO Box 990
Riyadh
Kingdom of Saudi Arabia 11421
966-1-491-4270
Fax: 966-1-491-7101
E-mail: registration@ais-r.edu.sa
http://www.aisr.org
Educate and inspire our students to be responsible, productive and ethical world citizens with the skills and passion to think creatively, reason critically, communicate effectively and learn continuously. We will accomplish this in an American educational environment characterized by high measurable standards and a clearly defined, appropriately interrelated college preparatory curriculum, implemented by a superior staff in partnership with parents and community.

Daryle Russell, EdD, Principal
Brian Matthews, Superintendent

1614 Saudia-Saudi Arabian International School

PO Box 167, CC 100
Jeddah 21231
Saudi Arabia
http://www.saudigazette.com
John Hazelton, Principal

1615 Sharjah English School

PO Box 1600
Sharjah
United Arab Emirates
971-655- 930
Fax: 971- 55- 930
E-mail: seschool@emirates.net.ae
http://www.seschool.ae
Not for profit school. It is self-supporting and financed by fees paid by parents for the education of their children.

David Throp, Principal
Jenefer Race, Primary Headteacher

1616 Sharjah Public School

PO Box 6125, Sharjah
United Arab Emirates
971-652- 124
http://www.sharjahpublicschool.ae
Nazim Khan, Principal

1617 St. Mary's Catholic High School

PO Box 52232
Dubai
United Arab Emirates
009-104-3370
Fax: 009-104-3368
E-mail: maryscol@emirates.net.ae
http://www.stmarysdubai.com
St. Mary's Catholic High School is reputed for its high standards in academic work and also in the standards of discipline which we try to inspire in the children.

Sr Anne Marie Quigg, Principal
U D'Souza, Vice Principal

1618 Sultan's School

PO Box 665
Seeb
Sultanate of Oman 00121
968-24 -367
Fax: 968-24 -362
E-mail: admissions@sultansschool.org
http://www.sultansschool.org
The Sultan's School is a co-educational school offering a bilingual Arabic-English education from early childhood to pre-university.

Anthony J Cashin, Principal

1619 Sunshine School

2 Dutcher Avenue
Pawling, NY 12564
845-855-9238
Fax: 845-855-0222
http://sunshineschool-pawling.org
Our goal is to provide a quality pre-school education for young children. We do this by addressing both the social and the intellectual development of the child.

David Brinded, Principal

1620 Tarsus American College and SEV Primary

Cengiz Topel Cd Caminur Mah 201 Sk
Tarsus/Mersin
Turkey 33440
90-324-613-5402
Fax: 90-324-624-6347
E-mail: info@tac.k12.tr
http://www.tac.k12.tr
The mission of Tarsus American Schools is to contribute to the growth of individuals who combine self-confidence with a firm sense of personal and social responsibility.

Bernard Mitchell, PhD, Superintendent
Jale Sever, Primary School Principal

1621 Universal American School

PO Box 17035
Khalidiya
Kuwait 72451
965-562-0297/561
Fax: 965-562-5343

E-mail: uas@qualitynet.net
http://www.uas.edu.kw
The Universal American School is a private, college-preparatory, N-12 school serving a multinational student body from the diverse populations residing in Kuwait

Nora Al-Ghanim, Administrative Director
Mike Church, Assistant Principal

1622 Uskudar American Academy
Vakif Sokak Number 1
Baglarbasi Istanbul
Turkey, TR
90-216-310-6823
Fax: 90-216-333-1818
E-mail: wshepard@uaa.k12.tr
http://www.uaa.k12.tr
The mission of SEV/ABH Schools is to contribute to the growth of individuals who combine self-confidence with a firm sense of personal, social, and environmental responsibility. We aim to enable our students to be strong bilinguals in English and Turkish, well-educated adults, lifelong learners, and efficient communicators, who have developed skills, accountability, and attitudes for leading a fulfilling life and for serving their country and humanity

Whitman Shepard, Director
Dilek Yakar, Primary Principal

1623 Walworth Barbour American International School in Israel
65 Hashomron Street
PO Box 484
Israel 40500
972-9-961-8100
Fax: 972-9-961-8111
E-mail: aisrael@wbais.org
http://www.american.hasharon.k12.il
Through a rigorous and dynamic American international curriculum, AIS, a private secular school in Israel, inspires each student to cultivate a respect for diversity, develop a passion for life-long learning, achieve academic potential, assume leadership, contribute actively to society, and resolve conflict through dialogue and understanding

Robert A Sills, Superintendent
John Chere, Chairman

Western Europe

1624 AC Montessori Kids
Route De Renipont 4
Lasne B-1380
Belgium
32-2-633-6652
Fax: 32-2-633-6652
E-mail: info@acmontessorikids.com
http://www.acmontessorikids.com
A bilingual English/French Montessori School for children aged18 months - 12 years.

Laurence Randoux, Director
Mark Ciepers, Director

1625 AFCENT Elementary & High School
Unit 21606
APO AE 09703
Brunssum, Netherlands
http://www.afcent.org

1626 Abbotsholme School
Rocester (Uttoxeter, Staffordshire)
ST14 5BS
England
01889-590217
Fax: 01889-590001
E-mail: admissions@abbotsholme.co.uk
http://www.abbotsholme.com

This interdenominational school offers an English-based curriculum for 78 day students and 166 boarding (152 boys; 92 girls), in grades 7-13.

Darrell J Farrant, MA, FRSA, Principal
Steve Fairclough, Head

1627 Academy-English Prep School
Apartado 1300 Palma D Mallorca
525 W 17th Street Bloomington
Spain, IN 47404
812-333-2882
Fax: 812-339-2253
http://www.theprepschool.info

CA Walker, Principal

1628 Ackworth School, Ackworth
Pontefract, West Yorkshire
England WF7 7
0977-611401
E-mail: admissions@ackworthschool.com
http://www.ackworthschool.com
This school offers an English-based curriculum to 264 day students and 111 boarding students (180 boys; 195 girls), ages 11-18 years of age.

Peter J Simpson, Head
Jeffrey Swales, Deputy Head, Curriculum

1629 Alconbury Elementary School
Unit 5570 Box 60
APO AE 09470
Great Britain
011-44-1480-843620
Fax: 011-44-1480-843172
E-mail:
AlconburyES.Principal@eu.dodea.edu
http://www.alco-es.eu.dodea.edu
To provide a safe and productive learning environment in which all students reach their fullest potential by developing knowledge and skills.

Teddy Emerson, Principal

1630 Alconbury High School
Unit 5570 Box 60
APO AE 09470
Great Britain
441- 80-4 36
Fax: 441- 80-4 31
http://www.alco-hs.eu.dodea.edu
To develop healthy, adaptable, independently thinking, and socially responsible members of the global community.

Teddy Emerson, Principal
Lance Posey, Assistant Principal

1631 Alexander M Patch Elementary School
Unit 30401
APO AE 09107
Germany
071- 68- 520
Fax: 071- 68- 713
http://www.patch-es.eu.dodea.edu
Provide a standards-based curriculum that develops lifelong learners and promotes highest student achievement in partnership with our community.

Robert Allen, Principal
Ronald Lathrop, Assistant. Principal

1632 Alexander M Patch High School
Unit 30401
APO AE 09107-0401
Germany
071- 68- 520
Fax: 071- 68- 713
http://www.patch-es.eu.dodea.edu
Prepares all students to exceed challenging academic standards, know how to learn, communicate effectively, and make responsible decisions so that they can be continuous

learners and productive citizens in a diverse society.

Robert Allen, Principal
Ronald Lathrop, Assistant. Principal

1633 Alfred T Mahan Elementary School
PSC 1003 Box 48
FPO Keflavik 09728
Iceland

Jan Long, Principal

1634 Alfred T Mahan High School
PSC 1003 Box 52
FPO Keflavik 09728 0352
Iceland

M Deatherage, Principal

1635 Amberg Elementary School
CMR 414
APO, Amberg 09173 0005
Germany

Letcher Connell, Principal

1636 Ambrit Rome International School
Via Filippo Tajani, 50
Rome, Italy 00149
39-06-559-5305
Fax: 39-06-559-5309
E-mail: ambrit@ambrit-rome.com
http://www.ambrit-rome.com
Grade levels Pre-K through 8, school year September - June

Bernard C Mullane, Director
Loretta Nanini, Admissions Director

1637 American College-Greece
6 Gravias Street
Aghia Paraskevi
Athens, Greece GR-15
30-1-600-9800
Fax: 30-1-600-9811
E-mail: info@acg.edu
http://www.acg.edu
Founded in 1875, combining the best of American education with the intellectual and cultural heritage of Greece, provide a unique foundation for international educational excellence.

David G Horner, President
Nicholas Jiavaras, Executive Vice President

1638 American Community School-Cobham
Heywood, Portsmouth Road
Cobham, Surrey
United Kingdom KT11
44-1932-869-744
Fax: 44-1932-869-789
E-mail: hayoub@acs-england.co.uk
http://www.acs-england.co.uk
Promotes a high standard of scholarship, responsibility, and citizenship in a supportive, international community.

Tom Lehman, Head of School
Heidi Ayoub, Dean of Admissions

1639 American Community School-Egham
Woodlee London Road (A30)
Egham, Surrey
United Kingdom TW20
44-1784-430-611
Fax: 44-1784-430-626
E-mail: jlove@acs-england.co.uk
http://www.acs-england.co.uk
Promotes high standards of scholarship, responsibility and citizenship in a supportive, international community

Julia Love, Dean of Admissions
Moyra Hadley, Head of School

101

1640 American Community School-Hillingdon

108 Vine Lane
Hillingdon, Middlesex
United Kingdom UB10
44-189-581-3734
Fax: 44-189-581-0634
E-mail:
HillingdonAdmissions@acs-england.co.uk
http://www.acs-england.co.uk
Foundes in 1978, has endeavoured to provide a quality education for a multi-national community in the London area.

Ginger Apple, Head of School
Rudianne Soltis, Dean of Admissions

1641 American Community Schools

108 Vine Court
Hillingdon, Uxbridge, Middlesex
UB100BE
England
44-189-581-3734
Fax: 44-189-581-0634
E-mail: hmulkey@acs-england.co.uk
http://www.acs-england.co.uk
This school serves the needs of the international business families in Greater London. Programs are nonsectarian, coeducational day schools with lower, middle and high school divisions offering coordinate college preparatory curricula from pre-kindergarten through grade twelve.

Paul Berg, Headmaster

1642 American Community Schools-Athens

129 Aghias Paraskevis Avenue and Ka
Halandri, Athens
Greece 15343
301-639-3200
Fax: 301-639-0051
E-mail: gialamas@acs.gr
http://www.acs.gr
Provides a student-centered environment where individuals excel academically and develop intellectually, socially and ethically to thrive as healthy, responsible members of global society.

Stefanos Gialamas, President
Steve Kakaris, Business Manager

1643 American Embassy School-Reykjavik

Lngulnu 8""
210 Gardab'r
Iceland
354-590-3106
Fax: 354-590-3110
E-mail: isi@internationalschool.is
http://www.internationalschool.is
The International School of Iceland (ISI)is a private elementary school housed in an Icelandic public school, Sjlandsskli. The school offers an international educational program to children in grades 1-7.

Berta Faber, Headmistress
Hanna Hilmarsdottir, Assistant Headmistress

1644 American International School-Carinthia

Friesacher Strasse 3 Audio ICC
A-9330 Althofen
Austria
http://www.cic-network.at

Ron Presswood, Principal

1645 American International School-Florence

Villa le Tavernule - via del Carota
Bagno a Ripoli, Florence
Italy, VA 50012
39-055-646-1007
Fax: 39-055-644-226
E-mail: admin.tav@isfitaly.org
http://www.isfitaly.org
Business Manager

Provide attendees

Christopher Maggio, Head of School
Marie Jos , Manzini

1646 American International School-Genoa

Via Quarto 13-C
Genoa
Italy 16148
39-010-386-528
Fax: 39-010-398-700
E-mail: info@aisge.it
http://www.aisge.it
Provides students of internationally-minded families with a high quality education in the English language, from Pre-School through to the 12th Grade.

Sheldon Friedman, Director
Raffaele Boccardo, President

1647 American International School-Lisbon

Rua Antonio Dos Reis, 95
Linho, 2710-301 Sintra
Portugal
351-21-923-98-00
Fax: 351-21-923-98-26
E-mail: tesc0893@mail.telepac.pt
http://www.ecis.org/aislisbon/index.html
An independent, coeducational day school which offers an educational program from early childhood through grade 12 for student of all nationalities.

Blannie M Curtis, Director

1648 American International School-Rotterdam

Verhulstlaan 21
3055 WJ Rotterdam
Netherlands
31-10-422-5351
Fax: 31-10-422-4075
E-mail: queries@aisr.nl
http://www.aisr.nl
Provides a comprehensive program of learning, with well-qualified and experienced faculty who prepare students Pre-School through Grade 12 for the ever-changing world in which we live.

Brian Atkins, Director
Anne-Marie Blitz, Elementary Principal

1649 American International School-Salzburg

Moosstrasse 106
Salzburg A-5020
Austria
43-662-824-617
Fax: 43-662-824-555
E-mail: office@ais.salzburg.at
http://www.ais-salzburg.at
A boarding and day school committed to the college-preparatory education of conscientious young men and women. The academic and boarding programs nurture the students' intellectual growth and artistic potential, as well as their social, physical, and personal development.

Paul McLean, Headmaster
Felicia Gundringer, Admissions Coordinator

1650 American International School-Vienna

Salmannsdorfer Strasse 47
A-1190 Vienna
Austria
43-1-401-320
Fax: 43-1-401-325
E-mail: info@ais.at
http://www.ais.at
Provide a culture of educational excellence, a nurturing environment, and an atmosphere of open communication and aims to prepare a diverse student body for higher education; to inspire the youth to realize their potential; to foster life-long learning, tolerance, personal integrity, and democratic values; and to prepare students to become responsible adults, with respect for different cultures and beliefs.

Ellen Stern, Director
Dr Greg Moncada, HS Principal

1651 American Overseas School-Rome

Via Cassia 811
Rome, IT 00189
39-06-3326-4841
Fax: 39-06-3326-2608
E-mail: aosr@aosr.org
http://www.aosr.org
An independent, coeducational day school for students of all nationalities in prekindergarten through grade 13 and offers a boarding program for select students in grades 9-12.

Beth Kempler, Head of School

1652 American School of the Hague

Rijksstraatweg 200
2241 BX Wassenaar
The Netherlands
31-70-512-1060
Fax: 31-70-511-2400
E-mail: info@ash.nl
http://www.ash.nl
educates students to excel in critical inquiry, creative thinking, clear communication, and commitment to others.

Paul De Minico, Superintendent
Douglas Buckley, Chair

1653 American School-Barcelona

Jaume Balmes 7
Esplugues de Llobregat
Spain 08950
34-93-371-4016
Fax: 34-93-473-4787
E-mail: info@a-s-b.com
http://www.a-s-b.com
fully develop each student's unique potential by providing a high quality American/Spanish curriculum in an English-language based, respectful and diverse environment

Nancy Boyd, Elementary School Principal
Bill Volckok, Secondary School Principal

1654 American School-Bilbao

Soparda Bidea 10
Berang (Bizkaia)
Spain 48640
34-94-668-0860
Fax: 34-94-668-0452
E-mail: asob@asob.es
http://www.asob.es/en
s a private, non-profit, International School, Offers students an American-style educational programme taught in English. The curriculum has an international focus and leads to the American High School Diploma

Roger West, Director

1655 American School-Las Palmas

Carretera de los Hoyos, Km 1.7
Las Palmas de Gran Canaria
Las Palmas, Spain 35017
34-928-430-023
Fax: 34-928-430-017
E-mail: info@dns.aslp.org
http://www.aslp.org

Supports students in becoming life long learners in the tradition of American education

Linnah Sanab, Director
Conchita Neyra, Assistant Director

1656 American School-London

One Waverly Place
London
United Kingdom NW8 0
44-207-449-1200
Fax: 44-207-449-1350
E-mail: admissions@asl.org
http://www.asl.org
is to develop the intellect and character of each student by providing an outstanding American education with a global perspective.

Jodi Coats, Dean of Admissions

1657 American School-Madrid

Apartado 80
Madrid
Spain 28080
34-91-740-1900
Fax: 34-91-357-2678
E-mail: info@asmadrid.org
http://www.amerschmad.org
Grade levels Pre-K through 12, school year September - June

Robert Thompson, Director
William O'Hale, Headmaster

1658 American School-Milan

Via K Marx 14
Noverasco di Opera, Milan
Italy 20090
39-02-530-001
Fax: 39-02-576-06274
E-mail: director@asmilan.org
http://www.asmilan.org
s to provide a fulfilling educational environment where learners can discover and develop their capacities and achieve personal excellence.

Alen P Austen, Director
Samer Khoury, High School Principal

1659 American School-Paris

41, rue Pasteur
Saint Cloud
France 92210
33-1-411-28282
Fax: 33-1-460-22390
E-mail: webteam@asparis.fr
http://www.asparis.org
We develop lifelong learners with an international focus who use their social, thinking and problem-solving skills to contribute constructively to a changing global society

Pilar Cabeza de Vaca, Headmistress
Jack Davis, Head of the School

1660 American School-Valencia

Avenida Sierra Calderona 29
Urb Los Monasterios, Puzol
Spain 46530
34-96-140-5412
Fax: 34-96-140-5039
E-mail: asvalencia@asvalencia.org
http://www.asvalencia.org
An international, private, bilingual, university- preparatory school that provides a broad and balanced curriculum in a safe and positive learning environment that encourages students to seek challenges.

Saara Tatem, Director
Ildefonso Segura, Financial Director

1661 American School-the Hague

Rijkstraatweg 200
BX Wassenaar
Netherlands 02241
31-70-514-0113
Fax: 31-70-511-2400
E-mail: info@ash.nl
http://www.ash.nl
Educates students to excel in critical inquiry, creative thinking, clear communication, and commitment to others.

Rick Spradling, Director

1662 Anatolia College

PO Box 21021
Pylea Thessaloniki
Greece 55510
30-31-398-201
Fax: 30-31-327-500
E-mail: admissions@act.edu
http://www.anatolia.edu.gr
Offers undergraduate and graduate programs of study characterized by reasoned and open inquiry, acquisition of the breadth and depth of knowledge associated with traditional university curricula, and achievement of the highest possible standards in student-centered teaching and faculty scholarship, with emphasis on individual growth.

Richard L Jackson, President
Panayiotis Kanellis, Executive Vice President

1663 Anglo-American School-Moscow

American Embassy
Itainen Puistotie 14
Finland 00140
7-095-231-4488
Fax: 7-095-231-4477
E-mail: director@aas.ru
http://www.aas.ru
An international learning community where students, teachers and parents demand excellence and engagement from one another.

Drew Alexander, Director
Nicolette Kirk, Admissions Officer

1664 Anglo-American School-St. Petersburg

c/o American Embassy
Itainen Puistotie 14, Box L, Helsinki
Finland
7-812-320-8925
Fax: 7-812-320-8926
E-mail: nastia.smirnova@aas.ru
http://www.aas.ru/stpetersburg
An international learning community where students, teachers and parents demand excellence and engagement from one another.

Ronald Gleason, Principal
Ellen D Stren, Director

1665 Ansbach Elementary School

Unit 28614 APO AE 09177
Germany
011-49 -802
Fax: 011-46 -802
E-mail: AnsbachES.Principal@eu.odedodea.edu
http://www.ansb-es.eu.dodea.edu
Provides many excellent opportunities to encouage and support all students intellectual, physical, social, emotional and creative developments and prepare them to meet the challengges of a dynamic and diverse world community.

Essie Grant, Principal

1666 Ansbach High School

Unit 28614
APO AE 09177
Germany
49-9802-223
Fax: 49-9802-1496
E-mail: AnsbachHS.Principal@eu.dodea.edu
http://www.ansb-hs.eu.dodea.edu

A public school serving the children of American Army units.

Jennifer Rowland, Principal

1667 Antwerp International School

Veltwijcklaan 180
2180 Ekeren-Antwerpen
Belgium
32-3-543-9300
Fax: 32-3-541-8201
E-mail: ais@ais-antwerp.be
http://www.ais-antwerp.be
Educates young people to be responsible, caring, and productive members of a democratic society in a global community, and to prepare them for continued education. It promotes integrity, self-realization, mutual respect and understanding in a multi-cultural environment of students and teachers.

Alun Cooper, Headmaster

1668 Argonner Elementary School

Unit 20193 Box 0015
APO, Hanau 09165 0015
Germany

Christine Holsten, Principal

1669 Athens College

420 Madison Avenue
New York, NY 10017
212-697-7071
Fax: 212-697-7093
E-mail: trustees@athenscollege.org
http://www.athenscollege.org
The mission of Athens College is to provide, by international standards, the highest quality education to the most deserving candidates and to cultivate in its students those habits of mind, body, and spirit necessary for responsible citizenship in GReece and the world; moral courage, intellectual discipline, compassion, and an unswerving devotion to justice and truth. Our goal is to instill in our students, by teaching and by example, a strong sense of measure.

Walter McCanny Eggleston, Principal
Dr Nicholas G Bacopoulos, President

1670 Aviano Elementary School

Unit 6210 Box 180
APO, AE 09604-0180
Italy
011-39-0434-660921
E-mail: avianoes.principal@eu.dodea.edu
http://www.avia-es.eu.dodea.edu

Lillian Hiyama, Principal
Phyllis Fuglaar, Assistant Principal

1671 Aviano High School

Unit 6210 Box 180
APO, AE 09604-0180
Italy
632-567-
Fax: 390- 34-6 09
E-mail: avianohs.principal@eu.dodea.edu
http://www.avia-hs.eu.dodea.edu

Debra K Johnson, Principal

1672 BEPS 2 Limal International School

23 Avenue Franklin Roosevelt
Brussels
Belgium 01050
32-10-417-227
Fax: 32-2-687-2968
E-mail: info@beps.com
http://www.beps.com
The schools share a common philosophy and approach to education. An average class size of 16 allows for a high level of individual attention in a caring and supportive environment.

Charles A Gellar, Head
Henny de Waal, Headmistress

1673 Babenhausen Elementary School
CMR 426 Unit 20219
APO, Babenhausen 09089 0005
Germany

Ida Rhodes, Principal

1674 Bad Kissingen Elementary School
CMR 464
APO, Bad Kissingen 09226 0005
Germany

Beatrice McWaters, Principal

1675 Bad Kreuznach Elementary School
CMR 441
APO, Bad Kreuznach 09525 0005
Germany

Peter Grenier, Principal

1676 Bad Kreuznach High School
Unit 24324
APO, Bad Krueznach 09252 0005
Germany

Jennifer Beckwith, Principal

1677 Bad Nauheim Elementary School
Unit 21103
APO, Bad Nauheim 09074 0005
Germany

Raymond Burkard, Principal

1678 Badminton School
Westbury-on-Trym, Bristol
BS9 3BA
England
0272-623141
E-mail:
admissions@badminton.bristol.sch.uk
http://www.badminton.bristol.sch.uk
The school combines excellent facilities
and teaching standards with a friendly atmosphere and a strong emphasis on pastoral care. Badminton is also focused on
ensuring that girls realise their potential so
that they can be capable of achieving whatever they want to be when they leave
school.

Jan Scarrow, Headmistress

1679 Bamberg Elementary School
USAG Bamberg, Unit 27539
APO AE 09139
Germany
469-761-
Fax: 095- 31-15
E-mail:
BambergES.Principal@eu.dodea.edu
http://www.bamb-es.eu.dodea.edu

John G Rhyne, Principal

1680 Bamberg High School
Unit 27539
APO AE 09139
Germany
469-088-
E-mail:
BambergHS.Principal@eu.dodea.edu
http://www.bamb-hs.eu.dodea.edu/
Preparing all students to achieve success
and personal fulfillment in a dynamic
global environment.

Dominick Calabria, Principal
Richard Jimenez, Assistant Principal

1681 Barrow Hills School
Roke Lane
Witley, Godalming
Surrey, England GU8 5
01428-683639
Fax: 01428-683639
E-mail: sec@barrowhills.org.uk
http://www.barrowhills.org.uk

Michael Connolly, Headmaster

1682 Baumholder High School
Unit 23816 Box 30
APO, AE 09034-0034
Germany
011-49 -783
Fax: 011-49 -783
E-mail:
BaumholderHS.Principal@eu.dodea.edu
http://www.baum-hs.eu.dodea.edu

Danny Robinson, Principal
Patrick McDonald, Assistant Principal

1683 Bavarian International School
Haputstrasse 1
Schloss Haimbausen
Haimhausen, Germany 85778
49-8133-9170
Fax: 49-8133-917-135
E-mail: k.lippacher@bis-school.com
http://www.bis-school.com
Inspiring young minds and challenging
young individuals to achieve their intellec-
tual and personal potential within a caring
international environment

Bryan Nixon, Director

1684 Bedales School
Church Road Steep
Petersfield Hampshire
England, UK GU32
01730-300100
Fax: 01730-300500
E-mail: admin@bedales.org.uk
http://www.bedales.org.uk

Keith Budge, Headmaster
Leo Winkley, Deputy Head

1685 Bedford School
De Parys Avenue Bedford
England, UK MK40
44-0-1234-362200
Fax: 44-0-1234-362283
E-mail: info@bedfordschool.org.uk
http://www.bedfordschool.org.uk
We pride ourselves on the pursuit of excellence, on encouraging boys to develop
their talent, discover new interests and prepare for the world beyond school.

John Moule, Head Master

1686 Bedgebury School
Goudhurst
Cranbrook
Kent TN17
0580-211954
E-mail: bedgebury@bell-centres.com
http://www.bedgeburyschool.co.uk
Our goal at Bell Bedgebury is a simple one
- to offer all our students the best possible
preparation for their future educational
careers.

Eric Squires, Headmaster
David Morse, Principal

**1687 Belgium Antwerp International
School**
Veltwijcklaan 180
Ekeren-Antwerp
Belgium 02180
32-3-543-9300
Fax: 32-3-541-8201
E-mail: ais@ais-antwerp.be
http://www.ais-antwerp.be
The school is concerned with the student's
social, physical, emotional and intellectual
development. It is committed to excellence
and to providing the best possible opportu-
nities for growth for each student.

Alun Cooper, Headmaster
Matthew Cox, Elementary School
Principal

1688 Benjamin Franklin International School
Martorell i Pena 9
Barcelona
Spain 08017
34-93-434-2380
Fax: 34-93-417-3633
E-mail: bfranklin@bfis.org
http://www.bfis.org
We view education as an opportunity for children
to live fully and become global citizens able to
build a more humane world.

David Penberg, Director
James Duval, Elementary Principal

1689 Berlin International School
Lentzeallee 8/14
Berlin
Germany 14195
49-30-790-00370
Fax: 49-30-3790-00370
E-mail: office@berlin-international-school.de
http://www.berlin-international-school.de
Berlin International School is a private,
non-profit, non-denominational day school offering student-centered learning to international and
local students from pre-school through university
entrance preparation.

Hubert Keulers, Acting Director
Michael Cunningham, Principal

1690 Berlin Potsdam International School
Am Hochwald 30, Haus 2
14 532 Kleinmachnow
Germany
49-332-086-760
Fax: 49-332-086-7612
E-mail: office@bpis.de
http://www.bpis.de
Grade levels N-12, school year August - June

Stephen Middlebrook, Director

1691 Bitburg Elementary School
52 MSG/CCSE-B Unit 3820 Box 45
APO, AE
Germany 09126-45
119-661-
Fax: 119- 61-
E-mail: BitburgES.Principal@eu.dodea.edu
http://www.bitb-es.eu.dodea.edu

Joseph Lovett, Principal

1692 Bitburg High School
52 MSG/CCSH-B Unit 3820 Box 50
APO, AE
Germany 09126-50
065-692-
Fax: 065- 90-0
E-mail: webmaster@eu.dodea.edu
http://www.bitb-hs.eu.dodea.edu

David W Carlisle, Principal
Jennifer Remoy, Assistant Principal

1693 Bitburg Middle School
52 MSG/CCSM-B Unit 3820 Box 55
APO, AE
Germany 09126
561-946-3200
Fax: 065-611-2091
E-mail: webmaster@eu.dodea.edu
http://www.bitb-ms.eu.dodea.edu

Douglas Carlson, Principal

1694 Bjorn's International School
Gartnerivej 5
Copenhagen
Denmark 02100
453-929-2937
Fax: 453-929-1938
E-mail: kontoret.101152@skolekom.dk
http://www.b-i-s.dk

Lea Kroghly, Principal

1695 Black Forest Academy

Postfach 1109
Kandern
Germany 79396
49-7626-91610
Fax: 49-7626-8821
http://www.bfacademy.com
Black Forest Academy's vision is globally-minded Christians changing their world for Christ.

George Durance, Principal
Tim Shuman, Director

1696 Bloxham School

Bloxham
Banbury
Oxfordshire, UK OX15
01295-720206
Fax: 01295-721897
E-mail: registar@bloxhamschool.com
http://www.bloxhamschool.com
As the largest group of Church of England Schools in the UK, Woodard was established in 1847 and today is known for providing academic excellence and an unrivalled supportive environment where individuals can flourish.

Mark Allbrook, Headmaster
B Hurst, Chairman

1697 Blue Coat School

Birmingham Street
Walsall
West Midlands, UK WS1 2
0121-456-3966
E-mail:
postbox@blue-coat-s.walsall.sch.uk
http://www.bluecoatschool.org

Brian Bissell, Principal
Ken Yeates, Headteacher

1698 Boeblingen Elementary School

Unit 30401
APO
AE 09107
070-1 1-2715
Fax: 070-1 2-1368
http://www.stut-esb.eu.dodea.edu
To inspire curiosity and ambition for life-long learning in every student.

Dale Moore, Principal
Toufy Haddad, Assistant Principal

1699 Bonn International School

Martin-Luther-King Strasse 14
Bonn
Germany 53175
49-228-308-540
Fax: 49-228-308-5420
E-mail: admin@bis.bonn.org
http://www.bis.bonn.org
The mission of Bonn International School is to inspire and empower students, aged 3-19, to become balanced, responsible global citizens who are successful, independent thinkers with a passion for learning.

Peter Murphy, Director
Diane Lewthwaite, Secondary School Principal

1700 Bordeaux International School

252 rue Jadaique
Bordeaux
France 33000
33-557-870-211
Fax: 33-556-790-047
E-mail: bis@bordeaux-school.com
http://www.bordeaux-school.com
Conveniently located in the centre of historic Bordeaux, the school is purpose-built around a secure, enclosed and partially covered courtyard, which provides a space for pupils across the school to socialise with each other.

Christine Cussac, Head Teacher

1701 Brillantmont International School

16, avenue Charles-Secretan
Lausanne
Switzerland, CH 01005
41-21-310-0400
Fax: 41-21-320-8417
E-mail: info@brillantmont.ch
http://www.brillantmont.ch
Brillantmont International School houses some 100 boarding boys and girls and about 50 day students.

Philippe Pasche, Director
Geraldine Boland, Deputy Director

1702 British Council School-Madrid

Prado de Somosaguas
Pozuelo de Alarcn
Madrid, UK 28223
34-91-337-3500
Fax: 34-91-337-3573
E-mail:
general.enquiries@britishcouncil.org
http://www.britishcouncil.org
The British Council School is one of the leading bilingual, bi-cultural schools in the world, offering the very best of British and Spanish education. The school is divided into three departments (Early Years, Primary and Secondary) and offers education from children aged three to eighteen years old.

Jack Cushman, Principal
Norman Roddom, Head of School

1703 British Kindergarten

Ctra Del La Coruna Km 17
Las Rozas, 28230 Madrid
Spain
http://www.britishnursery.com

Mary Jane Maybury, Principal

1704 British Primary School

Stationsstraat 3 Vossem
Tervuren, BE 03080
32-2-767-3098
Fax: 32-2-767-0351
E-mail: info@stpaulsbps.com
http://www.britishprimary.com
Our aim at St Paul's is to provide 'The Best Possible Start in Life '. We offer a secure, nurturing and truly caring environment for children, whether settling into a new country or going to school for the first time.

Katie Tyrie, Headteacher
Bruce Guy, Financial Manager

1705 British Primary School-Stockholm

Vossem
182 68 Djursholm
Sweden
468-755-2375
http://www.britishinternationalprimaryschool.se

Gaye Elliot, Principal

1706 British School-Amsterdam

Anthonie van Dijckstraat 1
Amsterdam, ME 01077
31-20-347-1111
Fax: 31-20-347-1222
http://www.britishschoolofamsterdam.nl
Our school is commited to providing the best possible eduction for our students. This is achieved in a calm, friendly, purposeful learning environment. Our strong and experieced team of teaching professionals are supported with excellent resources and facilities.

John Light, Principal
K McCarthy, Chairman

1707 British School-Bern

Hintere Dorfgasse 20
Gumligen
Switzerland 03073
41-31-951-2358
Fax: 41-31-951-1710
E-mail: britishschool@bluewin.ch
http://www.britishschool.ch
We aim to provide a high quality programme for children of all abilities that promotes the social, emotional, cognitive, moral, physical and aesthetic development of each child

Enid Potts, Head Teacher/Administrator
Joe Quinn, Support Staff

1708 British School-Brussels

Leuvensesteenweg 19
Tervuren
Belgium, BE 03080
322-767-4700
Fax: 322-767-8070
E-mail: reception@britishschool.be
http://www.britishschool.be
The British School of Brussels, situated 30 minutes from the city centre on a beautiful campus, offers a British education to International families in the heart of Europe, with pupils from some 70 nationalities on roll.

Roland Chant, Principal
Brenda Despontin, Principal

1709 British School-Netherlands

Wheatfields
Tarwekamp 3
Netherlands 02592
071-616958
Fax: 071-617144
E-mail: foundation@britishschool.nl
http://www.britishschool.nl
BSN provides the opportunity of becoming part of a student community defined by an ethos of mutual understanding and cultural harmony. We have high expectations of our students, so whilst appreciating the difference in the ability and achievement of individual children within the classroom, we expect the same high level of behaviour from all. Good behaviour, manners and a respect for teachers and other adults are everyday expectations of our students.

Martin Coles, Principal
Nigel Collins, Assistant Principal

1710 British School-Oslo

PO Box 7531, Skillebekk 0205
Oslo 2
Norway

Margaret Stark, Principal

1711 British School-Paris

21B Lavant Street
Petersfield
Hampshire GU32-3EL
01-34-80-45-94
Fax: 01-39-76-12-69
E-mail: ecis@ecis.org
http://www.ecis.org
The European Council of International Schools (ECIS) is a collaborative network promoting the ideals and best practice of international education.

Pilar Cabeza de Vaca, Executive Director
Mary Langford de Donoso, Deputy Executive Director

1712 Bromsgrove School

Worcester Road
Bromsgrove
Worcestershire B61-7DU
44-0-1527-579679
Fax: 44-0-1527-576177
E-mail:
headmaster@bromsgrove-school.co.uk
http://www.bromsgrove-school.co.uk
This school offers an English curriculum to 840 day students and 350 boarding (700 boys; 490 girls), ages 3 to 18. The curriculum is English based but french, german and

Spanish are also taught. Teachers from overseas are welcome with the length of stay being 1-2 years. Applications needed to teach include science, French, math, Spanish, reading, German, English and physical education.

Chris Edwards, Headmaster
John Rogers, Foundation Director

1713 Brooke House College

Market Harborough Leicestershire
Leicestershire
England LE16-7AU
44-0-1852-462452
Fax: 44-0-1858-462487
E-mail: enquiries@brookehouse.com
http://www.brookehouse.com
Brooke House College is a co-educational, international boarding college, specialising in preparing students from all over the globe, and from Britain, for entrance to the most prestigious universities to which they can aspire in both the U.K. and U.S.A

K Anderton, Academic Tutor
A Burditt, Diploma Personal Assistant

1714 Brussels American School

Unit 8100 Box 13
APO AE 09714-9998
Belgium, BE
320-271-9552
Fax: 302-717-9577
E-mail:
BrusselsEHS.Principal@eu.dodea.edu
http://www.brus-ehs.eu.dodea.edu
Brussels American School (BAS) serves students in Kindergarten through Grade 12. The elementary section of the school consists of Kindergarten through Grade 5. It is housed in one of the four major buildings and has a playground and special learning facilities. Grades 6-8 serve as transitional grades between the elementary and secondary programs; students attend classes in both the elementary and high school buildings

Walter G Seely, Principal
Cheryl A Aeillo, Assistant Principal

1715 Brussels English Primary School

23 Avenue Franklin Roosevelt
Brussels
Belgium 01050
62-010-41-72-27
Fax: 62-010-40-10-43
E-mail: info@beps.com
http://www.beps.com
Offering the Primary Years Programme, a prestigious programme supported by many international schools around the world (ages 3 to 11).

Henny de Waal, Head of School
Dominique Floridor, Secretary

1716 Bryanston School

Blandford
Dorset
UK DT11-0PX
0258-452411
E-mail: development@bryanston.co.uk
http://www.bryanston.co.uk
Bryanston they are those which encourage independence, individuality, and thinking, as well as being able to learn from living in a loving community which fast becomes, and remains, a family

Paul Speakman, Treasurer
Robert Ware, Chair

1717 Buckswood Grange International School

Broomham Hall Rye Road Guestling
Nr Hastings E Suxxex
England TN35-4LT

44-182-574-7000
Fax: 44-182-576-5010
E-mail: achieve@buckswood.co.uk
http://www.buckswood.co.uk
A multinational boarding school for British and foreign students which combines the British curriculum with specialist EFL tution and close attention to social skills in an international environment.

Michael Reiser, Principal
David Walker, Marketing Manager

1718 Butzbach Elementary School

CMR 452 Box 5500
APO, Butzbach 09045 0005
Germany

Carl Ford, Principal

1719 Byron Elementary School

202 New Dunbar Road
Byron, GA 31008
478-956-5020
Fax: 478-956-5910
E-mail: dmartin@peachschools.org
http://bes.peachschools.org
Our teachers are dedicated, hard working educators who are life learners themselves. An enriched, standards-based instruction is provided through collegial partnerships and staff development. Teachers continue to refine their instructional skills through book study discussions, grade level meetings, and attending various workshops.

Martin Dannelly, Principal
Dennis Teresia, Assistant Principal

1720 CIV International School-Sophia Antipolis

BP 97, 190 rue Frederic Mistral
Sophia Antipolis 06902
France
33-4-929-65224
Fax: 33-4-936-52215
E-mail: secretary@civissa.org
http://www.civissa.org
Grade levels 1-12, school year September-June

Andrew Derry, Head of Section

1721 Calpe College International School

Cta de Cadiz Km 171
29670 Malaga
Spain
95-278-1479
Fax: 95-278-9416
E-mail: info@calpeactivanet.es
http://www.calpeschool.com

Luis Proetta, Principal

1722 Campion School

PO Box 67484
Pallini GR-15302
Greece
301-813-5901
Fax: 301-813-6492
E-mail: dbaker@hol.gr
http://www.campionschool.in

Dennis MacKinnon, Principal

1723 Canadian College Italy-The Renaissance School

59 Macamo Courte
Maple, Ontario
Canada L6A-1G1
905-508-7108
800-422-0548
Fax: 905-508-5480
E-mail: cciren@rogers.com
http://www.ccilanciano.com
A unique source of highest-quality English-language education, preparing students for university entrance in the U.S.A., U.K., Canada and Europe, become one of

the pre-eminent high school boarding schools in Europe. Graduates from CCI's founding years earned acceptances, and a variety of scholarships

1724 Cascais International School

Rua Das Faias, Lt 7 Torre
2750 Cascais
Portugal
http://www.icsc.pt
An international nursery school, founded in 1996, that caters to children ages 1-6 years on a fulltime or part-time basis. The first language of the school is English and Portuguese is the second. Many other languages are spoken throughout the school. Offers an individual approach, flexible hours and transport. Total enrollment is 75 day students (45 boys; 30 girls).

Evan Lerven Sixma, Principal

1725 Castelli Elementary School

Via Dei Laghi, 8.60
Ligetta Di Marinus, Ag, 00047 Marina
Italy
39-06-9366-1311
Fax: 39-06-9366-1311
http://www.castelli-international.it

Diana Jaworska, Principal

1726 Castelli International School

Via Degli Scozzesi
13-Grottaferrata
Rome, Italy
39-06-943-15779
Fax: 39-06-943-15779
E-mail: maryac@castelli-international.it
http://www.castelli-international.it/
To provide a stimulating educational environment for international families living south of Rome and in the Castelli Romani area. CIS believes that the children, being naturally curious, are eager to learn, and that they learn best through inquiry, experience, and trial and error

Marianne Palladino, BA, MA, PhD, Director of Studies

1727 Casterton School

Kirkby Lonsdale, Via Carnforth
Lancashire, United Kingdom LA6-2SG
052-42-71202
E-mail: admissions@castertonschool.co.uk
http://www.castertonschool.co.uk
One of the most established academic girls boarding and day schools in the UK, with a national and international reputation.

P McLaughlin, Headmaster
G A Sykes, Deputy Head

1728 Caxton College

Ctra De Barcelona S/N 46530
Puzol Valencia
Spain
34-96-146-4500
Fax: 34-96142-0930
E-mail: caxton@caxtoncollege.com
http://www.caxtoncollege.com
Aim to provide pupils with the skills necessary to form independent opinions enabling them to make personal decisions in response to situations which will arise in their lives.

Amparo Gil, Principal
Marta Gil, Vice Principal

1729 Center Academy

92 St John's Hill Battersea
London SW11 1SH
England
071-821-5760
http://www.centeracademy.com
To provide students with a learning environment that facilitates the development of self-confidence, motivation, and academic skills, and gives students the opportunity to achieve success in life.

Robert Detweiler, Principal
Mack R Hicks, Founder and Chairman

1730 Centre International De Valbonne
Civ-bp 097 06902 Sophia
Antipolis Cedex
France
33-4-929-652-24
Fax: 33-4-936-522-15
E-mail: greta.antipolis languages @
ac-nice.fr
http://www.civfrance.com
Ian Hill, Principal

1731 Charters-Ancaster School
Penland Road, Bexhill on Sea
TN40 2JQ
England
0424-730499
Boarding girls ages eleven to eighteen; day school for boys three to eight and girls three-eighteen.
K Lewis, MA, Headmaster

1732 Children's House
Kornbergvegen 23-4050 Sola
Stavanger
Norway
http://www.hr.umich.edu
Christine Grov, Principal

1733 Cite Scolaire International De Lyon
2 Place De Montreal
69007 Lyon
France
33-04-78-69-60-06
Fax: 33-04-78-69-60-36
E-mail: csi-lyon-gerland@ac-lyon.fr
http://www.csilyon.fr
Grade levels 1-12.
Donna Galiana, Director

1734 Cobham Hall
Cobham (Nr Gravesend, Kent)
DA12 3BL
England, UK
0474-82-3371
E-mail: enquiries@cobhamhall.com
http://www.cobhamhall.com
Encouraged and supported to make the most of your talents, whether these are academic, musical, sporting ... or as yet undiscovered!
Paul Mitchel, Headmaster
C Sykes, Chairman

1735 Colegio Ecole
Santa Rosa 12
Lugo Llanera
Asturias 33690
985- 77-8
E-mail: ecole1@colegioecole.com
http://www.colegioecole.com
Patrick Wilson, Principal

1736 Colegio International-Meres
Apartado 107
33080 Oviedo, Asturias
Spain
985-792-427
Fax: 985-794-582
http://www.colegiomeres.com
Belen Orejas Fernandez, Principal

1737 Colegio International-Vilamoura
Apt 856, 8125 Vilamoura
Loule Algarve
Portugal
http://www.civ.com
Lawrence James, Principal

1738 College Du Leman International School
74 Route De Sauverny
CH-1290 Versoix, Geneva
Switzerland
41-22-775-5555
Fax: 41-22-775-5559
E-mail: admissions@cdl.ch
http://www.cdl.ch
Grade levels include N-13 with an enrollment of 1700.
Francis Clivaz, General Director
Cedric Chaffois, Director of Admission

1739 College International-Fontainebleau
48 Rue Guerin 77300
Fontainebleau
France
01-64-22-11-77
Fax: 01-64-23-43-17
E-mail: glenyskennedy@compuserve.com
http://www.fontainebleau.fr
Mrs. G Kennedy, Principal

1740 College Lycee Cevenol International
43400 Le Chambon sur Lignon
France
04-71-59-72-52
Fax: 04-71-65-87-38
E-mail: contact@lecevenol.org
http://www.lecevenol.org
he CollSge Lyc,e International C,venol (a private establishment under a contract of state sponsorship since 1971) today welcomes boarders and day students of local, regional, national and international origins.
Christiane Minssen, Principal
Robert Lassey, Headmaster

1741 Copenhagen International School
Hellerupvej 22-26
2900 Hellerup
Denmark
45-39-463-300
Fax: 45-39-612-230
E-mail: cis@cisdk.dk
http://www.cis-edu.dk
Develop the potential of each student in a stimulating environment of cultural diversity, academic excellence and mutual respect.
Peter Wellby, Director
Simon Watson, Senior School Principal

1742 Croughton High School
Unit 5485 Box 15
APO Croughton, 09494 0005
Great Britain
Dr. Charles Recesso, Principal

1743 Danube International School
Josef Gall-Gassee 2
1020 Vienna
Austria
00-43-1-720-3110
Fax: 43-1-720-3110-40
E-mail: info@ danubeschool.at
http://www.danubeschool.at
DIS started off life in 1992 in Schrutkagasse in the 13th District. The school had another name, then - 'Pawen International Community School' that now houses a Rudolf Steiner school
Peter Harding, Director
Sabine Biber-Brussmann, Registrar

1744 Darmstadt Elementary School
CMR 431
APO, Darmstadt 09175 0005
Germany
Sherry Templeton, Principal

1745 Darmstadt Junior High School
CMR 431
APO, Darmstadt 09175 0005
Germany
Daniel Basarich, Principal

1746 De Blijberg
Graaf Florisstraat 56
Rotterdam
Netherlands 3032C
010-448-2266
Fax: 010-448-2270
E-mail:
deblijberg_international@hotmail.com
http://www.blijberg.nl
Barbera Everaars, Director
Bart Loman, Director

1747 Dean Close School
Lansdown Road
Cheltenham
England GL51
0242-522640
E-mail: squirrels@deanclose.org.uk
http://www.deanclose.co.uk
Aim to provide a rich variety of opportunities that will enable your son or daughter to develop in confidence and independance within our happy and caring community.
Sue Bennett, Headmistress
Anthony R Barchand, Faculty Head

1748 Dexheim Elementary School
Unit 24027
APO, Dexheim 09110 0005
Germany
Gary Waltner, Principal

1749 Downside School
Stratton-on-the-Fosse, Bath (Avon)
Radstock Bath
England, UK BA3
0761-232-206
E-mail: admin@downside.co.uk
http://www.downside.co.uk
Downside is an independent Catholic co-educational boarding school for pupils aged 9 to 18.
Dom Leo Maidlow Davis, Head Master
AR Hobbs, Deputy Head Master

1750 Dresden International School
Annenstr 9
D-01067 Dresden
Germany
49-351-3400428
Fax: 49-351-3400430
E-mail: dis@dredsen-is.de
http://www.dresden-is.de
Committed to the aim of continuous improvement, which has been such a feature of the school since it opened in 1996.
Chrissie Sorenson, Director
Steve Ellis, Secondary School Principal

1751 ECC International School
Jacob Jordaensstraat 85-87
2018 Antwerp
Belgium
Dr. X Nieberding, Principal

1752 Ecole Active Bilingue
70 rue du Theatre
Paris
France 75015
01-44-37-00-80
Fax: 01-45-79-06-66
E-mail: info@eabjm.net
http://www.eabjm.net
An associated UNESCO school, EABJM is also contractually part of the French national education system. The high school prepares students for the French Baccalaureate, the French Baccalaureate with Option Internationale, or the International Baccalaureate. An official testing site for the SAT, EABJM is also accredited by the College Entrance Examination Board and the Cam-

bridge University Local Examination Syndicate.

Danielle Monod, Principal

1753 Ecole Active Bilingue Jeannine Manuel
70 rue du Theatre
75015 Paris
France 75015
45-44-37-00-80
Fax: 01-45-79-06-66
E-mail: info@eabjm.net
http://www.eabjm.com
Grade levels k-12.

Elizabeth Zeboulon, Directrice

1754 Ecole D'Humanite
CH-6085 Hasliberg-Goldern
Switzerland
41-33-972-9292
Fax: 41-33-972-9211
E-mail: us.office@ecole.ch
http://www.ecole.ch
150 boys and girls, aged 6 to 20 and faculty live in small family-style groups. International, inter-racial student body. Main language is German, with special classes for beginners.

Kathleen Hennessy, Interim Director
Arsheles Curturils, Director

1755 Ecole Des Roches & Fleuris
3961 Bluche
Valais
Switzerland

Marcel Clivez, Principal

1756 Ecole Lemania
Chemin de Preville 3
CP500 1001 Lausanne
Switzerland
41-0-21-320-15-01
Fax: 41-0-21-312-67-00
E-mail: info@lemania.com
http://www.lemania.com
This international college represents over 65 nationalities offering French and English intensive courses, summer programs, American academic studies at graduate and undergraduate levels, sports and cultural activities, and accommodation in boarding school. Total enrollment: 800 day students; 100 boarding (450 boys; 450 girls), in grades 1-10.

M JP du Pasquier, Principal

1757 Ecole Nouvelle Preparatoire
Route Du Lac 22, Ch-1094
Paudex
Switzerland

Marc Desmet, Principal

1758 Ecole Nouvelle de la Suisse Romande
Ch de Rovereaz 20, CP-161
CH-1000 Lausanne 12
Switzerland
41-21-654-65-00
Fax: 41-21-654-65-05
E-mail: info@ensr.ch
http://www.ensr.ch
The mission of the school is to prepare its students

Isabel Matos, Director
Administrative/Fina
Beth Krasna, President

1759 Edinburgh American School
29 Chester Street
Edinburgh EH37EN
Scotland

013-155- 460
Fax: 013-162- 499
http://www.edinburghacademy.org.uk

AW Morris, Principal

1760 Edradour School
Edradour House - Pitlochry
Perthshire PH165JW,
Scotland

JPA Romanes, Principal

1761 El Plantio International School Valencia
Urbanizacion El Plantio
Calle 233, N36, La Canada, Paterna
Spain
96-132-14-10
Fax: 96-132-18-41
E-mail: plantiointernational@retemail.es
http://www.plantiointernational.com
To educate young people who can adapt to their environment and therefore our objective is based on providing our students with the necessary skills to enable a better knowledge of the modem world and maximising the ability to communicate in an ever-changing and broadening society.

Anthony C Nelson, Principal

1762 Ellerslie School
Abbey Road, Malvern
WR14 3HF
England
0684-575701
http://www.ellerslie.school.nz

Elizabeth M Baker, BA, Headmaster

1763 English Junior School
Lilla Danska Vagen 1
412 74 Gothenburg
Sweden
31-401819

Patricia Gabrielsson, Principal

1764 English Kindergarten
Valenjanpolku 2
05880 Hyvinkaa
Finland
http://www.theenglishkindergarten.co.in

Riva Rentto, Principal

1765 English Montessori School
C/ de la Salle S/N
Aravaca, Madrid
Spain 28023
91-357-26-67
Fax: 91-307-15-43
E-mail: t.e.m.s@teleline.es
http://englishmontessorischool.com
Each year of school up to and including Year 10 at The English Montessori School is validated with the Spanish Educational System. The importance of this is that a students entering or leaving the school can transfer to the equivalent level in any other school.

Elaine Fitzpatrick, Headmistress
Milagros Alonso, Director

1766 English School-Helsinki
Mantytie 14
Helinski
Finland 00270
358-9-477-1123
Fax: 358-9-477-1980
E-mail: english.school@edu.hel.fi
http://www.eschool.edu.hel.fi
The English School is a private, national language school based on Christian values. The Ministry of Education has placed a special responsibility on the school to familiarize the students with Finnish and

English languages as well as the culture of Finnish and Anglo-Saxon language areas.

Erkki Lehto, Principal
Riitta Volanen, Secretary

1767 English School-Los Olivos
Avda Pino Panera 25, 46110 Godella
Valencia
Spain 46110
96-363-99-38
Fax: 96-364-48-63
http://www.school-losolivos.es

Jane Rodriguez, Principal

1768 European Business & Management School
Frederik de Merodestraat, 12-16
Antwerp
Belgium 02600
323-218-8182
Fax: 323-218-5868
E-mail: info@ebms.edu
http://www.ebms.edu
Once a year, European Business and Management School organizes a cross-cultural business tour, providing our students with another opportunity to strengthen their competencies in global thinking in international business.

Luc Van Meli, Director

1769 European School Culham
Thame Lane, Abingdon
Oxfordshire
Great Britain OX14
44 -235-5226
Fax: 44 -235-5546
E-mail: esculham@eursc.org
http://www.esculham.net
Educated side by side, untroubled from infancy by divisive prejudices, acquainted with all that is great and good in different cultures, it will be borne in upon them as they mature that they belong together.

T Hyem, Principal
Simon Sharron, Head

1770 European School-Brussels I
Avenue Du Vert Chasseur 46
Brussels
Belgium 01180
02-374-58-44
E-mail: kari.kivinen@eursc.org
http://www.eeb1.org
The European Schools fulfil a task that national schools are unable to fulfil: to teach pupils from different countries in their respective mother tongues and to instil in them the cultural values of their home country room a European perspective.

J Marshall, Principal
Kari Kivinen, Director

1771 European School-Italy
Via Montello 118
21100 Varese
Italy
32 -297-5990
http://www.ec.europa.eu

Jorg Hoffman, Principal

1772 Evangelical Christian Academy
Calle La Manda 47
Camarma de Esteruelas, Madrid
Spain 28816
34-91-741-2900
Fax: 34-91-320-8606
E-mail: secretary@ecaspain.com
http://www.ecaspain.com
The vision drives every facet of ECA's existence. ECA offers a challenging, college preperatory curriculum in an American-based system. Students at ECA study Bible each year, and a Chris-

tian worldview is integrated into every aspect of the curriculum.

Beth Hornish, Principal
Scot Musser, Business Manager

1773 Feltwell Elementary School

CCSE/F Unit 5185 Box 315
APO AE
Great Britain 09461-5315
011-44 -842
Fax: 018-2 8-7931
E-mail: feltwell.attendance@eu.dodea.edu
http://www.felt-es.eu.dodea.edu
School where teachers, parents, and community share the responsibility for each child's learning.

Tom LaRue, Principal

1774 Frankfurt International School

An der Waldlust 15
Oberursel
Germany 61440
49-6171-2020
Fax: 49-6171-202384
E-mail: admissions@fis.edu
http://www.fis.edu
To be the leading culturally diverse and family-oriented international school with English as the principal language of instruction. We inspire young individuals to develop their intellect, creativity and character to grow into adaptable, socially responsible global citizens by ensuring a dynamic, 21st-century, inquiry-driven education of the highest standard.

Jutta Kuehne, Director
Mark Ulfers, Head of School

1775 Frederiksborg Gymnasium

Carlsbergvej 15
3400 Hillerod
Denmark
800-055-7314
Fax: 482- 07-1
E-mail: post@frborg-gymhf.dk
http://www.frborg-gymhf.dk

Peter Kuhlman, Principal

1776 Friends School

Saffron Walden, Essex
England CB11
0642-722141
E-mail: admissions@friends.org.uk
http://www.friends.org.uk
Friends' School strives to be a unique community where the potential and talent of each individual is realised within a friendly and challenging environment based on Quaker principles.

Graham Wigley, Head

1777 Gaeta Elementary & Middle School

PSC Box 811
FPO Gaeta 09609 0005
Italy

Dr. Robert Kirkpatrick, Principal

1778 Garmisch Elementary School

Unit 24511
APO AE, Garmisch
Germany 09053
440-261-
Fax: 088-176-949
E-mail:
GarmischEMS.Webmaster@eu.dodea.edu
http://www.garm-es.eu.dodea.edu
To provide a challenging curriculum in an atmosphere respectful of individual needs and cultural diversity. All students will learn the academic and social skills necessary for their future success.

Debbie Strong, Principal

1779 Geilenkirchen Elementary School

Unit 8045
APO AE, Geilenkirchen 09104 0005
Germany 09104
024-1 9- 308
Fax: 024-1 9- 308
E-mail:
GeilenkirchenES.Webmaster@eu.dodea.edu
http://www.geil-es.eu.dodea.edu/
Educating our students to be responsible, productive and ethical citizens with the skills to think creatively, reason critically, communicate effectively and learn continuously.

James V Dierendonck, Principal

1780 Gelnhausen Elementary School

CMR 465
APO, Gelnhausen 09076 0005
Germany

Jim Harrison, Principal

1781 Geneva English School

36 Route de Malagny
1294 Genthod
Switzerland
41-22-755-18-55
Fax: 41-22-779-14-29
E-mail: admin@genevaenglishschool.ch
http://www.geneva-english-school.ch
A private, nonprofit primary school that is owned and managed by an association which is composed of parents whose children attend the school. The main objective of the school is to offer education on British lines for children of primary school age living in or near Geneva, and to prepare them for secondary education in any English-speaking school.

Denis Unsworth, Principal
Gareth Davies, Headmaster

1782 Giessen Elementary School

414th BSB GSN, Unit 20911
APO, Giessen 09169 0005
Germany
496-414-6265
496-414-8333
http://www.aoshs.org

Mary Ann Burkard, Principal

1783 Giessen High School

414th BSB GSB, Unit 20911
APO, Giessen 09169 0005
Germany
496-414-6266
http://www.aoshs.org

Gordon Gartner, Principal

1784 Grafenwoehr Elementary School

Unit 28127
APO AE
Germany 09114-8127
964-183-7133
Fax: 964- 32-4
E-mail:
GrafenwoehrES.Principal@eu.dodea.edu
http://www.graf-es.eu.dodea.edu
To maintain a meaningful partnership with the community through which physical well being, cognitive growth, and emotional support are provided to all learners.

Crystal Bailey, Principal
David Eldredge, Assistant Principal

1785 Greenwood Garden School

Via Vito Sinisi 5
Rome
Italy
39-06-332-66703
Fax: 39-06-332-66703
E-mail: greenwoodgarden@libero.it
http://www.greenwoodgardenschool.com
An international pre-school and kindergarten for children aging from 2-6 with teaching be-

ing done in English by mother-tongue educators experienced with young children

Donna Seibert, Directress

1786 Gstaad International School

Ahorn
Gstaad
Switzerland CH-37
41-33-744-2373
Fax: 41-33-744-3578
E-mail: gis@gstaad.ch
http://www.gstaadschool.ch
The school's mission includes the building of endurance and stamina in both academics and sports, as well as stimulating personal achievement by teaching the values of respect, gratitude, humour and real caring for others. Students are continually presented with challenges and the opportunities to achieve where perhaps before they thought impossible.

Alain Souperbiet, Director

1787 Haagsche School Vereeniging

Nassaulaan 26
Den Haag-2514
003-170-363
E-mail: info@hsvdenhaag.nl
http://www.hsvdenhaag.nl

HM Jongeling, Principal
Lorraine Dean, Director

1788 Hainerberg Elementary School

Unit 29647 Box 0086
APO AE, Wiesbaden
Germany 09096-86
337-516-
Fax: 011-49 -11 7
E-mail:
Wiesbadenes.principal@eu.dodea.edu
http://www.wies-esh.eu.dodea.edu
Provide exemplary educational programs that inspire and prepare all students for success in a global environment.

Maren James, Principal

1789 Halvorsen Tunner Elementary and Middle School

Unit 7565
APO, Rhein Main 09050 0005
Germany

Julie Gaski, Principal

1790 Hanau High School

Unit 20235
APO, Hanau 09165 0005
Germany

Allen Davenport, Principal

1791 Hanau Middle School

Unit 20193
APO, Hanau 09165 0016
Germany

Robert Sennett, Principal

1792 Harrow School

5 High Street
Harrow on the Hill
England HA1 3
01-423-2366
E-mail: harrow@harrowschool.org.uk
http://www.harrowschool.org.uk

Barnaby Lenon, Headmaster

1793 Hatherop Castle School

Hatherop, Cirencester
England GL7 3
028-575-206
http://www.hatheropcastle.com

Paul Easterbrook, Headmaster

1794 Heidelberg High School
Unit 29237
APO AE
Germany 09102
370-800-
Fax: 062-213- 587
http://www.heid-hs.eu.dodea.edu

Kevin J Brewer, Principal

1795 Heidelberg Middle School
Unit 29237
APO AE
Germany 09102
221-338-9310
http://www.heid-ms.eu.dodea.edu

Donald Johnson, Principal

1796 Hellenic College-London
67 Pont Street
London SWIX OBD
England
0171-581-5044
Fax: 0171-589-9055
E-mail: hellenic@rmplc.co.uk
http://www.rmplc.co.uk/eduweb/sites/hellenic

James Wardrobe, Principal

1797 Hellenic-American Education Foundation Athens College-Psychico College
15 Stefanou Delta
Psychico
Greece 154 5
30-1-671-2771
Fax: 30-1-674-8156
E-mail: info@haef.gr
http://www.haef.gr
Grade levels 1-12, school year September - June

David William Rupp, President

1798 Helsingin Suomalainen
Isonnevantie 8
Helinski, Finland 00320
358- 47-1
http://www.syk.fi
Helsingin Suomalainen Yhteiskoulu (SYK) is an independent coeducational, which prepares its students within for the national matriculation exam or the International Baccalaureate, both of which give a student general university entry qualifications.

Anja-Liisa Alanko, Principal

1799 Het Nederlands Lyceum
Wijndaelerduin 1
Hague, Netherlands 02554
070-338-4567
Fax: 070-328-2049
E-mail: primary@ishthehague.nl
http://www.ishthehague.nl
Offers young people of all nationalities between the ages of 4 and 18 top quality international education in a caring environment, which aim for academic success and encourage sporting and creative abilities in a community based on honesty, fairness, open-mindedness and tolerance.

Graeme Scott, Principal Primary School

1800 Het Rijnlands Lyceum
Appollolaan 1 2341 BA
Oegstgeest
Netherlands
31-3771-5155640
E-mail:
administratie@rijnlandslyceum-rlo.nl
http://www.rlo.nl
Lyceum is a state subsidized school with an international department offering IBMYP and IB. Offers an English/Dutch spoken curriculum to 1,190 day students and 60 boarding (650 boys; 600 girls), in grades 6 through 12. Student/teacher ratio is 15:1, and the school is willing to participate in a teacher exchange program, however, housing will not be provided by the school.

Drs LE Timmerman, Principal

1801 Hillhouse Montessori School
Avenida Alfonso Xiii 30 Y 34
Madrid 2
Spain
http://www.houseonthehill.com.sg

Judy Amick, Principal

1802 Hohenfels Elementary School
Unit 28214
APO AE
Germany 09173
466-400-
Fax: 094-2 8-32
http://www.hohe-es.eu.dodea.edu

Olaf Zwicker, Principal

1803 Hohenfels High School
CMR 414
APO, AE
Germany 09173
094-2 -9096
Fax: 094-2 8- 316
http://www.hohe-hs.eu.dodea.edu

Daniel J Mendoza, Principal

1804 Holmwood House
Chitts Hill, Lexden
Colchester, Essex
England CO3 9
44-0-1904-626183
Fax: 44-0-1904-670899
E-mail: hst@holmwood.essex.sch.uk
http://www.holmwood.essex.sch.uk
Holmwood House is an independent coeducational day and boarding preparatory school. The total enrollment of the school is 310 day students and 50 boarding students (240 boys and 120 girls), ages 4 1/2 to 13 1/2.

Alexander Mitchell, Headmaster

1805 Hvitfeldtska Gymnasiet
Rektorsgatan 2, SE-411 33
Goteborg
Sweden
46-31-367-0623
Fax: 46-31-367-0602
E-mail:
agneta.santesson@educ.goteborg.se
http://www.hvitfeldt.educ.goteborg.se
State school, founded 1647, offers the International Baccalaureate curriculum to a total enrollment of 90 girls and 90 boys, in grades 10-12.

Christen Holmstrom, Principal
Agneta Santesson, Deputy Headmaster

1806 Illesheim Elementary and Middle School
CMR 416 Box J
APO, Hohenfels 09140 0005
Germany
49-9841-8408
Fax: 49-9841-8987

Donald J Ness, Principal

1807 Independent Bonn International School
Tulpenbaumweg 42
Bonn 53177
Germany
49-228-32-31-66
Fax: 49-228-32-39-58
E-mail: ibis@ibis-school.com
http://www.ibis-school.com

IBIS is an international primary school.

Irene Bolik, Headteacher

1808 Independent Schools Information Service
Grosveror Gardens House 35-37
Frosvernor Gardens, London SW1W 0BS
England
020-77981575
Fax: 020-77981561
E-mail: national@isis.org.uk
http://www.isis.org.uk
Provides information on 1400 elementary and secondary schools in the United Kingdom and Ireland.

David J Woodhead

1809 Innsbruck International High School
Schonger, Austria A-6141
0-5225-4201
Fax: 0-5225-4202
An accredited coeducational boarding and day school. The school offers an American college preparatory high school curriculum for grades 9-12.

Gunther Wenko, Director
John E Wenrick, Headmaster

1810 Institut Alpin Le Vieux Chalet
1837 Chateau D'oex
Switzerland
212-338-9743
Fax: 212-949-7534
http://www.christusrex.org

Jean Bach, Principal

1811 Institut Auf Dem Rosenberg
Hohenweg 60-9000 St Gallen
Switzerland
417- 27-0777
Fax: 417- 27- 982
E-mail: info@instrosenberg.ch
http://www.instrosenberg.ch

Felicitas Scharli, Principal

1812 Institut Chateau Beau-Cedre
57 Av De Chillion
CH-1820 Territet Montreux
Switzerland
41-21-963-5341
Fax: 41-21-963-4783
E-mail: info@monterosaschool.com
This Institut is an exclusive boarding and finishing international school for girls. American high school with a general culture section for 30 boarding students in grades 9 through twelve. Languages spoken include French and English and the student/teacher ratio is 1:6.

Pierre Gay, Principal

1813 Institut Le Champ Des Pesses
1618 Chatel-st-denis
Montreux
Switzerland

PL Racloz, Principal

1814 Institut Le Rosey
Chateau du Rosey
1180 Rolle
Switzerland
41-21-822-5500
Fax: 41-21-822-5555
E-mail: rosey@rosey.ch
http://www.rosey.ch
Le Rosey's philosophy is inspired by what Harvard educationalist Howard Gardner has called multiple intelligences: its aim is to develop all Roseans' talents through academic, sporting and artistic programs.

Philippe Gudin, General Director
Michael Gray, Headmaster

**1815 Institut Montana
Bugerbug-American Schools**
Zugerberg
CH 6300 Zug
Switzerland
41-41-711-1722
Fax: 41-41-711-5465
E-mail: kob@montana.zug.ch
http://www.montana.zug.ch
Grade levels include 7-13 with a total enrollment of 111.

Daniel Fredez, Director

1816 Institut Monte Rosa
57, Ave de Chillon,
CH-1820 Territet/Montreux
Switzerland
021-963-5341
Fax: 021-963-4783
E-mail: info@monterosa.ch
http://www.monterosa.ch

Bernhard Gademann, BS, MS, Principal

1817 Inter-Community School
Strubenacher 3 Postfach
Zumikon
Switzerland 08126
41-1-919-8300
Fax: 41-1-919-8320
http://www.icsz.ch
The Inter-Community School is committed to providing a supportive and enabling learning environment in which all members of the community are challenged to achieve their individual potential, encouraged to pursue their passions, and expected to fulfil their responsibilities

Michael Matthews, Head of School
Martin Hall, Secondary Principal

1818 International Academy
Via di Grottarossa 295
00189 Rome
Italy
39-340-731-4195
E-mail: info@internationalacademy.in
http://www.internationalacademy.in

Joan Bafaloukas Bulgarini, Principal

1819 International College Spain
C/Vereda Norte 3
La Moraleja, Madrid
Spain 28109
34-91-650-2398
Fax: 34-91-650-1035
E-mail: admissions@icsmadrid.org
http://www.icsmadrid.com
The philosophy of the school is to provide students with a high quality international education which places a strong emphasis on fostering respect for the world's nations and cultures.

Terry Hedger, Director
Hubert Keulers, Head of Primary School

1820 International Management Institute
Garden Square Building, Block-C Laa
Antwerp
Belgium 02610
32-3-21-85-431
Fax: 32-3-21-85-868
E-mail: info@timi.edu
http://www.timi.edu
Our vision is to empower our students in terms of all the faculties required to pursue a career in the competitive globalized world. The focus of our curriculum is to enhance the learning perspective through customized modules and simulation exercises from globally renowned academicians and professionals.

Luc Van Mele, Director

1821 International Preparatory School
Rua Do Boror 12 Carcavelos
2775 Parede
Portugal
56-2-321-5800
Fax: 56-2-321-5821
E-mail: info@tipschool.com
http://www.tipschool.com

1822 International School Beverweerd
Beverweerdseweg 60, 3985 RE
Werkhoven
Netherlands
03437-1341
Fax: 03437-2079
http://www.isbeverweerd.nl

Ray Kern, BA, MA, Principal

1823 International School-Aberdeen
296 N Deeside Road
Milltimber, Aberdeen
Scotland, UK AB13
44-1224-732267
Fax: 44-1224-735648
E-mail: admin@isa.aberdeen.sch.uk
http://www.isa.aberdeen.sch.uk
The International School of Aberdeen (ISA) is an independent, non-profit school (K-12) that delivers excellence in education. We do this through a safe and caring learning environment where students are challenged to reach their maximum potential through academic success and personal growth, becoming socially responsible and active global citizens.

Daniel A Hovde PhD, Director
Don Newbury, Elementary Principal

1824 International School-Algarve
Apartado 80 Porches 8400
Lagoa Algarve
Portugal
http://www.algarveschool.com

Peter Maddison, Principal

1825 International School-Amsterdam
PO Box 920
AX Amstelveen
The Netherlands 01180
31-20-347-1111
Fax: 31-20-347-1222
E-mail: info@isa.nl
http://www.isa.nl
The International School of Amsterdam (ISA) was founded in 1964 to serve the educational needs of the children of the international community living in and around Amsterdam. ISA is a nonsectarian, non-profit coeducational day school, enrolling students in Pre-School through Grade 12 (from 3 to 18 years of age).

Dr Edward Greene, Director
Sarah Grace, Head of Lower School

1826 International School-Basel
Fleischbachstrasse 2
4153 Reinach BL
Switzerland
41-61-426-96-26
Fax: 41-61-426-96-25
http://www.isbasel.ch
mission of the International School Basel is to provide an international education to the highest recognized academic standards

Geoff Tomlinson, Principal

1827 International School-Bergen
Vilhelm Bjerknesvei 15
Bergen
Norway 05081
47-55-30-63-30
Fax: 47-55-30-63-31
E-mail: post@isob.no
http://www.isb.gs.hl.no

Provide an education for the children of expatriate oil company personnel in Bergen and to attract further corporate investment in the Bergen area.

June Murison, Director

1828 International School-Berne
170 Mattenstrasse
Gumligen
Switzerland 03073
41-31-951-2358
Fax: 41-31-951-1710
E-mail: office@isberne.ch
http://www.isberne.ch
Creative learning community for students from all over the world, within the framework of the three International Baccalaureate Programmes, guided by ISBerne teachers and staff, students aged 3 - 18 have the opportunity to become open-minded, principled, knowledgeable, confident lifelong learners and multilingual citizens of the world, who respect themselves and others.

Kevin Page, Director
Cory Etchberger, Chair

1829 International School-Brussels
Kattenberg 19
Brussels 1170
Belguim
32-2-661-4211
Fax: 32-2-661-4200
E-mail: admissions@isb.be
http://www.isb.be
Offers a challenging, inclusive international education designed to give every student opportunities for success within and beyond our school.

Kevin Bartlett, Director
Andrei Teixeira, Chairman

1830 International School-Cartagena
Manga Club Cp 30385 Cartagena
Los Belones Murcia
Spain
34-68-175000
E-mail: isc@sendanet.es
http://www.cartagenainternationalschool.com

Robert Risch, Principal

1831 International School-Curacao
PO Box 3090
Koninginnelaan Emmastad, Curacao
Netherlands Antilles
599-9-737-3633
Fax: 599-90737-3142
E-mail: iscmec@attglobal.net
http://www.isc.an
Offers a rigorous academic program in order to prepare students planning to pursue higher learning at colleges and universities around the world. The School's curriculum includes International Baccalaureate (IB) coursework that allows students the opportunity to receive the IB Diploma.

Margie Elhage, Director
Rene Romer, President

1832 International School-Dusseldorf
Niederrheinstrasse 336
Dusseldorf
Germany 40489
49-211-94066-799
Fax: 49-211-4080-744
E-mail: nmcw@isdedu.de
http://www.isdedu.eu
Provide the students of the International School of Dsseldorf with the best possible program of academic and personal development in a challenging and supportive environment.

Neil A McWilliam, Director
Michael Coffey, Senior School Principal

111

1833 International School-Eerde
Kasteellaan 1
PJ Ommen
The Netherlands 07731
031-0529-451452
Fax: 031-0529-456377
E-mail: info@eerde.nl
http://www.eerde.nl
Offers numerous programmes tailored to the individual needs of each student, including children with learning difficulties and dyslexia, as well as highly gifted children. Eerde carefully monitors the personal, academic, athletic and creative development of each individual student ages 4 to 19.

Herman Voogd, Principal

1834 International School-Friuli
Via Delle Grazie 1/A
Pordenone 33170
Italy
http://www.udineis.org

Susan Clarke, Principal

1835 International School-Geneva
62 route de Chene
Geneva
Switzerland CH-12
41-22-787-2400
Fax: 41-22-787-2410
E-mail: administration@ecolint.ch
http://www.ecolint.ch
Aims to provide a distinctive high quality international education that prepares pupils for membership of a world community based on mutual understanding, tolerance and shared humanitarian values.

Nicholas Tate, Director General
John Douglas, Director

1836 International School-Hamburg
Holmbrook 20
Hamburg
Germany 22605
49-40-883-1101
Fax: 49-40-1881-1405
E-mail: info@ishamburg.org
http://www.international-school-hamburg.de
A co-educational day school enrolling students from Primary 1 (age 3) to Grade 12. The school was founded in 1957 as the first international school in Germany.

Peter Gittin, Headmaster
Nick Ronai, Junior School Director

1837 International School-Hannover Region
Bruchmeisterstrasse 6
Hannover
Germany D-301
49-511-27041650
Fax: 49-511-557934
E-mail: adminoffice@is-hr.de
http://www.is-hr.de
Provides a high quality, balanced educational program in the English language for children of internationally-minded families.Offer a dynamic environment where each student is challenged and supported to become a dedicated learner for life and a contributing member of the local and global community.

Patricia Baier, Director
Steffen Stegeman, Business Manager

1838 International School-Helsinki
Selkamerenkatu 11
Helsinki
Finland 00180
358-9-686-6160
Fax: 358-9-685-6699

E-mail: mainoffice@ish.edu.hel.fi
http://www.ish.edu.hel.fi
Office Manager
Provide attendees
Bob Woods, Headmaster
Therese Thibault, Director

1839 International School-Iita
PMB 5320
Ibadan
Nigeria CR9 3
E-mail: iita@cgiar.org
http://www.iita.org
Provide a comprehensive, international curriculum in an environment which promotes confidence, caring and understanding, and prepares our students for successful learning here and in schools around the world.

Neil Jackson, Principal

1840 International School-Lausanne
Chemin de la Grangette 2
Le Mont-sur-Lausanne
Switzerland CH -
41-21-728-1733
Fax: 41-21-728-7868
E-mail: info@isl.ch
http://www.isl.ch
The school is committed to excellence in education, it strives to fulfill the unique potential of each student in a supportive and challenging holistic learning environment that prepares the student for continuing education and an active and responsible role in a multicultural world.

Lyn Cheetham, Director
John Ivett, Assistant Director

1841 International School-Le Chaperon Rouge
3963 Crans Sur Sierre
Crans/Montana
Switzerland
41-27-4812-500
Fax: 41-27-4812-502
http://www.chaperonrouge.ch

Prosper Bagnoud, Principal

1842 International School-London
139 Gunnersbury Avenue
London
England W3 8L
44-20-8992-5823
Fax: 44-20-8993-7012
E-mail: mail@ISLondon.com
http://www.islondon.com
Aims to maximize the achievement of its students throughout the curriculum and in personal and social fields. Drawing on the rich variety of cultures represented at the school, ISL aims to develop in each student a global outlook which seeks to understand and appreciate the attitudes and values of others.

Amin Makarem, Director
Sergio Pawel, Deputy Head, Curriculum

1843 International School-Lyon
80 chemin du Grand Roule
Ste-Foy-LSs-Lyon
France F-691
47 -86 -190
Fax: 47 -86 -198
E-mail: info@islyon.org
http://www.islyon.org
The school's curriculum is based on the programmes and pedagogy of the International Baccalaureate Organization which aims to develop in the students the skills, values and knowledge that will help them

to become responsible citizens in an increasingly interconnected world.

Donna Philip, Director
Michael Ford, Curriculum Coordinator

1844 International School-Naples
Viale della Liberazione, 1
Bagnoli, Napoli 80125
Italy
39-081-721-2037
Fax: 39-081-570-0248
E-mail: info@isnaples.it
http://www.isnaples.it
Provide a nurturing environment where students can grow intellectually, socially, psychologically and physically. Through a dedicated partnership of parents and educators, we strive to prepare our students to become productive, global citizens of the twenty-first century.

Josephine Sessa, Principal
Patricia Montesano, Vice Principal

1845 International School-Nice
15 Avenue Claude Debussy
Nice
France 06200
33-493-210-400
Fax: 33-493-216-911
E-mail: robert.silvetz@cote-azur.cci.fr
http://www.isn-nice.org
The school offers Pre-Kindergarten through grade 12 instruction and college preparatory education and provides an intellectually challenging programme of studies which aims to promote analytic understanding with an integrated view of the various academic disciplines and to encourage creativity and self-expression. Serves both the international community and local families who wish to offer their children an education in English, which is both international and versatile.

Wylie Michael, Director

1846 International School-Paris
6 Rue Beethoven
Paris
France 75016
33-1-422-40954
Fax: 33-1-452-71593
E-mail: info@isparis.edu
http://www.isparis.edu
ISP create a challenging and motivating English-speaking environment where students and staff from around the world use the programs of the International Baccalaureate Organisation and work in harmony to develop every student's full intellectual and human potential.

Audrey Peverelli, Headmaster
Catherine Hard, Head of Admissions

1847 International School-Sotogrande
Apartado 15
Sotogrande San Roque Cadiz
Spain 11310
34-956-79-59-02
Fax: 34-956-79-48-16
E-mail: director@sis.ac
http://www.sis.ac
Our school is a learning organisation with a passion for learning. Learning is a complex process and it is vitally important that our teachers know how pupils learn best and that they create exciting opportunities for learning to take place.

Geroge O'Brien, Headmaster
Christopher TJ Charleson, Head of School

1848 International School-Stavanger
Treskeveien 3
Hafrsfjord
Norway 04043
47-51-559-100
Fax: 47-51-552-962
E-mail: LDuevel@isstavanger.no
http://www.isstavanger.no

The International School of Stavanger is dedicated to providing its students with an English language education in a supportive, academically stimulating, and multi-cultural environment.

Linda Duevel, PhD, Director
Gareth Jones, High School Principal

1849 International School-Stockholm

Johannesgatan 18
Stockholm SE-111 38
Sweden
46-8-412-4000
Fax: 46-8-412-4001
E-mail: admin@intsch.se
http://www.intsch.se
SIS vision is to enable students to learn, develop, grow, and fulfill their potential in an international environment, which is student-centered, safe, nurturing and rich with opportunities to learn.

Chris Mockrish, Principal
Richard Mast, Director

1850 International School-Stuttgart

Sigmaringer Street 257
Stuttgart
Germany 70597
49-7-11-76-9600-0
Fax: 49-7-11-76-9600-0
E-mail: iss@issev.de
http://www.international-school-stuttgart.de

The International School of Stuttgart provides students of internationally-minded families with a high quality, English language education.

Timothy Kelley, Director
Sarah Kupke, Head of School

1851 International School-Trieste

Via Conconello 16 Opicina
Trieste Friuli - Venezia Giulia
Italy 34151
39-040-211-452
Fax: 39-040-213-122
E-mail: istrieste@interbusiness.it
http://www.istrieste.org
It is our mission to provide students from the international and local community with a broad, balanced education using English both in curricular and extra-curricular life of the school.

Peter Metzger, Principal
Jim Pastore, Director

1852 International School-Turin

Vicolo Tiziano 10
Moncalieri
Italy 10024
391- 45-9
Fax: 39 -11 -43 2
E-mail: info@acat-ist.it
http://www.acat-ist.it
The school's goal is to create self-motivated, independent learners who strive for excellence. The school community feels that this is best achieved in an environment which fosters trust and respect between the educational staff and the student body, demands accountability and team-work, while inspiring a general sense of well-being and self-confidence.

George Selby, BA, MA, Principal

1853 International School-Venice

Via Terraglio 30
Mestre, Venice
Italy 30174
04 -98 -711
Fax: 04 -98 -001
E-mail: info@isvenice.com
http://www.isvenice.com
The fundamental aim of The International School of Venice is to give its pupils a bilin-

gual education and an intellectual education based on tolerance, open-mindedness and an acceptance of diversity.

John Millerchip, Principal

1854 International School-Zug

Walterswil
Baar 6340
Switzerland
41-41-768-1188
Fax: 41-41-768-1189
E-mail: office@isoz.ch
http://www.iszl.ch
Grade levels include preK-8 with a total enrollment of 354.

Martin Latter, Head of School

1855 International Schule-Berlin, Potsdam

Seestrasse 45
14467 Potsdam
Germany
49-332-086-760
Fax: 49-332-086-7612
E-mail: office@isbp.p.bb.schule.de
http://www.shuttle.de/p/isbp
This school offers an English curriculum to 157 day students (87 boys and 64 girls) in grades PreK-12. Applications needed to teach include science, pre-school, math, social sciences, reading, English and physical education.

Matthias Truper, Principal

1856 International Secondary School-Eindhoven

Venetiestraat 43
RM Eindhoven
Netherlands 05632
040-413600
E-mail: isse@issehv.nl
http://www.issehv.nl
By striving for excellence in education and by engaging with the international community, the ISSE seeks to be an asset to Eindhoven and the Noord-Brabant region.

JM Westerhout, Principal
M Watts, Acting Head of School

1857 Internationale Schule Frankfurt-Rhein-Main

Strasse zur Internationalen Schule
Frankfurt
Germany 65931
49-69-954-3190
Fax: 49-69-954-31920
E-mail: isf@sabis.net
http://www.isf-net.de
ISF Internationale Schule-Rhein-Main, as a member of the SABISr School Network, is academically oriented without being highly selective.

Angus Slesser, School Director
Carl Bistany, Managing Director

1858 Interskolen

Engtoften 22
8260 Viby J
Denmark
45-8611-4560
Fax: 45-8614-9670
E-mail: adm@interskolen.dk
http://www.interskolen.dk
Coeducational day program for ages five to seventeen.

Tommy Schou Christensen, Principal

1859 John F Kennedy International School

CH-3792 Saanen
Switzerland 03792
41-33-744-1372
Fax: 41-33-744-8982

E-mail: lovell@jfk.ch
http://www.jfk.ch
Boarding day school for boys and girls aged 5-14 years.

William Lovell, Co-Director
Sandra Lovell, Co-Director

1860 John F Kennedy School-Berlin

Teltower Damm 87-93
Berlin
Germany 14167
49-30-6321-5711
Fax: 49-30-6321-6377
E-mail: jfks-el-adm@t-online.de
http://www.jfks.de
The John F. Kennedy School is a bilingual, bicultural German-American tuition-free public school.

Herr Ulrich Schurmann, Managing Principal
HR Roth, German Principal

1861 Joppenhof/Jeanne D'arc Clg

PO Box 4050, 6202 Rb Maastricht
Netherlands
47 -77 -000
http://www.paguro.net

L Spronck, Principal

1862 Kaiserslautern Elementary School

Unit 3240 Box 425
APO
Germany, AE 09021
080- -520
063- 99-46
Fax: 063- 58-06
http://www.kais-es.eu.dodea.edu

Bariett Prince, Principal

1863 Kaiserslautern High School

Unit 3240 Box 425
APO
Germany, AE 09021
801- 1-20
063- 99-47
Fax: 063- 99-46
http://www.kais-hs.eu.dodea.edu

Bariett Prince, Principal
Richard Nicholson, Assistant Principal

1864 Kaiserslautern Middle School

Unit 3240 Box 425
APO
Germany, AE 09021
802- 1-20
063- 99-48
Fax: 063- 99-25
http://www.kais-ms.eu.dodea.edu

Bariett Prince, Principal
Marion Sutton, Assistant Principal

1865 Kendale Primary International School

Via Gradoli 86, Via Cassia Km 10300
00189 Rome
Italy
39-06-332-676-08
Fax: 39-06-332-676-08
E-mail: kendale@diesis.com
http://www.diesis.com/kendale

Veronica Said Tani, Principal

1866 Kensington School

Carrer Dels Cavallers 31-33 Pedralb
Barcelona
Spain 08034
930-345-
Fax: 938-006-
E-mail: info@kensingtonschoolbcn.com
http://www.kensingtonschoolbcn.com

EP Giles, Principal

1867 King Fahad Academy
Bromyard Avenue, Acton
London
United Kingdom W3-7HD9
020-7259-3350
E-mail: academy@thekfa.org.uk
http://www.thekfa.org.uk
The idea for the establishment of an academy that caters for the educational needs of the Saudi Arabian, Arab and Muslim communities in the UK took its genesis in the creation of the King Fahad Academy in London in 1985 AD/1405 H

Dr. Ibtissam Al-Bassam, Dean
Mohammed Bin Na Al Saud, Chairman

1868 King's College
Paseo de los Andes, 35
Soto De Viuelas, Madrid
Spain
91-803-48-00
Fax: 91-803-65-57
E-mail: info@kingscollege.es
http://www.kingscollege.es
to sustain and develop an educational environment in which all students are able to fulfil their maximum potential, both as individuals and as members of a community.

CA Clark, Principal
David Johnson, Headmaster

1869 Kitzingen Elementary School
Unit 26124
APO, Kitzingen 09031 0005
Germany

Fred Paesel, Principal

1870 Kleine Brogel Elementary School
701 MUNSS
Unit 8150, APO AE
Belgium 09719
001-179-2527
Fax: 001-179-0091
E-mail: terry.emerson@eu.dodea.edu
http://www.kbro-es.eu.dodea.edu

Terry Emerson, Principal

1871 La Chataigneraie International School
Geneva La Chataigneraie, 1297
1208 Geneva
Switzerland
122-787-2400
http://www.ecolint.ch

Michael Lee, Principal

1872 La Maddalena Elementary School
PSC 816 Box 1755
FPO, La Maddalena, Sardinia 09612 0005
Italy
907-897- 820
http://www.aoshs.org

Janice Barber, Principal

1873 Lajes Elementary School
Unit 7725
APO AE
Portugal 09720
351-295-5741
Fax: 011-351-295
http://www.laje-ehs.eu.dodea.edu/index.htm

Mary Waller, Principal

1874 Lajes High School
Unit 7725
APO AE
Portugal 09720
351-295-5741
Fax: 351-295-5425

http://www.laje-hs.eu.dodea.edu/main1.htm

Virginia Briggs, Principal

1875 Lakenheath Elementary School
Unit 5185 Box 40
APO AE
Great Britain 09464-8540
016-805-3072
Fax: 016-8 5-3943
http://www.lake-es.eu.dodea.edu/index.htm
Lakenheath Elementary School serves the US Military overseas as part of the Department of Defense Dependent Schools

Charles Yahres, Principal
Rhonda Bennett, Assistant Principal

1876 Lakenheath High School
Unit 5185 Box 45
APO AE
Great Britain 09461-8545
044- 01- 852
Fax: 044- 01- 853
E-mail: lakenheathhs.attendance@eu.dodea.edu
http://www.lake-hs.eu.dodea.edu
Lakenheath High School (LHS) serves three U.S. Air Force bases located in the East Anglia region of England; about 1.5 hours drive northeast of London. LHS is coeducational.

Kent Worford, Principal
Barbara Lee, Assistant Principal

1877 Lakenheath Middle School
Unit 5185 Box 55
APO AE
Great Britain 09461-8555
011-44 -638
Fax: 226-737-
E-mail: LakenheathMS.Principal@eu.dodea.edu
http://www.lake-ms.eu.dodea.edu

Mary Zimmerman-Bayer, Principal
D J LaFon, Assistant Principal

1878 Lancing College
Lancing, West Sussex
BN15 ORW
England
0273-452213
Fax: 01273-464720
E-mail: admissions@lancing.org.uk
http://www.lancingcollege.co.uk
One of Britain's leading independent schools for boys and girls aged 13 to 18

Jonathan W J Gillespie, Headmaster
Harry Brunjes, Chairman

1879 Landstuhl Elementary and Middle School
CMR 402
APO AE
Germany 09180-402
637-192-6508
Fax: 637-192-6514
E-mail: LandstuhlEMS.Principal@eu.dodea.edu
http://www.lans-ems.eu.dodea.edu

Susan Ransom, Principal
Stephen Austin, Assistant Principal

1880 Leighton Park School
Shinfield Road
Reading RG2 7DH
England
4-118-987-9600
Fax: 44-118-987-9625
E-mail: info@leightonpark.com
http://www.leightonpark.com
Life at Leighton Park reflects the school's Quaker foundation and is influenced by

Quaker thinking and practice. We seek to create a community of tolerance and understanding within which a balance between discipline, especially self-discipline, freedom and exploration is maintained.

John Dunston, Headmaster
Elizabeth Thomas, Deputy Head

1881 Leipzig International School
Konneritzstrasse 47
Leipzig
Germany 04229
49-341-421-0574
Fax: 49-341-421-2154
E-mail: admin@intschool-leipzig.com
http://www.intschool-leipzig.com
The Leipzig International School provides a quality education conducted primarily in English for children of all nationalities and cultures living in the Leipzig region. We seek to give all students the opportunity to discover and develop their intellectual, creative, social and physical potential to the full.

Michael Webster, Headmaster
Clemens Gerteiser, Commercial Editor

1882 Lennen Bilingual School
65 Quai d'Orsay
Paris
France 75007
01-47-05-66-55
Fax: 01-47-05-17-18
http://www.lennenbilingual.com
This school teaches a curriculum in English and French to 120 day students. The school is willing to participate in a teacher exchange program with the length of stay being one year, with no housing provided by the school. Bilingual education is offered in the preschool and grade school (until Grade 3).

Michelle Lennen, Principal

1883 Leys School
The Leys School
Cambridge CB2 7AD
England
44-1223-508-900
Fax: 44-1223-505-333
E-mail: office@theleys.net
http://www.theleys.cambs.sch.uk
The Leys is one of England's premier independent schools.

Mark Slater, Headmaster

1884 Leysin American School
1854 Leysin
Switzerland
41-24-493-3777
Fax: 41-24-493-3790
E-mail: admissions@las.ch
http://www.las.ch
At the core of Leysin American School is a guiding set of principles and beliefs that set the highest standards for our efforts every day.

Steven Oh, Executive Director
Vladimir Kuskovski, Headmaster

1885 Livorno Elementary School
Unit 31301 Box 65
APO, Livorno 09613 0005
Italy
http://www.livo-ems.eu.dodea.edu

Dr. Robert Kethcart, Principal

1886 Livorno High School
Unit 31301 Box 65
APO, Livorno 09613 0005
Italy, AE 09613-5
http://www.livo-ems.eu.dodea.edu

Dr. Frank Calvano, Principal

1887 London Central High School
PSC 821 Box 119
APO, High Wycombe 09421 0005
Great Britain, AE 09421-5
http://www.londoncentral.org

Dr. Charles Recesso, Principal

1888 Lorentz International School
Groningensingel 1245, 6835HZ
Arnhem
Netherlands
31-26-320-0110
Fax: 31-26-320-0113

Jan M Meens, Principal

1889 Lusitania International College Foundation
Apartado 328
8600 Lagos
Portugal

Krisine Byrne, Principal

1890 Lyce International-American Section
BP 230, rue du Fer A Cheval
St Germain-En-Laye, 78104 Cedex
France
033-051-7485
Fax: 139-100-914
E-mail: american.lycee@wanadoo.fr
http://lycee-intl-american.org
pursues this mission through a rigorous and rewarding American curriculum which culminates in the French Baccalaureate with International Option, as well as through a broad and enriching co-curricular program including such activities as drama, community service, sports and student publications.

Sean Lynch, Director
Beth Heudebourg, President

1891 Lycee Francais De Belgique
9 Avenue Du Lycee Francais
1180 Brussels
Belgium
02-374-58-78
http://www.lyceefrancais-jmonnet.be

Jean-Claude Giudicelli, Principal

1892 Lyce International-American Section
BP 230, rue du Fer A Cheval
St. Germain-En-Laye, 78104 Cedex
France
33-1-345-17485
Fax: 33-1-308-70049
E-mail: american.lycee@wanadoo.fr
http://lycee-intl-american.org
Grade levels Pre-K through 12, school year September - June

Theodore Faunce, PhD, Director

1893 Malvern College
College Road, Malvern
Worcestershire WR14 3DF
England
01684-581-500
E-mail: inquiry@malcol.org
http://www.malcol.org

Roy de C Chapman, MA, Headmaster

1894 Mannheim Elementary School
Unit 29938
APO AE
09086
380-4705
Fax: 0621-723-905
E-mail: esmannattend@eu.dodea.edu
http://www.mann-es.eu.dodea.edu

Dr. Ardelle Hamilton PhD, Principal
Dr. Ellen Minette, Assistant Principal

1895 Mannheim High School
Unit 29939
APO AE
09267
380-409-
Fax: 062- 73-901
E-mail: MannheimHS.Principal@eu.dodea.edu
http://www.mann-hs.eu.dodea.edu
is to equip all students to be conscientiously contributing citizens through a challenging curriculum and effective instruction

Sharon O'Donnell, Principal

1896 Margaret Danyers College
N Downs Road, Cheadle Hulme
Cheadle SK8 5HA
England
061-485-4372

Harry Tomlinson, BA, MA, MS, Headmaster

1897 Mark Twain Elementary School
Unit 29237
APO, Heidelberg 09102 0005
Germany 80909
http://www.mtwain.k12.ca.us

Joseph Newbury, Principal

1898 Marymount International School-Rome
Via di Villa Lauchli 180
00191 Rome
Italy
33-1-462-41051
Fax: 33-1-463-70750
E-mail: marymount@marymountrome.org
http://www.marymountrome.org/
Marymount International School provides an education based on Christian values. Marymount is dedicated to fostering individual dignity in an atmosphere of love and respect in which students, faculty, staff and parents work and pray together.

Anne Marie Clancy, Headmistress

1899 Marymount International School-United Kingdom
George Road
Kingston upon Thames, Surrey, KT2 7PE
Surrey , United Kingdom KT2 7
44-20-8949-0571
Fax: 44-20-8336-2485
E-mail: admissions@marymount.kingston.sch.uk
http://www.marymountlondon.com/home.php
Marymount London is a vibrant and dynamic learning community where all are respected and encouraged to contribute,committed to developing individuals.

Cathleen Fagan, Headmistress

1900 Mattlidens Gymnasium
Mattliden 1
02230 Esbo
Finland
09 -16 -30 5
Fax: 09 -16 -30 5
E-mail: gun-maj.roiha@esbo.fi
http://www.mattliden.fi/gym/
Mattlidens Gymnasium is a coeducational Swedish-speaking upper secondary school

Tom Ginman, Headmaster

1901 Mayenne English School
Chateau les Courges 53420
Chailland
France

J Braillard, Principal

1902 Menwith Hill Estates & Middle School
PSC 45 Unit 8435
APO, High Wycombe 09468 0005
Great Britain
142-377-7778
Fax: 142-377-0236
http://www.mhil-ehs.eu.dodea.edu

Dr. Arnold Watland, Principal

1903 Millfield School
Butleigh Road Street
Somerset
England BA16-0YD
145-844-2291
E-mail: office@millfieldschool.com
http://www.millfieldschool.com
With its outstanding facilities, a staff:pupil ratio of 1:7.5, an extraordinary range of academic courses and the unrivalled strength of its extra-curricular programme, Millfield strives to move with the times whilst maintaining the important traditions of good manners, discipline and respect for others

Craig Considine, Headmaster
Adrian E White, Chairman of the Governors

1904 Monkton Combe School
Church Lane
Monkton Combe, Bath
England BA2-7HG
01225-721102
Fax: 01225-721208
E-mail: reception@monkton.org.uk
http://www.monktoncombeschool.com
Boarding and day school for girls and boys ages two to nineteen.

Chris Stafford, Headmaster
Richard Backhouse, Principal

1905 Monti Parioli English School
Via Monti Parioli 50
00197 Rome
Italy

Lynette Surtees, Principal

1906 Mougins School
615 Avenue Drive, Maurice Donat
BP 401, 06251 Mougins Cedex
France
33-4-93-90-15-47
Fax: 33-4-93-75-31-40
E-mail: information@mougins-school.com
http://www.mougins-school.com
The School has a capacity of 460 students, large enough to provide a stimulating environment and small enough to retain a caring family atmosphere. With thirty-five nationalities the School is culturally rich and its philosophy is designed to encourage pupils to develop morally, emotionally, culturally, intellectually and physically

Brian G Hickmore, Headmaster
Jane Hart, Deputy Head

1907 Mountainview School
Bosch 35-6331 Hunenberg
Switzerland

Brenda Moors, Principal

1908 Munich International School
Schloss Buchhof
Starnberg
Germany 82319
49-8151-366-100
Fax: 49-8151-366-109
E-mail: admissions@mis-munich.de
http://www.mis-munich.de
MIS caters for the physical, social, emotional and educational development of its children by providing a student-centred, in-

quiry-based learning environment which fosters an appreciation in its students of their cultural heritage and the cultural richness of the global community.

Mary Sepalla, Head of School
Maha Kattoura, Chairman

1909 Naples Elementary School
PSC 808 Box 39
FPO, AE
Italy 09618
011-39 -8108
Fax: 011-39 -8108
E-mail:
NaplesES.Principal@eu.dodea.edu
http://www.napl-es.eu.dodea.edu

Dr. Jacqueline Hulbert, Principal

1910 Naples High School
PSC 808 Box 15
FPO, AE
Italy 09618
011-39 -8108
Fax: 011-39 -8108
E-mail:
NaplesHS.Principal@eu.dodea.edu
http://www.napl-hs.eu.dodea.edu
Students will be prepared to be critical thinkers, effective communicators, and accountable members in a global society.

Carl Albrecht, Principal

1911 Neubruecke Elementary School
Unit 23825
APO, Neubruecke 09034 0005
Germany

Margaret Hoffman-Otto, Principal

1912 Neuchatel Junior College
44 Victoria Street
Suite 1310
Toronto, ON M5C-1Y2
038-25-27-00
800-263-2923
Fax: 038-24-42-59
E-mail: info@neuchatel.org
http://www.njc.ch
To provide students a rigorous university preparatory programme in a culturally rich and multi-lingual European setting where learning through educational travel, engagement with world affairs and service to others fosters personal growth and leadership.

Norman Southward, Principal
Dayle Leishman, Director

1913 New School Rome
Via Della Camilluccia 669
Roma
Italy 00135
39-329-4269
E-mail: info@newschoolrome.com
http://www.newschoolrome.com
The School is a non-profit making organisation run by the Academic Council (all staff and seven student representatives) which also elects the headteacher, and by the Executive Council (three elected teachers and four elected parents).

Josette Fusco, Head Teacher
Richard Lydiker, Executive Chairman

1914 Newton College
Av Ricardo Elas Aparicio 240
La Molina
Lima-Peru, PE
511-479-0460
Fax: 511-479-0430
E-mail: college@newton.edu.pe
http://www.newton.edu.pe

Newton College is an Anglo-Peruvian, co-educational, bilingual, day school for students aged 2 to 18.

David Few, Principal

1915 Norra Reals Gymnasium
Roslagsgatan 1
Stockholm
Sweden 113 5
087-420-
Fax: 087-328-
E-mail:
infonorrareal@utbildning.stockholm.se
http://www.norrareal.stockholm.se
Offers two preparatory study programs: the science and social science.

Per Engback, Principal
Maria Sellberg, Assistant Principal

1916 Numont School
C/ Parma 16
Madrid
Spain 28043
349-130-0243
Fax: 349-759-
E-mail: numont@telefonica.net
http://eoficina.e.telefonica.net
Provide a warm, happy and challenging atmosphere where children can derive pleasure from learning and achieving their personal goals. The emphasis is on the individual, so that all of the children, regardless of strengths and weaknesses, colour, creed or sex, feel valued and able to reach their full potential.

Margaret Ann Swanson, Principal

1917 Oak House School
Sant Pere Claver 12-18
Barcelona
Spain 08017
349-325- 402
Fax: 349-325- 402
E-mail: sec@oakhouseschool.com
http://www.oakhouseschool.com
The training of students both personal and social is one of the main objectives of the educational work.

Teresa Armadans, Director of Finance
Vicen Orobitg, Information Technology

1918 Oakham School
Chapel Close
Market Place
Oakham,Rutland, UK LE15
44-0-1572-758758
Fax: 44-0-1572-758595
E-mail: registrar@oakham.rutland.sch.uk
http://www.oakham.rutland.sch.uk
A pioneer of full co-education, a boarding and day school for boys and girls aged 10 to 18 years that has become widely known for developing new ideas and making them work to the benefit of all Oakham's pupils.

Joseph AF Spence, Headmaster
Jon Wills, Registrar

1919 Oporto British School
Rua Da Cerca 326/338
PORTO
Portugal 4150-
226-666-
E-mail: school@obs.edu.pt
http://www.obs.edu.pt
As the oldest British School in Continental Europe, the Oporto British School is committed to providing a high quality international education for its students.

Mark Rogers, Principal
David Butcher, Headmaster

1920 Oslo American School
Gml Ringeriksv 53, 1340 Bekkestua
Oslo
Norway 05507
http://www.oasalumni.org

James Mcneil, Principal

1921 Panterra American School
Via Ventre D'oca 41, Fontanella
Pescara 65131
Italy
http://www.panamterra.com

Virginia Simpson, Principal

1922 Paris American Academy
277 Rue Street Jacques
Paris
France 75005
001-449-
Fax: 01 -4 4- 99
http://www.parisamericanacademy.edu
To create and maintain a system of higher education that contributes to the transformation of students into

Peter Carman, President/Executive Director
Jean-Michel Ageron-Blanc, General Director

1923 Patrick Henry Elementary School
Unit 29237
APO, Heidelberg
Germany, AE 09102
388-905-
Fax: 062-1 7-5 49
E-mail:
PatrickHenryES.Principal@eu.dodea.edu
http://www.heid-esp.eu.dodea.edu
To educate all children by providing a nurturing environment and standards-based curriculum dedicated to meeting he diverse needs of every child.

Russ Claus, Principal
Marie Granger, Assistant Principal

1924 Perse School
Hills Road
Cambridge CB2 8QF
England
0223-248127
E-mail: office@perse.co.uk
http://www.perse.co.uk

Edward Elliott, Head of Politics
Dan Cross, Deputy Head

1925 Pinewood Schools of Thessaloniki
PO Box 21001
555 10 Pilea
Greece
30-31-301-221
Fax: 30-31-323-196
E-mail: pinewood@spark.net.gr
http://www.pinepeaceschool.k12.vi
Independent, coeducational schools which offer an educational program from prekindergarten through grade 12 and boarding facilities from grade 7 though grade 12 for students of all nationalities. The school year comprises 2 semesters extending from September to January and from January to June.

Peter B Baiter, Director

1926 Pordenone Elementary School
PSC 1
Aviano
Italy
39-0434-28462
Fax: 39-0434-28761

D Jean Waddell, Principal

1927 Priory School
West Bank, Dorking
Surrey RH4 3DG
England

130-688-7337
Fax: 130-688-8715
E-mail:
enquiries@staff.priorycofe.surrey.sch.uk
http://www.priorycofe.surrey.sch.uk
To provide an educational environment
which encourages pupils to become confident, competent, self-reliant and happy members of society, fully prepared for adult life
and the world of work

A C Sohatski, Headteacher
M Pinchin, Senior Deputy Headteacher

1928 Queen Elizabeth School
Queen's Road, Barnet
Hertfordshire
England, UK EN5 4
020-844-0464
Fax: 020-844-0750
E-mail: enquiries@qebarnet.co.uk
http://www.qebarnet.co.uk
To produce boys who are confident, able and
responsible.

John Marincowitz, Headmaster

1929 Queens College the English School
Juan De Saridakis 64
Palma de Malorca
Spain
809-393-2153
http://www.qc.cuny.edu
This Methodist affiliated school offers an
English-based curriculum to a total of 1,200
female students, grades K1-12. The school
does recruit from overseas, offering three
year contracts with housing provided for one
week at the beginning of the contract, while
they find accommodations. Applications
needed to teach include science, pre-school,
French, math, Spanish, English and physical
education.

Philip Cash, Principal

1930 Rainbow Elementary School
Unit 28614 Box 0040
APO, Ansbach 09177 0005
Germany
407-320-8450
http://www.rainbow.scps.k12.fl.us

Thomas Murdock, Principal

1931 Ramstein Elementary School
Unit 3240 Box 430
APO AE
Germany 09094
067-014-0 39
Fax: 067- 15- 835
http://www.rams-es.eu.dodea.edu
To provide a quality education for eligible
minor dipendents of DoD military and civil-
ian personnel stationed overseas.

Kathy Downs, Principal

1932 Ramstein High School
Unit 3240 Box 445
APO AE
Germany 09094-445
067-1 4-6095
Fax: 067-1 4-9 86
http://www.rams-hs.eu.dodea.edu
To provide a varied and challenging curriculum that will allow students to be life-long
learners and responsible participants in a
global community.

Greg Hatch, Principal

1933 Ramstein Intermediate School
Unit 3240 Box 600
APO AE
Germany 09094-600
067-1 4-6023
Fax: 067-1 5-238
http://www.rams-is.eu.dodea.edu

To provide an educational environment designed to maximize the potential of all
Students.

Stanley B Caldwell, Principal

1934 Ramstein Junior High School
86 SPTG CCSI R, Unit 3240 Box 455
APO, Ramstein 09094 0005
Germany

Richard Snell, Principal

1935 Rathdown School
Upper Glenageary Road Glenageary
Co Dublin
Ireland
01-853133
E-mail: admin@rathdownschool.ie
http://www.rathdownschool.ie/contact_us.p
hp
Our aim is to offer a high-quality, modern,
challenging and liberal education. In an inclusive and friendly environment, Rathdown
School hopes to foster a love of learning
which will enable each student to develop her
own unique potential. Our purpose is to support and promote the student's academic, cultural, sporting, creative, musical and
spiritual capabilities.

Barbara Ennis, Principal

1936 Rikkyo School in England
Guildford Road, Rudgwick, W Sussex
RH12 3BE
Great Britain
014-3 8-2107
Fax: 014-3 8-2535
E-mail: eikoku@rikkyo.w-sussex.sch.uk
http://www.rikkyo.co.uk

M Usuki, Principal

1937 Riverside School
Walterswil
6340 Baar
Switzerland
41-41-724-5690
Fax: 41-41-724-5692
E-mail: office.zug@iszl.ch
http://www.iszl.ch
The International School of Zug and Luzern
(ISZL) provides a high quality Pre-School to
Grade 12 international education to day stu-
dents resident in the Cantons of central
Switzerland.

Dominic Currer, Director
Elaine Tomlinson, Headmaster

1938 Robinson Barracks Elementary School
Unit 30401
APO
Germany, AE 09107
491-119-
Fax: 071- 85- 473
E-mail:
RobinsonBarracksES.Principal@eu.dodea.e
du
http://www.rbar-es.eu.dodea.edu
The Robinson Barrack's school community
provides a respectful environment where all
members learn to recognize their strengths
and gain confidence to become lifelong
learners and leaders in an ever-changing
world.

Shirley Sheck, Principal

1939 Rome International School
Via Panama 25
00198 Rome
Italy
039-06 -4482
Fax: 039-06 -4482
E-mail: office@romeinternationalschool.it
http://www.romeinternationalschool.it

Provides a nurturing environment, in which
children of all nationalities and faiths can explore and respect their own and each other's
cultural and religious heritage.

Patricia Martin-Smith, Principal Primary
School
Ivano Boragine, Managing Director

1940 Rosall School
Fleetwood
Lancashire
United Kingdom FY7 8
012- 37- 420
Fax: 012- 37- 205
E-mail: enquiries@rossallcorporation.co.uk
http://www.rossall.co.uk
Providing a unique educational experience
we offer a wide ranging choice of curricu-
lums underpinned by a commitment to aca-
demic excellence.

RDW Rhodes, Principal
GSH Penelley, Faculty Head

1941 Rosemead
East Street, Littlehampton
BN17 6AL
England
0903-716065

J Bevis, BA, Headmaster

1942 Rota Elementary School
PSC 819 Box 19
FPO AE 09645 0019
Spain
345-624-
Fax: 011-34 -56 8
E-mail: rotaes.principal@eu.dodea.edu
http://www.rota-es.eu.dodea.edu
Provides a standards-based educational pro-
gram, which creates lifelong learners and re-
sponsible citizens.

Charles Callahan, Principal

1943 Rota High School
PSC 819 Box 63
FPO AE 09645 0005
Spain
345-624-
Fax: 011-34 -56 8
E-mail: RotaHS.Principal@eu.dodea.edu
http://www.rota-hs.eu.dodea.edu

Lynne Michael, Principal

1944 Roudybush Foreign Service School
Place des Arcades, Sauveterre de
Rouergue (Averyon)
France
This European school prepares men for the
foreign service.

Franklin Roudybush, AB, MA, Headmaster

1945 Rugby School
Rugby, Warwickshire
United Kingdom CV22
44-178-854-3465
Fax: 44-178-856-9124
E-mail: enquiries@rugbyschool.net
http://www.rugbyschool.net
Rugby School is an educational community
whose philosophy embraces the challenges
of academic excellence, spiritual awareness,
responsibility and leadership, friendships
and relationships and participation in a wide
variety of activities

Patrick Derham, Headmaster
SK Fletcher, Deputy Head

1946 Runnymede College School
Calle Salvia 30
28109 La Moraleja, Madrid
Spain
34-91-650-8302
Fax: 34-91-650-8236

E-mail: office@runnymede-college.com
http://www.runnymede-college.com
Provides an all-round, academic, liberal humanist education to all students regardless of their sex, race, religion or nationality. There is no religious instruction.

Frank M Powell, Headmaster
FJ Murphy, Deputy Head

1947 Rygaards International School
Bernstorffsvej 54, DK-2900
Hellerup
Denmark
45-39-62-10-53
Fax: 45-39-62-10-81
E-mail: admin@rygaards.com
http://www.rygaards.com
Rygaards School is a private, Christian/Catholic, co-educational establishment. It is recognised by and subject to, Danish law and receives a subsidy from the Danish State.

Mathias Jepsen, Principal
Charles Dalton, Headmaster

1948 Salzburg International Preparatory School
Moosstrasse 106
A-5020 Salzburg
Austria
662-844485
Fax: 662-847711
http://www.ais-salzburg.a
A coeducational boarding school offering an American college preparatory high school curriculum for grades 7 to 12 as well as a post graduate course.

1949 Schiller Academy
51-55 Waterloo Road
London, SE1 8TX
United Kingdom
44-207-928-1372
Fax: 44-207-928-8089
E-mail: office@schiller-academy.org.uk
http://www.schiller-academy.org.uk
Grade levels 9-12, school year August - June

George Selby, Headmaster
Renee Miller, Director Studies

1950 Schools of England, Wales, Scotland & Ireland
J. Burrow & Company
Imperial House, Lypiatt Road
Cheltenham 50201
England

1951 Schweinfurt American Elementary School
CMR 457
AP, AE
Germany 09033
09721-81893
Fax: 09721-803905
E-mail:
schweinfurtes.principal@eu.dodea.edu
http://www.schw-es.eu.dodea.edu
The mission of Schweinfurt Elementary School is to help all students become respectful, responsible citizens and life-long learners.

Wilma Holt, Principal
Beverly Erdmann, Assistant Principal

1952 Schweinfurt Middle School
CMR 457
AP, AE
Germany 09033-5
354-681-1800
Fax: 097-1 8-363
E-mail:
SchweinfurtMS.Principal@eu.dodea.edu
http://www.schw-ms.eu.dodea.edu

Schweinfurt Middle School will engage all students in meaningful experiences that develop 21st Century Skills, preparing them to be successful and responsible citizens in a technological, global society.

Dr George P Carpenter, Principal

1953 Sembach Elementary School
Unit 4240 Box 325
APO, AE
Germany 09136
063- 67-0
Fax: 063-271-
E-mail:
SembachES.Principal@eu.dodea.edu
http://www.semb-es.eu.dodea.edu

Monica Harvey, Principal

1954 Sembach Middle School
Unit 4240 Box 320
APO, AE
Germany 09136
063- 67-0
Fax: 063-271-
E-mail:
SembachMS.Principal@eu.dodea.edu
http://www.semb-ms.eu.dodea.edu

Bonnie B Hannan, Principal

1955 Sevenoaks School
Sevenoaks
Kent TN13 IHU
England
44 -017-245
Fax: 44 -017-245
E-mail: enq@sevenoaksschool.org
http://www.sevenoaksschool.org
Sevenoaks School is an independent, co-educational boarding and day school, set in 100 acres in the heart of Southeast England. Half an hour from Central London, and half an hour from Gatwick International Airport, we are situated on the edge of Sevenoaks, overlooking the 15th century deer park of the Knole Estate.

Katy Ricks, Head of School
Tony Evans, Chairman

1956 Sevilla Elementary & Junior High School
496 ABS DODDS Unit 6585
APO Moron AB 09643 0005
Spain

Robert Ludwig, Principal

1957 Shape Elementary School
Unit 21420
APO, AE
Belgium 09705
011-32 -5044
Fax: 011-32 -31
E-mail:
ShapeES.Principal@eu.dodea.edu
http://www.shap-es.eu.dodea.edu
It is the mission of SHAPE Elementary School to educate all students in an integrated, multi-cultural environment to become productive thinkers, to achieve their maximum physical and mental potential, and to be literate, responsible members of a global society through excellence in teaching and learning.

Charlene Leister, Principal
Miles Shea, Assistant Principal

1958 Shape High School
Unit 21420
APO, AE
Belgium 09705
011-32 -5044
Fax: 011-32 -31

E-mail: david.tran@eu.dodea.edu
http://www.shap-hs.eu.dodea.edu

David Tran, Principal
Arlena Ray, Assistant Principal

1959 Shape International School
Avenue de Reijkjavik 717
SHAPE
Belgium 07010
65-44-52-83
http://www.nato.int/shape/community/school.htm
Performs the operational duties previously undertaken by Allied Command Europe and Allied Command Atlantic

Jacques Laurent, Principal

1960 Sidcot School
Winscombe
N Somerset BS25 1PD
England
44-193-484-3102
Fax: 44-193-484-4181
E-mail: addmissions@sidcot.org.uk
http://www.sidcot.org.uk
This friendly school with an international enrollment of 277 day students and 149 boarding students (255 boys; 171 girls), in grades K-12, is set in over one hundred acres of Somerset countryside. The school offers an English-based curriculum and the student/teacher ratio is 10:1.

John Walmsley, Headteacher
Ross Wallis, Head of Art

1961 Sierra Bernia School
La Caneta s/n
Alfaz del Pi Alicante
Spain 03580
96-687-51-49
Fax: 96-687-36-33
E-mail: duncan@ctv.es
http://sierraberniaschool.com/news.php
Forefront of modern education. Combining both traditional and innovative methods of teaching made possible by the wealth and immense knowledge base of its fully qualified teaching body

Duncan Allan, Owner/Director
Iain Macinnes, Headteacher

1962 Sigonella Elementary & High School
PSC 824 Box 2630
FPO Signoella, Sicily 09627 2630
Italy
624-440-
http://www.sigo-es.eu.dodea.edu/

Dr. Peter Price, Principal

1963 Sigtunaskolan Humanistiska Laroverket
Manfred Bjorkquists Alle 6
Box 508, Sigtuna
Sweden 19328
46-8-592-57100
Fax: 46-8-592-57250
E-mail: info@sshl.se
http://www.sshl.se
Grade levels include 7-12 with an enrollment of 543.

Kent Edberg, Principal
Rune Svaninger, Director

1964 Sir James Henderson School
Via Pisani Dossi 16
Milano
Italy 20134
39-02-264-13310
Fax: 39-02-264-13515
E-mail: sirjames@bbs.infosquare.it
http://www.sjhschool.com
To ensure that its diverse student body grows to its full potential as independent learners in a caring British and international community, uniting the best of British educational tradition with the val-

ues, practices and beliefs of the International Baccalaureate

Stephen Anson, Principal
Jim Noble, Chairman

1965 Skagerak Gymnas

PO Box 1545-Veloy
3206 Sandefjord
Norway
473-345-6500
http://www.skagerak.org

Elisabeth Norr, Principal

1966 Smith Elementary School

Unit 23814 Box 30
APO, AE
Germany 09034-3814
067-783-5693
Fax: 067-783-8874
E-mail: SmithES.Principal@eu.dodea.edu
http://www.baum-ess.eu.dodea.edu

Kent Bassett, Principal

1967 Southlands English School

Via Teleclide 40
Casalapalocco, Rome
Italy 00124
39 -605-5039
Fax: 06 -091-7192
http://www.southlands.it
Our aim is to give you a flavour of the quality educational experience available at Southlands and encourage you to visit the school so you can see for yourself the happy, successful community that Southlands nurtures.

Deryck M Wilson, Principal

1968 Spangdahlem Elementary School

52 MSG/CCSE S, Unit 3640 Box 50
APO, AE
Germany 09126-4050
065-056- 688
Fax: 065-056- 710
E-mail:
SpnagdahlemES.Principal@eu.dodea.edu
http://www.spang-es.eu.dodea.edu

Richard R Alix, Principal

1969 Spangdahlem Middle School

52 CSG CCSM, Unit 3640 Box 45
APO, AE
Germany 09126-4045
065-506- 725
Fax: 065-506-0279
E-mail:
SpangdahlemMS.Principal@eu.dodea.edu
http://www.spang-ms.eu.dodea.edu
Spangdhalem Middle School promotes high achievement and lifelong learning for all students through positive interactions and standards-based educational program.

Joseph Malloy, Principal

1970 Sportfield Elementary School

Unit 20193 Box 0014
APO, Hanau
Germany, AE 09165-14

John O'Reilly, Jr, Principal

1971 St. Andrew's College

19 Carillon Avenue
Newtown NSW
Australia 02042
02-9626-1999
E-mail:
principalassist@standrewscollege.edu.au
http://www.standrewscollege.edu.au
St Andrew's is proud of its reputation as a leading academic institution, fostering leaders within the community and moulding the leaders of tomorrow. The College places emphasis on academic and intellectual develop-

ment and excellence as core to the development of the individual.

Wayne Erickson, Principal
Donna Wiemann, Development Manager

1972 St. Anne's School

Jarama 9
Madrid 2
Spain
http://www.stannes.edu.in

Margaret Raines, Principal

1973 St. Anthony's International College

Camino de Coin km 53.5
Mijas-Costa, Malaga
Spain 29649
00 -09 -247
Fax: 00 -09 -046
E-mail: info@stanthonyscollege.com
http://www.stanthonyscollege.com
The school with its friendly, family atmosphere provides opportunities for our students to achieve their best. Trying not to cater just for high achievers we endeavour, through a broad and balanced education, to find courses for all abilities.

1974 St. Catherine's British School

PO Box 51019
Kifissia 145 10 Athens
Greece
301- 8-97
Fax: 301- 8-64
E-mail: administrator@stcatherines.gr
http://www.stcatherines.gr
The school endeavors to foster a love of learning through a well taught, appropriately challenging, clearly defined and balanced curriculum. Our aim is to fully develop intellectual, social, physical and creative potential, giving students the foundatin to develop into sensitive, informed, and capable global citizens of the future.

Michael Toman, Principal
R Morton, Headmaster & CEO

1975 St. Christopher School

Barrington Road, Letchworth
Hertfordshire SG6 3JZ
England
0462-679301
Fax: 0462-481578
E-mail: school.admin@stchris.co.uk
http://www.stchris.co.uk
St Christopher has a distinctive ethos, based on the development of each child's individuality whilst teaching a sense of responsibility towards others, towards the School and towards the local and global community.

Richard Palmer, Head of School
Emma-Kate Henry, Deputy Head of St Christophe

1976 St. Clare's Oxford

139 Banbury Road
Oxford OX2 7AL
England
44-186-555-2031
Fax: 44-186-551-3359
E-mail: admissions@stclares.ac.uk
http://www.stclares.ac.uk
St. Clare's welcomes students and staff of all nationalities and cultures who will benefit from, and contribute to, our learning community. Living and studying together, we learn from one another. We are enriched and challenged by a diversity of views and ideas.

Paula Holloway, Principal
Tom Walsh, Vice Principal

1977 St. David's School

Justin Hall, Beckenham Road
West Wickham BR4 0QS
England

01784-252494
Fax: 01784-252494
E-mail: office@stdavidsschool.com
http://www.sdsw.org
Boarding school for girls ages nine to eighteen; day school for girls ages four to eighteen.

Judith G Osborne, BA, Headmaster

1978 St. Dominic's International School

Outeiro de Polima-Arneiro
2785-816 Sao Domingos da Rana
Portugal
351-21-448-0550
351-214-5505
Fax: 351-21-444-3027
E-mail: school@dominics-int.org
http://www.dominics-int.org
Our school mission is to offer an international education of the highest calibre enriched and enlivened by the Dominican tradition of study and education; promoting the development of each student's potential: physical, emotional, social, intellectual, moral and spiritual.

Maria do Rosri Empis, Principal
Manuel Lucas, President of Supervision

1979 St. Dominic's Sixth Form College

Mount Park Avenue Harrow on the Hil
Middlesex HA1 3HX
England
020-84228084
208-422-3759
Fax: 020-8422-3759
E-mail: stdoms@stdoms.ac.uk
http://www.stdoms.ac.uk
St. Dominic's is a Roman Catholic Sixth Form College committed to the pesonal and spiritual growth of all its members based on Christian values, academic excellence and high quality pastoral care.

Patrick Harty, Principal

1980 St. Georges English School

Via Cassia Km 16
La Storta Rome
Italy 00123
06-3790141
Fax: 06-3792490
E-mail: Secretary@stgeorge.school.it
http://www.stgeorge.school.it
To develop the individual talents of young people and teach them to relate the experience of the classroom to the realities of the world outside.

Martyn Hales, Principal

1981 St. Georges School

Vila Goncalve, Quinta Loureiras
2750 Cascais
Portugal
112-602-4645
http://www.sgs.edu.in

MPB Hoare, Principal

1982 St. Georges School-Switzerland

Chemin de St Georges 19
Clarens Montreux
Switzerland 01815
21-964-34-11
Fax: 21-964-49-32
E-mail: office@st-georges.ch
http://www.st-georges.ch
St. George's School encourages students to lift their eyes and recognise positive qualities within themselves and others and to nurture a caring and dynamic attitude in today's demanding world.

Dr Ilya V Eigenbrot, Principal
Francis Kahn, President of Directors

1983 St. Gerard's School
Thornhill Road, Bray Co Wicklow
Republic of Ireland
353-001-2821
Fax: 353-001-2821
E-mail: info@stgerards.ie
http://www.stgerards.ie
To provide an opportunity for each student to realise his or her potential in all areas: academic, moral, personal, physical, social, spiritual and sporting.

Tom Geraghty, Headmaster
Victor Drummy, Deputy Principal

1984 St. Helen's School
Eastbury Road Northwood, Middlesex
England HA6-3AS
09274-28511
Fax: 0923-835824
E-mail: enquiries@sthn.co.uk
http://www.sthn.co.uk
We aim to give every pupil an academic, innovative and stimulating education, developing her intellectual, creative and physical talents to the full. We provide a friendly, supportive and well-ordered environment in which every girl is treated as an individual and where integrity, personal responsibility and respect for others are highly valued.

YA Burne, Principal

1985 St. John's International School
Dreve Richelle 146
Waterloo
Belguim 01410
32-2-352-0610
Fax: 32-2-352-0630
E-mail: contact@stjohns.be
http://www.stjohns.be
we exist to provide an English-speaking education that emphasizes Christian values, encourages academic excellence and stimulates social development within a culturally diverse environment. St. John's is also a caring environment where students are encouraged to reach their full potential, prepared to think globally, with a commitment to justice and challenged to act responsibly in a consistently changing society.

Joseph Doenges, Director
Judith Hoskins, Director Admissions

1986 St. Mary's School
Rhapta Road, PO Box 40580- 00100
Nairobi
Kenya
0990-23721
E-mail: info@stmarys.ac.ke
http://www.stmarys.ac.ke
We are a Catholic Private School committed to our international character in the provision of a spiritual, intellectual and physical education. We aim at developing the gifts of the young in an atmosphere which encourages the ethos of self-expression and mutual respect with a view to their facing the future responsibly, with confidence and courage.

M Mark Orchard, IBVM, BA, Principal

1987 St. Michael's School
Otford Court
Otford TN14 5SA
England
095-92-2137
http://www.stmichaels-otford.co.uk

Keith Crombie, Headmaster

1988 St. Stephen's School
Via Aventina 3
Rome
Italy 00153

39-06-575-0605
Fax: 39-06-574-1941
E-mail: ststephens@ststephens-rome.com
http://www.ststephens-rome.com

Philip Allen, Headmaster
Lesley Murphey, Head of the School

1989 Stavenger British School
Gauselbakken 107
4032 Gausel
Norway
475-195-0250
http://www.biss.no

Zelma Roisli, Principal

1990 Stover School
Newton Abbot
Devon
England TQ12
0626-54505
351-214-5505
E-mail: mail@stover.co.uk
http://www.stover.co.uk

Susan Bradley, Principal

1991 Stowe School
Stowe
Buckingham
England MK18
44-1280-818000
351-214-5505
Fax: 44-1280-818181
E-mail: enquiries@stowe.co.uk
http://www.stowe.co.uk
Our vision for Stowe, a co-educational independent boarding and day school in the heart of the English countryside, is of a school that delivers the highest academic and cultural achievement; and a school that continues to foster the development of Stoics who are as original and individual as their school.

Anthony Wallersteiner, Headmaster
GM Hornby, Faculty Head

1992 Summerfield School SRL
Via Tito Poggi 21 Divino Amore
00134 Rome
Italy
http://www.summerfields.co.in

Vivien Franceschini, Principal

1993 Summerhill School
Westward Ho
Leiston, Suffolk
England IP16
0728-830540
E-mail: zoe@summerhillschool.co.uk
http://www.summerhillschool.co.uk
A S Neill's Summerhill School, a co-educational boarding school in Suffolk, England, is the original alternative 'free' school. Founded in 1921, it continues to be an influential model for progressive, democratic education around the world.

Zoe Readhead, Principal

1994 Sunny View School
C/ Teruel No 32, Cerro del Toril
Torremolinos Malaga
Spain 29620
345-283-
Fax: 345-272-
E-mail: sunny@acade.es
http://www.sunnyviewschool.com
Sunny View is a privately owned day school, which accepts students of all nationalities from the age of 3 years to 18 years. It is a long-established International School.

Jane Barbadillo, Principal
David McConnell, HS Principal

1995 Sutton Park School
St Fintan's Road
Sutton, Dublin 13
Ireland
353-1-832-2940
Fax: 353-1-832-5929
E-mail: info@sps.ie
http://www.suttonparkschool.com
Sutton Park School aims to provide its pupils with an educational environment that is intellectually, physically and culturally challenging, so that they can grow into balanced, mature and confident adults.

Laurence J Finnegan, Chief Executive
Michael Moretta, Head of School

1996 Sutton Valence School
Maidstone
Kent
England ME17
0622-842281
E-mail: enquiries@svs.org.uk
http://www.svs.org.uk
Our aim today is to give our girls and boys an excellent all round education in an atmosphere of togetherness and trust, where day and boarding pupils benefit from the same supportive ethos.

Joe Davies, Headmaster
Kathy Webster, Admissions Officer

1997 Swans School
Capricho s/n
Marbella, Malaga
Spain 29600
95 -77 -248
Fax: 95 -77 -431
E-mail: info@swansschool.net
http://www.swansschool.net
Swans' motto is Constancy and Truth.

TJ Swan, Principal
Nick Lee, Head Teacher

1998 TASIS Hellenic International School
PO Box 51051
Kifissia Gr-145 10
Greece
30-1-623-3888
Fax: 30-1-623-3160
E-mail: info@tasis.edu.gr
http://www.tasis.com
Grade levels Pre-K through 12, school year September - June

Basile Daskalakis, President

1999 TASIS The American School in England
Coldharbour Lane
Thorpe, Surrey, TW20 8TE
England
44-1932-565-252
Fax: 44-1932-564-644
E-mail: ukadmissions@tasis.com
http://www.tasis.com
Grade levels Pre-K through 12, school year August - June

Barry Breen, Headmaster

2000 Taunus International Montessori School
Altkonigstrasse 1 6370
Oberursel
Germany
496-171-9133
http://www.tims-frankfurt.com

Kathleen Hauer, Principal

2001 Teach in Great Britain
5 Netherhall Gardens
London, NW3, England
http://www.teachaway.com

2002 Thessaloniki International High School & Pinewood Elementary School
PO Box 21001
555 10 Pilea, Thessaloniki
Greece
30-31-301-221
Fax: 30-31-323-196
E-mail: pinewood@spark.net.gr
http://www.users.otenet.gr/~pinewood
Grades preK-12, enrollment 256.

Peter B Baiter, Director

2003 Thomas Jefferson School
4100 South Lindbergh Boulevard
Saint Louis
Missouri, MO 63127
314-843-4151
http://www.tjs.org
The mission of Thomas Jefferson School is to give its students the strongest possible academic background, responsibility for their own learning, a concern for other people, and the resources to live happily as adults and become active contributors to society

William C Rowe, Head of School
Susan S Stepleton, Chair, Board of Trustees

2004 United Nations Nursery School
40 Rue Pierre Guerin
75016 Paris
France
33-1-452-72024
Fax: 33-1-428-87146
http://www.unns.net
Pre-K and kindergarten levels.

Brigitte Weill, Directrice

2005 United World College-Adriatic
Via Treste 29
Duino (TS)
Italy 34011
39 -40 -7391
Fax: 39 -40 -7392
http://www.uwcad.it
The United World Colleges offer students of all races and creeds the opportunity of developing international understanding through programmes which combine high quality academic study and activities which encourage

DB Sutcliffe, Principal
David Sutcliffe, Headmaster

2006 United World College-Atlantic
St Donats Castle Llantwit
Major S Glamorgan
United Kingdom
441- 46-9 90
http://www.atlanticcollege.org
a sense of adventure and social responsibility

Colin Jenkins, Principal

2007 Vajont Elementary School
PSC 1
Aviano
Italy
427-701553

Nick Suida, Principal

2008 Verdala International School
Fort Pembroke
Pembroke, STJ 14
Malta
356-332-361
Fax: 356-372-387
E-mail: vis@maltanet.net
http://www.verdala.org
An independent, coeducational day and boarding school which offers an educational program from play school through grade 12 for students of all nationalities.

Adam Pleasance, Headmaster
Charles Zerafa, Business Manager

2009 Verona Elementary School
1011 Lee Highway
Verona, VA 24482
540-248-0141
Fax: 540-248-0562
http://www.augusta.k12.va.us/veronaes/site/default.asp

Marguerite McDonald, Principal

2010 Vicenza Elementary School
Unit 31401 Box 11
APO, Vicenza
Italy 09630-5
011-390-444
Fax: 011-39 -444
E-mail: VicenzaES.Principal@eu.dodea.edu
http://www.vice-es.eu.dodea.edu/index.htm
Increase student achievement, we are committed to improving our children's ability to communicate in writing across all curricular areas, and to reason mathematically.

Martha Parsons, Principal

2011 Vicenza High School
Unit 31401 Box 11
APO, Vicenza
Italy 09630
011-390-444
Fax: 011-39 -444
E-mail:
VicenzaHS.Principal@eu.dodea.edu
http://www.vice-hs.eu.dodea.edu/

Lauri Kenney, Principal
Chris Beane, Assistant Principal

2012 Vicenza International School
Viale Trento 141
Vicenza 36100
Italy
39-0444-288-475
Fax: 39-0444-963-633
E-mail: vix-ib@vip.it
Grade levels 11-13, school year September - June

Dionigio Tanello, PhD, Director

2013 Vienna Christian School
Wagramerstrasse 175
Panthgasse 6A
Wien, Austria A-122
43-1-25122-501
351-214-5505
E-mail: office@vcs-austria.org
http://www.viennachristianschool.org/
VCS is an international school with a United States-based curriculum.

Ken Norman, Director
Nancy L Deibert, Athletic Director/PE

2014 Vienna International School
Strasse der Menschenrechte 1
Vienna, Austria 01220
43-1-203-5595
Fax: 43-1-203-0366
E-mail: visinfo@vis.ac.at.
http://www.vis.ac.at
To serve the children of the United Nations and diplomatic community in Vienna. It is also open to children of the international business community and of Austrian families.

James S Walbran, Director
Neil Tomalin, Head Primary School

2015 Vilseck Elementary School
Unit 28040
APO, Vilseck
Germany 09112-14
011-490-662
Fax: 011-490-662
E-mail: VilseckES.Principal@eu.dodea.edu
http://www.vils-es.eu.dodea.edu/
Vilseck Elementary School prepares students for lifelong learning within a safe, nurturing environment. Honoring the uniqueness of our military community, we foster respect for all people and for cultural diversity

Hammack, Principal, Assistant Principal

2016 Vilseck High School
Unit 20841
APO, Vilseck
Germany 09112-5
011-490-662
Fax: 011-490-662
E-mail: Duane.Werner@eu.dodea.edu
http://www.vils-hs.eu.dodea.edu/
VHS is home to approximately 520 students, grades 9-12, who have the opportunity to participate in Engaged Learning projects in academic areas. They have a wide range of choices in elective areas to include art, band, chorus, German, Spanish, home economics and technical education.

Duane Werner, Principal

2017 Violen School, International Department
Violenstraat 3, 1214
CJ Hilversum
Netherlands
035-621-6053
http://www.ipsviolen.nl
This school offers an enrollment of 240 day students (125 boys and 115 girls), in grades K through 6. The primary education is in the English language for international mobile families, set up and supported by the Dutch government.

Atse R Spoor, Principal

2018 Vogelweh Elementary School
Unit 3240 Box 435
APO
Germany, AE 09021
011-49 -3109
Fax: 011-49 -3105
http://www.voge-es.eu.dodea.edu
Vogelweh Elementary School is committed to creating an environment that supports lifelong learning in order for students to be successful in a global society.

Donna E Donaldson, Principal
Janie Page, Assistant Principal

2019 Volkel Elementary School
752 MUNSS Unit 6790
APO, Volkel 09717 5018
Netherlands
http://www.aoshs.org

Claudia Holtzclaw, Principal

2020 Westwing School
Kyneton House
Thornbury BS122JZ
England
0454-412311
http://westwing.dvusd.org

Marjorie Crane, MA, Headmaster

2021 Wetzel Elementary School
Unit 23815
APO, Baumholder 09034 0005
Germany
http://www.baum-esw.eu.dodea.edu

Robert Richards, Principal

2022 Wiesbaden Middle School
Unit 29647
APO, AE
Germany 09096
011-049- 110
Fax: 011-049- 110
E-mail:
wiesbadenMS.Webmaster@eu.dodea.edu
http://www.wies-ms.eu.dodea.edu

The entire WMS community strives to provide a positive school climate through which all students can mature socially, academically and physically, while developing a lifelong love of learning.

Alexia Venglik, Principal

2023 Wolfert Van Borselen
Bredewater 24, Postbus 501
2700 AM Zoetermeer
Netherlands
E-mail: info@owinsp.nl
http://http://www.wolfert.nl/
Gilles Schuilenburg, Principal

2024 Worksop College
Worksop, Nottinghamshire
S80 3AP
England
0909-472391
E-mail:
enquiries@worksopcollege.notts.sch.uk
http://http://www.worksopcollege.notts.sch.uk/
Worksop College was founded as St Cuthbert's School in 1890 by Nathaniel Woodard. As a parish priest working in London in the 1840s Woodard was dismayed by the ignorance of the middle classes and believed that there was a need for something comparable to the National School's Christian schools for the poor in order to serve the needs of the trade classes.

Roy Collard, Headmaster

2025 Worms Elementary School
CMR 455
APO, Worms 09058 0005
Germany
011-490-662
http://www.wikimapia.org
Charles Raglan, Principal

2026 Wuerzburg Elementary School
CMR 475 Box 6
APO, Wuerzburg 09244 6627
Germany
011-490-662
http://www.wikimapia.org
Dee Ann Edwards, Principal

2027 Wuerzburg High School
CMR 475 Box 8
APO, Wuerzburg 09036 0005
Germany
011-490-662
http://www.wikimapia.org
Robert Kubarek, Principal

2028 Wuerzburg Middle School
CMR 475 Box 7
APO, Wuerzburg 09036 0005
Germany
011-490-662
http://www.wikimapia.org
Karen Kroon, Principal

2029 Zurich International School
Steinacherstrasse 140
8820 Wadenswill
Switzerland
41-43-833-2222
Fax: 41-43-833-2223
E-mail: zis@zis.ch
http://www.zis.ch
Zurich International School is a co-educational international day school in the Zurich area for students aged 3 to 18 and is fully accredited by both the Council of International Schools and the New England

Association of Schools and Colleges and is an IB World School.

Peter C Mott, Director
Jennifer Saxe, Director Development

West Indies & Carribean

2030 American School-Santo Domingo
Apartado 20212
Santo Domingo
Dominican Republic
809-565-7946
809-549-5841
E-mail: info@assd.edu.do
http://www.assd.edu.do
The American School of Santo Domingo provides all students with quality educational opportunities to make life long learners while fostering moral values and physical development.

Lourdes Tomas, School Director

2031 Aquinas College
1607 Robinson Road SE
Grand Rapids, MI 49506-1799
616-632-8900
http://www.aquinas.edu
Emphasizes career preparation with a focus on leadership and service to others.

Vincent Ferguson, Principal

2032 Belair School
43 Decarteret Road
Mandeville
Jamaica
1-876-962-2168
Fax: 1-876-962-3396
E-mail: admissions@belairschool.com
http://www.belairschool.com
The Belair School seeks to promote the academic, social and emotional development of students and a value system of integrity through an integrated curriculum, so that students will become self-assured and responsible citizens.

Sylvan Shields, Director

2033 Bermuda High School
19 Richmond Road
Pembroke
Bermuda HM 08
1-441-295-6153
Fax: 1-441-295-2754
E-mail: info@bhs.bm
http://www.bhs.bm
This girls school offers an English-based curriculum for 620 total day students in grades 1-12.

Martina Harris, Primary Head
Jennifer Howarth, Primary Assistant

2034 Bermuda Institute-SDA
234 Middle Road
Southampton
Bermuda SN BX
441-238-1566
http://www.bermudainstitute.bm
The Bermuda Institute family exists to show children Jesus, nurture their love for Him and others, teach them to think, and empower them to serve.

Lois Tucker, Principal
Kathleen Allers, Elementary Vice Principal

2035 Bishop Anstey Junior School
Ariapita Road
Port of Spain
Trinidad and Tobago

868-624-1177
E-mail: admin@bishopansteyjunior.edu.tt
http://www.bishopansteyjunior.edu.tt
To stimulate learning within the spiritual, academic, social , cultural and sporting disciplines aimed at developing rounded individuals, within an environment that allows the flexibility to cope with the challenges of the changing education landscape.

Grace Campbell, Principal

2036 Capitol Christian School
C-11 #3 Urb Real Santo Domingo
Dominican Republic
916-856-5630
Fax: 916-856-5609
http://www.ccscougars.org
Stacy Lee Blossom, Principal

2037 Ecole Flamboyant
PO Box 1744-A Schweitzer Hosp
Port-au-Prince
Haiti
509-381-141/2
Fax: 509-381-141
E-mail: has-pap@acn.com
William Dunn, Principal

2038 International School-Aruba
Wayaca 238 A
Aruba
Dutch Caribbean
297-845-365
Fax: 297-847-341
E-mail: info@isaruba.com
http://www.isaruba.com
A nonprofit, coeducational English-speaking day school serving students from prekindergarten to grade 12.

Paul D Sibley, Headmaster
Mary B Sibley, Academic Dean/Counselor

2039 International School-Curacao
PO Box 3090
Koninginnelaan Emmastad, Curacao
Netherlands Antilles
5-999-737-3633
Fax: 5-999-737-3142
E-mail: iscmec@attglobal.net
http://www.isc.an
Offers a rigorous academic program in order to prepare students planning to pursue higher learning at colleges and universities around the world. The School's curriculum includes International Baccalaureate (IB) coursework that allows students the opportunity to receive the IB Diploma.

Margie Elhage PhD, Director
Rene Romer, President

2040 International School-West Indies
PO Box 278 Leeward
Providenciales
British West Indies
Alison Hodges, Principal

2041 Kingsway Academy
PO Box N-4378
Nassau
Bahamas
242-324-6887
Fax: 242-393-6917
http://www.kingswayacademy.com
Kingsway Academy endeavours to provide children with a sound education that is thoroughly Christian in its outlook and practices - Training Children in the King's Way .

Carol Harrison, Principal

2042 Mount Saint Agnes Academy
PO Box HM 1004
Hamilton HMDX
Bermuda

441-292-4134
Fax: 441-295-7265
E-mail: msaoffice@msa.bm
http://www.msa.bm
The Mission of Mount Saint Agnes Academy is to provide quality education in a caring, Christian environment. Belief in Christ and fidelity to the Roman Catholic Church form the foundation upon which all academic learning and social interaction take place. To this end we make a strong commitment to recognize each child as an individual and to help him/her to develop according to his/her own potential in order to become a responsible member of the community

Sue Moench, Principal
Margaret DiGiacomo, Assistant Principal

2043 Queens College
PO Box N7127
Nassau
Bahamas
242-393-1666
Fax: 242-393-3248
E-mail: info@qchenceforth.com
http://www.qchenceforth.com
Our interests lie not only in academic excellence but also in raising well-rounded, courteous, spiritually grounded global citizens.

Andrea Gibson, Principal

2044 Saltus Cavendish School
PO Box DV 209
Devonshire DV BX
Bermuda
441-236-3215
Fax: 441-292-0438
E-mail: head.cavendish@saltus.bm
http://www.saltus.bm
Saltus Grammar School is a co-educational, independent day school of excellent reputation. It is the premier independent school in Bermuda and is well known in the international community.

Susan Furr, Headteacher
Stephanie Queary, Secretary

2045 St. Andrew's School
16 Valleton Avenue
Marraval Trinidad West Indies
Trinidad and Tobago
868-622-2630
Fax: 868-628-1857
E-mail: principal@standrews.edu.tt
http://www.standrews.edu.tt
St. Andrew's is a progressive school that produces a caring, confident and responsible child. St. Andrew's also supports the development of social and moral values that allow the child to appreciate and respect diversity.

Sandra Farinha, Principal
Paula Moses, Vice Principal

2046 St. Anne's Parish School
PO Box SS6256
Nassau
Bahamas
868-622-2631
Fax: 868-628-1858
http://www.standrewsindia.com

Rev. Patrick Adderley, Principal

2047 St. John's College
PO Box N4858
Nassau
Bahamas
868-622-2632
Fax: 868-628-1859
http://www.standrewsindia.com

Arlene Ferguson, Principal

2048 St. Paul's Methodist College
PO Box F897
Freeport
Grand Bahamas
814-237-2163
http://stpaulsc.org

Annette Poitier, Principal

2049 Sunland Lutheran School
PO Box F2469
Freeport
Bahamas
http://www.sunlandbaptistacademy.org

J Pinder, Principal

2050 Tapion School
PO Box 511 La Toc
Castries, St Lucia
West Indies
758-452-2902
Fax: 758-453-0582
E-mail: tapionsch@candw.lc
http://tapionschool.com
The Tapion School will endeavour to produce individuals who would be empowered to meet the demands of a changing society.

Laurena Primus, Principal
Margaret Francois, Administration Officer

U.S. Branches

2051 Aisha Mohammed International School
Washington, DC 20521-1
http://www.joh.cam.ac.uk

Daryl Barker, Principal

2052 Albania Tirana International School
DOS/Administrative Officer
9510 Tirana Place
Washington, DC 20521-9510
355-436-5239
E-mail: qsialb@albaniaonline.net
http://www1.qsi.org/alb
Provides a quality education in the English language for expatriates living in Tirana and Albanian citizens who want their children to be educated in English.

Scott D'Alterio, Director
Sotiraq Trebicka, Administrative Coordinator

2053 Alexander Muss High School Israel
78 Randall Avenue
Rockville Centre, NY 11570
212-472-9300
800-327-5980
Fax: 212-472-9301
E-mail: info@amiie.org
http://amiie.org
Provide a superior Israel education experience to learners of all ages in Israel and within communities throughout North America and abroad. The Institute promotes, builds and strengthens lifelong bonds between Jews and Israel through education, experiences and understanding.

Gideon Shavit, CEO
Chaim Fischgrund, Headmaster

2054 Almaty International School
DOS/Administrative Officer
7030 Almaty Place
Washington, DC 20521-7030
E-mail: director@ais.almaty.kz
http://www.state.gov/www/about_state/schools/oalmaty.html
Grades preK-12, enrollment 169.

Robert B Draper, Director

2055 American School
Col Lomas del Guijarro Avenue Repb
Tegucigalpa
Honduras 02134
504-239-3333
Fax: 504-239-6162
E-mail: eagurcia@amschool.org
http://www.amschool.org
Provides a student-centered, enriching, college-preparatory education that emphasizes social responsibility in a safe, bicultural, and disciplined learning environment.

Liliana F Jenkins, Superintendent
David Mendoza, Business Administrator

2056 American Cooperative School
Calle 10 y Pasaje Kantutas, Calacot
c/o American Embassy, La Paz, Bolivia
La Paz, Bolivia
519-2-792-302
Fax: 591-2-797-218
E-mail: acs@acslp.org
http://www.acslp.org
Offers college prepatory North American education that enables our graduates to enter the best universities in the United States, Canada, Europe and Latin America.

Matthew Kirby, Superintendent
Robert Boni, Chair

2057 American Cooperative School of Tunis
6360 Tunis Place
Washington, DC 20521-6360
216-71-760-905
Fax: 216-71-761-412
E-mail: acst@acst.intl.tn
http://www.acst.net

Dennis Sheehan, Superintendent

2058 American Embassy School
Department of State/AES
9000 New Delhi Place
Washington, DC 20521-9000
91-11-611-7140
Fax: 91-11-687-3320
E-mail: aesindia@aes.ac.in
http://www.serve.com/aesndi
Grade levels Pre-K through 12, school year August - May

Rob Mochrish, PhD, Director

2059 American Embassy School of New Delhi
Chandragupta Marg
Chanakyapuri, New Delhi
India 11002
91-11-611-7140
Fax: 91-11-687-3320
E-mail: aesindia@del2.vsnl.net.in
http://aes.ac.in/splash.php
Serves students from the United States and other nations. It provides a quality American education that enables students to be inspired learners and responsible global citizens through the collaboration of a dedicated faculty and a supportive community.

Dr Robert Hetzel, Director
Linda McGinnis, Secretary, AES School Board

2060 American International School of Nouakchott
DOS/Administrative Officer
2430 Nouakchott Place
Washington, DC 20521-2430
222-2-52967
Fax: 222-2-52967
E-mail: aisnsahara@yahoo.com
http://www.aisn.mr
At the American International School of Nouakchott, a partnership of educators and parents is committed to providing our cultur-

ally diverse students a safe, nurturing and respectful learning environment. We promote academic achievement through a curriculum founded on an American educational philosophy.

Sharon Orlins PhD, Director

2061 American International School-Abuja
DOS/Administrative Officer
8300 Abuja Place
Washington, DC 20521-8300
234-9-413-4464
Fax: 234-9-413-4464
E-mail: info@aisabuja.com
http://www.aisabuja.com
Provide a quality education, utilizing an American curriculum for students of all nationalities from preschool through 12th grade.

Amy Uzoewulu, Director
Peter Williams, Primary Principal

2062 American International School-Bamako
DOS/Administrative Officer
2050 Bamako Place
Washington, DC 20189-2050
223-222-4738
Fax: 223-222-0853
E-mail: aisb@aisbmali.org
http://www.aisbmali.org
An independent, coeducational day school which offers an educational program from prekindergarten through grade 10. Supervised study using the University of Nebraska High School correspondence courses for grades 12 may also be arranged.

David Henry, Director
Rob Van Doeselaar, Chairman

2063 American International School-Chennai
100 Feet Road
Taramani
Chennai 00600-113
91-44-499-0881
Fax: 91-44-466-0636
E-mail: HeadofSchool@aisch.org
http://www.aisch.org
Embraces international diversity and strives to provide an academically challenging environment in order to foster intellectual curiosity and a sense of responsibility in our students. To fully educate the whole person, we are committed to cultivating lifelong learners and balanced, service-oriented citizens, who are thereby prepared to positively contribute in a globally competitive world.

Barry Clough, Head of School
Dr James R Fellabaum, High School Principal

2064 American International School-Costa Rica
Interlink 249
PO Box 02-5635
Miami, FL 33102
506-229-3256
Fax: 506-223-9062
E-mail: ais@aiscr.com
http://www.aiscr.com
A private, non-profit school that was founded in 1970 under the name of Costa Rica Academy. AIS serves approximately 200 students from pre-school through 12th grade.

Austin Briggs Jr, Headmaster
Neli Santiago, Principal

2065 American International School-Freetown
Department of State/MGT
2160 Freetown Place
Washington, DC 20521-2160
232-22-232-480
Fax: 232-22-225-471
E-mail: aisfinfo@yahoo.com
http://www.aisfreetown.websiteanimal.com
A private, non-profit, PreK-8th grade school providing an American curriculum to a multinational community in Freetown, Sierra Leone.

Ndye Njie, Director
Nielette Gordon, Administrative Assistant

2066 American International School-Kingston
1a Olivier Road
Kingston 8
Jamaica
876-977-3625
Fax: 876-977-3625
E-mail: aiskoff@cwjamaica.com
http://www.aisk.com
A non-profit, non-sectarian, private day school funded by tuition income receiving small annual grants from the U.S. Government through it Office of Overseas Schools.

Sean Goudie, Director
Anna Wallace, Lower School Coordinator

2067 American International School-Lesotho
DOS/Administrative Officer
2340 Maseru Place
Washington, DC 20521-2340
266-322-987
Fax: 266-311-963
E-mail: aisl@lesoff.co.za
http://www.aisl.lesoff.co.za
An independent, coeducational day school which offers an American education from preschool through grade 8. The school was founded in 1991 to serve the needs of the American community and other students seeking an English-language education.

Harvey Cohen, Principal

2068 American International School-Libreville
2270 Libreville Place
Washington, DC 20521-2270
241-76-20-03
Fax: 241-74-55-07
E-mail: aisl@internetgabon.com
http://www.aisa.or.ke

Paul Sicard, Director

2069 American International School-Lome
DOS/Administrative Officer
2300 Lome Place
Washington, DC 20521-2300
E-mail: aisl@cafe.tg
http://www.aisa.or.ke
Established in 1967 as a private, coeducational day school offering an educational program to students of all nationalities in pre-kindergarten through grade 8.

Clover Afokpa, Director
Warace Tchamsi, Administrative Assistant

2070 American International School-Lusaka
PO Box 31617
Lusaka
Zambia
260-1-260-509
Fax: 260-1-260-538
E-mail: SpecialPerson@aislusaka.org
http://www.aislusaka.org
Committed to being a leading IB World School, offering a balanced, academically rigorous and internationally recognized college preparatory education.

Chris Muller, Director
Shirley Mee, Business Manager

2071 American International School-Mozambique
DOS/Administrative Officer
2330 Maputo Place
Washington, DC 20521-2330
258-1-49-1994
Fax: 258-1-49-0596
E-mail: aism@aism-moz.com
http://www.aisa.or.ke

Don Reeser, Director

2072 American International School-N'Djamena
DOS/Administrative Officer
2410 N'Djamena Place
Washington, DC 20521-2410
235-52-2103
Fax: 235-51-5654
E-mail: aisn@intent.td
http://www.aisa.or.ke

Gay Mickle, Director

2073 American International School-Nouakchott
2430 Nouakchott Place
Washington, DC 20521-2430
222-2-52967
Fax: 222-2-52967
E-mail: aisnsahara@yahoo.com
http://www.aisn.mr
Committed to provide culturally diverse students a safe, nurturing and respectful learning environment and promotes academic achievement through a curriculum founded on an American educational philosophy.

Sharon Orlins PhD, Director

2074 American Nicaraguan School
c/o American Embassy
Unit No 2710 Box 7, APO AA 34021
Washington, DC 20521-3240
505-278-0029
Fax: 505-267-3088
E-mail: info@ans.edu.ni
http://www.ans.edu.ni
A private, nonsectarian coeducaitonal day school which offers an educaional program from prekindergarten through grade 12 for students of all nationalities.

Fredy Ramirez, Elementary School Principal
Joseph Azmeh, Secondary Principal

2075 American Samoa Department of Education
Pago Pago
American Samoa 96799
011-684-633-5237
Fax: 011-684-633-5733
http://www.doe.as
Is to ensure student success by providing high quality teaching and learning opportunities to all our children

Sili K Sataua

2076 American School Honduras
American Embassy Tegucigalpa
Department of State
Washington, DC 20521-3480
504-239-333
Fax: 504-239-6162
E-mail: admin_assistant@asamadagascar.org
http://www.amschool.org

A private, coeducational day school which offers an educational program from nursery through grade 12 for students of all nationalities.

James Szoka, Principal

2077 American School-Algiers

American Embassy Algiers
Washington, DC 20520-1
202-265-2800
Fax: 202-667-2174

Richard Gillogly, Principal

2078 American School-Antananarivo

2040 Antananarivo Place
Dulles, VA 20189-2040
261-20-22-420-39
Fax: 261-20-22-345-39
E-mail: miasaadm@gmail.com
http://www.asamadagascar.org
As the only English language institution in Madagascar offering a K-12 diploma program, we challenge our students to actively engage with the exceptional educational opportunities that are available to them in our school.

Jay Long, Director

2079 American School-Asuncion

Avenida Esapaa 1175
PO Box 10093
Asuncion, Paraguay
595-21-600-476
Fax: 595-21-603-518
E-mail: asagator@asa.edu.py
http://www.asa.edu.py
A bilingual learning community of International and Paraguayan families, is to prepare responsible proactive world citizens in a student-centered, caring environment through a college preparatory program that adheres to the highest U.S. and Paraguayan standards of excellence

Dennis Klumpp, Director
David Warken, Elementary Principal

2080 American School-Dschang

Washington, DC 20521-1

Jane French, Principal

2081 American School-Guatemala

11 Calle 1579 Zona 1511 calle 15-79
Guatemala
Guatemala
502-236- 079
Fax: 502-236- 833
E-mail: director@cag.edu.gt
http://www.cag.edu.gt
The school's goal is to educate independent, critical-thinking, responsible, bilingual individuals prepared to meet the challenges of the future.

Tracy Berry-Lazo, General Director
Fabio Corvaglia, High School Principal

2082 American School-Niamey

DOS/Administrative Officer
2420 Niamey Place
Dulles, VA 20189-2420
227-723-942
Fax: 227-723-457
E-mail: asniger@intnet.ne
http://www.geocities.com/asniamey
A coeducational day school offering an educational program from prekindergarten through grade 9, and 10-12 correspondence.

Deborah M Robinson, Director

2083 American School-Port Gentil

1100 Louisiana Street
Suite 2500
Houston, TX 77002-5215

Keith Marriott, Principal

2084 American School-Tegucigalpa

Coronel Lomas del Guijarro
Avenue Repblica Dominicana Calle Costa
Tegucigalpa, Honduras
504-239-3333
Fax: 504-239-6162
http://www.amschool.org
Provides a Student Centered, enriching, college-preparatory education that emphasizes social responsibility in a safe, bicultural, and disciplined learning enviroment

James Shepherd, Principal
Liliana Jerkins, Superintendent

2085 American School-Warsaw

Ul Warszawska 202
Konstancin-Jeziorna
Poland 05520
48-22-651-9611
Fax: 48-22-642-1506
E-mail: admissions@asw.waw.pl
http://www.asw.waw.pl
Offers a rigorous, supportive and balanced PK-12 program in English for the international community of Warsaw that is driven by a strong commitment to prepare students for lives as responsible world citizens

Tony Gerlicz, Director
Rebecca Brown, Finance/Operations Director

2086 American School-Yaounde

BP 7475
Yaounde
Cameroon
234-223-0421
Fax: 237-223-6011
E-mail: school@asoy.org
http://asoy.org
Ensures that all students achieve high academic success, demonstrate critical thinking skills, and become responsible and compassionate, global citizens prepared for their next stage in life; as gained through an enriched, American curriculum and offered in a challenging, secure, and diverse environment.

Nanci Shaw, School Director

2087 American-Nicaraguan School

Frente al Club Lomas de Monserrat
PO Box 2670, Managua
Nicaragua
505-2-782-565
Fax: 505-2-673-088
E-mail: elementary@ans.edu.ni
http://www.ans.edu.ni
Provides its multicultural student community with a US-accredited college preparatory program, based on democratic and universal values, that develops critical thinkers and ethical individuals capable of realizing their leadership potential by making meaningful contributions to society.

Stan Key, Director General
Roberto Cardenal, Director of Finance

2088 Amoco Galeota School

PO Box 4381
Houston, TX 77210-4381

Barbara Punch, Principal

2089 Andersen Elementary & Middle School

Unit 14057
APO, Mariana Islands 96543 4057
Guam
http://www.extranet.guam.pac.dodea.edu

2090 Anzoategui International School

PO Box 020010, M-42
Jet Cargo International
Miami, FL 33102-10

58-82-22683
Fax: 58-82-22683
E-mail: aishead@telcel.net.ve
http://www.anaco.net
Grade levels Pre-K through 12, school year August - June

Jorge Nelson EdD, Superintendent

2091 Armenia QSI International School-Yerevan

DOS/Administrative Officer
7020 Yerevan Place
Washington, DC 20521-7020
374-1-391-030
Fax: 374-1-151-438
E-mail: qsiy@arminco.com
http://www.qsi.org
An independent, coeducational day school which offers an educational program from preschool (3-4 years) through grade 12 for students of all nationalities. Enrollment 45.

Arthur W Hudson, Director

2092 Atlanta International School

2890 N Fulton Drive NE
Atlanta, GA 30305-3155
404-841-3840
Fax: 404-841-3873
E-mail: info@aischool.org
http://www.aischool.org
Continuing to develop and deserve a worldwide reputation as an exemplary center of teaching and learning, a school that achieves and sets, within the framework of the International Baccalaureate.Maintaining an optimal size composition of faculty and students so that opportunities for individual learning, mutual understanding, and community feeling are maximized.

Robert Brindley, Headmaster
Charlotte Smith, Executive Assistant

2093 Awty International School

7455 Awty School Lane
Houston, TX 77055-7222
713-686-4850
Fax: 713-686-4956
E-mail: admissions@awty.org
http://www.awty.org
Grade level prekindergarten through twelfth, with total enrollment of 900 students.

David Watson, Headmaster
John Ransom, Chairman

2094 Azerbaijan Baku International School

Darnagul Qasabasi Street Ajami Nakc
Block 3097
Baku, Azerbaijan 01108
994-12-90-63-52
Fax: 994-12-90-63-51
E-mail: baku@qsi.org
http://www.qsi.org
the primary purpose of the school is to meet the needs of the children in Baku who require this type of education with a view to continuing their education in their home countries with a minimum of adjustment problems.

Scott Root, Director
Arthur W Hudson, Director

2095 Baku International School

Darnagul Qasabasi Street Ajami Nakc
Block 3097
Baku, Azerbaijan, AZ 01108
994-12-656352
Fax: 991-12-4105951
E-mail: baku@qsi.org
http://www.qsi.org
the primary purpose of the school is to meet the needs of the children in Baku who require this type of education with a view to continu-

ing their education in their home countries with a minimum of adjustment problems.

Scott Root, Director
Arthur W Hudson, Director

2096 Ball Brothers Foundation
222 S Mulberry Street
Muncie, IN 47305
765-741-5500
Fax: 765-741-5518
E-mail: info@ballfdn.org
http://www.ballfdn.org
The Foundation's primary focus is Muncie and East Central Indiana.The Foundation has been a philanthropic leader, serving as initiator, convener, and catalyst among donors and nonprofit organizations. Within Muncie, the Foundation seeks to forge active partnerships with effective nonprofit agencies by providing consultation and financial support to promote their success.

Jud Fisher, Executive Director/ COO
John W Fisher, Chairman & President

2097 Banjul American Embassy School
2070 Banjul Place
Dulles, VA 20189-2070
220-495-920
Fax: 220-497-181
E-mail: baes@qanet.gm
http://www.baes.gm
The school demonstrates U.S. education abroad to a multi-ethnic, multi-cultural, diverse student body and otherwise increases mutual understanding through its emphasis on an American-based curriculum, use of American textbooks and supplemental materials, and its teaching staff, of whom four are American nationals trained in American universities.

Dianne Zemichael, Director
Leah Moore, Administrative Secretary

2098 Bingham Academy Ethiopia
SIM International
PO Box 4937
Addis Ababa, Ethiopia
East Africa
251-11 -791
Fax: 251-11 -791
E-mail: director@binghamacademy.net
http://www.binghamacademy.net
The purpose of Bingham Academy is to provide high quality, culturally sensitive education, within a Christian environment, which challenges each student to impact the world for God's glory.

Murray Overton, Director

2099 Bishkek International School
14A Tynystanova Street
Bishkek
Kyrgyzstan 72005
996-312-66-35-03
Fax: 996-312-66-35-03
E-mail: bishkek@qsi.org
http://www.qsi.org
The primary purpose of the school is to meet the needs of the children in Bishkek who require this type of education with a view to continuing their education in their home countries with a minimum of adjustment problems.

MaryKay Gudkova, Director

2100 Bosnia-Herzegovina QSI International School Sarajevo
Omladinska #12
Vogosca-Saravejo
Bosnia & Herzegovina 71320
387-33-434-756
Fax: 387-33-434-756
E-mail: saravejo@qsi.org
http://www.qsi.org

The primary purpose of the school is to meet the needs of the expatriate children living in Sarajevo who require this type of education.

Jay Hamric, Director
Arthur W Hudson, Director

2101 Bratislava American International School
American Embassy Bratislava
Karloveska 64
Bratislava
Slovak Republic 842-2
421-7-722-844
Fax: 721-7-722-844
E-mail: bratislava@qsi.org
http://www.qsi.sk
The primary purpose of the school is to meet the needs of the children in Bratislava who require this type of education with a view to continuing their education in their home countries with a minimum of adjustment problems.

Ronald Adams, Principal
Matthew Lake, Director

2102 Bulgaria Anglo-American School-Sofia
DOS/Administrative Officer
5740 Sophia Place
Washington, DC 20521-5740
359-2-974-4575
Fax: 359-2-974-4483
E-mail: aasregist@infotel.bg
http://www.geocities.com/angloamericans chool
An independent, coeducational day school which offers an educational program from prekindergarten through grade 8 for students of all nationalities. The school year comprises 2 semesters extending from August to December and from January to June. Enrollment 140.

Brian M Garton, Director
Arthur W Hudson, Director

2103 Burma International School Yangon
DOS/Administrative Officer
4250 Rangoon Place
Washington, DC 20521-4250
95-1-512-793/795
Fax: 95-1-525-020
E-mail: ISYDIRECTOR@mptmail.net.mm
http://www.internationalschoolyangon.or g
Grades PK-12, enrollment 331.

Merry Wade, Director

2104 Burns Family Foundation
410 N Michigan Avenue
Room 1600
Chicago, IL 60611-4213
Offers support in secondary school education, higher education and youth services.

2105 Caribbean American School
5 Gates Court
Cranbury, NJ 08512-2926
509-257-7961
http://www.isbi.com
Ernestine Rochelle, Principal
Ernestine Roche Robinson, Director

2106 Caribbean-American School
PO Box 407139
Lynx Air
Ft Lauderdale, FL 33340-7139
509-257-7961
http://www.isbi.com

Grade levels Pre-K through 12, school year September - June

Ernestine Roche Robinson, Director
Ernestine Rochelle, Principal

2107 Chinese American International School
150 Oak Street
San Francisco, CA 94102
415-865-6000
Fax: 415-865-6089
E-mail: caishead@aol.com
http://www.cais.org
Educates students for academic excellence, moral character and international perspective through immersion in American and Chinese culture and language.

Andrew W Corcoran, Executive Director

2108 Colegio Albania
PO Box 25573
Miami, FL 33102-5573
Eric Spindler, Principal

2109 Colegio Corazon de Maria
Ferrer y Ferrer-Santiago Igles
San Juan
Puerto Rico
M Cyril Stauss, Principal

2110 Colegio De Parvulos
263 Calle San Sebastian
San Juan 00901-1205
Puerto Rico
Maria Dolores Vice, Principal

2111 Colegio Del Buen Pastor
Camino Alejandrino Km 3.4
Rio Piedras 00927
Puerto Rico
http://www.colegiobuenpastor.com
Adria M Borges, Principal

2112 Colegio Del Sagrado Corazon
Obispado Final Urb La Alhambra
Ponce 00731
Puerto Rico
556- 14-2
http://www.sagradocorazon.edu.co
Joan G Dedapena, Principal

2113 Colegio Espiritu Santo
Box 191715 San Juan
Puerto Rico 00019-1715
787-754-0555
Fax: 754-715-
E-mail: admision@colespiritusanto.com
http://www.colespiritusanto.com
Carmen Jovet, Principal

2114 Colegio Inmaculada
Carr Militar 2 Km 49.6
Manati 00674
Puerto Rico
http://www.colegioinmaculada.es
Sor Nichlasa Maderea, Principal

2115 Colegio Inmaculada Concepcion
2 Calle Isabela
Guayanilla 00656-1703
Puerto Rico
http://www.colegioinmaculada.es
Sor Alejandrina Torres, Principal

2116 Colegio Internacional-Carabobo
VLN 1010
PO Box 025685
Miami, FL 33102-5685
58-41-421-807
Fax: 58-41-426-510
E-mail: admin@cic-valencia.org.ve
http://www.cic-valencia.org.ve

To develop young men and women of character through an international college-preparatory program, in English, based on high intellectual and moral standards

Frank Anderson, Superintendent
Joe Walker, Director

2117 Colegio Internacional-Caracas
PAKMAIL 6030
PO Box 025323
Miami, FL 33102-5304
58-2-945-0444
Fax: 58-2-945-0533
E-mail: cic@cic-caracas.org
http://www.cic-caracas.org
Colegio Internacional de Caracas is an English-medium, Pre-Nursery to Grade 12 school dedicated to the intellectual and personal development of each student in a caring and supportive environment. CIC offers a challenging program to prepare an international student body to excel in a variety of the world's finest schools and universities.

Alan Benson, Superintendent
Carmen Sweeting, Director of Academics

2118 Colegio Internacional-Puerto La Cruz
11010 NW 30th Street
Suite 104
Miami, FL 33172-5032
58-281-277-6051
Fax: 58-281-274-1134
E-mail: ciplc@telcel.net.ve
http://www.ciplc.net
Inspiring students to learn and serve by cultivating each student's full potential as an effective communicator, problem solver, and contributing global citizen.

Mike Martell, Superintendent
Frank Capuccio, Administrative Assistant

2119 Colegio La Inmaculada
1711 Ave Ponce De Leon
San Juan 00909-1905
Puerto Rico
787-754-0555
Fax: 754-715-
http://www.colegioinmaculada.es
Sor Teresa Del Rio, Principal

2120 Colegio La Milagrosa
107 Calle De Diego
San Juan 00925-3303
Puerto Rico
787-754-0555
Fax: 754-715-
http://www.colegioinmaculada.es
Maria Flores, Principal

2121 Colegio Lourdes
Box 190847
San Juan, PR 00919-847
787-767-6106
Fax: 787-767-5282
E-mail: clourdes@coqui.net
http://www.colegiolourdes.org
Forming strong Christian faith and critical, able to make a commitment within the society and the church that is open to the realities and needs of his time, able to integrate into an attitude of service in a democratic society, as understand and explain the Preamble to the Constitution of Puerto Rico.

Paz Asiain, Director
Thalia Lopez, Principal

2122 Colegio Madre Cabrini
1564 Calle Encarnacion
San Juan 00920-4739
Puerto Rico
787-792-6180
http://www.madrecabrini.com.b
Anne Marie Gavin, Principal

2123 Colegio Maria Auxiliadora
PO Box 797
Carolina 00986-0797
Puerto Rico
787-792-6181
http://www.auxiliadora.ne
Leles Rodriguez, Principal

2124 Colegio Marista
Final Santa Ana Alt Torrimar
Guaynabo 00969
Puerto Rico
http://www.marista.org.br
Hilario Martinez, Principal

2125 Colegio Marista El Salvador
PO Box 462
Manati 00674-0462
Puerto Rico
http://www.marista.org.br
Hnio Efrain Romo, Principal

2126 Colegio Mater Salvatoris
RR 3 Box 3080
San Juan 00926-9601
Puerto Rico
821- 99- 963
Fax: 821- 99- 973
http://www.matersalvatoris.org
Maria Luisa Benito, Principal

2127 Colegio Notre Dame Nivel
PO Box 967
Caguas 00726-0967
Puerto Rico
Francisca Suarez, Principal

2128 Colegio Nuestra Senora de La Caridad
PO Box 1164
Caparra Heigh 00920
Puerto Rico
http://www.colegiosdepr.com
Madre Esperanza Sanchez, Principal

2129 Colegio Nuestra Senora de La Merced
PO Box 4048
San Juan 00936-4048
Puerto Rico
http://www.colegiolamercedpr.com
Ivette Lopez, Principal

2130 Colegio Nuestra Senora de Lourdes
1050 Demetrio Odaly-Country Club
Rio Piedras 00924
Puerto Rico
Rita Manzano, Principal

2131 Colegio Nuestra Senora de Valvanera
53 Calle Jose I Quinton # 53
Coamo 00769-3108
Puerto Rico
Cruz Victor Colon, Principal

2132 Colegio Nuestra Senora del Carmen
RR 2, Box 9KK, Carr Trujillo Alt
Rio Piedras 00721
Puerto Rico
Candida Arrieta, Principal

2133 Colegio Nuestra Senora del Pilar
PO Box 387
Canovanas 00729-0387
Puerto Rico
Sor Leonilda Mallo, Principal

2134 Colegio Nuestra Senora del Rosario
Aa7 Calle 5
Bayamon 00959-3719
Puerto Rico
341-425-9781
http://www.maristasrosario.com
Theresita Miranda, Principal

2135 Colegio Nuestra Sra del Rosario
PO Box 1334
Ciales 00638-0414
Puerto Rico
787-871-1318
Fax: 787-871-5797
http://www.maristasrosario.com
Parrochial School - Prekindergarten to 9th grade.

Angel Mendoza, Principal
Padre Gabriel M Jorres, Director

2136 Colegio Padre Berrios
PO Box 7717
San Juan 00916-7717
Puerto Rico
http://www.colegiopadreberrios.webs.com
Sor Enedina Santos, Principal

2137 Colegio Parroquial San Jose
PO Box 7718
San Juan 00916-7718
Puerto Rico 00644
http://www.colegiopadreberrios.webs.com
Sor Enedina Santos, Principal

2138 Colegio Ponceno
PO Box 7718
San Juan 00916-7718
Puerto Rico 00644
809-848-2525
http://www.colegiopadreberrios.webs.com
Sor Enedina Santos, Principal

2139 Colegio Puertorriqueno de Ninas
Calle Turquessa 208
Golden Gate
Guaynabo, PR 00968
787-782-2618
Fax: 787-782-8370
E-mail: Info@cpnpr.org
http://www.cpnpr.org
Ivette Nter, School Director
Millie Suau, Principal

2140 Colegio Reina de Los Angeles
M-19 Calle Frontera
San Juan, PR 00926
787-761-7455
Fax: 787-761-7440
E-mail: info@reinaangeles.org
http://www.reinaangeles.org
Train Students education with a focus on physical, moral, intellectual, religious and social development within a framework of faith.

Victorina Ortega, Principal
Juana F Gomez, Director

2141 Colegio Rosa Bell
Calle Oviedo Number 42
Torrimar-Guaynabo, PR 00966
787-781-4240
Fax: 787-792-5415
E-mail: exalumno@rosabell.com
http://rosabell.wordpress.com
The purpose of a good education is to maximize the capabilities of the individual: intellectually, socially, emotionally and physically.

Rose Rodriguez, Director
Miguel Arzola-Barris, Executive Director

2142 Colegio Sacred Heart
Palma Real Urb, Univ Gardens
San Juan 00927
Puerto Rico
Paul Marie, CSB, Principal

2143 Colegio Sagrada Familia
7 Hostos
Ponce
Puerto Rico 00731
http://www.safa.edu.uy
Sor Pilar Becerra, Principal

2144 Colegio Sagrados Corazones
A Esmeralda Urb, Ponce De Leon
Guaynabo 00969
Puerto Rico
http://home.coqui.net/sagrado
Ana Arce de Marrer, Principal

2145 Colegio San Agustin
PO Box 4263
Bayamon 00958-1263
Puerto Rico
http://csa.edu.ph
Georgina Ortiz, Principal

2146 Colegio San Antonio
PO Box 21350
San Juan 00928-1350
Puerto Rico
809-764-0090
http://www.colegio-san-antonio.org
Rev. Paul S Brodie, Principal

2147 Colegio San Antonio Abad
PO Box 729
Humacao 00792-0729
Puerto Rico
809-764-0090
http://www.colegio-san-antonio.org
Padre Eduardo Torrella, Principal

2148 Colegio San Benito
PO Box 728
Humacao 00792-0728
Puerto Rico
http://www.csb.cl
Hermana Carmen Davila, Principal

2149 Colegio San Conrado (K-12)
PO Box 7111
Ponce 00732-7111
Puerto Rico
Fax: 787-841-7303
E-mail: sanconrado@pucpr.edu
Sister Nildred Rodriguez, Principal
Sister Wilma de Echevarria, Assistant
Principal

2150 Colegio San Felipe
566 Ave San Luis # 673
Arecibo 00612-3600
Puerto Rico
809-878-3532
http://www.colegiosanfelipe.edu.mx
Veronica Oravec, Principal

2151 Colegio San Francisco De Asis
PO Box 789
Barranquitas
Puerto Rico 00794
787-857-2123
Fax: 787-857-2123
E-mail: info@csfabarranquitas.com
http://www.csfabarranquitas.com
Founded in August 7, 1985
Hermana Maria Carbonell, Principal
Carlos Colon-Bernadi, Director

2152 Colegio San Gabriel
Gpo Box 347
San Juan 00936
Puerto Rico
http://www.sangabriel.cl
Sor Antonia Garatachea, Principal

2153 Colegio San Ignacio de Loyola
Urb Santa Mara, 1940 Calle Saco
San Juan
Puerto Rico 00927
787-765-3814
Fax: 787-758-4145
http://www.sanignacio.org
Dr Luis O Pino, Principal
Mario Alberto Torres, President

2154 Colegio San Jose
PO Box 21300
San Juan
Puerto Rico 00928-1300
787-751-8177
Fax: 787-767-7146
E-mail: sanjose@csj-rpi.org
http://www.csj-rpi.org
Bro Francisco T Gonzalez, Principal
Sra Elaine Torrens, Vice Principal

2155 Colegio San Juan Bautista
PO Box E
Orocovis 00720
Puerto Rico
787-751-8177
Fax: 787-767-7146
http://www.colegiosanjuanbautista.com
Sor Maria Antonia Miya, Principal

2156 Colegio San Juan Bosco
PO Box 14367
San Juan 00916-4367
Puerto Rico
http://www.sanjuanboscosalamanca.eu
Rev. P Jose Luis Gomez, Principal

2157 Colegio San Luis Rey
43 Final SE, Urb Reparto Metro
San Juan 00921
Puerto Rico
Rosario Maria, Principal

2158 Colegio San Miguel
GPO Box 1714
San Juan 00936
Puerto Rico
http://www.sanluisrey.edu.co
Elvira Gonzalez, Principal

2159 Colegio San Rafael
PO Box 301
Quebradillas 00678-0301
Puerto Rico
http://www.maristas.com.a

2160 Colegio San Vicente Ferrer
PO Box 455
Catano 00963-0455
Puerto Rico
Maria Soledad Colon, Principal

2161 Colegio San Vicente de Paul
Calle Bolivar 709, Parada 24
San Juan
Puerto Rico 00909
787-727-4273
Fax: 787-728-2263
http://www.csvp-sj.org
Dra Isabel C Machado, Principal
P Evaristo Oliveras, Director

2162 Colegio Santa Clara
Via 14-2JL-456 Villa Fontana
Carolina 00983
Puerto Rico

http://www.colegiostaclara.com
Elsie Mujica, Principal

2163 Colegio Santa Cruz
PO Box 235
Trujillo Alto 00977-0235
Puerto Rico
113-024-5197
http://www.santacruz.g12.br
Maria Ramon Santiago, Principal

2164 Colegio Santa Gema
PO Box 1705
Carolina 00984-1705
Puerto Rico
491-711-5093
http://www.colegio-santagema.es
Lilia Luna De Anaya, Principal

2165 Colegio Santa Rita
Calle 9, Apartado 1557
Bayamon 00958
Puerto Rico
http://www.colegiosantarita.com.br
Elba N Villalba, Principal

2166 Colegio Santa Rosa
Calle Marti, 15 Esquina Maceo
Bayamon 00961
Puerto Rico
http://www.colegiosantarosa-pa.com.br
Ana Josefa Colon, Principal

2167 Colegio Santa Teresita
342 Victoria
Ponce 00731
Puerto Rico
015-278-1202
http://www.santateresita.edu.pe
Mary Terence, Principal

2168 Colegio Santiago Apostol
Calle 23 Bloque 23 #17, Urb Sierra
Bayamon
Puerto Rico 00961
787-786- 917
Fax: 787-269-3965
E-mail: colegiosantiagoapostol@onlinkpr.net
http://www.colegiosantiagoapostol.net
Hilda Velazquez, Principal

2169 Colegio Santisimo Rosario
PO Box 26
Yauco 00698-0026
Puerto Rico
Judith Negron, Principal

2170 Colegio Santo Domingo
192 Calle Comerio
Bayamon 00959-5358
Puerto Rico
http://www.colegiosantodomingo.edu.do
Pura Huyke, Principal

2171 Colegio Santo Nino de Praga
PO Box 25
Penuelas 00624-0025
Puerto Rico
Aminta Santos, Principal

2172 Colegio Santos Angeles Custod
3 Sicilia Urb, San Jose
San Juan 00923
Puerto Rico
http://www.angelescustodios.com
Roberto Rivera, Principal

2173 Colegio de La Salle
PO Box 518
Bayamon 00960-0518
Puerto Rico

http://www.colsalle.edu.co
Wilfredo Perez De, Principal

2174 Commandant Gade Special Education School
St. Thomas, Virgin Islands 00801
Miss Jeanne Richards, Principal

2175 Community United Methodist School
PO Box 681
Frederiksted 00841-0681
Virgin Islands
Marva Oneal, Principal

2176 Country Day
RR 1 Box 6199
Kingshill, VI 00850
340-778-1974
Fax: 340-779-3331
E-mail: bsinfield@stxcountryday.com
http://www.stxcountryday.com
An independent, multicultural, college preparatory educational community set on a 34-acre tropical campus.
William Sinfield, Headmaster
Mariska Nurse, Dean of Guidance

2177 Croatia American International School-Zagreb
Vocarska 106
10 000 Zagreb
Croatia-5080
385-1-4680-133
Fax: 385-1-4680-171
E-mail: asz@asz.hr
http://www.aisz.hr
Grades K-8, enrollment 112.
Robin Heslip, Director

2178 Dallas International School
6039 Churchill Way
Dallas, TX 75230
972-991-6379
Fax: 972-991-6608
E-mail: rwkdis@metronet.com
http://www.dallasinternationalschool.org
DIS students will have the skills to continue their studies at universities in the United States or abroad and launch a professional career which will take advantage of all the opportunities created by globalization
Mea Ahlberg, Director of Admissions
MylSne Dumont, Middle School Coordinator

2179 Dominican Child Development Center
PO Box 5668
Agana
Guam 96910
617-477-7228
Fax: 671-472-4782
Kindergarten and nursery school.
Lednor Flores, Principal

2180 Dorado Academy
Urb Dorado del Mar Calle Madre Perl
Dorado
Puerto Rico 00646
787-796-2180
Fax: 787-796-7398
E-mail: mescabi@doradoacademy.org
http://www.doradoacademy.org
Its objective is to provide to all students an education that reflects the school's philosophy. The teachers strive to implement by instruction the school's philosophy and meet instructional goals and objectives.
Liutma Caballero, Principal
Nancy Escabi, Headmaster

2181 Dwight School
291 Central Park W
New York, NY 10024
212-724-7524
Fax: 212-724-2539
E-mail: admissions@dwight.edu
http://www.dwight.edu
Dwight's rigorous IB program and world-class faculty prepare a future generation of well-educated and ethical global leaders who will seek to create an environment of equality and respect for all human beings.
Marina Bernstein, Director Admissions
Alyson Waldman, Associate Director

2182 Educare
4235 Reserve Road
Unit 202
Lexington, KY 40514
859-396-7087
Fax: 859-201-1064
E-mail: mnaidu@educare.org
http://www.educare.org
To inspire children to achieve their very best; to educate children in character and leadership by drawing out their hidden character traits and leadership qualities.
Sara Connell, Principal

2183 Episcopal Cathedral School
PO Box 13305
Santurce
Puerto Rico 00908-3305
787-721-5478
Fax: 787-724-6668
E-mail: esc@gocougars.com
http://www.gocougars.com
Founded in 1946.
Gary J DeHope, Director

2184 Escole Tout Petit
PO Box 1248
San Juan 00902
Puerto Rico
Vivian Aviles, Principal

2185 Escuela Beata Imelda
PO Box 804
Guanica 00653-0804
Puerto Rico
P Salvador Barber, Principal

2186 Escuela Bella Vista
Avenido Cecilio Acosta Calle 67 Ent
Maracaibo
Venezuela
58-61-966-696
Fax: 58-61-969-417
E-mail: ebvnet@ebv.org.ve
http://www.ebv.org.ve
At EBV we offer an internationally enriched accredited U.S. program that prepares our students to participate actively, independently, cooperatively, and effectively in a multicultural, multilingual world. It is our commitment to educate each student to his/her maximum potential.
Steve Sibley, Superintendent
Todd Zukewich, High School Principal

2187 Escuela Campo Alegre
8424 NW 56th Street
Suite CCS 00007
Miami, FL 33166
58-2-993-3230
Fax: 58-2-993-0219
E-mail: info@eca.com.ve
http://www.eca.com.ve
ECA seeks to inspire its students toward the highest standards and expectations through a stimulating and comprehensive program of intellectual and personal development.
Bambi Betts, Director
Phil Redwine, Principal

2188 Escuela Campo Alegre-Venezuela
8424 NW 56th Street
Suite CCS00007
Miami, FL 33166
58-2-993-7135
Fax: 58-2-993-0219
E-mail: info@eca.com.ve
http://www.eca.com.ve
A private, coeducational day school offering a program for students from prekindergarten through grade 12.
Phil Redwine, Principal

2189 Escuela Caribe Vista School
8424 NW 56th Street
Suite CCS00007
Miami, FL 33166
765-668-4009
E-mail: info@eca.com.ve
http://www.eca.com.ve
Phil Redwine, Principal

2190 Escuela Las Morochas
Apartado Postal # 235
Ciudad Ojeda, Estado Zulia
Venezuela
58-265-6315-539
Fax: 58-265-6315-539
E-mail: jtrudeau@escuelalasmorochas.com
http://www.escuela-lasmorochas.com
Escuela Las Morochas is an English medium international school that offers a challenging U.S. education that encourages students to be life-long learners and responsible global citizens.
Jeff Trudeau, Director
Zulay Marcano, Assistant Secretary

2191 Escuela Nuestra Senora Del Carmen
PO Box 116, Playa De Ponce
Ponce 00731
Puerto Rico 00731
266-282-
Fax: 266-253-
http://www.colegionuestrasradelcarmen.edu
Paquita Alvarado, Principal

2192 Escuela Superior Catolica
PO Box 4245
Bayamon 00958-1245
Puerto Rico
Eledis Diaz, Principal

2193 Evangelical School for the Deaf
HC-01 Buzon 7111
Luquillo
Puerto Rico 00773-9602
787-889-3488
866-928-2836
E-mail: esdluquillo@gmail.com
http://www.esdluquillo.com
We believe that it is the obligation of the saved to witness by life and by words to the truths of Scripture, and to seek to proclaim the Gospel to all mankind.
Pamela Eadie, Principal
Hector Saroza, President

2194 Fajardo Academy
55 Calle Federico Garcia
PO Box 1146, Fajardo 00648
Puerto Rico
809-863-1001
http://fajardoacademy.org
Miguel A Rivera, BA, MA, MEd, Principal

2195 Freewill Baptist School
PO Box 6265
Christiansted 00823-6265
Virgin Islands
http://www.freewillschool.com
Joe Postlewaite, Principal

2196 French-American International School
150 Oak Street
San Francisco, CA 94102
415-558-2000
Fax: 415-558-2024
E-mail: fais@fais-ihs.org
http://www.fais-ihs.org
Grade levels preK-12, with total student enrollment of 813.
Jane Camblin, Head of School

2197 George D Robinson School
5 Nairn Condado
Santurce 00907
Puerto Rico
845-344-2292
http://www.orangeahrc.org
Daniel W Sheehan, Principal

2198 Georgetown American School
3170 Georgetown Place
Washington, DC 20521-3170
592-225-1595
Fax: 592-226-1459
E-mail: admin@amschoolguyana.net
http://www.geocities.com/Athens/Atlantis/6811
Thurston Riehl, Director

2199 Georgia QSI International School-Tbilisi
Village Zurgovani
Tbilisi
Republic of Georgia
995-32-982909
Fax: 995-32-322-607
E-mail: tbilisi@qsi.org
http://www.qsi.org/grg_home
A private non-profit organization, organizes and operates schools of excellence, identifies quality educators for these schools, and provides educational consulting services
Scott D'Alterio, Director
David Pera, Director Instruction

2200 Glynn Christian School
Club 6, Christian Hill
St Croix, Kingshill 00851
Virgin Islands
340-778-1932
http://www.virginislandsdailynews.com
Muriel Francis, Principal

2201 Good Hope School-St. Croix
Estate Good Hope Frederiksted
St Croix 00840
Virgin Islands
340-778-1932
http://www.virginislandsdailynews.com
Tanya L Nichols, Principal

2202 Good Shepherd School
PO Box 1069
St Croix, Kingshill 00851
Virgin Islands 00851
340-772-2280
Fax: 340-772-1021
http://www.virginislandsdailynews.com
Mary Ellen Mcencil, Director
Susan P Eversley, Assistant Director

2203 Grace Baptist Academy
7815 Shallowford Road
Chattanooga, TN 37421

423-892-8223
Fax: 423-892-1194
E-mail: jmccurdy@gracechatt.org
http://www.gracechatt.org
Helen Yasper, Principal

2204 Guam Adventist Academy
1200 Aguilar Road
Yoa
Guam 96915
617-789-1515
Fax: 617-789-3547
E-mail: Office@GAAsda.org
http://www.gaasda.org
Learn about God and His character through Bible study, aided by the study of nature and E.G. White's writings. Develop a personal friendship with Jesus Christ
John N Youngberg, Principal
Dori Talon, Accountant

2205 Guam Department of Education
PSC 455 Box 192
FPO, Mariana Islands 96540 1192
Guam 96915-1054
011-671-475-0457
Fax: 011-671-472-5003
http://www.gdoe.net
Develop a personal friendship with Jesus Christ
Rosie R Tainatongo, Director

2206 Guam High School
PSC 455 Box 192
FPO, Mariana Islands 96540 1192
Guam 96915-1054
671-475-0462
Fax: 671-472-5003
http://www.gdoe.net
Rosie R Tainatongo, Director

2207 Guam S Elementary & Middle School
PSC 455 Box 192
FPO, Mariana Islands 96540 1192
Guam 96915-1054
671-475-0462
Fax: 671-472-5003
http://www.gdoe.net
Rosie R Tainatongo, Director

2208 Guamani School
PO Box 3000
Guayama
Puerto Rico 00785
787-864-6880
Fax: 787-866-4947
E-mail: edelgado@guamani.com
http://www.guamani.com
A private non-profit, co-educational, non-sectarian school committed in offering an English-based academic college preparatory program geared in preparing students to become knowledgeable and responsible individuals for today's changing society.
Eduardo Delgado, Director
Pedro A Dominguez, Administrator

2209 Harvest Christian Academy
PO Box 23189
Barrigada
Guam 96921
671-477-6341
Fax: 671-477-7136
http://www.harvestministries.net
Harvest Christian Academy is a K-12th grade school. It is a ministry of Harvest Baptist Church.
John McGraw, Principal

2210 Hogar Colegio La Milagrosa
Ave Cotto 987 Barrio Cotto
Arecibo 00612
Puerto Rico 00612
787-878-0341
http://www.hogarcolegiolamilagrosa.com
Sor Trinidad Ibizarry, Principal

2211 India American Embassy School-New Delhi
Chandragupta Marg Chanakyapuri
New Delhi
India 11002
91-11-611-7140
Fax: 91-11-687-3320
E-mail: aesindia@aes.ac.in
http://aes.ac.in
The American Embassy School serves students from the United States and other nations. It provides a quality American education that enables students to be inspired learners and responsible global citizens through the collaboration of a dedicated faculty and a supportive community.
Bob Hetzel, Director

2212 India American International School-Bombay
6240 Mumbai Place
Dulles, VA 20189
91-22-652-1837
Fax: 91-22-652-1838
E-mail: personnel@asbindia.org
http://www.asbindia.org
We inspire all of our students to continuous inquiry, empowering them with the skills, courage, optimism, and integrity to pursue their dreams and enhance the lives of others.
Paul M Fochtman, Superintendent
Julie A Cox, Elementary School Principal

2213 Inter-American Academy
Suite 8227
6964 NW 50th Street
Miami, FL 33166-5632
593-4-871-790
Fax: 593-4-873-358
E-mail: bgoforth@acig.k12.ec
http://www.acig.k12.ec
Dr. Bruce Goforth, Executive Director

2214 International Community School-Abidjan
DOS/Administrative Officer
2010 Abidjan Place
Washington, DC 20521-2010
225-22-47-11-52
Fax: 225-22-47-19-96
E-mail: rmockrish@icsa.ac.ci
http://www.icsa.ac.ci
American style curriculum from kindergarten through grade 12 for children of all nationalities.
Rob Mockrish, Director

2215 International High School-Yangon
4250 Rangoon Place
Department of State
Washington, DC 20521-4250
95-1-512-793
Fax: 95-1-525-020
E-mail: isydirector@mptmail.net.mm
http://www.internationalschoolyangon.org
Merry Wade, Director

2216 International School of Port-of-Spain
#POS 1369 1601 NW 97th Avenue
PO Box 025307
Miami, FL 33102-5307
868-632-4591
Fax: 868-632-4595
E-mail: elarson@isps.edu.tt
http://www.isps.edu.tt
ISPS will provide an outstanding educational programme for both international and resident

families who want their children to pursue higher education.

Eric Larson, Director
John Horsfall, High School Principal

2217 International School-Conakry

2110 Conakry Place
Washington, DC 20521-2110
224-12-661-535
Fax: 224-41-15-22
E-mail: isc@biasy.net
http://www.iscguinea.org
A private, coeducational school offering an educational program from pre-kindergarten through grade 12 for children from expatriate and host country families. Develop pupils' academic knowledge; learning, thinking, social, and communication skills; international attitudes; and appreciation for cultural diversity.

Greg Hughes, Director
Robert Merritt, Management Officer

2218 International School-Dakar

BP 5136
Dakar
Senegal
221-033- 250
Fax: 221-033- 250
E-mail: admin_isd@orange.sn
http://www.isd.sn
An independent English-medium international school, which offers, in a nurturing environment, a rigorous, US-based, PK-12 curriculum enriched to reflect the needs and diversity of its international student body and faculty.

Wayne Rutherford, Director

2219 International School-Grenada

Washington, DC 20521-1
http://www.international-schoolfriends.com

Mary Delaney Dunn, Principal

2220 International School-Havana

Department of State
18 Street, 315 and 5th Avenue
Miramar, Havana City
Cuba 10600
053- 02- 281
Fax: 530-020-2740
E-mail: office@ish.co.cu
http://www.ishav.org
The school offer high quality education to the children of the expatriate community in Cuba. Serves and can admit students who have a foreign (non-Cuban) citizenship, and are temporarily living in Cuba with their parent(s) or guardian(s), and as such form part of the diplomatic or expatriate non-diplomatic community in the country.

Ian Morris, Principal
Richard Fluit, Head, Secondary School

2221 International School-Islamabad

H-9/1, PO Box 1124
Islamabad
Pakistan 44000
92-51-434-950
Fax: 92-51-440-193
E-mail: school@isoi.edu.pk
http://www.isoi.edu.pk
Offers an American- based curriculum to students of over 29 nationalities.

Rose C Puffer, Superintendent

2222 International School-Ouagadougou

s/c Ambassade des, Etats Unis
01 BP35, Ouagadougou
Burkina Faso
226-36-21-43
Fax: 226-36-22-28
E-mail: iso@iso.bf
http://www.iso.bf

ISO strives to cultivate a student's intellect and character in an English-speaking environment, offering strong academic programs and promoting cultural understanding.

Larry Ethier, Director
Kim Overton, Curriculum Coordinator

2223 International School-Port of Spain

1601 NW 97th Avenue
PO Box 025307
Miami, FL 33102-5307
868-633-4777
Fax: 868-632-4595
E-mail: elarson@isps.edu.tt
http://www.isps.edu.tt
Provides a college preparatory, holistic education for children in grades pre-kindergarten through grade 12, providing them with the skills, knowledge, and values necessary to be productive individuals in an interdependent world.

Eric Larson, Director
Jackie Fung-Kee-Fung, Admission Director/PR

2224 International School-Sfax

Brit Gas 1100 Louisiana
Houston, TX 77002

Sidney Norris, Principal

2225 International School-Yangon

20 Shwe Taungyar
Bahan Township, Yangon
Myanmar-1
512-93 -
Fax: 95 - 52-020
E-mail: director@isy.net.mm
http://www.isy.net.mm
We inspire students with a challenging, international education, based on an American curriculum, in a nurturing learning environment that promotes responbility and respect. We aim to develop socially engaged, self-motivated, creative, compassionate individuals who will be a force for positive change in their communities and the world.

DJ Condon, Middle/High School Principal
Dennis MacKinnon, Director

2226 Izmir American Institute

Friends-850 Third Avenue
18th Floor
New York, NY 10022
232-355-0555
http://www.aci.k12.tr

Richard Curtis, Principal

2227 John F Kennedy School-Queretaro

Sabinos #272, Jurica
Queretaro
Mexico 76100
442-218-0075
Fax: 442-218-1784
E-mail: admissions@jfk.edu.mx
http://www.jfk.edu.mx
The American School of Queretaro, is to provide the whole individual an opportunity for high quality U.S. type, bilingual education that recognizes individual talents and encourages lifelong learning

Dr. Francisco Galicia, Principal
Mirtha Stappung, General Director

2228 Jordan American Community School

PO Box 310, Dahiat Al-Amir Rashid
Amman 11831
Jordan
962-6-581-3944
Fax: 962-6-582-3357
E-mail: school@acsamman.edu.jo
http://www.acsamman.edu.jo

ACS is fully accredited K-12 by the Middle States Association of Colleges and Schools and is a member in good standing of NESA, the Near East South Asia Association of Overseas Schools

Dr. Gray Duckett, Superintendent

2229 Karachi American Society School

American Consulate General Karachi
610 Karachi Place
Washington, DC 20521-6150
92-21-453-909619
Fax: 92-21-453-7305
http://www.kas.edu.pk

David Holmer, Principal

2230 Kongeus Grade School

44-46 Gade
St Thomas 00802
Virgin Islands 00802

Veronica Miller, Principal

2231 Lincoln International School-Kampala

Co of State
Washington, DC 20521-1

Margaret Bell, Principal

2232 Lincoln School

Lincoln School 565-20
PO Box 025331
Miami, FL 33102-5331
506-224- 660
Fax: 506-224- 670
E-mail: director@ns.lincoln.ed.cr
http://www.lincoln.ed.cr
offer an integrated education, using English as the primary language of instruction, to motivate a continuing search for excellence and stimulate students to fully develop their potential to become responsible, enterprising, creative, open-minded citizens with solid ethical values, committed to democracy, and capable of being successful in a multicultural, global society.

Charles Prince, Principal

2233 Lincoln-Marti Schools

2700 SW 8 Street
Miami, FL 33135
305-643-4888
877-874-1999
Fax: 305-649-2767
E-mail: info@lincoln-marti.com
http://www.lincolnmarti.com
Lincoln-Mart is an institution dedicated to educating the future of our community, both academically and socially.

Demitrio Perez, President

2234 Little People's Learning Center

9605 SE 7th Street
Vancouver, WA 98664
360-892-7570
E-mail: info@lplc.net
http://www.lplc.net/home.html

Daphne Maynard, Principal
Becky Dolan, Director

2235 Little School House

47 Kongens Gade
St Thomas 00802
Virgin Islands
416-303-7282
http://www.littleschoolhouse.ca

Carol Struiell, Principal

2236 Luanda International School

Rua da Talatona Caixa 1566
Barrio da Talatona Luanda Sul Samba
Republica de Angola
244-2-44-3416
Fax: 244-2-44-3416

E-mail: officesec@lisluanda.com
http://www.lisluanda.com
offers a balanced, academically challenging, English language education to the international community of Luanda, designed to develop individuals who are both independent learners and international citizens.

Anthony Baron, Director
Di Atkinson, Senior Administrator

2237 Lutheran Parish School

#1 Lille Taarne Gade
Charlotte Aml 00802
Puerto Rico 00802

Nancy Gotwalt, Principal

2238 Manor School

236 La Grande Princesse
Christiansted, VI 00820-4449
340-718-1448
Fax: 340-718-3651
E-mail: jgadd@manorschoolstx.com
http://www.manorschoolstx.com
is dedicated to personal and academic growth in an extended-family environment. We promote academic confidence, creativity, community involvement and citizenship, a sense of respon-sibility, and positive decision- making. We strive to ensure that our graduates are person-ally and academically prepared to succeed in their future endeavors.

Judith C Gadd, Headmistress
Hanley Hamed, Office Manager

2239 Maranatha Christian Academy

9201 75th Avenue N
Brooklyn Park, MN 55428
612- 58- 285
Fax: 763-315-7294
E-mail: info@mca.lwcc.org
http://www.maranathachristianacademy.org
is to offer a pre-kindergarten through 12th grade traditional classroom education providing a quality educational experience, which encourages and enables students to mature spiritually, intellectually, physically, emotionally, and socially in accordanc

Rev. Gary Sprunger, Principal
Brian Sullivan, Chief Administrator

2240 Martin De Porress Academy

621 Elmont Road
Elmont, NY 11003
516-502-2840
Fax: 516-502-2841
E-mail: sfagin@mdp.org
http://www.mdp.org/
The Martin De Porress Academy program provides academic instruction based upon the NY State Learning Standards as well as hands on experiences in business enterprises, performing arts, home improvement skills, life skills, culinary arts, maintenance services and community services.

Raymond R Blixt, Executive Director
Philip E Chance, Assistant Executive Director

2241 Montessori House of Children

572 Dunholme Way
Suite 103
Sunnyvale, CA 94086
408-749-1602
http://www.sunnyvalemontessori.com
Our program is based on the premise that every child is an individual with his own needs and abilities. All children need affec-tion and friendliness. They require affirmation, encouragement and understanding

William Myers, Principal
Priya Medelberg, Founder-Director

2242 Moravian School

4313 Green Pond Road
Bethlehem
Virgin Islands
610-868-4744
http://www.moravianacademy.org
This Moravian affiliated school offers a curriculum based in English for 200 day students (96 boys; 104 girls), in grades K-6. The school is willing to participate in a teacher exchange program, with the length of stay being one year, with housing provided. Applications include science, Spanish and computer skills.

Condon L Joseph, Principal

2243 Morrocoy International

MUN 4051
PO Box 025352
Miami, FL 33102-5352
58-286-9520016
Fax: 58-286-9521861
E-mail: kempenich@telcel.net.ve
http://www.geocities.com/minaspov
Grade levels Pre-K through 10, school year August - June

Michael Kempenich, Headmaster

2244 Mount Carmel Elementary School

PO Box 7830
Agat 96928 0830
Guam-b830
256-852-7187
Fax: 256-852-0039
http://www.vrml.k12.la.us/mc
This Catholic school offers an English (primary) curriculum for 206 day students (100 boys; 106 girls), in Kinder 4 - 8th grade. Overseas teachers are accepted, with the length of stay being one year. Applications needed to teach include reading, English and counseling/counselor.

Bernadette Quintanilla, Sr, SSND, Principal
Augustin Gumataotao, Administrator

2245 Nazarene Christian School

385 Hazel Mill Road
Asheville, NC 28806
828-252-9713
E-mail: ncsoffice@ashevillefirstnazarene.org
http://www.ashevillefirstnazarene.org
The Nazarene International Center provides support services to more than 1.2 million members worshiping in more than 11,800 churches in the United States, Canada, and 135 other world areas

Peggy Neighbors, Administrator

2246 Nepal Lincoln School

Kathmandu (LS)
Department of State
Washington, DC 20521-6190
977-1-270-482
Fax: 977-1-272-685
E-mail: info@lsnepal.com.np
http://www.lsnepal.com
Lincoln School is an independent, international school in Kathmandu, Nepal with an American Curriculum. We are committed to nurture the individual student, excellence in all spheres of achievement, pursuit of personal responsibility, appreciation of diversity, and love of learning

Allan Bredy, Director
Craig Baker, Principal

2247 Northern Mariana Islands Department of Education

PO Box 501370 CK
Siapan, MP 96950
011-670-664-3720
Fax: 011-670-664-3798
http://www.cnmipss.org

Rita Hocog Inos, Commissioner

2248 Notre Dame High School

480 S San Miguel Street
Talofofo
Guam 96930-4699
671-789-1676
http://www.ndhs.org
Notre Dame is a co-educational, year-round high school run by the School Sisters of Notre Dame. This Roman Catholic affiliated school offers a curriculum in English for 191 day students and 9 boarding (32 boys; 168 girls), in grades 9-12. Student/teacher ratio is 10:1, and the applications needed to teach include science, math, social sciences, and English.

Regina Paulino, SSND, Principal

2249 Nuestra Senora de La Altagracia

672 Calle Felipe Gutierrez #672
San Juan 00924-2225
Puerto Rico

2250 Nuestra Senora de La Providencia

PO Box 11610
San Juan 00922-1610
Puerto Rico

2251 Okinawa Christian School

1835 Zakimi
Yomitan, Okinawa
Japan 904-0
098-958-3000
Fax: 098-958-6279
E-mail: info@ocsi.org
http://www.ocsi.org
A non-denominational mission whose purpose is to partner with families of the international community of Okinawa by offering an excellent Christian education in the English language.

Paul Gieschen, Principal

2252 Open Classroom

PO Box 4046
St Thomas 00803
Virgin Islands 00803
805-904-5931
805-289-1817
Fax: 852- 54- 133
http://www.openclassroom.stanford.edu

Janie Lang, Principal

2253 Osaka International School

4-16 Onohar Nishi 4-Chome
Mino, Osaki, 562-0032
Japan
072-727-5050
Fax: 072-727-5055
E-mail: addmissions@senri.ed.jp
http://www.senri.ed.jp
OIS is an english-language-based, preK-12 grade coeducational college-preparatory school.

John Searle, Head of School

2254 Palache Bilingual School

PO Box 1832
Arecibo 00613-1832
Puerto Rico

Rev. David Valez, Principal

2255 Peace Corp

1111 20th Street NW
Washington, DC 20526
202-692-1470
800-424-8580
Fax: 202-692-1897

E-mail: psa@peacecorps.gov
http://www.peacecorps.gov
Helping the people of interested countries in meeting their need for trained men and women. Helping promote a better understanding of Americans on the part of the peoples served

2256 Pine Peace School
PO Box 1657
St John, VI 00831
340-776-6595
E-mail: pinepeace@viaccess.net
http://www.pinepeaceschool.k12.vi
An independent, non-profit, English language school that serves students without regard to sex, race, religion, or nationality.

Beth Knight, Headmistress

2257 Ponce Baptist Academy
72 Calle 1 Belgica
Ponce 00731
Puerto Rico

Vivian Medina, Principal

2258 Prophecy Elementary School
PO Box 10497
APO St Thomas 00801-3497
Virgin Islands 00801
340-775-7223
Fax: 340-714-5354
E-mail: pai@prophecyacademy.org
http://www.prophecyacademy.net
Church of God of Prophecy Academy, Inc. offers a Christian atmosphere which develops the physical, spiritual, intellectual and the social skills of every student. Our primary purpose is to help train students while teaching them the Christian way of life.

Anne E Bramble-Johnson, Principal
VeronaCeleste Hutchinson,
Secretary/Office Manager

2259 Puerto Rico Department of Education
PO Box 190759
San Juan
Puerto Rico 00919-759
787-759-2000
http://www.de.gobierno.pr

Cesar A Rey-Hernandez, Secretary

2260 QSI International School-Chisinau
18 Anton Crihan Street
Chisinau
Moldova 20521-7080
373-24-2366
E-mail: chisinau@qsi.org
http://www.qsi.org
To keep this urge to learn alive in every child in QSI schools. Our schools are established to provide in the English language a quality education for students in the cities we serve.

Sandra Smith, Director

2261 QSI International School-Skopje
Inlindenska BB, Reon 55
1000 Skopie
Macedonia 20521-7120
389-91-367-678
Fax: 389-91-362-250
E-mail: skopje@qsi.org
http://www.qsi.org
To keep this urge to learn alive in every child in QSI schools. Our schools are established to provide in the English language a quality education for students in the cities we serve.

Robert Tower, Director
Aleksandar Kostadinovski, Finance Manager

2262 QSI International School-Vladivostok
DOS/Administrative Officer
5880 Vladivostok Place
Washington, DC 20521-5880
7-4232-321-292
Fax: 7-4232-313-684
E-mail: qsiisv@fastmail.vladivostok.ru
http://www.qsi.org
Grades preK-9, enrollment 18.

Harold M Strom Jr, Director

2263 Rainbow Development Center
PO Box 7618
Christiansted 00823-7618
Virgin Islands
408-215-1386
http://www.rainbowccc.com

Gloria Henry, Principal

2264 Rainbow Learning Institute
PO Box 75
Christiansted 00821-0075
Virgin Islands
408-215-1386
http://www.rainbowccc.com

Alda Lockhart, Principal

2265 Rainbow School
PO Box 422
Charlotte Aml 00801
Virgin Islands
408-215-1386
http://www.rainbowccc.com

Louise Thomas, Principal

2266 Robinson School
5 Nairn Street Condado
San Juan 00907
Puerto Rico 00907
1-787-728-6767
Fax: 1-787-727-7736
E-mail: robinson_school@hotmail.com
http://www.robinsonschool.org
The Heart of Educational Excellence. Robinson offers its students a solid foundation for their future academic and career pursuits.

Giberto Quintana, Executive Director
Hugh Andrews, President

2267 Roosevelt Roads Elementary School
PO Box 420132
Roosevelt Roads 00742-0132
Puerto Rico
787-865-3073
Fax: 787-865-4891
http://www.netdial.caribe.net

2268 Roosevelt Roads Middle & High School
PO Box 420131
Roosevelt Roads 00742-0131
Puerto Rico
787-865-4000
Fax: 787-865-4893
E-mail: wjames@caribe.net
http://www.antilles.odedodea.edu

Waynna James, Principal

2269 Saint Anthony School
529 Chalan San Antonio
Tamuning
Guam 96913
671-647-1140
Fax: 471-649-7130
http://stanthonyschoolguam.org/index.php
A Catholic co-educational elementary school in the Archdiocese of Agana, exists to educate the whole person by providing a rich integrated curriculum served by enabling adults.

Doris San Agustin, Principal
Elizabeth E San Nicolas, Vice-Principal

2270 Saint Eheresas Elementary School
2701 Indian Mound Trail
Coral Gables
American Samoa, F
305-446-1738
Fax: 305-446-2877
http://www.cotlf.org

Sister Katherine, Principal

2271 Saint Francis Elementary School
2701 Indian Mound Trail
Coral Gables
American Samoa, F
305-446-1738
Fax: 305-446-2877
http://www.cotlf.org

Sister Gaynor Ana, Principal

2272 Saint John's School
911 N Marine Corps Drive
Tumon Bay 96913
Guam
671-646-8080
Fax: 617-649-6791
E-mail: info@stjohns.edu.gu
http://www.stjohns.edu.gu
St. John's students on average score in the top 20% on national scholastic achievement tests in all academic subjects in all grades K-12, a tangible result of an integrated academic program supported by a dedicated faculty, many with advanced degrees in their respective areas of instruction

Glenn Chapin, Headmaster
Imelda D Santos, Dean of Students

2273 Saint John's School, Puerto Rico
1454-66 Ashford Avenue
San Juan 00907
Puerto Rico
787-728-5343
Fax: 787-268-1454
http://www.sjspr.org/home.aspx
Saint John's School is a college preparatory, nonsectarian, coeducational day school founded in 1915. The school, located in a residential area of the Condado, has an enrollment of approximately 750 students from preschool to grade twelve. 84% come from Hispanic backgrounds, 8% percent from diverse backgrounds and 8% from the continental United States. With the exception of Spanish and French classes, instruction is in English.

Louis R Christiansen, Principal
Barry Farnham, Headmaster

2274 Saints Peter & Paul High School
900 High Street
Easton, MD
410-822-2275
Fax: 410-822-1767
E-mail: jnemeth@ssppeaston.org
http://www.ssppeaston.org/schools/high_school
Saints Peter and Paul High School is a parochial, Catholic, college preparatory,

James Nemeth, Principal
Carolyn Hayman, Administrative Assistant

2275 Samoa Baptist Academy
Tafuna
Pago Pago 96799
American Samoa

Janice Yerton, Principal

2276 San Carlos & Bishop McManus High School
PO Box Loo 9, Yumet
Aguadilla 00605
Puerto Rico

504-246-5121
E-mail: questions@bishopmcmanus.ws
http://www.bishopmcmanus.ws
Nydia U Nieves, Principal

2277 San Vincente Elementary School
San Vincente School Drive
Soledad
Puerto Rico 96913
671-734-4242
http://www.soledad.monterey.k12.ca
This campus is on five acres of outside
Barrigada Village. The average enrollment
of 460 students consists of 234 boys and
226 girls in grades PreK-8. SVS holds a
Certificate of Accreditation from the Western Association of Schools and Colleges
until 1998. Length of stay for overseas
teachers is two years, with housing provided. Applications needed to teach include English and physical education.
Adrian Cristobal, Principal
Tarcisia Sablan SSND, Faculty Head

2278 Santa Barbara School
274A W Santa Barbara Avenue
Dededo
Guam 96929
671-632-5578
Fax: 671-632-1414
http://www.santabarbaraschool.org
To ensure that each student is given the opportunity to realize his or her full potential
according to God's design by recognizing
and affirming the gifts of each child.
Sr Jeanette Mar Pangelinan, Principal
Sr Maria Rosari Gaite, Vice Principal

2279 Santiago Christian School
PO Box 5600
Santiago
Dominican Republic, FL 33310-5600
809-570-6140
http://www.santiagochristianschool.org
Lloyd Haglund, Principal

2280 School of the Good Shepherd
1069 Kinghill
St Croix 00851
Virgin Islands 00851
http://www.goodshepherdtvm.org
Linda Navarro, Principal

2281 Seventh Day Adventist
PO Box 7909
St Thomas 00801-0909
Virgin Islands
Josiah Maynard, Principal

2282 Shekou International School
Jing Shan Villas, Nan Hai Road Shek
Guangdong Province
China 51806
86-755-2669-3669
Fax: 86-755-2667-4099
E-mail: sis@sis.org.cn
http://www.sis.org.cn
Shekou International School follows a rig-
orous college preparatory US style curricu-
lum and is dedicated to meeting the
outcomes of the Expected Student
Learning Results.
Robert Dunseth, Director
Jennifer Lees, Curriculum Coordinator

**2283 Slovak Republic QSI International
School of Bratislava**
Karloveska 64
Bratislava
Slovak Republic 84220
421-2-6541-1636
Fax: 421-2-6541-1646

E-mail: bratislava@qsi.org
http://www.qsi.sk
THE PRIMARY PURPOSE of the school is
to meet the needs of the children in
Bratislava who require this type of education with a view to continuing their education in their home countries with a
minimum of adjustment problems.
Ronald Adams, Principal
Matthew Lake, Director

**2284 Slovenia QSI International
School-Ljubljana**
Dolgi Most 6A
Ljubljana
Slovenia 01000
386-1-439-6300
Fax: 386-1-439-6305
E-mail: bratislava@qsi.org
http://www.qsi.org/sln_home
THE PRIMARY PURPOSE of the school is
to meet the needs of the children in
Ljubljana who require this type of educa-
tion with a view to continuing their educa-
tion in their home countries with a
minimum of adjustment problems.
Ronald Adams, Principal
Matthew Lake, Director

2285 South Pacific Academy
PO Box 520
Pago Pago 96799 0520
American Samoa
644-237-4072
http://www.spa.ac.nz
Tina Senrud, Principal

2286 Southern Peru Staff Schools-Peru
180 Maiden Lane
New York, NY 10038-4925
http://www.isbi.com
John Dansdill, Principal

2287 St. Croix Christian Academy
26-28 Golden Rock, Christiansted, S
PO Box 716
Virgin Islands, US 00821
340-718-4974
Fax: 340-718-6768
E-mail: stccacademy@vipowernet.net
http://www.stcroixchristianacademy.com
The mission of the school is to foster
knowledge of God and to give the children
a solid academic foundation, along with effective Christian training.
Linus Gittens, Principal

2288 St. Croix Country Day School
Rt-01, Box 6199
Kingshill
Virgin Islands, US 00850
1-340-778-1974
Fax: 1-340-779-3331
E-mail: bsinfield@stxcountryday.com
http://www.stxcountryday.com
It is dedicated to providing students with
an enriched and challenging education, en-
couraging them to love learning, grow as
individuals and be prepared for a produc-
tive and responsible future.
Bill Sinfield, Headmaster
Susan Gibbons, Business Manager

2289 St. Croix Moravian School
PO Box 117
St Thomas 00801
Virgin Islands
http://www.aavirginislands.org
Condon L Joseph, Principal

2290 St. Croix SDA School
PO Box 930
Kingshill 00851-0930
Virgin Islands
http://www.stcroixsdaschool.org
Peter Archer, Principal

2291 St. Joseph High School
PO Box 517
Frederiksted 00841-0517
Virgin Islands
Kevin Marin, Principal

2292 St. Patrick School
PO Box 988
Frderiksted 00841-0988
Virgin Islands
http://www.spsasansol.com
Juliette Clarke, Principal

2293 St. Peter & Paul Elementary School
PO Box 1706
St Thomas 00803
Virgin Islands
http://www.sppschool.org
Annamay Komment, Principal

2294 Sunbeam
36 Hospital Ground
St Thomas 00803
Virgin Islands
202-427-2383
Fax: 202-426-0308
http://www.sunbeaminfo.com
Ione Leonard, Principal

2295 Syria Damascus Community School
6110 Damascus Place
Dulles, VA 20189-6110
963-11-333-0331
Fax: 963-11-332-1457
E-mail: dcs-dam@net.sy
http://www.dcssyria.com
An independent, coeducational day school which
offers an American educational program from
preschool through grade 12 for students of all nationalities.
John Gates, Director
Maura Connelly, Chairman

2296 Tashkent International School
7117 Tashkent Place
Dulles, VA 20189-7110
998-71-191-9671
Fax: 998-71-120-6621
E-mail: office@tashschool.org
http://www.tashschool.org
To provide a high academic standard of education,
educating students to become ethical, responsible, productive citizens of the world with the
skills to think creatively, reason critically, and to
communicate effectively
John Thomas, Director

2297 Teaching in Austria
Austrian Institute
11 E 52nd Street
New York, NY 10022-5301
212-579-5165

2298 Temple Christian School
PO Box 3009
Agana 96910
Guam 96910
Rev. Ray Fagan, Principal

2299 Tirana International School-Albania
Kutia Postare
Tirana
Albania, DC 01527-9510
355-4-365-239
Fax: 335-4-227-734

E-mail: tirana@qsi.org
http://www.qsi.org
The school's educational philosophy, which includes a personalized approach to instruction, leads to teaching for mastery.

Ronald Adams, Principal
Matthew Lake, Director

2300 Trinity Christian School
1231 East Pleasant Run Road
Yiga 96929 0343
Cedar Hill, TX 75104
972-291-2505
Fax: 972-291-4739
http://www.trinitychristianschool.com
Being a Christian school means we assist parents in fulfilling their divine responsibility to thoroughly train each child to obey God in every area of life and make him or her a true disciple of Jesus Christ. Our program is designed to challenge and educate students of good moral character who are in the middle to upper range of academic ability

Kathleen L Watts, Superintendent
Rhonda Parker, Executive Assistant

2301 Turkmenistan Ashgabat International School
Box 2002
7070 Ashgabat Place
Washington, DC 20521-7070
967-1-234-437
Fax: 967-1-234-438
E-mail: director@ais.cat.glasnet.ru
Grades K-11, enrollment 75.

Scott Root, Director

2302 Ukraine Kiev International School-An American Institution
EOS/Administrative Officer
5850 Kiev Place
Washington, DC 20521-5850
380-44-452-2792
Fax: 380-44-452-2998
E-mail: kisukr@sovamua.com
http://www.kis.net.ua
An independent, coeducational day school which offers an educational program from prekindergarten through high school for students of all nationalities.

E Michael Tewalthomas, Director

2303 United Nations International School
24-50 FDR Drive
New York, NY 10010-4046
212-684-7400
Fax: 212-685-5023
E-mail: admissions@unis.org
http://www.unis.org
The United Nations International School provides an international education that emphasizes academic excellence within a caring community for kindergarten through twelfth grade students from families of the United Nations, as well as from other families seeking a similar education for their children

Kenneth Wrye, EdD, Executive Director
Satya Nandan, Chairperson

2304 University del Sagrado Corazon
PO Box 12383
San Juan
Puerto Rico 00914-383
787-728-1515
http://www.sagrado.edu

2305 Uruguayan American School
Av Saldn de Rodriguez
Montevideo
Uruguay, DC 11500-3360
598-2-600-7681
Fax: 598-2-600-1935
E-mail: info@uas.edu.uyuy
http://www.uas.edu.uy

Uruguayan American School is to provide, together with the family, a balanced college preparatory education. UAS integrates a US style curriculum with Uruguayan studies to equip our national and international students to be successful in a diverse, ever changing world

Thomas Oden, Director
Cecilia Burgueo, UP Coordinator

2306 Uruguayan American School-Montevideo
Av Saldn de Rodriguez
Montevideo
Uruguay, DC 11500-3360
598-2-600-7681
Fax: 598-2-606-1935
E-mail: info@uas.edu.uyuy
http://www.uas.edu.uy
Uruguayan American School is to provide, together with the family, a balanced college preparatory education. UAS integrates a US style curriculum with Uruguayan studies to equip our national and international students to be successful in a diverse, ever changing world

Thomas Oden, Director
Cecilia Burgueo, UP Coordinator

2307 Uzbekistan Tashkent International School
38 Sarikul Street
Tashkent, Uzbekistan 10000
998-71-191-9671
Fax: 998-71-120-6621
E-mail: office@tashschool.org
http://www.tashschool.org
Tashkent International School (TIS), an IB World School, is a private, not for profit, independent, co-educational day school governed by a Board of Directors elected and appointed from the parent community. TIS offers an American based international curriculum from Kindergarten - grade 12. TIS is an IB World School offering: the full International Baccalaureate Diploma in grades 11 - 12, the Primary Years Program for Kindergarten - grade 5, and is a candidate school for the Middle Years Program

Kevin Glass, Director
John Zohrab, Treasurer

2308 Venezuela Colegio Internacional-Carabobo
PO Box 025685
Miami, FL 33102-5685
58-41-426-551
Fax: 58-41-426-510
E-mail: admin@cic-valencia.org.ve
http://www.cic-valencia.org.ve
Colegio Internacional de Carabobo (CIC) is a school dedicated to the development of the whole child. Our teachers are innovative, skilled, and dedicated. Creativity and self-esteem are essential qualities for students to develop as they ascend the academic ladder.

Frank Anderson, Superintendent
Joe Walker, Director

2309 Venezuela Escuela Campo Alegre
8424 NW 56th Street
Suite CCS 00007
Miami, FL 33166
58-2-993-7135
Fax: 58-2-993-0219
E-mail: info@eca.com.ve
http://www.eca.com.ve
Escuela Campo Alegre is a private non-profit English language school, designed primarily to serve the needs of the children from ages 3-18 of its shareholding members.

Jean K Vahey, Superintendent

2310 Venezuela International School-Caracas
Pakmail 6030
PO Box 025304
Miami, FL 33102-5304
58-2-945-0422
Fax: 58-2-945-0533
E-mail: cic@cic-caracas.org
http://www.cic-caracus.org
Colegio Internacional de Caracas is an English-medium, Pre-Nursery to Grade 12 school dedicated to the intellectual and personal development of each student in a caring and supportive environment.

Alan Benson, Superintendent

2311 Virgin Island Montessori School
6936 Vessup Lane
Saint Thomas, VI 00802
340-775-6360
Fax: 340-775-3080
E-mail: info@vimontessori.com
http://www.vimontessori.com/
Virgin Islands Montessori School and International Academy offers a unique environment and learning experience to over 200 students from two years of age through High School

Shournagh Mcweeney, Administrator
Michael Bornn, President

2312 Virgin Islands Department of Education
44-46 Kongens Gade
Saint Thomas, Virgin Islands 00802
340-774-2810
Fax: 340-774-7153
http://www.doe.vi/
The mission of the Department of Education is to provide the Territory's students with an education that makes them competitive with their peers in the rest of the Caribbean,the United States, and the World; take advantage of our uniqueness of being geographically Caribbean and politically American; integrate all discipline; and educate the whole child.

LaVerne Terry, Commissioner
Donna Frett-Gregory, Assistant Commissioner

2313 Washington International School
3100 Macomb Street NW
Washington, DC 20008-3324
202-243-1800
Fax: 202-243-1802
E-mail: admissions@wis.edu
http://www.wis.edu
Washington International School (WIS) is a coeducational day school offering 890 students a challenging curriculum and rich language program from Pre-Kindergarten through Grade 12

Clayton W. Lewis, Head of School
Sandra Bourne, Middle School Principal

2314 We Care Child Development Center
PO Box 818
Christiansted 00821-0818
Virgin Islands
http://www.utexas.edu

Pauline Canton, Principal

2315 Wesleyan Academy
PO Box 1489
Guaynabo
Puerto Rico 00970-1489
787-008-
Fax: 787-790-0730
http://www.wesleyanacademy.org
We are a nonprofit, private, coeducational, English Christian school providing a Pre-Pre

Kinder through Twelfth grade college preparatory education.

Jack Mann, Principal

2316 Yakistan International School-Karachi

DOS/Administrative Officer
6150 Karachi Place
Washington, DC 20521-6150
92-21-453-9096
Fax: 92-21-454-7305
E-mail: ameschl@cyber.net.pk
http://www.isk.edu.pk
Grades N-12, enrollment 338.

Glen Shapin, Superintendent

2317 Zion Academy

7629 199th Street SW
Lynnwood, WA 98036
425-640-3311
E-mail: info@zionacademy.com
http://www.zionacademy.com
Zion Academy is a fully accredited private school. Consists of students that wish to work at home and desire complete oversight and administrative services.

Evelyn Williams, Principal
Marigene Lindsey, Founder and Headmaster

International

2318 Center for Strategic & International Studies

1800 K Street NW
Suite 400
Washington, DC 20006-2202
202-887-0200
Fax: 202-775-3199
E-mail: books@csis.org
http://www.csis.org
Provides strategic insights and policy solutions to decisionmakers in government, international institutions, the private sector, and civil society. A bipartisan, nonprofit organization headquartered in Washington, DC, CSIS conducts research and analysis and develops policy initiatives that look into the future and anticipate change.

John J Hamre, President/CEO
Sam Nunn, Cochairman & CEO

2319 Council for International Exchange of Scholars

3007 Tilden Street NW
Suite 5-L
Washington, DC 20008-3009
202-686-4000
Fax: 202-362-3442
E-mail: apprequest@cies.iie.org
http://www.cies.org
Helped administer the Fulbright Scholar Program on behalf of the United States Department of State, Bureau of Educational and Cultural Affairs.

Michael A Brintnall, Executive Director
Judy Pehrson, Director External Relations

2320 Defense Language Institute-English Language Branch

US Civil Service Commission, San Antonio Area
2235 Andrews Avenue
Lackland, TX 78236-5514
210-671-3783
Fax: 210-671-5362
http://www.dlielc.org
The DLIELC is a Department of Defense (DOD) agency responsible for the management and operation of the Defense English Language Program (DELP) to train international military and civilian personnel to speak and teach English, manage the English as a second language program for the US military

2321 Education Information Services which Employ Americans

Education Information Services
PO Box 620662
Newton, MA 02462-662
781-433-0125
Fax: 781-237-2842
http://www.alis.alberta.ca
Devoted to helping Americans who wish to teach in American overseas schools and International Schools in which English is the primary teaching language. Supports those wishing to teach English as a second language. Publish papers covering every country in the world, list of recruiting fairs, internships, volunteers, jobs, summer overseas jobs.

Frederic B Viaux, President

2322 Educational Information Services

PO Box 662
Newtown Lower Falls, MA 02162
617-964-4555
http://www.fulbright.jp
Offers information on employment opportunities including books, periodicals and more for the teaching professional who wishes to teach in American overseas schools, international schools, language (ESL) schools, and Department of Defense Dependencies Schools (DODDS).

Frederick B Viaux, President
Michelle V Curtin, Editor

2323 Educational Placement Sources-US

Education Information Services/Instant Alert
PO Box 620662
Newton, MA 02462-662
617-433-0125
Lists 100 organizations in the United States that find positions for teachers, educational administrators, counselors and other professionals. Listings are classified by type, listed alphabetically and offer all contact information.

4 pages Annual

FB Viaux, President

2324 Educational Staffing Program

International Schools Services
15 Roszel Road
PO Box 5910
Princeton, NJ 08543
609-452-0990
Fax: 609-452-2690
E-mail: edustaffing@iss.edu
http://www.iss.edu/edustaff/edstaffingprog.html
The Educational Staffing Program has placed almost 15,000 K-12 teachers and administrators in overseas schools since 1955. Most candidates obtain their overseas teaching positions by attending our US-based International Recruitment Center where ISS candidates have the potential to interview with overseas school heads seeking new staff. You must be an active ISS candidate to attend an IRC. Applicants must have a bachelor's degree and two years of current relevant experience.

2325 European Council of International Schools

21B Lavant Street
Petersfield, Hampshire GU3 23EL
United Kingdom GU32
44-0-1730-268244
Fax: 44-0-1730-267914
E-mail: ecis@ecis.org
http://www.ecis.org
The European Council of International Schools (ECIS) is a collaborative network promoting the ideals and best practice of international education.

T Michael Maybury, Executive Secretary
Pilar Cabeza de Vaca, CEO

2326 FRS National Teacher Agency

PO Box 298
Seymour, TN 37865-298
865-577-8143
http://www.ffiec.gov
Offers employment options to educators in the United States and abroad.

2327 Foreign Faculty and Administrative Openings

Education Information Services
PO Box 620662
Newton, MA 02462-662
617-433-0125
150 specific openings in administration, counseling, library and other professional positions for American teachers in American schools overseas and in international schools in which teaching language is English.

15 pages Every 6 Weeks

FB Viaux, Coordinating Education

2328 Fulbright Teacher Exchange

600 Maryland Avenue SouthWest
Suite 320
Washington, DC 20024-2520
202-314-3520
800-726-0479
Fax: 202-479-6806
E-mail: fulbright@grad.usda.gov
http://www.fulbrightexchanges.org
An organization that offers opportunities for two-year college faculty and secondary school teachers who would like to exchange with teachers in Eastern or Western Europe, Latin America, Australia, Africa, and Canada. To qualify, teachers must be US citizens, have three years full-time teaching experience and be employed in a full-time academic position.

2329 International Educators Cooperative

212 Alcott Road
East Falmouth, MA 02536-6803
508-540-8173
Fax: 508-540-8173
http://www.icemenlo.com
In addition to year round recruitment, International Educators Cooperative hosts Recruitment Centers in the United States each year.

Dr. Lou Fuccillo, Director

2330 National Association of Teachers' Agencies

National Association of Teachers' Agencies
799 Kings Highway
Fairfield, CT 06432
203-333-0611
Fax: 203-334-7224
E-mail: fairfieldteachers@snet.net
http://www.jobsforteachers.com
Provides placement services for those seeking professional positions at all levels of teaching/administration/support services worldwide.

Mark King, Secretary/Treasurer

2331 National Council of Independent Schools' Associations

112920th Street
PO Box 324
Australia

06-282-3488
Fax: 06-282-2926
http://www.nais.org
Services include career placement.

Fergus Thomson, President

2332 Overseas Employment Opportunities for Educators
Department of Defense, Office of Dependent Schools
2461 Eisenhower Avenue
Alexandria, VA 22331-3000
703-325-0867
This publication tells about teaching jobs in 250 schools operated for children of US military and civilian personnel stationed overseas. Applicants usually must qualify in two subject areas.

2333 Recruiting Fairs for Overseas Teaching
Education Information Services/Instant Alert
PO Box 620662
Newton, MA 02462-662

781-433-0125
Fax: 781-237-2842
Recruiting fairs and sponsors in the US and elsewhere for American educators who wish to teach outside of the United States.

FB Viaux, Coordinating Education

2334 UNI Overseas Recruiting Fair
University of Northern Iowa
102 Gilchrist Hall
Cedar Falls, IA 50614-390
319-273-2083
Fax: 319-273-6998
E-mail: overseas.placement@uni.edu
http://www.uni.edu/placement/overseas
UNI is home to the oldest international recruitment event in the world. The event began in 1976 after the UNI Career Services staff and several school headmasters recognized the need for more efficient and cost-effective recruitment techniques. It became readily apparent that UNI was meeting a need for school recruiters and interested educators all over the globe. In addition to inventing the international recruitment fair, UNI developed

fact sheets, credential files, vacancy listings, referral

February

Brian Atkins, Advisory Board
Susan Barba, Advisory Board

2335 WorldTeach
Center for International Development
79 John F Kennedy Street
Box 122
Cambridge, MA 02138
617-495-5527
800-483-2240
Fax: 617-495-1599
E-mail: info@worldteach.org
http://www.worldteach.org
WorldTeach is a non-profit, non-governmental organization that provides opportunities for individuals to make a meaningful contribution to international education by living and working as volunteer teachers in developing countries

Laurie Roberts Belton, Executive Director
Eric Weiss, Program Manager

Alabama

2336 Auburn University at Montgomery Library
PO Box 244023
Montgomery, AL 36124-4023
334-244-3649
Fax: 334-244-3720
http://www.aumnicat.aum.edu
Member of The Foundation Center network, maintaining a collection of private foundation tax returns which provide information on the scope of grants dispensed by that particular foundation.

R Best, Dean Administration
T Bailey, ILL/ Reference

2337 Benjamin & Roberta Russell Educational and Charitable Foundation
PO Box 272
Alexander City, AL 35010-0272
256-329-4224
http://www.non-profit-organizations.findthebest.com
Offers giving in the areas of higher and public education, youth programs and a hospital.

James D Nabors, Executive Director

2338 Birmingham Public Library
Government Documents
2100 Park Place
Birmingham, AL 35203-2794
205-226-3600
Fax: 205-226-3729
http://www.bplonline.org/resources/subjects/gov/deault
Member of The Foundation Center network, maintaining a collection of private foundation tax returns which provide information on the scope of grants dispensed by that particular foundation.

2339 Carolina Lawson Ivey Memorial Foundation
PO Box 340
Smiths, AL 36877-0340
334-826-5760
Scholarships are offered to college juniors and seniors who are pursuing careers of teaching social studies in middle or secondary grades. The grants are also offered to teachers in Alabama and west Georgia for curriculum planning and development, in-service training, the development of instructional materials for use in elementary and secondary schools, and other projects that focus on the cultural approach method of teaching.

2340 Huntsville Public Library
915 Monroe Street SW
Huntsville, AL 35801-5007
256-532-5940
http://www.hpl.lib.al.us/
Member of The Foundation Center network, maintaining a collection of private foundation tax returns which provide information on the scope of grants dispensed by that particular foundation.

Donna B Schremser, Library Director

2341 JL Bedsole Foundation
PO Box 1137
Mobile, AL 36633-1137
251-432-3369
Fax: 251-432-1134
http://www.jlbedsolefoundation.org
The foundation's primary interest is the support of educational institutions within the state of Alabama and civic and economic development which is limited to the geographical area of Southwest Alabama. The arts, social service and health programs receive limited grants. Organizations or projects outside of the State of Alabama are not considered for funding by the Foundation.

Mabel B Ward, Executive Director
Scott A Morton, Assistant Director

2342 Mildred Weedon Blount Educational and Charitable Foundation
PO Box 607
Tallassee, AL 36078-0007
334-283-4931
http://www.schoolsoup.com
Support for Catholic schools, public schools and a scholarship fund for secondary school students.

Arnold B Dopson, Executive Director

2343 Mitchell Foundation
PO Box 1126
Mobile, AL 36633
251-432-1711
Fax: 334-432-1712
http://www.cgmf.org
Places an emphasis on secondary and higher education, social services programs, youth agencies, and aid for the handicapped.

Augustine Meaher, Executive Director
Marilu Hastings, Director

2344 University of South Alabama
307 University Boulevard
Mobile, AL 36688-0002
251-460-7025
Fax: 251-460-7636
http://www.library.southalabama.edu

Richard Wood, Dean of Libraries

Alaska

2345 University of Alaska-Anchorage Library
3211 Providence Drive
Anchorage, AK 99508-8000
907-786-1848
Fax: 907-786-6050
http://www.lib.uaa.alaska.edu
Member of The Foundation Center network, maintaining a collection of private foundation tax returns which provide information on the scope of grants dispensed by that particular foundation.

Stephen J Rollins, Dean of Library

Arizona

2346 Arizona Department of Education
1535 W Jefferson Street
Phoenix, AZ 85007
602-542-5393
800-352-4558
Fax: 602-542-5440
http://www.ade.state.az.us
Implements procedures that ensure the proper allocation, distribution, and expenditure of all federal and state funds administerd by the department. The following links to our web pages contain information pertaining to educational grants funded from the state or federal programs.

Tom Horne, Superintendent

2347 Arizona Governor's Committee on Employment of People with Disabilities
Samaritan Rehabilitation Institute
1012 E Willetta Street
Phoenix, AZ 85006-3047
602-239-4762
Fax: 602-239-5256

Jim Bruzewski, Executive Director

2348 Education Services
Arizona Department of Education
1535 W Jefferson Street
Phoenix, AZ 85007-3280
602-364-1961
Fax: 602-542-5440
http://www.ade.state.az.us/edservices
Provides quality services and resources to schools, parent groups, government agencies, and community groups to enable them to achieve their goals.

Lillie Sly, Associate Superintendent

2349 Evo-Ora Foundation
2525 E Broadway Boulevard
Suite 111
Tucson, AZ 85716-5398
Giving is primarily aimed at education, especially Catholic high schools and universities.

2350 Flinn Foundation
1802 N Central Avenue
Suite 2300
Phoenix, AZ 85012-2513
602-744-6800
Fax: 602-744-6815
E-mail: info@flinn.org
http://www.flinn.org
Supports nonprofit organizations in the state of Arizona for programs in health care, as well as an annual awards competition for Arizona's principal arts institutions and a college scholarship program for Arizona high school graduates. Scholarship provides expenses for four years, two summers of study-related travel abroad and other benefits.

John W Murphy, Executive Director

2351 Phoenix Public Library
Business & Sciences Department
12 E McDowell Road
Phoenix, AZ 85004-1627
602-262-4636
Fax: 602-261-8836
http://www.phxlib.org
Member of The Foundation Center network, maintaining a collection of private foundation tax returns which provide information on the scope of grants dispensed by that particular foundation.

2352 Special Programs
721 Broadway
12th Floor
New York, NY 10003
212-998-1800
E-mail: tisch.special.info@nyu.edu
http://www.specialprograms.tisch.nyu.edu

Tom Horne, Superintendent

2353 Support Services
Arizona Department of Education
1535 W Jefferson Street
Phoenix, AZ 85007-3280
602-542-5393
Fax: 602-542-5440

Rachel Arroyo, School Finance

2354 Vocational Technological Education
Arizona Department of Education
1535 W Jefferson Street
Phoenix, AZ 85007-3280
602-542-5393
Fax: 602-542-5440

Tom Horne, Superintendent

Arkansas

2355 Charles A Frueauff Foundation
200 River Market Avenue
Suite 100
Little Rock, AR 72201-3848
501-324-2233
http://www.frueauff.org
Will review proposals from private four-year colleges and universities.

David Frueauff, President
Sue Frueauff, Chief Administrative Officer

2356 Northwest Arkansas Community College
Borham Library
One College Drive
Bentonville, AR 72904-7397
479-636-9222
800-995-6922
http://www.nwacc.edu
Member of The Foundation Center network, maintaining a collection of private foundation tax returns which provide information on the scope of grants dispensed by that particular foundation.

Daniel Shewmaker, Secretary
Ric Clifford, Chairman

2357 Roy and Christine Sturgis Charitable and Educational Trust
PO Box 92
Malvern, AR 72104-0092
501-337-5109
Giving is offered to Baptist and Methodist organizations, including schools, churches and higher and secondary education.

Katie Speer, Executive Director

2358 The Jones Center For Families
922 East Emma Avenue
Springdale, AR 72765
479-756-8090
http://www.thejonescenter.net
Focuses funds on education, medical resources and religious organizations in Arkansas.

HG Frost Jr, Executive Director
Grace Donoho, Director Of Education

2359 Walton Family Foundation
125 W Central Avenue
Room 217 Po Box 2030
Bentonville, AR 72712-5248
479-464-1570
Fax: 479-464-1580
http://www.wffhome.com
Offers giving for systemic reform of primary education (K-12) and early childhood development.

Stewart T Springfield, Executive Director

2360 William C & Theodosia Murphy Nolan Foundation
200 N Jefferson Avenue
Suite 308
El Dorado, AR 71730-5853
870-863-7118
Fax: 870-863-6528
Supports education and the arts (historic preservation, arts centers) as well as religious welfare and youth organizations in Northern Louisiana and Southern Arkansas.

William C Nolan, Executive Director

2361 Winthrop Rockefeller Foundation
225 East Markham Street
Suite 200
Little Rock, AR 72201-3999
501-376-6854
Fax: 501-374-4797

E-mail: webfeedback@wrfoundation.org
http://www.wrfoundation.org
Dedicated to improving the quality of life and education in Arkansas. Grants go to schools that work to involve teachers and parents in making decisions; to universities and local schools to strengthen both levels of education; and for projects that promote stakeholder participation in the development of educational policy.

Sherece Y West, President
Jackie Cox-New, Sr Program Officer

California

2362 Ahmanson Foundation
9215 Wilshire Boulevard
Beverly Hills, CA 90210-5538
310-278-0770
E-mail: info@theahmansonfoundation.org
http://www.theahmasonfoundation.org
Concentrates mainly on education, health and social services in Southern California.

Lee E Walcott, Executive Director
William H Ahmanson, President

2363 Alice Tweed Tuohy Foundation
205 E Carrillo Street
Suite 219
Santa Barbara, CA 93101-7186
805-962-6430
Priority consideration is given to applications from organizations serving: young people; education; selected areas of interest in health care and medicine; and community affairs.

Harris W Seed, President
Eleanor Van Cott, Executive VP

2364 Arrillaga Foundation
2560 Mission College Boulevard
Suite 101
Santa Clara, CA 95054-1217
408-980-0130
Fax: 408-988-4893
Giving is aimed at secondary schools and higher education in the state of California.

John Arrillaga, Executive Director

2365 Atkinson Foundation
1720 So.Amphlett Blvd
Suite 100
San Mateo, CA 94402-2710
650-357-1101
E-mail: atkinfdn@aol.com
http://www.atkinsonfdn.org
Provides opportunities for people in San Mateo County, California to reach their highest potential and to improve the quality of their lives and to assist educational institutions and supporting organizations with the implementation of effective programs that reach and serve their target populations.

Elizabeth H Curtis, Administrator

2366 BankAmerica Foundation
Bank of America Center
PO Box 37000
San Francisco, CA 94137-0001
800-678-2632
Fax: 818-507-4023
E-mail: banknote@bankamerica.com
http://www.bankamerica.com
Fields of interest include arts/cultural programs, higher education, community development and general federated giving programs.

Elizabeth Nachbaur, Program Director

2367 Bechtel Group Corporate Giving Program
Po Box 193965
San Francisco, CA 94119-3965
415-768-5974
Offers support for higher education and programs related to engineering and construction, math and science in grades K-12 and general charitable programs.

Kathryn M Bandarrae, Executive Director

2368 Bernard Osher Foundation
One Ferry Building
Suite 255
San Francisco, CA 94111
415-861-5587
Fax: 415-677-5868
E-mail: nagle@osherfoundation.org
http://www.osherfoundation.org
Funds in the arts, post-secondary education and environmental education on San Francisco and Alameda Counties.

Patricia Nagle, Sr VP
Jeanie Hirokane, Corporate Secretary and Exec

2369 Boys-Viva Supermarkets Foundation
955 Carrillo Drive
Suite 103
Los Angeles, CA 90048-5400
Wide range of support for education of school-aged children, especially the at-risk population, tutoring, and social opportunities.

Fred Snowden, Executive Director

2370 California Community Foundation
221 S Figueroa Street
Suite 400
Los Angeles, CA 90012-1638
213-413-4130
Fax: 213-383-2046
http://www.calfund.org
Improving human condition through nonprofit agencies in Los Angeles County. Integral parts of eligible proposals are, hosting conferences, incurring debt, individuals, sectarian purposes or regranting.

Judy Spiegel, Sr VP of Programs
Antonia Hernandez, President/CEO

2371 Carrie Estelle Doheny Foundation
707 Wilshire Boulevard
Suite 4960
Los Angeles, CA 90017-2659
213-488-1122
Fax: 213-488-1544
http://www.dohenyfoundation.org
This foundation funds a myriad of organizations ranging from the education and medicine field to public health and science areas.

Robert A Smith III, Executive Director

2372 Dan Murphy Foundation
PO Box 711267
Los Angeles, CA 90071-9767
213-623-3120
Fax: 213-623-1421
Funds Roman Catholic institutions, with a primary interest in religious orders and schools.

Daniel J Donohue, Executive Director

2373 David & Lucile Packard Foundation
343 Second Street
Los Altos Hills, CA 94022-3643
650-948-7658
Fax: 650-941-3151
http://www.packard.org
Concentrates on four categories: education, the arts, conservation and child health. Also

allocates funds to companies interested in public improvement and public policy.

Colburn S Wilbur, Executive Director

2374 Evelyn & Walter Haas Jr Fund
114 Sansome Street
Suite 600
San Francisco, CA 94104
415-856-1400
Fax: 415-856-1500
http://www.haasjr.org
Interested in strengthening neighborhoods, communities, and human services. Funds mainly in San Francisco Bay Area.

Ira Hirschfield, President
Clayton Juan, Grants Administrator

2375 Foundation Center-San Francisco
312 Sutter Street
Suite 606
San Francisco, CA 94108-4314
415-397-0902
Fax: 415-397-7670
http://www.fdncenter.org
One of five Foundation Centers nationwide, the Foundation Center - San Francisco is a library which collects information on private foundations, corporate philanthropy, nonprofit management, fundraising and other topics of interest to nonprofit organization representatives.

Melissa A Berman, President & CEO
John Colborn, Vice President

2376 Foundations Focus
Marin Community Foundation
5 Hamilton Landing
Suite 200
Novato, CA 94949
415-464-2500
Fax: 415-464-2555
http://www.marincf.org
Grants support projects that benefit residents of Marin County, CA.

Don Jen, Program Officer/Education
Thomas Peters, President/CEO

2377 Francis H Clougherty Charitable Trust
500 Newport Center Drive
Suite 910
Newport Beach, CA 92660-7009
Offers grants in the areas of elementary, secondary school and higher education in Southern California.

2378 Freitas Foundation
C/O Fiduciary Resources
874 Fourth St
Suite D
San Rafael, CA 94901-3246
Offers giving in the areas of elementary and secondary education, as well as theological education.

Margaret Boyden, Executive Director

2379 Fritz B Burns Foundation
4001 W Alameda Avenue
Suite 201
Burbank, CA 91505-4338
818-840-8802
Fax: 818-840-0468
Grants are primarily focused on education, hospitals and medical research organizations.

Joseph E Rawlinson, Executive Director

2380 George Frederick Jewett Foundation
235 Montgomery Street
Suite 612
San Francisco, CA 94104-2915

415-421-1351
Fax: 415-421-1351
Concerns itself mainly with voluntary, nonprofit organizations that promote human welfare.

2381 Grant & Resource Center of Northern California
2280 Benton Drive, Building C
Suite A
Redding, CA 96003
530-244-1219
Fax: 530-244-0905
E-mail: library@grcnc.org
Member of The Foundation Center network, maintaining a collection of private foundation tax returns which provide information on the scope of grants dispensed by that particular foundation.

2382 Greenville Foundation
PO Box 4667
Scottsdale, AZ 85261-4667
707-938-9377
Fax: 707-939-9311
This foundation focuses its support on education, the environment and human rights. The main focus of the educational grants lie within the areas of elementary, secondary and higher education.

Virginia Hubbell, Executive Director
Virginia Hubbell, Administrator

2383 HN & Frances C Berger Foundation
PO Box 3064
Arcadia, CA 91006
626-447-3351
http://www.hnberger.org
Provides scholarships and endowments to colleges and universities.

Ronald M Auen, President/CEO
Christopher M McGuire, Vice President of Programs

2384 Henry J Kaiser Family Foundation
Quadrus
2400 Sand Hill Road
Menlo Park, CA 94025-6941
650-854-9400
Fax: 650-854-4800
http://www.kff.org
Concentrates on health care, minority groups and South Africa.

Drew Altman, President/CEO
Susan V Berresford, Former President

2385 Hon Foundation
25200 La Paz Road
Suite 210
Laguna Hills, CA 92653-5110
949-586-4400
Offers giving in the areas of elementary, secondary and higher education in the states of Hawaii and California.

2386 Hugh & Hazel Darling Foundation
520 S Grand Avenue
7th Floor
Los Angeles, CA 90071-2645
213-683-5200
Fax: 213-627-7795
Supports education in California with special emphasis on legal education; no grants to individuals; grants only to 501(c)(3) organizations.

Richard L Stack, Trustee

2387 Ingraham Memorial Fund
C/O Emrys J. Ross
301 E Colorado Boulevard
Suite 900
Pasadena, CA 91101-1916
626-796-9123

Offers giving in the areas of elementary, secondary and higher education, as well as theological education in Claremont and Pasadena, California.

2388 James G Boswell Foundation
101 W Walnut Street
Pasadena, CA 91103-3636
626-583-3000
Fax: 626-583-3090
Funds hospitals, pre-college private schools, public broadcasting and youth organizations.

James G Boswell II, Chairman
Sherman Railsback, EVP/COO

2389 James Irvine Foundation
575 Market Street
Suite 3400
San Francisco, CA 94105-1017
415-777-2244
Fax: 415-777-0869
http://www.irvine.org
Giving is primarily aimed at the areas of education, youth and health.

James E Canales, President/CEO
Kristin Nelson, Executive Assistant

2390 James S Copley Foundation
7776 Ivanhoe Avenue #1530
La Jolla, CA 92037-4520
858-454-0411
Fax: 858-729-7629
Support is offered for higher and secondary education, child development, cultural programs and community services.

Anita A Baumgardner, Executive Director

2391 John Jewett & H Chandler Garland Foundation
PO Box 550
Pasadena, CA 91102-0550
Support given primarily for secondary and higher education, social services and cultural and historical programs.

GE Morrow, Executive Director

2392 Joseph Drown Foundation
1999 Avenue of the Stars
Suite 2330
Los Angeles, CA 90067-4611
310-277-4488
Fax: 310-277-4573
http://www.jdrown.org
The Foundation's goal is to assist individuals in becoming successful, self-sustaining, contributing citizens. The foundation is interested in programs that break down any barrier that prevents a person from continuing to grow and learn.

Norman Obrow, Executive Director

2393 Jules & Doris Stein Foundation
PO Box 30
Beverly Hills, CA 90213-0030
213-276-2101
Supports charitable organizations.

2394 Julio R Gallo Foundation
PO Box 1130
Modesto, CA 95353-1130
209-579-3373
Offers grants and support to secondary schools and higher education universities.

Sam Gallo, Chairman

2395 Kenneth T & Eileen L Norris Foundation
11 Golden Shore Street
Suite 450
Long Beach, CA 90802-4214
562-435-8444
Fax: 562-436-0584
E-mail: grants@ktn.org
http://www.norrisfoundation.org

Funding categories include medical, education/science, youth, cultural and community.

Ronald Barnes, Executive Director

2396 Koret Foundation
33 New Montgomery Street
Suite 1090
San Francisco, CA 94105-4526
415-882-7740
Fax: 415-882-7775
E-mail:
sandyedwards@koretfoundation.org
http://www.koretfoundation.org
Funding includes; public policy and selected programs in K-12 public education, higher education, youth programs, Jewish studies at colleges and universities, and Jewish education. The geographical area for grant-making is the San Francisco Bay area.

Tad Taube, President
Susan Koret, Board Chair

2397 Lane Family Charitable Trust
500 Almer Road
Apartment 301
Burlingame, CA 94010-3966
Offers giving in the areas of secondary schools and higher education facilities in California.

Ralph Lane, Trustee
Joan Lane, Trustee

2398 Levi Strauss Foundation
1155 Battery Street
Floor 7
San Francisco, CA 94111-1230
415-501-6000
Fax: 415-501-7112
http://www.levistrauss.com
Grants are made in four areas: AIDS prevention and care; economic empowerment; youth empowerment; and social justice. Grants are limited to communities where Levi Strauss and Company has plants or customer service centers.

Theresa Fay-Buslillos, Executive Director

2399 Louise M Davies Foundation
180 Montgomery St
Suite 1616
San Francisco, CA 94104-4235
Offers giving in the areas of elementary, secondary and higher education, as well as scholarship funding for California students.

Donald Crawford Jr, Executive Director

2400 Lowell Berry Foundation
3685 Mount Diablo Boulevard
Suite 269
Lafayette, CA 94549
925-284-4427
Fax: 925-284-4332
http://www.lowellberryfoundation.org
Assists Christian ministry at local church levels.

Debbie Coombe, Office Manager
Larry R Langdon, President

2401 Luke B Hancock Foundation
360 Bryant Street
Palo Alto, CA 94301-1409
650-321-5536
Fax: 650-321-0697
E-mail: lhancock@lukebhancock.org
http://www.fdcenter.org/grantmaker/hancock
Provides funding for programs which promote the well being of children and youth. Priority is given to programs which address the needs of youth who are at risk of school failure. Additional funding is provided for

early childhood development, music education and homeless families.

Ruth M Ramel, Executive Director

2402 Margaret E Oser Foundation
1911 Lyon Court
Santa Rosa, CA 95403-0974
949-553-4202
Offers grants in the areas of elementary and secondary and higher education, which will benefit women.

Carl Mitchell, Executive Director

2403 Marin Community Foundation
5 Hamilton Landing
Suite 200
Novato, CA 94949-1736
415-461-3333
Fax: 415-464-2555
http://www.marincf.org
Established as a nonprofit public benefit corporation to engage in educational and philanthropic activities in Marin County, California.

Thomas Peterson, President&CEO
Julie Absey, Vice President

2404 Mary A Crocker Trust
233 Post Street
Floor 2
San Francisco, CA 94108-5003
415-982-0138
Fax: 415-982-0141
E-mail: staff@mactrust.org
http://www.mactrust.org
Giving is aimed at precollegiate education, as well as conservation and environmental programs.

Barbaree Jernigan, Executive Director

2405 Maurice Amado Foundation
3940 Laurel Canyon Boulevard
Suite 809
Studio City, CA 91604
818-980-9190
Fax: 818-980-9190
E-mail: pkaizer@mauriceamadofdn.org
http://www.mauri
Concentrates on the Jewish heritage.

Pam Kaizer, Executive Director

2406 McConnell Foundation
PO Box 492050
800 Shasta View Drive
Redding, CA 96003
530-226-6200
Fax: 530-226-6210
http://www.mcconnellfoundation.org
Interested in cultural, community and health care related projects.

Ana Diaz, Program Assistant

2407 McKesson Foundation
1 Post Street
San Francisco, CA 94104-5203
415-983-8300
http://www.mckesson.com/foundation.html
Giving is primarily to programs for junior high school students and for emergency services such as food and shelter.

Marcia M Argyris, Executive Director

2408 Milken Family Foundation
C/O Foundations of the Milken Families
1250 4th Street
Floor 6
Santa Monica, CA 90401-1353
310-570-4800
Fax: 310-570-4801
http://www.mff.org
Offers support to the educational community to reward educational innovators, stimulate creativity among students, involve parents

and other citizens in the school system, and help disadvantaged youth.

Dr. Julius Lesner, Executive Director
Lowell Milken, Chairman & Co Founder

2409 Miranda Lux Foundation
57 Post Street
Suite 510
San Francisco, CA 94104-5020
415-981-2966
E-mail: admin@mirandalux.org
http://www.mirandalux.org
Offers support to promising proposals for pre-school through junior college programs in the fields of pre-vocational and vocational education and training.

Kenneth Blum, Executive Director

2410 Northern California Grantmakers
625 Market Street
3rd Floor
San Francisco, CA 94105
415-777-4111
Fax: 415-777-1714
E-mail: ncg@ncg.org
http://www.ncg.org
Northern California Grantmakers is an association of foundations, corporate contributions programs and other private grantmakers. Its mission is to jpromote the well being of people and their communities in balance with a healthy environment by the thoughtful and creative use of private wealth and resources for the public benefit. To this end, NCG works to enhance the effectiveness of philanthropy, including nonprofit organizations, government, business, media, academia and the public at large.

Colin Lacon, President

2411 Pacific Telesis Group Corporate Giving Program
130 Kearny Street
San Francisco, CA 94108-4818
415-394-3000
Primary areas of interest include K-12 education reform, education of minorities, women and disabled individuals in the math, science, engineering, education and MBA fields; and specific K-12 issues such as dropouts; information technology and parent involvement.

Jere A Jacobs, Executive Director

2412 Peninsula Community Foundation
11742 Jefferson Avenue
Suite 350
Newport News, VA 23606-3049
757-327-0862
Fax: 757-327-0865
http://www.pcfvirginia.org
Serving a population from Daly City to Mountain View, the foundations focus is on children and youth, adult services, programs serving homeless families and children, prevention of homelessness and civic and public benefit grants.

Sterling K Speirn, Executive Director
Gregory F Lawson, President

2413 Peter Norton Family Foundation
225 Arizona Avenue
Floor 2
Santa Monica, CA 90401-1243
310-576-7700
Fax: 310-576-7701
Offers giving in the areas of early childhood education, elementary school education, higher education, childrens services and AIDS research.

Anne Etheridge, ED, Executive Director

2414 RCM Capital Management Charitable Fund
4 Embarcadero Center
Suite 2900
San Francisco, CA 94111-4189
415-954-5474
Fax: 415-954-8200
http://www.rcm.com
Giving is offered in many areas including youth development, early childhood education and elementary education.

Jami Weinman, Executive Director

2415 Ralph M Parsons Foundation
888 West Sixth Street
Suite 700
Los Angeles, CA 90017-5600
213-362-7600
Fax: 213-482-8878
http://www.rmpf.org
Giving is focused on higher and pre-collegiate education, with an emphasis on engineering, technology, and science; social impact programs serving families, children and the elderly; health programs targeting underserved populations; civic and cultural programs.

Wendy G Hoppe, Executive Director
Walter B Rose, Vice Chairman

2416 Riordan Foundation
PO Box 491190
Los Angeles, CA 90049-3110
310-472-2020
Fax: 310-472-1414
E-mail: contact@riordanfoundation.org
http://www.riordanfoundation.org
Priorities of the foundation include early childhood literacy, youth programs, leadership programs, job training, direct medical services to young children, and cyclical, targeted mini-grants. When determining levels of support, priority is always given to programs which impact young children.

Jessica Flores, President
Jaime Kalenik, Program Coordinator

2417 Royal Barney Hogan Foundation
PMB 220,3000 S.Hulen
Ste 124
Forth Worth, TX
E-mail: RoyalHoganFoundation@yahoo.com
http://www.royalhoganfoundation.org
Offers grants specifically for secondary education in the state of California.

Jacque Hogan, President/Treasurer
Robert L Towery, Secretary/Chief Executive Of

2418 SH Cowell Foundation
595 Market Street
Suite 950
San Francisco, CA 94105-4303
415-397-0285
Fax: 415-986-6786
http://www.shcowell.org
Offers support for educational programs, including pre-school and primary public educational programs.

JD Erickson, Executive Director
Anna Alpers, President

2419 Sacramento Regional Foundation
555 Capitol Mall
Suite 550
Sacramento, CA 95814-4502
916-492-6510
Fax: 916-492-6515
http://www.sacregfoundation.org

Primary interests of this foundation include the arts, humanities and education.

Stephen F Boutin, President
Janice Gow Pettey, CEO

2420 San Diego Foundation
2508 Historic Decatur Rd
Suite 200
San Diego, CA 92106-2434
619-235-2300
Fax: 619-239-1710
E-mail: info@sdfoundation.org
http://www.sdfoundation.org
Offers grants in the areas of social services with emphasis on children and families, education and health for San Diego County.

Robert A Kelly, President/CEO
Rebecca Reichmann, VP Programs

2421 San Francisco Foundation
225 Bush Street
Suite 500
San Francisco, CA 94104-4224
415-733-8500
Fax: 415-477-2783
E-mail: rec@sff.org
http://www.sff.org
Addresses community needs in the areas of community health, education, arts and culture, neighborhood revitalization, and environmental justice. Works to support families and communities to help children and youth succeed in school and provide opportunities for them to become confident, caring and contributing adults.

Sandra R Hernandez MD, CEO
Sara Ying Kelley, Director Public Affairs

2422 Santa Barbara Foundation
1111 Chapala Street
Suite 200
Santa Barbara, CA 93101-2780
805-963-1873
Fax: 805-966-2345
http://www.sbfoundation.org
Offers a student aid program with no interest-1/2 loan and 1/2 scholarship. Funding limited to long-term Santa Barbara County residents.

Claudia Armann, Program Officer
Peter MacDougall, Chairman

2423 Sega Youth Education & Health Foundation
255 Shoreline Drive
Suite 200
Redwood City, CA 94065-1428
Offers support only to organizations that address and promote youth education and health issues.

Trizia Carpenter, Executive Director

2424 Sidney Stern Memorial Trust
PO Box 893
Pacific Palisades, CA 90272-0893
310-459-2117
E-mail: info@sidneysternmemorialtrust.org
http://www.sidneysternmemorialtrust.org
Funding offered includes education, community action groups, the arts and the disabled.

2425 Sol & Clara Kest Family Foundation
5150 Overland Avenue
Culver City, CA 90230-4914
213-204-2050
Offers support for Jewish organizations in the areas of education.

Sol Kest, Executive Director

2426 Szekely Family Foundation
3232 Dove Street
San Diego, CA 92103
619-295-2372
Offers giving in the areas of early childhood education, child development, elementary education, higher education, and adult and continuing education.

Deborah Szekely, Executive Director

2427 Thomas & Dorothy Leavey Foundation
10100 Santa Monica Boulevard
Suite 610
Los Angeles, CA 90067
310-551-9936
Focus is placed on college scholarships, medical research, youth groups and programs, and secondary and higher education purposes.

J Thomas McCarthy, Executive Director

2428 Times Mirror Foundation
202 West First Street
Los Angeles, CA 90012
213-237-3945
Fax: 213-237-2116
http://www.timesmirrorfoundation.org
Giving is largely for higher education purposes including liberal arts and business education.

Cassandra Malry, Executive Director

2429 Timken-Sturgis Foundation
7421 Eads Avenue
La Jolla, CA 92037-5037
619-454-2252
Offers support for education in Southern California and Nevada.

Joannie Barrancotto, Executive Director

2430 Toyota USA Foundation
19001 S Western Avenue
Torrance, CA 90501-1106
310-715-7486
800-331-4331
Fax: 310-468-7814
E-mail: b_pauli@toyota
http://www.toyota.com/foundation
Supports K-12 education programs, with strong emphasis on math and science.

William Pauli, National Manager

2431 Turst Funds Incorporated
100 Broadway Street
Floor 3
San Francisco, CA 94111-1404
415-434-3323
Offers grants for Catholic Schools, including elementary and secondary education, in the San Francisco Bay Area.

James T Healy, President

2432 Ventura County Community Foundation
Funding & Information Resource Center
4001 Mission Oaks Blvd
Suite 150
Camarillo, CA 93012-8504
805-988-0196
Fax: 805-484-2700
E-mail: vccf@vccf.org
http://www.vccf.org
Member of The Foundation Center network, maintaining a collection of private foundation tax returns which provide information on the scope of grants dispensed by that particular foundation.

Gary E Erickson, President/CEO
Virginia Weber, Program Officer

2433 WM Keck Foundation
550 S Hope Street
Suite 2500
Los Angeles, CA 90071
213-680-3833
Fax: 213-614-0934

E-mail: info@wmkeck.org
http://www.wmkeck.org
The Foundation also gives some consideration, limited to Southern California, for the support of arts and culture, civic and community services, health care and precollegiate education. The foundation's grant-making is focused primarily on pioneering research efforts in the areas of science, engineering and medical research, and on higher education, including liberal arts.

Dorothy Fleisher, Program Director
Allison Keller, Executive Director and Chief

2434 Walter & Elise Haas Fund
1 Lombard Street
Suite 305
San Francisco, CA 94111-1130
415-398-4474
Fax: 415-986-4779
http://www.haassr.org
Supports education, arts, environment, human services, humanities and public affairs; is especially in projects which have a wide impact within their respective fields through enhancing public education and access to information, serving a central organizing role, addressing public policy, demonstrating creative approaches toward meeting human needs, or supporting the work of a major institution in the field.

Pamela H David, Executive Director
Peter E Hass Jr, President

2435 Walter S Johnson Foundation
1660 Bush Street
Suite 300
San Francisco, CA 94025-3447
415-561-6540
Fax: 415-561-6477
http://www.wsjf.org
Giving is centered on education in public schools and social service agencies concerned with the quality of public education in Northern California and Washoe County, Nevada.

Pancho Chang, Executive Director

2436 Wayne & Gladys Valley Foundation
1939 Harrison Street
Suite 510
Oakland, CA 94612-3535
510-466-6060
Fax: 510-466-6067
Supports four areas: education, medical research, community services and special projects.

Michael D Desler, Executive Director

2437 Weingart Foundation
1055 W 7th Street
Suite 3200
Los Angeles, CA 90017-2509
213-688-7799
Fax: 213-688-1515
http://www.weingartfnd.org
Offers support for community services including a student loan program.

William C Allen, Chairman & CEO
Fred J Ali, President/Chief Adm. Officer

2438 Wells Fargo Foundation
550 California Street
7th Floor MAC A0112-073
San Francisco, CA 94104
415-396-5830
Fax: 415-975-6260
http://www.wellsfargo.com
Offers support for elementary school education, secondary school education and community development.

Tim Hanlon, Executive Director

2439 Wilbur D May Foundation
C/O Brookhill Corporation
2716 Ocean Park Boulevard
Suite 2011
Santa Monica, CA 90405
Gives to youth organizations and hospitals.

2440 William & Flora Hewlett Foundation
2121 Sand Hill Road
Menlo Park, CA 94025-3448
650-234-4500
Fax: 650-234-4501
http://www.hewlett.org
The Hewlett Foundation concentrates its resources on the performing arts, education, population issues, environmental issues, conflict resolution and family and community development. Grants in the education program, specifically the elementary and secondary education part of it, are limited to K-12 areas in California programs, with primary emphasis on public schools in the San Francisco Bay area. The program favors schools, school districts and universities.

Larry Kramer, President
Walter B Hewlett, Chairman

2441 William C Bannerman Foundation
9255 Sunset Boulevard
Suite 400
West Hollywood, CA 90069
310-273-9933
Fax: 310-273-9931
Offers grants in the fields of elementary school, secondary schools, education, human services and youth programs K-12 in Los Angeles County, Adult Education and Vocational Training.

Elliot Ponchick, President

2442 Y&H Soda Foundation
1635 School Street
Moraga, CA 94556
925-631-1133
Fax: 925-631-0248
E-mail: jNM@silcom.com
http://www.yhsodafoundation.org
Offers support in the areas of early childhood education, child development, elementary education and vocational and higher education.

Bob Uyeki, Executive Director

2443 Zellerbach Family Fund
575 Market Street
Suite 2950
San Francisco, CA 94105-4318
415-421-2629
Fax: 415-421-6713
http://www.zellerbachfamilyfoundation.org
Provides funds to nonprofit organizations in the San Francisco Bay Area.

Cindy Rambo, Executive Director
Linda Avidan, Program Director

Colorado

2444 Adolph Coors Foundation
4100 East Mississippi Avenue
Suite 1850
Denver, CO 80246
303-388-1636
Fax: 303-388-1684
http://www.adolphcoors.org
Giving is primarily offered for programs with an emphasis on education, human services, youth and health.

Sally W Rippey, Executive Director
Jeanne L Bistranin, Program Officers

2445 Boettcher Foundation
600 17th Street
Suite 2210
Denver, CO 80202-5422
303-534-1937
800-323-9640
http://www.boettcherfoundation.org
Offers grants to educational institutions, with an emphasis on scholarships and fellowships.

Timothy W Schultz, President/Executive Director

2446 Denver Foundation
55 Madison Street
8th Floor
Denver, CO 80206
303-300-1790
Fax: 303-300-6547
http://www.denverfoundation.org
The Foundation serves as the steward and the administrator of the endowment, charged with investing its earned income in programs that meet the community's growing and changing needs. The Foundation has a solid history of supporting a broad array of community efforts. Grants are awarded to nonprofit organizations that touch nearly every meaningful artistic, cultural, civic, educational, human service and health interest of metro Denver's citizens.

David Miller, President/CEO
Betsy Mangone, VP Philanthropic Services

2447 El Pomar Foundation
10 Lake Circle
Colorado Springs, CO 80906-4201
719-633-7733
800-554-7711
Fax: 719-577-5702
http://www.elpomar.org
Founded in 1937, the philosophy of this foundation is simply to help foster a climate for excellence in Colorado's third sector, the nonprofit community, as well as the foundation's own responsibility to improve the quality of life for all residents of Colorado. The foundation gives grants to the arts and humanities, civic and community, education, health, human services, and youth in community service.

William J Hybl, Executive Director

2448 Gates Foundation
500 Fifth Avenue North
Seattle, WA 98109
206-709-3100
E-mail: info@gatesfoundation.org
http://www.gatesfoundation.org
The purpose of this foundation is to aid, assist, encourage, initiate, or carry on activities that will promote the health, well-being, security and broad education of all people. Because of a deep concern for and confidence in the future of Colorado, the foundation will invest primarily in institutions and programs that will enhance the quality of life for those who live and work in the state.

Thomas C Stokes, Executive Director

2449 Ruth & Vernon Taylor Foundation
518 17th Street
Suite 1670
Denver, CO 80202
303-893-5284
Fax: 303-893-8263
Offers support for education, the arts, human services and conservation.

Friday A Green, Executive Director

2450 US West Foundation
915 Memorial Drive
Manitowoc, WI 54220

920-684-6110
Fax: 920-684-7381
E-mail: info@westfoundation.us
http://www.westfoundation.us
Grants are given in the areas of health and human services, including programs for youth, early childhood, elementary, secondary, higher and other.

Janet Rash, Executive Director
Thomas Bare, President

Connecticut

2451 Aetna Foundation
151 Farmington Avenue
Hartford, CT 06156-0001
860-273-0123
Fax: 860-273-4764
http://www.aetna.com/foundation/
Aetna gives grants in various areas that improve the community and its citizens. Certain areas include; children's health, education for at-risk students, and community initiatives. Geographic emphasis is placed on organizations and initiatives in Aetna's Greater Hartford headquarters communities; organizations in select communities across the country where Aetna has a significant local presence; and national organizations that can influence state, local or federal policies and programs.

Marilda L Gandara, President
Dave Wilmont, Executive Assistant

2452 Community Foundation of Greater New Haven
70 Audubon Street
New Haven, CT 06510-1248
203-777-2386
Fax: 203-787-6584
E-mail: contactus@cfgnh.org
http://www.cfgnh.org
Offers a wide variety of giving with an emphasis on social services, youth services, AIDS research and education.

William W Ginsberg, President/CEO
Ronda Maddox, Administrative Assistant

2453 Connecticut Mutual Financial Services
140 Garden Street
Hartford, CT 06154-0200
860-987-6500
Giving is aimed at education, primarily higher education, equal opportunity programs and social services.

Astrida R Olds, Executive Director

2454 Hartford Foundation for Public Giving
10 Columbus Boulevard
8th Floor
Hartford, CT 06106-2693
860-548-1888
Fax: 860-524-8346
E-mail: hpfg@hpfg.org
http://www.hfpg.org
Offers grants for demonstration programs and capital purposes with emphasis on educational institutions, social services and cultural programs.

Michael R Bangser, Executive Director
Edward Forand Jr, Chairman

2455 Loctite Corporate Contributions Program
Hartford Square North
10 Columbus Boulevard
5th Floor
Hartford, CT 06106-1976

860-571-5100
Fax: 860-571-5430
Offers support in various fields of interest including funding for educational programs for inner city youths in grades K-12.

Kiren Cooley, Corporate Contributions

2456 Louis Calder Foundation
125 Elm Street
New Canaan, CT 06840
203-966-8925
Fax: 203-966-5785
http://www.louiscalderfdn.org
Offers support to organizations who promote education, health and welfare of children and youth in New York City.

Holly Nuechterlein, Program Manager

2457 Sherman Fairchild Foundation
71 Arch Street
Greenwich, CT 06830-6544
203-661-9360
Fax: 203-661-9360
Offers grants in higher education, fine arts and cultural institutions.

Patricia A Lydon, Executive Director

2458 Smart Family Foundation
74 Pin Oak Lane
Wilton, CT 06897-1329
203-834-0400
Fax: 203-834-0412
The foundation is interested in educational projects that focus on primary and secondary school children.

Raymond Smart, Executive Director

2459 Worthington Family Foundation
P.O Box 4311
Traverse City, MI 49685
203-255-9400
http://www.worthington-family-foundation.org
Offers grants in the areas of elementary school education and secondary school education in Connecticut.

Worthington Johnson, Executive Director
Ruth Worthington, President

Delaware

2460 Crystal Trust
Po Box 39
Montchanin, DE 19710-0039
302-651-0533
Grants are awarded for higher and secondary education and social and family services.

Stephen C Doberstein, Executive Director

2461 HW Buckner Charitable Residuary Trust
JP Morgan Services
PO Box 8714
Wilmington, DE 19899-8714
302-633-1900
Focuses giving on educational and cultural organizations in New York, Rhode Island and Massachusetts.

2462 Longwood Foundation
100 W 10th Street
Suite 1109
Wilmington, DE 19801-1694
302-654-2477
Fax: 302-654-2323
Limited grants are offered to educational institutions and cultural programs.

David D Wakefield, Executive Director

District of Columbia

2463 Abe Wouk Foundation
3255 N Street NW
Washington, DC 20007-2845
Offers grants in elementary, secondary education and federated giving programs.

Herman Wouk, Executive Director

2464 Eugene & Agnes E Meyer Foundation
1250 Connecticut Avenue
Suite 800
Washington, DC 20036-2215
202-483-8294
Fax: 202-328-6850
http://www.meyerfoundation.org
Offers grants in the areas of development and housing, education and community services, arts and humanities, law and justice, health and mental health.

Julie L Rogers, President
Barbara Krumsiek, Chairman

2465 Foundation Center-District of Columbia
1627 K Street NW
3rd Floor
Washington, DC 20006-1708
202-331-1400
Fax: 202-331-1739
http://www.fdncenter.org/washington/index.jhtml
Member of The Foundation Center network, maintaining a collection of private foundation tax returns which provide information on the scope of grants dispensed to nonprofit organizations by those particular foundations.

2466 Foundation for the National Capitol Region
1201 15th Street NW
Suite 420
Washington, DC 20005
202-955-5890
Fax: 202-955-8084
http://www.cfncr.org
Grants are focused on organization strengthening and regional collaboration. The Foundation wishes to foster collaborations that identify, address, and increase awareness of regional issues, as well as help strengthen the region's existing nonprofit organizations to improve their financial stability. The Foundation welcomes requests from organizations serving the Greater Washington area that are tax-exempt under Section 501(c)(3) of the Internal Revenue Code.

Terry Lee Freeman, President

2467 Gilbert & Jaylee Mead Family Foundation
2700 Virginia Avenue NW #701
Washington, DC 20037-1908
202-338-0208
Offers support for education (K-12), the performing arts and community service programs for Washington, DC, Montgomery County, Maryland, and Geneva, Switzerland.

Linda Smith, Executive Director

2468 Hitachi Foundation
1509 22nd Street NW
Washington, DC 20037-1073
202-457-0588
Fax: 202-296-1098
http://www.hitachi.org
The majority of projects supported by the foundation: promote collaboration across sectors and among institutions, organizations and individuals; reflect multi-or-interdisciplinary perspectives; respect and value diversity of thought, action, and ethnicity. Grants are given in the areas

of community development, education, global citizenship and program related investments.

Barbara Dyer, President/CEO

2469 Morris & Gwendolyn Cafritz Foundation

1825 K Street NW
Suite 1400
Washington, DC 20006-1202
202-223-3100
Fax: 202-296-7567
http://www.cafritzfoundation.org
Gives grants to organizations in the metropolitan area, focusing on arts, humanities and scholarships.

Sara Cofrin, Program Assistant
Michael Bigley, Program Officer

2470 Public Welfare Foundation

1200 U Street NW
Washington, DC 20009-4443
202-965-1800
Fax: 202-265-8851
E-mail: info@publicwelfare.org
http://www.publicwelfare.org
Offers grants to grass roots organizations in the US and abroad with emphasis on the environment and education.

Larry Kressley, Executive Director
Teresa Langston, Director Of Programs

2471 Washington Post Company Educational Foundation

1150 15th Street NW
Washington, DC 20071-0002
202-334-6000
Offers support for pre-college and higher education including student scholarships and awards for academic excellence.

Eric Grant, Director Contributions

Florida

2472 Applebaum Foundation

1111 Biscaynees Boulevard
Tower 3, Room 853
North Miami, FL 33181
Offers an emphasis on higher education.

2473 Benedict Foundation for Independent Schools

607 Lantana Lane
Vero Beach, FL 32963-2315
http://www.thebenedictfoundation.org
Support is offered primarily for independent secondary schools that have been members of the National Association of Independent Schools for ten consecutive years.

Nancy H Benedict, Executive Director
Davis M Benedict, Vice President & Director

2474 Chatlos Foundation

PO Box 915048
Longwood, FL 32791-5048
407-862-5077
Fax: 407-862-0708
http://www.chatlos.org
Bible colleges and seminaries, liberal arts colleges, vocation and domestic education, medical education; children, elderly, disabled and learning disabled. The Foundation is non-receptive to primary or secondary education, the arts, medical research, individual churches. No direct scholarship support to individuals.

William J Chatlos, Executive Director

2475 Citibank of Florida Corporate Giving Program

8750 Doral Boulevard
7th Floor
Miami, FL 33718
305-599-5775
Fax: 305-599-5520
Offers support for K-12 education for at-risk children. Funding is also available through the program for housing and community development in the state of Florida.

Susan Yarosz, Executive Director

2476 Dade Community Foundation

200 S Biscayne Boulevard
Suite 505
Miami, FL 33131-2343
305-371-2711
Fax: 305-371-5342
http://www.dadecommunityfoundation.org
Offers support for projects in the fields of education, arts and culture.

Ruth Shack, Executive Director

2477 Innovating Worthy Projects Foundation

Lakeview Corporate Center
4045 Sheridan Avenue
Miami, FL 33140-2904
305-861-5352
Fax: 305-868-4293
E-mail: info@IWPF.org
http://www.iwpf.org
Offers grants and support for education in the areas of childhood education and elementary education.

Dr. Irving Packer, Executive Director

2478 Jacksonville Public Library

Business, Science & Documents
303 N Laura St
Jacksonville, FL 32202-3374
904-630-2665
Fax: 904-630-2431
http://www.jpl.coj.net
Member of The Foundation Center network, maintaining a collection of private foundation tax returns which provide information on the scope of grants dispensed by that particular foundation.

Gretchen Mitchell, Business/Science Department

2479 Jessie Ball duPont Fund

One Independent Drive
Suite 1400
Jacksonville, FL 32202-5011
904-353-0890
800-252-3452
Fax: 904-353-3870
E-mail: smagill@dupontfund.org
http://www.dupontfund.org
Grants limited to those institutions to which the donor contributed personally during the five year period ending December 31, 1964. Among the 325 institutions eligible to recieve funds are higher and secondary education intitutions, cultural and historic preservation programs, social services organizations, hospitals, health agencies, churches and church-related organizations and youth agencies.

Dr. Sherry P Magill, President
JoAnn Bennett, Director Administration

2480 Joseph & Rae Gann Charitable Foundation

10185 Collins Avenue
Apartment 317
Bal Harbour, FL 33154-1606
Offers support in the areas of elementary, secondary and theological education.

2481 Orlando Public Library-Orange County Library System

Social Sciences Department
101 E Central Boulivard
Orlando, FL 32801-2471
407-835-7323
Fax: 407-835-7646
E-mail: ajacobe@ocls.lib.fl.us
http://www.ocls.lib.fl.us
Member of The Foundation Center network, maintaining a collection on microfiche of Florida private foundation tax returns which provide information on the scope of grants dispensed by that particular foundation. Other available resources include directories of foundations, guide to funding, and materials on successful grant acquisition. FC Search Foundation Center CD Rom.

Angela C Jacobe, Head Social Science Dpt

2482 Peter D & Eleanore Kleist Foundation

12734 Kenwood Lane
Suite 89
Fort Myers, FL 33907-5638
Support is given to secondary school education and higher education.

Peter D Kleist, Executive Director

2483 Robert G Friedman Foundation

76 Isla Bahia Drive
Fort Lauderdale, FL 33316-2331
Giving is offered to elementary and high schools, with minor support to indigent individuals and charitable activities.

Robert G Friedman, Executive Director

2484 Southwest Florida Community Foundation

8771 College Parkway
Suite 201
Fort Myers, FL 33919
239-274-5900
Fax: 239-274-5930
E-mail: swflcfo@earthlink.net
http://www.floridacommunity.com
Offers grants and support in the areas of education, higher education, children and youth services and general charitable giving to Lee, Charlotte, Hendry, Glades, and Collier Counties, Florida.

Paul B Flynn, Executive Director
Carol McLaughlin, Program Director

2485 Student Help and Assistance Program to Education

C/O Michael Bienes
141 Bay Colony Drive
Fort Lauderdale, FL 33308-2024
Offers grants and support in the areas of elementary and secondary education, music and dance.

2486 Thomas & Irene Kirbo Charitable Trust

550 Water St
Suite 1327
Jacksonville, FL 32202-5113
904-354-7212
Favors smaller colleges in Florida and Georgia.

Murray Jenks, Executive Director

2487 Thompson Publishing Group

PO Box 26185
Tampa, FL 33623
800-876-0226
http://www.thompson.com or
www.grantsandfunding.com
Assists education administrators and grant seekers in successful fundraising in the public and private sectors.

Joel M Drucker, Executive Director

Georgia

2488 Atlanta-Fulton Public Library
Foundation Collection/Ivan Allen
Department
1 Margaret Mitchell Square NW
Atlanta, GA 30303-1089
404-730-1700
Fax: 404-730-1990
http://www.af.public.lib.ga.us.org
Member of The Foundation Center network, maintaining a collection of private foundation tax returns which provide information on the scope of grants dispensed by that particular foundation.

2489 BellSouth Foundation
C/O BellSouth Corporation
1155 Peachtree Street NE
Sutie 7H08
Atlanta, GA 30309-3600
404-249-2396
Fax: 404-249-5696
http://www.bellsouthfoundation.org
The foundation's purpose is to improve education in the South and to address the problem of the inadequate schooling in the region.

Mary D Boehm, President
Beverly Fleming, Administrative
Assistant

2490 Bradley Foundation
1241 North Franklin Place
Milwaukee, WI 53202-2901
414-291-9915
Fax: 414-291-9991
http://www.bradleyfdn.org
Focuses on higher educational facilities, elementary and secondary education, human services and federated giving programs.

Terry Considine, Chairman

2491 Callaway Foundation
209 W Broome Street
#790
Lagrange, GA 30241-3101
706-884-7348
Fax: 706-884-0201
http://www.callawayfoundation.org
Offers giving in the areas of elementary, higher and secondary education, including libraries and community giving.

JT Gresham, Executive Director

2492 Coca-Cola Foundation
Po Box 1734
Atlanta, GA 30301
404-676-2568
Fax: 404-676-8804
http://www.thecoca-colacompany.com
Committed to serving communities through education. The foundation supports programs for early childhood education, elementary and secondary schools, public and private colleges and universities, teacher training, adult learning and global education programs, among others.

Donald R Greene, Executive Director

2493 J Bulow Campbell Foundation
3050 Peachtree Road
Suite 270
Atlanta, GA 30305
404-658-9066
Fax: 404-659-4802
http://www.jbcf.org
The purpose of this foundation is to offer grants and support to privately supported

education, human welfare, youth services and the arts in the state of Georgia.

John W Stephenson, Executive Director

2494 JK Gholston Trust
C/O NationsBank of Georgia
PO Box 992
Athens, GA 30603-0992
706-357-6271
Support is offered to elementary school and higher education facilities in the Comer, Georgia area.

Janey M Cooley, Executive Director

2495 John & Mary Franklin Foundation
C/O Bank South N.A.
PO Box 4956
Atlanta, GA 30302
404-521-7397
Offers grants in secondary school/education, higher education and youth services.

Virlyn Moore Sr, Executive Director

2496 John H & Wilhelmina D Harland Charitable Foundation
2 Piedmont Center NE
Suite 710
Atlanta, GA 30305-1502
404-264-9912
Fax: 404-266-8834
E-mail: info@harlandfoundation.org
http://www.harlandfoundation.org
Children and higher education.

Jane G Hardesty, Executive Director
Gail G Byers, Grants Manager

2497 Joseph B Whitehead Foundation
191 Peachtree Street NE
Suite 3540
Atlanta, GA 30303-2916
404-522-6755
Fax: 404-522-7026
E-mail: fdns@woodruff.org
http://www.jbwhitehead.org
Offers grants in education, cultural programs, the arts and civic affairs.

Charles H McTier, Executive Director
James B William, Chairman

2498 Lettie Pate Evans Foundation
191 Peachtree Street NE
Suite 3540
Atlanta, GA 30303-2916
404-522-6755
Fax: 404-522-7026
E-mail: fdns@woodruff.org
http://www.lpevans.org
Offers grants in the areas of higher education, and support for educational and cultural institutions.

Charles H McTier, Executive Director
James B William, Chairman

2499 McCamish Foundation
1 Buckhead Loop NE #3060
Atlanta, GA 30326-1528
http://www.mccamish.com
Offers grants for conservation and educational institutions.

2500 Metropolitan Atlanta Community Foundation
50 Hurt Plaza
Suite 449
Atlanta, GA 30303
404-688-5525
Fax: 404-688-3060
http://www.atlcf.org
This foundation was organized for the administration of funds placed in trust for the purposes of improving education, commu-

nity development and civic health of the 19-county metropolitan area of Atlanta.

Winsome Hawkins Sr, Executive Director
Alicia Phillip, President

2501 Mill Creek Foundation
4400 Braselton Hwy
Hoschton, GA 30548-0190
478-237-0101
Fax: 478-237-6187
http://www.mccef.org
The foundation's primary interests are educational programs in all levels of study in Emanuel County, Georgia.

James H Morgan, Executive Director

2502 Mills Bee Lane Memorial Foundation
Nations Bank of Georgia
PO Box 9626
Savannah, GA 31412-9626
Offers support in various areas of education, including higher, secondary, and elementary.

2503 Peyton Anderson Foundation
577 Mulberry Street
Suite 830
Macon, GA 31201
478-743-5359
Fax: 912-742-5201
E-mail: grants@pafdn.org
http://www.peytonanderson.org
Supports organizations and programs that center on elementary education, higher education, adult education, literacy and basic skills and youth services, in Bibb County, Georgia only.

Juanita T Jordan, Executive Director
Karen Lambert, President

2504 Rich Foundation
11 Piedmont Avenue NE
Atlanta, GA 30303
404-262-2266
Funds are allocated to social services, health, the arts and education.

Anne Berg, Executive Director

2505 Robert & Polly Dunn Foundation
PO Box 723194
Atlanta, GA 31139-0194
404-816-2883
Fax: 404-237-2150
Offers support in the areas of child development, education, higher education, and children and youth services.

Karen C Wilbanks, Executive Director

2506 Sapelo Foundation
1712 Ellis Street
2nd Floor
Brunswick, GA 31520
912-265-0520
Fax: 912-265-1888
E-mail: sapelofoundation@mindspring.com
http://www.sapelofoundation.org
The Sapelo Foundation's scholarship program, The Richard Reynolds Scholarship Program offers college scholarships only to students who are legal residents of McIntosh County, Georgia.

Phyllis Bowen, Executive Director

2507 Tull Charitable Foundation
50 Hurt Plaza SE
Suite 1245
Atlanta, GA 30303-2916
404-659-7079
http://www.tullfoundation.org
Offers support to secondary schools, elementary schools and higher education facilities in the state of Georgia.

Barbara Cleveland, Executive Director

2508 Warren P & Ava F Sewell Foundation
PO Box 645
Bremen, GA 30110-0645
Offers support in elementary school, secondary school education and religion.

Jack Worley, Executive Director

Hawaii

2509 Barbara Cox Anthony Foundation
1132 Bishop Street #120
Honolulu, HI 96813-2807
Offers support to secondary schools, higher education, and human service organizations in Hawaii.

Barner Anthony, Executive Director

2510 Cooke Foundation
827 Fort Street Mall
Honolulu, HI 96813
808-537-6333
888-731-3863
Fax: 808-521-6286
E-mail: foundations@hcf-hawaii.org
http://www.hawaiicommunityfoundation.org
The environment, the arts, education and social services are the priority areas for this foundation.

Lisa Schiff, Private Foundation Service
Samuel Cooke, President & Trustee

2511 Harold KL Castle Foundation
1197 Auloa Road
Kailua, HI 96734-2835
808-263-7073
Fax: 808-261-6918
http://www.castlefoundation.org
Grants are given in the area of education, community and cultural/community affairs.

Terrence R George, Executive Director
H Mitchell D'Olier, President

2512 Hawaiian Electric Industries Charitable Foundation
PO Box 730
Honolulu, HI 96808-0730
808-532-5862
http://www.hei.com/heicf/heicf.html
Offers support for education, including higher education, business education, educational associations and secondary schools.

Scott Shirai, Executive Director
Robert F Clark, President

2513 James & Abigail Campbell Foundation
1001 Kamokila Boulevard
Kapolei, HI 96707-2014
808-674-3167
Fax: 808-674-3349
E-mail: keolal@jamescampbell.com
http://www.campbellfamilyfoundation.org
Offers support in education for schools and educational programs related to literacy or job training in Hawaii.

Theresia McMurdo, Public Relations
D. Keola Lloyd, Grants Manager

2514 Oceanic Cablevision Foundation
200 Akamainui Street
Mililani, HI 96789-3999
808-625-8359
Offers support in a variety of areas with an emphasis on education, especially early childhood and cultural programs.

Kit Beuret, Executive Director

2515 Samuel N & Mary Castle Foundation
733 Bishop Street
Suite 1275
Honolulu, HI 96813-2912
808-522-1101
Fax: 808-522-1103
E-mail: acastle@aloha.net
http://www.fdncenter.org
Funding is offered in the areas of education, human services and the arts for the state of Hawaii.

Annually

Al Castle, Executive Director

2516 University of Hawaii
Hamilton Library
2550 The Mall
Honolulu, HI 96822-2233
808-956-7214
Fax: 808-956-5968
http://www.libweb.hawaii.edu/uhmlib
Member of The Foundation Center network, maintaining a collection of private foundation tax returns which provide information on the scope of grants dispensed by that particular foundation.

Idaho

2517 Boise Public Library
715 S Capitol Boulevard
Boise, ID 83702-7115
208-384-4076
http://www.boisepubliclibrary.org
Member of The Foundation Center network, maintaining a collection of private foundation tax returns which provide information on the scope of grants dispensed by that particular foundation.

2518 Claude R & Ethel B Whittenberger Foundation
PO Box 1073
Caldwell, ID 83606-1073
208-459-0091
E-mail: whittfnd@cableone.net
http://www.whittenberger.org
Offers support for youth and children in higher and secondary education.

William J Rankin, Executive Director

2519 Walter & Leona Dufresne Foundation
1150 W State Street
Boise, ID 83702-5327
Offers support in the areas of secondary school education and higher education.

Royce Chigbrow, Executive Director

Illinois

2520 Ameritech Foundation
30 S Wacker Drive
Floor 34
Chicago, IL 60606-7487
312-750-5223
Fax: 312-207-1098
http://www.ntlf.com
A foundation that offers grants to elementary school/education, secondary school/education and higher education.

Michael E Kuhlin, Executive Director

2521 Carus Corporate Contributions Program
315 5th Street
Peru, IL 61354-2859
815-223-1500

Offers support for higher, secondary, elementary and early childhood education.

Robert J Wilmot, Executive Director

2522 Chauncey & Marion Deering McCormick Foundation
410 N Michigan Avenue
Suite 590
Chicago, IL 60611-4220
312-644-6720
Preschool education, journalism and the improvement of socio-economic condition of Metropolitan Chicago are the main areas of giving for this foundation.

Charles E Schroeder, Executive Director

2523 Chicago Community Trust
225 North Michigan Avenue
Suite 2200
Chicago, IL 60601-1088
312-616-8000
Fax: 312-616-7955
E-mail: sandy@cct.org
http://www.cct.org
A community foundation that offers support for general operating projects and specific programs and projects in areas including child development, education and higher education.

Sandy Chears, Grants Manager
Terry Mazany, President

2524 Coleman Foundation
651 West Washington Boulevard
Suite 306
Chicago, IL 60661-2515
312-902-7120
Fax: 312-902-7124
E-mail: info@colemanfoundation.org
http://www.colemanfoundation.org
A nonprofit, private foundation established in the state of Illinois in 1951. Major areas of support include health, educational, cultural, scientific and social programs. Grants generally focus on organizations within the Midwest and particularly within the state of Illinois and the Chicago Metropolitan area. No grants are made for programs outside of the United States. Ongoing support is not available, continuing programs must indicate how they will be sustained in the future.

Rosa Janus, Program Manager
Michael W Hennessy, President/CEO

2525 Dellora A & Lester J Norris Foundation
PO Box 4325
Saint Charles, IL 60174-9075
630-377-4111
Education, health and social services are the main concerns of this foundation, with Illinois, Colorado and Florida being their priority.

Eugene W Butler, Executive Director

2526 Dillon Foundation
PO Box 454
Boulder, MT 59632-0537
406-980-1588
E-mail: info@dillonfoundation.org
http://www.dillonfoundation.org
Offers support for educational purposes, including higher education and community services.

Peter W Dillon, Executive Director

2527 Dr. Scholl Foundation
1033 Skokie Boulevard
Suite 230
Northbrook, IL 60062
847-559-7430
http://www.drschollfoundation.com

Applications for grants are considered in the following areas: private education at all levels including elementary, secondary schools, colleges and universities and medical and nursing institutions; general charitable organizations and programs, including grants to hospitals and programs for children, developmentally disabled and senior citizens; civic, cultural, social services, health care, economic and religious activities.

Pamela Scholl, Executive Director

2528 Evanston Public Library
1703 Orrington Avenue
Evanston, IL 60201-3886
847-866-0300
Fax: 847-866-0313
http://www.evanston.lib.il.us
Member of The Foundation Center network, maintaining a collection of private foundation tax returns which provide information on the scope of grants dispensed by that particular foundation.

Neal J Ney, Director

2529 Farny R Wurlitzer Foundation
PO Box 418
Sycamore, IL 60178-0418
Offers support in the areas of education, including programs for minorities, early childhood, elementary and secondary institutions, music education and organizations.

William A Rolfing, Executive Director

2530 Grover Hermann Foundation
1000 Hill Grove
Suite 200
Western Springs, IL 60558-6306
708-246-8331
Focus of giving is on higher education and private schooling activities.

Paul K Rhoads, Executive Director

2531 Joyce Foundation
70 W Madison Street
Suite 2750
Chicago, IL 60602
312-782-2464
Fax: 312-782-4160
E-mail: info@joycefdn.org
http://www.joycefdn.org
Based in Chicago with assets of $1 billion, the Joyce foundation supports efforts to strengthen public policies in ways that improve the quality of life in the Great Lakes region. Last year the foundation made nearly $17 million in grants to groups working to improve public education in Chicago, Cleveland, Detroit and Milwaukee.

Ellen Alberding, President

2532 Lloyd A Fry Foundation
120 S Lasalle Street
Suite 1950
Chicago, IL 60603-3419
312-580-0310
Fax: 312-580-0980
http://www.fryfoundation.org
The foundation primarily supports education, higher education, the performing arts, and social service organizations.

Unmi Song, Executive Director

2533 Northern Trust Company Charitable Trust
Community Affairs Division
50 S Lasalle Street
Chicago, IL 60603-1006
312-630-6000
http://www.ntrs.com

Offers grants in the areas of community development, education and early childhood education.

Marjorie W Lundy, Executive Director

2534 Palmer Foundation
734 15th Street NW
Suite 600
Washington, DC 20005
202-595-1020
Fax: 202-833-5540
E-mail: admin@thepalmerfoundation.org
http://www.thepalmerfoundation.org
Offers grants in elementary and secondary education, as well as youth services and Protestant churches.

2535 Philip H Corboy Foundation
33 N Dearborn Street
Chicago, IL 60602-2502
312-346-3191
http://www.corboydemetrio.com
Offers grants in the areas of elementary, secondary, law school education and health care.

2536 Polk Brothers Foundation
20 W Kinzie Street
Suite 1100
Chicago, IL 60610-4600
312-527-4684
Fax: 312-527-4681
http://www.polkbrosfdn.org
Offers grants for new or ongoing programs to organizations whose work is based in the areas of education, social services and health care.

Nikki W Stein, Executive Director
Shiela A Robinson, Grants Administrator

2537 Prince Charitable Trust
303 West Madison Street
Suite 1900
Chicago, IL 60606-7407
312-419-8700
Fax: 312-419-8558
http://www.fdncenter.org/grantmaker/prince/chicago.html
Offers support for cultural programs, public school programming and social service organizations.

Benna B Wilde, Managing Director
Sharon L Robison, Grants Manager

2538 Regenstein Foundation
8600 W Bryn Mawr Avenue
Suite 705N
Chicago, IL 60631-3579
773-693-6464
Fax: 773-693-2480
Offers grants for educational and general charitable institutions within the metropolitan Chicago area and the state of Illinois.

Joseph Regenstein Jr, Executive Director

2539 Richard H Driehaus Foundation
333 N Michigan Avenue
Suite 510
Chicago, IL 60601-1604
312-641-5772
Fax: 312-641-5736
http://www.driehausfoundation.org
Offers support in elementary, secondary and higher education in the state of Illinois.

Susan Fischer, Executive Director
Peter Handler, Program Director

2540 Robert R McCormick Tribune Foundation
435 N Michigan Avenue
Suite 770
Chicago, IL 60611-4066

312-222-3512
Fax: 312-222-3523
http://www.rrmtf.org
Offers contributions for private higher education and rehabilitation services.

Nicholas Goodban, Senior VP/Philanthropy
Richard A Behrenhausen, President/CEO

2541 Sears-Roebuck Foundation
Sears Tower
Department 903-BSC 51-02
Chicago, IL 60684
312-875-8337
The foundation focuses its giving primarily on projects that address education and volunteerism.

Paula A Banke, Executive Director

2542 Spencer Foundation
875 N Michigan Avenue
Suite 3930
Chicago, IL 60611-1803
312-337-7000
Fax: 312-337-0282
http://www.spencer.org
Supports research aimed at the practice of understanding and expanding knowledge in the area of education.

Michael McPherson, President

2543 Sulzer Family Foundation
1940 W Irving Park Road
Chicago, IL 60613-2437
312-321-4700
Offers giving for education, including higher, secondary, elementary and adult education in the areas of Chicago, Illinois.

John J Hoellen, Executive Director

2544 United Airlines Foundation
1800 Massachusetts Avenue
Suite 400
Washington, DC 20036-0919
847-952-5714
http://www.unfoundation.org
Offers a wide variety of support programs with an emphasis on education and educational reform.

Eileen Younglove, Executive Director
Timothy E Wirth, President

2545 Valenti Charitable Foundation
Valenti Builders
PO Box 2534
Rancho Santa Fe, CA 92067-3311
858-759-9239
Fax: 858-759-1319
E-mail: Irene@valentifoundation.org
http://www.valentifoundation.org
Offers support in elementary education, secondary school education, higher education and children and youth services.

Valenti Sr Trustee, Executive Director

Indiana

2546 Allen County Public Library
900 Library Plaza
Fort Wayne, IN 46802-3699
260-421-1200
Fax: 260-421-1386
http://www.acpl.lib.in.us
Member of The Foundation Center network, maintaining a collection of private foundation tax returns which provide information on the scope of grants dispensed by that particular foundation.

2547 Arvin Foundation
1 Noblitt Plaza #3000
Columbus, IN 47201-6079
812-379-3207
Fax: 812-379-3688

Giving is offered primarily to primary, secondary and higher education and technical training.

E Fred Meyer, Executive Director

2548 Clowes Fund
320 N Meridian Street Suite 316
The Chamber of Commerce Building
Indianapolis, IN 46204-1722
800-943-7209
Fax: 800-943-7286
http://www.clowesfund.org
Offers giving for higher and secondary education; the performing arts; marine biology and social service organizations.

Elizabeth Casselman, Executive Director
Alexander W Clowes, President

2549 Dekko Foundation
PO Box 548
Kendallville, IN 46755-0548
260-347-1278
Fax: 260-347-7103
Offers support for all levels of education and human service organizations.

Linda Speakman, Executive Director

2550 Eli Lilly & Company Corporate Contribution Program
Lilly Corporate Center D.C. 1627
Indianapolis, IN 46285
317-276-2000
Offers support in the areas of secondary school/education, higher education and health care programs.

Thomas King, President

2551 Foellinger Foundation
520 E Berry Street
Fort Wayne, IN 46802-2002
260-422-2900
Fax: 260-422-9436
E-mail: info@foellinger.org
http://www.foellinger.org
Giving is aimed at higher education and other secondary and elementary projects, community programs and social service organizations.

Harry V Owen, Executive Director

2552 Indianapolis Foundation
615 N Alabama Street
Suite 119
Indianapolis, IN 46204-1498
317-634-2423
Fax: 317-684-0943
http://www.indyfund.org
Offers support in the areas of education and neighborhood services.

Kenneth Gladish, Executive Director

2553 John W Anderson Foundation
402 Wall Street
Valparaiso, IN 46383-2562
219-462-4611
Fax: 219-531-8954
Offers grants in the areas of higher education, youth programs, human services, and arts and humanities. Grants are limited primarily to Northwest Indian organizations.

William Vinovich, Vice Chairman/Trustee

2554 Lilly Endowment
2801 N Meridian Street
Indianapolis, IN 46208-0068
317-924-5471
Fax: 317-926-4431
http://www.lillyendowment.org
Supports the causes of religion, education and community development. Although the Endowment supports efforts of national significance, especially in the field of religion, it

is primarily committed to its hometown, Indianapolis, and home state, Indiana.

Sue Ellen Walker, Communications Associate

2555 Moore Foundation
1661 Page Mill Road
Palo Alto, CA 94304-2158
317-848-2013
Fax: 317-571-0744
E-mail: info@moore.org
http://www.moore.org
Offers support in elementary school and secondary school education, higher education, business school education and youth services in Indiana.

Eileen C Ryan, Executive Director
Gordon Moore, Chairman

2556 W Brooks Fortune Foundation
7933 Beaumont Green W Drive
Indianapolis, IN 46250-1652
317-842-1303
Support is limited to education-related programs in Indiana.

William Brooks Fortune, Executive Director

Iowa

2557 Cedar Rapids Public Library
Funding Information Center
500 1st Street SE
Cedar Rapids, IA 52401-2095
319-398-5123
Fax: 319-398-0476
http://www.crlibrary.org
Member of The Foundation Center network, maintaining a collection of private foundation tax returns which provide information on the scope of grants dispensed by that particular foundation.

Tamara Glise, Public Services Manager
Eileen C Ryan, Executive Director

2558 RJ McElroy Trust
425 Cedar Street
Suite 312
Waterloo, IA 50701
312
http://www.mcelroytrust.org
The trust funds grants to educational youth programs in the northeast quarter of Iowa. The trust guidelines do not include grants to individuals.

Linda L Klinger, Executive Director

Kansas

2559 Mary Jo Williams Charitable Trust
PO Box 660075
Dallas, TX 75266-0075
866-866-7509
Offers support in the areas of early childhood education, higher education, and children and youth services.

Michael E Collins, Executive Director

2560 Sprint Foundation
2330 Shawnee Mission Parkway
Westwood, KS 66205-2090
913-624-3343
http://www.sprint.com
Offers grants in a variety of areas with an emphasis on education, including business education, secondary education and higher education.

Don G Forsythe, Executive Director

2561 Wichita Public Library
223 S Main Street
Wichita, KS 67202-3795
316-261-8500
Fax: 316-262-4540
http://www.wichita.lib.ks.us
Member of The Foundation Center network, maintaining a collection of private foundation tax returns which provide information on the scope of grants dispensed by that particular foundation.

Kentucky

2562 Ashland Incorporated Foundation
50 E River Center Boulevard
Covington, KY 41012
859-815-3630
Fax: 859-815-4496
http://www.ashland.com
Offers support to educational organizations, colleges and universities, as well as giving an employee matching gift program to higher education and community funding.

James O'Brien, CEO

2563 Gheens Foundation
401 W Main Street
Suite 705
Louisville, KY 40202
502-584-4650
Fax: 502-584-4652
http://www.gheensfoundation.org
The foundation's support is aimed at higher and secondary education, ongoing teacher education, and social service agencies.

James N Davis, Executive Director
William G Duncan, Secretary

2564 James Graham Brown Foundation
4350 Brownsboro Road
Suite 200
Louisville, KY 40207
502-896-2440
Fax: 502-896-1774
E-mail: info@jgbf.org
http://www.jgbf.org
Offers grants in the areas of higher education and social services.

Mason Rummel, Executive Director
Dodie L McKenzie, Program Officer

2565 Louisville Free Public Library
301 York Street
Louisville, KY 40203-2257
502-574-1611
Fax: 502-574-1657
http://www.lfpl.org
Member of The Foundation Center network, maintaining a collection of private foundation tax returns which provide information on the scope of grants dispensed by that particular foundation.

2566 Margaret Hall Foundation
6685 Walnutwood Circle
Baltimore, MD 21212-1727
443-708-3548
http://www.margarethallfoundation.org
Awards grants and scholarships to private, nonprofit secondary schools for innovative programming.

Helen R Burg, Executive Director

2567 VV Cooke Foundation Corporation
220 Mount Mercy Drive
Pewee Valley, KY 40056-9068
502-241-0303
Offers support in education and youth services with an emphasis on Baptist church and school support.

John B Gray, Executive Director

149

Louisiana

2568 Baton Rouge Area Foundation
402 N 4th Street
Baton Rouge, LA 70802
225-387-6126
877-387-6126
Fax: 225-387-6153
http://www.braf.org
Offers grants in the area of elementary and secondary education and health.

John G Davies, President

2569 Booth-Bricker Fund
826 Union Street
Suite 300
New Orleans, LA 70112-1421
504-581-2430
Fax: 504-566-4785
Does not have a formal grant procedure or grant application form; nor does it publish an annual report. The Booth-Bricker Fund makes contributions for the purposes of promoting, developing and fostering religious, charitable, scientific, literary or educational programs, primarily in the state of Louisiana. It does not make contributions to individuals.

Gray S Parker, Chairman

2570 East Baton Rouge Parish Library
Centroplex Branch Grants Collection
7711 Goodwood Boulevard
Baton Rouge, LA 70806
225-231-3750
http://www.ebrpl.com
Member of The Foundation Center network, maintaining a collection of private foundation tax returns which provide information on the scope of grants dispensed by that particular foundation.

2571 Fred B & Ruth B Zigler Foundation
Zigler Foundation
PO Box 986
Zigler Building
Jennings, LA 70546-0986
337-824-2413
Fax: 337-824-2414
E-mail: frizler@bellsouth.net
http://www.ziglerfoundation.org
Offers support to higher, secondary and primary education.

Julie G Berry, President
Marie Romero, Secretary

2572 New Orleans Public Library
Business & Science Division
219 Loyola Avenue
New Orleans, LA 70112-2044
504-529-7323
Fax: 504-596-2609
http://www.nutrias.org
Member of The Foundation Center network, maintaining a collection of private foundation tax returns which provide information on the scope of grants dispensed by that particular foundation.

2573 Shreve Memorial Library
424 Texas Street
Shreveport, LA 71101-5452
318-226-5897
Fax: 318-226-4780
E-mail: webmaster@shreve-lib.org
http://www.shreve-lib.org
Member of The Foundation Center network, maintaining a collection of private Louisiana foundation tax returns which provide information on the scope of grants dispensed by that particular foundation.

Carlos Colon, Reference Supervisor

Maine

2574 Clarence E Mulford Trust
PO Box 290
Fryeburg, ME 04037-0290
207-935-2061
Fax: 207-935-3939
Offers grants to charitable, educational and scientific organizations for the purpose of improving education.

David R Hastings II, Executive Director

2575 Harold Alfond Trust
C/O Dexter Shoe Company
Two Monument Square
Portland, ME 04101-0353
207-828-7999
E-mail: info@haroldalfoundation.org
http://www.haroldalfondfoundation.org
Grants are offered to secondary and higher education in Maine and Maryland.

Keith Burden, Executive Director

Maryland

2576 Abell Foundation
111 S Calvert Street
Suite 2300
Baltimore, MD 21202-6182
410-547-1300
Fax: 410-539-6579
E-mail: abell@abell.org
http://www.abell.org
The foundation supports education with an emphasis on public education, including early childhood and elementary, research, and minority education.

Robert C Embry Jr, Executive Director
Ellen Mullan, Controller

2577 Aegon USA
1111 N Charles Street
Baltimore, MD 21201-5505
410-576-4571
Fax: 410-347-8685
http://www.aegonins.com
Offers grants in elementary school, secondary school, higher education and medical school education.

Larry G Brown, Executive Director

2578 Clarence Manger & Audrey Cordero Plitt Trust
C/O First National Bank of Maryland
25 S Charles St
Baltimore, MD 21201-3330
410-566-0914
Offers grants to educational institutions for student loans and scholarships.

Mary M Kirgan, Executive Director

2579 Clark-Winchcole Foundation
Air Rights Building
3 Bethesda Metro Center
Suite 550
Bethesda, MD 20814
301-654-3607
Fax: 301-654-3140
Offers grants in the areas of higher education and social service agencies.

Laura E Philips, Executive Director

2580 Commonwealth Foundation
9737 Colesville Road
Suite 800
Silver Spring, MD 20910
301-495-4400
Offers grants in the areas of early childhood education, child development, elementary schools, secondary schools and youth services.

Barbara Bainum, Executive Director

2581 Dresher Foundation
4940 Campbell Boulevard
Suite 110
Baltimore, MD 21236
410-933-0384
E-mail: web@jdgraphicdesign.com
http://www.jdgraphicdesign.com/dresher/dresherfoundation/
Offers giving in the areas of elementary school, early childhood education, meals on wheels, and food distribution.

2582 Edward E Ford Foundation
66 Pearl Street
Suite 322
Portland, ME 04101
207-774-2346
Fax: 207-774-2348
E-mail: office@eeford.org
http://www.eeford.org
Offers giving to secondary schools and private education in the US and its protectorates.

Robert Hallett, Executive Director

2583 Enoch Pratt Free Library
Social Science & History Department
400 Cathedral Street
Baltimore, MD 21201-4484
301-396-5430
http://www.pratt.lib.md.us
Member of The Foundation Center network, maintaining a collection of private foundation tax returns which provide information on the scope of grants dispensed by that particular foundation.

2584 France-Merrick Foundation
The Exchange
2 Hamill Rd, Quadrangle East
Suite 302
Baltimore, MD 21210-2139
410-464-2004
Fax: 410-832-5704
E-mail: rschaefer@france-merrickfdn-org
Offers grants in the areas of public education, private and higher education, health, social services and cultural activities.

Frederick W Lafferty, Executive Director

2585 Grayce B Kerr Fund
117 Bay Street
Easton, MD 21601-2769
410-822-6652
Fax: 410-822-4546
E-mail: office@gbkf.org
http://www.gbkf.org
The major area of interest to the fund is education, including higher, elementary and early childhood education for the state of Maryland with focus on the Eastern Shore Counties.

Margaret van den Berg, Administrative Assistant
John R Valliant, President

2586 Henry & Ruth Blaustein Rosenberg Foundation
Blaustein Building
10 East Baltimore Street
Suite 1111
Baltimore, MD 21202
410-347-7201
Fax: 410-347-7210
E-mail: info@blaufund.org
http://www.blaufund.org
Offers grants in the areas of secondary and higher education.

Betsy F Ringel, Executive Director
Henry A Rosenberg Jr, President

2587 James M Johnston Trust for Charitable and Educational Purposes
2 Wisconsin Circle
Suite 600
Chevy Chase, MD 20815-7003
301-907-0135
Grants are given to higher and secondary educational institutions located in Washington, DC and North Carolina.

Julie Sanders, Executive Director

2588 John W Kluge Foundation
15004 Sunflower CT
Rockville, MD 20853-0174
301-929-9340
Offers grants in higher education and secondary education.

2589 Marion I & Henry J Knott Foundation
3904 Hickory Avenue
Baltimore, MD 21211-1834
410-235-7068
Fax: 410-889-2577
E-mail: info@knottfoundation.org
http://www.knottfoundation.org
Grantmaking limited to private nonsectarian schools and Catholic schools geographically located within the Archdiocese of Baltimore, Maryland.

Greg Cantori, Executive Director

2590 Robert G & Anne M Merrick Foundation
The Exchange
1122 Kenilworth Drive
Suite 118
Baltimore, MD 21204-2142
410-832-5700
Fax: 410-832-5704
Offers grants for public education, higher education and social services.

Frederick W Lafferty, Executive Director

Massachusetts

2591 Associated Grantmakers of Massachusetts
55 Court Street
Suite 520
Boston, MA 02108-4304
617-426-2606
Fax: 617-426-2849
http://www.agmconnect.org
Member of The Foundation Center network, maintaining a collection of private foundation tax returns which provide information on the scope of grants dispensed by that particular foundation.

Ron Ancrum, President
Martha Moore, Director Center Philanthropy

2592 Boston Foundation
75 Arlington Street
10th Floor
Boston, MA 02116-4407
617-338-1700
Fax: 617-338-1604
http://www.tbf.org
Supports local educational, social and housing programs and institutions.

Paul Grogan, President

2593 Boston Globe Foundation II
135 Morrissey Boulevard
Boston, MA 02107
617-929-2895
Fax: 617-929-7889

http://www.bostonglobe.com/community/foundation/partner.stm
The foundation's highest priority is community based agencies which understand, represent and are part of the following populations; children and youth with disabilities, children and youth with AIDS, refugees, low-birth weight babies, pregnant and nursing mothers and incarcerated youth.

Suzanne W Maas, Executive Director
Leah P Bailey

2594 Boston Public Library
Social Sciences Reference
700 Boylston Street
Boston, MA 02116-2813
617-536-5400
http://www.bpl.org
Member of The Foundation Center network, maintaining a collection of private foundation tax returns which provide information on the scope of grants dispensed by that particular foundation.

Bernard Margolis, President

2595 Dean Foundation for Little Children
C/O Boston Safe Deposit & Trust Company
PO Box 185
Pittsburgh, PA 15230-0185
Giving is centered on little children age twelve and under for the care and relief of destitute children. Provides support for preschools, day care, summer camps and other programs.

Nancy Criscitiello, Executive Director

2596 Hyams Foundation
50 Federal Street
Floor 9
Boston, MA 02110-2210
617-426-5600
Fax: 617-426-5696
http://www.hyamsfoundation.org
The foundation seeks to promote understanding and appreciation of diversity, including race, ethnicity, gender, sexual orientation, age, physical ability, class and religion. The foundation's primary objective is to meet the needs of low-income and other underserved populations, striving to address the causes of those needs, whenever possible. Foundation supports low-income communities in their efforts to identify their own problems, solve these problems and improve people's lives.

Elizabeth B Smith, Executive Director
Angela Brown, Director of Programs

2597 Irene E & George A Davis Foundation
C/O Ann T Keiser
1 Monarch Place
Suite 1450
Springfield, MA 01144-1300
413-734-8336
Fax: 413-734-7845
E-mail: info@davisfdn.org
http://www.davisfdn.org
Education and social service organizations and programs in Western Massachusetts are the primary concern of this foundation.

Mary E Walachy, Executive Director

2598 James G Martin Memorial Trust
122 Pond Street
Jamaica Plain, MA 02130-2714
Giving is centered on elementary education and higher education in Massachusetts.

Ms Martin, Executive Director

2599 Jessie B Cox Charitable Trust
Grants Management Association
60 State Street
Boston, MA 02109-1899

617-227-7940
Fax: 617-227-0781
http://www.hemenwaybarnes.com/selectsrv/jbcox/cox.html
This trust makes grants for projects which will address important social issues in the trust's fields of interest and for which adequate funding from other sources cannot be obtained. The trust funds projects in New England in the areas of health, education and the environment. The trustees look to support special projects which will assist the applicants to achieve their long-range organizational goals.

Michaelle Larkins, Executive Director
Susan M Fish, Grants Administrator

2600 LG Balfour Foundation
Fleet Bank of Massachusetts
75 State Street
Boston, MA 02109-1775
617-346-4000
Offers support for scholarships and innovative projects designed to eliminate barriers and improve access to education for all potentially qualified students.

Kerry Herliney, Executive Director

2601 Little Family Foundation
33 Broad Street
Suite 10
Boston, MA 02109-4216
617-723-6771
Fax: 617-723-7107
Offers scholarships at various business schools and Junior Achievement programs in secondary schools.

Arthur D Little, Executive Director

2602 Rogers Family Foundation
10 Clay Street
Suite 200
Oakland, CA 94067-4501
510-899-7918
Fax: 978-685-1588
http://www.rogersfoundation.org
Offers support in the areas of secondary and higher education in the Lawrence, Massachusetts area.

Kathleen Rogers, President
Nicole Taylor, Secretary/Treasurer

2603 State Street Foundation
225 Franklin Street
12th Floor
Boston, MA 02110
617-664-1937
http://www.statestreet.com
Offers grants to organizations that help improve the quality of life in the greater Boston area. Interest includes human services, public and secondary education, vocational education, and arts and culture programs.

Madison Thompson, Executive Director

2604 Sudbury Foundation
326 Concord Road
Sudbury, MA 01776-1843
978-443-0849
Fax: 978-579-9536
http://www.sudburyfoundation.org
Offers college scholarships to local high school seniors who meet eligibility criteria.

Marilyn Martino, Executive Director
Tricia Brunner, Grants Administrator

2605 Trustees of the Ayer Home
PO Box 1865
Lowell, MA 01853-1865
978-452-5914
Fax: 978-452-5914

151

Funding (greater Lowell, MA only) educational programs (RLF, SMARTS). Primary interests are women and children.

D Donahue, Assistant Treasurer

2606 Weld Foundation
Peter Loring/Janice Palumbo
Loring, Wolcott & Coolidge
30 Congress Street
Boston, MA 02110-2409
617-523-6531
Fax: 617-523-6535
Grants are offered in the areas of elementary, secondary and higher education in Massachusetts.

2607 Western Massachusetts Funding Resource Center
65 Elliot Street
Springfield, MA 01105-1713
413-732-3175
Fax: 413-452-0618
http://www.diospringfield.org/wmfrc.html
Member of The Foundation Center network, maintaining a collection of private foundation tax returns which provide information on the scope of grants dispensed by that particular foundation.

Kathleen Dowd, Director
Jean Los, Administrative Assistant

2608 William E Schrafft & Bertha E Schrafft Charitable Trust
77 Summer Street
Boston, MA 02110
617-457-7327
http://www.schrafftcharitable.org
Giving is primarily allocated to educational programs in the Boston metropolitan area.

Arthur H Parker, Trustee
Lavinia B Chase, Trustee

2609 Woodstock Corporation
Woodstock Corporation
27 School Street
Suite 200
Boston, MA 02108-2301
617-227-0600
Fax: 617-523-0229
E-mail: info@woodstockcorp.com
http://www.woodstockcorp.com
Offers support in the area of secondary school education in the state of Massachusetts.

2610 Worcester Public Library
Grants Resource Center
3 Salem Square
Worcester, MA 01608
508-799-1655
Fax: 508-799-1652
http://www.worcpublib.org
Member of The Foundation Center network, maintaining a collection of private foundation tax returns which provide information on the scope of grants dispensed by that particular foundation.

J Peck, Director Grants Resource

Michigan

2611 Alex & Marie Manoogian Foundation
21001 Van Born Road
Taylor, MI 48180-1340
313-274-7400
Fax: 313-792-6657

Supports higher and secondary education, cultural programs and human service organizations.

Alex Manoogian, Executive Director

2612 Charles Stewart Mott Foundation
Office of Proposal Entry
503 S Saginaw Street
Suite 1200
Flint, MI 48502-1851
810-238-5651
800-645-1766
Fax: 810-237-4857
E-mail: infocenter@mott.org
http://www.mott.org
Grants are given to nonprofit organizations with an emphasis on programs of volunteerism, at-risk youth, environmental protection, economic development and education.

2613 Chrysler Corporate Giving Program
12000 Chrysler Drive
Detroit, MI 48288-0001
810-576-5741
Offers support for education, especially secondary education and leadership development.

Lynn A Feldhouse, Executive Director

2614 Community Foundation for Southeastern Michigan
333 W Fort Street
Suite 2010
Detroit, MI 48226-3134
313-961-6675
Fax: 313-961-2886
E-mail: cfsem@cfsem.orq
http://www.cfsem.org
Supports projects in the areas of education, culture and social services.

Mariam C Noland, President

2615 Community Foundation of Greater Flint
500 South Saginaw Street
Flint, MI 48502-2013
810-767-8270
Fax: 810-767-0496
E-mail: cfgf@cfgf.org
http://www.cfgf.org
A community foundation that makes grants to benefit residents of Genessee County, Michigan. Areas of interest include: arts, education, environment, community services and health and social services.

Kathi Horton, President
Evan M Albert, VP Program

2616 Cronin Foundation
203 E Michigan Avenue
Marshall, MI 49068-1545
616-781-9851
Fax: 616-781-2070
Offers support to expand educational, social and cultural needs of the community within the Marshall, Michigan school district.

Joseph E Schroeder, Executive Director

2617 Detroit Edison Foundation
2000 2nd Avenue
Room 1046
Detroit, MI 48226-1279
313-235-9271
Fax: 313-237-9271
http://www.my.dteenergy.com
Offers support for all levels of education, and local community social services and cultural organizations in Southeast Michigan.

Katharine W Hunt, Executive Director

2618 Ford Motor Company Fund
One American Road
PO Box 1899
Dearborn, MI 48126-2798
888-313-0102
Fax: 313-337-6680
http://www.ford.com
Ford Motor Company Fund continues the legacy of Henry Ford's commitment to innovative education at all levels. We remain dedicated to creating and enriching educational opportunities, especially in the areas of science, engineering, math and business, while promoting diversity in education.

Sandra E Ulsh, President
Jim Graham, Manager Education Programs

2619 Frey Foundation
40 Pearl Street NW
Suite 1100
Grand Rapids, MI 49503-3023
616-451-0303
Fax: 616-451-8481
http://www.freyfdn.org
Awards grants and supports the needs of children in their early years, support for environmental education and protection of our natural resources.

Milton W Rohwer, President
Teresa J Crawford, Grants Manager

2620 General Motors Foundation
PO Box 33170
Detroit, MI 48232-5170
313-556-4260
http://www.gm.com/company/gmability/philanthropy
Offers support for higher education, cultural programs and civic affairs.

Ronald L Theis, Executive Director

2621 Grand Rapids Foundation
185 Oakes St SW
Grand Rapids, MI 49503
616-454-1751
Fax: 616-454-6455
E-mail: grfound@grfoundation.org
http://www.grfoundation.org
A community foundation established in 1922. The foundation actively serves the people of Kent County by administering funds it receives and by making philanthropic grants to non-profit organizations in response to community needs. Various educational scholarships are offered on the basis of a competitive process which considers academic achievement, extracurricular activities, a statement of one's own personal aspirations and educational goals, and financial need. Kent County Residency required.

Ruth Bishop, Program Associate-Education
Diana Sieger, President

2622 Harry A & Margaret D Towsley Foundation
3055 Plymouth Road
Suite 200
Ann Arbor, MI 48105-3208
312-662-6777
Areas of support include pre-school education, social services, and continuing education.

Margaret Ann Riecker, Executive Director

2623 Henry Ford Centennial Library
Adult Services
16301 Michigan Avenue
Dearborn, MI 48126-2792
313-943-2330
Fax: 313-943-3063
http://www.dearborn.lib.mi.us/aboutus/adult.htm
Member of The Foundation Center network, maintaining a collection of private foundation tax returns which provide information on the scope of grants dispensed by that particular foundation.

2624 Herbert H & Grace A Dow Foundation
1018 W Main Street
Midland, MI 48640-4292
989-631-3699
Fax: 989-631-0675
http://www.hhdowfdn.org
Limited to organizations within Michigan. Has charter goals to improve the educational, religious, economic and cultural lives of Michigan's people.

Margaret Ann Riescker, President
Elysa M Rogers, Assistant VP

2625 Herrick Foundation
150 W Jefferson Avenue
Suite 2500
Detroit, MI 48226-4415
313-496-7585
Offers grants to colleges and universities, health agencies and social service organizations.

Dolores de Galleford, Executive Director

2626 Kresge Foundation
3215 W Big Beaver Road
Troy, MI 48084
248-643-9630
Fax: 313-643-0588
http://www.kresge.org
Giving is aimed at areas of interest including arts and humanities, social services and public policy.

John E Marshall III, Executive Director
Sandra McAlister Ambrozy, Senior Program Officer

2627 Malpass Foundation
PO Box 1206
East Jordan, MI 49727-1206
Offers giving in the areas of education and community development.

William J Lorne, Executive Director

2628 McGregor Fund
333 W Fort Street
Suite 2090
Detroit, MI 48226-3134
313-963-3495
Fax: 313-963-3512
E-mail: info@mcgregorfund.org
http://www.mcgregorfund.org
Social services, health and education grants awarded to organizations located in Ohio, primarily the Detroit area.

C David Campbell, President
Kate Levin Markel, Program Officer

2629 Michigan State University Libraries
Social Sciences/Humanities
366 W Circle Drive
East Lansing, MI 48824
517-353-8700
Fax: 517-432-3532
http://www.lib.msu.edu
Member of The Foundation Center network, maintaining a collection of private foundation tax returns which provide information on the scope of grants dispensed by that particular foundation.

2630 Richard & Helen DeVos Foundation
190 Muncie NW
Suite 500
Grand Rapids, MI 49503
616-454-4114
Fax: 616-454-4654
Strong geographical preference to Western Michigan. Funding includes Christian education, cultural, community, education (not an individual basis) and government services.

Donations are also made on a national level to organizations based in Washington, DC.

Stephanie Roy, Executive Director

2631 Rollin M Gerstacker Foundation
PO Box 1945
Midland, MI 48641-1945
989-631-6097
Fax: 517-832-8842
E-mail: lanphear@concentric.net
http://www.tamu.edu/baum/gerstack.html
Primary purpose of this foundation is to carry on, indefinitely, financial aid to charities concentrated in the states of Michigan and Ohio. Grants are given in the areas of community support, schools, education, social services, music and the arts, youth activities, health care and research, churches and other areas.

Carl A Gerstacker, Executive Director

2632 Steelcase Foundation
PO Box 1967, CH-4E
Grand Rapids, MI 49501-1967
616-246-4695
Fax: 616-475-2200
E-mail: sbroman@steelcse.com
http://www.steelcase.com
Offers support for human services and education, to improve the quality of life for children, the elderly and the disabled in the areas where there are manufacturing plants.

Susan Broman, Executive Director

2633 Wayne State University
Purdy-Kresge Library
5265 Cass Avenue
Detroit, MI 48202-3930
313-577-6424
http://www.lib.wayne.edu
Member of The Foundation Center network, maintaining a collection of private foundation tax returns which provide information on the scope of grants dispensed by that particular foundation.

2634 Whirlpool Foundation
2000 N M 63
MD 3106
Benton Harbor, MI 49022-2692
269-923-5584
Fax: 269-925-0154
http://www.whirlpoolcorp.com
Giving centers on learning, cultural diversity, adult education, and scholarships for children of corporation employees.

Ddaniel Hopp, President & Chairman
Pamela Silcox, Operations Manager

Minnesota

2635 Andersen Foundation
Andersen Corporation
100 4th Avenue N
Bayport, MN 55003-1058
651-264-5150
Fax: 651-264-5537
Grants are given in the areas of higher education, health, youth and the arts in Minnesota.

2636 Bush Foundation
E-900 First National Bank Building
332 Minnesota Street
Saint Paul, MN 55101-1314
651-227-0891
Fax: 651-297-6485
http://www.bushfoundation.org
The foundation is predominantly a regional grantmaking foundation, with broad interests in education, human services, health, arts and

humanities and in the development of leadership.

Anita M Pampusch, President
John Archabal, Senior Program Officer

2637 Cargill Foundation
PO Box 9300
Minneapolis, MN 55440-9300
952-742-4311
Fax: 612-742-7224
http://www.cargill.com
Offers grants in the areas of education, health, human service organizations, arts and cultural programs and social service agencies.

Audrey Tulberg, Executive Director

2638 Charles & Ellora Alliss Educational Foundation
800 Nicollet Mall
Minneapolis, MN 55402-1314
612-303-4411
Fax: 651-244-0860
E-mail: allissfoundation@usbank.com
http://www.allissfoundation.org
The foundation is organized exclusively for support of the education of young people, up to and including the period of postgraduate study. As a matter of policy, the foundation generally has limited its program to universities and colleges located in Minnesota. Grants are made to such institutions in support of undergraduate scholarship programs administered by their student aid offices. The foundation makes no direct grants to individuals.

John Bultena, Executive Director
Anita M Pampusch, Board of Trustee

2639 Duluth Public Library
520 W Superior Street
Duluth, MN 55802-1578
218-723-3802
Fax: 218-723-3815
http://www.duluth.lib.mn.us
Member of The Foundation Center network, maintaining a collection of private foundation tax returns which provide information on the scope of grants dispensed by that particular foundation.

Elizabeth Kelly, Library Director

2640 FR Bigelow Foundation
Center 55th Street East
Suite 600
St. Paul, MN 55101-1797
651-224-5463
800-875-6167
Fax: 651-224-8123
E-mail: info@frbiquelow.org
http://www.frbigelow.org
Offers support in early childhood education, elementary and secondary education, higher and adult education and human services.

Richard B Heydinger, Chair
Carleen K Rhodes, Secretary

2641 First Bank System Foundation
PO Box 522
Minneapolis, MN 55480-0522
612-973-2440
Offers support for public elementary and secondary education, arts and cultural programs.

Cheryl L Rantala, Executive Director

2642 Hiawatha Education Foundation
360 Vila Street
Winona, MN 55987-1500
507-453-5550
Giving is centered on Catholic high schools and colleges, as well as awarding scholar-

ships to college-bound high school graduates.

Robert Kierlin, Executive Director

2643 IA O'Shaughnessy Foundation
2001 Killebrew Drive
Suite 120
Bloomington, MN 55425-0704
952-698-0959
Fax: 952-698-0959
http://www.iaoshaughessyfdn.org
Giving is centered on cultural programs, secondary and higher education, human services and medical programs.

John Bultena, Executive Director
John F O'Shaughnessy, President

2644 Marbrook Foundation
730 2nd Avenue
Suite 1300
Minneapolis, MN 55402
612-752-1783
Fax: 612-752-1780
E-mail: jhara@marbrookfoundation.org
http://www.marbrookfoundation.org
Offers grants in the areas of the environment, the arts, social empowerment, spiritual endeavors, basic human needs and health.

Annual Report

Julie S Hara, Executive Director

2645 Medtronic Foundation
7000 Central Avenue NE
Minneapolis, MN 55432-3576
763-514-4000
800-328-2518
Fax: 763-514-8410
http://www.medtronic.com
Offers grants in the areas of education (especially at the pre-college level), community funding and social services.

Penny Hunt, Executive Director

2646 Minneapolis Foundation
800 Ids Center 80 S 8th Street
Minneapolis, MN 55402
612-672-3878
Fax: 612-672-3846
E-mail: mplsfoundation.org
http://www.minneapolisfoundation.org
The foundation strives to strengthen the community for the benefit of all citizens. Grants are awarded for the purposes of achieving this goal in the areas of early childhood education, child development, and education.

Karen Kelley-Ariwoola, VP Community Philanthropy

2647 Minneapolis Public Library
Music, Art, Sociology & Humanities
250 S Marquette
Minneapolis, MN 55401-2188
612-630-6000
Fax: 612-630-6220
http://www.mplib.org
Member of The Foundation Center network, maintaining a collection of private foundation tax returns which provide information on the scope of grants dispensed by that particular foundation.

Katherine G Hadle, Director

2648 Otto Bremer Foundation
445 Minnesota Street
Suite 2250
Saint Paul, MN 55101-2135
651-227-8036
888-291-1123
Fax: 651-312-3665
http://www.ottobremer.org

Offers support for post-secondary education, human services and community affairs.

John Kostishack, Executive Director
Karen Starr, Senior Program Officer

2649 Saint Paul Foundation
55 Fifth Street East
Suite 600
St. Paul, MN 55101-1797
651-224-5463
800-875-6167
Fax: 651-224-8123
E-mail: info@saintpaulfoundation.org
http://www.saintpaulfoundation.org
Offers support for educational, charitable and cultural purposes of a public nature.

Carleen K Rhodes, President
Mindy K Molumby, Grants Administrator

2650 TCF Foundation
Code EXO-02-C
200 Lake Street
East Wayzata, MN 55391-1693
952-745-2757
Fax: 612-661-8554
http://www.tcfexpress.com
Giving is primarily for education through grants and employee matching gifts, including secondary schools, higher education and organizations that increase public knowledge.

Neil I Whitehouse, Executive Director

Mississippi

2651 Foundation for the Mid South
134 East Amite Street
Jackson, MS 39201
601-355-8167
Fax: 601-355-6499
http://www.fndmidsouth.org
Makes grants in the area of education, as well as economic development and families and children.

George Penick, Executive Director
Kay Kelly Arnold, Vice Chairman

2652 Jackson-Hinds Library System
300 N State Street
Jackson, MS 39201-1705
601-968-5811
E-mail: reference@jhlibrary.com
http://www.jhlibrary.com
Member of The Foundation Center network, maintaining a collection of private foundation tax returns which provide information on the scope of grants dispensed by that particular foundation.

Carolyn McCallum, Executive Director

2653 Mississippi Power Foundation
PO Box 4079
Gulfport, MS 39502-4079
228-864-1211
http://www.mississippipower.com
The foundation is dedicated to the improvement and enhancement of education in Mississippi from kindergarten to twelfth grade.

Huntley Biggs, Executive Director

2654 Phil Hardin Foundation
2750 North Park Drive
Meridian, MS 39305-5800
601-483-4282
Fax: 601-483-5665
E-mail: info@philhardin.org
http://www.philhardin.org

Offers giving in Mississippi for schools and educational institutions and programs.

C Thompson Wacaster, Executive Director

Missouri

2655 Ameren Corporation Charitable Trust
Ameren Corporation
PO Box 66149
MC 100
Saint Louis, MO 63166-6149
314-554-2789
877-426-3736
Fax: 314-554-2888
E-mail: sbell@ameren.com
http://www.ameren.com
Offers giving in the areas of education, environment, youth and seniors; giving restricted to nonprofits located in Ameren service area in Missouri and Illinois.

Annually

Susan M Bell, Sr Community Relations
Otis Cowan, Community Relations Manger

2656 Clearinghouse for Midcontinent Foundations
University of Missouri
5110 Cherry Street
Suite 310
Kansas City, MO 64110-2426
816-253-1176
Fax: 816-235-5727
Member of The Foundation Center network, maintaining a collection of private foundation tax returns which provide information on the scope of grants dispensed by that particular foundation.

2657 Danforth Foundation
205 E Butterfield Road
Suite 410
Elmhurst, IL 60126-2733
630-501-1235
Fax: 314-588-0035
E-mail: meboozell@danforthfoundation.com
http://www.danforthfoundation.com
This foundation is aimed at enhancing human life through activities which emphasize the theme of improvement in teaching and learning. Serves the pre-collegiate education through grantmaking and program activities.

Dr. Bruce J Anderson, President

2658 Enid & Crosby Kemper Foundation
C/O UMB Bank, N.A.
PO Box 419692
Kansas City, MO 64141-6692
816-860-7711
Fax: 816-860-5690
Giving is primarily allocated to organizations and programs focusing on educational and cultural needs.

Stephen J Campbell, Executive Director

2659 Hall Family Foundation
Charitable & Crown Investment - 323
PO Box 419580
Kansas City, MO 64141-6580
816-274-8516
Fax: 816-274-8547
http://www.hallfamilyfoundation.org
Offers grants in the areas of all levels of education, performing and visual arts, community development, and children, youth and families.

William S Berkley, President & CEO
David A Warm, Executive Director

2660 James S McDonnell Foundation
1034 S Brentwood Boulevard
Suite 1850
Saint Louis, MO 63117-1284

314-721-1532
Fax: 314-721-7421
http://www.jsmf.org
Foundation Program, Cognitive Studies for Educational Practice, funding available through competition in broadly announced requests for proposals. Program grant guidelines are announced in 3 year cycles.

John T Bruer, President
Cheryl A Washington, Grants Manager

2661 Kansas City Public Library
14 West 10th Street
Kansas City, MO 64105
816-701-3400
Fax: 816-701-3401
http://www.kclibrary.org
Member of The Foundation Center network, maintaining a collection of private foundation tax returns which provide information on the scope of grants dispensed by that particular foundation.

Jonathan Kemper, President
David Mayta, Vice President

2662 Mary Ranken Jordan & Ettie A Jordan Charitable Foundation
Mercantile Bank
PO Box 387
Saint Louis, MO 63166-0387
314-231-7626
Giving is limited to charitable institutions with an emphasis on secondary education and cultural programs, as well as higher education and social services.

Fred Arnold, Executive Director

2663 McDonnell Douglas Foundation
PO Box 419692
M S 10203
Kansas City, MO 64141-6692
314-234-0360
Fax: 314-232-7654
Offers various grants with an emphasis on higher and other education and community funding.

AM Bailey, Executive Director

2664 Monsanto Fund
800 N Lindbergh Boulevard
Saint Louis, MO 63167-0001
314-694-1000
Fax: 314-694-7658
E-mail: monsanto.fund@monsanto.com
http://www.monsanto.com/monsanto/about
_us/monsanto_fund
Giving is offered primarily in the area of education, specifically science and math.

Deborah J Patterson, President

Montana

2665 Eastern Montana College Library
Special Collections-Grants
1500 N 30th Street
Billings, MT 59101-0245
406-657-1662
800-565-6782
Fax: 406-657-2037
http://www.msubillings.edu/library
Member of The Foundation Center network, maintaining a collection of private foundation tax returns which provide information on the scope of grants dispensed by that particular foundation.

Joan Bares, Grants Manager

2666 Montana State Library
Library Services
1500 University Drive
Billings, MT 59101-4542

406-657-2011
800-565-6782
Fax: 406-444-5612
http://www.msl.state.mt.us/
Member of The Foundation Center network, maintaining a collection of private foundation tax returns which provide information on the scope of grants dispensed by that particular foundation.

Barbara Duke, Administrative Assistant

Nebraska

2667 Dr. CC & Mabel L Criss Memorial Foundation
US Bank
PO Box 64713
Saint Paul, MN 55614-0713
800-441-2117
Fax: 402-348-6666
Offers support for educational and scientific purposes, including higher education.

2668 Thomas D Buckley Trust
PO Box 647
Chappell, NE 69129-0647
308-874-2212
Fax: 308-874-3491
Offers giving in the areas of education, health care and youth and religion. Grants awarded in Chappell, NE, community and surrounding area.

Connie Loos, Secretary

2669 W Dale Clark Library
Social Sciences Department
215 S 15th Street
Omaha, NE 68102-1601
402-444-4826
Fax: 402-444-4504
http://www.omahapubliclibrary.org
Member of The Foundation Center network, maintaining a collection of private foundation tax returns which provide information on the scope of grants dispensed by that particular foundation.

Angela Green-Garland, President
Arun K Agarwal, Vice President

Nevada

2670 Conrad N Hilton Foundation
30440 Agoura Road
Agoura Hills, CA 91301-1988
818-851-3700
Fax: 775-323-4150
http://www.hiltonfoundation.org
Founded in 1944 as a Trust, this foundation is dedicated to fulfilling and expanding Conrad Hilton's philanthropic vision by carrying out grantmaking activities. The foundation's giving is focused primarily in two areas: the alleviation of human suffering, particularly among disadvantaged children; and the human services works of the Catholic Sisters through a separate entity as described under Major Projects (supportive housing, disabled, education and prevention of domestic violence).

Donald H Hubbs, Executive Director
Steven M Hilton, President

2671 Cord Foundation
E.L. Cord Foundation Center For Learning Literacy
1664 N Virginia Street
Reno, NV 89557-0208
775-784-4951
Fax: 775-784-4758
http://www.unr.edu/cll

Offers support for secondary and higher education, including youth organizations and cultural programs.

Donald Bear, Director/Professor

2672 Donald W Reynolds Foundation
1701 Village Center Circle
Las Vegas, NV 89134-6303
702-804-6000
Fax: 702-804-6099
E-mail: generalquestions@dwrf.org
http://www.dwreynolds.org
Devotes funds to further the cause of free press and journalism education.

Fred Smith, Chairman
Wes Smith, Vice-Chairman

2673 EL Wiegand Foundation
Wiegand Center
165 W Liberty Street
Reno, NV 89501-1915
775-333-0310
Fax: 775-333-0314
Offers grants in of culture and the arts, organizations, health and medical institutions, with an emphasis on Roman Catholic organizations.

Kristen A Avansino, Executive Director

2674 Las Vegas-Clark County
Library District
7060 W Windmill Lane
Las Vegas, NV 89113-2030
702-382-5280
Fax: 702-382-5491
http://www.lvccld.org
Member of The Foundation Center network, maintaining a collection of private foundation tax returns which provide information on the scope of grants dispensed by that particular foundation.

Daniel L Walters, Executive Director
Kelly Benavidez, Chairman

2675 Washoe County Library
301 S Center Street
Reno, NV 89501-2102
775-327-8300
Fax: 775-327-8341
http://www.washoe.lib.nv.us/
Member of The Foundation Center network, maintaining a collection of private foundation tax returns which provide information on the scope of grants dispensed by that particular foundation.

Fred Lokken, Chairman

New Hampshire

2676 Lincolnshire
Liberty Lane
Hampton, NH 03842
Giving is primarily for secondary school education, business school education and recreation.

William Coffey, Executive Director

2677 New Hampshire Charitable Foundation
37 Pleasant Street
Concord, NH 03301-4005
603-225-6641
Fax: 603-225-1700
E-mail: info@nhcf.org
http://www.nhcf.org
Offers grants for charitable and educational purposes including college scholarships, existing charitable organizations, child welfare, community services, health and social

services and new programs that emphasize programs rather than capital needs.

Racheal Stuart, VP Program

2678 Plymouth State College
Herbert H. Lamson Library
17 High Street
Plymouth, NH 03264-1595
603-535-2258
Fax: 603-535-2445
http://www.plymouth.edu/psc/library
Member of The Foundation Center network, maintaining a collection of private foundation tax returns which provide information on the scope of grants dispensed by that particular foundation.

New Jersey

2679 Community Foundation of New Jersey
Knox Hill Road
PO Box 338
Morristown, NJ 07963-0338
973-267-5533
Fax: 973-267-2903
E-mail: cfnj@bellatlantic.net
http://www.cfnj.org
Offers support for programs that offer a path of solution of community problems in the areas of education, leadership development and human services.

Hans Dekker, President

2680 Fund for New Jersey
Kilmer Square
One Palmer Square East
Suite 303
Princeton, NJ 08542-1242
609-356-0241
Fax: 732-220-8654
http://www.fundfornj.org
Offers grants on projects which provide the basis of action in education, AIDS research, minorities/immigrants, public policy and community development.

Mark M Murphy, Executive Director
Kiki Jamieson, President

2681 Hoechst Celanese Foundation
Route 202-206 N
PO Box 2500
Somerville, NJ 08876
908-522-7500
Fax: 908-598-4424
Provides support for education, particularly in the sciences.

Lewis F Alpaugh, Executive Director

2682 Honeywell Foundation
101 Columbia Road
Morristown, NJ 07962-4658
973-455-2000
877-841-2840
Fax: 973-455-4807
http://www.honeywell.com/about/foundation.html
Offers support for education, including fellowship and scholarship aid to colleges.

2683 Hyde & Watson Foundation
31-F Mountain Boulevard
Warren, NJ 07059-1454
908-753-3700
Fax: 908-753-0004
E-mail: hydeandwatson@yahoo.com
http://www.fdncenter.org/grantmaker/hydeandwatson
Support of capital projects of lasting value which tend to increase quality, capacity, or efficiency of a grantee's programs or services, such as purchase or relocation of fa-

cilities, capital equipment, instructive materials development, and certain medical research areas. Broad fields include health, education, religion, social services, arts, and humanities. Geographic areas served include the New York City Metropolitan region and primarily Essex, Union, and Morris Counties in New Jersey.

Hunter W Corbin, President

2684 Mary Owen Borden Memorial Foundation
160 Hodge Road
Princeton, NJ 08540-3014
609-924-3637
Fax: 609-252-9472
E-mail: tborden@ibm.net
http://www.fdncenter.org/grantmaker/borden/index.htm
Offers grants in the areas of childhood education, child development, education, conservation and health and human services.

Thomas Borden, Executive Director

2685 Merck Company Foundation
1 Merck Drive #100
Whitehouse Station, NJ 08889-0100
908-423-2042
http://www.merck.com
Offers support of education, primarily medical through community programs, grants and matching gift programs for colleges and secondary education.

John R Taylor, Executive Director
Kenneth C Fraizer, Chairman,President& CEO

2686 Prudential Foundation
Prudential Plaza
751 Broad Street
Floor 15
Newark, NJ 07102-3714
973-802-4791
http://www.prudential.com
Focus is on children and youth for services that can better their lives. Grants are made in the areas of education, health and human services, community and urban development, business and civic affairs, culture and the arts. Emphasis is placed on programs that serve the city of Newark and the surrounding New Jersey urban centers, programs in cities where The Prudential has a substantial presence and national programs that further the company's objectives.

Barbara L Halaburda, Executive Director

2687 Turrell Fund
21 Van Vleck Street
Montclair, NJ 07042-2358
973-783-9358
Fax: 973-783-9283
E-mail: turrell@turrellfund.org
http://www.fdncenter.org/grantmaker/turrell
Offers grants to organizations and agencies that are dedicated to the care of children and youth under twelve years of age, with an emphasis on education, early childhood education, delinquency prevention and child and youth services.

E Belvin Williams, Executive Director

2688 Victoria Foundation
31 Mulberry Street
5th Floor
Newark, NJ 07102
973-792-9200
Fax: 793-792-1300
E-mail: cmcfarvic@aol.com
http://www.victoriafoundation.org
Grants are limited to Newark, New Jersey in the following areas: elementary and sec-

ondary education, after school enrichment programs, teacher training and academic enrichment.

Catherine M McFarland, Executive Officer
Nancy K Zimmerman, Senior Program Officer

2689 Warner-Lambert Charitable Foundation
201 Tabor Road
Morris Plains, NJ 07950-2614
212-573-2323
Fax: 212-573-7851
Grants are given in the areas of education, health care, culture and the arts. Supports higher institutions of learning which concentrate on pharmacy, medicine, dentistry, the sciences and mathematics. Current support is aimed at the higher levels of education, but the foundation has begun to place more of its attention on the growing needs that impact elementary and secondary training.

Evelyn Self, Community Affairs
Richard Keelty, VP Investor Affair

2690 Wilf Family Foundation
820 Morris Tpke
Short Hills, NJ 07078-2619
973-467-5000
Awards grants in the areas of Jewish higher education and religion.

Joseph Wilf, Executive Director

New Mexico

2691 Dale J Bellamah Foundation
PO Box 36600
Albuquerque, NM 87176-6600
858-756-1154
Fax: 858-756-3856
Offers grants for higher education including military academies, hospitals and social service organizations.

AF Potenziani, Executive Director

2692 New Mexico State Library
Information Services
1209 Camino Carlos Rey
Santa Fe, NM 87507
505-476-9700
Fax: 505-476-9701
http://www.stlib.state.nm.us
Member of The Foundation Center network, maintaining a collection of private foundation tax returns which provide information on the scope of grants dispensed by that particular foundation.

2693 RD & Joan Dale Hubbard Foundation
PO Box 1679
Ruidoso Downs, NM 88346-1679
505-378-4142
Giving is offered in the areas of childhood education, elementary, secondary and higher education as well as other cultural programs.

Jim Stoddard, Executive Director

New York

2694 Achelis Foundation
767 3rd Avenue
4th Floor
New York, NY 10017-2023
212-644-0322
Fax: 212-759-6510
E-mail: main@achelis-bodman-fnds.org
http://www.fdncenter.org/grantmaker/achelis-bodman
Grants include biomedical research at Rockefeller University, rebuilding the Hayden Planetarium at the American Museum of Natural History, support for the arts and culture, the charter school movement, youth organizations, and

special efforts to curb father absence and strengthen family life with awards.

Russell P Pennoyer, President
Joseph S Dolan, Executive Director

2695 Adrian & Jessie Archbold Charitable Trust
401 East 60th Street
New York, NY 10022
212-371-1152
Eastern United States educational institutions and health care service organizations are the main recipients of the Trust.

Myra Mahon, Executive Director

2696 Alfred P Sloan Foundation
630 5th Avenue
Suite 2550
New York, NY 10111-0100
212-649-1649
Fax: 212-757-5117
http://www.sloan.org
A nonprofit foundation offering Sloan Research Fellowships which are awarded in chemistry, computer science, economics, mathematics, neuroscience and physics. These are competitive grants given to young faculty members with high research potential on the recommendation of department heads and other senior scientists.

Ralph E Gomory, President

2697 Altman Foundation
521 5th Avenue
35th Floor
New York, NY 10175
212-682-0970
E-mail: info@altman.org
http://www.altmanfoundation.org
In education, the Altman Foundation supports programs that identify, sponsor and tutor talented disadvantaged youngsters and help them to obtain educations in non-public and independent schools. The Foundation awards grants only in New York State with an almost-exclusive focus on the five boroughs of New York City. The Foundation does not award grants or scholarships to individuals.

Karen L Rosa, VP/Executive Director

2698 Ambrose Monell Foundation
C/O Fulton, Duncombe & Rowe
1 Rockefeller Plaza
Room 301
New York, NY 10020-2002
212-586-0700
Fax: 212-245-1863
E-mail: info@monellvetlesen.org
http://www.monellvetlesen.org
Broad range of allocation including education, social service, cultural organizations and the environment.

Ambrose K Monell, Executive Director
George Rowe, President, Treasurer and Dire

2699 American Express Foundation
American Express Company
World Financial Center
New York, NY 10285
212-640-5661
http://www.home3.americanexpress.com/corp/philanthropy/contacts.asp
The foundation's giving focuses on three areas including community service, education and employment.

Mary Beth Salerno, Executive Director
Angela Woods, Philanthropic Program

2700 Andrew W Mellon Foundation
140 E 62nd Street
New York, NY 10065-8187

212-838-8400
Fax: 212-888-4172
http://www.mellon.org
Offers grants in the areas of higher education, cultural affairs and public affairs.

W.Taylor Revely, President
Lewis W Bernard, Chairman

2701 Arnold Bernhard Foundation
220 E 42nd Street
Floor 6
New York, NY 10017-5806
212-907-1500
Offers funding in the areas of education with the emphasis placed on college and universities as well as college preparatory schools.

Jean B Buttner, Executive Director

2702 Atran Foundation
23-25 East 21st Street
3rd Floor
New York, NY 10010
212-505-9677
Offers grants and funding to nonprofit educational and religious organizations.

2703 Beatrice P Delany Charitable Trust
The Chase Manhattan Bank
1211 Avenue of the Americas
34th Floor
New York, NY 10036
212-935-9935
Giving is offered for education, especially higher education and religion.

John HF Enteman, Executive Director

2704 Bodman Foundation
767 3rd Avenue
4th Floor
New York, NY 10017-2023
212-644-0322
Fax: 212-759-6510
E-mail: main@achelis-bodman-fnds.org
http://www.achelis-bodman-fnds.org
Grants include biomedical research at Rockefeller University, building the Congo Gorilla Forest Education Center at the Bronx Zoo through the Wildlife Conservation Society, rebuilding of the Hayden Planetarium for Science and Technology at the American Museum of Natural History, support for Symphony Space, the charter school movement, youth organizations, and the Rutgers University Foundation.

John N Irwin III, Chairman
John B Krieger, Executive Director

2705 Bristol-Myers Squibb Foundation
345 Park Avenue
Floor 43
New York, NY 10154-0004
212-546-4331
http://www.bms.com
Offers support for elementary and secondary school, math and science education reform, civic affairs and health care.

Cindy Johnson, Executive Director
Lamberto Andreotti, Chief Executive Officer

2706 Buffalo & Erie County Public Library
History Department
Lafayette Square
Buffalo, NY 14203
716-858-8900
Fax: 716-858-6211
http://www.buffalolib.org/libraries/central
Member of The Foundation Center network, maintaining a collection of private foundation tax returns which provide information on

the scope of grants dispensed by that particular foundation.

Michael C Mahaney, Director

2707 Caleb C & Julia W Dula Educational & Charitable Foundation
C/O Chemical Bank
112 S Hanley RD
St Louis, MO 63105-3418
212-270-9066
Offers grants to charities with an emphasis on secondary and higher education.

G Price-Fitch, Executive Director

2708 Capital Cities-ABC Corporate Giving Program
77 W 66th St
New York, NY 10023-6201
212-456-7498
Fax: 212-456-7909
Offers support in adult education, literary and basic skills, reading, and AIDS research.

Bernadette Longford Williams, Executive Director

2709 Carl & Lily Pforzheimer Foundation
950 Third Ave
30th Floor
New York, NY 10022-2705
212-764-0655
Offers support primarily for higher and secondary education, cultural programs, public administration, and health care.

Carl H Pforzheimer III, Executive Director

2710 Carnegie Corporation of New York
437 Madison Avenue
New York, NY 10022-7001
212-374-3200
Fax: 212-754-4073
http://www.carnegie.org
The foundation has several program goals including education and healthy development of children and youth, including early childhood health and education, early adolescence educational achievement, science education and education reform.

Janet L Robinson, President
Kurt L Schmoke, Vice-Chairman

2711 Chase Manhattan Corporation Philanthropy Department
1 Chase Manhattan Plaza
Floor 9
New York, NY 10005-1401
212-552-7087
Offers support to various organizations to enhance the well-being of the communities Chase Manahattan serves. Grants are awarded in the areas of education, youth services, community and economic development, homeless, library science, health care and housing development.

Steven Gelston, Executive Director

2712 Christian A Johnson Endeavor Foundation
1060 Park Avenue
New York, NY 10128-1008
212-534-6620
http://www.csuohio.edu/uored/funding/johnson.htm
Offers support to private institutions of higher education at the baccalaureate level and on educational outreach programs.

Wilmot H Kidd, Executive Director

2713 Cleveland H Dodge Foundation
420 Lexington Avenue
Suite 2331
New York, NY 10170-3292

212-972-2800
Fax: 212-972-1049
http://www.chdodgefoundation.org
Bestows funding for nonprofit organizations aimed at improving higher education and youth organizations.

William D Rueckert, President
Bayard Dodge, Vice-President

2714 Cowles Charitable Trust

P.O Box 219
Rumson, NJ 07760
732-936-9826
http://www1.mville.edu/Grants/GrantDescriptionPages/Cowles.htm
Funding for higher education and cultural organizations.

Gardner Cowles, President

2715 Daisy Marquis Jones Foundation

1600 S Avenue
Suite 250
Rochester, NY 14620-3921
585-461-4950
Fax: 585-461-9752
E-mail: mail@dmjf.org
http://www.dmjf.org
Offers grants for nonprofit organizations focusing on improving the lives of children, youth and the elderly, in Monroe and Yates counties in New York State.

Donald W Whitney, President
Marless A Honan, Administrative Assistant

2716 DeWitt Wallace-Reader's Digest Fund

5 Penn Plaza
7th Floor
New York, NY 10001-9301
212-251-9700
Fax: 212-679-6990
http://www.wallacefoundation.org
The mission of this foundation is to invest in programs and projects that enhance the quality of educational and career development opportunities for all school-age youth.

M Christine De Vita, President

2717 Edna McConnell Clark Foundation

415 Madison Avenue
10th Floor
New York, NY 10017
212-551-9100
Fax: 212-421-9325
http://www.emcf.org
Supports select youth, serving organizations working with children 9-24 during the non-school hours.

Michael Bailin, President

2718 Edward John Noble Foundation

32 E 57th Street
Floor 19
New York, NY 10022-2513
212-759-4212
Fax: 212-888-4531
Offers grants to major cultural organizations in New York City, especially for arts educational programs and management training internships.

June Noble Larkin, Chairman

2719 Edward W Hazen Foundation

333 Seventh Avenue
14 th Floor
New York, NY 10001
212-889-3034
Fax: 212-889-3039
E-mail: hazen@hazenfoundation.org
http://www.hazenfoundation.org

The foundation focuses giving on public education and youth development in the area of public education.

Lori Bezahler, President
Sonia Jarvis, Chairman

2720 Edwin Gould Foundation for Children

126 East 31st Street
New York, NY 10016
212-251-0907
Fax: 212-982-6886
Supports projects that promote the welfare and education of children. Interests lies in early childhood education, higher education, children and youth services and family services.

Michael W Osheowitz, Executive Director

2721 Elaine E & Frank T Powers Jr Foundation

81 Skunks Misery Road
Locust Valley, NY 11560-1306
Offers support in the areas of secondary and higher education as well as youth services.

2722 Elmer & Mamdouha Bobst Foundation

Elmer Holmes Bobst Library, NYU
70 Washington Square S
New York, NY 10012-1019
212-998-2440
Fax: 212-995-4070
Offers grants and funding in the areas of youth, community development and the arts.

2723 Equitable Foundation

3rd Floor Champaca II Building
162 L.P Leviste Street, Salcedo Village
Makati City 10019-6018
E-mail: mail@equitablefoundation.com
http://www.equitablefoundation.com
Offers grants in the areas of secondary school education, arts, community services, art and cultural programs, and higher education.

Kathleen A Carlson, Executive Director
Darlene Ramos, Administrative Assistant

2724 Ford Foundation

320 E 43rd Street
New York, NY 10017-4890
212-573-5000
Fax: 212-351-3677
E-mail: offsec@fordfound.rog
http://www.fordfound.org
Offers grants to advance public well-being and educational opportunities. Grants are given in the areas of education, secondary school/education, early childhood education, development services, human services, citizenship, academics and more.

Barron M Tenny, Secretary
Luis Ubinas, President

2725 Frances & Benjamin Benenson Foundation

C/O Door County Community Foundation
P.O. Box 802
Sturgeon Bay, WI 54235-1006
920-746-1786
Fax: 212-755-0021
http://www.benensoncapital.com
Offers grants in elementary/secondary education, higher education and human services.

Cynthia Green Colin, Executive Director

2726 George F Baker Trust

C/O JPMorgan Chase Bank
N.A Philanthropic Services
270 Park Avenue
New York, NY 10017
212-473-1587
Fax: 212-464-2305
E-mail: jonathan.q.horowitz@jpmchase.com
Offers giving in the areas of higher and secondary education, social services, civic affairs and international affairs.

Monica J Neal, Vice President

2727 George Link Jr Foundation

10 Rockefeller Plaza
16th Floor
New York, NY 10020
212-713-7654
Fax: 212-645-4055
Giving is primarily centered on higher education, secondary school/education and medical research.

Eve Weiss, Executive Director

2728 Gladys & Roland Harriman Foundation

51 Madison Avenue
30 th Floor
New York, NY 10010-1202
212-489-7700
Fax: 212-581-9541
E-mail: hlf1@hluce.org
Giving is centered on education and support for youth and social service agencies.

Michael Gilligan, President
Margaret B Fitzgerald, Chairman

2729 Gladys Brooks Foundation

1055 Franklin Avenue
Garden City, NY 11530
212-943-3217
http://www.gladysbrooksfoundation.org
The purpose of this foundation is to provide for the intellectual, moral and physical welfare of the people of this country by establishing and supporting nonprofit libraries, educational institutions, hospitals and clinics. In the area of education, grant applications will be considered generally for (a) educational endowments to fund scholarships based solely on leadership and academic ability of the student; (b) endowments to support salaries of educators.

Harman Hawkins, Chairman
Robert E Hill, Executive Director

2730 Green Fund

14 E 60th Street
Suite 702
New York, NY 10022-1006
212-755-2445
Fax: 212-755-0021
Offers grants in the area of higher and secondary education.

Cynthia Green Colin, Executive Director

2731 Hagedorn Fund

C/O JPMorgan Private Bank
Global Foundations Group
345 Park Avenue 4th Floor
New York, NY 10154
212-473-1587
http://www.fdncenter.org/grantmaker/hagedorn/
Offers support for higher and secondary education, youth agencies and social service agencies.

Monica J Neal, Vice President

2732 Hasbro Children's Foundation

10 Rockefeller Plaza
16th Floor
New York, NY 10020
212-713-7654
Fax: 212-645-4055
http://www.hasbro.org
Offers support to improve the quality of life for children. Areas of interest include education,

AIDS research, literacy, special education, and youth services.

Eve Weiss, Executive Director

2733 Henry Luce Foundation
111 W 50th Street
Room 3710
New York, NY 10020-1202
212-489-7700
Fax: 212-581-9541
http://www.hluce.org
Offers grants for specific programs and projects in the areas of higher education and scholarship, social sciences at private colleges and universities, American arts and public affairs.

Michael Gilligan, President

2734 Herman Goldman Foundation
61 Broadway
Floor 18
New York, NY 10006-2701
212-797-9090
Fax: 212-797-9161
This foundation offers grants in the areas of social, legal and organizational approaches to aid for deprived or handicapped people; education for new or improved counseling for effective pre-school, vocational, and paraprofessional training; and the arts.

Richard K Baron, Executive Director

2735 Hess Foundation
1185 Avenue of the Americas
New York, NY 10036-2601
212-997-8500
Fax: 212-536-8390
E-mail: webmaster@hess.com
http://www.hess.com
Offers grants that focus on higher education, performing arts, and welfare organizations.

Leon Hess, Executive Director

2736 Horace W Goldsmith Foundation
375 Park Avenue
Suite 1602
New York, NY 10152-1699
212-319-8700
800-319-2881
Fax: 212-319-2881
Offers giving and support for education, higher education, cultural programs and museums.

James C Slaughter, Executive Director

2737 IBM Corporate Support Program
Old Orchard Road
Armonk, NY 10504
914-765-1900
The mission of this fund is to improve the areas and the communities that IBM operates in. Grants are awarded in various areas including early childhood education, elementary education, secondary education, business school/education, and engineering school/education.

Stanley Litow, Executive Director

2738 JI Foundation
C/O Patterson, Belknap, Webb & Tyler
1133 Avenue of the Americas
New York, NY 10036
212-336-2000
Offers grants in the areas of elementary education, higher education, and general charitable giving.

2739 JP Morgan Charitable Trust
60 Wall Street
Floor 46
New York, NY 10005-2836
212-648-9673

Offers support in the area of education, housing, economic development, advocacy and international affairs.

Roberta Ruocco, Executive Director

2740 Joukowsky Family Foundation
410 Park Avenue
Suite 1610
New York, NY 10022-4407
212-355-3151
Fax: 212-355-3147
http://www.joukowsky.org
Giving is focused on higher and secondary education.

Nina J Koprulu, Director/President
Emily R Kessler, Executive Director

2741 Julia R & Estelle L Foundation
1 HSBC Center
Suite 3650
Buffalo, NY 14203-1217
716-856-9490
Fax: 716-856-9493
E-mail: info@oisheifdt.com
http://www.oisheifdt.org
This fund offers grants in the areas of higher and secondary education, medical research, social services and support agencies.

Thomas E Baker, President
James M Wadsworth, Chairman

2742 Leon Lowenstein Foundation
575 Madison Avenue
New York, NY 10022-3613
212-605-0444
Fax: 212-688-0134
Support is given for New York City public education and medical research.

John F Van Gorder, Executive Director

2743 Levittown Public Library
1 Bluegrass Lane
Levittown, NY 11756-1292
516-579-8585
Fax: 516-735-3168
http://www.nassaulibrary.org/levtown/
Member of The Foundation Center network, maintaining a collection of private foundation tax returns which provide information on the scope of grants dispensed by that particular foundation.

Margaret Santer, President

2744 Louis & Anne Abrons Foundation
C/O First Manhattan Company
437 Madison Avenue
New York, NY 10022-7001
212-756-3376
Fax: 212-832-6698
Offers support in the areas of education, improvement programs, environmental and cultural projects.

Richard Abrons, Executive Director

2745 Margaret L Wendt Foundation
40 Fountain Plaza
Suite 277
Buffalo, NY 14202-2200
716-855-2146
Fax: 716-855-2149
Offers various grants with an emphasis on education, the arts and social services in Buffalo and Western New York.

Robert J Kresse, Executive Director

2746 McGraw-Hill Foundation
1221 Avenue of the Americas
Room 2917
New York, NY 10020
212-512-6113
800-442-9685
http://www.mcgraw-hillresearchfoundation.org

Offers support to educational organizations in the areas of company operations or to national organizations.

Susan A Wallman, Executive Director

2747 New York Foundation
10 East 34th Street
10 th Floor
New York, NY 10016-2996
212-594-8009
Fax: 212-594-5918
E-mail: webmaster@nyf.org
http://www.nyf.org
Provides support for the implementation of programs that offer support for the quality of life including educational services, health organizations, centers and services, civil rights, public policy, research and more.

Maria Mottola, Executive Director
Melissa Hall, Operations Manager

2748 Palisades Educational Foundation
C/O Gibney, Anthony & Flaherty
665 5th Avenue
Floor 2
New York, NY 10022-5305
Offers support for secondary and higher education in New York, New Jersey and Connecticut.

Ralph F Anthony, Executive Director

2749 Robert Sterling Clark Foundation
135 E 64th Street
New York, NY 10065-7307
212-288-8900
Fax: 212-288-1033
E-mail: rscf@rsclark.org
http://www.rsclark.org
For more than 15 years, this foundation has provided support to New York City's cultural community. During this time, the Foundation has tried to structure a grants program so that it is flexible and meets the needs of the institutions and organizations. Grants are given in the areas of cultural institutions, arts advocacy, family planning services and supporting new initiatives in the area of arts and education.

Margaret C Ayers, President
James A Smith, Chairman

2750 Rochester Public Library
Business, Economics & Law
115 S Avenue
Rochester, NY 14604-1896
585-428-8045
Fax: 585-428-8353
http://www.rochester.lib.ny.us/central
Member of The Foundation Center network, maintaining a collection of private foundation tax returns which provide information on the scope of grants dispensed by that particular foundation.

Emeterio M Otero, President

2751 Ronald S Lauder Foundation
Rykestrasse 53
10405 Berlin
Berlin 10153-0023
212-572-6966
http://www.lauderfoundation.com
Offers giving in the areas of elementary/secondary education, human services and religion.

Marjorie S Federbush, Executive Director
Ronald S Lauder, Chairman & President

2752 SH & Helen R Scheuer Family Foundation
350 5th Avenue
Suite 3410
New York, NY 10118-0110

212-947-9009
Fax: 212-947-9770
Offers support in the areas of higher education, welfare funding and cultural programs.

2753 Samuel & May Rudin Foundation
345 Park Avenue
New York, NY 10154-0004
212-407-2544
Fax: 212-407-2540
Offers support for higher education, social services, religious welfare agencies, hospitals and cultural programs.

Susan H Rapaport, Executive Director

2754 Seth Sprague Educational and Charitable Foundation
C/O U.S. Trust Company of New York
114 W 47th Street
New York, NY 10036-1510
212-852-3683
Fax: 212-852-3377
Offers support in the areas of education, culture, the arts, human services, community development and government/public administration.

Maureen Augusciak, Executive Director

2755 Starr Foundation
399 Park Avenue
17th Floor
New York, NY 10022-0002
212-909-3600
Fax: 212-750-3536
http://www.fdncenter.org/grantmaker/starr
Support is given for educational projects with an emphasis on higher education, including scholarships under specific programs.

Ta Chun Hsu, Executive Director
Florence A Davis, President

2756 Tiger Foundation
101 Park Avenue
47th Floor
New York, NY 10178-0002
212-984-2565
Fax: 212-949-9778
E-mail: info@tigerfoundation.org
http://www.tigerfoundation.org
Support is given primarily for early childhood education, youth programs and job training.

Phoebe Boyer, Executive Director

2757 Tisch Foundation
667 Madison Avenue
New York, NY 10021-8029
212-545-2000
Support is given in the area of education, especially higher education, and includes institutions in Israel and research-related programs.

Laurence A Tisch, Executive Director

2758 Travelers Group
388 Greenwich Street
New York, NY 10013-2375
212-816-8000
Fax: 212-816-5944
The main purpose of this foundation is to support public education, offering grants in the communities that the company serves.

Dee Topol, Executive Director

2759 White Plains Public Library
100 Martine Avenue
White Plains, NY 10601-2599

914-422-1400
Fax: 914-422-1462
http://www.whiteplainslibrary.org
Member of The Foundation Center network, maintaining a collection of private foundation tax returns which provide information on the scope of grants dispensed by that particular foundation.

2760 William Randolph Hearst Foundation
300 West 57th Street
26th Floor
New York, NY 10019-3741
212-649-3750
Fax: 212-586-1917
E-mail: heart.ny@hearstfdn.org
http://www.hearstfdn.org
Offers support to programs that aid priority-level and minority groups, educational programs especially private secondary and higher education, health systems and cultural programs.

Paul DinoDinovitz, Executive Director
Ligia Cravo, Senior Program Officer

2761 William T Grant Foundation
570 Lexington Avenue
Floor 18
New York, NY 10022-6837
212-752-0071
Fax: 212-752-1398
E-mail: info@wtgrantfdn.org
http://www.wtgrantfoundation.org
The goal of the foundation is to help create a society that values people and helps them to reach their potenial. The Foundation is interested in environmentally friendly approaches

Edward Seidman, Senior VP Programs
Robert Granger, President

North Carolina

2762 AE Finley Foundation
P.O. Box 98266
Raleigh, NC 27624-8266
919-782-0565
Fax: 919-782-6978
E-mail: lesa@aeffinc.org
http://www.aefinleyfoundationinc.org
Private foundation contributing and supporting to charitable, scientific, literary, religious and educational organizations. It endeavors to contribute to soundly managed and operated qualifying organizations which fundamentally give service with a broad scope and impact, aid all kinds of people and contribute materially to the general welfare.

Robert C Brown, Executive Director

2763 Cannon Foundation
PO Box 548
Concord, NC 28026-0548
704-786-8216
Fax: 704-785-2052
E-mail: info@cannonfoundation.org
http://www.thecannonfoundationinc.org
Offers support for higher and secondary education, cultural programs, and grants to social service and youth agencies.

Frank Davis, Executive Director
William C Cannon Jr, President

2764 Dickson Foundation
301 S Tryon Street
Suite 1800
Charlotte, NC 28202
704-372-5404
Fax: 704-372-6409

Main focus is on areas of education & healthcare. Considers funding programs in the Southeast.

Susan Patterson, Secretary/Treasurer

2765 Duke Endowment
100 N Tryon Street
Suite 3500
Charlotte, NC 28202-4012
704-376-0291
Fax: 704-376-9336
http://www.dukeendowment.org
Support is given to higher education, children and youth services, churches and hospitals.

Eugene W Cochrane Jr, Executive Director
Minor M Shaw, Chairman

2766 First Union University
Two 1st Union Center
Charlotte, NC 28288
704-374-6868
Fax: 704-374-4147
Offers support for higher education and special programs for public elementary and secondary schools.

Ann D Thomas, Executive Director

2767 Foundation for the Carolinas
220 N Tryon Street
Charlotte, NC 28202
704-973-4500
800-973-7244
Fax: 704-376-1243
http://www.fftc.org
Offers support for education, the arts and health in North Carolina and South Carolina.

Ron Carter, President/CEO
Catherine P Bessant, Chairman

2768 Kathleen Price and Joseph M Bryan Family Foundation
3101 N Elm Street
Greensboro, NC 27408-3184
336-288-5455
Grants are primarily offered in the fields of higher, secondary, and early childhood education.

William Massey, Executive Director

2769 Mary Reynolds Babcock Foundation
2920 Reynolda Road
Winston Salem, NC 27106-4618
336-748-9222
Fax: 336-777-0095
http://www.mrbf.org
This foundation traditionally provides funds to programs in education, social services, the environment, the arts and citizen participation in the development of public policy. The foundation prefers to fund programs of two kinds: those particularly sensitive to the changing and emerging needs of society and those addressing society's oldest needs in new and imaginative ways.

Gayle W Dorman, Executive Director
Sandra H Mikush, Assitant Director

2770 Non-Profit Resource Center/Pack Memorial Library
Learning Resources Center
67 Haywood Street
Asheville, NC 28801-4897
828-254-4960
Fax: 828-251-2258
Cooperating collection of the Foundation Center. Other resources for non-profit organizations are also available.

Ed Sheary, Library Director

2771 State Library of North Carolina
Government & Business Services
109 E Jones Street
Raleigh, NC 27601-2806
919-807-7450
Fax: 919-733-5679
http://www.statelibrary.dcr.state.nc.us

Member of The Foundation Center network, maintaining a collection of private foundation tax returns which provide information on the scope of grants dispensed by that particular foundation.

2772 William R Kenan Jr Charitable Trust
Kenan Center
PO Box 3858
Chapel Hill, NC 27515-3858
919-962-0343
Fax: 919-962-3331
The focus of this foundation is on education, primarily at private institutions in the US. The emphasis now is on national literacy and the importance of early childhood education. Grants have just established an institute for the arts and an institute for engineering, technology and science. No grants are given to individuals for scholarships, for research or other special projects or for medical, public health or social welfare projects. This Trust does not accept unsolicited requests.

William C Friday, Executive Director

2773 Winston-Salem Foundation
860 W 5th Street
Winston Salem, NC 27101-2506
336-725-2382
Fax: 336-727-0581
http://www.wsfoundation.org
Educational grants and loans to residents of Forsyth County, North Carolina in most areas.

Scott Wierman, President
Donna Rader, VP Grants & Programs

2774 Z Smith Reynolds Foundation
102 West Third Street
Suite 1110
Winston Salem, NC 27101-3940
336-725-7541
800-443-8319
Fax: 336-725-6069
http://www.zsr.org
Grants are limited to the state of North Carolina. General purpose foundation provides for their current priorities including community economic development, women's issues, minority issues, environment and pre-collegiate education. No grants are given to individuals.

Thomas W Ross, Executive Director

North Dakota

2775 Myra Foundation
PO Box 13536
Grand Forks, ND 58208-3536
701-775-9420
E-mail: jbotsford@myrafoundation.org
http://www.myrafoundation.org
Offers grants in the areas of secondary school, and higher education to residents of Grand Forks County, North Dakota.

Edward C Gillig, Executive Director

2776 Tom & Frances Leach Foundation
1720 Burnt Boat Drive
PO Box 1136
Bismarck, ND 58502-1136
701-255-0479
http://www.leachfoundation.org
Offers grants in the areas of higher and other education in North Dakota.

Clement C Weber, Executive Director

Ohio

2777 Akron Community Foundation
345 W Cedar Street
Akron, OH 44307-2407
330-376-8522
Fax: 330-376-0202
E-mail: acf_fund@ix.netcom.com
http://www.akroncommunityfdn.org
The foundation receives donations to permanent endowment and makes grants to qualified nonprofit organizations within Summit County, Ohio.

Jody Bacon, President

2778 American Foundation Corporation
720 National City Bank Building
Cleveland, OH 44114
216-241-6664
Fax: 216-241-6693
Offers support in the areas of higher and secondary education, the arts and community funds.

Maria G Muth, Executive Director

2779 Burton D Morgan Foundation
22 Aurora Street
Hudson, OH 44236-1500
330-655-1660
Fax: 330-655-1673
E-mail: admin@bdmorganfdn.org
http://www.bdmorganfdn.org
The foundation's present areas of interest include economics, education, mental health and organizations principally located in Northeast Ohio. No grants are made to individuals and few grants are made to social service organizations.

Deborah D Hoover, President
Denise M Griggs, Chief Financial Officer

2780 Dayton Foundation
500 Kettering Tower
Dayton, OH 45423-1395
937-222-0410
Fax: 937-222-0636
E-mail: info@daytonfoundation.org
http://www.daytonfoundation.org
Educational and community service grants.

Michael M Parks, President
Ellen S Ireland, Vice-Chairman

2781 Eva L & Joseph M Bruening Foundation
1422 Euclid Avenue
Suite 966
Cleveland, OH 44115-1952
216-621-2632
Fax: 216-621-8198
http://www.fmscleveland.com/bruening
Support is offered in the fields of education, early childhood education, education fund-raising, higher education, youth services and health agencies.

Janet E Narten, Executive Director
Karen Noster, Chairman

2782 GAR Foundation
Andrew Jackson House
277 East Mill Street
Akron, OH 44308-1828
330-576-2926
800-686-2825
Fax: 330-437-2843
E-mail: info@garfdn.org
http://www.garfdn.org
Established in 1967 as a charitable trust, the foundation offers grants to organizations located primarily in Akron, Ohio area or, secondarily, in Northeastern Ohio or elsewhere in the United States at the discretion of the Distribution Committee. Grants for research projects of educational or scientific institutions, capital improvement projects, or matching campaigns are the priorities of this foundation.

Richard A Chenoweth, Executive Director
Robert W Briggs, Co-Trustee

2783 George Gund Foundation
1845 Guildhall Building
45 Prospect Avenue
West Cleveland, OH 44115
216-241-3114
Fax: 216-241-6560
E-mail: info@gundfdn.org
http://www.gundfdn.org
The primary interest of this foundation is in educational projects, with an emphasis on inventive movements in teaching and learning, and on increasing educational opportunities for the disadvantaged.

David Abbott, Executive Director
Marcia Egbert, Senior Program Officer

2784 Hoover Foundation
101 E Maple Street
North Canton, OH 44720-2517
330-499-9499
Fax: 330-497-5065
Offers grants for elementary education, secondary and higher education and youth agencies.

LR Hoover, Executive Director
Annette Bravard, Vice President of Marketing

2785 Kettering Fund
1480 Kettering Tower
Dayton, OH 45423-1001
937-228-1021
888-719-1185
http://www.cfketteringfamilies.com
Support is offered for social and educational studies and research as well as community development and cultural programs.

Judith M Thompson, Executive Director

2786 Kulas Foundation
Tower City Center
50 Public Square
Suite 600
Cleveland, OH 44113-2267
216-623-4770
Fax: 216-623-4773
http://www.fdncenter.org/grantmaker/kulas/
A major general interest foundation, but with an emphasis on music. Giving is limited to Cuyahoga County and its surrounding area. Provides support to musical educational programs at Baldwin Wallace College, Case Western Reserve University and Cleveland Institute of Music. Also provides tickets to cultural programs to students in 16 colleges and universities in the area. The Foundation does not provide grants or loans to individuals. Support is geared to local primary and secondary schools.

Nancy W McCann, President/Treasurer

2787 Louise H & David S Ingalls Foundation
20600 Chagrin Boulevard
Suite 301
Shaker Heights, OH 44122-5334
216-921-6000
Offers support to organizations whose primary interest in the improvement of the educational, physical and mental condition of humanity throughout the world. Grants are given in secondary, elementary, and educational research.

Jane W Watson, Executive Director

2788 Louise Taft Semple Foundation
425 Walnut Street
Suite 1800
Cincinnati, OH 45202-3948
513-381-2838
Fax: 513-381-0205
Support is offered in the areas of secondary school/education, higher education, human services and health care organizations.

Dudley S Taft, Executive Director

2789 Martha Holden Jennings Foundation
Advisory & Distribution Committee Office
1228 Euclid Avenue
Suite 710
Cleveland, OH 44115-1831
216-589-5700
Fax: 216-589-5730
http://www.mhjf.org
The purpose of this foundation is to foster the development of young people to the maximum possible extent through improving the quality of teaching in secular elementary and secondary schools.

William T Hiller, Executive Director
Kathy L Kooyman, Grants Manager

2790 Mead Corporation Foundation
Courthouse Plz NE
Dayton, OH 45463-0001
937-495-3883
Fax: 937-495-4103
Grants are given to elementary, secondary, higher and minority education.

Ronald F Budzik, Executive Director

2791 Nord Family Foundation
747 Milan Avenue
Amherst, OH 44001
440-984-3939
Fax: 440-984-3934
http://www.nordff.org
Offers support for a variety of programs, including giving for early childhood, secondary, and higher education, social services, cultural affairs and civic activities.

David R Ashenhurst, Executive Director

2792 Ohio Bell Telephone Contribution Program
45 Erieview Plaza
Room 870
Cleveland, OH 44114-1814
216-822-4445
800-257-0902
Offers support of elementary school/education, secondary school/education, higher education, literacy and basic skills.

William W Boag Jr, Executive Director

2793 Ohio State Library Foundation Center
Kent H. Smith Library
1480 West Lane Avenue
Columbus, OH 43221-2001
614-292-2141
Member of The Foundation Center network, maintaining a collection of private foundation tax returns which provide information on the scope of grants dispensed by that particular foundation.

John B Gerlach, Chairman & CEO
Martin Murrer, Vice-Chairman

2794 Owens-Corning Foundation
PO Box 1688
Toledo, OH 43603-1688
419-248-8000
Fax: 419-325-4273

Offers support for education, including religious schools and science and technology programs.

Emerson J Ross, Executive Director

2795 Procter & Gamble Fund
200 West Fourth Street
Cincinnati, OH 45202-2775
513-241-2880
Fax: 513-983-8250
E-mail: info@gcfdn.org
http://www.gcfdn.org
Always considers the interests of the company's employees helping in the community, the arts, improving of schools and universities and to meet the needs of the less-fortunate neighbors. Some donations into the education program include grants to the United Negro College Fund, The National Hispanic Scholarship Fund, The Leadership Conference on Civil Rights Education Fund and more than 600 colleges and universities.

RL Wehling, President
G Talbot, VP

2796 Public Library of Cincinnati
Grants Resource Center
800 Vine Street #Library
Cincinnati, OH 45202-2009
513-369-6900
Fax: 513-665-3384
http://www.cincinnatilibrary.org
Member of The Foundation Center network, maintaining a collection of private foundation tax returns which provide information on the scope of grants dispensed by that particular foundation.

Kimber L Fender, Director

2797 Thomas J Emery Memorial
Frost & Jacobs
201 E 5th Street
Suite 2500
Cincinnati, OH 45202-4113
513-621-3124
Offers support in secondary school/education, higher education, health care, human services and arts/cultural programs.

Henry W Hobson Jr, Executive Director

2798 Timken Foundation of Canton
200 Market Avenue N
Suite 210
Canton, OH 44702-1622
330-452-1144
Fax: 330-455-1752
Offers support to promote the broad civic betterment including the areas of education, conservation and recreation. Grants restricted to caption projects only.

Don D Dickes, Secretary
Nancy Kuvdsen

2799 Wolfe Associates
34 S 3rd Street
Columbus, OH 43215-4201
614-461-5220
Fax: 614-469-6126
The foundation supports those organizations whose programs educate the individual and cultivate the individual's ability to participate in and contribute to the community or which enhance the quality of life which the community can offer to its citizens. The foundation has six general program areas in which it focuses its support: health and medicine, religion, education, culture, community service and environment.

AK Pierce Jr, Executive Director

Oklahoma

2800 Grace & Franklin Bernsen Foundation
15 W 6th Street
Suite 1308
Tulsa, OK 74119-5407
918-584-4711
Fax: 918-584-4713
E-mail: gfbersen@aol.com
http://www.bernsen.org
The foundation is limited by its policies to support of nonprofit organizations within the metropolitan area of Tulsa. The foundation discourages applications for general support or reduction of debt or for continuing or additional support for the same programs, although a single grant may cover several years. No grant is made to individuals or for the benefit of specific individuals and the applications must be received before the twelfth of each month.

John Strong Jr, Trustee

2801 Mervin Bovaird Foundation
100 W 5th Street
Suite 800
Tulsa, OK 74103-4291
918-583-1777
Fax: 918-592-5809
Awards scholarships to the University of Tulsa. Recipients are selected by Tulsa Area high schools and by Tulsa Junior College. No individual grants are made.

R Casey Cooper, President

2802 Oklahoma City University
Dulaney Brown Library
2501 N Blackwelder Avenue
Oklahoma City, OK 73106-1493
405-521-5000
Fax: 405-521-5291
http://www.okcu.edu
Member of The Foundation Center network, maintaining a collection of private foundation tax returns which provide information on the scope of grants dispensed by that particular foundation.

Victoria Swinney, Director

2803 Public Service Company of Oklahoma Corporate Giving Program
212 E 6th Street #201
Tulsa, OK 74119-1295
918-586-0420
http://www.psoklahoma
Offers support in the areas of elementary, secondary and higher education.

Mary Polfer, Executive Director

2804 Samuel Roberts Noble Foundation
2510 Sam Noble Parkway
Ardmore, OK 73401-2180
580-223-5810
Fax: 580-224-6380
http://www.noble.org
Offers support in the areas of higher education, agricultural research, human services and educational grants for health research pertaining to degenerative diseases, cancer and for health delivery systems.

Michael A Cawley, Executive Director
Emily Bynum, Administrative Assistant

Oregon

2805 Collins Foundation
1618 SW 1st Avenue
Suite 305
Portland, OR 97201-5708
503-227-7171
Fax: 503-295-3794
http://www.collinsfoundation.org

Offers general support with an emphasis on higher education, hospices and health agencies, youth programs and arts and culture.

Cynthia G Adams, Executive Vice President
Cindy Knowles, Director Of Programs

2806 Ford Family Foundation
1600 NW Stewart Parkway
Roseburg, OR 97471-1957
541-957-5574
Fax: 541-957-5720
E-mail: info@tfff.org
http://www.tfff.org
Giving is centered on education, youth organizations and human service programs in Oregon and Siskiyou County in California.

Bart Howard, Director Scholarship Program
Sarah Reeve, Scholarship Program Officer

2807 Meyer Memorial Trust
425 NW 10th Avenue
Suite 400
Portland, OR 97209
503-228-5512
Fax: 503-228-5840
E-mail: mmt@mmt.org
http://www.mmt.org
The Trust operates three different funding programs, all of which are restricted primarily to Oregon: 1) a broad-based General Purpose program that provides funds for education, arts, and humanities, health, social welfare, community development, and other activities; 2) a Small Grants program that provides up to $12,000 for small projects in the general purpose categories; and 3) the Support for Teacher Initiatives program, which provides grants of up to $7,000- to teachers.

Doug Stamm, Executive Director
Cathie Glennon, Executive Assistant

2808 Multnomah County Library
Government Documents
801 SW 10th Avenue
Portland, OR 97205-2597
503-988-5123
Fax: 503-988-8014
http://www.multcolib.org
Member of The Foundation Center network, maintaining a collection of private foundation tax returns which provide information on the scope of grants dispensed by that particular foundation.

2809 Oregon Community Foundation
1221 SW Yamhill
Suite 100
Portland, OR 97205
503-227-6846
Fax: 503-274-7771
http://www.ocfl.org
The purpose of this foundation is to improve the cultural, educational and social needs in all levels of society throughout the state of Oregon.

Gregory A Chaille, Executive Director

2810 Tektronix Foundation
PO Box 1000
Wilsonville, OR 97070-1000
503-627-7111
http://www.tek.com
Offers support for education, especially science, math and engineering, and some limited art grants.

Jill Kirk, Executive Director

Pennsylvania

2811 Alcoa Foundation
201 Isabella Street
Pittsburgh, PA 15212-5858
412-553-4545
Fax: 412-553-4498
http://www.alcoa.com
Grants are given for education, arts and cultural programs.

F Worth Hobbs, Executive Director

2812 Annenberg Foundation
St. David's Center
2000 Avenue of the Stars
Suite 1000 S
Los Angeles, CA 90067-5293
310-209-4560
Fax: 310-209-1631
E-mail: info@annenbergfoundation.org
http://www.annenbergfoundation.org
Primary support is given to childhood and K-12 education.

Dr. Gail C Levin Sr, Executive Director
Wallis Annenberg, Chairman

2813 Arcadia Foundation
105 E Logan Street
Norristown, PA 19401-3058
215-275-8460
http://www.arcadiafoundation.org
Gives only in Eastern Pennsylvania, no personal scholarships, accepts proposals only between June 1-August 15. These will be considered for the following calendar year. Proposal has to be no more than 2 pages long and longer submissions will be discarded. Must have a copy of the IRS tax-identified letter with no other enclosures.

Marilyn Lee Steinbright, Executive Director

2814 Audrey Hillman Fisher Foundation
2000 Grant Building
Pittsburgh, PA 15219
412-338-3466
Fax: 412-338-3463
Offers support for secondary school/education, higher education, rehabilitation, science and engineering.

Ronald W Wertz, Executive Director

2815 Bayer Corporation
100 Bayer Court
Pittsburgh, PA 15205
412-777-2000
Fax: 412-777-3468
http://www.bayerus.com/about/community/
Support is given primarily in education, especially science programs, chemistry and the arts.

Rebecca Lucore, Executive Director

2816 Buhl Foundation
650 Smithfield Street
Pittsburgh, PA 15222-1207
412-566-2711
Fax: 412-566-2714
E-mail: buhl@buhlfoundation.org
http://www.buhlfoundation.org
Grants are given to colleges and universities, secondary schools and educational associations, community educational and training programs, and other community programs offering health and education to the community. Grants are not made for building funds, overhead costs, accumulated deficits, ordinary operating budgets, general fund-raising campaigns, loans, scholarships and fellowships, other foundations, nationally funded organized groups or individuals.

Dr. Doreen Boyce, President

2817 Connelly Foundation
One Tower Bridge
Suite 1450
West Conshohocken, PA 19428-2873
610-834-3222
Fax: 610-834-0866
http://www.connellyfdn.org
Offers support for education, health, human service, culture and civic programs to nonprofit organizations located in the city of Philadelphia and the greater Delaware Valley region.

Victoria K Flaville, VP Administration
Josephine C Mandeville, President/CEO

2818 Eden Hall Foundation
Pittsburgh Office And Research Park
600 Grant Street
Suite 3232
Pittsburgh, PA 15219
412-642-6697
Fax: 412-642-6698
http://www.edenhallfdn.org
This foundation offers support for higher education, social welfare and the improvement of conditions of the poor and needy.

Sylvia V Fields, Program Director
George C Greer, Chairman/President

2819 Erie County Library System
160 E Front Street
Erie, PA 16507-1554
814-451-6927
Fax: 814-451-6969
http://www.ecls.lib.pa.us
Member of The Foundation Center network, maintaining a collection of private foundation tax returns which provide information on the scope of grants dispensed by that particular foundation.

2820 Foundation Center-Carnegie Library of Pittsburgh
Foundation Collection
4400 Forbes Avenue
Pittsburgh, PA 15213-4080
412-622-6277
Fax: 412-454-7001
E-mail: foundati@carnegielibrary.org
http://www.clpgh.org/clp/Foundation
Member of the Foundation Center network, of cooperating collections; providing current, factual information about grants and grantmaking organizations, and other aspects of philanthropy to the local nonprofit community.

Jim Lutton, Manager
Herb Elish, Director

2821 HJ Heinz Company Foundation
PO Box 57
Pittsburgh, PA 15230-0057
412-456-5772
Fax: 412-456-7859
E-mail: heinz.foundation@hjheinz.com
http://www.heinz.com/jsp/foundation.jsp
Offers support for higher education, employee matching gifts, social service agencies and cultural programs.

Loretta M Oken, Executive Director

2822 John McShain Charities
540 N 17th Street
Philadelphia, PA 19130-3988
215-564-2322
Offers support for higher and secondary education, Roman Catholic church support and social welfare.

Mary McShain, Executive Director

2823 Mary Hillman Jennings Foundation
625 Stanwix Street
Apt 2203
Pittsburgh, PA 15222-1408

412-434-5606
Fax: 412-434-5907
Offers grants to schools, youth agencies, and hospitals and health associations.

Paul Euwer Jr, Executive Director

2824 McCune Foundation
750 Six PPG Place
Pittsburgh, PA 15222
412-644-8779
Fax: 412-644-8059
http://www.mccune-db.mccune.org
The foundation provides support to independent higher education and human services.

Henry S Beukema, Executive Director

2825 Pew Charitable Trusts
One Commerce Square
2005 Market Street
Suite 1700
Philadelphia, PA 19103-7077
215-575-9050
Fax: 215-575-4939
E-mail: info@pewtrusts.org
http://www.pewtrusts.com
Offers support for education (including theology), arts culture, as well as public policy and religion.

Rebecca W Rimel, Executive Director
Robert H Campbell, Board of Director

2826 Richard King Mellon Foundation
One Mellon Bank Center
500 Grant Street
Suite 4106
Pittsburgh, PA 15219-2502
412-392-2800
Fax: 412-392-2837
http://www.fdncenter.org/grantmaker/rkm
ellon/
Offers local grant programs with an emphasis on education, social services and the environment.

Seward Prosser Mellon,
Trustee/President
Bruce King Mell Henderson, President

2827 Rockwell International Corporation Trust
625 Liberty Avenue
Pittsburgh, PA 15222-3110
414-212-5200
Fax: 414-212-5201
Offers support in the areas of K-12 math and science education, and higher education in the field of engineering and science.

William R Fitz, Executive Director

2828 Samuel S Fels Fund
1528 Walnut Street
Suite 1002
Philadelphia, PA 19102-5308
215-731-9455
Fax: 215-731-9457
http://www.samfels.org
Offers grants in continuing support that help prevent, lessen or resolve contemporary social problems including education, arts/cultural programs, and community development.

Helen Cunningham, Executive Director
Robin N Culmer, Office Administrator

2829 Sarah Scaife Foundation
Three Mellon Bank Center
301 Grant Street
Suite 3900
Pittsburgh, PA 15219-6401
412-392-2900
http://www.scaife.com

Offers grants in the areas of education and community development.

Joanne B Beyer, Executive Director
Michael W Gleba, Executive Vice President

2830 Shore Fund
C/O Melton Bank N.A.
PO Box 185
Pittsburgh, PA 15230-0185
412-234-4695
Fax: 412-234-3551
Although the foundation appreciates funding opportunities within the field of education, most grants given out have been to schools with which the foundation's trustees have been personally involved.

Helen M Collins, Executive Director

2831 Stackpole-Hall Foundation
44 S Saint Marys Street
Saint Marys, PA 15857-1667
814-834-1845
Fax: 814-834-1869
E-mail: stackpolehall@windstream.net
http://www.stackpolehall.org
Offers support for higher education and secondary education, literacy and vocational projects, social services, arts and cultural programs, and community development.

William C Conrad, Executive Director

2832 United States Steel Foundation
600 Grant Street
Suite 639
Pittsburgh, PA 15219-2800
412-433-5237
Fax: 412-433-2792
http://www.psc.uss.com/usxfound
Grants are awarded for capital development, special projects or operating needs. Support is limited to organizations within the United States, with preference to those in the US Steel Corporation's operating areas. US Steel does not award grants for religious purposes. Additionally, grants are not awarded for conferences, seminars or symposia, travel, publication of papers, books or magazines, or production of films, videotapes or other audiovisual materials.

Craig D Mallick, General Manager
Pamela E DiNardo, Program Administrator

2833 William Penn Foundation
2 Logan Square11th Floor
100 North 18th Street
Philadelphia, PA 19103-2757
215-988-1830
Fax: 215-988-1823
E-mail:
grants@williampennfoundation.org
http://www.williampennfoundation.org
The foundation supports culture, environment, human development, including programs for youth and elderly, education, including early childhood, secondary, elementary and higher.

Kathryn J Engebretson, President
Bergen Bruce, Director of Finance and Admi

Rhode Island

2834 Champlin Foundations
2000 Chapel View Boulevard
Suite 350
Cranston, RI 02920
401-944-9200
Fax: 401-944-9299

E-mail: champlinfons@worldnet.att.net
http://www.fdncenter.org/grantmaker/champlin
Offers giving in the areas of higher, secondary and other education. Exclusively in Rhode Island.

David A King, Executive Director
Jonathan K Farnum, Distribution Committee Membe

2835 Providence Public Library
Reference Department
150 Empire Street
Providence, RI 02903-3219
401-455-8000
http://www.provlib.org
Member of The Foundation Center network, maintaining a collection of private foundation tax returns which provide information on the scope of grants dispensed by that particular foundation.

Dale Thompson, Director
Robert K Taylor, Chairman

2836 Rhode Island Foundation
One Union Station
Providence, RI 02903-4630
401-274-4564
Fax: 401-331-8085
http://www.rifoundation.org
Promotes charitable activities which tend to improve the living conditions and well-being of the residents of Rhode Island.

Ned Handy, President
David M Hirsch, Chairman

South Carolina

2837 Charleston County Library
68 Calhoun Street
Charleston, SC 29401
843-805-6930
Fax: 843-727-3741
http://www.ccpl.org
Member of The Foundation Center network, maintaining a collection of private foundation tax returns which provide information on the scope of grants dispensed by that particular foundation.

Janet Segal, Chairperson
Harlan Greene, Chairperson

2838 South Carolina State Library
1500 Senate Street
Columbia, SC 29201-3815
803-734-8666
Fax: 803-734-8676
http://www.state.sc.us/scsl/
Member of The Foundation Center network, maintaining a collection of private foundation tax returns which provide information on the scope of grants dispensed by that particular foundation.

James B Johnson Jr, Director

South Dakota

2839 South Dakota Community Foundation
1714 North Lincoln Ave
Box 296
Pierre, SD 57501-3159
605-224-1025
800-888-1842
Fax: 605-224-5364
http://www.sdcommunityfoundation.org
The mission of the foundation is to promote philanthropy, receive and administer charitable gifts and invest in a wide range of programs promoting the social and economic well being of the people of the South Dakota. Grants given in South Dakota only.

Bob Sutton, President
Stephanie Judson, Administrative Vice Presiden

2840 South Dakota State Library
Reference Department
800 Governors Drive
Pierre, SD 57501-2294
605-773-5070
Fax: 605-773-4950
http://www.sdstatelibrary.com
Member of The Foundation Center network, maintaining a collection of private foundation tax returns which provide information on the scope of grants dispensed by that particular foundation.

Tennesse

2841 Benwood Foundation
736 Market Street
Suite 1600
Chattanooga, TN 37402-4803
423-267-4311
Fax: 423-267-9049
http://www.benwood.org
The general purpose of this foundation is to support such religious, charitable, scientific, literary and educational activities as will promote the advancement of mankind in any part of the United States of America. It should be recognized by all prospective grantees that while the foundation is not limited to the Chattanooga, Tennessee area, the bulk of the grants are made to organizations in the immediate area.

Jean R McDaniel, Executive Director
Sarah Morgan, President

2842 Christy-Houston Foundation
1296 Dow Street
Murfreesboro, TN 37130-2413
615-898-1140
Fax: 615-895-9524
Offers grants for education, arts, culture and health care to residents and organizations of Rutherford County, Tennessee.

James R Arnhart, Executive Director

2843 Frist Foundation
3100 West End Avenue
Suite 1200
Nashville, TN 37203
615-292-3868
Fax: 615-292-5843
http://www.fristfoundation.org
Broad general-purposed charitable foundation whose grants are restricted primarily to Nashville.

Peter F Bird Jr, President/CEO
Thomas F Frist Jr, Chairman

2844 JR Hyde Foundation
17 West Pontotoc Ave
Suite 200
Memphis, TN 38103-0084
901-685-3400
Fax: 901-683-7478
E-mail: info@hydefoundation.org
http://www.hydefoundation.org
Offers grants for higher education, including scholarships for the children of Malone and Hyde employees, community funds, secondary education and youth services.

JR Hyde III, Executive Director

2845 Lyndhurst Foundation
517 E 5th Street
Chattanooga, TN 37403-1826
423-756-0767
Fax: 423-756-0770
http://www.lyndhurstfoundation.org
Support local arts and culture and downtown revitalzation efforts in Chattanooga. Support the protection and enhancement of the natural environment of the Southern Appalachian

Region. Support the elementary and secondary public schools in Chattanooga.

Jack E Murrah, President

2846 Nashville Public Library
Business Information Division
615 Church Street
Nashville, TN 37219
615-862-5800
http://www.library.nashville.org
Member of The Foundation Center network, maintaining a collection of private foundation tax returns which provide information on the scope of grants dispensed by that particular foundation.

Keith B Simmons, Board Chair

2847 Plough Foundation
6410 Poplar Avenue
Suite 710
Memphis, TN 38119-5736
901-761-9180
Fax: 901-761-6186
Offers grants for community projects, including a community fund, early childhood and elementary education, social service agencies and the arts.

Noris R Haynes Jr, Executive Director

2848 RJ Maclellan Charitable Trust
Provident Building
Suite 501
Chattanooga, TN 37402
423-755-1366
Supports higher and theological education, social services and youth programs.

Hugh O Maclellan Jr, Executive Director

Texas

2849 Albert & Ethel Herzstein Charitable Foundation
6131 Westview Drive
Houston, TX 77055-5421
713-681-7868
Fax: 713-681-3652
http://www.herzsteinfoundation.org
Concentrates support on temples and medical research with grants offered to medical schools.

L Michael Hajtman, President
Nathan H Topek, Chairman

2850 Burlington Northern Foundation
3800 Continental Plaza
777 Main Street
Fort Worth, TX 76102
817-352-6425
Fax: 817-352-7924
The major channel of philanthropy for Burlington Northern and its subsidiaries. The foundation administers a consistent contribution program in recognition of the company's opportunity to support and improve the general welfare and quality of life in communities it serves.

Beverly Edwards, President
Becky Blankenship, Grant Administrator

2851 Burnett Foundation
801 Cherry Street
Suite 1400
Fort Worth, TX 76102-6814
817-877-3344
Fax: 817-338-0448
Focus is on Fort Worth and Santa Fe, NM, seeking to be a positive force in the community, supporting the energy and creativity that exist in the nonprofit sector, and building capacity in organizations and people in the fields of education, health, community af-

fairs, human services and arts and humanities.

Thomas F Beech, Executive Director

2852 Cooper Industries Foundation
PO Box 4446
Houston, TX 77210-4446
713-209-8400
Fax: 713-209-8982
E-mail: evans@cooperindustries.com
http://www.cooperindustries.com
The policy of this foundation is to carry out the responsibilities of corporate citizenship, by supporting nonprofit organizations in areas where employees are located, which best serve the educational, health, welfare, civic, cultural and social needs of the foundation's communities. All gifts are consistent with the company's objectives to enhance the quality of life and to honor the principles and freedoms that have enabled the company to prosper and grow. Average Grant: $5,000.

Victoria Guennewig, President
Jennifer L Evans, Secretary

2853 Corpus Christi State University
Library-Reference Department
805 Comanche
Corpus Christi, TX 78401
361-880-7000
Fax: 361-880-7005
http://www.library.ci.corpus-christi.tx.us
Member of The Foundation Center network, maintaining a collection of private foundation tax returns which provide information on the scope of grants dispensed by that particular foundation.

Denise Landry

2854 Cullen Foundation
601 Jefferson Street
Floor 40
Houston, TX 77002-7900
713-651-8837
Fax: 713-651-2374
http://www.cullenfdn.org
Supports educational, medical purposes, community funds and conservation.

Alan M Stewart, Executive Director
Sue A Alexander, Grants Administrator

2855 Dallas Public Library
Urban Information
1515 Young Street
Dallas, TX 75201-5499
214-670-1400
Fax: 214-670-1451
http://www.dallaslibrary.org
Member of The Foundation Center network, maintaining a collection of private foundation tax returns which provide information on the scope of grants dispensed by that particular foundation.

2856 El Paso Community Foundation
333 North Oregon St
2nd Floor
El Paso, TX 79901
915-533-4020
Fax: 915-532-0716
http://www.epcf.org
Grants to 501(c)(3) organizations in the El Paso geographic area. Fields of interest are arts and humanities, education, environment, health and disabilities, human services and civic benefits. No grants to individuals are offered.

Janice Windle, President
Virginia Martinez, Executive VP

2857 Ellwood Foundation
PO Box 52482
Houston, TX 77052-2482
713-739-0763

Scholarships for social services and education.

H Wayne Hightower, Executive Director

2858 Eugene McDermott Foundation
1155 Union Circle
Suite 311580
Denton, TX 76203-5017
940-369-5200
Fax: 940-369-5248
http://www.tshaonline.org
Offers support primarily for higher and secondary education, health, cultural programs, and general community interests.

Eugene McDermott, Executive Director
Laurie E Jasinski, Research Editor

2859 Ewing Halsell Foundation
711 Navarro Street
Suite 535
San Antonio, TX 78205-1786
210-223-2649
Fax: 210-271-9089
http://www.ewinghalsell.org
Offers grants in the areas of art and cultural programs, education, medical research, human services and youth services.

Jackie Moczygemba

2860 Exxon Education Foundation
5959 Las Colinas Boulevard
Irving, TX 75039-2298
972-444-1106
Fax: 972-444-1405
http://www.exxon.mobile.com
Grants are given in the areas of environment, education, public information and policy research, united appeals and federated drives, health, civic and community service organizations, minority and women-oriented service organizations, arts, museums and historical associations. In the education area grants are awarded to mathematics education programs, elementary and secondary school improvement programs, undergraduate general education programs, research, training and support programs.

EF Ahnert, Executive Director

2861 Fondren Foundation
7 TCT 37
PO Box 2558
Houston, TX 77252
713-236-4403
Provides support in various areas of interest with an emphasis on higher and secondary education, social services and cultural organizations.

Melanie Scioneaus, Executive Director

2862 George Foundation
310 Morton Street
PMB Suite C
Richmond, TX 77469-3135
281-342-6109
Fax: 281-341-7635
http://www.thegeorgefoundation.org
Offers giving for religious, educational, charitable or scientific purposes.

Roland Adamson, Executive Director
Sandra Thompson, Chief Financial Officer

2863 Gordon & Mary Cain Foundation
8 E Greenway Plaza
Suite 702
Houston, TX 77046-0892
713-960-9283
Fax: 713-877-1824
The foundation is not limited to education but does contribute a large amount to that area. For a company to apply for a grant they must offer a statement of purpose or a summary of the project needing funding; budget with balance sheet, fund balance, distribution of funds, audited statement and number of employees; latest copy of IRS tax-exempt status letter 501(c)(3); current projects needing funding with amounts needed for entire project and the amount of the grant being requested.

James D Weaver, Executive Director

2864 Haggar Foundation
6113 Lemmon Avenue
Dallas, TX 75209-5715
214-352-8481
Fax: 214-956-4446
Offers support in various areas with an emphasis on higher and secondary education, including a program for children of company employees.

Mary Vaughan Rumble, Executive Director

2865 Hobby Foundation
2131 San Felipe Street
Houston, TX 77019-5620
713-521-4694
Fax: 713-521-3950
Offers grants to educational facilities in the state of Texas.

Oveta Culp Hobby, Executive Director

2866 Houston Endowment
600 Travis Street
Suite 6400
Houston, TX 77002-3000
713-238-8100
Fax: 713-238-8101
E-mail: info@houstonendowment.org
http://www.houstonendowment.org
Offers support for charitable, religious or educational organizations.

H Joe Nelson III, Executive Director
Ann B Stern, President

2867 Houston Public Library
Bibliographic Information Center
500 McKinney Street
Houston, TX 77002-2534
832-238-9640
Fax: 832-393-1383
http://www.hpl.lib.tx.us/hpl/hplhome
Member of The Foundation Center network, maintaining a collection of private foundation tax returns which provide information on the scope of grants dispensed by that particular foundation.

2868 James R Dougherty Jr Foundation
PO Box 640
Beeville, TX 78104-0640
361-358-3560
Fax: 361-358-9693
Offers support for Roman Catholic church-related industries including education, higher, secondary and other education.

Hugh Grove Jr, Executive Director

2869 Leland Fikes Foundation
3050 Lincoln Plaza
500 N Akard
Dallas, TX 75201
214-754-0144
Fax: 214-855-1245
Giving is focused on education, youth services, family planning, public interest and cultural programs.

Nancy Solana, Executive Director

2870 MD Anderson Foundation
1515 Holcombe Blvd
Houston, TX 77030-2558
713-658-2316
http://www.mdanderson.org
The purpose of this foundation is to improve lives in the areas of health care, education, human service, youth and research.

John W Lowrie, Executive Director

2871 Meadows Foundation
3003 Swiss Avenue
Wilson Historic Block
Dallas, TX 75204-6049
214-826-9431
800-826-9431
Fax: 214-824-0642
E-mail: besterline@mfi.org
http://www.mfi.org
Support is given in the area of arts and culture, civic and public affairs, education, health, including mental health, and human services.

Bruce Esterline, VP Grants
Carol Stabler, Director Communications

2872 Moody Foundation
2302 Post Office Street
Suite 704
Galveston, TX 77550-1994
409-797-1500
Fax: 409-763-5564
E-mail: info@moodyf.org
http://www.moodyf.org
Provides major support for two foundation-initiated projects: the Transitional Learning Center, a residential rehabilitation and research facility for the treatment of traumatic brain injury, and Moody Gardens, a world-class education and recreation complex that includes a 1-acre enclosed rainforest, the area's largest aquarium, a space museum, IMAX theater, and the Moody Hospitality Institute.

Peter M Moore, Grants Director
Robert L Moody, Sr.Chiarman

2873 Paul & Mary Haas Foundation
PO Box 2928
Corpus Christi, TX 78403-2928
361-887-6955
Offers scholastic grants to graduating high school seniors from Corpus Christi, Texas. The student must have above average grades and ability to prove financial need. The Foundation asks that the senior contact them in the Fall of his/her senior year in order to begin the in-house application process. The grant is a maximum of $1,500 per semester and is renewable for a total of eight semesters if the student maintains a 3.0 GPA. The student may attend college or university of his choice.

Karen Wesson, Executive Director

2874 Perot Foundation
12377 Merit Drive
Suite 1700
Dallas, TX 75251-2239
972-788-3000
Fax: 972-788-3091
Educational grants, medical research funding and grantmaking for the arts and cultural organizations.

Bette Perot, Executive Director

2875 RW Fair Foundation
PO Box 689
Tyler, TX 75710-0689
903-592-3811
Grants are given for secondary and higher education, church-related programs and legal education.

Wilton H Fair, Executive Director

2876 Sid W Richardson Foundation
309 Main Street
Fort Worth, TX 76102-4006
817-336-0494
Fax: 817-332-2176
E-mail: www.sidrichardson.org
http://www.sidrichardson.org

This foundation was established for the purpose of supporting organizations that serve the people of Texas. Grants are given in the areas of education, health, the arts and human services.

Valleau Wilkie Jr, Executive Director

2877 Strake Foundation
712 Main Street
Suite 3300
Houston, TX 77002-3210
713-546-2400
Fax: 713-216-2401
Foundation gives primarily in Texas in the areas of operating budgets, continuing support, annual campaigns, special projects, research, matching funds and general purposes.

George W Strake Jr, Executive Director

2878 Trull Foundation
404 4th Street
Palacios, TX 77465-4812
361-972-5241
Fax: 361-972-1109
E-mail: trullfdn@ncnet.net
http://www.trullfoundation.org
1. A concern for the needs of the Palacios, Matagorda county are, where the foundation has its roots. Local health care, the senior center, and other local projects were considered and supported. 2. A concern for children and families. Grants are given to direct and channel lives away from child abuse, neglect from hunger, and poverty. 3. A concern for those persons and families devastated by the effects of substance abuse.

Gail Purvis, Executive Director
Lucja White, Administrative Assistant

Utah

2879 Marriner S Eccles Foundation
79 S Main Street
Salt Lake City, UT 84111-1901
801-246-5155
General support for Utah's human services, education and the arts programs.

Erma E Hogan, Executive Director

2880 Ruth Eleanor Bamberger and John Ernest Bamberger Memorial Foundation
136 S Main Street
Salt Lake City, UT 84101-1690
801-364-2045
Fax: 801-322-5284
E-mail:
bambergermemfdn@qwestoffice.net
http://www.ruthandjohnbambergermemorial
fdn.org
Offers support for secondary education, especially undergraduate scholarships for student nurses and for schools.

William H Olwell, Executive Director

2881 Salt Lake City Public Library
210 East 400 south
Salt Lake City, UT 84111-3280
801-524-8200
Fax: 801-524-8272
http://www.slcpl.lib.ut.us
Member of The Foundation Center network, maintaining a collection of private foundation tax returns which provide information on the scope of grants dispensed by that particular foundation.

Dana Tumtowsky, Comm Relations Coordinator
Nancy Tessman, Director

Vermont

2882 Vermont Community Foundation
PO Box 30
Three Court Street
Middlebury, VT 05753-0030
802-388-3355
Fax: 802-388-3398
http://www.vermontcf.org
Offers support for the arts and education, the environment, preservation of the community, public affairs and more for the betterment of Vermont.

David F Finney, President/CEO
John Killacky, Executive Director

2883 Vermont Department of Libraries
Reference Services
109 State Street
Montpelier, VT 05609-0001
802-828-3268
Fax: 802-828-2199
http://www.dol.state.vt.us
Member of The Foundation Center network, maintaining a collection of private foundation tax returns which provide information on the scope of grants dispensed by that particular foundation.

2884 William T & Marie J Henderson Foundation
PO Box 600
Stowe, VT 05672-0600
Offers grants in the areas of elementary and secondary education.

William T Henderson, Executive Director

Virginia

2885 Beazley Foundation
3720 Brighton Street
Portsmouth, VA 23707-3902
757-393-1605
Fax: 757-393-4708
E-mail: info@beazleyfoundation.org
http://www.beazleyfoundation.org
The purpose of this foundation to further the causes of charity, education and religion. Offers support for higher, secondary and medical education, youth agencies, community agencies and development.

Judge Richard S Bray, President
Donna M Russell, Associate Director

2886 Flagler Foundation
PO Box 644
Richmond, VA 23205
804-648-5033
Offers support for secondary and higher education, cultural programs and restoration.

Lawrence Lewis Jr, Executive Director

2887 Hampton Public Library
22 Lincoln Street
Hampton, VA 23669-4200
757-727-6315
Fax: 757-728-3037
E-mail: council@hampton.gov
http://www.hampton.va.us
Member of The Foundation Center network, maintaining a collection of private foundation tax returns which provide information on the scope of grants dispensed by that particular foundation.

Molly Joseph Ward, Mayor
George E Wallace, Vice Mayor

2888 Jeffress Memorial Trust
Bank Of America Private Bank
Po Box 8795
Williamsburg, VA 23187-8795
804-788-3698
Fax: 804-788-2700
http://www.wm.edu/grants/opps/jeffress.ht
m
Funds research in higher education.

Richard B Brandt, Advisor

2889 Kentland Foundation
267 Kentlands Boulevard
Gaithesrsburg, MD 20878-5442
301-926-6636
E-mail: info@kentlands.org
http://www.kentlands.org
Focuses on civic affairs organizations and education.

Helene Walker, Executive Director

2890 Longview Foundation for Education in World Affairs/International Understanding
1069 West Broad Street
Suite 801
Falls Church, VA 22046
301-681-0899
Fax: 301-681-0925
E-mail: globaled@longviewfdn.org
http://www.longviewfdn.org
Offers grants and scholarships with an emphasis on pre-collegiate education, primarily elementary education, and also supports teacher education.

Betsy Devlin-Foltz, Director
Stevenson McIlvaine, President

2891 Richmond Public Library
Business, Science & Technology Department
3100 Ellwood Avenue
Richmond, VA 23221-2193
804-646-1139
Fax: 804-646-4757
http://www.richmondpubliclibrary.org
Member of The Foundation Center network, maintaining a collection of private foundation tax returns which provide information on the scope of grants dispensed by that particular foundation.

Peter Blake, Chairman
Brenda Drew, Vice-Chairman

2892 Virginia Foundation for Educational Leadership
2204 Recreation Drive
Virginia Beach, VA 23456-6178
757-430-2412
Fax: 757-430-3247

George E McGovern, Division Director

Washington

2893 Comstock Foundation
3010 Gull Road
Kalamazoo, MI 49048
269-250-8900
Fax: 269-250-8901
http://www.comstockps.org
The Foundation contributes only to 501(c)(3) organizations, limited to Spokane County and its environs. In the field of general education, Comstock Foundation favors grants only to private institutions of higher learning, and no grants are made to individuals.

Horton Herman, Trustee
Charles M Leslie, Trustee

2894 Foster Foundation
13 Central Way
Kirland, WA 98033
206-726-1815
E-mail: info@thefosterfoundation.org
http://www.thefosterfoundation.org
Offers support in art, culture, higher education, adult education, literacy and basic reading, health care and children and youth services.

Jill Goodsell, Executive Director

2895 MJ Murdock Charitable Trust
703 Broadway Street
Suite 701
Vancouver, WA 98660-3308
360-694-8415
Fax: 360-694-1819
http://www.murdock-trust.org
Offers support primarily for special projects of private organizations in the areas of education, higher education, human services and program development.

John Van Zytveld, Senior Program Director

2896 Seattle Foundation
1200 5th Avenue
Suite 1300
Seattle, WA 98101-3151
206-622-2294
Fax: 206-622-7673
http://www.seattlefoundation.org
A community foundation that facilitates charitable giving; administers charitable funds, trusts and bequests; and distributes grants to non-profit organizations that are making a positive difference in our community. Grants are awarded to organizations working in areas that include social service, children and youth, civic, culture, elderly, conservation, education and health/rehabilitation.

Phyllis J Campbell, President/CEO
Molly Stearns, Senior Vice President

2897 Seattle Public Library
Science, Social Science
1000 4th Avenue
Seattle, WA 98104-1109
206-386-4636
Fax: 206-386-4634
http://www.spl.org
Member of The Foundation Center network, maintaining a collection of private foundation tax returns which provide information on the scope of grants dispensed by that particular foundation.

2898 Spokane Public Library
Funding Information Center
906 West Main Street
Spokane, WA 99201-0903
509-444-5300
Fax: 509-444-5365
http://www.spokanelibrary.org
Member of The Foundation Center network, maintaining a collection of private foundation tax returns which provide information on the scope of grants dispensed by that particular foundation.

Pat Partovi, Director

West Virginia

2899 Clay Foundation
1426 Kanawha Boulevard E
Charleston, WV 25301-3084
304-344-8656
Fax: 304-344-3805

Private charitable foundation making grants for health, education and programs for the aging or disadvantaged children.

Charles M Avampao, Executive Director

2900 Kanawha County Public Library
123 Capitol Street
Charleston, WV 25301-2686
304-343-4646
Fax: 304-348-6530
http://www.kanawha.lib.wv.us
Member of The Foundation Center network, maintaining a collection of private foundation tax returns which provide information on the scope of grants dispensed by that particular foundation.

Michael Albert, President
Elizabeth O Lord, First Vice President

2901 Phyllis A Beneke Scholarship Fund
Security National Bank & Trust Company
PO Box 511
Wheeling, WV 26003-0064
Offers support and scholarships for secondary education.

GP Schramm Sr, Executive Director

Wisconsin

2902 Faye McBeath Foundation
101 W Pleasant Street
Suite 210
Milwaukee, WI 53212-3157
414-272-2626
Fax: 414-272-6235
E-mail: info@fayemcbeath.org
http://www.fayemcbeath.org
The purpose of the foundation is to provide Wisconsin people the best in education, child welfare, homes and care for the elderly and research in civics and government.

Scott E Gelzer, Executive Director
Aileen Mayer, Executive Assistant

2903 Lynde & Harry Bradley Foundation
1241 N Franklin Place
Milwaukee, WI 53202-2901
414-291-9915
Fax: 414-291-9991
http://www.bradleyfdn.org
The Foundation encourages projects that focus on cultivating a renewed, healthier and more vigorous sense of citizenship among the American people, and among peoples of all nations, as well. Grants are awarded to organizations and institutions exempt from federal taxation under Section 501(c)(3) and publicly supported under section 509(a), favor projects which are not normally financed by public tax funds, consider requests from religious organizations and institutions as well.

Michael W Grebe, President/CEO
Terry Considine, Chairman

2904 Marquette University Memorial Library
1355 West Wisconsin Avenue
Milwaukee, WI 53233-2287
414-288-7556
Fax: 414-288-5324
http://www.marquette.edu/library/
Member of The Foundation Center network, maintaining a collection of private foundation tax returns which provide information on the scope of grants dispensed by that particular foundation.

2905 Siebert Lutheran Foundation
300 N Corporate Dr
Suite 200
Brookfield, WI 53045-1392
262-754-9160
Fax: 262-754-9162
E-mail: contactus@siebertfoundation.org
http://www.siebertfoundation.org
Offers support in elementary and secondary, higher education and early childhood education.

Ronald D Jones, President
Deborah Engel, Administrative Assistant

2906 University of Wisconsin-Madison
Memorial Library
728 State Street
Madison, WI 53706-1418
608-262-3242
Fax: 608-262-8569
E-mail: grantsinfo@library.wisc.edu
http://www.grants.library.wisc.edu
Member of The Foundation Center network, maintaining a collection of private foundation tax returns which provide information on the scope of grants dispensed by that particular foundation.

Wyoming

2907 Natrona County Public Library
307 E 2nd Street
Casper, WY 82601-2598
307-237-4935
Fax: 307-266-3734
http://www.library.natrona.net
Member of The Foundation Center network, maintaining a collection of private foundation tax returns which provide information on the scope of grants dispensed by that particular foundation.

Grants, Federal & Private

2908 American Honda Foundation
PO Box 2205
Torrance, CA 90509-2205
310-781-4090
Fax: 310-781-4270
http://www.hondacorporate.com/community
Offers support for national organizations whose areas of interest include youth and scientific education. Grants reach private elementary, secondary, higher, vocational and scientific education.

Kathryn A Carey, Manager

2909 Awards for University Administrators and Librarians
Association of Commonwealth Universities
John Foster House
36 Gordon Square
London WC1H OPF, England
171 3878572
Fax: 171 3872655
E-mail: pubinfo@acu.ac.uk;
acusales@acu.ac.uk
Lists approximately 40 sources of financial assistance for administrative and library staff for universities worldwide. Includes name, address, phone, fax, tenure place and length, amount of aid, requirements for eligibility and application procedure, and frequency and number of grants available.

40 pages Biennial
ISSN: 0964-2714

Moira Hunter, Editor

2910 Awards for University Teachers and Research Workers
Association of Commonwealth Universities
36 Gordon Square
London
WC1H OPF, England
44-20-7380-6700
Fax: 44-20-7387-2655
E-mail: info@devry.edu
http://www.devry.edu
Lists approximately 740 awards open to university teachers and research workers in one country for research, study visits or teaching at a university in another country. Offers fellowships, visiting professorships and lectureships and travel grants.
364 pages Biennial
ISSN: 0964-2706

2911 Educational Foundation of America
55 Walls Drive
Fairfield, CT 06824-3515
203-226-6498
Fax: 203-227-0424
http://www.efaw.org
Funds projects in arts, education and programs benefiting Native Americans.
Diane M Allison, Executive Director
Lynn P Babicka, President

2912 Foundation Center
79 5th Avenue
Floor 8
New York, NY 10003-3076
212-620-4230
Fax: 212-807-3677
http://www.fdncenter.org
A national service organization which disseminates information on private giving through public service programs, publications, and through a national network of library reference collections for free public use. Over 100 network members have sets of private foundation information returns, and the New York, Washington, DC, Cleveland and San Francisco reference collections operated by the Foundation offer a wide variety of services and collections of information on foundations and grants.
Cheryl Loe, Director Of Communications
Laura Cascio, Fulfillment Management

2913 GTE Foundation
PO Box 152257
Irving, TX 75015-2257
972-507-5434
Fax: 972-615-4310
http://www.gte.com
The emphasis of giving for the foundation is on higher education in math, science and technology. It also sponsors scholarships and supports community funds and social service agencies that emphasize literacy training.
Maureen Gorman, VP

2914 George I Alden Trust
370 Main Street
Worcester, MA 01608-1714
508-459-8005
Fax: 508-459-8305
E-mail: trustees@aldentrust.org
http://aldentrust.org
Gives to higher education organizations and facilities with an emphasis on scholarship endowments.
Francis H Dewey III, Executive Director
Warner S Fletcher, Chairman

2915 Gershowitz Grant and Evaluation Services
505 Merle Hay Tower
Des Moines, IA 50310
515-270-1718
Fax: 515-270-8325
E-mail: gershowitz@netins.net
To give schools an edge in funding their technology programs
Michael V Gershowitz, PhD
Steve Panyan, PhD

2916 Grants and Contracts Service
Department of Education/Regional Office Building
7th & D Streets
Suite 3124
Washington, DC 20202-0001
202-401-2000
Fax: 202-260-7225
To support improvements in teaching and learning and to help meet special needs of schools and students in elementary and secondary education
Gary J Rasmussen, Director

2917 Grantsmanship Center
PO Box 17220
Los Angeles, CA 90017-0220
213-482-9860
Fax: 213-482-9863
E-mail: norton@tgci.com
http://www.tgci.com
The world's oldest and largest training organization for the nonprofit sector. Since it was founded in 1972, the has trained trains more than 75,000 staff members of public and private agencies; training provided includes grantsmanship, program management and fundraising. Center also produces publications on grantsmanship, fundraising, planning, management and personnel issues for nonprofit agencies.
Norton Kiritz, President

2918 John S & James L Knight Foundation
Wachovia Financial Center
Suite 3300
200south Biscayne Boulevard
Miami, FL 33131-2349
305-908-2600
Fax: 305-908-2698
E-mail: web@knightfoundation.org
http://www.knightfdn.org
The foundation makes national grants in journalism, education and the field of arts and culture. It also supports organizations in communities where the Knight brothers were involved in publishing newspapers but is wholly separate from and independent of those newspapers.
James D Spaniolo, Executive Director

2919 National Academy of Education
500 Fifth Street NW
Washington, DC 20001
212-998-9035
Fax: 212-995-4435
E-mail: info@naeducation.org
http://www.naeducation.org
Offers the Spencer Postdoctoral Fellowship which is designed to promote scholarship in the United States and abroad on matters relevant to the improvement of education in all its forms.
Debbie Leong-Childs, Executive Director

2920 National Science Foundation
4201 Wilson Boulevard
Arlington, VA 22230
703-292-5111
Fax: 703-292-9184
http://www.nsf.gov
Offers grants, workshops and curricula for all grade levels.
Arden L Bement Jr, Director

2921 Trust to Reach Education Excellence
1904 Association Drive
Reston, VA 20191-1537
703-860-0200
800-253-7746
Fax: 703-476-5432
E-mail: tree@principals.org
http://www.tree.principals.org
Founded to make grants to educators and students who would ordinarily not have access to outstanding NASSP programs, such as camps, programs and workshops on leadership, technology and school reform.
Dr. Anne Miller, Executive Director

2922 Union Carbide Foundation
39 Old Ridgebury Road
Danbury, CT 06817-0001
203-794-6945
Fax: 203-794-7031
http://www.unioncarbide.com
Offers grants in the areas of elementary and secondary education, with an emphasis on systemic reform; higher education with a focus on science and engineering; and environmental protection awareness.
Nancy W Deibler, Executive Director

2923 United States Institute of Peace
2301 Constitution Avenue
Washington, DC 20037
202-457-1700
Fax: 202-429-6063
http://www.usip.org
Includes grants, fellowships, a National Peace Essay Contest for high school students and teacher training institutes.
Richard H Solomon, President
Judy Ansley, Board of Director

2924 United States-Japan Foundation
145 E 32nd Street
Floor 12
New York, NY 10016-6055
212-481-8753
Fax: 212-481-8762
E-mail: info@us-jf.org
http://www.us-jf.org
A nonprofit, philanthropic organization with the principal mission of promoting a greater mutual knowledge between United States and Japan and to contribute to a strengthened understanding of important public policy issues of interest to both countries. Currently the focus is on precollegiate education, policy studies, and communications and public opinion.

2925 Westinghouse Foundation
Westinghouse Electric Corporation
Po Box 355
ECE 575C
Pittsburgh, PA 15230-0355
412-374-6824
Fax: 412-642-4874
http://www.westinghousenuclear.com
Makes charitable contributions to community priorities primarily where Westinghouse has a presence. Areas of emphasis include: education, health and welfare, culture and the arts and civic and social grants. Support for education is central to Westinghouse's contributions program, particularly higher education in the areas of engineering, applied science and business. Also encourages educational programs that strengthen public schools through enhanced student learning opportunities.
G Reynolds Clark, Executive Director

2926 Xerox Foundation
800 Long Ridge Road #1600
Stamford, CT 06902-1227

203-968-3445
http://www.xerox.com
Offers giving in the areas of higher education to prepare qualified men and women for careers in business, government and education.

Joseph M Cahalan, Executive Director

Fundraising

2927 A&L Fund Raising
29 Carriage Drive
South Windsor, CT 06074-1140
860-242-2476
800-286-7247
http://www.alstudentservices.com
Offers many successful fundraising programs including Christmas gifts, designer gift wraps from Ashley Taylor and Geoffrey Boehm chocolates. A&L sells only the highest quality items at affordable prices with great service to schools and organizations.

Anita Brown

2928 A+ Enterprises
1426 Route 33
Hamilton Square, NJ 08690-1704
609-587-1765
800-321-1765
A promotional corporation offering a variety of fundraising programs for schools and educational institutions, ranging from Christmas campaigns to chocolates, as well as magnets and gift campaigns.

2929 Aid for Education
CD Publications
8204 Fenton Street
Sliver Spring, MD 20910
301-588-6380
800-666-6380
Fax: 301-588-0519
E-mail: afe@cdpublications.com
http://www.cdpublications.com
18 pages Newsletter
ISSN: 1058-1324

Frank Kimko, Editor

2930 All Sports
21 Round Hill Road
Wethersfield, CT 06109
860-721-0273
800-829-0273
Fax: 860-257-9609
E-mail: shirts2graduationshirts.com
http://www.graduationshirts.com
Fundraising and school promotion company offering crew sweatshirts, hoods, tees, jackets, caps, gymwear and specialty signature shirts for graduating classes.

Wally Schultz, Owner

2931 Art to Remember
5535 Macy Drive
Indianapolis, IN 46235
317-826-0870
800-895-8777
Fax: 317-823-2822
E-mail: brackney@arttoremember.com
http://www.arttoremember.com
Raises funds for art departments and special school programs.

2932 Childrens Youth Funding Report
CD Publications
8204 Fenton Street
Sliver Spring, MD 20910
301-588-6380
800-666-6380
Fax: 301-588-6385

E-mail: cye@cdpublications.com
http://www.cdpublications.com
Detailed coverage of federal and private grant opportunities and legislative initiatives effecting childrens programs in such areas as child welfare, education healthcare.

18 pages Monthly
Steve Albright, Editor

2933 Dutch Mill Bulbs
PO Box 407
Hershey, PA 17033-1386
717-868-3120
800-533-8824
Fax: 800-556-0539
E-mail: info@dutchmillbulbs.com
http://www.dutchmillbulbs.com
Spring and Fall fundraising with flower bulbs program.

Jeffrey E Ellenberger, President

2934 E-S Sports Screenprint Specialists
47 Jackson Street
Holyoke, MA 01040-5512
413-534-5634
800-833-3171
Fax: 413-538-8648
Scholastic Spirit Division offers screenprinted T-shirts, sweatshirts, shorts and apparel. This program offers schools and organizations an easy way to increase school spirit with no risk, no minimum orders and prompt delivery.

Aaron Porchelli, Division Director

2935 Fundraising USA
1395 State Route 23
Butler, NJ 07405-1736
973-283-1946
800-428-6178
Fundraiser offering a variety of programs for schools and organizations including Walk-A-Thons. This program is fast becoming the most popular way for schools to raise money. The walks are designed to take place at your own school, and children are not responsible for collecting any money. Fundraising USA collects all donations through the mail.

2936 Gold Medal Products
10700 Medallion Drive
Cincinnati, OH 45241-4807
513-769-7676
800-543-0862
Fax: 513-769-8500
E-mail: info@gmpopcorn.com
http://www.gmpopcorn.copm
Offers a full line of fundraising products popcorn poppers and supplies and programs including candy, clothing and sports programs for schools and colleges.

Chris Petroff
Dan Kroeger, President

2937 Human-i-Tees
400 Columbus Avenue
Valhalla, NY 10595-1335
800-275-2638
Fax: 914-745-1799
http://www.humanitees.com
Environmental T-shirt fundraisers that provide large profits while raising environmental awareness for thousands of school, youth and service organizations across the country.

2938 Hummel Sweets
PO Box 232
Forestville, MD 20747
800-998-8115
Offer fundraising programs with 45% to 50% profit.

2939 M&M Mars Fundraising
800 High Street
Hackettstown, NJ 07840-1552
908-852-1000
Fax: 908-850-2734
Offers America's favorite candies for fundraising programs throughout the year.

2940 QSP
Subsidiary of the Reader's Digest Association
PO Box 2003
Ridgefield, CT 06877-0903
203-756-3022
800-667-2536
Fax: 800-844-3568
E-mail: customerservice@qsp.ca
http://www.qsp.ca
For twenty-seven years, this fundraiser has helped students raise more than $900,000,000 for extracurricular programs and projects that are essential to a meaningful, well-rounded education. With QSP programs, students earn money to fund worthwhile projects and learn about the business world at the same time. QSP offers various fundraising programs including: Family Reading Programs; The Music Package; Delightful Edibles; and The Parade of Gifts.

Robert L Metivier, Sales Manager

2941 Sally Foster Gift Wrap
PO Box 539
Duncan, SC 29334-0539
800-552-5875
Fax: 800-343-0809
http://www.sallyfoster.com
Fundraiser offers gift wrap packages to schools. Offers high quality merchandise, including the heaviest papers and foils available. This proven two-week program is quick, easy and profitable offering your school or organization the opportunity to raise thousands of dollars to buy computers, books, athletic equipment and more. Organizations and schools keep 50% of all the profits, and there are no up-front costs or risks.

Mark Metcalfe, Sr VP

2942 School Identifications
Chas. E. Petrie Comapny
PO Box 527
Woodburn, OR 97071-0012
503-982-0757
800-772-0798
Fax: 503-981-3038
E-mail: info@schoolidents.com
http://www.schoolidents.com
An easy fundraising project for schools, offering school identification cards and tags for students.

2943 School Memories Collection
Fundcraft Publishing
PO Box 340
Collierville, TN 38027
901-853-7070
800-853-1363
Fax: 901-853-6196
E-mail: info@fundcraft.com
http://www.schoolmemories.com
Memory books with games and activities.

Chris Bradley, Marketing Director

2944 Sports Shoes & Apparel
3 Moulton Drive
Londonderry, NH 03053-4061
603-437-7844
800-537-7844
Fax: 603-437-2300
Offers customized sweatshirts, T-shirts and beach towels at group discount, with several complete fund raising programs being available as well. Beach towels for fundraising.

Bill McMahon, Regional Manager

2945 Steve Wronker's Funny Business
39 Boswell Road
W Hartford, CT 06107-3708
860-233-6716
800-929-swfb
Fax: 860-561-8910
http://www.swfb.net/swfb.htm
Comedy and educational magic shows available for preschool and elementary school aged children. Award winning programs such as The Magic of Books and Magic from Around the World are available for any size audience. For middle schools and high schools, comedy hypnosis is a perfect venue for entertainment as a fundraising program, for high school after-prom parties, graduation parties, or just for an evening's entertainment.
Steve Wronker

2946 T-Shirt People/Wearhouse
10722 Hanna Street
Beltsville, MD 20705-2123
301-937-4843
800-638-7070
Fax: 301-937-2916
http://www.t-shirtpeople.com
Fundraiser offering customized T-shirts to boost school spirit, raise funds, instill school pride and save money.

2947 Troll Book Fairs
100 Corporate Drive
Mahwah, NJ 07430-2041
201-529-4000
Fax: 201-529-8282
A profit-making program designed to introduce children to the wonderful world of books.

2948 Union Pen Company
166 Wallins Corner Road
Amsterdam, NY 12010
800-203-9917
Fax: 800-688-4877
E-mail: unionpen@aol.com
http://www.unionpen.com
This company offers advertising gifts including customized pens and key chains that will increase confidence, school spirit and community goodwill in education. Group discounts are available.
Matt Roberts, General Manager
Morton Tenny, President

2949 www.positivepins.com
802 E 6th Streetve
PO Box 52528
Tulsa, OK 74152
918-587-2405
800-282-0085
Fax: 918-382-0906
E-mail: pinrus@aol.com
http://www.thepinman-pins.com
Fundraising organization used by educational organizations. Designer and manufacturer of lapel pins used for employee service, appreciation, volunteer recognition, donor incentives and recognition, public relations and spirit.
Bern L Gentry, President
Michelle Anderson, VP

Scholarships & Financial Aid

2950 AFL-CIO Guide to Union Sponsored Scholarships, Awards & Student Aid
AFL-CIO
1100 1st St NE
Suite 850
Washington, DC 20002-4104
202-637-5000
E-mail: info@unionprivelege.org
http://www.unionplus.org
Lists international and national unions, local unions, state federations and labor councils offering scholarships, awards or financial aid to students.
100 pages Annual

2951 American-Scandinavian Foundation
58 Park Avenue
New York, NY 10016
212-779-3587
E-mail: info@amscan.org
http://www.amscan.org
The Foundation provides information, scholarships and grants on the study programs in Scandinavia.
Edward Gallagher, President
Christian Sonne, Deputy Chairman

2952 Arts Scholarships
Jewish Foundation for Education of Women
430 Park Ave
Suite 3A
Highland Park, IL 60035-1827
212-288-3931
Fax: 212-288-5798
E-mail: fdnscholar@aol.com
http://www.scholarships.com
These scholarships are being offered at the Julliard School, Tisch School, of the Arts at New York University, and the Manhattan School of Music to qualified students enrolled in their programs. Faculty members will select recipients.
Marge Goldwater, Executive Director

2953 CUNY Teacher Incentive Program
Jewish Foundation for Education of Women
135 E 64th Street
New York, NY 10019-1827
212-288-3931
Fax: 212-288-5798
E-mail: fdnscholar@aol.com
http://www.jfew.org
Provide stipends to CUNY graduates who are studying for a master's degree in education and interested in a teaching career in the New York City public school system. Contact the office of the Vice Chancellor for Academic Affairs at CUNY for further information.
Marge Goldwater, Executive Director

2954 College Board
45 Columbus Avenue
New York, NY 10023-6917
212-713-8000
Fax: 212-713-8282
http://www.collegeboard.org
The College Board is a national, nonprofit membership association that supports educational transitions through programs and services in assessment, guidance, admission, placement, financial aid, and educational reform.
David Coleman, President

2955 Dissertation Fellowships in the Humanities
Jewish Foundation for Education of Women
135 E 64th Street
New York, NY 10065-1827
212-288-3931
Fax: 212-288-5798
E-mail: fdnscholar@aol.com
http://www.jfew.org
A small number of fellowships will be awarded through the CUNY Graduate Center to qualified applicants.
Marge Goldwater, Executive Director

2956 George & Mary Kremer Foundation
1100 5th Avenue S
Suite 411
Naples, FL 34102-7415
941-261-2367
Fax: 941-261-1494
http://www.kremerfoundation.com
Provides scholarship funding for needy children in elementary Catholic schools throughout the Continental United States.
Mary Anderson Goddard, Director
Sister MT Ballrach, Assistant Director

2957 Intel Science Talent Search Scholarship
1719 N Street NW
Washington, DC 20036-2888
202-785-2255
Fax: 202-785-1243
E-mail: sciedu@sciserv.org
http://www.sciserv.org
Offers a variety of services to teachers and students, including Intel Science Talent Search Scholarship competition, science fairs and publications.

2958 Jewish Foundation for Education of Women
Jewish Foundation for Education of Women
135 E 64th Street
New York, NY 10019-1827
212-288-3931
Fax: 212-288-5798
E-mail: fdnscholar@aol.com
http://www.jfew.org
The Jewish Foundation for Education of Women is a private, nonsectarian foundation providing scholarships to women for higher education in the New York City area. A variety of specific programs are available. Most programs are administered collaboratively with area schools and organizations; the Foundation's mission is to help women of all ages attain the education and training needed to make them productive, economically independent members of the community.
Marge Goldwater, Executive Director
Sharon L Weinberg, Chairman

2959 Octameron Associates
P.O Box 2748
Alexandria, VA 22301-0748
703-836-5480
Fax: 703-836-5650
E-mail: info@octameron.com
http://www.octameron.com
Octameron is a publishing and consulting firm with over 25 years experience in financial aid and admissions.
Anna Leider, Publisher

2960 Scholarship America
One Scholarship Way
Saint Peter, MN 56082-1556
507-931-1682
800-537-4180
Fax: 507-931-9250
E-mail: dsnatoff@aol.com
http://www.dollarsforscholars.org
Provides community volunteers with the tools and support to create, develop and sustain legally constituted community-based scholarship foundations. Over 15,000 volunteers are active on 760 Dollars for Scholars chapter boards and committees throughout the United States. In addition, 20,000 high school youth and community residents are active in fund-raising events and academic support programs. Since the late 1950's, over 155,000 students have received Dollars for Scholars scholarships.
David Bach, VP
Susan Ponwith, President&CEO

2961 Scholarships in the Health Professions

Jewish Foundation for Education of Women
135 E 64th Street
New York, NY 10021
212-288-3931
Fax: 212-288-5798
E-mail: fdnscholar@aol.com
http://www.jfew.org
Provides scholarships to emigres from the former Soviet Union who are studying medicine, dentistry, nursing, pharmacy, OT, PT, dental hygiene, and physician assistanceship.

Marge Goldwater, Executive Director

Federal Listings

2962 Accounting & Financial Management Services
Department of Education/1175 Main Building
400 Maryland Avenue SW
Washington, DC 20202-0001
Fax: 202-401-0207

Mitchell L Laine, Chief Officer

2963 Assistance to States Division
Department of Education/3042 Mary E. Switzer Bldg.
330 C Street
Washington, DC 20202
202-401-2000
Fax: 202-260-7225

Tom Irvin, Acting Director

2964 Brody Professional Development
Brody Communications Ltd.
115 West Avenue
Suite 114
Jenkintown, PA 19046
215-886-1688
Fax: 215-886-1699
E-mail: info@brodypro.com
http://www.brodypro.com
Brody offers tailored training programs, executive coaching and presentations in the areas of communication skills and professional development.

Miryam Roddy, Manager of Maximum Exposure

2965 Compensatory Education Program
US Department of Education
400 Maryland Avenue SW
Washington, DC 20202
202-260-0826
Fax: 202-260-7764

Mary Jean LeTendre, Director

2966 Elementary Secondary Bilingual & Research Branch
Department of Education/Regional Office Bldg.
7th & D Streets
Suite 3653
Washington, DC 20202
202-401-0113
Fax: 202-260-7225

Queenola Tyler, Bureau Chief

2967 Elementary, Secondary & Vocational Analysis
Department of Education
400 Maryland Avenue SW
3043 Main Building
Washington, DC 20202-0001
202-401-0318
Fax: 202-260-7225

Thomas Corwin, Division Director

2968 Management Services
Department of Education/3005 Main Building
400 Maryland Avenue SW
Washington, DC 20202-0001
202-401-0500
Fax: 202-260-7225

2969 National Center for Education Statistics
1990 K Street NW
Washington, DC 20006
202-502-7300
Fax: 202-260-7225
http://www.nces.ed.gov

Sean P. "Jack" Buckley, Commissioner

2970 National Council on Disability
1331 F Street NW
Suite 850
Washington, DC 20004-1107
202-272-2004
Fax: 202-272-2022
E-mail: ncd@ncd.gov
http://www.ncd.gov/
An independent federal agency comprised of 15 members appointed by the President and confirmed by the Senate.

Jonathan M. Young, Ph.D., Chairman
Aaron Bishop, Executive Director

2971 National Institute of Child Health and Human Development
Bldg.31, Room 2A32, MSC 2425
31 Center Drive
Bethesda, MD 20892-2425
800-370-2943
Fax: 866-760-5947
E-mail: NICHDInformationResourceCenter@mail.nih.gov
http://www.nichd.nih.gov
Develops research to solve problems in the physical and mental evolution of development. Including some of the most emotionally draining disorders, learning disabilities, behavioral disabilities, birth defects and infant mortality. Acts as a clearinghouse of materials, information and referrals and more.

Ellie Brown Hochman, Administrative Officer
Brenda Hanning, Program Management Officer

2972 National Library of Education
U.S. Department of Education
400 Maryland Avenue, SW
Washington, DC 20202
800-424-1616
Fax: 202-401-0547
E-mail: library@ed.gov
http://www.ed.gov

Dr. Rebecca Maynard, Commissioner

2973 National Trust for Historic Preservation: Office of Education Initiatives
1785 Massachusetts Avenue NW
Washington, DC 20036-2117
202-588-6000
800-944-6847
Fax: 202-588-6038
http://www.nationaltrust.org
Teaching with Historic Places, a program offered by the National Park Service's National Register of Historic Places, and the National Trust for Historic Preservation Press.

Stephanie Meeks, President & CEO

2974 No Child Left Behind
U.S. Department of Education
400 Maryland Avenue, SW
Washington, DC 20202
202-401-2000
800-872-5327
Fax: 202-401-0689
http://www.ed.gov/nclb
Provides education standards and incentives for states in adopting academic standards that prepare students to succeed in college and the workplace.

Arne Duncan, Secretary of Education
Tony Miller, Deputy Secretary

2975 Office for Civil Rights
U.S. Department of Education
400 Maryland Avenue SW
Lyndon Baines Johnson Dept of Ed Bldg.
Washington, DC 20202-1100
800-421-3481
Fax: 202-453-6012
E-mail: ocr@ed.gov
http://www.ed.gov

Russlynn Ali, Assistant Secretary
Ricardo Soto, Deputy Assistant Secretary

2976 Office of Bilingual Education and Minority Languages Affairs
U.S. Department of Education
600 Independence Avenue, SW
Washington, DC 20202-6510
202-205-5463
Fax: 202-260-7225
E-mail: askncbe@ncbe.gwu.edu

Delia Pompa, Director
Dang T. Pham, Deputy Director

2977 Office of Elementary & Secondary Education
U.S. Department of Education
400 Maryland Avenue SW
Washington, DC 20202
202-401-0113
Fax: 202-205-0310
E-mail: oese@ed.gov
http://www2.ed.gov

Thelma Melendez De Santa Ana, Assistant Secretary

2978 Office of Indian Education
U.S. Department of Education
400 Maryland Avenue SW
LBJ Building, 3E205
Washington, DC 20202-6335
202-260-3774
Fax: 202-260-7779
E-mail: indian.education@ed.gov
http://www.2.ed.gov

Jenelle Leonard, Acting Director
Terrie Nelson, Administrative Assistant

2979 Office of Legislation & Congressional Affairs
U.S. Department of Education
400 Maryland Avenue SW
Washington, DC 20202-3100
202-401-0020
Fax: 202-401-1438
E-mail: olca@ed.gov
http://www.2.ed.gov

Gabriella Gomez, Assistant Secretary
Lloyd Horwich, Deputy Assistant Secretary

2980 Office of Migrant Education
U.S. Department of Education
400 Maryland Avenue SW
Room 3E317 FOB-6
Washington, DC 20202-6135
202-260-1164
800-872-5327
Fax: 202-205-0089
http://www.2.ed.gov

Arne Duncan, Secretary Of Education
Lisa Ramirez, Director

2981 Office of Overseas Schools
US Department of State
Room H328, SA-1
Washington, DC 20522-0132
202-261-8200
Fax: 202-261-8224
E-mail: OverseasSchools@state.gov
http://www.state.gov
Maintains detailed information on 190 overseas elementary and secondary schools which receive some assistance from the US Department of State. These schools provide an American-type education which prepares students for schools, colleges and universities in the United States.

Dr. Keith D Miller, Director

2982 Office of Planning, Evaluation and Policy Development
U.S. Department of Education
330 C Street SW
Suite 4022
Washington, DC 20201-0001
202-205-9960
Fax: 202-260-7225
E-mail: judy.wurtzel.ed.gov
http://www.2.ed.gov

Carmel Martin, Assistant Secretary
Judy Wurtzel, Deputy Assistant Secretary

2983 Office of Special Education Programs
Department of Education/3086 Mary E. Switzer Bldg.
600 Independence Avenue SW
Washington, DC 20202-2570
202-205-5507
Fax: 202-260-7225
E-mail: thomas_hehir@ed.gov
http://www.ed.gov./offices/osers/idea/index.htm

Thomas Hehir, Director

2984 Office of Student Financial Assistance Programs
U.S. Department of Education
400 Maryland Avenue SW
Washington, DC 20202-0001
319-337-5665
800-433-3243

2985 Planning & Evaluation Service
Department of Education
Elementary Secondary Division
3127 Main Building, 400 Maryland
Washington, DC 20202
202-401-1968
Fax: 202-260-7225

Val Ptisko, Division Director

2986 Rehabilitation Services Administration
U.S. Department of Education
400 Maryland Avenue SW
Washington, DC 20202-2800
202-245-7488
Fax: 202-260-7225
E-mail: rsa.ed.gov
http://www.2.ed.gov

Lynnae M. Ruttledge, Commissioner
Edward Anthony, Deputy Commissioner

2987 Research to Practice Division
U.S. Department of Education
Ofc of Special Ed/Rehabilitative Sv
400 Maryland Avenue SW
Washington, DC 20202-7100
202-245-7459
http://www2.ed.gov

Alexa Posny, Assistant Secretary

2988 School Assistance Division
Department of Education/4200 Portals Building
1250 Maryland Avenue SW
Washington, DC 20024-2141
202-260-2270
Fax: 202-260-7225

Catherine Schagh, Division Director

2989 School Improvement Grants
U.S. Department Of Education
400 Maryland Avenue SW
Washington, DC 20202
800-872-5327
http://www.ed.gov

Arne Duncan, Secretary of Education
Tony Miller, Deputy Secretary

2990 School Improvement Programs-Equity and Educational Excellence Division
Department of Education/4500 Portals Building
1250 Maryland Avenue SW
Washington, DC 20024-2141
202-260-3693
Fax: 202-260-7225

Janice Williams-Madison, Division Director

2991 School Improvement Programs-Safe and Drug Free Schools
Office of Safe and Drug Free Schools
550 12th Street, SW
10th Floor
Washington, DC 20202-6450
202-245-7896
Fax: 202-485-0013
E-mail: osdfs.safeschl@ed.gov
http://www.ed.gov
Works to promote safe schools that are free from drug abuse and violence.

Kevin Jennings, Assistant Deputy Director
Tina Hunter, Executive Officer

2992 US Department of Defense Dependents Schools
2461 Eisenhower Avenue
Alexandria, VA 22331-3000
571-325-0867

Marilyn Witcher

2993 US Department of Education
400 Maryland Avenue SW
Washington, DC 20202
800-872-5327
Fax: 202-401-0689
E-mail: customerservice@inet.ed.gov
http://www.ed.gov
Ensures equal access to education and promotes educational excellence for all Americans.

Margaret Spellings, Secretary of Education

2994 Vocational & Adult Education
Department of Education/4090 Mary E. Switzer Bldg.
330 C Street
Washington, DC 20202
202-205-5451
Fax: 202-260-7225

Augusta Souza Kappner, Assistant Secretary

2995 Washington DC Department of Education
825 N Capitol Street NE
Suite 900
Washington, DC 20202-4210
202-442-5885
Fax: 202-442-5026

Paul L Varce, Superintendent

Alabama

2996 Alabama State Department of Education
50 N Ripley Street
PO Box 302101
Montgomery, AL 36104
334-242-9700
E-mail: astarks@alsde.edu
http://www.alsde.edu
Mission is to provide a state system of education which is committed to academic ex-

cellence and which provides education of the highest quality to all Alabama students, preparing them for the 21st century. For certification information contact the Alabama certification office at 334-242-9977.

Dr. Joseph B Morton, State Superintendent of Ed.
Dr. Craig Pouncey, Deputy State Superintendent

2997 General Counsel
Alabama Department of Education
50 N Ripley Street
Montgomery, AL 36130-0624
334-242-1899
E-mail: studor@alsde.edu
http://www.alsde.edu
Provides legal counsel to the State Superintendent of Education, State Board of Education and State Department of Education.

Larry Craven, General Counsel
Susan Tudor Crowther, Assoc General Counsel/Admin.

2998 Instructional Services
Alabama Department of Education
50 N Ripley Street
Montgomery, AL 36130-0624
334-242-9700
Fax: 334-242-9708

Charlie G Williams, Assistant Superintendent

2999 Professional Services
Alabama Department of Education
50 N Ripley Street
Montgomery, AL 36130-0624
334-242-9700
Fax: 334-242-9708

Eddie R Johnson, Assistant Superintendent

3000 Rehabilitation Services
Alabama Department of Rehabilitation Services
2129 E S Boulevard
PO Box 11586
Montgomery, AL 36111-0586
334-281-8780
800-441-7607
Fax: 334-281-1973
http://www.rehab.state.al.us
State agency that provides and services and assistance to Alabama's children and adults with disabilities and their families.

Steve Shrivers, Commissioner

3001 Special Education Services
Alabama Department of Education
50 N Ripley Street
Montgomery, AL 36130-0624
334-242-8114
Fax: 334-242-9192

Bill East, Division Director

3002 Student Instructional Services
Alabama Department of Education
50 N Ripley Street
Montgomery, AL 36130-0624
334-242-8256
Fax: 334-242-9708

Martha V Beckett, Assistant Superintendent

3003 Superintendent
Alabama Department of Education
50 N Ripley Street
Montgomery, AL 36130-0624
334-242-9700
Fax: 334-242-9708

Ed Richardson, Superintendent

3004 Vocational Education
Alabama Department of Education
50 N Ripley Street
Montgomery, AL 36130-0624

334-242-9111
Fax: 334-353-8861
Stephen B Franks, Division Director

Alaska

3005 Alaska Commission on Postsecondary Education

PO Box 110510
Juneau, AK 99811-0510
907-465-2962
800-441-2962
Fax: 907-465-5316
E-mail: customer.service@alaska.gov
http://www.akadvantage.alaska.gov
This state agency coordinates administration of state-funded educational financial assistance for students and their families. This agency is also responsible for licensing and regulating postsecondary institutions to operate in Alaska.

Diane Barrans, Executive Director
Kenneth Dodson, Dir. Information Support Svc

3006 Alaska Department of Education Administrative Services

801 W 10th Street
Suite 200
Juneau, AK 99801-1894
907-465-2802
Fax: 907-465-4156
For certification information visit www.eed.state.ak.us/TeacherCertification/ or contact 907-465-2831.

Shirley J Halloway, Commissioner

3007 Alaska Department of Education & Early Development

801 W 10th Street
Suite 200
Juneau, AK 99801
907-465-2800
Fax: 907-465-3452
http://www.educ.state.ak.us

Gerald Covey, Commissioner

3008 Libraries, Archives & Museums

Alaska Department of Education & Early Development
PO Box 110500
Juneau, AK 99811-0500
907-465-2800
Fax: 907-465-4156
E-mail: asl@alaska.gov
http://www.lam.alaska.gov
Summer reading programs

Linda Thibodeau, Director
Bob Banghart, Chief Curator

3009 School Finance & Data Management

Alaska Department of Education & Early Development
801 W 10th Street, Suite 200
PO Box 110500
Juneau, AK 99811-0500
907-465-2800
Fax: 907-465-4156
E-mail: eed.webmaster@alaska.gov
http://www.eed.state.ak.us
Public school funding programs

Cynthia Curran, Director
Paul Prussing, Deputy Director

3010 Teaching And Learning Support Program

Alaska Department of Education & Early Development
801 W 10th Street, Suite 200
PO Box 110500
Juneau, AK 99811-0500

907-465-2800
Fax: 907-465-4156
E-mail: eed.webmaster@alaska.gov
http://www.eed.state.ak.us
To improve students performance as well as the administering of a variety of federal, state and private programs that provide support to school district staff across the state.

Cynthia Curran, Director
Paul Prussing, Deputy Director

3011 Vocational Rehabilitation

Alaska Department of Labor & Workforce Development
801 W 10th Street
Suite A
Juneau, AK 99801-1894
907-465-2814
800-478-2815
Fax: 907-465-2856
E-mail: dawn.duval@alaska.gov
http://www.labor.state.ak.us
Helping individuals with disabilities to find employment

Cheryl Walsh, Director
John Cannon, Chairperson

Arkansas

3012 Arkansas Department of Education

4 Capitol Mall
Room 403-A
Little Rock, AR 72201-1071
501-683-4786
E-mail: virginia.hill@arkansas.gov
http://www.arkansased.org
Mission is to provide the highest quality leadership, service, and support to school districts and schools in order that they may provide equitable, quality education for all to ensure that all public schools comply with the standards.

Dr. Naccaman Williams, Chair
Virginia Hill, Administrative Assistant

3013 Arkansas Department of Education: Special Education

4 Capitol Mall
Room 403-A
Little Rock, AR 72201-1071
501-683-4786
E-mail: virginia.hill@arkansas.gov
http://www.arkansased.org

Dr. Naccaman Williams, Chair
Virginia Hill, Administrative Assistant

3014 Federal Programs

Arkansas Department of Education
4 Capitol Mall
Room 403-A
Little Rock, AR 72201-1011
501-682-4475
E-mail: virginia.hill@arkansas.gov
http://www.arkansased.org

Dr. Naccaman Williams, Chair
Virginia Hill, Administrative Assistant

California

3015 California Department of Education

1430 N Street
Sacramento, CA 95814-5901
916-319-0800
Fax: 916-657-4975
http://www.cde.ca.gov
Works to encourage the highest achievement for students by defining the knowledge, con-

cepts and skills that students should aquire in each grade level.

Tom Torlakson, St Superintendent Public Ins
Richard Zeiger, Chief Deputy Superintendent

3016 California Department of Education's Educational Resources Catalog

CDE Press Sales
1430 N Street
Suite 3207
Sacramento, CA 95814
916-323-4583
800-995-4099
Fax: 916-323-0823
E-mail: sales@cde.ca.gov
http://www.cde.ca.gov
Offers new techniques and fresh perspectives in handbooks, guides, videos and more.

Tom Torlakson, St Superintendent Public Ins

3017 California Department of Special Education

1430 N Street
Sacramento, CA 95814-5901
913-319-0800
Fax: 916-327-3516
Resources and information that serve the unique needs of persons with disabilities by helping them to meet or exceed high standards of achievement in both academic and nonacademic skills.

Tom Torlakson, St Superintendent Public Ins

3018 Curriculum & Instructional Leadership Branch

California Department of Education
1430 N Street
Sacramento, CA 95814
916-657-3043
http://www.cde.ca.gov
Works to improve students academic achievements

Harvey Hunt, Deputy

3019 Region 9: Education Department

San Diego COE
6401 Linda Vista Road
Suite 321
North San Diego, CA 92111
858-569-5304
E-mail: dbrashear@sdcoe.net
Part of a statewide system of school support established to meet state and federal requirements, the support system works within county offices offering intensive and sustained assistance to local schools and educational agencies receiving Title I funds, helping to increase the opportunity for all student's to meet the state academic content standards.

David Brashear, Director

3020 Specialized Programs Branch

California Department of Education
1430 N Street
Sacramento, CA 95814
916-319-0854
E-mail: mpayne@cde.ca.gov
http://www.cde.ca.gov
Works to ensure that all children have the opportunity to obtain high-quality education.

Tom Torlakson, St Superintendent Public Ins
Mary Payne, District/School Improvement

Colorado

3021 Colorado Department of Education
201 E Colfax Avenue
Denver, CO 80203-1799
303-866-6600
Fax: 303-866-6938
http://www.cde.state.co.us
For certification information visit
www.cde.state.co.us/index_license.htm or
contact 303-866-6628.

William T Moloney, Commissioner

3022 Educator Licensing Unit
Colorado Department of Education
201 E Colfax Avenue
Denver, CO 80203-1704
303-866-6628
Fax: 303-866-6866
Licensing applications for educators, career and technical education. Issues educators licenses, reviews content,
induction/professional development and
disciplinary actions

Ed Almon, Educator Licensing

**3023 Office of Federal Program
Administration**
Colorado Department of Education
1560 Broadway
Suite 1450
Denver, CO 80202-5149
303-866-6600
Fax: 303-866-6637
Administers funds under the elementary
and secondary education act as well as a variety of other state and federal competitive
awards and grants with the main goal to
help all students to reach proficiency in
English language arts, mathematics and
reading.

Patrick Chapman, Executive Director
Lynn Bamberry, Director

3024 State Library
Colorado Department of Education
201 E Colfax Avenue
Room 309
Denver, CO 80203-1704
303-866-6900
Fax: 303-866-6940
http://www.cde.state.co.us
Provides leadership and expertise in library related activities and policies and
provides assistance to public and academic
schools.

Eugene Hainer, Assistant Commissioner
Sharon Morris, Director

3025 Supplemental Educational Services
Colorado Department of Education
1560 Broadway
Suite 1450
Denver, CO 80202
303-866-6600
Fax: 303-866-6637
E-mail: medler_l@cde.state.co.us
http://www.cde.state.co.us
SES offers tutoring outside the regular
school day that is designed to increase the
academic achievement in reading/mathe-
matics and language arts to low-income
students in low-income schools

Patrick Chapman, Executive Director
Lisa Medler, Title IIA Coordinator

Connecticut

3026 Connecticut Early Childhood Unit
Connecticut State Department of
Education
165 Capital Avenue
Hartford, CT 06106
860-713-6740
Fax: 860-713-7018
E-mail: www.sde.ct.gov
Offers programs for children, infants and
toddlers with disabilities.

Steven Adamowski, Superintendent

**3027 Connecticut Governor's
Committee on Employment of the
Handicapped**
Labor Department Building
200 Folly Brook Boulevard
Wethersfield, CT 06109-1153
860-263-6774
Fax: 860-263-6039
http://www.dol.gov

**3028 Connecticut State Department of
Education**
165 Capitol Avenue
Hartford, CT 06106
860-713-6543
Fax: 860-722-8502
http://www.sde.ct.gov

Steven Adamowski, Superintendent

3029 Education Programs & Services
Connecticut Department of Education
25 Industrial Park Road
Middletown, CT 06457-1520
860-807-2005
Fax: 860-635-7125

Theodore S Sergi, Division Director

3030 Finance & Grants Department
Connecticut State Department of
Education
Grants Management
165 Capitol Avenue
Hartford, CT 06106
860-713-0466
Fax: 860-713-7046
http://www.sde.ct.gov

Eugene Croce, Manager
Candace Madison, Secretary

**3031 Office of State Coordinator of
Vocational Education for Disabled
Students**
Vocational Prgs. for the Disabled &
Disadvantaged
PO Box 2219
Hartford, CT 06145
860-807-2001
Fax: 860-807-2196

3032 Teaching & Learning Division
Connecticut State Department of
Education
165 Capital Avenue
Hartford, CT 06106-1659
860-713-6740
Fax: 860-713-7018
E-mail: ciquest@ct.gov
http://www.sde.ct.gov

George Coleman, Acting Commissioner

**3033 Vocational-Technical School
Systems**
Connecticut Technical High School
System
25 Industrial Park Road
Middletown, CT 06457-1520
800-822-6832
Fax: 860-807-2196

E-mail: cthsinternet@ct.gov
http://www.cttech.org
Patricia Ciccone, Superintendent
Robert Lombardi, Assistant

Delaware

**3034 Assessments & Accountability Branch
Delaware Department of Education**
John G. Townsend Bldg.
401 Federal St (Federal & Lockerman Sts)
Dover, DE 19901
302-735-4000
Fax: 302-739-4654
http://www.doe.k12.de.us
Teri Quinn Gray, Ph.D., President/St. Board Of
Educ.
Jorge L. Melendez, VP, State Board of
Education

3035 Delaware Department of Education
John G. Townsend Bldg.
401 Federal St (Federal & Lockerman Sts)
Dover, DE 19901
302-735-4000
Fax: 302-739-4654
E-mail: dedoe@doe.k12.de.us
http://www.doe.k12.de.us
Our mission is to promote the highest quality education for every Delaware student by providing
visionary leadership and superior service.

Teri Quinn Gray, Ph.D., President State Board
of Ed.
Jorge L. Melendez, VP State Board of Ed

**3036 Delaware Department of Education:
Administrative Services**
John G. Townsend Bldg.
401 Federal St (Federal & Lockerman Sts)
Dover, DE 19901
302-735-4000
Fax: 302-739-4654
E-mail: dedoe@doe.k12.de.us
http://www.doe.k12.de.us
Teri Quinn Gray, Ph.D., President State Board
of Ed
Jorge L. Melendez, VP State Board of Ed

**3037 Improvement & Assistance Branch
Delaware Department of Education**
John G. Townsend Bldg.
401 Federal St (Federal & Lockerman Sts)
Dover, DE 19901
302-735-4000
Fax: 302-739-4654
E-mail: dedoe@doe.k12.de.us
http://www.doe.k12.de.us
Teri Quinn Gray, Ph.D., President School Board
of Ed
Jorge J. Melendez, VP State Board of Ed

District of Columbia

3038 DC Office of Special Education
District of Columbia Public Schools
1200 First Street, NE
9th Floor
Washington, DC 20002
202-442-4800
http://www.ocp.dc.gov

Richard Nyankori, Deputy Chancellor

**3039 District of Columbia Department of
Education**
1200 First Street, NE
Washington, DC 20002
202-442-5885
Fax: 202-442-5026

E-mail: ocao.dc.gov
http://www.ocp.dc.gov

Dr. Carey Wright, Chief Academic Officer

Florida

3040 Florida Department of Education
Turlington Building Suite 1514
325 West Gaines Street
Tallahassee, FL 32399
850-245-0505
Fax: 850-245-9667
E-mail: commissioner@fldoe.org
http://www.fldoe.org
Offers information on community colleges, vocational education, public schools, human resources, financial assistance, adult education and more.

Dr. Eric J. Smith, Commissioner/Fl. Dept of Ed

Georgia

3041 Georgia Department of Education
2054 Twin Towers East
205 Jesse Hill Jr. Drive SE
Atlanta, GA 30334
404-656-2800
800-311-3627
Fax: 404-651-6867
E-mail: askdoe@doe.k12.ga.us
http://www.gadoe.org
Among many other features, this organization offers agriculture education, federal programs, Leadership Development Academy, school and community nutrition progams, Spanish language and cultural program, technology/career (vocational) education and more.

Dr. John D. Barge, Superintendent
Sue Goodman, Manager

Hawaii

3042 Career & Technical Education Center
University of Hawaii
Lunalilo Portable 1
Lower Campus Road
Honolulu, HI 96822-2489
808-956-7461
Fax: 808-956-9096
E-mail: hicte@hawaii.edu
http://www.hawaii.edu/cte

Angela Meixell, Interim Director

3043 Hawaii Department of Education
1390 Miller Street
PO Box 2360
Honolulu, HI 96804
808-586-3230
Fax: 808-586-3314
E-mail: doe_info@notes.k12.hi.us
http://www.doe.k12.hi.us

Kathryn Matayoshi, Superintendent

3044 Information & Telecommunications Services Branch
Hawaii Department of Education
1390 Miller St., Room 417
PO Box 2360
Honolulu, HI 96804
808-586-3222
Fax: 808-586-3227
E-mail: doe_info@notes.k12.hi.us
http://www.doe.k12.hi.us

Kathryn Matayoshi, Superintendent

3045 Office of Curriculum, Instruction and Student Support
Hawaii Department of Education
Queen Liliuokalani Bldg, Rm 316
1390 Miller St,
Honolulu, HI 96813
808-586-3446
Fax: 808-586-3429
E-mail: doe_info@notes.k12.hi.us
http://www.ociss.k12.hi.us

Kathryn Matayoshi, Superintendent

3046 Special Education Department
Hawaii Department of Education
475 22nd Ave, Room 115
Ofc Curriculum/Instruction/Student Supp.
Honolulu, HI 96804
808-203-5560
Fax: 808-733-4475
E-mail: doe_info@notes.k12.hi.us
http://www.doe.k12.hi.us

Kathryn Matayoshi, Superintendent
Debra Farmer, Administrator

3047 State Public Library System
Hawaii State Public Library System
478 South King Street
Honolulu, HI 96813-2901
808-586-3617
Fax: 808-586-3314
http://www.librarieshawaii.org

Richard P. Burns, State Librarian

Idaho

3048 Idaho State Department of Education
650 West State Street
PO Box 83720
Boise, ID 83720-0027
208-332-6800
800-432-4601
Fax: 208-334-2228
E-mail: trluna@sde.idaho.gov
http://www.sde.idaho.gov

Tom Luna, Superintendent

3049 Special Education Division
Idaho State Department of Education
650 W. State Street
PO Box 83720
Boise, ID 83720-0027
208-332-6806
E-mail: rhenderson@sde.idaho.gov
http://www.sde.idaho.gov
Committed to empower people with disabilities with appropriate resources to make informed choices about their futures.

Richard Henderson, Director
Casandra Myers, Administrative Assistant

Illinois

3050 Educator & School Development
Illinois Department of Education
100 N. 1st Street
Springfield, IL 62777
217-782-4321
866-262-6663
http://www.isbe.state.il.us

Dr. Christopher Koch, State Superintendent
Jesse Ruiz, Board Chair

3051 Educator Certification
Illinois Department of Education
100 N. 1st Street
Springfield, IL 62777

217-782-4321
866-262-6663
http://www.isbe.state.il.us

Dr. Christopher Koch, State Superintendent
Jesse Ruiz, Board Chair

3052 Finance & Support Services
Illinois Department of Education
100 N. 1st Street
Springfield, IL 62777
217-782-4321
866-262-6663
E-mail: finance@isbe.net
http://www.isbe.state.il.us

Dr. Christopher Koch, State Superintendent
Jesse Ruiz, Board Chair

3053 Illinois Department of Education
100 N 1st Street
Springfield, IL 62777
217-782-4321
866-262-6663
http://www.isbe.state.il.us

Dr. Christopher Koch, State Superintendent
Jesse Ruiz, Board Chair

3054 School Finance
Illinois State Department of Education
100 N. 1st Street
Springfield, IL 62777
217-782-4321
866-262-6663
E-mail: finance@isbe.net
http://www.isbe.state.il.us

Dr. Christopher Koch, State Superintendent
Jesse Ruiz, Board Chair

3055 School Improvement & Assessment Services
Illinois State Board of Education
100 N 1st Street
Springfield, IL 62777
217-782-4321
866-262-6663
http://www.isbe.state.il.us

Chris Koch, Superintendent

3056 Special Education
Illinois State Board of Education
100 N 1st Street
Springfield, IL 62777
217-782-4321
866-262-6663
http://www.isbe.state.il.us

Dr. Christopher Koch, State Superintendent

Indiana

3057 Center for School Assessment & Research
Indiana Department of Education
100 N Capitol Avenue, Room 229
Indianapolis, IN 46204-2203
317-232-9050
Fax: 317-233-2196

Wes Bruce, Director

3058 Community Relations & Special Populations
Indiana Department of Education
100 N Capitol Avenue, Room 229
Indianapolis, IN 46204-2203
317-232-0520
Fax: 317-233-6502

Linda Miller, Senior Officer

3059 External Affairs
Indiana Department of Education
100 N Capitol Avenue, Room 229
Indianapolis, IN 46204-2203

317-232-6614
Fax: 317-232-8004
Joe DiLaura, Division Director

3060 Indiana Department of Education
200 W Washington Street
State House, Room 229
Indianapolis, IN 46204-2798
317-232-6665
Fax: 317-232-8004
http://www.doe.state.in.us
For certification information visit
www.in.gov/psb or contact 866-542-3672.

Suellen K Reed, Superintedent

3061 Office of Legal Affairs
Indiana Department of Education
Office of Legal Affairs
151 West Ohio Street
Indianapolis, IN 46204-2203
317-232-6676
Fax: 317-232-0744
E-mail: legal@doe.in.gov
http://www.doe.in.gov

Dr. Tony Bennett, Superintendent
Susie Langston, Office Manager

3062 Office of School Financial Management
Indiana Department of Education
151 West Ohio Street
Indianapolis, IN 46204-2203
317-232-0840
Fax: 317-232-0504
E-mail: webmaster@doe.in.gov
http://www.doe.in.gov

Dr. Tony Bennett, Superintendent

3063 Office of the Deputy Superintendent
Indiana Department of Education
100 N Capitol Avenue, Room 229
Indianapolis, IN 46204-2203
317-232-0510
Fax: 317-232-0589

Robert Dalton, Division Director

3064 School Improvement & Performance Center
Indiana Department of Education
100 N Capitol Avenue, Room 229
Indianapolis, IN 46204-2203
317-232-9100
Fax: 317-232-9121

Phyllis Land Usher, Division Director

Iowa

3065 Community Colleges Division
Iowa Department of Education
14th E & Grand Streets
Des Moines, IA 50319-0001
515-281-8260

Harriet Custer, Division Director

3066 Division of Library Services
Iowa Department of Education
14th E & Grand Streets
Des Moines, IA 50319-0001
515-281-4105

Sharman B Smith, Administrator

3067 Educational Services for Children & Families
Iowa Department of Education
14th E & Grand Streets
Des Moines, IA 50319-0001
515-281-3575

Susan J Donielson, Administrator

3068 Elementary & Secondary Education
Iowa Department of Education
400 E. 14th Street
Des Moines, IA 50319-0146
515-281-5294
http://www.iowa.gov
Strives for higher levels of learning and achievement for students in public elementary and secondary schools

Jason Glass, Director
Kathy Petosa, Administrative Assistant

3069 Financial & Information Services
Iowa Department of Education
Grimes State Office Buildings
Des Moines, IA 50319-0001
515-281-5293
Fax: 515-242-5988
E-mail: lee.tack@ed.state.ia.us
http://www.state.ia.us/educate

Leland Tack, Administrator

3070 Iowa Department of Education
Grimes State Office Building
400 E 14th & Grand Streets
Des Moines, IA 50319-0146
515-281-5294
Fax: 515-281-5988
E-mail: webmaster@ed.state.ia.us
http://www.state.ia.us/educate
Serves the students of Iowa by providing leadership and resources for schools, area education agencies and community colleges. For certification information visit www.state.ia.us/boee or contact 515-281-3245.

Ted Stilwill, Director

3071 Iowa Public Television
Iowa Department of Education
14th E & Grand Streets
Des Moines, IA 50319-0001
515-242-3150

David Bolender, Executive Director

3072 Vocational Rehabilitation Services
Iowa Department of Education
14th E & Grand Streets
Des Moines, IA 50319-0001
515-281-6731

Margaret Knudsen, Administrator

Kansas

3073 Kansas Department of Education
120 SE Tenth Avenue
Topeka, KS 66612-1182
785-296-3201
Fax: 785-796-7933
E-mail: ddebacker@ksde.org
http://www.ksde.org

Dr. Diane DeBacker, Commissioner of Education

3074 Office of the Commissioner
Kansas State Department of Education
120 SE 10th Avenue
Topeka, KS 66612-1182
785-296-3201
Fax: 785-296-7933
E-mail: price@ksde.org
http://www.ksde.org

Dr. Diane DeBacker, Commissioner of Education
Penny Rice, Administrative Officer

3075 Special Education Services Department
Kansas State Department of Education
120 SE 10th Avenue
Topeka, KS 66612-1182
785-296-3201
Fax: 785-296-7933
E-mail: khaag@ksde.org
http://www.ksde.org

Dr. Diane DeBacker, Commissioner of Education
Kerry Haag, SES Assistant Director

3076 Teacher Education & Licensure
Kansas State Department of Education
120 SE 10th Avenue
Topeka, KS 66612-1182
785-296-3201
Fax: 785-296-7933
E-mail: pcoleman@ksde.org
http://www.ksde.org

Dr. Diane DeBacher, Commissioner of Education
Pamela Coleman, Director

Kentucky

3077 Communications Services
Kentucky Department of Education
15 Fountain Place
Frankfort, KY 40601-1957
502-564-2020
E-mail: andrew.liaupsin@education.ky.gov
http://www.education.ky.gov

Terry Holliday, Ph.D, Commissioner of Education
Andrew Liaupsin

3078 Curriculum, Assessment & Accountability Council
Kentucky Department of Education
500 Mero Street
18th Floor
Frankfort, KY 40601-1957
502-564-4394
Fax: 502-564-7749
E-mail: rhonda.sims@education.ky.gov

Terry Holliday, Ph.D, Commissioner of Education
Rhonda Sims

3079 Education Technology Office
Kentucky Department of Education
500 Mero Street
16th Floor CPT
Frankfort, KY 40601-1957
502-564-1976
E-mail: lauren.moore@education.ky.gov
http://www.education.ky.gov

Terry Holliday, Ph.D, Commissioner of Education
Lauren Moore

3080 Kentucky Department of Education
500 Mero Street
Capital Plaza Tower
Frankfort, KY 40601-1957
502-564-3141
Fax: 502-564-5680
http://www.education.ky.gov
For certification information visit www.kyepsb.net or contact 502-573-4606.

Terry Holliday PhD, Commissioner

3081 Regional Services Centers
Kentucky Department of Education
500 Mero Street
18th Floor CPT
Frankfort, KY 40601-1957

502-564-2106
E-mail: michael.miller@education.ky.gov
http://www.kde.state.ky.us
Terry Holliday, Ph.D, Commissioner of
Education
Michael Miller

3082 Special Education Services
Kentucky Department of Education
500 Mero Street
8th Floor
Frankfort, KY 40601-1957
502-564-4970
Fax: 502-564-6721
E-mail: larry.taylor@education.ky.gov
http://www.education.ky.gov
Terry Holliday, Ph.D, Commissioner of
Education
Larry Taylor, Special Education Services

3083 Teacher Education & Certification
Kentucky Department of Education
500 Mero Street, 17th Floor
Frankfort, KY 40601-1957
502-564-7056
E-mail:
annie.rooney-french@education.ky.gov
http://www.education.ky.gov
Terry Holliday, Ph.D, Commissioner of
Education

Louisiana

3084 Academic Programs Office
Louisiana Department of Education
PO Box 94064
Baton Rouge, LA 70804-9064
877-453-2721
Fax: 225-342-0193
E-mail: customerservice@la.gov
http://www.louisianaschools.net
Paul Pastorek, State Superintendent of
Educ
Rene Greer, Director, Public Affairs

3085 Louisiana Department of Education
2758-D Brightside Drive
PO Box 94064
Baton Rouge, LA 70804-9064
504-342-3607
Fax: 504-342-7316
http://www.doe.state.la.us
Provides leadership and enacts policies that
result in improved academic achievement
and responsible citizenship for all students.
For certification information visit
www.louisianaschools.net or contact
225-342-3490.
Cecil J Picard, Superintendent

3086 Management & Finance Office
Louisana State Department of Education
PO Box 64064
Baton Rouge, LA 70804-9064
225-342-3617
877-453-2721
Fax: 225-219-7538
E-mail: mlangley@doe.state.la.us
http://www.doe.state.la.us
Marlyn J Langley, Deputy Superintendent

3087 Office of Educator Support
Louisiana Department of Education
PO Box 94064
Baton Rouge, LA 70804-9064
877-453-2721
Fax: 225-342-0193

E-mail: customerservice@la.gov
http://www.louisianaschools.net
Paul Pastorek, State Superintendent of
Educ
Karen Burke, Acting Asst. Superintendent

3088 Special Education Services
Louisiana Department of Education
PO Box 94064
Baton Rouge, LA 70804-9064
877-453-2721
Fax: 225-342-0193
E-mail: customerservice@la.gov
http://www.louisianaschools.net
Paul Pastorek, State Superintendent of
Educ
Rene Greer, Director, Public Affairs

**3089 Standards, Assessments &
Accountability**
Louisiana Department of Education
PO Box 94064
Baton Rouge, LA 70804-9064
877-453-2721
Fax: 225-342-3600
E-mail: customerservice@la.gov
http://www.louisianaschools.net
Paul Pastorek, State Superintendent of
Educ
Scott Norton, Assistant Superintendent

Maine

**3090 Administrator and Teacher
Certification**
Maine Department of Education
Certification Office
23 State House Station
Augusta, ME 04333-0023
207-624-6603
Fax: 207-624-6604
E-mail: cert.doe@maine.gov
http://www.maine.gov
Angela Faherty, Commissioner
Mark Cyr, Team Coordinator

3091 Adult Education
Maine Department of Education
23 State House Station
Augusta, ME 04333-0023
207-624-6600
Fax: 207-624-6700
E-mail: jeff.fantine@maine.gov
http://www.maine.gov
Angela Faherty, Commissioner
Jeff Fantine, State Director Adult Educ.

3092 Maine Department of Education
23 State House Station
Augusta, ME 04333-0023
207-624-6620
Fax: 207-624-6601
http://www.state.me.us/education
Susan Gendron, Commissioner

Maryland

3093 Career & Technology Education
Maryland State Department of Education
200 W Baltimore Street
Baltimore, MD 21201
410-767-0186
Fax: 410-333-2099
E-mail: pmikos@msde.state.md.us
http://www.marylandpublicschools.org
Pat Mikos, Program Manager

3094 Certification & Accreditation
Maryland State Department of Education
200 W. Baltimore Street
Baltimore, MD 21201-2502
410-767-0412
866-772-8922
http://www.marylandpublicschools.org
Nancy S. Grasmick, St Superintendent of
Schools

3095 Instruction Division
Maryland State Department of Education
200 W Baltimore Street
Baltimore, MD 21201-2502
410-767-0316
http://www.marylandpublicschools.org
Mary Cary, Assistant Superintendent

3096 Library Development & Services
Maryland State Department of Education
200 West Baltimore Street
Baltimore, MD 21201-2502
410-333-2113
E-mail: www.marylandpublicschools.org
Irene Padilla, Asst St Superintendent Lib.

3097 Maryland Department of Education
200 W Baltimore Street
Baltimore, MD 21201-2502
410-767-0600
888-246-0016
Fax: 410-333-6033
http://www.msde.state.md.us
Mission of MSDE is to provide leadership,
support, and accountability for effective systems of public education, library services and
rehabilitation services. For certification information visit www.certifica-
tion.msde.state.md.us or contact
410-767-0412.
Nancy S Grasmick, Superintendent

**3098 Office of Special Education and
Rehabilitative Services**
U.S. Department of Education
400 Maryland Avenue SW
Washington, DC 20202-7100
202-245-7459
http://www.2.ed.gov
Melody Musgrove, Director
Bill Wolf, Acting Deputy Director

**3099 Special Education/Early Intervention
Services Division**
Maryland State Department of Education
200 W Baltimore Street
9th Floor
Baltimore, MD 21201-2502
410-767-0261
800-535-0182
Fax: 410-333-8165
http://www.marylandpublicschools.org
Nancy S. Grasmick, St Superintendent of
Schools

Massachusetts

**3100 Massachusetts Department of
Education**
350 Main Street
Malden, MA 02148-5023
781-338-3000
Fax: 781-338-3770
http://www.doe.mass.edu
David P Driscoll, Commissioner

**3101 Massachusetts Department of
Educational Improvement**
350 Main Street
Malden, MA 02148-5089

781-388-3300

Andrea Perrault, Division Director

3102 Region 1: Education Department
J.W. McCormick Post Office &
Courthouse
540 McCormick Courthouse
Boston, MA 02109-4557
617-223-9317
Fax: 617-223-9324

Michael Sentance

Michigan

3103 Administrative Services Office
Michigan Department of Education
608 W Allegan Street
Lansing, MI 48933-1524
517-373-3324
Fax: 517-335-4565
http://www.michigan.gov

Calvin C Cupidore, Director

3104 Adult Extended Learning Office
Michigan Department of Education
608 W Allegan Street
Lansing, MI 48933-1524
517-373-3324
Fax: 517-335-4565
http://www.michigan.gov

Ronald Gillum, Director

3105 Career & Technical Education
Michigan Department of Education
608 W Allegan Street
Lansing, MI 48933-1524
517-373-3324
Fax: 517-373-8776
http://www.michigan.gov

William Welsgerber, Director

3106 Higher Education Management Office
Michigan Department of Education
608 W Allegan Street
Lansing, MI 48933-1524
517-373-3324
Fax: 517-373-2759
http://www.michigan.gov

Ronald L Root, Director

3107 Instructional Programs
Michigan Department of Education
608 W Allegan Street
Lansing, MI 48933-1524
517-373-3324
Fax: 517-335-4565
http://www.michigan.gov

3108 Michigan Department of Education
608 W Allegan Street
PO Box 30008
Lansing, MI 48909
517-373-3324
Fax: 517-335-4565
E-mail: MDEweb@michigan.gov
http://www.michigan.gov/mde

Thomas D Watkins, Superintendent

3109 Office of School Management
Michigan Department of Education
608 W Allegan Street
Lansing, MI 48933-1524
517-373-3324
Fax: 517-335-4565
http://www.michigan.gov

Roger Lynas, Director

3110 Office of the Superintendent
Michigan Department of Education
608 W Allegan Street
Lansing, MI 48933-1524
517-373-3324
Fax: 517-335-4565
http://www.michigan.gov

3111 Postsecondary Services
Michigan Department of Education
608 W Allegan Street
Lansing, MI 48909
517-373-3324
Fax: 517-335-4565
http://www.michigan.gov

3112 School Program Quality
Michigan Department of Education
608 W Allegan Street
Lansing, MI 48933-1524
517-373-3324
Fax: 517-335-4565
http://www.michigan.gov

Anne Hansen, Division Director

3113 Special Education
Michigan Department of Education
608 W Allegan Street
Lansing, MI 48933-1524
517-373-3324
Fax: 581-733-5456

Richard Baldwin, Director

3114 Student Financial Assistance
Michigan Department of Education
608 W Allegan Street
Lansing, MI 48933-1524
517-373-3324
Fax: 517-335-4565

Jack Nelson, Director

3115 Teacher & Administrative Preparation
Michigan Department of Education
608 W Allegan Street
Lansing, MI 48933-1524
514-373-3324
Fax: 517-335-4565
http://www.michigan.gov

Carolyn Logan, Director

Minnesota

3116 Data & Technology
Minnesota Department of Education
550 Cedar Street
Saint Paul, MN 55101-2233
612-297-3151

Mark Manning, Division Director

3117 Data Management
Minnesota Department of Education
1500 Highway 39 W
Roseville, MN 55113
651-582-8296
Fax: 651-582-8873

Carol Hokenson, Manager Data
Management

3118 Education Funding
Minnesota Department of Education
550 Cedar Street
Saint Paul, MN 55101-2233
651-297-2194

Tom Melcher, Division Director

3119 Financial Conditions & Aids Payment
Minnesota Department of Education
550 Cedar Street
Saint Paul, MN 55101-2233

612-296-4431

Gary Farland, Division Director

3120 Government Relations
Minnesota Department of Education
550 Cedar Street
Saint Paul, MN 55101-2233
612-296-5279

Sliv Carlson, Division Director

3121 Human Resources Office
Minnesota Department of Education
550 Cedar Street
Saint Paul, MN 55101-2233
651-582-8200

William O'Neill, Division Director

3122 Minnesota Department of Children, Families & Learning
1500 Highway 36 W
Roseville, MN 55113-4266
651-582-8204
Fax: 651-582-8724
http://cfl.state.mn.us
Works to help communities to measurably improve the well-being of children through programs that focus on education, community services, prevention, and the preparation of young people for the world of work. All department efforts emphasize the achievement of positive results for children and their families.

Dr.Cheri Pierson, Commissioner

3123 Minnesota Department of Education
1500 Highway 36 W
Roseville, MN 55113-4266
651-582-8204
Fax: 651-582-8724
http://www.education.state.mn.us

Christine Jax, Commissioner

3124 Residential Schools
Minnesota Department of Education
550 Cedar Street
Saint Paul, MN 55101-2233
507-332-3363

Wade Karli, Division Director

Mississippi

3125 Community Outreach Services
Mississippi Department of Education
PO Box 771
Jackson, MS 39205-1113
601-359-3513
Fax: 601-359-3033

Sarah Beard, Division Director

3126 Educational Innovations
Mississippi Department of Education
PO Box 771
Jackson, MS 39205-0771
601-359-3499
Fax: 601-359-2587

David Robinson, Division Director

3127 External Relations
Mississippi Department of Education
PO Box 771
372 Central High Building
Jackson, MS 39201
601-359-3515
Fax: 601-359-3033

Andrew P Mullins, Division Director

3128 Management Information Systems
Mississippi Department of Education
PO Box 771
Jackson, MS 39205

601-359-3487
Fax: 601-359-3033
Rusty Purvis, Division Director

3129 Mississippi Department of Education
359 NW Street
PO Box 771
Jackson, MS 39205-0771
601-359-3512
Fax: 601-359-3242
http://www.mde.k12.ms.us
Dr.Henry Johnson, Superintendent

3130 Mississippi Employment Security Commission
PO Box 1699
Jackson, MS 39215-1699
601-961-7400
Fax: 601-961-7405
http://www.mesc.state.ms

3131 Office of Accountability
Mississippi Department of Education
PO Box 771
Jackson, MS 39205
601-359-2038
Fax: 601-359-1748
Judy Rhodes, Division Director

3132 Vocational Technical Education
Mississippi Department of Education
359 NW Street
PO Box 771
Jackson, MS 39292
601-359-3090
Fax: 601-359-3989
Samuel McGee, Division Director

Missouri

3133 Deputy Commissioner
Missouri Department of Education
205 Jefferson Street
PO Box 480 Floor 6
Jefferson City, MO 65101-2901
573-751-3503
Fax: 573-751-1179
Dr.Bert Schulte, Deputy Commissioner

3134 Division of Instruction
Missouri Department of Education
205 Jefferson Street
Floor 6
Jefferson City, MO 65101-2901
573-751-4234
Fax: 573-751-8613
Otis Baker, Division Director

3135 Missouri Department of Education
205 Jefferson Street, 6th Floor
PO Box 480
Jefferson City, MO 65102-0480
573-751-4212
Fax: 573-751-8613
E-mail: pubinfo@mail.dese.state.mo.us
http://www.dese.state.mo.us
A team of dedicated individuals working for the continuous improvement of education and services for all citizens. We believe that we can make a positive difference in the quality of life for all Missourians by providing exceptional service to students, educators, schools and citizens.
D Kent King, Commissioner

3136 Region 7: Education Department
10220 NW Executive Hills Boulevard
Kansas City, MO 64153-2312
816-891-7972
Fax: 816-891-7972

3137 Special Education Division
Missouri Department of Education
205 Jefferson Street
PO Box 480 Floor 6
Jefferson City, MO 65102-2901
573-751-5739
Fax: 573-526-4404
John F Allan, Division Director

3138 Urban & Teacher Education
Missouri Department of Education
205 Jefferson Street
Floor 6
Jefferson City, MO 65101-2901
573-751-2931
Fax: 573-751-8613
L Celestine Ferguson, Division Director

3139 Vocational & Adult Education
Missouri Department of Education
205 Jefferson Street, 5th Floor
PO Box 480
Jefferson City, MO 65102-0480
573-751-2660
Fax: 573-526-4261
E-mail: nheadrick@mail.dese.state.mo.us
http://www.dese.state.mo.us
Nancy J Headrick, Assistant Commissioner

3140 Vocational Rehabilitation
Missouri Department of Education
3024 Dupont Circle
Jefferson City, MO 65109-0525
573-751-3251
Fax: 573-751-1441
Don L Gann, Division Director

Montana

3141 Accreditation & Curriculum Services Department
Montana Department of Education
106 State Capitol
Helena, MT 59620
406-444-5726
Fax: 406-444-2893
Dr.Linda Vrooman, Administrator

3142 Division of Information-Technology Support
Montana Department of Education
106 State Capitol
Helena, MT 59620
406-444-4326
Fax: 406-444-2893
Scott Buswell, Division Director

3143 Montana Department of Education
1227 11th Avenue
PO Box 202501
Helena, MT 59620-2501
406-444-3095
Fax: 406-444-2893
http://www.opi.state.mt.us
For certification information visit www.opi.state.mt.us or contact 406-444-3150.
Linda McCulloch, Superindtendent

3144 Operations Department
Montana Department of Education
106 State Capitol
Helena, MT 59620
406-444-3095
Fax: 406-444-2893

Nebraska

3145 Administrative Services Office
Nebraska Department of Education
301 Centennial Mall S
Lincoln, NE 68508-2529
402-471-2295
Fax: 402-471-6351
http://www.nde.state.ne.us/ADSS/index.html
To provide quality services and support in the areas of finance human resource management continuous quality improvement, office/building services,and technical assistant.
Mike Stefkovich, Division Director

3146 Division of Education Services
Nebraska Department of Education
301 Centennial Mall S
Lincoln, NE 68508-2529
402-471-2783
Fax: 402-471-0117
Marge Harouff, Division Director

3147 Nebraska Department of Education
301 Centennial Mall S
PO Box 94987
Lincoln, NE 68509-4987
402-471-5020
Fax: 402-471-4433
http://www.nde.state.ne.us
Douglas D Christensen, Commissioner

3148 Rehabilitation Services Division
Nebraska Department of Education
301 Centennial Mall S 6th Floor
PO Box 94987
Lincoln, NE 68509-2529
402-471-3649
877-637-3422
Fax: 402-471-0788
http://www.bocrehab.state.ne.us
Frank C Lloyd, Director

Nevada

3149 Administrative & Financial Services
Nevada Department of Education
400 W King St
Carson City, NV 89703-4204
775-687-9102
888-590-6726
Fax: 702-486-5803
Douglas Thunder

3150 Instructional Services Division
Nevada Department of Education
400 W King St
Carson City, NV 89703-4204
775-687-3104
Mary L Peterson, Division Director

3151 Nevada Department of Education
700 E 5th Street
Carson City, NV 89701-5096
775-687-9200
Fax: 775-687-9101
http://www.nsn.k12.nv.us
Mission is to lead Nevada's citizens in accomplishing lifelong learning and educational excellence.
Jack McLaughlin, Superintendent

New Hampshire

3152 Information Services
New Hampshire Department of Education
101 Pleasent Street
Concord, NH 03301-3852
603-271-2778
Fax: 603-271-1953
http://www.ed.state.nh.us
New Hampshire schools enrollment, financial, assessment information.

Dr.Judith Fillion, Division Director

3153 New Hampshire Department of Education
101 Pleasant Street
State Office Park S
Concord, NH 03301-3860
603-271-3494
800-339-9900
Fax: 603-271-1953
E-mail: llovering@ed.state.nh.us
http://www.state.nh.us/doe
Mission is to provide educational leadership and services which promote equal educational opportunities and quality practices and programs than enable New Hampshire residents to become fully productive members of society.

Nicholas C Donohue, Commissioner

3154 New Hampshire Division of Instructional Services
101 Pleasant Street
Concord, NH 03301-3852
603-271-3880

William B Evert, Division Director

3155 Standards & Certification Division
New Hampshire Dept of Education
101 Pleasant St
Concord, NH 03301-3852
603-271-3453
Fax: 603-271-8709

Judith D Fillion, Divisions Director

New Jersey

3156 New Jersey Department of Education
100 Riverview Plaza
PO Box 500
Trenton, NJ 08625-0500
609-292-4450
Fax: 609-777-4099
http://www.state.nj.us/education
Develops and implements policies that address the major education issues in New Jersey. The State Board will engage in an effort to ensure that all children receive a quality public education that prepares them to succeed as responsible, productive citizens in a global society.

William L Librera, Commissioner

3157 New Jersey Department of Education: Finance
100 Riverview Plaza
PO Box 500
Trenton, NJ 08625-0500
609-292-4421
Fax: 609-292-6794
http://www.state.nj.us/education

Richard Rosenberg, Assistant Commissioner

3158 New Jersey Division of Special Education
100 Riverview Plaza
PO Box 500
Trenton, NJ 08625
609-292-0147
Fax: 609-984-8422

Jeffrey Osowski, Divsion Director

3159 New Jersey State Library
PO Box 520
Trenton, NJ 08625-0520
609-292-6200
Fax: 609-292-2746
E-mail: nblake@njstatelib.org
http://www.njstatelib.org

Norma E Blake, State Librarian

3160 Professional Development & Licensing
New Jersey Department of Education
100 Riverview Plaza, PO Box 500
Trenton, NJ 08625
609-292-2070
Fax: 609-292-3768

Hilda Hidalgo, Division Director

3161 Urban & Field Services
New Jersey Department of Education
100 Riverview Plaza, PO Box 500
Trenton, NJ 08625
609-292-4442
Fax: 609-292-3830

Elena Scambio, Division Director

New Mexico

3162 Agency Support
New Mexico Department of Education
300 Don Gaspar, Education Building
Santa Fe, NM 87501-2786
505-827-6330

Tres Giron, Division Director

3163 Learning Services
New Mexico Department of Education
300 Don Gaspar, Education Building
Santa Fe, NM 87501
505-827-6508
Fax: 505-827-6689

Albert Zamora, Division Director

3164 New Mexico Department of Education
300 Don Gaspar
Education Building
Santa Fe, NM 87501-2786
505-827-6688
Fax: 505-827-6520
http://www.sde.state.nm.us

Michael J Davis, Superintendent

3165 New Mexico Department of School-Transportation & Support Services
300 Don Gaspar, Education Building
Santa Fe, NM 87501
505-827-6683

Susan Brown, Division Director

3166 School Management Accountability
New Mexico Department of Education
300 Don Gaspar, Education Building
Santa Fe, NM 87501
505-827-3876
Fax: 505-827-6689

Michael J Davis, Division Director

3167 Vocational Education
New Mexico Department of Education
300 Don Gaspar, Education Building
Santa Fe, NM 87501
505-827-6511

Tom Trujillo, Division Director

New York

3168 Cultural Education
New York Department of Education
Madison Avenue
Albany, NY 12230
518-474-5976
Fax: 518-474-2718
E-mail: CISINFO@mail.nysed.gov

Carole F Huxley, Division Director

3169 Elementary, Middle & Secondary Education
New York Department of Education
89 Washington Avenue
Room 875 EBA
Albany, NY 12234-0001
518-474-5915
Fax: 518-474-2718
E-mail: emscgen@mail.nysed.gov

James Kadamus, Deputy

3170 Higher & Professional Education
New York Department of Education
111 Education Avenue W Mezzanine
2nd Floor
Albany, NY 12234-0001
518-474-5851
Fax: 518-474-2718

Johanna Duncan-Poitier, Deputy Commissioner

3171 New York Department of Education
89 Washington Avenue
Education Building, Room 111
Albany, NY 12234
518-474-5844
Fax: 518-473-4909
E-mail: rmills@mail.nysed.gov
http://www.nysed.gov

Richard P Mills, President

3172 Professional Responsibility Office
New York Department of Education
89 Wolf Road Suite 204
Albany, NY 12205-2643
518-485-9350
Fax: 518-485-9361

3173 Region 2: Education Department
75 Park Place
New York, NY 10007
212-264-7005
Fax: 212-264-4427

3174 Vocational & Educational Services for Disabled
New York Department of Education
80 Wolf Road Suite 200
Albany, NY 12205
518-473-8097
800-272-5448
Fax: 518-457-4562

David Segalla, Regional Coordinator

North Carolina

3175 Auxiliary Services
North Carolina Department of Education
301 N Wilmington Street
Raleigh, NC 27601-2825

919-733-1110
Fax: 919-733-5279

Charles Weaver, Division Director

3176 Financial & Personnel Services
North Carolina Department of Education
301 N Wilmington Street
Raleigh, NC 27601-2825
919-807-3600

James O Barber, Division Director

3177 North Carolina Department of Education
301 N Wilmington Street
Raleigh, NC 27601-2825
919-715-1299
Fax: 919-807-3279
http://www.ncpublicschools.org

Bob R Etheridge, Division Director

3178 North Carolina Department of Instructional Services
301 N Wilmington Street
Raleigh, NC 27601-2825
919-715-1506
Fax: 919-807-3279

Henry Johnson, Division Director

3179 Staff Development & Technical Assistance
North Carolina Department of Education
301 N Wilmington Street
Raleigh, NC 27601-2825
919-715-1315

Nancy Davis, Division Director

North Dakota

3180 North Dakota Department of Education
600 E Boulevard Avenue
State Capitol Building, Floor 11
Bismarck, ND 58505-0440
701-328-4572
Fax: 701-328-2461
http://www.state.nd.us/espb

Wayne G Sanstead, Superintendent

3181 North Dakota Department of Public Instruction Division
600 E Boulevard Avenue, Dept. 201
Floor 9,10, & 11
Bismarck, ND 58505-0440
701-328-2260
Fax: 701-328-2461
E-mail: wsanstea@mail.dpi.state.nd.us
http://www.dpi.state.nd.us/dpi/index.htm

Dr. Wayne G Sanstead, State Superintendent

3182 North Dakota State Board for Vocational & Technical Education
600 E Boulevard Avenue
Floor 15
Bismarck, ND 58505-0660
701-224-2259
Fax: 701-328-2461

Reuben Guenthner, Division Director

3183 Study & State Film Library
North Dakota Department of Education
600 E Boulevard Avenue
Floor 11
Bismarck, ND 58505-0660
701-237-7282

Robert Stone, Division Director

Ohio

3184 Blind School
Ohio Department of Education
65 S Front Street
Columbus, OH 43215-4131
614-466-3641
Fax: 614-752-1713

Dennis Holmes, Division Director

3185 Curriculum, Instruction & Professional Development
Ohio Department of Education
65 S Front Street
Columbus, OH 43215-4131
614-466-2761
Fax: 704-992-5168

Nancy Eberhart, Division Director

3186 Early Childhood Education
Ohio Department of Education
65 S Front Street
Columbus, OH 43215-4131
614-466-0224
Fax: 614-728-2338

Jane Wiechel, Division Director

3187 Federal Assistance
Ohio Department of Education
65 S Front Street
Columbus, OH 43215-4131
614-466-4161
Fax: 704-992-5168

William Henry, Division Director

3188 Ohio Department of Education
25 S Front Street
7th Floor
Columbus, OH 43215-4183
614-466-7578
877-644-6338
Fax: 614-728-4781
http://www.ode.state.oh.us
Works in partnership with school districts to assure high achievements for all learners, promote a safe and orderly learning environment, provide leadership, support, and build capacity, and provide support to school districts particularly those who need it most.

Susan T Zelman, Superintendent

3189 Personnel Services
Ohio Department of Education
65 S Front Street
Columbus, OH 43215-4131
614-466-3763
Fax: 704-992-5168

Larry Cathell, Division Director

3190 School Finance
Ohio Department of Education
65 S Front Street
Columbus, OH 43215-4131
614-466-6266
Fax: 704-992-5168
E-mail: sf_tavakolia@ode.ohio.gov
http://www.ode.state.ohio.us/foundation/www_.html

Susan Tavakolian, Division Director

3191 School Food Service
Ohio Department of Education
65 S Front Street
Columbus, OH 43215-4131
614-466-2945
Fax: 704-992-5168

Lorita Myles, Division Director

3192 School for the Deaf
Ohio Department of Education
65 S Front Street
Columbus, OH 43215-4131
614-466-3641
Fax: 704-992-5168

Edward C Corbett Jr, Division Director

3193 Special Education
Ohio Department of Education
933 High Street
Worthington, OH 43085
614-466-2650
Fax: 704-992-5168
E-mail: se_herner@ode.ohio.gov

John Herner, Director Special Education

3194 Student Development
Ohio Department of Education
65 S Front Street
Columbus, OH 43215-4131
614-466-3641
Fax: 704-992-5168

Hazel Flowers, Division Director

3195 Teacher Education & Certification
Ohio Department of Education
65 S Front Street
Columbus, OH 43215-4131
614-466-3430
Fax: 704-992-5168

Darrell Parks, Division Director

3196 Vocational & Career Education
Ohio Department of Education
65 S Front Street
Columbus, OH 43215-4131
614-466-3430
Fax: 704-992-5168

Darrell Parks, Division Director

Oklahoma

3197 Accreditation & Standards Division
Oklahoma Department of Education
2500 N Lincoln Boulevard
Oklahoma City, OK 73105-4503
405-521-3333
Fax: 405-521-6205

Sharon Lease, Division Director

3198 Federal/Special/Collaboration Services
Oklahoma Department of Education
2500 N Lincoln Boulevard
Oklahoma City, OK 73105-4503
405-521-4873
Fax: 405-522-3503

Sid Hudson, Division Director

3199 Oklahoma Department of Career and Technology Education
1500 W 7th Avenue
Stillwater, OK 74074-4398
405-743-5444
Fax: 405-743-5541

Roy Peters Jr, Division Director

3200 Oklahoma Department of Education
2500 N Lincoln Boulevard
Hodge Education Building
Oklahoma City, OK 73105-4599
405-521-4485
Fax: 405-521-6205
http://http://sde.state.ok.us

Sandy Garrett, Superindentdent

3201 Oklahoma Department of Education; Financial Services
Oklahoma Department of Education
2500 N Lincoln Boulevard
Oklahoma City, OK 73105-4503
405-521-3371
Fax: 405-521-6205

Don Shive, Division Director

3202 Professional Services
Oklahoma Department of Education
2500 N Lincoln Boulevard
Oklahoma City, OK 73105-4503
405-521-4311
Fax: 405-521-6205

Paul Simon, Division Director

3203 School Improvement
Oklahoma Department of Education
2500 N Lincoln Boulevard
Oklahoma City, OK 73105-4503
405-521-4869
Fax: 405-521-6205

Hugh McCrabb, Division Director

Oregon

3204 Assessment & Evaluation
Oregon Department of Education
255 Capitol Street NE
Salem, OR 97310-0203
503-378-3600
Fax: 503-378-5156
E-mail: firstname.lastname@state.or.us
http://www.ode.state.or.us

Doug Kosty, Assistant Superintendent

3205 Community College Services
Oregon Department of Education
225 Capitol Street NE
Salem, OR 97310-1341
503-378-3600
Fax: 503-378-5156

Stan Bunn, Superintendent

3206 Compensatory Education Office
Oregon Department of Education
225 Capitol Street NE
Salem, OR 97310-1341
503-378-3569
Fax: 503-378-5156

Jerry Fuller, Division Director

3207 Deputy Superintendent Office
Oregon Department of Education
225 Capitol Street NE
Salem, OR 97310-1341
503-378-3573
Fax: 503-378-5156

Bob Burns, Division Director

3208 Early Childhood Council
Oregon Department of Education
225 Capitol Street NE
Salem, OR 97310-1341
503-378-5585
Fax: 503-378-5156

Judy Miller, Division Director

3209 Government Relations
Oregon Department of Education
225 Capitol Street NE
Salem, OR 97310-1341
503-378-8549
Fax: 503-378-5156

Greg McMurdo, Division Director

3210 Management Services
Oregon Department of Education
225 Capitol Street NE
Salem, OR 97310-1341
503-378-8549
Fax: 503-378-5156

Chris Durham, Division Director

3211 Office of Field, Curriculum & Instruction Services
Oregon Department of Education
225 Capitol Street NE
Salem, OR 97310-1341
503-378-8004
Fax: 503-378-5156

Roberta Hutton, Division Director

3212 Oregon Department of Education
225 Capitol Street NE
Salem, OR 97310-0203
503-378-3569
Fax: 503-378-5156
E-mail: ode.frontdesk@ode.state.or.us
http://www.ode.state.or.us

Susan Castillo, Superintendent

3213 Professional Technical Education
Oregon Department of Education
225 Capitol Street NE
Salem, OR 97310-1341
503-378-3584
Fax: 503-378-5156

JD Hoye, Division Director

3214 Special Education
Oregon Department of Education
225 Capitol Street NE
Salem, OR 97310-1341
503-378-3600
Fax: 503-378-5156
http://www.ode.state.or.us

Steve Johnson, Division Director

3215 Student Services Office
Oregon Department of Education
225 Capitol Street NE
Salem, OR 97310-1341
503-378-5585
Fax: 503-378-5156

Judy Miller, Division Director

3216 Twenty First Century Schools Council
Oregon Department of Education
225 Capitol Street NE
Salem, OR 97310-1341
503-378-3600
Fax: 503-378-5156

Joyce Reinke, Division Director

Pennsylvania

3217 Chief Counsel
Pennsylvania Department of Education
333 Market Street
Harrisburg, PA 17101-2210
717-787-5500
Fax: 717-783-0347

Jeffrey Champagne, Division Director

3218 Chief of Staff Office
Pennsylvania Department of Education
333 Market Street
Harrisburg, PA 17101-2210
717-787-9744
Fax: 717-787-7222

Terry Dellmuth, Chief of Staff

3219 Higher Education/Postsecondary Office
Pennsylvania Department of Education
333 Market Street
Harrisburg, PA 17101-2210
717-787-5041
Fax: 717-783-0583

Charles Fuget, Division Director

3220 Office of Elementary and Secondary Education
Pennsylvania Department of Education
333 Market Street
5th Floor
Harrisburg, PA 17101
717-787-2127
Fax: 717-783-6802
E-mail: dhaines@state.pa.us
http://www.pde.state.pa.us

Debra Haines, Executive Secretary

3221 Office of the Comptroller
Pennsylvania Department of Education
333 Market Street
Harrisburg, PA 17101-2210
717-787-5506
Fax: 717-787-3593

William Hardenstine, Division Director

3222 Pennsylvania Department of Education
333 Market Street
Harrisburg, PA 17126
717-783-6788
Fax: 717-787-7222
http://www.education.state.pa.us

Ronald J Tomalis, Acting Secretary

3223 Region 3: Education Department
3535 Market Street
Philadelphia, PA 19104-3309
215-596-1001

Rhode Island

3224 Career & Technical Education
Rhode Island Department of Education
255 Westminster Street
Providence, RI 02903-3414
401-222-4600
Fax: 401-222-2537
http://www.ridoe.net

Frank M Santoro, Division Director

3225 Equity & Access Office
Rhode Island Department of Education
255 Westminster Street
Providence, RI 02903-3414
401-222-4600
Fax: 401-222-2537
http://www.ridoe.net

Frank R Walker III, Division Director

3226 Human Resource Development
Rhode Island Department of Education
255 Westminster Street
Providence, RI 02903-3414
401-222-4600
Fax: 401-222-2537
http://www.ridoe.net

Paula A Rossi, Division Director

3227 Instruction Office
Rhode Island Department of Education
255 Westminster Street
Providence, RI 02903-3414
401-222-4600
Fax: 401-222-2537
http://www.ridoe.net

Marie C DiBiasio, Division Director

3228 Office of Finance
Rhode Island Department of Education
255 Westminster Street
Providence, RI 02903-3414
401-222-4600
Fax: 401-222-2537
http://www.ridoe.net

Frank A Pontarelli, Division Director

3229 Outcomes & Assessment Office
Rhode Island Department of Education
255 Westminster Street
Providence, RI 02903-3414
401-222-4600
Fax: 401-222-2537
http://www.ridoe.net

Pasquale J DeVito, Division Director

3230 Resource Development
Rhode Island Department of Education
255 Westminster Street
Providence, RI 02903-3414
401-222-4600
Fax: 401-222-6033
http://www.ridoe.net

Edward T Costa, Division Director

3231 Rhode Island Department of Education
255 Westminster Street
Providence, RI 02903
401-222-4600
Fax: 401-222-6178
E-mail: ride0001@ride.ri.net
http://www.ridoe.net
Goal of all our work is to improve student performance and help all students meet or exceed a high level of performance. Standards, instruction, and assessment intertwine to provide a system that ensures a strong education for our students.

Peter McWalters, Commissioner

3232 School Food Services Administration
Rhode Island Department of Education
255 Westminster Street
Providence, RI 02903-3414
401-222-4600
Fax: 401-222-3080
http://www.ridoe.net

Virginia da Mora, Dir Integrated Soc Service

3233 Special Needs Office
Rhode Island Department of Education
255 Westminster Street
Providence, RI 02903-3414
401-456-9331
Fax: 401-456-8699
http://www.ridoe.net

Dr.Frances Gallo, Acting Dirctor

3234 Teacher Education & Certification Office
Rhode Island Department of Education
255 Westminster Street
Providence, RI 02903-3414
401-222-4600
Fax: 401-222-2048
http://www.ridoe.net

Louis E DelPapa, Division Director

South Carolina

3235 Budgets & Planning
South Carolina Department of Education
1201 Main Street
Suite 950
Columbia, SC 29201-3730

803-734-2280
Fax: 803-734-0645

Les Boles, Division Director

3236 Communications Services
South Carolina Department of Education
1429 Senate Street
Columbia, SC 29201-3730
803-734-8500
Fax: 803-734-3389

Jerry Adams, Division Director

3237 General Counsel
South Carolina Department of Education
1429 Senate Street
Columbia, SC 29201-3730
803-734-8500
Fax: 803-734-4384

Shelly Carrigg, Esq, Division Director

3238 Internal Administration
South Carolina Department of Education
1429 Senate Street
Columbia, SC 29201-3730
803-734-8500
Fax: 803-734-6225

Jackie Rosswurm, Division Director

3239 Policy & Planning
South Carolina Department of Education
1429 Senate Street
Columbia, SC 29201-3730
803-734-8500
Fax: 803-734-8624

Valerie Truesdale, Division Director

3240 South Carolina Department of Education
1429 Senate Street
Columbia, SC 29201
803-734-8492
Fax: 803-734-3389
http://www.state.sc.us
Provides leadership and services to ensure a system of public education in which all students become educated, responsible, and contributing citizens. For certification information visit www.myscschools.com or contact 803-734-5280.

Inez M Tenenbaum, Superintendent

3241 Support Services
South Carolina Department of Education
1429 Senate Street
Columbia, SC 29201-3730
803-734-8500
Fax: 803-734-8254

Donald Tudor, Division Director

South Dakota

3242 Finance & Management
South Dakota Department of Education
700 Governors Drive
Pierre, SD 57501-2291
605-773-3248
Fax: 605-773-6139

Stacy Krusemark, Division Director

3243 Services for Education
South Dakota Department of Education
700 Governors Drive
Pierre, SD 57501-2291
605-773-4699
Fax: 605-773-3782

Donlynn Rice, Division Director

3244 South Dakota Department of Education & Cultural Affairs
700 Governors Drive
Pierre, SD 57501-2291
605-773-2291
Fax: 605-773-6139
E-mail: ray.christensen@state.sd.us
http://www.state.sd.us/deca/
Advocates for education, facilitate the delivery of statewide educational and cultural services, and promote efficient, appropriate, and quality educational opportunities for all persons residing in South Dakota.

Ray Christensen, Secretary
Patrick Keating, Division Director

3245 South Dakota State Historical Society
South Dakota Dept of Education & Cultural Affairs
900 Governors Drive
Pierre, SD 57501-2291
605-773-3458
Fax: 605-773-6041
E-mail: jay.vogt@state.sd.us
http://www.state.sd.us/deca/
Program areas: Archaeology, archives, historic preservation, museum, research, and publishing

Jay D Vogt, History Manager

3246 Special Education Office
South Dakota Department of Education
700 Governors Drive
Pierre, SD 57501-2291
605-773-3678
Fax: 605-773-3782

Michelle Powers, Division Director

Tennessee

3247 Special Education
Tennessee Department of Education
710 John Robertson Parkway
6th Floor
Nashville, TN 37243
615-741-2851
Fax: 615-532-9412

Joe Fisher, Division Director

3248 Teaching and Learning
Tennessee Department of Education
710 James Robertson Parkway
5th Floor
Nashville, TN 37243
615-532-6195
Fax: 615-741-1837
E-mail: wprotoe@mail.state.tn.us
http://www.state.tn.us/education

Wilma Protoe, Assitant Commissioner

3249 Tennessee Department of Education
710 James Robertson Parkway
6th Floor
Nashville, TN 37243-0375
615-741-2731
Fax: 615-741-6236
E-mail: jwalters@mail.state.tn.us
http://www.state.tn.us/education

Lana Seivers, Commissioner

3250 Vocational Education
Tennessee Department of Education
710 John Robertson Parkway
4th Floor
Nashville, TN 37243-0383
615-532-2800
Fax: 615-532-8226

Ralph Barnett, Assistant Commissioner

Texas

3251 Accountability Reporting and Research
Texas Education Agency
1701 Congress Avenue
WBT Building Room 3-111
Austin, TX 78701-1494
512-475-3523
Fax: 512-475-0028
E-mail: ccloudt@tmail.tea.state.tx.us
http://www.tea.state.tx.us
Criss Cloudt, Associate Commissioner

3252 Chief Counsel
Texas Department of Education
1701 Congress Avenue
Austin, TX 78701-1402
512-463-9720
Fax: 512-463-9838
Kewin O'Hanlon, Division Director

3253 Continuing Education
Texas Education Agency
1701 Congress Avenue
Austin, TX 78701-1402
512-463-9322
Fax: 512-463-6782
E-mail: wtillian@tea.state.tx.us
Walter Tillian, Manager

3254 Curriculum Development & Textbooks
Texas Department of Education
1701 Congress Avenue
Austin, TX 78701-1402
512-463-9581
Fax: 512-463-8057
Ann Smisko, Division Director

3255 Curriculum, Assessment & Professional Development
Texas Department of Education
1701 Congress Avenue
Austin, TX 78701-1402
512-463-9328
Fax: 512-475-3640
Linda Cimusz, Division Director

3256 Curriculum, Assessment and Technology
Texas Department of Education
1701 Congress Avenue
Austin, TX 78701-1402
512-463-9087
Fax: 512-475-3667
E-mail: asmisko@tea.tetn.net
Ann Smisko, Associate Commissioner

3257 Education of Special Populations & Adults
Texas Department of Education
1701 Congress Avenue
Austin, TX 78701-1402
512-463-8992
Fax: 512-463-9176
Jay Cummings, Division Director

3258 Field Services
Texas Department of Education
1701 Congress Avenue
Austin, TX 78701-1402
512-463-9354
Fax: 512-463-9227

3259 Internal Operations
Texas Department of Education
1701 Congress Avenue
Austin, TX 78701-1402
512-463-9437
Fax: 512-475-4293

3260 Operations & School Support
Texas Department of Education
1701 Congress Avenue
Austin, TX 78701-1494
512-463-8994
Fax: 512-463-9227
Roberto Zamora, Division Director

3261 Permanent School Fund
Texas Department of Education
1701 Congress Avenue
Room 5-120
Austin, TX 78701-1402
512-463-9169
Fax: 512-463-9432
Carlos Resendez, Division Director

3262 Region 6: Education Department
1200 Main Tower
Dallas, TX 75202-4325
214-767-3626

3263 Texas Department of Education
1701 N Congress Avenue
William B Travis Building
Austin, TX 78701-1494
512-463-8985
Fax: 512-463-9008
http://www.sbec.state.tx.us
Dr.Shirley Neeley, Commissioner

Utah

3264 Applied Technology Education Services
Utah Department of Education
250 E 500 S
Salt Lake City, UT 84111-4200
801-538-7840
Fax: 801-538-7868
E-mail: rbrems@usoe.kiz.ut.us
http://www.usoe.k12.ut.us
State agency for career and technical education.
Rod Brems, Associate Superintendent
Leslee Andelean, Administrative Assistant

3265 Instructional Services Division
Utah Department of Education
250 E 500 S
Salt Lake City, UT 84111-3204
801-538-7515
Fax: 801-538-7768
Jerry P Peterson, Division Director

3266 Schools for the Deaf & Blind
Utah Department of Education
250 E 500 S
Salt Lake City, UT 84111-3204
801-629-4700
Fax: 801-629-4896
Wayne Glaus, Division Director

3267 Utah Office of Education
250 E 500 South
PO Box 144200
Salt Lake City, UT 84111
801-538-7510
Fax: 801-538-7768
http://www.usoe.k12.ut.us
Steven O Laing, Superintendent

3268 Utah Office of Education; Agency Services Division
250 E 500 S
PO Box 144200
Salt Lake City, UT 84114-4200

801-538-7500
Fax: 801-538-7768
http://www.usoe.k12.ut.us
Patrick Ogden, Associate Superintendent

Vermont

3269 Career & Lifelong Learning
Vermont Department of Education
120 State Street
Montpelier, VT 05620-0001
802-828-3101
Fax: 802-828-3146
Charles Stander, Division Director

3270 Core Services
Vermont Department of Education
120 State Street
Montpelier, VT 05620-0001
802-828-3135
Fax: 802-828-3140
Eleanor Perry, Division Director

3271 Family & School Support
Vermont Department of Education
120 State Street
Montpelier, VT 05620-0001
802-828-2447
Fax: 802-828-3140
Jo Busha, Division Director

3272 Financial Management Team
Vermont Department of Education
120 State Street
Montpelier, VT 05620-0001
802-828-3155
Fax: 802-828-3140
Mark O'Day, Division Director

3273 School Development & Information
Vermont Department of Education
120 State Street
Montpelier, VT 05620-0001
802-828-2756
Fax: 802-828-3140
Douglas Chiappetta, Division Director

3274 Teaching & Learning
Vermont Department of Education
120 State Street
Montpelier, VT 05620-0001
802-828-3111
Fax: 802-828-3140
Marguerite Meyer, Division Director

3275 Vermont Department of Education
120 State Street
Montpelier, VT 05620-2501
802-828-3135
Fax: 802-828-3140
http://Vermont.gov
For certification information visit www.pen.k12.va.us or contact 804-225-2022.
Richard Cate, Commissioner

3276 Vermont Special Education
120 State Street
Montpelier, VT 05602-2703
802-828-3141
Theodore Riggen, Division Director

Virginia

3277 Administrative Services
Virginia Department of Education
14th & Franklin Streets
PO Box 2120
Richmond, VA 23216

804-225-3252
Fax: 804-786-5828

Edward W Carr, Division Director

3278 Policy, Assessment, Research & Information Systems
Virginia Department of Education
101 N 4th Street
PO Box 2120
Richmond, VA 23218-2120
804-225-2102
800-292-3820
Fax: 804-371-8978
E-mail: charris@pen.k12.va.us
http://www.pen.k12.va.us

Anne Wescott, Assistant Superintendent

3279 Student Services
Virginia Department of Education
14th & Franklin Streets
PO Box 2120
Richmond, VA 23216
804-225-2757
Fax: 804-786-5828

Dr.Cynthia Cave, Division Director

3280 Virginia Centers for Community Education
Virginia Department of Education
PO Box 2120
Richmond, VA 23218-2120
804-225-2293
Fax: 804-786-5828

Dr. Lenox L McLendon, Division Director

3281 Virginia Department of Education
James Monroe Building
101 N 14th Street
Richmond, VA 23219
804-225-2023
800-292-3820
Fax: 804-371-2099
E-mail: rlayman@pen.k12.va.us
http://www.pen.k12.va.us

Jo Lynne DeMary, Superintendent

Washington

3282 Region 10: Education Department
915 2nd Avenue
Room 3362
Seattle, WA 98174-1001
206-220-7800
Fax: 202-220-7806
http://www.ed.gov

3283 Washington Department of Education
PO Box 47200
Olympia, WA 98504-7200
360-725-6000
Fax: 360-753-6712
http://www.k12.wa.us

Theresa Bergeson, Superintendent

3284 Washington Department of Education; Instruction Program
PO Box 47200
Olympia, WA 98504-7200
206-753-1545
Fax: 360-586-0247

John Pearson, Division Director

3285 Washington Department of Education; Commission on Student Learning Administration
PO Box 47200
Olympia, WA 98504-7200

360-664-3155
Fax: 360-664-3028

Terry Bergeson, Division Director

3286 Washington Department of Education; Executive Services
PO Box 47200
Olympia, WA 98504-7200
360-586-9056
Fax: 360-753-6754

Ken Kanikeberg, Division Director

3287 Washington Department of Education; School Business & Administrative Services
PO Box 47200
Olympia, WA 98504-7200
206-753-6742

David Moberly, Division Director

West Virginia

3288 Division of Administrative Services
West Virginia Department of Education
1900 Kanawha Boulevard E
Building 6
Charleston, WV 25305-0009
304-558-2441
Fax: 304-558-8867

Carolyn Arrington, Division Director

3289 Research, Accountability & Professional
West Virginia Department of Education
1900 Kanawha Boulevard E
Building 6
Charleston, WV 25305-0009
304-558-3762
Fax: 304-558-8867

William J Luff Jr, Division Director

3290 Student Services & Instructional Services
West Virginia Department of Education
1900 Kanawha Boulevard E
Building 6
Charleston, WV 25305-0009
304-558-2691
Fax: 304-558-8867

Keith Smith, Division Director

3291 Technical & Adult Education Services
West Virginia Department of Education
1900 Kanawha Boulevard E
Building 6
Charleston, WV 25305-0009
304-558-2346
Fax: 304-558-8867

Adam Sponaugle, Division Director

3292 West Virginia Department of Education
1900 Kanawha Boulevard E
Building 6, Room B-358
Charleston, WV 25305-0330
304-558-2681
Fax: 304-558-0048
http://www.wvde.state.wv.us
The constitutional mission is to provide supervision of the K-12 education system.

David Stewart, Superintendent
Audrey Horne, President

Wisconsin

3293 Division for Learning Support: Equity & Advocacy
Wisconsin Department of Education
125 S Webster Street
PO Box 7841
Madison, WI 53707-7841
608-266-1649
Fax: 608-267-3746
http://www.dpi.state.wi.us

Carolyn Stanford-Taylor, Division Director

3294 Instructional Services Division
Wisconsin Department of Education
125 S Webster Street
PO Box 7841
Madison, WI 53707-7841
608-266-3361
Fax: 608-267-3746
http://www.dpi.state.wi.us

Pauline Nikolay, Division Director

3295 Library Services Division
Wisconsin Department of Education
125 S Webster Street
PO Box 7841
Madison, WI 53707-7841
608-266-2205
Fax: 608-267-3746
http://www.dpi.state.wi.us

William Wilson, Division Director

3296 School Financial Resources & Management
Wisconsin Department of Education
125 S Webster Street
PO Box 7841
Madison, WI 53707-7841
608-266-3851
Fax: 608-267-3746
http://www.dpi.state.wi.us

Bambi Statz, Division Director

3297 Wisconsin College System Technical
310 Price Place
PO Box 7874
Madison, WI 53707-7874
608-266-1770
Fax: 608-266-1285
E-mail: wtcsb@board.tec.wi.us
http://www.board.tec.wi.us

Richard Carpenter, President

3298 Wisconsin Department of Public Instruction
125 S Webster Street
PO Box 7841
Madison, WI 53707-7841
608-266-1771
800-441-4563
Fax: 608-266-5188
E-mail: statesuperintendent@dpi.wi.gov
http://www.dpi.wi.gov

Tony Evers, Superintendent
Mike Thompson, Deputy State Superintendent

Wyoming

3299 Accounting, Personnel & School Finance Unit
Wyoming Department of Education
2300 Capitol Avenue
Floor 2
Cheyenne, WY 82001-3644
307-777-6392
Fax: 307-777-6234

Barry Nimmo, Division Director

3300 Applied Data & Technology Unit
Wyoming Department of Education
2300 Capitol Avenue
Floor 2
Cheyenne, WY 82001-3644
307-777-6213
Fax: 307-777-6234

Steven King, Division Director

3301 Services for Individuals with Hearing Loss
Wyoming Department of Education
2300 Capitol Avenue
Floor 2
Cheyenne, WY 82001-3644

307-777-4686
Fax: 307-777-6234

Tim Sanger, Division Director

3302 Support Programs & Quality Results Division
Wyoming Department of Education
2300 Capitol Avenue
Floor 2
Cheyenne, WY 82001-3644
307-777-6213
Fax: 307-777-6234

Dr. Alan Sheinker, Division Director

3303 Wyoming Department of Education
2300 Capitol Avenue
Hathaway Building, 2nd Floor
Cheyenne, WY 82002-0050
307-777-7675
Fax: 307-777-6234
http://www.k12.wy.us

Dr.Trent Blankenship, Superintendent

Associations

3304 Agency for Instructional Technology
1800 N StoneLake Drive
Box A
Bloomington, IN 47402-0120
812-339-2203
800-457-4509
Fax: 812-333-4218
E-mail: info@ait.net
http://www.ait.net
AIT's mission is to be the premier provider of services and products to enhance student learning. A nonprofit organization and is one of the largest providers of instructional TV programs in North America.

Ruth Blankenbaker, Vice Chair
Chuck Wilson, Executive Director

3305 American Association for Higher Education & Accreditation
2020 Pennsylvania Avenue NW
#975
Washington, DC 20006
202-293-6440
Fax: 877-510-4240
E-mail: admin@aahea.org
http://www.aahea.org
The individual membership organization that promotes the changes higher education must make to ensure its effectiveness in a complex, interconnected world. The association equips individuals and institutions committed to such changes with the knowledge they need to bring those changes about.

Jose Luis Gomez, President

3306 American Association of Colleges for Teacher Education
1307 New York Avenue NW
Suite 300
Washington, DC 20005
202-293-2450
Fax: 202-457-8095
E-mail: aacte@aacte.org
http://www.aacte.org
A national alliance of educator preparation programs dedicated to the highest quality professional development of teachers and school leaders in order to enhance PK-12 student learning.

Sharon P Robinson, President/CEO
Sandy L Monroe, Executive Assistant

3307 American Educational Research Association
1430 K Street NW
Suite 1200
Washington, DC 20005
202-238-3200
Fax: 202-238-3250
E-mail: flevine@aera.net
http://www.aera.net
Supports improvement of the educational process through the encouragement of scholarly inquiry related to education, the dissemination of research results, and their practical application. Holds a conference and publishes books, videos, and magazines.

Kris D Gutierrez, President
Felice J Levine PhD, Executive Director

3308 American Educational Studies Association
Department of Education
235 Morton Hall
Huntsville, AL 35899
330-972-7111
http://www.educationalstudies.org
An international learned society for students, teachers, research scholars, and administrators who are interested in the foundations of education. A society primarily comprised of college and university professors who teach and research in the field of education utilizing one or more of the liberal arts disciplines of philosophy, history, politics, sociology, anthropology, or economics as well as comparative/international and cultural studies.

Audrey Thompson, President
Sofia Villenas, President-Elect/Prog Chair

3309 American Foundation for Negro Affairs
117 S 17th Street
Suite 1200
Philadelphia, PA 19103-5011
215-854-1470
Fax: 215-854-1487
Offers a model for educational programs preparing minority students for professional careers.

Samuel L Evans, President

3310 American Society for Training and Development Information Center
1640 King Street
Box 1443
Alexandria, VA 22313-1443
703-683-8100
800-628-2783
Fax: 703-683-8103
E-mail: customercare@astd.org
http://www.astd.org
Dedicated to workplace learning and performance professionals. Members come from more than 100 countries and connect locally in more than 130 U.S. chapters and with more than 30 international partners.

Tony Bingham, President/CEO

3311 Association of Teacher Educators
8503 Euclid Avenue
Suite 3
Manassas Park, VA 20111-2407
703-331-0911
Fax: 703-331-3666
E-mail: info@ate1.org
http://www.ate1.org
The mission of the Association of Teacher Educators is to improve the effectiveness of teacher education through leadership in the development of quality programs to prepare teachers, by analyzing issues and practices relating to professional development, and by providing opportunities for the personal and professional growth of Association members.

David A Ritchey PhD, Executive Director
Terrell Peace, President

3312 Center for Rural Studies
University of Vermont
206 Morrill Hall
146 University Place
Burlington, VT 05405
802-656-3021
Fax: 802-656-1423
E-mail: crs@uvm.edu
http://www.uvm.edu/crs
A nonprofit, fee-for-service research and resource center that works with people and communities to address social, economic, and resource-based challenges. CRS supports the research and teaching missions of the university through its work in applied research, community outreach, program evaluation, and consulting services.

Jane Kolodinsky, Director
Fred Schmidt, Founder/Director Emeritus

3313 Committee on Continuing Education for School Personnel
Kean College of New Jersey
Academic Services
Union, NJ 07083
908-737-5326
Fax: 908-737-5845
Develops activities for professional and personal growth among teachers and educators.

George Sisko, Director

3314 Council for Learning Disabilities
11184 Antioch Road
PO Box 405
Overland Park, KS 66210
913-491-1011
Fax: 913-491-1012
E-mail: CLDInfo@ie-events.com
http://www.cldinternational.org
An international organization that promotes evidence-based teaching, collaboration, research, leadership, and advocacy. Comprised of professionals who represent diverse disciplines and are committed to enhancing the education and quality of life for individuals with learning disabilities and others who experience challenges in learning.

Cari Dunn, President
Linda Nease, President-Elect

3315 Council of Administrators of Special Education
Osigian Office Centre
101 Katelyn Circle, Suite E
Warner Robins, GA 31088
478-333-6892
Fax: 478-333-2453
E-mail: lpurcell@casecec.org
http://www.casecec.org
An international professional educational organization which is affiliated with the Council for Exceptional Children (CEC) whose members are dedicated to the enhancement of the worth, dignity, potential, and uniqueness of each individual in society.

Dr Mary V Kealy, President
Luann Purcell, Executive Director

3316 Distance Education & Training Council
1601 18th Street NW
Suite 2
Washington, DC 20009
202-234-5100
Fax: 202-332-1386
E-mail: mike@detc.org
http://www.detc.org
A voluntary, non-governmental, educational organization that was founded to promote sound educational standards and ethical business practices within the correspondence field.

Michael P Lambert, Executive Director

3317 ERIC Clearinghouse on Teaching and Teacher Education
American Association of Colleges for Teacher Ed.
1307 New York Avenue NW
Suite 300
Washington, DC 20005-4701
202-293-2450
Fax: 202-457-8095
E-mail: aacte@aacte.org
http://www.aacte.org
To promote the learning of all PK-12 students through high-quality, evidence-based preparation and continuing education for all school personnel.

Mary Dilworth, Director
Deborah Newby, Associate Director

3318 Educational Leadership Institute
4455 Connecticut Avenue NW
Suite 310
Washington, DC 20008
202-822-8405
Fax: 202-872-4050
E-mail: iel@iel.org
http://www.iel.org
A non-profit, nonpartisan organization that envisions a society that uses its resources effectively to achieve better futures for all children and youth. IEL's mission continues to be to build the capacity of individuals and organizations in education and related fields to work together, across policies, programs and sectors.

Martin J Blank, President
Louise A Clark, Chief Administrative Officer

3319 International Council on Education for Teaching
National-Louis University
1000 Capitol Drive
Wheeling, IL 60090
847-947-5881
Fax: 847-947-5881
E-mail: contact@icet4u.org
http://icet4u.org
An international association of policy and decision-makers in education, government and business dedicated to global development through education. ICET provides programs and services that give its members access to a worldwide resource base of organizations, programs, specialized consultative services and research and training opportunities at the university level.

Darrell Bloom, President

3320 National Association of State Directors of Teacher Education & Certification
1225 Providence Road
PMB #116
Whitinsville, MA 01588
508-380-1202
Fax: 508-278-5342
E-mail: rje@nasdtec.com
http://www.nasdtec.org
The organization that represents professional standards boards and commissions and state departments of education in all 50 states, the District of Columbia, the Department of Defense Education Activity, the U.S. Territories, Alberta, British Columbia, and Ontario that are responsible for the preparation, licensure, and discipline of educational personnel.

Roy Einreinhofer, Executive Director

3321 National Center for Community Education
1017 Avon Street
Flint, MI 48503-2797
810-238-0463
800-811-1105
Fax: 810-238-9211
E-mail: info@nccenet.org
http://www.nccenet.org
It is the mission of the National Center for Community Education to promote community and educational change emphasizing community schools by providing state-of-the-art leadership development, training and technical assistance.

Maxine Murray, Operations Director
Marion Baldwin, Chief Administrator

3322 National Middle School Association
4151 Executive Parkway
Suite 300
Westerville, OH 43081
614-895-4730
800-528-6672
Fax: 614-895-4750
E-mail: info@nmsa.org
http://www.nmsa.org
NMSA has been a voice for those committed to the educational and developmental needs of young adolescents. NMSA is the only national education association dedicated exclusively to those in the middle level grades.

Joan Jarrett, President
Dr Drew Allbritten, Executive Director

3323 National Staff Development Council
504 S Locust Street
Oxford, OH 45056
513-523-6029
800-727-7288
Fax: 513-523-0638
E-mail: NSDCoffice@nsdc.org
http://www.nsdc.org
The largest non-profit professional association committed to ensuring success for all students through staff development and school improvement. The purpose of the NSDC is that every educator engages in effective professional learning every day so every student achieves.

Stephanie Hirsh, Executive Director
Carol Francois, Director of Learning

3324 National Women's Studies Association
7100 Baltimore Avenue
Suite 203
College Park, MD 20740
301-403-0407
Fax: 301-403-4137
E-mail: nwsaoffice@nwsa.org
http://www.nwsa.org
A professional organization dedicated to leading the field of women's studies and gender studies, as well as its teaching, learning, research and service wherever they be found.

Allison Kimmich, Executive Director
Bonnie Thornton Dill, President

3325 Recruiting New Teachers
385 Concord Avenue
Suite 103
Belmont, MA 02478-3037
617-489-6000
800-45 -EACH
Fax: 617-489-6005
E-mail: rnt@rnt.org
http://www.rnt.org/channels/clearinghouse
Conducts public service advertising campaign encouraging people to consider teaching careers.

Mildred Hudson, CEO

3326 Search Associates
PO Box 636
Dallas, PA 18612-636
570-696-4600
Fax: 570-696-9500
E-mail: SearchCentralHQ@cs.com
http://www.search-associates.com
Each year Search Associates places over 1,500 teachers, administrators and interns in international schools throughout the world, making us the largest of the International School placement organizations. However, it is our personalized approach to the schools and candidates we serve which we would most like to emphasize.

John Magagna, Founding Director

Awards & Honors

3327 Apple Education Grants
Apple Computer
1 Infinite Loop
Cupertino, CA 95014
408-996-1010
800-800-2775
Fax: 512-919-2992
http://www.apple.com
Awarded each year to teams of K-12 educators working on educational technology plans. Potential awardees find innovative uses of technology in the classroom and come from schools that would otherwise have limited access to technology.

3328 Bayer/NSF Award for Community Innovation
105 Terry Drive
Suite 120
Newtown, PA 18940
215-579-8590
800-291-6020
Fax: 215-579-8589
E-mail: success@edumedia.com
A community-based science and technology competition to give all sixth, seventh and eighth-graders a hands-on experience with real-world problems using the scientific method.

Stephanie Hallman, Program Manager
Stacey Gall, Competition Coordinator

3329 Excellence in Teaching Cabinet Grant
Curriclum Associates
PO Box 2001
North Billerica, MA 01862
800-225-0248
Fax: 800-366-1158
Awarded to educators who wish to implement unique educational projects. Potential awardees propose projects using a variety of teaching tools, including technology and print.

3330 Magna Awards
American School Board Journal
1680 Duke Street
Alexandria, VA 22314
703-838-6722
http://www.asbj.com
A national recognition program co-sponsored by American School Board Journal, the National School Boards Association, and Sodexo School Services that honors school board best practices and innovative programs that advance student learning.

3331 NSTA Fellow Award
National Science Teachers Association
1840 Wilson Boulevard
Arlington, VA 22201
703-243-7100
Fax: 703-243-7177
http://www.nsta.org
This award recognizes NSTA members who have made extraordinary contributions to science education through personal commitment to education, specifically science teaching or science; educational endeavors and original work that position recipients as exemplary leaders in their field; significant contributions to the profession that reflect dedication to NSTA as well the entire educational community.

Dr Alan J McCormack, President
Dr Francis Q Eberle, Executive Director

3332 NSTA Legacy Award
National Science Teachers Association
1840 Wilson Boulevard
Arlington, VA 22201
703-243-7100
Fax: 703-243-7177
http://www.nsta.org

This NSTA award posthumously recognizes long-standing members of NSTA for significant lifelong service to NSTA and contributions to science education.

Dr Alan J McCormack, President
Dr Francis Q Eberle, Executive Director

3333 National Teachers Hall of Fame

National Teachers Hall of Fame
1200 Commercial
Box 4017
Emporia, KS 66801
620-341-5660
800-968-3224
Fax: 620-341-5912
E-mail: hallfame@emporia.edu
http://www.nthf.org
The mission of The National Teachers Hall of Fame is to recognize and honor exceptional career teachers, encourage excellence in teaching, and preserve the rich heritage of the teaching profession in the United States.

Roberts T Jones, President
Dr Anne L Bryant, Executive Director

3334 Presidential Awards for Excellence in Mathematics and Science Teaching

National Science Foundation
4201 Wilson Boulevard
Arlington, VA 22230
703-292-8620
Fax: 703-292-9044
E-mail: msaul@nsf.gov
http://www.ehr.nsf.gov
This award is the nation's highest commendation for K-12 math and science teachers. Approximately 108 teachers are recognized annually with this prestigious award.

Mark Saul, Director

3335 Senior Researcher Award

Music Education Research Council
Deptartment of Music
138 Fine Arts Center
Columbia, MO 65211
573-884-1604
Fax: 573-884-7444
For recognition of a significant scholarly achievement maintained over a period of years.

3336 Toyota Tapestry Grants for Teachers

National Science Teachers Association
1840 Wilson Boulevard
Arlington, VA 22201
703-243-7100
Fax: 703-243-7177
http://www.nsta.org
Awards 50 grants of up to $10,000 each to K-12 teachers of science in the fields of environmental science education.

Dr Alan J McCormack, President
Dr Francis Q Eberle, Executive Director

Conferences

3337 AASA National Conference on Education

American Association of School Administrators
801 N Quincy Street
Suite 700
Arlington, VA 22203-1730
703-528-0700
Fax: 703-841-1543
E-mail: info@aasa.org
http://www.aasa.org
Where America's school leaders go for a vision of the future in public education; to explore new thinking, new products, new services and new technologies.

February

Daniel A Domenech, Executive Director
Christopher Daw, Meetings Director

3338 ACE Fellows Program

American Council on Education
One Dupont Circle NW
Washington, DC 20036-1193
202-939-9420
E-mail: fellows@ace.nche.edu
http://www.acenet.edu
The nation's premier higher education leadership development program in preparing senior leaders to serve American colleges and universities. Enables participants to immerse themselves in the culture, policies, and decision-making processes of another institution.

Sharon A McDade, Director
Brian Madden, Program Coordinator

3339 AFT Convention

American Federation of Teachers AFL-CIO
555 New Jersey Avenue NW
Washington, DC 20001
202-879-4400
E-mail: online@aft.org
http://www.aft.org
The AFT represents one million teachers, school support staff, higher education faculty and staff, health care professionals, and state and municipal employees. AFT is an affiliated international union of the AFL-CIO.

Randi Weingarten, President

3340 Alaska Department of Education Bilingual& Bicultural Education Conference

University of Alaska, Conference & Special Events
117 Eielson Building
Fairbanks, AK 99775-7680
907-474-7436
Fax: 907-474-6586
http://www.uaf.edu/anla/contact-us/
Stresses the importance of literacy and multicultural education for Alaskan educators.

February

Gary Holton, Director

3341 American Association of Collegiate Registrars & Admissions Officers

American Assoc of Collegiate Registrars/Admissions
1 Dupont Circle NW
Suite 520
Washington, DC 20036
202-293-9161
Fax: 202-872-8857
E-mail: meetings@aacrao.org
http://www.aacrao.org
Provides the opportunity to reflect on where the association has been, where it currently stands, and what we can do to lead our colleagues, our students, and our institutions into the future.

March

Jerome Sullivan, Executive Director
Melissa Ficek, Meeetings/Conferences

3342 American Society for Training & Development International Conference & Exposition

American Society for Training & Development
1640 King Street
Box 1443
Alexandria, VA 22313-1443
703-683-8100
Fax: 703-683-8103
E-mail: customercare@astd.org
http://www.astd.org
This premier event for workplace learning and performance professionals welcomes attendees from more than 70 countries. The conference features 200+ educational sessions from industry leading experts, and a world-class EXPO filled with the latest products and services available from top suppliers.

Annual/May

Tony Bingham, President/CEO

3343 Annual Building Championship Schools Conference

Center for Peak Performing Schools
2021 Clubhouse Drive
Greeley, CO 80634
970-339-9277
Interested in curriculum development and instructional assessment. Members include administrators at all levels of education.

February

3344 Annual New England Kindergarten Conference

Lesley University
29 Everett Street
Cambridge, MA 02138
617-349-8544
800-999-1959
Fax: 617-349-8125
E-mail: hr@lesley.edu
http://www.lesley.edu
Committed to active learning, scholarly research, critical inquiry, and diverse forms of artistic practice through close mentoring relationships among students, faculty, and practitioners in the field

November
1000 attendees

Mary Mindess, Conference Coordinator
Kari Nygaard, Conference Manager

3345 Annual State Convention of Association of Texas Professional Educators

Association of Texas Professional Educators
305 E Huntland Drive
Suite 300
Austin, TX 78752
800-777-2873
Fax: 512-467-2203
E-mail: meetings@atpe.org
http://www.atpe.org
A member-owned, member-governed professional association with more than 112,000 members leading educators' association in the state and the largest independent association for public school educators in the nation.

March
100 booths with 1,300 attendees

Doug Rogers, Executive Director
Andrea Davis, Meetings/Conferences

3346 Association for Educational Communications & Technology Annual Convention

Assoc for Educational Communications & Technology
1800 N Stonelake Drive, Suite 2
PO Box 2447
Bloomington, IN 47402-2447
812-335-7675
Fax: 812-335-7678
E-mail: aect@aect.org
http://www.aect.org
Provide leadership in educational communications and technology by linking a wide range of professionals holding a common in-

terest in the use of educational technology and its application learning process.

November

Dr Phillip Harris, Executive Director

3347 Association for Library & Information Science Education Annual Conference
ALISE
65 E Wacker Place
Suite 1900
Chicago, IL 60601-7246
312-795-0996
Fax: 312-419-8950
E-mail: contact@alise.org
http://www.alise.org
Promotes excellence in education for library and information sciences as a means of increasing library services.

January

Kathleen Combs, Executive Director
Ewanya Clark, Executive Assistant

3348 Association of Teacher Educators Annual Meeting
Association of Teacher Educators
PO Box 793
Manassas, VA 20113
703-331-0911
Fax: 703-331-3666
E-mail: info@ate1.org
http://www.ate1.org

February

David A Ritchey, Executive Director
Terrell Peace, President

3349 CASE Annual Convention
Colorado Association of School Executives
4101 S Bannock Street
Englewood, CO 80110-4606
303-762-8762
Fax: 303-762-8697
E-mail: case@co-case.org
http://www.co-case.org

July

Bruce Caughey, Executive Director

3350 CCAE/COABE National Conference
California Council for Adult Education
19332 Peachtree Lane
Huntington Beach, CA 92648
626-825-9363
Fax: 714-960-8764
E-mail: sprantalos@socal.rr.com
http://www.ccaestate.org

April
1200 attendees

Steve Prantalos, Executive Director

3351 CSBA Education Conference & Trade Show
California School Boards Association
3100 Beacon Boulevard
West Sacramento, CA 95691
800-266-3382
Fax: 916-371-3407
E-mail: dfernandes@csba.org
http://www.csba.org
Premier continuing education program - delivering practical solutions to help governance teams from districts and county offices of education improve student learning and achievement.

Annual/December
200 booths

Deanna Fernandes, Conference Coordinator
Laura Bohannon, Exhibit Manager

3352 California Kindergarten Conference and PreConference Institute
California Kindergarten Association
1014 Chippendale Way
Roseville, CA 95661
916-780-5331
Fax: 916-780-5330
E-mail: cka@ckanet.org
http://www.ckanet.org
The original conference for teachers by teachers.

January
120 booths with 2,000 attendees and 100 exhibits

Laura Darcy, Conference Co-Chair
Meredith Yeh, Principal

3353 Careers Conference
University of Wisconsin-Madison
Center on Education & Work
1025 W Johnson Street, Room 964
Madison, WI 53706-1796
608-265-6700
800-862-1071
Fax: 608-262-3063
E-mail: cewconf@education.wisc.edu
http://www.cew.wisc.edu
Designed to serve everyone and anyone who is involved with career development, careers education, and related fields. This national conference presents learning opportunities at all levels, from a basic introduction for those starting out. to the very latest practices, strategies, and resources for those who are advanced in the field.

Annual/Januaray
40 booths with 1500 attendees

Carol Edds, Conference Manager

3354 Center for Play Therapy Fall Conference
University of North Texas
1400 Highland Street
Room 114
Denton, TX 76203-0829
940-565-3864
Fax: 940-565-4461
E-mail: cpt@unt.edu
http://cpt.unt.edu
Features a one day workshop led by a recognized authority in the field of play therapy. This workshop enables professionals in the field of mental health to broaden their knowledge and clinical skills in play therapy.

Annual/October
350 attendees

Sue Bratton, Director

3355 Central States Conference on the Teaching of Foreign Languages
Central States Conference on the Teaching
PO Box 251
Milwaukee, WI 53201-0251
414-405-4645
Fax: 414-276-4650
E-mail: csctfl@aol.com
http://www.csctfl.org
Includes approximately 140 workshops and sessions presented by world language teachers at all levels of instruction. Serves Arkansas, Colorado, Illinois, Indiana, Iowa, Kansas, Kentucky, Michigan, Minnesota, Missouri, Nebraska, North Dakota, Ohio, Oklahoma, South Dakota, Tennessee and Wisconsin.

Annual/March

Patrick T Raven, Executive Director

3356 Chicago Principals Association Education Conference
221 N Lasalle Street
Suite 3316
Chicago, IL 60601-1505
312-263-7767
Fax: 312-263-2012
Educational or fund raising products including copy machines, computers, book companies, etc.

February

Beverly Tunney, Conference Coordinator

3357 Classroom Connect
6277 Sea Harbor Drive
Orlando, FL 32887
800-638-1639
888-801-8299
Fax: 650-351-5300
E-mail: help@classroom.com
http://www.classroom.com
A leading provider of professional development programs and online instructional content for K-12 education.

October

Jim Bowler, President
Melinda Cook, Vice President Sales

3358 Florida Elementary School Principals Association Conference
206 S Monroe Street
Suite B
Tallahassee, FL 32301-1801
800-593-3626
Fax: 850-224-3892
Exhibitors from fundraisers to computer companies.

November
50 booths

Lisa Begue, Conference Coordinator

3359 Florida School Administrators Association Summer Conference
Florida Association of School Administrators
326 Williams Street
Tallahassee, FL 32303
850-224-3626
800-593-3626
Fax: 850-224-3892
http://www.fasa.net
Exhibits include computer software, textbooks and school supplies, fundraising companies, schoolyear book and ring companies, video and audio companies, furniture suppliers and other school related products.

Annual/July

Juhan Mixon, Executive Director

3360 Florida Vocational Association Conference
1420 N Paul Russell Road
Tallahassee, FL 32301-4835
850-878-6860
Fax: 850-878-5476
Curriculum materials, industrial equipment and supplies, computer hardware and software, medical equipment and other materials utilized by vocational educators.

July
150 booths

Donna Harper, Conference Coordinator

3361 Foundation for Critical Thinking Annual Conference
PO Box 196
Tomales, CA 94971
707-878-9100
800-833-3645
Fax: 707-878-9111
E-mail: cct@criticalthinking.org
http://www.criticalthinking.org
Provides a unique opportunity to improve understanding of critical thinking, as well as one's abil-

ity to foster it in the classroom and other aspects in work/life.

July-August
1200 attendees

Dr. Richard Paul, Fellow
Dr. Linda Elder, Fellow

3362 IASB Convention

Iowa Association of School Boards
6000 Grand Avenue
Des Moines, IA 50312-1417
515-288-1991
800-795-4272
Fax: 515-243-4992
http://www.ia-sb.org
IASB is an organization of elected school board members dedicated to assisting school boards in achieving their goal of excellence and equity in public education.

Annual/November

LouAnn Gvist, Convention Director
Veronica Stalker, Interim Executive Director

3363 IASB Joint Annual Conference

Illinois Association of School Boards
2921 Baker Drive
Springfield, IL 62703-5929
217-528-9688
http://www.iasb.com
Recognized as one of the nation's largest state education conferences, the event was open to local school board members, superintendents and secretaries, school administrators, state and regional educators and officials, school attorneys, university professors, exhibitors, and guests.

November
235 booths with 9500+ attendees

Dr Michael D Johnson, Executive Director Emeritus
Sandra Boston, Asst Director/Exhibit Mgr

3364 IASSIST Annual Conference

Int'l Assoc for Social Science Info Service & Tech
405 Hilgard Avenue
Attn: Wendy Treadwell
Los Angeles, CA 90095-9000
612-624-4389
Fax: 612-626-9353
E-mail: melanie@essex.ac.uk
http://www.iassistdata.org
IASSIST is an international organization of professionals working with information technology and data services to support research and teaching in the social sciences. Its 300 members work in a variety of settings, including data archives, statistical agencies, research centers, libraries, academic departments, government departments, and non-profit organizations.

May-June

Melanie Wright, President
William Block, Vice President

3365 ISBA/IAPSS Annual Conference

Indiana School Board Association
1 N Capitol Avenue
Suite 1215
Indianapolis, IN 46204-2225
317-639-0330
Fax: 317-639-3591
E-mail: mwagers@isba-ind.org
http://www.isba-ind.org
Jointy sponsored by the Indiana School Boards Association and Indiana Association of Public School Superintendents. A comprehensive program, designed by the ISBA and IAPPS, that brings the latest information and

some of the most informed experts on current topics in education.

Fall

Dr Frank A Bush, Executive Director
Leanne R Waters, Conference Coordinator

3366 Illinois Assistant Principals Conference

Illinois Principals Association
2940 Baker Drive
Springfield, IL 62703
217-525-1383
Fax: 217-525-7264
E-mail: support@ilprincipals.org
http://www.ilprincipals.org
Where assistant principals and deans attend annually to hear outstanding educational leaders; participate in educational sessions and to network with colleagues across the state

Annual/February
120 booths with 200 attendees

Jason Leahy, Executive Director
Jean Smith, Professional Development Dir

3367 Illinois Resource Center Conference of Teachers of Linguistically Diverse Students

Illinois Resource Center
2626 Clearbrook Drive
Arlington Heights, IL 60005-4626
224-366-8555
Fax: 847-649-0551
http://www.thecenterweb.org/irc/
A conference that caters to those educators involved with teaching multi-licensed pupils.

March

3368 Iowa Council Teachers of Math Conference

Iowa Council of Teachers of Mathematics
1712 55th Street
Des Moines, IA 50310-1548
515-242-7846
http://www.iowamath.org
Math teachers conference.

Annual/February
48 booths

Ruth Avazian, President

3369 Iowa Reading Association Conference

Iowa Reading Association
512 Lynn Avenue
Ames, IA 50014-7320
712-754-3636
E-mail: jneal@jefferson0scranton.k12.ia.us
http://www.iowareading.org
Nationally prominent speakers, published authors, and experienced instructors will anchor the conference, sharing current research and creative reading strategies.

Annual/April

Julie Neal, Conference Chair
Clark Goltz, Executive Director

3370 KSBA Annual Conference

Kentucky School Boards Association
260 Democrat Drive
Frankfort, KY 40601
800-372-2962
Fax: 502-695-5451
http://www.ksba.org

February

William G Scott, Executive Director

3371 Kansas School Boards Association Conference

1420 SW Arrowhead Road
Topeka, KS 66604-4024

785-273-3600
800-432-2471
Fax: 785-273-7580
E-mail: ahartzell@kasb.org
http://www.kasb.org
Wide variety of school district vendors and contacts for products and services.

December
70 booths

Dennis Depew, President
Frank Henderson, President-Elect

3372 Kentucky School Superintendents Association Meeting

152 Consumer Lane
Frankfort, KY 40601
502-875-3411
800-928-5272
Fax: 502-875-4634
E-mail: webmaster@kasa.org
http://www.kasa.org
KASA is dedicated to serving school administrators throughout Kentucky through advocacy, professional development, research and leadership.

June
36 booths

Dr. Roland Haun, Conference Contact
Wayne Young, Executive Director

3373 LSBA Convention

Louisiana School Boards Association
7912 Summa Avenue
Baton Rouge, LA 70809
225-769-3191
877-664-5722
Fax: 225-769-6108
http://www.lsba.com

Annual/March

Nolton Senegal, Executive Director

3374 Lilly Conference on College Teaching

Miami University
303 S Patterson Ave
Oxford, OH 45056
513-529-9266
Fax: 513-529-9984
E-mail: lillycon@muohio.edu
http://www.units.muohio.edu/lillycon
One of the nation's most renowned conferences presenting the scholarship of teaching and learning. Teacher-scholars from across the U.S. and internationally gather to share innovative pedagogies and discuss questions, challenges, and insights about teaching and learning.

Annual/November
660 attendees

Melody Barton, Administrative Associate
Milton Cox, Conference Director

3375 MASB Annual Fall Conference

Michigan Association of School Boards
1001 Centennial Way
Suite 400
Lansing, MI 48917-8249
517-327-5900
Fax: 517-327-0775
E-mail: info@masb.org
http://www.masb.org
The premier leadership event that features nationally acclaimed speakers addressing current education topics.

October
110 booths with 500 attendees and 110 exhibits

Kathy Hayes, Executive Director
Deborah Keys, Conference Director

3376 MESPA Spring Conference
Massachusetts Elementary School
Principals Assoc
28 Lord Road
Suite 125
Marlborough, MA 01752
508-624-0500
Fax: 508-485-9965
E-mail: mespa@mespa.org
http://www.mespa.org
Features nationally-known speakers, numerous workshops on relevant topics, awards presentation, and an outstanding exhibition of school-related vendors.

Annual/May
100 booths

Nadya Aswad Higgins, Executive
Director
Eileen Gallant, Exhibit Coordinator

3377 MNEA Fall Conference
Missouri National Education Association
1810 E Elm Street
Jefferson City, MO 65101
573-634-3202
Fax: 573-634-5646
E-mail: chris.guinther@mnea.org
http://www.mnea.org
Free and open to the public. Includes workshops, exhibits and features a keynote address presented by Diane Ravitch

Annual/November
95 booths with 1,500 attendees

Chris Guinther, President

3378 MSBA Annual Conference
Missouri School Boards Association
2100 I-70 Drive SW
Columbia, MO 65203
800-221-6722
Fax: 573-445-9981
E-mail: info@msbanet.org
http://www.msbanet.org

September/October
125 booths

Dr Carter Ward, Executive Director
Jaime Fessler, Conference/Events
Manager

**3379 Maine Principals Association
Conference**
50 Industrial Drive
PO Box 2468
Augusta, ME 04330-2468
207-622-0217
Fax: 207-622-1513
E-mail: mpa@mpa.cc
http://www.mpa.cc
To assure a quality education for all students, promote the principalship

April

Barbara Proko, Conference Contact
Mary Martin, President

**3380 Massachusetts School Boards
Association Meeting**
One Mckinley Square
Boston, MA 02109-1650
617-523-8454
800-392-6023
http://www.masc.org

May
100 booths

Capt. Edward Bryant, NCCC, Conference
Contact
Glen Koocher, Executive Director

**3381 Michigan Association of
Elementary and Middle School
Principals Conference**
1980 N College Road
Mason, MI 48854

517-694-8955
Fax: 517-694-8945
http://www.memspa.org
Exhibits offer books, fundraisers, camps, insurance groups and non-profit organizations.

October
100 booths

William Hays, Jr, Conference Contact

**3382 Michigan Science Teachers
Association Annual Conference**
Michigan Science Teachers Association
1390 Eisenhower Place
Ann Arbor, MI 48108
734-973-0433
Fax: 734-677-3287
http://www.msta-mich.org
A conference that aims to supply science teachers with information and research.

February

Robby Cramer, Executive Director
Paul Drummond, Conference Chair

**3383 Mid-South Educational Research
Association Annual Meeting**
Louisiana State University, School of
Dentistry
1100 Florida Avenue
#223
New Orleans, LA 70119-2714
504-619-8700
Fax: 504-619-8740
http://www.dtm10.cep.msstate.edu/
Focuses on assessment and involvement in education by releasing research and statistics.

November

Diana Gardiner PhD, Conference Contact

**3384 Middle States Council for the
Social Studies Annual Regional
Conference**
P.O Box 1196
Savona, NY 14879
717-865-2117
http://www.mscssonline.org
Seeks to develop and implement new curriculum into the social studies area.

April

Dan Sidelnick, Conference Contact
Rebecca Herndon, President

**3385 Minnesota Leadership Annual
Conference**
Minnesota School Boards Association
1900 W Jefferson Avenue
Saint Peter, MN 56082-3015
507-934-2450
800-324-4459
Fax: 507-931-1515
E-mail: gabbott@mnmsba.org
http://www.mnmsba.org
The purpose of the Association is to support, promote and enhance the work of public school boards

January
200+ booths with 2,000+ attendees

Kent Thiesse, President
Greg Abbott, MSBA Dir. of
Communications

**3386 Minnesota School Administrators
Association**
1884 Como Avenue
Saint Paul, MN 55108-2715
651-645-6272
866-444-5251
Fax: 651-645-7518
E-mail: members@mnasa.org
http://www.mnasa.org

MASA's Educational Leaderswill establish the statewide agenda for children, serve as the preeminent voice for public education and empower members through quality services and support.

October
70 booths

Gary Amoroso, Executive Director
Mia Urick, Director of Communications

**3387 Minnesota School Boards Association
Annual Meeting**
1900 W Jefferson Street
Saint Peter, MN 56082-3015
507-934-2450
800-324-4459
Fax: 507-931-1515
http://www.mnmsba.org
School supplies and services as diverse as buses and architectural services.

January
190 booths

Mike Torkelson, Conference Contact
Kent Thiesse, President

**3388 Missouri State Teachers Association
Conference**
PO Box 458
Columbia, MO 65205-458
573-442-3127
800-392-0532
Fax: 573-443-5079
E-mail: membercare@msta.org
http://www.msta.org
Educational materials.

November
280 booths

Kent King, Conference Contact

**3389 Montana Association of Elementary
School Principals Conference**
1134 Butte Avenue
Helena, MT 59601-5178
406-442-2510
Fax: 406-442-2518

January/Febuary
20 booths

Loran Frazier, Conference Contact

3390 NAAEE Annual Conference
North American Assoc for Environmental
Education
2000 P Street NW
Suite 540
Washington, DC 20036
202-419-0412
Fax: 202-419-0415
E-mail: communicator@naaee.org
http://www.naaee.org

October

Brian A Day, Executive Director
Bridget Chicholm, Conference Manager

3391 NCASA Annual Conference
North Carolina Association of School
Administrator
PO Box 27711
Raleigh, NC 27611
919-828-1426
Fax: 919-828-6099
E-mail: info@ncasa.net
http://www.ncasa.net
Delivers a powerful agenda packed with essential training and sessions led by key education leaders and political insiders in the state and nation.

March-April
40 booths

Bill McNeal, Executive Director
Katherine Joyce, Assistant Executive Director

3392 NCTM Annual Meeting & Exposition

National Council of Teachers of Mathematics
1906 Association Drive
Reston, VA 20191-1502
703-620-9840
800-235-7566
Fax: 703-476-2970
E-mail: nctm@nctm.org
http://www.nctm.org
Covers topics like differentiated instruction, common core standards, intervention, technology and more

April
650 booths with 18M attendees

Michael J Shaughnessy, President
Kichoon Yang, Executive Director

3393 NELMS Annual Conference

New England League of Middle Schools
120 Water Street
Suite 403
North Andover, MA 01845
978-557-9311
Fax: 978-557-9312
E-mail: nelms@nelms.org
http://www.nelms.org

April
160+ booths with 3800+ attendees

Brenda Needham, Executive Director

3394 NMSA Annual Education Conference & Exhibit

National Middle School Association
4151 Executive Parkway
Suite 300
Westerville, OH 43016
614-895-4730
800-528-6678
Fax: 614-895-4750
E-mail: info@nmsa.org
http://www.nmsa.org
Provides information, tools, and encouragement necessary to provide a high-quality education for every young adolescent.

November

Dr Betty Greene Bryant, Interim Executive Director
Sally Ann DeBolt, Meetings/Events Manager

3395 NSBA Annual Confernce & Exposition

National School Boards Association
1680 Duke Street
Alexandria, VA 22314
703-838-6722
Fax: 703-683-7590
E-mail: conference@nsba.org
http://www.nsba.org
The largest national gathering of elected officials and offers an impressive collection of professional development opportunities for school board members and other education leaders. Offers a great opportunity to improve leadership skills and learn what is happening in public education.

April
550 booths

Dr Anne L Bryant, Executive Director
Robin Preston, Conference Management

3396 NSTA National Conference

National Science Teachers Association
1840 Wilson Boulevard
Arlington, VA 22201
703-312-9232
Fax: 703-243-7177
E-mail: conferences@nsta.org
http://www.nsta.org

March

Dr Alan J McCormack, President
Dr Francis Q Eberle, Executive Director

3397 NYSSBA Annual Convention & Expo

New York School Board Association
24 Century Hill Drive
Suite 200
Latham, NY 12210-2125
518-783-0200
Fax: 518-783-0211
E-mail: info@nyssba.org
http://www.nyssba.org
Join your fellow school board colleagues from all corners of the state for an unsurpassed opportunity to learn, network with peers, and hear about the latest products and services impacting education at this all-important event.

October

Kate Chauvin, Trade Show Manager

3398 National Association of Secondary School Principals Annual Convention and Exposition

1904 Association Drive
Reston, VA 20191-1537
703-860-0200
800-253-7746
Fax: 703-476-5432
E-mail: membership@principals.org
http://www.nassp.org
Offers workshops for principals on leadership training, student personnel services, and how to deal with at-risk students. Convention highlights include more than 200 educational sessions, special interest forums and luncheons and spotlights on the latest education products and services.

Phoenix
March
290 booths

Gayle Mercer, Conference Contact

3399 National Association of State Boards of Education Conference

National Association of State Boards of Education
2121 Crystal Drive
Suite 350
Arlington, VA 22202
703-684-4000
Fax: 703-836-2313
E-mail: boards@nasbe.org
http://www.nasbe.org
Aims are to study problems of mutual interest and concern, improve communication among state boards, and exchange and collect information concerning all aspects of education.

October
24 booths with 150 attendees

Doris Cruel, Conventions/Meetings Dir

3400 National Career Development Association Conference

National Career Development Association
305 N Beech Circle
Broken Arrow, OK 74012
918-663-7060
Fax: 918-663-7058
E-mail: webeditor@ncda.org
http://www.ncda.org

Deneen Pennington, Executive Director
Bobbi Carter, Convention/Education Dir

3401 National Conference on Education

American Association of School Administrators
801 N Quincy Street
Suite 700
Arlington, VA 22203-1730
703-528-0700
E-mail: info@aasa.org
http://www.aasa.org
Rich with content about the issues and challenges in public education. Take this opportunity to hear recognized speakers discuss solutions, beest practices, challenges and more.

Annual/February

Molly O'Neill, Meetings Manager

3402 National Conference on Standards and Assessment

National School Conference Institute
Riviera Hotel
Las Vegas, NV 89101
602-371-8655
Fax: 602-371-8790
http://www.nscinet.com
Two pre-conference workshops: The five most important things that educators need to know when using information for continuous program improvement, and The key to sustained leadership effectiveness. Conference will also hold over 60 breakout sessions.

April

Bill Daggett
Bob Marzano

3403 National Council for Geographic Education Annual Meeting

National Council for Geographic Education
1710 Sixteenth Street NW
Washington, DC 20009-3198
202-360-4237
Fax: 202-234-2744
http://www.ncge.org
Where geography educators from across the country and around the world meet to exchange ideas, research, resources, and best practices in geogrpahy education.

October
45 booths with 800 attendees

Jacqueline Waite, Program Manager

3404 National Council for History Education Conference

National Council for History Education
7100 Baltimore Avenue
Suite 510
College Park, MD 20740
440-835-1776
E-mail: nche@nche.net
http://www.nche.net
bring school and university people together to tackle all the issues that concern them—from curricular design, K to Ph.D., through state, local, and university standards and requirements, teacher education, certification, and professional development, to the implications of the assessment movement, of new technologies, and of school re-structuring.

March-April
750 attendees and 75 exhibits

Peter Seibert, Executive Director
John Csepegi, Conferences/Events Director

3405 National Council for Social Studies Annual Conference

National Council for the Social Studies
8555 Sixteenth Street
Suite 500
Silver Spring, MD 20910
301-588-1800
Fax: 301-588-2049

195

E-mail: sgriffin@ncss.org
http://www.socialstudies.org
Provides new ideas, resources, techniques, and skills that will pay off in the classroom, school, district, and invigorate your career. Features more than 400 sessions, workshops, poster presentations, clinics, tours, speakers and panels, and social events.

December

David Bailor, Meetings/Exhibits Director
Susan Griffin, Executive Director

3406 National Council of English Teachers Conference

National Council of Teachers of English
1111 W Kenyon Road
Urbana, IL 61801-1096
217-328-3870
800-369-6283
Fax: 217-328-9645
E-mail: public_info@ncte.org
http://www.ncte.org

Annual/November

Keith Gilyard, Program Chair

3407 National Education Association Annual Meeting

National Education Association (NEA)
1201 16th Street NW
Washington, DC 20036-3290
202-833-4000
Fax: 202-822-7974
E-mail: ncuea@nea.org
http://www.nea.org
A general conference that addresses all facets and concerns of the educator.

July

Gloria Durgin, Conference Contact
Dennis Van Roekel, President

3408 National Educational Computing Conference

Washington State Convention & Trade Center
Walter E Washington Convention Cent
Washington, DC 20001
800-336-5191
Fax: 206-694-5399
E-mail: neccinfo@iste.org
http://www.center.uoregon.edu/ISTE
NECC has been the premier forum in which to learn, exchange, and survey the field of educational technology.

June
417 booths with 12,500 attendees

Dr Heidi Rogers, First Executive Director
Trina Davis, President

3409 National Occupational Information Coordinating Committee Conference

2100 M Street NW
Suite 156
Washington, DC 20037-1207
202-653-7680
Focuses on policy, social issues and social services addressing career development and occupational information.

August

Mary Susan Vickers, Conference Contact

3410 New Mexico School Boards Association Conference

New Mexico School Boards Association
300 Galisteo Street
Suite 204
Santa Fe, NM 87501
505-983-5041
Fax: 505-983-2450
E-mail: nmsba1@nm.net
http://www.nmsba.org

The New Mexico School Boards Association aspires to be recognized as the premier source of development and support for local boards of education in New Mexico.

February
20 booths

Elizabeth Egelhoff, Programs Director

3411 New York School Superintendents Association Annual Meeting

111 Washington Avenue
Suite 404
Albany, NY 12210-2210
518-449-1063
Fax: 518-426-2229
Provides leadership and membership services through a professional organization of school superintendents.

October
50 booths

Dr. Claire Brown, Conference Contact

3412 New York Science Teachers Association Annual Meeting

2449 Union Boulevard
Apartment 20B
Islip, NY 11751-3117
516-783-5432
Fax: 516-783-5432
Education related publications, equipment, supplies and services.

November
110 booths

Harold Miller, Conference Contact

3413 New York State United Teachers Conference

159 Wolf Road
Albany, NY 12205-1106
518-213-6000
Fax: 518-213-6415
http://www.nysut.org

February
40 booths

Anthony Bifaro, Conference Contact

3414 New York Teachers Math Association Conference

92 Governor Drive
Scotia, NY 12302-4802
518-399-0149

October-November
50 booths

Phil Reynolds, Conference Contact

3415 North Carolina Association for Career and Technical Education Conference

Association for Career and Technical Education
1410 King Street
Alexandria, VA 22314
703-683-3311
800-826-9972
Fax: 703-683-7424
http://www.acteonline.org

July
110 booths with 3000 + attendees

Gary Moore, President
Tom H Jones, Executive Director

3416 North Central Association Annual Meeting

North Central Association Commission on Accred.
9115 Westside Parkway
Alpharetta, GA 30009-1008
866-837-2229
800-525-9517
Fax: 480-773-6901

E-mail: denz@ncacasi.org
http://www.ncacasi.org
Founded in 1895, NCA CASI accredits over 8,500 public and private schools in 19 states, the Navajo Nation, and the Department of Defense Schools. NCA CASI is an accreditation division of AdvancED.

April
30 booths with 1,800 attendees

William Fisher, CEO
Jay Cummings, Dean, College of Education,

3417 North Central Conference on Summer Sessions Conference

North Central Conference on Summer Sessions
University of Wisconsin
410 S 3rd Street
River Falls, WI 54022
715-425-3851
Fax: 715-425-3785
http://www.nccss.org
This conference attracts a wide variety range of attendees, from faculty, admissions personnel, registrars, business office and marketing representatives, and a wide variety of academic and student affairs administrators with responsibility for overseeing or direecting some aspect of their institution's summer session activities.

Annual/March

William V Weber, President
Robert Griggs, President-Elect

3418 Northeast Conference on the Teaching of Foreign Languages

Northeast Conference at Dickinson College
PO Box 1773
Carlisle, PA 17013-2896
717-243-5121
800-644-1773
Fax: 717-245-1976
E-mail: nectfl@dickinson.edu
http://www.nectfl.org
NECTFL aspires to serve the diverse community of language professionals through responsive leadership in its outreach activities and its annual conference.

April
160 booths with 2500 attendees

Rebecca Kline, Executive Director
Susan M Shaffer, Associate Executive Director

3419 Northeast Teachers Foreign Language Conference

Northeast Conference at Dickinson College
PO Box 1773
Carlisle, PA 17013-2896
717-243-5121
800-644-1773
Fax: 802-654-2595
E-mail: nectfl@dickinson.edu
http://www.nectfl.org
Foreign language textbooks, supplementary materials, audio equipment, computer software, travel abroad program materials and other related teaching aids and publications.

April
130 booths

Rebecca Kline, Executive Director

3420 Northwest Association of Schools & Colleges Annual Meeting

1910 University Drive
Boise, ID 83725-1060
208-426-1000
Fax: 208-334-3228
http://www.boisestate.edu
The university offers more than 190 fields of interest. Undergraduate, graduate and technical programs are available in seven colleges: Arts and Sciences, Business and Economics, Education, Engineering, Graduate Studies, Health Sciences, and Social Sciences and Public Affairs. Students

can also study abroad and participate in one of the largest internship programs in the Northwest.

December
120 attendees

Bob Kustra, President
Martin Schimpf, Vice President for Academic

3421 Northwest Regional Educational Laboratory Conference

101 SW Main Street
Suite 500
Portland, OR 97204-3213
503-275-9500
800-547-6339
Fax: 503-275-0660
E-mail: info@nwrel.org
http://www.nwrel.org
The mission of the Northwest Regional Educational Laboratory (NWREL) is to improve learning by building capacity in schools, families, and communities through applied research and development

October/November

Jeffrey Weldon, Chairperson
Steve Bradshaw, Vice Chairperson

3422 Ohio Business Teachers Association

Wright State University, Lake Campus
2350 Westbelt Drive
Colcumbus, OH 43228-2921
419-586-0337
Fax: 419-586-0368
E-mail: MCWhite@itt-tech.edu
http://www.obta-ohio.org
Promote among educators the desire to find better techniques and methods in an effort to improve instruction in the field of business so that the students are well prepared to take their place in the business world.

October
40 booths

Daniel McCarthy, President
Stella Hull, Treasurer

3423 Ohio Public School Employees Association Convention

6805 Oak Creek Drive
Columbus, OH 43229
614-890-4770
800-786-2773
Fax: 614-890-3540
http://www.oapse.org
Committed in developing the most effective programs in the labor movement today.

May
15 booths

Joseph P Rugola, Executive Director
JoAnn Johntony, State President

3424 Ohio Secondary School Administrators Association Conference

Ohio Association of Secondary School Administrator
8050 N High Street
Suite 180
Columbus, OH 43235-6484
614-430-8311
Fax: 614-430-8315
http://www.oassa.org
Offers school secretaries the opportunity to network with colleagues while gaining valuable information that will add to their performance. Current administrators, representatives from the business community, OASSA legal counsel, and fellow secre-

taries combine to update these valuable employees.

April
42 booths

James J Harbuck, Executive Director
JoAnne Rubsam, Conference Secretary

3425 Oklahoma School Boards Association & School Administrators Conference

2801 N Lincoln Boulevard
Suite 125
Oklahoma City, OK 73105-4223
405-528-3571
888-528-3571
Fax: 405-528-5695
http://www.ossba.org
The mission of the Oklahoma State School Boards Association shall be to offer services to safeguard,represent and improve public education.The Association shall represent the interests of public school boards before the legislature; provide training programs for school board members; provide school system services; and provide to the individual school board members a variety of other services and information that will improve the quality of educational leadership for each school district in Okla

August
195 booths

Joann Yandell, Conference Contact
Beth Schieber, President

3426 Oregon School Boards Association Annual Convention

Oregon School Boards Association
1201 Court Street NE
Suite 400
Salem, OR 97301
503-588-2800
800-578-6722
Fax: 503-588-2813
E-mail: info@osba.org
http://www.osba.org
To improve student achievement through advocacy, leadership and services to Oregon public school boards.

November

Kevin McCann, Executive Director

3427 PDK International Conference

Int'l Honor and Professional Assoc in Education
PO Box 7888
Bloomington, IN 47407-7888
812-339-1156
800-766-1156
Fax: 812-339-0018
E-mail: plt@pdkintl.org
http://www.pilambda.org
Conference on Innovations in Teaching and Learning was selected because of its relevance to educators everywhere as new and effective educational practices continue to emerge. Includes interactive sessions, research presentations, and networking events.

Annual/February
400 attendees

Bill Bushaw, Executive Director

3428 PSBA School Board Secretaries and Affiliates Conference

Pennsylvania School Boards Association
PO Box 2042
Mechanicsburg, PA 17055
717-506-2450
Fax: 717-506-2451
http://www.psba.org

To promote excellence in school board governance through leadership, service and advocacy for public education.

October
140 booths

Thomas J Gentzel, Executive Director

3429 Pacific Northwest Council on Languages Annual Conference

5290 University of Oregon
Eugene, OR 97403
541-346-5699
Fax: 541-346-6303
E-mail: pncfl@uoregon.edu
http://www.pncfl.org
The Pacific Northwest Council for Languages unites, serves, and supports all world language educators in Alaska, Idaho, Montana, Oregon, Washington, and Wyoming.

April

Brenda Gaver, President
Laura Kiolet, Executive Director

3430 Pennsylvania Council for the Social Studies Conference

Pennsylvania Council for the Social Studies
1212 Smallman Street
Senator John Heinz Regional Histiry Cnt
Pittsburgh, PA 15222-4200
717-238-8768
E-mail: JKEARNEY@CBSD.ORG
http://www.pcssonline.org
The PCSS promotes quality Social Studies education from kindergarten to higher learning by advocating the Social Studies at all levels of education in Pennsylvania.

October
50 booths with 500 attendees

David Trevaskis, President elect
Don Imler, Executive Secretary

3431 Pennsylvania Science Teachers Association

Center for Science & Technology Education
PO Box 330
Shippenville, PA 16254-330
814-782-6301
http://www.pascience.org
Work towards the advancement, improvement, and coordination of science education in all areas of science at all educational levels.

December
70 booths

Keith Butler, President
Kathleen Conn, President-Elect

3432 Principals' Center Spring Institute Conference

Harvard Graduate School of Education
6 Appian Way
#336
Cambridge, MA 02138-3704
617-495-1825
Fax: 617-495-5900
http://www.gse.harvard.edu
Administrative professionals get together to discuss issues, policy and procedures.

April

Nindy Leroy, Conference Contact

3433 Restructuring Curriculum Conference

National School Conference Institute
PO Box 35099
Phoenix, AZ 85069-5099
602-674-8990
Presents research, studies, and new information relevant to curriculum development.

January

3434 SAI Annual Conference
School Administrators of Iowa
12199 Stratford Drive
Clive, IA 50325
515-267-1115
Fax: 515-267-1066
E-mail: dsmith@sai-iowa.org
http://www.sai-iowa.org
August
Dr Dan Smith, Executive Director

3435 SchoolTech Forum
Miller Freeman
600 Harrison Street
San Francisco, CA 94109
415-947-6657
Fax: 415-947-6015
National forum for educational technology
professional development and exhibits, devoted to intensive instruction by today's
leading practitioners, eye-opening special
events, unparalleled networking opportunities, and exposure to products and
services.

**3436 South Carolina Library
Association Conference**
South Carolina Library Association
PO Box 1763
Columbia, SC 29202
803-252-1087
Fax: 803-252-0589
E-mail: scla@capconsc.com
http://www.scla.org
Annual/October
125 booths with 350 attendees
Adam Haigh, President
Donald Wood, Executive Secretary

**3437 Southern Association Colleges &
Schools**
1866 Southern Lane
Decatur, GA 30033-4097
404-679-4500
Fax: 404-679-4556
http://www.sacs.org
Exhibits publications, data and word pro-
cessing equipment, school photography,
charter bus services and more.
December
50 booths with 3700 attendees
Dr. James Rogers, Chief Academic
Officer

**3438 Southern Early Childhood Annual
Convention**
Southern Early Childhood Association
PO Box 55930
Little Rock, AR 72215-5930
501-221-1648
800-305-7322
Fax: 501-227-5297
E-mail:
info@southernearlychildhood.org
http://www.southernearlychildhood.org
Southern Early Childhood Association has
brought together preschool, kindergarten,
and primary teachers and administrators,
caregivers, program directors, and individuals working with and for families, to promote quality care and education for young
children.
January
2,500 attendees
Janie Humphries, President
Glenda Bean, Executive Director

3439 Superintendents Work Conference
Teachers College, Columbia University
525 W 120th Street
PO Box 179
New York, NY 10027-6696
212-678-7449
Fax: 212-678-3682
E-mail: swc@tc.columbia.edu
http://www.superintendentsworkconferen
ce.com
Offers practicing school superintendents a
unique opportunity for professional
growth in stimulating surroundings.
July
60 attendees
Thomas Sobol, Conference Chair
Gibran Matdalany, Associate Chair

3440 TASA/TASB Convention
Texas Association of School Boards
PO Box 400
Austin, TX 78767-0400
512-467-0222
800-580-8272
Fax: 512-467-3554
E-mail: tasb@tasb.org
http://www.tasb.org
Offers school board members and school
administrators the opportunity to earn almost 17 hours of continuing education
credit, hear outstnading keynote speakers,
explore a tradeshow with hundreds of exhibitors, and network with more than 6,000
public school officials.
September-October
James B Crow, Executive Director

**3441 Teachers Association in Instruction
Conference**
150 W Market Street
Indianapolis, IN 46204-2806
317-634-1515
Exhibits a wide variety of teaching materi-
als and information from Grades K-12.
October
150 booths
Barbara Stainbrook, Conference Contact

**3442 Tennessee School Boards
Association Conference**
525 Brick Church Park Drive
Nashville, TN 37207-2884
615-815-3900
800-448-6465
Fax: 615-815-3911
E-mail: webadmin@tsba.net
http://www.tsba.net
The mission of the Tennessee School
Boards Associationis to assisst school
boards in effectively governing school dis-
tricts.
November
60 booths with 1,000 attendees
Tammy Grissom, Executive Director
David Pickler, President

**3443 Texas Middle School Association
Conference**
Texas Middle School Association
PO Box 152499
Austin, TX 78715-2499
512-462-1105
888-529-8672
Fax: 512-462-0991
E-mail: tmsa@austin.rr.com
http://www.tmsanet.org
To promote the implementation of stu-
dent-centered programs and highly effec-
tive practices by providing vision,
knowledge, and resources which meet the
unique individual needs of adolescents in
an ever-changing society.
February
Cecil Floyd, Executive Director

3444 Texas State Teachers Association
316 W 12th Street
Austin, TX 78701-1815
877-275-8782
Fax: 512-476-9555
http://www.tsta.org
The Texas State Teachers Association will unite,
organize and empower public education advocates to shape public education in Texas thus providing a quality public school for every child
April
120 booths
Carla Bond, Conference Contact
Rita Haecker, President

3445 Training & Presentations
Chief Manufacturing, Inc.
6436 City West Parkway
Eden Prairie, MN 55344-4839
612-894-6280
800-582-6480
Fax: 877-894-6918
E-mail: chief@chiefmfg.com
http://www.chiefmfg.com
Providing top quality mounting solutions for pro-
jectors, monitors, and flat panel TVs. Committed
to responding to industry needs in Commercial,
Residential and Workstation/IT markets, Chief is
dedicated to producing solutions that packed with
form, function, and flexibility
Chicago, Illinois
February
Kris Murray, Director Customer Service/Pr
Yvette Danz, Manager Customer Service

3446 UPCEA Annual Conference
University Professional/Continuing Education
Assoc
One Dupont Circle
Suite 615
Washington, DC 20036
202-659-3130
Fax: 202-785-0374
E-mail: nkats@upcea.edu
http://www.ucea.edu
The largest single gathering of higher education
professionals who develop, implement, and pro-
mote professional and continuing education and
online learning in North America.
April
70 booths with 1,000 attendees
Robert Hansen, CEO/Executive Director
Natalia Kats, Conference Director

3447 USA Kansas Annual Convention
United School Administrators of Kansas
515 S Kansas Avenue
Suite 201
Topeka, KS 66603
785-232-6566
Fax: 785-232-9776
E-mail: usaoffice@usa-ks.org
http://www.usakansas.org
Offers quality professional development opportu-
nities for education administrators and leaders.
During the convention, administrators are able to
participate in professional workshops or learning
clusters.
180 booths
Cheryl Semmel, Executive Director

3448 VAIS Conference
Virginia Association of Independent Schools
6802 Paragon Place
Suite 525
Richmond, VA 23230
804-282-3592
Fax: 804-282-3596
E-mail: info@vais.org
http://www.vais.org
The Virginia Association of Independent Schools
is a service organization that promotes educa-
tional, ethical and professional excellence.

Through its school evaluation/accreditation program, attention to professional development and insistence on integrity, the Association safeguards the interests of its member schools.

November
1,500 attendees

Dr Sally K Boese, Executive Director

3449 Virginia ASCD Conference

Virginia ASCD
513 Half Mile Branch
Crozet, VA 22932
434-960-7732
E-mail: annetchison@earthlink.net
http://vaascd.org
Dedicated to advancing excellence in Teaching, Learning and Leadership.

December
30 booths with 600 attendees

Ann Etchison, Executive Director
Judy Lam, Administrative Coordinator

3450 Virginia Association of Elementary School Principals Conference

Virginia Assoc of Elementary School
Principals
1805 Chantilly Street
Richmond, VA 23230
804-355-6791
Fax: 804-355-1196
E-mail: info@vaesp.org
http://www.vaesp.org
Nonprofit professional association advocating for public education and equal educational opportunities. Promotes leadership of school administrators, principal as educational leaders, and provides professional development opportunities.

50 booths with 300 attendees

James Baldwin, Interim Executive Director

3451 Virginia School Boards Association Conference

Virginia School Boards Association
200 Hansen Road
Charlottesville, VA 22911
434-295-8722
800-446-8722
Fax: 434-295-8785
http://www.vsba.org
A voluntary, self-supporting and nonpartisan organization that promotes quality education through its services for local school boards. Provides member boards with services, training, and advocacy so that they may exercise effective leadership in public school governance on behalf of public education for all the children of the Commonwealth.

Annual/November

Barbara J Coyle, Executive Director
Gina G Patterson, Assistant Executive Director

3452 Wisconsin Association of School Boards Annual Conference

Wisconsin Association of School Boards
122 W Washington Avenue
Suite 400
Madison, WI 53703
608-257-2622
Fax: 608-257-8386
E-mail: convention@wasb.org
http://www.wasb.org
The WASB provides background and support for elected school leaders as they do the difficult work of democracy: weighing and balancing the unique values of their communities.

January
370 booths with 3,000 attendees

John Ashley, Executive Director

3453 Wisconsin Association of School District Administrators Conference

Wisconsin Assoc of School District
Administrators
4797 Hayes Road
Suite 201
Madison, WI 53704
608-242-1090
Fax: 608-242-1290
E-mail: mturner@wasda.org
http://www.wasda.org
The premiere collaborative leadership association, serves superintendents by providing professional support and expanding their capacity to be effective, innovative leaders.

Annual/May
70 booths

Miles Turner, Executive Director
Nancy Lund, Executive Assistant

3454 Wisconsin School Administrators Association Conference

Association of Wisconsin School
Administrators
4797 Hayes Road
Suite 103
Madison, WI 53704
608-241-0300
Fax: 608-249-4973
E-mail: patricia@awsa.org
http://www.awsa.org
The Association of Wisconsin School Administrators exists to coordinate the collective interests and needs of school administrators and to enhance their professional growth and competency for the purpose of improving the quality of educational opportunities for the youth of Wisconsin

October
60 booths

Jim Lynch, Executive Director
Kelly Meyers, Associate Executive Director

Directories & Handbooks

3455 American Association of Colleges for Teacher Education-Directory

American Association of Colleges for
Teacher Ed.
1307 New York Avenue NW
Suite 300
Washington, DC 20005
202-293-2450
Fax: 202-457-8095
E-mail: aacte@aacte.org
http://www.aacte.org
Promote the learning of all PK-12 students through high-quality, evidence-based preparation and continuing education for all school personnel.

144 pages Annual
ISSN: 0516-9313

Sharon P Robinson, President/CEO
Jeannette Knight-Mills, Associate Director Executive

3456 American Society for Training/Development-Training Video

American Society for Training &
Development
1640 King Street
Box 1443
Alexandria, VA 22313-1443
703-683-8100
800-628-2783
Fax: 703-683-8103
E-mail: customercare@astd.org
http://www.astd.org

Serves as the educational society for persons engaged in training and development of business, industry, education and government personnel.

Tony Bingham, President/CEO
Cindy Huggett, Chair

3457 Appropriate Inclusion and Paraprofessionals

National Education Association (NEA)
1201 16th Street NW
Washington, DC 20036-3290
202-833-4000
Fax: 202-822-7974
E-mail: ncuea@nea.org
http://www.nea.org
A book offering information on mainstreaming disabled students and the work of paraprofessionals in the education process.

10 pages

Dennis Van Roekel, President
Lily Eskelsen, Vice President

3458 Assessing Student Performance: Exploring the Purpose and Limits of Testing

Jossey-Bass/Pfeiffer
989 Market Street
San Francisco, CA 94103-1741
415-433-1740
Fax: 415-433-0499
E-mail: info@wiley.com
http://www.josseybass.com
Clarifies the limits of testing in an assessment system. Analyzes problematic practices in test design and formats that prevent students from explaining their answers by showing that assessment is more than testing and intellectual performance is more than right answers.

336 pages Softcover
ISBN: 0-7879-5047-5

3459 Association for Continuing Higher Education Directory

1700 Asp Avenue
Norman, OK 73072-6400
405-329-0249
800-807-2243
Fax: 405-325-7196
E-mail: admin@acheinc.org
http://www.acheinc.org
Dedicated to promoting lifelong learning and excellence in continuing higher education. Encourage professional development, research and exchange of information for its members and continuing higher education as a means of enhancing and improving society.

102 pages Annual/March
10 booths with 250 attendees

James P Pappas, Executive VP
Rick E Osborn, President

3460 BBX Teacher Clearinghouse

175 Norwood Road
Silver Spring, MD 20905
301-628-9776
Fax: 301-989-9606
E-mail: CEO@BBXOnline.com
http://www.teachersclearinghouse.com
BBX's Teacher Clearinghouse is a comprehensive resume databank where elementary and secondary school teachers, administrators, and education majors can post their resumes at no charge for review by subscribing school districts. Subscribers are public and private schools with an interest in receiving applications from, and importantly, a commitment to hiring, members of the African American/Black communities.

J R Moore, Administrator

3461 Before the School Bell Rings
Phi Delta Kappa Educational Foundation
320 W Eight Street
Suite 216
Bloomington, IN 47404
812-339-1156
800-766-1156
Fax: 812-339-0018
E-mail: memberservices@pdkintl.org
http://www.pdkintl.org
Early childhood teachers and administrators, childcare providers and parents will enjoy and learn from this practical, insightful book.

84 pages Paperback
ISBN: 0-87367-476-6

Carol B Hillman, Author
George Kersey, Executive Director
Donovan R Walling, Editor, Special Publications

3462 Beyond Tracking: Finding Success in Inclusive Schools
Phi Delta Kappa Educational Foundation
PO Box 7888
Bloomington, IN 47407-7888
812-339-1156
800-766-1156
Fax: 812-339-0018
E-mail: memberservices@pdkintl.org
http://www.pdkintl.org
Research data, practical ideas and reports from educators involved in untracking schools make this an authoritative and useful collection of important articles.

293 pages Hardcover
ISBN: 0-87367-470-7

Harbison Pool and Jane A Page, Author
George Kersey, Executive Director
Donovan R Walling, Dir Publications/Research

3463 Book of Metaphors, Volume II
AEE and Kendall/Hunt Publishing Company
4050 Westmark Drive
P.O Box 1840
Dubuque, IA 52004-1840
563-589-1000
800-228-0810
Fax: 800-772-9165
E-mail: orders@kendallhunt.com
http://www.kendallhunt.com
A compilation of presentations designed to enhance learning for those participating in adventure-based programs. Practitioners share how they prepare experiences for presentations.

256 pages Paperback
ISBN: 0-7872-0306-8

AEE, Author
Karen Berger, Customer Service Assistant

3464 Brief Legal Guide for the Independent Teacher
441 Vine Street
Suite 505
Cincinnati, OH 45202-2811
Offering insights into the most common legal issues faced by independent music teachers.

28 pages

3465 Building Life Options: School-Community Collaborations
Academy for Educational Development
1255 23rd Street NW
Washington, DC 20037-1125
202-884-8800
Fax: 202-884-8400

A handbook for family life educators on how to prevent pregnancy in the middle grades.

3466 Closing the Achievement Gap
Master Teacher
Leadership Lane
PO Box 1207
Manhattan, KS 66505-1207
785-539-0555
800-669-9633
Fax: 800-669-1132
http://www.masterteacher.com
A complete step-by-step approach to building a system that narrows the gap between student potenial and student performance— between success and failure.

162 pages
ISBN: 0-914607-73-1

Kristy Meeks, Author

3467 Coming Up Short? Practices of Teacher Educators Committed to Character
Character Education Partnership
1025 Connecticut Avenue NW
Suite 1011
Washington, DC 20036
202-296-7743
800-988-8081
Fax: 202-296-7779
E-mail: rsipos@character.org
http://www.character.org
Nonprofit, nonpartisan, nonsectarian coalition of organizations and individuals committed to fostering effective character education in our nation's K-12 schools.

Henry Huffman, Author
Rebecca Sipos, Director Communications
Anne Bryant, Executive Director

3468 Competency-Based Framework for Professional Development of Certified Health Specialists
Nat'l Health Education Credentialing
1541 Alta Drive
Suite 303
Whitehall, PA 18052-5642
484-223-0770
888-624-3248
Fax: 800-813-0727
http://www.nchec.org
Aims to help the health education profession provide the leadership necessary for improving health in a rapidly changing, culturally pluralistic and technologically complex society. Provides universities, professional organizations, and accreditation a common basis of skills for the development, assessment, and improvement of professional preparation for health educators.

Linda Lysoby, Executive Director
Melissa Rehrig, Communication Director

3469 Contracting Out: Strategies for Fighting Back
National Education Association (NEA)
1201 16th Street NW
Washington, DC 20036-3290
202-833-4000
Fax: 202-822-7974
E-mail: ncuea@nea.org
http://www.nea.org
The voice of education professionals. Advocate for education professionals

John I Wilson, Executive Director
Dennis Van Roekel, President

3470 Directory of Curriculum Materials Centers
PO Box 399
Addison, IL 60101-0399
630-833-5300
877-850-2300
Fax: 630-833-5303
E-mail: info@telusys.net
http://www.telusys.com
Listing of over 275 centers that have collections of curriculum materials to aid in elementary and secondary teaching preparation.

200 pages

Jackie Bedell, Supervisor
Ruth Miller, Supervisor

3471 Distance Learning Directory
Virginia A Ostendorf
PO Box 2896
Littleton, CO 80161-2896
303-797-3131
Fax: 303-797-3524
E-mail: ostendorf@vaostendorf.com
Comprehensive list of distance learning practitioners and vendors. Each listing includes names, addresses, e-mail, fax and phones, credits awarded, program content, peripherals and technologies used, class configurations and more. Includes a lists of vendors offering descriptions of distance learning products, services and programming.

308 pages Annual

Virginia A Ostendorf, President
Ronald Ostendorf, VP

3472 Education Index
H.W. Wilson Company
950 University Avenue
Bronx, NY 10452-4224
718-588-8400
800-367-6770
Fax: 718-590-1617
E-mail: rsky@hwwilson.com
http://www.hwwilson.com
Contains more than 456,000 citations to articles, interviews, editorials and letters, reviews of books, educational films, and software in the field of education. Available electronically on the Web with index, abstracts and full text versions.

Monthly

Roseward Sky, Assistant Manager/Marketing
Harold Regan, President

3473 Educational Administration Resource Centre Database
3-300 Edmonton Clinic Health Academy
11405-87 Ave
Edmonton, AB G1C9
780-492-0560
Fax: 780-492-0364
E-mail: school.publichealth@ualberta.ca
http://www.publichealth.ualberta.ca
Over 3,650 bibliographic descriptions of the Centre's collection of educational administration print and audiovisual materials.

Laing Lory, Interim Dean

3474 Ethical Issues in Experiential Education
AEE and Kendall/Hunt Publishing Company
4050 Westmark Drive
Dubuque, IA 52002-2624
319-589-1000
800-228-0810
Fax: 800-772-9165
http://www.kendallhunt.com
An examination of ethical issues in the field of adventure programming and experiential education. Topics include ethical theory, informed consent,

sexual issues, student rights, environmental concerns and programming practices.

144 pages
ISBN: 0-7872-93083

Karen Berger, Customer Service Assistant

3475 Finishing Strong: Your Personal Mentoring & Planning Guide for the Last 60 Days of Teaching

Master Teacher
Leadership Lane
PO Box 1207
Manhattan, KS 66505-1207
785-539-0555
800-669-9633
Fax: 800-669-1132
http://www.masterteacher.com
In this book we've selected from the 32 years of The Master Teacher, the writings we know you would most like your teachers to have to support that last 60 days of the school year.

132 pages
ISBN: 1-58992-095-3

Robert L De Bruyn, Author

3476 How to Plan and Develop a Career Center

Center on Education and Work
1025 W Johnson Street
Room 964
Madison, WI 53706-1796
608-265-6700
800-862-1071
Fax: 608-262-3063
E-mail: cewmail@education.wisc.edu
http://www.cew.wisc.edu
High school, postsecondary, adult, and virtual career centers-a comprehensive blueprint that covers all the bases.

3477 How to Raise Test Scores

Skylight Professional Development
1900 E Lake Avenue
Glenview, IL 60025
847-657-7450
800-348-4474
Fax: 847-486-3183
E-mail: info@skylightedu.com
http://www.skylightedu.com
Addresses the teaching and learning process at its most basic and important level-the classroom.

30 pages Softcover
ISBN: 1575171635

Robin Fogarty, Author

3478 Inclusion: The Next Step DVD

Master Teacher
Leadership Lane
PO Box 1207
Manhattan, KS 66505-1207
785-539-0555
800-669-9633
Fax: 800-669-1132
http://www.masterteacher.com
Offers practical help for regular classroom teachers and special education teachers in meeting the challenges of inclusion.

225 pages
ISBN: 0-914607-69-3

Wendy Dover, Author

3479 Law of Teacher Evaluation: A Self-Assessment Handbook

Phi Delta Kappa Educational Foundation
PO Box 7888
Bloomington, IN 47407-7888
812-339-1156
800-766-1156

Fax: 812-339-0018
http://www.pdkintl.org
This handy guidebook provides a concise, authoritative overview of US state statutes, regulations and guidelines regarding the performance evaluation of educators.

51 pages Paperback
ISBN: 0-87367-488-X

Perry A. Zirkel, Author
DR Walling, Director Publications/Resear

3480 Learning for Life

1329 W Walnut Hill Lane
PO Box 152225
Irving, TX 75015-2225
972-580-2433
855-806-9992
Fax: 972-580-2137
E-mail: exploring@lflmail.org
http://www.learning-for-life.org
Learning for Life is designed to support schools and other youth-serving organizations in their efforts toward preparing youth to successfully handle the complexities of today's society and to enhance their self-confidence, motivation, and self-worth.

Diane E Thornton, National Director
William E Taylor, Director of Criminal Justice

3481 Lesson Plans for the Substitue Teacher: Elementary Edition

Master Teacher
Po Box 1207
Manhattan, KS 66505-1207
785-539-0555
800-669-9633
Fax: 800-669-1132
http://www.masterteacher.com
Gives you more than 100 lessons developed and tested by teachers across the curriculum and at all grade levels.

145 pages
ISBN: 1-58992-107-0

Robert L DeBruyn, Author

3482 Libraries Unlimited

PO Box 1911
Santa Barbara, CA 93116-1911
800-368-6868
800-225-5800
Fax: 805-968-1911
E-mail: CustomerService@abc-clio.com
http://www.lu.com
Publisher of resource books written by educators for educators. The books offer innovative ideas, practical lessons, and classroom-tested activities in the areas of math, science, social studies, whole language literature and library connections.

Debby LaBoon, Manager of Authors/Workshops

3483 Life Skills Training

711 Westchester Avenue
White Plains, NY 10604
914-421-2525
800-293-4969
Fax: 914-421-2007
E-mail: lstinfo@nhpamail.com
http://www.LifeSkillsTraining.com
Botvin LifeSkills Training (LST) is a research-validated substance abuse prevention program proven to reduce the risks of alcohol, tobacco, drug abuse, and violence by targeting the major social and psychological factors that promote the initiation of substance use and other risky behaviors.

Gilbert J Botvin, Developer

3484 List of Regional, Professional & Specialized Accrediting Association

Educational Information Services
PO Box 662
Newton Lower Falls, MA 02162
617-964-4555
A list of those associations involved in accreditation for the education fields.

3485 MacMillan Guide to Correspondence Study

MacMillan Publishing Company
1633 Broadway
New York, NY 10019
212-512-2000
Fax: 800-835-3202
Listing of 175 colleges, accredited trade, technical and vocational schools that offer home study courses.

500 pages

3486 Middle Grades Education in an Era of Reform

Academy for Educational Development
1255 23rd Street NW
Washington, DC 20037-1125
202-884-8800
Fax: 202-884-8400
Reviews middle-grades educational reform policies and practices.

3487 Middle School Teachers Guide to FREE Curriculum Materials

Educators Progress Service
214 Center Street
Randolph, WI 53956-1408
920-326-3126
888-951-4469
Fax: 920-326-3127
E-mail: epsinc@centurytel.net
http://www.freeteachingaids.com
Lists and describes free supplementary teaching aids for the middle school and junior high level.

290 pages Annual
ISBN: 87708-401-7

Kathy Nehmer, President

3488 NASDTEC Knowledge Base

1629 K Street NW
Suite 300
Washington, DC 20006
202-204-2208
Fax: 202-204-2210
E-mail: rje@nasdtec.com
http://www.nasdtec.org
It is the organization that represents professional standards boards and commissions and state departments of education in all 50 states, the District of Columbia, the Department of Defense Education Activity, the U.S. Territories, Alberta, British Columbia, and Ontario that are responsible for the preparation, licensure, and discipline of educational personnel.

Annually
ISBN: 0-9708628-3-0

Phillip Rogers, Executive Director

3489 Orators & Philosophers: A History of the Idea of Liberal Education

College Board Publications
45 Columbus Avenue
New York, NY 10023-6992
212-713-8165
800-323-7155
Fax: 212-713-8143
E-mail: aces@info.collegeboard.org
http://www.collegeboard.org
A cogent study of the historical evolution of the idea of liberal education. Clearly and forcefully argued, the book portrays this evolution as a struggle between two contending

points of view, one oratorical and the other philosophical.

308 pages

Bruce A Kimball, Author
David Coleman, President

3490 Parent Training Resources

PACER Center
8161 Normandale Boulevard
Bloomington, MN 55437
952-838-0190
800-537-2237
Fax: 952-838-0199
E-mail: pacer@pacer.org
http://www.pacer.org
A Minnesota nonprofit, tax-exempt organization that provides information, training, and assistance to parents of children and young adults with all disabilities; physical, learning, cognitive, emotional, and health

130 pages

Paula F Goldberg, Executive Director
Mary Schrock, Chief Operating and Developm

3491 Personal Planner and Training Guide for the Paraprofessional

Master Teacher
Po Box 1207
Manhattan, KS 66505-1207
785-539-0555
800-669-9633
Fax: 800-669-1132
http://www.masterteacher.com
Includes numerous forms which allow each para to keep track of vital information he or she will need in working with specific teachers and their special students.

128 pages
ISBN: 0-914607-39-1

Wendy Dover, Author

3492 Practical Handbook for Assessing Learning Outcomes in Continuing Education

International Association for Continuing Education
1760 Old Meadow Road
Suite 500
McLean, VA 22102
703-506-3275
Fax: 703-506-3266
http://www.iacet.org
Innovative guide offers readers a series of steps to help select an assessment plan which will work for any organization.

Michael Todd Shinholster, President
Kristopher Newbauer, President-Elect

3493 Principles of Good Practice in Continuing Education

International Association for Continuing Education
1760 Old Meadow Road
Suite 500
McLean, VA 22102
703-506-3275
Fax: 703-506-3266
http://www.iacet.org
Principles from many sources for the field of continuing education, placing a pervasive emphasis on learning outcomes for the individual learner.

Michael Todd Shinholster, President
Kristopher Newbauer, President-Elect

3494 Professional Learning Communities at Work

National Educational Service
65 West Shore Drive
Enfield, CT 06082

860-763-2609
800-733-6786
Fax: 812-336-7790
E-mail: nes@nesonline.com
http://www.nesonline.com
This publication provides specific, practical, how-to information on the best practices in use in schools through the US and Canada for curriculum development, teacher preparation, school leadership, professional development programs, school-parent partnerships, assessment practices and much more.

3495 Programs for Preparing Individuals for Careers in Special Education

The Council for Exceptional Children
1920 Association Drive
Reston, VA 20191-1545
703-620-3660
800-232-7323
Fax: 703-264-1637
This directory offers over 600 colleges and universities with programs in special education. Information includes institution name, address, contact person, telephone, fax, Internet, accreditation status, size of faculty, level of program, and areas of specialty.

256 pages

3496 Quality School Teacher

National Professional Resources
25 South Regent Street
Port Chester, NY 10573-8295
914-937-8897
800-453-7461
Fax: 914-937-8879
E-mail: service@nprinc.com
http://www.nprinc.com
Provides the specifics that classroom teachers are asking for as they begin the move to quality schools. It is written for educators who are trying to give up the old system of boss-managing, and to create classrooms that produce quality work.

144 pages
ISBN: 0060-952857

William Glasser, Author
Robert Hanson, President
Helene Hanson, VP

3497 Requirements for Certification of Teachers & Counselors

University of Chicago Press
5801 S Ellis Avenue
Floor 4
Chicago, IL 60637-5418
312-702-7700
800-621-2736
Fax: 800-621-8476
A list of state and local departments of education for requirements including teachers, counselors, librarians, and administrators for elementary and secondary schools.

256 pages Annual
ISBN: 0-226-42850-8

Elizabeth Kaye, Author
John Tryneski, Coordinating Education

3498 Research for Better Schools Publications

123 South Broad Street
Philadelphia, PA 19109-2471
215-568-6150
Fax: 215-568-7260
E-mail: info@rbs.org
http://www.rbs.org
RBS is a private, nonprofit educational organization funded primarily through grants and contracts from the U.S. Department of Education, the National Science

Foundation, Mid-Atlantic state departments of education, institutions of higher education, foundations, and school districts.

Dr. Keith M Kershner, Executive Director
Rev. John F Bloh, President

3499 Resources for Teaching Middle School Science

National Academy Press
901 D Street SW
Suite 704B
Washington, DC 20024-403
202-633-2966
Fax: 202-287-7309
E-mail: shulers@si.edu
http://www.nsrconline.org
The NSRC is an intermediary organization that bridges research on how children learn with best practices for the classroom.

496 pages

National Science Resources Center, Author
Sally Goetz Shuler, Executive Director
Tanya Miller, Executive Assistant

3500 Restructuring in the Classroom: Teaching, Learning, and School Organization

Jossey-Bass/Pfeiffer
989 Market Street
San Francisco, CA 94103-1741
415-433-1740
Fax: 415-433-0499
http://www.josseybass.com
Teaching, learning and school organization.

288 pages Hardcover
ISBN: 0-7879-0239-X

Riched Elmore, Penelope Peterson & Sara McCarthey, Author

3501 Revolution Revisited: Effective Schools and Systemic Reform

Phi Delta Kappa Educational Foundation
320 W Eight Street
Suite 216
Bloomington, IN 47404-3800
812-339-1156
800-766-1156
Fax: 812-339-0018
E-mail: memberservices@pdkintl.org
http://www.pdkintl.org
The authors examine the Effective Schools movement of the past quarter century as a school reform philosophy and renewal process for today and for the coming years.

132 pages Paperback
ISBN: 0-873674-83-9

BO Taylor and P Bullard, Author
Donovan R Walling, Director Publications/Resear
Kathleen Andreson, President

3502 Seminar Information Service

250 El Camino Real
Suite 112
Tustin, CA 92780-4469
714-508-0340
877-736-4636
Fax: 714-734-8027
E-mail: info@seminarinformation.com
http://www.seminarinformation.com
In 1981, Catherine Bellizzi and Mona Piontkowski founded Seminar Information Service, Inc. (SIS). Their idea was to fill a void - thousands of seminars were taking place, but there wasn't any one central source to tell someone where and when they were being held.

1,000 pages Annual

Mona Pointkowski, Co-Founder
Catherine Bellizzi, Co-Founder

3503 Service-Learning and Character Education: One Plus One is More Than Two
Character Education Partnership
1025 Connecticut Avenue NW
Suite 1011
Washington, DC 20036
202-296-7743
800-988-8081
Fax: 202-296-7779
E-mail: jmazzola@character.org
http://www.character.org
Leading the nation in helping schools develop people of good character for a just and compassionate society.

Rebecca Sipos, Director Communications
Joe Mazzola, Executive Director

3504 Teacher Created Resources
Teacher Created Resources
6421 Industry Way
Westminster, CA 92683-3652
888-343-4335
800-662-4321
Fax: 800-525-1524
E-mail: custserv@teachercreated.com
http://www.teachercreated.com
We publish quality resource books at the early childhood, elementary, and middle school levels. Our books cover all aspects of the curriculum—language arts, social studies, math, science, technology, and the arts.

Ina Levin, Managing Editor
Karen Goldfluss, Managing Editor

3505 Teachers as Educators of Character: Are the Nations Schools of Education Coming Up Short?
Character Education Partnership
1025 Connecticut Avenue NW
Suite 1011
Washington, DC 20036
202-296-7743
800-988-8081
Fax: 202-296-7779
E-mail: rsipos@character.org
http://www.character.org
Leading the nation in helping schools develop people of good character for a just and compassionate society.

Henry Huffman, Author
Rebecca Sipos, Director Communications
Joseph W Mazzola, Executive Director

3506 Teachers as Leaders
Phi Delta Kappa Educational Foundation
PO Box 7888
Bloomington, IN 47407-7888
812-339-1156
800-766-1156
Fax: 812-339-0018
http://www.pdkintl.org
Examines teacher recruitment, retention, professional development and leadership. The central theme of these twenty essays is excellence in education and how to achieve it.

320 pages Hardcover
ISBN: 0-873674-68-5

Donovan R Walling, Author
Donovan R Walling, Director Publications/Resear

3507 Teachers in Publishing
Pike Publishing Company
221 Town Center W
Suite 112
Santa Maria, CA 93458-5083
Editorial, research, sales, consulting, in office positions or travel to learn teachers' needs and instruct new texts.

3508 Teaching About Islam & Muslims in the Public School Classroom
9300 Gardenia Avenue
#B3
Fountain Valley, CA 92708-2253
714-839-2929
Fax: 714-839-2714
117 pages
ISBN: 1-930109-008

Susan Douglas, Author
Shabbir Mansuri, Founding Director

3509 Teaching as the Learning Profession: Handbook of Policy and Practice
Jossey-Bass/Pfeiffer
989 Market Street
San Francisco, CA 94103-1741
415-433-1740
Fax: 415-433-0499
Provides the best essays about the status of teaching, and the contributing writers are among the best thinkers in education today.

426 pages Hardcover

Linda Darling-Hammond, Editor
Gary Sykes, Editor

3510 Teaching for Results
Master Teacher
Leadership Lane
PO Box 1207
Manhattan, KS 66505-1207
800-669-9633
Fax: 800-669-1132
http://www.masterteacher.com
An easy-to-implement powerful method for helping to ensure sucess in the classroom.

45 pages
ISBN: 1-58992-120-8

3511 Their Best Selves: Building Character Education and Service Learning Together
Character Education Partnership
1025 Connecticut Avenue NW
Suite 1011
Washington, DC 20036
202-296-7743
800-988-8081
Fax: 202-296-7779
E-mail: rsipos@character.org
http://www.character.org
Character Education Partnership (CEP) is one of the world's premier character education organizations. It is recognized as a leader in the field and a foremost advocate for developing young people of good character and civic virtue

Joseph Mazzola, Executive Director
David W Fisher, Chairman

3512 Theory of Experiential Education
AEE and Kendall/Hunt Publishing Company
4050 Westmark Drive
PO Box 1840
Dubuque, IA 52004-2624
319-589-1000
800-228-0810
Fax: 563-589-1253
http://www.kendallhunt.com
This groundbreaking resource looks at the theoretical foundations of experiential education from philosophical, historical, psychological, social and ethical perspectives.

496 pages
ISBN: 0-7872-0262-2

AEE, Author
Karen Berger, Customer Service Assistant

3513 Time to Teach, Time to Learn: Changing the Pace of School
1615 Duke Street
Alexandria, VA 22314
703-528-0700
800-360-6332
Fax: 413-774-1129
E-mail: info@aasa.org
Giving students the chance to learn and their teachers the chance to teach.

322 pages Softcover

Chip Wood, Author

3514 Top Quality School Process (TQSP)
National School Services
390 Holbrook Drive
Wheeling, IL 60090-5812
847-541-2768
800-262-4511
Fax: 847-541-2553
A customized School Improvement Program that incorporates input from all stakeholders in the educational process to establish baseline data, implement a continuous process of school improvement, and select quality programs for professional development.

3515 US Department of Education: Office of Educational Research & Improvement
National Library of Education
555 New Jersey Avenue NW
Washington, DC 20208-5573
202-219-2230
Fax: 202-219-2030
http://www2.ed.gov/pubs/TeachersGuide/oeri.html
Offers a variety of publications for professional development. The list of sources includes statistical reports, topical reports and effective programs, schools and practices.

John Blake, Reference/Information
Nancy Cavanaugh, Collection Development

3516 Understanding and Relating To Parents Professionally
Master Teacher
Leadership Lane
PO Box 1207
Manhattan, KS 66505-1207
800-669-9633
Fax: 800-669-1132
http://www.masterteacher.com
From one man with a mission to over sixty employees and growing, The MASTER Teacher has developed and matured. We will continue to provide educators with cutting-edge professional development solutions as we advance into the future.

70 pages
ISBN: 0-914607-65-0

Robert L DeBruyn, Author

3517 Welcome to Teaching and our Schools
Master Teacher
Leadership Lane
PO Box 1207
Manhattan, KS 66505-1207
800-669-9633
800-669-9633
Fax: 800-669-1132
http://www.masterteacher.com
Sets the stage for teachers so that they can have an enthusiastic and successful year in the classroom.

50 pages
ISBN: 0-914607-49-9

Robert L DeBryon, Author

3518 World Exchange Program Directory
Center for U.N. Studies, GPO Box 2786
Ramna
Dacca 1000, Bangladesh
Offers listings, by geographical location, of exchange programs available to United States and abroad students. Listings include all contact information, schedules, fields and levels of study and bilingual information.
Biennial

3519 You Can Handle Them All
Master Teacher
Leadership Lane
PO Box 1207
Manhattan, KS 66505-1207
800-669-9633
Fax: 800-669-1132
http://www.masterteacher.com
Encyclopedia of student misbehaviors offering answers that work. one hundred seventeen student misbehaviors are covered.
320 pages
ISBN: 0-914607-04-9
Robert L DeBruyn, Author

3520 Your Personal Mentoring & Planning Guide forthe First 60 Days of Teaching
Master Teacher
Leadership Lane
PO Box 1207
Manhattan, KS 66505-1207
800-669-9633
Fax: 800-669-1132
http://www.masterteacher.com
In this book we've selected from 32 years of The Master Teacher, the writings we know you would most like your teachers to have to support the first 60 days of the school year.
116 pages
ISBN: 1-58992-056-2

Periodicals

3521 AACTE Briefs
American Association of Colleges for Teacher Ed.
1307 New York Avenue NW
Suite 300
Washington, DC 20005-4701
202-293-2450
Fax: 202-457-8095
E-mail: aacte@aacte.org
http://www.aacte.org
To promote the learning of all PK-12 students through high-quality, evidence-based preparation.
4-12 pages Monthly
ISSN: 0731-602x
Kristin McCabe, Publications Specialist/Edit
Aimee J Hall, Meetings Coordinator

3522 ATEA Journal
American Technical Education Association
Dunwoody College of Technology
818 Dunwoody Blvd
Minneapolis, MN 55043
612-381-3315
Fax: 701-671-2260
E-mail: skrebsbach@dunwoody.edu
http://www.ateaonline.org
To be recognized as the preeminent international organization dedicated to the professional growth and development of postsecondary educators and industrial trainers. Provide leadership in assessing the needs of targeted technology initiatives and providing an array of professional growth and development opportunities to meet or exceed the expectation of institutional and individual members.
32 pages Quarterly
ISSN: 0889-6488
Sandra Krebsbach, Executive Director
DeeAnn Bilben, Administrative Assistant

3523 Action in Teacher Education
University of Georgia, College of Education
820 Van Vleet Oval
Rome 100
Norman, OK 73019
405-325-1081
Fax: 706-542-4277
E-mail: educationinformation@ou.edu
http://www.ou.edu/action
The official publication of the Association of Teacher Educators, serving as a forum for the exchange of information and ideas related to the improvement of teacher education at all levels.
Quarterly
John J Chiodo, Editor
Laura Bolf-Beliveau, Editor

3524 American Educational Research Journal
Columbia University Teachers College
PO Box 51
New York, NY 10027
212-678-3498
Fax: 212-678-4048
http://www.aer.sagepub.com
Publishes research articles that explore the processes and outcomes of teaching, learning, and human development at all educational levels and in both formal and informal settings.
Quarterly
Lois Weis, Editor
Philip Altbach, Associate Editor

3525 American Educator
American Federation of Teachers
555 New Jersey Avenue NW
Washington, DC 20001-2029
202-879-4420
E-mail: amered@aft.org
http://www.aft.org/pubs-reports/american_educator/index.htm
Professional journal of the American Federation of Teachers, is a quarterly magazine published for classroom teachers and other education professionals from preschool through university
Quarterly
Elizabeth McPike, Editor
Mary Kearney, Advertising/Sales

3526 Arts Management in Community Institutions: Summer Training
National Guild of Community Schools of the Arts
520 8th Avenue
Suite 302
New York, NY 10018
212-268-3337
Fax: 212-268-3995
E-mail: info@natguild.org
http://www.nationalguild.org
Advances high-quality, community arts education so all people may participate in the arts according to their interests and abilities. Support the creation and development of community arts education organizations by providing research and information resources, professional development and networking opportunities, advocacy, and high-profile leadership.
June
Jonathan Herman, Executive Director
Kenneth T Cole, Associate Director

3527 Balance Sheet
ITP South-Western Publishing
5101 Madison Road
Cincinnati, OH 45227-1427
513-271-8811
800-824-5179
Fax: 800-487-8488
Informational publication for high school accounting educators. Articles contain information about innovations in teaching accounting, producing an extensive line of educational texts and software for K-postsecondary markets.
2x Year
Larry Qualls, Editor
Carol Bross-McMahon, Coordinating Editor

3528 Better Teaching
The Parent Institute
PO Box 7474
Fairfax Station, VA 22039-7474
703-323-9170
800-756-5525
Fax: 703-323-9173
http://www.parent-institute.com
Newsletter for teachers (grades 1-12) that offers tips and techniques to improve student learning.
Monthly
ISSN: 1061-1495
John Wherry, President

3529 C/S Newsletter
Center for Instructional Services
Purdue University
W. Lafayette, IN 47907
317-494-9454
Contains descriptions of CIS services and articles about instructional techniques.
4 pages 7x Year
Vickie Lojek

3530 Curriculum Brief
International Technology Education Association
1914 Association Drive
Reston, VA 20191-1538
703-860-2100
Fax: 703-860-0353
Seeks to advance technological literacy through professional development activities and publications.
4x Year
Kendall Starkweather, Executive Director

3531 Education & Treatment of Children
Pressley Ridge School
PO Box 6295
Morgantown, WV 26506-3016
304-293-8400
Fax: 304-293-6585
E-mail: fdowney@wvu.edu
http://www.educationandtreatmentofchildren.net

A journal devoted to the dissemination of information concerning the development and improvement of services for children and youth. Its primary criterion for publication is that the material be of direct value to educators and other child care professionals in improving their teaching/training effectiveness. Various types of material are appropriate for publication including originial experimental research, experimental replications, adaptations of previously reported research and reviews.
Quarterly
Bernie Fabry, Managing Editor
Daniel E Hursh, Senior Editor

3532 Educational Placement Sources-US
Education Information Services/Instant
Alert
PO Box 620662
Newton, MA 2462-662
617-433-0125
Lists 100 organizations in the United States
that find positions for teachers, educational
administrators, counselors and other professionals. Listings are classified by type, listed
alphabetically and offers all contact
information.

4 pages Annual

FB Viaux, President

**3533 Exceptional Child Education
Resources**
The Council for Exceptional Children
1920 Association Drive
Reston, VA 20191-1545
703-620-3660
800-328-0272
Fax: 703-264-1637
E-mail: askeric@ericir.syr.edu
A quarterly abstract journal that helps teachers stay abreast of the book, nonprint media,
and journal literature in special and gifted education.

Quarterly
ISSN: 0160-4309

**3534 Extensions - Newsletter of the
High/Scope Curriculum**
High/Scope Educational Research
Foundation
600 N River Street
Ypsilanti, MI 48198-2898
734-485-2000
800-40P-RESS
Fax: 734-485-0704
E-mail: info@highscope.org
http://www.highscope.org
Teacher guide for users of the High/Scope
curriculum. Articles on classroom strategies,
training techniques, problem-solving ideas,
and news from the field. Also includes updated training data.

8 pages BiMonthly
ISSN: 0892-5135

Sharon Adams-Taylor, Associate Executive
Director
A Clay Shouse, Vice President

3535 Guild Notes Bi-Monthly Newswletter
National Guild of Community Schools of
the Arts
520 8th Avenue
Suite 302, 3rd Floor
New York, NY 10018
212-268-3337
Fax: 212-268-3995
E-mail: info@natguild.org
http://www.nationalguild.org

Bi-Monthly

Noah Xifr, Director Membership/Operatio

**3536 Infocus: A Newsletter of the
University Continuing Education
Association**
University Continuing Education
Association
1 Dupont Circle NW
Suite 615
Washington, DC 20036-1134
202-659-3130
Fax: 202-785-0374
E-mail: kjkohl@ucea.edu
http://www.ucea.edu
Reports on higher education activities, fed-
eral legislation and government agencies, in-
novative programming at institutions across
the country; member institutions; trends in
continuing and part-time education; re-

sources; professional development opportunities within the field; and changes in
member personnel.

12-20 pages Monthly

Roger Whitaker, President
Kay J Kohl, Executive Director/CEO

3537 Innovator
University of Michigan Association
4001 School of Education Building
Ann Arbor, MI 48104
734-764-0394
Fax: 734-763-6934
For professional educators and alumni of
University of Michigan's School of Educa-
tion.

20 pages Quarterly

Eric Warden, Contact

**3538 International Journal of
Instructional Media**
Westwood Press
149 Goose Lane
Tolland, CT 6084-3822
860-875-5484
E-mail: PLSleeman@aol.com
http://www.adprima.com/ijim.htm
A professional journal directly responsive to
the need for precise information on the application of media to your instructional and
training needs.

Quarterly

Dr Phillip J Sleeman, Executive Editor
Dr Bruce R Ledford, Associate Editor

3539 Intervention in School and Clinic
Pro-Ed., Inc.
8700 Shoal Creek Boulevard
Austin, TX 78757-6897
512-451-3246
800-897-3202
Fax: 800-397-7633
E-mail: general@proedinc.com
http://www.proedinc.com
The hands-on how-to resource for teachers
and clinicians working with students (especially LD and BD) for whom minor curiculum
and environmental medications are
ineffective.

64 pages 5x Year Magazine
ISSN: 1053-4512

Judith K Voress, Periodicals Director
Brenda Smith Myles, Editor

3540 Journal of Classroom Interaction
University of Houston-University Park
442 Farish Hall
University of Houston
Houston, TX 77204-5026
713-743-5919
Fax: 713-743-8664
E-mail: jci@bayou.uh.edu
http://cmcd.coe.uh.edu/coejci/index.htm
The Journal is a semi-annual publication devoted to empirical investigations and theoretical papers dealing with observation
techniques, research on student and teacher
behavior, and other issues relevant to the do-
main of classroom interaction.

Bi-Annually

Dr. Jerome Freiberg, Editor
Stacey Lamb, Assistant to the Editor

3541 Journal of Economic Education
Heldref Publications
1319 18th Street NW
Washington, DC 20036-1802
202-296-6267
800-365-9753
Fax: 202-296-5149
http://www.indiana.edu/~econed/index.html

The Journal of Economic Education offers
original articles on innovations in and evaluations of teaching techniques, materials, and
programs in economics

Quarterly

William E Becker, Executive Editor

3542 Journal of Experiential Education
Association for Experiential Education
3775 Iris Avenue
Suite 4
Boulder, CO 80301-2043
303-440-8844
866-522-8337
Fax: 303-440-9581
E-mail: webmaster@aee.org
http://www.aee.org
Association for Experiential Education develops and promotes experiential education.
The association is committed to supporting
professional development, theoretical advancement and the evaluation of experiential
education worldwide.

64 pages 3x Year
ISSN: 1053-8259

Paul Limoges, CEO
Laurie Frank, President

**3543 Journal on Excellence in College
Teaching**
Miami University
Miami University
Oxford, OH 45056
513-529-9265
Fax: 531-529-9264
E-mail: wentzegw@muohio.edu
http://celt.muohio.edu/ject
A peer-reviewed journal published by and for
faculty at colleges and universities to increase student learning through effective
teaching, interest in and enthusiasm for the
profession of teaching, and communication
among faculty about their classroom experiences. The Journal provides a scholarly forum for faculty to share proven, innovative
pedagogies and thoughtful, inspirational
insights about teaching.

Journal 3x/Yr
ISSN: 1052-4800

Gregg Wentzell, Author
Gregg Wentzell, Managing Editor
Milton Cox, Editor-in-Chief

3544 Journalism Education Association
Kansas State University
103 Kedzie Hall
Manhattan, KS 66506-1505
785-532-5532
866-532-5532
Fax: 785-532-5563
E-mail: jea@spub.ksu.edu
http://www.jea.org
Among JEA's 2,100 members are journalism
teachers and publications advisers, media
professionals, press associations, adviser organizations, libraries, yearbook companies,
newspapers, radio stations and departments
of journalism.

April & November
25-30 booths with 4700 attendees

Jack Kennedy, President
Bob Bair, Vice President

3545 NCRTL Special Report
National Center for Research on Teacher
Education
Michigan State University
East Lansing, MI 48824
517-355-9302
E-mail: floden@msu.edu
http://www.ncrtb.msu.edu
Membership news and updates.

205

3546 NCSIE Inservice
National Council of States on Inservice Education
Syracuse University
402 Huntington Hall
Syracuse, NY 13244
315-443-1870
Fax: 315-443-9082
Professional development, staff development and inservice education.

20 pages Quarterly

James Collins

3547 On The Go! for the Educational Office Professional
Master Teacher
Leadership Lane
PO Box 1207
Manhattan, KS 66505-1207
800-669-9633
Fax: 800-669-1132
http://www.masterteacher.com
Positive, practical, and successful insights and techniques to help you manage and work with your support staff.

1 pages Monthly Newsletter

Tracey H DeBruyn, Executive Editor

3548 On-The-Go For Educational Office Professionals
Master Teacher
Leadership Lane
PO Box 1207
Manhattan, KS 66505-1207
785-539-0555
800-669-9633
Fax: 800-669-1132
http://www.masterteacher.com
The publication that provides you with great articles to complete your in-house newsletters and newsletters to parents, without fear of copyright violations.

1 pages Monthly Newsletter

Erica Parkinson, Executive Editor

3549 Paraeducator's Guide to Instructional & Curricular Modifications
Master Teacher
Leadership Lane
PO Box 1207
Manhattan, KS 66505-1207
800-669-9633
Fax: 800-669-1132
http://www.masterteacher.com
An indispensible tool your paras can use to understand, plan for and carry out appropriate modification for students with all types of special needs.

100 pages
ISBN: 0-914607-88-X

Wendy Dover, Author

3550 Pennsylvania Education
Pennsylvania Department of Education
333 Market Street
Harrisburg, PA 17126-2210
717-783-6788
Fax: 717-783-8230
http://www.pde.state.pa.us
The mission of the Pennsylvania Department of Education is to assist the General Assembly, the Governor, the Secretary of Education and Pennsylvania educators in providing for the maintenance and support of a thorough and efficient system of education.

8-10 pages 8x Year

Gary Tuma, Press Secretary
Beth Boyer, Information Specialist

3551 Performance Improvement Journal
International Society for Performance
1400 Spring Street
Suite 260
Silver Spring, MD 20910-2753
301-587-8570
Fax: 301-587-8573
E-mail: info@ispi.org
http://www.ispi.org
To develop and recognize the proficiency of its members and advocate the use of Human Performance Technology.

48 pages Monthly
ISSN: 1090-8811

April Davis, Executive Director
Matthew T Peters, President

3552 Preventing School Failure
Heldref Publications
1319 Eighteenth Street, NW
Washington, DC 20036-1802
202-296-6267
800-365-9753
Fax: 202-296-5149
E-mail: psf@heldref.org
http://www.heldref.org
The journal for educators and parents seeking strategies to promote the success of students who have learning and behavior problems. It includes practical examples of programs and practices that help children and youth in schools, clinics, correctional institutions, and other settings. Articles are written by educators and concern teaching children with various kinds of special needs.

48 pages Quarterly
ISSN: 1045-988X

Mary O'Donnell, Managing Editor

3553 Prevention Researcher
Integrated Research
66 Club Road
Suite 370
Eugene, OR 97401
541-683-9278
800-929-2955
Fax: 541-683-2621
E-mail: orders@TPRonline.org
http://www.TPRonline.org
A quarterly journal that uses a straightforward and easy-to-read approach to present the most current research and developments in adolescent behavioral research. In addition to cutting-edge, evidence-based research it also examines exemplary prevention programs and strategies that can help youth workers see which of today's best practices are most successful.

24 pages Magazine/Quarterly
ISSN: 1086-4385

Steven Ungerleider PhD, Editor
Jasmine Hunter, Office Manager & Contributin

3554 Progressive Teacher
Progressive Publishing Company
2678 Henry Street
Augusta, GA 30904-4656
770-868-1691
Offers new information and updates for the improvement and development of higher education.

Quarterly
ISSN: 0033-0825

MS Adcock

3555 Retaining Great Teachers
Master Teacher
Leadership Lane
PO Box 1207
Manhattan, KS 66505-1207
800-669-9633
Fax: 800-669-1132
http://www.masterteacher.com
The Retaining Great Teachers Book is a systemic approach for attracting, mentoring, supporting, and retaining new and veteran teacher.

85 pages
ISBN: 1-58992-097-X

Michael J Lovett PhD, Author

3556 Rural Educator-Journal for Rural and Small Schools
National Rural Education Association
Colorado State University
Fort Collins, CO 80523-1588
970-491-6444
Fax: 970-491-1317
E-mail: presofc@lamar.colostate.edu
http://www.colostate.edu
Official journal of the NREA. A nationally recognized publication that features timely and informative articles written by leading rural educators from all levels of education. All NREA members are encouraged to submit research articles and items of general information for publication.

40 pages Quarterly Magazine
ISSN: 0273-446X

Joseph T Newlin, Editor
Anthony A Frank, President

3557 TED Newsletter
The Council for Exceptional Children
1920 Association Drive
Reston, VA 20191-1545
703-620-3660
888-232-7733
Fax: 703-264-9494
Newsletter of the Teacher Education Division offering information about TED activities, upcoming events, current trends and practices, state and national legislation, recently published materials and practical information of interest to persons involved in the preparation and continuing professional development of effective professionals in special education and related service fields.

3x Year

Diana Hammitte, Co-Editor
Laurence O'Shea, Editor

3558 TESOL Journal: A Journal of Teaching and Classroom Research
Teachers of English to Speakers of Other Languages
1600 Cameron Street
Suite 300
Alexandria, VA 22314-2705
703-836-0774
Fax: 703-836-7864
E-mail: tescol@tesol.edu
http://www.tesol.edu
TESOL's mission is to develop the expertise of its members and others involved in teaching English to speakers of other languages to help them foster communication in diverse settings. The association advances standards for professional preparation and employment, continuing education, and student programs, produces programs, services, and products, and promotes advocacy to further the profession. TESOL has 91 affiliates worldwide.

50 pages Quarterly

Christian J Faltis, Editor
Marilyn Kupetz, Managing Editor

3559 Teacher Education Reports
Feistritzer Publishing
4401-A Connecticut Avenue NW
#212
Washington, DC 20008-2302
202-362-3444
Fax: 202-362-3493

Covers the field of teacher education for elementary and secondary schools, including pre-service preparation, in-service training and professional development, related federal programs, legislation and funding.

8 pages BiWeekly

David T Chester, Editor

3560 Teacher Education and Special Education
The Council for Exceptional Children
1920 Association Drive
Reston, VA 20191-1545
703-620-3660
Fax: 352-392-7159
Contains information on current research, exemplary practices, timely issues, legislation, book reviews, and new programs and materials relative to the preparation and continuing professional development of effective professionals in special education and related service fields.

Quarterly

Vivian Correa, Editor

3561 Teacher Magazine
6935 Arlington Road
Suite 100
Bethesda, MD 20814-5233
301-280-3100
800-346-1834
Fax: 301-280-3250
E-mail: webeditors@epe.org
http://www.edweek.org
Our primary mission is to help raise the level of awareness and understanding among professionals and the public of important issues in American education.

Anthony Rebora, Managing Editor
Elizabeth Rich, Online Editor

3562 Teacher's Guide to Classroom Management
Economics Press
12 Daniel Road
Fairfield, NJ 7004-2507
973-227-1224
Bulletins showing teachers how to solve problems and avoid problematic situations.

BiWeekly

Robert Guder

3563 Teachers in Touch
ISM Independent School Management
1316 N Union Street
Wilmington, DE 19806-2534
302-656-4944
800-955-4944
Fax: 302-656-0647
Faculty professional development publication with strategies for career satisfaction, good teaching practices and stress-reducing techniques. The forum for professional sharing for private-independent school educators.

4 pages 5x Year

Rozanne S Elliott, Publisher
Kelly Rawlings, Editor

3564 Teaching Education
University of South Carolina, College of Education
Wardlaw College
Room 231
Columbia, SC 29208-1
803-777-6301
Fax: 803-777-3068
Focuses on the actual profession of teaching and new methodology by which to learn.

2x Year

James T. Sears, PhD, Editor

3565 Techniques-Connecting Education and Careers
Association for Career and Technical Education
1410 King Street
Alexandria, VA 22314-2749
703-683-3111
800-826-9972
Fax: 703-683-7424
E-mail: sackley@acteonline.org
http://www.acteonline.org
To provide leadership in developing an educated, prepared, adaptable and competitive workforce.

Newsletter/Magazine

Peter Magnuson, Director of Programs/Communi
Jan Bray, Executive Director

3566 Technology Integration for Teachers
Master Teacher
Po Box 1207
Manhattan, KS 66505-1207
785-539-0555
800-669-9633
Fax: 800-669-1132
http://www.masterteacher.com
The publication that provides teachers with innovative strategies for integratinjg technology into the classroom.

Monthly Newsletter

Brad Roberts, Executive Editor

3567 The Board
Master Teacher
Po Box 1207
Manhattan, KS 66505-1207
785-539-0555
800-669-9633
Fax: 800-669-1132
http://www.masterteacher.com
A complete program of in-service training for school board members.

Robert DeBruyn, Executive Editor

3568 The Professor In The Classroom
Master Teacher
Leadership Lane
PO Box 1207
Manhattan, KS 66505-1207
785-539-0555
800-669-9633
Fax: 800-669-1132
http://www.masterteacher.com
From one man with a mission to over sixty employees and growing, The MASTER Teacher has developed and matured. We will continue to provide educators with cutting-edge professional development solutions as we advance into the future.

1 pages Semi-Monthly

Robert DeBruyn, Author

3569 Today's Catholic Teacher
2621 Dryden Road
Suite 300
Dayton, OH 45439
937-293-1415
800-523-4625
Fax: 937-293-1310
E-mail: service@peterli.com
http://www.catholicteacher.com
Today's Catholic Teacher magazine is written for you, a teacher in a Catholic school. Each issue is filled with information that will help you succeed in the classroom

72 pages Bimonthly
ISSN: 0040-8441

Mary C Noschang, Editor-in-chief
Peter Li, President/Publisher

3570 Training Research Journal: The Science and Practice of Training
Educational Technology Publications
700 Paliside Avenue
Englewood Cliffs, NJ 7632
Fax: 201-871-4009
Peer-reviewed publication, published once yearly by Educational Technology Publications, is now in its fourth volume. Provides a high-quality, peer-reviewed forum for theoretical and empirical work relevant to training.

Annually

Software, Hardware & Internet Resources

3571 Analog & Digital Peripherals
PO Box 499
Troy, OH 45373-3585
937-339-2241
800-758-1041
Fax: 937-339-0070
E-mail: info@adpi.com
Established in 1978 to provide OEM manufacturers and end users with practical solutions in data logging, storage, and retrieval as well as program loading and back-up.

Lyle Ellicott

3572 E-Z Grader Software
E-Z Grader Company
PO Box 23608
Chagrin Falls, OH 44023
800-432-4018
http://www.ezgrader.com
Electronic guidebook designed by teachers for teachers.

3573 K12jobs.Com
PO Box 210811
West Palm Beach, FL 33421
E-mail: beth@k12jobs.com
To provide schools with an efficient and cost-effective recruiting tool, providing service and opportunities to institutions and job seekers alike.

Also: K-12jobs.Com

Beth Jones, CSR & General Information

3574 KidsCare Childcare Management Software
770 Cochituate Road
Framingham, MA 1701-4672
508-875-3451
Sells software programs to education professionals involved in childcare to aid their development and understanding.

3575 Mental Edge
Learning ShortCuts
PO Box 382367
Germantown, TN 38183-2367
901-218-8163
Fax: 309-406-5358
E-mail: feedback@learningshortcuts.com
http://www.learningshortcuts.com
The Mental Edge is specifically designed to facilitate review and reinforcement. It is the quickest, easiest, and most thorough way to bring the things that have been learned back to mind in preparation for any testing scenario.

3576 The Center For The Future Of Teaching And Learning
Center for the Future of Teaching & Learning
133 Mission Street
Suite 220
Santa Cruz, CA 95060

831-427-3628
Fax: 831-427-1612
E-mail: info@cftl.org
http://www.cftl.org
A not-for-profit organization dedicated to strengthening teacher development policy and practice.

Margaret Gaston, President/Executive Director
Harvey Hunt, Vice President

3577 www.aasa.org
American Association of School Administrators
801 N Quincy Street
Suite 700
Arlington, VA 22203-1730
703-528-0700
Fax: 703-841-1543
E-mail: info@aasa.org
http://www.aasa.org
Supports and develops effective school system leaders who are dedicated to the highest quality public education for all children.

Randall H Collins, President
Mark T Bielang, President-Elect

3578 www.classbuilder.Com
Class Builder

http://www.classbuilder.com
Free teachers toolbox! Grade book, Create tests, Reports, Lessons, Distance Learning Courseware, and more.

Internet Only Access

Edhelper.Com, Author

3579 www.ed.gov/free
Federal Resources for Educational Excellence
Teaching and learning resources from Federal Agencies

3580 www.eduverse.com
eduverse.com
Leading Internet e-Knowledge software developer building core technologies for powering international distance education.

3581 www.freeteachingaids.com
Free Teaching Aids.com
214 Center Street
Randolph, WI 53956
888-951-4469
http://www.freeteachingaids.com
Guides for finding free resources for teachers.

3582 www.gsn.org
Global Schoolhouse
132 N El Camino Real
Suite 395
Encinitas, CA 92024
760-635-0001
Fax: 760-635-0003
E-mail: helper2009@globalschoolnet.org
http://www.gsn.org
Collaborative projects, communication tools and professional development.

Yvonne Marie Andres, President
John St. Clair, Vice President

3583 www.imagescape.com/helpweb/www/oneweb.html
An Overview of the World Wide Web
E-mail: help@imagescape.com
http://www.imagescape.com/helpweb/www/oneweb.html

3584 www.learningpage.com
1840 E River Road
Suite 320
Tucson, AZ 85718
E-mail: learningpage@learningpage.com.
http://www.learningpage.com
LearningPage provides a huge collection of professionally produced instructional materials you can download and print.

3585 www.mmhschool.com
McGraw Hill School Division
220 E Danieldale Road
Desoto, TX 75115
800-442-9685
Fax: 972-228-1982
http://www.mhschool.com
Dedicated to educating children and to helping educational professionals by providing the highest quality materials and services.

John Predmore, Privacy Official

3586 www.nprinc.com
National Professional Resources
25 S Regent Street
Port Chester, NY 10573
800-453-7461
Fax: 914-937-9327
E-mail: service@nprinc.com
http://www.nprinc.com
Produces videos/DVDs and publishes books on the most significant and current topical areas in the educational arena. New to this product line are laminated reference guides that provide a succinct summary of the topic being addressed.

Angela Hanson, Director of Marketing

3587 www.onlinelearning.net
OnlineLearning.net
12975 Coral Tree Place
Los Angeles, CA 90066
800-784-8436
E-mail:
customerservice@laureate-inc.com
http://www.onlinelearning.net
Source for teacher education online.

Susan Ko, Vice President

3588 www.pagestarworld.com
Pagestar
E-mail: orders@pagestarworld.com
http://www.scrase.com/pagestar
Software products that are specifically designed for teachers. Over 600 electronic forms that are commonly used by teachers for planning, administering, delivering and assessing student learning.

3589 www.pbs.org
PBS TeacherSource
http://www.pbs.org
Offers all Americans the opportunity to explore new ideas and new worlds through television and online content.

3590 www.pbs.org/uti/quicktips.html
QuickTips
On understanding and using the Internet, you'll find tips on navigating the Web.

3591 www.rhlschool.com
RHL School
E-mail: contact2@rhlschool.com
http://www.rhlschool.com
Free ready to use quality worksheets for teaching, reinforcement,and review.

3592 www.sanjuan.edu/select/structures.html
San Juan Select - Structures
A Web site that examines various ways to structure and facilitate student projects using Internet capabilities. Each suggestion is accompanied by a specific example of how that structure can be or is being used on the Internet.

3593 www.schoolrenaissance.com
School Renaissance Model
PO Box 8036
Wisconsin Rapids, WI 54495-8036
715-424-3636
800-338-4204
Fax: 715-424-4242
E-mail: answers@renlearn.com
http://www.renlearn.com
Advance technology for essential practice. Makes the practice component of reading, math, and writing curriculum more personalized and effective.

3594 www.teachingjobs.com
The Teachers Employment Network
http://
Leading resource for education employment.

3595 www.usajobs.opm.gov/b1c.htm
Overseas Employment Info- Teachers
US Office of Personnel Management

Covers eligibility, position categories and special requirements, application procedures, program information and entitlement, housing, living/working conditions, shipment of household goods, and complete application forms and guidance.

3596 www.webworkshops.com
Web Work Shops
http://www.webworkshops.com
A series of on-line courses, designed to prepare teachers to integrate both the Internet and classroom computer applications into daily lessons.

Training Materials

3597 At-Risk Students: Identification and Assistance Strategies
Center for the Study of Small/Rural Schools
555 E Constitution Street
Room 138
Norman, OK 73072-7820
405-325-1450
Fax: 405-325-7075
E-mail: jcsimmons@ou.edu
http://cssrs.ou.edu
The Center for the Study of Small/Rural Schools is a cooperative effort between the University of Oklahoma's Colleges of Education and Continuing Education. Endorsed by the National Rural Education Association as one of its five recognized rural education research

Video

Jan C Simmons, Program Director

3598 Character Education: Making a Difference
Character Education Partnership
1025 Connecticut Avenue NW
Suite 1011
Washington, DC 20036
202-296-7743
800-988-8081
Fax: 202-296-7779
http://www.character.org
Leading the nation in helping schools develop people of good character for a just and compassionate society.

Rebecca Sipos, Director Communications
Joseph W Mazzola, Executive Director

3599 Character Education: Restoring Respect & Responsibility in our Schools
Master Teacher
Po Box 1207
Manhattan, KS 66505-1207
785-539-0555
800-669-9633
Fax: 800-669-1132
http://www.masterteacher.com
Provides a comprehensive model for character education in our nations schools. Specific classroom stategies as well as school wide approaches are outlines in a clear and compelling fashion.

Thomas Lickona PhD, Author

3600 Cisco Educational Archives
University of North Carolina at Chapel Hill
170 W Tasman Drive
San Jose, CA 95134-3455
408-526-4000
800-553-6387
http://www.cisco.com/web/siteassets
Focus on business operations, product innovation and design, and customer solutions. We develop products with minimal environmental impact and extend our technology to reduce environmental footprints globally.

John T Chambers, Chairman / CEO
Frank Calderoni, Executive VP/CFO

3601 Classroom Teacher's Guide for Working with Paraeducators Video Set
Master Teacher
Po Box 1207
Manhattan, KS 66505-1207
785-539-0555
800-669-9633
Fax: 800-669-1132
http://www.masterteacher.com
Covers a range of nuts-and-bolts topics including why the job duties of paras have changed so much over the years, what a classroom teacher needs to know to get started working effectively with a para. Useful tips for managing another adult, and how para factor into the planning process.

Wendy Dover, Author

3602 Clinical Play Therapy Videos: Child-Centered Developmental & Relationship Play Therapy
University of North Texas
PO BOX 310829
Denton, TX 76203-829
940-565-3864
Fax: 940-565-4461
E-mail: cpt@unt.edu
http://www.centerforplaytherapy.com
Encourage the unique development and emotional growth of children through the process of play therapy, a dynamic interpersonal relationship between a child and a therapist trained in play therapy procedures.

Garry Landreth PhD, Founder
Sue Bratton PhD, Director

3603 Conferencing with Students & Parents Video Series
Master Teacher
PO Box 1207
Manhattan, KS 66505-1207
800-669-9633
800-669-9633
Fax: 800-669-1132
http://www.masterteacher.com

Will help teachers turn both formal and informal conferences with students and parents into opportunities for student success.

Robert L DeBruyn, Author/Publisher

3604 Conflict Resolution Strategies in Schools
Center for the Study of Small/Rural Schools
555 E Constitution Street
Room 138
Norman, OK 73072-7820
405-325-1450
Fax: 405-325-7075
E-mail: jcsimmons@ou.edu
http://cssrs.ou.edu
Series IV
Video

Jan C Simmons, Director

3605 Conover Company
4 Brookwood Court
Appleton, WI 54914-8618
800-933-1933
Fax: 800-933-1943
E-mail: sales@conovercompany.com
http://www.conovercompany.com
Developing training programs for industry. Provide off-the-shelf as well as custom sales and marketing, training, presentation, and application programs that connect learning to the workplace

Rebecca Schmitz, Member

3606 Cooperative Learning Strategies
Center for the Study of Small/Rural Schools
555 E Constitution Street
Room 138
Norman, OK 73072-7820
405-325-1450
Fax: 405-325-7075
E-mail: jcsimmons@ou.edu
http://cssrs.ou.edu
Series I
Video

Jan C Simmons, Program Director

3607 Creating Schools of Character Video Series
Master Teacher
PO Box 1207
Manhattan, KS 66505-1207
785-539-0555
800-669-9633
Fax: 800-669-1132
http://www.masterteacher.com
Visit a Blue Ribbon School of excellence and hear staff and others discuss how to create or improve a whole school charecter education program.

ISBN: 0-914607-90-1

3608 Crisis Management in Schools
Center for the Study of Small/Rural Schools
555 E Constitution Street
Room 138
Norman, OK 73072-7820
405-325-1450
Fax: 405-325-7075
E-mail: jcsimmons@ou.edu
http://cssrs.ou.edu
Series IV
Video

Jan C Simmons, Director

3609 Critical Thinking Video Set
Master Teacher
PO Box 1207
Manhattan, KS 66505-1207
785-539-0555
800-669-9633
Fax: 800-669-1132
http://www.masterteacher.com

Will help teachers challange students to think in a new way. Research shows that when we engage students in critical and creative though, retention increases tremendously.

ISBN: 1-58992-079-1

3610 Curriculum Alignment: Improving Student Learning
Center for the Study of Small/Rural Schools
555 E Constitution Street
Room 138
Norman, OK 73072-7820
405-325-1450
Fax: 405-325-7075
E-mail: jcsimmons@ou.edu
http://cssrs.ou.edu
Series I
Video

Jan C Simmons, Director

3611 Datacad
20 Tower Lane
Avon, CT 6001
860-677-4004
800-394-2231
Fax: 860-677-2610
E-mail: info@datacad.com
http://www.datacad.com
DATACAD's product development, sales, and marketing activities are managed at the corporate headquarters in Avon, Connecticut

Mark F Madura, President/CEO
David A Giessleman, Senior Vice President and CT

3612 Discipline Techniques you can Master in a Minute Video Series
Master Teacher
Leadership Lane
PO Box 1207
Manhattan, KS 66505-1207
800-669-9633
Fax: 800-669-1132
http://www.masterteacher.com
he MASTER Teacher provides essential solutions to meet the professional development needs of educators at all levels-from the paraeducator to the superintendent. For over 30 years, we have provided practical strategies to inspire, enrich, and motivate educators.

ISBN: 1-58992-040-6

Robert L DeBruyn, Founder

3613 Educational Productions Inc
7101 Wisconsin Avenue
Suite 700
Bethesda, MD 20814
800-950-4949
800-950-4949
Fax: 301-634-0826
E-mail: custserv@edpro.com
http://www.edpro.com
To increase the skills and understanding of the adults who work with, teach and care for young children.

Linda Freedman, President
Rae Latham, Vice-President

3614 Eleven Principals of Effective Character Education
Master Teacher
Leadership Lane
PO Box 1207
Manhattan, KS 66505-1207
800-669-9633
Fax: 800-669-1132
http://www.masterteacher.com
Takes you to schools in Maryland, New York, and Missouri, where quality character educa-

tion programs are being implemented by skilled and resourceful staff.

ISBN: 1-887943-13-7

Thomas Lickona PhD, Author

3615 Eleven Principles of Effective Character Education
Character Education Partnership
1025 Connecticut Avenue NW
Suite 1011
Washington, DC 20036
202-296-7743
800-988-8081
Fax: 202-296-7779
E-mail: jmazzola@character.org
http://www.character.org
Leading the nation in helping schools develop people of good character for a just and compassionate society.

Rebecca Sipos, Director Communications
Joseph W Mazzola, Executive Director

3616 Eye on Education
6 Depot Way West
Larchmont, NY 10538
888-299-5350
Fax: 914-833-0761
E-mail: customer-service@eyeoneducation.com
http://www.eyeoneducation.com
Books on performance-based learning and assessment.

3617 Great Classroom Management Series DVD
Master Teacher
Leadership Lane
PO Box 1207
Manhattan, KS 66505-1207
800-669-9633
Fax: 800-669-1132
http://www.masterteacher.com
Effestive classroom management is getting more difficult everday. teachers face increasing demands and expectations in ebery aspect of their jobs.

ISBN: 0-914607-90-1

3618 Great Classroom Management Video Series VHS
Master Teacher
Leadership Lane
PO Box 1207
Manhattan, KS 66505-1207
800-669-9633
Fax: 800-669-1132
http://www.masterteacher.com
Effective classroom management is getting more difficult everyday. teachers face increasing demands and expectations in everyday. Teachers face increasing demands and expectations in every aspect of their jobs.

ISBN: 1-58992-121-6

3619 Handling Chronically Disruptive Students at Risk Video Series
Master Teacher
Leadership Lane
PO Box 1207
Manhattan, KS 66505-1207
800-669-9633
Fax: 800-669-1132
http://www.masterteacher.com
Implement and utlize a CARE couscil, develop and individual Action plan, strategies for enhancing individual action plan.

ISBN: 1-58992-031-7

3620 Hearlihy & Company
Po Box 1747
Pittaburg, KS 66762-1747

866-622-1003
Fax: 800-443-2260
E-mail: kbolte@hearlihy.com
http://www.hearlihy.com
Training and installation for schools purchasing modular labratories.

Kevin Bolte, Contact

3621 Improving Parent/Educator Relationships
Center for the Study of Small/Rural Schools
555 E Constitution Street
Room 138
Norman, OK 73072-7820
405-325-1450
Fax: 405-325-7075
E-mail: jcsimmons@ou.edu
http://cssrs.ou.edu
Series I

Video

Jan C Simmons, Director

3622 Improving Student Thinking in the Content Area
Center for the Study of Small/Rural Schools
555 E Constitution Street
Room 138
Norman, OK 73072-7820
405-325-1450
Fax: 405-325-7075
E-mail: jcsimmons@ou.edu
http://cssrs.ou.edu
Series II

Video

Jan C Simmons, Director

3623 Inclusion: The Next Step the Video Series
Master Teacher
Leadership Lane
PO Box 1207
Manhattan, KS 66505-1207
800-669-9633
Fax: 800-669-1132
http://www.masterteacher.com
Will help you propel your inclusion efforts to a new level of success giving you the necessary insights and stagies for building consensus; weighing your program, curriculum, and instructional options.

ISBN: 1-58992-012-0

Wendy Dover, Author

3624 Integrating Technology into the Curriculum Video Series
Master Teacher
Leadership Lane
PO Box 1207
Manhattan, KS 66505-1207
800-669-9633
Fax: 800-669-1132
http://www.masterteacher.com
Gives teachers the tools and strategies they need to make information technology work for then and for students while empowering then to teach the skills necessary for students to be productive in a technology driven world.

ISBN: 1-58992-007-Y

3625 International Clearinghouse for the Advancement of Science Teaching
University of Maryland
Benjamin Building
Room 226
College Park, MD 20742-1100
301-405-3161
Fax: 301-314-9055

Provides curriculum information about science and mathematics teaching.

Dr. David Lockard, Director

3626 Lesson Plans and Modifications for Inclusionand Collaborative Classrooms
Master Teacher
Leadership Lane
PO Box 1207
Manhattan, KS 66505-1207
800-669-9633
Fax: 800-669-1132
http://www.masterteacher.com
Discover specific strategies lesson plans and activity modifications to enhance learning for all students in the inclusive classroom.

ISBN: 1-58992-022-8

3627 Managing Students Without Coercion
Center for the Study of Small/Rural Schools
555 E Constitution Street
Room 138
Norman, OK 73072-7820
405-325-1450
Fax: 405-325-7075
E-mail: jcsimmons@ou.edu
http://cssrs.ou.edu
Series II

Video

Jan C Simmons, Director

3628 Mentoring Teachers to Mastery Video Series
Master Teacher
Leadership Lane
PO Box 1207
Manhattan, KS 66505-1207
800-669-9633
Fax: 800-669-1132
http://www.masterteacher.com
The MASTER Teacher's e-learning solutions provide cost-effective, subscription-based systems that help meet educators' time demands and continuous learning needs.

ISBN: 1-58992-001-5

3629 Motivating Students in the Classroom Video Series
Master Teacher
Leadership Lane
PO Box 1207
Manhattan, KS 66505-1207
800-669-9633
Fax: 800-669-1132
http://www.masterteacher.com
The MASTER Teacher has developed and matured.We will continue to provide educators with cutting-edge professional development solutions as we advance into the future

ISBN: 1-58992-074-0

3630 Multicultural Education: Teaching to Diversity
Center for the Study of Small/Rural Schools
555 E Constitution Street
Room 138
Norman, OK 73072-7820
405-325-1450
Fax: 405-325-7075
E-mail: jcsimmons@ou.edu
http://cssrs.ou.edu
Series II

Video

Jan C Simmons, Director

3631 Outcome-Based Education: Making it Work
Center for the Study of Small/Rural Schools
555 E Constitution Street
Room 138
Norman, OK 73072-7820

405-325-1450
Fax: 405-325-7075
E-mail: jcsimmons@ou.edu
http://cssrs.ou.edu
Series III

Video

Jan C Simmons, Director

3632 Overview of Prevention: A Social Change Model
Center for the Study of Small/Rural Schools
555 E Constitution Street
Room 138
Norman, OK 73072-7820
405-325-1450
Fax: 405-325-7075
E-mail: jcsimmons@ou.edu
http://cssrs.ou.edu
Prevention Series

Video

Jan C Simmons, Director

3633 Quality School
Center for the Study of Small/Rural Schools
555 E Constitution Street
Room 138
Norman, OK 73072-7820
405-325-1450
Fax: 405-325-7075
E-mail: jcsimmons@ou.edu
http://cssrs.ou.edu
Series II

Video

Jan C Simmons, Director

3634 SAP Today
Performance Resource Press
1270 Rankin Drive
Suite F
Troy, MI 48083-2843
800-453-7733
Fax: 800-499-5718
Overview offers the basics of student assistance.

3635 School-Wide Strategies for Retaining Great Teachers Video Series
Master Teacher
Leadership Lane
PO Box 1207
Manhattan, KS 66505-1207
800-669-9633
Fax: 800-669-1132
http://www.masterteacher.com
You will hear proven strategies for supporting new teachers through all those typical expirences that cansabatage their efforts and cause them to leave your district or even abandon teaching all together.

ISBN: 1-58992-098-8

3636 Site-Based Management
Center for the Study of Small/Rural Schools
555 E Constitution Street
Room 138
Norman, OK 73072-7820
405-325-1450
Fax: 405-325-7075
E-mail: jcsimmons@ou.edu
http://cssrs.ou.edu
Series III

Video

Jan C Simmons, Director

3637 Strategic Planning for Outcome-Based Education
Center for the Study of Small/Rural Schools
555 E Constitution Street
Room 138
Norman, OK 73072-7820
405-325-1450
Fax: 405-325-7075

E-mail: jcsimmons@ou.edu
http://cssrs.ou.edu
Series II

Video

Jan C Simmons, Director

3638 Strengthening the Family: An Overview of a Holistic Family Wellness Model
Center for the Study of Small/Rural Schools
555 E Constitution Street
Room 138
Norman, OK 73072-7820
405-325-1450
Fax: 405-325-7075
E-mail: jcsimmons@ou.edu
http://cssrs.ou.edu
Prevention Series

Video

Jan C Simmons, Director

3639 Students-at-Risk Video Series
Master Teacher
Leadership Lane
PO Box 1207
Manhattan, KS 66505-1207
800-669-9633
Fax: 800-669-1132
http://www.masterteacher.com
Gives you specific stategies for reaching those students who are giving up.

ISBN: 1-58992-060-0

Mildred Odom Bradley, Author

3640 Superintendent/School Board Relationships
Center for the Study of Small/Rural Schools
555 E Constitution Street
Room 138
Norman, OK 73072-7820
405-325-1450
Fax: 405-325-7075
E-mail: jcsimmons@ou.edu
http://cssrs.ou.edu
Series I

Video

Jan C Simmons, Director

3641 TQM: Implementing Quality Management in Your School
Center for the Study of Small/Rural Schools
555 E Constitution Street
Room 138
Norman, OK 73072-7820
405-325-1450
Fax: 405-325-7075
E-mail: jcsimmons@ou.edu
http://cssrs.ou.edu
Series III

Video

Jan C Simmons, Program Director

3642 Teachers as Heros
Center for the Study of Small/Rural Schools
555 E Constitution Street
Room 138
Norman, OK 73072-7820
405-325-1450
Fax: 405-325-7075
E-mail: jcsimmons@ou.edu
http://cssrs.ou.edu
Series IV

Video

Jan C Simmons, Director

3643 Teaching for Intelligent Behavior
Center for the Study of Small/Rural Schools
555 E Constitution Street
Room 138
Norman, OK 73072-7820

405-325-1450
Fax: 405-325-7075
E-mail: jcsimmons@ou.edu
http://cssrs.ou.edu
Series IV

Video

Jan C Simmons, Director

3644 The Master Teacher
Master Teacher
Leadership Lane
PO Box 1207
Manhattan, KS 66505-1207
800-669-9633
Fax: 800-669-1132
http://www.masterteacher.com
From one man with a mission to over sixty employees and growing, The MASTER Teacher has developed and matured. We will continue to provide educators with cutting-edge professional development solutions as we advance into the future.

2 pages Weekly

3645 Training Video Series for the Substitute Teacher
Master Teacher
Leadership Lane
PO Box 1207
Manhattan, KS 66505-1207
800-669-9633
Fax: 800-669-1132
http://www.masterteacher.com
From one man with a mission to over sixty employees and growing, The MASTER Teacher has developed and matured. We will continue to provide educators with cutting-edge professional development solutions as we advance into the future.

ISBN: 0-914607-95-2

3646 Voices in the Hall: High School Principals at Work
Phi Delta Kappa Educational Foundation
PO Box 789
408 N Union Street
Bloomington, IN 47405-3800
812-339-1156
800-766-1156
Fax: 812-339-0018
E-mail: customerservice@pdkintl.org
http://www.pdkintl.org
The mission of Phi Delta Kappa International is to promote high-quality education, in particular publicly supported education, as essential to the development and maintenance of a democratic way of life. This mission is accomplished through leadership, research, and service in education

William E Webster, Author
Donovan R Walling, Director
Publications/Resear
John Amato, President

3647 Wavelength
4753 N Broadway
Suite 808
Chicago, IL 60640
773-784-1012
877-528-47 2
Fax: 773-784-1079
E-mail: info@wavelengthinc.com
http://www.wavelengthinc.com
Wavelength offers a fresh perspective on the key challenges in education today. Our programs are founded on the tenet that humor heals and enlightens. Of course, we also realized that by focusing our humor on education, we'd never run out of material

3648 You Can Handle Them All Discipline Video Series
Master Teacher
Leadership Lane
PO Box 1207
Manhattan, KS 66505-1207
800-669-9633
Fax: 800-669-1132
http://www.masterteacher.com
Based upon the best selling books You Can Handle Them All and BEfore you can Discipline by Robert L Debruyn. It contains the vital professional foundations that must underpin and solid philosophy of discipline.

ISBN: 1-58992-035-X

Robert L DeBruyn, Author

Workshops & Programs

3649 ACE Fellows Program
American Council on Education
1 Dupont Circle NW
Washington, DC 20036-1193
202-939-9300
Fax: 202-785-8056
E-mail: comments@ace.nche.edu
http://www.acenet.edu
Provides comprehensive leadership development for senior faculty and administrators of universities and colleges. Offers mentor-intern relationships programs. Special institutional grants available for candidates from community colleges, tribal colleges and private historical black universities and colleges.

Andrew K Benton, Chairman
Judy Genshaft, Vice Chair

3650 ART New England Summer Workshops
Massachusetts College of Art and De
621 Huntington Avenue
Boston, MA 2115-5801
617-879-7175
E-mail: Nancy.Mccarthy@massart.edu
http://massart.edu/ane
Offers painting, drawing, photography, jewelry making, sculpting, computer imaging and ceramics.

Nancy McCarthy, Administrator

3651 Annual Conductor's Institute of South Carolina
University of South Carolina
School of Music
Columbia, SC 29208
803-777-7500
Fax: 803-777-9774
E-mail: CI@mozart.sc.edu
http://www.conductorsinstitute.com
Since its inception, more than 600 conductors have traveled to Columbia to study with guest conductors and composers. Academic credit is available.

Donald Portnoy, Director

3652 Annual Summer Institute for Secondary Teachers
Rock and Roll Hall of Fame
E-mail: soehler@rockhall.org
http://www.rockhall.com/programs/institute.asp
The institute provides teachers with the knowledge and tools needed to bring popular music into the curriculum. The program includes a rock and roll history survey; guest speakers; discussions and workshops.

June

Susan Oehler, Education Programs Manager

3653 Ball State University
2000 W University Avenue
Muncie, IN 47306
765-289-1241
800-382-8540
E-mail: askus@bsu.edu
http://cms.bsu.edu
At Ball State, we're more than just educators-we're educational entrepreneurs. Combining top-flight talent with thetop-notch resources Ball State has to offer, our students and faculty inject endless energy and creativity into what they teach and how they learn. The result-a university The Princeton Review calls one of the best in the Midwest.

Jo Ann M Gora, President
Terry King, Provost and Vice President f

3654 Bryant and Stratton College
1259 Central Avenue
Albany, NY 12205-142
518-437-1802
Fax: 716-821-9343
E-mail: rpferrell@bryantstratton.edu
http://www.bryantstratton.edu
For 150 years, Bryant & Stratton College has been helping students develop meaningful career skills in a concise, contemporary and effective manner - providing graduates with the marketable job skills they need to succeed in an increasingly competitive marketplace

Bryant H Prentice, Chairman of the Board
David J Ament, Managing Partner

3655 Center for Educational Leadership Trinity University
Trinity University
One Trinity Place
San Antonio, TX 78212-7200
210-999-7207
Fax: 210-999-8164
E-mail: admissions@trinity.edu
http://www.carme.cs.trinity.edu/education/index.asp
Offers three Masters degree programs for Arts, Teaching, Psychology and School Administration. The school also offers summer institutes and training programs for educators and administrators. Also see information regarding the Master of Education: School Administration at http://carme.cs.trinity.edu/education/graduate/medschoolleadership.htm

Paul Kelleher, Chairman
Sonia L Mireles, Senior Secretary

3656 Center for Global Education
Augsbury College
2211 Riverside Avenue
Minneapolis, MN 55454-1350
612-330-1159
800-299-8889
Fax: 612-330-1695
E-mail: globaled@augsburg.edu
http://www.augsburg.edu/global
To provide cross-cultural educational opportunities in order to foster critical analysis of local and global conditions so that personal and systemic change takes place leading to a more just and sustainable world.

Orval Gingerich, Associate Dean
Regina McGoff, Associate Director

3657 Center for Image Processing in Education
PO Box 13750
Tucson, AZ 85732-3750
520-322-0118
800-322-9884
Fax: 520-327-0175
E-mail: kRISR@evisual.org
http://www.cipe.com
CIPE promotes computer-aided visualization as a tool for inquiry-based learning. In support of that mission, it develops instructional materials and conducts workshops that use digital image analysis and geographic information systems technologies as platforms for teaching about science, mathematics, and technology.

Steve Moore, Chief Executive Director
Kristine Rees, Secretary/Treasurer

3658 Center for Learning Connections
Highline Community College
PO Box 98000
Des Moines, WA 98198-9800
206-870-3759
Fax: 206-870-5915
E-mail: jjacob@highline.edu
http://www.learningconnections.org
The mission of the Center for Learning Connections is to prepare learners to manage change and create successful futures.

3659 Center for Occupational Research & Development
601 Lake Air Drive
PO Box 21689
Waco, TX 76710
254-772-8756
800-231-3015
Fax: 254-772-8972
E-mail: twarner@cord.org
http://www.cord.org
The Center for Occupational Research and Development (CORD) is a national nonprofit organization dedicated to leading change in education

Teemus Warner, Coordinator Professional Dev
Richard Hinckley, President and CEO

3660 Center for Play Therapy
University of North Texas
PO Box 310829
Denton, TX 76203-829
940-565-3864
Fax: 940-565-4461
E-mail: cpt@unt.edu
http://www.centerforplaytherapy.com
Encourages the unique development and emotional growth of children through the process of play therapy, a dynamic interpersonal relationship between a child and a therapist trained in play therapy procedures. Provides training, research, publications, counseling services and acts as a clearinghouse for literature in the field.

Sue Bratton, Director
Garry Landreth, Founder

3661 Classroom Connect
6277 Sea Harbor Drive
Orlando, FL 32887
800-638-1639
888-801-8299
Fax: 650-351-5300
E-mail: help@classroom.com
http://www.classroom.com
A leading provider of professional development programs and online instructional content for K-12 education.

October

Jim Bowler, President
Melinda Cook, Vice President Sales

3662 College of the Ozarks
PO Box 17
Point Lookout, MO 65726

417-334-6411
800-222-0525
Fax: 417-335-2618
E-mail: webmaster@cofo.edu
http://www.cofo.edu
The College of the Ozarks began as a dream. In 1905, young Presbyterian missionary James Forsythe was assigned to serve the region that encompassed Sparta, Mansfield, and Forsyth, Missouri

Jerry C Davis, President

3663 Connect
Synergy Learning
116 Birge Street
PO Box 60
Brattleboro, VT 5302-60
800-769-6199
800-769-6199
Fax: 802-254-5233
E-mail: info@synergylearning.org
http://www.synergylearning.org
To engage in publishing and professional development for educators, pre-K through middle school

28 pages
ISSN: 1041-682X

Casey Murrow, Director
Susan Hathaway, Circulation Manager

3664 Critical Issues in Urban Special Education: The Implications of Whole-School Change
Harvard Graduate School of Education
44 Brattle Street
Fifth Floor
Cambridge, MA 2138
617-495-3572
800-545-1849
Fax: 617-496-8051
E-mail: ppe@gse.harvard.edu
http://www.gse.harvard.edu/~ppe
A one-week summer seminar that examines the implications of whole-school change on students with disabilities, policy, procedure, and practice. The program will clarify competing agendas, illuminate various models, and identify unified approaches to ensuring measurable benefits to all children.

Genet Jeanjean, Program Coordinator
Al Written, Interim Director

3665 Critical and Creative Thinking in the Classroom
National Center for Teaching Thinking
815 Washington Street
Suite 8
Newtonville, MA 2460
617-965-4604
Fax: 617-965-4674
A unique summer program of courses for K-12 teachers, curriculum developers, staff-development specialists, school/district administrators, teacher educators and college faculty.

3666 Curriculum Center - Office of Educational Services
3430 Constitution Drive
Suite 114
Springfield, IL 62707-9402
217-786-3010
Fax: 217-786-3020
E-mail: oesiscc@siu.edu
http://www.oes.siu.edu
Programs in vocational areas, career awareness, career development, integration, technology, tech preparation.

3667 Darryl L Sink & Associates
1 Cielo Vista Place
Suite 101
Monterey, CA 93940

831-649-8384
800-650-7465
Fax: 831-649-3914
E-mail: jane@dsink.com
http://www.dsink.com
DSA encourages customers to evaluate such adult learning strategies as cognitive apprenticeship, problem-based learning, goal-based scenarios, and real world authentic learning activities as the cornerstones of efficient, effective, and appealing learning experiences.

3668 DeVry University
One Tower Lane
Oakbrook Terrace, IL 60181
602-216-7700
800-295-8694
Fax: 602-943-4108
http://www.devry.edu
Subjects include communications, computer technology, electronics, graphic communications, and training and development.

Peter Anderson, Chief Strategist
Richard L Ehrlickman, Executive Vice President

3669 Delmar Thomson Learning
3 Columbia Circle
Albany, NY 12212
518-464-3500
Fax: 518-464-7000
E-mail: info@delmar.com
http://www.delmar.com
Subjects include welding, HVAC-R, electrical, electronics, automotive, CADD and drafting, construction, blueprint reading, and fire science.

3670 Depco
3305 Airport Drive
PO Box 178
Pittsburg, KS 66762
620-231-0019
800-767-1062
Fax: 620-231-0024
E-mail: tcoon@depcollc.com
http://www.depcoinc.com
DEPCO (Dependable Education Products Company) was introduced as a manufacturers' representative organization, which represented manufacturers of vocational education products

3671 Eastern Illinois University School of Technology
600 Lincoln Avenue
Charleston, IL 61920
217-581-3226
Fax: 217-581-6607
http://www.eiu-edu/~tech1
Subjects include manufacturing, construction, electronics, graphic communications, training and development.

3672 Edison Welding Institute
EWI
1250 Arthur E Adams Drive
Columbus, OH 43221-3585
614-688-5000
Fax: 614-688-5001
E-mail: info@ewi.org
http://www.ewi.org
The NJC's mission is to enhance the life-cycle affordability and mission capability of critical Navy weapon systems through the implementation of materials joining technology

Henry Cialone, President/CEO
Jim Tighe, CFO/Vice-President

3673 Educational Summit
The Principals' Center
20 Nassau Street
Suite 211
Princeton, NJ 8542-4509

609-497-1907
Fax: 609-497-1927
An educational summit held in August for school principals to explore, debate and design new models for schooling in America with implications for choice, charters and the community.

3674 Effective Strategies for School Reform
Harvard Graduate School of Education
44 Brattle Street
5th Floor
Cambridge, MA 2138
617-495-3572
800-545-1849
Fax: 617-496-8051
E-mail: ppe@gse.harvard.edu
http://www.gse.harvard.edu/~ppe
To enrich the professional practice of individuals and institutions worldwide that share our commitment to improving education.

Rosanne Boyle, Program Coordinator
Jennifer Stine, Managing Director/Profession

3675 Electronics Industries Alliance/CEA
2500 Wilson Boulevard
Arlington, VA 22201-3834
703-907-7670
Fax: 703-907-7968
http://www.CEMAweb.org
Electronics workshops.

3676 Elementary Education Professional Development School
Pennsylvania State University
148 Chambers Building
Pennsylvania State University
University Park, PA 16802
814-865-2243
E-mail: n78@psu.edu
http://www.ed.psu.edu/pds
The first goal is to enhance the educational experiences of all children. The second goal focuses on ensuring high quality field experiences for new teachers.

James Nolan, Professor of Education

3677 Emco Maier Corporation
2841 Charter Street
Columbus, OH 43228
614-771-5991
Fax: 614-771-5990
E-mail: info@emcomaier-usa.com
http://www.emcomaier-usa.com
The EMCO success story began in 1947 with the production of conventional lathes. In the years to follow, EMCO repeatedly impressed the market with extraordinary, innovative solutions.

Josh Dack, Sales Manager
Karen Fahy, Sales/Marketing Coordinator

3678 Energy Concepts
404 Washington Boulevard
Mundelein, IL 60060
847-837-8191
800-621-1247
Fax: 847-837-8171
http://www.energy-concepts-inc.com
Subjects include material science technology, principles of technology year I&II.

3679 Fastech
1750 Westfield Drive
Findlay, OH 45840
419-425-2233
Fax: 419-425-9431
E-mail: info@fastechinc.net
http://www.fastechinc.net
Subjects include mastercam training, and FMMT CD's.

3680 Festo Corporation
395 Moreland Road
PO Box 18023
Hauppauge, NY 11788
631-435-0800
Fax: 631-435-8026
E-mail: customer.service@us.festo.com
http://www.festo-usa.com
Subjects include fluid power, PLC, industrial automation.

Fred Zieram, Sales Manager
Petra Milks, Product Coordinator

3681 Foundation for Critical Thinking
PO Box 196
Tomales, CA 94971
707-878-9100
800-833-3645
Fax: 707-878-9111
E-mail: cct@criticalthinking.org
http://www.criticalthinking.org
The work of the Foundation is to integrate the Center's research and theoretical developments, and to create events and resources designed to help educators improve their instruction. Materials developed through the Foundation for Critical Thinking include books, thinker's guides, videos, and other teaching and learning resources.

Dr Richard Paul, Fellow
Dr Linda Elder, Fellow

3682 Four State Regional Technology Conference
Pittsburg State University
College of Technology
1701 S Broadway
Pittsburg, KS 66762
620-235-4365
800-854-7488
Fax: 620-235-4343
E-mail: tbaldwin@pittstate.edu
http://www.pittstate.edu
Subjects include educational technology and technology management.

November
30 booths with 250 attendees
Tom Baldwin, Dean, College of Technology

3683 Graduate Programs for Professional Educators
North Central Association of Colleges & Schools
Walden University
155 5th Avenue S
Minneaoplis, MN 55401
800-444-6795
Fax: 941-498-4266
E-mail: request@waldenu.edu
Both the MS and PhD in Education allow study from home or work. The Master of Science in Education serves classroom teachers and the PhD in education serves the advanced learning needs of educators from a wide range that serves practice fields and levels.

3684 Grand Canyon University College of Education
3300 W Camelback Road
Phoenix, AZ 85017-1097
602-639-7500
877-860-3951
Fax: 312-263-7462
E-mail: cmosby@gcu.edu
http://www.gcu.edu
Prepares learners to become global citizens, critical thinkers, effective communicators, and responsible leaders by providing an academically challenging,

values-based curriculum from the context of our Christian heritage.

Kathy Player, Provots and Chief Academic O
Cheri St Arnauld, Senior VP of Academic Affair

3685 Harvard Institute for School Leadership
Harvard Graduate School of Education
44 Brattle Street
Fifth Floor
Cambridge, MA 2138
617-495-3572
800-545-1849
Fax: 617-496-8051
E-mail: ppe@harvard.edu
http://www.gse.harvard.edu/ppe
An intensive residential program for leadership teams from school districts. Participants will gain new perspectives on the processes and goals of school reform and practical skills for leading change in their districts.

July

3686 Harvard Seminar for Superintendents
Harvard Graduate School of Education
44 Brattle Street
Fifth Floor
Cambridge, MA 2138
617-495-3572
800-545-1849
Fax: 617-496-8051
E-mail: ppe@harvard.edu
http://www.gse.harvard.edu/ppe
Veteran superintendents from around the country participate in a week of intellectually stimulating conversations with Harvard faculty and networking with colleagues. Topics discussed include the arts, science, social science, and current events.

July

Julia Bean, Program Assistant

3687 Hobart Institute of Welding Technology
400 Trade Square East
Troy, OH 45373
800-332-9448
Fax: 937-332-5200
http://www.welding.org
Preparation course for CWI/CWE exams. Instructor course devoted to welding theory and hand-son practice.

Elmer Swank, Contact

3688 Indiana University-Purdue University of Indianapolis, IUPUI
Department of Construction Technology
799 W Michigan Street
ET 209
Indianapolis, IN 46202-5160
317-274-2533
Fax: 317-274-4567
E-mail: pmay2@iupui.edu
http://www.engr.iupui.edu/cnt
Subjects include architectural technology, civil engineering technology, construction technology, interior design.

H Tner Yurtseven, Dean
Lisa Jones, Administrative Assistant

3689 Industrial Training Institute
3385 Wheeling Road
Lancaster, OH 43130
740-687-5262
800-638-4180
Fax: 740-687-5262
E-mail: drbillstevens1@msn.com
http://www.trainingrus.com

Subjects include basic electricity, motors, controls, PLC's, NEC and process control; custom designed training and consulting.

3690 Institute of Higher Education
General Board of Higher Education & Ministry/UMC
1001 19th Avenue S
Nashville, TN 37212
615-340-7406
Fax: 615-340-7379
E-mail: scu@gbhem.org
http://www.gbhem.org/highed.html
An annual seminar for administrators and faculty of United Methodist-related educational institutions addressing current themes related to the college's mission.

June
125 attendees

Cynthia Bond Hopson, Assistant General Secretary
Wanda Bigham, Interim Associate General

3691 International Curriculum Management Audit Center
Phi Delta Kappa International
320 W Eight Street
Suite 216
Bloomington, IN 47404
812-339-1156
800-766-1156
Fax: 812-339-0018
E-mail: memberservices@pdkintl.org
http://www.pdkintl.org
The mission of Phi Delta Kappa International is to promote high-quality education, in particular publicly supported education, as essential to the development and maintenance of a democratic way of life. This mission is accomplished through leadership, research, and service in education.

William Bushaw, Executive Director
Diana Daugherty, Administrative Assistant

3692 International Graduate School
Berne University
35 Center Street
Suite 18
Wolfeboro Falls, NH 03896-1080
603-569-8648
866-755-5557
Fax: 603-569-4052
E-mail: berne@berne.edu
http://www.berne.edu
Doctoral Degrees in one to two years, Specialist Diplomas in six to twelve months in: business, education (all specialties), government, health services, international relations, psychology, religion, social work and human services.

3693 International Workshops
187 Aqua View Road
Cedarburg, WI 53012
262-377-7062
Fax: 262-377-7096
E-mail: thintz@internationalworkshops.org
http://www.internationalworkshops.org
International Workshops creates an international community of artists and teachers in a site that combines touristic and cultural interest.

400 attendees

Tori Hintz, Manager
Gerald F Fischbach, Director

3694 Island Drafting & Technical Institute
128 Broadway
Amityville, NY 11701-2704
631-691-8733
Fax: 631-691-8738
E-mail: info@idti.edu
http://www.idti.edu
Our aim is to graduate students well-trained and technically qualified so that they may enter their

chosen field or continue their education at the baccalaureate or higher level.

John G Diliberto, VP

3695 Janice Borla Vocal Jazz Camp

N Central College, Music Department
30 N Brainard Street
Naperville, IL 60540
630-416-3911
Fax: 630-416-6249
E-mail: jborla@aol.com
http://www.janiceborlavocaljazzcamp.org
The camp's mission is to enable jazz vocalists to develop and enhance their individual performing skills and musical creativity, regardless of prior experience level, by studying with and attending performances of professional artists actively engaged in the field of jazz performance.

Janice Borla, Director
Jay Clayton, Faculty

3696 Jefferson State Community College

2601 Carson Road
Birmingham, AL 35215
205-853-1200
800-239-5900
Fax: 205-856-8572
E-mail: workforcedev@jeffstateonline.com
http://www.jeffstateonline.com
Certificate and degree programs in automated manufacturing, electromechanical systems, industrial maintenance, and CAD.

3697 July in Rensselaer

St Joseph's College, Graduate Dept
PO Box 984
Rensselaer, IN 47978
219-866-6352
Fax: 219-866-6102
E-mail: jamesc@saintjoe.edu
Solo, ensemble, liturgy, accompanying, history, improvisation, private lessons, technique, repertoire, sight reading, workshops, theory and sacred choral music.

Rev. James Challancin, Director

3698 K'nex Education Division

2990 Bergey Road
PO Box 700
Hatfield, PA 19440
888-ABC-KNEX
Fax: 215-996-4222
E-mail: abcknex@knex.com
http://www.knexeducation.com
Introductory, set specific, regional and design your own professional development programs offered for any/all K-12 technology, math and science sets.

3699 Kaleidoscope

Consulting Psychologists Press
3803 E Bayshore Road
Palo Alto, CA 94303-4300
800-624-1765
Fax: 650-969-8608
An institute for educators that develops insights into teaching styles and learning styles; administers and interprets the Myers-Briggs Type Indicator (personality inventory); learn new techniques to help children understand and value their unique qualities; create and deliver lessons that enlighten all students and more.

July

3700 Kent State University

375 Terrace Drive
Van Deusen Hall
Kent, OH 44242
330-672-2892
Fax: 330-672-2894
E-mail: lepps@kent.edu
http://www.tech.kent.edu

Subjects include aeronautics, electronics, manufacturing engineering, computer technology, and automotive engineering technology.

Verna Fitzsimmons, Interim Dean
Isaac Richmond Nettey, Associate Dean

3701 Kentucky State University

400 East Main Street
Frankfort, KY 40601
502-597-6000
Fax: 502-227-6236
E-mail: webadmin@kysu.edu
http://www.kysu.edu
Associates in applied science in drafting and design technology and applied science in electronics technology.

Mary Evans Sias, President
Stephen Mason, Executive Assistant to the P

3702 Kodaly Teaching Certification Program

DePaul University, School of Music
804 West Belden Avenue
Chicago, IL 60614
773-325-4355
Fax: 773-325-7263
Music education, pedagogy and workshops.

Robert Krueger, Director Operations

3703 Lab Volt Systems

1710 State Highway 34
Farmingdale, NJ 07727
732-938-2000
800-522-2658
Fax: 732-774-8573
E-mail: us@labvolt.com
http://www.labvolt.com
Global leader in the design and manufacture of hands-on training laboratories for public education, industry, and the military.

Eric Maynard, Contact

3704 Leadership and the New Technologies

Harvard Graduate School of Education
44 Brattle Street
Fifth Floor
Cambridge, MA 02138
800-545-1849
800-545-1849
Fax: 617-496-8051
E-mail: ppe@gse.harvard.edu
http://www.gse.harvard.edu/~ppe
Programs designed to help teams of school leaders anticipate the far-reaching impacts that new technologies can have on students, teachers, curriculum, and communication. Participants make long-term plans for the use of technology in their schools and districts and learn how to take advantage of federal and state technology initiatives.

July

Ann Doyle, Program Coordinator

3705 Learning & The Enneagram

National Enneagram Institute at Milton Academy
230 Atherton Street
Milton, MA 02186-2424
617-898-1798
Fax: 617-898-1712
An educational enterprise dedicated to guiding individuals and organizations in the most responsible and effective format for their needs. Programs include exploration of what every educator needs to know; why we learn in the way we do; and how we teach.

July

Regina Pyle, Coordinator

3706 Learning Materials Workshop

58 Henry Street
Burlington, VT 05401
800-693-7164
Fax: 802-862-8399
E-mail: info@learningmaterialswork.com
http://www.learningmaterialswork.com
Learning Materials Workshop Blocks are learning tools in the hands of young children. They are open-ended, yet carefully designed in a variety of colors, sizes, shapes, and textures that stimulate and develop perpetual, motor, and language skills. Learning Materials Workshops are designed for early childhood/primary grade teachers, paraprofessionals, curriculum coordinators, special education teachers, ESL teachers, and teachers of the gifted and talented to help develop the learning process.

Karen Hewitt, President

3707 Light Machines

444 E Industrial Park Avenue
Manchester, NH 03109-5317
800-221-2763
Fax: 603-625-2137
E-mail: industrialsales@intelitek_usa.com
http://www.lightmachines.com
Subjects include demonstrations and comprehensive training on CNC routers, turning machines and milling machines, and CAD/CAM software.

3708 MPulse Maintenance Software

PO Box 22906
Eugene, OR 97402
541-302-6677
800-944-1796
Fax: 541-302-6680
E-mail: info@mpulsesoftware.com
http://www.mpulsesoftware.com
Deliver simply better EAM/CMMS software that is easier to use and faster to implement. Keep it affordable by controlling the cost of sales and marketing. Design it to keep up with their needs today, their challenges of tomorrow, while maintaining the history of what they did yesterday. And do it better than anyone else

Steve Brous, President & CEO

3709 Marcraft International Corporation

1350 Spaulding Ave
Suite 302
Kennwick, WA 99352
509-374-1951
800-441-6006
Fax: 509-374-9250
E-mail: sales@marcraft.com
http://www.marcraft.com
s to develop exceptional products for effectively teaching and training people the technical IT, computer, and electronics training skills in demand today and in the future.

Robert Krug, National Sales Manager

3710 Maryland Center for Career and Technology Education

1415 Key Highway
Baltimore, MD 21230
410-685-1648
Fax: 410-685-0032
Subjects include technology education and occupational education certification.

3711 Media and American Democracy

Harvard Graduate School of Education
Programs in Professional Education
Appian Way
Cambridge, MA 02138
617-495-3572
800-545-1849
Fax: 617-496-8051

E-mail: ppe@harvard.edu
http://www.gse.harvard.edu/~ppe
Participants learn about the interaction between the media and American democratic process, develop curriculum units, and examine ways to help students become thoughtful consumers of media messages about politics. Designed for secondary school teachers of history, social studies, English, journalism, and humanities.

August

Tracy Ryder, Program Assistant

3712 Millersville University
PO Box 1002
1 South George Street
Millersvile, PA 17551
717-872-3011
800-426-4553
Fax: 877-327-8132
http://www.millersville.edu
With a student population of 7,259 undergraduate and 1,047 graduate students, Millersville University offers all the advantages you would expect from a university: competitive programs, great facilities, a diverse student community and a variety of campus programming all offered in an accessible, intimate and close-knit atmosphere more frequently found at a smaller college

Michael G Warfel, Chairman
Paul G Wedel, Vice Chairman

3713 Morehead State University
150 University Boulevard
Morehead, KY 40351
606-783-2221
Fax: 606-783-5000
E-mail: admissions@moreheadstate.edu
http://www.morehead-st.edu
Morehead State University was founded upon and continues to embrace the ideal that all persons should have opportunity to participate in higher education. With immense pride in its past and great promise for its future, the University intends to emerge in the first decade of the 21st century as an even stronger institution recognized for superb teaching and learning with exemplary programs in teacher education, space-related science and technology, entrepreneurship, visual and performing arts.

Beth Patrick, Vice President
Dayna Seelig, Special Assistant to the Pre

3714 Musikgarten
507 Arlington Street
Greensboro, NC 27406
336-272-5303
800-216-6864
Fax: 336-272-0581
E-mail: musgarten@aol.com
http://www.musikgarten.org
Early childhood music education workshops teaching music and understanding children.

Lorna Heyge, President

3715 NASA Educational Workshop
NSTA
1840 Wilson Boulevard
Arlington, VA 22201-3000
703-243-7100
888-400-6782
Fax: 703-243-7177
E-mail: businessoffice@nsta.org
http://www.nsta.org
Two week workshop at a NASA Center, professional development opportunity for K-12 teachers in mathematics, science, and technology, teachers and curriculum specialists at the K-12 levels; media special-

ists, resource teachers, elementary curriculum developers, counselors, and others with special interest in mathematics, science, technology, and geography.

Karen Ostlund, President
Bill Badders, President-Elect

3716 NCSS Summer Workshops
National Council for the Social Studies
8555 Sixteenth Street
Suite 500
Silver Spring, MD 20910
301-588-1800
800-683-0812
Fax: 301-588-2049
E-mail: sgriffin@ncss.org
http://www.socialstudies.org
Social studies educators teach students the content knowledge, intellectual skills, and civic values necessary for fulfilling the duties of citizenship in a participatory democracy.

July

Susan Griffin, Executive Director
Sojan Alex, Finance Assistant

3717 National Center for Construction Education & Research
13614 Progress Boulevard
Alachua, FL 32615
386-518-6500
888-622-3720
Fax: 386-518-6303
E-mail: info@nccer.org
http://www.nccer.org
Our mission is to build a safe, productive, and sustainable workforce of craft professionals.

Don Whyte, President
Cathy Tyler, Executive Assistant

3718 National Computer Systems
4401 L Street NW
Suite 550
Edina, MN 55435
612-995-8997
800-328-6172
Fax: 952-830-8564
http://www.ncsus.net
Programs offer skills to teach technology in the classroom.

3719 National Head Start Association
1651 Prince Street
Alexandria, VA 22314-2818
703-739-0875
Fax: 703-739-0878
http://www.nhsa.org
The National Head Start Association is a private not-for-profit membership organization dedicated exclusively to meeting the needs of Head Start children and their families.

Ron Herndon, Chairman
Linda Broyles, Vice- Chairperson

3720 Northern Arizona University
South San Francisco Street
Flagstaff, AZ 86011
928-523-9011
Fax: 520-523-6395
E-mail: tlc2@dana.ucc.nau.edu
http://www.nau.edu
Provide an outstanding undergraduate residential education strengthened by research, graduate and professional programs, and sophisticated methods of distance delivery.

John D Haeger, President
Tracy Cooper, Lab Assistant

3721 Orff-Schulwerk Teacher Certification Program
DePaul University, School of Music
804 West Belden Avenue
Chicago, IL 60614
773-325-7260
Fax: 773-325-7264
E-mail: ahutchen@wppost.depaul.edu.
Music education, pedagogy and workshops.

Judy Bundra, Associate Dean

3722 Owens Community College
PO Box 10000
Toledo, OH 43699-1947
567-661-7000
800-466-9367
Fax: 419-661-7664
http://www.owens.edu
We believe in serving our students and our communities. Your success is our misssion.

Diana H Talmage, Chairman
R J Molter, Vice Chair

3723 Paideia Group
608 Garden Leaf Court
St. Louis, MO 63011
636-220-9300
Fax: 919-932-3905
E-mail: bethsymes@psideiagroup.com
http://www.paideiagroup.com
To help people understand what it means to be customer-focused. Participants focus on the skills, attitudes, and automatic behaviors that must be developed to reach a common goal of becoming a customer-focused organization.

Beth Symes, Principal and Founder

3724 Pamela Sims & Associates
54 Mozart Crescent
Brampton, Ontario
Canada L6Y-2W7
905-455-7331
888-610-7467
Fax: 905-455-0207
E-mail: loveofkids@aol.com
http://www.pamelasims.com
Seminars and workshops for educators and parents.

Pamela Sims, President
Kelly Smith, Marketing Director

3725 Pennsylvania State University-Workforce Education & Development Program
411D Keller Building
University Park, PA 16802
814-863-3858
Fax: 814-863-7532
E-mail: eif1@psu.edu
http://www.ed.psu.edu/wfed
To promote excellence, opportunity, and leadership among professionals in the workforce education and development field including, but not limited to, those employed in secondary or postsecondary education institutions, social services industries, and employee groups and private businesses.

Edgar I Farmer, Department Head
Judith A Kolb, Professor-in-Charge

3726 Performance Learning Systems
72 Lone Oak Drive
Cadiz, KY 42211
270-522-2000
866-757-2527
Fax: 270-522-2010
E-mail: info@plsweb.com
http://www.plsweb.com
The mission of Performance Learning Systems, Inc. is to enhance education through the development of educational services.

Jackie Futrell, Resource Manager
Stephen G Barkley, Master teacher-of-teachers

3727 Piano Workshop
Goshen College
1700 S Main Street
Goshen, IN 46526
574-535-7000
Fax: 574-535-7949
E-mail: beverlykl@goshen.edu
http://www.goshen.edu/music/Piano%20Workshop/Main
The Goshen College Piano Workshop and Academy comprises lectures, master classes and recital performances presented by distinguished clinicians, composers and performers. Teachers participating in the Workshop hear inspiring lectures relevant to piano pedagogy, performance and literature.

Beverly K Lapp, Associate Professor of Music

3728 Pittsburg State University
College of Technology
1701 S Broadway
Pittsburg, KS 66762
620-231-7000
800-854-7488
Fax: 620-235-4343
E-mail: psuinfo@pittstate.edu
http://www.pittstate.edu
A comprehensive regional university, provides undergraduate and graduate programs and services to the people of southeast Kansas, but also to others who seek the benefits offered.

Bruce Dallman, Dean, College of Technology
Steve Scott, President

3729 Polaroid Education Program
565 Technology Square
#3B
Cambridge, MA 02139-3539
781-386-2000
Fax: 781-386-3925
This program offers workshops for professional educators, preK-12; the Visual Learning Workshop and an Instant Image Portfolio Workshop.

3730 Professional Development Institutes
Center for Professional Development & Services
2730 University Boulevard
Suite 301
Kensington, MD 20895
301-949-1771
800-766-1156
Fax: 301-949-5441
E-mail: info@pditraining.net
http://www.pditraining.net
Offers a wide variety of courses for Real Estate professionals around the US to meet their pre-licensing, post-licensing, and continuing education needs. Also offers non-credit courses on Technology, Business, Accounting, and Project Management, among others to further any career.

3731 Professional Development Workshops
Rebus
4111 Jackson Road
Ann Arbor, MI 48103
734-668-4870
800-435-3085
Fax: 734-668-4728
http://www.rebusinc.com
Workshops that promote success by assessing children in the context of active learning.

June/July

Sam Meisels, CEO
Linda Borgsdorf, President

3732 Project Zero Classroom
Harvard Graduate School of Education
Programs in Professional Education
Appian Way
Cambridge, MA 02138
617-495-3572
800-545-1849
Fax: 617-496-8051
E-mail: ppe@harvard.edu
http://www.gse.harvard.edu/~ppe
Renowned educators Howard Gardner and David Perkins and their Project Zero colleagues work with K-12 educators to help them reshape their classroom practices to promote student understanding. The week focuses on five concepts: teaching for understanding, multiple intelligences, the thinking classroom, authentic assessment, and learning with and through the arts.

July

Tracy Ryder, Program Assistant

3733 Robert McNeel & Associates
3670 Woodland Park Avenue N
Seattle, WA 98103
206-545-7000
Fax: 206-545-7321
E-mail: bob@mcneelcom
http://www.en.na.mcneel.com
3D modeling workshop for design, drafting, graphics, and technology educators.

3734 Rockford Systems
4620 Hydraulic Road
Rockford, IL 61109-2695
815-874-7891
800-922-7533
Fax: 815-874-6144
E-mail: sales@rockfordsystems.com
http://www.rockfordsystems.com
Machine safegaurding seminar for technology educators.

3735 SUNY College at Oswego
7060 Route 104
Oswego, NY 13126-3599
315-312-2500
Fax: 315-312-2863
E-mail: stanley@oswego.edu
http://www.oswego.edu
The chief goal of the Oswego College Foundation, Inc. is to raise and manage private support to advance SUNY Oswego's mission.

October
26 booths with 350-400 attendees

Deborah F Stanley, President
Howard Gordon, Executive Assistant to Presi

3736 School of Music
Georgia State University
PO Box 4097
Atlanta, GA 30302-4097
404-413-5900
Fax: 404-413-5910
E-mail: music@gsu.edu
http://www.music.gsu.edu
The mission of the School of Music is to provide a comprehensive, rigorous, and innovative academic program that is consistent with the urban context and mission of Georgia State University, and that serves the pursuit of artistic, professional, and scholarly excellence through experiences of lasting value to all stakeholders.

W Dwight Coleman, Director
Robert J Ambrose, Associate Director

3737 Southern Polytechnic State University
1100 S Marietta Parkway
Marietta, GA 30060-2896
678-915-7778
800-635-3204

Fax: 678-915-7490
E-mail: coned@spsu.edu
http://www.oce.spsu.edu
Specialize in the delivery of comprehensive real-world training on a grand scale. Whether it be High-Tech, Business Professional or Engineering

3738 Southwestern Oklahoma State University
Industrial and Engineering Technology Department
100 Campus Drive
Weatherford, OK 73096
580-774-3063
Fax: 580-774-3795
E-mail: admissions@swosu.edu
http://www.swosu.edu
The mission of Southwestern Oklahoma State University is to provide educational opportunities in higher education that meet the needs of the state and region; contribute to the educational, economic, and cultural environment; and support scholarly activity.

Gary Bell, Chair
Jeff Short, Program Coordinator

3739 Specialized Solutions
24703 US Highway 19-N
Suite 200
Clearwater, FL 33763
240-252-5070
888-840-2378
Fax: 877-200-5959
E-mail: cameron@specializedsolutions.com
http://www.specializedsolutions.com
Technology based training and certification self study programs.

Sheri Nash, Contact

3740 Staff Development Workshops & Training Sessions
National School Conference Institute
PO Box 37527
Phoenix, AZ 85069-7527
602-371-8655
Fax: 602-371-8790
Offers twenty relevant and leading edge programs including curriculum instruction assessment, restructuring your school, improving student performance and gifted at-risk students. Ten monthly sessions of each program are available, with monthly feedback to follow-up. Accelerates restructuring efforts and also offers graduate credit.

3741 Standards and Accountability: Their Impact on Teaching and Assessment
Harvard Graduate School of Education
Programs in Professional Education
339 Gutman Library
Cambridge, MA 02138
617-495-3572
800-545-1849
Fax: 617-496-8051
E-mail: ppe@harvard.edu
http://www.gse.harvard.edu/~ppe
Examines educational and policy issues by new approaches to standards, assessment, and accountability. Focuses on issues of excellence and equity, aligning assessments with standards, strengthening professional development, impacts of challenges on school communities, and political and legal issues surrounding standards and forms of accountability. Designed for public school leaders whose responsibilities include evaluation and testing.

July

Tracy Ryder, Program Assistant

3742 Storytelling for Educational Enrichment The Magic of Storytelling
2709 Oak Haven Drive
San Marcos, TX 78666-5065
512-392-0669
800-322-3199
Fax: 512-392-9660
E-mail: krieger@corridor.net
Teacher in-service and training in story-telling and puppetry for teachers of Pre-K through third grades. The Magic of Story-telling is for all ages and levels, specializing in original stories of enlightenment and environmental education. Over ten years experiences with many national and regional conferences and training.

Cherie Krieger, President

3743 Summer Institute in Siena
University of Siena-S/American Universities
595 Prospect Road
Waterbury, CT 06706
203-754-5741
Fax: 203-753-8105
E-mail: siena@sienamusic.org
http://www.sienamusic.org
Programs offered in cooperation with the University of Siena-S and American Universities and Colleges. The program in Siena Italy is open to qualified graduates, undergraduates, professionals, teachers, 19 years of age or above. Special diploma; credit or non-credit; in-service credit; auditions; trips to Rome, Florence, Assisi, Venice, Pisa, three days in Switzerland; a Puccini Opera.

Joseph Del Principe, Music Director

3744 Summer Programs for School Teams
National Association of Elementary School Principa
1615 Duke Street
Alexandria, VA 22314-3345
703-684-3345
800-386-2377
Fax: 703-518-6281
http://www.naesp.org
Events focused on the key to exceptional instruction. Effective teaching and learning for school teams, must include the principal.

Ann R Walker, Assistant Executive Director
Herrie Hahn, Director Programs

3745 Supplemental Instruction, Supervisor Workshops
University of Missouri-Kansas City
5100 Rockhill Road
SASS 210
Kansas City, MO 64110-2499
816-235-1174
Fax: 816-235-5156
E-mail: cad@umkc.edu
http://www.umkc.edu/cad/si
Supplemental Instruction (SI) is an academic assistance program that utilizes peer-assisted study sessions.

Kim Wilcox, Coordinator of Training
Glen Jacobs, Executive Director

3746 THE Institute & Knowvation
1105 Media 9201 Oakdale Avenue
Suite 101
Chatsworth, CA 91311
818-734-1520
800-840-0003
Fax: 818-734-1522
E-mail: kodell@1105media.com
http://www.thejournal.com/institute

T.H.E. Institute believes that in order for students to be successful in the 21st century, technology must be an integral part of every aspect of education.

Geoffrey H Fletcher, Executive Director

3747 TUV Product Service
Westendstrae 199
Munich, MA D-806
49 -9 5-91 0
800-TUV-0123
Fax: 978-762-7637
E-mail: info@tuev-sued.de
http://www.tuvglobal.com
As process partners with comprehensive industry knowledge our teams of specialists provide early consultation and continuous guidance, thus achieving the optimisation of technology, systems and expertise

Axel Stepken, Chief Executive Officer
Manfred Bayerlein, Chief Operations Officer

3748 Teacher Education Institute
1079 W Morse Boulevard
Suite A
Winter Park, FL 32789-3751
800-331-2208
Fax: 800-370-2600
E-mail: tei@teachereducation.com
http://www.teachereducation.com
TEI was founded in 1981 to meet the needs of classroom teachers for quality education and training in practical, proven skills and methods that make a tangible and positive difference in their relationships and interactions with students and colleagues.

Vince Welsh, President

3749 Teachers College: Columbia University
Center for Technology & School Change
525 W 120th Street
New York, NY 10027
212-678-3000
Fax: 212-678-4048
E-mail: webcomments@tc.columbia.edu
http://www.tc.columbia.edu
bring educational opportunities to all members of society, and whose faculty and students, time and again during more than a century of leadership, have demonstrated the power of ideas to change the world.

Howard Budin, Director Center for Technolo
Susan H Fuhrman, President

3750 Technology Training for Educators
Astronauts Memorial Foundation
Kennedy Space Center
, FL 32899
321-452-2887
800-792-3494
Fax: 321-452-6244
E-mail: amfreg@amfcse.org
http://www.amfcse.org
Microsoft NT Administration; Technology Specialist; Management of Technology; Advanced Technology Specialist.

3751 Tooling University
3615 Superior Avenue
Building 44,6th Floor
Cleveland, OH 44114-3898
216-706-6600
866-706-8665
Fax: 216-706-6601
E-mail: info@toolingu.com
http://www.toolingu.com
Toolingu.com is the leading online training provider focused on the unique needs of manufacturers. Our roots are in manufac-

turing, and our business started by recognizing the industry's specific needs

Gene Jones, Director Marketing

3752 Total Quality Schools Workshop
Pennsylvania State University
302F Rackley Building
University Park, PA 16802
814-843-3765
E-mail: hli@psu.edu
http://www.ed.psu.edu/ctqs/index.html
Designed for public school educators at the state, national, and international level, this training program provides information in the philosophy, tools, and techniques of total quality management in education. The three day-six week program focuses on leadership, reform models, and education decision making.

William Hartman, Director

3753 University of Arkansas at Little Rock
2801 S University Avenue
Little Rock, AR 72204-1099
501-683-7302
Fax: 501-683-7304
E-mail: admissions@ualr.edu
http://www.ualr.edu
With more than 100 programs of study, UALR has an academic program to suit your interests. We offer everything from computer science to fine arts, and we're sure you will find your niche on our campus

Sandra Bates, President
Tammy Starks, Vice President

3754 University of Central Florida
3100 Technology Parkway
Suite 264
Orlando, FL 32826-3281
407-823-4910
Fax: 407-207-4911
E-mail: distrib@ucf.edu
http://www.distrib.ucf.edu
The University of Central Florida is one of the most dynamic universities in the country. Offering 223 degree programs, it has become an academic and research leader in numerous fields, such as optics, modeling and simulation, engineering and computer science, business administration, education, science, hospitality management and digital media.

John C Hitt, President/Corporate Secretar
John Schell, Vice President

3755 University of Michigan-Dearborn Center for Corporate & Professional Development
4901 Evergreen Road
CCPD-2000
Dearborn, MI 48128-2406
313-593-5000
Fax: 313-593-5111
E-mail: info@umich.edu
http://www.umd.umich.edu
We offer undergraduate, graduate, and professional education to a diverse, highly motivated, and talented student body. Our programs are responsive to the changing needs of society; relevant to the goals of our students and community partners; rich in opportunities for independent and collaborative study, research, and practical application; and reflective of the traditions of excellence, innovation, and leadership that distinguish the University of Michigan

Daniel Little, Chancellor
Ray Metz, Chief of Staff

3756 Wavelength
4753 N Broadway
Suite 808
Chicago, IL 60640
773-784-1012
877-528-47 2
Fax: 773-784-1079

E-mail: info@wavelengthinc.com
http://www.wavelengthinc.com
Wavelength offers a fresh perspective on the key challenges in education today. Our programs are founded on the tenet that humor heals and enlightens.

3757 Wids Learning Design System

1 Foundation Circle
Waunakee, WI 53597
800-677-9437
800-821-6313
Fax: 608-849-2468
E-mail: info@wids.org
http://www.wids.org
WIDS strives to enhance the quality of learning through the development, implementation, support, and continuous improvement of the WIDS Learning Design System, a comprehensive methodology, supported by application and professional development tools, for designing and planning performance-based assessment learning and teaching.

Lisa Laabs, Office Manager
Judy Neill, Director

3758 Workforce Education and Development

Southern Illinois University Carbondale
475 Clocktower Drive
Mailcode 4605
Carbondale, IL 62901-4605
618-453-3321
Fax: 618-453-1909
E-mail: wed@siu.edu
http://www.wed.siu.edu/Public/
The Department of Workforce Education and Development is one of the largest education, training, and development departments in the United States. A recent external evaluation team recognized the Department as among the top ten in the nation.

Keith Waugh, Associate
Professor/Chairman

Directories & Handbooks / General

3759 106 Ways Parents Can Help Students Achieve
American Association of School Administrators
801 N Quincy Street
Suite 700
Arlington, VA 22203-1730
703-528-0700
Fax: 703-841-1543
http://www.aasa.org
Provides parents with useful information about the importance of parental involvement, concrete ways to work with children and schools to promote success, and a list of resources for further reading.
Set of 10
ISBN: 0-8108-4220-3

3760 A Personal Planner & Training Guide for the Substitute Teacher
Master Teacher
Leadership Lane
PO Box 1207
Manhattan, KS 66505-1207
800-669-9633
Fax: 800-669-1132
http://www.masterteacher.com
Helps substitute teachers set the tone for a positive experience.
90 pages
ISBN: 0-914607-89-8
John Eller, Author

3761 Academic Year & Summer Programs Abroad
American Institute for Foreign Study
102 Greenwich Avenue
Greenwich, CT 06830-5504
203-869-9090
800-727-2437
Fax: 203-399-5590
E-mail: college.info@aifs.com
http://www.aifs.com
Offers school names, addresses, courses offered, tuition and fee information.
224 pages Annual

3762 Accredited Institutions of Postsecondary Education
MacMillan Publishing Company
1633 Broadway
New York, NY 10019
212-654-8500
Fax: 800-835-3202
Lists over 5,000 accredited institutions and programs for postsecondary education in the United States.
600 pages Annual

3763 Activities and Strategies for Connecting Kids with Kids: Elementary Edition
Master Teacher
Leadership Lane
PO Box 1207
Manhattan, KS 66505-1207
800-669-9633
Fax: 800-669-1132
http://www.masterteacher.com
Activities, lesson plans, and strategies that celebrate each student's individual differences while developing cooperation, tolerance, understanding, sharing and caring.
159 pages
ISBN: 0-914607-74-X

3764 Activities and Strategies for Connecting Kids with Kids: Secondary Edition
Master Teacher
Leadership Lane
PO Box 1207
Manhattan, KS 66505-1207
800-669-9633
Fax: 800-669-1132
http://www.masterteacher.com
Activities, lesson plans, and strategies that celebrate each student's individual differences while developing cooperation, tolerance, understanding, sharing and caring.
136 pages
ISBN: 0-914607-75-8

3765 American School Directory
PO Box 20002
Murfreesboro, TN 37129
866-273-2797
Fax: 800-929-3408
E-mail: asdwebmaster@asd.com
http://www.asd.com
More than 104,000 school sites are loaded with pictures, art, calendars, menus, local links and notes from students, parents and alumni. Choose the school by name, state list, or by ASD number.

3766 Amusing and Unorthodox Definitions
Careers/Consultants Consultants in Education
3050 Palm Aire Drive N
#310
Pompano Beach, FL 33069
954-974-5477
Fax: 954-974-5477
E-mail: carconed@aol.com
Collection of amusing and unorthodox definitions. The meanings, purposes and implications assigned to the words appearing here will delight audiences, enliven conversations and keep you chuckling.
ISBN: 0-7392-0089-5
ISSN: 99-94623
Dr. Robert M Bookbinder, President/Author

3767 Associated Schools Project in Education for International Co-operation
UNESCO Associated Schools Project Network
7 Place de Fontenoy
F-75700 Paris
France
1-45681000
Lists 1,970 secondary and primary schools, teacher training institutions and nursery schools in 95 countries that participate in the UNESCO Associated School Project.
200 pages Annual

3768 Association for Community-Based Education Directory of Members
Association for Community Based Education
1805 Florida Avenue NW
Washington, DC 20009-1708
202-462-6333
Offers information on 100 private community organizations concerned with alternative education including colleges that award degrees without residency requirements and more.
115 pages Annual

3769 Awakening Brilliance: How to Inspire Children to Become Successful Learners
Pamela Sims & Associates
54 Mozart Crescent
Canada L6Y 2W7
905-455-7331
888-610-7467
Fax: 905-455-0207
E-mail: loveofkids@aol.com
http://www.pamelasims.com
Seminars and workshops for educators and parents. Upcoming workshops include themes of awakening students' potential and team leadership skills.
248 pages Paperback
ISBN: 0-9651126-0-8
Pamela Sims, Author/Editor
Kelly Smith, Marketing Director

3770 Beyond the Bake Sale
Master Teacher
Leadership Lane
PO Box 1207
Manhattan, KS 66505-1207
800-669-9633
Fax: 800-669-1132
http://www.masterteacher.com
A notebook containing 101 detailed plans that not only provide you with fundraising ideas, but get you started, keep you on track, and lead your team through the finishing touches.
101 pages
ISBN: 1-58992-119-4

3771 Biographical Membership Directory
American Educational Research Association
1230 17th Street NW
Washington, DC 20036-3078
202-223-9485
Fax: 202-775-1824
Membership directory of more than 23,000 persons involved in education research and development, including the names, addresses, phone numbers, highest degree held and year received, occupational specialization areas, e-mail addresses and more.
420 pages Bi-Annual
Thomas J Campbell, Director Publications

3772 CASE Directory of Advancement Professionals in Education
Council for Advancement & Support of Education
1307 New York Avenue NW
Suite 1000
Washington, DC 20005-4701
202-328-2273
Fax: 202-387-4973
E-mail: info@case.org
http://www.case.org
Membership directory of 16,000 professionals in alumni relations, communications and fund raising at educational institutions worldwide.
Publication Date: 1995 200 pages Annual
ISBN: 0-899643-10-8
Cedric Calhoun, Membership Director

3773 Cabells Directory of Publishing Opportunities in Educational Curriculum & Methods
Cabell Publishing Company
Box 5428
Tobe Hahn Station
Beaumont, TX 77726
409-898-0575
Fax: 409-866-9554
E-mail: publish@cabells.com
http://www.cabells.com
Provides information on editor's contact information, manuscript guidelines, acceptance rate, re-

view information and circulation data for over 350 academic journals.

799 pages Annual
ISBN: 0-911753-27-3
David WE Cabell, Editor
Deborah L English, Editor

3774 Cadet Gray: Your Guide to Military Schools-Military Colleges & Cadet Programs
Reference Desk Books
PO Box 22925
Santa Barbara, CA 93121
805-772-8806
This is a comprehensive reference book which describes 55 American military schools, grade schools, high schools, junior colleges, senior colleges, and the federal service academies. Descriptions include school histories, academic requirements, military environment, extracurricular activities and costs.

Publication Date: 1990 212 pages
ISBN: 0-962574-90-2

3775 Character Education Evaluation Tool Kit
Character Education Partnership
1025 Connecticut Avenue NW
Suite 1011
Washington, DC 20036
202-296-7743
800-988-8081
Fax: 202-296-7779
http://www.character.org
Julea Posey, Matthew Davison, Meg Korpi, Author
Andrea Grenadier, Director Communications
Esther Schaeffer, CEO/Executive Director

3776 Character Education Kit: 36 Weeks of Success: Elementary Edition
Master Teacher
Leadership Lane
PO Box 1207
Manhattan, KS 66505-1207
800-669-9633
Fax: 800-669-1132
http://www.masterteacher.com
Takes the guesswork out of delivering your character education message by providing you with all the pieces of a well-rounded program including important components for 36 character traits.

428 pages
ISBN: 1-58992-096-1

3777 Choosing Your Independent School in the United Kingdom & Ireland
Independent Schools Information Service
56 Buckingham Gate
London SW1E 6AG
England
71-63087934
1,400 independent schools in the United Kingdom and Ireland with contact information, entry requirements, fees, scholarships available, subjects and exam boards.

293 pages Annual/September

3778 Classroom Teacher's Guide for Working with Paraeducators
Master Teacher
Leadership Lane
PO Box 1207
Manhattan, KS 66505-1207
800-669-9633
Fax: 800-669-1132
http://www.masterteacher.com
This workbook includes numerous forms that allow teachers to communicate more effec-

tively to paras the vital information they will need in working with special students.

60 pages
ISBN: 1-58992-127-5
Wendy Dover, Author

3779 Commonwealth Universities Yearbook
Association of Commonwealth Universities
36 Gordon Square
London WC1H 0PF
England
44-20-7380-6700
Fax: 44-20-738-2655
E-mail: info@acu.ac.uk
http://www.acu.ac.uk
Offers information on over 700 university institutions of recognized academic standing in 36 Commonwealth countries or regions, including Africa, Asia, Australia, Britain, Canada and the Pacific.

2,600 pages Annual
ISBN: 0-85143-188-7
ISSN: 0069-7745

3780 Complete Learning Disabilities Directory
Grey House Publishing
185 Millerton Road
Millerton, NY 12546
518-789-8700
800-562-2139
Fax: 518-789-0545
E-mail: books@greyhouse.com
http://www.greyhouse.com
A one-stop sourcebook for people of all ages with learning disabilities and those who work with them. This comprehensive database in print includes information about associations and organizations, schools, government agencies, testing materials, camps, books, newsletters and more.

800 pages Annual/Softcover
ISBN: 1-59237-049-7
Leslie Mackenzie, Publisher
Richard Gottlieb, Editor

3781 Computer and Web Resources for People with Disabilities
Alliance for Technology Access/Hunter House
1304 Southpoint Boulevard
Suite 240
Petaluma, CA 94954
707-778-3011
800-914-3017
Fax: 707-765-2080
E-mail: atainfo@ataccess.org
http://www.ataccess.org
This directory shows how America's forty-five million people with disabilities can potentially benefit from using computer technology to achieve goals and change their lives. Written by experts in the field, this important work provides a comprehensive, step-by-step guide to approaching computer innovations. It explains how to identify the appropriate technology, how to seek funding, how to set it up and what to consider.

Publication Date: 1996 400 pages Paperback/CD ROM
ISBN: 0-89793-433-4
Libbie Butler, Information/Referral Assista

3782 Conservation Education and Outreach Techniques
North American Assoc for Environmental Education
2000 P Street NW
Suite 540
Washington, DC 20036

202-419-0412
Fax: 212-419-0415
E-mail: info@naaee.org
http://www.naaee.org
Presents the theory and practice for creating effective education and outreach programmes for conservation. An exciting array of techniques for enhancing school resources, marketing environmental messages, using mass media, developing partnerships for conservation, and designing on-site programmes for natural areas and community centres.

ISBN: 0-19-856772-3
Susan Jacobson, Author
Martha C Monroe, Author

3783 Contemporary World Issues: Public Schooling in America
ABC-CLIO
130 Cremona Drive
#1911
Santa Barbara, CA 93117-5599
805-963-4221
800-368-6868
Fax: 805-685-9685
Offers information on organizations and agencies involved with public education systems.

3784 Cornocopia of Concise Quotations
Careers/Consultants Consultants in Education
3050 Palm Aire Drive N
#310
Pompano Beach, FL 33069
954-974-5477
Fax: 954-974-5477
E-mail: carconed@aol.com
Wealth of practical reminders of the enduring ideas. The book furthers humane understandings by gathering and preserving the wisdom of the wise and experienced.

ISBN: 0-7392-0275-8
ISSN: 99-95201
Dr. Robert M Bookbinder, President

3785 Council for Educational Development and Research Directory
National Education Association (NEA)
1201 16th Street NW
Washington, DC 20036-3290
202-833-4000
Fax: 202-822-7974
E-mail: ncuea@nea.org
http://www.nea.org
Offers 15 member educational research and development institutions.

50 pages Annual

3786 Digest of Supreme Court Decisions
Phi Delta Kappa Educational Foundation
PO Box 789
408 N Union Street
Bloomington, IN 47402-0789
812-339-1156
800-786-1156
Fax: 812-339-0018
http://www.pdkintl.org
Designed as a ready reference, this edition of a popular digest provides a concise set of individual summaries of cases decided by the Supreme Court. Fully indexed.

256 pages Paperback
ISBN: 0-87367-835-4
Perry A Zirkel, Author
George Kersey, Executive Director
Donovan R Walling, Dir Publications/Research

3787 Directory for Exceptional Children
Porter Sargent Publishers, Inc.
11 Beacon Street
Suite 1400
Boston, MA 02108-3028
617-523-1670
800-342-7470
Fax: 617-523-1021
E-mail: info@portersargent.com
http://www.portersargent.com
A comprehensive survey of 2,500 schools, facilities and organizations across the country serving children and young adults with developmental, physical and medical disabilities. With 15 distinct chapters covering a range of disabilities, this work is an invaluable aid to parents and professionals seeking the optimal environment for special-needs children. Hardcover.

Publication Date: 1994 1152 pages BiAnnual
ISSN: 0070-5012

Dan McKeever, Senior Editor

3788 Directory of Catholic Special Educational Programs & Facilities
National Catholic Educational Association
1077 30th Street NW
Suite 100
Washington, DC 20007-3829
202-337-6232
Fax: 202-333-6706
Lists approximately 950 Catholic schools and day and residential school programs for children and adolescents with special education needs.

Publication Date: 1989 100 pages

3789 Directory of Central Agencies for Jewish Education
Jewish Education Service of North America
111 8th Avenue
New York, NY 10011
212-284-6882
Fax: 212-284-6951
E-mail: info@jesna.org
http://www.jesna.org
Offers educational resources for professionals in Jewish education, including general education information, materials and services.

Rika Levin, Director
Marketing/Communica

3790 Directory of College Cooperative Education Programs
National Commission for Cooperative Education
360 Huntington Avenue
#384CP
Boston, MA 02115-5096
617-373-3770
Fax: 617-373-3463
E-mail: ncce@neu.edu
http://www.co-op.edu
A publication providing detailed information on cooperative education programs at 460 colleges throughout the United States.

Publication Date: 1962 219 pages
ISBN: 0-89774-998-4

Polly Hutcheson, VP
Paul Stonely, President

3791 Directory of ERIC Information Service Providers
Educational Resources Information
Ctr./Access ERIC
1600 Research Boulevard
Rockville, MD 20850-3172
301-656-9723

Offers information on more than 1,000 government agencies, nonprofit and profit organizations, individuals and foreign organizations that provide access to ERIC microfiche collections, search services and abstract journal collections.

100 pages Biennial

3792 Directory of Graduate Programs
Graduate Record Examinations Program/
ETS
PO Box 6014
Princeton, NJ 08541-6014
609-951-1542
Accredited institutions that offer graduate degrees.

1,400 pages 4 Volumes

3793 Directory of Indigenous Education
Floyd Beller - Wested
730 Harrison Street
San Francisco, CA 94107
415-565-3000
877-4we-sted
Fax: 415-565-3012
E-mail: fbeller@WestEd.org
http://www.wested.org
This revised and expanded edition incorporates a wider scope of information, including a list of Head Start, Child Care and Title IX programs and JOM contractors, which enhances our principal goal of improving educational services to native students and communities.

Publication Date: 1998 94 pages

Floyd Beller, Research Associate

3794 Directory of International Internships: A World of Opportunities
International Studies & Programs
209 International Center
Michigan State University
East Lansing, MI 48824-1035
517-353-5589
Fax: 517-353-7254
E-mail: gliozzo@msu.edu
http://www.isp.msu.edu
A directory containing information about a wide range of overseas internship oppotunities. Over 500 entries of international internships sponsored by educational institutions, government agencies, and private organizations. There are indexes of topics in geographical areas listed by countries and geographical areas listed by topic.

Charles Gliozzo

3795 Directory of Member Institutions and Institutional Representatives
Council of Graduate Schools
1 Dupont Circle NW
Suite 430
Washington, DC 20036-1136
202-223-3791
Fax: 202-331-7157
Offers listings of over 400 member graduate schools in the US and Canada.

85 pages Annually

Nancy A Goffney, Administrator/Editor
Kathy Baker, Assistant

3796 Directory of Overseas Educational Advising Centers
College Board Publications
45 Columbus Avenue
New York, NY 10023-6917
212-713-8165
800-323-7155
Fax: 800-525-5562
http://www.collegeboard.org

This directory has been developed as a means through which institutions of higher education can communicate directly with overseas education advisers and through which advisers can communicate more directly with each other.

Publication Date: 1995 165 pages

3797 Directory of Postsecondary Institutions
National Center for Education Statistics
K Street NW
Washington, DC 20006
202-502-7300
877-4ED-PUBS
Fax: 301-470-1244
E-mail: edpubs@inet.ed.gov
http://www.ed.pubs/
Postsecondary institutions in the US, Puerto Rico, Virgin Islands and territories in the Pacific United States. Two volumes: Volume I Degree-Granting Institutions, Volume II Non-Degree-Granting Institutions.

Publication Date: 1990 500 pages Biennial

3798 Directory of Youth Exchange Programs
UN Educational, Scientific & Cultural Association
Youth Division, 1 Rue Miollis
Paris F-75015
France
1-4563842
Offers about 370 nonprofit organizations and governmental agencies in 95 countries that organize youth and student exchanges, study tours and correspondence exchanges.

Publication Date: 1992 225 pages

3799 Diversity, Accessibility and Quality
College Board Publications
45 Columbus Avenue
New York, NY 10023-6917
212-713-8165
800-323-7155
Fax: 800-525-5562
http://www.collegeboard.org
Primarily for non-Americans, this overview is designed to examine aspects of US education that have particular importance in programs of student exchange.

Publication Date: 1995 47 pages
ISBN: 0-874474-24-8

Clifford F Sjogren, Author

3800 Education Sourcebook: Basic Information about National Education Expectations and Goals
Omnigraphics
615 Griswold Street
Detroit, MI 48226
313-961-1340
800-234-1340
Fax: 313-961-1383
E-mail: info@omnigraphics.com
http://www.omnigraphics.com
A collection of education-related documents and articles for parents and students.

1123 pages
ISBN: 0-7808-0179-2

Jeanne Gough, Author
Paul Rogers, Publicity Associate

3801 Educational Placement Sources-Abroad
Education Information Services/Instant Alert
PO Box 620662
Newton, MA 02462-0662
617-433-0125
Lists 150 organizations, arranged by type, in the United States and abroad that place English-speaking teachers and education administrators in positions abroad.

19 pages Annual

FB Viaux, President

3802 Educational Rankings Annual
Gale Group
27500 Drake Road
Farmington Hills, MI 48331-3535
248-699-GALE
800-414-5043
Fax: 248-699-8069
E-mail: galeord@galegroup.com
http://www.galegroup.com
Top 10 lists from popular and scholarly periodicals, government publications, and others. The lists cover all facets of education.
890 pages Annual Hardcover
ISBN: 0-7876-7419-2

Lynn C Hattendorf Westney, Author
Kathleen Maki Petts, Coordinating Editor

3803 Educational Resources Catalog
CDE Press
PO Box 271
Sacramento, CA 95812-0271
916-445-1260
800-995-4099
Fax: 916-323-0823
http://www.cde.ca.gov/cdepress
Resource catalog from the California Department of Education.

3804 Educator's Desk Reference: A Sourcebook of Educational Information & Research
MacMillan Publishing Company
1633 Broadway
New York, NY 10019
212-654-8500
Fax: 800-835-3202
Directory includes national and regional education organizations.
Publication Date: 1989

3805 Educator's Scrapbook
Careers/Consultants Consultants in Education
3050 Palm Aire Drive N
#310
Pompano Beach, FL 33069
954-974-5477
Fax: 954-974-5477
E-mail: carconed@aol.com
Collection of education morsels offered to those who who would seek to redefine and clarify the aims and purposes of today's education. The book attepts to help its readers refocus upon the real purposes of education and their relationships to current education practices.
ISBN: 0-9703623-0-7
ISSN: 00-93185

Dr. Robert M Bookbinder, President

3806 Educators Guide to FREE Computer Materials and Internet Resources
Educators Progress Service
214 Center Street
Randolph, WI 53956-1408
920-326-3126
888-951-4469
Fax: 920-326-3127
E-mail: epsinc@centurytel.net
http://www.freeteachingaids.com
Lists and describes almost 2000 web sites of educational value. Available in two grade specific editions.
317 pages Annual
ISBN: 87708-362-2

Kathy Nehmer, President

3807 Educators Guide to FREE Films, Filmstrips and Slides
Educators Progress Service
214 Center Street
Randolph, WI 53956-1408
920-326-3126
888-951-4469
Fax: 920-326-3127
E-mail: epsinc@centurytel.net
http://www.freeteachingaids.com
Lists and describes free and free-loan films, filmstrips, slides, and audiotapes for all age levels.
135 pages Annual
ISBN: 87708-400-9

Kathy Nehmer, President

3808 Educators Guide to FREE Multicultural Material
Educators Progress Service
214 Center Street
Randolph, WI 53956-1408
920-326-3126
888-951-4469
Fax: 920-326-3127
E-mail: epsinc@centurytel.net
http://www.freeteachingaids.com
Lists and describes FREE films, videotapes, filmstrips, slides, web sites, and hundreds of free printed materials in the field of multicultural and diversity education for all age levels.
198 pages Annual
ISBN: 87708-412-2

Kathy Nehmer, President

3809 El-Hi Textbooks and Serials in Print
RR Bowker Reed Reference
121 Chanlon Road
New Providence, NJ 07974-1541
908-464-6800
Fax: 908-665-6688
Listing of about 995 publishers of elementary and secondary level textbooks and related teaching materials.
Annual

3810 Environmental Education Materials: Guidelines for Excellence
North American Assoc for Environmental Education
2000 P Street NW
Suite 540
Washington, DC 20036
202-419-0412
Fax: 212-419-0415
E-mail: info@naaee.org
http://www.naaee.org
A set of recommendations for developing and selecting environmental education materials. These guidelines aim to help developers of activity guides, lesson plans, and other instructional materials produce high wuality products, and to provide educators with a tool to evaluate the wide array of available environmental education materials.
23 pages
ISBN: 1-884008-41-0

Bora Simmons, Author

3811 Evaluating Your Environmental Education Programs: A Workbook for Practitioners
North American Assoc for Environmental Education
2000 P Street NW
Suite 540
Washington, DC 20036
202-419-0412
Fax: 212-419-0415
E-mail: info@naaee.org
http://www.naaee.org
Walks you through how to design and conduct an evaluation. Throughout the workbook, 23 exercises as you to check your understanding (the answers are included). In addition, 47 application exercises point you to tasks that will help you develop your own evaluation.

Julie A Ernst, Author
Martha C Monroe, Author

3812 Excellence in Environmental Education: Guidelines for Learning (PreK-12)
North American Assoc for Environmental Education
2000 P Street NW
Suite 540
Washington, DC 20036
202-419-0412
Fax: 212-419-0415
E-mail: info@naaee.org
http://www.naaee.org
The guidelines support state and local environmental education efforts by: setting expectations for performance and achievement in fourth, eighth, and twelfth grades; suggesting a framework for effective and comprehensive environmental education programs and curricula; demonstrating how environmental edcuation can be used to meet standards set by the traditional disciplines and to give students opportunities to synthesize knowledge and experience across disciplines.
121 pages
ISBN: 1-884008-75-5

Bora Simmons, Author

3813 Exceptional Children Education Resources
The Council for Exceptional Children
110 N Glebe Road
Suite 300
Arlington, VA 22201-5704
703-620-3660
800-232-7323
Fax: 703-264-9494
E-mail: cec@cec.sped.org
http://www.cec.sped.org/bk/catalog/journals.htm
A proprietary database that includes bibliographic data and abstract information on journal articles, and audiovisual materials in special education, and gifted education.
ISSN: 0160-4309

3814 Family Services Report
CD Publications
8204 Fenton Street
Sliver Spring, MD 20910
301-588-6380
301-666-6380
Fax: 301-588-0519
E-mail: fsr@cdpublications.com
http://cdpublications.com
Private grants for family service programs
18 pages
ISSN: 1524-9484

Ray Sweeney, Editor

3815 Fifty State Educational Directories
Career Guidance Foundation
8090 Engineer Road
San Diego, CA 92111-1906
619-508-8051
A collection on microfiche consisting of reproductions of the state educational directories published by each individual state department of education.

3816 Funny School Excuses
Careers/Consultants Consultants in Education
3050 Palm Aire Drive N
#310
Pompano Beach, FL 33069

954-974-5477
Fax: 954-974-5477
E-mail: carconed@aol.com
Collection of illustrations, cartoons and excuses gathered from authentic notes written by parents and sometimes their children. The book is wonderfully entertaining and recommended for its unusual humor, variety, and revelations of human nature.

ISBN: 0-7392-0309-6
ISSN: 99-95349

Dr. Robert M Bookbinder, President

3817 Ganley's Catholic Schools in America

Fisher Publishing Company
PO Box 15070
Scottsdale, AZ 85267-5070
800-759-7615
Fax: 480-657-9422
E-mail:
publisher@ganleyscatholicschools.com
http://www.ganleyscatholicschool.com
Comprehensive listings on all Catholic Schools in America. Listings include phone numbers, addresses, names of administrators, number of students, complete diocesan, state, regional and national statistics. Includes an extensive analysis of demographic trends within Catholic elementary and secondary education, prepared by the National Catholic Education Association.

450+ pages Annual/June
ISBN: 1-558331-59-0

Millard T Fischer, Publisher

3818 Graduate & Undergraduate Programs & Courses in Middle East Studies in the US, Canada

Middle East Studies Association of North America
University of Arizona
1643 E Helen Street
Tucson, AZ 85721
520-621-5850
Fax: 520-626-9095
E-mail: mesana@u.arizona.edu
http://www.acls.org

3819 Guide to International Exchange, Community Service & Travel for Persons with Disabilities

Mobility International USA
45 W Broadway Suite 202
PO Box 10767
Eugene, OR 97401
541-343-1284
Fax: 541-343-6812
E-mail: info@miusa.org
http://www.miusa.org
This directory lists an impressive array of information regarding international study, living, travel, funding and contact organizations for people with disabilities.

Publication Date: 1997
ISBN: 1-880034-24-7

Christa Bucks, Editor

3820 Guide to Schools and Departments of Religion and Seminaries

MacMillan Publishing Company
1633 Broadway
New York, NY 10019
800-858-7674
Fax: 201-767-5029
Over 700 accredited programs and institutions granting degrees in theology, divinity and religion.

3821 Guide to Summer Camps & Schools

Porter Sargent Publishers
11 Beacon Street
Suite 1400
Boston, MA 02108-3028
617-523-1670
800-342-7470
Fax: 617-523-1021
E-mail: info@portersargent.com
http://www.portersargent.com
Covers the broad spectrum of recreational and educational summer opportunities. Current facts from 1,500 camps and schools, as well as programs for those with special needs or learning disabilities, makes the guide a comprehensive and convenient resource.

816 pages Biannual
ISBN: 0-875581-33-1

HJ Lane Coordinating Editor, Author
J Yonce, General Manager
Daniel McKeever, Sr Editor

3822 Guidelines for Effective Character Education Through Sports

Character Education Partnership
1025 Connecticut Avenue NW
Suite 1011
Washington, DC 20036
202-296-7743
800-988-8081
Fax: 202-296-7779
http://www.character.org
Guidelines for turning sports and physical education programs into the powerful, positive forces they should be.

Andrea Grenadier, Director Communications
Esther Schaeffer, CEO/Executive Director

3823 Guidelines for the Preparation and Professional Development of Environmental Educato

North American Assoc for Environmental Education
2000 P Street NW
Suite 540
Washington, DC 20036
202-419-0412
Fax: 212-419-0415
E-mail: info@naaee.org
http://www.naaee.org
Recommendations about the basic knowledge and abilities educators need to provide high quality environmental education. The guidelines are designed to apply: within the context of pre-service teacher education programs and environmental education courses offered to students with varied backgrounds such as environmental studies, geography, liberal studies, or natural resources.

43 pages
ISBN: 1-884008-78-X

Bora Simmons, Author

3824 Handbook of Private Schools

Porter Sargent Publishers
11 Beacon Street
Suite 1400
Boston, MA 02108-3028
617-523-1670
800-342-7470
Fax: 617-523-1021
E-mail: info@portersargent.com
http://www.portersargent.com
Continuing a tradition that began in 1915, this handbook provides optimal guidance in the choice of educational environments and opportunities for students. Totally revised and updated, this 83rd edition pres-

ents current facts on 1,700 elementary and secondary boarding and day schools across the United States. Complete statistical data on enrollments, tuition, graduates, administrators and faculty have been compiled and objectively reported. Hardcover.

1472 pages Annual
ISBN: 0-875581-44-7

J Yonce, General Manager
Daniel McKeever, Sr Editor

3825 Handbook of United Methodist-Related Schools, Colleges, Universities & Theological Schools

General Board of Higher Education & Ministry/UMC
1001 19th Avenue
PO Box 340007
Nashville, TN 37203-0007
615-340-7406
Fax: 615-340-7379
E-mail: scu@gbhem.org
http://www.gbhem.org/highed.html
Includes two pages of information about each of United Methodist's 123 institutions, a chart indicating major areas of study, information about United Methodist loan and scholarship programs, as well as information about how to select a college. Published every four years.

344 pages Paperback

Dr. James A Noseworthy, Assistant General Secretary

3826 Hidden America

Place in the Woods
3900 Glenwood Avenue
Golden Valley, MN 55422-5302
763-374-2120
Fax: 952-593-5593
E-mail: placewoods@aol.com
Set of five reference-essay books on American minorities (African America; Hispanic America, the People (Native Americans); American women; My Own Book! classroom reference for elementary through secondary).

36+ pages Paperback Book

Roger Hammer, Publisher

3827 Higher Education Directory

Higher Education Publications
6400 Arlington Boulevard
Suite 648
Falls Church, VA 22042-2342
703-532-2300
888-349-7915
Fax: 703-532-2305
E-mail: info@hepinc.com
http://www.hepinc.com
Lists over 4,364 degree granting colleges and universities accredited by approved agencies, recognized by the US Secretary of Education successor to the Department of Education's: Education Directory, Colleges and Universities and Council for Higher Education Accreditation (CHEA).

Publication Date: 1994 1,040 pages Annual/Paperback
ISBN: 0-914927-44-2
ISSN: 0736-0197

Jeanne Burke, Editor
Fred Hafner JR, Vice President Operations

3828 Higher Education Opportunities for Women & Minorities: Annotated Selections

U.S. Office of Postsecondary Education
400 Maryland Avenue SW
Room 3915
Washington, DC 20202-0001
202-708-9180
Programs of public and private organizations and state and federal government agencies that offer

loans, scholarships and fellowship opportunities for women and minorities.

143 pages Biennial

3829 Home from Home (Educational Exchange Programs)

Central Bureau for Educational Visits & Exchanges
10 Spring Gardens
London, SW1A 2BN, England
171-389-4004
Fax: 171-389-4426
150 organizations and agencies worldwide that arrange stays with families for paying guests or on an exchange basis. Organizations are geographically listed including a description of program, costs, insurance information, overseas representation and language instruction.

216 pages

3830 Homeschooler's Guide to FREE Teaching Aids

Educators Progress Service
214 Center Street
Randolph, WI 53956-1408
920-326-3126
888-951-4469
Fax: 920-326-3127
E-mail: epsinc@centurytel.net
http://www.freeteachingaids.com
Lists and describes free print materials specifically available to homeschoolers with students of all age levels.

277 pages
ISBN: 87708-375-4

Kathy Nehmer, President

3831 Homeschooler's Guide to FREE Videotapes

Educators Progress Service
214 Center Street
Randolph, WI 53956-1408
920-326-3126
888-951-4469
Fax: 920-326-3127
E-mail: epsinc@centurytel.net
http://www.freeteachingaids.com
Lists and describes free and free-loan videotapes specifically available to homeschoolers with students of all age levels.

248 pages Annual
ISBN: 87708-411-4

Kathy Nehmer, President

3832 IIEPassport: Academic Year Abroad 2007

Institute of International Education
809 United Nations Plaza
New York, NY 10017-3580
412-741-0930
Fax: 212-984-5496
E-mail: iiebooks@abdintl.com
http://www.iiebooks.org
Over 3,100 undergraduate and graduate study-abroad programs conducted worldwide during the academic year by United States and foreign colleges, universities, and private organizations.

Publication Date: 2007 Annual
ISBN: 87206-279-1

Marie O'Sullivan, Author
Daniel Obst, Sr Editor

3833 ISS Directory of Overseas Schools

International Schools Services
15 Roszel Road
PO Box 5910
Princeton, NJ 08540-6729
609-452-0990
Fax: 609-452-2690

E-mail: jlarsson@iss.edu
http://www.iss.edu
The only comprehensive guide to American and international schools around the world. The Directory is carefully researched and compiled to include current and complete information on over 600 international schools.

590 pages Paperback
ISBN: 0-913663-13-1

Jane Larsson, Director Of Education

3834 Inclusion Guide for Handling Chronically Disruptive Behavior

Master Teacher
Leadership Lane
PO Box 1207
Manhattan, KS 66505-1207
800-669-9633
Fax: 800-669-1132
http://www.masterteacher.com
A comprehensive process for ensuring that no disruptive behavior is tolerated, no student is turned away, and all students are served.

150 pages
ISBN: 0-914607-40-5

Teresa VanDover, Author

3835 Incorporating Multiple Intelligences into the Curriculum and into the Classroom: Elementary

Master Teacher
Leadership Lane
PO Box 1207
Manhattan, KS 66505-1207
800-669-9633
Fax: 800-669-1132
http://www.masterteacher.com
Contains lesson plans and teaching methods that address the needs of students and help them identify their strengths according to the domains of multiple intelligences.

181 pages
ISBN: 0-914607-63-4

3836 Incorporating Multiple Intelligences into the Curriculum and into the Classroom: Secondary

Master Teacher
Leadership Lane
PO Box 1207
Manhattan, KS 66505-1207
800-669-9633
Fax: 800-669-1132
http://www.masterteacher.com
Contains lesson plans and teaching methods that address the needs of students and help them identify their strengths according to the domains of multiple intelligences.

147 pages
ISBN: 0-914607-64-2

3837 Independent Schools Association of the Southwest-Membership List

Independent Schools Association of the Southwest
PO Box 52297
Tulsa, OK 74152-0297
817-569-9200
Fax: 817-569-9103
A geographical index of 65 independent elementary and secondary schools accredited by the association.

5 pages Annual/August

Richard W Ekdahl, Coordinating Education

3838 Independent Study Catalog

Peterson's Guides
PO Box 2123
Princeton, NJ 08543-2123
800-338-3282
Fax: 609-896-4531

A comprehensive listing of over 10,000 correspondence course offerings at 100 accredited colleges and universities nationwide, for those seeking the flexibility and convenience of at-home study.

293 pages
ISBN: 1-560794-60-7

3839 International Federation of Organizations for School Correspondence/Exchange

FIOCES
29, rue d'ulm, F-75230 Paris
F-75230 Paris
France
Governmental agencies and other organizations concerned with scholastic correspondence and student exchange programs.

Publication Date: 1991 3 pages

3840 International Schools Directory

European Council of International Schools
21B Lavant Street, Petersfield,
Hampshire GU3 23EL
United Kingdom
1730-268244
Fax: 1730-267914
E-mail: 100412.242@compuserve.com
Over 420 ECIS schools in more than 90 countries; 300 affiliated colleges and universities worldwide; educational publishers and equipment suppliers.

550 pages Annual

JS Henleu, Coordinating Education

3841 International Study Telecom Directory

WorldWide Classroom
PO Box 1166
Milwaukee, WI 53201-1166
414-224-3476
Fax: 414-224-3466
E-mail: info@worldwide.edu
http://www.worldwide.edu
Comprehensive directory for locating educational resources both internationally and throughout the US Provides contact information on educational institutions including address, phone, fax, e-mail and URL. New icon system offers additional information on the type of programs offered. Resource guide at beginning includes useful web sites, airline and car rental contact numbers, currency converters, international organizations and international publications.

Mike Witley, President
Stacy Hargarten, Classroom Publications

3842 International Voluntary Service Directory

Volunteers for Peace
1034 Tiffany Road
Belmont, VT 05730
802-259-2759
Fax: 802-259-2922
E-mail: vfp@vfp.org
http://www.vfp.org
Comprehensive listing of over 3,400 workcamps in 100 countries around the world. Organized by country.

289 pages Annual
ISBN: 0-945617-20-B

Peter Coldwell, Director

3843 International Who's Who in Education

International Biographical Centre/Melrose Press
3 Regal Lane, Soham, Ely
Cambridgeshire CB7 5BA
United Kingdom
353-721091

Lists about 5,000 persons at all levels of teaching and educational administration.

1,000 pages

3844 International Yearbook of Education: Education in the World
UN Educational, Scientific & Cultural Assn.
7, place de Fontenoy
F-75700 Paris
France
1-45681000
Describes and offers information on educational systems worldwide.

Publication Date: 1989 200 pages

3845 Job Search Handbook for Educators
American Association for Employment in Education
3040 Riverside Drive
Suite 117
Columbus, OH 43221
614-485-1111
Fax: 360-244-7802
E-mail: execdir@aaee.org
http://www.aaee.org
Resume writing, interviewing tips, as well as articles on how to select the kind of school system you want, job fair networking and other related articles.

212 pages Bi-Annually

Neil Shnider, Executive Director
Diane Sledden Reed, Board President

3846 Legal Basics: A Handbook for Educators
Phi Delta Kappa International
408 N Union Street
PO Box 789
Bloomington, IL 47402-0789
812-339-1156
800-766-1156
Fax: 812-339-0018
http://www.pdkintl.org
Superintendents, principals, counselors, teachers, and paraprofessionals need to pay close attention to their actions in schools and classrooms because, from a legal standpoint, those settings may contain hazardous conditions. Legal Basics points out the pitfalls and how to avoid them.

Publication Date: 1998 120 pages Paperback
ISBN: 0-8736-806-0

Evelyn B Kelly, Author
DR Walling, Dir Publications/Research

3847 Lesson Plans and Modifications for Inclusion and Collaborative Classrooms
Master Teacher
Leadership Lane
PO Box 1207
Manhattan, KS 66505-1207
800-669-9633
Fax: 800-669-1132
http://www.masterteacher.com
Each modification is a complete lesson plan that gives the teacher a description of the activity and objective the materials need and a step-by-step guide of how to carry out the learning process.

Publication Date: 0 242 pages
ISBN: 0-914607-37-5

3848 Lesson Plans for Character Education: Elementary Edition
Master Teacher
Leadership Lane
PO Box 1207
Manhattan, KS 66505-1207

800-669-9633
Fax: 800-669-1132
http://www.masterteacher.com
Gives you more than 140 practical lessons developed and tested by teachers across the curriculum and in all grade levels.

207 pages
ISBN: 0-914607-53-7

3849 List of Over 70 Higher Education Association
Educational Information Services
PO Box 662
Newton Lower Falls, MA 02162
617-964-4555
Provides descriptions and contact information on associations for individuals in higher education.

3850 List of State Boards of Higher Education
Educational Information Services
PO Box 662
Newton Lower Falls, MA 02162
617-964-4555
A compilation of the boards of education for all the states in the union.

3851 List of State Community & Junior College Board Offices
Educational Information Services
PO Box 662
Newton Lower Falls, MA 02162
617-964-4555
A list of the board officers and state officers within community, junior and university institutions.

3852 MDR School Directory
Market Data Retrieval
1 Forest Parkway
Shelton, CT 06484-6216
203-926-4800
800-333-8802
Fax: 203-929-5253
E-mail: msubrizi@dnb.com
MDR's school directories provide comprehensive data on every public school district and school, Catholic and other independent schools, regional and county centers in all fifty states and the District of Columbia. Updated each year, each state directory contains current names and job titles of key decision makers, school and district addresses, phone numbers, current enrollments and much more. Also available on CD-ROM and diskette.

51 Volume Set

Mike Subrizi, Director Marketing

3853 Minority Student Guide to American Colleges
Paoli Publishing
1708 E Lancaster Avenue
Suite 287
Paoli, PA 19301-1553
215-640-9889
Covers colleges, military schools, and financial aid information for minority students.

89 pages

3854 Monograph 1-Using a Logic Model to Review and Analyze an Environmental Education Program
North American Assoc for Environmental Education
2000 P Street NW
Suite 540
Washington, DC 20036
202-419-0412
Fax: 212-419-0415

E-mail: info@naaee.org
http://www.naaee.org
Reviews and analyzes a long-standing and well-documented program in environmental education, Hungerford et al.'s issue-and-action instruction program (1973-). Logic models provide conceptual guidance and visual support for this review and analysis. These models were adapted from work in Aquatic Resource Education by Peyton, and the literature on logic modeling in program evaluation.

72 pages
ISBN: 1-884008-86-0

Thomas C Marcinkowski, Author

3855 Monograph 2-Preparing Effective Environmental Educators
North American Assoc for Environmental Education
2000 P Street NW
Suite 540
Washington, DC 20036
202-419-0412
Fax: 212-419-0415
E-mail: info@naaee.org
http://www.naaee.org
Focuses on the methods used to prepare those who teach environmental education. Research and evaluation related to three main audiences for environmental education preparedness training - pre-service teachers, in-service teachers, and nonformal education - are examined. The five papers presented represent an interesting and instructive array of research and evaluation that can be used to spur our thinking about the preparation of environmental educators.

89 pages
ISBN: 1-884008-88-7

Bora Simmons, Author

3856 NAFSA's Guide to Education Abroad for Advisers & Administrators
NAFSA: Association of International Educators
1307 New York Avenue NW
8th Floor
Washington, DC 20005-4701
202-737-3699
800-836-4994
Fax: 202-737-3657
E-mail: inbox@nafsa.org
http://www.nafsa.org

Marlene M Johnson, Director/CEO

3857 NEA Almanac of Higher Education
National Education Association (NEA)
1201 16th Street NW
Washington, DC 20036-3207
202-833-4000
Fax: 202-822-7624
E-mail: nche@nea.org
http://www.nea.org
Annually
ISSN: 0743-670X

Con Lehane, Author

3858 National Directory of Children, Youth & Families Services
Contexo Media
2755 E Cottonwood Parkway
Suite 400
Salt Lake City, UT 84120
800-343-6681
Fax: 801-365-0710
E-mail: customersupport@contexomedia.com
http://www.contexomedia.com
Organized by state and county, this directory lists over 30,000 organizations and 46,000 contacts that focus on helping anyone who is committed to

providing the best possible service to our nation's at-risk children, youth and families.

Publication Date: 0 1456 pages Annually

Treavor Peterson, President
Kim Luna, Product Manager

3859 National Guide to Educational Credit for Training Programs

American Council on Education
1 Dupont Circle NW
Suite 535
Washington, DC 20036-1110
202-939-9430
Fax: 202-833-4762
More than 4,500 courses offered by over 280 government agencies, business firms and nonprofit groups.

1,018 pages Annual

3860 National Reference Directory of Year-Round Education Programs

National Association for Year-Round Education
PO Box 711386
San Diego, CA 92171-1386
619-276-5296
Fax: 858-571-5754
E-mail: info@nayre.org
http://www.nayre.org
Six hundred fifty school districts in the US with year-round programs are covered in this directory, listed by geographical location, including all contact information and descriptions.

178 pages Annual Paperback

Shirley Jennings, Directory Editor
Samuel Pepper, Executive Director

3861 National Schools of Character: Best Practices and New Perspectives

Character Education Partnership
1025 Connecticut Avenue NW
Suite 1011
Washington, DC 20036
202-296-7743
800-988-8081
Fax: 202-296-7779
http://www.character.org

Andrea Grenadier, Director
Communications
Esther Schaeffer, CEO/Executive Director

3862 National Schools of Character: Practices to Adopt & Adapt

Character Education Partnership
1025 Connecticut Avenue NW
Suite 1011
Washington, DC 20036
202-296-7743
800-988-8081
Fax: 202-296-7779
http://www.character.org

Andrea Grenadier, Director
Communications
Esther Schaeffer, CEO/Executive Director

3863 National Society for Experiential Education

515 King Street
Suite 420
Alexandria, VA 22314
703-706-9552
Fax: 703-684-6048
E-mail: info@nsee.org
http://www.nsee.org

28 pages Quarterly

Linda Goff, Author

3864 New England Association of Schools and Colleges

New England Association of Schools and Colleges
209 Burlington Road
Bedford, MA 01730-1433
781-271-0022
Fax: 781-271-0950
Listing of over 1,575 institutions of higher education, public and independent schools and vocational-technical schools in New England.

65 pages Annual

3865 Nonformal Environmental Education Programs: Guidelines for Excellence

North American Assoc for Environmental Education
2000 P Street NW
Suite 540
Washington, DC 20036
202-419-0412
Fax: 212-419-0415
E-mail: info@naaee.org
http://www.naaee.org
A set of recommendations for developing and administering high quality nonformal environmental education programs. These recommendations provide a tool that can be used to ensure a firm foundation for new programs or to trigger improvements in existing ones. The overall goal of these guidelines is to facilitate a superior educational process leading to the environmental quality that people desire.

ISBN: 1-884008-89-5

Bora Simmons, Author

3866 Overseas American-Sponsored Elementary and Secondary Schools

US Department of State, Office Overseas Schools
Room 245, SA-29
Washington, DC 20522
202-647-4000
Fax: 202-261-8224
Lists nearly 180 independent schools overseas and 10 regional associations of schools.

30 pages Annual

3867 Paradigm Lost: Leading America Beyond It's Fear of Educational Change

American Association of School Administrators
801 N Quincy Street
Suite 700
Arlington, VA 22203-1730
703-528-0700
Fax: 703-841-1543
E-mail: info@aasa.org
http://www.aasa.org
Explores the beliefs and assumptions upon which schools operate, provides powerful and practical insights and improvement strategies.

Publication Date: 1998 158 pages Softcover
ISBN: 0-87652-232-0

William G Spady, Editor

3868 Patterson's American Education

Educational Directories Inc
Po Box 68097
Schaumburg, IL 60168
847-459-0605
800-357-6183
Fax: 847-891-0945
E-mail: info@ediusa.com
http://www.ediusa.com
Lists more than 11,000 public school districts; 300 parochial superintendents; 400 territorial schools; 400 state department of education personnel; and 400 educational as-

sociations in one easy to use consistent format. Arranged alphabetically by state then by city. City listings include the city name, telephone area code, city population, county name, public school district name, enrollment, grade range, superintendent's name, address and phone number. Index of secondary schools included.

Publication Date: 1994 974 pages Annual
ISBN: 0-9771602-3-8
ISSN: 0079-0230

Linda Moody, Office Manager

3869 Patterson's Schools Classified

Educational Directories Inc.
1025 W Wise Road
PO Box 68097
Schaumburg, IL 60168
847-891-1250
800-357-6183
Fax: 847-891-0945
E-mail: info@ediusa.org
http://www.ediusa.org
Contains 7,000 accredited postsecondary schools, the broadest assortment available in a single directory. Universities, colleges, community colleges, junior colleges, career schools and teaching hospitals are co-mingled under 50 academic disciplines but retain their school type identification. School professional accreditation is shown in 32 classifications. The basic entry includes school name, mailing address and contact person, with additional descriptive material supplied by the school.

Publication Date: 2006 302 pages Annual
ISBN: 0-9771602-2-X

Wayne Moody, Coordinating Education

3870 Persons as Resources

World Council for Curriculum & Instruction
School of Education
Indiana University
Bloomington, IN 47405
812-336-4702
Fax: 812-856-8088
Listing of about 600 member individuals and institutions concerned with curriculum and instruction in schools, colleges, universities and non-school agencies.

75 pages Triennial

3871 Peterson's Competitive Colleges

Peterson's, A Nelnet Company
Princeton Pike Corporate Center
2000 Lenox Drive PO Box 67005
Lawrenceville, NJ 08648
609-896-1800
800-338-3282
Fax: 609-896-4531
E-mail: custsvc@petersons.com
http://www.petersons.com
The most trusted source of advice for excellent students searching for high-quality schools. Provides objective criteria to compare more than 440 leading colleges and universities.

524 pages
ISBN: 1-560795-98-0

3872 Peterson's Guide to Four-Year Colleges

Peterson's, A Nelnet Company
Princeton Pike Corporate Center
2000 Lenox Drive PO Box 67005
Lawrenceville, NJ 08648
609-896-1800
800-338-3282
Fax: 609-896-1811
E-mail: custsvc@petersons.com
http://www.petersons.com

Includes descriptions of over 2,000 colleges, providing guidance on selecting the right school, getting in and financial aid.

2,922 pages

3873 Peterson's Guide to Two-Year Colleges

Peterson's, A Nelnet Company
Princeton Pike Corporate Center
2000 Lenox Drive PO Box 67005
Lawrenceville, NJ 08648
609-896-1800
800-338-3282
Fax: 609-896-4531
E-mail: custsvc@petersons.com
http://www.petersons.com
The only two-year college guide available, this new and expanded directory is the most complete source of information on institutions that grant an associate as their highest degree.

Publication Date: 2006 712 pages
ISBN: 1-560796-05-7

3874 Peterson's Regional College Guide Set

Peterson's, A Nelnet Company
Princeton Pike Corporate Center
2000 Lenox Drive PO Box 67005
Lawrenceville, NJ 08648
609-896-1800
800-338-3282
Fax: 609-896-4531
E-mail: custsvc@petersons.com
http://www.petersons.com
Six individual regional guides that help students compare colleges in a specific geographic area.

3875 Power of Public Engagement Book Set

Master Teacher
Leadership Lane
PO Box 1207
Manhattan, KS 66505-1207
800-669-9633
Fax: 800-669-1132
http://www.masterteacher.com
Learn how to engage your community to make the changes needed to ensure the best education for its children.

ISBN: 1-58992-128-3

William G O'Callaghan Jr, Author

3876 PreK-12 Excellence In Environmental Educatio Education

North American Assoc for Environmental Education
2000 P Street NW
Suite 540
Washington, DC 20036
202-419-0412
Fax: 212-419-0415
E-mail: info@naaee.org
http://www.naaee.org
Offers a vision of environmental education and promotes progress toward sustaining a healthy environment and quality of life. The Guidelines support state and local environmental efforts by: setting expectations for performance and achievement in fourth, eighth, and twelfth grades; suggesting a framework for effective and comprehensive environmental education programs.

ISBN: 1-884008-77-1

Bora Simmons, Author

3877 Private Independent Schools

Bunting & Lyon
238 N Main Street
Wallingford, CT 06492-3728
203-269-3333
Fax: 203-269-5697
E-mail: BuntingandLyon@aol.com
http://www.buntingandlyon.com
Provides information on more than 1,100 elementary and secondary private schools and summer programs in the United States and abroad. This annual guide, now in its 56th edition, is the most concise, current resource available on private school programs.

Publication Date: 1996 644 pages Annual Hardcover
ISBN: 0-913094-56-0
ISSN: 0079-5399

Peter G Bunting, Publisher

3878 Private School Law in America

Progressive Business Publications
370 Technology Drive
Malvern, PA 19355
800-220-5000
Fax: 610-647-8089
E-mail: customer_service@pbp.com
http://www.pbp.com
An up-to-date compilation of summarized federal and state appellate court decisions which affect private education. The full legal citation is supplied for each case. A brief introductory note on the American judicial system is provided along with updated appendices of recent US Supreme Court cases and recently published law review articles. Also included are portions of the US Constitution which are most frequently cited in private education cases.

500 pages Annually
ISBN: 0-939675-80-3

3879 Public Schools USA: A Comparative Guide to School Districts

Peterson's, A Nelnet Company
Princeton Pike Corporate Center
2000 Lenox Drive PO Box 67005
Lawrenceville, NJ 08648
609-896-1800
800-338-3282
Fax: 609-896-4531
E-mail: custsvc@petersons.com
http://www.petersons.com
Lists over 400 school districts in 52 metropolitan areas throughout the United States.

490 pages Annual

Charles Hampton Harrison, Author

3880 School Foodservice Who's Who

Information Central
PO Box 3900
Prescott, AZ 86302-3900
520-778-1513
Listing of over 2,500 food service programs in public and Catholic school systems.

110 pages Triennial

3881 School Guide

School Guide Publications
210 N Avenue
New Rochelle, NY 10801-6402
914-632-7771
800-433-7771
Fax: 914-632-3412
E-mail: info@schoolguides.com
http://schoolguides.com
Listing of over 3,000 colleges, vocational schools and nursing schools in the US.

280 pages Annual/Paperback
ISBN: 1-893275-30-2

Janette Aiello, Editor

3882 Schools Abroad of Interest to Americans

Porter Sargent Publishers
11 Beacon Street
Suite 1400
Boston, MA 02108-3028
617-523-1670
800-342-7470
Fax: 617-523-1021
E-mail: info@portersargent.com
http://www.portersargent.com
Lists and authoritatively describes 800 elementary and secondary schools in 130 countries. Written for the educator, personnel advisor, student and parent as well as diplomatic and corporate officials, this unique guide is an indispensable reference for American students seeking preparatory schooling overseas. Hardcover.

Publication Date: 1991 544 pages BiAnnual

J Yonce, General Manager
Daniel McKeever, Sr Editor

3883 Schools-Business & Vocational Directory

American Business Directories
5711 S 86th Circle
Omaha, NE 68127-4146
402-593-4600
888-999-1307
Fax: 402-331-5481
A complete listing of business and vocational schools nationwide. Includes phone numbers, contact names, employee sizes and more.

Annual

Jerry Venner, Coordinating Education

3884 Treasury of Noteworthy Proverbs

Careers/Consultants Consultants in Education
3050 Palm Aire Drive N
#310
Pompano Beach, FL 33069
954-974-5477
Fax: 954-974-5477
E-mail: carconed@aol.com
Tapestry of maxims, aphorisims, and pithy sayings. A revealing picture of the wisdom, philosophy, and humor of the people of this and many other nations throughout the world.

ISBN: 0-7392-0208-1
ISSN: 99-943-75

Dr. Robert M Bookbinder, President

3885 US Supreme Court Education Cases

Progressive Business Publications
370 Technology Drive
Malvern, PA 19355
800-220-5000
Fax: 610-647-8089
E-mail: customer_service@pbp.com
http://www.pbp.com
A compilation of summarized US Supreme Court decisions since 1954 which affect education. The full legal citation is supplied for each case. Also included are portions of the US Constitution which are most frequently cited in education cases.

Annually

3886 VincentCurtis Educational Register

Vincent-Curtis
PO Box 724
Falmouth, MA 02541-0724
508-457-6473
Fax: 508-457-6499
E-mail: stan@vincentcurtis.com
http://www.vincentcurtis.com
An online guide to a variety of private boarding and day schools and resident summer programs in the United States, Canada and Europe, together with articles by school heads and camp directors of interest to educators and parents of students 10-18.

Publication Date: 1994 236 pages Annual/June

Stan Vincent, Editor

3887 Western Association of Schools and Colleges
Western Association of Schools and Colleges
3060 Valencia Avenue
#70
Aptos, CA 95003-4126
831-688-7575
Listing of schools and colleges in California, Hawaii, Guam, American Samoa and East Asia.

130 pages Annual

3888 What's Fair Got to Do With It
North American Assoc for Environmental Education
2000 P Street NW
Suite 540
Washington, DC 20036
202-419-0412
Fax: 212-419-0415
E-mail: info@naaee.org
http://www.naaee.org
Educators will find these cases a powerful tool for professional development. Each case is a candid, dramatic, and highly readable first-person account that makes concrete the challenges of fairness, expectations, respect, and communication when people who share goals, perhaps, but not cultures, interact.

119 pages
ISBN: 0-914409-20-4

Tania D Madfes, Editor

3889 Whole Nonprofit Catalog
Grantmanship Center
PO Box 17720
Los Angeles, CA 90017
Offers information on training programs offered by the Center, publications and other services available to the nonprofit sector.

3890 Working Together: A Guide to Community-Based Educational Resources
Research, Advocacy & Legislation/Council of LaRaza
810 1st Street NE
Suite 300
Washington, DC 20002-4227
202-289-1380
Listing of about 30 community-based organizations nationwide providing educational services to Hispanic Americans.

35 pages

3891 World of Learning
Gale Group
27500 Drake Road
Farmington Hills, MI 48331
248-699-4253
800-877-4253
Fax: 248-699-8064
E-mail: galeord@galegroup.com
http://www.galegroup.com
Contains information for over 26,000 universities, colleges, schools of art and music, libraries, archives, learned societies, research institutes, museums and art galleries in more than 180 countries.

ISBN: 0-7876-5004-8

Allen W Paschal, President

Directories & Handbooks / Administration

3892 American Association of Collegiate Registrars & Admissions Officers
American Association of Collegiate Registrars
1 Dupont Circle NW
Suite 330
Washington, DC 20036-1137
202-293-9161
Fax: 202-872-8857
Offers more than 2,300 member institutions and 8,400 college and university registrars, financial aid information and admissions officers.

Publication Date: 1995 224 pages Annual

3893 American School & University - Who's Who Directory & Buyer's Guide
Prism Business Media
9800 Metcalf Avenue
Overland Park, KS 66212-2286
913-967-1960
Fax: 913-967-1905
E-mail: jagron@asumag.com
http://www.asumag.com
Comprehensive directory of suppliers and products for facility needs; listings of architects by region; listing of associations affiliated with the education industry; article index for quick and easy reference; in-depth calendar of events.

Annual

Joe Agron, Editor-In-Chief
Susan Lustig, Executive Editor

3894 Bricker's International Directory
Peterson's, A Nelnet Company
Princeton Pike Corporate Center
2000 Lenox Drive PO Box 67005
Lawrenceville, NJ 08648
609-896-1800
800-338-3282
Fax: 609-896-4531
E-mail: custsvc@petersons.com
http://www.petersons.com
Offers over 400 residential management development programs at academic institutions in the United States and abroad.

Annual

3895 Cabells Directory of Publishing Opportunities in Educational Psychology and Administration
Cabell Publishing Company
Box 5428
Tobe Hahn Station
Beaumont, TX 77726
409-898-0575
Fax: 409-866-9554
E-mail: publish@cabells.com
http://www.cabells.com
Provides information on editor contact information, manuscript guidelines, acceptance rate, review information and circulation data for over 225 academic journals.

799 pages Annual
ISBN: 0-911753-28-1

David WE Cabell, Editor
Deborah L English, Associate Editor

3896 Character Education Questions & Answers
Character Education Partnership
1025 Connecticut Avenue NW
Suite 1011
Washington, DC 20036
202-296-7743
800-988-8081
Fax: 202-296-7779
http://www.character.org
Andrea Grenadier, Director
Communications
Esther Schaeffer, CEO/Executive Director

3897 Character Education Resource Guide
Character Education Partnership
1025 Connecticut Avenue NW
Suite 1011
Washington, DC 20036
202-296-7743
800-988-8081
Fax: 202-296-7779
http://www.character.org
Andrea Grenadier, Director
Communications
Esther Schaeffer, CEO/Executive Director

3898 Character Education: The Foundation for Teacher Education
Character Education Partnership
1025 Connecticut Avenue NW
Suite 1011
Washington, DC 20036
202-296-7743
800-988-8081
Fax: 202-296-7779
http://www.character.org
Andrea Grenadier, Director
Communications
Esther Schaeffer, CEO/Executive Director

3899 Continuing Education Guide
International Association for Continuing Education
Department #3087
Washington, DC 20042-0001
202-463-2905
Fax: 202-463-8498
Explores how to interpret and use the Continuing Education Unit or other criteria used for continuing education programs. This guide, written by continuing education and training consultant, Louis Phillips, is a reference source complete with sample forms, charts, checklists and everything you need to plan, develop and evaluate your school's continuing education program.

3900 Creating Quality Reform: Programs, Communities and Governance
Pearson Education Communications
1 Lake Street
Upper Saddle River, NJ 07458
201-236-7000
Fax: 877-260-2530
E-mail: communications@pearsoned.com
http://www.pearsoned.com

Publication Date: 2002

J Thomas Owens, Editor
Jan C Simmons, Editor

3901 Designing & Implementing a Leadership Academy in Character Education
Character Education Partnership
1025 Connecticut Avenue NW
Suite 1011
Washington, DC 20036
202-296-7743
800-988-8081
Fax: 202-296-7779
http://www.character.org
Andrea Grenadier, Director
Communications
Esther Schaeffer, CEO/Executive Director

3902 Deskbook Encyclopedia of American School Law
Progressive Business Publications
370 Technology Drive
Malvern, PA 19355
800-220-5000
Fax: 610-647-8089
E-mail: customer_service@pbp.com
http://www.pbp.com
An up-to-date compilation of summarized federal and state appellate court decisions which affect education. The full legal citation is supplied for each case with a brief introductory note on the American judicial system is provided along with updated appendices of recent US Supreme Court cases and recently published law review articles.

Annually

3903 Developing a Character Education Program
Character Education Partnership
1025 Connecticut Avenue NW
Suite 1011
Washington, DC 20036
202-296-7743
800-988-8081
Fax: 202-296-7779
http://www.character.org

Henry Huffman, Author
Andrea Grenadier, Director Communications
Esther Schaeffer, CEO/Executive Director

3904 Development Education: A Directory of Non-Governmental Practitioners
U.N. Non-Governmental Liaison Service
Palais des Nations, CH 1211
Geneva 10
Switzerland
Lists about 800 national non-governmental organizations in industrialized countries and international non-governmental networks concerned with developmental education.

Publication Date: 1992 400 pages

3905 Directory of Chief Executive Officers of United Methodist Schools, Colleges & Universities
General Board of Higher Education & Ministry/UMC
1001 19th Avenue
PO Box 340007
Nashville, TN 37203-0007
615-340-7406
Fax: 615-340-7379
E-mail: scu@gbhem.org
http://www.gbhem.org/highed.html
123 United Methodist educational institutions including theology schools, professional schools, two year colleges and colleges and universities with all contact information arranged by institution type. Paperback.

32 pages Annual

Dr. James A Noseworthy, Assistant General Secretary

3906 Directory of Organizations in Educational Management
ERIC Clearinghouse on Educational Management
1787 Agate Street
Eugene, OR 97403-1923
541-346-5043
800-438-8841
Fax: 541-346-2334
E-mail: sales@oregon.uoregon.edu
http://www.eric.uoregon.edu

Offers listings of 163 organizations in the field of educational management at the elementary and secondary school levels.

Dr. Philip Piele, Director
Stuart C Smith, Associate Director

3907 Directory of State Education Agencies
Council of Chief State School Officers
1 Massachusette Avenue NW
Suite 700
Washington, DC 20001-1431
202-336-7000
Fax: 202-408-8072
http://www.ccsso.org
A reference to state and national education agency contracts. Arranged state-by-state, it includes state education agency personnel titles, addresses, phone numbers, and fax numbers when applicable. National information includes key contacts and information for 33 national education associations and 5 pages of names, titles, addresses, and numbers for the US Department of Education.

103 pages
ISBN: 1-884037-66-6

Kathleen Neary, Editor

3908 Educating for Character
Master Teacher
Leadership Lane
PO Box 1207
Manhattan, KS 66505-1207
800-669-9633
Fax: 800-669-1132
http://www.masterteacher.com
Dr. Licona has developed a 12 point program that offers practical strategies designed to create a working coalition of parents, teachers and communities.

428 pages
ISBN: 0-553-37052-9

Thomas Lickona PhD, Author

3909 Educating for Character: How Our Schools Can Teach Respect and Responsibility
Character Education Partnership
1025 Connecticut Avenue NW
Suite 1011
Washington, DC 20036
202-296-7743
800-988-8081
Fax: 202-296-7779
http://www.character.org

Tom Likona, Author
Andrea Grenadier, Director Communications
Esther Schaeffer, CEO/Executive Director

3910 Education Budget Alert
Committee for Education Funding
122 C Street NW
Suite 280
Washington, DC 20001-2109
202-383-0083
Fax: 202-383-0097
E-mail: jchang@cef.org
http://www.cef.org
Federal programs currently help over 63 million Americans to engage in formal learning. This guidebook explains what these programs do, what types of activities are supported, the reasons the federal government initiated these programs, and their level at funding.

150 pages Annually

Jennifer Chang, Administrative Assistant
Michael Pons, Editor

3911 Educational Consultants Directory
American Business Directories, Inc.
5711 S 86th Circle
PO Box 27347
Omaha, NE 68127
402-593-4600
800-555-6124
Fax: 402-331-5481
E-mail: directory@abi.com
A list of more than 5,000 entries, including name, address, phone, size of advertisement, name of owner or manager and number of employees.

3912 Educational Dealer-Buyers' Guide Issue
Fahy-Williams Publishing
171 Reed Street
Geneva, NY 14456-2137
315-789-0458
Fax: 315-789-4263
List of approximately 2,000 suppliers of educational materials and equipment.

Annual

3913 Executive Summary Set
Master Teacher
Leadership Lane
PO Box 1207
Manhattan, KS 66502
800-669-9633
Fax: 800-669-1132
http://www.masterteacher.com
An easy, effective and practical way to orient new board members before they attend their first meeting. Executive Summary Sets cover the vital information board members must have in eight areas: tenets of education; powers and responsibilities; decision making; communication for maximum results; resource management; assessment of programs; assessment of personnel and conflict resolution.

Robert DeBruyn, Editor

3914 Grants and Contracts Handbook
Association of School Business Officials Int'l
11401 N Shore Drive
Reston, VA 20190-4232
703-478-0405
Fax: 703-478-0205
This is a basic reference for grant applicants, executors, project managers, administrators and staff. The ideas are school-tested and based on information gathered from institutions and agencies over the past two decades.

32 pages
ISBN: 0-910170-52-5

Peg D Kirkpatrick, Editor/Publisher
Robert Gluck, Managing Editor

3915 Hispanic Yearbook-Anuario Hispano
TIYM Publishing
6718 Whittier Avenue
Suite 130
McLean, VA 22101
703-734-1632
Fax: 703-356-0787
E-mail: TIYM@aol.com
http://www.tiym.com
This guide lists Hispanic organizations, publications, radio and TV stations, through not specifically for grant-giving purposes.

Annually

John O Zavala, COO
Ramon Palencia, Director PR

3916 Leading to Change: The Challenge of the New Superintendency
Jossey-Bass/Pfeiffer
989 Market Street
San Francisco, CA 94103-1741
415-433-1740
Fax: 415-433-0499
http://www.josseybass.com

The challenge of the new superintendency.

352 pages
ISBN: 0-7879-0214-4

Susan Moore Johnson, Author

3917 Legal Basics: A Handbook for Educators
Phi Delta Kappa International
PO Box 789
Bloomington, IL 47402-0789
812-339-1156
Fax: 812-339-0018
http://www.pdkintl.org
Superintendents, principals, counselors, teachers, and paraprofessionals need to pay close attention to their actions in schools and classrooms because, from a legal standpoint, those settings may contain hazardous conditions. Legal Basics points out the pitfalls and how to avoid them.

120 pages Paperback
ISBN: 8-87367-806-0

Evelyn B Kelly, Author
DR Walling, Dir Publications/Research

3918 Legal Issues and Education Technology
National School Board Association
PO Box 161
Annapolis Junction, MD 20701
800-706-6722
Fax: 703-683-7590
Helps administrators craft an acceptable-use policy.

Publication Date: 1999
ISSN: 0314510

3919 Lifeworld of Leadership: Creating Culture, Community, and Personal Meaning in Our Schools
Jossey-Bass Publishers
989 Market Street
San Francisco, CA 94103-1741
415-433-1740
Fax: 415-433-0499
http://www.josseybass.com
Explores the crucial link between school improvement and school character.

Publication Date: 2004 240 pages Paperback
ISBN: 0-7879-7277-6

Thomas J Sergiovanni

3920 Looking at Schools: Instruments & Processes for School Analysis
Research for Better Schools
112 N Broad Street
Philadelphia, PA 19102
215-568-6150
Fax: 215-568-7260
http://www.rbs.org
Thirty-five institutions that offer instruments and processes to assess the performance of students, teachers and administrators, school climate effectiveness and school-community relations.

Publication Date: 1991 140 pages

Carol Crociante, Executive Secretary
Keith M Kershner, Executive Co-Director

3921 Market Data Retrieval-National School Market Index
Market Data Retrieval
1 Forest Parkway
Shelton, CT 06484-0947
203-926-4800
800-333-8802
Fax: 203-929-5253
E-mail: msubrizi@dnb.com
An annual report on school spending patterns for instructional materials in the United States. The Index now in its twenty-fifth year of publication, lists the expenditures for in-

structional materials for all 15,000 US senior districts.

Publication Date: 1996
ISBN: 0-897708-25-3

Mike Subrizi, Marketing Director

3922 National Association of Principals of Schools for Girls Directory
National Association of Principals/Girls Schools
4050 Little River Road
Hendersonville, NC 28739-8317
828-693-8248
Fax: 828-693-1490
List of 575 principals and deans of private and secondary schools for girls and coeducational schools, colleges and admissions officers.

Annual

3923 National School Public Relations Association Directory
National School Public Relations Association
1501 Lee Highway
Arlington, VA 22209-1109
703-528-6713
Lists over 2,800 school system public relations directors and school administration officers.

100 pages Annual

3924 National School Supply & Equipment Association Membership/Buyers' Guide Directory
National School Supply & Equipment Association
830 Colesville Road
Suite 250
Silver Spring, MD 20910
301-495-0240
800-395-5550
Fax: 301-495-3330
E-mail: awatts@nssea.org
http://www.nssea.org
Lists 1,500 member dealers, manufacturers and manufacturers' representatives for school supplies, equipment and instructional materials.

200 pages Annual

Adrienne Watts, Author
Adrienne Watts, VP Marketing
Kathy Jentz, Director Communications

3925 National Schools of Character
Character Education Partnership
1025 Connecticut Avenue NW
Suite 1011
Washington, DC 20036
202-296-7743
800-988-8081
Fax: 202-296-7779
http://www.character.org

Andrea Grenadier, Director Communications
Esther Schaeffer, CEO/Executive Director

3926 Proactive Leadership in the 21st Century
Master Teacher
Leadership Lane
PO Box 1207
Manhattan, KS 66505-1207
800-669-9633
Fax: 800-669-1132
http://www.masterteacher.com
Contain the laws and principals of leadership and people management as they had never been defined and described before giving

school administrators a set of guidelines that if followed would guarantee success.

ISBN: 0-914607-44-8

Robert L DeBruyn, Author

3927 QED's State School Guides
Quality Education Data
1625 Broadway Street
Suite 250
Denver, CO 80203
303-860-1832
800-525-5811
Fax: 303-209-9444
E-mail: info@qeddata.com
http://www.qeddata.com
Complete directories of every US school district and public, Catholic and private school. Directories are available for individual states, geographic regions and the entire United States. Each directory includes names of district administrators, school principals and school librarians, as well as addresses, phone numbers and enrollment information. QED's State school guide also includes key demographic and instructional technology data for each district and school.

Publication Date: 1993 Yearly
ISBN: 0-887476-49-0

Liz Stephens, Marketing

3928 School Promotion, Publicity & Public Relations: Nothing but Benefits
Master Teacher
Leadership Lane
PO Box 1207
Manhattan, KS 66505-1207
785-539-0555
800-669-9633
Fax: 785-539-7739
http://www.masterteacher.com
Contains the vital foundations an administrator must have to understand and implement a program of publicity, promotion and public relations, in a school or school district.

327 pages
ISBN: 0-914607-25-1

Tracey H DeBruyn, Author

3929 Schoolwide Discipline Strategies that Make a Difference in Teaching & Learning
Master Teacher
Leadership Lane
PO Box 1207
Manhattan, KS 66505-1207
800-669-9633
Fax: 800-669-1132
http://www.masterteacher.com
This approach to discipline will help your school or district eliminate the dependecy on one individual, provide guidance for present and new teachers, allow disipline to become a K-12 program, an bring about consistancy in the handling of all student misbehaviors.

150 pages
ISBN: 1-58992-000-7

Larry Dixon, Author

3930 The Teaching Professor
Magna Publications
2718 Dryden Drive
Madison, WI 53704
608-246-3590
Fax: 608-246-3597
E-mail: billh@magnapubs.com
http://www.magnapubs.com
This newsletter has been a leading source of information and inspiration for educators

committed to creating a better learning environment.

Publication Date: 1995 530 pages Paperback
November
1000 attendees and 10+ exhibits

William Haight, President
Jody Glynn Patrick, Vice President

Directories & Handbooks / Early Childhood Education

3931 Early Childhood Environmental Education Programs: Guidelines for Excellence
North American Assoc for Environmental Education
2000 P Street NW
Suite 540
Washington, DC 20036
202-419-0412
Fax: 212-419-0415
E-mail: info@naaee.org
http://www.naaee.org
A set of recommendations for developing and administering high-quality environmental education programs for young children from birth to age eight, with a focus on ages three to six. These guidelines provide a tool that can be used to ensure a firm foundation for new programs or to trigger improvements in existing ones.

Bora Simmons, Author

Directories & Handbooks / Elementary Education

3932 Educational Impressions
PO Box 77
Hawthorne, NJ 07507-0077
973-423-4666
800-451-7450
Fax: 973-423-5569
E-mail: awpeller@worldnet.att.net
Educational workbooks, activity books, literature guides, and audiovisuals. Grades K-8, with emphasis on intermediate and middle grades.

Paperback/Video/Audi

Neil Peller, Marketing Director
Lori Brown, Sales/Marketing

3933 Educators Guide to FREE Videotapes-Elementary/ Middle School Edition
Educators Progress Service
214 Center Street
Randolph, WI 53956-1408
920-326-3126
888-951-4469
Fax: 920-326-3127
E-mail: epsinc@centurytel.net
http://www.freeteachingaids.com
Lists and describes free and free-loan videotapes for the elementary and middle school level.

Annual
ISBN: 0-877082-67-7

Kathy Nehmer, President

3934 Educators Guide to FREE Videotapes-Secondary Edition
Educators Progress Service
214 Center Street
Randolph, WI 53956-1408
920-326-3126
888-951-4469

Fax: 920-326-3127
E-mail: epsinc@centurytel.net
http://www.freeteachingaids.com
Lists and describes free and free-loan videotapes for the elementary and middle school level.

Annual
ISBN: 0-877082-67-7

Kathy Nehmer, President

3935 Elementary Teachers Guide to FREE Curriculum Materials
Educators Progress Service
214 Center Street
Randolph, WI 53956-1408
920-326-3126
888-951-4469
Fax: 920-326-3127
E-mail: epsinc@centurytel.net
http://www.freeteachingaids.com
Lists and describes free supplementary teaching aids for the elementary level.

Annual
ISBN: 0-877082-64-2

Kathy Nehmer, President

3936 KIDSNET Media Guide and News
KIDSNET
6856 Eastern Avenue NW
Suite 208
Washington, DC 20012
202-291-1400
Fax: 202-882-7315
E-mail: kidsnet@kidsnet.org
http://www.kidsnet.org
Contains children's television, radio and video listings. Also lists related teaching materials and copyright guidelines.

150 pages Monthly

3937 Lesson Plans, Integrating Technology into the Classroom: Elementary Edition
Master Teacher
Leadership Lane
PO Box 1207
Manhattan, KS 66505-1207
800-669-9633
Fax: 800-669-1132
http://www.masterteacher.com
Gives teachers practical lessons developed and tested by teachers across the curriculum, with students of all levels of ability in using technology.

130 pages
ISBN: 0-914607-59-6

3938 Nursery Schools & Kindergartens Directory
American Business Directories
5711 S 86th Circle
Omaha, NE 68127-4146
402-593-4600
888-999-1307
Fax: 402-331-5481
A geographical listing of 34,900 nursery schools and kindergartens including all contact information, first year in Yellow Pages and descriptions. Also available are regional editions and electronic formats.

Annual

Jerry Venner, Coordinating Education

3939 Parent Involvement Facilitator: Elementary Edition
Master Teacher
Leadership Lane
PO Box 1207
Manhattan, KS 66505-1207
800-669-9633
Fax: 800-669-1132
http://www.masterteacher.com

Packed with ideas for you and your teachers to implement along with the exact steps for you to follow.

169 pages
ISBN: 0-914607-45-6

3940 Patterson's Elementary Education
Educational Directories Inc.
1025 W Wise Road
PO Box 68097
Schaumberg, IL 60168
847-891-1250
800-357-6183
Fax: 847-891-0945
E-mail: info@ediusa.org
http://www.ediusa.org
A directory to more than 13,000 public school districts; 71,000 public, private and Catholic elementary and middle schools; 1,600 territorial schools; and 400 state department of education personnel in one easy to use consistent format. Arranged alphabetically by state then city. City listings include city name, telephone area code, city population, county name, public school district name, enrollment, grade range, superintendent's name, address and phone number.

Publication Date: 1994 870 pages Annual
ISBN: 0-910536-59-7

Douglas Moody, Coordinating Education

3941 Teaching Our Youngest-A Guide for Preschool Teachers and Child Care and Family Providers
PO Box 1398
Jessup, MD 20794-1398
877-4ED-PUBS
Fax: 301-470-1244
E-mail: edpubs@inet.ed.gov
http://www.edpubs.org
This booklet draws from scientifically based research about what can be done to help children develop their language abilities, increase their knowledge, become familiar with books and other printed materials,learn letters and sounds, recognize numbers and learn to count.

Directories & Handbooks / Employment

3942 AAEE Job Search Handbook for Educators
American Association for Employment in Education
3040 Riverside Drive
Suite 117
Columbus, OH 43221
614-485-1111
Fax: 614-485-9609
E-mail: aaee@osu.edu
http://www.aaee.org
Information for those pursuing work as educators.

72 pages Annually

Neil Shnider, Executive Director
Diane Sledden Reed, Board President

3943 Cabell's Directory of Publishing Opportunities in Education
Cabell Publishing
Box 5428
Tobe Hahn Station
Beaumont, TX 77726-5428
409-898-0575
Fax: 409-866-9554
E-mail: publish@cabells.com
http://www.cabells.com
Includes list of more than 430 education journals that consider manuscripts for publication. Includes contact names and addresses for submit-

ting manuscripts, topics considered, publication guidelines, fees, and circulation information.

1,200 pages

David WE Cabell, Editor
Deborah L English, Associate Editor

3944 Cabell's Directory of Publishing Opportunities in Accounting
Cabell Publishing Company
Box 5428
Tobe Hahn Station
Beaumont, TX 77726
409-898-0575
Fax: 409-866-9554
E-mail: publish@cabells.com
http://www.cabells.com
Contains information on 130 journal. Entries include manuscript guidelines for authors: editor's address, phone, fax and e-mail. Review process and the time required, acceptance rates, readership circulation and subscription prices. The Index classifies journals by 15 topics areas and provides information on type of review, acceptance rate and review time.

425 pages Annual
ISBN: 0-911753-13-3

David WE Cabell, Editor
Deborah L English, Editor

3945 Cabell's Directory of Publishing Opportunities in Economics & Finance
Cabell Publishing Company
Box 5428
Tobe Hahn Station
Beaumont, TX 77726-5428
409-898-0575
Fax: 409-866-9554
E-mail: publish@cabells.com
http://www.cabells.com
Contains information on 350 journals. Each journal entry includes manuscript guidelines for authors: editor's address, phone, fax and e-mail, review process and time required, acceptance rates, readership, circulation and subscription prices. The Index classifies journals by 15 topic areas and provides information on type of review, acceptance rate and review time.

Publication Date: 1995 1100 pages Annual
ISBN: 0-911753-14-1

David WE Cabell, Editor
Deborah L English, Associate Editor

3946 Cabells Directory of Publishing Opportunities in Management
Cabell Publishing Company
Box 5428
Tobe Hahn Station
Beaumont, TX 77726
409-898-0575
Fax: 409-866-9554
E-mail: publish@cabells.com
http://www.cabells.com
Provides editor contact information, acceptance rates, review information, manuscript guidelines and circulation data for over 540 academic journals.

Publication Date: 1973 648 pages
ISBN: 0-911753-15-X

David WE Cabell, Editor
Deborah L English, Associate Editor

3947 Career Book
VGM Career Books
4255 W Touhy Avenue
Lincolnwood, IL 60712
732-329-6991
Fax: 732-329-6994

Offers information on educational employment opportunities in America and abroad.

BiAnnual Hard/Paper

Joyce Lain Kennedy & Darryl Laramore, Author

3948 Career Development Activities for Every Classroom
University of Wisconsin-Madison
1025 W Johnson Street
Madison, WI 53706-1796
608-263-3696
800-446-0399
Fax: 608-262-9197
E-mail: cewmail@soemadison.wisc.edu
http://www.cew.wisc.edu
Four volumes containing hundreds of career development activities, and separate activity masters to duplicate. All lessons are keyed to National Career Development Guidelines Competencies and subject matter areas. Each volume is available individually.

3949 Career Information Center; 13 Volumes
MacMillan Publishing Company
1633 Broadway
New York, NY 10019
212-512-2000
Fax: 800-835-3202
13 volumes covering 3,000 careers, 633 job summaries with 800 photos. Up-to-date information on salaries and occupational outlooks for nearly 3,000 careers.

2.6M pages Triennial
ISBN: 0-028974-52-2

3950 Careers Information Officers in Local Authorities
Careers Research & Advisory Centre/Hobsons Pub.
Bateman Street
Cambridge CB2 1LZ England
223-354551
1,100 United Kingdom institutions offering collections of career information and audio-visual materials covering career opportunities and current job markets. Arranged alphabetically listing address, phone, contact name and titles, type of materials held and a description of the facilities.

165 pages 12.95 pounds

3951 Certification and Accreditation Programs Directory
Gale Research
27500 Drake Road
Farmington Hills, MI 48331-3535
248-699-4253
800-877-4253
Fax: 248-699-8064
E-mail: galeord@gale.com
http://www.galegroup.com
Directory of private organizations that offer more than 1,700 voluntary certification programs and approximately 300 accreditation programs. Also on CD-ROM.

Publication Date: 1995 620 pages
ISSN: 1084-2128

Allen W Paschal, President

3952 Council of British Independent Schools in the European Communities-Members Directory
Lucy's Hill
Hythe, Kent CT21 5ES
England
44-1303-260857
Fax: 44-1303-260857

E-mail: secretariat@cobisec.org
http://www.cobisec.org

Annual

Roger Fry CBE, Chairman
Sybil Melchers MBE, Honorary Secretary

3953 Directory of English Language Schools in Japan Hiring English Teachers
Information Career Opportunities Research Center
Box 1100, Station F
Toronto M4Y 2T7
Canada
416-925-8878
English-language schools in Japan.

15 pages Annual

3954 Directory of International Internships Michigan State University
MSU: Dean's Office of Int'l Studies and Programs
209 International Center
East Lansing, MI 48824
517-355-2350
Fax: 517-353-7254
E-mail: gliozzo@pilot.msu.edu
http://www.isp.msu.edu
International internships sponsored by academic institutions, private corporations and the federal government.

Publication Date: 1994 168 pages Paperback

Charles A Gliozzo, Coordinating Editor

3955 Directory of Schools, Colleges, and Universities Overseas
Overseas Employment Services
EBSCO Industries
PO Box 1943
Birmingham, AL 35201
205-991-1330
Fax: 205-995-1582
Directory of 300 educational institutions worldwide that hire teachers to teach different subjects in English.

21 pages Annual

Leonard Simcoe, Editor

3956 Directory of Work and Study in Developing Countries
Vacation-Work Publishers
9 Park End Street
Oxford OX1 1HJ
England
865-241978
Offers information on about 420 organizations worldwide offering employment and study opportunities in over 100 developing countries.

215 pages

3957 Earn & Learn: Cooperative Education Opportunities
Octameron Associates
1900 Mount Vernon Avenue
PO Box 2748
Alexandria, VA 22301-0748
703-836-5480
Fax: 703-836-5650
E-mail: info@octameron.com
http://www.octameron.com
Explains how students may participate in co-operative work-study education programs with federal government agencies.

Publication Date: 1997 48 pages BiAnnual
ISBN: 1-57509-023-6

3958 English in Asia: Teaching Tactics for New English Teachers
Global Press
697 College Parkway
Rockville, MD 20850-1135
303-393-7645
Directory covering 1,000 private English-language schools in Asia, to which applications can be sent to teach.
Publication Date: 1992 180 pages

3959 European Council of International Schools Directory
European Council of International Schools
21 Lavant Street, Petersfield
Hampshire GU3 23EL
United Kingdom
44-1730-26-8244
Fax: 44-1730-267914
E-mail: 100412.242@compuserve.com
More than 420 member elementary and secondary international schools in Europe and worldwide.
480 pages Annual
JS Henley, President

3960 Faculty Exchange Center Directory and House Exchange Supplement
Faculty Exchange Center
962 Virginia Avenue
Lancaster, PA 17603-3116
717-393-1130
Offers information for college and faculty members wishing to exchange positions and/or homes temporarily with faculty members at other institutions.
35 pages Annual

3961 Foreign Faculty and Administrative Openings
Education Information Services
PO Box 620662
Newton, MA 02462-0662
617-433-0125
150 specific openings in administration, counseling, library and other professional positions for American teachers in American schools overseas and in international schools in which teaching language is English.
15 pages Every 6 Weeks
FB Viaux, Coordinating Education

3962 Guide to Educational Opportunities in Japan
Embassy of Japan
2520 Massachusetts Avenue NW
Washington, DC 20008
202-238-6700
Fax: 202-328-2187
http://www.embjapan.org
This guide describes opportunities for study in Japan and outlines different forms of financial assistance.

3963 How to Create a Picture of Your Ideal Job or Next Career
Ten Speed Press
PO Box 7123
Berkeley, CA 94707-0123
415-845-8414
800-841-BOOK
Fax: 510-524-4588
Offers handy tips on how to choose the right career, and then go out and get it.
Publication Date: 1989
Richard Nelson Bolles, Author

3964 How to Plan and Develop a Career Center
Center on Education and Work
964 Educational Sciences Building
1025 W Johnson Street
Madison, WI 53706-1796
800-446-0399
Fax: 608-262-9197
E-mail: cewmail@soemadison.wisc.edu
http://www.cew.wisc.edu
High school, postsecondary, adult, and virtual career centers-a comprehensive blueprint that covers all the bases.

3965 Leading Educational Placement Sources in the US
Educational Information Services
PO Box 662
Newton Lower Falls, MA 02162
617-964-4555
An index of the host placement agencies in America for education professionals.

3966 List of Over 200 Executive Search Consulting Firms in the US
Educational Information Services
PO Box 662
Newton Lower Falls, MA 02162
617-964-4555
Covers companies with active search committees in America.

3967 List of Over 600 Personnel & Employment Agencies
Educational Information Services
PO Box 662
Newton Lower Falls, MA 02162
617-964-4555
Contains information on personnel and employment agencies.

3968 Living in China: A Guide to Studying, Teaching & Working in the PRC & Taiwan
China Books & Periodicals
360 Swift Avenue
Suite 48
South San Francisco, CA 94080
650-872-7076
800-818-2017
Fax: 650-872-7808
E-mail: info@chinabooks.com
http://www.chinabooks.com
America's #1 source of publications about China since 1960.
284 pages Paperback
ISBN: 0835125823
November
Chellis Ying, Marketing Director
Jane Lau, Customer Support Specialist

3969 National Directory of Internships
National Society for Experiential Education
3509 Haworth Drive
Suite 207
Raleigh, NC 27609-7235
631-728-9100
Fax: 631-728-9228
E-mail: info@nsee.org
http://www.nsee.org
Directory contains internship descriptions for hundreds of organizations in 85 fields in nonprofit organizations, government and corporations. Lists work and service experiences for high school, college and graduate students, people entering the job market, mid-career professionals and retired persons. Includes indexes by field of interest, location and host organization.
Publication Date: 1995 703 pages
ISBN: 0-536-01123-0

3970 Opening List in US Colleges, Public & Private Schools
Education Information Services/Instant Alert
PO Box 620662
Newton, MA 02462-0662
617-433-0125
Offers about 150 current professional openings in US colleges and public and private schools.
10 pages Every 6 weeks
FB Viaux, Coordinating Education

3971 Opening List of Professional Openings in American Overseas Schools
Education Information Services/Instant Alert
PO Box 620662
Newton, MA 02462-0662
617-433-0125
About 150 current professional openings for teachers, administrators, counselors, librarians and educational specialists in American overseas schools and international schools at which the teaching language is primarily English.
FB Viaux, Coordinating Education

3972 Overseas Employment Opportunities for Educators
Department of Defense, Office of Dependent Schools
2461 Eisenhower Avenue
Alexandria, VA 22331-3000
703-325-0867
This publication tells about teaching jobs in 250 schools operated for children of US military and civilian personnel stationed overseas. Applicants usually must qualify in two subject areas.

3973 Private School, Community & Junior College Four Year Colleges & Universities
Educational Information Services
PO Box 662
Newton Lower Falls, MA 02162
617-964-4555
Names, addresses and phones for any state or region in the United States offering employment opportunities.

3974 Research, Study, Travel, & Work Abroad
US Government Printing Office
732 N Capitol Street NW
Washington, DC 20401
202-512-1999
Fax: 202-512-1293
E-mail: admin@access.gpo.gov
http://www.access.gpo.gov

3975 Teaching Overseas
KSJ Publishing Company
PO Box 2311
Sebastopol, CA 95473-2311
A directory of information on how to find jobs teaching overseas.
Publication Date: 1992 89 pages 2nd Edition
ISBN: 0-962044-55-5

3976 Thirty-Four Activities to Promote Careers in Special Education
The Council for Exceptional Children
1920 Association Drive
Reston, VA 20191-1545
703-620-3660
800-232-7323
Fax: 703-264-1637
This guide introduces individuals to the opportunities, rewards and delights of working with children with exceptionalities. It provides directions on how to plan, develop, and implement activities in the school and community that will increase people's awareness of careers in special education and related services.
Publication Date: 1996 120 pages
ISBN: 0-865862-77-0

3977 VGM's Careers Encyclopedia
VGM Career Books/National Textbook
Company
4255 W Touhy Avenue
Lincolnwood, IL 60646-1933
708-679-5500
A list of over 200 professional associations
that provide career guidance information.

**3978 Work Abroad: The Complete Guide
to Finding a Job Overseas**
Transitions Abroad
PO Box 745
Bennington, VT 05201
802-442-4827
Fax: 802-442-4827
E-mail: editor@transitionsabroad.com
http://www.transitionsabroad.com
Resource for finding both short- and
long-term jobs abroad. Organized by region
and country, includes websites and phone
numbers.

**3979 Workforce Preparation: An
International Perspective**
PO Box 8623
Ann Arbor, MI 48107-8623
800-530-9673
Fax: 734-975-2787
Excellent collection of material by 20 promi-
nent educators describes efforts in developed
and developing countries worldwide to pre-
pare youth and adults for work.

3980 World of Learning
Europa Publications
18 Bedford Square
London WC1B 3JN
England
171-580-8236
Fax: 171-636-1664
Details over 26,000 educational, cultural and
scientific institutions throughout the world,
together with an exhaustive directory of over
150,000 people active within them.

2,072 pages Annual
ISBN: 0-946653-92-5

Directories & Handbooks / Financial Aid

**3981 Catalog of Federal Domestic
Assistance**
Office of Management & Budget
Washington, DC 20402
Offers information from all federal agencies
that have assistance programs (loans, scholarships and technical assistance as well as
grants) and compiles these into the CFDA.
The individual entries are grouped by Department of Agency and includes an excellent set
of instructions and several indices. Indices
allow the user to search for grants by subject
matter, agency, deadline date or eligibility
criteria.

3982 Chronicle Financial Aid Guide
Chronicle Guidance Publications
66 Aurora Street
Moravia, NY 13118-3576
315-497-0330
800-622-7284
Fax: 315-497-3359
E-mail:
customerservice@chronicleguidance.com
http://www.chronicleguidance.com
Financial aid programs offered primarily by
noncollegiate organizations, independent
and AFL-CIO affiliated labor unions and federal and state governments for high school se-

niors and undergraduate and graduate
students.

460 pages Annual
ISBN: 1-5563-310-1

Janet Seemann, Author
Janet Seemann, Author/Editor

**3983 College Costs and Financial Aid
Handbook**
College Board Publications
PO Box 869010
Plano, TX 75074-6917
800-323-7155
Fax: 888-321-7183
http://www.collegeboard.org
A step-by-step guide providing the most
up-to-date facts on costs plus financial aid
and scholarship availability at 3,200 two- and
four-year institutions.

Publication Date: 2003
ISBN: 0-874476-83-6

3984 College Financial Aid Annual
Arco/Macmillan
1633 Broadway
Floor 7
New York, NY 10019-6708
212-654-8933
Lists of private businesses, academic institutions and other organizations that provide
awards and scholarships for financial aid;
guide to federal and state financial aid.

**3985 Directory of Educational Contests
for Students K-12**
ABC-CLIO
130 Cremona Drive
#1911
Santa Barbara, CA 93117-5599
805-968-1911
800-368-6868
Fax: 805-685-9685
Offers about 200 competitive scholarship
programs and other educational contests for
elementary and secondary school students.

Publication Date: 1991 253 pages

**3986 Directory of Financial Aid for
Women**
Reference Service Press
5000 Windplay Drive
Suite 4
El Dorado Hills, CA 95762
916-939-9620
Fax: 916-939-9626
E-mail: rspinfo@aol.com
http://www.rspfunding.com
Offers information on more than 1,500 schol-
arships, fellowships, loan sources, grants,
awards and internships.

490 pages

**3987 Directory of Institutional Projects
Funded by Office of Educational
Research**
U.S. Office of Educational Research &
Improvement
555 New Jersey Avenue NW
Washington, DC 20001-2029
202-219-2050

Publication Date: 1990 60 pages

**3988 Directory of International Grants &
Fellowships in the Health Sciences**
National Institutes of Health
31 Center Drive MSC 2220
Building 31, Room B2C29
Bethesda, MD 20892-2220
301-496-2075
Fax: 301-594-1211
E-mail: ficinfo@nih.gov
http://www.nih.gov/fic

Fellowships and grants listed separately in
this guide. Each listing includes a complete
program description with contact information.

**3989 Don't Miss Out: The Ambitous
Students Guide to Financial Aid**
Octameron Associates
1900 Mt Vernon Avenue
Alexandria, VA 22301-0748
703-836-5480
Fax: 703-836-5650
E-mail: info2octameon.com
http://www.octameron.com

Publication Date: 0 192 pages Anually

**3990 Fellowships in International
Affairs-A Guide to Opportunities in
the US & Abroad**
Lynne Rienner Publishing
1800 30th Street
Suite 314
Boulder, CO 80301
303-444-6684
Fax: 303-444-0824
E-mail: questions@rienner.com
http://www.rienner.com
This guide lists fellowships meant to encour-
age women to pursue careers in international
security.

**3991 Fellowships, Scholarships and
Related Opportunities**
Center for International Ed./University of
TN
201 Aconda Court
Knoxville, TN 37996
865-974-1000
Fax: 865-974-2985
140 grants, scholarships and fellowships
available to citizens of the United States for
study or research abroad.

50 pages Biennial

**3992 Financial Aid for Research &
Creative Activities Abroad**
Reference Service Press
5000 Windplay Drive
Suite 4
El Dorado Hills, CA 95762
916-939-9620
Fax: 916-939-9626
E-mail: webagent@rspfunding.com
http://www.rspfunding.com
This book lists opportunities fir high school
students and undergraduates, graduates,
postdoctoral students, professionals and
others.

432 pages
ISBN: 1588410625

Gail Schlachter, Author
R.David Weber, Author

**3993 Financial Aid for Study Abroad: a
Manual for Advisers &
Administrators**
NAFSA: Association of International
Educators
1307 New York Avenue NW
8th Floor
Washington, DC 20005-4701
202-737-3699
800-836-4994
Fax: 202-737-3657
E-mail: inbox@nafsa.org
http://www.nafsa.org

Publication Date: 1989 105 pages

Marlene M Johnson, Director/CEO

3994 Financial Resources for International Study
Institute of International Education
809 United Nations Plaza
New York, NY 10017-3580
412-741-0930
Fax: 212-984-5452
E-mail: iiebooks@abdintl.com
http://www.iiebooks.org
Directory of more than 600 awards that can be used for international study.
Publication Date: 1996 320 pages
ISBN: 087206-220-1

3995 Foundation Grants to Individuals
Foundation Center
79 Fifth Avenue
New York, NY 10003-3076
212-260-4230
Fax: 212-807-3677
Features current information for grant seekers.

3996 Free Money for College: Fifth Edition
Facts On File
132 West 31st Street
17th Floor
New York, NY 10001
800-678-3633
E-mail: llikoff@factsonfile.com
http://www.factsonfile.com
1,000 grants and scholarships.
Publication Date: 1999 240 pages Annual Hardcover
ISBN: 081603947X

Laurie Blum, Author
Laurie Likoff, Editorial Director

3997 Free Money for Foreign Study: A Guide to 1,000 Grants for Study Abroad
Facts On File
132 West 31st Street
17th Floor
New York, NY 10001
800-678-3633
E-mail: llikoff@factsonfile.com
http://www.factsonfile.com
Lists organizations and institutions worldwide offering scholarships and grants for study outside the United States.
262 pages

Laurie Likoff, Editorial Director

3998 Fulbright and Other Grants for USIA Graduate Study Abroad
U.S. Student Programs Division
809 United Nations Plaza
New York, NY 10017-3503
212-984-5330
Fax: 212-984-5325
http://www.iie.org
Mutual educational exchange grants for pre-doctoral students offered by foreign governments.
90 pages Annual

3999 Fund Your Way Through College: Uncovering 1,100 Opportunities in Aid
Visible Ink Press/Gale Research
830 Penobscot Building
Detroit, MI 48226
313-961-2242
1,100 scholarships, grants, loans, awards and prizes for undergraduate students.
470 pages

4000 German-American Scholarship Guide-Exchange Opportunities for Historians and Social Scientist
German Historical Institute
1607 New Hampshire Avenue NW
Washington, DC 20009-2562
202-387-3355
Fax: 202-483-3430
http://www.ghi-dc.org
This guide is divided into two sections: scholarships for study and research in the US and scholarships for study and research in Germany.

4001 Getting Funded: The Complete Guide to Writing Grant Proposals
Continuing Education Press
PO Box 1394
Portland, OR 97207-1394
503-725-4891
866-647-7377
Fax: 503-725-4715
E-mail: press@pdx.edu
http://www.cep.pdx.edu
A step-by-step guide to writing successful grants and proposals. An indispensible reference for experienced and first-time grant writers alike.
180 pages Paperback
ISBN: 0-87678-071-0

Mary Hall, Author
Mary Hall, Author

4002 Graduate Scholarship Book
Pearson Education
1 Lake Street
Upper Saddle River, NJ 07458
201-909-6200
Fax: 201-767-5029
A complete guide to scholarships, grants and loans for graduate and professional study.
441 pages Biennial

4003 Grant Opportunities for US Scholars & Host Opportunities for US Universities
International Research & Exchange Board
2121 K Street NW
Suite 700
Washington, DC 20037
202-628-8188
Fax: 202-628-8189
E-mail: irex@irex.org
http://www.irex.org
This pamphlet lists programs in advanced research, language and development, short-term travel, special projects and institutional opportunities.

4004 Grant Writing Beyond The Basics: Proven Strategies Professionals Use To Make Proposals
Continuing Education Press
PO Box 1394
Portland, OR 97207-1394
503-725-4891
866-647-7377
Fax: 503-725-4840
E-mail: press@pdx.edu
http://www.cep.pdx.edu
Designed to inspire those with grant writing experience who want to take their development strategies to the next level.
128 pages Paperback
ISBN: 0-87678-117-2

Michael K Wells, Author
Alba Scholz, Manager
Martha Ketchum, Customer Service

4005 Grants & Awards Available to American Writers
PEN American Center
588 Broadway
Suite 303
New York, NY 10012
212-334-1660
Fax: 212-334-2181
E-mail: ftw@pen.org
http://www.pen.org
Includes a full program description and is then broken down by type of writing. Awards for work in a particular country are listed alphabetically by country.
340 pages Paperback
ISBN: 0-934638-20-9

4006 Grants Register
St. Martin's Press
175 5th Avenue
New York, NY 10010
212-674-5151
888-330-8477
Fax: 800-672-2054
E-mail: firstname.lastname@stmartins.com
http://www.vhpsva.com
This directory offers a comprehensive list of programs organized alphabetically with special attention to eligibility requirements. Index by subject.

4007 Grants, Fellowships, & Prizes of Interest to Historians
American Historical Association
400 A Street SE
Washington, DC 20003-3889
202-544-2422
Fax: 202-544-8307
E-mail: aha@theaha.org
http://www.theaha.org
This guide offers information on awards for historians from undergraduate to postgraduate grants, fellowships, prizes, internships and awards.

4008 Guide to Department of Education Programs
US Department of Education
400 Maryland Avenue SW
Washington, DC 20202-0001
202-401-0765
Programs of financial aid offered by the Department of Education.
35 pages Annual

4009 Harvard College Guide to Grants
Office of Career Services
Harvard University
54 Dunster Street
Cambridge, MA 02138
617-495-2595
Fax: 617-496-6880
http://www.ocs.fas.harvard.edu
This guide describes national and regional grants and fellowships for study in the US, study abroad and work and practical experience.
234 pages Paperback

4010 How to Find Out About Financial Aid & Funding
Reference Service Press
5000 Windplay Drive
Suite 4
El Dorado Hills, CA 95762
916-939-9620
Fax: 916-939-9626
E-mail: rspinfo@aol.com
http://www.rspfunding.com
Over 700 financial aid directories and Internet sites described and evaluated.
432 pages Hardcover
ISBN: 1588410935

Gail A Schlachter, Author

4011 International Foundation Directory
Europa Publications
11 New Fetter Lane
London
England EC4P 4EE
44-0-20-7842-2110
Fax: 44-0-20-7842-2249
http://www.europapublications.co.uk
A world directory of international foundations, trusts and similar non-profit institutions. Provides detailed information on over 1,200 institutions in some 70 countries throughout the world.
Publication Date: 1994 736 pages
ISBN: 1-857430-01-8
Paul Kelly, Editorial Director

4012 International Scholarship Book: The Complete Guide to Financial Aid
Pearson Education
1 Lake Street
Upper Saddle River, NJ 07458
201-909-6200
Fax: 201-767-5029
Offers information on private organizations providing financial aid for university students interested in studying in foreign countries.
335 pages Cloth

4013 Journal of Student Financial Aid
University of Notre Dame
Office of Financial Aid
Notre Dame, IN 46556
574-631-6436
Offers a listing of private and federal sources of financial aid for college bound students.
3x Year
Joseph A Russo, Editor

4014 Loans and Grants from Uncle Sam
Octameron Associates
1900 Mount Vernon Avenue
PO Box 2748
Alexandria, VA 22301-0748
703-836-5480
Fax: 703-836-5650
E-mail: info@octameron.com
http://www.octameron.com
Offers information on federal student loan and grant programs and state loan guarantee agencies.
72 pages Annual
ISBN: 1-57509-097-X
Anna Leider, Author

4015 Money for Film & Video Artists
American for the Art
1000 Vermont Avenue NW
6th Floor
Washington, DC 20005
202-371-2830
Fax: 202-371-0424
http://www.artsusa.org
The listings are organized by sponsoring organization and entries include basic application and program information.

4016 Money for International Exchange in the Arts
American for the Art
1000 Vermont Avenue NW
12th Floor
Washington, DC 20005
202-371-2830
Fax: 202-371-0424
http://www.artsusa.org
A guide to the various resources available to support artists and arts organizations in international work.

4017 Money for Visual Artists
America for the Art
1000 Vermont Avenue NW
6th Floor
Washington, DC 20005
202-371-2830
Fax: 202-371-0424
http://www.artsusa.org
Programs are listed alphabetically by sponsor with detailed program description.

4018 National Association of State Scholarship and Grant Program Survey Report
National Association of State Scholarship Programs
660 Boas Street
Harrisburg, PA 17102-1324
717-257-2794
Listing of over 50 member state agencies administering scholarship and grant programs for student financial aid.
150 pages

4019 National Association of Student Financial Aid Administrators Directory
1129 20th Street NW
Suite 400
Washington, DC 20036-5001
202-785-0453
Fax: 202-785-1487
Offers information on over 3,000 institutions of postsecondary education and their financial aid administrators.
230 pages Annual

4020 Need A Lift?
The American Legion
700 N Pennsylvania Street
PO Box 1055
Indianapolis, IN 46206-1050
317-630-1200
888-453-4466
Fax: 317-630-1223
http://www.EMBLEM.legion.org
Sources of career, scholarship and loan information or assistance.
144 pages Annual/Paperback
Robert Caudell, Author

4021 Peterson's Grants for Graduate and Postdoctoral Study
Peterson's, A Nelnet Company
Princeton Pike Corporate Center
2000 Lenox Drive PO Box 67005
Lawrenceville, NJ 08648
609-698-1800
800-338-3282
Fax: 609-896-4531
E-mail: custsvc@petersons.com
http://www.petersons.com
Only comprehensive source of current information on grants and fellowships exclusively for graduate and postdoctoral students.
Publication Date: 1998 5th Edition
ISBN: 1-560794-01-1

4022 Peterson's Sports Scholarships and College Athletic Programs
Peterson's, A Nelnet Company
Princeton Pike Corporate Center
2000 Lenox Drive
Lawrenceville, NJ 08648
609-896-1800
800-338-3282
Fax: 609-896-4531
E-mail: custsvc@petersons.com
http://www.petersons.com

A college-by-college look at scholarships designated exclusively for student athletes in 32 men's and women's sports.
Publication Date: 2004 624 pages 5th Edition
ISBN: 0768915244

4023 Scholarship Handbook
The College Board
45 Columbus Avenue
New York, NY 10023
800-323-7155
http://www.collegeboard.org
Useful text for college-bound students, their families and guidance counselors. Offers more than 2,000 descriptions of national and state level award programs, public and private education loan programs, intership opportunities and more.

4024 Scholarships for Emigres Training for Careers in Jewish Education
Jewish Foundation for Education of Women
135 E 64th Street
New York, NY 10021
212-288-3931
Fax: 212-288-5798
E-mail: fdnscholar@aol.com
http://www.jfew.org
Open to emigres from the former Soviet Union who are pursuing careers in Jewish education. Candidates in Jewish education, rabbinical and cantorial studies, and Jewish studies are invited to write the Foundation.
Marge Goldwater, Executive Director

4025 Scholarships, Fellowships and Loans
Gale Research
PO Box 33477
Detroit, MI 48232-5477
800-877-GALE
Fax: 800-414-5043
http://www.galegroup.com
Written especially for professionals, students, counselors, parents and others interested in education. This resource provides more than 3,700 sources of education-related financial aid and awards at all levels of study.
Publication Date: 1995 1,290 pages Annual
ISBN: 0-810391-14-7

4026 Student Guide
Federal Student Aid Information Center
PO Box 84
Washington, DC 20044-0084
800-433-3243
800-433-3243
Describes the federal student aid programs, and general information about the eligibility criteria, application procedures and award levels, and lists important deadlines and phone numbers.
54 pages
John J McCarthy, Director

4027 Study Abroad
U.N. Educational, Scientific & Cultural Assn.
7, place de Fontenoy
F-75700 Paris
France
1-45681123
Listing of over 200,000 scholarships, fellowships and educational exchange opportunities offered for study in 124 countries.
1,300 pages Biennial

4028 Write Now: A Complete Self-Teaching Programfor Better Handwriting
Continuing Education Press
PO Box 1394
Portland, OR 97207-1394

503-725-4891
866-647-7377
Fax: 503-725-4840
E-mail: press@pdx.edu
http://www.cep.pdx.edu
A step-by-step guide to improving one's handwriting. Develop clean and legible italic handwriting with regular practice.

128 pages Paperback
ISBN: 0-87678-089-3

Barbara Getty & Inga Dubay, Author
Alba Scholz, Manager
Martha Ketchum, Customer Service

Directories & Handbooks / Guidance & Counseling

4029 Accredited Institutions of Postsecondary Education
MacMillan Publishing Company
1633 Broadway
New York, NY 10019
212-512-2000
Fax: 800-835-3202
Lists over 5,000 accredited institutions and programs for postsecondary education in the United States.

600 pages Annual

4030 Adolescent Pregnancy Prevention Clearinghouse
Children's Defense Fund Education & Youth Develop.
122 C Street NW
#400
Washington, DC 20001-2109
202-628-8787
Fax: 202-662-3560
Provides information and clarification on the connection between pregnancy and broader life questions for youth.

Marian Wright Edelman, Coordinating Education

4031 COLLEGESOURCE
Career Guidance Foundation
8090 Engineer Road
San Diego, CA 92111-1906
800-854-2670
Fax: 858-278-8960
http://www.collegesource.org
CD-ROM and Web College Catalog Collection. Contains colleges and universitie's catalogs from throughout the US, over 2,600. Also a college search program that can be searched by major, tuition costs, and more. Foreign catalogs available.

Annette Crone, Account Coordinator
David Hunt, Account Coordinator

4032 Cabells Directory of Publishing Opportunities in Educational Psychology and Administration
Cabell Publishing Company
Box 5428
Tobe Hahn Station
Beaumont, TX 77726
409-898-0575
Fax: 409-866-9554
E-mail: publish@cabells.com
http://www.cabells.com
Provides information on editor contact information, manuscript guidelines, acceptance rate, review information and

circulation data for over 225 academic journals.

799 pages Annual
ISBN: 0-911753-19-2

David WE Cabell, Editor
Deborah L English, Associate Editor

4033 Career & Vocational Counseling Directory
American Business Directories
5711 S 86th Circle
Omaha, NE 68127-4146
402-593-4600
888-999-1307
Fax: 402-331-5481
Nationwide listing of 3,300 companies/consultants available in print, computer magnetic tape and diskette, mailing labels, and index cards listing the name, address, phone, size of advertisement, contact person and number of employees.

Annual

Jerry Venner, Coordinating Education

4034 College Handbook
College Board Publications
45 Columbus Avenue
New York, NY 10023-6992
212-713-8000
Fax: 800-525-5562
E-mail: puborderinfo@collegeboard.org
http://www.collegeboard.org
Descriptions of 3,200 colleges and universities.

Publication Date: 1994 1728 pages Annually

Kea Waithe, Director Customer Service

4035 College Handbook Foreign Student Supplement
College Board Publications
45 Columbus Avenue
New York, NY 10023-6917
212-713-8000
Fax: 800-525-5562
Lists about 2,800 colleges and universities that are open to foreign students.

Publication Date: 1994 288 pages Annual
ISBN: 0-877474-83-3

4036 College Transfer Guide
School Guide Publications
210 N Avenue
New Rochelle, NY 10801-6402
914-632-7771
800-433-7771
Fax: 914-632-3412
Five hundred four-year colleges in the Northeast and Midwest that accept transfer students listing transfer requirements, deadlines, fees, enrollment, costs and contact information. Circulation, 60,000.

125 pages Annual/January

4037 Community College Exemplary Instructional Programs
Massachusetts Bay Community College Press
50 Oakland Street
Wellsley Hills, MA 02181
781-237-1100
Fax: 781-237-1061
Community college programs identified as outstanding by the National Council of Instructional Administrators.

4038 Comparative Guide to American Colleges for Students, Parents & Counselors
HarperCollins
10 E 53rd Street
New York, NY 10022-5244

212-207-7000
Fax: 212-207-7145
Accredited four-year colleges in the United States.

800 pages Cloth

4039 Directory of Play Therapy Training
University of North Texas
PO Box 310829
Denton, TX 76203
940-565-3864
Fax: 940-565-4461
E-mail: cpt@coefs.coe.unt.edu
http://www.centerforplaytherapy.com
Provides training, research publications and serves as a clearinghouse for literature in the field.

Paperback

Rinda Thomas, Office Manager
Sue C Bratton, Center Director

4040 Educators Guide to FREE Guidance Materials
Educators Progress Service
214 Center Street
Randolph, WI 53956-1408
920-326-3126
888-951-4469
Fax: 920-326-3127
E-mail: epsinc@centurytel.net
http://www.freeteachingaids.com
Lists and describes free films, videotapes, filmstrips, slides, web sites, and hundreds of free printed materials in the field of career education and guidance for all age levels.

190 pages Annual
ISBN: 87708-406-8

Kathy Nehmer, President

4041 Index of Majors and Graduate Degrees
College Board Publications
45 Columbus Avenue
New York, NY 10023-6992
212-713-8000
Fax: 800-525-5562
http://www.collegeboard.org
Includes descriptions of over 600 majors and identifies the 3,200 colleges, universities, and graduate schools that offer them.

Annual
ISBN: 0-87447-592-9

4042 Tests: a Comprehensive Reference for Psychology, Education & Business
PRO-ED
8700 Shoal Creek Boulevard
Austin, TX 78757-6897
512-451-3246
800-897-3202
Fax: 800-397-7633
E-mail: info@proedinc.com
http://www.proedinc.com
This fifth edition groups updated information on approximately 2,000 assessment instruments into three primary classifications-psychology, education, and business-and 89 subcategories, enabling users to readily identify the tests that meet their assessment needs. Each entry contains a statement of the instrument's purpose, a concise description of the instrument, scoring procedures, cost, and publisher information.

Publication Date: 1991 809 pages Paperback/Hardcover
ISBN: 0-89079-709-9

Taddy Maddox, General Editor

4043 Vocational Biographies
PO Box 31
Sauk Centre, MN 56378-0031
320-352-6516
800-255-0752
Fax: 320-352-5546
E-mail: careers@vocbio.com
http://www.vocbio.com

Real life career success stories of persons in every walk of life that allow students to see a career through the eyes of a real person. New for 2005: Internet Access to 1001 Career Success Stories.

Toby Behnen, President
Roxann Behnen, Customer Service/Sales

4044 What Works and Doesn't With at Risk Students
BKS Publishing
3109 150th Place SE
Mill Creek, WA 98012-4864
425-745-3029
Fax: 425-337-4837
E-mail: DocBlokk@aol.com
http://www.literacyfirst.com
Publication Date: 1919 162 pages Paperback
ISBN: 0-9656713-0-5

Jan Glaes, Author
Bill Blokker, Owner

4045 World of Play Therapy Literature
Center for Play Therapy
PO Box 311337
Denton, TX 76203
940-565-3864
Fax: 940-565-4461
E-mail: cpt@coefs.coe.unt.edu
http://www.centerforplaytherapy.com
Author and topical listings of over 6,000 books, dissertations, documents, and journal articles on play therapy, updated every two years.
Publication Date: 1995 306 pages

Landreth, Homeyer, Bratton, Kale, Hipl, Schumann, Author

Directories & Handbooks / Language Arts

4046 Classroom Strategies for the English Language Learner
Master Teacher
Leadership Lane
PO Box 1207
Manhattan, KS 66505-1207
800-669-9633
Fax: 800-669-1132
http://www.masterteacher.com
A practical model for accelerating both oral language and literacy development, based on the latest research for effective instruction of both Native English speakers and English language learners.
266 pages
ISBN: 1-58992-068-6

Socrro Herrera EdD, Author

4047 Italic Handwriting Series-Book A
Continuing Education Press
PO Box 1394
Portland, OR 97207-1394
503-725-4891
866-647-7377
Fax: 503-725-4840
E-mail: press@pdx.edu
http://www.cep.pdx.edu
Book A is the first workbook of a seven-part series. Designed for the beginning reader and writer, it introduces the alphabet one letter at a time. Illustrated.
64 pages Paperback
ISBN: 0-87678-092-3

Barbara Getty & Inga Dubay, Author
Alba Scholz, Manager

4048 Italic Handwriting Series-Book B
Continuing Education Press
PO Box 1394
Portland, OR 97207-1394
503-725-4891
866-647-7377
Fax: 503-725-4840
E-mail: press@pdx.edu
http://www.cep.pdx.edu
Book B is the second workbook of a seven-part series. Designed for the beginning reader and writer. Introduces words and sentences, lowercase and capitol print script, one letter per page. Illustrated.
59 pages Paperback
ISBN: 0-87678-093-1

Barbara Getty & Inga Dubay, Author
Alba Scholz, Manager

4049 Italic Handwriting Series-Book C
Continuing Education Press
PO Box 1394
Portland, OR 97207-1394
503-725-4891
866-647-7377
Fax: 503-725-4840
E-mail: press@pdx.edu
http://www.cep.pdx.edu
Book C is the third workbook of a seven-part series. Covers basic italic and introduces the cursive. Words and sentences include days of week, months of year, modes of transportation, and tongue twisters. Illustrated.
60 pages Paperback
ISBN: 0-87678-094-X

Barbara Getty & Inga Dubay, Author
Alba Scholz, Manager

4050 Italic Handwriting Series-Book D
Continuing Education Press
PO Box 1394
Portland, OR 97207-1394
503-725-4891
866-647-7377
Fax: 503-725-4840
E-mail: press@pdx.edu
http://www.cep.pdx.edu
Book D is the fourth workbook of a seven-part series. Reviews basic italic and covers the total cursive program. Includes prefixes, suffixes, capitalization, and playful poems. Explores history of the alphabet. Illustrated.
80 pages Paperback
ISBN: 0-87678-095-8

Barbara Getty & Inga Dubay, Author
Alba Scholz, Manager

4051 Italic Handwriting Series-Book E
Continuing Education Press
PO Box 1394
Portland, OR 97207-1394
503-725-4891
866-647-7377
Fax: 503-725-4840
E-mail: press@pdx.edu
http://wwww.cep.pdx.edu
Book E is the fifth workbook of a seven-part series. Reviews basic italic and covers the total cursive program. Writing practice covers natural history— plants, volcanoes, cities. Explores history of the alphabet. Illustrated.
56 pages Paperback
ISBN: 0-87678-096-6

Barbara Getty & Inga Dubay, Author
Alba Scholz, Manager

4052 Italic Handwriting Series-Book F
Continuing Education Press
PO Box 1394
Portland, OR 97207-1394
503-725-4891
866-647-7377

Fax: 503-725-4840
E-mail: press@pdx.edu
http://;.cep.pdx.edu
Book F is the sixth workbook of a seven-part series. Reviews basic italic and covers the total cursive program. Writing practice emphasizes figures of speech (e.g. homophones, puns, metaphors, acronyms). Explores history of the alphabet. Illustrated.
56 pages Paperback
ISBN: 0-87678-097-4

Barbara Getty & Inga Dubay, Author
Alba Scholz, Manager

4053 Italic Handwriting Series-Book G
Continuing Education Press
PO Box 1394
Portland, OR 97207-1394
503-725-4891
866-647-7377
Fax: 503-725-4840
E-mail: press@pdx.edu
http://www.cep.pdx.edu
Book G is the seventh workbook of a seven-part series. A comprehensive self-instruction program in basic and cursive italic. Writing content follows a central theme-the history of our alphabet. Suitable for older students. Illustrated.
56 pages Paperback
ISBN: 0-87678-098-2

Barbara Getty & Inga Dubay, Author
Alba Scholz, Manager

4054 Language Schools Directory
American Business Directories
5711 S 86th Circle
Omaha, NE 68127-4146
402-593-4600
888-999-1307
Fax: 402-331-5481
A listing of language schools, arranged by geographic location, offering contact information which is updated on a continual basis, and printed on request. Directory is also available in electronic formats.

Jerry Venner, Coordinating Education

4055 Picture Book Learning Volume-1
Picture Book Learning Inc.
PO Box 270075
Louisville, CO 80027
303-548-2809
E-mail: todd@picturebooklearning.com
http://www.picturebooklearning.com
Teachers can use this fun method of teaching elementary children basic language arts skills through the use of picture books.
60 pages
ISBN: 0-9760725-0-5

Todd Osborne, Co-President
Corinne Osborne, Editor

4056 Process of Elimination - a Method of Teaching Basic Grammar - Teacher Ed
Scott & McCleary Publishing Company
2482 11th Street SW
Akron, OH 44314-1712
702-566-8756
800-765-3564
Fax: 702-568-1378
E-mail: jscott7576@aol.com
http://www.scottmccleary.com
Series of 7 steps designed to teach basic grammar skills to students in middle grades

through college. Available in a teacher edition and a student workbook.

50 pages
ISBN: 0-9636225-2-8
ISSN: 0-9636225-

Milton Metheny, Author
Janet Scott, Publisher
Sheila McCleary, Publisher

4057 Process of Elimination: A Method of Teaching Basic Grammar - Student Ed
Scott & McCleary Publishing Company
2482 11th Street SW
Akron, OH 44314-1712
702-566-8756
800-765-3564
Fax: 702-568-1378
E-mail: jscott7576@aol.com
http://www.scottmccleary.com
Series of 7 steps designed to teach basic grammar skills to students in middle grades through college. Available in a teacher edition and a student workbook.

Milton Metheny, Author
Janet Scott, Publisher
Sheila McCleary, Publisher

4058 Put Reading First: The Research Building Blocks For Teaching Children To Read
PO Box 1398
Jessup, MD 20794-1398
877-4ED-PUBS
Fax: 301-470-1244
E-mail: edpubs@inet.ed.gov
http://www.edpubs.org
Provides analysis and discussion in five areas of reading instruction: phonemic awareness, phonics, fluency, vocabulary and text comprehension.

4059 Write Now: A Complete Self Teaching Program for Better Handwriting
Continuing Education Press
PO Box 1394
Portland, OR 97207-1394
503-725-4891
866-647-7377
Fax: 503-725-4840
E-mail: press@pdx.edu
http://www.cep.pdx.edu
Finally, a handwriting improvement book for adults. Teach yourself to write legibly and retain it over time using this step-by-step guide to modern italic handwriting with complete instructions as well as practice exercises and tips. The secret to legible handwriting is the absence of loops in letterform, making it easier to write and easier to read.

96 pages Paperback
ISBN: 0-87678-089-3

Barbara Getty & Inga Dubay, Author
Alba Scholz, Manager
Wendi Johnson, Customer Service

Directories & Handbooks / Library Services

4060 Directory of Manufacturers & Suppliers
Special Libraries Association
331 S Patrick Street
Alexandria, VA 22314-3501
703-647-4900
Fax: 703-647-4901
E-mail: sla@sla.org
http://www.sla.org

The SLA network consists of nearly 15,000 librarians and information professionals who specialize in the arts, communication, business, social science, biomedical sciences, geosciences and environmental studies, and industry, business, research, educational and technical institutions, government, special departments of public and university libraries, newspapers, museums, and public or private organizations that provide or require specialized information.

4061 Directory of Members of the Association for Library and Information Science Education
1009 Commerce Park Drive Suite 150
PO Box 4219
Oak Ridge, TN 37830
865-425-0155
Fax: 865-481-0390
E-mail: contact@alise.org
http://www.alise.org
The Directory is designed to serve as a handbook for the association, including a list of officers, committees, and interest groups and strategic planning information for the association. Also listed are graduate schools of library and information science and their faculty.

Annual Paperback

Rand Price, Executive Director
Maureen Thompson, Administrator

4062 Libraries Unlimited Academic Catalog
88 Post Road W
Westport, CT 06881
203-226-3571
Fax: 203-222-1502
E-mail: lu-books@lu.com
http://www.lu.com
Catalog includes reference, collection development, library management, cataloging, and technology.

4063 Managing Info Tech in School Library Media Center
Libraries Unlimited
88 Post Road West
Westport, CT 06881
203-226-3571
800-225-5800
Fax: 203-222-1502
E-mail: lu-books@lu.com
http://www.lu.com

Publication Date: 2000 290 pages Hardcover
ISBN: 1-56308-724-3

L Anne Clyde

4064 Managing Media Services Theory and Practice
Libraries Unlimited
88 Post Road West
Westport, CT 06881
203-226-3571
800-225-5800
Fax: 203-222-1502
E-mail: lu-books@lu.com
http://www.lu.com

Publication Date: 2002 418 pages Cloth
ISBN: 1-56308-530-5

L Anne Clyde

Directories & Handbooks / Music & Art

4065 College Guide for Visual Arts Majors
Peterson's, A Nelnet Company
Princeton Pike Corporate Center
2000 Lenox Drive PO Box 67005
Lawrenceville, NJ 08648
609-896-1800
800-338-3282
Fax: 609-896-4531
E-mail: custsvc@petersons.com
http://www.petersons.com
Offers descriptions of over 700 accredited US colleges and universities, music conservatories, and art/design schools that grant undergraduate degrees in the areas of studio art.

Publication Date: 2006 404 pages
ISBN: 1-560795-36-0

4066 Community Outreach and Education for the Arts Handbook
Music Teachers National Association
441 Vine Street
Cincinnati, OH 45202
513-421-1420
888-512-5278
Fax: 513-421-2503
E-mail: mtnanet@mtaa.org
http://www.mtaa.org
Resource booklet for independent music teachers.

Paperback
March
150 booths with 2500 attendees

Chad Schwatbach, Pr/Marketing Associate

4067 Italic Letters
Continuing Education Press
PO Box 1394
Portland, OR 97207-1394
503-725-4891
866-647-7377
Fax: 503-725-4840
E-mail: press@pdx.edu
http://www.cep.pdx.edu
Italic Letters is for professional and amateur calligraphers, art teachers, and enthusiasts of the book arts. Numerous tips on letter shapes, spacing, slant, pen edge angle, and other secrets to handsome writing.

128 pages Paperback
ISBN: 0-87678-091-5

Barbara Getty & Inga Dubay, Author
Alba Scholz, Manager

4068 Money for Film & Video Artists
American for the Art
1000 Vermont Avenue NW
6th Floor
Washington, DC 20005
202-371-2830
Fax: 202-371-0424
http://www.artsusa.org
The listings are organized by sponsoring organization and entries include basic application and program information.

4069 Money for Visual Artists
America for the Art
1000 Vermont Avenue NW
12th Floor
Washington, DC 20005
202-371-2830
Fax: 202-371-0424
http://www.artsusa.org
Programs are listed alphabetically by sponsor with detailed program description.

4070 Music Teachers Guide to Music Instructional Software
Music Teachers National Association
441 Vine Street
Suite 505
Cincinnati, OH 45202-2811
888-512-5278
Fax: 513-421-2503
E-mail: mtnanet@mtna.org
http://www.mtna.org
Evaluations of music software for the macintosh and PC, including CD-ROMs, music skills and keyboard technique drill software, sequencers and soundequipment controllers.

4071 Resource Booklet for Independent Music Teachers
Music Teachers National Association
441 Vine Street
Suite 505
Cincinnati, OH 45202-2811
888-512-5278
Fax: 513-421-2503
E-mail: mtnanet@mtna.org
http://www.mtna.org
A booklet for organizing information about community resources.

4072 School Arts
50 Portland Street
Worcester, MA 01608
800-533-2847
Fax: 508-753-3834
Companies offering products, materials, and art education resources or programs that focus on the history of art, multicultural resources such as Fine Art, reproductions, CD-Roms, museum education, programs, slides, books, videos, exhibits, architecture, timelines, and resource kits.

Directories & Handbooks / Physical Education

4073 Educators Guide to FREE HPER Materials
Educators Progress Service
214 Center Street
Randolph, WI 53956-1408
920-326-3126
888-951-4469
Fax: 920-326-3127
E-mail: epsinc@centurytel.net
http://www.freeteachingaids.com
Lists and describes free films, videotapes, filmstrips, slides, web sites, and hundreds of free printed materials in the field of health, physical education, and recreation for all age levels.

184 pages Annual
ISBN: 87708-407-6

Kathy Nehmer, President

4074 Schools & Colleges Directory
Association for Experiential Education
3775 Iris Avenue
Suite 4
Boulder, CO 80301-2043
303-440-8844
Fax: 303-440-9581
E-mail: publications@aee.org
http://www.aee.org
Provides information about many schools, colleges and universities that have programs or offer degrees related to the field of outdoor/experiential education. Listings include programs in high schools and independent or-

ganizations as well as institutions of higher learning. Paperback.

Publication Date: 1995 Paperback

Natalie Kurylke, Publications Manager

Directories & Handbooks / Reading

4075 Diagnostic Reading Inventory for Bilingual Students in Grades 1-8
Scott & McCleary Publishing Company
2482 11th Street SW
Akron, OH 44314-1712
702-566-8756
800-765-3564
Fax: 702-568-1378
E-mail: jscott7576@aol.com
http://www.scottmccleary.com
Series of 13 tests designed to access reading performance. IRI, spelling, phonics, visual and auditory discrimination and listening comprehension are just some of the tests included.

155 pages
ISBN: 0-9636225-1-X

Janet M Scott, Co-Author
Sheila C McCleary, Co-Author

4076 Diagnostic Reading Inventory for Primary and Intermediate Grades K-8
Scott & McCleary Publishing Company
2482 11th Street SW
Akron, OH 44314-1712
702-566-8756
800-765-3564
Fax: 702-568-1378
E-mail: jscott7576@aol.com
http://www.scottmccleary.com
Designed to assess reading performance in grades K-8. Tests include: word recognition, oral reading inventory, comprehension, listening comprehension, auditory and visual discrimination, auditory and visual memory, learning modalities inventory, phonics mastery tests, structural analysis, word association and a diagnostic spelling test.

260 pages
ISBN: 0-9636225-4-4

Janet M Scott, Co-Author
Sheila C McCleary, Co-Author

4077 Educational Leadership
Assn. for Supervision & Curriculum Dev. (ASCD)
1703 N Beauregard Street
Alexandria, VA 22311-1714
703-578-9600
800-933-2723
Fax: 703-575-5400
E-mail: el@ascd.org
http://www.ascd.org
For educators by educators. With a circulation of 175,000, Educational Leadership is acknowledged throughout the world as an authoritative source of information about teaching and learning, new ideas and practices relevant to practicing educators, and the latest trends and issues affecting prekindergarten through higher education.

Marge Scherer, Executive Editor

4078 Laubach Literacy Action Directory
Laubach Literacy Action
1320 Jamesville Avenue
Syracuse, NY 13210
315-422-9121
888-528-2224
Fax: 315-422-6369

E-mail: info@laubach.org
http://www.laubach.org
Listing of over 1,100 local literacy councils and associates who teach the Laubach Method.

90 pages Annual

4079 Ready to Read, Ready to Learn
PO Box 1398
Jessup, MD 20794-1398
877-4ED-PUBS
Fax: 301-470-1244
E-mail: edpubs@inet.ed.gov
http://www.edpubs.org

4080 Tips for Reading Tutors
PO Box 1398
Jessup, MD 20794-1398
877-4ED-PUBS
Fax: 301-470-1244
E-mail: edpubs@inet.ed.gov
http://www.edpubs.org
Basic tips for reading tutors

Directories & Handbooks / Secondary Education

4081 College Board Guide to High Schools
College Board Publications
45 Columbus Avenue
New York, NY 10023-6917
212-713-8165
800-323-7155
Fax: 800-525-5562
http://www.collegeboard.org
Offers listings and information on over 25,000 public and private high schools nationwide.

Publication Date: 1994 2,024 pages
ISBN: 0-874474-66-3

4082 Compendium of Tertiary & Sixth Forum Colleges
SCOTVIC: S McDonald, Principal
Ridge College
Manchester
England
61-4277733
Offers listings of over 200 Sixth Form and Tertiary Colleges in the United Kingdom offering courses preparing secondary students for university study.

Publication Date: 1990 200 pages Biennial

4083 Directory of Public Elementary and Secondary Education Agencies
US National Center for Education Statistics
555 New Jersey Avenue NW
Washington, DC 20208-5651
202-219-1916
800-424-1616
Fax: 202-502-7466
Directory of approximately 17,000 local education agencies that operate their own schools or pay tuition to other local education agencies.

400 pages Annual

John Sietsema, Statistician
Lena McDowell, Contact

4084 Educators Guide to FREE Family and Consumer Education Materials
Educators Progress Service
214 Center Street
Randolph, WI 53956-1408
920-326-3126
888-951-4469
Fax: 920-326-3127
E-mail: epsinc@centurytel.net
http://www.freeteachingaids.com

Lists and describes free films, videotapes, filmstrips, slides, web sites, and hundreds of free printed materials in the field of home econominics and consumer education for all age levels.

161 pages Annual
ISBN: 87708-408-4

Kathy Nehmer, President

4085 Focus on School
ABC-CLIO
130 Cremona Drive
#1911
Santa Barbara, CA 93117-5599
805-968-1911
800-368-6868
Fax: 805-685-9685
Hotlines, print and nonprint resources on education for young adults.

Publication Date: 1990

4086 Great Source Catalog
Great Source Education Group
PO Box 7050
Wilmington, MA 01887
800-289-4490
Fax: 800-289-3994
http://www.greatsource.com
Alternative, affordable, student-friendly K-12 materials to make teaching and learning fun for educators and students.

4087 Helping Your Child Succeed In School: Elementary and Secondary Editions
Master Teacher
Po Box 1207
Manhattan, KS 66505-1207
785-539-0555
800-669-9633
Fax: 800-669-1132
http://www.masterteacher.com
Provides a way for school administrators to help parents help their children succeed in school. Published in English and Spanish.

Erica Paronson, Executive Editor

4088 Lesson Plans for Integrating Technology into the Classroom: Secondary Edition
Master Teacher
Leadership Lane
PO Box 1207
Manhattan, KS 66505-1207
800-669-9633
Fax: 800-669-1132
http://www.masterteacher.com
Gives teachers practical lessons developed and tested by teachers across the curriculum, with students of all levels of ability in using technology.

104 pages
ISBN: 1-58992-152-6

4089 Lesson Plans for Problem-Based Learning: Secondary Edition
Master Teacher
Leadership Lane
PO Box 1207
Manhattan, KS 66505-1207
800-669-9633
Fax: 800-669-1132
http://www.masterteacher.com
An instructional technique which organizes the curriculum around a major problem that students work to solve over the weeks or months.

117 pages
ISBN: 0-914607-87-1

4090 Lesson Plans for the Substitute Teacher: Secondary Edition
Master Teacher
Leadership Lane
PO Box 1207
Manhattan, KS 66505-1207
800-669-9633
Fax: 800-669-1132
http://www.masterteacher.com
Gives you more than 100 lessons developed and tested by teachers across the curriculum and at all grade levels.

177 pages
ISBN: 1-58992-108-9

4091 Peterson's Private Secondary Schools
Peterson's, A Nelnet Company
Princeton Pike Corporate Center
2000 Lenox Drive PO Box 67005
Lawrenceville, NJ 08648-2123
609-896-1800
800-338-3282
Fax: 609-896-4531
E-mail: custsvc@petersons.com
http://www.petersons.com
Listing of over 1,400 accredited and state-approved private secondary schools in the US and abroad.

1,300 pages Annual

4092 Secondary Teachers Guide to FREE Curriculum Materials
Educators Progress Service
214 Center Street
Randolph, WI 53956-1408
920-326-3126
888-951-4469
Fax: 920-326-3127
E-mail: epsinc@centurytel.net
http://www.freeteachingaids.com
Lists and describes free supplementary teaching aids for the high school and college level.

296 pages Annual
ISBN: 87708-399-1

Kathy Nehmer, President

Directories & Handbooks / Science

4093 Earth Education: A New Beginning
Institute for Earth Education
Cedar Cove
PO Box 115
Greenville, WV 24945
304-832-6404
Fax: 304-832-6077
E-mail: iee1@aol.com
http://www.eartheducation.org
This book proposes another direction-an alternative that many environmental leaders and teachers around the world have already taken. It is called The Earth Education Path, and anyone can follow it in developing a genuine program made up of magical learning adventures.

334 pages Paperback
ISBN: 0917011023

Steve Van Matre, Chairman

4094 Earthkeepers
Institute for Earth Education
Cedar Cove
PO Box 115
Greenville, WV 24945
304-832-6404
Fax: 304-832-6077
E-mail: iee1@aol.com
http://www.eartheducation.org

This book will give you the best picture of what a complete earth education program involves. Even if you can't set up the complete Earthkeepers program, there are many activities you can use to build an earth education program in your own settting and situation.

108 pages Paperback
ISBN: 0917011015

Bruce Johnson, Chairman

4095 Educators Guide to FREE Science Materials
Educators Progress Service
214 Center Street
Randolph, WI 53956-1408
920-326-3126
888-951-4469
Fax: 920-326-3127
E-mail: epsinc@centurytel.net
http://www.freeteachingaids.com
Lists and describes free films, videotapes, filmstrips, slides, web sites, and hundreds of free printed materials in the field of science for all age levels.

Annual

Kathy Nehmer, President

4096 K-6 Science and Math Catalog
Carolina Biological Supply Co.
2700 York Road
Burlington, NC 27215-3398
336-584-0381
800-334-5551
Fax: 800-222-7112
http://www.carolina.com
Service teaching materials for grades Pre K through 8, including charts, computers, software, books, living animals and plants, microscopes, microscope slides, models, teaching kits and more.

4097 Science for All Children; A Guide to Improving Science Education
National Academy Press
Arts & Industries Bldg Room 1201
900 Jefferson Drive SW
Washington, DC 20560-0403
202-287-2063
Fax: 202-287-2070
E-mail: outreach@nas.edu
http://www.si.edu/nsrc
Provides concise and practical guidelines for implementing science education reform at local level, including the elements of an effective, inquiry-based, hands-on science program. Produced by the National Science Resources Center. Published by National Academy Press.

240 pages
ISBN: 0-309-05297-1

National Science Resources Center, Author
Douglas Lapp, Executive Director

4098 Sunship Earth
Institute for Earth Education
Cedar Cove
PO Box 115
Greenville, WV 24945
304-832-6404
Fax: 304-832-6077
E-mail: iee1@aol.com
http://www.eartheducation.org
Contains clear descriptions of key ecological concepts and concise reviews of important learning principals, plus over 200 additional pages of ideas, activities and guidelines for setting up a complete Sunship Earth Study Station.

265 pages Paperback
ISBN: 0876030460

Bruce Johnson, Chairman

4099 Sunship III
Institute for Earth Education
Cedar Cove
PO Box 115
Greenville, WV 24945
304-832-6404
Fax: 304-832-6077
E-mail: iee1@aol.com
http://www.eartheducation.org
Examines perception and choice in our daily habits and routines. It is about exploration and discovery in the larger context of where and how we live, and examining alteratives and making sacrifices on behalf of a healthier home planet.
133 pages Paperback
ISBN: 0917011031
Bruce Johnson, Chairman

4100 UNESCO Sourcebook for Out-of-School Science & Technology Education
U.N. Educational, Scientific & Cultural Assn.
7, place de Fontenoy
F-75700 Paris
France
Offers information on science clubs, societies and congresses, science fairs and museums.
145 pages

Directories & Handbooks / Social Studies

4101 Directory of Central America Classroom Resources
Central American Resource Center
317 17th Avenue SE
Minneapolis, MN 55414-2012
612-627-9445
Offers information on suppliers of education resource materials about Central America, including curricula, materials, directories and organizations providing related services.
Publication Date: 1990 200 pages

4102 Educators Guide to FREE Social Studies Materials
Educators Progress Service
214 Center Street
Randolph, WI 53956-1408
920-326-3126
888-951-4469
Fax: 920-326-3127
E-mail: epsinc@centurytel.net
http://www.freeteachingaids.com
Lists and describes free films, videotapes, filmstrips, slides, web sites, and hundreds of free printed materials in the field of social studies for all age levels.
287 pages Annual
ISBN: 87708-405-X
Kathy Nehmer, President

4103 Geography: A Resource Guide for Secondary Schools
ABC-CLIO
130 Cremona Drive
#1911
Santa Barbara, CA 93117-5599
805-968-1911
800-368-6868
Fax: 805-685-9685
List of organizations and associations to use as resources for secondary education geography studies.

Directories & Handbooks / Technology in Education

4104 American Trade Schools Directory
Croner Publications
10951 Sorrento Valley Road
Suite 1D
San Diego, CA 92121
858-546-1954
800-441-4033
Fax: 858-546-1955
E-mail: paul@croner.com
http://ww.croner.com
Loose leaf binder directory listing trade and technical schools throughout the United States, in alphabetical order, by state, then city, then school name.
411 pages
ISBN: 0-875140-02-5
Rosa Padilla, Office Manager

4105 Association for Educational Communications & Technology: Membership Directory
Association for Educational Communications & Tech.
1025 Vermont Avenue NW
Suite 820
Washington, DC 20005-3516
202-965-2059
Five thousand audiovisual and instructional materials specialists and school media specialists, with audio-visual and TV production personnel. Also listed are committees, task force divisions, auxiliary affiliates, state organizations and directory of corporate members.
200 pages Annual/Spring

4106 Chronicle Vocational School Manual
Chronicle Guidance Publications
66 Aurora Street
Moravia, NY 13118-3569
315-497-0330
800-899-0454
Fax: 315-497-3359
E-mail: customerservice@chronicleguidance.com
http://www.chronicleguidance.com
A geographical index of more than 3,500 vocational schools including all contact information, programs, admissions requirements, costs, financial aid programs and student services.
Publication Date: 1996 300 pages Annual
ISBN: 1-556312-50-4
Patricia F Hammon, Research Associate
Stephen Thompson, Managing Editor

4107 Directory of Public Vocational-Technical Schools & Institutes in the US
Media Marketing Group
PO Box 611
DeKalb, IL 60115-0611
360-576-5864
Offers information on over 1,400 post secondary vocational and technical education programs in public education; private trade and technical schools are not included.
Publication Date: 1994 400 pages Biennial
ISBN: 0-933474-51-2

4108 Directory of Vocational-Technical Schools
Media Marketing Group
PO Box 611
DeKalb, IL 60115-0611
360-576-5864

Offers information on public, postsecondary schools offering degree and non-degree occupational education.
Publication Date: 1996 450 pages Biennial
ISBN: 0-933474-52-0

4109 Educational Film & Video Locator
RR Bowker Reed Reference
121 Chanlon Road
New Providence, NJ 07974-1541
908-464-6800
Fax: 908-665-6688
Producers and distributors of educational films.
Publication Date: 1990

4110 Guide to Vocational and Technical Schools East & West
Peterson's, A Nelnet Company
Princeton Pike Corporare Center
2000 Lenox Drive PO Box 67005
Lawrenceville, NJ 08648
609-896-1800
800-338-3282
Fax: 690-896-4531
E-mail: custsvc@petersons.com
http://www.petersons.com
These two directories cover the full range of training programs in over 240 career fields divided into the categories of Business, Technology, Trade, Personal Services, and Health Care. East edition covers East of Mississippi; West edition covers West of the Mississippi.
Publication Date: 2006 579 pages Per Volume

4111 Industrial Teacher Education Directory
National Assn. of Industrial Teacher Educators
University of Northern Iowa
Cedar Falls, IA 50614-0001
319-273-2561
Fax: 319-273-5818
http://www.uni.edu/indtech
Listing of about 2,800 industrial education faculty members at 250 universities and four-year colleges in the United States, Canada, Australia, Japan and Taiwan.
108 pages Annual
M Fahmy, Professor/Head of Department
Charles Johnson, Coordinator of Tech Ed. Prog

4112 Information Literacy: Essential Skills for the Information Age
Syracuse University
4-194 Center for Science & Tech.
Syracuse, NY 13244-0001
315-443-3640
800-464-9107
Fax: 315-443-5448
E-mail: eric@ericir.sye.edu
Traces history, development, and economic necessity of information literacy. Reports on related subject matter standards. Includes reports on the National Educational Goals (1991), the Secretary's Commission on Achieving Necessary Skills Report (1991), and the latest updates from ALA's Information Power (1998).
377 pages
ISBN: 0-937597-44-9
Kathleen L Spitzer, Editor

4113 Internet Resource Directory for Classroom Teachers
Regulus Communications
140 N 8th Street
Suite 201
Lincoln, NE 68508-1358
402-432-2680
Directory offering information on all resources available on-line for classroom

teachers, including e-mail addresses, Home Page URL's, phone and fax numbers, surface-mail addresses, classroom contacts and teaching resources. Available in paper and electronic formats.

Publication Date: 1996 272 pages Paper Format

Jane A Austin, Coordinating Education

4114 K-12 District Technology Coordinators

Quality Education Data
1625 Broadway
Suite 250
Denver, CO 80202-4715
303-860-1832
800-525-5811
Fax: 303-209-9444
E-mail: info@qeddata.com
http://www.qeddata.com
The first in QED's National Educator Directories, this comprehensive directory of technology coordinators combines QED's exclusive database of technology and demographic data with names of technology coordinators in the 7,000 largest US school districts. The directory includes district phone number, number of students in the district, number of computers, student/computer ratio and predominant computer brand.

Publication Date: 1994 400 pages

Laurie Christensen, Coordinating Education

4115 NetLingo Internet Dictionary

805-794-8687
E-mail: info@netlingo.com
http://www.netlingo.com
A smart looking easy-to-understand dictionary of 3000 internet terms, 1200 chat acronyms, and much more. Modem reference book for international students, educators, industry professionals and online businesses and organizations.

Publication Date: 0

Erin Jansen, Author

4116 Quick-Source

AM Educational Publishing
3745 Suffolk Drive
Suite D
Tallahassee, FL 32308-3048
850-668-4148
Educational technology directory with over 1,100 names, addresses, phones/faxes, and brief descriptions of the products/services of companies/organizations; supports major works/word processors (MS-DOS/MAC); conferences and other educational technology listings.

Annual/September

4117 Schools Industrial, Technical & Trade Directory

American Business Directories
5711 S 86th Circle
Omaha, NE 68127-4146
402-593-4600
888-999-1307
Fax: 402-331-5481
A geographical listing of over 3,750 schools with all contact information, size of advertisement and first year in Yellow Pages. Also available in electronic formats.

Annual

Jerry Venner, Coordinating Education

4118 TESS: The Educational Software Selector

EPIE Institute
103 W Montauk Highway
PO Box 590
Hampton Bays, NY 11946-4003
631-728-9100
Fax: 631-728-9228
E-mail: kkomoski@epie.org
http://www.epie.org
A list of over 1,200 suppliers of educational software and over 18,000 educational software products (on CD-ROM) for pre-school through college information. Includes description of program, grade level data, price, platform and review citations.

Nancy Boland, Coordinating Education

4119 Tech Directions-Directory of Federal & Federal and State Officials Issue

Prakken Publications
416 Longshore Drive
Ann Arbor, MI 48105-1624
313-577-4042
Fax: 313-577-1672
Listing of federal and state officials concerned with vocational, technical, industrial trade and technology education in the United States and Canada.

Annual

4120 Technology in Public Schools

Quality Education Data
1624 Broadway
Suite 250
Denver, CO 80202-4715
303-860-1832
800-525-5811
Fax: 303-209-9444
E-mail: info@qeddata.com
http://www.qeddata.com
Annual survey of instructional technology represents more than 67% of all US K-12 students. Includes computer brand and processor type market share, CD-ROM, networks, LAN, modem, cable and in-depth internet access installed base information.

Publication Date: 1994 160 pages Yearly
ISBN: 0-88947-925-1

Liz Stephens, Marketing Coordinator

Periodicals / General

4121 AACS Newsletter

American Association of Christian Schools
4500 S Selsa Road
Blue Springs, MO 64015-2221
816-252-9900
Fax: 703-252-6700
Association news offering the most up-to-date information relating to Christian education.

4 pages Monthly

Dr. Carl Herbster, Contact

4122 AAHE Bulletin

American Association for Higher Education
1 Dupont Circle
Suite 360
Washington, DC 20036
202-293-6440
Fax: 202-293-0073
http://www.aahebulletin.com
Electronic newsletter

16 pages Monthly

Vicky Hendly Dobin, Manager

4123 ACJS Today

Academy of Criminal Justice Services
7339 Hanover Parkway
Suite A
Greenbelta, MD 20770
301-446-6300
800-757-2257
Fax: 301-446-2819
http://www.acjs.org
Provides upcoming events, news releases, ACJS activities, ads, book reviews and miscellaneous information.

24-32 pages Quarterly

Laura Myers, Editor
Laura Monaco, Association Manager

4124 ASCD Update

Assn. for Supervision & Curriculum Development
1703 N Beauregard Street
Alexandria, VA 22311
703-578-9600
Fax: 703-575-5400
News on contemporary education issues and information on ASCD programs.

Ronald Brandt, Publisher
John O'Neil, Editor

4125 ASSC Newsletter

Arkansas School Study Council
255 Graduate Education Building
Fayetteville, AR 72701
479-442-8464
Fax: 479-442-2038
Monthly up-date on education, finance, new legislation, mandates for Arkansas public schools.

3-10 pages

Martin Schoppmeyer, Editor

4126 AV Guide Newsletter

Educational Screen
380 E NW Highway
Des Plaines, IL 60016-2201
847-298-6622
Fax: 847-390-0408
Provides concise and practical information on audiovisually oriented products with an emphasis on new ideas and methods of using learning media, including educational computer software.

Monthly
ISSN: 0091-360X

HS Gillette, Publisher
Natalie Ferguson, Editor

4127 Academe

American Association of University Professors
1012 14th Street NW
Suite 500
Washington, DC 20005-3406
202-737-5900
Fax: 202-737-5526
E-mail: academe@aaup.org
http://www.aaup.org
A thoughtful and provocative review of developments affecting higher education faculty. With timely features and informative departments, Academe delivers the latest on the state of the profession, legal and legislative trends, and issues in academia.

BiMonthly

Lawrence Hanley, Editor, Author
Gwendolyn Bradley, Managing Co-Director
Wendi Maloney, Managing Editor

4128 Aero Gramme

Alternative Education Resource Organizations
417 Roslyn Road
Roslyn Heights, NY 11577-2620
516-621-2195
800-769-4171
Fax: 516-625-3257

Networks all forms of educational alternatives, from public and private alternative schools to homeschooling.

Quarterly

Jerry Mintz, Editor

4129 Agenda: Jewish Education
Jewish Education Service of North America
111 Eighth Avenue
Suite 11E
New York, NY 10011
212-284-6950
Fax: 212-284-6951
E-mail: info@jesna.org
http://www.jesna.org
Seeks to create a community of discourse on issues of Jewish public policy dealing with Jewish education and the indications of policy options for the practice of Jewish education.

Quarterly
ISSN: 1072-1150

Amy Skin, Dir Marketing/Communication

4130 American Council on Education: GED Testing Service
American Council on Education
1 Dupont Circle NW
Suite 800
Washington, DC 20036-1193
202-939-9300
Fax: 202-833-4760
Information relating to GED items and testing.

8 pages 5x Year

Colleen Allen, Contact

4131 American Journal of Education
University of Chicago
5835 S Kimbark Avenue
Chicago, IL 60637
773-702-1555
Fax: 773-702-6207
E-mail: aje@uchicago.edu

Quarterly

Robert Dreeben and Zalman Usiskin, Author
John E Craig, Editor
Susan S Stodolsky, Editor

4132 American Scholar
1785 Massachusetts Avenue NW
4th Floor
Washington, DC 20036-2117
202-265-3808
A general interest magazine that includes articles on science, literature, and book reviews.

Quarterly

Anne Fadiman, Editor

4133 American Students & Teachers Abroad
US Government Printing Office
732 N Capitol Street NW
Washington, DC 20401
202-512-0000
Fax: 202-512-1293
E-mail: admin@access.gpo.gov
http://www.access.gpo.gov

4134 Annual Report
Jessie Ball duPont Fund
One Dependent Drive
Suite 1400
Jacksonville, FL 32202-5011
904-353-0890
800-252-3452
Fax: 904-353-3870
E-mail: contactus@dupontfund.org
http://www.dupontfund.org

Focused on a variety of good work aimed at growing the capacity of the nonprofit sector.

Publication Date: 0 Annually

4135 Association of Orthodox Jewish Teachers of the New York Public Schools
Association of Orthodox Jewish Teachers of the NY
1577 Coney Island Avenue
Brooklyn, NY 11230
718-258-3585
Fax: 718-258-3586
E-mail: aojt@juno.com
Newsletter representing observant Jewish teachers in the New York City Public Schools.

8-12 pages Quarterly Newsletter

Max Zakon, Executive Director

4136 Between Classes-Elderhostel Catalog
Elderhostel
75 Federal Street
Boston, MA 02110-1913
617-426-7788
Fax: 617-426-8351
http://www.elderhostel.org
Seasonal listings of elderhostel educational programs offered by educational cultural institutions in the US and 60 countries overseas.

120 pages Quarterly

Heather Baynes, Contact

4137 Blumenfeld Education Newsletter
PO Box 45161
Boise, ID 83711-5161
Providing knowledge to parents and educators who want to save children of America from destructive forces that endanger them. Children in public schools are at grave risk in 4 ways: academically, spiritually, morally, physically, and only a well-informed public will be able to reduce these risks.

8 pages

Peter F Watt, Publisher
Samuel L Blumenfeld, Editor

4138 Brighton Times
Brighton Academy/Foundation of Human Understanding
1121 NE 7th Street
Grants Pass, OR 97526-1421
541-474-6865
Fax: 541-474-6866
Home schooling information.

Monthly

Cynthia Coumoyer, Contact

4139 Brochure of American-Sponsored Overseas Schools
Office of Overseas Schools, Department of State
Room 245
SA-29
Washington, DC 20522
202-261-8200
Fax: 202-261-8224

4140 Business-Education Insider
Heritage Foundation
214 Massachusetts Avenue NE
Washington, DC 20002-4958
202-546-4400
Fax: 202-546-8328
Deals with issues relating to the corporate/business world, and the effects it has on education.

Monthly

Jeanne Allen, Contact

4141 CBE Report
Association for Community Based Education
1806 Vernon Street NW
Washington, DC 20009-1217
202-462-6333
Educational institutions covering news, workshops and resources.

Monthly

4142 CEDS Communique
The Council for Exceptional Children
1920 Association Drive
Reston, VA 20191-1545
703-620-3660
888-232-7733
Fax: 703-264-9494
Reports on the activities of the Council for Educational Diagnostic Services and information about special programs, upcoming events, current trends and practices, and other topical matters.

Quarterly

Lamoine Miller, Contact

4143 Center Focus
Center of Concern
1225 Otis Street NE
Washington, DC 20017-2516
202-635-2757
Fax: 202-832-9494
E-mail: coc@coc.org
http://www.coc.org
Newsletters addressing the everchanging needs and concerns in the education field.

6 pages BiMonthly

Jane Deren, Publisher/Editor

4144 Center for Continuing Education of Women Newsletter
University of Michigan
Ann Arbor, MI 48109
734-763-1400
Fax: 734-936-1641
Association news focusing on the concerns of women in education.

4 pages

4145 Center for Parent Education Newsletter
81 Wyman Street
Wapham, MA 02160
617-964-2442
Offers information and tips to address parent involvement in the education of their children.

BiMonthly

4146 Change
Heldref Publications
1319 18th Street NW
Washington, DC 20036-1802
202-296-6267
800-365-9753
Fax: 202-296-5149
http://www.heldref.org
Perspectives on the critical issues shaping the world of higher education. It is not only issue-oriented and reflective, but challenges the status quo in higher education.

BiMonthly

Margaret A Miller, President
Theodore J Marchese, VP/Editor

4147 Clearing House: A Journal of Educational Research
Heldref Publications
1319 18th Street NW
Washington, DC 20036-1826
202-296-6267
800-365-9753

Fax: 202-296-5149
E-mail: tch@heldfred.org
Each issue offers a variety of articles for teachers and administrators of middle schools and junior and senior high schools. It includes experiments, trends and accomplishments in courses, teaching methods, administrative procedures and school programs.

4 pages BiMonthly
ISSN: 0009-8655

Deborah N Cohen, Promotions Manager
Judy Cusick, Managing Editor

4148 Commuter Perspectives
National Clearinghouse for Commuter Programs
1195 Stamp Union
College Park, MD 30314-9634
301-405-0986
Fax: 301-314-9874
E-mail: nccp@accmail.umd.edu
http://www.umd.edu/NCCP
A quarterly newsletter published by the National Clearinghouse for Commuter Programs for professionals who work for, with, and on behalf of commuter students.

8 pages Quarterly

Barbara Jacoby, Contact

4149 Congressional Digest
Congressional Digest Corp.
4416 East West Highway
Suite 400
Bethesda, MD 20814-4568
301-634-3113
800-637-9915
Fax: 301-634-3189
E-mail: griff.thomas@pro-and-con.org
http://www.pro-and-con.org
An independent publication featuring controversies in Congress, pro-and-con.

ISSN: 0010-5899

Delores Baisden, Assistant

4150 ConneXions
Association of International Schools in Africa
Peponi Road
PO Box 14103, Nairobi
Kenya 00800
254-20-2697442
Fax: 254-20-4183272
E-mail: info@aisa.or.ke
http://www.aisa.or.ke
Published twice per year, ConneXions is AISA's print and online newsletter

Peter Bateman, Executive Director
Thomas Shearer, Chairperson

4151 Contemporary Education
Indiana State University, School of Education
SE 1005th
Terre Haute, IN 47809-0001
877-856-8005
Fax: 812-856-8088
A readable and currently informative journal of topics in the mainstream of educational thought.

Quarterly
ISSN: 0010-7476

Todd Whitaker, Editor
Beth Whitaker, Editor

4152 Creative Child & Adult Quarterly
Nat'l Assn. for Creative Children & Adults
8080 Springvalley Drive
Cincinnati, OH 45236-1352

513-631-1777
Quarterly

Anne Fabe Isaacs, Editor

4153 Creativity Research Journal
Lawrence Erlbaum Associates
10 Industrial Avenue
Mahwah, NJ 07430-2262
201-258-2200
800-926-6579
Fax: 201-236-0072
E-mail: journals@erlbaum.com
http://www.erlbaum.com
A peer-reviewed journal covering a full range of approaches including behavioral, cognitive, clinical developmental, educational, social and organizational. Online access is available by visiting LEAonline.com

Quarterly
ISSN: 1040-0419

Mark A Runco, PhD., Editor

4154 Currents
Council for Advancement & Support of Education
1307 New York Avenue NW
Suite 1000
Washington, DC 20005-4726
703-379-4611
Fax: 202-387-4973
E-mail: memberservicecenter@case.org
http://www.case.org
Published nine times a year and distributed to 19,000 professional members, Currents delivers essential information, insight and ideas that empower those who support education to master challenges and act decisively to create a better future for their institutions and the world.

Liz Reilly, Editor-in-Chief

4155 DCDT Network
The Council for Exceptional Children
1920 Association Drive
Reston, VA 20191-1545
703-620-3660
888-232-7733
Fax: 703-264-9494
Newsletter of the Division on Career Development and Transition. Provides the latest information on legislation, projects, resource materials and implementation strategies in the field of career development and transition for persons with disabilities and/or who are gifted. Carries information about Division activities, upcoming events, announcements and reports of particular interest to DCDT members.

3x Year

Sherrilyn Fisher, Contact

4156 DECA Dimensions
1908 Association Drive
Reston, VA 20191-1503
703-860-5000
Fax: 703-860-4013
http://www.deca.org
An educational nonprofit association news management for marketing education students across the country, Canada, Guam and Puerto Rico. Offers information on DECA activities, leadership, business and career skills, which help develop future leaders in business, marketing and management.

36 pages Quarterly
ISSN: 1060-6106

Carol Lund, Author

4157 DLD Times
The Council for Exceptional Children
1920 Association Drive
Reston, VA 20191-1589
703-620-3660
800-CEC-SPED
Fax: 703-264-1637
Information concerning education and welfare of children and youth with learning disabilities.

8 pages TriQuarterly

Katherine Garnett, Editor

4158 Decision Line
Decision Sciences Institute
University Plaza
Atlanta, GA 30303
404-651-4000
Fax: 404-651-2896
Contains articles on education, business and decision sciences as well as available positions and textbook advertising.

32 pages 5x Year

K Roscoe Davis

4159 Desktop Presentations & Publishing
Doron & Associates
1213 Ridgecrest Circle
Denton, TX 76205-5421
940-320-0068
Fax: 940-591-9586
Computer generated presentations and visual aids for education and business.

16 pages BiMonthly

Tom Doron, Contact

4160 Development and Alumni Relations Report
LRP Publications
1901 N Moore Street
Suite 700
Arlington, VA 22209
703-516-7002
800-341-7874
Fax: 703-516-9313
E-mail: custserve@lrp.com
http://www.lrp.com
Provides colleges and universities with innovative ideas for improving: alumni relations; the involvement of alumni in clubs and chapters; annual giving; endowment and capital campaigns; and planned giving. Plus, you can recieve free e-mail updates on crucial news affecting your job with your paid subscription.

Monthly Newsletter

4161 Different Books
Place in the Woods
3900 Glenwood Avenue
Golden Valley, MN 55422-5302
763-374-2120
Fax: 952-593-5593
E-mail: differentbooks@aol.com
Special imprint of books by, for and about persons on a different path. Features main characters with disabilities as heroes and heroines in storyline. For hi-lo reading in early elementary grades (3-7).

Paperback

Roger Hammer, Publisher

4162 Directions
AFS Intercultural Programs USA
198 Madison Avenue
Floor 8
New York, NY 10016
212-299-9000
Fax: 212-299-9090
News of AFS US volunteers.

6 pages Monthly

Pedro Valez, Contact

4163 Disability Compliance for Higher Education
LRP Publications
1901 N Moore Street
Suite 700
Arlington, VA 22209
703-516-9313
800-341-7874
Fax: 703-516-9313
E-mail: custserve@lrp.com
http://www.lrp.com
Newsletter helps colleges determine if they're complying with the Americans with Disabilities Act (ADA) and Section 504 of the Rehabilitation Act- so they can avoid costly litigation. Gives tips on how to provide reasonable accommodations in test-taking, grading, admissions, and accessibility to programs and facilities.

Monthly
ISSN: 1086-1335

Edward Filo, Author

4164 Diversity 2000
Holocaust Resource Center
Kean College
1000 Morris Avenue
Union, NJ 07083
Offers ideas and issues on multicultural school education programs.

BiMonthly

J Preill, Contact

4165 ERIC/CRESS Bulletin
AEL, Inc.
PO Box 1348
Charleston, WV 25325-1348
304-347-0437
800-624-9120
Fax: 304-347-0467
E-mail: ericrc@ael.org
Announces new developments in the ERIC system nationally, and publications and events relevant to American Indians, Alaska Natives, Mexican Americans, migrants, outdoor education and rural, small schools.

3x Year Newsletter

Patricia Hammer Cahape, Associate Director

4166 Eagle Forum
Eagle Education Fund
8383 E 123rd Avenue
Brighton, CO 80601-8110
News on the Eagle Education Fund.

Quarterly

Jayne Schindler, Editor

4167 EdPress News
Association of Educational Publishers
510 Heron Drive
Suite 201
Logan Township, NJ 08085
856-241-7772
Fax: 856-241-0709
E-mail: mail@edpress.org
http://www.edpress.org
The Association supports the growth of educational publishing and it's positive effects on learning and teaching. EdPress provides information and analysis of markets and trends, education and legislative policy, learning and teaching research, and intellectual property. The Association also provides training and staff development programs, promotes supplemental learning resources as essential curriculum materials, and advocates on issues relevant to its constituents.

Charlene F Gaynor, Executive Director
Stacey Pusey, Communications Director

4168 Education
Project Innovation
1362 Santa Cruz Court
Chula Vista, CA 91910-7114
760-630-9938
E-mail: rcassel5@aol.com
http://www.rcassel.com
Original investigations and theoretical articles dealing with education. Preference given to innovations, real or magical, which promise to improve learning.

160 pages Quarterly
ISSN: 0013-1172

Dr. Russell Cassel, Editor
Lan Mieu Cassel, Managing Editor

4169 Education Digest
Prakken Publications
PO Box 8623
3970 Varsity Drive
Ann Arbor, MI 48107-8623
734-975-2800
800-530-9673
Fax: 734-975-2787
E-mail: publisher@techdirectories.com
http://www.eddigest.com
Offers outstanding articles condensed for quick review from over 200 magazines, monthlies, books, newsletters and journals, timely and important for professional educators and others interested in the field.

80 pages Monthly
ISSN: 0013-127X

George F Kennedy, Publisher
Kenneth Schroeder, Managing Editor

4170 Education Hotline
6935 Arlington Road
Suite 100
Bethesda, MD 20814
301-280-3100
800-346-1834
Fax: 301-280-3250
E-mail: ads@epe.org
http://www.edweek.org
Education newsletter.

4171 Education Newsletter Library Counterpoint
LRP Publications
1901 N Moore Street
Suite 700
Alington, VA 22209
703-516-7002
800-341-7874
Fax: 703-516-9313
E-mail: custserve@lrp.com
http://www.lrp.com
Offers its readers concise, informative and timely articles covering innovative practices in special education. Covers: special education news from the states; updates on curriculum; developments in special education technology; classified ads; descriptions of new products and publications; and more.

On-Line

4172 Education Newsline
National Association of Christian Educators
PO Box 3200
Costa Mesa, CA 92628-3200
949-251-9333
Articles pertinent to public education for teachers and parents, current trends and solutions and the work of Citizens for Excellence in Education.

8 pages BiMonthly

Robert Simonds, Publisher
Kathi Hudson, Editor

4173 Education Now and in the Future
Northwest Regional Educational Laboratory
101 SW Main Street
Suite 500
Portland, OR 97204-3213
503-275-9500
800-597-6339
Fax: 503-275-0458
E-mail: info@nwrel.org
http://www.nwrel.org
Contains articles about products, events, research and publications produced or sponsored by the NW Regional Educational Laboratory, a private nonprofit educational institution whose mission is to help schools improve outcomes for all students.

Carol F Thomas, CEO

4174 Education Quarterly
New Jersey State Department of Education
100 Riverview Plaza
PO Box 500
Trenton, NJ 08625
609-292-4040
New Jersey education information and updates.

6 pages Quarterly

Richard Vespucci, Contact

4175 Education USA
LRP Publications
1901 N Moore Street
Suite 1106
Arlington, VA 22209
703-516-7002
800-341-7874
Fax: 703-516-9313
E-mail: custserve@lrp.com
http://www.lrp.com
Offers information on court decisions, federal funding, the national debate over standards, education research, school finance, and more. Subscribers receive biweekly reports on Education Department policies on Title I, special education, bilingual education, drug-free schools and other issues affecting schools nationwide.

8-10 pages BiWeekly

4176 Education Update
Heritage Foundation
214 Massachusetts Avenue NE
Washington, DC 20002-4958
202-546-4400
Fax: 202-544-7330
http://www.heritage.org
Contains analyses of policy issues and trends in US education.

4177 Education Week
6935 Arlington Road
Suite 100
Bethesda, MD 20814
301-280-3100
800-346-1834
Fax: 301-280-3250
E-mail: ads@epe.org
http://www.edweek.org
For principals, superintendents, director, managers and other administrators.

4178 Education in Focus
Books for All Times
PO Box 2
Alexandria, VA 22313-0002
703-548-0457
E-mail: jdavid@bfat.com
Examines failures and successes of public and private education by looking beneath the surface for answers and explanations.

6 pages BiAnnually
ISSN: 1049-7250

Joe David, Editor

4179 Educational Forum
University of Colorado-Denver, School of
Education
PO Box 173364
Campus Box 106
Denver, CO 80217-3364
303-556-3402
Fax: 303-556-4479
E-mail: education@cudenver.edu
http://www.cudenver.edu/sehd
The university is recognized as one of the
leading public universities in the nation
and offers a broad range of academic op-
portunities to students.

Quarterly

Hank Brown, President
Michel Dahlin, Interim Vice President

**4180 Educational Freedom Spotlight On
Homeschooling**
Clonlara Home Based Education
Programs
1289 Jewett Street
Ann Arbor, MI 48104-6201
734-769-4511
Fax: 734-769-9629
E-mail: clonlara@wash.k12.mi.us
http://www.clonlara.org
Clonlara School is committed to illuminat-
ing educational rights and freedoms
through our actions and deep dedication to
human rights and dignity.

12 pages Monthly

Susan Andrews, Editor
Carmen Amabile, Coordinator

4181 Educational Horizons
P. Lambda Theta, Int'l Honor &
Professional Assn.
PO Box 6626
Bloomington, IN 47407-6626
812-339-3411
Fax: 812-339-3462
E-mail: root@pilambda.org
http://www.pilambda.org
Founded in the spirit of academic excellence in order to provide leadership in addressing educational, social and cultural
issues of national and international significance and to enhance the status of educators by providing a recognized forum for
sharing new perspectives, research
findings and scholarly essays.

48 pages Quarterly
ISSN: 0013-175X

Juli Knutson, Editor

4182 Educational Research Forum
American Educational Research
Association
1230 17th Street NW
Washington, DC 20036-3078
202-223-9485
Fax: 202-775-1824
E-mail: aera@gmu.edu
Contains news and information on educa-
tional research, teaching, counseling and
school administration.

4183 Educational Researcher
American Educational Research
Association
1230 17th Street NW
Washington, DC 20036-3078
202-223-9485
Fax: 202-775-1824
E-mail: aera@gmu.edu
Publishes research news and commentary
on events in the field of educational re-

search and articles of a wide interest to anyone involved in education.

9x Year

Robert Donmoyer, Editor
Leannah Harding, Managing Editor

4184 Educational Theory
University of Illinois at Urbana
1310 S 6th Street
Champaign, IL 61820-6925
217-333-3003
Fax: 217-244-3711
E-mail: edtheory@uiuc.edu
http://www.ed.uiuc.edu/educational-theor
y
The purpose of this journal is to foster the
continuing development of educational
theory and encourage wide and effective
discussion of theoretical problems with the
educational profession. Publishes articles
and studies in the foundations of education
and in related disciplines outside the field
of education which contribute to the
advancement of education theory.

570 pages Quarterly
ISSN: 0013-2004

Nicholas C Burbules, Editor
Diane E Beckett, Business Manager

4185 Exceptional Children
The Council for Exceptional Children
2900 Crystal Drive
Suite 100
Arlington, VA 22202-3557
703-620-3660
888-232-7733
Fax: 703-264-3494
E-mail: service@cec.sped.org
http://www.cec.sped.org
Original research on the education and development of infants, toddlers, children
and youth with exceptionalities and articles on professional issues of concern to
special educators. Published quarterly,
free to members or $86.00 per year to
individuals.

Quarterly
ISSN: 0014-4029

Margo Mastropieri, Editor
Thomas Scruggs, Editor

4186 Focus on Autism
Pro-Ed., Inc.
8700 Shoal Creek Boulevard
Austin, TX 78757-6816
512-451-3246
800-897-3202
Fax: 512-302-9129
http://www.proedinc.com
Hands-on tips, techniques, methods and
ideas from top authorities for improving
the quality of assessment, instruction and
management.

Brenda Smith Myles, PhD, Editor

4187 Focus on Research
The Council for Exceptional Children
1920 Association Drive
Reston, VA 20191-1545
703-620-3660
888-232-7733
Fax: 703-264-9494
Contains member opinion articles, debates
on research issues, descriptions and dates
of specific projects, notices of funded program priorities in special education, the
availability of research dollars, and the discussion of emerging issues that may affect
research in special education.

3x Year

Mavis Donahue, Co-Editor
Eileen Ball, Co-Editor

4188 Foreign Student Service Council
2263 12th Place NW
Washington, DC 20009-4405
202-232-4979
Non-profit organization dedicated to promoting
understanding between international students and
Americans.

Quarterly

4189 Fortune Education Program
105 Terry Drive
Suite 120
Newtown, PA 18940-1872
800-448-3399
Fax: 215-579-8589
Professional program that offers 75% off the
cover price of Fortune magazine, a free educator's
desk reference, a free 2-page teaching guide, fast
delivery, choice of billing options. Plus quality
customer service.

Pat Sproehnle, Editor

4190 Forum
Educators for Social Responsibility
23 Garden Street
Cambridge, MA 02138-3623
617-492-1764
Fax: 617-864-5164
E-mail: educators@esrnational.org
http://www.esrnational.org
Edited for educators concerned with teaching in
the nuclear age.

12 pages Quarterly

Susan Pittman, Contact

**4191 Foundation for Exceptional Children:
Focus**
The Council for Exceptional Children
1920 Association Drive
Reston, VA 20191-1545
703-620-3660
888-232-7733
Fax: 703-264-9494
Membership and association news.

6 pages TriQuarterly

Ken Collins, Contact

4192 Fulbright News
Metro International Program Services of New
York
285 W Broadway
Room 450
New York, NY 10013-2269
212-431-1195
Fax: 212-941-6291
A four page newsletter distributed 5 times a year
to visiting Fulbright scholars in the New York
area. Contains a scholar profile, information
about activities, tips for living in the United
States, events in the New York area, and relevant
announcements.

4 pages

Kristen Pendleton, Publisher

4193 GED Items
Center for Adult Learning & Education
Credentials
1 Dupont Circle NW
Washington, DC 20036-1110
202-939-9490
Newsletter of the GED Testing Service with articles focusing on adult education programs, teaching tips, GED graduate success stories and
administration of GED testing.

12 pages BiMonthly

4194 Gifted Child Society Newsletter
190 Rock Road
Glen Rock, NJ 07452-1736
201-444-6530
Fax: 201-444-9099

E-mail: admin@gifted.org
http://www.gifted.org
Provides educational enrichment and support for gifted children through national advocacy and various programs.

Bi-Annual

Janet L Chen, Executive Director

4195 Harvard Education Letter
8 Story Street
5th Floor
Cambridge, MA 02138
617-495-3432
800-513-0763
Fax: 617-496-3584
E-mail: editor@edletter.org
http://www.edletter.org
Published by the Harvard Graduate School of Education and reports on current research and innovative practice in PreK-12.

8 pages Bi-Monthly
ISSN: 8755-3716

Douglas Clayton, Publisher
David T Gordon, Editor

4196 Health in Action
American School Health Association
PO Box 708
Kent, OH 44240-0013
330-678-1601
800-445-2742
Fax: 330-678-4526
E-mail: asha@ashaweb.org
http://www.ashaweb.org

24 pages Quarterly
ISSN: 1540-2479

Tom Reed, Assistant Executive Director

4197 Help! I'm in Middle School... How Will I Survive?
NRS Publications
1482 51st Road
Douglass, KS 67039
620-986-5472
E-mail: info@englishthrough.com
http://www.nsrpublications.com
The goal of NRS Publications is the success of every child. We provide a varity of books, educational games, posters, educational dice, overhead tiles, science kits, the SHAPES parts of speech learning system and creative play toys to help meet that goal.

Merry L Gumm, President
Tanya L Hein, Vice President

4198 Higher Education & National Affairs
American Council on Education
1 Dupont Circle NW
Suite 800
Washington, DC 20036-1132
202-939-9365
National newsletter with Capitol Hill and Administration updates on issues that affect colleges and universities. Includes stories on the federal budget, student financial aid, tax laws, Education Department regulations and research, legal issues and minorities in higher education.

Janetta Hammock, Contact

4199 History of Education Quarterly
Indian University
School of Education
Bloomington, IN 47405
812-855-9334
Fax: 812-855-3631
Discusses current and historical movements in education.

Quarterly

Amy Schutt, Editor

4200 Homeschooling Marketplace Newsletter
13106 Patrici Circle
Omaha, NE 68164
Offers information, strategies and tips for homeschooling.

Clarice Routh, Contact

4201 IDRA Newsletter
Intercultural Development Research Association
5835 Callaghan Road
Suite 350
San Antonio, TX 78228-1125
210-444-1710
Fax: 210-444-1714
E-mail: idra@txdirect.net
http://www.idra.org
Mini-journal covering topics in the education of minority, poor and language-minority students in public institutions. It provides research-based solutions and editorial materials for education.

Monthly

Maria Robledo Montecel, Executive Director

4202 IEA Reporter
Idaho Education Association
620 N 6th Street
Boise, ID 83702-5542
208-344-1341
Fax: 208-336-6967
http://www.idahoea.org

Quarterly

Diana Mikesell, VP
Kathy Phelan, President

4203 Inclusive Education Programs
LRP Publications
1901 N Moore Street
Suite 700
Arlington, VA 22209
703-516-7002
800-341-7874
Fax: 703-516-9313
E-mail: custserve@lrp.com
http://www.lrp.com
Newsletter covers the legal and practical issues of educating children with disabilities in regular education environments. It provides practical, how-to-advice, real life examples, and concise case summaries of the most recent judicial case laws.

Monthly
ISSN: 1076-8548

4204 Independent Scholar
National Coalition of Independent Scholars
PO Box 5743
Berkeley, CA 94705-0743
510-704-0990
A newsletter for independent scholars and their organizations.

Quarterly

Murray Wax, Contact

4205 Innovative Higher Education
Kluwer Academic/Human Sciences Press
233 Spring Street
New York, NY 10013
212-620-8000
800-221-9369
Fax: 212-463-0742
http://www.wkpa.nl
Provides educators and scholars with the latest creative strategies, programs and innovations designed to meet contemporary challenges in higher education. Professionals throughout the world contribute high-quality papers on the changing rules of vocational and liberal arts education, the needs of adults reentering the education process, and the rec-

onciliation of faculty desires to economic realities, among other topics.

Quarterly
ISSN: 0742-5627

Carol Bischoff, Publisher
Ronald Simpson, Editor

4206 Insight
Independent Education Consultants Association
3251 Old Lee Highway
Suite 510
Fairfax, VA 22030-1504
703-591-4850
800-888-4322
Fax: 703-591-4860
E-mail: requests@IECAonline.com
http://www.IECAonline.com
Publication of national professional association of educational counselors working in private practice. Association provides counseling in college, secondary schools, learning disabilities and wilderness therapy programs.

Rebecca Peek, Author
Mark H Sklarow, Executive Director

4207 International Debates
Congressional Digest Corp.
4416 East West Highway
Suite 400
Bethesda, MD 20814-4568
301-634-3113
800-637-9915
Fax: 301-634-3189
E-mail: griff.thomas@pro-and-con.org
http://www.pro-and-con.org
An independent publication featuring global controversies in the United Nations and other international forums, pro and cons.

ISSN: 1542-0345

Delores Baisden, Assistant

4208 International Education
University of Tennessee
College of Education
Health & Human Services
Knoxville, TN 37996-3400
865-974-5252
Fax: 865-974-8718
E-mail: scarey@utk.edu
Publishes articles related to various international topics.

Publication Date: 1997 BiAnnual/Paperback
ISSN: 0160-5429

Sue Carey, Managing Editor

4209 International Journal of Qualitive Studies in Education
Sanchez 310
University of Texas at Austin
Austin, TX 78712
512-232-1552
Fax: 512-471-5975
E-mail: 8se@uts.cc.utexas.edu
http://www.tandF.co.uk/journals
Aims to enhance the theory of qualitative research in education.

6 Issues Per Year

Jim Scheurich, Editor
Angela Valenzuela, Editor

4210 International Volunteer
Volunteers for Peace
1034 Tiffany Road
Belmont, VT 05730-9988
802-259-2759
Fax: 802-259-2922
E-mail: vfp@vfp.org
http://www.vfp.org

Newsletter of Volunteers for Peace, which provides intercultural education and community services.

8 pages Annual

Peter Coldwell, Author

4211 Issues in Integrative Studies

Association for Integrative Studies
Miami University
Oxford, OH 45056
513-529-2659
Fax: 513-529-5849
E-mail: aisorg@muohio.edu
http://www.units.muohio.edu/aisorg
An annual, refereed professional journal for members.

ISBN: 1081-4760

Rick Szostak, Editor

4212 It Starts in the Classroom

National School Public Relations Association
1501 Lee Highway
Suite 201
Arlington, VA 22209-1109
703-528-5840
Devoted to classroom and teacher public relations techniques and ideas.

8 pages Monthly

Joseph Scherer, Publisher
Judi Cowan, Editor

4213 Journal of Behavioral Education

Kluwer Academic/Human Sciences Press
233 Spring Street
New York, NY 10013
212-620-8000
800-221-9369
Fax: 212-463-0742
http://www.wkpa.nl
Provides the first single-source forum for the publication of research on the application of behavioral principles and technology to education. Publishes original empirical research and brief reports covering behavioral education in regular, special and adult education settings. Subject populations include handicapped, at-risk, and non-handicapped students of all ages.

Quarterly
ISSN: 1053-0819

Carol Bischoff, Publisher
Christopher Skinner, Co-Editor

4214 Journal of Creative Behavior

Creative Education Foundation
289 Bay Road
Hadley, MA 01035
413-559-6614
800-447-2774
Fax: 413-559-6615
E-mail: contact@creativeeducationfoundation.org
http://www.cef-cpsi.org
Devoted to the serious general reader with vocational/avocational interests in the fields of creativity and problem solving. Its articles are authored not only by established writers in the field, but by up-and coming contributors as well. The criteria for selecting articles include reference, clarity, interest and overall quality.

Quarterly

Grace A Guzzetta, Managing Editor
Mary Pokojowczyk, Circulation Manager

4215 Journal of Curriculum Theorizing

Colgate University
Department of Education
Hamilton, NY 13346

315-228-1000
Fax: 315-228-7998
Analyzes and provides insights to curriculum movements and evolution.

Quarterly

JoAnne Pagano, Editor

4216 Journal of Disability Policy Studies

Pro-Ed., Inc.
8700 Shoal Creek Boulevard
Austin, TX 78757-6816
512-451-3246
800-897-3202
Fax: 512-302-9129
E-mail: proed1@aol.com
http://www.proedinc.com
Devoted exclusively to disability policy topics and issues.

Quarterly Magazine
ISSN: 1044-2073

Craig R Fiedler, JD, PhD, Editor
Billie Jo Rylance, PhD, Editor

4217 Journal of Educational Research

Heldref Publications
1319 18th Street NW
Washington, DC 20036-1826
202-296-6267
800-365-9753
Fax: 202-296-5149
http://www.heldref.org
Since 1920, this journal has contributed to the advancement of educational practice in elementary and secondary schools. Authors experiment with new procedures, evaluate traditional practices, replicate previous research for validation and perform other work central to understanding and improving the education of today's students and teachers. This Journal is a valuable resource for teachers, counselors, supervisors, administrators, planners and educational researchers.

64 pages BiMonthly
ISSN: 0022-0671

Deborah Cohen, Promotions Editor

4218 Journal of Experimental Education

Heldref Publications
1319 18th Street NW
Washington, DC 20036-1826
202-296-6267
800-365-9753
Fax: 202-296-5149
E-mail: jxe@heldref.org
http://www.heldref.org
Aims to improve educational practice by publishing basic and applied research studies using the range of quantitative and qualitative methodologies found in the behavioral, cognitive and social sciences. Published studies address all levels of schooling, from preschool through graduate and professional education, and various educational context, including public and private education in the United States and abroad.

96 pages Quarterly

Paige Jackson, Managing Editor

4219 Journal of Law and Education

University of South Carolina Law School
Columbia, SC 29208
803-777-4155
Fax: 803-777-9405
A periodical offering information on the newest laws and legislation affecting education.

Quarterly

Eldon D Wedlock Jr, Editor

4220 Journal of Learning Disabilities

Pro-Ed., Inc.
8700 Shoal Creek Boulevard
Austin, TX 78757-6816
512-451-3246
800-897-3202
Fax: 512-302-9129
E-mail: proed1@aol.com
http://www.proedinc.com
Special series, feature articles and research articles.

Bi-Monthly Magazine
ISSN: 0022-2194

Wayne P Hresko, PhD, Editor-in-Chief

4221 Journal of Negro Education

Howard University
PO Box 311
Washington, DC 20059-0001
202-806-8120
Fax: 202-806-8434
E-mail: jne@howard.edu
A Howard University quarterly review of issues incident to the education of Black people; tracing educational developments and presenting research on issues confronting Black students in the US and around the world.

120+ pages Quarterly
ISSN: 0022-2984

D. Kamili Anderson, Associate Editor
Dr. Sylvia T. Johnson, Editor-in-Chief

4222 Journal of Positive Behavior Interventions

Pro-Ed., Inc.
8700 Shoal Creek Boulevard
Austin, TX 78757-6816
512-451-3246
800-897-3202
Fax: 512-302-9129
http://www.proedinc.com
Sound, research-based principles of positive behavior support for use in home, school and community settings for people with challenges in behavioral adaptation.

Glen Dunlap, PhD, Editor
Robert L Koegel, PhD, Editor

4223 Journal of Research and Development in Education

University of Georgia, College of Education
427 Tucker Hall
Athens, GA 30602
404-542-1154
A magazine offering insight and experimental and theoretical studies in education.

Quarterly

4224 Journal of Research in Character Education

Character Education Partnership
1025 Connecticut Avenue NW
Suite 1011
Washington, DC 20036
202-296-7743
800-988-8081
Fax: 202-296-7779
http://www.character.org

Andrea Grenadier, Director Communications
Esther Schaeffer, CEO/Executive Director

4225 Journal of Research in Rural Education

University of Maine, College of Education
5766 Shibles Hall
Orono, ME 04469-5766
207-581-2493
Fax: 207-581-2423
http://www.umaine.edu

Publishes the results of educational research relevant to rural settings.

3x Year Journal

Theodore Coladarci, Editor
Sara Sheppard, Managing Editor

4226 Journal of School Health

American School Health Association
PO Box 708
Kent, OH 44240-0013
330-678-1601
800-445-2742
Fax: 330-678-4526
E-mail: asha@ashaweb.org
http://www.ashaweb.org
Contains material related to health promotion in school settings. A non-profit organization founded in 1927, ASHA's mission is to protect and improve the health and well-being of children and youth by supporting comprehensive, preschool-12 school health programs. ASHA and its 4,000 members (school nurses, health educators, and physicians) work to improve school health services and school health environments.

40 pages Monthly
ISSN: 0022-4391

Tom Reed, Assistant Executive Director

4227 Journal of Special Education

Pro-Ed., Inc.
8700 Shoal Creek Boulevard
Austin, TX 78757-6816
512-451-3246
800-897-3202
Fax: 512-302-9129
http://www.proedinc.com
Timely, sound special education research.

Lynn S Fuchs, PhD, Editor
Douglas Fuchs, PhD, Editor

4228 Journal of Urban & Cultural Studies

University of Massachusetts at Boston
Department of English
Harbor Campus
Boston, MA 02125
617-287-5760
Fax: 617-287-6511
Explores various issues in education that deal with urban and cultural affairs.

Donaldo Macedo, Editor

4229 Kaleidoscope

Evansville-Vanderburgh School Corporation
1 SE 9th Street
Evansville, IN 47708-1821
812-435-8453
A staff publication for and about employees of the Evansville-Vanderburgh School Corporation.

8 pages Monthly

Patti S Coleman, Contact

4230 LD Forum

Council for Learning Disabilities
PO Box 40303
Overland Park, KS 68204
913-492-8755
Fax: 913-492-2546
Provides updated information and research on the activities of the Council for Learning Disabilities.

60 pages Quarterly
ISSN: 0731-9487

4231 Learning Disability Quarterly

Council for Learning Disabilities
PO Box 40303
Overland Park, KS 66204-4303
913-492-8755
Fax: 913-492-2546

Aimed at learning disabled students, their parents and educators. Accepts advertising.

Quarterly

4232 Learning Point Magazine Laboratory

North Central Regional Educational Laboratory
1900 Spring Road
Suite 300
Oak Brook, IL 60523-1447
630-649-6500
Fax: 630-649-6700
E-mail: info@ncrel.org
http://www.ncrel.org
Applies research and technology to learning.

16 pages Quarterly

Jeri Nowakowski, Director

4233 Learning Unlimited Network of Oregon

31960 SE Chin Street
Boring, OR 97009-9708
503-663-5153
Cuts through all barriers to communication and learning; institutional, personal, physical, psychological, spiritual. It focuses on basic communication/language skills but sets no limits on means or tools, subjects or participants in seeking maximum balance and productivity for all.

10 pages 9x Year

Gene Lehman, Contact

4234 Let It Grow. Let It Grow. Let It Grow. Hands-on Activities to Explore the Planet Kingdom

NSR Publications
1482 51st Road
Douglass, KS 67039
620-986-5472
E-mail: info@englishthrough.com
http://www.nsrpublications.com
The goal of NSR Publication is the success of every child. We provide a variety of books, educational games, posters, educational dice, overhead tiles, science kits, the SHAPES parts of speech learning system and creative play toys to help meet that goal.

58 pages

Merry L Gumm, President
Tanya L Hein, Vice President

4235 Liaison Bulletin

National Assn. of State Directors of Special Ed.
1800 Diagonal Road
Suite 320
Alexandria, VA 22314-2840
703-519-3800
Fax: 703-519-3808
Membership news for persons affiliated with the National Association of State Directors of Special Education.

BiWeekly

Dr. William Schipper, Editor

4236 Liberal Education

Association of American Colleges & Universities
1818 R Street NW
Washington, DC 20009-1604
202-387-3760
Fax: 202-265-9532
http://www.aacu-edu.org
Concentrates on issues currently affecting American higher education. Promotes and strengthens undergraduate curriculum, classroom teaching and learning, collaborative leadership, faculty leadership, diversity. Other publications on higher education include books, monographs, peer review, and on campus with women.

64 pages Quarterly
ISSN: 0024-1822

Bridget Puzon, Editor
Debra Humphreys, Comm/Public Affairs VP

4237 Link

AEL, Inc.
PO Box 1348
Charleston, WV 25325-1348
304-347-0400
800-624-9120
Fax: 304-347-0487
E-mail: aelinfo@ael.org
http://www.ael.org
A newsletter for educators providing research summaries, education news, and news of AEL products, services and events.

12 pages Quarterly Newsletter

Carolyn Luzader, Communications Associate

4238 Lisle-Interaction

433 W Sterns Street
Temperance, MI 48182-9568
734-847-7126
800-477-1538
Fax: 512-259-0392
Reports on domestic and international programs, annual meetings and board meetings of the Lisle Fellowship which seeks to broaden global awareness and appreciation of different cultures. Occasional special articles on topics such as racism, book reviews. News of members are also included.

16 pages Quarterly

Mark Kinney, Executive Director
Dianne Brause, VP

4239 MEA Today

Montana Education Association
1232 E 6th Avenue
Helena, MT 59601-3927
406-442-4250
Fax: 406-443-5081
National and state association news, legislative policies, and classroom features.

8 pages Monthly

Nancy Robbins

4240 Massachusetts Home Learning Association Newsletter

23 Mountain Street
Sharon, MA 02067-2234
781-784-8006
A source for information gleaned from all the major national magazines and many state newsletters. Calendar of events for Massachusetts homeschooling and several feature articles on legal, educational or familial issues.

24 pages Quarterly

Sharon Terry, Editor
Patrick Terry, Editor

4241 Mel Gabler's Newsletter

Educational Research Analysts
PO Box 7518
Longview, TX 75607-7518
972-753-5993
Educational information pertaining to curricula used in schools.

8 pages SemiAnnually

Mel Gabler, Publisher
Chad Rosenberger, Editor

4242 Minnesota Education Update
Office of Library Development & Services
440 Capital Square
550 Cedar Street
St. Paul, MN 55101
651-296-2821
Policies and activities in elementary and secondary education in the state of Minnesota.
8 pages Monthly
James Lee

4243 Missouri Schools
Missouri Department of Education
PO Box 480
Jefferson City, MO 65102-0480
573-751-3469
Fax: 573-751-8613
State education policy.
28 pages BiMonthly
James L Morris

4244 Momentum
National Catholic Educational Association
1077 30th Street NW
Suite 100
Washington, DC 20007-3852
202-337-6232
Fax: 202-333-6706
http://www.ncea.org
The association offers a quarterly publication, conducts research, works with voluntary groups and government agencies on educational problems, conducts seminars and workshops for all levels of educators.
Quarterly
Catherine T McNamee, CSJ, Publisher

4245 Montana Schools
Montana Office of Public Instruction
State Capitol
Helena, MT 59620
406-444-3095
Fax: 406-444-2893
Information about people and programs in the Montana education system.
12 pages 5x Year
Ellen Meloy

4246 Montessori Observer
International Montessori Society
9525 Georgia Avenue
Suite 200
Silver Spring, MD 20910-4570
301-589-1127
800-301-3131
Fax: 301-589-0733
E-mail: havis@erols.com
http://http://imsmontessori.org
Provides news and information about Montessori education and the work of the International Montessori Society.
ISSN: 0889-5643
Lee Havis, Editor

4247 NAEIR Advantage
Nat'l Assn. for Exchange of Industrial Resources
560 McClure Street
Galesburg, IL 61401-4286
309-343-0704
800-562-0955
Fax: 309-343-3519
E-mail: member.naeir@misslink.net
http://www.freegoods.com
News of the National Association for the Exchange of Industrial Resources, which collects donations of new excess inventory from corporations and redistributes them to American schools and nonprofits.
8 pages BiMonthly
Gary C Smith, President/CEO
Jack Zavada, Communications Director

4248 NAEN Bulletin
Nort American Association of Education Negotiators
NAEN
PO Box 1068
Salem, OR 97308
503-588-2800
Fax: 503-588-2813
E-mail: naen@osba.org
http://www.naen.org
Association news and notes.
Members Only

4249 NAFSA Newsletter
NAFSA: Association of International Educators
1875 Connecticut Avenue NW
8th Floor
Washington, DC 20009-5728
202-737-3699
800-836-4994
Fax: 202-737-3657
E-mail: inbox@nafsa.org
http://www.nafsa.org
Publishes news and information related to international education and exchange.
40 pages Weekly & Quarterly
Marlene M Johnson, Director/CEO

4250 NAPSEC News
Assn. of Private Schools for Exceptional Children
1522 K Street NW
Suite 1032
Washington, DC 20005-1202
202-408-3338
Fax: 202-408-3340
Association news and events.
8-12 pages Quarterly
Sherry L Kolbe, Executive Director/CEO
Barb DeGroot, Manager

4251 NEA Higher Education Advocate
National Education Association (NEA)
1201 16th Street NW
Washington, DC 20036-3207
202-822-7364
Fax: 202-822-7624
E-mail: ncuea@nea.org
http://www.nea.org
Reports on NEA and general higher education news.
4 pages Monthly
Alicia Sandoual, Publisher
Rebecca Robbins, Editor

4252 NEA Today
National Education Association (NEA)
1201 16th Street NW
Washington, DC 20036-3290
202-822-7364
Fax: 202-822-7624
E-mail: ncuea@nea.org
http://www.nea.org
Contains news and features of interest to classroom teachers and other employees of schools.
8x Year
Bill Fischer, Editor
Suzanne Wade, Advertising Coordinator

4253 NEWSLINKS
International Schools Services
15 Roszel Road
Princeton, NJ 08540-6248
609-452-0990
Fax: 609-452-2690
E-mail: newslinks@iss.edu
http://www.iss.edu
Regularly published newspaper of International Schools Services that is distributed free of charge to overseas teachers, school administrators and libraries, US universities, educational organizations, multinational corporations, school supply companies and educational publishers.
32-40 pages Quarterly
Judy Seltz, Director Communications

4254 NJEA Review
New Jersey Education Association
180 W State Street
PO Box 1211
Trenton, NJ 08607
609-599-4561
Fax: 609-392-6321
Monthly educational journal of the New Jersey Education Association which focuses on educational news and issues related to New Jersey public schools. Its readers are active and retired teaching staff members and support staff, administrators, board members, teacher education students, and others in New Jersey public schools and colleges.
80 pages Monthly
ISSN: 0027-6758
Martha O DeBlieu, Editor
Rosemary Kaub, Conference Manager

4255 NREA News
National Rural Education Association
Education Room 246
Fort Collins, CO 80523-0001
Fax: 970-491-1317
E-mail: jnewlin@lamar.colostate.edu
http://www.colostate.edu
Keeps all members up-to-date on Association activities, events, rural education conferences and meetings, and research projects in progress.
8 pages Quarterly Newsletter
ISSN: 0273-4460
Joseph T Newlin, Editor

4256 National Accrediting Commission of Cosmetology, Arts and Sciences
National Accrediting Commission of Cosmetology
901 N Stuart Street
Suite 900
Arlington, VA 22203-1816
703-527-7600
Fax: 703-379-2200
E-mail: naccas@naccas.org
http://www.naccas.org
Information on accreditation, cosmetology schools and any federal regulations affecting accreditation and postsecondary education.
20 pages 6x Year
Clifford A Culbreath, Editor

4257 National Alliance of Black School Educators (NABSE)
2816 Georgia Avenue NW
Washington, DC 20001-3819
202-483-1549
800-221-2654
Fax: 202-608-6319
E-mail: nabse@nabse.org
http://www.nabse.org
For teachers, principals, specialists, superintendents, school board members and higher education personnel.
15-25 pages 3x Year

4258 National Homeschool Association Newsletter
National Homeschool Association
PO Box 290
Hartland, MI 48353-0290
425-432-1544
Information on what's happening in the homeschooling community.

28 pages Quarterly

4259 National Monitor of Education
CA Monitor of Education
1331 Fairmount Avenue
Suite 61
El Cerrito, CA 94530
510-527-4430
Fax: 510-528-9833
E-mail: jsod@aol.com
http://www.e-files.org
Supports traditional moral and academic values in education. Reports on litigation and reviews various education publications. Issues reported on include parents' rights and movement to restore basic academics.

8 pages Bi-Monthly/Paperback

Susan O'Donnell, Publisher
Susan Sweet, Newsletter Design

4260 New Hampshire Educator
National Education Association, New Hampshire
103 N State Street
Concord, NH 03301-4334
603-224-7751
Fax: 603-224-2648
Reports on the advancements in education in the state and nation and promotes the welfare of educators.

10 pages Monthly

Carol Carstarphen

4261 New Images
METCO
55 Dimock Street
Boston, MA 02119-1029
617-427-1545
Mailed to METCO parents and educational institutions local and national.

4 pages Quarterly

JM Mitchell

4262 New York Teacher
New York State United Teachers
PO Box 15008
Albany, NY 12212-5008
518-213-6000
800-342-9810
Fax: 518-213-6415
Edited primarily for teaching personnel in elementary, intermediate and high schools and colleges. News and features cover organizations' development, progress of legislation affecting education at local state and national levels and news of the labor movement.

BiWeekly

Nicki Rhue, Advertising Director
Bob Fitzpatrick, Production Manager

4263 News N' Notes
NTID at Rochester Institute of Technology
LBJ 2264
Box 9687
Rochester, NY 14623
716-475-6201
Convention news, membership information, education legislation advocacy and personal contributions to the scholarly society.

12 pages Quarterly

Judy Egleston

4264 Non-Credit Learning News
Learning for All Seasons
6 Saddle Club Road
#579X
Lexington, MA 02420-2115
781-861-0379
Marketing information for directors and marketers of non-credit programs.

8 pages 10x Year

Susan Capon

4265 Notes from the Field
Jessie Ball duPont Fund
One Dependent Drive
Suite 1400
Jacksonville, FL 32202-5011
904-353-0890
800-252-3452
Fax: 904-353-3870
E-mail: contactus@dupontfund.org
http://www.dupontfund.org
Provides information on the various organizations and institutes the Jessie Ball duPont Fund reaches out to every year.

Publication Date: 0 3x

4266 Occupational Programs in California Community Colleges
Leo A Myer Associates/LAMA Books
2381 Sleepy Hollow Avenue
Hayward, CA 94545
510-785-1091
888-452-6244
Fax: 510-785-1099
E-mail: lama@lmabooks.com
http://www.lamabooks.com
Writers and publishers of HVAC books.

186 pages Bi-Annually
ISBN: 0-88069

Steve Meyer, President

4267 Our Children: The National PTA Magazine
330 N Wabash Avenue
Suite 2100
Chicago, IL 60611-3603
312-670-6782
Fax: 312-670-6783
http://www.pta.org
Written by, for and about the National PTA. A nonprofit organization of parents, educators, students, and other citizens active in their schools and communities.

5x Year

Douglas Seibold, Editor
Laura Martinelli, Graphic Designer

4268 PTA National Bulletin
National Association of Hebrew Day School PTA'S
160 Broadway
New York, NY 10038-4201
212-227-1000
Fax: 212-406-6934
Educational events in day school relating to PTA movement. News of national and regional groups.

Quarterly

4269 PTA in Pennsylvania
Pennsylvania PTA
4804 Derry Street
Harrisburg, PA 17111-3440
717-564-8985
Fax: 717-564-9046
E-mail: info@papta.org
http://www.papta.org
Topical articles about issues affecting education and children, such as safety and health, AIDS, parents involvement and guidance, environmental concerns and special education.

24 pages Quarterly
ISSN: 1072-3242
250 attendees and 40-50 exhibits

Peg Fallon, Executive Director
Mary Hess, Membership Coordinator

4270 Parents as Teachers National Center
2228 Ball Drive
Saint Louis, MO 63146
314-432-4330
Fax: 314-432-8963
E-mail: patnc@patnc.org
http://www.patnc.org
Provides information, training and technical assistance for those interested in adopting the home-school-community partnership program. Offers parents the information and support needed to give their children the best possible start in life.

Quarterly

Julie Robbens, Editor, Author
Susan S Stepleton, President/CEO
Cheryl Dyle-Palmer, Director Operations

4271 Passing Marks
San Bernadino City Unified School District
777 N F Street
San Bernardino, CA 92410-3017
909-381-1250
Fax: 909-388-1451
Educational resume of school activities, covering instruction, personnel, administration, board of education, etc.

12 pages Monthly

Jan Bell

4272 Pennsylvania Home Schoolers Newsletter
RR 2 Box 117
Kittanning, PA 16201-9311
724-783-6512
Fax: 724-783-6512
A support newsletter directed to homeschooling families in Pennsylvania. Articles, reviews of curriculum, advice, calendar, support group listing, children's writing section.

32 pages Quarterly

Howard Richman, Publisher
Susan Richman, Editor

4273 Pennsylvania State Education Association
400 N 3rd Street
Harrisburg, PA 17101-1346
717-255-7000
Fax: 717-255-7124
http://www.psea.org

16 pages 9x Year
ISSN: 0896-6605

William H Johnson, Editor

4274 Phi Delta Kappa Educational Foundation
PO Box 789
Bloomington, IN 47402-0789
812-339-1156
800-766-1156
Fax: 812-339-0018
E-mail: information@pdkintl.org
http://www.pdkintl.org

Articles concerned with educational research, service, and leadership; issues, trends and policy are emphazied.

350 pages 10x Year
ISBN: 0-87367-835-4
November
600 attendees and 30 exhibits

Perry A. Zirkel, Author
William Bushaw, Executive Director
Donovan Walling, Director Publications

4275 Phi Delta Kappan

Phi Delta Kappa International
408 N Union Street
Bloomington, IN 47405
812-339-1156
800-766-1156
Fax: 812-339-0018
E-mail: customerservice@pdkintl.org
http://www.pdkintl.org
Published 8 times a year and is Phi Delta Kappa International's professional education magazine distributed to more than 35,000 individuals. Addresses policy/practice for teachers, administrators, education faculty. Advocates research-based school reform and covers professinal development, research, federal policy, and standards. Includes annual PDK/Gallup poll on public education and features full text of current issues available to online subscribers.

ISBN: 0031-7217

Joan Richardson, Editor

4276 Planning for Higher Education

Society for College and University Planning (SCUP)
399 East Liberty Street
Suite 300
Ann Arbor, MI 48104
734-998-7832
Fax: 734-998-6532
E-mail: info@scup.org
http://www.scup.org/phe
A quarterly, peer-reviewed journal devoted to the advancement and application of the best planning practices for colleges and universities.

70+ pages Quarterly Journal
ISSN: 0736-0983
July
150 booths with 1,200 attendees and 150 exhibits

Tom Longin, Executive Editor
Chantelle Neumann, Managing Editor

4277 Policy & Practice

American Public Human Services Association
810 1st Street NE
Suite 500
Washington, DC 20002-4207
202-682-0100
Fax: 202-289-6555
http://www.aphsa.org
This quarterly magazine presents a comprehensive look at issues important to public human services administrators. It also features a wide spectrum of views by the best thinkers in social policy.

52 pages Quarterly
ISSN: 1520-801X

Sybil Walker Barnes, Editor

4278 Population Educator

Population Connection
1400 16th Street NW
Suite 320
Washington, DC 20036-2215
202-332-2200
800-767-1956
Fax: 202-332-2302

E-mail:
poped@populationconnection.org
http://www.populationeducation.org
Offers population education news, classroom activities and workshop schedules for grades K-12.

4 pages Quarterly
Pamela Wasseman

4279 Public Education Alert

Public Education Association
39 W 32nd Street
New York, NY 10001-3803
212-868-1640
Fax: 212-302-0088
E-mail: info@peaonline
http://www.pea-online.org
Provides information and consumer-oriented analysis of law policy issues and current developments in New York City public education. PEA Alert back issues; e-guide to New York City's public high school offering comparative data.

Ray Domanico, Publisher
Jessica Wolfe, Editor

4280 QEG

Friends Council on Education
1507 Cherry Street
Philadelphia, PA 19102-1403
215-241-7245
Informal news sheet for Quaker schools.

4 pages BiMonthly
Irene McHenry

4281 QUIN: Quarterly University International News

University of Minnesota, Office in Education
149 Nicholson Hall
Minneapolis, MN 55455
612-625-1915
Fax: 612-624-6839
International campus update for students, faculty, staff and the community.

TriQuarterly
Gayla Marty

4282 Reclaiming Children and Youth

Pro-Ed., Inc.
8700 Shoal Creek Boulevard
Austin, TX 78757-6816
512-451-3246
800-897-3202
Fax: 512-302-9129
E-mail: proed1@aol.com
http://www.proedinc.com
Provides positive, creative solutions to professionals serving youth in conflict.

Quarterly Magazine
Nicholas J Long, PhD, Editor
Larry K Brendtro, PhD, Editor

4283 Recognition Review

Awards and Recognition Association
4700 W Lake Avenue
Glenview, IL 60025
847-375-4800
Fax: 877-734-9380
E-mail: rbloch@accessgroup.com
http://www.ara.org
Published monthly by the Awards and Recognition Association. Recognition Review is the leading voice of the awards, engraving and recognition industry.

Monthly
Stacy McTaggert, Editor

4284 Regional Spotlight

Southern Regional Education Board
592 10th Street NW
Atlanta, GA 30318-5776

404-875-9211
News of educational interest directed to 15 SREB-member states.

9 pages
Margaret Sullivan

4285 Remedial and Special Education

Pro-Ed., Inc.
8700 Shoal Creek Boulevard
Austin, TX 78757-6816
512-451-3246
800-897-3202
Fax: 512-302-9129
E-mail: proed1@aol.com
http://www.proedinc.com
Highest-quality interdisciplinary scholarship that bridges the gap between theory and practice involving the education of individuals for whom typical instruction is not effective.

Bi-Monthly Magazine
ISSN: 0741-9325

Edward A Polloway, EdD, Editor-in-Chief

4286 Renaissance Educator

Renaissance Educational Associates
4817 N County Road 29
Loveland, CO 80538-9515
970-679-4300
Quarterly publication highlighting educators around the world who are revealing the effectiveness of integrity in education.

8 pages Quarterly
Kristy Clark

4287 Research in Higher Education

Kluwer Academic/Human Sciences Press
233 Spring Street
New York, NY 10013
212-620-8000
800-221-9369
Fax: 212-463-0742
http://www.wkpa.nl
Essential source of new information for all concerned with the functioning of postsecondary educational institutions. Publishes original, quantitative research articles which contribute to an increased understanding of an institution, aid faculty in making more informed decisions about current or future operations, and improve the efficiency of an institution.

Bimonthly
ISSN: 0361-0365

Carol Bischoff, Publisher
John C Smart, Editor

4288 Research in the Schools

Mid-South Educational Research Association
University of Alabama
Tuscaloosa, AL 35487-0001
Fax: 205-348-6873
A nationally refereed journal sponsored by the Mid-South Educational Research Association and the University of Alabama. RITS publishes original contributions in the following areas: 1) Research in practice; 2) Topical Articles; 3) Methods and Techniques; 4) Assessment and 5) Other topics of interest dealing with school-based research. Contributions should follow the guidelines in the latest edition of the Publications Manual of the American Psychological Association.

James E McLean, Co-Editor
Alan S Kaufman, Co-Editor

4289 Roeper Review: A Journal on Gifted Education

Roeper Institute
PO Box 329
Bloomfield Hills, MI 48303-0329
248-203-7321
Fax: 248-203-7310
E-mail: tcross@bsu.edu
http://www.roeperreview.org

A journal that focuses on gifted and talented education, the Roeper Review applies the highest standards of peer review journalism to cover a broad range of issues. For professionals who work with teachers and for professionals who work directly with gifted and talented children and their families, the journal provides readable coverage of policy issues. Each issue covers one or more subjects. Regular departments include research reports and book reviews.

60-80 pages Quarterly
ISSN: 0278-3193

Tracy L Cross PhD, Editor
Vicki Rossbach, Subsciption

4290 Rural Educator: Journal for Rural and Small Schools

National Rural Education Association
246 E Ed Building
Colorado State University
Fort Collins, CO 80523-1588
970-491-7022
Fax: 970-491-1317
E-mail: jnewlin@lamar.colostate.edu
http://www.colostate.edu
Official journal of the NREA. A nationally recognized publication that features timely and informative articles written by leading rural educators from all levels of education. All NREA members are encouraged to submit research articles and items of general information for publication.

40 pages TriAnnual

Joseph T Newlin, Editor

4291 SEDL Letter

Southwestern Educational Development Laboratory
4700 Mueller Boulevard
Austin, TX 78701
512-476-6861
800-476-6861
Fax: 512-476-2286
E-mail: info@sedl.org
http://www.sedl.org
A biannual letter that complements and draws on work and performed by SEDL under a variety of funding sources, including the US Department of Education and the US government.

ISBN: 520-7315

Laura Shankland, Editor

4292 SKOLE: A Journal of Alternative Education

Down-To-Earth Books
72 Philip Street
Albany, NY 12202-1729
518-432-1578
Publishes articles, poems, and research by people engaged in alternative education.

200 pages SemiAnnually

Mary Leue

4293 SNEA Impact: The Student Voice of the Teaching Profession

National Education Association (NEA)
1201 16th Street NW
Washington, DC 20036-3207
202-822-7131
Fax: 202-822-7624
Offers articles and views on current events and the educational system through students' eyes for education professionals.

7x Year

4294 Safety Forum

Safety Society
1900 Association Drive
Reston, VA 20191-1502
703-476-3440

Offers articles and up-to-date information on school safety.

4 pages TriQuarterly

Linda Moore

4295 School Bus Fleet

Bobit Business Media
3520 Challenger Street
Torrance, CA 90503
310-533-2400
Fax: 310-533-2512
E-mail: sbf@bobit.com
http://www.schoolbusfleet.com
Coverage of federal vehicle and education regulations that affect pupil transportation, policy and management issues and, of course, how to improve the safety of children riding yellow buses. Special sections include how to transport students with disabilities, a state report on regulations and legislation, and various other departments. School officials that manage finance operations at school districts, private contractors, school bus manufacturers are the audience.

Frank Di Giacomo, Publisher
Steve Hirano, Editor/Associate Publisher

4296 School Foodservice & Nutrition

1600 Duke Street
Floor 7
Alexandria, VA 22314-3421
703-739-3900
800-877-8822
Fax: 703-739-3915
For foodservice professionals presenting current articles on industry issues, management events, legislative issues, public relations programs and professional development news.

11x Year

Adrienne Gall Tufts, Editor

4297 School Law Bulletin

Quinlan Publishing
23 Drydock Avenue
Boston, MA 02210-2336
617-542-0048
Covers cases and laws pertaining to schools.

8 pages Monthly

4298 School Safety

National School Safety Center
141 Duesenberg Drive
Suite 11
Westlake Village, CA 91362-3815
805-373-9977
800-453-7461
Fax: 805-373-9277
E-mail: rstephens@nssc1.org
http://www.nssc1.org
For educators, law enforcers, judges and legislators on the prevention of drugs, gangs, weapons, bullying, discipline problems and vandalism; also on-site security and character development as they relate to students and schools.

Monthly

Dr. Ronald D Stephens, Executive Director
June Lane Arnette, Editor

4299 School Transportation News

STN Media Company Inc.
700 Torrance Boulevard
Suite C
Redondo Beach, CA 90277
310-792-2226
Fax: 310-792-2231
E-mail: bpaul@stnonline.com
http://www.stnonline.com
Covers school district and contractor fleets, special needs and prekindergarten transportation, Head Start, and more on a monthly basis. Reports developments affecting public

school transportation supervisors and directors, state directors of school transportation, school bus contractors, special needs transportation, Head Start transportation, private school transportation, school business officials responsible for transportation and industry suppliers.

Magazine/Monthly
100 booths

Bill Paul, Author
Colette Paul, VP
Bill Paul, Publisher/Editor

4300 School Zone

West Aurora Public Schools, District 129
80 S River Street
#14
Aurora, IL 60506-5178
630-844-4400
Informs the community of what is happening in their schools, with their students, and with their tax dollars.

4 pages 5x Year

Laurel Chivari

4301 Shaping the Future

Lutheran Education Association
7400 Augusta Street
River Forest, IL 60305-1402
708-209-3343
Fax: 708-209-3458
E-mail: lea@lea.org
http://www.lea.org
Newsletter for LEA members to focus on the unique spiritual and professional needs of church workers and to celebrate life in the ministry. Resource information for the organization, upcoming events, encouragement for pre-planning.

Dr. Johnathan Laabs, Contact

4302 Sharing Space

Creative Urethanes, Children's Creative Response
PO Box 271
Nyack, NY 10960-0271
845-358-4601
Trains all those working with children to communicate positivity and cooperation.

12 pages TriAnnually

4303 Special Education Leadership

LifeWay Church Resources
One LifeWay Plaza
Nashville, TN 37234
615-251-2000
Fax: 615-251-5933
Covers special education issues relating to religious education.

52 pages Quarterly

Ben Garner, Editor-in-Chief
Ellen Beene, Editor

4304 Special Educator

LRP Publications
1901 N Moore Street
Suite 700
Arlington, VA 22209
703-516-7002
800-341-7874
Fax: 703-516-9313
E-mail: custserve@lrp.com
http://www.lrp.com
Covers important issues in the field of special education, including such topics as law and administrative policy.

22 pages 22 Issues Per Year
ISSN: 1047-1618

4305 Star News

Jefferson Center for Character Education
PO Box 1283
Monrovia, CA 91017-1283

949-770-7602
Fax: 949-450-1100
Mission is to produce and promote programs to teach children the concepts, skills and behavior of good character, common core values, personal and civic responsibility, workforce readiness and citizenship.

Quarterly
Robert Jamieson, CEO
Sharon McClenahan, Administrative Assistant

4306 Statewise: Statistical & Research Newsletter
State Board of Education, Planning & Research
PO Box 1402
Dover, DE 19903-1402
302-736-4601
Fax: 302-739-4654
Statistical data relating to Delaware public schools.

2 pages

4307 Street Scenes
(APO Street College of Education
610 W 112th Street
New York, NY 10025-1898
212-222-6700
Fax: 212-222-6700
New ideas in education.

8 pages SemiAnnually
Renee Creange

4308 Supreme Court Debates
Congressional Digest Corp.
4416 East West Highway
Suite 400
Bethesda, MD 20814-4568
301-634-3113
800-637-9915
Fax: 301-634-3189
E-mail: griff.thomas@pro-and-con.org
http://www.pro-and-con.org
An independent publication featuring controversies before the U.S. Supreme Court, pro-and-con.

ISSN: 1099-5390
Delores Baisden, Assistant

4309 Teacher$ Talk
Teachers Insurance and Annuity Association
730 3rd Avenue
New York, NY 10017-3206
212-490-9000
Fax: 800-914-8922
Offers timely information and helpful hints about savings, investments, finance and insurance for teachers and educators.

Quarterly
Robert D Williams, Editor

4310 Teaching Exceptional Children
Council for Exceptional Children
2900 Crystal Drive
Suite 1000
Arlington, VA 22202-3557
703-620-3660
888-232-7733
Fax: 703-264-9494
E-mail: service@cec.sped.org
http://www.cec.sped.org
Features practical articles that present methods and materials for classroom use as well as current issues in special education teaching and learning. Published four times per year, free with membership or $86.00 for individual subscription.

Marilyn Friend, President
Bruce Ramirez, Executive Director

4311 Telluride Newsletter
217 W Avenue
Ithaca, NY 14850-3980
607-273-5011
Fax: 607-272-2667
News of interest to alumni of Telluride Association sponsored programs.

8 pages TriQuarterly
Eric Lemer

4312 Tennessee Education
University of Tennessee
College of Education
Knoxville, TN 37996-0001
865-974-5252
Fax: 865-974-8718
E-mail: scarey@utk.edu
Publishes articles on topics related to K through higher education.

BiAnnually
ISSN: 0739-0408
Sue Carey, Editor

4313 Tennessee School Board Bulletin
Tennessee School Boards Association
500 13th Avenue N
Nashville, TN 37203-2884
Articles of interest to boards of education.

6 pages
Daniel Tollett, Publisher
Holly Hewitt, Editor

4314 The Sounds and Spelling Patterns of English: P Honics for Teachers and Parents
Oxton House Publishers, LLC
Po Box 209
Farmington, ME 04938
207-779-1923
800-539-7323
Fax: 207-779-0623
E-mail: info@oxtonhouse.com
http://www.oxtonhouse.com
A clear, concise, practical, jargon-free overview of the sounds that make up the English language and the symbols that we use to represent them in writing. It includes a broad range of strategies for helping beginning readers develop fluent decoding skills.

62 pages
William Berlinghoff, Managing Editor
Bobby Brown, Marketing Director

4315 Theory Into Practice
Ohio State University, College of Education
122 Ramseyer Hall
29 W Woodruff Avenue
Columbus, OH 43210
614-292-3407
Fax: 614-292-7900
E-mail: tip@osu.edu
http://www.coe.ohio-state.edu
Nationally recognized for excellence in educational journalism; thematic format, providing comprehensive discussion of single topic with many diverse points of view.

Quarterly
ISSN: 0040-5841
Anita Woolfolk Hey, Author

4316 This Active Life
National Education Association (NEA)
1201 16th Street NW
Washington, DC 20036-3207
202-822-7125
Fax: 202-822-7624
http://www.nea.org/retired

Serves as a resource in the maintenance of quality public education.

20 pages Bi-Monthly
ISSN: 1526-9342
John O'Neil, Editor

4317 Three R'S for Teachers: Research, Reports & Reviews
Master Teacher
Po Box 1207
Manhattan, KS 66502
785-539-0555
800-669-9633
Fax: 800-669-1132
http://www.masterteacher.com
The publication that synthesizes the most recent educational research, data and trends on specific topics for teachers.

Quarterly
Alice King, Executive Editor

4318 Tidbits
Assn. for Legal Support of Alternative Schools
PO Box 2823
Santa Fe, NM 87504-2823
505-471-6928
Information and legal advice to those involved in non-public educational facilities.

12 pages Quarterly
Ed Nagel

4319 Transitions Abroad: The Guide to Learning, Living, & Working Abroad
Transitions Abroad
PO Box 745
Bennington, VT 05201
802-442-4827
Fax: 802-442-4827
E-mail: editor@transitionsabroad.com
http://www.transitionsabroad.com
This magazine contains articles and bibliographies on travel, study, teaching, internships and work abroad.

Bi-Monthly

4320 Unschoolers Network
2 Smith Street
Farmingdale, NJ 07727-1006
732-938-2473
Information and support for families teaching their children at home.

14 pages Monthly
Nancy Plent

4321 VSBA Newsletter
Vermont School Boards Association
2 Prospect Street
Montpelier, VT 05602-3555
802-223-3580
General information.

16 pages Monthly
Donald Jamieson

4322 WCER Highlights
Wisconsin Center for Education Research
1025 W Johnson Street
Suite 785
Madison, WI 53706-1706
608-263-8814
Fax: 608-263-6448
News about research conducted at the Wisconsin Center for Education Research.

8 pages Quarterly
ISSN: 1073-1882
Paul Baker, Editor

4323 WestEd: Focus
WestEd
730 Harrison Street
San Francisco, CA 94107-1242

415-615-3144
877-493-7833
Fax: 415-512-2024
E-mail: info@WestEd .org
http://www.WestEd.org
Improving education through research, development and service.

Mark Kerr, Manager of Organizational
Danny Torres, Publications Manager

4324 Western Journal of Black Studies
Washington State University
Heritage House
Pullman, WA 99164-0001
509-335-8681
Fax: 509-335-8338
A journal which canvasses topical issues affecting Black studies and education.

Quarterly

Talmadge Anderson, Editor

4325 World Gifted
World Council for Gifted & Talented
Children
Purdue University
1446 S Campus
West Lafayette, IN 47907
Offers information and articles on gifted education for the professional.

4326 Young Audiences Newsletter
115 E 92nd Street
New York, NY 10128-1688
212-831-8110
Fax: 212-289-1202
Organization news of performing arts education programs in schools and communities.

Annual

Jane Bak

Periodicals / Administration

4327 AACRAO Data Dispenser
American Association of Collegiate
Registrars
1 Dupont Circle NW
Suite 330
Washington, DC 20036-1137
202-293-9161
Fax: 202-872-8857
Association newsletter for US and foreign postsecondary education institution professionals involved in admissions, records and registration.

12 pages 10x Year

Eileen Kennedy, Editor

4328 AASA Bulletin
American Association of School
Administrators
801 N Quincy Street
Suite 700
Arlington, VA 22203-1730
703-528-0700
Fax: 703-841-1543
E-mail: info@aasa.org
http://www.aasa.org
The AASA Bulletin is a supplement to The School Administrator. It contains the Job Bulletin and information for school leaders about the many products, services and events available to them from AASA.

Ginger O'Neil, Editor
Kari Arfstrom, Project Director

4329 ACCT Advisor
Association of Community College Trustees
1233 20th Street NW
Suite 605
Washington, DC 20036-2907

202-775-4667
Fax: 202-223-1297
http://www.acct.org
Provides news of association events, federal regulations, activities, state activities, legal issues and other news of interest to community college governing board members.

Ray Taylor, ACCT President
Alvin Major II, Director
Mktg/Communications

4330 AVA Update
Association for Volunteer Administration
PO Box 4584
Boulder, CO 80306-4584
303-447-0558
Information of value to administrators of volunteer services.

4 pages BiMonthly

Martha Martin

4331 Accreditation Fact Sheet
NAPNSC Accrediting Commission for
Higher Education
182 Thompson Road
Grand Junction, CO 81503-2246
970-243-5441
Fax: 970-242-4392
E-mail: director@napnsc.org
http://www.napnsc.org
Newsletter reporting on the origin, history, developments, procedures and changes of educational institution accreditation.

Annually

H. Earl Heusser, Author
H Earl Heusser, Executive Director

4332 Administrative Information Report
Nat'l Association of Secondary School
Principles
1904 Association Drive
Reston, VA 20191-1502
703-860-0200
800-253-7746
Fax: 703-620-6534
Offers school statistics and administrative updates for secondary school principals and management officers.

4 pages Monthly

Thomas Koerner, Editor

4333 American School & University
Magazine
Intertec Publishing
PO Box 12960
Overland Park, KS 66282-2960
913-967-1960
Fax: 913-967-1905
Directed at business and facilities administrators in the nation's public and private schools.

Monthly

Joe Agron, Editor

4334 American School Board Journal
National School Boards Association
1680 Duke Street
Alexandria, VA 22314-3455
703-838-6722
Fax: 703-549-6719
E-mail: editor@asbj.com
Published primarily for school board members and school system superintendents serving public elementary and secondary schools in the United States and Canada.

Monthly

Anne L Bryant, Executive Publisher
Harold P Seamon, Deputy Executive
Publisher

4335 Board
Master Teacher
Leadership Lane
PO Box 1207
Manhattan, KS 66502
800-669-9633
Fax: 800-669-1132
http://www.masterteacher.com
Designed to be a continuous form of communication to help board members know and understand the duties, responsibilities, and commitments of the office; view the superintendent of schools as the educational leader; improve administrator-board working relationships; better understand the purpose of education; and work at their responsibilities in a prudent, calm, and rational manner.

Monthly

Robert DeBruyn, Editor

4336 Building Leadership Bulletin
2990 Baker Drive
Springfield, IL 62703-2800
217-525-1383
Fax: 217-525-7264
http://www.ipa.vsta.net
Topical, timely issues.

8 pages 11x Year

Julie Weichert, Associate Director

4337 Business Education Forum
National Business Education Association
1914 Association Drive
Reston, VA 20191-1538
703-860-8300
Fax: 703-620-4483
A journal of distinctive articles dealing with current issues and trends, future directions and exemplary programs in business education at all instructional levels. Articles focus on international business, life-long learning, cultural diversity, critical thinking, economics, state-of-the-art technology and the latest research in the field.

200 pages Quarterly

Janet M Treichel, Executive Director
Regina McDowell, Editor

4338 CASE Currents
1307 New York Avenue NW
Suite 1000
Washington, DC 20036-1226
202-328-2273
Fax: 202-387-4973
Covers the world of fund raising, alumni administration, public relations, periodicals, publications and student recruitment in higher education.

10x Year

Karla Taylor, Editor

4339 CASE Newsletter
The Council for Exceptional Children
1920 Association Drive
Reston, VA 20191-1545
703-620-3660
888-232-7733
Fax: 703-264-9494
News about CASE activities, upcoming events, current trends and practices, state and national legislation, and other practical information relevant to the administration of special education programs.

5x Year

Jo Thomason, Editor

4340 CASE in Point
The Council for Exceptional Children
1920 Association Drive
Reston, VA 20191-1545

703-620-3660
888-232-7733
Fax: 703-264-9494
A journal reporting on emerging promising practices, current research, contact points for expanded information, and field-based commentary relevant to the administration of special education programs.

BiAnnual

Donnie Evans, Editor

4341 California Schools Magazine
California School Boards Association
3100 Beacon Boulevard
West Sacramento, CA 95691
916-371-4691
Fax: 916-372-3369
For school board members, superintendents and school business managers, responsible for the operation of California's public schools. Articles of interest to parents, teachers, community members and anyone else concerned with public education.

20 pages Quarterly
ISSN: 1081-8936

Mina G Fasulo, Executive Editor

4342 Clearing House: A Journal of Educational Research
Heldref Publications
1319 18th Street NW
Washington, DC 20036-1826
202-296-6267
800-365-9753
Fax: 202-296-5149
E-mail: tch@heldfred.org
Each issue offers a variety of articles for teachers and administrators of middle schools and junior and senior high schools. It includes experiments, trends and accomplishments in courses, teaching methods, administrative procedures and school programs.

4 pages BiMonthly
ISSN: 0009-8655

Deborah N Cohen, Promotions Manager
Judy Cusick, Managing Editor

4343 Connection
National Association of State Boards of Education
277 S Washington Street
Suite 100
Alexandria, VA 22314
703-684-4000
Fax: 703-836-2313
Quarterly magazine for state board of education members.

10 pages

David Kysilko, Editor

4344 Developer
National Staff Development Council
PO Box 240
Oxford, OH 45056-0240
513-523-6029
Fax: 513-523-0638
Devoted to staff development for educational personnel.

8 pages 10x Year

Dennis Sparks

4345 ERS Spectrum
Educational Research Service
1001 N. Fairfax Street
Suite 500
Arlington, VA 22314-1587
703-243-2100
800-791-9308
Fax: 703-243-1985

E-mail: ers@ers.org
http://www.ers.org
A quarterly journal of school research and information. Publishes practical research and information for school decisions. Authors include practicing administrators and other educators in local school districts.

48 pages Quarterly
ISSN: 0740-7874

John C Draper, Ed.D., CEO
Katherine A Behrens, COO

4346 Education Daily
LRP Publications
1901 N Moore Street
Suite 1106
Arlington, VA 22209
703-516-7002
800-341-7874
Fax: 703-516-9313
E-mail: custserve@lrp.com
http://www.lrp.com
News on national education policy. Offers daily reports of Education Department policies, initiatives and priorities— how they are developed and how they affect school programs.

6-8 pages Daily

4347 Educational Administration Quarterly
University of Wisconsin, Milwaukee
PO Box 413
Milwaukee, WI 53201-0413
414-229-4740
Fax: 414-229-5300
Deals with administrative issues and policy.

Quarterly

Dr. James Cibulka, Editor

4348 Electronic Learning
Scholastic
555 Broadway
New York, NY 10012-3919
212-343-6100
800-724-6527
Fax: 212-343-4801
Published for the administrative level, education professionals who are directly responsible for the implementing of electronic technology at the district, state and university levels.

8x Year

Lynn Diamond, Advertising Director
Therese Mageau, Editor

4349 Enrollment Management Report
LRP Publications
1901 N Moore Street
Suite 700
Arlington, VA 22209
703-516-7002
800-341-7874
Fax: 703-516-9313
E-mail: custserve@lrp.com
http://www.lrp.com
Provides colleges and universities with solutions and strategies for recruitment, admissions, retention and financial aid. Reviews the latest trends, research studies and their findings and gives a profile on how other institutions are handling their enrollment management issues.

Monthly
ISSN: 1094-3757

4350 Galileo For Superintendents And District Level Administrators
Master Teacher
Po Box 1207
Manhattan, KS 66505-1207

785-539-0555
800-669-9633
Fax: 800-669-1132
http://www.masterteacher.com
The monthly web and print service provides direction & strategies for superintendents and district level administrators.

Monthly Newsletter

Rick Stultz, Executive Editor

4351 HR on Campus
LRP Publications
1901 N Moore Street
Suite 700
Arlington, VA 22209
703-516-7002
800-341-7874
Fax: 703-516-9313
E-mail: custserve@lrp.com
http://www.lrp.com
This monthly newsletter provides coverage of the latest and most inovative programs higher education institutions use to handle their human resource challenges. Plus, you can recieve free e-mail updates on crucial news affecting your job with your paid subscription.

Monthly
ISSN: 1098-9293

4352 IPA Newsletter
2990 Baker Drive
Springfield, IL 62703-2800
217-525-1383
Fax: 217-525-7264
http://www.ipa.vsta.net
Provides current information on Illinois principals and the profession.

8 pages 11x Year

David Turner, Author
Julie Weichert, Associate Director

4353 Integrated Pathways
Association of Integrative Studies
Miami University
Oxford, OH 45056
513-529-2659
Fax: 513-529-5849
E-mail: aisorg@muohio.edu
http://www.units.muohio.edu/aisorg
AIS news, including updates on AIS conferences, decisions of the AIS Board of Directors, and membership announcements. Published quarterly.

ISSN: 1081-647X

William H Newell, Editor

4354 Journal of Curriculum & Supervision
Association for Supervision & Curriculum Develop.
1703 N Beauregard Street
Alexandria, VA 22311-1714
512-471-4611
Fax: 512-471-8460
E-mail: oldavisjr@mail.uteyas.edu
http://www.ascd.org/framejcs.html
Offers professional updates and news as well as membership/association information.

Quarterly Paperback

OL Davis Jr, Editor

4355 Journal of Education for Business
Heldref Publications
1319 18th Street NW
Washington, DC 20036-1802
202-296-6267
800-365-9753
Fax: 202-296-5149
http://www.heldref.org
Offers information to instructors, supervisors, and administrators at the secondary, postsecondary and collegiate levels. The journal features basic and applied research-based articles in accounting, communications, economics, fi-

nance, information systems, management, marketing and other business disciplines.

BiMonthly

4356 Keystone Schoolmaster Newsletter

Pennsylvania Assn. of Secondary School Principals
PO Box 953
Easton, PA 18044-0953
215-253-8516
Reports achievements, honors, problems and innovations by officers and established authorities.

4 pages Monthly

Joseph Mamana, Contact

4357 LSBA Quarter Notes

Louisiana School Boards Association
7912 Summa Avenue
Baton Rouge, LA 70809-3416
News articles relative to the association, feature stories on research.

6 pages BiMonthly

Victor Hodgkins

4358 Legal Notes for Education

Progressive Business Publications
370 Technology Drive
Malvern, PA 19355
800-220-5000
Fax: 610-647-8089
E-mail: customer_service@pbp.com
http://www.pbp.com
Reports the latest school law cases and late-breaking legislation along with the most recent law review articles affecting education. Federal and state appellate court decisions are summarized and the full legal citation is supplied for each case.

Monthly

4359 Maintaining Safe Schools

LRP Publications
1901 N Moore Street
Suite 700
Arlington, VA 22209
703-516-7002
800-341-7874
Fax: 703-516-9313
E-mail: custserve@lrp.com
http://www.lrp.com
Focuses on the legal and practical issues involved in preventing and responding to violent acts by students in schools, and highlights successful violence prevention programs in school districts across the country. Offers strategies for mediation, discipline and crisis managment.

Monthly
ISSN: 1082-4774

4360 Managing School Business

LRP Publications
1901 N Moore Street
Suite 700
Arlington, VA 22209
703-516-7002
800-341-7874
Fax: 703-516-9313
E-mail: custserve@lrp.com
http://www.lrp.com
Newsletter provides school business managers with tips on how to solve the problems they face in managing finance, operations, personnel, and their own career.

Biweekly
ISSN: 1092-2229

Angela Childers, Author

4361 Memo to the President

American Assn. of State Colleges & Universities
1307 New York Avenue
Washington, DC 20005
202-293-7070
Fax: 202-296-5819
http://www.aascu.org
Monitors public policies at national, state and campus level on higher education issues. Reports on activities of the Association and member institutions.

20 pages Monthly
November

Susan Chilcott, Director Communications

4362 NASPA Forum

National Assn. of Student Personnel Administrators
1875 Connecticut Avenue NW
Suite 418
Washington, DC 20009-5737
202-265-7500
Fax: 202-797-1157
Offers information for personnel administrators and strategies, updates and tips on the education system.

Monthly

Sybil Walker, Editor

4363 National Faculty Forum

National Faculty of Humanities, Arts & Sciences
1676 Clifton Road NE
Atlanta, GA 30329-4050
404-727-5788
Offers administrative news and updates for persons in higher education.

TriQuarterly

4364 Network

National School Public Relations Association
1501 Lee Highway
Suite 201
Arlington, VA 22209-1109
301-519-0496
Fax: 301-519-0494
E-mail: nspra@nspra.org
http://www.nspra.org
Monthly newsletter for and about our members. Some articles about school public relations, issues that affect school public relations people.

Andy Grunig, Editorial Coordinator
Tommy Jones, Advertising/Sales

4365 OASCD Journal

Oklahoma Curriculum Development
3705 S. 98th East Avenue
Tulsa, OK 74146
918-627-4403
Fax: 918-627-4433
A refereed journal which prints contributions on curriculum theory and practices, leadership in education, staff development and supervision. The Editorial Board welcomes photographs, letters to the editor, program descriptions, interviews, research reports, theoretical pieces, reviews of books and non-print media, poetry, humor, cartoons, satire and children's art and writing, as well as expository articles.

Annual

Blaine Smith, Executive Secretary

4366 On Board

New York State School Boards Association
24 Century Hill Drive
Suite 200
Latham, NY 12110-2125
518-783-0200
800-342-3360

Fax: 518-783-0211
E-mail: info@nyssba.org
http://www.nyssba.org
Contains general educational news, state and federal legislative activity, legal and employee relations issues, commentary, issues in education, and successful education programs around the state.

21x Year

4367 Perspectives for Policymakers

New Jersey School Boards Association
413 W State Street
#909
Trenton, NJ 08618-5617
609-695-7600
Each issue focuses on a specific topic in education providing background, activities and resources.

8 pages SemiAnnually

Missy Martin

4368 Planning & Changing

Illinois State University
Dept. of Ed. Admin. & Foundations
Normal, IL 61790-5900
309-438-2399
Fax: 309-438-8683
http://http://coe.ilstu.edu/eafdept/pandc.htm

An educational leadership and policy journal. This journal attempts to disseminate timely and useful reports of practice and theory with particular emphasis on change, and planning in K-12 educational settings and higher education settings. Paperback.

64 pages Quarterly
ISSN: 0032-0684

Judith Mogilka, Editor
Lilly J Meiner, Publications Manager

4369 Principal

Nat'l Association of Elementary School Principals
1615 Duke Street
Alexandria, VA 22314-3406
703-684-3345
Fax: 800-396-2377
A professional magazine edited for elementary and middle school principals and others interested in education.

5x Year

Leon E Greene, Editor
Louanne M Wheeler, Production Manager

4370 Principal Communicator

National School Public Relations Association
15948 Derwood Road
Rockville, MD 20855
301-519-0496
Fax: 301-519-0494
E-mail: nspra@nspra.org
http://www.napra.org
Tips for building public relations people.

6 pages Monthly

Andy Grunig, Manager of Communications

4371 Private Education Law Report

Progressive Business Publications
370 Technology Drive
Malvern, PA 19355
800-220-5000
Fax: 610-647-8089
E-mail: customer_service@pbp.com
http://www.pbp.com
Reports the latest school law cases and late-breaking legislation along with the most recent law review articles affecting private education. Federal and state appellate court

decisions are summarized and the full legal citation is supplied for each case.

Monthly

4372 Public Personnel Management
International Personnel Management Association
1617 Duke Street
Alexandria, VA 22314-3406
703-549-7100
Fax: 703-684-0948
Caters to those professionals in human resource management.

Quarterly

Sarah Al Shiffert, Editor

4373 Rural Educator-Journal for Rural and Small Schools
National Rural Education Association
246 E Ed Building
Colorado State University
Ft. Collins, CO 80523-1588
970-491-7022
Fax: 970-491-1317
E-mail: jnewlin@lamar.colostate.edu
http://www.colostate.edu
Official journal of the NREA. A nationally recognized publication that features timely and informative articles written by leading rural educators from all levels of education. All NREA members are encouraged to submit research articles and items of general information for publication.

40 pages Quarterly Magazine
ISSN: 0273-446X

Joseph T Newlin, Editor

4374 School Administrator
American Association of School Administrators
801 N Quincy Street
Suite 700
Arlington, VA 22203-1730
703-528-0700
Fax: 703-841-1543
E-mail: info@aasa.org
http://www.aasa.org
Ensures the highest quality education systems for all learners through the support and development of leadership on the building, district and state levels.

52 pages Monthly

Paul D Houston, Executive Director

4375 School Business Affairs
Association of School Business Officials Int'l
11401 N Shore Drive
Reston, VA 20190-4232
703-478-0405
Fax: 703-478-0205
For school business administrators responsible for the administration and purchase of products and services for the schools.

Monthly

Peg D Kirkpatrick, Editor/Publisher
Robert Gluck, Managing Editor

4376 School Law Briefings
LRP Publications
1901 N Moore Street
Suite 700
Arlington, VA 22209
703-516-7002
800-341-7874
Fax: 703-516-9313
E-mail: custserve@lrp.com
http://www.lrp.com
Gives you summaries of general education, special education, and early childhood

court cases, as well as administrative hearings.

Monthly
ISSN: 1094-3749

4377 School Law News
LPR Publications
1901 N Moore Street
Suite1106
Arlington, VA 22209
703-516-7002
800-341-7874
Fax: 703-516-9313
E-mail: custserve@lrp.com
http://www.lrp.com
Advises administrators to avoid legal pitfalls by monitoring education-related court action across the nation. With School Law News, administrators receive the latest information on issues like sexual harassment liability, special education, religion in the schools, affirmative action, youth violence, student-faculty rights, school finance, desegregation and much more.

8-10 pages Monthly

4378 School Planning & Management
Peter Li Education Group
330 Progress Road
Dayton, OH 45449-2322
937-293-1415
800-523-4625
Fax: 415-626-0554
For the business needs of school administrators featuring issues, ideas and technology at work in public, private and independent schools.

Monthly
ISSN: 1086-4628

Peter J Li, Publisher
Deborah Moore, Editor

4379 Section 504 Compliance Advisor
LRP Publications
1901 N Moore Street
Suite 700
Arlington, VA 22209
703-516-7002
800-341-7874
Fax: 703-516-9313
E-mail: custserve@lrp.com
http://www.lrp.com
Newsletter examines the requirements of Section 504 of the Rehabilitation Act and analyzes their impact on disciplining students. Provides educators and administrators with detailed tips and advice to help them solve the discipline problems they face everyday and keep their policies and programs in compliance.

Monthly
ISSN: 1094-3730

4380 Special Education Law Monthly
LRP Publications
1901 N Moore Street
Suite 700
Arlington, VA 22209
703-516-7002
800-341-7874
Fax: 703-516-9313
E-mail: custserve@lrp.com
http://www.lrp.com
Covers court decisions and administrative rulings affecting the education of students with disabilities.

Monthly
ISSN: 1094-3773

4381 Special Education Law Report
Progressive Business Publications
370 Technology Drive
Malvern, PA 19355

800-220-5000
Fax: 610-647-8089
E-mail: customer_service@pbp.com
http://www.pbp.com
Reports the latest school law cases and late-breaking legislation along with the most recent law review articles affecting special education. Federal and state appellate court decisions are summarized and the full legal citation is supplied for each case.

Monthly

4382 Special Education Report
LPR Publications
1901 N Moore Street
Suite 1106
Arlington, VA 22209
703-516-7002
800-341-7874
Fax: 703-516-9313
E-mail: custserve@lrp.com
The special education administrator's direct pipeline to federal legislation, regulation and funding of programs for children and youths with disabilities.

6-8 pages Monthly

4383 Student Affairs Today
LRP Publications
1901 N Moore Street
Suite 700
Arlington, VA 22209
703-516-7002
800-341-7874
Fax: 703-516-9313
E-mail: custserve@lrp.com
http://www.lrp.com
Newsletter provides strategies and tips for handling higher education institutions' student affairs challenges and problems involving: sexual harassment, binge drinking, fraternity and sorority activities, student housing and more. Gives profiles of other colleges programs.

Monthly
ISSN: 1098-5166

4384 Superintendents Only Notebook
Master Teacher
Leadership Lane
PO Box 1207
Manhattan, KS 66502
800-669-9633
Fax: 800-669-1132
http://www.masterteacher.com
Offers superintendents hundreds of solid ideas to help their jobs run more smoothly. Written by practicing superintendents and business executives, this publication saves hundreds of hours of anguish over the course of the year.

Monthly

4385 THE Journal Technology Horizons in Education
T.H.E Journal
16261 Laguna Canyon Road
Suite 130
Irvine, CA 92618
949-265-1520
Fax: 949-265-1528
E-mail: wladuke@1105media.com
http://www.thejournal.com
A forum for administrators and managers in school districts to share their experiences in the use of technology-based educational aids.

Wendy LaDuke, Publisher/CEO
Matthew Miller, Editor

4386 Thrust for Educational Leadership
Association of California School Administrators
1517 L Street
Sacramento, CA 95814-4004
916-444-3216
Fax: 916-444-3245

Designed for school administrators who must stay abreast of educational developments, management and personnel practices, social attitudes and issues that impact schools.

7x Year

Tom DeLapp, Communications Director
Susan Davis, Editor

4387 Title I Handbook
Thompson Publishing Group, Inc.
Customer Service Center
PO Box 26185
Tampa, FL 33623-6185
800-677-3789
Fax: 800-759-7179
http://www.titleionline.com
Two-volume looseleaf provides complete, up-to-date coverage of Title I, the largest federal program of aid for elementary and secondary education. The book contains all the laws, regulations and guidance needed to sucessfully operate the grant program, and insightful articles on key Title I topics, ongoing budget coverage, and special reports on issues like Title I testing, schoolwide programs, and audits. Also included is a compilation of official Title I policy letters, found nowhere else.

1,500 pages Quarterly

Cheryl L. Sattler, Author

4388 Title I Monitor
Thompson Publishing Group, Inc.
Customer Service Center
PO Box 26185
Tampa, FL 33623-6185
202-872-4000
800-876-0226
Fax: 202-739-9578
http://www.titleionline.com
This newsletter provides continuing coverage of Title I, the largest federal program of aid for elementary and secondary education. Title I is at the heart of the debate over education reform, and the Monitor ensures that educators have the most up-to-date information about developments in this ever-changing program. Breaking news about the Title I budget, new legislation and regulations, court cases and other issues.

Monthly
ISSN: 1086-2455

Cheryl L Sattler, Author

4389 Training Magazine
Lakewood Publications
50 S 9th Street
Minneapolis, MN 55402-3118
612-333-0471
800-328-4329
Fax: 612-333-6526
Focuses on corporate training and employee development, as well as management and human performance issues.

Monthly

Jack Gordon, Editor

4390 Updating School Board Policies
National School Boards Association
1680 Duke Street
Alexandria, VA 22314-3455
703-838-6722
Fax: 703-683-7590
Offers information and statistics for school boards and administrative offices across the country.

16 pages BiMonthly
ISSN: 1081-8286

Michael Wessely, Editor

Periodicals / Early Childhood Education

4391 Child Development
Arizona State University
Department of Psychology
Tempe, AZ 85287
480-965-3326
Fax: 480-965-8544
http://www.asu.edu
Offers professionals working with children news on childhood education, books, reviews, questions and answers and professional articles of interest.

BiMonthly

Susan C Somerville

4392 Child Study Journal
Buffalo State College
1300 Elmwood Avenue
#306
Buffalo, NY 14222-1004
716-878-5302
Articles of interest related to childhood education.

Quarterly

Donald E Carter

4393 Children Today
ACF Office of Public Affairs
370 Lenfant Plaza SW
Floor 7
Washington, DC 20560-0002
202-401-9218
Fax: 202-205-9688
An interdisciplinary magazine published by the Administration for Children and Families (ACF). The content is a mix of theory and practice, research and features, news and opinions for its audience.

Quarterly

4394 Children and Families
National Head Start Association
1651 Prince Street
Alexandria, VA 22314-2818
703-739-0875
Fax: 703-739-0878
http://www.nhsa.org
Designed to support the Head Start programs, directors, staff, parents and volunteers.

Quarterly
ISSN: 1091-7578

Julie Konieczny, Editor

4395 Division for Children with Communication Disorders Newsletter
The Council for Exceptional Children
1920 Association Drive
Reston, VA 20191-1545
703-620-3660
800-232-7323
Fax: 703-264-1637
Information concerning education and welfare of children with communication disorders.

12 pages SemiAnnually

Christine DeSouza, Editor

4396 Early Childhood Education Journal
Kluwer Academic/Human Sciences Press
233 Spring Street
New York, NY 10013
212-620-8000
Fax: 212-463-0742
http://www.wkpa.nl
Provides professional guidance on instructional methods and materials, child develop-

ment trends, funding and administrative issues and the politics of day care.

Quarterly
ISSN: 1082-3301

Carol Bischoff, Publisher
Mary Renck Jalongo, Editor

4397 Early Childhood Report
LRP Publications
1901 N Moore Street
Suite 700
Arlington, VA 22209
703-516-7002
800-341-7874
Fax: 703-516-9313
E-mail: custserve@lrp.com
http://www.lrp.com
Educational newsletter for parents and professionals involved at the local state and federal levels responsible for the design and implementation of early childhood programs.

Monthly
ISSN: 1058-6482

4398 Early Childhood Research Quarterly
Department of Individuals & Family Syudies
111 Alison Annex
University of Delaware
Newark, DE 19716
302-831-8552
Fax: 302-831-8776
Addresses various topics in the development and education of young children.

Quarterly

Dr. Marion Hyson, Editor

4399 Early Childhood Today
Scholastic
555 Broadway
New York, NY 10012
212-343-6100
800-724-6527
Fax: 212-343-4801
E-mail: ect@scholastic.com
http://www.scholastic.com
The magazine for all early childhood professionals working with infants to six-year-olds. Each issue provides child development information resources, staff development information and parent communication information.

8x Year
ISSN: 1070-1214

Ellen Christian, Publisher
Jill Strauss, Managing Editor

4400 Highlights for Children
PO Box 269
Columbus, OH 43216
800-255-9517
Magazine featuring Fun with a Purpose, to all children preschool to preteen. Features stories, hidden pictures, reading and thinking exercises, crafts, puzzles, and more.

4401 Journal of Early Intervention
The Council for Exceptional Children
1920 Association Drive
Reston, VA 20191-1545
703-620-3660
800-232-7323
Fax: 703-264-1637

Quarterly
ISSN: 0885-3460

4402 Journal of Research in Childhood Education
Association for Childhood Education International
17904 Georgia Avenue
Suite 215
Olney, MD 20832

301-570-2111
800-423-3563
Fax: 301-570-2212
Current research in education and related fields. It is intended to advance knowledge and theory of the education of children, from infancy through early adolescence. The journal seeks to stimulate the exchange of research ideas through publication of: reports of empirical research; theroretical articles; ethnographic and case studies; cross-cultural studies and studies addressing international concerns; participant observation studies and, studies, deriving data collected.

142 pages BiAnnual
ISSN: 0256-8543

4403 NHSA Journal
National Head Start Association
1651 Prince Street
Alexandria, VA 22314-2818
703-739-0875
Fax: 703-739-0878
Edited for Head Start communities serving children 3 to 5 years of age throughout the country. The journal is an invaluable resource containing current research, innovative programming ideas, details on the Head Start conferences and training events.

Quarterly

Ethan Salwen, Editor

4404 National Guild of Community Schools of the Arts
National Guild of Community Schools of the Arts
520 8th Avenue
Suite 302, 3rd Floor
New York, NY 10018
212-268-3337
Fax: 212-268-3995
E-mail: info@natguild.org
http://www.nationalguild.org
National association of community based arts education institutions employment opportunities, guildnotes newsletter, and publications catalog. See www.nationalguild.org.

Monthly

Noah Xifr, Director Membership/Oper.

4405 Parents Make the Difference!: School Readiness Edition
The Parent Institute
PO Box 7474
Fairfax Station, VA 22039-7474
703-323-9170
Fax: 703-323-9173
http://www.parent-institute.com
Newsletter focusing on parent involvement in education. Focuses on parents of children ages infant to five.

Monthly
ISSN: 1089-3075

John Wherry, Publisher

4406 Pre-K Today
Scholastic
555 Broadway
New York, NY 10012-3919
212-343-6100
800-724-6527
Fax: 212-343-4801
Edited to serve the needs of early childhood professionals, owners, directors, teachers and administrators in preschools and kindergarten.

8x Year

Ellen Christian, Editor

4407 Report on Preschool Programs
Business Publishers
8737 Colesville Road
Suite 1100
Silver Spring, MD 20910-3928
301-587-6300
800-274-6737
Fax: 301-585-9075
E-mail: bpinews@bpinews.com
http://www.bpinews.com
Reports on information about Head Start regulations, federal funding policies, state trends in Pre-K and research news. Also covers information on grant and contract opportunities.

8 pages BiWeekly

Eric Easton, Publisher
Chuck Devarics, Editor

4408 Topics in Early Childhood Special Education
Pro-Ed
8700 Shoal Creek Boulevard
Austin, TX 78757-6816
512-451-3246
800-897-3202
Fax: 512-302-9129
http://www.proedinc.com
Provides program developers, advocates, researchers, higher education faculty and other leaders with the most current, relevant research on all aspects of early childhood education for children with special needs.

Judith J Carta, PhD, Editor

4409 Totline Newsletter
Frank Schaffer Publications
23740 Hawthorne Boulevard
Torrance, CA 90505
310-378-1137
800-421-5533
Fax: 800-837-7260
E-mail: fspcustsrv@aol.com
http://www.frankschaffer.com
Creative activities for working with toddlers and preschool children.

32 pages BiMonthly

4410 Vision
SERVE
PO Box 5367
Greensboro, NC 27435
336-315-7400
800-755-3277
Fax: 336-315-7457
E-mail: cahearn@serve.org
http://www.serve.org
Publication of the Regional Educational Laboratories, an educational research and development organization supported by contracts with the US Education Department, National Institute for Education Sciences. Specialty area: Extended Learning Opportunity including Before and After School programs and Early Childhood.

Quarterly

Charles Ahearn, Author
Jack Sanders, Executive Director

Periodicals / Elementary Education

4411 Children's Literature in Education
Kluwer Academic/Human Sciences Press
233 Spring Street
New York, NY 10013
212-620-8000
Fax: 212-463-0742
http://www.wkpa.nl

Source for stimulating articles and interviews on noted children's authors, incisive critiques of classic and contemporary writing for young readers, and original articles describing successful classroom reading projects. Offers timely reviews on a variety of reading-related topics for teachers and teachers-in-training, librarians, writers and interested parents.

Quarterly
ISSN: 0045-6713

Margaret Mackey & Geoff Fox, Editors, Author
Carol Bischoff, Publisher

4412 Creative Classroom
Creative Classroom Publishing
149 5th Avenue
12th Floor
New York, NY 10010
212-353-3639
Fax: 212-353-8030
http://www.creativeclassroom.com
A magazine for teachers of K-8, containing innovative ideas, activities, classroom management tips and information on contemporary social problems facing teachers and students.

BiMonthly

Susan Eveno, Editorial Director
Laura Axler, Associate Editor

4413 Dragonfly
National Science Teachers Association
1840 Wilson Boulevard
Arlington, VA 22201-3000
703-243-7100
800-782-6782
Fax: 703-243-7177
http://www.nsta.org
A fun-filled interdisciplinary magazine for children grades 3-6. A teacher's companion is also available. The teacher's companion is designed to help you integrate Dragonfly into your curriculum.

Dr. Gerald Wheeler, Executive Director
Shelley Johnson Carey, Managing Editor

4414 Educate@Eight
US Department of Education, Region VIII
1244 Speer Boulevard
Suite 310
Denver, CO 80204-3582
303-844-3544
Fax: 303-844-2524
http://www.ed.gov

8 pages

Helen Littlejohn, Author

4415 Elementary School Journal
University of Missouri
1507 E Broadway
Hillcrest Hall
Columbia, MO 65211
573-882-7889
Academic journal publishing primarily original studies but also reviews of research and conceptual analyses for researchers and practitioners interested in elementary schooling. Emphasizes papers dealing with educational theory and research and their implications.

5x Year

Thomas L Good, Editor
Gail M Hinkel, Managing Editor

4416 Elementary Teacher's Ideas and Materials Workshop
Princeton Educational Publishers
117 Cuttermill Road
Great Neck, NY 11021-3101
516-466-9300
Articles on teaching for elementary schools.

16 pages 10x Year

Barry Pavelec

4417 Helping Your Child Succeed in Elementary School
Rowman & Littlfield Education
4501 Forbes Boulevard
Suite 200
Lanham, MD 20706
301-459-3366
Fax: 301-429-5748
http://www.rowmaneducation.com
Provides parents with useful information about the importance of parental involvement, concrete ways to work with children and schools to promote success, and a list of resources for further reading.

4418 Highlights for Children
PO Box 269
Columbus, OH 43216-0269
800-255-9517
Fax: 614-876-8564
Magazine featuring Fun with a Purpose, to all children preschool to preteen. Features stories, hidden pictures, reading and thinking exercises, crafts, puzzles, and more.

4419 Independent School
National Association of Independent Schools
75 Federal Street
Boston, MA 02110-1913
617-451-2444
Contains information and opinion about secondary and elementary education in general and independent education in particular.

TriAnnually

Thomas W Leonhardt, Editor
Kurt R Murphy, Advertising/Editor

4420 Instructor
Scholastic
555 Broadway
New York, NY 10012-3919
212-343-6100
800-724-6527
Fax: 212-343-4801
http://www.scholastic.com/instructor
Edited for teachers, curriculum coordinators, principals and supervisors of primary grades through junior high school.

Monthly

Claudia Cohl, Publisher
Lynn Diamond, Advertising Director

4421 Journal of Research in Childhood Education
Association for Childhood Education International
17904 Georgia Avenue
Suite 215
Olney, MD 20832
301-570-2111
800-423-3563
Fax: 301-570-2212
Current research in education and related fields. It is intended to advance knowledge and theory of the education of children, from infancy through early adolescence. The journal seeks to stimulate the exchange of research ideas through publication of: reports of empirical research; theroretical articles; ethnographic and case studies; cross-cultural studies and studies addressing international concerns; participant observation studies and, studies, deriving data collected.

142 pages BiAnnual
ISSN: 0256-8543

4422 Montessori LIFE
American Montessori Society
281 Park Avenue S
6th Floor
New York, NY 10010
212-358-1250
Fax: 212-358-1256

E-mail: kate@amshq.org
http://www.amshq.org
Magazine for parents and educators.

Quarterly
ISSN: 1054-0040

Joy Turner, Author
Eileen Roper, Executive Assistant

4423 Parents Make the Difference!
The Parent Institute
PO Box 7474
Fairfax Station, VA 22039-7474
703-323-9170
Fax: 703-323-9173
http://www.parent-institute.com
Newsletter focusing on parent involvement in children's education. Focuses on parents of preschool-aged children.

9x Year

John Wherry, Publisher

4424 Teaching K-8 Magazine
Early Years
40 Richards Avenue
Norwalk, CT 06854-2319
203-855-2650
800-249-9363
Fax: 203-855-2656
E-mail: patricia@teachingk-8.com
http://www.teachingk-8.com
Written for teachers in the elementary grades, kindergarten through eighth, offering classroom tested ideas and methods.

Monthly Magazine
ISSN: 0891-4508
November-December

Allen A Raymond, Publisher
Patricia Broderick, Editorial Director

Periodicals / Employment

4425 AACE Careers Update
American Association for Career Education
2900 Amby Place
Hermosa Beach, CA 90254
310-376-7378
Fax: 310-376-2926
Connects careers, education and work through career education for all ages. Career awareness, exploration, decision making, and preparation. Employability, transitions, continuing education, paid and nonpaid work, occupations, career tips, resources, partnerships, conferences and workshops. Awards and recognition, trends and futures. A newsletter is published.

8+ pages Quarterly/Newsletter
ISBN: 1074-9551

Dr.Pat Nellor Wickwire, Author

4426 Career Development for Exceptional Individuals
The Council for Exceptional Children
1920 Association Drive
Reston, VA 20191-1545
703-620-3660
888-232-7733
Fax: 703-264-9494
Contains articles dealing with the latest research activities, model programs, and issues in career development and transition planning for individuals with disabilities and/or who are gifted.

2x Year

Gary Greene, Executive Editor

4427 Career Education News
Diversified Learning
72300 Vallat Road
Rancho Mirage, CA 92270-3906

619-346-3336
Reports on programs, materials and training for career educators.

4 pages BiWeekly

Webster Wilson Jr, Publisher
Webster Wilson, Editor

4428 Careers Bridge Newsletter
St. Louis Public Schools
901 Locust Street
Saint Louis, MO 63101-1401
314-231-3720
Available to educators and business/community persons on collaborative activities and promotion of career and self-awareness education in preschool to grade 12.

BiMonthly

Susan Katzman, Contact

4429 Chronicle of Higher Education
Subscription Department
PO Box 1955
Marion, OH 43305-1955
800-347-6969
Newspaper published weekly advertising many teaching opportunities overseas.

Weekly

4430 Current Openings in Education in the USA
Education Information Services
PO Box 620662
Newton, MA 02462-0662
617-433-0125
This publication is a booklet listing about 140 institutions or school systems, each with one to a dozen or more openings for teachers, librarians, counselors and other personnel.

15 pages Every 6 Weeks

F Viaux, Coordinating Education

4431 Education Jobs
National Education Service Center
PO Box 1279
Riverton, WY 82501-1279
307-856-0170
Offers information on employment in the education field.

Weekly

Lucretia Ficht, Contact

4432 Employment Opportunities
National Guild of Community Schools of the Arts
520 8th Avenue
Suite 302, 3rd Floor
New York, NY 10018
212-268-3337
Fax: 212-268-3995
E-mail: info@natguild.org
http://www.nationalguild.org

Monthly

Noah Xifr, Director Membership/Oper.

4433 Faculty, Staff & Administrative Openings in US Schools & Colleges
Educational Information Services
PO Box 662
Newton Lower Falls, MA 02162
617-964-4555
A listing of available positions in the educational system in the United States.

Monthly

4434 International Educator
PO Box 513
Cummaquid, MA 02637-0513
508-580-1880
A newspaper listing over 100 teaching positions overseas.

Quarterly

4435 Jobs Clearinghouse
Association for Experiential Education
2305 Canyon Boulevard
Suite 100
Boulder, CO 80302-5651
303-440-8844
Fax: 303-440-9581
E-mail: jch@aee.org
http://www.aee.org
A newsletter that is one of the most comprehensive and widely-used monthly listings of full-time, part-time, and seasonal employment and internship opportunities in the experiential/adventure education field for both employers and job seekers.
Monthly
Kristen Cherry

4436 Journal of Cooperative Education
University of Waterloo
200 University Avenue
Waterloo, ON N2L 3G1 Canada
519-885-1211
Dedicated to the publication of thoughtful and timely articles concerning work-integrated education. It invites manuscripts which are essays that analyze issues, reports of research, descriptions of innovative practices.
3x Year
Patricia M Rowe, Editor

4437 Journal of Vocational Education Research
Colorado State University
202 Education
Fort Collins, CO 80523-0001
970-491-6835
Fax: 970-491-1317
Publishes refereed articles dealing with research and research-related topics in vocational education. Manuscripts based on original investigations, comprehensive reviews of literature, research methodology and theoretical constructs in vocational education are encouraged.
Quarterly
Brian Cobb, Editor

4438 New Jersey Education Law Report
Whitaker Newsletters
313 S Avenue
#340
Fanwood, NJ 07023-1364
908-889-6336
800-359-6049
Fax: 908-889-6339
Court decisions and rulings on employment in New Jersey schools.
8 pages
ISSN: 0279-8557
Joel Whitaker, Publisher
Fred Rossu, Editor

4439 SkillsUSA Champions
Vocational Industrial Clubs of America
PO Box 3000
Leesburg, VA 20177-0300
703-777-8810
Fax: 703-777-8999
E-mail: anyinfo@skillsusa.org
http://www.skillsusa.org
To individuals interested in cultivating leaderships skills, SkillsUSA is a dynamic resource that inspires and connencts all

members creating a virtual community through its revalent and useful content.
28 pages Quarterly
ISSN: 1040-4538
E Thomas Hah, Director Office Publications
Timothy W Lawrence, Executive Director

4440 VEWAA Newsletter
Vocational Evaluation & Work Adjustment Assn.
1234 Haley Circle
Auburn University
Auburn, AL 36849
334-844-3800
News and information about the practice of vocational evaluation and work adjustment.
8 pages Quarterly
Ronald Fru, Publisher
Clarence D Brown, Editor

4441 Views & Visions
Wisconsin Vocational Association
44 E Mifflin Street
Suite 104
Madison, WI 53703-2800
608-283-2595
Fax: 608-283-2589
For teachers of vocational and adult education.
8 pages BiMonthly
Linda Stemper

4442 Vocational Training News
Aston Publications
701 King Street
Suite 444
Alexandria, VA 22314-2944
703-683-4100
800-453-9397
Fax: 703-739-6517
Contains timely, useful reports on the federal Job Training Partnership Act and the Carl D Perkins Vocational Education Act. Other areas include literacy, private industry councils and training initiatives.
10 pages Weekly
Cynthia Carter, Publisher
Matthew Dembicki, Editor

Periodicals / Financial Aid

4443 American-Scandinavian Foundation Magazine
American-Scandinavian Foundation
58 Park Avenue
New York, NY 10016-5025
212-779-3587
E-mail: info@amscan.org
http://www.amscan.org
Covers politics, culture and lifestyles of Denmark, Finland, Iceland, Norway and Sweden.
100 pages Quarterly Magazine
Edward P Gallagher, President
Christian Sonne, Deputy Chairman

4444 Education Grants Alert
LPR Publications
1901n Moore Street
Suite 700
Arlington, VA 22209-2944
703-516-7002
800-341-7874
Fax: 703-516-9313
E-mail: custserve@lrp.com
http://www.lrp.com

Dedicated to helping schools increase funding for K-12 programs. This newsletter will uncover new and recurring grant competitions from federal agencies that fund school projects, plus scores of corporate and foundation sources.
Weekly

4445 Federal Research Report
Business Publishers
8737 Colesville Road
Suite 1100
Silver Spring, MD 20910-3928
301-587-6300
800-274-6737
Fax: 301-585-9075
E-mail: bpinews@bpinews.com
http://www.bpinews.com
Identifies critical funding sources supplying administrator's with contact names, addresses, telephone numbers, RFP numbers and other vital details.
8 pages Weekly
Eric Easton, Publisher
Leonard Eiserer, Editor

4446 Foundation & Corporate Grants Alert
LRP Publishing
1901 N Moore Street
Suite 1106
Arlington, VA 22209
703-516-7002
800-341-7874
Fax: 703-516-9313
E-mail: custserve@lrp.com
http://www.lrp.com
Offers information on funding trends, new foundations and hard-to-find regional funders. You'll also get to foundation and corporate funders from the inside, with foundation profiles and interviews with program officers.
Monthly

4447 Grants for School Districts Monthly
Quinlan Publishing
23 Drydock Avenue
Boston, MA 02210-2336
617-542-0048
Listing of grants available for schools across the country.
Monthly

4448 Informativo
LASPAU (Latin America Scholarship Program)
25 Mount Auburn Street
Cambridge, MA 02138-6028
617-495-5255
Administers scholarships for staff members nominated by Latin American and Caribbean education and development organizations and other public and private sector entities.
8 pages SemiAnnually
Carole Biederman, Contact

4449 NASFAA Newsletter
National Assn. of Student Financial Aid Admin.
1920 L Street NW
Suite 200
Washington, DC 20036-5010
202-785-0453
Fax: 202-785-1487
News covering student financial aid legislation and regulations.
24 pages SemiMonthly
Madeleine McLean, Editor

4450 United Student Aid Funds Newsletter
PO Box 6180
Indianapolis, IN 46206-6180
317-578-6094

USA Funds Education Loan products and services information.

8 pages BiMonthly

Nelson Scharadin, Publisher
Dena Weisbard, Editor

Periodicals / Guidance & Counseling

4451 ASCA Counselor
American Counseling Association
5999 Stevenson Avenue
Alexandria, VA 22304-3302
703-823-9800
Fax: 703-823-0252
Aimed at the guidance counselor.

16 pages BiMonthly

Dolores Ehrlich, Editor

4452 Adolescence
Libra Publishers
3089C Clairemont Drive
San Diego, CA 92117-6802
858-571-1414
Fax: 858-571-1414
E-mail: librapublishers@juno.com
Articles contributed by professionals spanning issues relating to teenage education, counseling and guidance. Paperback.

256 pages Quarterly
ISSN: 0001-8449

Jon Kroll, Editor
William Kroll, Author

4453 Association for Play Therapy Newsletter
2050 N Winery Avenue
Suite 101
Fresno, CA 93703-2831
559-252-2278
Fax: 559-252-2297
E-mail: info@a4pt.org
http://www.a4pt.org
Dedicated to the advancement of play therapy. APT is interdisciplinary and defines play therapy as a distinct group of interventions which use play as an integral component of the therapeutic process.

Quarterly

William S Burns CAE, Executive Director
Kathryn Lebby MS, General Manager

4454 Attention
CHADD
8181 Professional Place
Suite 150
Landover, MD 20785
301-306-7070
800-233-4050
Fax: 301-306-7090
E-mail: attention@chadd.org
http://www.chadd.org
Magazine for children and adults with Attention Deficit/Hyperactivity Disorder, and their families.

48 pages Bi-Monthly
ISSN: 1551-0980
70+ booths with 1,400 attendees and 70+ exhibits

Marsha Bokman, Manager

4455 Before You Can Discipline
Master Teacher
Leadership Lane
PO Box 1207
Manhattan, KS 66505-1207
800-669-9633
Fax: 800-669-1132
http://www.masterteacher.com

Understand exactly how student's primary and secondary needs can and do influence acceptable and unacceptable behavior. Develop professional attitudes toward discipline problems and learn the laws and principals of managing people.

170 pages
ISBN: 0-914607-03-0
Robert L DeBruyn, Author

4456 Child Psychiatry & Human Development
Kluwer Academic/Human Sciences Press
233 Spring Street
New York, NY 10013
212-620-8000
800-221-9369
Fax: 212-463-0742
http://www.wkpa.nl
Interdisciplinary international journal serving the groups represented by child psychiatry, clinical child/pediatric/family psychology, pediatrics, social science, and human development. Publishes research on diagnosis, assessment, treatment, epidemiology, development, advocacy, training, cultural factors, ethics, policy, and professional issues as related to clinical disorders in children, adolescents and families.

Quarterly
ISSN: 0009-398X

Carol Bischoff, Publisher
Kenneth J Tarnowski, Editor

4457 Child Welfare
Child Welfare League of America
440 1st Street NW
Suite 310
Washington, DC 20001-2085
202-638-2952
Fax: 202-638-4004

BiMonthly

Eve Klein, Editor

4458 Child and Adolescent Social Work Journal
Kluwer Academic/Human Sciences Press
233 Spring Street
New York, NY 10013
212-620-8000
800-221-9369
Fax: 212-463-0742
http://www.wkpa.nl
Features original articles that focus on clinical social work practice with children, adolescents and their families. The journal addresses current issues in the field of social work drawn from theory, direct practice, research, and social policy, as well as focuses on problems affecting specific populations in special settings.

Bimonthly
ISSN: 0738-0151

Carol Bischoff, Publisher
Thomas Kenemore, Editor

4459 College Board News
College Board Publications
45 Columbus Avenue
New York, NY 10023-6992
212-713-8165
800-323-7155
Fax: 800-525-5562
http://www.collegeboard.org
Sent free to schools and colleges several times a year, the News reports on the activities of the College Board. Its articles inform readers about the Board's services in such areas as high school, guidance, college admission, curriculum and placement, testing, financial aid, adult education and research.

4460 College Board Review
College Board Publications
45 Columbus Avenue
New York, NY 10023-6992
212-713-8165
800-323-7155
Fax: 800-525-5562
http://www.collegeboard.org
Each issue of the Review probes key problems and trends facing education professionals concerned with student transition from high school to college.

4461 College Times
College Board Publications
45 Columbus Avenue
New York, NY 10023-6917
212-713-8165
800-323-7155
Fax: 800-525-5562
http://www.collegeboard.org
This annual magazine is a one-stop source to college admission. It provides valuable advice to help students through the complex college selection, application and admission process.

Publication Date: 1995 32 pages Package of 50

4462 Communique
National Association of School Psychologists
4340 EW Highway
Suite 402
Bethesda, MD 20814
301-657-0270
Fax: 301-657-0275
E-mail: center@naspweb.org
http://www.nasponline.org

50 pages 8x Year
ISSN: 0164-775X

4463 Counseling & Values
American Counseling Association
5999 Stevenson Avenue
Alexandria, VA 22304-3302
703-823-9800
Fax: 703-823-0252
Editorial content focuses on the roles of values and religion in counseling and psychology.

3x Year

Stephen Brooks, Advertising Director
Susan Lausch, Advertising/Sales

4464 Counseling Today
American Counseling Association
5999 Stevenson Avenue
Alexandria, VA 22304-3302
703-823-9800
Fax: 703-823-0252
Covers national and international counseling issues and reports legislative and governmental activities affecting counselors.

Monthly

Kathy Maguire, Advertising Director
Mary Morrissey, Editor-in-Chief

4465 Counselor Education & Supervision
American Counseling Association
5999 Stevenson Avenue
Alexandria, VA 22304-3302
703-823-9800
Fax: 703-823-0252
Covers counseling theories, techniques and skills, teaching and training.

Quarterly

Stephen Brooks, Advertising Director
Susan Lausch, Advertising/Sales

4466 ERIC Clearinghouse on Counseling & Student Services
201 Ferguson Building UNCG
Greensboro, NC 27402-6171
336-334-4114
800-414-9769
Fax: 336-334-4116
E-mail: ericcass@uncg.edu.edu
http://ericcass.uncg.edu
Covers news about ERIC and the counseling clearinghouse and developments in the fields of education and counseling.

4 pages Quarterly

Garry R Walz, Co-Director
Jeanne C Bleuer, Co-Director

4467 Educational & Psychological Measurement
Sage Publications
2455 Telle Road
Thousand Oaks, CA 91320
805-499-9774
Fax: 805-375-1700
E-mail: order@sagepub.com
http://www.sagepub.com

Quarterly

4468 Elementary School Guidance & Counseling
American Counseling Association
5999 Stevenson Avenue
Alexandria, VA 22304-3300
703-823-9800
Fax: 703-823-0252
http://www.counseling.org
Journal concerned with enhancing the role of the elementary, middle school and junior high school counselor.

Quarterly
ISSN: 0013-5976

Michael Comlish, Editor

4469 Family Relations
Miami University
Family & Child Studies Center
Oxford, OH 45056
513-529-4909
Fax: 513-529-7270

Quarterly

Timothy H Brubaker, Editor

4470 Family Therapy: The Journal of the California Graduate School of Family Psychology
Libra Publishers
3089C Clairemont Drive
PNB 383
San Diego, CA 92117-6802
858-571-1414
Fax: 858-571-1414
Articles contributed by professionals spanning issues relating to teenage education, counseling and guidance. Paperback.

96 pages Quarterly
ISSN: 0091-6544

William Kroll, Editor

4471 Health & Social Work
National Association of Social Workers
750 First Street NE
Suite 700
Washington, DC 20002-4241
202-408-8600
800-638-8799
Fax: 202-336-8311
http://www.socialworkers.org
Covers practice, innovation, research, legislation, policy, planning, and all the professional issues relevant to social work services in all levels of education.

Mal Milburn, Marketing/Sales Associate
Lyn Carter, Advertising Specialist

4472 ICA Quarterly
Western Illinois University
Counseling Center
Memorial Hall
Macomb, IL 61455
309-298-2453
Fax: 309-298-3253
Official publication of the Illinois Counseling Association. Focus is on material of interest and value to professional counselors.

Quarterly

Michael Illovsky, Editor

4473 International Journal of Play Therapy
2050 N Winery Avenue
Suite 101
Fresno, CA 93703-2831
559-252-2278
Fax: 559-252-2297
E-mail: info@a4pt.org
http://www.a4pt.org
Dedicated to the advancement of play therapy. APT is interdisciplinary and defines play therapy as a distinct group of interventions which use play as an integral component of the therapeutic process.

Publication Date: 1982 BiAnnual

William S Burns CAE, Executive Director
Kathryn Lebby MS, General Manager

4474 Journal for Specialists in Group Work
American Counseling Association
5999 Stevenson Avenue
Alexandria, VA 22304-3302
703-823-9800
Fax: 703-823-0252
Contains theory, legal issues and current literature reviews.

Quarterly

Stephen Brooks, Editor

4475 Journal of At-Risk Issues
Clemson University
209 Martin Street
Clemson, SC 29631-1555
864-656-2599
800-443-6392
Fax: 864-656-0136
E-mail: NDPC@clemson.edu
http://www.dropoutprevention.org

36 pages
ISBN: 1098-1608

Dr. Judy Johnson, Author
Dr. Alice Fisher, Editor

4476 Journal of Child and Adolescent Group Therapy
Kluwer Academic/Human Sciences Press
233 Spring Street
New York, NY 10013
212-620-8000
800-221-9369
Fax: 212-463-0742
http://www.wkpa.nl
Addresses the whole spectrum of professional issues relating to juvenile and parent group treatment. Promotes the exchange of new ideas from a wide variety of disciplines concerned with enhancing treatments for this special population. The multidisciplinary contributions include clinical reports, illustrations of new technical methods, and studies that contribute to the advancement of therapeutic results,

as well as articles on theoretical issues, applications, and the group process.

Quarterly
ISSN: 1053-0800

Carol Bischoff, Publisher
Edward S Soo, Editor

4477 Journal of College Admission
Nat'l Association for College Admission Counseling
1631 Prince Street
Alexandria, VA 22314-2818
703-836-2222
Fax: 703-836-8015
http://www.nacac.com
Membership association offering information to counselors and guidance professionals working in the college admissions office.

32 pages Quarterly
ISSN: 0734-6670

Elaina Loveland, Author
Shanda T Ivory, Chief Officer Communications
Amy C Vogt, Assistant Director

4478 Journal of Counseling & Development
American Counseling Association
5999 Stevenson Avenue
Alexandria, VA 22304
703-823-9800
Fax: 703-823-0252
E-mail: jc-d@psu.edu
http://www.counseling.org
A quarterly journal that publishe articles that have broad interest for a readership composed mostly of couselors and other mental health professionals who work in private practice, schools, colleges, community agencies, hospitals and government.

ISBN: 0748-9633

Spencer Niles, Editor

4479 Journal of Counseling and Development
American Counseling Association
5999 Stevenson Avenue
Alexandria, VA 22304-3302
703-823-9800
Fax: 703-823-0252
Edited for counseling and human development specialists in schools, colleges and universities.

Monthly

Stephen Brooks, Editor

4480 Journal of Drug Education
California State University
Department of Health Science
Northridge, CA 91330-8285
818-677-3101
Fax: 818-677-2045
Offers information to counselors and guidance professionals dealing with areas of drug and substance abuse education in the school system.

Quarterly

Robert Huff, Contact

4481 Journal of Emotional and Behavioral Disorders
Pro-Ed
8700 Shoal Creek Boulevard
Austin, TX 78757-6816
512-451-3246
800-897-3202
Fax: 512-302-9129
http://www.proedinc.com
Presents high-quality interdisciplinary scholarship in the area of emotional and behavioral disabilities. Explores issues including youth violence, emotional problems among minority children, long-term foster care placement, mental health services, social development and educational strategies.

Michael H Epstein, EdD, Editor
Douglas Cullinan, EdD, Editor

4482 Journal of Employment Counseling
American Counseling Association
5999 Stevenson Avenue
Alexandria, VA 22304-3302
703-823-9800
Fax: 703-823-0252
Editorial content includes developing trends in case studies and newest personnel practices.
Quarterly
Stephen Brooks, Editor

4483 Journal of Humanistic Education and Development
Ohio University
201 McCracken Hall
Athens, OH 45701
740-593-4000
Fax: 740-593-0569
Focuses on the humanities and promotes their place in the educational system.
Quarterly

4484 Journal of Multicultural Counseling & Development
American Counseling Association
5999 Stevenson Avenue
Alexandria, VA 22304-3302
703-823-9800
Fax: 703-823-0252
Contains articles with focus on research, theory and program application related to multicultural counseling.
Quarterly
Stephen Brooks, Editor

4485 Journal of Sex Education & Therapy
American Association of Sex Educators
PO Box 5488
Richmond, VA 23220-0488
804-644-3288
Fax: 804-644-3290
E-mail: aasect@worldnet.att.net
http://www.aasect.org
Provides education and training in all areas of sexual health.
110 pages Quarterly
ISSN: 0161-4576
Michael Plant, Author

4486 Measurement & Evaluation in Counseling and Development
American Counseling Association
5999 Stevenson Avenue
Alexandria, VA 22304-3302
703-823-9800
Fax: 703-823-0252
Editorial focuses on research and applications in counseling and guidance.
Quarterly
Stephen Brooks, Editor
Susan Lausch, Advertising/Sales

4487 NACAC Bulletin
Nat'l Association for College Admission Counseling
1631 Prince Street
Alexandria, VA 22314-2818
703-836-2222
Fax: 703-836-8015
http://www.nacac.com
Membership association offering information to counselors and guidance professionals working in the college admissions office.
Monthly
Shanda T Ivory, Chief Officer Communications
Amy C Vogt, Assistant Director

4488 NASW News
National Association of Social Workers
PO Box 431
Annapolis Junction, MD 20701-0431
301-317-8688
800-638-8799
Fax: 301-206-7989
Features in-depth coverage of developments in social work practice, news of national social policy developments, political and legislative news in social services, noteworthy achievements of social workers and association news.
Monthly
Scott Moss, Editor

4489 National Coalition for Sex Equity in Education
PO Box 534
Annandale, NJ 08801
908-735-5045
Fax: 908-735-9674
E-mail: info@ncsee.org
http://www.ncsee.org
The only national organization for gender equity specialists and educators. Individuals and organizations committed to reducing sex role stereotyping for females and males. Services include an annual national training conference, a quarterly newsletter and a membership directory. Members may join task forces dealing with equity related topics such as computer/technology issues, early childhood, male issues, sexual harassment prevention, sexual orientation and vocational issues.
Quarterly Newsletter
Theodora Martin, Business Manager

4490 New Horizons
National Registration Center for Study Abroad
PO Box 1393
Milwaukee, WI 53201-1393
414-278-0631
Fax: 414-271-8884
E-mail: info@nrcsa.com
http://www.nrcsa.com
Provides information about member institution's programs and establishes standards for treatment of visitors from abroad including the appointment of bilingual housing officers and counselors to deal with culture shock.
16 pages Quarterly
ISBN: 1-977864-43-3
Anne Wittig, Author
Mike Wittig, General Manager

4491 Rehabilitation Counseling Bulletin
Pro-Ed
8700 Shoal Creek Boulevard
Austin, TX 78757-6816
512-451-3246
800-897-3202
Fax: 512-302-9129
E-mail: proed1@aol.com
http://www.proedinc.com
International journal providing original empirical research, essays of a theoretical nature, methodological treatises and comprehensive reviews of the literature, intensive case studies and research critiques.
Quarterly Magazine
ISSN: 0034-3552
Douglas Strohmer, PhD, Editor

4492 School Counselor
American Counseling Association
5999 Stevenson Avenue
Alexandria, VA 22304-3302
703-823-9800
Fax: 703-823-0252

Includes current issues and information affecting teens and how counselors can deal with them.
5x Year
Stephen Brooks, Editor
Susan Lausch, Advertising/Sales

4493 School Psychology Review
National Association of School Psychologists
4340 EW Highway
Suite 402
Bethesda, MD 20814
301-657-0270
Fax: 301-657-0275
E-mail: center@naspweb.org
http://www.nasponline.org
170 pages Quarterly
ISSN: 0279-6015

4494 Social Work Research Journal
National Association of Social Workers
750 1st Street NE
Suite 700
Washington, DC 20002-4241
202-408-8600
800-638-8799
Fax: 202-336-8311
http://www.socialworkers.org
Contains orginal research papers that contribute to knowledge about social work issues and problems. Topics include new technology, strategies and methods, and resarch results.
Quarterly
ISSN: 1070-5309
Stuart A Kirk, Editor

4495 Social Work in Education
National Association of Social Workers
750 1st Street NE
Suite 700
Washington, DC 20002-4241
202-408-8600
Fax: 202-336-8310
http://www.socialworkers.org
Covers practice, innovation, research, legislation, policy, planning, and all the professional issues relevant to social work services in all levels of education.
Mal Milburn, Marketing/Sales Associate
Lyn Carter, Advertising Specialist

4496 SocialWork
National Association of Social Workers
750 1st Street NE
Suite 700
Washington, DC 20002-4241
202-408-8600
800-638-8799
Fax: 202-336-8311
http://www.socialworkers.org
Covers important research findings, critical analyses, practice issues, and information on current social issues such as AIDS, homelessness, and federal regulation of social programs. Case management, third-party reimbursement, credentialing, and other professional issues are addressed.
Mal Milburn, Marketing/Sales Associate
Lyn Carter, Advertising Specialist

4497 Today's School Psychologist
LRP Publications
1901 N Moore Street
Suite 700
Arlington, VA 22209
703-516-7002
800-341-7874
Fax: 703-516-9313
E-mail: custserve@lrp.com
http://www.lrp.com/ed

An in-depth guide to a school psychologist's job, offering practical strategies and tips for handling day-to-day responsibilites, encouraging change, and improving professional standing and performance.

Monthly
ISSN: 1098-9277

4498 Washington Counseletter

Chronicle Guidance Publications
66 Aurora Street
Moravia, NY 13118-1190
315-497-0330
800-622-7284
Fax: 315-497-3359
E-mail:
customerservice@chronicleguidance.com
http://www.chronicleguidance.com
Monthly report highlighting federal, state, and local developments affecting the counseling and education professions. Items list events, programs, activities and publications of interest to counselors and educators.

8 pages 8x Year

Gary Fickeisen, President
Priscilla Lorah, Coordinator

Periodicals / Language Arts

4499 AATF National Bulletin

American Association of Teachers of French
Mailcode 4510
Southern Illinois University
Carbondale, IL 62901
618-453-5731
Fax: 618-453-5733
E-mail: abrate@siu.edu
http://www.frenchteachers.org
Announcements and short articles relating to the association on French language and cultural activities.

30-50 pages 5x Year

Jayne Abrate, Executive Director
Marie-Christine Koop, President

4500 ACTFL Newsletters

American Council on the Teaching of Foreign Lang.
6 Executive Plaza
Yonkers, NY 10701-6832
914-963-8830
Fax: 914-963-1275
A quarterly newsletter containing topical and timely information on matters of interest to foreign language educators. Regular columns include Languages in the News and Washington Watch.

20 pages Quarterly

C Edward Scebold, C-Editor
Jamie Draper, Co-Editor

4501 ADE Bulletin

Association of Departments of English
26 Broadway
Third Floor
New York, NY 10004-1789
646-576-5133
Fax: 646-458-0033
http://www.ade.org
This bulletin concentrates on developments in scholarship, curriculum and teachers in English.

64 pages
ISSN: 0001-0888

4502 Beyond Words

1534 Wells Drive NE
Albuquerque, NM 87112-6383

505-275-2558
Offers information on literature, language arts and English for the teaching professional.

10x Year

4503 Bilingual Research Journal

National Association for Bilingual Education
1030 15th Street NW
Suite 470
Washington, DC 20005-4018
202-898-1829
Fax: 202-789-2866
E-mail: nabe@nabe.org
http://www.nabe.org
Journal published by National Association for Bilingual Education.

Quarterly
8,000 attendees

Delia Pompa, Executive Director
Alicia Sosa, Membership Director

4504 Bilingual Review Press

Arizona State University
Hispanic Research Center
Tempe, AZ 85287
480-965-3990
Fax: 480-965-0315
Offers information and reviews on books, materials and the latest technology available to bilingual educators.

3x Year

Gary D Keller, Editor

4505 CEA Forum

College English Association
English Department
Youngstown State University
Youngstown, OH 44555-0001
330-941-3415
Fax: 330-941-2304
E-mail: Daniel.Robinson@widener.edu
http://www.as.ysu.edu/~english/cea/forum1.htm
Publishes articles on professional issues and pedagogy related to the teaching of English. Subscription includes CEA Critic, a scholarly journal that appears 3x annually.

Newsletter
ISSN: 0007-8034

Daniel Robinson, Editor

4506 Classroom Notes Plus

National Council of Teachers of English
1111 W Kenyon Road
Urbana, IL 61801-1010
217-328-3870
800-369-6283
Fax: 217-278-3761
E-mail: notesplus@ncte.org
http://www.ncte.org
Secondary periodical for English/Language Arts featuring usable teaching ideas for teachers by teachers.

16 pages Quarterly

Felice Kaufmann, Communications Director

4507 Communication Disorders Quarterly

Pro-Ed., Inc.
8700 Shoal Creek Boulevard
Austin, TX 78757-6816
512-451-3246
800-897-3202
Fax: 512-302-9129
E-mail: proed1@aol.com
http://www.proedinc.com

Research, intervention and practice in speech, language and hearing.

Quarterly Magazine
ISSN: 1525-7401

Alejandro Brice, Editor

4508 Communication: Journalism Education Today

Truman High School
3301 S Noland Road
Independence, MO 64055-1318
816-521-2710
Fax: 816-521-2913
Provides educational perspectives to JEA members— mostly high schools journalism editors— on a wide variety of topics such as teaching/advising issues, scholastic media strategy, pedagogical updates, current journalism research and other professional and technological concerns.

Quarterly
ISBN: 1536
ISSN: 9129

Bradley Wilson, Editor

4509 Composition Studies Freshman English News

De Paul University
802 W Belden Avenue
Chicago, IL 60614
312-362-8000
Fax: 773-325-7328
Theoretical and practical articles on rhetorical theory.

44 pages SemiAnnually

Peter Vandenberg, English Department

4510 Council-Grams

National Council of Teachers of English
1111 W Kenyon Road
Urbana, IL 61801-1010
217-328-3870
800-369-6283
Fax: 217-328-9645
http://www.ncte.org
Offers information and updates in the areas of English, language arts and reading.

16 pages 5x Year

Michael Spooner

4511 Counterforce

Society for the Advancement of Good English
4501 Riverside Avenue
#30
Anderson, CA 96007-2759
530-365-8026
Offers updates and information for English teachers and professors.

Quarterly

4512 English Education

New York University
635 E Building
New York, NY 10003
212-998-8857
Fax: 212-995-4376
Offers updates and information for reading and English teachers, and professors.

Quarterly

Gordon M Pradl, Editor

4513 English Journal

National Council of Teachers of English
1111 W Kenyon Road
Urbana, IL 61801-1010
217-328-3870
800-369-6283
Fax: 217-328-9645
http://www.ncte.org

An ideal magazine for middle school, junior and senior high school English teachers.

Biannual
ISSN: 0013-8274

Carrie Stewart, Editor

4514 English Leadership Quarterly

National Council of Teachers of English
1111 W Kenyon Road
Urbana, IL 61801-1010
217-328-3870
800-369-6283
Fax: 217-328-9645
http://www.ncte.org
Teaching of English for secondary school English Department chairpersons.

12 pages Quarterly

James Strickland

4515 English for Specific Purposes

University of Michigan
Ann Arbor, MI 48109
619-594-6331
Fax: 619-594-6530
Concerned with English education and its importance to the developing student.

3x Year

John Swales, Editor

4516 Foreign Language Annals

American Council on the Teaching of Foreign Lang.
6 Executive Plaza
Yonkers, NY 10701-6832
914-963-8830
Fax: 914-963-1275
Dedicated to advancing all areas of the profession of foreign language teaching. It seeks primarily to serve the interests of teachers, administrators and researchers, regardless of educational level of the language with which they are concerned. Preference is given in this scholarly journal to articles that describe innovative and successful teaching methods, that report educational research or experimentation, or that are relevant to the concerns and problems of the profession.

128 pages Quarterly

C Edward Scebold, Executive Director

4517 Journal of Basic Writing

City University of NY, Instructional Resource Ctr.
535 E 80th Street
New York, NY 10021-0767
212-794-5445
Fax: 212-794-5706
Publishes articles of theory, research and teaching practices related to basic writing. Articles are referred by members of the Editorial Board and the editors.

Spring & Fall

Karen Greenberg, Editor
Trudy Smoke, Editor

4518 Journal of Children's Communication Development

The Council for Exceptional Children
1920 Association Drive
Reston, VA 20191-1545
703-620-3660
800-232-7323
Fax: 703-264-1637
Provides in-depth research and practical application articles in communication assessment and intervention. The journal frequently contains a practitioner's section that addresses professional questions, reviews tests and therapy materials, and de-

scribes innovative programs and service delivery models.

2x Year
ISSN: 0735-3170

Richard Nowell, Editor

4519 Journal of Teaching Writing

Indiana Teachers of Writing
IUPUI Department of English CA502L
425 University Boulevard
Indianapolis, IN 46202-5148
317-278-2054
Fax: 317-278-1287
E-mail: sfox@iupui.edu
http://www.iupui.edu/~jtw
A refereed journal for classroom teachers and researchers at all academic levels whose interest or emphasis is the teaching of writing. Appearing semiannually, JTW publishes articles on the theory, practice, and teaching of writing throughout the curriculum. Each issue covers a range of topics, from composition theory and discourse analysis to curriculum development and innovative teaching techniques. Contributors are reminded to tailor their writing for a diverse readership.

12-20 pages Semiannually

4520 Journalism Quarterly

George Washington University
School of Journalism
Washington, DC 20052-0001
202-994-6227
Fax: 202-994-5806
Information on all facets of writing and journalism for the student and educator.

Quarterly

Jean Folkerts, Editor

4521 Language & Speech

Kingston Press Services, Ltd.
43 Derwent Road, Whitton
Twickenham, Middlesex TW2 7HQ
United Kingdom
0-20-8893-3015
Fax: 208-893-3015
E-mail: sales@kingstonepress.com
http://www.kingstonepress.com
Includes psychological research articles, speech perception, speech production, psycholinguistics and reading.

Quarterly

4522 Language Arts

National Council of Teachers of English
1111 W Kenyon Road
Urbana, IL 61801-1010
217-328-3870
800-369-6283
Fax: 217-328-9645
http://www.ncte.org
Edited for instructors in language arts at the elementary level.

Monthly

Kent Williamson, Editor

4523 Language, Speech & Hearing Services in School

Ohio State University
110 Pressey Hall
1070 Carmack Road
Columbus, OH 43210
614-292-8207
Fax: 614-292-7504
Interested in innovative technology and growth in language development in schools.

Wayne A Secord, PhD, Editor

4524 Merlyn's Pen: Fiction, Essays and Poems by America's Teens

PO Box 910
East Greenwich, RI 02818-0964
401-885-5175
800-247-2027
Fax: 401-885-5199
E-mail: merlynspen@aol.com
http://www.merlynspen.com
Merlyns' Pen magazine is a selective publisher of model writing by America's students in grades 6-12. Products include Merlyn's Pen magazine (a reproducible annual magazine) and the American Teen Writer Series, collections of anthologized short fiction and nonfiction by brilliant teen writers. Used for models, inspiration, and instruction in literature and writing.

100 pages Annually
ISSN: 0882-2050

Jim Stahl, Editor

4525 Modern Language Journal

Case Western Reserve University
Department of Modern Languages
Cleveland, OH 44106
216-368-2000
Fax: 216-368-2216

Quarterly

David P Benseler, Editor

4526 NABE News

National Association for Bilingual Education
1030 15th Street NW
Suite 470
Washington, DC 20005-4018
202-898-1829
Fax: 202-789-2866
E-mail: nabe@nabe.org
http://www.nabe.org
Magazine published by the National Association for Bilingual Education.

Bi-Monthly

Delia Pompa, Executive Director
Alicia Sosa, Membership Director

4527 NASILP Journal

National Assn. of Self-Instructional Language
Temple University
Philadelphia, PA 19122
215-204-7000
Articles, news and book reviews on language instructional methodology.

12 pages SemiAnnually

Dr. John Means

4528 National Clearinghouse for Bilingual Education Newsletter

George Washington University
2121 K Street NW
Suite 260
Washington, DC 20037-1214
202-467-0867
800-321-6223
E-mail: askncbe@ncbe.gwu.edu
http://www.ncbe.gwu.edu
Provides information to practitioners on the education of language minority students.

Weekly

Dr. Minerva Gorena, Director

4529 PCTE Bulletin

Pennsylvania Council of Teachers of English
Williamsport Area Community College
Williamsport, PA 17701
Focuses on Pennsylvania literacy issues.

SemiAnnually

Robert Ulrich

4530 Quarterly Journal of Speech
National Communication Association
1765 N Street NW
Washington, DC 20036
202-464-4622
Fax: 202-464-4600
http://www.natcom.org
Main academic journal in the speech/communication field of education.

Quarterly

James Gaudino, Executive Director

4531 Quarterly Review of Doublespeak
National Council of Teachers of English
1111 W Kenyon Road
Urbana, IL 61801-1010
217-328-3870
800-369-6283
Fax: 217-328-9645
http://www.ncte.org
Provides information on the misuses and abuse of language.

8 pages Quarterly

Harry Brent

4532 Quarterly of the NWP
National Writing Project
2105 Bancroft Way
Suite 1042
Berkeley, CA 94720-1042
510-642-0963
Fax: 510-642-4545
E-mail: writingproject.org
http://www.writingproject.org
Journal on the research in and practice of teaching writing at all grade levels.

40 pages Quarterly Magazine
ISSN: 0896-3592

Art Peterson, Amy Bauman; Editors,
Author
Art Peterson, Senior Editor
Amy Bauman, Managing Editor

4533 Quill and Scroll
University of Iowa School of Journalism
100 Adler Journalism Builing
Room E346
Iowa City, IA 52242
319-335-3457
Fax: 319-335-3989
E-mail: quill-scroll@uiowa.edu
http://www.uiowa.edu/~quill-sc
Founded and distributed for the purpose of encouraging and rewarding individual achievements in journalism and allied fields. This magazine is published bimonthly during the school year and has a variety of pamphlets and lists of publications available as resources.

BiMonthly

Richard P Johns, Executive Director

4534 Research in the Teaching of English
Harvard Graduate School of Education
Larsen Hall
Appian Way
Cambridge, MA 02138
617-495-3521
Fax: 617-495-0540
A research journal devoted to original research on the relationships between teaching and learning for language development in reading, writing and speaking at all age levels.

Quarterly

Sandra Stotsky, Editor

4535 Rhetoric Review
University of Arizona
Department of English
Tucson, AZ 85721-0001
520-621-3371
Fax: 520-621-7397
http://http://members.aol.com/sborrowman/rr/html
A journal of rhetoric and composition publishing scholarly and historical studies, theoretical and practical articles, views of the profession, review essays of professional books, personal essays about writing and poems.

200+ pages Quarterly
ISSN: 0735-0198

Theresa Enos, Editor

4536 Slate Newsletter
National Council of Teachers of English
1111 W Kenyon Road
Urbana, IL 61801-1010
217-328-3870
800-369-6283
Fax: 217-328-9645
http://www.ncte.org
Short articles on topics such as censorship, trends and issues and testing.

4537 Studies in Second Language Acquisition
Cambridge University Press
1105 Atwater
Bloomington, IN 47401-5020
812-855-6874
Fax: 812-855-2386
E-mail: ssla@indiana.edu
http://www.indiana.edu/~ssla
Referred journal devoted to problems and issues in second and foreign language acquisition of any language.

140 pages Quarterly Paperback
ISSN: 0272-2631

Albert Valdman, Editor

4538 TESOL Journal: A Journal of Teaching and Classroom Research
Teachers of English to Speakers of Other Languages
1600 Cameron Street
Suite 300
Alexandria, VA 22314-2705
703-836-0774
Fax: 703-836-7864
E-mail: tescol@tesol.edu
http://www.tesol.edu
TESOL's mission is to develop the expertise of its members and others involved in teaching English to speakers of other languages to help them foster communication in diverse settings. The association advances standards for professional preparation and employment, continuing education, and student programs, produces programs, services, and products, and promotes advocacy to further the profession. TESOL has 91 affiliates worldwide.

50 pages Quarterly

Christian J Faltis, Editor
Marilyn Kupetz, Managing Editor

4539 TESOL Quarterly
Teachers of English to Speakers of Other Languages
1600 Cameron Street
Suite 300
Alexandria, VA 22314-2705
703-836-0774
Fax: 703-836-7864
E-mail: tesol@tesol.edu
http://www.tesol.com
TESOL Quarterly is our scholarly journal containing articles on academic research, theory, reports, reviews. Articles about linguistics, ethnographies, and more describe the theoretic basis for ESL/EFL teaching

practices. Readership is approximately 23,400.

830 pages Quarterly

Carol Chapelle, Editor

4540 Writing Lab Newsletter
Purdue University, Department of English
500 Oval Drive
W. Lafayette, IN 47907-2038
765-494-7268
Fax: 765-494-3780
E-mail: wln@purdue.edudue.edu
http://www.owl.english.purdue.edu/lab/newsletter/index.html
Monthly newsletter for readers involved in writing centers and/or one-to-one instruction in writing skills.

16 pages Monthly/Newsletter
ISSN: 1040-3779

Muriel Harris, Editor
Shawna McCaw, Managing Editor

Periodicals / Library Services

4541 ALA Editions Catalog
Membership Services American Library Association
50 E Huron Street
Chicago, IL 60611
800-545-2433
Fax: 312-836-9958
http://www.ala.org
Contains over 1,000 job listings, news and reports on the latest technologies in 11 issues annually. Also scholarships, grants and awards are possibilities.

Annually

4542 American Libraries
American Library Association
50 E Huron Street
Chicago, IL 60611-2795
312-944-6780
800-545-2433
Fax: 312-440-9374
E-mail: ala@ala.org
http://www.ala.org
The magazine of the American Library Association that is published six times a year and distributed to more than 65,000 individuals.

ISBN: 0002-9769

Leonard Kniffel, Editor

4543 Booklist
American Library Association
50 E Huron Street
Chicago, IL 60611-5295
312-944-6780
Fax: 312-440-9374
http://www.ala.org/booklist
A guide to current print and audiovisual materials worthy of consideration for purchase by small and medium-sized public libraries and school library media centers.

Semimonthly

Bill Ott, Editor

4544 Catholic Library World
Catholic Library Association
461 W Lancaster Avenue
Haverford, PA 19041-1412
734-722-7185
A periodical geared toward the professional librarian in order to keep them abreast of new publications, library development, association news and technology.

Quarterly

Allen Gruenke, Executive Director

4545 Choice
Current Reviews for Academic Libraries
100 Riverview Center
Middletown, CT 06457-3445
860-347-6933
Fax: 860-346-8586
E-mail: adsales@ala-choice.org
http://www.ala.org/acrl/choice
A magazine distributed to librarians and other organizations that analyzes various materials, offers book reviews and information on the latest technology available for the library acquisitions departments.

11x Year

Steven Conforti, Subscriptions Manager
Stuart Foster, Advertising Manager

4546 Emergency Librarian
Ken Haycock and Associates
101-1001 W Braodway
Vancouver
British Columbia
604-925-0266
604-925-056
Professional journal targeted to the specific needs and concerns of teachers and teacher-librarians.

5x Year

Dr. Ken Haycock

4547 ILA Reporter
33 W Grand Avenue
Suite 301
Chicago, IL 60610-4306
312-644-1896
Fax: 312-644-1899
E-mail: ila@ila.org
http://www.ila.org
30 pages
ISSN: 0018-9979

Robert P Doyle, Arthor

4548 Information Technology & Libraries
University of the Pacific
William Knox Holt Library
Stockton, CA 95211-0001
209-946-2434
Fax: 209-946-2805
Offers information on the latest technology, systems and electronics offered to the library market.

Quarterly

Thomas W Leonhardt, Editor
Karen Hope

4549 Journal of Education for Library and Information Sciences
Kent State University
School of Library Science
Kent, OH 44242-0001
330-672-2782
Fax: 330-672-7965
The latest information on books, publications, electronics and technology for the librarian.

Quarterly

4550 Libraries & Culture
University of Texas at Austin/Univ. of Texas Press
PO Box 7819
Austin, TX 78713-7819
512-232-7618
Fax: 512-232-7178
E-mail: dgdavis@gslis.utexas.edu
An interdisciplinary journal that explores the significance of collections of recorded knowledge. Scholarly articles and book reviews cover international topics dealing with libraries, books, reviews, archives, personnel, and their history; for scholars, librarians,

historians, readers interested in the history of books and libraries.

100 pages Quarterly
ISSN: 0894-8631

Dr. Donald G Davis Jr, Editor
Colleen Daly, Assistant Editor

4551 Library Collections, Acquisitions & Technical Services
Pergamon Press, Elsevier Science
The Boulevard, Lanngford Lane
Kidlington, Oxford
United Kingdom
614-292-4738
Fax: 614-292-7859
E-mail: deidrichs.1@osu.edu
http://www.elsvier.com
Offers information on policy, practice, and research on the collection management and technical service areas of libraries.

500 pages Quarterly
ISSN: 1464-9055

Carol Pitts Diedrichs, Editor

4552 Library Issues: Briefings for Faculty and Administrators
Mountainside Publishing Company
PO Box 8330
Ann Arbor, MI 48107-8330
734-662-3925
Fax: 734-662-4450
E-mail: apdougherty@compuserve.com
http://www.libraryissues.com
Offers overviews of the trends and problems affecting campus libraries. Explained in layman's terms as they relate to faculty, administrators and the parent institution.

4-6 pages Bi-Monthly
ISSN: 0734-3035

Dr. Richard M Dougherty, Editor
Ann Dougherty, Managing Editor

4553 Library Quarterly
Indiana University, School of Library Science
Lib 013
Bloomington, IN 47405
812-855-5113
Fax: 812-855-6166
Updates, information, statistics, book reviews and publications for librarians.

Quarterly

Stephen P Harter, Editor

4554 Library Resources & Technical Services
Columbia University, School of Library Sciences
516 Butler Library
New York, NY 10027
212-854-3329
Fax: 212-854-8951

Quarterly

Richard P Smirgalia, Editor

4555 Library Trends
Grad. School Library & Info. Science
501 E Daniel Street
Champaign, IL 61820
217-333-1359
Fax: 217-244-7329
E-mail: puboff@alexia.lis.uiuc.edu
http://www.edfu.lis.uiuc.edu/puboff
A scholarly quarterly devoted to invited papers in library and information science. Each issue is devoted to a single theme.

208 pages Quarterly

FW Lancaster, Editor
James Dowling, Managing Editor

4556 Media & Methods Magazine
American Society of Educators
1429 Walnut Street
Philadelphia, PA 19102-3218
215-563-6005
Fax: 215-587-9706
E-mail: claudette@media-methods.com
http://www.media-methods.com
Leading pragmatic magazine for K-12 educators and administrators. The focus is on how to integrate today's technologies and presentation tools into the curriculum. Very up-to-date and well respected national source publication. Loyal readers are media specialists, school librarians, technology coordinators, administrators and classroom teachers.

5x Year

Michele Sokoloff, Publisher
Christine Weiser, Editor

4557 NEWSletter
New Jersey Library Association
PO Box 1534
Trenton, NJ 08607
609-394-8032
Fax: 609-394-8164
E-mail: ptumulty@njla.org
http://www.njla.org
A quarterly newsletter and distributed to more than 1,800 members, serves as a vehicle for communication of library issues and activities among members of NJLA.

Anita O'Malley, Production Manager

4558 Read, America!
Place in the Woods
3900 Glenwood Avenue
Golden Valley, MN 55422-5302
763-374-2120
Fax: 952-593-5593
E-mail: readamerica10732@aol.com
News, book reviews, ideas for librarians and reading program leaders; short stories and poetry pages for adults and children; and an annual Read America! collection with selections of new books solicited from 350 publishers.

12 pages Quarterly Newsletter
ISSN: 0891-4214

Roger Hammer, Editor/Publisher

4559 School Library Journal
360 Park Avenue
New York, NY 10010
646-746-6759
Fax: 646-746-6689
E-mail: slj@reedbusiness.com
http://www.schoollibraryjournal.com
For children, young adults and school librarians.

Francine Fialkoff, Editorial Director
Brian Kenney, Editor-in-Chief

4560 School Library Media Activities Monthly
LMS Associates
17 E Henrietta Street
Baltimore, MD 21230-3910
301-685-8621

Monthly

Paula Montgomery, Editor

4561 School Library Media Quarterly
American Library Association
50 E Huron Street
Chicago, IL 60611-5295
312-944-6780
Fax: 312-280-3255
For elementary and secondary building level library media specialists, district supervisors

and others concerned with the selection and purchase of print and nonprint media.

Quarterly

Judy Pitts, Editor
Barbara Stripling, Editor

4562 Southeastern Librarian (SELn)

Southeastern Library Association
PO Box 950
Rex, GA 30273
770-961-3520
Fax: 770-961-3712
E-mail: gordonbaker@clayton.edu
http://seaonline.org
This quarterly publication seeks to publish articles, announcements and news of professional interest to the library community in the southeast. The publication also represents a significant means for addressing the Association's research objective. Two newsletter-style issues serve as a vehicle for conducting Association business, and two issues include juried articles.

Perry Bratcher, Editor

4563 Special Libraries

Special Libraries Association
1700 18th Street NW
Washington, DC 20009-2514
202-234-4700
Fax: 202-265-9317
Includes information and manuscripts on the administration, organization and operation of special libraries.

Quarterly

Maria Barry, Editor

4564 Specialist

Special Libraries Association
1700 18th Street NW
Washington, DC 20009-2514
202-234-4700
Fax: 202-265-9317
Contains news and information about the special library/information field.

Monthly

Alisa Nesmith Cooper, Editor

4565 TLACast

Texas Library Association
3355 Bee Cave Road
Suite 401
Austin, TX 78746
512-328-1518
800-580-2852
Fax: 512-328-8852
E-mail: tla@txla.org
http://www.txla.org
The association's online newsletter that is published several times a year to keep members informed on TLA issues and events.

Patricia A Smith, Executive Director
Gloria Meraz, Communications Director

4566 Texas Library Journal

Texas Library Association
3355 Bee Cave Road
Suite 401
Austin, TX 78746
512-328-1518
800-580-2852
Fax: 512-328-8852
E-mail: tla@txla.org
http://www.txla.org
ISBN: 0040-4446

Patricia A Smith, Executive Director
Gloria Meraz, Editor

Periodicals / Mathematics

4567 Focus on Learning Problems in Math

Center for Teaching/Learning Math
PO Box 3149
Framingham, MA 01701-3149
508-877-7895
Fax: 508-788-3600
E-mail: msharma@rea.com
An interdisciplinary journal. Edited jointly by the Research Council for Diagnostic and Prescription Mathematics and the Center for Teaching/Learning of Mathematics. The objective of focus is to make available the current research, methods of identification, diagnosis, and remediation of learning problems in mathematics. Contribution from the fields of education psychology and mathematics having the potential to import on classroom or clinical practice are valued.

64-96 pages Quarterly

Mahesh Sharma, Editor

4568 Journal for Research in Mathematics Education

National Council of Teachers of Mathematics
1906 Association Drive
Reston, VA 20191-1502
703-620-9840
Fax: 703-476-2970
E-mail: nctm@nctm.org
http://www.nctm.org
A forum for disciplined inquiry into the teaching and learning of math at all levels— from preschool through adult. Available in print or online version.

5x Year
ISSN: 0021-8251

Harry B Tunis, Publications Director
Rowena G Martelino, Promotions Manager

4569 Journal of Computers in Math & Science

PO Box 2966
Charlottesville, VA 22902-2966
804-973-3087
Fax: 703-997-8760

Quarterly

4570 Journal of Recreational Mathematics

4761 Bigger Road
Kettering, OH 45440-1829
631-691-1470
Fax: 631-691-1770
Promotes the creative practice of mathematics for educational learning.

Quarterly

Joseph S Madachy, Editor

4571 Math Notebook

Center for Teacher/Learning Math
PO Box 3149
Framingham, MA 01705-3149
508-877-7895
Fax: 508-788-3600
A publication for teachers and parents to improve mathematics instruction.

4x/5x Year

Mahesh Sharma, Editor

4572 Mathematics & Computer Education

MAYTC Journal
PO Box 158
Old Bethpage, NY 11804-0158
516-822-5475
Contains a variety of articles pertaining to the field of mathematics.

TriAnnually

George Miller, Editor

4573 Mathematics Teacher

National Council of Teachers of Mathematics
1906 Association Drive
Reston, VA 20191-1502
703-620-9840
Fax: 703-295-0973
E-mail: nctm@nctm.org
http://www.nctm.org
Devoted to the improvement of mathematics instruction in grades 9 and higher.

Monthly
ISSN: 0025-5769

Harry B Tunis, Publications Director
Rowena G Martelino, Promotions Manager

4574 Mathematics Teaching in the Middle School

National Council of Teachers of Mathematics
1906 Association Drive
Reston, VA 20191-1593
703-620-9840
Fax: 703-476-2970
E-mail: nctm@nctm.org
http://www.nctm.org
Addresses the learning needs of students in grades 5-9.

Monthly
ISSN: 1072-0839

Harry B Tunis, Publications Director
Rowena G Martelino, Promotions Manager

4575 NCTM News Bulletin

National Council of Teachers of Mathematics
1906 Association Drive
Reston, VA 20191-9988
703-620-9840
Fax: 703-476-2970
E-mail: nctm@nctm.org
http://www.nctm.org
Publication that reaches all of NCTM's individual and institutional members of more than 107,000 math teachers and school personnel.

Harry B Tunis, Director Publications
Krista Hopkins, Director Marketing Services

4576 Notices of the American Mathematical Society

American Mathematical Society
PO Box 6248
Providence, RI 02940-6248
401-455-4000
Fax: 401-331-3842
Announces programs, meetings, conferences and symposia of the AMS and other mathematical groups.

10x Year

Dr. John S Bradley, Managing Editor
Anne Newcomb, Avertising Coordinator

4577 SSMart Newsletter

School Science & Mathematics Association
Curriculum & Foundations
Bloomsburg, PA 17815
570-389-3894
Fax: 570-389-3894
Membership news offering information, updates, reviews, articles and association news for professionals in the science and mathematics fields of education.

8 pages Quarterly

Darrel Fyffe, Publisher
Norbert Kuenzi, Editor

4578 Teaching Children Mathematics
National Council of Teachers of
Mathematics
1906 Association Drive
Reston, VA 20191-1502
703-620-9840
Fax: 703-476-2970
E-mail: nctm@nctm.org
http://www.nctm.org
Concerned primarily with the teaching of
mathematics from Pre-K through grade 6.

Monthly
ISSN: 1073-5836

Harry B Tunis, Publications Director
Rowena G Martelino, Promotions Manager

Periodicals / Music & Art

**4579 American Academy of Arts &
Sciences Bulletin**
Norton Woods, 136 Irving Street
Cambridge, MA 02138
617-576-5000
Fax: 617-576-5050
Covers current news of the Academy as well
as developments in the arts and sciences.

Alexandra Oleson

4580 Art Education
National Art Education Association
1916 Association Drive
Reston, VA 20191-1590
703-860-8000
Fax: 703-860-2960
A professional journal in the field of art education devoted to articles on all education
levels.

6x Year

Thomas A Hatfield, Editor
Beverly Jeanne Davis, Managing Editor

4581 Arts & Activities
Arts & Activities Magazine
12345 World Trade Drive
San Diego, CA 92128
858-605-0242
E-mail: subs@artsandactivities.com
http://www.artsandactivities.com
For classroom teachers, art teachers and other
school personnel teaching visual art from
kindergarten through college levels.

Monthly
ISSN: 0004-3931

4582 Arts Education Policy Review
Heldref Publications
1319 18th Street NW
Washington, DC 20036-1826
202-296-6267
800-365-9753
Fax: 202-296-5149
http://www.heldref.org
Discusses major policy issues concerning
K-12 education in the various arts. The journal presents a variety of views rather than taking sides and emphasizes analytical
exploration. Its goal is to produce the most insightful, comprehensive and rigorous exchange of ideas ever available on arts
education. The candid discussions are a valuable resource for all those involved in the arts
and concerned about their role in education.

40 pages BiWeekly
ISSN: 1063-2913

Leila Saad, Managing Editor

4583 CCAS Newsletter
Council of Colleges of Arts & Sciences
186 University Hall
Columbus, OH 43210

614-292-1882
Fax: 614-292-8666
Membership newsletter to inform deans
about arts and sciences issues in education.

4-10 pages BiMonthly

Richard J Hopkins, Contact

4584 Choral Journal
American Choral Directors Association
PO Box 6310
Lawton, OK 73506-0310
903-935-7963
Fax: 903-934-8114
E-mail: jmoore@etbu.edu
Publishes scholarly, practical articles and
regular columns of importance to professionals in the fields of choral music and music education. Articles explore conducting
teachnique, rehearsal strategies, historical
performance practice, choral music history
and teaching materials.

Monthly

James A Moore, President

4585 Clavier
200 Northfield Road
Northfield, IL 60093
847-446-5000
Fax: 847-446-6263
Published 10 times each year for piano and
organ teachers, with issues in all months except June and August.

Monthly

4586 Dramatics
Educational Theatre Association
2343 Auburn Avenue
Cincinnati, OH 45219-2815
513-421-3900
Fax: 513-421-7055
E-mail: info@etassoc.org
http://www.etassoc.org
Magazine published by Educational Theatre
Association, a professional association for
theatre educators/artists.

Monthly

David LaFleche, Dir
Membership/Leadership

4587 Flute Talk
200 Northfield Road
Northfield, IL 60093
847-446-5000
Fax: 847-446-6263
Published 10 times each year for flute teachers and intermediate or advanced students,
with issues every month except June and
August.

Monthly

4588 Instrumentalist
200 Northfield Road
Northfield, IL 60093
847-446-5000
Fax: 847-446-6263
Published 12 times each year for band and or-
chestra directors and teachers of instruments
in these groups.

Monthly

4589 Journal of Experiential Education
Association of Experiential Education
2305 Canyon Boulevard
Suite 100
Boulder, CO 80302
303-440-8844
Fax: 303-440-9581
E-mail: aewert@indiana.edu
http://www.aee.org
A professional journal that publishes articles
in outdoor adventure programming, service
learning, environmental education, therapeutic applications, research and theory, the cre-

ative arts, and much more. An invaluable reference tool for anyone in the field of
experiential education.

3x Year
ISSN: 1053-8259

Alan Ewert, Editor

**311 Journal of the American
Musicological Society**
American Musicological Society
6010 College Station
Brunswick, ME 04011
207-798-4243
877-679-7648
Fax: 207-798-4254
E-mail: ams@ams-net.org
http://www.ams-net.org
One of the premier journals in the field, the
Journal of the American Musicological Soci-
ety(JAMS) publishes scholarship from all
fields of musicalinquiry:from historical mu-
sicology, critical theory, music analysis,
iconographyand organology, to performance
practice, aesthetics and hermeneutics,
ethnomusicology, gender and sexuality,
popular music and cultural studies.

ISBN: 0003
ISSN: 0139

Annegret Fauser, Editor-in-Chief
Louise Goldberg, Assistant Editor

4590 Music Educators Journal
National Association for Music Education
1806 Robert Fulton Drive
Reston, VA 20191-4348
703-860-4000
Fax: 703-860-1531
http://www.menc.org
Offers informative, timely and accurate articles, editorials, and features to a national audience of music educators.

BiMonthly
ISSN: 0027-4321

Frances Ponick, Editor, Author

**4591 Music Educators Journal and
Teaching Music**
National Association for Music Education
1806 Robert Fulton Drive
Reston, VA 20191-4348
703-860-4000
Fax: 703-860-4826
http://www.menc.org
Informative, timely and accurate articles, editorials, and features to a national audience of
music educators.

BiMonthly
ISSN: 1069-7446

Jeanne Spaeth, Editor

4592 NAEA News
National Art Education Association
1916 Association Drive
Reston, VA 20191-1502
703-860-8000
Fax: 703-860-2960
E-mail: naea@dgs.dgsys.com
http://www.naea-reston.org
National, state and local news affecting vi-
sual arts education.

24 pages BiMonthly

Dr. Thomas Hatfield, Executive Director

**4593 National Guild of Community
Schools of the Arts**
National Guild of Community Schools of
the Arts
520 8th Avenue
Suite 302, 3rd Floor
New York, NY 10018
212-268-3337
Fax: 212-268-3995

E-mail: info@natguild.org
http://www.nationalguild.org
National association of community based arts education institutions employment opportunities, guildnotes newsletter, and publications catalog.

Monthly

Noah Xifr, Director Membership/Oper.

4594 Oranatics Journal
Educational Theatre Association
2343 Auburn Avenue
Cincinnati, OH 45219-2815
513-451-3900
Fax: 513-421-7077
http://www.etassoc.org
Promotes and strengthens theatre in education - primarily middle school and high school. Sponsors an honor society, various events, numerous publications, and arts education advocacy activities.

9x Year

David LaFleche, Director Membership

4595 SchoolArts Davis Publications
50 Portland Street
Worcester, MA 01682
800-533-2847
Fax: 508-791-0779
http://www.davis-art.com/
Davis has promoted and advocated for art education at both the local and national levels, providing good ideas for teachers and celebrating cultural diversity and the contributions of world cultures through a wide range of art forms.

Wyatt Wade, Publisher
Claire Mowbray Golding, Managing Editor

4596 SchoolArts Magazine
Davis Publications
50 Portland Street
Worcester, MA 01608-2013
508-754-7201
800-533-2847
Fax: 508-791-0779
Aimed at art educators in public and private schools, elementary through high school. Articles offer ideas and information involving art media for the teaching profession and for use in classroom activities.

Monthly
ISSN: 0036-3463

Wyatt Wade, Publisher
Eldon Katter, Editor

4597 Studies in Art Education
Louisiana State University, Dept. of Curriculum
Baton Rouge, LA 70803-0001
225-578-3202
Fax: 225-578-9135
Reports on developments in art education.

Quarterly

Karen A Hamblen, Editor

4598 Teaching Journal
Educational Theatre Association
2343 Auburn Avenue
Cincinnati, OH 45219-2815
513-421-3900
Fax: 513-421-7055
E-mail: info@etassoc.org
http://www.etassoc.org
Journal published by Educational Theatre Association, a professional association for theatre educators/artists.

Quarterly

David LaFleche, Dir Membership/Leadership

4599 Teaching Music
National Association for Music Education
1806 Robert Fulton Drive
Reston, VA 20191-4348
703-860-4000
Fax: 703-860-4826
http://www.menc.org
Offers informative, timely and accurate articles, editorials, and features to a national audience of music educators.

BiMonthly
ISSN: 1069-7446

Christine Stinson, Editor

4600 Ultimate Early Childhood Music Resource
Miss Jackie Music Company
10001 El Monte Street
Shawnee Mission, KS 66207-3631
913-381-3672
Designed to assist parents and teachers engaged in early childhood.

16 pages Quarterly

Jackie Weissman, Publisher
Emily Smith, Editor

Periodicals / Physical Education

4601 Athletic Director
National Association for Sport & Physical Ed.
1900 Association Drive
Reston, VA 20191-1502
703-476-3410
Fax: 703-476-8316
Of interest to athletic directors and coaches.

4 pages SemiAnnually

4602 Athletic Management
College Athletic Administrator
2488 N Triphammer Road
Ithaca, NY 14850-1014
607-272-0265
Fax: 607-273-0701
Offers information on how athletic managers can improve their operations, focusing on high school and college athletic departments.

BiMonthly

Mark Goldberg, Publisher
Eleanor Frankel, Editor

4603 Athletic Training
National Athletic Trainers' Association
2952 N Stemmons Freeway
Dallas, TX 75247-6103
214-637-6282
800-879-6282
Fax: 214-637-2206
http://www.nata.org
Edited for athletic trainers.

100 pages Quarterly Magazine

4604 Athletics Administration
NACDA
PO Box 16428
Cleveland, OH 44116
440-892-4000
Fax: 440-892-4007
E-mail: jwork@nacda.com
http://www.nacda.com
The official publication of the National Association of Collegiate Directors of Athletics (NACDA), Athletics Administration focuses on athletics facilities, new ideas in marketing, promotions, development, le-

gal ramifications and other current issues in collegiate athletics administrations.

44-48 pages BiMonthly
ISSN: 0044-9873

Julie Work, Editor

4605 Journal of Environmental Education
Heldref Publications
1319 18th Street NW
Washington, DC 20036-1826
202-296-6267
800-365-9753
Fax: 202-296-5149
E-mail: jee@heldref.org
http://www.heldref.org
An excellent resource for department chairpersons and directors of programs in environmental, resources, and outdoor education.

48 pages Quarterly
ISSN: 0095-8964

B Alison Panko, Managing Editor

4606 Journal of Experiential Education
Association for Experiential Education
2305 Canyon Boulevard
Suite 100
Boulder, CO 80302
303-440-8844
800-787-7979
Fax: 303-440-9581
E-mail: simps_sv@mail.uwlax.edu
http://www.aee.org
A professional journal that publishes articles in outdoor adventure programming, service learning, environmental education, therapeutic applications, research and theory, the creative arts, and much more. An invaluable reference tool for anyone in the field of experiential education.

3x Year

Steve Simpson, Editor

4607 Journal of Physical Education, Recreation and Dance
American Alliance for Health, Phys. Ed. & Dance
1900 Association Drive
Reston, VA 20191-1502
703-476-3495
Fax: 703-476-9527
Presents new books, teaching aids, facilities, equipment, supplies, news of the profession and related groups.

9x Year

Fran Rowan, Editor

4608 Journal of Teaching in Physical Education
Human Kinetics Incorporation
1607 N Market Street
Champaign, IL 61820
217-351-5076
800-747-4457
Fax: 217-351-2674
http://www.humankinetics.com/jtpe
Journal for in-service and pre-service teachers, teacher educators, and administrators, that presents research articles based on classroom and laboratory studies, descriptive and survey studies, summary and review articles, as well as discussions of current topics.

132 pages Quarterly
ISSN: 0273-5024

M Solmon, Author/Editor
R McBride, Author/Editor

4609 Marketing Recreation Classes
Learning Resources Network
1550 Hayes Drive
Manhattan, KS 66502-5068
785-539-5376
800-678-5376

Successful new class ideas and promotion techniques for recreation instructors.

8 pages Monthly

William Draves, Publisher
Julie Coates, Production Manager

4610 National Association for Sport & Physical Education News

National Association for Sport & Physical Ed.
1900 Association Drive
Reston, VA 20191-1502
703-476-3410
800-321-0789
Fax: 703-476-8316
News of conventions, new publications, workshops, and more, all tailored for people in the field of sports, physical education, coaching, etc. Legislative issues are covered as well as news about the over 20 structures in NASPE.

12 pages Monthly

Paula Kun, Editor

4611 National Standards for Dance Education News

National Dance Association
1900 Association Drive
Reston, VA 20191-1502
703-476-3400
Fax: 703-476-9527
E-mail: nda@aahperd.org
http://www.aahperd.org/nda
News of the National Dance Association activities, national events in dance education and topics of interest to recreation and athletic directors.

12 pages Quarterly

Barbara Hernandez, Executive Director

4612 Physical Education Digest

11 Cerilli Crescent
Sudbury
Ontario, Canada P3E5R5
705-523-3331
800-455-8782
Fax: 705-523-3331
E-mail: coach@pedigest.com
http://www.pedigest.com
Edited for physical educators and scholastic coaches. Condenses practical ideas from periodicals and books.

36 pages Quarterly
ISSN: 0843-2635

Dick Moss, Editor

4613 Physical Educator

Arizona State University
Editorial Office
Department of ESPE
Tempe, AZ 85287
480-965-3875
Fax: 480-965-2569
Offers articles for the physical educator.

Quarterly

Robert Pangrazi, Editor

4614 Quest

Louisiana State University/Dept. of Kinesiology
Huey Room 112
Baton Rouge, LA 70803-0001
225-388-2036
Fax: 225-388-3680
Publishes articles concerning issues critical to physical education in higher education. Its purpose is to stimulate professional development within the field.

Quarterly

4615 Teaching Elementary Physical Education

Human Kinetics Publishers
1607 N Market Street
Champaign, IL 61820-2220
217-351-5076
800-747-4457
Fax: 217-351-2674
A resource for elementary physical educators, by physical educators. Each 32-page issue includes informative articles on current trends, teaching hints, activity ideas, current resources and events, and more.

32 pages BiMonthly Magazine
ISSN: 1045-4853

G Jake Jaquet, Director Journal Division
Margery Robinson, Managing Editor

Periodicals / Reading

4616 Beyond Words

1534 Wells Drive NE
Albuquerque, NM 87112-6383
505-275-2558
Offers information on literature, language arts and English for the teaching professional.

10x Year

4617 Christian Literacy Outreach

Christian Literacy Association
541 Perry Highway
Pittsburgh, PA 15229-1851
412-364-3777
Association news offering membership information, convention news, books and articles for the Christian education professional.

4 pages Quarterly

Joseph Mosca

4618 Exercise Exchange

Appalachian State University
222 Duncan Hall
Boone, NC 28608-0001
828-262-2234
Fax: 828-262-2128
Bi-annual journal which features classroom-tested approaches to the teaching of English language arts from middle school through college; articles are written by classroom practitioners.

BiAnnual
ISSN: 0531-531X

Charles R Duke, Editor

4619 Forum for Reading

Fitchburg State College, Education Department
160 Pearl Street
Fitchburg, MA 01420-2631
978-343-2151
Offers articles, reviews, question and answer columns and more for educators and students.

2x Year

Rona F Flippo, Editor

4620 Journal of Adolescent & Adult Literacy

International Reading Association
800 Barksdale Road
#8139
Newark, DE 19714
302-731-1600
800-336-7323
Fax: 302-731-1057
E-mail: journals@reading.org
http://www.reading.org
Carries articles and departments for those who teach reading in adolescent and adult programs. Applied research, instructional techniques, program descriptions, training of teachers and professional issues.

80-96 pages 8x Year
ISSN: 1081-3004

John Elleins, Editor

4621 Journal of Reading Recovery

Reading Recovery Council of North America
500 W. Wilson Bridge Road
Suite 250
Worthington, OH 43085-5218
614-310-7323
Fax: 614-310-7345
E-mail: jjohnson@readingrecovery.org
http://www.readingrecovery.org
The Journal of Reading Recovery is published twice per year, and is primarily a practitioners journal offering current information on Reading Recovery teaching theory, implementation and research for K-6 classroom literacy.

Jady Johnson, Executive Director
Linda Wilson, Executive Assistant

4622 Laubach LitScape

Laubach Literacy Action
1320 Jamesville Avenue
Syracuse, NY 13210
315-422-9121
888-528-2224
Fax: 315-422-6369
E-mail: info@laubach.org
http://www.laubach.org
Includes articles about national literacy activities as well as support and information on tutoring, resources, training, new readers, program management, and recruitment and retention of students and volunteers.

12 pages Quarterly

Linda Church, Managing Editor

4623 Literacy Advocate

Laubach Literacy Action
1320 Jamesville Avenue
Syracuse, NY 13210
315-422-9121
888-528-2224
Fax: 315-422-6369
E-mail: info@laubach.org
http://www.laubach.org
Covers United States and international programs and membership activities.

8 pages Quarterly

Beth Kogut, Editor

4624 News for You

Laubach Literacy Action
1320 Jamesville Avenue
Syracuse, NY 13210
315-422-9121
888-528-2224
Fax: 315-422-6369
E-mail: info@laubach.org
http://www.laubach.org
A newspaper for older teens and adults with special reading needs. Includes US and world news written at a 4th to 6th grade reading level.

4 pages Weekly
ISSN: 0884-3910

Heidi Stephens, Editor

4625 Phonics Institute

PO Box 98785
Tacoma, WA 98498-0785
253-588-3436
E-mail: mah@readingstore.com
http://www.readingstore.com
Restoration of intensive phonics to beginning reading instruction.

8 pages 5x Year

4626 RIF Newsletter
Smithsonian Institution
900 Jefferson Drive SW
Washington, DC 20560-0004
202-357-2888
Fax: 202-786-2564
Describes RIF's nationwide reading motivation program.
TriQuarterly

4627 Read, America!
Place in the Woods
3900 Glenwood Avenue
Golden Valley, MN 55422-5302
763-374-2120
Fax: 952-593-5593
E-mail: readamerica10732@aol.com
News, book reviews, ideas for librarians and reading program leaders; short stories and poetry pages for adults and children; and an annual Read America! collection with selections of new books solicited from 350 publishers.
12 pages Quarterly Newsletter
ISSN: 0891-4214

Roger Hammer, Editor/Publisher

4628 Reading Improvement
Project Innovation of Mobile
PO Box 8508
Mobile, AL 36689-0508
334-633-7802
A journal dedicated to improving reading and literacy in America.
Quarterly

Dr. Phil Feldman, Editor

4629 Reading Psychology
Texas A&M University, College of Education
Department of Education
College Station, TX 77843-0001
979-845-7093
Fax: 979-845-9663
Quarterly

Dr. William H. Rupley, Editor

4630 Reading Research Quarterly
Ohio State University
1945 N High Street
Columbus, OH 43210-1120
614-292-8054
Fax: 614-292-1816
Delves into reading ratings and special concerns in the field of literacy.
Quarterly

Dr. Robert Tierney, Editor

4631 Reading Research and Instruction
Appalachian State University, College of Education
Dept. of Curriculum & Instruction
Boone, NC 28608-0001
828-262-6055
Quarterly

William E Blanton, Editor

4632 Reading Teacher
International Reading Association
800 Barksdale Road
#8139
Newark, DE 19711-3204
302-731-1600
800-336-READ
Fax: 301-731-1057
Carries articles and departments for those who teach reading in preschool and elementary schools. Applied research, instructional techniques, program descriptions, the training of teachers, professional issues and special feature re-

views of children's books and ideas for classroom practice.
8x Year

Dr. James Baumann, Journal Editor
Linda Hunter, Advertising Manager

4633 Reading Today
International Reading Association
800 Barksdale Road
#8139
Newark, DE 19711-3204
302-731-1600
800-336-READ
Fax: 302-731-1057
Edited for IRA individual and institutional members offering information for teachers, news of the education profession and information for and relating to parents, councils and international issues.
36-44 pages BiMonthly

Linda Hunter, Advertising Manager
John Mickles, Editor

4634 Recording for the Blind & Dyslexic
69 Mapleton Road
Princeton, NJ 08540
609-750-1830
Fax: 609-750-9653
E-mail: scampbell@rfbd.org
http://www.rfbd.org
Textbooks on tape for students who cannot read standard print.

Stephanie Campbell, Executive Director

4635 Report on Literacy Programs
Business Publishers
8737 Colesville Road
Suite 1100
Silver Spring, MD 20910-3928
301-587-6300
800-274-6737
Fax: 301-585-9075
E-mail: bpinews@bpinews.com
http://www.bpinews.com
Reports on the efforts of business and government to provide literacy training to adults— focusing on the effects of literacy on the workforce.
8-10 pages BiWeekly

Eric Easton, Publisher
Dave Speights, Editor

4636 Visual Literacy Review & Newsletter
International Visual Literacy Association
Virginia Tech
Old Security Building
Blacksburg, VA 24061
540-231-8992
Forum for sharing research and practice within an educational context in the area of visual communication.
8 pages BiMonthly

Richard Couch

4637 WSRA Journal
University of Wisconsin - Oshkosh
1863 Doty Street
Oshkosh, WI 54901-6978
920-424-7231
Fax: 920-326-6280
E-mail: wsra@centurytel.net
A quarterly publication of the Wisconsin State Reading Association that publishes articles about literacy for academicians, teachers, libraries and literary workers.
Quarterly

Dr. Margaret Humadi Genisio, Editor

4638 What's Working in Parent Involvement
The Parent Institute
PO Box 7474
Fairfax Station, VA 22039-7474
703-323-9170
Fax: 703-323-9173
http://www.parent-institute.com
Focuses on parent involvement in children's reading education.
10x Year

John Wherry, Publisher

Periodicals / Secondary Education

4639 ACTIVITY
American College Testing
2201 Dodge
Iowa City, IA 52243-0001
319-337-1410
Fax: 319-337-1014
Distributed free of charge to more than 100,000 persons concerned with secondary and postsecondary education. ACT, an independent nonprofit organization provides a broad range of educational programs and services throughout this country and abroad.
Quarterly

Dan Lechay, Editor

4640 Adolescence
Libra Publishers
3089C Clairemont Drive
PNB 383
San Diego, CA 92117-6802
858-571-1414
Fax: 858-571-1414
Articles contributed by professionals spanning issues relating to teenage education, counseling and guidance. Paperback.
256 pages Quarterly
ISSN: 0001-8449

William Kroll, Editor

4641 American Secondary Education
Bowling Green State University
Education Room 531
Bowling Green, OH 43403-0001
419-372-7379
Fax: 419-372-8265
Serves those involved in secondary education— administrators, teachers, university personnel and others. Examines and reports on current issues in secondary education and provides readers with information on a wide range of topics that impact secondary education professionals. Professionals are provided with the most up-to-date theories and practices in their field.
Quarterly

Gregg Brownell, Editor
Madu Ireh, Graduate Editor

4642 Child and Youth Care Forum
Kluwer Academic/Human Sciences Press
233 Spring Street
New York, NY 10013
212-620-8000
800-221-9369
Fax: 212-463-0742
http://www.wkpa.nl
Independent, professional publication committed to the improvement of child and youth care practice in a variety of day and residential settings and to the advancement of this field. Designed to serve child and youth care practitioners, their supervisors, and other personnel in child and youth care settings, the journal provides a channel of communication and debate including material on

practice, selection and training, theory and research, and professional issues.

Bimonthly
ISSN: 1053-1890

Carol Bischoff, Publisher
Doug Magnuson, Co-Editor

4643 Family Therapy: The Journal of the California Graduate School of Family Psychology
Libra Publishers
3089C Clairemont Drive
PNB 383
San Diego, CA 92117-6802
858-571-1414
Fax: 858-571-1414
Articles contributed by professionals spanning issues relating to teenage education, counseling and guidance. Paperback.

96 pages Quarterly
ISSN: 0091-6544

William Kroll, Editor

4644 High School Journal
University of North Carolina
212-D #3500
Chapel Hill, NC 27599-0001
919-962-1395
Fax: 919-962-1533
The Journal publishes articles dealing with adolescent growth, development, interests, beliefs, values, learning, etc., as they effect school practice. In addition, it reports on research dealing with teacher, administrator and student interaction within the school setting. The audience is primarily secondary school teachers and administrators, as well as college level educators.

60 pages Quarterly
ISSN: 0018-1498

Dr. George Noblit, Editor

4645 Independent School
National Association of Independent Schools
75 Federal Street
Boston, MA 02110-1913
617-451-2444
Contains information and opinion about secondary and elementary education in general and independent education in particular.

TriAnnually

Thomas W Leonhardt, Editor
Kurt R Murphy, Advertising/Editor

4646 Journal of At-Risk Issues
Clemson University
209 Martin Street
Clemson, SC 29631-1555
864-656-2599
800-443-6392
Fax: 864-656-0136
E-mail: NDPC@clemson.edu
http://www.dropoutprevention.org

Publication Date: 0 36 pages
ISBN: 1098-1608

Dr. Judy Johnson, Author
Dr. Judy Johnson, Author
Dr. Alice Fisher, Editor

4647 NASSP Bulletin
National Assn. of Secondary School Principals
1904 Association Drive
Reston, VA 20191-1537
703-860-0200
800-253-7746
Fax: 703-620-6534
E-mail: nassp@nassp.org

For administrators at the secondary school level dealing with subjects that range from the philosophical to the practical.

TriAnnual

Eugenia Cooper Potter, Editor

4648 Parents Still Make the Difference!
The Parent Institute
PO Box 7474
Fairfax Station, VA 22039-7474
703-323-9170
Fax: 703-323-9173
http://www.parent-institute.com
Newsletter focusing on parent involvement in children's education. Focuses on parents of children in grades 7-12.

Monthly
ISSN: 1523-2395

Betsie Millar, Author
John Wherry, Publisher

4649 Parents Still Make the Difference!: Middle School Edition
The Parent Institute
PO Box 7474
Fairfax Station, VA 22039-7474
703-323-9170
Fax: 703-323-9173
http://www.parent-institute.com
Newsletter focusing on parent involvement in children's education. Focuses on parents of children in grades 7-12.

Monthly
ISSN: 1071-5118

John Wherry, Publisher

Periodicals / Science

4650 American Biology Teacher
National Association of Biology Teachers
12030 Sunrise Valley Drive
Reston, VA 20191
703-264-9696
800-406-0775
Fax: 703-264-7778
E-mail: office@nabt.org
http://www.nabt.org
Edited for elementary, secondary school, junior college, four-year college and university teachers of biology.

80 pages 9 times a year

Cheryl Merrill, Managing Editor
Kay Acevedo, Publications Specialist

4651 AnthroNotes
Smithsonian Institution Anthropology Outreach Offi
PO Box 37012
Washington, DC 20013-7012
202-633-1917
Fax: 202-357-2208
E-mail: anthroutreach@si.edu
http://www.nmnsi.edu/anthro
Offers archeological, anthropological research in an engaging style.

20 pages

Ann Krupp, Editor

4652 Appraisal: Science Books for Young People
Children's Science Book Review Committee
Boston University
School of Education
Boston, MA 02215
617-353-4150
This is a journal dedicated to the review of science books for children and young adults. Now in its 27th year of publication, Appraisal reviews nearly all of the science books pub-

lished yearly for pre-school through high-school age young people. Each book is examined by a children's librarian and by a specialist in its particular discipline.

Quarterly

Diane Holzheimer, Editor

4653 Association of Science-Technology Centers Dimensions
1025 Vermont Avenue NW
Suite 500
Washington, DC 20005-3516
202-783-7200
Fax: 202-783-7207
E-mail: info@astc.org
http://www.astc.org

20 pages
ISSN: 1528-820X

Carolyn Sutterfield, Author
Bonnie VanDorn, Executive Director
Wendy Pollock, Dir Communication/Research

4654 CCAS Newsletter
Council of Colleges of Arts & Sciences
186 University Hall
Columbus, OH 43210
614-292-1882
Fax: 614-292-8666
Membership newsletter to inform deans about arts and sciences issues in education.

4-10 pages BiMonthly

Richard J Hopkins, Contact

4655 Cream of the Crop
California Foundation for Agriculture
2300 River Plaza Drive
Sacramento, CA 95833-3293
916-561-5625
800-700-2482
Fax: 916-561-5697
E-mail: info@learnaboutag.org
http://www.LearnAboutAg.org
E-newsletter released monthly with articles about agriculture related resources, ideas, information and CFAITC event overviews.

Judy Culbertson, Executive Director
Mindy DeRohan, Communications Coordinator

4656 Journal of College Science Teaching
National Science Teachers Association
1840 Wilson Boulevard
Arlington, VA 22201-3000
703-243-7100
800-782-6782
Fax: 703-243-7177
http://www.nsta.org
Professional journal for college and university teachers of introductory and advanced science with special emphasis on interdisciplinary teaching of nonscience majors. Contains feature articles and departments including a science column, editorials, lab demonstrations, problem solving techniques and book reviews.

6x Year

Dr. Gerald Wheeler, Executive Director
Michael Byrnes, Managing Editor

4657 Journal of Environmental Education
Heldref Publications
1319 18th Street NW
Washington, DC 20036-1826
202-296-6267
800-365-9753
Fax: 202-296-5149
A vital research journal for everyone teaching about the environment. Each issue features case studies of relevant projects, evaluation of new research, and discussion of public policy and philosophy in the area of environmental education. The Journal is an

excellent resource for department chairpersons and directors of programs in outdoor education.

Quarterly

Kerri P Kilbane, Editor

4658 Journal of Research in Science Teaching

Wiley InterScience
Wiley Corporate Headquarters
111 River Street
Hoboken, NJ 07030-5774
201-748-6000
Fax: 201-748-6088
http://www.interscience.wiley.com

10x Year

4659 NSTA Reports!

National Science Teachers Association
1840 Wilson Boulevard
Arlington, VA 22201-3000
703-243-7100
800-782-6782
Fax: 703-243-7177
http://www.nsta.org
The association's timely source of news on issues of interest to science teachers of all levels. Includes national news, information on teaching materials, announcements of programs for teachers and students, and advance notice about all NSTA programs, conventions and publications.

52 pages BiMonthly

Dr. Gerald Wheeler, Executive Director
Jodi Peterson, Editor

4660 Odyssey

Cobblestone Publishing
30 Grove Street
Suite C
Peterborough, NH 03458-1453
603-924-7209
800-821-0115
Fax: 603-924-7380
E-mail: custsvc@cobblestonepub.org
http://www.odysseymagazine.com
Secrets of science are probed with each theme issues's articles, interviews, activities and math puzzles. Astronomical concepts are experienced with Jack Horkheimer's Star Gazer cartoon and Night-Sky Navigation.

48 pages Monthly
ISSN: 0163-0946

Elizabeth E Lindstrom, Editor

4661 Physics Teacher

American Association of Physics Teachers
One Physics Ellipse
College Park, MD 20740-3845
301-209-3300
Fax: 301-209-0845
E-mail: aapt-web@aapt.org
http://www.aapt.org
Published by the American Association of Physics Teachers and dedicated to the improvement of the teaching of introductory physics at all levels.

9x Year

Karl C Mamola, Editor
Pamela R Brown, Senior Editorial Associate

4662 Quantum

National Science Teachers Association
1840 Wilson Boulevard
Arlington, VA 22201-3000
703-243-7100
800-782-6782
Fax: 703-243-7177
http://www.nsta.org

Illustrated magazine containing material translated from Russian magazine Kvant as well as original material specifically targeted to American students. In addition to feature articles and department pieces, Quantum offers olympiad-style problems and brainteasers. Each issue also contains an answer section.

BiMonthly

Dr. Gerald Wheeler, Executive Director
Mike Donaldson, Managing Editor

4663 Reports of the National Center for Science Education

National Center for Science Education
925 Kearney Street
El Cerrito, CA 94530-2810
510-601-7203
800-290-6006
Fax: 510-601-7204
E-mail: ncse@ncseweb.org
http://www.ncseweb.org
An examination of issues and current events in science education with a focus on evolutionary science, and the evolution/creation controversy.

36-44 pages BiMonthly Newsletter
ISSN: 1064-2358

Eugenie C Scott, PhD, Publisher
Andrew J Petto PhD, Editor

4664 Science Activities

Heldref Publications
1319 18th Street NW
Washington, DC 20036-1826
202-296-6267
800-365-9753
Fax: 202-296-5149
E-mail: sa@heldref.org
http://www.heldref.org
A storehouse of up-to-date creative science projects and curriculum ideas for the K-12 classroom teacher. A one-step source of experiments, projects and curriculum innovations in the biological, physical and behavioral sciences, the journal's ideas have been teacher tested, providing the best of actual classroom experiences. Regular departments feature news notes, computer news, book reviews and new products and resources for the classroom.

48 pages Quarterly
ISSN: 0036-8121

Betty Bernard, Managing Editor

4665 Science News Magazine

1719 N Street NW
Washington, DC 20036-2888
202-785-2255
Fax: 202-659-0365
Information and programs in all areas of science.

Weekly

4666 Science Scope

National Science Teachers Association
1840 Wilson Boulevard
Arlington, VA 22201-3000
703-243-7100
800-782-6782
Fax: 703-243-7177
http://www.nsta.org
Specifically for middle-school and junior-high science teachers. Science Scope addresses the needs of both new and veteran teachers. The publication includes classroom activities, posters and teaching tips, along with educational theory on the way adolescents learn.

8x Year

Dr. Gerald Wheeler, Executive Director
Ken Roberts, Managing Editor

4667 Science Teacher

National Science Teachers Association
1840 Wilson Boulevard
Arlington, VA 22201-3000
703-243-7100
800-782-6782
Fax: 703-243-7177
http://www.nsta.org
Professional journal for junior and senior high school science teachers. Offers articles on a wide range of scientific topics, innovative teaching ideas and experiments, and current research news. Also offers reviews, posters, information on free or inexpensive materials, and more.

9x Year

Dr. Gerald Wheeler, Executive Director
Shelley Johnson Carey, Managing Editor

4668 Science and Children

National Association of Science Teachers
1840 Wilson Boulevard
Arlington, VA 22201-3000
703-243-7100
800-782-6782
Fax: 703-243-7177
http://www.nsta.org
Dedicated to preschool through middle school science teaching provides lively how-to articles, helpful hints, software and book reviews, colorful posters and inserts, think pieces and on-the-scene reports from classroom teachers.

8x Year

Dr. Gerald Wheeler, Executive Director
Linda L Roswog, Managing Editor

4669 Sea Frontiers

International Oceanographic Foundation
4600 Rickenbacker Causeway
Key Biscayne, FL 33149-1031
305-361-4888
A general interest magazine about science education including underwater studies.

BiMonthly

Bonnie Gordon, Editor

4670 Teacher Resource Guide

California Foundation for Agriculture
2300 River Plaza Drive
Sacramento, CA 95833
916-561-5625
800-722-2482
Fax: 916-561-5697
E-mail: infolearnaboutag.org
http://www.LearnAboutAg.org
This is a must have tool for professional and volunteers encouraging the agriculturalliteracy of California's youth. Resources that assist in teaching about agriculture are plentiful. This guide provides an all-encompassing look at the array of materials that readily support such an endeavor.

Judy Culbertson, Executive Director
Mindy DeRohan, Communications Coordinator

4671 Universe in the Classroom

Astronomical Society of the Pacific
390 Ashton Avenue
San Francisco, CA 94112-1722
415-337-1100
Fax: 415-337-5205
E-mail: astroed@astrosociety.org
http://www.astrosociety.org/uitc
On teaching astronomy in grades 3-12, including astronomical news, plain-English explanations, teaching resources and classroom activities.

8 pages Quarterly

Noel Encaracian, Customer Service

Periodicals / Social Studies

4672 Alumni Newsletter
Jewish Labor Committee
25 E 21st Street
Floor 2
New York, NY 10010-6207
212-477-0707
Fax: 212-477-1918
Newsletter of American public secondary school teachers who teach about the Holocaust and Jewish Resistance to the Nazis during World War II.

8 pages SemiAnnually

Arieh Lebowitz

4673 American Sociological Review
Pennsylvania State University
206 Oswald Tower, Sociology Dept
University Park, PA 16802
814-865-5021
Fax: 814-865-0705
Addresses most aspects of sociology in a general range of categories for academic and professional sociologists.

Bimonthly

Glenn Firebaugh, Editor

4674 AnthroNotes
Anthropology Outreach Office
PO Box 37012
Washington, DC 20013-7012
202-357-1592
Fax: 202-357-2208
Offers archeological, anthropological research in an engaging style.

4675 AppleSeeds
Cobblestone Publishing
30 Grove Street
Suite C
Peterborough, NH 03458-1453
603-924-7209
800-821-0115
Fax: 603-924-7380
E-mail: custsvc@cobblestonepub.com
http://www.cobblestonepub.com
A delightful way to develop love of non-fiction reading in grades 2-4. Full color articles, photographs, maps, activities that grab student and teacher interest. Children's doings and thinking around the world in Mail Bag.

32 pages Monthly
ISSN: 1099-7725

Susan Buckey, Barb Burt, Editors, Author
Lou Waryncia, Managing Editor

4676 Boletin
Center for the Teaching of the Americas
Immaculata College
Immaculata, PA 19345
610-647-4400
School teaching of the Americas.

Quarterly

Sr. Mary Consuela

4677 California Weekly Explorer
California Weekly Reporter
285 E Main Street
Suite 3
Tustin, CA 92780-4429
714-730-5991
Fax: 714-730-3548
Resources, events, awards and reviews relating to California history.

16 pages Weekly

Don Oliver

4678 Calliope
Cobblestone Publishing
30 Grove Street
Suite C
Peterborough, NH 03458-1453
603-924-7209
800-821-0115
Fax: 603-924-7380
E-mail: custsvc@cobblestonepub.com
http://www.cobblestonepub.com
Invests in world history with reality not only through articles, stories and maps but also current events and resource lists. Calliope's themes are geared to topics studied in world history classrooms.

48 pages Monthly
ISSN: 1058-7086

Lou Waryncia, Managing Editor
Charles F Baker, Editors

4679 Capitalism for Kids
National Schools Commitee for Economic Education
330 East 70th Street
Suite 5J
New York, NY 10021-8641
212-535-9534
Fax: 212-535-4167
E-mail: info@nscee.org
http://www.nscee.org
Teaches young people about capitalism and the free enterprise system in a clear and entertaining styl. Disscusses the practical aspects of starting a small business.

247 pages

John E Donnelly, Executive Director

4680 Cobblestone
Cobblestone Publishing
30 Grove Street
Suite C
Peterborough, NH 03458-1445
603-924-7209
800-821-0115
Fax: 603-924-7380
E-mail: custsvc@cobblestonepub.com
http://www.cobblestonepub.com
Blends sound information with excellent writing, a combination that parents and teachers appreciate. Cobblestone offers imaginative approaches to introduce young readers to the world of American history.

48 pages Monthly
ISSN: 0199-5197

Lou Waryncia, Managing Editor
Meg Chorlian, Editor

4681 Colloquoy on Teaching World Affairs
World Affairs Council of North California
312 Sutter Street
Suite 200
San Francisco, CA 94108-4311
415-982-3263
Fax: 415-982-5028
Offers information, articles and updates for the history teacher.

3x Year

Cassie Todd

4682 Faces
Cobblestone Publishing
30 Grove Street
Suite C
Peterborough, NH 03458-1453
603-924-7209
800-821-0115
Fax: 603-924-7380
E-mail: custsvc@cobblestonepub.com
http://www.cobblestonepub.com
The world is brought to the classroom through the faces of its people. World culture encourages young readers' perspectives through history, folk tales, news and activities.

48 pages Monthly
ISSN: 0749-1387

Lou Waryncia, Managing Editor
Elizabeth Crooker Carpentiere, Editor

4683 Focus
Freedoms Foundation at Valley Forge
PO Box 706
Valley Forge, PA 19482-0706
215-933-8825
800-896-5488
Fax: 610-935-0522
E-mail: tsueta@ffvf.org
http://www.ffvf.org
Strives to teach America and promote responsible citizenship through educational programs and awards designed to recognize outstanding Americans.

6 pages Quarterly

Thomas M Sueat, Editor

4684 Footsteps
Cobblestone Publishing
30 Grove Street
Suite C
Peterborough, NH 03458-1453
603-924-7209
800-821-0115
Fax: 603-924-7380
E-mail: custsvc@cobblestonepub.com
http://www.cobblestonepub.com
Celebrates heritage of African Americans and explores their contributions to culture from colonial times to present. Courage, perserverance mark struggle for freedom and equality in articles, maps, photos, etc.

48 pages 9x Year
ISSN: 1521-5865

Lou Waryncia, Managing Editor
Charles Baker, Editor

4685 History Matters Newsletter
National Council for History Education
26915 Westwood Road
Suite B-2
Westlake, OH 44145-4657
440-835-1776
Fax: 440-835-1295
E-mail: nche@nche.nett
http://www.history.org/nche
Serves as a resource to help members improve the quality and quantity of history learning.

8 pages Monthly
ISSN: 1090-1450

Elaine W Reed, Executive Director

**4686 Inquiry in Social Studies:
Curriculum, Research & Instruction**
University of North Carolina-Charlotte
Dept of Curriculum & Instruction
Charlotte, NC 28223
704-547-4500
Fax: 704-547-4705
An annual journal of North Carolina Council for the Social Studies with a readership of 1,400.

Annual

John A Gretes, Editor
Jeff Passe, Editor

4687 Journal of American History
Organization of American Historians
121 N Bryan Street
Bloomington, IN 47408-4136
812-855-7311
800-446-8923
Fax: 812-855-0696

Contains articles and essays concerning the study and investigation of American history.

Quarterly

Tamzen Meyer, Editor

4688 Journal of Economic Education

Heldref Publications
1319 18th Street NW
Washington, DC 20036-1826
202-296-6267
800-365-9753
Fax: 202-296-5149
Offers original articles on innovations in and evaluations of teaching techniques, materials and programs in economics.

Quarterly
ISSN: 0022-4085

4689 Journal of Geography

National Council for Geographic Education
700 Pelham Road N
Jacksonville, AL 36265
256-782-5293
Fax: 256-782-5336
E-mail: ncge@jsu.edu
http://www.ncge.org
Stresses the essential value of geographic education and knowledge in schools.

Quarterly
ISSN: 0022-1341

Michal LeVasseur, Executive Director
Allison Newton, Associate Director

4690 Magazine of History

Organizations of American History
112 N Bryan Avenue
Bloomington, IN 47408-4199
812-855-7311
800-446-8923
Fax: 812-855-0696
E-mail: oah@oah.org
http://www.oah.org
Includes informative articles, lesson plans, current historiography and reproducible classroom materials on a particular theme. In addition to topical articles, such columns as Dialogue, Studentspeak and History Headlines allow for the exchange of ideas from all levels of the profession.

70-90 pages Quarterly Magazine
ISSN: 0882-228X

Michael Regoli, Managing Editor

4691 New England Journal of History

Bentley College
Dept of History
Waltham, MA 02254
781-891-2509
Fax: 781-891-2896
Covers all aspects of American history for the professional and student.

3x Year

Joseph Harrington, Editor

4692 News & Views

Pennsylvania Council for the Social Studies
11533 Clematis Boulevard
Pittsburgh, PA 15235-3105
717-238-8768
E-mail: lguru1@aol.com
http://www.pcss.org
Offers news, notes, and reviews of interest to social studies educators.

20 pages 5x Year
ISSN: 0894-8712

Jack Suskind, Executive Secretary
Leo R West, Editor

4693 Perspective

Association of Teachers of Latin American Studies
PO Box 620754
Flushing, NY 11362-0754
718-428-1237
Fax: 718-428-1237
Promotes the teaching of Latin America in US schools and colleges.

10 pages BiMonthly

Daniel Mugan

4694 Social Education

National Council for the Social Studies
8555 Sixteenth Street
Suite 500
Silver Spring, MD 20910
301-588-1800
800-683-0812
Fax: 301-588-2049
E-mail: sgriffin@ncss.org
http://www.socialstudies.org
Journal for the social studies profession serves middle school, high school and college and university teachers. Social Education features research on significant topics relating to social studies, lesson plans that can be applied to various disciplines, techniques for using teaching materials in the classroom and information on the latest instructional technology.

7x Year
ISSN: 0337-7724

Michael Simpson, Editor
Robin Hayes, Manager

4695 Social Studies

Heldref Publications
1319 18th Street NW
Washington, DC 20036-1826
202-296-6267
800-365-9753
Fax: 202-296-5149
Offers K-12 classroom teachers, teacher educators and curriculum administrators an independent forum for publishing their ideas about the teaching of social studies at all levels. The journal presents teachers' methods and classroom-tested suggestions for teaching social studies, history, geography and the social sciences.

48 pages BiMonthly

Helen Kress, Managing Editor

4696 Social Studies Journal

Pennsylvania Council for the Social Studies
11533 Clematis Boulevard
Pittsburgh, PA 15235-3105
717-238-8768
E-mail: lguru1@aol.com
http://www.pcss.org
Delves into matters of social studies, history, research and statistics for the education professional and science community.

80 pages Annual

Leo R West, Editor
Dr. Saundra McKee, Editor

4697 Social Studies Professional

National Council for the Social Studies
8555 Sixteenth Street
Suite 500
Silver Spring, MD 20910
301-588-1800
800-683-0812
Fax: 301-588-2049
E-mail: sgriffin@ncss.org
http://www.socialstudies.org
Newsletter focusing on strategies, tips and techniques for the social studies educator. New product announcements, professional development opportunities, association news, state and regional meetings.

6 Times

Terri Ackermann, Editor

4698 Social Studies and the Young Learner

National Council for the Social Studies
8555 Sixteenth Street
Suite 500
Silver Spring, MD 20910
301-588-1800
800-683-0812
Fax: 301-588-2049
E-mail: sgriffin@ncss.org
http://www.socialstudies.org
This publication furthers creative teaching in grades K-6, meeting teachers' needs for new information and effective teaching activities.

Quarterly

Steven S. Lapham, Editor

4699 Society For History Education/History Teacher

California State University - Long Beach
CSULB, 1250 Bellflower Blvd.
Long Beach, CA 90840-1601
562-985-2573
Fax: 562-985-5431
E-mail: historytacherjournal@gmail.com
http://www.thehistoryteacher.org
The most widely recognized journal in the United States suppoting all areas of history education, pre-collegiate through university level, with practical and insightful professional analyses of both traditional and innovative teaching techniques.

150 pages Quarterly
ISSN: 0018-2745

Jane Dabel, Editor
Elisa Herrera, Executive Director

4700 Teaching Georgia Government Newsletter

Carl Vinson Institute of Government
201 N Milledge Avenue
Athens, GA 30602-5027
706-542-2736
Fax: 706-542-6239
Substantive and supplementary material for social studies teachers in Georgia. Topics of government, history, archaeology, geography, citizenship, etc. are covered. Publications available and upcoming social studies meetings in the state are also announced.

8 pages TriAnnually

Inge Whittle, Editor
Ed Jackson, Editor

4701 Theory and Research in Social Education

National Council for the Social Studies
8555 Sixteenth Street
Suite 500
Silver Spring, MD 20910
301-588-1800
800-683-0812
Fax: 301-588-2049
E-mail: sgriffin@ncss.org
http://www.socialstudies.org
Features articles covering a variety of topics: teacher training, learning theory, and child development research; instructional strategies; the relationship of the social sciences, philosophy, history and the arts to social education; models and theories used in developing social studies curriculum; and schemes for student participation and social action.

Quarterly

4702 Wall Street Journal - Classroom Edition

PO Box 7019
Chicopee, MA 01021

800-544-0522
Fax: 413-598-2332
E-mail: classroom.edition@wsj.com
http://www.wsjclassroom.com
Monthly student newspaper, with stories drawn from the daily journal that show international, business, economic, and social issues affect students' lives and futures. The newspaper is supported by posters, monthly teacher guides, and videos. Regular features on careers, enterprise, marketing, personal finance and technology. Helps teachers prepare students for the world of work by combining timely articles with colorful graphics, etc.

Monthly

Krishnan Anantharamanz, Editor

4703 Women's History Project News
National Women's History Project
3343 Industrial Drive
Suite #4
Santa Rosa, CA 95403
707-636-2888
Fax: 707-636-2909
E-mail: nwhp@aol.com
http://www.nwhp.org
Monthly E-mail newsletter about US women's history, for educators, researchers, program planners, and general women's history enthusiasts.

Monthly

Molly Murphy MacGregor, Exec. Dir./Co-Founder

Periodicals / Technology in Education

4704 Cable in the Classroom
CCI/Crosby Publishing
214 Lincoln Street
Suite 112
Boston, MA 02134
617-254-9481
Fax: 617-254-9776
http://www.ciconline.org
Most comprehensive guide to integrating educational video with the Internet and other curriculum resources for K-12 educators.

54 pages Monthly
ISSN: 1054-5409

Stephen P Crosby, Publisher
Al Race, Executive Editor

4705 Connections/EdTech News
Commonwealth of Learning
1055 W. Hastings Street
Suite 1200
Vancouver BC-V6E
604-775-8200
Fax: 604-775-8210
E-mail: info@col.org
http://www.col.org/connections
Published three times per year to, these newsletters provide a continually updated mailing list of over 9,000 government officials, education leaders and international agencies with information on COL's work with its partners as well as other developments worldwide.

Dave Wilson, Editor-In-Chief

4706 E-School News
7920 Norfolk Avenue
Suite 900
Bethesda, MD 20814
301-913-0115
800-394-0115
Fax: 301-913-0119
http://www.eschoolnews.com

Monthly newspaper dedicated to providing news and information to help educators use technology to improve education.

Monthly

Gregs Downey, Publisher

4707 EDUCAUSE Quarterly
EDUCAUSE
4772 Walnut Street
Suite 206
Boulder, CO 80301-2538
303-544-5665
Fax: 303-440-0461
E-mail: pdeblois@educause.edu
http://www.educause.edu
Strategic policy advocacy; teaching and learning initiatives; applied research; special interest collaboration communities; awards for leadership and exemplary practices; and extensive online information services.

Quarterly Magazine
ISSN: 1528-5324

Nancy Hays, Author
Peter DeBlois, Director Communications

4708 EDUCAUSE Review
EDUCAUSE
4772 Walnut Street
Suite 206
Boulder, CO 80301-2408
303-544-5665
Fax: 303-440-0461
E-mail: pdeblois@educause.edu
http://www.educause.edu
Strategic policy advocacy; teaching and learning initiatives applied research; special interest collaboration communities; awards for leadership and exemplary practices; and extensive online information services.

Monthly
ISSN: 1527-6619

Nancy Hays, Author
Peter DeBlois, Director Communications

4709 Education Technology News
Business Publishers
8737 Colesville Road
Suite 1100
Silver Spring, MD 20910-3928
301-587-6300
800-274-6737
Fax: 301-585-9075
E-mail: bpinews@bpinews.com
http://www.bpinews.com
Offers information on computer hardware, multimedia products, software applications, public and private funding and integration of technology into K-12 classrooms.

8 pages BiWeekly

Eric Easton, Publisher
Brian Love, Editorial Coordinato

4710 Educational Technology
700 E Palisade Avenue
Englewood Cliffs, NJ 07632-3040
201-871-4007
800-952-BOOK
Fax: 201-871-4009
Published since 1961, periodical covering the entire field of educational technology. Issues feature essays by leading authorities plus a Research Section. With many special issues covering aspects of the field in depth. Readers are found in some 120 countries.

9x Year

Lawrence Lipsitz, Editor

4711 Electronic Learning
Scholastic
555 Broadway
New York, NY 10012-3919

212-343-6100
800-724-6527
Fax: 212-343-4801
Published for the administrative level, education professionals who are directly responsible for the implementing of electronic technology at the district, state and university levels.

8x Year

Lynn Diamond, Advertising Director
Therese Mageau, Editor

4712 Electronic School
1680 Duke Street
Alexandria, VA 22314
703-838-6722
Fax: 703-683-7590
E-mail: cwilliams@nsba.org
http://www.electronic-school.com
The school technology authority.

Cheryl S Williams, Director
Ann Lee Flynn, Director Education

4713 Information Searcher
Datasearch Group
14 Hadden Road
Scarsdale, NY 10583-3328
914-723-1995
Fax: 914-723-1995
http://www.infosearcher.com
Quarterly newsletter for the Internet and curriculum-technology integration in school.

32 pages

Pam Berger, President
Bill Berger, Treasurer

4714 Journal of Computing in Childhood Education
AACE
PO Box 2966
Charlottesville, VA 22902-2966
757-623-7588
Fax: 703-997-8760
Discusses the realm of software and technology now merging with primary education.

Quarterly

4715 Journal of Educational Technology Systems
58 New Mill Road
Smithtown, NY 11787-3342
516-632-8767
A compendium of articles submitted by professionals regarding the newest technology in the educational field.

Quarterly

Dr. Thomas Liao, Editor

4716 Journal of Information Systems Education
Bryant University
1150 Douglas Pike
Smithfield, RI 02917-1291
401-232-6393
Fax: 401-232-6319
Publishes original articles on current topics of special interest to Information Systems Educators and Trainers. Focus is applications-oriented articles describing curriculum, professional development or facilities issues. Topics include course projects/cases, lecture materials, curriculum design and/or implementation, workshops, faculty/student intern/extern programs, hardware/software selection and industry relations.

Quarterly

Richard Glass, Contact

4717 Journal of Research on Computing in Education
International Society for Technology in Education
480 Charnelton Street
Eugene, OR 97401-2626
541-302-3777
800-336-5191
Fax: 541-302-3778
E-mail: cust_serv@ccmail.uoregon.edu
http://www.iste.org
A quarterly journal of original research and detailed system and project evaluations. It also defines the state of the art and future horizons of educational computing.
Quarterly
Diane McGrath, Editor

4718 Journal of Special Education Technology
The Council for Exceptional Children
1920 Association Drive
Reston, VA 20191-1545
703-620-3660
888-232-7733
Fax: 703-264-9494
Provides professionals in the field with information on new technologies, current research, exemplary practices, relevant issues, legislative events and more concerning the availability and effective use of technology and media for individuals with disabilities and/or who are gifted.
Quarterly
Herbert Rieth, Editor

4719 Matrix Newsletter
Department of CCTE, Teachers
College/Communication
PO Box 8
New York, NY 10027-0008
212-678-3344
Fax: 212-678-8227
Newsletter describing activities and interests of Department of Communication, Computing and Technology.
14 pages SemiAnnually
Marie Sayer

4720 MultiMedia Schools
Information Today
143 Old Marlton Pike
Medford, NJ 08055-8750
609-654-6266
800-300-9868
Fax: 609-654-4309
E-mail: custserv@infotoday.com
http://www.infotoday.com
A practical journal of multimedia, CD-Rom, online and Internet in K-12.
Thomas H Hogan, Publisher
Ferdi Serim, Editor

4721 National Forum of Instructional Technology Journal
McNeese State University
324 Prewitt Street
Lake Charles, LA 70601-5915

337-475-5000
Fax: 318-475-5467
Dr. J Mark Hunter, Editor

4722 Society for Applied Learning Technology
50 Culpeper Street
Warrenton, VA 20186
540-347-0055
800-457-6812
Fax: 540-349-3169
E-mail: info@lti.org
http://www.salt.org
Quarterly

4723 TAM Connector
The Council for Exceptional Children
1920 Association Drive
Reston, VA 20191-1545
703-620-3660
888-232-7733
Fax: 703-264-9494
Contains information about upcoming events, current trends and practices, state and national legislation, recently published materials and practical information relative to the availability and effective use of technology and media for individuals who are gifted or are disabled.
Quarterly
Cynthia Warger, Editor

4724 TECHNOS Quarterly for Education & Technolgy
Agency for Instructional Technology
PO Box A
Bloomington, IN 47402-0120
812-339-2203
Fax: 812-333-4218
E-mail: info@technos.net
http://www.technos.net
TECHNOS Quarterly is a forum for the discussion of ideas about the use of technology in education, with a focus on reform.
36 pages Quarterly
ISSN: 1060-5649
Michael F Sullivan, Executive Director
Carole Novak, Manager TECHNOS Press

4725 Tech Directions
Prakken Publications
275 Meity Drive
Suite 1
Ann Arbor, MI 48107
734-975-2800
Fax: 734-975-2787
E-mail: publisher@techdirections.com
http://www.eddigest.com
Issues programs, projects for educators in career-technical and technology education and monthly features on technology, computers, tech careers.
Monthly
ISSN: 1062-9351
Tom Bowden, Managing Editor

4726 Technology & Learning
CMP Media
600 Harrison Street
San Francisco, CA 94107

516-562-5000
800-607-4410
Fax: 516-562-7013
http://www.techlearning.com
Product reviews; hard-hitting, straightforward editorial features; ideas on challenging classroom activities; and more. Tailor made to the special needs of a professional and an educator.
60-80 pages Monthly Magazine
ISSN: 1053-6728
March & October
Susan McLester, Author
Judy Salpeter, Editor-in-Chief
Jo-Ann McDevitt, Publisher

4727 Technology Integration for Teachers
Master Teacher
Leadership Lane
PO Box 1207
Manhattan, KS 66505-1207
800-669-9633
Fax: 800-669-1132
http://www.masterteacher.com
4 pages Monthly

4728 Technology Teacher
International Technology Education Association
1914 Association Drive
Suite 201
Reston, VA 20191-1538
703-860-2100
Fax: 703-860-0353
E-mail: itea@iris.org
http://www.iteawww.org
Seeks to advance technological literacy through professional development activities and publications.
40 pages 8x Year
Kendall Starkweather, Executive Director
Kathleen de la Paz, Editor

4729 Technology in Education Newsletter
111 E 14th Street
#140
New York, NY 10003-4103
800-443-7432
This newsletter for K-12 educators and administrators, covers national trends of technology in education.

4730 Web Feet Guides
Thomson Gale
Thomson Gale World Headquarters
27500 Drake Road
Farmington Hills, MI 48331-3535
248-699-4253
http://www.webfeetguides.com
The premier subject guides to the Internet, rigorously reviewed by librarians and educators, fully annotated, expanded and updated monthly. Appropriate for middle school through adult. Available in print, online, or MARC records. For more information, free trials and free samples.
Monthly

General

4731 ABC Feelings Adage Publications
Po Box 7280
Ketchum, ID 83340
208-788-5399
Fax: 208-788-4195
E-mail: info@abcfeelings.com
http://www.abcfeelings.com
Interactive line of children's products that relate feelings to each letter of the alphabet. Encourages dialogue, understanding, communication, enhances self-esteem. Books, audiotape, poster, placemats, charts, activity cards, t-shirts and multicultural activity guides, floor puzzles, feelings dictionary, carpets.

Ages 3-10

Dr. Alexandra Delis-Abrams, President

4732 ABDO Publishing Company
P.O Box 398166
Minneapolis, MN 55439-5300
452-831-2120
800-800-1312
Fax: 800-862-3480
E-mail: info@abdopublishing.com
http://www.abdopub.com
K-8 nonfiction books, including Abdo and Daughters imprint, high/low books for reluctant readers and Checkerboard Library with K-3 science, geography, and biographics for beginning readers. Sand Castle for pre-K to second grade, graduated reading program.

Jill Abdo Hansen, President
James Abdo, Publisher

4733 AGS
4201 Woodland Road
Circle Pines, MN 55014-1796
763-786-4343
800-328-2560
Fax: 800-471-8457
Major test publisher and distributor of tests for literature, reading, English, mathematics, sciences, aptitude, and various other areas of education. Includes information on timing, scoring, teacher's guides and student's worksheets.

4734 AIMS Education Foundation
1595 S Chestnut Avenue
Fresno, CA 93702-4706
559-255-4094
888-733-2467
Fax: 559-255-6396
E-mail: aimsed@fresno.edu
http://www.aimsedu.org
A nonprofit educational foundation that focuses on preparing materials for science and mathematics areas of education.

4735 Ablex Publishing Corporation
PO Box 811
Stamford, CT 06904-0811
201-767-8450
Fax: 201-767-8450
Publishes academic books and journals dealing with many different subject areas. Some of these include: education, linguistics, psychology, library science, computer and cognitive science, writing research and sociology.

Kristin K Butter, President

4736 Acorn Naturalists
155 El Camino Real
Tustin, CA 92780
714-838-4888
800-422-8886
Fax: 714-838-5309
http://www.acornnaturalists.com

Publishes and distributes science and environmental education materials for teachers, naturalists and outdoor educators. A complete catalog is available.

World Wildlife Fund, Author
Jennifer Rigby, Director
Mika Stonehawk, Operations Manager

4737 Active Child
PO Box 2346
Salem, OR 97308-2346
503-371-0865
Publishes creative curriculum for young children.

4738 Active Learning
10744 Hole Avenue
Riverside, CA 92505-2867
909-689-7022
Fax: 909-689-7142
Interactive learning center publishing materials for childhood education.

4739 Active Parenting Publishers
1220 Kennestone Circle
Suite 130
Marietta, GA 30066-6022
770-429-0565
800-825-0060
Fax: 770-429-0334
E-mail: cservice@activeparenting.com
http://www.activeparenting.com
Produces and sells books and innovative video-based programs for use in parent education, self-esteem education and loss education groups/classes.

4740 Addison-Wesley Publishing Company
2725 Sand Hill Road
Menlo Park, CA 94025-7019
650-854-0300
Publisher and distributor of a wide range of fiction, nonfiction and textbooks for grades K-12 in the areas of mathematics, reading, language arts, science, social studies and counseling.

4741 Advance Family Support & Education Program
301 S Frio Street
Suite 103
San Antonio, TX 78207-4422
210-270-4630
Fax: 210-270-4612
Offers books and publications on counseling and support for the family, student and educator.

4742 Alarion Press
PO Box 1882
Boulder, CO 80306-1882
303-443-9039
800-523-9177
Fax: 303-443-9098
E-mail: info@alarion.com
http://www.alarion.com
Video programs, posters, activities, manuals and workbooks dealing with History Through Art and Architecture for grades K-12.

4743 Albert Whitman & Company
250 South Northwest Highway
Suite 320
Park Ridge, IL 60068-2723
847-232-2800
800-255-7675
Fax: 847-581-0039
E-mail: mail@awhitmanco.com
http://www.albertwhitman.com
Children's books.

4744 Allyn & Bacon
160 Gould Street
Needham Heights, MA 02194
781-455-1250
Fax: 781-455-1220
Publisher of college textbooks and professional reference books.

4745 Alpha Publishing Company
1910 Hidden Point Road
Annapolis, MD 21401-6002
410-757-5404
Educational materials for K-12 curricula.

4746 American Association for State & Local History
1717 Church Street
Nashville, TN 37203-2921
615-320-3203
Fax: 615-327-9013
http://www.aaslh.org
How-to books for anyone teaching history or social studies.

4747 American Association of School Administrators
1615 Duke Street
Alexandria, VA 22314-1813
703-528-0700
Fax: 703-528-2146
E-mail: info@aasa.org
http://www.aasa.org

Paul Houston, Executive Director

4748 American Guidance Service
4201 Woodland Road
Circle Pines, MN 55014-1796
612-786-4343
800-328-2560
Fax: 763-783-4658
Largest distributor of educational materials focusing on guidance counselors and educators in the field of counseling. Materials include books, pamphlets, workshops and information on substance abuse, childhood education, alcoholism, inner-city subjects and more.

Matt Keller, Marketing Director

4749 American Institute of Physics
2 Huntington Quadrangle
Suite 1NO1
Melville, NY 11747
516-576-2200
Fax: 516-349-9704
http://www.aip.org
Physics books.

Marc Brodsky, Executive Director

4750 American Nuclear Society
Outreach Department
555 N Kensington Avenue
La Grange Park, IL 60526-5592
708-352-6611
800-323-3044
Fax: 708-352-0499
E-mail: outreach@ans.org
http://www.aboutnuclear.com
Nuclear science and technology, supplemental educational materials for grades K-12. Re-Actions newsletters.

4751 American Physiological Society
9650 Rockville Pike
Bethesda, MD 20814-3991
301-530-7132
Fax: 301-634-7098
http://www.the-aps.org
Videotapes, tracking materials and free teacher resource packets.

4752 American Technical Publishers
10100 Orland Parkway
Suite 200
Orland Parkway, IL 60467-5756
708-957-1100
800-323-3471
Fax: 708-957-1101
E-mail: service@americantech.net
http://www.go2atp.com
Offers instructional materials for a variety
of vocational and technical training areas.

4753 American Water Works Association
6666 W Quincy Avenue
Denver, CO 80235-3098
303-794-7711
800-926-7337
Fax: 303-347-0804
http://www.awwa.org
Activity books, teacher guides and more on
science education.

Gary McCoy, Director-at-large

4754 Ampersand Press
750 Lake Street
Port Townsend, WA 98368
360-379-5187
800-624-4263
Fax: 360-379-0324
E-mail: info@ampersandpress.com
http://www.ampersandpress.com
Nature and science educational games.

Lou Haller, Owner

4755 Amsco School Publications
315 Hudson Street
New York, NY 10013-1085
212-886-6500
800-969-8398
Fax: 212-675-7010
http://www.amscopub.com
Basal textbooks, workbooks and supplementary materials for grades 7-12.

4756 Anderson's Bookshops
123 West Jefferson
Naperville, IL 60540-3832
630-355-2665
Fax: 630-355-3470
http://www.andersonsbookshop.com
The very latest and best trade books to use
in the classroom.

4757 Annenberg/CPB Project
1301 Pennsylvania Avenue NW
Suite 302
Washington, DC 20004-2037
202-783-0500
Fax: 202-783-0333
E-mail: order@learner.org
http://www.learner.org
Offers teaching resources in chemistry, ge-
ology, physics and environmental science.

Pete Neal, General Manager
Larisa M Kirgan, Operations Officer

4758 Art Image Publications
PO Box 160
Derby Line, VT 05830-0568
800-361-2598
Fax: 800-559-2598
http://www.artimagepublications.com
Offers various products including art appreciation kits, art image mini-kits and visual arts programs for grades K-12.

Rachel Ross, President
Rachel Ross, Art Educational Consultant

4759 Art Visuals
PO Box 925
Orem, UT 84059-0925
801-226-6115
Fax: 801-226-6115

E-mail: artvisuals@sisna.com
http://www.artvisuals.tripod.com
Social studies and art history products including an Art History Timeline, 20 feet
long that represents over 50 different
styles, ranging from prehistoric to contemporary art; Modern Art Styles, set of 30
posters depicting 20th century styles;
Multicultural Posters, Africa, India,
China, Japan and the World of Islam, with
18 posters in each culture. Sets on women
artists and African American Artists. Each
set is printed on hard cardstock, laminated
and ultraviolet protected.

Diane Asay, Owner

4760 Asian American Curriculum Project
529 East Third Avenue
San Mateo, CA 94401
650-375-8286
800-874-2242
Fax: 650-375-8797
E-mail: aacpinc@best.com
http://www.asianamericanbooks.com
Develops, promotes and disseminates
Asian-American books to schools, libraries and Asian-Americans. Over 1,500
titles.

Florence M Hongo, General Manager

4761 Association for Science Teacher Education
University of Florida
11000 University Parkway
Pensacola, FL 32514-5732
850-474-2000
Fax: 850-474-3205
http://www.theaste.org
Yearbooks, journals, newsletters and information on AETS.

John Tilloston, President

4762 Association for Supervision & Curriculum Development
ASCD
1703 N Beauregard Street
Alexandria, VA 22311-1717
703-578-9600
800-933-2723
Fax: 703-575-5400
E-mail: member@ascd.org
http://www.ascd.org
Publishers of educational leadership
books, audios and videos focusing on
teaching and learning in all subjects and
grade levels.

4763 Association of American Publishers
71 5th Avenue
Floor 12
New York, NY 10003
212-255-0200
Fax: 212-255-7007
http://www.publishers.org
Association for the book publishing industry.

4764 Atheneum Books for Children
MacMillan Publishing Company
1633 Broadway
New York, NY 10019
212-512-2000
Fax: 800-835-3202
Hardcover trade books for children and
young adults.

4765 Australian Press-Down Under Books
15235 Brand Boulevard
Suite A107
Mission Hills, CA 91345-1423
818-837-3755

Big Books, models for writing, small books and
teacher's ideas books from Australia.

4766 Avon Books
1350 Avenue of the Americas
New York, NY 10019-4702
212-481-5600
Fax: 212-532-2172
Focuses on middle grade paperbacks for the class-
room and features authors such as Cleary, Avi,
Borks, Hous, Reeder, Hobbs, Hahn, Taylor and
Prish.

4767 Ballantine/Del Rey/Fawcett/Ivy
201 E 50th Street
New York, NY 10022-7703
212-782-9000
800-638-6460
Fax: 212-782-8438
Offer paperback books for middle school and junior and senior high.

4768 Barron's Educational Series
250 Wireless Boulevard
Hauppauge, NY 11788-3924
631-434-3311
800-645-3476
Fax: 631-434-3217
E-mail: barrons@barronseduc.com
http://www.barronseduc.com
Educational books, including a full line of juvenile fiction and non-fiction, and titles for test prep
and guidance, ESL, foreign language, art history
and techniques, business, and reference.

Frederick Glasser, Director School/Library Sale

4769 Baylor College of Medicine
One Baylor Plaza
Houston, TX 77030
713-798-4951
Fax: 713-798-6521
http://www.bcm.edu
Offers materials and programs in the scientific
area from Texas Scope, Sequence and Coordination projects.

Peter G Traber, President
Robert H Allen, Chairman

4770 Beech Tree Books
1350 Avenue of the Americas
New York, NY 10019-4702
212-261-6500
Fax: 212-261-6518
Curriculum offering reading materials, fiction
and nonfiction titles.

4771 Black Butterfly Children's Books
625 Broadway
Floor 10
New York, NY 10012-2611
212-982-3158
A wide variety of books focusing on children,
hardcover and paperback.

4772 Blake Books
2222 Beebee Street
San Luis Obispo, CA 93401-5505
805-543-7314
800-727-8550
Fax: 805-543-1150
Photo books on nature, endangered species, habitats, etc. for ages 10 and up.

Paige Torres, President

4773 Bluestocking Press Catalog
Bluestocking Press
PO Box 1014
Placerville, CA 95997-1014
530-622-8586
800-959-8586
Fax: 530-642-9222
E-mail: Jane@bluestockingpress.com
http://www.bluestockingpress.com

Approximately 800 items with a concentration in American History, economics and law. That includes fiction, nonfiction, primary source material, historical documents, facsimile newspapers, historical music, hands-on-kits, audio history, coloring books and more.

Jane A Williams, Coordinating Editor

4774 Boyds Mill Press
815 Church Street
Honesdale, PA 18431-1889
570-253-1164
Fax: 570-253-0179
Publishes books for children from preschool to young adult.

4775 BridgeWater Books
100 Corporate Drive
Mahwah, NJ 07430-2041
Distinctive children's hardcover books featuring award-winning authors and illustrators, including Laurence Yep, Babette Cole, Joseph Bruchac and others. An imprint of Troll Associates.

4776 Bright Ideas Charter School
2507 Central Freeway East
Wichita Falls, TX 76302-5802
940-767-1561
Fax: 940-767-1904
E-mail: lydiaplmr@aol.com
K-12 curriculum framework for educators struggling to move toward a global tomorrow.

Lynda Plummer, President

4777 Brown & Benchmark Publishers
25 Kessel Court
Madison, WI 63711
608-273-0040
College textbooks in language arts and reading.

4778 Bureau for At-Risk Youth Guidance Channel
Guidance Channel
135 Dupont Street
PO Box 760
Plainview, NY 11803-0760
516-349-5520
800-999-6884
Fax: 800-262-1886
E-mail: info@at-risk.com
http://www.at-risk.com
Publisher and distributor of educational curriculums, videos, publications and products for at-risk youth and the counselors and others who work with them. Bureau products focus on areas such as violence and drug prevention, character education, parenting skills and more.

Sally Germain, Editor-in-Chief

4779 Business Publishers
PO Box 17592
Baltimore, MD 21297
301-587-6300
800-274-6737
Fax: 301-585-9075
E-mail: bpinews@bpinews.com
http://www.bpinews.com
Publishes education related materials.

4780 CLEARVUE/eav
6465 N Avondale Avenue
Chicago, IL 60631
773-775-9433
800-253-2788
Fax: 773-775-9855
E-mail: slucas@clearvue.com
http://www.clearvue.com
CLEARVUE/eav offers educators the largest line of curriculum-oriented media in the industry. CLEARVUE/eav programs have, and will continue to enhance students' interest, learning, motivation and skills.

Sarah M Lucas, Communications Coordinator
Kelli Campbell, VP

4781 Calculators
7409 Fremont Avenue S
Minneapolis, MN 55423-3971
800-533-9921
Fax: 612-866-9030
Calculators and calculator books for K thru college level instruction. Calculator products by Texas Instruments, Casio, Sharp and Hewlett-Packard.

Richard Nelson, President

4782 Cambridge University Press
Edinburgh Building
Shaftesbury Road
Cambridge, England CB22RU
http://www.cup.cam.ac.uk
Curriculum materials and textbooks for science education for grades K-12.

4783 Candlewick Press
2067 Massachusetts Avenue
Cambridge, MA 02140-1340
617-661-3330
Fax: 617-661-0565
High quality trade hardcover and paperback books for children and young adults.

4784 Capstone Press
151 Good Counsel Drive
Mankato, MN 56001-3143
952-224-0529
888-262-6135
Fax: 888-262-0705
E-mail: timadsen@capstone-press.com
http://www.capstonepress.com
PreK-12 Nonfiction publisher

Tim Mandsen, Director Marketing

4785 Careers/Consultants in Education Press
3050 Palm Aire Drive N
#310
Pompano Beach, FL 33069
954-974-3511
Fax: 954-974-5477
E-mail: carconed@aol.com
Current education job lists for teacher and administrator positions in schools and colleges. Plus nine differently titled desk/reference paperback books.

Dr. Robert M Bookbinder, President

4786 Carolrhoda Books
A Division of Lerner Publishing Group
241 1st Avenue N
Minneapolis, MN 55401-1607
612-332-3344
800-328-4929
Fax: 612-332-7615
http://www.lernerbooks.com
Fiction and nonfiction for readers K through grade 6. List includes picture books, biographies, nature and science titles, multicultural and introductory geography books, and fiction for beginning readers.

Rebecca Poole, Submissions Editor

4787 Carson-Dellosa Publishing Company
PO Box 35665
Greensboro, NC 27425-5665
336-632-0084
800-321-0943
Fax: 336-632-087
Textbooks, manuals, workbooks and materials aimed at increasing students reading skills.

4788 Center for Play Therapy
University of North Texas
PO Box 311337
Denton, TX 76203
940-565-3864
Fax: 940-565-4461
E-mail: cpt@coefs.coe.unt.edu
http://www.centerforplaytherapy.com
Encourages the unique development and emotional growth of children through the process of play therapy, a dynamic interpersonal relationship between a child and a therapist trained in play therapy procedures. Provides training, research, publications, counseling services and acts as a clearinghouse for literature in the field.

Garry Landreth PhD, Director

4789 Central Regional Educational Laboratory
2550 S Parker Road
Suite 500
Aurora, CO 80014
303-337-0990
Fax: 303-337-3005
E-mail: twaters@mcrel.org
The Regional Educational Laboratories are educational research and development organizations supported by contracts with the US Education Department, Office of Educational Research and Improvement. Specialty area: curriculum, learning and instruction.

Dr. J Timothy Waters, Executive Director

4790 Charles Scribner & Sons
MacMillan Publishing Company
1633 Broadway
New York, NY 10019
212-632-4944
Fax: 800-835-3202
Hardcover trade books for children and young adults.

4791 Chicago Board of Trade
141 W Jackson Boulevard
Chicago, IL 60604-2992
312-435-3500
Educational materials including a new economics program entitled Commodity Challenge.

4792 Children's Book Council
12 West 37th Street
2nd Floor
New York, NY 10018-7480
212-966-1990
800-999-2160
Fax: 212-966-2073
E-mail: staff@cbcbooks.org
http://www.cbcbooks.org
The Children's Book Council, Inc is the non-profit trade association of publishers and packagers of trade books and related materials for children and young adults.

JoAnn Sabatino-Falkenstein, VP Marketing

4793 Children's Press
Grolier Publishing
90 Sherman Turnpike
Danbury, CT 06816
800-621-1115
Fax: 800-374-4329
http://publishing.grolier.com
Leading supplier of reference and children's nonfiction and fiction books.

4794 Children's Press/Franklin Watts
PO Box 1330
Danbury, CT 06813-1330
203-797-3500
Fax: 203-797-3197
K-12 curriculum materials.

4795 Children's Television Workshop
1 Lincoln Plaza
New York, NY 10023-7129
212-875-6809
Fax: 212-875-7388
Hands-on books for elementary school use
in the area of science education.

Brenda Pilson, Review Coordinator
Elaine Israel, Editor-in-Chief

4796 Chime Time
2440-C Pleasantdale Road
Atlanta, GA 30340-1562
770-662-5664
Early childhood products and publications.

4797 Choices Education Project
Watson Institute for International Studies
Brown University
PO Box 1948
Providence, RI 02912-1948
401-863-3155
Fax: 401-863-1247
E-mail: choices@brown.edu
http://www.choices.edu
Develops interactive, supplementary curriculum resources on current and historical international issues. Makes complex current and historic international issues accessible for secondary school students. Materials are low-cost, reproducible, updated annually.

Annually

4798 Close Up Publishing
44 Canal Center Plaza
Alexandria, VA 22314-1592
800-765-3131
Fax: 703-706-3564
Offers textbooks, workbooks and other publications focusing on self-esteem, learning and counseling.

4799 Cognitive Concepts
PO Box 1363
Evanston, IL 60204-1363
888-328-8199
Fax: 847-328-5881
http://www.cogcon.com
Leading provider of language and literacy software, books, internet services and staff development. Specialize in integrating technology with scientific principles and proven instructional methods to offer effective and affordable learning solutions for educators, specialists and families.

4800 College Board
45 Columbus Avenue
New York, NY 10023-6992
212-713-8000
Fax: 212-713-8282
http://www.collegeboard.org
Publishers of books of interest to educational researchers, policymakers, students, counselors, teachers; products to prepare students for college and test prep materials.

4801 Coloring Concepts
1732 Jefferson Street
Suite 7
Napa, CA 94559-1737
707-257-1516
800-257-1516
Fax: 707-253-2019
E-mail: chris@coloringconcepts.com
http://www.coloringconcepts.com
Colorable active learning books for middle school through college that combine scientifically correct text with colorable illustrations to provide an enjoyable and educational experience that helps the user retain more information than during normal reading. Subjects include Anatomy, Marine Biology, Zoology, Botany, Human Evolution, Human Brain, Microbiology and biology.

Christopher Elson, Operations

4802 Comprehensive Health Education Foundation
22419 Pacific Hwy S
Seattle, WA 98198-5106
206-824-2907
800-833-6388
E-mail: info@chef.org
http://www.chef.org
Primarily Health gives K-3 kids a dynamic, hands-on health program while teaching academic skills.

Larry Clark, President
Marvin Hamanishi, Vice President

4803 Computer Learning Foundation
PO Box 60007
Palo Alto, CA 94306-0007
408-720-8898
Fax: 408-730-1191
E-mail: clf@computerlearning.org
http://www.computerlearning.org
Publishes books and videos on using technology.

4804 Computer Literacy Press
Computer Literacy Press
PO Box 562
Earlysville, VA 22936
513-600-3455
513-530-0110
Fax: 800-833-5413
E-mail: info@complitpress.com
http://www.complitpress.com
Instructional materials using hands-on, step-by-step format, appropriate for courses in adult and continuing education, business education, computer literacy and applications, curriculum integration, Internet instruction, and training and staff development. Products are available for ranging from middle school through high school as well as post secondary, teacher training and adult/senior courses.

Robert First, President

4805 Concepts to Go
PO Box 10043
Berkeley, CA 94709-5043
510-848-3233
Fax: 510-486-1248
Develops and distributes manipulative activities for language arts and visual communications for ages 3-8.

4806 Congressional Quarterly
1414 22nd Street NW
Washington, DC 20037-1003
202-887-8500
Fax: 202-293-1487
Comprehensive publications and reference and paperback books pertaining to Congress, US Government and politics, the presidency, the Supreme Court, national affairs and current issues.

4807 Continental Press
520 E Bainbridge Street
Elizabethtown, PA 17022-2299
717-367-1836
800-233-0759
Fax: 717-367-5660
E-mail:
cpeducation@continentalpress.com
http://www.continentalpress.com
Publisher of print for PreK-12 (plus adult education). Programs relate to skill areas in reading, math, comprehension, phonics, etc. Producers of Testlynx Software.

4808 Cottonwood Press
107 Cameron Drive
Suite 398
Fort Collins, CO 80525
970-204-0715
800-864-4297
Fax: 970-204-0761
E-mail: cottonwood@cottonwwodpress.com
http://www.cottonwoodpress.com
Publishes books focusing on teaching language arts and writing, grades 5-12.

Cheryl Thurston

4809 Council for Exceptional Children
The Council for Exceptional Children
2900 Crystal Drive
Suite 1000
Arlington, VA 22202-3557
703-620-3660
888-232-7733
Fax: 703-264-9494
E-mail: service@cec.sped.org
http://www.cec.sped.org
The Council for Exceptional Children is a major publisher of special education literature and produces a catalog semiannually.

Marilyn Friend, President
Bruce Ramirez, Executive Director

4810 Creative Teaching Press
Po Box 2723
Huntington Beach, CA 92647-0723
800-287-8879
Fax: 800-229-9929
E-mail: customerservice@creativeteaching.com
http://www.creativeteaching.com
Offers language and literature-based books including Teaching Basic Skills through Literature, Literature-Based Homework Activities, I Can Read! I Can Write!, Multicultural Art Activities, Responding to Literature, and Linking Math and Literature.

Jim Connelly, President
Luella Connelly, Co-Founder

4811 Cricket Magazine Group
315 5th Street
Peru, IL 61354-2859
815-223-1500
Magazines of high quality children's literature.

4812 Curriculum Associates
PO Box 2001
North Billerica, MA 01862-0901
978-667-8000
800-225-0248
Fax: 800-366-1158
E-mail: cainfo@curriculumassociates.com
http://www.curriculumassociates.com
Supplementary educational materials; cross-curriculum, language arts, reading, study skills, test preparation, diagnostic assessments, emergent readers, videos, and software.

4813 DC Heath & Company
125 Spring Street
Lexington, MA 02421-7801
781-862-6650
Publishes resources for all academic levels ranging from textbooks, fiction and nonfiction titles to business and college guides.

4814 DLM Teaching Resources
PO Box 4000
Allen, TX 75013-1302
972-248-6300
800-527-4747
Offers a variety of teacher's resources and guides for testing in all areas of education.

4815 Dawn Publications
14618 Tyler Foote Road
Nevada City, CA 95959-9316

530-478-7540
800-545-7475
Fax: 530-478-0112
Specializes in nature, children and health and
healing books, tapes and videos and dedicated to helping people experience unity and
harmony.

Bob Rinzler, Publisher
Glenn Hoveman, Editor

4816 Delta Education
80 Northwest Blvd.
Nashua, NH 03061-3000
800-258-1302
Fax: 800-282-9560
Science programs, materials and curriculum
kits.

4817 Dial Books for Young Readers
345 Hudson Street
New York, NY 10014-3658
212-366-2800
Fax: 212-366-2938
http://www.penguinputnam.com
General hardcover, children's books, from
toddler through young adult, fiction and nonfiction.

4818 Didax Educational Resources
PO Box 507
Rowley, MA 01969-0907
978-948-2340
800-458-0024
Fax: 978-948-2813
E-mail: info@didaxinc.com
http://www.didaxinc.com
High quality educational materials featuring
Unifix and hundreds of math and reading sup-
plements.

Brian Scarlett, President
Martin Kennedy, VP

4819 Dinah-Might Activities
PO Box 39657
San Antonio, TX 78218-6657
210-698-0123
Fax: 210-698-0095
Learn how to integrate language arts, math,
map and globe skills and more into a science
curriculum. Books include The Big Book of
Books and Activities, Organizing the Inte-
grated Classroom, Write Your Own Thematic
Units and Reading and Writing All Day Long.

4820 Dinocardz Company
146 5th Avenue
San Francisco, CA 94118-1310
415-751-5809
Dinosaur curriculums for grades 1-3 and 4-6.

4821 Disney Press
Disney Juvenile Publishing
114 5th Avenue
New York, NY 10011-5604
212-633-4400
Fax: 212-633-5929
Hardcover trade and library editions and pa-
perback books for children, grades K-12.

Liisa-Ann Fink, President

4822 Dominic Press
1949 Kellogg Avenue
Carlsbad, CA 92008-6582
619-481-3838
Offers a range of materials for the Reading
Recovery Program and Chapter 1 programs.

4823 Dorling Kindorley Company
95 Madison Avenue
New York, NY 10016
212-213-4800
Fax: 212-689-5254
Science books for all grade levels.

4824 Dover Publications
31 E 2nd Street
Mineola, NY 11501
516-294-7000
Fax: 516-742-6953
Fun and educational storybooks, coloring,
activity, cut-and-assemble toy books, science
for children.

Clarence Strowbridge, President

4825 Dutton Children's Books
375 Hudson Street
New York, NY 10014-3658
212-366-2000
Fax: 212-366-2948
General hardcover children's books from
toddler through young adult, fiction and nonfiction.

4826 DynEd International
1350 Bayshore Highway
Suite 850
Burlingame, CA 94010
800-765-4375
Fax: 650-375-7017
http://www.dyned.com
Pre-K-adult listening and speaking skill development English language acquisition
software.

Steven Kearney, Sales
Sue Young, Operations

5078 EBSCO Publishing
EBSCO Publishing
10 Estes Street
Ipswich, MA 01938
800-653-2726
Fax: 978-356-6565
E-mail: information@ebscohost.com
http://www.ebscohost.com
Database and eBook provider for libraries
and other institutions — more than 375
full-text and secondary research databases
and more than 300,000 eBooks available via
the EBSCOhost platform. EBSCO's content
services K-12 students to public library patrons, from academic, corporate and medical
researchers to clinicians and governments
around the world.

Tim Collins, President
Sam Brooks, EVP Sales/Marketing

4827 ETA - Math Catalog
620 Lakeview Parkway
Vernon Hills, IL 60061-1828
847-816-5050
800-445-5985
Fax: 847-816-5066
E-mail: info@etauniverse.com
http://www.etauniverse.com
Offers a full line of mathematics products,
materials, books, textbooks and workbooks
for grades K-12.

Mary Cooney, Product Development
Manager
Monica Butler, Director Marketing

4828 ETR Associates
4 Carbonero Way
Scotts Valley, CA 95066
831-438-4060
800-321-4407
Fax: 800-435-8433
http://www.etr.org
ETR Associate's mission is to enhance the
well-being of individuals, families and communities by providing leadership, educational resources, training and research in
health promotion with an emphasis on sexuality and health education.

Robert Keet, President
Arnold W. Kriegel, Vice President

4829 EVAN-Motor Corporation
18 Lower Ragsdale Drive
Monterey, CA 93940-5728
831-649-5901
Fax: 800-777-4332
Resource materials for K-6 science educational programs.

4830 Early Start-Fun Learning
PO Box 350187
Jacksonville, FL 32235-0187
904-641-6138
Preschool materials for the educator.

4831 Earth Foundation
5151 Mitchelldale
B11
Houston, TX 77092-7200
713-686-9453
Fax: 713-686-6561
Join the largest active network of educators
working to save endangered ecosystems and
their species! Multi-disciplinary, hands-on
curriculum and videos for the classroom.

Cynthia Everage, President

4832 Editorial Projects in Education
6935 Arlington Road
Suite 100
Bethesda, MD 20814-5233
301-280-3100
800-346-1834
Fax: 301-280-3250
E-mail: customercare@epe.org
http://www2.edweek.org
Publishes various newsletters and publications in the fields of history and education.

Christopher B Swanson, Director
Carole Vinograd Bausell, Assistant
Director

4833 Edmark
Riverdeep Inc.
100 Pine Street
Suite 1900
San Francisco, CA 94111
415-659-2000
888-242-6747
Fax: 415-659-2020
E-mail: info@riverdeep.net
http://www.edmark.com
Develops innovative and effective educa-
tional materials for children.

Barry O'Callaghan, Chairman
Tony Mulderry, Executive Vice President

4834 Education Center
3515 W Market Street
Greensboro, NC 27403-1309
336-273-9409
Publishers of the Mailbox, teacher's helper
magazines, learning centers clubs, classroom
beautiful bulletin board clubs, the storybook
club and more.

4835 Educational Marketer
SIMBA Information
11 Riverbend Drive
PO Box 4234
Stamford, CT 06907-0234
800-307-2529
Fax: 203-358-5824
Contains a range of print and electronic tools,
including software and multimedia materials
for educational institutions.

4836 Educational Press Association of
America
Glassboro State College
Glassboro, NJ 08028
609-445-7349
Offers various publications and biblio-
graphic data focusing on all aspects of educa-
tion.

4837 Educational Productions
9000 SW Gemini Drive
Beaverton, OR 97008
503-644-7000
800-950-4949
Fax: 503-350-7000
E-mail: custserv@edpro.com
http://www.edpro.com
Video training programs that help increase parenting skills and help every teacher meet performance standards. Offers training on preventing discipline problems, increasing parenting skills, supporting literacy efforts and more.

4838 Educational Teaching Aids
620 Lakeview Pkwy
Vernon Hills, IL 60061-1838
847-816-5050
800-445-5985
Fax: 847-816-5066
E-mail: info@etauniverse.com
http://www.etauniverse.com
Manipulatives to enhance understanding of basic concepts and to help bridge the gap between the concrete and the abstract.

4839 Educators Progress Service
214 Center Street
Randolph, WI 53956
920-326-3127
888-951-4469
Fax: 920-326-3126
http://www.freeteachingaids.com
A complete spectrum of curriculum and mixed media resources for all grade levels.

4840 Educators Publishing Service
31 Smith Place
Cambridge, MA 02138-1089
617-547-6706
800-225-5750
Fax: 617-547-0412
http://www.epsbooks.com
Supplementary workbooks and teaching materials in reading, spelling, vocabulary, comprehension, and elementary math, as well as materials for assessment and learning differences.

4841 Edumate-Educational Materials
2231 Morena Boulevard
San Diego, CA 92110-4134
619-275-7117
Multicultural and multilingual materials in the form of toys, puzzles, books, videos, music, visuals, games, dolls and teacher resources. Special emphasis on Spanish and other languages. Literature offered from North and South America.

Gustavo Blankenburg, President

4842 Ellis
406 W 10600 S
Suite 610
Salt Lake City, UT 84003
801-374-3424
888-756-1570
Fax: 801-374-3495
http://www.ellis.com
Publish software that teaches English.

4843 Encyclopaedia Britannica
333 N La Salle Street
Chicago, IL 60610
312-347-7159
800-323-1229
Fax: 312-294-2104
http://www.britannica.com
Books and related educational materials.

4844 Energy Learning Center
USCEA
1776 I Street NW
Suite 400
Washington, DC 20006-3700
703-741-5000
Fax: 703-741-6000
Energy learning materials.

4845 Essential Learning Products
PO Box 2590
Columbus, OH 43216-2590
800-357-3570
Fax: 614-487-2272
Publishers of phonics workbooks.

4846 Ethnic Arts & Facts
PO Box 20550
Oakland, CA 94620-0550
510-465-0451
888-278-5652
Fax: 510-465-7488
E-mail: eaf@ethnicartsnfacts.com
http://www.ethnicartsnfacts.com
Kit titles include: Traditional Africa, Urban Africa, China, Guatemala, Peru, Huichol Indians of Mexico, Chinese Shadow Puppet Kit. African-American Music History Mini-Kit. Artifact kits/resource booklets designed to enhance appreciation of cultural diversity, improve geographic literacy and sharpen critical thinking and writing skills.

Susan Drexler, Curriculum Specialist

4847 Evan-Moor Corporation
18 Lower Ragsdale Drive
Monterey, CA 93940-5728
How to Make Books with Children and other fine teacher resources and reproducible materials for all curriculum areas grades PreK-6.

4848 Everyday Learning Corporation
PO Box 812960
Chicago, IL 60681-2960
800-382-7670
Fax: 312-233-7860
University of Chicago school mathematics project. Everyday Mathematics enriched curriculum for grades K-6.

4849 Exploratorium
3601 Lyon Street
San Francisco, CA 94123-1099
415-563-7337
Fax: 415-561-0307
http://www.exploratorium.edu
Exploratorium is dedicated to the formal and informal teaching of science using innovative interactive methods of inquiry. It publishes materials for educators and provides professional development opportunities both in print and online.

Quarterly/Monthly

4850 Extra Editions K-6 Math Supplements
PO Box 38
Urbana, IL 61803-0038
Fax: 614-794-0107
Special needs math supplements offering 70 single-topic units from K-6 that reach students your basic math program misses. Extra Editions newspaper-like format uses animation with a hands-on approach to show real life necessity for computational skills, time, money, problem solving, critical thinking, etc. Ideal for Chapter One, Peer-Tutoring, Parental Involvement, Home Use, and more.

Craig Rucker, General Manager
Earl Ockenga, Author/Owner

4851 F(G) Scholar
Future Graph
538 Street Road
Suite 200
Southhampton, PA 18966-3780
215-396-0721
Fax: 215-396-0724
A revolutionary program for teaching, learning and using math. This single program allows students and teachers easy answers to Algebra, Trigonometry, Pre-Calculus, Calculus, Statistics, Probability and more. It combines all of the power of a graphing calculator, spreadsheet, drawing tools, mathematics and programming/scripting language and much more, and makes it simple and fun to use.

4852 Facts on File
11 Penn Plaza
New York, NY 10001
212-967-8800
800-322-8755
Fax: 212-967-9196
E-mail: llikoff@factsonfile.com
http://www.factsonfile.com
Reference books for teacher education, software, hardware and educational computer systems.

9 Hardcover Books

Laurie Likoff, Editorial Director

4853 Farrar, Straus & Giroux
19 Union Square W
New York, NY 10003-3304
212-741-6900
Fax: 212-633-9385
Children's, young adult and adult trade books in hardcover and paperback, including Sunburst Books, Aerial Miraso/libros juveniles and Hill and Wang.

4854 First Years
1 Kiddie Drive
Avon, MA 02322-1171
508-588-1220
Early childhood books, hardcover and paperback.

4855 Forbes Custom Publishing
60 5th Avenue
New York, NY 10011-8802
513-229-1000
800-355-9983
Fax: 800-451-3661
E-mail: fcpinfo@forbes.com
http://www.forbescp.com
Offers educators and teachers the opportunity to select unique teaching material to create a book designed specifically for their courses.

4856 Formac Distributing
5502 Atlantic Street
Halifax, NS E3HIG-4
902-421-7022
800-565-1905
Fax: 902-425-0166
Contemporary and historical fiction for ages 6-15. Multicultural themes featuring Degrassi Y/A series; first novel chapter books.

4857 Frank Schaffer Publications
3195 Wilson Drive NW
Grand Rapids, MI 49534
800-417-3261
Fax: 888-203-9361
E-mail: cpg_custserve@schoolspecialty.com
http://www.frankschaffer.com
Best-selling supplemental materials including charts, literature notes, resource materials and more.

4858 Franklin Watts
Grolier Publishing
Sherman Turnpike
Danbury, CT 06816

800-621-1115
800-843-3749
Fax: 800-374-4329
Publisher of library bound books, paperback and Big Books for literature based, multicultural classrooms and school libraries.

4859 Free Spirit Publishing

217 Fifth Avenue North
Suite 200
Minneapolis, MN 55401-1299
612-338-2068
800-736-7323
Fax: 612-337-5050
Free Spirit is the leading publisher of learning tools that support young people's social and emotional health.

4860 Frog Publications

PO Box 280996
Tampa, FL 33682
813-935-5845
Fax: 813-935-3764
http://www.frog.com
An organized system of cooperative games for K-5 reading, language arts, thinking skills, math, social studies, Spanish and multicultural studies. Parental Involvement Program, Learning Centers, Test Preperation, Afterschool Program Materials. Drops in the Bucket daily practice books.

4861 Gareth Stevens

330 W Olive Street
Suite 100
Milwaukee, WI 53212
414-332-3520
800-542-2595
Fax: 414-336-0156
E-mail: info@gsinc.com
http://garethstevens.com
Complete display of supplemental children's reading material for grades K-6, including our New World Almanac Library imprint grades 6-12.

Bi-Annually
ISSN: 0-8368

Mark Sachner, Author
Juanita Jones, Marketing Manager
Jonathan Strickland, National Sales Manager

4862 Glencoe/Div. of Macmillan/McGraw Hill

936 Eastwind Drive
Westerville, OH 43081-3329
708-615-3360
800-442-9685
Fax: 972-228-1982
Secondary science programs.

4863 Goethe House New York

1014 5th Avenue
New York, NY 10028-0104
Teaching materials on Germany for the social studies classroom in elementary, middle and high schools.

4864 Goodheart-Willcox Publisher

18604 W Creek Drive
Tinley Park, IL 60477-6243
800-323-0440
Fax: 888-409-3900
E-mail: custerv@goodheartwillcox.com
http://www.goodheartwillcox.com
Comprehensive text designed to help young students learn about themselves, others, and the environment. Readers will develop skills in clothing, food, decision making, and life management. Case studies throughout allow students to apply learning to real-life situations.

4865 Greenhaven Press

PO Box 9187
Farmington Hills, MI 48333-9187
800-231-5163
800-231-5163
Fax: 248-699-8035
E-mail: info@greenhaven.com
Publishers of the Opposing Viewpoints Series, presenting viewpoints in an objective, pro/con format on some of today's controversial subjects.

4866 Greenwillow Books

1350 Avenue of the Americas
New York, NY 10019-4702
212-261-6500
Fax: 212-261-6518
Offers publications for all reading levels.

4867 Grey House Publishing

4419 Route 22
Amenia, NY 12501
518-789-8700
800-562-2139
Fax: 518-789-0545
E-mail: books@greyhouse.com
http://www.greyhouse.com
Publisher of educational reference directories, and encyclopedias.

Richard Gottlieb, President
Leslie Mackenzie, Publisher

4868 Grolier Publishing

90 Sherman Turnpike
Danbury, CT 06816
203-797-3500
800-621-1115
Fax: 203-797-3197
http://www.publishing.grolier.com
Publisher of library bound and paperback books in the areas of social studies, science, reference, history, and biographies for schools and libraries for grades K-12.

4869 Gryphon House

Gryphon House
PO Box 275
Mount Rainier, MD 20712-0275
301-779-6200
Fax: 301-595-0051
E-mail: info@ghbooks.com
http://www.ghbooks.com
Resource and activity books for early childhood teachers and directors.

Cathy Callootte, Marketing Director

4870 Hands-On Prints

PO Box 5899-268
Berkeley, CA 94705
510-601-6279
Fax: 510-601-6278
Specializes in cultural and language materials for children with an emphasis on internationalism and multiculturalism.

Christina Cheung, President

4871 Hardcourt Religion Publishers

6277 Sea Harbor Drive
Orlando, FL 32887
563-557-3700
800-922-7696
Fax: 563-557-3719
E-mail: hardcourtreligion.com
Publishers of religion education materials for schools and parishes.

4872 Hazelden Educational Materials

PO Box 176
Center City, MN 55012-0176
651-257-4010
Fax: 651-213-4590
Educational publisher of materials supporting both students and faculty in areas of substance abuse and related topics.

4873 Heinemann

361 Hanover Street
Portsmouth, NH 03801-3959
603-431-7894
Fax: 203-750-9790
Holistic/student-centered publications, videotapes and workshops for parents, teachers and administrators.

4874 Henry Holt & Company

175 Fifth Avenue
New York, NY 10010
646-307-5095
800-628-9658
Fax: 212-633-0748
Books and materials for classroom teachers, grades 6-adult, including programs on science literacy.

4875 Henry Holt Books for Young Readers

115 W 18th Street
New York, NY 10011-4113
800-628-9658
Fax: 212-647-0490
Hardcover and paperback trade books for preschool through young adult, fiction and nonfiction. Also, big books and promotional materials are available.

4876 High Touch Learning

PO Box 754
Houston, MN 55943-0754
507-896-3500
800-255-0645
Fax: 507-896-3243
Classroom interactive learning maps promoting the hands-on approach to the teaching of social studies.

4877 High/Scope Educational Research Foundation

600 N River Street
Ypsilanti, MI 48198-2821
734-485-2000
800-40 -RESS
Fax: 734-485-4467
Early childhood, elementary, movement and music, and adolescent materials. Over 300 titles of books, videos, cassettes and CDs from which to choose. Research and training materials as well as curriculum and development materials are based on the acclaimed High/Scope active learning approach.

Emily Koepp, President

4878 Holiday House

425 Madison Avenue
New York, NY 10017-1110
212-688-0085
Fax: 212-688-0395
Hardcover and paperback children's books. General fiction and nonfiction, preschool through high school.

4879 Hoover's

5800 Airport
Dallas, TX 78752-3812
512-374-4500
Fax: 512-374-4501
Everything educational, for the early childhood and K-12 market. As a partner for over 100 years, the company is eager to extend their commitment to produce quality, timely shipping and customer service to the public. Offer over 10,000 products for infants, toddlers, pre-school and school age educational needs.

4880 Horn Book Guide

Horn Book
56 Roland Street
Suite 200
Boston, MA 02129

617-628-0225
800-325-1170
Fax: 617-628-0882
E-mail: info@hbook.com
http://www.hbook.com
The most comprehensive review source of children's and young adult books available. Published each spring and fall, the Guide contains concise, critical reviews of almost every hardcover trade children's and young adult book published in the United States - nearly 2,000 books each issue.

BiAnnually
ISSN: 1044-405X

Anne Quirk, Marketing Manager
Roger Sutton, Editor

4881 Houghton Mifflin Books for Children

222 Berkeley Street
Boston, MA 02116-3748
617-351-5000
800-225-3362
Fax: 617-351-1111
http://www.hmco.com
Wide variety of children's and young adult books, fiction and nonfiction.

4882 Houghton Mifflin Company: School Division

222 Berkeley Street
Boston, MA 02116-3748
617-351-5000
Fax: 617-651-1106
Children's literature; K-12 reading and language arts print and software programs; and testing and evaluation for K-12.

4883 Hyperion Books for Children

114 5th Avenue
New York, NY 10011-5604
212-633-4400
Fax: 212-633-5929
Children's books in paperback and hardcover editions.

4884 ITP South-Western Publishing Company

5101 Madison Road
Cincinnati, OH 45227-1427
800-824-5179
Fax: 800-487-8488
Innovative instructional materials for teaching integrated science.

4885 Idea Factory

10710 Dixon Drive
Riverview, FL 33569-7406
813-677-6727
Teacher resource books, science project ideas, materials and more for elementary and middle school teachers.

4886 Institute for Chemical Education

University of Wisconsin
1101 University Avenue
Madison, WI 53706-1322
608-262-3033
800-991-5534
Fax: 608-265-8094
E-mail: ice@chem.wisc.edu
http://ice.chem.wisc.edu
Hands-on activities, publications, kits and videos.

4887 Institute for Educational Leadership

1001 Connecticut Avenue NW
Suite 310
Washington, DC 20036-5541
202-822-8405
Fax: 202-872-4050

The Institute's list of publications on educational trends and policies is available to the public.

Michael C Usdan, President

4888 IntelliTools

1720 Corporate Circle
Petaluma, CA 94954
707-773-2000
800-899-6687
Fax: 707-773-2001
http://www.intellitools.com
Provider of hardware and software giving students with special needs comprehensive access to learning.

4889 Intellimation

130 Cremona Drive
Santa Barbara, CA 93117-5599
805-968-2291
800-346-8355
Fax: 805-968-8899
Educational materials in all areas of curriculum for early learning through college level. Over 400 titles are available in video, and software and multimedia exclusively for the Macintosh. Free catalogs avaiable.

Karin Fisher, Marketing Associate
Marlene Carlyle, Marketing Supervisor

4890 Intercultural Press

100 City Hall Plaza
Suite 501
Boston, MA 02108
617-523-3801
888-273-2539
Fax: 617-523-3708
E-mail: books@interculturalpress.com
http://www.interculturalpress.com
Publishes over 100 titles.

Judy Carl-Hendrick, Managing Editor

4891 J Weston Walch, Publisher

PO Box 658
Portland, ME 04104-0658
207-772-2846
800-558-2846
Fax: 207-772-3105
http://www.walch.com
Walch Publishing is an independent, family-owned publisher of educational supplemental materials for grades 3 through 12 and adult makets.

4892 Jacaranda Designs

3000 Jefferson Street
Boulder, CO 80304-2638
707-374-2543
Fax: 707-374-2543
Authentic African children's books from Kenya, including modern concept stories for K-3 in bilingual editions, folktales, and traditional cultural stories for older readers. All books are written and illustrated by African Kenyans.

Carrie Jenkins Williams, President

4893 Jarrett Publishing Company

PO Box 1460
Ronkonkoma, NY 11779
631-981-4248
Fax: 631-588-4722
Offers a wide range of books for today's educational needs.

4894 JayJo Books

Guidance Channel
135 Dupont Street
PO Box 760
Plainview, NY 11803
516-349-5520
800-999-6884
Fax: 516-349-5521
E-mail:

jayjobooks@guidancechannel.com
http://www.jayjo.com
Publisher of books to help teachers, parents and children cope with chronic illnesses, special needs and health education in classroom, family and social settings.

Sally Germain, Editor-in-Chief

4895 John Wiley & Sons

111 River Street
Hoboken, NJ 07030-5774
201-748-6000
Fax: 201-748-6088
Publish science and nature books for children and adults.

4896 Jossey-Bass: An Imprint of Wiley

Jossey-Bass/Pfeiffer
989 Market Street
San Francisco, CA 94103-1741
415-433-1740
Fax: 415-433-0499
http://www.josseybass.com
Creating educational incentives that work.

Adrianne Biggs, Publicity/Manager
Jennifer A O'Day, Editor

4897 Junior Achievement

1 Education Way
Colorado Springs, CO 80906-4477
719-540-8000
Fax: 719-540-6127
Provides business and economics-related materials and programs to students in grades K-12. All programs feature volunteers from the local business community. Materials are free, but available only from local Junior Achievement offices.

4898 Kaeden Corporation

PO Box 16190
19915 Lake Road
Rocky River, OH 44116
440-356-0030
800-890-7323
Fax: 440-356-5081
E-mail: lcowan@kaedeen.com
http://www.kaeden.com
Books for emergent readers at the K, 1 and 2 levels, ideal for Title 1 and Reading Recovery and other at-risk reading programs.

Laura Cowan, Sales Manager
Joan Hoyer, Office Manager

4899 Kane/Miller Book Publishers

PO Boxn 8515
La Jolla, CA 92038-0529
858-456-0540
Fax: 858-456-9641
E-mail: info@kanemiller.com
http://www.kanemiller.com
English translation of foreign children's picture books. Distributors of Spanish language children's books.

Byron Parnell, Sales Manager
Kira Lynn, President

4900 Keep America Beautiful

1010 Washington Boulevard
Stamford, CT 06901
203-323-8987
Fax: 203-325-9199
E-mail: info@kab.org
http://www.kab.org
K-12 curriculum specializing in litter prevention and environmental education. Education posters with lesson plans printed right on the back of each poster and school recycling guides.

4901 Kendall-Hunt Publishing Company

4050 Westmark Drive
Dubuque, IA 52002-2624
319-589-1000
800-228-0810
Fax: 800-772-9165

E-mail: webmaster@kendallhunt.com
http://www.kendallhunt.com
A leading custom publisher in the United States with over 6,000 titles in print. Kendall/Hunt publishes educational materials for kindergarten through college to continuing education creditation and distance learning courses.

Karen Berger, Customer Service Assistant

4902 Knowledge Adventure
2377 Crenshaw Blvd
Suite 302
Torrance, CA 90501
310-533-3400
Fax: 310-533-3700
E-mail: editorial@education.com
http://www.knowledgeadventure.com
Develops, publishes, and distributes best-selling multimedia educational software for use in both homes and schools.

4903 Knowledge Unlimited
PO Box 52
Madison, WI 53701-0052
800-356-2303
Fax: 608-831-1570
http://www.newscurrents.com
NewsCurrents, the most effective current events programs for grades 3-12. Now available on DVD or Online.

4904 Kraus International Publications
358 Saw Mill River Road
Millwood, NY 10546-1035
914-762-2200
800-223-8323
Fax: 914-762-1195
Offers teacher resource notebooks with complete resource information for teachers and administrators at all levels. Great for program planning, quick reference, inservice training. Also offers books on early childhood education, English/language arts, mathematics, science, health education and visual arts.

Barry Katzen, President

4905 Lake Education
AGS/Lake Publishing Company
500 Harbor Boulevard
Belmont, CA 94002-4075
650-592-1606
800-328-2560
Fax: 800-471-8457
Alternative learning materials for under-achieving students grades 6-12, RSL and adult basic education. High interest, low readability fiction, adapted classic literature, lifeskills and curriculum materials to supplement and support many basal programs.

Phil Schlenter
Carol Hegarty, VP Editorial

4906 Langenseheidt Publishing
515 Valley Street
Maplewood, NJ 07040-1337
800-526-4953
Fax: 908-206-1104
E-mail: edusales@hammond.com
http://www.hammondmap.com
World maps, atlases, general reference guides and CD-Roms.

4907 Lawrence Hall of Science
University of California
Berkeley, CA 94720
510-642-5132
Fax: 510-642-1055
E-mail: lhsinfo@uclink.berkeley.edu
http://www.lawrencehallofscience.org
Offers programs and materials in the field of science and math education for teachers, families and interested citizens. Exhibits include Equals, Family Math, CePUP and FOSS.

Linda Schneider, Marketing Manager
Mike Salter, Marketing/PR Associate

4908 Leap Frog Learning Materials
6401
Suite 100
Emeryville, CA 94608-1071
510-596-3333
800-701-5327
Learning materials, books, posters, games and toys for children.

4909 Learning Connection
19 Devane Street
Frostproof, FL 33843-2017
863-635-5610
800-338-2282
Fax: 863-635-4676
Thematic, literature-based units with award-winning books, media and hands-on for PK-12 including parent involvement, early childhood, bilingual, literacy, math, writing, science and multicultural.

4910 Learning Disabilities Association of America
Learning Disabilities Association of America
4156 Library Road
Pittsburgh, PA 15234-1349
412-341-1515
888-300-6710
Fax: 412-344-0224
E-mail: info@ldaamerica.org
http://www.ldaamerica.org
Has 50 state affiliates with more than 300 local chapters. The national office has a resource center of over 500 publications for sale.

4911 Learning Links
2300 Marcus Avenue
New Hyde Park, NY 11042-1083
516-437-9075
800-724-2616
Fax: 516-437-5392
E-mail: learningLx@aol.com
http://www.learinglinks.com
All you need for literature based instruction; Noveltie, study guides, thematic units books and more.

4912 Lee & Low Books
95 Madison Avenue
Suite 606
New York, NY 10016-3303
212-779-4400
Fax: 212-683-1894
E-mail: info@leeandlow.com
http://www.leeandlow.com
A multicultural children's book publisher. Our primary focus is on picture books, especially stories set in contemporary America. Spanish language titles are available.

Craig Low, VP Publisher
Louise May, Executive Editor

4913 Leo A Myer Associates/LAMA Books
20956 Corsair Boulevard
Hayward, CA 94545-1002
510-785-1091
Fax: 510-785-1099
E-mail: lama@lmabooks.com
Writers and publishers of HVAC books.

Barbara Ragura, Marketing Assistant

4914 Lerner Publishing Group
A Division Lerner Publications Group
241 1st Avenue N
Minneapolis, MN 55401-1607
612-332-3344
800-328-4929
Fax: 612-332-7615
http://www.lernerbooks.com
Primarily nonfiction for readers of all grade levels. List includes titles encompassing nature, geography, natural and physical science, current events, ancient and modern history, world art, special interests, sports, world cultures, and numerous biography series. Some young adult and middle grade fiction.

Jennifer Martin, Submissions Editor

4915 Linden Tree Children's Records & Books
170 State Street
Los Altos Hills, CA 94022-2863
650-949-3390
Fax: 650-949-0346
Offers a wide variety of books, audio cassettes and records for children.

4916 Listening Library
One Park Avenue
Old Greenwich, CT 06870-1727
203-637-3616
800-243-4504
Fax: 800-454-0606
E-mail: moreinfo@listeninglib.com
http://www.listeninglib.com
A producer of quality unabridged audiobooks for listeners of all ages. Specializing in children's literature and adult classics.

BiAnnually

Annette Imperati, Director Sales/Marketing

4917 Little, Brown & Company
3 Center Plaza
Boston, MA 02108-2084
617-227-0730
Fax: 617-263-2854
Trade books for children and young adults, hardcover and paper, including Sierra Club Books for Children.

4918 Lodestar Books
375 Hudson Street
New York, NY 10014-3658
212-366-2000
General hardcover children's books from toddler through young adult, fiction and nonfiction.

4919 Lothrop, Lee & Shepard Books
1350 Avenue of the Americas
New York, NY 10019-4702
212-261-6500
Fax: 212-261-6518
Children's books.

4920 Lynne Rienner Publishing
1800 30th Street
Suite 314
Boulder, CO 80301
303-333-3003
800-803-8488
Fax: 303-333-4037
E-mail: karen-hemmes@mindspring.com
http://www.fireflybooks.com
Publishes academic-level books with a focus on international and domestic social sciences.

Karen Hemmes, Publicist
Mary Kay Opicka, Publicist

4921 MHS
PO Box 950
North Tonawanda, NY 14120-0950
416-492-2627
800-456-3003
Fax: 416-492-3343
E-mail: customer_service@mhs.com
http://www.mhs.com

Publishers and distributors of professional assessment materials.

Steven J Stein, PhD, President

4922 MacMillan Children's Books
1633 Broadway
New York, NY 10019
212-512-2000
Fax: 800-835-3202
Hardcover trade books for children and young adults.

4923 MacMillan Reference
1633 Broadway
New York, NY 10019
212-512-2000
Fax: 800-835-3202
A wide variety of titles for students and teachers of all grade levels.

4924 Macmillan/McGraw-Hill School Division
1633 Broadwaty
New York, NY 10019
212-654-8500
800-442-9685
Fax: 800-835-3202
Quality literature for the student and excellent support for the teacher. Programs and educational materials for all grade levels.

4925 Macro Press
18242 Peters Court
Fountain Valley, CA 92708-5873
310-823-9556
Fax: 310-306-2296
Includes resources to conduct thematic hands-on science lessons and integrated curriculum; and, student materials offering a Scientist's Notebook and reading materials to integrate hands-on (grade specific) scientific thinking, problem solving and documenting skills to benefit all students. Nine award-winning K-6 teachers (200+ years combined experience) joined together to address the real needs of today's high student load.

Leigh Hoven Swenson, President

4926 Magna Publications
2718 Dryden Drive
Madison, WI 53704
608-227-8109
800-206-4805
Fax: 608-246-3597
E-mail: carriej@magnapubs.com
http://www.magnapubs.com
Produces eight subscriptions newsletters in the field of higher education.

Carrie Jenson, Conference Manager
David Burns, Associate Publisher

4927 Major Educational Resources Corporation
10153 York Road
Suite 107
Hunt Valley, MD 21030-3340
800-989-5353
Multimedia curriculum tools for educators.

4928 Margaret K McElderry Books
1633 Broadway
New York, NY 10019
212-512-2000
Fax: 800-835-3202
Hardcover trade books for children and young adults.

4929 Mari
3215 Pico Boulevard
Santa Monica, CA 90405-4603
310-829-2212
800-955-9494

Fax: 310-829-2317
http://www.mariinc.com
The best literature learning materials for K-12. Offers Mini-Units for writing and critical thinking skills, Literature Extenders that extend literature across the curriculum and Basic Skills Through Literature that combine literature and skill work.

4930 MasterTeacher
Leadership Lane
PO Box 1207
Manhattan, KS 66505-1207
800-669-9633
Fax: 800-669-1132
http://www.masterteacher.com
A publisher of videotapes for the professional. Offers programs on inclusion, tests and testing, student motivation, discipline and more.

4931 MathSoft
101 Main Street
Cambridge, MA 02142
617-577-1017
800-628-4223
Fax: 617-577-8829
http://www.mathsoft.com
Provider of math, science and engineering software for business, academia, research and government.

4932 McCracken Educational Services
PO Box 3588
Blaine, WA 98231
360-332-1881
800-447-1462
Fax: 360-332-7332
E-mail: mes@mccrackened.com
http://www.mccrackened.com
Materials for beginning reading, writing and spelling. Big Books, manipulative materials, teacher resource books, spelling through phonics, posters and both audio and video tapes.

Robert & Marlene McCracken, Author

4933 McGraw Hill Children's Publishing
PO Box 1650
Grand Rapids, MI 49501-1650
616-363-1290
Fax: 800-543-2690
New self-esteem literature based reading and multicultural literature based reading.

4934 Mel Bay Publications
4 Industrial Drive
PO Box 66
Pacific, MO 63069-0066
637-257-3970
800-863-5229
Fax: 636-257-5062
E-mail: email@melbay.com
http://www.melbay.com
Music supply distributors.

Sheri Stephens, Customer Service Supervisor

4935 Merriam-Webster
47 Federal Street
#281
Springfield, MA 01105-3805
413-734-3134
Fax: 413-734-0257
A wide variety of titles for students and teachers of all grade levels.

4936 Millbrook Press
1251 Washington Avenue N
Minneapolis, MN 55401
203-740-2220
800-328-4929

Fax: 800-332-1132
http://www.millbrookpress.com
Exceptional nonfiction juvenile and young adult books for schools and public libraries.

4937 Milton Roy Company
820 Linden Avenue
Rochester, NY 14625-2710
716-248-4000
Teacher support materials, scientific kits and manuals.

4938 Mimosa Publications
90 New Montgomery Street
San Francisco, CA 94105-4501
415-982-5350
A language based K-3 math program featuring big books, language and activity based math topics and multicultural math activities.

4939 Model Technologies
2420 Van Layden Way
Modesto, CA 95356-2454
209-575-3445
Curriculum guides and scientific instruction kits.

4940 Mondo Publishing
980 Avenue Of The Americas
New York, NY 10018
Fax: 888-532-4492
E-mail: mondopub@aol.com
http://www.mondopub.com
Offers multicultural big books and music cassettes: Folk Tales from Around the World series; Exploring Habitats series; and, Let's Write and Sing a Song, whole language activities through music.

4941 Morning Glory Press
6595 San Haroldo Way
Buena Park, CA 90620-3748
714-828-1998
888-612-8254
Fax: 714-828-2049
E-mail: info@morningglorypress.com
http://www.morningglorypress.com
Publishes books and materials for teenage parents.

Quarterly

Jeanne Lindsay, President
Carole Blum, Promotion Director

4942 Music for Little People
PO Box 1460
Redway, CA 95560-1460
707-923-3991
Fax: 707-923-3241
Science and environmental education materials set to music for younger students.

4943 N&N Publishing Company
18 Montgomery Street
Middletown, NY 10940-5116
Low-cost texts and workbooks.

4944 NASP Publications
National Association of School Psychologists
4340 EW Highway
Suite 402
Bethesda, MD 20814
301-657-0270
Fax: 301-657-0275
E-mail: center@naspweb.org
http://www.naspionline.org
Over 100 hard-to-find books and videos centering on counseling, psychology and guidance for students.

Betty Somerville, President

4945 NCTM Educational Materials
National Council of Teachers of Mathematics
1906 Association Drive
Reston, VA 20191-1502

703-620-9840
Fax: 703-476-2970
E-mail: nctm@nctm.org
http://www.nctm.org
Publications, videotapes, software, posters and information to improve the teaching and learning of mathematics.

Harry B Tunis, Publications Director
Cynthia C Rosso, Director Marketing Services

4946 NYSTROM

3333 N Elston Avenue
Chicago, IL 60618-5898
773-463-1144
800-621-8086
Fax: 773-463-0515
Maps, globes, hands-on geography and history materials.

4947 Narrative Press

PO Box 145
Crabtree, OR 97335
800-315-9005
Fax: 541-259-2154
E-mail: service@narrativepress.com
http://www.narrativepress.com
Publisher of first person narratives of adventure and exploration.

Vickie Zimmer, Editor

4948 National Aeronautics & Space Administration

NASA Headquarters
300 E Street SW
Washington, DC 20546
202-358-0000
Fax: 202-358-3251
Over 10 different divisions offering a wide variety of classroom and educational materials in the areas of science, physics, aeronautics and more.

4949 National Center for Science Teaching & Learning/Eisenhower Clearinghouse

1929 Kenny Road
Columbus, OH 43210-1015
Collects and creates the most up-to-date listing of science and mathematics curriculum materials in the nation.

4950 National Council for the Social Studies

8555 Sixteenth Street
Suite 500
Silver Spring, MD 20910
301-588-1800
800-683-0812
Fax: 301-588-2049
E-mail: sgriffin@ncss.org
http://www.ncss.org
Publishes books, videotapes and journals in the area of social education and social studies.

4951 National Council of Teachers of English

1111 W Kenyon Road
Urbana, IL 61801-1096
217-328-3870
800-369-6283
Fax: 217-328-9645
E-mail: public_info@ncte.org
http://www.ncte.org
Devoted to the advancement of English language and literature studies at all levels of education. Publishes 12 periodicals, a member newspaper, and 20-25 books a year, and holds conventions and workshops.

Lori Bianchini, Public Affairs

4952 National Council on Economic Education

1140 Avenue of the Americas
New York, NY 10036-5803
212-730-7007
Offers various programs including their latest, US History: Eyes on the Economy, a council program for secondary education teachers.

4953 National Geographic School Publishing

1145 17th Street NW
Washington, DC 20036
800-368-2728
Fax: 515-362-3366
Books, magazines, videos, and software in the areas of science, geography and social studies.

4954 National Geographic Society

PO Box 10041
Des Moines, IA 50340-0597
800-548-9797
Fax: 301-921-1575
http://www.nationalgeographic.com
Science materials, videos, CD-ROM's and telecommunications program.

4955 National Head Start Association

1651 Prince Street
Alexandria, VA 22314-2818
703-739-0875
Fax: 703-739-0878
http://www.nhsa.org
Dedicated to promoting and protecting the Head Start program. Advocates on the behalf of America's low-income children and families. Publishes many books, periodicals and resource guides. Offers a legislative hotline as well as training programs through the NHSA Academy.

Ron Herndon, President
Blanche Russ-Glover, VP

4956 National Textbook Company

4255 W Touhy Avenue
Lincolnwood, IL 60646-1975
847-679-5500
800-323-4900
Fax: 847-679-2494
Offers various textbooks for students grades K-college level.

4957 National Women's History Project

3343 Industrial Drive
Suite #4
Santa Rosa, CA 95403
707-636-2888
Fax: 707-636-2909
E-mail: nwhp@aol.com
http://www.nwhp.org
Non-profit organization, the clearinghouse for information about multicultural US women's history. Initiated March as National Women's History Month; issues a catalog of women's history materials. Provides teacher-training nationwide; coordinates the Women's History Network; produces videos, posters, curriculum units and other curriculum materials.

Molly Murphy MacGregor, Exec. Dir./Co-Founder

4958 National Writing Project

University of California, Berkeley
2105 Bancroft Way
#1042
Berkeley, CA 94720-1042
510-642-6096
Fax: 510-642-4545
http://www.writingproject.org
Technical reports and occasional paper series: a series of research reports and essays on the research in and practice of teaching writing at all grade levels.

4959 New Canaan Publishing Company

PO Box 752
New Canaan, CT 06840
203-966-3408
800-705-5698
Fax: 203-966-3408
http://www.newcanaanpublishing.com
Children's publications.

4960 New Press

38 Greene Street
4th Floor
New York, NY 10013
212-629-8802
Fax: 212-629-8617
Multicultural teaching materials, focusing on the social studies.

4961 NewsBank

5020 Tamiami Trail N
Suite 110
Naples, FL 34103-2837
941-263-6004
Electronic information services that support the science curriculum.

4962 North South Books

11 E 26th Street
17 Floor
New York, NY 10010-2007
212-706-4545
Fax: 212-706-4544
Publisher of quality children's books by authors and illustrators from around the world.

4963 Nystrom, Herff Jones

3333 N Elston Avenue
Chicago, IL 60618-5811
913-432-8100
Fax: 913-432-3958
Charts for earth, life and physical science for upper elementary and high school grades.

4964 Options Publishing

PO Box 1749
Merrimack, NH 03054
603-429-2698
800-782-7300
Fax: 603-424-4056
E-mail: serviceoptionspublishing.com m
http://www.optionspublishing.com
Publishers of supplemental materials in reading, math and language arts.

Marty Furlong, VP

4965 Organization of American Historians

112 N Bryan Avenue
Bloomington, IN 47408-4136
812-855-7311
800-446-8923
Fax: 812-855-0696
E-mail: oah@oah.org
http://www.oah.org
Offers various products and literature dealing with American history, as well as job registries, Magazine of History, Journal of American History, OAH Newsletter, and more.

Damon Freeman, Marketing Manager
Michael Regoli, Publications Director

4966 Oxton House Publishers, LLC

Po Box 209
Farmington, ME 04938
207-779-1923
800-539-7323
Fax: 207-779-0623
E-mail: info@oxtonhouse.com
http://www.oxtonhouse.com
Publishes high quality, innovative, affordable materials for teaching, reading and

mathematics and for dealing with learning disabilities.

William Berlinghoff, Managing Editor
Bobby Brown, Marketing Director

4967 PF Collier
1315 W 22nd Street
Suite 250
Oak Brook, IL 60523-2061
A leading educational publisher for more than 110 years, creating the home learning center. Products include: Collier's Encyclopedia, Quickstart and Early Learning Fun.

4968 PRO-ED
8700 Shoal Creek Boulevard
Austin, TX 78757-6897
512-451-3246
800-897-3202
Fax: 800-397-7633
E-mail: info@proedinc.com
http://www.proedinc.com
A leading publisher of assessments, therapy materials and resource/reference books in the areas of speech, language, and hearing; psychology; special education; and occupational therapy.

4969 Parenting Press
PO Box 75267
11065 5th Avenue NE
Seattle, WA 98125-0267
206-364-2900
800-992-6657
Fax: 206-364-0702
E-mail: office@ParentingPress.com
http://www.ParentingPress.com
Publishes books for parents, children, and professionals who work with them. Nonfiction books include topics on parenting, problem solving, dealing with feelings, safety, and special issues.

Carolyn J Threadgill, Publisher

4970 Penguin USA
375 Hudson Street
New York, NY 10014-3658
212-366-2000
Fax: 212-366-2934
http://www.penguinputnam.com
Children's and adult hardcover and paperback general trade books, including classics and multiethnic literature.

4971 Perfection Learning Corporation
Perfection Learning
10520 New York Avenue
Des Moines, IA 50322
303-333-3003
800-803-8488
Fax: 303-333-4037
E-mail: karen-hemmes@mindspring.com
http://www.fireflybooks.com
Perfection Learning publishes high interest-low reading level fiction and non-fiction books for young adults.

Karen Hemmes, Publicist
Mary Kay Opicka, Publicist

4972 Perma Bound Books
E Vandalia Road
Jacksonville, IL 62650
217-243-5451
800-637-6581
Fax: 800-551-1169
Thematically arranged for K-12 classroom use with 480,000 titles available in durable Perma-Bound bindings; related library services also available.

Ben Mangum, President

4973 Personalizing the Past
1534 Addison Street
Berkeley, CA 94703-1454
415-388-9351
Museum quality artifact history kits complete with integrated lesson plan teachers guide. Copy-ready student worksheets, literature section, videos and audio tapes. United States and ancient world history.

4974 Perspectives on History Series
Discovery Enterprises, Ltd.
31 Laurelwood Drive
Carlisle, MA 01741
978-287-5401
800-729-1720
Fax: 978-287-5402
E-mail: ushistorydocs@aol.com
http://www.ushistorydocs.com
Primary and secondary source materials for middle school to college levels; bibliographies; plays for grades 5-9 on American history topics. Educators curriculum guides for using primary source documents. 75-volumes of primary source documents on American history may be purchased individually or in sets. New Researching American History Series presents documents with summaries and vocabulary on each page (20 volumes) sold individually or in sets.

JoAnne Deitch, President

4975 Peytral Publications Inc
PO Box 1162
Minnetonka, MN 55345
952-949-8707
877-739-8725
Fax: 952-906-9777
E-mail: inquiry@peytral.com
http://www.peytral.com
Books and videos for educators.

Peggy Hammeken, Owner

4976 Phelps Publishing
PO Box 22401
Cleveland, OH 44122
216-752-4938
Fax: 216-752-4941
E-mail: earl@phelpspublishing.com
http://www.phelpspublishing.com
Publisher of art instruction books for ages 8 to 108.

Earl Phelps, President

4977 Phoenix Learning Resources
12 W 31st Street
New York, NY 10001-4415
212-629-3887
800-221-1274
Fax: 212-629-5648
Phoenix Learning Resources provides all students with the skills to be successful, lifelong learners.

Alexander Burke, President
John Rothermich, Executive VP

4978 Pleasant Company Publications
8400 Fairway Pl
Middleton Branch, WI 53562-2554
608-836-4848
800-233-0264
Fax: 800-257-3865
The American Girls Collection historical fiction series.

4979 Pocket Books/Paramount Publishing
1230 Avenue of the Americas
New York, NY 10020-1513
212-698-7000
Books for children and young adults in hardcover and paperback originals and reprints of bestselling titles.

4980 Population Connection
1400 16th Street NW
Suite 320
Washington, DC 20036-2290
800-767-1956
Fax: 202-332-2302
E-mail: poped@populationconnection.org
http://www.populationconnection.org
Curriculum materials for grades K-12 to teach students about population dynamics and their social, political and environmental effects in the United States and the world.

Pamela Wasserman, Director Education

4981 Prentice Hall School Division
340 Rancheros Drive
Suite 160
San Marcos, CA 92069
760-510-0222
Fax: 760-510-0230
Superb language arts textbooks and ancillaries for students grades 6-12.

4982 Prentice Hall School Division - Science
1 Lake Street
Upper Saddle River, NJ 07458
201-236-7000
Fax: 201-236-3381
Science textbooks and ancillaries for grades 6-12 and advanced placement students.

4983 Prentice Hall/Center for Applied Researchin Education
1 Lake Street
Upper Saddle River, NJ 07458
201-236-7000
Fax: 201-236-3381
Publisher of practical, time and work saving teaching/learning resources for PreK-12 teachers and specialists in all content areas.

4984 Project Learning Tree
American Forest Foundation
1111 19th Street NW
Suite 780
Washington, DC 20036-3603
202-463-2462
Fax: 202-463-2461
Pre-K through grade 12 curriculum materials containing hundreds of hands-on science activities. PLT uses the forest as a window into the natural world to increase students' understanding of our complex environment. Stimulates critical and creative thinking; develops the ability to make informed decisions on environmental issues; and instills the confidence and commitment to take action on them.

Kathy McGlauflin, President

4985 Prufrock Press
PO Box 8813
Waco, TX 76714
800-998-2208
Fax: 800-240-0333
http://www.prufrock.com
Exciting classroom products for gifted and talented education.

4986 Puffin Books
375 Hudson Street
New York, NY 10014-3658
212-366-2819
Fax: 212-366-2040
Offers the Puffin Teacher Club set.

Lisa Crosby, President

4987 RR Bowker
ProQuest
121 Chanlon Road
New Providence, NJ 07974-1541
908-464-6800
Fax: 908-665-6688
A leading information provider to schools and libraries for over one hundred years, RR Bowker

provides quality resources to help teachers and librarians make informed reading selections for children and young adults.

4988 Raintree/Steck-Vaughn

Harcourt Achieve
6277 Sea Harbor Drive
Orlando, FL 32887
800-531-5015
Fax: 800-699-9459
http://www.steck-vaughn.com
Reference materials for K-8 students and texts for underachieving students K-12.

Tim McEwen, President
Martijn Tel, Chief Financial Officer

4989 Rand McNally

8255 Central Park Avenue
Skokie, IL 60076-2970
847-674-2151
Cross-curricular products featuring reading/language arts in the social studies.

4990 Random House

201 E 50th Street
New York, NY 10022-7703
212-751-2600
Fax: 212-572-8700
Offers a line of science trade books for grades K-8.

4991 Random House/Bullseye/Alfred A Knopf/Crown Books for Young Readers

201 E 50th Street
New York, NY 10022-7703
212-751-2600
Fax: 212-572-8700
Publisher of hardcover books, paperbacks, books and cassettes and videos for children.

4992 Recorded Books

270 Skipjack Road
Prince Frederick, MD 20678-3410
800-638-1304
Professionally narrated, unabridged books on standard-play audio cassettes, classroom ideas and combinations of print book, cassettes and teacher's guides.

Linda Hirshman, President

4993 Redleaf Press

10 Yorkton Court
Saint Paul, MN 55117-1065
800-428-8309
Fax: 800-641-0115
E-mail: jward@redleafpress.org
http://www.redleafpress.org
Publisher of curriculum, activity, and childrens books for early childhood professionals.

Sid Farrer, Editor In Chief
JoAnne Voltz, Marketing Manager

4994 Reference Desk Books

430 Quintana Road
Suite 146
Morro Bay, CA 93442-1948
805-772-8806
Offers a variety of books for the education professional.

4995 Rhythms Productions

PO Box 34485
Los Angeles, CA 90034-0485
310-836-4678
800-544-7244
Fax: 310-837-1534
Producer and publisher of songs and games for learning through music. Cassettes, CDs, books for birth through elementary featuring rhythms, puppet play, art activities, and more. Titles include Lullabies, Singing Games, Watch Me Grow series, Mr. Windbag

concept stories, phonics, First Reader's Kit, Hear-See-Say-Do Musical Math series, Themes, and more. Also publishes a line of folk dances from elementary through adult.

Audio

Ruth White, President

4996 Richard C Owen Publishers

PO Box 585
Katonah, NY 10536
914-232-3903
800-336-5588
Fax: 914-232-3977
E-mail: mfrund@rcowen.com
http://www.rcowen.com
Focus child-centered learning, Books for Young Learners, professional books, the Learning Network and Meet the Author series.

Mary Frundt, Marketing

4997 Riverside Publishing Company

425 Spring Lake Drive
Ithaca, IL 60143
630-467-7000
800-323-9540
Fax: 630-467-7192
http://www.riverpub.com
Offers a full line of reading materials, including fiction and nonfiction titles for all grade levels.

4998 Roots & Wings Educational Catalog-Australiafor Kids

PO Box 19678
Boulder, CO 80308-2678
303-776-4796
800-833-1787
Fax: 303-776-6090
E-mail: roos@boulder.net
http://www.rootsandwingscatalog.com/
www.australiaforkids.com
Catalog company providing materials for the education of the young child, specializing in the following topics: Australia, multiculturalism, parenting and families, teaching, special needs, environment and peace.

Susan Ely, President/Sales
Anne Wilson, VP/Marketing

4999 Rosen Publishing Group

29 E 21st Street
New York, NY 10010-6209
212-777-3017
800-237-9932
Fax: 888-436-4643
Nonfiction books on self-help and guidance for young adults. Books also available for reluctant readers on self-esteem, values and drug abuse prevention.

5000 Routledge/Europa Library Reference

Taylor & Francis Books
29 W 35 Street
New York, NY 10001-2299
212-216-7800
800-634-7064
Fax: 212-564-7854
E-mail: reference@routledge-ny.com
http://www.reference.routlege-ny.com
Publisher of a wide range of print and online library reference titles, including the renowned Europa World Yearbook and the award-winning Routledge Encyclopedia of Philosophy (both available in online and print formats), Garland Encyclopedia of World Music, Routledge Religion and Society Encyclopedias, Chronological History of US Foreign Relations, and many other acclaimed resources.

Koren Thomas, Sr Marketing/Library Ref
Elizabeth Sheehan, Marketing/Library Reference

5001 Runestone Press

A Divisions of Lerner Publishing Group
241 1st Avenue N
Minneapolis, MN 55401-1607
612-332-3344
800-328-4929
Fax: 612-332-7615
http://www.lernerbooks.com
Nonfiction for readers in Grades 5 and up. Newly revised editions of previously out-of-print books. List includes Buried Worlds archaeology series and titles of Jewish and Native American interest. Complete catalog is available.

Harry J Lerner, President
Mary M Rodgers, Editorial Director

5002 Saddleback Educational

Three Watson
Irvine, CA 92618-2767
949-860-2500
800-637-8715
Fax: 888-734-4010
Supplementary curriculum materials for K-12 and adult students.

5003 SafeSpace Concepts

1424 N Post Oak Road
Houston, TX 77055-5401
713-956-0820
800-622-4289
Fax: 713-956-6416
E-mail: safespacec@aol.com
http://www.safespaceconcepts.com
Manufactures young children's play equipment and furnishings.

Barbara Carlson, PhD, President
Jerry Johnson, Marketing Director

5004 Sage Publications

Sage Publications
2455 Teller Road
Thousand Oaks, CA 91320
303-333-3003
800-803-8488
Fax: 303-333-4037
E-mail: karen-hemmes@mindspring.com
http://www.fireflybooks.com
Sage Publications publishes handbooks and guides with a focus on research and science.

Karen Hemmes, Publicist
Mary Kay Opicka, Publicist

5079 Salem Press

Grey House Publishing
2 University Plaza
Suite 310
Hackensack, NJ 07601
201-968-0500
Fax: 201-968-0511
E-mail: sales@salempress.com
http://www.salempress.com
Salem Press delivers award-winning literary, historical, medical and science reference content to the public library, academic and high school markets.

Richard Gottlieb, President
Pam Bronke, Sales Manager

5005 Santillana Publishing

901 W Walnut Street
Compton, CA 90220-5109
310-763-0455
800-245-8584
Fax: 305-591-9145
Publishers of K-12 and adult titles in Spanish.Imprints include: Altea, Alfagunea, Taurus and Aguilar.

Marla Norman, Publisher/Trade Book
Antonio de Marco, President

5006 Scholastic

555 Broadway
New York, NY 10012

212-343-6100
800-724-6527
Fax: 212-343-4801
http://www.scholastic.com
Publisher and distributor of children's books. Provides professional and classroom resources for K-12.

5007 School Book Fairs
PO Box 835105
Richardson, TX 75083
972-231-9838
A children's book publisher that provides distribution of leisure reading materials to elementary and middle schools through book fair fund-raising events via a North American network with 97 locations.

5008 Science Inquiry Enterprises
14358 Village View Lane
Chino Hills, CA 91709-1706
530-295-3338
Fax: 530-295-3334
Selected science teaching materials.

5009 Scott & McCleary Publishing Company
2482 11th Street SW
Akron, OH 44314-1712
702-566-8756
800-765-3564
Fax: 702-568-1378
E-mail: jscott7576@aol.com
http://www.scottmccleary.com
Diagnostic reading and testing material.

Janet M Scott, Publisher
Sheila C McCleary, Publisher

5010 Scott Foresman Company
1900 E Lake Avenue
Glenview, IL 60025-2086
800-554-4411
Fax: 800-841-8939
Science tests and reading/language arts materials for teachers and students. Celebrate Reading! is the K-8 literature-based reading/integrated language arts program designed to meet the needs of all children. Book Festival is a literature learning center that offers teachers a collection of trade books for independent reading.

Bert Crossland, Reading Product Manager
Jim Fitzmaurice, VP Editor Group

5011 Sharpe Reference
M.E. Sharpe, Inc.
80 Business Park Drive
Armonk, NY 10504
914-273-1800
800-541-6563
Fax: 914-273-2106
E-mail: custserv@mesharpe.com
http://www.mesharpe.com
Historical, political, geographical and art reference books.

Diana McDermott, Director Marketing

5012 Signet Classics
375 Hudson Street
New York, NY 10014-3658
212-366-2000
Fax: 212-366-2888
Publishes books on literature, poetry and reading.

5013 Silver Moon Press
160 5th Avenue
Suite 622
New York, NY 10010-7003
212-242-6499
800-874-3320
Fax: 212-242-6799

Informational and entertaining books for young readers. Subjects include history, multiculturalism and science.

5014 Simon & Schuster Children's Publishing
1230 Avenue of the Americas
New York, NY 10020
212-698-7000
Fax: 212-698-7007
http://www.simonsayskids.com
Fiction and nonfiction, in hardcover and paperback editions, for preschool through young adult.

5015 Social Issues Resources Series
1100 Holland Drive
Boca Raton, FL 33487-2701
561-994-0079
Fax: 561-994-2014
Provides information systems in print format and CD-ROM format.

5016 Social Science Education Consortium
Box 21270
Boulder, CO 80308-4270
303-492-8154
Fax: 303-449-3925
E-mail: singletl@stripe.colorado.edu
http://www.ssecinc.org
Produces curriculum guides, instructional units and collections of lesson plans on US history, law-related education, global studies, public issues and geography. Develops projects for social studies teachers and evaluates social studies programs.

James Cooks, Executive Director
Laurel Singleton, Associate Director

5017 Social Studies School Service
10200 Jefferson Boulevard
Culver City, CA 90232-3598
310-839-2436
800-421-4246
Fax: 310-839-2249
E-mail: access@socialstudies.com
http://www.socialstudies.com
Supplemental materials in all areas of social studies, language arts.

5018 Special Education & Rehabilitation Services
330 C Street
Washington, DC 20202
202-205-5465
Fax: 202-260-7225

Judith E Heuman, Assistant Secretary

5019 Speech Bin
1965 25th Avenue
Vero Beach, FL 32960-3000
561-770-0007
800-477-3324
Fax: 561-770-0006
Publisher and distributor of books and materials for professionals in rehabilitation, speech-language pathology, occupational and physical therapy, special education, and related fields. Major product lines include professional and children's books, computer software, diagnostic tests.

Jan J Binney, VP

5020 Stack the Deck Writing Program
PO Box 5352
Chicago, IL 60680-0429
312-675-1000
Fax: 312-765-0453
E-mail: stackthedeck@sbcglobal.net
http://www.stackthedeck.com
Composition textbooks, grades 1-12, plus computer software.

5021 Stenhouse Publishers
477 Congress Street
Suite 4B
Portland, ME 04101-3417
888-363-0566
Fax: 800-833-9164
http://www.stenhouse.com
Professional materials for teachers by teachers.

5022 Story Teller
PO Box 921
Salem, UT 84653-0921
801-423-2560
Fax: 801-423-2568
E-mail: patti@thestoryteler.com
http://www.thestoryteller.com
Felt board stories books and educational sets.

Patti Gardner, VP Sales

5023 Summit Learning
7755 Rockwell Avenue
PO Box 755
Fort Atkinson, WI 53538-0755
800-777-8817
800-777-8817
Fax: 800-317-2194
E-mail: info@summitlearning.com
http://www.summitlearning.com
Summit learning is a distributor of manipulative-based math and science materials, provides you with a carefully selected group of the most popular high-quality products at low prices.

Gary Otto, Marketing Manager

5024 Sunburst Technology
1550 Executive Drive
Elgin, IL 60123
914-747-3310
800-338-3457
Fax: 914-747-4109
http://www.sunburst.com
K-12 educational software, guidance and health materials, and online teacher resources.

5025 Sundance Publishing
234 Taylor Street
PO Box 1326
Littleton, MA 01460
978-486-9201
800-343-8204
Fax: 978-486-8759
E-mail: kjasmine@sundancepub.com
http://www.sindancepub.com
A supplementary educational publisher of instructional materials for shared, guided, and independent reading, phonics, and comprehension skills for grades K-9. Some of its programs include AlphKids, SunLit Fluency, Popcorns and Little Readers. Its Second Chance Reading Program for below-level readers features high-interest titles, written for upper elementary/middle school students. It also distributes paperback editions of some of the most widely taught literature titles for grades K-1

Katherine Jasmine, VP Marketing

5026 Synergistic Systems
2297 Hunters Run Drive
Reston, VA 20191-2834
703-758-9213
Science education curriculum materials.

5027 TASA
PO Box 382
Brewster, NY 10509-0382
845-277-8100
800-800-2598
Fax: 845-277-3548
Degrees of Literacy Power Program; English Language Profiles, primary, standard and advanced DRP tests, Degrees of World Meaning Tests.

5028 TL Clark Incorporated
5111 SW Avenue
St. Louis, MO 63110
314-865-2525
800-859-3815
Fax: 314-865-2240
E-mail: general@tlclarkinc.com
http://www.tlclarkinc.com
Educational products for grades Pre-K-3. Rest time products including cots and mats, sand and water play tubs, active play items including tunnels, tricycles and foam play items.

Jim Fleminla, President

5029 TMC/Soundprints
353 Main Avenue
Norwalk, CT 06851-1508
203-846-2274
800-228-7839
Fax: 203-846-1776
E-mail: sndprnts@ixinctcom.com
http://www.soundprints.com
Children's story books for children ages 4 through 8 under the license of the Smithsonian Institute and the National Wildlife Federation. Each 32 page four color book highlights a unique aspect of the animal featured in the book so as to provide education while still being entertaining. Each book can be bought with an audiocassette read-a-long and plush toy. Over 80 books in print.

Ashley Anderson, Associate Publisher
Chelsea Shriver

5030 Tambourine Books
1350 Avenue of the Americas
New York, NY 10019-4702
212-261-6500
Fax: 212-261-6518
A wide variety of books to increase creativity and reading skills in students.

5031 Taylor & Francis Publishers
7625 Empire Drive
Florence, KY 41042
800-624-7064
Fax: 800-248-4724
Publisher of professional texts and references in several fields including the behavioral sciences; arts, humanities, social sciences, science technology and medicine.

Chris Smith, Customer Service Manager

5032 Teacher's Friend Publications
3240 Trade Center Drive
Riverside, CA 92507
909-682-4748
800-343-9680
Fax: 909-682-4680
Complete line of the original monthly and seasonal Creative Idea Books. Plus, two new cooperative-learning language series and much more.

Karen Sevaly, Author
Richard Sevaly, President/CEO
Kim Marsh, National Sales Manager

5033 Teaching Comprehension: Strategies for Stories
Oxton House Publishers, LLC
Po Box 209
Farmington, ME 04938
207-779-1923
800-539-7323
Fax: 207-779-0623
E-mail: info@oxtonhouse.com
http://www.oxtonhouse.com
A detailed roadmap for providing students with effective strategies for comprehending and remembering stories. It includes story-line masters for helping students to organize their thinking and to accurately depict character and sequence events.

62 pages

William Berlinghoff, Managing Editor
Bobby Brown, Marketing Director

5034 Theme Connections
Perfection Learning
PO Box 500
Logan, IA 51546-0500
800-831-4190
Fax: 712-644-2392
Features 135 best-selling literature titles and related theme libraries for students to develop lifelong learning strategies.

5035 Ther-A-Play Products
PO Box 2030
Lodi, CA 95241-2030
209-368-6787
800-308-6749
Fax: 209-365-2157
E-mail: madgic@attbi.com
Children's books, play therapy books, sandplay and sandtray manipulatives, puppets, games, doll houses and furniture. Playmobile and educational toys, specializing in counselors' tools. Books on abuses, illness, death, behavior and parenting.

Madge Geiszler, Owner

5036 Thomson Learning
115 5th Avenue
New York, NY 10003-1004
212-979-2210
800-880-4253
Fax: 248-699-8061
Book publisher of library and classroom-oriented educational resources for children and young adults. Over 200 books are available in 30 different subjects.

5037 Time-Life Books
2000 Duke Street
Alexandria, VA 22314-3414
703-838-7000
Fax: 703-838-7166
A wide-ranging selection of quality reference and supplemental books for students from elementary to high school.

5038 Tiny Thought Press
1427 S Jackson Street
Louisville, KY 40208-2720
502-637-6916
Fax: 502-634-1693
Children's books that build character and self-esteem.

5039 Tom Snyder Productions
80 Coolidge Hill Road
Watertown, MA 02472
800-342-0236
Fax: 800-304-1254
E-mail: ask@tomsynder.com
http://www.tomsynder.com
Developer and publisher of educational software.

John McAndrews, Contact

5040 Tor Books/Forge/SMP
175 5th Avenue
New York, NY 10010-7703
212-388-0100
Fax: 212-388-0191
Science-fiction and fantasy children's books, mysteries, Westerns, general fiction and classics publications.

5041 Tricycle Press
PO Box 7123
Berkeley, CA 94707-0123
510-559-1600
800-841-2665
Fax: 510-559-1637
Publisher of books and posters for children ages 2-12 and their grown-ups. Catalog available.

Christine Longmuir, Publicity/Marketing

5042 Troll Associates
100 Corporate Drive
Mahwah, NJ 07430-2322
201-529-4000
Fax: 201-529-8282
Publisher of children's books and products, including paperbacks and hardcovers, special theme units, read-alongs, videos, software and big books.

5043 Trumpet Club
1540 Broadway
New York, NY 10036-4039
212-492-9595
School book club featuring hardcover and paperback books, in class text sets and author video visits.

5044 Turn-the-Page Press
203 Baldwin Avenue
Roseville, CA 95678-5104
916-786-8756
800-959-5549
Fax: 916-786-9261
E-mail: mleeman@ibm.net
http://www.turnthepage.com
Books, cassettes and videos focusing on early childhood education.

Michael Leeman, President

5045 USA Today
1000 Wilson Boulevard
Arlington, VA 22209-3901
703-276-3400
Fax: 703-854-2103
Educational programs focusing on social studies.

5046 Upstart Books
PO Box 800
Fort Atkinson, WI 53538-0800
920-563-9571
800-558-2110
Fax: 920-563-7395
http://www.hpress.highsmith.com
Publishes teacher activity resources, reading activities, library and information seeking skills, Internet.

Matt Mulder, Director
Virginia Harrison, Editor

5047 Useful Learning
711 Meadow Lane Court
Apartment 12
Mount Vernon, IA 52314-1549
319-895-6155
800-962-3855
The Useful Spelling Textbook series for Grades 2-8, represents a curriculum based upon the scientific knowledge of research studies conducted during the past 80 years at The University of Iowa, Iowa City, IA. Incorporates the New Iowa Spelling Scale and is composed of qualitative curriculum, qualitative learning practices and qualitative instructional procedures.

Larry D. Zenor, PhD, President
Bradley M Loomer, PhD, Board Chairman

5048 VIDYA Books
PO Box 7788
Berkeley, CA 94707-0788
510-527-9932
Fax: 510-527-2936
Supplemental materials about India and the surrounding region for K-12 lesson plans.

5049 Viking Children's Books
375 Hudson Street
New York, NY 10014-3658
212-941-8780
General hardcover children's books, from
toddler through young adult, fiction and
nonfiction.

5050 Vision 23
Twenty-Third Publications
185 Willow Street
Mystic, CT 06355-2636
860-536-2611
Fax: 800-572-0788
A wide variety of children's products in-
cluding books, games, clothing and toys.

5051 WH Freeman & Company
41 Madison Avenue
New York, NY 10010-2202
212-576-9400
Fax: 212-481-1891
Books relating to the world of mathematics.

**5052 Wadsworth Publishing School
Group**
10 Davis Drive
Belmont, CA 94002-3002
650-595-2350
Fax: 800-522-4923
College and advanced placement/honors
high school materials in biology, chemistry
and environmental science.

5053 Walker & Company
104 Fifth Avenue
New York, NY 10011
212-727-8300
800-289-2553
Fax: 212-727-0984
http://www.walkerbooks.com
Hardcover and paperback trade titles for
Pre-K-12th grade, including picture books,
photo essays, fiction and nonfiction titles
appropriate for every curriculum need.

5054 Warren Publishing House
11625-G Airport Road
Everett, WA 98204-3790
425-353-3100
New Totline Teaching Tales with related
activities plus quality whole language
teacher activity books including Alphabet
Theme-A-Saurus and Piggyback Songs.

5055 Waterfront Books
85 Crescent Road
Burlington, VT 05401-4126
802-658-7477
800-639-6063
Fax: 802-860-1368
E-mail: helpkids@waterfrontbooks.com
http://www.waterfrontbooks.com
Publishes and distributes books on special
issues for children: barriers to learning,
coping skills, mental health, prevention
strategies, family/parenting, etc. for
grades K-12. Titles include: The Divorce
Workbook; Josh, a Boy with Dyslexia;
What's a Virus, Anyway? The Kids' Book
About AIDS and more.

Sherrill N Musty, Publisher
Michelle Russell, Order Fulfillment

5056 Web Feet Guides
Rock Hill Communications
14 Rock Hill Road
Bala Cynwyd, PA 19004
610-667-2040
888-762-5445
Fax: 610-667-2291
E-mail:
info@rockhillcommunications.com
http://www.webfeetguides.com

The premier subject guides to the Internet,
rigorously reviewed by librarians and educators, fully annotated, expanded and updated monthly. Appropriate for middle
school through adult. Available in print,
online, or marc records. For more information, free trials and Web casts, and free interactive Web Quests for your K-8
students, visit our Web site.

Linda Smith, Marketing Coordinator

5057 West Educational Publishing
620 Opperman Drive
#645779
Saint Paul, MN 55123-1340
A leader in quality social studies textbooks
and ancillaries for grades K-12.

5058 Western Psychological Services
12031 Wilshire Boulevard
Los Angeles, CA 90025-1251
310-478-2061
800-648-8857
Fax: 310-478-7838
http://www.wpspublish.com
Assessment tools for professionals in education, psychology and allied fields. Offer
a variety of tests, books, software and therapeutic games.

5059 Wildlife Conservation Society
Bronx Zoo
Education Department
2300 Southern Boulevard
Bronx, NY 10460
718-220-5131
800-937-5131
Fax: 718-733-4460
E-mail: sscheio@wes.org
http://www.wcs.com
Environmental science and conservation
biology curriculum materials and information regarding teacher training programming for Grades K-12, on site or off site,
nationally and locally. Science programming for grades pre-K-12 available on site.

Sydell Schein, Manager/Program
Services
Ann Robinson, Director National
Programs

5060 William Morrow & Company
1350 Avenue of the Americas
New York, NY 10019-4702
212-261-6500
Fax: 212-261-6518
High quality hardcover and paperback
books for children.

5061 Winston Derek Publishers
101 French Landing Drive
Nashville, TN 37228-1511
615-321-0535
A cross section of African American books
and educational materials, including pre-
school and primary grade books.

5062 Wolfram Research, Inc.
100 Trade Center Drive
Champaign, IL 61820-7237
217-398-0700
800-965-3726
Fax: 217-398-0747
E-mail: info@wolfram.com
http://www.wolfram.com
Offers mathematics publications, statistics
and information to educators of grades
K-12.

Stephen Wolfram, Founder/CEO
Jean Buck, Dir., Corp Communications

5063 Workman Publishing
708 Broadway
New York, NY 10003-9508

212-254-5900
Fax: 212-254-8098
Children's curriculum, books, textbooks, work-
books, fiction and nonfiction titles.

5064 World & I
News World Communications
2800 New York Avenue NE
Washington, DC 20002-1945
202-636-3365
800-822-2822
Fax: 202-832-5780
E-mail: ckim@worldandimag.com
http://www.worldandi.com
With over 40 articles each month, The World & I
presents an enlightening look at our changing
world through the eyes of noted scholars and experts covering current issues, the arts, science,
book reviews, lifestyles, cultural perspectives,
philosophical trends, and the millennium. For educators, students and libraries. Free teacher's
guides year round. Also, online archives available
at www.worldandi.com.

Charles Kim, Business Director

**5065 World Association of Publishers,
Manufacturers& Distributors**
Worlddidac
Bollwerk 21, PO Box 8866 CH-3001
Berne
Switzerland
41-31-3121744
Fax: 41-31-3121744
E-mail: info@worlddidac.org
A worldwide listing of over 330 publishers, manu-
facturers and distributors of educational materi-
als. Listings include all contact information,
products and school levels/grades.

160 pages Annual

Beat Jost, Coordinating Education

5066 World Bank
1818 H Street NW
Room T-8061
Washington, DC 20433-0002
202-477-1234
Fax: 202-477-6391
Maps, poster kits, case studies and videocassettes
that teach about life in developing countries.

5067 World Book Educational Products
525 W Monroe Street
20th Floor
Chicago, IL 60661
312-729-5800
Fax: 312-729-5600
Reference books and the World Book Encyclopedia on CD-Rom.

5068 World Eagle
111 King Street
Littleton, MA 01460-1527
978-486-9180
800-854-8273
Fax: 978-486-9652
E-mail: info@ibaradio.org
http://www.worldeagle.com
Publishes an online, social studies educational resource magazine: comparative data, graphs, maps
and charts on world issues. Publishes world regional atlases, and supplies maps and curriculum
materials.

Valentina Bardawil Powers, Author
Martine Crandall-Hollick, President

5069 World Resources Institute
10 G Street, NE
Suite 800
Washington, DC 20002
202-729-7600
Fax: 202-729-7610
The world Resources Institute is an
environmental think tank that goes beyond research to create practical ways to protect the Earth

and improve people's lives. our mission is to move human society to live in ways that protect Earth's environment for surrent and future generations.

Jonathan Lash, President

5070 World Scientific Publishing Company

27 Warren Street
Suite 401-402
Hackensack, NJ 07601
201-487-9655
Fax: 201-487-9695
E-mail: wspc@wspc.com
http://www.wspc.com
This is one of the world's leading academic publishers. It now publishes more than 400 books and 100 journals a year in diverse fields of science technology, medicine, business and management.

Ruth Zhou, Marketing Executive

5071 World of Difference Institute

Anti-Defamation League
823 United Nations Plaza
New York, NY 10017-3518
212-490-2525
Fax: 212-867-0779
E-mail: webmaster@adl.org
http://www.adl.org
Materials and training, as well as Pre K-12 curriculum resources, Anti-bias and diversity.

Lindsay J Friedman, Director

5072 Worth Publishers

33 Irving Plaza
New York, NY 10003-2332
212-475-6000
Fax: 212-689-2383
A balanced and comprehensive account of the U.S. past is accompanied by an extensive set of supplements.

5073 Wright Group

19201 120th Avenue NE
Bothell, WA 98011-9507
800-523-2371
Fax: 425-486-7704
http://www.wrightgroup.com
Supplementary program materials for reading education.

5074 Write Source Educational Publishing House

PO Box 460
Burlington, WI 53105-0460
262-763-8258
Fax: 262-763-2651
Publishes Writers Express, a writing, thinking and learning handbook series for grades 4 and 5. Also offer the latest editions of Write Source 2000 and Writers INC for grades 6-8 and 9-12.

5075 Zaner-Bloser K-8 Catalog

2200 W 5th Avenue
Columbus, OH 43215
614-486-0221
800-421-3018
Fax: 614-487-2699
http://www.zaner-bloser.com
Publisher of handwriting materials and reading, writing, spelling and study skills programs.

Robert Page, President

5076 Zephyr Press

814 North Franklin Street
Chicago, IL 60610-3109
312-337-5985
800-232-2187
Fax: 312-337-5985
E-mail: neways2learn@zephyrpress.com
http://www.zephyrpress.com
Zephyr Press publishes effective, state-of-the-art-teaching materials for classroom use.

Joey Tanner MEd, President

5077 ZooBooks

ZooBooks/Wildlife Education. Ltd.
12233 Thatcher Court
Poway, CA 92064-6880
619-513-7600
800-477-5034
Fax: 858-513-7660
E-mail: animals@zoobooks.com
http://www.zoobooks.com
Reference books offering fascinating insights into the world of wildlife. Created in collaboration with leading scientists and educators, these multi-volume Zoobooks make important facts and concepts about nature, habitat and wildlife understandable to children. From alligators to zebras, aquatic to exotic, each Zoobook is colorful, scientifically accurate and easy to read.

General

5080 AVKO Educational Research Foundation

3084 Willard Road
Birch Run, MI 48415-9404
810-686-9283
866-285-6612
Fax: 810-686-1101
E-mail: avkoemail@aol.com
http://www.avko.org
Comprised of teachers and individuals interested in helping others learn to read and spell. Develops reading training materials for individuals with dyslexia or other learning disabilities using a method involving audio, visual, kinesthetic and oral diagnosis and remediation. Conducts research into the causes of reading, spelling, and writing disabilities.

Don McCabe, Research Director
Devorah Wolf, President

5081 Assistive Technology Clinics

Children's Hospital
1056 E 19th Avenue
#030
Denver, CO 80218-1007
303-861-6250
Fax: 303-764-8214
A diagnostic clinic providing evaluation, information and support to families with children with disabilities in the areas of seating and mobility. Offers augmentative communication and assistive technology access.

Tracey Kovach, Coordinator

5082 Center for Equity and Excellence in Education

George Washington University
1555 Wilson Boulevard
Suite 515
Arlington, VA 22209-2004
703-528-3588
800-925-3223
Fax: 703-528-5973
E-mail: ceeeinfo@ceee.gwu.edu
http://www.ceee.gwu.edu
Mission is to advance education reform so that all students achieve high standards. Operates under the umbrella of the Institute for Education Policy Studies within the Graduate School of Education and Human Development. Designs and conducts program evaluation for states, districts and schools and conducts program evalutaion, policy and applied research effecting equitable educational opportunities for all students.

Charlene Rivera, Executive Director
Kristina Anstrom, Assistant Director

5083 Center for Learning

The Center for Learning
PO Box 910
2105 Evergreen Road
Villa Maria, PA 16155
724-964-8083
800-767-9090
Fax: 724-964-8992
E-mail:
customerservice@centerforlearning.org
http://www.centerforlearning.org
To improve education by writing and publishing values-based curriculum materials that enable teachers to foster student responsibility for learning

5084 Center for Organization of Schools

Johns Hopkins University
2701 N Charles Street
Suite 300
Baltimore, MD 21218-2404
410-516-8810
Fax: 410-516-8890
E-mail: mmaushard@csos.jhu.edu
http://www.csos.jhu.edu
Conduct research, development, evaluation, and dissemination of replicable strategies designed to transform low-performing schools so that al lstudents graduate ready for college, career and life. Products include curricula that help all students achieve at a high level. Programs in early learning; school, family and community partnerships; a financial literacy program called Stocks ain the Future, and the Baltimore Education Research Consotrium, plus Talent development Secondary reform

James McPartland, Co-Director
Mary Maushard, Communication Director

5085 Center for Research on the Context of Teaching

Stanford University
CERAS Building
4th Floor 520 Galvez Mall
Stanford, CA 94305-3084
650-725-1845
Fax: 650-736-2296
http://www.stanford.edu/group/CRC/
Conducts research on ways in which secondary school teaching and learning are affected by their contexts.

Milbrey W McLaughlin, Co-Director
Joan E Talbert, Co-Director

5086 Center for Social Organization of Schools

Johns Hopkins University
3003 N Charles Street
Suite 200
Baltimore, MD 21218-3888
410-516-8800
Fax: 410-516-8890
E-mail: jmcpartland@csos.jhu.edu
http://www.csos.jhu.edu
Conduct programmatic research to improve the education system, as well as full-time support staff engaged in developing curricula and providing technical assistance to help schools use the Center's research.

Jim McPartland, Director
Mary Maushard, Communication Director

5087 Center for Technology in Education

Bank Street College of Education
6740 Alexander Bell Drive
Suite 302
Columbia, MD 21046-1898
410-516-9800
Fax: 410-516-9818
E-mail: cte@jhu.edu
http://cte.jhu.edu
Improve the quality of life of children and youth, particularly those with special needs, through teaching, research, and leadership in the use of technology.

Jacqueline A Nunn, Director
K Lynne Harper Mainzer, Deputy Director

5088 Center for the Study of Reading

University of Illinois
158 Children's Research Center
51 Gerty Drive
Champaign, IL 61820
217-333-2552
Fax: 217-244-4501
E-mail: csrrca@uiuc.edu
http://csr.ed.uiuc.edu
Conduct reading research and development must be to discover and put into practice the means for reaching children who are failing to read.

Richard C Anderson, Director
Kim Nguyen-Jahiel, Associate Director

5089 Center for the Study of Small/Rural Schools

University of Oklahoma
555 E Constitution Street
Suite 138
Norman, OK 73072-7820
405-325-1450
Fax: 405-325-7075
E-mail: jcsimmons@ou.edu
http://cssrs.ou.edu
Assists small and rural schools in building and maintaining necessary knowledge bases, founded on state-of-the-art research in the areas of school improvement and reform, restructuring, staff development, administration, and teaching.

Jan C Simmons, Director

5090 Center on Families, Schools, Communities & Children's Learning

Northeastern University
50 Nightingale Hall
Boston, MA 02215
617-373-2595
Fax: 617-373-8924
Examines how families, communities and schools can work in partnership to promote children's motivation, learning and development, including disseminating information.

Nancy Ames, Vice President

5091 Center on Organization & Restructuring of Schools

1025 W Johnson Street
Madison, WI 53706-1706
608-263-7575
Fax: 608-263-6448
Focuses on restructuring K-12 schools in various areas of student development and progress.

Fred M Newman, Director

5092 Council for Educational Development and Research

National Education Association (NEA)
1201 16th Street NW
Washington, DC 20036-3290
202-833-4000
Fax: 202-822-7974
http://www.nea.org
The voice of education professionals. Advocate for education professionals

John I Wilson, Executive Director
Dennis Van Roekel, President

5093 Curriculum Research and Development Group

1776 University Avenue
Honolulu, HI 96822-2463
808-956-4949
800-799-8111
Fax: 808-956-6730
E-mail: crdg@hawaii.edu
http://www.hawaii.edu/crdg
Conducts research and creates, evaluates, disseminates, and supports educational programs that serve students, teachers, parents, and other educators in grades preK-12.

Helen Au, Assistant Director

5094 Division for Research

The Council for Exceptional Children
2000 Broadway
Oakland, CA 94612

510-891-3400
http://www.dor.kaiser.org
The Division of Research aims to conduct, publish, and disseminate high-quality epidemiologic and health services research to improve the health and medical care of Kaiser Permanente members and the society at large.

Joe Selby, Director
Morris Collen, Founder

5095 Educational Information & Resource Center
Research Department
606 Delsea Drive
Sewell, NJ 08080-9399
856-582-7000
Fax: 856-582-4206
E-mail: info@eirc.org
http://www.eirc.org
EIRC is committed to continuously improving the education, safety, physical and emotional health of children. EIRC meets this commitment by developing and delivering a comprehensive array of support services to those who teach, raise, care for and mentor children.

Charles Ivory, Executive Director
John Henry, Program Director

5096 Educational Research Service
1001 N Fairfax Street
Suite 500
Alexandria, VA 22314-1587
703-243-2100
800-791-9308
Fax: 703-243-1985
E-mail: ers@ers.org
http://www.ers.org
For over 30 years Educational Research Service has been the nonprofit organization serving the research and information needs of the nation's K-12 education leaders and the public.

John C Draper EdD, CEO
Katherine A Behrens, Chief Operating Officer

5097 Educational Testing Service
Rosedale Road
Princeton, NJ 08541
609-921-9000
Fax: 609-734-5410
http://www.ets.org
To advance quality and equity in education by providing fair and valid assessments, research and related services. Our products and services measure knowledge and skills, promote learning and educational performance, and support education and professional development for all people worldwide.

Susan Keipper, Program Director
Kurt Landgraf, President and CEO

5098 Florida Atlantic University-Multifunctional Resource Center
1515 W Commercial Boulevard
Suite 303
Boco Raton, FL 33309-3095
561-297-3000
800-328-6721
Fax: 561-297-2141
Provides training and technical assistance to Title VII-funded classroom instructional projects and other programs serving limited-English proficient students.

Dr Ann C Willig, Director
Elaine Sherr, Research Assistant

5099 Higher Education Center
National Education Association (NEA)
1201 16th Street NW
Washington, DC 20036-3290

202-833-4000
Fax: 202-822-7974
E-mail: ncuea@nea.org
http://www.nea.org
The center provides data and other research products to NEA higher education affiliates. The Research Advisory Group, composed of higher education leaders and staff, meets twice a year to review products from the NEA Research Center for Higher Education and make recommendations about additional research needs. The center currently provides salary reports, Higher Education Contract Analysis System, and budget analysis.

Dennis Van Roekel, President
John I Wilson, Executive Director

5100 Information Center on Education
Eba Room 385
Albany, NY 12234-1
518-474-8716
Fax: 518-473-7737
Coordinates data collection procedures within the New York State Education Department.

Leonard Powell, Director

5101 Information Exchange
Maine State Library
64 State House Station
Augusta, ME 04333-64
207-287-5620
800-322-8899
Fax: 207-287-5624
Provides access to the latest education research and information for teachers.

Edna M Comstock, Director

5102 Institute for Research in Learning Disabilities
The University of Kansas
3060 Robert
Lawrence, KS 66045-1
785-864-4780
Fax: 785-864-5728
Although the focus of the Institute's research is children, they have a sizeable publication list with some of their research having relevance for adults.

5103 Instructional Materials Laboratory
University of Missouri-Columbia
8 London Hall
Columbia, MO 65211-2230
800-669-2465
800-669-2465
Fax: 573-882-1992
E-mail: iml@missouri.edu
http://www.iml.missouri.edu/
Prepares and disseminates instructional materials for the vocational education community.

Dana Tannehill, Director
Richard Branton, Assistant Director

5104 Learning Research and Development Center
University of Pittsburgh
3939 O'Hara Street
Pittsburgh, PA 15260
412-624-7487
Fax: 412-624-3051
E-mail: lrangel@pitt.edu
http://www.lrdc.pitt.edu
LRDC fosters an environment in which research initiatives relating to the science, practice, organization and technology of learning, teaching and training are born and thrive.

Charles Perfetti, Director
Alan Lesgold, Senior Scientist/Research Sc

5105 Life Lab Science Program
1156 High Street
Santa Cruz, CA 95064
831-459-2001
Fax: 831-459-3483
E-mail: lifelab@lifelab.org
http://www.lifelab.org
Life Lab Science Program is nationally acknowledged as an expert leader in the development and dissemination of garden-centered educational programs.

Gail Harlamoff, Executive Director
Whitney Cohen, Education Director

5106 Merrimack Education Center
101 Mill Road
Chelmsford, MA 01824-4899
978-256-3985
Fax: 978-256-6890
E-mail: cjeffers@meccorp.mec.edu
http://www.mec.edu/
Merrimack Education Center (MEC) is a diversified educational and technological resource for schools, cities and towns and other non-profit organizations. MEC offers a broad range of special education, professional development, facilities management and technology programs and solutions.

John Barranco, Director

5107 Mid-Atlantic Regional Educational Laboratory
1301 Cecil B Moore Avenue
Philadelphia, PA 19122-6091
215-204-3000
Fax: 215-204-5130
E-mail: robert.sullivan@temple.edu
http://www.temple.edu/lss
The Regional Educational Laboratories are educational research and development organizations supported by contracts with the US Education Department. Specialty area: Education Leadership.

William Evans, Director

5108 Mid-Continent Regional Educational Laboratory
2550 S Parker Road
Suite 500
Aurora, CO 80014-1678
303-337-0990
Fax: 303-337-3005
Focuses on improvement of education practices in Colorado, Kansas, Missouri, Nebraska, Wyoming, North Dakota and South Dakota.

C. Lawrence Hutchins, Director

5109 Midwestern Regional Educational Laboratory
1900 Spring Road
Suite 300
Oak Brook, IL 60521
630-649-6500
Fax: 630-649-6700
E-mail: nowakows@ncrel.org
The Regional Educational Laboratories are educational research and development organizations supported by contracts with the US Education Department, Office of Educational Research and Improvement. Specialty area: Technology.

Dr. Jeri Nowakowski, Executive Director

5110 Missouri LINC
401 E Stewart Road
Columbia, MO 65211
573-882-2733
800-392-0533
Fax: 573-882-5071
Serves students with special needs through a resource and technical assistance center.

Linda Bradley, Director

5111 Music Teachers National Association
441 Vine Street
Suite 3100
Cincinnatti, OH 45202-3004
513-421-1420
888-512-5278
Fax: 513-421-2503
E-mail: mtnanet@mtna.org
http://www.mtna.org
Research reports dealing with any aspects of music, music teaching, music learning and related subjects.

Rachel Kramer, Member Liaison

5112 NEA Foundatrion for the Improvement of Education
1201 16th Street NW
Washington, DC 20036
202-822-7840
Fax: 202-822-7779
E-mail: info@neafoundation@list.nea.org
http://www.neafoundation.org
The NEA Foundation, through the unique strength of its partnership with educators, advances student achievement by investing in public education that will prepare each of America's children to learn and thrive in a rapidly changing world.

Aaron J Pope, Communications Associate
John I Wilson, Executive Director

5113 National Black Child Development Institute
1313 L Street, NW
Suite 110
Washington, DC 20005-4110
202-833-2220
800-556-2234
Fax: 202-833-8222
E-mail: moreinfo@nbcdi.org
http://www.nbcdi.org
NBCDI's mission is to improve and protect the quality of life of Black children and families.

Carol Brunson Day, President
Gillian Shurland, Contact

5114 National Center for Improving Science Education
2000 L Street NW
Suite 616
Washington, DC 20036-4917
202-467-0652
Fax: 202-467-0659
Promotes change in state and local policies and practices in science curricula, teaching, and assessment.

Senta A Raizen, Director

5115 National Center for Research in Mathematical Sciences Education
University of Wisconsin-Madison
1025 W Johnson Street
#557
Madison, WI 53706-1706
608-263-4285
Fax: 608-263-3406
Provides a research base for the reform of school mathematics.

Thomas A Romberg, Director

5116 National Center for Research in Vocational Education
University of California, Berkeley
2030 Addison Street
Suite 500
Berkeley, CA 94720-1674
510-642-4004
800-762-4093
Fax: 510-642-2124

E-mail: NCRVE@berkeley.edu
http://vocserve.berkeley.edu
The mission of the National Center for Research in Vocational Education (NCRVE) is to strengthen education to prepare all individuals for lasting and rewarding employment and lifelong learning.

David Stern, Director
Phyllis Hudecki, Associate Director

5117 National Center for Research on Teacher Learning
Michigan State University, College of Education
116 Erickson Hall
East Lansing, MI 48824-1034
517-355-9302
Fax: 517-432-2795
E-mail: floden_@_msu.edu
http://ncrtl.msu.edu
The NCRTL extended its findings about learning from students-as-learners to teachers-as-learners in order to understand how teachers learn to teach.

Robert E Floden, Director
G Williamson McDiarmid, Director

5118 National Center for Science Teaching & Learning
Ohio State University
1314 Kinnear Road
Columbus, OH 43212-1156
614-292-3339
Fax: 614-292-0263
Seeks to understand how non-curricular factors affect how science is taught in grades K-12.

Arthur L White, Director

5119 National Center for the Study of Privatizationin Education
525 W 120th Street
Box 181, 230 Thompson Hall
New York, NY 10027-6696
212-678-3259
Fax: 212-678-3474
E-mail: ncspe@columbia.edu
http://www.ncspe.org
The goal of the National Center for the Study of Privatization in Education is to provide an independent, non-partisan source of analysis and information on privatization in education.

Henry M Levin, Director
Clive Belfield, Associate Director

5120 National Center on Education & the Economy
555 13th Street, NW
Suite 500 W
Washington, DC 20004
202-783-3668
888-361-6233
Fax: 202-783-3672
E-mail: info@ncee.org
http://www.ncee.org
NCEE is committed not just to research, analysis and advocacy, but also to following through on its recommendations by creating the training, professional development, technical assistance and materials that professionals in the system need to implement the proposals we make.

Marc Tucker, President/Founder
Rich Moglia Cannon, Chief Financial Officer

5121 National Center on Education in the Inner Cities
Temple University
13th Street & Cecil B Moore Avenue
Philadelphia, PA 19122

215-893-8400
Fax: 215-735-9718
Conducts systematic studies of innovative initiatives for improving the quality and outcomes of schooling and broad-based efforts to strengthen and improve education.

Margaret C Wang, Director

5122 National Child Labor Committee
1501 Broadway
Suite 1908
New York, NY 10036-5592
212-840-1801
Fax: 212-768-0963
E-mail: info@nationalchildlabor.org
http://www.nationalchildlabor.org
The National Child Labor Committee (NCLC) is a private, non-profit organization founded in 1904 and incorporated by an Act of Congress in 1907 with the mission of promoting the rights, awareness, dignity, well-being and education of children and youth as they relate to work and working.

Jeffrey F Newman, President/Executive Director
Erik Butler, President

5123 National Clearinghouse for Alcohol & Drug Information
PO Box 2345
Rockville, MD 20847-2345
240-221-4019
800-729-6686
Fax: 240-221-4292
http://ncadi.samhsa.gov
SAMHSA's National Clearinghouse for Alcohol and Drug Information (NCADI) is the Nation's one-stop resource for information about substance abuse prevention and addiction treatment.

John Noble, Director

5124 National Clearinghouse for Bilingual Education
George Washington University
2011 Eye Street NW
Suite 300
Washington, DC 20006
202-467-0867
800-321-6223
Fax: 202-467-4283
E-mail: askncela@ncela.gwu.edu
http://www.ncela.gwu.edu
OELA's National Clearinghouse collects, coordinates and conveys a broad range of research and resources in support of an inclusive approach to high quality education for ELLs.

Nancy Zelasko, Director
Minerva Gorena, Director

5125 National Clearinghouse for Information on Business Involvement in Education
National Association for Industry-Education Co-op
235 Hendricks Boulevard
Buffalo, NY 14226-3304
716-834-7047
Fax: 718-834-7047
E-mail: www2.pecom/naiec
http://www2.pecom.net/naiec
Seeks to foster industry-education cooperation in the US and Canada in the areas of school improvement, career education and human resource/economic development.

Dr. Donald Clark, Director

5126 National Dropout Prevention Center
Clemson University
209 Martin Street
Clemson, SC 29631-1555
864-656-2599
Fax: 864-656-0136
E-mail: ndpc@clemson.edu
http://www.dropoutprevention.org

Provide knowledge and promote networking for researchers, practitioners, policymakers, and families to increase opportunities for youth in at-risk situations to receive the quality education and services to successfully graduate from high school.

Jay Smink, Executive Director
Marty Duckenfield, Public Information Director

5127 National Early Childhood Technical Assistance System

517 S Greensboro Street
Carrboro, NC 27510
919-962-2001
919-843-3269
Fax: 919-966-7463
E-mail: nectac@unc.edu
http://www.nectac.org
NECTAC is the national early childhood technical assistance center supported by the U.S. Department of Education's Office of Special Education Programs.

Lynne Kahn, Director
Joan Danaher, Associate Director

5128 National Information Center for Educational Media

PO Box 8640
Albuquerque, NM 87198-8640
505-998-0800
800-926-8328
Fax: 505-256-1080
E-mail: mhlava@accessinn.com
http://www.nicem.com
The world's most comprehensive audiovisual database for over 35 years and a crucial reference tool for librarians, media specialists, training directors, faculty, teachers and researchers.

Marjorie Hlava, President
Jay Van Eman, Chief Executive Officer

5129 National Research Center on the Gifted & Talented

University of Connecticut
2131 Hillside Road
Unit 3007
Storrs, CT 06269-3007
860-486-4826
Fax: 860-486-2900
http://www.gifted.uconn.edu
Studies focusing on meeting the needs of gifted and talented youth have received national and international attention for over 40 years.

Joseph S Renzulli, Director
Phillip E Austin, President

5130 National Resource Center on Self-Care & School-Age Child Care

American Home Economics Association
1555 King Street
Alexandria, VA 22314-2738
703-706-4620
800-252-SAFE
Fax: 703-706-4663
Provides materials to parents, educators, child care professionals and others concerned about the number of latchkey children and about quality school-age child care.

Dr. Margaret Plantz, Director

5131 National School Boards Association Library

1680 Duke Street
Alexandria, VA 22314-3455
703-838-6731
Fax: 703-683-7590
Maintains up-to-date collection of resources concerning education issues, with an emphasis on school board policy issues.

Adria Thomas, Director

5132 National School Safety Center

141 Duesenberg Drive
Suite 11
Westlake Village, CA 91362-3815
805-373-9977
Fax: 805-373-9277
E-mail: info@schoolsafety.us
http://www.schoolsafety.us
Serves as an advocate for safe, secure and peaceful schools worldwide and as a catalyst for the prevention of school crime and violence.

Ronald D Stephens, Executive Director
June Lane Arnette, Associate Director

5133 National Science Resources Center

901 D Street SW
Suite 704B
Washington, DC 20024
202-633-2966
Fax: 202-287-2070
E-mail: nsrcinfo@si.edu
http://www.nsrconline.org
Intermediary organization that bridges research on how children learn with best practices for the classroom.

Sally Shuler, Executive Director
Jennifer Childress, Director

5134 North Central Regional Educational Laboratory

1120 East Diehl Road
Suite 200
Naperville, IL 60563-1486
630-649-6500
Fax: 630-649-6700
E-mail: info@ncrel.org
http://www.ncrel.org
Being an educator is a great responsibility. At Learning Point Associates, we accept responsibility in order to deserve the trust that has been placed in us and our work

Gina Burkhard, Chief Executive Officer
Robert Davis, Chief Financial Officer

5135 Northeast Regional Center for Drug-Free Schools & Communities

12 Overton Avenue
Sayville, NY 11782-2437
718-930-7000
Fax: 516-589-7894
Works to support the prevention of alcohol and other drug use in the northeast region of the United States.

Dr. Gerald Edwards, Director

5136 Northeast and Islands Regional Educational Laboratory

222 Richmond Street
Suite 300
Providence, RI 02903
401-274-9548
800-521-9550
Fax: 401-421-7650
E-mail: info@lab.brown.edu
Promotes educational change to provide all students equitable opportunities to succeed. We advocate for populations whose access to excellent education has been limited or denied.

Oaxaca Schroder, Administrative Assistant
Sunitha Appikatla, Senior Programmer/Analyst

5137 Northwest Regional Educational Laboratory

101 SW Main Street
Suite 500
Portland, OR 97204-3213
503-275-9500
800-547-6339
Fax: 503-275-0660

E-mail: info@nwrel.org
http://www.nwrel.org
The mission of the Northwest Regional Educational Laboratory (NWREL) is to improve learning by building capacity in schools, families, and communities through applied research and development

Jerry Colonna, Chairperson
Rob Larson, Vice Chairperson

5138 Pacific Regional Educational Laboratory

1099 Alakea Street
Suite 2500
Honolulu, HI 96813
808-969-3482
Fax: 808-969-3483
E-mail: kofelj@prel.hawaii.edu
The Regional Educational Laboratories are educational research and development organizations supported by contracts with the U.S. Education Department, Office of Educational Research and Improvement. Specialty area: Language and Cultural Diversity.

Dr. John Kofel, Executive Director

5139 Parent Educational Advocacy Training Center

100 N Washington Street
Suite 234
Falls Church, VA 22046
804-819-1999
E-mail: partners@peatc.org
http://www.peatc.org
Mission is to build positive futures for children in Virginia by working collaboratively with families, schools and communities in order to improve opportunities for excellence in education and success in school and community life.

Cathy Healy, CEO
Michael Heaney, President

5140 Parents as Teachers National Center

2228 Ball Drive
Saint Louis, MO 63146
314-432-4330
866-728-4968
Fax: 314-432-8963
E-mail: info@parentsasteachers.org
http://www.patnc.org
To provide the information, support and encouragement parents need to help their children develop optimally during the crucial early years of life.

Sue Stepleton, President/CEO
Cheryl Dyle-Palmer, COO

5141 Public Education Fund Network

601 13th Street NW
Suite 710 S
Washington, DC 20005-3808
202-628-7460
Fax: 202-628-1893
E-mail: PEN@PublicEducation.org
http://www.publiceducation.org
To build public demand and mobilize resources for quality public education for all children through a national constituency of local education funds and individuals.

Wendy D Puriefoy, Director
Richard J. Vierk, Chairman

5142 Quality Education Data

1050 Seventeenth Street
Suite 1100
Denver, CO 80265
303-209-9400
800-525-5811
Fax: 303-209-9444
E-mail: info@qeddata.com
http://www.qeddata.com
Gathers information about K-12 schools, colleges and other educational institutions, of-

fers an on-line database on education, directories of public and nonpublic schools and research reports.

Jeanne Hayes, President
Katie Bukovsky, Sales Executive

5143 Regional Laboratory for Educational Improvement of the Northeast
555 New Jersey Ave NW
Washington, DC 20208
800-347-4200
Fax: 781-481-1120
Seeks to improve education in Connecticut, Maine, Massachusetts, New Hampshire, New York, Rhode Island, Vermont, Puerto Rico and the Virgin Islands.

David P Crandall, Director

5144 Research for Better Schools
112 N Broad Street
Philadelphia, PA 19102-2471
215-568-6150
Fax: 215-568-7260
E-mail: info@rbs.org
http://www.rbs.org
RBS is a private, nonprofit educational organization funded primarily through grants and contracts from the U.S. Department of Education, the National Science Foundation, Mid-Atlantic state departments of education, institutions of higher education, foundations, and school districts.

Dr. Keith M Kershner, Executive Director
Rev. John F Bloh, President

5145 SERVE
PO Box 5367
Greensboro, NC 27435
336-315-7400
800-755-3277
Fax: 336-315-7457
E-mail: info@serve.org
http://www.serve.org
Its mission is to support and promote teaching and learning excellence in the Pre-kindergarten to Grade 12 education community.

Ludwig Van Broekhuizen, Executive Director
Francena Cummings, Director, Technical Assistan

5146 SIGI PLUS
Educational Testing Service
105 Terry Drive
Suite 120
Newtown, PA 18940-1872
800-257-7444
Fax: 215-579-8589
A computerized career guidance program developed by Educational Testing Service. Covers all the major aspects of career decision making and planning through a carefully constructed system of nine separate but interrelated sections, including a Tech Prep module and Internet Hydrolink Connectivity.

Annie Schofer, Sales Manager

5147 Satellite Educational Resources Consortium
939 S Stadium Road
Columbia, SC 29201-4724
803-252-2782
Fax: 803-252-5320
http://www.adec.edu
Seeks to expand educational opportunities by employing the latest telecommunication technologies to make quality education in math, science, and foreign languages available equally and cost-effectively to stu-

dents regardless of their geographic location.

Wilbur H Hinton, Executive Director

5148 Scientific Learning
300 Frank H Ogawa Plaza
Suite 600
Oakland, CA 94612-2040
888-665-9707
888-665-9707
Fax: 510-444-3580
E-mail: customerservice@scilearn.com
http://www.scientificlearning.com
Scientific Learning bases their products and services on neuroscience research and scientifically validated efficacy and deliver them using the most efficient technologies. We also provide beneficial products and services to our customers that are easy to use and access.

Robert C Bowen, Chairman/CEO
Andy Myers, President/COO

5149 Smithsonian Institution/Office of Elementary & Secondary Education
PO Box 37012
SI Building, Room 153, MRC 010
Washington, DC 20013-7012
202-633- 100
Fax: 202-357-2116
E-mail: info@si.edu
http://si.edu
Helps K-12 teachers incorporate museums and other community resources into their curricula.

Ann Bay, Director
G Wayne Clough, Secretary

5150 Society for Research in Child Development
University of Chicago Press
2950 S State Street
Suite 401
Ann Arbor, MI 48104
734-926-0600
Fax: 734-926-0601
E-mail: info@srcd.org
http://www.srcd.org
The Society is a multidisciplinary, not-for-profit, professional association with a membership

Barbara Kahn, Business Manager
Lonnie Sherrod, Executive Director

5151 Southeast Regional Center for Drug-Free Schools & Communities
Spencerian Office Plaza
Louisville, KY 40292-1
502-588-0052
800-621-7372
Fax: 502-588-1782
Works to support the prevention of alcohol and drug use among youth in the Southeast region.

Nancy J Cunningham, Director

5152 Southern Regional Education Board
592 10th Street NW
Atlanta, GA 30318-5776
404-875-9211
Fax: 404-872-1477
E-mail: evalutech@sreb.org
http://www.sreb.org
Nonprofit, nonpartisan organization that helps government and education leaders in its 16 member states work together to advance education and improve the social and economic life of the region.

Mark D Musick, Director
David S Spence, President

5153 Southwest Comprehensive Regional Assistance Center-Region IX
New Mexico Highlands University
121 Tijeras Avenue NE
Suite 2100
Albuquerque, NM 87102-3461
800-247-4269
Fax: 505-243-4456
National network of 15 technical assistance centers, funded through the US Department of Education, designed to support federally funded educational programs. Specifically, these centers will provide comprehensive training and technical assistance under the Improving America's Schools Act (IASA) to States, Tribes, community based organizations, local education agencies, schools and other recipients of funds under the Act.

Paul E Martinez EdD, Director

5154 Southwestern Educational Development Laboratory
4700 Mueller Boulevard
Austin, TX 78723
512-476-6861
800-476-6861
Fax: 512-476-2286
E-mail: info@sedl.org
http://www.sedl.org
SEDL is a private, nonprofit corporation dedicated to fulfilling its mission with clients and other education stakeholders on a national, regional, state, and local basis through diverse and interrelated funding, partnerships, and projects.

Dr. Wesley A Hoover, Executive Director
Christine A Moses, Director of Communications

5155 Special Interest Group for Computer Science Education
Computer Science Department
University of Texas at Austin
Austin, TX 78712
512-471-9539
Fax: 512-471-8885
http://www.sigcse.org
Provides a forum for solving problems common in developing, implementing and evaluating computer science education programs and courses.

Nell B Dale, Director

5156 TACS/WRRC
1268 University of Oregon
Eugene, OR 97403
541-346-5641
Fax: 541-346-0322
E-mail: wrrc@oregon.uoregon.edu
http://wrrc.uoregon.edu/tacs
Supports state education agencies in their task of ensuring quality programs and services for children with disabilities and their families.

Richard Zeller, Co-Director
Caroline Moore, Project Director

5157 TERC
2067 Massachusetts Avenue
Cambridge, MA 2140-1340
617-873-9600
Fax: 617-873-9601
E-mail: communications@terc.edu
http://www.terc.edu
We imagine a future in which learners from diverse communities engage in creative, rigorous, and reflective inquiry as an integral part of their lives.

24 pages
ISSN: 0743-0221

Ken Mayer, Communications Director
Arthur Nelson, Chairman/Founder

5158 UCLA Statistical Consulting
University of California, Los Angeles
8130 MSB, UCLA
PO Box 951554
Los Angeles, CA 90095-1554
310-825-8299
Fax: 310-206-5658
http://www.ats.ucla.edu
Provides statistical consulting services to UCLA and off-campus students. The staff is faculty members, graduate students and the Department of Statistics. Specializes in the quantitative analysis of research problems in a wide variety of fields.

Debbie Barrera, Administrator
Richard Berk, Director

Audio Visual Materials

5159 AGC/United Learning
Discovery Education
1560 Sherman Avenue
Suite 100
Evanston, IL 60201
847-328-6700
800-323-9084
Fax: 847-328-6706
http://www.discoveryed.com
A publisher/producer of educational videos and digital content K-College curriculum based.

Coni Rechner, Director Marketing
Ronald Reed, Sr. Vice President

5160 Active Parenting Publishing
810 Franklin Court
Suite B
Marietta, GA 30067
800-825-0060
Fax: 770-429-0334
E-mail: cservice@activeparenting.com
http://www.activeparenting.com
Videos and books on parenting, character education, substance abuse prevention, divorce and step-parenting, ADHD and more.

5161 Agency for Instructional Technology/AIT
PO Box A
Bloomington, IN 47402-0120
800-457-4509
Videodiscs, videocassettes, films and electronics.

5162 Allied Video Corporation
PO Box 702618
Tulsa, OK 74170-2618
918-587-6477
800-926-5892
Fax: 918-587-1550
E-mail: allied@farpointer.net
http://www.alliedvd.com
Produces the educational video series, The Assistant Professor. Animations and three-dimensional graphics clearly illustrate concepts in mathematics, science and music. Companion supplementary materials are also available.

Video

Charles Brown, President

5163 Altschul Group Corporation
1560 Sherman Avenue
Suite 100
Evanston, IL 60201-4817
800-323-9084
Video and film educational programs.

5164 Ambrose Video Publishing Inc
145 West 45th Street
New York, NY 10036
212-768-7373
800-526-4663
Fax: 212-768-9282
http://www.ambrosevideo.com
A leading distributor of broadcast quality documentation/educational videos to individuals (in the home) and schools, libraries and other institutions. The company also sells through catalog, sales staff and television advertising.

5165 Anchor Audio
3415 Lomita Boulevard
Torrance, CA 90505-5010
310-784-2300
800-262-4671
Fax: 310-784-0533
http://www.anchoraudio.com

Various audio visual products for the school and library.

5166 Association for Educational Communications & Technology
1025 Vermont Avenue NW
Suite 820
Washington, DC 20005-3516
202-347-7834
Offers a full line of videotapes and films for the various educational fields including language arts, science and social studies.

5167 BUILD Sucess Through the Values of Excellence
Center for the Study of Small/Rural Schools
555 E Constitution Street
Room 138
Norman, OK 73072-7820
405-325-1450
Fax: 405-325-7075
E-mail: jcsimmons@ou.edu
http://cssrs.ou.edu
Series IV

Video

Jan C Simmons, Director

5168 Bergwall Productions
540 Baltimore Pike
Chadds Ford, PA 19317-9304
800-645-3565
Educational videotapes and films.

5169 Cedrus
1420 Buena Vista Avenue
McLean, VA 22101-3510
703-883-0986
Videodiscs, videocassettes and filmstrips for educational purposes.

5170 Character Education
Center for the Study of Small/Rural Schools
555 E Constitution Street
Room 138
Norman, OK 73072-7820
405-325-1450
Fax: 405-325-7075
E-mail: jcsimmons@ou.edu
http://cssrs.ou.edu
Series IV

Video

Jan C Simmons, Director

5171 Chip Taylor Communications
2 E View Drive
Derry, NH 03038-5728
603-434-9262
800-876-2447
Fax: 603-432-2723
E-mail: sales@chiptaylor.com
http://www.chiptaylor.com
Quality educational videotapes and DVDs and multimedia in all areas of interest.

Video

Chip Taylor, President

5172 Churchill Media
6677 N NW Highway
Chicago, IL 60631-1304
310-207-6600
800-334-7830
Fax: 800-624-1678
Videos, videodiscs and curriculum packages for schools and libraries.

5173 College Board Publications
College Board Publications
45 Columbus Avenue
New York, NY 10023-6992
212-713-8165
800-323-7155

Fax: 800-525-5562
http://www.collegeboard.org
Offers a variety of educational videotapes and publications focusing on college issues.

5174 Computer Prompting & Captioning Company
1010 Rockville Pike
Suite 306
Rockville, MD 20852-3035
301-738-8487
800-977-6678
Fax: 301-738-8488
E-mail: info@cpcweb.com
http://www.cpcweb.com
Closed captioning systems and service.

Sid Hoffman, Project Manager

5175 Concept Media
2493 Du Bridge Avenue
Irvine, CA 92606-5022
949-660-0727
800-233-7078
Fax: 949-660-0206
E-mail: info@conceptmedia.com
http://www.conceptmedia.com
Videos for students and professionals focused on child development, early childhood education, and the challenges facing many young children. Effective educational media for development specialists, regular and special education staff in elementary school, preschool teachers, childcare providers, health care workers and parents.

Dennis Timmerman, Sr Account Executive

5176 Crystal Productions
PO Box 2159
Glenview, IL 60025-6159
847-657-8144
800-255-8629
Fax: 800-657-8149
E-mail: custserv@crystalproductions.com
http://www.crystalproductions.com
Producer and distributor of educational resource material in art and sciences. Resources include videotapes, posters, books, videodiscs, CD-Rom, reproductions, games.

132 pages

Amy Woodworth, President

5177 Dukane Corporation
Audio Visual Products Division
2900 Dukane Drive
St Charles, IL 60174-3395
630-584-2300
Fax: 630-584-5156
Full line of audio visual products, LCD display panels, computer data projectors, overhead projectors, microfilm readers and silent and sound filmstrip projectors.

Stew deLacey

5178 Early Advantage
270 Monroe Turnpike
PO Box 4063
Monroe, CT 06468-4063
888-999-4670
Fax: 800-301-9268
E-mail: customerservice@early-advantage.com
http://www.earlyadvantage.com
Features the Muzzy video collection for teaching children beginning second language skills.

5179 Educational Video Group
291 S Wind Way
Greenwood, IN 46142-9190
317-888-6581
Fax: 317-888-5857
E-mail: evg@insightbb.com
http://www.evgonline.com

Award-winning video programs and text-books in education, presenting new offerings in speech, government and historic documentaries.

Roger Cook, President

5180 English as a Second Language Video Series
Master Teacher
Leadership Lane
PO Box 1207
Manhattan, KS 66505-1207
800-669-9633
Fax: 800-669-1132
http://www.masterteacher.com
Assessing the needs of culturally diverse learners, you will learn what must be done to evaluate the learning needs and progress of ESL students.
ISBN: 1-58992-045-7

5181 Fase Productions
4801 Wilshire Boulevard
Suite 215
Los Angeles, CA 90010-3813
213-965-8794
Educational videotapes and films.

5182 Films for Humanities & Sciences
PO Box 2053
Princeton, NJ 08543-2053
609-419-8000
800-257-5126
Fax: 609-419-8071
A leading publisher/distributor of over four thousand educational programs, including NOVA and TV Ontario, for school and college markets. Also a leader in the production and distribution of videotapes and videodiscs to the educational, institutional and government markets.

5183 First Steps/Concepts in Motivation
18105 Town Center Drive
Olney, MD 20832-1479
301-774-9429
800-947-8377
Educational videotapes and accessories promoting physical fitness for preschoolers and young children. Using choreographed dance movement, familiar and fun children's music, colorful mats, bean bags and rhythm sticks, First Steps teaches balance, gross and fine motor skills, rhythm, coordination, and primary learning skills.

Dale Rimmey, Marketing Director
Larry Rose, President/Owner

5184 Future of Rural Education
Center for the Study of Small/Rural Schools
555 E Constitution Street
Room 138
Norman, OK 73072-7820
405-325-1450
Fax: 405-325-7075
E-mail: jcsimmons@ou.edu
http://cssrs.ou.edu
Series I
Video
Jan C Simmons, Director

5185 GPN Year 2005 Literacy Catalog
GPN Educational Media
PO Box 80669
Lincoln, NE 68501-0669
402-472-2007
800-228-4630
Fax: 402-472-4076
E-mail: gpn@unl.edu
http://www.gpn.unl.edu
DVD, VHS, CD-ROM and slides for K-12 libraries and higher education. Free previews and satisfaction guaranteed. The sole source

of Reading Rainbow and many other quality programs seen on PBS.
Annually/Video
Stephen C Lenzen, Executive Director
John Vondracek, Director Marketing

5186 Gangs in Our Schools: Identification, Response, and Prevention Strategies
Center for the Study of Small/Rural Schools
555 E Constitution Street
Room 138
Norman, OK 73072-7820
405-325-1450
Fax: 405-325-7075
E-mail: jcsimmons@ou.edu
http://cssrs.ou.edu
Series III
Video
Jan C Simmons, Director

5187 Guidance Associates
PO Box 1000
Mount Kisco, NY 10549-7000
800-431-1242
Fax: 914-666-5319
E-mail: sales@guidanceassociates.com
http://www.guidanceassociates.com
Curriculum based videos in health/guidance, social studies, math, science, English, the humanities and career education.

Will Goodman, President

5188 Health Connection
55 W Oak Ridge Drive
Hagerstown, MD 21740
800-548-8700
Fax: 888-294-8405
E-mail: sales@healthconnection.org
http://www.healthconnection.org
Tools for freedom from tobacco and other drugs.

5189 Human Relations Media
175 Tompkins Avenue
Pleasantville, NY 10570-3144
800-431-2050
Fax: 914-244-0485
Offers a wide variety of videotapes and videodiscs in the areas of guidance, social services, human relations, self-esteem and student services.

5190 IIEPassport: Short Term Study Abroad
Institute of International Education
809 United Nations Plaza
New York, NY 10017-3580
412-741-0930
Fax: 212-984-5496
E-mail: iiebooks@abdintl.com
http://www.iiebooks.org
Over 2,900 short-term study abroad programs offered by universities, schools, associations and other organizations.
Annual
ISBN: 087206-296-1
Daniel Obst, Sr Editor

5191 INSIGHTS Visual Productions
374-A N Highway 101
Encinitas, CA 92024-2527
760-942-0528
Fax: 760-944-7793
Science video for K-12 and teacher training.

5192 INTELECOM Intelligent Telecommunications
150 E Colorado Boulevard
Suite 300
Pasadena, CA 91105-3710
626-796-7300
Fax: 626-577-4282

Videos and educational films.
Bob Miller, VP Marketing/Sale

5193 In Search of Character
Performance Resource Press
1270 Rankin Drive
Suite F
Troy, MI 48083-2843
800-453-7733
Fax: 800-499-5718
http://www.pronline.net
Character education videos.

5194 Instructional Resources Corporation
1819 Bay Ridge Avenue
Annapolis, MD 21403-2835
American History Videodisc.

5195 Intermedia
1165 Eastlake Ave East
Suite 400
Seattle, WA 98109-3571
206-284-2995
800-553-8336
Fax: 206-283-0778
http://www.intermedia-inc.com
Distributes a wide range of high-quality, social interest videos on topics such as teen pregnancy prevention, substance abuse prevention, domestic violence, sexual harassment, dating violence, date rape, gang education, cultural diversity, AIDS prevention and teen patenting. Offer free 30 day previews of the programs which are developed to address the needs of educators who must deal with the pressing social problems of today.
Paperback/Video
Susan Hoffman, President
Ted Fitch, General Manager

5196 International Historic Films
3533 S Archer Avenue
Chicago, IL 60609-1135
773-927-2900
Fax: 773-927-9211
E-mail: info@ihffilm.com
http://www.ihffilm.com
Military, political and social history of the 20th century.
Video/Audio

5197 January Productions
PO Box 66
Hawthorne, NJ 07507-0066
973-423-4666
800-451-7450
Fax: 973-423-5569
E-mail: anpeller@worldnet.att.net
Educational videotapes, read-a-long books, and CD-Rom.
Paperback/Video/Audi
Lori Brown, Sales/Marketing

5198 Karol Media
350 N Pennsylvania Avenue
Wilkes Barre, PA 18702-4415
570-822-8899
Fax: 570-822-8226
Science videos.

5199 Kimbo Educational
PO Box 477
Long Branch, NJ 07740-0477
800-631-2187
Manufacturer of children's audio-musical learning fun. Also offers videos and music by other famous children's artists such as Raffi, Sharon, Lois and Bram.

5200 Leadership: Rethinking the Future
Center for the Study of Small/Rural Schools
555 E Constitution Street
Room 138
Norman, OK 73072-7820

307

405-325-1450
Fax: 405-325-7075
E-mail: jcsimmons@ou.edu
http://cssrs.ou.edu
Series IV

Video

Jan C Simmons, Director

5201 MPC Multimedia Products Corp
1010 Sherman Avenue
Hamden, CT 06514
203-407-4623
800-243-2108
Fax: 203-407-4636
E-mail: sales@800-pickmpc.com
http://www.800-pickmpc.com
Over 5,000 most frequently requested high
quality audio, visual and video products
and materials offered at deep discount
prices. Manufacturer of high quality tape
records,CD's record players, PA systems,
headphones

148 pages BiAnnual

T. Guercia, Author
T Guercia, VP
A Melillo, Sales Manager

5202 Main Street Foundations: Building Community Teams
Center for the Study of Small/Rural
Schools
555 E Constitution Street
Room 138
Norman, OK 73072-7820
405-325-1450
Fax: 405-325-7075
E-mail: jcsimmons@ou.edu
http://cssrs.ou.edu
Prevention Series

Video

Jan C Simmons, Director

5203 Marshmedia
Marsh Media
8025 Ward Parkway Plaza
Kansas City, MO 64114
816-523-1059
800-821-3303
Fax: 816-333-7421
E-mail: order@marshmedia.com
http://www.marshmedia.com
Children's educational videotapes, books
and teaching guides.

32 pages Bi-Annual
ISBN: 1-55942-xxx

Joan K Marsh, President

5204 Media Projects
5215 Homer Street
Dallas, TX 75206-6623
214-826-3863
Fax: 214-826-3919
E-mail: mediaprojects@noval.net
http://www.mediaprojects.org
Educational videotapes in all areas of interest, including drug education, violence
prevention, women's studies, history,
youth issues and special education.

5205 Middle School: Why and How
Center for the Study of Small/Rural
Schools
555 E Constitution Street
Room 138
Norman, OK 73072-7820
405-325-1450
Fax: 405-325-7075
E-mail: jcsimmons@ou.edu
http://cssrs.ou.edu
Series III

Video

Jan C Simmons, Director

5206 Multicultural Educations: Valuing Diversity
Center for the Study of Small/Rural
Schools
555 E Constitution Street
Room 138
Norman, OK 73072-7820
405-325-1450
Fax: 405-325-7075
E-mail: jcsimmons@ou.edu
http://cssrs.ou.edu
Series I

Video

Jan C Simmons, Director

5207 NUVO, Ltd.
PO Box 1729
Chula Vista, CA 91912
619-426-8440
Fax: 619-691-1525
E-mail: nuvoltd@aol.com
Produces and distributes how-to video-
tapes for teens and adults on beginning
reading and decorative napkin folding use-
ful in classroom instruction and individual
practice. Also distributes two bilingual
(Spanish/English) books by psychologist
Dr. Jorge Espinoza.

5208 National Film Board
1251 Avenue of the Americas
New York, NY 10020-1104
800-542-2164
Fax: 845-774-2945
Educational films and videos ranging from
documentaries on nature and science to social issues such as teen pregnancy.

5209 National Geographic School Publishing
PO Box 10579
Washington, DC 20090-8019
800-368-2728
Fax: 515-362-3366
Offers a wide variety of videodiscs, videotapes and educational materials in the area
of social studies, geography, science and
social sciences.

5210 PBS Video
1320 Braddock Pl
Alexandria, VA 22314-1649
703-739-5380
800-424-7963
Fax: 703-739-5269
Award-winning programs from PBS, public television's largest video distributors.
Video and multimedia programming including interactive videodiscs for schools,
colleges and libraries. The PBS Video Resource Catalog is organized into detailed
subject categories.

5211 PICS Authentic Foreign Video
University of Iowa
270 International Center
Iowa City, IA 52242-1802
319-335-2335
800-373-PICS
Fax: 319-335-0280
Provides educators with authentic foreign
language videos in French, German and
Spanish on videotapes and videodisc. Also
offers software to accompany the videodiscs as well as written materials in the
form of transcripts and videoguides with
pedagogical hints and tips.

Becky Bohde, German Coll Editor
Anny Ewing, French Coll Editor

5212 Penton Overseas
2470 Impala Drive
Carlsbad, CA 92008-7226

800-748-5804
Fax: 760-431-8110
Educational videotapes and videodiscs in a wide
variety of interests for classroom use.

5213 Phoenix Films/BFA Educ Media/Coronet/MII
Phoenix Learning Group
2349 Chaffee Drive
St. Louis, MO 63146
314-569-0211
800-777-8100
Fax: 314-569-2834
E-mail: phoenixdealer@aol.com
http://www.phoenixlearninggroup.com
Educational multi-media - VHS, CD-Rom, DVD,
streaming & broadcast.

Video

Kathy Longsworth, Vice President, Market Dev

5214 Presidential Classroom
119 Oronoco Street
Alexandria, VA 22314-2015
703-683-5400
800-441-6533
Fax: 703-548-5728
E-mail: eriedel@presidentialclassroom.org
http://www.presidentialclassroom.org
Video of civic education programs in Washington,
DC for high school juniors and seniors. Each one
week program provides students with an inside
view of the federal government in action and their
role as responsible citizens and future leaders.

Annual
400 attendees

Jack Buechner, President/CEO
Emily Davisriedel, Director Marketing

5215 Rainbow Educational Media Charles Clark Company
4540 Preslyn Drive
Raleigh, NC 27616
919-954-7550
800-331-4047
Fax: 919-954-7554
E-mail: karencf@rainbowedumedia.com
http://www.rainbowedumedia.com
Educational videocassettes and CD-Roms.

Karen C Francis, Business Analyst

5216 Rainbow Educational Video
170 Keyland Court
Bohemia, NY 11716-2638
800-331-4047
Producer and distributor of educational videos.

Wesley Clark, Marketing Director

5217 Reading & O'Reilly: The Wilton Programs
PO Box 302
Wilton, CT 06897-0302
800-458-4274
Producers and distributors of award-winning audiovisual educational programs in art appreciation, history, multicultural education, social
studies and music. Titles include: African-American Art and the Take-a-Bow, musical production
series. Free catalog is available of full product
line.

Lee Reading, President
Gretchen O'Reilly, VP

5218 SAP Today
Performance Resource Press
1270 Rankin Drive
Suite F
Troy, MI 48083-2843
800-453-7733
Fax: 800-499-5718
Overview offers the basics of student assistance.

5219 SVE: Society for Visual Education
55 E Monroe Street
Suite 3400
Chicago, IL 60603-5710
312-849-9100
800-829-1900
Fax: 800-624-1678
Producer and distributor of curriculum based instructional materials including videodisc, microcomputer software, video cassettes and filmstrips for grade levels PreK-12.

5220 Slow Learning Child Video Series
Master Teacher
Leadership Lane
PO Box 1207
Manhattan, KS 66505-1207
800-669-9633
Fax: 800-669-1132
http://www.masterteacher.com
Provides a full understandging of the slow learning child and allows all educators to share in the excitment of teaching this invidual in ways that develop his or her emerging potenial to the fullest.
ISBN: 1-58992-157-0
Mildred Odom Bradley, Author

5221 Spoken Arts
PO Box 100
New Rochelle, NY 10802-0100
727-578-7600
Literature-based audio and visual products for library and K-12 classrooms.

5222 Teacher's Video Company
8150 S Krene Road
Tempe, AZ 85284
800-262-8837
Fax: 800-434-5638
http://www.teachersvideo.com
Video for teachers.

5223 Teen Court: An Alternative Approach to Juvenile Justice
Center for the Study of Small/Rural Schools
555 E Constitution Street
Room 138
Norman, OK 73072-7820
405-325-1450
Fax: 405-325-7075
E-mail: jcsimmons@ou.edu
http://cssrs.ou.edu
Prevention Series
Video
Jan C Simmons, Director

5224 Tools to Help Youth
529 S 7 Street
Suite 570
Minneapolis, MN 55415
800-328-0417
Fax: 612-342-2388
http://www.communityintervention.com
Books and videos on counseling, character education, anger management, life skills, and achohol, tobacco and other drug uses.

5225 Training Video Series for the Professional School Bus Driver
Master Teacher
Leadership Lane
PO Box 1207
Manhattan, KS 66505-1207
800-669-9633
Fax: 800-669-1132
http://www.masterteacher.com
Will help you provide bus drivers with consistent direction and training for the many situations thay will encounter beyond driving safety.
ISBN: 1-58992-082-1

5226 True Colors
Center for the Study of Small/Rural Schools
555 E Constitution Street
Room 138
Norman, OK 73072-7820
405-325-1450
Fax: 405-325-7075
E-mail: jcsimmons@ou.edu
http://cssrs.ou.edu
Series III
Video
Jan C Simmons, Director

5227 United Transparencies
435 Main Street
Johnson City, NY 13790-1935
607-729-6368
800-477-6512
Fax: 607-729-4820
A full line of overhead transparencies for Junior-Senior high school and colleges and technical programs.
D Hetherington

5228 Video Project
200 Estates Drive
Ben Lomond, CA 95005
800-475-2638
Fax: 905-278-2801
E-mail: videoproject@igc.org
http://www.videoproject.org
Distributor of environmental videos with a collection of over 500 programs for all grade levels, including Oscar and Emmy award winners. Many videotapes come with teacher's guides. Free catalogs available.
Terry Thiermann, Administrative Director
Ian Thiermann, Executive Director

5229 Weston Woods Studios
265 Post Road West
Westport, CT 06880
203-845-0197
800-243-5020
Fax: 203-845-0498
E-mail: wstnwoods@aol.com
Audiovisual adaptations of classic children's literature.
Video
Cindy Cardozo, Marketing Coordinator

Classroom Materials

5230 ABC School Supply
3312 N Berkeley Lake Road NW
Duluth, GA 30096-3024
Instructional materials and supplies.

5231 ADP Lemco
5970 W Dannon Way
West Jordan, UT 84088
801-280-4000
800-575-3626
Fax: 801-280-4040
E-mail: sales@adplemco.com
http://www.adplemco.com
Announcement boards, schedule boards, chalkboards, tackboard, marker boards, trophy cases, athletic equipment, gym divider curtains and basketball backstops.
David L Hall, Sr VP

5232 APCO
388 Grant Street SE
Atlanta, GA 30312-2227
404-688-9000
Fax: 404-577-3847
Classroom supplies including announcement and chalkboards.
Anne M Gallup

5233 AbleNet
2808 Fairview Avenue N
Roseville, MN 55113-1308
651-294-2200
800-322-0956
Fax: 651-294-2259
http://www.ablenetinc.com
Adaptive devices for students with disabilities from Pre-K through adult, as well as activities and games for students of all abilities.

5234 Accounter Systems USA
1107 S Mannheim Road
Suite 305
Westchester, IL 60154-2560
800-229-8765
Sports timers and clocks and classroom supplies.

5235 Accu-Cut Systems
1035 E Dodge Street
Fremont, NE 68025
402-721-4134
800-288-1670
Fax: 402-721-5778
E-mail: info@accucut.com
http://www.accucut.com
Manufacturer of die cutting machines dies.

5236 Airomat Corporation
2916 Engle Road
Fort Wayne, IN 46809-1198
260-747-7408
800-348-4905
Fax: 260-747-7409
E-mail: airomat@airomat.com
http://www.airomat.com
Mats and matting.
Jody Feasel, VP
Janie Feasel, President/CEO

5237 Airspace USA
89 Patton Avenue
Asheville, NC 28801
828-258-1319
800-872-1319
Fax: 828-258-1390
E-mail: sales@airspace-usa.com
http://www.airspacesolutions.com
Airspace Soft Center Play and Learn Systems provide a comprehensive range of play, learning and physical development opportunities using commercial grade and foam filled play equipment. Play manual provided.
Daniel Brenman, VP Sales/Marketing
Tracy Syxes, Administrator

5238 All Art Supplies
Art Supplies Wholesale
4 Enon Street
North Beverly, MA 01915
800-462-2420
Fax: 800-462-2420
E-mail: info@allartsupplies.com
http://www.allartsupplies.com
Art supplies at wholesale prices.

5239 American Foam
HC 37 Box 317 H
Lewisburg, WV 24901
304-497-3000
800-344-8997
Fax: 304-497-3001
http://www.bfoam.com
Carving blocks of foam.

5240 American Plastics Council
1300 Wilson Boulevard
Arlington, VA 22209
800-243-5790
http://www.plastics.org
Offers classroom materials on recycling and environmental education.

5241 Anatomical Chart Company
8221 Kimball Avenue
Skokie, IL 60076-2956
847-679-4700
http://www.anatomical.com
Maps and charts for educational purposes.

5242 Angels School Supply
600 E Colorado Boulevard
Pasadena, CA 91101-2006
626-584-0855
Fax: 626-584-0888
http://www.angelschoolsupply.com
School and classroom supplies.

Jennifer , Sales Representitive

5243 Aol@School
22070 Broderick Drive
Dulles, VA 20166
888-468-3768
E-mail: aol at school@aol.com
http://www.school.aol.com
Age-appropriate, high-quality educational
content tailored for K-12 students and educators. Aol@School focuses and filters the
Web for us, providing appropriate, developmental access to the vast educational
resources on the internet.

5244 Armada Art Materials
Armada Art Inc.
142 Berkeley Street
Boston, MA 02116
617-859-3800
800-435-0601
Fax: 617-859-3808
E-mail: info@armadaart.com
http://www.armadaart.com

5245 Art Materials Catalog
United Art and Education
PO Box 9219
Fort Wayne, IN 46899
800-322-3247
Fax: 800-858-3247
http://www.unitednow.com
Art materials.

5246 Art Supplies Wholesale
4 R Enon Street
N Beverly, MA 01915
800-462-2420
Fax: 978-922-1495
E-mail: info@allartsupplies.com
http://www.allartsupplies.com
Wholesale art supplies.

5247 Art to Remember
10625 Deme Drive
Unit E
Indianapolis, IN 46236
317-826-0870
800-895-8777
Fax: 317-823-2822
http://www.arttoremember.com
A unique program that encourages your
students' artisic creativity while providing
an opportunity to raise funds for schools.

5248 Artix
PO Box 25008
Kelowna, BC V1W3Y
250-861-5345
800-665-5345
http://www.artix.bc.ca
Papermaking kits.

5249 Assessories by Velma
PO Box 2580
Shasta, CA 96087-2580
Multicultural education-related products.

5250 At-Risk Resources
135 Dupont Street
PO Box 760
Plainview, NY 11803-0706
800-999-6884
Fax: 800-262-1886
Dealing with drug violence prevention,
character education, self-esteem, teen sexuality, dropout prevention, safe schoolks,
career development, parenting crisis and
trauma, and professional development.

5251 Atlas Track & Tennis
19495 SW Teton Avenue
Tualatin, OR 97062-8846
800-423-5875
Fax: 503-692-0491
Specialty sport surfaces; synthetic running
tracks, tennis courts, and athletic flooring
for schools.

5252 Audio Forum
69 Broad Street
Guildford, CT 06437
203-453-9794
Fax: 203-453-9774
E-mail: info@audioforum.com
http://www.audioforum.com
Cassettes, CD's and books for language
study.

5253 Badge-A-Minit
PO Box 800
La Salle, IL 61301-0800
815-883-8822
800-223-4103
Fax: 815-883-9696
E-mail: questions@badgeaminit.com
http://www.badgeaminit.com
Awards, trophies, emblems and badges for
educational purposes.

5254 Bag Lady School Supplies
9212 Marina Pacifica Drive N
Long Beach, CA 90803-3886
Classroom supplies.

5255 Bale Company
PO Box 6400
Providence, RI 02940-6400
800-822-5350
Fax: 401-831-5500
http://www.bale.com
Awards, medals, pins, plaques and tro-
phies.

5256 Bangor Cork Company
William & D Streets
Pen Argyl, PA 18072
610-863-9041
Fax: 610-863-6275
Announcement boards.

Janice Cory, Customer Services Rep

5257 Baumgarten's
144 Ottley Drive
Atlanta, GA 30324-4016
404-874-7675
800-247-5547
Fax: 800-255-5547
E-mail: mlynch@baumgartens.com
http://www.baumgartens.com
Products available include pencil sharpen-
ers, pencil grips, pocket binders, dispos-
able aprons, American flags, practical
colorful clips, fastening devices in a variety of shapes and sizes, identification security items, lamination, magnifiers and key
chains.

Michael Lynch, National Sales Manager

5258 Best Manufacturing Sign Systems
PO Box 577
Montrose, CO 81402-0577

970-249-2378
800-235-2378
Fax: 970-249-0223
E-mail: sales@bestsigns.com
http://www.bestsigns.com
Architectural and ADA signs, announcement
boards.

Mary Phillips, Sales Manager

5259 Best-Rite
201 N Crockett Avenue
#713
Cameron, TX 76520-3376
254-778-4727
800-749-2258
Fax: 866-888-7483
E-mail: boards@bestrite.com
http://www.bestrite.com
Quality visual display products which include a
complete line of chalk, marker, tack, bulletin, fabric and projection boards. Display and trophy
cases, beginner boards, reversible boards, mobile
easels, desk-top and floor carrels and early childhood products are also manufactured.

Bob Wilson, VP
Greg Moore, Executive VP

5260 Binney & Smith
1100 Church Lane
Easton, PA 18044
610-253-6271
800-CRA-YOLA
Fax: 610-250-5768
http://www.crayola.com
Crayons.

5261 Black History Month
Guidance Channel
135 Dupont Street
PO Box 760
Plainview, NY 44803-0706
800-999-6884
Fax: 800-262-1886
Products to celebrate Black history, multicututral
resources.

5262 Blackboard Resurfacing Company
50 N 7th Street
Bangor, PA 18013-1731
610-588-0965
Fax: 610-863-1997
Chalk and announcement boards.

Karin Karpinski, Administrative Assistant

5263 Bob's Big Pencils
1848 E 27th Street
Hays, KS 67601-2108
Large novelty pencils, plaques, bookends and
many pencil related items.

5264 Book It!/Pizza Hut
9111 E Douglas Avenue
Wichita, KS 67207-1205
316-687-8401
National reading incentive program with materials, books and incentive display items to get students interested in reading.

5265 Borden
Home & Professional Products Group
180 E Broad Street
Columbus, OH 43215-3799
614-225-7479
Fax: 614-225-7167
Arts and crafts supplies, maintenance and repair
supplies.

5266 Bulman Products
1650 McReynolds NW
Grand Rapids, MI 49504
616-363-4416
Fax: 616-363-0380
E-mail: bulman@macatawa.com
Art craft paper.

5267 Bydee Art
8603 Yellow Oak Street
Austin, TX 78729-3739
512-474-4343
Fax: 512-474-5749
Prints, books, T-shirts with the Bydee People focusing on education.

5268 C-Thru Ruler Company
6 Britton Drive
Bloomfield, CT 06002-3632
860-243-0303
Fax: 860-243-1856
http://www.CThruRuler.com
Arts, crafts and classroom supplies.

Ross Zachs, Manager

5269 CHEM/Lawrence Hall of Science
University of California
Berkeley, CA 94720
510-642-6000
Fax: 510-642-1055
E-mail: lhsinfo@uclink.berkley.edu
http://www.lawrencehallofscience.org
Activities for grades 5-6 and helps students understand the use of chemicals in our daily lives.

Linda Schnieder, Marketing Manager
Mike Slater, Marketing/PR Associate

5270 CORD Communications
324 Kelly Street
Waco, TX 76710-5709
254-776-1822
Fax: 254-776-3906
Instructional materials for secondary and postsecondary applications in science education.

5271 Califone International
21300 Superior Street
Chatsworth, CA 91311-4328
818-407-2400
800-722-0500
Fax: 818-407-2491
http://www.califone.com
Multisensory, supplemental curricula on magnetic cards for use with all Card Reader/Language master equipment.

Nelly Spievak, Sales Coordinator

5272 Cardinal Industries
PO Box 1430
Grundy, VA 24614-1430
276-935-4545
800-336-0551
Fax: 276-935-4970
Awards, emblems, trophies and badges.

5273 Carousel Productions
1100 Wilcrest Drive
Suite 100
Houston, TX 77042-1642
281-568-9300
Fax: 281-568-9498
Moments in History T-shirts, as well as other various educational gifts and products.

5274 Cascade School Supplies
1 Brown Street
PO Box 780
North Adams, MA 01247
800-628-5078
Fax: 413-663-3719
Offers a variety of school supplies and more.

5275 Celebrate Diversity
Guidance Channel
135 Dupont Street
PO Box 760
Plainview, NY 44803-0706
800-999-6884
Fax: 800-262-1886
Educational resources that celebrate diversity.

5276 Celebrate Earth Day
Guidance Channel
135 Dupont Street
PO Box 760
Plainview, NY 44803-0706
800-999-6884
Fax: 800-262-1886
Educational resources for celebrating earth day.

5277 Center Enterprises
PO Box 33161
West Hartford, CT 06110
860-953-4423
Fax: 800-373-2923
Clifford individual curriculum and storybook stamp sets, individual, grading, curriculum based and Sweet Arts rubber stamp line, stamp pads, embossing inks and powders.

5278 Center for Learning
21590 Center Ridge Road
Rocky River, OH 44116-3963
440-331-1404
800-767-9090
Fax: 888-767-8080
E-mail: cfl@stratos.net
http://www.centerforlearning.org
Supplementary curriculum units for all grade levels in biography, language arts, novel/drama and social studies.

5279 Center for Teaching International Relations
University of Denver
Denver, CO 80208
303-871-3106
Reproducible teaching activities and software promoting multicultural understanding and international relations in the classroom for grades K-adult.

5280 Childcraft Education Corporation
20 Kilmer Avenue
Edison, NJ 08817
732-572-6100
Distributes children's toys, products, materials and publications to schools.

5281 Childswork/Childsplay
The Guidance Channel
135 Dupont Street
PO Box 760
Plainview, NY 11803-0760
800-962-1141
Fax: 800-262-1886
http://www.childswork.com
Contains over 450 resources to address the social and emotional needs of children and adolescents.

Lawrence C Shapiro, PhD, President
Constance H Logan, Development Coordinator

5282 Chroma
205 Bucky Drive
Lititz, PA 17543
717-626-8866
800-257-8278
Fax: 717-626-9292
http://www.chromaonline.com
Tempera and acrylic paints.

5283 Chroma-Vision Sign & Art System
PO Box 434
Greensboro, NC 27402-0434
336-275-0602
Refillable and renewable felt tip markers used with non-toxic, water soluable, fast drying colors for making signs, posters, and general art work with no messy cleanup.

S Gray, President

5284 Citizenship Through Sports and Fine Arts Curriculum
National Federation of State High School Assoc.
PO Box 20626
Kansas City, MO 64195-0626
816-464-5400
800-776-3462
Fax: 816-891-2414
http://www.nfhs.org
High school activities curriculum package that includes an introductory video, Rekindling the Spirit, along with the Overview booklet, plus two insightful books covering eight targets of the curriculum.

5285 Claridge Products & Equipment
Claridge Products & Equipment
601 Highway 62-65 S
PO Box 910
Harrison, AR 72601-0910
870-743-2200
Fax: 870-743-1908
E-mail: claridge@claridgeproducts.com
http://www.claridgeproducts.com
Claridge manufactures chalkboards, markerboards, bulletin boards, display and trophy cases, bulletin and directory board cabinets, easels, lecterns, speakers' stands, wood lecture units with matching credenzas and much more.

Terry McCutchen, Sales Manager

5286 Collins & Aikman Floorcoverings
311 Smith Industrial Boulevard
Dalton, GA 30722
800-248-2878
Fax: 706-259-2666
E-mail: tellis@powerbond.com
http://www.powerbond.com
An alternative to conventional carpet to improve indoor air quality and reduce maintenance cost. Powerboard floor covering.

T Ellis, General Manager/Edu Markets

5287 Columbia Cascade Company
1975 SW 5th Avenue
Portland, OR 97201-5293
503-223-1157
Fax: 503-223-4530
E-mail: hq@timberform.com
http://www.timberform.com
Playground equipment and site furniture.

Dale Gordon, Sales Manager

5288 Creative Artworks Factory
19031 McGuire Road
Perris, CA 92570-8305
909-780-5950
Screenprinted T-shirts, posters and gifts for educational purposes.

5289 Creative Educational Surplus
9801 James Avenue S
#C
Bloomington, MN 55431-2919
Art and classroom materials.

5290 Crizmac Art & Cultural Education Materials Inc
PO Box 65928
Tucson, AZ 85728
520-323-8555
800-913-8555
Fax: 520-323-6194
E-mail: customerservice@crizmac.com
http://www.crizmac.com
Publisher of art and cultural education materials includes curriculum, books, music, and folk art.

Stevie Mack, President

5291 Crown Mats & Matting
2100 Commerce Drive
Fremont, OH 43420-1048
419-332-5531
800-628-5463
Fax: 800-544-2806
E-mail: sales@crown-mats.com
http://www.crown-mats.com
Mats, matting and flooring for schools.

5292 Dahle USA
375 Jaffrey Road
Peterborough, NH 03458
603-924-0003
800-243-8145
Fax: 603-924-1616
E-mail: info@dahleusa.com
http://www.dahleusa.com
Arts and crafts supplies, school and office products, office shreddars and more.

5293 Designer Artwear I
8475 C-1 Highway 6 N
Houston, TX 77095
281-446-6641
Specialty clothing, accessories, etc. all educationally designed.

5294 Dexter Educational Toys
Dexter Educational Toys, Inc.
PO Box 630861
Aventura, FL 33163-0861
305-931-7426
Fax: 305-931-0552
Manufacturer and distributor of education material. Dress-ups for children 2-7 years. Multicultural hand puppets, finger puppets, head masks puppet theaters, rag dolls, dress-ups for teddy bears and dolls, cloth books, export manufacturing under special designs and orders.

Genny Silverstein, VP Secretary

5295 Dick Blick Art Materials
PO Box 1267
Galesburg, IL 61402
800-828-4584
Fax: 800-621-8293
E-mail: info@dickblick.com
http://www.dickblick.com
Classroom art supplies.

5296 Dinorock Productions
407 Granville Drive
Silver Spring, MD 20901-3238
301-588-9300
Musical, Broadway puppet shows for early childhood fun and education.

5297 Discovery Toys
12443 Pine Creek Road
Cerritos, CA 90703-2044
562-809-0331
Fax: 562-809-0331
http://www.discoverytoyslink.com/elizab
eth
Emphasizes child physical, social and educational development through creative play. Educational toys, games and books are available for all ages. Services include home demonstrations, fund raisers, phone and catalog orders. New Book of Knowledge Encyclopedia and patenting video tapes are also available.

5298 Disney Educational Productions
500 S Buena Vista Street
Burbank, CA 91521-0001
800-777-8100
Creates and manufactures classroom aids for the educational field.

5299 Dixie Art Supplies
2612 Jefferson Highway
New Orleans, LA 70121
800-783-2612
Fax: 504-831-5738
http://www.dixieart.com
Fine art supplier.

5300 Dr. Playwell's Game Catalog
Guidance Channel
135 Dupont Street
PO Box 760
Plainview, NY 44803-0706
800-999-6884
Fax: 800-262-1886
Games that develop character and life skills.

5301 Draper
125 S Pearl Street
Spiceland, IN 47385
765-987-7999
800-238-7999
Fax: 765-987-7142
E-mail: draper@draper.com
http://www.draperinc.com
Projection screens, video projector mounts and lifts, plasma display mounts, presentation easels, window shades and gymnasium equipment.

Chris Broome, Contract Market Manager
Bob Mathes, AV/Video Market Manager

5302 Draw Books
Peel Productions
PO Box 546
Columbus, NC 28722-0546
828-859-3879
800-345-6665
Fax: 801-365-9898
http://www.drawbooks.com
How-to-draw books for elementary and middle school.
Paperback
ISBN: 0-939217

5303 Dupont Company
Corlan Products
CRP-702
Wilmington, DE 19880
302-774-1000
800-436-7426
Fax: 800-417-1266
Arts and crafts supplies.

5304 Durable Corporation
75 N Pleasant Street
Norwalk, OH 44857-1218
419-668-8138
800-537-1603
Fax: 419-668-8068
Furniture, classroom supplies, arts and crafts and educational products.

5305 EZ Grader
PO Box 23608
Chagrin Falls, OH 44023
800-732-4018
Fax: 800-689-2772
Electronic gradebook designed by teachers for teachers. It is an incredible time saver and computes percentage scores accurately, quickly and easily.

5306 Early Ed
3110 Sunrise Drive
Crown Point, IN 46307-8905
Teacher sweatshirts, cardigans, T-shirts, tote bags and jewelry.

5307 Education Department
Wildlife Conservation Society
2300 Southern Boulevard
Bronx, NY 10460
718-220-5131
800-937-5131
Fax: 718-733-4460
http://www.wcs.com

Year round programs for school and general audience. Teacher training, grades K-12.

Sydell Schein, Manager/Program Services
Ann Robinson, Director/National Programs

5308 Educational Equipment Corporation of Ohio
845 Overholt Road
Kent, OH 44240-7529
330-673-4881
Fax: 330-673-4915
E-mail: mkaufman@mkco.com
Chalkboards, tackboards, trophy cases, announcement boards.

Michael Kaufman, General Manager
Eric Baughman, Sales Manager

5309 Electronic Book Catalog
Franklin Learning Resources
1 Franklin Plaza
Burlington, NJ 08016-4908
800-BOO-MAN
Fax: 609-387-1787
Electronic translation machines, calculators and supplies.

5310 Ellison Educational Equipment
25862 Commercentre Drive
Lake Forest, CA 92630-8804
800-253-2238
Fax: 888-270-1200
E-mail: info@ellison.com
http://www.ellison.com
Serves the educational and craft community with time-saving equipment, supplies and ideas.

5311 Endura Rubber Flooring
2 University Office Park
Waltham, MA 02453-3421
781-647-5375
Fax: 781-647-4543
Floorcoverings, mats and matting for schools.

5312 Fairgate Rule Company
22 Adams Avenue
Cold Spring, NY 10516-1501
845-265-3677
Fax: 845-265-4128
Arts and crafts supplies.

5313 Family Reading Night Kit
Renaissance Learning
PO Box 8036
Wisconsin Rapids, WI 54495-8036
715-424-3636
800-338-4204
Fax: 715-424-4242
E-mail: answers@renlearn.com
http://www.renlearn.com
Kit to start a family reading night where parents and children spent quality time together sharing enthusiasm over books.

5314 Fascinating Folds
PO Box 10070
Glendale, AZ 85318
602-375-9979
Fax: 602-375-9978
http://www.fascinating-folds.com
World's large supplier of origami and paper arts products.

5315 Fiskars Corporation
636 Science Drive
Madison, WI 53711
608-233-1649
Fax: 608-294-4790
http://www.fiskars.com
School scissors.

5316 Fox Laminating Company
84 Custer Street
W Hartford, CT 06110-1955
860-953-4884
800-433-2468

Fax: 860-953-1277
E-mail: sales@foxlam.com
http://www.foxlam.com
Easy, simple, and inexpensive do-it-yourself laminators. A piece of paper can be laminated for just pennies. Badges, ID's and luggage tags can also be made. Also laminated plaques for awards, diplomas, and mission statements.

Joe Fox, President
John Mills, Marketing Manager

5317 George F Cram Company
PO Box 426
Indianapolis, IN 46206-0426
317-635-5564
Fax: 317-687-2845
Classroom geography maps, state maps, social studies skills and globes.

5318 Gift-in-Kind Clearinghouse
PO Box 850
Davidson, NC 28036-0850
704-892-7228
Fax: 704-892-3825
Educational and classroom supplies, computers and gifts for teachers.

5319 Gold's Artworks
2100 N Pine
Lumberton, NC 28358
910-739-9605
800-356-2306
Fax: 910-739-9605
http://www.goldsartworks.20m.com
Papermaking supplies.

5320 Golden Artist Colors
188 Bell Road
New Berlin, NY 13411-9527
800-959-6543
E-mail: goldenart@goldenpaints.com
http://www.goldenpaints.com
Acrylic paints.

5321 Graphix
19499 Miles Road
Cleveland, OH 44128-4109
216-581-9050
Fax: 216-581-9041
E-mail: sales@grafixarts.com
http://www.grafixarts.com
Art and crafts supplies and a source for creative plastic films.

Tanya Lutz, National Sales Manager

5322 Grolier Multimedial Encyclopedia
Grolier Publishing
PO Box 1716
Danbury, CT 06816
203-797-3703
800-371-3908
Fax: 203-797-3899
Encyclopedia software.

5323 Hands-On Equations
Borenson & Associates
PO Box 3328
Allentown, PA 18106
800-993-6284
Fax: 610-398-7863
http://www.borenson.com
System to teach algebraic concepts to elementary and middle school students.

5324 Harrisville Designs
Center Village
PO Box 806
Harrisville, NH 03450
603-827-3333
800-938-9415
Fax: 603-827-3335
http://www.harrisville.com
Award-winning weaving products for children.

5325 Hayes School Publishing
321 Penwood Avenue
Pittsburgh, PA 15221
800-245-6234
Fax: 800-543-8771
E-mail: info@hayespub.com
http://www.hayespub.com
Suppliers of certificates and awards.

5326 Henry S Wolkins Company
605 Myles Standish Boulevard
Taunton, MA 02780
800-233-1844
Fax: 877-965-5467
http://www.wolkins.com
Art and craft materials, teaching aids, early learning products, furniture, general school equipment.

5327 Hooked on Phonics Classroom Edition
665 3rd Street
Suite 225
San Francisco, CA 94107
714-437-3450
800-222-3334
E-mail: customerservice@hop.com
http://www.hop.com
Program that teaches students to learn letters and sounds to decoding words, and then reading books.

5328 Hydrus Galleries
PO Box 4944
San Diego, CA 92164-4944
800-493-7299
Fax: 619-283-7466
E-mail: info@hydra9.com
http://www.hydra9.com
Curriculum-based classroom activities including papyrus outlines for students to paint.

5329 Insect Lore
PO Box 1535
Shafter, CA 93263
800-548-3284
Fax: 661-746-0334
E-mail: livebug@insectlore.com
http://www.insectlore.com
Science materials for elementary and preschool students.

5330 J&A Handy-Crafts
165 S Pennsylvania Avenue
Lindenhurst, NY 11757-5058
631-226-2400
888-252-1130
Fax: 631-226-2564
E-mail: info@jacrafts.com
http://www.jacrafts.com
Arts, crafts and educational supplies.

Paul Siegelman, Marketing

5331 Jiffy Printers Products
35070 Maria Road
Cathedral City, CA 92234
760-321-7335
Fax: 760-770-1955
E-mail: jiffyprod@aol.com
Adhesive wax sticks.

Ivan Zwelling, Owner

5332 Key-Bak
Division of West Coast Chain Manufacturing Co.
4245 Pacific Privado
Ontario, CA 91761
909-923-7800
800-685-2403
Fax: 800-565-6202
E-mail: sales@keybak.com
http://www.keybak.com
Badges, awards and emblems for educational purposes.

5333 Keyboard Instructor
Advanced Keyboard Technology, Inc.
PO Box 2418
Paso Robles, CA 93447-2418
805-237-2055
Fax: 805-239-8973
http://www.keyboardinstructor.com
Mobile keyboarding lab with individualized instruction.

5334 Kids Percussion Buyer's Guide
Percussion Marketing Council
818-753-1310
E-mail: DLevine360@aol.com
http://www.playdrums.com
This guide is divided into two sections- recreational instruments and those for beginning traditional drummers.

5335 Kids at Heart & School Art Materials
PO Box 94082
Seattle, WA 98124-9482
Classroom and art materials.

5336 Kidstamps
PO Box 18699
Cleveland Heights, OH 44118-0699
216-291-6884
Fax: 216-291-6887
E-mail: kidstamps@apk.net
http://www.kidstamps.com
Rubber stamps, T-shirts, bookplates and mugs designed by leading children's illustrators.

5337 Knex Education Catalog
Knex Education
2990 Bergey Road
PO Box 700
Hatfield, PA 19440-0700
888-ABC-KNEX
E-mail: abcknex@knex.com
http://www.knexeducation.com
Hands-on, award-winning curriculum supported K-12 math, science and technology sets.

5338 Lauri
PO Box 0263
Smethport, PA 16749
800-451-0520
Fax: 207-639-3555
Lacing puppets craft kits, crepe rubber picture puzzles, phonics kits and math manipulatives for pre-K and up. Catalog offers 200 manipulatives for early childhood.

5339 Learning Materials Workshop
274 N Winooski Avenue
Burlington, VT 05401-3621
802-802-8399
800-693-7164
Fax: 802-862-0794
E-mail: mail@learningmaterialswork.com
http://www.learningmaterialswork.com
Designs and produces open-ended blocks and construction sets for early childhood classrooms. An education guide and video, as well as training workshops are offered.

Karen Hewitt, President

5340 Learning Needs Catalog
Riverdeep Interactive Learning
PO Box 97021
Redmond, WA 98073-9721
800-362-2890
http://www.learningneeds.com
Hardware, software and print products designed for specialized student needs for Pre-K to grade 12.

5341 Learning Power and the Learning Power Workbook
Great Source Education Group
181 Ballardvale
Willmington, MA 01887
800-289-4490
Student materials for 8th and 9th grade critical thinking, study skills, life management, and other student success course.

218 pages
ISBN: 0-963813-33-1

5342 Learning Well
111 Kane Street
Baltimore, MD 21224-1728
800-645-6564
Fax: 800-413-7442
E-mail: learningwell@wclm.com
Drawing compass/ruler.

5343 Linray Enterprises
167 Corporation Road
Hyannis, MA 02601-2204
800-537-9752
Mats and matting for gym classes.

5344 Loew-Coenell
563 Chestnut Avenue
Teaneck, NJ 07666-2491
201-836-8110
Fax: 201-836-7070
E-mail: sales@loew-cornell.com
http://www.loew-cornell.com
Leader in art and craft brushes, painting accessories and artists' tools.

5345 Longstreth
PO Box 475
Parker Ford, PA 19457-0475
610-495-7022
Fax: 610-495-7023
Awards, emblems, badges and trophies, sports timers and clocks.

5346 Love to Teach
693 Glacier Pass
Westerville, OH 43081-1295
614-899-2118
800-326-8361
Fax: 614-899-2070
http://www.lovetoteach.com
Gifts for teachers.

Linda Vollmer, Contact

5347 Lyra
78 Browne Street
Suite 3
Brookline, MA 02146
888-PEN-LYRA
E-mail: mshoham@aol.com
Drawing supplies.

5348 MPI School & Instructional Supplies
PO Box 24155
Lansing, MI 48909-4155
517-393-0440
Fax: 517-393-8884
School and classroom supplies, arts and crafts.

5349 Magnetic Aids
133 N 10th Street
Paterson, NJ 07522-1220
973-790-1400
800-426-9624
Fax: 973-790-1425
E-mail: magneticaids@worldnet.att.com
http://www.magneticaids.com
Announcement and chalkboards, office supplies and equipment. Magnetic book supports.

Paul Pecka, VP Sales

5350 Mailer's Software
970 Calle Negocio
San Clemente, CA 92673-6201
949-492-7000
Fax: 949-589-5211
Charts, maps, globes and software for the classroom.

5351 Marsh Industries
Div. of Marsh Lumber Company
PO Box 509
Dover, OH 44622-1935
330-343-8825
800-426-4244
Fax: 330-343-9515
E-mail: wdsinghaus@marsh-ind.com
http://www.marsh-ind.com
Marker boards chalkboards, and tacknoards for new rennovative construction projects. Glass enclosed bulletin and directory boards. Map rail and accessories.

William Singhaus, Sales Manager

5352 Master Woodcraft
1312 College Street
Oxford, NC 27565
919-693-8811
800-333-2675
Fax: 919-693-1707
Announcement and classroom chalkboards, arts and craft supplies. Cork bulletin boards, dry erase melamine boards, easels, floor and table top.

J Moss, VP

5353 Material Science Technology
Energy Concepts
595 Bond Street
Lincolnshire, IL 60069
800-621-1247
http://www.energy-concepts-inc.com
Provides practical knowledge of the use and development of materials in todays world. Each unit combines theory with hands-on experience.

5418 Math Through the Ages: A Gentle History for Teachers and Others
Oxton Publishers, LLC
Po Box 209
Farmington, ME 04938
207-779-1923
800-539-7323
Fax: 207-779-0623
E-mail: info@oxtonhouse.com
http://www.oxtonhouse.com
An easy-to-use tool for teachers who want some history for their math classes, this book contains 25 independent 4-to-6 page historical summaries of particular topics from elementary and secondary math, a 56-page overview and an extensive bibliography.

224 pages

William Berlinghoff, Managing Editor
Bobby Brown, Marketing Director

5354 Midwest Publishers Supply
4640 N Olcott Avenue
Harwood Heights, IL 60706
800-621-1507
Fax: 800-832-3189
E-mail: info@mps-co.com
http://www.mps-co.com
Arts and crafts supplies.

Bonnie Cready, Sales Manager

5355 Miller Multiplex
1555 Larkin Williams Road
Fenton, MO 63026-3008
636-343-5700
800-325-3350
Fax: 636-326-1716
E-mail: info@millermultiplex.com

Announcement boards, classroom displays, charts and photography, books towers, posters, frames, kiosk displays, presentation displays.

12 pages Annually

Kathy Webster, Director Marketing

5356 Monsanto Company
800 N Lindbergh Boulevard
Saint Louis, MO 63167-0001
314-694-3902
Fax: 314-694-7625
Arts and crafts supplies.

5357 Morrison School Supplies
304 Industrial Road
San Carlos, CA 94070-6285
650-592-3000
Fax: 650-592-1679
School supplies, classroom equipment, furniture and toys.

5358 Names Unlimited
2300 Spikes Lane
Lansing, MI 48906-3996
Chalkboard and markerboard slates and tablets.

5359 Nasco Arts & Crafts Catalog
Nasco
901 Janesville Avenue
PO Box 901
Fort Atkinson, WI 53538-0901
920-563-2446
800-558-9595
Fax: 920-563-8296
http://www.eNASCO.com
Complete line of arts and craft materials for the art educator and individual artist.

Kris Bakke, Arts & Crafts Director

5360 Nasco Early Learning & Afterschool Essential Catalogs
Nasco
901 Janesville Avenue
PO Box 901
Fort Atkinson, WI 53538-0901
920-563-2446
800-558-9595
Fax: 920-563-8296
E-mail: info@enasco.com
http://www.eNasco.com
Features low prices on classroom supplies, materials, furniture and equipment for early childhood and afterschool programs.

Scott J Beyer, Director, Sales & Marketing

5361 Nasco Math Catalog
Nasco
901 Janesville
PO Box 901
Fort Atkinson, WI 53538-0901
920-563-2446
800-558-9595
Fax: 920-563-8296
http://www.nascofa.com
Features hands-on manipulatives and real-life problem-solving projects.

5362 National Teaching Aids
PO Box 2121
Fort Collins, CO 80522
970-484-7445
800-289-9299
Fax: 970-484-1198
E-mail: bevans@amep.com
http://www.hubbardscientific.com
Learning math, alphabet, and geography skills is easy with our Clever Catch Balls. These colorful 24-inch inflatable vinyl balls provide an excellent way for children to practice math, alphabet and geography skills. Excellent learning tool in organized classroom activities, on the playground, or at home.

Barbara Evans, Customer Service Manager
Candy Coffman, National Sales Manger

5363 New Hermes
2200 Northmont Parkway
Duluth, GA 30096
770-623-0331
800-843-7637
Fax: 800-533-7637
E-mail: sales@newhermes.com
http://www.newhermes.com
Announcement boards, trophies, badges, emblems.

5364 Newbridge Discovery Station
PO Box 5267
Clifton, NH 07015
Monthly quick tips and activities for teachers.

5365 Newbridge Jumbo Seasonal Patterns
PO Box 5267
Clifton, NJ 07015
Art projects, games, bulletin boards, flannel boards, story starters, learning center displays, costumes, masks and more for grades Pre K-3.

5366 NewsCurrents
Knowledge Unlimited
PO Box 52
Madison, WI 53701
800-356-2303
Fax: 608-831-1570
E-mail: sales@newscurrents.com
http://www.newscurrents.com
Current issues discussion programs for grades 3 and up.

5367 Partners in Learning Programs
1065 Bay Boulevard
Suite H
Chula Vista, CA 91911-1626
619-407-4744
Fax: 619-407-4755
Manufacturers and produces books, manuals, materials, supplies and gifts, such as banners for classroom purposes.

5368 Pearson Education Technologies
827 W Grove Avenue
Mesa, AZ 85210
520-615-7600
800-222-4543
Fax: 520-615-7601
http://www.pearsonedtech.com
SuccessMaker is a multimedia K-Adult learning system which includes math, reading, language arts and science courseware.

5369 Pentel of America
2805 Columbia Street
Torrance, CA 90509-3800
310-320-3831
800-421-1419
Fax: 310-533-0697
http://www.pentel.com
Office supplies and equipment.

5370 Pin Man
Together Inc.
802 E 6th Street
PO Box 52528
Tulsa, OK 74105-3264
918-587-2405
800-282-0085
Fax: 918-382-0906
http://www.thepinmanok.com
Manufacturer of custom designed lapel pins, totes for Chapter 1, reading, scholastic achievement, honor roll, parent involvement, staff awards and incentives with over 25,000 items available for imprint.

Bern Gentry, CEO

5371 PlayConcepts
2275 Huntington Drive
#305
San Marino, CA 91108-2640
800-261-2584
Fax: 626-795-1177
Creative, 3-D scenery that stimulates dramatic play. The scenes complement integrated curriculum. They are age and developmentally appropriate, non-biased, and effective for groups or individuals.

5372 Polyform Products Company
1901 Estes Avenue
Elk Grove Village, IL 60007
847-427-0020
Fax: 847-427-0020
E-mail: polyform@sculpey.com
http://www.sculpey.com
Manufacturer of sculpey modeling clay.

5373 Presidential Classroom
119 Oronoco Street
Alexandria, VA 22314-2015
703-683-5400
800-441-6533
Fax: 703-548-5728
E-mail: eriedel@presidentialclassroom.org
http://www.presidentialclassroom.org
Civic education programs in Washington, DC for high school juniors and seniors. Each one week program provides students with an inside view of the federal government in action and their role as responsible citizens and future leaders.

Jan-March, June+July
400 attendees

Jack Buechner, President/CEO
Ginger King, Dean

5374 Professor Weissman's Software
Professor Weissman's Software
246 Crafton Avenue
Staten Island, NY 10314-4227
718-698-5219
Fax: 718-698-5219
E-mail: mathprof@hotmail.com
http://www.math911.com
Algebra comic books, learn by example algebra flash cards, step-by-step software tutorials for algebra, trigonometry, precalculus, statistics, network versions for all software.

Martin Weissman, Owner
Keith Morse, VP

5375 Pumpkin Masters
PO Box 61456
Denver, CO 80206-8456
303-860-8006
Fax: 303-860-9826
Classroom pumpkin carving kits featuring whole language curriculum with safer and easier carving tools and patterns.

5376 Puppets on the Pier
Pier 39
Box H4
San Francisco, CA 94133
415-781-4435
800-443-4463
Fax: 415-379-9544
E-mail: onepuppet@earthlink.net
http://www.puppetdream.com
Puppets, arts, crafts and other creative educational products for children.

Arthur Partner

5377 Qwik-File Storage Systems
1000 Allview Drive
Crozet, VA 22932-3144
804-823-4351
Schedule boards and classroom supplies.

5378 RC Musson Rubber Company
1320 E Archwood Avenue
Akron, OH 44306-2825
330-773-7651
800-321-3281
Fax: 330-773-3254
E-mail: info@mussonrubber.com
http://www.mussonrubber.com
Rubber floorcoverings, mats and athletic matting.

Mark Reese, Customer Service Manager
Robert Segers, VP

5379 RCA Rubber Company
1833 E Market Street
Akron, OH 44305-4214
330-784-1291
Fax: 330-784-2899
Floorcoverings, athletic mats and more for the physical education class.

5380 Reading is Fundamental
600 Maryland Avenue SW
Suite 600
Washington, DC 20024-2520
202-673-1641
Fax: 202-673-1633
Distributor of posters, bookmarks, and parent guide brochures.

5381 Reconnecting Youth
National Educational Service
304 W Kirkwood Avenue
Suite 2
Bloomington, IN 47404-5132
812-336-7700
800-733-6786
Fax: 812-336-7790
E-mail: nes@nesonline.com
http://www.nesonline.com
Curriculum to help discouraged learners achieve in school, manage their anger, and decrease drug use, depression, and suicide risk. The program was piloted for five years with over 600 urban Northwestern public high school students with funding from the National Institute on Drug Abuse and the National Institute of Mental Health, and has since been successful in many educational settings.

3 Ring Binder Circul
ISBN: 1-879639-42-4

Jane St. John, Sales Marketing Director

5382 Red Ribbon Resources
135 Dupont Street
PO Box 760
Plainview, NY 11803
800-646-7999
Fax: 800-262-1886
http://ww.redribbonresources.com
Over 250 low cost giveaways to promote your safe and drug-free school and community.

5383 Renaissance Graphic Arts
69 Steamwhistle Drive
Ivyland, PA 18974
888-833-3398
Fax: 215-357-5258
E-mail: pat@printmaking-materials.com
http://www.printmaking-materials.com
Tools, papers, plates, inks and assorted products necessary for printmaking.

5384 Rock Paint Distributing Corporation
PO Box 482
Milton, WI 53563
608-868-6873
Fax: 800-715-7625
E-mail: handyart@handyart.com
http://www.handyart.com
Tempera paint, India ink, acrylic paint, block inc, washable paint, fabric paint.

5385 S&S Worldwide
S&S Arts & Crafts
75 Mill Street
Department 2030
Colchester, CT 06415-1263
800-243-9232
Fax: 800-566-6678
Arts and crafts, classroom games and group paks.

5386 Safe & Drug Free Catalog
Performance Resource Press
1270 Rankin Drive
Suite F
Troy, MI 48083-2843
800-453-7733
Fax: 800-499-5718
http://www.pronline.net
Books, videos, CD-Roms, phamlets and posters toassist students with social skills, counseling, drug and violence prevention.

5387 Sakura of America
30780 San Clemente Street
Hayward, CA 94544-7131
510-475-8880
800-776-6257
Fax: 510-475-0973
E-mail: express@sakuraofamerica.com
http://www.gellyroll.com
Gelly Roll pens, Cray pas oil pastels, Fantasia watercolors, Pigma micron pens, Pentouch and Aqua Wipe markers and other art supplies for the classroom.

John Crook
Donna Wilson, Marketing Director

5388 Sanford Corporation
A Lifetime of Color
2711 Washington Boulevard
Bellwood, IL 60104-1970
708-547-6650
800-323-0749
Fax: 708-547-6719
E-mail:
consumer.service@sanfordcorp.com
http://www.sanfordcorp.com
Writing instruments, art supplies.

Angela Nigl, Author
Sharon Meyers, PR Manager

5389 Sax Visual Art Resources
Sax Arts and Crafts
2725 S Moorland Road
bept. SA
New Berlin, WI 53151
800-558-6696
Fax: 800-328-4729
E-mail: catalog@saxfcs.com
http://www.saxfcs.com
Variety of resources for slides, books, videos, fine art posters and CD-Roms.

5390 School Mate
PO Box 2225
Jackson, TN 38302
731-935-2000
Fax: 800-668-7610
E-mail: school@schoolmateinc.com
Pre-school and elementary art products.

5391 SchoolMatters
Current
The Current Building
Colorado Springs, CO 80941-0001
800-525-7170
Fax: 800-993-3232
Offers a variety of creative classroom ideas including stickers, mugs, posters, signs and more for everyday and holidays and everyday of the year.

5392 Scott Sign Systems
PO Box 1047
Tallevast, FL 34270-1047

941-355-5171
800-237-9447
Fax: 941-351-1787
E-mail: mail@scottsigns.com
http://www.scottsigns.com
Educational supplies including announcement, letters, signs, graphics and chalkboards.

5393 Scratch-Art Company
PO Box 303
Avon, MA 02322
508-583-8085
800-377-9003
Fax: 508-583-8091
E-mail: info@scratchart.com
http://www.scratchart.com
Offers materials for drawing, sketching and rubbings.

5394 Sea Bay Game Company
PO Box 162
Middletown, NJ 07748-0162
732-583-7902
Fax: 732-583-7284
Manufacturer and distributor of products, games and creative play to nursery schools and preschools.

5395 Seton Identification Products
20 Thompson Road
PO Box 819
Branford, CT 06405
203-488-8059
800-243-6624
Fax: 203-488-4114
http://www.seton.com
Manufacturer of all types of identification products including signs, tags, labels, traffic control, OSHA, ADA and much more.

5396 Shapes, Etc.
PO Box 400
Dansville, NY 14437-0400
585-335-6619
Fax: 585-335-6070
Notepads and craft materials for creative writing projects. Coordinates with literature themes. Perfect for storystarters, bulletin boards, awards and motivators.

5397 Sign Product Catalog
Scott Sign Systems, Inc.
PO Box 1047
Tallevast, FL 34270-1047
845-355-5171
800-237-9447
Fax: 941-351-1787
E-mail: scottsigns@mindspring.com
http://www.scottsigns.com
Educational supplies including announcement, letters, signs, graphics and chalkboards.

Robert Lew, Account Executive

5398 Small Fry Originals
2700 S Westmoreland Road
Dallas, TX 75233-1312
214-330-8671
800-248-9443
Children's original artwork preserved in plastic plates and mugs.

5399 Southwest Plastic Binding Corporation
109 Millwell Drive
Maryland Heights, MO 63043-2509
800-986-2001
Fax: 800-942-2010
Overhead transparencies, maps, charts and classroom supplies.

5400 Spectrum Corporation
10048 Easthaven Boulevard
Houston, TX 77075-3298

800-392-5050
Fax: 713-944-1290
Announcement boards, scoreboards and sports equipment, sports timers and clocks.

5401 Speedball Art Products Company
2226 Speedball Road
PO Box 5157
Statesville, NC 28687
704-838-1475
800-898-7224
Fax: 704-838-1472
E-mail: tonyahill@speedballart.com
http://www.speedballart.com
Art products for stamping, calligraphy, printmaking, drawing and painting.

Rita Madsen, Manager
Tonya Hill, Director of Sales

5402 Sponge Stamp Magic
525 S Anaheim Hills Road
Apartment C314
Anaheim, CA 92807-4726
Rubber stamps and games for classroom use.

5403 Staedtler
PO Box 2196
Chatsworth, CA 91313-2196
818-882-6000
800-776-5544
Fax: 818-882-3767
E-mail: rhoye@staedtler-usa.com
http://www.staedtler-usa.com
Arts and crafts supplies, office supplies and equipment.

Dick Hoye, National Sales Manager

5404 Sylvan Learning Systems
1000 Lancaster Street
Baltimore, MD 21202
410-843-6828
888-779-5826
Fax: 410-783-3832
http://www1.sylvan.net
Provides public school academic programs that are traditional sylvan programs modified to fit the needs of individual school districts and performance guarantees.

Jody Madron, Contact

5405 Tandy Leather Company
PO Box 791
Fort Worth, TX 76101-0791
817-451-1480
Fax: 817-451-5254
Arts and crafts supplies, computer peripherals and systems.

5406 Teacher Appreciation
Guidance Channel
135 Dupont Street
PO Box 760
Plainview, NY 44803-0706
800-999-6884
Fax: 800-262-1886
Products for celebrating teacher appreciation week.

5407 Teachers Store
PO Box 24155
Lansing, MI 48909-4155
517-393-0440
Fax: 517-393-8884
School and classroom supplies, arts and crafts.

5408 Texas Instruments
12500 TI Boulevard
Dallas, TX 75243-4136
800-336-5236
Fax: 972-995-4360
http://www.ti.com
Manufacturer of calculators.

5409 Triarco Arts & Crafts
14650 28th Avenue N
Plymouth, MN 55447
763-559-5590
800-328-3360
Fax: 736-559-2215
E-mail: info@triarcoarts.com
Art supplies.

5410 Vanguard Crafts
1081 E 48th Street
Brooklyn, NY 11234
718-377-5188
800-662-7238
Fax: 888-692-0056
Arts and crafts supplier.

5411 Wagner Zip-Change
3100 W Hirsch Avenue
Melrose Park, IL 60160-1741
800-323-0744
Fax: 708-681-4165
Non-lighted changeable letter message activity signs, changeable letters in all sizes and colors.

CJ Krasula, Marketing VP
Jim Leone, Sales Manager

5412 Walker Display
6520 Grand Avenue
Duluth, MN 55807-2242
218-624-8990
Fax: 888-695-4647
Arts, crafts, classroom supplies and displays.

5413 Wellness Reproductions
Guidance Channel
135 Dupont Street
PO Box 760
Plainview, NY 44803-0706
800-999-6884
Fax: 800-262-1886
Mental and life skills educational materials.

5414 Wikki Stix One-of-a-Kind Creatables
Omnicor
2432 W Peoria Avenue #1188
Suite 1188
Phoenix, AZ 85029-4735
602-870-9937
800-869-4554
Fax: 602-870-9877
E-mail: info@wikkistix.com
http://www.wikkistix.com
Unique, one-of-a-kind twistable, stickable, creatable, hands-on teaching tools. Ideal for Pre-K through 8 for science, language arts, math, arts and crafts, positive behavior rewards, rainy day recess, classroom display, diagrams and 3-D work. Self-stick; no glue needed.

Kem Clark, President

5415 Wilson Language Training
175 W Main Strete
Millbury, MA 01527-1441
508-865-5699
Fax: 508-865-9644
Multisensory language program.

5416 Wilton Art Appreciation Programs
Reading & O'Reilley
PO Box 646
Botsford, CT 06404
203-270-6336
800-458-4274
Fax: 203-270-5569
E-mail: ror@wiltonart.com
http://www.wiltonart.com
Materials for art appreciation including CD-ROMS, videos, fine art prints, slides, workbooks, teacher' guides, lessons, puzzles and games.

Diana O'Neill, President

5417 Young Explorers
1810 E Eisenhower Boulevrd
Loveland, CO 80539
800-239-7577
Fax: 888-876-8847
http://www.youngexplorers.com
Educational material for children.

Electronic Equipment

5419 AIMS Multimedia
9710 De Soto Avenue
Chatsworth, CA 91311-4409
818-773-4300
800-367-2467
Fax: 818-341-6700
E-mail: info@aimsmultimedia.com
http://www.aimsmultimedia.com
Film, video, laserdisc producer and distributor, offering a free catalog available materials. Also provides internet video streaming.

David Sherman, President
Biff Sherman, President

5420 Advance Products Company
1101 E Central Avenue
Wichita, KS 67214-3922
316-263-4231
Fax: 316-263-4245
Manufacturer of steel mobile projection and television tables, video cabinets, easels, computer furniture, wall and ceiling TV mounts, and study tables and carrels.

Paul Keck

5421 All American Scoreboards
Everbrite
401 S Main Street
Pardeeville, WI 53954
608-429-2121
800-356-8146
Fax: 608-429-9216
E-mail: score@everbrite.com
http://www.allamericanscoreboards.com
Scoreboards.

Doug Winkelmann, Product Manager

5422 American Time & Signal Company
140 3rd Avenue S
Dassel, MN 55325
800-328-8996
Fax: 800-789-1882
Sports timers and clocks.

5423 Arts & Entertainment Network
235 E 45th Street
Floor 9
New York, NY 10017-3354
212-210-1400
Fax: 212-210-9755
Cable network offering free educational programming to schools.

5424 Barr Media/Films
12801 Schabarum Avenue
Irwindale, CA 91706-6808
626-338-7878
K-12 film, video and interactive Level I and III laserdisc programs.

5425 Buhl Optical Company
1009 Beech Avenue
Pittsburgh, PA 15233-2013
412-321-0076
Fax: 412-322-2640
Overhead projectors and transparencies.

5426 C-SPAN Classroom
4000 N Capitol Street NW
Washington, DC 20001
800-523-7586
Fax: 202-737-6226

C-SPAN School Bus travels through more than 80 communities during each school year. This bus is a mobile television production studio and learning center designed to give hands-on experience with C-SPAN's programming.

5427 CASIO
570 Mount Pleasant Avenue
Dover, NJ 07801-1631
973-361-5400
Fax: 570-868-6898
Cameras, overhead projectors and electronics.

5428 CASPR
100 Park Center Plaza
Suite 550
San Jose, CA 95113-2204
800-852-2777
http://www.caspr.com
Leader in the field of library automation for schools. Integrated library automation-cross platforms: Macintosh, Windows, Apple IIe/IIGS. Multimedia source.

Norman Kline, President

5429 Cable in the Classroom
1800 N Beauregard Street
Suite 100
Alexandria, VA 22311-1710
703-845-1400
Fax: 703-845-1409
http://www.ciconline.org
Represents the cable tele-communications industry's commitment to improving teaching and learning for children in schools, at home and in their communities.

5430 Canon USA
1 Canon Plaza
New Hyde Park, NY 11042-1198
516-488-1400
Fax: 516-328-5069
School equipment and supplies including a full line of electronics, cameras, calculators and other technology.

5431 Caulastics
5955 Mission Street
Daly City, CA 94014-1397
415-585-9600
Overhead projectors, transparencies and electronics.

5432 Cheshire Corporation
Cheshire Corporation
PO Box 61109
Denver, CO 80206-8109
303-333-3003
Fax: 303-333-4037
E-mail: karen-hemmes@mindspring.com
Cheshire corporation is a publicist for book, video, CD-ROM and internet publishers in the school and library market.

Karen Hemmes, Publicist
Mary Kay Opicka, Publicist

5433 Chief Manufacturing
14310 Ewing Avenue S
Burnsville, MN 55306-4839
612-894-6280
800-582-6480
Fax: 877-894-6918
E-mail: chief@chiefmfg.com
http://www.chiefmfg.com
Manufacturer of Communications Support Systems for audio visual and video equipment. Chief's product includes a full-line of mounts, electric lifts, carts, and accessories for LCD/DLP projectors, plasma displays and TV/monitors.

Liz Sorensen, Marketing Assistant
Sharon McCubbin, Marketing Manager

5434 Chisholm
7019 Realm Drive
San Jose, CA 95119-1321
800-888-4210
Computer peripherals, overhead projectors and overhead transparencies.

5435 Daktronics
331 32nd Avenue
Brookings, SD 57006-4704
605-697-4300
888-325-8766
Fax: 605-697-4300
E-mail: sales@daktronics.com
http://www.daktronics.com
Scoreboards, electronic message displays statistics software.

Gary Gramm, HSPR Market Manager

5436 Depco- Millennium 3000
3305 Airport Drive
PO Box 178
Pittsburg, KS 66762
316-231-0019
800-767-1062
Fax: 316-231-0024
E-mail: sales@depcoinc.com
http://www.depcoinc.com
Program tracks and schedules for you, the test taker delivers tests electronically, as well as, automatic final exams. There are workstation security features to help keep students focused on their activities.

5437 Discovery Networks
7700 Wisconsin Avenue
Bethesda, MD 20814-3578
301-986-0444
Manages and operates The Discovery Channel, offering the finest in nonfiction documentary programming, as well as The Learning Channel, representing a world of ideas to learners of all ages.

5438 Echolab
175 Bedford Street
Burlington, MA 01803-2794
781-273-1512
Fax: 978-250-3335
Cameras, equipment, projectors and electronics.

5439 Eiki International
Audio Visual/Video Products
26794 Vista Terrace Drive
Lake Forest, CA 92630
949-457-0200
Fax: 949-457-7878
Video projectors, overhead projectors and transparencies.

5440 Elmo Manufacturing Corporation
1478 Old Country Road
Plainview, NY 11803-5034
516-501-1400
800-654-7628
Fax: 516-501-0429
Overhead projectors and transparencies.

5441 Fair-Play Scoreboards
1700 Delaware Avenue
Des Moines, IA 50317-2999
800-247-0265
Fax: 515-265-3364
E-mail: sales@fair-play.com
http://www.fair-play.com
Scoreboards and sports equipment.

5442 Festo Corporation
395 Moreland Road
PO Box 18023
Hauppauge, NY 11788
631-435-0800
Fax: 631-435-3847
http://www.festo-usa.com

5443 General Audio-Visual
333 W Merrick Road
Valley Stream, NY 11580-5219
516-825-8500
Fax: 516-568-2057
Offers a full line of audio-visual equipment and supplies, cameras, projectors and various other electronics for the classroom.

5444 Hamilton Electronics
2003 W Fulton Street
Chicago, IL 60612-2365
312-421-5442
Fax: 312-421-0818
Electronics, equipment and supplies.

5445 JR Holcomb Company
3205 Harvard Avenue
Cleveland, OH 44101
216-341-3000
800-362-9907
Fax: 216-341-5151
A full line of electronics including calculators, overhead projectors and overhead transparencies.

5446 JVC Professional Products Company
41 Slater Drive
Elmwood Park, NJ 07407-1311
201-794-3900
Electronics line including cameras, projectors, transparencies and other technology for the classroom.

5447 Labelon Corporation
10 Chapin Street
Canandaigua, NY 14424-1589
585-394-6220
800-428-5566
Fax: 585-394-3154
Electronics, supplies and equipment for schools.

5448 Learning Channel
7700 Wisconsin Avenue
Bethesda, MD 20814
800-346-0032
Offers educational programming for schools.

5449 Learning Station/Hug-a-Chug Records
3950 Bristol Court
Melbourne, FL 32904-8712
321-728-8773
800-789-9990
Fax: 321-722-9121
http://www.learningstationmusic.com
Early childhood products including OMH, cassettes, CD's and videos. Also, the Learning Station performs children and family concerts and are internationally acclaimed for their concert/keynote presentations for early childhood conferences and other educational organizations.

Don Monopoli, President
Laurie Monopoli, VP

5450 Learning Well
2200 Marcus Avenue
#3759
New Hyde Park, NY 11042-1042
800-645-6564
Fax: 800-638-6499
Instructional material including computer and board games, videos, cassettes, audio tapes, theme units, manipulatives for grades PreK-8.

Mona Russo, President

5451 Leightronix
2330 Jarco Drive
Holt, MI 48842-1210

517-694-5589
Fax: 517-694-1600
Educational cable programming for schools and institutions.

5452 MCM Electronics
650 Congress Park Drive
Centerville, OH 45459
800-543-4330
Fax: 800-765-6960
http://www.mcmelectronics.com
Offers a full line of electronics products and components for use in the classroom or at home. Over 40,000 parts.

5453 Magna Plan Corporation
1320 Route 9
Champlain, NY 12919-5007
518-298-8404
800-361-1192
Fax: 518-298-2368
E-mail: info@visualplanning.com
http://www.visualplanning.com
Overhead projectors.

Joseph P Josephson, Managing Director
Joel Boloten, Manager Consultation Service

5454 Mitsubishi Professional Electronics
200 Cottontail Lane
Somerset, NJ 08873-1231
732-563-9889
Video projectors and electronics.

5455 Multi-Video
PO Box 35444
Charlotte, NC 28235-5444
704-563-4279
800-289-0111
Fax: 704-568-0219
Cameras, projectors and equipment.

5456 Naden Scoreboards
505 Fair Avenue
PO Box 636
Webster City, IA 50595-0636
515-832-4290
800-467-4290
Fax: 515-832-4293
E-mail: naden@ncn.net
http://www.naden.com
Electronic scoreboards for sports.

Russ Naden, President

5457 Neumade Products Corporation
30 Pecks Lane
Newtown, CT 06470-2361
203-270-1100
Fax: 203-270-7778
E-mail: neumadeGJ@aol.com
http://www.neumade.com
Overhead projectors, overhead transparencies, video projectors and electronics.

Gregory Jones, VP Sales

5458 Nevco Scoreboard Company
301 E Harris Avenue
Greenville, IL 62246-2151
618-664-0360
800-851-4040
Fax: 618-664-0398
E-mail: info@nevco.com
http://www.nevco.com
Nevco is a premier manufacturer and distributor of scoreboards, message centers and video displays.

Phil Robertson, Sales Manager

5459 Panasonic Communications & System Company
1 Panasonic Way
Secaucus, NJ 07094-2917
201-392-4818
800-524-1064
Fax: 201-392-4044

Cameras, projectors, equipment, players, CD-ROM equipment and school supplies.

5460 Quickset International
3650 Woodhead Drive
Northbrook, IL 60062-1895
800-247-6563
Fax: 847-498-1258
Telecommunication equipment, cameras, projectors and electronics.

5461 RMF Products
PO Box 520
Batavia, IL 60510-0520
630-879-0020
Fax: 630-879-6749
E-mail: mail@rmfproducts.com
http://www.rmfproducts.com
Complete line of slide-related products including two and three-projector dissolve controls, programmers, multi-track tape recorders, audio-visual cables, remote controls and slide mounts.

Richard Frieders, President

5462 RTI-Research Technology International
4700 W Chase Avenue
Lincolnwood, IL 60646-1608
800-323-7520
Fax: 800-784-6733
TapeChek Videotape Cleaner/Inspector/Rewinders make videotapes last longer and perform better. Find damage before tape is circulated. Also available is videotape/laser disc storage, shipping and care products.

Bill Wolavka, Marketing Director

5463 Recreation Equipment Unlimited
PO Box 4700
Pittsburgh, PA 15206-0700
412-731-3000
Fax: 412-731-3052
Scoreboards and sports/recreation equipment.

5464 Reliance Plastics & Packaging
25 Prospect Street
Newark, NJ 07105-3300
973-473-7200
Fax: 973-589-6440
Vinyl albums for audio or video cassettes, video discs, slides, floppy disks, CDs Protect, store and circulate valuable media properly.

5465 Resolution Technology
26000 Avenida Aeropuerto Spc 22
San Juan Capistrano, CA 92675-4736
949-661-6162
Fax: 949-661-0114
Video systems and videomicroscopy equipment.

5466 RobotiKits Direct
17141 Kingsview Avenue
Suite B
Carson, CA 90746
310-515-6800
877-515-6652
Fax: 310-515-0927
E-mail: info@owirobot.com
http://www.robotikitsdirect.com
New science and robotic kits for the millenium.

Craig Morioka, President
Armer Amante, General Manger

5467 S'Portable Scoreboards
3058 Alta Vista Drive
Fallbrook, CA 92028-8738
800-323-7745
Fax: 270-759-0066

Portable scoreboards, manual and electronic, sports timers and clocks.

5468 SONY Broadcast Systems Product Division
1 Sony Drive
Park Ridge, NJ 07656
800-472-SONY
Interactive videodisc players for multimedia applications, VTRs, monitors, projection systems, video cameras, editing systems, printers and scanners, video presentation stands, audio cassette duplicators and video library systems.

5469 Scott Resources/ Hubbard Scientific
National Training Aids
PO Box 2121
Fort Collins, CO 80522-2121
970-484-7445
800-289-9299
Fax: 970-484-1198
E-mail: sgranger@amep.com
http://www.hubbardscientific.com
Microslide system is a comprehensive, classroom-ready to help students learn. The microslide system combines superb photo-materials with detailed curriculum material and reproducible student activity sheets at an affrdable price.

Shelley Granger, OEM/Retail Sales Manager
Candy Coffman, National Sales Manager

5470 Shure Brothers
222 Hartrey Avenue
Evanston, IL 60202-3696
847-866-2200
Fax: 847-866-2551
Electronics, hardware and classroom supplies.

5471 Swift Instruments
1190 N 4th Street
San Jose, CA 95112
408-293-2380
800-523-4544
Fax: 408-292-7967
http://www.swiftmicroscope.com
Capture live or still microscopic images through your compound or stereo microscope and background sound images through your VCR or computer.

5472 Tech World
Lab-Volt
PO Box 686
Farmingdale, NJ 07727
732-938-2000
800-522-8658
Fax: 732-774-8573
E-mail: us@labvolt.com
http://www.labvolt.com
Tech World provides superior hands-on instruction using state-of-the-art technology and equipment. Lab-Volt also offers a full line of attractive, durable, and flexible modular classroom furniture.

5473 Technical Education Systems
814 Chestnut Street
PO Box 1203
Rockford, IL 61102
815-966-2525
800-451-2169
Fax: 815-965-4836
http://www.tii-tech.com
Hands-on application-oriented training systems integrating today's real world technologies in a flexible and easy-to-understand curriculum format.

5474 Telex Communications
12000 Portland Avenue S
Burnsville, MN 55337

952-884-4051
800-828-6107
Fax: 952-884-0043
http://www.telex.com
Telex manufactures a variety of products for the educational market, including multimedia headphones, headsets and microphones; LCD computer and multimedia projection panels, group listening centers, video projectors, slide projectors, portable sound systems, wired and wireless intercoms, and wired and wireless microphones.

Dawn Wiome, Marketing Coordinator

5475 The Transcription Studio
The Transcription Studio, LLC
210 N. Pass Avenue
Suite 206
Burbank, CA 91505
818-846-8973
Fax: 818-846-8933
E-mail: www.transcriptionstudio.com
http://jeff@transcriptionstudio.com
We transcribe and provide closed-captioning services to the education and academic fields.

Jeff Zedlar, CEO
Deborah Hargreaves, Director of Operations

5476 Three M Visual Systems
3M Austin Center
6801 River Place Boulevard
Austin, TX 78726-4530
800-328-1371
Fax: 512-984-6529
Overhead projectors, audiovisual carts and tables, and overhead transparencies.

5477 Tom Snyder Productions
80 Coolidge Hill Road
Watertown, MA 02472-7013
617-926-6000
800-342-0236
Fax: 800-304-1254
E-mail: ask@tpmsnyder.com
http://www.tomsnyder.com
Educational videotapes, videodiscs and computer programs.

5478 Varitronics Systems
PO Box 234
Minneapolis, MN 55440
800-637-5461
Fax: 800-543-8966
Computer electronics, hardware, software and systems.

5479 Wholesale Educational Supplies
PO Box 120123
East Haven, CT 06512-0123
800-243-2518
Fax: 800-452-5956
E-mail: wes4@snet.net
http://www.discountav.com
Over 5,000 audio visual and video equipment and supplies offered at deep discount prices. Free 148 page catalog.

J Fields, President

Furniture & Equipment

5480 ASRS of America
225 W 34th Street
Suite 1708
New York, NY 10122-0049
212-760-1607
Fax: 212-714-2084
E-mail: elecompack@erols.com
http://www.elecompack.com
Offers Elecompack, high density compact shelving which offers double storage capac-

ity, automatic passive safety systems and custom front panels.

Walter M Kaufman

5481 Adden Furniture
26 Jackson Street
Lowell, MA 01852-2199
978-454-7848
800-625-3876
Fax: 978-453-1449
E-mail: fsafran@addenfurniture.com
http://www.addenfurniture.com
Manufacturer of dormitory furniture, bookcases and shelving products.

Frank Safran, Education/Sales Director

5482 Air Technologies Corporation
27130 Paseo Espada
Suite 1405-A
San Juan Capistrano, CA 92675
949-661-5060
800-759-5060
Fax: 949-661-2454
E-mail: sales@airtech.net
http://www.airtech.net
Develop and manufacture professional ergonomic computer products.

5483 Alma Industries
1300 Prospect Street
High Point, NC 27260-8329
336-578-5700
Fax: 336-578-0105
Bookcases and shelving for educational purposes.

5484 Angeles Group
Dailey Industrial Park
9 Capper Drive
Pacific, MO 63069
636-257-0533
Fax: 636-257-5473
http://www.angeles-group.com
Housekeeping furniture and children play kitchen's made of durable and sturdy molded polyethylene. Baseline Furniture: tables, chairs, lockers, cubbies, bookcases, bookracks, silver rider trikes, spaceline cots, basic trikes, and bye bye buggies.

Dianna Pritcjett, Customer Service Manager
Tami Warren, Customer Service Manager

5485 Anthro Corporation Technology Furniture
10450 SW Manhasset
Tualatin, OR 97062
503-691-2556
800-325-3841
Fax: 800-325-0045
http://www.anthro.com
Durable computer workstations and accessories; educational discounts; and dozens of shapes and sizes.

Mila Graham, Educational Sales

5486 Architectural Precast
10210 Winstead Lane
Cincinnati, OH 45231
513-772-4670
Fax: 513-772-4672
Furniture, tables, playground equipment, desks.

5487 Blanton & Moore Company
PO Box 70
Barium Springs, NC 28010-0070
704-528-4506
Fax: 704-528-6519
http://www.blantonandmoore.com
Standard and custom library furniture crafted from fine hardwoods.

Billy Galliher, Manager Sales Administration

5488 Borroughs Corporation
3002 N Burdick Street
Kalamazoo, MI 49004-3483
616-342-0161
800-627-6767
Bookcases and shelving products for educational purposes.

5489 Brady Office Machine Security
11056 S Bell Avenue
Chicago, IL 60643-3935
773-779-8349
800-326-8349
Fax: 773-779-9712
E-mail: b.brady1060@aol.com
The Brady Office Machine Security physically protects all office machines, computer components, faxes, printers, VCRs, have wall and ceiling mounts for TVs.

Bernadette Brady, President
Don Brady, VP

5490 Bretford Manufacturing
9715 Soreng Avenue
Schiller Park, IL 60176-2186
540-678-2545
Manufacturer of a full line of AV and computer projection screens, television mounts, wood office furniture and a full line of combination wood shelving and steel library shelving.

5491 Brixey
30414 Ganado Drive
Suite A
Palos Verdes Estates, CA 90275-6221
310-544-6098
Furniture for the classroom.

5492 Brodart Company, Automation Division
500 Arch Street
Williamsport, PA 17701
570-326-2461
800-233-8467
Fax: 570-327-9237
E-mail: salesmkt@brodart.com
http://www.brodart.com
Brodart's Automation Division has been providing library systems, software, and services for over 25 years. Products include: library management systems, media management systems, Internet solutions, cataloged web sites, cataloging resource tools, union catalog solutions, public access catalogs, and bibliographic services.

Kasey Dibble, Marketing Coordinator
Sally Wilmoth, Director Marketing/Sales

5493 Buckstaff Company
Buckstaff Company
1127 S Main Street
PO Box 2506
Oshkosh, WI 54902
920-235-5890
800-755-5890
Fax: 920-235-2018
E-mail: tmugerauer@buckstaff.com
http://www.buckstaff.com
The premier manufacturer of library furniture in the United States. Quality and durability has been the Buckstaff trademark for 150 years.

Tom Mugerauer, Sales Manager, National

5494 Carpets for Kids Etc...
115 SE 9th Avenue
Portland, OR 97214-1301
503-232-1203
Fax: 503-232-1394
http://www.carpetforkids.com
Carpets, flooring and floorcoverings for educational purposes.

5495 Children's Factory
505 N Kirkwood Road
Saint Louis, MO 63122-3913
314-821-1441
Fax: 877-726-1714
Manufactures children's indoor play furniture.

5496 Children's Furniture Company
Gressco Ltd.
328 Moravian Valley Road
Waunakee, WI 53597
800-697-3408
Fax: 608-849-6300
E-mail: caroline@gresscoltd.com
http://www.gressco.com
Commercial quality furniture for children of all ages.

Robert Childers, President
Caroline Ashmore, Marketing/Sales

5497 Community Playthings
PO Box 901
Rifton, NY 12471-0901
800-777-4244
Fax: 800-336-5948
E-mail: sales@bruderhof.com
Unstructured maple toys and furniture including innovative products, especially for infants and toddlers.

5498 Continental Film
PO Box 5126
Chattanooga, TN 37406-0126
423-622-1193
888-909-3456
Fax: 423-629-0853
E-mail: cfpc@chattanooga.net
http://www.continentalfilm.com
LCD projectors, distance learning systems, interactive white boards, document cameras.

Jim Webster, President
Courtney Sisk, VP

5499 Counterpoint
17237 Van Wagoner Road
Spring Lake, MI 49456-9702
800-628-1945
Fax: 616-847-3109
Audiovisual carts and tables.

5500 CyberStretch By Jazzercise
2460 Impala Drive
Carlsbad, CA 92008
760-476-1750
Fax: 760-602-7180
E-mail: cyberstretch@cyberstretch.com
http://www.jazzercize.com
To foster and promote wellness through the production of free interactive software programs for business, government, educational and personal use.

Kathy Missett, Contact

5501 Da-Lite Screen Company
3100 N Detroit Street
Warsaw, IN 46582
574-267-8101
800-622-3737
Fax: 574-267-7804
E-mail: info@dalite.com
http://www.da-lite.com
Projection screens, monitor mounts, audiovisual carts and tables, overhead projectors and transparencies.

5502 DeFoe Furniture 4 Kids
910 S Grove Avenue
Ontario, CA 91761-8011
909-947-4459
Fax: 909-947-3377
Furniture, floorcoverings, toys, constructive playthings and more for children grades PreK-5.

5503 Decar Corporation
7615 University Avenue
Middleton Branch, WI 53562-3142
606-836-1911
Library shelving, storage facilities and furniture.

5504 DecoGard Products
Construction Specialties
Route 405
PO Box 400
Muncy, PA 17756
570-546-5941
Fax: 570-546-5169
Physical fitness and athletic floor coverings and mats.

5505 Engineering Steel Equipment Company
1307 Boissevain Avenue
Norfolk, VA 23507-1307
757-627-0762
Fax: 757-625-5754
Audiovisual carts and tables, bookcases and library shelving.

5506 Environments
PO Box 1348
Beaufort, SC 29901-1348
843-846-8155
800-348-4453
Fax: 843-846-2999
Publishes a catalog featuring equipment and materials for child care and early education. Offers durable and easy-to-maintain products with values that promote successful preschool, kindergarden, special needs and multi-age programs.

5507 Flagship Carpets
PO Box 1189
Chatsworth, GA 30705-1189
Carpets, flooring and floorcoverings.

5508 Fleetwood Group
PO Box 1259
Holland, MI 49422-1259
616-396-1142
800-257-6390
Fax: 616-820-8300
E-mail: www.fleetwoodfurniture.com
Offers library and school furniture including shelving, check out desks and multimedia units.

5509 Fordham Equipment Company
3308 Edson Avenue
New York, NY 10469
718-379-7300
800-249-5922
Fax: 718-379-7312
E-mail: alrobbi@attglobal.net
http://www.fordhamequip.com
Distributor and manufacturer of complete line of library supplies. Specialize in professional library shelving and furniture (wood and metal), mobile shelving and displayers. Catalog on request.

Al Robbins, President

5510 Good Sports
6031 Broad Street Mall
Pittsburgh, PA 15206-3009
412-661-9500
Mats, matting, floorcoverings and athletic training mats.

5511 Grafco
ERD
PO Box 71
Catasauqua, PA 18032-0071
800-367-6169
Fax: 610-782-0813
E-mail: info@grafco.com
http://www.grafco.com

GRAFCO manufacturers sturdy and durable computer furniture and tables designed for the educational environment.

Art Grafenberg, President

5512 Grammer
6989 N 55th Street
Suite A
Oakdale, MN 55128
651-770-6515
800-367-7328
http://www.grammerusa.com
Leading manufacturer and designer of ergonomically sound seating. Offers a chair designed especially for children.

5513 Greeting Tree
2709 Oak Haven Drive
San Marcos, TX 78666
512-392-0669
800-322-3199
Fax: 512-392-9660
E-mail: krieger@corridor.net
http://www.greetingtree.com
Solid wood furniture for Reading Recovery, Reading Library, Primary and Early Childhood. Specializes in quality and customized furniture for today's classroom. Kitchen learning centers, storage units of all sizes and sorts, easels with over fourteen different display front possibilities.

BiAnnually

Cherie Krieger, Owner

5514 Gressco Ltd.
Gressco
328 Moravian Valley Road
PO Box 339
Waunakee, WI 53597
608-849-6300
800-345-3480
Fax: 608-849-6304
E-mail: custserv@gresscoltd.com
http://www.gressco.com
Gressco is a supplier of a complete line of commercial children's HABA furniture and library displays for all types of medias. Kwik-case for the security protection of CDs, videos, and audiocassettes. Catalog available.

Caroline Ashmore, Marketing/Sales

5515 H Wilson Company
555 W Taft Drive
South Holland, IL 60473-2071
708-339-5111
800-245-7224
Fax: 800-245-8224
E-mail: sales@wilson.com
http://www.hwilson.com
Manufacturer of furniture for audio, video, and computers. Complete line of TV wall and ceiling mounts. Makers of the famous Tuffy color carts.

Matthew Glowiak, Director
Sales/Marketing

5516 HON Company
200 Oak Street
#769
Muscatine, IA 52761-4341
563-264-7100
Fax: 563-264-7505
Bookcases and shelving units.

5517 Haworth
One Haworth Center
Holland, MI 49423-9570
616-393-3000
800-344-2600
Fax: 616-393-1570
http://www.haworth.com

Steel and wood desks, systems furniture, seating, files, bookcases, shelving units, and tables.

5518 Joy Carpets
104 W Forrest Road
Fort Oglethorpe, GA 30742-3675
706-866-3335
800-645-2787
Fax: 706-866-7928
E-mail: joycarpets@joycarpets.com
http://www.joycarpets.com
Manufacturer of recreational and educational carpet for the classroom, home, or business. With a 10 year wear warranty, Class #1 Flammability rating, anti-stain and anti-bacterial treatment.

Joy Dobosh, Director Marketing

5519 KI
PO Box 8100
Green Bay, WI 54308-8100
920-468-8100
Fax: 920-468-2232
Library shelving, furniture, bookcases and more.

5520 Kensington Technology Group
2855 Campus Drive
San Mateo, CA 94403
650-572-2700
Fax: 650-572-9675
http://www.kensington.com
Offers several ergonomic mice.

5521 Kimball Office Furniture Company
1600 Royal Street
Jasper, IN 47549-1022
812-482-1600
Fax: 812-482-8300
Bookcases, office equipment and shelving units for educational institutions.

5522 Lee Metal Products
PO Box 6
Littlestown, PA 17340-0006
717-359-4111
Fax: 717-359-4414
http://www.leemetal.com
Carts, tables, bookcases and storage cabinets.

Richard Kemper, President

5523 Library Bureau
172 Industrial Road
Fitchburg, MA 01420
978-345-7942
800-221-6638
Fax: 978-345-0188
E-mail: melvil@librarybureau.com
http://www.librarybureau.com
Library shelving, bookcases, cabinets, circulation desks, carrels, computer workstations, upholstered seating.

Dennis Ruddy, Sr Project Manager

5524 Library Store
Library Store
112 E S Street
PO Box 964
Tremont, IL 61568
309-925-5571
800-548-7204
Fax: 800-320-7706
E-mail: libstore@thelibrarystore.com
http://www.thelibrarystore.com
The Library Store offers through its full-line catalog, supplies and furniture items for librarians, schools, and churches. Free catalog available containing special product discounts.

Janice Smith, Marketing Director

5525 Little Tikes Company
2180 Barlow Road
Hudson, OH 44236-4199
330-656-3906
800-321-4424
Fax: 330-650-3221
Offers a wide variety of furniture, educational games and toys and safety products for young children.

5526 Lucasey Manufacturing Company
2744 E 11th Street
Oakland, CA 94601-1429
510-534-1435
800-582-2739
Fax: 510-534-6828
E-mail: janrence@lucasey.com
Audiovisual carts , tables, and TV mounts

Jan RenceTurnbull, National Accountant

5527 Lundia
600 Capitol Way
Jacksonville, IL 62650-1096
800-726-9663
Fax: 800-869-9663
Bookcases and shelving products, as well as furniture for educational institutions.

5528 Lyon Metal Products
PO Box 671
Aurora, IL 60507-0671
630-892-8941
Fax: 630-892-8966
Bookcases and library shelving.

5529 Mateflex-Mele Corporation
1712 Erie Street
Utica, NY 13502-3337
315-733-4600
800-926-3539
Fax: 315-733-3183
http://www.mateflex.com
Manufacturers of Mateflex gymnasium flooring for basketball/gym courts. Mateflex II tennis court surfaces and Mateflex/Versaflex gridded safety floor tiles.

Gabe Martini, Sales Manager

5530 Microsoft Corporation
One Microsoft Way
Redmond, WA 98502-6399
425-882-8080
Fax: 206-703-2641
http://www.microsoft.com
Strives to produce innovative products and services that meet our costomers' evolving needs.

5531 Miller Multiplex
1555 Larkin Williams Road
Fenton, MO 63026-3008
636-343-5700
800-325-3350
Fax: 636-326-1716
E-mail: info@millermultiplex.com
Announcement boards, classroom displays, charts and pghtography, books towers, posters, frames, kiosk displays, presentation displays.

12 pages

Kathy Webster, Director Marketing

5532 ModuForm
ModuForm, Inc.
172 Industry Road
Fitchburg,, MA 01420
978-345-7942
800-221-6638
Fax: 978-345-0188
E-mail: guestlog@moduform.com
http://www.moduform.com

Residence hall furniture, loung seating, tables, stacking chairs, fully upholstered seating.

Robert Kushnir, Nationals Sales Manager
Darlene Bailey, VP Sales/Marketing

5533 Morgan Buildings, Pools, Spas, RV's
PO Box 660280
Dallas, TX 75266-0280
972-864-7300
800-935-0321
Fax: 972-864-7382
E-mail: rmoran@morganusa.com
http://www.morganusa.com
Classrooms, campus and other buildings custom designed to meet your projects needs. Permanent and relocatable modular classrooms or complete custom facilities. Rent, lease or purchase options available.

5534 Norco Products
Division of USA McDonald Corporation
PO Box 4227
Missoula, MT 59806
406-251-3800
800-662-2300
Fax: 406-251-3824
E-mail: john@norcoproducts.com
http://www.norcoproducts.com
Mobile cabinets, YRE furniture, tables, science labs, home economics displays, bookcases and shelving units, laboratory equipment, casework, cabinets, computer labs, podiums, award display cabinets, flags and flag poles.

Jim McDonald, President
John Schrom, Office Manger

5535 Nova
421 W Industrial Avenue
PO Box 725
Effingham, IL 62401
800-730-6682
Fax: 800-940-6682
E-mail: novadesk@effingham.net
http://www.novadesk.com
Patented furniture solution for computer mounting incorporates the downward gaze, our visual system's natural way of viewing close objects. Scientific evidence indicates that viewing a computer monitor at a downward gaze angle is a better solution than with traditional monitor placement.

5536 Oscoda Plastics
5585 N Huron Avenue
PO Box 189
Oscoda, MI 48750
989-739-6900
800-544-9538
Fax: 800-548-7678
E-mail: sales@oscodaplastics.com
http://www.oscodaplastics.com
Oscoda Plastics manufactures Protect-All Specialty Flooring from 100% recycled post-industrial vinyls. Protect-All is perfect for use in locker rooms, kitchen/walk-in cooler floors, fitness areas, weight rooms, gym floors, or as a temporary gym floor cover.

Joe Brinn, National Sales Manager
Rick Maybury, Sales Coordinator

5537 Palmer Snyder
201 High Street
Conneautville, PA 16406
814-587-6313
800-762-0415
Fax: 814-587-2375
Tables are built with the highest quality materials for long life and low maintenance. A complete range of rugged options.

5538 Paragon Furniture
2224 E Randol Mill Road
Arlington, TX 76011
817-633-3242
800-451-8546
Fax: 817-633-2733
E-mail: customerservice@paragoninc.com
http://www.paragoninc.com
Offers a line of furniture for classroom, labs, science, and libraries.

Carl Brockway, VP Sales
Mark Hubbard, President

5539 Pawling Corporation
Borden Lane
Wassaic, NY 12592
845-373-9300
800-431-3456
Fax: 800-451-2200
E-mail: sales@pawling.com
Pawling is an approved manufacturer by E&I co-operative buying for athletic flooring, traffic safety products, wall and corner protection and entrance mat systems.

Richard Meyer, Sales Manager

5540 Peerless Sales Company
1980 N Hawthorne Avenue
Melrose Park, IL 60160-1167
708-865-8870
Fax: 708-865-2941
Auidovisual carts and tables.

5541 RISO
300 Rosewood Drive
Suite 210
Danvers, MA 01923-4527
978-777-7377
800-876-7476
Fax: 978-777-2517
The Risograph digital printer offers high speed copy/duplicating at up to 130 pages per minute. A 50-sheet document feeder lets people print multi-page documents quickly and inexpensively. Specifically designed to handle medium run length jobs that are too strenuous for copiers. Offers various other products and office equipment available to the education community.

5542 Research Technology International
4700 Chase Avenue
Lincolnwood, IL 60646-1689
847-677-3000
800-323-7520
Fax: 847-677-1311
E-mail: sales@rtico.com
http://www.ritco.com
Tape check, Video tape cleaner, disk chack optical, disc rejestor.

5543 Russ Bassett Company
8189 Byron Road
Whittier, CA 90606-2615
800-350-2445
Fax: 562-689-8972
Shelving units, furniture and bookcases for educational institutions.

5544 SNAP-DRAPE
2045 Westgate
Suite 100
Carrollton, TX 75006-5116
972-466-1030
800-527-5147
Fax: 800-230-1330
E-mail: mecton@snapdrape.com
http://www.snapdrape.com
Table and stage skirting

Melissa Acton, Marketing/Sales Assistant

5545 Screen Works
2201 W Fulton Street
Chicago, IL 60612

312-243-8265
800-294-8111
Fax: 312-243-8290
E-mail: daveh@thescreenworks.com
http://www.thescreenworks.com
Manufacturers the E-Z Fold brand of portable projection screens and offers a full line of portable presentation accessories and services, including: an extensive screen rental inventory; audio-visula roll carts; lecterns and PaperStand flip charts. Custom screen sizes, screen surface cleaning and frame repair service also available.

David Hull, National Sales Manager

5546 Spacemaster Systems
155 W Central Avenue
Zeeland, MI 49464-1601
616-772-2406
Fax: 616-772-2100
Standard and Custom Shelving Systems and USEFUL AISLE Storage Systems.

5547 Spacesaver Corporation
1450 Janesville Avenue
Fort Atkinson, WI 53538-2798
920-563-6362
800-492-3434
Fax: 920-563-2702
E-mail: ssc@spacesaver.com
http://www.spacesaver.com
Flexible Spacesaver custom designs high-density mobile storage systems. Will double your storage and filing capacity while increasing usable floor space. Store files, supplies, manuals, books, drawings, multi-media, etc.

5548 Synsor Corporation
1920 Merrill Creek Pkwy
Everett, WA 98203-5859
800-426-0193
Fax: 425-551-1313
Offers a full line of educational furniture.

5549 Tab Products Company
1400 Page Mill Road
Palo Alto, CA 94304-1124
800-672-3109
Fax: 920-387-1802
Bookcases and shelving products for library/media centers.

5550 Tepromark International
206 Mosher Avenue
Woodmere, NY 11598-1662
516-569-4533
800-645-2622
Fax: 516-295-5991
Trolley Rail wall guards, corner guards, wall guards with hand rails, door plates, chair rolls, kick plates, vinyl floor mats and carpet mats. All mats promote safety from slipping in wet areas.

Robert Rymers

5551 Tesco Industries
1038 E Hacienda Street
Bellville, TX 77418-2828
979-865-3176
Fax: 979-865-9026
Bookcases and shelving units.

5552 Texwood Furniture
1353 N 2nd Street
Taylor, TX 76574
512-352-3000
888-878-0000
Fax: 512-352-3084
E-mail: ajohnson@texwood.com
http://www.texwood.com

Wood library furniture, shelving, computer tables and circulation desks and early childhood furniture.

Andrea Johnson, Director Marketing
Dave Gaskers, VP Sales/Marketing

5553 Tot-Mate by Stevens Industries
704 W Main Street
Teutopolis, IL 62467-1212
217-857-6411
800-397-8687
Fax: 217-857-3638
E-mail: timw@stevens.com
Early learning furniture manufactured by Stevens Industries. Features include 16 color choices, plastic laminate surfacing, rounded corners, beveled edges, safe and strong designs. Items offered include change tables, storage shelving, book displays, teacher cabinets, housekeeping sets and locker cubbies.

Randy Ruholl, Sales Representative
Paul Jones, Customer Service

5554 University Products
University Products
517 Main Street
PO Box 101
Holyoke, MA 01041-0101
413-532-3372
800-628-1912
Fax: 413-532-9281
E-mail: info@universityproducts.com
http://www.universityproducts.com
University Products specializes in top-quality archival materials for conservation and preservation as well as library and media centers supplies, equipment, and furnishings.

John A Dunphy

5555 W. C. Heller & Company
Heller
201 W Wabash Avenue
Montpelier, OH 43543
419-485-3176
Fax: 419-485-8694
E-mail: wcheller@hotmail.com
Complete line of wood library furniture in oak and birch, custom cabinetry and special modifications. Over 110 years in business.

Robert L Heller II, VP Sales

5556 Wheelit
PO Box 352800
Toledo, OH 43635-2800
419-531-4900
800-523-7508
Fax: 419-531-6415
Carts and storage containers.

5557 White Office Systems
50 Boright Avenue
Kenilworth, NJ 07033-1015
908-272-8888
Fax: 908-931-0840
Shelving, bookcases, furniture and products for libraries, media centers, schools and offices.

5558 Whitney Brothers Company
PO Box 644
Keene, NH 03431-0644
603-352-2610
Fax: 603-357-1559
Manufactures children's furniture products for preschools and day care centers.

5559 Winsted Corporation
10901 Hampshire Avenue S
Minneapolis, MN 55438-2385
952-944-9050
800-447-2257
Fax: 800-421-3839
E-mail: racks@winsted.com
http://www.winsted.com

Video furniture, accessories, tape storage systems and lan rack systems.

Randy Smith, President

5560 Wood Designs
PO Box 1308
Monroe, NC 28111-1308
704-283-7508
800-247-8465
Fax: 704-289-1899
E-mail: p.schneider@tip-me-not.com
Manufactures wooden educational equipment and teaching toys for early learning environments. Sold through school supply dealers and stores.

Dennis Gosney, President
Paul Schneider, VP Sales/Marketing

5561 Worden Company
199 E 17th Street
Holland, MI 49423-4298
800-748-0561
Fax: 616-392-2542
Furniture for office, business, school or library.

Maintenance

5562 American Locker Security Systems
608 Allen Street
Jamestown, NY 14701-3966
716-664-9600
800-828-9118
Fax: 716-664-2949
E-mail: 103303.1432@compuserve.com
http://www.americanlocker.com
Lockers featuring coin operated lockers.

David L Henderson, VP/General Manager

5563 Atlantic Fitness Products
PO Box 300
Linthicum Hts, MD 21090-0300
800-445-1855
School lockers and fitness/physical education products and equipment.

5564 Barco Products
11 N Batavia Avenue
Batavia, IL 60510-1961
800-338-2697
Maintenance and safety products made from recycled materials.

Kitt Pittman, Office Manager
Judy Leonard, Marketing Manager

5565 Blaine Window Hardware
17319 Blaine Drive
Hagerstown, MD 21740-2394
800-678-1919
Fax: 301-797-2510
E-mail: user533955@aol.com
http://www.blainewindow.com
Window and door parts including window repair hardware, custom screens locker hardware, chair glides, panic exit hardware, balance systems, door closers and motorized operators.

William Pasquerette, VP
Robert Slick, Purchasing Agent

5566 Bleacherman, M.A.R.S.
105 Mill Street
Corinth, NY 12822-1021
518-654-9084
School lockers.

5567 Burkel Equipment Company
14670 Hanks Drive
Red Bluff, CA 96080-9475
800-332-3993
School lockers, hardware and security equipment, maintenance and repair supplies.

5568 Chemtrol
Santa Barbara Control Systems
5375 Overpass Road
Santa Barbara, CA 93111-5879
800-621-2279
Fax: 805-683-1893
E-mail: chemtrol@slocontrol.com
http://www.chemtrolcontrol.com
Maintenance supplies for educational institutions.

Kevin R Smith, Sales Manager

5569 Contact East
335 Willow Street S
N Andover, MA 01845-5995
978-682-2000
800-225-5370
Fax: 978-688-7829
E-mail: sales@contacteast.com
http://www.contacteast.com
Maintenance supplies and equipment.

5570 DeBourgh Manufacturing Company
27505 Otero Avenue
La Junta, CO 81050-9403
719-384-8161
Fax: 719-384-7713
Security equipment, hardware, storage and school lockers.

5571 Dow Corning Corporation
PO Box 0994
Midland, MI 48686-0001
989-496-4000
Fax: 989-496-4572
Maintenance supplies and equipment.

5572 Dri-Dek Corporation
2706 Horseshoe Drive S
Naples, FL 34104-6142
941-643-0578
800-348-2378
Fax: 800-828-4248
E-mail: dri-dek@kictr.com
http://www.dri-dek.com
Oxy-BI vinyl compound in the Dri-Dek flooring systems helps halt the spread of infectious fungus and bacteria in areas with barefooted traffic. This compound makes Dri-Dek's anti-skid, self-draining surface ideal for use in the wettest conditions.

5573 Esmet
Tufloc Group
1406 5th Street SW
Canton, OH 44702-2062
330-452-9132
Fax: 330-452-2557
Lockers for the educational institution.

5574 Ex-Cell Metal Products
11240 Melrose Avenue
Franklin, IL 60131
847-451-0451
Fax: 847-451-0458
Maintenance supplies and repair equipment.

5575 Facilities Network
PO Box 868
Mahopac, NY 10541-0868
845-621-1664
School lockers and security system units.

5576 Fibersin Industries
37031 E Wisconsin Avenue
Oconomowoc, WI 53066
262-567-4427
Fax: 262-567-4814
School lockers and maintenance supplies. Desks, cradenzas, bookcases for school adm. Tables for cafeteria and adm.

5577 Flagpole Components
4150A Kellway Circle
Addison, TX 75001-4205
972-250-0893
800-634-4926
Fax: 972-380-5143
Maintenance and repair supplies and equipment.

5578 Flexi-Wall Systems
PO Box 89
Liberty, SC 29657-0089
Maintenance and repair supplies for educational institutions.

5579 Flo-Pac Corporation
700 Washington Avenue N
Suite 400
Minneapolis, MN 55401-1130
612-332-6240
Fax: 612-344-1663
Maintenance and repair supplies.

5580 Four Rivers Software Systems
2400 Ardmore Boulevard
7th Floor
Pittsburgh, PA 15221-1451
412-273-6400
Fax: 412-273-6420
Maintenance and repair supplies, business and administrative software and supplies.

5581 Friendly Systems
3878 Oak Lawn Avenue
#1008-300
Dallas, TX 75219-4460
972-857-0399
Maintenance and repair supplies.

5582 GE Capitol Modular Space
40 Liberty Boulevard
Malvern, PA 19355
610-225-2836
800-523-7918
Fax: 610-225-2762
School lockers, shelving and storage facilities.

5583 Glen Products
13765 Alton Parkway
Suite A
Irvine, CA 92618-1627
800-486-4455
Storage facilities, lockers and security systems.

5584 Global Occupational Safety
22 Harbor Park Drive
Port Washington, NY 11050-4650
516-625-4466
Safety storage facilities, shelving, lockers and hardware.

5585 Graffiti Gobbler Products
6428 Blarney Stone Court
Springfield, VA 22152-2106
800-486-2512
Educational maintenance and repair supplies and equipment.

5586 H&H Enterprises
PO Box 585
Grand Haven, MI 49417-9430
616-846-8972
800-878-7777
Fax: 616-846-1004
E-mail: hhenterprises@novagate.com
Maintenance and repair supplies.

5587 HAZ-STOR
2454 Dempster Street
Des Plaines, IL 60016
217-345-4422
800-727-2067
Fax: 217-345-4475
E-mail: info@hazstor.com
http://www.hazstor.com
Manufacturer of pre-fabricated steel structures including hazardous material storage buildings and outdoor flammables lockers as well as waste compactors and drum crushers, secondary containment products and process shelters.

Roger Quinlan, National Sales Manager
Antoinette Balthazor, Marketing Coordinator

5588 HOST/Racine Industries
1405 16th Street
Racine, WI 53403-2249
800-558-9439
Fax: 262-637-1624
Maintenance and repair supplies.

5589 Hako Minuteman
111 S Rohlwing Road
Addison, IL 60101-4244
630-627-6900
Fax: 630-627-1130
Maintenance and repair supplies for educational institutions.

5590 Haws Corporation
PO Box 2070
Sparks, NV 89432-2070
775-359-4712
Fax: 775-359-7424
E-mail: haws@hawsco.com
http://www.hawsco.com
Manufacturer of drinking fountains, electric water coolers, emergency drench showers and eyewashes.

Jim Bowers, Marketing Manager

5591 Honeywell
Home & Building Control
PO Box 524
Minneapolis, MN 55440-0524
973-455-2001
Fax: 973-455-4807
Maintenance and cleaning products for educational purposes.

5592 Insta-Foam Products
2050 N Broadway Street
Joliet, IL 60435-2571
800-800-FOAM
Fax: 800-326-1054
Maintenance supplies, cleaning products and repair hardware.

5593 Interstate Coatings
1005 Highway 301 S
Wilson, NC 27895
800-533-7663
Hardware, repair, maintenance and cleaning supplies.

5594 J.A. Sexauer
PO Box 1000
White Plains, NY 10602-1000
800-431-1872
Fax: 856-439-1333
Cleaning and maintenance supplies for educational institutions.

5595 Karnak Corporation
330 Central Avenue
Clark, NJ 07066-1199
732-388-0300
800-526-4236
Fax: 732-388-9422
Maintenance and cleaning supplies.

5596 Kool Seal
Unifex Professional Maintenance Products
1499 Enterprise Pkwy
Twinsburg, OH 44087-2241
800-321-0572
Fax: 330-425-9778
Maintenance, repair and cleaning supplies.

5597 LDSystems
9535 Monroe Road
Suite 140
Charlotte, NC 28270
704-847-1338
Fax: 704-847-1354
E-mail: ds@starkpr.com
http://www.bottompump.com
Environmentally-safe bottom pump air powered spray containers to dispense cleaning supplies such as window sprays, for cooling during workouts and general storage containers.

Dick Stark

5598 List Industries
401 NW 12th Avenue
Deerfield Beach, FL 33442-1707
954-429-9155
Fax: 954-428-3843
School lockers and storage facilities.

5599 Maintenance
1051 W Liberty Street
Wooster, OH 44691-3307
330-264-6262
800-892-6701
Fax: 800-264-2578
Provides pavement maintenance products for parking lots, driveways, tennis courts, etc.

Robert E Huebner

5600 Master Bond
PO Box 522
Teaneck, NJ 07666
201-343-8983
Fax: 201-343-2132
E-mail: main@masterbond.com
http://www.masterbond.com
Repair hardware, maintenance and cleaning products for schools.

5601 Master Builders
Admixture Division
23700 Chagrin Boulevard
Cleveland, OH 44122-5554
216-831-5500
Fax: 216-839-8815
School hardware, maintenance and repair supplies and equipment.

5602 Medart
Division of Carriage Industries
PO Box 435
Garrettsville, OH 44231-0435
662-453-2506
School lockers.

5603 Modular Hardware
8190 N Brookshire Court
Tucson, AZ 85741-4037
520-744-4424
800-533-0042
Fax: 800-533-7942
School hardware, for repair and maintenance purposes.

5604 Penco Products
99 Brower Avenue
PO Box 378
Oaks, PA 19456-0378
610-666-0500
800-562-1000
Fax: 610-666-7561
E-mail: general@pencoproducts.com
http://www.pencoproducts.com
School lockers.

5605 Permagile Industries
910 Manor Lane
Bay Shore, NY 11706-7512
516-349-1100
Maintenance and cleaning products and supplies.

5606 Powr-Flite Commercial Floor Care Equipment
3301 Wichita Court
Fort Worth, TX 76140
817-551-0700
800-880-2913
Fax: 817-551-0719
http://www.powrflite.com
School maintenance supplies focusing on floor care equipment products, accessories and parts.

Curtis Walton, Contact

5607 ProCoat Products
260 Centre Street
Suite D
Holbrook, MA 02343-1074
781-767-2270
Fax: 781-767-2271
E-mail: info@procoat.com
http://www.procoat.com
Designed to restore aged and discolored acoustical ceiling tiles. Acoustical and fire retarding qualities are maintained. Ceiling restoration is cost effective, time efficient and avoids solid waste disposal. Products available also for preventative maintenance programs.

Kenneth Woolf, President

5608 Rack III High Security Bicycle Rack Company
675 Hartz Avenue
Suite 306
Danville, CA 94526-3859
800-733-1971
Lockers, bicycle racks, storage facilities and hardware.

5609 Republic Storage Systems Company
1038 Belden Avenue NE
Canton, OH 44705-1454
330-438-5800
Fax: 330-452-5071
Storage facilities, containers, maintenance products, shelving and lockers.

5610 Safety Storage
2301 Bert Drive
Hollister, CA 95023-2547
800-344-6539
Fax: 831-637-7405
Equipment, supplies and storage containers for maintenance and educational purposes.

5611 Salsbury Industries
1010 E 62nd Street
Los Angeles, CA 90001-1598
800-624-5269
Fax: 800-624-5299
E-mail: salsbury@mailboxes.com
http://www.mailboxes.com
School lockers, maintenance products and storage facilities.

5612 Servicemaster
Education Management Services
One Servicemaster Way
Downers Grove, IL 60515
800-926-9700
http://www.servicemaster.com
A provider of facility management support services to education.

5613 Sheffield Plastics
DSM Engineered Plastics Company
119 Salisbury Road
Sheffield, MA 01257-9706
413-229-8711
Maintenance and cleaning products for schools.

5614 Southern Sport Surfaces
PO Box 1817
Cumming, GA 30028-1817
770-887-3508
800-346-1632
Maintenance and cleaning products for schools.

5615 System Works
3301 Windy Ridge Parkway
Marietta, GA 30067
770-952-8444
800-868-0497
Fax: 770-955-2977
Addresses the capacity, quality and safety requirements of maintenance operations. Comprehensive and interactive it maximizes maintenance resources, people, tools and replacement parts, for increased productivity and equipment reliability, reduced inventories and accurate cost accounting.

Karen Kharlead

5616 TENTEL Corporation
4475 Golden Foothill Parkway
El Dorado Hills, CA 95762-9638
800-538-6894
Fax: 916-939-4114
Cleaning, repair and maintenance products for educational institutions.

5617 Tiffin Systems
450 Wall Street
Tiffin, OH 44883-1366
419-447-8414
800-537-0983
Fax: 419-447-8512
E-mail: tiffin@bpsom.com
http://www.tiffinmetal.com
Lockers, storage containers and shelving.

5618 Topog-E Gasket Company
1224 N Utica Avenue
Tulsa, OK 74110-4682
918-587-6649
Fax: 918-587-6961
Maintenance supplies and products.

5619 Tru-Flex Recreational Coatings
Touraine Paints
1760 Revere Beach Pkwy
Everett, MA 02149-5906
800-325-0017
Maintenance, floor care, coatings and repair supplies for upkeep of schools and institutions.

5620 Wagner Spray Tech Corporation
1770 Fernbrook Lane N
Plymouth, MN 55447-4663
763-553-7000
Fax: 763-553-7288
Maintenance supplies, floor care, cleaning and repair products and equipment.

5621 Wilmar
303 Harper Drive
Moorestown, NJ 08057
609-439-1222
800-523-7120
Fax: 800-220-3291
Maintenance and repair products, hardware and supplies.

5622 Witt Company
4454 Steel Place
Cincinnati, OH 45209-1184
513-979-3127
800-543-7417
Fax: 513-979-3134
Lockers, maintenance supplies and storage containers for educational purposes.

5623 Zep Manufacturing
1310 Seaboard Industrial Blvd NW
Atlanta, GA 30318-2807
404-352-1680
Maintenance and cleaning supplies.

Scientific Equipment

5624 Adventures Company
435 Main Street
Johnson City, NY 13790-1935
607-729-6512
800-477-6512
Fax: 607-729-4820
A full line of supplies and equipment for science and technology education.

D Hetherington

5625 Alfa Aesar
30 Bond Street
Ward Hill, MA 01835-8042
800-343-0660
Laboratory equipment and supplies.

5626 American Chemical Society
1155 16th Street NW
Washington, DC 20036-4800
202-872-4600
800-ACS-5558
Fax: 202-833-7732
Exhibits hands-on activities and programs for K-12 and college science curriculum.

5627 Arbor Scientific
PO Box 2750
Ann Arbor, MI 48106-2750
800-367-6695
Fax: 734-477-9570
E-mail: mail@arborsci.com
http://www.arborsci.com
Innovative products for Science Education.

56 pages Bi-Annual Catalog

Dave Barnes, Marketing Director

5628 Astronomy to Go
1115 Melrose Avenue
Melrose Park, PA 19027-3017
215-782-8970
Fax: 215-831-0486
E-mail: astro2go@aol.com
http://www.astronomytogo.com
Programs include Starlab Planetarium presentations, hands-on demonstrations, slides and lecture shows and energy observing sessions with our many telescopes. We are funded through our traveling museum shop which carries a large assortment of t-shirts, jewelry, gifts, books, and teaching supplies as well as an extensive selection of meteorites.

Bob Summerfield, Director

5629 CEM Corporation
3100 Smith Farm Road
Matthews, NC 28104-5044
704-821-7015
Fax: 704-821-7894
Laboratory and scientific supplies, furniture, casework and equipment.

5630 Carolina Biological Supply Company
2700 York Road
Burlington, NC 27215-3398
336-584-0381
800-334-5551
Fax: 800-222-7112
E-mail: carolina@carolina.com
http://www.carolina.com
Educational products for teachers and students of biology, molecular biology, biotechnology, chemistry, earth science, space science, physics, and mathematics. Carolina serves elementary schools through universities with living and preserved animals and plants, prepared microscope slides, microscopes, audiovisuals, books, charts, models, computer software, games, apparatus, and much more.

5631 Challenger Center for Space Science Education
1250 N Pitt Street
Alexandria, VA 22314
703-683-9740
Fax: 703-683-7546
E-mail: mail@challenger.org
http://www.challenger.org
Is a global not-for-profit education organization created in 1986 by families of the astronauts tragically lost during the last flight of the Challenger Space Shuttle. Dedicated to the educational spirit of that mission, Challenger center develops Learning Centers and other educational programs worldwide to continue the mission to engage students in science and math education

Glenn Ono, Marketing/Communications
Tracy Martin, Marketing Assistant

5632 ChronTrol Corporation
9975 Businesspark Avenue
San Diego, CA 92131-1644
619-282-8686
Fax: 619-563-6563
Scientific equipment, laboratory supplies and furniture.

5633 Classic Modular Systems
1911 Columbus Street
Two Rivers, WI 54241-2898
920-793-2269
800-558-7625
Fax: 920-793-2896
E-mail: cms@dataplusnet.com
http://www.dct.com/cms
Laboratory equipment, shelving, cabinets and markerboards.

Cathy Albers, Advertising Manager

5634 Columbia University's Biosphere 2 Center
Highway 77 & Biosphere Road
Oracle, AZ 85623
520-896-6200
Fax: 520-896-6471
Educational programs and products.

5635 Connecticut Valley Biological Supply Company
82 Valley Road
PO Box 326
Southampton, MA 01073-9536
413-527-4030
800-628-7748
Fax: 800-355-6813
E-mail: connval@ctvalleybio.com
Cultures and specimens, instruments, equipment, hands-on kits, books, software, audiovisuals, models and charts for teaching botany, zoology, life science, anatomy, physiology, genetics, astronomy, entomology, microscopy, AP Biology, microbiology, horticulture, biotechnology, earth science, natural history and environmental science.

5636 Crow Canyon Archaeological Center
23390 County Road K
Cortez, CO 81321-9408
970-565-8975
800-422-8975
Fax: 970-565-4859
E-mail: jsimpson@crowcanyon.org
http://www.crowcanyon.org
Experiential education programs in archaeology and Native American history.

Programs offered for school groups, teachers and other adults.

ISBN: 0-7872-6748-1

M Elaine Davis and Marjorie R Connelly, Author
Joyce Simpson, Director Marketing
Elaine Davis, Director Education

5637 Cuisenaire Company of America
10 Bank Street
#5026
White Plains, NY 10606-1933
914-997-2600
Fax: 914-684-6137
Science materials and equipment.

5638 DISCOVER Science Program
105 Terry Drive
Suite 120
Newtown, PA 18940-1872
800-448-3399
Fax: 215-579-8589
Features the newest developments in a wide range of science topics and provides an easy way for teachers to stay current and up-to-date in the world of science. The DISCOVER Program offers the DISCOVER magazine at the lowest possible price.

5639 Delta Biologicals
PO Box 26666
Tucson, AZ 85726-6666
520-790-7737
800-821-2502
Fax: 520-745-7888
E-mail: sales@deltabio.com
http://www.deltabio.com
Products and supplies for science and biology educators for over 30 years. Preserves specimens, laboratory furniture, microscopes, anatomy models, balances and scales, dissection supplies, lab safety supplies, multimedia, plant presses.

Lynn Hugins, Marketing
Darlene Harris, Customer Service Manager

5640 Delta Biologicals Catalog
PO Box 26666
Tucson, AZ 85726-6666
520-790-7737
800-821-2502
Fax: 520-745-7888
E-mail: sales@deltabio.com
http://www.deltabio.com

96 pages

Lynn Hugins, Marketing
Darlene Harris, Customer Service Manager

5641 Detecto Scale Corporation
203 E Daugherty Street
Webb City, MO 64870-1929
417-673-4631
800-641-2008
Fax: 417-673-5001
E-mail: detecto@cardet.com
http://www.detectoscale.com
Scientific equipment and supplies for educational laboratories.

5642 Dickson Company
930 S Westwood Avenue
Addison, IL 60101-4997
630-543-3747
Laboratory instruments, electronics, furniture and equipment.

5643 Donald K. Olson & Associates
PO Box 858
Bonsall, CA 92003-0858
Mineral and fossil samples for educational purposes.

5644 Dranetz Technologies
1000 Durham Road
Edison, NJ 08818

732-287-3680
Fax: 732-287-9014
Laboratory instruments, equipment and supplies.

5645 Edmund Scientific - Scientifics Catalog
E726 Edscorp Building
Department 16A1
Barrington, NJ 08007
856-547-3488
Fax: 856-573-6295
Over 5,000 products including a wide selection of microscopes, telescopes, astronomy aids, fiber optic kits, demonstration optics, magnets and science discover products used in science fair projects.

Nancy McGonigle, President

5646 Educational Products
1342 N I35 E
Carrollton, TX 75006
972-245-9512
Fax: 972-245-5468
Science display boards, workshop materials and science fair accessories.

5647 Edwin H. Benz Company
73 Maplehurst Avenue
Providence, RI 02908-5324
401-331-5650
Fax: 401-331-5685
E-mail: sales@benztesters.com
http://www.benztesters.com
Laboratory equipment.

5648 Electro-Steam Generator Corporation
1000 Bernard Street
Alexandria, VA 22314-1299
703-549-0664
800-634-8177
Fax: 703-836-2581
E-mail: jharlineclectrostream.com
http://www.electrosteam.com
Laboratory equipment and supplies. Manufacture steam generators for sterilizers, autoclaves, clean rooms, pure steam humidification, laboratories, steam rooms, and cleaning of all kinds.

Jack Harlin, Sales/Marketing Associate

5649 Estes-Cox Corporation
1295 H Street
Penrose, CO 81240-9676
719-372-6565
800-820-0202
Fax: 719-372-3217
E-mail: info@esteseducator.com
http://www.esteseducator.com
Supplier of model rockets, engines and supporting videos, curriculums and educational publications for K-12.

Ann Grimm, Director Education

5650 FOTODYNE
950 Walnut Ridge Drive
Hartland, WI 53029-9388
262-369-7000
800-362-3642
Fax: 262-369-7017
Biotechnology curriculum equipment.

5651 First Step Systems
PO Box 2304
Jackson, TN 38302-2304
800-831-0877
Fax: 216-361-0829
Developed an effective, safe and less expensive approach to blood exposure safety for schools and classrooms that both help comply with OSHA requirements and is easy to purchase and resupply.

Susan Staples, Account Manager
Renee Carr, Bid Support

5652 Fisher Scientific Company
1410 Wayne Avenue
Indiana, PA 15701-3940
724-357-1000
Fax: 724-357-1019
A full line of laboratory and scientific supplies and equipment for educational institutions.

5653 Fisher Scientific/EMD
3970 John Creek Court
Suite 500
Suwanee, GA 30024
770-871-4500
800-766-7000
Fax: 800-926-1166
Supplier of chemistry, biology and physics laboratory supplies and equipment.

5654 Fisons Instruments
8 Forge Parkway
Franklin, MA 02038-3157
978-524-1000
Laboratory equipment and instruments for the scientific classroom.

5655 Flinn Scientific
PO Box 219
Batavia, IL 60510-0219
630-879-6900
800-452-1261
Fax: 630-879-6962
Laboratory safety supplies.

5656 Forestry Supplies
PO Box 8397
Jackson, MS 39284-8397
601-354-3565
800-647-5368
Fax: 800-543-4203
E-mail: fsi@forestry-suppliers.com
http://www.forestry-suppliers.com
Field and lab equipment for earth, life and environmental sciences.

Ken Peacock, VP Marketing
Debbie Raddin, Education Specialist

5657 Frank Schaffer Publications
23740 Hawthorne Boulevard
Torrance, CA 90505-5927
310-378-1133
800-421-5565
Fax: 800-837-7260
Charts, animal posters, floor puzzles, resource books and more.

5658 Frey Scientific
905 Hickory Lane
Mansfield, OH 44905-2862
800-225-FREY
Fax: 419-589-1522
Name brand scientific products including Energy Physics, Earth Science, Chemistry and Applied Science. Over 12,000 products and kits for grades 5-14 are available.

5659 Great Adventure Tours
1717 Old Topanga Canyon Road
Topanga, CA 90290-3934
800-642-3933
Educational science field trips and adventures.

5660 Guided Discoveries
PO Box 1360
Claremont, CA 91711-1360
Outdoor educational science programs.

5661 HACH Company
PO Box 389
Loveland, CO 80539-0389
970-669-3050
Fax: 970-669-2932
Water and soil test kits for field and laboratory work.

5662 Heathkit Educational Systems
455 Riverview Drive
Benton Harbor, MI 49022-5015
616-925-6000
800-253-0570
Fax: 616-925-3895
Electronics educational products from basic electricity to high-tech lasers and microscopes and beyond. Comprehensive line of different media to fit varied applications. Including Computer-Aided Instruction and Computer-Aided Troubleshooting services and Heathkit's PC Servicing, Troubleshooting and Networking courses.

Carolyn Feltner, Sales Coordinator
Patrick Beckett, Marketing Manager

5663 Holometrix
25 Wiggins Avenue
Bedford, MA 01730-2314
781-275-3300
Fax: 781-275-3705
Laboratory instruments.

5664 Howell Playground Equipment
1714 E Fairchild Street
Danville, IL 61832-3616
217-442-0482
800-637-5075
Fax: 217-442-8944
E-mail: howellequipment@aol.com
http://www.primestripe.com
Playground equipment and bicycle racks.

Nina Payne, President

5665 Hubbard Scientific
PO Box 2121
Fort Collins, CO 80522-2121
Earth science and life science models, kits, globes and curriculum materials.

5666 Innova Corporation
115 George Lamb Road
Bernardston, MA 01337-9742
Science kits and globes.

5667 Insect Lore
PO Box 1535
Shafter, CA 93263-1535
661-746-6047
800-548-3284
Fax: 661-746-0334
E-mail: orders@insectlore.com
http://www.insectlore.com
Science and nature materials for preschool through grade 6. Raises butterflies, frogs, ladybugs and more. Features books, curriculum units, videos, puppet, posters, and other nature oriented products.

5668 Insights Visual Productions
PO Box 230644
Encinitas, CA 92023-0644
800-942-0528
Laboratory instruments, manuals, and supplies.

5669 Instron Corporation
100 Royall Street
Canton, MA 02021-1089
781-828-2500
Fax: 781-575-5776
Laboratory and scientific equipment, supplies and furniture.

5670 Johnsonite
16910 Munn Road
Chagrin Falls, OH 44023-5493
800-899-8916
Fax: 440-632-5643
Physical education mats, matting and
floors.

5671 Justrite Manufacturing Company
2454 E Dempster Street
Des Plaines, IL 60016-5315
847-298-9250
Fax: 847-298-3429
E-mail: justrite@justritemfg.com
http://www.justritemfg.com
Supplies and equipment aimed at the scientific classroom or laboratory.

5672 KLM Bioscientific
8888 Clairemont Mesa Boulevard
Suite D
San Diego, CA 92123
858-571-5562
Fax: 858-571-5587
A mail order company that provides high
quality, reasonably priced, on time living
and preserved biological specimens. The
Biology Store also carries a wide range of
instructional materials including books,
charts, models and videos. Also available
is a wide range of general labware.

Loli Victorio, President

**5673 Ken-a-Vision Manufacturing
Company**
5615 Raytown Road
Kansas City, MO 64133-3388
816-353-4787
Fax: 816-358-5072
E-mail: info@ken-a-vision.com
http://www.ken-a-vision.com
Video Flex, Vison Viewer, Pupil CAM, Microscopes and Microrojectors

Steve Dunn, Domestic/International Op.
Ben Hoke, Sales Manger

5674 Kepro Circuit Systems
3640 Scarlet Oak Boulevard
Kirkwood, MO 63122-6606
800-325-3878
Fax: 636-861-9109
Laboratory equipment.

5675 Kewaunee Scientific Corporation
2700 W Front Street
Statesville, NC 28677-2894
704-873-7202
Fax: 704-873-1275
E-mail: humanresources@kewaunee.com
http://www.kewaunee.com
Science and laboratory supplies.

Bob Neals, Human Resources

5676 Knex Education Catalog
Knex Education
2990 Bergey Road
PO Box 700
Hatfield, PA 19440-0700
888-ABC-KNEX
E-mail: abcknex@knex.com
http://www.knexeducation.com
Hands-on, award-winning curriculum supported K-12 math, science and technology
sets.

5677 Koffler Sales Company
100A Oakwood Road e
Lake Zurich, IL 60047-1524
847-438-1152
800-323-0951
Fax: 847-438-1514
http://www.kofflersales.com
Floor mats, Matting and stair treads.

5678 Komodo Dragon
PO Box 822
The Dalles, OR 97058-0822
541-773-5808
Museum-quality fossils and minerals.

5679 Kreonite
715 E 10th Street N
Wichita, KS 67214-2918
316-263-1111
Fax: 316-263-6829
Laboratory equipment, furniture and hardware.

5680 Kruger & Eckels
1406 E Wilshire Avenue
Santa Ana, CA 92705-4423
714-547-5165
Fax: 714-547-2009
Laboratory and scientific instruments for
institutional or educational use.

5681 LEGO Data
PO Box 1600
Enfield, CT 06083-1600
860-749-2291
Fax: 860-763-7477
Curriculum programs and materials for science education.

5682 LINX System
Science Source
PO Box 727
Waldoboro, ME 04572-0727
207-832-6344
800-299-5469
Fax: 207-832-7281
E-mail: info@thesciencesource.com
http://www.thesciencesource.com
A building system that integrates science,
mathematics and technology at the K-9
level.

5683 Lab Safety Supply
PO Box 1368
Janesville, WI 53547-1368
608-754-2345
Fax: 800-543-9910
Extensive variety of school products, including lab and safety apparel and
floorcoverings.

5684 Lab Volt Systems
PO Box 686
Farmingdale, NJ 07727-0686
Educational materials and equipment for
the science educator.

5685 Lab-Aids
17 Colt Center
Ronkonkoma, NY 11779-6949
631-737-1133
800-381-8003
Fax: 631-737-1286
E-mail: mkt@lab-aids.com
http://www.lab-aids.com
Science kits, published curriculum materials.

John Weatherby, Sales/Marketing
Director
David M Frank, President

5686 Labconco Corporation
8811 Prospect Avenue
Kansas City, MO 64132-2696
816-333-8811
Fax: 816-363-0130
Laboratory equipment and supplies.

5687 Lakeside Manufacturing
1977 S Allis Street
Milwaukee, WI 53207-1295
414-481-3900
Fax: 414-481-9313

Laboratory and scientific instruments, equipment, furniture and supplies.

5688 Lane Science Equipment Company
225 W 34th Street
Suite 1412
New York, NY 10122-1496
212-563-0663
Fax: 212-465-9440
Scientific equipment, technology and supplies.

5689 Lasy USA
1309 Webster Avenue
Fort Collins, CO 80524-2756
800-444-2126
Fax: 970-221-4352
Building sets that encourage children to encounter technology through problem solving activities, planning, co-operation and perseverance.
Allows students to build and learn programming
skills in areas of communication, construction,
manufacturing and transportation.

Dave Nayak

5690 Learning Technologies
40 Cameron Avenue
Somerville, MA 02144-2404
617-628-1459
800-537-8703
Fax: 617-628-8606
E-mail: starlab@starlab.com
http://www.starlab.com
STARLAB portable planetarium systems and the
Project STAR hands-on science materials.

Jane Sadler, President

5691 Leica Microsystems EAD
PO Box 123
Buffalo, NY 14240-0123
716-686-3000
Fax: 716-686-3085
Educational microscopes for elementary through
university applications.

5692 Life Technologies
7335 Executive Way
Suite A
Frederick, MD 21704-8354
716-774-6700
800-952-9166
Fax: 716-774-6727
Supplier of biology and cell culture products.

5693 Lyon Electric Company
1690 Brandywine Avenue
Chula Vista, CA 91911-6021
619-216-3400
Fax: 619-216-3434
Electrical tabletop incubators for science classrooms and tabletop animal intensive care units,
hatchers and brooders.

Caroline Vazquez, Sales Manager
Jose Madrigal, Marketing Manager

5694 Magnet Source
607 S Gilbert Street
Castle Rock, CO 80104-2221
303-688-3966
888-293-9190
Fax: 303-688-5303
E-mail: magnet@magnetsource.com
http://www.magnetsource.com
Educational magnetic products and magnetic toys
designed to stimulate creativity and encourage exploration of science with fun magnets. Kits include experiments, fun games, activities and
powerful magnets. Moo Magnets, rare earth magnets, horseshoes, and bulk magnets.

Jim Madsen, Sales Manager

5695 Meiji Techno America
Meiji Techno America
2186 Bering Drive
San Jose, CA 95131-2041

408-428-9654
800-832-0060
Fax: 408-428-0472
http://www.meijitechno.com
A full line of elementary, secondary, grade school and college-level microscopes and accessories.

James J Dutkiewicz, General Manager

5696 Metrologic Instruments
Coles Road at Route 42
Blackwood, NJ 08012
800-436-3876
Fax: 856-228-0653
Manufactures low-power lasers and laser accessories for the classroom, a range of helium-neon lasers, a modulated VLD laser, optics lab, sandbox holography kit, speed of light lab, optics bench system and digital laser power meter, as well as a selection of pin carriers, mounting pins, lenses and mirrors. Sponsors the Physics Bowl, a yearly national physics competition for high school students by the American Association of Physics Teachers.

Betty Williams

5697 Modern School Supplies
PO Box 958
Hartford, CT 06143-0958
860-243-9565
Fax: 800-934-7206
Products for hands-on science education.

5698 Mohon International
1600 Porter Court
Paris, TN 38242
731-642-4251
Fax: 731-642-4262
Classroom equipment and supplies, directed at the scientific classroom and laboratory.

5699 Museum Products Company
84 Route 27
Mystic, CT 06355-1226
860-536-6433
800-395-5400
Fax: 860-572-9589
E-mail: museumprod@aol.com
http://www.museumproducts.net
Field guides, rock collections, environmental puzzles, posters, charts, books, magnets, magnifiers, microscopes and other lab equipment. Also weather simulators, physics demonstration, games, toys in space, animal track replicas and fossils. Free catalog.

John Bannister, President

5700 Nalge Company
PO Box 20365
Rochester, NY 14602-0365
585-586-8800
800-625-4327
Fax: 585-586-8987
Plastic labware and safety products for the scientific classroom.

5701 National Instruments
6504 Bridge Point Parkway
Austin, TX 78730-5039
512-794-0100
Fax: 512-683-5794
Laboratory/scientific instruments.

5702 National Optical & Scientific Instruments
11113 Landmark 35 Drive
San Antonio, TX 78233-5786
210-590-7010
800-275-3716
Fax: 210-590-1104
E-mail: natlopt@sbcglobal.net
http://www.nationaloptical.com

Wholesale distributor of national comppound, stero and digital miocroscopes for K-12 and college.

Michael Hart, Director Sales/Marketing

5703 Ohaus Corporation
19 A Chapin Road
Pine Brook, NJ 07058-1408
973-377-9000
800-672-7722
Fax: 973-593-0359
Scientific supplies and equipment for the classroom or laboratory.

5704 PASCO Scientific
10101 Foothills Boulevard
Roseville, CA 95747-7100
916-786-3800
800-772-8700
Fax: 916-786-7565
E-mail: jbrown@pasco.com
http://www.pasco.com
US manufacturers of physics apparatus and probe warer that enable teachers to improve science literacy and meet the standards

Justine Brown, Copy Writer

5705 Quest Aerospace Education
350 E 18th Street
Yuma, AZ 85364
602-595-9506
Fax: 520-783-9534
A complete line of model rockets and related teaching materials.

5706 Resources for Teaching Elementary School Science
National Academy Press
Arts & Industries Bldg Room 1201
900 Jefferson Drive SW
Washington, DC 20560-0403
202-287-2063
Fax: 202-287-2070
E-mail: outreach@nas.edu
http://www.si.edu
Resource guides for elementary, middle school, and high school science teachers. Annotated guides to hands-on, inquiry-centered curriculum materials and sources of help in teaching science from kindergarten through sixth grades. Produced by the National Science Resources Center.

National Science Resources Center, Author
Douglas Lapp, Executive Director

5707 Rheometrics
1 Possumtown Road
Piscataway, NJ 08854-2100
732-560-8550
Laboratory/science supplies and equipment.

5708 SARUT
107 Horatio Street
New York, NY 10014-1569
212-691-9453
Science and nature-related educational tools.

5709 Safe-T-Rack Systems
4325 Dominguez Road
Suite A
Rocklin, CA 95677-2146
916-632-1121
Fax: 916-632-1173
Laboratory furniture, safety storage containers and equipment.

5710 Sargent-Welch Scientific Company
911 Commerce Court
Buffalo Grove, IL 60089-2375
847-459-6625
Models, books and instruments for the scientific classroom.

5711 Science Instruments Company
6122 Reisterstown Road
Baltimore, MD 21215-3423
410-358-7810
Develops, manufactures and markets unique hands-on programs in biotechnology, biomedical instrumentation, telecommunications, electronics and industrial controls.

5712 Science Source
PO Box 727
Waldoboro, ME 04572-0727
207-832-6344
800-299-5469
Fax: 207-832-7281
E-mail: info@thesciencesource.com
http://www.thesciencesource.com
Design technology books, teacher resource and student books on design and technology, design technology materials, equipment and supplies used in the construction of design challenges.

Michelle Winter, Sales/Marketing Support
Rudolf Graf, President

5713 Science for Today & Tomorrow
1840 E 12th Street
Mishawaka, IN 46544
574-258-5397
Fax: 574-258-5594
Hands-on science activities packaged for K-3 students.

5714 Scientific Laser Connection, Incorporated
5021 N 55th Avenue
Suite 10
Glendale, AZ 85301-7535
623-939-6711
877-668-7844
Fax: 623-939-3369
E-mail: sales@slclaser.com
http://www.slclasers.com
Laser education modules.

Don Morris, President
Travis Gatrin, Service

5715 Shain/Shop-Bilt
509 Hemlock Street
Philipsburg, PA 16866-2937
814-342-2820
Fax: 814-342-6180
Laboratory casework and cabinets.

5716 Sheldon Lab Systems
PO Box 836
Crystal Springs, MS 39059-0836
601-892-2731
Fax: 601-892-4364
Laboratory casework and technical equipment for K-12, college and university level.

5717 Skilcraft
CRAFT House Corporation
328 N Westwood Avenue
Toledo, OH 43607-3317
419-537-9090
Fax: 419-537-9160
Microchemistry sets.

5718 Skullduggery Kits
624 S B Street
Tustin, CA 92780-4318
800-336-7745
Fax: 714-832-1215
Social studies kits offers hands-on learning, art projects, complete lesson plans, authentic replicas, and challenging products designed for small groups of students with increasing levels of difficulty.

5719 Skulls Unlimited International
10313 S Sunnylane Road
Oklahoma City, OK 73160

405-794-9300
800-659-SKUL
Fax: 405-794-6985
E-mail: sales@skullsunlimited.com
http://www.skullsunlimited.com
Leading supplier of specimen supplies to the educational community.

5720 Society of Automotive Engineers

400 Commonwealth Drive
Warrendale, PA 15086-7511
724-776-4841
877-606-7323
Fax: 724-776-5760
E-mail: info@sae.org
http://www.sae.org
Award-winning science unit for grades 4-6.

Steve Yaeger, Corporate PR Manager
Kathleen O'Conner, K-12 Education Program Mgr

5721 Southern Precision Instruments Company

3419 E Commerce Street
San Antonio, TX 78220-1322
210-212-5055
800-417-5055
Fax: 210-212-5062
E-mail: spico@flash.net
http://www.flash.net/spico
Microscopes and microprojectors for grades K-1-K-12 and college levels. Stereo and compound microscopes, along with CCTV color systems.

Victor Spiroff, VP/General Manager

5722 Southland Instruments

17741 Metzler Lane
Unit A
Huntington Beach, CA 92647-6246
714-847-5007
Fax: 714-893-3613
Microscopes.

5723 Spectronics Corporation

956 Brush Hollow Road
Westbury, NY 11590-1714
516-333-4840
800-274-8888
Fax: 800-491-6868
E-mail: vvvv@aol.com
http://www.spectroline.com
Laboratory and scientific classroom equipment, hardware and shelving.

Gloria Blusk, Manager Customer Service
Vincent McKenna, Publicist

5724 Spitz

Transnational Industries
PO Box 198
Chadds Ford, PA 19317-0198
215-459-5200
Offers scientific and laboratory instruments and accessories.

5725 Swift Instruments

1190 N 4th Street
San Jose, CA 95112-4946
408-293-2380
Educational microscopes and other laboratory instruments.

5726 TEDCO

498 S Washington Street
Hagerstown, IN 47346-1596
765-489-4527
800-654-6357
Fax: 765-489-5752
E-mail: sales@tedcotoys.com
http://www.tedcotoys.com
Bill Nye Extreme Gyro, Prisms, Educational Toys Solar Science Kit.

Jane Shadle

5727 Telaire Systems

6489 Calle Real
Goleta, CA 93117-1538
805-964-1699
Fax: 805-964-2129
Laboratory instruments and hardware.

5728 Tooltron Industries

103 Parkway
Boerne, TX 78006-9224
830-249-8277
800-293-8134
Fax: 830-755-8134
E-mail: easyleut@gvtc.comt
http://www.tooltron.com
Scientific hardware and laboratory equipment, including instruments and accessories. School scissors and craft supplies.

Thomas Love, Owner/VP Marketing

5729 Triops

PO Box 10852
Pensacola, FL 32524-0852
850-479-4415
800-200-DINO
Fax: 850-479-3315
E-mail: triopsinc@aol.com
http://www.triops.com
Classroom activities and kits in environmental, ecological and biological sciences.

Dr. Eugene Hull, President
Peter Bender, Office Manager

5730 Trippense Planetarium Company

Science First
95 Botsford Place
Buffalo, NY 14216
716-874-0133
800-875-3214
Fax: 716-874-9853
E-mail: info@sciencefirst.com
http://www.sciencefirst.com
Astronomy and earth science models and materials, including the Trippense planetarium, Elementary planetarium, Copernican and Ptolemic solar systems, Milky Way model, Explore Celestial Globes and the patented top quality educational astronomy models since 1905.

Kris Spors, Customer Service Manager
Nancy Bell, President

5731 Unilab

967 Mabury Road
San Jose, CA 95133
800-288-9850
Fax: 408-975-1035
E-mail: unilab@richnet.net
http://www.unilabinc.com
Designs and manufactures products for teaching science and technology.

Gerald A Beer, VP

5732 Vibrac Corporation

16 Columbia Drive
Amherst, NH 03031-2304
603-882-6777
Fax: 603-271-3454
Scientific instruments and hardware.

5733 Wild Goose Company

5181 S 300 W
Murray, UT 84107-4709
801-466-1172
Hands-on science kits for elementary-aged students 3 and up and resource books for all levels of general science.

5734 Wildlife Supply Company

95 Botsford Place
Buffalo, NY 14216-d
716-877-9518
800-799-8301
Fax: 716-874-9853
E-mail: goto@wildco.com
http://www.wildco.com
Aquatic sampling equipment including Fieldmaster Field Kits, Water Bottle Kits, Secchi Disks, line and messengers and a NEW Mini Ponar bottom grab. Also, a variety of professional Wildco bottom grabs, water bottles, plankton nets, hand corers and other materials.

Aaron Bell, Product Manager
Bruce Izard, Customer Service Manager

5735 WoodKrafter Kits

PO Box 808
Yarmouth, ME 04096-0808
207-846-3722
Fax: 207-846-1019
Science kits, hands-on curriculum-based science kits for ages 4 and up, classroom packs, supplies and science materials also available.

Sports & Playground Equipment

5736 American Playground Corporation

6406 Production Drive
Anderson, IN 46013-9408
765-642-0288
800-541-1602
Fax: 765-649-7162
E-mail: sales@american-playgroud.com
http://www.american-playground.com
Playground equipment and supplies.

Julie Morson, Inside Sales Manager
Marty Bloyd, General Manager

5737 American Swing Products

2533 N Carson Street
Suite 1062
Carson City, NV 89706-0147
800-433-2573
800-433-2573
Fax: 775-883-4874
E-mail: play@americanswing.com
http://www.americanswing.com
Replacement playground parts, including commercial and residential swing sets, swing hangers for pipes and wood beams, spring animals, S-hooks, spring connectors, and more.

Susan Watson, President

5738 BCI Burke Company

660 Van Dyne Road
Fond Du Lac, WI 54937-1447
920-921-9220
Fax: 920-921-9566
Playground equipment.

5739 Belson Manufacturing

111 N River Road
North Aurora, IL 60542-1396
800-323-5664
Playground equipment.

5740 Colorado Time Systems

1551 E 11th Street
Loveland, CO 80537-5056
970-667-1000
800-279-0111
Fax: 970-667-5876
E-mail: sales@coloradotimes.com
http://www.coloradotime.com
Been the system of choice for sports timing and scoring. Has a timing system for almost every sport including swimming, basketball, football, baseball, track, soccer and most others. Has a wide variety of displays ranging from fixed digit scoreboards to animation LED boards to fullcolor video displays and ribbon boards.

Randy Flint, Sr Sales Representative
Rick Connell, CDS Sales Manager

5741 Constructive Playthings
1227 E 119th Street
Grandview, MO 64030-1178
Playground, recreational and indoor fun equipment for children grades PreK-3.

5742 Creative Outdoor Designs
142 Pond Drive
Lexington, SC 29073-8009
803-957-9259
Fax: 803-957-7152
Playground equipment.

5743 Curtis Marketing Corporation
2550 Rigel Road
Venice, FL 34293-3200
941-493-8085
Playground equipment.

5744 GameTime
PO Box 680121
Fort Payne, AL 35968-0099
256-845-5610
800-235-2440
Fax: 256-845-9361
E-mail: info@gametime.com
http://www.gametime.com
Playground equipment.

Doris Dellinger, Marketing Service Manager

5745 Gared Sports
707 N 2nd Street
Suite 220
Saint Louis, MO 63102
800-325-2682
Fax: 314-421-6014
E-mail: laura@garedsports.com
http://www.garedsports.com
Basketball, Volleyball, Soccer, Equipment and training aids for indoor and outdoor facilities.

Laura St George, Sales/Marketing Manager

5746 Gerstung/Gym-Thing
6308 Blair Hill Lane
Baltimore, MD 21209-2102
800-922-3575
Physical education mats, matting and floorcoverings.

5747 Grounds for Play
1401 E Dallas Road
Mansfield, TX 76063
817-477-5482
800-552-7529
Fax: 817-477-1140
E-mail: jimdempsey@groundsforplay.com
http://www.groundsforplay.com
Playground equipment, flooring, floorcoverings, play eviroment design, lanscape architecure, insatllation, and safety insepection.

Jim Dempsey, Senior VP
Emily Smith, Office Manager

5748 Iron Mountain Forge
One Iron Mountain Drive
Farmington, MO 63640
800-325-8828
Fax: 573-760-7441
Playground equipment.

5749 JCH International
978 E Hermitage Road NE
Rome, GA 30161-9641
800-328-9203
Coverings, mats and physical education matting.

5750 Jaypro
Jaypro Sports
976 Hartford Tpke
Waterford, CT 06385-4002
860-447-3001
800-243-0533
Fax: 860-444-1779
E-mail: info@jaypro.com
http://www.jaypro.com
Sports equipment.

Linda Andels, Marketing Manager
Bill Wild, VP Sales/Marketing

5751 Kidstuff Playsystems
5400 Miller Avenue
Gary, IN 46403-2844
800-255-0153
Fax: 219-938-3340
E-mail: rhagelberg@kidstuffplaysystems.com
http://www.fun-zone.com
Preschool and grade school playground equipment, Health Trek Fitness Course, park site furnishings.

Dick Hagelberg, CEO

5752 Kompan
7717 New Market Street
Olympia, WA 98501
360-943-6374
800-426-9788
Fax: 360-943-5575
http://www.kompan.com
Unique playgrond equipment.

Tom Grover, Marketing Director

5753 LA Steelcraft Products
1975 Lincoln Avenue
Pasadena, CA 91103-1395
626-798-7401
800-371-2438
Fax: 626-798-1482
E-mail: info@lasteelcraft.com
http://www.lasteelcraft.com
Manufacturer of quality athletic, park and playground equipment for schools, parks and industry. Features indoor/outdoor fiberglass furniture, court and field equipment, site furnishings, bike racks, flagpoles, baseball and basketball backstops.

James D Holt, President
John C Gaudesi, COO

5754 Landscape Structures
PO Box 198
Delano, MN 55328-0198
612-972-3391
Playground equipment.

5755 MMI-Federal Marketing Service
PO Box 241367
Montgomery, AL 36124-1367
334-286-0700
Fax: 334-286-0711
Playground equipment, sports timers, clocks and school supplies.

5756 Matworks
Division of Janitex Rug Service Corporation
11900 Old Baltimore Pike
Beltsville, MD 20705-1265
800-523-5179
Fax: 301-595-0740
Mats, matting and floorcoverings for entrances, gymnasiums, and all other facilities where the potential for slip and fall exists.

5757 Miracle Recreation Equipment Company
PO Box 420
Monett, MO 65708-0420
417-235-6917
Fax: 417-235-6816
Playground and recreation equipment.

5758 National Teaching Aids
PO Box 2121
Fort Collins, CO 80522
970-484-7445
800-289-9299
Fax: 970-484-1198
E-mail: bevans@amep.com
http://www.hubbardscientific.com
Learning math, alphabet, and geography skills is easy with our Clever Catch Balls. These colorful 24-inch inflatable vinyl balls provide an excellent way for children to practice math, alphabet and geography skills. Excellent learning tool in organized classroom activities, on the playground, or at home.

Barbara Evans, Customer Service Manager
Candy Coffman, National Sales Manger

5759 New Braunfels General Store International
3150 Interstate H 35 S
New Braunfels, TX 78130-7927
830-620-4000
Fax: 830-620-0598
Playground equipment, supplies and classroom supplies.

5760 Outback Play Centers
1280 W Main Street
Sun Prairie, WI 53590-0010
608-825-2140
800-338-0522
Fax: 608-825-2114
http://www.outbackplaycenters.com
Playground equipment.

Jack Garczynskl, President

5761 PlayDesigns
1000 Buffalo Road
Lewisburg, PA 17837-9795
800-327-7571
Fax: 570-522-3030
E-mail: webmaster@playdesigns.com
http://www.playdesigns.com
Playground and recreational equipment, flooring and matting.

5762 Playground Environments
22 Old Country Road
PO Box 578
Quogue, NY 11959
631-231-1300
800-662-0922
Fax: 631-231-1329
E-mail: peplay@mindspring.com
Designs and manufactures integrated play and recreational areas for children, providing them with new experiences in a safe, accessible, educationally supportive and fun environment.

5763 Playnix
3530 S Logan Street
Englewood, CO 80110-3731
303-761-5630
Fax: 303-781-6749
Wood products and playground equipment.

5764 Playworld Systems
1000 Buffalo Road
Lewisburg, PA 17837-9795
570-522-9800
800-233-8404
Fax: 570-522-3030
E-mail: webmaster@playworldsystems.com
http://www.playworldsystems.com
Playground and recreational equipment.

5765 Porter Athletic Equipment Company
Porter Athletic Equipment Company
2500 S 25th Avenue
Broadview, IL 60155-3870
708-338-2000
800-947-6783
Fax: 708-338-2060
E-mail: porter@porter-ath.com
http://www.porter-ath.com

Athletic equipment, floorcoverings, mats and supplies.

Dan Morgan, VP Sales/Marketing

5766 Quality Industries
PO Box 765
Hillsdale, MI 49242-0765
800-766-9458
Fax: 517-439-1878
Recycled plastic park and playground equipment.

5767 Real ACT Prep Guide
Peterson's, A Nelnet Company
Princeton Pike Corporate Center
2000 Lenox Drive PO Box 67005
Lawrenceville, NJ 08648
609-896-1800
800-338-3282
Fax: 609-896-4531
Familiarizes students with the test's format, reviews skills, and provides the all-important practice that helps build confidence.

621 pages
ISBN: 0-768919-75-4

Elaine Bender, Mark Weinfeld, et al., Author

5768 Recreation Creations
PO Box 955
Hillsdale, MI 49242-0955
517-439-0300
800-888-0977
Fax: 517-439-0303
Heavy duty park and playground equipment for school and public use. Equipment is both colorful and safe.

DC Shaneour

5769 Roppe Corporation
1602 N Union Street
Fostoria, OH 44830-1958
419-435-8546
Fax: 419-435-1056
Floorcoverings, mats and matting.

5770 Safety Play
10460 Roosevelt Boulevard
#295
St Petersburgh, FL 33716-3818
727-522-0061
888-878-0244
Fax: 727-522-0061
http://www.mindspring.com
Playground and recreational accident consultants. Experienced in insepctions, design, expert witness. Creators of Playground Safety Signs as required to be on the playground.

Scott Burmon, Contact

5771 Sport Court
939 S 700 W
Salt Lake City, UT 84104-1504
801-972-0260
800-421-8112
Fax: 801-975-7752
E-mail: info@sportcourt.com
http://www.sportcourt.com
Sport flooring, portable flooring, outdoor-indoor educational institutions.

Finnika Lundmark, Director Marketing

5772 Sport Floors
PO Box 1478
Cartersville, GA 30120-1478
800-322-3567
Fax: 574-293-2381
Sport floors, flooring, floorcoverings, mats and matting.

5773 Sportmaster
6031 Broad Street Mall
Pittsburgh, PA 15206-3009
412-243-5100
Fax: 412-731-3052
Playground equipment, sports timers and clocks.

5774 Stackhouse Athletic Equipment Company
1505 Front Street NE
Salem, OR 97303-6949
503-363-1840
Fax: 503-363-0511
E-mail: bob@stackhouseathletic.com
http://www.stackhouseathletic.com
Volleyball, soccer, football and baseball hardgoods.

Greg Henshaw, VP Marketing

5775 Swedes Systems - HAGS Play USA
2180 Stratingham Drive
Dublin, OH 43016-8907
Fax: 614-889-9026
Playground safety consultants.

5776 Ultra Play Systems
Parek Stuff
425 Sycamore Street
Anderson, IN 46016-1000
800-45 -LTRA
Playground and recreational equipment.

5777 Wausau Tile
PO Box 1520
Wausau, WI 54402-1520
715-359-3121
800-388-8728
Fax: 715-355-4627
E-mail: wtile@wausautile.com
http://www.wausautile.com
Playground and recreation equipment.

Rob Geurink, Furnishings Division Manager

5778 Wear Proof Mat Company
2156 W Fulton Street
Chicago, IL 60612-2392
312-733-4570
Fax: 800-322-7105
http://www.notracks.com
Mats, matting and floorcoverings for the physical education class.

5779 Wolverine Sports
745 State Circle
Ann Arbor, MI 48108-1647
734-761-5690
Fax: 800-654-4321
Playground, sports and physical fitness furniture and equipment.

General

5780 A-V Online
National Information Center for Educational Media
PO Box 8640
Albuquerque, NM 87198
505-265-3591
800-926-8328
Fax: 505-256-1080
E-mail: nicem@nicem.com
http://www.nicem.com
A CD-ROM that contains over 400,000 citations with abstracts, to non-print educational materials for all educational levels. It is available on an annual subscription basis and comes with semiannual updates.

Lisa Savard, Marketing and Sales

5781 AASA Daily News
American Association of School Administrators
801 N Quincy Street
Suite 700
Arlington, VA 22203-1730
703-528-0700
Fax: 703-841-1543
E-mail: info@aasa.org
http://www.aasa.org

Jay Goldman, Editor

5782 ACT
2201 N Dodge Street
PO Box 168
Iowa City, IA 52243-0168
319-337-1000
Fax: 319-339-3021
http://www.act.org
Help individuals and organizations make informed decisions about education and work.

5783 AMX Corporation
11995 Forestgate Drive
Dallas, TX 75243-5481
972-644-3048
Fax: 972-624-7153
Multiple products, equipment and supplies.

5784 ASC Electronics
2 Kees Pl
Merrick, NY 11566-3625
516-623-3206
Fax: 516-378-2672
High tech multimedia system. Completely software driven, featuring interactive video, audio and data student drills. Novell network. System includes CD-ROM, laserdisc and digital voice card technology.

5785 Accelerated Math
Renaissance Learning
PO Box 8036
Wisconsin Rapids, WI 54495-8036
715-424-3636
800-338-4204
Fax: 715-424-4242
E-mail: answers@renlearn.com
http://www.renlearn.com
Math management software that helps teachers increase student math achievement in grades 1 through calculus.

5786 Accelerated Reader
Renaissance Learning
PO Box 8036
Wisconsin Rapids, WI 54495-8036
715-424-3636
800-338-4204
Fax: 715-424-4242
E-mail: answers@renlearn.com
http://www.renlearn.com
Software program that helps teachers manage literature-based reading.

5787 Actrix Systems
6315 San Ignacio Avenue
San Jose, CA 95119-1202
800-422-8749
Fax: 509-744-2851
Computer networks.

5788 Allen Communications
5 Triac Center
5th Floor
Salt Lake Cty, UT 84180
801-537-7800
Fax: 801-537-7805
Software.

5789 Alltech Electronics Company
602 Garrison Street
Oceanside, CA 92054-4865
760-721-0093
Fax: 760-732-1460
Computer hardware.

5790 Anchor Pad Products
Anchor Pad Products
11105 Dana Circle
Cypress, CA 90630-5133
714-799-4071
800-626-2467
Fax: 714-799-4094
E-mail: kris@anchor.com
http://www.anchorpad.com
Cost effective physical security systems for computers, computer peripherals and office equipment.

Kris Jones, Marketing Associate
Melanie Rustle, Marketing Associate

5791 Apple Computer
1 Infinite Loop
Cupertino, CA 95014-2084
408-996-1010
Fax: 408-974-2786
Offers a wide selection of software systems and programs for the student, educator, professional and classroom use. Program areas include reading, science, social studies, history, language arts, mathematics and more.

5792 Ascom Timeplex
400 Chestnut Ridge Road
Woodcliff Lake, NJ 07675-7604
201-646-1571
Fax: 201-646-0485
Computer networks.

5793 BGS Systems
128 Technology Drive
Waltham, MA 02453-8909
617-891-0000
Facility planning and evaluation software.

5794 BLS Tutorsystems
5153 W Woodmill Drive
Wilmington, DE 19808-4067
800-545-7766
Computer software.

5795 Broderbund Software
500 Redwood Boulevard
Novato, CA 94947-6921
319-395-9626
800-223-8941
Fax: 319-395-7449
Educational software.

5796 Bulletin Boards for Busy Teachers
http://www.geocities.com/VisionTeacherwv/
Bulletin board tips and education links.

5797 CASL Software
6818 86th Street E
Puyallup, WA 98371-6450
206-845-7738

Educational software for schools and institutions in all areas of interest.

5798 CCU Software
PO Box 6724
Charleston, WV 25362-0724
800-843-5576
Fax: 800-321-4297
Educational software.

5799 CCV Software
5602 36th Street S
Fargo, ND 58104-6768
800-541-6078
Fax: 800-457-6953
All varieties of software and hardware for the educational fields of interest including language arts, math, social studies, science, history and more.

5800 Cambridge Development Laboratory
86 West Street
Waltham, MA 02451-1110
800-637-0047
Fax: 781-890-2894
E-mail: customerservice@edumatch.com
http://www.edumatch.com
Meets all educational software needs in language arts, mathematics, science, social studies early learning and special education.

5801 Chariot Software Group
123 Camino De La Reina W Building
San Diego, CA 92108-3002
619-298-0202
800-242-7468
Fax: 619-491-0021
E-mail: info@chariot.com
http://www.chariot.com
Academic software.

5802 Child's Play Software
5785 Emporium Square
Columbus, OH 43231-2802
614-833-1836
Fax: 614-833-1837
Markets learning games and creative software to schools.

5803 Claris Corporation
5201 Patrick Henry Drive
Santa Clara, CA 95054-1171
800-747-7483
Educational software.

5804 Classroom Direct
20200 E 9 Mile Road
Saint Clair Shores, MI 48080-1791
800-777-3642
Fax: 800-628-6250
Full line of hardware and software for Mac, IBM and Apple II at discount prices.

5805 College Board/SAT
45 Columbus Avenue
New York, NY 10023-6992
217-713-8000
http://http://sat.org/

5806 Computer City Direct
2000 Two Tandy Center
Fort Worth, TX 76102
800-538-0586
Hardware.

5807 Computer Friends
10200 SW Eastridge Street
Portland, OR 97225
800-547-3303
Fax: 503-643-5379
E-mail: cfi@cfriends.com
http://www.cfriends.com
Computer hardware, software and networks, printer support products.

Jimmy Moglia, Marketing Director

5808 Data Command
PO Box 548
Kankakee, IL 60901-0548
800-528-7390
Educational software.

5809 Davidson & Associates
19840 Pioneer Avenue
Torrance, CA 90503-1690
800-545-7677
Educational software and systems.

5810 Dell Computer Corporation
9595 Arboretum Boulevard
Austin, TX 78759-6337
512-338-4400
800-388-1450
Hardware.

5811 Digital Divide Network
http://www.digitaldividenetwork.org
Knowledge to help everyone succeed in the digital age.

5812 Digital Equipment Corporation
Educational Computer Systems Group
2 Iron Way
Marlboro, MA 01752
Computer hardware and networks.

5813 Don Johnston Developmental Equipment
1000 N Rand Road
Suite 115
Wauconda, IL 60084-1190
847-526-2682
800-999-4660
Develops educational software for special needs. Products include the Ukandu Series for emergent literacy, LD, ESL, students Co-Writer and Write: OutLoud.

5814 Edmark Corporation
6727 185th Avenue NE
PO Box 97021
Redmond, WA 98052-5037
425-556-8400
800-691-2986
Fax: 425-556-8430
Markets educational software.

5815 EduQuest, An IBM Company
PO Box 2150
Atlanta, GA 30301-2150
Offers exciting educational software in various fields of interest including history, social studies, reading, math and language arts, as well as computers.

5816 Educational Activities
1937 Grand Avenue
Baldwin, NY 11510-2889
516-223-4666
800-645-3739
Fax: 516-623-9282
http://www.edact.com
Supplemental materials.

Roni Hofbauer, Office Manager
Carol Stern, VP

5817 Educational Resources
1550 Executive Drive
Elgin, IL 60123-9330
630-213-8681
Fax: 630-213-8681
The largest distributor of educational software and technology in the education market. Features Mac, APL, ligs and IBM school versions, lab packs, site licenses, networking and academic versions. Hardware, accessories and multimedia is also available.

5818 Electronic Specialists Inc.
PO Box 389
Natick, MA 01760-0004
508-655-1532
810-225-4876
Fax: 508-653-0268
E-mail: esp@elect-spec.com
http://www.elect-spec.com
Computer and electronics, including networks and computer systems plus transformers and power converters.

F Stifter, President

5819 Environmental Systems Research Institute
380 New York Street
Redlands, CA 92373-8118
Demonstrates a full range of geographic information system software products.

5820 Eversan Inc.
34 Main Street
Whitesboro, NY 13492
800-383-6060
Fax: 315-736-4058
E-mail: sales&eversan.com
http://www.eversan.com
Announcement boards, scoreboards and classroom supplies, sports timers and clocks.

Michelle Moran, Sales Representative
Elsa Kucherna, Sales Representative

5821 GAMCO Educational Materials
PO Box 1911
Big Spring, TX 79721-1911
800-351-1404
Publishes software in math, language arts, reading, social studies, early childhood education and teacher tools for Macintosh, Apple, IBM and MS-DOS compatible.

5822 Games2Learn
1936 East Deere Avenue
Suite 120
Santa Ana, CA 92705
714-751-4263
888-713-4263
Fax: 714-442-0869
E-mail: CustomerService@Games2Learn.com
http://www.games2learn.com
Develops, markets and provides children and adults with quality, fun, interactive educational products designed to increase their skills in language, math and general knowledge. Creator of The Phonics Game.

5823 Gateway Learning Corporation
665 3rd Street
Suite 225
San Francisco, CA 94107
800-544-7323
http://www.hop.com
Develop and sell innovative educational products for home learning.

5824 Greene & Associates
1834 E Manhatton Drive
Tempe, AZ 85282-5857
480-491-1151
Educational software.

5825 Grolier
PO Box 1716
Danbury, CT 06816
800-371-3908
Fax: 800-456-4402
Multimedia software for education.

5826 Hubbell
Kellems Division
14 Lords Hill Road
Stonington, CT 06378-2604
860-535-5350
Fax: 860-535-1719
Computer hardware, software, systems, and networks.

5827 Indiana Cash Drawer
1315 S Miller Street
Shelbyville, IN 46176-2424
317-398-6643
Fax: 317-392-0958
Computer peripherals.

5828 Ingenuity Works
1123 Fir Avenue
Blaine, WA 98230-9702
604-412-1555
800-665-0667
Fax: 604-431-7996
E-mail: info@ingenuityworks.com
http://www.ingenuityworks.com
Publishes K-12 educational software for classroom use. Key curriculum areas include geography, keyboarding, and math (K-9). Network and district licenses are available.

Brigetta , Director Marketing

5829 Instructional Design
WIDS-Worldwide Instructional Design System
1 Foundation Circle
Waunakee, WI 53597-8914
608-849-2411
800-677-9437
Fax: 608-849-2468
E-mail: info@wids.org
http://www.wids.org
Performance-based curriculum design software and professional devlopment tools. Use software to write curriculum, implement standards, create assessments, and build in learning styles. Excellent upfront online design tool.

Robin Nickel, Associate Director

5830 Instructor
Scholastic
555 Broadway
New York, NY 10012-3919
212-343-6100
800-724-6527
Fax: 212-343-4801
http://www.scholastic.com/instructor
Edited for teachers, curriculum coordinators, principals and supervisors of primary grades through junior high school.

Monthly

Claudia Cohl, Publisher
Lynn Diamond, Advertising Director

5831 Jostens Learning Corporation
4920 Pacific Heights Boulevard
Suite 500
San Diego, CA 92121
858-587-0087
800-521-8538
Fax: 858-587-1629
Educational software and CD-ROM's.

5832 Journey Education
1325 Capital Parkway
Suite 130
Carrollton, TX 75006
800-874-9001
Fax: 972-245-3585
E-mail: sales@journeyed.com
http://www.journeyed.com
Software for students.

5833 Ken Cook Education Systems
9929 W Silver Spring Drive
PO Box 25267
Milwaukee, WI 53225-1024
800-362-2665
Fax: 414-466-0840
Classroom curricular software.

334

5834 Kensington Microwave
2855 Campus Drive
San Mateo, CA 94403-2510
650-572-2700
800-535-4242
Fax: 650-572-9675
http://www.kensington.com
Computer systems and peripherals.

5835 Lapis Technologies
1100 Marina Village Parkway
Alameda, CA 94501-1043
510-748-1600
Computer peripherals.

5836 Laser Learning Technologies
120 Lakeside Avenue
#3240
Seattle, WA 98122-6533
800-722-3505
Educational CD-ROM's and interactive videos.

5837 Lawrence Productions
1800 S 35th Street
Galesburg, MI 49053-9687
800-421-4157
Fax: 616-665-7060
More than 60 proven software titles for PreK to adult, covering problem solving, early learning and leadership skills.

5838 Learning Company
500 Redwood Boulevard
Novato, CA 94947
800-825-4420
Fax: 877-864-2275
http://www.learningcompanyschool.com
School educational software.

5839 Library Corporation, Sales & Marketing
1501 Regency Way
Woodstock, GA 30189-5487
Computer networks.

5840 LinkNet
Introlink
1400 E Touhy Avenue
Suite 260
Des Plaines, IL 60018-3339
847-390-8700
Fax: 847-390-9435
Computer networks.

5841 MECC
6160 Summit Drive N
Minneapolis, MN 55430-2100
800-685-MECC
Educational software, hardware and overhead projectors.

5842 Mamopalire of Vermont
PO Box 24
Warren, VT 05674
802-496-4095
888-496-4094
Fax: 802-496-4096
E-mail: bethumpd@wcvt.com
http://www.bethumpd.com
Provides quality educational books and board games for the whole family.

Rebecca Cahilly, President
Glenn Cahilly, CEO

5843 McGraw-Hill Educational Resources
11 W 19th Street
New York, NY 10011-4209
800-442-9685
Fax: 972-228-1982
Educational software for all areas of interest including social studies, science, mathematics and reading.

5844 Microsoft Corporation
1 Microsoft Way
Redmond, WA 98052-8300
425-882-8080
Fax: 425-936-7329
One of the largest publishers and distributors of educational software, hardware, equipment and supplies.

5845 Misty City Software
11866 Slater Avenue NE
Kirkland, WA 98034-4103
206-820-2219
800-795-0049
Fax: 425-820-4298
Publisher of Grade Machine, gradebook software for Macintosh, MS-DOS, and Apple II. Grade Machine used by thousands of teachers in hundreds of schools worldwide. Grade Machine has full-screen editing, flexible reports, large class capacity, excellent documentation and reasonable cost.

Roberta Spiro, Business Manager
Russell Cruickshanks, Sales Manager

5846 NCR Corporation
1700 S Patterson Boulevard
Dayton, OH 45479-0002
937-445-5000
Computer networks, systems (large, mini, micro, medium and personal).

5847 NetLingo The Internet Dictionary
PO Box 627
Ojai, CA 93024
805-640-3754
Fax: 805-640-3654
E-mail: info@netlingo.com
http://www.NetLingo.com
A smart-looking and easy to understand dictionary of 3000 internet terms, 1200 chat acronyms, and much more. NetLingo is a modern reference book fo international students, educators, industry professionals, and online businesses and organizations.

528 pages Paperback
ISBN: 0-9706396-7-8

Erin Jansen, Author
Erin Jansen, Author/Publisher

5848 NetZero
2555 Townsgate Road
Westlake Village, CA 91361-2650
805-418-2020
Fax: 805-418-2075
http://www.netzero.com
Free Internet access.

5849 New Century Education Corporation
220 Old New Brunswick Road
Piscataway, NJ 08854
732-981-0820
800-833-6232
Fax: 732-981-0552
E-mail: jharrison@ncecorp.com
http://www.ncecorp.com
ILS systems.

Janice Harrison, Marketing Representative

5850 OnLine Educator
http://faldo.atmos.uiuc.edu/CLA
A comprehensive archive of educational sites with useful search capabilities and descriptions of the sites.

5851 Online Computer Systems
1 Progress Drive
Horsham, PA 19044-3502
CD-ROM networking, CD-ROM titles and CD-ROM tower units.

5852 PBS TeacherSource
http://www.pbs.org/teachersource

Includes an on-line inventory of more than 1,000 free lesson plans, teacher guides and other activities designed to complement PBS television programs.

5853 Parent Link
Parlant Technology
290 N University Avenue
Provo, UT 84601
801-373-9669
800-735-2930
Fax: 801-373-9697
E-mail: info@parlant.com
http://www.parlant.com
School to home communication systems allow scholls to create messages — emails, telephone calls, web content, printed letters, about student information, grades, attendance, homework, and activities. Also provides inbound access via internet and telephone.

George Joeckel, Marketing

5854 Peopleware
1621 114th Avenue SE
Suite 120
Bellevue, WA 98004-6905
425-454-6444
Fax: 425-454-7634
Classroom curricular software.

5855 Phillips Broadband Networks
100 Fairgrounds Drive
Manlius, NY 13104-2437
315-682-9105
Fax: 315-682-1022
Computer networks.

5856 Pioneer New Media Technologies
2265 E 220th Street
Long Beach, CA 90810-1639
800-LAS-R ON
DRM-604X CD-ROM mini-changer, world's fastest CD-ROM drive for multimedia. Also offers special packages including The Mystery Reading Bundle, CLD-V2400RB which includes the CLD-V2400 LaserDisc player, educator's remote control, UC-V109BC barcode reader and membership in the Pioneers in Learning Club and The Case of the Missing Mystery Writer videodisc from Houghton Mifflin.

5857 Polaroid Corporation
575 Tech Square
Cambridge, MA 02139
781-386-2000
Fax: 781-386-3925
Computer repair, hardware and peripherals, equipment and various size systems.

5858 Power Industries
37 Walnut Street
Wellsley Hills, MA 02181
800-395-5009
Educational software.

5859 Quetzal Computers
1708 E 4th Street
Brooklyn, NY 11223-1925
718-375-1186
Computer systems and networks, peripherals and hardware.

5860 RLS Groupware
Realtime Learning Systems
2700 Connecticut Avenue NW
Washington, DC 20008-5330
202-483-1510
Classroom curricular software.

5861 Radio Shack
100 Throckmorton Street
Suite 1800
Ft. Worth, TX 76102

817-415-3700
Fax: 817-415-2335
Computer networks and peripherals.
Laura Moore, Sr VP Public Relations

5862 Rose Electronics
10850 Wilcrest Drive
Suite 900
Houston, TX 77099-3599
281-933-7673
Fax: 281-933-0044
Computer peripherals and hardware.

5863 STAR Reading & STAR Math
Renaissance Learning
PO Box 8036
Wisconsin Rapids, WI 54495-8036
715-424-3636
800-338-4204
Fax: 715-424-4242
E-mail: answers@renlearn.com
http://www.renlearn.com
Computer-adaptive tests provide instructional levels, grade equivalents and percentile ranks.

5864 SVE & Churchill Media
6677 N NW Highway
Chicago, IL 60631
773-775-9550
800-829-1900
Fax: 773-775-5091
E-mail: slucas@svemedia.com
http://www.svemedia.com
Has brought innovative media technology into america's pre-K through high school classrooms. By producing programs to satisfy state curriculum standards, SVE consistently provides educators with high-quality and award-winning videos, CD-ROMs, eLMods, and DVDs in science, social studies, english and health/guidance.

Sarah M Lucas, Communications Coordinator
Kelli Campbell, VP Marketing/Development

5865 School Cruiser
Time Cruiser Computing Corporation
9 Law Drive
3rd Floor, Ottawa, Ontario
Canada K1N 7G1
613-562-9847
877-450-9482
Fax: 613-562-4768
http://www.epals.com
School Cruiser provides online tools and resources to promote academic and community interaction. It lets you access and share school calenders, lesson plans, homework assignments, announcements and other school related information.

5866 SchoolHouse
http://www.encarta.msn.com/schoolhouse/maincontent.asp
The Encarta Lesson Collection and other educational resources.

5867 Seaman Nuclear Corporation
7315 S 1st Street
Oak Creek, WI 53154-2095
414-762-5100
Fax: 414-762-5106
Facility planning and evaluation software.

5868 Skills Bank Corporation
7104 Ambassador Road
Suite 1
Baltimore, MD 21244-2732
800-451-5726
Educational manufacturing company offering computer and electronic resources,

software, programs and systems focusing on home education and tutoring.

5869 Sleek Software Corporation
2404 Rutland Drive
Suite 600
Austin, TX 78758
800-337-5335
Fax: 888-353-2900
http://www.sleek.com
Specializes in Algorithm-Based tutorial and test-generating software.

5870 Smartstuff Software
PO Box 82284
Portland, OR 97282-0284
415-763-4799
800-671-3999
Fax: 877-278-7456
E-mail: info@smartstuff.com
http://www.smartstuff.com
Foolproof Security is a dual platform desktop security product that prevents unwanted changes to the desktop and a product line for the internet that protects browser settings, filters content, and allows guided activities.

5871 Society for Visual Education
1345 W Diversey Parkway
Chicago, IL 60614-1249
773-775-9550
Fax: 800-624-1678
Educational software dealing specifically with special education.

5872 SofterWare
540 Pennsylvania Avenue
Suite 200
Fort Washington, PA 19034-3388
215-628-0400
800-220-4111
Fax: 215-628-0585
E-mail: info@softerware.com
http://www.softerware.com
Offers software, support and administrative solutions to four markets: childcare centers, public and private schools, non-profit organizations and institutions, and camps.

5873 SpecialNet
GTE Educational Network Services
5525 N Macarthur Boulevard
Suite 320
Irving, TX 75038-2600
214-518-8500
800-927-3000
Fax: 757-852-8277
Contains news and information on trends and developments in educational services and programs. Databases, bulletin boards, school packages, student/teacher packages, online magazines, distance learning, vocational education, school health, educational laws, and more.

5874 Student Software Guide
800-874-9001
E-mail: journey.com
Discounts on a variety of software materials.

5875 Sun Microsystems
2550 Garcia Avenue
#6-13
Mountain View, CA 94043-1100
714-643-2688
800-555-9786
Fax: 650-934-9776
Computer networks and peripherals.

5876 Sunburst/Wings for Learning
101 Castleton Street
Pleasantville, NY 10570-3405

914-747-3310
800-338-3457
Fax: 914-747-4109
Educational materials, including software, print materials, videotapes, videodisc and interdisciplinary packages.

5877 Support Systems International Corporation
136 S 2nd Street
Richmond, CA 94804-2110
510-234-9090
800-777-6269
Fax: 510-233-8888
E-mail: info@support-systems-intl.com
http://www.fiberopticcableshop.com
Fiber optic patch cables, converters, and switches.

Ben Parsons, General Manager

5878 Surfside Software
PO Box 1112
East Orleans, MA 02643-1112
800-942-9008
Educational software.

5879 Target Vision
1160 Pittsford Victor Road
Suite K
Pittsford, NY 14534-3825
800-724-4044
Fax: 585-248-2354
TVI DeskTop expands your show directly to desktop PC utilizing existing LANS. View information by topics or as a screen saver. Features: graphic importing, VCR interface, advanced scheduling and more.

5880 Teacher Universe
5900 Hollis Street
Suite A
Emeryville, CA 94608
877-248-3224
Fax: 415-763-4917
E-mail: info@teacheruniverse.com
http://www.teacheruniverse.com
Creates technology-rich solutions for improving the quality of life and work for teachers worldwide.

5881 Technolink Corporation
24 Depot Square
Tuckahoe, NY 10707-4004
914-961-1900
Computer systems and electronics.

5882 Tom Snyder Productions
80 Coolidge Hill Road
Watertown, MA 02472
800-342-0236
Fax: 800-304-1254
E-mail: ask@tomsnyder.com
http://www.tomsnyder.com
Educational CD-ROM products and Internet services for schools.

5883 Tripp Lite
500 N Orleans Street
Chicago, IL 60610-4117
312-329-1601
Peripherals, hardware and computer systems.

5884 True Basic
12 Commerce Avenue
West Lebanon, NH 03784-1669
800-436-2111
Fax: 603-298-7015
E-mail: john@truebasic.com
http://www.truebasic.com
Educational software.

5885 U.S. Public School Universe Database
U.S. National Center for Education Statistics
555 New Jersey Avenue NW
Washington, DC 20001-2029

202-219-1335
85,000 public schools of elementary and secondary levels, public special education, vocational/technical education and alternative education schools.

5886 USA CityLink Project
USA CityLink Project
Floppies for Kiddies
4060 Highway 59
Mandeville, LA 70471
985-898-2158
Fax: 985-892-8535
Collects used and promotional disketts from the masses for redistribution to school groups and nonprofits throughout the county.

Carol Blake, Contact

5887 Unisys
PO Box 500
Blue Bell, PA 19424-0001
215-986-3501
Fax: 215-986-3279
A full line of computers (sizes ranging from mini/micro to medium/large and personal).

5888 Ventura Educational Systems
910 Ramona Avenue
Suite E
Grover Beach, CA 93433-2154
805-473-7383
800-336-1022
Fax: 805-473-7382
E-mail: sales@venturaes.com
http://www.venturaes.com
Publishers of curriculum based educational software for all grade levels, specializing in interactive math and science software. Programs include teacher's guide with student worksheets.

5889 Viziflex Seels
16 E Lafayette Street
Hackensack, NJ 07601-6895
201-487-8080
Peripherals, hardware and electronics, floorcoverings, mats and matting.

5890 Waterford Institute
1590 E 9400 S
Sandy, UT 84093-3009
800-767-9976
Fax: 801-572-1667
Produces children's educational software for math and reading.

5891 Web Connection
Education Week
301-280-3100
E-mail: ads@epe.org
http://www.edweek.org
Information about education suppliers.

5892 Wiremold Company
60 Woodlawn Street
W Hartford, CT 06110-2383
800-243-8421
Computer networks and peripherals.

5893 Wisconsin Technical College System Foundation
1 Foundation Cir
Waunakee, WI 53597-8914
800-821-6313
Fax: 608-849-2468
E-mail: foundation@wtcsf.tec.wi.us
Interactive videodiscs, self-paced instruction or with barcodes. Students learn faster, become more motivated and retain more information. Math, algebra and electronics courseware are also available.

5894 Word Associates
3226 Robincrest Drive
Northbrook, IL 60062-5125

847-291-1101
Fax: 847-291-0931
E-mail: microlrn@aol.com
http://www.wordassociates.com
Software tutorials featuring lessons in question format, with tutorial and test mode. 15 titles include Math SAT, 2 English SAT; US Constitution Tutor; Phraze Maze; Geometry: Planely Simple, Concepts and Proofs, Right Triangles; Life Skills Math; Algebra; Reading: Myths and More Myths, Magic and Monsters; Economics; American History. Windows, Macintosh, CD's or disks.

Software

Myrna Helfand, President
Sherry Azaria, Marketing

5895 Ztek Company
PO Box 11768
Lexington, KY 40577-1768
859-281-1611
800-247-1603
Fax: 859-281-1521
E-mail: cs@ztek.com
http://www.ztek.com
Offers physics multimedia lessons on CD-ROM, DVD, videodisc and videotape. Also, carries Pioneer New Media DVD and videodisc players as well as Bretford Manufacturing's line of audio-visual furniture.

5896 ePALS.com
Classroom Exchange
http://www.epals.com
World's largest online classroom community, connecting over 3 million students and teachers through 41,044 profiles.

5897 http://ericir.syr.edu
AskERIC
Ask a question about education and receive a personalized e-mail response in two business days.

5898 http://gsn.bilkent.edu.tr
Ballad of an EMail Terrorist
Global SchoolNet Foundation

One pitfall of the internet is danger of vulgarity and/or obscenity to a child via e-mail.

5899 http://suzyred.home.texas.net
The Little Red School House
Offers sections on music, writing, quotes, web quests, jokes, poetry, games, activities and more.

5900 www.FundRaising.Com
FundRaising.Com
800-443-5353
Internet fundraising company.

5901 www.abcteach.com
E-mail: sandkems@abcteach.com
Offers ideas and activities for kids, parents, students and teachers. Features section on many topics in education, including writing, poetry, word searches, crosswords, games, maps, mazes and more.

5902 www.abctooncenter.com
ABC Toon Center
This family orientated site offers games, cartoons, storybook, theater, information stations and more. This site is open to children of differnt languages. Can be translated into Italian, French, Spanish, German and Russian.

5903 www.americatakingaction.com
America Taking Action
Provides every school with a free, 20 page website with resources for teachers, parents, students and the community. Created entirely by involved parents, teachers and community leaders as a public service.

5904 www.awesomelibrary.org
Awesome Library
Organizes the Web with 15,000 carefully reviewed resources, including the top 5 percent in education. Offers sections of mathematics, science, social studies, english, health, physical education, technology, languages, special education, the arts and more. Features a section involved with today's current issues facing our world, like pollution, gun control, tobacco, and other changing 'hot' topics. Site can be browsed in English, German, Spanish, French or Portuguese.

5905 www.bigchalk.com
Big Chalk-The Education Network
Educational web site tailored to fit teachers' and students' needs.

5906 www.brunchbunch.org
Brunch Bunch
The foundation names all of the grants it makes after teachers who have demonstrated excellence. The foundation regularly makes significant grants to aid teachers' efforts.

5907 www.busycooks.com
BusyCooks.com
A hit with home economics teachers, enjoying free recipes and online cooking shows. Tapping into the experience of thousands to nuture your culinary creativity.

5908 www.chandra.harvard.edu
Chandra X-ray Observatory Center
Find teacher-developed, classroom-ready materials based on results from the Chandra mission. Classroom-ready activities, interactive games, activities, quizzes, and printable activities which will keep students absorbed with interest.

5909 www.cherrydale.com
Cherrydale Farms
Website offers company information, fund raising products and information, online mega mall, card shop, career opportunities and much more. Produces fine chocolates and confections. Many opportunities for schools to raise funds with various Cherrydale programs.

5910 www.cleverapple.com
Education Station
Offers links to many sites involved with education.

5911 www.edhelper.com
edhelper.com
Keeps you up to date with the latest educational news.

5912 www.education-world.com
Education World
Features and education-specific search engine with links to over 115,000 sites. Offers monthly reviews of other educational web sites, and other original content on a weekly basis.

5913 www.eduverse.com
Software developer building core technologies for powering international distance education. Features an online distance education engine, product information, news releases and more.

5914 www.efundraising.com
efundraising.com
Provides non-profit groups with quality products, low prices and superior service. Helping thousands of schools, youth sports

teams and community groups reach their fundraising goals each year.

5915 www.embracingthechild.com
Embracing the Child
Educational resource for teachers and parents that provides a structural resource for home and classroom use, lesson planning, as well as a child-safe site, for children's research, classroom use and homework fulfillment.

5916 www.enc.org
Eisenhower National Clearinghouse
For math and science teachers-anywhere in the K-12 spectrum. This organization contains a wealth of information, activities, resources, and demonstrations for the sciences and math.

5917 www.englishhlp.com
English Help
E-mail: englishhlpr@hotmail.com
This page is a walk through of Microsoft Power Point. The goal is to show in a few simple steps how to make your own website. Created by Rebecca Holland.

5918 www.expage.com/Just4teachers
Just 4 Teachers
The ultimate website for educators! Teaching tips, resources, themeunits, search engines, classroom management and sites for kids.

5919 www.fraboom.com
Fraboom
This site's tools let you specify areas within your state's standards and search for a list of 'Flying Rhinoceros' lessons that meet your criteria. Offers other information sources for teachers and students.

5920 www.globalschoolnet.org
Global Schoolhouse
Connects teachers, administrators, and parents with options and possibilities the Internet has to offer the schools of the world.

5921 www.gradebook.org/
The Classroom
Dedicated to the students and teachers of the world.

5922 www.homeworkspot.com
HomeworkSpot
A free online homework resource center developed by educators, students, parents and journalists for K-12 students. It simplifies the search for homework help, features a top-notch reference cetner, current events, virtual field trips and expeditions, extracurricular activities and study breaks, parent and teacher resources and much more.

5923 www.iearn.org
iEARN USA
Utilizes projects for students ages 6 through 19. Projects are concerned with the environment as well as arts, politics, and the health and welfare of all the Earth's citizens.

5924 www.jasonproject.org
Jason Project
Founded in 1989 as a tool for live, interactive programs for students in the fourth through eighth grades. Annual projects are funded through a variety of public corporations and governmental organizations.

5925 www.junebox.com
JuneBox.com
A classroom superstore that features the leading suppliers of educational products and services. A gateway to project ideas and educational links.

5926 www.k12planet.com
Chancery Software
Chancery Software is announcing a new school to home extension that will provide student information systems to give parents, students, and educators access to accurate information about students in one, easy-to-use website.

5927 www.kiddsmart.com
Institute for Child Development
E-mail: dcornell@kiddsmart.com
The ICD develops educational materials and resources designed to facilitate children's social and emotional development. Offers the previous materials as well as research summaries, lesson plans, training, workshops, games, multi-cultural materials and other resources to teachers, educational centers, parents, counselors, corporations, non-profits and others involved in the child-care professions.

5928 www.lessonplansearch.com
Lesson Plan Search
220 lesson plans from cooking to writing.

5929 www.lessonplanspage.com
A collection of over 1,000 free lesson plans for teachers to use in their classrooms. Lesson plans are organized by subject and grade level.

5930 www.library.thinkquest.org
Think Quest Library of Entries
The Arti FAQS 2100 Project is designed to predict how art will influence our lives in the next hundred years. Students can use available data to make reasonable predictions for the future.

5931 www.ncspearson.com
NCS Pearson
E-mail: info@ncs.com
NCS Pearson is at the forefront of the education space with curriculum, contant, tools, assessment, and interface to enterprise systems

5932 www.negaresa.org
LearningGate
For teachers, electronic web-based grade book aplication eGRader 2000. Many educational resource links as well has discussion groups, a news and events section, and even links to online shopping.

5933 www.netrover.com/~kingskid/108.html
Room 108

An educational activity center for kids. Offers lots of fun for children with educational focus; like songs, art, math, kids games, children's stories and much more. Sections with pen pal information, puzzles, crosswords, teachers store, spelling, kids sites, email, music, games and more.

5934 www.pcg.cyberbee.com
Postcard Geography
Offered to classes all over the world via the internet. Your class commits to exchanging picture postcards with all other participants. Appropriate for all ages, for public and private schools, for youth groups and for home- schools.

5935 www.pitt.edu
EdIndex
E-mail: poole@pitt.edu
A web resource for teachers and students, offers course information, MS Office tutorials, personal and professional pages, and more.

5936 www.riverdeep.net
Riverdeep Interactive Learning
Riverdeep's interactive science, language and math arts programs deliver high quality educational experiences.

5937 www.safedayeducation.com
Safe Day Education
The leader in bully prevention and street proofing education for kids; safe dating preparation programs for teens; and re-empowerment and assault prevention training for women.

5938 www.safekids.com/child_safety.htm
SafeKids.Com
Cyberspace is a fabulous tool for learning, but some of it can be exploitative and even criminal.

5939 www.sdcoe.k12.ca.us
Researches a coral reef and creates a diorama for The Cay by Theodore Taylor.

5940 www.shop2gether.com
Collective Publishing Service
We are committed to helping all schools buy better by shopping together. Building upon a scalable, dynamic procurement platform and group buying technology, we also provide a unique ecommerce system, delivering next generation procurement services over the Internet.

5941 www.spaceday.com
Space Day
Program engineered to build problem-solving and teamwork skills.

5942 www.specialednews.com
Special Education News
E-mail: info@specialednews.com
Consists of breaking news stories from Washington and around the country. These stories are complied together in the Special Education News letter is sent via e-mail once a week.

5943 www.straightscoop.org
Straight Scoop News Bureau
SSNB increases the frequency of anti-drug themes and messages in junior high and high school student media.

5944 www.tcta.org
Texas Classroom Teachers Association
Compromised of Texas educators, provides interest for teachers everywhere. Education laws and codes are presented here.

5945 www.teacherszone.com
TeachersZone.Com
Lesson plans, free stuff for teachers, contests, sites for kids, conferences and workshops, schools and organizations, job listings, products for school.

5946 www.teacherweb.com
TeacherWeb
TeacherWeb, your free personal website that's as easy to use as the bulletin board in your classroom. This site offers a secure, password-protected service.

5947 www.teachingheart.com
Teaching is A Work of Heart
Chock-full of ideas, projects, motivational thoughts, behavior ideas.

5948 www.thelearningworkshop.com
Learning Workshop.com
Services for teachers, students, and parents.
For teachers online gradebooks and grade
tracking, students can check their grades online, parents enjoy articles written expressly
for them and a tutor search by zip code.

5949 www.tutorlist.com
TutorList.com
Offers information on tips on how to find and
choose a tutor, what a tutor does, educational
news and more.

5950 www.worksafeusa.org
WorkSafeUSA
Addresses the alarming injury and death rates
experienced by America's adolescent workers. This non-profit site publishes and distributes A Teen Guide to Workplace Safety,
available in English and Spanish.

5951 www1.hp.com
Compaq Computer Corporation
Compaq is one of the leading corporations in
educational technology, working on developing solutions that will connect students,
teachers and the community.

Administration

5952 ASQC
611 E Wisconsin Avenue
Milwaukee, WI 53202-4695
800-248-1946
Fax: 414-272-1734
Business and administrative software.

5953 Anchor Pad
Anchor Pad Products
11105 Dana Cir
Cypress, CA 90630-5133
714-799-4071
800-626-2467
Fax: 714-799-4094
E-mail: anchor@anchor.com
http://www.anchorpad.com
Computer and office security

Caroline Jones, COO
Melanie Ruste, Sales/Marketing Associate

5954 Applied Business Technologies
4631 W Chester Pike
Newtown Square, PA 19073-2225
610-359-0700
800-220-2281
Fax: 610-359-9420
Computer networks and administrative software.

5955 AskSam Systems
121 S Jefferson Street
Perry, FL 32347-3232
850-584-6590
800-800-1997
Fax: 850-584-7481
E-mail: info@asksam.com
http://www.asksam.com
Business and administrative free form database software.

Dottie Sheffield, Sales Manager

5956 Autodesk Retail Products
1725 220th Street
Suite C101
Bothell, WA 98021-8809
425-487-2233
Fax: 425-486-1636
Administrative and business software.

5957 Avcom Systems
250 Cox Lane
PO Box 977
Cutchogue, NY 11935-1303
631-734-5080
800-645-1134
Fax: 631-734-7204
Supplies for making and mounting transparencies. Products includes economy and
self-adhesive mounts; transparent rolls and
sheets; markers, pens and cleaners; thermo,
computer graphics and plain-paper copier
transparency films and laminating supplies.

Joseph K Lukas

5958 Bobbing Software
67 Country Oaks Drive
Buda, TX 78610-9338
800-688-6812
Administrative software and systems.

5959 Bull HN Information Systems
Technology Park
Billerica, MA 01821
978-294-6000
Fax: 978-294-7999
Computer networks, computers (large, me-
dium, micro and mini), and supplies.

5960 Bureau of Electronic Publishing
745 Alexander Road
#728
Princeton, NJ 08540-6343
973-808-2700
Administrative software, hardware and systems.

5961 CRS
17440 Dallas Parkway
Suite 120
Dallas, TX 75287-7307
800-433-9239
Administrative software and systems.

5962 Campus America
900 E Hill Avenue
Suite 205
Knoxville, TN 37915-2580
865-523-4477
877-536-0222
Fax: 617-492-9081
http://www.campus.com
Computer supplies, equipment, systems and
networks.

5963 Century Consultants
150 Airport Road
Suite 1500
Lakewood, NJ 08701-3309
732-363-9300
Fax: 732-363-9374
E-mail: marketing@centuryltd.com
http://www.centuryltd.com
Develops, markets, and services Oracle
based web-enabled Management software,
STAR_BASE, for school districts K-12.

5964 Computer Resources
PO Box 60
Barrington, NH 03825-0060
603-664-5811
Fax: 603-664-5864
The Modular Management System for
Schools is a school administrative software
system designed to handle all student record
keeping and course scheduling needs. A totally integrated modular system built around
a central Student Master File. Additional
modules handle student scheduling, grades,
attendance and discipline reporting.

Raymond J Perreault, VP Marketing
Robert W Cook, National Sales Manager

5965 Cyborg Systems
2 N Riverside Plaza
Chicago, IL 60606-2600
312-454-1865
Administrative and business software programs.

5966 Diskovery Educational Systems
1860 Old Okeechobee Road
Suite 105
West Palm Beach, FL 33409-5281
561-683-8410
800-331-5489
Fax: 561-683-8416
http://www.diskovery.com
Computer supplies, equipment, and various
size systems.

5967 Doron Precision Systems
Doron Precision Systems
174 Court Street
PO Box 400
Binghamton, NY 13902-0400
607-772-1610
Fax: 607-772-6760
http://www.doronprecision.com
Business and classroom curriculum software.
Driving Simulation Systems and Entertain-
ment Simulation Systems.

5968 Educational Data Center
180 De La Salle Drive
Romeoville, IL 60446-1895
800-451-7673
Fax: 815-838-9412
Administration software.

**5969 EnrollForecast: K-12 Enrollment
Forecasting Program**
Association of School Business Officials
Int'l
11401 N Shore Drive
Reston, VA 20190-4232
703-478-0405
Fax: 703-478-0205
A powerful planning tool that helps project
student enrollment.

Peg D Kirkpatrick, Editor/Publisher
Robert Gluck, Managing Editor

5970 Epson America
20770 Madrona Avenue
Torrance, CA 90503-3778
800-289-3776
Computer repair and peripherals.

**5971 FMJ/PAD.LOCK Computer Security
Systems**
741 E 223rd Street
Carson, CA 90745-4111
310-549-3221
800-322-3365
Fax: 310-549-2921
E-mail: info@fmjpadlock.com
Computer peripherals, supplies and equip-
ment.

Tom Separa

5972 Geist
Geist Manufacturing
1821 Yolande Avenue
Lincoln, NE 68521-1835
402-474-3400
Fax: 402-474-4369
E-mail: products@geistmfg.com
http://www.geistmfg.com
Power distribution for racks, cabinets and
data centers.

Terri Rockeman, Customer Service
Supervisor

5973 Global Computer Supplies
11 Harbor Park Drive
Port Washington, NY 11050-4622

516-625-6200
Fax: 516-484-8533
Computer supplies, equipment, hardware, software and systems.

5974 Harrington Software
658 Ridgewood Road
Maplewood, NJ 07040-2536
201-761-5914
Administrative and business software.

5975 Information Design
7009 S Potomac Street
Suite 110
Englewood, CO 80112
303-792-2990
800-776-2469
Fax: 303-792-2378
E-mail: sales@idesgninc.com
http://www.idesigninc.com
Administrative and business software including systems focusing on payroll, personnel, financial accounting, purchasing, budgeting, fixed asset accounting and salary administration.

5976 International Rotex
7171 Telegraph Road
Los Angeles, CA 90040-3227
800-648-1871
Computer supplies.

5977 Jay Klein Productions Grade Busters
1695 Summit Point Court
Colorado Springs, CO 80919-3444
719-599-8786
Fax: 719-599-8312
A line of teacher productivity tools, the most highly recognized integrated gradebooks, attendance records, seating charts and scantron packages in K-12 education today (Mac, DOS, Windows, Apple II).

Jay A Klein, President
Angela C Wormley, Office Manager

5978 Jostens Learning Corporation
5521 Norman Center Drive
Minneapolis, MN 55437-1040
800-635-1429
The leading provider of comprehensive multimedia instruction, including hardware, software and service.

5979 MISCO Computer Supplies
1 Misco Plaza
Holmdel, NJ 07733-1033
800-876-4726
Computer supplies, networks, equipment and accessories.

5980 Mathematica
Wolfram Research, Inc.
100 Trade Centre Drive
Champaign, IL 61820-7237
217-398-0700
800-965-3726
Fax: 217-398-0747
E-mail: info@wolfram.com
http://www.wolfram.com
Classroom curricular software and business/administrative software.

Stephen Wolfram, Founder/CEO
Jean Buck, Dir., Corp Communications

5981 Media Management & Magnetics
N94W14376 Garwin Mace Drive
Menomonee Falls, WI 53051-1629
262-251-5511
800-242-2090
Fax: 262-251-4737
E-mail: medmgt@execpc.com
http://www.computersupplypeople.com

Computer supplies, equipment and systems, Koss headphones.

John Schimberg, Education Sales

5982 MicroAnalytics
Student Transportation Systems
2300 Clarendon Boulevard
Suite 404
Arlington, VA 22201-3331
703-841-0414
Fax: 703-527-1693
Automates bus routing and scheduling for school districts with fleets of 5 to 500 buses. BUSTOPS is flexible, affordable and easy to use. Offers color maps and graphics, efficient routing, report writing, planning and more to improve your pupil transportation system.

Mary Buchanan, Sales Manager

5983 MicroLearn Tutorial Series
Word Associates
3226 Robincrest Drive
Northbrook, IL 60062-5125
847-291-1101
Fax: 847-291-0931
E-mail: microlrn@aol.com
http://www.wordassociates.com
Software tutorials featuring lessons in question format, with tutorial and test mode. 15 titles include Math SAT, 2 English SAT; US Constitution Tutor; Phraze Maze; Geometry: Planely Simple, Concepts and Proofs, Right Triangles; Life Skills Math; Algebra; Reading: Myths and More Myths, Magic and Monsters; Economics; American History. Windows, Macintosh, CD's or disks.

Software

Myrna Helfand, President

5984 NCS Marketing
11000 Prairie Lakes Drive
Eden Prairie, MN 55344-3885
800-447-3269
Fax: 612-830-7788
http://www.ncspearson.com
OpScan optical mark reading scanners from NCS process data at speeds of up to 10,000 sheets per hour for improved accuracy and faster turnaround. Also provides software and scanning applications and services that manage student, financial, human resources, instructional and assessment information.

Sheryl Kyweriga

5985 National Computer Systems
11000 Prairie Lakes Drive
Minneapolis, MN 55440
800-447-3269
Fax: 952-830-8564
Administrative software and systems.

5986 Parlant Technologies
290 N University Avenue
Provo, UT 84601-2821
800-735-2930
Fax: 801-373-9697
Administrative software and systems.

5987 Quill Corporation
100 Schelter Road
Lincolnshire, IL 60069-3621
847-634-4800
Fax: 847-634-5708
Computer and office supplies and equipment.

5988 Rauland Borg
3450 Oakton Street
Skokie, IL 60076-2958
847-679-0900
Fax: 800-217-0977

Administrative software and systems.

5989 Rediker Administration Software
2 Wileraham Road
Hampden, MA 01036-9685
800-882-2994
Fax: 413-566-2274
E-mail: sales@rediker.com
School administrative software for the teaching professional.

5990 Scantron Corporation
PO Box 2411
Tustin, CA 92781-2411
714-259-8887
Computer peripherals, administrative software and services.

5991 SourceView Software International
PO Box 578
Concord, CA 94522-0578
925-825-1248
Classroom curricular, business and administrative software.

5992 Systems & Computer Technology Services
4 Country View Road
Malvern, PA 19355-1408
610-647-5930
Fax: 610-578-7778
Administrative and business software programs and services.

5993 Trapeze Software
23215 Commerce Park Drive
Suite 200
Beachwood, OH 44122
216-595-3100
Fax: 216-595-3113
E-mail: clint@mail.trapezesoftware.com
http://www.trapezesoftware.com
Computerized bus routing, boundary planning and redistricting software and services, and AVL (automatic vehicle locator software).

Clint Rooley, Director of Sales

5994 University Research Company
4724 W 2100 N
Cedar City, UT 84720-7846
800-526-4972
Supplies Quiz-A-Matic electronics for quiz competitions.

5995 Velan
4153 24th Street
Suite 1
San Francisco, CA 94114-3667
415-949-9150
Administrative software and systems.

5996 WESTLAW
West Group
610 Opperman Drive
Eagan, MN 55123-1340
612-687-7000
800-757-9378
Fax: 651-687-5827
http://www.westlaw.com
Online service concerning the complete text of U.S. federal court decisions, state court decisions from all 50 states, regulations, specialized files, and texts dealing with education.

5997 http://teacherfiles.homestead.com/index~ns4
Offers sections on clip art, quotes, slogans, lesson plans, organizations, web quests, political involvement, grants, publications, special education, professional development, humor and more.

5998 www.abcteach.com
Abcteach
E-mail: sandkems@abcteach.com

Free printable materials for kids, parents, student teachers and teachers. Theme units, spelling word searches, research help, writing skills and much more.

5999 www.apple.com
PowerSchool
PowerSchool's web-based architecture makes it easy to learn and easy to use.

6000 www.atozteacherstuff.com
A to Z Teacher Stuff
E-mail: webmaster@atozteacherstuff.com
Features quick indexes to online lesson plans and teacher resources, educational sites for teachers, articles, teacher store and more.

6001 www.awesomelibrary.org
Awesome Library
Organizes the Web with 15,000 carefully reviewed resources, including the top 5 percent in education. Offers sections of mathematics, science, social studies, english, health, physical education, technology, languages, special education, the arts and more. Features a section involved with today's current issues facing our world, like pollution, gun control, tobacco, and other changing 'hot' topics. Site can be browsed in English, German, Spanish, French or Portuguese.

6002 www.easylobby.com
EasyLobby
The complete electronic visitor management system.

6003 www.fraboom.com
Stan D. Bird's WhizBang Thang
This site's tools let's you specify areas within your state's standards and search for a list of 'Flying Rhinoceros' lessons that meet your criteria. Offers other information sources for teachers and students.

6004 www.fundraising.com
800-443-5353
http://www.fundraising.com
Internet fundraising company.

6005 www.hoagiesgifted.org
Hoagies Gifted Education Page
Features the latest research on parenting and educating gifted children. Offers ideas, solutions and other things to try for parents of gifted children. Sections with world issues facing children and other important social topics.

6006 www.kiddsmart.com
Institute for Child Development
E-mail: dcornell@kiddsmart.com
The ICD develops educational materials and resources designed to facilitate children's social and emotional development. Offers the previous materials as well as research summaries, lesson plans, training, workshops, games, multi-cultural materials and other resources to teachers, educational centers, parents, counselors, corporations, non-profits and others involved in the child-care professions.

6007 www.nycteachers.com
NYCTeachers.com
Designed for NYC teachers that work within public school systems. Speaks out on controversial issues facing the broadening, funding, development, staffing and other concerns about public schools. Welcomes your suggestions and comments about the site and the issues involved.

6008 www.songs4teachers.com
O'Flynn Consulting
E-mail: oflynn4@home.com

Offers many resources for teachers including songs made especially for your classroom. Sections with songs and activities for holidays, seasons and more. Features books and audios with 101 theme songs for use in the classroom or anywhere children gather to sing.

6009 www.thecanadianteacher.com
Free Stuff for Canadian Teachers
Site where educators can find the latest links to free resources, materials, lesson plans, software, samples and computers. Some links are for Canadians only.

6010 www.welligent.Com
Welligent
A web-based software program that improves student health management and your school's finances at the same time.

Early Childhood Education

6011 Jump Start Math for Kindergartners
Knowledge Adventure
Torrance, CA
800-545-7677
http://www.knowledgeadventure.com
The program covers important and essential kindergarten math skills such as, writing numbers, sorting, and problem solving/following directions.

6012 Mindplay
160 W Fort Lowell Road
Tucson, AZ 85705
520-888-1800
800-221-7911
Fax: 520-888-7904
E-mail: mail@mindplay.com
http://www.mindplay.com
Educational software focusing on early childhood education and adult literacy.

Stacie Johnson, Communication Coordinator

6013 Nordic Software
PO Box 5403
Lincoln, NE 68505
402-489-1557
800-306-6502
Fax: 402-489-1560
E-mail: info@nordicsoftware.com
http://www.nordicsoftware.com
Specializes in developing and publishing educational software titles. Well-known for its software titles that make it easy for children to learn while playing on the computer. Develops and publishes elementary software products for the Macintosh and Windows platforms. Products include Turbo Math Facts, Clock Shop, Coin Critters, Language Explorer and Preschool Parade, and more.

Tammy Hurlbut, Finance/Operations

6014 Personalized Software
PO Box 359
Phoenix, OR 97535
541-535-8085
Fax: 541-535-8889
Offers a full line of childcare management and development software programs.

6015 Science for Kids
9950 Concord Church Road
Lewisville, NC 27023-9720
336-945-9000
800-572-4362
Fax: 336-945-2500
E-mail: sci4kids@aol.com
http://www.scienceforkids.com
Developers and publishers of CD-ROM science and early learning programs for children

ages 5-14; for Macintosh and Windows computers; school and home programs available.

Charles Moyer, Executive VP

6016 http://daycare.about.com/parenting/daycare
About Parenting/Family Daycare

6017 www.booksofwonder.com
New and vintage childrens books.

6018 www.lil-fingers.com
Lil' Fingers
A computer storybook site for toddlers. Parents and children are encouraged to enjoy the colorful drawings and animations. Offers games, storybooks, coloring pages, the Lil' Store and more.

Elementary Education

6019 Educational Institutions Partnership Program
Defense Information Systems Agency
Automation Resources Information
701 S Courthouse Road
Arlington, VA 22204-2199
703-607-6900
Fax: 703-607-4371
Makes available used computer equipment for donation of transfer to eligible schools, including K-12 schools recognized by the US Department of Education, Universities, colleges, Minority Institutions and nonporfit groups.

6020 Houghton Mifflin Company
222 Berkeley Street
Boston, MA 02116-3748
617-351-5000
Fax: 617-351-1106
Offers literature-based technology products for grades K-8 including CD's Story Time, a Macintosh based CD-ROM programs for grades 1 and 2 and Channel R.E.A.D., a videodisc series for grades 3-8.

6021 Kid Keys 2.0
Knowledge Adventure
800-545-7677
Keyboarding for grades K-2.

6022 Kinder Magic
1680 Meadowglen Lane
Encinitas, CA 92024-5652
760-632-6693
Fax: 760-632-9995
Educational software for ages 4-11.

Dr. Ilse Ortabasi, President

6023 Micrograms Publishing
9934 N Alpine Road
Suite 108
Machesney Park, IL 61115-8240
800-338-4726
Fax: 815-877-1482
http://www.micrograms.com
Micrograms develops educational software for schools and homes.

6024 Tudor Publishing Company
17218 Preston Road
Suite 400
Dallas, TX 75252-4018
Grade level evaluation (GLE) is a computer-adaptive assessment program for elementary and secondary students.

6025 Wordware Publishing
2320 Los Rios Boulevard
#200
Plano, TX 75074-8157

214-423-0090
Fax: 972-881-9147
Publisher of computer reference tutorials, regional Texas and Christian books. Educational division produces a diagnostic and remediation software for grade levels 3-8. Content covers over 3,000 objectives in reading, writing and math. Contact publisher for dealer information.

Eileen Schnett, Product Manager

6026 World Classroom
Global Learning Corporation
PO Box 201361
Arlington, TX 76006-1361
214-641-3356
800-866-4452
An educational telecommunications network that prepares students, K-12 to use real-life data to make real-life decisions about themselves and their environment. Participating countries have included Argentina, Australia, Belgium, Canada, Denmark, France, Germany, Hungary, Iceland, Indonesia, Kenya, Russia, Lithuania, Mexico, Singapore, Taiwan, the Netherlands, the United States and Zimbabwe.

6027 http://k-6educators....education/k-6 educators
About Education Elementary Educators

6028 http://www.etacuisenaire.com/index.htm
ETA Cuisenaire
Over 5,000 manipulative-based education and supplemental materials for grades K-12.

6029 http://www.wnet.org/wnetschool
wNet School
212-560-2713
Helps K-12 teachers by providing free standards based lesson plans, classroom activities, multimedia primers, online mentors, links to model technology schools, and more. Online workshops are also included in the WNET TV site.

6030 www.cherrydale.com/
Cherrydale Farms
Website offers company information, fund raising products and information, online mega mall, card shop, career opportunities and much more. Produces fine chocolates and confections. Many opportunities for schools to raise funds with various Cherrydale programs.

6031 www.efundraising.com
eFundraising
Provides non-profit groups with quality products, low prices and superior service. Helping thousands of schools, youth sports teams and community groups reach their fundraising goals each year.

6032 www.hoagiesgifted.org
Hoagies' Gifted Education Page
Features the latest research on parenting and educating gifted children. Offers ideas, solutions and other things to try for parents of gifted children. Sections with world issues facing children and other important social topics.

6033 www.netrover.com/~kingskid/108.html
Room 108
An educational activity center for kids. Offers lots of fun for children with educational focus; like songs, art, math, kids games, children's stories and much more. Sections with pen pal information, puzzles, crosswords, teachers store, spelling, kids sites, email, music, games and more.

6034 www.netrox.net
Dr. Labush's Links to Learning
General links for teachers with internet help, coloring pages, and enrichment programs.

6035 www.primarygames.com
PrimaryGames.com
Contains educational games for elementary students.

6036 www.usajobs.opm.gov/b1c.htm
Overseas Employment Info-Teachers

Employment

6037 Educational Placement Service
90 S Cascade
Suite 1110
Colorado Springs, CO 80903
http://www.teacherjobs.com
Largest teacher placement service in the U.S.

6038 Job Bulletin
American Association of School Administrators
801 N Quincy Street
Arlington, VA 22203-1730
703-528-0700
Fax: 703-841-1543
E-mail: info@aasa.org
http://www.aasa.org
The Job Bulletin was made to help employers and job candidates save time finding one another.

Jay Goldman, Editor

6039 Teachers@Work
PO Box 430
Vail, CO 81658
970-476-5008
Fax: 970-476-1496
http://www.teachersatwork.com
Electronic employment service designed to match the professional staffing needs of schools with teacher applicants.

6040 www.SchoolJobs.com
SchoolJobs.com
Provides principals, superintendents and other administrators the ability to market their job openings to a national pool of candidates, also gives educational professionals the chance to search for opportunities matching their skills.

6041 www.aasa.org
American Association of School Administrators
801 N Quincy Street
Suite 700
Arlington, VA 22203-1730
703-528-0700
Fax: 703-841-1543
E-mail: info@aasa.org
http://www.aasa.org
Leadership news online.

Guidance & Counseling

6042 Alcohol & Drug Prevention for Teachers, Law Enforcement & Parent Groups
PO Box 4656
Reading, PA 19606
610-582-2090
Fax: 610-404-0406
E-mail: nodrugs@earthlink.net
http://www.nodrugs.com
Local organizations and international groups against drugs.

6043 Live Wire Media
3450 Sacramento Street
619
San Francisco, CA 94118
800-359-5437
Fax: 415-665-8006
E-mail: info@livewiremedia.com
http://www.livewiremedia.com/
Videos for youth guidance and character development, and teacher training.

Christine Hollander, Director Marketing

6044 Phillip Roy Multimedia Materials
PO Box 130
Indian Rocks Beach, FL 34635
727-593-2700
800-255-9085
Fax: 727-595-2685
E-mail: info@philliproy.com
http://www.philliproy.com
Multimedia materials for use with alternative education, Chapter 1, dropout prevention, Even Start, Head Start, JTPA/PIC, special education students, at-risk students, transition to work programs. Focuses on basic skills, conflict resolution, remediation, vocational education, critical thinking skills, communication skills, reasoning and decision making skills. Materials can be duplicated networked at no cost.

Phil Padol, Consultant
Regina Jacques, Customer Support

6045 www.goodcharacter.com
Character Education
Teaching guides for k-12 character education, packed with discussion questions, assignments, and activities that you can use as your own lesson plans.

International

6046 www.aed.org
Academy for Educational Development
The site provides information on international exchange, fellowshipand training.

6047 www.asce.org
American Society of Civil Engineers
This site lists scholarships and fellowships available only to ASCE members.

6048 www.cie.uci.edu
International Opportunities Program
Valuable links for exploring opportunities for study and research abroad.

6049 www.ciee.org
Council on International Educational Exchange
Study abroad programs by region, work abroad opportunities, international volunteer projects and Council-administered financial aid and grant information .

6050 www.cies.org
Council for International Exchange of Scholars
Information on the Fulbright Senior Scholar Program which is made available to Fulbright alumni,grantees, prospective applicants and public at large.

6051 www.daad.org
German Academic Exchange Service (DADD)
Promotes international academic relations and contains links to research grants, summer language grants,annual grants, grants in German studies andspecial programs.

6052 www.ed.gov
US Department of Education
Office of Higher Education Programs

This site describes programs and fellowships offered by the International Education and Graduate Programs office of the US Department of Education.

6053 www.finaid.org
FinAid
A free, comprehensive, independent and ojective guide to student financial aid.

6054 www.iie.org
Institute of International Education
809 United Nations Plaza
New York, NY 10017-3580
412-741-0930
Fax: 212-984-5452
E-mail: iiebooks@abdintl.com
http://www.iiebooks.org
The largest not-for-profit international educational organization in the United States. This site provides information regarding IIE's programs, services and resources, including the Filbright Fellowship.

6055 www.iiepasspport.org
Institute of International Education
IIE Passport: Study Abroad
1350 Edgmont Avenue Suite 1100
Chester, PA 19013
877-404-0338
Fax: 610-499-9205
E-mail: info@iiepassport.org
http://www.iiepassport.org
A student guide on the web to 5,000 learning oppurtunities worldwide.

6056 www.irex.org
International Research and Exchange Board
Academic exchanges between the United States and Russia. Lists a variety of programs as well as grant and fellowship oppurtunities.

6057 www.isp.msu.edu/ncsa
Michigan State University
National Consortium for Study
in Africa

Provides a comprehensive lists of sponsors for African exchange.

6058 www.istc.umn.edu/
University of Minnesota
International Study and Travel
Center

Comprehensive and searchable links to study, work and travel abroad opportunities.

6059 www.languagetravel.com
Language Travel Magazine
Resource for finding study abroad language immersion courses.

6060 www.nsf.gov/
National Science Foundation

Encourages exchange in science and engineering. The site has inter-national component, providing links with valuable information on fellowships grants and awards, summer institutes, workshops,research and education projects and international programs.

6061 www.si.edu/
Smithsonian Institution
Fellowships link to Smithsonian Oppurtunities for research and study.

6062 www.studiesinaustralia.com/study
Studies in Australia
Listing of study abroad oppurtunities in Australia, providing details of academic and training institutions and the programs they offer to prospective international students and education professionals.

6063 www.studyabroad.com/
Educational Directories Unlimited, Inc.
Study abroad information resource listing study abroad programs worldwide.

6064 www.studyabroad.com/.
StudyAbroad.com
A commercial site with thousands of study abroad programs in over 100 countries with links to study abroad program home pages.

6065 www.ucis.pitt.edu/crees
University of Pittsburgh
Center for Russian/European Studies

Index of electronic resources for the student interested in Russian and European language and culture study.

6066 www.upenn.edu/oip/scholarships.html
University of Pennsylvania
Scholarships/Graduate Study Abroad

Provides links for graduate study abroad and scholarship opportunities.

6067 www.usc.edu
University of Southern California
Resources for Colleges and
Universities in International Exchange

Links for browsing all aspects of international exchange, including study, research, work and teaching abroad, financial aid, grants and scholarships.

6068 www.usinfo.state/gov
US Department of State International
Information Programs

Comprehensive desriptions of all IIP programs, sections on policy issues, global and regional issues and IIP publications.

6069 www.wes.org
World Education Services
Features information on WES' foreign credentials evaluation services, world education workshops, and the journals World Education and News Reviews.

6070 www.world-arts-resources.com/
World Wide Arts Resources
Focuses solely on the arts, this site provides links for funding sources, university programs and arts organizations all over the world.

6071 www.yfu.org/
Youth for Understanding (YFU)
Oppurtunities for young people around the world to spend a summer, semester or year with a host family in another country.

6072 wwww.sas.upenn.edu
African Studies Center, University of
Pennsylvania
African Studies WWW

Links to Africa-related internet sources, African Studies Association and UPenn African Studies Center.

Language Arts

6073 Advantage Learning Systems
Renaissance Learning
PO Box 8036
Wisconsin Rapids, WI 54495-8036
715-424-3636
800-338-4204
Fax: 715-424-4242
E-mail: answers@renlearn.com
http://www.renlearn.com
Accelerated Reader software and manuals that motivate K-12 students to read more and better books. The program boosts reading scores and library circulation. Lets educators quickly and accurately assess student reading while motivating students to read more and better books.

6074 Bytes of Learning Incorporated
150 Consumers Road
Suite 2021
Willowdale, ON, Canada, M2 J 1P9
800-465-6428
Single and site licensed software for Macintosh, Apple II, DOS and Windows-network compatible too. Keyboarding, language arts, career exploration and more on diskette and CD-ROM.

6075 Humanities Software
408 Columbia Street
#950
Hood River, OR 97031-2044
503-386-6737
800-245-6737
Fax: 541-386-1410
Over 150 whole language, literature-based language arts software titles for grades K-12.

Karen Withrow, Marketing Assistant
Charlotte Arnold, Marketing Director

6076 Teacher Support Software
3542 NW 97th Boulevard
Gainesville, FL 32606-7322
352-332-6404
800-228-2871
Fax: 352-332-6779
E-mail: tss@tssoftware.com
http://www.tssoftware.com
Language arts, Title 1, special ed, at-risk and ESL, curriculum-based networkable software for grades K-12. Vocabulary software that develops sight word recognition, provides basal correlated databases, tests reading comprehension, tracks student's progress and provides powerful teacher tools.

6077 Weaver Instructional Systems
6161 28th Street SE
Grand Rapids, MI 49546-6931
616-942-2891
Fax: 616-942-1796
Reading and language arts computer software programs for K-college.

6078 www.caslt.org
Canadian Association of Second Language Teachers
Promotes the advancement of second language education throughout Canada.

6079 www.riverdeep.net
Riverdeep Interactive Learning
Riverdeep's interactive science, language and math arts programs deliver high quality educational experiences.

6080 www.signit2.com
Aylmer Press
Website hosted by Aylmer Press which produces video's to teach kids sign language as well as music.

6081 www.usajobs.opm.gov/b1c.htm1
Overseas Employment Info- Teachers
US Office of Personnel Management

Library Services

6082 American Econo-Clad Services
2101 N Topeka
Topeka, KS 66601
800-255-3502
Fax: 785-233-3129
A full service supplier of educational materials for the library, curriculum and software resource needs including MatchMaker, CD-ROM and ABLE (Analytically Budgeted Library Expenditures) computer systems.

6083 Anchor Audio
3415 Lomita Boulevard
Torrance, CA 90505-5010
310-784-2300
800-262-4671
Fax: 310-784-0533
http://www.anchoraudio.com
Various audio visual products for the school and library.

6084 Baker & Taylor
8140 Lehigh Avenue
Morton Grove, IL 60053-2627
847-965-8060
Nation's leading wholesale supplier of audio, computer software, books, videocassettes and other accessories to schools and libraries.

6085 Brodart Company, Automation Division
500 Arch Street
Williamsport, PA 17701
570-326-2461
800-233-8467
Fax: 570-327-9237
E-mail: salesmkt@brodart.com
http://www.brodart.com
Brodart's Automation Division has been providing library systems, software, and services for over 25 years. Products include: library management systems, media management systems, Internet solutions, cataloged web sites, cataloging resource tools, union catalog solutions, public access catalogs, and bibliographic services.

Kasey Dibble, Marketing Coordinator
Sally Wilmoth, Director Marketing/Sales

6086 Catalog Card Company
12219 Nicollet Avenue
Burnsville, MN 55337-1650
612-882-8558
800-442-7332
Fax: 785-290-1223
MARC records compatible with all software for retrospective conversions and new book orders. Catalog Card's conversion services include barcode labels to complement circulation software. MARC records generated from Dewey/Sears and Library of Congress databases are in standard USMARC or MicroLIF format.

6087 Chancery Student Management Solutions
3001 Wayburne Drive
Burnbay
Canada V5G 4W3
604-294-1233
800-999-9931
Fax: 604-294-2225
http://www.chancery.com
Online catalog searches and checking materials in and out.

6088 Data Trek
5838 Edison Place
Carlsbad, CA 92008-6519
800-876-5484
Turn-key library automation systems and computer networks.

6089 Demco
PO Box 7488
Madison, WI 53707-7488
800-356-1200
Fax: 608-241-1799
A leader in educational and library supplies for more than 80 years, Demco offers library audio and visual supplies and equipment plus display furniture.

6090 Dewey Decimal Classification
OCLC Forest Press
6565 Frantz Road
Dublin, OH 43017-3395
800-848-5878
Fax: 888-339-3921
E-mail: orders@oclc.org
http://www.oclc.org/fp
OCLC Forest Press publishes the Dewey Decimal Classification (DDC) system and many related print and CD-ROM products that teach librarians and library users about the DDC.

Libble Clawford, Marketing Manager

6091 Ebsco Subscription Services
International Headquarters
PO Box 1943
Birmingham, AL 35201-1943
205-991-1480
Fax: 205-980-6700
Periodical subscription and ordering and customer service equipment, computer and CD-ROM supplies, products and hardware for libraries.

Shannon Hayslip

6092 Electronic Bookshelf
5276 S Country Road, 700 W
Frankfort, IN 46041
765-324-2182
Fax: 765-324-2183
Reading motivation, testing management system and various computer systems and networks for educational purposes.

Rosalie Carter

6093 Filette Keez Corporation/Colorworks Diskette Organizing System
3204 Channing Lane
Bedford, TX 76021-6506
817-283-5428
Produces ten filing inventions for classroom library, lab and district technology resources management. SelecTsideS folders store multimedia in Press-an-Inch Technology Slings and keep instruction, printouts, pamphlets and blackliners altogether. The diskette/CD portfolio color coordinates with the student/magazine Spbinder, plastic LaceLox fastener and all systems paper supplies: CD envelopes, storage box dividers, sheeted cards, perforated tractor labels and keys, available in 7 tech colors.

Roxanne Kay Harbert, Founder/President
Ray L Harbert, VP

6094 Follett Software Company
1391 Corporate Drive
McHenry, IL 60050
815-344-8700
800-323-3397
Fax: 815-344-8774
E-mail: marketing@fsc.follett.com
http://www.fsc.follett.com

Helping K-12 schools and districts create a vital library-to-classroom link to improve student achievement. FSC combines award-winning library automation with practical applications of the Internet. From OPAC data enhancement and easy-to-implement Internet technology to innovative information literacy solutions, FSC helps simplify resource management, increase access to resources inside and outside your collection and provide tools to integrate technology into the curriculum.

Patricia Yonushonis, Marketing Manager
Ann Reist, Conference Manager

6095 Foundation for Library Research
1200 Bigley Avenue
Charleston, WV 25302-3752
304-343-6480
Fax: 304-343-6489
The Automated Library Systems integrated library automation software.

Robert Evans

6096 Gaylord Brothers
PO Box 4901
Syracuse, NY 13221-4901
800-448-6160
Fax: 315-457-8387
Library, AV supplies and equipment; security systems; and library furniture.

Tim Krein

6097 Highsmith Company
W5527 Highway 106
Fort Atkinson, WI 53538
414-563-9571
Catalog of microcomputer and multimedia curriculum products and software.

Barbara R Endl

6098 Information Access Company
362 Lakeside Drive
Foster City, CA 94404-1171
800-227-8431
Offers automation products and electronics for library/media centers.

6099 LePAC NET
Brodart Automation
500 Arch Street
Williamsport, PA 17705
570-326-2461
800-233-8467
Fax: 570-327-9237
E-mail: salesmkt@brodart.com
http://www.brodart.com
Software for searching thousands of library databases with a single search. Schools can use to take multiple individual library databases and consolidate them, while deleting duplicate listings, into a union database.

Shawn Knight, Assistant Marketing Manager
Denise Macafee, Marketing Manager

6100 Library Corporation
Library Corporation
Research Park
Inwood, WV 25428-9733
800-325-7759
http://www.tlcdelivers.com
Web-based library management systems allows patrons to have easy and immediate access to books and other library resources.

6101 Lingo Fun
International Software
PO Box 486
Westerville, OH 43086-0486
800-745-8258
Providers of microcomputer software including CD-ROM's for Macintosh and MPC, on-line dictionaries, translation assistants; teaching programs for elementary presentation, review and

reinforcement, test preparation, and literary exploration.

6102 MARCIVE
PO Box 47508
San Antonio, TX 78265-7508
210-646-6161
800-531-7678
Fax: 210-646-0167
E-mail: info@marcive.com
http://www.marcive.com
Economical, fast 100% conversion. Full MARC records with SEARS or LC headings. Free authorities processing smart barcode labels, reclassification, MARC Record enrichment

6103 Medianet/Dymaxion Research Limited
5515 Cogswell Street
Halifax, Nova Scotia, B3 J 1R2
902-422-1973
Fax: 902-421-1267
E-mail: info@medianet.ns.ca
http://www.medianet.ns.ca
Medianet is the scheduling system for equipment and media that has consistently been rated as best in its class. Features include book library system integration, time-of-day booking, catalog production, WWW and touch tone phone booking by patrons.

Peter Mason, President

6104 Mitinet/Marc Software
6409 Odana Road
Madison, WI 53719-1125
800-824-6272
Fax: 608-270-1107
Import/export USMARC, MICROLIF to USMARC conversions.

6105 Orange Cherry Software
69 Westchester Avenue
PO Box 390
Pound Ridge, NY 10576-1702
914-764-4104
800-672-6002
Fax: 914-764-0104
http://www.orangecherry.com
Educational software products for libraries and media centers.

Biannual

Nicholas Vazzana, President

6106 Right on Programs
778 New York Avenue
Huntington, NY 11743-4240
631-424-7777
Fax: 631-424-7207
E-mail: friends@rightonprograms.com
http://www.rightonprograms.com
Computer software for Windows and networks for library management including circulation, cataloging, periodicals, catalog cardmaking, inventory and thirty more. Used in more than 24,000 schools and libraries of all sizes.

D Farren, VP

6107 SOLINET, Southeastern Library Network
1438 W Peachtree Street NW
Suite 200
Atlanta, GA 30309-2955
404-892-0943
800-999-8558
Fax: 404-892-7879
E-mail: information@solinet.net
http://www.solinet.net
SOLINET provides access, training and support for OCLC products and services; offers discounted library products and services, including licensed databases; provides electronic information solutions; workflow consulting, training and customized workshops; and supports a regional preservation of materials program.

Cathie Gharing, Marketing Coordinator
Liz Hornsby, Editor

6108 Sirsi Corporation
101 Washington Street SE
Huntsville, AL 35801-4827
256-704-7000
800-917-4774
Fax: 256-704-7007
E-mail: sales@sirsi.com
http://www.sirsi.com
Unicorn Collection Management Systems are fully integrated UNIX-based library systems, automating all of a library's operation. Modules include: cataloging, authority control, public access, materials booking, circulation, academic reserves, acquisitions, serials control, reference database manager and electronic mail. Modules can be configured for all types and sizes of libraries.

Vicki Smith, Communication Specialist

6109 Social Issues Resources Series
PO Box 2348
Boca Raton, FL 33427
561-994-0079
800-232-SIRS
Fax: 561-994-4704
Publisher of CD-ROM reference systems for PC and Macintosh computers. Databases of full-text articles carefully selected from 1,000 domestic and international sources. Also provides PC-compatible and stand-alone and network packages.

Paula Jackson, Marketing Director
Suzanne Panek, Customer Service

6110 TekData Systems Company
1111 W Park Avenue
Libertyville, IL 60048-2952
847-367-8800
Fax: 847-367-0235
E-mail: tekdata@tekdata.com
http://www.tekdata.com
Scheduling and booking systems for intranets and internets.

Randy Kick, Sales Manager

6111 Three M Library Systems
Three M Center
Building 225-4N-14
St. Paul, MN 55144
800-328-0067
Fax: 800-223-5563
Materials Flow Management system is the first comprehensive system for optimizing the handling, processing and security of your library materials - from processing to check-out to check-in. The SelfCheck System and Staff Workstation automate the processing of virtually all of your library materials, while the Tattle-Tape Security Strips and Detection Systems help ensure the security of those materials.

6112 UMI
300 N Zeeb Road
Ann Arbor, MI 48103-1553
800-521-0600
Fax: 800-864-0019
Information products in microform, CD-ROM, online and magnetic tape.

6113 University Products
517 Main Street
#101
Holyoke, MA 01040-5514
413-532-3372
800-628-1912
Fax: 413-452-0618
Complete selection of library and media center supplies and equipment.

Juhn Dunpay

6114 WLN
PO Box 3888
Lacey, WA 98509-3888
360-923-4000
800-342-5956
Fax: 360-923-4009
School and media librarians experience 95% hit rates with WLN's LaserCat, CD-ROM database, a cataloging product and MARC record service.

6115 Winnebago Software Company
457 E S Street
Caledonia, MN 55921-1356
800-533-5430
Fax: 507-725-2301
E-mail: sales@winnebago.com
http://www.winnebago.com
Comprehensive, user-friendly circulation and catalog software for Windows, Mac OS, and MS-DOS systems-plus Internet technology, online periodical databases, outstanding customer support, and retrospective conversion services-all developed within the quality guidelines of Winnebago's ISO 9001 certification with TickIT accreditation.

6116 www.awesomelibrary.org
Awesome Library
Organizes the Web with 15,000 carefully reviewed resources, including the top 5 percent in education. Offers sections of mathematics, science, social studies, english, health, physical education, technology, languages, special education, the arts and more. Features a section involved with today's current issues facing our world, like pollution, gun control, tobacco, and other changing 'hot' topics. Site can be browsed in English, German, Spanish, French or Portuguese.

6117 www.techlearning.com
Technology & Learning
Open 24 hours, every day of the week, with an extensive and up-to-date catalog of over 53,000 software and hardware products. Powerful search engine will help you find the right education-specific products.

Mathematics

6118 Accelerated Math
Renaissance Learning
PO Box 8036
Wisconsin Rapids, WI 54495-8036
715-424-3636
800-338-4204
Fax: 715-424-4242
E-mail: answers@renlearn.com
http://www.renlearn.com
Accelerated Math provides 17 different reports, providing individualized, constructive feedback to students, parents, and teachers.

6119 Applied Mathematics Program
Prime Technology Corporation
PO Box 2407
Minneola, FL 34755-2407
352-394-7558
Fax: 352-394-3778
http://www.primetechnology.net
Provides students with comprehensive instruction in 11 math areas. In working with this program, students develop employment and life skills. The program will also lead the student to greater success on the mathematics sections of any standardized test.

Paul Scime, President

6120 CAE Software
3608 Shepherd Street
Chevy Chase, MD 20815-4132
301-907-9845
800-354-3462
Provides educational software for mathematics, grades 3-12. Simulations, tutorials, games, and problem solving. Titles include Mathematics Life Skills Services, Reading and Making Graphs Series, MathLab Series, Meaning of Fractions, Using Fractions and Using Decimals, ALG Football, GEO Pool and GEO Billiards, Paper Route, Mathematics Achievement Project, and others.

Alan R Chap, President

6121 EME Corporation
PO Box 1949
Stuart, FL 34995-1949
800-848-2050
Fax: 561-219-2209
E-mail: emecorp@aol.com
http://www.emescience.com
Publishers of award-winning science and math software, elementary through high school levels.

6122 Logal Software
125 Cambridgepark Drive
Cambridge, MA 02140-2329
617-491-4440
Fax: 617-491-5855
Math and science products for high school through college.

Martha Cheng, President

6123 MathType
Design Science
4028 E Broadway
Long Beach, CA 90803-1502
562-433-0685
800-827-0685
Fax: 562-433-6969
http://www.mathtype.com
Designed to make the creation of complex equations on a computer simple and fast. It works in conjunction with the software applications you already own, such as word processing programs, graphics programs, presentation programs, and web-authoring applications. Create research papers, tests, slides, books or web pages quickly and easily. MathType is the powerful, professional version of the Equation Editor in Microscoft Word, and Wordperfect.

Bruce Virga, VP Sales/Marketing
Nicole Jessey, Sale/Marketing Coordinator

6124 Mathematica
Wolfram Research, Inc.
100 Trade Center Drive
Champaign, IL 61820-7237
217-398-0700
800-965-3726
Fax: 217-398-0747
E-mail: info@wolfram.com
http://www.wolfram.com
Mathematica is an indispensable tool for finding and communicating solutions quickly and easily.

Stephen Wolfram, Founder/CEO
Jean Buck, Dir., Corp Communications

6125 MindTwister Math
Edmark Corporation
PO Box 97021
Redmond, WA 98073-9721
425-556-8400
800-691-2986
Fax: 425-556-8430
E-mail: edmarkteam@edmark.com
http://www.edmark.com

Software to help students in grade 3 and 4 build math fact fluency, practice mental math and improve estimating skills as they compete in a series of math challenges.

6126 Multimedia - The Human Body
Sunburst Technology
101 Castleton Street
Pleasantville, NY 10570
914-747-3310
800-321-7511
Fax: 914-747-4109
http://www.sunburst.com
Multimedia production of the intricate workings of the human body.

6127 Texas Instruments
Consumer Relations
PO Box 53
Lubbock, TX 79408-0053
800-842-2737
Fax: 972-917-0874
Instructional calculators offer features matched to math concepts taught at each of conceptional development. Classroom accessories and teacher support programs that support the Texas Instruments products enhance instruction and learning. TI also offers a complete range of powerful notebook computers and laser printers for every need.

6128 William K. Bradford Publishing Company
35 Forest Ridge Road
Concord, MA 01742-5414
800-421-2009
Fax: 978-318-9500
http://www.wkbradford.com
Educational software for grades K-12. Especially math and grade book.

Hal Wexler, VP

6129 www.mathgoodies.com
Mrs. Glosser's Math Goodies
Free educational site featuring interactive math lessons. Use a problem-solving approach and actively engage students in the learning process.

6130 www.mathstories.com
MathStories.com
The goal of this site is to help grade school children improve their math problem-solving and critical thinking skills. Offers over 4000 math word problems for children.

6131 www.riverdeep.net
Riverdeep Interactive Learning
Riverdeep's interactive science, language and math arts programs deliver high quality educational experiences.

6132 www.themathemagician.8m.com
The Mathemagician
Offers the help of a real live person to help students correct and understand math and other home work problems.

Music & Art

6133 Harmonic Vision
68 E Wacker Place
Chicago, IL 60610
312-332-9200
800-474-0903
http://www.harmonicvision.com
Leading musical education software to teach effectiveness of music in the home, school and studio.

6134 Midnight Play
Simon & Schuster Interactive
800-793-9972
http://www.simonandschuster.com
Electronic picture book with an unusual look at creativity.

6135 Music Teacher Find
33 W 17th Street
10th Floor
New York, NY 10011
212-242-2464
http://www.MusicTeacherFind.com
Comprehensive Music Teacher Database designed to help music students find quality teachers in their neighborhood.

6136 Music and Guitar
http://www.nl-guitar.com
Original music programs for schools, courses and encounterswith music.

6137 Pure Gold Teaching Tools
PO Box 16622
Tuscon, AZ 85732
520-747-5600
866-692-6500
Fax: 520-571-9077
E-mail: info@puregoldteachingtools.com
http://www.puregoldteachingtools.com
Exciting teaching methods and fabulous gifts for teachers, parents, students, pre-schoolers, homeschoolers and music therapists.

Heidi Goldman, President

6138 http://library.thinkquest.org
Think Quest
The Arti FAQS 2100 Project is designed to predict how art will influence our lives in the next hundred years. Students can use available data to make reasonable predictions for the future.

6139 http://members.truepath.com/headoftheclass
Head of The Class
Offers three galleries with clip art for teachers and children, several lesson plans, teaching tips, songs for teachers, lounge laughs, teacher tales and more.

6140 www.billharley.com
BillHarley.com
Humerous, yet meaningful songs which chronicle the lives of children at school and at home. His recordings of songs and stories can be used most effectively in the classroom as inspirational tools for the motivation of learning.

6141 www.sanford-artedventures.com
Sanford- A Lifetime of Color
800-323-0749
Teaches students about art and color theory while they play a game. Lessons plans, newsletter and product information.

6142 www.songs4teachers.com
O'Flynn Consulting
E-mail: oflynn4@home.com
Offers many resources for teachers including songs made especially for your classroom. Sections with songs and activities for holidays, seasons and more. Features books and audios with 101 theme songs for use in the classroom or anywhere children gather to sing.

6143 www.ushistory.com
History Happens
Teaches integrating art, music, literature, science, math, library skills, and American history. The Primary source is stories from American history presented in musci video style.

Physical Education

6144 InfoUse
2560 9th Street
Suite 216
Berkeley, CA 94710-2557
510-549-6520
Fax: 510-549-6512
An award-winning, multimedia development and products firm, features CD-ROM, websites on health, education and disability. For training, education or presentations, our services include: research, instructional design, interface design, graphics, animation, content acquisition, videoing, analog and digital editing and evaluation. Products include SafeNet, (HIV prevention for fifth and sixth grade children), Place Math and Math Pad (math tools and lessons for students with disabilities).

Lewis E Kraus, VP
Susan Stoddard, President

6145 www.sports-media.org
Sports Media
A tool for p.e. teachers, coaches, students and everyone who is interested in p.e./fitness and sports. Interactive p.e. lesson plans, sports pen-apls for the kids, European p.e. mailing list, and developing teaching skills in physical education.

Reading

6146 Accelerated Reader
Renaissance Learning
PO Box 8036
Wisconsin Rapids, WI 54495-8036
715-424-3636
800-338-4204
Fax: 715-424-4242
E-mail: answers@renlearn.com
http://www.renlearn.com
Helps teachers increase literature-based reading practice for all k-12 students

Secondary Education

6147 New York Times
New York, NY
646-698-8000
Fax: 646-698-8344
http://www.nytimes.com/learning
A resource for educators, parents and students in grades six through 12. Provides a daily lesson plan and comprehensive interactive resources based on newspaper content.

Rob Larson, Education Editor
Diane Morgan, Director Marketing

6148 Wm. C. Brown Communications
2460 Kerper Boulevard
Dubuque, IA 52001-2224
College textbooks, software, CD-ROM and more for grades 10-12.

6149 http://adulted.about.com/education/adulted
Adult/Continuing Education

6150 http://englishhlp.www5.50megs.com
English Help
E-mail: englishhlpr@hotmail.com
This page is a walk through of Microsoft Power Point. The goal is to show in a few simple steps how to make your own website. Created by Rebecca Holland.

6151 www.number2.com
Number2.com
Currently offer SAT and GRE prep along with a vocabulary builder. Practice questions and word drill are adapted to the ability level of the user.

Science

6152 Academic Software Development Group
University of Maryland
University of Maryland
Computer Science Center
College Park, MD 20742-0001
301-405-5100
Fax: 301-405-0726
Offers BioQuest Library which is a set of peer-reviewed resources for science education.

6153 Accu-Weather
385 Science Park Road
State College, PA 16803-2215
814-237-0309
Fax: 814-238-1339
Offers a telecommunications weather and oceanography database.

6154 AccuLab Products Group
614 Senic Drive
Suite 104
Modesto, CA 95350
209-522-8874
Fax: 209-522-8875
Science laboratory software.

6155 Learning Team
10 Long Pond Road
Armonk, NY 10504-2625
914-273-2226
800-793-TEAM
Fax: 914-273-2227
Offers CD-ROM, including MathFinder, Science Helper and Small Blue Planet and Redshift, the Learning Team edition.

Thomas Laster

6156 Problem Solving Concepts
611 N Capitol Avenue
Indianapolis, IN 46204-1205
317-267-9827
800-755-2150
Fax: 317-262-5044
Pro Solv provides students with a new approach to learning introductory physics problem solving techniques. Multi-experiential exercises with supporting text introduce students to relevant variables and their interrelations, principles, graphing and the development of problem solving skills through the quiz/tutorial mode.

Thomas D Feigenbaum, President
Gean R Shelor, Administrative Assistant

6157 Quantum Technology
PO Box 8252
Searcy, AR 72145-8252
A microcomputer database collection system that allows users to perform experiments in chemistry, biology and applied physics.

6158 SCI Technologies
SCI Technologies
105 Terry Drive
Suite 120
Newtown, PA 18940
215-579-8590
800-421-9881
Fax: 215-579-8589
E-mail: cgreenblatt@scitechnologies.com
http://www.scitechnologies.com

A computer-based interface with an integrated hardware and software package that allows the focus of a science lab to shift from data collection to data analysis and experiment design.

Colleen Greenblatt, Sales Manager
Michelle Trexler, Event Coordinator

6159 Videodiscovery
1700 Westlake Avenue N
Suite 600
Seattle, WA 98109-3040
206-285-5400
800-548-3472
Fax: 206-285-9245
Publishers of award winning science videodiscs and multimedia software for kindergarten through post-secondary classes.

6160 www.kidsastronomy.com
KidsAstronomy.com
Offers information on astronomy, deep space, the solar system, space exploration, a teachers corner and more.

6161 www.riverdeep.net
Riverdeep Interactive Learning
Riverdeep's interactive science, language and math arts programs deliver high quality educational experiences.

Social Studies

6162 AccuNet/AP Multimedia Archive
AccuWeather, Inc.
385 Science Park Road
State College, PA 16803
814-235-8600
800-566-6606
Fax: 814-231-0453
E-mail: salesmail@accuwx.com
http://www.ap.accuweather.com
The Photo Archive is an on-line database containing almost a half-million of Associated Press's current and historic images for the last 150 years.

Michael Warfield, Southeastern Sales Manager
Richard Towne, Northeastern Sales Manager

6163 Gale Research
PO Box 33477
Detroit, MI 48232-5477
800-877-GALE
Fax: 800-414-5043
Offers CD-Rom information that offer students contextual understanding of the most commonly-studies persons, events and social movements in U.S. history; concepts, theories, discoveries and people involved in the study of science; current geopolitical data with cultural information on 200 nations of the world as well as all U.S. states and dependencies; poetry and literary information; and more in various databases for education.

6164 World Geography Web Site
ABC-CLIO Schools
130 Cremona Drive
#1911
Santa Barbara, CA 93117-5599
805-968-1911
800-368-6868
Fax: 805-685-9685
Provides convenient internet access to curriculum-based reference and research materials for media specialist, educators and students.

CD-ROM

Judy Fay, Managing Editor
Valerie Mercado, Customer Service

6165 WorldView Software
76 N Broadway
Suite 4009
Hicksville, NY 11801-4241
516-681-1773
800-347-8839
Fax: 516-681-1775
E-mail: history@worldviewsoftware.com
WorldView Software's interactive social studies programs for middle school and high school are comprehensive, curriculum-based tools that may be used along with or in place of textbooks. Each dynamic program contains Socratic learning sessions, writing activities and exams with instant feedback. Resource materials in every program include sketches and artwork. Used nationally in classrooms, computer labs and learning centers.

Grades 7-12

Jerrold Kleinstein, President

6166 http://faculty.acu.edu
M.I. Smart Program
Site designed for teacher and students. Offers electronic resources for historical and cultural geography. Features games, quizzes, trivia and virtual tours for students and thier teachers.

Technology in Education

6167 BLINKS.Net
PO Box 79321
Atlanta, GA 30357
404-243-5202
Fax: 404-241-4992
E-mail: info@blinks.net
http://www.blinks.net
Fastest growing free Internet service provider and community portal for information and resources for the African American, Caribbean, Latino, and African markets.

6168 Boyce Enterprises
360 Sharry Lane
Santa Maria, CA 93455
805-937-4353
Fax: 805-934-1765
Development of computer-based vocational curriculums.

6169 Center for Educational Outreach and Innovation
Teachers College-Columbia University
525 W 120th Street
Box 132
New York, NY 10027
212-678-3987
800-209-1245
Fax: 212-678-8417
E-mail: ceoi-mail@tc.columbia.edu
http://www.tc.columbia.edu
Lifelong learning programs, including distance learning courses, certificates and workshoops in education related topics.

6170 Depco
3305 Airport Drive
PO Box 178
Pittsburg, KS 66762
316-231-0019
800-767-1062
Fax: 316-231-0024
E-mail: sales@depcoinc.com
http://www.depcoinc.com
Program tracks and schedules for you, the test taker delivers tests electronically, as well as, automatic final exams. There are workstation security features to help keep students focused on their activities.

6171 Dialog Information Services
Worldwide Headquaters
3460 Hillview Avenue
#10010
Palo Alto, CA 94304-1338
415-858-3785
800-334-2564
Fax: 650-858-7069
The world's most comprehensive online information source offering over 450 databases containing over 330 million articles, abstracts and citations - covering an unequaled variety of topics, with particular emphasis on news, business, science and technology. Dialog has offices throughout the United States and around the world.

6172 Distance Education Database
International Centre for Distance Learning
Open University, Walton Hall
Milton Keynes
England
441-085-3537
Fax: 441-086-4173
Contains information on distance education, including more than 22,000 distance-taught programs and courses in the Commonwealth of Learning, an organization created by the Commonwealth Heads of Government. On-line and CD-Rom versions of the database contain detailed information on over 30,000 distance-taught courses, 900 distance teaching instructions, and nearly 9,000 books, journals, reports and papers.

Keith Harry, Director

6173 EDUCAUSE
1112 16th Street NW
Suite 600
Washington, DC 20036-4822
202-872-4200
Fax: 202-872-4318
http://www.educause.edu
Aims to link practitioners in primary and secondary education through computer-mediated communications networks.

John Clement, Director

6174 Educational Structures
NCS Pearson
827 W Grove Avenue
Mesa, AZ 85210
800-736-4357
http://www.ncspearson.com
Features complete lesson plans and resources in social studies, mathematics, science, and language arts.

6175 Gibson Tech Ed
1216 S 1580 West
Building C
Orem, UT 84058
800-422-1100
Fax: 800-470-1606
E-mail: gary@gibsonteched.com
http://www.gibsonteched.com
Educational materials to teach electronics, from middle, junior, high school and college.

Gary Gibson, Manager
Tim Gibson, President

6176 Grolier Interactive
Grolier Publishing
90 Sherman Turnpike
Danbury, CT 06816
800-371-3908
Fax: 800-456-4402
http://http://publishing.grolier.com
Instructional software including reference, science, mathematics, music, social studies, early learning, art and art history, language arts/literature.

6177 Heifner Communications
4451 Interstate 70 Drive NW
Columbia, MO 65202-3271
573-445-6163
800-445-6164
Fax: 512-527-2395
Offers educational-merit, cable-programming available via satellite. HCI Distance Learning systems are designed for dependable services and ease of operation and competitive prices.

Vicky Roberts

6178 In Focus
27700 B SW Parkway Avenue
Wilsonville, OR 97070-9215
503-685-8887
800-294-6400
Fax: 503-685-8887
LCD panels, video projectors and systems.

6179 JonesKnowledge.com
9697 E Mineral Avenue
Englewood, CO 80112
800-701-6463
For administrators, that means and integrated solution-with no minimum commitment, or upfront investment. For instructors, it means getting your course online your way, without being a web expert, and for students it means, an accessible and convenient online experience.

6180 Mastercam
CNC Software
5717 Wollochet Drive NW
Suite 2A
Gig Harbor, WA
800-275-6226
Fax: 253-858-6737
E-mail: mcinfo@mastercam.com
http://www.mastercamedu.com

6181 Merit Audio Visual
Merit Software
132 W 21st Street
New York, NY 10011-3203
212-675-8567
800-753-6488
Fax: 212-675-8607
E-mail: sales@meritsoftware.com
http://www.merutsoftware.com
Easy to use, interactive basic skills software for Windows 9x/ME/NT/2000/XP computers. Lessons for reading, writing, grammar and math with appropriate graphics for teens and adults.

Ben Weintraub, Marketing Manager

6182 National Information Center for Educational Media
PO Box 8640
Albuquerque, NM 87198
505-265-3591
800-926-8328
Fax: 505-256-1080
E-mail: nicem@nicem.com
http://www.nicem.com
NICEM maintains a comprehensive database describing educational media materials for all ages and subjects. It is available on CD-ROM and online.

Lisa Savard, Sales/Marketing Director

6183 NoRad Corporation
4455 Torrance Boulevard
#2806513
Torrance, CA 90503-4398
310-605-0808
Fax: 323-934-2101
Mini, personal, medium and large computer systems for educational institutions.

6184 Proxima Corporation
9440 Carroll Park Drive
San Diego, CA 92121
858-457-5500
800-294-6400
Fax: 503-685-7239
http://www.proxima.com
Proxima Corporation is a global leader in the multimedia projection market, providing world class presentation solutions to corporate enterprises, workgroups, mobile professionals, trainers, and professional public speakers.

Kim Gallagher, Public Relations Manager
Kathy Bankerd, Director Marketing Programs

6185 RB5X: Education's Personal Computer Robot
General Robotics Corporation
760 S Youngfield Court
Suite 8
Lakewood, CO 80228-2813
303-988-5636
800-422-4265
Fax: 303-988-5303
E-mail: cbrown@generalrobotics.com
http://www.edurobot.com
RB5X: Education's Personal Computer Robot. All grade levels. Self learn, self teach, hands on modular system. Problem solving, basic learning skills, increases self-esteem. Expanable open-ended, motivation at its best.

Constant Brown, President

6186 SEAL
550 Spring Street
Naugatuck, CT 06770-1906
203-729-5201
Complete line of systems and electronics for schools.

6187 Sharp Electronics Corporation
LCD Products Group
Sharp Plaza
Mall Stop One
Mahwah, NJ 07430
201-529-8731
Fax: 201-529-9636
E-mail: prolcd@sharpsec.com
http://www.sharplcd.com
Offers a full line of LCD-based video and computer multimedia projectors and projection panels for use in a wide range of educational applications. Sharp's product line also includes industrial VHS format VCRs, color TV monitors.

J Ganguzza, Director/Marketing

6188 Valiant
PO Box 3171
S Hackensack, NJ 07606-1171
800-631-0867
Fax: 201-814-0418
Distributors of LCD projection panels, P/A systems, overhead/slide and filmstrip projectors, cassette recorders, classroom record players, laser pointers, laminating equipment, lecturns, listening centers and headphones.
Sheldon Goldstein

6189 Vernier Software
8565 SW Beaverton Hillsdale Hwy
Portland, OR 97225-2429
Laboratory interacting software for the Macintosh, IBM and Apple II.

6190 Websense
10240 Sorrento Valley Road
San Diego, CA 92121
858-320-8000
800-723-1166
Fax: 858-458-2950
http://www.websense.com
Internet filtering.

6191 http://di...elearn/cs/eductechnology/index.htm
About Education Distance Learning

6192 http://futurekids.com
FUTUREKIDS School Technology Solutions
http://www.futurekids.com
Helping schools use technology to transform education.

6193 http://online.uophx.edu
University of Phoenix Online
Offers you the convenience and flexibility of attending classes from your personal computer. Students are discussing issues, sharing ideas, testing theories, essentially enjoying all of the advantages of an on-campus degree programs. Interaction is included like e-mail, so you practice at your convenience.

6194 http://www.crossteccorp.com
NetOp
800-675-0729
Fax: 561-391-5820
http://www.crossteccorp.com
A powerful combination of seven essential tools for networked classrooms. Based on the award winning technology of NetOp Remote Control and is easy-to-use software only solution.

6195 http://www.growsmartbrains.com
GrowSmartBrains.com
Website for parents and educators who want research based information and practical stradegies for raising children in a media age.

6196 http://www.zdnet.com
ZDNet
Full-service destination for people looking to buy, use and learn more about technology.

6197 www.21ct.org
Twenty First Century Teachers Network
A nationwide, non-profit initiative of the McGuffey Project, dedicated to assisting k-12 teachers learn, use and effectively integrate technology in the curriculum for improved student learning.

6198 www.aboutonehandtyping.com/
One Hand Typing and Keyboarding Resources
This site dishes up a blend of messages and stories, resources for one-hand typists, links to alternative keyboards, teaching links, and more.

6199 www.digitaldividenetwork.org
Digital Divide Network
E-mail: ddivide@benton.org
The goal of bridging the divide is to use communications technology to help improve the quality of life of all communities and their citizens; provide them with the tools, skills and information they need to help them realize their socioeconomic, educational and cultural potential.

6200 www.getquizzed.com
GetQuizzed
Designed as a free service that provides a database that allows users to create, store and edit Multiple Choice or Question and Answer quizzes, under password protected conditions.

6201 www.guidetogeekdom.com
Guide to Geekdom
E-mail: info@guidetogeekdom.com
Designed especially for Homeschoolers, step-by-step lessons teach students how to use the computer and troubleshoot computer problems. Offers workbooks, sample lesson and more.

6202 www.happyteachers.com
HappyTeachers.com
Information about technical and vocational education programs, products and curriculum.

6203 www.integratingit.com
Integrating Information Technology for the Classroom, School, & District

Dedicated to providing the education community a place to find real world strategies, solutions, and resources for integrating technology. Organized by the perspective of the classroom teacher, the school administrator, and the district.

6204 www.livetext.com
LiveText Curriculum Manager
Provides tools for engaged learning classroom projects and provides online professional development for teachers.

6205 www.ncrel.org
North Central Regional Educational Laboratory
Offers research results regarding the effective use of technology.

6206 www.ncrtec.org
N Central Regional Technology in Education Consortiums

Provides a variety of tools and information to improve technology-related professional development programs.

349

Elementary Education

6207 Curriculum Associates
153 Rangeway Road
No. Billerica, MA 01862
800-225-0248
Fax: 800-366-1158
http://www.curriculumassociates.com
Test preparation material with a guarantee of success; skill instruction and assessment.

6208 Diagnostic Reading Inventory for Primaryand Intermediate Grades K-8
Scott and McCleary Publishing Co.
2482 11th Street SW
Akron, OH 44314-1712
702-566-8756
800-765-3564
Fax: 702-568-1378
E-mail: jscott7576@aol.com
http://www.scottmccleary.com
A series of 13 tests at each grade level, 10 can be given in a group setting. 3 Forms of the IRI teacher friendly. Easy to administer.
Spiral Paperback
ISBN: 0-9636225-4-4
Janet M. Scott and Sheila C. McCleary, Author
Janet Scott, Co-Author
Sheila McCleary, Co-Author

6209 Lexia Learning Systems
PO Box 466
Lincoln, MA 01773-0466
781-259-8752
Fax: 781-259-1349
E-mail: info@lexialearning.com
http://www.lexialearning.com
Reading software and assessment programs for children and adults, professional development programs for teachers, principals and administrators.

6210 LinguiSystems
3100 4th Avenue
East Moline, IL 61244-9700
800-776-4332
Fax: 800-577-4555
E-mail: service@linguisystems.com
http://www.linguisystems.com
Offers tests and print materials for speech language pathologists, teachers of the learning disabled, middle school language arts and reading teachers.

6211 National Study of School Evaluation
1699 E Woodfield Road
Suite 406
Schaumburg, IL 60173-4958
847-995-9080
800-843-6773
Fax: 847-995-9088
E-mail: schoolimprovement@nsse.org
http://www.nsse.org
Provides educational leaders with state-of-the-art assessment and evaluation materials to enhance and promote student growth and school improvement.
Dr. Kathleen A. Fitzpatrick, Executive Director

6212 Testing Miss Malarky
Walker And Company
435 Hudson Street
New York, NY 10014
212-727-8300
800-289-2553
Fax: 212-727-0984
http://www.walkerbooks.com

Author and artist exploit the mania that accompanies the classes first standardized test.
32 pages
ISBN: 0-8027-8737-1
Judy Finchler, Contact

Language Arts

6213 CTB/McGraw-Hill
20 Ryan Ranch Road
Monterey, CA 93940-5703
831-393-0700
800-538-9547
Fax: 800-282-0266
http://www.ctb.com
K-12 achievement tests, early literacy assessment, language proficiency evaluation, adult basic skills tests, and test management and instructional planning software.

6214 SLEP Program Office
PO Box 6155
Princeton, NJ 08541-6155
Offers information on the Secondary Level English Proficiency Test.

Mathematics

6215 Psychological Assessment Resources
PO Box 998
Odessa, FL 33556
800-331-TEST
Fax: 800-727-9329
http://www.parinc.com
Catalog of professional testing resources.

6216 Summing It Up: College Board Mathematics Assessment Programs
College Board Publications
45 Columbus Avenue
New York, NY 10023-6917
212-713-8165
800-323-7155
Fax: 800-525-5562
http://www.collegeboard.org
An overview of SAT I: Reasoning Tests and PSAT/NMSQT, SAT II: Subject Tests, Descriptive Tests of Mathematical Skills (DTMS), CPTs in Mathematics, CLEP Mathematics Examinations, AP Exams in Mathematics, AP Exams in Computer Sciences, and Pacesetter Mathematics.
30 pages

Music & Art

6217 A&F Video's Art Catalog
PO Box 264
Geneseo, NY 14454
http://www.aandfvideo.com
New listing of titles for Art Teachers and Art Lovers.

6218 All Art Supplies
Art Supplies Wholesale
4 Enon Street
North Beverly, MA 01915
800-462-2420
http://www.allartsupplies.com
Art supplies at wholesale prices.

6219 American Art Clay Company
6060 Guion Road
Indianapolis, IN 46254

317-244-6871
800-374-1600
Fax: 317-248-9300
E-mail: catalog@amaco.com
http://www.amaco.com
Provides ceramic materials and equipment.

6220 Arnold Grummer
PO Box 13245
Milwaukee, WI 53213
800-453-1485
Fax: 414-453-1495
E-mail: webmaster@arnoldgrummer.com
http://www.arnoldgrummer.com
Products and information to meet most any papermaking need.

6221 Arrowmont School of Arts & Crafts
556 Parkway
Gainsburg, TN 37738
865-438-5860
Fax: 865-438-4101
http://www.arrowmont.org
The art school of tomorrow.

6222 Art & Creative Materials Institute
PO Box 479
Hanson, MA 02341
781-293-4100
Fax: 781-294-0808
E-mail: debbieg@acminec.org
http://www.acminec.org
A non-profit trade association whose memebers are manufacturers of art and creative materials. Sponsors a certification program to ensure that art materials are non-toxic or affixed with health warning labels where appropriate. Publishes a booklet on the safe use of art materials and a listing of products that are approved under its certification program. Both of these publications are free of charge.
Deborah Fanning, Executive Vice President
Deborah Gustafson, Associate Director

6223 Art Instruction Schools
3309 Broadway Street NW
Minneapolis, MN 55413
http://www.artists-ais.com

6224 Art to Remember
10625 Deme Drive
Unit E
Indianapolis, IN 46236
317-826-0870
800-895-8777
Fax: 317-823-2822
http://www.arttoremember.com
A unique program that encourages your students' artisic creativity while providing an oppurtunity to raise funds for schools.

6225 ArtSketchbook.com
487 Hulsetown Road
Campbell Hall, NY 10916
845-496-4709
http://www.artsketchbook.com
Provides instructions and work examples by an elementary student, secondary student and a professional artist.

6226 Arts Institutes International
Education Management Corporation
300 6th Avenue
Suite 800
Pittsburgh, PA 15222
800-275-2440
Post-secondary career education. Offers associate's, bachelor's and non-degree programs in design, media arts, technology, culinary arts and fashion.

6227 Museum Stamps
PO Box 356
New Canaan, CT 06840

800-659-2787
Fax: 203-966-2729
http://www.museumstamps.com
Rubber stamps of famous works of art, stamp accessories, classroom projects.

6228 Music Ace 2

Harmonic Vision
68 E Wacker Place
8th Floor
Chicago, IL 60610
312-332-9200
800-474-0903
Fax: 312-726-1946
http://www.harmonicvision.com
Introduces concepts such as standard notation, rhythm, melody, time signatures, harmony, intervals and more.

6229 http://www.ilford.com

Ilford
Partners in imaging.

6230 www.schoolrenaissance.com

School Renaissance Model
The School Renaissance Model combines the #1 software in education with professional development and consulting services to help you dramatically improve student performance.

6231 www.speedballart.com

Speedball lesson plans and teaching aids for calligraphy, stamping, printmaking, drawing, painting and more.

Reading

6232 Advantage Learning Systems

2911 Peach Street
PO Box 8036
Wisconsin Rapids, WI 54495-8036
800-338-4204
Fax: 715-424-4242
http://www.advlearn.com
New computer-adaptive tests that assess student reading and math levels in just 15 minutes or less.

6233 Educational Testing Service/Library

Test Collection
Rosedale Road
Princeton, NJ 08541
609-734-5686
Fax: 609-734-5410
Provides information on tests and related materials to those in research and advisory services and educational activities.

Janet Williams, President

6234 National Foundation for Dyslexia

4801 Hermitage Road
Richmond, VA 23227-3332
804-262-0586
800-SOS-READ
Provides screenings for schools or individuals and assists individuals with IEP's. Provides information about support groups and organizations and teacher training workshops.

Jo Powell, Executive Director

6235 Psychological Assessment Resources

PO Box 998
Odessa, FL 33556
800-331-TEST
Fax: 800-727-9329
http://www.parinc.com
Catalog of professional testing resources.

6236 www.schoolrenaissance.com

Renaissance Learning and School Renaissance Inst.
The School Renaissance Model combines the #1 software in education with professional development and consulting services to help you dramatically improve student performance.

6237 www.voyagerlearning.com

Voyager Expanded Learning
Improves students performance in reading for those at different grade levels.

Secondary Education

6238 ACT

PO Box 4060
Iowa City, IA 52243-0001
319-337-1000
800-498-6065
Offers a full-service catalog of tests for intermediate and secondary schools organized by assessment, career and educational planning, study skills, surveys and research services.

Catalog

6239 Admission Officer's Handbook for the New SAT Program

College Board Publications
45 Columbus Avenue
New York, NY 10023-6917
212-713-8165
800-323-7155
Fax: 800-525-5562
http://www.collegeboard.org
Designed to help college admission staff quickly find information on the new SAT program, the Handbook has detailed descriptions of score reports and special services for colleges.

56 pages

6240 American College Testing

ACT
2201 Dodge
#168
Iowa City, IA 52243-0001
319-337-1028
Fax: 319-337-1014
E-mail: gullettk@act.org
http://www.act.org
Provides educational assessment services to students and their parents, high schools, colleges and professional associations. Also workforce development services, including a network of ACT Centers and the Workkeys program.

Ken Gullette, Director, Media Relations

6241 College-Bound Seniors

College Board Publications
45 Columbus Avenue
New York, NY 10023-6917
212-713-8165
800-323-7155
Fax: 800-525-5562
http://www.collegeboard.org
Profile of SAT and achievement test takers, national report.

13 pages

6242 CollegeChoice, StudentChoice

College Board Publications
45 Columbus Avenue
New York, NY 10023-6917
212-713-8165
800-323-7155
Fax: 800-525-5562
http://www.collegeboard.org
This video provides a reassuring perspective on the SAT's importance and how the college

admission process really works. It shows how SAT scores are only one of many elements in the admission picture and emphasizes academic preparation for college and discusses the SAT within the context of the entire admission process.

15 Minutes

6243 Counselor's Handbook for the SAT Program

College Board Publications
45 Columbus Avenue
New York, NY 10023-6917
212-713-8165
800-323-7155
Fax: 800-525-5562
http://www.collegeboard.org
Easy-to-use reference provides details on the new SAT program tests and services.

64 pages

6244 Destination College: Planning with the PSAT/NMSQT

College Board Publications
45 Columbus Avenue
New York, NY 10023-6917
212-713-8165
800-323-7155
Fax: 800-525-5562
http://www.collegeboard.org
This new video offers schools an ideal format for explaining the features and benefits of the PSAT/NMSQT Score Report to groups of students.

18 Minutes

6245 Educational Testing Service

Rosedale Road
MS 26-C
Princeton, NJ 08541
609-921-9000
Fax: 609-734-5410
Private educational measurement institution and a leader in educational research.

Susan Keipper, Program Director

6246 Focus on the SAT: What's on it, How to Prepare & What Colleges Look For

College Board Publications
45 Columbus Avenue
New York, NY 10023-6917
212-713-8165
800-323-7155
Fax: 800-525-5562
http://www.collegeboard.org
The authoritative video for students on how to prepare for the SAT and PSAT/NMSQT. It provides test-taking tips, sample test questions, and an explanation of how SAT is developed.

20 Minutes

6247 GED Testing Service

American Council on Education
1 Dupont Cir NW
Washington, DC 20036-1110
202-939-9490
Fax: 202-775-8578
The largest testing service in the United States. Maintains a full line of tests and testing resources for all areas of education and all grade levels K-college level testing.

6248 Guide to the College Board Validity Study Service

College Board Publications
45 Columbus Avenue
New York, NY 10023-6917
212-713-8165
800-323-7155
Fax: 800-525-5562
http://www.collegeboard.org

The purpose of this manual is to assist Validity Study Service users in designing and interpreting validity studies. It provides design suggestions, sample admission and placement studies, advice on interpreting studies, and a discussion of basic statistical concepts.

60 pages

6249 Look Inside the SAT I: Test Prep from the Test Makers Video
College Board Publications
45 Columbus Avenue
New York, NY 10023-6917
212-713-8165
800-323-7155
Fax: 800-525-5562
http://www.collegeboard.org
Brings the College Board's test-taking tips to life through interviews with people from different backgrounds who recount their SAT experiences.

30 Minutes
ISBN: 0-874475-29-5

6250 Master The GMAT
Peterson's, A Nelnet Company
Princeton Pike Corporate Center
2000 Lenox Drive PO Box 67005
Lawrenceville, NJ 08648
609-896-1800
800-338-3282
Fax: 690-896-4531
E-mail: custsvc@petersons.com
http://www.petersons.com
Helps test takers get ready, develop test-preparation strategies and manage test anxiety constructively, whether they have seven weeks to prepare or just one day.

672 pages Book & Disk

Martinson, Author

6251 Master The SAT
Peterson's, A Nelnet Company
Princeton Pike Corporate Center
2000 Lenox Drive PO Box 67005
Lawrenceville, NJ 08648
609-896-1800
800-338-3282
Fax: 609-896-4531
E-mail: custsvc@petersons.com
http://www.petersons.com
Features easily accessible Red Alert sections offering essential tips for test-taking success. Provides students with the critical skills they need to tackle the SAT.

821 pages Book & Disk
ISBN: 1-560796-06-5

John Davenport Carris with Michael R. Crystal, Author

6252 National Center for Fair & Open Testing
342 Broadway
Cambridge, MA 02139-1843
617-864-4810
Fax: 617-497-2224
Dedicated to ensuring that America's students and workers are assessed using fair, accurate, relevant and open tests.

Cinthia Schuman, President

6253 National Study of School Evaluation
1699 E Woodfield Road
Suite 406
Schaumburg, IL 60173-4958
847-995-9080
800-843-6773
Fax: 847-995-9088

E-mail: schoolimprovement@nsse.org
http://www.nsse.org
Provides educational leaders with state-of-the-art assessment and evaluation materials to enhance and promote student growth and school improvement.

Dr. Kathleen A. Fitzpatrick, Executive Director

6254 Official Guide to the SAT II: Subject Tests
College Board Publications
45 Columbus Avenue
New York, NY 10023-6917
212-713-8165
800-323-7155
Fax: 800-525-5562
http://www.collegeboard.org
The authoritative preparation guide for students taking the SAT II: Subject Tests. The guide includes full-length practice Subject Tests, along with answer sheets, answer keys, and scoring instructions for Writing, Literature, American History, World History, Math I, Math IIC, Biology, Chemistry and Physics. It also includes minitests in French (reading only), German (reading only), Italian, Latin, Modern Hebrew, and Spanish.

380 pages
ISBN: 0-874474-88-4

6255 One-On-One with the SAT
College Board Publications
45 Columbus Avenue
New York, NY 10023-6917
212-713-8165
800-323-7155
Fax: 800-525-5562
http://www.collegeboard.org
Gives students easy access to proven advice and test-taking strategies directly from the test makers, as well as a unique chance to take a real SAT on computer. This program also includes password protection for each student record and toll-free technical support.

Home License

6256 Panic Plan for the SAT
Peterson's, A Nelnet Company
Princeton Pike Corporate Center
2000 Lenox Drive PO Box 67005
Lawrenceville, NJ 08648
609-896-1800
800-338-3282
Fax: 609-896-4531
E-mail: custsvc@petersons.com
http://www.petersons.com
An excellent, two-week review, featuring actual questions from the SAT. Helps students make the most out of the limited time they have left to study.

368 pages
ISBN: 1-560794-32-1

Michael R Crystal, Author

6257 Preventing School Failure
Heldref Publications
1319 Eighteenth Street NW
Washington, DC 20036-1802
202-296-6267
800-365-9753
Fax: 202-296-5149
http://www.heldref.org
The articles cover a broad array of specific topics, from important technical aspects and adaptions of functional behavioral assessment to descriptions of projects in which functional behavioral assessment is being used to provide technical assistance to preschools, schools, and families who

must deal eith children and adolescents who present serious challenging behaviors.

Quarterly
ISSN: 1045-988X

Sheldon Braaten, Executive Editor

6258 Psychological Corporation
555 Academic Court
San Antonio, TX 78204-2498
210-921-8701
Assessment materials for teachers in all areas of curricula.

6259 Psychometric Affiliates
PO Box 807
Murfreeboro, TN 37133
615-890-6296
Testing instruments for use by educational institutions.

Jeannette Heritage

6260 Real SAT's
College Board Publications
45 Columbus Avenue
New York, NY 10023-6917
212-713-8165
800-323-7155
Fax: 800-525-5562
http://www.collegeboard.org
The only preparation guide that contains actual scorable tests. It has been developed to help the millions of students taking the tests each year to do their best on the PSAT/NMSQT and SAT and to improve their scores.

396 pages
ISBN: 0-874475-11-2

6261 Registration Bulletin
College Board Publications
45 Columbus Avenue
New York, NY 10023-6917
212-713-8165
800-323-7155
Fax: 800-525-5562
http://www.collegeboard.org
Available in five regional and a New York State edition, the Bulletin provides information on how to register for the SAT I and SAT II, and on how to use the related services.

24 pages

6262 SAT Services for Students with Disabilities
College Board Publications
45 Columbus Avenue
New York, NY 10023-6917
212-713-8165
800-323-7155
Fax: 800-525-5562
http://www.collegeboard.org
Describes arrangements for students with physical, hearing, visual and learning disabilities who wish to take the SAT I and/or SAT II.

6 pages

6263 Scholastic Testing Service
480 Meyer Road
Bensenville, IL 60106-1617
630-766-7150
800-642-6STS
Fax: 630-766-8054
E-mail: stslh25@aol.com
http://www.ststesting.com
Publisher of assessment materials from birth into adulthood, ability and achievement tests for kindergarten through grade twelve. Tests are also constructed on contract for educational agencies and school districts. Publish the Torrance Tests of Creative Thinking, Thinking Creatively in Action and Movement, the STS High School Placement Test and Educational Development Series.

OF Anderhalter, President
John D Kauffman, VP Marketing

6264 TOEFL Test and Score Manual
College Board Publications
45 Columbus Avenue
New York, NY 10023-6917
212-713-8165
800-323-7155
Fax: 800-525-5562
http://www.collegeboard.org
Focuses on information that college admissions officers, foreign student advisers and other users of TOEFL score reports need to know about the operation of the TOEFL program, the test itself, and the interpretation of scores.

48 pages

6265 Taking the SAT I: Reasoning Test
College Board Publications
45 Columbus Avenue
New York, NY 10023-6917
212-713-8165
800-323-7155
Fax: 800-525-5562
http://www.collegeboard.org
A complete guide for students who plan to take the SAT I: Reasoning Test.

80 pages

6266 Taking the SAT II: The Official Guide to the SAT II: Subject Tests
College Board Publications
45 Columbus Avenue
New York, NY 10023-6917
212-713-8165
800-323-7155
Fax: 800-525-5562
http://www.collegeboard.org
Provides information about the content and format of each of the SAT II: Subject Tests, as well as test-taking advice and sample questions.

95 pages

6267 TestSkills
College Board Publications
45 Columbus Avenue
New York, NY 10023-6917
212-713-8165
800-323-7155
Fax: 800-525-5562
http://www.collegeboard.org
A preparation program for the PSAT/NMSQT that helps students, particularly those from minority and disadvantaged groups, sharpen skills and increase confidence needed to succeed on the tests.

Spiral-Bound

6268 Think Before You Punch: Using Calculators on the New SAT I and PSAT/NMSQT
College Board Publications
45 Columbus Avenue
New York, NY 10023-6917
212-713-8165
800-323-7155
Fax: 800-525-5562
http://www.collegeboard.org
This video looks at the pros and cons of calculators usage on a test. In it, students talk about using them, and College Board and ETS staff explain the new calculator policy. It works through math questions that may or may not best be answered with the help of a calculator.

12 Minutes

EDUCATION STATISTICS

Percentage of persons age 25 and over and of persons 25 to 29 years old with high school completion or higher and a bachelor's or higher degree, by race/ethnicity and sex: Selected years, 1910 through 2011

Age, year, and sex	Total		White[1]		Black[1]		Hispanic		Asian[2]	
	High school completion or higher[3]	Bachelor's or higher degree[4]	High school completion or higher[3]	Bachelor's or higher degree[4]	High school completion or higher[3]	Bachelor's or higher degree[4]	High school completion or higher[3]	Bachelor's or higher degree[4]	High school completion or higher[3]	Bachelor's or higher degree[4]
1	2	3	4	5	6	7	8	9	10	11
Total, 25 and over										
1910[5]	13.5 (—)	2.7 (—)	— (†)	— (†)	— (†)	— (†)	— (†)	— (†)	— (†)	— (†)
1920[5]	16.4 (—)	3.3 (—)	— (†)	— (†)	— (†)	— (†)	— (†)	— (†)	— (†)	— (†)
1930[5]	19.1 (—)	3.9 (—)	— (†)	— (†)	— (†)	— (†)	— (†)	— (†)	— (†)	— (†)
April 1940	24.5 (—)	4.6 (—)	26.1 (—)	4.9 (—)	7.7 (—)	1.3 (—)	— (†)	— (†)	— (†)	— (†)
April 1950	34.3 (—)	6.2 (—)	36.4 (—)	6.6 (—)	13.7 (—)	2.2 (—)	— (†)	— (†)	— (†)	— (†)
April 1960	41.1 (—)	7.7 (—)	43.2 (—)	8.1 (—)	21.7 (—)	3.5 (—)	— (†)	— (†)	— (†)	— (†)
March 1970	55.2 (—)	11.0 (—)	57.4 (—)	11.6 (—)	36.1 (—)	6.1 (—)	— (†)	— (†)	— (†)	— (†)
March 1975	62.5 (—)	13.9 (—)	65.8 (—)	14.9 (—)	42.6 (—)	6.4 (—)	38.5 (—)	6.6 (—)	— (†)	— (†)
March 1980	68.6 (0.20)	17.0 (0.16)	71.9 (0.21)	18.4 (0.18)	51.4 (0.81)	7.9 (0.44)	44.5 (1.18)	7.6 (0.63)	— (†)	— (†)
March 1985	73.9 (0.18)	19.4 (0.16)	77.5 (0.19)	20.8 (0.19)	59.9 (0.74)	11.1 (0.47)	47.9 (0.99)	8.5 (0.55)	— (†)	— (†)
March 1986	74.7 (0.18)	19.4 (0.16)	78.2 (0.19)	20.9 (0.19)	62.5 (0.72)	10.9 (0.47)	48.5 (0.96)	8.4 (0.53)	— (†)	— (†)
March 1987	75.6 (0.17)	19.9 (0.16)	79.0 (0.18)	21.4 (0.19)	63.6 (0.71)	10.8 (0.46)	50.9 (0.94)	8.6 (0.53)	— (†)	— (†)
March 1988	76.2 (0.17)	20.3 (0.16)	79.8 (0.18)	21.8 (0.19)	63.5 (0.70)	11.2 (0.46)	51.0 (0.92)	10.0 (0.55)	— (†)	— (†)
March 1989	76.9 (0.17)	21.1 (0.16)	80.7 (0.18)	22.8 (0.19)	64.7 (0.69)	11.7 (0.46)	50.9 (0.89)	9.9 (0.53)	82.3 (1.17)	41.5 (1.51)
March 1990	77.6 (0.17)	21.3 (0.16)	81.4 (0.17)	23.1 (0.19)	66.2 (0.67)	11.3 (0.45)	50.8 (0.88)	9.2 (0.51)	84.2 (1.09)	41.7 (1.47)
March 1991	78.4 (0.16)	21.4 (0.16)	82.4 (0.17)	23.3 (0.19)	66.8 (0.66)	11.5 (0.45)	51.3 (0.86)	9.7 (0.51)	84.2 (1.05)	40.3 (1.42)
March 1992	79.4 (0.16)	21.4 (0.16)	83.4 (0.16)	23.2 (0.19)	67.7 (0.65)	11.9 (0.45)	52.6 (0.85)	9.3 (0.49)	83.7 (1.02)	39.3 (1.35)
March 1993	80.2 (0.16)	21.9 (0.16)	84.1 (0.16)	23.8 (0.19)	70.5 (0.63)	12.2 (0.45)	53.1 (0.83)	9.0 (0.48)	84.2 (1.00)	42.1 (1.35)
March 1994	80.9 (0.15)	22.2 (0.16)	84.9 (0.16)	24.3 (0.19)	73.0 (0.61)	12.9 (0.46)	53.3 (0.78)	9.1 (0.45)	84.8 (0.98)	41.3 (1.34)
March 1995	81.7 (0.15)	23.0 (0.16)	85.9 (0.16)	25.4 (0.19)	73.8 (0.61)	13.3 (0.47)	53.4 (0.78)	9.3 (0.45)	83.8 (1.06)	38.5 (1.40)
March 1996	81.7 (0.16)	23.6 (0.17)	86.0 (0.16)	25.9 (0.20)	74.6 (0.53)	13.8 (0.42)	53.1 (0.68)	9.3 (0.40)	83.5 (0.82)	42.3 (1.09)
March 1997	82.1 (0.14)	23.9 (0.16)	86.3 (0.15)	26.2 (0.19)	75.3 (0.52)	13.3 (0.41)	54.7 (0.54)	10.3 (0.33)	85.2 (0.75)	42.6 (1.04)
March 1998	82.8 (0.14)	24.4 (0.16)	87.1 (0.14)	26.6 (0.19)	76.4 (0.50)	14.8 (0.42)	55.5 (0.53)	11.0 (0.33)	84.9 (0.74)	42.3 (1.02)
March 1999	83.4 (0.14)	25.2 (0.16)	87.7 (0.14)	27.7 (0.19)	77.4 (0.49)	15.5 (0.43)	56.1 (0.52)	10.9 (0.33)	84.7 (0.73)	42.4 (1.01)
March 2000	84.1 (0.13)	25.6 (0.16)	88.4 (0.14)	28.1 (0.19)	78.9 (0.48)	16.6 (0.44)	57.0 (0.51)	10.6 (0.32)	85.7 (0.71)	44.4 (1.00)
March 2001	84.3 (0.13)	26.1 (0.16)	88.7 (0.13)	28.6 (0.19)	79.5 (0.47)	16.1 (0.43)	56.5 (0.50)	11.2 (0.32)	87.8 (0.60)	48.0 (0.92)
March 2002	84.1 (0.09)	26.7 (0.11)	88.7 (0.10)	29.4 (0.14)	79.2 (0.34)	17.2 (0.31)	57.0 (0.34)	11.1 (0.21)	87.7 (0.44)	47.7 (0.66)
March 2003	84.6 (0.09)	27.2 (0.11)	89.4 (0.09)	30.0 (0.14)	80.3 (0.33)	17.4 (0.31)	57.0 (0.33)	11.4 (0.21)	87.8 (0.44)	50.0 (0.67)
March 2004	85.2 (0.09)	27.7 (0.11)	90.0 (0.09)	30.6 (0.14)	81.1 (0.32)	17.7 (0.31)	58.4 (0.32)	12.1 (0.21)	86.9 (0.44)	49.7 (0.66)
March 2005[6]	85.2 (0.14)	27.7 (0.23)	90.1 (0.16)	30.6 (0.29)	81.4 (0.44)	17.6 (0.45)	58.5 (0.53)	12.0 (0.31)	87.7 (0.62)	50.4 (0.93)
March 2006[6]	85.5 (0.15)	28.0 (0.20)	90.5 (0.15)	31.0 (0.25)	81.2 (0.43)	18.6 (0.47)	59.3 (0.58)	12.4 (0.32)	87.5 (0.71)	50.0 (1.06)
March 2007[6]	85.7 (0.15)	28.7 (0.21)	90.6 (0.15)	31.8 (0.27)	82.8 (0.39)	18.7 (0.51)	60.3 (0.56)	12.7 (0.31)	87.9 (0.81)	52.5 (1.03)
March 2008[6]	86.6 (0.15)	29.4 (0.21)	91.5 (0.15)	32.6 (0.26)	83.3 (0.40)	19.7 (0.51)	62.3 (0.58)	13.3 (0.29)	88.8 (0.64)	52.9 (0.97)
March 2009[6]	86.7 (0.15)	29.5 (0.21)	91.6 (0.15)	32.9 (0.26)	84.2 (0.44)	19.4 (0.45)	61.9 (0.56)	13.2 (0.34)	88.3 (0.63)	52.8 (0.95)
March 2010[6]	87.1 (0.13)	29.9 (0.19)	92.1 (0.14)	33.2 (0.24)	84.7 (0.41)	20.0 (0.51)	62.9 (0.53)	13.9 (0.31)	89.1 (0.68)	52.8 (1.09)
March 2011[6]	87.6 (0.13)	30.4 (0.19)	92.4 (0.14)	34.0 (0.24)	84.8 (0.41)	20.2 (0.50)	64.3 (0.54)	14.1 (0.34)	88.7 (0.57)	50.8 (0.96)
Total, 25 to 29										
1920[5]	— (†)	— (†)	22.0 (—)	4.5 (—)	6.3 (—)	1.2 (—)	— (†)	— (†)	— (†)	— (†)
April 1940	38.1 (—)	5.9 (—)	41.2 (—)	6.4 (—)	12.3 (—)	1.6 (—)	— (†)	— (†)	— (†)	— (†)
April 1950	52.8 (—)	7.7 (—)	56.3 (—)	8.2 (—)	23.6 (—)	2.8 (—)	— (†)	— (†)	— (†)	— (†)
April 1960	60.7 (—)	11.0 (—)	63.7 (—)	11.8 (—)	38.6 (—)	5.4 (—)	— (†)	— (†)	— (†)	— (†)
March 1970	75.4 (—)	16.4 (—)	77.8 (—)	17.3 (—)	58.4 (—)	10.0 (—)	— (†)	— (†)	— (†)	— (†)
March 1975	83.1 (—)	21.9 (—)	86.6 (—)	23.8 (—)	71.1 (—)	10.5 (—)	53.1 (—)	8.8 (—)	— (†)	— (†)
March 1980	85.4 (0.40)	22.5 (0.47)	89.2 (0.40)	25.0 (0.55)	76.7 (1.64)	11.6 (1.24)	58.0 (2.59)	7.7 (1.39)	— (†)	— (†)
March 1985	86.1 (0.37)	22.2 (0.45)	89.5 (0.38)	24.4 (0.53)	80.5 (1.42)	11.6 (1.15)	60.9 (2.17)	11.1 (1.39)	— (†)	— (†)
March 1986	86.1 (0.37)	22.4 (0.45)	89.6 (0.37)	25.2 (0.53)	83.5 (1.32)	11.8 (1.15)	59.1 (2.07)	9.0 (1.21)	— (†)	— (†)
March 1987	86.0 (0.37)	22.0 (0.44)	89.4 (0.38)	24.6 (0.53)	83.4 (1.32)	11.5 (1.13)	59.8 (2.04)	8.7 (1.17)	— (†)	— (†)
March 1988	85.9 (0.37)	22.7 (0.45)	89.7 (0.38)	25.1 (0.54)	80.9 (1.39)	12.0 (1.15)	62.3 (1.96)	11.3 (1.28)	— (†)	— (†)
March 1989	85.5 (0.38)	23.4 (0.45)	89.3 (0.38)	26.3 (0.55)	81.7 (1.35)	12.6 (1.17)	61.0 (1.92)	10.1 (1.19)	89.7 (2.31)	45.1 (3.77)
March 1990	85.7 (0.38)	23.2 (0.46)	90.1 (0.37)	26.4 (0.55)	81.7 (1.37)	13.4 (1.20)	58.2 (1.94)	8.1 (1.07)	91.5 (2.09)	43.0 (3.71)
March 1991	85.4 (0.39)	23.2 (0.46)	89.8 (0.39)	26.7 (0.56)	81.8 (1.36)	11.0 (1.10)	56.7 (1.96)	9.2 (1.15)	92.5 (2.00)	41.6 (3.74)
March 1992	86.3 (0.38)	23.6 (0.47)	90.7 (0.38)	27.2 (0.58)	80.9 (1.41)	11.0 (1.12)	60.9 (1.93)	9.5 (1.16)	95.7 (1.53)	44.6 (3.77)
March 1993	86.7 (0.38)	23.7 (0.48)	91.2 (0.37)	27.2 (0.59)	82.6 (1.36)	13.3 (1.22)	60.9 (1.90)	8.3 (1.08)	94.4 (1.69)	44.6 (3.67)
March 1994	86.1 (0.39)	23.3 (0.47)	91.1 (0.38)	27.1 (0.60)	84.1 (1.31)	13.6 (1.23)	60.3 (1.75)	8.0 (0.97)	92.2 (1.92)	45.9 (3.58)
March 1995	86.8 (0.39)	24.7 (0.49)	92.5 (0.36)	28.8 (0.62)	86.7 (1.23)	15.4 (1.31)	57.1 (1.80)	8.9 (1.04)	90.8 (2.26)	43.1 (3.87)
March 1996	87.3 (0.40)	27.1 (0.53)	92.6 (0.38)	31.6 (0.67)	86.0 (1.14)	14.6 (1.16)	61.1 (1.58)	10.0 (0.97)	90.0 (1.68)	49.9 (2.80)
March 1997	87.4 (0.37)	27.8 (0.50)	92.9 (0.35)	32.6 (0.63)	86.0 (1.10)	14.2 (1.14)	61.8 (1.24)	11.0 (0.80)	90.6 (1.60)	51.2 (2.74)
March 1998	88.1 (0.36)	27.3 (0.50)	93.6 (0.34)	32.3 (0.64)	88.2 (1.04)	15.8 (1.18)	62.8 (1.23)	10.4 (0.78)	90.5 (1.60)	43.1 (2.70)
March 1999	87.8 (0.37)	28.2 (0.51)	93.0 (0.35)	33.6 (0.66)	88.7 (1.03)	15.0 (1.16)	61.6 (1.26)	8.9 (0.74)	93.4 (1.31)	51.3 (2.65)
March 2000	88.1 (0.37)	29.1 (0.52)	94.0 (0.33)	34.0 (0.67)	86.8 (1.13)	17.8 (1.28)	62.8 (1.22)	9.7 (0.75)	93.7 (1.27)	54.3 (2.60)
March 2001	87.7 (0.38)	28.6 (0.52)	93.3 (0.36)	33.0 (0.68)	87.0 (1.11)	17.8 (1.27)	63.2 (1.23)	11.1 (0.80)	95.2 (1.06)	54.8 (2.46)
March 2002	86.4 (0.28)	29.3 (0.37)	93.0 (0.26)	35.9 (0.50)	87.6 (0.80)	18.0 (0.94)	62.4 (0.78)	8.9 (0.46)	95.4 (0.76)	55.9 (1.80)
March 2003	86.5 (0.27)	28.4 (0.36)	93.7 (0.25)	34.2 (0.49)	88.5 (0.78)	17.5 (0.93)	61.7 (0.75)	10.0 (0.47)	97.3 (0.60)	62.1 (1.77)
March 2004	86.6 (0.27)	28.7 (0.36)	93.3 (0.26)	34.5 (0.49)	88.7 (0.76)	17.1 (0.90)	62.4 (0.75)	10.9 (0.48)	96.6 (0.67)	62.6 (1.78)
March 2005[6]	86.2 (0.42)	28.8 (0.55)	92.8 (0.39)	34.5 (0.78)	87.0 (1.03)	17.6 (1.21)	63.3 (1.32)	11.2 (0.81)	95.5 (0.92)	62.1 (2.25)

See notes at end of table.

Percentage of persons age 25 and over and of persons 25 to 29 years old with high school completion or higher and a bachelor's or higher degree, by race/ethnicity and sex: Selected years, 1910 through 2011—Continued

Age, year, and sex	Total				White[1]				Black[1]				Hispanic				Asian[2]			
	High school completion or higher[3]		Bachelor's or higher degree[4]		High school completion or higher[3]		Bachelor's or higher degree[4]		High school completion or higher[3]		Bachelor's or higher degree[4]		High school completion or higher[3]		Bachelor's or higher degree[4]		High school completion or higher[3]		Bachelor's or higher degree[4]	
1	2		3		4		5		6		7		8		9		10		11	
March 2006[6]	86.4	(0.36)	28.4	(0.52)	93.4	(0.35)	34.3	(0.78)	86.3	(1.09)	18.7	(1.33)	63.2	(1.17)	9.5	(0.66)	96.6	(0.86)	61.9	(2.44)
March 2007[6]	87.0	(0.36)	29.6	(0.54)	93.5	(0.33)	35.5	(0.75)	87.7	(1.16)	19.5	(1.21)	65.0	(1.06)	11.6	(0.61)	97.5	(0.73)	61.5	(2.26)
March 2008[6]	87.8	(0.36)	30.8	(0.51)	93.7	(0.38)	37.1	(0.70)	87.5	(1.29)	20.4	(1.35)	68.3	(1.16)	12.4	(0.69)	95.8	(0.91)	60.2	(2.32)
March 2009[6]	88.6	(0.36)	30.6	(0.57)	94.6	(0.33)	37.2	(0.85)	88.9	(0.98)	18.9	(1.36)	68.9	(1.16)	12.2	(0.80)	95.8	(0.95)	60.3	(2.28)
March 2010[6]	88.8	(0.32)	31.7	(0.51)	94.5	(0.31)	38.6	(0.72)	89.6	(0.93)	19.4	(1.20)	69.4	(1.22)	13.5	(0.80)	94.0	(1.24)	55.8	(2.47)
March 2011[6]	89.0	(0.34)	32.2	(0.62)	94.4	(0.34)	39.2	(0.88)	88.1	(0.98)	20.1	(1.25)	71.5	(1.12)	12.8	(0.73)	95.3	(0.91)	57.2	(2.52)
Males, 25 and over																				
April 1940	22.7	(—)	5.5	(—)	24.2	(—)	5.9	(—)	6.9	(—)	1.4	(—)	—	(†)	—	(†)	—	(†)	—	(†)
April 1950	32.6	(—)	7.3	(—)	34.6	(—)	7.9	(—)	12.6	(—)	2.1	(—)	—	(†)	—	(†)	—	(†)	—	(†)
April 1960	39.5	(—)	9.7	(—)	41.6	(—)	10.3	(—)	20.0	(—)	3.5	(—)	—	(†)	—	(†)	—	(†)	—	(†)
March 1970	55.0	(—)	14.1	(—)	57.2	(—)	15.0	(—)	35.4	(—)	6.8	(—)	—	(†)	—	(†)	—	(†)	—	(†)
March 1980	69.2	(0.30)	20.9	(0.26)	72.4	(0.31)	22.8	(0.29)	51.2	(1.23)	7.7	(0.66)	44.9	(1.74)	9.2	(1.01)	—	(†)	—	(†)
March 1990	77.7	(0.24)	24.4	(0.25)	81.6	(0.25)	26.7	(0.29)	65.8	(1.03)	11.9	(0.70)	50.3	(1.27)	9.8	(0.76)	86.0	(1.49)	45.9	(2.14)
March 1995	81.7	(0.22)	26.0	(0.25)	86.0	(0.22)	28.9	(0.29)	73.5	(0.91)	13.7	(0.71)	52.9	(1.11)	10.1	(0.67)	85.8	(1.46)	42.3	(2.06)
March 1996	81.9	(0.23)	26.0	(0.26)	86.1	(0.23)	28.8	(0.30)	74.6	(0.80)	12.5	(0.61)	53.0	(0.97)	10.3	(0.59)	86.2	(1.10)	46.9	(1.59)
March 1997	82.0	(0.21)	26.2	(0.24)	86.3	(0.21)	29.0	(0.28)	73.8	(0.79)	12.5	(0.60)	54.9	(0.76)	10.6	(0.47)	87.5	(1.00)	48.0	(1.51)
March 1998	82.8	(0.20)	26.5	(0.24)	87.1	(0.21)	29.3	(0.28)	75.4	(0.77)	14.0	(0.62)	55.7	(0.74)	11.1	(0.47)	87.9	(0.98)	46.0	(1.50)
March 1999	83.4	(0.20)	27.5	(0.24)	87.7	(0.20)	30.6	(0.28)	77.2	(0.74)	14.3	(0.62)	56.0	(0.75)	10.7	(0.46)	86.9	(1.00)	46.3	(1.48)
March 2000	84.2	(0.19)	27.8	(0.24)	88.5	(0.20)	30.8	(0.28)	79.1	(0.72)	16.4	(0.65)	56.6	(0.73)	10.7	(0.45)	88.4	(0.94)	48.1	(1.47)
March 2001	84.4	(0.19)	28.0	(0.24)	88.6	(0.19)	30.9	(0.28)	80.6	(0.69)	15.9	(0.64)	55.6	(0.72)	11.1	(0.45)	90.6	(0.78)	52.9	(1.33)
March 2002	83.8	(0.14)	28.5	(0.17)	88.5	(0.14)	31.7	(0.20)	79.0	(0.51)	16.5	(0.47)	56.1	(0.48)	11.0	(0.30)	89.8	(0.58)	51.5	(0.96)
March 2003	84.1	(0.13)	28.9	(0.17)	89.0	(0.14)	32.3	(0.20)	79.9	(0.50)	16.8	(0.47)	56.3	(0.46)	11.2	(0.29)	89.8	(0.59)	54.2	(0.98)
March 2004	84.8	(0.13)	29.4	(0.17)	89.9	(0.13)	32.9	(0.20)	80.8	(0.49)	16.6	(0.46)	57.3	(0.45)	11.8	(0.30)	88.8	(0.60)	54.0	(0.95)
March 2005[6]	84.9	(0.19)	28.9	(0.29)	89.9	(0.20)	32.4	(0.37)	81.4	(0.60)	16.0	(0.64)	57.9	(0.69)	11.8	(0.43)	90.5	(0.66)	54.3	(1.13)
March 2006[6]	85.0	(0.20)	29.2	(0.24)	90.2	(0.21)	32.8	(0.31)	80.7	(0.63)	17.5	(0.63)	58.5	(0.77)	11.9	(0.40)	89.7	(0.86)	53.1	(1.35)
March 2007[6]	85.0	(0.21)	29.5	(0.25)	90.2	(0.22)	33.2	(0.33)	82.5	(0.55)	18.1	(0.62)	58.2	(0.80)	11.8	(0.37)	90.1	(0.82)	55.8	(1.32)
March 2008[6]	85.9	(0.19)	30.1	(0.25)	91.1	(0.20)	33.8	(0.33)	82.1	(0.61)	18.7	(0.67)	60.9	(0.72)	12.6	(0.39)	90.8	(0.69)	56.1	(1.24)
March 2009[6]	86.2	(0.19)	30.1	(0.28)	91.4	(0.20)	33.9	(0.36)	84.2	(0.60)	17.9	(0.57)	60.6	(0.72)	12.5	(0.41)	90.7	(0.68)	56.5	(1.17)
March 2010[6]	86.6	(0.17)	30.3	(0.23)	91.8	(0.19)	34.2	(0.30)	84.2	(0.57)	17.9	(0.59)	61.4	(0.68)	12.9	(0.37)	91.5	(0.79)	56.2	(1.30)
March 2011[6]	87.1	(0.18)	30.8	(0.23)	92.0	(0.17)	35.0	(0.29)	84.2	(0.55)	18.4	(0.64)	63.6	(0.71)	13.1	(0.44)	90.6	(0.69)	54.0	(1.21)
Females, 25 and over																				
April 1940	26.3	(—)	3.8	(—)	28.1	(—)	4.0	(—)	8.4	(—)	1.2	(—)	—	(†)	—	(†)	—	(†)	—	(†)
April 1950	36.0	(—)	5.2	(—)	38.2	(—)	5.4	(—)	14.7	(—)	2.4	(—)	—	(†)	—	(†)	—	(†)	—	(†)
April 1960	42.5	(—)	5.8	(—)	44.7	(—)	6.0	(—)	23.1	(—)	3.6	(—)	—	(†)	—	(†)	—	(†)	—	(†)
March 1970	55.4	(—)	8.2	(—)	57.7	(—)	8.6	(—)	36.6	(—)	5.6	(—)	—	(†)	—	(†)	—	(†)	—	(†)
March 1980	68.1	(0.28)	13.6	(0.21)	71.5	(0.30)	14.4	(0.23)	51.5	(1.10)	8.1	(0.60)	44.2	(1.66)	6.2	(0.80)	—	(†)	—	(†)
March 1990	77.5	(0.23)	18.4	(0.22)	81.3	(0.24)	19.8	(0.25)	66.5	(0.92)	10.8	(0.60)	51.3	(1.25)	8.7	(0.70)	82.5	(1.57)	37.8	(2.01)
March 1995	81.6	(0.21)	20.2	(0.22)	85.8	(0.22)	22.1	(0.26)	74.1	(0.81)	13.0	(0.62)	53.8	(1.09)	8.4	(0.61)	81.9	(1.54)	35.0	(1.90)
March 1996	81.6	(0.22)	21.4	(0.23)	85.9	(0.22)	23.2	(0.27)	74.6	(0.71)	14.8	(0.58)	53.3	(0.97)	8.3	(0.53)	81.0	(1.21)	38.0	(1.50)
March 1997	82.2	(0.20)	21.7	(0.21)	86.3	(0.20)	23.7	(0.25)	76.5	(0.68)	14.0	(0.56)	54.6	(0.76)	10.1	(0.46)	82.9	(1.11)	37.4	(1.43)
March 1998	82.9	(0.19)	22.4	(0.21)	87.1	(0.20)	24.1	(0.25)	77.1	(0.67)	15.4	(0.58)	55.3	(0.75)	10.9	(0.47)	82.3	(1.09)	38.9	(1.39)
March 1999	83.3	(0.19)	23.1	(0.22)	87.6	(0.19)	25.0	(0.26)	77.5	(0.66)	16.5	(0.59)	56.3	(0.73)	11.0	(0.46)	82.8	(1.06)	39.0	(1.37)
March 2000	84.0	(0.19)	23.6	(0.22)	88.4	(0.19)	25.5	(0.26)	78.7	(0.64)	16.8	(0.59)	57.5	(0.71)	10.6	(0.44)	83.4	(1.03)	41.0	(1.37)
March 2001	84.2	(0.18)	24.3	(0.22)	88.8	(0.19)	26.5	(0.26)	78.6	(0.64)	16.3	(0.58)	57.4	(0.70)	11.3	(0.45)	85.2	(0.91)	43.4	(1.26)
March 2002	84.4	(0.13)	25.1	(0.15)	88.9	(0.13)	27.3	(0.19)	79.4	(0.45)	17.7	(0.42)	57.9	(0.48)	11.2	(0.31)	85.7	(0.64)	44.2	(0.91)
March 2003	85.0	(0.13)	25.7	(0.15)	89.7	(0.13)	27.9	(0.19)	80.7	(0.44)	18.0	(0.43)	57.8	(0.46)	11.6	(0.30)	86.1	(0.64)	46.3	(0.92)
March 2004	85.4	(0.12)	26.1	(0.15)	90.1	(0.12)	28.4	(0.19)	81.2	(0.43)	18.5	(0.43)	59.5	(0.46)	12.3	(0.31)	85.1	(0.64)	45.7	(0.90)
March 2005[6]	85.5	(0.15)	26.5	(0.23)	90.3	(0.18)	28.9	(0.30)	81.5	(0.53)	18.9	(0.51)	59.1	(0.63)	12.1	(0.42)	85.2	(0.78)	46.8	(1.10)
March 2006[6]	85.9	(0.16)	26.9	(0.22)	90.8	(0.17)	29.3	(0.28)	81.5	(0.51)	19.5	(0.55)	60.1	(0.59)	12.9	(0.39)	85.6	(0.81)	47.3	(1.15)
March 2007[6]	86.4	(0.15)	28.0	(0.23)	91.0	(0.16)	30.6	(0.29)	83.0	(0.49)	19.2	(0.59)	62.5	(0.56)	13.7	(0.44)	86.0	(0.97)	49.5	(1.10)
March 2008[6]	87.2	(0.17)	28.8	(0.24)	91.8	(0.18)	31.5	(0.29)	84.2	(0.49)	20.5	(0.58)	63.7	(0.61)	14.1	(0.37)	87.0	(0.78)	50.1	(1.02)
March 2009[6]	87.1	(0.16)	29.1	(0.21)	91.9	(0.17)	31.9	(0.26)	84.2	(0.48)	20.6	(0.56)	63.3	(0.59)	14.0	(0.41)	86.3	(0.75)	49.7	(1.02)
March 2010[6]	87.6	(0.15)	29.6	(0.21)	92.3	(0.17)	32.4	(0.26)	85.0	(0.46)	21.6	(0.63)	64.4	(0.59)	14.9	(0.42)	87.1	(0.75)	49.9	(1.19)
March 2011[6]	88.0	(0.15)	30.1	(0.22)	92.8	(0.16)	33.1	(0.28)	85.3	(0.50)	21.7	(0.60)	65.1	(0.57)	15.2	(0.43)	87.0	(0.66)	48.0	(1.07)

—Not available.

†Not applicable.

[1]Includes persons of Hispanic ethnicity for years prior to 1980.

[2]Includes Pacific Islanders for years prior to 2003.

[3]Data for years prior to 1993 are for persons with 4 or more years of high school. Data for later years are for high school completers—i.e., those persons who graduated from high school with a diploma, as well as those who completed high school through equivalency programs, such as a GED program.

[4]Data for years prior to 1993 are for persons with 4 or more years of college.

[5]Estimates based on Census Bureau reverse projection of 1940 census data on education by age.

[6]Beginning in 2005, standard errors were computed using replicate weights, which produced more precise values than the methodology used in prior years. For more information, see Appendix A: Guide to Sources.

NOTE: Totals include other racial/ethnic groups not separately shown. Race categories exclude persons of Hispanic ethnicity except where otherwise noted. Standard errors appear in parentheses.

SOURCE: U.S. Department of Commerce, Census Bureau, *U.S. Census of Population: 1960*, Vol. I, Part 1; J.K. Folger and C.B. Nam, *Education of the American Population* (1960 Census Monograph); Current Population Reports, Series P-20, various years; and Current Population Survey (CPS), March 1970 through March 2011. (This table was prepared September 2011.)

Number of persons age 18 and over, by highest level of educational attainment, sex, race/ethnicity, and age: 2011

[In thousands]

Sex, race/ethnicity, and age	Total	Elementary		High school			College					
		Less than 7 years	7 or 8 years	1 to 3 years	4 years, no completion	Completion	Some college	Associate's degree	Bachelor's degree	Master's degree	First-professional degree	Doctor's degree
1	2	3	4	5	6	7	8	9	10	11	12	13
Total, 18 and over	231,194 (100.8)	6,295 (135.8)	4,554 (120.1)	16,545 (214.1)	3,458 (100.9)	70,316 (378.3)	45,245 (313.6)	20,611 (204.1)	41,943 (287.9)	16,154 (201.8)	2,993 (89.8)	3,079 (99.6)
18 and 19 years old	8,125 (86.1)	58 (14.0)	83 (12.3)	2,786 (61.8)	619 (35.6)	2,109 (66.8)	2,373 (66.9)	62 (11.1)	26 (7.1)	#	#	‡ (†)
20 to 24 years old	21,525 (25.1)	205 (20.6)	225 (24.5)	1,392 (60.3)	444 (35.4)	6,296 (127.9)	8,670 (143.6)	1,503 (62.4)	2,631 (90.4)	139 (22.9)	13 ! (5.3)	‡ (†)
25 years old and over	201,543 (59.3)	6,031 (128.3)	4,246 (109.1)	12,368 (189.6)	2,395 (78.1)	61,911 (350.0)	34,203 (277.9)	19,047 (194.2)	39,286 (280.3)	16,015 (198.0)	2,980 (89.4)	3,062 (99.3)
25 to 29 years old	21,382 (34.6)	390 (29.3)	261 (22.1)	1,363 (56.0)	330 (27.1)	5,757 (110.4)	4,277 (94.5)	2,126 (71.8)	5,398 (122.4)	1,134 (58.3)	213 (22.4)	133 (18.0)
30 to 34 years old	20,202 (40.1)	526 (35.7)	282 (23.8)	1,191 (48.2)	214 (20.7)	5,493 (95.3)	3,564 (86.6)	2,079 (66.3)	4,549 (109.8)	1,715 (59.3)	302 (26.9)	287 (25.5)
35 to 39 years old	19,255 (29.3)	523 (34.9)	277 (22.6)	1,089 (44.6)	227 (22.0)	5,117 (89.5)	3,280 (76.8)	2,031 (60.4)	4,385 (78.0)	1,745 (59.5)	252 (23.1)	328 (27.9)
40 to 49 years old	42,576 (40.9)	1,122 (50.4)	577 (37.5)	2,417 (66.2)	488 (33.1)	12,774 (155.6)	6,985 (120.9)	4,501 (96.2)	8,907 (126.0)	3,559 (87.1)	669 (37.2)	579 (34.3)
50 to 59 years old	41,519 (55.9)	1,101 (44.7)	564 (34.9)	2,172 (73.0)	466 (30.5)	13,190 (153.1)	7,106 (109.2)	4,247 (70.8)	7,974 (126.8)	3,475 (92.5)	576 (37.2)	649 (34.6)
60 to 64 years old	17,430 (97.0)	470 (29.3)	338 (25.3)	863 (44.0)	191 (20.1)	5,355 (92.8)	3,105 (81.3)	1,676 (70.8)	3,066 (85.6)	1,685 (63.1)	343 (31.9)	339 (28.9)
65 years old and over	39,179 (81.6)	1,899 (68.5)	1,948 (68.5)	3,272 (95.6)	479 (36.9)	14,225 (153.4)	5,886 (119.7)	2,387 (70.7)	5,008 (113.6)	2,703 (87.7)	624 (41.8)	748 (51.8)
Males, 18 and over	112,301 (88.5)	3,161 (85.0)	2,303 (79.6)	8,449 (140.7)	1,853 (67.5)	35,082 (267.9)	21,393 (202.7)	8,905 (142.7)	20,137 (184.8)	7,231 (131.5)	1,870 (66.6)	1,916 (70.2)
18 and 19 years old	4,121 (64.1)	32 (16.1)	56 (9.3)	1,521 (47.4)	326 (24.5)	988 (49.6)	1,024 (40.0)	27 (7.9)	13 ! (4.7)	#	‡ (†)	‡ (†)
20 to 24 years old	10,960 (22.6)	127 (16.4)	131 (19.6)	759 (43.2)	253 (26.5)	2,705 (92.7)	4,232 (105.5)	697 (45.0)	1,107 (54.9)	50 (11.6)	#	‡ (†)
25 years old and over	97,220 (58.2)	3,002 (82.3)	2,115 (72.3)	6,169 (126.7)	1,274 (53.9)	30,370 (249.8)	16,137 (169.9)	8,182 (133.0)	19,017 (182.8)	7,181 (129.1)	1,862 (66.2)	1,911 (70.0)
25 to 29 years old	10,917 (34.1)	250 (25.0)	142 (17.1)	782 (41.5)	194 (20.8)	3,352 (87.5)	2,153 (69.9)	946 (52.3)	2,541 (82.4)	418 (36.9)	90 (14.5)	50 (12.2)
30 to 34 years old	10,067 (39.8)	293 (26.9)	163 (17.9)	694 (34.1)	122 (16.5)	3,092 (72.5)	1,722 (58.6)	929 (46.1)	2,101 (57.7)	652 (38.8)	148 (19.6)	151 (18.7)
35 to 39 years old	9,542 (29.9)	279 (33.8)	147 (15.8)	565 (31.7)	120 (16.8)	2,847 (64.8)	1,548 (50.9)	883 (40.1)	2,087 (52.5)	762 (38.6)	117 (15.8)	186 (18.7)
40 to 49 years old	20,972 (40.5)	592 (30.4)	314 (27.1)	1,276 (47.2)	298 (26.9)	6,798 (110.6)	3,285 (83.5)	1,908 (62.6)	4,193 (85.7)	1,571 (56.9)	399 (27.3)	340 (25.9)
50 to 59 years old	20,194 (38.6)	539 (30.2)	277 (23.4)	1,146 (57.0)	239 (23.7)	6,502 (109.7)	3,362 (79.7)	1,797 (59.3)	3,948 (89.5)	1,614 (59.4)	382 (27.9)	385 (26.9)
60 to 64 years old	8,447 (87.8)	220 (20.4)	151 (17.1)	426 (30.7)	109 (15.6)	2,347 (63.2)	1,534 (56.0)	755 (41.9)	1,632 (82.7)	792 (39.4)	250 (26.4)	230 (24.0)
65 years old and over	17,081 (81.5)	829 (44.5)	921 (46.6)	1,280 (56.8)	193 (20.9)	5,432 (97.9)	2,533 (75.7)	964 (49.9)	2,515 (71.3)	1,371 (61.0)	476 (36.9)	568 (41.0)
Females, 18 and over	118,893 (57.3)	3,134 (87.6)	2,251 (71.8)	8,096 (137.6)	1,605 (63.9)	35,234 (235.1)	23,852 (213.7)	11,706 (143.3)	21,806 (196.1)	8,923 (141.9)	1,123 (50.4)	1,163 (55.7)
18 and 19 years old	4,005 (55.8)	26 (7.6)	26 (7.3)	1,265 (45.4)	293 (24.0)	1,121	1,349 (47.9)	36 (6.9)	13 ! (5.5)	#	#	‡ (†)
20 to 24 years old	10,565 (6.9)	78 (12.8)	94 (14.1)	633 (39.1)	191 (20.0)	3,591	4,437 (83.2)	806 (41.0)	1,524 (66.8)	89 (18.8)	#	‡ (†)
25 years old and over	104,323 (11.5)	3,030 (83.5)	2,130 (67.8)	6,198 (117.3)	1,121 (49.0)	31,541	18,065 (185.5)	10,865 (139.4)	20,269 (185.9)	8,834 (137.2)	1,118 (50.3)	1,151 (55.5)
25 to 29 years old	10,464 (6.3)	140 (15.7)	119 (14.5)	581 (32.7)	137 (15.8)	2,405	2,123 (58.5)	1,180 (49.3)	2,857 (73.9)	717 (45.1)	124 (16.6)	83 (15.2)
30 to 34 years old	10,135 (5.4)	233 (20.3)	119 (13.5)	497 (28.0)	93 (13.1)	2,401	1,842 (56.2)	1,151 (47.6)	2,447 (62.8)	1,062 (43.6)	154 (15.1)	135 (17.9)
35 to 39 years old	9,713 (6.0)	244 (19.8)	130 (15.5)	524 (28.0)	108 (13.3)	2,270	1,732 (48.9)	1,149 (45.7)	2,298 (51.1)	983 (38.5)	135 (15.1)	142 (16.4)
40 to 49 years old	21,604 (6.5)	530 (31.7)	262 (24.1)	1,142 (42.1)	190 (16.6)	5,976	3,700 (73.1)	2,593 (58.8)	4,715 (87.5)	1,988 (58.3)	270 (23.2)	239 (19.5)
50 to 59 years old	21,325 (38.1)	562 (29.2)	286 (24.1)	1,026 (41.7)	227 (20.9)	6,688	3,743 (81.0)	2,449 (72.5)	4,026 (85.8)	1,860 (63.4)	194 (20.3)	264 (23.2)
60 to 64 years old	8,983 (38.0)	250 (20.5)	186 (20.1)	437 (30.6)	82 (13.8)	3,008	1,571 (57.2)	920 (49.5)	1,434 (48.5)	892 (45.9)	93 (16.6)	109 (13.6)
65 years old and over	22,098 (0.4)	1,070 (44.7)	1,028 (46.3)	1,992 (64.0)	286 (25.9)	8,793	3,354 (80.6)	1,423 (50.9)	2,492 (75.3)	1,332 (57.4)	148 (19.5)	180 (21.9)
White, 18 and over	156,709 (115.8)	1,069 (59.9)	2,304 (90.6)	8,503 (147.8)	1,484 (65.2)	47,765 (316.8)	31,211 (281.5)	14,947 (198.0)	32,065 (272.6)	12,662 (185.2)	2,374 (86.1)	2,325 (88.7)
18 and 19 years old	4,735 (71.9)	26 ! (10.2)	44 (9.2)	1,624 (45.1)	293 (22.8)	1,253 (55.0)	1,432 (56.3)	36 (9.3)	18 ! (5.6)	#	#	‡ (†)
20 to 24 years old	12,829 (30.0)	27 ! (8.8)	75 (17.8)	560 (39.3)	145 (18.6)	3,552 (107.3)	5,434 (125.4)	965 (53.0)	1,965 (82.3)	96 (18.6)	13 ! (5.3)	‡ (†)
25 years old and over	139,146 (91.3)	1,017 (60.8)	2,185 (83.4)	6,320 (144.2)	1,046 (56.6)	42,960 (291.9)	24,345 (247.7)	13,945 (188.6)	30,082 (264.4)	12,566 (184.2)	2,371 (86.2)	2,310 (88.4)
25 to 29 years old	12,782 (31.8)	38 (9.5)	87 (14.7)	494 (36.1)	94 (14.0)	3,141 (71.9)	2,519 (71.9)	1,399 (58.6)	3,972 (105.8)	810 (51.3)	130 (17.4)	98 (16.6)
30 to 34 years old	12,078 (43.1)	43 (12.5)	84 (13.2)	410 (31.6)	50 (10.0)	3,016 (72.4)	2,195 (72.2)	1,406 (51.9)	3,241 (77.8)	1,207 (50.2)	227 (24.2)	198 (23.0)
35 to 39 years old	11,531 (34.8)	46 ! (13.1)	79 (14.0)	393 (31.3)	58 (11.9)	2,810 (63.8)	2,082 (64.3)	1,370 (53.2)	3,057 (72.5)	1,251 (50.4)	178 (18.7)	207 (22.6)
40 to 49 years old	28,202 (43.8)	95 (19.1)	174 (20.5)	1,111 (47.6)	196 (21.8)	8,308 (125.0)	4,757 (104.7)	3,258 (74.8)	6,738 (110.4)	2,652 (76.6)	510 (34.1)	403 (27.7)
50 to 59 years old	30,244 (50.3)	143 (18.7)	258 (26.5)	1,153 (55.8)	221 (25.0)	9,722 (142.0)	5,373 (106.5)	3,220 (90.5)	6,269 (117.7)	2,912 (86.6)	484 (35.7)	489 (32.8)
60 to 64 years old	13,258 (88.4)	80 (14.5)	156 (21.2)	487 (36.4)	108 (16.4)	4,054 (83.8)	2,460 (78.0)	1,347 (62.5)	2,566 (85.2)	1,429 (60.4)	299 (30.0)	271 (26.7)
65 years old and over	31,052 (85.7)	571 (42.8)	1,348 (60.0)	2,271 (85.8)	320 (31.3)	11,908 (145.9)	4,958 (112.5)	1,946 (67.2)	4,240 (107.3)	2,305 (78.2)	543 (41.3)	643 (48.3)
Black, 18 and over	26,684 (63.4)	412 (34.5)	473 (32.5)	2,895 (87.8)	622 (43.2)	9,062 (130.5)	6,006 (116.0)	2,456 (70.3)	3,214 (87.3)	1,199 (47.3)	176 (15.5)	168 (20.9)
18 and 19 years old	1,209 (32.8)	#	15 ! (5.7)	478 (27.0)	114 (15.6)	290 (23.7)	300 (23.9)	7 ! (3.6)	‡ (†)	#	‡ (†)	#
20 to 24 years old	2,996 (20.1)	12 ! (5.7)	30 (8.9)	264 (27.2)	82 (14.2)	945 (43.0)	1,252 (45.9)	201 (25.0)	198 (21.6)	#	#	‡ (†)
25 years old and over	22,479 (48.5)	400 (32.6)	428 (31.3)	2,153 (72.1)	426 (31.9)	7,826 (118.6)	4,455 (96.9)	2,247 (66.5)	3,012 (82.3)	1,188 (46.8)	175 (15.6)	168 (20.9)
25 to 29 years old	2,782 (20.0)	9 ! (3.7)	22 (6.5)	236 (22.1)	64 (13.6)	925 (43.9)	698 (35.4)	269 (25.3)	448 (34.6)	78 (12.2)	29 (7.8)	13 ! (5.5)
30 to 34 years old	2,564 (17.6)	16 ! (6.0)	10 ! (4.3)	183 (18.8)	48 (7.8)	897 (38.5)	579 (38.2)	271 (24.5)	411 (27.5)	124 (17.4)	12 ! (4.7)	24 (7.0)
35 to 39 years old	2,351 (16.2)	21 ! (9.8)	16 ! (5.7)	174 (19.1)	25 ! (7.8)	810 (35.8)	497 (28.3)	268 (21.7)	365 (27.0)	132 (15.5)	17 ! (9.3)	35 (10.2)
40 to 49 years old	5,103 (21.3)	35 (8.2)	31 (6.9)	374 (27.4)	101 (13.9)	1,822 (59.5)	1,024 (43.9)	557 (34.7)	758 (36.4)	316 (20.6)	48 (9.3)	38 (8.4)
50 to 59 years old	4,604 (44.6)	58 (10.8)	65 (10.8)	461 (27.4)	86 (12.4)	1,595 (46.5)	894 (36.6)	522 (30.8)	624 (31.8)	228 (21.7)	31 (8.4)	38 (5.8)
60 to 64 years old	1,762 (41.1)	29 (6.6)	42 (9.6)	183 (18.3)	31 (7.5)	667 (32.6)	318 (23.6)	169 (18.1)	164 (15.1)	123 (14.6)	19 (5.7)	17 ! (7.4)
65 years old and over	3,314 (21.1)	233 (19.3)	242 (21.0)	542 (28.2)	70 (10.9)	1,109 (35.1)	444 (23.2)	190 (17.0)	241 (18.7)	187 (16.7)	19 (5.0)	37 (7.4)

See notes at end of table.

Number of persons age 18 and over, by highest level of educational attainment, sex, race/ethnicity, and age: 2011—Continued

[In thousands]

Sex, race/ethnicity, and age	Total	Elementary		High school			Some college	College				
		Less than 7 years	7 or 8 years	1 to 3 years	4 years, no completion	Completion		Associate's degree	Bachelor's degree	Master's degree	First-professional degree	Doctor's degree
1	2	3	4	5	6	7	8	9	10	11	12	13
Hispanic, 18 and over	32,434 (32.5)	4,291 (106.3)	1,524 (60.2)	4,258 (94.3)	1,103 (51.2)	9,825 (131.4)	5,388 (100.3)	2,049 (60.4)	2,895 (77.7)	780 (40.1)	147 (16.7)	174 (16.3)
18 and 19 years old	1,589 (31.8)	26 ! (8.6)	19 ! (5.7)	523 (27.5)	156 (15.9)	432 (23.9)	419 (22.8)	13 ! (4.6)	‡	# (†)	# (†)	# (†)
20 to 24 years old	4,173 (7.9)	153 (16.4)	107 (15.4)	483 (31.8)	195 (21.9)	1,436 (48.8)	1,326 (45.9)	238 (21.0)	224 (18.8)	8 ! (3.7)	‡ (†)	# (†)
25 years old and over	26,672 (11.1)	4,112 (102.2)	1,398 (56.7)	3,251 (83.6)	752 (38.8)	7,957 (118.8)	3,642 (84.7)	1,799 (56.3)	2,669 (75.0)	772 (39.4)	144 (16.6)	174 (16.3)
25 to 29 years old	4,182 (28.9)	333 (26.8)	148 (16.2)	558 (33.6)	154 (17.6)	1,366 (45.2)	761 (37.8)	327 (24.6)	424 (28.4)	76 (12.7)	21 ! (6.7)	14 ! (4.9)
30 to 34 years old	3,948 (29.2)	457 (33.1)	176 (19.3)	541 (33.6)	101 (14.4)	1,236 (40.9)	584 (31.8)	281 (22.0)	432 (26.5)	105 (12.8)	21 (5.7)	14 (4.2)
35 to 39 years old	3,715 (27.1)	429 (29.7)	173 (17.9)	470 (28.2)	125 (16.0)	1,172 (31.8)	504 (28.8)	236 (19.3)	464 (27.7)	96 (11.7)	19 (5.6)	24 (6.1)
40 to 49 years old	6,317 (35.7)	910 (42.9)	324 (25.0)	801 (39.3)	148 (17.8)	1,963 (51.8)	826 (40.8)	432 (28.2)	634 (33.8)	205 (17.3)	33 (7.3)	41 (8.4)
50 to 59 years old	4,201 (38.7)	802 (35.9)	201 (18.6)	416 (29.8)	121 (14.2)	1,176 (39.4)	558 (30.1)	288 (20.1)	440 (29.0)	139 (15.6)	24 (6.0)	36 (7.9)
60 to 64 years old	1,453 (34.2)	330 (22.3)	110 (13.0)	142 (13.6)	38 (8.7)	385 (23.2)	175 (17.2)	94 (12.2)	102 (13.5)	51 (9.0)	10 ! (3.8)	15 ! (4.4)
65 years old and over	2,857 (3.1)	851 (40.9)	265 (22.9)	322 (23.8)	66 (10.3)	659 (28.9)	235 (20.3)	141 (16.2)	173 (16.5)	100 (14.2)	16 (4.4)	30 (7.6)
Asian, 18 and over	10,819 (71.3)	473 (47.5)	195 (20.0)	428 (32.2)	172 (18.7)	2,242 (74.3)	1,555 (55.2)	676 (32.9)	3,158 (76.9)	1,299 (54.5)	257 (22.3)	364 (28.8)
18 and 19 years old	305 (16.3)	‡ (†)	‡ (†)	77 (11.1)	32 (7.1)	41 (7.8)	138 (14.8)	‡ (†)	‡ (†)	# (†)	‡ (†)	‡ (†)
20 to 24 years old	948 (19.8)	‡ (†)	‡ (†)	30 (7.0)	14 ! (5.1)	146 (17.1)	458 (22.4)	65 (12.4)	188 (20.2)	22 ! (7.2)	‡ (†)	‡ (†)
25 years old and over	9,566 (66.2)	455 (39.0)	182 (19.2)	321 (27.9)	127 (18.1)	2,055 (69.4)	969 (42.6)	606 (30.5)	2,967 (73.6)	1,277 (53.2)	254 (22.1)	363 (28.9)
25 to 29 years old	1,101 (27.3)	10 ! (4.0)	‡ (†)	28 (7.5)	12 ! (4.6)	159 (16.9)	179 (18.7)	82 (13.0)	438 (27.3)	146 (17.5)	30 (7.7)	16 (4.8)
30 to 34 years old	1,159 (31.0)	‡ (†)	9 ! (4.3)	22 (6.1)	10 ! (4.2)	200 (18.9)	104 (12.9)	69 (9.9)	393 (23.9)	249 (18.6)	35 (7.7)	57 (10.8)
35 to 39 years old	1,239 (29.3)	26 ! (9.2)	8 ! (4.0)	24 ! (7.1)	11 ! (5.0)	207 (18.9)	105 (12.1)	88 (12.0)	431 (27.4)	238 (22.3)	73 (9.5)	64 (11.0)
40 to 49 years old	2,192 (40.5)	77 (14.1)	42 (8.2)	76 (14.7)	34 (9.1)	453 (26.8)	190 (16.6)	160 (16.7)	658 (33.7)	336 (27.0)	30 (11.5)	92 (12.8)
50 to 59 years old	1,751 (42.1)	93 (12.9)	26 (7.2)	71 (12.5)	31 (7.9)	468 (27.7)	159 (15.2)	113 (13.5)	536 (28.2)	157 (17.6)	30 (6.6)	67 (10.6)
60 to 64 years old	677 (28.0)	25 (5.8)	19 (5.4)	29 ! (9.4)	11 ! (4.1)	168 (16.2)	82 (13.1)	32 (7.5)	207 (18.6)	62 (9.9)	10 ! (4.4)	34 (8.2)
65 years old and over	1,446 (27.6)	213 (21.3)	75 (11.9)	72 (13.4)	17 (4.6)	400 (29.3)	141 (15.9)	62 (10.4)	305 (23.7)	89 (13.1)	40 (9.1)	33 (7.8)

#Rounds to zero.
†Not applicable.
!Interpret data with caution. The coefficient of variation (CV) for this estimate is 30 percent or greater.
‡Reporting standards not met. Either there are too few cases or the coefficient of variation (CV) is 50 percent or greater.
NOTE: Total includes other racial/ethnic groups not shown separately. Although cells with fewer than 75,000 weighted persons are subject to relatively wide sampling variation, they are included in the table to permit various types of aggregations.

Race categories exclude persons of Hispanic ethnicity. Detail may not sum to totals because of rounding. Standard errors appear in parentheses and were computed using replicate weights. For more information, see Appendix A: Guide to Sources.
SOURCE: U.S. Department of Commerce, Census Bureau, Current Population Survey (CPS), March 2011. (This table was prepared September 2011.)

Persons age 25 and over who hold a bachelor's or higher degree, by sex, race/ethnicity, age group, and field of bachelor's degree: 2009

| Field of bachelor's degree | Total | | Sex | | | | Race/ethnicity | | | | | | | | | Age | | | | | |
| | | | Males | | Females | | White | | Black | | Hispanic | | Asian/Pacific Islander | | American Indian/Alaska Native | | 25 to 29 years old | | 30 to 49 years old | | 50 years old and over | |
1	2	(†)	3	(†)	4	(†)	5	(†)	6	(†)	7	(†)	8	(†)	9	(†)	10	(†)	11	(†)	12	(†)
Total population, 25 and over (in thousands)	201,998	(49.3)	97,493	(28.6)	104,505	(29.7)	139,972	(16.8)	22,537	(21.7)	26,116	(15.9)	9,582	(16.0)	1,182	(10.7)	21,459	(20.9)	84,501	(30.0)	96,038	(31.7)
Percent of population with bachelor's degree	27.9	(0.01)	28.4	(0.07)	27.4	(0.06)	31.1	(0.06)	17.7	(0.12)	12.7	(0.11)	48.9	(0.23)	13.7	(0.33)	29.9	(0.14)	30.3	(0.09)	25.3	(0.06)
Bachelor's degree holders											Number (in thousands)											
Total	56,375	(126.9)	27,692	(70.4)	28,682	(71.4)	43,510	(84.1)	3,993	(26.4)	3,309	(28.1)	4,685	(23.3)	162	(4.3)	6,418	(30.8)	25,617	(75.5)	24,340	(57.1)
Agriculture/forestry	619	(7.6)	448	(6.5)	171	(4.3)	531	(7.3)	19	(1.5)	26	(1.8)	38	(2.0)	1	(0.4)	59	(2.9)	262	(4.7)	299	(5.6)
Art/architecture	2,606	(16.8)	1,125	(12.9)	1,481	(12.9)	2,094	(15.5)	108	(3.7)	159	(4.9)	197	(5.0)	6	(1.0)	391	(8.5)	1,232	(12.9)	983	(10.6)
Business/management	11,292	(38.6)	6,572	(29.4)	4,720	(23.1)	8,547	(32.0)	925	(13.8)	776	(11.5)	888	(9.7)	30	(2.0)	1,291	(13.7)	5,760	(28.0)	4,241	(22.1)
Communications	1,984	(17.5)	846	(9.7)	1,138	(12.8)	1,594	(16.9)	165	(5.5)	115	(4.6)	73	(2.9)	5	(0.8)	372	(8.5)	1,139	(12.6)	473	(8.0)
Computer and information sciences	1,495	(16.3)	1,057	(13.3)	439	(6.6)	910	(12.1)	145	(5.0)	96	(4.4)	315	(7.2)	3	(0.5)	259	(6.2)	972	(12.7)	265	(5.6)
Education	7,974	(36.0)	1,998	(18.2)	5,976	(28.9)	6,633	(27.7)	585	(9.0)	408	(7.9)	250	(5.6)	26	(1.7)	577	(8.7)	2,494	(17.4)	4,902	(26.8)
Engineering	4,453	(24.0)	3,882	(21.0)	570	(8.8)	3,101	(20.2)	166	(4.4)	305	(7.3)	819	(11.2)	9	(1.4)	436	(8.6)	2,099	(14.0)	1,917	(13.8)
English/literature	1,953	(15.3)	674	(8.4)	1,279	(11.4)	1,623	(14.0)	104	(3.9)	73	(3.8)	122	(4.4)	4	(0.7)	200	(5.3)	812	(9.9)	942	(10.3)
Foreign languages	618	(8.6)	179	(5.0)	439	(6.7)	477	(8.1)	21	(1.9)	53	(2.6)	56	(2.7)	1	(0.3)	68	(3.3)	250	(6.1)	301	(5.7)
Health sciences	3,806	(23.9)	697	(9.7)	3,109	(22.2)	2,843	(20.3)	304	(6.7)	183	(4.9)	424	(7.9)	12	(1.2)	348	(6.8)	1,714	(14.8)	1,744	(16.1)
Liberal arts/humanities	1,016	(11.8)	415	(7.6)	601	(9.2)	778	(10.8)	69	(3.3)	75	(2.9)	71	(3.3)	5	(0.6)	117	(4.4)	456	(7.8)	443	(7.7)
Mathematics/statistics	868	(10.0)	522	(7.3)	346	(6.5)	678	(8.3)	47	(2.4)	31	(2.2)	101	(3.9)	2	(0.4)	70	(3.2)	325	(6.8)	473	(6.3)
Natural sciences (biological and physical)	3,845	(24.8)	2,296	(17.9)	1,549	(14.6)	2,906	(19.9)	197	(5.3)	177	(5.3)	505	(7.4)	9	(1.1)	455	(7.2)	1,755	(16.2)	1,635	(13.4)
Philosophy/religion/theology	804	(11.4)	561	(8.6)	243	(5.4)	647	(10.5)	60	(3.1)	37	(2.7)	46	(2.3)	2	(0.6)	89	(4.0)	297	(7.1)	419	(7.1)
Pre-professional	815	(11.6)	509	(8.8)	306	(6.5)	586	(9.2)	122	(4.5)	72	(3.4)	18	(1.7)	6	(0.9)	135	(4.5)	472	(8.3)	209	(4.9)
Psychology	2,576	(17.5)	843	(10.4)	1,733	(14.4)	2,015	(15.7)	210	(5.6)	174	(4.5)	124	(4.5)	10	(1.1)	371	(7.6)	1,239	(12.8)	965	(8.3)
Social sciences/history	5,626	(29.3)	3,223	(18.5)	2,403	(18.4)	4,483	(22.9)	386	(7.4)	305	(6.5)	359	(7.7)	15	(1.4)	645	(9.0)	2,445	(18.9)	2,536	(18.8)
Other fields	4,022	(26.1)	1,844	(16.0)	2,178	(20.3)	3,065	(21.5)	359	(8.4)	244	(6.7)	279	(6.2)	18	(1.4)	535	(8.8)	1,895	(17.8)	1,592	(13.4)
Total											Percentage distribution, by field											
Total	100.0	(†)	100.0	(†)	100.0	(†)	100.0	(†)	100.0	(†)	100.0	(†)	100.0	(†)	100.0	(†)	100.0	(†)	100.0	(†)	100.0	(†)
Agriculture/forestry	1.1	(0.01)	1.6	(0.02)	0.6	(0.01)	1.2	(0.02)	0.5	(0.04)	0.8	(0.05)	0.8	(0.04)	0.8	(0.23)	0.9	(0.04)	1.0	(0.02)	1.2	(0.02)
Art/architecture	4.6	(0.03)	4.1	(0.05)	5.2	(0.04)	4.8	(0.03)	2.7	(0.09)	4.8	(0.15)	4.2	(0.11)	3.5	(0.61)	6.1	(0.13)	4.8	(0.05)	4.0	(0.04)
Business/management	20.0	(0.06)	23.7	(0.10)	16.5	(0.07)	19.6	(0.07)	23.2	(0.29)	23.4	(0.30)	19.0	(0.19)	18.6	(1.09)	20.1	(0.18)	22.5	(0.09)	17.4	(0.09)
Communications	3.5	(0.03)	3.1	(0.03)	4.0	(0.04)	3.7	(0.04)	4.1	(0.13)	3.5	(0.13)	1.6	(0.06)	2.8	(0.48)	5.8	(0.13)	4.4	(0.05)	1.9	(0.03)
Computer and information sciences	2.7	(0.03)	3.8	(0.04)	1.5	(0.02)	2.1	(0.03)	3.6	(0.13)	2.9	(0.13)	6.7	(0.16)	1.7	(0.33)	4.0	(0.09)	3.8	(0.05)	1.1	(0.02)
Education	14.1	(0.05)	7.2	(0.06)	20.8	(0.09)	15.2	(0.06)	14.6	(0.17)	12.3	(0.22)	5.3	(0.11)	16.2	(1.00)	9.0	(0.13)	9.7	(0.06)	20.1	(0.09)
Engineering	7.9	(0.04)	14.0	(0.07)	2.0	(0.03)	7.1	(0.04)	4.2	(0.11)	9.2	(0.20)	17.5	(0.22)	5.3	(0.86)	6.8	(0.12)	8.2	(0.05)	7.9	(0.06)
English/literature	3.5	(0.03)	2.4	(0.03)	4.5	(0.04)	3.7	(0.03)	2.6	(0.10)	2.2	(0.11)	2.6	(0.09)	2.4	(0.41)	3.1	(0.08)	3.2	(0.04)	3.9	(0.04)
Foreign languages	1.1	(0.01)	0.6	(0.02)	1.5	(0.02)	1.1	(0.02)	0.5	(0.05)	1.6	(0.08)	1.2	(0.06)	0.6	(0.19)	1.1	(0.05)	1.0	(0.02)	1.2	(0.02)
Health sciences	6.8	(0.04)	2.5	(0.03)	10.8	(0.07)	6.5	(0.04)	7.6	(0.16)	5.5	(0.14)	9.0	(0.16)	7.4	(0.70)	5.4	(0.11)	6.7	(0.05)	7.2	(0.06)
Liberal arts/humanities	1.8	(0.02)	1.5	(0.03)	2.1	(0.03)	1.8	(0.03)	1.7	(0.08)	2.3	(0.09)	1.5	(0.07)	2.8	(0.38)	1.8	(0.07)	1.8	(0.03)	1.8	(0.03)
Mathematics/statistics	1.5	(0.02)	1.9	(0.03)	1.2	(0.02)	1.6	(0.02)	1.2	(0.06)	0.9	(0.07)	2.2	(0.08)	1.2	(0.25)	1.1	(0.05)	1.3	(0.03)	1.9	(0.03)
Natural sciences (biological and physical)	6.8	(0.04)	8.3	(0.06)	5.4	(0.05)	6.7	(0.04)	4.9	(0.13)	5.4	(0.14)	10.8	(0.15)	5.3	(0.64)	7.1	(0.10)	6.9	(0.06)	6.7	(0.05)
Philosophy/religion/theology	1.4	(0.02)	2.0	(0.03)	0.8	(0.02)	1.5	(0.02)	1.5	(0.08)	1.1	(0.08)	1.0	(0.05)	1.5	(0.36)	1.4	(0.06)	1.2	(0.03)	1.7	(0.03)
Pre-professional	1.4	(0.02)	1.8	(0.03)	1.1	(0.02)	1.3	(0.02)	3.1	(0.11)	2.2	(0.10)	0.4	(0.04)	3.7	(0.52)	2.1	(0.07)	1.8	(0.03)	0.9	(0.02)
Psychology	4.6	(0.03)	3.0	(0.04)	6.0	(0.05)	4.6	(0.04)	5.3	(0.14)	5.3	(0.13)	2.7	(0.10)	6.0	(0.61)	5.8	(0.12)	4.8	(0.05)	4.0	(0.03)
Social sciences/history	10.0	(0.05)	11.6	(0.06)	8.4	(0.06)	10.3	(0.05)	9.7	(0.18)	9.2	(0.18)	7.7	(0.15)	9.5	(0.89)	10.1	(0.13)	9.5	(0.07)	10.4	(0.07)
Other fields	7.1	(0.04)	6.7	(0.05)	7.6	(0.07)	7.0	(0.05)	9.0	(0.22)	7.4	(0.19)	6.0	(0.13)	10.9	(0.80)	8.3	(0.13)	7.4	(0.07)	6.5	(0.05)

†Not applicable.
NOTE: Race categories exclude persons of Hispanic ethnicity. Detail may not sum to totals because of rounding. Standard errors appear in parentheses.

SOURCE: U.S. Department of Commerce, Census Bureau, American Community Survey, 2009, unpublished tabulations. (This table was prepared April 2012.)

Percentage of persons 18 to 24 years old and 25 and over, by educational attainment and state: 2000 and 2007–09

State	Percent of 18- to 24-year-olds who were high school completers[1]		Percent of population 25 years old and over, by educational attainment											
			2000					2007–09 (3-year average)[2]					
					Bachelor's or higher degree				High school completion or higher		Bachelor's or higher degree		
	2000	2007–09 (3-year average)[2]	Less than high school completion	High school completion or higher	Total	Bachelor's degree	Graduate degree	Less than high school completion	Total	High school only	Total	Bachelor's degree	Graduate degree
1	2	3	4	5	6	7	8	9	10	11	12	13	14
United States	74.7 (0.02)	83.2 (0.06)	19.6 (0.01)	80.4 (0.01)	24.4 (0.01)	15.5 (0.01)	8.9 (#)	15.0 (0.03)	85.0 (0.03)	29.0 (0.04)	27.8 (0.04)	17.6 (0.03)	10.2 (0.02)
Alabama	72.2 (0.15)	80.3 (0.41)	24.7 (0.06)	75.3 (0.06)	19.0 (0.05)	12.1 (0.04)	6.9 (0.03)	18.5 (0.18)	81.5 (0.18)	31.6 (0.19)	21.9 (0.17)	14.1 (0.13)	7.8 (0.10)
Alaska	76.9 (0.40)	81.7 (1.13)	11.7 (0.12)	88.3 (0.12)	24.7 (0.16)	16.1 (0.13)	8.6 (0.10)	8.6 (0.33)	91.4 (0.33)	28.7 (0.53)	26.6 (0.49)	17.0 (0.47)	9.6 (0.32)
Arizona	69.2 (0.19)	77.4 (0.41)	19.0 (0.06)	81.0 (0.06)	23.5 (0.07)	15.1 (0.06)	8.4 (0.04)	16.2 (0.12)	83.8 (0.12)	25.3 (0.16)	25.5 (0.13)	16.3 (0.12)	9.2 (0.08)
Arkansas.................	75.4 (0.19)	81.6 (0.53)	24.7 (0.07)	75.3 (0.07)	16.7 (0.06)	11.0 (0.05)	5.7 (0.04)	18.1 (0.20)	81.9 (0.20)	35.0 (0.23)	19.0 (0.21)	12.8 (0.17)	6.3 (0.11)
California	70.7 (0.07)	81.9 (0.16)	23.2 (0.03)	76.8 (0.03)	26.6 (0.03)	17.1 (0.02)	9.5 (0.02)	19.4 (0.07)	80.6 (0.07)	21.5 (0.06)	29.9 (0.07)	19.2 (0.06)	10.7 (0.04)
Colorado	75.1 (0.15)	83.4 (0.37)	13.1 (0.05)	86.9 (0.05)	32.7 (0.06)	21.6 (0.06)	11.1 (0.04)	10.9 (0.12)	89.1 (0.12)	23.2 (0.19)	35.7 (0.19)	23.1 (0.15)	12.6 (0.12)
Connecticut..............	78.2 (0.21)	87.2 (0.43)	16.0 (0.06)	84.0 (0.06)	31.4 (0.08)	18.1 (0.07)	13.3 (0.06)	11.5 (0.16)	88.5 (0.16)	28.4 (0.22)	35.4 (0.23)	20.1 (0.18)	15.3 (0.15)
Delaware	77.6 (0.41)	82.7 (0.95)	17.4 (0.14)	82.6 (0.14)	25.0 (0.16)	15.6 (0.14)	9.4 (0.11)	12.8 (0.35)	87.2 (0.35)	32.0 (0.47)	26.9 (0.41)	16.3 (0.35)	10.7 (0.26)
District of Columbia	79.4 (0.40)	84.7 (0.88)	22.2 (0.18)	77.8 (0.18)	39.1 (0.21)	18.1 (0.17)	21.0 (0.18)	13.5 (0.43)	86.5 (0.43)	20.5 (0.43)	48.4 (0.41)	20.9 (0.36)	27.4 (0.37)
Florida...................	71.7 (0.11)	81.1 (0.25)	20.1 (0.04)	79.9 (0.04)	22.3 (0.04)	14.2 (0.03)	8.1 (0.02)	14.8 (0.07)	85.2 (0.07)	30.5 (0.09)	25.7 (0.08)	16.7 (0.06)	9.0 (0.05)
Georgia	70.0 (0.15)	79.0 (0.34)	21.4 (0.05)	78.6 (0.05)	24.3 (0.05)	16.0 (0.05)	8.3 (0.04)	16.5 (0.11)	83.5 (0.11)	29.6 (0.12)	27.3 (0.12)	17.6 (0.10)	9.7 (0.08)
Hawaii....................	85.8 (0.25)	90.2 (0.79)	15.4 (0.10)	84.6 (0.10)	26.2 (0.12)	17.8 (0.10)	8.4 (0.08)	9.8 (0.22)	90.2 (0.22)	29.1 (0.34)	29.3 (0.36)	19.3 (0.31)	10.0 (0.22)
Idaho.....................	77.3 (0.25)	84.3 (0.72)	15.3 (0.09)	84.7 (0.09)	21.7 (0.10)	14.9 (0.09)	6.8 (0.06)	11.9 (0.23)	88.1 (0.23)	29.0 (0.32)	24.2 (0.30)	16.6 (0.26)	7.5 (0.19)
Illinois....................	76.0 (0.09)	84.5 (0.22)	18.6 (0.03)	81.4 (0.03)	26.1 (0.03)	16.6 (0.03)	9.5 (0.02)	13.9 (0.09)	86.1 (0.09)	27.9 (0.12)	30.2 (0.12)	18.8 (0.10)	11.4 (0.08)
Indiana...................	76.5 (0.15)	80.9 (0.37)	17.9 (0.05)	82.1 (0.05)	19.4 (0.05)	12.2 (0.04)	7.2 (0.04)	13.8 (0.12)	86.2 (0.12)	36.0 (0.17)	22.5 (0.13)	14.6 (0.11)	7.9 (0.09)
Iowa	81.4 (0.16)	89.2 (0.49)	13.9 (0.06)	86.1 (0.06)	21.2 (0.07)	14.7 (0.06)	6.5 (0.04)	9.8 (0.14)	90.2 (0.14)	34.2 (0.24)	24.5 (0.23)	17.1 (0.21)	7.4 (0.14)
Kansas...................	78.3 (0.18)	86.1 (0.52)	14.0 (0.06)	86.0 (0.06)	25.8 (0.08)	17.1 (0.06)	8.7 (0.05)	10.6 (0.15)	89.4 (0.15)	28.8 (0.24)	29.5 (0.24)	19.5 (0.18)	10.0 (0.16)
Kentucky.................	74.9 (0.15)	82.9 (0.39)	25.9 (0.06)	74.1 (0.06)	17.1 (0.05)	10.2 (0.04)	6.9 (0.03)	18.9 (0.18)	81.1 (0.18)	34.7 (0.21)	20.3 (0.19)	12.2 (0.13)	8.1 (0.11)
Louisiana................	72.3 (0.17)	79.3 (0.47)	25.2 (0.06)	74.8 (0.06)	18.7 (0.05)	12.2 (0.04)	6.5 (0.04)	18.8 (0.17)	81.2 (0.17)	34.9 (0.21)	20.8 (0.18)	14.1 (0.14)	6.7 (0.11)
Maine	78.9 (0.28)	86.6 (0.74)	14.6 (0.08)	85.4 (0.08)	22.9 (0.10)	15.0 (0.09)	7.9 (0.06)	10.2 (0.23)	89.8 (0.23)	35.4 (0.37)	26.0 (0.30)	16.8 (0.27)	9.2 (0.20)
Maryland.................	79.6 (0.16)	85.8 (0.35)	16.2 (0.05)	83.8 (0.05)	31.4 (0.07)	18.0 (0.06)	13.4 (0.05)	12.1 (0.13)	87.9 (0.13)	26.7 (0.15)	35.4 (0.15)	19.8 (0.13)	15.6 (0.12)
Massachusetts...........	82.2 (0.13)	87.8 (0.27)	15.2 (0.05)	84.8 (0.05)	33.2 (0.06)	19.5 (0.05)	13.7 (0.04)	11.3 (0.11)	88.7 (0.11)	26.7 (0.15)	38.2 (0.17)	22.1 (0.15)	16.2 (0.12)
Michigan.................	76.5 (0.10)	84.6 (0.29)	16.6 (0.03)	83.4 (0.03)	21.8 (0.04)	13.7 (0.03)	8.1 (0.02)	12.2 (0.10)	87.8 (0.10)	31.7 (0.14)	24.7 (0.12)	15.2 (0.10)	9.5 (0.07)
Minnesota...............	79.3 (0.13)	86.7 (0.36)	12.1 (0.04)	87.9 (0.04)	27.4 (0.06)	19.1 (0.05)	8.3 (0.03)	8.7 (0.12)	91.3 (0.12)	27.8 (0.20)	31.6 (0.19)	21.4 (0.17)	10.2 (0.14)
Mississippi	71.3 (0.18)	79.4 (0.61)	27.1 (0.08)	72.9 (0.08)	16.9 (0.06)	11.1 (0.05)	5.8 (0.04)	20.0 (0.21)	80.0 (0.21)	30.8 (0.27)	19.6 (0.19)	12.6 (0.16)	6.9 (0.11)
Missouri..................	76.5 (0.13)	82.7 (0.41)	18.7 (0.05)	81.3 (0.05)	21.6 (0.05)	14.0 (0.04)	7.6 (0.03)	13.7 (0.14)	86.3 (0.14)	32.4 (0.17)	25.2 (0.15)	16.0 (0.13)	9.2 (0.10)
Montana..................	78.6 (0.31)	84.2 (1.14)	12.8 (0.10)	87.2 (0.10)	24.4 (0.13)	17.2 (0.11)	7.2 (0.08)	9.1 (0.28)	90.9 (0.28)	31.9 (0.47)	27.0 (0.41)	18.5 (0.33)	8.4 (0.30)
Nebraska	80.0 (0.21)	86.8 (0.67)	13.4 (0.07)	86.6 (0.07)	23.7 (0.09)	16.4 (0.08)	7.3 (0.06)	10.2 (0.22)	89.8 (0.22)	30.1 (0.28)	27.0 (0.26)	18.5 (0.23)	8.6 (0.20)
Nevada	66.7 (0.32)	76.8 (0.63)	19.3 (0.10)	80.7 (0.10)	18.2 (0.10)	12.1 (0.08)	6.1 (0.06)	16.3 (0.20)	83.7 (0.20)	29.4 (0.27)	21.8 (0.22)	14.5 (0.18)	7.2 (0.12)
New Hampshire	77.8 (0.29)	87.5 (0.71)	12.6 (0.08)	87.4 (0.08)	28.7 (0.11)	18.7 (0.10)	10.0 (0.07)	9.3 (0.23)	90.7 (0.23)	30.2 (0.34)	32.5 (0.35)	21.2 (0.31)	11.3 (0.22)
New Jersey	76.3 (0.14)	85.9 (0.30)	17.9 (0.04)	82.1 (0.04)	29.8 (0.05)	18.8 (0.04)	11.0 (0.04)	12.6 (0.10)	87.4 (0.10)	29.9 (0.15)	34.4 (0.13)	21.5 (0.11)	12.9 (0.09)
New Mexico	70.5 (0.24)	76.8 (0.89)	21.1 (0.09)	78.9 (0.09)	23.5 (0.09)	13.7 (0.07)	9.8 (0.06)	17.5 (0.27)	82.5 (0.27)	27.3 (0.37)	24.8 (0.24)	14.3 (0.17)	10.5 (0.17)
New York	76.1 (0.09)	84.7 (0.19)	20.9 (0.03)	79.1 (0.03)	27.4 (0.04)	15.6 (0.03)	11.8 (0.03)	15.7 (0.07)	84.3 (0.07)	28.1 (0.08)	32.2 (0.09)	18.4 (0.07)	13.8 (0.07)
North Carolina	74.2 (0.11)	82.9 (0.22)	21.9 (0.04)	78.1 (0.04)	22.5 (0.04)	15.3 (0.04)	7.2 (0.03)	16.3 (0.10)	83.7 (0.10)	28.1 (0.11)	26.3 (0.13)	17.7 (0.10)	8.7 (0.07)
North Dakota	84.4 (0.24)	90.5 (0.79)	16.1 (0.10)	83.9 (0.10)	22.0 (0.12)	16.5 (0.10)	5.5 (0.06)	10.5 (0.31)	89.5 (0.31)	27.9 (0.47)	26.1 (0.56)	19.7 (0.47)	6.4 (0.29)
Ohio	76.8 (0.09)	83.9 (0.31)	17.0 (0.03)	83.0 (0.03)	21.1 (0.03)	13.7 (0.03)	7.4 (0.02)	12.7 (0.08)	87.3 (0.08)	35.8 (0.13)	24.1 (0.12)	15.3 (0.10)	8.8 (0.07)
Oklahoma	74.8 (0.16)	82.1 (0.50)	19.4 (0.06)	80.6 (0.06)	20.3 (0.06)	13.5 (0.05)	6.8 (0.04)	14.7 (0.14)	85.3 (0.14)	32.4 (0.19)	22.5 (0.20)	15.2 (0.18)	7.2 (0.10)
Oregon...................	74.2 (0.17)	84.0 (0.59)	14.9 (0.05)	85.1 (0.05)	25.1 (0.06)	16.4 (0.06)	8.7 (0.04)	11.3 (0.14)	88.7 (0.14)	25.7 (0.19)	28.7 (0.21)	18.3 (0.17)	10.4 (0.13)
Pennsylvania	79.8 (0.09)	86.7 (0.25)	18.1 (0.03)	81.9 (0.03)	22.4 (0.03)	14.0 (0.03)	8.4 (0.02)	12.6 (0.09)	87.4 (0.09)	37.9 (0.13)	26.2 (0.12)	16.2 (0.09)	10.0 (0.08)
Rhode Island	81.3 (0.32)	87.4 (0.70)	22.0 (0.13)	78.0 (0.13)	25.6 (0.14)	15.9 (0.12)	9.7 (0.10)	16.3 (0.29)	83.7 (0.29)	28.4 (0.36)	30.1 (0.37)	18.6 (0.29)	11.5 (0.22)
South Carolina	74.3 (0.18)	81.3 (0.43)	23.7 (0.07)	76.3 (0.07)	20.4 (0.07)	13.5 (0.06)	6.9 (0.04)	17.1 (0.14)	82.9 (0.14)	31.0 (0.17)	24.0 (0.17)	15.6 (0.14)	8.4 (0.12)
South Dakota	78.2 (0.33)	83.5 (1.06)	15.4 (0.12)	84.6 (0.12)	21.5 (0.13)	15.5 (0.12)	6.0 (0.08)	10.6 (0.33)	89.4 (0.33)	33.5 (0.49)	24.8 (0.47)	17.7 (0.39)	7.0 (0.28)
Tennessee	75.1 (0.16)	83.3 (0.43)	24.1 (0.06)	75.9 (0.06)	19.6 (0.06)	12.8 (0.05)	6.8 (0.03)	17.4 (0.14)	82.6 (0.14)	33.2 (0.15)	22.5 (0.15)	14.8 (0.13)	7.8 (0.09)
Texas	68.6 (0.08)	79.9 (0.20)	24.3 (0.03)	75.7 (0.03)	23.2 (0.03)	15.6 (0.03)	7.6 (0.02)	20.4 (0.07)	79.6 (0.07)	25.9 (0.07)	25.6 (0.08)	17.1 (0.07)	8.4 (0.04)
Utah	80.3 (0.16)	87.2 (0.45)	12.3 (0.07)	87.7 (0.07)	26.1 (0.09)	17.8 (0.08)	8.3 (0.06)	9.5 (0.18)	90.5 (0.18)	25.5 (0.29)	28.7 (0.28)	19.4 (0.22)	9.3 (0.14)
Vermont	83.0 (0.28)	89.6 (0.87)	13.6 (0.10)	86.4 (0.10)	29.4 (0.13)	18.3 (0.11)	11.1 (0.09)	9.6 (0.36)	90.4 (0.36)	32.0 (0.64)	33.3 (0.71)	20.4 (0.54)	12.9 (0.47)
Virginia	79.4 (0.13)	86.9 (0.27)	18.5 (0.05)	81.5 (0.05)	29.5 (0.06)	17.9 (0.05)	11.6 (0.04)	13.9 (0.11)	86.1 (0.11)	25.9 (0.14)	33.7 (0.15)	19.9 (0.12)	13.8 (0.10)
Washington	75.3 (0.16)	83.3 (0.42)	12.9 (0.05)	87.1 (0.05)	27.7 (0.06)	18.4 (0.05)	9.3 (0.04)	10.3 (0.11)	89.7 (0.11)	24.4 (0.16)	30.7 (0.15)	19.9 (0.14)	10.8 (0.11)
West Virginia	78.2 (0.22)	83.1 (0.73)	24.8 (0.09)	75.2 (0.09)	14.8 (0.07)	8.9 (0.06)	5.9 (0.05)	18.1 (0.23)	81.9 (0.23)	40.8 (0.29)	17.1 (0.24)	10.4 (0.19)	6.7 (0.17)
Wisconsin	78.9 (0.13)	87.5 (0.34)	14.9 (0.04)	85.1 (0.04)	22.4 (0.05)	15.2 (0.04)	7.2 (0.03)	10.5 (0.10)	89.5 (0.10)	34.1 (0.19)	25.6 (0.18)	16.8 (0.14)	8.7 (0.11)
Wyoming.................	79.0 (0.41)	86.3 (1.08)	12.1 (0.13)	87.9 (0.13)	21.9 (0.16)	14.9 (0.14)	7.0 (0.10)	8.7 (0.43)	91.3 (0.43)	31.0 (0.47)	23.6 (0.57)	15.6 (0.49)	8.0 (0.33)

#Rounds to zero.

[1]High school completers include diploma recipients and those completing high school through alternative credentials, such as a GED.

[2]Use of a 3-year average increases the sample size, thereby reducing the size of sampling errors and producing more stable estimates.

NOTE: Detail may not sum to totals because of rounding. Standard errors appear in parentheses.

SOURCE: U.S. Department of Commerce, Census Bureau, Census 2000 Summary File 3, retrieved October 11, 2006, from http://factfinder.census.gov/servlet/DatasetMain PageServlet?_ds_name=DEC_2000_SF3_U&_program=DEC&_lang=en; Census Briefs, *Educational Attainment: 2000*; and 2007-2009 American Community Survey (ACS) 3-Year Public Use Microdata Sample (PUMS) data. (This table was prepared June 2011.)

Percentage of persons age 25 and over with high school completion or higher and a bachelor's or higher degree, by race/ethnicity and state: 2007–09

State	Percent with high school completion or higher								Percent with bachelor's degree or higher							
	Total	White	Black	Hispanic	Asian	Native Hawaiian/ Pacific Islander	American Indian/ Alaska Native	Two or more races	Total	White	Black	Hispanic	Asian	Native Hawaiian/ Pacific Islander	American Indian/ Alaska Native	Two or more races
1	2	3	4	5	6	7	8	9	10	11	12	13	14	15	16	17
United States	85.0 (0.03)	90.0 (0.03)	80.8 (0.06)	60.7 (0.11)	85.6 (0.09)	86.1 (0.50)	79.6 (0.25)	88.0 (0.17)	27.8 (0.04)	30.9 (0.04)	17.5 (0.07)	12.7 (0.07)	50.0 (0.14)	14.9 (0.62)	13.5 (0.20)	25.5 (0.23)
Alabama	81.5 (0.18)	83.8 (0.19)	76.6 (0.35)	57.3 (1.65)	86.1 (1.28)	‡ (†)	76.2 (2.32)	81.2 (1.29)	21.9 (0.17)	24.3 (0.21)	14.5 (0.31)	11.6 (1.03)	49.3 (1.97)	‡ (†)	13.4 (1.63)	17.5 (1.52)
Alaska	91.4 (0.33)	94.7 (0.27)	90.3 (2.50)	81.1 (3.19)	85.7 (2.04)	86.9 (5.72)	80.0 (1.01)	87.8 (1.87)	26.6 (0.49)	32.2 (0.63)	14.9 (3.40)	15.9 (2.00)	24.1 (2.50)	12.2 (0.91)	5.0 (0.61)	20.8 (2.49)
Arizona	83.8 (0.12)	92.5 (0.12)	87.3 (0.80)	60.5 (0.38)	88.1 (0.81)	89.0 (1.95)	71.7 (0.87)	90.8 (1.03)	25.5 (0.13)	31.3 (0.19)	23.2 (0.85)	9.8 (0.24)	53.0 (1.03)	13.1 (2.87)	8.0 (0.52)	23.0 (1.35)
Arkansas	81.9 (0.20)	84.4 (0.20)	77.3 (0.57)	48.5 (1.74)	79.1 (2.12)	59.8 (7.61)	83.8 (2.61)	80.0 (1.94)	19.0 (0.21)	20.5 (0.23)	12.4 (0.57)	8.5 (0.73)	34.7 (2.81)	‡ (†)	18.4 (2.77)	13.5 (1.45)
California	80.6 (0.07)	93.2 (0.06)	87.2 (0.23)	56.5 (0.18)	85.7 (0.14)	84.3 (0.96)	84.0 (0.80)	90.1 (0.40)	29.9 (0.07)	38.6 (0.10)	21.2 (0.22)	10.0 (0.09)	47.9 (0.21)	15.4 (1.10)	16.3 (0.80)	31.0 (0.52)
Colorado	89.1 (0.12)	94.7 (0.09)	87.4 (0.74)	63.1 (0.54)	85.5 (0.98)	79.6 (5.70)	85.8 (2.32)	92.4 (0.92)	35.7 (0.19)	41.1 (0.21)	21.8 (0.97)	12.0 (0.34)	48.1 (1.10)	18.3 (4.55)	17.9 (1.75)	32.0 (1.70)
Connecticut	88.5 (0.16)	91.9 (0.14)	81.1 (0.58)	66.9 (0.73)	89.2 (1.03)	‡ (†)	73.5 (5.50)	90.4 (1.34)	35.4 (0.23)	38.7 (0.25)	18.6 (0.58)	14.7 (0.49)	63.0 (1.51)	‡ (†)	18.1 (3.30)	32.4 (2.14)
Delaware	87.2 (0.35)	90.0 (0.32)	83.9 (0.83)	57.7 (2.85)	89.8 (1.68)	‡ (†)	77.5 (6.18)	89.6 (3.26)	26.9 (0.41)	29.1 (0.43)	17.3 (0.98)	12.9 (1.58)	62.4 (2.42)	‡ (†)	10.0 ! (3.95)	22.8 (3.73)
District of Columbia	86.5 (0.43)	98.9 (0.18)	81.2 (0.69)	60.7 (2.69)	92.0 (1.59)	‡ (†)	89.2 (7.41)	97.7 (1.12)	48.4 (0.41)	87.6 (0.64)	21.3 (0.61)	34.9 (2.59)	75.3 (2.77)	‡ (†)	‡ (†)	57.8 (4.72)
Florida	85.2 (0.07)	90.2 (0.07)	77.4 (0.23)	73.5 (0.22)	85.7 (0.45)	86.1 (4.73)	81.8 (1.53)	86.1 (0.80)	25.7 (0.08)	28.4 (0.09)	15.9 (0.24)	20.8 (0.20)	46.2 (0.68)	18.1 (5.38)	18.7 (1.56)	25.3 (0.89)
Georgia	83.5 (0.11)	87.3 (0.14)	81.3 (0.21)	54.6 (0.72)	85.7 (0.59)	92.3 (3.67)	85.0 (2.78)	87.1 (1.19)	27.3 (0.12)	31.3 (0.16)	19.1 (0.25)	13.6 (0.43)	51.1 (0.94)	8.4 ! (3.58)	21.5 (2.40)	28.0 (1.62)
Hawaii	90.2 (0.22)	95.5 (0.29)	97.4 (1.20)	88.4 (1.03)	86.8 (0.40)	85.4 (1.05)	94.8 (2.33)	92.3 (0.52)	29.3 (0.36)	41.3 (0.70)	31.2 (3.22)	18.6 (1.13)	29.8 (0.48)	12.2 (0.91)	24.1 (7.17)	18.9 (0.73)
Idaho	88.1 (0.23)	91.1 (0.23)	91.1 (3.20)	54.1 (1.48)	85.8 (2.01)	‡ (†)	84.4 (1.96)	85.9 (2.15)	24.2 (0.30)	25.6 (0.35)	22.9 (5.37)	8.2 (0.71)	39.9 (2.98)	‡ (†)	11.5 (2.29)	20.6 (2.27)
Illinois	86.1 (0.09)	91.4 (0.09)	81.3 (0.27)	58.9 (0.44)	90.7 (0.38)	95.0 (4.75)	84.9 (7.11)	89.4 (0.86)	30.2 (0.12)	33.6 (0.14)	18.7 (0.30)	11.8 (0.27)	61.7 (0.55)	60.9 (9.81)	25.4 (3.28)	31.7 (1.34)
Indiana	86.2 (0.12)	87.8 (0.13)	81.4 (0.55)	61.6 (1.07)	87.3 (1.05)	‡ (†)	81.1 (2.69)	84.4 (1.14)	22.5 (0.13)	23.3 (0.15)	14.2 (0.50)	11.7 (0.59)	56.4 (1.52)	‡ (†)	15.4 (2.95)	18.9 (1.49)
Iowa	90.2 (0.14)	91.6 (0.13)	78.8 (1.59)	58.3 (1.77)	83.2 (1.84)	‡ (†)	88.3 (3.17)	88.9 (1.73)	24.5 (0.23)	24.8 (0.24)	16.6 (1.53)	11.6 (1.13)	50.2 (2.52)	‡ (†)	20.5 (5.26)	14.7 (2.10)
Kansas	89.4 (0.15)	92.4 (0.13)	86.7 (0.87)	57.5 (1.12)	82.6 (1.63)	‡ (†)	90.0 (1.63)	88.7 (1.39)	29.5 (0.24)	31.4 (0.26)	17.6 (1.20)	11.7 (0.63)	49.2 (2.00)	‡ (†)	24.3 (2.23)	18.9 (1.55)
Kentucky	81.1 (0.18)	81.3 (0.19)	81.6 (0.75)	64.2 (2.14)	88.1 (1.55)	‡ (†)	78.8 (3.43)	79.4 (2.07)	20.3 (0.19)	20.5 (0.20)	13.8 (0.61)	14.1 (1.29)	56.6 (2.31)	‡ (†)	14.0 (2.81)	18.7 (1.91)
Louisiana	81.2 (0.17)	84.9 (0.17)	74.1 (0.38)	71.6 (1.16)	73.2 (1.80)	‡ (†)	67.0 (3.08)	83.3 (1.54)	20.8 (0.18)	24.3 (0.18)	12.1 (0.31)	19.4 (1.05)	39.3 (1.91)	‡ (†)	11.1 (1.86)	18.0 (1.64)
Maine	89.8 (0.23)	90.2 (0.22)	78.1 (4.61)	78.8 (4.10)	82.4 (3.44)	‡ (†)	79.0 (3.17)	80.2 (3.75)	26.0 (0.23)	26.2 (0.30)	11.6 ! (4.27)	21.4 (3.65)	37.3 (4.63)	‡ (†)	11.6 (3.01)	14.8 (3.34)
Maryland	87.9 (0.13)	91.1 (0.13)	85.9 (0.26)	61.8 (0.82)	89.0 (0.53)	‡ (†)	84.2 (2.85)	90.8 (0.96)	35.4 (0.15)	39.8 (0.21)	24.4 (0.35)	20.7 (0.63)	60.1 (0.83)	‡ (†)	20.4 (2.71)	31.8 (1.77)
Massachusetts	88.7 (0.11)	91.5 (0.11)	82.5 (0.62)	64.6 (0.69)	83.1 (0.54)	‡ (†)	79.9 (3.74)	86.3 (1.08)	38.2 (0.17)	40.2 (0.18)	22.8 (0.74)	15.8 (0.56)	56.4 (0.76)	‡ (†)	24.5 (3.66)	32.6 (1.62)
Michigan	87.8 (0.10)	89.8 (0.10)	81.2 (0.37)	62.9 (0.92)	88.4 (0.73)	91.3 (7.31)	83.2 (1.30)	85.7 (0.90)	24.7 (0.12)	25.7 (0.13)	14.3 (0.29)	14.0 (0.60)	62.7 (1.05)	29.0 ! (9.91)	12.9 (1.32)	21.1 (1.17)
Minnesota	91.3 (0.12)	93.4 (0.10)	79.8 (1.40)	58.7 (1.43)	80.3 (1.19)	‡ (†)	80.4 (1.58)	87.8 (1.62)	31.6 (0.19)	32.5 (0.21)	19.8 (1.05)	15.1 (0.93)	43.8 (1.48)	‡ (†)	13.7 (1.50)	24.4 (2.06)
Mississippi	80.0 (0.21)	84.6 (0.24)	72.3 (0.36)	59.4 (2.07)	75.4 (2.90)	‡ (†)	75.6 (3.14)	83.9 (2.54)	19.6 (0.19)	23.4 (0.25)	12.4 (0.28)	12.7 (1.44)	37.3 (3.02)	‡ (†)	9.0 (1.88)	19.8 (3.11)
Missouri	86.3 (0.14)	87.6 (0.15)	80.6 (0.51)	66.1 (1.33)	86.3 (1.22)	85.2 (5.34)	83.3 (2.05)	83.1 (1.05)	25.2 (0.15)	26.2 (0.16)	15.6 (0.55)	16.7 (0.99)	56.7 (1.48)	5.1 ! (3.33)	15.6 (1.90)	18.9 (1.29)
Montana	90.9 (0.28)	91.9 (0.27)	89.3 (5.53)	82.1 (2.89)	79.7 (6.11)	‡ (†)	77.3 (1.83)	89.5 (2.72)	27.0 (0.41)	28.1 (0.45)	31.3 ! (9.82)	14.0 (2.72)	31.2 (5.76)	‡ (†)	12.6 (1.36)	18.4 (2.84)
Nebraska	89.8 (0.22)	92.9 (0.20)	84.9 (1.60)	49.3 (1.69)	86.6 (2.05)	‡ (†)	84.4 (2.54)	89.1 (2.35)	27.0 (0.26)	28.6 (0.27)	16.3 (1.59)	6.8 (0.78)	47.5 (3.22)	‡ (†)	12.2 (2.89)	23.5 (3.21)
Nevada	83.7 (0.20)	91.5 (0.19)	86.5 (0.76)	56.2 (0.74)	89.1 (0.65)	89.3 (2.12)	84.9 (1.43)	90.3 (1.14)	21.8 (0.22)	25.0 (0.28)	16.7 (0.83)	8.1 (0.34)	38.4 (0.91)	8.7 (2.30)	13.3 (1.74)	24.4 (1.65)
New Hampshire	90.7 (0.23)	91.1 (0.25)	87.1 (3.16)	75.3 (2.80)	91.7 (1.72)	‡ (†)	67.4 (7.60)	88.1 (2.20)	32.5 (0.35)	32.3 (0.36)	21.8 (3.74)	24.8 (2.69)	58.8 (2.87)	‡ (†)	24.8 (7.24)	27.2 (3.26)
New Jersey	87.4 (0.10)	91.4 (0.09)	83.8 (0.35)	69.3 (0.47)	92.2 (0.28)	‡ (†)	84.5 (2.58)	88.7 (1.11)	34.4 (0.13)	37.4 (0.17)	19.8 (0.42)	15.6 (0.29)	66.8 (0.46)	21.7 ! (8.42)	18.8 (2.73)	34.5 (1.42)
New Mexico	82.5 (0.27)	93.4 (0.22)	88.8 (1.66)	70.4 (0.53)	88.9 (1.36)	‡ (†)	74.5 (1.04)	93.9 (1.08)	24.8 (0.24)	37.0 (0.38)	23.1 (2.01)	12.6 (0.37)	46.5 (3.09)	‡ (†)	9.2 (0.56)	30.4 (2.85)
New York	84.3 (0.07)	90.8 (0.06)	80.2 (0.20)	63.5 (0.28)	78.0 (0.34)	77.6 (5.85)	81.4 (1.63)	86.1 (0.74)	32.2 (0.09)	37.4 (0.12)	20.3 (0.22)	15.2 (0.22)	45.2 (0.42)	26.0 (7.34)	15.9 (1.51)	33.5 (0.95)
North Carolina	83.7 (0.10)	87.3 (0.11)	79.8 (0.26)	52.0 (0.72)	84.5 (0.85)	95.6 (2.47)	67.4 (1.27)	86.5 (1.18)	26.3 (0.13)	29.6 (0.13)	16.9 (0.28)	12.3 (0.41)	50.8 (1.12)	15.3 ! (6.91)	10.5 (0.83)	24.4 (1.24)
North Dakota	89.5 (0.31)	90.0 (0.32)	75.7 (9.55)	78.1 (3.82)	78.9 (5.82)	‡ (†)	84.8 (1.75)	93.6 (2.29)	26.1 (0.56)	26.4 (0.61)	11.5 ! (5.57)	16.8 (4.82)	52.3 (9.92)	‡ (†)	19.1 (2.76)	34.6 (7.07)

See notes at end of table.

Percentage of persons age 25 and over with high school completion or higher and a bachelor's or higher degree, by race/ethnicity and state: 2007–09—Continued

State	Percent with high school completion or higher								Percent with bachelor's degree or higher							
	Total	White	Black	Hispanic	Asian	Native Hawaiian/ Pacific Islander	American Indian/ Alaska Native	Two or more races	Total	White	Black	Hispanic	Asian	Native Hawaiian/ Pacific Islander	American Indian/ Alaska Native	Two or more races
1	2	3	4	5	6	7	8	9	10	11	12	13	14	15	16	17
Ohio	87.3 (0.08)	88.6 (0.09)	80.2 (0.33)	69.5 (0.95)	89.6 (0.72)	76.3 (9.14)	77.7 (2.79)	85.5 (0.99)	24.1 (0.12)	24.8 (0.13)	14.5 (0.29)	16.6 (0.80)	62.2 (1.10)	12.0 ! (5.48)	15.9 (2.16)	19.9 (0.96)
Oklahoma	85.3 (0.14)	87.8 (0.14)	84.8 (0.64)	54.2 (1.14)	83.9 (1.38)	89.0 (3.01)	83.3 (0.73)	85.9 (0.69)	22.5 (0.20)	24.3 (0.23)	16.8 (0.68)	10.3 (0.62)	40.8 (2.16)	12.8 ! (5.65)	15.2 (0.59)	18.2 (0.79)
Oregon	88.7 (0.14)	92.0 (0.13)	88.1 (1.13)	53.8 (1.11)	87.2 (0.78)	84.5 (4.06)	84.4 (1.41)	88.4 (0.77)	28.7 (0.21)	30.0 (0.23)	22.0 (1.69)	11.0 (0.51)	46.4 (1.15)	23.1 (4.78)	13.2 (1.52)	22.8 (1.18)
Pennsylvania	87.4 (0.09)	89.1 (0.08)	81.4 (0.38)	65.5 (0.78)	83.2 (0.69)	82.5 (4.79)	81.7 (2.85)	88.0 (1.07)	26.2 (0.12)	27.3 (0.12)	14.3 (0.38)	13.6 (0.55)	53.3 (1.00)	15.9 ! (6.04)	19.7 (2.88)	22.8 (1.29)
Rhode Island	83.7 (0.29)	86.9 (0.29)	77.7 (1.98)	58.3 (1.78)	79.3 (2.22)	‡ (†)	74.6 (7.13)	88.0 (2.15)	30.1 (0.37)	32.2 (0.43)	19.7 (1.67)	12.7 (0.96)	47.9 (2.70)	‡ (†)	‡ (†)	18.9 (3.40)
South Carolina	82.9 (0.14)	86.8 (0.17)	75.7 (0.35)	57.1 (1.11)	84.3 (1.14)	81.9 (7.76)	75.5 (3.26)	82.9 (1.73)	24.0 (0.17)	28.2 (0.20)	13.2 (0.29)	12.0 (0.68)	48.7 (1.65)	18.5 ! (10.93)	12.9 (2.39)	19.0 (2.13)
South Dakota	89.4 (0.33)	90.7 (0.38)	83.1 (8.82)	73.1 (4.74)	87.4 (5.35)	‡ (†)	76.6 (1.87)	88.3 (2.87)	24.8 (0.47)	25.9 (0.51)	17.3 (4.57)	16.9 (3.24)	45.7 (7.03)	‡ (†)	10.4 (1.19)	16.0 (3.85)
Tennessee	82.6 (0.14)	84.1 (0.14)	79.4 (0.36)	54.9 (1.30)	86.5 (1.04)	‡ (†)	78.9 (3.12)	79.1 (1.37)	22.5 (0.15)	23.8 (0.15)	15.5 (0.36)	11.3 (0.61)	50.4 (1.69)	‡ (†)	14.6 (2.14)	18.8 (1.46)
Texas	79.6 (0.07)	91.4 (0.07)	84.1 (0.19)	57.1 (0.18)	86.8 (0.29)	92.5 (1.77)	87.6 (0.97)	90.1 (0.55)	25.6 (0.08)	33.7 (0.11)	18.3 (0.26)	11.0 (0.10)	54.1 (0.51)	14.7 (2.72)	21.0 (1.17)	27.8 (0.86)
Utah	90.5 (0.18)	94.0 (0.16)	86.3 (1.89)	63.8 (1.06)	86.7 (1.30)	89.7 (2.79)	78.7 (2.35)	91.1 (2.42)	28.7 (0.28)	30.8 (0.30)	27.3 (3.84)	11.0 (0.56)	42.7 (1.99)	11.6 (2.28)	10.3 (1.55)	23.4 (3.07)
Vermont	90.4 (0.36)	90.6 (0.36)	89.3 (6.06)	90.2 (3.28)	80.1 (5.50)	‡ (†)	61.2 (8.24)	89.8 (3.37)	33.3 (0.71)	33.5 (0.68)	28.0 ! (10.71)	25.1 (5.25)	43.0 (6.06)	‡ (†)	14.4 ! (7.65)	19.9 (4.99)
Virginia	86.1 (0.11)	89.1 (0.11)	79.3 (0.28)	67.3 (0.86)	88.7 (0.54)	89.0 (4.16)	83.2 (2.00)	90.0 (1.09)	33.7 (0.15)	37.1 (0.17)	17.9 (0.34)	22.8 (0.61)	56.8 (0.76)	24.8 (6.64)	18.4 (2.02)	36.5 (1.57)
Washington	89.7 (0.11)	93.0 (0.10)	86.6 (0.78)	58.5 (0.71)	85.5 (0.44)	85.7 (1.78)	81.4 (1.16)	91.5 (0.61)	30.7 (0.15)	32.0 (0.19)	19.2 (0.90)	12.3 (0.40)	45.8 (0.66)	8.5 (1.42)	14.1 (0.94)	26.2 (1.09)
West Virginia	81.9 (0.23)	81.7 (0.24)	86.1 (1.16)	78.7 (2.96)	89.9 (2.09)	‡ (†)	83.2 (5.97)	81.7 (2.48)	17.1 (0.24)	16.9 (0.25)	13.2 (1.18)	18.9 (2.48)	65.2 (3.34)	‡ (†)	12.4 ! (4.42)	19.5 (2.56)
Wisconsin	89.5 (0.10)	91.6 (0.11)	78.2 (0.90)	59.9 (1.20)	81.2 (1.65)	‡ (†)	84.8 (1.60)	85.4 (1.73)	25.6 (0.18)	26.6 (0.18)	13.3 (0.78)	11.7 (0.57)	45.9 (2.24)	‡ (†)	11.0 (1.30)	19.9 (2.05)
Wyoming	91.3 (0.43)	93.0 (0.36)	93.7 (3.61)	69.8 (4.06)	91.1 (5.07)	‡ (†)	84.5 (3.47)	89.4 (3.77)	23.6 (0.57)	24.8 (0.60)	17.4 ! (6.56)	9.7 (2.43)	42.8 (6.79)	‡ (†)	6.2 ! (2.04)	21.4 (4.36)

†Not applicable.

!Interpret data with caution. The coefficient of variation (CV) for this estimate is 30 percent or greater.

‡Reporting standards not met (too few cases).

NOTE: Estimates are 3-year averages of 2007–09 data. Use of a 3-year average increases the sample size, thereby reducing the size of sampling errors and producing more stable estimates. Race categories exclude persons of Hispanic ethnicity. Standard errors appear in parentheses.
SOURCE: U.S. Department of Commerce, Census Bureau, 2007–2009 American Community Survey (ACS) 3-Year Public Use Microdata Sample (PUMS) data. (This table was prepared July 2011.)

Percentage of persons age 25 and over with high school completion or higher and a bachelor's or higher degree, by sex and state: 2007–09

State	Number of persons 25 years old and over (in thousands)						Percent with high school completion or higher						Percent with bachelor's or higher degree					
	Total		Males		Females		Total		Male		Female		Total		Male		Female	
1	2		3		4		5		6		7		8		9		10	
United States ...	199,756	(30.2)	96,327	(17.0)	103,429	(18.2)	85.0	(0.03)	84.3	(0.04)	85.6	(0.03)	27.8	(0.04)	28.4	(0.04)	27.2	(0.04)
Alabama.............	3,084	(1.8)	1,454	(1.6)	1,630	(1.5)	81.5	(0.18)	81.0	(0.22)	81.9	(0.22)	21.9	(0.17)	22.3	(0.23)	21.5	(0.18)
Alaska...............	422	(1.3)	218	(1.0)	204	(0.8)	91.4	(0.33)	91.1	(0.44)	91.6	(0.43)	26.6	(0.49)	25.0	(0.64)	28.3	(0.69)
Arizona..............	4,171	(1.7)	2,057	(1.6)	2,114	(1.3)	83.8	(0.12)	82.9	(0.17)	84.7	(0.15)	25.5	(0.13)	26.4	(0.19)	24.6	(0.18)
Arkansas...........	1,889	(1.8)	906	(1.4)	984	(1.3)	81.9	(0.20)	81.0	(0.29)	82.7	(0.26)	19.0	(0.21)	19.1	(0.27)	18.9	(0.28)
California...........	23,459	(4.6)	11,540	(3.9)	11,920	(3.6)	80.6	(0.07)	80.1	(0.09)	81.0	(0.07)	29.9	(0.07)	30.6	(0.08)	29.1	(0.08)
Colorado............	3,225	(1.7)	1,602	(1.7)	1,623	(1.5)	89.1	(0.12)	88.4	(0.19)	89.7	(0.12)	35.7	(0.19)	36.3	(0.23)	35.1	(0.23)
Connecticut........	2,353	(1.2)	1,118	(1.0)	1,235	(1.1)	88.5	(0.16)	88.2	(0.20)	88.6	(0.19)	35.4	(0.23)	36.4	(0.28)	34.5	(0.28)
Delaware...........	587	(0.5)	278	(0.6)	309	(0.5)	87.2	(0.35)	86.4	(0.44)	87.8	(0.44)	26.9	(0.41)	27.2	(0.49)	26.7	(0.48)
District of Columbia ...	408	(0.5)	190	(0.5)	218	(0.4)	86.5	(0.43)	86.7	(0.61)	86.4	(0.52)	48.4	(0.41)	50.0	(0.60)	46.9	(0.51)
Florida................	12,677	(3.1)	6,098	(3.2)	6,579	(2.5)	85.2	(0.07)	84.3	(0.10)	86.0	(0.09)	25.7	(0.08)	27.0	(0.11)	24.5	(0.11)
Georgia..............	6,156	(3.5)	2,942	(2.9)	3,214	(2.2)	83.5	(0.11)	82.4	(0.16)	84.6	(0.13)	27.3	(0.12)	27.6	(0.17)	27.0	(0.16)
Hawaii................	872	(0.7)	430	(0.8)	442	(0.6)	90.2	(0.22)	90.8	(0.28)	89.5	(0.28)	29.3	(0.36)	29.1	(0.47)	29.5	(0.48)
Idaho.................	948	(1.0)	468	(0.9)	479	(0.8)	88.1	(0.23)	87.8	(0.27)	88.5	(0.33)	24.2	(0.30)	25.5	(0.42)	22.9	(0.36)
Illinois...............	8,370	(2.8)	4,030	(2.9)	4,340	(2.3)	86.1	(0.09)	85.6	(0.12)	86.5	(0.11)	30.2	(0.12)	30.8	(0.15)	29.6	(0.16)
Indiana..............	4,156	(1.8)	2,002	(1.6)	2,154	(1.6)	86.2	(0.12)	85.7	(0.16)	86.6	(0.16)	22.5	(0.13)	23.1	(0.17)	21.9	(0.16)
Iowa..................	1,969	(1.4)	951	(1.3)	1,018	(1.4)	90.2	(0.14)	89.5	(0.22)	90.9	(0.18)	24.5	(0.23)	24.5	(0.33)	24.5	(0.29)
Kansas..............	1,798	(1.8)	873	(1.4)	925	(1.3)	89.4	(0.15)	88.8	(0.19)	90.0	(0.19)	29.5	(0.24)	30.2	(0.31)	28.9	(0.27)
Kentucky............	2,852	(1.7)	1,362	(1.5)	1,490	(1.6)	81.1	(0.18)	79.8	(0.26)	82.2	(0.19)	20.3	(0.19)	20.4	(0.23)	20.2	(0.21)
Louisiana	2,848	(1.9)	1,346	(1.6)	1,503	(1.5)	81.2	(0.17)	79.8	(0.22)	82.4	(0.22)	20.8	(0.18)	20.4	(0.23)	21.1	(0.23)
Maine................	924	(0.9)	440	(1.0)	484	(0.8)	89.8	(0.23)	88.6	(0.30)	90.8	(0.28)	26.0	(0.30)	24.8	(0.36)	27.1	(0.40)
Maryland............	3,765	(1.6)	1,775	(1.7)	1,990	(1.6)	87.9	(0.13)	86.9	(0.17)	88.7	(0.16)	35.4	(0.15)	36.3	(0.19)	34.7	(0.20)
Massachusetts	4,447	(2.0)	2,112	(1.8)	2,335	(1.5)	88.7	(0.11)	88.2	(0.16)	89.1	(0.11)	38.2	(0.17)	38.8	(0.22)	37.8	(0.20)
Michigan............	6,623	(2.9)	3,192	(2.7)	3,431	(2.0)	87.8	(0.10)	87.1	(0.14)	88.4	(0.14)	24.7	(0.12)	25.4	(0.15)	24.0	(0.13)
Minnesota..........	3,448	(2.0)	1,692	(2.0)	1,755	(1.6)	91.3	(0.12)	90.9	(0.16)	91.7	(0.15)	31.6	(0.19)	31.8	(0.26)	31.5	(0.25)
Mississippi	1,856	(1.9)	868	(1.6)	988	(1.3)	80.0	(0.21)	78.7	(0.28)	81.0	(0.30)	19.6	(0.19)	19.2	(0.23)	19.9	(0.25)
Missouri.............	3,925	(2.4)	1,869	(1.8)	2,055	(1.9)	86.3	(0.14)	86.3	(0.19)	86.4	(0.17)	25.2	(0.15)	25.7	(0.19)	24.7	(0.20)
Montana............	643	(0.9)	316	(0.8)	326	(0.9)	90.9	(0.28)	90.2	(0.41)	91.6	(0.39)	27.0	(0.41)	27.0	(0.50)	26.9	(0.54)
Nebraska...........	1,144	(1.2)	555	(1.1)	589	(1.1)	89.8	(0.22)	89.3	(0.30)	90.4	(0.26)	27.0	(0.26)	26.9	(0.35)	27.2	(0.36)
Nevada..............	1,702	(1.1)	859	(1.2)	843	(0.9)	83.7	(0.20)	83.2	(0.26)	84.3	(0.25)	21.8	(0.22)	22.4	(0.31)	21.1	(0.27)
New Hampshire.........	898	(0.9)	436	(0.8)	462	(0.8)	90.7	(0.23)	89.7	(0.33)	91.7	(0.27)	32.5	(0.35)	33.6	(0.44)	31.5	(0.45)
New Jersey.........	5,865	(2.0)	2,804	(2.2)	3,062	(1.6)	87.4	(0.10)	87.1	(0.14)	87.6	(0.13)	34.4	(0.13)	35.9	(0.19)	32.9	(0.17)
New Mexico	1,281	(1.4)	621	(1.2)	660	(1.2)	82.5	(0.27)	81.6	(0.35)	83.4	(0.34)	24.8	(0.24)	24.9	(0.34)	24.8	(0.33)
New York............	13,110	(3.4)	6,206	(3.0)	6,903	(3.1)	84.3	(0.07)	84.1	(0.10)	84.6	(0.08)	32.2	(0.09)	32.4	(0.12)	32.1	(0.10)
North Carolina	6,063	(2.5)	2,881	(2.1)	3,182	(2.0)	83.7	(0.10)	81.9	(0.16)	85.2	(0.13)	26.3	(0.13)	26.2	(0.15)	26.4	(0.17)
North Dakota	411	(0.8)	202	(0.7)	209	(0.6)	89.5	(0.31)	88.6	(0.47)	90.3	(0.37)	26.1	(0.56)	25.1	(0.70)	27.0	(0.64)
Ohio...................	7,711	(2.6)	3,673	(2.3)	4,037	(2.3)	87.3	(0.08)	87.0	(0.13)	87.6	(0.11)	24.1	(0.12)	25.0	(0.15)	23.3	(0.14)
Oklahoma...........	2,354	(1.9)	1,132	(1.3)	1,222	(1.5)	85.3	(0.14)	84.6	(0.19)	85.8	(0.20)	22.5	(0.20)	23.1	(0.23)	21.8	(0.24)
Oregon..............	2,550	(1.5)	1,246	(1.3)	1,304	(1.3)	88.7	(0.14)	87.8	(0.20)	89.5	(0.16)	28.7	(0.21)	29.6	(0.23)	27.8	(0.27)
Pennsylvania............	8,558	(2.7)	4,067	(2.2)	4,490	(2.5)	87.4	(0.09)	87.3	(0.12)	87.5	(0.11)	26.2	(0.12)	27.3	(0.15)	25.2	(0.15)
Rhode Island	714	(0.6)	337	(0.6)	377	(0.6)	83.7	(0.29)	82.9	(0.46)	84.4	(0.32)	30.1	(0.37)	31.3	(0.51)	28.9	(0.45)
South Carolina...........	2,974	(1.5)	1,404	(1.3)	1,570	(1.3)	82.9	(0.14)	81.7	(0.20)	84.1	(0.16)	24.0	(0.17)	24.5	(0.23)	23.5	(0.21)
South Dakota...........	521	(1.1)	253	(1.0)	267	(0.8)	89.4	(0.33)	88.3	(0.44)	90.5	(0.41)	24.8	(0.47)	24.7	(0.61)	24.8	(0.61)
Tennessee..........	4,169	(2.0)	1,983	(1.6)	2,185	(1.9)	82.6	(0.14)	81.6	(0.18)	83.4	(0.18)	22.5	(0.15)	23.1	(0.21)	22.0	(0.18)
Texas................	15,050	(4.6)	7,364	(3.3)	7,685	(3.5)	79.6	(0.07)	78.8	(0.10)	80.4	(0.08)	25.6	(0.08)	26.4	(0.10)	24.8	(0.11)
Utah..................	1,537	(1.4)	762	(1.2)	775	(0.9)	90.5	(0.18)	90.1	(0.23)	91.0	(0.20)	28.7	(0.28)	31.6	(0.40)	25.8	(0.31)
Vermont	424	(0.8)	204	(0.7)	220	(0.6)	90.4	(0.36)	89.1	(0.49)	91.6	(0.47)	33.3	(0.71)	32.1	(0.80)	34.5	(0.82)
Virginia..............	5,149	(2.6)	2,470	(2.8)	2,679	(2.2)	86.1	(0.11)	85.1	(0.16)	86.9	(0.12)	33.7	(0.15)	34.5	(0.18)	33.0	(0.20)
Washington.........	4,369	(1.6)	2,142	(1.9)	2,227	(1.6)	89.7	(0.11)	89.2	(0.16)	90.1	(0.12)	30.7	(0.15)	31.8	(0.20)	29.7	(0.19)
West Virginia...........	1,258	(1.0)	601	(0.8)	657	(0.8)	81.9	(0.23)	80.8	(0.35)	82.9	(0.28)	17.1	(0.24)	17.0	(0.31)	17.2	(0.26)
Wisconsin...........	3,727	(2.6)	1,823	(2.0)	1,904	(1.8)	89.5	(0.10)	88.8	(0.16)	90.2	(0.13)	25.6	(0.18)	25.6	(0.22)	25.6	(0.22)
Wyoming............	347	(0.7)	174	(0.8)	173	(0.7)	91.3	(0.43)	90.9	(0.55)	91.7	(0.46)	23.6	(0.57)	24.0	(0.76)	23.1	(0.67)

NOTE: Estimates are 3-year averages of 2007–09 data. Use of a 3-year average increases the sample size, thereby reducing the size of sampling errors and producing more stable estimates. Standard errors appear in parentheses. Detail may not sum to totals because of rounding.

SOURCE: U.S. Department of Commerce, Census Bureau, 2007–2009 American Community Survey (ACS) 3-Year Public Use Microdata Sample (PUMS) data. (This table was prepared July 2011.)

Educational Attainment

Number of persons age 25 and over in metropolitan areas with populations greater than 1 million and percentage with high school completion or higher and a bachelor's or higher degree, by sex: 2011

Metropolitan area	Number of persons 25 years old and over (in thousands)			Percent with high school completion or higher			Percent with bachelor's or higher degree		
	Total	Males	Females	Total	Male	Female	Total	Male	Female
1	2	3	4	5	6	7	8	9	10
Atlanta-Sandy Springs-Marietta, GA CBSA	3,510 (230.5)	1,684 (115.0)	1,826 (120.9)	90.4 (1.26)	88.6 (1.58)	92.0 (1.24)	36.0 (2.18)	37.0 (2.63)	35.1 (2.37)
Austin-Round Rock, TX CBSA	1,151 (86.4)	558 (49.6)	592 (42.8)	87.5 (3.20)	85.7 (3.40)	89.2 (3.40)	43.9 (3.92)	43.3 (4.95)	44.4 (4.17)
Birmingham-Hoover, AL CBSA	837 (64.3)	395 (34.7)	442 (34.6)	90.5 (2.22)	89.9 (3.02)	91.0 (2.31)	24.2 (3.83)	25.9 (4.03)	22.7 (4.79)
Boston-Worcester-Manchester, MA-NH-CT-ME CSA[1]	3,894 (104.8)	1,875 (63.6)	2,020 (54.8)	93.1 (0.78)	93.1 (0.95)	93.1 (1.02)	43.9 (2.10)	46.3 (2.43)	41.6 (2.23)
Buffalo-Niagara Falls, NY CSA	728 (55.5)	381 (33.4)	347 (32.5)	92.6 (1.69)	91.4 (2.35)	93.8 (2.15)	34.7 (3.63)	34.3 (4.60)	35.1 (4.75)
Charlotte-Gastonia-Concord, NC-SC CBSA	1,230 (80.3)	603 (45.5)	626 (42.5)	89.4 (1.93)	86.3 (2.58)	92.4 (1.75)	36.1 (3.47)	39.0 (4.03)	33.3 (3.53)
Chicago-Naperville-Michigan City, IL-IN-WI CSA	6,309 (256.0)	3,084 (135.3)	3,225 (130.4)	89.0 (0.81)	89.0 (1.04)	89.0 (0.92)	36.4 (1.58)	35.7 (1.87)	37.2 (1.76)
Cincinnati-Middletown, OH-KY-IN CBSA[1]	1,272 (76.0)	584 (41.9)	688 (42.9)	88.3 (1.91)	88.4 (3.00)	88.2 (2.21)	26.5 (2.98)	26.4 (3.24)	26.6 (3.30)
Cleveland-Akron-Elyria, OH CSA	1,913 (79.1)	947 (48.5)	966 (41.8)	91.9 (1.13)	92.5 (1.35)	91.3 (1.62)	27.2 (2.47)	26.5 (3.05)	27.8 (2.70)
Columbus, OH CSA	1,150 (67.4)	530 (35.4)	620 (37.6)	90.4 (1.70)	91.4 (2.32)	89.6 (2.18)	29.6 (3.10)	29.3 (3.78)	29.8 (3.32)
Dallas-Fort Worth-Arlington, TX CBSA	4,281 (159.5)	2,182 (97.3)	2,099 (77.5)	81.9 (1.51)	80.5 (1.70)	83.4 (1.62)	32.3 (1.66)	33.1 (1.95)	31.4 (1.90)
Denver-Aurora-Boulder, CO CSA	1,946 (44.9)	975 (31.1)	971 (21.8)	91.6 (1.04)	92.3 (1.25)	90.8 (1.18)	47.6 (2.09)	49.8 (2.49)	45.3 (2.25)
Detroit-Warren-Flint, MI CSA	3,530 (187.4)	1,679 (90.9)	1,851 (101.1)	88.8 (1.03)	88.0 (1.37)	89.5 (1.20)	32.3 (1.77)	33.4 (2.09)	31.3 (2.04)
Fresno-Madera, CA CSA	723 (187.1)	364 (82.4)	360 (106.1)	77.2 (3.69)	74.0 (5.62)	80.5 (3.06)	16.5 (3.58)	17.7 (4.20)	15.3 (3.41)
Grand Rapids-Muskegon-Holland, MI CSA	887 (167.7)	429 (77.8)	458 (91.2)	89.9 (1.86)	89.9 (2.45)	89.9 (1.78)	25.6 (3.37)	27.5 (3.44)	23.8 (4.16)
Greensboro-Winston-Salem-High Point, NC CSA	911 (61.0)	413 (32.5)	498 (36.7)	87.6 (2.24)	89.9 (2.96)	85.8 (2.49)	28.2 (3.49)	28.9 (5.04)	27.6 (3.64)
Hartford-West Hartford, CT CBSA	780 (40.9)	381 (21.4)	398 (22.6)	92.5 (1.18)	92.3 (1.33)	92.7 (1.35)	43.7 (2.99)	45.0 (3.42)	42.4 (3.11)
Houston-Baytown-Sugarland, TX CBSA	3,784 (158.0)	1,863 (88.7)	1,921 (82.7)	82.6 (1.43)	82.3 (1.59)	82.9 (1.68)	31.0 (2.05)	32.0 (2.40)	30.0 (2.28)
Indianapolis-Anderson-Columbus, IN CSA	1,198 (143.4)	579 (72.7)	619 (74.5)	91.4 (1.33)	91.6 (1.88)	91.2 (1.59)	31.3 (3.73)	32.3 (4.87)	30.3 (3.49)
Jacksonville, FL CBSA	1,000 (69.6)	485 (35.2)	515 (40.4)	93.8 (1.45)	94.3 (1.66)	93.4 (2.28)	28.7 (3.54)	28.1 (4.33)	29.2 (4.43)
Kansas City, MO-KS CSBA	1,273 (63.9)	609 (36.5)	663 (34.5)	90.5 (1.38)	89.5 (2.16)	91.4 (1.55)	34.9 (2.44)	33.3 (3.05)	36.3 (2.76)
Las Vegas-Paradise, NV CBSA	1,241 (35.4)	634 (23.0)	607 (16.6)	88.6 (1.15)	88.9 (1.38)	88.3 (1.34)	25.4 (1.64)	25.8 (1.84)	25.8 (1.96)
Los Angeles-Long Beach-Riverside, CA CSA	11,476 (137.1)	5,594 (89.6)	5,882 (68.4)	80.3 (0.84)	80.5 (1.01)	80.2 (0.90)	30.2 (1.09)	30.2 (1.30)	29.3 (1.13)
Louisville, KY-IN CBSA[1]	835 (71.4)	397 (36.5)	438 (38.1)	89.7 (1.73)	91.0 (2.05)	88.5 (2.20)	26.0 (2.90)	24.8 (3.73)	24.8 (4.11)
Memphis, TN-MS-AR CBSA[1]	915 (64.9)	469 (39.4)	446 (34.2)	87.8 (2.41)	87.8 (3.40)	87.8 (2.55)	31.5 (3.44)	31.2 (4.02)	31.9 (3.79)
Miami-Fort Lauderdale-Miami Beach, FL CBSA	3,824 (140.0)	1,803 (80.0)	2,020 (73.4)	87.9 (1.10)	87.3 (1.43)	88.4 (1.09)	32.7 (1.67)	35.3 (2.15)	30.3 (1.86)
Milwaukee-Racine-Waukesha, WI CSA	1,190 (157.7)	570 (83.7)	620 (75.7)	89.9 (1.45)	89.1 (1.49)	90.6 (1.88)	33.0 (2.88)	34.6 (3.45)	31.4 (2.96)
Minneapolis-St. Paul-St. Cloud, MN-WI CSA[1]	2,180 (45.7)	1,056 (28.9)	1,125 (28.3)	93.8 (0.68)	94.2 (0.98)	93.5 (0.87)	38.4 (1.70)	38.8 (2.18)	38.0 (1.77)
Nashville-Davidson-Murfreesboro, TN CBSA	1,088 (180.9)	527 (83.6)	561 (99.8)	87.6 (2.20)	87.9 (2.49)	87.3 (3.30)	37.4 (3.39)	38.8 (4.18)	34.8 (3.75)
New Orleans-Metairie-Kenner, LA CBSA	741 (54.1)	345 (30.4)	396 (29.5)	85.3 (3.16)	82.5 (3.92)	87.8 (3.44)	35.5 (3.44)	37.3 (4.43)	34.0 (3.81)
New York-Newark, NY-NJ-PA CSA	14,498 (198.0)	6,893 (111.2)	7,605 (115.4)	87.2 (0.54)	87.2 (0.72)	87.3 (0.58)	38.2 (0.89)	38.4 (1.09)	37.9 (1.00)
Oklahoma City, OK CBSA	882 (51.5)	407 (25.4)	475 (28.9)	90.1 (1.60)	90.6 (1.98)	89.6 (1.84)	28.3 (2.52)	28.5 (3.44)	28.2 (2.51)
Orlando, FL CBSA	1,382 (93.6)	666 (52.0)	716 (50.1)	86.0 (2.04)	82.6 (2.82)	89.1 (2.10)	33.2 (2.71)	29.7 (3.22)	36.5 (2.96)
Philadelphia-Camden-Vineland, PA-NJ-DE-MD CSA	3,909 (91.2)	1,856 (58.1)	2,053 (49.6)	90.8 (0.95)	91.4 (1.15)	90.2 (1.08)	33.7 (1.52)	33.4 (1.87)	34.0 (1.88)
Phoenix-Mesa-Scottsdale, AZ CBSA	2,775 (242.4)	1,390 (124.6)	1,386 (122.3)	88.4 (1.40)	88.4 (1.64)	88.5 (1.58)	33.6 (2.86)	33.8 (3.27)	33.3 (3.03)
Pittsburgh-New Castle, PA CSA	1,638 (68.0)	746 (38.5)	892 (40.1)	91.8 (1.17)	92.3 (1.44)	91.3 (1.47)	33.8 (2.17)	37.1 (3.34)	31.0 (2.31)
Portland-Vancouver-Beaverton, OR-WA CBSA	1,442 (57.1)	687 (32.6)	755 (31.1)	92.8 (1.00)	93.4 (1.41)	92.3 (1.20)	40.1 (2.23)	39.5 (2.94)	40.6 (2.37)
Providence-Fall River-Warwick, RI-MA CBSA	884 (45.0)	426 (22.0)	458 (26.1)	85.5 (1.19)	86.2 (1.28)	84.9 (1.60)	31.1 (1.96)	30.9 (2.47)	31.2 (2.12)
Raleigh-Durham-Cary, NC CSA	1,111 (67.3)	515 (37.1)	596 (39.6)	87.7 (2.20)	83.5 (3.42)	91.3 (1.60)	34.7 (3.59)	33.6 (4.46)	35.6 (3.91)
Richmond, VA CBSA	954 (61.5)	442 (32.2)	513 (36.5)	89.3 (1.99)	87.3 (2.85)	91.1 (2.27)	33.8 (3.34)	36.2 (4.89)	31.7 (3.20)
Rochester, NY CBSA	686 (48.9)	310 (26.3)	376 (31.8)	91.2 (2.97)	91.4 (2.65)	91.1 (3.90)	32.7 (3.82)	31.7 (5.31)	32.1 (3.86)
Sacramento-Arden-Arcade-Roseville, CA CBSA	1,364 (70.8)	651 (41.2)	713 (39.5)	83.0 (2.39)	83.9 (2.97)	82.3 (2.60)	30.9 (2.57)	31.7 (3.26)	30.1 (2.79)
Salt Lake City-Ogden-Clearfield, UT CSA	1,014 (44.3)	490 (25.0)	523 (23.5)	91.3 (1.22)	90.8 (1.33)	91.7 (1.79)	32.7 (2.43)	37.5 (3.12)	28.3 (2.53)
San Antonio, TX CSA	1,328 (89.2)	615 (45.5)	712 (49.5)	79.0 (2.87)	78.7 (3.70)	79.3 (2.72)	25.9 (3.04)	25.9 (3.99)	26.0 (2.96)
San Diego-Carlsbad-San Marcos, CA CBSA	1,889 (88.3)	936 (51.1)	953 (45.2)	87.9 (1.86)	88.5 (2.19)	87.3 (1.96)	37.3 (2.68)	36.7 (3.29)	37.8 (2.87)
San Jose-San Francisco-Oakland, CA CSA	5,309 (192.3)	2,671 (108.7)	2,638 (100.6)	88.0 (1.00)	87.9 (1.13)	88.0 (1.08)	44.2 (1.60)	46.0 (1.88)	42.3 (1.75)
Seattle-Tacoma-Olympia, WA CSA	2,796 (75.9)	1,402 (48.4)	1,393 (39.6)	93.1 (0.88)	93.1 (1.05)	93.0 (1.15)	36.1 (1.78)	37.4 (2.30)	34.8 (1.92)
St. Louis, MO-IL CSA	1,929 (83.9)	923 (49.6)	1,006 (44.1)	92.3 (0.99)	90.6 (1.56)	93.8 (1.13)	30.5 (2.19)	33.8 (2.62)	27.4 (2.49)
Tampa-St. Petersburg-Clearwater, FL CBSA	1,944 (184.7)	937 (89.0)	1,006 (101.6)	93.5 (1.16)	93.1 (1.64)	93.8 (1.26)	28.2 (2.37)	31.0 (2.89)	25.5 (2.70)
Virginia Beach-Norfolk-Newport News, VA-NC CBSA[1]	1,013 (67.1)	453 (35.4)	559 (36.6)	94.9 (1.29)	94.5 (1.93)	95.3 (1.15)	30.3 (3.14)	29.3 (4.13)	31.0 (3.19)
Washington-Baltimore-Northern Virginia, DC-MD-VA-WV CSA[1]	5,588 (108.3)	2,687 (66.9)	2,902 (51.4)	91.6 (0.68)	91.1 (1.01)	92.1 (0.62)	47.7 (1.23)	47.4 (1.52)	47.9 (1.41)

[1]Information on metropolitan status was suppressed for a small portion of sample observations. As a result, population estimates for these areas may be slightly underestimated.

NOTE: CSA = Combined Statistical Area; CBSA = Core Based Statistical Area. Detail may not sum to totals because of rounding. Standard errors appear in parentheses and were computed using replicate weights. For more information, see Appendix A: Guide to Sources.

SOURCE: U.S. Department of Commerce, Census Bureau, Current Population Survey (CPS), March 2011. (This table was prepared September 2011.)

Average reading scale score, by age and selected student and school characteristics: Selected years, 1971 through 2008

Selected student and school characteristic	1971		1975		1980		1984		1988		1990		1994		1996		1999		2004		2008	
1	2		3		4		5		6		7		8		9		10		11		12	
9-year-olds																						
All students	208	(1.0)	210	(0.7)	215	(1.0)	211	(0.8)	212	(1.1)	209	(1.2)	211	(1.2)	212	(1.0)	212	(1.3)	216	(1.0)	220	(0.9)
Sex																						
Male	201	(1.1)	204	(0.8)	210	(1.1)	207	(1.0)	207	(1.4)	204	(1.7)	207	(1.3)	207	(1.4)	209	(1.6)	212	(1.1)	216	(1.1)
Female	214	(1.0)	216	(0.8)	220	(1.1)	214	(0.9)	216	(1.3)	215	(1.2)	215	(1.4)	218	(1.1)	215	(1.5)	219	(1.1)	224	(0.9)
Race/ethnicity																						
White	214[1]	(0.9)	217	(0.7)	221	(0.8)	218	(0.9)	218	(1.4)	217	(1.3)	218	(1.3)	220	(1.2)	221	(1.6)	224	(0.9)	228	(1.0)
Black	170[1]	(1.7)	181	(1.2)	189	(1.8)	186	(1.3)	189	(2.4)	182	(2.9)	185	(2.3)	191	(2.6)	186	(2.3)	197	(1.8)	204	(1.7)
Hispanic	[2]	(†)	183	(2.2)	190	(2.3)	187	(3.0)	194	(3.5)	189	(2.3)	186	(3.9)	195	(3.4)	193	(2.7)	199	(1.5)	207	(1.5)
Region																						
Northeast	213	(1.7)	215	(1.3)	221	(2.1)	216	(2.2)	215	(2.6)	217	(2.2)	217	(2.9)	220	(1.8)	222	(3.5)	221	(2.5)	225	(1.6)
Southeast	194	(2.9)	201	(1.2)	210	(2.3)	204	(2.0)	207	(2.1)	197	(3.2)	208	(3.0)	206	(2.8)	205	(2.3)	214	(1.6)	220	(2.1)
Central	215	(1.2)	215	(1.2)	217	(1.4)	215	(1.9)	218	(2.2)	213	(2.0)	214	(2.3)	215	(2.6)	215	(3.9)	217	(2.5)	218	(1.6)
West	205	(2.0)	207	(2.0)	213	(1.8)	209	(2.0)	208	(2.6)	210	(2.8)	205	(2.8)	210	(1.9)	206	(1.8)	213	(1.6)	218	(1.3)
13-year-olds																						
All students	255	(0.9)	256	(0.8)	258	(0.9)	257	(0.6)	257	(1.0)	257	(0.8)	258	(0.9)	258	(1.0)	259	(1.0)	257	(1.0)	260	(0.8)
Sex																						
Male	250	(1.0)	250	(0.8)	254	(1.1)	253	(0.7)	252	(1.3)	251	(1.1)	251	(1.2)	251	(1.2)	254	(1.3)	252	(1.1)	256	(1.0)
Female	261	(0.9)	262	(0.9)	263	(0.9)	262	(0.7)	263	(1.0)	263	(1.1)	266	(1.2)	264	(1.2)	265	(1.2)	262	(1.2)	264	(0.9)
Race/ethnicity																						
White	261[1]	(0.7)	262	(0.7)	264	(0.7)	263	(0.6)	261	(1.1)	262	(0.9)	265	(1.1)	266	(1.0)	267	(1.2)	265	(1.0)	268	(1.0)
Black	222[1]	(1.2)	226	(1.2)	233	(1.5)	236	(1.2)	243	(2.4)	241	(2.2)	234	(2.4)	234	(2.6)	238	(2.4)	239	(1.9)	247	(1.6)
Hispanic	[2]	(†)	232	(3.0)	237	(2.0)	240	(2.0)	240	(3.5)	238	(2.3)	235	(1.9)	238	(2.9)	244	(2.9)	241	(2.1)	242	(1.5)
Parents' highest level of education																						
Did not finish high school	—	(†)	—	(†)	239	(1.1)	240	(1.2)	246	(2.1)	241	(1.8)	237	(2.4)	239	(2.8)	238	(3.4)	238	(2.3)	239	(1.9)
Graduated high school	—	(†)	—	(†)	253	(0.9)	253	(0.8)	253	(1.2)	251	(0.9)	251	(1.4)	251	(1.5)	251	(1.8)	249	(1.1)	251	(1.1)
Some education after high school	—	(†)	—	(†)	268	(1.0)	266	(1.1)	265	(1.7)	267	(1.7)	266	(1.9)	268	(2.3)	269	(2.4)	261	(1.4)	265	(1.1)
Graduated college	—	(†)	—	(†)	273	(0.9)	268	(0.9)	265	(1.6)	267	(1.1)	269	(1.2)	269	(1.4)	270	(1.2)	266	(1.2)	270	(1.2)
Region																						
Northeast	261	(2.0)	259	(1.8)	260	(1.8)	261	(0.8)	259	(2.4)	259	(1.8)	269	(2.0)	259	(2.6)	263	(2.9)	264	(2.5)	266	(1.7)
Southeast	245	(1.7)	249	(1.5)	253	(1.6)	256	(1.9)	258	(2.2)	256	(2.2)	253	(2.5)	251	(3.3)	254	(2.4)	253	(1.8)	258	(1.9)
Central	260	(1.8)	261	(1.4)	265	(1.4)	258	(1.3)	256	(2.0)	257	(1.5)	259	(3.3)	267	(1.8)	261	(1.9)	259	(1.8)	262	(1.9)
West	254	(1.3)	253	(1.7)	256	(2.0)	254	(1.1)	258	(2.1)	256	(1.6)	253	(2.1)	257	(1.7)	259	(2.2)	253	(1.7)	256	(1.5)
17-year-olds																						
All students	285	(1.2)	286	(0.8)	285	(1.2)	289	(0.8)	290	(1.0)	290	(1.1)	288	(1.3)	288	(1.1)	288	(1.3)	283	(1.1)	286	(0.9)
Sex																						
Male	279	(1.2)	280	(1.0)	282	(1.3)	284	(0.8)	286	(1.5)	284	(1.6)	282	(2.2)	281	(1.3)	281	(1.6)	276	(1.4)	280	(1.1)
Female	291	(1.3)	291	(1.0)	289	(1.2)	294	(0.9)	294	(1.5)	296	(1.2)	295	(1.5)	295	(1.2)	295	(1.4)	289	(1.2)	291	(1.0)
Race/ethnicity																						
White	291[1]	(1.0)	293	(0.6)	293	(0.9)	295	(0.9)	295	(1.2)	297	(1.2)	296	(1.5)	295	(1.2)	295	(1.4)	289	(1.2)	295	(1.0)
Black	239[1]	(1.7)	241	(2.0)	243	(1.8)	264	(1.2)	274	(2.4)	267	(2.3)	266	(3.9)	266	(2.7)	264	(1.7)	262	(1.9)	266	(2.4)
Hispanic	[2]	(†)	252	(3.6)	261	(2.7)	268	(2.9)	271	(4.3)	275	(3.6)	263	(4.9)	265	(4.1)	271	(3.9)	267	(2.5)	269	(1.3)
Parents' highest level of education																						
Did not finish high school	—	(†)	—	(†)	262	(1.5)	269	(1.4)	267	(2.0)	270	(2.8)	268	(2.7)	267	(3.2)	265	(3.6)	259	(2.7)	266	(2.1)
Graduated high school	—	(†)	—	(†)	277	(1.0)	281	(0.8)	282	(1.3)	283	(1.4)	276	(1.9)	273	(1.7)	274	(2.1)	271	(1.4)	274	(1.4)
Some education after high school	—	(†)	—	(†)	295	(1.2)	298	(0.9)	299	(2.2)	295	(1.9)	294	(1.6)	295	(2.2)	295	(1.8)	285	(1.5)	288	(1.1)
Graduated college	—	(†)	—	(†)	301	(1.0)	302	(0.9)	300	(1.4)	302	(1.5)	300	(1.7)	299	(1.5)	298	(1.3)	295	(1.2)	298	(1.1)
Region																						
Northeast	291	(2.8)	289	(1.7)	286	(2.4)	291	(2.5)	295	(2.9)	296	(1.8)	297	(4.2)	292	(2.8)	295	(4.0)	286	(2.1)	290	(1.6)
Southeast	271	(2.4)	277	(1.4)	280	(2.2)	284	(2.1)	286	(2.1)	285	(2.5)	283	(2.8)	279	(2.6)	279	(2.4)	278	(1.6)	281	(1.8)
Central	291	(2.1)	292	(1.4)	287	(2.2)	290	(1.8)	291	(1.9)	294	(2.4)	286	(3.7)	293	(2.1)	292	(1.5)	289	(1.8)	290	(2.1)
West	284	(1.8)	282	(1.9)	287	(2.1)	289	(1.6)	289	(1.8)	287	(2.6)	288	(2.8)	287	(2.4)	286	(3.0)	280	(2.7)	284	(1.5)

—Not available.

†Not applicable.

[1]Data for 1971 include persons of Hispanic ethnicity.

[2]Test scores of Hispanics were not tabulated separately.

NOTE: The NAEP reading scores have been evaluated at certain performance levels. Scale ranges from 0 to 500. Students scoring 150 (or higher) are able to follow brief written directions and carry out simple, discrete reading tasks. Students scoring 200 are able to understand, combine ideas, and make inferences based on short uncomplicated passages about specific or sequentially related information. Students scoring 250 are able to search for specific information, interrelate ideas, and make generalizations about literature, science, and social studies materials. Students scoring 300 are able to find, understand, summarize, and explain relatively complicated literary and informational material. Includes public and private schools. Excludes persons not enrolled in school and students who were unable to be tested due to limited proficiency in English or due to a disability. Beginning in 2004, data are for a revised assessment format that provides accommodations for students with disabilities and English language learners. Race categories exclude persons of Hispanic ethnicity, except where noted. Totals include other racial/ethnic groups not shown separately. Some data have been revised from previously published figures. Standard errors appear in parentheses. SOURCE: U.S. Department of Education, National Center for Education Statistics, National Assessment of Educational Progress (NAEP), *NAEP 2004 Trends in Academic Progress*; and 2008 NAEP Long-Term Trend Reading Assessment, retrieved May 4, 2009, from Long-Term Trend NAEP Data Explorer (http://nces.ed.gov/nationsreportcard/naepdata/). (This table was prepared May 2009.)

Average reading scale score and standard deviation, by sex, race/ethnicity, percentile, and grade: Selected years, 1992 through 2011

Race/ethnicity, percentile, and grade	1992[1]	1994[1]	1998	2000	2002	2003	2005	2007	2009	2011 Total	2011 Male	2011 Female
1	2	3	4	5	6	7	8	9	10	11	12	13
	Average reading scale score[2]											
All students												
4th grade	217 (0.9)	214 (1.0)	215 (1.1)	213 (1.3)	219 (0.4)	218 (0.3)	219 (0.2)	221 (0.3)	221 (0.3)	221 (0.3)	218 (0.3)	225 (0.3)
8th grade	260 (0.9)	260 (0.8)	263 (0.8)	— (†)	264 (0.4)	263 (0.3)	262 (0.2)	263 (0.2)	264 (0.3)	265 (0.2)	261 (0.3)	270 (0.2)
12th grade	292 (0.6)	287 (0.7)	290 (0.6)	— (†)	287 (0.7)	— (†)	286 (0.6)	— (†)	288 (0.7)	— (†)	— (†)	— (†)
Race/ethnicity												
4th grade												
White	224 (1.2)	224 (1.3)	225 (1.0)	224 (1.1)	229 (0.3)	229 (0.2)	229 (0.2)	231 (0.2)	230 (0.3)	231 (0.2)	228 (0.3)	234 (0.3)
Black	192 (1.7)	185 (1.8)	193 (1.9)	190 (1.8)	199 (0.5)	198 (0.4)	200 (0.3)	203 (0.4)	205 (0.5)	205 (0.5)	200 (0.5)	210 (0.6)
Hispanic	197 (2.6)	188 (3.4)	193 (3.2)	190 (2.9)	201 (1.3)	200 (0.6)	203 (0.5)	205 (0.5)	206 (0.5)	206 (0.5)	203 (0.7)	209 (0.6)
Asian/Pacific Islander	216 (2.9)	220 (3.8)	215 (5.6)	225 (5.2)	224 (1.6)	226 (1.2)	229 (0.7)	232 (1.0)	235 (1.0)	235 (1.2)	231 (1.3)	238 (1.6)
Asian	— (†)	— (†)	— (†)	— (†)	— (†)	— (†)	— (†)	— (†)	— (†)	236 (1.3)	233 (1.3)	239 (1.6)
Native Hawaiian/Pacific Islander	— (†)	— (†)	— (†)	— (†)	— (†)	— (†)	— (†)	— (†)	— (†)	216 (1.9)	213 (3.1)	219 (2.9)
American Indian/Alaska Native	‡ (†)	211 (6.6)	‡ (†)	214 (6.0)	207 (2.0)	202 (1.4)	204 (1.3)	203 (1.2)	204 (1.3)	202 (1.3)	196 (1.9)	208 (1.6)
8th grade												
White	267 (1.1)	267 (1.0)	270 (0.9)	— (†)	272 (0.4)	272 (0.2)	271 (0.2)	272 (0.2)	273 (0.2)	274 (0.2)	269 (0.3)	279 (0.3)
Black	237 (1.7)	236 (1.8)	244 (1.2)	— (†)	245 (0.7)	244 (0.5)	243 (0.4)	245 (0.4)	246 (0.4)	249 (0.5)	243 (0.6)	254 (0.5)
Hispanic	241 (1.6)	243 (1.2)	243 (1.7)	— (†)	247 (0.8)	245 (0.7)	246 (0.4)	247 (0.4)	249 (0.6)	252 (0.5)	249 (0.6)	256 (0.6)
Asian/Pacific Islander	268 (3.9)	265 (3.0)	264 (7.1)	— (†)	267 (1.7)	270 (1.1)	271 (0.8)	271 (1.1)	274 (1.1)	275 (1.0)	271 (1.0)	280 (1.3)
Asian	— (†)	— (†)	— (†)	— (†)	— (†)	— (†)	— (†)	— (†)	— (†)	277 (1.0)	273 (1.1)	282 (1.4)
Native Hawaiian/Pacific Islander	— (†)	— (†)	— (†)	— (†)	— (†)	— (†)	— (†)	— (†)	— (†)	254 (2.2)	247 (2.8)	260 (3.2)
American Indian/Alaska Native	‡ (†)	248 (4.7)	‡ (†)	— (†)	250 (3.5)	246 (3.0)	249 (1.4)	247 (1.2)	251 (1.2)	252 (1.2)	247 (1.6)	256 (1.8)
12th grade												
White	297 (0.6)	293 (0.7)	297 (0.7)	— (†)	292 (0.7)	— (†)	293 (0.7)	— (†)	296 (0.6)	— (†)	— (†)	— (†)
Black	273 (1.4)	265 (1.6)	269 (1.4)	— (†)	267 (1.3)	— (†)	267 (1.2)	— (†)	269 (1.1)	— (†)	— (†)	— (†)
Hispanic	279 (2.7)	270 (1.7)	275 (1.5)	— (†)	273 (1.5)	— (†)	272 (1.2)	— (†)	274 (1.0)	— (†)	— (†)	— (†)
Asian/Pacific Islander	290 (3.2)	278 (2.4)	287 (2.7)	— (†)	286 (2.0)	— (†)	287 (1.9)	— (†)	298 (2.4)	— (†)	— (†)	— (†)
American Indian/Alaska Native	‡ (†)	274 (5.8)	‡ (†)	— (†)	‡ (†)	— (†)	279 (6.3)	— (†)	283 (3.7)	— (†)	— (†)	— (†)
Percentile[3]												
4th grade												
10th	170 (1.9)	159 (1.5)	163 (2.1)	159 (2.3)	170 (0.9)	169 (0.5)	171 (0.4)	174 (0.4)	175 (0.5)	174 (0.4)	169 (0.5)	180 (0.4)
25th	194 (1.1)	189 (1.1)	191 (1.7)	189 (1.4)	196 (0.5)	195 (0.4)	196 (0.3)	199 (0.3)	199 (0.4)	200 (0.4)	196 (0.4)	203 (0.5)
50th	219 (1.3)	219 (1.4)	217 (1.3)	218 (1.7)	221 (0.5)	221 (0.3)	221 (0.2)	224 (0.3)	223 (0.3)	224 (0.3)	221 (0.5)	227 (0.4)
75th	242 (1.1)	243 (1.3)	242 (0.9)	243 (0.8)	244 (0.5)	244 (0.3)	244 (0.3)	246 (0.3)	245 (0.3)	246 (0.3)	243 (0.4)	248 (0.4)
90th	261 (1.4)	263 (1.7)	262 (0.9)	262 (1.4)	263 (0.4)	263 (0.4)	264 (0.3)	264 (0.3)	264 (0.4)	264 (0.4)	262 (0.3)	267 (0.5)
8th grade												
10th	213 (1.2)	211 (1.9)	216 (1.7)	— (†)	220 (0.5)	217 (0.6)	216 (0.3)	217 (0.4)	219 (0.5)	221 (0.3)	215 (0.4)	227 (0.6)
25th	237 (1.1)	236 (1.1)	241 (0.7)	— (†)	244 (0.5)	242 (0.3)	240 (0.2)	242 (0.3)	243 (0.3)	244 (0.3)	240 (0.4)	249 (0.4)
50th	262 (1.1)	262 (0.7)	266 (0.7)	— (†)	267 (0.5)	266 (0.2)	265 (0.2)	265 (0.2)	267 (0.2)	267 (0.2)	263 (0.4)	271 (0.3)
75th	285 (0.8)	286 (1.1)	288 (1.0)	— (†)	288 (0.4)	288 (0.4)	286 (0.2)	287 (0.2)	288 (0.4)	289 (0.3)	284 (0.3)	293 (0.3)
90th	305 (1.3)	305 (1.2)	306 (0.8)	— (†)	305 (0.5)	306 (0.2)	305 (0.2)	305 (0.2)	305 (0.4)	307 (0.4)	302 (0.5)	311 (0.4)
12th grade												
10th	249 (0.8)	239 (0.9)	240 (0.6)	— (†)	237 (1.5)	— (†)	235 (1.1)	— (†)	238 (0.8)	— (†)	— (†)	— (†)
25th	271 (0.8)	264 (0.9)	267 (0.8)	— (†)	263 (1.3)	— (†)	262 (0.8)	— (†)	264 (0.8)	— (†)	— (†)	— (†)
50th	294 (0.8)	290 (0.6)	293 (0.6)	— (†)	289 (0.7)	— (†)	288 (0.8)	— (†)	291 (0.7)	— (†)	— (†)	— (†)
75th	315 (0.5)	313 (0.8)	317 (0.7)	— (†)	312 (0.6)	— (†)	313 (1.1)	— (†)	315 (0.9)	— (†)	— (†)	— (†)
90th	333 (0.7)	332 (1.2)	336 (0.8)	— (†)	332 (0.9)	— (†)	333 (1.1)	— (†)	335 (0.9)	— (†)	— (†)	— (†)
	Standard deviation[4] of the reading scale score											
All students												
4th grade	36 (0.6)	41 (0.6)	39 (0.7)	42 (0.9)	36 (0.3)	37 (0.2)	36 (0.1)	36 (0.2)	35 (0.2)	36 (0.1)	37 (0.2)	35 (0.2)
8th grade	36 (0.3)	37 (0.4)	35 (0.5)	— (†)	34 (0.3)	35 (0.2)	35 (0.1)	35 (0.2)	34 (0.2)	34 (0.1)	35 (0.2)	33 (0.2)
12th grade	33 (0.4)	37 (0.5)	38 (0.4)	— (†)	37 (0.4)	— (†)	38 (0.4)	— (†)	38 (0.3)	— (†)	— (†)	— (†)

—Not available.
†Not applicable.
‡Reporting standards not met (too few cases).
[1]Accommodations were not permitted for this assessment.
[2]Scale ranges from 0 to 500.
[3]The percentile represents a specific point on the percentage distribution of all students ranked by their reading score from low to high. For example, 10 percent of students scored at or below the 10th percentile score, while 90 percent of students scored above it.
[4]The standard deviation provides an indication of how much the test scores varied. The lower the standard deviation, the closer the scores were clustered around the average score. About two-thirds of the student scores can be expected to fall within the range of one standard deviation above and one standard deviation below the average score. For example, the average score for all 4th-graders in 2011 was 221, and the standard deviation was 36. This means that we would expect about two-thirds of the students to have scores between 257 (one standard deviation above the average) and 185 (one standard deviation below). Standard errors also must be taken into account when making comparisons of these ranges. For a discussion of standard errors, see Appendix A: Guide to Sources.
NOTE: Includes public and private schools. For 1998 and later years, includes students tested with accommodations (1 to 10 percent of all students, depending on grade level and year); excludes only those students with disabilities and English language learners who were unable to be tested even with accommodations (2 to 6 percent of all students). Race categories exclude persons of Hispanic ethnicity. Standard errors appear in parentheses.
SOURCE: U.S. Department of Education, National Center for Education Statistics, National Assessment of Educational Progress (NAEP), 1992, 1994, 1998, 2000, 2002, 2003, 2005, 2007, 2009, and 2011 Reading Assessments, retrieved November 1, 2011, from the Main NAEP Data Explorer (http://nces.ed.gov/nationsreportcard/naepdata/). (This table was prepared November 2011.)

Average reading scale score, by grade and selected student and school characteristics: Selected years, 1992 through 2011

Grade and selected student or school characteristic	1992[1]		1994[1]		1998		2000		2002		2003		2005		2007		2009		2011	
1	2		3		4		5		6		7		8		9		10		11	
4th grade, all students	**217**	**(0.9)**	**214**	**(1.0)**	**215**	**(1.1)**	**213**	**(1.3)**	**219**	**(0.4)**	**218**	**(0.3)**	**219**	**(0.2)**	**221**	**(0.3)**	**221**	**(0.3)**	**221**	**(0.3)**
Sex																				
Male	213	(1.2)	209	(1.3)	212	(1.3)	208	(1.3)	215	(0.4)	215	(0.3)	216	(0.2)	218	(0.3)	218	(0.3)	218	(0.3)
Female	221	(1.0)	220	(1.1)	217	(1.3)	219	(1.4)	222	(0.5)	222	(0.3)	222	(0.3)	224	(0.3)	224	(0.3)	225	(0.3)
Eligibility for free or reduced-price lunch																				
Eligible	—	(†)	—	(†)	196	(1.7)	193	(1.7)	203	(0.7)	201	(0.3)	203	(0.3)	205	(0.3)	206	(0.3)	207	(0.3)
Not eligible	—	(†)	—	(†)	227	(0.9)	226	(1.2)	230	(0.4)	229	(0.3)	230	(0.2)	232	(0.3)	232	(0.3)	235	(0.3)
Unknown	—	(†)	—	(†)	223	(2.7)	225	(2.3)	226	(1.6)	230	(0.9)	232	(0.9)	233	(1.3)	236	(1.3)	235	(0.8)
Read for fun on own																				
Almost every day	223	(1.2)	223	(1.2)	219	(1.5)	218	(1.7)	225	(0.5)	225	(0.3)	225	(0.3)	227	(0.3)	228	(0.4)	228	(0.4)
1–2 times a week	218	(1.2)	213	(1.1)	217	(1.2)	216	(1.2)	220	(0.5)	219	(0.3)	220	(0.3)	223	(0.3)	221	(0.4)	221	(0.4)
1–2 times a month	210	(1.6)	208	(2.1)	211	(1.9)	212	(1.6)	210	(0.8)	211	(0.5)	213	(0.4)	216	(0.4)	214	(0.4)	214	(0.4)
Never or hardly ever	199	(1.8)	197	(1.9)	202	(1.9)	201	(1.8)	208	(0.5)	207	(0.4)	208	(0.3)	211	(0.4)	210	(0.3)	210	(0.5)
Magazines in home																				
Yes	221	(1.2)	220	(1.1)	221	(1.0)	219	(1.3)	223	(0.5)	223	(0.3)	223	(0.3)	225	(0.3)	224	(0.3)	226	(0.3)
No	207	(1.1)	201	(1.3)	202	(1.6)	203	(1.7)	209	(0.6)	209	(0.5)	210	(0.3)	213	(0.4)	215	(0.4)	216	(0.4)
Unknown	214	(2.1)	206	(2.1)	210	(1.9)	209	(2.4)	214	(0.6)	214	(0.4)	215	(0.4)	218	(0.4)	219	(0.4)	217	(0.4)
Control of school																				
Public	215	(1.0)	212	(1.1)	213	(1.2)	211	(1.4)	217	(0.5)	216	(0.3)	217	(0.2)	220	(0.3)	220	(0.3)	220	(0.3)
Private	232	(1.7)	231	(2.5)	‡	(†)	231	(1.8)	234	(0.9)	235	(0.8)	‡	(†)	234	(1.1)	235	(1.0)	234	(0.8)
8th grade, all students	**260**	**(0.9)**	**260**	**(0.8)**	**263**	**(0.8)**	**—**	**(†)**	**264**	**(0.4)**	**263**	**(0.3)**	**262**	**(0.2)**	**263**	**(0.2)**	**264**	**(0.3)**	**265**	**(0.2)**
Sex																				
Male	254	(1.1)	252	(1.0)	256	(1.0)	—	(†)	260	(0.5)	258	(0.3)	257	(0.2)	258	(0.3)	259	(0.3)	261	(0.3)
Female	267	(1.0)	267	(1.0)	270	(0.8)	—	(†)	269	(0.5)	269	(0.3)	267	(0.2)	268	(0.3)	269	(0.3)	270	(0.2)
Eligibility for free or reduced-price lunch																				
Eligible	—	(†)	—	(†)	245	(1.0)	—	(†)	249	(0.5)	247	(0.4)	247	(0.3)	247	(0.3)	249	(0.3)	252	(0.3)
Not eligible	—	(†)	—	(†)	269	(1.0)	—	(†)	272	(0.4)	271	(0.3)	270	(0.2)	271	(0.3)	273	(0.3)	275	(0.3)
Unknown	—	(†)	—	(†)	272	(2.0)	—	(†)	271	(1.4)	272	(1.0)	275	(1.1)	277	(1.3)	280	(1.3)	283	(0.9)
Read for fun on own																				
Almost every day	277	(1.1)	277	(1.4)	277	(1.0)	—	(†)	279	(0.6)	279	(0.4)	279	(0.3)	281	(0.4)	282	(0.4)	284	(0.4)
1–2 times a week	263	(1.0)	264	(1.1)	267	(1.1)	—	(†)	266	(0.5)	265	(0.4)	265	(0.3)	265	(0.3)	267	(0.4)	268	(0.3)
1–2 times a month	258	(1.2)	257	(0.8)	263	(0.9)	—	(†)	264	(0.6)	262	(0.3)	261	(0.3)	261	(0.4)	261	(0.4)	263	(0.3)
Never or hardly ever	246	(1.4)	246	(1.1)	251	(1.1)	—	(†)	255	(0.4)	253	(0.3)	252	(0.3)	253	(0.3)	253	(0.4)	255	(0.3)
Magazines in home																				
Yes	265	(0.9)	264	(0.8)	267	(0.8)	—	(†)	269	(0.4)	268	(0.3)	267	(0.2)	268	(0.2)	269	(0.3)	272	(0.2)
No	243	(1.3)	243	(1.5)	248	(1.1)	—	(†)	254	(0.7)	252	(0.4)	252	(0.3)	255	(0.3)	257	(0.4)	261	(0.3)
Unknown	242	(2.0)	237	(2.5)	240	(2.2)	—	(†)	246	(0.8)	245	(0.9)	247	(0.6)	248	(0.5)	252	(0.5)	253	(0.4)
Parents' highest level of education																				
Did not finish high school	243	(1.4)	238	(1.9)	242	(1.6)	—	(†)	248	(1.0)	245	(0.7)	244	(0.5)	245	(0.5)	248	(0.6)	248	(0.6)
Graduated high school	251	(1.4)	252	(1.2)	254	(1.3)	—	(†)	257	(0.5)	254	(0.4)	252	(0.4)	253	(0.4)	254	(0.4)	254	(0.4)
Some education after high school ..	265	(1.1)	266	(1.3)	268	(1.1)	—	(†)	268	(0.5)	267	(0.4)	265	(0.3)	266	(0.3)	267	(0.3)	267	(0.4)
Graduated college	271	(1.0)	270	(0.9)	273	(0.9)	—	(†)	274	(0.4)	273	(0.3)	272	(0.2)	273	(0.2)	274	(0.3)	275	(0.3)
Control of school																				
Public	258	(1.0)	257	(0.8)	261	(0.8)	—	(†)	263	(0.5)	261	(0.2)	260	(0.2)	261	(0.2)	262	(0.3)	264	(0.2)
Private	278	(2.0)	279	(1.4)	‡	(†)	—	(†)	281	(0.9)	282	(0.7)	‡	(†)	280	(0.9)	282	(0.9)	282	(0.7)
12th grade, all students	**292**	**(0.6)**	**287**	**(0.7)**	**290**	**(0.6)**	**—**	**(†)**	**287**	**(0.7)**	**—**	**(†)**	**286**	**(0.6)**	**—**	**(†)**	**288**	**(0.7)**	**—**	**(†)**
Sex																				
Male	287	(0.7)	280	(0.8)	282	(0.8)	—	(†)	279	(0.9)	—	(†)	279	(0.8)	—	(†)	282	(0.7)	—	(†)
Female	297	(0.7)	294	(0.8)	298	(0.8)	—	(†)	295	(0.7)	—	(†)	292	(0.7)	—	(†)	294	(0.8)	—	(†)
Eligibility for free or reduced-price lunch																				
Eligible	—	(†)	—	(†)	270	(1.1)	—	(†)	273	(1.4)	—	(†)	271	(1.0)	—	(†)	273	(0.7)	—	(†)
Not eligible	—	(†)	—	(†)	293	(0.6)	—	(†)	289	(0.9)	—	(†)	290	(0.7)	—	(†)	294	(0.8)	—	(†)
Unknown	—	(†)	—	(†)	295	(1.6)	—	(†)	294	(1.5)	—	(†)	295	(1.9)	—	(†)	296	(2.4)	—	(†)
Read for fun on own																				
Almost every day	304	(0.9)	302	(1.1)	304	(1.0)	—	(†)	304	(1.1)	—	(†)	302	(1.2)	—	(†)	305	(0.9)	—	(†)
1–2 times a week	296	(0.7)	294	(1.0)	298	(0.9)	—	(†)	292	(1.1)	—	(†)	292	(1.0)	—	(†)	295	(1.0)	—	(†)
1–2 times a month	290	(0.9)	285	(1.0)	289	(0.7)	—	(†)	288	(0.9)	—	(†)	285	(0.8)	—	(†)	288	(0.8)	—	(†)
Never or hardly ever	279	(1.0)	273	(1.1)	275	(1.0)	—	(†)	275	(1.0)	—	(†)	274	(0.8)	—	(†)	275	(0.6)	—	(†)
Magazines in home																				
Yes	295	(0.6)	291	(0.7)	294	(0.6)	—	(†)	292	(0.7)	—	(†)	292	(0.6)	—	(†)	294	(0.7)	—	(†)
No	278	(1.2)	271	(1.2)	277	(1.2)	—	(†)	277	(1.0)	—	(†)	276	(1.0)	—	(†)	281	(0.7)	—	(†)
Unknown	264	(3.5)	256	(4.2)	247	(5.2)	—	(†)	255	(3.4)	—	(†)	260	(2.8)	—	(†)	263	(1.6)	—	(†)
Parents' highest level of education																				
Did not finish high school	275	(1.4)	266	(1.5)	268	(1.8)	—	(†)	268	(1.5)	—	(†)	268	(1.7)	—	(†)	269	(1.0)	—	(†)
Graduated high school	283	(0.8)	277	(1.3)	279	(1.2)	—	(†)	278	(1.1)	—	(†)	274	(0.9)	—	(†)	276	(0.7)	—	(†)
Some education after high school ..	294	(0.8)	289	(1.0)	291	(1.0)	—	(†)	289	(1.0)	—	(†)	287	(0.8)	—	(†)	287	(0.7)	—	(†)
Graduated college	301	(0.8)	298	(1.0)	300	(0.7)	—	(†)	296	(0.8)	—	(†)	297	(0.7)	—	(†)	299	(0.8)	—	(†)
Control of school																				
Public	290	(0.7)	286	(0.7)	289	(0.7)	—	(†)	285	(0.7)	—	(†)	285	(0.7)	—	(†)	287	(0.8)	—	(†)
Private	308	(1.3)	301	(1.9)	‡	(†)	—	(†)	‡	(†)	—	(†)	‡	(†)	—	(†)	‡	(†)	—	(†)

—Not available.
†Not applicable.
‡Reporting standards not met. Participation rates fell below the required standards for reporting.
[1]Accommodations were not permitted for this assessment.
NOTE: Scale ranges from 0 to 500. Includes public and private schools. For 1998 and later years, includes students tested with accommodations (1 to 10 percent of all students, depending on grade level and year); excludes only those students with disabilities and English language learners who were unable to be tested even with accommodations (2 to 6 percent of all students). Race categories exclude persons of Hispanic ethnicity. Standard errors appear in parentheses.
SOURCE: U.S. Department of Education, National Center for Education Statistics, National Assessment of Educational Progress (NAEP), 1992, 1994, 1998, 2000, 2002, 2003, 2005, 2007, 2009, and 2011 Reading Assessments, retrieved November 2, 2011, from the Main NAEP Data Explorer (http://nces.ed.gov/nationsreportcard/naepdata/). (This table was prepared November 2011.)

Average reading scale scores and percentage distribution of 9-, 13-, and 17-year-olds, by amount of reading for school, frequency of reading for fun, and time spent doing homework and watching TV/video: Selected years, 1984 through 2008

Average scale score

Time spent on reading and homework	9-year-olds 1984	1994	1999	2004	2008	13-year-olds 1984	1994	1999	2004	2008	17-year-olds 1984	1994	1999	2004	2008
(column)	2	3	4	5	6	7	8	9	10	11	12	13	14	15	16
Pages read daily in school and for homework															
5 or fewer	208 (0.9)	203 (2.3)	202 (1.8)	206 (1.5)	210 (1.1)	250 (0.8)	249 (1.7)	249 (2.0)	245 (1.4)	250 (1.2)	273 (0.8)	271 (1.9)	273 (2.7)	269 (1.4)	271 (1.3)
6–10	215 (1.0)	214 (1.7)	212 (2.4)	217 (1.4)	219 (1.3)	261 (0.6)	261 (1.8)	262 (1.7)	257 (1.5)	258 (1.2)	287 (0.9)	284 (2.1)	285 (2.1)	283 (1.5)	284 (1.4)
11–15	220 (1.4)	217 (2.9)	214 (2.0)	220 (1.6)	224 (1.5)	264 (1.4)	266 (2.3)	263 (2.1)	263 (1.5)	263 (1.5)	294 (1.1)	288 (2.9)	285 (2.1)	286 (2.0)	290 (1.5)
16–20	215 (1.4)	209 (2.9)	214 (2.0)	220 (1.1)	225 (1.5)	263 (1.1)	266 (2.3)	264 (2.6)	266 (1.9)	267 (1.3)	296 (1.1)	298 (2.8)	292 (2.9)	298 (1.6)	296 (1.5)
More than 20	215 (1.6)	217 (2.4)	217 (2.1)	218 (1.1)	226 (1.2)	261 (1.5)	261 (2.0)	265 (2.0)	261 (1.6)	267 (1.4)	300 (1.2)	304 (2.2)	302 (1.9)	298 (1.9)	303 (1.3)
Frequency of reading for fun															
Almost every day	214 (1.1)	215 (2.3)	215 (2.4)	‡	225 (1.2)	264 (1.4)	272 (3.2)	272 (3.2)	‡	274 (1.4)	302 (1.7)	302 (4.2)	301 (4.9)	‡	302 (1.7)
Once or twice a week	212 (1.7)	215 (2.3)	215 (2.6)	‡	221 (1.2)	255 (2.1)	255 (3.7)	260 (3.7)	‡	265 (0.6)	290 (1.9)	286 (4.5)	286 (4.8)	‡	291 (1.7)
Once or twice a month	204 (3.7)	213 (5.8)	211 (4.2)	‡	221 (1.7)	255 (2.1)	252 (5.4)	260 (4.4)	‡	254 (1.3)	283 (2.7)	281 (8.2)	283 (4.4)	‡	287 (1.5)
A few times a year	197 (4.2)	193 (3.9)	‡	‡	211 (3.1)	252 (2.5)	237 (5.1)	242 (5.3)	‡	247 (0.9)	279 (2.7)	258 (5.2)	262 (5.0)	‡	269 (1.1)
Never or hardly ever	198 (2.7)	193 (3.9)	195 (3.3)	‡	211 (2.7)	239 (2.5)	237 (5.1)	242 (5.3)	‡	247 (0.9)	269 (2.4)	258 (5.2)	262 (5.0)	‡	269 (1.1)
Time spent on homework yesterday															
No homework assigned	212 (1.0)	213 (2.0)	210 (1.9)	215 (1.5)	219 (1.7)	254 (1.0)	250 (1.7)	251 (2.0)	248 (1.7)	251 (1.2)	276 (0.8)	273 (2.3)	275 (2.3)	268 (1.6)	272 (1.3)
Didn't do assignment	199 (2.3)	200 (4.3)	204 (4.4)	194 (3.0)	201 (2.6)	247 (1.7)	243 (5.6)	249 (4.2)	245 (2.1)	242 (0.9)	287 (1.4)	288 (2.1)	291 (3.1)	277 (1.7)	288 (1.7)
Less than 1 hour	217 (0.8)	217 (1.4)	214 (1.5)	214 (1.9)	221 (0.9)	261 (0.8)	261 (1.4)	258 (1.2)	258 (1.4)	260 (0.9)	279 (0.9)	281 (1.7)	286 (2.8)	286 (1.5)	295 (1.1)
1 to 2 hours	216 (1.0)	214 (3.1)	215 (3.5)	218 (3.6)	207 (3.1)	267 (0.8)	269 (2.4)	266 (3.0)	266 (2.3)	277 (1.9)	296 (0.8)	306 (3.1)	300 (2.8)	294 (2.4)	306 (2.2)
More than 2 hours	201 (1.9)	192 (2.7)	198 (1.7)	198 (3.6)	205 (3.1)	264 (1.2)	270 (3.0)	269 (1.8)	259 (2.3)	277 (1.9)	303 (1.4)	300 (3.1)	300 (2.8)	300 (2.4)	306 (2.2)
TV/video watched on school day															
None	212 (3.4)	212 (4.8)	221 (4.6)	‡	223 (3.0)	264 (2.7)	270 (5.1)	265 (6.0)	‡	267 (3.0)	300 (1.6)	308 (3.4)	308 (2.8)	‡	292 (2.4)
1 hour or less	217 (1.2)	216 (2.2)	208 (2.7)	‡	225 (1.1)	269 (1.1)	268 (1.4)	270 (1.5)	‡	266 (1.3)	294 (0.9)	292 (2.0)	298 (2.0)	‡	290 (1.1)
2 hours	220 (1.5)	218 (2.2)	214 (2.3)	‡	227 (1.3)	264 (0.8)	262 (1.6)	268 (1.5)	‡	262 (1.3)	288 (1.0)	284 (2.0)	282 (2.3)	‡	284 (1.3)
3 hours	214 (1.4)	214 (2.2)	218 (2.4)	‡	219 (2.4)	262 (0.8)	264 (2.2)	262 (2.4)	‡	255 (2.6)	277 (1.0)	276 (4.1)	273 (3.8)	‡	276 (2.3)
4 hours or more	199 (0.8)	192 (2.7)	208 (3.0)	‡	205 (1.2)	245 (1.0)	234 (3.0)	238 (1.8)	‡	238 (1.4)	269 (1.5)	256 (3.7)	256 (5.2)	‡	256 (2.3)

Percentage distribution

Time spent on reading and homework	9-year-olds 1984	1994	1999	2004	2008	13-year-olds 1984	1994	1999	2004	2008	17-year-olds 1984	1994	1999	2004	2008
Pages read daily in school and for homework															
5 or fewer	36 (0.8)	28 (1.4)	28 (1.4)	25 (0.9)	25 (0.9)	27 (0.7)	26 (0.9)	23 (1.0)	25 (0.8)	26 (0.8)	26 (0.8)	21 (1.2)	23 (1.4)	31 (0.9)	30 (0.9)
6–10	25 (0.6)	24 (0.7)	24 (0.7)	25 (0.6)	24 (0.5)	34 (0.5)	31 (0.8)	18 (0.8)	25 (0.7)	24 (0.5)	31 (0.9)	25 (0.8)	24 (0.6)	24 (0.6)	23 (0.5)
11–15	14 (0.4)	14 (0.5)	15 (0.7)	14 (0.6)	14 (0.4)	18 (0.4)	18 (0.6)	16 (0.8)	16 (0.5)	17 (0.5)	18 (0.8)	18 (0.6)	17 (0.6)	15 (0.5)	16 (0.4)
16–20	13 (0.4)	14 (0.9)	13 (0.6)	13 (0.6)	14 (0.6)	11 (0.5)	13 (0.8)	16 (0.7)	12 (0.5)	13 (0.4)	14 (0.3)	13 (0.6)	14 (0.6)	11 (0.5)	12 (0.5)
More than 20	13 (0.5)	17 (0.9)	19 (1.0)	29 (1.0)	28 (0.6)	11 (0.5)	14 (0.8)	21 (1.0)	21 (0.7)	22 (0.9)	11 (0.5)	22 (1.5)	22 (1.2)	19 (0.9)	19 (0.7)
Frequency of reading for fun															
Almost every day	53 (1.0)	58 (1.6)	54 (1.6)	‡	48 (0.7)	35 (1.0)	32 (1.8)	28 (1.7)	‡	26 (0.7)	30 (1.0)	30 (2.6)	25 (2.7)	‡	20 (0.6)
Once or twice a week	28 (0.6)	25 (1.5)	26 (1.5)	‡	23 (0.3)	35 (1.2)	37 (2.1)	36 (1.7)	‡	25 (0.6)	33 (1.1)	31 (1.9)	28 (2.7)	‡	22 (0.5)
Once or twice a month	7 (0.6)	5 (0.6)	6 (0.7)	‡	8 (0.4)	14 (0.8)	14 (1.2)	17 (1.6)	‡	13 (0.4)	14 (0.8)	15 (1.5)	15 (1.7)	‡	17 (0.5)
A few times a year	3 (0.5)	3 (0.6)	4 (0.7)	‡	14 (0.6)	8 (0.6)	10 (0.8)	10 (1.4)	‡	21 (0.7)	8 (0.6)	12 (1.4)	12 (2.4)	‡	16 (0.6)
Never or hardly ever	9 (0.5)	9 (0.8)	10 (0.8)	‡	14 (0.6)	9 (0.6)	8 (0.6)	12 (1.4)	‡	24 (0.7)	19 (0.6)	12 (1.4)	16 (2.4)	‡	24 (0.6)
Time spent on homework yesterday															
No homework assigned	35 (1.3)	32 (2.1)	26 (1.6)	23 (1.5)	18 (1.3)	22 (0.7)	26 (1.4)	24 (1.2)	20 (1.2)	23 (1.2)	28 (0.9)	23 (1.4)	26 (1.0)	26 (1.0)	28 (0.8)
Didn't do assignment	41 (1.0)	48 (0.4)	53 (0.7)	55 (0.3)	60 (1.3)	36 (0.6)	34 (1.0)	37 (1.4)	27 (0.8)	43 (1.2)	26 (0.4)	27 (0.6)	26 (1.0)	19 (0.7)	27 (0.5)
Less than 1 hour	16 (0.2)	11 (0.7)	15 (0.5)	13 (0.2)	15 (0.5)	29 (0.5)	28 (1.0)	28 (0.8)	42 (0.7)	21 (0.7)	22 (0.5)	26 (0.9)	26 (0.8)	21 (0.7)	22 (0.5)
1 to 2 hours	6 (0.4)	6 (0.4)	7 (0.7)	13 (0.3)	6 (0.3)	13 (0.3)	11 (0.7)	11 (0.8)	24 (0.5)	6 (0.4)	13 (0.3)	13 (0.9)	12 (0.9)	10 (0.6)	10 (0.5)
More than 2 hours	30 (0.7)	20 (0.8)	22 (1.2)	29 (1.0)	26 (0.8)	10 (0.4)	13 (0.9)	16 (1.0)	21 (1.0)	13 (0.4)	19 (0.6)	19 (1.2)	19 (1.2)	19 (0.7)	19 (0.7)
TV/video watched on school day															
None	3 (0.2)	2 (0.2)	4 (0.8)	4 (0.8)	4 (0.3)	3 (0.2)	4 (0.3)	4 (0.6)	5 (0.3)	5 (0.3)	5 (0.3)	6 (0.8)	6 (0.3)	6 (0.3)	6 (0.3)
1 hour or less	14 (0.4)	23 (0.7)	24 (0.9)	24 (0.5)	24 (0.5)	12 (0.5)	27 (0.7)	26 (0.8)	26 (0.5)	25 (0.5)	26 (0.5)	31 (0.8)	34 (0.9)	33 (0.6)	33 (0.6)
2 hours	16 (0.3)	21 (0.7)	21 (0.9)	18 (0.6)	24 (0.5)	18 (0.5)	22 (0.7)	22 (0.8)	18 (0.6)	18 (0.5)	20 (0.3)	26 (0.6)	26 (0.7)	27 (0.7)	27 (0.6)
3 hours	12 (0.3)	11 (0.5)	14 (0.4)	14 (0.6)	13 (0.4)	12 (0.4)	12 (0.6)	11 (0.6)	10 (0.4)	10 (0.4)	17 (0.3)	18 (0.6)	17 (0.7)	18 (0.6)	16 (0.5)
4 hours or more	30 (0.7)	20 (0.8)	22 (1.2)	26 (0.4)	26 (0.8)	13 (0.4)	10 (0.9)	5 (0.6)	13 (0.4)	13 (0.4)	30 (0.7)	5 (0.4)	5 (0.4)	8 (0.4)	8 (0.2)
6 hours or more												6 (0.2)	4 (0.4)	4 (0.6)	6 (0.4)

—Not available.
†Not applicable.
‡Reporting standards not met (too few cases).
NOTE: The NAEP reading scores have been evaluated at certain performance levels. Scale ranges from 0 to 500. Students scoring 150 (or higher) are able to follow brief written directions and carry out simple, discrete reading tasks. Students scoring 200 are able to understand, combine ideas, and make inferences based on short uncomplicated passages about specific or sequentially related information. Students scoring 250 are able to search for specific information, interrelate ideas, and make generalizations about literature, science, and social studies materials. Students scoring 300 are able to find, understand, summarize, and explain relatively complicated literary and informational material. Includes public and private schools. Excludes persons not enrolled in school and students who were unable to be tested due to limited proficiency in English or due to a disability. Beginning in 2004, data are for a revised assessment format that provides accommodations for students with disabilities and English language learners. Detail may not sum to totals because of rounding. Some data have been revised from previously published figures. Standard errors appear in parentheses.
SOURCE: U.S. Department of Education, National Center for Education Statistics, National Assessment of Educational Progress (NAEP), NAEP Trends in Academic Progress, 1996 and 1999; and 2004 and 2008 NAEP Long-Term Trend Reading Assessments, retrieved June 24, 2009, from the Long-Term Trend NAEP Data Explorer (http://nces.ed.gov/nationsreportcard/naepdata/). (This table was prepared June 2009.)

Percentage of students at or above selected reading score levels, by age, sex, and race/ethnicity: Selected years, 1971 through 2008

Selected characteristic	1971		1975		1980		1984		1988		1990		1992		1994		1996		1999		2004		2008	
1	2		3		4		5		6		7		8		9		10		11		12		13	
9-year-olds																								
Total																								
Level 150	91	(0.5)	93	(0.4)	95	(0.4)	92	(0.4)	93	(0.7)	90	(0.9)	92	(0.4)	92	(0.7)	93	(0.6)	93	(0.7)	94	(0.5)	96	(0.4)
Level 200	59	(1.0)	62	(0.8)	68	(1.0)	62	(0.8)	63	(1.3)	59	(1.3)	62	(1.1)	63	(1.4)	64	(1.3)	64	(1.4)	69	(1.0)	73	(0.9)
Level 250	16	(0.6)	15	(0.6)	18	(0.8)	17	(0.7)	17	(1.1)	18	(1.0)	16	(0.8)	17	(1.2)	17	(0.8)	16	(1.0)	19	(0.7)	21	(0.8)
Male																								
Level 150	88	(0.7)	91	(0.5)	93	(0.5)	90	(0.5)	90	(0.9)	88	(1.4)	90	(0.8)	90	(1.0)	92	(0.8)	91	(1.1)	92	(0.6)	94	(0.6)
Level 200	53	(1.2)	56	(1.0)	63	(1.1)	58	(1.0)	58	(1.8)	54	(1.9)	57	(1.6)	59	(1.5)	58	(2.0)	61	(1.8)	64	(1.3)	70	(1.2)
Level 250	12	(0.6)	12	(0.6)	15	(0.9)	16	(0.8)	16	(1.4)	16	(1.2)	14	(1.0)	15	(1.2)	14	(1.3)	15	(1.3)	17	(0.8)	19	(1.0)
Female																								
Level 150	93	(0.5)	95	(0.3)	96	(0.4)	94	(0.5)	95	(1.0)	92	(1.1)	94	(0.6)	94	(0.8)	95	(0.8)	95	(0.8)	96	(0.5)	97	(0.4)
Level 200	65	(1.1)	68	(0.8)	73	(1.0)	65	(1.0)	67	(1.4)	64	(1.2)	67	(1.2)	67	(1.9)	70	(1.6)	67	(1.6)	73	(1.2)	77	(1.1)
Level 250	19	(0.8)	18	(0.8)	21	(1.0)	18	(0.8)	19	(1.2)	21	(1.2)	18	(1.1)	18	(1.5)	19	(1.3)	17	(1.3)	20	(1.0)	22	(1.1)
White																								
Level 150	94 [1]	(0.4)	96	(0.3)	97	(0.2)	95	(0.3)	95	(0.7)	94	(0.9)	96	(0.5)	96	(0.5)	96	(0.6)	97	(0.4)	97	(0.4)	98	(0.4)
Level 200	65 [1]	(1.0)	69	(0.8)	74	(0.7)	69	(0.9)	68	(1.6)	66	(1.4)	69	(1.2)	70	(1.5)	71	(1.5)	73	(1.6)	77	(1.0)	81	(1.0)
Level 250	18 [1]	(0.7)	17	(0.7)	21	(0.9)	21	(0.8)	20	(1.5)	23	(1.2)	20	(1.0)	20	(1.5)	20	(1.1)	20	(1.4)	24	(0.8)	27	(1.1)
Black																								
Level 150	70 [1]	(1.7)	81	(1.1)	85	(1.4)	81	(1.2)	83	(2.4)	77	(2.7)	80	(2.2)	79	(2.4)	84	(1.9)	82	(2.5)	88	(1.7)	91	(1.1)
Level 200	22 [1]	(1.5)	32	(1.5)	41	(1.9)	37	(1.5)	39	(2.9)	34	(3.4)	37	(2.2)	38	(2.8)	42	(3.2)	36	(3.0)	50	(2.3)	58	(2.3)
Level 250	2 [1]	(0.5)	2	(0.3)	4	(0.6)	5	(0.5)	6	(1.2)	5	(1.5)	5	(0.8)	4	(1.5)	6	(1.1)	4	(1.1)	7	(0.8)	9	(0.9)
Hispanic																								
Level 150	[2]	(†)	81	(2.5)	84	(1.8)	82	(3.0)	86	(3.5)	84	(1.8)	83	(2.6)	80	(4.6)	86	(2.4)	87	(3.3)	89	(1.3)	93	(0.8)
Level 200	[2]	(†)	35	(3.0)	42	(2.6)	40	(2.7)	46	(3.3)	41	(2.7)	43	(3.5)	37	(4.6)	48	(3.8)	44	(3.4)	53	(1.7)	62	(1.7)
Level 250	[2]	(†)	3	(0.5)	5	(1.4)	4	(0.6)	9	(2.3)	6	(2.0)	7	(2.3)	6	(1.6)	7	(3.2)	6	(1.7)	7	(0.8)	10	(1.2)
13-year-olds																								
Total																								
Level 200	93	(0.5)	93	(0.4)	95	(0.4)	94	(0.3)	95	(0.6)	94	(0.6)	93	(0.7)	92	(0.6)	92	(0.7)	93	(0.7)	92	(0.6)	94	(0.4)
Level 250	58	(1.1)	59	(1.0)	61	(1.1)	59	(0.8)	59	(1.3)	59	(1.0)	62	(1.4)	60	(1.2)	60	(1.3)	61	(1.5)	59	(1.1)	63	(0.8)
Level 300	10	(0.5)	10	(0.5)	11	(0.5)	11	(0.4)	11	(0.8)	11	(0.6)	15	(0.9)	14	(0.8)	14	(1.0)	15	(1.1)	12	(0.8)	13	(0.5)
Male																								
Level 200	91	(0.7)	91	(0.5)	93	(0.6)	92	(0.4)	93	(1.0)	91	(0.9)	90	(1.1)	89	(1.1)	89	(1.2)	91	(0.9)	89	(0.8)	92	(0.6)
Level 250	52	(1.2)	52	(1.1)	56	(1.2)	54	(0.9)	52	(1.9)	52	(1.5)	55	(2.0)	53	(1.9)	53	(1.6)	55	(1.9)	55	(1.3)	59	(1.2)
Level 300	7	(0.5)	7	(0.4)	9	(0.7)	9	(0.5)	9	(0.9)	8	(0.8)	13	(1.1)	10	(0.7)	10	(1.0)	11	(1.1)	11	(0.9)	11	(0.7)
Female																								
Level 200	95	(0.4)	96	(0.4)	96	(0.4)	96	(0.3)	97	(0.6)	96	(0.6)	95	(0.7)	95	(0.6)	95	(0.6)	96	(0.7)	95	(0.6)	96	(0.5)
Level 250	64	(1.1)	65	(1.2)	65	(1.1)	64	(0.8)	65	(1.4)	65	(1.5)	68	(1.4)	68	(1.7)	66	(1.6)	66	(1.9)	65	(1.3)	66	(1.0)
Level 300	12	(0.6)	13	(0.7)	13	(0.6)	13	(0.6)	13	(0.9)	14	(0.9)	18	(1.1)	18	(1.1)	17	(1.3)	18	(1.7)	14	(1.0)	16	(0.9)
White																								
Level 200	96 [1]	(0.3)	96	(0.2)	97	(0.2)	96	(0.2)	96	(0.6)	96	(0.6)	96	(0.6)	95	(0.7)	95	(0.5)	96	(0.6)	95	(0.5)	96	(0.4)
Level 250	64 [1]	(0.9)	65	(0.9)	68	(0.8)	65	(0.8)	64	(1.5)	65	(1.2)	68	(1.4)	68	(1.3)	69	(1.4)	69	(1.7)	68	(1.1)	72	(1.2)
Level 300	11 [1]	(0.5)	12	(0.5)	14	(0.6)	13	(0.6)	12	(0.9)	13	(0.9)	18	(1.1)	17	(1.0)	17	(1.3)	18	(1.4)	16	(0.9)	18	(0.8)
Black																								
Level 200	74 [1]	(1.7)	77	(1.3)	84	(1.7)	85	(1.2)	91	(2.2)	88	(2.3)	82	(2.7)	81	(2.3)	82	(3.2)	85	(2.3)	86	(1.5)	91	(1.1)
Level 250	21 [1]	(1.2)	25	(1.6)	30	(2.0)	35	(1.3)	40	(2.3)	42	(3.5)	38	(2.7)	38	(3.5)	34	(3.9)	38	(2.7)	40	(2.3)	48	(2.3)
Level 300	1 [1]	(0.2)	2	(0.3)	2	(0.5)	3	(0.6)	5	(1.2)	5	(0.8)	6	(1.4)	4	(1.2)	3	(0.9)	5	(1.4)	4	(0.7)	6	(0.8)
Hispanic																								
Level 200	[2]	(†)	81	(2.3)	87	(2.4)	86	(1.7)	87	(2.6)	86	(2.4)	83	(3.5)	82	(2.7)	85	(3.2)	89	(2.8)	85	(1.9)	87	(1.3)
Level 250	[2]	(†)	32	(3.6)	35	(2.6)	39	(2.3)	38	(4.4)	37	(2.9)	41	(5.1)	34	(3.9)	38	(3.7)	43	(3.8)	44	(2.3)	44	(1.8)
Level 300	[2]	(†)	2	(1.0)	2	(0.6)	4	(1.0)	4	(1.9)	4	(1.2)	6	(1.9)	4	(1.8)	5	(1.7)	6	(1.8)	5	(1.2)	5	(0.6)
17-year-olds																								
Total																								
Level 250	79	(0.9)	80	(0.7)	81	(0.9)	83	(0.6)	86	(0.8)	84	(1.0)	83	(0.8)	81	(1.0)	82	(0.8)	82	(1.0)	79	(0.9)	80	(0.6)
Level 300	39	(1.0)	39	(0.8)	38	(1.1)	40	(1.0)	41	(1.5)	41	(1.0)	43	(1.1)	41	(1.2)	39	(1.4)	40	(1.4)	36	(1.2)	39	(0.8)
Male																								
Level 250	74	(1.0)	76	(0.8)	78	(1.0)	80	(0.7)	83	(1.4)	80	(1.4)	78	(1.2)	76	(1.5)	77	(1.2)	77	(1.5)	73	(1.2)	76	(0.8)
Level 300	34	(1.1)	34	(1.0)	35	(1.3)	36	(1.0)	37	(2.3)	36	(1.5)	38	(1.6)	36	(1.9)	34	(1.9)	34	(1.7)	32	(1.2)	35	(0.9)
Female																								
Level 250	83	(1.0)	84	(0.9)	84	(1.0)	87	(0.6)	88	(1.1)	89	(1.0)	87	(1.1)	86	(1.2)	87	(1.0)	87	(1.0)	84	(0.8)	84	(0.8)
Level 300	44	(1.2)	44	(0.9)	41	(1.2)	45	(1.1)	44	(2.0)	47	(1.3)	48	(1.5)	46	(1.5)	45	(1.7)	45	(1.8)	41	(1.6)	43	(1.0)
White																								
Level 250	84 [1]	(0.7)	86	(0.6)	87	(0.6)	88	(0.5)	89	(0.9)	88	(1.1)	88	(0.9)	86	(1.1)	87	(0.8)	87	(1.3)	83	(0.9)	87	(0.6)
Level 300	43 [1]	(0.9)	44	(0.8)	43	(1.1)	47	(1.1)	45	(1.6)	48	(1.2)	50	(1.4)	48	(1.4)	46	(1.5)	46	(1.5)	42	(1.3)	47	(1.0)
Black																								
Level 250	40 [1]	(1.6)	43	(1.6)	44	(2.0)	65	(1.5)	76	(2.4)	69	(2.8)	61	(2.3)	66	(4.1)	68	(4.0)	66	(2.5)	64	(2.2)	67	(2.4)
Level 300	8 [1]	(0.9)	8	(0.7)	7	(0.8)	16	(1.0)	25	(3.1)	20	(1.8)	17	(2.5)	22	(3.7)	18	(2.2)	17	(1.7)	16	(1.8)	21	(1.5)
Hispanic																								
Level 250	[2]	(†)	53	(4.1)	62	(3.1)	68	(2.4)	71	(4.8)	75	(4.7)	69	(4.0)	63	(4.4)	65	(4.2)	68	(4.3)	67	(2.4)	70	(1.5)
Level 300	[2]	(†)	13	(2.7)	17	(2.1)	21	(3.0)	23	(3.7)	27	(3.3)	27	(3.2)	20	(3.0)	20	(4.8)	24	(3.8)	23	(2.1)	22	(1.0)

†Not applicable.

[1] Data for 1971 include persons of Hispanic ethnicity.

[2] Test scores of Hispanics were not tabulated separately.

NOTE: The NAEP reading scores have been evaluated at certain performance levels. Scale ranges from 0 to 500. Students scoring 150 (or higher) are able to follow brief written directions and carry out simple, discrete reading tasks. Students scoring 200 are able to understand, combine ideas, and make inferences based on short uncomplicated passages about specific or sequentially related information. Students scoring 250 are able to search for specific information, interrelate ideas, and make generalizations about literature, science, and social studies materials. Students scoring 300 are able to find, understand, summarize, and explain relatively complicated literary and informational material. Includes public and private schools. Excludes persons not enrolled in school and students who were unable to be tested due to limited proficiency in English or due to a disability. Beginning in 2004, data are for a revised assessment format that provides accommodations for students with disabilities and English language learners. Race categories exclude persons of Hispanic ethnicity, except where noted. Standard errors appear in parentheses.

SOURCE: U.S. Department of Education, National Center for Education Statistics, National Assessment of Educational Progress (NAEP), *NAEP 1999 Trends in Academic Progress*; and 2004 and 2008 Long-Term Trend Reading Assessments, retrieved May 12, 2009, from the Long-Term Trend NAEP Data Explorer (http://nces.ed.gov/nationsreportcard/naepdata/). (This table was prepared May 2009.)

Average scores in NAEP reading for fourth-grade public school students, by state/jurisdiction: Various years, 1992–2011

State/jurisdiction	Accommodations not permitted			Accommodations permitted						
	1992	1994	1998	1998	2002	2003	2005	2007	2009	2011
Nation (public)	215*	212*	215*	213*	217*	216 *	217*	220	220	220
Alabama	207*	208*	211*	211*	207*	207 *	208*	216*	216*	220
Alaska	—	—	—	—	—	212	211	214*	211	208
Arizona	209	206*	207*	206*	205*	209 *	207*	210	210	212
Arkansas	211*	209*	209*	209*	213*	214	217	217	216	217
California	202*	197*	202*	202*	206	206 *	207*	209	210	211
Colorado	217*	213*	222	220	—	224	224	224	226	223
Connecticut	222*	222*	232	230	229	228	226	227	229	227
Delaware	213*	206*	212*	207*	224	224	226	225	226	225
Florida	208*	205*	207*	206*	214*	218 *	219*	224	226	225
Georgia	212*	207*	210*	209*	215*	214 *	214*	219	218	221
Hawaii	203*	201*	200*	200*	208*	208 *	210*	213	211*	214
Idaho	219	—	—	—	220	218 *	222	223*	221	221
Illinois	—	—	—	—	—	216	216	219	219	219
Indiana	221	220	—	—	222	220	218	222	223	221
Iowa	225*	223	223	220	223	223	221	225*	221	221
Kansas	—	—	222	221	222	220 *	220	225	224	224
Kentucky	213*	212*	218*	218*	219*	219 *	220*	222	226	225
Louisiana	204*	197*	204*	200*	207	205 *	209	207	207	210
Maine	227*	228*	225*	225	225	224	225*	226*	224	222
Maryland	211*	210*	215*	212*	217*	219 *	220*	225*	226*	231
Massachusetts	226*	223*	225*	223*	234*	228 *	231*	236	234*	237
Michigan	216	—	217	216	219	219	218	220	218	219
Minnesota	221	218*	222	219	225	223	225	225	223	222
Mississippi	199*	202*	204*	203*	203*	205 *	204*	208	211	209
Missouri	220	217	216*	216*	220	222	221	221	224*	220
Montana	—	222	226	225	224	223	225	227	225	225
Nebraska	221	220	—	—	222	221	221	223	223	223
Nevada	—	—	208*	206*	209*	207 *	207*	211	211	213
New Hampshire	228	223*	226*	226*	—	228 *	227*	229	229	230
New Jersey	223*	219*	—	—	—	225 *	223*	231	229	231
New Mexico	211	205	206	205	208	203 *	207	212*	208	208
New York	215*	212*	216*	215*	222	222	223	224	224	222
North Carolina	212*	214*	217*	213*	222	221	217*	218*	219	221
North Dakota	226	225	—	—	224	222 *	225	226	226	226
Ohio	217*	—	—	—	222	222	223	226	225	224
Oklahoma	220*	—	220*	219*	213	214	214	217	217	215
Oregon	—	—	214	212*	220	218	217	215	218	216
Pennsylvania	221*	215*	—	—	221*	219 *	223*	226	224	227
Rhode Island	217*	220	218*	218*	220*	216 *	216*	219*	223	222
South Carolina	210*	203*	210*	209*	214	215	213	214	216	215
South Dakota	—	—	—	—	—	222	222*	223*	222*	220
Tennessee	212	213	212	212	214	212	214	216	217	215
Texas	213*	212*	217	214	217	215	219	220	219	218
Utah	220	217	215*	216*	222	219	221	221	219	220
Vermont	—	—	—	—	227	226	227	228	229	227
Virginia	221*	213*	218*	217*	225	223	226	227	227	226
Washington	—	213*	217*	218	224	221	223	224	221	221
West Virginia	216	213	216	216	219*	219 *	215	215	215	214
Wisconsin	224	224*	224*	222	—	221	221	223	220	221
Wyoming	223	221	219*	218*	221*	222	223	225	223	224
Other jurisdictions										
District of Columbia	188*	179*	182*	179*	191*	188*	191*	197*	202	201
DoDEA[1]	—	—	222*	220*	224*	224*	226*	229	228	229

— Not available. The state/jurisdiction did not participate or did not meet the minimum participation guidelines for reporting.

* Significantly different (p < .05) from 2011 when only one state/jurisdiction or the nation is being examined.

[1] Elepartment of Defense Education Activity (overseas and domestic schools).

SOURCE: U.S. Department of Education, Institute of Education Sciences, National Center for Education Statistics, National Assessment of Educational Progress (NAEP), various years, 1992-2011 Reading Assessments.

Average scores and achievement-level results in NAEP reading for fourth-grade public school students, by state/jurisdiction: 2011

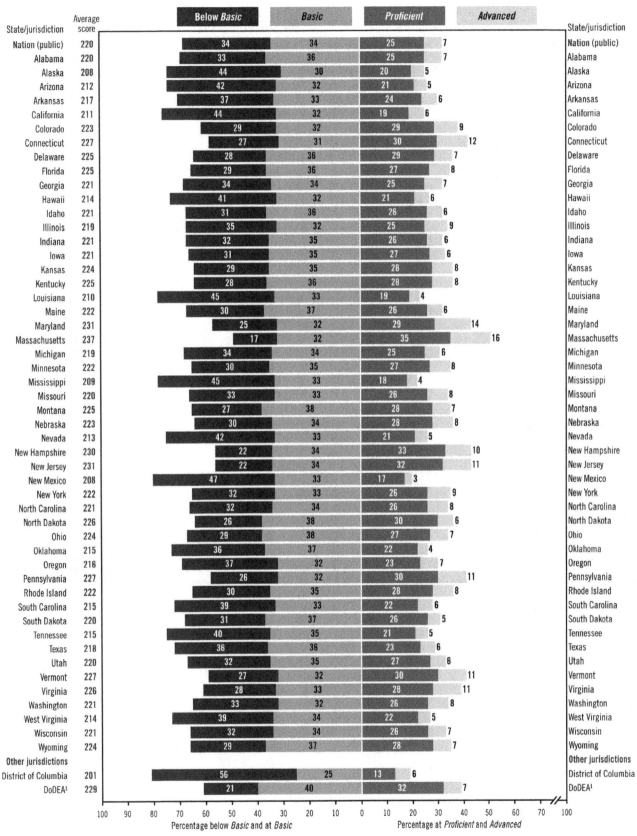

State/jurisdiction	Average score	Below Basic	Basic	Proficient	Advanced
Nation (public)	220	34	34	25	7
Alabama	220	33	36	25	7
Alaska	208	44	30	20	5
Arizona	212	42	32	21	5
Arkansas	217	37	33	24	6
California	211	44	32	19	6
Colorado	223	29	32	29	9
Connecticut	227	27	31	30	12
Delaware	225	28	36	29	7
Florida	225	29	36	27	8
Georgia	221	34	34	25	7
Hawaii	214	41	32	21	6
Idaho	221	31	36	26	6
Illinois	219	35	32	25	9
Indiana	221	32	35	26	6
Iowa	221	31	35	27	6
Kansas	224	29	35	28	8
Kentucky	225	28	36	28	8
Louisiana	210	45	33	19	4
Maine	222	30	37	26	6
Maryland	231	25	32	29	14
Massachusetts	237	17	32	35	16
Michigan	219	34	34	25	6
Minnesota	222	30	35	27	8
Mississippi	209	45	33	18	4
Missouri	220	33	33	26	8
Montana	225	27	38	28	7
Nebraska	223	30	34	28	8
Nevada	213	42	33	21	5
New Hampshire	230	22	34	33	10
New Jersey	231	22	34	32	11
New Mexico	208	47	33	17	3
New York	222	32	33	26	9
North Carolina	221	32	34	26	8
North Dakota	226	26	38	30	6
Ohio	224	29	38	27	7
Oklahoma	215	36	37	22	4
Oregon	216	37	32	23	7
Pennsylvania	227	26	32	30	11
Rhode Island	222	30	35	28	8
South Carolina	215	39	33	22	6
South Dakota	220	31	37	26	5
Tennessee	215	40	35	21	5
Texas	218	36	36	23	6
Utah	220	32	35	27	6
Vermont	227	27	32	30	11
Virginia	226	28	33	28	11
Washington	221	33	32	26	8
West Virginia	214	39	34	22	5
Wisconsin	221	32	34	26	7
Wyoming	224	29	37	28	7
Other jurisdictions					
District of Columbia	201	56	25	13	6
DoDEA[1]	229	21	40	32	7

Percentage below *Basic* and at *Basic* — Percentage at *Proficient* and *Advanced*

[1] Department of Defense Education Activity (overseas and domestic schools).

NOTE: The shaded bars are graphed using unrounded numbers. Detail may not sum to totals because of rounding.

SOURCE: U.S. Department of Education, Institute of Education Sciences, National Center for Education Statistics, National Assessment of Educational Progress (NAEP), 2011 Reading Assessment.

Average scores and achievement-level results in NAEP reading for fourth-grade public school students, by race/ethnicity and state/jurisdiction: 2011

State/jurisdiction	White Average scale score	Below Basic	At or above Basic	At or above Proficient	At Advanced	Black Average scale score	Below Basic	At or above Basic	At or above Proficient	At Advanced	Hispanic Average scale score	Below Basic	At or above Basic	At or above Proficient	At Advanced
Nation (public)	**230**	**23**	**77**	**42**	**10**	**205**	**51**	**49**	**16**	**2**	**205**	**50**	**50**	**18**	**2**
Alabama	230	21	79	41	9	204	52	48	14	2	205	50	50	16	2
Alaska	223	29	71	36	8	206	50	50	20	3	212	40	60	24	5
Arizona	225	28	72	38	9	204	53	47	20	5	203	52	48	16	2
Arkansas	224	28	72	38	8	197	60	40	11	1	204	50	50	18	3
California	229	24	76	40	10	208	47	53	19	4	198	58	42	12	1
Colorado	236	16	84	51	13	207	47	53	18	2	203	51	49	18	3
Connecticut	239	15	85	55	17	204	52	48	14	2	204	50	50	17	3
Delaware	234	17	83	47	11	215	40	60	23	3	214	41	59	22	3
Florida	235	17	83	48	12	209	46	54	17	2	220	33	67	30	6
Georgia	231	22	78	43	11	208	49	51	19	3	214	40	60	25	4
Hawaii	226	26	74	38	9	215	40	60	26	7	209	44	56	22	4
Idaho	225	26	74	37	7	‡	‡	‡	‡	‡	201	54	46	15	2
Illinois	231	22	78	45	12	198	58	42	12	2	204	51	49	18	2
Indiana	226	26	74	38	8	203	56	44	13	2	203	49	51	17	1
Iowa	225	27	73	37	7	193	62	38	11	1	201	52	48	15	2
Kansas	229	24	76	42	10	204	54	46	18	3	209	45	55	19	2
Kentucky	226	27	73	37	8	210	48	52	19	2	222	32	68	35	6
Louisiana	223	30	70	33	6	197	61	39	11	1	208	44	56	22	4
Maine	223	29	71	33	7	192	60	40	14	1	‡	‡	‡	‡	‡
Maryland	242	13	87	56	19	213	43	57	22	4	226	29	71	37	8
Massachusetts	243	11	89	59	18	216	39	61	24	3	216	38	62	23	4
Michigan	225	26	74	37	7	192	67	33	8	1	206	51	49	20	3
Minnesota	229	22	78	42	10	199	56	44	16	3	201	55	45	12	2
Mississippi	220	32	68	30	6	198	60	40	12	1	203	53	47	25	3
Missouri	226	27	73	39	10	199	57	43	14	2	209	46	54	23	5
Montana	229	22	78	39	8	‡	‡	‡	‡	‡	217	34	66	23	2
Nebraska	230	23	77	42	10	199	56	44	15	1	208	46	54	20	2
Nevada	224	29	71	36	8	202	55	45	15	1	203	51	49	17	2
New Hampshire	231	21	79	44	10	‡	‡	‡	‡	‡	217	38	62	26	6
New Jersey	239	12	88	53	14	216	39	61	25	4	216	38	62	25	4
New Mexico	225	28	72	34	8	208	47	53	17	2	202	54	46	15	1
New York	232	21	79	46	12	208	48	52	18	3	209	46	54	20	3
North Carolina	232	19	81	45	12	206	50	50	16	2	207	48	52	20	4
North Dakota	228	23	77	38	7	220	33	67	29	5	214	40	60	22	2
Ohio	229	22	78	39	8	204	54	46	13	1	211	41	59	19	1
Oklahoma	221	29	71	31	5	199	55	45	13	1	207	47	53	18	4
Oregon	222	30	70	35	8	202	51	49	18	3	196	60	40	12	2
Pennsylvania	233	19	81	47	13	204	52	48	19	3	202	52	48	17	3
Rhode Island	230	22	78	43	10	208	42	58	23	2	204	51	49	16	1
South Carolina	226	27	73	39	9	199	56	44	12	2	208	43	57	20	3
South Dakota	225	25	75	35	6	204	52	48	18	2	207	44	56	21	3
Tennessee	221	32	68	31	6	198	59	41	11	1	201	52	48	16	2
Texas	233	19	81	45	11	210	45	55	18	3	210	46	54	19	2
Utah	226	26	74	38	7	‡	‡	‡	‡	‡	196	59	41	13	2
Vermont	228	26	74	42	11	205	50	50	24	6	‡	‡	‡	‡	‡
Virginia	235	19	81	49	15	210	45	55	19	2	209	45	55	21	3
Washington	229	24	76	42	10	209	44	56	19	1	199	55	45	16	2
West Virginia	216	38	62	28	5	196	58	42	14	1	‡	‡	‡	‡	‡
Wisconsin	227	26	74	39	8	196	61	39	12	2	202	52	48	13	1
Wyoming	227	25	75	38	8	‡	‡	‡	‡	‡	213	42	58	21	3
Other jurisdictions															
District of Columbia	255	8	92	74	37	193	63	37	12	2	202	52	48	19	4
DoDEA[1]	233	17	83	44	9	222	27	73	29	3	226	24	76	33	5

See notes at end of table.

Average scores and achievement-level results in NAEP reading for fourth-grade public school students, by race/ethnicity and state/jurisdiction: 2011—Continued

	Asian/Pacific Islander					American Indian/Alaska Native				
	Average scale score	Percentage of students				Average scale score	Percentage of students			
		Below *Basic*	At or above *Basic*	At or above *Proficient*	At *Advanced*		Below *Basic*	At or above *Basic*	At or above *Proficient*	At *Advanced*
State/jurisdiction										
Nation (public)	**234**	**21**	**79**	**49**	**17**	**204**	**51**	**49**	**19**	**4**
Alabama	‡	‡	‡	‡	‡	‡	‡	‡	‡	‡
Alaska	197	58	42	13	1	175	74	26	8	1
Arizona	226	28	72	42	14	185	70	30	8	2
Arkansas	220	37	63	34	7	‡	‡	‡	‡	‡
California	233	20	80	48	15	‡	‡	‡	‡	‡
Colorado	234	20	80	51	13	‡	‡	‡	‡	‡
Connecticut	241	17	83	57	21	‡	‡	‡	‡	‡
Delaware	240	17	83	57	17	‡	‡	‡	‡	‡
Florida	244	12	88	57	25	‡	‡	‡	‡	‡
Georgia	242	13	87	57	21	‡	‡	‡	‡	‡
Hawaii	211	44	56	25	5	‡	‡	‡	‡	‡
Idaho	224	29	71	43	11	‡	‡	‡	‡	‡
Illinois	237	17	83	52	18	‡	‡	‡	‡	‡
Indiana	‡	‡	‡	‡	‡	‡	‡	‡	‡	‡
Iowa	227	27	73	45	13	‡	‡	‡	‡	‡
Kansas	228	27	73	43	15	‡	‡	‡	‡	‡
Kentucky	249	6	94	67	26	‡	‡	‡	‡	‡
Louisiana	‡	‡	‡	‡	‡	‡	‡	‡	‡	‡
Maine	219	29	71	28	5	‡	‡	‡	‡	‡
Maryland	251	10	90	67	31	‡	‡	‡	‡	‡
Massachusetts	243	15	85	56	25	‡	‡	‡	‡	‡
Michigan	236	19	81	48	15	‡	‡	‡	‡	‡
Minnesota	217	37	63	32	10	195	60	40	14	2
Mississippi	‡	‡	‡	‡	‡	‡	‡	‡	‡	‡
Missouri	233	28	72	52	21	‡	‡	‡	‡	‡
Montana	‡	‡	‡	‡	‡	200	57	43	14	2
Nebraska	234	23	77	56	15	‡	‡	‡	‡	‡
Nevada	222	33	67	32	8	‡	‡	‡	‡	‡
New Hampshire	234	22	78	47	14	‡	‡	‡	‡	‡
New Jersey	247	12	88	64	27	‡	‡	‡	‡	‡
New Mexico	222	31	69	39	11	193	64	36	12	2
New York	235	20	80	49	17	‡	‡	‡	‡	‡
North Carolina	236	19	81	48	19	192	62	38	10	2
North Dakota	‡	‡	‡	‡	‡	206	50	50	15	2
Ohio	‡	‡	‡	‡	‡	‡	‡	‡	‡	‡
Oklahoma	225	31	69	38	11	212	40	60	25	4
Oregon	230	28	72	47	16	213	39	61	28	7
Pennsylvania	242	18	82	60	24	‡	‡	‡	‡	‡
Rhode Island	232	18	82	47	12	‡	‡	‡	‡	‡
South Carolina	‡	‡	‡	‡	‡	‡	‡	‡	‡	‡
South Dakota	‡	‡	‡	‡	‡	197	58	42	13	2
Tennessee	234	24	76	51	15	‡	‡	‡	‡	‡
Texas	247	8	92	59	24	‡	‡	‡	‡	‡
Utah	217	37	63	32	7	187	66	34	14	4
Vermont	‡	‡	‡	‡	‡	‡	‡	‡	‡	‡
Virginia	236	20	80	50	19	‡	‡	‡	‡	‡
Washington	227	30	70	43	15	202	54	46	19	6
West Virginia	‡	‡	‡	‡	‡	‡	‡	‡	‡	‡
Wisconsin	225	32	68	39	11	‡	‡	‡	‡	‡
Wyoming	‡	‡	‡	‡	‡	192	65	35	11	2
Other jurisdictions										
District of Columbia	‡	‡	‡	‡	‡	‡	‡	‡	‡	‡
DoDEA[1]	231	18	82	40	9	‡	‡	‡	‡	‡

‡ Reporting standards not met. Sample size insufficient to permit a reliable estimate.
[1] Department of Defense Education Activity (overseas and domestic schools).
NOTE: Black includes African American, Hispanic includes Latino, and Pacific Islander includes Native Hawaiian. Race categories exclude Hispanic origin. Results are not shown for students of two or more races. Detail may not sum to totals because of rounding.
SOURCE: U.S. Department of Education, Institute of Education Sciences, National Center for Education Statistics, National Assessment of Educational Progress (NAEP), 2011 Reading Assessment.

Average scores and achievement-level results in NAEP reading for fourth-grade public school students, by gender and state/jurisdiction: 2011

| | Male | | | | | Female | | | | |
| | Percentage of students | | | | | | Percentage of students | | | |
State/jurisdiction	Average scale score	Below Basic	At or above Basic	At or above Proficient	At Advanced	Average scale score	Below Basic	At or above Basic	At or above Proficient	At Advanced
Nation (public)	**217**	**37**	**63**	**30**	**6**	**223**	**30**	**70**	**35**	**9**
Alabama	218	35	65	30	6	223	30	70	33	7
Alaska	204	48	52	23	4	212	40	60	28	6
Arizona	209	45	55	24	4	216	38	62	29	7
Arkansas	214	40	60	28	6	219	34	66	32	6
California	209	46	54	23	4	214	41	59	26	7
Colorado	219	33	67	33	7	228	25	75	44	11
Connecticut	224	30	70	38	10	232	23	77	46	14
Delaware	223	31	69	33	7	228	25	75	39	8
Florida	221	33	67	32	7	228	25	75	39	10
Georgia	216	39	61	28	5	226	28	72	37	9
Hawaii	208	46	54	24	5	219	35	65	30	7
Idaho	218	34	66	30	6	224	28	72	35	7
Illinois	217	37	63	31	7	222	32	68	36	10
Indiana	217	36	64	29	5	225	28	72	37	8
Iowa	218	34	66	31	6	224	28	72	36	7
Kansas	219	33	67	32	6	228	25	75	41	10
Kentucky	223	31	69	33	7	227	26	74	38	9
Louisiana	206	49	51	20	3	215	40	60	25	5
Maine	219	34	66	30	6	225	27	73	35	7
Maryland	227	29	71	39	12	234	22	78	47	16
Massachusetts	234	20	80	47	13	239	15	85	54	18
Michigan	216	38	62	29	6	222	31	69	33	7
Minnesota	219	33	67	33	7	225	27	73	38	9
Mississippi	204	51	49	18	3	215	39	61	26	5
Missouri	215	38	62	30	6	225	28	72	38	11
Montana	222	30	70	32	6	229	23	77	39	9
Nebraska	220	33	67	33	7	226	27	73	40	10
Nevada	210	45	55	23	4	216	38	62	28	5
New Hampshire	226	27	73	38	8	235	17	83	50	13
New Jersey	229	24	76	42	10	233	20	80	46	13
New Mexico	205	50	50	19	3	211	43	57	22	4
New York	219	35	65	32	8	226	29	71	38	10
North Carolina	217	36	64	30	7	225	28	72	38	10
North Dakota	223	29	71	32	5	228	24	76	39	7
Ohio	222	31	69	32	6	226	26	74	35	8
Oklahoma	213	39	61	25	4	219	33	67	28	5
Oregon	212	42	58	26	5	221	33	67	35	9
Pennsylvania	223	31	69	38	9	232	22	78	45	13
Rhode Island	218	34	66	32	6	227	26	74	39	9
South Carolina	210	43	57	25	5	220	34	66	32	7
South Dakota	217	35	65	28	4	223	28	72	35	7
Tennessee	211	44	56	23	4	219	35	65	29	6
Texas	216	38	62	26	5	220	34	66	30	6
Utah	218	35	65	31	6	223	28	72	36	7
Vermont	224	29	71	38	9	230	24	76	45	13
Virginia	223	32	68	35	9	230	24	76	43	12
Washington	216	38	62	30	6	226	29	71	39	10
West Virginia	210	45	55	23	4	219	34	66	31	6
Wisconsin	219	35	65	32	6	224	29	71	36	8
Wyoming	221	33	67	31	5	228	24	76	38	8
Other jurisdictions										
District of Columbia	194	62	38	16	4	208	50	50	22	7
DoDEA[1]	226	25	75	34	5	233	16	84	44	9

[1] Department of Defense Education Activity (overseas and domestic schools).
NOTE: Detail may not sum to totals because of rounding.
SOURCE: U.S. Department of Education, Institute of Education Sciences, National Center for Education Statistics, National Assessment of Educational Progress (NAEP), 2011 Reading Assessment.

Average reading scale score of 4th-grade public school students and percentage attaining reading achievement levels, by state: Selected years, 1992 through 2011

State	1992	1994	1998	2002	2003	2005	2007	2009	2011	At or above Basic [2]	At or above Proficient [3]	At Advanced [4]
1	2	3	4	5	6	7	8	9	10	11	12	13
United States	215 (1.0)	212 (1.1)	212 (1.2)	217 (0.5)	216 (0.3)	217 (0.2)	220 (0.3)	220 (0.3)	220 (0.3)	66 (0.4)	32 (0.4)	7 (0.2)
Alabama	207 (1.7)	208 (1.5)	211 (1.9)	207 (1.4)	207 (1.7)	208 (1.2)	216 (1.3)	216 (1.2)	220 (1.3)	67 (1.7)	31 (1.5)	7 (0.8)
Alaska	— (†)	— (†)	— (†)	— (†)	212 (1.6)	211 (1.4)	214 (1.0)	211 (1.2)	208 (1.1)	56 (1.4)	26 (1.1)	5 (0.7)
Arizona	209 (1.2)	206 (1.9)	206 (1.4)	205 (1.5)	209 (1.2)	207 (1.6)	210 (1.6)	210 (1.2)	212 (1.2)	58 (1.4)	26 (1.3)	5 (0.6)
Arkansas	211 (1.2)	209 (1.7)	209 (1.6)	213 (1.4)	214 (1.4)	217 (1.1)	217 (1.2)	216 (1.1)	217 (1.0)	63 (1.2)	30 (1.1)	6 (0.6)
California[5,6]	202 (2.0)	197 (1.8)	202 (2.5)	206 (2.5)	206 (1.2)	207 (0.7)	209 (1.0)	210 (1.5)	211 (1.8)	56 (2.1)	25 (2.0)	6 (1.0)
Colorado	217 (1.1)	213 (1.3)	220 (1.4)	— (†)	224 (1.2)	224 (1.1)	224 (1.1)	226 (1.2)	223 (1.3)	71 (1.4)	39 (1.5)	9 (0.9)
Connecticut	222 (1.3)	222 (1.6)	230 (1.6)	229 (1.1)	228 (1.1)	226 (1.0)	227 (1.3)	229 (1.1)	227 (1.3)	73 (1.5)	42 (1.5)	12 (0.9)
Delaware[7]	213 (0.6)	206 (1.1)	207 (1.7)	224 (0.6)	224 (0.7)	226 (0.8)	225 (0.7)	226 (0.5)	225 (0.7)	72 (1.0)	36 (1.2)	7 (0.7)
District of Columbia	188 (0.8)	179 (0.9)	179 (1.2)	191 (0.9)	188 (0.9)	191 (1.0)	197 (0.9)	202 (1.0)	201 (0.8)	44 (0.9)	19 (0.8)	6 (0.6)
Florida	208 (1.2)	205 (1.7)	206 (1.4)	214 (1.4)	218 (1.1)	220 (0.9)	224 (0.8)	226 (1.0)	225 (1.1)	71 (1.4)	35 (1.4)	8 (0.7)
Georgia	212 (1.5)	207 (2.4)	209 (1.4)	215 (1.0)	214 (1.3)	214 (1.2)	219 (0.9)	218 (1.1)	221 (1.1)	66 (1.4)	32 (1.3)	7 (0.6)
Hawaii	203 (1.7)	201 (1.7)	200 (1.5)	208 (0.9)	208 (1.4)	210 (1.0)	213 (1.1)	211 (1.0)	214 (1.0)	59 (1.2)	27 (1.1)	6 (0.7)
Idaho	219 (0.9)	‡ (†)	— (†)	220 (1.1)	218 (1.0)	222 (0.9)	223 (0.8)	221 (0.9)	221 (0.8)	69 (1.1)	33 (1.0)	6 (0.6)
Illinois	— (†)	220 (1.3)	‡ (†)	‡ (†)	216 (1.6)	217 (1.2)	219 (1.2)	219 (1.4)	219 (1.1)	65 (1.2)	33 (1.2)	9 (0.7)
Indiana	221 (1.3)	220 (1.3)	— (†)	222 (1.4)	220 (1.0)	218 (1.1)	222 (0.9)	223 (1.3)	221 (0.9)	68 (1.2)	33 (1.0)	6 (0.6)
Iowa[5,6]	225 (1.1)	223 (1.3)	220 (1.6)	223 (1.1)	223 (1.1)	221 (0.9)	225 (1.1)	221 (1.2)	221 (0.8)	69 (0.9)	33 (0.9)	6 (0.6)
Kansas[5,6]	— (†)	— (†)	221 (1.4)	222 (1.4)	220 (1.2)	221 (1.3)	225 (1.1)	224 (1.3)	224 (1.0)	71 (1.1)	36 (1.5)	8 (0.7)
Kentucky	213 (1.3)	212 (1.6)	218 (1.5)	219 (1.1)	219 (1.3)	220 (1.1)	222 (1.1)	226 (1.1)	225 (1.0)	72 (1.3)	35 (1.5)	8 (0.7)
Louisiana	204 (1.2)	197 (1.3)	200 (1.6)	207 (1.7)	205 (1.4)	209 (1.3)	207 (1.6)	207 (1.1)	210 (1.4)	55 (1.8)	23 (1.4)	4 (0.5)
Maine	227 (1.1)	228 (1.3)	225 (1.4)	225 (1.1)	224 (0.9)	225 (0.9)	226 (0.9)	224 (0.9)	222 (0.7)	70 (1.0)	32 (1.3)	6 (0.5)
Maryland	211 (1.6)	210 (1.5)	212 (1.6)	217 (1.5)	219 (1.4)	220 (1.3)	225 (1.1)	226 (1.4)	231 (0.9)	75 (1.0)	43 (1.2)	14 (1.0)
Massachusetts[5]	226 (0.9)	223 (1.3)	223 (1.4)	234 (1.1)	228 (1.2)	231 (0.9)	236 (1.1)	234 (1.1)	237 (1.0)	83 (1.2)	50 (1.5)	16 (1.1)
Michigan	216 (1.5)	‡ (†)	216 (1.5)	219 (1.1)	219 (1.2)	218 (1.5)	220 (1.4)	218 (1.0)	219 (1.2)	66 (1.4)	31 (1.4)	6 (0.7)
Minnesota[5,6]	221 (1.2)	218 (1.4)	219 (1.7)	225 (1.1)	223 (1.1)	225 (1.3)	225 (1.3)	223 (1.3)	222 (1.2)	70 (1.4)	35 (1.5)	8 (0.8)
Mississippi	199 (1.3)	202 (1.6)	203 (1.3)	203 (1.3)	205 (1.3)	204 (1.4)	208 (1.0)	211 (1.1)	209 (1.2)	55 (1.4)	22 (1.2)	4 (0.5)
Missouri	220 (1.2)	217 (1.5)	216 (1.3)	220 (1.3)	222 (1.2)	221 (0.9)	221 (1.1)	224 (1.1)	220 (0.9)	67 (1.0)	34 (1.1)	8 (0.6)
Montana[5,6,8]	— (†)	222 (1.4)	225 (1.5)	224 (1.8)	223 (1.2)	225 (1.1)	227 (1.0)	225 (0.8)	225 (0.6)	73 (1.0)	36 (1.1)	7 (0.6)
Nebraska[7,8]	221 (1.1)	220 (1.5)	— (†)	222 (1.5)	221 (1.0)	221 (1.2)	223 (1.3)	223 (1.0)	223 (1.0)	70 (1.1)	36 (1.4)	8 (0.7)
Nevada	— (†)	— (†)	206 (1.8)	209 (1.2)	207 (1.2)	207 (1.2)	211 (1.2)	211 (1.1)	213 (1.0)	58 (1.3)	25 (1.1)	5 (0.5)
New Hampshire[5,7,8]	228 (1.2)	223 (1.5)	226 (1.7)	— (†)	228 (1.0)	227 (0.9)	229 (0.9)	229 (1.0)	230 (0.8)	78 (0.8)	43 (1.1)	10 (0.6)
New Jersey[7]	223 (1.4)	219 (1.2)	— (†)	— (†)	225 (1.2)	223 (1.3)	231 (1.2)	229 (0.9)	231 (1.2)	78 (1.5)	44 (1.4)	11 (0.7)
New Mexico	211 (1.5)	205 (1.7)	205 (1.4)	208 (1.6)	203 (1.5)	207 (1.3)	212 (1.3)	208 (1.4)	208 (1.0)	53 (1.5)	21 (0.9)	3 (0.5)
New York[5,6,7]	215 (1.4)	212 (1.4)	215 (1.6)	222 (1.5)	222 (1.1)	223 (1.1)	224 (1.0)	224 (1.0)	222 (1.1)	68 (1.3)	35 (1.4)	9 (0.8)
North Carolina	212 (1.1)	214 (1.5)	213 (1.6)	222 (1.0)	221 (1.0)	217 (1.0)	218 (0.9)	219 (1.1)	221 (1.2)	68 (1.2)	34 (1.4)	8 (0.8)
North Dakota[6]	226 (1.1)	225 (1.2)	— (†)	224 (1.0)	222 (0.9)	225 (0.9)	226 (0.9)	226 (0.9)	226 (0.5)	74 (1.0)	36 (0.9)	6 (0.4)
Ohio	217 (1.3)	— (†)	— (†)	222 (1.3)	222 (1.2)	223 (1.4)	226 (1.1)	225 (1.1)	224 (1.0)	71 (1.1)	34 (1.5)	7 (0.7)
Oklahoma	220 (0.9)	— (†)	219 (1.2)	213 (1.2)	214 (1.2)	214 (1.1)	217 (1.1)	217 (1.1)	215 (1.1)	64 (1.5)	27 (1.2)	4 (0.4)
Oregon	— (†)	— (†)	212 (1.8)	220 (1.4)	218 (1.4)	217 (1.4)	215 (1.4)	218 (1.2)	216 (1.1)	63 (1.3)	30 (1.4)	7 (0.5)
Pennsylvania[8]	221 (1.3)	215 (1.6)	— (†)	221 (1.2)	219 (1.3)	223 (1.3)	226 (1.0)	224 (1.4)	227 (1.2)	74 (1.3)	41 (1.4)	11 (0.9)
Rhode Island[8]	217 (1.8)	220 (1.3)	218 (1.4)	220 (1.2)	216 (1.3)	216 (1.2)	219 (1.0)	223 (1.1)	222 (0.8)	70 (1.3)	35 (1.0)	8 (0.6)
South Carolina	210 (1.3)	203 (1.4)	209 (1.4)	214 (1.3)	215 (1.3)	213 (1.3)	214 (1.2)	216 (1.1)	215 (1.2)	61 (1.2)	28 (1.5)	6 (0.6)
South Dakota	— (†)	— (†)	— (†)	— (†)	222 (1.2)	222 (0.5)	223 (1.0)	222 (0.6)	220 (0.9)	69 (1.0)	31 (1.0)	5 (0.6)
Tennessee[6,8]	212 (1.4)	213 (1.7)	212 (1.4)	214 (1.2)	212 (1.6)	214 (1.4)	216 (1.2)	217 (1.2)	218 (1.5)	60 (1.5)	26 (1.3)	5 (0.6)
Texas	213 (1.6)	212 (1.9)	214 (1.9)	217 (1.7)	215 (1.4)	219 (0.8)	220 (0.9)	219 (1.2)	218 (1.5)	64 (1.8)	28 (1.8)	6 (1.0)
Utah	220 (1.1)	217 (1.3)	216 (1.2)	222 (1.0)	219 (1.0)	221 (1.1)	221 (1.2)	219 (1.0)	220 (1.2)	68 (1.2)	33 (1.3)	6 (0.6)
Vermont	— (†)	— (†)	— (†)	227 (1.1)	226 (0.9)	227 (0.9)	228 (0.8)	229 (0.8)	227 (0.6)	73 (0.9)	41 (0.9)	11 (0.6)
Virginia	221 (1.4)	213 (1.5)	217 (1.2)	225 (1.3)	223 (1.5)	226 (0.8)	227 (1.1)	227 (1.2)	226 (1.1)	72 (1.4)	39 (1.4)	11 (0.9)
Washington[6]	— (†)	213 (1.5)	213 (1.5)	218 (1.4)	224 (1.2)	221 (1.1)	224 (1.1)	221 (1.2)	221 (1.1)	67 (1.3)	34 (1.3)	8 (0.9)
West Virginia	216 (1.3)	213 (1.7)	216 (1.7)	219 (1.2)	219 (1.0)	215 (0.8)	215 (1.1)	215 (1.0)	214 (0.8)	61 (1.1)	27 (1.0)	5 (0.5)
Wisconsin[5,6,8]	224 (1.0)	224 (1.1)	222 (1.1)	‡ (†)	221 (0.8)	221 (1.0)	223 (1.2)	220 (1.1)	221 (0.8)	68 (1.1)	34 (1.1)	7 (0.7)
Wyoming	223 (1.1)	221 (1.2)	218 (1.5)	221 (1.0)	222 (0.8)	223 (0.7)	225 (0.5)	223 (0.7)	224 (0.8)	71 (1.3)	34 (1.1)	7 (0.6)
Department of Defense dependents schools[9]	— (†)	— (†)	220 (0.7)	224 (0.4)	224 (0.5)	226 (0.6)	229 (0.5)	228 (0.5)	229 (0.5)	79 (0.9)	39 (1.3)	7 (0.5)

—Not available.

†Not applicable.

‡Reporting standards not met. Participation rates fell below the required standards for reporting.

[1]Scale ranges from 0 to 500.

[2]Basic denotes partial mastery of the knowledge and skills that are fundamental for proficient work at the 4th-grade level.

[3]Proficient represents solid academic performance for 4th-graders. Students reaching this level have demonstrated competency over challenging subject matter.

[4]Advanced signifies superior performance.

[5]Did not satisfy one or more of the guidelines for school participation in 1998. Data are subject to appreciable nonresponse bias.

[6]Did not satisfy one or more of the guidelines for school participation in 2002. Data are subject to appreciable nonresponse bias.

[7]Did not satisfy one or more of the guidelines for school participation in 1992. Data are subject to appreciable nonresponse bias.

[8]Did not satisfy one or more of the guidelines for school participation in 1994. Data are subject to appreciable nonresponse bias.

[9]Prior to 2005, NAEP divided the Department of Defense (DoD) schools into two jurisdictions, domestic and overseas. In 2005, NAEP began combining the DoD domestic and overseas schools into a single jurisdiction. Data shown in this table for years prior to 2005 were recalculated for comparability.

NOTE: With the exception of 1992 and 1994, includes public school students who were tested with accommodations; excludes only those students with disabilities (SD) and English language learners (ELL) who were unable to be tested even with accommodations. SD and ELL populations, accommodation rates, and exclusion rates vary from state to state. Race categories exclude persons of Hispanic ethnicity. Standard errors appear in parentheses.

SOURCE: U.S. Department of Education, National Center for Education Statistics, National Assessment of Educational Progress (NAEP), 1992, 1994, 1998, 2002, 2003, 2005, 2007, 2009, and 2011 Reading Assessments, retrieved November 2, 2011, from the Main NAEP Data Explorer (http://nces.ed.gov/nationsreportcard/naepdata/). (This table was prepared November 2011.)

Average reading scale score and percentage of 4th-grade public school students, by race/ethnicity and state: 2011

	Average scale score[1]						Percent of students					
State	White	Black	Hispanic	Asian	Native Hawaiian/ Pacific Islander	American Indian/ Alaska Native	White	Black	Hispanic	Asian	Native Hawaiian/ Pacific Islander	American Indian/ Alaska Native
1	2	3	4	5	6	7	8	9	10	11	12	13
United States	230 (0.3)	205 (0.4)	205 (0.5)	236 (1.3)	214 (1.8)	204 (1.3)	52 (0.4)	16 (0.3)	23 (0.4)	5 (0.2)	# (†)	1 (0.1)
Alabama	230 (1.2)	204 (2.1)	205 (3.1)	‡ (†)	‡ (†)	‡ (†)	60 (1.9)	32 (1.9)	5 (0.7)	1 (0.2)	# (†)	1 (0.4)
Alaska	223 (1.1)	206 (4.3)	212 (3.7)	199 (3.2)	192 (5.8)	175 (2.4)	50 (1.1)	4 (0.3)	6 (0.4)	6 (0.4)	2 (0.2)	23 (1.0)
Arizona	225 (1.6)	204 (4.7)	203 (1.3)	225 (5.1)	‡ (†)	185 (4.0)	43 (1.6)	5 (0.5)	43 (1.8)	3 (0.3)	# (†)	5 (0.5)
Arkansas....................	224 (1.0)	197 (1.7)	204 (2.7)	‡ (†)	‡ (†)	‡ (†)	65 (1.2)	21 (1.3)	10 (0.8)	2 (0.2)	# (†)	# (†)
California	229 (2.3)	208 (3.5)	198 (1.3)	233 (4.0)	‡ (†)	‡ (†)	25 (1.7)	7 (1.1)	54 (2.2)	12 (1.7)	1 (0.2)	# (†)
Colorado	236 (1.1)	207 (3.3)	203 (1.9)	234 (4.3)	‡ (†)	‡ (†)	56 (1.3)	4 (0.4)	33 (1.3)	3 (0.3)	# (†)	# (†)
Connecticut.................	239 (1.1)	204 (2.7)	204 (2.9)	241 (3.4)	‡ (†)	‡ (†)	60 (1.9)	13 (1.6)	20 (1.2)	5 (0.5)	# (†)	# (†)
Delaware....................	234 (1.1)	215 (1.4)	214 (1.9)	240 (3.1)	‡ (†)	‡ (†)	49 (0.8)	32 (0.7)	12 (0.7)	4 (0.3)	# (†)	1 (0.1)
District of Columbia	255 (2.8)	193 (1.1)	202 (2.8)	‡ (†)	‡ (†)	‡ (†)	8 (0.4)	77 (0.5)	12 (0.4)	2 (0.2)	# (†)	# (†)
Florida.......................	235 (1.2)	209 (1.8)	220 (1.4)	246 (4.2)	‡ (†)	‡ (†)	40 (1.7)	25 (1.8)	29 (1.4)	2 (0.3)	# (†)	# (†)
Georgia......................	231 (1.1)	208 (1.8)	214 (2.4)	242 (4.8)	‡ (†)	‡ (†)	45 (1.7)	36 (1.8)	12 (1.2)	4 (0.4)	# (†)	# (†)
Hawaii........................	226 (1.7)	215 (4.5)	209 (4.2)	221 (1.4)	201 (1.7)	‡ (†)	15 (1.0)	3 (0.4)	5 (0.3)	36 (1.1)	33 (1.2)	1 (0.1)
Idaho.........................	225 (0.8)	‡ (†)	201 (1.8)	227 (5.9)	‡ (†)	‡ (†)	78 (0.9)	1 (0.2)	16 (0.8)	2 (0.2)	# (†)	2 (0.6)
Illinois.......................	231 (1.3)	198 (2.1)	204 (1.8)	237 (2.6)	‡ (†)	‡ (†)	53 (1.4)	20 (1.0)	19 (0.8)	4 (0.5)	# (†)	# (†)
Indiana.......................	226 (0.9)	203 (2.4)	203 (2.1)	‡ (†)	‡ (†)	‡ (†)	72 (1.5)	12 (1.4)	10 (1.0)	1 (0.2)	# (†)	# (†)
Iowa..........................	225 (0.8)	193 (2.2)	201 (2.1)	227 (4.1)	‡ (†)	‡ (†)	80 (1.0)	6 (0.5)	9 (0.7)	2 (0.2)	# (†)	# (†)
Kansas.......................	229 (1.1)	204 (2.8)	209 (1.8)	228 (4.4)	‡ (†)	‡ (†)	68 (1.3)	7 (0.6)	16 (1.2)	3 (0.4)	# (†)	1 (0.2)
Kentucky.....................	226 (1.0)	210 (2.0)	222 (4.4)	250 (4.8)	‡ (†)	‡ (†)	84 (0.9)	9 (0.7)	3 (0.3)	1 (0.3)	# (†)	# (†)
Louisiana.....................	223 (1.5)	197 (1.7)	208 (4.4)	‡ (†)	‡ (†)	‡ (†)	47 (2.1)	46 (2.0)	3 (0.4)	1 (0.2)	# (†)	1 (0.2)
Maine.........................	223 (0.6)	192 (4.8)	‡ (†)	217 (5.5)	‡ (†)	‡ (†)	92 (0.7)	3 (0.5)	2 (0.2)	2 (0.2)	# (†)	# (†)
Maryland.....................	242 (1.3)	213 (1.1)	226 (2.1)	252 (3.0)	‡ (†)	‡ (†)	45 (1.3)	35 (1.0)	9 (0.7)	6 (0.8)	# (†)	# (†)
Massachusetts.............	243 (0.7)	216 (2.0)	216 (1.5)	243 (2.8)	‡ (†)	‡ (†)	68 (1.7)	9 (1.0)	14 (1.3)	6 (0.5)	# (†)	# (†)
Michigan.....................	225 (1.0)	192 (2.4)	206 (3.1)	236 (6.1)	‡ (†)	‡ (†)	70 (1.4)	17 (1.2)	6 (0.6)	3 (0.6)	# (†)	1 (0.5)
Minnesota...................	229 (1.0)	199 (2.8)	201 (3.0)	218 (5.7)	‡ (†)	195 (5.4)	73 (1.6)	9 (1.0)	9 (1.2)	5 (0.4)	# (†)	2 (0.3)
Mississippi..................	220 (1.3)	198 (1.6)	203 (6.2)	‡ (†)	‡ (†)	‡ (†)	50 (1.8)	46 (1.9)	3 (0.4)	1 (0.2)	# (†)	# (†)
Missouri......................	226 (1.0)	199 (1.9)	209 (3.5)	234 (6.6)	‡ (†)	‡ (†)	75 (1.1)	17 (1.2)	5 (0.7)	2 (0.3)	# (†)	# (†)
Montana......................	229 (0.7)	‡ (†)	217 (3.8)	‡ (†)	‡ (†)	200 (2.9)	82 (1.0)	1 (0.1)	3 (0.3)	1 (0.1)	# (†)	11 (1.0)
Nebraska	230 (0.9)	199 (3.4)	208 (2.6)	234 (5.6)	‡ (†)	‡ (†)	70 (1.1)	8 (0.6)	15 (0.9)	2 (0.2)	# (†)	1 (0.3)
Nevada	224 (1.3)	202 (2.2)	203 (1.5)	223 (2.6)	‡ (†)	‡ (†)	37 (1.0)	10 (0.6)	42 (1.2)	6 (0.5)	1 (0.2)	1 (0.3)
New Hampshire	231 (0.8)	‡ (†)	217 (4.0)	234 (3.9)	‡ (†)	‡ (†)	91 (0.4)	2 (0.2)	3 (0.3)	3 (0.2)	# (†)	# (†)
New Jersey	239 (1.0)	216 (2.7)	216 (2.3)	248 (2.9)	‡ (†)	‡ (†)	54 (1.9)	14 (1.4)	22 (1.8)	9 (1.1)	# (†)	# (†)
New Mexico	225 (1.5)	208 (3.8)	202 (1.1)	222 (5.2)	‡ (†)	193 (2.8)	28 (1.1)	2 (0.2)	59 (1.2)	2 (0.2)	# (†)	9 (0.9)
New York	232 (1.3)	208 (1.8)	209 (1.8)	235 (2.9)	‡ (†)	‡ (†)	48 (2.2)	20 (1.7)	20 (1.2)	10 (0.8)	# (†)	1 (†)
North Carolina	232 (1.3)	206 (1.5)	207 (2.4)	236 (4.5)	‡ (†)	192 (4.3)	54 (1.3)	26 (1.1)	12 (0.8)	3 (0.4)	# (†)	1 (0.1)
North Dakota	228 (0.5)	220 (4.3)	214 (3.8)	‡ (†)	‡ (†)	206 (2.5)	85 (0.4)	2 (0.3)	3 (0.2)	1 (0.2)	# (†)	9 (0.3)
Ohio..........................	229 (1.1)	204 (1.9)	211 (3.3)	‡ (†)	‡ (†)	‡ (†)	72 (1.6)	18 (1.7)	4 (0.6)	2 (0.3)	# (†)	# (†)
Oklahoma	221 (1.3)	199 (3.9)	207 (3.2)	228 (6.1)	‡ (†)	212 (2.2)	56 (1.2)	11 (0.8)	12 (1.1)	2 (0.2)	# (†)	18 (0.8)
Oregon.......................	222 (1.2)	202 (5.3)	196 (1.4)	233 (5.5)	‡ (†)	213 (5.7)	65 (1.0)	3 (0.4)	21 (0.9)	4 (0.5)	1 (0.1)	2 (0.2)
Pennsylvania...............	233 (1.1)	204 (2.2)	202 (2.8)	244 (3.8)	‡ (†)	‡ (†)	74 (1.7)	13 (1.4)	8 (1.0)	3 (0.4)	# (†)	# (†)
Rhode Island	230 (0.9)	208 (2.7)	204 (1.8)	233 (3.9)	‡ (†)	‡ (†)	64 (0.9)	8 (0.5)	22 (0.9)	3 (0.3)	# (†)	# (†)
South Carolina	226 (1.2)	199 (1.7)	208 (2.8)	‡ (†)	‡ (†)	‡ (†)	54 (1.4)	36 (1.5)	6 (0.5)	1 (0.1)	# (†)	# (†)
South Dakota...............	225 (0.8)	204 (4.3)	207 (4.1)	‡ (†)	‡ (†)	197 (3.0)	78 (0.8)	3 (0.3)	3 (0.3)	1 (0.1)	# (†)	14 (0.7)
Tennessee..................	221 (1.3)	198 (1.6)	201 (3.1)	‡ (†)	‡ (†)	‡ (†)	68 (1.5)	23 (1.6)	7 (0.7)	2 (0.3)	# (†)	# (†)
Texas........................	233 (2.2)	210 (1.6)	210 (1.4)	247 (6.1)	‡ (†)	‡ (†)	31 (1.8)	14 (1.1)	51 (2.1)	3 (0.7)	# (†)	# (†)
Utah..........................	226 (1.0)	‡ (†)	196 (2.1)	226 (6.9)	206 (4.3)	187 (6.3)	79 (1.1)	1 (0.2)	14 (1.0)	2 (0.2)	2 (0.2)	1 (0.2)
Vermont	228 (0.7)	205 (5.6)	‡ (†)	‡ (†)	‡ (†)	‡ (†)	92 (0.3)	2 (0.2)	1 (0.2)	2 (0.2)	# (†)	# (†)
Virginia......................	235 (1.2)	210 (1.6)	209 (2.8)	236 (4.1)	‡ (†)	‡ (†)	56 (1.6)	21 (1.1)	11 (1.0)	7 (0.7)	# (†)	# (†)
Washington..................	229 (1.3)	209 (2.7)	199 (2.3)	230 (3.7)	‡ (†)	202 (4.1)	58 (1.4)	5 (0.6)	21 (1.4)	7 (0.6)	1 (0.2)	2 (0.2)
West Virginia...............	216 (0.8)	196 (3.0)	‡ (†)	‡ (†)	‡ (†)	‡ (†)	92 (0.7)	5 (0.6)	1 (0.2)	1 (0.2)	# (†)	# (†)
Wisconsin...................	227 (0.9)	196 (1.8)	202 (1.9)	224 (2.9)	‡ (†)	‡ (†)	75 (1.3)	9 (0.7)	10 (0.9)	4 (0.4)	# (†)	2 (0.8)
Wyoming.....................	227 (0.8)	‡ (†)	213 (1.9)	‡ (†)	‡ (†)	192 (3.6)	80 (0.5)	1 (0.2)	14 (0.4)	1 (0.2)	# (†)	3 (0.2)
Department of Defense dependents schools.....	233 (0.8)	222 (1.7)	226 (1.6)	233 (2.3)	‡ (†)	‡ (†)	48 (0.6)	16 (0.4)	17 (0.5)	6 (0.3)	1 (0.2)	1 (0.2)

†Not applicable.
#Rounds to zero.
‡Reporting standards not met (too few cases).
[1]Scale ranges from 0 to 500.
NOTE: Includes public school students who were tested with accommodations; excludes only those students with disabilities (SD) and English language learners (ELL) who were unable to be tested even with accommodations. SD and ELL populations, accommodation rates, and exclusion rates vary from state to state. Race/ethnicity based on school records. Race categories exclude persons of Hispanic ethnicity. Detaail may not sum to totals because of rounding and because table does not include students classified as "Two or more races." Standard errors appear in parentheses.
SOURCE: U.S. Department of Education, National Center for Education Statistics, National Assessment of Educational Progress (NAEP), 2011 Reading Assessment, retrieved November 22, 2011, from the Main NAEP Data Explorer (http://nces.ed.gov/nationsreport card/ naepdata/). (This table was prepared November 2011.)

Average scores in NAEP reading for eighth-grade public school students, by state/jurisdiction: Various years, 1998-2011

State/jurisdiction	Accommodations not permitted 1998	Accommodations permitted						
	1998	1998	2002	2003	2005	2007	2009	2011
Nation (public)	**261***	**261***	**263**	**261***	**260***	**261***	**262***	**264**
Alabama	255	255	253*	253*	252*	252*	255	258
Alaska	—	—	—	256*	259*	259	259	261
Arizona	261	260	257	255*	255*	255*	258	260
Arkansas	256*	256*	260	258	258	258	258	259
California	253	252	250*	251*	250*	251*	253	255
Colorado	264*	264*	—	268	265*	266*	266*	271
Connecticut	272*	270*	267*	267*	264*	267*	272*	275
Delaware	256*	254*	267	265	266	265	265	266
Florida	253*	255*	261	257*	256*	260	264	262
Georgia	257*	257*	258*	258*	257*	259*	260	262
Hawaii	250*	249*	252*	251*	249*	251*	255*	257
Idaho	—	—	266	264*	264*	265*	265*	268
Illinois	—	—	—	266	264	263*	265	266
Indiana	—	—	265	265	261*	264	266	265
Iowa	—	—	—	268*	267	267*	265	265
Kansas	268	268	269	266	267	267	267	267
Kentucky	262*	262*	265*	266	264*	262*	267	269
Louisiana	252	252	256	253	253	253	253	255
Maine	273	271	270	268	270	270	268	270
Maryland	262*	261*	263*	262*	261*	265*	267*	271
Massachusetts	269*	269*	271*	273	274	273	274	275
Michigan	—	—	265	264	261*	260*	262*	265
Minnesota	267	265*	—	268	268	268	270	270
Mississippi	251	251	255	255	251	250*	251	254
Missouri	263*	262*	268	267	265	263*	267	267
Montana	270*	271	270*	270*	269*	271	270*	273
Nebraska	—	—	270	266	267	267	267	268
Nevada	257	258	251*	252*	253*	252*	254*	258
New Hampshire	—	—	—	271	270	270	271	272
New Jersey	—	—	—	268*	269*	270*	273	275
New Mexico	258	258	254	252*	251*	251*	254	256
New York	266	265	264	265	265	264	264	266
North Carolina	264	262	265	262	258*	259*	260*	263
North Dakota	—	—	268	270	270	268	269	269
Ohio	—	—	268	267	267	268	269	268
Oklahoma	265*	265*	262	262	260	260	259	260
Oregon	266	266	268*	264	263	266	265	264
Pennsylvania	—	—	265	264	267	268	271	268
Rhode Island	262*	264	262*	261*	261*	258*	260*	265
South Carolina	255*	255*	258	258	257*	257*	257	260
South Dakota	—	—	—	270	269	270	270	269
Tennessee	259	258	260	258	259	259	261	259
Texas	262	261	262	259	258*	261	260	261
Utah	265	263*	263*	264*	262*	262*	266	267
Vermont	—	—	272	271*	269*	273	272	274
Virginia	266	266	269	268	268	267	266	267
Washington	265	264*	268	264*	265	265	267	268
West Virginia	262*	262*	264*	260*	255	255	255	256
Wisconsin	266	265	—	266	266	264*	266	267
Wyoming	262*	263*	265*	267*	268	266*	268	270
Other jurisdictions								
District of Columbia	236*	236*	240	239*	238*	241	242	242
DoDEA[1]	269*	269*	273	272	271	273	272	272

— Not available. The state/jurisdiction did not participate or did not meet the minimum participation guidelines for reporting.

* Significantly different ($p < .05$) from 2011 when only one state/jurisdiction or the nation is being examined.

[1] Department of Defense Education Activity (overseas and domestic schools).

SOURCE: U.S. Department of Education, Institute of Education Sciences, National Center for Education Statistics, National Assessment of Educational Progress (NAEP), various years, 1998-2011 Reading Assessments.

Average scores and achievement-level results in NAEP reading for eighth-grade public school students, by state/jurisdiction: 2011

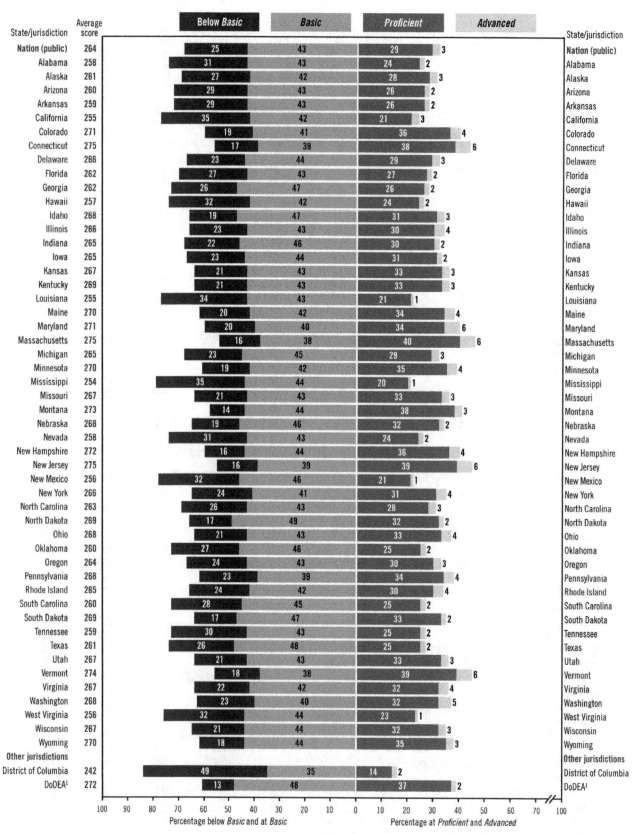

State/jurisdiction	Average score	Below Basic	Basic	Proficient	Advanced
Nation (public)	264	25	43	29	3
Alabama	258	31	43	24	2
Alaska	261	27	42	28	3
Arizona	260	29	43	26	2
Arkansas	259	29	43	26	2
California	255	35	42	21	3
Colorado	271	19	41	36	4
Connecticut	275	17	39	38	6
Delaware	266	23	44	29	3
Florida	262	27	43	27	2
Georgia	262	26	47	26	2
Hawaii	257	32	42	24	2
Idaho	268	19	47	31	3
Illinois	266	23	43	30	4
Indiana	265	22	46	30	2
Iowa	265	23	44	31	2
Kansas	267	21	43	33	3
Kentucky	269	21	43	33	3
Louisiana	255	34	43	21	1
Maine	270	20	42	34	4
Maryland	271	20	40	34	6
Massachusetts	275	16	38	40	6
Michigan	265	23	45	29	3
Minnesota	270	19	42	35	4
Mississippi	254	35	44	20	1
Missouri	267	21	43	33	3
Montana	273	14	44	38	3
Nebraska	268	19	46	32	2
Nevada	258	31	43	24	2
New Hampshire	272	16	44	36	4
New Jersey	275	16	39	39	6
New Mexico	256	32	46	21	1
New York	266	24	41	31	4
North Carolina	263	26	43	28	3
North Dakota	269	17	49	32	2
Ohio	268	21	43	33	4
Oklahoma	260	27	46	25	2
Oregon	264	24	43	30	3
Pennsylvania	268	23	39	34	4
Rhode Island	265	24	42	30	4
South Carolina	260	28	45	25	2
South Dakota	269	17	47	33	2
Tennessee	259	30	43	25	2
Texas	261	26	48	25	2
Utah	267	21	43	33	3
Vermont	274	18	38	39	6
Virginia	267	22	42	32	4
Washington	268	23	40	32	5
West Virginia	256	32	44	23	1
Wisconsin	267	21	44	32	3
Wyoming	270	18	44	35	3
Other jurisdictions					
District of Columbia	242	49	35	14	2
DoDEA[1]	272	13	48	37	2

Percentage below *Basic* and at *Basic*   Percentage at *Proficient* and *Advanced*

[1] Department of Defense Education Activity (overseas and domestic schools).

NOTE: The shaded bars are graphed using unrounded numbers. Detail may not sum to totals because of rounding.

SOURCE: U.S. Department of Education, Institute of Education Sciences, National Center for Education Statistics, National Assessment of Educational Progress (NAEP), 2011 Reading Assessment.

Average scores and achievement-level results in NAEP reading for eighth-grade public school students, by race/ethnicity and state/jurisdiction: 2011

State/jurisdiction	White					Black					Hispanic				
	Average scale score	Percentage of students				Average scale score	Percentage of students				Average scale score	Percentage of students			
		Below Basic	At or above Basic	At or above Proficient	At Advanced		Below Basic	At or above Basic	At or above Proficient	At Advanced		Below Basic	At or above Basic	At or above Proficient	At Advanced
Nation (public)	272	16	84	41	4	248	42	58	14	1	251	37	63	18	1
Alabama	268	20	80	34	3	243	49	51	11	#	246	44	56	16	2
Alaska	274	15	85	42	4	252	34	66	17	1	260	26	74	24	1
Arizona	272	18	82	41	4	248	42	58	18	1	251	37	63	17	#
Arkansas	267	21	79	35	2	238	54	46	9	#	253	36	64	21	1
California	268	21	79	35	5	243	47	53	11	1	245	44	56	14	1
Colorado	278	11	89	49	5	257	34	66	22	2	254	35	65	22	1
Connecticut	283	9	91	54	9	255	34	66	21	1	255	34	66	22	1
Delaware	273	15	85	42	5	254	34	66	18	1	259	27	73	26	2
Florida	270	18	82	38	3	248	43	57	14	1	259	29	71	27	2
Georgia	272	15	85	38	2	251	39	61	14	#	258	30	70	21	1
Hawaii	273	16	84	41	4	261	27	73	25	2	246	44	56	17	1
Idaho	271	16	84	37	3	‡	‡	‡	‡	‡	254	33	67	17	1
Illinois	274	15	85	44	5	249	38	62	15	1	257	31	69	23	2
Indiana	269	18	82	36	2	247	41	59	14	1	255	32	68	22	2
Iowa	267	20	80	35	2	247	43	57	12	1	251	38	62	20	1
Kansas	272	16	84	41	3	248	42	58	15	1	254	34	66	19	#
Kentucky	271	18	82	39	4	248	42	58	13	#	264	25	75	30	2
Louisiana	264	24	76	31	2	241	49	51	10	#	249	42	58	19	2
Maine	271	19	81	39	4	248	45	55	21	2	‡	‡	‡	‡	‡
Maryland	282	10	90	52	8	255	34	66	21	1	262	29	71	30	3
Massachusetts	282	9	91	53	8	255	32	68	20	2	248	41	59	18	1
Michigan	269	18	82	36	3	244	46	54	11	#	260	25	75	26	1
Minnesota	274	14	86	44	4	246	42	58	15	1	257	31	69	23	2
Mississippi	267	18	82	33	1	240	52	48	9	#	‡	‡	‡	‡	‡
Missouri	271	17	83	40	3	244	44	56	12	#	258	30	70	26	5
Montana	275	12	88	44	3	‡	‡	‡	‡	‡	262	24	76	27	3
Nebraska	272	14	86	39	3	250	36	64	15	1	252	37	63	20	1
Nevada	269	19	81	37	3	250	38	62	17	2	247	42	58	16	#
New Hampshire	273	15	85	41	3	‡	‡	‡	‡	‡	253	37	63	16	1
New Jersey	284	8	92	56	8	256	34	66	21	1	257	29	71	22	1
New Mexico	270	17	83	36	2	248	39	61	14	#	251	37	63	16	1
New York	276	14	86	46	6	251	37	63	18	1	251	38	62	20	1
North Carolina	271	17	83	40	4	247	42	58	14	#	256	33	67	22	1
North Dakota	272	13	87	37	2	‡	‡	‡	‡	‡	‡	‡	‡	‡	‡
Ohio	274	15	85	43	4	247	42	58	14	1	252	35	65	17	#
Oklahoma	265	22	78	32	2	247	40	60	13	1	251	37	63	15	#
Oregon	269	19	81	37	3	248	41	59	19	1	250	39	61	16	1
Pennsylvania	275	15	85	46	5	244	46	54	13	#	250	40	60	16	1
Rhode Island	272	17	83	41	5	248	42	58	17	1	248	43	57	14	1
South Carolina	269	18	82	37	3	246	44	56	11	#	257	31	69	22	2
South Dakota	273	12	88	39	2	256	30	70	17	1	256	32	68	22	1
Tennessee	265	23	77	31	3	240	52	48	12	#	255	32	68	24	1
Texas	274	13	87	42	3	252	37	63	15	At	254	32	68	17	1
Utah	272	16	84	40	3	‡	‡	‡	‡	‡	247	42	58	13	#
Vermont	274	17	83	45	6	‡	‡	‡	‡	‡	‡	‡	‡	‡	‡
Virginia	273	16	84	43	5	251	38	62	16	1	259	28	72	24	1
Washington	272	18	82	42	5	254	34	66	22	1	250	40	60	17	1
West Virginia	256	31	69	24	1	249	43	57	19	1	‡	‡	‡	‡	‡
Wisconsin	272	16	84	40	3	240	51	49	11	#	248	40	60	13	1
Wyoming	272	16	84	40	3	‡	‡	‡	‡	‡	258	31	69	26	1
Other jurisdictions															
District of Columbia	292	6	94	66	15	239	52	48	12	1	239	50	50	16	1
DoDEA[1]	277	9	91	46	3	263	19	81	25	1	268	16	84	32	1

See notes at end of table.

Average scores and achievement-level results in NAEP reading for eighth-grade public school students, by race/ethnicity and state/jurisdiction: 2011—Continued

	Asian/Pacific Islander					American Indian/Alaska Native				
		Percentage of students					Percentage of students			
State/jurisdiction	Average scale score	Below *Basic*	At or above *Basic*	At or above *Proficient*	At *Advanced*	Average scale score	Below *Basic*	At or above *Basic*	At or above *Proficient*	At *Advanced*
Nation (public)	**275**	**18**	**82**	**46**	**8**	**253**	**36**	**64**	**22**	**2**
Alabama	‡	‡	‡	‡	‡	‡	‡	‡	‡	‡
Alaska	261	28	72	29	3	234	56	44	10	1
Arizona	269	19	81	34	8	241	50	50	15	1
Arkansas	‡	‡	‡	‡	‡	‡	‡	‡	‡	‡
California	271	21	79	41	6	‡	‡	‡	‡	‡
Colorado	285	11	89	60	12	‡	‡	‡	‡	‡
Connecticut	282	11	89	55	9	‡	‡	‡	‡	‡
Delaware	285	10	90	56	11	‡	‡	‡	‡	‡
Florida	279	16	84	48	10	‡	‡	‡	‡	‡
Georgia	277	12	88	48	6	‡	‡	‡	‡	‡
Hawaii	255	34	66	23	2	‡	‡	‡	‡	‡
Idaho	‡	‡	‡	‡	‡	‡	‡	‡	‡	‡
Illinois	280	12	88	53	11	‡	‡	‡	‡	‡
Indiana	‡	‡	‡	‡	‡	‡	‡	‡	‡	‡
Iowa	266	23	77	38	5	‡	‡	‡	‡	‡
Kansas	269	24	76	46	7	‡	‡	‡	‡	‡
Kentucky	‡	‡	‡	‡	‡	‡	‡	‡	‡	‡
Louisiana	‡	‡	‡	‡	‡	‡	‡	‡	‡	‡
Maine	‡	‡	‡	‡	‡	‡	‡	‡	‡	‡
Maryland	294	5	95	68	19	‡	‡	‡	‡	‡
Massachusetts	288	10	90	61	14	‡	‡	‡	‡	‡
Michigan	279	20	80	53	14	‡	‡	‡	‡	‡
Minnesota	267	26	74	37	6	258	33	67	30	5
Mississippi	‡	‡	‡	‡	‡	‡	‡	‡	‡	‡
Missouri	‡	‡	‡	‡	‡	‡	‡	‡	‡	‡
Montana	‡	‡	‡	‡	‡	257	33	67	25	2
Nebraska	‡	‡	‡	‡	‡	‡	‡	‡	‡	‡
Nevada	264	25	75	34	4	‡	‡	‡	‡	‡
New Hampshire	280	18	82	49	14	‡	‡	‡	‡	‡
New Jersey	291	8	92	66	15	‡	‡	‡	‡	‡
New Mexico	273	20	80	40	9	242	48	52	16	1
New York	276	17	83	50	6	‡	‡	‡	‡	‡
North Carolina	274	17	83	44	8	245	48	52	16	3
North Dakota	‡	‡	‡	‡	‡	245	48	52	13	2
Ohio	‡	‡	‡	‡	‡	‡	‡	‡	‡	‡
Oklahoma	‡	‡	‡	‡	‡	256	31	69	23	1
Oregon	263	31	69	38	9	256	34	66	30	7
Pennsylvania	285	15	85	62	13	‡	‡	‡	‡	‡
Rhode Island	261	26	74	31	4	‡	‡	‡	‡	‡
South Carolina	‡	‡	‡	‡	‡	‡	‡	‡	‡	‡
South Dakota	‡	‡	‡	‡	‡	244	48	52	14	1
Tennessee	‡	‡	‡	‡	‡	‡	‡	‡	‡	‡
Texas	284	8	92	59	6	‡	‡	‡	‡	‡
Utah	257	33	67	30	1	244	43	57	18	#
Vermont	‡	‡	‡	‡	‡	‡	‡	‡	‡	‡
Virginia	282	11	89	55	8	‡	‡	‡	‡	‡
Washington	279	17	83	51	10	254	40	60	24	4
West Virginia	‡	‡	‡	‡	‡	‡	‡	‡	‡	‡
Wisconsin	271	22	78	39	7	‡	‡	‡	‡	‡
Wyoming	‡	‡	‡	‡	‡	‡	‡	‡	‡	‡
Other jurisdictions										
District of Columbia	‡	‡	‡	‡	‡	‡	‡	‡	‡	‡
DoDEA[1]	272	16	84	39	2	‡	‡	‡	‡	‡

Rounds to zero.

‡ Reporting standards not met. Sample size insufficient to permit a reliable estimate.

[1] Department of Defense Education Activity (overseas and domestic schools).

NOTE: Black includes African American, Hispanic includes Latino, and Pacific Islander includes Native Hawaiian. Race categories exclude Hispanic origin. Results are not shown for students of two or more races. Detail may not sum to totals because of rounding.

SOURCE: U.S. Department of Education, Institute of Education Sciences, National Center for Education Statistics, National Assessment of Educational Progress (NAEP), 2011 Reading Assessment.

Average scores and achievement-level results in NAEP reading for eighth-grade public school students, by gender and state/jurisdiction: 2011

State/jurisdiction	Male					Female				
		Percentage of students					Percentage of students			
	Average scale score	Below Basic	At or above Basic	At or above Proficient	At Advanced	Average scale score	Below Basic	At or above Basic	At or above Proficient	At Advanced
Nation (public)	**259**	**30**	**70**	**27**	**2**	**268**	**21**	**79**	**36**	**4**
Alabama	254	36	64	22	1	263	26	74	29	3
Alaska	256	32	68	24	1	267	22	78	38	4
Arizona	255	34	66	24	1	265	24	76	33	3
Arkansas	254	34	66	23	1	264	25	75	33	2
California	249	41	59	19	1	261	28	72	28	4
Colorado	268	20	80	36	2	274	18	82	45	6
Connecticut	270	20	80	40	5	279	14	86	50	8
Delaware	260	27	73	26	2	271	19	81	40	5
Florida	257	31	69	25	1	267	22	78	34	3
Georgia	258	31	69	23	1	267	21	79	32	2
Hawaii	252	37	63	22	1	263	26	74	30	3
Idaho	264	22	78	29	1	272	16	84	39	4
Illinois	261	28	72	29	3	271	18	82	39	5
Indiana	260	27	73	27	1	270	18	82	36	3
Iowa	261	27	73	28	1	269	19	81	37	3
Kansas	263	26	74	31	2	272	17	83	40	4
Kentucky	264	25	75	31	2	274	16	84	42	4
Louisiana	251	39	61	18	1	259	30	70	26	2
Maine	265	23	77	33	3	275	16	84	44	6
Maryland	267	23	77	35	4	275	17	83	45	7
Massachusetts	271	19	81	41	5	280	12	88	51	8
Michigan	260	28	72	25	2	271	18	82	39	4
Minnesota	266	21	79	35	3	274	16	84	44	5
Mississippi	249	41	59	17	#	259	29	71	25	1
Missouri	261	26	74	29	2	272	17	83	42	4
Montana	268	19	81	35	2	278	10	90	48	4
Nebraska	264	23	77	30	2	272	15	85	40	3
Nevada	252	36	64	19	1	264	25	75	34	4
New Hampshire	268	20	80	34	2	276	13	87	46	5
New Jersey	270	19	81	39	5	280	13	87	51	8
New Mexico	252	36	64	19	1	260	29	71	26	2
New York	261	28	72	30	3	270	19	81	40	5
North Carolina	256	33	67	25	2	270	19	81	37	4
North Dakota	264	20	80	28	1	273	14	86	41	3
Ohio	263	26	74	32	3	273	15	85	42	4
Oklahoma	256	31	69	22	1	264	24	76	32	2
Oregon	260	29	71	28	2	269	20	80	38	4
Pennsylvania	263	26	74	32	3	272	19	81	44	6
Rhode Island	260	29	71	28	2	271	20	80	39	5
South Carolina	255	33	67	22	1	265	23	77	31	3
South Dakota	265	20	80	30	1	273	15	85	41	3
Tennessee	255	34	66	22	2	264	25	75	32	3
Texas	260	27	73	25	1	263	24	76	28	2
Utah	262	25	75	30	1	272	17	83	41	4
Vermont	268	22	78	37	4	280	13	87	52	8
Virginia	263	25	75	31	3	271	19	81	41	5
Washington	261	28	72	30	3	274	18	82	44	7
West Virginia	250	39	61	19	1	263	25	75	30	2
Wisconsin	262	26	74	30	2	272	17	83	40	4
Wyoming	265	22	78	32	2	274	14	86	43	4
Other jurisdictions										
District of Columbia	234	56	44	12	1	249	42	58	20	2
DoDEA[1]	268	16	84	34	1	276	10	90	45	3

Rounds to zero.

[1] Department of Defense Education Activity (overseas and domestic schools).

NOTE: Detail may not sum to totals because of rounding.

SOURCE: U.S. Department of Education, Institute of Education Sciences, National Center for Education Statistics, National Assessment of Educational Progress (NAEP), 2011 Reading Assessment.

Average reading scale score of 8th-grade public school students and percentage attaining reading achievement levels, by locale and state: Selected years, 2003 through 2011

State	Average scale score[1]					Percent attaining reading achievement levels, 2011			Average scale score[1] by school location, 2011			
	2003	2005	2007	2009	2011	At or above Basic[2]	At or above Proficient[3]	At Advanced[4]	City	Suburb	Town	Rural
1	2	3	4	5	6	7	8	9	10	11	12	13
United States	261 (0.2)	260 (0.2)	261 (0.2)	262 (0.3)	264 (0.2)	75 (0.3)	32 (0.3)	3 (0.1)	257 (0.4)	267 (0.4)	263 (0.5)	266 (0.4)
Alabama	253 (1.5)	252 (1.4)	252 (1.0)	255 (1.1)	258 (1.5)	69 (1.8)	26 (1.6)	2 (0.4)	252 (2.5)	266 (3.0)	259 (2.2)	259 (2.3)
Alaska	256 (1.1)	259 (0.9)	259 (1.0)	259 (0.9)	261 (0.9)	73 (1.1)	31 (1.1)	3 (0.3)	‡ (†)	‡ (†)	‡ (†)	‡ (†)
Arizona	255 (1.4)	255 (1.0)	255 (1.2)	258 (1.2)	260 (1.2)	71 (1.5)	28 (1.5)	2 (0.6)	257 (1.7)	268 (2.5)	257 (3.2)	259 (2.5)
Arkansas.....................	258 (1.3)	258 (1.1)	258 (1.0)	258 (1.2)	259 (0.9)	71 (1.1)	28 (1.6)	2 (0.4)	260 (2.2)	263 (3.4)	258 (1.8)	258 (1.7)
California[5]	251 (1.3)	250 (0.6)	251 (0.8)	253 (1.2)	255 (1.0)	65 (1.2)	24 (1.2)	3 (0.5)	251 (1.5)	257 (1.6)	262 (3.2)	261 (3.4)
Colorado	268 (1.2)	265 (1.1)	266 (1.0)	266 (0.8)	271 (1.4)	81 (1.5)	40 (2.0)	4 (0.8)	264 (3.1)	274 (2.2)	267 (4.3)	275 (1.8)
Connecticut.................	267 (1.1)	264 (1.3)	267 (1.6)	272 (0.9)	275 (0.9)	83 (1.0)	45 (1.3)	6 (0.8)	261 (1.7)	278 (1.2)	279 (4.7)	284 (1.8)
Delaware	265 (0.7)	266 (0.6)	265 (0.6)	265 (0.7)	266 (0.6)	77 (0.8)	33 (1.2)	3 (0.5)	264 (2.1)	263 (1.2)	265 (1.1)	273 (1.5)
District of Columbia	239 (0.8)	238 (0.9)	241 (0.7)	242 (0.9)	242 (0.9)	51 (1.0)	16 (0.9)	2 (0.4)	242 (0.9)	‡ (†)	‡ (†)	‡ (†)
Florida........................	257 (1.3)	256 (1.2)	260 (1.2)	264 (1.2)	262 (1.0)	73 (1.4)	30 (1.4)	2 (0.4)	261 (2.4)	263 (1.3)	259 (3.2)	263 (2.8)
Georgia.......................	258 (1.1)	257 (1.3)	259 (1.0)	260 (1.0)	262 (1.1)	74 (1.3)	28 (1.5)	2 (0.4)	251 (5.6)	264 (1.5)	263 (2.6)	264 (1.3)
Hawaii	251 (0.9)	249 (0.9)	251 (0.8)	255 (0.6)	257 (0.7)	68 (1.2)	26 (1.1)	2 (0.4)	263 (1.3)	256 (1.4)	254 (1.5)	257 (1.3)
Idaho..........................	264 (0.9)	264 (1.1)	265 (0.9)	265 (0.9)	268 (0.7)	81 (1.1)	34 (1.1)	3 (0.4)	269 (1.5)	266 (1.5)	271 (1.4)	265 (1.4)
Illinois	266 (1.0)	264 (1.0)	263 (1.0)	265 (1.2)	266 (0.8)	77 (1.1)	34 (1.4)	4 (0.4)	260 (1.5)	268 (1.5)	264 (2.8)	270 (2.4)
Indiana	265 (1.0)	261 (1.1)	264 (1.1)	266 (1.0)	265 (1.0)	78 (1.0)	32 (1.6)	2 (0.5)	259 (2.2)	268 (1.7)	266 (2.2)	267 (1.7)
Iowa	268 (0.8)	267 (0.9)	267 (0.9)	265 (0.9)	265 (1.0)	77 (1.1)	33 (1.5)	2 (0.4)	258 (1.5)	269 (2.3)	263 (2.1)	268 (1.6)
Kansas[5]	266 (1.5)	267 (0.9)	267 (0.8)	267 (1.1)	267 (1.0)	79 (1.0)	35 (1.4)	3 (0.6)	262 (2.1)	274 (2.4)	264 (2.0)	271 (1.4)
Kentucky	266 (1.3)	264 (1.1)	262 (1.0)	267 (0.9)	269 (0.8)	79 (1.1)	36 (1.2)	3 (0.5)	264 (1.7)	269 (2.6)	268 (1.6)	271 (1.3)
Louisiana	253 (1.6)	253 (1.6)	253 (1.1)	253 (1.6)	255 (1.5)	66 (2.2)	22 (1.4)	1 (0.3)	257 (2.5)	255 (2.4)	244 (4.7)	260 (2.0)
Maine	268 (1.0)	270 (1.0)	270 (0.8)	268 (0.7)	270 (0.8)	80 (0.9)	39 (1.4)	4 (0.5)	270 (2.4)	279 (1.9)	265 (1.4)	269 (1.3)
Maryland......................	262 (1.4)	261 (1.2)	265 (1.2)	267 (1.1)	271 (1.2)	80 (1.2)	40 (1.6)	6 (0.8)	266 (1.9)	269 (1.6)	275 (3.8)	281 (2.3)
Massachusetts..............	273 (1.0)	274 (1.0)	273 (1.0)	274 (1.2)	275 (1.0)	84 (0.9)	46 (1.5)	6 (0.9)	262 (2.2)	278 (1.1)	‡ (†)	279 (4.0)
Michigan	264 (1.8)	261 (1.2)	260 (1.2)	262 (1.4)	265 (0.9)	77 (1.2)	32 (1.3)	3 (0.5)	260 (3.1)	267 (1.0)	263 (3.7)	269 (1.6)
Minnesota	268 (1.1)	268 (1.2)	268 (0.9)	270 (1.0)	270 (1.0)	81 (1.2)	39 (1.3)	4 (0.5)	265 (2.6)	272 (1.6)	269 (2.1)	272 (1.8)
Mississippi	255 (1.4)	251 (1.3)	250 (1.1)	251 (1.0)	254 (1.2)	65 (1.6)	21 (1.4)	1 (0.3)	253 (3.4)	263 (1.7)	248 (1.7)	254 (2.0)
Missouri	267 (1.0)	265 (1.0)	263 (1.0)	267 (1.0)	267 (1.1)	79 (1.1)	35 (1.7)	3 (0.5)	260 (4.6)	268 (1.8)	267 (1.9)	269 (1.6)
Montana.......................	270 (1.0)	269 (0.7)	271 (0.8)	270 (0.6)	273 (0.6)	86 (0.7)	42 (1.0)	3 (0.5)	274 (1.2)	‡ (†)	271 (1.1)	274 (1.1)
Nebraska	266 (0.9)	267 (0.9)	267 (0.9)	267 (0.9)	268 (0.7)	81 (0.8)	35 (1.2)	2 (0.5)	264 (1.1)	268 (2.2)	270 (1.3)	270 (1.4)
Nevada	252 (0.8)	253 (0.9)	252 (0.8)	254 (0.9)	258 (0.9)	69 (1.2)	26 (1.2)	2 (0.3)	257 (1.6)	252 (1.9)	267 (2.1)	265 (1.7)
New Hampshire	271 (0.9)	270 (1.2)	270 (0.9)	271 (1.0)	272 (0.7)	84 (1.1)	40 (1.2)	4 (0.4)	257 (2.0)	272 (1.4)	273 (1.9)	277 (1.1)
New Jersey	268 (1.2)	269 (1.2)	270 (1.1)	273 (1.3)	275 (1.2)	84 (1.3)	45 (1.3)	6 (0.5)	259 (4.9)	277 (1.2)	‡ (†)	280 (1.6)
New Mexico	252 (0.9)	251 (1.0)	251 (0.8)	254 (1.2)	256 (0.9)	68 (1.3)	22 (1.3)	1 (0.3)	255 (1.4)	258 (2.0)	258 (1.5)	253 (1.6)
New York	265 (1.3)	265 (1.0)	264 (1.1)	264 (1.2)	266 (1.1)	76 (1.2)	35 (1.5)	4 (0.5)	256 (1.8)	273 (2.0)	270 (4.2)	274 (2.4)
North Carolina	262 (1.0)	258 (0.9)	259 (1.1)	260 (1.2)	263 (0.9)	74 (1.2)	31 (1.5)	3 (0.5)	264 (2.2)	265 (2.6)	257 (3.4)	264 (1.3)
North Dakota	270 (0.8)	270 (0.6)	268 (0.7)	269 (0.6)	269 (0.7)	83 (1.0)	34 (1.3)	2 (0.4)	270 (1.6)	273 (1.9)	266 (1.3)	268 (1.0)
Ohio...........................	267 (1.3)	267 (1.3)	268 (1.2)	269 (1.3)	268 (1.1)	79 (1.2)	37 (1.6)	4 (0.5)	252 (2.5)	272 (2.1)	268 (2.3)	273 (2.0)
Oklahoma	262 (0.9)	260 (1.1)	260 (0.8)	259 (0.9)	260 (1.1)	73 (1.5)	27 (1.4)	2 (0.3)	257 (2.5)	263 (2.3)	261 (2.1)	260 (1.5)
Oregon........................	264 (1.2)	263 (1.1)	266 (0.9)	265 (1.0)	264 (0.9)	76 (1.1)	33 (1.4)	3 (0.4)	265 (1.4)	269 (1.7)	259 (2.0)	263 (2.3)
Pennsylvania................	264 (1.2)	267 (1.3)	268 (1.2)	271 (0.8)	268 (1.3)	77 (1.6)	38 (1.5)	4 (0.6)	252 (2.9)	271 (2.2)	269 (2.8)	273 (2.5)
Rhode Island	261 (0.7)	261 (0.7)	258 (0.9)	260 (0.6)	265 (0.7)	76 (0.8)	33 (1.0)	4 (0.5)	255 (1.4)	269 (0.9)	‡ (†)	271 (2.1)
South Carolina	258 (1.3)	257 (1.1)	257 (0.9)	257 (1.2)	260 (0.9)	72 (1.1)	27 (1.4)	2 (0.3)	264 (3.1)	264 (1.9)	256 (1.7)	258 (1.4)
South Dakota	270 (0.8)	269 (0.6)	270 (0.7)	270 (0.5)	269 (0.8)	83 (1.0)	35 (1.2)	2 (0.5)	270 (1.4)	‡ (†)	272 (1.1)	267 (1.0)
Tennessee	258 (1.2)	259 (0.9)	259 (1.0)	261 (1.1)	259 (1.0)	70 (1.2)	27 (1.3)	2 (0.6)	252 (2.0)	266 (2.4)	258 (2.1)	262 (1.5)
Texas	259 (1.1)	258 (0.6)	261 (0.9)	260 (1.1)	261 (1.4)	74 (1.4)	27 (1.3)	2 (0.4)	259 (1.3)	263 (1.9)	260 (3.5)	265 (2.4)
Utah	264 (0.8)	262 (0.8)	262 (1.0)	266 (0.8)	267 (0.8)	79 (1.1)	35 (1.6)	3 (0.5)	264 (1.6)	269 (1.2)	266 (2.3)	265 (2.1)
Vermont	271 (0.8)	269 (0.7)	273 (0.8)	272 (0.6)	274 (0.9)	82 (0.8)	44 (1.3)	6 (0.7)	‡ (†)	‡ (†)	‡ (†)	‡ (†)
Virginia.......................	268 (1.1)	268 (1.0)	267 (1.1)	266 (1.1)	267 (1.2)	78 (1.2)	36 (1.7)	4 (0.5)	264 (2.6)	275 (1.8)	260 (4.6)	263 (2.1)
Washington..................	264 (0.9)	265 (1.3)	265 (0.9)	267 (1.1)	268 (1.0)	77 (1.0)	37 (1.2)	5 (0.7)	265 (2.7)	270 (1.3)	266 (3.2)	267 (2.4)
West Virginia	260 (1.0)	255 (1.2)	255 (1.0)	255 (0.9)	256 (0.9)	68 (1.1)	24 (1.2)	1 (0.4)	258 (2.2)	262 (2.1)	255 (1.6)	253 (1.4)
Wisconsin	266 (1.3)	266 (1.1)	264 (1.0)	266 (1.0)	267 (0.9)	79 (1.0)	35 (1.3)	3 (0.7)	257 (1.9)	275 (1.4)	269 (2.2)	269 (1.9)
Wyoming......................	267 (0.5)	268 (0.7)	266 (0.7)	268 (1.0)	270 (1.0)	82 (1.0)	38 (1.6)	3 (0.5)	269 (1.6)	‡ (†)	271 (1.3)	268 (1.5)
Department of Defense dependents schools[6]	272 (0.6)	271 (0.7)	273 (1.0)	272 (0.7)	272 (0.7)	87 (1.1)	39 (1.3)	2 (0.5)	270 (2.9)	270 (1.9)	‡ (†)	‡ (†)

†Not applicable.

‡Reporting standards not met. Either there are too few cases or item response rates fell below the required standards for reporting.

[1]Scale ranges from 0 to 500.

[2]Basic denotes partial mastery of the knowledge and skills that are fundamental for proficient work at the 8th-grade level.

[3]Proficient represents solid academic performance for 8th-graders. Students reaching this level have demonstrated competency over challenging subject matter.

[4]Advanced signifies superior performance.

[5]Did not satisfy one or more of the guidelines for school participation in 2003. Data are subject to appreciable nonresponse bias.

[6]Prior to 2005, NAEP divided the Department of Defense (DoD) schools into two jurisdictions, domestic and overseas. In 2005, NAEP began combining the DoD domestic and overseas schools into a single jurisdiction. Data shown in this table for years prior to 2005 were recalculated for comparability.

NOTE: Includes public school students who were tested with accommodations; excludes only those students with disabilities (SD) and English language learners (ELL) who were unable to be tested even with accommodations. SD and ELL populations, accommodation rates, and exclusion rates vary from state to state. Standard errors appear in parentheses.

SOURCE: U.S. Department of Education, National Center for Education Statistics, National Assessment of Educational Progress (NAEP), 2003, 2005, 2007, 2009, and 2011 Reading Assessments, retrieved November 1, 2011, from the Main NAEP Data Explorer (http://nces.ed.gov/nationsreportcard/naepdata/). (This table was prepared November 2011.)

Average reading scale scores of 4th- and 8th-grade public school students and percentage at or above selected reading achievement levels, by race/ethnicity and jurisdiction or specific urban district: 2007, 2009, and 2011

Grade level and jurisdiction or specific urban district	Average reading scale score[1]										Percent of students	
	2007	2009				2011					2011	
	All students	All students	White	Black	Hispanic	All students	White	Black	Hispanic	Asian	At or above Basic[2]	At or above Proficient[3]
1	2	3	4	5	6	7	8	9	10	11	12	13
4th grade												
United States	220 (0.3)	220 (0.3)	229 (0.3)	204 (0.5)	204 (0.5)	220 (0.3)	230 (0.3)	205 (0.4)	205 (0.5)	236 (1.3)	66 (0.4)	32 (0.4)
Large city	208 (0.7)	210 (0.7)	233 (1.4)	201 (0.9)	202 (0.8)	211 (0.7)	232 (0.9)	202 (0.7)	203 (0.8)	225 (2.5)	55 (1.0)	24 (0.7)
Albuquerque	— (†)	— (†)	— (†)	— (†)	— (†)	209 (1.6)	231 (2.5)	‡ (†)	201 (1.7)	‡ (†)	53 (1.9)	24 (1.6)
Atlanta	207 (1.5)	209 (1.5)	253 (2.9)	201 (1.6)	‡ (†)	212 (1.4)	251 (1.9)	203 (1.6)	215 (3.4)	‡ (†)	54 (1.6)	24 (1.7)
Austin	218 (2.0)	220 (1.8)	245 (2.0)	211 (3.0)	208 (2.3)	224 (2.3)	249 (3.3)	215 (4.5)	210 (2.6)	‡ (†)	68 (2.3)	36 (2.5)
Baltimore City	— (†)	202 (1.7)	220 (4.8)	200 (1.7)	‡ (†)	200 (1.7)	221 (3.3)	198 (1.7)	‡ (†)	‡ (†)	40 (2.5)	11 (1.2)
Boston	210 (1.9)	215 (1.2)	231 (2.9)	212 (1.5)	209 (2.0)	217 (0.8)	241 (2.5)	211 (1.7)	214 (1.1)	226 (3.8)	62 (1.5)	26 (1.3)
Charlotte	222 (1.5)	225 (1.6)	243 (1.6)	211 (2.3)	212 (2.8)	224 (1.2)	244 (1.5)	211 (1.9)	212 (2.6)	233 (5.3)	70 (1.5)	36 (1.7)
Chicago	201 (1.5)	202 (1.5)	228 (3.5)	194 (1.8)	203 (2.1)	203 (1.3)	229 (2.4)	197 (1.9)	201 (1.5)	228 (4.2)	48 (1.4)	18 (1.2)
Cleveland	198 (1.7)	194 (2.0)	209 (3.4)	189 (2.2)	200 (4.4)	193 (0.9)	209 (2.6)	187 (1.1)	196 (3.3)	‡ (†)	32 (1.4)	8 (1.0)
Dallas	— (†)	— (†)	— (†)	— (†)	— (†)	204 (1.6)	237 (6.9)	204 (2.0)	200 (1.4)	‡ (†)	46 (2.1)	14 (1.7)
Detroit	— (†)	187 (1.9)	‡ (†)	186 (2.1)	190 (2.8)	191 (2.0)	‡ (†)	190 (2.5)	199 (5.5)	‡ (†)	31 (2.8)	7 (1.4)
District of Columbia	197 (0.9)	203 (1.2)	257 (2.9)	195 (1.3)	207 (3.2)	201 (1.0)	255 (3.0)	191 (1.3)	204 (3.3)	‡ (†)	44 (1.1)	20 (1.3)
Fresno	— (†)	197 (1.7)	217 (3.0)	193 (3.4)	194 (1.8)	194 (2.4)	216 (3.9)	191 (4.3)	190 (2.5)	195 (3.0)	37 (2.1)	11 (1.4)
Hillsborough County (FL)	— (†)	— (†)	— (†)	— (†)	— (†)	231 (1.7)	242 (1.8)	218 (2.5)	223 (2.4)	‡ (†)	77 (1.8)	44 (2.4)
Houston	206 (1.2)	211 (1.7)	243 (4.7)	210 (2.5)	206 (1.9)	213 (1.6)	243 (3.0)	207 (1.7)	209 (1.6)	245 (6.3)	57 (1.8)	24 (1.8)
Jefferson County (KY)	— (†)	219 (1.8)	230 (2.1)	203 (2.0)	‡ (†)	223 (1.3)	230 (1.4)	208 (2.1)	221 (3.9)	256 (5.7)	68 (1.7)	35 (1.5)
Los Angeles	196 (1.3)	197 (1.1)	222 (3.5)	195 (3.3)	193 (1.1)	201 (1.2)	225 (3.7)	196 (4.2)	196 (1.1)	226 (4.2)	45 (1.7)	15 (1.4)
Miami-Dade	— (†)	221 (1.2)	238 (3.4)	205 (2.1)	224 (1.1)	221 (1.5)	240 (3.4)	210 (2.1)	222 (1.8)	‡ (†)	67 (1.7)	32 (1.7)
Milwaukee	— (†)	196 (2.0)	223 (4.6)	187 (2.4)	198 (2.7)	195 (1.7)	216 (3.9)	187 (2.0)	198 (2.7)	206 (3.3)	38 (1.9)	13 (1.3)
New York City	213 (1.1)	217 (1.4)	235 (2.8)	208 (1.6)	208 (1.9)	216 (1.2)	235 (3.3)	209 (1.7)	207 (1.5)	230 (3.6)	61 (1.4)	29 (1.4)
Philadelphia	— (†)	195 (1.8)	215 (4.2)	191 (2.1)	187 (4.6)	199 (1.8)	217 (3.3)	195 (1.9)	191 (3.5)	212 (5.2)	43 (2.1)	13 (1.6)
San Diego	210 (1.8)	213 (2.1)	236 (2.8)	206 (4.1)	193 (2.6)	215 (1.7)	240 (2.3)	205 (3.0)	201 (2.2)	225 (3.3)	61 (1.7)	31 (1.6)
8th grade												
United States	261 (0.2)	262 (0.3)	271 (0.2)	245 (0.4)	248 (0.6)	264 (0.2)	272 (0.3)	248 (0.5)	251 (0.5)	277 (1.1)	75 (0.3)	32 (0.3)
Large city	250 (0.7)	252 (0.5)	272 (1.0)	243 (0.7)	245 (0.9)	255 (0.5)	273 (1.0)	245 (0.8)	249 (0.8)	271 (1.5)	65 (0.6)	23 (0.5)
Albuquerque	— (†)	— (†)	— (†)	— (†)	— (†)	254 (1.2)	271 (2.2)	‡ (†)	248 (1.6)	‡ (†)	64 (1.4)	22 (1.5)
Atlanta	245 (1.4)	250 (1.5)	292 (3.9)	246 (1.7)	‡ (†)	253 (1.0)	287 (3.2)	249 (1.2)	‡ (†)	‡ (†)	63 (1.8)	17 (0.9)
Austin	257 (2.0)	261 (2.0)	282 (2.5)	247 (2.5)	251 (2.1)	261 (1.5)	285 (1.8)	246 (3.6)	251 (2.2)	‡ (†)	71 (1.8)	30 (1.5)
Baltimore City	— (†)	245 (1.7)	‡ (†)	243 (1.6)	‡ (†)	246 (1.6)	267 (3.7)	242 (1.7)	‡ (†)	‡ (†)	54 (2.0)	12 (1.2)
Boston	254 (1.6)	257 (1.5)	282 (3.0)	248 (2.4)	251 (2.1)	255 (1.2)	281 (4.3)	246 (2.0)	245 (2.3)	280 (3.4)	63 (1.6)	24 (1.1)
Charlotte	260 (1.2)	259 (1.0)	276 (2.4)	249 (1.2)	254 (3.7)	265 (0.9)	283 (1.8)	253 (1.6)	256 (2.5)	264 (5.3)	75 (1.4)	34 (1.5)
Chicago	250 (1.5)	249 (1.6)	272 (3.1)	243 (1.8)	249 (2.5)	253 (1.1)	271 (3.5)	245 (1.9)	255 (1.3)	262 (13.1)	64 (1.4)	21 (1.5)
Cleveland	246 (1.5)	242 (1.6)	258 (3.4)	239 (2.2)	237 (3.5)	240 (1.7)	260 (3.1)	234 (2.2)	241 (3.8)	‡ (†)	48 (2.6)	11 (1.3)
Dallas	— (†)	— (†)	— (†)	— (†)	— (†)	248 (1.0)	276 (4.1)	244 (2.8)	246 (1.1)	‡ (†)	58 (1.5)	13 (1.4)
Detroit	— (†)	232 (2.4)	‡ (†)	232 (2.6)	232 (4.7)	237 (1.0)	‡ (†)	235 (1.1)	244 (4.2)	‡ (†)	43 (1.4)	7 (0.9)
District of Columbia	241 (0.7)	240 (1.5)	‡ (†)	235 (1.5)	249 (5.3)	237 (1.2)	290 (3.4)	231 (1.2)	232 (3.8)	‡ (†)	46 (1.4)	15 (1.3)
Fresno	— (†)	240 (2.4)	263 (3.8)	232 (3.4)	235 (2.7)	238 (1.8)	257 (3.2)	230 (3.5)	234 (2.2)	241 (3.4)	45 (2.2)	12 (1.1)
Hillsborough County (FL)	— (†)	— (†)	— (†)	— (†)	— (†)	264 (1.5)	276 (1.5)	247 (2.4)	258 (2.3)	‡ (†)	75 (2.1)	32 (2.3)
Houston	252 (1.4)	252 (1.2)	280 (3.6)	243 (2.2)	250 (1.2)	252 (0.9)	283 (2.2)	247 (2.4)	249 (1.3)	‡ (†)	64 (1.3)	18 (1.0)
Jefferson County (KY)	— (†)	259 (1.0)	267 (1.4)	245 (2.1)	‡ (†)	260 (1.1)	269 (1.7)	245 (1.7)	‡ (†)	‡ (†)	70 (1.6)	27 (1.9)
Los Angeles	240 (1.0)	244 (1.1)	271 (3.4)	239 (3.6)	239 (1.0)	246 (1.1)	273 (3.6)	242 (3.3)	241 (1.2)	269 (4.5)	56 (1.5)	16 (1.1)
Miami-Dade	— (†)	261 (1.4)	273 (3.2)	250 (2.4)	261 (1.6)	260 (1.4)	275 (2.4)	246 (1.8)	262 (1.5)	‡ (†)	71 (1.9)	28 (1.8)
Milwaukee	— (†)	241 (2.0)	265 (3.4)	233 (2.3)	249 (2.9)	238 (1.6)	255 (3.0)	232 (2.0)	243 (2.9)	248 (5.5)	46 (2.1)	10 (1.3)
New York City	249 (1.9)	252 (1.4)	271 (2.4)	246 (1.9)	243 (2.2)	254 (1.8)	271 (3.6)	248 (2.3)	246 (2.4)	273 (3.3)	65 (2.1)	24 (1.8)
Philadelphia	— (†)	247 (2.5)	266 (5.2)	241 (1.9)	241 (3.7)	247 (1.5)	264 (3.8)	244 (1.9)	239 (3.0)	258 (4.7)	56 (2.1)	16 (1.6)
San Diego	250 (1.2)	254 (2.8)	273 (3.4)	239 (5.0)	242 (3.8)	256 (2.1)	275 (2.6)	238 (4.8)	245 (3.2)	268 (4.2)	68 (2.2)	27 (2.2)

—Not available.
†Not applicable.
‡Reporting standards not met (too few cases).
[1]Scale ranges from 0 to 500.
[2]Basic denotes partial mastery of prerequisite knowledge and skills that are fundamental for proficient work at a given grade.
[3]Proficient represents solid academic performance. Students reaching this level have demonstrated competency over challenging subject matter.
NOTE: Beginning in 2009, if the results for charter schools are not included in a school district's Adequate Yearly Progress (AYP) report to the U.S. Department of Education under the Elementary and Secondary Education Act, they are excluded from that district's results. This change had little or no impact on differences between any participating district's 2007 and 2009 average reading scores except those of the District of Columbia at grade 8. For details, see the Technical Notes in The Nation's Report Card: Reading 2009 Trial Urban District Assessment (NCES 2010-459). Race categories exclude persons of Hispanic ethnicity. Totals include racial/ethnic groups not shown separately. Standard errors appear in parentheses.
SOURCE: U.S. Department of Education, National Center for Education Statistics, National Assessment of Educational Progress (NAEP), 2007, 2009, and 2011 Reading Assessments, retrieved May 20, 2010, and December 7, 2011, from the Main NAEP Data Explorer (http://nces.ed.gov/nationsreportcard/naepdata/). (This table was prepared December 2011.)

Average reading scale scores of 4th- and 8th-graders in public schools and percentage scoring at or above selected reading achievement levels, by English language learner status and state: 2011

State	4th-graders							8th-graders						
	English language learners				Not English language learners			English language learners				Not English language learners		
	Percent of all students assessed	Average scale score[1]	Percent		Average scale score[1]	Percent		Percent of all students assessed	Average scale score[1]	Percent		Average scale score[1]	Percent	
			At or above Basic[2]	At or above Proficient[3]		At or above Basic[2]	At or above Proficient[3]			At or above Basic[2]	At or above Proficient[3]		At or above Basic[2]	At or above Proficient[3]
1	2	3	4	5	6	7	8	9	10	11	12	13	14	15
United States	11 (0.3)	188 (0.8)	30 (1.1)	7 (0.4)	224 (0.3)	70 (0.3)	35 (0.4)	5 (0.2)	223 (1.0)	29 (1.4)	3 (0.4)	266 (0.2)	77 (0.3)	33 (0.3)
Alabama	2 (0.4)	189 (6.0)	32 (8.8)	5 (3.0)	221 (1.4)	68 (1.8)	32 (1.5)	1 (0.2)	‡ (†)	‡ (†)	‡ (†)	259 (1.5)	70 (1.8)	26 (1.6)
Alaska	13 (0.8)	153 (3.5)	9 (1.8)	2 (0.8)	216 (1.1)	63 (1.5)	29 (1.2)	10 (0.5)	215 (4.3)	22 (4.4)	5 (2.0)	267 (0.8)	79 (1.0)	34 (1.1)
Arizona	12 (1.0)	171 (2.8)	14 (2.6)	1 (1.0)	218 (1.0)	64 (1.3)	29 (1.3)	2 (0.2)	‡ (†)	‡ (†)	‡ (†)	261 (1.2)	72 (1.5)	29 (1.5)
Arkansas	8 (0.8)	197 (2.9)	41 (3.6)	14 (2.6)	218 (1.0)	65 (1.3)	31 (1.3)	5 (0.5)	239 (3.3)	47 (5.3)	8 (2.2)	260 (1.0)	72 (1.1)	29 (1.7)
California	31 (1.9)	186 (1.6)	27 (2.3)	5 (0.9)	223 (1.9)	70 (2.0)	33 (2.5)	17 (1.0)	220 (1.9)	26 (2.7)	3 (0.9)	262 (1.1)	73 (1.2)	28 (1.5)
Colorado	16 (1.2)	184 (2.5)	28 (2.8)	5 (1.4)	231 (1.2)	79 (1.2)	45 (1.7)	7 (0.6)	224 (3.2)	28 (4.2)	2 (†)	274 (1.3)	85 (1.3)	43 (2.1)
Connecticut	5 (0.7)	178 (5.0)	22 (5.2)	3 (2.0)	230 (1.2)	76 (1.4)	44 (1.6)	4 (0.5)	224 (5.6)	24 (6.2)	3 (†)	277 (0.9)	85 (1.0)	46 (1.3)
Delaware	3 (0.8)	187 (4.1)	22 (5.6)	4 (2.6)	226 (0.7)	74 (0.9)	37 (1.2)	1 (0.2)	‡ (†)	‡ (†)	‡ (†)	266 (0.7)	78 (0.8)	33 (1.2)
District of Columbia	7 (0.4)	179 (3.9)	22 (4.6)	5 (1.8)	202 (0.9)	45 (1.0)	20 (0.9)	5 (0.3)	215 (3.4)	25 (5.1)	3 (1.7)	244 (0.9)	52 (1.0)	17 (1.0)
Florida	8 (0.6)	195 (2.0)	35 (3.3)	7 (1.8)	227 (1.1)	75 (1.4)	38 (1.5)	4 (0.3)	225 (3.9)	28 (5.8)	4 (1.7)	264 (1.0)	75 (1.4)	31 (1.5)
Georgia	4 (0.5)	191 (3.2)	31 (4.4)	5 (3.4)	222 (1.0)	68 (1.4)	34 (1.3)	1 (0.3)	‡ (†)	‡ (†)	‡ (†)	263 (1.1)	75 (1.3)	28 (1.5)
Hawaii	10 (0.7)	180 (2.4)	21 (3.4)	3 (1.4)	217 (1.0)	64 (1.3)	30 (1.2)	8 (0.3)	220 (3.1)	26 (3.6)	3 (1.3)	260 (0.7)	72 (1.2)	28 (1.1)
Idaho	4 (0.4)	166 (3.1)	12 (3.1)	2 (†)	223 (0.7)	71 (1.2)	34 (1.0)	3 (0.2)	231 (2.9)	39 (5.8)	2 (†)	269 (0.7)	82 (1.1)	35 (1.1)
Illinois	7 (0.7)	180 (3.0)	23 (3.9)	5 (1.6)	223 (1.1)	69 (1.2)	36 (1.3)	4 (0.4)	224 (3.3)	32 (5.9)	2 (†)	267 (0.9)	78 (1.1)	35 (1.4)
Indiana	7 (1.0)	197 (3.2)	42 (4.1)	14 (3.7)	223 (0.9)	70 (1.2)	34 (1.1)	3 (0.5)	235 (4.6)	45 (7.5)	6 (4.1)	266 (1.0)	79 (1.0)	33 (1.6)
Iowa	5 (0.6)	189 (3.7)	35 (4.3)	7 (2.3)	223 (0.8)	71 (1.0)	35 (1.0)	3 (0.5)	231 (4.3)	39 (6.7)	6 (2.9)	266 (1.0)	78 (1.1)	34 (1.5)
Kansas	11 (1.3)	203 (2.2)	48 (2.9)	16 (2.1)	226 (1.1)	73 (1.2)	39 (1.6)	6 (0.7)	242 (3.0)	49 (4.3)	11 (3.5)	269 (0.9)	81 (0.9)	37 (1.4)
Kentucky	1 (0.2)	‡ (†)	‡ (†)	‡ (†)	225 (1.0)	72 (1.3)	36 (1.5)	1 (0.2)	‡ (†)	‡ (†)	‡ (†)	269 (0.8)	80 (1.0)	37 (1.2)
Louisiana	2 (0.4)	197 (6.1)	44 (7.0)	9 (5.1)	211 (1.4)	56 (1.8)	23 (1.5)	1 (0.3)	‡ (†)	‡ (†)	‡ (†)	255 (1.6)	66 (2.2)	22 (1.4)
Maine	3 (0.5)	186 (5.1)	34 (6.7)	7 (†)	223 (0.7)	71 (1.0)	33 (1.3)	2 (0.2)	‡ (†)	‡ (†)	‡ (†)	271 (0.8)	81 (0.9)	39 (1.4)
Maryland	3 (0.4)	205 (3.2)	47 (5.6)	15 (4.4)	232 (0.9)	76 (1.0)	44 (1.2)	1 (0.3)	‡ (†)	‡ (†)	‡ (†)	272 (1.1)	81 (1.1)	40 (1.6)
Massachusetts	7 (0.7)	204 (2.4)	46 (4.6)	12 (2.6)	239 (1.0)	86 (1.1)	53 (1.5)	3 (0.3)	211 (3.9)	17 (3.9)	1 (†)	277 (1.0)	87 (0.9)	48 (1.5)
Michigan	3 (0.8)	192 (2.9)	33 (5.0)	7 (3.4)	220 (1.2)	67 (1.4)	32 (1.4)	2 (0.3)	237 (4.8)	48 (10.0)	8 (4.2)	266 (0.9)	78 (1.2)	33 (1.3)
Minnesota	10 (1.3)	187 (3.1)	30 (3.2)	5 (1.6)	226 (1.1)	74 (1.3)	39 (1.5)	5 (0.5)	233 (3.7)	38 (5.6)	6 (2.2)	272 (1.0)	83 (1.2)	41 (1.3)
Mississippi	2 (0.4)	‡ (†)	‡ (†)	‡ (†)	210 (1.2)	55 (1.4)	22 (1.2)	1 (0.2)	‡ (†)	‡ (†)	‡ (†)	254 (1.2)	65 (1.6)	21 (1.4)
Missouri	3 (0.8)	189 (5.5)	29 (5.7)	11 (3.3)	221 (1.0)	68 (1.3)	35 (1.1)	1 (0.2)	‡ (†)	‡ (†)	‡ (†)	267 (1.1)	79 (1.1)	35 (1.7)
Montana	2 (0.3)	174 (5.1)	18 (6.0)	4 (†)	226 (0.6)	75 (1.0)	36 (1.1)	1 (0.2)	‡ (†)	‡ (†)	‡ (†)	273 (0.6)	86 (0.8)	42 (1.0)
Nebraska	7 (0.8)	191 (4.4)	32 (4.4)	7 (2.4)	226 (0.8)	73 (1.1)	38 (1.4)	2 (0.3)	‡ (†)	‡ (†)	‡ (†)	268 (0.7)	82 (0.7)	36 (1.3)
Nevada	27 (1.0)	193 (1.8)	36 (2.0)	10 (1.0)	220 (1.1)	67 (1.4)	31 (1.4)	10 (0.4)	215 (2.8)	20 (3.1)	2 (1.0)	263 (0.8)	75 (1.2)	29 (1.3)
New Hampshire	2 (0.2)	203 (4.7)	45 (7.0)	14 (4.7)	231 (0.7)	79 (0.9)	44 (1.1)	1 (0.2)	‡ (†)	‡ (†)	‡ (†)	273 (0.8)	84 (1.1)	40 (1.3)
New Jersey	2 (0.4)	‡ (†)	‡ (†)	‡ (†)	232 (1.2)	79 (1.4)	45 (1.4)	1 (0.3)	‡ (†)	‡ (†)	‡ (†)	276 (1.2)	85 (1.4)	45 (1.4)
New Mexico	15 (0.7)	171 (2.0)	14 (2.3)	2 (0.9)	214 (1.0)	60 (1.5)	24 (1.0)	10 (0.5)	218 (2.3)	22 (3.1)	1 (†)	260 (0.8)	73 (1.2)	25 (1.3)
New York	8 (0.6)	187 (3.2)	29 (4.5)	5 (2.2)	226 (1.0)	72 (1.2)	38 (1.4)	5 (0.5)	216 (2.6)	21 (2.9)	1 (0.8)	268 (1.2)	79 (1.2)	37 (1.6)
North Carolina	7 (0.6)	189 (3.4)	32 (4.0)	7 (2.0)	224 (1.1)	71 (1.2)	36 (1.4)	4 (0.3)	233 (3.4)	38 (5.0)	3 (†)	264 (1.0)	75 (1.2)	32 (1.6)
North Dakota	2 (0.2)	198 (4.1)	38 (6.8)	9 (4.0)	226 (0.5)	75 (1.0)	36 (0.9)	1 (0.2)	‡ (†)	‡ (†)	‡ (†)	269 (0.7)	84 (1.0)	34 (1.4)
Ohio	3 (0.5)	206 (2.8)	53 (4.6)	14 (3.7)	224 (1.0)	72 (1.1)	34 (1.5)	1 (0.2)	224 (7.6)	27 (11.1)	5 (†)	269 (1.1)	80 (1.2)	37 (1.6)
Oklahoma	5 (0.7)	186 (4.7)	26 (4.8)	7 (2.7)	217 (1.1)	66 (1.5)	28 (1.3)	2 (0.4)	‡ (†)	‡ (†)	‡ (†)	261 (1.1)	74 (1.5)	27 (1.4)
Oregon	14 (0.8)	183 (2.0)	25 (2.2)	4 (0.9)	222 (1.1)	69 (1.3)	35 (1.5)	6 (0.6)	215 (3.5)	22 (5.0)	1 (†)	267 (0.9)	79 (1.1)	35 (1.4)
Pennsylvania	2 (0.3)	183 (4.7)	26 (7.2)	10 (3.7)	228 (1.2)	75 (1.4)	42 (1.4)	2 (0.3)	220 (6.0)	23 (6.9)	2 (1.1)	269 (1.2)	78 (1.5)	39 (1.5)
Rhode Island	6 (0.5)	180 (3.1)	20 (4.6)	3 (1.4)	225 (0.7)	73 (1.3)	37 (1.0)	3 (0.2)	219 (4.8)	30 (4.9)	3 (1.8)	267 (0.7)	77 (0.8)	34 (1.1)
South Carolina	5 (0.5)	207 (3.5)	56 (4.9)	20 (3.8)	215 (1.2)	62 (1.3)	29 (1.6)	4 (0.4)	251 (3.5)	63 (5.0)	18 (4.2)	261 (0.9)	72 (1.2)	27 (1.4)
South Dakota	4 (0.4)	175 (4.8)	20 (4.0)	2 (1.5)	222 (0.8)	71 (0.9)	33 (1.0)	1 (0.2)	‡ (†)	‡ (†)	‡ (†)	270 (0.8)	83 (0.9)	36 (1.2)
Tennessee	3 (0.5)	177 (4.9)	21 (6.7)	5 (†)	216 (1.1)	62 (1.5)	26 (1.3)	1 (0.2)	‡ (†)	‡ (†)	‡ (†)	260 (1.0)	71 (1.2)	27 (1.3)
Texas	18 (1.2)	197 (2.0)	38 (2.9)	9 (1.4)	223 (1.5)	70 (1.8)	33 (2.0)	7 (0.9)	225 (3.0)	27 (5.1)	1 (0.6)	264 (0.9)	78 (1.3)	29 (1.4)
Utah	6 (0.5)	167 (3.5)	14 (2.7)	2 (1.2)	224 (0.9)	72 (1.2)	35 (1.3)	4 (0.3)	222 (2.5)	23 (4.1)	2 (†)	269 (0.8)	81 (1.1)	37 (1.6)
Vermont	2 (0.2)	189 (6.4)	36 (7.0)	16 (5.9)	228 (0.6)	74 (1.0)	42 (0.9)	1 (0.2)	‡ (†)	‡ (†)	‡ (†)	274 (0.9)	83 (0.9)	45 (1.3)
Virginia	7 (0.8)	190 (2.8)	30 (3.9)	7 (2.2)	229 (1.0)	75 (1.3)	41 (1.4)	5 (0.5)	241 (5.3)	54 (7.2)	7 (2.9)	269 (1.1)	79 (1.2)	37 (1.7)
Washington	11 (0.9)	172 (2.9)	15 (2.7)	2 (0.9)	226 (1.0)	73 (1.2)	38 (1.4)	5 (0.5)	222 (3.5)	25 (4.3)	4 (1.6)	270 (0.9)	80 (1.0)	39 (1.2)
West Virginia	1 (0.1)	‡ (†)	‡ (†)	‡ (†)	214 (0.8)	61 (1.1)	27 (1.0)	# (†)	‡ (†)	‡ (†)	‡ (†)	256 (0.9)	68 (1.1)	24 (1.2)
Wisconsin	8 (0.8)	195 (2.6)	39 (3.1)	10 (2.3)	223 (0.8)	70 (1.2)	36 (1.1)	5 (0.5)	240 (3.3)	47 (5.8)	9 (2.8)	269 (0.9)	80 (1.0)	36 (1.3)
Wyoming	3 (0.2)	190 (3.4)	32 (5.8)	5 (3.3)	225 (0.8)	73 (1.3)	35 (1.1)	1 (0.2)	‡ (†)	‡ (†)	‡ (†)	270 (1.0)	82 (1.0)	38 (1.6)
Department of Defense dependents schools	5 (0.3)	211 (3.0)	53 (5.4)	17 (4.0)	230 (0.5)	81 (0.8)	40 (1.3)	4 (0.3)	‡ (†)	‡ (†)	‡ (†)	273 (0.8)	88 (1.0)	40 (1.2)

†Not applicable.
#Rounds to zero.
‡Reporting standards not met (too few cases).
[1]Scale ranges from 0 to 500.
[2]Basic denotes partial mastery of the knowledge and skills that are fundamental for proficient work at a given grade.
[3]Proficient represents solid academic performance. Students reaching this level have demonstrated competency over challenging subject matter.
NOTE: The results for English language learners are based on students who were assessed and cannot be generalized to the total population of such students. Although testing accommodations were permitted, some English language learners—making up about 1 percent of all public school students at both grade 4 and grade 8—did not have a sufficient level of English proficiency to participate in the 2011 Reading Assessment. Standard errors appear in parentheses.
SOURCE: U.S. Department of Education, National Center for Education Statistics, National Assessment of Educational Progress (NAEP), 2011 Reading Assessment, retrieved November 2, 2011, from the Main NAEP Data Explorer (http://nces.ed.gov/nationsreport card/naep-data/). (This table was prepared November 2011.)

Average writing scale score and percentage of students attaining writing achievement levels, by selected student characteristics and grade level: 2002 and 2007

Grade, year, and achievement level	All students	Sex		Race/ethnicity					Parents' highest level of education				Free or reduced-price lunch eligibility		
		Male	Female	White	Black	Hispanic	Asian/ Pacific Islander	American Indian/ Alaska Native	Did not finish high school	Graduated high school	Some education after high school	Graduated college	Eligible	Not eligible	Information not available
1	2	3	4	5	6	7	8	9	10	11	12	13	14	15	16
Average scale score[1]															
4th-graders, 2002	154 (0.4)	146 (0.6)	163 (0.4)	161 (0.3)	140 (0.7)	141 (1.6)	167 (1.5)	139 (1.9)	— (†)	— (†)	— (†)	— (†)	141 (0.8)	163 (0.5)	161 (1.5)
8th-graders 2002	153 (0.5)	143 (0.6)	164 (0.6)	161 (0.6)	135 (0.7)	137 (0.9)	161 (2.0)	137 (2.9)	136 (0.9)	144 (0.6)	156 (0.6)	165 (0.6)	136 (0.5)	162 (0.7)	161 (1.5)
8th-graders 2007	156 (0.2)	146 (0.3)	166 (0.3)	164 (0.2)	141 (0.4)	142 (0.6)	167 (1.2)	143 (1.3)	139 (0.6)	147 (0.5)	158 (0.4)	166 (0.3)	141 (0.3)	164 (0.3)	170 (1.2)
12th-graders 2002	148 (0.8)	136 (0.8)	160 (0.9)	154 (0.8)	130 (1.3)	136 (1.5)	151 (2.4)	‡ (†)	129 (1.7)	139 (1.1)	149 (0.9)	158 (1.0)	132 (1.4)	152 (1.0)	156 (1.5)
12th-graders 2007	153 (0.6)	144 (0.6)	162 (0.7)	159 (0.6)	137 (1.0)	139 (1.0)	160 (1.7)	140 (3.9)	134 (1.0)	141 (0.8)	152 (0.7)	163 (0.6)	138 (0.7)	157 (0.6)	165 (1.5)
Percent attaining achievement levels															
4th-graders, 2002															
Below Basic	14 (0.4)	19 (0.5)	9 (0.3)	10 (0.2)	23 (0.8)	23 (1.6)	7 (1.1)	25 (2.6)	— (†)	— (†)	— (†)	— (†)	22 (0.8)	8 (0.3)	10 (1.1)
At or above Basic[2]	86 (0.4)	81 (0.5)	91 (0.3)	90 (0.2)	77 (0.8)	77 (1.6)	93 (1.1)	75 (2.6)	— (†)	— (†)	— (†)	— (†)	78 (0.8)	92 (0.3)	90 (1.1)
At or above Proficient[3]	28 (0.4)	20 (0.5)	36 (0.6)	34 (0.4)	14 (0.7)	17 (0.9)	41 (2.1)	15 (1.7)	— (†)	— (†)	— (†)	— (†)	15 (0.5)	36 (0.6)	34 (1.6)
At Advanced[4]	2 (0.1)	1 (0.1)	3 (0.2)	3 (0.1)	1 (0.2)	1 (0.2)	4 (0.6)	1 (0.5)	— (†)	— (†)	— (†)	— (†)	1 (0.1)	3 (0.2)	3 (0.3)
8th-graders 2002															
Below Basic	15 (0.4)	21 (0.6)	9 (0.3)	10 (0.4)	26 (1.0)	27 (1.0)	12 (1.3)	27 (3.9)	26 (1.3)	19 (0.7)	11 (0.6)	9 (0.4)	26 (0.6)	9 (0.4)	11 (0.7)
At or above Basic[2]	85 (0.4)	79 (0.6)	91 (0.3)	90 (0.4)	74 (1.0)	73 (1.0)	88 (1.3)	73 (3.9)	74 (1.3)	81 (0.7)	89 (0.6)	91 (0.4)	74 (0.6)	91 (0.4)	89 (0.7)
At or above Proficient[3]	31 (0.6)	21 (0.6)	42 (0.8)	38 (0.6)	13 (0.6)	16 (1.1)	40 (2.6)	16 (2.5)	14 (1.0)	20 (0.6)	31 (0.8)	43 (0.8)	16 (0.6)	39 (0.8)	39 (1.7)
At Advanced[4]	2 (0.1)	1 (0.1)	3 (0.2)	3 (0.2)	# (†)	1 (0.2)	4 (0.8)	1 (#)	# (†)	1 (0.2)	1 (0.4)	4 (0.2)	1 (0.1)	3 (0.2)	4 (0.6)
8th-graders 2007															
Below Basic	12 (0.2)	17 (0.3)	7 (0.2)	7 (0.2)	19 (0.5)	20 (0.6)	8 (0.8)	21 (1.3)	21 (1.0)	16 (0.5)	9 (0.4)	7 (0.2)	20 (0.3)	7 (0.2)	5 (0.6)
At or above Basic[2]	88 (0.2)	83 (0.3)	93 (0.2)	93 (0.2)	81 (0.5)	80 (0.6)	92 (0.8)	79 (1.3)	79 (1.0)	84 (0.5)	91 (0.4)	93 (0.2)	80 (0.3)	93 (0.2)	95 (0.6)
At or above Proficient[3]	33 (0.3)	22 (0.3)	43 (0.4)	41 (0.3)	16 (0.6)	18 (0.5)	46 (1.4)	20 (1.6)	14 (0.6)	21 (0.6)	33 (0.5)	44 (0.4)	17 (0.3)	41 (0.4)	49 (1.8)
At Advanced[4]	2 (0.1)	1 (†)	3 (0.1)	3 (0.1)	# (†)	1 (0.1)	5 (0.5)	1 (0.4)	# (†)	1 (†)	1 (0.1)	3 (0.1)	# (†)	3 (0.1)	4 (0.5)
12th-graders 2002															
Below Basic	26 (0.7)	37 (1.0)	15 (0.7)	21 (0.7)	41 (1.7)	36 (1.8)	24 (2.3)	‡ (†)	43 (2.1)	32 (1.2)	23 (1.0)	18 (0.9)	40 (1.5)	23 (0.8)	19 (1.3)
At or above Basic[2]	74 (0.7)	63 (1.0)	85 (0.7)	79 (0.7)	59 (1.7)	64 (1.8)	76 (2.3)	‡ (†)	57 (2.1)	68 (1.2)	77 (1.0)	82 (0.9)	60 (1.5)	77 (0.8)	81 (1.3)
At or above Proficient[3]	24 (0.8)	14 (0.8)	33 (1.0)	28 (0.9)	9 (1.0)	13 (1.4)	25 (2.8)	‡ (†)	8 (1.4)	14 (1.1)	22 (1.3)	32 (1.0)	11 (1.0)	26 (1.0)	29 (1.6)
At Advanced[4]	2 (0.2)	1 (0.1)	3 (0.3)	2 (0.3)	# (†)	1 (0.2)	3 (1.1)	‡ (†)	# (†)	# (†)	1 (0.2)	3 (0.4)	1 (0.2)	2 (0.3)	2 (0.4)
12th-graders 2007															
Below Basic	18 (0.5)	26 (0.6)	11 (0.5)	14 (0.5)	31 (1.2)	29 (1.1)	14 (1.5)	30 (5.3)	34 (1.5)	27 (1.1)	16 (0.7)	12 (0.4)	31 (1.0)	15 (0.5)	10 (1.0)
At or above Basic[2]	82 (0.5)	74 (0.6)	89 (0.5)	86 (0.5)	69 (1.2)	71 (1.1)	86 (1.5)	70 (5.3)	66 (1.5)	73 (1.1)	84 (0.7)	88 (0.4)	69 (1.0)	85 (0.5)	90 (1.0)
At or above Proficient[3]	24 (0.6)	16 (0.6)	32 (0.8)	30 (0.6)	9 (0.8)	11 (0.9)	30 (2.2)	12 (2.6)	8 (1.0)	13 (0.6)	20 (0.7)	34 (0.8)	11 (0.5)	27 (0.7)	36 (2.1)
At Advanced[4]	1 (0.1)	# (†)	1 (0.2)	1 (0.2)	# (†)	# (†)	1 (†)	# (†)	# (†)	# (†)	# (†)	2 (0.2)	# (†)	1 (0.2)	2 (0.4)

—Not available.
†Not applicable.
#Rounds to zero.
‡Reporting standards not met (too few cases).
[1]Scale ranges from 1 to 300 for all three grades, but scores cannot be compared across grades. For example, a score of 156 at grade 8 does not denote higher performance than a score of 153 at grade 12.
[2]Basic denotes partial mastery of the knowledge and skills that are fundamental for proficient work at a given grade.
[3]Proficient represents solid academic performance. Students reaching this level have demonstrated competency over challenging subject matter.
[4]Advanced signifies superior performance for a given grade.

NOTE: Includes public and private schools. Excludes persons unable to be tested due to limited proficiency in English or due to a disability (if the accommodations provided were not sufficient to enable the test to properly reflect the students' writing proficiency). In 2002, the NAEP national samples of 4th- and 8th-graders were obtained by aggregating the samples from each state, rather than by independently selecting national samples for grades 4 and 8. As a consequence, the size of the national samples increased for these grade levels, and smaller differences were found to be statistically significant than would have been detected in previous assessments. Grade 4 was not included in the 2007 survey. Race categories exclude persons of Hispanic ethnicity. Some data have been revised from previously published figures. Detail may not sum to totals because of rounding. Standard errors appear in parentheses.

SOURCE: U.S. Department of Education, National Center for Education Statistics, National Assessment of Educational Progress (NAEP), 2002 and 2007 Writing Assessments, retrieved May 6, 2008, from the NAEP Data Explorer (http://nces.ed.gov/nationsreportcard/nde/). (This table was prepared May 2008.)

Average arts scale score of 8th-graders, percentage distribution by frequency of instruction, and percentage participating in selected activities, by subject and selected student and school characteristics: 2008

| Selected student or school characteristic | Average score | | | Percentage distribution of students by school-reported frequency of instruction | | | | | | | | Percent of students reporting participation in musical activities in school | | |
	Music,[1] responding scale score (0 to 300)	Visual arts[2] Responding scale score (0 to 300)	Visual arts[2] Creating task score (0 to 100)	Music Subject not offered	Music Less than once a week	Music Once or twice a week	Music At least 3 or 4 times a week	Visual arts Subject not offered	Visual arts Less than once a week	Visual arts Once or twice a week	Visual arts At least 3 or 4 times a week	Play in band	Play in orchestra	Sing in chorus or choir
1	2	3	4	5	6	7	8	9	10	11	12	13	14	15
All students	150 (1.2)	150 (1.2)	52 (0.6)	8 (2.0)	8 (2.0)	27 (3.1)	57 (3.2)	14 (2.4)	10 (2.5)	30 (3.5)	47 (3.9)	16 (0.9)	5 (0.5)	17 (1.2)
Sex														
Male	145 (1.3)	145 (1.4)	49 (0.7)	9 (2.1)	8 (2.1)	27 (3.1)	56 (3.2)	14 (2.6)	10 (2.5)	30 (3.6)	46 (4.1)	18 (1.0)	3 (0.5)	9 (1.2)
Female	155 (1.4)	155 (1.2)	54 (0.7)	8 (2.0)	7 (1.9)	28 (3.2)	57 (3.2)	13 (2.3)	10 (2.5)	29 (3.3)	48 (3.8)	14 (1.0)	6 (0.6)	26 (1.8)
Race/ethnicity														
White	161 (1.3)	160 (1.2)	55 (0.5)	6 (2.5)	8 (2.5)	29 (4.0)	57 (3.6)	11 (2.6)	11 (3.4)	34 (4.4)	44 (4.6)	19 (1.2)	5 (0.6)	19 (1.6)
Black	130 (2.0)	129 (2.4)	43 (1.5)	10 (2.9)	8 (4.5)	26 (5.5)	56 (7.0)	18 (4.9)	10 (4.9)	24 (4.4)	49 (5.7)	13 (1.2)	4 (1.0)	21 (1.9)
Hispanic	129 (1.9)	134 (1.9)	46 (1.1)	14 (4.3)	6 (2.3)	21 (4.1)	59 (4.5)	17 (4.5)	5 (2.0)	23 (4.7)	56 (6.0)	8 (1.2)	3 (0.6)	10 (1.6)
Asian/Pacific Islander	159 (4.7)	156 (4.2)	54 (2.0)	7 (4.1)	8 (3.4)	25 (6.6)	60 (8.7)	5 (2.5)	11 (4.6)	29 (6.0)	54 (8.4)	21 (3.5)	6 (2.1)	16 (2.9)
Free or reduced-price lunch eligibility														
Eligible	132 (1.3)	132 (1.4)	46 (1.0)	10 (2.1)	6 (2.1)	26 (3.4)	58 (3.9)	18 (3.4)	9 (3.2)	26 (3.7)	47 (4.7)	12 (1.2)	3 (0.6)	15 (1.4)
Not eligible	161 (1.4)	161 (1.2)	55 (0.6)	8 (2.6)	8 (2.6)	26 (4.0)	59 (4.0)	10 (2.4)	10 (3.2)	30 (4.1)	50 (4.6)	19 (1.0)	5 (0.6)	19 (1.6)
Unknown	156 (5.6)	156 (5.9)	57 (2.6)	4 (†)	19 (8.7)	54 (11.5)	23 (10.5)	16 (10.3)	13 (8.4)	47 (13.6)	24 (10.6)	14 (6.3)	5 (2.3)	13 (2.0)
Control of school														
Public	149 (1.3)	149 (1.2)	51 (0.7)	8 (2.1)	7 (2.1)	24 (3.2)	61 (3.5)	13 (2.4)	10 (2.7)	26 (3.5)	51 (4.2)	17 (0.9)	5 (0.5)	18 (1.3)
Private	163 (2.8)	159 (5.2)	60 (1.3)	10 (6.0)	15 (6.9)	71 (8.8)	3 (†)	17 (8.2)	10 (6.1)	70 (10.2)	3 (0.9)	9 (1.9)	1 (0.4)	13 (2.1)
School location														
City	142 (2.0)	144 (2.1)	49 (1.2)	13 (4.0)	10 (3.8)	24 (5.7)	52 (5.6)	12 (2.6)	9 (3.5)	24 (4.9)	55 (5.4)	14 (1.0)	4 (0.6)	13 (1.3)
Suburban	155 (1.9)	155 (1.8)	54 (0.7)	3 (2.2)	7 (3.5)	32 (5.6)	57 (6.3)	10 (3.1)	10 (4.6)	33 (6.4)	46 (6.1)	14 (1.5)	6 (1.0)	16 (1.6)
Town	156 (3.5)	149 (2.8)	50 (1.2)	4 (1.0)	# (†)	18 (9.0)	78 (9.0)	16 (8.4)	# (†)	23 (9.2)	60 (10.5)	23 (3.0)	4 (1.3)	23 (3.4)
Rural	150 (2.6)	151 (3.0)	52 (1.5)	13 (5.0)	8 (4.8)	29 (5.7)	50 (7.7)	20 (7.3)	17 (6.8)	35 (7.8)	28 (6.7)	18 (2.5)	3 (1.0)	21 (3.4)
Region														
Northeast	154 (3.1)	160 (2.3)	52 (0.9)	10 (5.3)	13 (5.8)	40 (9.0)	37 (8.6)	5 (3.3)	5 (†)	50 (6.2)	39 (9.3)	16 (2.7)	6 (0.9)	17 (2.6)
Midwest	158 (2.9)	155 (2.3)	53 (1.3)	12 (6.6)	# (†)	25 (7.2)	63 (5.8)	9 (2.0)	15 (7.7)	26 (6.7)	50 (7.3)	22 (2.1)	6 (1.3)	24 (3.1)
South	147 (1.9)	147 (2.2)	51 (1.0)	6 (1.8)	10 (4.0)	25 (3.9)	59 (5.7)	19 (5.3)	9 (3.8)	26 (5.0)	46 (6.4)	16 (1.2)	4 (0.6)	16 (2.0)
West	144 (2.0)	143 (2.1)	51 (1.1)	8 (3.7)	8 (3.5)	24 (6.9)	60 (5.4)	15 (4.9)	9 (4.0)	25 (9.0)	51 (8.2)	9 (1.2)	3 (0.6)	12 (1.7)
Frequency of instruction														
Subject not offered	139 (6.3)	138 (4.2)	—	‡	‡	‡	‡	‡	‡	‡	‡	17 (4.0)	4 (1.5)	11 (2.1)
Less than once a week	149 (6.4)	154 (5.3)	—	‡	‡	‡	‡	‡	‡	‡	‡	11 (2.4)	4 (1.5)	10 (2.0)
Once or twice a week	152 (2.8)	154 (2.6)	—	‡	‡	‡	‡	‡	‡	‡	‡	12 (1.7)	3 (0.8)	17 (2.2)
At least 3 or 4 times a week	149 (1.8)	149 (1.8)	—	‡	‡	‡	‡	‡	‡	‡	‡	17 (1.4)	5 (0.7)	20 (1.6)

—Not available.
†Not applicable.
#Rounds to zero.
‡Reporting standards not met.
[1]Students were asked to analyze and describe aspects of music they heard, critique instrumental and vocal performances, and demonstrate their knowledge of standard musical notation and music's role in society.
[2]Responding questions asked students to analyze and describe works of art and design, while creating questions required students to create works of art and design of their own.

NOTE: Excludes students unable to be tested due to limited proficiency in English or due to a disability (if the accommodations provided were not sufficient to enable the test to properly reflect the students' music or visual arts proficiency). Detail may not sum to totals because of rounding. Race categories exclude persons of Hispanic ethnicity. Totals include other racial/ethnic groups not shown separately. Standard errors appear in parentheses.
SOURCE: U.S. Department of Education, National Center for Education Statistics, National Assessment of Educational Progress (NAEP), 2008 Arts Assessment, retrieved June 30, 2009, from the Main NAEP Data Explorer (http://nces.ed.gov/nationsreportcard/naepdata/). (This table was prepared June 2009.)

Average U.S. history scale score, standard deviation, and percentage of students attaining U.S. history achievement levels, by grade level, selected student characteristics, and percentile: Selected years, 1994 through 2010

Selected student characteristic	4th-graders				8th-graders				12th-graders			
	1994[1]	2001	2006	2010	1994[1]	2001	2006	2010	1994[1]	2001	2006	2010
1	2	3	4	5	6	7	8	9	10	11	12	13
Average U.S. history scale score[2]												
All students	205 (1.0)	208 (0.9)	211 (1.1)	214 (0.8)	259 (0.6)	260 (0.8)	263 (0.8)	266 (0.8)	286 (0.8)	287 (0.9)	290 (0.7)	288 (0.8)
Sex												
Male	203 (1.5)	207 (1.1)	211 (1.2)	215 (1.0)	259 (0.8)	261 (0.9)	264 (0.9)	268 (0.8)	288 (0.8)	288 (1.1)	292 (0.9)	290 (0.8)
Female	206 (1.1)	209 (1.2)	211 (1.1)	213 (0.9)	259 (0.7)	260 (0.9)	261 (0.8)	263 (0.8)	285 (0.9)	286 (0.9)	288 (0.8)	286 (1.0)
Race/ethnicity												
White	214 (1.3)	217 (1.3)	223 (1.1)	224 (1.1)	266 (0.8)	268 (0.9)	273 (0.6)	274 (0.7)	292 (0.8)	292 (1.0)	297 (0.8)	296 (0.7)
Black	176 (1.6)	186 (2.0)	191 (1.9)	198 (1.9)	238 (1.6)	240 (1.9)	244 (1.2)	250 (1.1)	265 (0.9)	267 (1.4)	270 (1.3)	268 (1.5)
Hispanic	175 (2.6)	184 (2.6)	194 (1.9)	198 (1.2)	243 (1.4)	248 (2.0)	248 (1.2)	252 (1.1)	267 (1.7)	271 (1.9)	275 (1.0)	275 (1.3)
Asian/Pacific Islander	204 (3.6)	216 (3.7)	214 (5.1)	221 (2.4)	261 (5.0)	264 (2.8)	270 (3.0)	275 (1.8)	283 (3.5)	294 (6.0)	296 (2.6)	293 (2.5)
American Indian/Alaska Native	‡ (†)	‡ (†)	190 (5.9)	193 (6.2)	245 (3.4)	255 (4.4)	244 (6.3)	259 (5.0)	272 (3.0)	283 (4.2)	278 (4.1)	278 (4.2)
Parents' highest level of education												
Did not finish high school	— (†)	— (†)	— (†)	— (†)	241 (1.3)	241 (2.8)	244 (1.2)	249 (0.9)	263 (1.4)	266 (1.6)	268 (1.3)	268 (1.7)
Graduated high school	— (†)	— (†)	— (†)	— (†)	251 (0.8)	251 (1.0)	252 (1.3)	255 (0.9)	276 (1.1)	274 (1.1)	278 (1.0)	277 (1.0)
Some education after high school	— (†)	— (†)	— (†)	— (†)	264 (0.8)	264 (1.0)	265 (0.9)	267 (0.9)	287 (1.2)	286 (0.8)	290 (0.8)	286 (0.8)
Graduated college	— (†)	— (†)	— (†)	— (†)	270 (0.8)	273 (0.9)	274 (0.8)	276 (0.8)	296 (0.9)	298 (1.2)	300 (0.8)	298 (0.8)
Eligibility for free or reduced-price lunch												
Eligible	— (†)	188 (1.4)	195 (1.1)	199 (0.9)	— (†)	242 (1.3)	247 (1.1)	253 (0.7)	— (†)	269 (1.4)	273 (1.0)	273 (1.0)
Not eligible	— (†)	219 (1.4)	224 (1.0)	227 (0.8)	— (†)	267 (1.1)	273 (0.7)	275 (0.8)	— (†)	289 (1.2)	295 (0.8)	294 (0.7)
Unknown	— (†)	217 (2.8)	227 (3.9)	225 (6.1)	— (†)	266 (2.0)	281 (2.7)	278 (2.0)	— (†)	294 (2.1)	300 (2.4)	300 (2.5)
Percentile[3]												
10th	147 (2.1)	157 (1.4)	165 (2.3)	169 (1.4)	216 (1.1)	216 (1.30)	221 (1.4)	227 (1.2)	243 (1.2)	244 (1.2)	249 (1.3)	246 (1.3)
25th	180 (1.5)	184 (1.4)	189 (1.3)	192 (1.6)	239 (0.9)	239 (0.9)	243 (0.9)	246 (0.9)	265 (1.2)	266 (1.1)	270 (1.0)	267 (1.3)
50th	210 (0.9)	211 (1.1)	213 (1.0)	216 (0.6)	261 (1.1)	262 (1.1)	265 (0.7)	267 (0.9)	288 (0.9)	288 (1.1)	291 (0.9)	290 (0.7)
75th	234 (1.2)	234 (1.0)	235 (1.1)	238 (0.9)	282 (1.0)	284 (1.0)	285 (0.7)	286 (0.7)	309 (1.0)	309 (1.0)	312 (0.7)	311 (0.6)
90th	253 (1.4)	254 (1.4)	254 (1.0)	256 (1.4)	299 (0.6)	302 (0.7)	302 (1.0)	302 (1.1)	326 (1.0)	326 (1.5)	329 (0.9)	328 (1.0)
Standard deviation of the U.S. history scale score[4]												
All students	41 (0.7)	38 (0.7)	34 (0.5)	34 (0.7)	32 (0.3)	33 (0.4)	32 (0.4)	29 (0.3)	32 (0.4)	32 (0.6)	31 (0.3)	32 (0.4)
Percent of students achieving U.S. history achievement levels												
Achievement level												
Below Basic	36 (1.1)	34 (1.2)	30 (1.3)	27 (0.8)	39 (0.9)	38 (1.0)	35 (1.0)	31 (1.0)	57 (1.1)	57 (1.2)	53 (1.1)	55 (1.0)
At or above Basic[5]	64 (1.1)	66 (1.2)	70 (1.3)	73 (0.8)	61 (0.9)	62 (1.0)	65 (1.0)	69 (1.0)	43 (1.1)	43 (1.2)	47 (1.1)	45 (1.0)
At or above Basic by race/ethnicity												
White	73 (1.3)	76 (1.5)	84 (1.2)	83 (1.0)	70 (1.1)	71 (1.1)	79 (0.8)	80 (0.9)	50 (1.1)	49 (1.3)	56 (1.3)	55 (1.2)
Black	35 (1.5)	41 (2.3)	46 (2.5)	54 (2.6)	32 (2.4)	35 (2.1)	40 (1.7)	48 (2.1)	17 (2.4)	19 (1.5)	20 (1.6)	20 (1.2)
Hispanic	36 (3.2)	40 (2.8)	49 (2.7)	56 (1.6)	41 (2.2)	36 (2.6)	46 (2.2)	52 (1.7)	22 (2.2)	24 (2.3)	27 (1.4)	28 (1.4)
Asian/Pacific Islander	62 (4.3)	74 (4.5)	71 (4.8)	82 (3.1)	60 (6.9)	65 (3.0)	75 (4.4)	78 (2.1)	40 (6.3)	51 (6.7)	54 (3.5)	50 (3.2)
American Indian/Alaska Native	‡ (†)	‡ (†)	41 (7.7)	49 (5.4)	42 (6.6)	57 (6.5)	43 (6.1)	61 (6.3)	21 (6.3)	37 (7.8)	32 (7.3)	29 (5.9)
At or above Proficient[6]	17 (1.0)	18 (0.9)	18 (1.0)	20 (0.7)	14 (0.6)	16 (0.7)	17 (0.8)	17 (0.8)	11 (0.7)	11 (0.9)	13 (0.7)	12 (0.5)
At Advanced[7]	2 (0.3)	2 (0.3)	2 (0.3)	2 (0.3)	1 (0.1)	1 (0.2)	1 (0.1)	1 (0.1)	1 (0.2)	1 (0.3)	1 (0.2)	1 (0.1)

—Not available.
†Not applicable.
‡Reporting standards not met (too few cases).
[1]Accommodations were not permitted for this assessment.
[2]Scale ranges from 0 to 500.
[3]The percentile represents a specific point on the percentage distribution of all students ranked by their U.S. history score from low to high. For example, 10 percent of students scored at or below the 10th percentile score, while 90 percent of students scored above it.
[4]The standard deviation provides an indication of how much the test scores varied. The lower the standard deviation, the closer the scores were clustered around the average score. About two-thirds of the student scores can be expected to fall within the range of one standard deviation above and one standard deviation below the average score. For example, the average score for all 4th-graders in 2010 was 214, and the standard deviation was 34. This means that we would expect about two-thirds of the students to have scores between 248 (one standard deviation above the average) and 180 (one standard deviation below). Stan-

dard errors also must be taken into account when making comparisons of these ranges. For a discussion of standard errors, see Appendix A: Guide to Sources.
[5]Basic denotes partial mastery of the knowledge and skills that are fundamental for proficient work.
[6]Proficient represents solid academic performance. Students reaching this level have demonstrated competency over challenging subject matter.
[7]Advanced signifies superior performance.
NOTE: For 2001 and later years, includes students tested with accommodations (3 to 13 percent of all students, depending on grade level and year); excludes only those students with disabilities and English language learners who were unable to be tested even with accommodations (2 to 3 percent of all students). Race categories exclude persons of Hispanic ethnicity. Standard errors appear in parentheses.
SOURCE: U.S. Department of Education, National Center for Education Statistics, National Assessment of Educational Progress (NAEP), 1994, 2001, 2006, and 2010 U.S. History Assessments, retrieved June 27, 2010, from the Main NAEP Data Explorer (http://nces.ed.gov/nationsreportcard/naepdata/). (This table was prepared June 2011.)

Average civics scale score and percentage of students attaining civics achievement levels, by grade level and selected student characteristics: 1998, 2006, and 2010

Selected student characteristic	Average scale score[1] 1998		2006		2010		At or above Basic[2] 1998		2010		At or above Proficient[3] 1998		2010		At Advanced[4] 1998		2010	
1	2		3		4		5		6		7		8		9		10	
4th-graders	150	(0.7)	154	(1.0)	157	(0.8)	69	(1.0)	77	(1.0)	23	(0.9)	27	(0.9)	2	(0.3)	2	(0.2)
Sex																		
Male	149	(1.0)	153	(1.1)	153	(1.0)	68	(1.2)	73	(1.3)	22	(1.2)	24	(1.0)	2	(0.4)	1	(0.3)
Female	151	(0.9)	155	(1.1)	160	(0.8)	70	(1.0)	81	(1.0)	23	(1.2)	30	(1.2)	1	(0.4)	2	(0.3)
Race/ethnicity																		
White	158	(0.9)	164	(0.9)	167	(0.8)	78	(1.3)	87	(0.9)	29	(1.2)	37	(1.3)	2	(0.4)	2	(0.3)
Black	130	(1.1)	140	(1.5)	143	(1.2)	45	(1.7)	62	(2.2)	7	(1.1)	12	(1.1)	1	(0.3)	#	(†)
Hispanic	123	(2.2)	138	(1.3)	140	(1.6)	40	(2.8)	58	(2.3)	6	(1.1)	10	(1.2)	#	(†)	#	(†)
Asian/Pacific Islander	147	(4.0)	154	(3.8)	164	(2.0)	66	(5.5)	82	(2.3)	20	(3.5)	37	(4.4)	2	(0.9)	3	(1.4)
American Indian/Alaska Native	‡	(†)	124	(7.6)	143	(7.0)	‡	(†)	63	(10.9)	‡	(†)	12	(7.4)	‡	(†)	#	(†)
Free or reduced-price lunch eligibility																		
Eligible	132	(0.9)	139	(1.1)	143	(0.9)	49	(1.3)	62	(1.3)	9	(0.9)	11	(0.9)	#	(†)	#	(†)
Not eligible	160	(1.1)	166	(0.8)	169	(0.8)	80	(1.4)	90	(0.9)	30	(1.3)	40	(1.4)	2	(0.5)	3	(0.4)
Unknown	154	(2.2)	167	(2.1)	171	(2.7)	72	(3.1)	89	(2.9)	27	(2.5)	44	(3.4)	2	(0.9)	5	(1.4)
8th-graders	150	(0.7)	150	(0.8)	151	(0.8)	70	(0.9)	72	(1.0)	22	(0.8)	22	(0.8)	2	(0.2)	1	(0.1)
Sex																		
Male	148	(0.9)	149	(1.0)	150	(0.9)	67	(1.1)	70	(1.1)	22	(1.0)	22	(0.9)	2	(0.3)	1	(0.2)
Female	152	(0.8)	151	(0.8)	152	(0.8)	73	(1.2)	74	(1.1)	22	(1.1)	22	(0.9)	1	(0.3)	1	(0.2)
Race/ethnicity																		
White	158	(0.9)	161	(0.8)	160	(0.8)	78	(1.1)	82	(1.0)	28	(1.0)	29	(1.0)	2	(0.3)	2	(0.2)
Black	131	(1.2)	133	(1.5)	135	(1.6)	49	(1.7)	53	(2.3)	7	(1.0)	9	(1.1)	#	(†)	#	(†)
Hispanic	127	(1.3)	131	(1.1)	137	(1.1)	44	(2.3)	56	(1.4)	7	(1.0)	11	(0.9)	#	(†)	#	(†)
Asian/Pacific Islander	151	(8.9)	154	(3.2)	158	(2.5)	69	(9.5)	78	(2.5)	25	(5.8)	30	(3.1)	3	(1.3)	2	(0.8)
American Indian/Alaska Native	‡	(†)	127	(7.3)	136	(12.6)	‡	(†)	56	(18.0)	‡	(†)	11	(6.0)	‡	(†)	1	(†)
Parents' highest level of education[5]																		
Did not finish high school	123	(3.2)	129	(1.6)	134	(1.3)	40	(3.8)	52	(2.1)	4	(1.2)	6	(1.2)	#	(†)	#	(†)
Graduated high school	144	(1.2)	140	(1.3)	139	(1.1)	65	(2.0)	60	(1.8)	14	(1.4)	10	(0.7)	#	(†)	#	(†)
Some education after high school	143	(1.0)	153	(1.0)	155	(1.1)	64	(1.5)	78	(1.5)	15	(1.2)	22	(1.3)	1	(0.2)	1	(0.4)
Graduated college	160	(0.8)	162	(0.9)	162	(0.8)	80	(1.0)	83	(1.0)	32	(1.2)	32	(1.2)	3	(0.4)	2	(0.3)
Free or reduced-price lunch eligibility																		
Eligible	131	(1.1)	132	(1.0)	136	(0.9)	48	(1.6)	54	(1.4)	8	(0.8)	9	(0.6)	#	(0.2)	#	(†)
Not eligible	157	(1.0)	160	(0.8)	163	(0.7)	78	(1.2)	85	(0.8)	27	(1.2)	31	(1.0)	2	(0.3)	2	(0.3)
Unknown	156	(2.2)	171	(2.4)	166	(2.3)	76	(2.7)	88	(2.5)	29	(2.1)	35	(3.5)	3	(0.6)	3	(0.9)
12th-graders	150	(0.8)	151	(0.9)	148	(0.8)	65	(0.9)	64	(1.0)	26	(0.9)	24	(0.9)	4	(0.4)	4	(0.3)
Sex																		
Male	148	(1.1)	150	(1.1)	148	(0.9)	62	(1.2)	63	(1.0)	27	(1.2)	25	(0.9)	5	(0.6)	5	(0.5)
Female	152	(0.8)	152	(1.0)	148	(0.9)	68	(1.2)	64	(1.3)	26	(1.1)	22	(1.1)	3	(0.4)	3	(0.4)
Race/ethnicity																		
White	157	(1.0)	158	(1.0)	156	(0.9)	73	(1.1)	73	(1.0)	32	(1.3)	30	(1.1)	5	(0.6)	5	(0.4)
Black	130	(1.6)	131	(1.4)	127	(1.6)	41	(2.0)	38	(1.9)	9	(1.3)	8	(0.9)	1	(0.3)	1	(0.2)
Hispanic	132	(1.1)	134	(1.1)	137	(1.4)	45	(1.9)	50	(1.8)	10	(1.2)	13	(1.4)	1	(0.3)	2	(0.4)
Asian/Pacific Islander	149	(5.2)	155	(3.1)	153	(2.6)	63	(4.8)	70	(3.1)	27	(6.6)	29	(2.8)	5	(2.3)	5	(1.4)
American Indian/Alaska Native	‡	(†)	131	(3.5)	134	(14.6)	‡	(†)	47	(17.3)	‡	(†)	16	(9.0)	‡	(†)	1	(†)
Parents' highest level of education[5]																		
Did not finish high school	124	(2.1)	126	(1.8)	128	(1.4)	38	(2.6)	40	(2.3)	6	(1.6)	8	(1.2)	#	(†)	#	(†)
Graduated high school	140	(1.2)	138	(1.0)	137	(1.2)	54	(1.8)	51	(1.7)	14	(1.4)	13	(1.1)	#	(†)	1	(0.4)
Some education after high school	145	(1.1)	150	(0.9)	147	(1.1)	60	(1.3)	63	(1.5)	20	(1.4)	20	(1.4)	2	(0.4)	3	(0.6)
Graduated college	160	(0.9)	162	(1.1)	158	(0.9)	75	(1.0)	75	(1.0)	36	(1.3)	33	(1.2)	7	(0.8)	6	(0.5)
Free or reduced-price lunch eligibility																		
Eligible	130	(1.4)	133	(1.0)	132	(1.0)	42	(2.1)	44	(1.4)	10	(1.7)	11	(0.8)	1	(0.4)	1	(0.2)
Not eligible	153	(1.0)	156	(1.0)	155	(0.9)	69	(1.1)	72	(1.0)	29	(1.3)	29	(1.2)	5	(0.5)	5	(0.4)
Unknown	153	(1.3)	160	(2.4)	159	(3.3)	68	(1.6)	75	(3.3)	29	(1.5)	35	(3.7)	5	(0.7)	7	(1.6)

#Rounds to zero.
†Not applicable.
‡Reporting standards not met (too few cases).
[1]Scale ranges from 0 to 300 for all three grades, but scores cannot be compared across grades. For example, the average score of 167 for White 4th-graders in 2010 does not denote higher performance than the score of 160 for White 8th-graders.
[2]*Basic* denotes partial mastery of the knowledge and skills that are fundamental for proficient work at a given grade.
[3]*Proficient* represents solid academic performance. Students reaching this level have demonstrated competency over challenging subject matter.
[4]*Advanced* signifies superior performance for a given grade.

[5]These data are based on students' responses to questions about their parents' education level. Because the wording of the questions was different in 1998 than in the later assesssment years, data from 1998 are not directly comparable to data from 2006 and 2010.
NOTE: Includes students tested with accommodations (1 to 13 percent of all students, depending on grade level and year); excludes only those students with disabilities and English language learners who were unable to be tested even with accommodations (1 to 5 percent of all students). Race categories exclude persons of Hispanic ethnicity. Standard errors appear in parentheses.
SOURCE: U.S. Department of Education, National Center for Education Statistics, National Assessment of Educational Progress (NAEP), 1998, 2006, and 2010 Civics Assessments, retrieved May 25, 2011, from the Main NAEP Data Explorer (http://nces.ed.gov/nations reportcard/naepdata/). (This table was prepared May 2011.)

Average economics scale score of 12th-graders, percentage attaining economics achievement levels, and percentage with different levels of economics coursework, by selected student and school characteristics: 2006

Selected student or school characteristic	Average scale score[1]	Percent of students attaining achievement levels				Percentage distribution of students by highest level of economics coursework taken				
		Below Basic	At or above Basic[2]	At or above Proficient[3]	At Advanced[4]	No economics courses	Combined course	Consumer economics/business	General economics	Advanced economics[5]
1	2	3	4	5	6	7	8	9	10	11
All students	150 (0.9)	21 (0.8)	79 (0.8)	42 (1.1)	3 (0.3)	13 (0.9)	12 (0.7)	11 (0.7)	49 (1.4)	16 (0.7)
Sex										
Male	152 (1.0)	21 (0.8)	79 (0.8)	45 (1.3)	4 (0.5)	13 (1.0)	10 (0.6)	10 (0.7)	50 (1.4)	16 (0.8)
Female	148 (0.9)	21 (0.9)	79 (0.9)	38 (1.3)	2 (0.3)	12 (0.9)	13 (0.9)	11 (0.8)	48 (1.6)	15 (0.8)
Race/ethnicity										
White	158 (0.8)	13 (0.7)	87 (0.7)	51 (1.2)	4 (0.4)	15 (1.1)	12 (0.8)	11 (0.8)	49 (1.6)	13 (0.9)
Black	127 (1.2)	43 (1.9)	57 (1.9)	16 (1.3)	# (†)	8 (0.8)	11 (0.9)	11 (1.2)	49 (1.7)	21 (1.1)
Hispanic	133 (1.2)	36 (1.6)	64 (1.6)	21 (1.2)	# (†)	8 (1.7)	13 (1.1)	7 (0.9)	55 (2.6)	18 (1.2)
Asian/Pacific Islander	153 (3.5)	20 (4.0)	80 (4.0)	44 (4.5)	4 (1.4)	13 (1.8)	10 (1.8)	10 (1.4)	45 (4.1)	22 (1.9)
American Indian/Alaska Native	137 (4.1)	28 (5.6)	72 (5.6)	26 (4.8)	2 (—)	11 (3.9)	18 (2.7)	17 (3.2)	41 (4.9)	13 (3.1)
Parents' highest level of education										
Not high school graduate	129 (1.4)	41 (2.1)	59 (2.1)	17 (1.7)	# (†)	10 (1.7)	13 (1.4)	10 (1.4)	53 (3.2)	14 (1.3)
Graduated high school	138 (1.2)	31 (1.5)	69 (1.5)	27 (1.4)	1 (0.3)	11 (1.2)	12 (1.0)	12 (1.0)	52 (1.7)	13 (0.9)
Some college	150 (0.8)	18 (1.1)	82 (1.1)	39 (1.4)	1 (0.4)	11 (1.0)	13 (0.9)	12 (1.0)	51 (1.9)	14 (1.0)
Graduated college	160 (0.9)	13 (0.8)	87 (0.8)	54 (1.3)	5 (0.6)	14 (1.0)	11 (0.8)	10 (0.7)	47 (1.5)	17 (1.0)
Free or reduced-price lunch eligibility										
Eligible	132 (0.9)	38 (1.1)	62 (1.1)	20 (1.1)	1 (0.2)	9 (0.7)	13 (1.1)	10 (0.9)	50 (1.6)	18 (0.8)
Not eligible	155 (0.9)	16 (0.8)	84 (0.8)	48 (1.2)	4 (0.4)	13 (1.1)	12 (0.8)	12 (0.9)	48 (1.6)	16 (0.9)
Not available	157 (1.9)	14 (1.7)	86 (1.7)	50 (2.8)	4 (1.1)	16 (3.0)	12 (1.6)	7 (1.1)	54 (3.1)	11 (1.4)
School location										
Central city	148 (1.4)	24 (1.3)	76 (1.3)	39 (1.8)	3 (0.7)	10 (1.3)	12 (1.2)	9 (1.0)	51 (2.7)	18 (1.3)
Urban fringe	152 (1.2)	20 (1.1)	80 (1.1)	44 (1.6)	3 (0.5)	14 (1.5)	12 (0.9)	11 (0.9)	47 (1.8)	17 (1.2)
Rural	149 (1.3)	20 (1.5)	80 (1.5)	40 (1.7)	2 (0.4)	12 (1.9)	12 (1.3)	13 (1.3)	51 (2.6)	12 (1.2)
Region										
Northeast	153 (2.0)	19 (1.7)	81 (1.7)	46 (2.6)	4 (0.9)	26 (2.6)	7 (1.1)	11 (1.3)	43 (3.2)	13 (1.4)
Midwest	153 (1.5)	17 (1.4)	83 (1.4)	45 (2.0)	3 (0.6)	12 (2.2)	12 (1.6)	15 (1.5)	51 (2.6)	10 (1.0)
South	147 (1.4)	23 (1.4)	77 (1.4)	37 (1.7)	2 (0.5)	6 (1.1)	14 (1.2)	9 (1.3)	49 (2.0)	22 (1.5)
West	‡ (†)	‡ (†)	‡ (†)	‡ (†)	‡ (†)	‡ (†)	‡ (†)	‡ (†)	‡ (†)	‡ (†)

—Not available.
†Not applicable.
#Rounds to zero.
‡Reporting standards not met. Item response rates fell below the required standards for reporting.
[1]Scale ranges from 0 to 300.
[2]Basic denotes partial mastery of the knowledge and skills that are fundamental for proficient work at a given grade.
[3]Proficient represents solid academic performance. Students reaching this level have demonstrated competency over challenging subject matter.
[4]Advanced signifies superior performance for a given grade.

[5]Advanced economics includes Advanced Placement, International Baccalaureate, and honors courses.
NOTE: Includes public and private schools. Excludes persons unable to be tested due to limited proficiency in English or due to a disability (if the accommodations provided were not sufficient to enable the test to properly reflect the students' economics proficiency). Detail may not sum to totals due to rounding. Race categories exclude persons of Hispanic ethnicity. Totals include other racial/ethnic groups not shown separately. Standard errors appear in parentheses.
SOURCE: U.S. Department of Education, National Center for Education Statistics, National Assessment of Educational Progress (NAEP), 2006 Economics Assessment, retrieved August 23, 2007, from the NAEP Data Explorer (http://nces.ed.gov/nationsreportcard/nde/). (This table was prepared August 2007.)

Average geography scale score, standard deviation, and percentage of students attaining geography achievement levels, by grade level, selected student characteristics, and percentile: 1994, 2001, and 2010

Selected student characteristic	4th-graders						8th-graders						12th-graders					
	1994[1]		2001		2010		1994[1]		2001		2010		1994[1]		2001		2010	
1	2		3		4		5		6		7		8		9		10	
	Average geography scale score[2]																	
All students	206	(1.2)	208	(0.9)	213	(0.8)	260	(0.7)	260	(1.0)	261	(0.7)	285	(0.7)	284	(0.8)	282	(0.6)
Sex																		
Male	208	(1.4)	210	(1.0)	215	(0.9)	262	(0.9)	262	(1.2)	263	(0.8)	288	(0.8)	287	(1.0)	285	(0.6)
Female	203	(1.4)	206	(1.3)	211	(0.9)	258	(0.8)	258	(1.0)	259	(0.8)	281	(0.9)	281	(0.8)	280	(0.8)
Race/ethnicity																		
White	218	(1.5)	219	(1.1)	224	(0.9)	269	(0.8)	269	(1.4)	272	(0.6)	290	(0.8)	291	(0.8)	290	(0.5)
Black	166	(2.4)	180	(1.8)	192	(1.3)	229	(1.7)	233	(1.6)	241	(1.1)	258	(1.4)	258	(1.5)	261	(1.2)
Hispanic	177	(3.3)	185	(2.5)	197	(1.2)	238	(2.0)	237	(2.0)	244	(1.0)	269	(1.7)	268	(1.6)	270	(1.2)
Asian/Pacific Islander	211	(4.0)	214	(3.5)	224	(3.3)	262	(5.3)	264	(2.7)	268	(2.7)	283	(3.1)	284	(5.0)	285	(1.7)
American Indian/Alaska Native	‡	(†)	‡	(†)	201	(3.5)	251	(5.5)	261	(5.3)	250	(3.9)	‡	(†)	‡	(†)	277	(2.5)
Parents' highest level of education																		
Did not finish high school	—	(†)	—	(†)	—	(†)	238	(1.7)	236	(1.8)	243	(1.3)	263	(1.2)	266	(1.7)	263	(1.2)
Graduated high school	—	(†)	—	(†)	—	(†)	250	(1.2)	251	(1.2)	251	(1.1)	274	(1.1)	275	(0.9)	274	(0.8)
Some education after high school	—	(†)	—	(†)	—	(†)	265	(1.0)	264	(1.1)	262	(1.0)	286	(1.0)	284	(0.9)	280	(0.7)
Graduated college	—	(†)	—	(†)	—	(†)	272	(1.0)	273	(1.0)	272	(0.7)	294	(0.9)	293	(1.0)	291	(0.7)
Eligibility for free or reduced-price lunch																		
Eligible	—	(†)	185	(1.4)	197	(0.7)	—	(†)	239	(1.3)	246	(0.9)	—	(†)	268	(1.7)	269	(0.8)
Not eligible	—	(†)	221	(1.1)	227	(0.8)	—	(†)	269	(1.2)	272	(0.7)	—	(†)	287	(1.0)	288	(0.5)
Unknown	—	(†)	219	(2.8)	227	(3.7)	—	(†)	265	(2.3)	276	(2.6)	—	(†)	288	(1.6)	289	(2.2)
Percentile[3]																		
10th	146	(1.9)	159	(2.6)	169	(1.8)	213	(1.3)	213	(1.2)	220	(1.2)	244	(0.9)	246	(1.1)	247	(0.8)
25th	179	(1.5)	184	(1.4)	192	(1.2)	237	(1.0)	238	(1.3)	241	(0.7)	265	(1.1)	266	(1.2)	265	(0.8)
50th	211	(1.1)	211	(1.0)	216	(1.1)	263	(1.1)	264	(1.2)	263	(0.9)	287	(0.9)	286	(0.9)	284	(0.7)
75th	237	(1.3)	235	(1.4)	236	(0.7)	285	(0.9)	285	(1.1)	284	(0.9)	306	(1.0)	304	(0.9)	301	(0.7)
90th	257	(2.0)	254	(1.3)	253	(0.9)	302	(1.9)	302	(1.1)	300	(0.7)	321	(1.0)	319	(1.3)	315	(0.7)
	Standard deviation of the geography scale score[4]																	
All students	44	(0.8)	37	(0.8)	33	(0.4)	35	(0.4)	35	(0.5)	31	(0.3)	30	(0.4)	28	(0.4)	26	(0.3)
	Percent of students achieving geography achievement levels																	
Achievement level																		
Below *Basic*	30	(1.1)	27	(1.0)	21	(0.9)	29	(1.0)	28	(1.2)	26	(0.9)	30	(0.9)	29	(1.0)	30	(0.9)
At or above *Basic*[5]	70	(1.1)	73	(1.0)	79	(0.9)	71	(1.0)	72	(1.2)	74	(0.9)	70	(0.9)	71	(1.0)	70	(0.9)
At or above *Basic* by sex																		
Male	71	(1.3)	74	(0.9)	80	(1.0)	72	(1.3)	73	(1.5)	75	(1.0)	73	(1.1)	74	(1.3)	73	(1.0)
Female	68	(1.4)	71	(1.5)	78	(1.1)	69	(1.1)	71	(1.1)	73	(1.1)	67	(1.2)	68	(1.2)	66	(1.2)
At or above *Basic* by race/ethnicity																		
White	81	(1.3)	84	(1.1)	89	(1.0)	81	(0.9)	82	(1.5)	86	(0.7)	78	(0.9)	81	(0.9)	81	(0.8)
Black	33	(2.4)	43	(2.5)	57	(2.1)	34	(3.0)	39	(2.4)	49	(1.7)	33	(2.3)	33	(2.0)	36	(1.8)
Hispanic	44	(3.1)	50	(3.1)	64	(1.7)	49	(3.8)	45	(2.5)	55	(1.5)	48	(3.0)	48	(2.9)	52	(2.0)
Asian/Pacific Islander	72	(4.4)	77	(4.2)	87	(3.2)	72	(6.7)	77	(3.6)	80	(3.3)	67	(3.8)	70	(6.2)	73	(2.7)
American Indian/Alaska Native	‡	(†)	‡	(†)	68	(6.4)	62	(7.7)	74	(4.8)	62	(7.2)	‡	(†)	‡	(†)	62	(5.1)
At or above *Proficient*[6]	22	(1.2)	20	(0.9)	21	(0.8)	28	(1.0)	29	(1.3)	27	(0.8)	27	(1.2)	24	(1.2)	20	(0.8)
At *Advanced*[7]	3	(0.4)	2	(0.3)	2	(0.2)	4	(0.4)	4	(0.5)	3	(0.2)	2	(0.5)	1	(0.3)	1	(0.1)

—Not available.
†Not applicable.
‡Reporting standards not met (too few cases).
[1]Accommodations were not permitted for this assessment.
[2]Scale ranges from 0 to 500.
[3]The percentile represents a specific point on the percentage distribution of all students ranked by their geography score from low to high. For example, 10 percent of students scored at or below the 10th percentile score, while 90 percent of students scored above it.
[4]The standard deviation provides an indication of how much the test scores varied. The lower the standard deviation, the closer the scores were clustered around the average score. About two-thirds of the student scores can be expected to fall within the range of one standard deviation above and one standard deviation below the average score. For example, the average score for all 4th-graders in 2010 was 213, and the standard deviation was 33. This means that we would expect about two-thirds of the students to have scores between 246 (one standard deviation above the average) and 180 (one standard deviation below). Standard errors also must be taken into account when making comparisons of these ranges. For a discussion of standard errors, see Appendix A: Guide to Sources.
[5]*Basic* denotes partial mastery of the knowledge and skills that are fundamental for proficient work.
[6]*Proficient* represents solid academic performance. Students reaching this level have demonstrated competency over challenging subject matter.
[7]*Advanced* signifies superior performance.
NOTE: For 2001 and later years, includes students tested with accommodations (3 to 13 percent of all students, depending on grade level and year); excludes only those students with disabilities and English language learners who were unable to be tested even with accommodations (1 to 4 percent of all students). Race categories exclude persons of Hispanic ethnicity. Detail may not sum to totals because of rounding. Standard errors appear in parentheses.
SOURCE: U.S. Department of Education, National Center for Education Statistics, National Assessment of Educational Progress (NAEP), 1994, 2001, and 2010 Geography Assessments, retrieved July 22, 2011, from the Main NAEP Data Explorer (http://nces.ed.gov/nationsreportcard/naepdata/). (This table was prepared July 2011.)

Average mathematics scale score, by age and selected student and school characteristics: Selected years, 1973 through 2008

Selected student and school characteristic	1973		1978		1982		1986		1990		1992		1994		1996		1999		2004		2008	
1	2		3		4		5		6		7		8		9		10		11		12	
9-year-olds																						
All students	219	(0.8)	219	(0.8)	219	(1.1)	222	(1.0)	230	(0.8)	230	(0.8)	231	(0.8)	231	(0.8)	232	(0.8)	239	(0.9)	243	(0.8)
Sex																						
Male	218	(0.7)	217	(0.7)	217	(1.2)	222	(1.1)	229	(0.9)	231	(1.0)	232	(1.0)	233	(1.2)	233	(1.0)	239	(1.0)	242	(0.9)
Female	220	(1.1)	220	(1.0)	221	(1.2)	222	(1.2)	230	(1.1)	228	(1.0)	230	(0.9)	229	(0.7)	231	(0.9)	240	(1.0)	243	(1.0)
Race/ethnicity																						
White	225	(1.0)	224	(0.9)	224	(1.1)	227	(1.1)	235	(0.8)	235	(0.8)	237	(1.0)	237	(1.0)	239	(0.9)	245	(0.8)	250	(0.8)
Black	190	(1.8)	192	(1.1)	195	(1.6)	202	(1.6)	208	(2.2)	208	(2.0)	212	(1.6)	212	(1.4)	211	(1.6)	221	(2.1)	224	(1.9)
Hispanic	202	(2.4)	203	(2.2)	204	(1.3)	205	(2.1)	214	(2.1)	212	(2.3)	210	(2.3)	215	(1.7)	213	(1.9)	229	(2.0)	234	(1.2)
Region																						
Northeast	227	(1.9)	227	(1.9)	226	(1.8)	226	(2.7)	236	(2.1)	235	(1.9)	238	(2.2)	236	(2.0)	242	(1.7)	243	(2.5)	248	(1.5)
Southeast	208	(1.3)	209	(1.2)	210	(2.5)	218	(2.5)	224	(2.4)	221	(1.7)	229	(1.4)	227	(2.0)	226	(2.6)	236	(1.7)	237	(1.9)
Central	224	(1.5)	224	(1.5)	221	(2.7)	226	(2.3)	231	(1.3)	234	(1.6)	233	(1.8)	233	(2.3)	233	(1.4)	240	(1.9)	244	(1.2)
West	216	(2.2)	213	(1.3)	219	(1.8)	217	(2.4)	228	(1.8)	229	(2.3)	226	(1.6)	229	(1.3)	228	(1.7)	239	(1.7)	243	(1.1)
13-year-olds																						
All students	266	(1.1)	264	(1.1)	269	(1.1)	269	(1.2)	270	(0.9)	273	(0.9)	274	(1.0)	274	(0.8)	276	(0.8)	279	(1.0)	281	(0.9)
Sex																						
Male	265	(1.3)	264	(1.3)	269	(1.4)	270	(1.1)	271	(1.2)	274	(1.1)	276	(1.3)	276	(0.9)	277	(0.9)	279	(1.0)	284	(1.0)
Female	267	(1.1)	265	(1.1)	268	(1.1)	268	(1.5)	270	(0.9)	272	(1.0)	273	(1.0)	272	(1.0)	274	(1.1)	278	(1.2)	279	(1.0)
Race/ethnicity																						
White	274	(0.9)	272	(0.8)	274	(1.0)	274	(1.3)	276	(1.1)	279	(0.9)	281	(0.9)	281	(0.9)	283	(0.8)	287	(0.9)	290	(1.2)
Black	228	(1.9)	230	(1.9)	240	(1.6)	249	(2.3)	249	(2.3)	250	(1.9)	252	(3.5)	252	(1.3)	251	(2.6)	257	(1.8)	262	(1.2)
Hispanic	239	(2.2)	238	(2.0)	252	(1.7)	254	(2.9)	255	(1.8)	259	(1.8)	256	(1.9)	256	(1.6)	259	(1.7)	264	(1.5)	268	(1.2)
Parents' highest level of education																						
Did not finish high school	—	(†)	245	(1.2)	251	(1.4)	252	(2.3)	253	(1.8)	256	(1.0)	255	(2.1)	254	(2.4)	256	(2.8)	263	(1.9)	268	(1.3)
Graduated high school	—	(†)	263	(1.0)	263	(0.8)	263	(1.2)	263	(1.2)	263	(1.2)	266	(1.1)	267	(1.1)	264	(1.1)	270	(1.3)	272	(1.1)
Some education after high school	—	(†)	273	(1.2)	275	(0.9)	274	(0.8)	277	(1.0)	278	(1.0)	277	(1.6)	277	(1.4)	279	(0.9)	282	(1.4)	285	(1.1)
Graduated college	—	(†)	284	(1.2)	282	(1.5)	280	(1.4)	280	(1.0)	283	(1.0)	285	(1.2)	283	(1.2)	286	(1.0)	289	(1.1)	291	(1.0)
Region																						
Northeast	275	(2.4)	273	(2.4)	277	(2.0)	277	(2.2)	275	(2.3)	274	(2.2)	284	(1.5)	275	(2.1)	279	(2.7)	282	(2.5)	285	(1.6)
Southeast	255	(3.2)	253	(3.3)	258	(2.2)	263	(1.4)	266	(1.9)	271	(2.5)	269	(2.0)	270	(1.8)	270	(2.3)	276	(2.4)	277	(1.8)
Central	271	(1.8)	269	(1.8)	273	(2.1)	266	(4.5)	272	(2.4)	275	(1.5)	275	(3.4)	280	(1.3)	278	(1.8)	281	(1.7)	284	(2.2)
West	262	(1.9)	260	(1.9)	266	(2.4)	270	(2.1)	269	(1.6)	272	(1.4)	272	(1.7)	273	(1.9)	276	(1.4)	278	(1.5)	281	(1.3)
17-year-olds																						
All students	304	(1.1)	300	(1.0)	298	(0.9)	302	(0.9)	305	(0.9)	307	(0.9)	306	(1.0)	307	(1.2)	308	(1.0)	305	(0.7)	306	(0.6)
Sex																						
Male	309	(1.2)	304	(1.0)	301	(1.0)	305	(1.2)	306	(1.1)	309	(1.1)	309	(1.4)	310	(1.3)	310	(1.4)	307	(0.9)	309	(0.7)
Female	301	(1.1)	297	(1.0)	296	(1.0)	299	(1.0)	303	(1.1)	305	(1.1)	304	(1.1)	305	(1.4)	307	(1.0)	304	(0.8)	303	(0.8)
Race/ethnicity																						
White	310	(1.1)	306	(0.9)	304	(0.9)	308	(1.0)	309	(1.0)	312	(0.8)	312	(1.1)	313	(1.4)	315	(1.1)	311	(0.7)	314	(0.7)
Black	270	(1.3)	268	(1.3)	272	(1.2)	279	(2.1)	289	(2.8)	286	(2.2)	286	(1.8)	286	(1.7)	283	(1.5)	284	(1.4)	287	(1.2)
Hispanic	277	(2.2)	276	(2.3)	277	(1.8)	283	(2.9)	284	(2.9)	292	(2.6)	291	(3.7)	292	(2.1)	293	(2.5)	292	(1.2)	293	(1.1)
Parents' highest level of education																						
Did not finish high school	—	(†)	280	(1.2)	279	(1.0)	279	(2.3)	285	(2.2)	285	(2.3)	284	(2.4)	281	(2.4)	289	(1.8)	287	(1.2)	292	(1.3)
Graduated high school	—	(†)	294	(0.8)	293	(0.8)	293	(1.0)	294	(0.9)	298	(1.7)	295	(1.1)	297	(2.4)	299	(1.6)	294	(0.9)	296	(1.2)
Some education after high school	—	(†)	305	(0.9)	304	(0.9)	305	(1.2)	308	(1.0)	308	(1.1)	305	(1.3)	307	(1.5)	308	(1.6)	305	(0.9)	306	(0.8)
Graduated college	—	(†)	317	(1.0)	312	(1.0)	314	(1.4)	316	(1.3)	316	(1.0)	318	(1.4)	317	(1.3)	317	(1.2)	315	(0.9)	316	(0.7)
Region																						
Northeast	312	(1.8)	307	(1.8)	304	(2.0)	307	(1.9)	304	(2.1)	311	(2.0)	313	(2.9)	309	(3.0)	313	(2.4)	306	(1.6)	308	(1.4)
Southeast	296	(1.8)	292	(1.7)	292	(2.1)	297	(1.4)	301	(2.3)	301	(1.9)	301	(1.6)	303	(2.1)	300	(1.4)	300	(1.2)	303	(1.5)
Central	306	(1.8)	305	(1.9)	302	(1.4)	304	(1.9)	311	(2.1)	312	(2.0)	307	(2.2)	314	(2.0)	310	(2.0)	310	(1.3)	309	(1.6)
West	303	(2.0)	295	(1.8)	294	(1.9)	299	(2.7)	302	(1.5)	303	(2.3)	305	(2.4)	304	(2.3)	310	(2.0)	305	(1.6)	305	(1.1)

—Not available.
†Not applicable.
NOTE: Scale ranges from 0 to 500. Students scoring 150 (or higher) know some basic addition and subtraction facts. Students scoring 200 have considerable understanding of two-digit numbers and know some basic multiplication and division facts. Students scoring 250 have an initial understanding of the four basic operations and are developing an ability to analyze simple logical relations. Students scoring 300 can perform reasoning and problem solving involving fractions, decimals, percents, elementary geometry, and simple algebra. Students scoring 350 can perform reasoning and problem solving involving geometry, algebra, and beginning statistics and probability. Includes public and private schools. Excludes persons not enrolled in school and students who were unable to be tested due to limited proficiency in English or due to a disability. Beginning in 2004, data are for a revised assessment format that provides accommodations for students with disabilities and English language learners. Race categories exclude persons of Hispanic ethnicity. Totals include other racial/ethnic groups not shown separately. Some data have been revised from previously published figures. Standard errors appear in parentheses.
SOURCE: U.S. Department of Education, National Center for Education Statistics, National Assessment of Educational Progress (NAEP), *NAEP 2004 Trends in Academic Progress*; and 2008 NAEP Long-Term Trend Mathematics Assessment, retrieved May 4, 2009, from the Long-Term Trend NAEP Data Explorer (http://nces.ed.gov/nationsreportcard/naepdata/). (This table was prepared May 2009.)

Percentage of students at or above selected mathematics proficiency levels, by age, sex, and race/ethnicity: Selected years, 1978 through 2008

Selected characteristic	9-year-olds			13-year-olds			17-year-olds		
	Simple arithmetic facts[1]	Beginning skills and understanding[2]	Numerical operations and beginning problem solving[3]	Beginning skills and understanding[2]	Numerical operations and beginning problem solving[3]	Moderately complex procedures and reasoning[4]	Numerical operations and beginning problem solving[3]	Moderately complex procedures and reasoning[4]	Multistep problem solving and algebra[5]
1	2	3	4	5	6	7	8	9	10
Total									
1978	96.7 (0.25)	70.4 (0.92)	19.6 (0.73)	94.6 (0.46)	64.9 (1.18)	18.0 (0.73)	92.0 (0.50)	51.5 (1.14)	7.3 (0.44)
1982	97.1 (0.35)	71.4 (1.18)	18.8 (0.96)	97.7 (0.37)	71.4 (1.18)	17.4 (0.95)	93.0 (0.50)	48.5 (1.28)	5.5 (0.43)
1986	97.9 (0.29)	74.1 (1.24)	20.7 (0.88)	98.6 (0.25)	73.3 (1.59)	15.8 (1.01)	95.6 (0.48)	51.7 (1.43)	6.5 (0.52)
1990	99.1 (0.21)	81.5 (0.96)	27.7 (0.86)	98.5 (0.21)	74.7 (1.03)	17.3 (0.99)	96.0 (0.52)	56.1 (1.43)	7.2 (0.63)
1992	99.0 (0.24)	81.4 (0.80)	27.8 (0.90)	98.7 (0.25)	77.9 (1.06)	18.9 (1.01)	96.6 (0.52)	59.1 (1.26)	7.2 (0.63)
1994	99.0 (0.24)	82.0 (0.66)	29.9 (1.12)	98.5 (0.33)	78.1 (1.07)	21.3 (1.35)	96.5 (0.50)	58.6 (1.35)	7.4 (0.76)
1996	99.1 (0.18)	81.5 (0.76)	29.7 (1.02)	98.8 (0.20)	78.6 (0.87)	20.6 (1.24)	96.8 (0.42)	60.1 (1.72)	7.4 (0.77)
1999	98.9 (0.17)	82.5 (0.84)	30.9 (1.07)	98.7 (0.25)	78.8 (1.02)	23.2 (0.95)	96.8 (0.45)	60.7 (1.63)	8.4 (0.83)
2004	98.7 (0.19)	87.0 (0.77)	40.9 (0.89)	98.1 (0.19)	81.1 (0.98)	27.8 (1.09)	95.8 (0.40)	58.3 (1.12)	6.1 (0.47)
2008	99.0 (0.18)	89.1 (0.69)	44.5 (1.01)	98.2 (0.19)	83.4 (0.63)	30.0 (1.08)	96.0 (0.37)	59.4 (0.87)	6.2 (0.40)
Male									
1978	96.2 (0.48)	68.9 (0.98)	19.2 (0.64)	93.9 (0.49)	63.9 (1.32)	18.4 (0.85)	93.0 (0.52)	55.1 (1.21)	9.5 (0.57)
1982	96.5 (0.55)	68.8 (1.29)	18.1 (1.06)	97.5 (0.55)	71.3 (1.44)	18.9 (1.18)	93.9 (0.58)	51.9 (1.51)	6.9 (0.70)
1986	98.0 (0.51)	74.0 (1.45)	20.9 (1.10)	98.5 (0.32)	73.8 (1.76)	17.6 (1.12)	96.1 (0.63)	54.6 (1.78)	8.4 (0.91)
1990	99.0 (0.26)	80.6 (1.05)	27.5 (0.96)	98.2 (0.34)	75.1 (1.75)	19.0 (1.24)	95.8 (0.77)	57.6 (1.42)	8.8 (0.76)
1992	99.0 (0.29)	81.9 (1.05)	29.4 (1.21)	98.8 (0.42)	78.1 (1.60)	20.7 (1.13)	96.9 (0.56)	60.5 (1.80)	9.1 (0.73)
1994	99.1 (0.27)	82.3 (0.87)	31.5 (1.59)	98.3 (0.45)	78.9 (1.49)	23.9 (1.59)	97.3 (0.57)	60.2 (2.08)	9.3 (1.04)
1996	99.1 (0.20)	82.5 (1.10)	32.7 (1.74)	98.7 (0.25)	79.8 (1.43)	23.0 (1.64)	97.0 (0.66)	62.7 (1.77)	9.5 (1.32)
1999	98.8 (0.28)	82.6 (0.92)	32.4 (1.25)	98.5 (0.27)	79.3 (1.12)	25.4 (1.19)	96.5 (0.81)	63.1 (2.12)	9.8 (1.09)
2004	98.3 (0.27)	86.1 (0.89)	40.7 (1.03)	97.7 (0.29)	80.5 (1.08)	29.9 (1.27)	95.6 (0.45)	60.8 (1.31)	7.3 (0.68)
2008	99.0 (0.27)	88.4 (0.87)	44.4 (1.18)	98.2 (0.28)	84.3 (0.75)	33.4 (1.29)	96.2 (0.47)	62.9 (0.96)	7.6 (0.61)
Female									
1978	97.2 (0.27)	72.0 (1.05)	19.9 (1.00)	95.2 (0.49)	65.9 (1.17)	17.5 (0.75)	91.0 (0.57)	48.2 (1.29)	5.2 (0.66)
1982	97.6 (0.33)	74.0 (1.30)	19.6 (1.11)	98.0 (0.27)	71.4 (1.29)	15.9 (1.00)	92.1 (0.56)	45.3 (1.37)	4.1 (0.42)
1986	97.8 (0.38)	74.3 (1.32)	20.6 (1.28)	98.6 (0.31)	72.7 (1.95)	14.1 (1.31)	95.1 (0.65)	48.9 (1.73)	4.7 (0.59)
1990	99.1 (0.26)	82.3 (1.26)	27.9 (1.31)	98.9 (0.18)	74.4 (1.32)	15.7 (1.00)	96.2 (0.84)	54.7 (1.84)	5.6 (0.79)
1992	99.0 (0.33)	80.9 (1.15)	26.3 (1.52)	98.6 (0.23)	77.7 (1.06)	17.2 (1.39)	96.3 (0.82)	57.7 (1.63)	5.2 (0.75)
1994	98.9 (0.31)	81.7 (0.91)	28.3 (1.28)	98.7 (0.31)	77.3 (0.99)	18.7 (1.39)	96.0 (0.65)	57.2 (1.40)	5.5 (0.87)
1996	99.1 (0.36)	80.7 (0.93)	26.7 (1.07)	98.8 (0.27)	77.4 (1.09)	18.4 (1.48)	96.7 (0.57)	57.6 (2.21)	5.3 (0.80)
1999	99.0 (0.19)	82.5 (1.15)	29.4 (1.36)	99.0 (0.40)	78.4 (1.22)	21.0 (1.38)	97.2 (0.40)	58.5 (1.89)	7.1 (1.06)
2004	99.0 (0.22)	87.8 (0.96)	41.1 (1.13)	98.4 (0.25)	81.7 (1.10)	25.7 (1.24)	95.9 (0.58)	55.9 (1.18)	4.9 (0.48)
2008	99.0 (0.21)	89.9 (0.78)	44.6 (1.18)	98.2 (0.25)	82.5 (0.86)	26.7 (1.13)	95.7 (0.43)	55.8 (1.25)	4.6 (0.34)
White									
1978	98.3 (0.19)	76.3 (1.00)	22.9 (0.87)	97.6 (0.27)	72.9 (0.85)	21.4 (0.73)	95.6 (0.30)	57.6 (1.14)	8.5 (0.48)
1982	98.5 (0.25)	76.8 (1.22)	21.8 (1.13)	99.1 (0.14)	78.3 (0.94)	20.5 (1.00)	96.2 (0.33)	54.7 (1.41)	6.4 (0.54)
1986	98.8 (0.24)	79.6 (1.33)	24.6 (1.03)	99.3 (0.27)	78.9 (1.69)	18.6 (1.17)	98.0 (0.36)	59.1 (1.69)	7.9 (0.68)
1990	99.6 (0.16)	86.9 (0.86)	32.7 (1.04)	99.4 (0.14)	82.0 (1.01)	21.0 (1.23)	97.6 (0.28)	63.2 (1.59)	8.3 (0.73)
1992	99.6 (0.14)	86.9 (0.68)	32.4 (1.01)	99.6 (0.18)	84.9 (1.10)	22.8 (1.28)	98.3 (0.36)	66.4 (1.40)	8.7 (0.87)
1994	99.6 (0.16)	87.0 (0.84)	35.3 (1.33)	99.3 (0.22)	85.5 (0.93)	25.6 (1.64)	98.4 (0.36)	67.0 (1.40)	9.4 (1.06)
1996	99.6 (0.15)	86.6 (0.80)	35.7 (1.38)	99.6 (0.16)	86.4 (1.02)	25.4 (1.50)	98.7 (0.37)	68.7 (2.18)	9.2 (1.02)
1999	99.6 (0.12)	88.6 (0.78)	37.1 (1.35)	99.4 (0.29)	86.7 (0.92)	29.0 (1.26)	98.7 (0.40)	69.9 (1.96)	10.4 (1.07)
2004	99.2 (0.18)	91.9 (0.61)	47.2 (0.97)	99.1 (0.16)	89.3 (0.82)	35.1 (1.21)	97.5 (0.28)	66.8 (1.08)	7.6 (0.63)
2008	99.6 (0.12)	94.0 (0.52)	52.9 (1.29)	98.9 (0.17)	90.4 (0.83)	39.2 (1.60)	98.2 (0.26)	70.5 (1.09)	8.1 (0.55)
Black									
1978	88.4 (1.01)	42.0 (1.44)	4.1 (0.64)	79.7 (1.48)	28.7 (2.06)	2.3 (0.48)	70.7 (1.73)	16.8 (1.57)	0.5 (—)
1982	90.2 (0.97)	46.1 (2.35)	4.4 (0.81)	90.2 (1.60)	37.9 (2.51)	2.9 (0.96)	76.4 (1.47)	17.1 (1.51)	0.5 (—)
1986	93.9 (1.37)	53.4 (2.47)	5.6 (0.92)	95.4 (0.95)	49.0 (3.70)	4.0 (1.42)	85.6 (2.53)	20.8 (2.83)	0.2 (—)
1990	96.9 (0.88)	60.0 (2.76)	9.4 (1.72)	95.4 (1.10)	48.7 (3.56)	3.9 (1.61)	92.4 (2.20)	32.8 (4.49)	2.0 (1.04)
1992	96.6 (1.12)	59.8 (2.82)	9.6 (1.42)	95.0 (1.35)	51.0 (2.73)	4.0 (0.69)	89.6 (2.53)	29.8 (3.94)	0.9 (—)
1994	97.4 (0.98)	65.9 (2.56)	11.1 (1.71)	95.6 (1.60)	51.0 (3.91)	6.4 (2.37)	90.6 (1.79)	29.8 (3.38)	0.4 (—)
1996	97.3 (0.84)	65.3 (2.38)	10.0 (1.24)	96.2 (1.27)	53.7 (2.56)	4.8 (1.08)	90.6 (1.33)	31.2 (2.51)	0.9 (—)
1999	96.4 (0.64)	63.3 (2.11)	12.3 (1.48)	96.5 (1.06)	50.8 (4.01)	4.4 (1.37)	88.6 (1.95)	26.6 (2.70)	1.0 (—)
2004	97.1 (0.65)	74.3 (2.61)	22.0 (1.72)	95.3 (0.78)	61.5 (2.47)	9.7 (1.35)	89.1 (1.63)	29.4 (2.07)	0.4 (—)
2008	96.9 (0.86)	75.6 (2.31)	24.6 (1.67)	96.6 (0.68)	67.6 (1.69)	10.2 (1.17)	90.6 (1.42)	31.8 (1.60)	0.8 (0.23)
Hispanic									
1978	93.0 (1.20)	54.2 (2.80)	9.2 (2.49)	86.4 (0.94)	36.0 (2.92)	4.0 (0.95)	78.3 (2.29)	23.4 (2.67)	1.4 (0.58)
1982	94.3 (1.19)	55.7 (2.26)	7.8 (1.74)	95.9 (0.95)	52.2 (2.48)	6.3 (0.97)	81.4 (1.86)	21.6 (2.16)	0.7 (0.36)
1986	96.4 (1.29)	57.6 (2.95)	7.3 (2.81)	96.9 (1.43)	56.0 (5.01)	5.5 (1.15)	89.3 (2.52)	26.5 (4.48)	1.1 (—)
1990	98.0 (0.76)	68.4 (3.03)	11.3 (3.49)	96.8 (1.06)	56.7 (3.32)	6.4 (1.70)	85.8 (4.18)	30.1 (3.09)	1.9 (0.78)
1992	97.2 (1.29)	65.0 (2.94)	11.7 (2.53)	98.1 (0.70)	63.3 (2.67)	7.0 (1.15)	94.1 (2.21)	39.2 (4.86)	1.2 (—)
1994	97.2 (1.15)	63.5 (3.08)	9.7 (1.82)	97.1 (1.31)	59.2 (2.17)	6.4 (1.78)	91.8 (3.57)	38.3 (5.50)	1.4 (—)
1996	98.1 (0.73)	67.1 (2.14)	13.8 (2.26)	96.2 (0.78)	58.3 (2.28)	6.7 (1.17)	92.2 (2.24)	40.1 (3.47)	1.8 (—)
1999	98.1 (0.71)	67.5 (2.47)	10.5 (1.63)	97.2 (0.60)	62.9 (2.50)	8.2 (1.37)	93.6 (2.21)	37.7 (4.15)	3.1 (1.12)
2004	98.0 (0.46)	80.5 (2.03)	30.2 (2.17)	96.4 (0.66)	68.5 (1.86)	13.7 (1.44)	92.3 (1.05)	38.1 (2.12)	1.9 (0.60)
2008	98.9 (0.28)	85.1 (1.25)	33.5 (1.46)	97.0 (0.44)	73.3 (1.71)	14.4 (1.09)	92.2 (1.10)	41.1 (1.69)	1.5 (0.41)

—Not available.
[1] Scale score of 150 or above.
[2] Scale score of 200 or above.
[3] Scale score of 250 or above.
[4] Scale score of 300 or above.
[5] Scale score of 350 or above.
NOTE: Excludes persons not enrolled in school and students who were unable to be tested due to limited proficiency in English or due to a disability. Beginning in 2004, data are for a revised assessment format that provides accommodations for students with disabilities and English language learners. Totals include other racial/ethnic groups not shown separately. Race categories exclude persons of Hispanic ethnicity. Standard errors appear in parentheses.
SOURCE: U.S. Department of Education, National Center for Education Statistics, National Assessment of Educational Progress (NAEP), *NAEP 1999 Trends in Academic Progress*; and 2004 and 2008 Long-Term Trend Mathematics Assessments, retrieved May 4, 2009, from the Long-Term Trend NAEP Data Explorer (http://nces.ed.gov/nationsreportcard/naepdata/). (This table was prepared June 2009.)

Mathematics performance of 17-year-olds, by highest mathematics course taken, sex, and race/ethnicity: Selected years, 1978 through 2008

Year, sex, and race/ethnicity	Percent of students		Average scale score by highest mathematics course taken												Percent of students at or above score levels							
			All students		Prealgebra or general mathematics		Algebra I		Geometry		Algebra II		Precalculus or calculus		200		250		300		350	
1	2		3		4		5		6		7		8		9		10		11		12	
1978																						
All students	100	(†)	300	(1.0)	267	(0.8)	286	(0.7)	307	(0.7)	321	(0.7)	334	(1.4)	100	(†)	92	(0.5)	52	(1.1)	7	(0.4)
Sex																						
Male	49	(0.5)	304	(1.0)	269	(1.0)	289	(0.9)	310	(1.0)	325	(0.8)	337	(2.0)	100	(†)	93	(0.5)	55	(1.2)	10	(0.6)
Female	51	(0.5)	297	(1.0)	264	(0.9)	284	(1.0)	304	(0.8)	318	(0.9)	329	(1.8)	100	(†)	91	(0.6)	48	(1.3)	5	(0.7)
Race/ethnicity																						
White	83	(1.3)	306	(0.9)	272	(0.6)	291	(0.6)	310	(0.6)	325	(0.6)	338	(1.1)	100	(†)	96	(0.3)	58	(1.1)	8	(0.5)
Black	12	(1.1)	268	(1.3)	247	(1.6)	264	(1.5)	281	(1.9)	292	(1.4)	297	(6.5)	99	(0.3)	71	(1.7)	17	(1.6)	#	(†)
Hispanic	4	(0.5)	276	(2.3)	256	(2.3)	273	(2.8)	294	(4.4)	303	(2.9)	‡	(†)	99	(0.4)	78	(2.3)	23	(2.7)	1	(0.6)
Other[1]	1	(0.1)	313	(3.3)	‡	(†)	‡	(†)	‡	(†)	323	(2.9)	‡	(†)	100	(†)	94	(2.6)	65	(4.9)	15	(3.2)
1990																						
All students	100	(†)	305	(0.9)	273	(1.1)	288	(1.2)	299	(1.5)	319	(1.0)	344	(2.7)	100	(†)	96	(0.5)	56	(1.4)	7	(0.6)
Sex																						
Male	49	(0.9)	306	(1.1)	274	(1.7)	291	(1.6)	302	(1.6)	323	(1.2)	347	(2.4)	100	(†)	96	(0.8)	58	(1.4)	9	(0.8)
Female	51	(0.9)	303	(1.1)	271	(1.8)	285	(1.8)	296	(1.8)	316	(1.1)	340	(4.0)	100	(†)	96	(0.8)	55	(1.8)	6	(0.8)
Race/ethnicity																						
White	73	(0.5)	309	(1.0)	277	(1.1)	292	(1.6)	304	(1.3)	323	(0.9)	347	(2.8)	100	(†)	97	(0.3)	63	(1.6)	8	(0.7)
Black	16	(0.3)	289	(2.8)	264	(2.2)	278	(4.0)	285	(3.5)	302	(3.2)	‡	(†)	100	(†)	92	(2.2)	33	(4.5)	2	(1.0)
Hispanic	7	(0.4)	284	(2.9)	‡	(†)	‡	(†)	‡	(†)	306	(3.3)	‡	(†)	100	(†)	86	(4.2)	30	(3.1)	2	(0.8)
Other[1]	4	(0.5)	312	(5.2)	‡	(†)	‡	(†)	‡	(†)	321	(3.8)	‡	(†)	100	(†)	98	(‡)	62	(7.0)	16	(4.3)
1994																						
All students	100	(†)	306	(1.0)	272	(1.2)	288	(1.4)	297	(1.7)	316	(1.0)	340	(2.2)	100	(†)	97	(0.5)	59	(1.4)	7	(0.8)
Sex																						
Male	49	(1.3)	309	(1.4)	274	(1.8)	289	(1.6)	301	(2.1)	320	(1.5)	343	(2.6)	100	(†)	97	(0.6)	60	(2.1)	9	(1.0)
Female	51	(1.3)	304	(1.1)	268	(1.9)	286	(1.9)	293	(1.8)	313	(1.1)	337	(2.8)	100	(†)	96	(0.6)	57	(1.4)	6	(0.9)
Race/ethnicity																						
White	73	(0.5)	312	(1.1)	275	(1.4)	292	(1.7)	301	(1.5)	320	(1.0)	344	(2.0)	100	(†)	98	(0.4)	67	(1.4)	9	(1.1)
Black	15	(0.3)	286	(1.8)	‡	(†)	275	(3.3)	283	(3.8)	297	(2.5)	‡	(†)	100	(†)	91	(1.8)	30	(3.4)	#	(†)
Hispanic	9	(0.3)	291	(3.7)	‡	(†)	‡	(†)	‡	(†)	304	(4.1)	‡	(†)	100	(†)	92	(3.6)	38	(5.5)	1	(—)
Other[1]	3	(0.3)	313	(4.5)	‡	(†)	‡	(†)	‡	(†)	323	(3.5)	‡	(†)	100	(†)	97	(‡)	66	(6.6)	12	(3.6)
1996																						
All students	100	(†)	307	(1.2)	269	(1.9)	283	(1.3)	298	(1.3)	316	(1.3)	339	(1.7)	100	(†)	97	(0.4)	60	(1.7)	7	(0.8)
Sex																						
Male	50	(1.2)	310	(1.3)	272	(2.5)	286	(1.5)	302	(1.7)	320	(1.7)	342	(2.3)	100	(†)	97	(0.7)	63	(1.8)	9	(1.3)
Female	50	(1.2)	305	(1.4)	265	(2.2)	278	(2.2)	294	(1.5)	313	(1.4)	335	(2.2)	100	(†)	97	(0.6)	58	(2.2)	5	(0.8)
Race/ethnicity																						
White	71	(0.6)	313	(1.4)	273	(2.3)	287	(2.0)	304	(1.6)	320	(1.4)	342	(1.9)	100	(†)	99	(0.4)	69	(2.2)	9	(1.0)
Black	15	(0.3)	286	(1.7)	‡	(†)	272	(2.4)	280	(3.0)	299	(2.2)	‡	(†)	100	(†)	91	(1.3)	31	(2.5)	1	(—)
Hispanic	9	(0.7)	292	(2.1)	‡	(†)	‡	(†)	‡	(†)	306	(2.8)	‡	(†)	100	(†)	92	(2.2)	40	(3.5)	2	(—)
Other[1]	4	(0.7)	312	(5.7)	‡	(†)	‡	(†)	‡	(†)	‡	(†)	‡	(†)	100	(†)	97	(1.2)	64	(7.2)	14	(5.0)
1999																						
All students	100	(†)	308	(1.0)	278	(2.8)	285	(1.7)	298	(1.2)	315	(0.8)	341	(1.4)	100	(†)	97	(0.5)	61	(1.6)	8	(0.8)
Sex																						
Male	48	(1.0)	310	(1.4)	281	(3.2)	288	(2.6)	301	(1.8)	317	(1.3)	343	(1.9)	100	(†)	96	(0.8)	63	(2.1)	10	(1.1)
Female	52	(1.0)	307	(1.0)	274	(3.2)	282	(2.5)	295	(1.3)	314	(1.1)	340	(2.0)	100	(†)	97	(0.4)	58	(1.9)	7	(1.1)
Race/ethnicity																						
White	72	(0.5)	315	(1.1)	282	(3.4)	290	(2.2)	303	(1.5)	320	(0.9)	343	(1.5)	100	(†)	99	(0.4)	70	(2.0)	10	(1.1)
Black	15	(0.4)	283	(1.5)	‡	(†)	267	(2.9)	281	(2.5)	293	(1.4)	‡	(†)	100	(†)	89	(2.0)	27	(2.7)	1	(—)
Hispanic	10	(0.5)	293	(2.5)	‡	(†)	‡	(†)	‡	(†)	308	(3.0)	‡	(†)	100	(†)	94	(2.2)	38	(4.1)	3	(1.1)
Other[1]	4	(0.2)	320	(4.0)	‡	(†)	‡	(†)	‡	(†)	320	(4.4)	‡	(†)	100	(†)	100	(†)	76	(6.3)	14	(4.1)
2008																						
All students	100	(†)	306	(0.6)	270	(1.9)	280	(1.1)	295	(0.8)	307	(0.7)	333	(0.8)	—	(†)	96	(0.4)	59	(0.9)	6	(0.4)
Sex															—	(†)						
Male	50	(0.5)	309	(0.7)	273	(2.9)	283	(1.5)	300	(0.8)	310	(0.8)	336	(1.1)	—	(†)	96	(0.5)	63	(1.0)	8	(0.6)
Female	50	(0.5)	303	(0.8)	267	(2.8)	276	(1.6)	289	(1.0)	303	(0.8)	331	(0.9)	—	(†)	96	(0.4)	56	(1.3)	5	(0.3)
Race/ethnicity															—	(†)						
White	59	(1.5)	314	(0.7)	275	(2.3)	287	(1.3)	301	(0.9)	314	(0.8)	337	(0.8)	—	(†)	98	(0.3)	71	(1.1)	8	(0.5)
Black	14	(1.4)	287	(1.2)	‡	(†)	266	(2.6)	282	(1.6)	291	(1.5)	312	(2.6)	—	(†)	91	(1.4)	32	(1.6)	1	(0.2)
Hispanic	19	(1.2)	293	(1.1)	261	(3.2)	274	(2.3)	289	(1.3)	296	(1.2)	320	(1.9)	—	(†)	92	(1.1)	41	(1.7)	1	(0.4)
Other[1]	7	(0.5)	316	(1.8)	‡	(†)	‡	(†)	297	(2.8)	311	(1.9)	340	(2.2)	—	(†)	98	(0.7)	71	(2.2)	13	(1.8)

—Not available.
†Not applicable.
#Rounds to zero.
‡Reporting standards not met (too few cases).
[1]Includes Asians/Pacific Islanders and American Indians/Alaska Natives.
NOTE: Score level 200 indicates ability to perform simple additive reasoning and problem solving. Score level 250 indicates ability to perform simple multiplicative reasoning and two-step problem solving. Score level 300 indicates ability to perform reasoning and problem solving involving fractions, decimals, percents, elementary geometry, and simple algebra. Score level 350 indicates ability to perform reasoning and problem solving involving geometry, algebra, and beginning statistics and probability. Scale ranges from 0 to 500. Excludes persons

not enrolled in school and students who were unable to be tested due to limited proficiency in English or due to a disability. Beginning in 2008, data are for a revised assessment format that provides accommodations for students with disabilities and English language learners. Includes public and private schools. Race categories exclude persons of Hispanic ethnicity. Detail may not sum to totals because of rounding. Standard errors appear in parentheses.
SOURCE: U.S. Department of Education, National Center for Education Statistics, National Assessment of Educational Progress (NAEP), *NAEP Trends in Academic Progress*, 1996 and 1999; and 2004 and 2008 Long-Term Trend Mathematics Assessments, retrieved June 4, 2009, from the Long-Term Trend NAEP Data Explorer (http://nces.ed.gov/nationsreport card/naepdata/). (This table was prepared June 2009.)

Average mathematics scale score, by grade and selected student and school characteristics: Selected years, 1990 through 2011

Grade and selected student or school characteristic	1990[1]		1992[1]		1996		2000		2003		2005		2007		2009		2011	
1	2		3		4		5		6		7		8		9		10	
4th grade, all students	213	(0.9)	220	(0.7)	224	(1.0)	226	(0.9)	235	(0.2)	238	(0.1)	240	(0.2)	240	(0.2)	241	(0.2)
Sex																		
Male	214	(1.2)	221	(0.8)	224	(1.1)	227	(1.0)	236	(0.3)	239	(0.2)	241	(0.2)	241	(0.3)	241	(0.2)
Female	213	(1.1)	219	(1.0)	223	(1.1)	224	(0.9)	233	(0.2)	237	(0.2)	239	(0.2)	239	(0.3)	240	(0.2)
Race/ethnicity																		
White	220	(1.0)	227	(0.8)	232	(1.0)	234	(0.8)	243	(0.2)	246	(0.1)	248	(0.2)	248	(0.2)	249	(0.2)
Black	188	(1.8)	193	(1.4)	198	(1.6)	203	(1.2)	216	(0.4)	220	(0.3)	222	(0.3)	222	(0.3)	224	(0.4)
Hispanic	200	(2.2)	202	(1.5)	207	(1.9)	208	(1.5)	222	(0.4)	226	(0.3)	227	(0.3)	227	(0.4)	229	(0.3)
Asian[2]	225	(4.1)	231	(2.1)	229	(4.2)	‡	(†)	246	(1.1)	251	(0.7)	253	(0.8)	255	(1.0)	257	(1.0)
Native Hawaiian/Pacific Islander	[2]	(†)	[2]	(†)	[2]	(†)	[2]	(†)	[2]	(†)	[2]	(†)	[2]	(†)	[2]	(†)	236	(2.1)
American Indian/Alaska Native	‡	(†)	‡	(†)	217	(5.6)	208	(3.5)	223	(1.0)	226	(0.9)	228	(0.7)	225	(0.9)	225	(0.9)
Eligibility for free or reduced-price lunch																		
Eligible	—	(†)	—	(†)	207	(1.3)	208	(0.9)	222	(0.3)	225	(0.2)	227	(0.2)	227	(0.2)	229	(0.2)
Not eligible	—	(†)	—	(†)	232	(0.8)	235	(1.1)	244	(0.3)	248	(0.2)	249	(0.2)	250	(0.3)	252	(0.2)
Unknown	—	(†)	—	(†)	231	(2.8)	237	(1.6)	241	(0.7)	244	(0.7)	246	(0.9)	246	(1.1)	249	(0.9)
Control of school																		
Public	212	(1.1)	219	(0.8)	222	(1.1)	224	(1.0)	234	(0.2)	237	(0.2)	239	(0.2)	239	(0.2)	240	(0.2)
Private	224	(2.6)	228	(1.1)	235	(1.9)	238	(0.8)	244	(0.7)	‡	(†)	246	(0.8)	246	(0.8)	247	(0.8)
Amount of math homework teacher assigns per day																		
None	—	(†)	—	(†)	227	(5.4)	227	(2.4)	234	(1.0)	—	(†)	236	(0.9)	236	(0.9)	234	(0.9)
15 minutes	—	(†)	—	(†)	227	(1.7)	229	(1.2)	237	(0.4)	—	(†)	242	(0.2)	242	(0.3)	243	(0.3)
30 minutes	—	(†)	—	(†)	223	(1.9)	225	(1.4)	234	(0.4)	—	(†)	239	(0.3)	239	(0.4)	240	(0.3)
45 minutes	—	(†)	—	(†)	217	(4.7)	214	(2.7)	229	(1.2)	—	(†)	233	(0.9)	235	(1.0)	235	(1.1)
1 hour	—	(†)	—	(†)	‡	(†)	225	(4.7)	225	(2.2)	—	(†)	233	(2.5)	228	(3.0)	230	(1.9)
More than 1 hour	—	(†)	—	(†)	‡	(†)	‡	(†)	217	(3.0)	—	(†)	233	(4.4)	222	(5.9)	232	(2.5)
8th grade, all students	263	(1.3)	268	(0.9)	270	(0.9)	273	(0.8)	278	(0.3)	279	(0.2)	281	(0.3)	283	(0.3)	284	(0.2)
Sex																		
Male	263	(1.6)	268	(1.1)	271	(1.1)	274	(0.9)	278	(0.3)	280	(0.2)	282	(0.3)	284	(0.3)	284	(0.3)
Female	262	(1.3)	269	(1.0)	269	(1.1)	272	(0.9)	277	(0.3)	278	(0.2)	280	(0.3)	282	(0.4)	283	(0.2)
Race/ethnicity																		
White	270	(1.3)	277	(1.0)	281	(1.1)	284	(0.8)	288	(0.3)	289	(0.2)	291	(0.3)	293	(0.3)	293	(0.2)
Black	237	(2.7)	237	(1.3)	240	(1.9)	244	(1.2)	252	(0.5)	255	(0.4)	260	(0.4)	261	(0.5)	262	(0.5)
Hispanic	246	(4.3)	249	(1.2)	251	(1.7)	253	(1.3)	259	(0.6)	262	(0.4)	265	(0.4)	266	(0.6)	270	(0.5)
Asian[2]	275	(5.0)	290	(5.9)	‡	(†)	288	(3.5)	291	(1.3)	295	(0.9)	297	(0.9)	301	(1.2)	305	(1.1)
Native Hawaiian/Pacific Islander	[2]	(†)	[2]	(†)	[2]	(†)	[2]	(†)	[2]	(†)	[2]	(†)	[2]	(†)	[2]	(†)	269	(2.4)
American Indian/Alaska Native	‡	(†)	‡	(†)	‡	(†)	‡	(†)	259	(7.5)	263	(1.8)	264	(0.9)	264	(1.2)	266	(1.1)	265	(0.9)
Eligibility for free or reduced-price lunch																		
Eligible	—	(†)	—	(†)	250	(1.7)	253	(1.1)	259	(0.4)	262	(0.3)	265	(0.3)	266	(0.3)	269	(0.3)
Not eligible	—	(†)	—	(†)	277	(1.3)	283	(1.1)	287	(0.3)	288	(0.2)	291	(0.3)	294	(0.3)	296	(0.3)
Unknown	—	(†)	—	(†)	279	(2.3)	276	(1.6)	285	(1.0)	289	(1.2)	291	(1.7)	295	(1.4)	296	(1.1)
Parents' highest level of education																		
Did not finish high school	242	(2.0)	249	(1.7)	250	(2.0)	253	(1.4)	257	(0.6)	259	(0.5)	263	(0.5)	265	(0.6)	265	(0.6)
Graduated high school	255	(1.6)	257	(1.2)	260	(1.3)	261	(1.0)	267	(0.4)	267	(0.3)	270	(0.4)	270	(0.5)	271	(0.4)
Some education after high school	267	(1.6)	271	(1.1)	277	(1.2)	277	(1.1)	280	(0.4)	280	(0.3)	283	(0.4)	284	(0.4)	285	(0.3)
Graduated college	274	(1.5)	281	(1.2)	281	(1.2)	286	(1.0)	286	(0.3)	290	(0.2)	292	(0.3)	295	(0.3)	295	(0.3)
Control of school																		
Public	262	(1.4)	267	(1.0)	269	(1.0)	272	(0.9)	276	(0.3)	278	(0.2)	280	(0.3)	282	(0.3)	283	(0.2)
Private	271	(2.5)	281	(2.2)	285	(1.8)	286	(1.2)	292	(1.2)	‡	(†)	293	(1.3)	296	(1.2)	296	(0.9)
Amount of math homework teacher assigns per day																		
None	—	(†)	—	(†)	—	(†)	—	(†)	—	(†)	—	(†)	—	(†)	263	(2.0)	264	(1.8)
Less than 1 hour	—	(†)	—	(†)	—	(†)	—	(†)	—	(†)	—	(†)	—	(†)	284	(0.3)	285	(0.3)
About 1 hour	—	(†)	—	(†)	—	(†)	—	(†)	—	(†)	—	(†)	—	(†)	284	(0.8)	287	(0.7)
About 2–3 hours	—	(†)	—	(†)	—	(†)	—	(†)	—	(†)	—	(†)	—	(†)	274	(3.0)	277	(3.3)
More than 3 hours	—	(†)	—	(†)	—	(†)	—	(†)	—	(†)	—	(†)	—	(†)	269	(5.0)	264	(2.9)
12th grade, all students	[3]	(†)	[3]	(†)	[3]	(†)	[3]	(†)	—	(†)	150	(0.6)	—	(†)	153	(0.7)	—	(†)
Sex																		
Male	[3]	(†)	[3]	(†)	[3]	(†)	[3]	(†)	—	(†)	151	(0.7)	—	(†)	155	(0.9)	—	(†)
Female	[3]	(†)	[3]	(†)	[3]	(†)	[3]	(†)	—	(†)	149	(0.7)	—	(†)	152	(0.7)	—	(†)
Race/ethnicity																		
White	[3]	(†)	[3]	(†)	[3]	(†)	[3]	(†)	—	(†)	157	(0.6)	—	(†)	161	(0.6)	—	(†)
Black	[3]	(†)	[3]	(†)	[3]	(†)	[3]	(†)	—	(†)	127	(1.1)	—	(†)	131	(0.8)	—	(†)
Hispanic	[3]	(†)	[3]	(†)	[3]	(†)	[3]	(†)	—	(†)	133	(1.3)	—	(†)	138	(0.8)	—	(†)
Asian/Pacific Islander	[3]	(†)	[3]	(†)	[3]	(†)	[3]	(†)	—	(†)	163	(2.0)	—	(†)	175	(2.7)	—	(†)
American Indian/Alaska Native	[3]	(†)	[3]	(†)	[3]	(†)	[3]	(†)	—	(†)	134	(4.1)	—	(†)	144	(2.8)	—	(†)
Eligibility for free or reduced-price lunch																		
Eligible	[3]	(†)	[3]	(†)	[3]	(†)	[3]	(†)	—	(†)	132	(1.1)	—	(†)	137	(0.8)	—	(†)
Not eligible	[3]	(†)	[3]	(†)	[3]	(†)	[3]	(†)	—	(†)	155	(0.7)	—	(†)	160	(0.4)	—	(†)
Unknown	[3]	(†)	[3]	(†)	[3]	(†)	[3]	(†)	—	(†)	162	(1.8)	—	(†)	159	(2.6)	—	(†)
Parents' highest level of education																		
Did not finish high school	[3]	(†)	[3]	(†)	[3]	(†)	[3]	(†)	—	(†)	130	(1.5)	—	(†)	135	(1.0)	—	(†)
Graduated high school	[3]	(†)	[3]	(†)	[3]	(†)	[3]	(†)	—	(†)	138	(1.1)	—	(†)	142	(0.7)	—	(†)
Some education after high school	[3]	(†)	[3]	(†)	[3]	(†)	[3]	(†)	—	(†)	148	(0.8)	—	(†)	150	(0.7)	—	(†)
Graduated college	[3]	(†)	[3]	(†)	[3]	(†)	[3]	(†)	—	(†)	161	(0.6)	—	(†)	164	(0.8)	—	(†)

—Not available.
†Not applicable.
‡Reporting standards not met. Either there are too few cases or participation rates fell below the required standards for reporting.
[1]Accommodations were not permitted for this assessment.
[2]For assessment years prior to 2011, Native Hawaiian/Pacific Islander students are included with Asian students.
[3]Because of major changes to the framework and content of the grade 12 assessment, scores from 2005 and later assessment years cannot be compared with scores from earlier assessment years. Therefore, this table does not include scores from the earlier grade 12 assessment years (1990, 1992, 1996, and 2000). For data pertaining to comparisons between earlier years, see the *Digest of Education Statistics 2009*, table 138 (http://nces.ed.gov/programs/digest/d09/tables/dt09_138.asp).

NOTE: For the grade 4 and grade 8 assessments, scale ranges from 0 to 500. For the grade 12 assessment, scale ranges from 0 to 300. Includes public and private schools. For 1996 and later years, includes students tested with accommodations (1 to 12 percent of all students, depending on grade level and year); excludes only those students with disabilities and English language learners who were unable to be tested even with accommodations (2 to 4 percent of all students). Race categories exclude persons of Hispanic ethnicity. Some data have been revised from previously published figures. Standard errors appear in parentheses. SOURCE: U.S. Department of Education, National Center for Education Statistics, National Assessment of Educational Progress (NAEP), 1990, 1992, 1996, 2000, 2003, 2005, 2007, 2009, and 2011 Mathematics Assessments, retrieved November 2, 2011, from the Main NAEP Data Explorer (http://nces.ed.gov/nationsreportcard/naepdata/). (This table was prepared November 2011.)

Average mathematics scale score of 8th-graders and percentage reporting various attitudes toward mathematics work, by frequency of attitude and selected student and school characteristics: 2011

Student or school characteristic	Math work is engaging and interesting				Math work is challenging				Math work is too easy			
	Never or hardly ever	Sometimes	Often	Always/ almost always	Never or hardly ever	Sometimes	Often	Always/ almost always	Never or hardly ever	Sometimes	Often	Always/ almost always
1	2	3	4	5	6	7	8	9	10	11	12	13
	Average scale score[1]											
All students	280 (0.3)	284 (0.3)	289 (0.3)	286 (0.5)	293 (0.4)	285 (0.3)	283 (0.3)	274 (0.6)	284 (0.4)	283 (0.2)	287 (0.4)	289 (0.7)
Sex												
Male	281 (0.4)	285 (0.4)	289 (0.5)	287 (0.7)	295 (0.6)	286 (0.4)	284 (0.5)	272 (0.8)	283 (0.6)	283 (0.3)	289 (0.5)	292 (0.8)
Female	278 (0.4)	283 (0.4)	288 (0.5)	286 (0.6)	290 (0.6)	284 (0.3)	283 (0.4)	276 (0.7)	285 (0.5)	282 (0.3)	285 (0.5)	286 (1.1)
Race/ethnicity												
White	286 (0.3)	294 (0.3)	299 (0.3)	300 (0.7)	300 (0.6)	294 (0.3)	293 (0.3)	285 (0.6)	291 (0.4)	293 (0.2)	297 (0.4)	298 (0.7)
Black	261 (0.9)	263 (0.6)	265 (0.7)	265 (0.7)	274 (1.1)	265 (0.5)	262 (0.7)	253 (1.0)	262 (0.8)	261 (0.6)	266 (0.6)	270 (1.2)
Hispanic	267 (0.7)	269 (0.7)	274 (0.7)	274 (1.0)	277 (1.2)	271 (0.6)	270 (0.8)	262 (1.2)	268 (1.2)	269 (0.6)	275 (0.8)	275 (1.8)
Asian	300 (2.1)	304 (1.5)	309 (1.5)	309 (2.3)	317 (2.6)	306 (1.4)	303 (1.7)	295 (4.1)	312 (2.8)	303 (1.2)	307 (1.7)	312 (3.1)
Native Hawaiian/ Pacific Islander	272 (5.8)	267 (3.3)	276 (4.6)	272 (6.0)	268 (11.9)	273 (3.1)	271 (4.4)	257 (6.0)	272 (4.3)	271 (3.1)	268 (4.6)	277 (9.5)
American Indian/ Alaska Native	263 (2.1)	267 (2.1)	269 (1.8)	268 (2.8)	275 (3.6)	267 (1.6)	266 (1.6)	260 (3.7)	267 (3.0)	265 (1.3)	267 (2.0)	275 (4.5)
Eligibility for free or reduced-price lunch												
Eligible	266 (0.5)	269 (0.4)	273 (0.4)	271 (0.6)	279 (0.7)	271 (0.4)	268 (0.4)	258 (0.6)	266 (0.6)	268 (0.3)	274 (0.5)	276 (1.1)
Not eligible	288 (0.4)	296 (0.4)	301 (0.4)	301 (0.6)	303 (0.6)	296 (0.3)	295 (0.4)	289 (0.7)	295 (0.5)	295 (0.3)	299 (0.6)	301 (0.9)
Unknown	290 (1.5)	296 (1.2)	301 (1.5)	301 (2.2)	305 (1.7)	298 (1.5)	295 (1.3)	286 (2.7)	295 (1.7)	295 (1.1)	300 (1.5)	304 (3.2)
Control of school												
Public	279 (0.3)	283 (0.3)	287 (0.3)	285 (0.5)	292 (0.4)	284 (0.3)	282 (0.3)	273 (0.6)	283 (0.4)	282 (0.2)	286 (0.4)	288 (0.7)
Private	290 (1.2)	296 (1.0)	301 (1.2)	300 (1.9)	305 (1.6)	298 (1.2)	295 (1.0)	286 (2.1)	295 (1.3)	295 (0.9)	301 (1.3)	304 (2.7)
	Percent of students											
All students	23 (0.2)	36 (0.2)	27 (0.2)	14 (0.2)	12 (0.2)	46 (0.2)	31 (0.2)	10 (0.1)	17 (0.2)	54 (0.2)	21 (0.2)	8 (0.1)
Sex												
Male	23 (0.3)	35 (0.3)	28 (0.3)	14 (0.2)	13 (0.2)	46 (0.3)	31 (0.3)	10 (0.2)	15 (0.2)	54 (0.3)	23 (0.3)	9 (0.2)
Female	23 (0.2)	38 (0.2)	26 (0.2)	13 (0.2)	12 (0.2)	47 (0.3)	30 (0.3)	10 (0.1)	19 (0.2)	55 (0.3)	19 (0.3)	7 (0.2)
Race/ethnicity												
White	26 (0.3)	37 (0.2)	26 (0.2)	11 (0.2)	13 (0.2)	46 (0.3)	31 (0.3)	10 (0.1)	20 (0.2)	54 (0.2)	19 (0.2)	7 (0.1)
Black	18 (0.4)	34 (0.5)	28 (0.4)	20 (0.4)	12 (0.4)	45 (0.5)	31 (0.4)	13 (0.3)	15 (0.3)	55 (0.5)	21 (0.4)	9 (0.3)
Hispanic	19 (0.5)	38 (0.5)	29 (0.5)	14 (0.3)	11 (0.3)	48 (0.5)	32 (0.5)	10 (0.3)	12 (0.3)	56 (0.5)	24 (0.4)	8 (0.4)
Asian	15 (0.6)	36 (0.9)	32 (0.9)	18 (0.9)	16 (1.0)	50 (1.2)	27 (1.1)	7 (0.6)	10 (0.6)	49 (1.0)	29 (0.8)	12 (0.6)
Native Hawaiian/ Pacific Islander	12 (1.9)	36 (3.2)	36 (3.2)	15 (2.0)	12 (2.7)	45 (4.4)	32 (3.5)	10 (1.3)	8 (1.0)	48 (3.6)	37 (3.3)	7 (1.5)
American Indian/ Alaska Native	23 (1.4)	37 (1.5)	27 (1.2)	13 (1.0)	11 (0.9)	44 (1.5)	33 (1.6)	12 (1.0)	15 (1.0)	59 (1.6)	19 (1.0)	6 (0.6)
Eligibility for free or reduced-price lunch												
Eligible	21 (0.3)	36 (0.3)	27 (0.3)	15 (0.2)	12 (0.2)	47 (0.3)	31 (0.3)	11 (0.2)	14 (0.2)	55 (0.3)	23 (0.3)	8 (0.2)
Not eligible	25 (0.2)	37 (0.2)	27 (0.3)	12 (0.2)	13 (0.2)	46 (0.3)	31 (0.3)	10 (0.1)	18 (0.2)	54 (0.2)	20 (0.2)	8 (0.1)
Unknown	23 (0.7)	36 (0.8)	28 (0.7)	13 (0.6)	11 (0.5)	44 (0.8)	35 (0.8)	10 (0.5)	22 (0.8)	56 (0.9)	17 (0.7)	5 (0.4)
Control of school												
Public	23 (0.2)	37 (0.2)	27 (0.2)	14 (0.2)	13 (0.2)	47 (0.2)	30 (0.2)	10 (0.1)	16 (0.2)	54 (0.2)	22 (0.2)	8 (0.2)
Private	24 (0.6)	35 (0.6)	28 (0.5)	13 (0.4)	11 (0.4)	44 (0.6)	35 (0.6)	10 (0.4)	21 (0.6)	56 (0.7)	17 (0.5)	5 (0.3)

[1]Scale ranges from 0 to 500.

NOTE: Includes public and private schools. Includes students tested with accommodations (10 percent of all 8th-grade students); excludes only those students with disabilities and English language learners who were unable to be tested even with accommodations (2 percent of all 8th-grade students). Race categories exclude persons of Hispanic ethnicity. Detail may not sum to totals because of rounding. Standard errors appear in parentheses.

SOURCE: U.S. Department of Education, National Center for Education Statistics, National Assessment of Educational Progress (NAEP), 2011 Mathematics Assessment, retrieved November 1, 2011, from the Main NAEP Data Explorer (http://nces.ed.gov/nationsreportcard/naepdata/). (This table was prepared November 2011.)

Average scores in NAEP mathematics for fourth-grade public school students, by state/jurisdiction:
Various years, 1992–2011

State/jurisdiction	Accommodations not permitted			Accommodations permitted					
	1992	1996	2000	2000	2003	2005	2007	2009	2011
Nation (public)	**219***	**222***	**226***	**224***	**234***	**237***	**239***	**239***	**240**
Alabama	208*	212*	218*	217*	223*	225*	229	228*	231
Alaska	—	224*	—	—	233*	236	237	237	236
Arizona	215*	218*	219*	219*	229*	230*	232*	230*	235
Arkansas	210*	216*	217*	216*	229*	236	238	238	238
California	208*	209*	214*	213*	227*	230*	230*	232	234
Colorado	221*	226*	—	—	235*	239*	240*	243	244
Connecticut	227*	232*	234*	234*	241	242	243	245	242
Delaware	218*	215*	—	—	236*	240	242*	239	240
Florida	214*	216*	—	—	234*	239	242	242	240
Georgia	216*	215*	220*	219*	230*	234*	235*	236*	238
Hawaii	214*	215*	216*	216*	227*	230*	234*	236*	239
Idaho	222*	—	227*	224*	235*	242	241	241	240
Illinois	—	—	225*	223*	233*	233*	237	238	239
Indiana	221*	229*	234*	233*	238*	240*	245	243	244
Iowa	230*	229*	233*	231*	238*	240*	243	243	243
Kansas	—	—	232*	232*	242*	246	248	245	246
Kentucky	215*	220*	221*	219*	229*	231*	235*	239	241
Louisiana	204*	209*	218*	218*	226*	230	230	229	231
Maine	232*	232*	231*	230*	238*	241*	242	244	244
Maryland	217*	221*	222*	222*	233*	238*	240*	244*	247
Massachusetts	227*	229*	235*	233*	242*	247*	252	252	253
Michigan	220*	226*	231*	229*	236	238	238	236	236
Minnesota	228*	232*	235*	234*	242*	246*	247	249	249
Mississippi	202*	208*	211*	211*	223*	227*	228	227	230
Missouri	222*	225*	229*	228*	235*	235*	239	241	240
Montana	—	228*	230*	228*	236*	241*	244	244	244
Nebraska	225*	228*	226*	225*	236*	238	238	239	240
Nevada	—	218*	220*	220*	228*	230*	232*	235	237
New Hampshire	230*	—	—	—	243*	246*	249*	251	252
New Jersey	227*	227*	—	—	239*	244*	249	247	248
New Mexico	213*	214*	214*	213*	223*	224*	228*	230*	233
New York	218*	223*	227*	225*	236	238	243*	241*	238
North Carolina	213*	224*	232*	230*	242*	241*	242*	244	245
North Dakota	229*	231*	231*	230*	238*	243*	245	245	245
Ohio	219*	—	231*	230*	238*	242	245	244	244
Oklahoma	220*	—	225*	224*	229*	234*	237	237	237
Oregon	—	223*	227*	224*	236	238	236	238	237
Pennsylvania	224*	226*	—	—	236*	241*	244	244	246
Rhode Island	215*	220*	225*	224*	230*	233*	236*	239*	242
South Carolina	212*	213*	220*	220*	236	238	237	236	237
South Dakota	—	—	—	—	237*	242	241	242	241
Tennessee	211*	219*	220*	220*	228*	232	233	232	233
Texas	218*	229*	233*	231*	237*	242	242	240	241
Utah	224*	227*	227*	227*	235*	239*	239*	240	243
Vermont	—	225*	232*	232*	242*	244*	246	248	247
Virginia	221*	223*	230*	230*	239*	240*	244	243	245
Washington	—	225*	—	—	238*	242	243	242	243
West Virginia	215*	223*	225*	223*	231*	231*	236	233	235
Wisconsin	229*	231*	—	—	237*	241*	244	244	245
Wyoming	225*	223*	229*	229*	241*	243	244	242*	244
Other jurisdictions									
District of Columbia	193*	187*	193*	192*	205*	211*	214*	219*	222
DoDEA[1]	—	224*	228*	227*	237*	239*	240	240	241

— Not available. The state/jurisdiction did not participate or did not meet the minimum participation guidelines for reporting.

* Significantly different ($p < .05$) from 2011 when only one state/jurisdiction or the nation is being examined.

[1] Department of Defense Education Activity (overseas and domestic schools).

SOURCE: U.S. Department of Education, Institute of Education Sciences, National Center for Education Statistics, National Assessment of Educational Progress (NAEP), various years, 1992–2011 Mathematics Assessments.

Average scores and achievement-level results in NAEP mathematics for fourth-grade public school students, by state/jurisdiction: 2011

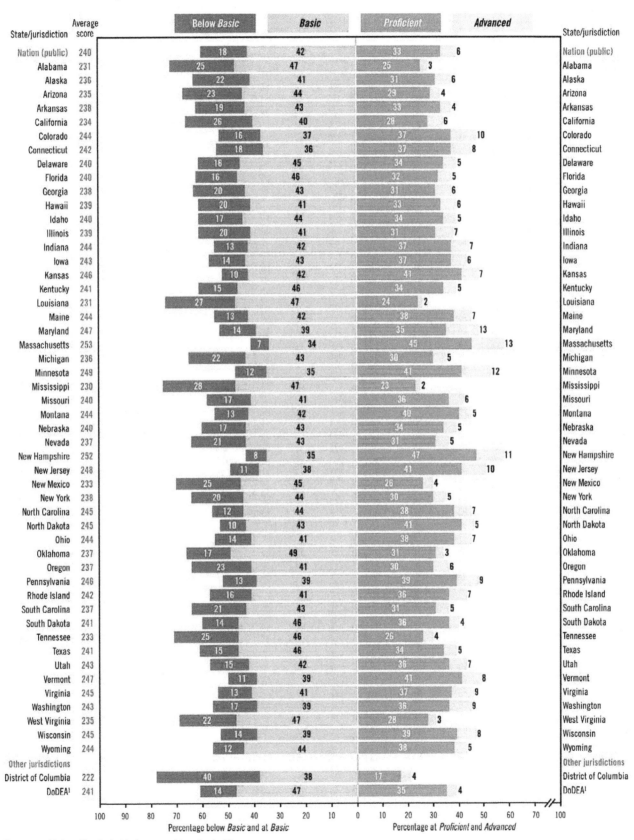

State/jurisdiction	Average score	Below Basic	Basic	Proficient	Advanced
Nation (public)	240	18	42	33	6
Alabama	231	25	47	25	3
Alaska	236	22	41	31	6
Arizona	235	23	44	29	4
Arkansas	238	19	43	33	4
California	234	26	40	28	6
Colorado	244	16	37	37	10
Connecticut	242	18	36	37	8
Delaware	240	16	45	34	5
Florida	240	16	46	32	5
Georgia	238	20	43	31	6
Hawaii	239	20	41	33	6
Idaho	240	17	44	34	5
Illinois	239	20	41	31	7
Indiana	244	13	42	37	7
Iowa	243	14	43	37	6
Kansas	246	10	42	41	7
Kentucky	241	15	46	34	5
Louisiana	231	27	47	24	2
Maine	244	13	42	38	7
Maryland	247	14	39	35	13
Massachusetts	253	7	34	45	13
Michigan	236	22	43	30	5
Minnesota	249	12	35	41	12
Mississippi	230	28	47	23	2
Missouri	240	17	41	36	6
Montana	244	13	42	40	5
Nebraska	240	17	43	34	5
Nevada	237	21	43	31	5
New Hampshire	252	8	35	47	11
New Jersey	248	11	38	41	10
New Mexico	233	25	45	26	4
New York	238	20	44	30	5
North Carolina	245	12	44	38	7
North Dakota	245	10	43	41	5
Ohio	244	14	41	38	7
Oklahoma	237	17	49	31	3
Oregon	237	23	41	30	6
Pennsylvania	246	13	39	39	9
Rhode Island	242	16	41	36	7
South Carolina	237	21	43	31	5
South Dakota	241	14	46	36	4
Tennessee	233	25	46	26	4
Texas	241	15	46	34	5
Utah	243	15	42	36	7
Vermont	247	11	39	41	8
Virginia	245	13	41	37	9
Washington	243	17	39	36	9
West Virginia	235	22	47	28	3
Wisconsin	245	14	39	39	8
Wyoming	244	12	44	38	5
Other jurisdictions					
District of Columbia	222	40	38	17	4
DoDEA[1]	241	14	47	35	4

Percentage below *Basic* and at *Basic* — Percentage at *Proficient* and *Advanced*

[1] Department of Defense Education Activity (overseas and domestic schools).

NOTE: The shaded bars are graphed using unrounded numbers. Detail may not sum to totals because of rounding.

SOURCE: U.S. Department of Education, Institute of Education Sciences, National Center for Education Statistics, National Assessment of Educational Progress (NAEP), 2011 Mathematics Assessment.

Average scores and achievement-level results in NAEP mathematics for fourth-grade public school students, by race/ethnicity and state/jurisdiction: 2011

State/jurisdiction	White					Black					Hispanic				
	Average scale score	| Percentage of students |				Average scale score	| Percentage of students |				Average scale score	| Percentage of students |			
		Below Basic	At or above Basic	At or above Proficient	At Advanced		Below Basic	At or above Basic	At or above Proficient	At Advanced		Below Basic	At or above Basic	At or above Proficient	At Advanced
Nation (public)	**249**	**9**	**91**	**52**	**9**	**224**	**34**	**66**	**17**	**1**	**229**	**28**	**72**	**24**	**2**
Alabama	240	14	86	37	4	215	46	54	9	#	227	29	71	21	#
Alaska	248	10	90	50	9	225	32	68	15	2	239	18	82	36	5
Arizona	246	11	89	49	8	224	38	62	22	3	227	30	70	21	1
Arkansas	244	12	88	45	6	219	42	58	16	1	233	24	76	28	3
California	252	8	92	57	12	225	32	68	19	1	222	38	62	17	1
Colorado	254	7	93	60	14	225	34	66	21	1	230	28	72	26	3
Connecticut	253	7	93	60	11	220	41	59	15	1	222	38	62	19	2
Delaware	250	7	93	53	7	227	29	71	19	1	231	24	76	25	1
Florida	250	8	92	52	9	226	30	70	18	1	236	19	81	31	3
Georgia	249	9	91	51	10	224	35	65	18	1	233	24	76	29	3
Hawaii	248	11	89	53	10	233	25	75	32	4	237	22	78	39	4
Idaho	244	12	88	44	6	‡	‡	‡	‡	‡	223	36	64	17	1
Illinois	249	10	90	51	10	219	42	58	14	2	226	30	70	20	1
Indiana	249	9	91	51	9	223	35	65	15	#	234	21	79	29	3
Iowa	246	11	89	47	6	224	37	63	18	2	229	27	73	24	1
Kansas	251	7	93	56	9	227	28	72	18	1	235	17	83	26	1
Kentucky	243	13	87	41	6	225	31	69	17	1	236	18	82	30	3
Louisiana	241	13	87	40	4	219	41	59	12	1	230	25	75	20	#
Maine	246	11	89	47	8	212	55	45	10	1	‡	‡	‡	‡	‡
Maryland	258	6	94	64	18	230	27	73	23	2	245	13	87	43	9
Massachusetts	258	4	96	67	15	235	19	81	27	3	236	20	80	32	4
Michigan	242	14	86	41	5	211	53	47	8	#	228	31	69	21	2
Minnesota	255	6	94	60	14	225	37	63	23	3	230	27	73	28	2
Mississippi	241	14	86	38	3	217	44	56	10	#	229	25	75	22	2
Missouri	246	11	89	48	7	216	47	53	14	1	231	23	77	24	1
Montana	247	9	91	50	6	‡	‡	‡	‡	‡	237	18	82	31	3
Nebraska	247	10	90	48	7	213	49	51	7	1	226	32	68	20	1
Nevada	247	11	89	48	8	226	33	67	23	1	229	29	71	24	1
New Hampshire	252	7	93	59	10	235	19	81	27	3	235	23	77	30	2
New Jersey	256	5	95	64	12	231	23	77	24	2	234	21	79	28	2
New Mexico	247	11	89	48	8	226	32	68	19	3	228	29	71	23	2
New York	245	11	89	46	7	224	35	65	17	1	226	31	69	20	1
North Carolina	253	5	95	58	10	229	25	75	18	#	238	14	86	33	2
North Dakota	249	6	94	52	6	‡	‡	‡	‡	‡	233	20	80	24	2
Ohio	249	9	91	53	8	226	32	68	20	2	233	24	76	27	4
Oklahoma	243	11	89	41	3	224	34	66	14	#	227	28	72	19	2
Oregon	243	16	84	43	7	215	50	50	14	2	220	42	58	15	1
Pennsylvania	251	8	92	56	11	224	33	67	17	1	226	31	69	20	2
Rhode Island	249	9	91	53	10	225	31	69	20	2	224	33	67	21	1
South Carolina	248	10	90	52	9	220	39	61	13	#	234	20	80	28	2
South Dakota	246	9	91	46	5	227	32	68	21	1	226	29	71	18	2
Tennessee	239	18	82	36	5	216	45	55	12	1	228	28	72	19	1
Texas	253	6	94	60	9	232	23	77	25	1	235	19	81	29	2
Utah	247	10	90	49	8	‡	‡	‡	‡	‡	223	36	64	17	1
Vermont	248	10	90	50	8	‡	‡	‡	‡	‡	‡	‡	‡	‡	‡
Virginia	251	8	92	56	11	229	27	73	20	1	237	17	83	31	4
Washington	249	11	89	53	10	227	29	71	20	2	226	32	68	22	2
West Virginia	235	21	79	32	3	227	30	70	20	2	‡	‡	‡	‡	‡
Wisconsin	251	8	92	55	10	217	45	55	12	1	228	29	71	22	1
Wyoming	246	9	91	47	6	‡	‡	‡	‡	‡	235	20	80	31	2
Other jurisdictions															
District of Columbia	272	1	99	84	33	215	46	54	13	1	223	36	64	21	2
DoDEA[1]	246	9	91	47	5	228	27	73	19	#	236	18	82	30	2

See notes at end of table.

Average scores and achievement-level results in NAEP mathematics for fourth-grade public school students, by race/ethnicity and state/jurisdiction: 2011—Continued

State/jurisdiction	Asian/Pacific Islander					American Indian/Alaska Native				
	Average scale score	Percentage of students				Average scale score	Percentage of students			
		Below Basic	At or above Basic	At or above Proficient	At Advanced		Below Basic	At or above Basic	At or above Proficient	At Advanced
Nation (public)	256	9	91	62	20	227	32	68	24	2
Alabama	‡	‡	‡	‡	‡	‡	‡	‡	‡	‡
Alaska	234	23	77	29	3	213	50	50	14	1
Arizona	249	13	87	53	14	216	45	55	14	1
Arkansas	247	17	83	53	13	‡	‡	‡	‡	‡
California	256	9	91	63	19	‡	‡	‡	‡	‡
Colorado	246	21	79	55	15	‡	‡	‡	‡	‡
Connecticut	255	10	90	62	18	‡	‡	‡	‡	‡
Delaware	262	4	96	69	24	‡	‡	‡	‡	‡
Florida	257	4	96	64	17	‡	‡	‡	‡	‡
Georgia	263	6	94	70	29	‡	‡	‡	‡	‡
Hawaii	237	21	79	37	6	‡	‡	‡	‡	‡
Idaho	247	16	84	52	12	‡	‡	‡	‡	‡
Illinois	257	7	93	63	19	‡	‡	‡	‡	‡
Indiana	‡	‡	‡	‡	‡	‡	‡	‡	‡	‡
Iowa	248	15	85	52	14	‡	‡	‡	‡	‡
Kansas	253	5	95	59	11	‡	‡	‡	‡	‡
Kentucky	261	6	94	66	27	‡	‡	‡	‡	‡
Louisiana	‡	‡	‡	‡	‡	‡	‡	‡	‡	‡
Maine	246	15	85	48	11	‡	‡	‡	‡	‡
Maryland	267	5	95	74	33	‡	‡	‡	‡	‡
Massachusetts	267	2	98	76	30	‡	‡	‡	‡	‡
Michigan	263	7	93	71	25	‡	‡	‡	‡	‡
Minnesota	253	12	88	57	16	233	26	74	30	4
Mississippi	‡	‡	‡	‡	‡	‡	‡	‡	‡	‡
Missouri	252	10	90	57	17	‡	‡	‡	‡	‡
Montana	‡	‡	‡	‡	‡	220	43	57	16	1
Nebraska	241	15	85	40	10	‡	‡	‡	‡	‡
Nevada	252	11	89	58	12	‡	‡	‡	‡	‡
New Hampshire	264	5	95	70	29	‡	‡	‡	‡	‡
New Jersey	265	4	96	75	29	‡	‡	‡	‡	‡
New Mexico	254	11	89	63	18	219	42	58	15	2
New York	252	12	88	58	17	‡	‡	‡	‡	‡
North Carolina	263	3	97	71	26	225	36	64	20	3
North Dakota	‡	‡	‡	‡	‡	221	39	61	15	1
Ohio	254	8	92	58	11	‡	‡	‡	‡	‡
Oklahoma	252	4	96	55	10	234	22	78	29	3
Oregon	249	16	84	51	17	220	41	59	21	3
Pennsylvania	264	4	96	75	25	‡	‡	‡	‡	‡
Rhode Island	251	8	92	49	13	‡	‡	‡	‡	‡
South Carolina	‡	‡	‡	‡	‡	‡	‡	‡	‡	‡
South Dakota	‡	‡	‡	‡	‡	220	40	60	15	#
Tennessee	249	13	87	51	13	‡	‡	‡	‡	‡
Texas	263	3	97	69	27	‡	‡	‡	‡	‡
Utah	236	22	78	31	8	214	46	54	14	1
Vermont	‡	‡	‡	‡	‡	‡	‡	‡	‡	‡
Virginia	262	4	96	70	24	‡	‡	‡	‡	‡
Washington	256	10	90	62	20	223	37	63	20	1
West Virginia	‡	‡	‡	‡	‡	‡	‡	‡	‡	‡
Wisconsin	242	20	80	42	12	231	29	71	34	5
Wyoming	‡	‡	‡	‡	‡	223	38	62	23	2
Other jurisdictions										
District of Columbia	‡	‡	‡	‡	‡	‡	‡	‡	‡	‡
DoDEA[1]	244	13	87	45	6	‡	‡	‡	‡	‡

Rounds to zero.

‡ Reporting standards not met. Sample size insufficient to permit a reliable estimate.

[1] Department of Defense Education Activity (overseas and domestic schools).

NOTE: Black includes African American, Hispanic includes Latino, and Pacific Islander includes Native Hawaiian. Race categories exclude Hispanic origin. Results are not shown for students of two or more races. Detail may not sum to totals because of rounding.

SOURCE: U.S. Department of Education, Institute of Education Sciences, National Center for Education Statistics, National Assessment of Educational Progress (NAEP), 2011 Mathematics Assessment.

Average scores and achievement-level results in NAEP mathematics for fourth-grade public school students, by gender and state/jurisdiction: 2011

State/jurisdiction	Male					Female				
		Percentage of students					Percentage of students			
	Average scale score	Below Basic	At or above Basic	At or above Proficient	At Advanced	Average scale score	Below Basic	At or above Basic	At or above Proficient	At Advanced
Nation (public)	**241**	**18**	**82**	**41**	**7**	**239**	**18**	**82**	**39**	**6**
Alabama	231	26	74	28	3	232	25	75	27	2
Alaska	237	22	78	38	6	235	22	78	35	5
Arizona	237	21	79	36	5	234	24	76	31	3
Arkansas	238	20	80	37	5	238	19	81	37	4
California	235	25	75	35	7	234	27	73	33	6
Colorado	246	16	84	49	11	243	16	84	45	8
Connecticut	243	17	83	46	9	241	19	81	44	7
Delaware	241	16	84	40	6	239	16	84	37	4
Florida	240	17	83	38	6	240	16	84	36	5
Georgia	238	22	78	37	7	239	19	81	37	6
Hawaii	238	21	79	39	6	240	18	82	40	6
Idaho	241	16	84	41	6	239	18	82	38	5
Illinois	240	19	81	39	8	238	21	79	37	6
Indiana	245	12	88	46	8	242	15	85	42	6
Iowa	244	14	86	44	6	242	15	85	42	5
Kansas	247	10	90	48	7	246	10	90	47	7
Kentucky	242	14	86	39	6	240	16	84	38	5
Louisiana	231	28	72	26	2	231	26	74	26	2
Maine	246	12	88	48	8	243	14	86	42	6
Maryland	248	14	86	50	14	246	14	86	45	11
Massachusetts	255	8	92	60	16	252	7	93	57	11
Michigan	238	21	79	37	6	235	22	78	33	4
Minnesota	250	12	88	54	13	248	12	88	52	11
Mississippi	229	29	71	25	2	231	26	74	25	2
Missouri	240	18	82	42	6	241	16	84	41	5
Montana	245	12	88	48	6	242	14	86	43	4
Nebraska	241	17	83	41	6	239	18	82	37	4
Nevada	238	20	80	38	5	236	22	78	33	4
New Hampshire	252	8	92	58	11	251	7	93	56	10
New Jersey	249	11	89	53	11	247	11	89	49	9
New Mexico	234	24	76	31	4	232	26	74	28	4
New York	238	20	80	37	6	237	20	80	34	4
North Carolina	245	12	88	44	8	244	12	88	44	6
North Dakota	246	10	90	49	7	244	10	90	44	4
Ohio	245	14	86	47	9	243	13	87	44	5
Oklahoma	237	18	82	34	3	238	16	84	33	3
Oregon	237	23	77	37	7	237	22	78	36	6
Pennsylvania	247	14	86	49	10	245	13	87	46	8
Rhode Island	242	17	83	43	8	242	15	85	42	6
South Carolina	237	23	77	36	6	238	19	81	36	5
South Dakota	242	14	86	42	5	240	15	85	37	3
Tennessee	233	24	76	30	4	232	25	75	29	3
Texas	241	15	85	39	5	241	15	85	39	4
Utah	244	14	86	46	9	241	16	84	40	5
Vermont	248	11	89	52	9	245	12	88	46	6
Virginia	247	12	88	48	10	244	13	87	44	8
Washington	244	17	83	46	10	242	17	83	43	8
West Virginia	235	21	79	33	4	234	22	78	29	3
Wisconsin	245	14	86	49	9	244	14	86	45	7
Wyoming	245	12	88	46	6	243	13	87	42	5
Other jurisdictions										
District of Columbia	220	42	58	21	4	223	38	62	22	4
DoDEA[1]	242	14	86	40	4	240	14	86	37	3

[1] Department of Defense Education Activity (overseas and domestic schools).
NOTE: Detail may not sum to totals because of rounding.
SOURCE: U.S. Department of Education, Institute of Education Sciences, National Center for Education Statistics, National Assessment of Educational Progress (NAEP), 2011 Mathematics Assessment.

Average mathematics scale score of 4th-grade public school students and percentage attaining mathematics achievement levels, by state: Selected years, 1992 through 2011

State	Average scale score[1]														Percent attaining mathematics achievement levels, 2011							
	1992		2000		2003		2005		2007		2009		2011		Below Basic		At or above Basic[2]		At or above Proficient[3]		At Advanced[4]	
1	2		3		4		5		6		7		8		9		10		11		12	
United States	219	(0.8)	224	(1.0)	234	(0.2)	237	(0.2)	239	(0.2)	239	(0.2)	240	(0.2)	18	(0.2)	82	(0.2)	40	(0.3)	6	(0.2)
Alabama	208	(1.6)	217	(1.2)	223	(1.2)	225	(0.9)	229	(1.3)	228	(1.1)	231	(1.0)	25	(1.5)	75	(1.5)	27	(1.6)	3	(0.5)
Alaska..........................	—	(†)	—	(†)	233	(0.8)	236	(1.0)	237	(1.0)	237	(0.9)	236	(0.9)	22	(1.1)	78	(1.1)	37	(1.5)	6	(0.7)
Arizona	215	(1.1)	219	(1.3)	229	(1.1)	230	(1.1)	232	(1.0)	230	(1.1)	235	(1.1)	23	(1.1)	77	(1.1)	34	(1.7)	4	(0.6)
Arkansas......................	210	(0.9)	216	(1.1)	229	(0.9)	236	(0.9)	238	(1.1)	238	(0.9)	238	(0.8)	19	(0.9)	81	(0.9)	37	(1.2)	4	(0.6)
California[5]	208	(1.6)	213	(1.6)	227	(0.9)	230	(0.6)	230	(0.7)	232	(1.2)	234	(1.4)	26	(1.3)	74	(1.3)	34	(1.8)	6	(1.1)
Colorado	221	(1.0)	—	(†)	235	(1.0)	239	(1.1)	240	(1.0)	243	(1.0)	244	(0.9)	16	(0.8)	84	(0.8)	47	(1.5)	10	(0.9)
Connecticut..................	227	(1.1)	234	(1.1)	241	(0.8)	242	(0.8)	243	(1.1)	245	(1.0)	242	(1.3)	18	(1.6)	82	(1.6)	45	(1.6)	8	(0.7)
Delaware......................	218	(0.8)	—	(†)	236	(0.5)	240	(0.5)	242	(0.4)	239	(0.5)	240	(0.6)	16	(0.9)	84	(0.9)	39	(1.1)	5	(0.5)
District of Columbia	193	(0.5)	192	(1.1)	205	(0.8)	211	(0.8)	214	(0.8)	219	(0.7)	222	(0.7)	40	(1.0)	60	(1.0)	22	(0.7)	4	(0.4)
Florida..........................	214	(1.5)	—	(†)	234	(1.1)	239	(0.7)	242	(0.8)	242	(1.0)	240	(0.8)	16	(1.1)	84	(1.1)	37	(1.3)	5	(0.5)
Georgia........................	216	(1.2)	219	(1.1)	230	(1.0)	234	(1.0)	235	(0.8)	236	(0.9)	238	(0.7)	20	(0.9)	80	(0.9)	37	(1.2)	6	(0.5)
Hawaii..........................	214	(1.3)	216	(1.0)	227	(1.0)	230	(0.8)	234	(0.8)	236	(1.1)	239	(0.7)	20	(0.8)	80	(0.8)	40	(1.0)	6	(0.5)
Idaho[5].........................	222	(1.0)	224	(1.4)	235	(0.7)	242	(0.7)	241	(0.7)	241	(0.8)	240	(0.6)	17	(0.8)	83	(0.8)	39	(1.1)	5	(0.5)
Illinois[5]........................	—	(†)	223	(1.9)	233	(1.1)	233	(1.0)	237	(1.1)	238	(1.1)	239	(1.1)	20	(1.1)	80	(1.1)	38	(1.5)	7	(0.7)
Indiana[5].......................	221	(1.0)	233	(1.1)	238	(0.9)	240	(0.9)	245	(0.8)	243	(0.9)	244	(1.0)	13	(1.1)	87	(1.1)	44	(1.6)	7	(0.9)
Iowa[5]...........................	230	(1.0)	231	(1.2)	238	(0.7)	240	(0.7)	243	(0.8)	243	(0.8)	243	(0.8)	14	(0.8)	86	(0.8)	43	(1.5)	6	(0.6)
Kansas[5].......................	—	(†)	232	(1.6)	242	(1.0)	246	(1.0)	248	(0.9)	245	(1.0)	246	(0.9)	10	(0.8)	90	(0.8)	48	(1.7)	7	(0.7)
Kentucky	215	(1.0)	219	(1.4)	229	(1.1)	232	(0.9)	235	(1.0)	239	(1.1)	241	(0.8)	15	(0.9)	85	(0.9)	39	(1.2)	5	(0.5)
Louisiana......................	204	(1.5)	218	(1.4)	226	(1.0)	230	(0.9)	230	(1.0)	229	(1.0)	231	(1.0)	27	(1.4)	73	(1.4)	26	(1.4)	2	(0.3)
Maine[5].........................	232	(1.0)	230	(1.0)	238	(0.7)	241	(0.8)	242	(0.8)	244	(0.8)	244	(0.7)	13	(0.8)	87	(0.8)	45	(1.3)	7	(0.6)
Maryland......................	217	(1.3)	222	(1.2)	233	(1.3)	238	(1.0)	240	(0.9)	244	(0.9)	247	(0.9)	14	(0.9)	86	(0.9)	48	(1.4)	13	(0.9)
Massachusetts..............	227	(1.2)	233	(1.2)	242	(0.8)	247	(0.8)	252	(0.8)	252	(0.9)	253	(0.8)	7	(0.7)	93	(0.7)	58	(1.2)	13	(0.9)
Michigan[5].....................	220	(1.7)	229	(1.6)	236	(0.9)	238	(1.2)	238	(1.3)	236	(1.0)	236	(1.1)	22	(1.2)	78	(1.2)	35	(1.5)	5	(0.8)
Minnesota[5]...................	228	(0.9)	234	(1.3)	242	(0.9)	246	(1.0)	247	(1.0)	249	(1.1)	249	(0.9)	12	(0.8)	88	(0.8)	53	(1.3)	12	(0.9)
Mississippi	202	(1.1)	211	(1.1)	223	(1.0)	227	(0.9)	228	(1.0)	227	(1.0)	230	(0.9)	28	(1.2)	72	(1.2)	25	(1.3)	2	(0.4)
Missouri	222	(1.2)	228	(1.2)	235	(0.9)	235	(0.9)	239	(0.9)	241	(1.2)	240	(0.9)	17	(1.0)	83	(1.0)	41	(1.3)	6	(0.6)
Montana[5]......................	—	(†)	228	(1.7)	236	(0.8)	241	(0.8)	244	(0.8)	244	(0.7)	244	(0.6)	13	(0.7)	87	(0.7)	45	(1.2)	5	(0.5)
Nebraska......................	225	(1.2)	225	(1.8)	236	(0.8)	238	(0.9)	238	(1.1)	239	(0.9)	240	(1.0)	17	(1.2)	83	(1.2)	39	(1.6)	5	(0.6)
Nevada.........................	—	(†)	220	(1.0)	228	(0.8)	230	(0.8)	232	(0.9)	235	(0.9)	237	(0.8)	21	(1.0)	79	(1.0)	36	(1.3)	5	(0.5)
New Hampshire	230	(1.2)	—	(†)	243	(0.9)	246	(0.9)	249	(0.8)	251	(0.8)	252	(0.6)	8	(0.7)	92	(0.7)	57	(1.1)	11	(0.7)
New Jersey	227	(1.5)	—	(†)	239	(1.1)	244	(1.1)	249	(1.1)	247	(1.0)	248	(0.9)	11	(1.0)	89	(1.0)	51	(1.5)	10	(0.7)
New Mexico	213	(1.4)	213	(1.5)	223	(1.1)	224	(0.8)	228	(0.9)	230	(1.0)	233	(0.8)	25	(1.0)	75	(1.0)	30	(1.1)	4	(0.5)
New York[5]....................	218	(1.2)	225	(1.4)	236	(0.9)	238	(0.9)	243	(0.8)	241	(0.7)	238	(0.8)	20	(1.0)	80	(1.0)	36	(1.0)	5	(0.5)
North Carolina	213	(1.1)	230	(1.1)	242	(0.8)	241	(0.9)	242	(0.8)	244	(0.8)	245	(0.7)	12	(0.8)	88	(0.8)	44	(1.4)	7	(0.5)
North Dakota	229	(0.8)	230	(1.2)	238	(0.7)	243	(0.5)	245	(0.8)	245	(0.6)	245	(0.6)	10	(0.7)	90	(0.7)	46	(1.2)	5	(0.6)
Ohio[5]...........................	219	(1.2)	230	(1.5)	238	(1.0)	242	(1.0)	245	(1.0)	244	(1.1)	244	(0.8)	14	(1.0)	86	(1.0)	45	(1.5)	7	(0.6)
Oklahoma	220	(1.0)	224	(1.0)	229	(1.0)	234	(1.0)	237	(0.8)	237	(0.9)	237	(0.8)	17	(1.3)	83	(1.3)	33	(1.3)	3	(0.5)
Oregon[5].......................	—	(†)	224	(1.8)	236	(0.9)	238	(0.8)	236	(0.9)	238	(0.9)	237	(0.9)	23	(1.2)	77	(1.2)	37	(1.3)	6	(0.8)
Pennsylvania................	224	(1.3)	—	(†)	236	(1.1)	241	(1.2)	244	(0.8)	244	(1.1)	246	(1.1)	13	(1.2)	87	(1.2)	48	(1.7)	9	(0.8)
Rhode Island	215	(1.5)	224	(1.1)	230	(1.0)	233	(0.9)	236	(0.9)	239	(0.8)	242	(0.7)	16	(0.8)	84	(0.8)	43	(1.2)	7	(0.7)
South Carolina..............	212	(1.1)	220	(1.4)	236	(0.9)	238	(0.9)	237	(0.8)	236	(0.9)	237	(1.0)	21	(1.2)	79	(1.2)	36	(1.7)	5	(0.6)
South Dakota................	—	(†)	—	(†)	237	(0.7)	242	(0.5)	241	(0.7)	242	(0.5)	241	(0.6)	14	(0.8)	86	(0.8)	40	(1.2)	4	(0.5)
Tennessee	211	(1.4)	220	(1.4)	228	(1.0)	232	(1.2)	233	(0.9)	232	(1.1)	233	(0.9)	25	(1.0)	75	(1.0)	30	(1.3)	4	(0.6)
Texas	218	(1.2)	231	(1.1)	237	(0.9)	242	(0.6)	242	(0.7)	240	(0.7)	241	(1.1)	15	(1.1)	85	(1.1)	39	(1.9)	5	(0.8)
Utah.............................	224	(1.0)	227	(1.3)	235	(0.8)	239	(0.8)	239	(0.9)	240	(1.0)	243	(0.8)	15	(0.8)	85	(0.8)	43	(1.4)	7	(0.8)
Vermont[5]......................	—	(†)	232	(1.6)	242	(0.8)	244	(0.5)	246	(0.5)	248	(0.4)	247	(0.5)	11	(0.7)	89	(0.7)	49	(1.0)	8	(0.6)
Virginia.........................	221	(1.3)	230	(1.0)	239	(1.1)	241	(0.9)	244	(0.9)	243	(1.0)	245	(0.8)	13	(0.8)	87	(0.8)	46	(1.4)	9	(0.8)
Washington...................	—	(†)	—	(†)	238	(1.0)	242	(0.9)	243	(1.0)	242	(0.8)	243	(0.9)	17	(1.0)	83	(1.0)	45	(1.5)	9	(0.8)
West Virginia................	215	(1.1)	223	(1.3)	231	(0.8)	231	(0.7)	236	(0.9)	233	(0.8)	235	(0.7)	22	(1.0)	78	(1.0)	31	(1.0)	3	(0.4)
Wisconsin[5]..................	229	(1.1)	—	(†)	237	(0.9)	241	(0.9)	244	(0.9)	244	(0.9)	245	(0.8)	14	(0.8)	86	(0.8)	47	(1.5)	8	(0.8)
Wyoming.......................	225	(0.9)	229	(1.1)	241	(0.6)	243	(0.6)	244	(0.5)	242	(0.6)	244	(0.4)	12	(0.7)	88	(0.7)	44	(1.3)	5	(0.4)
Department of Defense dependents schools[6] .	—	(†)	227	(0.6)	237	(0.4)	239	(0.5)	240	(0.4)	240	(0.5)	241	(0.4)	14	(0.8)	86	(0.8)	39	(1.2)	4	(0.4)

—Not available.
†Not applicable.
[1]Scale ranges from 0 to 500.
[2]*Basic* denotes partial mastery of the knowledge and skills that are fundamental for proficient work at the 4th-grade level.
[3]*Proficient* represents solid academic performance for 4th-graders. Students reaching this level have demonstrated competency over challenging subject matter.
[4]*Advanced* signifies superior performance.
[5]Did not meet one or more of the guidelines for school participation in 2000. Data are subject to appreciable nonresponse bias.
[6]Prior to 2005, NAEP divided the Department of Defense (DoD) schools into two jurisdictions, domestic and overseas. In 2005, NAEP began combining the DoD domestic and overseas schools into a single jurisdiction. Data shown in this table for years prior to 2005 were recalculated for comparability.

NOTE: With the exception of 1992, includes public school students who were tested with accommodations; excludes only those students with disabilities (SD) and English language learners (ELL) who were unable to be tested even with accommodations. SD and ELL populations, accommodation rates, and exclusion rates vary from state to state. Detail may not sum to totals because of rounding. Standard errors appear in parentheses.
SOURCE: U.S. Department of Education, National Center for Education Statistics, National Assessment of Educational Progress (NAEP), 1992, 2000, 2003, 2005, 2007, 2009, and 2011 Mathematics Assessments, retrieved November 1, 2011, from the Main NAEP Data Explorer (http://nces.ed.gov/nationsreportcard/naepdata). (This table was prepared November 2011.)

Average scores in NAEP mathematics for eighth-grade public school students, by state/jurisdiction: Various years, 1990-2011

State/jurisdiction	Accommodations not permitted				Accommodations permitted					
	1990	1992	1996	2000	2000	2003	2005	2007	2009	2011
Nation (public)	**262***	**267***	**271***	**274***	**272***	**276***	**278***	**280***	**282***	**283**
Alabama	253*	252*	257*	262*	264*	262*	262*	266	269	269
Alaska	—	—	278*	—	—	279*	279*	283	283	283
Arizona	260*	265*	268*	271*	269*	271*	274*	276*	277	279
Arkansas	256*	256*	262*	261*	257*	266*	272*	274*	276*	279
California	256*	261*	263*	262*	260*	267*	269*	270	270	273
Colorado	267*	272*	276*	—	—	283*	281*	286*	287*	292
Connecticut	270*	274*	280*	282*	281*	284*	281*	282*	289	287
Delaware	261*	263*	267*	—	—	277*	281*	283	284	283
Florida	255*	260*	264*	—	—	271*	274*	277	279	278
Georgia	259*	259*	262*	266*	265*	270*	272*	275*	278	278
Hawaii	251*	257*	262*	263*	262*	266*	266*	269*	274*	278
Idaho	271*	275*	—	278*	277*	280*	281*	284*	287	287
Illinois	261*	—	—	277*	275*	277*	278*	280	282	283
Indiana	267*	270*	276*	283	281*	281*	282*	285	287	285
Iowa	278*	283	284	—	—	284	284	285	284	285
Kansas	—	—	—	284*	283*	284*	284*	290	289	290
Kentucky	257*	262*	267*	272*	270*	274*	274*	279*	279	282
Louisiana	246*	250*	252*	259*	259*	266*	268*	272	272	273
Maine	—	279*	284*	284*	281*	282*	281*	286*	286*	289
Maryland	261*	265*	270*	276*	272*	278*	278*	286	288	288
Massachusetts	—	273*	278*	283*	279*	287*	292*	298	299	299
Michigan	264*	267*	277	278	277	276	277	277	278	280
Minnesota	275*	282*	284*	288*	287*	291*	290*	292*	294	295
Mississippi	—	246*	250*	254*	254*	261*	262*	265*	265*	269
Missouri	—	271*	273*	274*	271*	279*	276*	281	286*	282
Montana	280*	—	283*	287*	285*	286*	286*	287*	292	293
Nebraska	276*	278*	283	281	280*	282	284	284	284	283
Nevada	—	—	—	268*	265*	268*	270*	271*	274*	278
New Hampshire	273*	278*	—	—	—	286*	285*	288*	292	292
New Jersey	270*	272*	—	—	—	281*	284*	289*	293	294
New Mexico	256*	260*	262*	260*	259*	263*	263*	268*	270*	274
New York	261*	266*	270*	276	271*	280	280	280	283	280
North Carolina	250*	258*	268*	280*	276*	281*	282*	284	284	286
North Dakota	281*	283*	284*	283*	282*	287*	287*	292	293	292
Ohio	264*	268*	—	283*	281*	282*	283*	285*	286*	289
Oklahoma	263*	268*	—	272*	270*	272*	271*	275*	276*	279
Oregon	271*	—	276*	281	280	281	282	284	285	283
Pennsylvania	266*	271*	—	—	—	279*	281*	286	288	286
Rhode Island	260*	266*	269*	273*	269*	272*	272*	275*	278*	283
South Carolina	—	261*	261*	266*	265*	277*	281	282	280	281
South Dakota	—	—	—	—	—	285*	287*	288*	291	291
Tennessee	—	259*	263*	263*	262*	268*	271*	274	275	274
Texas	258*	265*	270*	275*	273*	277*	281*	286*	287*	290
Utah	—	274*	277*	275*	274*	281*	279*	281	284	283
Vermont	—	—	279*	283*	281*	286*	287*	291*	293	294
Virginia	264*	268*	270*	277*	275*	282*	284*	288	286	289
Washington	—	—	276*	—	—	281*	285*	285	289	288
West Virginia	256*	259*	265*	271*	266*	271	269*	270*	270*	273
Wisconsin	274*	278*	283*	—	—	284*	285*	286*	288	289
Wyoming	272*	275*	275*	277*	276*	284*	282*	287	286	288
Other jurisdictions										
District of Columbia	231*	235*	233*	234*	235*	243*	245*	248*	254*	260
DoDEA[1]	—	—	274*	278*	277*	285*	284*	285*	287	288

— Not available. The state/jurisdiction did not participate or did not meet the minimum participation guidelines for reporting.

* Significantly different ($p < .05$) from 2011 when only one state/jurisdiction or the nation is being examined.

[1] Department of Defense Education Activity (overseas and domestic schools).

SOURCE: U.S. Department of Education, Institute of Education Sciences, National Center for Education Statistics, National Assessment of Educational Progress (NAEP), various years, 1990-2011 Mathematics Assessments.

Average scores and achievement-level results in NAEP mathematics for eighth-grade public school students, by state/jurisdiction: 2011

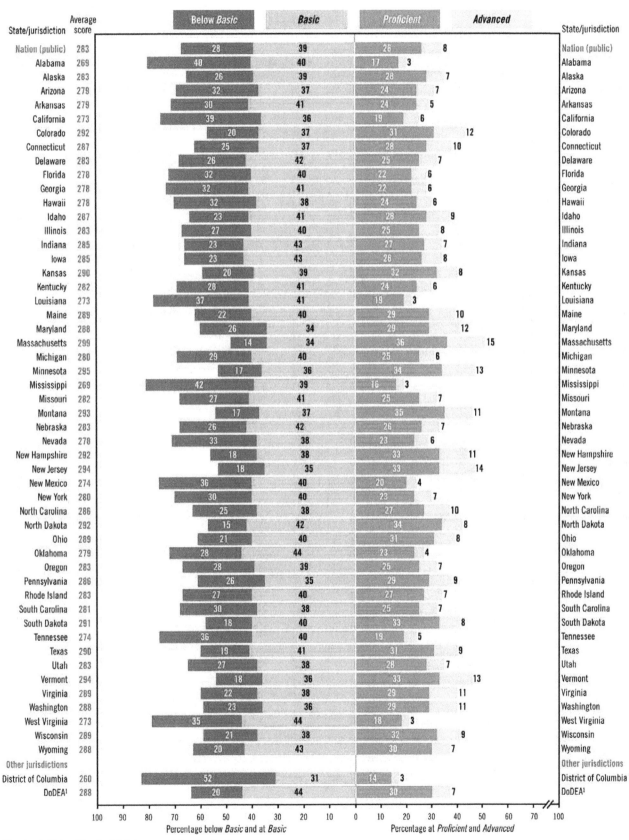

State/jurisdiction	Average score	Below Basic	Basic	Proficient	Advanced
Nation (public)	283	28	39	26	8
Alabama	269	40	40	17	3
Alaska	283	26	39	28	7
Arizona	279	32	37	24	7
Arkansas	279	30	41	24	5
California	273	39	36	19	6
Colorado	292	20	37	31	12
Connecticut	287	25	37	28	10
Delaware	283	26	42	25	7
Florida	278	32	40	22	6
Georgia	278	32	41	22	6
Hawaii	278	32	38	24	6
Idaho	287	23	41	28	9
Illinois	283	27	40	25	8
Indiana	285	23	43	27	7
Iowa	285	23	43	26	8
Kansas	290	20	39	32	8
Kentucky	282	28	41	24	6
Louisiana	273	37	41	19	3
Maine	289	22	40	29	10
Maryland	288	26	34	29	12
Massachusetts	299	14	34	36	15
Michigan	280	29	40	25	6
Minnesota	295	17	36	34	13
Mississippi	269	42	39	16	3
Missouri	282	27	41	25	7
Montana	293	17	37	35	11
Nebraska	283	26	42	26	7
Nevada	278	33	38	23	6
New Hampshire	292	18	38	33	11
New Jersey	294	18	35	33	14
New Mexico	274	36	40	20	4
New York	280	30	40	23	7
North Carolina	286	25	38	27	10
North Dakota	292	15	42	34	8
Ohio	289	21	40	31	8
Oklahoma	279	28	44	23	4
Oregon	283	28	39	25	7
Pennsylvania	286	26	35	29	9
Rhode Island	283	27	40	27	7
South Carolina	281	30	38	25	7
South Dakota	291	18	40	33	8
Tennessee	274	36	40	19	5
Texas	290	19	41	31	9
Utah	283	27	38	28	7
Vermont	294	18	36	33	13
Virginia	289	22	38	29	11
Washington	288	23	36	29	11
West Virginia	273	35	44	18	3
Wisconsin	289	21	38	32	9
Wyoming	288	20	43	30	7
Other jurisdictions					
District of Columbia	260	52	31	14	3
DoDEA[1]	288	20	44	30	7

Percentage below *Basic* and at *Basic*   Percentage at *Proficient* and *Advanced*

[1] Department of Defense Education Activity (overseas and domestic schools).

NOTE: The shaded bars are graphed using unrounded numbers. Detail may not sum to totals because of rounding.

SOURCE: U.S. Department of Education, Institute of Education Sciences, National Center for Education Statistics, National Assessment of Educational Progress (NAEP), 2011 Mathematics Assessment.

403

Average scores and achievement-level results in NAEP mathematics for eighth-grade public school students, by race/ethnicity and state/jurisdiction: 2011

	White					Black					Hispanic				
		Percentage of students					Percentage of students					Percentage of students			
State/jurisdiction	Average scale score	Below Basic	At or above Basic	At or above Proficient	At Advanced	Average scale score	Below Basic	At or above Basic	At or above Proficient	At Advanced	Average scale score	Below Basic	At or above Basic	At or above Proficient	At Advanced
Nation (public)	**293**	**17**	**83**	**43**	**10**	**262**	**50**	**50**	**13**	**1**	**269**	**40**	**60**	**20**	**3**
Alabama	280	26	74	28	4	250	64	36	7	#	255	60	40	9	1
Alaska	296	12	88	47	10	273	34	66	17	1	277	33	67	25	5
Arizona	294	17	83	46	12	269	39	61	18	1	266	45	55	18	2
Arkansas	287	21	79	37	6	257	56	44	9	1	272	36	64	20	2
California	290	20	80	41	11	254	58	42	12	1	260	51	49	13	1
Colorado	302	10	90	55	16	270	39	61	17	2	271	38	62	20	3
Connecticut	297	14	86	48	13	262	50	50	11	2	262	51	49	13	1
Delaware	294	15	85	43	10	266	44	56	14	1	274	32	68	21	2
Florida	287	21	79	37	8	258	54	46	11	1	274	35	65	22	3
Georgia	291	18	82	40	9	262	49	51	12	1	277	31	69	25	5
Hawaii	290	18	82	41	7	277	28	72	26	5	263	52	48	19	2
Idaho	291	18	82	41	10	‡	‡	‡	‡	‡	267	42	58	16	3
Illinois	294	16	84	44	11	260	52	48	10	1	272	36	64	19	3
Indiana	290	18	82	40	8	264	46	54	11	1	275	32	68	21	3
Iowa	288	20	80	37	9	258	52	48	11	1	269	38	62	14	1
Kansas	295	14	86	47	10	269	41	59	16	2	274	35	65	22	2
Kentucky	284	25	75	33	7	261	53	47	12	1	269	39	61	18	1
Louisiana	283	25	75	31	4	259	54	46	10	1	269	39	61	16	1
Maine	290	21	79	40	11	265	42	58	18	3	‡	‡	‡	‡	‡
Maryland	303	11	89	56	18	267	45	55	18	3	273	39	61	27	4
Massachusetts	304	9	91	58	17	275	35	65	26	4	273	36	64	21	3
Michigan	286	22	78	35	6	250	66	34	7	#	274	36	64	23	5
Minnesota	302	11	89	55	16	266	45	55	18	1	270	41	59	18	3
Mississippi	283	24	76	30	5	255	60	40	8	#	273	30	70	20	2
Missouri	288	21	79	36	8	254	60	40	8	#	267	42	58	16	#
Montana	297	13	87	49	12	‡	‡	‡	‡	‡	285	23	77	31	7
Nebraska	290	18	82	39	8	255	58	42	8	1	261	52	48	11	1
Nevada	292	17	83	43	10	259	55	45	12	1	266	45	55	15	2
New Hampshire	293	17	83	45	11	‡	‡	‡	‡	‡	266	45	55	15	2
New Jersey	304	9	91	59	17	272	37	63	21	3	274	33	67	24	3
New Mexico	290	19	81	40	8	265	49	51	16	2	269	41	59	18	2
New York	291	18	82	40	9	264	47	53	13	1	263	49	51	13	1
North Carolina	296	15	85	48	13	267	43	57	15	2	275	34	66	23	4
North Dakota	296	11	89	47	9	‡	‡	‡	‡	‡	‡	‡	‡	‡	‡
Ohio	295	14	86	46	10	263	50	50	12	1	273	39	61	26	4
Oklahoma	286	19	81	34	5	262	48	52	11	1	264	44	56	14	1
Oregon	287	22	78	37	9	263	51	49	18	1	268	42	58	17	2
Pennsylvania	294	17	83	47	11	257	56	44	9	1	269	42	58	22	3
Rhode Island	292	18	82	42	10	256	52	48	12	1	261	49	51	13	2
South Carolina	293	17	83	43	10	263	50	50	14	2	273	37	63	25	4
South Dakota	295	13	87	47	10	270	40	60	21	1	274	34	66	20	3
Tennessee	281	27	73	28	6	252	62	38	9	1	266	44	56	15	1
Texas	304	8	92	58	15	277	29	71	21	4	283	24	76	31	4
Utah	289	20	80	41	8	‡	‡	‡	‡	‡	257	57	43	9	1
Vermont	295	18	82	47	13	‡	‡	‡	‡	‡	‡	‡	‡	‡	‡
Virginia	297	15	85	48	14	268	42	58	18	1	279	31	69	27	5
Washington	294	17	83	46	12	265	44	56	15	2	269	42	58	22	3
West Virginia	274	34	66	22	3	260	51	49	10	#	‡	‡	‡	‡	‡
Wisconsin	295	15	85	47	11	256	57	43	11	1	270	40	60	21	3
Wyoming	291	16	84	41	8	‡	‡	‡	‡	‡	271	37	63	20	2
Other jurisdictions															
District of Columbia	319	3	97	76	32	256	56	44	13	2	261	50	50	17	2
DoDEA[1]	295	13	87	46	10	274	32	68	17	2	282	26	74	29	4

See notes at end of table.

Average scores and achievement-level results in NAEP mathematics for eighth-grade public school students, by race/ethnicity and state/jurisdiction: 2011—Continued

State/jurisdiction	Asian/Pacific Islander					American Indian/Alaska Native				
	Average scale score	Percentage of students				Average scale score	Percentage of students			
		Below Basic	At or above Basic	At or above Proficient	At Advanced		Below Basic	At or above Basic	At or above Proficient	At Advanced
Nation (public)	**302**	**15**	**85**	**55**	**22**	**266**	**45**	**55**	**17**	**4**
Alabama	‡	‡	‡	‡	‡	‡	‡	‡	‡	‡
Alaska	282	29	71	32	8	258	52	48	15	3
Arizona	302	11	89	58	17	253	60	40	12	3
Arkansas	‡	‡	‡	‡	‡	‡	‡	‡	‡	‡
California	298	17	83	50	19	‡	‡	‡	‡	‡
Colorado	313	8	92	67	30	‡	‡	‡	‡	‡
Connecticut	307	8	92	60	20	‡	‡	‡	‡	‡
Delaware	311	7	93	67	24	‡	‡	‡	‡	‡
Florida	312	8	92	65	25	‡	‡	‡	‡	‡
Georgia	302	12	88	52	24	‡	‡	‡	‡	‡
Hawaii	277	33	67	29	6	‡	‡	‡	‡	‡
Idaho	‡	‡	‡	‡	‡	‡	‡	‡	‡	‡
Illinois	314	8	92	67	31	‡	‡	‡	‡	‡
Indiana	‡	‡	‡	‡	‡	‡	‡	‡	‡	‡
Iowa	291	23	77	45	11	‡	‡	‡	‡	‡
Kansas	300	15	85	53	22	‡	‡	‡	‡	‡
Kentucky	‡	‡	‡	‡	‡	‡	‡	‡	‡	‡
Louisiana	‡	‡	‡	‡	‡	‡	‡	‡	‡	‡
Maine	‡	‡	‡	‡	‡	‡	‡	‡	‡	‡
Maryland	311	9	91	65	27	‡	‡	‡	‡	‡
Massachusetts	320	6	94	72	39	‡	‡	‡	‡	‡
Michigan	310	13	87	63	31	‡	‡	‡	‡	‡
Minnesota	282	27	73	35	7	263	49	51	11	4
Mississippi	‡	‡	‡	‡	‡	‡	‡	‡	‡	‡
Missouri	‡	‡	‡	‡	‡	‡	‡	‡	‡	‡
Montana	‡	‡	‡	‡	‡	264	47	53	19	5
Nebraska	‡	‡	‡	‡	‡	‡	‡	‡	‡	‡
Nevada	287	27	73	41	11	‡	‡	‡	‡	‡
New Hampshire	303	16	84	60	24	‡	‡	‡	‡	‡
New Jersey	318	6	94	73	36	‡	‡	‡	‡	‡
New Mexico	‡	‡	‡	‡	‡	258	56	44	7	1
New York	302	14	86	55	21	‡	‡	‡	‡	‡
North Carolina	314	12	88	71	38	265	46	54	22	5
North Dakota	‡	‡	‡	‡	‡	264	46	54	15	2
Ohio	‡	‡	‡	‡	‡	‡	‡	‡	‡	‡
Oklahoma	304	13	87	60	19	273	36	64	21	3
Oregon	297	18	82	49	18	260	55	45	16	3
Pennsylvania	310	14	86	62	33	‡	‡	‡	‡	‡
Rhode Island	287	23	77	41	7	‡	‡	‡	‡	‡
South Carolina	‡	‡	‡	‡	‡	‡	‡	‡	‡	‡
South Dakota	‡	‡	‡	‡	‡	263	48	52	14	2
Tennessee	‡	‡	‡	‡	‡	‡	‡	‡	‡	‡
Texas	316	3	97	69	30	‡	‡	‡	‡	‡
Utah	284	24	76	35	7	244	73	27	4	2
Vermont	‡	‡	‡	‡	‡	‡	‡	‡	‡	‡
Virginia	313	7	93	65	32	‡	‡	‡	‡	‡
Washington	302	16	84	55	25	256	51	49	12	2
West Virginia	‡	‡	‡	‡	‡	‡	‡	‡	‡	‡
Wisconsin	290	24	76	43	16	‡	‡	‡	‡	‡
Wyoming	‡	‡	‡	‡	‡	‡	‡	‡	‡	‡
Other jurisdictions										
District of Columbia	‡	‡	‡	‡	‡	‡	‡	‡	‡	‡
DoDEA[1]	290	17	83	40	8	‡	‡	‡	‡	‡

\# Rounds to zero.

‡ Reporting standards not met. Sample size insufficient to permit a reliable estimate.

[1] Department of Defense Education Activity (overseas and domestic schools).

NOTE: Black includes African American, Hispanic includes Latino, and Pacific Islander includes Native Hawaiian. Race categories exclude Hispanic origin. Results are not shown for students of two or more races. Detail may not sum to totals because of rounding.

SOURCE: U.S. Department of Education, Institute of Education Sciences, National Center for Education Statistics, National Assessment of Educational Progress (NAEP), 2011 Mathematics Assessment.

Average scores and achievement-level results in NAEP mathematics for eighth-grade public school students, by gender and state/jurisdiction: 2011

State/jurisdiction	Male					Female				
	Average scale score	Percentage of students				Average scale score	Percentage of students			
		Below Basic	At or above Basic	At or above Proficient	At Advanced		Below Basic	At or above Basic	At or above Proficient	At Advanced
Nation (public)	**283**	**28**	**72**	**34**	**9**	**282**	**28**	**72**	**33**	**7**
Alabama	269	40	60	21	3	269	40	60	19	2
Alaska	283	26	74	36	7	284	25	75	35	7
Arizona	282	30	70	34	9	276	34	66	29	6
Arkansas	280	30	70	31	6	278	31	69	28	4
California	273	38	62	26	7	273	39	61	25	6
Colorado	291	21	79	44	12	292	19	81	43	13
Connecticut	288	24	76	39	11	286	26	74	37	9
Delaware	282	27	73	31	7	284	25	75	33	7
Florida	278	32	68	29	6	277	32	68	27	5
Georgia	279	33	67	29	7	278	30	70	27	5
Hawaii	277	33	67	30	6	279	31	69	30	6
Idaho	287	23	77	37	9	286	23	77	36	8
Illinois	283	28	72	33	10	283	26	74	32	7
Indiana	285	24	76	34	7	285	23	77	34	6
Iowa	286	23	77	34	8	284	24	76	33	7
Kansas	291	19	81	41	9	289	21	79	40	8
Kentucky	282	29	71	32	7	281	28	72	29	5
Louisiana	272	39	61	22	3	274	34	66	22	3
Maine	288	23	77	38	11	289	20	80	39	10
Maryland	289	25	75	42	13	287	26	74	38	10
Massachusetts	299	15	85	52	17	298	14	86	51	14
Michigan	282	28	72	33	7	279	30	70	29	5
Minnesota	295	17	83	47	14	295	16	84	48	12
Mississippi	267	45	55	18	3	272	39	61	20	3
Missouri	283	27	73	33	7	281	28	72	30	6
Montana	293	18	82	46	12	293	16	84	45	10
Nebraska	284	25	75	35	8	282	26	74	31	5
Nevada	279	32	68	29	7	277	34	66	28	5
New Hampshire	292	19	81	44	11	292	18	82	44	11
New Jersey	294	19	81	48	15	294	17	83	46	12
New Mexico	275	35	65	24	4	274	36	64	24	3
New York	280	30	70	30	7	281	30	70	30	7
North Carolina	285	26	74	37	10	287	23	77	37	9
North Dakota	293	15	85	45	9	291	16	84	40	7
Ohio	290	21	79	40	9	288	22	78	37	8
Oklahoma	280	28	72	29	5	278	29	71	26	3
Oregon	285	26	74	35	9	280	30	70	30	6
Pennsylvania	287	26	74	40	10	285	26	74	38	9
Rhode Island	283	27	73	35	8	283	26	74	33	6
South Carolina	280	31	69	31	7	282	28	72	32	7
South Dakota	291	19	81	42	9	290	17	83	41	7
Tennessee	276	35	65	26	6	272	37	63	22	3
Texas	291	19	81	41	10	290	18	82	39	7
Utah	285	26	74	37	8	281	28	72	33	5
Vermont	294	19	81	46	14	294	17	83	46	12
Virginia	289	23	77	40	12	289	22	78	40	10
Washington	288	25	75	41	11	288	22	78	40	11
West Virginia	274	34	66	22	3	272	36	64	21	3
Wisconsin	290	20	80	43	11	287	22	78	39	8
Wyoming	290	18	82	41	9	285	21	79	34	5
Other jurisdictions										
District of Columbia	259	54	46	17	4	262	50	50	17	3
DoDEA[1]	289	20	80	37	8	287	20	80	36	6

[1] Department of Defense Education Activity (overseas and domestic schools).
NOTE: Detail may not sum to totals because of rounding.
SOURCE: U.S. Department of Education, Institute of Education Sciences, National Center for Education Statistics, National Assessment of Educational Progress (NAEP), 2011 Mathematics Assessment.

Average mathematics scale score of 8th-grade public school students and percentage attaining mathematics achievement levels, by state: Selected years, 1990 through 2011

State	Average scale score[1]								Percent attaining mathematics achievement levels, 2011			
	1990[2]	1996[3]	2000	2003	2005	2007	2009	2011	Below Basic	At or above Basic[4]	At or above Proficient[5]	At Advanced[6]
1	2	3	4	5	6	7	8	9	10	11	12	13
United States	262 (1.4)	271 (1.2)	272 (0.9)	276 (0.3)	278 (0.2)	280 (0.3)	282 (0.3)	283 (0.2)	28 (0.3)	72 (0.3)	34 (0.2)	8 (0.2)
Alabama	253 (1.1)	257 (2.1)	264 (1.8)	262 (1.5)	262 (1.5)	266 (1.5)	269 (1.2)	269 (1.4)	40 (1.9)	60 (1.9)	20 (1.5)	3 (0.5)
Alaska.............................	— (†)	278 (1.8)	— (†)	279 (0.9)	279 (0.8)	283 (1.1)	283 (1.0)	283 (0.8)	26 (0.8)	74 (0.8)	35 (1.1)	7 (0.6)
Arizona[7]	260 (1.3)	268 (1.6)	269 (1.8)	271 (1.2)	274 (1.1)	276 (1.2)	277 (1.4)	279 (1.0)	32 (1.2)	68 (1.2)	31 (1.5)	7 (0.7)
Arkansas	256 (0.9)	262 (1.5)	257 (1.5)	266 (1.2)	272 (1.2)	274 (1.1)	276 (1.1)	279 (1.0)	30 (1.4)	70 (1.4)	29 (1.2)	5 (0.7)
California[7]	256 (1.3)	263 (1.9)	260 (2.1)	267 (1.2)	269 (0.7)	270 (0.8)	270 (1.3)	273 (1.2)	39 (1.4)	61 (1.4)	25 (1.2)	6 (0.8)
Colorado	267 (0.9)	276 (1.1)	— (†)	283 (1.1)	281 (1.2)	286 (0.9)	287 (1.4)	292 (1.1)	20 (1.1)	80 (1.1)	43 (1.3)	12 (0.9)
Connecticut.....................	270 (1.0)	280 (1.1)	281 (1.3)	284 (1.2)	281 (1.4)	282 (1.5)	289 (1.0)	287 (1.1)	25 (1.3)	75 (1.3)	38 (1.5)	10 (1.0)
Delaware	261 (0.9)	267 (0.9)	— (†)	277 (0.7)	281 (0.6)	283 (0.6)	284 (0.5)	283 (0.7)	26 (0.8)	74 (0.8)	32 (1.1)	7 (0.8)
District of Columbia	231 (0.9)	233 (1.3)	235 (1.1)	243 (0.8)	245 (0.9)	248 (0.9)	254 (0.9)	260 (1.0)	52 (1.0)	48 (1.0)	17 (0.8)	3 (0.4)
Florida.............................	255 (1.2)	264 (1.8)	— (†)	271 (1.5)	274 (1.1)	277 (1.3)	279 (1.1)	278 (0.8)	32 (0.9)	68 (0.9)	28 (1.0)	6 (0.5)
Georgia	259 (1.3)	262 (1.6)	265 (1.2)	270 (1.2)	272 (1.1)	275 (1.0)	278 (0.9)	278 (1.0)	32 (1.1)	68 (1.1)	28 (1.5)	6 (0.7)
Hawaii	251 (0.8)	262 (1.0)	262 (1.4)	266 (0.8)	266 (0.7)	269 (0.8)	274 (0.7)	278 (0.7)	32 (0.9)	68 (0.9)	30 (0.9)	6 (0.4)
Idaho[7]	271 (0.8)	— (†)	277 (1.0)	280 (0.9)	281 (0.9)	284 (0.9)	287 (0.8)	287 (0.8)	23 (1.0)	77 (1.0)	37 (1.1)	9 (0.8)
Illinois[7]	261 (1.7)	— (†)	275 (1.7)	277 (1.2)	278 (1.1)	280 (1.1)	282 (1.2)	283 (1.1)	27 (1.2)	73 (1.2)	33 (1.3)	8 (0.7)
Indiana[7]	267 (1.2)	276 (1.4)	281 (1.4)	281 (1.1)	282 (1.0)	285 (1.1)	287 (0.9)	285 (1.0)	23 (1.2)	77 (1.2)	34 (1.2)	7 (0.8)
Iowa................................	278 (1.1)	284 (1.3)	— (†)	284 (0.8)	284 (0.9)	285 (0.9)	284 (1.0)	285 (0.9)	23 (1.2)	77 (1.2)	34 (1.3)	8 (0.7)
Kansas[7]	— (†)	— (†)	283 (1.7)	284 (1.3)	284 (1.0)	290 (1.1)	289 (1.0)	290 (0.9)	20 (0.9)	80 (0.9)	41 (1.4)	8 (0.8)
Kentucky	257 (1.2)	267 (1.1)	270 (1.3)	274 (1.2)	274 (1.2)	279 (1.1)	279 (1.1)	282 (0.9)	28 (1.2)	72 (1.2)	31 (1.2)	6 (0.6)
Louisiana	246 (1.2)	252 (1.6)	259 (1.5)	266 (1.5)	268 (1.4)	272 (1.1)	272 (1.6)	273 (1.2)	37 (1.4)	63 (1.4)	22 (1.2)	3 (0.4)
Maine[7]...........................	— (†)	284 (1.3)	281 (1.1)	282 (0.9)	281 (0.8)	286 (0.8)	286 (0.7)	289 (0.8)	22 (0.8)	78 (0.8)	39 (1.1)	10 (0.7)
Maryland	261 (1.4)	270 (2.1)	272 (1.7)	278 (1.0)	278 (1.1)	286 (1.2)	288 (1.1)	288 (1.2)	26 (1.3)	74 (1.3)	40 (1.4)	12 (0.8)
Massachusetts.................	— (†)	278 (1.7)	279 (1.5)	287 (0.9)	292 (0.9)	298 (1.3)	299 (1.3)	299 (0.8)	14 (0.8)	86 (0.8)	51 (1.0)	15 (0.9)
Michigan[7]	264 (1.2)	277 (1.8)	277 (1.9)	276 (2.0)	277 (1.5)	277 (1.4)	278 (1.6)	280 (1.4)	29 (1.6)	71 (1.6)	31 (1.7)	6 (0.8)
Minnesota	275 (0.9)	284 (1.3)	287 (1.4)	291 (1.1)	290 (1.2)	292 (1.0)	294 (1.0)	295 (1.0)	17 (1.0)	83 (1.0)	48 (1.1)	13 (0.8)
Mississippi	— (†)	250 (1.2)	254 (1.1)	261 (1.1)	263 (1.2)	265 (0.8)	265 (1.2)	269 (1.4)	42 (2.0)	58 (2.0)	19 (1.2)	3 (0.6)
Missouri	— (†)	273 (1.4)	271 (1.5)	279 (1.1)	276 (1.3)	281 (1.0)	286 (1.0)	282 (1.1)	27 (1.4)	73 (1.4)	32 (1.3)	7 (0.7)
Montana[7]	280 (0.9)	283 (1.3)	285 (1.4)	286 (0.8)	286 (0.7)	287 (0.7)	292 (0.9)	293 (0.6)	17 (0.9)	83 (0.9)	46 (0.9)	11 (0.7)
Nebraska	276 (1.0)	283 (1.0)	280 (1.2)	282 (0.9)	284 (1.0)	284 (1.0)	284 (1.1)	283 (0.8)	26 (1.3)	74 (1.3)	33 (1.2)	7 (0.7)
Nevada	— (†)	— (†)	265 (0.8)	268 (0.8)	270 (0.8)	271 (0.8)	274 (0.7)	278 (0.8)	33 (1.2)	67 (1.2)	29 (1.3)	6 (0.7)
New Hampshire	273 (0.9)	— (†)	— (†)	286 (0.8)	285 (0.8)	288 (0.7)	292 (0.9)	292 (0.7)	18 (1.0)	82 (1.0)	44 (0.9)	11 (0.6)
New Jersey	270 (1.1)	— (†)	— (†)	281 (1.1)	284 (1.4)	289 (1.2)	293 (1.4)	294 (1.2)	18 (1.0)	82 (1.0)	47 (1.5)	14 (1.0)
New Mexico	256 (0.7)	262 (1.2)	259 (1.3)	263 (1.0)	263 (0.9)	268 (0.9)	270 (1.1)	274 (0.8)	36 (1.0)	64 (1.2)	24 (0.9)	4 (0.4)
New York[7]	261 (1.4)	270 (1.7)	271 (2.2)	280 (1.1)	280 (0.9)	280 (1.2)	283 (1.2)	280 (0.9)	30 (1.1)	70 (1.1)	30 (1.3)	7 (0.6)
North Carolina	250 (1.1)	268 (1.4)	276 (1.3)	281 (1.0)	282 (0.9)	284 (1.1)	284 (1.3)	286 (1.0)	25 (1.3)	75 (1.3)	37 (1.3)	10 (0.8)
North Dakota	281 (1.2)	284 (0.9)	282 (1.1)	287 (0.8)	287 (0.6)	292 (0.7)	293 (0.7)	292 (0.6)	15 (0.9)	85 (0.9)	43 (1.4)	8 (0.8)
Ohio	264 (1.0)	— (†)	281 (1.6)	282 (1.3)	283 (1.1)	285 (1.2)	286 (1.0)	289 (1.0)	21 (1.2)	79 (1.2)	39 (1.4)	8 (0.9)
Oklahoma	263 (1.3)	— (†)	270 (1.3)	272 (1.1)	271 (1.0)	275 (0.9)	276 (1.0)	279 (1.0)	28 (1.3)	72 (1.3)	27 (1.2)	4 (0.6)
Oregon[7]	271 (1.2)	276 (1.6)	280 (1.5)	281 (1.3)	282 (1.0)	284 (1.1)	285 (1.0)	283 (1.0)	28 (1.2)	72 (1.2)	33 (1.2)	7 (0.8)
Pennsylvania...................	266 (1.6)	— (†)	— (†)	279 (1.1)	281 (1.5)	286 (1.1)	288 (1.3)	286 (1.2)	26 (1.4)	74 (1.4)	39 (1.1)	9 (0.8)
Rhode Island	260 (0.6)	269 (0.9)	269 (1.3)	272 (0.7)	272 (0.8)	275 (0.7)	278 (0.8)	283 (0.5)	27 (0.9)	73 (0.9)	34 (0.9)	7 (0.6)
South Carolina.................	— (†)	261 (1.5)	265 (1.5)	277 (1.3)	281 (0.9)	282 (1.0)	280 (1.3)	281 (1.1)	30 (1.3)	70 (1.3)	32 (1.2)	7 (0.7)
South Dakota	— (†)	— (†)	— (†)	285 (0.8)	287 (0.6)	288 (0.8)	291 (0.5)	291 (0.5)	18 (0.7)	82 (0.7)	42 (1.0)	8 (0.6)
Tennessee	— (†)	263 (1.4)	262 (1.5)	268 (1.8)	271 (1.1)	274 (1.1)	275 (1.4)	274 (1.2)	36 (1.5)	64 (1.5)	24 (1.3)	5 (0.7)
Texas	258 (1.4)	270 (1.4)	273 (1.6)	277 (1.1)	281 (0.6)	286 (1.0)	287 (1.3)	290 (0.9)	19 (1.1)	81 (1.1)	40 (1.5)	9 (0.7)
Utah	— (†)	277 (1.0)	274 (1.2)	281 (1.0)	279 (0.7)	281 (0.9)	284 (0.9)	283 (0.8)	27 (1.0)	73 (1.0)	35 (1.0)	7 (0.7)
Vermont[7]	— (†)	279 (1.0)	281 (1.5)	286 (0.8)	287 (0.8)	291 (0.7)	293 (0.6)	294 (0.7)	18 (1.1)	82 (1.1)	46 (1.1)	13 (0.8)
Virginia	264 (1.5)	270 (1.6)	275 (1.3)	282 (1.3)	284 (1.1)	288 (1.1)	286 (1.1)	289 (1.1)	22 (1.3)	78 (1.3)	40 (1.5)	11 (1.0)
Washington......................	— (†)	276 (1.3)	— (†)	281 (0.9)	285 (1.0)	285 (1.0)	289 (1.0)	288 (1.0)	23 (0.9)	77 (0.9)	40 (1.3)	11 (0.8)
West Virginia	256 (1.0)	265 (1.0)	266 (1.2)	271 (1.2)	269 (1.0)	270 (1.0)	270 (1.0)	273 (0.7)	35 (1.1)	65 (1.1)	21 (0.8)	3 (0.4)
Wisconsin	274 (1.3)	283 (1.5)	— (†)	284 (1.3)	285 (1.2)	286 (1.1)	288 (0.9)	289 (1.0)	21 (0.9)	79 (0.9)	41 (1.3)	9 (0.8)
Wyoming	272 (0.7)	275 (0.9)	276 (1.0)	284 (0.7)	282 (0.8)	287 (0.7)	286 (0.6)	288 (0.6)	20 (1.0)	80 (1.0)	37 (1.2)	7 (0.7)
Department of Defense dependents schools[8] ...	— (†)	274 (0.9)	277 (1.1)	285 (0.7)	284 (0.7)	285 (0.8)	287 (0.9)	288 (0.8)	20 (1.0)	80 (1.0)	37 (1.4)	7 (0.8)

—Not available.
†Not applicable.
[1]Scale ranges from 0 to 500.
[2]Accommodations were not permitted for this assessment.
[3]The 1996 data in this table do not include students who were tested with accommodations. Data for students tested with accommodations are not available at the state level for 1996.
[4]Basic denotes partial mastery of the knowledge and skills that are fundamental for proficient work at the 8th-grade level.
[5]Proficient represents solid academic performance for 8th-graders. Students reaching this level have demonstrated competency over challenging subject matter.
[6]Advanced signifies superior performance.
[7]Did not meet one or more of the guidelines for school participation in 2000. Data are subject to appreciable nonresponse bias.

[8]Prior to 2005, NAEP divided the Department of Defense (DoD) schools into two jurisdictions, domestic and overseas. In 2005, NAEP began combining the DoD domestic and overseas schools into a single jurisdiction. Data shown in this table for years prior to 2005 were recalculated for comparability.
NOTE: For 2000 and later years, includes public school students who were tested with accommodations; excludes only those students with disabilities (SD) and English language learners (ELL) who were unable to be tested even with accommodations. SD and ELL populations, accommodation rates, and exclusion rates vary from state to state. Detail may not sum to totals because of rounding. Standard errors appear in parentheses.
SOURCE: U.S. Department of Education, National Center for Education Statistics, National Assessment of Educational Progress (NAEP), 1990, 1996, 2000, 2003, 2005, 2007, 2009, and 2011 Mathematics Assessments, retrieved November 2, 2011, from the Main NAEP Data Explorer (http://nces.ed.gov/nationsreportcard/naepdata). (This table was prepared November 2011.)

Average mathematics scale score of 8th-grade public school students, by race/ethnicity, level of parental education, and state: 2011

State	White		Black		Hispanic		Asian		Native Hawaiian/ Pacific Islander		American Indian/ Alaska Native		Did not finish high school		Graduated high school		Some education after high school		Graduated college	
1	2		3		4		5		6		7		8		9		10		11	
United States	293	(0.2)	262	(0.5)	269	(0.5)	305	(1.1)	265	(2.5)	266	(1.0)	265	(0.6)	271	(0.5)	285	(0.3)	294	(0.3)
Alabama	280	(1.5)	250	(1.7)	255	(3.1)	‡	(†)	‡	(†)	‡	(†)	257	(2.7)	258	(2.0)	275	(1.6)	278	(1.8)
Alaska..........................	296	(1.2)	273	(2.8)	277	(2.9)	287	(2.6)	‡	(†)	258	(2.2)	‡	(†)	‡	(†)	‡	(†)	‡	(†)
Arizona	294	(1.5)	269	(3.2)	266	(1.3)	303	(4.2)	‡	(†)	253	(3.1)	267	(2.4)	264	(1.8)	281	(2.0)	296	(1.4)
Arkansas	287	(0.9)	257	(1.7)	272	(2.2)	‡	(†)	‡	(†)	‡	(†)	269	(2.1)	268	(1.5)	283	(2.0)	288	(1.5)
California	290	(1.9)	254	(3.2)	260	(1.0)	301	(2.7)	‡	(†)	‡	(†)	254	(1.9)	261	(2.4)	281	(1.6)	290	(1.8)
Colorado	302	(1.1)	270	(2.6)	271	(1.5)	313	(4.1)	‡	(†)	‡	(†)	264	(2.7)	272	(1.9)	293	(1.7)	304	(1.3)
Connecticut..................	297	(1.0)	262	(1.8)	262	(1.8)	307	(3.9)	‡	(†)	‡	(†)	259	(3.0)	268	(2.2)	284	(1.7)	298	(1.3)
Delaware......................	294	(1.0)	266	(1.0)	274	(2.0)	311	(3.5)	‡	(†)	‡	(†)	269	(2.9)	274	(1.7)	286	(1.3)	290	(1.1)
District of Columbia	319	(2.6)	256	(0.8)	261	(2.4)	‡	(†)	‡	(†)	‡	(†)	255	(3.3)	251	(2.0)	266	(1.7)	269	(1.4)
Florida.........................	287	(1.2)	258	(1.7)	274	(1.0)	314	(4.3)	‡	(†)	‡	(†)	265	(1.9)	268	(1.6)	282	(1.7)	286	(1.3)
Georgia	291	(1.3)	262	(1.1)	277	(2.3)	303	(5.0)	‡	(†)	‡	(†)	268	(2.5)	264	(2.0)	282	(1.7)	288	(1.4)
Hawaii	290	(1.6)	277	(4.3)	263	(3.3)	288	(1.2)	263	(1.4)	‡	(†)	261	(3.8)	267	(1.5)	282	(1.9)	286	(1.1)
Idaho...........................	291	(0.8)	‡	(†)	267	(1.9)	‡	(†)	‡	(†)	‡	(†)	267	(2.1)	274	(1.7)	288	(1.7)	297	(1.0)
Illinois.........................	294	(1.4)	260	(1.5)	272	(1.5)	315	(3.5)	‡	(†)	‡	(†)	271	(2.2)	268	(1.6)	285	(1.6)	294	(1.5)
Indiana	290	(1.0)	264	(2.3)	275	(2.4)	‡	(†)	‡	(†)	‡	(†)	270	(2.5)	274	(1.5)	285	(1.9)	295	(1.3)
Iowa	288	(1.0)	258	(3.3)	269	(2.9)	293	(6.0)	‡	(†)	‡	(†)	268	(2.5)	274	(1.8)	283	(1.7)	295	(1.1)
Kansas	295	(1.0)	269	(2.1)	274	(1.9)	302	(5.5)	‡	(†)	‡	(†)	272	(2.8)	278	(1.9)	290	(1.6)	298	(1.2)
Kentucky	284	(1.0)	261	(1.8)	269	(3.5)	‡	(†)	‡	(†)	‡	(†)	267	(1.9)	272	(1.7)	281	(1.4)	293	(1.2)
Louisiana	283	(1.2)	259	(1.6)	269	(4.4)	‡	(†)	‡	(†)	‡	(†)	262	(2.4)	267	(1.8)	278	(1.8)	278	(1.3)
Maine...........................	290	(0.8)	265	(5.1)	‡	(†)	‡	(†)	‡	(†)	‡	(†)	269	(3.1)	274	(1.9)	289	(1.8)	298	(1.0)
Maryland.......................	303	(1.3)	267	(1.5)	273	(3.1)	313	(3.4)	‡	(†)	‡	(†)	264	(4.0)	271	(2.1)	288	(1.8)	298	(1.3)
Massachusetts................	304	(0.8)	275	(3.0)	273	(1.7)	321	(3.9)	‡	(†)	‡	(†)	271	(2.7)	285	(1.7)	295	(1.8)	307	(0.9)
Michigan	286	(1.2)	250	(2.4)	274	(4.3)	311	(7.0)	‡	(†)	‡	(†)	260	(3.9)	266	(1.9)	278	(2.2)	291	(1.7)
Minnesota	302	(0.9)	266	(2.8)	270	(2.6)	282	(4.2)	‡	(†)	263	(3.7)	267	(3.9)	275	(2.3)	294	(1.8)	305	(1.0)
Mississippi	283	(1.2)	255	(1.6)	273	(4.7)	‡	(†)	‡	(†)	‡	(†)	260	(2.7)	257	(2.1)	276	(1.7)	276	(1.6)
Missouri	288	(1.0)	254	(2.7)	267	(2.9)	‡	(†)	‡	(†)	‡	(†)	265	(2.6)	270	(1.8)	283	(1.6)	291	(1.4)
Montana.......................	297	(0.6)	‡	(†)	285	(4.1)	‡	(†)	‡	(†)	264	(3.2)	272	(4.1)	281	(1.8)	291	(1.8)	302	(0.7)
Nebraska......................	290	(0.8)	255	(3.1)	261	(1.7)	‡	(†)	‡	(†)	‡	(†)	262	(2.6)	271	(2.2)	280	(1.6)	294	(1.0)
Nevada	292	(1.3)	259	(2.2)	266	(1.1)	292	(3.1)	‡	(†)	‡	(†)	262	(2.1)	269	(1.6)	285	(1.8)	290	(1.3)
New Hampshire	293	(0.7)	‡	(†)	266	(3.4)	305	(5.5)	‡	(†)	‡	(†)	269	(3.2)	281	(1.7)	290	(2.0)	300	(0.9)
New Jersey....................	304	(1.1)	272	(2.5)	274	(2.3)	318	(2.8)	‡	(†)	‡	(†)	273	(3.4)	280	(2.3)	287	(2.3)	304	(1.2)
New Mexico...................	290	(1.4)	265	(4.3)	269	(0.9)	‡	(†)	‡	(†)	258	(2.7)	259	(2.0)	267	(1.7)	279	(1.6)	287	(1.0)
New York......................	291	(1.2)	264	(1.8)	263	(1.3)	302	(2.9)	‡	(†)	‡	(†)	266	(2.0)	270	(1.6)	282	(1.6)	289	(1.1)
North Carolina	296	(1.0)	267	(1.6)	275	(1.9)	316	(4.4)	‡	(†)	265	(4.8)	273	(2.7)	272	(1.6)	289	(1.4)	295	(1.3)
North Dakota.................	296	(0.6)	‡	(†)	‡	(†)	‡	(†)	‡	(†)	264	(2.5)	‡	(†)	276	(1.8)	291	(1.8)	298	(0.7)
Ohio.............................	295	(1.0)	263	(1.7)	273	(4.0)	‡	(†)	‡	(†)	‡	(†)	266	(2.8)	277	(1.4)	290	(1.5)	297	(1.3)
Oklahoma.....................	286	(1.1)	262	(2.6)	264	(2.8)	305	(4.7)	‡	(†)	273	(1.9)	264	(2.4)	267	(1.9)	280	(1.3)	292	(1.3)
Oregon.........................	287	(1.2)	263	(4.6)	268	(1.8)	302	(5.0)	‡	(†)	260	(5.6)	266	(2.0)	273	(2.0)	286	(1.9)	295	(1.2)
Pennsylvania.................	294	(1.0)	257	(2.1)	269	(3.4)	312	(4.8)	‡	(†)	‡	(†)	261	(4.7)	274	(1.3)	289	(1.9)	296	(1.5)
Rhode Island	292	(0.7)	256	(2.7)	261	(1.8)	287	(4.9)	‡	(†)	‡	(†)	263	(2.6)	269	(2.0)	281	(1.8)	296	(0.9)
South Carolina..............	293	(0.9)	263	(1.8)	273	(3.5)	‡	(†)	‡	(†)	‡	(†)	262	(2.3)	269	(1.6)	283	(1.7)	290	(1.4)
South Dakota................	295	(0.6)	270	(4.2)	274	(3.7)	‡	(†)	‡	(†)	263	(2.1)	269	(2.5)	275	(1.3)	291	(1.6)	298	(0.7)
Tennessee	281	(1.2)	252	(2.4)	266	(2.8)	‡	(†)	‡	(†)	‡	(†)	262	(3.4)	265	(1.5)	277	(1.6)	284	(1.6)
Texas	304	(1.2)	277	(1.7)	283	(1.2)	317	(3.8)	‡	(†)	‡	(†)	281	(1.9)	285	(1.4)	293	(1.6)	301	(1.3)
Utah.............................	289	(0.9)	‡	(†)	257	(1.9)	‡	(†)	‡	(†)	244	(6.5)	253	(2.6)	265	(1.9)	280	(1.8)	295	(1.0)
Vermont.......................	295	(0.8)	‡	(†)	‡	(†)	‡	(†)	‡	(†)	‡	(†)	270	(3.3)	276	(2.0)	295	(1.7)	305	(0.9)
Virginia........................	297	(1.4)	268	(1.7)	279	(1.8)	313	(3.1)	‡	(†)	‡	(†)	267	(2.6)	272	(2.0)	287	(1.7)	300	(1.3)
Washington...................	294	(1.1)	265	(3.4)	269	(2.4)	306	(3.3)	‡	(†)	256	(6.5)	267	(2.0)	276	(2.0)	288	(1.8)	301	(1.4)
West Virginia.................	274	(0.8)	260	(3.1)	‡	(†)	‡	(†)	‡	(†)	‡	(†)	253	(3.0)	264	(1.2)	277	(1.4)	283	(1.1)
Wisconsin.....................	295	(1.0)	256	(3.0)	270	(2.3)	289	(5.0)	‡	(†)	‡	(†)	258	(3.2)	274	(1.8)	288	(1.9)	299	(1.0)
Wyoming.......................	291	(0.7)	‡	(†)	271	(2.5)	‡	(†)	‡	(†)	‡	(†)	268	(4.0)	276	(1.8)	288	(1.4)	297	(0.9)
Department of Defense dependents schools.....	295	(1.2)	274	(1.9)	282	(1.7)	292	(2.4)	‡	(†)	‡	(†)	‡	(†)	276	(1.8)	287	(1.8)	293	(1.1)

†Not applicable.
‡Reporting standards not met. Either there are too few cases or item response rates fell below the required standards for reporting.
[1]Excludes students who responded "I don't know" to the question about educational level of parents.
NOTE: Scale ranges from 0 to 500. Includes public school students who were tested with accommodations; excludes only those students with disabilities (SD) and English language learners (ELL) who were unable to be tested even with accommodations. SD and ELL populations, accommodation rates, and exclusion rates vary from state to state. Detail may not sum to totals because of rounding. Standard errors appear in parentheses.
SOURCE: U.S. Department of Education, National Center for Education Statistics, National Assessment of Educational Progress (NAEP), 2011 Mathematics Assessment, retrieved November 2, 2011, from the Main NAEP Data Explorer (http://nces.ed.gov/nationsreport card/naepdata/). (This table was prepared November 2011.)

Average mathematics scale scores of 4th- and 8th-grade public school students and percentage at or above selected mathematics achievement levels, by race/ethnicity and jurisdiction or specific urban district: 2007, 2009, and 2011

Grade level and jurisdiction or specific urban district	Average reading scale score[1]											Percent of students	
	2007	2009				2011						2011	
	All students	All students	White	Black	Hispanic	All students	White	Black	Hispanic	Asian		At or above Basic[2]	At or above Proficient[3]
1	2	3	4	5	6	7	8	9	10	11		12	13
4th grade													
United States	239 (0.2)	239 (0.2)	248 (0.2)	222 (0.3)	227 (0.4)	240 (0.2)	249 (0.2)	224 (0.4)	229 (0.3)	257 (1.1)		82 (0.2)	40 (0.3)
Large city	230 (0.5)	231 (0.5)	250 (1.0)	219 (0.6)	226 (0.5)	233 (0.6)	251 (0.8)	222 (0.5)	228 (0.6)	249 (2.1)		74 (0.7)	30 (0.8)
Albuquerque	— (†)	— (†)	— (†)	— (†)	— (†)	235 (1.3)	254 (1.9)	‡ (†)	229 (1.3)	‡ (†)		76 (1.4)	34 (1.7)
Atlanta	224 (0.9)	225 (0.8)	266 (1.8)	218 (1.0)	222 (3.7)	228 (0.7)	269 (1.4)	219 (0.8)	230 (2.8)	‡ (†)		66 (1.2)	25 (0.9)
Austin	241 (1.2)	240 (1.0)	262 (1.5)	226 (2.7)	233 (1.1)	245 (1.1)	266 (1.5)	232 (2.7)	237 (1.5)	‡ (†)		87 (1.8)	46 (1.8)
Baltimore City	— (†)	222 (1.0)	240 (3.5)	220 (1.0)	‡ (†)	226 (1.1)	244 (2.6)	223 (1.2)	‡ (†)	‡ (†)		68 (1.7)	17 (1.6)
Boston	233 (1.1)	236 (0.7)	251 (2.2)	231 (1.2)	232 (1.1)	237 (0.6)	255 (1.8)	230 (1.1)	234 (1.2)	259 (2.5)		81 (1.1)	33 (1.8)
Charlotte	244 (1.1)	245 (1.3)	263 (1.3)	231 (1.4)	235 (1.8)	247 (1.1)	264 (1.4)	232 (1.4)	240 (1.6)	259 (3.7)		88 (1.1)	48 (2.0)
Chicago	220 (1.0)	222 (1.2)	242 (3.2)	212 (1.8)	226 (1.3)	224 (0.9)	246 (2.5)	217 (1.9)	223 (1.3)	246 (3.2)		64 (1.7)	20 (1.1)
Cleveland	215 (1.6)	213 (1.0)	228 (2.3)	209 (1.3)	217 (2.3)	216 (0.7)	232 (2.0)	211 (0.9)	218 (1.8)	‡ (†)		53 (1.8)	11 (0.9)
Dallas	— (†)	— (†)	— (†)	— (†)	— (†)	233 (1.3)	258 (3.5)	225 (2.0)	234 (1.2)	‡ (†)		79 (1.7)	25 (2.2)
Detroit	— (†)	200 (1.7)	‡ (†)	199 (1.8)	206 (3.5)	203 (1.4)	‡ (†)	201 (1.5)	215 (2.4)	‡ (†)		34 (2.2)	3 (0.9)
District of Columbia	214 (0.8)	220 (0.8)	270 (2.3)	212 (0.9)	227 (2.8)	222 (1.0)	272 (1.8)	212 (1.2)	223 (2.6)	‡ (†)		59 (1.3)	23 (0.9)
Fresno	— (†)	219 (1.4)	237 (2.5)	213 (3.1)	216 (1.7)	218 (0.9)	238 (2.2)	214 (2.3)	214 (1.0)	222 (2.0)		56 (1.5)	15 (0.9)
Hillsborough County (FL)...	— (†)	— (†)	— (†)	— (†)	— (†)	243 (1.1)	253 (1.7)	228 (1.9)	239 (1.2)	‡ (†)		86 (1.4)	43 (1.9)
Houston	234 (1.1)	236 (1.2)	260 (2.5)	227 (1.9)	235 (1.2)	237 (0.8)	259 (2.1)	229 (1.4)	236 (0.9)	265 (3.4)		82 (1.3)	32 (1.3)
Jefferson County (KY)	— (†)	233 (1.6)	243 (1.7)	216 (1.7)	226 (3.5)	235 (0.9)	243 (1.2)	221 (1.3)	238 (3.1)	256 (4.3)		78 (1.4)	32 (1.4)
Los Angeles	221 (0.9)	222 (1.2)	245 (3.3)	209 (3.0)	218 (1.1)	223 (0.8)	243 (1.6)	215 (3.0)	220 (0.8)	251 (2.6)		63 (1.4)	20 (0.9)
Miami-Dade	— (†)	236 (1.3)	253 (2.0)	222 (1.6)	239 (1.1)	236 (1.0)	255 (2.0)	225 (1.5)	237 (1.0)	‡ (†)		79 (1.1)	33 (1.5)
Milwaukee	— (†)	220 (1.5)	242 (3.0)	211 (2.0)	226 (1.5)	220 (1.0)	239 (1.9)	211 (1.4)	221 (1.8)	230 (3.2)		58 (1.8)	14 (1.2)
New York City	236 (1.3)	237 (1.0)	254 (1.9)	227 (1.2)	230 (1.2)	234 (1.2)	248 (3.2)	226 (1.1)	227 (1.7)	252 (2.0)		76 (1.2)	32 (1.4)
Philadelphia	— (†)	222 (1.4)	239 (2.6)	216 (1.7)	221 (2.1)	225 (1.2)	243 (3.0)	220 (0.9)	223 (2.4)	251 (2.8)		66 (1.5)	20 (1.8)
San Diego	234 (1.4)	236 (1.6)	255 (2.3)	222 (2.8)	224 (1.7)	239 (1.3)	258 (2.1)	222 (2.7)	229 (1.4)	248 (2.5)		80 (1.3)	39 (1.8)
8th grade													
United States	280 (0.3)	282 (0.3)	292 (0.2)	260 (0.4)	266 (0.6)	283 (0.2)	293 (0.2)	262 (0.5)	269 (0.5)	305 (1.1)		72 (0.3)	34 (0.2)
Large city	269 (0.7)	271 (0.7)	294 (1.1)	256 (0.8)	264 (1.2)	274 (0.7)	295 (1.1)	261 (0.9)	267 (1.0)	298 (2.3)		63 (0.7)	26 (0.7)
Albuquerque	— (†)	— (†)	— (†)	— (†)	— (†)	275 (1.0)	291 (2.3)	‡ (†)	269 (1.2)	‡ (†)		63 (1.3)	26 (1.9)
Atlanta	256 (1.5)	259 (1.6)	‡ (†)	255 (1.5)	‡ (†)	266 (1.3)	309 (2.8)	262 (1.4)	264 (3.5)	‡ (†)		54 (1.9)	16 (1.2)
Austin	283 (1.1)	287 (0.9)	312 (1.8)	274 (3.4)	274 (1.2)	287 (1.1)	313 (1.8)	265 (5.3)	276 (1.7)	‡ (†)		74 (1.4)	38 (1.5)
Baltimore City	— (†)	257 (1.9)	‡ (†)	255 (1.6)	‡ (†)	261 (1.3)	280 (4.0)	259 (1.5)	‡ (†)	‡ (†)		48 (2.1)	13 (1.3)
Boston	276 (1.0)	279 (1.3)	311 (2.5)	268 (2.0)	269 (1.9)	282 (0.9)	305 (3.1)	272 (1.6)	271 (1.6)	319 (3.6)		69 (1.4)	34 (1.2)
Charlotte	283 (1.2)	283 (0.9)	304 (1.4)	270 (1.4)	272 (2.5)	285 (0.8)	311 (1.3)	268 (1.2)	272 (2.6)	304 (6.4)		72 (1.2)	37 (1.2)
Chicago	260 (1.9)	264 (1.4)	289 (3.8)	252 (1.9)	268 (1.6)	270 (1.0)	296 (4.3)	260 (1.4)	271 (1.4)	296 (3.3)		60 (1.5)	20 (1.1)
Cleveland	257 (1.7)	256 (1.0)	275 (2.7)	252 (1.1)	250 (5.4)	256 (2.1)	277 (3.4)	249 (2.1)	258 (4.4)	‡ (†)		41 (2.5)	10 (1.4)
Dallas	— (†)	— (†)	— (†)	— (†)	— (†)	274 (0.9)	306 (4.5)	264 (2.2)	276 (1.1)	‡ (†)		64 (1.6)	22 (1.6)
Detroit	— (†)	238 (2.7)	‡ (†)	237 (2.9)	255 (5.8)	246 (1.2)	‡ (†)	244 (1.4)	258 (2.8)	‡ (†)		29 (1.5)	4 (0.6)
District of Columbia	248 (0.9)	251 (1.3)	‡ (†)	244 (1.3)	263 (5.2)	255 (0.9)	322 (3.0)	249 (1.2)	253 (2.8)	‡ (†)		42 (1.3)	15 (1.0)
Fresno	— (†)	258 (1.2)	282 (3.8)	246 (3.6)	253 (1.4)	256 (0.9)	281 (2.6)	243 (2.6)	251 (1.2)	265 (2.9)		43 (1.3)	10 (1.0)
Hillsborough County (FL)...	— (†)	— (†)	— (†)	— (†)	— (†)	282 (1.5)	293 (2.1)	263 (1.9)	274 (2.4)	‡ (†)		72 (1.8)	32 (1.9)
Houston	273 (1.2)	277 (1.2)	311 (2.8)	266 (1.9)	275 (1.0)	279 (1.0)	309 (3.0)	271 (1.9)	278 (1.1)	310 (5.2)		72 (1.2)	27 (1.2)
Jefferson County (KY)	— (†)	271 (0.9)	284 (1.1)	252 (1.4)	‡ (†)	274 (1.0)	285 (1.5)	257 (1.4)	270 (4.5)	‡ (†)		62 (1.8)	25 (1.5)
Los Angeles	257 (1.1)	258 (1.0)	287 (3.4)	247 (3.2)	254 (0.9)	261 (1.3)	291 (4.6)	246 (3.9)	255 (1.3)	297 (3.9)		49 (1.7)	16 (1.2)
Miami-Dade	— (†)	273 (1.1)	291 (2.5)	260 (2.7)	274 (1.2)	272 (1.1)	288 (3.1)	256 (2.2)	274 (1.0)	‡ (†)		61 (1.3)	22 (1.2)
Milwaukee	— (†)	251 (1.5)	271 (4.6)	244 (1.6)	256 (3.5)	254 (1.7)	274 (4.2)	246 (1.8)	259 (3.3)	271 (5.6)		41 (2.0)	10 (1.4)
New York City	270 (1.8)	273 (1.5)	295 (3.0)	261 (1.9)	261 (2.1)	272 (1.6)	292 (3.2)	262 (2.1)	261 (1.6)	304 (3.2)		59 (1.7)	24 (1.6)
Philadelphia	— (†)	265 (2.0)	284 (3.9)	256 (1.7)	258 (3.1)	265 (2.0)	281 (3.9)	260 (2.3)	256 (3.1)	295 (5.4)		52 (2.7)	18 (1.8)
San Diego	272 (1.4)	280 (2.0)	301 (2.6)	263 (4.3)	265 (2.0)	278 (1.7)	302 (2.3)	256 (4.0)	263 (2.6)	293 (3.3)		66 (3.0)	31 (1.6)

—Not available.
†Not applicable.
‡Reporting standards not met (too few cases).
[1]Scale ranges from 0 to 500.
[2]*Basic* denotes partial mastery of the knowledge and skills that are fundamental for proficient work at a given grade.
[3]*Proficient* represents solid academic performance. Students reaching this level have demonstrated competency over challenging subject matter.
NOTE: Beginning in 2009, if the results for charter schools are not included in a school district's Adequate Yearly Progress (AYP) report to the U.S. Department of Education under the Elementary and Secondary Education Act, they are excluded from that district's results. This change had little or no impact on differences between any participating district's 2007 and 2009 average mathematics scores except those of the District of Columbia at grade 8. For details, see the Technical Notes in *The Nation's Report Card: Mathematics 2009 Trial Urban District Assessment* (NCES 2010-452). Race categories exclude persons of Hispanic ethnicity. Totals include racial/ethnic groups not shown separately. Standard errors appear in parentheses.
SOURCE: U.S. Department of Education, National Center for Education Statistics, National Assessment of Educational Progress (NAEP), 2007, 2009, and 2011 Mathematics Assessments, retrieved April 14 and 26 and June 7, 2010, and December 7, 2011, from the Main NAEP Data Explorer (http://nces.ed.gov/nationsreportcard/naepdata/). (This table was prepared December 2011.)

Average scores and achievement-level results in NAEP science for eighth-grade public school students, by state/jurisdiction: 2011

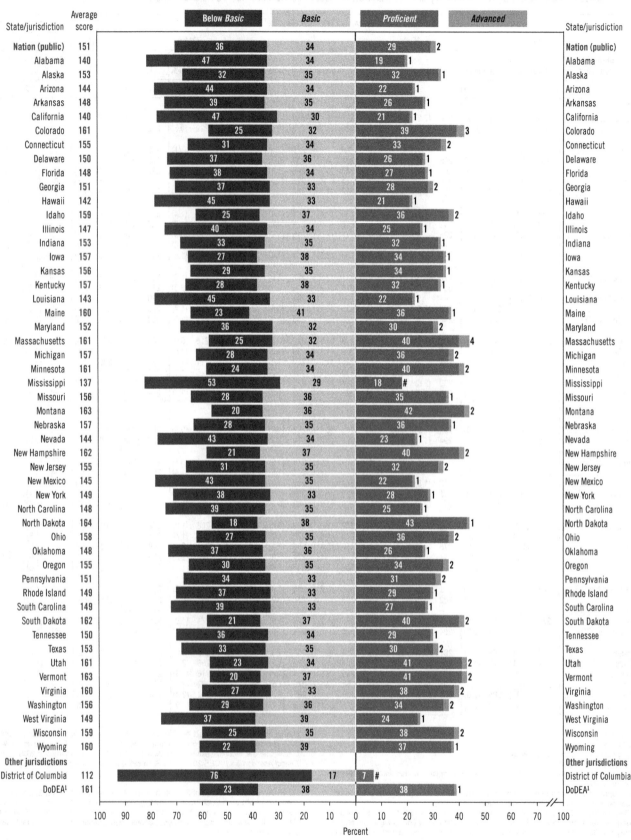

State/jurisdiction	Average score	Below Basic	Basic	Proficient	Advanced
Nation (public)	151	36	34	29	2
Alabama	140	47	34	19	1
Alaska	153	32	35	32	1
Arizona	144	44	34	22	1
Arkansas	148	39	35	26	1
California	140	47	30	21	1
Colorado	161	25	32	39	3
Connecticut	155	31	34	33	2
Delaware	150	37	36	26	1
Florida	148	38	34	27	1
Georgia	151	37	33	28	2
Hawaii	142	45	33	21	1
Idaho	159	25	37	36	2
Illinois	147	40	34	25	1
Indiana	153	33	35	32	1
Iowa	157	27	38	34	1
Kansas	156	29	35	34	1
Kentucky	157	28	38	32	1
Louisiana	143	45	33	22	1
Maine	160	23	41	36	1
Maryland	152	36	32	30	2
Massachusetts	161	25	32	40	4
Michigan	157	28	34	36	2
Minnesota	161	24	34	40	2
Mississippi	137	53	29	18	#
Missouri	156	28	36	35	1
Montana	163	20	36	42	2
Nebraska	157	28	35	36	1
Nevada	144	43	34	23	1
New Hampshire	162	21	37	40	2
New Jersey	155	31	35	32	2
New Mexico	145	43	35	22	1
New York	149	38	33	28	1
North Carolina	148	39	35	25	1
North Dakota	164	18	38	43	1
Ohio	158	27	35	36	2
Oklahoma	148	37	36	26	1
Oregon	155	30	35	34	2
Pennsylvania	151	34	33	31	2
Rhode Island	149	37	33	29	1
South Carolina	149	39	33	27	1
South Dakota	162	21	37	40	2
Tennessee	150	36	34	29	1
Texas	153	33	35	30	2
Utah	161	23	34	41	2
Vermont	163	20	37	41	2
Virginia	160	27	33	38	2
Washington	156	29	36	34	2
West Virginia	149	37	39	24	1
Wisconsin	159	25	35	38	2
Wyoming	160	22	39	37	1
Other jurisdictions					
District of Columbia	112	76	17	7	#
DoDEA[1]	161	23	38	38	1

Percent

Rounds to zero.

[1] Department of Defense Education Activity (overseas and domestic schools).

NOTE: The bars in this figure were graphed using unrounded numbers. Detail may not sum to totals because of rounding.

SOURCE: U.S. Department of Education, Institute of Education Sciences, National Center for Education Statistics, National Assessment of Educational Progress (NAEP), 2011 Science Assessment.

Average science scale score, standard deviation, and percentage of students attaining science achievement levels, by grade level, selected student and school characteristics, and percentile: 2009

Selected characteristic, percentile, and achievement level	Grade 4			Grade 8			Grade 12		
	Total, all students	Male	Female	Total, all students	Male	Female	Total, all students	Male	Female
1	2	3	4	5	6	7	8	9	10
	(0.3)	(0.3)	(0.3)	(0.3)	(0.4)	(0.3)	(0.8)	(0.9)	(0.9)
Average science scale score[1]									
All students	150 (0.3)	151 (0.3)	149 (0.3)	150 (0.3)	152 (0.4)	148 (0.3)	150 (0.8)	153 (0.9)	147 (0.9)
Race/ethnicity									
White	163 (0.2)	164 (0.3)	162 (0.3)	162 (0.2)	164 (0.3)	160 (0.3)	159 (0.7)	162 (0.9)	156 (0.8)
Black	127 (0.4)	126 (0.6)	128 (0.5)	126 (0.4)	125 (0.6)	126 (0.5)	125 (1.2)	127 (1.6)	123 (1.5)
Hispanic	131 (0.5)	132 (0.7)	130 (0.6)	132 (0.6)	134 (0.8)	130 (0.7)	134 (1.2)	138 (2.3)	130 (1.5)
Asian/Pacific Islander	160 (1.2)	159 (1.4)	160 (1.4)	160 (1.0)	162 (1.3)	158 (1.3)	164 (3.0)	161 (2.9)	166 (3.8)
American Indian/Alaska Native	135 (1.3)	135 (1.5)	135 (1.8)	137 (1.4)	141 (1.8)	133 (2.0)	144 (3.7)	‡ (†)	‡ (†)
Parents' highest level of education[2]									
Did not finish high school	— (†)	— (†)	— (†)	131 (0.6)	135 (1.0)	128 (0.7)	131 (1.4)	136 (1.9)	128 (1.8)
Graduated high school	— (†)	— (†)	— (†)	139 (0.4)	141 (0.6)	137 (0.5)	138 (1.2)	140 (1.5)	136 (1.4)
Some education after high school	— (†)	— (†)	— (†)	152 (0.4)	154 (0.5)	150 (0.4)	147 (0.9)	150 (1.3)	144 (1.1)
Graduated college	— (†)	— (†)	— (†)	161 (0.4)	162 (0.5)	159 (0.3)	161 (0.7)	163 (0.9)	159 (1.0)
Eligibility for free or reduced-price lunch									
Eligible	134 (0.3)	134 (0.4)	133 (0.3)	133 (0.4)	135 (0.5)	131 (0.4)	132 (1.0)	135 (1.1)	130 (1.1)
Not eligible	163 (0.3)	164 (0.3)	163 (0.3)	161 (0.3)	163 (0.4)	159 (0.3)	157 (0.9)	159 (1.1)	154 (1.0)
Unknown	162 (1.3)	163 (1.7)	161 (1.3)	164 (1.2)	167 (1.4)	161 (1.2)	156 (2.7)	156 (3.6)	156 (3.0)
School type									
Public	149 (0.3)	149 (0.3)	148 (0.3)	149 (0.3)	151 (0.4)	147 (0.3)	— (†)	— (†)	— (†)
Private	163 (0.9)	165 (1.2)	162 (1.0)	164 (0.9)	167 (1.2)	161 (1.0)	—	—	—
School location									
City	142 (0.6)	142 (0.6)	142 (0.7)	142 (0.6)	144 (0.7)	141 (0.7)	146 (1.8)	148 (1.6)	144 (2.2)
Suburban	154 (0.4)	154 (0.6)	153 (0.4)	154 (0.5)	155 (0.6)	152 (0.5)	154 (1.4)	157 (1.8)	150 (1.5)
Town	150 (0.6)	151 (0.6)	149 (0.5)	149 (1.0)	152 (1.1)	147 (1.0)	150 (1.2)	153 (1.5)	146 (1.6)
Rural	155 (0.5)	156 (0.7)	154 (0.5)	154 (0.4)	156 (0.5)	152 (0.5)	150 (1.2)	153 (1.5)	146 (1.4)
Science courses taken by 12th-graders									
Biology, chemistry, and physics	— (†)	— (†)	— (†)	— (†)	— (†)	— (†)	166 (1.0)	169 (1.0)	163 (1.4)
Biology and chemistry	— (†)	— (†)	— (†)	— (†)	— (†)	— (†)	148 (0.9)	151 (1.4)	147 (1.0)
Biology only or other	— (†)	— (†)	— (†)	— (†)	— (†)	— (†)	133 (0.9)	136 (1.1)	128 (1.2)
Percentile[2]									
10th	104 (0.6)	103 (0.6)	104 (0.5)	103 (0.6)	103 (0.7)	103 (0.6)	104 (1.2)	106 (1.8)	103 (1.1)
25th	128 (0.4)	128 (0.6)	128 (0.5)	128 (0.4)	130 (0.5)	127 (0.5)	126 (0.8)	128 (1.0)	125 (1.5)
50th	153 (0.3)	154 (0.4)	152 (0.4)	153 (0.3)	156 (0.4)	151 (0.3)	151 (1.1)	154 (1.4)	148 (1.1)
75th	175 (0.3)	176 (0.3)	174 (0.4)	175 (0.2)	178 (0.3)	172 (0.2)	174 (1.0)	178 (1.2)	171 (1.1)
90th	192 (0.3)	194 (0.4)	191 (0.5)	192 (0.3)	195 (0.2)	188 (0.4)	194 (1.0)	198 (0.9)	190 (1.4)
Standard deviation of the science scale score[3]									
All students	35 (0.2)	36 (0.2)	34 (0.2)	35 (0.2)	36 (0.2)	34 (0.2)	35 (0.4)	36 (0.5)	34 (0.5)
Percent of students attaining science achievement levels									
Achievement level									
Below *Basic*	28 (0.3)	27 (0.4)	28 (0.3)	37 (0.4)	35 (0.5)	38 (0.4)	40 (1.0)	37 (1.1)	42 (1.3)
At or above *Basic*[4]	72 (0.3)	73 (0.4)	72 (0.3)	63 (0.4)	65 (0.5)	62 (0.4)	60 (1.0)	63 (1.1)	58 (1.3)
At or above *Proficient*[5]	34 (0.3)	35 (0.3)	32 (0.3)	30 (0.3)	34 (0.4)	27 (0.3)	21 (0.8)	24 (1.0)	18 (0.8)
At *Advanced*[6]	1 (0.1)	1 (0.1)	1 (0.1)	2 (0.1)	2 (0.1)	2 (0.1)	1 (0.2)	2 (0.3)	1 (0.2)

—Not available.

†Not applicable.

‡Reporting standards not met (too few cases).

[1]Scale ranges from 0 to 300 for all three grades, but scores cannot be compared across grades. For example, the average score of 163 for White 4th-graders does not denote higher performance than the score of 159 for White 12th-graders.

[2]The percentile represents a specific point on the percentage distribution of all students ranked by their science score from low to high. For example, 10 percent of students scored at or below the 10th percentile score, while 90 percent of students scored above it.

[3]The standard deviation provides an indication of how much the test scores varied. The lower the standard deviation, the closer the scores were clustered around the average score. About two-thirds of the student scores can be expected to fall within the range of one standard deviation above and one standard deviation below the average score. For example, the average score for all 4th-graders was 150, and the standard deviation was 35. This means that we would expect about two-thirds of the students to have scores between 185 (one standard deviation above the average) and 115 (one standard deviation below). Standard errors also must be taken into account when making comparisons of these ranges. For a discussion of standard errors, see Appendix A: Guide to Sources.

[4]*Basic* denotes partial mastery of the knowledge and skills that are fundamental for proficient work.

[5]*Proficient* represents solid academic performance. Students reaching this level have demonstrated competency over challenging subject matter.

[6]*Advanced* signifies superior performance.

NOTE: Includes students tested with accommodations (7 to 11 percent of all students, depending on grade level); excludes only those students with disabilities and English language learners who were unable to be tested even with accommodations (2 to 3 percent of all students). Race categories exclude persons of Hispanic ethnicity. Standard errors appear in parentheses.

SOURCE: U.S. Department of Education, National Center for Education Statistics, National Assessment of Educational Progress (NAEP), 2009 Science Assessment, retrieved May 25, 2011, from the Main NAEP Data Explorer (http://nces.ed.gov/nationsreportcard/naepdata/). (This table was prepared May 2011.)

Average science scale scores of 4th- and 8th-grade public school students, by race/ethnicity and state: 2009

State	Grade 4											Grade 8										
	Total, all students		White		Black		Hispanic		Asian/Pacific Islander			Total, all students		White		Black		Hispanic		Asian/Pacific Islander	
1	2		3		4		5		6			7		8		9		10		11	
United States	149	(0.3)	162	(0.3)	127	(0.4)	130	(0.5)	160	(1.2)		149	(0.3)	161	(0.2)	125	(0.4)	131	(0.6)	159	(1.0)
Alabama	143	(1.2)	155	(1.1)	121	(1.6)	125	(4.2)	‡	(†)		139	(1.1)	152	(1.1)	115	(1.8)	129	(3.5)	‡	(†)
Alaska	—	(†)	—	(†)	—	(†)	—	(†)	—	(†)		—	(†)	—	(†)	—	(†)	—	(†)	—	(†)
Arizona	138	(1.2)	155	(1.2)	129	(4.0)	124	(1.7)	156	(4.1)		141	(1.3)	157	(1.3)	126	(3.2)	127	(1.5)	159	(5.5)
Arkansas	146	(1.2)	157	(1.1)	117	(1.8)	136	(3.2)	152	(5.0)		144	(1.3)	154	(0.9)	111	(2.1)	134	(3.0)	‡	(†)
California	136	(1.6)	157	(2.3)	122	(3.3)	121	(1.5)	160	(3.9)		137	(1.4)	157	(2.0)	122	(2.8)	122	(1.3)	154	(2.2)
Colorado	155	(1.2)	166	(1.2)	128	(4.3)	134	(1.8)	162	(3.5)		156	(1.0)	166	(1.0)	135	(3.7)	137	(1.6)	161	(3.7)
Connecticut	156	(1.1)	167	(0.8)	129	(2.5)	128	(2.1)	164	(3.7)		155	(0.9)	164	(0.8)	126	(2.3)	128	(1.8)	169	(3.5)
Delaware	153	(0.5)	166	(0.7)	135	(1.2)	142	(1.8)	169	(3.7)		148	(0.6)	159	(0.9)	133	(1.0)	141	(2.2)	160	(4.3)
District of Columbia	—	(†)	—	(†)	—	(†)	—	(†)	—	(†)		—	(†)	—	(†)	—	(†)	—	(†)	—	(†)
Florida	151	(1.1)	163	(1.5)	131	(1.4)	144	(1.3)	158	(3.8)		146	(1.0)	158	(1.4)	126	(1.4)	139	(1.2)	163	(4.1)
Georgia	144	(1.1)	159	(1.2)	126	(1.7)	133	(2.5)	167	(3.5)		147	(1.0)	161	(1.2)	129	(1.3)	137	(2.2)	172	(2.7)
Hawaii	140	(1.2)	159	(2.4)	134	(4.8)	134	(5.9)	138	(1.2)		139	(0.7)	153	(1.5)	133	(5.0)	148	(4.3)	136	(1.0)
Idaho	154	(0.9)	159	(0.8)	‡	(†)	128	(1.7)	156	(4.7)		158	(0.9)	162	(0.9)	‡	(†)	137	(1.4)	‡	(†)
Illinois	148	(1.3)	164	(1.2)	120	(1.7)	129	(1.9)	166	(3.2)		148	(1.4)	162	(1.2)	118	(1.5)	131	(1.5)	167	(3.2)
Indiana	153	(1.0)	158	(1.0)	129	(2.2)	136	(3.7)	‡	(†)		152	(1.2)	159	(1.0)	126	(3.9)	135	(3.5)	‡	(†)
Iowa	157	(0.9)	161	(0.9)	130	(4.4)	134	(1.8)	156	(5.1)		156	(0.9)	160	(0.8)	127	(3.5)	133	(3.2)	‡	(†)
Kansas	—	(†)	—	(†)	—	(†)	—	(†)	—	(†)		—	(†)	—	(†)	—	(†)	—	(†)	—	(†)
Kentucky	161	(1.1)	164	(1.1)	135	(1.9)	150	(4.0)	172	(5.3)		156	(0.8)	159	(0.9)	137	(1.8)	145	(3.5)	‡	(†)
Louisiana	141	(1.4)	159	(1.3)	123	(1.8)	144	(4.5)	‡	(†)		139	(1.7)	155	(1.5)	120	(1.9)	‡	(†)	‡	(†)
Maine	160	(0.8)	161	(0.8)	139	(4.9)	‡	(†)	‡	(†)		158	(0.8)	159	(0.8)	126	(4.5)	‡	(†)	‡	(†)
Maryland	150	(1.1)	164	(1.4)	131	(1.3)	143	(1.8)	164	(2.8)		148	(1.1)	164	(1.2)	127	(1.5)	136	(2.8)	169	(2.5)
Massachusetts	160	(1.2)	169	(0.9)	138	(2.0)	132	(2.3)	167	(4.5)		160	(1.1)	167	(1.1)	132	(2.6)	131	(2.7)	168	(4.1)
Michigan	150	(1.2)	160	(1.3)	118	(1.8)	138	(2.8)	162	(5.0)		153	(1.4)	162	(1.0)	121	(2.1)	139	(3.4)	‡	(†)
Minnesota	158	(1.1)	166	(0.7)	129	(2.7)	134	(3.2)	147	(4.2)		159	(1.0)	166	(0.9)	128	(2.8)	132	(3.7)	141	(3.0)
Mississippi	133	(1.2)	152	(1.2)	116	(1.2)	142	(4.5)	‡	(†)		132	(1.2)	150	(1.2)	114	(1.1)	‡	(†)	‡	(†)
Missouri	156	(1.4)	164	(1.1)	127	(2.9)	141	(4.1)	‡	(†)		156	(1.1)	161	(0.9)	129	(2.5)	150	(3.8)	167	(4.7)
Montana	160	(0.8)	164	(0.8)	‡	(†)	149	(4.1)	‡	(†)		162	(0.7)	166	(0.7)	‡	(†)	155	(3.3)	‡	(†)
Nebraska	—	(†)	—	(†)	—	(†)	—	(†)	—	(†)		—	(†)	—	(†)	—	(†)	—	(†)	—	(†)
Nevada	141	(1.0)	156	(1.0)	122	(2.1)	128	(1.2)	151	(3.1)		141	(0.7)	153	(0.9)	127	(2.4)	129	(1.0)	148	(2.4)
New Hampshire	163	(0.8)	165	(0.8)	‡	(†)	139	(3.9)	171	(4.3)		160	(0.8)	161	(0.8)	‡	(†)	131	(4.2)	‡	(†)
New Jersey	155	(1.0)	166	(1.1)	133	(1.9)	136	(1.9)	173	(3.4)		155	(1.5)	165	(1.0)	127	(3.3)	138	(2.7)	174	(2.6)
New Mexico	142	(1.1)	163	(1.8)	134	(4.9)	134	(1.2)	‡	(†)		143	(1.4)	163	(1.4)	‡	(†)	135	(1.4)	‡	(†)
New York	148	(0.8)	161	(0.8)	127	(1.8)	130	(1.4)	156	(2.5)		149	(1.2)	164	(1.0)	123	(1.8)	125	(1.7)	161	(2.3)
North Carolina	148	(1.1)	162	(1.2)	126	(1.5)	132	(1.7)	163	(3.9)		144	(1.3)	158	(1.3)	121	(1.6)	132	(2.3)	165	(7.1)
North Dakota	162	(0.6)	165	(0.6)	‡	(†)	‡	(†)	‡	(†)		162	(0.5)	166	(0.6)	‡	(†)	‡	(†)	‡	(†)
Ohio	157	(1.2)	165	(1.0)	129	(2.4)	140	(4.4)	‡	(†)		158	(1.0)	164	(0.9)	126	(2.1)	140	(4.6)	‡	(†)
Oklahoma	148	(0.9)	156	(0.8)	125	(2.2)	131	(2.8)	‡	(†)		146	(0.9)	155	(1.0)	124	(2.6)	127	(2.6)	‡	(†)
Oregon	151	(1.0)	157	(1.0)	131	(4.1)	128	(1.9)	159	(3.2)		154	(1.0)	160	(1.1)	135	(4.1)	130	(1.8)	160	(3.5)
Pennsylvania	154	(1.4)	164	(1.2)	121	(2.6)	125	(4.2)	166	(4.6)		154	(1.1)	162	(0.9)	123	(2.0)	121	(4.4)	159	(4.1)
Rhode Island	150	(1.0)	161	(1.0)	126	(2.2)	124	(2.2)	152	(3.8)		146	(0.6)	155	(0.8)	125	(2.6)	119	(1.9)	146	(5.3)
South Carolina	149	(1.2)	163	(1.1)	128	(1.8)	140	(4.8)	‡	(†)		143	(1.6)	158	(1.1)	124	(1.7)	129	(4.2)	‡	(†)
South Dakota	157	(0.6)	162	(0.7)	‡	(†)	145	(3.4)	‡	(†)		161	(0.6)	165	(0.6)	141	(5.5)	135	(4.1)	‡	(†)
Tennessee	148	(1.2)	159	(1.2)	121	(2.0)	134	(3.8)	‡	(†)		148	(1.2)	157	(0.9)	122	(2.0)	139	(3.8)	‡	(†)
Texas	148	(1.2)	168	(2.0)	139	(2.1)	136	(1.0)	163	(5.1)		150	(1.2)	167	(1.4)	133	(2.5)	141	(1.5)	170	(3.6)
Utah	154	(1.2)	161	(0.9)	‡	(†)	129	(2.7)	147	(4.1)		158	(1.0)	164	(1.1)	‡	(†)	129	(1.7)	147	(3.9)
Vermont	—	(†)	—	(†)	—	(†)	—	(†)	—	(†)		—	(†)	—	(†)	—	(†)	—	(†)	—	(†)
Virginia	162	(1.2)	172	(1.0)	141	(1.9)	152	(2.3)	174	(4.0)		156	(1.1)	166	(1.1)	135	(2.0)	144	(2.2)	168	(3.1)
Washington	151	(1.4)	160	(1.2)	127	(4.2)	125	(2.2)	156	(3.1)		155	(1.0)	161	(1.1)	135	(3.7)	132	(2.3)	157	(3.0)
West Virginia	148	(1.0)	150	(1.0)	130	(2.7)	‡	(†)	‡	(†)		145	(0.8)	146	(0.8)	127	(2.8)	‡	(†)	‡	(†)
Wisconsin	157	(1.0)	164	(1.0)	121	(2.4)	138	(2.1)	153	(3.6)		157	(0.9)	165	(0.8)	120	(1.5)	134	(3.9)	152	(3.5)
Wyoming	156	(0.7)	159	(0.8)	‡	(†)	140	(1.9)	‡	(†)		158	(0.7)	162	(0.7)	‡	(†)	137	(1.8)	‡	(†)
Department of Defense dependents schools	159	(0.6)	166	(0.7)	141	(1.8)	153	(1.9)	161	(2.4)		162	(0.7)	170	(1.0)	144	(1.4)	155	(2.0)	160	(2.3)

—Not available.
†Not applicable.
‡Reporting standards not met.(too few cases)
NOTE: Scale ranges from 0 to 300. Includes students tested with accommodations (10 to 11 percent of all students, depending on grade level); excludes only those students with disabilities and English language learners who were unable to be tested even with accommodations (2 percent of all students at both grades). Race categories exclude persons of Hispanic eth-nicity. Totals include other racial/ethnic groups not shown separately. Standard errors appear in parentheses.
SOURCE: U.S. Department of Education, National Center for Education Statistics, National Assessment of Educational Progress (NAEP), 2009 Science Assessment, retrieved May 26, 2011, from the Main NAEP Data Explorer (http://nces.ed.gov/nationsreportcard/naepdata/). (This table was prepared May 2011.)

Average science scale scores of 12th-graders reporting various educational goals and attitudes toward science, and percentages of students reporting these goals and attitudes, by selected student characteristics: 2009

Student characteristic	Educational goals[1]				Like science				Take science only because required			
	Graduate high school	Some education after high school	Graduate college	Go to graduate school	Strongly disagree	Disagree	Agree	Strongly agree	Strongly disagree	Disagree	Agree	Strongly agree
1	2	3	4	5	6	7	8	9	10	11	12	13
Average scale score[2]												
All students	114 (1.9)	131 (1.3)	148 (0.6)	171 (1.0)	132 (1.3)	141 (0.9)	153 (0.9)	172 (1.1)	169 (1.1)	159 (0.9)	142 (0.9)	134 (1.0)
Sex												
Male	121 (2.6)	134 (1.8)	152 (0.8)	177 (1.3)	130 (1.7)	141 (1.4)	155 (1.2)	175 (1.3)	172 (1.4)	162 (1.2)	143 (1.2)	134 (1.3)
Female	103 (2.6)	127 (1.9)	143 (0.8)	166 (1.2)	133 (1.8)	141 (1.1)	150 (0.9)	169 (1.8)	165 (1.8)	156 (0.9)	140 (1.2)	134 (1.4)
Race/ethnicity												
White	127 (2.1)	140 (1.6)	156 (0.7)	178 (1.0)	140 (1.6)	150 (1.1)	161 (0.9)	180 (1.0)	176 (1.1)	167 (0.8)	151 (1.0)	143 (1.4)
Black	89 (3.6)	107 (3.2)	124 (1.1)	144 (1.8)	113 (2.0)	120 (2.0)	128 (1.5)	142 (2.6)	140 (2.6)	135 (2.3)	121 (1.6)	115 (1.7)
Hispanic	106 (3.7)	122 (2.7)	136 (1.1)	154 (2.3)	123 (2.6)	127 (1.5)	135 (1.8)	157 (2.4)	152 (2.9)	143 (1.7)	128 (1.6)	125 (2.3)
Asian/Pacific Islander	‡ (†)	‡ (†)	154 (2.9)	181 (3.4)	141 (5.2)	149 (3.8)	166 (2.9)	188 (4.5)	181 (4.2)	171 (3.3)	154 (3.2)	141 (4.5)
American Indian/Alaska Native	‡ (†)	‡ (†)	‡ (†)	‡ (†)	‡ (†)	‡ (†)	‡ (†)	‡ (†)	‡ (†)	‡ (†)	‡ (†)	‡ (†)
Eligibility for free or reduced-price lunch												
Eligible	105 (2.9)	120 (2.0)	134 (0.8)	151 (2.0)	120 (1.8)	125 (1.4)	135 (1.1)	152 (2.0)	147 (2.7)	142 (1.4)	127 (1.1)	121 (1.6)
Not eligible	122 (2.0)	138 (1.8)	153 (0.8)	176 (1.0)	137 (1.5)	148 (1.1)	159 (1.1)	179 (1.3)	175 (1.2)	165 (1.0)	148 (1.1)	140 (1.4)
Unknown	‡ (†)	‡ (†)	151 (2.4)	169 (3.5)	139 (3.1)	146 (3.6)	158 (2.9)	177 (3.8)	175 (3.6)	164 (3.3)	149 (2.6)	138 (3.3)
Parents' highest level of education												
Did not finish high school	112 (3.7)	124 (2.8)	134 (1.5)	145 (3.1)	119 (2.7)	125 (2.5)	134 (2.0)	153 (3.5)	147 (3.1)	138 (2.5)	127 (2.3)	121 (2.2)
Graduated high school	109 (2.8)	129 (2.7)	141 (1.3)	158 (2.1)	124 (2.2)	132 (1.3)	141 (1.3)	158 (2.7)	149 (2.7)	149 (1.6)	133 (1.8)	126 (1.9)
Some education after high school	126 (4.0)	135 (2.2)	146 (0.9)	162 (2.1)	133 (1.5)	138 (1.2)	149 (1.2)	168 (1.7)	164 (2.3)	156 (1.3)	140 (1.1)	133 (1.7)
Graduated college	120 (3.9)	140 (2.4)	155 (0.8)	177 (0.9)	141 (1.7)	151 (1.3)	163 (1.0)	181 (1.3)	180 (1.3)	168 (1.0)	152 (1.0)	143 (1.2)
Percent of students												
All students	5 (0.3)	7 (0.3)	59 (0.7)	26 (0.8)	14 (0.4)	21 (0.4)	48 (0.5)	16 (0.3)	15 (0.4)	34 (0.5)	31 (0.4)	19 (0.4)
Sex												
Male	6 (0.4)	9 (0.4)	59 (0.8)	22 (0.8)	12 (0.5)	18 (0.5)	52 (0.7)	18 (0.5)	17 (0.5)	37 (0.6)	29 (0.7)	17 (0.5)
Female	4 (0.3)	6 (0.4)	58 (0.9)	31 (1.0)	16 (0.5)	25 (0.6)	45 (0.7)	14 (0.5)	14 (0.6)	31 (0.7)	33 (0.6)	21 (0.6)
Race/ethnicity												
White	4 (0.3)	7 (0.3)	60 (0.7)	26 (0.8)	13 (0.5)	21 (0.5)	49 (0.7)	17 (0.5)	17 (0.5)	36 (0.6)	29 (0.6)	18 (0.5)
Black	6 (0.8)	6 (0.6)	60 (1.3)	25 (1.4)	20 (1.0)	23 (0.9)	43 (1.3)	14 (0.9)	11 (0.8)	28 (1.2)	33 (1.0)	28 (1.1)
Hispanic	7 (0.7)	12 (0.8)	59 (1.4)	18 (1.1)	13 (0.7)	24 (0.9)	49 (1.1)	14 (0.9)	12 (0.8)	31 (1.1)	38 (1.0)	19 (0.9)
Asian/Pacific Islander	3 (0.8)	2 (0.5)	42 (2.6)	50 (2.8)	9 (1.0)	18 (1.7)	55 (1.5)	18 (1.6)	19 (1.6)	40 (1.3)	28 (1.9)	13 (1.1)
American Indian/Alaska Native	‡ (†)	‡ (†)	‡ (†)	‡ (†)	‡ (†)	‡ (†)	‡ (†)	‡ (†)	‡ (†)	‡ (†)	‡ (†)	‡ (†)
Eligibility for free or reduced-price lunch												
Eligible	8 (0.5)	10 (0.6)	60 (1.2)	18 (1.1)	16 (0.7)	23 (0.9)	47 (1.0)	14 (0.6)	13 (0.7)	30 (0.8)	34 (0.7)	22 (0.8)
Not eligible	4 (0.3)	7 (0.4)	59 (0.8)	29 (0.9)	13 (0.4)	21 (0.5)	49 (0.6)	17 (0.4)	16 (0.5)	35 (0.6)	30 (0.6)	18 (0.5)
Unknown	2 (0.7)	4 (1.0)	56 (2.4)	35 (2.7)	13 (1.2)	21 (1.3)	48 (1.9)	18 (1.6)	16 (1.6)	36 (2.3)	29 (1.8)	19 (1.6)
Parents' highest level of education												
Did not finish high school	11 (1.1)	13 (1.0)	53 (2.2)	16 (1.8)	19 (1.4)	22 (1.4)	47 (1.7)	13 (1.2)	13 (1.2)	30 (1.6)	35 (1.7)	23 (1.3)
Graduated high school	10 (0.6)	12 (0.8)	62 (1.4)	13 (1.0)	16 (0.8)	25 (1.0)	46 (1.2)	12 (0.7)	12 (0.7)	31 (1.3)	35 (1.1)	22 (1.1)
Some education after high school	4 (0.4)	9 (0.5)	65 (1.0)	20 (1.1)	15 (0.8)	22 (0.9)	48 (0.9)	15 (0.8)	14 (0.9)	33 (1.0)	32 (0.9)	21 (0.8)
Graduated college	2 (0.2)	4 (0.3)	56 (0.8)	37 (0.9)	12 (0.6)	19 (0.6)	50 (0.7)	19 (0.5)	18 (0.4)	37 (0.7)	28 (0.6)	17 (0.6)

†Not applicable.
‡Reporting standards not met (too few cases).
[1]The educational goals columns exclude the 1 percent of students who reported that they would not finish high school and the 2 percent who reported that they did not know how much education they would complete.
[2]Scale ranges from 0 to 300.

NOTE: Includes students tested with accommodations (7 percent of all 12th-graders); excludes only those students with disabilities and English language learners who were unable to be tested even with accommodations (3 percent of all 12th-graders). Race categories exclude persons of Hispanic ethnicity. Standard errors appear in parentheses.
SOURCE: U.S. Department of Education, National Center for Education Statistics, National Assessment of Educational Progress (NAEP), 2009 Science Assessment, retrieved May 26, 2011, from the Main NAEP Data Explorer (http://nces.ed.gov/nationsreportcard/naepdata/). (This table was prepared May 2011.)

SAT mean scores of college-bound seniors, by race/ethnicity: Selected years, 1986–87 through 2010–11

Race/ethnicity	1986–87	1990–91	1996–97	1999–2000	2000–01	2001–02	2002–03	2003–04	2004–05	2005–06	2006–07	2007–08	2008–09	2009–10	2010–11	Score change 1986–87 to 1996–97	Score change 2000–01 to 2010–11	Score change 2005–06 to 2010–11	Score change 2009–10 to 2010–11
1	2	3	4	5	6	7	8	9	10	11	12	13	14	15	16	17	18	19	20
SAT—Critical reading																			
All students	507	499	505	505	506	504	507	508	508	503	502	502	501	501	497	-2	-9	-6	-4
White	524	518	526	528	529	527	529	528	532	527	527	528	528	528	528	2	-1	1	0
Black	428	427	434	434	433	430	431	430	433	434	433	430	429	429	428	6	-5	-6	-1
Mexican American	457	454	451	453	451	446	448	451	453	454	455	454	453	454	451	-6	0	-3	-3
Puerto Rican	436	436	454	456	457	455	456	457	460	459	459	456	452	454	452	18	-5	-7	-2
Other Hispanic	464	458	466	461	460	458	457	461	463	458	459	455	455	454	451	2	-9	-7	-3
Asian/Pacific Islander	479	485	496	499	501	501	508	507	511	510	514	513	516	519	517	17	16	7	-2
American Indian/Alaska Native	471	470	475	482	481	479	480	483	489	487	487	485	486	485	484	4	3	-3	-1
Other	480	486	512	508	503	502	501	494	495	494	497	496	494	494	493	32	-10	-1	-1
SAT—Mathematics																			
All students	501	500	511	514	514	516	519	518	520	518	515	515	515	516	514	10	0	-4	-2
White	514	513	526	530	531	533	534	531	536	536	534	537	536	536	535	12	4	-1	-1
Black	411	419	423	426	426	427	426	427	431	429	429	426	426	428	427	12	1	-2	-1
Mexican American	455	459	458	460	458	457	457	458	463	465	466	463	463	467	466	3	8	1	-1
Puerto Rican	432	439	447	451	451	451	453	452	457	456	454	453	450	452	452	15	1	-4	0
Other Hispanic	462	462	468	467	465	464	464	465	469	463	463	461	461	462	462	6	-3	-1	0
Asian/Pacific Islander	541	548	560	565	566	569	575	577	580	578	578	581	587	591	595	19	29	17	4
American Indian/Alaska Native	463	468	475	481	479	483	482	488	493	494	494	491	493	492	488	12	9	-6	-4
Other	482	492	514	515	512	514	513	508	513	513	512	512	514	514	517	32	5	4	3
SAT—Writing																			
All students	†	†	†	†	†	†	†	†	†	497	494	494	493	492	489	†	†	-8	-3
White	†	†	†	†	†	†	†	†	†	519	518	518	517	516	516	†	†	-3	0
Black	†	†	†	†	†	†	†	†	†	428	425	424	421	420	417	†	†	-11	-3
Mexican American	†	†	†	†	†	†	†	†	†	452	450	447	446	448	445	†	†	-7	-3
Puerto Rican	†	†	†	†	†	†	†	†	†	448	447	445	443	443	442	†	†	-6	-1
Other Hispanic	†	†	†	†	†	†	†	†	†	450	450	448	448	447	444	†	†	-6	-3
Asian/Pacific Islander	†	†	†	†	†	†	†	†	†	512	513	516	520	526	528	†	†	16	2
American Indian/Alaska Native	†	†	†	†	†	†	†	†	†	474	473	470	469	467	465	†	†	-9	-2
Other	†	†	†	†	†	†	†	†	†	493	493	494	493	494	492	†	†	-1	0

†Not applicable.

NOTE: Data for 2009–10 and earlier years are for seniors who took the SAT any time during their high school years through March of their senior year. Data for 2010–11 are for seniors who took the SAT any time during their high school years through June of their senior year. If a student took a test more than once, the most recent score was used. The SAT was formerly known as the Scholastic Assessment Test and the Scholastic Aptitude Test. Possible scores on each part of the SAT range from 200 to 800. The critical reading section was formerly known as the verbal section. The writing section was introduced in March 2005.

SOURCE: College Entrance Examination Board, *College-Bound Seniors: Total Group Profile [National] Report*, selected years, 1986–87 through 2010–11, retrieved September 14, 2011, from http://professionals.collegeboard.com/profdownload/cbs2011_total_group_report.pdf. (This table was prepared September 2011.)

SAT mean scores of college-bound seniors, by sex: 1966–67 through 2010–11

School year	SAT[1] Critical reading score			Mathematics score			Writing score[2]			Scholastic Aptitude Test (old scale) Verbal score			Mathematics score		
	Total	Male	Female	Total	Male	Female	Total	Male	Female	Total	Male	Female	Total	Male	Female
1	2	3	4	5	6	7	8	9	10	11	12	13	14	15	16
1966–67	543	540	545	516	535	495	†	†	†	466	463	468	492	514	467
1967–68	543	541	543	516	533	497	†	†	†	466	464	466	492	512	470
1968–69	540	536	543	517	534	498	†	†	†	463	459	466	493	513	470
1969–70	537	536	538	512	531	493	†	†	†	460	459	461	488	509	465
1970–71	532	531	534	513	529	494	†	†	†	455	454	457	488	507	466
1971–72	530	531	529	509	527	489	†	†	†	453	454	452	484	505	461
1972–73	523	523	521	506	525	489	†	†	†	445	446	443	481	502	460
1973–74	521	524	520	505	524	488	†	†	†	444	447	442	480	501	459
1974–75	512	515	509	498	518	479	†	†	†	434	437	431	472	495	449
1975–76	509	511	508	497	520	475	†	†	†	431	433	430	472	497	446
1976–77	507	509	505	496	520	474	†	†	†	429	431	427	470	497	445
1977–78	507	511	503	494	517	474	†	†	†	429	433	425	468	494	444
1978–79	505	509	501	493	516	473	†	†	†	427	431	423	467	493	443
1979–80	502	506	498	492	515	473	†	†	†	424	428	420	466	491	443
1980–81	502	508	496	492	516	473	†	†	†	424	430	418	466	492	443
1981–82	504	509	499	493	516	473	†	†	†	426	431	421	467	493	443
1982–83	503	508	498	494	516	474	†	†	†	425	430	420	468	493	445
1983–84	504	511	498	497	518	478	†	†	†	426	433	420	471	495	449
1984–85	509	514	503	500	522	480	†	†	†	431	437	425	475	499	452
1985–86	509	515	504	500	523	479	†	†	†	431	437	426	475	501	451
1986–87	507	512	502	501	523	481	†	†	†	430	435	425	476	500	453
1987–88	505	512	499	501	521	483	†	†	†	428	435	422	476	498	455
1988–89	504	510	498	502	523	482	†	†	†	427	434	421	476	500	454
1989–90	500	505	496	501	521	483	†	†	†	424	429	419	476	499	455
1990–91	499	503	495	500	520	482	†	†	†	422	426	418	474	497	453
1991–92	500	504	496	501	521	484	†	†	†	423	428	419	476	499	456
1992–93	500	504	497	503	524	484	†	†	†	424	428	420	478	502	457
1993–94	499	501	497	504	523	487	†	†	†	423	425	421	479	501	460
1994–95	504	505	502	506	525	490	†	†	†	428	429	426	482	503	463
1995–96	505	507	503	508	527	492	†	†	†	—	—	—	—	—	—
1996–97	505	507	503	511	530	494	†	†	†	—	—	—	—	—	—
1997–98	505	509	502	512	531	496	†	†	†	—	—	—	—	—	—
1998–99	505	509	502	511	531	495	†	†	†	—	—	—	—	—	—
1999–2000	505	507	504	514	533	498	†	†	†	†	†	†	†	†	†
2000–01	506	509	502	514	533	498	†	†	†	†	†	†	†	†	†
2001–02	504	507	502	516	534	500	†	†	†	†	†	†	†	†	†
2002–03	507	512	503	519	537	503	†	†	†	†	†	†	†	†	†
2003–04	508	512	504	518	537	501	†	†	†	†	†	†	†	†	†
2004–05	508	513	505	520	538	504	†	†	†	†	†	†	†	†	†
2005–06	503	505	502	518	536	502	497	491	502	†	†	†	†	†	†
2006–07	502	504	502	515	533	499	494	489	500	†	†	†	†	†	†
2007–08	502	504	500	515	533	500	494	488	501	†	†	†	†	†	†
2008–09	501	503	498	515	534	499	493	486	499	†	†	†	†	†	†
2009–10	501	503	498	516	534	500	492	486	498	†	†	†	†	†	†
2010–11	497	500	495	514	531	500	489	482	496	†	†	†	†	†	†

—Not available.

†Not applicable.

[1]Data for 1966–67 to 1985–86 were converted to the recentered scale by using a formula applied to the original mean and standard deviation. For 1986–87 to 1994–95, individual student scores were converted to the recentered scale and then the mean was recomputed. For 1995–96 to 1998–99, nearly all students received scores on the recentered scale; any score on the original scale was converted to the recentered scale prior to recomputing the mean. From 1999–2000 on, all scores have been reported on the recentered scale.

[2]Writing data are based on students who took the SAT writing section, which was introduced in March 2005.

NOTE: Data for 1966–67 through 1970–71 are estimates derived from the test scores of all participants. Data for 1971–72 through 2009–10 are for seniors who took the SAT any time during their high school years through March of their senior year. Data for 2010-11 are for seniors who took the SAT any time during their high school years through June of their senior year. If a student took a test more than once, the most recent score was used. The SAT was formerly known as the Scholastic Assessment Test and the Scholastic Aptitude Test. Possible scores on each part of the SAT range from 200 to 800. The critical reading section was formerly known as the verbal section.

SOURCE: College Entrance Examination Board, *College-Bound Seniors: Total Group Profile [National] Report*, selected years, 1966–67 through 2010–11, retrieved September 14, 2011, from http://professionals.collegeboard.com/profdownload/cbs2011_total_group_report.pdf. (This table was prepared September 2011.)

SAT mean scores and percentage distribution of college-bound seniors, by selected student characteristics: Selected years, 1995–96 through 2010–11

Selected student characteristic	1995–96			2000–01			2005–06				2009–10				2010–11			
	Critical reading score[1]	Mathematics score	Percentage distribution	Critical reading score[1]	Mathematics score	Percentage distribution	Critical reading score[1]	Mathematics score	Writing score[2]	Percentage distribution	Critical reading score[1]	Mathematics score	Writing score[2]	Percentage distribution	Critical reading score[1]	Mathematics score	Writing score[2]	Percentage distribution
1	2	3	4	5	6	7	8	9	10	11	12	13	14	15	16	17	18	19
All students	**505**	**508**	**100**	**506**	**514**	**100**	**503**	**518**	**497**	**100**	**501**	**516**	**492**	**100**	**497**	**514**	**489**	**100**
High school rank																		
Top decile	591	606	22	588	607	24	580	604	577	31	578	606	575	34	575	606	572	35
Second decile	530	539	22	526	540	23	516	537	511	25	514	535	505	27	510	535	503	27
Second quintile	494	496	28	490	497	26	484	498	476	20	484	499	472	19	482	498	470	18
Third quintile	455	448	24	454	452	22	—	—	—	—	—	—	—	—	—	—	—	—
Fourth quintile	429	418	4	423	417	4	—	—	—	—	—	—	—	—	—	—	—	—
Fifth quintile	411	401	1	407	401	1	—	—	—	—	—	—	—	—	—	—	—	—
Bottom three quintiles[3]	—	—	—	—	—	—	443	449	435	23	441	450	429	23	438	448	426	20
High school grade point average																		
A+ (97–100)	617	632	6	609	626	6	602	621	599	7	599	621	596	6	596	620	595	6
A (93–96)	573	583	14	566	581	17	563	582	559	18	563	584	558	19	560	583	556	19
A- (90–92)	545	554	15	540	552	17	534	552	529	18	531	550	525	19	528	548	521	19
B (80–89)	486	485	49	482	486	47	479	489	471	46	473	483	462	45	469	480	458	45
C (70–79)	432	426	15	428	425	12	426	428	414	11	418	424	405	10	416	421	401	10
D, E, or F (below 70)	414	408	#	403	404	#	406	413	389	#	411	422	399	#	409	425	398	#
High school type																		
Public	502	506	83	502	510	83	500	514	492	83	498	511	488	84	494	506	483	84
Private, religiously affiliated	525	510	12	530	523	12	531	529	528	11	533	534	530	11	531	533	528	10
Private, independent	547	556	5	549	567	5	544	573	550	5	557	583	560	6	541	579	550	6
Intended college major[4]																		
Agriculture and related sciences	491	484	2	487	484	1	481	485	469	1	476	485	464	1	475	484	461	1
Architecture/environmental design	492	519	3	493	521	2	488	528	485	3	492	536	487	2	490	534	485	2
Area, ethnic, cultural and gender studies	†	†	†	†	†	†	†	†	†	†	555	523	540	#	545	513	531	#
Arts: visual/performing	520	497	6	518	501	8	516	502	507	9	513	501	503	8	508	497	499	8
Biological sciences	546	545	6	545	549	5	540	554	532	6	544	560	536	6	540	557	533	6
Business and commerce	483	500	13	489	511	14	486	511	481	15	490	523	487	12	488	522	484	11
Communications and journalism	527	497	4	527	506	4	522	504	520	4	524	506	520	3	519	502	516	3
Computer or information sciences	497	522	3	501	533	3	503	534	482	7	510	539	486	4	511	539	485	2
Construction trades	†	†	†	†	†	†	†	†	†	†	416	452	398	#	422	451	399	#
Education	487	477	8	483	481	9	480	484	478	8	481	486	477	6	480	487	476	6
Engineering	525	569	8	523	572	9	519	577	506	8	531	587	516	8	528	584	513	8
Engineering technologies/technicians	†	†	†	†	†	†	463	509	446	2	463	509	446	2	464	511	447	2
English language and literature/letters	605	545	1	606	549	1	597	541	584	2	587	532	572	2	584	529	570	1
Family and consumer sciences/human sciences[5]	458	452	#	459	458	#	462	466	461	#	459	465	455	#	456	461	452	#
Foreign languages, literatures, and linguistics	556	534	#	557	540	1	572	549	563	1	572	545	562	1	567	542	557	1
General/interdisciplinary	576	553	†	554	539	†	542	532	532	#	558	505	519	1	558	505	519	1
Health and allied services	500	505	19	494	502	15	485	498	483	18	489	503	485	18	487	502	484	19
History	†	†	†	†	†	†	†	†	†	†	545	516	516	1	542	510	511	1
Legal professions and studies	†	†	†	†	†	†	†	†	†	†	511	506	499	3	512	507	500	3
Liberal arts and sciences, general studies, and humanities	554	512	†	574	504	†	579	509	542	†	559	539	549	1	552	532	541	1
Library and archival sciences	†	†	†	†	†	†	†	†	†	†	564	505	516	#	564	505	516	#
Mathematics	552	628	1	549	625	1	539	624	537	1	522	606	522	1	518	603	519	1
Mechanic and repair technologies/technician	†	†	†	†	†	†	†	†	†	†	419	452	402	#	421	451	400	#
Military sciences	503	505	†	507	511	†	510	521	487	†	501	504	469	#	467	471	433	#
Multi/interdisciplinary studies	†	†	†	†	†	†	†	†	†	†	605	598	592	#	582	580	570	#
Natural resources and conservation	†	†	†	†	†	†	†	†	†	†	528	528	510	1	525	524	506	1

See notes at end of table.

SAT mean scores and percentage distribution of college-bound seniors, by selected student characteristics: Selected years, 1995–96 through 2010–11—Continued

Selected student characteristic	1995–96			2000–01			2005–06				2009–10				2010–11			
	Critical reading score[1]	Mathematics score	Percentage distribution	Critical reading score[1]	Mathematics score	Percentage distribution	Critical reading score[1]	Mathematics score	Writing score[2]	Percentage distribution	Critical reading score[1]	Mathematics score	Writing score[2]	Percentage distribution	Critical reading score[1]	Mathematics score	Writing score[2]	Percentage distribution
1	2	3	4	5	6	7	8	9	10	11	12	13	14	15	16	17	18	19
Parks, recreation, leisure, and fitness studies	†	†	†	†	†	†	†	†	†	†	448	474	439	1	444	468	435	1
Personal and culinary services	†	†	†	†	†	†	†	†	†	†	457	460	443	#	457	456	440	#
Philosophy/religious studies	560	536	1	561	539	1	557	537	535	1	563	540	540	#	557	535	530	#
Physical sciences	575	595	#	568	588	1	557	589	542	2	558	588	540	1	553	582	537	1
Precision production	†	†	†	†	†	†	†	†	†	†	436	464	417	#	436	468	422	#
Psychology	458	448	3	461	455	3	462	461	454	3	505	492	496	5	505	494	497	5
Public affairs and services	†	†	†	†	†	†	†	†	†	†	469	459	462	#	467	459	462	#
Security and protective services	†	†	†	†	†	†	†	†	†	†	448	459	438	2	445	454	432	2
Social sciences and history	532	509	11	531	512	10	539	519	525	9	†	†	†	†	†	†	†	†
Social sciences	†	†	†	†	†	†	†	†	†	†	574	558	559	2	573	558	559	2
Technical and vocational	435	441	1	444	451	1	437	454	421	1	†	†	†	†	†	†	†	†
Theology and religious vocations	†	†	†	†	†	†	†	†	†	†	539	524	515	#	539	522	513	#
Transportation and materials moving	†	†	†	†	†	†	†	†	†	†	464	465	451	#	465	462	446	#
Other	†	†	†	†	†	†	439	456	436	2	456	465	447	2	453	462	443	2
Undecided	500	507	7	515	524	7	512	530	502	7	532	548	524	7	530	545	522	8
Degree-level goal																		
Certificate program	434	439	1	443	455	1	443	462	435	1	442	463	432	1	445	464	434	1
Associate's degree	422	415	2	419	416	2	416	420	409	2	414	421	405	1	412	416	400	1
Bachelor's degree	476	476	23	478	483	25	477	487	469	25	477	488	466	28	478	490	467	30
Master's degree	514	518	29	516	526	29	512	525	505	30	509	524	501	30	506	524	499	29
Doctor's or related degree	548	552	24	547	554	24	539	553	532	21	534	551	529	21	534	550	527	21
Other	430	438	1	438	449	1	439	456	436	1	431	452	427	1	425	451	423	1
Undecided	502	503	20	511	517	19	515	528	508	22	516	529	507	18	509	522	499	16
Family income																		
Less than $20,000	—	—	—	—	—	—	—	—	—	—	437	460	432	11	434	460	429	13
$20,000, but less than $40,000	—	—	—	—	—	—	—	—	—	—	465	479	455	16	464	480	454	16
$40,000, but less than $60,000	—	—	—	—	—	—	—	—	—	—	490	500	478	15	487	499	475	15
$60,000, but less than $80,000	—	—	—	—	—	—	—	—	—	—	504	514	492	14	502	512	489	14
$80,000, but less than $100,000	—	—	—	—	—	—	—	—	—	—	518	529	505	12	515	527	503	12
$100,000, but less than $120,000	—	—	—	—	—	—	—	—	—	—	528	541	518	10	526	539	515	10
$120,000, but less than $140,000	—	—	—	—	—	—	—	—	—	—	533	546	523	5	530	544	520	5
$140,000, but less than $160,000	—	—	—	—	—	—	—	—	—	—	540	554	531	4	538	552	529	4
$160,000, but less than $200,000	—	—	—	—	—	—	—	—	—	—	547	561	540	5	543	557	536	5
More than $200,000	—	—	—	—	—	—	—	—	—	—	568	586	567	7	568	586	567	7
Highest level of parental education																		
No high school diploma	414	439	4	411	438	4	418	445	418	4	422	446	419	5	421	449	418	6
High school diploma	475	474	35	472	476	32	467	478	460	31	464	475	453	31	463	476	452	31
Associate's degree	489	487	8	489	491	9	484	493	474	8	482	491	469	9	480	489	466	8
Bachelor's degree	525	529	28	525	533	29	522	536	514	30	521	536	512	30	522	538	514	31
Graduate degree	556	558	25	559	567	26	558	571	552	27	561	575	554	26	559	574	554	25

—Not available.
†Not applicable.
#Rounds to zero.
[1] Prior to 2006, the critical reading section was known as the verbal section.
[2] Writing data are based on students who took the SAT writing section, which was introduced in March 2005.
[3] Beginning in 2005–06, the College Board has reported third, fourth, and fifth quintiles as the bottom three quintiles instead of reporting them separately as in previous years.
[4] Data may not be comparable over time because of additions to the list of majors and changes in subspecialties within majors.
[5] Prior to 2006–07, family and consumer sciences/human sciences was called home economics.

NOTE: Data for 2009–10 and earlier years are for seniors who took the SAT any time during their high school years through March of their senior year. Data for 2010–11 are for seniors who took the SAT any time during their high school years through June of their senior year. If a student took a test more than once, the most recent score was used. The SAT was formerly known as the Scholastic Assessment Test and the Scholastic Aptitude Test. Possible scores on each part of the SAT range from 200 to 800. The critical reading section was formerly known as the verbal section. Detail may not sum to totals because of rounding.
SOURCE: College Entrance Examination Board, College-Bound Seniors: Total Group Profile [National] Report, selected years, 1995–96 through 2010–11, retrieved September 15, 2011, from http://professionals.collegeboard.com/data-reports-research/sat/cb-seniors-2011. (This table was prepared September 2011.)

SAT mean scores of college-bound seniors and percentage of graduates taking SAT, by state: Selected years, 1995–96 through 2010–11

State	1995–96		2000–01		2005–06			2008–09			2009–10			2010–11			Percent of graduates taking SAT, 2009–10[1]	Percent of graduates taking SAT, 2010–11[1]
	Critical reading	Mathematics	Critical reading	Mathematics	Critical reading	Mathematics	Writing[2]	Critical reading	Mathematics	Writing[2]	Critical reading	Mathematics	Writing[2]	Critical reading	Mathematics	Writing[2]		
1	2	3	4	5	6	7	8	9	10	11	12	13	14	15	16	17	18	19
United States	**505**	**508**	**506**	**514**	**503**	**518**	**497**	**501**	**515**	**493**	**501**	**516**	**492**	**497**	**514**	**489**	**47**	**—**
Alabama	565	558	559	554	565	561	565	557	552	549	556	550	544	546	541	536	7	8
Alaska....................	521	513	514	510	517	517	493	520	516	492	518	515	491	515	511	487	48	52
Arizona..................	525	521	523	525	521	528	507	516	521	497	519	525	500	517	523	499	25	28
Arkansas................	566	550	562	550	574	568	567	572	572	556	566	566	552	568	570	554	4	5
California	495	511	498	517	501	518	501	500	513	498	501	516	500	499	515	499	50	53
Colorado	536	538	539	542	558	564	548	568	575	555	568	572	555	570	573	556	18	19
Connecticut	507	504	509	510	512	516	511	509	513	512	509	514	513	509	513	513	84	87
Delaware................	508	495	501	499	495	500	484	495	498	484	493	495	481	489	490	476	71	74
District of Columbia ...	489	473	482	474	487	472	482	466	451	461	474	464	466	469	457	459	76	79
Florida....................	498	496	498	499	496	497	480	497	498	480	496	498	479	487	489	471	59	64
Georgia..................	484	477	491	489	494	496	487	490	491	479	488	490	475	485	487	473	74	80
Hawaii...................	485	510	486	515	482	509	472	479	502	469	483	505	470	479	500	469	58	64
Idaho.....................	543	536	543	542	543	545	525	541	540	520	543	541	517	542	539	517	19	20
Illinois...................	564	575	576	589	591	609	586	588	604	583	585	600	577	599	617	591	6	5
Indiana..................	494	494	499	501	498	509	486	496	507	480	494	505	477	493	501	475	64	68
Iowa......................	590	600	593	603	602	613	591	610	615	588	603	613	582	596	606	575	3	3
Kansas...................	579	571	577	580	582	590	566	581	589	564	590	595	567	580	591	563	6	7
Kentucky	549	544	550	550	562	562	555	573	573	561	575	575	563	576	572	563	6	6
Louisiana...............	559	550	564	562	570	571	571	563	558	555	555	550	547	555	550	546	7	8
Maine[3]..................	504	498	506	500	501	501	491	468	467	455	468	467	454	469	469	453	92	93
Maryland................	507	504	508	510	503	509	499	*500	502	495	501	506	495	499	502	491	70	74
Massachusetts.........	507	504	511	515	513	524	510	514	526	510	512	526	509	513	527	509	86	89
Michigan................	557	565	561	572	568	583	555	584	603	575	585	605	576	583	604	573	5	5
Minnesota..............	582	593	580	589	591	600	574	595	609	578	594	607	580	593	608	577	7	7
Mississippi.............	569	557	566	551	556	541	562	567	554	559	566	548	552	564	543	553	3	4
Missouri.................	570	569	577	577	587	591	582	595	600	584	593	595	580	592	593	579	4	5
Montana.................	546	547	539	539	538	545	524	541	542	519	538	538	517	539	537	516	24	26
Nebraska................	567	568	562	568	576	583	566	587	594	572	585	593	568	585	591	569	4	5
Nevada..................	508	507	509	515	498	508	481	501	505	479	496	501	473	494	496	470	43	47
New Hampshire	520	514	520	516	520	524	509	523	523	510	520	524	510	523	525	511	77	77
New Jersey	498	505	499	513	496	515	496	496	513	496	495	514	497	495	516	497	76	78
New Mexico	554	548	551	542	557	549	543	553	546	534	553	549	534	548	541	529	11	12
New York	497	499	495	505	493	510	483	485	502	478	484	499	478	485	499	476	85	89
North Carolina	490	486	493	499	495	513	485	495	511	480	497	511	477	493	508	474	63	67
North Dakota	596	599	592	599	610	617	588	590	593	566	580	594	559	586	612	561	4	3
Ohio......................	536	535	534	539	535	544	521	537	546	523	538	548	522	539	545	522	21	21
Oklahoma...............	566	557	567	561	576	574	563	575	571	557	569	568	547	571	565	547	5	6
Oregon..................	523	521	526	526	523	529	503	523	525	499	523	524	499	520	521	499	54	56
Pennsylvania...........	498	492	500	499	493	500	483	493	501	483	492	501	480	493	501	479	71	73
Rhode Island	501	491	501	499	495	502	490	498	496	494	494	495	488	495	493	489	67	68
South Carolina........	480	474	486	488	487	498	480	486	496	470	484	495	468	482	490	464	66	70
South Dakota	574	566	577	582	590	604	578	589	600	569	592	603	571	584	591	562	3	4
Tennessee	563	552	562	553	573	569	572	571	565	565	576	571	565	575	568	567	10	10
Texas	495	500	493	499	491	506	487	486	506	475	484	505	473	479	502	465	53	58
Utah	583	575	575	570	560	557	550	559	558	540	568	559	547	563	559	545	6	6
Vermont	506	500	511	506	513	519	502	518	518	506	519	521	506	515	518	505	66	67
Virginia..................	507	496	510	501	512	513	500	511	512	498	512	512	497	512	509	495	67	71
Washington............	519	519	527	527	527	532	511	524	531	507	524	532	508	523	529	508	54	57
West Virginia...........	526	506	527	512	519	510	515	511	501	499	515	507	500	514	501	497	16	17
Wisconsin	577	586	584	596	588	600	577	594	608	582	595	604	579	590	602	575	4	5
Wyoming................	544	544	547	545	548	555	537	567	568	550	570	567	546	572	569	551	5	5

—Not available
[1]Participation rate is based on the projection of high school graduates by the Western Inter-state Commission for Higher Education (WICHE), and the number of seniors who took the SAT in each state.
[2]Writing data are based on students who took the SAT writing section, which was introduced in March 2005.
[3]Beginning with the spring SAT administration in 2006, all Maine high school juniors, including all students in their third year of high school, are required to take SAT tests in critical reading, writing, and mathematics.
NOTE: Data for 2009–10 and earlier years are for seniors who took the SAT any time during their high school years through March of their senior year. Data for 2010–11 are for seniors who took the SAT any time during their high school years through June of their senior year. If a student took a test more than once, the most recent score was used. The SAT was formerly known as the Scholastic Assessment Test and the Scholastic Aptitude Test. Possible scores on each part of the SAT range from 200 to 800. The critical reading section was formerly known as the verbal section.
SOURCE: College Entrance Examination Board, College-Bound Seniors Tables and Related Items, selected years, 1995–96 through 2010–11, retrieved September 14, 2011, from http://professionals.collegeboard.com/profdownload/SAT_Trends_Report_9_12_2011.pdf. (This table was prepared September 2011.)

ACT score averages and standard deviations, by sex and race/ethnicity, and percentage of ACT test takers, by selected composite score ranges and planned fields of study: Selected years, 1995 through 2011

Score type and test-taker characteristic	1995	2000	2001	2002	2003	2004	2005	2006	2007	2008	2009	2010	2011
1	2	3	4	5	6	7	8	9	10	11	12	13	14
Total test takers													
Number (in thousands) ...	945	1,065	1,070	1,116	1,175	1,171	1,186	1,206	1,301	1,422	1,480	1,569	1,623
Percent of graduates	37.5	37.6	37.6	38.4	39.0	38.4	38.2	38.6	40.6	42.9	44.6	47.2	49.5
						Average test score[1]							
Composite score, total ...	20.8	21.0	21.0	20.8	20.8	20.9	20.9	21.1	21.2	21.1	21.1	21.0	21.1
Sex													
Male	21.0	21.2	21.1	20.9	21.0	21.0	21.1	21.2	21.2	21.2	21.3	21.2	21.2
Female	20.7	20.9	20.9	20.7	20.8	20.9	20.9	21.0	21.0	21.0	20.9	20.9	21.0
Race/ethnicity													
White	—	22.7	21.8	21.7	21.7	21.8	21.9	22.0	22.1	22.1	22.2	22.3	22.4
Black	—	17.8	16.9	16.8	16.9	17.1	17.0	17.1	17.0	16.9	16.9	16.9	17.0
Hispanic	—	—	—	18.4	18.5	18.5	18.6	18.6	18.7	18.7	18.7	18.6	18.7
Asian/Pacific Islander........	—	22.4	21.7	21.6	21.8	21.9	22.1	22.3	22.6	22.9	23.2	23.4	—
Asian	—	—	—	—	—	—	—	—	—	—	—	—	23.6
Native Hawaiian/Pacific Islander	—	—	—	—	—	—	—	—	—	—	—	—	19.5
American Indian/Alaska	—	20.4	18.8	18.6	18.7	18.8	18.7	18.8	18.9	19.0	18.9	19.0	18.6
Two or more races	—	—	—	—	—	—	—	—	—	—	—	—	21.1
Subject-area scores													
English	20.2	20.5	20.5	20.2	20.3	20.4	20.4	20.6	20.7	20.6	20.6	20.5	20.6
Male	19.8	20.0	20.0	19.7	19.8	19.9	20.0	20.1	20.2	20.1	20.2	20.1	20.2
Female	20.6	20.9	20.8	20.6	20.7	20.8	20.8	21.0	21.0	21.0	20.9	20.8	20.9
Mathematics	20.2	20.7	20.7	20.6	20.6	20.7	20.7	20.8	21.0	21.0	21.0	21.0	21.1
Male	20.9	21.4	21.4	21.2	21.2	21.3	21.3	21.5	21.6	21.6	21.6	21.6	21.6
Female	19.7	20.2	20.2	20.1	20.1	20.2	20.2	20.3	20.4	20.4	20.4	20.5	20.6
Reading	21.3	21.4	21.3	21.1	21.2	21.3	21.3	21.4	21.5	21.4	21.4	21.3	21.3
Male	21.1	21.2	21.1	20.9	21.0	21.1	21.0	21.1	21.2	21.2	21.3	21.1	21.1
Female	21.4	21.5	21.5	21.3	21.4	21.5	21.5	21.6	21.6	21.5	21.4	21.4	21.4
Science reasoning	21.0	21.0	21.0	20.8	20.8	20.9	20.9	20.9	21.0	20.8	20.9	20.9	20.9
Male	21.6	21.6	21.6	21.3	21.3	21.3	21.4	21.4	21.4	21.3	21.4	21.4	21.4
Female	20.5	20.6	20.6	20.4	20.4	20.5	20.5	20.5	20.5	20.4	20.4	20.5	20.5
						Standard deviation[2]							
Composite score, total ...	—	4.7	4.7	4.8	4.8	4.8	—	4.8	5.0	5.0	5.1	5.2	5.2
Sex													
Male	—	4.9	4.9	5.0	5.0	5.0	5.0	—	—	—	—	—	—
Female	—	4.6	4.6	4.7	4.7	4.7	4.7	—	—	—	—	—	—
Subject-area scores													
English	—	5.5	5.6	5.8	5.8	5.9	—	5.9	6.0	6.1	6.3	6.4	6.5
Male	—	5.6	5.6	5.8	5.8	5.9	6.0	—	—	—	—	—	—
Female	—	5.5	5.6	5.7	5.8	5.8	5.9	—	—	—	—	—	—
Mathematics	—	5.0	5.0	5.0	5.1	5.0	—	5.0	5.1	5.2	5.3	5.3	5.3
Male	—	5.2	5.2	5.3	4.8	5.3	5.3	—	—	—	—	—	—
Female	—	4.8	4.7	4.8	5.3	4.8	4.8	—	—	—	—	—	—
Reading	—	6.1	6.0	6.1	6.1	6.0	—	6.0	6.1	6.1	6.2	6.2	6.2
Male	—	6.1	6.1	6.3	5.3	6.1	6.1	—	—	—	—	—	—
Female	—	6.0	6.0	6.1	4.8	5.9	6.0	—	—	—	—	—	—
Science reasoning	—	4.5	4.6	4.6	4.6	4.6	—	4.6	4.9	4.9	5.0	5.1	5.1
Male	—	4.8	4.9	4.9	4.9	4.9	4.9	—	—	—	—	—	—
Female	—	4.3	4.3	4.3	4.3	4.3	4.3	—	—	—	—	—	—
						Percent of ACT test takers							
Obtaining composite scores of—													
28 or above	—	10	10	10	10	10	10	11	11	12	12	12	13
17 or below	—	25	25	27	27	26	26	25	25	26	27	28	28
Planned major field of study													
Business[3]	13	11	11	10	10	9	9	9	8	11	12	11	10
Education[4]	8	9	8	8	7	7	6	6	5	6	7	7	6
Engineering[5]	8	8	7	7	7	6	6	6	5	7	8	8	8
Health sciences and technologies	—	17	16	15	16	17	16	15	14	17	19	20	19
Social sciences[6]	9	9	9	8	8	7	7	6	5	6	7	7	8

—Not available.

[1] Minimum score is 1 and maximum score is 36.

[2] Standard deviations not available for racial/ethnic groups.

[3] For years prior to 2011, includes business and management, business and office, and marketing and distribution.

[4] For years prior to 2011, includes education and teacher education.

[5] Includes engineering and engineering-related technologies.

[6] Includes social sciences and philosophy, religion, and theology. For 2011, also includes law.

NOTE: Data are for high school graduates who took the ACT during their sophomore, junior, or senior year. If a student took a test more than once, the most recent score was used. Race categories exclude persons of Hispanic ethnicity. Some data have been revised from previously published figures.

SOURCE: ACT, *High School Profile Report*, selected years, 1995 through 2011. U.S. Department of Education, National Center for Education Statistics, Common Core of Data (CCD), "State Nonfiscal Survey of Public Elementary/Secondary Education," 1995–96 through 2008–09; Private School Universe Survey (PSS), 1995 through 2007; and *Projections of Education Statistics to 2020*. (This table was prepared September 2011.)

Percentage distribution of elementary and secondary school children, by average grades and selected child and school characteristics: 1996, 2003, and 2007

Distribution of children, by parental reports of average grades in all subjects

Selected characteristic of children and schools	1996				2003				2007			
	Mostly A's	Mostly B's	Mostly C's	Mostly D's or F's	Mostly A's	Mostly B's	Mostly C's	Mostly D's or F's	Mostly A's	Mostly B's	Mostly C's	Mostly D's or F's
1	2	3	4	5	6	7	8	9	10	11	12	13
All students	39.5 (0.53)	37.8 (0.56)	18.5 (0.41)	4.2 (0.22)	43.6 (0.62)	37.0 (0.58)	15.9 (0.52)	3.6 (0.24)	47.2 (0.75)	35.0 (0.80)	14.1 (0.72)	3.8 (0.36)
Sex of child												
Male	32.5 (0.68)	38.3 (0.82)	23.5 (0.62)	5.7 (0.36)	36.4 (0.72)	38.6 (0.86)	19.8 (0.74)	5.2 (0.40)	40.3 (1.01)	37.1 (1.17)	17.0 (1.25)	5.7 (0.64)
Female	46.9 (0.79)	37.2 (0.77)	13.2 (0.60)	2.7 (0.27)	51.0 (0.84)	35.3 (0.76)	11.9 (0.61)	1.9 (0.24)	54.7 (0.99)	32.7 (0.97)	11.0 (0.62)	1.7 (0.24)
Race/ethnicity of child												
White	43.7 (0.66)	36.1 (0.60)	16.5 (0.48)	3.7 (0.27)	47.8 (0.86)	35.2 (0.75)	14.0 (0.63)	3.1 (0.25)	53.9 (0.97)	32.2 (0.91)	11.7 (0.68)	2.1 (0.27)
Black	27.0 (1.40)	41.0 (1.48)	26.2 (1.51)	5.8 (0.67)	34.5 (1.75)	39.5 (1.65)	20.9 (1.33)	5.0 (0.82)	28.3 (2.04)	40.5 (2.75)	24.9 (2.89)	6.3 (1.41)
Hispanic	31.7 (1.41)	43.8 (1.50)	19.6 (1.17)	4.9 (0.71)	34.9 (1.14)	42.3 (1.24)	18.6 (1.03)	4.2 (0.48)	40.8 (1.68)	39.2 (1.66)	14.1 (1.24)	6.0 (1.15)
Asian/Pacific Islander	55.5 (3.46)	35.0 (3.35)	8.3 (1.93)	‡ (†)	62.0 (3.47)	25.5 (2.76)	11.3 (3.06)	‡ (†)	— (†)	— (†)	— (†)	— (†)
Asian	— (†)	— (†)	— (†)	— (†)	— (†)	— (†)	— (†)	— (†)	74.5 (3.67)	20.7 (3.60)	3.2! (1.10)	‡ (†)
Pacific Islander	— (†)	— (†)	— (†)	— (†)	— (†)	— (†)	— (†)	— (†)	‡ (†)	70.5 (18.20)	‡ (†)	‡ (†)
American Indian/Alaska Native	30.2 (3.90)	31.9 (4.78)	29.3 (4.92)	8.7! (3.82)	29.5 (6.53)	53.3 (6.42)	12.1! (4.90)	5.1! (2.54)	39.7 (9.13)	29.2 (8.22)	19.9! (6.67)	‡ (†)
Other	40.7 (2.98)	33.3 (3.35)	20.1 (2.85)	5.8! (1.96)	41.4 (4.34)	36.2 (3.91)	18.8 (2.81)	3.5! (1.38)	— (†)	50.2! (21.33)	‡ (†)	‡ (†)
Two or more races	— (†)	— (†)	— (†)	— (†)	— (†)	— (†)	— (†)	— (†)	44.3 (3.92)	38.2 (4.13)	11.3 (2.25)	6.2 (1.77)
Highest education level of parents												
Less than high school	28.7 (1.87)	39.2 (1.89)	24.0 (1.68)	8.1 (1.04)	27.8 (2.17)	41.6 (2.05)	22.7 (2.27)	7.8 (1.46)	26.8 (3.18)	41.9 (4.27)	22.0 (2.55)	9.3 (2.02)
High school/GED	30.5 (0.90)	40.5 (1.09)	23.1 (0.91)	5.9 (0.52)	32.1 (1.20)	41.4 (1.23)	21.7 (1.12)	4.8 (0.57)	32.9 (1.70)	39.8 (1.64)	21.9 (2.02)	5.4 (0.82)
Vocational/technical or some college	35.2 (1.25)	41.3 (1.20)	19.4 (0.82)	4.1 (0.52)	39.8 (3.49)	38.3 (1.36)	17.2 (0.95)	4.7 (0.58)	40.7 (1.65)	38.6 (2.03)	16.6 (1.43)	4.0 (0.78)
Associate's degree	41.5 (1.83)	36.9 (1.88)	18.0 (1.53)	3.5 (0.68)	46.7 (2.13)	34.5 (1.94)	16.4 (1.51)	2.4 (0.57)	40.3 (2.27)	38.4 (2.00)	15.7 (1.76)	5.5! (2.10)
Bachelor's degree/some graduate school	52.7 (1.32)	32.9 (1.16)	12.5 (0.92)	1.9 (0.31)	53.0 (1.26)	34.2 (1.29)	11.1 (0.85)	1.7 (0.28)	58.9 (1.62)	32.2 (1.52)	7.3 (0.85)	1.6 (0.38)
Graduate/professional degree	59.1 (1.40)	30.4 (1.26)	9.5 (0.99)	1.0 (0.24)	61.9 (1.71)	30.5 (1.75)	6.7 (0.67)	0.9 (0.24)	68.2 (1.59)	24.1 (1.37)	6.6 (1.33)	1.2! (0.38)
Family income (in current dollars)												
$5,000 or less	28.9 (2.50)	38.8 (2.39)	23.3 (2.35)	8.9 (1.67)	31.8 (4.43)	38.9 (4.27)	21.0 (3.53)	8.3! (3.25)	22.9 (4.72)	31.0 (5.89)	32.6 (7.04)	13.6 (3.93)
$5,001 to $10,000	26.6 (1.97)	41.9 (2.30)	24.6 (2.33)	6.9 (1.15)	31.6 (2.90)	40.1 (3.70)	24.9 (2.70)	3.4 (0.98)	26.4 (4.16)	51.1 (5.45)	17.2 (3.65)	5.3! (1.97)
$10,001 to $15,000	27.6 (2.00)	40.0 (2.33)	26.1 (1.95)	6.3 (1.10)	33.4 (3.49)	35.1 (2.85)	23.9 (2.67)	7.5 (1.44)	34.7 (3.80)	38.9 (4.35)	21.1 (3.21)	5.3 (1.44)
$15,001 to $20,000	32.7 (2.34)	38.4 (1.99)	21.6 (1.81)	7.3 (1.35)	34.6 (2.28)	41.1 (2.41)	18.8 (2.00)	5.4 (1.26)	30.0 (4.45)	35.7 (4.69)	29.5 (7.46)	4.8 (1.45)
$20,001 to $25,000	34.4 (1.92)	40.8 (2.19)	20.6 (1.77)	4.2 (0.88)	33.5 (2.51)	42.1 (2.93)	19.8 (1.99)	4.7 (0.96)	32.3 (3.13)	39.8 (3.38)	20.2 (3.49)	7.7 (1.85)
$25,001 to $30,000	33.0 (1.88)	42.0 (2.05)	19.8 (1.41)	5.2 (0.76)	34.5 (2.67)	42.6 (3.13)	17.9 (1.92)	5.0 (1.21)	38.5 (4.05)	39.2 (4.27)	16.2 (2.91)	6.1! (2.01)
$30,001 to $35,000	40.0 (1.88)	38.0 (1.66)	18.1 (1.44)	3.9 (0.69)	35.1 (2.76)	43.1 (2.57)	16.9 (1.84)	5.0 (1.09)	44.2 (3.61)	32.7 (3.44)	18.7 (3.83)	4.4! (1.67)
$35,001 to $40,000	40.4 (1.70)	37.3 (1.69)	19.4 (1.22)	2.8 (0.65)	39.6 (3.20)	37.8 (2.79)	19.1 (1.78)	3.6 (0.93)	37.6 (3.35)	36.4 (3.56)	19.8 (2.89)	6.1 (1.75)
$40,001 to $50,000	43.2 (1.49)	36.0 (1.51)	16.8 (1.09)	4.0 (0.57)	43.9 (2.06)	35.8 (1.95)	15.8 (1.51)	4.4 (0.75)	37.9 (2.57)	39.4 (2.92)	15.9 (1.76)	6.9! (2.57)
$50,001 to $75,000	50.2 (1.05)	32.7 (1.04)	14.9 (0.86)	2.2 (0.34)	48.0 (1.29)	35.0 (1.22)	14.0 (0.81)	3.0 (0.45)	53.0 (1.50)	33.8 (1.42)	11.0 (0.97)	2.2 (0.42)
Over $75,000	51.0 (1.58)	36.8 (1.55)	10.9 (0.93)	1.3 (0.31)	54.0 (1.19)	33.8 (1.18)	11.0 (0.78)	1.2 (0.19)	59.4 (1.13)	31.3 (1.09)	8.0 (0.70)	1.3 (0.25)
Child attending public school	38.2 (0.54)	37.9 (0.56)	19.3 (0.44)	4.6 (0.23)	41.8 (0.64)	37.5 (0.62)	16.8 (0.57)	3.8 (0.26)	45.5 (0.80)	35.5 (0.84)	14.9 (0.77)	4.1 (0.39)
Elementary (kindergarten to grade 8)	43.2 (0.75)	36.6 (0.69)	16.3 (0.55)	3.9 (0.26)	46.1 (0.80)	35.9 (0.84)	14.6 (0.74)	3.4 (0.32)	50.0 (0.99)	33.1 (1.00)	13.4 (1.12)	3.5 (0.43)
Secondary (grades 9 to 12)	29.6 (0.89)	40.2 (1.00)	24.5 (0.89)	5.7 (0.46)	34.6 (0.96)	40.2 (0.97)	20.6 (0.94)	4.6 (0.46)	38.6 (1.36)	39.1 (1.27)	17.2 (1.08)	5.2 (0.71)
Child attending private school	50.6 (1.64)	36.3 (1.58)	11.9 (0.96)	1.3! (0.40)	57.6 (1.72)	33.0 (1.68)	8.1 (0.91)	1.3! (0.45)	60.6 (2.79)	30.8 (2.85)	7.8 (1.73)	0.9! (0.35)
Elementary (kindergarten to grade 8)	55.5 (2.02)	35.5 (1.90)	7.5 (0.86)	1.4! (0.57)	61.6 (2.39)	30.3 (2.28)	7.3 (1.03)	0.8! (0.28)	66.1 (3.73)	26.6 (4.05)	6.6 (1.66)	‡ (†)
Secondary (grades 9 to 12)	40.9 (2.89)	37.7 (2.39)	20.4 (2.29)	1.0! (0.44)	48.8 (3.22)	38.9 (2.94)	10.0 (1.77)	‡ (†)	51.2 (3.91)	37.8 (3.43)	9.8! (3.87)	‡ (†)

—Not available.
†Not applicable.
!Interpret data with caution. The coefficient of variation (CV) for this estimate is 30 percent or greater.
‡Reporting standards not met. Either there are too few cases or the coefficient of variation (CV) is 50 percent or greater.

NOTE: Includes children enrolled in kindergarten through grade 12. Excludes children whose programs have no classes with lettered grades. Race categories exclude persons of Hispanic ethnicity. Detail may not sum to totals because of rounding. Standard errors appear in parentheses. Some data have been revised from previously published figures.
SOURCE: U.S. Department of Education, National Center for Education Statistics, Parent and Family Involvement in Education/Civic Involvement Survey and Parent and Family Involvement in Education Survey of the National Household Education Surveys Program (PFI/CI-NHES:1996 and PFI-NHES:2003 and 2007). (This table was prepared August 2008.)

Enrollment in public elementary and secondary schools, by state or jurisdiction: Selected years, fall 1990 through fall 2014

State or jurisdiction	Total												Fall 2008			Fall 2009			Percent change in total enrollment, 2004 to 2009	Projected fall 2011 enrollment	Projected fall 2014 enrollment
	Fall 1990	Fall 1995	Fall 1998	Fall 1999	Fall 2000	Fall 2001	Fall 2002	Fall 2003	Fall 2004	Fall 2005	Fall 2006	Fall 2007	Total	Prekindergarten to grade 8[1]	Grades 9 to 12[2]	Total	Prekindergarten to grade 8[1]	Grades 9 to 12[2]			
1	2	3	4	5	6	7	8	9	10	11	12	13	14	15	16	17	18	19	20	21	22
United States	41,216,683	44,840,481	46,538,585	46,857,149	47,203,539	47,671,870	48,183,086	48,540,215	48,795,465	49,113,298	49,315,842	49,292,507	49,265,572	34,285,564	14,980,008	49,373,307	34,417,985	14,955,322	1.2	49,422,000	50,268,000
Alabama	721,806	746,149	747,980	740,732	739,992	737,190	739,366	731,220	730,140	741,761	743,632	744,865	745,668	528,078	217,590	748,889	529,394	219,495	2.6	741,000	740,000
Alaska	113,903	127,618	135,373	134,391	133,356	134,349	134,364	133,933	132,970	133,288	132,608	131,029	130,662	89,263	41,399	131,661	90,824	40,837	-1.0	133,000	141,000
Arizona	639,853	743,566	848,262	852,612	877,696	922,180	937,755	1,012,068	1,043,298	1,094,454	1,068,249	1,087,447	1,087,817	771,749	316,068	1,077,831	760,420	317,411	3.3	1,136,000	1,209,000
Arkansas	436,286	453,257	452,256	451,034	449,959	449,805	450,985	454,523	463,115	474,206	476,409	479,016	478,965	341,603	137,362	480,559	344,209	136,350	3.8	484,000	490,000
California	4,950,474	5,536,406	5,926,037	6,038,590	6,140,814	6,247,726	6,353,667	6,413,867	6,441,557	6,437,202	6,406,750	6,343,471	6,322,528	4,306,258	2,016,270	6,263,449	4,264,033	1,999,416	-2.8	6,329,000	6,425,000
Colorado	574,213	656,279	699,135	708,109	724,508	742,145	751,862	757,693	765,976	779,826	794,026	801,867	818,443	580,304	238,139	832,368	591,378	240,990	8.7	856,000	897,000
Connecticut	469,123	517,935	544,698	553,993	562,179	570,228	570,023	577,203	577,390	575,059	575,100	570,626	567,198	392,218	174,980	563,985	389,965	174,020	-2.3	552,000	545,000
Delaware	99,658	108,461	113,262	112,836	114,676	115,555	116,342	117,668	119,091	120,937	122,254	122,574	125,430	86,811	38,619	126,801	87,710	39,091	6.5	128,000	133,000
District of Columbia	80,694	79,802	71,889	77,194	68,925	75,392	76,166	78,057	76,714	76,876	72,850	78,422	68,681	50,779	17,902	69,433	51,656	17,777	-9.5	72,000	73,000
Florida	1,861,592	2,176,222	2,337,633	2,381,396	2,434,821	2,500,478	2,539,929	2,587,628	2,639,336	2,675,024	2,671,513	2,666,811	2,631,020	1,849,295	781,725	2,634,522	1,850,901	783,621	-0.2	2,586,000	2,617,000
Georgia	1,151,687	1,311,126	1,401,291	1,422,762	1,444,937	1,470,634	1,496,012	1,522,611	1,553,437	1,598,461	1,629,157	1,649,589	1,655,792	1,185,684	470,108	1,667,685	1,194,751	472,934	7.4	1,686,000	1,733,000
Hawaii	171,708	187,180	188,069	185,860	184,360	184,546	183,829	183,609	183,185	182,818	180,728	179,897	179,478	125,910	53,568	180,196	127,477	52,719	-1.6	180,000	182,000
Idaho	220,840	243,097	244,722	245,136	245,117	246,521	248,604	252,120	256,084	261,982	267,380	272,119	275,051	193,554	81,497	276,299	194,728	81,571	7.9	286,000	300,000
Illinois	1,821,407	1,943,623	2,011,530	2,027,600	2,048,792	2,071,391	2,084,187	2,100,961	2,097,503	2,111,706	2,118,276	2,112,805	2,119,707	1,479,195	640,512	2,104,175	1,463,713	640,462	0.3	2,115,000	2,118,000
Indiana	954,525	977,263	989,001	988,702	989,267	996,133	1,003,875	1,011,130	1,021,348	1,035,074	1,045,940	1,046,766	1,046,147	730,021	316,126	1,046,661	730,599	316,062	2.5	1,044,000	1,046,000
Iowa	483,652	502,343	498,214	497,301	495,080	485,932	482,210	481,226	478,319	483,482	483,122	485,115	487,559	335,566	151,993	491,842	341,333	150,509	2.8	487,000	494,000
Kansas	437,034	463,008	472,353	472,188	470,610	470,205	470,957	470,490	469,136	467,525	469,506	468,295	471,060	331,079	139,981	474,489	332,997	141,492	1.1	476,000	487,000
Kentucky	636,401	659,821	655,687	648,180	665,850	654,363	660,782	663,369	674,796	679,878	683,152	666,225	670,030	472,204	197,826	680,089	484,466	195,623	0.8	671,000	673,000
Louisiana	784,757	797,366	768,734	756,579	743,089	731,328	730,464	727,709	724,281	654,526	675,851	681,038	684,873	504,213	180,660	690,915	509,883	181,032	-4.6	686,000	683,000
Maine	215,149	213,569	211,051	209,253	207,037	205,586	204,337	202,084	198,820	195,498	193,996	196,245	192,935	129,324	63,611	189,225	128,646	60,579	-4.8	189,000	188,000
Maryland	715,176	805,544	841,671	846,582	852,920	860,640	866,743	869,113	865,561	860,020	851,640	845,700	843,861	576,473	267,388	848,412	581,785	266,627	-2.0	837,000	850,000
Massachusetts	834,314	915,007	962,317	971,425	975,150	973,139	982,989	980,459	975,574	971,909	968,661	962,958	958,910	666,538	292,372	957,053	666,551	290,502	-1.9	938,000	924,000
Michigan	1,584,431	1,641,456	1,720,287	1,725,639	1,720,626	1,730,669	1,785,160	1,757,604	1,751,290	1,742,282	1,722,656	1,692,739	1,659,921	1,118,569	541,352	1,649,082	1,114,611	534,471	-5.8	1,581,000	1,555,000
Minnesota	756,374	835,166	856,455	854,034	854,340	851,384	846,891	842,854	838,503	839,243	840,565	837,578	836,048	560,184	275,864	837,053	564,661	272,392	-0.2	846,000	874,000
Mississippi	502,417	506,272	502,379	500,716	497,871	493,507	492,645	493,540	495,376	494,954	495,026	494,122	491,962	351,807	140,155	492,481	351,652	140,829	-0.6	487,000	483,000
Missouri	816,558	889,881	913,494	914,110	912,744	909,792	906,499	905,941	905,449	917,705	920,353	917,188	917,871	635,411	282,460	917,982	638,082	279,900	1.4	910,000	917,000
Montana	152,974	165,547	159,988	157,556	154,875	151,947	149,995	148,356	146,705	145,416	144,418	142,823	141,899	96,869	45,030	141,807	97,868	43,939	-3.3	141,000	143,000
Nebraska	274,081	289,744	291,140	288,261	286,199	285,095	285,402	285,542	285,761	286,646	287,580	291,244	292,590	202,912	89,678	295,368	206,860	88,508	3.4	298,000	305,000
Nevada	201,316	265,041	311,061	325,610	340,706	356,814	369,498	385,401	400,083	412,395	424,766	429,362	433,371	308,328	125,043	428,947	305,512	123,435	7.2	458,000	486,000
New Hampshire	172,785	194,171	204,713	206,783	208,461	206,847	207,671	207,417	206,852	205,767	203,572	200,772	197,934	132,995	64,939	197,140	132,768	64,372	-4.7	190,000	187,000
New Jersey	1,089,646	1,197,381	1,268,996	1,289,256	1,313,405	1,341,656	1,367,438	1,380,753	1,393,347	1,395,602	1,388,850	1,382,348	1,381,420	956,765	424,655	1,396,029	968,332	427,697	0.2	1,373,000	1,375,000
New Mexico	301,881	329,640	328,753	324,495	320,306	320,260	320,234	323,066	326,102	326,758	328,220	329,040	330,245	231,415	98,830	334,419	235,343	99,076	2.6	336,000	348,000
New York	2,598,337	2,813,230	2,877,143	2,887,776	2,882,188	2,872,132	2,888,233	2,864,775	2,836,337	2,815,581	2,809,649	2,765,435	2,740,592	1,843,080	897,512	2,766,052	1,847,003	919,049	-2.5	2,641,000	2,598,000
North Carolina	1,086,871	1,183,090	1,254,821	1,275,925	1,293,638	1,315,363	1,335,954	1,360,209	1,385,754	1,416,436	1,444,481	1,489,492	1,488,645	1,058,926	429,719	1,483,397	1,053,801	429,596	7.0	1,541,000	1,598,000
North Dakota	117,825	119,100	114,927	112,751	109,201	106,047	104,225	102,233	100,513	98,283	96,670	95,059	94,728	63,955	30,773	95,073	64,576	30,497	-5.4	93,000	93,000

See notes at end of table.

Enrollment in public elementary and secondary schools, by state or jurisdiction: Selected years, fall 1990 through fall 2014—Continued

State or jurisdiction	Fall 1990	Fall 1995	Fall 1998	Fall 1999	Fall 2000	Fall 2001	Fall 2002	Fall 2003	Fall 2004	Fall 2005	Fall 2006	Fall 2007	Fall 2008 Total	Fall 2008 Prekindergarten to grade 8[1]	Fall 2008 Grades 9 to 12[2]	Fall 2009 Total	Fall 2009 Prekindergarten to grade 8[1]	Fall 2009 Grades 9 to 12[2]	Percent change in total enrollment, 2004 to 2009	Projected fall 2011 enrollment	Projected fall 2014 enrollment
1	2	3	4	5	6	7	8	9	10	11	12	13	14	15	16	17	18	19	20	21	22
Ohio	1,771,089	1,836,015	1,842,163	1,836,554	1,835,049	1,830,985	1,838,285	1,845,428	1,840,032	1,839,683	1,836,722	1,827,184	1,817,163	1,239,494	577,669	1,764,297	1,225,346	538,951	-4.1	1,778,000	1,765,000
Oklahoma	579,087	616,393	628,492	627,032	623,110	622,139	624,548	626,160	629,476	634,739	639,391	642,065	645,108	467,960	177,148	654,802	476,962	177,840	4.0	653,000	664,000
Oregon	472,394	527,914	542,809	545,033	546,231	551,480	554,071	551,273	552,505	552,194	562,574	565,586	575,393	395,421	179,972	582,839	404,451	178,388	5.5	580,000	598,000
Pennsylvania	1,667,834	1,787,533	1,816,414	1,816,716	1,814,311	1,821,627	1,816,747	1,821,146	1,828,089	1,830,684	1,871,060	1,801,971	1,775,029	1,194,327	580,702	1,786,103	1,200,502	585,601	-2.3	1,720,000	1,706,000
Rhode Island	138,813	149,799	154,785	156,454	157,347	158,046	159,205	159,375	156,498	153,422	151,612	147,629	145,342	97,983	47,359	145,118	98,184	46,934	-7.3	139,000	138,000
South Carolina	622,112	645,586	664,600	666,780	677,411	676,198	694,389	699,198	703,736	701,544	708,021	712,317	718,113	507,602	210,511	723,143	512,124	211,019	2.8	725,000	738,000
South Dakota	129,164	144,685	132,495	131,037	128,603	127,542	130,048	125,537	122,798	122,012	121,158	121,606	126,429	87,477	38,952	123,713	85,745	37,968	0.7	130,000	133,000
Tennessee	824,595	893,770	905,454	916,202	909,161	924,899	927,608	936,682	941,091	953,928	978,368	964,259	971,950	684,549	287,401	972,549	686,668	285,881	3.3	979,000	998,000
Texas	3,382,887	3,748,167	3,945,367	3,991,783	4,059,619	4,163,447	4,259,823	4,331,751	4,405,215	4,525,394	4,599,509	4,674,832	4,752,148	3,446,511	1,305,637	4,850,210	3,520,348	1,329,862	10.1	5,011,000	5,313,000
Utah	446,652	477,121	481,176	480,255	481,485	484,684	489,262	495,981	503,607	508,430	523,386	576,244	559,778	404,469	155,309	582,793	421,336	161,457	15.7	572,000	589,000
Vermont	95,762	105,565	105,120	104,559	102,049	101,179	99,978	99,103	98,352	96,638	95,399	94,038	93,625	62,994	30,631	92,431	62,850	29,581	-6.0	89,000	90,000
Virginia	998,601	1,079,854	1,124,022	1,133,994	1,144,915	1,163,091	1,177,229	1,192,092	1,204,739	1,213,616	1,220,440	1,230,857	1,235,795	855,008	380,787	1,245,340	864,020	381,320	3.4	1,245,000	1,273,000
Washington	839,709	956,572	998,053	1,003,714	1,004,770	1,009,200	1,014,798	1,021,349	1,020,005	1,031,985	1,026,774	1,030,247	1,037,018	704,794	332,224	1,035,347	705,387	329,960	1.5	1,057,000	1,098,000
West Virginia	322,389	307,112	297,530	291,811	286,367	282,885	282,455	281,215	280,129	280,866	281,939	282,535	282,729	199,477	83,252	282,662	200,313	82,349	0.9	282,000	280,000
Wisconsin	797,621	870,175	879,542	877,753	879,476	879,361	881,231	880,031	864,757	875,174	876,700	874,633	873,750	589,528	284,222	872,436	593,436	279,000	0.9	865,000	876,000
Wyoming	98,226	99,859	95,241	92,105	89,940	88,128	88,116	87,462	84,733	84,409	85,193	86,422	87,161	60,635	26,526	88,155	61,825	26,330	4.0	91,000	96,000
Bureau of Indian Education	—	—	50,125	49,076	46,938	46,476	46,126	45,828	45,828	50,938	—	—	40,927	30,612	10,315	41,351	31,381	9,970	-9.8	—	—
DoD, overseas	—	—	78,170	108,035[3]	73,581	73,212	72,889	71,053	68,327	62,543	60,891	57,247	56,768	43,931	12,837	—	—	—	—	—	—
DoD, domestic	—	—	—	—	34,174	32,847	32,115	30,603	29,151	28,329	26,631	27,548	28,013	25,255	2,758	—	—	—	—	—	—
Other jurisdictions																					
American Samoa	12,463	14,576	15,372	15,477	15,702	15,897	15,984	15,893	16,126	16,438	16,400	—	15,984	—	—	—	—	—	—	—	—
Guam	26,391	32,960	32,222	32,951	32,473	31,992	—	31,572	30,605	30,986	—	—	—	—	—	—	—	—	—	—	—
Northern Marianas	6,449	8,809	9,498	9,732	10,004	10,479	11,251	11,244	11,601	11,718	11,695	11,299	10,913	7,816	3,097	10,961	7,743	3,218	-5.5	—	—
Puerto Rico	644,734	627,620	613,862	613,019	612,725	604,177	596,502	584,916	575,648	563,490	544,138	526,565	503,635	355,115	148,520	493,393	347,638	145,755	-14.3	—	—
U.S. Virgin Islands	21,750	22,737	20,976	20,866	19,459	18,780	18,333	17,716	16,429	16,750	16,284	15,903	15,768	10,567	5,201	15,493	10,409	5,084	-5.7	—	—

—Not available.
[1]Includes elementary unclassified.
[2]Includes secondary unclassified.
[3]Includes both overseas and domestic schools.

NOTE: DoD = Department of Defense. Detail may not sum to totals because of rounding. Some data have been revised from previously published figures.
SOURCE: U.S. Department of Education, National Center for Education Statistics, Common Core of Data (CCD), "State Nonfiscal Survey of Public Elementary/Secondary Education," 1990–91 through 2009–10, and Projections of Education Statistics to 2020. (This table was prepared May 2011.)

Enrollment in public elementary and secondary schools, by level, grade, and state or jurisdiction: Fall 2009

State or jurisdiction	Total, all grades	Prekindergarten through grade 8 and elementary ungraded												Grades 9 through 12 and secondary ungraded					
		Total	Prekinder-garten	Kinder-garten	Grade 1	Grade 2	Grade 3	Grade 4	Grade 5	Grade 6	Grade 7	Grade 8	Elementary ungraded	Total	Grade 9	Grade 10	Grade 11	Grade 12	Secondary ungraded
1	2	3	4	5	6	7	8	9	10	11	12	13	14	15	16	17	18	19	20
United States	49,373,307	34,417,985	1,224,498	3,678,831	3,729,681	3,665,560	3,707,808	3,701,246	3,652,886	3,644,768	3,642,152	3,651,917	118,638	14,955,322	4,080,743	3,809,972	3,541,891	3,432,741	89,975
Alabama	748,889	529,394	7,774	57,019	57,821	56,628	58,608	59,512	58,656	58,231	58,118	57,027	0	219,495	63,338	57,794	50,199	48,164	0
Alaska	131,661	90,824	2,475	9,804	9,926	9,827	10,032	10,046	9,864	9,567	9,657	9,626	0	40,837	10,112	10,072	10,874	9,779	0
Arizona	1,077,831	760,420	9,175	84,191	85,725	84,033	84,060	83,686	83,193	81,987	82,050	82,163	157	317,411	82,461	80,281	75,372	79,283	14
Arkansas	480,559	344,209	13,504	38,115	37,665	36,934	36,903	36,479	36,489	35,958	36,113	35,715	334	136,350	37,556	35,523	32,567	30,567	137
California	6,263,449	4,264,033	71,783	471,058	470,783	459,334	459,813	465,866	460,248	461,382	466,895	472,856	4,015	1,999,416	524,681	506,192	487,688	478,503	2,352
Colorado	832,368	591,378	29,701	64,190	66,076	63,948	63,558	62,929	61,547	60,631	59,669	59,129	0	240,990	64,106	60,394	57,964	58,526	0
Connecticut	563,985	389,965	15,682	39,873	41,889	40,270	41,209	41,510	41,729	42,506	42,305	42,992	0	174,020	46,377	43,850	42,754	41,039	0
Delaware	126,801	87,710	755	9,537	10,160	9,794	9,740	9,672	9,511	9,562	9,460	9,519	0	39,091	11,726	10,321	8,727	8,317	0
District of Columbia	69,433	51,656	8,499	5,190	5,023	4,908	4,995	4,893	4,513	4,520	4,394	4,452	269	17,777	6,181	4,431	3,684	3,301	180
Florida	2,634,522	1,850,901	51,495	196,057	197,882	198,479	209,068	199,322	198,980	198,789	202,584	198,245	0	783,621	219,705	199,162	192,433	172,321	0
Georgia	1,667,685	1,194,751	41,940	131,325	128,857	128,712	132,515	130,091	128,457	126,060	122,710	124,084	0	472,934	144,918	122,022	108,215	97,779	0
Hawaii	180,196	127,477	1,547	15,970	14,684	14,298	13,619	14,249	13,681	13,287	13,076	12,967	99	52,719	15,327	14,223	12,459	10,621	89
Idaho	276,299	194,728	2,646	21,605	21,901	21,734	21,604	21,337	21,364	20,815	20,703	21,019	0	81,571	21,763	20,615	19,943	19,250	0
Illinois	2,104,175	1,463,713	84,727	148,097	152,352	152,042	155,488	154,405	152,701	154,420	154,478	155,003	0	640,462	176,457	170,612	146,917	146,476	0
Indiana	1,046,661	730,599	12,444	78,224	80,067	79,092	82,178	79,992	78,871	79,048	79,700	80,983	0	316,062	84,235	80,905	77,923	72,999	0
Iowa	491,842	341,333	21,804	38,956	35,222	34,823	34,992	35,225	35,006	34,939	35,127	35,239	0	150,509	37,359	37,494	36,971	38,685	0
Kansas	474,489	332,997	10,509	36,461	36,524	35,617	35,853	35,782	35,336	34,978	34,161	34,596	3,180	141,492	37,450	35,672	33,596	33,522	1,252
Kentucky	680,089	484,466	27,909	51,276	52,066	50,541	53,071	51,027	50,075	49,934	49,005	49,298	264	195,623	54,798	50,703	46,917	43,097	108
Louisiana	690,915	509,883	29,447	53,763	55,612	54,189	53,922	59,998	49,658	51,348	49,128	52,818	0	181,032	56,163	45,587	40,454	38,828	0
Maine	189,225	128,646	3,783	13,704	13,451	13,372	13,653	13,769	13,888	14,239	14,349	14,438	0	60,579	15,259	15,324	14,750	15,246	0
Maryland	848,412	581,785	28,626	61,428	62,691	62,079	60,064	61,183	60,168	61,292	61,664	62,590	0	266,627	74,731	68,025	62,598	61,273	0
Massachusetts	957,053	666,551	27,871	68,369	70,941	70,025	70,700	71,078	71,052	72,201	71,399	72,093	822	290,502	78,771	73,298	70,460	67,973	0
Michigan	1,649,082	1,114,611	29,850	126,313	116,606	115,054	117,622	118,702	118,082	119,934	120,994	121,463	9,991	534,471	140,781	136,697	125,872	126,181	4,940
Minnesota	837,053	564,661	13,933	63,111	61,983	60,407	61,343	60,640	60,257	60,207	61,499	61,281	0	272,392	65,006	65,871	66,983	74,532	0
Mississippi	492,481	351,652	3,607	39,148	38,903	38,512	38,833	39,651	37,798	36,802	37,125	36,577	4,696	140,829	40,164	36,215	32,189	28,943	3,318
Missouri	917,982	638,082	25,584	69,016	68,133	67,357	68,045	68,730	67,901	68,577	67,309	67,430	0	279,900	74,943	70,126	67,577	67,254	0
Montana	141,807	97,868	1,209	10,960	10,848	10,691	10,707	10,499	10,674	10,635	10,734	10,911	0	43,939	11,563	11,072	10,741	10,563	0
Nebraska	295,368	206,860	11,954	23,577	22,483	22,088	21,831	21,517	21,047	20,776	20,753	20,834	0	88,508	22,765	22,073	21,404	22,266	0
Nevada	428,947	305,512	3,953	32,038	33,759	33,698	33,935	33,664	33,635	33,778	33,298	33,291	463	123,435	33,735	34,330	29,420	25,935	15
New Hampshire	197,140	132,768	2,987	11,969	14,165	14,215	14,246	14,560	14,682	15,082	15,345	15,517	0	64,372	17,108	16,277	15,399	15,588	0
New Jersey	1,396,029	968,332	33,937	95,251	100,792	98,370	100,138	99,911	100,675	100,866	101,248	100,749	36,395	427,697	108,577	104,572	100,966	98,733	14,849
New Mexico	334,419	235,343	7,406	26,266	26,165	25,985	25,781	25,358	25,406	24,473	24,377	24,126	0	99,076	29,715	26,763	22,448	20,150	0
New York	2,766,052	1,847,003	51,251	190,741	197,592	192,032	191,006	193,473	190,719	192,170	194,440	198,690	54,889	919,049	238,626	234,375	196,709	188,377	60,962
North Carolina	1,483,397	1,053,801	26,688	104,954	118,565	117,054	120,190	116,876	115,079	112,838	111,155	109,864	538	429,596	128,454	111,955	100,204	88,983	0
North Dakota	95,073	64,576	1,285	7,472	7,149	6,727	6,841	6,547	6,905	7,092	7,250	7,308	0	30,497	7,588	7,701	7,571	7,637	0
Ohio	1,764,297	1,225,346	29,329	131,114	132,572	131,009	133,405	133,751	132,768	133,678	133,551	134,169	0	538,951	156,711	139,964	123,404	118,872	0
Oklahoma	654,802	476,962	39,784	51,037	52,447	49,167	48,601	48,457	47,633	47,472	45,886	45,268	1,210	177,840	48,847	45,882	42,591	40,046	474
Oregon	582,839	404,451	21,143	40,563	42,439	41,881	42,660	43,059	43,181	43,425	42,839	43,261	0	178,388	44,788	44,090	43,422	46,088	0
Pennsylvania	1,786,103	1,200,502	15,239	128,947	128,565	127,268	130,380	132,213	132,528	132,538	134,436	137,072	1,316	585,601	151,739	149,834	141,898	140,845	1,285
Rhode Island	145,118	98,184	2,109	10,254	10,817	10,789	10,873	10,188	9,803	11,083	10,993	11,275	0	46,934	13,137	12,245	10,855	10,697	0

See notes at end of table.

Enrollment in public elementary and secondary schools, by level, grade, and state or jurisdiction: Fall 2009—Continued

State or jurisdiction	Total, all grades	Prekindergarten through grade 8 and elementary ungraded												Grades 9 through 12 and secondary ungraded					
		Total	Prekindergarten	Kindergarten	Grade 1	Grade 2	Grade 3	Grade 4	Grade 5	Grade 6	Grade 7	Grade 8	Elementary ungraded	Total	Grade 9	Grade 10	Grade 11	Grade 12	Secondary ungraded
1	2	3	4	5	6	7	8	9	10	11	12	13	14	15	16	17	18	19	20
South Carolina	723,143	512,124	24,425	53,615	54,538	54,158	55,491	55,671	54,346	53,869	53,300	52,711	0	211,019	62,997	55,250	48,408	44,364	0
South Dakota	123,713	85,745	1,367	10,560	9,518	9,234	9,062	9,245	9,172	9,117	9,219	9,251	0	37,968	10,286	9,767	9,174	8,741	0
Tennessee	972,549	686,668	16,506	76,745	76,356	74,825	75,705	75,052	74,810	73,420	72,199	71,050	0	285,881	77,576	73,927	68,012	66,366	0
Texas	4,850,210	3,520,348	239,030	369,433	383,572	374,560	373,653	368,175	361,413	352,562	351,426	346,524	0	1,329,862	393,182	335,262	310,288	291,130	0
Utah	582,793	421,336	9,820	48,472	48,876	47,307	46,670	46,258	45,387	44,164	42,810	41,572	0	161,457	41,440	40,523	39,538	39,956	0
Vermont	92,431	62,850	4,887	6,281	6,275	6,224	6,324	6,305	6,533	6,624	6,677	6,720	0	29,581	7,456	7,494	7,219	7,412	0
Virginia	1,245,340	864,020	30,600	92,281	93,977	93,141	93,366	93,708	91,852	92,014	91,006	92,075	0	381,320	104,717	97,969	90,795	87,839	0
Washington	1,035,347	705,387	11,037	74,547	77,266	75,912	77,707	78,270	78,158	77,666	77,618	77,206	0	329,960	85,551	81,220	79,585	83,604	0
West Virginia	282,662	200,313	13,894	21,454	20,741	20,885	20,394	20,790	20,347	20,793	20,499	20,516	0	82,349	23,702	20,696	19,263	18,688	0
Wisconsin	872,436	593,436	47,054	61,094	60,197	59,557	60,661	61,242	60,413	60,656	60,814	61,748	0	279,000	69,323	68,291	70,144	71,242	0
Wyoming	88,155	61,825	534	7,406	7,064	6,774	6,693	6,683	6,695	6,763	6,607	6,606	0	26,330	6,792	7,031	6,347	6,160	0
Bureau of Indian Education	41,351	31,381	91	4,528	3,941	3,711	3,484	3,423	3,192	3,157	2,994	2,860	0	9,970	2,818	2,749	2,215	2,188	0
DoD, overseas	—	—	—	—	—	—	—	—	—	—	—	—	—	—	—	—	—	—	—
DoD, domestic	—	—	—	—	—	—	—	—	—	—	—	—	—	—	—	—	—	—	—
Other jurisdictions																			
American Samoa	—	—	—	—	—	—	—	—	—	—	—	—	—	—	—	—	—	—	—
Guam	10,961	7,743	462	632	766	813	839	862	819	891	782	823	54	3,218	976	827	780	635	—
Northern Marianas	—	—	—	—	—	—	—	—	—	—	—	—	—	—	—	—	—	—	—
Puerto Rico	493,393	347,638	270	31,976	36,254	35,389	37,306	38,583	38,452	38,553	41,773	39,143	9,939	145,755	38,831	38,853	33,727	29,374	4,970
U.S. Virgin Islands	15,493	10,409	(¹)	1,006	1,048	1,162	1,150	1,212	1,209	1,160	1,359	1,103	0	5,084	1,685	1,242	1,133	1,024	0

—Not available.
¹No prekindergarten pupils reported.
NOTE: DoD = Department of Defense. The total ungraded counts of students were prorated to the elementary and secondary levels based on prior reports.

SOURCE: U.S. Department of Education, National Center for Education Statistics, Common Core of Data (CCD), "State Non-fiscal Survey of Public Elementary/Secondary Education," 2009–10. (This table was prepared May 2011.)

Enrollment in public elementary and secondary schools, by level and grade: Selected years, fall 1980 through fall 2009

Grade	Fall 1980	Fall 1985	Fall 1990	Fall 1992	Fall 1993	Fall 1994	Fall 1995	Fall 1996	Fall 1997	Fall 1998	Fall 1999	Fall 2000	Fall 2001	Fall 2002	Fall 2003	Fall 2004	Fall 2005	Fall 2006	Fall 2007	Fall 2008	Fall 2009
1	2	3	4	5	6	7	8	9	10	11	12	13	14	15	16	17	18	19	20	21	22
Number (in thousands)																					
All grades	40,877	39,422	41,217	42,823	43,465	44,111	44,840	45,611	46,127	46,539	46,857	47,204	47,672	48,183	48,540	48,795	49,113	49,316	49,293	49,266	49,373
Elementary	27,647	27,034	29,876	31,086	31,502	31,896	32,338	32,762	33,071	33,344	33,486	33,686	33,936	34,114	34,201	34,178	34,204	34,235	34,205	34,286	34,418
Prekindergarten	96	151	303	505	545	603	637	670	695	729	751	776	865	915	950	990	1,036	1,084	1,081	1,180	1,224
Kindergarten	2,593	3,041	3,306	3,313	3,377	3,444	3,536	3,532	3,503	3,443	3,397	3,382	3,379	3,434	3,503	3,544	3,619	3,631	3,609	3,640	3,679
1st grade	2,894	3,239	3,499	3,542	3,529	3,593	3,671	3,770	3,755	3,727	3,684	3,636	3,614	3,594	3,613	3,663	3,691	3,751	3,750	3,708	3,730
2nd grade	2,800	2,941	3,327	3,431	3,429	3,440	3,507	3,600	3,689	3,681	3,656	3,634	3,593	3,565	3,544	3,560	3,606	3,641	3,704	3,699	3,666
3rd grade	2,893	2,895	3,297	3,361	3,437	3,439	3,445	3,524	3,597	3,696	3,691	3,676	3,653	3,623	3,611	3,580	3,586	3,627	3,659	3,708	3,708
4th grade	3,107	2,771	3,248	3,342	3,361	3,426	3,431	3,454	3,507	3,592	3,686	3,711	3,695	3,669	3,619	3,612	3,578	3,586	3,624	3,647	3,701
5th grade	3,130	2,776	3,197	3,325	3,350	3,372	3,438	3,453	3,458	3,520	3,604	3,707	3,727	3,711	3,685	3,635	3,633	3,602	3,600	3,629	3,653
6th grade	3,038	2,789	3,110	3,303	3,356	3,381	3,395	3,494	3,492	3,497	3,564	3,663	3,769	3,788	3,772	3,735	3,670	3,660	3,628	3,614	3,645
7th grade	3,085	2,938	3,067	3,299	3,355	3,404	3,422	3,464	3,520	3,530	3,541	3,629	3,720	3,821	3,841	3,818	3,777	3,716	3,701	3,653	3,642
8th grade	3,086	2,982	2,979	3,129	3,249	3,302	3,356	3,403	3,415	3,480	3,497	3,538	3,616	3,709	3,809	3,825	3,802	3,766	3,709	3,692	3,652
Elementary ungraded	924	511	541	536	513	492	500	399	440	449	415	334	304	285	255	215	205	170	139	117	119
Secondary	13,231	12,388	11,341	11,737	11,963	12,215	12,502	12,849	13,056	13,195	13,371	13,517	13,736	14,069	14,339	14,618	14,909	15,081	15,087	14,980	14,955
9th grade	3,377	3,439	3,169	3,352	3,487	3,604	3,704	3,801	3,819	3,856	3,935	3,963	4,012	4,105	4,190	4,281	4,287	4,260	4,200	4,123	4,081
10th grade	3,368	3,230	2,896	3,027	3,050	3,131	3,237	3,323	3,376	3,382	3,415	3,491	3,528	3,584	3,675	3,750	3,866	3,882	3,863	3,822	3,810
11th grade	3,195	2,866	2,612	2,656	2,751	2,748	2,826	2,930	2,972	3,021	3,034	3,083	3,174	3,229	3,277	3,369	3,454	3,551	3,558	3,548	3,542
12th grade	2,925	2,550	2,381	2,431	2,424	2,488	2,487	2,586	2,673	2,722	2,782	2,803	2,863	2,990	3,046	3,094	3,180	3,277	3,375	3,400	3,433
Secondary ungraded	366	303	284	272	250	244	247	208	216	214	205	177	159	161	150	122	121	110	92	87	90
Percentage distribution																					
All grades	100.0	100.0	100.0	100.0	100.0	100.0	100.0	100.0	100.0	100.0	100.0	100.0	100.0	100.0	100.0	100.0	100.0	100.0	100.0	100.0	100.0
Elementary	67.6	68.6	72.5	72.6	72.5	72.3	72.1	71.8	71.7	71.6	71.5	71.4	71.2	70.8	70.5	70.0	69.6	69.4	69.4	69.6	69.7
Prekindergarten	0.2	0.4	0.7	1.2	1.3	1.4	1.4	1.5	1.5	1.6	1.6	1.6	1.8	1.9	2.0	2.0	2.1	2.2	2.2	2.4	2.5
Kindergarten	6.3	7.7	8.0	7.7	7.8	7.8	7.9	7.7	7.6	7.4	7.3	7.2	7.1	7.1	7.2	7.3	7.4	7.4	7.3	7.4	7.5
1st grade	7.1	8.2	8.5	8.3	8.1	8.1	8.2	8.3	8.1	8.0	7.9	7.7	7.6	7.5	7.4	7.5	7.5	7.6	7.6	7.5	7.6
2nd grade	6.8	7.5	8.1	8.0	7.9	7.8	7.8	7.9	8.0	7.9	7.8	7.7	7.5	7.4	7.3	7.3	7.3	7.4	7.5	7.5	7.4
3rd grade	7.1	7.3	8.0	7.8	7.9	7.8	7.7	7.7	7.8	7.9	7.9	7.8	7.7	7.5	7.4	7.3	7.3	7.4	7.4	7.5	7.5
4th grade	7.6	7.0	7.9	7.8	7.7	7.8	7.7	7.6	7.6	7.7	7.9	7.9	7.8	7.6	7.5	7.4	7.3	7.3	7.4	7.4	7.5
5th grade	7.7	7.0	7.8	7.8	7.7	7.6	7.7	7.6	7.5	7.6	7.7	7.9	7.8	7.7	7.6	7.4	7.4	7.3	7.3	7.4	7.4
6th grade	7.4	7.1	7.5	7.7	7.7	7.7	7.6	7.7	7.6	7.5	7.6	7.8	7.9	7.9	7.8	7.7	7.5	7.4	7.4	7.3	7.4
7th grade	7.5	7.5	7.4	7.7	7.7	7.7	7.6	7.6	7.6	7.6	7.6	7.7	7.8	7.9	7.9	7.8	7.7	7.5	7.5	7.4	7.4
8th grade	7.5	7.6	7.2	7.3	7.5	7.5	7.5	7.5	7.4	7.5	7.5	7.5	7.6	7.7	7.8	7.8	7.7	7.6	7.5	7.5	7.4
Elementary ungraded	2.3	1.3	1.3	1.3	1.2	1.1	1.1	0.9	1.0	1.0	0.9	0.7	0.6	0.6	0.5	0.4	0.4	0.3	0.3	0.2	0.2
Secondary	32.4	31.4	27.5	27.4	27.5	27.7	27.9	28.2	28.3	28.4	28.5	28.6	28.8	29.2	29.5	30.0	30.4	30.6	30.6	30.4	30.3
9th grade	8.3	8.7	7.7	7.8	8.0	8.2	8.3	8.3	8.3	8.3	8.4	8.4	8.4	8.5	8.6	8.8	8.7	8.6	8.5	8.4	8.3
10th grade	8.2	8.2	7.0	7.1	7.0	7.1	7.2	7.3	7.3	7.3	7.3	7.4	7.4	7.4	7.6	7.7	7.9	7.9	7.8	7.8	7.7
11th grade	7.8	7.3	6.3	6.2	6.3	6.2	6.3	6.4	6.4	6.5	6.5	6.5	6.7	6.7	6.8	6.9	7.0	7.2	7.2	7.2	7.2
12th grade	7.2	6.5	5.8	5.7	5.6	5.6	5.5	5.7	5.8	5.8	5.9	5.9	6.0	6.2	6.3	6.3	6.5	6.6	6.8	6.9	7.0
Secondary ungraded	0.9	0.8	0.7	0.6	0.6	0.6	0.6	0.5	0.5	0.5	0.4	0.4	0.3	0.3	0.3	0.3	0.2	0.2	0.2	0.2	0.2

NOTE: Because of changes in reporting practices and imputation of data for nonrespondents since 1992, prekindergarten enrollment data for 1992 and later years are not comparable to prekindergarten enrollment data for prior years. The total ungraded counts of students were prorated to the elementary and secondary levels based on prior reports. Detail may not sum to totals because of rounding.

SOURCE: U.S. Department of Education, National Center for Education Statistics, *Statistics of Public Elementary and Secondary School Systems, 1980–81*; Common Core of Data (CCD), "State Nonfiscal Survey of Public Elementary/Secondary Education," 1985–86 through 2009–10. (This table was prepared May 2011.)

Number and percentage of homeschooled students ages 5 through 17 with a grade equivalent of kindergarten through 12th grade, by selected child, parent, and household characteristics: 1999, 2003, and 2007

Selected characteristic	1999 Number of students[1] (in thousands)	1999 Number homeschooled (in thousands)	1999 Percent homeschooled	2003 Number of students[1] (in thousands)	2003 Number homeschooled (in thousands)	2003 Percent homeschooled	2007 Number of students[1] (in thousands)	2007 Number homeschooled (in thousands)	2007 Percent homeschooled
1	2	3	4	5	6	7	8	9	10
Total	50,188 (72.7)	850 (71.1)	1.7 (0.14)	50,707 (89.3)	1,096 (92.3)	2.2 (0.18)	51,135 (155.3)	1,508 (117.9)	2.9 (0.23)
Sex of child									
Male	25,515 (233.9)	417 (43.9)	1.6 (0.17)	25,819 (286.8)	569 (61.9)	2.2 (0.24)	26,286 (355.6)	633 (75.2)	2.4 (0.28)
Female	24,673 (238.7)	434 (46.1)	1.8 (0.19)	24,888 (277.7)	527 (58.2)	2.1 (0.23)	24,849 (386.9)	875 (97.7)	3.5 (0.39)
Race/ethnicity of child									
White	32,474 (168.2)	640 (62.3)	2.0 (0.19)	31,584 (187.2)	843 (77.5)	2.7 (0.25)	29,815 (197.9)	1159 (101.6)	3.9 (0.34)
Black	8,047 (102.3)	84 (24.8)	1.0 (0.31)	7,985 (45.7)	103 ! (33.9)	1.3 ! (0.42)	7,523 (114.0)	61 ! (21.2)	0.8 ! (0.28)
Hispanic	7,043 (85.5)	77 (17.7)	1.1 (0.25)	8,075 (35.1)	59 ! (21.1)	0.7 ! (0.26)	9,589 (84.8)	147 (27.5)	1.5 (0.29)
Other	2,623 (114.2)	49 ! (17.2)	1.9 ! (0.65)	3,063 (161.1)	91 ! (31.5)	3.0 ! (1.02)	4,208 (170.6)	141 (36.1)	3.3 (0.86)
Grade equivalent[2]									
Kindergarten through 5th grade	24,428 (20.5)	428 (48.1)	1.8 (0.20)	24,269 (24.7)	472 (55.3)	1.9 (0.23)	23,529 (68.1)	717 (83.8)	3.0 (0.36)
Kindergarten	3,790 (20.0)	92 (19.7)	2.4 (0.52)	3,643 (24.7)	98 (23.5)	2.7 (0.64)	3,669 (67.9)	114 ! (35.4)	3.1 ! (0.96)
Grades 1 through 3	12,692 (6.2)	199 (36.7)	1.6 (0.29)	12,098 (#)	214 (33.3)	1.8 (0.28)	11,965 (2.4)	406 (64.5)	3.4 (0.54)
Grades 4 through 5	7,946 (1.3)	136 (22.5)	1.7 (0.28)	8,528 (30.1)	160 (30.1)	1.9 (0.35)	7,895 (2.1)	197 (41.4)	2.5 (0.52)
Grades 6 through 8	11,788 (3.4)	186 (28.0)	1.6 (0.24)	12,472 (6.5)	302 (44.9)	2.4 (0.36)	12,435 (0.7)	359 (64.9)	2.9 (0.52)
Grades 9 through 12	13,954 (70.5)	235 (33.2)	1.7 (0.24)	13,958 (81.8)	315 (47.0)	2.3 (0.33)	15,161 (129.3)	422 (58.2)	2.8 (0.38)
Number of children in the household									
One child	8,226 (153.8)	120 (20.3)	1.5 (0.24)	8,033 (218.1)	110 (22.3)	1.4 (0.27)	8,463 (227.1)	187 (31.4)	2.2 (0.37)
Two children	19,883 (211.4)	207 (27.1)	1.0 (0.14)	20,530 (319.4)	306 (45.1)	1.5 (0.22)	20,694 (295.3)	412 (67.3)	2.0 (0.33)
Three or more children	22,078 (241.2)	523 (65.2)	2.4 (0.30)	22,144 (362.8)	679 (80.2)	3.1 (0.36)	21,979 (331.0)	909 (102.4)	4.1 (0.46)
Number of parents in the household									
Two parents	33,007 (203.8)	683 (68.3)	2.1 (0.21)	35,936 (315.1)	886 (82.7)	2.5 (0.23)	37,262 (302.1)	1348 (111.5)	3.6 (0.30)
One parent	15,454 (209.4)	142 (25.0)	0.9 (0.16)	13,260 (319.2)	196 (42.6)	1.5 (0.32)	11,734 (299.2)	115 (28.4)	1.0 (0.24)
Nonparental guardians	1,727 (86.0)	‡ (†)	‡ (†)	1,511 (100.1)	‡ (†)	‡ (†)	2,139 (203.2)	45 ! (17.3)	2.1 ! (0.81)
Parent participation in the labor force									
Two parents—both in labor force	22,880 (241.5)	237 (39.8)	1.0 (0.17)	25,108 (373.1)	274 (44.1)	1.1 (0.18)	26,075 (318.9)	509 (76.8)	2.0 (0.30)
Two parents—one in labor force	9,628 (194.4)	444 (53.8)	4.6 (0.55)	10,545 (297.2)	594 (73.7)	5.6 (0.67)	10,776 (284.8)	808 (94.3)	7.5 (0.82)
One parent—in labor force	13,907 (220.0)	98 (21.8)	0.7 (0.16)	12,045 (267.9)	174 (39.8)	1.4 (0.33)	9,989 (277.2)	127 (29.5)	1.3 (0.30)
No parent participation in labor force	3,773 (162.3)	71 (18.8)	1.9 (0.48)	3,008 (171.4)	54 ! (23.7)	1.8 ! (0.78)	4,296 (228.0)	64 ! (20.6)	1.5 ! (0.48)
Highest education level of parents									
High school diploma or less	18,334 (217.3)	160 (26.5)	0.9 (0.15)	16,106 (272.3)	269 (51.6)	1.7 (0.32)	14,303 (292.6)	206 (35.6)	1.4 (0.24)
Vocational/technical or some college	15,177 (215.2)	287 (37.3)	1.9 (0.24)	16,068 (323.4)	338 (57.7)	2.1 (0.36)	14,584 (326.3)	549 (77.3)	3.8 (0.52)
Bachelor's degree/some graduate school	9,412 (179.0)	230 (36.3)	2.4 (0.37)	10,849 (275.0)	309 (48.5)	2.8 (0.45)	12,321 (281.6)	502 (70.1)	4.1 (0.57)
Graduate/professional degree	7,264 (179.9)	173 (39.9)	2.4 (0.54)	7,683 (239.5)	180 (41.6)	2.3 (0.55)	9,927 (242.9)	251 (41.0)	2.5 (0.41)
Household income									
$25,000 or less	16,776 (116.9)	262 (45.0)	1.6 (0.27)	12,375 (53.6)	283 (56.0)	2.3 (0.45)	11,544 (123.8)	239 (49.9)	2.1 (0.43)
$25,001 to $50,000	15,220 (232.7)	278 (36.7)	1.8 (0.24)	13,220 (270.2)	311 (49.9)	2.4 (0.37)	10,592 (236.4)	364 (56.9)	3.4 (0.52)
$50,001 to $75,000	8,576 (189.3)	162 (25.5)	1.9 (0.30)	10,961 (282.2)	264 (51.1)	2.4 (0.46)	10,289 (232.9)	405 (57.9)	3.9 (0.56)
Over $75,000	9,615 (211.2)	148 (26.5)	1.5 (0.28)	14,150 (261.7)	238 (45.8)	1.7 (0.33)	18,710 (232.6)	501 (74.9)	2.7 (0.40)
Urbanicity									
City	— (†)	—	—	—	— (†)	— (†)	15,998 (292.3)	327 (40.4)	2.0 (0.26)
Suburb	— (†)	—	—	—	— (†)	— (†)	18,988 (291.3)	503 (78.8)	2.6 (0.41)
Town	— (†)	—	—	—	— (†)	— (†)	5,574 (209.4)	165 (37.2)	3.0 (0.66)
Rural	— (†)	—	—	—	— (†)	— (†)	10,576 (110.9)	513 (75.5)	4.9 (0.71)

—Not available.
†Not applicable.
#Rounds to zero.
!Interpret data with caution. The coefficient of variation (CV) for this estimate is 30 percent or greater. The coefficient of variation (CV) for this estimate is 50 percent or greater.
‡Reporting standards not met.
[1]Refers to all students in public and private schools and homeschooled students.
[2]Students whose grade equivalent was "ungraded" were excluded from the grade analysis. The percentage of students with an "ungraded" grade equivalent was 0.03 percent in 1999 and 0.02 percent in 2003 and 2007.

NOTE: The number and percentage of homeschoolers exclude students who were enrolled in school for more than 25 hours a week; also excluded in 1999 and 2003 are students who were homeschooled only due to a temporary illness and, in 2007, students who were homeschooled primarily due to a temporary illness. Detail may not sum to totals because of rounding. Some data have been revised from previously published figures. Race categories exclude persons of Hispanic ethnicity. Standard errors appear in parentheses.
SOURCE: U.S. Department of Education, National Center for Education Statistics, *Homeschooling in the United States: 2003*; and Parent Survey (Parent:1999) and Parent and Family Involvement in Education Survey (PFI:2003 and PFI:2007) of the National Household Education Surveys Program. (This table was prepared July 2010.)

Percentage distribution of students ages 5 through 17 attending kindergarten through 12th grade, by school type or participation in homeschooling and selected child, parent, and household characteristics: 1999, 2003, and 2007

Selected characteristic	1999 Public school Assigned	1999 Public school Chosen	1999 Private school	1999 Homeschooled[1]	2003 Public school Assigned	2003 Public school Chosen	2003 Private school	2003 Homeschooled[1]	2007 Public school Assigned	2007 Public school Chosen	2007 Private school	2007 Homeschooled[1]
1	2	3	4	5	6	7	8	9	10	11	12	13
Total	74.1 (0.45)	14.3 (0.33)	10.0 (0.28)	1.7 (0.14)	72.1 (0.57)	15.0 (0.41)	10.8 (0.39)	2.2 (0.18)	70.6 (0.70)	15.0 (0.55)	11.4 (0.45)	2.9 (0.23)
Sex of child												
Male	74.8 (0.60)	13.9 (0.44)	9.7 (0.34)	1.6 (0.17)	72.1 (0.70)	15.0 (0.56)	10.7 (0.48)	2.2 (0.24)	70.7 (1.05)	15.3 (0.79)	11.5 (0.73)	2.4 (0.28)
Female	73.4 (0.61)	14.6 (0.45)	10.3 (0.41)	1.8 (0.19)	72.1 (0.78)	14.9 (0.54)	10.8 (0.51)	2.1 (0.23)	70.5 (0.88)	14.7 (0.64)	11.2 (0.54)	3.5 (0.39)
Race/ethnicity of child												
White	75.0 (0.54)	11.2 (0.35)	11.8 (0.39)	2.0 (0.19)	72.7 (0.67)	12.4 (0.47)	12.2 (0.48)	2.7 (0.25)	69.9 (0.80)	12.0 (0.46)	14.2 (0.61)	3.9 (0.34)
Black	70.2 (1.24)	22.6 (1.22)	6.2 (0.47)	1.0 (0.31)	66.6 (1.49)	23.4 (1.45)	8.6 (0.85)	1.3 ! (0.42)	68.4 (2.30)	23.0 (2.20)	7.8 (1.33)	0.8 ! (0.28)
Hispanic	76.0 (1.02)	17.6 (0.91)	5.2 (0.40)	1.1 (0.25)	77.2 (1.17)	15.0 (0.99)	7.1 (0.66)	0.7 ! (0.26)	74.6 (1.41)	17.5 (1.25)	6.3 (0.57)	1.5 (0.29)
Other	69.5 (2.20)	17.6 (1.99)	11.0 (1.35)	1.9 ! (0.65)	67.1 (2.59)	18.7 (1.94)	11.3 (1.61)	3.0 ! (1.02)	70.4 (2.23)	16.7 (1.79)	9.4 (1.12)	3.3 (0.86)
Disability status of child as reported by parent												
Has a disability	74.8 (0.93)	15.3 (0.78)	8.0 (0.49)	1.8 (0.27)	72.4 (1.12)	16.2 (0.75)	9.2 (0.70)	2.2 (0.35)	72.7 (1.35)	14.0 (0.91)	10.5 (0.96)	2.6 (0.48)
Does not have a disability	73.9 (0.51)	14.0 (0.36)	10.5 (0.34)	1.7 (0.16)	72.0 (0.67)	14.5 (0.51)	11.3 (0.44)	2.1 (0.21)	69.9 (0.76)	15.3 (0.63)	11.7 (0.48)	3.1 (0.28)
Grade equivalent[2]												
Kindergarten through 5th grade	71.5 (0.61)	15.1 (0.43)	11.6 (0.41)	1.8 (0.20)	70.1 (0.70)	16.2 (0.56)	11.8 (0.53)	1.9 (0.23)	68.5 (1.16)	16.2 (1.04)	12.2 (0.69)	3.0 (0.36)
Kindergarten	66.2 (1.67)	15.4 (1.13)	15.9 (1.29)	2.4 (0.52)	69.0 (1.50)	15.5 (1.18)	12.8 (1.21)	2.7 (0.64)	66.4 (2.20)	14.7 (1.60)	15.8 (1.61)	3.1 ! (0.96)
Grades 1 through 3	72.2 (0.87)	15.3 (0.67)	10.9 (0.53)	1.6 (0.29)	70.0 (1.18)	16.2 (0.96)	12.1 (0.73)	1.8 (0.28)	68.4 (1.68)	15.9 (1.63)	12.3 (0.93)	3.4 (0.54)
Grades 4 through 5	72.9 (1.17)	14.6 (0.79)	10.7 (0.77)	1.6 (0.28)	70.7 (1.03)	16.5 (0.96)	10.9 (0.76)	1.9 (0.35)	69.7 (1.62)	17.5 (1.34)	10.3 (1.08)	2.5 (0.52)
Grades 6 through 8	77.4 (0.79)	11.5 (0.65)	9.5 (0.47)	1.6 (0.24)	73.3 (1.03)	14.1 (0.81)	10.2 (0.59)	2.4 (0.36)	74.4 (1.44)	11.6 (0.81)	11.0 (1.14)	2.9 (0.52)
Grades 9 through 12	75.7 (0.75)	15.1 (0.60)	7.5 (0.44)	1.7 (0.24)	74.6 (0.97)	13.6 (0.76)	9.5 (0.63)	2.3 (0.33)	70.8 (1.07)	15.9 (0.84)	10.5 (0.75)	2.8 (0.38)
Number of parents in the household												
Two parents	74.5 (0.54)	12.0 (0.35)	11.5 (0.37)	2.1 (0.21)	71.8 (0.67)	13.6 (0.51)	12.1 (0.47)	2.5 (0.23)	69.5 (0.73)	13.8 (0.49)	12.9 (0.52)	3.6 (0.30)
One parent	73.5 (0.78)	18.2 (0.55)	7.3 (0.47)	0.9 (0.16)	72.9 (1.09)	18.0 (0.98)	7.6 (0.67)	1.5 (0.32)	73.6 (1.39)	17.2 (1.14)	8.1 (1.18)	1.0 (0.24)
Nonparental guardians	71.6 (2.70)	21.9 (2.72)	5.1 (0.84)	‡ (†)	73.2 (3.05)	20.1 (2.59)	5.8 (1.36)	‡ (†)	72.2 (5.91)	23.0 (6.19)	2.6 (0.74)	2.1 ! (0.81)
Highest education level of parents												
Less than a high school diploma	79.1 (1.38)	18.0 (1.46)	2.7 (0.51)	0.2 ! (0.10)	76.9 (2.06)	18.9 (1.76)	2.9 ! (1.18)	‡ (†)	83.3 (2.03)	12.7 (1.53)	3.5 ! (1.81)	0.5 ! (0.23)
High school diploma or GED	79.0 (0.84)	14.3 (0.72)	5.6 (0.44)	1.1 (0.19)	77.8 (1.01)	15.5 (0.89)	4.9 (0.45)	1.8 (0.34)	78.8 (1.90)	15.1 (1.84)	4.1 (0.63)	1.9 (0.36)
Vocational/technical or some college	75.8 (0.72)	14.7 (0.63)	7.7 (0.40)	1.9 (0.24)	74.0 (0.97)	15.5 (0.74)	8.3 (0.58)	2.1 (0.36)	72.0 (1.03)	15.3 (0.99)	8.8 (0.70)	3.8 (0.52)
Bachelor's degree/some graduate school	68.6 (1.06)	13.2 (0.75)	15.8 (0.75)	2.4 (0.37)	67.1 (1.00)	13.2 (0.84)	16.8 (0.90)	2.8 (0.45)	66.8 (1.24)	14.8 (1.02)	14.3 (0.87)	4.1 (0.57)
Graduate/professional degree	65.0 (1.14)	12.4 (0.77)	20.2 (0.91)	2.4 (0.54)	63.6 (1.50)	13.5 (1.14)	20.5 (1.28)	2.3 (0.55)	59.2 (1.37)	15.9 (1.01)	22.4 (1.22)	2.5 (0.41)
Poverty status of household												
Below poverty	74.8 (1.16)	19.2 (1.06)	4.3 (0.50)	1.7 (0.34)	76.3 (1.28)	17.7 (1.10)	3.7 (0.67)	2.3 (0.58)	76.6 (2.48)	17.8 (2.35)	3.7 (1.04)	1.8 (0.40)
Between poverty and 200 percent of poverty	76.8 (0.79)	15.3 (0.70)	5.9 (0.48)	2.0 (0.31)	75.1 (1.17)	16.0 (0.87)	5.9 (0.69)	3.1 (0.50)	74.4 (1.45)	16.2 (1.15)	5.2 (0.69)	4.1 (0.69)
At or above 200 percent of poverty	72.5 (0.57)	11.8 (0.34)	14.0 (0.47)	1.6 (0.18)	69.8 (0.70)	13.8 (0.54)	14.6 (0.54)	1.8 (0.21)	67.6 (0.75)	13.8 (0.48)	15.7 (0.54)	2.9 (0.30)
Urbanicity												
City	— (†)	— (†)	— (†)	— (†)	— (†)	— (†)	— (†)	— (†)	61.7 (1.46)	22.1 (1.38)	14.2 (0.97)	2.0 (0.26)
Suburb	— (†)	— (†)	— (†)	— (†)	— (†)	— (†)	— (†)	— (†)	72.7 (0.95)	11.8 (0.67)	12.8 (0.68)	2.6 (0.41)
Town	— (†)	— (†)	— (†)	— (†)	— (†)	— (†)	— (†)	— (†)	77.3 (1.77)	12.4 (1.43)	7.1 (0.75)	3.0 (0.66)
Rural	— (†)	— (†)	— (†)	— (†)	— (†)	— (†)	— (†)	— (†)	76.7 (1.36)	11.5 (1.03)	6.8 (1.09)	4.9 (0.71)
Region												
Northeast	72.8 (1.06)	13.4 (0.78)	12.6 (0.63)	1.1 (0.30)	71.6 (1.42)	11.9 (1.02)	14.6 (1.03)	1.8 ! (0.58)	72.5 (1.42)	11.8 (1.11)	13.6 (0.98)	2.1 (0.47)
South	75.4 (0.65)	13.2 (0.52)	9.3 (0.43)	2.0 (0.28)	74.2 (0.88)	14.9 (0.72)	8.3 (0.58)	2.6 (0.39)	71.9 (1.15)	13.6 (0.96)	10.8 (0.58)	3.7 (0.46)
Midwest	74.3 (0.80)	13.4 (0.72)	10.9 (0.61)	1.4 (0.24)	69.9 (1.27)	14.4 (0.92)	13.8 (1.04)	2.0 (0.37)	70.8 (1.54)	14.2 (1.06)	12.8 (1.14)	2.2 (0.53)
West	72.7 (0.95)	17.7 (0.73)	7.5 (0.49)	2.0 (0.34)	71.9 (1.07)	17.9 (0.97)	8.3 (0.59)	2.0 (0.34)	67.0 (1.40)	20.3 (1.17)	9.4 (0.75)	3.1 (0.42)

—Not available.
†Not applicable.
‡Reporting standards not met. The coefficient of variation (CV) for this estimate is 50 percent or greater.
!Interpret data with caution. The coefficient of variation (CV) for this estimate is 30 percent or greater.
[1]Excludes students who were enrolled in school for more than 25 hours a week; also excluded in 1999 and 2003 are students who were homeschooled only due to a temporary illness and, in 2007, students who were homeschooled primarily due to a temporary illness.
[2]Students whose grade equivalent was "ungraded" were excluded from the grade analysis. The percentage of students with an "ungraded" grade equivalent was 0.03 percent in 1999 and 0.02 percent in 2003 and 2007.
NOTE: Data are based on parent reports. Race categories exclude persons of Hispanic ethnicity. Detail may not sum to totals because of rounding. Some data have been revised from previously published figures. Standard errors appear in parentheses.
SOURCE: U.S. Department of Education, National Center for Education Statistics, Parent Survey (Parent:1999) and Parent and Family Involvement in Education Survey (PFI:2003 and PFI:2007) of the National Household Education Surveys Program. (This table was prepared July 2010.)

Percentage distribution of enrollment in public elementary and secondary schools, by race/ethnicity and state or jurisdiction: Fall 1999 and fall 2009

State or jurisdiction	Percentage distribution, fall 1999						Percentage distribution, fall 2009						
	Total	White	Black	Hispanic	Asian/ Pacific Islander	American Indian/ Alaska Native	Total	White	Black	Hispanic	Asian/ Pacific Islander	American Indian/ Alaska Native	Other[1]
1	2	3	4	5	6	7	8	9	10	11	12	13	14
United States	**100.0**	**62.1**	**17.2**	**15.6**	**4.0**	**1.2**	**100.0**	**54.1**	**16.8**	**22.1**	**5.1**	**1.2**	**0.7**
Alabama	100.0	61.1	36.4	1.1	0.7	0.7	100.0	58.7	35.0	4.3	1.3	0.8	—
Alaska	100.0	62.2	4.5	3.2	5.2	24.9	100.0	53.2	3.8	5.8	8.0	23.0	6.2
Arizona	100.0	54.0	4.6	32.7	1.9	6.8	100.0	44.1	6.0	41.4	3.1	5.5	—
Arkansas	100.0	72.2	23.5	3.0	0.9	0.5	100.0	65.3	21.9	9.2	1.8	0.7	1.0
California	100.0	37.0	8.6	42.4	11.1	0.9	100.0	27.0	6.9	50.4	11.6	0.7	3.4
Colorado	100.0	69.5	5.7	20.8	2.8	1.2	100.0	60.6	5.9	28.6	3.7	1.2	—
Connecticut	100.0	70.5	13.7	12.8	2.7	0.3	100.0	63.7	13.9	17.6	4.4	0.4	—
Delaware	100.0	61.6	30.6	5.4	2.2	0.2	100.0	51.6	33.3	11.3	3.5	0.4	—
District of Columbia	100.0	4.1	86.2	8.3	1.5	0.0	100.0	6.7	80.2	11.5	1.6	0.1	—
Florida	100.0	54.3	25.4	18.2	1.9	0.3	100.0	45.9	23.9	27.2	2.7	0.4	—
Georgia	100.0	55.5	38.2	4.0	2.1	0.2	100.0	45.0	37.4	11.3	3.3	0.3	2.8
Hawaii	100.0	20.5	2.4	4.6	72.2	0.4	100.0	19.7	2.3	4.6	72.7	0.6	—
Idaho	100.0	86.6	0.7	10.2	1.2	1.3	100.0	80.4	1.2	15.0	1.8	1.7	—
Illinois	100.0	60.7	21.3	14.6	3.3	0.2	100.0	54.2	19.5	21.7	4.3	0.2	—
Indiana	100.0	84.3	11.5	3.1	0.9	0.2	100.0	77.8	12.8	7.4	1.7	0.3	—
Iowa	100.0	90.8	3.8	3.2	1.7	0.5	100.0	82.2	5.1	8.1	2.1	0.5	2.0
Kansas	100.0	79.7	8.7	8.3	2.1	1.2	100.0	68.8	7.7	15.7	2.5	1.2	4.0
Kentucky	100.0	88.1	10.5	0.8	0.5	0.1	100.0	84.3	11.0	3.3	1.3	0.1	—
Louisiana	100.0	49.2	47.6	1.3	1.3	0.6	100.0	48.5	46.0	3.2	1.5	0.8	—
Maine	100.0	96.8	1.0	0.5	1.0	0.7	100.0	93.4	2.9	1.2	1.7	0.7	—
Maryland	100.0	54.3	36.8	4.4	4.2	0.3	100.0	45.5	37.9	10.0	6.1	0.4	—
Massachusetts	100.0	76.6	8.6	10.2	4.3	0.3	100.0	69.1	8.2	14.8	5.4	0.3	2.2
Michigan	100.0	74.4	19.6	3.2	1.7	1.0	100.0	71.1	20.3	4.9	2.7	0.9	—
Minnesota	100.0	84.0	6.2	2.9	4.9	2.0	100.0	75.0	9.7	6.7	6.3	2.2	—
Mississippi	100.0	47.5	51.0	0.6	0.6	0.1	100.0	46.1	50.1	2.2	0.9	0.2	0.5
Missouri	100.0	79.7	17.3	1.6	1.1	0.3	100.0	75.7	17.8	4.1	2.0	0.5	—
Montana	100.0	86.5	0.6	1.7	0.9	10.4	100.0	83.1	1.1	2.8	1.2	11.8	—
Nebraska	100.0	86.0	5.7	5.7	1.3	1.3	100.0	73.8	8.0	14.3	2.2	1.7	—
Nevada	100.0	58.9	10.1	23.9	5.4	1.8	100.0	41.4	11.4	37.5	8.2	1.5	—
New Hampshire	100.0	95.9	1.1	1.6	1.2	0.2	100.0	90.8	2.0	3.5	2.5	0.3	0.7
New Jersey	100.0	60.8	18.1	14.9	6.1	0.2	100.0	53.0	17.1	20.6	8.6	0.2	0.4
New Mexico	100.0	36.2	2.3	49.4	1.1	11.0	100.0	25.5	2.1	59.9	1.3	10.4	0.8
New York	100.0	55.2	20.3	18.3	5.8	0.4	100.0	50.8	19.1	21.7	8.0	0.5	—
North Carolina	100.0	61.8	31.3	3.7	1.8	1.5	100.0	53.9	31.0	11.1	2.6	1.4	—
North Dakota	100.0	89.4	0.9	1.3	0.8	7.6	100.0	84.5	2.4	2.5	1.2	9.4	—
Ohio	100.0	81.1	16.1	1.6	1.1	0.1	100.0	78.1	17.0	3.0	1.7	0.1	—
Oklahoma	100.0	66.2	10.7	5.4	1.4	16.3	100.0	56.4	11.0	11.2	2.2	19.3	—
Oregon	100.0	81.9	2.8	9.5	3.8	2.1	100.0	70.0	2.9	20.3	4.8	2.0	—
Pennsylvania	100.0	78.8	14.9	4.2	1.9	0.1	100.0	73.1	15.8	7.9	3.1	0.2	—
Rhode Island	100.0	75.5	7.7	13.1	3.2	0.5	100.0	68.0	9.2	18.6	3.4	0.9	—
South Carolina	100.0	55.2	42.2	1.5	0.9	0.2	100.0	53.7	38.4	5.8	1.6	0.4	—
South Dakota	100.0	87.0	1.1	1.1	0.9	9.8	100.0	81.3	2.6	2.8	1.4	12.0	—
Tennessee	100.0	72.9	24.4	1.5	1.1	0.2	100.0	68.2	24.3	5.5	1.8	0.2	—
Texas	100.0	43.1	14.4	39.6	2.6	0.3	100.0	33.3	14.0	48.6	3.7	0.4	—
Utah	100.0	86.9	0.9	8.0	2.6	1.6	100.0	79.1	1.5	14.6	3.3	1.4	—
Vermont	100.0	96.8	1.0	0.5	1.1	0.5	100.0	93.5	1.8	1.2	1.6	0.2	1.7
Virginia	100.0	64.3	27.2	4.3	3.9	0.3	100.0	57.7	26.2	9.7	6.1	0.3	—
Washington	100.0	75.3	5.2	9.6	7.2	2.7	100.0	66.1	5.8	16.5	9.1	2.5	—
West Virginia	100.0	94.8	4.2	0.4	0.5	0.1	100.0	92.4	5.3	1.0	0.7	0.1	0.4
Wisconsin	100.0	81.4	9.8	4.1	3.2	1.4	100.0	76.0	10.4	8.4	3.7	1.5	—
Wyoming	100.0	88.4	1.0	6.8	0.8	2.9	100.0	81.4	1.2	12.1	0.9	3.2	1.2
Bureau of Indian Education	100.0	0.0	0.0	0.0	0.0	100.0	100.0	0.0	0.0	0.0	0.0	100.0	—
DoD, overseas	—	—	—	—	—	—	—	—	—	—	—	—	—
DoD, domestic	100.0	59.4	21.4	7.5	10.8	1.0	—	—	—	—	—	—	—
Other jurisdictions													
American Samoa	100.0	0.0	0.0	0.0	100.0	0.0	—	—	—	—	—	—	—
Guam	100.0	1.9	0.4	0.2	97.4	0.1	—	—	—	—	—	—	—
Northern Marianas	100.0	0.7	0.0	0.0	99.3	0.0	100.0	0.6	0.0	0.0	99.4	0.0	—
Puerto Rico	100.0	0.0	0.0	100.0	0.0	0.0	100.0	0.1	0.0	99.8	#	#	—
U.S. Virgin Islands	100.0	0.9	83.6	15.2	0.1	0.1	100.0	1.3	82.7	15.5	0.3	0.1	—

—Not available.
#Rounds to zero.
[1]Includes data for states reporting students of two or more races.
NOTE: Percentage distribution based on students for whom race/ethnicity was reported, which may be less than the total number of students in the state. Race categories exclude persons of Hispanic ethnicity. DoD = Department of Defense. Detail may not sum to totals because of rounding.
SOURCE: U.S. Department of Education, National Center for Education Statistics, Common Core of Data (CCD), "State Nonfiscal Survey of Public Elementary/Secondary Education," 1999–2000 and 2009–10. (This table was prepared August 2011.)

Number and percentage of public school students eligible for free or reduced-price lunch, by state: Selected years, 2000–01 through 2009–10

State	Number of students				Number of students eligible for free/reduced-price lunch				Percent of students eligible for free/reduced-price lunch			
	2000–01	2005–06	2008–09	2009–10	2000–01	2005–06	2008–09	2009–10	2000–01	2005–06	2008–09	2009–10
1	2	3	4	5	6	7	8	9	10	11	12	13
United States	46,579,068 [1]	48,403,390	48,168,458	48,684,948 [1]	17,839,867 [1]	20,333,474	21,501,568	23,103,677 [1]	38.3 [1]	42.0	44.6	47.5 [1]
Alabama	728,351	741,544	742,997	748,836	335,143	383,219	389,252	411,067	46.0	51.7	52.4	54.9
Alaska...........................	105,333	103,498	130,662	131,661	32,468	41,872	44,578	47,678	30.8	40.5	34.1	36.2
Arizona.........................	877,696 [2]	955,320	1,075,949	1,060,622	274,277 [2]	492,450	515,916	501,512	31.2 [2]	51.5	47.9	47.3
Arkansas.......................	449,959	474,206	478,965	480,060	205,058	250,641	273,549	286,477	45.6	52.9	57.1	59.7
California	6,050,753	6,311,900	6,180,511	6,100,133	2,820,611	3,063,627	3,267,160	3,393,827	46.6	48.5	52.9	55.6
Colorado	724,349	779,825	816,922	831,906	195,148	258,264	289,326	319,404	26.9	33.1	35.4	38.4
Connecticut...................	562,179 [2]	575,051	552,978	556,498	143,030 [2]	152,669	169,742	179,586	25.4 [2]	26.5	30.7	32.3
Delaware.......................	114,676	120,937	122,622	124,809	37,766	43,682	48,982	58,375	32.9	36.1	39.9	46.8
District of Columbia	68,380	66,498	66,511	66,849	47,839	41,050	46,102	48,330	70.0	61.7	69.3	72.3
Florida..........................	2,434,755	2,674,998	2,631,020	2,634,522	1,079,009	1,224,228	1,304,324	1,408,677	44.3	45.8	49.6	53.5
Georgia.........................	1,444,937	1,598,461	1,655,792	1,667,685	624,511	795,394	877,701	934,899	43.2	49.8	53.0	56.1
Hawaii...........................	184,357	184,925	179,406	180,196	80,657	74,926	74,895	77,947	43.8	40.5	41.7	43.3
Idaho............................	244,755	260,343	274,672	276,299	85,824	99,093	109,071	118,932	35.1	38.1	39.7	43.0
Illinois..........................	2,048,792 [2]	1,976,077	1,977,007	1,953,713	759,973 [2]	785,715	832,946	901,912	37.1 [2]	39.8	42.1	46.2
Indiana..........................	977,219	1,034,719	1,045,833	1,046,357	285,267	373,433	437,293	474,326	29.2	36.1	41.8	45.3
Iowa.............................	492,021	481,094	482,735	482,123	131,553	154,416	165,830	179,921	26.7	32.1	34.4	37.3
Kansas..........................	462,594	466,263	470,397	469,218	154,693	180,919	202,060	214,437	33.4	38.8	43.0	45.7
Kentucky.......................	626,723	641,682	660,419	674,953	298,334	336,287	345,926	370,264	47.6	52.4	52.4	54.9
Louisiana.......................	741,162	654,388	684,745	690,741	433,068	400,596	444,562	454,338	58.4	61.2	64.9	65.8
Maine............................	198,532	189,572	187,484	184,232	60,162	65,877	71,407	76,715	30.3	34.8	38.1	41.6
Maryland........................	852,911	860,018	840,506	848,412	255,872	272,069	292,398	324,904	30.0	31.6	34.8	38.3
Massachusetts.................	979,590	971,907	958,910	957,053	237,871	274,515	294,681	315,153	24.3	28.2	30.7	32.9
Michigan........................	1,703,260	1,711,532	1,629,880	1,617,262	504,044	609,754	681,764	742,273	29.6	35.6	41.8	45.9
Minnesota......................	854,154	838,998	826,121	836,936	218,867	253,938	270,777	296,756	25.6	30.3	32.8	35.5
Mississippi	497,421	494,744	491,129	492,165	319,670	344,107	336,113	348,050	64.3	69.6	68.4	70.7
Missouri.........................	912,247	915,844	917,871	908,056	315,608	358,428	354,973	401,947	34.6	39.1	38.7	44.3
Montana.........................	154,438	143,093	140,430	140,553	47,415	50,172	52,021	56,201	30.7	35.1	37.0	40.0
Nebraska	286,138	286,610	291,805	295,368	87,045	99,387	112,293	121,915	30.4	34.7	38.5	41.3
Nevada..........................	282,621	410,531	422,250	419,967	92,978	170,039	169,185	181,688	32.9	41.4	40.1	43.3
New Hampshire	206,919	203,998	197,934	197,140	31,212	35,087	40,496	46,246	15.1	17.2	20.5	23.5
New Jersey	1,312,983	1,395,600	1,377,573	1,370,083	357,728	373,946	414,582	445,174	27.2	26.8	30.1	32.5
New Mexico	320,303	326,755	322,363	327,689	174,939	181,916	202,758	218,130	54.6	55.7	62.9	66.6
New York........................	2,859,927	2,812,964	2,717,371	2,766,052 [2]	1,236,945	1,260,933	1,226,247	1,248,215 [2]	43.3	44.8	45.1	45.1 [2]
North Carolina	1,194,371	1,356,570	1,076,134	1,445,761	470,316	603,316	493,946	720,798	39.4	44.5	45.9	49.9
North Dakota	109,201	98,284	94,728	95,073	31,840	29,064	29,963	32,163	29.2	29.6	31.6	33.8
Ohio..............................	1,745,237	1,836,982	1,813,999	1,762,315	494,829	597,517	661,151	710,381	28.4	32.5	36.4	40.3
Oklahoma.......................	623,110	632,812	643,640	654,167	300,179	346,070	362,090	384,448	48.2	54.7	56.3	58.8
Oregon..........................	535,617	534,814	553,825	541,789	186,203	230,737	255,795	272,196	34.8	43.1	46.2	50.2
Pennsylvania...................	1,798,977	1,813,760	1,638,671	1,737,649	510,121	574,951	591,250	663,132	28.4	31.7	36.1	38.2
Rhode Island	157,347	151,686	139,922	143,674	52,209	53,521	57,174	60,179	33.2	35.3	40.9	41.9
South Carolina.................	677,411	700,397	717,001	721,532	320,254	361,567	376,735	394,018	47.3	51.6	52.5	54.6
South Dakota...................	128,598	121,999	124,323	122,264	37,857	39,059	43,836	45,956	29.4	32.0	35.3	37.6
Tennessee	909,161 [2]	934,444	949,964	948,128	436,298 [2]	448,431	485,590	516,176	48.0 [2]	48.0	51.1	54.4
Texas	4,059,353	4,523,575	4,751,003	4,850,003	1,823,029	2,181,697	2,317,239	2,450,265	44.9	48.2	48.8	50.5
Utah.............................	470,265	508,399	553,040	580,718	135,428	164,255	174,729	244,458	28.8	32.3	31.6	42.1
Vermont.........................	102,049	96,638	85,842	85,339	23,986	25,487	27,115	29,529	23.5	26.4	31.6	34.6
Virginia..........................	1,067,710	1,167,860	1,235,143	1,219,806	320,233	377,725	408,336	444,715	30.0	32.3	33.1	36.5
Washington.....................	1,004,770 [2]	1,031,967	997,244	996,612	326,295 [2]	376,198	396,602	428,263	32.5 [2]	36.5	39.8	43.0
West Virginia...................	286,285	280,699	282,718	282,661	143,446	137,878	141,448	147,036	50.1	49.1	50.0	52.0
Wisconsin.......................	859,276	864,207	872,338	871,156	219,276	256,645	292,609	323,634	25.5	29.7	33.5	37.1
Wyoming........................	89,895	84,402	87,153	88,152	43,483	26,707	27,050	31,054	48.4	31.6	31.0	35.2

[1] U.S. total includes imputation for nonreporting states.
[2] Imputation for survey nonresponse. State-level imputations for 2000–01 were based on the reported percentages for 2001–02 applied to the 2000–01 enrollments. The state-level imputation for 2009–10 was based on the reported percentage for 2008–09 applied to the 2009–10 enrollment.

NOTE: Table reflects counts of students enrolled in schools for which both enrollment data and free/reduced-price lunch eligibility data were reported.
SOURCE: U.S. Department of Education, National Center for Education Statistics, Common Core of Data (CCD), "Public Elementary/Secondary School Universe Survey," 2000–01, 2005–06, 2008–09, and 2009–10. (This table was prepared August 2011.)

Children 3 to 21 years old served under Individuals with Disabilities Education Act, Part B, by type of disability: Selected years, 1976–77 through 2009–10

Type of disability	1976–77	1980–81	1990–91	1995–96	1999–2000	2000–01	2001–02	2002–03	2003–04	2004–05	2005–06	2006–07	2007–08[1]	2008–09[1]	2009–10
1	2	3	4	5	6	7	8	9	10	11	12	13	14	15	16
						Number served (in thousands)									
All disabilities	**3,694**	**4,144**	**4,710**	**5,572**	**6,195**	**6,296**	**6,407**	**6,523**	**6,634**	**6,719**	**6,713**	**6,686**	**6,606**	**6,483**	**6,481**
Autism	—	—	—	28	65	94	114	137	163	191	223	258	296	336	378
Deaf-blindness	—	3	1	1	2	1	2	2	2	2	2	2	2	2	2
Developmental delay	—	—	—	—	19	178	242	283	305	332	339	333	358	354	368
Emotional disturbance	283	347	389	437	469	481	483	485	489	489	477	464	442	420	407
Hearing impairments	88	79	58	67	71	78	78	78	79	79	79	80	79	78	79
Intellectual disability	961	830	534	571	600	624	616	602	593	578	556	534	500	478	463
Multiple disabilities	—	68	96	93	111	133	136	138	140	140	141	142	138	130	131
Orthopedic impairments	87	58	49	63	71	83	83	83	77	73	71	69	67	70	65
Other health impairments[2]	141	98	55	133	253	303	350	403	464	521	570	611	641	659	689
Preschool disabled[3]	†	†	390	544	581	†	†	†	†	†	†	†	†	†	†
Specific learning disabilities	796	1,462	2,129	2,578	2,834	2,868	2,861	2,848	2,831	2,798	2,735	2,665	2,573	2,476	2,431
Speech or language impairments	1,302	1,168	985	1,022	1,080	1,409	1,391	1,412	1,441	1,463	1,468	1,475	1,456	1,426	1,416
Traumatic brain injury	—	—	—	9	14	16	22	22	23	24	24	25	25	26	25
Visual impairments	38	31	23	25	26	29	28	29	28	29	29	29	29	29	29
						Percentage distribution of children served									
All disabilities	**100.0**	**100.0**	**100.0**	**100.0**	**100.0**	**100.0**	**100.0**	**100.0**	**100.0**	**100.0**	**100.0**	**100.0**	**100.0**	**100.0**	**100.0**
Autism	—	—	—	0.5	1.0	1.5	1.8	2.1	2.5	2.8	3.3	3.9	4.5	5.2	5.8
Deaf-blindness	—	0.1	#	#	#	#	#	#	#	#	#	#	#	#	#
Developmental delay	—	—	—	—	0.3	2.8	3.8	4.3	4.6	4.9	5.1	5.0	5.4	5.5	5.7
Emotional disturbance	7.7	8.4	8.3	7.8	7.6	7.6	7.5	7.4	7.4	7.3	7.1	6.9	6.7	6.5	6.3
Hearing impairments	2.4	1.9	1.2	1.2	1.1	1.2	1.2	1.2	1.2	1.2	1.2	1.2	1.2	1.2	1.2
Intellectual disability	26.0	20.0	11.3	10.2	9.7	9.9	9.6	9.2	8.9	8.6	8.3	8.0	7.6	7.4	7.1
Multiple disabilities	—	1.6	2.0	1.7	1.8	2.1	2.1	2.1	2.1	2.1	2.1	2.1	2.1	2.0	2.0
Orthopedic impairments	2.4	1.4	1.0	1.1	1.1	1.3	1.3	1.3	1.2	1.1	1.1	1.0	1.0	1.1	1.0
Other health impairments[2]	3.8	2.4	1.2	2.4	4.1	4.8	5.5	6.2	7.0	7.7	8.5	9.1	9.7	10.2	10.6
Preschool disabled[3]	†	†	8.3	9.8	9.4	†	†	†	†	†	†	†	†	†	†
Specific learning disabilities	21.5	35.3	45.2	46.3	45.7	45.5	44.7	43.7	42.7	41.6	40.7	39.9	39.0	38.2	37.5
Speech or language impairments	35.2	28.2	20.9	18.3	17.4	22.4	21.7	21.6	21.7	21.8	21.9	22.1	22.0	22.0	21.8
Traumatic brain injury	—	—	—	0.2	0.2	0.2	0.3	0.3	0.4	0.4	0.4	0.4	0.4	0.4	0.4
Visual impairments	1.0	0.7	0.5	0.4	0.4	0.5	0.4	0.4	0.4	0.4	0.4	0.4	0.4	0.4	0.4
						Number served as a percent of total enrollment[4]									
All disabilities	**8.3**	**10.1**	**11.4**	**12.4**	**13.2**	**13.3**	**13.4**	**13.5**	**13.7**	**13.8**	**13.7**	**13.6**	**13.4**	**13.2**	**13.1**
Autism	—	—	—	0.1	0.1	0.2	0.2	0.3	0.3	0.4	0.5	0.5	0.6	0.7	0.8
Deaf-blindness	—	#	#	#	#	#	#	#	#	#	#	#	#	#	#
Developmental delay	—	—	—	—	#	0.4	0.5	0.6	0.6	0.7	0.7	0.7	0.7	0.7	0.7
Emotional disturbance	0.6	0.8	0.9	1.0	1.0	1.0	1.0	1.0	1.0	1.0	1.0	0.9	0.9	0.9	0.8
Hearing impairments	0.2	0.2	0.1	0.1	0.2	0.2	0.2	0.2	0.2	0.2	0.2	0.2	0.2	0.2	0.2
Intellectual disability	2.2	2.0	1.3	1.3	1.3	1.3	1.3	1.2	1.2	1.2	1.1	1.1	1.0	1.0	0.9
Multiple disabilities	—	0.2	0.2	0.2	0.2	0.3	0.3	0.3	0.3	0.3	0.3	0.3	0.3	0.3	0.3
Orthopedic impairments	0.2	0.1	0.1	0.1	0.2	0.2	0.2	0.2	0.2	0.2	0.1	0.1	0.1	0.1	0.1
Other health impairments[2]	0.3	0.2	0.1	0.3	0.5	0.6	0.7	0.8	1.0	1.1	1.2	1.2	1.3	1.3	1.4
Preschool disabled[3]	†	†	0.9	1.2	1.2	†	†	†	†	†	†	†	†	†	†
Specific learning disabilities	1.8	3.6	5.2	5.8	6.0	6.1	6.0	5.9	5.8	5.7	5.6	5.4	5.2	5.0	4.9
Speech or language impairments	2.9	2.9	2.4	2.3	2.3	3.0	2.9	2.9	3.0	3.0	3.0	3.0	3.0	2.9	2.9
Traumatic brain injury	—	—	—	#	#	#	#	#	#	#	0.1	0.1	0.1	0.1	0.1
Visual impairments	0.1	0.1	0.1	0.1	0.1	0.1	0.1	0.1	0.1	0.1	0.1	0.1	0.1	0.1	0.1

—Not available.
†Not applicable.
#Rounds to zero.
[1]Data do not include Vermont, for which 2007–08 and 2008–09 data were not available. In 2006–07, the total number of 3- to 21-year-olds served in Vermont was 14,010.
[2]Other health impairments include having limited strength, vitality, or alertness due to chronic or acute health problems such as a heart condition, tuberculosis, rheumatic fever, nephritis, asthma, sickle cell anemia, hemophilia, epilepsy, lead poisoning, leukemia, or diabetes.
[3]Prior to 1990–91 and after 1999–2000, preschool children are included in the counts by disability condition. For other years, preschool children are not included in the counts by disability condition, but are separately reported.
[4]Based on the total enrollment in public schools, prekindergarten through 12th grade.
NOTE: Prior to October 1994, children and youth with disabilities were served under Chapter 1 of the Elementary and Secondary Education Act as well as under the Individuals with Disabilities Education Act (IDEA), Part B. Data reported in this table for years prior to 1994–95 include children ages 0–21 served under Chapter 1. Data are for the 50 states and the District of Columbia only. Increases since 1987–88 are due in part to new legislation enacted in fall 1986, which added a mandate for public school special education services for 3- to 5-year-old children with disabilities. Some data have been revised from previously published figures. Detail may not sum to totals because of rounding.
SOURCE: U.S. Department of Education, Office of Special Education Programs, *Annual Report to Congress on the Implementation of the Individuals with Disabilities Education Act*, selected years, 1979 through 2006; and Individuals with Disabilities Education Act (IDEA) database, retrieved September 14, 2011, from http://www.ideadata.org/PartBdata.asp. National Center for Education Statistics, *Statistics of Public Elementary and Secondary School Systems*, 1977–78 and 1980–81; Common Core of Data (CCD), "State Nonfiscal Survey of Public Elementary/Secondary Education," 1990–91 through 2009–10. (This table was prepared September 2011.)

Percentage distribution of students 6 to 21 years old served under Individuals with Disabilities Education Act, Part B, by educational environment and type of disability: Selected years, fall 1989 through fall 2009

Type of disability	All environments	Regular school, time outside general class			Separate school for students with disabilities		Separate residential facility		Parentally placed in regular private schools	Homebound/ hospital placement	Correctional facility
		Less than 21 percent	21–60 percent	More than 60 percent	Public	Private	Public	Private			
1	2	3	4	5	6	7	8	9	10	11	12
All students with disabilities											
1989	100.0	31.7	37.5	24.9	3.2	1.3	0.7	0.3	—	0.6	—
1990	100.0	33.1	36.4	25.0	2.9	1.3	0.6	0.3	—	0.5	—
1994	100.0	44.8	28.5	22.4	2.0	1.0	0.5	0.3	—	0.6	—
1995	100.0	45.7	28.5	21.5	2.1	1.0	0.4	0.3	—	0.5	—
1996	100.0	46.1	28.3	21.4	2.0	1.0	0.4	0.3	—	0.5	—
1997	100.0	46.8	28.8	20.4	1.8	1.0	0.4	0.3	—	0.5	—
1998	100.0	46.0	29.9	20.0	1.8	1.1	0.4	0.3	—	0.5	—
1999	100.0	45.9	29.8	20.3	1.9	1.0	0.4	0.3	—	0.5	—
2000	100.0	46.5	29.8	19.5	1.9	1.1	0.4	0.3	—	0.5	—
2001	100.0	48.2	28.5	19.2	1.7	1.2	0.4	0.4	—	0.4	—
2002	100.0	48.2	28.7	19.0	1.7	1.2	0.3	0.4	—	0.5	—
2003	100.0	49.9	27.7	18.5	1.7	1.1	0.3	0.4	—	0.5	—
2004	100.0	51.5	26.5	17.9	1.8	1.2	0.3	0.3	—	0.4	—
2005	100.0	54.2	25.1	16.7	1.8	1.2	0.3	0.3	—	0.4	—
2006	100.0	54.8	23.8	16.4	2.9 [1]	([1])	0.4 [1]	([1])	1.0 [2]	0.4	0.4
2007											
All students with disabilities	**100.0**	**56.8**	**22.4**	**15.4**	**3.0** [1]	**([1])**	**0.4** [1]	**([1])**	**1.1** [2]	**0.4**	**0.4**
Autism	100.0	34.6	18.2	37.0	8.7 [1]	([1])	0.7 [1]	([1])	0.6 [2]	0.3	#
Deaf-blindness	100.0	20.1	13.4	34.4	20.9 [1]	([1])	8.5 [1]	([1])	0.3 [2]	2.2	0.1
Developmental delay	100.0	61.4	20.8	16.3	0.7 [1]	([1])	0.1 [1]	([1])	0.4 [2]	0.2	#
Emotional disturbance	100.0	37.3	19.7	24.1	13.1 [1]	([1])	2.1 [1]	([1])	0.4 [2]	1.2	2.0
Hearing impairments	100.0	51.8	17.6	16.8	8.1 [1]	([1])	4.3 [1]	([1])	1.1 [2]	0.2	0.1
Intellectual disability	100.0	15.9	27.6	48.9	6.0 [1]	([1])	0.4 [1]	([1])	0.3 [2]	0.5	0.3
Multiple disabilities	100.0	12.9	16.1	45.2	20.6 [1]	([1])	1.9 [1]	([1])	0.5 [2]	2.5	0.3
Orthopedic impairments	100.0	49.9	17.4	24.5	5.5 [1]	([1])	0.2 [1]	([1])	0.8 [2]	1.5	0.1
Other health impairments[3]	100.0	58.9	25.3	11.7	1.6 [1]	([1])	0.2 [1]	([1])	0.9 [2]	1.0	0.3
Specific learning disabilities	100.0	59.0	29.7	9.2	0.6 [1]	([1])	0.1 [1]	([1])	0.8 [2]	0.2	0.4
Speech or language impairments	100.0	86.6	5.7	4.6	0.3 [1]	([1])	# [1]	([1])	2.7 [2]	#	#
Traumatic brain injury	100.0	43.9	24.7	22.5	5.7 [1]	([1])	0.7 [1]	([1])	0.7 [2]	1.6	0.2
Visual impairments	100.0	59.9	14.3	12.8	6.6 [1]	([1])	4.5 [1]	([1])	1.3 [2]	0.6	0.1
2008											
All students with disabilities	**100.0**	**58.5**	**21.4**	**14.9**	**2.9** [1]	**([1])**	**0.4** [1]	**([1])**	**1.1** [2]	**0.4**	**0.4**
Autism	100.0	36.3	18.2	35.7	8.3 [1]	([1])	0.6 [1]	([1])	0.6 [2]	0.3	#
Deaf-blindness	100.0	31.2	16.3	28.5	15.2 [1]	([1])	6.8 [1]	([1])	0.6 [2]	1.3	0.1
Developmental delay	100.0	61.8	20.6	16.2	0.7 [1]	([1])	0.1 [1]	([1])	0.5 [2]	0.2	#
Emotional disturbance	100.0	39.3	19.3	23.1	13.0 [1]	([1])	2.0 [1]	([1])	0.2 [2]	1.0	1.9
Hearing impairments	100.0	53.7	17.1	15.7	8.2 [1]	([1])	3.9 [1]	([1])	1.2 [2]	0.2	0.1
Intellectual disability	100.0	17.3	26.9	48.2	6.1 [1]	([1])	0.4 [1]	([1])	0.2 [2]	0.5	0.3
Multiple disabilities	100.0	13.7	16.4	45.9	19.0 [1]	([1])	1.9 [1]	([1])	0.3 [2]	2.5	0.2
Orthopedic impairments	100.0	51.5	16.5	24.7	4.9 [1]	([1])	0.2 [1]	([1])	0.8 [2]	1.4	0.1
Other health impairments[3]	100.0	60.3	24.4	11.2	1.6 [1]	([1])	0.2 [1]	([1])	1.0 [2]	1.0	0.3
Specific learning disabilities	100.0	61.6	27.9	8.4	0.6 [1]	([1])	0.1 [1]	([1])	0.8 [2]	0.2	0.4
Speech or language impairments	100.0	86.5	5.7	4.7	0.3 [1]	([1])	# [1]	([1])	2.8 [2]	#	#
Traumatic brain injury	100.0	45.0	23.1	23.0	5.9 [1]	([1])	0.6 [1]	([1])	0.6 [2]	1.5	0.2
Visual impairments	100.0	62.2	13.7	11.8	6.5 [1]	([1])	4.0 [1]	([1])	1.2 [2]	0.6	0.1
2009											
All students with disabilities	**100.0**	**59.4**	**20.7**	**14.6**	**3.0** [1]	**([1])**	**0.4** [1]	**([1])**	**1.2** [2]	**0.4**	**0.4**
Autism	100.0	37.4	18.3	34.8	8.0 [1]	([1])	0.6 [1]	([1])	0.7 [2]	0.3	#
Deaf-blindness	100.0	21.6	13.3	33.3	19.1 [1]	([1])	9.9 [1]	([1])	0.6 [2]	2.3	0.2
Developmental delay	100.0	61.6	20.5	16.2	0.9 [1]	([1])	0.1 [1]	([1])	0.6 [2]	0.2	#
Emotional disturbance	100.0	40.6	18.8	22.2	13.2 [1]	([1])	2.0 [1]	([1])	0.2 [2]	1.1	2.0
Hearing impairments	100.0	54.6	17.0	14.7	8.2 [1]	([1])	4.0 [1]	([1])	1.3 [2]	0.2	0.1
Intellectual disability	100.0	17.4	26.7	48.2	6.3 [1]	([1])	0.4 [1]	([1])	0.3 [2]	0.5	0.3
Multiple disabilities	100.0	13.2	16.2	45.5	19.6 [1]	([1])	1.9 [1]	([1])	0.4 [2]	2.9	0.2
Orthopedic impairments	100.0	52.2	16.3	23.6	5.1 [1]	([1])	0.2 [1]	([1])	0.9 [2]	1.7	0.1
Other health impairments[3]	100.0	61.4	23.8	10.8	1.6 [1]	([1])	0.2 [1]	([1])	1.1 [2]	0.9	0.3
Specific learning disabilities	100.0	63.3	26.6	8.0	0.6 [1]	([1])	0.1 [1]	([1])	0.9 [2]	0.2	0.4
Speech or language impairments	100.0	86.3	5.6	4.6	0.3 [1]	([1])	# [1]	([1])	3.1 [2]	0.1	#
Traumatic brain injury	100.0	46.4	23.8	21.5	5.2 [1]	([1])	0.6 [1]	([1])	0.7 [2]	1.7	0.2
Visual impairments	100.0	62.6	13.5	12.0	6.2 [1]	([1])	3.6 [1]	([1])	1.4 [2]	0.7	#

—Not available.

#Rounds to zero.

[1]Data for 2006 and later years combine public and private schools and combine public and private residential facilities.

[2]Students who are enrolled by their parents or guardians in regular private schools and have their basic education paid through private resources, but receive special education services at public expense. These students are not included under "Regular school, time outside general class" (columns 3 through 5).

[3]Other health impairments include having limited strength, vitality, or alertness due to chronic or acute health problems such as a heart condition, tuberculosis, rheumatic fever, nephritis, asthma, sickle cell anemia, hemophilia, epilepsy, lead poisoning, leukemia, or diabetes.

NOTE: Data are for the 50 United States, the District of Columbia, and the Bureau of Indian Education schools. Some data have been revised from previously published figures. Detail may not sum to totals because of rounding.

SOURCE: U.S. Department of Education, Office of Special Education Programs, Individuals with Disabilities Education Act (IDEA) database. Retrieved September 15, 2011, from https://www.ideadata.org/DACAnalyticTool/Intro_2.asp. (This table was prepared September 2011.)

Number and percentage of children served under Individuals with Disabilities Education Act, Part B, by age group and state or jurisdiction: Selected years, 1990–91 through 2009–10

State or jurisdiction	3- to 21-year-olds served						As a percent of public school enrollment, 2009–10[1]	Percent change in number served, 2000–01 to 2009–10	3- to 5-year-olds served					
	1990–91	2000–01	2005–06	2007–08	2008–09	2009–10			1990–91	2000–01	2005–06	2007–08	2008–09	2009–10
1	2	3	4	5	6	7	8	9	10	11	12	13	14	15
United States	4,710,089	6,295,816	6,712,605	6,605,695	6,483,372	6,480,540	13.1	2.9	389,751	592,087	698,608	699,841	699,966	716,175
Alabama	94,601	99,828	92,635	84,772	82,861	82,997	11.1	-16.9	7,154	7,554	8,218	7,111	7,079	7,258
Alaska	14,390	17,691	17,997	17,535	17,662	17,893	13.6	1.1	1,458	1,637	2,082	1,954	1,941	1,987
Arizona	56,629	96,442	124,504	131,136	124,793	125,866	11.7	30.5	4,330	9,144	14,062	14,097	14,028	14,340
Arkansas	47,187	62,222	67,314	65,965	64,719	65,039	13.5	4.5	4,626	9,376	10,286	11,795	12,288	12,865
California	468,420	645,287	676,318	670,904	671,095	673,428	10.8	4.4	39,627	57,651	66,653	68,002	70,497	71,783
Colorado	56,336	78,715	83,498	83,077	83,577	83,765	10.1	6.4	4,128	8,202	10,540	10,802	11,255	11,327
Connecticut	63,886	73,886	71,968	68,987	68,853	68,738	12.2	-7.0	5,466	7,172	7,881	7,660	7,911	8,019
Delaware	14,208	16,760	18,857	19,435	19,084	19,348	15.3	15.4	1,493	1,652	2,073	2,264	2,237	2,572
District of Columbia	6,290	10,559	11,738	10,863	10,671	11,371	16.4	7.7	411	374	507	567	543	683
Florida	234,509	367,335	398,916	391,092	384,975	376,576	14.3	2.5	14,883	30,660	34,350	32,819	33,796	34,944
Georgia	101,762	171,292	197,596	189,424	179,707	177,070	10.6	3.4	7,098	16,560	20,728	18,454	16,185	16,491
Hawaii	12,705	23,951	21,963	20,441	20,130	19,957	11.1	-16.7	809	1,919	2,423	2,477	2,501	2,455
Idaho	21,703	29,174	29,021	27,989	27,930	27,787	10.1	-4.8	2,815	3,591	4,043	3,976	3,981	3,932
Illinois	236,060	297,316	323,444	321,668	318,529	313,583	14.9	5.5	22,997	28,787	35,454	36,957	36,997	36,962
Indiana	112,949	156,320	177,826	179,076	176,114	172,095	16.4	10.1	7,243	15,101	19,228	19,530	18,834	18,602
Iowa	59,787	72,461	72,457	69,204	67,362	66,636	13.5	-8.0	5,421	5,580	6,118	5,872	5,944	6,267
Kansas	44,785	61,267	65,595	65,712	65,730	66,219	14.0	8.1	3,881	7,728	9,267	9,608	9,896	10,354
Kentucky	78,853	94,572	108,798	109,187	107,732	106,045	15.6	12.1	10,440	16,372	21,317	20,591	19,755	18,865
Louisiana	72,825	97,938	90,453	88,153	86,022	85,119	12.3	-13.1	6,703	9,957	10,597	10,151	9,860	9,952
Maine	27,987	35,633	36,522	34,425	33,284	32,766	17.3	-8.0	2,895	3,978	4,348	3,889	3,700	3,843
Maryland	88,017	112,077	110,959	104,585	103,451	103,018	12.1	-8.1	7,163	10,003	12,148	11,752	12,203	12,532
Massachusetts	149,743	162,216	162,654	166,747	168,497	167,297	17.5	3.1	12,141	14,328	15,195	15,920	16,311	16,271
Michigan	166,511	221,456	243,607	236,576	232,444	227,973	13.8	2.9	14,547	19,937	24,290	24,097	24,488	24,245
Minnesota	79,013	109,880	116,511	119,332	119,991	121,359	14.5	10.4	8,646	11,522	13,402	14,286	14,361	14,706
Mississippi	60,872	62,281	68,099	65,717	64,407	63,988	13.0	2.7	5,642	6,944	8,319	8,422	8,968	9,649
Missouri	101,166	137,381	143,204	138,292	132,946	129,886	14.1	-5.5	4,100	11,307	15,268	15,629	15,245	15,720
Montana	16,955	19,313	19,259	18,158	17,645	17,213	12.1	-10.9	1,751	1,635	1,925	1,971	1,954	1,722
Nebraska	32,312	42,793	45,239	45,687	44,038	43,470	14.7	1.6	2,512	3,724	4,665	5,179	4,522	3,712
Nevada	18,099	38,160	47,794	48,332	48,328	48,115	11.2	26.1	1,401	3,676	5,492	5,715	6,170	6,872
New Hampshire	19,049	30,077	31,782	32,274	30,156	30,210	15.3	0.4	1,468	2,387	2,902	2,523	2,891	3,090
New Jersey	178,870	221,715	249,385	250,099	223,910	229,066	16.4	3.3	14,741	16,361	19,329	19,580	15,379	16,451
New Mexico	36,000	52,256	50,322	46,384	45,957	45,782	13.7	-12.4	2,210	4,970	6,441	6,337	6,487	6,585
New York	307,366	441,333	447,422	453,715	444,339	461,470	16.7	4.6	26,266	51,665	58,297	63,040	61,799	64,903
North Carolina	122,942	173,067	192,820	191,668	187,728	184,893	12.5	6.8	10,516	17,361	20,543	19,914	18,682	18,144
North Dakota	12,294	13,652	13,883	13,616	13,278	13,262	13.9	-2.9	1,164	1,247	1,520	1,560	1,576	1,660
Ohio	205,440	237,643	266,447	269,742	264,878	263,396	14.9	10.8	12,487	18,664	22,702	23,137	23,209	23,336
Oklahoma	65,457	85,577	96,601	95,323	93,936	95,186	14.5	11.2	5,163	6,393	8,149	7,617	7,431	7,808
Oregon	54,422	75,204	77,376	78,264	79,404	80,062	13.7	6.5	2,854	6,926	8,167	8,572	9,008	8,946
Pennsylvania	214,254	242,655	288,733	293,865	294,958	294,595	16.5	21.4	17,982	21,477	25,964	28,145	29,496	30,186
Rhode Island	20,646	30,727	30,681	29,033	27,596	26,332	18.1	-14.3	1,682	2,614	2,815	2,967	2,930	2,903
South Carolina	77,367	105,922	110,219	103,731	101,896	101,039	14.0	-4.6	7,948	11,775	11,603	10,472	10,763	10,878
South Dakota	14,726	16,825	17,631	17,971	17,867	17,907	14.5	6.4	2,105	2,286	2,747	2,683	2,734	2,688
Tennessee	104,853	125,863	120,122	120,925	118,425	119,016	12.2	-5.4	7,487	10,699	12,008	12,264	12,325	12,858
Texas	344,529	491,642	507,405	472,749	452,311	444,198	9.2	-9.7	24,848	36,442	40,236	37,528	38,169	40,706
Utah	46,606	53,921	60,526	63,066	65,084	67,781	11.6	25.7	3,424	5,785	7,462	8,023	8,366	8,679
Vermont	12,160	13,623	13,917	—	—	14,163	15.3	4.0	1,097	1,237	1,556	—	—	1,750
Virginia	112,072	162,212	174,640	168,496	166,689	164,771	13.2	1.6	9,892	14,444	17,480	16,845	17,124	17,057
Washington	83,545	118,851	124,498	123,698	125,334	126,024	12.2	6.0	9,558	11,760	13,429	13,529	14,006	13,858
West Virginia	42,428	50,333	49,677	47,855	46,978	46,169	16.3	-8.3	2,923	5,445	5,833	5,849	5,899	5,754
Wisconsin	85,651	125,358	130,076	126,496	125,304	125,503	14.4	0.1	10,934	14,383	16,077	14,867	15,153	15,729
Wyoming	10,852	13,154	13,696	14,254	14,767	15,098	17.1	14.8	1,221	1,695	2,469	2,842	3,083	3,276
Bureau of Indian Education	6,997	8,448	7,795	7,057	6,730	6,747	16.3	-20.1	1,092	338	330	325	330	394
Other jurisdictions	38,986	70,670	93,256	105,451	108,751	126,702	—	79.3	3,892	8,168	5,149	10,205	8,708	15,263
American Samoa	363	697	1,211	1,171	1,087	1,106	—	58.7	48	48	80	169	106	177
Guam	1,750	2,267	2,480	2,259	2,189	2,088	—	-7.9	198	205	171	162	201	182
Northern Marianas	411	569	750	784	816	870	7.9	52.9	211	53	70	78	80	78
Palau	—	131	—	—	—	—	—	—	—	10	—	—	—	—
Puerto Rico	35,129	65,504	87,125	99,680	103,118	121,159	24.6	85.0	3,345	7,746	4,677	9,644	8,185	14,681
U.S. Virgin Islands	1,333	1,502	1,690	1,557	1,541	1,479	9.5	-1.5	90	106	151	152	136	145

—Not available.

[1]Percentage of students with disabilities is based on the total enrollment in public schools, prekindergarten through 12th grade.

NOTE: Prior to October 1994, children and youth with disabilities were served under Chapter 1 of the Elementary and Secondary Education Act as well as under the Individuals with Disabilities Education Act (IDEA), Part B. Data reported in this table for 1990–91 include children ages 0–21 served under Chapter 1. U.S. totals for 2007–08 and 2008–09 do not include data for Vermont.

SOURCE: U.S. Department of Education, Office of Special Education Programs, *Annual Report to Congress on the Implementation of the Individuals with Disabilities Education Act*, selected years, 1992 through 2006, and Individuals with Disabilities Education Act (IDEA) database, retrieved September 14, 2011, from http://www.ideadata.org/PartBdata.asp. National Center for Education Statistics, Common Core of Data (CCD), "State Nonfiscal Survey of Public Elementary/ Secondary Education," 2009–10. (This table was prepared September 2011.)

Percentage of gifted and talented students in public elementary and secondary schools, by sex, race/ethnicity, and state: 2004 and 2006

State	Total 2004	Total 2006	Male 2004	Male 2006	Female 2004	Female 2006	White 2004	White 2006	Black 2004	Black 2006	Hispanic 2004	Hispanic 2006	Asian/Pacific Islander 2004	Asian/Pacific Islander 2006	American Indian/Alaska Native 2004	American Indian/Alaska Native 2006
	2	3	4	5	6	7	8	9	10	11	12	13	14	15	16	17
United States	6.7 (0.05)	6.7 (0.04)	6.3 (0.05)	6.3 (0.04)	7.0 (0.06)	7.0 (0.05)	7.9 (0.07)	8.0 (0.07)	3.5 (0.05)	3.6 (0.05)	4.3 (0.05)	4.2 (0.04)	11.9 (0.20)	13.1 (0.29)	5.2 (0.20)	5.2 (0.24)
Alabama	4.8 (0.11)	5.5 (0.06)	4.6 (0.11)	5.2 (0.06)	4.9 (0.11)	5.7 (0.07)	6.3 (0.16)	7.1 (0.11)	2.4 (0.09)	2.8 (0.06)	2.3 (0.17)	2.9 (0.09)	9.4 (0.50)	10.2 (0.45)	4.9 (0.54)	4.9 (0.43)
Alaska	4.1 (0.19)	5.1 (0.09)	3.9 (0.17)	3.9 (0.19)	4.2 (0.19)	4.3 (0.09)	5.8 (0.22)	5.8 (0.22)	2.1 (0.03)	2.5 (0.02)	2.5 (0.11)	2.5 (0.13)	4.5 (0.45)	5.0 (0.52)	1.0 (0.08)	1.1 (0.12)
Arizona	5.9 (0.17)	6.3 (0.11)	5.9 (0.17)	6.3 (0.12)	5.9 (0.17)	6.3 (0.11)	9.1 (0.26)	9.1 (0.21)	3.5 (0.14)	3.4 (0.06)	3.5 (0.13)	3.5 (0.07)	13.9 (0.54)	14.2 (0.21)	4.0 (1.09)	3.7 (0.92)
Arkansas	9.9 (0.65)	9.5 (0.43)	8.8 (0.63)	8.6 (0.41)	11.0 (0.67)	10.5 (0.50)	11.2 (0.80)	10.9 (0.73)	7.1 (0.90)	7.3 (0.73)	5.8 (2.39)	5.8 (2.29)	10.6 (0.78)	10.3 (0.62)	4.7 (1.21)	8.2 (1.35)
California	8.4 (0.18)	8.3 (0.21)	8.0 (0.16)	8.0 (0.21)	8.8 (0.20)	8.6 (0.23)	12.0 (0.36)	11.9 (0.42)	4.6 (0.16)	4.3 (0.16)	5.1 (0.13)	4.8 (0.11)	14.6 (0.56)	16.1 (0.89)	6.5 (0.56)	5.8 (0.62)
Colorado	6.7 (0.11)	6.8 (0.11)	6.6 (0.11)	6.9 (0.11)	6.8 (0.12)	6.8 (0.11)	7.9 (0.14)	8.2 (0.16)	5.2 (0.03)	5.0 (0.02)	3.9 (0.14)	3.8 (0.07)	9.6 (0.11)	10.4 (0.09)	4.5 (0.39)	4.3 (0.29)
Connecticut	3.0 (0.32)	3.0 (0.41)	2.9 (0.31)	3.5 (0.40)	3.2 (0.34)	4.0 (0.44)	3.5 (0.38)	4.3 (0.44)	1.7 (0.44)	1.8 (0.59)	1.4 (0.33)	1.8 (0.42)	5.7 (0.68)	5.7 (0.95)	4.3 (0.44)	4.3 (2.37)
Delaware[1]	3.6	5.6	4.0	4.7	— (0.05)	—	6.8	6.1 (0.11)	3.6	2.0 (0.02)	3.5	4.4 (0.03)	11.5	9.3 (0.06)	3.4 (†)	5.0 (0.15)
District of Columbia	—	4.7	—	4.5	—	4.8 (0.05)	—	5.7	—	2.0 (0.02)	—	4.0	—	8.8	4.6 (0.12)	4.6
Florida	4.5 (0.06)	4.7 (0.05)	4.5 (0.06)	4.7 (0.05)	4.5	4.8	5.7 (0.11)	6.1 (0.10)	2.0 (0.02)	2.0 (0.02)	4.0 (0.02)	4.4 (0.03)	8.8 (0.08)	9.3 (0.06)	4.6 (0.12)	5.0 (0.15)
Georgia	8.9 (0.30)	9.3 (0.35)	8.3 (0.29)	8.6 (0.33)	9.5 (0.31)	10.0 (0.39)	13.6 (0.59)	14.1 (0.69)	4.1 (0.15)	4.1 (0.15)	2.6 (0.25)	3.1 (0.17)	18.8 (0.41)	19.3 (0.71)	7.6 (0.49)	9.6 (0.65)
Hawaii[2]	5.7 (0.57)	6.2 (†)	5.1 (0.42)	5.1 (†)	7.0 (0.74)	7.5 (0.39)	7.7 (0.95)	9.7 (0.23)	2.9 (0.53)	2.0 (0.14)	3.9 (0.36)	3.9 (0.12)	5.5 (0.38)	5.8 (0.46)	4.3 (0.76)	4.8 (0.28)
Idaho	3.9 (0.23)	4.2 (0.20)	3.9 (0.21)	3.9 (0.20)	3.9 (0.24)	3.9 (0.21)	4.4 (0.26)	4.7 (0.23)	2.0 (0.20)	2.0 (0.14)	1.3 (0.13)	1.3 (0.12)	6.9 (0.38)	6.1 (0.46)	1.2 (0.28)	1.0 (0.23)
Illinois	5.4 (0.22)	5.8 (0.24)	5.0 (0.20)	5.4 (0.23)	5.8 (0.24)	6.3 (0.28)	6.7 (0.33)	7.0 (0.39)	2.5 (0.18)	4.2 (0.40)	2.8 (0.34)	3.1 (0.08)	13.1 (0.98)	14.1 (0.97)	5.4 (1.15)	5.1 (0.83)
Indiana	7.1 (0.49)	7.9 (0.40)	6.3 (0.44)	5.8 (0.36)	7.9 (0.55)	7.9 (0.49)	7.7 (0.52)	8.7 (0.50)	3.8 (0.78)	4.1 (0.54)	3.9 (0.66)	3.9 (0.39)	15.5 (2.71)	14.1 (2.08)	6.7 (1.64)	3.9 (0.56)
Iowa	8.5 (0.38)	9.0 (0.26)	8.2 (0.37)	7.9 (0.25)	8.9 (0.40)	8.9 (0.29)	9.0 (0.41)	8.8 (0.30)	4.6 (0.33)	3.9 (0.11)	3.1 (0.61)	3.1 (0.38)	13.5 (1.10)	12.2 (0.97)	3.6 (0.35)	2.9 (0.25)
Kansas	3.3 (0.11)	3.0 (0.12)	3.5 (0.11)	3.2 (0.13)	3.1 (0.11)	3.1 (0.13)	3.9 (0.15)	3.6 (0.16)	1.1 (0.05)	1.0 (0.04)	0.8 (0.08)	0.8 (0.04)	5.5 (0.17)	5.4 (0.25)	1.5 (0.19)	1.8 (0.20)
Kentucky	13.0 (0.32)	14.6 (0.50)	13.2 (0.31)	13.2 (0.47)	16.1 (0.34)	16.1 (0.60)	14.2 (0.62)	14.8 (0.64)	5.2 (0.54)	7.0 (0.60)	5.7 (0.46)	5.7 (0.38)	20.2 (1.48)	21.3 (1.14)	6.6 (1.24)	7.2 (0.96)
Louisiana	3.9 (0.32)	4.3 (0.13)	3.8 (0.31)	3.8 (0.13)	4.0 (0.34)	4.0 (0.14)	5.5 (0.60)	4.8 (0.60)	1.6 (0.07)	1.6 (0.04)	3.3 (0.34)	3.3 (0.18)	11.7 (0.91)	11.7 (0.34)	2.6 (1.04)	2.7 (0.78)
Maine	3.0 (0.30)	3.2 (0.19)	3.1 (0.30)	3.1 (0.18)	3.2 (0.36)	3.4 (0.22)	3.1 (0.37)	3.3 (0.20)	1.1 (0.22)	1.1 (0.12)	2.3 (0.27)	2.3 (0.54)	3.8 (0.80)	5.6 (0.60)	0.8 (0.35)	3.1 (1.29)
Maryland[1]	13.8 (0.13)	16.1 (0.10)	12.9	15.0 (0.08)	14.7 (0.14)	14.7 (0.15)	17.0 (0.14)	21.1 (0.12)	6.7 (0.13)	7.0 (0.05)	14.5 (0.21)	14.7 (0.05)	33.8 (0.30)	37.8 (0.24)	9.8 (0.25)	12.6 (0.13)
Massachusetts	3.9 (0.37)	3.4 (0.10)	3.6 (0.35)	3.2 (0.08)	4.3 (0.40)	3.7 (0.15)	4.1 (0.41)	3.8 (0.34)	1.9 (0.62)	1.9 (0.44)	2.7 (0.54)	1.4 (0.18)	8.1 (1.56)	8.1 (1.30)	0.9 (0.25)	0.5 (0.19)
Michigan	2.2 (0.18)	2.8 (0.29)	2.0 (0.17)	2.6 (0.28)	2.3 (0.19)	3.2 (0.32)	2.7 (0.41)	3.8 (0.11)	0.8 (0.07)	0.8 (0.09)	1.5 (0.10)	1.4 (0.09)	10.1 (0.33)	13.5 (1.14)	1.4 (0.57)	4.6 (0.54)
Minnesota	8.1 (0.37)	6.9 (0.13)	7.7 (0.36)	6.7 (0.26)	8.6 (0.38)	8.6 (0.16)	8.3 (0.44)	8.0 (0.64)	5.2 (0.34)	6.7 (0.11)	5.4 (0.34)	5.4 (0.18)	13.7 (0.33)	16.5 (0.98)	3.8 (1.04)	3.7 (0.64)
Mississippi	6.0 (0.19)	6.1 (0.20)	5.7 (0.18)	5.8 (0.19)	6.3 (0.22)	6.4 (0.22)	8.7 (0.37)	8.7 (0.30)	2.9 (0.21)	2.9 (0.11)	5.0 (0.43)	4.5 (0.37)	10.7 (0.80)	13.5 (1.47)	6.7 (0.35)	3.7 (0.64)
Missouri	3.8 (0.12)	3.6 (0.11)	3.5 (0.12)	3.5 (0.11)	3.8 (0.13)	3.6 (0.11)	4.3 (0.15)	4.0 (0.14)	1.7 (0.05)	1.5 (0.08)	1.3 (0.10)	1.3 (0.09)	9.0 (0.33)	9.1 (0.36)	2.0 (0.22)	2.4 (0.20)
Montana	5.6 (0.28)	2.7 (0.17)	5.4 (0.26)	2.8 (0.10)	5.3 (0.31)	5.3 (0.31)	6.0 (0.31)	5.7 (0.31)	2.8 (0.21)	4.8 (0.22)	3.3 (0.22)	3.9 (0.29)	9.9 (0.77)	8.2 (0.62)	2.1 (0.38)	2.1 (0.23)
Nebraska	11.4 (0.31)	11.4 (0.24)	10.9 (0.30)	11.0 (0.24)	11.8 (0.32)	11.9 (0.27)	12.8 (0.38)	13.3 (0.33)	6.4 (0.06)	4.8 (0.05)	4.5 (0.32)	3.9 (0.24)	17.0 (0.25)	18.2 (0.28)	4.6 (0.94)	3.1 (0.36)
Nevada	1.9 (0.18)	1.9 (0.13)	2.1 (0.17)	2.1 (0.07)	1.8 (0.18)	1.8 (0.11)	2.8 (0.01)	2.6 (0.01)	0.8 (#)	0.9 (0.11)	0.8 (0.01)	0.8 (†)	2.8 (0.02)	3.1 (†)	1.0 (0.07)	1.1 (†)
New Hampshire	2.3 (0.55)	2.6 (0.54)	2.1 (0.49)	2.5 (0.56)	2.7 (0.62)	2.7 (0.54)	2.3 (0.56)	2.6 (0.58)	0.6 (0.11)	1.1 (0.19)	1.0 (0.56)	0.9 (0.10)	5.8 (1.25)	5.9 (1.07)	0.9 (0.09)	3.3 (†)
New Jersey	6.9 (0.38)	7.0 (0.35)	6.2 (0.34)	6.1 (0.31)	7.7 (0.42)	7.9 (0.43)	8.4 (0.53)	8.4 (0.55)	3.3 (0.35)	3.5 (0.36)	3.4 (0.39)	3.5 (0.33)	12.2 (1.13)	13.9 (1.50)	4.8 (0.59)	3.3 (0.61)
New Mexico	10.7 (0.45)	4.0 (0.14)	10.9 (0.27)	13.1 (0.15)	10.5 (0.50)	10.5 (0.26)	12.6 (0.42)	16.6 (0.31)	9.6 (0.18)	2.8 (0.11)	11.4 (0.37)	2.4 (0.15)	13.6 (1.09)	12.0 (1.34)	2.1 (0.17)	1.5 (0.25)
New York	2.2 (0.18)	2.0 (0.13)	2.0 (0.17)	2.6 (0.12)	2.3 (0.19)	2.3 (0.15)	3.4 (0.31)	3.3 (0.14)	0.8 (0.07)	0.8 (0.09)	1.5 (0.29)	1.5 (0.04)	1.7 (0.18)	5.5 (0.04)	2.5 (0.29)	2.1 (0.04)
North Carolina	10.9 (0.83)	10.8 (0.42)	10.3 (0.81)	10.2 (0.40)	11.6 (0.85)	11.3 (0.47)	15.7 (1.17)	15.4 (0.68)	4.3 (0.27)	4.3 (0.20)	3.0 (0.29)	3.1 (0.18)	16.5 (2.76)	17.3 (0.98)	6.3 (1.39)	6.3 (0.36)
North Dakota	3.1 (0.30)	2.6 (0.18)	3.0 (0.30)	2.9 (0.19)	3.2 (0.32)	3.2 (0.25)	2.8 (0.23)	2.6 (0.20)	1.7 (0.05)	1.2 (0.13)	1.4 (0.01)	1.4 (0.13)	8.1 (0.38)	5.4 (0.26)	3.3 (3.34)	7.0 (1.46)
Ohio	7.4 (0.40)	7.3 (0.33)	7.3 (0.40)	7.2 (0.34)	7.6 (0.40)	7.6 (0.35)	7.6 (0.48)	7.8 (0.42)	4.7 (0.37)	4.7 (0.37)	3.3 (0.26)	3.3 (0.28)	13.6 (1.44)	14.0 (1.64)	5.6 (0.62)	5.4 (0.60)
Oklahoma	14.0 (0.45)	13.7 (0.39)	13.1 (0.41)	13.0 (0.36)	15.0 (0.50)	15.0 (0.47)	16.6 (0.56)	16.2 (0.55)	7.7 (0.22)	7.4 (0.23)	7.0 (0.27)	6.8 (0.23)	23.6 (0.56)	21.5 (0.60)	11.3 (0.67)	11.8 (0.72)
Oregon	7.1 (0.18)	6.9 (0.19)	7.3 (0.17)	7.3 (0.17)	6.9 (0.21)	6.6 (0.16)	8.3 (0.24)	8.0 (0.24)	3.5 (0.07)	3.5 (0.09)	2.0 (0.38)	2.0 (0.12)	11.1 (0.14)	11.1 (0.21)	3.6 (0.29)	3.9 (0.31)
Pennsylvania	4.8 (0.19)	4.9 (0.17)	4.5 (0.20)	4.5 (0.17)	4.8 (0.19)	4.8 (0.18)	5.0 (0.24)	5.0 (0.22)	2.4 (0.16)	2.4 (0.15)	1.8 (0.38)	1.7 (0.12)	9.5 (0.87)	9.7 (0.96)	2.2 (0.42)	2.2 (0.36)
Rhode Island	1.8 (0.38)	1.6 (0.21)	1.6 (0.35)	2.0 (0.18)	2.1 (0.41)	1.6 (0.24)	2.0 (0.44)	1.5 (0.25)	1.5 (0.47)	1.2 (0.09)	1.0 (0.48)	1.0 (0.13)	2.2 (0.60)	2.3 (0.30)	0.9 (0.34)	0.3 (0.10)
South Carolina	12.7 (0.98)	11.0 (0.57)	11.7 (0.89)	10.1 (0.52)	13.9 (1.07)	11.9 (0.68)	17.8 (0.93)	15.9 (0.95)	5.1 (0.70)	5.1 (0.39)	4.6 (0.93)	4.6 (0.56)	21.6 (1.29)	19.3 (2.33)	8.3 (1.29)	8.2 (2.52)
South Dakota	2.2 (0.20)	2.7 (0.17)	2.3 (0.20)	2.8 (0.18)	2.1 (0.20)	2.5 (0.20)	2.4 (0.21)	2.9 (0.13)	0.9 (0.16)	0.7 (0.03)	0.6 (0.15)	0.6 (0.04)	3.3 (0.37)	4.2 (0.31)	2.9 (0.41)	1.6 (0.70)
Tennessee	3.3 (0.10)	1.7 (0.10)	3.1 (0.10)	3.5 (0.10)	3.5 (0.11)	1.9 (0.09)	2.9 (0.21)	2.9 (0.13)	0.7 (0.15)	0.7 (0.03)	1.6 (0.15)	0.6 (0.04)	7.9 (0.77)	4.2 (0.37)	2.9 (0.27)	2.9 (0.20)
Texas	8.0 (0.10)	7.6 (0.07)	7.5 (0.10)	7.2 (0.07)	8.5 (0.11)	8.0 (0.08)	11.2 (0.21)	10.8 (0.06)	4.4 (0.14)	4.4 (0.11)	5.6 (0.11)	5.5 (0.07)	16.4 (0.28)	16.0 (0.13)	7.1 (0.27)	7.1 (0.24)
Utah	4.6 (0.29)	5.0 (0.05)	4.3 (0.30)	4.6 (0.05)	5.0 (0.29)	5.5 (0.06)	4.5 (0.29)	4.9 (0.06)	4.6 (0.26)	4.6 (0.03)	4.1 (0.37)	4.1 (0.05)	11.7 (0.81)	12.0 (0.06)	2.6 (0.36)	2.7 (0.03)
Vermont	0.8 (0.17)	0.9 (0.15)	0.8 (0.17)	0.9 (0.16)	0.9 (0.17)	0.9 (0.16)	0.8 (0.17)	0.8 (0.16)	0.4 (0.16)	0.5 (0.11)	1.3 (0.65)	1.3 (0.57)	0.2 (0.10)	1.4 (0.41)	# (2.41)	# (2.61)
Virginia	12.1 (0.38)	12.6 (0.32)	11.5 (0.36)	13.1 (0.15)	12.8 (0.40)	12.8 (0.37)	14.9 (0.55)	15.6 (0.50)	4.6 (0.21)	5.2 (0.35)	6.7 (0.12)	7.5 (0.12)	24.5 (0.83)	26.4 (0.46)	8.3 (0.21)	13.3 (0.10)
Washington	3.8 (0.19)	3.9 (0.13)	3.6 (0.19)	3.7 (0.12)	3.9 (0.19)	3.9 (0.16)	4.2 (0.14)	4.4 (0.19)	1.4 (0.02)	1.4 (0.07)	1.7 (0.12)	1.7 (0.09)	5.0 (1.90)	5.8 (0.12)	1.6 (0.28)	1.6 (0.82)
West Virginia	6.8 (0.47)	6.4 (0.35)	6.4 (0.44)	6.1 (0.33)	6.8 (0.51)	6.8 (0.41)	7.8 (0.55)	7.1 (0.45)	4.4 (0.14)	3.7 (0.25)	5.5 (0.23)	3.5 (0.21)	16.4 (0.55)	10.9 (0.44)	7.1 (2.04)	3.2 (1.23)
Wisconsin	6.8 (0.47)	2.2 (0.35)	6.4 (0.44)	2.8 (0.32)	7.1 (0.51)	2.3 (0.39)	3.5 (1.14)	2.3 (0.39)	1.5 (0.47)	1.5 (0.19)	2.4 (0.23)	0.9 (0.11)	6.7 (0.55)	6.7 (1.35)	4.6 (2.04)	1.0 (0.16)
Wyoming	3.2 (1.04)	2.2 (0.35)	2.8 (0.90)	2.0 (0.32)	3.7 (1.19)	3.7 (0.39)	3.5 (1.14)	2.3 (0.39)	1.5 (0.47)	3.7 (0.25)	1.2 (0.29)	0.9 (0.11)	3.6 (0.31)	6.7 (1.35)	4.6 (†)	1.0 (†)

—Not available.
†Not applicable.
#Rounds to zero.
! Interpret data with caution. The coefficient of variation (CV) for this estimate is 30 percent or greater.
‡ Reporting standards not met. Either there are too few cases or the coefficient of variation (CV) is 50 percent or greater.
[1]Data are based on universe counts of schools and school districts; therefore, these figures do not have standard errors.
[2]Data for 2006 are based on universe counts of schools and school districts; therefore, these figures do not have standard errors.
NOTE: Race categories exclude persons of Hispanic ethnicity. Standard errors appear in parentheses.
SOURCE: U.S. Department of Education, Office for Civil Rights, Civil Rights Data Collection: 2004 and 2006. (This table was prepared June 2008.)

433

Enrollment in grades 9 through 12 in public and private schools compared with population 14 to 17 years of age: Selected years, 1889–90 through fall 2011

[In thousands]

Year	All schools	Enrollment, grades 9 to 12[1]												Population 14 to 17 years of age[2]	Enrollment as a ratio of population 14 to 17 years of age[3]
		Public schools						Private schools							
		Total	9th grade	10th grade	11th grade	12th grade	Secondary ungraded	Total	9th grade	10th grade	11th grade	12th grade	Secondary ungraded		
1	2	3	4	5	6	7	8	9	10	11	12	13	14	15	16
1889–90	298	203	—	—	—	—	—	95	—	—	—	—	—	5,355	5.6
1899–1900	630	519	—	—	—	—	—	111	—	—	—	—	—	6,152	10.2
1909–10	1,032	915	—	—	—	—	—	117	—	—	—	—	—	7,220	14.3
1919–20	2,414	2,200	917	576	396	312	0	214	—	—	—	—	—	7,736	31.2
1929–30	4,741	4,399	1,627	1,192	880	701	0	341 [4]	—	—	—	—	—	9,341	50.7
1939–40	7,059	6,601	2,011	1,767	1,486	1,282	55	458 [5]	—	—	—	—	—	9,720	72.6
1949–50	6,397	5,725	1,761	1,513	1,275	1,134	42	672	—	—	—	—	—	8,405	76.1
Fall 1959	9,306	8,271	—	—	—	—	—	1,035	—	—	—	—	—	11,155	83.4
Fall 1963	12,170	10,883	—	—	—	—	—	1,287	—	—	—	—	—	13,492	90.2
Fall 1965	13,002	11,602	3,215	2,993	2,741	2,477	176	1,400 [6]	—	—	—	—	—	14,146	91.9
Fall 1966	13,280	11,880	3,318	3,111	2,756	2,508	187	1,400 [6]	—	—	—	—	—	14,398	92.2
Fall 1967	13,647	12,247	3,395	3,221	2,879	2,525	226	1,400 [6]	—	—	—	—	—	14,727	92.7
Fall 1968	14,123	12,723	3,508	3,310	2,986	2,650	268	1,400 [6]	—	—	—	—	—	15,170	93.1
Fall 1969	14,337	13,037	3,568	3,405	3,047	2,732	285	1,300 [6]	—	—	—	—	—	15,549	92.2
Fall 1970	14,647	13,336	3,654	3,458	3,128	2,775	321	1,311	—	—	—	—	—	15,924	92.0
Fall 1971	15,053	13,753	3,781	3,571	3,200	2,864	337	1,300 [6]	—	—	—	—	—	16,328	92.2
Fall 1972	15,148	13,848	3,779	3,648	3,248	2,873	299	1,300 [6]	—	—	—	—	—	16,639	91.0
Fall 1973	15,344	14,044	3,801	3,650	3,323	2,918	352	1,300 [6]	—	—	—	—	—	16,867	91.0
Fall 1974	15,403	14,103	3,832	3,675	3,302	2,955	339	1,300 [6]	—	—	—	—	—	17,035	90.4
Fall 1975	15,604	14,304	3,879	3,723	3,354	2,986	362	1,300 [6]	—	—	—	—	—	17,128	91.1
Fall 1976	15,656	14,314	3,825	3,738	3,373	3,015	363	1,342	—	—	—	—	—	17,119	91.5
Fall 1977	15,546	14,203	3,779	3,686	3,388	3,026	324	1,343	—	—	—	—	—	17,045	91.2
Fall 1978	15,441	14,088	3,726	3,610	3,312	3,023	416	1,353	—	—	—	—	—	16,946	91.1
Fall 1979	14,916	13,616	3,526	3,532	3,241	2,969	348	1,300 [6]	—	—	—	—	—	16,611	89.8
Fall 1980	14,570	13,231	3,377	3,368	3,195	2,925	366	1,339	—	—	—	—	—	16,143	90.3
Fall 1981	14,164	12,764	3,286	3,218	3,039	2,907	314	1,400 [6]	—	—	—	—	—	15,609	90.7
Fall 1982	13,805	12,405	3,248	3,137	2,917	2,787	315	1,400 [6]	—	—	—	—	—	15,057	91.7
Fall 1983	13,671	12,271	3,330	3,103	2,861	2,678	299	1,400	—	—	—	—	—	14,740	92.7
Fall 1984	13,704	12,304	3,440	3,145	2,819	2,599	300	1,400 [6]	—	—	—	—	—	14,725	93.1
Fall 1985	13,750	12,388	3,439	3,230	2,866	2,550	303	1,362	—	—	—	—	—	14,888	92.4
Fall 1986	13,669	12,333	3,256	3,215	2,954	2,601	308	1,336 [6]	—	—	—	—	—	14,824	92.2
Fall 1987	13,323	12,076	3,143	3,020	2,936	2,681	296	1,247	—	—	—	—	—	14,502	91.9
Fall 1988	12,893	11,687	3,106	2,895	2,749	2,650	288	1,206 [6]	—	—	—	—	—	14,023	91.9
Fall 1989	12,524	11,393	3,141	2,868	2,629	2,473	281	1,131	303	284	267	273	5	13,536	92.5
Fall 1990	12,476	11,341	3,169	2,896	2,612	2,381	284	1,136 [6]	—	—	—	—	—	13,329	93.6
Fall 1991	12,675	11,544	3,313	2,915	2,645	2,392	278	1,131	309	286	272	260	4	13,491	94.0
Fall 1992	12,862	11,737	3,352	3,027	2,656	2,431	272	1,125 [6]	—	—	—	—	—	13,775	93.4
Fall 1993	13,081	11,963	3,487	3,050	2,751	2,424	250	1,118	312	286	266	249	5	14,096	92.8
Fall 1994	13,354	12,215	3,604	3,131	2,748	2,488	244	1,138 [6]	—	—	—	—	—	14,637	91.2
Fall 1995	13,665	12,502	3,704	3,237	2,826	2,487	247	1,163	325	304	276	255	2	15,013	91.0
Fall 1996	14,027	12,849	3,801	3,323	2,930	2,586	208	1,178 [6]	—	—	—	—	—	15,443	90.8
Fall 1997	14,241	13,056	3,819	3,376	2,972	2,673	216	1,185	326	306	283	266	4	15,769	90.3
Fall 1998	14,407	13,195	3,856	3,382	3,021	2,722	214	1,212 [6]	—	—	—	—	—	15,829	91.0
Fall 1999	14,600	13,371	3,935	3,415	3,034	2,782	205	1,229	336	313	295	280	5	16,007	91.2
Fall 2000	14,781	13,517	3,963	3,491	3,083	2,803	177	1,264 [6]	—	—	—	—	—	16,144	91.6
Fall 2001	15,032	13,736	4,012	3,528	3,174	2,863	159	1,296	350	333	316	293	3	16,280	92.3
Fall 2002	15,374	14,069	4,105	3,584	3,229	2,990	161	1,306 [6]	—	—	—	—	—	16,506	93.1
Fall 2003	15,651	14,339	4,190	3,675	3,277	3,046	150	1,311	351	334	317	304	5	16,694	93.8
Fall 2004	15,949	14,618	4,281	3,750	3,369	3,094	122	1,331 [6]	—	—	—	—	—	17,054	93.5
Fall 2005	16,258	14,909	4,287	3,866	3,454	3,180	121	1,349	356	348	326	315	3	17,358	93.7
Fall 2006	16,441	15,081	4,260	3,882	3,551	3,277	110	1,360 [6]	—	—	—	—	—	17,549	93.7
Fall 2007	16,451	15,087	4,200	3,863	3,558	3,375	92	1,364	357	347	334	324	2	17,597	93.5
Fall 2008	16,322	14,980	4,123	3,822	3,548	3,400	87	1,342 [6]	—	—	—	—	—	17,395	93.8
Fall 2009	16,265	14,955	4,081	3,810	3,542	3,433	90	1,309	333	330	324	319	3	17,232	94.4
Fall 2010[7]	15,975	14,668	4,049	3,734	3,446	3,355	85	1,306	—	—	—	—	—	17,063	93.6
Fall 2011[7]	15,797	14,530	4,039	3,685	3,429	3,293	85	1,266	—	—	—	—	—	—	—

—Not available.

[1] Includes a relatively small number of secondary ungraded students.
[2] Data for 1890 through 1950 are from the decennial censuses of population. Later data are Census Bureau estimates as of July 1 preceding the opening of the school year.
[3] Gross enrollment ratio based on school enrollment of all ages in grades 9 to 12 divided by the 14- to 17-year-old population. Differs from enrollment rates in other tables, which are based on the enrollment of persons in the given age group only.
[4] Data are for 1927–28.
[5] Data are for 1940–41.
[6] Estimated.
[7] Projected.
NOTE: Includes enrollment in public schools that are a part of state and local school systems and also in most private schools, both religiously affiliated and nonsectarian. Some data have been revised from previously published figures. Detail may not sum to totals because of rounding.

SOURCE: U.S. Department of Education, National Center for Education Statistics, *Annual Report of the Commissioner of Education*, 1890 through 1910; *Biennial Survey of Education in the United States*, 1919–20 through 1949–50; *Statistics of State School Systems*, 1951–52 through 1957–58; *Statistics of Public Elementary and Secondary School Systems*, 1959 through 1980; *Statistics of Nonpublic Elementary and Secondary Schools*, 1959 through 1980; Common Core of Data (CCD), "State Nonfiscal Survey of Public Elementary/Secondary Education," 1981–82 through 2009–10; Schools and Staffing Survey, Private School Data File, 1987–88; Private School Universe Survey (PSS), 1989–90 through 2009–10; *Projections of Education Statistics to 2020*; and unpublished data. U.S. Department of Commerce, Census Bureau, Current Population Reports, Series P-25, Nos. 1000, 1022, 1045, 1057, 1059, 1092, and 1095; and 2000 through 2010 Population Estimates, retrieved February 15, 2012, from http://www.census.gov/popest/data/intercensal/national/nat2010.html. (This table was prepared February 2012.)

High school graduates, by sex and control of school: Selected years, 1869–70 through 2020–21

	High school graduates							Averaged freshman graduation rate for public schools[3]	Population 17 years old[4]	Graduates as a ratio of 17-year-old population
		Sex		Control						
				Public[2]			Private			
School year	Total[1]	Males	Females	Total	Males	Females	Total			
1	2	3	4	5	6	7	8	9	10	11
1869–70	16,000	7,064	8,936	—	—	—	—	—	815,000	2.0
1879–80	23,634	10,605	13,029	—	—	—	—	—	946,026	2.5
1889–90	43,731	18,549	25,182	21,882	—	—	21,849 [5]	—	1,259,177	3.5
1899–1900	94,883	38,075	56,808	61,737	—	—	33,146 [5]	—	1,489,146	6.4
1909–10	156,429	63,676	92,753	111,363	—	—	45,066 [5]	—	1,786,240	8.8
1919–20	311,266	123,684	187,582	230,902	—	—	80,364 [5]	—	1,855,173	16.8
1929–30	666,904	300,376	366,528	591,719	—	—	75,185 [5]	—	2,295,822	29.0
1939–40	1,221,475	578,718	642,757	1,143,246	538,273	604,973	78,229 [5]	—	2,403,074	50.8
1949–50	1,199,700	570,700	629,000	1,063,444	505,394	558,050	136,256 [5]	—	2,034,450	59.0
1959–60	1,858,023	895,000	963,000	1,627,050	791,426	835,624	230,973	—	2,672,000	69.5
1969–70	2,888,639	1,430,000	1,459,000	2,588,639	1,285,895	1,302,744	300,000 [5]	78.7	3,757,000	76.9
1974–75	3,132,502	1,542,000	1,591,000	2,822,502	1,391,519	1,430,983	310,000 [5]	74.9	4,256,000	73.6
1975–76	3,142,120	1,552,000	1,590,000	2,837,129	1,401,064	1,436,065	304,991	74.9	4,272,000	73.6
1976–77	3,139,536	1,551,000	1,589,000	2,837,340	—	—	302,196	74.4	4,272,000	73.5
1977–78	3,128,824	1,546,000	1,583,000	2,824,636	—	—	304,188	73.2	4,286,000	73.0
1978–79	3,101,152	1,532,000	1,569,000	2,801,152	—	—	300,000 [5]	71.9	4,327,000	71.7
1979–80	3,042,214	1,503,000	1,539,000	2,747,678	—	—	294,536	71.5	4,262,000	71.4
1980–81	3,020,285	1,492,000	1,528,000	2,725,285	—	—	295,000 [5]	72.2	4,212,000	71.7
1981–82	2,994,758	1,479,000	1,515,000	2,704,758	—	—	290,000 [5]	72.9	4,134,000	72.4
1982–83	2,887,604	1,426,000	1,461,000	2,597,604	—	—	290,000 [5]	73.8	3,962,000	72.9
1983–84	2,766,797	—	—	2,494,797	—	—	272,000 [5]	74.5	3,784,000	73.1
1984–85	2,676,917	—	—	2,413,917	—	—	263,000 [5]	74.2	3,699,000	72.4
1985–86	2,642,616	—	—	2,382,616	—	—	260,000 [5]	74.3	3,670,000	72.0
1986–87	2,693,803	—	—	2,428,803	—	—	265,000 [5]	74.3	3,754,000	71.8
1987–88	2,773,020	—	—	2,500,020	—	—	273,000 [5]	74.2	3,849,000	72.0
1988–89	2,743,743	—	—	2,458,800	—	—	284,943	73.4	3,842,000	71.4
1989–90[6]	2,574,162	—	—	2,320,337	—	—	253,825 [7]	73.6	3,505,000	73.4
1990–91	2,492,988	—	—	2,234,893	—	—	258,095	73.7	3,417,913	72.9
1991–92	2,480,399	—	—	2,226,016	—	—	254,383 [7]	74.2	3,398,884	73.0
1992–93	2,480,519	—	—	2,233,241	—	—	247,278	73.8	3,449,143	71.9
1993–94	2,463,849	—	—	2,220,849	—	—	243,000 [5]	73.1	3,442,521	71.6
1994–95	2,519,084	—	—	2,273,541	—	—	245,543	71.8	3,635,803	69.3
1995–96	2,518,109	—	—	2,273,109	—	—	245,000 [5]	71.0	3,640,132	69.2
1996–97	2,611,988	—	—	2,358,403	—	—	253,585	71.3	3,792,207	68.9
1997–98	2,704,050	—	—	2,439,050	1,187,647	1,251,403	265,000 [5]	71.3	4,008,416	67.5
1998–99	2,758,655	—	—	2,485,630	1,212,924	1,272,706	273,025	71.1	3,917,885	70.4
1999–2000	2,832,844	—	—	2,553,844	1,241,631	1,312,213	279,000 [5]	71.7	4,056,639	69.8
2000–01	2,847,973	—	—	2,569,200	1,251,931	1,317,269	278,773	71.7	4,023,686	70.8
2001–02	2,906,534	—	—	2,621,534	1,275,813	1,345,721	285,000 [5]	72.6	4,023,968	72.2
2002–03	3,015,735	—	—	2,719,947	1,330,973	1,388,974	295,788	73.9	4,125,087	73.1
2003–04[6,8]	3,054,438	—	—	2,753,438	1,347,800	1,405,638	301,000 [5]	74.3	4,113,074	74.3
2004–05	3,106,499	—	—	2,799,250	1,369,749	1,429,501	307,249	74.7	4,120,073	75.4
2005–06[6]	3,122,544	—	—	2,815,544	1,376,458	1,439,086	307,000 [5]	73.4	4,200,554	74.3
2006–07	3,199,650	—	—	2,893,045	1,414,069	1,478,976	306,605	73.9	4,297,239	74.5
2007–08	3,312,337	—	—	3,001,337	1,467,180	1,534,157	311,000 [5]	74.7	4,436,955	74.7
2008–09[6]	3,347,828	—	—	3,039,015	1,490,317	1,548,698	308,813	75.5	4,336,950	77.2
2009–10[9]	3,321,380	—	—	3,013,400	—	—	307,980	76.3	4,311,831	77.0
2010–11[9]	3,282,200	—	—	2,981,520	—	—	300,680	—	4,226,622	77.7
2011–12[9]	3,220,050	—	—	2,926,440	—	—	293,610	—	—	—
2012–13[9]	3,197,300	—	—	2,912,480	—	—	284,820	—	—	—
2013–14[9]	3,153,500	—	—	2,874,500	—	—	279,000	—	—	—
2014–15[9]	3,132,400	—	—	2,867,400	—	—	265,000	—	—	—
2015–16[9]	3,164,790	—	—	2,904,410	—	—	260,380	—	—	—
2016–17[9]	3,182,750	—	—	2,930,530	—	—	252,220	—	—	—
2017–18[9]	3,231,350	—	—	2,983,130	—	—	248,220	—	—	—
2018–19[9]	3,224,820	—	—	2,983,780	—	—	241,040	—	—	—
2019–20[9]	3,182,520	—	—	2,950,880	—	—	231,640	—	—	—
2020–21[9]	3,209,510	—	—	2,981,170	—	—	228,340	—	—	—

—Not available.

[1] Includes graduates of public and private schools.

[2] Data for 1929–30 and preceding years are from *Statistics of Public High Schools* and exclude graduates from high schools that failed to report to the Office of Education. Includes estimates for jurisdictions not reporting counts of graduates by sex.

[3] The averaged freshman graduation rate provides an estimate of the percentage of students who receive a regular diploma within 4 years of entering ninth grade. The rate uses aggregate student enrollment data to estimate the size of an incoming freshman class and aggregate counts of the number of diplomas awarded 4 years later. Averaged freshman graduation rates in this table are based on reported totals of enrollment by grade and high school graduates, rather than on details reported by race/ethnicity.

[4] Derived from Current Population Reports, Series P-25. For years 1869–70 through 1989–90, 17-year-old population is an estimate of the October 17-year-old population based on July data. Data for 1990–91 and later years are October resident population estimates prepared by the Census Bureau.

[5] Estimated.

[6] Includes imputations for nonreporting states.

[7] Projected by private schools.

[8] Includes estimates for public schools in New York and Wisconsin. Without estimates for these two states, the averaged freshman graduation rate for the remaining 48 states and the District of Columbia is 75.0 percent.

[9] Projected by NCES.

NOTE: Includes graduates of regular day school programs. Excludes graduates of other programs, when separately reported, and recipients of high school equivalency certificates. Some data have been revised from previously published figures. Detail may not sum to totals because of rounding.

SOURCE: U.S. Department of Education, National Center for Education Statistics, *Annual Report of the Commissioner of Education*, 1870 through 1910; *Biennial Survey of Education in the United States*, 1919–20 through 1949–50; *Statistics of State School Systems*, 1951–52 through 1957–58; *Statistics of Public Elementary and Secondary School Systems*, 1958–59 through 1980–81; *Statistics of Nonpublic Elementary and Secondary Schools*, 1959 through 1980; Common Core of Data (CCD), "State Nonfiscal Survey of Public Elementary/Secondary Education," 1981–82 through 2009–10; *Public School Graduates and Dropouts from the Common Core of Data*, 2007–08 and 2008–09; Private School Universe Survey (PSS), 1989 through 2009; and *Projections of Education Statistics to 2020*. U.S. Department of Commerce, Census Bureau, Population Estimates, retrieved August 11, 2011, from http://www.census.gov/popest/national/asrh/2009-nat-res.html. (This table was prepared August 2011.)

Public high school graduates, by state or jurisdiction: Selected years, 1980–81 through 2009–10

State or jurisdiction	1980–81	1989–90	1999–2000	2002–03	2003–04	2004–05	2005–06	2006–07	2007–08	2008–09	Projected 2009–10 graduates	Percent change, 1999–2000 to 2009–10
1	2	3	4	5	6	7	8	9	10	11	12	13
United States	**2,725,285**	**2,320,337** [1]	**2,553,844**	**2,719,947**	**2,753,438** [1]	**2,799,250**	**2,815,544** [1]	**2,893,045**	**3,001,337**	**3,039,015** [1]	**3,013,400**	**18.0**
Alabama	44,894	40,485	37,819	36,741	36,464	37,453	37,918	38,912	41,346	42,082	40,630	7.4
Alaska	5,343	5,386	6,615	7,297	7,236	6,909	7,361	7,666	7,855	8,008	8,360	26.4
Arizona	28,416	32,103	38,304	49,986	45,508	59,498	54,091	55,954	61,667	62,374	60,610	58.2
Arkansas	29,577	26,475	27,335	27,555	27,181	26,621	28,790	27,166	28,725	28,057	28,510	4.3
California	242,172	236,291	309,866	341,097	343,480	355,217	343,515	356,641	374,561	372,310 [2]	383,680	23.8
Colorado	35,897	32,967	38,924	42,379	44,777	44,532	44,424	45,628	46,082	47,459	47,740	22.6
Connecticut	38,369	27,878	31,562	33,667	34,573	35,515	36,222	37,541	38,419	34,968	37,750	19.6
Delaware	7,349	5,550	6,108	6,817	6,951	6,934	7,275	7,205	7,388	7,839	8,140	33.3
District of Columbia[3]	4,848	3,626	2,695	2,725	3,031	2,781	3,150 [4]	2,944	3,352	3,517	3,010	11.7
Florida	88,755	88,934	106,708	127,484	131,418	133,318	134,686	142,284	149,046	153,461	144,250	35.2
Georgia	62,963	56,605	62,563	66,890	68,550	70,834	73,498	77,829	83,505	88,003	85,370	36.5
Hawaii	11,472	10,325	10,437	10,013	10,324	10,813	10,922	11,063	11,613	11,508	10,700	2.5
Idaho	12,679	11,971	16,170	15,858	15,547	15,768	16,096	16,242	16,567	16,807	17,220	6.5
Illinois	136,795	108,119	111,835	117,507	124,763	123,615	126,817	130,220	135,143	131,670	133,710	19.6
Indiana	73,381	60,012	57,012	57,897	56,008	55,444	57,920	59,887	61,901	63,663	62,440	9.5
Iowa	42,635	31,796	33,926	34,860	34,339	33,547	33,693	34,127	34,573	33,926	33,510	-1.2
Kansas	29,397	25,367	29,102	29,963	30,155	30,355	29,818	30,139	30,737	30,368	30,060	3.3
Kentucky	41,714	38,005	36,830	37,654	37,787	38,399	38,449	39,099	39,339	41,851	40,980	11.3
Louisiana	46,199	36,053	38,430	37,610	37,019	36,009	33,275	34,274	34,401	35,622	34,570	-10.0
Maine	15,554	13,839	12,211	12,947	13,278	13,077	12,950	13,151	13,150 [5]	14,093 [5]	13,970	14.4
Maryland	54,050	41,566	47,849	51,864	52,870	54,170	55,536	57,564	59,171	58,304	58,150	21.5
Massachusetts	74,831	55,941 [6]	52,950	55,987	58,326	59,665	61,272	63,903	65,197	65,258	63,650	20.2
Michigan	124,372	93,807	97,679	100,301	98,823	101,582	102,582	111,838	115,183	112,742	112,740	15.4
Minnesota	64,166	49,087	57,372	59,432	59,096	58,391	58,898	59,497	60,409	59,729	59,700	4.1
Mississippi	28,083	25,182	24,232	23,810	23,735	23,523	23,848	24,186	24,795	24,505	25,970	7.2
Missouri	60,359	48,957	52,848	56,925	57,983	57,841	58,417	60,275	61,717	62,969	63,720	20.6
Montana	11,634	9,370	10,903	10,657	10,500	10,335	10,283	10,122	10,396	10,077	9,940	-8.8
Nebraska	21,411	17,664	20,149	20,161	20,309	19,940	19,764	19,873	20,035	19,501	20,070	-0.4
Nevada	9,069	9,477	14,551	16,378	15,201	15,740	16,455	17,149	18,815	19,904 [2]	18,540	27.4
New Hampshire	11,552	10,766	11,829	13,210	13,309	13,775	13,988	14,452	14,982	14,757	14,480	22.4
New Jersey	93,168	69,824	74,420	81,391	83,826	86,502	90,049	93,013	94,994	95,085	94,660	27.2
New Mexico	17,915	14,884	18,031	16,923	17,892	17,353	17,822	16,131	18,264	17,931	18,130	0.5
New York	198,465	143,318	141,731	143,818	142,526 [7]	153,203	161,817	168,333	176,310	180,917	177,260	25.1
North Carolina	69,395	64,782	62,140	69,696	72,126	75,010	76,710	76,031	83,307	86,712	85,490	37.6
North Dakota	9,924	7,690	8,606	8,169	7,888	7,555	7,192	7,159	6,999	7,232	6,780	-21.2
Ohio	143,503	114,513	111,668	115,762	119,029	116,702	117,356	117,658	120,758	122,203	120,180	7.6
Oklahoma	38,875	35,606	37,646	36,694	36,799	36,227	36,497	37,100	37,630	37,219	38,110	1.2
Oregon	28,729	25,473	30,151	32,587	32,958	32,602	32,394	33,446	34,949	35,138	34,860	15.6
Pennsylvania	144,645	110,527	113,959	119,933	123,474	124,758	127,830 [4]	128,603	130,298	130,658	121,890	7.0
Rhode Island	10,719	7,825	8,477	9,318	9,258	9,881	10,108	10,384	10,347	10,028	9,480	11.8
South Carolina	38,347	32,483	31,617	32,482	33,235	33,439	34,970 [4]	35,108	35,303	39,114	38,590	22.1
South Dakota	10,385	7,650	9,278	8,999	9,001	8,585	8,589	8,346	8,582	8,123	8,640	-6.9
Tennessee	50,648	46,094	41,568	44,113	46,096	47,967	50,880	54,502	57,486	60,368	58,180	40.0
Texas	171,665	172,480	212,925	238,111	244,165	239,717	240,485	241,193	252,121	264,275	265,660	24.8
Utah	19,886	21,196	32,501	29,527	30,252	30,253	29,050	28,276	28,167	30,463	26,390	-18.8
Vermont	6,424	6,127	6,675	6,970	7,100	7,152	6,779	7,317	7,392	7,209	7,070	5.9
Virginia	67,126	60,605	65,596	72,943	72,042	73,667	69,597	73,997	77,369	79,651	78,440	19.6
Washington	50,046	45,941	57,597	60,435	61,274	61,094	60,213	62,801	61,625	62,764	64,510	12.0
West Virginia	23,580	21,854	19,437	17,287	17,339	17,117	16,763	17,407	17,489	17,690	17,520	-9.9
Wisconsin	67,743	52,038	58,545	63,272	62,784 [7]	63,229	63,003	63,968	65,183	65,410	64,040	9.4
Wyoming	6,161	5,823	6,462	5,845	5,833	5,616	5,527	5,441	5,494	5,493	5,390	-16.6
Bureau of Indian Education	—	—	—	—	—	—	—	—	—	—	—	—
DoD, overseas	—	—	2,642	2,641	2,766	—	—	—	—	—	—	—
DoD, domestic	—	—	560	590	584	—	—	—	—	—	—	—
Other jurisdictions												
American Samoa	—	703	698	832	852	905	879	954	—	—	—	—
Guam	—	1,033	1,406	1,502	1,346	1,179	—	—	—	—	—	—
Northern Marianas	—	227	360	422	575	614	670	643	—	—	—	—
Puerto Rico	—	29,049	30,856	31,408	30,083	29,071	31,896	31,718	30,016	29,286	—	—
U.S. Virgin Islands	—	1,260	1,060	886	816	940	—	820	820	940	—	—

—Not available.

[1] U.S. total includes estimates for nonreporting states.

[2] Estimated high school graduates from NCES 2011-312, *Public School Graduates and Dropouts from the Common Core of Data: School Year 2008–09.*

[3] Beginning in 1989–90, graduates from adult programs are excluded.

[4] Projected data from NCES 2009-062, *Projections of Education Statistics to 2018.*

[5] Includes 1,161 graduates in 2007–08 and 1,169 graduates in 2008–09 from private high schools that received a majority of their funding from public sources.

[6] Projected data from NCES 91-490, *Projections of Education Statistics to 2002.*

[7] Estimated high school graduates from NCES 2006-606rev, *The Averaged Freshman Graduation Rate for Public High Schools From the Common Core of Data: School Years 2002–03 and 2003–04.*

NOTE: Data include regular diploma recipients, but exclude students receiving a certificate of attendance and persons receiving high school equivalency certificates. DoD = Department of Defense. Some data have been revised from previously published figures. Detail may not sum to totals because of rounding.

SOURCE: U.S. Department of Education, National Center for Education Statistics; *Projections of Education Statistics to 2020;* Common Core of Data (CCD), "State Nonfiscal Survey of Public Elementary/Secondary Education," 1981–82 through 2009–10; and *Public School Graduates and Dropouts from the Common Core of Data: School Years 2007–08 and 2008–09.* (This table was prepared August 2011.)

Averaged freshman graduation rates for public secondary schools, by state or jurisdiction: Selected years, 1990–91 through 2008–09

State or jurisdiction	1990–91	1995–96	1996–97	1997–98	1998–99	1999–2000	2000–01	2001–02	2002–03	2003–04	2004–05	2005–06	2006–07	2007–08	2008–09
1	2	3	4	5	6	7	8	9	10	11	12	13	14	15	16
United States	73.7	71.0	71.3	71.3	71.1	71.7	71.7	72.6	73.9	74.3 [1]	74.7	73.4 [2]	73.9	74.7	75.5 [2]
Alabama	69.8	62.7	62.4	64.4	61.3	64.1	63.7	62.1	64.7	65.0	65.9	66.2	67.1	69.0	69.9
Alaska	74.6	68.3	67.9	68.9	70.0	66.7	68.0	65.9	68.0	67.2	64.1	66.5	69.0	69.1	72.6
Arizona	76.7	60.8	65.3	65.6	62.3	63.6	74.2	74.7	75.9	66.8	84.7	70.5	69.6	70.7	72.5
Arkansas	76.6	74.2	70.6	73.9	73.7	74.6	73.9	74.8	76.6	76.8	75.7	80.4	74.4	76.4	74.0
California	69.6	67.6	68.8	69.6	71.1	71.7	71.6	72.7	74.1	73.9	74.6	69.2	70.7	71.2	71.0 [3]
Colorado	76.3	74.8	74.7	73.9	73.4	74.1	73.2	74.7	76.4	78.7	76.7	75.5	76.6	75.4	77.6
Connecticut	80.2	76.1	76.7	76.9	76.0	81.9	77.5	79.7	80.9	80.7	80.9	80.9	81.8	82.2	75.4
Delaware	72.5	70.4	71.7	74.1	70.4	66.8	71.0	69.5	73.0	72.9	73.0	76.3	71.9	72.1	73.7
District of Columbia	54.5	49.7	54.6	53.9	52.0	54.5	60.2	68.4	59.6	68.2	66.3	65.4 [4]	54.8	56.0	62.4
Florida	65.6	62.3	62.7	62.1	61.4	61.0	61.2	63.4	66.7	66.4	64.6	63.6	65.0	66.9	68.9
Georgia	70.3	61.9	62.0	58.2	57.5	59.7	58.7	61.1	60.8	61.2	61.7	62.4	64.1	65.4	67.8
Hawaii	75.9	74.5	69.1	68.8	67.5	70.9	68.3	72.1	71.3	72.6	75.1	75.5	75.4	76.0	75.3
Idaho	79.6	80.5	80.1	79.7	79.5	79.4	79.6	79.3	81.4	81.5	81.0	80.5	80.4	80.1	80.6
Illinois	76.6	75.2	76.1	76.8	76.0	76.3	75.6	77.1	75.9	80.3	79.4	79.7	79.5	80.4	77.7
Indiana	76.9	73.6	74.0	73.8	74.3	71.8	72.1	73.1	75.5	73.5	73.2	73.3	73.9	74.1	75.2
Iowa	84.4	84.3	84.6	83.9	83.3	83.1	82.8	84.1	85.3	85.8	86.6	86.9	86.5	86.4	85.7
Kansas	80.8	77.1	76.9	76.0	76.7	77.1	76.5	77.1	76.9	77.9	79.2	77.5	78.8	79.0	80.2
Kentucky	72.9	71.3	71.1	70.2	70.0	69.7	69.8	69.8	71.7	73.0	75.9	77.2	76.4	74.4	77.6
Louisiana	57.5	61.7	59.3	61.3	61.1	62.2	63.7	64.4	64.1	69.4	63.9	59.5	61.3	63.5	67.3
Maine	80.7	73.7	75.2	78.5	74.7	75.9	76.4	75.6	76.3	77.6	78.6	76.3	78.5	79.1 [5]	79.9 [5]
Maryland	77.5	78.3	76.6	76.2	76.6	77.6	78.7	79.7	79.2	79.5	79.3	79.9	80.0	80.4	80.1
Massachusetts	79.1	78.0	78.4	78.3	77.9	78.0	78.9	77.6	75.7	79.3	78.7	79.5	80.8	81.5	83.3
Michigan	72.1	71.4	73.5	74.6	73.9	75.3	75.4	72.9	74.0	72.5	73.0	72.2	77.0	76.3	75.3
Minnesota	90.8	86.1	78.6	85.0	86.0	84.9	83.6	83.9	84.8	84.7	85.9	86.2	86.5	86.4	87.4
Mississippi	63.3	59.7	59.6	59.8	59.2	59.4	59.7	61.2	62.7	62.7	63.3	63.5	63.5	63.9	62.0
Missouri	76.0	75.0	74.7	75.2	75.8	76.3	75.5	76.8	78.3	80.4	80.6	81.0	81.9	82.4	83.1
Montana	84.4	83.9	83.2	82.2	81.3	80.8	80.0	79.8	81.0	80.4	81.5	81.9	81.5	82.0	82.0
Nebraska	86.7	85.6	84.8	85.6	87.3	85.7	83.8	83.9	85.2	87.6	87.8	87.0	86.3	83.8	82.9
Nevada	77.0	65.8	73.2	70.6	71.0	69.7	70.0	71.9	72.3	57.4	55.8	55.8	54.2	56.3	56.3 [3]
New Hampshire	78.6	77.5	77.3	76.7	75.3	76.1	77.8	77.8	78.2	78.7	80.1	81.1	81.7	83.3	84.3
New Jersey	81.4	82.8	83.9	76.3	77.5	83.6	85.4	85.8	87.0	86.3	85.1	84.8	84.4	84.6	85.3
New Mexico	70.1	63.7	62.5	61.6	63.3	64.7	65.9	67.4	63.1	67.0	65.4	67.3	59.1	66.8	64.8
New York	66.1	63.6	65.3	63.4	62.5	61.8	61.5	60.5	60.9	60.9 [6]	65.3	67.4	68.9	70.9	73.5
North Carolina	71.3	66.5	65.5	65.6	65.4	65.8	66.5	68.2	70.1	71.4	72.6	71.8	68.6	72.8	75.1
North Dakota	87.6	89.5	87.8	86.7	85.6	86.0	85.4	85.0	86.4	86.1	86.3	82.2	83.1	83.8	87.4
Ohio	77.5	74.5	76.4	77.0	75.0	75.2	76.5	77.5	79.0	81.3	80.2	79.2	78.7	79.0	79.6
Oklahoma	76.5	75.6	74.8	75.1	76.4	75.8	75.8	76.0	76.0	77.0	76.9	77.8	77.8	78.0	77.3
Oregon	72.7	68.3	69.1	69.0	68.2	69.6	68.3	71.0	73.7	74.2	74.2	73.0	73.8	76.7	76.5
Pennsylvania	79.7	80.0	79.8	79.4	79.1	78.7	79.0	80.2	81.7	82.2	82.5	83.5 [4]	83.0	82.7	80.5
Rhode Island	75.0	72.7	72.9	72.5	72.2	72.8	73.5	75.7	77.7	75.9	78.4	77.8	78.4	76.4	75.3
South Carolina	66.6	60.9	59.6	59.3	59.1	58.6	56.5	57.9	59.7	60.6	60.1	61.0 [4]	58.9	62.2	66.0
South Dakota	83.8	84.5	84.2	77.7	74.2	77.6	77.4	79.0	83.0	83.7	82.3	84.5	82.5	84.4	81.7
Tennessee	69.8	66.6	61.6	58.4	58.5	59.5	59.0	59.6	63.4	66.1	68.5	70.7	72.6	74.9	77.4
Texas	72.2	66.1	67.0	69.4	69.2	71.0	70.8	73.5	75.5	76.7	74.0	72.5	71.9	73.1	75.4
Utah	77.5	76.9	81.1	80.7	81.6	82.5	81.6	80.5	80.2	83.0	84.4	78.6	76.6	74.3	79.4
Vermont	79.5	85.3	83.6	83.9	81.9	81.0	80.2	82.0	83.6	85.4	86.5	82.3	88.5	89.3	89.6
Virginia	76.2	76.2	76.6	76.6	76.3	76.9	77.5	76.7	80.6	79.3	79.6	74.5	75.5	77.0	78.4
Washington	75.7	75.5	74.0	73.3	73.2	73.7	69.2	72.2	74.2	74.6	75.0	72.9	74.8	71.9	73.7
West Virginia	76.6	77.0	76.7	77.4	77.9	76.7	75.9	74.2	75.7	76.9	77.3	76.9	78.2	77.3	77.0
Wisconsin	85.2	83.6	83.7	83.1	82.6	82.7	83.3	84.8	85.8	85.8 [6]	86.7	87.5	88.5	89.6	90.7
Wyoming	81.1	77.7	78.4	77.1	76.6	76.3	73.4	74.4	73.9	76.0	76.7	76.1	75.8	76.0	75.2
Other jurisdictions															
American Samoa	85.3	79.7	79.7	76.6	80.4	71.9	77.0	82.9	81.0	80.2	81.1	81.0	84.6	—	—
Guam	48.2	44.6	45.4	39.5	54.7	52.9	51.7	—	56.3	48.4	—	—	—	—	—
Northern Marianas	—	63.3	68.9	63.4	63.5	61.1	62.7	65.2	65.2	75.3	75.4	80.3	73.6	—	—
Puerto Rico	60.9	60.8	61.5	61.9	63.6	64.7	65.7	66.2	67.8	64.8	61.7	68.6	66.7	63.1	62.1
U.S. Virgin Islands	53.2	54.2	62.0	58.6	58.6	53.8	57.3	48.7	53.5	—	—	—	57.8	57.8	68.1

—Not available.

[1] Includes estimates for New York and Wisconsin. Without estimates for these two states, the averaged freshman graduation rate for the remaining 48 states and the District of Columbia is 75.0 percent.

[2] U.S. total includes estimates for nonreporting states.

[3] Estimated high school graduates from NCES 2011-312, *Public School Graduates and Dropouts from the Common Core of Data: School Year 2008–09.*

[4] Projected high school graduates from NCES 2009-062, *Projections of Education Statistics to 2018.*

[5] Includes 1,161 graduates in 2007–08 and 1,169 graduates in 2008–09 from private high schools that received a majority of their funding from public sources.

[6] Estimated high school graduates from NCES 2006-606rev, *The Averaged Freshman Graduation Rate for Public High Schools From the Common Core of Data: School Years 2002–03 and 2003–04.*

NOTE: The averaged freshman graduation rate provides an estimate of the percentage of students who receive a regular diploma within 4 years of entering ninth grade. The rate uses aggregate student enrollment data to estimate the size of an incoming freshman class and aggregate counts of the number of diplomas awarded 4 years later. Averaged freshman graduation rates in this table are based on reported totals of enrollment by grade and high school graduates, rather than on details reported by race/ethnicity. Some data have been revised from previously published figures.

SOURCE: U.S. Department of Education, National Center for Education Statistics, Common Core of Data (CCD), "State Nonfiscal Survey of Public Elementary/Secondary Education," 1986–87 through 2009–10; *The Averaged Freshman Graduation Rate for Public High Schools From the Common Core of Data: School Years 2002–03 and 2003–04; Public School Graduates and Dropouts from the Common Core of Data, 2007–08 and 2008–09; and Projections of Education Statistics to 2019.* (This table was prepared August 2011.)

Public high school graduates and dropouts, by race/ethnicity and state or jurisdiction: 2008–09

State or other jurisdiction	High school graduates, by race/ethnicity, 2008–09[1]							Event dropout rates (percent of 9th- to 12th-graders who dropped out) during 2008–09, by race/ethnicity						
	Total	White	Black	Hispanic	Asian/ Pacific Islander	American Indian/ Alaska Native	Two or more races	Total	White	Black	Hispanic	Asian/ Pacific Islander	American Indian/ Alaska Native	Two or more races
1	2	3	4	5	6	7	8	9	10	11	12	13	14	15
United States	3,020,619	1,883,382	451,384	481,698	163,575	32,213	‡	4.1	2.7	6.6	6.0	2.4	6.3	‡
Alabama	42,033	26,380	13,884	799	509	461	—	1.5	1.4	1.7	1.6	0.7	1.2	—
Alaska	8,008	4,874	283	364	588	1,508	391	7.0	—	—	—	—	—	—
Arizona	62,374	31,895	3,519	21,607	2,007	3,346	—	8.3	6.1	10.1	10.2	5.0	12.9	—
Arkansas	28,057	19,872	5,939	1,599	442	205	—	4.1	3.5	5.7	4.7	3.8	4.5	—
California	372,310	134,816	25,420	147,717	54,701	2,890	6,766	5.0	3.2	9.2	6.2	2.4	6.8	5.5
Colorado	47,459	33,272	2,619	9,364	1,738	466	—	6.1	3.7	9.6	11.4	3.4	12.3	—
Connecticut	34,968	25,561	4,221	3,861	1,248	77	—	3.1	1.4	6.8	7.4	0.9	2.4	—
Delaware	7,839	4,602	2,438	522	246	31	—	5.1	4.1	6.9	6.6	2.3	5.4	—
District of Columbia	3,517	131	3,084	245	55	2	—	7.0	4.8	6.9	8.3	5.3	0.0	—
Florida	150,066	78,933	32,167	34,079	4,436	451	—	2.6	1.8	4.3	3.0	0.9	2.9	—
Georgia	86,163	45,921	31,949	5,052	3,101	140	—	4.2	3.4	5.3	4.7	1.8	2.3	—
Hawaii	11,508	2,065	226	487	8,673	57	—	4.9	5.3	4.6	4.8	4.6	6.6	—
Idaho	16,807	14,353	181	1,778	297	198	—	1.6	1.4	1.3	3.1	2.0	2.7	—
Illinois	130,094	82,749	21,887	19,616	5,600	242	—	—	—	—	—	—	—	—
Indiana	62,312	52,568	6,070	2,700	834	140	—	1.7	1.5	2.7	2.3	1.0	3.0	—
Iowa	33,926	30,418	1,344	1,353	657	154	—	3.1	2.7	7.9	5.3	2.4	6.0	—
Kansas	29,702	23,569	2,321	2,655	739	418	—	2.1	1.8	3.1	3.0	1.3	3.0	—
Kentucky	41,390	36,044	4,213	710	417	6	—	2.9	2.6	4.8	4.0	2.2	3.0	—
Louisiana	35,622	19,589	14,346	718	682	287	—	6.8	4.7	9.4	8.5	3.1	6.6	—
Maine	14,093	13,397	274	116	216	90	—	3.6	3.5	4.5	4.4	2.8	8.9	—
Maryland	58,304	30,269	20,581	3,842	3,426	186	—	3.0	2.3	3.9	4.1	1.1	5.3	—
Massachusetts	65,258	48,694	5,240	6,972	3,279	171	902	2.9	1.8	5.6	7.5	1.8	4.3	3.4
Michigan	112,084	85,642	19,219	3,538	2,812	873	—	3.8	2.6	7.9	5.6	1.6	6.4	—
Minnesota	59,729	49,455	3,969	1,997	3,407	901	—	1.9	1.2	4.7	5.0	1.9	8.5	—
Mississippi	24,505	12,079	11,837	313	239	37	0	4.2	3.2	5.2	3.2	1.9	3.9	0.0
Missouri	62,969	49,938	10,111	1,591	1,058	271	—	4.3	3.1	9.6	4.9	2.2	5.0	—
Montana	10,077	8,844	65	190	115	863	—	5.0	4.1	7.5	8.3	3.5	12.3	—
Nebraska	19,501	16,275	1,054	1,617	328	227	—	2.4	1.7	6.0	4.7	1.7	5.5	—
Nevada	19,904	10,723	1,849	5,014	2,054	264	—	5.1	3.7	6.9	6.6	3.4	5.8	—
New Hampshire	14,757	13,892	359	192	276	38	—	1.7	1.7	6.0	2.1	0.7	3.1	—
New Jersey	95,085	56,875	15,220	14,808	7,776	136	270	1.6	0.9	3.4	2.9	0.3	3.5	0.7
New Mexico	17,931	6,298	478	8,760	277	2,118	—	4.9	3.8	5.2	5.0	3.1	7.1	—
New York	180,594	105,632	30,441	29,529	14,346	646	—	4.2	2.0	7.6	7.1	2.5	6.7	—
North Carolina	84,847	52,487	24,103	5,067	2,088	1,102	—	5.3	4.6	6.0	7.3	2.1	7.7	—
North Dakota	7,232	6,507	138	89	75	423	—	2.5	1.7	5.5	5.2	1.0	8.7	—
Ohio	119,883	100,117	15,630	2,113	1,835	188	—	4.2	2.8	9.9	7.8	1.7	7.6	—
Oklahoma	37,219	22,976	3,643	2,664	902	7,034	—	2.5	2.3	2.7	3.7	1.9	2.6	—
Oregon	34,022	26,558	826	4,250	1,695	693	—	3.4	2.9	6.1	5.1	2.4	6.4	—
Pennsylvania	130,242	103,712	16,424	6,509	3,428	169	—	2.3	1.6	4.6	5.9	1.5	3.4	—
Rhode Island	10,028	7,324	836	1,519	286	63	—	4.4	3.5	6.3	7.2	3.7	5.4	—
South Carolina	38,933	22,453	14,541	1,227	605	107	—	3.4	3.2	3.6	3.9	1.4	6.3	—
South Dakota	8,123	7,192	141	137	99	554	—	1.8	1.2	0.8	3.5	0.8	6.2	—
Tennessee	60,368	43,360	14,221	1,762	916	109	—	3.2	2.0	6.4	3.9	1.7	2.7	—
Texas	264,275	112,016	35,982	104,854	10,462	961	—	3.2	1.5	5.0	4.2	1.0	2.2	—
Utah	30,358	25,801	344	2,707	1,086	420	—	3.3	2.6	5.3	6.7	2.8	7.4	—
Vermont	7,209	6,822	99	61	150	39	38	2.6	—	—	—	—	—	—
Virginia	78,409	49,490	18,961	4,960	4,758	240	—	2.5	1.7	3.9	5.0	1.1	3.2	—
Washington	61,932	45,496	2,961	6,398	5,860	1,217	—	4.7	4.0	7.2	6.7	3.1	9.4	—
West Virginia	17,690	16,644	741	140	149	16	—	4.1	4.1	4.4	4.8	1.2	8.4	—
Wisconsin	65,410	53,987	4,920	3,122	2,533	848	—	2.3	1.3	8.0	5.2	2.0	4.9	—
Wyoming	5,493	4,815	65	414	69	130	—	1.1	0.7	2.7	2.7	0.3	4.5	—
Bureau of Indian Education	—	—	—	—	—	—	—	—	—	—	—	—	—	—
DoD, overseas	—	—	—	—	—	—	—	—	—	—	—	—	—	—
DoD, domestic	—	—	—	—	—	—	—	—	—	—	—	—	—	—
Other jurisdictions														
American Samoa	—	—	—	—	—	—	—	—	—	—	—	—	—	—
Guam	—	—	—	—	—	—	—	—	—	—	—	—	—	—
Northern Marianas	—	—	—	—	—	—	—	—	—	—	—	—	—	—
Puerto Rico	—	—	—	—	—	—	—	—	—	—	—	—	—	—
U.S. Virgin Islands	940	6	833	97	1	3	—	7.4	8.3	7.2	9.2	0.0	12.5	—

—Not available.
#Rounds to zero.
‡Reporting standards not met (too few cases).
[1]Data differ slightly from figures reported in other tables due to varying reporting practices for racial/ethnic survey data.
NOTE: Includes only graduates for whom race/ethnicity was reported. Race categories exclude persons of Hispanic ethnicity. Event dropout rates measure the percentage of public school stu-dents in grades 9 through 12 who dropped out of school between one October and the next.
DoD = Department of Defense.
SOURCE: U.S. Department of Education, National Center for Education Statistics, Common Core of Data (CCD), *Public School Graduates and Dropouts from the Common Core of Data, 2007–08 and 2008–09.* (This table was prepared August 2011.)

General Educational Development (GED) test takers and test passers, by age: 1971 through 2010

Year	Number of test takers (in thousands)			Percentage distribution of test passers, by age[1]				
	Total[2]	Completing test battery[3]	Passing tests[4]	16 to 18 years old	19 to 24 years old	25 to 29 years old	30 to 34 years old	35 years old or over
1	2	3	4	5	6	7	8	9
1971[5]	377	—	227	—	—	—	—	—
1972[5]	419	—	245	—	—	—	—	—
1973[5]	423	—	249	—	—	—	—	—
1974	—	—	294	35 [6]	27 [6]	13	9	17
1975	—	—	340	33 [6]	26 [6]	14	9	18
1976	—	—	333	31 [6]	28 [6]	14	10	17
1977	—	—	330	40 [6]	24 [6]	13	8	14
1978	—	—	381	31 [6]	27 [6]	13	10	18
1979	—	—	426	37 [6]	28 [6]	12	13	11
1980	—	—	479	37 [6]	27 [6]	13	8	15
1981	—	—	489	37 [6]	27 [6]	13	8	14
1982	—	—	486	37 [6]	28 [6]	13	8	15
1983	—	—	465	34 [6]	29 [6]	14	8	15
1984	—	—	427	32 [6]	28 [6]	15	9	16
1985	—	—	413	32 [6]	26 [6]	15	10	16
1986	—	—	428	32 [6]	26 [6]	15	10	17
1987	—	—	444	33 [6]	24 [6]	15	10	18
1988	—	—	410	35 [6]	22 [6]	14	10	18
1989	632	541	357	22	37	13	—	—
1990	714	615	410	22	39	13	10	15
1991	755	657	462	20	40	13	10	16
1992	739	639	457	22	39	13	9	17
1993	746	651	469	22	38	13	10	16
1994	774	668	491	25	37	13	9	15
1995	787	682	504	27	36	13	9	15
1996	824	716	488	27	37	13	9	14
1997	785	681	460	31	36	12	8	13
1998	776	673	481	32	36	11	7	13
1999	808	702	498	32	37	11	7	13
2000	811	699	487	33	37	11	7	13
2001[7]	1,016	928	648	29	38	11	8	14
2002[7]	557	467	330	38	36	10	6	11
2003	657	552	387	35	37	10	7	11
2004	666	570	406	35	38	11	6	10
2005	681	588	424	34	37	12	7	11
2006	676	580	398	35	36	12	6	11
2007	692	600	429	35	35	12	7	11
2008	737	642	469	34	35	13	7	11
2009	748	645	448	31	36	13	8	12
2010	720	623	452	27	37	14	9	14

—Not available.

[1] People who did not report their age were excluded from this calculation. Age data for 1988 and prior years are for all test takers and may not be comparable to data for later years.
[2] All people taking the GED tests (one or more subtests).
[3] People completing the entire GED battery of five tests.
[4] Data for 2002 and later years are for people passing the GED tests (i.e., earning both a passing total score on the test battery and a passing score on each individual test). Data for 2001 and prior years are for high school equivalency credentials issued by the states to GED test passers. In order to receive high school equivalency credentials in some states, GED test passers must meet additional state requirements (e.g., complete an approved course in civics or government).
[5] Includes other jurisdictions, such as Puerto Rico, Guam, and American Samoa.

[6] For 1988 and prior years, 19-year-olds are included with the 16- to 18-year-olds instead of the 19- to 24-year-olds.
[7] A revised GED test was introduced in 2002. In 2001, test takers were required to successfully complete all five components of the GED or else begin the five-part series again with the new test that was introduced in 2002.
NOTE: Data are for the United States only and exclude other jurisdictions, except where noted. Detail may not sum to totals because of rounding.
SOURCE: American Council on Education, General Educational Development Testing Service, the GED annual *Statistical Report*, 1971 through 1992; *Who Took the GED?* 1993 through 2001; *Who Passed the GED Tests?* 2002 through 2005; and *GED Testing Program Statistical Report*, 2006 through 2010. Retrieved July 15, 2011, from http://www.acenet.edu/Content/NavigationMenu/ged/pubs/GED_ASR_2010.pdf. (This table was prepared July 2011.)

Percentage of high school dropouts among persons 16 through 24 years old (status dropout rate), by sex and race/ethnicity: Selected years, 1960 through 2010

Year	Total status dropout rate				Male status dropout rate				Female status dropout rate			
	All races[1]	White	Black	Hispanic	All races[1]	White	Black	Hispanic	All races[1]	White	Black	Hispanic
1	2	3	4	5	6	7	8	9	10	11	12	13
1960[2]	27.2 (—)	— (†)	— (†)	— (†)	27.8 (—)	— (†)	— (†)	— (†)	26.7 (—)	— (†)	— (†)	— (†)
1967[3]	17.0 (—)	15.4 (—)	28.6 (—)	— (†)	16.5 (—)	14.7 (—)	30.6 (—)	— (†)	17.3 (—)	16.1 (—)	26.9 (—)	— (†)
1968[3]	16.2 (—)	14.7 (—)	27.4 (—)	— (†)	15.8 (—)	14.4 (—)	27.1 (—)	— (†)	16.5 (—)	15.0 (—)	27.6 (—)	— (†)
1969[3]	15.2 (—)	13.6 (—)	26.7 (—)	— (†)	14.3 (—)	12.6 (—)	26.9 (—)	— (†)	16.0 (—)	14.6 (—)	26.7 (—)	— (†)
1970[3]	15.0 (0.29)	13.2 (0.30)	27.9 (1.22)	— (†)	14.2 (0.42)	12.2 (0.42)	29.4 (1.82)	— (†)	15.7 (0.41)	14.1 (0.42)	26.6 (1.65)	— (†)
1971[3]	14.7 (0.28)	13.4 (0.29)	24.0 (1.14)	— (†)	14.2 (0.41)	12.6 (0.41)	25.5 (1.70)	— (†)	15.2 (0.40)	14.2 (0.42)	22.6 (1.54)	— (†)
1972	14.6 (0.28)	12.3 (0.29)	21.3 (1.07)	34.3 (2.22)	14.1 (0.40)	11.6 (0.40)	22.3 (1.59)	33.7 (3.23)	15.1 (0.39)	12.8 (0.41)	20.5 (1.44)	34.8 (3.05)
1973	14.1 (0.27)	11.6 (0.28)	22.2 (1.06)	33.5 (2.24)	13.7 (0.38)	11.5 (0.39)	21.5 (1.53)	30.4 (3.16)	14.5 (0.38)	11.8 (0.39)	22.8 (1.47)	36.4 (3.16)
1974	14.3 (0.27)	11.9 (0.28)	21.2 (1.05)	33.0 (2.08)	14.2 (0.39)	12.0 (0.40)	20.1 (1.51)	33.8 (2.99)	14.3 (0.38)	11.8 (0.39)	22.1 (1.45)	32.2 (2.90)
1975	13.9 (0.27)	11.4 (0.27)	22.9 (1.06)	29.2 (2.02)	13.3 (0.37)	11.0 (0.38)	23.0 (1.56)	26.7 (2.84)	14.5 (0.38)	11.8 (0.39)	22.9 (1.44)	31.6 (2.86)
1976	14.1 (0.27)	12.0 (0.28)	20.5 (1.00)	31.4 (2.01)	14.1 (0.38)	12.1 (0.39)	21.2 (1.49)	30.3 (2.94)	14.2 (0.37)	11.8 (0.39)	19.9 (1.35)	32.3 (2.76)
1977	14.1 (0.27)	11.9 (0.28)	19.8 (0.99)	33.0 (2.02)	14.5 (0.38)	12.6 (0.40)	19.5 (1.45)	31.6 (2.89)	13.8 (0.37)	11.2 (0.38)	20.0 (1.36)	34.3 (2.83)
1978	14.2 (0.27)	11.9 (0.28)	20.2 (1.00)	33.3 (2.00)	14.6 (0.38)	12.2 (0.40)	22.5 (1.52)	33.6 (2.88)	13.9 (0.37)	11.6 (0.39)	18.3 (1.31)	33.1 (2.78)
1979	14.6 (0.27)	12.0 (0.28)	21.1 (1.01)	33.8 (1.98)	15.0 (0.39)	12.6 (0.40)	22.4 (1.52)	33.0 (2.83)	14.2 (0.37)	11.5 (0.38)	20.0 (1.35)	34.5 (2.77)
1980	14.1 (0.26)	11.4 (0.27)	19.1 (0.97)	35.2 (1.89)	15.1 (0.39)	12.3 (0.40)	20.8 (1.47)	37.2 (2.72)	13.1 (0.36)	10.5 (0.37)	17.7 (1.28)	33.2 (2.61)
1981	13.9 (0.26)	11.3 (0.27)	18.4 (0.93)	33.2 (1.80)	15.1 (0.38)	12.5 (0.40)	19.9 (1.40)	36.0 (2.61)	12.8 (0.35)	10.2 (0.36)	17.1 (1.24)	30.4 (2.48)
1982	13.9 (0.27)	11.4 (0.29)	18.4 (0.97)	31.7 (1.93)	14.5 (0.40)	12.0 (0.42)	21.2 (1.50)	30.5 (2.73)	13.3 (0.38)	10.8 (0.40)	15.9 (1.26)	32.8 (2.71)
1983	13.7 (0.27)	11.1 (0.29)	18.0 (0.97)	31.6 (1.93)	14.9 (0.41)	12.2 (0.43)	19.9 (1.46)	34.3 (2.84)	12.5 (0.37)	10.1 (0.39)	16.2 (1.28)	29.1 (2.61)
1984	13.1 (0.27)	11.0 (0.29)	15.5 (0.91)	29.8 (1.91)	14.0 (0.40)	11.9 (0.43)	16.8 (1.37)	30.6 (2.78)	12.3 (0.37)	10.1 (0.39)	14.3 (1.22)	29.0 (2.63)
1985	12.6 (0.27)	10.4 (0.29)	15.2 (0.92)	27.6 (1.93)	13.4 (0.40)	11.1 (0.42)	16.1 (1.37)	29.9 (2.76)	11.8 (0.37)	9.8 (0.39)	14.3 (1.23)	25.2 (2.68)
1986	12.2 (0.27)	9.7 (0.28)	14.2 (0.90)	30.1 (1.88)	13.1 (0.40)	10.3 (0.42)	15.0 (1.33)	32.8 (2.66)	11.4 (0.37)	9.1 (0.39)	13.5 (1.21)	27.2 (2.63)
1987	12.6 (0.28)	10.4 (0.30)	14.1 (0.90)	28.6 (1.84)	13.2 (0.40)	10.8 (0.43)	15.0 (1.35)	29.1 (2.57)	12.1 (0.38)	10.0 (0.41)	13.3 (1.21)	28.1 (2.64)
1988	12.9 (0.30)	9.6 (0.31)	14.5 (1.00)	35.8 (2.30)	13.5 (0.44)	10.3 (0.46)	15.0 (1.48)	36.0 (3.19)	12.2 (0.42)	8.9 (0.43)	14.0 (1.36)	35.4 (3.31)
1989	12.6 (0.31)	9.4 (0.32)	13.9 (0.98)	33.0 (2.19)	13.6 (0.45)	10.3 (0.47)	14.9 (1.46)	34.4 (3.08)	11.7 (0.42)	8.5 (0.43)	13.0 (1.32)	31.6 (3.11)
1990	12.1 (0.29)	9.0 (0.30)	13.2 (0.94)	32.4 (1.91)	12.3 (0.42)	9.3 (0.44)	11.9 (1.30)	34.3 (2.71)	11.8 (0.41)	8.7 (0.42)	14.4 (1.34)	30.3 (2.70)
1991	12.5 (0.30)	8.9 (0.31)	13.6 (0.95)	35.3 (1.93)	13.0 (0.43)	8.9 (0.44)	13.5 (1.37)	39.2 (2.74)	11.9 (0.41)	8.9 (0.43)	13.7 (1.31)	31.1 (2.70)
1992[4]	11.0 (0.28)	7.7 (0.29)	13.7 (0.95)	29.4 (1.86)	11.3 (0.41)	8.0 (0.42)	12.5 (1.32)	32.1 (2.67)	10.7 (0.39)	7.4 (0.40)	14.8 (1.36)	26.6 (2.56)
1993[4]	11.0 (0.28)	7.9 (0.29)	13.6 (0.94)	27.5 (1.79)	11.2 (0.40)	8.2 (0.42)	12.6 (1.32)	28.1 (2.54)	10.9 (0.40)	7.6 (0.41)	14.4 (1.34)	26.9 (2.52)
1994[4]	11.4 (0.26)	7.7 (0.27)	12.6 (0.75)	30.0 (1.16)	12.3 (0.38)	8.0 (0.38)	14.1 (1.14)	31.6 (1.60)	10.6 (0.36)	7.5 (0.37)	11.3 (0.99)	28.1 (1.66)
1995[4]	12.0 (0.27)	8.6 (0.28)	12.1 (0.74)	30.0 (1.15)	12.2 (0.38)	9.0 (0.40)	11.1 (1.05)	30.0 (1.59)	11.7 (0.37)	8.2 (0.39)	12.9 (1.05)	30.0 (1.66)
1996[4]	11.1 (0.27)	7.3 (0.27)	13.0 (0.80)	29.4 (1.19)	11.4 (0.38)	7.3 (0.38)	13.5 (1.18)	30.3 (1.67)	10.9 (0.38)	7.3 (0.39)	12.5 (1.08)	28.3 (1.69)
1997[4]	11.0 (0.27)	7.6 (0.28)	13.4 (0.80)	25.3 (1.11)	11.9 (0.39)	8.5 (0.41)	13.3 (1.16)	27.0 (1.55)	10.1 (0.36)	6.7 (0.37)	13.5 (1.11)	23.4 (1.59)
1998[4]	11.8 (0.27)	7.7 (0.28)	13.8 (0.81)	29.5 (1.12)	13.3 (0.40)	8.6 (0.41)	15.5 (1.24)	33.5 (1.59)	10.3 (0.36)	6.9 (0.37)	12.2 (1.05)	25.0 (1.56)
1999[4]	11.2 (0.26)	7.3 (0.27)	12.6 (0.77)	28.6 (1.11)	11.9 (0.38)	7.7 (0.39)	12.1 (1.10)	31.0 (1.58)	10.5 (0.36)	6.9 (0.37)	13.0 (1.08)	26.0 (1.54)
2000[4]	10.9 (0.26)	6.9 (0.26)	13.1 (0.78)	27.8 (1.08)	12.0 (0.38)	7.0 (0.37)	15.3 (1.20)	31.8 (1.56)	9.9 (0.35)	6.9 (0.37)	11.1 (1.00)	23.5 (1.48)
2001[4]	10.7 (0.25)	7.3 (0.26)	10.9 (0.71)	27.0 (1.06)	12.2 (0.38)	7.9 (0.39)	13.0 (1.12)	31.6 (1.55)	9.3 (0.34)	6.7 (0.36)	9.0 (0.90)	22.1 (1.42)
2002[4]	10.5 (0.24)	6.5 (0.24)	11.3 (0.70)	25.7 (0.93)	11.8 (0.35)	6.7 (0.35)	12.8 (1.07)	29.6 (1.32)	9.2 (0.32)	6.3 (0.34)	9.9 (0.91)	21.2 (1.27)
2003[4,5]	9.9 (0.23)	6.3 (0.24)	10.9 (0.69)	23.5 (0.90)	11.3 (0.34)	7.1 (0.35)	12.5 (1.05)	26.7 (1.29)	8.4 (0.30)	5.6 (0.32)	9.5 (0.89)	20.1 (1.23)
2004[4,5]	10.3 (0.23)	6.8 (0.24)	11.8 (0.70)	23.8 (0.89)	11.6 (0.34)	7.1 (0.35)	13.5 (1.08)	28.5 (1.30)	9.0 (0.31)	6.4 (0.34)	10.2 (0.92)	18.5 (1.18)
2005[4,5]	9.4 (0.22)	6.0 (0.23)	10.4 (0.66)	22.4 (0.87)	10.8 (0.33)	6.6 (0.34)	12.0 (1.02)	26.4 (1.26)	8.0 (0.29)	5.3 (0.31)	9.0 (0.86)	18.1 (1.16)
2006[4,5]	9.3 (0.22)	5.8 (0.23)	10.7 (0.66)	22.1 (0.86)	10.3 (0.33)	6.4 (0.33)	9.7 (0.91)	25.7 (1.25)	8.3 (0.30)	5.3 (0.31)	11.7 (0.96)	18.1 (1.15)
2007[4,5]	8.7 (0.21)	5.3 (0.22)	8.4 (0.59)	21.4 (0.83)	9.8 (0.32)	6.0 (0.32)	8.0 (0.82)	24.7 (1.22)	7.7 (0.29)	4.5 (0.28)	8.8 (0.84)	18.0 (1.13)
2008[4,5]	8.0 (0.20)	4.8 (0.21)	9.9 (0.63)	18.3 (0.78)	8.5 (0.30)	5.4 (0.30)	8.7 (0.85)	19.9 (1.12)	7.5 (0.28)	4.2 (0.28)	11.1 (0.93)	16.7 (1.08)
2009[4,5]	8.1 (0.20)	5.2 (0.21)	9.3 (0.61)	17.6 (0.76)	9.1 (0.31)	6.3 (0.33)	10.6 (0.93)	19.0 (1.10)	7.0 (0.27)	4.1 (0.27)	8.1 (0.80)	16.1 (1.06)
2010[4,5,6]	7.4 (0.27)	5.1 (0.30)	8.0 (0.76)	15.1 (0.87)	8.5 (0.40)	5.9 (0.42)	9.5 (1.11)	17.3 (1.24)	6.3 (0.28)	4.2 (0.35)	6.7 (0.85)	12.8 (0.97)

—Not available.
†Not applicable.
[1]Includes other racial/ethnic categories not separately shown.
[2]Based on the April 1960 decennial census.
[3]White and Black include persons of Hispanic ethnicity.
[4]Because of changes in data collection procedures, data may not be comparable with figures for years prior to 1992.
[5]White and Black exclude persons identifying themselves as two or more races.
[6]Beginning in 2010, standard errors were computed using replicate weights, which produced more precise values than the methodology used in prior years. For more information, see Appendix A: Guide to Sources.

NOTE: "Status" dropouts are 16- to 24-year-olds who are not enrolled in school and who have not completed a high school program, regardless of when they left school. People who have received GED credentials are counted as high school completers. All data except for 1960 are based on October counts. Data are based on sample surveys of the civilian noninstitutionalized population, which excludes persons in prisons, the military, and other persons not living in households. Race categories exclude persons of Hispanic ethnicity except where otherwise noted. Standard errors appear in parentheses.
SOURCE: U.S. Department of Commerce, Census Bureau, Current Population Survey (CPS), October 1967 through October 2010. (This table was prepared July 2011.)

Percentage of high school dropouts among persons 16 through 24 years old (status dropout rate), by income level, and percentage distribution of status dropouts, by labor force status and educational attainment: 1970 through 2010

Year	Status dropout rate	Status dropout rate, by family income quartile				Percentage distribution of status dropouts, by labor force status				Percentage distribution of status dropouts, by years of school completed				
		Lowest quartile	Middle low quartile	Middle high quartile	Highest quartile	Total	Employed[1]	Unemployed	Not in labor force	Total	Less than 9 years	9 years	10 years	11 or 12 years
1	2	3	4	5	6	7	8	9	10	11	12	13	14	15
1970	15.0 (0.29)	28.0 (0.92)	21.2 (0.65)	11.7 (0.50)	5.2 (0.34)	100.0 (†)	49.8 (1.06)	10.3 (0.65)	39.9 (1.04)	100.0 (†)	28.5 (0.96)	20.6 (0.86)	26.8 (0.94)	24.0 (0.91)
1971	14.7 (0.28)	28.8 (0.90)	20.7 (0.63)	10.9 (0.49)	5.1 (0.32)	100.0 (†)	49.5 (1.05)	10.9 (0.65)	39.6 (1.02)	100.0 (†)	27.9 (0.94)	21.7 (0.86)	27.8 (0.94)	22.7 (0.88)
1972	14.6 (0.28)	27.6 (0.85)	20.8 (0.62)	10.2 (0.46)	5.4 (0.33)	100.0 (†)	51.2 (1.03)	10.2 (0.63)	38.6 (1.01)	100.0 (†)	27.5 (0.92)	20.8 (0.84)	29.0 (0.94)	22.7 (0.87)
1973	14.1 (0.27)	28.0 (0.85)	19.6 (0.60)	9.9 (0.45)	4.9 (0.31)	100.0 (†)	53.2 (1.04)	9.2 (0.60)	37.5 (1.01)	100.0 (†)	26.5 (0.92)	20.9 (0.84)	27.4 (0.93)	25.3 (0.90)
1974	14.3 (0.27)	— (†)	— (†)	— (†)	— (†)	100.0 (†)	51.8 (1.02)	12.3 (0.67)	35.9 (0.98)	100.0 (†)	25.4 (0.89)	20.1 (0.82)	28.7 (0.93)	25.8 (0.90)
1975	13.9 (0.27)	28.8 (0.82)	18.0 (0.58)	10.2 (0.45)	5.0 (0.30)	100.0 (†)	46.0 (1.02)	15.6 (0.74)	38.4 (1.00)	100.0 (†)	23.5 (0.87)	21.1 (0.84)	27.5 (0.92)	27.9 (0.92)
1976	14.1 (0.27)	28.1 (0.79)	19.2 (0.60)	10.1 (0.45)	4.9 (0.29)	100.0 (†)	48.8 (1.01)	16.0 (0.74)	35.2 (0.97)	100.0 (†)	24.3 (0.87)	20.1 (0.81)	27.8 (0.91)	27.8 (0.91)
1977	14.1 (0.27)	28.5 (0.80)	19.0 (0.60)	10.4 (0.46)	4.5 (0.29)	100.0 (†)	52.9 (1.02)	13.6 (0.70)	33.6 (0.96)	100.0 (†)	24.3 (0.87)	21.7 (0.84)	27.3 (0.91)	26.6 (0.90)
1978	14.2 (0.27)	28.2 (0.80)	18.9 (0.60)	10.5 (0.46)	5.5 (0.31)	100.0 (†)	54.3 (1.01)	12.4 (0.67)	33.3 (0.95)	100.0 (†)	22.9 (0.85)	20.2 (0.81)	28.2 (0.91)	28.8 (0.91)
1979	14.6 (0.27)	28.1 (0.79)	18.5 (0.60)	11.5 (0.47)	5.6 (0.32)	100.0 (†)	54.0 (0.99)	12.7 (0.66)	33.3 (0.94)	100.0 (†)	22.6 (0.83)	21.0 (0.81)	28.6 (0.90)	27.8 (0.89)
1980	14.1 (0.26)	27.0 (0.77)	18.1 (0.60)	10.7 (0.46)	5.7 (0.32)	100.0 (†)	50.4 (1.01)	17.0 (0.76)	32.6 (0.95)	100.0 (†)	23.6 (0.86)	19.7 (0.80)	29.8 (0.93)	27.0 (0.90)
1981	13.9 (0.26)	26.4 (0.75)	17.8 (0.57)	11.1 (0.47)	5.2 (0.30)	100.0 (†)	49.8 (1.01)	18.3 (0.78)	31.9 (0.94)	100.0 (†)	24.3 (0.86)	18.6 (0.78)	30.2 (0.92)	26.9 (0.89)
1982	13.9 (0.27)	27.2 (0.78)	18.3 (0.63)	10.2 (0.48)	4.4 (0.29)	100.0 (†)	45.2 (1.06)	21.1 (0.87)	33.7 (1.01)	100.0 (†)	22.9 (0.90)	20.8 (0.87)	28.8 (0.96)	27.6 (0.95)
1983	13.7 (0.27)	26.5 (0.77)	17.8 (0.62)	10.5 (0.50)	4.1 (0.29)	100.0 (†)	48.4 (1.08)	18.2 (0.83)	33.4 (1.02)	100.0 (†)	23.0 (0.91)	19.3 (0.85)	28.8 (0.98)	28.8 (0.98)
1984	13.1 (0.27)	25.9 (0.76)	16.5 (0.61)	9.9 (0.48)	3.8 (0.29)	100.0 (†)	49.7 (1.11)	17.3 (0.84)	32.9 (1.05)	100.0 (†)	23.6 (0.95)	21.4 (0.91)	27.5 (1.00)	27.5 (0.99)
1985	12.6 (0.27)	27.1 (0.78)	14.7 (0.60)	8.3 (0.46)	4.0 (0.29)	100.0 (†)	50.1 (1.15)	17.5 (0.88)	32.4 (1.08)	100.0 (†)	23.9 (0.98)	21.0 (0.94)	27.9 (1.03)	27.2 (1.03)
1986	12.2 (0.27)	25.4 (0.75)	14.8 (0.60)	8.0 (0.45)	3.4 (0.28)	100.0 (†)	51.1 (1.18)	16.4 (0.87)	32.5 (1.10)	100.0 (†)	25.4 (1.03)	21.5 (0.97)	25.7 (1.03)	27.4 (1.05)
1987	12.6 (0.28)	25.5 (0.76)	16.6 (0.63)	8.0 (0.46)	3.6 (0.28)	100.0 (†)	52.4 (1.16)	13.6 (0.80)	34.0 (1.10)	100.0 (†)	25.9 (1.02)	20.7 (0.94)	26.0 (1.02)	27.5 (1.04)
1988	12.9 (0.30)	27.2 (0.85)	15.4 (0.68)	8.2 (0.51)	3.4 (0.30)	100.0 (†)	52.9 (1.27)	‡ (†)	‡ (†)	100.0 (†)	28.9 (1.15)	19.3 (1.00)	25.1 (1.10)	26.8 (1.12)
1989	12.6 (0.31)	25.0 (0.84)	16.2 (0.71)	8.7 (0.52)	3.3 (0.31)	100.0 (†)	53.2 (1.30)	13.8 (0.90)	33.0 (1.22)	100.0 (†)	29.4 (1.18)	20.8 (1.05)	24.9 (1.12)	25.0 (1.13)
1990	12.1 (0.29)	24.3 (0.82)	15.1 (0.65)	8.7 (0.51)	2.9 (0.28)	100.0 (†)	52.5 (1.29)	13.3 (0.88)	34.2 (1.23)	100.0 (†)	28.6 (1.17)	20.9 (1.05)	24.4 (1.11)	26.1 (1.14)
1991	12.5 (0.30)	25.9 (0.83)	15.5 (0.66)	7.7 (0.49)	3.0 (0.29)	100.0 (†)	47.5 (1.28)	15.8 (0.93)	36.7 (1.23)	100.0 (†)	28.6 (1.15)	20.5 (1.03)	26.1 (1.12)	24.9 (1.10)
1992[2]	11.0 (0.28)	23.4 (0.79)	12.9 (0.62)	7.3 (0.48)	2.4 (0.26)	100.0 (†)	47.6 (1.36)	15.0 (0.97)	37.4 (1.32)	100.0 (†)	21.6 (1.12)	17.5 (1.04)	24.4 (1.17)	36.5 (1.31)
1993[2]	11.0 (0.28)	22.9 (0.80)	12.7 (0.62)	6.6 (0.46)	2.9 (0.26)	100.0 (†)	48.7 (1.37)	12.8 (0.91)	38.5 (1.33)	100.0 (†)	20.5 (1.10)	16.6 (1.02)	24.1 (1.17)	38.8 (1.33)
1994[2]	11.4 (0.26)	20.7 (0.71)	13.7 (0.58)	8.7 (0.45)	4.9 (0.33)	100.0 (†)	49.5 (1.21)	13.0 (0.81)	37.5 (1.17)	100.0 (†)	23.9 (1.18)	16.2 (0.89)	20.3 (0.97)	39.6 (1.18)
1995[2]	12.0 (0.27)	23.2 (0.69)	13.8 (0.59)	8.3 (0.46)	3.6 (0.29)	100.0 (†)	48.9 (1.19)	14.2 (0.83)	37.0 (1.14)	100.0 (†)	22.2 (0.99)	17.0 (0.89)	22.5 (1.06)	38.3 (1.15)
1996[2]	11.1 (0.27)	22.0 (0.72)	13.6 (0.60)	7.0 (0.45)	3.2 (0.28)	100.0 (†)	47.3 (1.28)	15.0 (0.91)	37.7 (1.24)	100.0 (†)	20.3 (1.03)	17.7 (0.98)	22.6 (1.07)	39.4 (1.25)
1997[2]	11.0 (0.27)	21.8 (0.71)	13.5 (0.59)	6.2 (0.42)	3.4 (0.29)	100.0 (†)	53.3 (1.22)	13.2 (0.86)	33.5 (1.21)	100.0 (†)	19.9 (1.02)	15.7 (0.93)	22.3 (1.06)	42.1 (1.26)
1998[2]	11.8 (0.27)	22.3 (0.71)	14.9 (0.62)	7.7 (0.45)	3.5 (0.29)	100.0 (†)	55.1 (1.22)	10.3 (0.74)	34.6 (1.17)	100.0 (†)	21.0 (1.00)	14.9 (0.87)	21.4 (1.01)	42.6 (1.21)
1999[2]	11.2 (0.26)	21.0 (0.70)	14.3 (0.60)	7.4 (0.44)	3.9 (0.30)	100.0 (†)	55.6 (1.24)	10.0 (0.75)	34.4 (1.18)	100.0 (†)	22.2 (1.03)	16.3 (0.92)	22.5 (1.04)	39.0 (1.21)
2000[2]	10.9 (0.26)	20.7 (0.70)	12.8 (0.56)	8.3 (0.46)	3.5 (0.29)	100.0 (†)	56.9 (1.24)	12.3 (0.82)	30.8 (1.16)	100.0 (†)	21.5 (1.03)	15.3 (0.90)	23.1 (1.06)	40.0 (1.23)
2001[2]	10.7 (0.25)	19.3 (0.68)	13.4 (0.57)	9.0 (0.47)	3.2 (0.27)	100.0 (†)	58.3 (1.24)	14.8 (0.89)	26.9 (1.11)	100.0 (†)	18.4 (0.97)	16.8 (0.94)	23.8 (1.07)	40.9 (1.23)
2002[2]	10.5 (0.24)	18.8 (0.62)	12.3 (0.53)	8.4 (0.43)	3.8 (0.28)	100.0 (†)	57.4 (1.18)	13.3 (0.81)	29.2 (1.09)	100.0 (†)	22.8 (1.00)	17.1 (0.90)	21.3 (0.98)	38.9 (1.17)
2003[2]	9.9 (0.23)	19.5 (0.64)	10.8 (0.49)	7.3 (0.40)	3.4 (0.26)	100.0 (†)	53.5 (1.22)	13.7 (0.84)	32.9 (1.15)	100.0 (†)	21.2 (1.00)	18.2 (0.94)	20.7 (0.99)	40.0 (1.20)
2004[2]	10.3 (0.23)	18.0 (0.60)	12.7 (0.52)	8.2 (0.42)	3.7 (0.27)	100.0 (†)	53.0 (1.19)	14.3 (0.83)	32.7 (1.12)	100.0 (†)	21.4 (0.97)	15.9 (0.87)	22.5 (0.99)	40.3 (1.17)
2005[2]	9.4 (0.22)	17.9 (0.60)	11.5 (0.51)	7.1 (0.39)	2.7 (0.23)	100.0 (†)	56.9 (1.23)	11.9 (0.80)	31.2 (1.15)	100.0 (†)	18.9 (0.97)	16.8 (0.93)	21.4 (1.02)	42.9 (1.23)
2006[2]	9.3 (0.22)	16.5 (0.58)	12.1 (0.51)	6.3 (0.37)	3.8 (0.27)	100.0 (†)	56.4 (1.23)	11.7 (0.80)	32.0 (1.16)	100.0 (†)	22.1 (1.03)	13.4 (0.85)	20.7 (1.01)	43.9 (1.23)
2007[2]	8.7 (0.21)	16.7 (0.59)	10.5 (0.48)	6.4 (0.36)	3.2 (0.25)	100.0 (†)	55.5 (1.27)	11.2 (0.80)	33.3 (1.20)	100.0 (†)	21.2 (1.04)	16.9 (0.96)	22.9 (1.07)	39.0 (1.24)
2008[2]	8.0 (0.20)	16.4 (0.58)	9.4 (0.45)	5.4 (0.34)	2.2 (0.21)	100.0 (†)	46.8 (1.33)	16.3 (0.98)	36.9 (1.28)	100.0 (†)	18.4 (1.03)	15.2 (0.96)	23.8 (1.13)	42.6 (1.32)
2009[2]	8.1 (0.20)	15.8 (0.57)	9.7 (0.45)	5.4 (0.34)	2.5 (0.22)	100.0 (†)	43.2 (1.31)	19.9 (1.06)	36.9 (1.28)	100.0 (†)	17.7 (1.01)	13.6 (0.91)	24.4 (1.14)	44.3 (1.32)
2010[2,3]	7.4 (0.27)	13.8 (0.83)	8.9 (0.54)	5.1 (0.48)	2.5 (0.31)	100.0 (†)	45.8 (1.64)	18.7 (1.38)	35.5 (1.70)	100.0 (†)	19.2 (1.48)	13.1 (1.07)	22.5 (1.59)	45.2 (1.89)

—Not available.
†Not applicable.
‡Reporting standards not met.
[1]Includes persons employed, but not currently working.
[2]Because of changes in data collection procedures, data may not be comparable with figures for years prior to 1992.
[3]Beginning in 2010, standard errors were computed using replicate weights, which produced more precise values than the methodology used in prior years. For more information, see Appendix A: Guide to Sources.

NOTE: "Status" dropouts are 16- to 24-year-olds who are not enrolled in school and who have not completed a high school program, regardless of when they left school. People who have received GED credentials are counted as high school completers. Data are based on sample surveys of the civilian noninstitutional population, which excludes persons in prisons, persons in the military, and other persons not living in households. Detail may not sum to totals because of rounding. Standard errors appear in parentheses
SOURCE: U.S. Department of Commerce, Census Bureau, Current Population Survey (CPS), October 1970 through October 2010. (This table was prepared July 2011.)

Number of 14- through 21-year-old students served under Individuals with Disabilities Education Act, Part B, who exited school, by exit reason, age, and type of disability: 2007–08 and 2008–09

Age and type of disability	Total	Exiting school					Transferred to regular education[3]	Moved, known to be continuing[4]
		Graduated with diploma	Received a certificate of attendance	Reached maximum age[1]	Dropped out[2]	Died		
1	2	3	4	5	6	7	8	9
2007–08								
Total............................	366,964	216,738	53,092	5,622	89,999	1,513	51,087	211,924
Age								
14..........................	3,598	3	9	†	3,385	201	13,015	43,003
15..........................	7,915	24	32	†	7,588	271	11,691	47,908
16..........................	20,170	1,881	625	†	17,365	299	11,559	49,587
17..........................	135,299	92,434	15,862	†	26,711	292	9,674	41,311
18..........................	136,144	90,836	20,995	980	23,100	233	3,881	21,760
19..........................	40,174	22,905	8,222	515	8,429	103	885	5,958
20..........................	14,139	5,955	4,266	1,240	2,604	74	262	1,738
21..........................	9,525	2,700	3,081	2,887	817	40	120	659
Type of disability								
Autism........................	7,188	4,544	1,722	398	499	25	544	2,853
Deaf-blindness.............	89	52	18	8	8	3	9	43
Emotional disturbance..........	42,469	19,385	3,971	580	18,385	148	5,189	44,148
Hearing impairments.........	4,183	2,913	733	64	464	9	534	1,785
Intellectual disability..........	41,604	15,643	14,811	1,955	8,908	287	1,713	19,574
Multiple disabilities...........	8,198	3,745	2,095	651	1,442	265	236	4,146
Orthopedic impairments........	3,327	2,060	603	142	437	85	371	1,260
Other health impairments[5]........	38,535	25,635	3,831	234	8,618	217	7,224	22,073
Specific learning disabilities..........	208,380	133,985	23,645	1,460	48,891	399	27,338	108,668
Speech or language impairments........	9,270	6,183	1,140	32	1,879	36	7,651	6,076
Traumatic brain injury............	2,256	1,464	371	65	328	28	119	810
Visual impairments.............	1,465	1,129	152	33	140	11	159	488
2008–09								
Total............................	407,441	246,990	61,486	6,107	91,198	1,660	66,211	218,964
Age								
14..........................	3,658	40	17	†	3,366	235	16,937	42,164
15..........................	7,784	88	36	†	7,394	266	14,867	48,895
16..........................	22,057	3,062	932	†	17,747	316	14,188	50,699
17..........................	151,382	105,331	18,505	†	27,202	344	12,446	43,532
18..........................	152,942	104,261	24,337	882	23,230	232	5,815	23,990
19..........................	42,767	24,113	9,282	498	8,738	136	1,336	6,809
20..........................	15,626	6,643	4,714	1,427	2,754	88	452	2,112
21..........................	11,225	3,452	3,663	3,300	767	43	170	763
Type of disability								
Autism........................	9,892	6,374	2,390	488	609	31	1,017	3,570
Deaf-blindness.............	77	49	8	10	7	3	4	27
Emotional disturbance..........	45,813	21,729	4,769	565	18,587	163	7,061	44,841
Hearing impairments.........	4,893	3,510	785	75	515	8	736	1,876
Intellectual disability..........	42,908	16,606	15,313	2,204	8,500	285	2,021	19,498
Multiple disabilities...........	8,916	4,286	2,299	705	1,323	303	316	4,052
Orthopedic impairments........	3,807	2,330	706	146	520	105	472	1,334
Other health impairments[5]........	46,422	31,248	5,204	282	9,460	228	9,519	23,741
Specific learning disabilities..........	230,461	151,016	28,190	1,473	49,294	488	35,365	112,511
Speech or language impairments........	10,085	6,887	1,236	44	1,895	23	9,326	6,099
Traumatic brain injury............	2,416	1,641	363	76	320	16	147	810
Visual impairments.............	1,751	1,314	223	39	168	7	227	605

†Not applicable.

[1]Students may exit special education services due to maximum age beginning at age 18 depending on state law or practice or order of any court.

[2]"Dropped out" is defined as the total who were enrolled at some point in the reporting year, were not enrolled at the end of the reporting year, and did not exit for any of the other reasons described. Includes students previously categorized as "moved, not known to continue."

[3]"Transferred to regular education" was previously labeled "no longer receives special education."

[4]"Moved, known to be continuing" is the total number of students who moved out of the administrative area or transferred to another district and are known to be continuing in an educational program.

[5]Other health impairments include having limited strength, vitality, or alertness due to chronic or acute health problems such as a heart condition, tuberculosis, rheumatic fever, nephritis, asthma, sickle cell anemia, hemophilia, epilepsy, lead poisoning, leukemia, or diabetes.

NOTE: Data are for the 50 states, the District of Columbia, and the Bureau of Indian Education schools.

SOURCE: U.S. Department of Education, Office of Special Education Programs, Individuals with Disabilities Education Act (IDEA) database. Retrieved September 19, 2011, from https://www.ideadata.org/DACAnalyticTool/Intro_2.asp. (This table was prepared September 2011.)

Number and percentage distribution of private elementary and secondary students, teachers, and schools, by orientation of school and selected school and student characteristics: Fall 1999, fall 2007, and fall 2009

Selected school and student characteristics	Fall 1999, total number	Fall 2007, total number	Fall 2009 Total Number	Percent	Catholic Number	Percent	Other religious Number	Percent	Nonsectarian Number	Percent
1	2	3	4	5	6	7	8	9	10	11
Students[1]										
Total................	6,018,280 (30,179)	5,910,210 (28,363)	5,488,490 (35,857)	100.0 (†)	2,160,220 (3,494)	100.0 (†)	2,076,220 (32,751)	100.0 (†)	1,252,050 (8,849)	100.0 (†)
Level of school										
Elementary............	3,595,020 (11,516)	3,228,310 (17,116)	2,937,090 (26,807)	53.5 (0.24)	1,454,540 (3,244)	67.3 (0.17)	883,640 (24,501)	42.6 (0.67)	598,910 (6,684)	47.8 (0.27)
Secondary.............	806,640 (2,395)	827,390 (10,804)	785,810 (4,810)	14.3 (0.11)	587,350 (4,408)	27.2 (0.18)	106,880 (1,871)	5.1 (0.09)	91,580 (907)	7.3 (0.06)
Combined.............	1,616,620 (23,949)	1,854,510 (19,370)	1,765,590 (15,909)	32.2 (0.21)	118,330 (250)	5.5 (0.01)	1,085,700 (15,429)	52.3 (0.64)	561,560 (3,495)	44.9 (0.25)
School enrollment										
Less than 50	238,980 (5,691)	260,030 (7,147)	296,000 (22,889)	5.4 (0.39)	6,800 (550)	0.3 (0.03)	170,890 (21,993)	8.2 (0.96)	118,320 (4,552)	9.5 (0.34)
50 to 149	939,110 (10,717)	982,810 (13,267)	950,050 (12,053)	17.3 (0.18)	148,240 (1,003)	6.9 (0.04)	448,670 (8,484)	21.6 (0.35)	353,140 (5,440)	28.2 (0.35)
150 to 299	1,615,970 (7,315)	1,535,540 (13,069)	1,423,220 (9,951)	25.9 (0.17)	638,300 (808)	29.5 (0.05)	518,820 (8,930)	25.0 (0.44)	266,110 (3,949)	21.3 (0.25)
300 to 499	1,419,360 (13,203)	1,254,690 (4,667)	1,154,950 (10,730)	21.0 (0.19)	577,950 (3,534)	26.8 (0.12)	377,020 (9,656)	18.2 (0.44)	199,980 (3,066)	16.0 (0.24)
500 to 749	917,670 (2,330)	860,950 (4,374)	768,540 (†)	14.0 (0.09)	412,610 (†)	19.1 (0.03)	233,810 (†)	11.3 (0.18)	122,130 (†)	9.8 (0.07)
750 or more............	887,190 (18,232)	1,016,180 (16,638)	895,720 (6,538)	16.3 (0.12)	376,330 (†)	17.4 (0.03)	327,020 (6,538)	15.8 (0.30)	192,370 (†)	15.4 (0.11)
Student race/ethnicity[2]										
White....................	4,061,870 (24,242)	3,779,030 (22,170)	3,410,360 (31,067)	72.6 (0.20)	1,423,200 (3,216)	70.8 (0.05)	1,337,600 (30,282)	76.3 (0.41)	649,560 (3,480)	69.2 (0.34)
Black....................	494,530 (5,079)	496,580 (4,455)	430,970 (2,579)	9.2 (0.07)	151,300 (76)	7.5 (0.01)	180,090 (1,594)	10.3 (0.19)	99,580 (1,470)	10.6 (0.12)
Hispanic	435,890 (1,592)	487,770 (7,435)	443,290 (4,113)	9.4 (0.09)	267,120 (258)	13.3 (0.03)	107,760 (1,311)	6.2 (0.12)	68,410 (2,970)	7.3 (0.28)
Asian....................	239,510 (877)	276,380 (3,537)	239,320 (1,894)	5.1 (0.05)	91,110 (85)	4.5 (0.01)	72,620 (342)	4.1 (0.07)	75,590 (1,822)	8.1 (0.17)
Pacific Islander	[3] (†)	[3] (†)	28,020 (884)	0.6 (0.02)	11,300 (8)	0.6 (#)	12,490 (884)	0.7 (0.05)	4,220 (14)	0.5 (#)
American Indian/ Alaska Native....	22,690 (164)	32,730 (1,217)	21,080 (162)	0.4 (#)	8,640 (†)	0.4 (#)	7,190 (115)	0.4 (0.01)	5,250 (114)	0.6 (0.01)
Two or more races....	— (†)	— (†)	127,090 (781)	2.7 (0.02)	56,960 (127)	2.8 (0.01)	34,270 (680)	2.0 (0.05)	35,860 (282)	3.8 (0.03)
Type of locale										
City......................	— (†)	2,429,570 (13,222)	2,252,780 (12,708)	41.0 (0.31)	996,640 (2,097)	46.1 (0.15)	762,410 (4,502)	36.7 (0.57)	493,730 (8,446)	39.4 (0.57)
Suburban	— (†)	2,382,550 (12,070)	2,137,800 (20,891)	39.0 (0.34)	868,610 (5,048)	40.2 (0.17)	757,590 (16,094)	36.5 (0.68)	511,600 (7,716)	40.9 (0.58)
Town....................	— (†)	411,700 (5,477)	387,920 (9,565)	7.1 (0.17)	182,610 (†)	8.5 (0.01)	153,540 (9,129)	7.4 (0.41)	51,780 (2,888)	4.1 (0.23)
Rural....................	— (†)	686,390 (21,308)	709,990 (26,462)	12.9 (0.42)	112,360 (301)	5.2 (0.02)	402,680 (25,172)	19.4 (0.98)	194,940 (4,207)	15.6 (0.32)
Teachers[4]										
Total...................	408,400 (2,977)	456,270 (2,897)	437,410 (3,222)	100.0 (†)	142,620 (393)	100.0 (†)	171,870 (3,140)	100.0 (†)	122,930 (654)	100.0 (†)
Level of school										
Elementary............	200,910 (735)	207,230 (1,433)	194,480 (1,878)	44.5 (0.25)	88,760 (190)	62.2 (0.25)	62,940 (1,815)	36.6 (0.63)	42,780 (336)	34.8 (0.18)
Secondary.............	62,740 (229)	69,240 (767)	67,530 (553)	15.4 (0.14)	43,380 (486)	30.4 (0.27)	11,050 (317)	6.4 (0.16)	13,090 (157)	10.7 (0.09)
Combined.............	144,750 (2,682)	179,800 (2,184)	175,410 (1,853)	40.1 (0.26)	10,480 (51)	7.3 (0.04)	97,870 (1,797)	56.9 (0.64)	67,060 (348)	54.5 (0.18)
School enrollment										
Less than 50	25,970 (488)	32,060 (847)	34,120 (1,642)	7.8 (0.34)	1,070 (202)	0.7 (0.14)	19,350 (1,572)	11.3 (0.79)	13,690 (467)	11.1 (0.36)
50 to 149	70,800 (983)	84,590 (1,566)	82,460 (1,102)	18.9 (0.23)	12,950 (120)	9.1 (0.08)	39,280 (759)	22.9 (0.44)	30,240 (548)	24.6 (0.39)
150 to 299	102,240 (486)	109,660 (982)	107,490 (1,873)	24.6 (0.33)	41,550 (79)	29.1 (0.09)	41,190 (1,856)	24.0 (0.86)	24,740 (286)	20.1 (0.21)
300 to 499	90,010 (1,316)	90,540 (331)	86,850 (751)	19.9 (0.19)	37,160 (381)	26.1 (0.21)	28,990 (607)	16.9 (0.40)	20,690 (224)	16.8 (0.19)
500 to 749	57,930 (79)	62,250 (537)	56,920 (†)	13.0 (0.10)	25,410 (†)	17.8 (0.05)	17,900 (†)	10.4 (0.19)	13,620 (†)	11.1 (0.06)
750 or more............	61,440 (2,143)	77,170 (1,618)	69,570 (566)	15.9 (0.13)	24,480 (†)	17.2 (0.05)	25,150 (566)	14.6 (0.29)	19,940 (†)	16.2 (0.09)
Type of locale										
City......................	— (†)	185,530 (1,253)	176,740 (799)	40.4 (0.33)	65,000 (237)	45.6 (0.21)	62,410 (311)	36.3 (0.62)	49,320 (505)	40.1 (0.35)
Suburban	— (†)	177,160 (1,322)	166,170 (2,463)	38.0 (0.41)	56,090 (460)	39.3 (0.24)	62,230 (2,264)	36.2 (0.92)	47,840 (544)	38.9 (0.37)
Town....................	— (†)	32,490 (917)	30,390 (663)	6.9 (0.15)	13,040 (†)	9.1 (0.03)	12,510 (610)	7.3 (0.34)	4,840 (392)	3.9 (0.32)
Rural....................	— (†)	61,090 (2,025)	64,120 (1,960)	14.7 (0.39)	8,480 (52)	5.9 (0.04)	34,720 (1,807)	20.2 (0.87)	20,930 (417)	17.0 (0.34)
Schools										
Total...................	33,000 (301)	33,740 (370)	33,370 (834)	100.0 (†)	7,110 (22)	100.0 (†)	15,620 (804)	100.0 (†)	10,630 (190)	100.0 (†)
Level of school										
Elementary............	22,300 (242)	21,870 (293)	21,420 (745)	64.2 (0.70)	5,680 (19)	79.8 (0.36)	8,900 (721)	57.0 (1.84)	6,840 (130)	64.3 (0.86)
Secondary.............	2,540 (62)	2,930 (67)	2,780 (39)	8.3 (0.23)	1,100 (28)	15.4 (0.36)	780 (33)	5.0 (0.31)	900 (24)	8.5 (0.21)
Combined.............	8,150 (160)	8,940 (160)	9,160 (153)	27.5 (0.54)	340 (7)	4.8 (0.09)	5,940 (170)	38.0 (1.64)	2,890 (124)	27.2 (0.92)
School enrollment										
Less than 50	9,160 (210)	10,060 (287)	11,070 (801)	33.2 (1.61)	230 (28)	3.2 (0.38)	6,460 (769)	41.4 (2.85)	4,380 (200)	41.1 (1.25)
50 to 149	10,260 (134)	10,800 (160)	10,470 (154)	31.4 (0.81)	1,410 (15)	19.8 (0.19)	4,980 (111)	31.9 (1.56)	4,080 (74)	38.4 (0.99)
150 to 299	7,440 (34)	7,220 (75)	6,690 (46)	20.1 (0.24)	2,920 (4)	41.0 (0.13)	2,490 (39)	16.0 (0.83)	1,280 (21)	12.1 (0.23)
300 to 499	3,730 (41)	3,270 (12)	3,010 (30)	9.0 (0.24)	1,490 (9)	21.0 (0.17)	1,000 (28)	6.4 (0.37)	520 (8)	4.9 (0.11)
500 to 749	1,530 (3)	1,430 (8)	1,280 (†)	3.8 (0.10)	690 (†)	9.7 (0.03)	380 (†)	2.5 (0.13)	200 (†)	1.9 (0.03)
750 or more............	870 (20)	960 (17)	850 (7)	2.5 (0.06)	370 (†)	5.2 (0.02)	300 (7)	1.9 (0.10)	180 (†)	1.6 (0.03)
Type of locale										
City......................	— (†)	11,210 (100)	10,810 (171)	32.4 (0.88)	2,970 (26)	41.7 (0.28)	4,200 (77)	26.9 (1.42)	3,640 (105)	34.2 (0.92)
Suburban	— (†)	12,670 (198)	11,610 (176)	34.8 (0.94)	2,580 (16)	36.2 (0.25)	4,390 (110)	28.1 (1.52)	4,640 (113)	43.6 (0.97)
Town....................	— (†)	3,300 (130)	3,340 (154)	10.0 (0.50)	960 (†)	13.5 (0.04)	1,670 (96)	10.7 (0.77)	710 (158)	6.7 (1.42)
Rural....................	— (†)	6,560 (263)	7,610 (799)	22.8 (1.86)	610 (7)	8.6 (0.10)	5,350 (782)	34.3 (3.32)	1,650 (78)	15.5 (0.79)

—Not available.
†Not applicable.
#Rounds to zero.
[1]Includes students in prekindergarten through grade 12 in schools that offer kindergarten or higher grade.
[2]Race/ethnicity is not known for prekindergarten students (788,000 in fall 2009). Percentage distribution is calculated based on the students for whom race/ethnicity is known.
[3]Included under Asian.

[4]Reported in full-time equivalents (FTE). Excludes teachers who teach only prekindergarten students.
NOTE: Includes special education, vocational/technical education, and alternative schools. Tabulation includes schools that offer kindergarten or higher grade. Detail may not sum to totals because of rounding. Standard errors appear in parentheses.
SOURCE: U.S. Department of Education, National Center for Education Statistics, Private School Universe Survey (PSS), 1999–2000, 2007–08, and 2009–10. (This table was prepared July 2011.)

Private elementary and secondary enrollment, number of schools, and average tuition, by school level, orientation, and tuition: 1999–2000, 2003–04, and 2007–08

School orientation and tuition	Kindergarten through 12th-grade enrollment[1]				Schools				Average tuition charged to students[2] (in current dollars)			
	Total	Elementary	Secondary	Combined	Total	Elementary	Secondary	Combined	Total	Elementary	Secondary	Combined
1	2	3	4	5	6	7	8	9	10	11	12	13
1999–2000												
Total	5,262,850 (131,001)	2,920,680 (55,057)	818,920 (34,102)	1,523,240 (88,816)	27,220 (239)	16,560 (278)	2,580 (126)	8,080 (276)	$4,978 (157.3)	$3,737 (248.6)	$6,085 (174.6)	$6,762 (260.9)
Catholic	2,548,710 (23,352)	1,810,330 (18,134)	616,200 (25,935)	122,190 (15,613)	8,100 (24)	6,650 (54)	1,130 (57)	330 (26)	3,344 (57.2)	2,597 (47.3)	4,835 (91.9)	6,889 (690.1)
Other religious	1,871,850 (86,782)	831,060 (41,035)	115,010 (10,981)	925,780 (66,926)	13,270 (237)	7,020 (231)	790 (78)	5,460 (252)	4,439 (153.5)	4,072 (129.7)	6,402 (455.6)	4,524 (280.1)
Nonsectarian	842,290 (61,373)	279,290 (28,987)	87,720 (11,774)	475,270 (43,377)	5,850 (76)	2,900 (155)	670 (100)	2,290 (154)	11,120 (774.7)	10,128 (1,921.0)	14,447 (1,460.6)	11,089 (801.5)
2003–04												
Total	5,059,450 (104,287)	2,675,960 (55,714)	832,320 (54,051)	1,551,170 (82,059)	28,380 (262)	17,330 (262)	2,660 (206)	8,400 (217)	$6,600 (144.5)	$5,049 (119.5)	$8,412 (433.4)	$8,302 (289.7)
Catholic	2,320,040 (49,156)	1,645,680 (41,231)	584,250 (32,236)	90,110 (14,746)	7,920 (35)	6,530 (50)	1,060 (39)	320 (39)	4,254 (95.9)	3,533 (105.9)	6,046 (130.6)	5,801 (883.0)
Other religious	1,746,460 (63,090)	714,960 (28,936)	107,980 (33,776)	923,630 (48,379)	13,660 (203)	7,280 (200)	640 (175)	5,740 (182)	5,839 (143.9)	5,398 (161.4)	9,537 (962.6)	5,748 (230.3)
Nonsectarian	992,940 (71,519)	315,430 (30,820)	140,080 (27,556)	537,440 (59,332)	6,810 (136)	3,510 (141)	960 (108)	2,340 (144)	13,419 (379.1)	12,169 (468.5)	17,413 (1,987.6)	13,112 (480.4)
2007–08												
Total	5,165,280 (104,435)	2,462,980 (58,830)	850,750 (38,553)	1,851,550 (91,348)	28,220 (328)	16,370 (291)	3,040 (149)	8,810 (254)	$8,549 (176.0)	$6,733 (180.6)	$10,549 (355.5)	$10,045 (371.6)
Less than $2,499	455,850 (33,102)	271,960 (21,952)	‡	173,660 (24,693)	6,100 (347)	3,450 (229)	‡	2,370 (226)	1,670 (80.6)	1,938 (80.7)	†	1,313 (175.7)
$2,500 to $3,499	666,450 (42,950)	478,050 (33,030)	‡	168,440 (26,113)	3,930 (257)	2,820 (225)	‡	1,020 (119)	3,428 (41.0)	3,453 (43.2)	†	3,416 (116.5)
$3,500 to $5,999	1,790,410 (77,850)	1,066,750 (45,444)	143,510 (19,815)	580,150 (53,528)	9,110 (341)	6,100 (263)	550 (76)	2,460 (192)	5,206 (41.6)	5,218 (49.3)	5,081 (80.0)	5,214 (89.0)
$6,000 to $9,999	1,155,290 (60,342)	366,470 (37,396)	455,840 (33,376)	332,980 (36,574)	4,460 (232)	2,390 (188)	1,050 (85)	1,020 (114)	8,264 (100.6)	9,231 (286.7)	7,657 (104.7)	8,031 (191.9)
$10,000 or more	1,097,280 (67,145)	279,740 (31,540)	221,210 (23,837)	596,320 (60,614)	4,630 (232)	1,620 (156)	1,070 (96)	1,940 (150)	20,272 (513.4)	19,510 (1,006.4)	21,202 (1,081.1)	20,285 (712.1)
Catholic	2,224,470 (49,385)	1,457,960 (32,114)	620,840 (32,581)	145,680 (25,445)	7,400 (34)	5,950 (57)	1,080 (46)	370 (39)	6,018 (180.3)	4,944 (211.6)	7,826 (231.8)	9,066 (964.2)
Less than $2,499	190,800 (20,946)	174,580 (20,080)	‡	‡	1,130 (102)	1,050 (96)	‡	‡	2,144 (75.7)	2,166 (74.7)	†	†
$2,500 to $3,499	428,610 (35,795)	396,980 (32,130)	‡	‡	1,680 (131)	1,630 (126)	‡	‡	3,352 (42.8)	3,385 (45.8)	†	†
$3,500 to $5,999	826,120 (37,974)	683,980 (32,576)	111,770 (16,043)	‡	3,040 (131)	2,680 (117)	280 (43)	‡	4,896 (48.8)	4,864 (56.7)	5,150 (80.2)	†
$6,000 to $9,999	607,980 (49,329)	165,120 (28,123)	395,900 (30,158)	‡	1,170 (102)	470 (72)	630 (49)	‡	7,682 (116.3)	7,785 (240.4)	7,660 (116.7)	†
$10,000 or more	170,960 (27,585)	‡	‡	‡	380 (62)	‡	‡	‡	16,536 (1,704.9)	‡	‡	‡
Other religious	1,975,980 (81,216)	709,730 (36,666)	128,550 (15,136)	1,137,700 (75,038)	13,350 (282)	7,170 (228)	960 (85)	5,820 (192)	7,117 (237.1)	6,576 (241.5)	10,493 (1,336.5)	7,073 (358.7)
Less than $2,499	221,810 (25,272)	94,820 (10,131)	‡	122,880 (21,602)	4,160 (294)	2,320 (215)	‡	1,780 (185)	1,577 (129.3)	1,552 (178.6)	†	1,601 (185.7)
$2,500 to $3,499	208,200 (24,333)	77,840 (11,714)	‡	129,590 (23,401)	2,020 (208)	1,120 (175)	‡	880 (115)	3,520 (84.3)	3,758 (170.4)	†	3,380 (74.7)
$3,500 to $5,999	860,370 (59,588)	340,150 (27,800)	‡	489,390 (49,116)	5,030 (257)	2,640 (170)	‡	2,160 (175)	5,372 (74.8)	5,568 (110.6)	†	5,269 (100.8)
$6,000 to $9,999	384,850 (39,687)	103,280 (15,561)	57,150 (10,809)	224,420 (33,273)	1,640 (137)	680 (94)	370 (65)	600 (72)	8,045 (155.1)	8,807 (429.9)	7,683 (187.6)	7,787 (163.8)
$10,000 or more	300,750 (34,146)	93,640 (19,216)	‡	171,400 (31,330)	1,100 (114)	420 (72)	‡	420 (81)	17,497 (759.9)	15,209 (632.4)	†	18,008 (1,196.0)
Nonsectarian	964,830 (55,074)	295,280 (25,191)	101,370 (12,739)	568,180 (48,321)	6,860 (119)	3,240 (143)	1,010 (87)	2,620 (138)	17,316 (555.2)	15,945 (702.2)	27,302 (1,506.3)	16,247 (795.3)
Less than $2,499	43,250 (6,840)	‡	‡	‡	800 (113)	‡	‡	‡	54 (33.2)	‡	†	‡
$2,500 to $3,499	‡	‡	‡	‡	‡	‡	‡	‡	‡	‡	†	†
$3,500 to $5,999	103,930 (18,494)	42,610 (7,809)	‡	‡	1,040 (143)	770 (139)	‡	‡	6,289 (352.1)	8,094 (687.4)	†	‡
$6,000 to $9,999	162,450 (24,872)	98,070 (16,434)	‡	‡	1,650 (168)	1,250 (151)	‡	‡	10,963 (530.4)	12,111 (792.2)	†	‡
$10,000 or more	625,570 (45,837)	148,810 (20,542)	90,480 (12,886)	386,280 (43,701)	3,150 (177)	1,070 (129)	660 (77)	1,410 (131)	22,628 (703.0)	21,232 (1,046.6)	30,265 (1,589.3)	21,377 (983.4)

†Not applicable.

‡Reporting standards not met (too few cases).

[1]Only includes kindergarten students who attend schools that offer first or higher grade.

[2]Each school reports the highest annual tuition charged for a full-time student; this amount does not take into account discounts that individual students may receive. This amount is weighted by the number of students enrolled in each school and averaged.

NOTE: Excludes schools not offering first or higher grade. Elementary schools have grade 6 or lower and no grade higher than 8. Secondary schools have no grade lower than 7. Combined schools have grades lower than 7 and higher than 8.

Excludes prekindergarten students. Includes a small percentage of schools reporting tuition of 0: these private schools are often under contract to public school districts to provide special education services. Detail may not sum to totals because of rounding and cell suppression. Some data have been revised from previously published figures. Standard errors appear in parentheses.

SOURCE: U.S. Department of Education, National Center for Education Statistics, Schools and Staffing Survey (SASS), "Private School Questionnaire," 1999–2000, 2003–04, and 2007–08. (This table was prepared in January 2012.)

Private elementary and secondary school full-time-equivalent (FTE) staff and student to FTE staff ratios, by orientation of school, school level, and type of staff: 2007–08

Type of staff	Total				Catholic			
	Total	Elementary[1]	Secondary[2]	Combined[3]	Total	Elementary[1]	Secondary[2]	Combined[3]
1	2	3	4	5	6	7	8	9
Number of schools	28,220 (328)	16,370 (291)	3,040 (149)	8,810 (254)	7,400 (34)	5,950 (57)	1,080 (46)	370 (39)
Enrollment (in thousands)	5,165 (104)	2,463 (59)	851 (39)	1,852 (91)	2,224 (49)	1,458 (32)	621 (33)	146 (25)
Number of FTE staff								
Total FTE staff	778,610 (16,146)	326,320 (8,044)	126,490 (5,809)	325,810 (14,362)	250,380 (6,211)	157,980 (3,488)	70,240 (3,582)	22,150 (3,520)
Principals	30,430 (463)	15,260 (316)	3,360 (168)	11,810 (398)	7,730 (101)	5,950 (75)	1,240 (63)	530 (67)
Assistant principals	13,000 (485)	4,860 (287)	2,840 (194)	5,290 (337)	3,980 (191)	1,940 (123)	1,670 (117)	360 (79)
Other managers	25,940 (947)	9,150 (443)	5,160 (357)	11,630 (775)	7,010 (387)	3,100 (196)	3,180 (242)	730 (168)
Instruction coordinators	7,770 (535)	2,620 (274)	1,570 (217)	3,590 (391)	2,060 (252)	1,020 (179)	820 (156)	220 ! (88)
Teachers	433,400 (8,589)	186,870 (4,498)	68,840 (2,748)	177,690 (8,011)	146,120 (3,316)	92,210 (2,001)	41,910 (2,054)	12,010 (1,874)
Teacher aides	52,960 (2,577)	26,740 (1,390)	1,740 (352)	24,480 (2,237)	14,730 (997)	12,820 (548)	270 (55)	1,640 ! (779)
Other aides	11,160 (1,243)	4,780 (517)	710 (206)	5,660 (1,254)	2,580 (351)	2,440 (355)	110 ! (56)	20 ! (11)
Guidance counselors	11,620 (504)	2,290 (131)	4,140 (211)	5,190 (439)	5,040 (257)	1,600 (93)	2,880 (160)	570 (119)
Librarians/media specialists	11,960 (346)	5,680 (202)	1,900 (106)	4,380 (293)	4,730 (137)	3,230 (116)	1,160 (63)	340 (58)
Library/media center aides	4,030 (254)	1,910 (161)	600 (84)	1,520 (178)	1,770 (149)	1,200 (126)	420 (67)	140 (39)
Nurses	8,160 (396)	3,350 (163)	1,580 (181)	3,240 (281)	2,970 (153)	2,180 (121)	600 (62)	190 ! (62)
Student support staff[4]	24,500 (1,227)	7,900 (569)	4,690 (523)	11,900 (1,030)	6,080 (507)	3,670 (282)	1,500 (230)	910 ! (350)
Secretaries/clerical staff	50,010 (1,437)	19,230 (684)	9,730 (532)	21,050 (1,111)	15,940 (541)	8,840 (261)	5,730 (384)	1,380 (262)
Food service personnel	27,610 (1,008)	11,900 (490)	5,420 (461)	10,290 (814)	11,220 (476)	6,920 (341)	3,300 (264)	1,000 (195)
Custodial and maintenance	45,170 (1,464)	17,590 (596)	8,340 (526)	19,250 (1,369)	14,800 (483)	9,120 (284)	4,320 (319)	1,360 (248)
Other employees[5]	20,880 (2,707)	6,180 (784)	5,870 ! (2,016)	8,840 (1,345)	3,620 (642)	1,730 (366)	1,140 ! (378)	‡ (†)
Students per FTE staff member								
Total FTE staff	7 (0.1)	8 (0.1)	7 (0.2)	6 (0.1)	9 (0.1)	9 (0.1)	9 (0.2)	7 (0.6)
Principals	170 (2.9)	161 (4.2)	253 (12.5)	157 (5.7)	288 (5.9)	245 (4.9)	500 (23.5)	273 (33.8)
Assistant principals	397 (12.5)	506 (24.5)	300 (17.1)	350 (17.6)	559 (22.0)	750 (41.9)	371 (17.1)	401 (60.3)
Other managers	199 (6.0)	269 (11.1)	165 (9.1)	159 (8.2)	317 (14.7)	470 (29.0)	195 (11.2)	201 (39.1)
Instruction coordinators	664 (43.6)	942 (91.0)	544 (83.9)	515 (55.3)	1,080 (147.3)	1,431 (279.8)	759 (183.2)	‡ (†)
Teachers	12 (0.1)	13 (0.1)	12 (0.3)	10 (0.2)	15 (0.1)	16 (0.2)	15 (0.2)	12 (0.7)
Teacher aides	98 (4.9)	92 (4.5)	489 (123.0)	76 (7.2)	151 (10.0)	114 (4.6)	2,329 (617.7)	‡ (†)
Other aides	463 (53.6)	515 (57.9)	1,190 ! (407.3)	327 (87.8)	864 (141.3)	598 (103.4)	‡ (†)	‡ (†)
Guidance counselors	444 (16.5)	1,073 (55.9)	206 (6.9)	357 (24.4)	441 (17.9)	912 (49.6)	216 (5.9)	256 (34.1)
Librarians/media specialists	432 (9.7)	434 (12.8)	447 (19.7)	423 (18.3)	470 (11.5)	451 (15.7)	535 (21.4)	431 (55.7)
Library/media center aides	1,283 (77.5)	1,288 (106.6)	1,427 (202.0)	1,219 (142.7)	1,258 (107.6)	1,210 (124.6)	1,475 (256.0)	1,027 ! (371.4)
Nurses	633 (26.9)	736 (33.2)	539 (57.7)	572 (46.1)	750 (38.6)	668 (33.3)	1,041 (117.0)	775 ! (324.2)
Student support staff[4]	211 (10.2)	312 (21.7)	181 (20.4)	156 (13.9)	366 (28.0)	397 (27.3)	414 (64.1)	‡ (†)
Secretaries/clerical staff	103 (2.1)	128 (3.0)	87 (3.6)	88 (3.2)	140 (3.2)	165 (4.0)	108 (4.6)	106 (12.9)
Food service personnel	187 (6.4)	207 (8.7)	157 (13.1)	180 (11.7)	198 (7.4)	211 (9.8)	188 (14.1)	146 (22.0)
Custodial and maintenance	114 (2.8)	140 (3.4)	102 (5.3)	96 (5.2)	150 (3.5)	160 (4.3)	144 (7.0)	107 (10.3)
Other employees[5]	247 (29.7)	399 (49.5)	145 ! (55.5)	209 (32.7)	614 (120.7)	841 (193.8)	547 ! (233.0)	‡ (†)

See notes at end of table.

Private elementary and secondary school full-time-equivalent (FTE) staff and student to FTE staff ratios, by orientation of school, school level, and type of staff: 2007–08—Continued

Type of staff	Other religious orientation — Total (10)	Elementary[1] (11)	Secondary[2] (12)	Combined[3] (13)	Nonsectarian — Total (14)	Elementary[1] (15)	Secondary[2] (16)	Combined[3] (17)
Number of schools	13,950 (282)	7,170 (228)	960 (85)	5,820 (192)	6,860 (119)	3,240 (143)	1,010 (87)	2,620 (138)
Enrollment (in thousands)	1,976 (81)	710 (37)	129 (15)	1,138 (75)	965 (55)	295 (25)	101 (13)	568 (48)

Number of FTE staff

Type of staff	Other religious orientation — Total (10)	Elementary[1] (11)	Secondary[2] (12)	Combined[3] (13)	Nonsectarian — Total (14)	Elementary[1] (15)	Secondary[2] (16)	Combined[3] (17)
Total FTE staff	293,830 (10,433)	105,540 (4,977)	22,270 (2,241)	166,020 (10,154)	234,410 (10,902)	62,790 (4,761)	33,980 (4,014)	137,630 (9,797)
Principals	14,860 (343)	6,000 (236)	1,080 (106)	7,780 (336)	7,840 (264)	3,310 (184)	1,040 (107)	3,500 (234)
Assistant principals	4,860 (300)	1,650 (150)	560 (88)	2,650 (238)	4,160 (272)	1,270 (168)	610 (116)	2,280 (194)
Other managers	8,940 (479)	3,040 (256)	860 (145)	5,050 (393)	9,990 (661)	3,010 (314)	1,120 (175)	5,850 (628)
Instruction coordinators	2,520 (237)	640 (100)	260 ! (113)	1,610 (194)	3,190 (421)	950 (185)	490 (109)	1,760 (355)
Teachers	172,830 (6,093)	61,040 (2,838)	12,730 (1,389)	99,070 (5,822)	114,440 (5,551)	33,630 (2,610)	14,200 (1,498)	66,610 (5,111)
Teacher aides	15,280 (902)	7,260 (671)	240 ! (79)	7,780 (778)	22,950 (2,039)	6,650 (959)	1,230 (327)	15,060 (1,839)
Other aides	3,050 (387)	1,530 (306)	‡ (†)	1,480 (222)	5,540 (1,295)	820 ! (250)	560 ! (206)	4,160 ! (1,261)
Guidance counselors	3,380 (267)	420 (73)	600 (81)	2,360 (227)	3,200 (369)	280 (61)	670 (86)	2,260 (364)
Librarians/media specialists	4,280 (235)	1,530 (125)	360 ! (66)	2,380 (217)	2,950 (200)	910 (115)	380 (63)	1,660 (167)
Library/media center aides	1,550 (183)	570 (91)	70 ! (22)	910 (156)	710 (108)	140 ! (41)	100 ! (48)	470 (85)
Nurses	2,230 (177)	780 (84)	230 (58)	1,220 (143)	2,970 (289)	380 (71)	760 (142)	1,830 (236)
Student support staff[4]	5,750 (633)	1,910 (245)	470 ! (146)	3,360 (602)	12,670 (999)	2,320 (437)	2,720 (472)	7,630 (871)
Secretaries/clerical staff	19,530 (802)	6,870 (435)	1,760 (231)	10,910 (692)	14,530 (992)	3,520 (385)	2,250 (296)	8,760 (887)
Food service personnel	10,510 (727)	3,720 (298)	910 (171)	5,880 (653)	5,880 (606)	1,270 (209)	1,210 (321)	3,400 (483)
Custodial and maintenance	17,270 (1,073)	5,770 (355)	1,470 ! (225)	10,020 (1,002)	13,110 (1,009)	2,700 (337)	2,550 (429)	7,860 (919)
Other employees[5]	6,980 (950)	2,800 (601)	‡ (†)	3,540 (748)	10,280 (2,232)	1,640 (356)	4,090 ! (1,918)	4,550 (1,049)

Students per FTE staff member

Type of staff	Other religious orientation — Total (10)	Elementary[1] (11)	Secondary[2] (12)	Combined[3] (13)	Nonsectarian — Total (14)	Elementary[1] (15)	Secondary[2] (16)	Combined[3] (17)
Total FTE staff	7 (0.1)	7 (0.2)	7 (0.4)	7 (0.2)	7 (0.1)	5 (0.2)	3 (0.3)	4 (0.2)
Principals	133 (4.7)	118 (6.9)	119 (13.8)	146 (6.9)	123 (5.8)	89 (6.3)	98 (11.1)	162 (10.6)
Assistant principals	407 (22.3)	430 (28.8)	230 (47.6)	430 (30.3)	232 (15.6)	233 (28.9)	167 (30.1)	249 (21.1)
Other managers	221 (10.4)	234 (16.5)	150 (23.6)	225 (14.1)	97 (5.2)	98 (8.0)	90 (12.5)	97 (7.6)
Instruction coordinators	784 (72.1)	1,102 (175.4)	‡ (†)	705 (90.8)	302 (33.7)	310 (50.1)	209 (53.1)	324 (60.6)
Teachers	11 (0.2)	12 (0.3)	11 (0.7)	11 (0.2)	8 (0.2)	9 (0.3)	7 (0.5)	9 (0.2)
Teacher aides	129 (7.5)	98 (7.4)	‡ (†)	146 (12.8)	42 (4.4)	44 (6.5)	82 ! (29.7)	38 (5.7)
Other aides	648 (83.3)	464 (103.6)	‡ (†)	767 (123.2)	174 (49.2)	361 ! (139.0)	‡ (†)	137 ! (60.7)
Guidance counselors	585 (39.0)	1,689 (247.6)	216 (18.5)	481 (38.8)	301 (28.0)	1,072 (297.2)	152 (20.3)	252 (30.2)
Librarians/media specialists	462 (18.7)	463 (25.3)	354 (50.3)	478 (30.0)	327 (15.3)	324 (36.0)	267 (29.4)	342 (17.1)
Library/media center aides	1,274 (145.0)	1,243 (207.8)	1,820 ! (798.8)	1,251 (234.4)	1,363 (220.2)	2,172 ! (876.5)	‡ (†)	1,216 (231.0)
Nurses	887 (64.5)	906 (90.6)	567 ! (174.4)	933 (104.7)	325 (30.3)	775 (151.0)	134 (30.3)	310 (36.4)
Student support staff[4]	344 (39.1)	371 (48.7)	271 ! (111.5)	338 (61.8)	76 (6.8)	127 (27.7)	37 (7.8)	74 (10.1)
Secretaries/clerical staff	101 (3.0)	103 (4.3)	73 (6.9)	104 (4.2)	66 (3.6)	84 (5.4)	45 (5.3)	65 (4.7)
Food service personnel	188 (12.0)	191 (15.9)	142 (32.0)	193 (17.8)	164 (15.1)	233 (34.9)	84 ! (32.3)	167 (19.8)
Custodial and maintenance	114 (5.8)	123 (6.7)	87 (9.1)	113 (9.2)	74 (4.3)	109 (10.7)	40 (5.3)	72 (5.6)
Other employees[5]	283 (39.1)	254 (55.1)	‡ (†)	321 (84.4)	94 (20.6)	180 (44.9)	‡ (†)	125 (30.8)

†Not applicable.

!Interpret data with caution. The coefficient of variation (CV) for this estimate is 30 percent or greater.

‡Reporting standards not met. The coefficient of variation (CV) for this estimate is 50 percent or greater.

[1]Includes schools beginning with grade 6 or below and with no grade higher than 8.

[2]Schools with no grade lower than 7.

[3]Schools with grades lower than 7 and higher than 8.

[4]Includes student support services professional staff, such as school psychologists, social workers, and speech therapists or pathologists.

[5]Includes other employees not identified by function.

NOTE: FTE staff consists of the total number of full-time staff, plus 48 percent of the part-time staff; this percentage was estimated based on the number of hours that part-time staff reported working. Data are based on a sample survey and may not be strictly comparable with data reported elsewhere. Excludes all prekindergarten students attending schools that offer first or higher grade. Includes only schools that offer first or higher grade. Standard errors appear in parentheses. Detail may not sum to totals because of rounding.

SOURCE: U.S. Department of Education, National Center for Education Statistics, Schools and Staffing Survey (SASS), "Private School Questionnaire," 2007–08. (This table was prepared October 2009.)

Enrollment and instructional staff in Catholic elementary and secondary schools, by level: Selected years, 1919–20 through 2010–11

	Number of schools			Enrollment[1]				Instructional staff[2]		
School year	Total	Elementary[3]	Secondary	Total	Pre-kindergarten	Elementary	Secondary	Total	Elementary[3]	Secondary
1	2	3	4	5	6	7	8	9	10	11
1919–20	8,103	6,551	1,552	1,925,521	([4])	1,795,673	129,848	49,516	41,592	7,924
1929–30	10,046	7,923	2,123	2,464,467	([4])	2,222,598	241,869	72,552	58,245	14,307
1939–40	10,049	7,944	2,105	2,396,305	([4])	2,035,182	361,123	81,057	60,081	20,976
1949–50	10,778	8,589	2,189	3,066,387	([4])	2,560,815	505,572	94,295	66,525	27,770
Fall 1960	12,893	10,501	2,392	5,253,791	([4])	4,373,422	880,369	151,902	108,169	43,733
1969–70	11,352	9,366	1,986	4,367,000	([4])	3,359,000	1,008,000	195,400 [5]	133,200 [5]	62,200 [5]
1970–71	11,350	9,370	1,980	4,363,566	([4])	3,355,478	1,008,088	166,208	112,750	53,458
1974–75	10,127	8,437	1,690	3,504,000	([4])	2,602,000	902,000	150,179	100,011	50,168
1975–76	9,993	8,340	1,653	3,415,000	([4])	2,525,000	890,000	149,276	99,319	49,957
1979–80	9,640	8,100	1,540	3,139,000	([4])	2,293,000	846,000	147,294	97,724	49,570
1980–81	9,559	8,043	1,516	3,106,000	([4])	2,269,000	837,000	145,777	96,739	49,038
1981–82	9,494	7,996	1,498	3,094,000	([4])	2,266,000	828,000	146,172	96,847	49,325
1982–83	9,432	7,950	1,482	3,007,189	([4])	2,211,412	795,777	146,460	97,337	49,123
1983–84	9,401	7,937	1,464	2,969,000	([4])	2,179,000	790,000	146,913	98,591	48,322
1984–85	9,325	7,876	1,449	2,903,000	([4])	2,119,000	784,000	149,888	99,820	50,068
1985–86	9,220	7,790	1,430	2,821,000	([4])	2,061,000	760,000	146,594	96,741	49,853
1986–87	9,102	7,693	1,409	2,726,000	([4])	1,998,000	728,000	141,930	93,554	48,376
1987–88	8,992	7,601	1,391	2,690,668	67,637	1,942,148	680,883	139,887	93,199	46,688
1988–89	8,867	7,505	1,362	2,627,745	76,626	1,911,911	639,208	137,700	93,154	44,546
1989–90	8,719	7,395	1,324	2,588,893	90,023	1,892,913	605,957	136,900	94,197	42,703
1990–91	8,587	7,291	1,296	2,575,815	100,376	1,883,906	591,533	131,198	91,039	40,159
1991–92	8,508	7,239	1,269	2,550,863	107,939	1,856,302	586,622	153,334	109,084	44,250
1992–93	8,423	7,174	1,249	2,567,630	122,788	1,860,937	583,905	154,816	109,825	44,991
1993–94	8,345	7,114	1,231	2,576,845	132,236	1,859,947	584,662	157,201	112,199	45,002
1994–95	8,293	7,055	1,238	2,618,567	143,360	1,877,782	597,425	164,219	117,620	46,599
1995–96	8,250	7,022	1,228	2,635,210	144,099	1,884,461	606,650	166,759	118,753	48,006
1996–97	8,231	7,005	1,226	2,645,462	148,264	1,885,037	612,161	153,276	107,548	45,728
1997–98	8,223	7,004	1,219	2,648,859	150,965	1,879,737	618,157	152,259	105,717	46,542
1998–99	8,217	6,990	1,227	2,648,844	152,356	1,876,211	620,277	153,081	105,943	47,138
1999–2000	8,144	6,923	1,221	2,653,038	152,622	1,877,236	623,180	157,134	109,404	47,730
2000–01	8,146	6,920	1,226	2,647,301	155,742	1,863,682	627,877	160,731	111,937	48,794
2001–02	8,114	6,886	1,228	2,616,330	159,869	1,827,319	629,142	155,658	108,485	47,173
2002–03	8,000	6,785	1,215	2,553,277	157,250	1,765,893	630,134	163,004	112,884	50,120
2003–04	7,955	6,727	1,228	2,484,252	150,422	1,708,501	625,329	162,337	112,303	50,034
2004–05	7,799	6,574	1,225	2,420,590	150,905	1,642,868	626,817	160,153	107,764	52,389
2005–06	7,589	6,386	1,203	2,325,220	146,327	1,568,687	610,206	152,502 [6]	103,481 [6]	49,021 [6]
2006–07	7,498	6,288	1,210	2,320,651	152,429	1,544,695	623,527	159,135	107,682	51,453
2007–08	7,378	6,165	1,213	2,270,913	152,980	1,494,979	622,954	160,075	107,217	52,858
2008–09	7,248	6,028	1,220	2,192,531	153,325	1,434,949	604,257	157,615	105,518	52,097
2009–10	7,094	5,889	1,205	2,119,341	150,262	1,375,982	593,097	154,316	103,460	50,856
2010–11	6,980	5,774	1,206	2,065,872	152,846	1,336,560	576,466	151,473	102,365	49,108

[1]Elementary enrollment is for kindergarten through grade 8, and secondary enrollment is for grades 9 through 12.
[2]From 1919–20 through fall 1960, includes part-time teachers. From 1969–70 through 1993–94, excludes part-time teachers. Beginning in 1994–95, reported in full-time equivalents (FTE). Prekindergarten teachers not counted separately but may be included with elementary teachers.
[3]Includes middle schools.
[4]Prekindergarten enrollment was not reported separately, but may be included in elementary enrollment.
[5]Includes estimates for the nonreporting schools.

[6]Excludes the Archdiocese of New Orleans.
NOTE: Data collected by the National Catholic Educational Association and data collected by the National Center for Education Statistics are not directly comparable because survey procedures and definitions differ.
SOURCE: National Catholic Educational Association, *A Statistical Report on Catholic Elementary and Secondary Schools for the Years 1967–68 to 1969–70; A Report on Catholic Schools, 1970–71 through 1973–74; A Statistical Report on U.S. Catholic Schools, 1974–75 through 1980–81;* and *United States Catholic Elementary and Secondary Schools, 1981–82 through 2010–11,* retrieved May 24, 2011, from http://www.ncea.org/news/AnnualDataReport.asp. (This table was prepared May 2011.)

447

Private elementary and secondary schools, enrollment, teachers, and high school graduates, by state: Selected years, 1999 through 2009

State	Schools, fall 2009	Enrollment in prekindergarten through grade 12												Teachers,[1] fall 2009		High school graduates, 2008–09	
		Fall 1999		Fall 2001		Fall 2003		Fall 2005		Fall 2007		Fall 2009					
1	2	3		4		5		6		7		8		9		10	
United States	33,370	(834)	6,018,280	(30,179)	6,319,650	(40,272)	6,099,220	(41,219)	6,073,240	(42,446)	5,910,210	(28,363)	5,488,490	(35,857)	437,410	(3,222)	308,810	(1,359)
Alabama................	580	(110)	81,040	(†)	92,380	(3,926)	99,580	(12,130)	92,280	(5,892)	83,840	(103)	95,570	(11,745)	8,780	(2,112)	5,280	(368)
Alaska..................	120 !	(65)	6,980	(†)	7,420	(†)	7,370	(424)	7,500	(1,028)	4,990	(†)	7,510 !	(2,740)	530	(108)	190	(†)
Arizona.................	360	(†)	58,740	(2,591)	78,660	(18,218)	75,360	(16,426)	66,840	(†)	64,910	(†)	55,390	(†)	3,910	(†)	2,760	(†)
Arkansas..............	220	(55)	29,400	(†)	32,570	(†)	31,300	(†)	35,390	(5,858)	40,120	(11,961)	28,900	(1,371)	2,390	(164)	1,330	(†)
California..............	3,640	(55)	724,010	(1,403)	757,750	(8,415)	740,460	(8,703)	737,490	(15,529)	703,810	(6,129)	623,150	(4,185)	45,740	(286)	35,250	(71)
Colorado..............	490	(85)	65,690	(†)	64,700	(†)	62,080	(476)	70,770	(1,160)	64,740	(†)	63,720	(3,486)	4,790	(110)	2,840	(99)
Connecticut..........	410	(15)	80,060	(391)	82,320	(†)	102,960	(25,024)	76,220	(1,619)	85,150	(9,241)	72,540	(464)	7,430	(60)	6,230	(†)
Delaware..............	140	(†)	26,940	(†)	31,690	(1,023)	33,020	(2,649)	29,830	(†)	32,520	(2,701)	26,640	(†)	2,060	(†)	1,850	(†)
District of Columbia.......	90	(†)	17,000	(†)	33,660 !	(14,373)	23,510	(6,121)	19,880	(†)	19,640	(†)	17,810	(†)	1,890	(†)	1,340	(†)
Florida.................	1,960	(36)	349,180	(4,957)	365,890	(8,301)	398,720	(14,590)	396,790	(7,429)	391,660	(6,123)	343,990	(1,023)	26,580	(63)	18,220	(†)
Georgia................	820	(75)	137,420	(9,460)	137,060	(4,550)	144,850	(6,527)	152,600	(10,394)	157,430	(9,185)	150,300	(6,251)	13,250	(420)	8,320	(108)
Hawaii.................	140	(†)	35,550	(746)	42,980	(220)	39,940	(†)	32,810	(†)	37,300	(290)	37,130	(†)	3,040	(†)	2,660	(†)
Idaho..................	200 !	(63)	12,720	(†)	12,050	(†)	12,570	(†)	15,320	(2,518)	24,700 !	(11,608)	18,680	(4,814)	1,360	(296)	550	(59)
Illinois................	1,730	(105)	347,750	(700)	357,390	(19,293)	316,430	(1,698)	317,940	(4,263)	312,270	(6,638)	289,720	(9,237)	20,290	(927)	15,110	(251)
Indiana................	910	(144)	121,960	(†)	129,240	(326)	124,500	(455)	139,370	(17,870)	119,910	(2,284)	120,770	(5,919)	8,420	(476)	5,230	(105)
Iowa...................	230	(†)	54,640	(844)	51,540	(†)	53,850	(4,634)	60,960	(8,311)	47,820	(†)	45,160	(†)	3,220	(†)	2,250	(†)
Kansas................	260	(51)	56,840	(12,716)	51,540	(8,341)	47,710	(2,151)	47,130	(1,654)	47,780	(2,414)	44,680	(1,668)	3,370	(214)	2,170	(†)
Kentucky..............	360	(19)	89,300	(6,657)	85,230	(3,227)	82,100	(1,525)	78,880	(1,228)	76,140	(2,074)	70,590	(2,132)	5,280	(206)	3,940	(†)
Louisiana.............	460	(51)	148,020	(†)	159,910	(11,381)	155,780	(3,515)	138,270	(525)	137,460	(†)	147,040	(9,890)	10,060	(622)	8,140	(54)
Maine.................	160	(†)	19,820	(261)	20,820	(174)	24,740	(3,629)	20,680	(337)	21,260	(143)	18,310	(†)	1,890	(†)	2,360	(†)
Maryland..............	790	(14)	166,570	(1,030)	175,740	(†)	172,360	(†)	170,350	(4,201)	165,760	(1,160)	145,690	(160)	13,210	(21)	9,230	(†)
Massachusetts......	830	(27)	154,060	(147)	177,490	(9,836)	164,390	(6,636)	157,770	(3,273)	151,640	(2,516)	137,110	(1,169)	14,920	(198)	10,630	(†)
Michigan..............	1,070	(200)	208,470	(4,965)	198,380	(†)	180,080	(†)	166,950	(407)	159,100	(2,047)	153,230	(5,828)	10,890	(386)	8,520	(†)
Minnesota............	520	(†)	101,360	(†)	112,310	(2,993)	106,010	(3,011)	104,730	(3,467)	101,740	(3,903)	89,530	(†)	6,420	(†)	4,240	(†)
Mississippi...........	320	(69)	67,200	(14,096)	67,380	(10,106)	57,110	(2,981)	57,930	(4,104)	55,270	(†)	54,650	(2,458)	4,510	(226)	3,360	(61)
Missouri...............	690	(72)	131,750	(†)	138,140	(4,321)	141,530	(9,966)	137,810	(10,580)	125,610	(3,685)	117,970	(2,065)	9,030	(220)	7,040	(42)
Montana...............	150 !	(52)	10,170	(487)	12,930	(1,895)	12,510	(2,091)	35,980	(22,655)	15,030 !	(5,465)	10,390	(1,221)	880	(80)	370	(†)
Nebraska..............	220	(†)	44,560	(†)	45,590	(618)	41,650	(†)	42,420	(†)	40,320	(†)	39,040	(†)	2,660	(†)	2,000	(†)
Nevada................	160	(†)	17,350	(†)	20,370	(385)	23,930	(†)	29,120	(†)	29,820	(2,009)	25,060	(†)	1,600	(†)	820	(†)
New Hampshire	290	(†)	36,480	(†)	38,650	(†)	33,780	(†)	33,220	(†)	30,920	(†)	26,470	(†)	2,610	(†)	2,460	(†)
New Jersey...........	1,380	(137)	237,540	(2,316)	282,450	(4,182)	269,530	(7,577)	256,160	(8,439)	253,250	(5,016)	232,020	(16,536)	19,020	(1,712)	14,350	(477)
New Mexico...........	190	(14)	28,570	(220)	26,510	(†)	29,310	(3,928)	25,030	(141)	27,290	(1,388)	23,730	(507)	2,020	(42)	1,390	(†)
New York..............	2,020	(33)	542,520	(4,368)	559,670	(1,669)	515,620	(4,071)	510,750	(3,596)	518,850	(7,196)	486,310	(5,211)	41,970	(476)	31,280	(357)
North Carolina.......	670	(54)	104,370	(1,403)	116,500	(4,112)	126,230	(11,439)	117,280	(11,681)	121,660	(2,226)	110,740	(1,851)	9,960	(192)	5,730	(24)
North Dakota.........	50	(†)	7,730	(†)	7,180	(†)	6,840	(†)	7,290	(†)	7,430	(†)	7,750	(†)	580	(†)	450	(†)
Ohio...................	1,760 !	(783)	280,930	(1,730)	290,370	(7,180)	270,660	(7,094)	254,530	(9,821)	239,520	(2,741)	246,250	(24,214)	16,790	(1,661)	13,300	(35)
Oklahoma.............	250	(49)	45,660	(7,770)	46,570	(8,723)	34,300	(2,013)	35,350	(1,194)	40,320	(5,032)	34,000	(716)	2,940	(124)	1,530	(†)
Oregon................	500	(56)	61,000	(5,195)	71,500	(15,519)	54,320	(†)	69,620	(14,139)	66,260	(5,188)	56,820	(3,502)	4,370	(480)	3,140	(141)
Pennsylvania.........	2,270	(21)	392,060	(6,679)	374,490	(†)	357,580	(3,364)	332,740	(3,918)	324,020	(6,253)	301,640	(5,036)	23,700	(527)	18,660	(1,133)
Rhode Island.........	160	(†)	29,570	(†)	30,970	(†)	31,960	(†)	30,600	(†)	28,260	(1,096)	24,940	(†)	2,300	(†)	1,820	(†)
South Carolina	400	(12)	86,810	(18,537)	70,950	(†)	73,800	(†)	70,240	(1,797)	71,430	(1,043)	62,320	(311)	5,060	(25)	3,070	(†)
South Dakota........	70	(†)	10,120	(†)	11,740	(†)	11,980	(†)	12,700	(†)	12,280	(†)	11,470	(†)	850	(†)	520	(†)
Tennessee............	520	(24)	104,150	(5,281)	98,790	(†)	93,390	(†)	105,240	(2,531)	117,540	(12,851)	98,310	(4,176)	8,580	(365)	6,220	(†)
Texas..................	1,850	(178)	277,770	(2,338)	314,210	(12,244)	271,380	(2,758)	304,170	(20,453)	296,540	(4,132)	313,360	(11,968)	25,660	(1,044)	12,900	(224)
Utah...................	180	(25)	15,900	(†)	20,040	(†)	19,990	(†)	21,220	(†)	20,860	(†)	21,990	(1,558)	1,850	(90)	1,270	(†)
Vermont...............	120	(†)	15,010	(1,829)	14,090	(†)	12,730	(†)	11,530	(†)	12,600	(232)	10,350	(†)	1,320	(†)	1,170	(†)
Virginia................	920	(152)	116,110	(215)	129,470	(†)	131,160	(6,936)	155,220	(14,290)	143,140	(7,988)	128,140	(2,581)	11,360	(380)	6,510	(†)
Washington	660	(33)	88,080	(1,493)	91,150	(2,028)	101,130	(7,935)	119,640	(13,187)	104,070	(3,054)	94,340	(625)	6,960	(66)	4,450	(†)
West Virginia.........	140	(†)	16,370	(†)	16,560	(†)	15,300	(†)	16,120	(†)	14,980	(†)	13,860	(†)	1,280	(†)	740	(†)
Wisconsin.............	890	(†)	154,340	(1,581)	162,220	(9,080)	159,240	(11,743)	142,280	(137)	138,290	(1,597)	130,510	(†)	9,580	(†)	5,610	(†)
Wyoming..............	40	(†)	2,640	(†)	2,430	(†)	2,600	(†)	2,310	(†)	2,930	(†)	2,910	(†)	270	(†)	30	(†)

†Not applicable.

!Interpret data with caution. The coefficient of variation (CV) for this estimate is 30 percent or greater.

[1]Reported in full-time equivalents (FTE). Excludes teachers who teach only prekindergarten students.

NOTE: Includes special education, vocational/technical education, and alternative schools. Tabulation includes schools that offer kindergarten or higher grade. Includes enrollment of students in prekindergarten through grade 12 in schools that offer kindergarten or higher grade. Detail may not sum to totals because of rounding. Standard errors appear in parentheses.

SOURCE: U.S. Department of Education, National Center for Education Statistics, Private School Universe Survey (PSS), various years, 1999–2000 through 2009–10. (This table was prepared August 2011.)

Revenues for public elementary and secondary schools, by source of funds: Selected years, 1919–20 through 2008–09

School year	Total (in thousands)	Federal (in thousands)	Federal revenue per student		State (in thousands)	Local (including intermediate)[1] (in thousands)	Percentage distribution			
			Current dollars	Constant 2009–10 dollars			Total	Federal	State	Local (including intermediate)[1]
1	2	3	4	5	6	7	8	9	10	11
1919–20	$970,121	$2,475	#	$1	$160,085	$807,561	100.0	0.3	16.5	83.2
1929–30	2,088,557	7,334	#	4	353,670	1,727,553	100.0	0.4	16.9	82.7
1939–40	2,260,527	39,810	$2	24	684,354	1,536,363	100.0	1.8	30.3	68.0
1941–42	2,416,580	34,305	1	19	759,993	1,622,281	100.0	1.4	31.4	67.1
1943–44	2,604,322	35,886	2	19	859,183	1,709,253	100.0	1.4	33.0	65.6
1945–46	3,059,845	41,378	2	21	1,062,057	1,956,409	100.0	1.4	34.7	63.9
1947–48	4,311,534	120,270	5	47	1,676,362	2,514,902	100.0	2.8	38.9	58.3
1949–50	5,437,044	155,848	6	57	2,165,689	3,115,507	100.0	2.9	39.8	57.3
1951–52	6,423,816	227,711	9	71	2,478,596	3,717,507	100.0	3.5	38.6	57.9
1953–54	7,866,852	355,237	12	99	2,944,103	4,567,512	100.0	4.5	37.4	58.1
1955–56	9,686,677	441,442	14	116	3,828,886	5,416,350	100.0	4.6	39.5	55.9
1957–58	12,181,513	486,484	15	112	4,800,368	6,894,661	100.0	4.0	39.4	56.6
1959–60	14,746,618	651,639	19	137	5,768,047	8,326,932	100.0	4.4	39.1	56.5
1961–62	17,527,707	760,975	20	146	6,789,190	9,977,542	100.0	4.3	38.7	56.9
1963–64	20,544,182	896,956	22	157	8,078,014	11,569,213	100.0	4.4	39.3	56.3
1965–66	25,356,858	1,996,954	47	322	9,920,219	13,439,686	100.0	7.9	39.1	53.0
1967–68	31,903,064	2,806,469	64	408	12,275,536	16,821,063	100.0	8.8	38.5	52.7
1969–70	40,266,923	3,219,557	71	406	16,062,776	20,984,589	100.0	8.0	39.9	52.1
1970–71	44,511,292	3,753,461	82	446	17,409,086	23,348,745	100.0	8.4	39.1	52.5
1971–72	50,003,645	4,467,969	97	511	19,133,256	26,402,420	100.0	8.9	38.3	52.8
1972–73	52,117,930	4,525,000	99	501	20,699,752	26,893,180	100.0	8.7	39.7	51.6
1973–74	58,230,892	4,930,351	108	504	24,113,409	29,187,132	100.0	8.5	41.4	50.1
1974–75	64,445,239	5,811,595	129	540	27,060,563	31,573,079	100.0	9.0	42.0	49.0
1975–76	71,206,073	6,318,345	141	551	31,602,885	33,284,840	100.0	8.9	44.4	46.7
1976–77	75,332,532	6,629,498	150	552	32,526,018	36,177,019	100.0	8.8	43.2	48.0
1977–78	81,443,160	7,694,194	177	611	35,013,266	38,735,700	100.0	9.4	43.0	47.6
1978–79	87,994,143	8,600,116	202	639	40,132,136	39,261,891	100.0	9.8	45.6	44.6
1979–80	96,881,165	9,503,537	228	637	45,348,814	42,028,813	100.0	9.8	46.8	43.4
1980–81	105,949,087	9,768,262	239	598	50,182,659	45,998,166	100.0	9.2	47.4	43.4
1981–82	110,191,257	8,186,466	204	471	52,436,435	49,568,356	100.0	7.4	47.6	45.0
1982–83	117,497,502	8,339,990	211	465	56,282,157	52,875,354	100.0	7.1	47.9	45.0
1983–84	126,055,419	8,576,547	218	465	60,232,981	57,245,892	100.0	6.8	47.8	45.4
1984–85	137,294,678	9,105,569	232	476	67,168,684	61,020,425	100.0	6.6	48.9	44.4
1985–86	149,127,779	9,975,622	253	504	73,619,575	65,532,582	100.0	6.7	49.4	43.9
1986–87	158,523,693	10,146,013	255	497	78,830,437	69,547,243	100.0	6.4	49.7	43.9
1987–88	169,561,974	10,716,687	268	501	84,004,415	74,840,873	100.0	6.3	49.5	44.1
1988–89	192,016,374	11,902,001	296	530	91,768,911	88,345,462	100.0	6.2	47.8	46.0
1989–90	208,547,573	12,700,784	313	535	98,238,633	97,608,157	100.0	6.1	47.1	46.8
1990–91	223,340,537	13,776,066	334	541	105,324,533	104,239,939	100.0	6.2	47.2	46.7
1991–92	234,581,384	15,493,330	368	578	108,783,449	110,304,605	100.0	6.6	46.4	47.0
1992–93	247,626,168	17,261,252	403	613	113,403,436	116,961,481	100.0	7.0	45.8	47.2
1993–94	260,159,468	18,341,483	422	625	117,474,209	124,343,776	100.0	7.1	45.2	47.8
1994–95	273,149,449	18,582,157	421	607	127,729,576	126,837,717	100.0	6.8	46.8	46.4
1995–96	287,702,844	19,104,019	426	598	136,670,754	131,928,071	100.0	6.6	47.5	45.9
1996–97	305,065,192	20,081,287	440	600	146,435,584	138,548,321	100.0	6.6	48.0	45.4
1997–98	325,925,708	22,201,965	481	645	157,645,372	146,078,370	100.0	6.8	48.4	44.8
1998–99	347,377,993	24,521,817	527	694	169,298,232	153,557,944	100.0	7.1	48.7	44.2
1999–2000	372,943,802	27,097,866	578	740	184,613,352	161,232,584	100.0	7.3	49.5	43.2
2000–01	401,356,120	29,100,183	616	763	199,583,097	172,672,840	100.0	7.3	49.7	43.0
2001–02	419,501,976	33,144,633	695	846	206,541,793	179,815,551	100.0	7.9	49.2	42.9
2002–03	440,111,653	37,515,909	779	927	214,277,407	188,318,337	100.0	8.5	48.7	42.8
2003–04	462,026,099	41,923,435	864	1,006	217,384,191	202,718,474	100.0	9.1	47.1	43.9
2004–05	487,753,525	44,809,532	918	1,038	228,553,579	214,390,414	100.0	9.2	46.9	44.0
2005–06	520,621,788	47,553,778	968	1,095	242,151,076	230,916,934	100.0	9.1	46.5	44.4
2006–07	555,710,762	47,150,608	957	1,042	263,608,741	244,951,413	100.0	8.5	47.4	44.1
2007–08[2]	584,683,686	47,788,467	971	1,031	282,622,523	254,272,697	100.0	8.2	48.3	43.5
2008–09	593,061,181	56,730,664	1,158	1,185	277,079,518	259,250,999	100.0	9.6	46.7	43.7

#Rounds to zero.

[1]Includes a relatively small amount from nongovernmental private sources (gifts and tuition and transportation fees from patrons). These sources accounted for 2.1 percent of total revenues in 2008–09.

[2]Revised from previously published figures.

NOTE: Beginning in 1980–81, revenues for state education agencies are excluded. Beginning in 1988–89, data reflect new survey collection procedures and may not be entirely comparable with figures for earlier years. With the exception of federal revenue per student, data are not adjusted for changes in the purchasing power of the dollar due to inflation. Detail may not sum to totals because of rounding.

SOURCE: U.S. Department of Education, National Center for Education Statistics, *Biennial Survey of Education in the United States*, 1919–20 through 1955–56; *Statistics of State School Systems*, 1957–58 through 1969–70; *Revenues and Expenditures for Public Elementary and Secondary Education*, 1970–71 through 1986–87; and Common Core of Data (CCD), "National Public Education Financial Survey," 1987–88 through 2008–09. (This table was prepared June 2011.)

Revenues for public elementary and secondary schools, by source and state or jurisdiction: 2008–09

State or jurisdiction	Total (in thousands)	Federal			State		Local and intermediate		Private[1]	
		Amount (in thousands)	Per student	Percent of total	Amount (in thousands)	Percent of total	Amount (in thousands)	Percent of total	Amount (in thousands)	Percent of total
1	2	3	4	5	6	7	8	9	10	11
United States	$593,061,181	$56,730,664	$1,158	9.6	$277,079,518	46.7	$247,056,935	41.7	$12,194,064	2.1
Alabama	7,239,083	777,591	1,052	10.7	4,166,018	57.5	1,992,298	27.5	303,176	4.2
Alaska	2,262,964	314,949	2,410	13.9	1,459,658	64.5	465,579	20.6	22,777	1.0
Arizona	9,771,972	1,137,316	1,046	11.6	4,594,648	47.0	3,798,559	38.9	241,449	2.5
Arkansas	4,823,956	556,500	1,162	11.5	2,684,309	55.6	1,437,641	29.8	145,506	3.0
California	70,687,012	9,185,270	1,453	13.0	40,605,913	57.4	20,368,059	28.8	527,770	0.7
Colorado	8,353,849	578,233	707	6.9	3,670,240	43.9	3,777,087	45.2	328,289	3.9
Connecticut	9,871,755	440,826	777	4.5	3,842,177	38.9	5,462,465	55.3	126,286	1.3
Delaware	1,755,133	142,428	1,136	8.1	1,094,909	62.4	499,023	28.4	18,773	1.1
District of Columbia	1,651,014	175,732	2,559	10.6	†	†	1,464,435	88.7	10,848	0.7
Florida	26,322,090	2,694,579	1,024	10.2	9,047,588	34.4	13,612,475	51.7	967,448	3.7
Georgia	18,017,477	1,688,274	1,020	9.4	7,780,725	43.2	8,069,989	44.8	478,489	2.7
Hawaii	2,689,757	392,837	2,189	14.6	2,205,032	82.0	66,726	2.5	25,163	0.9
Idaho	2,243,784	229,156	833	10.2	1,509,815	67.3	466,957	20.8	37,856	1.7
Illinois	26,512,711	3,146,741	1,552	11.9	7,324,750	27.6	15,531,406	58.6	509,814	1.9
Indiana	12,569,782	1,432,813	1,370	11.4	4,964,928	39.5	5,830,641	46.4	341,401	2.7
Iowa	5,519,854	443,827	943	8.0	2,545,360	46.1	2,383,358	43.2	147,308	2.7
Kansas	5,757,927	453,608	963	7.9	3,323,346	57.7	1,856,661	32.2	124,312	2.2
Kentucky	6,641,128	731,351	1,123	11.0	3,802,150	57.3	1,990,051	30.0	117,576	1.8
Louisiana	8,099,981	1,264,057	1,846	15.6	3,740,262	46.2	3,027,466	37.4	68,196	0.8
Maine	2,575,516	245,719	1,274	9.5	1,127,032	43.8	1,158,487	45.0	44,278	1.7
Maryland	13,097,508	694,847	823	5.3	5,698,735	43.5	6,398,354	48.9	305,572	2.3
Massachusetts	15,102,480	1,276,250	1,331	8.5	6,036,202	40.0	7,585,205	50.2	204,823	1.4
Michigan	19,585,635	2,253,644	1,358	11.5	10,904,987	55.7	6,102,408	31.2	324,596	1.7
Minnesota	10,542,303	632,057	756	6.0	6,914,839	65.6	2,669,453	25.3	325,954	3.1
Mississippi	4,360,702	675,972	1,374	15.5	2,334,355	53.5	1,234,198	28.3	116,176	2.7
Missouri	10,042,753	833,909	934	8.3	3,425,716	34.1	5,426,763	54.0	356,364	3.5
Montana	1,595,197	199,017	1,412	12.5	774,091	48.5	562,804	35.3	59,285	3.7
Nebraska	3,455,794	280,666	997	8.1	1,213,317	35.1	1,808,600	52.3	153,210	4.4
Nevada	4,450,741	434,484	1,003	9.8	1,362,123	30.6	2,524,226	56.7	129,908	2.9
New Hampshire	2,717,115	147,318	744	5.4	1,003,249	36.9	1,516,311	55.8	50,236	1.8
New Jersey	25,283,290	1,040,733	753	4.1	10,525,550	41.6	13,174,940	52.1	542,066	2.1
New Mexico	3,820,116	569,047	1,723	14.9	2,675,916	70.0	521,818	13.7	53,334	1.4
New York	55,558,190	3,220,417	1,175	5.8	25,346,556	45.6	26,630,218	47.9	360,999	0.6
North Carolina	13,322,946	1,406,049	960	10.6	8,401,249	63.1	3,231,841	24.3	283,807	2.1
North Dakota	1,102,479	161,484	1,705	14.6	408,004	37.0	485,412	44.0	47,578	4.3
Ohio	22,956,215	1,685,617	947	7.3	10,917,974	47.6	9,660,733	42.1	691,892	3.0
Oklahoma	5,729,610	770,745	1,195	13.5	3,042,487	53.1	1,661,176	29.0	255,202	4.5
Oregon	6,145,206	670,547	1,165	10.9	3,117,303	50.7	2,210,170	36.0	147,187	2.4
Pennsylvania	25,632,072	1,868,034	1,052	7.3	9,920,340	38.7	13,443,213	52.4	400,487	1.6
Rhode Island	2,232,149	215,514	1,483	9.7	817,590	36.6	1,177,531	52.8	21,514	1.0
South Carolina	7,702,962	762,297	1,062	9.9	3,679,907	47.8	3,014,155	39.1	246,603	3.2
South Dakota	1,241,892	203,354	1,608	16.4	410,179	33.0	591,747	47.6	36,612	2.9
Tennessee	8,283,928	935,135	962	11.3	3,809,467	46.0	3,095,648	37.4	443,677	5.4
Texas	46,962,119	5,014,820	1,055	10.7	19,973,129	42.5	21,030,167	44.8	944,003	2.0
Utah	4,542,690	565,022	1,027	12.4	2,387,698	52.6	1,401,061	30.8	188,910	4.2
Vermont	1,571,006	102,785	1,098	6.5	1,346,300	85.7	99,007	6.3	22,915	1.5
Virginia	14,964,444	914,524	740	6.1	6,303,648	42.1	7,456,028	49.8	290,243	1.9
Washington	11,903,510	1,385,449	1,350	11.6	7,146,394	60.0	3,059,180	25.7	312,487	2.6
West Virginia	3,281,385	366,038	1,295	11.2	1,938,999	59.1	946,034	28.8	30,313	0.9
Wisconsin	10,832,105	1,302,449	1,502	12.0	4,809,185	44.4	4,478,422	41.3	242,049	2.2
Wyoming	1,675,896	110,634	1,276	6.6	945,167	56.4	600,751	35.8	19,344	1.2
Other jurisdictions										
American Samoa	79,922	68,432	—	85.6	11,282	14.1	137	0.2	71	0.1
Guam	262,823	50,170	—	19.1	0	0.0	211,886	80.6	767	0.3
Northern Marianas	65,538	30,711	2,814	46.9	34,602	52.8	225	0.3	0	0.0
Puerto Rico	3,542,658	1,076,147	2,137	30.4	2,462,725	69.5	12	#	3,775	0.1
U.S. Virgin Islands	243,079	40,037	2,539	16.5	0	0.0	163,537	67.3	39,505	16.3

—Not available.
†Not applicable.
#Rounds to zero.
[1]Includes revenues from gifts, and tuition and fees from patrons.

NOTE: Excludes revenues for state education agencies. Detail may not sum to totals because of rounding.
SOURCE: U.S. Department of Education, National Center for Education Statistics, Common Core of Data (CCD), "National Public Education Financial Survey," 2008–09. (This table was prepared June 2011.)

Total expenditures for public elementary and secondary education, by function and state or jurisdiction: 2008–09

[In thousands of current dollars]

Columns 3–14 fall under "Current expenditures for elementary and secondary programs"; columns 5–12 fall under "Support services."

State or jurisdiction	Total	Elementary/ secondary current expenditures, total	Instruction	Support services — Total	Student support[4]	Instructional staff	General administration	School administration	Operation and maintenance	Student transportation	Other support services	Food services	Enterprise operations[3]	Other current expenditures[1]	Capital outlay[2]	Interest on school debt
1	2	3	4	5	6	7	8	9	10	11	12	13	14	15	16	17
United States	$610,109,923	$518,997,430	$316,345,253	$181,622,348	$28,104,003	$24,988,164	$10,323,926	$29,092,503	$50,639,590	$21,685,125	$16,789,038	$19,805,134	$1,224,695	$8,539,329	$65,881,936	$16,691,228
Alabama	7,866,617	6,683,843	3,897,501	2,337,967	373,911	311,959	173,277	416,151	610,997	320,755	130,918	448,376	0	115,007	927,145	140,621
Alaska	2,359,510	2,006,114	1,123,574	820,206	161,052	113,309	29,706	121,084	261,004	60,126	73,924	53,355	8,979	7,966	304,504	40,926
Arizona	10,451,060	8,625,276	5,205,607	2,978,397	530,369	231,809	124,720	419,035	973,667	318,706	380,091	394,913	46,359	51,625	1,242,591	531,568
Arkansas	4,862,688	4,240,839	2,462,105	1,534,972	210,994	336,688	103,551	222,227	404,085	152,065	105,361	239,472	4,291	28,502	473,438	119,909
California	72,059,482	60,080,929	35,942,432	21,753,530	3,067,163	3,928,377	572,688	4,010,200	6,150,391	1,472,636	2,552,076	2,236,786	148,182	1,235,054	8,844,862	1,898,637
Colorado	8,732,152	7,187,267	4,141,866	2,761,981	334,618	394,998	117,909	489,394	699,155	214,033	511,873	244,032	39,387	56,266	1,048,756	439,864
Connecticut	9,904,492	8,708,294	5,441,636	2,975,808	539,182	272,889	182,451	498,983	849,063	437,208	196,032	215,038	75,811	146,086	893,667	156,445
Delaware	1,843,876	1,518,786	925,411	532,632	76,345	17,749	19,397	88,877	157,576	97,419	75,270	60,742	0	20,920	258,087	46,083
District of Columbia	1,865,053	1,352,905	624,116	685,775	138,818	88,290	39,250	120,413	124,747	88,538	85,719	41,386	1,627	24,754	474,140	13,254
Florida	29,197,311	23,328,028	14,104,997	8,195,582	1,087,761	1,512,924	210,878	1,332,838	2,500,985	947,681	602,516	1,027,449	0	510,550	4,523,261	835,471
Georgia	18,989,232	15,976,945	10,013,104	5,121,083	766,374	808,520	234,531	933,393	1,185,832	660,665	531,767	795,964	46,793	36,743	2,714,768	260,776
Hawaii	2,423,593	2,225,437	1,384,466	736,148	211,127	73,175	11,688	137,433	166,205	62,619	73,901	104,823	0	25,231	69,864	103,060
Idaho	2,370,488	1,957,740	1,192,267	668,144	113,401	81,142	45,261	109,581	184,705	92,622	41,433	96,900	430	4,266	352,323	56,159
Illinois	27,273,680	23,495,271	13,813,130	8,949,552	1,508,922	1,084,402	976,876	1,182,234	2,199,235	1,129,961	867,922	732,589	0	165,318	2,884,296	728,796
Indiana	11,069,893	9,680,895	5,652,947	3,619,385	451,616	357,410	204,041	558,674	1,155,276	563,551	328,816	408,563	0	142,523	929,150	317,325
Iowa	5,517,616	4,731,463	2,897,898	1,617,639	268,931	214,072	124,570	274,472	424,493	166,920	144,182	211,267	4,660	27,506	677,328	81,318
Kansas	5,389,538	4,805,310	2,902,869	1,683,298	276,623	224,562	147,283	278,983	451,954	186,685	117,208	219,144	0	6,268	409,651	168,308
Kentucky	6,839,799	5,886,890	3,486,673	2,042,628	260,815	310,156	125,985	330,122	547,636	335,246	132,668	344,230	13,359	86,735	714,321	151,852
Louisiana	8,269,661	7,276,651	4,218,540	2,664,645	334,256	394,418	185,137	407,148	729,088	393,372	221,227	393,243	224	54,859	829,054	109,097
Maine	2,579,168	2,350,447	1,414,747	851,795	147,738	112,710	93,647	126,609	240,565	109,552	20,972	83,850	55	27,881	156,303	44,537
Maryland	12,753,441	11,591,965	7,147,477	3,979,493	529,879	596,948	78,538	802,912	1,078,237	570,850	322,129	304,976	160,019	25,038	988,894	147,544
Massachusetts	15,081,541	13,942,586	9,072,483	4,505,468	956,365	662,050	179,899	563,110	1,262,220	551,549	330,275	364,636	0	65,704	793,699	279,552
Michigan	19,897,270	17,217,584	9,843,731	6,810,105	1,306,870	820,143	352,864	993,486	1,787,713	742,718	806,311	563,748	0	339,221	1,469,393	871,072
Minnesota	11,332,655	9,270,281	6,042,279	2,831,683	247,591	424,726	369,889	372,858	679,799	483,691	253,129	372,592	23,726	422,034	1,215,827	424,514
Mississippi	4,402,170	3,967,232	2,327,535	1,398,665	186,883	182,341	117,437	229,664	414,227	180,014	88,097	240,748	285	28,517	333,562	72,858
Missouri	10,466,632	8,827,224	5,304,123	3,127,460	414,203	406,271	279,832	502,570	876,773	443,929	203,883	395,641	0	195,440	1,129,253	314,714
Montana	1,624,979	1,436,062	862,843	511,489	81,182	54,966	40,524	77,712	155,356	67,239	34,510	59,207	2,523	9,036	161,935	17,946
Nebraska	3,579,827	3,053,575	1,982,560	863,350	112,011	87,034	90,352	152,571	272,526	84,034	64,822	123,337	84,328	3,242	449,965	73,045
Nevada	4,550,664	3,606,035	2,142,723	1,345,410	173,167	188,597	83,654	259,658	383,827	153,352	128,154	117,902	0	22,291	633,569	288,769
New Hampshire	2,655,947	2,490,623	1,600,157	822,153	173,945	78,609	83,924	134,348	220,207	105,787	25,333	68,313	0	7,225	112,508	45,591
New Jersey	25,623,867	23,589,224	13,929,759	8,910,366	2,187,782	756,515	546,390	1,565,022	2,453,912	1,258,842	141,903	525,349	223,751	249,594	1,432,051	352,997
New Mexico	3,912,992	3,186,252	1,837,760	1,215,387	324,958	95,441	69,963	196,954	320,854	112,072	95,145	131,500	1,605	4,229	722,373	138
New York	54,766,076	48,635,363	33,644,194	13,968,400	1,629,616	1,361,331	916,311	2,014,531	4,218,196	2,568,077	1,260,339	1,022,769	0	2,103,039	2,908,659	1,119,015
North Carolina	14,242,947	12,470,470	7,900,594	3,893,531	572,903	472,377	170,085	768,246	1,043,229	503,762	362,930	676,345	0	72,203	1,693,306	6,967
North Dakota	1,046,126	928,528	541,896	308,827	38,023	28,752	41,600	46,839	90,196	40,263	23,155	49,773	28,031	9,129	95,376	13,093
Ohio	22,901,610	19,397,511	11,049,442	7,701,222	1,180,645	1,261,165	582,662	1,110,923	1,807,485	896,796	861,547	645,308	1,538	470,118	2,556,351	477,631
Oklahoma	5,622,898	5,082,062	2,908,376	1,828,735	342,773	184,305	148,430	276,346	579,842	158,208	138,832	298,388	46,563	12,794	472,558	55,484
Oregon	6,624,906	5,529,831	3,218,961	2,119,694	397,276	238,764	75,675	351,366	460,928	240,911	354,774	188,987	2,189	23,268	803,068	268,739
Pennsylvania	26,001,339	21,831,816	13,201,013	7,778,904	1,086,621	852,409	651,573	952,843	2,310,842	1,109,260	815,356	758,229	93,670	599,517	2,468,875	1,101,131
Rhode Island	2,259,628	2,139,317	1,280,778	806,377	266,637	69,384	55,355	105,391	182,792	84,232	42,586	52,081	81	57,046	25,523	37,742
South Carolina	8,378,028	6,626,763	3,826,821	2,441,544	487,739	437,172	79,535	395,185	617,719	216,135	208,058	339,378	19,020	74,810	1,317,674	358,781
South Dakota	1,273,647	1,080,054	626,773	391,593	61,302	44,605	37,864	53,784	116,036	37,844	40,158	56,746	4,943	3,630	167,299	22,694
Tennessee	8,645,029	7,768,052	4,874,867	2,508,101	321,372	452,226	151,729	446,506	706,404	281,361	148,503	385,084	0	65,622	636,113	175,242
Texas	52,980,125	40,688,181	24,415,370	14,155,735	1,971,160	2,120,068	596,482	2,254,343	4,593,772	1,106,854	1,513,056	2,117,077	0	303,178	9,293,157	2,695,608
Utah	4,754,524	3,638,775	2,352,270	1,078,296	138,666	157,909	45,066	216,969	324,720	112,747	82,219	190,117	18,092	104,773	891,455	119,521

See notes at end of table.

Total expenditures for public elementary and secondary education, by function and state or jurisdiction: 2008–09—Continued

[In thousands of current dollars]

State or jurisdiction	Total	Elementary/ secondary current expenditures, total	Total expenditures — Current expenditures for elementary and secondary programs — Instruction	Support services — Total	Student support[4]	Instructional staff[5]	General administration	School administration	Operation and maintenance	Student transportation	Other support services	Food services	Enterprise operations[3]	Other current expenditures[1]	Capital outlay[2]	Interest on school debt
1	2	3	4	5	6	7	8	9	10	11	12	13	14	15	16	17
Vermont	1,501,278	1,413,329	881,772	492,311	103,821	56,216	33,092	95,999	121,630	47,342	34,212	38,520	725	10,119	64,522	13,308
Virginia	15,155,776	13,505,290	8,194,326	4,813,707	655,441	906,450	214,391	799,234	1,324,723	691,335	222,133	495,745	1,512	77,601	1,418,910	153,975
Washington	12,226,885	9,940,056	5,981,819	3,512,391	660,150	443,977	185,121	579,763	882,009	391,809	369,562	324,730	121,116	57,389	1,811,236	418,204
West Virginia	3,196,380	3,059,420	1,825,237	1,065,622	113,038	123,211	73,795	161,598	324,806	218,795	50,379	168,560	0	41,145	83,357	12,458
Wisconsin	11,135,130	9,696,228	5,935,538	3,422,525	448,911	470,984	249,525	485,249	886,881	356,477	524,487	338,068	97	301,023	631,446	506,432
Wyoming	1,650,665	1,268,407	745,889	482,637	73,057	83,660	24,524	68,670	125,061	58,484	49,182	39,156	725	7,289	372,510	2,460
Other jurisdictions																
American Samoa	71,468	65,436	32,737	17,540	1,799	3,372	928	6,093	2,631	1,225	1,493	15,158	0	1,980	4,052	0
Guam	265,065	235,711	135,903	87,369	26,318	6,113	3,613	13,663	33,190	1,011	3,462	12,438	0	0	22,800	6,555
Northern Marianas	65,766	62,787	28,625	28,094	7,857	5,138	1,354	4,912	5,161	1,264	2,408	488	5,580	1,576	1,403	0
Puerto Rico	4,026,886	3,502,757	1,738,493	1,417,946	227,299	168,157	125,230	185,627	421,380	100,516	189,737	346,319	0	101,921	417,112	5,096
U.S. Virgin Islands	207,633	201,326	116,671	76,159	11,687	4,560	7,266	9,144	9,290	14,182	20,031	8,496	0	1,677	4,630	0

[1]Includes expenditures for adult education, community colleges, private school programs funded by local and state education agencies, and community services.

[2]Includes expenditures for property and for buildings and alterations completed by school district staff or contractors.

[3]Includes expenditures for operations funded by sales of products or services (e.g., school bookstore or computer time). Also includes small amounts for direct program support made by state education agencies for local school districts.

[4]Includes expenditures for health, attendance, and speech pathology services.

[5]Includes expenditures for curriculum development, staff training, libraries, and media and computer centers.

NOTE: Excludes expenditures for state education agencies. Detail may not sum to totals because of rounding.

SOURCE: U.S. Department of Education, National Center for Education Statistics, Common Core of Data (CCD), "National Public Education Financial Survey," 2008–09. (This table was prepared June 2011.)

Total and current expenditures per pupil in public elementary and secondary schools: Selected years, 1919–20 through 2008–09

School year	Expenditure per pupil in average daily attendance				Expenditure per pupil in fall enrollment[1]				
	Unadjusted dollars		Constant 2009–10 dollars[2]		Unadjusted dollars		Constant 2009–10 dollars[2]		
	Total expenditure[3]	Current expenditure	Total expenditure[3]	Current expenditure	Total expenditure[3]	Current expenditure	Total expenditure[3]	Current expenditure	Annual percent change in current expenditure
1	2	3	4	5	6	7	8	9	10
1919–20	$64	$53	$727	$606	$48	$40	$544	$454	—
1929–30	108	87	1,374	1,098	90	72	1,138	909	—
1931–32	97	81	1,456	1,219	82	69	1,233	1,032	—
1933–34	76	67	1,248	1,104	65	57	1,060	938	—
1935–36	88	74	1,387	1,172	74	63	1,173	991	—
1937–38	100	84	1,508	1,269	86	72	1,295	1,089	—
1939–40	106	88	1,640	1,366	92	76	1,421	1,184	—
1941–42	110	98	1,529	1,367	94	84	1,310	1,170	—
1943–44	125	117	1,551	1,455	105	99	1,307	1,226	—
1945–46	146	136	1,733	1,621	124	116	1,476	1,381	—
1947–48	205	181	1,906	1,688	179	158	1,664	1,474	—
1949–50	260	210	2,383	1,925	231	187	2,114	1,708	—
1951–52	314	246	2,593	2,029	275	215	2,271	1,776	—
1953–54	351	265	2,829	2,134	312	236	2,515	1,898	—
1955–56	387	294	3,120	2,372	354	269	2,852	2,168	—
1957–58	447	341	3,396	2,589	408	311	3,097	2,361	—
1959–60	471	375	3,474	2,767	440	350	3,246	2,585	—
1961–62	517	419	3,729	3,021	485	393	3,499	2,835	—
1963–64	559	460	3,926	3,235	520	428	3,654	3,011	—
1965–66	654	538	4,441	3,652	607	499	4,123	3,391	—
1967–68	786	658	5,012	4,195	732	612	4,662	3,903	—
1969–70	955	816	5,479	4,682	879	751	5,044	4,310	—
1970–71	1,049	911	5,726	4,971	970	842	5,293	4,596	6.6
1971–72	1,128	990	5,940	5,213	1,034	908	5,448	4,781	4.0
1972–73	1,211	1,077	6,129	5,452	1,117	993	5,654	5,029	5.2
1973–74	1,364	1,207	6,340	5,612	1,244	1,101	5,781	5,117	1.7
1974–75	1,545	1,365	6,464	5,710	1,423	1,257	5,955	5,261	2.8
1975–76	1,697	1,504	6,633	5,876	1,563	1,385	6,108	5,411	2.9
1976–77	1,816	1,638	6,707	6,047	1,674	1,509	6,180	5,572	3.0
1977–78	2,002	1,823	6,929	6,308	1,842	1,677	6,373	5,801	4.1
1978–79	2,210	2,020	6,992	6,393	2,029	1,855	6,421	5,871	1.2
1979–80	2,491	2,272	6,953	6,342	2,290	2,088	6,392	5,830	-0.7
1980–81	2,742 [4]	2,502	6,861 [4]	6,259	2,529 [4]	2,307	6,329 [4]	5,773	-1.0
1981–82	2,973 [4]	2,726	6,848 [4]	6,277	2,754 [4]	2,525	6,343 [4]	5,815	0.7
1982–83	3,203 [4]	2,955	7,074 [4]	6,526	2,966 [4]	2,736	6,550 [4]	6,043	3.9
1983–84	3,471 [4]	3,173	7,392 [4]	6,757	3,216 [4]	2,940	6,848 [4]	6,260	3.6
1984–85	3,722 [4]	3,470	7,627 [4]	7,111	3,456 [4]	3,222	7,081 [4]	6,603	5.5
1985–86	4,020 [4]	3,756	8,006 [4]	7,480	3,724 [4]	3,479	7,418 [4]	6,930	5.0
1986–87	4,308 [4]	3,970	8,394 [4]	7,736	3,995 [4]	3,682	7,784 [4]	7,174	3.5
1987–88	4,654 [4]	4,240	8,707 [4]	7,933	4,310 [4]	3,927	8,064 [4]	7,347	2.4
1988–89	5,108	4,645	9,135	8,306	4,737	4,307	8,471	7,703	4.8
1989–90	5,547	4,980	9,468	8,500	5,172	4,643	8,828	7,925	2.9
1990–91	5,882	5,258	9,519	8,509	5,484	4,902	8,875	7,933	0.1
1991–92	6,072	5,421	9,522	8,501	5,626	5,023	8,823	7,877	-0.7
1992–93	6,279	5,584	9,549	8,491	5,802	5,160	8,824	7,846	-0.4
1993–94	6,489	5,767	9,619	8,549	5,994	5,327	8,884	7,896	0.6
1994–95	6,723	5,989	9,688	8,630	6,206	5,529	8,943	7,967	0.9
1995–96	6,959	6,147	9,763	8,623	6,441	5,689	9,036	7,981	0.2
1996–97	7,297	6,393	9,953	8,719	6,761	5,923	9,222	8,079	1.2
1997–98	7,701	6,676	10,319	8,945	7,139	6,189	9,567	8,293	2.7
1998–99	8,115	7,013	10,690	9,238	7,531	6,508	9,920	8,572	3.4
1999–2000	8,589	7,394	10,996	9,466	8,030	6,912	10,280	8,849	3.2
2000–01	9,180	7,904	11,363	9,783	8,572	7,380	10,610	9,135	3.2
2001–02	9,611	8,259	11,690	10,045	8,993	7,727	10,938	9,399	2.9
2002–03	9,950	8,610	11,842	10,247	9,296	8,044	11,064	9,574	1.9
2003–04	10,308	8,900	12,005	10,365	9,625	8,310	11,210	9,679	1.1
2004–05	10,779	9,316	12,187	10,533	10,078	8,711	11,395	9,849	1.8
2005–06	11,338	9,778	12,349	10,650	10,603	9,145	11,549	9,960	1.1
2006–07	12,015	10,336	12,757	10,974	11,252	9,679	11,946	10,276	3.2
2007–08 [5]	12,759	10,982	13,063	11,243	11,965	10,298	12,249	10,543	2.6
2008–09	13,015	11,231	13,141	11,339	12,274	10,591	12,393	10,694	1.4

—Not available.

[1] Data for 1919–20 to 1953–54 are based on school-year enrollment.

[2] Constant dollars based on the Consumer Price Index, prepared by the Bureau of Labor Statistics, U.S. Department of Labor, adjusted to a school-year basis.

[3] Excludes "Other current expenditures," such as community services, private school programs, adult education, and other programs not allocable to expenditures per student at public schools.

[4] Estimated.

[5] Revised from previously published figures.

NOTE: Beginning in 1980–81, state administration expenditures are excluded from both "total" and "current" expenditures. Current expenditures include instruction, student support services, food services, and enterprise operations. Total expenditures include current expenditures, capital outlay, and interest on debt. Beginning in 1988–89, extensive changes were made in the data collection procedures.

SOURCE: U.S. Department of Education, National Center for Education Statistics, *Biennial Survey of Education in the United States*, 1919–20 through 1955–56; *Statistics of State School Systems*, 1957–58 through 1969–70; *Revenues and Expenditures for Public Elementary and Secondary Education*, 1970–71 through 1986–87; and Common Core of Data (CCD), "National Public Education Financial Survey," 1987–88 through 2008–09. (This table was prepared June 2011.)

Total and current expenditures per pupil in fall enrollment in public elementary and secondary education, by function and state or jurisdiction: 2008–09

State or jurisdiction	Total[1]	Current expenditures, capital expenditures, and interest on school debt													Capital outlay[2]	Interest on school debt
		Current expenditures														
		Total	Instruction	Support services								Food services	Enterprise operations[3]		
				Total	Student support[4]	Instructional staff[5]	General administration	School administration	Operation and maintenance	Student transportation	Other support services				
1	2	3	4	5	6	7	8	9	10	11	12	13	14	15	16
United States	$12,274	$10,591	$6,456	$3,706	$574	$510	$211	$594	$1,033	$443	$343	$404	$25	$1,344	$341
Alabama	10,486	9,042	5,273	3,163	506	422	234	563	827	434	177	607	0	1,254	190
Alaska	17,996	15,353	8,599	6,277	1,233	867	227	927	1,998	460	566	408	69	2,330	313
Arizona	9,559	7,929	4,785	2,738	488	213	115	385	895	293	349	363	43	1,142	489
Arkansas	10,092	8,854	5,140	3,205	441	703	216	464	844	317	220	500	9	988	250
California	11,202	9,503	5,685	3,441	485	621	91	634	973	233	404	354	23	1,399	300
Colorado	10,600	8,782	5,061	3,375	409	483	144	598	854	262	625	298	48	1,281	537
Connecticut	17,203	15,353	9,594	5,247	951	481	322	880	1,497	771	346	379	134	1,576	276
Delaware	14,534	12,109	7,378	4,246	609	142	155	709	1,256	777	600	484	0	2,058	367
District of Columbia	26,753	19,698	9,087	9,985	2,021	1,286	571	1,753	1,816	1,289	1,248	603	24	6,904	193
Florida	10,900	8,867	5,361	3,115	413	575	80	507	951	360	229	391	0	1,719	318
Georgia	11,446	9,649	6,047	3,093	463	488	142	564	716	399	321	481	28	1,640	157
Hawaii	13,361	12,399	7,714	4,102	1,176	408	65	766	926	349	412	584	0	389	574
Idaho	8,601	7,118	4,335	2,429	412	295	165	398	672	337	151	352	2	1,281	204
Illinois	13,374	11,592	6,815	4,415	744	535	482	583	1,085	557	428	361	0	1,423	360
Indiana	10,444	9,254	5,404	3,460	432	342	195	534	1,104	539	314	391	0	888	303
Iowa	11,667	10,055	6,159	3,438	572	455	265	583	902	355	306	449	10	1,439	173
Kansas	11,427	10,201	6,162	3,573	587	477	313	592	959	396	249	465	0	870	357
Kentucky	10,365	9,038	5,353	3,136	400	476	193	507	841	515	204	528	21	1,097	233
Louisiana	11,995	10,625	6,160	3,891	488	576	270	594	1,065	574	323	574	0	1,211	159
Maine	13,222	12,183	7,333	4,415	766	584	485	656	1,247	568	109	435	0	810	231
Maryland	15,083	13,737	8,470	4,716	628	707	93	951	1,278	676	382	361	190	1,172	175
Massachusetts	15,659	14,540	9,461	4,699	997	690	188	587	1,316	575	344	380	0	828	292
Michigan	11,781	10,373	5,930	4,103	787	494	213	599	1,077	447	486	340	0	885	525
Minnesota	13,046	11,088	7,227	3,387	296	508	442	446	813	579	303	446	28	1,454	508
Mississippi	8,889	8,064	4,731	2,843	380	371	239	467	842	366	179	489	1	678	148
Missouri	11,507	9,891	5,943	3,504	464	455	314	563	982	497	228	443	0	1,265	353
Montana	11,463	10,189	6,122	3,629	576	390	288	551	1,102	477	245	420	18	1,149	127
Nebraska	12,703	10,846	7,042	3,066	398	309	321	542	968	298	230	438	300	1,598	259
Nevada	10,449	8,321	4,944	3,105	400	435	135	599	886	354	296	272	0	1,462	666
New Hampshire	13,381	12,583	8,084	4,154	879	397	424	679	1,113	534	128	345	0	568	230
New Jersey	18,367	17,076	10,084	6,450	1,584	548	396	1,133	1,776	911	103	380	162	1,037	256
New Mexico	11,835	9,648	5,565	3,680	984	289	212	596	972	339	288	398	5	2,187	0
New York	19,212	17,746	12,276	5,097	595	497	334	735	1,539	937	460	373	0	1,061	408
North Carolina	9,679	8,518	5,397	2,660	391	323	116	525	713	344	248	462	0	1,157	5
North Dakota	10,947	9,802	5,721	3,260	401	304	439	494	952	425	244	525	296	1,007	138
Ohio	12,592	10,902	6,210	4,328	664	709	327	624	1,016	504	484	363	1	1,437	268
Oklahoma	8,696	7,878	4,508	2,835	531	286	230	428	899	245	215	463	72	733	86
Oregon	11,473	9,611	5,594	3,684	690	415	132	611	801	419	617	328	4	1,396	467
Pennsylvania	14,308	12,299	7,437	4,382	612	480	367	537	1,302	625	459	427	53	1,391	620
Rhode Island	15,154	14,719	8,812	5,548	1,835	477	381	725	1,258	580	293	358	1	176	260
South Carolina	11,562	9,228	5,329	3,400	679	609	111	550	860	301	290	473	26	1,835	500
South Dakota	10,045	8,543	4,958	3,097	485	353	299	425	918	299	318	449	39	1,323	179
Tennessee	8,825	7,992	5,016	2,580	331	465	156	459	727	289	153	396	0	654	180
Texas	11,085	8,562	5,138	2,979	415	446	126	474	967	233	318	445	0	1,956	567
Utah	8,446	6,612	4,275	1,959	252	287	82	394	590	205	149	345	33	1,620	217
Vermont	15,925	15,096	9,418	5,258	1,109	600	353	1,025	1,299	506	365	411	8	689	142
Virginia	12,201	10,928	6,631	3,895	530	733	173	647	1,072	559	180	401	1	1,148	125
Washington	11,860	9,688	5,830	3,423	643	433	180	565	860	382	360	316	118	1,765	408
West Virginia	11,159	10,821	6,456	3,769	400	436	261	572	1,149	774	178	596	0	295	44
Wisconsin	12,491	11,183	6,846	3,947	518	543	288	560	1,023	411	605	390	0	728	584
Wyoming	18,922	14,628	8,602	5,566	843	965	283	792	1,442	674	567	452	8	4,296	28
Other jurisdictions															
American Samoa	—	—	—	—	—	—	—	—	—	—	—	—	—	—	—
Guam	—	—	—	—	—	—	—	—	—	—	—	—	—	—	—
Northern Marianas	5,882	5,753	2,623	2,574	720	471	124	450	473	116	221	45	511	129	0
Puerto Rico	7,790	6,955	3,452	2,815	451	334	249	369	837	200	377	688	0	828	10
U.S. Virgin Islands	13,062	12,768	7,399	4,830	741	289	461	580	589	899	1,270	539	0	294	0

—Not available.

[1] Excludes "Other current expenditures," such as community services, private school programs, adult education, and other programs not allocable to expenditures per pupil in public schools.

[2] Includes expenditures for property and for buildings and alterations completed by school district staff or contractors. Excludes capital outlay related to "Other current expenditures."

[3] Includes expenditures for operations funded by sales of products or services (e.g., school bookstore or computer time).

[4] Includes expenditures for health, attendance, and speech pathology services.

[5] Includes expenditures for curriculum development, staff training, libraries, and media and computer centers.

NOTE: Excludes expenditures for state education agencies. "0" indicates none or less than $0.50. Detail may not sum to totals because of rounding.

SOURCE: U.S. Department of Education, National Center for Education Statistics, Common Core of Data (CCD), "National Public Education Financial Survey," 2008–09. (This table was prepared June 2011.)

Number of public school districts and public and private elementary and secondary schools: Selected years, 1869–70 through 2009–10

School year	Regular public school districts[1]	Total, all public and private schools	Total, all public schools[4]	Total, schools with reported grade spans[5]	Schools with elementary grades — Total	Schools with elementary grades — One-teacher	Schools with secondary grades	Total, all private schools	Private — Schools with elementary grades	Private — Schools with secondary grades
1	2	3	4	5	6	7	8	9	10	11
1869–70	—	—	116,312	—	—	—	—	—	—	—
1879–80	—	—	178,122	—	—	—	—	—	—	—
1889–90	—	—	224,526	—	—	—	—	—	—	—
1899–1900	—	—	248,279	—	—	—	—	—	—	—
1909–10	—	—	265,474	—	—	212,448	—	—	—	—
1919–20	—	—	271,319	—	—	187,948	—	—	—	—
1929–30	—	—	248,117	—	238,306	148,712	23,930	—	9,275 [6]	3,258 [6]
1939–40	117,108 [7]	—	226,762	—	—	113,600	—	—	11,306 [6]	3,568 [6]
1949–50	83,718 [7]	—	—	—	128,225	59,652	24,542	—	10,375 [6]	3,331 [6]
1951–52	71,094 [7]	—	—	—	123,763	50,742	23,746	—	10,666 [6]	3,322 [6]
1959–60	40,520 [7]	—	—	—	91,853	20,213	25,784	—	13,574 [6]	4,061 [6]
1961–62	35,676 [7]	125,634	107,260	—	81,910	13,333	25,350	18,374	14,762 [6]	4,129 [6]
1963–64	31,705 [7]	—	104,015	—	77,584	9,895	26,431	—	—	4,451 [6]
1965–66	26,983 [7]	117,662	99,813	—	73,216	6,491	26,597	17,849 [6]	15,340 [6]	4,606 [6]
1967–68	22,010 [7]	—	—	94,197	70,879	4,146	27,011	—	—	—
1970–71	17,995 [7]	—	—	89,372	65,800	1,815	25,352	—	14,372 [6]	3,770 [6]
1973–74	16,730 [7]	—	—	88,655	65,070	1,365	25,906	—	—	—
1975–76	16,376 [7]	—	88,597	87,034	63,242	1,166	25,330	—	—	—
1976–77	16,271 [7]	—	—	86,501	62,644	1,111	25,378	19,910 [6]	16,385 [6]	5,904 [6]
1978–79	16,014 [7]	—	—	84,816	61,982	1,056	24,504	19,489 [6]	16,097 [6]	5,766 [6]
1979–80	15,944 [7]	—	87,004	—	—	—	—	—	—	—
1980–81	15,912 [7]	106,746	85,982	83,688	61,069	921	24,362	20,764 [6]	16,792 [6]	5,678 [6]
1982–83	15,824 [7]	—	84,740	82,039	59,656	798	23,988	—	—	—
1983–84	15,747 [7]	111,872	84,178	81,418	59,082	838	23,947	27,694	20,872	7,862
1984–85	—	—	84,007	81,147	58,827	825	23,916	—	—	—
1985–86	—	—	—	—	—	—	—	25,616	20,252	7,387
1986–87	15,713	—	83,421	82,316	60,811	763	23,481	—	—	—
1987–88	15,577	110,055	83,248	81,416	59,754	729	23,841	26,807	22,959	8,418
1988–89	15,376	—	83,165	81,579	60,176	583	23,638	—	—	—
1989–90	15,367	110,137	83,425	81,880	60,699	630	23,461	26,712	24,221	10,197
1990–91	15,358	109,228	84,538	82,475	61,340	617	23,460	24,690	22,223	8,989
1991–92	15,173	110,576	84,578	82,506	61,739	569	23,248	25,998	23,523	9,282
1992–93	15,025	—	84,497	82,896	62,225	430	23,220	—	—	—
1993–94	14,881	111,486	85,393	83,431	62,726	442	23,379	26,093	23,543	10,555
1994–95	14,772	—	86,221	84,476	63,572	458	23,668	—	—	—
1995–96	14,766	121,519	87,125	84,958	63,961	474	23,793	34,394	32,401	10,942
1996–97	14,841	—	88,223	86,092	64,785	487	24,287	—	—	—
1997–98	14,805	123,403	89,508	87,541	65,859	476	24,802	33,895	31,408	10,779
1998–99	14,891	—	90,874	89,259	67,183	463	25,797	—	—	—
1999–2000	14,928	125,007	92,012	90,538	68,173	423	26,407	32,995	30,457	10,693
2000–01	14,859	—	93,273	91,691	69,697	411	27,090	—	—	—
2001–02	14,559	130,007	94,112	92,696	70,516	408	27,468	35,895	33,191	11,846
2002–03	14,465	—	95,615	93,869	71,270	366	28,151	—	—	—
2003–04	14,383	130,407	95,726	93,977	71,195	376	28,219	34,681	31,988	11,188
2004–05	14,205	—	96,513	95,001	71,556	338	29,017	—	—	—
2005–06	14,166	132,436	97,382	95,731	71,733	326	29,705	35,054	32,127	12,184
2006–07	13,856	—	98,793	96,362	72,442	313	29,904	—	—	—
2007–08	13,838	132,656	98,916	97,654	73,011	288	30,542	33,740	30,808	11,870
2008–09	13,809	—	98,706	97,119	72,771	237	29,971	—	—	—
2009–10	13,629	132,183	98,817	97,521	72,870	217	30,381	33,366	30,590	11,941

—Not available.

[1] Includes operating and nonoperating districts.

[2] Schools with both elementary and secondary programs are included under elementary schools and also under secondary schools.

[3] Data for most years prior to 1976–77 are partly estimated. Prior to 1995–96, excludes schools with highest grade of kindergarten.

[4] Includes regular schools and special schools not classified by grade span.

[5] Includes elementary, secondary, and combined elementary/secondary schools.

[6] These data cannot be compared directly with the data for years after 1980–81.

[7] Because of expanded survey coverage, data are not directly comparable with figures after 1983–84.

SOURCE: U.S. Department of Education, National Center for Education Statistics, *Annual Report of the Commissioner of Education*, 1870 through 1910; *Biennial Survey of Education in the United States*, 1919–20 through 1949–50; *Statistics of State School Systems*, 1951–52 through 1967–68; *Statistics of Public Elementary and Secondary School Systems*, 1970–71 through 1980–81; *Statistics of Public and Nonpublic Elementary and Secondary Day Schools*, 1968–69; *Statistics of Nonpublic Elementary and Secondary Schools*, 1970–71; *Private Schools in American Education*; Schools and Staffing Survey (SASS), "Private School Questionnaire," 1987–88 and 1990–91; Private School Universe Survey (PSS), 1989–90 through 2009–10; and Common Core of Data (CCD), "Local Education Agency Universe Survey" and "Public Elementary/Secondary School Universe Survey," 1982–83 through 2009–10. (This table was prepared August 2011.)

Selected statistics on enrollment, teachers, dropouts, and graduates in public school districts enrolling more than 15,000 students: Selected years, 1990 through 2009

Name of district	State	Enrollment, fall 1990	Enrollment, fall 2000	Enrollment, fall 2009	Number of English language learners, 2009	Percent eligible for free or reduced-price lunch, 2009	White	Black	Hispanic	Asian/ Pacific Islander	American Indian/ Alaska Native	Two or more races	Number of classroom teachers	Pupil/ teacher ratio	Total number of staff	Student/ staff ratio	Teachers as a percentage of total staff	Percent dropping out of grades 9-12	Number of dropouts from grades 9-12	Averaged freshman graduation rate (AFGR)[1]	Number of high school graduates[2]	Number of schools, fall 2009
1	2	3	4	5	6	7	8	9	10	11	12	13	14	15	16	17	18	19	20	21	22	23
Districts with more than 15,000 students[3]	†	16,835,912	20,228,367	21,603,515	2,979,388	52.2	37.6	23.0	30.9	7.0	0.7	0.7	1,317,442	16.4	2,475,106	8.7	53.2	—	—	—	—	32,385
Baldwin County	AL	17,479	22,656	27,880	728	41.4	79.3	14.5	4.7	0.8	0.6	—	1,685	16.5	3,037	9.2	55.5	0.7	56	72.5	1,549	46
Birmingham City	AL	41,710	37,843	26,721	584	85.0	1.0	96.1	2.7	0.2	#	—	1,631	16.4	2,954	9.0	55.2	4.3	349	47.4	1,210	80
Huntsville City	AL	24,024	22,832	23,374	966	45.8	47.6	43.3	5.9	2.6	0.5	—	1,738	13.4	2,853	8.2	60.9	1.5	105	68.1	1,351	50
Jefferson County	AL	40,752	40,726	36,058	795	47.2	52.8	42.1	4.5	0.5	0.1	—	2,269	15.9	4,192	8.6	54.1	1.5	164	68.9	2,194	58
Madison County	AL	13,861	15,675	20,046	161	30.1	72.1	18.5	2.3	1.7	5.4	—	1,232	16.3	2,182	9.2	56.5	1.9	112	71.7	1,142	28
Mobile County	AL	67,286	64,976	62,767	1,057	66.8	43.8	51.1	1.7	2.4	1.0	—	3,689	17.0	7,110	8.8	51.9	1.4	253	65.2	3,369	110
Montgomery County	AL	35,973	33,267	31,764	1,019	70.5	15.7	78.6	2.9	2.6	0.2	—	1,935	16.4	3,707	8.6	52.2	0.6	49	52.4	1,279	63
Shelby County	AL	16,096	20,129	27,717	1,576	29.2	75.9	13.9	8.1	1.8	0.1	—	1,798	15.4	3,239	8.6	55.5	0.6	48	83.3	1,597	39
Tuscaloosa County	AL	14,514	15,666	17,644	259	50.0	68.8	27.6	2.9	0.6	0.1	—	1,097	16.1	1,932	9.1	56.8	2.9	139	69.4	878	33
Anchorage	AK	41,992	49,526	49,592	5,400	38.0	48.1	6.3	9.9	14.2	9.0	12.6	2,913	17.0	6,161	8.0	47.3	4.7	717	74.9	2,967	98
Matanuska-Susitna Borough	AK	9,810	13,008	16,770	413	36.0	80.7	1.3	2.4	1.8	10.8	3.0	985	17.0	1,889	8.9	52.1	7.0	370	76.4	1,012	43
Amphitheater Unified	AZ	13,834	16,857	15,020	814	3.1	51.8	4.6	37.5	4.2	1.8	—	917	16.4	1,837	8.2	49.9	4.8	247	75.9	1,039	20
Cartwright Elementary	AZ	14,368	17,746	18,351	5,672	76.1	4.4	3.8	90.2	0.5	1.1	—	921	19.9	2,061	8.9	44.7	†	†	†	†	21
Chandler Unified	AZ	11,041	21,703	38,147	1,727	26.4	56.6	7.0	26.5	8.5	1.5	—	1,985	19.2	3,725	10.2	53.3	4.1	423	85.6	2,083	41
Deer Valley Unified	AZ	15,899	27,158	36,241	986	19.8	77.3	3.5	14.1	4.1	1.0	—	1,882	19.3	3,285	11.0	57.3	2.7	295	76.3	2,182	38
Dysart Unified	AZ	3,804	5,459	24,430	924	43.2	50.5	9.4	35.8	3.2	1.1	—	1,235	19.8	2,075	11.8	59.5	3.7	231	88.4	1,084	24
Gilbert Unified	AZ	10,862	29,188	38,800	392	22.8	71.9	5.0	17.1	5.1	0.9	—	2,098	18.5	3,755	10.3	55.9	4.1	497	84.8	2,503	42
Kyrene Elementary	AZ	10,483	19,446	17,756	343	23.3	57.7	10.9	18.5	8.9	3.9	—	1,009	17.6	1,726	10.3	58.5	†	†	†	†	26
Mesa Unified	AZ	62,748	73,587	67,471	6,024	53.9	51.2	4.6	37.4	2.5	4.3	—	3,472	19.4	7,026	9.6	49.4	5.3	1,054	68.8	4,068	91
Paradise Valley Unified	AZ	26,695	34,882	33,146	2,023	29.1	67.4	4.0	23.6	3.9	1.1	—	1,783	18.6	3,045	10.9	58.6	2.0	209	78.7	2,263	47
Peoria Unified	AZ	20,850	32,608	37,500	1,114	35.5	62.3	6.0	26.9	3.5	1.4	—	2,022	18.5	3,466	10.8	58.3	2.1	255	80.9	2,679	40
Phoenix Union High	AZ	18,297	22,192	25,187	2,542	78.0	6.1	10.1	78.2	2.4	3.2	—	1,494	16.9	2,379	10.6	62.8	4.1	1,006	—	4,260	16
Scottsdale Unified	AZ	19,752	26,958	26,588	1,109	17.0	72.7	3.4	17.0	4.9	2.0	—	1,494	17.8	2,619	10.2	57.0	2.2	195	89.1	1,924	31
Sunnyside Unified	AZ	13,067	14,518	17,497	3,542	77.2	5.1	2.3	87.5	0.8	4.4	—	976	17.9	2,018	8.7	48.4	8.0	362	57.0	746	23
Tucson Unified	AZ	56,174	61,869	55,369	4,025	54.9	29.1	7.5	56.2	2.7	4.5	—	3,106	17.8	5,727	9.7	54.2	4.5	769	69.0	3,317	125
Washington Elementary	AZ	22,446	24,723	23,288	—	50.8	35.3	7.8	49.4	3.5	4.0	—	1,236	18.8	2,473	9.4	50.0	†	†	†	†	32
Little Rock	AR	25,813	25,502	25,837	1,739	70.3	21.8	67.9	8.1	1.9	0.3	0.0	1,889	13.7	3,958	6.5	47.7	3.0	229	65.6	1,355	48
Pulaski Co. Spec. School Dist.	AR	21,495	18,735	17,734	308	56.0	49.5	43.9	4.6	1.8	0.3	0.0	1,411	12.6	2,883	6.2	48.9	5.5	257	59.6	875	37
Springdale	AR	7,877	11,422	18,727	7,410	61.7	43.9	2.4	42.9	8.9	0.6	1.3	1,168	16.0	2,209	8.5	52.9	4.0	186	74.2	868	25
ABC Unified	CA	20,972	22,303	20,750	6,088	45.5	8.0	10.2	40.9	38.8	0.2	1.9	896	23.2	1,276	16.3	70.3	—	—	—	—	31
Alhambra Unified	CA	20,313	19,776	18,541	8,244	69.4	3.5	0.7	41.5	53.4	0.1	0.8	725	25.6	1,201	15.4	60.3	—	—	—	—	18
Alvord Unified	CA	14,853	17,664	20,026	8,961	71.8	12.8	4.2	76.2	5.2	0.3	1.4	857	23.4	1,212	16.5	70.7	—	—	—	—	22
Anaheim City	CA	14,972	22,275	19,312	14,813	88.9	5.3	1.8	85.2	7.1	0.3	0.4	875	22.1	1,257	15.4	69.6	—	—	—	—	24
Anaheim Union High	CA	23,096	29,363	33,187	15,964	63.2	15.3	2.9	62.9	16.6	0.3	2.0	1,377	24.1	1,972	16.8	69.8	—	—	—	—	22
Antelope Valley Union High	CA	10,937	19,056	26,255	7,009	62.8	23.1	20.9	51.3	3.7	0.6	0.4	1,110	23.7	1,802	14.6	61.6	—	—	—	—	14
Antioch Unified	CA	13,045	20,018	19,007	3,298	56.0	24.2	23.1	35.7	11.8	0.8	4.4	930	20.4	1,380	13.8	67.4	—	—	—	—	29
Apple Valley Unified	CA	11,245	13,292	15,097	1,281	60.3	45.9	10.9	37.7	3.6	0.8	1.4	622	24.3	1,078	14.0	57.7	—	—	—	—	18
Bakersfield City	CA	24,911	27,674	27,267	10,815	89.0	11.0	9.9	75.8	1.6	0.8	0.8	1,362	20.0	1,864	14.6	73.1	†	†	†	†	42
Baldwin Park Unified	CA	15,878	17,473	20,379	9,115	90.7	3.2	2.9	86.5	6.0	0.2	0.9	924	22.1	1,295	15.7	71.4	—	—	—	—	23
Burbank Unified	CA	12,057	16,170	16,733	3,778	32.3	45.8	2.6	38.3	10.0	0.2	3.2	703	23.8	1,127	14.8	62.4	—	—	—	—	22
Cajon Valley Union	CA	17,328	19,059	16,140	5,799	59.7	46.2	6.7	35.0	3.8	0.6	7.7	742	21.8	1,022	15.8	72.6	—	—	—	—	30
Capistrano Unified	CA	26,852	45,074	53,381	8,202	19.7	61.1	1.2	24.5	7.0	0.4	5.7	2,030	26.3	2,668	20.0	76.1	—	—	—	—	61
Chaffey Joint Union High	CA	13,505	19,851	25,414	6,752	41.1	20.8	9.7	60.6	7.3	0.4	1.2	980	25.9	1,421	17.9	69.0	—	—	—	—	11
Chino Valley Unified	CA	23,257	31,763	31,992	6,156	36.3	24.6	3.9	53.5	14.9	0.2	2.9	1,286	24.9	1,742	18.4	73.8	—	—	—	—	34
Chula Vista Elementary	CA	17,604	23,132	27,473	11,217	42.5	39.1	4.2	41.7	13.5	0.5	0.9	1,413	19.4	1,821	15.1	77.6	†	†	†	†	45
Clovis Unified	CA	23,224	32,717	38,004	4,189	33.9	48.6	3.6	29.1	15.2	0.9	2.5	1,677	22.7	2,013	18.9	83.3	†	†	†	†	46
Coachella Valley Unified	CA	9,091	12,636	18,186	11,622	84.4	1.4	0.3	97.1	0.3	0.4	0.4	914	19.9	1,118	16.3	81.7	†	†	†	†	22
Colton Joint Unified	CA	16,415	22,118	23,608	8,685	74.8	9.2	6.8	79.6	3.8	0.5	0.3	1,090	21.7	1,606	14.7	67.8	—	—	—	—	27

See notes at end of table.

Selected statistics on enrollment, teachers, dropouts, and graduates in public school districts enrolling more than 15,000 students: Selected years, 1990 through 2009—Continued

Name of district	State	Enrollment, fall 1990	Enrollment, fall 2000	Enrollment, fall 2009	Number of English language learners, 2009	Percent eligible for free or reduced-price lunch, 2009	White	Black	Hispanic	Asian/Pacific Islander	American Indian/Alaska Native	Two or more races	Number of classroom teachers	Pupil/teacher ratio	Total number of staff	Student/staff ratio	Teachers as a percentage of total staff	Percent dropping out of grades 9-12	Number of dropouts from grades 9-12	Averaged freshman graduation rate (AFGR)[1]	Number of high school graduates[2]	Number of schools, fall 2009
1	2	3	4	5	6	7	8	9	10	11	12	13	14	15	16	17	18	19	20	21	22	23
Compton Unified	CA	27,585	31,037	26,221	13,552	81.9	0.2	19.2	77.2	0.7	0.1	2.6	1,400	18.7	1,965	13.3	71.2	—	—	—	—	40
Conejo Valley Unified	CA	17,209	20,999	21,199	2,865	17.9	64.3	1.7	21.6	10.2	0.6	1.7	922	23.0	1,315	16.1	70.1	—	—	—	—	27
Corona-Norco Unified	CA	23,036	37,487	52,052	7,974	43.7	31.1	6.0	48.9	9.2	0.3	4.5	2,238	23.3	3,214	16.2	69.6	—	—	—	—	51
Cupertino Union	CA	12,227	15,670	18,010	3,918	5.7	21.4	1.2	5.0	71.8	0.2	0.3	801	22.5	1,129	15.9	70.9	†	†	†	†	25
Desert Sands Unified	CA	16,058	23,500	29,323	11,275	56.9	25.7	2.2	68.0	2.7	0.4	1.1	1,237	23.7	1,743	16.8	70.9	—	—	—	—	34
Downey Unified	CA	15,418	21,474	22,702	6,910	62.5	8.9	3.4	83.1	4.1	0.4	0.1	957	23.7	1,366	16.6	70.1	—	—	—	—	20
East Side Union High	CA	21,973	24,282	26,915	5,255	39.3	9.5	3.9	48.2	37.4	0.3	0.7	1,119	24.1	1,523	17.7	73.5	—	—	—	—	20
Elk Grove Unified	CA	27,246	47,736	62,483	16,755	51.7	24.5	16.9	25.1	27.4	0.5	5.7	2,954	21.1	3,945	15.8	74.9	—	—	—	—	66
Escondido Union	CA	14,663	19,312	19,337	10,407	70.9	22.7	2.4	62.6	4.7	0.4	7.2	928	20.8	1,319	14.7	70.3	—	—	—	—	25
Fairfield-Suisun Unified	CA	20,227	22,263	21,972	4,041	34.7	11.6	10.2	34.0	10.2	1.0	33.0	1,001	22.0	1,571	14.0	63.7	—	—	—	—	27
Folsom-Cordova Unified	CA	12,656	16,277	19,182	3,031	33.0	60.3	8.0	16.5	13.1	0.7	1.5	781	24.6	1,231	15.6	63.4	—	—	—	—	35
Fontana Unified	CA	27,043	37,244	41,004	21,320	73.2	5.9	7.0	83.9	2.8	0.3	0.1	1,685	24.3	2,479	16.5	68.0	—	—	—	—	45
Fremont Unified	CA	27,172	31,078	32,304	9,090	19.0	20.7	4.6	14.2	57.0	0.4	3.1	1,447	22.3	1,793	18.0	80.7	—	—	—	—	41
Fresno Unified	CA	71,500	79,007	75,468	27,053	80.9	13.7	10.6	61.1	13.9	0.7	#	3,811	19.8	5,362	14.1	71.1	—	—	—	—	105
Fullerton Joint Union High	CA	12,729	15,165	15,130	2,474	34.7	23.3	2.2	50.9	22.0	0.3	1.2	564	26.9	894	16.9	63.0	—	—	—	—	8
Garden Grove Unified	CA	37,969	48,742	47,950	21,818	71.0	11.9	0.9	53.1	33.8	0.2	0.2	1,963	24.4	2,847	16.8	69.0	—	—	—	—	68
Glendale Unified	CA	25,456	30,329	26,574	11,231	43.8	56.1	1.3	22.2	19.5	0.2	0.7	1,163	22.9	1,812	14.7	64.2	—	—	—	—	33
Grossmont Union High	CA	18,647	23,639	25,466	4,126	35.2	51.3	8.9	30.5	5.2	1.3	2.7	970	26.3	1,609	15.8	60.3	—	—	—	—	20
Hacienda La Puente Unified	CA	23,267	24,646	21,290	5,655	73.1	4.4	1.2	79.5	14.1	0.2	0.6	1,021	20.9	1,445	14.7	70.6	—	—	—	—	37
Hayward Unified	CA	19,122	24,205	21,878	7,258	67.7	8.7	14.7	55.9	19.0	0.5	1.1	994	22.0	1,328	16.5	74.8	—	—	—	—	33
Hemet Unified	CA	12,811	17,451	22,257	3,462	71.2	39.2	7.3	47.0	3.3	1.4	1.7	957	23.2	1,565	14.2	61.2	—	—	—	—	27
Hesperia Unified	CA	13,113	15,360	22,836	5,640	60.1	31.6	8.4	56.0	2.1	0.6	1.2	858	26.6	1,468	15.6	58.4	—	—	—	—	31
Huntington Beach Union High	CA	14,039	14,359	16,162	3,099	21.1	43.8	1.2	22.9	24.4	6.5	1.1	629	25.7	1,129	14.3	55.7	—	—	—	—	9
Irvine Unified	CA	20,735	23,961	26,822	4,872	9.7	36.7	2.1	8.6	44.6	0.2	7.5	1,026	26.1	1,420	18.9	72.2	—	—	—	—	35
Jurupa Unified	CA	15,419	19,839	20,425	9,441	71.7	15.5	2.1	79.0	2.0	0.9	0.6	896	22.8	1,401	14.6	64.0	—	—	—	—	25
Kern Union High	CA	20,183	29,333	37,928	10,098	60.3	28.9	7.4	58.5	3.7	0.7	0.7	1,481	25.6	2,475	15.3	59.8	—	—	—	—	24
Lake Elsinore Unified	CA	11,000	17,178	22,244	3,536	50.2	37.3	5.3	50.9	3.3	0.8	2.5	959	23.2	1,439	15.5	66.6	—	—	—	—	27
Lodi Unified	CA	23,954	27,339	30,942	10,251	58.3	28.8	8.5	52.6	13.5	0.8	1.2	1,405	22.0	2,027	15.3	69.3	—	—	—	—	54
Long Beach Unified	CA	71,342	93,694	86,283	26,736	68.1	15.9	16.7	52.6	13.5	0.2	1.1	3,917	22.0	5,605	15.4	69.9	—	—	—	—	92
Los Angeles Unified	CA	625,073	721,346	670,746	210,539	77.0	8.8	10.2	73.7	5.8	0.3	1.1	31,316	21.4	44,316	15.1	70.7	—	—	—	—	870
Madera Unified	CA	13,728	15,957	19,418	9,991	81.6	11.2	2.7	82.8	1.5	0.8	1.1	852	22.8	1,240	15.7	68.7	—	—	—	—	27
Manteca Unified	CA	13,356	19,746	23,314	6,586	53.0	26.8	9.4	47.7	5.9	1.2	0.5	912	25.6	1,295	18.0	70.4	—	—	—	—	29
Modesto City Elementary	CA	17,405	18,740	15,188	6,088	82.3	21.9	4.2	65.1	8.6	0.9	#	778	19.5	1,061	14.3	73.3	†	†	†	†	27
Modesto City High	CA	10,697	14,547	15,456	1,978	50.6	35.8	5.5	47.3	5.5	0.7	1.1	582	26.5	967	16.0	60.2	—	—	—	—	7
Montebello Unified	CA	32,938	34,794	32,739	10,923	78.1	2.1	0.3	94.0	3.1	0.3	2.1	1,329	24.6	1,924	17.0	69.1	—	—	—	—	29
Moreno Valley Unified	CA	29,064	32,730	36,822	9,751	70.2	11.7	18.6	63.3	4.8	0.4	2.1	1,496	24.6	2,053	17.9	72.9	—	—	—	—	38
Mount Diablo Unified	CA	32,840	36,648	34,316	9,566	35.8	45.8	4.9	34.3	13.0	0.4	0.1	1,507	22.8	2,117	16.2	71.2	—	—	—	—	56
Murrieta Valley Unified	CA	3,990	12,065	22,274	976	23.7	51.0	5.8	31.9	9.1	0.6	1.3	910	24.5	1,347	16.5	67.5	—	—	—	—	20
Napa Valley Unified	CA	13,705	16,392	17,959	6,591	40.2	34.3	2.1	49.8	7.9	0.5	1.4	826	21.7	1,147	15.7	72.0	—	—	—	—	35
Newport-Mesa Unified	CA	16,434	21,658	21,718	7,042	40.7	50.3	1.5	41.8	6.2	0.5	0.9	969	22.6	1,387	15.7	69.2	—	—	—	—	32
Norwalk-La Mirada Unified	CA	19,179	23,610	20,685	4,438	61.0	11.5	3.0	78.9	7.0	0.3	#	925	22.4	1,386	14.9	66.8	—	—	—	—	27
Oakland Unified	CA	52,095	54,863	46,099	18,465	70.8	7.5	32.6	38.9	15.1	0.4	5.5	2,446	18.8	3,108	14.8	78.7	—	—	—	—	139
Oceanside Unified	CA	17,034	22,354	21,122	4,019	59.5	26.8	6.7	55.0	3.1	0.5	3.8	942	22.4	1,444	14.6	65.2	—	—	—	—	25
Ontario-Montclair Elementary	CA	21,033	26,407	22,685	13,088	68.8	5.4	3.1	88.6	1.4	0.3	0.6	1,135	20.0	1,530	14.8	74.2	†	†	†	†	33
Orange Unified	CA	25,224	31,097	30,210	9,273	39.9	34.5	1.4	47.4	12.2	0.4	3.1	1,183	25.5	1,931	15.6	61.3	—	—	—	—	42
Oxnard	CA	12,212	16,249	15,554	9,567	73.0	5.4	1.9	88.6	3.4	0.2	0.5	659	23.6	954	16.3	69.1	†	†	†	†	22
Oxnard Union High	CA	11,512	14,552	16,856	6,880	49.6	17.1	2.7	71.7	7.5	0.5	0.6	651	25.9	1,074	15.7	60.7	—	—	—	—	8
Pajaro Valley Unified	CA	16,355	19,864	19,381	9,352	71.9	18.0	0.5	78.9	2.0	0.2	0.4	825	23.5	1,137	17.1	72.5	—	—	—	—	33
Palm Springs Unified	CA	14,427	20,847	23,943	11,542	79.2	17.4	5.6	67.7	3.9	0.6	0.6	1,013	23.6	1,510	15.9	67.1	—	—	—	—	27
Palmdale Elementary	CA	13,199	20,853	21,296	6,565	77.3	9.4	16.8	49.2	2.6	0.5	2.9	897	23.7	1,288	16.5	69.7	†	†	†	†	28
Panama-Buena Vista Union	CA	10,066	12,843	16,529	2,058	58.1	30.1	11.3	67.7	8.6	0.8	0.2	703	23.5	1,243	13.3	56.5	†	†	†	†	23
Paramount Unified	CA	12,855	16,862	15,836	5,659	91.8	2.1	9.6	85.4	2.4	0.2	#	704	22.5	1,101	14.4	64.0	—	—	—	—	19
Pasadena Unified	CA	21,802	23,559	20,084	6,227	65.6	13.8	17.8	58.5	4.7	0.3	4.9	963	20.9	1,498	13.4	64.3	—	—	—	—	33

See notes at end of table.

457

Selected statistics on enrollment, teachers, dropouts, and graduates in public school districts enrolling more than 15,000 students: Selected years, 1990 through 2009—Continued

Name of district	State	Enrollment, fall 1990	Enrollment, fall 2000	Enrollment, fall 2009	Number of English language learners, 2009	Percent eligible for free or reduced-price lunch, 2009	White	Black	Hispanic	Asian/ Pacific Islander	American Indian/ Alaska Native	Two or more races	Number of classroom teachers	Pupil/ teacher ratio	Total number of staff	Student/ staff ratio	Teachers as a percentage of total staff	Percent dropping out of grades 9-12	Number of dropouts from grades 9-12	Averaged freshman graduation rate (AFGR)[1]	Number of high school graduates[2]	Number of schools, fall 2009
1	2	3	4	5	6	7	8	9	10	11	12	13	14	15	16	17	18	19	20	21	22	23
Placentia-Yorba Linda Unified	CA	21,438	26,046	25,920	5,292	29.8	48.6	1.7	35.5	12.0	0.2	1.9	1,059	24.5	1,868	13.9	56.7	—	—	—	—	34
Pomona Unified	CA	26,918	34,479	29,044	12,348	81.3	4.6	5.9	82.4	5.8	0.2	1.0	1,266	22.9	1,832	15.9	69.1	—	—	—	—	45
Poway Unified	CA	24,662	32,532	33,797	3,882	12.5	54.2	2.9	11.4	24.1	0.4	7.0	1,285	26.3	2,185	15.5	58.8	—	—	—	—	37
Redlands Unified	CA	16,002	19,411	21,810	2,843	49.9	35.3	7.2	42.8	11.4	0.6	2.8	885	24.7	1,215	18.0	72.8	—	—	—	—	24
Rialto Unified	CA	19,794	28,060	27,170	8,708	80.9	5.4	15.9	75.6	2.0	0.3	0.8	1,152	23.6	1,801	15.1	64.0	—	—	—	—	29
Riverside Unified	CA	31,326	38,124	42,696	8,589	62.3	28.6	8.4	55.4	4.9	0.4	2.2	1,821	23.5	2,435	17.5	74.8	—	—	—	—	49
Rowland Unified	CA	19,143	18,972	15,980	7,374	62.2	3.5	2.1	63.0	29.8	0.1	1.4	710	22.5	1,120	14.3	63.4	—	—	—	—	23
Sacramento City Unified	CA	49,557	52,734	47,890	15,924	66.7	18.3	18.2	35.7	21.3	0.9	5.6	2,243	21.3	2,886	16.6	77.7	—	—	—	—	85
Saddleback Valley Unified	CA	25,130	35,199	32,387	4,263	19.0	56.5	1.8	27.6	10.1	0.3	3.7	1,308	24.8	1,809	17.9	72.3	—	—	—	—	35
San Bernardino City Unified	CA	40,589	52,031	53,837	24,249	86.9	9.8	15.3	70.4	2.7	0.7	1.1	2,598	20.7	3,483	15.5	74.6	—	—	—	—	74
San Diego Unified	CA	121,107	141,804	131,417	37,161	64.7	23.5	11.7	46.0	15.3	0.4	3.2	6,519	20.2	8,513	15.4	76.6	—	—	—	—	218
San Francisco Unified	CA	61,688	59,979	55,140	20,872	56.9	10.7	11.0	23.7	47.1	0.4	7.0	3,125	17.6	4,144	13.3	75.4	—	—	—	—	116
San Jose Unified	CA	29,630	33,015	32,423	11,418	45.0	26.7	3.4	51.5	15.5	0.8	2.2	1,511	21.5	2,006	16.2	75.3	—	—	—	—	52
San Juan Unified	CA	47,690	50,266	47,327	4,122	39.1	65.1	8.0	17.7	7.1	1.7	0.4	2,171	21.8	2,990	15.8	72.6	—	—	—	—	76
San Marcos Unified	CA	9,108	12,204	17,940	3,439	43.1	40.1	3.2	46.9	8.6	0.6	0.6	712	25.2	1,343	13.4	53.0	—	—	—	—	19
San Ramon Valley Unified	CA	16,119	20,742	27,937	1,180	2.8	56.2	2.2	8.6	26.5	0.2	6.3	1,223	22.8	1,887	14.8	64.8	—	—	—	—	35
Santa Ana Unified	CA	45,964	60,643	56,937	31,873	83.8	3.0	0.6	93.2	3.0	#	0.2	2,347	24.3	2,929	19.4	80.1	—	—	—	—	60
Simi Valley Unified	CA	18,262	21,181	20,415	3,516	26.8	60.2	1.4	26.8	8.9	0.6	1.6	845	24.2	1,396	14.6	60.6	—	—	—	—	29
Stockton Unified	CA	32,687	37,573	38,141	10,485	80.5	9.1	12.2	57.5	16.7	4.1	0.4	1,915	19.9	2,577	14.8	74.3	—	—	—	—	59
Sweetwater Union High	CA	27,894	35,330	42,209	19,042	52.7	9.1	3.8	74.1	11.2	0.4	1.3	1,796	23.5	2,912	14.5	61.7	—	—	—	—	30
Temecula Valley Unified	CA	7,596	18,980	30,184	3,041	15.9	49.5	4.4	29.8	10.1	0.9	5.2	1,345	22.4	2,024	14.9	66.4	—	—	—	—	31
Torrance Unified	CA	19,645	24,118	24,614	5,196	20.8	32.7	3.9	20.2	36.1	0.6	6.5	979	25.2	1,965	12.5	49.8	—	—	—	—	31
Tracy Joint Unified	CA	7,626	13,816	17,494	5,279	39.8	28.1	7.7	44.2	16.7	0.6	2.8	817	21.4	1,173	14.9	69.6	—	—	—	—	25
Tustin Unified	CA	10,831	16,963	22,454	5,848	37.9	33.1	2.2	44.2	18.5	0.3	1.7	831	27.0	1,249	18.0	66.6	—	—	—	—	28
Twin Rivers Unified	CA	—	—	31,213	11,079	79.5	32.4	15.3	35.1	11.9	1.0	4.4	1,484	21.0	2,052	15.2	72.4	—	—	—	—	59
Val Verde Unified	CA	19,049	11,242	19,636	7,882	77.1	6.3	15.1	71.7	3.9	0.7	2.7	754	26.0	1,000	19.6	75.4	—	—	—	—	21
Vallejo City Unified	CA	15,383	20,270	16,169	2,996	58.0	10.3	31.0	32.3	23.1	0.7	2.7	737	21.9	1,055	15.3	69.9	—	—	—	—	29
Ventura Unified	CA	21,309	17,527	17,507	3,429	47.0	45.7	1.8	45.5	3.5	1.0	2.5	769	22.8	1,213	14.4	63.4	—	—	—	—	32
Visalia Unified	CA	18,499	23,989	26,964	4,238	58.8	29.8	2.6	59.5	5.0	1.9	1.2	1,109	24.3	1,578	17.1	70.3	—	—	—	—	37
Vista Unified	CA	31,292	27,651	26,145	9,570	52.2	29.2	4.9	57.7	5.2	0.7	2.3	1,226	21.3	1,836	14.2	66.8	—	—	—	—	34
West Contra Costa Unified	CA	—	34,499	30,087	9,809	65.5	11.6	22.6	48.3	16.9	0.2	0.4	1,437	20.9	1,991	15.1	72.2	—	—	—	—	61
William S. Hart Union High	CA	10,278	17,001	26,320	2,074	15.4	49.5	5.2	31.7	11.5	0.6	1.6	953	27.6	1,437	18.3	66.3	—	—	—	—	19
Academy, No. 20	CO	10,986	17,628	22,620	269	10.4	80.9	4.2	8.6	5.5	0.7	—	1,376	16.4	2,757	8.2	49.9	1.1	81	93.1	1,554	32
Adams 12 Five Star Schools	CO	20,838	30,079	41,949	4,716	32.2	60.2	2.7	30.8	5.4	0.9	—	2,078	20.2	4,283	9.8	48.5	10.3	1,188	69.1	1,950	53
Aurora, Joint District No. 28	CO	25,897	30,453	36,967	13,235	61.3	23.5	20.2	50.8	4.7	0.9	—	1,908	19.4	4,329	8.5	44.1	13.2	1,206	52.6	1,360	55
Boulder Valley, No. RE2	CO	21,502	27,508	29,011	2,547	17.0	75.3	1.5	15.4	7.1	0.7	—	1,716	16.9	3,797	7.6	45.2	2.4	219	92.5	2,114	54
Cherry Creek, No. 5	CO	29,210	42,320	51,786	3,654	24.4	62.2	14.7	13.9	8.6	0.6	—	2,959	17.5	6,162	8.4	48.0	5.4	817	86.9	3,337	57
Colorado Springs, No. 11	CO	30,000	32,699	29,673	2,517	50.5	61.0	10.9	23.4	3.0	1.7	—	1,733	17.1	3,814	7.8	45.4	6.3	556	78.3	1,872	59
Denver	CO	59,013	70,847	77,267	22,249	70.5	24.9	16.1	54.4	4.7	1.1	—	4,573	16.9	9,795	7.9	46.7	14.0	2,601	55.1	2,893	148
Douglas County, No. RE1	CO	13,125	34,918	59,932	1,500	8.5	82.5	3.0	9.3	4.7	0.5	—	3,089	19.4	6,712	8.9	46.0	2.8	445	97.5	3,347	78
Greeley, No. 6	CO	11,657	15,998	19,151	4,137	57.4	43.8	1.6	52.4	1.3	0.9	—	1,104	17.3	2,232	8.6	49.5	5.7	292	69.8	980	31
Jefferson County, No. R-1	CO	76,275	87,703	86,282	5,288	28.7	73.5	2.0	19.3	3.9	1.3	—	4,891	17.6	10,652	8.1	45.9	3.6	979	81.2	5,767	164
Littleton, No. 6	CO	15,524	16,516	15,753	658	18.4	82.5	2.1	11.3	3.4	0.7	—	886	17.8	1,869	8.4	47.4	1.7	94	91.7	1,222	23
Mesa County Valley, No. 51	CO	17,024	19,688	22,050	1,007	44.3	76.2	1.6	19.7	1.2	1.3	—	1,280	17.2	2,751	8.0	46.5	6.2	409	81.8	1,336	44
Poudre, No. R-1	CO	18,589	24,052	26,520	1,650	26.7	76.5	2.2	16.4	3.8	1.1	—	1,556	17.0	3,315	8.0	46.9	2.7	215	89.3	1,813	52
Pueblo, No. 60	CO	18,364	17,636	18,325	660	68.6	34.7	2.8	60.8	0.8	0.9	—	1,059	17.3	2,025	9.0	52.3	8.7	470	69.7	978	39
Saint Vrain Valley, No. RE1J	CO	15,070	19,620	26,724	3,235	32.6	66.7	1.2	27.3	3.9	0.8	—	1,552	17.2	3,020	8.8	51.4	4.8	349	81.0	1,394	49
Thompson, No. R-2J	CO	12,019	14,766	15,225	444	26.2	80.5	1.3	15.5	1.8	0.9	—	896	17.0	1,957	7.8	45.8	4.1	205	87.6	1,106	31

See notes at end of table.

Selected statistics on enrollment, teachers, dropouts, and graduates in public school districts enrolling more than 15,000 students: Selected years, 1990 through 2009—Continued

Name of district	State	Enrollment, fall 1990	Enrollment, fall 2000	Enrollment, fall 2009	Number of English language learners, 2009	Percent eligible for free or reduced-price lunch, 2009	White	Black	Hispanic	Asian/ Pacific Islander	American Indian/ Alaska Native	Two or more races	Number of classroom teachers	Pupil/ teacher ratio	Total number of staff	Student/ staff ratio	Teachers as a percentage of total staff	Percent dropping out of grades 9-12	Number of dropouts from grades 9-12	Averaged freshman graduation rate (AFGR)[1]	Number of high school graduates[2]	Number of schools, fall 2009
1	2	3	4	5	6	7	8	9	10	11	12	13	14	15	16	17	18	19	20	21	22	23
Bridgeport	CT	19,687	22,432	20,161	2,655	98.2	8.6	40.5	48.0	2.9	0.1	—	1,425	14.2	3,053	6.6	46.7	9.8	517	53.4	937	37
Hartford	CT	25,418	22,543	21,216	3,710	92.1	7.4	38.2	52.3	1.9	0.2	—	1,538	13.8	3,198	6.6	48.1	10.8	618	50.6	909	49
New Haven	CT	17,881	19,549	19,853	2,393	70.4	13.1	47.7	37.1	1.9	0.2	—	1,536	12.9	3,361	5.9	45.8	8.7	453	59.7	911	47
Stamford	CT	11,574	14,791	15,036	2,037	39.9	39.4	20.9	32.2	7.4	0.1	—	1,210	12.4	2,200	6.8	55.0	2.5	117	88.6	1,018	21
Waterbury	CT	13,323	16,282	18,152	1,989	79.7	25.5	28.1	44.3	1.8	0.3	—	1,367	13.3	2,839	6.4	48.1	6.3	279	68.9	857	31
Christina	DE	17,872	19,882	16,980	1,410	58.9	37.1	42.3	15.4	4.9	0.2	0.2	1,194	14.2	2,751	6.2	43.4	10.8	440	51.7	877	30
Red Clay Consolidated	DE	14,551	15,827	15,674	1,890	47.3	48.0	24.8	22.4	4.7	0.2	0.2	991	15.8	1,885	8.3	52.6	5.3	200	60.9	814	27
District of Columbia	DC	80,694	68,925	43,866	4,203	71.9	8.9	75.5	13.4	2.2	0.1	—	4,017	10.9	8,180	5.4	49.1	8.6	1,055	65.0	2,679	134
Alachua	FL	26,387	29,712	27,783	438	48.5	50.6	38.3	6.4	4.5	0.2	—	1,898	14.6	4,175	6.7	45.5	3.0	262	76.2	1,864	63
Bay	FL	21,875	25,755	25,897	445	50.1	76.9	15.9	4.5	2.2	0.5	—	1,879	13.8	3,254	8.0	57.7	0.9	65	69.5	1,532	42
Brevard	FL	56,639	70,597	72,412	1,777	39.0	72.6	15.8	9.2	2.4	0.3	—	5,268	13.7	9,254	7.8	56.9	0.7	148	79.8	4,931	123
Broward	FL	161,100	251,129	256,137	24,400	53.0	27.7	39.2	29.1	3.6	0.3	—	17,819	14.4	30,062	8.5	59.3	2.4	1,873	70.9	15,663	308
Charlotte	FL	13,030	17,170	16,940	187	57.7	78.3	9.9	9.7	1.7	0.5	—	1,253	13.5	2,537	6.7	49.4	3.3	197	90.0	1,402	24
Citrus	FL	11,697	15,199	16,082	233	52.4	85.3	5.2	7.1	1.8	0.6	—	1,276	12.6	2,513	6.4	50.8	1.6	83	73.8	1,056	25
Clay	FL	21,933	28,115	35,956	482	33.8	74.5	13.9	8.4	3.0	0.2	—	2,655	13.5	4,850	7.4	54.7	1.3	144	84.8	2,469	42
Collier	FL	20,878	34,203	42,714	6,566	53.9	42.0	12.3	44.2	1.2	0.3	—	2,994	14.3	5,517	7.7	54.3	2.4	306	69.3	2,477	68
Dade	FL	292,000	368,625	345,804	59,423	68.0	8.9	25.2	64.6	1.3	0.1	—	21,756	15.9	37,604	9.2	57.9	4.7	4,770	61.6	19,207	506
Duval	FL	111,100	125,846	122,586	3,661	48.1	41.5	45.9	8.0	4.4	0.2	—	7,881	15.6	12,609	9.7	62.5	5.9	1,992	59.9	5,958	180
Escambia	FL	43,091	45,012	40,613	372	59.7	55.0	38.0	3.3	2.9	0.8	—	3,135	13.0	5,682	7.1	55.2	2.7	322	56.6	2,116	73
Hernando	FL	12,861	17,215	22,901	666	55.4	75.7	7.5	14.8	1.6	0.5	—	1,672	13.7	3,103	7.4	53.9	3.1	211	68.8	1,338	28
Hillsborough	FL	123,900	164,311	193,265	22,255	53.7	43.5	23.0	29.9	3.3	0.3	—	14,296	13.5	26,637	7.3	53.7	1.1	605	69.1	10,415	292
Indian River	FL	11,838	14,979	17,750	1,093	50.3	62.6	16.4	19.0	1.6	0.4	—	1,248	14.2	2,279	7.8	54.8	1.6	90	76.6	1,108	30
Lake	FL	21,065	29,293	41,050	1,842	50.5	61.5	16.0	18.9	2.6	0.9	—	2,805	14.6	5,612	7.3	50.0	3.2	374	78.0	2,354	54
Lee	FL	43,240	58,401	80,484	6,594	59.8	51.7	15.8	30.7	1.5	0.2	—	5,246	15.3	9,320	8.6	56.3	1.7	379	71.2	4,258	118
Leon	FL	27,241	32,050	32,733	540	40.7	49.2	42.9	4.4	3.3	0.2	—	2,402	13.6	4,680	7.0	51.3	3.6	334	73.6	1,857	58
Manatee	FL	26,326	36,569	42,939	4,058	51.8	56.0	15.6	26.4	1.8	0.2	—	2,602	16.5	5,418	7.9	48.0	4.3	516	71.6	2,438	79
Marion	FL	29,577	38,562	42,005	1,974	65.1	62.0	20.5	15.1	1.8	0.6	—	3,018	13.9	6,351	6.6	47.5	3.1	406	64.5	2,421	62
Martin	FL	11,808	16,308	18,010	2,343	36.8	69.7	8.0	20.7	1.5	0.2	—	1,271	14.2	2,325	7.7	54.7	0.7	44	76.8	1,242	37
Okaloosa	FL	26,140	30,344	28,828	581	33.5	77.7	13.1	5.8	2.9	0.5	—	1,888	15.3	2,949	9.8	64.0	0.8	78	80.7	2,089	53
Orange	FL	103,000	150,681	173,259	30,032	50.9	33.7	28.1	33.1	4.6	0.5	—	10,683	16.2	21,264	8.1	50.2	1.2	595	70.0	9,946	240
Osceola	FL	19,570	34,566	52,139	9,562	64.6	31.0	11.8	53.8	2.8	0.6	—	3,369	15.5	6,460	8.1	52.1	1.2	190	75.7	3,202	66
Palm Beach	FL	106,000	153,871	172,897	18,117	46.9	38.3	29.3	28.6	2.5	0.7	—	13,457	12.8	22,526	7.7	59.7	2.9	1,533	73.3	10,654	248
Pasco	FL	33,891	49,704	67,147	2,869	50.1	74.2	5.7	17.2	2.5	0.3	—	4,971	13.5	9,901	6.8	50.2	1.4	265	65.9	3,611	106
Pinellas	FL	94,364	113,027	105,238	4,136	48.2	65.4	20.0	10.0	4.3	0.3	—	7,629	13.8	14,042	7.5	54.3	2.6	896	65.8	6,711	161
Polk	FL	65,218	79,477	94,530	8,906	63.0	51.6	22.6	24.0	1.6	0.2	—	7,414	12.8	14,158	6.7	52.4	5.0	1,312	68.4	4,884	156
Saint Johns	FL	12,080	20,090	30,018	246	20.8	83.0	8.8	5.2	2.9	0.2	—	1,807	16.6	3,388	8.9	53.3	1.2	105	84.9	1,840	44
Saint Lucie	FL	22,224	29,540	39,013	2,778	59.7	45.0	31.4	21.2	1.9	0.5	—	2,405	16.2	4,705	8.3	51.1	1.8	208	67.6	2,052	52
Santa Rosa	FL	15,741	22,633	25,577	140	36.7	89.1	5.5	2.8	1.9	0.7	—	1,627	15.7	2,469	10.4	65.9	2.1	167	80.9	1,664	38
Sarasota	FL	27,888	35,533	41,281	2,356	46.1	74.1	9.9	13.5	2.2	0.3	—	3,108	13.3	5,859	7.0	53.0	2.1	259	74.5	2,607	63
Seminole	FL	49,027	60,869	64,457	2,434	39.2	61.1	14.6	19.8	4.2	0.2	—	4,537	14.2	7,562	8.5	60.0	0.4	84	76.1	4,373	74
Volusia	FL	48,403	61,517	62,306	2,880	52.2	64.3	15.1	18.4	1.9	0.3	—	4,367	14.3	8,435	7.4	51.8	1.4	270	63.9	3,633	90
Atlanta	GA	60,795	58,230	48,909	1,475	77.5	11.2	81.1	5.4	0.8	0.1	1.5	3,760	13.0	6,962	7.0	54.0	9.5	1,196	53.3	2,033	106
Bibb County	GA	24,413	24,739	25,109	359	76.6	21.5	72.9	2.6	1.6	0.1	1.4	1,649	15.2	3,763	6.7	43.8	7.1	461	49.0	979	44
Chatham County	GA	34,100	35,344	34,668	681	70.0	27.6	64.3	5.0	2.3	0.2	0.6	2,692	12.9	4,900	7.1	54.9	4.7	408	55.3	1,528	58
Cherokee County	GA	16,086	26,043	38,293	1,306	27.9	75.6	6.8	12.7	1.7	0.4	2.7	2,516	15.2	4,656	8.2	54.0	4.2	416	70.2	1,880	40
Clayton County	GA	34,754	46,930	50,204	3,804	80.4	3.9	71.4	16.7	4.7	0.2	3.0	3,519	14.3	7,641	6.6	46.1	5.8	773	45.8	1,944	67
Cobb County	GA	69,441	95,781	107,245	8,710	40.6	46.2	32.3	15.9	5.1	0.4	4.9	7,989	13.4	14,299	7.5	55.9	3.5	1,148	77.9	6,833	117
Columbia County	GA	14,096	18,756	23,328	278	29.3	67.7	16.8	6.6	3.6	0.3	0.0	1,470	15.9	3,067	7.6	47.9	3.6	251	74.1	1,380	31
Coweta County	GA	10,430	16,766	22,560	473	40.1	66.5	21.6	6.6	1.5	0.3	3.5	1,461	15.4	3,106	7.3	47.0	3.3	210	74.1	1,217	29
DeKalb County	GA	74,404	95,958	99,406	9,696	68.9	10.7	72.0	11.1	4.4	0.2	1.5	6,761	14.7	13,797	7.2	49.0	6.0	1,736	63.1	5,129	145
Dougherty County	GA	18,877	16,799	16,134	137	80.0	9.4	87.2	1.4	1.0	0.1	0.9	1,070	15.1	2,452	6.6	43.6	3.3	137	59.1	752	29
Douglas County	GA	14,002	17,489	24,951	913	56.0	36.3	47.5	10.5	1.4	0.1	4.2	1,743	14.3	3,438	7.3	50.7	2.7	207	77.6	1,459	36

See notes at end of table.

Selected statistics on enrollment, teachers, dropouts, and graduates in public school districts enrolling more than 15,000 students: Selected years, 1990 through 2009—Continued

Name of district	State	Enrollment, fall 1990	Enrollment, fall 2000	Enrollment, fall 2009	Number of English language learners, 2009	Percent eligible for free or reduced-price lunch, 2009	White	Black	Hispanic	Asian/Pacific Islander	American Indian/Alaska Native	Two or more races	Number of classroom teachers	Pupil/teacher ratio	Total number of staff	Student/staff ratio	Teachers as a percentage of total staff	Percent dropping out of grades 9-12	Number of dropouts from grades 9-12	Averaged freshman graduation rate (AFGR)[1]	Number of high school graduates[2]	Number of schools, fall 2009
1	2	3	4	5	6	7	8	9	10	11	12	13	14	15	16	17	18	19	20	21	22	23
Fayette County	GA	13,105	19,590	21,727	516	20.4	57.9	22.8	8.3	4.3	0.3	6.4	1,481	14.7	2,953	7.4	50.1	1.0	77	90.1	1,829	29
Forsyth County	GA	7,742	17,131	34,208	1,544	18.3	76.8	2.3	11.9	6.0	0.5	2.6	2,176	15.7	4,160	8.2	52.3	2.1	171	83.7	1,555	35
Fulton County	GA	41,935	68,583	90,399	5,038	42.5	34.4	42.2	11.0	8.7	0.1	3.6	6,443	14.0	12,590	7.2	51.2	4.6	1,195	81.5	5,090	103
Gwinnett County	GA	64,980	110,075	159,296	20,604	49.9	32.7	27.5	25.2	10.3	0.5	3.9	10,777	14.8	20,359	7.8	52.9	3.4	1,575	71.5	8,327	124
Hall County	GA	13,833	20,330	25,777	4,316	57.0	55.2	4.8	36.1	1.7	0.2	1.9	1,740	14.8	3,223	8.0	54.0	3.3	237	62.2	1,273	35
Henry County	GA	10,929	23,601	40,951	864	43.9	41.2	44.7	7.1	2.7	0.2	4.0	2,652	15.4	5,099	8.0	52.0	5.1	635	77.8	2,395	51
Houston County	GA	16,249	21,529	26,787	789	49.9	51.9	35.4	7.1	2.4	0.2	3.0	1,858	14.4	3,796	7.1	48.9	3.6	279	76.8	1,523	38
Muscogee County	GA	30,125	32,916	32,458	427	61.8	30.9	57.6	0.0	2.0	0.2	9.2	2,349	13.8	5,266	6.2	44.6	3.3	320	64.7	1,791	63
Newton County	GA	8,054	11,734	19,637	538	60.8	39.9	50.3	4.9	0.8	0.1	3.9	1,362	14.4	2,774	7.1	49.1	2.9	153	62.4	858	26
Paulding County	GA	7,604	16,587	28,444	405	37.0	67.6	20.1	7.2	0.9	0.4	3.8	1,906	14.9	3,645	7.8	52.3	3.5	271	71.8	1,349	35
Richmond County	GA	33,660	35,424	32,449	141	72.2	20.1	74.3	2.1	1.3	0.1	2.0	2,240	14.5	4,586	7.1	48.8	3.7	343	52.9	1,529	59
Rockdale County	GA	10,942	13,519	15,777	607	59.9	25.2	58.2	11.6	1.7	0.2	3.0	1,086	14.5	2,263	7.0	48.0	2.9	150	69.5	1,033	19
Hawaii Department of Education	HI	159,285	184,360	180,196	18,097	43.3	19.7	2.3	4.6	72.7	0.6	—	11,403	15.8	21,649	8.3	52.7	4.9	2,602	75.3	11,508	289
Boise	ID	23,394	26,598	25,453	1,820	38.3	82.1	3.2	9.2	4.8	0.6	—	1,468	17.3	2,624	9.7	55.9	1.2	99	86.9	1,809	53
Meridian Joint District	ID	14,802	23,854	34,233	1,239	25.9	85.6	1.3	9.4	2.8	0.8	—	1,809	18.9	3,465	9.9	52.2	1.4	142	80.7	1,887	54
Nampa	ID	7,878	11,403	15,331	1,423	57.9	67.8	1.1	29.1	1.4	0.7	—	779	19.7	1,372	11.2	56.8	0.8	31	70.4	761	29
Carpentersville (CUSD 300)	IL	11,196	16,711	20,341	2,479	36.7	59.6	5.1	29.2	5.9	0.2	—	1,175	17.3	1,407	14.5	83.5	8.7	508	91.4	1,326	27
City of Chicago	IL	408,830	435,261	407,157	51,992	87.1	9.1	45.0	42.1	3.6	0.2	—	24,760	16.4	28,350	14.4	87.3	15.0	17,564	60.8	20,082	633
Elgin (SD U-46)	IL	27,726	36,767	41,446	9,402	51.7	38.0	7.3	46.2	8.4	0.2	—	2,327	17.8	2,646	15.7	87.9	9.1	1,107	80.2	2,455	58
Indian Prairie (CUSD 204)	IL	7,670	23,173	29,733	2,359	10.4	62.8	9.7	7.9	19.5	0.1	—	1,909	15.6	2,244	13.2	85.0	5.5	475	1.2	25	33
Naperville (CUSD 203)	IL	16,212	18,762	17,977	640	10.9	74.2	4.9	5.3	15.4	0.1	—	1,055	17.0	1,302	13.8	81.1	5.4	331	100.0 [4]	1,579	21
Oswego (CUSD 308)	IL	4,108	6,846	16,314	546	21.2	67.1	8.5	17.8	6.3	0.2	—	830	19.7	954	17.1	87.0	6.0	229	93.3	795	20
Plainfield (SD 202)	IL	3,324	11,986	29,254	2,715	14.8	64.8	9.3	20.1	5.6	0.1	—	1,700	17.2	2,011	14.6	84.6	8.1	642	96.9	1,643	30
Rockford (SD 205)	IL	27,255	27,399	29,071	3,174	76.0	39.4	32.3	24.6	3.6	0.1	—	1,839	15.8	2,178	13.3	84.5	22.7	1,700	55.0	1,367	54
Springfield (SD 186)	IL	15,813	15,387	15,110	55	63.3	55.2	40.4	2.0	6.8	0.3	—	1,130	13.4	1,361	11.1	83.0	11.0	437	59.6	684	35
Valley View (CUSD 365)	IL	11,781	13,558	18,133	1,874	52.8	33.4	23.7	36.0	6.8	0.1	—	1,058	17.1	1,275	14.2	83.0	13.7	764	84.6	1,140	20
Waukegan (CUSD 60)	IL	12,116	15,510	16,660	5,471	72.8	6.2	17.4	74.8	1.5	0.1	—	1,092	15.3	1,302	12.8	83.9	17.8	767	65.2	811	24
Carmel Clay Schools	IN	8,449	12,073	15,593	407	8.5	83.4	3.2	2.4	10.9	0.1	0.1	775	20.1	2,254	6.9	34.4	0.5	21	90.9	916	17
Evansville Vanderburgh	IN	22,918	22,875	22,527	321	55.7	80.7	15.6	2.1	1.3	0.3	5.1	1,476	15.3	3,018	7.5	48.9	1.8	123	75.7	1,416	42
Fort Wayne	IN	31,611	31,843	31,549	2,281	65.0	55.4	27.0	13.2	3.8	0.6	5.9	1,864	16.9	3,822	8.3	48.8	0.8	77	70.8	1,898	54
Hamilton Southeastern Schools	IN	3,113	8,777	17,937	528	11.1	84.3	7.0	3.1	5.3	0.2	3.0	885	20.3	1,967	9.1	45.0	0.5	23	94.6	863	20
Indianapolis	IN	48,140	41,008	33,372	3,880	82.6	24.2	58.6	16.7	0.4	0.1	1.0	2,296	14.5	5,183	6.4	44.3	5.1	416	35.0	1,159	64
MSD Lawrence Township	IN	11,066	15,692	15,711	1,392	48.3	45.0	41.6	11.6	1.6	0.2	3.0	858	18.3	2,096	7.5	40.9	1.6	84	77.6	1,079	18
MSD Wayne Township	IN	12,229	13,263	15,807	1,949	67.4	49.0	33.1	16.4	1.3	0.2	3.0	933	16.9	1,953	8.1	47.8	2.4	114	67.6	786	17
South Bend Community	IN	21,425	21,536	21,093	2,574	68.7	42.9	37.6	17.6	1.4	0.5	5.5	1,288	16.4	3,289	6.4	39.2	3.2	199	66.3	1,109	38
Vigo County	IN	16,982	16,545	16,014	178	51.5	91.1	6.1	1.1	1.6	0.1	7.7	1,011	15.8	1,950	8.2	51.8	0.1	5	71.6	952	29
Cedar Rapids	IA	17,003	17,780	17,399	318	41.3	77.8	15.4	3.6	2.5	0.6	0.1	1,108	15.7	2,778	6.3	39.9	5.6	306	76.3	1,071	34
Davenport	IA	17,846	16,874	17,013	271	55.3	61.8	18.0	12.5	2.1	0.5	5.1	1,122	15.2	2,154	7.9	52.1	9.4	448	72.7	930	34
Des Moines Independent	IA	30,888	32,435	32,749	4,541	64.3	50.6	17.1	20.6	5.4	0.5	5.9	2,232	14.7	4,545	7.2	49.1	7.6	645	64.9	1,607	60
Blue Valley	KS	9,433	17,111	21,359	329	6.1	81.4	2.9	4.1	8.4	0.3	3.0	1,358	15.7	2,588	8.3	52.5	0.5	31	94.4	1,412	33
Kansas City	KS	22,118	21,173	20,524	5,710	85.2	15.0	40.1	39.7	3.7	0.4	1.0	1,219	16.8	2,466	8.3	49.4	3.3	173	53.9	911	44
Olathe	KS	14,870	20,703	27,020	1,254	22.9	73.8	6.4	11.9	4.6	0.3	3.0	1,866	14.5	3,639	7.4	51.3	0.8	62	95.0	1,788	50
Shawnee Mission	KS	30,619	30,765	27,395	1,830	30.6	69.0	7.7	14.4	3.1	0.4	5.5	1,870	14.6	3,499	7.8	53.5	2.2	199	87.1	2,061	48
Wichita	KS	47,222	48,228	48,324	7,223	72.5	38.1	19.3	28.2	5.1	1.7	7.7	2,958	16.3	5,685	8.5	52.0	2.9	376	72.0	2,635	93
Boone County	KY	9,911	13,445	19,088	768	30.1	89.9	3.4	3.8	2.7	0.2	0.2	1,162	16.4	2,967	6.4	39.2	1.5	75	80.9	1,079	23
Fayette County	KY	32,083	33,130	36,988	2,365	46.8	61.0	24.7	10.1	4.0	0.2	—	2,682	13.8	6,586	5.6	40.7	3.5	361	78.0	2,101	71
Jefferson County	KY	91,450	96,660	98,808	4,895	59.1	53.7	37.6	5.7	2.9	0.1	—	6,409	15.4	17,952	5.5	35.7	5.7	1,689	69.5	5,506	176

See notes at end of table.

Selected statistics on enrollment, teachers, dropouts, and graduates in public school districts enrolling more than 15,000 students: Selected years, 1990 through 2009—Continued

Name of district	State	Enrollment, fall 1990	Enrollment, fall 2000	Enrollment, fall 2009	Number of English language learners, 2009	Percent eligible for free or reduced-price lunch, 2009	Percentage distribution of enrollment, by race, fall 2009						Teachers and staff, fall 2009					Dropouts and graduates, 2008–09				Number of schools, fall 2009
							White	Black	Hispanic	Asian/Pacific Islander	American Indian/Alaska Native	Two or more races	Number of classroom teachers	Pupil/teacher ratio	Total number of staff	Student/staff ratio	Teachers as a percentage of total staff	Percent dropping out of grades 9–12	Number of dropouts from grades 9–12	Averaged freshman graduation rate (AFGR)[1]	Number of high school graduates[2]	
1	2	3	4	5	6	7	8	9	10	11	12	13	14	15	16	17	18	19	20	21	22	23
Ascension Parish	LA	13,001	15,038	19,460	340	44.6	63.5	30.2	5.0	1.1	0.2	—	1,385	14.1	2,742	7.1	50.5	4.8	253	78.9	1,083	28
Bossier Parish	LA	17,804	18,797	20,186	580	45.8	62.3	29.7	5.9	1.8	0.3	—	1,334	15.1	2,798	7.2	47.7	5.3	273	71.2	1,041	36
Caddo Parish	LA	51,375	45,119	41,757	399	64.6	33.1	63.9	1.6	1.2	0.3	—	2,911	14.3	6,713	6.2	43.4	10.0	1,128	60.5	2,126	72
Calcasieu Parish	LA	32,917	32,261	32,905	269	57.8	61.0	35.9	1.9	1.0	0.3	—	2,491	13.2	5,113	6.4	48.7	3.5	296	69.9	1,695	61
East Baton Rouge Parish	LA	61,669	54,246	42,307	1,301	79.8	11.9	82.1	3.2	2.8	0.1	—	3,180	13.3	6,382	6.6	49.8	9.9	1,045	51.7	1,839	83
Jefferson Parish	LA	58,177	50,891	44,713	3,858	76.8	31.4	49.0	13.7	5.1	0.8	—	3,076	13.8	6,871	6.5	47.2	8.1	878	59.7	2,093	89
Lafayette Parish	LA	29,403	28,931	29,905	857	59.6	50.9	43.5	3.4	1.9	0.3	—	2,076	14.4	4,329	6.9	48.0	6.6	536	70.9	1,652	46
Livingston Parish	LA	16,310	19,723	24,301	279	46.5	90.5	6.5	2.3	0.5	0.2	—	1,652	14.7	3,315	7.3	49.8	4.0	248	73.1	1,203	41
Ouachita Parish	LA	17,667	17,479	19,359	163	55.5	65.2	32.6	1.2	0.8	0.2	—	1,309	14.8	3,008	6.4	43.5	6.8	349	68.9	1,057	35
Rapides Parish	LA	24,765	23,467	23,770	410	68.7	52.6	42.9	2.3	1.4	0.8	—	1,694	14.0	3,388	7.0	50.0	7.7	464	64.2	1,134	51
Saint Landry Parish	LA	17,213	15,457	15,135	109	76.9	40.7	57.6	1.1	0.5	0.1	—	1,115	13.6	2,234	6.8	49.9	7.3	263	66.3	738	37
Saint Tammany Parish	LA	27,522	32,392	36,021	574	44.8	75.3	19.3	3.4	1.6	0.4	—	2,598	13.9	5,350	6.7	48.6	4.6	473	77.2	2,132	55
Tangipahoa Parish	LA	16,724	18,197	19,369	243	72.7	49.2	47.6	2.4	0.7	0.2	—	1,190	16.3	2,622	7.4	45.4	5.4	282	65.5	995	39
Terrebonne Parish	LA	21,116	19,774	18,869	282	64.9	57.7	28.9	3.0	1.2	9.2	—	1,416	13.3	2,745	6.9	51.6	6.7	334	69.6	1,003	41
Anne Arundel County	MD	65,011	74,491	74,776	2,414	25.8	65.3	23.0	7.0	4.2	0.5	—	4,837	15.5	9,337	8.0	51.8	—	—	81.2	4,908	125
Baltimore City	MD	108,663	99,859	82,866	1,810	84.0	8.0	87.8	3.1	0.9	0.3	—	5,662	14.6	10,960	7.6	51.9	—	—	56.4	4,285	192
Baltimore County	MD	86,737	106,898	103,324	3,379	39.5	47.9	40.6	4.7	6.2	0.6	—	7,437	13.9	14,334	7.2	51.9	—	—	81.1	7,299	172
Calvert County	MD	10,398	16,170	17,006	159	18.8	77.7	17.0	2.6	2.1	0.6	—	1,092	15.6	2,207	7.7	49.5	—	—	89.4	1,356	26
Carroll County	MD	21,835	27,528	27,721	164	14.6	90.8	4.3	2.6	2.1	0.3	—	1,910	14.5	3,582	7.7	53.3	—	—	93.5	2,359	48
Cecil County	MD	12,868	15,905	16,205	122	34.6	83.6	11.0	3.7	1.3	0.4	—	1,160	14.0	2,215	7.3	52.3	—	—	78.1	1,080	29
Charles County	MD	18,708	23,468	26,779	173	27.0	37.4	54.5	3.6	3.5	0.9	—	1,735	15.4	3,331	8.0	52.1	—	—	93.4	2,172	37
Frederick County	MD	26,848	36,885	40,159	1,291	20.9	73.3	12.6	8.7	5.0	0.4	—	2,645	15.2	5,353	7.5	49.4	—	—	92.3	3,022	64
Harford County	MD	31,500	39,520	38,636	437	26.3	71.8	20.5	3.9	3.3	0.6	—	2,724	14.2	5,191	7.4	52.5	—	—	80.7	2,666	53
Howard County	MD	29,949	44,946	50,641	1,959	14.6	55.5	22.1	5.8	16.3	0.3	—	3,822	13.2	7,456	6.8	51.3	—	—	90.4	3,711	73
Montgomery County	MD	103,757	134,180	141,722	15,996	29.2	38.1	23.2	22.7	15.6	0.3	—	9,524	14.9	19,935	7.1	47.8	—	—	89.0	10,129	205
Prince George's County	MD	108,868	133,723	127,039	13,549	53.3	4.6	72.2	19.6	3.1	0.4	—	8,347	15.2	17,040	7.5	49.0	—	—	69.5	8,266	205
Saint Mary's County	MD	12,549	15,151	17,186	137	26.1	69.1	20.4	6.9	3.1	0.6	—	1,059	16.2	2,093	8.2	50.6	—	—	79.7	1,093	27
Washington County	MD	17,778	19,782	21,902	376	42.6	78.9	14.5	4.2	2.1	0.4	—	1,530	14.3	2,952	7.4	51.8	—	—	88.4	1,546	46
Boston	MA	60,543	63,024	55,371	6,599	75.6	13.1	36.5	39.6	8.7	0.4	1.8	4,170	13.3	7,396	7.5	56.4	7.2	1,308	71.3	3,549	131
Brockton	MA	14,529	16,791	15,501	2,361	72.0	28.5	50.8	14.1	2.8	0.6	3.2	1,100	14.1	2,010	7.7	54.7	5.4	234	69.8	909	22
Springfield	MA	24,194	26,526	25,141	2,926	81.4	14.7	22.3	56.7	2.2	0.1	4.1	2,144	11.7	3,768	6.7	56.9	9.6	670	52.7	1,099	45
Worcester	MA	21,066	25,828	23,988	6,126	71.7	37.5	13.8	37.3	8.1	0.3	3.0	1,716	14.0	3,166	7.6	54.2	5.1	350	78.7	1,535	45
Ann Arbor	MI	14,190	16,539	16,646	934	21.7	62.7	15.9	5.4	15.6	0.4	—	1,041	16.0	3,543	4.7	29.4	1.7	95	92.8	1,289	32
Chippewa Valley	MI	9,340	12,329	16,116	490	21.7	87.3	7.9	2.0	2.5	0.3	—	780	20.7	1,475	10.9	52.9	1.7	81	90.5	1,124	20
Dearborn City	MI	13,380	17,129	18,725	5,916	62.5	92.0	4.9	2.0	0.8	0.3	—	1,089	17.2	2,163	8.7	50.4	1.9	108	75.4	1,220	36
Detroit City	MI	168,956	162,194	90,499	6,722	79.1	2.5	88.2	8.1	0.9	0.3	—	5,346	16.9	12,203	7.4	43.8	6.0	1,860	45.1	5,634	182
Grand Rapids	MI	26,871	25,625	18,652	3,740	86.0	25.3	50.6	21.0	1.8	1.3	—	1,225	15.2	2,812	6.6	43.6	6.5	346	45.7	808	74
Livonia	MI	16,543	18,347	16,607	190	21.7	87.8	7.5	1.7	3.0	0.1	—	906	18.3	1,930	8.6	46.9	1.0	65	89.9	1,393	26
Plymouth-Canton Community	MI	14,955	16,518	16,607	588	15.3	76.5	9.3	2.0	11.8	0.4	—	954	20.3	1,938	10.0	49.2	2.0	126	93.7	1,379	26
Rochester Community	MI	11,350	13,862	15,111	447	13.3	80.3	5.6	2.4	11.5	0.1	—	824	18.3	1,761	8.6	46.8	0.4	22	97.2	1,182	22
Utica Community	MI	23,960	27,786	29,525	1,183	23.1	91.1	4.2	1.6	3.0	0.1	—	1,432	20.6	2,981	9.9	48.0	0.9	88	93.1	2,236	45
Walled Lake	MI	9,555	14,438	15,656	1,413	19.7	83.0	8.3	2.5	6.0	0.3	—	864	18.1	1,649	9.5	52.4	2.4	124	90.1	1,193	22
Warren Consolidated	MI	14,336	14,602	16,003	2,087	46.6	79.3	12.2	0.9	7.1	0.4	—	796	20.1	1,533	10.4	51.9	2.2	124	88.8	1,136	25
Anoka-Hennepin	MN	34,524	41,314	39,904	2,337	29.0	78.8	9.6	3.9	6.4	1.3	—	2,291	17.4	4,637	8.6	49.4	1.6	220	85.0	2,870	58
Minneapolis	MN	41,050	48,834	35,076	7,400	64.8	30.9	37.6	18.4	8.4	4.7	—	2,396	14.6	5,536	6.3	43.3	5.8	612	55.1	1,724	98
Osseo	MN	19,579	22,017	21,114	1,912	35.3	55.8	22.8	7.0	14.5	0.8	—	1,171	18.0	2,560	8.2	45.7	0.7	49	78.2	1,353	29
Rochester	MN	19,579	15,929	16,278	2,081	32.0	70.5	11.8	7.3	10.1	0.4	—	919	17.7	1,846	8.8	49.8	1.4	71	84.2	1,194	40
Rosemount-Apple Valley-Eagan	MN	20,547	28,330	27,599	1,314	18.2	76.6	9.1	5.7	7.9	0.7	—	1,696	16.3	3,388	8.1	50.1	0.8	69	92.7	2,109	35
Saint Paul	MN	35,932	45,115	38,531	13,903	73.2	24.7	30.1	13.8	29.6	1.8	—	2,461	15.7	5,614	6.9	43.8	3.9	476	73.0	2,409	109
South Washington County	MN	11,417	14,953	17,194	654	15.6	77.0	7.7	5.2	9.5	0.6	—	1,024	16.8	1,974	8.7	51.9	0.6	29	97.7	1,248	26

See notes at end of table.

Selected statistics on enrollment, teachers, dropouts, and graduates in public school districts enrolling more than 15,000 students: Selected years, 1990 through 2009—Continued

Name of district	State	Enrollment, fall 1990	Enrollment, fall 2000	Enrollment, fall 2009	Number of English language learners, 2009	Percent eligible for free or reduced-price lunch, 2009	Percentage distribution of enrollment, by race, fall 2009						Teachers and staff, fall 2009					Dropouts and graduates, 2008-09				Number of schools, fall 2009
							White	Black	Hispanic	Asian/ Pacific Islander	American Indian/ Alaska Native	Two or more races	Number of classroom teachers	Pupil/ teacher ratio	Total number of staff	Student/ staff ratio	Teachers as a percentage of total staff	Percent dropping out of grades 9–12	Number of dropouts from grades 9–12	Averaged freshman graduation rate (AFGR)[1]	Number of high school graduates[2]	
1	2	3	4	5	6	7	8	9	10	11	12	13	14	15	16	17	18	19	20	21	22	23
Desoto County	MS	13,470	19,812	31,213	1,008	46.7	62.9	29.8	5.7	1.5	0.1	#	1,786	17.5	3,784	8.2	47.2	1.4	122	70.7	1,551	38
Jackson	MS	33,546	31,351	30,609	135	87.2	1.5	97.5	0.7	0.1	#	0.1	1,891	16.2	4,608	6.6	41.0	5.9	491	51.6	1,274	61
Rankin County	MS	12,824	15,013	18,613	239	40.1	74.6	21.7	1.8	1.3	0.1	0.5	1,294	14.4	2,296	8.1	56.4	3.0	147	66.9	890	27
Columbia 93	MO	12,786	16,178	17,396	593	35.9	66.6	23.9	4.2	5.7	0.7	—	1,308	13.3	2,439	7.1	53.6	4.1	218	91.5	1,213	31
Fort Zumwalt R-II	MO	10,110	16,521	18,840	186	17.6	88.2	6.6	2.5	2.6	0.2	—	1,212	15.5	2,470	7.6	49.1	3.2	192	87.0	1,297	24
Francis Howell R-III	MO	13,391	19,497	19,707	157	15.3	88.1	6.3	2.2	3.3	0.2	—	1,214	16.2	2,096	9.4	58.0	1.8	107	96.5	1,488	23
Hazelwood	MO	16,985	18,855	18,839	301	53.9	27.8	69.2	1.6	1.2	0.1	—	1,212	15.5	2,453	7.7	49.4	2.6	165	75.1	1,386	30
Kansas City 33	MO	34,486	37,298	18,839	3,105	76.4	8.8	62.8	25.6	2.6	0.4	—	1,528	12.3	3,409	5.5	44.8	5.4	242	43.3	1,032	58
Lee's Summit R-VII	MO	7,132	14,340	17,521	135	15.6	80.7	12.4	4.2	2.3	0.4	—	1,180	14.9	2,520	7.0	46.8	3.1	170	90.1	1,189	27
North Kansas City 74	MO	15,732	17,258	18,523	1,063	43.1	69.5	13.9	10.2	5.1	1.3	—	1,300	14.2	3,316	5.6	39.2	3.1	176	93.4	1,268	32
Parkway C-2	MO	21,542	20,433	17,386	475	11.2	70.0	15.9	2.5	11.3	0.3	—	1,179	14.7	2,610	6.7	45.2	1.4	83	92.0	1,418	28
Rockwood R-VI	MO	15,608	21,203	22,657	248	6.6	82.6	10.0	1.8	5.4	0.2	—	1,499	15.1	3,182	7.1	47.1	1.3	93	94.5	1,721	31
Saint Louis City	MO	43,284	44,412	26,311	2,050	78.1	13.8	80.4	3.0	2.6	0.3	—	2,225	11.8	3,211	8.2	69.3	25.9	2,334	51.9	1,643	78
Springfield R-XII	MO	23,631	24,630	24,681	470	47.3	85.6	7.9	3.3	2.6	0.6	—	1,632	15.1	3,391	7.3	48.1	4.9	356	82.7	1,673	55
Lincoln	NE	27,986	31,354	34,915	2,699	42.6	76.2	9.6	8.1	4.5	1.7	—	2,529	13.8	5,249	6.7	48.2	3.9	388	79.4	1,954	69
Millard	NE	16,764	19,160	22,647	381	14.0	87.6	3.2	4.3	4.5	0.4	—	1,497	15.1	2,612	8.7	57.3	0.9	62	96.8	1,583	37
Omaha	NE	41,699	45,197	48,692	6,607	67.4	38.5	30.7	26.8	2.6	1.4	—	3,369	14.5	7,468	6.5	45.0	5.6	733	57.7	2,293	97
Clark County	NV	121,994	231,655	307,059	51,579	44.5	34.1	14.5	41.0	9.6	0.7	—	15,472	19.8	17,983	17.1	86.0	—	—	—	—	358
Washoe County	NV	38,466	56,268	64,838	12,032	40.7	53.2	3.9	33.8	6.7	2.5	—	3,429	18.9	3,856	16.8	88.9	—	—	—	—	106
Elizabeth	NJ	15,266	19,674	22,068	2,425	85.0	8.7	22.9	66.4	2.0	#	0.0	2,066	10.7	3,881	5.7	53.2	6.7	336	62.2	928	34
Jersey City	NJ	28,585	31,347	27,670	2,393	75.0	10.9	34.2	38.0	16.1	0.8	0.0	2,852	9.7	5,362	5.2	53.2	6.4	441	71.1	1,471	38
Newark	NJ	48,433	42,150	39,443	3,257	84.1	7.5	55.9	36.6	0.9	0.1	0.0	2,685	14.7	6,741	5.9	39.8	4.2	461	75.4	2,421	73
Paterson	NJ	22,109	24,629	24,080	4,503	85.7	5.4	31.1	60.0	3.3	0.1	0.0	2,230	10.8	3,664	6.6	60.9	4.3	218	52.7	991	39
Toms River Regional	NJ	16,002	17,621	17,372	166	19.7	81.1	4.6	8.7	4.0	0.1	1.5	1,194	14.5	2,201	7.9	54.2	2.2	129	89.2	1,315	18
Albuquerque	NM	88,295	85,276	96,572	14,977	60.2	24.1	2.5	64.4	2.1	4.3	2.6	6,529	14.8	13,162	7.3	49.6	2.7	761	61.9	4,784	172
Las Cruces	NM	19,216	22,185	24,872	3,343	60.7	23.1	2.7	72.1	1.3	0.8	#	1,655	15.0	3,328	7.5	49.7	6.6	478	63.3	1,268	37
Rio Rancho	NM	—	10,219	16,550	494	44.6	26.6	2.7	66.5	1.8	2.4	0.0	1,053	15.7	2,022	8.2	52.1	3.9	184	75.8	915	19
Brentwood Union Free	NY	11,749	15,565	16,517	4,005	65.3	9.2	15.9	72.5	2.1	0.2	—	1,189	13.9	2,331	7.1	51.0	2.0	94	73.1	1,029	17
Buffalo City	NY	47,224	45,721	34,526	3,236	77.4	23.0	56.9	15.1	3.5	1.4	—	3,032	11.4	5,439	6.3	55.7	9.3	944	61.4	1,538	58
New York City	NY	943,969	1,066,516	1,014,020	141,908	—	16.5	29.4	39.0	14.7	0.4	—	70,163	14.5	129,106	7.9	54.3	7.4	22,914	—	56,655	1,531
Rochester City	NY	32,730	36,294	32,516	3,085	84.8	10.5	64.0	22.3	2.8	0.3	—	2,806	11.6	6,163	5.3	54.5	11.3	1,147	43.9	1,406	62
Syracuse City	NY	22,561	23,015	21,320	2,075	75.4	28.7	53.5	11.3	5.1	1.4	—	1,770	12.0	4,112	5.2	43.0	11.0	615	52.3	847	34
Yonkers City	NY	18,621	26,237	24,956	3,325	71.9	18.1	24.3	51.4	5.9	0.2	—	1,003	24.9	2,675	9.3	37.5	4.7	319	64.3	1,361	38
Alamance-Burlington	NC	10,322	20,729	22,763	2,760	50.8	53.3	26.6	18.2	1.5	0.3	0.3	1,492	15.3	2,807	8.1	53.1	8.0	542	72.3	1,349	35
Buncombe County	NC	22,026	24,708	25,625	1,944	49.1	78.2	10.8	9.1	1.6	0.4	0.4	1,627	15.8	3,832	6.7	42.4	4.7	380	75.2	1,628	41
Cabarrus County	NC	12,853	19,115	28,242	1,937	37.2	64.3	21.5	11.7	2.2	0.4	0.4	1,866	15.1	3,530	8.0	52.9	5.0	394	80.4	1,591	35
Catawba County	NC	12,770	16,250	17,338	1,580	45.4	73.0	9.8	9.7	7.2	0.3	0.4	1,077	16.1	2,055	8.4	52.4	4.2	232	81.8	1,166	28
Charlotte-Mecklenburg	NC	77,069	103,336	136,969	15,227	51.7	33.5	45.4	15.9	4.9	0.4	0.2	8,949	15.3	17,799	7.7	50.3	6.3	2,364	69.2	7,052	171
Cleveland County	NC	8,131	9,663	16,420	304	42.0	65.6	30.0	3.4	0.9	0.2	0.2	1,113	14.7	2,219	7.4	50.2	8.1	419	68.6	1,027	29
Cumberland County	NC	44,612	50,850	53,035	1,235	53.3	36.3	52.2	7.5	2.0	2.0	0.2	3,674	14.4	7,378	7.2	49.8	3.8	615	76.4	3,327	87
Davidson County	NC	16,426	19,136	20,757	403	39.1	89.0	4.9	4.7	1.1	0.2	0.2	1,234	16.8	2,405	8.6	51.3	6.4	395	77.7	1,289	33
Durham	NC	18,517	29,728	32,470	4,564	55.5	21.4	56.6	19.2	2.6	0.2	0.2	2,210	14.7	4,375	7.4	50.5	5.1	500	70.1	1,813	53
Forsyth County	NC	37,625	44,769	52,795	6,399	50.9	44.5	35.3	17.9	2.1	0.2	0.2	3,869	13.6	7,291	7.2	53.1	6.0	922	78.3	3,150	81
Gaston County	NC	29,631	30,603	32,351	1,510	55.1	67.7	22.6	8.0	1.5	0.2	0.2	1,935	16.7	3,886	8.3	49.8	6.1	607	72.6	2,035	54
Guilford County	NC	24,575	63,417	72,758	5,957	51.6	38.8	45.7	9.5	5.6	0.5	0.5	4,900	14.8	10,074	7.2	48.6	3.1	702	80.4	4,616	119
Harnett County	NC	11,890	16,338	19,291	1,413	54.7	53.8	31.9	12.7	0.7	1.0	0.2	1,256	15.4	2,322	8.3	54.1	6.3	347	73.1	1,108	27
Iredell-Statesville	NC	10,610	17,235	21,488	1,089	41.0	71.3	16.6	9.2	2.7	0.2	0.2	1,325	16.2	2,584	8.3	51.3	3.6	243	85.9	1,407	35
Johnston County	NC	14,647	21,334	31,960	2,972	41.5	61.7	21.4	15.7	0.7	0.5	0.5	2,162	14.8	3,928	8.1	55.0	5.3	446	74.0	1,625	42

See notes at end of table.

Selected statistics on enrollment, teachers, dropouts, and graduates in public school districts enrolling more than 15,000 students: Selected years, 1990 through 2009—Continued

Name of district	State	Enrollment, fall 1990	Enrollment, fall 2000	Enrollment, fall 2009	Number of English language learners, 2009	Percent eligible for free or reduced-price lunch, 2009	White	Black	Hispanic	Asian/Pacific Islander	American Indian/Alaska Native	Two or more races	Number of classroom teachers	Pupil/teacher ratio	Total number of staff	Student/staff ratio	Teachers as a percentage of total staff	Percent dropping out of grades 9–12	Number of dropouts from grades 9–12	Averaged freshman graduation rate (AFGR)[1]	Number of high school graduates[2]	Number of schools, fall 2009
1	2	3	4	5	6	7	8	9	10	11	12	13	14	15	16	17	18	19	20	21	22	23
Nash-Rocky Mount	NC	11,653	18,342	17,812	908	62.3	35.0	55.4	7.9	1.2	0.5	—	1,083	16.4	2,245	7.9	48.3	7.0	368	70.8	1,049	27
New Hanover County	NC	19,090	21,605	24,505	982	40.7	63.6	28.0	6.3	1.7	0.5	—	1,601	15.3	3,420	7.2	46.8	5.8	424	72.1	1,462	40
Onslow County	NC	18,605	20,984	24,075	346	43.4	60.6	30.1	6.9	1.6	0.8	—	1,473	16.3	3,062	7.9	48.1	4.7	312	81.9	1,472	35
Pitt County	NC	17,693	20,040	23,382	1,033	52.6	38.6	52.0	7.8	1.4	0.2	—	1,581	14.8	3,045	7.7	51.9	6.6	467	69.2	1,298	36
Randolph County	NC	13,572	17,271	18,954	1,460	50.8	79.1	7.1	11.9	1.2	0.6	—	1,206	15.7	2,385	7.9	50.6	6.3	343	69.2	1,035	31
Robeson County	NC	23,251	23,911	23,937	1,516	77.0	16.8	29.4	9.4	0.6	43.8	—	1,516	15.8	3,193	7.5	47.5	6.7	461	70.3	1,389	42
Rowan-Salisbury	NC	16,403	20,472	20,887	1,564	56.1	65.6	22.7	10.3	1.3	0.3	—	1,393	15.0	2,765	7.6	50.4	6.1	396	75.9	1,352	35
Union County	NC	12,864	22,862	39,395	2,140	32.7	68.8	17.1	12.2	1.6	0.3	—	2,490	15.8	4,996	7.9	49.8	3.3	342	87.6	2,136	52
Wake County	NC	64,266	98,950	140,558	12,281	32.0	51.0	30.7	11.9	6.1	0.3	—	8,924	15.8	16,346	8.6	54.6	4.3	1,689	84.7	8,186	159
Wayne County	NC	13,653	19,279	19,458	1,495	57.1	44.2	42.0	12.6	1.0	0.2	—	1,288	15.1	2,535	7.7	50.8	5.6	316	75.5	1,170	31
Akron City	OH	33,213	31,464	23,643	747	71.9	44.4	50.7	1.8	3.0	0.1	—	1,774	13.3	5,700	4.1	31.1	6.3	478	65.0	1,484	56
Cincinnati City	OH	51,148	46,562	33,449	1,141	73.2	25.6	71.0	2.4	0.9	0.1	—	1,829	18.3	4,535	7.4	40.3	5.3	578	52.7	1,723	59
Cleveland Municipal	OH	70,019	75,684	48,392	2,466	61.1	15.4	71.3	12.5	0.6	0.3	—	3,554	13.6	8,165	5.9	43.5	12.9	1,986	42.3	2,187	112
Columbus Municipal	OH	64,280	64,511	52,810	5,023	64.0	28.5	62.9	6.3	2.0	0.2	—	3,339	15.8	7,556	7.0	44.2	2.2	343	55.0	2,709	127
Hilliard City	OH	6,533	12,423	15,293	1,150	19.5	83.3	5.8	4.5	6.2	0.2	—	857	17.8	1,719	8.9	49.8	1.1	49	86.4	968	23
Lakota Local	OH	9,356	14,659	18,212	957	19.2	80.9	9.6	3.5	5.8	0.1	—	879	20.7	1,821	10.0	48.3	1.6	87	95.1	1,232	20
South-Western City	OH	16,605	19,216	20,573	2,595	49.9	75.6	11.9	10.5	1.8	0.2	—	1,111	18.5	2,435	8.4	45.6	3.7	242	70.4	1,220	33
Toledo City	OH	40,452	37,738	25,699	379	71.0	43.0	47.4	8.9	0.7	0.1	—	1,918	13.4	3,761	6.8	51.0	4.2	331	48.9	1,276	61
Broken Arrow	OK	13,872	14,990	16,618	736	30.8	74.0	5.9	7.1	3.1	9.9	—	953	17.4	2,022	8.2	47.1	3.6	162	78.7	921	23
Edmond	OK	13,041	17,084	20,750	888	23.6	73.8	11.9	5.4	5.0	4.0	—	1,175	17.7	2,421	8.6	48.5	0.6	39	89.2	1,331	23
Lawton	OK	17,727	17,338	16,398	776	57.5	45.6	31.9	12.0	2.6	7.8	—	1,118	14.7	2,424	6.8	46.1	3.4	151	77.5	1,013	35
Moore	OK	16,630	18,101	21,675	834	39.7	66.7	8.0	10.5	5.2	10.5	—	1,286	16.9	2,490	8.7	51.6	3.4	199	80.0	1,233	29
Oklahoma City	OK	36,066	39,750	42,549	10,686	83.4	20.7	30.2	41.3	2.7	5.1	—	2,590	16.4	5,118	8.3	50.6	4.9	467	58.3	1,657	95
Putnam City	OK	18,071	19,506	18,700	1,839	65.9	46.9	27.2	16.5	5.0	4.4	—	1,200	15.6	2,125	8.8	56.5	2.1	112	73.6	1,182	26
Tulsa	OK	40,732	42,812	41,493	5,454	81.3	32.3	33.4	21.9	1.7	10.7	—	2,739	15.1	6,191	6.7	44.2	0.4	40	58.0	1,652	88
Union	OK	9,563	13,054	15,010	2,110	47.0	48.2	15.0	20.1	7.0	9.6	—	866	17.3	1,827	8.2	47.4	4.1	179	81.8	919	17
Beaverton	OR	24,874	33,600	38,120	5,769	35.5	59.0	3.1	22.6	14.7	0.6	—	2,025	18.8	3,926	9.7	51.6	2.8	325	83.0	2,459	55
Bend-Lapine	OR	9,481	13,128	15,835	656	45.6	87.4	0.8	10.0	0.7	1.1	—	739	21.4	1,557	10.2	47.5	2.6	128	86.1	1,131	27
Eugene	OR	17,904	18,432	17,475	465	37.9	78.6	2.9	11.1	5.3	2.2	—	858	20.4	1,910	9.1	44.9	1.5	87	91.3	1,353	41
Hillsboro	OR	10,396	18,315	20,796	3,179	45.2	55.8	2.4	33.4	7.8	0.7	—	984	21.1	2,111	9.8	46.6	2.0	119	85.3	1,293	34
North Clackamas	OR	12,403	14,876	17,620	2,263	44.7	74.7	2.1	14.8	7.3	1.0	—	844	20.9	1,829	9.6	46.1	3.7	219	81.8	1,113	34
Portland	OR	53,042	53,141	45,748	4,776	45.9	57.9	14.3	15.8	10.6	1.4	—	2,475	18.5	5,284	8.7	46.8	8.6	992	68.4	2,320	91
Salem-Keizer	OR	27,756	35,108	40,259	7,785	58.0	55.3	1.2	37.7	4.3	1.5	—	2,132	18.9	4,478	9.0	47.6	4.5	552	81.7	2,474	68
Allentown City	PA	13,519	16,424	17,465	2,054	74.8	17.0	17.4	64.0	1.4	0.1	—	1,161	15.0	2,216	7.9	52.4	9.1	485	67.3	1,068	22
Central Bucks	PA	10,286	17,305	20,436	94	6.0	90.8	1.8	2.5	4.7	0.1	—	1,202	17.0	2,347	8.7	51.2	0.4	28	96.2	1,529	23
Philadelphia City	PA	190,979	201,190	165,694	12,172	81.6	14.0	61.3	17.8	6.8	0.2	—	11,104	14.9	22,306	7.4	49.8	7.0	3,324	53.5	8,377	273
Pittsburgh	PA	39,896	38,560	27,945	366	74.0	36.5	60.0	1.4	2.0	0.1	—	2,229	12.5	4,564	6.1	48.8	5.6	463	64.8	1,716	69
Reading	PA	11,965	15,487	17,869	3,521	91.6	10.2	11.6	77.4	0.7	#	—	1,149	15.5	2,200	8.1	52.2	10.0	483	55.5	760	24
Providence	RI	20,908	26,937	23,847	3,224	85.5	11.6	22.1	60.0	5.7	0.7	—	1,629	14.6	3,016	7.9	54.0	7.5	562	66.9	1,462	51
Aiken 01	SC	23,970	25,147	24,632	1,121	55.4	57.5	35.9	5.6	0.8	0.2	—	1,471	16.7	2,144	11.5	68.6	4.7	350	62.5	1,276	41
Beaufort 01	SC	12,518	16,721	19,786	2,953	49.2	44.9	34.4	19.1	1.3	0.3	—	1,350	14.7	1,755	11.3	76.9	0.9	49	63.7	995	30
Berkeley 01	SC	27,384	26,635	29,104	1,583	51.7	55.4	35.0	6.6	2.6	0.4	—	1,789	16.3	2,592	11.2	69.0	5.5	446	64.6	1,422	38
Charleston 01	SC	43,063	44,767	43,063	2,244	51.1	43.4	48.5	6.1	1.7	0.3	—	2,989	14.4	4,130	10.4	72.4	2.8	341	60.2	2,158	76
Dorchester 02	SC	13,735	16,678	22,388	598	38.4	59.8	32.2	4.5	2.9	0.7	—	1,280	17.5	1,748	12.8	73.2	4.2	271	67.4	1,136	20
Florence 01	SC	14,731	13,930	15,794	205	59.0	43.8	52.5	1.7	1.8	0.2	—	1,054	15.0	1,719	9.2	61.3	2.2	103	67.3	900	23
Greenville 01	SC	51,434	59,875	70,966	6,573	46.3	60.2	26.1	10.8	2.6	0.3	—	4,404	16.1	6,156	11.5	71.5	3.5	725	69.0	3,805	94
Horry 01	SC	24,080	29,894	37,790	2,172	60.7	66.9	23.6	7.3	1.6	0.6	—	2,498	15.1	3,794	10.0	65.8	4.8	529	72.1	2,091	49
Lexington 01	SC	11,202	17,285	22,300	790	34.8	81.5	10.6	4.8	2.5	0.6	—	1,503	14.8	2,170	10.3	65.8	1.4	87	73.7	1,206	26
Lexington 05	SC	11,683	15,064	16,694	387	28.6	65.4	29.2	2.4	2.8	0.1	—	1,188	14.1	1,571	10.6	75.6	1.7	92	80.8	1,186	19

See notes at end of table.

Selected statistics on enrollment, teachers, dropouts, and graduates in public school districts enrolling more than 15,000 students: Selected years, 1990 through 2009—Continued

Name of district	State	Enrollment, fall 1990	Enrollment, fall 2000	Enrollment, fall 2009	Number of English language learners, 2009	Percent eligible for free or reduced-price lunch, 2009	Percentage distribution of enrollment, by race, fall 2009						Teachers and staff, fall 2009					Dropouts and graduates, 2008–09				Number of schools, fall 2009
							White	Black	Hispanic	Asian/Pacific Islander	American Indian/Alaska Native	Two or more races	Number of classroom teachers	Pupil/teacher ratio	Total number of staff	Student/staff ratio	Teachers as a percentage of total staff	Percent dropping out of grades 9–12	Number of dropouts from grades 9–12	Averaged freshman graduation rate (AFGR)[1]	Number of high school graduates[2]	
1	2	3	4	5	6	7	8	9	10	11	12	13	14	15	16	17	18	19	20	21	22	23
Pickens 01	SC	14,289	15,938	16,594	568	45.0	84.4	9.8	3.8	1.6	0.4	—	1,015	16.4	1,412	11.8	71.9	4.0	194	62.9	855	25
Richland 01	SC	27,051	27,061	24,460	586	64.6	18.4	77.3	3.1	1.1	0.1	—	1,828	13.4	2,371	10.3	77.1	4.0	281	58.8	1,251	50
Richland 02	SC	12,788	17,409	24,949	1,389	39.8	30.3	60.6	5.7	3.3	0.2	—	1,676	14.9	2,037	12.2	82.3	2.9	213	74.4	1,347	27
York 03	SC	12,685	14,925	17,717	856	48.7	53.9	36.7	5.9	1.9	1.7	—	1,180	15.0	1,519	11.7	77.6	2.8	148	67.5	997	28
Sioux Falls	SD	16,092	19,097	20,843	1,502	38.5	76.0	9.0	6.3	2.8	5.9	—	1,398	14.9	2,600	8.0	53.8	0.6	42	75.6	1,289	49
Davidson County	TN	68,452	67,669	75,080	7,926	67.9	32.7	47.5	15.8	3.8	0.1	—	5,324	14.1	10,701	7.0	49.8	5.7	1,180	70.4	3,978	139
Hamilton County	TN	22,785	39,915	41,832	1,155	54.7	59.6	32.5	5.6	2.1	0.2	—	2,876	14.5	4,965	8.4	57.9	4.9	570	71.8	2,367	76
Knox County	TN	50,750	51,944	56,758	1,188	40.8	78.8	14.8	4.0	2.1	0.3	—	3,848	14.8	7,087	8.0	54.3	4.0	678	79.2	3,500	86
Memphis City	TN	107,103	113,730	109,300	5,549	81.4	7.0	85.0	6.5	1.3	0.1	—	6,871	15.9	12,526	8.7	54.9	10.5	3,567	67.3	6,559	206
Montgomery County	TN	16,591	23,339	29,138	587	46.7	60.8	27.7	8.0	2.9	0.6	—	1,969	14.8	3,789	7.7	52.0	1.1	92	86.3	1,826	36
Rutherford County	TN	17,996	25,356	37,679	1,352	37.8	70.4	16.8	8.4	4.2	0.4	—	2,476	15.2	3,975	9.5	62.3	1.4	177	88.7	2,649	44
Shelby County	TN	37,675	46,972	48,211	930	31.3	52.3	37.8	4.6	4.9	0.4	—	3,064	15.7	5,490	8.8	55.8	0.3	37	76.1	2,727	52
Sumner County	TN	19,630	22,347	27,158	415	36.9	84.6	9.6	4.2	1.4	0.2	—	1,901	14.3	3,672	7.4	51.8	1.4	115	82.6	1,689	46
Williamson County	TN	11,472	19,545	30,652	396	10.2	88.0	4.5	3.2	4.2	0.1	—	1,962	15.6	3,634	8.4	54.0	0.8	78	100.0[4]	2,300	37
Wilson County	TN	10,175	11,430	15,163	187	26.8	87.5	7.4	3.1	1.7	0.3	—	927	16.4	1,915	7.9	48.4	1.6	83	91.4	1,175	20
Abilene ISD	TX	18,217	18,118	17,016	482	62.5	43.8	14.2	39.3	2.0	0.7	—	1,215	14.0	2,419	7.0	50.2	2.7	117	69.7	879	38
Aldine ISD	TX	41,372	52,520	62,792	15,538	84.3	3.0	28.3	66.9	1.7	0.1	—	4,238	14.8	8,635	7.3	49.1	5.6	839	59.0	2,652	73
Alief ISD	TX	29,774	42,151	45,553	14,061	78.0	3.8	33.8	49.3	12.6	0.5	—	3,081	14.8	6,129	7.4	50.3	5.0	590	64.6	2,270	46
Allen ISD	TX	5,240	10,604	18,242	1,238	15.6	62.2	11.2	13.0	13.0	0.7	—	1,216	15.0	2,172	8.4	56.0	0.3	13	98.5	1,230	22
Alvin ISD	TX	9,323	11,324	16,788	2,113	51.6	37.1	12.5	42.5	7.5	0.4	—	1,087	15.4	2,255	7.4	48.2	3.2	141	79.6	808	22
Amarillo ISD	TX	27,374	28,908	31,890	3,497	64.3	41.8	11.6	42.1	4.1	0.5	—	2,190	14.6	4,026	7.9	54.4	3.1	250	73.8	1,706	55
Arlington ISD	TX	44,958	58,866	63,487	10,388	59.7	28.8	24.0	39.6	7.2	0.4	—	4,124	15.4	8,079	7.9	51.0	2.9	510	68.1	3,441	77
Austin ISD	TX	65,885	77,816	84,676	22,292	63.3	25.8	11.3	58.9	3.6	0.3	—	5,976	14.2	11,571	7.3	51.6	4.9	994	68.6	3,914	122
Beaumont ISD	TX	20,627	20,696	19,551	1,333	72.7	16.2	64.1	16.4	3.1	0.2	—	1,443	13.5	2,869	6.8	50.3	3.1	171	70.2	1,091	33
Birdville ISD	TX	18,477	21,246	22,897	2,148	52.1	52.5	7.2	33.7	5.7	0.9	—	1,489	15.4	2,855	8.0	52.2	3.6	230	70.7	1,297	32
Brownsville ISD	TX	37,489	40,898	49,121	15,748	72.1	1.8	0.2	97.7	0.3	0.1	—	3,365	14.6	7,543	6.5	44.6	2.3	293	68.7	2,524	58
Bryan ISD	TX	11,413	13,501	15,579	2,598	70.4	29.4	23.2	46.7	0.5	0.1	—	1,060	14.7	2,224	7.0	47.6	4.4	166	72.1	747	27
Carrollton-Farmers Branch ISD	TX	17,561	24,134	25,920	5,544	59.4	21.5	15.4	51.9	10.9	0.3	—	1,727	15.0	3,201	8.1	54.0	1.6	120	73.7	1,553	46
Clear Creek ISD	TX	22,372	29,875	37,611	2,205	22.7	58.8	9.2	21.3	10.4	0.3	—	2,630	14.3	4,865	7.7	54.0	0.9	105	83.5	2,412	44
Comal ISD	TX	5,883	10,695	16,700	667	31.5	64.9	2.7	30.5	1.5	0.4	—	1,098	15.2	2,236	7.5	49.1	1.3	61	100.0[4]	1,072	28
Conroe ISD	TX	23,288	34,928	49,629	4,677	34.9	60.8	6.8	28.1	3.6	0.7	—	3,141	15.8	6,047	8.2	51.9	0.9	120	84.2	2,931	53
Corpus Christi ISD	TX	41,881	39,138	38,196	1,865	68.1	15.3	5.2	77.4	1.9	0.2	—	2,395	15.9	5,031	7.6	47.6	2.8	287	69.4	2,079	61
Crowley ISD	TX	5,832	9,137	15,126	1,042	48.8	28.9	40.6	25.4	4.4	0.7	—	967	15.6	1,848	8.2	52.3	3.1	132	74.1	808	21
Cypress-Fairbanks ISD	TX	41,196	63,497	104,231	13,921	43.0	35.5	16.5	39.0	8.8	0.3	—	6,725	15.5	12,860	8.1	52.3	1.2	347	85.9	5,614	80
Dallas ISD	TX	135,000	161,548	157,111	52,405	86.5	4.6	26.4	67.6	1.2	0.2	—	10,704	14.7	19,526	8.0	54.8	6.0	2,257	57.1	6,671	231
Denton ISD	TX	10,690	13,645	22,825	3,132	39.7	54.7	12.2	29.6	2.7	0.7	—	1,827	12.5	3,217	7.1	56.8	0.8	45	78.8	1,081	33
Eagle Mount-Saginaw ISD	TX	4,691	6,567	16,126	1,009	37.9	52.0	11.2	32.1	4.3	0.4	—	1,022	15.8	1,923	8.4	53.1	1.7	67	93.9	821	24
Ector County ISD	TX	26,993	26,831	27,435	3,004	55.9	27.9	5.3	65.1	1.0	0.8	—	1,712	16.0	3,416	8.0	50.1	4.4	323	61.6	1,270	38
Edinburg CISD	TX	15,645	22,005	32,011	9,595	18.3	1.7	0.4	97.1	0.8	0.1	—	2,057	15.6	4,389	7.3	46.9	3.7	296	74.9	1,494	38
El Paso ISD	TX	64,092	62,325	63,378	14,005	68.6	12.0	4.9	81.3	1.4	0.4	—	4,404	14.4	8,818	7.2	49.9	4.8	883	66.0	3,396	97
Fort Bend ISD	TX	36,286	53,999	69,374	7,819	34.8	22.4	31.4	24.1	21.8	0.2	—	4,385	15.8	9,047	7.7	48.5	1.5	338	83.5	4,636	69
Fort Worth ISD	TX	69,163	79,661	80,209	21,637	74.8	13.0	24.5	60.5	1.7	0.3	—	5,069	15.8	10,959	7.3	46.3	6.5	1,243	62.4	3,568	140
Frisco ISD	TX	1,419	7,234	33,973	1,390	12.7	61.4	12.2	13.1	12.6	0.7	—	2,494	13.6	4,456	7.6	56.0	0.2	15	100.0[4]	1,270	45
Galena Park ISD	TX	15,593	18,885	21,536	5,822	76.4	6.0	18.6	74.1	1.1	0.4	—	1,573	13.7	3,094	7.0	50.8	4.0	244	81.1	1,298	24
Garland ISD	TX	37,978	50,312	57,861	10,793	56.5	27.2	18.8	45.3	8.3	0.4	—	3,720	15.6	7,394	7.8	50.3	2.7	459	80.0	3,562	74
Goose Creek CISD	TX	17,654	18,003	20,954	2,231	63.0	27.9	17.9	52.5	1.4	0.5	—	1,463	14.3	2,875	7.3	50.9	2.8	160	68.1	1,103	27
Grand Prairie ISD	TX	16,482	20,257	26,395	5,242	69.5	15.1	17.7	63.1	3.7	0.1	—	1,612	16.4	3,300	8.0	48.9	4.4	303	67.2	1,266	40
Harlingen CISD	TX	14,863	15,857	18,205	2,287	76.7	8.7	0.7	89.7	0.8	0.1	—	1,230	14.8	2,609	7.0	47.2	4.2	206	68.9	960	31
Houston ISD	TX	194,000	208,462	202,773	57,747	59.4	7.9	27.1	61.6	3.3	0.1	—	12,027	16.9	24,737	8.2	48.6	4.6	2,191	59.2	8,595	297
Humble ISD	TX	19,560	24,684	34,923	2,636	32.4	51.3	18.3	26.4	3.6	0.4	—	2,426	14.4	4,762	7.3	50.9	1.7	176	92.0	2,140	40
Hurst-Euless-Bedford ISD	TX	18,740	19,203	20,762	1,645	49.0	48.7	15.9	26.4	9.7	1.0	—	1,310	15.9	2,454	8.5	53.4	0.9	53	90.3	1,323	32
Irving ISD	TX	23,509	29,097	33,679	12,038	78.2	13.8	12.9	68.7	4.2	0.4	—	2,428	13.9	4,299	7.8	56.5	3.0	261	68.9	1,648	39
Judson ISD	TX	13,145	16,603	21,750	1,434	60.4	20.9	28.2	47.9	2.6	0.4	—	1,423	15.3	2,932	7.4	48.5	4.5	259	75.0	1,154	28

See notes at end of table.

Selected statistics on enrollment, teachers, dropouts, and graduates in public school districts enrolling more than 15,000 students: Selected years, 1990 through 2009—Continued

Name of district	State	Enrollment, fall 1990	Enrollment, fall 2000	Enrollment, fall 2009	Number of English language learners, 2009	Percent eligible for free or reduced-price lunch, 2009	Percentage distribution of enrollment, by race, fall 2009						Teachers and staff, fall 2009					Dropouts and graduates, 2008–09				Number of schools, fall 2009
							White	Black	Hispanic	Asian/Pacific Islander	American Indian/Alaska Native	Two or more races	Number of classroom teachers	Pupil/teacher ratio	Total number of staff	Student/staff ratio	Teachers as a percentage of total staff	Percent dropping out of grades 9-12	Number of dropouts from grades 9-12	Averaged freshman graduation rate (AFGR)[1]	Number of high school graduates[2]	
1	2	3	4	5	6	7	8	9	10	11	12	13	14	15	16	17	18	19	20	21	22	23
Katy ISD	TX	19,507	34,503	59,078	6,705	28.9	47.8	10.1	31.0	10.9	0.2	—	4,120	14.3	7,585	7.8	54.3	1.0	169	93.3	3,539	56
Keller ISD	TX	8,212	17,083	31,569	1,495	18.2	66.7	8.1	16.2	7.7	1.4	—	1,952	16.2	3,514	9.0	55.6	1.4	117	87.8	1,736	36
Killeen ISD	TX	22,131	29,687	39,603	2,544	52.3	33.5	36.8	25.1	3.9	0.8	—	2,729	14.5	5,770	6.9	47.3	2.6	233	69.1	1,660	54
Klein ISD	TX	26,220	32,376	44,824	4,659	36.2	42.9	15.5	32.5	8.9	0.3	—	2,938	15.3	5,724	7.8	51.3	2.8	371	79.7	2,760	44
La Joya ISD	TX	9,844	17,641	28,004	12,482	36.2	0.5	0.0	99.2	#	0.2	—	1,906	14.7	3,924	7.1	48.6	4.0	262	69.7	1,190	34
Lamar CISD	TX	12,335	15,159	23,864	2,369	20.1	30.6	19.1	44.4	5.5	0.3	—	1,457	16.4	2,966	8.0	49.1	2.7	166	82.7	1,228	36
Laredo ISD	TX	23,304	22,547	24,707	15,722	47.6	0.5	0.1	99.2	0.2	0.0	—	1,603	15.4	3,877	6.4	41.3	2.9	173	62.3	1,068	30
Leander ISD	TX	5,419	14,499	30,454	1,333	22.5	67.9	5.2	20.8	5.5	0.6	—	2,086	14.6	3,996	7.6	52.3	2.5	182	92.7	1,477	37
Lewisville ISD	TX	20,776	39,096	50,840	5,817	25.5	57.5	9.4	22.4	10.2	0.5	—	3,745	13.6	6,406	7.9	58.5	1.2	175	82.8	3,158	64
Lubbock ISD	TX	30,991	29,026	28,680	524	61.8	32.1	15.0	50.7	1.9	0.3	—	2,024	14.2	3,522	8.1	57.5	6.2	466	75.2	1,603	61
Mansfield ISD	TX	7,570	14,888	31,662	2,789	36.2	44.4	27.4	21.0	6.5	0.7	—	1,928	16.4	3,749	8.1	51.4	2.1	183	81.1	1,666	40
McAllen ISD	TX	21,120	21,747	25,172	6,561	26.8	5.4	0.6	91.9	1.8	0.2	—	1,681	15.0	3,378	7.5	49.8	4.2	278	68.9	1,306	35
Mesquite ISD	TX	25,920	32,334	37,272	5,068	62.2	37.2	12.7	45.2	3.7	0.6	—	2,369	15.7	4,590	8.1	51.6	1.4	151	88.3	1,234	47
Midland ISD	TX	21,082	20,522	21,374	1,663	52.8	34.2	9.4	54.8	1.1	0.4	—	1,440	14.8	2,816	7.6	51.1	4.8	286	73.1	1,212	37
Mission CISD	TX	11,032	12,464	15,412	4,884	42.7	1.0	0.1	98.7	0.1	#	—	1,027	15.0	2,282	6.8	45.0	1.4	57	70.1	756	22
North East ISD	TX	39,909	50,875	65,498	4,250	49.8	36.8	9.4	49.4	4.1	0.3	—	4,374	15.0	8,554	7.7	51.1	1.3	234	81.0	3,961	75
Northside ISD	TX	50,229	63,739	92,335	5,734	78.7	23.4	8.0	64.4	3.8	0.3	—	5,921	15.6	12,590	7.3	47.0	1.1	279	80.4	5,000	106
Pasadena ISD	TX	37,643	42,577	52,303	12,920	24.4	11.5	7.5	77.6	3.2	0.2	—	3,442	15.2	7,147	7.3	48.2	5.0	686	63.8	2,428	65
Pearland ISD	TX	6,739	10,618	18,308	1,161	49.0	46.5	17.1	25.9	10.1	0.3	—	1,087	16.8	2,168	8.4	50.1	1.6	75	90.6	991	24
Pflugerville ISD	TX	6,482	14,545	22,060	2,784	23.5	29.4	22.2	38.9	9.1	0.3	—	1,475	15.0	2,528	8.7	58.3	4.0	251	84.3	1,271	26
Pharr-San Juan-Alamo ISD	TX	18,773	22,537	31,329	12,719	54.9	0.8	0.3	98.6	0.2	#	—	2,040	15.4	4,282	7.3	47.6	1.6	125	78.6	1,594	41
Plano ISD	TX	30,585	47,161	54,939	5,506	28.3	49.0	11.2	18.8	20.7	0.4	—	3,941	13.9	6,762	8.1	58.3	0.8	127	86.6	3,449	76
Richardson ISD	TX	32,555	35,138	34,843	5,008	51.9	31.4	25.0	35.9	7.3	0.4	—	2,504	13.9	4,735	7.4	52.9	1.9	177	75.6	1,922	58
Round Rock ISD	TX	19,636	31,536	43,008	8,790	28.3	51.0	10.7	26.3	11.7	0.2	—	2,920	14.7	5,423	7.9	53.8	1.9	225	88.2	2,545	51
San Antonio ISD	TX	60,161	57,273	55,327	8,272	93.1	2.7	7.4	89.5	0.6	0.2	—	3,402	16.3	7,477	7.4	45.5	9.0	1,221	55.7	2,270	100
Socorro ISD	TX	14,350	26,711	41,357	5,424	75.2	4.0	1.9	93.1	0.6	0.2	—	2,493	16.6	4,877	8.5	51.1	2.0	236	77.7	2,336	42
Spring Branch ISD	TX	26,495	31,659	32,502	8,272	57.2	30.4	6.5	56.6	6.4	0.2	—	2,298	14.1	4,375	7.4	52.5	2.3	196	78.0	1,818	49
Spring ISD	TX	18,537	23,034	35,350	5,424	68.1	15.7	40.1	39.6	4.5	0.2	—	2,353	15.0	5,001	7.1	47.0	3.5	323	76.1	1,718	37
Tyler ISD	TX	16,182	16,626	18,408	3,438	65.2	27.5	31.3	39.4	1.5	0.3	—	1,360	13.5	2,584	7.1	52.6	3.7	179	66.5	901	27
United ISD	TX	12,553	27,556	40,885	17,251	75.2	1.3	0.2	98.1	0.4	#	—	2,538	16.1	6,083	6.7	41.7	0.4	42	80.4	2,140	42
Waco ISD	TX	14,304	15,433	15,337	2,072	87.9	12.2	33.8	53.5	0.4	0.2	—	1,073	14.3	2,157	7.1	49.7	7.5	291	66.9	722	33
Weslaco ISD	TX	11,903	13,407	17,279	4,029	87.9	1.6	0.1	97.9	0.3	#	—	1,077	16.0	2,370	7.3	45.5	2.3	104	67.6	801	21
Ysleta ISD	TX	49,974	46,394	44,620	9,925	59.6	5.2	2.3	91.7	0.3	0.5	—	3,041	14.7	6,375	7.0	47.7	4.0	549	77.9	2,915	61
Alpine District	UT	38,854	47,117	65,918	2,613	30.8	87.4	0.8	8.9	2.4	0.5	—	2,850	23.1	5,332	12.4	53.5	2.2	368	76.4	3,032	74
Cache County	UT	12,280	13,026	15,161	713	34.6	90.8	0.6	7.2	1.2	0.3	—	620	24.4	1,509	10.0	41.1	1.3	56	90.0	904	27
Canyons District	UT	—	—	33,678	1,996	31.9	84.8	1.4	9.8	3.3	0.7	—	1,451	23.2	2,589	13.0	56.0	—	—	—	—	51
Davis District	UT	54,558	59,578	69,689	2,895	32.3	87.0	1.6	7.9	2.8	0.6	—	2,845	24.5	5,886	11.8	48.3	2.9	534	83.9	3,837	101
Granite District	UT	78,554	71,328	70,595	14,095	56.3	58.3	2.6	29.8	7.7	1.7	—	2,973	23.7	5,958	11.8	49.9	4.9	968	67.2	3,601	117
Jordan District	UT	64,991	73,158	48,853	2,487	29.7	84.8	1.1	10.4	3.4	0.4	—	2,053	23.8	4,096	11.9	50.1	2.1	496	85.0	4,982	53
Nebo District	UT	16,393	21,094	29,579	1,149	43.5	87.4	0.7	9.7	1.4	0.9	—	1,241	23.8	2,654	11.1	46.8	2.2	160	86.2	1,540	46
Salt Lake District	UT	24,766	25,367	25,447	7,041	68.2	43.3	4.8	41.0	8.9	2.0	—	1,168	21.8	2,590	9.8	45.1	7.6	505	66.7	1,117	44
Washington District	UT	13,264	18,374	25,915	1,994	45.1	82.9	0.8	11.9	2.4	1.9	—	1,153	22.5	2,245	11.5	51.3	2.8	191	76.7	1,280	48
Weber District	UT	25,661	27,783	30,900	932	37.5	85.9	1.4	10.0	2.0	0.7	—	1,333	23.2	2,548	12.1	52.3	2.3	207	82.5	1,816	49
Arlington County	VA	14,825	18,870	20,268	5,331	32.6	48.3	13.0	27.3	11.2	0.1	—	1,321	15.3	3,695	5.5	35.8	2.7	152	82.3	1,124	33
Chesapeake City	VA	29,533	37,645	39,883	538	28.1	56.4	36.2	3.6	3.3	0.4	—	2,131	18.7	6,184	6.4	34.5	1.8	237	78.5	2,871	47
Chesterfield County	VA	44,480	51,212	59,509	2,309	28.0	59.2	28.5	8.4	3.6	0.4	—	3,089	19.3	7,665	7.8	40.3	1.7	328	85.7	4,103	65
Fairfax County	VA	128,840	156,012	171,956	34,030	24.5	48.7	11.1	19.7	20.2	0.3	—	8,720	19.7	31,548	5.5	27.6	2.0	1,086	89.6	12,003	212
Hampton City	VA	21,383	23,290	21,571	289	46.7	29.6	64.0	2.3	3.7	0.4	—	1,252	17.2	3,409	6.3	36.7	4.2	281	65.6	1,357	35
Hanover County	VA	11,328	16,611	18,854	104	16.6	85.7	10.1	1.9	1.9	0.4	—	1,044	18.1	3,060	6.2	34.1	1.1	69	88.1	1,446	26
Henrico County	VA	32,638	41,655	49,407	2,253	32.8	48.2	39.2	5.2	7.0	0.4	—	2,695	18.3	6,490	7.6	41.5	3.3	499	80.0	3,090	72
Loudoun County	VA	14,485	31,804	60,003	4,741	14.5	63.5	8.1	13.6	14.5	0.3	—	3,317	18.1	10,438	5.7	31.8	1.0	147	95.1	3,389	76
Newport News City	VA	28,925	33,008	30,869	676	52.6	30.8	58.6	7.2	2.8	0.5	—	1,729	17.9	5,459	5.7	31.7	4.7	441	68.0	1,852	46
Norfolk City	VA	36,541	37,349	34,011	623	61.3	24.6	67.8	4.5	2.8	0.2	—	2,171	15.7	6,229	5.5	34.9	5.6	511	52.9	1,560	54

See notes at end of table.

Selected statistics on enrollment, teachers, dropouts, and graduates in public school districts enrolling more than 15,000 students: Selected years, 1990 through 2009—Continued

Name of district	State	Enrollment, fall 1990	Enrollment, fall 2000	Enrollment, fall 2009	Number of English language learners, 2009	Percent eligible for free or reduced-price lunch, 2009	White	Black	Hispanic	Asian/Pacific Islander	American Indian/Alaska Native	Two or more races	Number of classroom teachers	Pupil/teacher ratio	Total number of staff	Student/staff ratio	Teachers as a percentage of total staff	Percent dropping out of grades 9-12	Number of dropouts from grades 9-12	Averaged freshman graduation rate (AFGR)[1]	Number of high school graduates[2]	Number of schools, fall 2009
1	2	3	4	5	6	7	8	9	10	11	12	13	14	15	16	17	18	19	20	21	22	23
Portsmouth City	VA	18,405	16,473	15,289	35	56.2	23.5	73.2	2.1	0.9	0.2	—	780	19.6	2,274	6.7	34.3	7.4	320	57.9	826	25
Prince William County	VA	41,888	54,646	76,861	13,569	34.1	41.7	24.2	25.7	8.2	0.3	—	3,994	19.2	9,623	8.0	41.5	2.2	485	78.5	4,590	85
Richmond City	VA	27,021	27,237	22,994	954	72.3	8.2	85.4	5.7	0.7	0.1	—	1,305	17.6	4,082	5.6	32.0	5.1	317	52.2	991	52
Spotsylvania County	VA	12,227	18,876	24,062	753	26.8	67.6	20.4	8.7	3.0	0.3	—	1,349	17.8	2,667	9.0	50.6	2.2	176	83.1	1,669	34
Stafford County	VA	12,555	21,124	27,060	996	20.3	65.0	21.6	9.6	3.5	0.4	—	1,495	18.1	4,100	6.6	36.5	1.5	132	88.4	1,960	30
Virginia Beach City	VA	70,266	76,586	71,182	1,052	30.4	57.6	28.5	6.4	7.0	0.4	—	3,954	18.0	10,566	6.7	37.4	1.9	439	75.7	4,789	88
Bellevue	WA	14,971	15,431	17,578	1,228	21.5	56.4	3.3	9.9	30.0	0.4	—	909	19.3	1,725	10.2	52.7	1.1	66	87.1	1,219	30
Bethel	WA	11,319	16,029	17,651	199	41.0	63.4	12.0	12.7	8.8	3.1	—	834	21.2	1,724	10.2	48.3	6.6	388	66.6	981	37
Edmonds	WA	18,452	22,067	20,609	1,351	27.9	64.7	6.4	10.5	16.8	1.6	—	969	21.3	1,938	10.6	50.0	5.5	383	75.5	1,355	40
Everett	WA	14,846	18,683	19,049	1,407	40.8	67.4	4.6	12.8	13.9	1.2	—	929	20.5	1,735	11.0	53.6	2.2	129	75.8	1,102	33
Evergreen (Clark)	WA	14,242	21,650	25,933	1,616	41.4	75.8	3.7	9.6	9.7	1.1	—	1,405	18.5	2,492	10.4	56.4	7.4	589	70.7	1,317	37
Federal Way	WA	17,263	22,623	21,390	2,274	51.8	44.6	13.6	21.2	19.3	1.3	—	1,180	18.1	2,219	9.6	53.2	3.4	251	64.0	1,291	45
Highline	WA	15,900	18,024	17,563	2,683	62.6	31.3	14.1	30.3	22.0	2.3	—	959	18.3	1,835	9.6	52.3	4.0	222	56.8	847	48
Issaquah	WA	8,533	14,259	16,948	459	7.9	68.6	2.6	5.5	22.7	0.6	—	791	21.4	1,502	11.3	52.7	1.5	75	88.7	1,146	26
Kennewick	WA	11,147	13,629	15,898	1,427	50.0	63.3	2.3	30.9	2.6	0.9	—	767	20.7	1,501	10.6	51.1	4.0	200	74.8	886	26
Kent	WA	20,212	26,535	27,196	3,110	43.5	51.1	12.3	14.6	20.8	1.2	—	1,409	19.3	2,626	10.4	53.7	5.8	513	64.3	1,533	42
Lake Washington	WA	22,431	23,662	24,178	983	15.3	71.6	2.5	7.6	17.7	0.6	—	1,253	19.3	2,204	11.0	56.8	1.6	115	86.0	1,597	54
Northshore	WA	17,213	20,255	19,707	735	15.0	74.9	2.1	9.1	13.1	0.8	—	946	20.8	1,782	11.1	53.1	1.9	126	88.8	1,491	34
Puyallup	WA	14,325	19,757	20,957	429	27.4	71.0	11.7	8.5	7.2	1.6	—	1,003	20.9	1,937	10.8	51.8	7.1	485	81.9	1,419	37
Seattle	WA	40,917	47,575	46,522	4,168	41.2	44.1	20.9	11.5	21.7	1.8	—	2,532	18.4	4,942	9.4	51.2	6.7	904	77.0	2,661	100
Spokane	WA	27,965	31,725	28,327	794	53.8	82.6	4.2	4.5	4.5	4.1	—	1,664	17.0	3,101	9.1	53.7	8.3	755	62.7	1,622	50
Tacoma	WA	29,465	34,093	28,890	1,527	60.5	47.2	22.9	14.2	13.7	1.9	—	1,642	17.6	3,166	9.1	51.8	6.3	568	54.3	1,460	67
Vancouver	WA	15,943	21,892	22,655	1,499	50.5	73.0	5.4	14.1	6.1	1.4	—	1,083	20.9	2,275	10.0	47.6	4.7	331	72.8	1,285	41
Berkeley County	WV	10,415	13,076	17,446	306	45.2	80.9	11.6	5.3	1.1	0.2	0.9	1,241	14.1	2,433	7.2	51.0	4.2	204	79.2	1,018	29
Kanawha County	WV	34,284	29,250	28,481	222	52.8	84.6	13.0	0.7	1.5	0.1	0.2	1,961	14.5	3,788	7.5	51.8	5.3	428	75.4	1,656	72
Appleton Area	WI	12,876	14,793	15,081	1,599	36.1	77.4	3.9	6.7	11.2	0.8	—	910	16.6	1,513	10.0	60.2	2.1	105	94.6	1,159	37
Green Bay Area	WI	18,048	20,104	20,332	4,068	54.3	59.7	7.7	19.9	7.5	5.1	—	1,399	14.5	2,406	8.5	58.1	5.8	368	83.8	1,381	38
Kenosha	WI	16,219	20,099	22,933	1,777	46.3	59.9	16.6	21.1	1.9	0.4	—	1,448	15.8	2,619	8.8	55.3	3.7	255	82.1	1,482	44
Madison Metropolitan	WI	23,214	25,087	24,628	3,811	46.6	50.3	23.6	14.9	10.4	0.8	—	1,774	13.9	3,556	6.9	49.9	3.6	273	82.5	1,674	54
Milwaukee	WI	92,789	97,985	82,096	7,996	79.0	15.2	56.5	22.7	4.8	0.4	—	4,636	17.7	10,233	8.0	45.3	8.9	2,206	65.0	4,745	200
Racine	WI	22,159	21,102	21,276	2,084	56.7	48.0	27.3	22.8	1.5	0.4	—	1,382	15.4	2,580	8.2	53.6	5.6	369	73.9	1,250	35

—Not available.
†Not applicable.
#Rounds to zero.
[1]The averaged freshman graduation rate provides an estimate of the percentage of students who receive a regular diploma within 4 years of entering ninth grade. The rate uses aggregate student enrollment data to estimate the size of an incoming freshman class and aggregate counts of the number of diplomas awarded 4 years later.
[2]Includes regular diplomas only.
[3]Total for districts reporting data.

[4]Reported data indicated an averaged freshman graduation rate of greater than 100.0 percent.
NOTE: Total enrollment, staff, and teacher data in this table reflect totals reported by school districts and may differ from data derived from summing school-level data to school district aggregates. ISD = independent school district. CISD = consolidated independent school district. Race categories exclude persons of Hispanic ethnicity. Detail may not sum to totals because of rounding.
SOURCE: U.S. Department of Education, National Center for Education Statistics, Common Core of Data (CCD), "Public Elementary/Secondary School Universe Survey," 2009–10; "Local Education Agency Universe Survey," 1990–91, 2000–01, and 2009–10; and "Local Education Agency-Level Public-Use Data File on Public School Dropouts: School Year 2008–09". (This table was prepared August 2011.)

Enrollment, poverty, and federal funds for the 100 largest school districts, by enrollment size in 2009: Fall 2009, 2008–09, and federal fiscal year 2011

Name of district	State	Rank order	Enrollment, fall 2009	5- to 17-year-old population, 2009	5- to 17-year-olds in poverty, 2009[1]	Poverty rate of 5- to 17-year-olds, 2009[1]	Total (in thousands)	Federal (in thousands)	Federal as a percent of total	Federal revenue per student[8]	Title I basic and concentration grants	School lunch	Individuals with Disabilities Education Act (IDEA)	Eisenhower math and science	Vocational education	Drug-free schools	Title I Total	Basic grants	Concentration grants	Targeted grants	Education finance incentive grants
1	2	3	4	5	6	7	8	9	10	11	12	13	14	15	16	17	18	19	20	21	22
New York City	NY	1	1,014,020	1,309,885	348,043	26.6	$21,165,693	$1,817,770	8.6	$1,852	$839,467	$310,964	$268,809	—	$29,217	$18,733	$803,902	$302,301	$76,641	$233,174	$191,787
Los Angeles Unified	CA	2	670,746	793,226	195,073	24.6	9,695,990	1,427,027	14.7	2,076	441,998	253,986	139,423	49,498	11,506	6,586	366,598	123,204	31,282	100,786	111,327
City of Chicago	IL	3	407,157	483,644	138,378	28.6	5,028,161	1,182,403	23.5	2,806	393,955	139,166	95,230	50,979	7,895	13,401	300,333	103,589	25,740	80,665	90,338
Dade	FL	4	345,804	405,678	90,563	22.3	3,531,152	455,555	12.9	1,318	144,352	91,936	102,280	17,895	7,209	1,830	131,632	49,824	12,182	37,586	32,040
Clark County	NV	5	307,059	348,928	54,406	15.6	3,179,037	286,412	9.0	916	68,126	53,274	41,114	11,991	3,257	842	75,870	30,048	7,346	21,391	17,084
Broward	FL	6	256,137	293,644	43,896	14.9	2,513,314	252,590	10.1	985	65,039	55,766	55,131	10,189	4,331	1,121	61,779	24,601	6,052	16,803	14,323
Houston ISD	TX	7	202,773	266,882	75,600	28.3	2,098,480	288,212	13.7	1,439	110,205	73,084	41,413	18,447	4,503	1,163	115,196	41,576	10,165	30,815	32,640
Hillsborough	FL	8	193,265	206,536	43,351	21.0	1,905,911	269,224	14.1	1,402	54,594	54,340	40,890	7,707	3,075	800	60,548	24,170	5,909	16,448	14,021
Hawaii Department of Education	HI	9	180,196	201,374	25,040	12.4	2,689,758	392,837	14.6	2,189	54,851	34,123	57,331	16,872	3,660	1,760	47,557	20,445	4,419	11,290	11,403
Orange	FL	10	173,259	185,306	31,667	17.1	1,810,528	162,745	9.0	945	37,607	41,907	36,864	7,059	2,624	712	43,034	17,535	4,433	11,492	9,574
Palm Beach	FL	11	172,897	191,605	35,681	18.6	1,944,936	159,995	8.2	937	39,763	34,996	43,607	—	1,953	472	48,517	19,828	4,848	12,870	10,971
Fairfax County	VA	12	171,956	181,395	10,981	6.1	2,371,152	94,869	4.0	561	18,754	18,412	35,310	3,865	1,648	554	18,997	7,767	1,899	4,297	5,034
Philadelphia City	PA	13	165,694	252,401	77,073	30.5	2,671,065	326,710	12.2	2,044	155,708	65,657	—	24,196	6,213	1,691	195,070	64,144	16,349	51,030	63,546
Gwinnett County	GA	14	159,296	169,838	25,823	15.2	1,666,446	111,335	6.7	708	—	42,465	—	—	—	—	39,039	15,546	3,801	9,790	9,901
Dallas ISD	TX	15	157,111	201,590	63,281	31.4	1,615,590	229,315	14.2	1,457	86,416	64,159	36,350	8,717	2,536	1,162	94,486	34,647	8,471	25,105	26,262
Montgomery County	MD	16	141,722	167,869	11,850	7.1	2,508,088	91,702	3.7	658	21,412	18,311	28,388	4,313	1,165	472	22,896	9,661	2,362	5,456	5,418
Wake County	NC	17	140,558	166,628	17,048	10.2	1,945,241	77,473	4.0	560	16,235	18,742	27,422	3,562	1,357	363	22,703	9,140	2,235	5,490	5,839
Charlotte-Mecklenburg	NC	18	136,969	163,361	29,514	18.1	1,699,290	113,623	6.7	841	32,803	35,226	25,642	3,964	1,681	470	40,564	15,850	3,875	10,097	10,740
San Diego Unified	CA	19	131,417	154,349	30,198	19.6	1,511,821	200,987	13.3	1,520	42,639	35,775	25,043	9,289	1,183	603	45,243	17,734	4,502	11,656	11,351
Prince George's County	MD	20	127,039	146,247	12,940	8.8	1,914,801	117,996	6.2	922	28,538	31,110	25,568	6,956	1,346	441	25,261	10,566	2,583	6,077	6,035
Duval	FL	21	122,586	145,051	29,748	20.5	1,148,276	115,263	10.0	940	34,892	26,787	24,155	5,246	1,368	569	39,849	16,431	4,017	10,473	8,928
Memphis	TN	22	109,300	133,461	41,743	31.3	1,045,848	150,238	14.4	1,342	53,312	41,096	26,252	—	3,497	740	60,862	22,343	5,463	15,043	18,014
Cobb County	GA	23	107,245	122,264	14,321	11.7	1,107,472	75,246	6.8	705	—	21,115	—	—	—	—	21,144	8,731	2,135	5,111	5,169
Pinellas	FL	24	105,238	120,650	20,106	16.7	1,068,296	100,985	9.5	952	26,973	20,652	30,179	5,059	3,239	495	26,605	11,168	2,730	6,859	5,847
Cypress-Fairbanks ISD	TX	25	104,231	75,969	10,239	13.5	860,846	54,706	6.4	543	9,180	18,510	17,374	1,544	597	188	12,739	5,625	1,375	3,059	2,679
Baltimore County	MD	26	103,324	124,043	10,522	8.5	1,482,453	75,829	5.1	735	20,662	16,903	22,847	3,340	1,137	489	20,871	8,886	2,173	4,923	4,889
DeKalb County	GA	27	99,406	115,416	25,488	22.1	1,168,643	112,405	9.6	1,127	—	33,884	—	—	—	—	42,532	16,338	4,148	10,626	11,420
Jefferson County	KY	28	98,808	118,378	23,647	20.0	1,095,123	119,409	10.9	1,209	—	28,493	—	—	—	—	37,032	14,394	3,519	9,009	10,109
Albuquerque	NM	29	96,572	108,634	20,528	18.9	1,029,988	103,711	10.1	1,081	31,619	35	21,444	5,673	1,852	814	31,142	12,169	2,975	7,507	8,491
Polk	FL	30	94,530	99,731	22,679	22.7	915,097	97,511	10.7	1,030	25,101	27,778	20,041	3,578	1,532	277	30,227	12,607	3,082	7,848	6,690
Northside ISD	TX	31	92,335	80,225	12,414	15.5	814,677	60,016	7.4	674	14,686	20,638	15,896	2,604	770	232	17,282	7,182	1,823	4,264	4,012
Detroit City	MI	32	90,499	185,632	80,645	43.4	1,294,223	249,063	19.2	2,552	123,013	—	24,228	—	3,910	1,360	171,468	56,335	14,359	44,656	56,119
Fulton County	GA	33	90,399	100,622	15,380	15.3	1,043,327	64,160	6.1	727	—	18,324	—	—	—	—	22,567	9,272	2,267	5,483	5,545
Long Beach Unified	CA	34	86,283	95,836	24,388	25.4	906,642	163,484	18.0	1,868	45,366	25,791	14,872	6,276	1,138	709	37,244	14,745	3,744	9,542	9,213
Jefferson County, No. R-1	CO	35	86,282	88,451	8,000	9.0	853,041	40,579	4.8	472	11,310	8,394	13,728	2,517	449	198	10,533	4,616	1,129	2,344	2,444

See notes at end of table.

Enrollment, poverty, and federal funds for the 100 largest school districts, by enrollment size in 2009: Fall 2009, 2008–09, and federal fiscal year 2011—Continued

Name of district	State	Rank order	Enrollment, fall 2009	5- to 17-year-old population, 2009	5- to 17-year-olds in poverty, 2009[1]	Poverty rate of 5- to 17-year-olds, 2009[1]	Total (in thousands)	Federal (in thousands)	Federal as a percent of total	Federal revenue per student[8]	Title I basic and concentration grants	School lunch	Individuals with Disabilities Education Act (IDEA)	Eisenhower math and science	Vocational education	Drug-free schools	Title I Total	Basic grants	Concentration grants	Targeted grants	Education finance incentive grants
1	2	3	4	5	6	7	8	9	10	11	12	13	14	15	16	17	18	19	20	21	22
Austin ISD	TX	36	84,676	105,185	25,074	23.8	1,067,343	92,541	8.7	1,109	31,202	25,234	17,601	4,346	1,226	391	34,155	13,795	3,373	8,669	8,319
Baltimore City	MD	37	82,866	97,612	24,889	25.5	1,382,981	152,921	11.1	1,859	65,736	25,359	21,920	7,783	2,596	700	56,294	21,778	5,442	14,363	14,711
Milwaukee	WI	38	82,096	114,114	41,586	36.4	1,240,232	287,789	23.2	3,371	100,234	31,487	30,910	—	2,261	—	83,284	30,468	7,701	19,888	25,227
Lee	FL	39	80,484	84,066	13,244	15.8	858,184	71,100	8.3	895	15,820	19,758	16,192	—	926	257	17,154	7,357	1,868	4,342	3,588
Fort Worth ISD	TX	40	80,209	106,561	30,519	28.6	769,865	111,504	14.5	1,406	42,412	24,398	18,377	7,791	1,429	497	41,859	16,734	4,091	10,687	10,347
Denver	CO	41	77,267	88,358	22,855	25.9	879,654	88,281	10.0	1,190	29,633	20,175	12,280	5,349	1,305	496	37,201	14,226	3,614	9,170	10,191
Prince William County	VA	42	76,861	75,747	5,608	7.4	934,669	39,731	4.3	538	6,109	11,259	12,657	2,524	731	65	7,849	3,948	0	1,885	2,016
Fresno Unified	CA	43	75,468	87,652	30,318	34.6	835,948	144,700	17.3	1,889	55,165	27,397	14,433	6,725	1,480	645	48,077	18,838	4,783	12,388	12,068
Davidson County	TN	44	75,080	93,710	20,720	22.1	740,320	85,967	11.6	1,157	27,261	23,841	16,596	—	1,221	—	33,431	12,785	3,246	8,246	9,155
Anne Arundel County	MD	45	74,776	86,527	6,776	7.8	1,031,083	45,403	4.4	616	10,358	7,458	15,680	2,506	1,602	234	12,121	5,456	1,334	2,675	2,656
Guilford County	NC	46	72,758	81,643	15,778	19.3	745,883	90,906	12.2	1,246	17,499	36,378	20,708	3,013	1,143	330	20,848	8,443	2,064	5,011	5,330
Brevard	FL	47	72,412	79,472	11,694	14.7	675,705	53,392	7.9	730	14,203	12,567	15,185	—	728	244	14,792	6,474	1,583	3,636	3,100
Virginia Beach City	VA	48	71,182	75,906	6,879	9.1	830,709	54,992	6.6	769	11,871	9,825	14,951	2,727	1,090	246	11,099	4,899	1,198	2,408	2,594
Greenville 01	SC	49	70,969	81,218	14,693	18.1	687,992	63,278	9.2	898	19,867	15,214	21,924	2,242	1,115	263	22,694	8,806	2,153	5,186	6,549
Granite District	UT	50	70,595	80,672	10,739	13.3	494,431	56,596	11.4	807	10,983	14,237	17,252	2,752	2,228	321	14,573	5,848	1,430	3,230	4,064
Davis District	UT	51	69,689	70,431	5,286	7.5	492,176	57,822	11.7	868	2,712	9,952	9,807	1,399	560	126	5,811	2,878	0	1,366	1,568
Fort Bend ISD	TX	52	69,374	83,137	7,598	9.1	594,526	35,455	6.0	516	6,294	8,132	11,962	1,466	531	140	9,338	4,328	1,058	2,168	1,783
Mesa Unified	AZ	53	67,471	107,503	20,893	19.4	611,366	56,657	9.3	805	16,803	17,163	10,637	1,849	1,777	374	28,967	11,379	2,782	7,028	7,779
Pasco	FL	54	67,147	72,462	12,529	17.3	647,083	56,762	8.8	850	13,924	15,708	12,302	—	455	3,272	15,964	6,939	1,697	3,956	3,372
Alpine District	UT	55	65,918	73,558	6,718	9.1	442,458	53,892	12.2	865	3,940	7,874	8,403	1,513	586	123	8,456	3,671	897	1,802	2,086
North East ISD	TX	56	65,498	66,090	10,114	15.3	655,626	40,396	6.2	637	9,935	12,132	13,434	1,518	620	169	12,723	5,599	1,369	3,041	2,715
Washoe County	NV	57	64,838	70,803	10,392	14.7	647,707	71,010	11.0	1,085	10,642	10,786	10,619	1,494	695	0	12,938	5,800	1,418	3,197	2,524
Seminole	FL	58	64,457	71,686	9,565	13.3	580,536	41,198	7.1	635	9,395	10,805	12,364	2,370	523	203	11,777	5,275	1,290	2,813	2,398
Arlington ISD	TX	59	63,487	78,477	14,838	18.9	549,822	54,829	10.0	870	14,920	17,340	13,777	2,225	788	262	19,285	8,122	1,986	4,774	4,403
El Paso ISD	TX	60	63,378	66,730	21,755	32.6	607,374	101,448	16.7	1,628	35,130	20,101	13,750	6,843	1,345	429	32,664	12,859	3,277	8,551	7,977
Aldine ISD	TX	61	62,792	60,109	18,651	31.0	586,222	69,548	11.9	1,130	18,096	26,053	10,867	2,898	902	199	24,854	10,247	2,505	6,233	5,869
Mobile County	AL	62	62,767	74,402	18,579	25.0	580,220	76,629	13.2	1,225	29,748	21,636	16,092	4,695	2,367	548	26,373	10,267	2,607	6,457	7,042
Elk Grove Unified	CA	63	62,483	51,649	8,532	16.5	585,025	66,400	11.3	1,068	9,951	13,497	9,812	2,670	396	190	11,435	5,227	1,278	2,755	2,174
Volusia	FL	64	62,306	69,865	14,469	20.7	627,597	53,288	8.5	846	14,964	13,741	14,088	3,336	897	242	18,834	8,080	1,975	4,739	4,040
Loudoun County	VA	65	60,003	62,373	1,984	3.2	799,102	17,746	2.2	312	1,415	4,328	7,386	775	710	100	1,411	1,411	0	0	0
Douglas County, No. RE1	CO	66	59,932	62,470	2,057	3.3	568,232	14,609	2.6	249	1,096	1,821	9,274	600	155	74	1,151	1,151	0	0	0
Chesterfield County	VA	67	59,509	60,895	4,626	7.6	638,573	26,138	4.1	442	4,927	5,125	10,622	1,154	525	138	6,343	3,249	0	1,502	1,591
Katy ISD	TX	68	59,078	41,793	4,800	11.5	538,776	25,014	4.6	440	2,696	7,222	8,457	603	327	63	4,913	2,666	0	1,245	1,001
Garland ISD	TX	69	57,861	59,089	12,017	20.3	498,512	46,232	9.3	804	9,694	13,687	13,881	1,862	666	147	15,207	6,566	1,605	3,706	3,329
Santa Ana Unified	CA	70	56,937	62,182	13,089	21.0	608,210	93,784	15.4	1,633	23,321	22,895	10,921	4,028	574	546	17,834	7,497	1,903	4,412	4,021

See notes at end of table.

Enrollment, poverty, and federal funds for the 100 largest school districts, by enrollment size in 2009: Fall 2009, 2008–09, and federal fiscal year 2011—Continued

Name of district (1)	State (2)	Rank order (3)	Enrollment, fall 2009 (4)	5- to 17-year-old population, 2009 (5)	5- to 17-year-olds in poverty, 2009[1] (6)	Poverty rate of 5- to 17-year-olds, 2009[1] (7)	Revenues total (in thousands) (8)	Federal (in thousands) (9)	Federal as a percent of total (10)	Federal revenue per student[3] (11)	Title I basic and concentration grants (12)	School lunch (13)	IDEA (14)	Eisenhower math and science (15)	Vocational education (16)	Drug-free schools (17)	Title I allocations Total (18)	Basic grants (19)	Concentration grants (20)	Targeted grants (21)	Education finance incentive grants (22)
Knox County	TN	71	56,758	67,918	10,754	15.8	465,157	43,940	9.4	791	14,689	10,950	11,290	—	1,335	280	14,070	5,900	1,442	3,266	3,463
Boston	MA	72	55,371	76,610	18,756	24.5	1,232,829	118,739	9.6	2,123	42,851	12,937	18,767	—	1,605	—	45,571	16,428	4,187	10,884	14,073
Tucson Unified	AZ	73	55,369	85,345	19,745	23.1	504,272	60,749	12.0	1,059	21,587	15,234	10,450	3,477	1,621	1,251	27,867	10,977	2,684	6,752	7,455
San Antonio ISD	TX	74	55,327	71,926	24,702	34.3	550,221	103,261	18.8	1,888	35,116	27,395	12,260	7,201	865	399	34,069	13,739	3,419	8,631	8,280
San Francisco Unified	CA	75	55,140	76,178	11,056	14.5	723,906	97,792	13.5	1,772	16,819	12,670	—	6,107	462	246	14,714	6,435	1,581	3,584	3,113
Plano ISD	TX	76	54,939	88,311	6,084	6.9	637,364	23,785	3.7	439	3,425	5,586	10,451	1,099	497	113	6,265	3,339	0	1,615	1,311
San Bernardino City Unified	CA	77	53,837	60,525	21,017	34.7	647,553	102,481	15.8	1,873	35,607	20,807	10,427	5,366	714	373	29,748	12,214	2,986	7,553	6,994
Capistrano Unified	CA	78	53,381	55,119	3,940	7.1	455,566	43,032	9.4	817	3,405	4,043	10,586	1,101	220	93	4,016	2,256	0	1,011	749
Cumberland County	NC	79	53,035	52,293	12,196	23.3	474,346	65,174	13.7	1,201	18,591	14,868	12,494	2,495	1,002	222	15,940	6,599	1,613	3,745	3,983
Columbus City	OH	80	52,810	74,674	28,241	37.8	894,781	110,268	12.3	2,060	—	17,147	15,515	—	2,634	481	55,022	20,205	4,940	12,849	17,028
Forsyth County	NC	81	52,795	62,512	12,048	19.3	573,416	49,670	8.7	939	13,651	12,539	12,672	2,392	819	181	15,507	6,436	1,574	3,633	3,864
Pasadena ISD	TX	82	52,303	52,066	12,700	24.4	489,209	53,924	11.0	1,045	12,892	18,709	8,204	2,238	756	156	16,284	6,977	1,706	3,988	3,613
Osceola	FL	83	52,139	53,391	10,844	20.3	500,150	48,462	9.7	933	10,883	15,040	10,083	—	590	287	13,693	6,037	1,476	3,336	2,844
Corona-Norco Unified	CA	84	52,052	50,375	5,995	11.9	477,608	43,869	9.2	841	3,804	10,259	8,225	1,149	195	162	6,413	3,493	0	1,691	1,229
Cherry Creek, No. 5	CO	85	51,786	47,626	4,519	9.5	517,942	19,570	3.8	382	3,228	5,776	7,910	1,100	201	100	4,946	2,548	0	1,174	1,224
Lewisville ISD	TX	86	50,840	64,196	4,370	6.8	503,399	22,703	4.5	452	2,849	6,092	9,001	974	346	101	4,421	2,422	0	1,111	888
Howard County	MD	87	50,641	54,753	2,501	4.6	835,108	21,029	2.5	421	2,761	3,054	9,108	1,185	706	88	2,018	2,018	0	0	0
Clayton County	GA	88	50,204	58,422	12,741	21.8	543,400	59,270	10.9	1,197	—	20,622	—	—	—	—	18,482	7,716	1,887	4,414	4,464
Conroe ISD	TX	89	49,629	52,750	6,398	12.1	423,607	26,195	6.2	546	5,388	7,148	8,875	1,455	447	124	7,561	3,552	868	1,732	1,409
Anchorage	AK	90	49,592	51,549	4,255	8.3	649,717	65,775	10.1	1,347	14,330	10,503	11,665	4,941	1,015	462	11,644	4,970	0	3,315	3,358
Henrico County	VA	91	49,407	50,214	5,355	10.7	510,259	30,446	6.0	621	5,394	7,292	12,740	1,452	893	144	7,489	3,781	0	1,794	1,914
Brownsville ISD	TX	92	49,121	46,011	21,320	46.3	475,144	81,470	17.1	1,677	34,576	24,457	8,689	3,529	1,036	239	29,594	11,618	2,949	7,806	7,220
Atlanta	GA	93	48,909	82,365	24,857	30.2	857,196	85,634	10.0	1,746	—	18,342	—	—	—	—	38,754	15,025	3,673	9,432	10,623
Jordan District	UT	94	48,853	40,663	3,158	7.8	295,008	32,955	11.2	866	2,788	4,740	7,280	987	372	85	3,370	1,770	0	757	843
Omaha	NE	95	48,692	60,697	11,589	19.1	550,528	74,603	13.6	1,554	17,599	15,845	12,497	3,706	917	212	22,319	8,487	2,075	4,845	6,913
Cleveland Municipal	OH	96	48,392	82,041	33,114	40.4	912,022	128,877	14.1	2,580	—	20,017	15,279	—	3,229	565	63,900	23,259	5,776	14,945	19,920
Wichita	KS	97	48,324	58,649	12,112	20.7	583,235	58,211	10.0	1,232	21,299	14,835	—	—	—	379	23,898	8,825	2,158	5,051	7,864
Shelby County	TN	98	48,211	44,432	4,439	10.0	380,894	24,776	6.5	522	3,621	5,956	10,353	—	465	126	5,107	2,661	0	1,247	1,200
Garden Grove Unified	CA	99	47,950	53,273	9,944	18.7	457,636	61,519	13.4	1,267	13,552	14,861	8,484	2,308	407	186	13,329	5,693	1,816	3,113	2,707
Sacramento City Unified	CA	100	47,890	63,709	16,544	26.0	542,503	91,696	16.9	1,904	23,701	14,477	9,687	4,123	1,018	317	23,127	9,839	2,405	5,922	4,961

—Not available.

[1] Poverty is defined based on the number of persons and related children in the family and their income. For information on poverty thresholds for 2009, see http://www.census.gov/hhes/www/poverty/threshld/thresh09.html.

[2] Fiscal year 2010 Department of Education funds available for spending by school districts in the 2011–12 school year.

[3] Federal revenue per student is based on fall enrollment collected through the "School District Finance Survey (Form F-33)."

NOTE: Detail may not sum to totals because of rounding. ISD = independent school district.

SOURCE: U.S. Department of Education, National Center for Education Statistics, Common Core of Data (CCD), "School District Finance Survey (Form F-33)," 2008–09, and "Local Education Agency Universe Survey," 2009–10; and unpublished Department of Education budget data. (This table was prepared September 2011.)

Public elementary and secondary schools, by level of school: Selected years, 1967–68 through 2009–10

Year	Total, all public schools	Schools with reported grade spans											
		Total	Elementary schools				Secondary schools					Combined elementary/ secondary schools[2]	Other schools[1]
			Total[3]	Middle schools[4]	One-teacher schools	Other elementary schools	Total[5]	Junior high[6]	3-year or 4-year high schools	5-year or 6-year high schools	Other secondary schools		
1	2	3	4	5	6	7	8	9	10	11	12	13	14
1967–68	—	94,197	67,186	—	4,146	63,040	23,318	7,437	10,751	4,650	480	3,693	—
1970–71	—	89,372	64,020	2,080	1,815	60,125	23,572	7,750	11,265	3,887	670	1,780	—
1972–73	—	88,864	62,942	2,308	1,475	59,159	23,919	7,878	11,550	3,962	529	2,003	—
1974–75	—	87,456	61,759	3,224	1,247	57,288	23,837	7,690	11,480	4,122	545	1,860	—
1975–76	88,597	87,034	61,704	3,916	1,166	56,622	23,792	7,521	11,572	4,113	586	1,538	1,563
1976–77	—	86,501	61,123	4,180	1,111	55,832	23,857	7,434	11,658	4,130	635	1,521	—
1978–79	—	84,816	60,312	5,879	1,056	53,377	22,834	6,282	11,410	4,429	713	1,670	—
1980–81	85,982	83,688	59,326	6,003	921	52,402	22,619	5,890	10,758	4,193	1,778	1,743	2,294
1982–83	84,740	82,039	58,051	6,875	798	50,378	22,383	5,948	11,678	4,067	690	1,605	2,701
1983–84	84,178	81,418	57,471	6,885	838	49,748	22,336	5,936	11,670	4,046	684	1,611	2,760
1984–85	84,007	81,147	57,231	6,893	825	49,513	22,320	5,916	11,671	4,021	712	1,596	2,860
1986–87	83,421	82,316	58,835	7,483	763	50,589	21,505	5,109	11,430	4,196	770	1,976	1,105 [7]
1987–88	83,248	81,416	57,575	7,641	729	49,205	21,662	4,900	11,279	4,048	1,435	2,179	1,832 [7]
1988–89	83,165	81,579	57,941	7,957	583	49,401	21,403	4,687	11,350	3,994	1,372	2,235	1,586 [7]
1989–90	83,425	81,880	58,419	8,272	630	49,517	21,181	4,512	11,492	3,812	1,365	2,280	1,545 [7]
1990–91	84,538	82,475	59,015	8,545	617	49,853	21,135	4,561	11,537	3,723	1,314	2,325	2,063
1991–92	84,578	82,506	59,258	8,829	569	49,860	20,767	4,298	11,528	3,699	1,242	2,481	2,072
1992–93	84,497	82,896	59,676	9,152	430	50,094	20,671	4,115	11,651	3,613	1,292	2,549	1,601
1993–94	85,393	83,431	60,052	9,573	442	50,037	20,705	3,970	11,858	3,595	1,282	2,674	1,962
1994–95	86,221	84,476	60,808	9,954	458	50,396	20,904	3,859	12,058	3,628	1,359	2,764	1,745
1995–96	87,125	84,958	61,165	10,205	474	50,486	20,997	3,743	12,168	3,621	1,465	2,796	2,167
1996–97	88,223	86,092	61,805	10,499	487	50,819	21,307	3,707	12,424	3,614	1,562	2,980	2,131
1997–98	89,508	87,541	62,739	10,944	476	51,319	21,682	3,599	12,734	3,611	1,738	3,120	1,967
1998–99	90,874	89,259	63,462	11,202	463	51,797	22,076	3,607	13,457	3,707	1,305	3,721	1,615
1999–2000	92,012	90,538	64,131	11,521	423	52,187	22,365	3,566	13,914	3,686	1,199	4,042	1,474
2000–01	93,273	91,691	64,601	11,696	411	52,494	21,994	3,318	13,793	3,974	909	5,096	1,582
2001–02	94,112	92,696	65,228	11,983	408	52,837	22,180	3,285	14,070	3,917	908	5,288	1,416
2002–03	95,615	93,869	65,718	12,174	366	53,178	22,599	3,263	14,330	4,017	989	5,552	1,746
2003–04	95,726	93,977	65,758	12,341	376	53,041	22,782	3,251	14,595	3,840	1,096	5,437	1,749
2004–05	96,513	95,001	65,984	12,530	338	53,116	23,445	3,250	14,854	3,945	1,396	5,572	1,512
2005–06	97,382	95,731	66,026	12,545	326	53,155	23,998	3,249	15,103	3,910	1,736	5,707	1,651
2006–07	98,793	96,362	66,458	12,773	313	53,372	23,920	3,112	15,043	4,048	1,717	5,984	2,431
2007–08	98,916	97,654	67,112	13,014	288	53,810	24,643	3,117	16,146	3,981	1,399	5,899	1,262
2008–09	98,706	97,119	67,148	13,060	237	53,851	24,348	3,037	16,246	3,761	1,304	5,623	1,587
2009–10	98,817	97,521	67,140	13,163	217	53,760	24,651	2,953	16,706	3,778	1,214	5,730	1,296

—Not available.

[1] Includes special education, alternative, and other schools not reported by grade span.
[2] Includes schools beginning with grade 6 or lower and ending with grade 9 or above.
[3] Includes schools beginning with grade 6 or below and with no grade higher than 8.
[4] Includes schools with grade spans beginning with 4, 5, or 6 and ending with 6, 7, or 8.
[5] Includes schools with no grade lower than 7.
[6] Includes schools with grades 7 and 8 or grades 7 through 9.
[7] Because of revision in data collection procedures, figures not comparable to data for other years.

SOURCE: U.S. Department of Education, National Center for Education Statistics, *Statistics of State School Systems,* 1967–68 and 1975–76; *Statistics of Public Elementary and Secondary Day Schools,* 1970–71, 1972–73, 1974–75, and 1976–77 through 1980–81; and Common Core of Data (CCD), "Public Elementary/Secondary School Universe Survey," 1982–83 through 2009–10. (This table was prepared May 2011.)

Public elementary and secondary schools, by level, type, and state or jurisdiction: 1990–91, 2000–01, and 2009–10

State or jurisdiction	Total, all schools, 1990–91	Total, all schools, 2000–01	Schools by level, 2009–10								Selected types of schools, 2009–10			
			Total, all schools	Elementary[1]	Secondary[2]	Combined elementary/secondary[3]				Other[4]	Alternative[5]	Special education[5]	Charter[5]	One-teacher schools[5]
						Total	Prekindergarten, kindergarten, or 1st grade to grade 12	Other schools ending with grade 12	Other combined schools					
1	2	3	4	5	6	7	8	9	10	11	12	13	14	15
United States	**84,538**	**93,273**	**98,817**	**67,140**	**24,651**	**5,730**	**2,861**	**2,193**	**676**	**1,296**	**6,293**	**2,089**	**4,952**	**217**
Alabama....................	1,297	1,517	1,600	964	423	183	122	57	4	30	117	41	0	0
Alaska......................	498	515	506	193	85	228	211	14	3	0	51	2	25	7
Arizona	1,049	1,724	2,248	1,361	718	149	80	43	26	20	82	20	504	5
Arkansas..................	1,098	1,138	1,120	715	392	11	4	2	5	2	11	4	38	0
California..................	7,913	8,773	10,068	6,917	2,608	517	398	89	30	26	1,375	146	813	40
Colorado	1,344	1,632	1,793	1,273	413	107	40	55	12	0	95	9	158	2
Connecticut...............	985	1,248	1,165	838	282	32	8	18	6	13	44	56	18	0
Delaware..................	173	191	217	152	38	24	19	4	1	3	10	19	18	0
District of Columbia	181	198	233	168	40	15	3	6	6	10	11	10	99	0
Florida.....................	2,516	3,316	4,043	2,662	657	577	230	318	29	147	422	170	412	1
Georgia....................	1,734	1,946	2,461	1,784	437	51	16	25	10	189	140	72	63	0
Hawaii	235	261	289	209	51	27	23	3	1	2	1	3	31	0
Idaho.......................	582	673	742	442	227	73	45	18	10	0	83	15	36	8
Illinois.....................	4,239	4,342	4,405	3,198	1,040	148	53	81	14	19	188	147	39	0
Indiana....................	1,915	1,976	1,961	1,415	447	67	18	36	13	32	19	38	53	0
Iowa........................	1,588	1,534	1,468	1,005	423	40	4	36	0	0	51	7	9	4
Kansas.....................	1,477	1,430	1,419	962	405	37	11	23	3	15	1	10	35	0
Kentucky	1,400	1,526	1,542	990	428	123	31	90	2	1	170	10	0	0
Louisiana	1,533	1,530	1,488	981	307	195	115	73	7	5	184	38	77	0
Maine	747	714	649	486	150	13	9	4	0	0	2	1	0	1
Maryland...................	1,220	1,383	1,447	1,119	268	39	17	15	7	21	62	40	42	1
Massachusetts..............	1,842	1,905	1,836	1,355	367	41	12	24	5	73	19	23	62	1
Michigan	3,313	3,998	3,879	2,475	1,044	236	114	101	21	124	312	197	294	6
Minnesota	1,590	2,362	2,433	1,276	862	280	140	118	22	15	480	276	181	1
Mississippi	972	1,030	1,085	620	335	116	66	48	2	14	64	3	1	0
Missouri	2,199	2,368	2,427	1,581	655	171	82	83	6	20	112	68	48	0
Montana...................	900	879	828	479	349	0	0	0	0	0	4	2	0	58
Nebraska	1,506	1,326	1,120	742	349	29	16	12	1	0	5	28	0	11
Nevada	354	511	636	465	137	34	7	26	1	0	32	10	35	11
New Hampshire	439	526	484	378	106	0	0	0	0	0	0	0	15	1
New Jersey	2,272	2,410	2,590	1,899	551	42	21	14	7	98	103	73	70	0
New Mexico	681	765	855	600	235	20	7	9	4	0	40	6	72	3
New York	4,010	4,336	4,730	3,308	1,090	235	87	96	52	97	28	105	140	0
North Carolina	1,955	2,207	2,550	1,873	526	137	73	57	7	14	4	14	96	0
North Dakota	663	579	517	298	185	0	0	0	0	34	0	34	0	5
Ohio........................	3,731	3,916	3,796	2,600	1,021	165	40	65	60	10	6	64	323	0
Oklahoma	1,880	1,821	1,795	1,240	552	3	0	3	0	0	5	4	18	0
Oregon.....................	1,199	1,273	1,301	917	317	66	49	15	2	1	43	2	102	12
Pennsylvania..............	3,260	3,252	3,244	2,293	823	117	55	40	22	11	13	12	134	0
Rhode Island	309	328	321	237	74	4	3	1	0	6	9	3	12	0
South Carolina.............	1,097	1,127	1,206	900	272	25	8	15	2	9	21	10	39	0
South Dakota	802	769	714	437	254	21	8	12	1	2	27	7	0	20
Tennessee	1,543	1,624	1,772	1,290	354	127	58	38	31	1	28	19	20	0
Texas	5,991	7,519	8,619	5,871	2,130	615	277	217	121	3	1,076	25	536	0
Utah........................	714	793	1,046	628	353	65	28	11	26	0	92	86	72	3
Vermont....................	397	393	323	238	68	17	11	6	0	0	1	0	0	1
Virginia....................	1,811	1,969	2,164	1,514	405	20	9	8	3	225	190	42	3	0
Washington................	1,936	2,305	2,318	1,433	569	316	155	82	79	0	315	103	0	4
West Virginia..............	1,015	840	759	566	132	61	45	14	2	0	32	3	0	0
Wisconsin..................	2,018	2,182	2,242	1,554	596	88	23	61	4	4	89	9	206	6
Wyoming...................	415	393	363	239	101	23	10	7	6	0	24	3	3	5
Bureau of Indian Education..................	—	189	173	107	19	47	39	4	4	0	0	0	0	5
DoD, domestic	—	71	66	57	7	2	1	1	0	0	0	0	0	0
DoD, overseas	—	156	125	85	28	12	9	3	0	0	0	0	0	0
Other jurisdictions														
American Samoa	30	31	30	22	6	0	0	0	0	2	0	1	0	0
Guam......................	35	38	40	35	5	0	0	0	0	0	0	0	0	0
Northern Marianas.......	26	29	30	23	6	0	0	0	0	1	0	0	0	0
Puerto Rico	1,619	1,543	1,509	907	402	178	4	6	168	22	8	25	0	0
U.S. Virgin Islands.......	33	36	32	22	9	1	0	0	1	0	0	0	0	0

—Not available.
[1]Includes schools beginning with grade 6 or below and with no grade higher than 8.
[2]Includes schools with no grade lower than 7.
[3]Includes schools beginning with grade 6 or below and ending with grade 9 or above.
[4]Includes schools not reported by grade span.
[5]Schools are also included under elementary, secondary, combined, or other as appropriate.
NOTE: DoD = Department of Defense.
SOURCE: U.S. Department of Education, National Center for Education Statistics, Common Core of Data (CCD), "Public Elementary/Secondary School Universe Survey," 1990–91, 2000–01, and 2009–10. (This table was prepared May 2011.)

Public elementary schools, by grade span, average school size, and state or jurisdiction: 2009–10

State or jurisdiction	Total, all elementary schools	Total, all regular elementary schools[1]	Prekindergarten, kindergarten, or 1st grade to grades 3 or 4	Prekindergarten, kindergarten, or 1st grade to grade 5	Prekindergarten, kindergarten, or 1st grade to grade 6	Prekindergarten, kindergarten, or 1st grade to grade 8	Grade 4, 5, or 6 to grade 6, 7, or 8	Other grade spans	All elementary schools	Regular elementary schools[1]
1	2	3	4	5	6	7	8	9	10	11
United States	67,140	65,947	4,906	25,264	11,207	6,205	13,163	6,395	473	478
Alabama	964	952	86	300	168	68	225	117	485	487
Alaska	193	192	2	39	95	21	21	15	334	334
Arizona	1,361	1,337	55	267	339	437	196	67	511	514
Arkansas	715	713	125	141	184	5	154	106	423	424
California	6,917	6,663	153	2,481	2,152	859	1,056	216	557	572
Colorado	1,273	1,268	29	597	222	105	240	80	426	426
Connecticut	838	820	92	286	94	91	154	121	433	439
Delaware	152	149	14	76	7	7	37	11	550	555
District of Columbia	168	160	10	56	17	38	25	22	290	294
Florida	2,662	2,594	20	1,636	150	157	563	136	668	683
Georgia	1,784	1,780	42	1,063	32	20	462	165	658	656
Hawaii	209	208	0	84	87	10	27	1	540	543
Idaho	442	438	35	149	136	23	78	21	383	385
Illinois	3,198	3,158	307	794	343	690	584	480	432	436
Indiana	1,415	1,411	147	541	327	35	269	96	466	467
Iowa	1,005	1,002	122	344	167	15	228	129	310	310
Kansas	962	959	94	302	230	79	186	71	310	311
Kentucky	990	973	29	486	121	82	202	70	478	482
Louisiana	981	920	84	330	126	107	216	118	464	472
Maine	486	485	64	94	57	86	92	93	250	250
Maryland	1,119	1,106	15	645	105	77	221	56	507	511
Massachusetts	1,355	1,340	194	480	127	102	288	164	453	454
Michigan	2,475	2,385	213	942	271	208	511	330	411	414
Minnesota	1,276	1,122	108	341	340	71	229	187	408	446
Mississippi	620	617	60	130	113	39	144	134	499	500
Missouri	1,581	1,569	147	477	307	139	307	204	373	374
Montana	479	476	20	53	215	112	53	26	177	177
Nebraska	742	732	42	179	293	44	96	88	259	260
Nevada	465	459	7	256	86	16	88	12	627	634
New Hampshire	378	378	56	113	36	48	80	45	340	340
New Jersey	1,899	1,894	278	551	159	292	365	254	472	473
New Mexico	600	589	20	237	141	14	126	62	363	368
New York	3,308	3,306	272	1,295	391	203	743	404	523	523
North Carolina	1,873	1,873	73	1,085	66	117	447	85	542	542
North Dakota	298	297	10	57	129	60	27	15	190	191
Ohio	2,600	2,570	340	699	405	233	551	372	418	422
Oklahoma	1,240	1,236	65	402	91	301	247	134	370	371
Oregon	917	911	42	387	156	120	177	35	386	387
Pennsylvania	2,293	2,292	288	731	454	192	427	201	461	461
Rhode Island	237	235	28	79	48	4	41	37	382	384
South Carolina	900	897	39	454	58	29	229	91	550	551
South Dakota	437	433	16	131	80	99	92	19	189	190
Tennessee	1,290	1,284	103	434	179	238	265	71	503	504
Texas	5,871	5,713	593	2,609	547	122	1,332	668	554	566
Utah	628	589	12	86	412	27	37	54	552	574
Vermont	238	238	12	30	105	64	17	10	219	219
Virginia	1,514	1,511	54	852	151	9	315	133	545	546
Washington	1,433	1,361	43	539	401	83	226	141	428	441
West Virginia	566	566	79	263	35	38	116	35	344	344
Wisconsin	1,554	1,548	140	607	167	155	309	176	361	362
Wyoming	239	238	27	54	85	14	42	17	220	221
Bureau of Indian Education	107	107	6	5	24	67	4	1	201	201
DoD, domestic	57	57	15	15	4	2	10	11	—	—
DoD, overseas	85	85	5	28	22	7	18	5	—	—
Other jurisdictions										
American Samoa	22	22	0	0	0	22	0	0	—	—
Guam	35	35	0	25	0	0	8	2	—	—
Northern Marianas	23	23	0	2	10	0	2	9	281	281
Puerto Rico	907	906	53	7	797	2	26	22	251	251
U.S. Virgin Islands	22	22	1	0	19	0	2	0	378	378

—Not available.

[1]Excludes special education and alternative schools.

[2]Average for schools reporting enrollment data. Enrollment data were available for 66,706 out of 67,140 public elementary schools in 2009–10.

NOTE: Includes schools beginning with grade 6 or below and with no grade higher than 8. Excludes schools not reported by grade level, such as some special education schools for the disabled. DoD = Department of Defense.

SOURCE: U.S. Department of Education, National Center for Education Statistics, Common Core of Data (CCD), "Public Elementary/Secondary School Universe Survey," 2009–10. (This table was prepared May 2011.)

Public secondary schools, by grade span, average school size, and state or jurisdiction: 2009–10

State or jurisdiction	Total, all secondary schools	Total, all regular secondary schools[1]	Schools, by grade span							Vocational schools[2]	Average number of students per school[3]	
			Grades 7 to 8 and 7 to 9	Grades 7 to 12	Grades 8 to 12	Grades 9 to 12	Grades 10 to 12	Other spans ending with grade 12	Other grade spans		All secondary schools	Regular secondary schools[1]
1	2	3	4	5	6	7	8	9	10	11	12	13
United States	24,651	19,604	2,953	3,176	602	15,961	745	403	811	1,417	693	798
Alabama	423	321	42	84	11	242	33	3	8	72	691	712
Alaska	85	66	15	20	1	48	1	0	0	3	466	562
Arizona	718	486	78	32	6	569	8	8	17	207	576	715
Arkansas.....................	392	360	57	130	10	137	35	2	21	23	475	485
California	2,608	1,586	379	308	13	1,794	65	32	17	75	884	1,318
Colorado	413	349	52	55	2	288	5	3	6	6	605	688
Connecticut.................	282	209	39	15	5	185	15	13	10	16	690	864
Delaware.....................	38	29	2	2	24	10	0	0	0	6	998	1,057
District of Columbia	40	31	2	2	0	29	0	1	6	4	414	478
Florida........................	657	481	18	52	34	523	8	8	14	53	1,224	1,544
Georgia.......................	437	425	17	6	6	376	3	1	28	1	1,099	1,121
Hawaii	51	50	11	7	0	33	0	0	0	0	1,189	1,210
Idaho..........................	227	150	34	52	0	119	20	0	2	11	429	578
Illinois........................	1,040	831	152	67	20	684	17	53	47	53	727	824
Indiana	447	409	70	87	3	280	3	1	3	29	859	877
Iowa	423	374	47	75	0	284	9	3	5	0	393	435
Kansas	405	400	58	88	5	245	8	0	1	1	414	417
Kentucky	428	245	27	42	6	341	4	5	3	124	727	827
Louisiana	307	252	36	46	71	124	17	1	12	6	609	696
Maine	150	121	12	9	3	98	1	27	0	27	490	498
Maryland......................	268	202	14	6	4	227	1	8	8	24	1,073	1,280
Massachusetts..............	367	315	31	38	10	283	1	1	3	39	848	868
Michigan	1,044	751	88	99	28	751	25	21	32	38	575	704
Minnesota	862	488	49	291	27	387	51	45	12	11	399	602
Mississippi	335	239	32	62	4	207	22	2	6	90	635	637
Missouri	655	570	68	180	2	359	19	11	16	66	534	541
Montana......................	349	346	178	0	0	171	0	0	0	0	164	166
Nebraska	349	339	30	188	1	118	5	7	0	0	357	357
Nevada	137	121	23	10	4	95	1	4	0	1	961	1,048
New Hampshire	106	106	16	0	0	87	1	0	2	0	650	650
New Jersey	551	404	59	40	19	378	13	12	30	55	863	1,081
New Mexico	235	204	41	29	1	149	7	0	8	1	491	537
New York	1,090	1,045	69	141	9	774	21	2	74	6	835	853
North Carolina	526	525	23	14	3	446	5	4	31	1	820	821
North Dakota	185	175	12	95	1	71	3	1	2	9	208	209
Ohio...........................	1,021	932	135	129	49	655	17	14	22	73	613	631
Oklahoma	552	547	73	0	0	428	35	3	13	0	354	355
Oregon	317	286	35	46	4	222	6	3	1	0	592	644
Pennsylvania................	823	726	105	153	12	461	63	9	20	87	836	846
Rhode Island	74	59	13	1	0	60	0	0	0	11	779	839
South Carolina..............	272	222	22	12	2	212	16	3	5	39	982	990
South Dakota	254	240	72	0	0	179	2	0	1	4	166	170
Tennessee	354	324	18	41	9	273	8	2	3	21	868	909
Texas	2,130	1,517	307	176	85	1,225	48	36	253	0	701	947
Utah...........................	353	244	97	49	14	74	79	18	22	6	705	897
Vermont	68	52	8	17	0	28	0	0	15	15	545	555
Virginia.......................	405	344	33	6	32	323	6	0	5	49	1,158	1,193
Washington..................	569	388	70	76	57	320	18	9	19	15	655	868
West Virginia................	132	107	2	27	3	99	0	0	1	31	591	723
Wisconsin....................	596	527	61	56	1	429	17	27	5	8	497	547
Wyoming	101	84	21	15	1	61	3	0	0	0	318	371
Bureau of Indian Education....	19	19	1	5	1	12	0	0	0	0	311	311
DoD, domestic	7	7	2	0	0	5	0	0	0	0	—	—
DoD, overseas	28	28	1	11	0	16	0	0	0	0	—	—
Other jurisdictions												
American Samoa	6	5	0	0	0	6	0	0	0	1	—	—
Guam	5	5	0	0	0	5	0	0	0	0	—	—
Northern Marianas........	6	6	1	1	0	4	0	0	0	0	740	740
Puerto Rico	402	371	197	26	1	5	161	0	12	29	490	478
U.S. Virgin Islands..........	9	8	4	0	0	5	0	0	0	1	868	868

—Not available.
[1]Excludes vocational, special education, and alternative schools.
[2]Vocational schools are also included under appropriate grade span.
[3]Average for schools reporting enrollment data. Enrollment data were available for 23,053 out of 24,651 public secondary schools in 2009–10.

NOTE: Includes schools with no grade lower than 7. Excludes schools not reported by grade level, such as some special education schools for the disabled. DoD = Department of Defense.
SOURCE: U.S. Department of Education, National Center for Education Statistics, Common Core of Data (CCD), "Public Elementary/Secondary School Universe Survey," 2009–10. (This table was prepared May 2011.)

Age range for compulsory school attendance and special education services, and policies on year-round schools and kindergarten programs, by state: Selected years, 2000 through 2011

State	Compulsory attendance							Compulsory special education services, 2004[1]	Year-round schools, 2008		Kindergarten programs, 2011		
	2000	2002	2004	2006	2008	2009	2010		Has policy on year-round schools	Has districts with year-round schools	School districts required to offer Program	Full-day program	Attendance required
1	2	3	4	5	6	7	8	9	10	11	12	13	14
Alabama	7 to 16	7 to 16	7 to 16 [2]	7 to 16	7 to 16	7 to 16	7 to 17	6 to 21		Yes	X	X	
Alaska	7 to 16	7 to 16	7 to 16	7 to 16	7 to 16	7 to 16	7 to 16	3 to 22		Yes			
Arizona	6 to 16 [2]	6 to 16 [2]	6 to 16 [2]	6 to 16 [2]	6 to 16 [2]	6 to 16 [2]	6 to 16 [2]	3 to 21	—	—	X		
Arkansas	5 to 17 [2,3]	5 to 17 [2,3]	5 to 17 [2,3]	5 to 17 [2,3]	5 to 17 [2,3]	5 to 17 [2,3]	5 to 17 [2,3]	5 to 21	X	Yes	X	X	X
California	6 to 18 [2]	6 to 18	6 to 18	6 to 18	6 to 18	6 to 18	6 to 18	Birth to 21 [4]	X	Yes	X		
Colorado	—	—	7 to 16	7 to 16	6 to 17	6 to 17	6 to 17	3 to 21		Yes	X		
Connecticut	7 to 16	7 to 16 [2]	7 to 18 [2]	5 to 18 [3]	5 to 18 [3]	5 to 18 [3]	5 to 18 [3]	3 to 21		—	X		X
Delaware	5 to 16	5 to 16	5 to 16	5 to 16	5 to 16	5 to 16	5 to 16	Birth to 20		Yes	X	X	X
District of Columbia	—	5 to 18 [5]	5 to 18	5 to 18	5 to 18	5 to 18	5 to 18	—	—	—	X		X
Florida	6 to 16 [5]	6 to 16 [5]	6 to 16 [5]	6 to 16 [5]	6 to 16 [5]	6 to 16 [5]	6 to 16 [5]	3 to 21	X	Yes	X		
Georgia	6 to 16	6 to 16	6 to 16	6 to 16	6 to 16	6 to 16	6 to 16	Birth to 21 [6]		Yes	X	X	
Hawaii	6 to 18	6 to 18	6 to 18	6 to 18	6 to 18	6 to 18	6 to 18	Birth to 19		(7)	X		
Idaho	7 to 16	7 to 16	7 to 16	7 to 16	7 to 16	7 to 16	7 to 16	3 to 21		Yes			
Illinois	7 to 16	7 to 16	7 to 17	7 to 17	7 to 17	7 to 17	7 to 17	3 to 21	X	Yes	X		
Indiana	7 to 16	7 to 16	7 to 16	7 to 18 [2]	7 to 18 [2]	7 to 18 [2]	7 to 18 [2]	3 to 22		Yes	X		
Iowa	6 to 16 [2]	6 to 16 [2]	6 to 16	6 to 16	6 to 16	6 to 16	6 to 16	Birth to 21	X	Yes	X		
Kansas	7 to 18 [2]	7 to 18 [2]	7 to 18 [2]	7 to 18 [2]	7 to 18 [2]	7 to 18 [2]	7 to 18 [2]	3 to 21 [8]		—	X		
Kentucky	6 to 16	6 to 16	6 to 16 [2]	6 to 16	6 to 16	6 to 16	6 to 16	Birth to 21		Yes	X		
Louisiana	7 to 17	7 to 17	7 to 17 [2]	7 to 17 [2]	7 to 17 [2]	7 to 18 [2]	7 to 18 [2]	3 to 21 [9]		Yes	X	X	X
Maine	7 to 17	7 to 17	7 to 17 [2]	7 to 17 [2]	7 to 17 [2]	7 to 17 [2]	7 to 17 [2]	5 to 19 [9,10]		—	X		
Maryland	5 to 16	5 to 16	5 to 16	5 to 16	5 to 16 [3]	5 to 16 [3]	5 to 16 [3]	Birth to 21	X	—	X	X	X
Massachusetts	6 to 16	6 to 16	6 to 16	6 to 16 [2]	6 to 16 [2]	6 to 16 [2]	6 to 16 [2]	3 to 21 [6]	(11)	—	X		
Michigan	6 to 16	6 to 16	6 to 16	6 to 16	6 to 16	6 to 16	6 to 18	Birth to 25	X	Yes	X		
Minnesota	7 to 18 [2]	7 to 16	7 to 16	7 to 16 [2]	7 to 16 [2]	7 to 16 [2]	7 to 16 [2]	Birth to 21	X	Yes	X		
Mississippi	6 to 17	6 to 17	6 to 16	6 to 16	6 to 17	6 to 17	6 to 17	Birth to 20		—	X	X	
Missouri	7 to 16	7 to 16	7 to 16	7 to 16	7 to 16	7 to 16	7 to 17	Birth to 20		Yes [12]	X		
Montana	7 to 16 [2]	7 to 16 [2]	7 to 16 [2]	7 to 16 [2]	7 to 16 [2]	7 to 16 [2]	7 to 16 [2]	3 to 18 [9]		—	X		
Nebraska	7 to 16	7 to 16	7 to 16	6 to 18	6 to 18	6 to 18	6 to 18	Birth to 20		Yes	X		
Nevada	7 to 17	7 to 17	7 to 17	7 to 17	7 to 18 [2]	7 to 18 [2]	7 to 18 [2]	Birth to 21 [4]		Yes	X		X
New Hampshire	6 to 16	6 to 16	6 to 16	6 to 16	6 to 16	6 to 16	6 to 18	3 to 21		—			
New Jersey	6 to 16	6 to 16	6 to 16	6 to 16	6 to 16	6 to 16	6 to 16	5 to 21		—	X		
New Mexico	5 to 18	5 to 18	5 to 18 [2]	5 to 18 [2]	5 to 18 [2]	5 to 18 [2]	5 to 18 [2]	3 to 21	X	Yes	X		X
New York	6 to 16 [2]	6 to 16	6 to 16	6 to 16 [13]	6 to 16 [13]	6 to 16 [13]	6 to 16 [13]	Birth to 20		—	X		
North Carolina	7 to 16	7 to 16	7 to 16	7 to 16	7 to 16	7 to 16	7 to 16	5 to 20	X	Yes	X	X	
North Dakota	7 to 16	7 to 16	7 to 16	7 to 16	7 to 16	7 to 16	7 to 16	3 to 21		No			
Ohio	6 to 18	6 to 18	6 to 18	6 to 18	6 to 18	6 to 18	6 to 18	3 to 21	X	—	X	X [14]	X
Oklahoma	5 to 18	5 to 18	5 to 18	5 to 18	5 to 18	5 to 18	5 to 18	Birth to 21 [9]		Yes	X	(15)	X
Oregon	7 to 18	7 to 18	7 to 18 [2]	7 to 18	7 to 18	7 to 18	7 to 18 [2]	3 to 20		Yes	X		
Pennsylvania	8 to 17	8 to 17	8 to 17 [2]	8 to 17 [2]	8 to 17 [2]	8 to 17 [2]	8 to 17 [2]	6 to 21	X [12]	— [12]			
Rhode Island	6 to 16	6 to 16	6 to 16	6 to 16	6 to 16	6 to 16	6 to 16	3 to 21		—	X		X
South Carolina	5 to 16	5 to 16	5 to 16	5 to 17 [3]	5 to 17 [3]	5 to 17 [3]	5 to 17 [3]	3 to 21 [16]		—	X	X [17]	X
South Dakota	6 to 16	6 to 16	6 to 16	6 to 16	6 to 16	6 to 16 [2,18]	6 to 18 [2,18]	Birth to 21	X	—	X		X
Tennessee	6 to 17	6 to 17	6 to 17	6 to 17 [3]	6 to 17 [3]	6 to 17 [3]	6 to 17	3 to 21 [4]	X	Yes	X		X
Texas	6 to 18	6 to 18	6 to 18	6 to 18	6 to 18	6 to 18	6 to 18	3 to 21	X	Yes	X		X
Utah	6 to 18	6 to 18	6 to 18	6 to 18	6 to 18	6 to 18	6 to 18	3 to 22		Yes	X		
Vermont	7 to 16	6 to 16	6 to 16	6 to 16 [2]	6 to 16 [2]	6 to 16 [2]	6 to 16 [2]	3 to 21		— [12]	X		
Virginia	5 to 18	5 to 18	5 to 18	5 to 18 [2]	5 to 18 [2]	5 to 18 [2,3]	5 to 18 [2,3]	2 to 21 [4]	X	Yes	X		X
Washington	8 to 17 [2]	8 to 17 [2]	8 to 16 [2]	8 to 18	8 to 18	8 to 18	8 to 18	3 to 21 [16]		Yes	X		
West Virginia	6 to 16	6 to 16	6 to 16	6 to 16	6 to 16	6 to 16	6 to 17	5 to 21 [19]	X	Yes	X	X	X
Wisconsin	6 to 18	6 to 18	6 to 18	6 to 18	6 to 18	6 to 18	6 to 18	3 to 21		Yes	X		
Wyoming	6 to 16 [2]	6 to 16 [2]	7 to 16 [2]	7 to 16 [2]	7 to 16 [2]	7 to 16 [2]	7 to 16 [2]	3 to 21		—	X		

—Not available.

X Denotes that the state has a policy. A blank denotes that the state does not have a policy.

[1] Most states have a provision whereby education is provided up to a certain age or completion of secondary school, whichever comes first.

[2] Child may be exempted from compulsory attendance if he/she meets state requirements for early withdrawal with or without meeting conditions for a diploma or equivalency.

[3] Parent/guardian may delay child's entry until a later age per state law/regulation.

[4] Student may continue in the program if 22nd birthday falls before the end of the school year.

[5] Attendance is compulsory until age 18 for Manatee County students, unless they earn a high school diploma prior to reaching their 18th birthday.

[6] Through age 21 or until child graduates with a high school or special education diploma or equivalent.

[7] Some districts operate on a multitrack system; the schools are open year-round, but different cohorts start and end at different times.

[8] To be determined by rules and regulations adopted by the state board.

[9] Children from birth through age 2 are eligible for additional services.

[10] Must be age 5 before October 15, and not age 20 before start of school year.

[11] Policies about year-round schools are decided locally.

[12] State did not participate in 2008 online survey. Data are from 2006.

[13] New York City and Buffalo require school attendance until age 17 unless employed; Syracuse requires kindergarten attendance at age 5.

[14] State requires districts with full-day programs to allow half-day attendance.

[15] Beginning in 2011–12, it will be mandatory for all districts in Oklahoma to offer full-day kindergarten.

[16] Student may complete school year if 21st birthday occurs while attending school.

[17] Parents may request either a full-day or a half-day program. For students enrolled in half-day programs, child care must be provided for the remainder of the school day.

[18] Compulsory attendance beginning at age 5 effective July 1, 2010.

[19] Severely handicapped children may begin receiving services at age 3.

NOTE: The Education of the Handicapped Act (EHA) Amendments of 1986 make it mandatory for all states receiving EHA funds to serve all 3- to 18-year-old disabled children.

SOURCE: Council of Chief State School Officers, *Key State Education Policies on PK–12 Education*, 2000, 2002, 2004, and 2008; Education Commission of the States (ECS), ECS StateNotes, *Compulsory School Age Requirements*, retrieved August 9, 2010, from http://www.ecs.org/clearinghouse/86/62/8662.pdf; ECS StateNotes, *Special Education: State Special Education Definitions, Ages Served*, retrieved August 9, 2010, from http://www.ecs.org/clearinghouse/52/29/5229.pdf; ECS StateNotes, *State Characteristics: Kindergarten*, retrieved August 24, 2011, from http://www.ecs.org/clearinghouse/90/71/9071.pdf; ECS StateNotes, *District Offering of Full-Day Kindergarten*, retrieved August 24, 2011, from http://ecs.force.com/ecsforum/mbtab2?rep=KD33&SID=a0i70000000XkGj&Q=Q2207&Q1=Q2208; and supplemental information retrieved from various state websites. (This table was prepared September 2011.)

Minimum amount of instructional time per year and policy on textbook selection, by state: 2000, 2006, 2008, and 2011

	Minimum amount of instructional time per year				State policy on textbook selection, 2008					
	In days			In hours	State recommends or selects textbooks				State standards used in recommendation or selection	
State	2000	2006	2011	2011	Recommends	Selects	Either recommends or selects	Local decision	State standards used	State
1	2	3	4	5	6	7	8	9	10	11
Alabama	175	175	180				X		X	Alabama
Alaska	180	180	170[1]	740 (K–3); 900 (4–12)				X		Alaska
Arizona	175[2]	180	180[3]	356 (K); 712 (1–3); 890 (4–6); 1,000 (7–8); 720[4] (9–12)				X		Arizona
Arkansas	178	178	178[1]		X				X	Arkansas
California	175	180	180/175[5]	600 (K); 840 (1–3); 900 (4–8); 1,080 (9–12)	X					California
Colorado	[6]	160	160	435/870 (K); 968 (1–5); 1,056 (6–12)				X		Colorado
Connecticut	180	180	180	450/900 (K); 900 (1–12)				X		Connecticut
Delaware	[6]	†	†	440 (K); 1,060 (1–11); 1,032 (12)				X		Delaware
District of Columbia	180[7]	180	178							District of Columbia
Florida	180	180	180	720[8] (K–3); 900[8] (4–12)	X				X	Florida
Georgia	180[7]	180	180	810 (K–3); 900 (4–5); 990 (6–12)	X				X	Georgia
Hawaii	184	179	180[9]	915 (K–6)[9,10]; 990 (7–12)[9,11]	X				X	Hawaii
Idaho	180	†	†	450[12] (K); 810[12] (1–3); 900[12] (4–8); 990[12,13] (9–12)	X				X	Idaho
Illinois	180[14]	176	176	†				X		Illinois
Indiana	180	180	180	†	X				X	Indiana
Iowa	180	180	180	†				X		Iowa
Kansas	186	186 (K–11); 181 (12)	186 (K–11); 181 (12)	465 (K); 1,116 (1–11); 1,086 (12)				X		Kansas
Kentucky	175	175	175[1]	1,062	X				X	Kentucky
Louisiana	175	177	177[1]	1,062			X			Louisiana
Maine	175	175	175[1]					X		Maine
Maryland	180	180	180	1,080				X		Maryland
Massachusetts	180	180	180	425 (K); 900 (1–5); 990 (6–12)				X		Massachusetts
Michigan	180	†	165	1,098				X		Michigan
Minnesota	[6]	[6]	†	425 (K); 935 (1–6); 1,020 (7–12)				X		Minnesota
Mississippi	180	180	180	†		X				Mississippi
Missouri	174	174	174/142[15]	1,044	—	—	—	—	—	Missouri
Montana	180	90 (K); 180 (K–12)	†	360/720[1] (K); 720[1] (1–3); 1,080[1,13] (4–12)				X		Montana
Nebraska	[6]	†	†	400 (K); 1,032 (1–8); 1,080 (9–12)				X		Nebraska
Nevada	180	180	180							Nevada
New Hampshire	180	180	180	945 (1–5); 990 (6–12)				X		New Hampshire
New Jersey	180	180	180	†				X		New Jersey
New Mexico	180	180	180	450/990[16] (K); 990[16] (1–6); 1,080 (7–12)		X		X	X	New Mexico
New York	180[7]	180	180	†	X			X		New York
North Carolina	180	180	180	1,000	X			X		North Carolina
North Dakota	173	173	175[1]	951.5 (K–8); 1,038 (9–12)				X		North Dakota
Ohio	182	182	182[12]	910				X		Ohio
Oklahoma	180	180	180[12]	900[12] (1–6); 1,080[12] (7–12)		X			X	Oklahoma
Oregon	[6]	†	†	405 (K); 810 (1–3); 900 (4–8); 990[13] (9–12)			X		X	Oregon
Pennsylvania	180	180	180	450 (K); 900 (1–8); 990 (9–12)	—	—		—	—	Pennsylvania
Rhode Island	180	180	180	†				X		Rhode Island
South Carolina	180	180	180[1]	†			X	X	X	South Carolina
South Dakota	—	†	†	437.5 (K); 875 (1–3); 962.5[13] (4–12)				X		South Dakota
Tennessee	180	180	180[1]	†		X			X	Tennessee
Texas	187	180	180	†			X			Texas
Utah	180	180	180	450 (K); 810 (1); 990 (2–12)			X			Utah
Vermont	175	175	175							Vermont
Virginia	180	180	180	540 (K); 990 (1–12)	X			X	X	Virginia
Washington	180[14]	180	180	450 (K); 1,000 (1–6); 1,080 (7–12)				X	X	Washington
West Virginia	180	180	180	†			X			West Virginia
Wisconsin	180	180	180	437 (K); 1,050 (1–6); 1,137 (7–12)				X		Wisconsin
Wyoming	175	175	180	†				X		Wyoming

---Not available.

†Not applicable.

X Denotes that the state has a policy. A blank denotes that the state does not have a policy.

[1]Does not include time for in-service or staff development or parent-teacher conferences.

[2]1994 data.

[3]Or an equivalent number of minutes of instruction per year.

[4]Students must enroll in at least 4 subjects that meet at least 720 hours.

[5]Through 2014–15, charter schools and districts are allowed to shorten the 180-day instructional year to 175 days without fiscal penalty.

[6]No statewide policy; varies by district.

[7]1996 data.

[8]For schools on double-session or approved experimental calendar: 630 (K–3); 810 (4–12).

[9]Does not apply to charter and multitrack schools.

[10]Beginning in the 2012–13 school year.

[11]For the 2014–15 and 2015–16 school years.

[12]Includes time for in-service or staff development or parent-teacher conferences.

[13]Instructional time for graduating seniors may be reduced.

[14]1998 data.

[15]174 days required for a 5-day week; 142 days required for a 4-day week.

[16]Teachers may use 33 hours of the full-day kindergarten program and 22 hours of the grades 1 through 5 programs for home visits or parent-teacher conferences.

NOTE: Minimum number of instructional days refers to the actual number of days that pupils have contact with a teacher. Some states allow for different types of school calendars by setting instructional time in both days and hours, while others use only days or only hours. For states in which the number of days or hours varies by grade, the relevant grade(s) appear in parentheses.

SOURCE: Council of Chief State School Officers, *Key State Education Policies on PK–12 Education*, 2000, 2006, and 2008; Education Commission of the States, StateNotes, *Number of Instructional Days/Hours in the School Year* (August 2011 revision), retrieved September 22, 2011, from http://www.ecs.org/clearinghouse/95/05/9505.pdf; and supplemental information retrieved September 24, 2010, from the New Hampshire Department of Education, http://www.education.nh.gov/standards/faq.htm; retrieved September 24, 2010, from the South Dakota Department of Education, http://doe.sd.gov/oatq/districtaccrediation.asp; and retrieved September 29, 2010, from the Pennsylvania State Code, http://pacode.com/secure/data/022/Chapter11/s11.3.html. (This table was prepared September 2011.)

Credit requirements and exit exam requirements for a standard high school diploma and the use of other high school completion credentials, by state: 2008 and 2011

State	Course credits (in Carnegie units), 2008						High school exit exams, 2011				Other completion credentials, 2011	
	Total required credits for standard diploma, all courses	Required credits in selected subject areas					Exit exam required for standard diploma	Characteristics of required exams			Advanced recognition for exceeding standard requirements	Alternative credential for not meeting all standard requirements
		English/ language arts	Social studies	Science	Mathematics	Other credits		Subjects tested[1]	Exam based on standards for 10th grade or higher	Appeals or alternative route to standard diploma if exam failed		
1	2	3	4	5	6	7	8	9	10	11	12	13
Alabama	24.0	4.0	4.0	4.0	4.0	8.0	Yes	EMSH	Yes	Yes	Yes	Yes
Alaska	21.0	4.0	3.0	2.0	2.0	10.0	Yes	EM	Yes	Yes	No	Yes
Arizona	20.0	4.0	3.0	2.0	3.0	8.0	Yes	EM	Yes	Yes	Yes	No
Arkansas	22.0	4.0	3.0	3.0	4.0	8.0	Yes	M	No	Yes	No	No
California	13.0	3.0	3.0	2.0	2.0	3.0	Yes	EM	Yes	Yes	Yes	Yes
Colorado	†[2]	†[2]	†[2]	†[2]	†[2]	†[2]	No	†	†	†	No	No
Connecticut	20.0	4.0	3.0	2.0	3.0	8.0	No [3]	†	†	†	No	No
Delaware	22.0	4.0	3.0	3.0	3.0	9.0	No	†	†	†	No	Yes
District of Columbia	24.0	4.0	4.0	4.0	4.0	8.0	No	†	†	†	No	Yes
Florida	24.0 or 18.0 [4]	4.0	3.0	3.0	4.0 or 3.0 [4]	10.0 or 5.0 [4]	Yes	EM	Yes	Yes	No	Yes
Georgia	23.0	4.0	3.0	4.0	4.0	8.0	Yes	EMSH	Yes	Yes	Yes	Yes
Hawaii	22.0	4.0	4.0	3.0	3.0	8.0	No	†	†	†	Yes	Yes
Idaho	42.0 [5]	9.0 [5]	5.0	4.0	4.0	20.0 [5]	Yes	EM	Yes	Yes	No	No
Illinois	18.0	3.0	2.0	1.0	3.0	9.0	No	†	†	†	No	No
Indiana	40.0 [5]	8.0 [5]	6.0 [5]	6.0 [5]	6.0 [5]	14.0 [5]	Yes	EM	No	Yes	Yes	No
Iowa	†[2]	†[2]	1.5	†[2]	†[2]	†[2]	No	†	†	†	Yes	No
Kansas	21.0	4.0	3.0	3.0	3.0	8.0	No	†	†	†	No	No
Kentucky	22.0	4.0	3.0	3.0	3.0	9.0	No	†	†	†	No	Yes
Louisiana	23.0	4.0	3.0	3.0	3.0	10.0	Yes	EMSH [6]	Yes	Yes	Yes	Yes
Maine	16.0	4.0	2.0	2.0	2.0	6.0	No	†	†	†	No	Yes
Maryland	21.0	4.0	3.0	3.0	3.0	8.0	Yes	EMSH	Yes	Yes	Yes	Yes
Massachusetts	†[2]	†[2]	†[2]	†[2]	†[2]	†[2]	Yes	EMS	Yes	Yes	Yes	Yes
Michigan	†[2]	4.0	3.0	3.0	4.0	†[2]	No	†	†	†	No	Yes
Minnesota	21.5	4.0	3.5	3.0	3.0	8.0	Yes	EM [7]	Yes	Yes	No	No
Mississippi	20.0	4.0	3.0	3.0	3.0	7.0	Yes	EMSH	Yes	Yes	No	Yes
Missouri	22.0 [8]	4.0 [8]	2.0 [8]	2.0 [8]	2.0 [8]	12.0 [8]	No	†	†	†	Yes	No
Montana	20.0	4.0	2.0	2.0	2.0	10.0	No	†	†	†	No	No
Nebraska	200.0 [9]	†[2]	†[2]	†[2]	†[2]	†[2]	No	†	†	†	No	No
Nevada	22.5	4.0	2.0	2.0	3.0	11.5	Yes	EMS	Yes	Yes	No	Yes
New Hampshire	20.0	4.0	2.5	2.0	3.0	8.5	No	†	†	†	Yes	Yes
New Jersey	22.0	4.0	3.0	3.0	3.0	9.0	Yes	EM	Yes	Yes	No	No
New Mexico	24.0	4.0	3.0	3.0	4.0	10.0	Yes	EMSH	No	Yes	No	Yes
New York	22.0	4.0	4.0	3.0	3.0	8.0	Yes	EMSH	Yes	Yes	Yes	Yes
North Carolina	20.0	4.0	3.0	3.0	4.0	6.0	No	†	†	†	Yes	Yes
North Dakota	21.0	†[2]	†[2]	†[2]	†[2]	†[2]	No	†	†	†	No	No
Ohio	20.0	4.0	3.0	3.0	3.0	7.0	Yes	EMSH	Yes	Yes	Yes	No
Oklahoma	23.0	4.0	3.0	3.0	3.0	10.0	No [10]	†	†	†	Yes	No
Oregon	22.0	3.0	3.0	2.0	2.0	12.0	No	†	†	†	No	Yes
Pennsylvania	†[2,8]	†[2,8]	†[2,8]	†[2,8]	†[2,8]	†[2,8]	No	†	†	†	Yes	No
Rhode Island	20.0	4.0	3.0	3.0	4.0	6.0	No [11]	†	†	†	No	Yes
South Carolina	24.0	4.0	3.0	3.0	4.0	10.0	Yes	EM	Yes	No	Yes	Yes
South Dakota	22.0	4.0	3.0	3.0	3.0	9.0	No	†	†	†	Yes	No
Tennessee	20.0	4.0	3.0	3.0	3.0	7.0	Yes	EMS	Yes	No	Yes	Yes
Texas	24.0	4.0	5.0	3.0	3.0	9.0	Yes	EMSH	Yes	No	Yes	Yes
Utah	24.0	3.0	2.5	2.0	2.0	14.5	No	†	†	†	No	Yes
Vermont	20.0 [8]	8z [8]	3.0 [8]	3.0 [8]	3.0 [8]	7.0 [8]	No	†	†	†	No	No
Virginia	22.0	4.0	3.0	3.0	3.0	9.0	Yes	EMSH [12]	Yes	Yes	Yes	Yes
Washington	20.0	3.0	2.5	2.0	3.0	9.5	Yes	E [13]	Yes	Yes	No	No
West Virginia	24.0	4.0	4.0	3.0	4.0	9.0	No	†	†	†	No	Yes
Wisconsin	21.5 [14]	4.0	3.0	2.0	2.0	10.5	No	†	†	†	No	Yes
Wyoming	22.0	4.0	3.0	3.0	3.0	9.0	No	†	†	†	Yes	No

†Not applicable.

[1]Exit exam subjects tested: E = English (including writing), M = Mathematics, S = Science, and H = History/social studies.

[2]Graduation requirements are determined locally.

[3]Requirement takes effect for class of 2018.

[4]Florida offers three graduation programs: one 4-year, 24-credit program, and two 3-year, 18-credit programs. The 4-year program requires 4 credits of mathematics, and both 3-year programs require 3 credits of mathematics.

[5]Expressed in semester credits instead of Carnegie units.

[6]Students must pass either the science or social studies components of the Graduation Exit Examination (GEE) to receive a standard diploma.

[7]For the graduating classes of 2010 through 2014, students can graduate by passing statewide reading and writing assessments and either passing mathematics assessments or meeting other requirements.

[8]State did not participate in the 2008 online survey; data are from 2006.

[9]Expressed in credit hours instead of Carnegie units.

[10]Requirement takes effect for class of 2012.

[11]Requirement takes effect for class of 2014.

[12]To receive the standard diploma, students must earn at least six verified credits by passing end-of-course assessments. One of those credits may be earned by passing a student-selected test in computer science, technology, career and technical education, or other areas.

[13]For the graduating class of 2011, students must pass an exit exam in reading and writing. Students in the class of 2013 will be required to pass reading, writing, math, and science assessments.

[14]Determined locally, but state encourages school boards to adopt this requirement.

NOTE: Local school districts frequently have other graduation requirements in addition to state requirements. The Carnegie unit is a standard of measurement that represents one credit for the completion of a 1-year course.

SOURCE: Council of Chief State School Officers, *Key State Education Policies on PK–12 Education, 2008*, table 7, retrieved October 6, 2010, from http://www.ccsso.org/Documents/2008/Key_State_Education_Policies_2008.pdf; *Education Week* and Editorial Projects in Education Research Center, *Diplomas Count 2008*, Graduation Briefs, retrieved October 6, 2010, from http://www.edweek.org/ew/toc/2008/06/05/index.html; and *Diplomas Count 2011*, "Graduation Policies" table, retrieved July 19, 2011, from http://www.edweek.org/media/dc11-graduationpolicies.pdf. (This table was prepared July 2011.)

States that use criterion-referenced tests (CRTs) aligned to state standards, by subject area and level: 2006–07

State	Aligned to state standards		Off-the-shelf/ norm-referenced test (NRT)[1]	Criterion-referenced tests,[2] by subject area and level			
	Custom-developed test (CRT)[2]	Augmented or hybrid test[3]		English/ language arts	Mathematics	Science	Social studies/ history
1	2	3	4	5	6	7	8
Alabama	X		X	ES, MS, HS	ES, MS, HS	HS	HS
Alaska	X		X	ES, MS, HS	ES, MS, HS		
Arizona	X	X	X	ES, MS, HS	ES, MS, HS		
Arkansas	X		X	ES, MS, HS	ES, MS, HS	ES, MS	
California	X		X	ES, MS, HS	ES, MS, HS	ES, MS, HS	MS, HS
Colorado	X		X	ES, MS, HS	ES, MS, HS	ES, MS, HS	
Connecticut	X			ES, MS, HS	ES, MS, HS	HS	
Delaware		X		ES, MS, HS	ES, MS, HS	ES, MS, HS	ES, MS, HS
District of Columbia	X			ES, MS, HS	ES, MS, HS		
Florida	X		X	ES, MS, HS	ES, MS, HS	ES, MS, HS	
Georgia	X		X	ES, MS, HS	ES, MS, HS	ES, MS, HS	ES, MS, HS
Hawaii		X		ES, MS, HS	ES, MS, HS		
Idaho	X			ES, MS, HS	ES, MS, HS		
Illinois	X	X		ES, MS, HS	ES, MS, HS	HS	
Indiana	X			ES, MS, HS	ES, MS, HS	ES, MS	
Iowa			X	ES, MS, HS	ES, MS, HS	ES, MS, HS	
Kansas	X			ES, MS, HS	ES, MS, HS		
Kentucky	X		X	ES, MS, HS	ES, MS, HS	ES, MS, HS	ES, MS, HS
Louisiana	X	X		ES, MS, HS	ES, MS, HS	ES, MS, HS	ES, MS, HS
Maine	X		X	ES, MS, HS	ES, MS, HS	ES, MS	
Maryland	X	X		ES, MS, HS	ES, MS, HS	HS	HS
Massachusetts	X			ES, MS, HS	ES, MS, HS	ES, MS, HS	
Michigan	X		X	ES, MS, HS	ES, MS, HS	ES, MS, HS	MS, HS
Minnesota	X			ES, MS, HS	ES, MS, HS		
Mississippi	X		X	ES, MS, HS	ES, MS, HS	ES, MS, HS	HS
Missouri		X		ES, MS, HS	ES, MS, HS		
Montana	X		X	ES, MS, HS	ES, MS, HS		
Nebraska	X			ES, MS, HS			
Nevada	X		X	ES, MS, HS	ES, MS, HS		
New Hampshire	X			ES, MS	ES, MS		
New Jersey	X			ES, MS, HS	ES, MS, HS	ES, MS	
New Mexico	X		X	ES, MS, HS	ES, MS, HS	ES, MS, HS	
New York	X			ES, MS, HS	ES, MS, HS	ES, MS, HS	ES, MS, HS
North Carolina	X			ES, MS, HS	ES, MS, HS	HS	HS
North Dakota	X			ES, MS, HS	ES, MS, HS	ES, MS, HS	
Ohio	X			ES, MS, HS	ES, MS, HS	ES, MS, HS	ES, MS, HS
Oklahoma	X			ES, MS, HS	ES, MS, HS	ES, MS, HS	ES, MS, HS
Oregon	X			ES, MS, HS	ES, MS, HS	MS, HS	
Pennsylvania	X			ES, MS, HS	ES, MS, HS		
Rhode Island	X	X		ES, MS, HS	ES, MS, HS		
South Carolina	X			ES, MS, HS	ES, MS, HS	ES, MS, HS	ES, MS, HS
South Dakota		X	X	ES, MS, HS	ES, MS, HS	ES, MS, HS	
Tennessee	X			ES, MS, HS	ES, MS, HS	ES, MS, HS	ES, MS, HS
Texas	X			ES, MS, HS	ES, MS, HS	ES, MS, HS	MS, HS
Utah	X		X	ES, MS, HS	ES, MS, HS	ES, MS, HS	
Vermont	X			ES, MS	ES, MS		
Virginia	X			ES, MS, HS	ES, MS, HS	ES, MS, HS	ES, MS, HS
Washington	X			ES, MS, HS	ES, MS, HS	ES, MS, HS	
West Virginia	X		X	ES, MS, HS	ES, MS, HS	ES, MS, HS	ES, MS
Wisconsin		X		ES, MS, HS	ES, MS, HS	ES, MS, HS	ES, MS, HS
Wyoming	X			ES, MS, HS	ES, MS, HS		

X State has a test.

[1] Off-the-shelf/norm-referenced tests (NRTs) are commercially developed tests that have not been modified to reflect state content standards.

[2] Custom-developed criterion-referenced tests (CRTs) are explicitly designed to measure state content standards.

[3] Augmented or hybrid tests incorporate elements of both NRTs and CRTs. These tests include NRTs that have been augmented or modified to reflect state standards.

NOTE: ES = elementary school, MS = middle school, and HS = high school.

SOURCE: Quality Counts 2007, Cradle to Career, *Education Week*, 2007. (This table was prepared September 2008.)

States requiring testing for initial certification of elementary and secondary teachers, by skills or knowledge assessment and state: 2010 and 2011

State	Assessment for certification, 2010				Assessment for certification, 2011			
	Basic skills exam	Subject-matter exam	Knowledge of teaching exam	Assessment of teaching performance	Basic skills exam	Subject-matter exam	Knowledge of teaching exam	Assessment of teaching performance
1	2	3	4	5	6	7	8	9
Alabama	X	X	X	X	X	X	X	X
Alaska	X				X			
Arizona		X	X			X	X	
Arkansas	X	X	X	X	X	X	X	X
California	X	—		X	X	—		X
Colorado		X				X		
Connecticut	X	X	X	X	X	X	X	X
Delaware	X	X			X	X		
District of Columbia	X	X	—	—	X	X	X	
Florida	X			X	X			X
Georgia	X	X			X	X		
Hawaii	X	X	X	—	X	X	X	—
Idaho		X	X	X		X		X
Illinois	X	X	X		X	X	X	
Indiana	X	X		X	X	X		X
Iowa	—		—	—	—		—	—
Kansas		X	X			X	X	
Kentucky	X	X	X	X	X	X	X	X
Louisiana	X	X	X	X	X	X	X	X
Maine	—	—	—	—	—		—	—
Maryland	X	X	X	X	X	X	X	X
Massachusetts	X	X		X	X	X		X
Michigan	X	X		X	X	X		X
Minnesota	X	X	X		X	X	X	
Mississippi	—	—	—	—	—	—	—	—
Missouri	X	X		X	X	X		X
Montana								
Nebraska	X				X			
Nevada	—	X	—	—	—	X	—	—
New Hampshire	X	X			X	X		
New Jersey	—	—	—	—	—	—	—	—
New Mexico	X	X	X	X	X	X	X	X
New York		X	X			X	X	
North Carolina	—	—	—	—	—	—	—	—
North Dakota		X	—	—		X	—	—
Ohio		X	X	X		X	X	X
Oklahoma	—	—	—	—	—	—	—	—
Oregon	X	X	—	—	X	X		X
Pennsylvania	X	X	X	X	X	X	X	X
Rhode Island			X	X			X	X
South Carolina		X	X			X	X	
South Dakota	X	X	X	X	X	X	X	X
Tennessee	X	X	X		X	X	X	
Texas	—	—	—	—	—	—	—	—
Utah		X		X		X		X
Vermont	X	X			X	X		
Virginia	X	X	X		X	X	X	
Washington	X	X		X	X	X		X
West Virginia	X	X	X	X	X	X	X	X
Wisconsin	X	X			X	X		
Wyoming	—		—	—	—		—	—

—Not available.
X Denotes that the state requires testing. A blank denotes that the state does not require testing.

SOURCE: National Association of State Directors of Teacher Education and Certification, NASDTEC Knowledgebase, retrieved June 23, 2011, from https://www.nasdtec.info/. (This table was prepared June 2011.)

Percentage of schools with various security measures, by school control and selected characteristics: 2007–08

School control and selected characteristic	Total schools		Percent of schools with security measures											
	Number	Percentage distribution	Controlled access to school buildings[1]	Controlled access to school grounds[2]	School uniforms	Strict dress code	Daily metal detector checks[3]	Random metal detector checks	Closed lunch[4]	Random dog sniffs	Random drug sweeps	Daily presence of police or security	Security cameras	Badges required
1	2	3	4	5	6	7	8	9	10	11	12	13	14	15
Public total	90,500 (540)	100.0 (†)	88.8 (0.63)	44.9 (1.12)	16.5 (0.83)	54.0 (0.99)	2.3 (0.31)	5.9 (0.45)	60.8 (1.07)	25.0 (0.68)	14.8 (0.76)	27.2 (0.99)	51.8 (0.94)	7.5 (0.53)
School enrollment														
Under 300	26,400 (910)	29.2 (0.96)	86.0 (1.41)	38.2 (2.05)	15.9 (1.60)	49.0 (2.13)	5.1 (0.84)	6.5 (0.88)	58.8 (2.06)	24.0 (1.72)	19.3 (1.76)	17.6 (1.57)	43.3 (1.82)	4.9 (0.80)
300 to 499	25,900 (970)	28.6 (1.04)	90.6 (1.06)	42.7 (2.23)	16.0 (1.51)	50.9 (2.25)	0.8 (0.23)	3.6 (0.77)	57.2 (2.04)	18.0 (1.44)	10.3 (1.09)	15.5 (1.31)	50.1 (2.19)	3.7 (0.67)
500 to 999	29,100 (870)	32.1 (0.98)	90.5 (1.01)	49.7 (1.92)	18.2 (1.33)	57.2 (1.94)	0.8 ! (0.28)	5.4 (0.84)	61.1 (2.04)	23.5 (1.42)	11.0 (1.07)	30.7 (1.74)	53.8 (1.84)	8.5 (1.19)
1,000 to 1,499	5,400 (350)	6.0 (0.39)	88.5 (2.08)	50.1 (3.79)	16.4 (3.57)	66.6 (3.19)	2.3 ! (0.84)	9.8 (1.94)	75.5 (2.48)	48.7 (3.97)	27.5 (3.20)	66.4 (3.64)	69.5 (3.60)	18.2 (3.08)
1,500 or more	3,700 (240)	4.1 (0.26)	83.7 (2.78)	63.6 (3.16)	11.1 (3.02)	67.5 (3.34)	3.9 ! (1.49)	15.6 (2.39)	75.5 (3.17)	57.4 (3.28)	25.5 (2.91)	92.7 (1.80)	81.8 (3.89)	28.2 (3.28)
Percent of students approved for free or reduced-price school lunch														
School does not participate	3,900 (420)	4.3 (0.46)	70.2 (5.54)	38.9 (4.76)	16.9 (3.97)	43.2 (5.52)	‡	8.2 ! (3.37)	44.0 (5.66)	13.8 (3.02)	20.2 (4.48)	23.4 (3.94)	43.5 (4.86)	10.2 (2.33)
0 to 25 percent	25,000 (920)	27.6 (1.03)	89.7 (1.35)	36.9 (2.02)	4.7 (0.86)	44.7 (2.08)	0.5 ! (0.18)	1.8 (0.35)	60.0 (2.04)	25.0 (1.83)	10.1 (1.12)	25.2 (1.60)	53.1 (2.22)	5.5 (0.78)
26 to 50 percent	24,800 (920)	27.4 (0.98)	90.6 (0.94)	41.1 (1.88)	8.2 (1.00)	53.4 (2.03)	0.7 (0.22)	4.3 (0.65)	63.8 (1.59)	30.3 (1.51)	13.5 (1.11)	26.5 (1.85)	56.8 (2.00)	7.4 (0.80)
51 to 75 percent	19,600 (690)	21.6 (0.73)	89.2 (1.38)	48.7 (2.26)	19.3 (1.80)	57.7 (2.28)	2.7 (0.52)	7.4 (1.06)	61.1 (2.26)	27.7 (1.94)	17.5 (2.05)	26.2 (1.98)	52.6 (2.30)	7.7 (1.03)
76 to 100 percent	17,300 (660)	19.1 (0.74)	89.2 (1.63)	59.0 (2.42)	42.2 (3.04)	66.5 (2.40)	6.1 (1.17)	11.9 (1.65)	61.1 (2.56)	16.6 (1.78)	19.2 (1.91)	33.1 (2.74)	43.6 (2.59)	9.6 (1.57)
School locale														
City	21,600 (730)	23.8 (0.81)	89.4 (1.45)	55.6 (2.31)	36.5 (2.33)	63.2 (2.33)	4.1 (0.76)	9.7 (1.14)	61.3 (2.57)	14.5 (1.50)	13.2 (1.51)	37.1 (1.97)	45.3 (1.96)	11.5 (1.43)
Suburban	25,900 (920)	28.6 (1.01)	89.7 (1.19)	44.9 (2.32)	13.5 (1.33)	50.4 (2.17)	2.2 ! (0.70)	5.3 (0.97)	57.9 (2.06)	25.0 (1.56)	10.5 (1.37)	29.3 (1.76)	55.9 (1.77)	8.9 (0.93)
Town	13,900 (670)	15.3 (0.74)	90.2 (1.35)	41.2 (2.55)	10.0 (1.56)	51.9 (2.43)	2.3 (0.60)	5.3 (1.01)	63.6 (2.48)	30.1 (2.14)	16.2 (1.73)	22.5 (1.86)	53.7 (2.79)	5.0 (1.03)
Rural	29,200 (1,010)	32.2 (1.07)	87.0 (1.13)	38.8 (1.78)	7.4 (0.85)	51.3 (1.87)	1.0 ! (0.31)	3.8 (0.67)	61.6 (1.86)	37.0 (1.48)	19.2 (1.32)	20.2 (1.60)	51.9 (1.78)	4.4 (0.71)
Level[5]														
Elementary	62,300 (580)	68.9 (0.54)	92.1 (0.71)	45.7 (1.61)	17.5 (1.05)	50.0 (1.38)	0.3 ! (0.14)	3.0 (0.48)	57.5 (1.47)	13.2 (0.83)	7.6 (0.84)	16.2 (1.14)	46.1 (1.29)	4.1 (0.57)
Secondary	21,600 (460)	23.8 (0.46)	82.1 (1.42)	43.3 (1.53)	12.1 (1.19)	64.4 (1.87)	5.2 (1.03)	11.9 (1.05)	68.5 (1.68)	54.6 (1.59)	30.5 (1.59)	58.3 (1.93)	68.7 (1.77)	16.8 (1.15)
Combined	6,600 (360)	7.3 (0.40)	79.8 (2.50)	42.6 (3.33)	21.4 (2.51)	57.3 (3.13)	11.3 (1.84)	13.4 (1.80)	66.0 (2.96)	39.1 (2.91)	31.7 (3.22)	29.0 (2.90)	50.1 (2.70)	9.2 (1.95)
Private total	28,000 (330)	100.0 (†)	81.5 (1.15)	42.4 (1.22)	55.4 (1.19)	76.3 (1.08)	0.6 ! (0.19)	1.1 (0.24)	44.0 (1.06)	3.9 (0.43)	8.8 (0.69)	6.4 (0.54)	32.9 (1.21)	2.9 (0.42)
School enrollment														
Under 300	22,800 (390)	81.7 (0.85)	80.6 (1.39)	41.7 (1.40)	51.9 (1.46)	73.7 (1.30)	0.6 ! (0.21)	1.3 (0.28)	41.3 (1.30)	2.5 (0.44)	9.0 (0.83)	4.3 (0.58)	27.9 (1.36)	1.7 (0.44)
300 to 499	3,000 (190)	10.6 (0.70)	88.6 (1.95)	45.7 (3.07)	73.4 (3.13)	85.8 (2.14)	‡	‡ (†)	55.4 (2.90)	6.5 (1.32)	7.5 (1.50)	10.1 (1.70)	49.5 (3.22)	7.8 (1.61)
500 to 999	1,800 (120)	6.3 (0.44)	83.0 (2.44)	43.4 (3.43)	69.4 (3.39)	89.4 (2.29)	#	‡ (†)	59.3 (3.58)	17.1 (2.42)	8.2 (1.96)	17.3 (2.21)	61.0 (3.32)	7.8 (1.90)
1,000 or more	400 (50)	1.4 (0.19)	77.4 (5.07)	52.7 (7.16)	61.2 (6.89)	94.6 (2.34)	#	#	49.9 (7.21)	9.7 (3.78)	13.2 ! (4.95)	50.5 (6.78)	67.1 (5.69)	11.6 ! (4.08)
Percent of students approved for free or reduced-price school lunch														
School does not participate	19,700 (400)	70.3 (1.05)	78.9 (1.43)	41.6 (1.45)	52.2 (1.48)	74.7 (1.34)	0.4 ! (0.14)	0.6 ! (0.20)	41.3 (1.48)	3.8 (0.48)	8.6 (0.80)	6.6 (0.58)	28.8 (1.32)	2.9 (0.52)
0 to 25 percent	4,600 (230)	16.3 (0.81)	89.7 (2.03)	40.5 (3.06)	67.6 (2.83)	85.6 (2.08)	#	‡ (†)	53.2 (3.04)	6.0 (1.42)	6.5 (1.44)	5.1 (1.47)	42.9 (3.21)	3.5 ! (1.17)
26 to 100 percent	3,700 (230)	13.3 (0.84)	85.5 (2.44)	48.8 (3.14)	57.3 (3.35)	72.8 (3.11)	‡	4.7 ! (1.61)	47.0 (3.86)	2.3 ! (1.09)	12.7 (2.11)	7.0 (1.76)	42.1 (3.52)	‡ (†)
Level[5]														
Elementary	16,100 (300)	57.6 (0.81)	84.1 (1.35)	45.6 (1.50)	62.2 (1.68)	75.9 (1.48)	#	‡ (†)	42.0 (1.39)	0.4 ! (0.20)	2.1 (0.42)	4.3 (0.61)	31.4 (1.65)	1.6 (0.38)
Secondary	2,900 (170)	10.5 (0.59)	76.9 (2.83)	34.7 (3.37)	42.8 (3.22)	75.3 (3.36)	‡	‡ (†)	56.7 (3.25)	17.0 (2.32)	26.0 (3.64)	11.8 (2.46)	43.1 (3.64)	6.2 (1.27)
Combined	8,900 (270)	31.9 (0.88)	78.4 (2.11)	39.2 (2.27)	47.2 (2.23)	77.3 (1.72)	‡	2.9 (0.70)	43.5 (2.46)	6.0 (1.00)	15.4 (1.54)	8.3 (1.13)	32.1 (1.99)	4.2 (1.00)

†Not applicable.
#Rounds to zero.
!Interpret data with caution. The coefficient of variation (CV) for this estimate is 30 percent or greater.
‡Reporting standards not met. The coefficient of variation (CV) for this estimate is 50 percent or greater.
[1]Access to buildings is controlled during school hours (e.g., by locked or monitored doors).
[2]Access to grounds is controlled during school hours (e.g., by locked or monitored gates).
[3]All students must pass through a metal detector each day.
[4]All or most students are required to stay on school grounds during lunch.
[5]Elementary schools have grade 6 or below, with no grade higher than 8; secondary schools have no grade lower than 7; and combined schools have grades lower than 7 and higher than 8.

NOTE: Detail may not sum to totals because of rounding. Standard errors appear in parentheses.
SOURCE: U.S. Department of Education, National Center for Education Statistics, Schools and Staffing Survey (SASS), "Public School Principal Questionnaire" and "Private School Principal Questionnaire," 2007–08. (This table was prepared October 2009.)

Number and percentage of public schools reporting crime incidents, and number and rate of incidents, by school characteristics and type of incident: 1999–2000, 2007–08, and 2009–10

Type of crime incident	All public schools, 1999–2000	All public schools, 2007–08	2009–10							
			All public schools	Instruction level of school			Size of enrollment			
				Primary	Middle	High	Less than 300	300 to 499	500 to 999	1,000 or more
1	2	3	4	5	6	7	8	9	10	11
Number of public schools (in thousands)										
All schools	82 (#)	83 (0.4)	83 (0.5)	49 (0.3)	15 (0.1)	12 (0.1)	19 (0.4)	25 (0.2)	30 (0.1)	9 (0.1)
Schools with incident	71 (1.0)	71 (0.8)	70 (1.0)	38 (0.9)	15 (0.1)	12 (0.1)	15 (0.6)	21 (0.5)	26 (0.5)	9 (0.1)
Percent of schools with incident	86.3 (1.23)	85.5 (0.87)	85.0 (1.07)	77.9 (1.69)	96.2 (0.66)	98.3 (0.49)	78.4 (2.84)	83.5 (2.06)	87.0 (1.55)	96.9 (1.10)
Violent incidents[1]	71.4 (1.37)	75.5 (1.09)	73.8 (1.07)	64.4 (1.63)	90.5 (1.10)	90.9 (1.21)	62.8 (3.25)	71.3 (2.34)	76.4 (1.75)	95.4 (1.22)
Serious violent incidents[2]	19.7 (0.98)	17.2 (1.06)	16.4 (0.94)	13.0 (1.42)	18.9 (1.46)	27.6 (1.35)	10.4 (2.11)	15.7 (2.14)	15.9 (1.42)	32.8 (1.61)
Rape or attempted rape[3]	0.7 (0.10)	0.8 (0.17)	0.5 (0.10)	— (†)	1.3! (0.42)	2.0 (0.41)	‡ (†)	‡ (†)	0.6 (0.17)	1.8 (0.43)
Sexual battery other than rape[4]	2.5 (0.33)	2.5 (0.33)	2.3 (0.34)	1.0! (0.38)	3.2 (0.56)	5.1 (0.73)	‡ (†)	4.8 (1.08)	2.5 (0.54)	7.2 (0.96)
Physical attack or fight with weapon[5]	5.2 (0.60)	3.0 (0.33)	3.9 (0.48)	3.0 (0.68)	3.9 (0.75)	7.1 (1.02)	2.3! (1.08)	8.0 (1.51)	3.1 (0.63)	7.2 (1.16)
Threat of attack with weapon[6]	11.1 (0.70)	9.3 (0.77)	7.7 (0.72)	6.8 (1.11)	10.3 (1.04)	10.0 (0.99)	3.8! (1.40)	8.0 (1.40)	8.3 (1.08)	12.8 (1.24)
Robbery[7] with a weapon	0.5! (0.15)	0.5! (0.14)	0.2 (0.05)	— (†)	0.5! (0.20)	1.0 (0.30)	— (†)	0.2! (0.09)	0.2! (0.09)	1.3 (0.37)
Robbery[7] without a weapon	5.3 (0.56)	5.2 (0.56)	4.4 (0.49)	2.7 (0.66)	5.5 (0.74)	10.6 (0.87)	2.9! (1.17)	2.7 (0.69)	4.1 (0.67)	13.7 (1.16)
Physical attack or fight without a weapon	63.7 (1.52)	72.7 (1.07)	70.5 (1.11)	60.3 (1.65)	88.8 (1.13)	88.4 (1.36)	58.1 (3.45)	67.3 (2.59)	74.2 (1.70)	93.6 (1.24)
Threat of attack without weapon	52.2 (1.47)	47.8 (1.19)	46.4 (1.33)	38.0 (1.94)	61.5 (1.73)	61.9 (1.58)	34.3 (3.46)	44.6 (2.51)	47.8 (2.30)	72.5 (1.49)
Theft/larceny[8]	45.6 (1.37)	47.3 (1.30)	44.1 (1.31)	25.7 (1.82)	65.2 (1.48)	82.6 (1.35)	30.7 (3.35)	36.4 (2.52)	46.7 (1.74)	84.9 (1.80)
Other incidents[9]	— (†)	67.4 (1.13)	68.1 (1.12)	57.3 (1.72)	81.9 (1.25)	92.2 (1.10)	55.3 (2.97)	63.3 (2.47)	72.5 (1.80)	94.3 (1.32)
Possess firearm/explosive device[10]	5.5 (0.44)	4.7 (0.38)	4.7 (0.52)	3.5 (0.81)	5.8 (0.79)	9.4 (1.20)	2.5! (1.16)	4.5 (1.11)	4.5 (0.89)	10.5 (1.25)
Possess knife or sharp object	42.6 (1.28)	40.6 (1.10)	39.7 (1.06)	33.5 (1.51)	51.5 (1.94)	55.2 (1.51)	26.4 (2.85)	33.4 (2.11)	45.5 (1.74)	66.3 (1.82)
Distribution, possession, or use of illegal drugs	— (†)	23.2 (0.68)	24.6 (0.57)	3.5 (0.69)	44.7 (1.17)	77.2 (1.51)	11.7 (1.28)	15.0 (1.30)	24.6 (0.97)	78.4 (1.77)
Distribution, possession, or use of alcohol	— (†)	14.9 (0.57)	14.1 (0.50)	2.1 (0.52)	19.7 (1.31)	51.6 (1.60)	6.2 (1.22)	8.7 (1.09)	11.3 (0.82)	55.5 (1.64)
Inappropriate distribution, possession, or use of prescription drugs	— (†)	— (†)	12.1 (0.47)	1.5! (0.48)	18.8 (1.13)	43.0 (1.64)	5.1 (1.10)	5.5 (1.02)	12.4 (0.94)	44.5 (1.60)
Vandalism[11]	51.5 (1.61)	49.3 (1.16)	45.8 (1.12)	37.9 (1.69)	55.5 (1.38)	62.5 (1.86)	33.9 (2.89)	43.7 (2.45)	47.2 (1.93)	72.4 (1.80)
Number of incidents (in thousands)	2,259 (117.0)	2,041 (65.4)	1,877 (50.9)	626 (39.6)	548 (23.6)	590 (19.3)	169 (19.3)	386 (31.8)	704 (40.1)	617 (21.7)
Violent incidents[1]	1,466 (103.7)	1,332 (62.1)	1,184 (44.4)	482 (37.3)	375 (19.3)	264 (12.9)	111 (17.2)	274 (25.1)	488 (35.6)	310 (16.1)
Serious violent incidents[2]	61 (7.0)	58 (6.6)	52 (5.5)	22 (3.8)	14 (2.4)	14 (1.7)	6! (2.1)	14 (3.6)	16 (2.4)	16 (2.1)
Rape or attempted rape[3]	1 (0.1)	1 (0.2)	1 (0.1)	— (†)	# (†)	# (†)	# (†)	# (†)	# (†)	# (†)
Sexual battery other than rape[4]	4 (1.1)	4 (0.6)	4 (0.6)	1! (0.4)	1 (0.2)	1 (0.2)	‡ (†)	# (†)	1 (0.3)	1 (0.3)
Physical attack or fight with weapon[5]	12 (2.5)	14 (3.9)	14 (3.6)	8! (2.9)	2! (0.7)	3 (0.7)	‡ (†)	6! (2.8)	4! (1.2)	1 (0.3)
Threat of attack with weapon[6]	21 (1.9)	20 (2.6)	19 (2.9)	8 (1.9)	8 (1.9)	3 (0.6)	1! (0.3)	6! (1.9)	7 (1.2)	6 (1.6)
Robbery[7] with a weapon	‡ (†)	1! (0.2)	# (0.2)	# (†)	# (†)	# (†)	— (†)	# (†)	# (†)	# (†)
Robbery[7] without a weapon	20 (3.2)	19 (3.1)	14 (1.9)	6! (1.9)	3 (0.6)	6 (0.8)	‡ (†)	2! (0.5)	4 (1.2)	7 (1.1)
Physical attack or fight without a weapon	807 (59.6)	812 (45.7)	725 (27.8)	295 (24.0)	239 (12.7)	157 (10.6)	63 (8.8)	157 (17.0)	314 (23.5)	191 (12.4)
Threat of attack without weapon	599 (52.7)	462 (29.4)	406 (23.0)	165 (21.6)	123 (8.8)	94 (5.4)	42 (10.2)	103 (14.3)	157 (17.1)	103 (7.4)
Theft/larceny[8]	218 (9.2)	269 (9.5)	259 (8.6)	42 (5.7)	69 (4.8)	125 (5.1)	21 (3.2)	41 (6.3)	82 (5.5)	115 (4.4)
Other incidents[9]	— (†)	440 (11.2)	435 (11.1)	102 (6.4)	104 (4.4)	200 (7.7)	37 (3.3)	71 (5.3)	135 (6.7)	192 (8.6)
Possess firearm/explosive device[10]	9 (2.2)	5 (0.5)	5 (0.6)	2 (0.4)	1 (0.3)	2 (0.2)	1! (0.2)	1 (0.3)	2 (0.3)	1 (0.1)
Possess knife or sharp object	86 (4.0)	77 (2.4)	72 (2.6)	29 (1.7)	18 (0.9)	22 (1.5)	7 (0.8)	15 (1.1)	28 (1.7)	22 (1.6)
Distribution, possession, or use of illegal drugs	— (†)	107 (4.1)	116 (4.7)	3 (0.8)	25 (1.6)	79 (3.6)	6 (1.1)	9 (1.4)	27 (1.7)	73 (3.7)
Distribution, possession, or use of alcohol	— (†)	38 (1.4)	41 (1.8)	1 (0.3)	7 (0.6)	29 (1.5)	2 (0.5)	4 (0.5)	11 (1.2)	24 (1.5)
Inappropriate distribution, possession, or use of prescription drugs	— (†)	— (†)	29 (1.9)	1! (0.3)	6 (0.6)	19 (1.5)	2! (0.5)	3 (0.5)	9 (0.8)	16 (1.7)
Vandalism[11]	211 (13.6)	212 (8.8)	172 (7.3)	66 (5.8)	46 (3.1)	49 (4.5)	19 (2.4)	39 (4.0)	58 (4.4)	56 (5.0)

See notes at end of table.

Number and percentage of public schools reporting crime incidents, and number and rate of incidents, by school characteristics and type of incident: 1999–2000, 2007–08, and 2009–10—Continued

Type of crime incident	All public schools, 1999–2000	All public schools, 2007–08	2009–10								
			All public schools	Instruction level of school			Size of enrollment			
				Primary	Middle	High	Less than 300	300 to 499	500 to 999	1,000 or more
1	2	3	4	5	6	7	8	9	10	11
Number of incidents per 100,000 students	4,849 (252.4)	4,270 (134.1)	3,965 (103.7)	2,766 (172.3)	5,840 (249.6)	4,773 (149.9)	4,135 (452.2)	3,731 (312.0)	3,610 (199.3)	4,610 (168.1)
Violent incidents[1]	3,147 (223.8)	2,788 (127.9)	2,500 (90.9)	2,131 (163.6)	3,997 (203.9)	2,141 (105.3)	2,718 (408.2)	2,650 (244.2)	2,501 (177.7)	2,316 (119.2)
Serious violent incidents[2]	130 (15.2)	122 (13.8)	111 (11.5)	97 (16.8)	145 (25.2)	110 (13.7)	149 ! (50.8)	138 (34.6)	84 (12.3)	118 (15.0)
Rape or attempted rape[3]	1 (0.2)	2 (0.4)	1 (0.3)	— (†)	3 ! (1.0)	3 (0.6)	‡ (†)	# (†)	2 (0.5)	2 (0.4)
Sexual battery other than rape[4]	9 (2.4)	8 (1.3)	8 (1.3)	4 ! (2.0)	10 (2.4)	11 (1.8)	‡ (†)	‡ (†)	8 (1.7)	10 (1.9)
Physical attack or fight[5] with weapon[6]	26 (5.4)	29 (8.2)	30 (7.5)	34 ! (13.0)	19 ! (7.4)	23 (5.5)	‡ (†)	62 ! (27.3)	18 ! (5.9)	10 (2.1)
Threat of attack with weapon[6]	45 (4.1)	42 (5.4)	41 (6.1)	34 (8.4)	81 (20.4)	26 (4.8)	20 ! (7.1)	56 ! (18.7)	34 (6.2)	44 (12.1)
Robbery[7] with a weapon[6]	‡ (†)	1 ! (0.5)	1 ! (0.3)	— (†)	‡ (†)	‡ (†)	— (†)	‡ (†)	‡ (†)	1 ! (0.4)
Robbery[7] without a weapon	43 (6.8)	39 (6.6)	30 (4.1)	25 ! (8.2)	31 (6.2)	45 (6.5)	‡ (†)	15 ! (4.9)	22 (6.2)	51 (8.0)
Physical attack or fight without a weapon	1,732 (128.8)	1,699 (93.8)	1,532 (57.9)	1,305 (106.9)	2,545 (132.7)	1,271 (85.0)	1,537 (208.3)	1,514 (162.2)	1,612 (117.4)	1,428 (91.7)
Threat of attack without weapon	1,285 (113.2)	967 (61.5)	857 (47.4)	730 (94.0)	1,307 (94.3)	760 (45.4)	1,032 (244.6)	999 (140.6)	805 (86.8)	771 (56.4)
Theft/larceny[8]	468 (20.2)	563 (20.1)	546 (18.5)	185 (24.8)	736 (50.7)	1,012 (43.5)	522 (73.4)	395 (61.9)	419 (28.5)	855 (36.3)
Other incidents[9]	— (†)	920 (23.5)	918 (23.2)	450 (27.9)	1,108 (47.1)	1,620 (60.8)	894 (87.1)	687 (53.0)	690 (33.6)	1,438 (66.9)
Possess firearm/explosive device[10]	18 (4.8)	11 (1.0)	11 (1.2)	8 (1.9)	15 (2.8)	13 (1.9)	13 ! (5.7)	14 (3.3)	9 (1.8)	9 (1.1)
Possess knife or sharp object	184 (8.7)	161 (4.7)	153 (5.2)	126 (7.3)	193 (9.8)	175 (12.5)	182 (19.1)	145 (10.9)	145 (8.6)	161 (12.1)
Distribution, possession, or use of illegal drugs	— (†)	225 (8.3)	245 (9.8)	14 (3.4)	262 (17.4)	637 (28.9)	151 (29.6)	91 (13.5)	139 (9.0)	547 (28.8)
Distribution, possession, or use of alcohol	— (†)	79 (2.9)	86 (3.9)	5 (1.3)	77 (6.9)	238 (13.7)	57 (12.6)	34 (4.9)	55 (6.1)	180 (12.0)
Inappropriate distribution, possession, or use of prescription drugs	— (†)	— (†)	62 (4.0)	4 ! (1.3)	68 (6.5)	157 (12.4)	39 ! (13.8)	25 (4.6)	45 (4.2)	122 (12.1)
Vandalism[11]	453 (28.6)	444 (19.0)	362 (15.3)	293 (25.6)	492 (32.4)	400 (35.4)	453 (61.2)	378 (38.9)	296 (22.4)	419 (38.5)

See notes at end of table.

Number and percentage of public schools reporting crime incidents, and number and rate of incidents, by school characteristics and type of incident: 1999–2000, 2007–08, and 2009–10—Continued

2009–10

Type of crime incident	Urbanicity				Combined percent Black, Hispanic, Asian/Pacific Islander, and American Indian/Alaska Native enrollment				Percent of students eligible for free/reduced-price lunch		
	City	Suburban	Town	Rural	Less than 5	5 to less than 20	20 to less than 50	50 or more	0 to 25	26 to 50	51 or more
1	12	13	14	15	16	17	18	19	20	21	22
Number of public schools (in thousands)											
All schools	22 (0.2)	24 (0.2)	12 (0.1)	25 (0.3)	12 (1.0)	21 (1.1)	20 (0.7)	30 (1.3)	14 (0.7)	26 (1.2)	43 (1.1)
Schools with incident	19 (0.4)	20 (0.6)	11 (0.3)	21 (0.5)	10 (0.8)	17 (1.0)	17 (0.7)	27 (1.4)	10 (0.7)	23 (1.1)	38 (1.2)
Percent of schools with incident	86.9 (1.71)	84.3 (2.07)	89.4 (2.63)	82.1 (2.04)	82.1 (3.23)	79.9 (2.44)	85.1 (1.89)	89.7 (1.55)	73.0 (3.28)	85.8 (1.78)	88.4 (1.30)
Violent incidents[1]	74.9 (2.12)	73.5 (2.21)	80.3 (3.14)	70.2 (1.91)	69.6 (3.33)	67.9 (2.82)	75.9 (2.14)	78.2 (1.75)	61.7 (3.40)	74.6 (2.04)	77.2 (1.66)
Serious violent incidents[2]	21.7 (2.12)	15.5 (1.80)	15.6 (2.33)	13.2 (1.51)	12.6 (2.52)	9.9 (1.29)	18.6 (1.58)	21.1 (1.82)	10.5 (1.41)	15.4 (1.65)	18.9 (1.50)
Rape or attempted rape[3]	0.7 ! (0.26)	0.6 ! (0.25)	0.6 ! (0.28)	0.3 ! (0.13)	‡ (†)	0.5 ! (0.17)	0.5 ! (0.17)	0.7 ! (0.22)	0.4 ! (0.20)	0.6 (0.17)	0.5 (0.15)
Sexual battery other than rape[4]	3.2 (0.76)	1.6 (0.32)	2.7 ! (0.82)	1.9 ! (0.68)	2.6 ! (1.21)	1.1 (0.26)	2.6 (0.71)	2.7 (0.57)	1.4 (0.33)	2.7 (0.72)	2.3 (0.44)
Physical attack or fight with weapon[5]	5.5 (1.18)	4.6 (1.00)	4.1 ! (1.28)	1.8 (0.48)	‡ (†)	4.8 (0.57)	4.8 (1.04)	5.3 (0.95)	2.3 ! (0.77)	3.6 (0.69)	4.6 (0.73)
Threat of attack with weapon[6]	10.2 (1.69)	7.7 (1.15)	6.3 (1.57)	6.2 (1.13)	5.9 (1.49)	4.8 (0.96)	8.6 (1.11)	9.8 (1.42)	4.7 (1.06)	5.9 (0.72)	9.7 (1.32)
Robbery[7] with a weapon[6]	0.6 ! (0.19)	0.2 ! (0.10)	‡ (†)	— (†)	— (†)	‡ (†)	0.3 ! (0.12)	0.4 ! (0.13)	‡ (†)	0.2 ! (0.09)	0.3 ! (0.09)
Robbery[7] without a weapon	6.5 (0.84)	3.4 (0.55)	3.0 (1.05)	4.3 (0.97)	‡ (†)	2.3 (0.73)	4.4 (0.80)	7.0 (0.90)	3.4 (0.74)	4.5 (0.86)	4.7 (0.74)
Physical attack or fight without a weapon	71.7 (2.02)	69.9 (2.11)	76.8 (2.93)	67.2 (2.26)	65.3 (3.73)	63.6 (2.67)	72.2 (2.32)	76.3 (1.78)	57.9 (3.19)	70.4 (2.30)	74.6 (1.63)
Threat of attack without weapon	48.6 (2.43)	46.3 (2.44)	56.2 (3.86)	40.0 (2.15)	38.6 (3.19)	43.6 (3.12)	48.2 (2.49)	50.3 (2.10)	34.7 (2.84)	47.7 (2.21)	49.4 (1.97)
Theft/larceny[8]	47.6 (2.70)	43.1 (1.97)	46.2 (3.22)	41.1 (2.51)	40.8 (3.33)	38.3 (2.37)	46.2 (2.45)	48.0 (2.35)	38.0 (2.26)	48.8 (2.50)	43.1 (1.98)
Other incidents[9]	73.5 (2.39)	66.1 (2.23)	74.1 (2.97)	62.6 (2.62)	59.0 (3.65)	61.2 (2.19)	69.7 (2.23)	75.5 (2.33)	54.8 (3.31)	67.3 (2.10)	72.9 (1.79)
Possess firearm/explosive device[10]	6.0 (0.99)	4.9 (0.89)	3.8 ! (1.37)	3.8 (1.01)	4.3 ! (1.42)	2.1 (0.51)	3.6 (0.67)	7.4 (1.02)	3.1 (0.64)	3.3 (0.58)	6.0 (0.93)
Possess knife or sharp object	41.1 (2.36)	38.7 (1.75)	49.8 (3.16)	34.7 (2.13)	25.6 (3.01)	34.6 (2.00)	44.2 (2.29)	45.8 (1.99)	26.7 (2.20)	38.0 (1.96)	44.8 (1.72)
Distribution, possession, or use of illegal drugs	27.8 (1.22)	22.4 (0.83)	25.5 (1.42)	23.4 (1.17)	21.0 (1.82)	21.8 (1.37)	26.4 (1.35)	26.6 (1.39)	20.3 (1.39)	27.9 (1.67)	23.8 (0.96)
Distribution, possession, or use of alcohol	14.9 (1.14)	15.5 (0.92)	12.8 (1.17)	12.7 (1.03)	11.8 (1.61)	12.2 (0.94)	15.4 (1.32)	15.5 (0.92)	14.7 (1.01)	16.5 (1.21)	12.5 (0.76)
Inappropriate distribution, possession, or use of prescription drugs	10.3 (0.92)	12.1 (0.79)	12.3 (1.12)	13.5 (1.18)	12.9 (1.55)	13.5 (1.01)	14.5 (1.24)	9.2 (0.89)	13.1 (1.20)	15.2 (0.98)	9.8 (0.76)
Vandalism[11]	56.9 (2.11)	47.2 (2.44)	44.7 (3.54)	35.7 (2.25)	38.7 (3.64)	38.6 (2.29)	44.7 (1.96)	54.4 (2.43)	38.5 (2.96)	47.0 (2.27)	47.5 (1.92)
Number of incidents (in thousands)	642 (32.5)	585 (37.5)	255 (23.1)	395 (19.5)	165 (24.3)	326 (20.0)	481 (24.2)	905 (51.8)	211 (15.1)	560 (25.6)	1,106 (51.1)
Violent incidents[1]	396 (27.4)	371 (33.0)	166 (21.2)	250 (15.9)	108 (20.3)	193 (15.5)	294 (21.0)	589 (43.7)	110 (10.6)	322 (20.5)	752 (43.2)
Serious violent incidents[2]	17 (2.8)	16 (3.1)	6 (1.4)	13 (2.9)	5 ! (2.1)	7 (1.5)	15 (3.0)	25 (4.4)	6 (1.4)	13 (2.0)	33 (5.4)
Rape or attempted rape[3]	# (†)	# (†)	# (†)	# (†)	‡ (†)	# (†)	# (†)	# (†)	# (†)	1 ! (0.5)	# (†)
Sexual battery other than rape[4]	1 (0.4)	1 (0.2)	# (†)	1 ! (0.4)	‡ (†)	# (†)	1 (0.2)	2 (0.4)	# (†)	3 (0.9)	2 (0.4)
Physical attack or fight with weapon[5]	3 ! (1.0)	5 ! (2.1)	3 ! (1.0)	‡ (†)	‡ (†)	1 ! (0.3)	‡ (†)	6 (1.6)	1 ! (0.3)	5 (1.3)	10 ! (3.6)
Threat of attack with weapon[6]	7 (1.8)	7 (1.5)	2 ! (1.1)	3 (0.9)	2 ! (0.8)	3 (0.8)	5 (1.2)	9 (2.4)	2 ! (0.7)	4 (1.2)	12 (2.7)
Robbery[7] with a weapon[6]	# (†)	# (†)	# (†)	— (†)	— (†)	‡ (†)	# (†)	# (†)	# (†)	# (†)	# (†)
Robbery[7] without a weapon	6 (0.9)	3 (0.7)	1 ! (0.3)	5 ! (1.6)	‡ (†)	2 ! (1.1)	4 (1.1)	8 (1.3)	3 ! (0.9)	4 (1.2)	8 (1.4)
Physical attack or fight without a weapon	249 (19.7)	232 (17.9)	93 (15.1)	152 (10.7)	68 (15.4)	110 (8.0)	181 (15.7)	367 (24.1)	68 (5.9)	194 (14.3)	464 (27.5)
Threat of attack without weapon	130 (10.7)	123 (17.0)	67 (9.4)	86 (7.1)	35 (5.8)	77 (11.0)	98 (8.3)	197 (22.0)	36 (4.6)	115 (11.7)	255 (20.8)
Theft/larceny[8]	85 (7.0)	81 (4.0)	33 (3.3)	59 (4.6)	23 (2.4)	53 (4.3)	74 (5.4)	108 (8.1)	41 (3.3)	96 (5.7)	121 (8.4)
Other incidents[9]	160 (9.2)	133 (6.4)	55 (4.0)	86 (4.5)	34 (3.8)	80 (5.0)	113 (5.6)	208 (10.1)	60 (4.1)	142 (7.2)	233 (11.7)
Possess firearm/explosive device[10]	2 (0.3)	2 (0.3)	1 ! (0.2)	1 ! (0.3)	1 ! (0.9)	1 (0.1)	1 (0.2)	3 (0.5)	1 (0.1)	1 (0.2)	3 (0.5)
Possess knife or sharp object	21 (1.3)	22 (1.9)	12 (0.9)	17 (1.3)	6 (0.9)	14 (1.0)	20 (1.2)	33 (2.4)	7 (0.6)	22 (1.3)	44 (4.4)
Distribution, possession, or use of illegal drugs	44 (4.0)	36 (2.0)	15 (1.5)	20 (1.5)	8 (1.1)	20 (1.6)	31 (2.1)	56 (4.0)	17 (1.4)	42 (2.6)	56 (4.4)
Distribution, possession, or use of alcohol	14 (1.3)	14 (1.1)	5 (0.8)	8 (0.9)	3 (0.5)	10 (1.2)	12 (1.1)	16 (1.4)	9 (0.9)	16 (1.3)	15 (1.3)
Inappropriate distribution, possession, or use of prescription drugs	7 (0.9)	10 (1.2)	5 (0.9)	8 (0.9)	4 (1.0)	9 (1.2)	9 (1.1)	8 (0.9)	5 (0.6)	13 (1.5)	11 (1.1)
Vandalism[11]	72 (5.7)	49 (3.6)	18 (1.8)	32 (3.5)	13 (1.7)	27 (2.1)	41 (3.0)	91 (6.6)	21 (2.6)	47 (3.4)	103 (6.9)

See notes at end of table.

Number and percentage of public schools reporting crime incidents, and number and rate of incidents, by school characteristics and type of incident: 1999–2000, 2007–08, and 2009–10—Continued

	2009–10										
	Urbanicity				Combined percent Black, Hispanic, Asian/Pacific Islander, and American Indian/Alaska Native enrollment				Percent of students eligible for free/reduced-price lunch		
Type of crime incident	City	Suburban	Town	Rural	Less than 5	5 to less than 20	20 to less than 50	50 or more	0 to 25	26 to 50	51 or more
1	12	13	14	15	16	17	18	19	20	21	22
Number of incidents per 100,000 students[1]	4,672 (250.7)	3,527 (210.5)	4,320 (350.6)	3,554 (184.8)	3,551 (391.8)	2,910 (140.2)	3,777 (203.7)	4,825 (222.7)	2,220 (131.3)	3,613 (149.4)	4,950 (200.9)
Violent incidents[1]	2,885 (210.8)	2,236 (192.4)	2,820 (335.6)	2,250 (149.0)	2,329 (362.2)	1,721 (118.6)	2,306 (176.0)	3,140 (196.2)	1,153 (93.1)	2,081 (127.4)	3,364 (177.9)
Serious violent incidents[2]	126 (21.3)	98 (18.4)	107 (23.2)	113 (26.4)	117 ! (44.0)	58 (12.7)	119 (23.2)	135 (22.6)	62 (14.3)	86 (13.2)	149 (24.4)
Rape or attempted rape[3]	1 ! (0.5)	1 ! (0.5)	2 ! (0.9)	1 ! (0.3)	‡ (†)	1 ! (0.5)	1 ! (0.3)	2 ! (0.5)	1 ! (0.4)	1 ! (0.3)	2 (0.5)
Sexual battery other than rape[4]	11 (2.7)	4 (1.2)	8 (2.5)	8 ! (3.5)	‡ (†)	3 (0.8)	7 (1.7)	10 (2.3)	3 (0.8)	8 (2.9)	9 (1.8)
Physical attack or fight[5] with weapon[6]	22 ! (7.5)	32 ! (12.7)	43 ! (16.7)	‡ (†)	47 ! (16.6)	7 ! (2.6)	‡ (†)	32 (8.5)	9 ! (3.1)	21 (6.1)	46 ! (16.0)
Threat of attack with weapon[6]	49 (13.2)	40 (9.2)	38 ! (17.9)	31 (7.6)	‡ (†)	27 (7.4)	38 (9.4)	49 (12.5)	22 ! (7.7)	30 (8.3)	56 (12.3)
Robbery[7] with a weapon[6]	2 ! (1.2)	# (†)	# (†)	— (†)	— (†)	# (†)	# (†)	2 ! (0.9)	# (†)	# (†)	2 ! (0.7)
Robbery[7] without a weapon[6]	40 (6.6)	19 (4.3)	15 ! (4.6)	43 ! (14.3)	‡ (†)	20 ! (9.7)	33 (8.6)	41 (6.9)	28 ! (9.6)	25 (7.6)	35 (6.3)
Physical attack or fight without a weapon	1,814 (148.1)	1,398 (104.3)	1,571 (242.2)	1,364 (100.3)	1,459 (289.4)	980 (62.5)	1,420 (132.1)	1,956 (119.8)	713 (49.9)	1,251 (89.8)	2,076 (117.2)
Threat of attack without weapon	945 (81.4)	741 (100.8)	1,142 (154.3)	773 (64.6)	753 (101.6)	683 (93.3)	767 (66.8)	1,049 (100.0)	378 (44.0)	744 (73.4)	1,139 (86.5)
Theft/larceny[8]	622 (53.0)	488 (21.6)	565 (52.2)	528 (40.7)	487 (42.0)	476 (36.4)	584 (41.8)	577 (40.8)	436 (34.0)	619 (37.3)	542 (36.2)
Other incidents[9]	1,166 (62.6)	803 (32.2)	935 (65.7)	776 (42.2)	735 (55.8)	712 (36.8)	887 (42.0)	1,108 (52.4)	631 (41.1)	914 (37.1)	1,044 (46.9)
Possess firearm/explosive device[10]	13 (2.2)	10 (1.8)	10 ! (3.5)	9 (2.4)	11 ! (3.5)	5 (1.3)	8 (1.4)	16 (2.3)	6 (1.1)	7 (1.2)	15 (2.3)
Possess knife or sharp object	156 (9.7)	131 (10.9)	208 (15.1)	151 (10.1)	125 (15.9)	122 (7.4)	154 (9.0)	177 (11.7)	72 (5.4)	140 (6.6)	196 (11.2)
Distribution, possession, or use of illegal drugs	321 (27.1)	220 (10.4)	250 (25.6)	184 (13.5)	177 (16.8)	181 (13.4)	246 (15.9)	299 (22.9)	183 (13.8)	273 (15.8)	251 (18.4)
Distribution, possession, or use of alcohol	100 (9.9)	85 (6.2)	82 (14.2)	72 (8.0)	66 (9.6)	86 (10.5)	91 (8.6)	87 (7.6)	95 (10.6)	105 (8.6)	69 (5.7)
Inappropriate distribution, possession, or use of prescription drugs	48 (6.4)	60 (7.2)	84 (15.3)	70 (8.3)	87 (19.9)	78 (10.2)	68 (9.1)	42 (4.7)	55 (6.2)	83 (9.3)	50 (4.8)
Vandalism[11]	527 (40.4)	297 (20.5)	301 (30.3)	289 (32.3)	269 (30.8)	240 (15.9)	320 (23.0)	487 (34.1)	221 (27.0)	305 (18.2)	462 (29.6)

—Not available.
†Not applicable.
#Rounds to zero.
!Interpret data with caution. The coefficient of variation (CV) for this estimate is 30 percent or greater.
‡Reporting standards not met. The coefficient of variation (CV) for this estimate is 50 percent or greater.
[1]Violent incidents include serious violent incidents (i.e., rape or attempted rape, sexual battery other than rape, physical attack or fight with a weapon, and robbery with or without a weapon) plus physical attack or fight without a weapon and threat of physical attack without a weapon.
[2]Serious violent incidents include rape or attempted rape, sexual battery other than rape, physical attack or fight with a weapon, and robbery with or without a weapon.
[3]Rape was defined for respondents as "forced sexual intercourse (vaginal, anal, or oral penetration). This includes penetration from a foreign object. Both male and female students can be victims of rape."
[4]Sexual battery was defined for respondents as an "incident that includes threatened rape, fondling, indecent liberties, child molestation, or sodomy. Both male and female students can be victims of sexual battery. Classification of these incidents should take into consideration the age and developmentally appropriate behavior of the offender(s)."
[5]Physical attack or fight was defined for respondents as an "actual and intentional touching or striking of another person against his or her will, or the intentional causing of bodily harm to an individual."
[6]Weapon was defined for respondents as "any instrument or object used with the intent to threaten, injure, or kill. Includes look-alikes if they are used to threaten others."
[7]Robbery was defined for respondents as "the taking or attempting to take anything of value that is owned by another person or organization, under confrontational circumstances by force or threat of force or violence and/or by putting the victim in fear. A key difference between robbery and theft/larceny is that robbery involves a threat or battery."

[8]Theft/larceny (taking things over $10 without personal confrontation) was defined for respondents as "the unlawful taking of another person's property without personal confrontation, threat, violence, or bodily harm. Included are pocket picking, stealing purse or backpack (if left unattended or no force was used to take it from owner), theft from a building, theft from a motor vehicle or motor vehicle parts or accessories, theft of bicycles, theft from vending machines, and all other types of thefts."
[9]Other incidents include possession of a firearm or explosive device; possession of a knife or sharp object; distribution, possession, or use of illegal drugs or alcohol; inappropriate distribution, possession, or use of prescription drugs; and vandalism.
[10]Firearm/explosive device was defined as "any weapon that is designed to (or may readily be converted to) expel a projectile by the action of an explosive. This includes guns, bombs, grenades, mines, rockets, missiles, pipe bombs, or similar devices designed to explode and capable of causing bodily harm or property damage."
[11]Vandalism was defined for respondents as "the willful damage or destruction of school property including bombing, arson, graffiti, and other acts that cause property damage. Includes damage caused by computer hacking."
NOTE: Either the school principal or the person most knowledgeable about discipline issues at school completed the questionnaire. Includes incidents happening in school buildings, on school grounds, on school buses, and at places that are holding school-sponsored events or activities. Covers times during normal school hours or when school activities/events were in session. Primary schools are defined as schools in which the lowest grade is not higher than grade 3 and the highest grade is not higher than grade 8. Middle schools are defined as schools in which the lowest grade is not lower than grade 4 and the highest grade is not higher than grade 9. High schools are defined as schools in which the lowest grade is not lower than grade 9 and the highest grade is not higher than grade 12. All public schools also includes schools with other combinations of grades (including K–12 schools), which are not shown separately. Detail may not sum to totals because of rounding. Standard errors appear in parentheses.
SOURCE: U.S. Department of Education, National Center for Education Statistics, School Survey on Crime and Safety (SSOCS), 2000, 2008, and 2010. (This table was prepared August 2011.)

Percentage of students suspended and expelled from public elementary and secondary schools, by sex, race/ethnicity, and state: 2006

Standard errors appear in parentheses.

State	Percent suspended[1] Total	Male	Female	White	Black	Hispanic	Asian/Pacific Islander	American Indian/Alaska Native	Percent expelled[2] Total	Male	Female	White	Black	Hispanic	Asian/Pacific Islander	American Indian/Alaska Native
(col)	2	3	4	5	6	7	8	9	10	11	12	13	14	15	16	17
United States	**6.9 (0.04)**	**9.1 (0.06)**	**4.5 (0.03)**	**4.8 (0.04)**	**15.0 (0.14)**	**6.8 (0.07)**	**2.7 (0.04)**	**7.9 (0.49)**	**0.31 (0.003)**	**0.14 (0.004)**	**0.11 (0.002)**	**0.21 (0.002)**	**0.47 (0.011)**	**0.22 (0.004)**	**0.07 (0.002)**	**0.26 (0.013)**
Alabama	10.1 (0.11)	13.3 (0.15)	6.8 (†)	5.8 (0.10)	18.3 (0.32)	4.3 (0.10)	3.2 (0.14)	4.8 (0.49)	0.24 (0.003)	0.33 (0.006)	0.18 (0.006)	0.09 (0.003)	0.33 (0.009)	0.16 (0.006)	0.13 (0.001)	0.01 (0.001)
Alaska	5.9 (0.35)	8.0 (0.47)	3.6 (0.21)	4.6 (0.13)	10.0 (0.10)	5.9 (0.29)	4.6 (0.50)	8.2 (1.18)	0.20 (0.005)	0.07 (0.007)	0.13 (0.006)	0.13 (0.004)	# (0.003)	0.16 (0.006)	# (0.011)	0.10 (0.009)
Arizona	5.9 (0.14)	8.4 (0.19)	3.3 (0.10)	4.5 (0.10)	11.8 (0.10)	6.4 (0.14)	2.5 (0.05)	10.0 (2.19)	0.11 (0.004)	0.03 (0.012)	0.03 (0.001)	0.12 (0.008)	0.45 (0.006)	0.08 (0.004)	0.07 (0.031)	0.08 (0.015)
Arkansas	7.3 (0.30)	10.2 (0.43)	4.3 (0.17)	5.0 (0.28)	15.9 (0.96)	4.9 (0.48)	3.5 (0.35)	4.7 (0.63)	0.15 (0.004)	0.06 (0.012)	0.06 (0.008)	0.14 (0.016)	0.14 (0.016)	0.09 (0.025)	0.03 (0.006)	0.03 (0.002)
California	7.5 (0.18)	10.5 (0.25)	4.4 (0.12)	6.0 (0.18)	17.1 (0.82)	7.9 (0.22)	3.3 (0.13)	12.2 (2.33)	0.48 (0.010)	0.31 (0.015)	0.28 (0.005)	0.61 (0.013)	0.30 (0.030)	0.32 (0.013)	0.11 (0.006)	0.46 (0.068)
Colorado	6.0 (0.09)	8.3 (0.13)	3.7 (0.06)	4.5 (0.09)	13.2 (0.05)	8.1 (0.14)	3.2 (0.03)	8.7 (0.89)	0.43 (0.026)	0.43 (0.012)	0.20 (0.007)	0.56 (0.005)	0.40 (0.005)	0.40 (0.022)	0.12 (0.003)	0.60 (0.138)
Connecticut	6.8 (0.52)	8.9 (0.65)	4.7 (0.39)	4.0 (0.37)	17.2 (2.39)	11.4 (1.39)	2.4 (0.22)	5.2 (0.95)	0.36 (0.026)	0.14 (0.034)	0.14 (0.022)	0.66 (0.016)	0.45 (0.126)	0.79 (0.079)	0.10 (0.017)	0.15 (0.069)
Delaware[3]	10.9 (†)	13.8 (†)	7.9 (†)	6.4 (†)	20.1 (†)	9.2 (†)	3.3 (†)	5.5 (†)	0.30 (†)	0.10 (†)	0.10 (†)	0.32 (†)	0.30 (†)	0.06 (†)	0.06 (†)	0.00 (†)
District of Columbia[3]	0.4 (0.14)	0.3 (0.17)	0.3 (0.11)	0.2 (†)	0.4 (0.34)	0.2 (†)	0.2 (†)	0.0 (†)	0.25 (†)	0.20 (†)	0.03 (†)	0.25 (†)	0.25 (†)	0.17 (†)	0.01 (†)	0.00 (0.012)
Florida	10.5 (0.14)	13.4 (0.17)	7.3 (0.11)	7.9 (0.16)	19.3 (0.34)	7.7 (0.08)	2.9 (0.03)	7.2 (0.59)	0.06 (0.003)	0.02 (0.004)	0.04 (0.001)	0.06 (0.003)	0.06 (0.005)	0.02 (0.001)	0.01 (#)	0.06 (0.068)
Georgia	8.8 (0.23)	11.4 (0.29)	6.1 (0.16)	4.8 (0.21)	15.0 (0.36)	5.4 (0.27)	2.8 (0.07)	3.7 (0.21)	0.33 (0.011)	0.12 (0.017)	0.18 (0.006)	0.32 (0.013)	# (0.015)	0.11 (0.011)	0.04 (0.005)	0.08 (0.035)
Hawaii[3]	5.5 (0.15)	7.2 (0.26)	3.6 (0.16)	4.9 (0.22)	7.0 (0.35)	5.7 (0.39)	5.5 (0.28)	6.0 (2.90)	0.00 (#)	0.00 (#)	0.00 (#)	0.00 (#)	# (#)	0.00 (0.018)	0.00 (#)	0.00 (#)
Idaho[3]	3.6 (0.15)	5.3 (0.26)	1.7 (0.10)	3.3 (0.19)	3.5 (0.21)	5.1 (0.19)	1.6 (0.07)	8.6 (2.41)	0.14 (0.005)	0.00 (0.008)	0.07 (0.004)	0.32 (0.005)	0.20 (0.005)	0.20 (0.004)	0.03 (0.005)	0.37 (0.111)
Illinois	6.4 (0.15)	8.4 (0.20)	4.4 (0.10)	3.8 (0.17)	14.5 (0.53)	6.0 (0.19)	2.6 (0.08)	2.9 (0.40)	0.20 (0.007)	0.07 (0.008)	0.03 (0.006)	0.32 (0.011)	0.11 (0.011)	0.11 (0.004)	0.03 (0.005)	0.07 (0.008)
Indiana	7.4 (0.28)	9.9 (0.37)	4.7 (0.20)	6.0 (0.27)	17.3 (1.18)	7.4 (0.87)	1.8 (0.24)	6.1 (0.70)	0.85 (0.039)	0.40 (0.053)	0.54 (0.028)	1.24 (0.039)	1.11 (0.111)	0.70 (0.077)	0.19 (0.038)	0.60 (0.168)
Iowa	3.0 (0.11)	4.0 (0.14)	1.9 (0.08)	2.4 (0.11)	11.4 (0.31)	3.2 (0.27)	1.6 (0.18)	5.2 (0.25)	0.07 (0.008)	0.01 (0.013)	0.04 (0.004)	0.07 (0.008)	0.12 (0.012)	0.06 (0.022)	0.12 (0.001)	0.09 (0.090)
Kansas	5.1 (0.18)	6.9 (0.26)	3.1 (0.11)	3.8 (0.20)	13.3 (0.27)	6.6 (0.22)	2.9 (0.10)	5.8 (0.59)	0.25 (0.014)	0.10 (0.015)	0.12 (0.014)	0.68 (0.017)	0.19 (0.019)	0.19 (0.011)	0.12 (0.013)	0.04 (#)
Kentucky	6.6 (0.36)	8.7 (0.48)	4.3 (0.24)	5.8 (0.35)	13.3 (1.27)	4.0 (0.33)	1.5 (0.19)	3.8 (0.94)	0.11 (0.017)	0.52 (0.021)	0.07 (0.021)	1.42 (0.012)	# (#)	# (#)	0.03 (0.013)	0.12 (0.021)
Louisiana	10.3 (0.41)	13.2 (0.51)	7.3 (0.31)	7.1 (0.56)	14.6 (0.48)	4.7 (0.16)	2.6 (0.14)	6.8 (0.24)	1.23 (0.037)	0.55 (0.054)	0.53 (0.021)	0.32 (0.012)	0.56 (0.056)	0.47 (0.020)	0.17 (0.011)	0.14 (0.070)
Maine	4.6 (0.28)	6.6 (0.41)	2.4 (0.15)	4.5 (0.28)	9.0 (0.38)	5.7 (1.11)	2.9 (0.18)	6.4 (1.13)	0.13 (0.012)	0.04 (0.015)	0.09 (0.011)	0.09 (0.012)	0.22 (0.022)	0.05 (0.002)	0.05 (0.038)	0.09 (0.004)
Maryland[3]	7.1 (0.28)	8.9 (0.33)	5.2 (0.22)	3.7 (0.30)	12.4 (0.79)	6.9 (0.51)	2.5 (0.13)	3.7 (0.70)	0.27 (†)	0.18 (0.006)	0.08 (0.003)	0.31 (0.005)	0.09 (0.009)	0.27 (0.009)	0.03 (0.003)	0.09 (0.003)
Massachusetts	5.6 (0.34)	7.1 (0.26)	3.9 (0.22)	4.2 (0.19)	10.3 (0.21)	12.0 (0.31)	2.5 (0.12)	8.3 (0.47)	0.09 (0.004)	0.06 (0.014)	0.03 (0.005)	0.24 (0.007)	0.04 (0.004)	0.13 (0.009)	0.04 (0.012)	0.04 (0.003)
Michigan	8.2 (0.18)	10.8 (0.43)	5.4 (0.27)	6.1 (0.29)	17.8 (1.48)	7.4 (0.83)	2.2 (0.05)	4.5 (0.97)	0.19 (0.010)	0.13 (0.010)	0.09 (0.003)	0.32 (0.012)	0.40 (0.040)	0.15 (0.023)	0.06 (0.012)	0.12 (0.041)
Minnesota	3.7 (0.15)	5.0 (0.14)	2.4 (0.10)	2.4 (0.14)	14.4 (0.33)	5.4 (0.28)	2.6 (0.19)	10.0 (1.08)	0.05 (0.006)	0.05 (0.010)	0.04 (0.003)	0.32 (0.007)	0.05 (0.014)	0.04 (0.007)	0.08 (0.011)	0.14 (0.048)
Mississippi	10.2 (0.33)	13.3 (0.41)	7.0 (0.24)	5.5 (0.26)	14.8 (0.55)	4.3 (0.44)	3.0 (0.47)	12.7 (3.08)	0.42 (0.015)	0.16 (0.025)	0.16 (0.006)	0.46 (0.020)	0.19 (0.019)	0.07 (0.007)	0.08 (0.013)	0.09 (0.009)
Missouri	7.3 (0.24)	9.8 (0.32)	4.6 (0.16)	4.6 (0.17)	20.2 (1.07)	5.4 (0.32)	2.9 (0.10)	7.0 (0.51)	0.05 (0.004)	0.01 (0.005)	0.03 (0.003)	0.04 (0.005)	0.03 (0.003)	0.02 (0.001)	0.01 (0.001)	0.04 (0.040)
Montana	4.5 (0.18)	6.1 (0.24)	2.7 (0.11)	3.7 (0.17)	4.9 (0.17)	3.5 (0.19)	2.3 (0.16)	9.6 (1.05)	0.12 (0.007)	0.02 (0.013)	0.05 (0.005)	0.92 (0.007)	0.04 (0.004)	0.32 (0.018)	0.13 (0.013)	0.24 (0.121)
Nebraska	3.7 (0.08)	4.9 (0.11)	2.4 (0.05)	2.6 (0.06)	12.6 (0.45)	5.0 (0.30)	1.9 (0.04)	6.7 (0.89)	0.32 (0.008)	0.12 (0.008)	0.13 (0.002)	0.86 (0.004)	0.04 (0.014)	0.35 (0.017)	0.22 (0.001)	0.76 (0.070)
Nevada[3]	7.4 (0.37)	9.5 (0.45)	5.2 (0.31)	5.1 (0.33)	15.5 (0.33)	8.5 (0.40)	3.9 (0.19)	6.6 (2.24)	0.55 (0.060)	0.16 (0.081)	0.26 (0.005)	0.52 (0.007)	0.01 (0.065)	0.05 (0.007)	0.36 (0.004)	0.36 (0.002)
New Hampshire	5.6 (0.32)	7.2 (0.46)	3.9 (0.18)	5.4 (0.33)	8.7 (0.32)	5.7 (0.23)	2.2 (0.19)	4.8 (0.45)	0.08 (0.021)	0.04 (0.024)	0.06 (0.020)	0.28 (0.021)	# (0.001)	0.07 (0.007)	0.03 (0.001)	0.17 (0.011)
New Jersey	5.7 (0.26)	7.5 (0.33)	3.7 (0.19)	3.7 (0.30)	12.4 (0.79)	6.9 (0.51)	1.4 (0.13)	3.7 (0.70)	0.03 (0.008)	# (0.016)	0.01 (0.002)	0.03 (0.006)	0.09 (0.009)	0.03 (0.015)	0.17 (0.006)	0.22 (0.038)
New Mexico	5.3 (0.14)	6.9 (0.26)	3.5 (0.14)	4.0 (0.14)	7.0 (0.21)	5.4 (0.31)	2.5 (0.12)	8.3 (0.47)	0.12 (0.005)	0.03 (0.009)	0.03 (0.003)	0.13 (0.003)	0.02 (0.002)	0.06 (0.006)	# (#)	0.29 (0.021)
New York	3.8 (0.10)	5.1 (0.17)	2.5 (0.11)	3.4 (0.14)	8.8 (0.24)	2.8 (0.45)	1.9 (0.05)	4.5 (0.97)	0.05 (0.006)	0.01 (0.010)	0.03 (0.003)	0.04 (0.003)	0.02 (0.014)	0.01 (0.002)	0.03 (0.004)	0.47 (0.070)
North Carolina	10.8 (0.52)	14.3 (0.66)	7.0 (0.37)	6.5 (0.33)	18.9 (1.41)	7.2 (0.40)	2.7 (0.19)	8.0 (1.80)	0.21 (0.014)	0.21 (0.011)	0.04 (0.005)	0.05 (0.007)	0.14 (0.034)	0.05 (0.007)	0.08 (0.013)	0.04 (0.004)
North Dakota	2.2 (0.32)	2.9 (0.21)	1.4 (1.00)	1.5 (0.10)	14.6 (0.16)	3.1 (0.35)	7.2 (0.12)	12.7 (2.92)	0.05 (0.006)	# (0.024)	# (0.020)	0.02 (0.002)	# (0.001)	# (0.007)	0.10 (0.007)	0.19 (0.020)
Ohio	6.2 (0.24)	8.2 (0.30)	4.2 (0.17)	4.6 (0.21)	14.6 (0.99)	6.0 (0.83)	2.1 (0.24)	3.7 (0.45)	0.61 (0.020)	0.32 (0.026)	0.47 (0.014)	1.69 (0.029)	0.72 (0.078)	0.20 (0.035)	0.09 (0.014)	0.21 (0.038)
Oklahoma	4.9 (0.17)	6.7 (0.24)	3.0 (0.11)	3.9 (0.18)	12.1 (0.60)	5.3 (0.18)	1.8 (0.07)	4.0 (1.19)	0.47 (0.013)	0.21 (0.019)	0.28 (0.010)	0.94 (0.014)	0.23 (0.014)	0.16 (0.009)	0.29 (0.039)	0.55 (0.221)
Oregon	4.9 (0.18)	7.1 (0.26)	2.4 (0.05)	4.8 (0.19)	8.8 (0.24)	5.5 (0.37)	2.1 (0.08)	7.2 (0.36)	0.52 (0.025)	0.15 (0.044)	0.32 (0.006)	0.58 (0.093)	0.41 (0.015)	0.17 (0.017)	0.17 (0.009)	0.47 (0.014)
Pennsylvania	6.8 (0.37)	8.7 (0.45)	4.8 (0.29)	4.2 (0.33)	18.9 (1.41)	8.7 (0.79)	2.7 (0.19)	3.4 (0.64)	0.39 (0.008)	0.10 (0.011)	0.09 (0.008)	0.58 (0.031)	0.16 (0.016)	0.21 (0.017)	0.08 (0.013)	0.29 (0.004)
Rhode Island	8.4 (0.44)	10.7 (1.00)	5.9 (0.47)	6.7 (0.83)	14.6 (2.07)	12.6 (0.65)	7.2 (0.26)	11.8 (2.92)	0.07 (0.021)	0.04 (0.011)	0.02 (0.005)	0.22 (0.001)	0.01 (0.001)	0.06 (0.002)	0.04 (#)	0.19 (0.020)
South Carolina	11.9 (0.44)	15.1 (0.56)	8.6 (0.35)	6.9 (0.36)	14.6 (0.89)	6.5 (1.05)	2.9 (0.31)	9.6 (4.26)	0.08 (0.019)	0.03 (0.031)	0.05 (0.026)	1.26 (0.020)	0.20 (0.091)	0.20 (0.078)	0.09 (0.047)	0.42 (0.169)
South Dakota	2.7 (0.16)	3.7 (0.22)	1.6 (0.11)	1.9 (0.12)	13.9 (0.24)	4.3 (0.16)	3.0 (0.06)	6.8 (1.19)	0.16 (0.014)	0.05 (0.025)	0.08 (0.024)	0.08 (0.014)	0.09 (0.038)	0.23 (0.014)	0.16 (0.039)	0.55 (0.221)
Tennessee	7.2 (0.15)	9.6 (0.22)	4.8 (0.08)	5.3 (0.27)	12.8 (0.38)	5.4 (0.22)	3.7 (0.15)	3.4 (0.36)	0.47 (0.014)	0.15 (0.016)	0.31 (0.006)	0.70 (0.016)	0.11 (0.011)	0.29 (0.011)	0.17 (0.009)	0.29 (0.021)
Texas	5.6 (0.06)	8.7 (0.08)	3.6 (0.04)	4.2 (0.06)	21.5 (4.03)	5.7 (0.08)	1.6 (0.01)	3.1 (1.98)	0.39 (0.008)	0.04 (0.008)	0.07 (0.005)	0.58 (0.007)	0.16 (0.016)	0.26 (0.005)	0.08 (0.002)	0.47 (0.070)
Utah	3.2 (0.04)	4.5 (0.05)	1.9 (0.03)	2.4 (0.04)	7.8 (0.04)	6.7 (0.07)	4.2 (0.04)	6.9 (0.09)	0.18 (0.001)	0.02 (0.002)	0.04 (0.005)	0.22 (0.001)	0.16 (0.001)	0.06 (0.002)	0.04 (#)	0.19 (0.020)
Vermont	4.0 (0.18)	5.5 (0.25)	2.4 (0.18)	4.0 (0.18)	5.8 (0.50)	4.1 (0.55)	1.8 (0.23)	5.7 (0.77)	0.08 (0.019)	0.02 (0.031)	0.05 (0.008)	0.03 (0.020)	0.01 (0.013)	0.09 (0.005)	0.06 (0.003)	0.10 (0.045)
Virginia	7.2 (0.24)	9.4 (0.31)	4.9 (0.18)	4.7 (0.17)	13.9 (0.73)	5.6 (0.16)	1.8 (0.06)	4.0 (0.34)	0.15 (0.014)	0.03 (0.025)	0.08 (0.003)	0.48 (0.014)	0.10 (0.010)	0.50 (0.035)	0.16 (0.002)	0.69 (0.130)
Washington	5.6 (0.37)	7.1 (0.45)	4.8 (0.29)	5.3 (0.27)	12.0 (0.09)	7.2 (0.39)	3.7 (0.54)	11.3 (1.98)	0.53 (0.014)	0.14 (0.021)	0.31 (0.007)	0.09 (0.016)	0.04 (0.034)	0.29 (0.011)	0.47 (0.009)	0.29 (0.014)
West Virginia	10.2 (1.02)	13.8 (1.31)	6.4 (0.70)	9.7 (0.91)	21.5 (4.03)	11.2 (3.07)	2.4 (0.07)	13.5 (5.23)	0.09 (0.012)	0.04 (0.015)	0.07 (0.011)	0.09 (0.011)	0.34 (0.016)	0.05 (0.005)	0.20 (0.002)	0.30 (0.105)
Wisconsin	5.0 (0.16)	6.3 (0.20)	3.6 (0.13)	2.7 (0.12)	19.7 (0.60)	7.5 (0.18)	2.1 (0.07)	6.4 (1.37)	0.23 (0.008)	0.10 (0.012)	0.12 (0.010)	0.12 (0.009)	0.16 (0.006)	0.09 (0.020)	0.06 (0.008)	0.19 (0.004)
Wyoming	2.8 (0.34)	4.0 (0.33)	† (†)	2.7 (0.34)	3.2 (0.26)	3.1 (0.43)	1.7 (0.26)	6.4 (1.37)	0.18 (0.018)	0.02 (0.027)	0.11 (0.016)	0.23 (0.001)	0.06 (0.006)	0.09 (0.005)	0.10 (0.007)	0.30 (0.105)

† Not applicable.
# Rounds to zero.
! Interpret data with caution. The coefficient of variation (CV) for this estimate is 30 percent or greater.
‡ Reporting standards not met. The coefficient of variation (CV) for this estimate is 50 percent or greater.
[1] A student is counted only once, even if suspended more than once during the same school year.
[2] A student is counted only once, even if expelled more than once during the same school year.
[3] Data are based on universe counts of schools and school districts; therefore, these figures do not have standard errors.

NOTE: Suspension is excluding a student from school for disciplinary reasons for 1 school day or longer. Expulsion is the exclusion of a student from school for disciplinary reasons that results in the student's removal from school attendance rolls or that meets the criteria for expulsion as defined by the appropriate state or local civil authority. Race categories exclude persons of Hispanic ethnicity. Standard errors appear in parentheses.

SOURCE: U.S. Department of Education, Office for Civil Rights, Civil Rights Data Collection: 2006. (This table was prepared May 2008.)

Percentage of students in grades 9 through 12 who reported experience with drugs and violence on school property, by race/ethnicity, grade, and sex: Selected years, 1997 through 2009

						2009							
								Race/ethnicity			Grade			
Type of violence or drug-related behavior, and sex	1997 total	1999 total	2003 total	2005 total	2007 total	Total	White	Black	Hispanic	9th	10th	11th	12th
1	2	3	4	5	6	7	8	9	10	11	12	13	14
Felt too unsafe to go to school[1]	**4.0 (0.6)**	**5.2 (1.3)**	**5.4 (0.41)**	**6.0 (0.61)**	**5.5 (0.39)**	**5.0 (0.34)**	**3.5 (0.33)**	**6.3 (0.76)**	**8.1 (0.60)**	**5.8 (0.44)**	**5.0 (0.53)**	**5.3 (0.60)**	**3.4 (0.42)**
Male	4.1 (0.8)	4.8 (1.6)	5.5 (0.51)	5.7 (0.56)	5.4 (0.44)	4.6 (0.43)	3.3 (0.43)	5.9 (0.77)	7.9 (1.06)	5.4 (0.61)	4.6 (0.66)	4.9 (0.72)	3.4 (0.63)
Female	3.9 (0.7)	5.7 (1.5)	5.3 (0.51)	6.3 (0.77)	5.6 (0.53)	5.3 (0.38)	3.8 (0.43)	6.6 (1.12)	8.3 (0.77)	6.4 (0.73)	5.3 (0.64)	5.8 (0.84)	3.3 (0.46)
Carried a weapon on school property[1,2]	**8.5 (1.5)**	**6.9 (1.2)**	**6.1 (0.56)**	**6.5 (0.46)**	**5.9 (0.37)**	**5.6 (0.32)**	**5.6 (0.44)**	**5.3 (0.74)**	**5.8 (0.58)**	**4.9 (0.46)**	**6.1 (0.57)**	**5.2 (0.44)**	**6.0 (0.57)**
Male	12.5 (2.9)	11.0 (2.1)	8.9 (0.77)	10.2 (0.82)	9.0 (0.65)	8.0 (0.52)	8.3 (0.76)	6.6 (1.06)	7.9 (0.90)	6.4 (0.74)	8.9 (0.91)	7.9 (0.77)	9.1 (1.03)
Female	3.7 (0.7)	2.8 (0.7)	3.1 (0.51)	2.6 (0.31)	2.7 (0.33)	2.9 (0.24)	2.4 (0.28)	4.0 (0.83)	3.7 (0.52)	3.2 (0.39)	3.1 (0.55)	2.3 (0.35)	2.9 (0.40)
Threatened or injured with a weapon on school property[3]	**7.4 (0.9)**	**7.7 (0.8)**	**9.2 (0.77)**	**7.9 (0.36)**	**7.8 (0.44)**	**7.7 (0.37)**	**6.4 (0.43)**	**9.4 (0.80)**	**9.1 (0.61)**	**8.7 (0.53)**	**8.4 (0.72)**	**7.9 (0.60)**	**5.2 (0.53)**
Male	10.2 (1.4)	9.5 (1.6)	11.6 (0.97)	9.7 (0.41)	10.2 (0.59)	9.6 (0.59)	7.8 (0.65)	11.2 (1.25)	12.0 (1.07)	9.5 (0.92)	11.1 (1.16)	10.7 (0.89)	6.5 (0.73)
Female	4.0 (0.6)	5.8 (1.2)	6.5 (0.61)	6.1 (0.41)	5.4 (0.41)	5.5 (0.37)	4.9 (0.47)	7.4 (0.84)	6.3 (0.60)	7.7 (0.61)	5.2 (0.74)	4.8 (0.59)	3.8 (0.52)
Engaged in a physical fight on school property[3]	**14.8 (1.3)**	**14.2 (1.3)**	**12.8 (0.77)**	**13.6 (0.56)**	**12.4 (0.48)**	**11.1 (0.54)**	**8.6 (0.58)**	**17.4 (0.99)**	**13.5 (0.82)**	**14.9 (0.98)**	**12.1 (0.83)**	**9.5 (0.63)**	**6.6 (0.59)**
Male	20.0 (2.0)	18.5 (1.4)	17.1 (0.92)	18.2 (0.92)	16.3 (0.60)	15.1 (1.05)	12.4 (1.25)	22.2 (1.40)	17.7 (1.26)	19.7 (1.75)	16.4 (1.66)	13.3 (0.97)	9.3 (0.95)
Female	8.6 (1.5)	9.8 (1.9)	8.0 (0.71)	8.8 (0.51)	8.5 (0.62)	6.7 (0.42)	4.3 (0.40)	12.5 (1.45)	9.3 (0.93)	9.5 (0.72)	7.3 (0.73)	5.5 (0.70)	3.8 (0.47)
Cigarette use on school property[1]	**14.6 (1.5)**	**14.0 (1.9)**	**8.0 (0.71)**	**6.8 (0.41)**	**5.7 (0.50)**	**5.1 (0.31)**	**5.8 (0.50)**	**2.6 (0.46)**	**4.8 (0.36)**	**3.7 (0.32)**	**4.7 (0.47)**	**6.2 (0.65)**	**6.5 (0.60)**
Male	15.9 (1.7)	14.8 (2.0)	8.2 (0.66)	7.4 (0.41)	6.5 (0.53)	6.2 (0.48)	6.6 (0.69)	4.0 (0.85)	5.9 (0.66)	4.2 (0.47)	5.6 (0.84)	7.1 (0.91)	8.4 (0.85)
Female	13.0 (2.2)	13.2 (2.0)	7.6 (0.92)	6.2 (0.61)	4.8 (0.56)	4.0 (0.32)	4.7 (0.52)	1.2 (0.34)	3.7 (0.44)	3.0 (0.37)	3.5 (0.51)	5.1 (0.66)	4.4 (0.65)
Smokeless tobacco use on school property[4]	**5.1 (1.4)**	**4.2 (1.8)**	**5.9 (1.53)**	**5.0 (0.61)**	**4.9 (0.71)**	**5.5 (0.59)**	**7.0 (0.90)**	**2.6 (0.48)**	**3.2 (0.40)**	**4.1 (0.56)**	**5.1 (0.75)**	**6.2 (0.71)**	**6.7 (0.90)**
Male	9.0 (2.5)	8.1 (3.5)	8.5 (1.48)	9.2 (1.12)	8.9 (1.31)	9.4 (1.16)	12.1 (1.83)	4.1 (0.84)	5.3 (0.77)	6.2 (0.99)	8.8 (1.37)	11.0 (1.39)	12.6 (1.74)
Female	0.4 (0.2)	0.3 (0.2)	3.3 (1.68)	0.8 (0.15)	1.0 (0.20)	1.1 (0.16)	1.1 (0.24)	1.0 (0.29)	1.2 (0.31)	1.6 (0.35)	0.9 (0.26)	1.1 (0.37)	0.6 (0.17)
Alcohol use on school property[1]	**5.6 (0.7)**	**4.9 (0.7)**	**5.2 (0.46)**	**4.3 (0.31)**	**4.1 (0.32)**	**4.5 (0.29)**	**3.3 (0.27)**	**5.4 (0.59)**	**6.9 (0.70)**	**4.4 (0.37)**	**4.8 (0.46)**	**4.6 (0.44)**	**4.1 (0.44)**
Male	7.2 (1.3)	6.1 (1.1)	6.0 (0.61)	5.3 (0.41)	4.6 (0.35)	5.3 (0.41)	4.1 (0.48)	5.9 (0.80)	7.9 (0.91)	4.3 (0.51)	5.9 (0.82)	5.7 (0.66)	5.4 (0.64)
Female	3.6 (0.7)	3.6 (0.7)	4.2 (0.41)	3.3 (0.31)	3.6 (0.37)	3.6 (0.34)	2.3 (0.34)	4.8 (0.76)	5.9 (0.79)	4.5 (0.52)	3.5 (0.45)	3.4 (0.54)	2.7 (0.40)
Marijuana use on school property[1]	**7.0 (1.0)**	**7.2 (1.4)**	**5.8 (0.66)**	**4.5 (0.31)**	**4.5 (0.46)**	**4.6 (0.35)**	**3.8 (0.38)**	**5.6 (0.64)**	**6.5 (0.76)**	**4.3 (0.38)**	**4.6 (0.50)**	**5.0 (0.55)**	**4.6 (0.49)**
Male	9.0 (1.3)	10.1 (2.6)	7.6 (0.87)	6.0 (0.46)	5.9 (0.61)	6.3 (0.54)	5.1 (0.60)	8.3 (1.03)	8.7 (0.91)	5.2 (0.67)	6.4 (0.77)	6.9 (0.80)	7.0 (0.85)
Female	4.6 (1.1)	4.4 (0.8)	3.7 (0.46)	3.0 (0.31)	3.0 (0.39)	2.8 (0.32)	2.3 (0.38)	2.9 (0.52)	4.2 (0.86)	3.4 (0.53)	2.5 (0.48)	3.0 (0.55)	2.1 (0.36)
Offered, sold, or given an illegal drug on school property[3]	**31.7 (1.8)**	**30.2 (2.4)**	**28.7 (1.94)**	**25.4 (1.07)**	**22.3 (1.04)**	**22.7 (1.04)**	**19.8 (1.13)**	**22.2 (1.42)**	**31.2 (1.53)**	**22.0 (1.32)**	**23.7 (1.11)**	**24.3 (1.44)**	**20.6 (1.21)**
Male	37.4 (2.3)	34.7 (3.3)	31.9 (2.09)	28.8 (1.22)	25.7 (1.15)	25.9 (1.36)	22.7 (1.55)	25.7 (1.90)	35.1 (1.59)	22.9 (1.94)	27.3 (1.70)	27.8 (2.05)	25.8 (1.46)
Female	24.7 (2.4)	25.7 (2.4)	25.0 (1.94)	21.8 (1.02)	18.7 (1.16)	19.3 (1.01)	16.5 (1.11)	18.8 (2.02)	27.1 (1.96)	21.1 (1.40)	19.6 (1.25)	20.5 (1.46)	15.4 (1.36)

[1]One or more times during the 30 days preceding the survey.
[2]Such as a gun, knife, or club.
[3]One or more times during the 12 months preceding the survey.
[4]Used chewing tobacco or snuff one or more times during the 30 days preceding the survey.

NOTE: Totals include other racial/ethnic groups not shown separately and students whose racial/ethnic group or grade was not reported. Race categories exclude persons of Hispanic ethnicity. Standard errors appear in parentheses.
SOURCE: U.S. Department of Health and Human Services, Centers for Disease Control and Prevention, Youth Risk Behavior Survey (YRBS), 2009 National YRBS Data Files, retrieved June 21, 2010, from http://www.cdc.gov/HealthyYouth/YRBS/data/index.htm. (This table was prepared June 2010.)

Percentage of 12- to 17-year-olds reporting use of illicit drugs, alcohol, and cigarettes during the past 30 days and the past year, by substance used, sex, and race/ethnicity: Selected years, 1985 through 2009

Year, sex, and race/ethnicity	Percent reporting use during past 30 days					Percent reporting use during past year				
	Illicit drugs			Alcohol	Cigarettes	Illicit drugs			Alcohol	Cigarettes
	Any[1]	Marijuana	Cocaine			Any[1]	Marijuana	Cocaine		
1	2	3	4	5	6	7	8	9	10	11
1985	13.2 (—)	10.2 (—)	1.5 (—)	41.2 (—)	29.4 (—)	20.7 (—)	16.7 (—)	3.4 (—)	52.7 (—)	29.9 (—)
1990	7.1 (—)	4.4 (—)	0.6 (—)	32.5 (—)	22.4 (—)	14.1 (—)	9.6 (—)	1.9 (—)	41.8 (—)	26.2 (—)
1993	5.7 (—)	4.0 (—)	0.4 (—)	23.9 (—)	18.5 (—)	11.9 (—)	8.5 (—)	0.7 (—)	35.9 (—)	22.5 (—)
1994	8.2 (—)	6.0 (—)	0.3 (—)	21.6 (—)	18.9 (—)	15.5 (—)	11.4 (—)	1.1 (—)	36.2 (—)	24.5 (—)
1995	10.9 (—)	8.2 (—)	0.8 (—)	21.1 (—)	20.2 (—)	18.0 (—)	14.2 (—)	1.7 (—)	35.1 (—)	26.6 (—)
1996	9.0 (—)	7.1 (—)	0.6 (—)	18.8 (—)	18.3 (—)	16.7 (—)	13.0 (—)	1.4 (—)	32.7 (—)	24.2 (—)
1997	11.4 (—)	9.4 (—)	1.0 (—)	20.5 (—)	19.9 (—)	18.8 (—)	15.8 (—)	2.2 (—)	34.0 (—)	26.4 (—)
1998	9.9 (—)	8.3 (—)	0.8 (—)	19.1 (—)	18.2 (—)	16.4 (—)	14.1 (—)	1.7 (—)	31.8 (—)	23.8 (—)
1999	9.8 (0.23)	7.2 (0.20)	0.5 (0.06)	16.5 (0.30)	14.9 (0.31)	19.8 (0.32)	14.2 (0.29)	1.6 (0.10)	34.1 (0.41)	23.4 (0.37)
2000	9.7 (0.24)	7.2 (0.21)	0.6 (0.07)	16.4 (0.29)	13.4 (0.28)	18.6 (0.31)	13.4 (0.27)	1.7 (0.12)	33.0 (0.39)	20.8 (0.34)
2001	10.8 (0.26)	8.0 (0.24)	0.4 (0.06)	17.3 (0.33)	13.0 (0.28)	20.8 (0.36)	15.2 (0.32)	1.5 (0.10)	33.9 (0.39)	20.0 (0.35)
2002	11.6 (0.29)	8.2 (0.24)	0.6 (0.07)	17.6 (0.32)	13.0 (0.30)	22.2 (0.38)	15.8 (0.32)	2.1 (0.13)	34.6 (0.42)	20.3 (0.35)
2003	11.2 (0.27)	7.9 (0.24)	0.6 (0.06)	17.7 (0.33)	12.2 (0.29)	21.8 (0.36)	15.0 (0.31)	1.8 (0.11)	34.3 (0.42)	19.0 (0.36)
2004	10.6 (0.27)	7.6 (0.23)	0.5 (0.06)	17.6 (0.32)	11.9 (0.30)	21.0 (0.34)	14.5 (0.31)	1.6 (0.11)	33.9 (0.41)	18.4 (0.35)
2005	9.9 (0.25)	6.8 (0.22)	0.6 (0.06)	16.5 (0.32)	10.8 (0.28)	19.9 (0.35)	13.3 (0.30)	1.7 (0.11)	33.3 (0.41)	17.3 (0.36)
2006	9.8 (0.27)	6.7 (0.21)	0.4 (0.05)	16.6 (0.32)	10.4 (0.26)	19.6 (0.37)	13.2 (0.31)	1.6 (0.11)	32.9 (0.42)	17.0 (0.35)
2007	9.5 (0.27)	6.7 (0.22)	0.4 (0.05)	15.9 (0.34)	9.8 (0.26)	18.7 (0.35)	12.5 (0.30)	1.5 (0.11)	31.8 (0.42)	15.7 (0.34)
2008	9.3 (0.24)	6.7 (0.22)	0.4 (0.05)	14.6 (0.31)	9.1 (0.24)	19.0 (0.35)	13.0 (0.29)	1.2 (0.10)	30.8 (0.40)	15.0 (0.31)
Sex										
Male	9.5 (0.33)	7.3 (0.30)	0.5 (0.08)	14.2 (0.41)	9.0 (0.33)	19.0 (0.45)	13.6 (0.41)	1.3 (0.13)	29.6 (0.55)	14.8 (0.41)
Female	9.1 (0.36)	6.0 (0.32)	0.3 (0.06)	15.0 (0.46)	9.2 (0.36)	18.9 (0.52)	12.4 (0.42)	1.2 (0.14)	32.1 (0.60)	15.1 (0.47)
Race/ethnicity										
White	9.8 (0.32)	7.2 (0.28)	0.5 (0.06)	16.3 (0.41)	10.6 (0.31)	19.7 (0.44)	13.8 (0.37)	1.4 (0.13)	33.1 (0.52)	17.0 (0.41)
Black	8.2 (0.59)	5.9 (0.51)	0.1 (0.06)	10.1 (0.68)	5.0 (0.49)	17.6 (0.89)	12.5 (0.73)	0.1 (0.07)	25.5 (0.95)	9.7 (0.67)
Hispanic	8.9 (0.66)	6.1 (0.59)	0.5 (0.16)	14.8 (0.82)	7.9 (0.64)	18.8 (0.95)	12.2 (0.76)	1.3 (0.26)	31.0 (1.07)	14.0 (0.84)
Asian	2.7 (0.87)	1.0 (0.35)	# (†)	5.7 (1.11)	3.8 (1.16)	9.8 (1.76)	3.1 (1.00)	0.6 (0.37)	15.5 (2.01)	5.9 (1.29)
Native Hawaiian/Pacific Islander	‡ (†)	‡ (†)	‡ (†)	‡ (†)	‡ (†)	‡ (†)	‡ (†)	‡ (†)	‡ (†)	‡ (†)
American Indian/Alaska Native	18.2 (4.64)	‡ (†)	‡ (†)	17.2 (4.57)	18.9 (2.54)	31.3 (4.53)	26.8 (4.28)	‡ (†)	41.7 (4.64)	28.9 (3.92)
Two or more races	13.5 (1.88)	10.6 (1.74)	0.3 (0.22)	13.6 (1.90)	13.1 (2.19)	24.8 (2.50)	17.2 (2.07)	2.0 (0.88)	30.3 (2.58)	18.1 (2.29)
2009	10.0 (0.27)	7.3 (0.24)	0.3 (0.05)	14.7 (0.32)	8.9 (0.26)	19.5 (0.36)	13.6 (0.31)	1.0 (0.09)	30.3 (0.42)	15.0 (0.33)
Sex										
Male	10.6 (0.38)	8.3 (0.35)	0.3 (0.08)	15.1 (0.46)	9.2 (0.35)	20.2 (0.51)	15.0 (0.47)	1.2 (0.14)	30.6 (0.58)	15.8 (0.46)
Female	9.4 (0.38)	6.3 (0.30)	0.2 (0.06)	14.3 (0.43)	8.6 (0.36)	18.9 (0.50)	12.1 (0.40)	0.8 (0.11)	30.1 (0.56)	14.1 (0.43)
Race/ethnicity										
White	9.6 (0.32)	7.2 (0.28)	0.3 (0.05)	16.1 (0.41)	10.6 (0.35)	19.2 (0.46)	13.7 (0.39)	1.1 (0.12)	32.0 (0.52)	16.7 (0.42)
Black	10.8 (0.72)	7.3 (0.63)	‡ (†)	10.6 (0.71)	5.1 (0.49)	20.1 (0.96)	12.3 (0.78)	0.1 (0.07)	24.2 (0.96)	9.3 (0.69)
Hispanic	11.4 (0.74)	8.1 (0.62)	0.7 (0.21)	15.2 (0.82)	7.5 (0.60)	20.9 (0.91)	15.2 (0.87)	1.5 (0.27)	32.4 (1.04)	15.9 (0.87)
Asian	5.5 (1.13)	2.9 (0.83)	# (†)	6.5 (1.34)	2.5 (0.71)	11.2 (1.50)	4.9 (1.00)	0.4 (0.27)	17.3 (2.01)	4.7 (1.02)
Native Hawaiian/Pacific Islander	‡ (†)	‡ (†)	‡ (†)	‡ (†)	‡ (†)	‡ (†)	‡ (†)	‡ (†)	‡ (†)	‡ (†)
American Indian/Alaska Native	14.6 (2.77)	11.5 (2.41)	‡ (†)	11.9 (2.13)	11.6 (2.12)	29.5 (4.16)	19.8 (3.23)	2.2 (1.28)	31.3 (3.88)	21.0 (3.09)
Two or more races	11.7 (1.85)	9.6 (1.71)	# (†)	16.7 (2.22)	12.9 (1.99)	24.0 (2.58)	17.3 (2.20)	1.1 (0.43)	30.6 (2.73)	16.9 (2.19)

—Not available.
†Not applicable.
#Rounds to zero.
‡Reporting standards not met (too few cases).
[1]Includes other illegal drug use not shown separately—specifically, the use of heroin, hallucinogens, and inhalants, as well as the nonmedical use of prescription-type pain relievers, tranquilizers, stimulants, and sedatives.
NOTE: Marijuana includes hashish usage. Data for 1999 and later years were gathered using Computer Assisted Interviewing (CAI) and may not be directly comparable to previous years. Because of survey improvements in 2002, the 2002 data constitute a new baseline for tracking trends. Valid trend comparisons can be made for 1985 through 1998, 1999 through 2001, and 2002 through 2009. Race categories exclude persons of Hispanic ethnicity. Standard errors appear in parentheses.

SOURCE: U.S. Department of Health and Human Services, Substance Abuse and Mental Health Services Administration, National Household Survey on Drug Abuse: Main Findings, selected years, 1985 through 2001, and National Survey on Drug Use and Health, 2002 through 2009. Retrieved May 20, 2011, from http://www.oas.samhsa.gov/WebOnly.htm#NSDUHtabs. (This table was prepared May 2011.)

Percentage of high school seniors reporting drug use, by type of drug and reporting period: Selected years, 1975 through 2010

Type of drug	Class of 1975	Class of 1980	Class of 1985	Class of 1990	Class of 1995	Class of 2000	Class of 2003	Class of 2004	Class of 2005	Class of 2006	Class of 2007	Class of 2008	Class of 2009	Class of 2010
1	2	3	4	5	6	7	8	9	10	11	12	13	14	15
Percent reporting having ever used drugs														
Alcohol[1]	90.4 (0.69)	93.2 (0.46)	92.2 (0.48)	89.5 (0.57)	80.7 (0.73)	80.3 (0.80)	76.6 (0.80)	76.8 (0.80)	75.1 (0.81)	72.7 (0.85)	72.2 (0.83)	71.9 (0.85)	72.3 (0.85)	71.0 (0.84)
Any illicit drug	55.2 (1.68)	65.4 (1.23)	60.6 (1.26)	47.9 (1.33)	48.4 (1.32)	54.0 (1.44)	51.1 (1.35)	51.1 (1.35)	50.4 (1.35)	48.2 (1.37)	46.8 (1.33)	47.4 (1.35)	46.7 (1.36)	48.2 (1.33)
Marijuana only	19.0 (1.32)	26.7 (1.15)	20.9 (1.05)	18.5 (1.03)	20.3 (1.06)	25.0 (1.25)	23.4 (1.15)	22.4 (1.13)	23.0 (1.14)	21.3 (1.12)	21.3 (1.09)	22.5 (1.13)	22.7 (1.15)	23.5 (1.13)
Any illicit drug other than marijuana[2]	36.2 (1.33)	38.7 (1.04)	39.7 (1.04)	29.4 (0.99)	28.1 (0.97)	29.0 (1.08)	27.7 (0.99)	28.7 (1.00)	27.4 (0.99)	26.9 (1.00)	25.5 (0.95)	24.9 (0.96)	24.0 (0.96)	24.7 (0.94)
Use of selected drugs														
Cocaine	9.0 (0.73)	15.7 (0.72)	17.3 (0.74)	9.4 (0.59)	6.0 (0.48)	8.6 (0.62)	7.7 (0.55)	8.1 (0.56)	8.0 (0.56)	8.5 (0.58)	7.8 (0.54)	7.2 (0.53)	6.0 (0.49)	5.5 (0.46)
Heroin	2.2 (0.21)	1.1 (0.12)	1.2 (0.12)	1.3 (0.13)	1.6 (0.14)	2.4 (0.19)	1.5 (0.14)	1.5 (0.14)	1.5 (0.14)	1.4 (0.14)	1.5 (0.14)	1.3 (0.13)	1.2 (0.13)	1.6 (0.14)
LSD	11.3 (0.81)	9.3 (0.57)	7.5 (0.52)	8.7 (0.57)	11.7 (0.64)	11.1 (0.69)	5.9 (0.49)	4.6 (0.43)	3.5 (0.38)	3.3 (0.37)	3.4 (0.37)	4.0 (0.40)	3.1 (0.36)	4.0 (0.40)
Marijuana/hashish	47.3 (1.68)	60.3 (1.27)	54.2 (1.83)	40.7 (1.30)	41.7 (1.30)	48.8 (1.45)	46.1 (1.35)	45.7 (1.35)	44.8 (1.34)	42.3 (1.36)	41.8 (1.31)	42.6 (1.34)	42.0 (1.35)	43.8 (1.32)
PCP	— (†)	9.6 (0.33)	4.9 (0.24)	2.8 (0.19)	2.7 (0.18)	3.4 (0.23)	2.5 (0.18)	1.6 (0.15)	2.4 (0.18)	2.2 (0.17)	2.1 (0.17)	1.8 (0.16)	1.7 (0.15)	1.8 (0.15)
Percent reporting use of drugs in the past 12 months														
Alcohol[1]	84.8 (0.84)	87.9 (0.59)	85.6 (0.63)	80.6 (0.73)	73.7 (0.81)	73.2 (0.89)	70.1 (0.86)	70.6 (0.86)	68.6 (0.87)	66.5 (0.90)	66.4 (0.88)	65.5 (0.90)	66.2 (0.90)	65.2 (0.88)
Any illicit drug	45.0 (1.64)	53.1 (1.26)	46.3 (1.26)	32.5 (1.21)	39.0 (1.26)	40.9 (1.39)	39.3 (1.29)	38.8 (1.29)	38.4 (1.28)	36.5 (1.29)	35.9 (1.25)	36.6 (1.27)	36.5 (1.29)	38.3 (1.26)
Marijuana only	18.8 (1.29)	22.7 (1.06)	18.9 (0.99)	14.6 (0.91)	19.6 (1.02)	20.5 (1.14)	19.5 (1.05)	18.3 (1.02)	18.8 (1.03)	17.3 (1.01)	17.4 (0.99)	18.3 (1.02)	19.5 (1.06)	21.0 (1.06)
Any illicit drug other than marijuana[2]	26.2 (1.15)	30.4 (0.92)	27.4 (0.89)	17.9 (0.79)	19.4 (0.81)	20.4 (0.90)	19.8 (0.83)	20.5 (0.85)	19.7 (0.83)	19.2 (0.84)	18.5 (0.80)	18.3 (0.81)	17.0 (0.79)	17.3 (0.78)
Use of selected drugs														
Cocaine	5.6 (0.52)	12.3 (0.58)	13.1 (0.59)	5.3 (0.40)	4.0 (0.35)	5.0 (0.43)	4.8 (0.39)	5.3 (0.41)	5.1 (0.40)	5.7 (0.43)	5.2 (0.40)	4.4 (0.38)	3.4 (0.34)	2.9 (0.30)
Heroin	1.0 (0.13)	0.5 (0.07)	0.6 (0.07)	0.5 (0.07)	1.1 (0.10)	1.5 (0.13)	0.8 (0.09)	0.9 (0.10)	0.8 (0.09)	0.8 (0.09)	0.9 (0.09)	0.7 (0.08)	0.7 (0.09)	0.9 (0.09)
LSD	7.2 (0.59)	6.5 (0.43)	4.4 (0.36)	5.4 (0.41)	8.4 (0.49)	6.6 (0.49)	1.9 (0.25)	2.2 (0.27)	1.8 (0.24)	1.7 (0.24)	2.1 (0.26)	2.7 (0.30)	1.9 (0.25)	2.6 (0.29)
Marijuana/hashish	40.0 (1.61)	48.8 (1.27)	40.6 (1.24)	27.0 (1.15)	34.7 (1.23)	36.5 (1.36)	34.9 (1.26)	34.3 (1.25)	33.6 (1.24)	31.5 (1.24)	31.7 (1.21)	32.4 (1.24)	32.8 (1.25)	34.8 (1.24)
PCP	— (†)	4.4 (0.20)	2.9 (0.16)	1.2 (0.11)	1.8 (0.13)	2.3 (0.16)	1.3 (0.11)	0.7 (0.08)	1.3 (0.11)	0.7 (0.09)	0.9 (0.09)	1.1 (0.11)	1.0 (0.10)	1.0 (0.10)
Percent reporting use of drugs in the past 30 days														
Alcohol[1]	68.2 (1.10)	72.0 (0.81)	65.9 (0.85)	57.1 (0.92)	51.3 (0.92)	50.0 (1.01)	47.5 (0.94)	48.0 (0.94)	47.0 (0.94)	45.3 (0.95)	44.4 (0.92)	43.1 (0.93)	43.5 (0.95)	41.2 (0.91)
Any illicit drug	30.7 (1.35)	37.2 (1.09)	29.7 (1.03)	17.2 (0.87)	23.8 (0.98)	24.9 (1.09)	24.1 (1.01)	23.4 (1.00)	23.1 (0.99)	21.5 (0.98)	21.9 (0.96)	22.3 (0.98)	23.3 (1.01)	23.8 (0.99)
Marijuana only	15.3 (1.06)	18.8 (0.88)	14.8 (0.80)	9.2 (0.67)	13.8 (0.79)	14.5 (0.89)	19.5 (0.93)	18.3 (0.91)	12.8 (0.78)	11.7 (0.77)	12.4 (0.76)	13.0 (0.79)	14.7 (0.84)	15.2 (0.83)
Any illicit drug other than marijuana[2]	15.4 (0.80)	18.4 (0.66)	14.9 (0.60)	8.0 (0.47)	10.0 (0.52)	10.4 (0.58)	10.4 (0.54)	10.8 (0.55)	10.3 (0.54)	9.8 (0.54)	9.5 (0.51)	9.3 (0.52)	8.6 (0.50)	8.6 (0.49)
Use of selected drugs														
Cocaine	1.9 (0.25)	5.2 (0.31)	6.7 (0.35)	1.9 (0.20)	1.8 (0.19)	2.1 (0.23)	2.1 (0.21)	2.3 (0.22)	2.3 (0.22)	2.5 (0.23)	2.0 (0.20)	1.9 (0.20)	1.3 (0.17)	1.3 (0.16)
Heroin	0.4 (0.08)	0.2 (0.04)	0.3 (0.05)	0.2 (0.04)	0.6 (0.08)	0.7 (0.09)	0.4 (0.06)	0.5 (0.07)	0.5 (0.07)	0.4 (0.06)	0.4 (0.06)	0.4 (0.06)	0.4 (0.06)	0.4 (0.06)
LSD	2.3 (0.28)	2.3 (0.21)	1.6 (0.18)	1.9 (0.20)	4.0 (0.28)	1.6 (0.20)	0.6 (0.11)	0.7 (0.12)	0.7 (0.12)	0.6 (0.12)	0.6 (0.11)	1.1 (0.15)	0.5 (0.11)	0.8 (0.13)
Marijuana/hashish	27.1 (1.30)	33.7 (1.07)	25.7 (0.98)	14.0 (0.80)	21.2 (0.94)	21.6 (1.04)	21.2 (0.96)	19.9 (0.94)	19.8 (0.94)	18.3 (0.92)	18.8 (0.90)	19.4 (0.93)	20.6 (0.96)	21.4 (0.95)
PCP	— (†)	1.4 (0.11)	1.6 (0.12)	0.4 (0.06)	0.6 (0.08)	0.9 (0.10)	0.6 (0.08)	0.4 (0.06)	0.7 (0.08)	0.4 (0.06)	0.5 (0.07)	0.6 (0.08)	0.5 (0.07)	0.8 (0.09)

—Not available.
†Not applicable.
[1]Survey question changed in 1993; later data are not comparable to figures for earlier years.
[2]Other illicit drugs include any use of LSD or other hallucinogens, crack or other cocaine, or heroin, or any use of other narcotics, amphetamines, barbiturates, or tranquilizers not under a doctor's orders.

NOTE: Detail may not sum to totals because of rounding. Standard errors were calculated from formulas to perform trend analysis over an interval greater than 1 year (for example, a comparison between 1975 and 1990). A revised questionnaire was used in 1982 and later years to reduce the inappropriate reporting of nonprescription stimulants. This slightly reduced the positive responses for some types of drug abuse. SOURCE: University of Michigan, Institute for Social Research, Monitoring the Future, selected years, 1975 through 2010, retrieved May 20, 2011, from http://monitoringthefuture.org/data/10data.html#2010data-drugs. (This table was prepared May 2011.)

Public and private elementary and secondary teachers, enrollment, and pupil/teacher ratios: Selected years, fall 1955 through fall 2020

Year	Teachers (in thousands)			Enrollment (in thousands)			Pupil/teacher ratio		
	Total	Public	Private	Total	Public	Private	Total	Public	Private
1	2	3	4	5	6	7	8	9	10
1955	1,286	1,141	145 [1]	35,280	30,680	4,600 [1]	27.4	26.9	31.7 [1]
1960	1,600	1,408	192 [1]	42,181	36,281	5,900 [1]	26.4	25.8	30.7 [1]
1965	1,933	1,710	223	48,473	42,173	6,300	25.1	24.7	28.3
1970	2,292	2,059	233	51,257	45,894	5,363	22.4	22.3	23.0
1971	2,293	2,063	230 [1]	51,271	46,071	5,200 [1]	22.4	22.3	22.6 [1]
1972	2,337	2,106	231 [1]	50,726	45,726	5,000 [1]	21.7	21.7	21.6 [1]
1973	2,372	2,136	236 [1]	50,445	45,445	5,000 [1]	21.3	21.3	21.2 [1]
1974	2,410	2,165	245 [1]	50,073	45,073	5,000 [1]	20.8	20.8	20.4 [1]
1975	2,453	2,198	255 [1]	49,819	44,819	5,000 [1]	20.3	20.4	19.6 [1]
1976	2,457	2,189	268	49,478	44,311	5,167	20.1	20.2	19.3
1977	2,488	2,209	279	48,717	43,577	5,140	19.6	19.7	18.4
1978	2,479	2,207	272	47,637	42,551	5,086	19.2	19.3	18.7
1979	2,461	2,185	276 [1]	46,651	41,651	5,000 [1]	19.0	19.1	18.1 [1]
1980	2,485	2,184	301	46,208	40,877	5,331	18.6	18.7	17.7
1981	2,440	2,127	313 [1]	45,544	40,044	5,500 [1]	18.7	18.8	17.6 [1]
1982	2,458	2,133	325 [1]	45,166	39,566	5,600 [1]	18.4	18.6	17.2 [1]
1983	2,476	2,139	337	44,967	39,252	5,715	18.2	18.4	17.0
1984	2,508	2,168	340 [1]	44,908	39,208	5,700 [1]	17.9	18.1	16.8 [1]
1985	2,549	2,206	343	44,979	39,422	5,557	17.6	17.9	16.2
1986	2,592	2,244	348 [1]	45,205	39,753	5,452 [1]	17.4	17.7	15.7 [1]
1987	2,631	2,279	352	45,488	40,008	5,479	17.3	17.6	15.6
1988	2,668	2,323	345	45,430	40,189	5,242 [1]	17.0	17.3	15.2 [1]
1989	2,713	2,357	356	46,141	40,543	5,599	17.0	17.2	15.7
1990	2,759	2,398	361 [1]	46,864	41,217	5,648 [1]	17.0	17.2	15.6 [1]
1991	2,797	2,432	365	47,728	42,047	5,681	17.1	17.3	15.6
1992	2,823	2,459	364 [1]	48,694	42,823	5,870 [1]	17.2	17.4	16.1 [1]
1993	2,868	2,504	364	49,532	43,465	6,067	17.3	17.4	16.7
1994	2,922	2,552	370 [1]	50,106	44,111	5,994 [1]	17.1	17.3	16.2 [1]
1995	2,974	2,598	376	50,759	44,840	5,918	17.1	17.3	15.7
1996	3,051	2,667	384 [1]	51,544	45,611	5,933 [1]	16.9	17.1	15.5 [1]
1997	3,138	2,746	391	52,071	46,127	5,944	16.6	16.8	15.2
1998	3,230	2,830	400 [1]	52,526	46,539	5,988 [1]	16.3	16.4	15.0 [1]
1999	3,319	2,911	408	52,875	46,857	6,018	15.9	16.1	14.7
2000	3,366	2,941	424 [1]	53,373	47,204	6,169 [1]	15.9	16.0	14.5 [1]
2001	3,440	3,000	441	53,992	47,672	6,320	15.7	15.9	14.3
2002	3,476	3,034	442 [1]	54,403	48,183	6,220 [1]	15.7	15.9	14.1 [1]
2003	3,490	3,049	441	54,639	48,540	6,099	15.7	15.9	13.8
2004	3,538	3,091	447 [1]	54,882	48,795	6,087 [1]	15.5	15.8	13.6 [1]
2005	3,593	3,143	450	55,187	49,113	6,073	15.4	15.6	13.5
2006	3,622	3,166	456 [1]	55,307	49,316	5,991 [1]	15.3	15.6	13.2 [1]
2007	3,634	3,178	456	55,203	49,293	5,910	15.2	15.5	13.0
2008	3,670	3,222	448 [1]	54,973	49,266	5,707 [1]	15.0	15.3	12.8 [1]
2009	3,647	3,210	437	54,862	49,373	5,488	15.0	15.4	12.5
2010 [2]	3,668	3,240	428	54,704	49,306	5,398	14.9	15.2	12.6
2011 [2]	3,679	3,253	426	54,746	49,422	5,324	14.9	15.2	12.5
2012 [2]	3,696	3,274	422	54,905	49,642	5,263	14.9	15.2	12.5
2013 [2]	3,725	3,306	419	55,133	49,914	5,219	14.8	15.1	12.4
2014 [2]	3,752	3,334	419	55,455	50,268	5,187	14.8	15.1	12.4
2015 [2]	3,782	3,364	418	55,836	50,659	5,176	14.8	15.1	12.4
2016 [2]	3,814	3,395	419	56,214	51,038	5,176	14.7	15.0	12.4
2017 [2]	3,846	3,425	420	56,617	51,430	5,187	14.7	15.0	12.3
2018 [2]	3,876	3,454	422	57,009	51,803	5,206	14.7	15.0	12.3
2019 [2]	3,910	3,485	425	57,438	52,204	5,234	14.7	15.0	12.3
2020 [2]	3,939	3,510	429	57,939	52,666	5,273	14.7	15.0	12.3

[1]Estimated.
[2]Projected.
NOTE: Data for teachers are expressed in full-time equivalents (FTE). Counts of private school teachers and enrollment include prekindergarten through grade 12 in schools offering kindergarten or higher grades. Counts of public school teachers and enrollment include prekindergarten through grade 12. The pupil/teacher ratio includes teachers for students with disabilities and other special teachers, while these teachers are generally excluded from class size calculations. Ratios for public schools reflect totals reported by states and differ from totals reported for schools or school districts. Some data have been revised from previously published figures. Detail may not sum to totals because of rounding.
SOURCE: U.S. Department of Education, National Center for Education Statistics, *Statistics of Public Elementary and Secondary Day Schools*, 1955–56 through 1980–81; Common Core of Data (CCD), "State Nonfiscal Survey of Public Elementary/Secondary Education," 1981–82 through 2009–10; Private School Universe Survey (PSS), 1989–90 through 2009–10; *Projections of Education Statistics to 2020*; and unpublished data. (This table was prepared February 2012.)

Public elementary and secondary teachers, by level and state or jurisdiction: Selected years, fall 2000 through fall 2009

State or jurisdiction	Fall 2000	Fall 2005	Fall 2006	Fall 2007	Fall 2008[1]				Fall 2009			
					Total	Elementary	Secondary	Ungraded	Total	Elementary	Secondary	Ungraded
1	2	3	4	5	6	7	8	9	10	11	12	13
United States	2,941,461 [1]	3,143,003 [1]	3,166,391 [1]	3,178,142 [1]	3,222,154 [1]	1,760,865 [1]	1,234,197	227,092	3,209,637 [1]	1,777,149 [1]	1,227,484	205,004
Alabama	48,194 [2]	57,757	56,134	50,420	47,818	27,193	20,625	0	47,492	27,075	20,417	0
Alaska........................	7,880	7,912	7,903	7,613	7,927	4,111	3,816	0	8,083	4,264	3,819	0
Arizona......................	44,438	51,376	52,625	54,032	54,696	39,077	15,619	0	51,947	37,008	14,939	0
Arkansas...................	31,947	32,997	35,089	33,882	37,162	19,656	14,525	2,981	37,240	19,705	14,577	2,958
California...................	298,021 [2]	309,222 [2]	307,366 [2]	305,230 [2]	303,647 [2]	206,996 [2]	88,190	8,461	313,795 [2]	224,644 [2]	89,151	0
Colorado....................	41,983	45,841	46,973	47,761	48,692	27,679	21,013	0	49,060	28,071	20,989	0
Connecticut................	41,044	39,687	39,115	39,304	48,463	31,808	15,602	1,053	43,593	28,303	14,236	1,054
Delaware....................	7,469	7,998	8,038	8,198	8,322	4,093	4,229	0	8,640	4,262	4,378	0
District of Columbia	4,949	5,481 [3]	5,383 [3]	6,347	5,321	2,768	2,263	290	6,370	3,782	2,291	297
Florida.......................	132,030	158,962	162,851	168,737	186,361	75,396	66,343	44,622	183,827	74,156	65,821	43,851
Georgia......................	91,043	108,535	113,597	116,857	118,839	72,537	46,233	69	115,918	70,513	45,344	61
Hawaii.......................	10,927	11,226	11,271	11,397	11,295	6,058	5,194	43	11,404	6,213	5,151	40
Idaho........................	13,714	14,521	14,770	15,013	15,148	7,951	7,197	0	15,201	8,024	7,177	0
Illinois......................	127,620	133,857	140,988	136,571	135,704	93,183	42,518	3	138,483	93,414	45,062	8
Indiana......................	59,226	60,592	61,346	62,334	62,668	34,007	28,296	365	62,258	33,685	28,171	402
Iowa.........................	34,636	35,181	35,653	36,089	35,961	19,603	16,358	0	35,842	19,793	16,049	0
Kansas......................	32,742	33,608	35,297	35,359	35,883	16,957	18,769	157	34,700	17,017	16,816	867
Kentucky...................	39,589	42,413	43,371	43,536	43,451	21,609	10,117	11,725	44,371	21,986	10,329	12,056
Louisiana...................	49,915	44,660	45,951	48,610	49,377	34,573	14,804	0	49,646	34,292	15,355	0
Maine........................	16,559	16,684	16,826	16,558	15,912	10,881	5,031	0	16,275	11,122	5,154	0
Maryland....................	52,433	56,685	58,443	59,320	58,940	34,396	24,544	0	58,235	34,288	23,948	0
Massachusetts.............	67,432	73,596	73,157	70,719	70,398	46,585	23,813	0	69,909	46,235	23,674	0
Michigan....................	97,031	98,069	98,037	96,204	94,754	37,702	37,761	19,291	92,691	36,937	36,706	19,047
Minnesota..................	53,457	51,107	51,880	52,975	53,083	27,327	24,124	1,632	52,839	27,459	23,884	1,496
Mississippi.................	31,006	31,433	32,351	33,560	33,358	15,891	13,291	4,176	33,103	15,755	13,270	4,078
Missouri....................	64,735	67,076	67,521	68,430	68,015	34,870	33,145	0	67,796	34,931	32,865	0
Montana....................	10,411	10,369	10,398	10,519	10,467	7,079	3,388	0	10,521	7,133	3,388	0
Nebraska...................	20,983	21,359	21,459	21,930	22,057	14,202	7,855	0	22,256	13,774	8,482	0
Nevada	18,293	21,744	22,908	23,423	21,993	11,283	7,892	2,818	22,104	11,179	7,982	2,942
New Hampshire............	14,341	15,536	15,515	15,484	15,661	10,649	5,012	0	15,491	10,531	4,960	0
New Jersey.................	99,061	112,673	112,301	111,500	114,713	53,374	48,663	12,676	115,248	62,091	40,615	12,542
New Mexico.................	21,042	22,021	22,016	22,300	22,825	13,473	5,127	4,225	22,724	9,976	8,657	4,090
New York....................	206,961	218,989	218,879	211,854	217,944	105,446	73,282	39,216	214,804	103,684	72,408	38,712
North Carolina	83,680	95,664	112,304	106,562	109,634	56,823	49,063	3,748	105,046 [4]	55,601 [4]	47,923	1,522
North Dakota	8,141	8,003	8,007	8,068	8,181	5,132	3,049	0	8,366	5,242	3,123	0
Ohio.........................	118,361	117,982	110,459	109,766	112,845	54,741	53,743	4,361	111,378	54,398	53,016	3,963
Oklahoma..................	41,318	41,833	42,206	46,735	46,571	22,386	19,770	4,415	42,678	22,891	19,788	0
Oregon......................	28,094	28,346	29,940	30,013	30,152	20,886	9,266	0	28,751	20,148	8,604	0
Pennsylvania...............	116,963	122,397	123,114	135,234	129,708	61,395	59,464	8,849	130,984	61,921	59,973	9,089
Rhode Island	10,645	14,180 [2]	11,381	11,271	11,316	5,386	5,930	0	11,365	5,443	5,922	0
South Carolina.............	45,380	48,212	49,284	47,382	49,941	33,282	14,272	2,387	46,980	32,922	14,058	0
South Dakota	9,397	9,129	9,070	9,416	9,244	5,791	2,553	900	9,326	5,877	2,566	884
Tennessee..................	57,164	59,596	62,176	64,659	64,926	44,397	18,848	1,681	65,361	44,584	18,946	1,832
Texas	274,826	302,425	311,649	321,929	327,905	163,514	127,161	37,230	333,164	166,632	131,239	35,292
Utah	22,008	22,993	23,640	24,336	23,657	11,658	9,563	2,436	25,474	12,827	9,979	2,667
Vermont	8,414	8,851	8,859	8,749	8,766	3,333	3,551	1,882	8,734	3,352	3,563	1,819
Virginia......................	86,977 [2]	103,944	79,688	71,861	71,415	35,233	36,182	0	70,827	35,179	35,649	0
Washington.................	51,098	53,508	53,743	53,960	54,428	26,775	22,372	5,281	53,448	27,306	22,852	3,290
West Virginia...............	20,930	19,940	19,633	20,306	20,209	9,452	10,757	0	20,299	9,474	10,825	0
Wisconsin..................	60,165	60,127	59,089	58,914	59,401	28,622	30,660	119	58,426	28,319	29,962	145
Wyoming....................	6,783	6,706	6,737	6,915	7,000	3,646	3,354	0	7,166	3,734	3,431	0
Bureau of Indian Education .	—	—	—	—	—	—	—	—	—	—	—	—
DoD, overseas	5,105	5,726	5,204	4,147	4,551	1,581	1,532	1,438	—	—	—	—
DoD, domestic	2,399	2,033	2,033	2,243	2,145	974	423	748	—	—	—	—
Other jurisdictions												
American Samoa	820	989	971	—	—	—	—	—	—	—	—	—
Guam	1,975	1,804	—	—	—	—	—	—	—	—	—	—
Northern Marianas........	526	614	579	550	514	280	230	4	552	295	254	3
Puerto Rico	37,620	42,036	40,163	40,826	39,356	19,065	15,031	5,260	39,102	18,303	15,295	5,504
U.S. Virgin Islands..........	1,511	1,434	1,531	1,518	1,331	632	472	227	1,425	602	463	360

—Not available.
[1]Includes imputed values for states.
[2]Includes imputations for underreporting of prekindergarten teachers.
[3]Imputed.
[4]Includes imputations for underreporting of kindergarten teachers.

NOTE: Distribution of elementary and secondary teachers determined by reporting units. Teachers reported in full-time equivalents (FTE). DoD = Department of Defense. Some data have been revised from previously published figures.
SOURCE: U.S. Department of Education, National Center for Education Statistics, Common Core of Data (CCD), "State Nonfiscal Survey of Public Elementary/Secondary Education," 2000–01 through 2009–10. (This table was prepared February 2012.)

Teachers, enrollment, and pupil/teacher ratios in public elementary and secondary schools, by state or jurisdiction: Selected years, fall 2000 through fall 2009

State or jurisdiction	Pupil/teacher ratio				Fall 2007			Fall 2008			Fall 2009		
	Fall 2000	Fall 2004	Fall 2005	Fall 2006	Teachers	Enrollment	Pupil/teacher ratio	Teachers	Enrollment	Pupil/teacher ratio	Teachers	Enrollment	Pupil/teacher ratio
1	2	3	4	5	6	7	8	9	10	11	12	13	14
United States	**16.0** [1]	**15.8** [1]	**15.6** [1]	**15.6** [1]	**3,178,142** [1]	**49,292,507** [1]	**15.5** [1]	**3,222,154** [1]	**49,265,572** [1]	**15.3** [1]	**3,209,637** [1]	**49,373,307** [1]	**15.4** [1]
Alabama	15.4 [2]	14.2	12.8	13.2	50,420	744,865	14.8	47,818	745,668	15.6	47,492	748,889	15.8
Alaska	16.9	17.1	16.8	16.8	7,613	131,029	17.2	7,927	130,662	16.5	8,083	131,661	16.3
Arizona	19.8	21.3	21.3	20.3	54,032	1,087,447	20.1	54,696	1,087,817	19.9	51,947	1,077,831	20.7
Arkansas	14.1	14.8	14.4	13.6	33,882	479,016	14.1	37,162	478,965	12.9	37,240	480,559	12.9
California	20.6 [2]	21.1 [2]	20.8 [2]	20.8 [2]	305,230 [2]	6,343,471 [2]	20.8 [2]	303,647 [2]	6,322,528 [2]	20.8 [2]	313,795 [2]	6,263,449	20.0 [2]
Colorado	17.3	17.0	17.0	16.9	47,761	801,867	16.8	48,692	818,443	16.8	49,060	832,368	17.0
Connecticut	13.7	14.9	14.5	14.7	39,304	570,626	14.5	48,463	567,198	11.7	43,593	563,985	12.9
Delaware	15.4	15.2	15.1	15.2	8,198	122,574	15.0	8,322	125,430	15.1	8,640	126,801	14.7
District of Columbia	13.9	14.2	14.0 [3]	13.5 [3]	6,347	78,422	12.4	5,321	68,681	12.9	6,370	69,433	10.9
Florida	18.4	17.0	16.8	16.4	168,737	2,666,811	15.8	186,361	2,631,020	14.1	183,827	2,634,522	14.3
Georgia	15.9	14.8	14.7	14.3	116,857	1,649,589	14.1	118,839	1,655,792	13.9	115,918	1,667,685	14.4
Hawaii	16.9	16.4	16.3	16.0	11,397	179,897	15.8	11,295	179,478	15.9	11,404	180,196	15.8
Idaho	17.9	17.9	18.0	18.1	15,013	272,119	18.1	15,148	275,051	18.2	15,201	276,299	18.2
Illinois	16.1	16.0	15.8	15.0	136,571	2,112,805	15.5	135,704	2,119,707	15.6	138,483	2,104,175	15.2
Indiana	16.7	16.9	17.1	17.0	62,334	1,046,766	16.8	62,668	1,046,147	16.7	62,258	1,046,661	16.8
Iowa	14.3	13.8	13.7	13.6	36,089	485,115	13.4	35,961	487,559	13.6	35,842	491,842	13.7
Kansas	14.4	14.2	13.9	13.3	35,359	468,295	13.2	35,883	471,060	13.1	34,700	474,489	13.7
Kentucky	16.8	16.3	16.0	15.8	43,536	666,225	15.3	43,451	670,030	15.4	44,371	680,089	15.3
Louisiana	16.6	16.6	16.6	16.6	48,610	681,038	16.6	49,377	684,873	16.6	49,646	690,915	16.6
Maine	12.5	11.9	11.7	11.5	16,558	196,245	11.9	15,912	192,935	12.1	16,275	189,225	11.6
Maryland	16.3	15.7	15.2	14.6	59,320	845,700	14.3	58,940	843,861	14.3	58,235	848,412	14.6
Massachusetts	14.5	13.3	13.2	13.2	70,719	962,958	13.6	70,398	958,910	13.6	69,909	957,053	13.7
Michigan	17.7 [2]	17.4	17.8	17.6	96,204	1,692,739	17.6	94,754	1,659,921	17.5	92,691	1,649,082	17.8
Minnesota	16.0	16.1	16.4	16.2	52,975	837,578	15.8	53,083	836,048	15.7	52,839	837,053	15.8
Mississippi	16.1	15.8	15.7	15.3	33,560	494,122	14.7	33,358	491,962	14.7	33,103	492,481	14.9
Missouri	14.1	13.8	13.7	13.6	68,430	917,188	13.4	68,015	917,871	13.5	67,796	917,982	13.5
Montana	14.9	14.3	14.0	13.9	10,519	142,823	13.6	10,467	141,899	13.6	10,521	141,807	13.5
Nebraska	13.6	13.5	13.4	13.4	21,930	291,244	13.3	22,057	292,590	13.3	22,256	295,368	13.3
Nevada	18.6	19.1	19.0	18.5	23,423	429,362	18.3	21,993	433,371	19.7	22,104	428,947	19.4
New Hampshire	14.5	13.5	13.2	13.1	15,484	200,772	13.0	15,661	197,934	12.6	15,491	197,140	12.7
New Jersey	13.3	12.1	12.4	12.4	111,500	1,382,348	12.4	114,713	1,381,420	12.0	115,248	1,396,029	12.1
New Mexico	15.2	15.0	14.8	14.9	22,300	329,040	14.8	22,825	330,245	14.5	22,724	334,419	14.7
New York	13.9	13.0	12.9	12.8	211,854	2,765,435	13.1	217,944	2,740,592	12.6	214,804	2,766,052	12.9
North Carolina	15.5	15.0	14.8	12.9	106,562	1,489,492	14.0	109,634	1,488,645	13.6	105,046 [4]	1,483,397	14.1
North Dakota	13.4	12.5	12.3	12.1	8,068	95,059	11.8	8,181	94,728	11.6	8,366	95,073	11.4
Ohio	15.5	15.6	15.6	16.6	109,766	1,827,184	16.6	112,845	1,817,163	16.1	111,378	1,764,297	15.8
Oklahoma	15.1	15.6	15.2	15.1	46,735	642,065	13.7	46,571	645,108	13.9	42,678	654,802	15.3
Oregon	19.4	20.1	19.5	18.8	30,013	565,586	18.8	30,152	575,393	19.1	28,751	582,839	20.3
Pennsylvania	15.5	15.1	15.0	15.2	135,234	1,801,971	13.3	129,708	1,775,029	13.7	130,984	1,786,103	13.6
Rhode Island	14.8	13.3	10.8	13.3	11,271	147,629	13.1	11,316	145,342	12.8	11,365	145,118	12.8
South Carolina	14.9	15.0	14.6	14.4	47,382	712,317	15.0	49,941	718,113	14.4	46,980	723,143	15.4
South Dakota	13.7	13.5	13.4	13.4	9,416	121,606	12.9	9,244	126,429	13.7	9,326	123,713	13.3
Tennessee	15.9 [2]	15.7 [2]	16.0	15.7	64,659	964,259	14.9	64,926	971,950	15.0	65,361	972,549	14.9
Texas	14.8	15.0	15.0	14.8	321,929	4,674,832	14.5	327,905	4,752,148	14.5	333,164	4,850,210	14.6
Utah	21.9	22.6 [2]	22.1	22.1	24,336	576,244	23.7	23,657	559,778	23.7	25,474	582,793	22.9
Vermont	12.1	11.3	10.9	10.8	8,749	94,038	10.7	8,766	93,625	10.7	8,734	92,431	10.6
Virginia	13.2 [2]	12.9	11.7	15.3	71,861	1,230,857	17.1	71,415	1,235,795	17.3	70,827	1,245,340	17.6
Washington	19.7	19.2	19.3	19.1	53,960	1,030,247	19.1	54,428	1,037,018	19.1	53,448	1,035,347	19.4
West Virginia	13.7	14.0	14.1	14.4	20,306	282,535	13.9	20,209	282,729	14.0	20,299	282,662	13.9
Wisconsin	14.6	14.3	14.6	14.8	58,914	874,633	14.8	59,401	873,750	14.7	58,426	872,436	14.9
Wyoming	13.3	12.7	12.6	12.6	6,915	86,422	12.5	7,000	87,161	12.5	7,166	88,155	12.3
Bureau of Indian Education	—	—	—	—	—	—	—	—	—	—	—	—	—
DoD, overseas	14.4	14.0	10.9	11.7	4,147	57,247	13.8	4,551	56,768	12.5	—	—	—
DoD, domestic	14.2	14.6	13.9	13.1	2,243	27,548	12.3	2,145	28,013	13.1	—	—	—
Other jurisdictions													
American Samoa	19.1	17.1	16.6	16.9	—	—	—	—	—	—	—	—	—
Guam	16.4	18.3	17.2	—	—	—	—	—	—	—	—	—	—
Northern Marianas	19.0	20.0	19.1	20.2	550	11,299	20.5	514	10,913	21.2	552	10,961	19.9
Puerto Rico	16.3	13.4	13.4	13.5	40,826	526,565	12.9	39,356	503,635	12.8	39,102	493,393	12.6
U.S. Virgin Islands	12.9	10.6	11.7	10.6	1,518	15,903	10.5	1,331	15,768	11.8	1,425	15,493	10.9

—Not available.
[1] Includes imputed values for states.
[2] Includes imputations for underreporting of prekindergarten teachers/enrollment.
[3] Imputed.
[4] Includes imputations for underreporting of kindergarten teachers.
NOTE: Teachers reported in full-time equivalents (FTE). DoD = Department of Defense. The pupil/teacher ratio includes teachers for students with disabilities and other special teachers, while these teachers are generally excluded from class size calculations. Ratios reflect totals reported by states and differ from totals reported for schools or school districts. Some data have been revised from previously published figures.
SOURCE: U.S. Department of Education, National Center for Education Statistics, Common Core of Data (CCD), "State Nonfiscal Survey of Public Elementary/Secondary Education," 2000–01 through 2009–10. (This table was prepared February 2012.)

Highest degree earned, years of full-time teaching experience, and average class size for teachers in public elementary and secondary schools, by state: 2007–08

State	Total number of teachers (in thousands)	Percent of teachers, by highest degree earned[1]				Percent of teachers, by years of full-time teaching experience				Average class size, by level of instruction[2]	
		Bachelor's	Master's	Education specialist[3]	Doctor's	Less than 3	3 to 9	10 to 20	Over 20	Elementary	Secondary
1	2	3	4	5	6	7	8	9	10	11	12
United States	3,404.5 (43.98)	47.4 (0.59)	44.5 (0.55)	6.4 (0.25)	0.9 (0.08)	13.4 (0.59)	33.6 (0.52)	29.3 (0.55)	23.7 (0.60)	20.0 (0.14)	23.4 (0.16)
Alabama	53.2 (3.03)	44.3 (3.32)	46.9 (2.84)	6.9 (1.15)	0.6 (0.24)	14.4 (1.40)	31.3 (1.85)	36.1 (2.36)	18.2 (1.43)	18.9 (0.64)	25.3 (1.00)
Alaska	8.1 (1.00)	56.3 (3.04)	36.3 (2.72)	5.4 (0.98)	0.7 (0.27)	12.0 (1.33)	27.5 (2.54)	39.7 (2.74)	20.7 (1.95)	19.0 (0.81)	21.6 (0.67)
Arizona	66.5 (4.13)	49.1 (2.67)	41.6 (2.56)	7.1 (1.30)	0.7 (0.38)	21.0 (2.63)	34.6 (2.62)	26.1 (2.22)	18.4 (2.26)	23.5 (0.66)	25.6 (0.76)
Arkansas	35.8 (1.30)	58.6 (2.67)	34.1 (2.26)	5.3 (1.06)	0.2 (0.14)	10.7 (1.31)	25.7 (1.91)	32.1 (2.20)	31.6 (2.16)	19.8 (0.49)	20.3 (0.61)
California	310.0 (17.05)	52.7 (1.94)	34.3 (1.77)	10.2 (1.16)	1.9 (0.43)	13.5 (1.41)	35.9 (1.70)	30.3 (1.51)	20.3 (1.48)	21.5 (0.44)	30.0 (0.57)
Colorado	50.1 (2.19)	42.9 (2.61)	48.4 (2.54)	6.9 (1.41)	1.4 (0.56)	17.2 (1.73)	37.9 (2.55)	28.1 (2.54)	16.8 (1.88)	21.2 (0.70)	23.9 (0.69)
Connecticut	50.1 (2.85)	19.2 (1.88)	64.3 (1.94)	15.0 (1.72)	0.9 (0.42)	12.2 (1.26)	29.7 (2.19)	31.1 (2.18)	27.1 (2.16)	19.4 (0.84)	21.3 (0.79)
Delaware	8.2 (0.59)	38.2 (3.13)	53.0 (3.05)	6.2 (1.79)	1.2 (0.70)	10.6 (2.42)	43.3 (4.14)	27.9 (3.25)	18.2 (2.55)	21.4 (1.35)	22.0 (0.69)
District of Columbia	4.4 (0.39)	41.3 (3.83)	45.3 (3.96)	7.1 (1.93)	5.9 (1.64)	20.0 (3.26)	29.9 (3.61)	24.6 (2.84)	25.5 (3.46)	19.0 (0.76)	19.1 (1.58)
Florida	177.2 (9.43)	60.9 (2.40)	34.1 (2.42)	3.1 (0.76)	1.1 (0.52)	14.8 (1.66)	35.0 (2.24)	27.4 (2.11)	22.8 (2.09)	18.3 (0.48)	24.2 (0.63)
Georgia	121.9 (5.22)	38.8 (2.65)	43.4 (2.67)	15.0 (1.97)	2.3 (0.77)	10.3 (1.92)	32.4 (3.27)	35.9 (3.70)	21.4 (3.01)	17.6 (0.50)	22.6 (0.82)
Hawaii	12.8 (1.44)	46.9 (3.40)	32.6 (3.23)	17.7 (2.56)	1.4 (1.25)	18.6 (3.61)	34.3 (3.63)	28.6 (3.07)	18.6 (3.21)	20.6 (1.01)	23.6 (1.37)
Idaho	16.2 (1.32)	66.1 (2.57)	29.7 (2.38)	2.7 (0.91)	0.8 (0.60)	12.5 (1.20)	31.0 (2.46)	33.6 (2.42)	22.8 (2.05)	23.7 (0.54)	23.0 (0.55)
Illinois	145.0 (5.62)	45.5 (2.39)	49.8 (2.35)	4.0 (0.93)	0.3 (0.19)	13.4 (1.43)	35.6 (2.32)	29.3 (1.82)	21.6 (2.16)	21.4 (0.78)	23.2 (0.70)
Indiana	68.4 (2.99)	37.4 (2.78)	57.0 (2.92)	4.9 (1.34)	0.4 (0.21)	9.2 (1.37)	32.3 (2.26)	29.1 (2.14)	29.4 (2.38)	21.3 (0.42)	25.5 (0.75)
Iowa	39.6 (3.67)	59.8 (2.51)	37.9 (2.54)	1.4 (0.62)	‡ (†)	11.4 (1.44)	30.5 (2.05)	29.9 (2.34)	28.2 (2.04)	20.0 (0.62)	21.0 (0.73)
Kansas	37.7 (2.13)	53.0 (2.69)	41.8 (2.72)	4.7 (1.16)	0.2 (0.17)	13.0 (1.95)	30.2 (2.35)	27.2 (2.65)	29.6 (2.23)	19.5 (0.64)	21.0 (0.94)
Kentucky	44.4 (2.88)	20.9 (2.22)	57.5 (3.42)	18.9 (2.47)	0.7 (0.31)	10.2 (1.59)	33.5 (2.90)	30.1 (3.53)	24.2 (2.46)	22.1 (0.64)	24.3 (0.90)
Louisiana	48.1 (3.63)	71.9 (2.34)	23.5 (2.18)	3.7 (0.86)	0.4 (0.16)	12.7 (1.94)	33.3 (2.08)	27.6 (2.54)	26.3 (2.12)	18.1 (1.01)	20.9 (0.57)
Maine	17.8 (0.81)	54.4 (2.57)	37.9 (2.45)	5.1 (0.95)	0.6 (0.21)	12.3 (2.19)	27.0 (2.17)	31.5 (3.38)	29.1 (2.51)	16.9 (0.69)	19.9 (1.36)
Maryland	59.9 (3.67)	42.6 (3.60)	47.0 (3.56)	8.2 (1.94)	1.5 (0.64)	12.0 (2.05)	37.1 (2.80)	26.2 (2.83)	24.8 (2.55)	20.2 (1.35)	23.1 (0.75)
Massachusetts	80.4 (2.91)	30.6 (2.73)	62.0 (2.99)	5.6 (1.19)	0.7 (0.36)	11.1 (1.58)	39.9 (2.66)	27.2 (2.63)	21.8 (2.77)	18.7 (1.02)	20.6 (0.50)
Michigan	98.3 (6.60)	37.2 (2.81)	57.6 (2.56)	4.4 (1.34)	0.3 (0.22)	9.4 (1.66)	32.5 (2.69)	36.3 (3.06)	21.8 (1.98)	24.5 (1.04)	26.7 (0.78)
Minnesota	64.0 (5.32)	41.6 (2.00)	51.4 (2.11)	6.1 (1.09)	0.8 (0.34)	12.7 (1.61)	28.5 (2.28)	35.3 (2.54)	23.6 (1.93)	23.3 (0.74)	25.8 (0.64)
Mississippi	35.5 (1.49)	56.6 (2.34)	37.2 (2.29)	4.2 (0.89)	0.7 (0.24)	17.1 (1.42)	31.8 (2.00)	26.1 (1.90)	25.1 (2.51)	19.3 (0.55)	19.9 (0.65)
Missouri	73.3 (3.52)	47.2 (3.34)	47.5 (2.90)	3.9 (1.18)	0.6 (0.45)	13.3 (1.57)	34.2 (2.43)	31.6 (2.80)	20.8 (1.68)	19.4 (0.53)	20.6 (0.61)
Montana	12.7 (0.58)	62.8 (2.34)	33.4 (2.19)	3.5 (1.06)	‡ (†)	11.0 (1.70)	26.9 (2.23)	28.8 (2.31)	33.3 (2.07)	18.2 (0.57)	18.5 (0.84)
Nebraska	23.2 (1.18)	53.1 (2.42)	44.2 (2.42)	2.0 (0.70)	‡ (†)	11.4 (1.52)	24.2 (1.79)	30.2 (2.10)	34.2 (1.98)	18.8 (0.49)	18.7 (0.73)
Nevada	23.7 (0.88)	41.5 (2.67)	49.5 (2.58)	7.5 (1.68)	1.0 (1.25)‡	15.6 (2.01)	37.3 (3.01)	27.8 (3.10)	19.4 (2.81)	21.5 (0.67)	26.5 (1.01)
New Hampshire	17.4 (0.70)	49.4 (2.60)	45.4 (2.51)	4.5 (1.08)	‡ (†)	13.3 (2.12)	31.7 (2.33)	29.1 (2.85)	26.0 (2.97)	19.0 (0.50)	21.7 (0.68)
New Jersey	124.5 (8.59)	55.8 (3.56)	36.5 (3.11)	6.3 (1.78)	1.4 (0.52)	12.3 (1.91)	40.8 (3.16)	22.8 (2.58)	24.1 (2.39)	19.8 (1.29)	23.0 (1.11)
New Mexico	22.7 (1.44)	66.5 (2.73)	39.5 (2.74)	5.4 (1.48)	1.5 (0.80)	13.3 (1.86)	35.6 (2.81)	29.6 (2.76)	21.5 (1.95)	18.8 (0.50)	22.5 (0.67)
New York	228.1 (17.70)	11.8 (1.61)	77.6 (2.19)	8.9 (1.62)	1.1 (0.49)	12.8 (1.67)	38.0 (2.69)	28.5 (2.78)	20.6 (2.35)	18.0 (0.73)	21.0 (0.53)
North Carolina	96.0 (4.48)	64.6 (3.22)	28.0 (2.88)	5.4 (1.22)	0.4 (0.26)	15.6 (1.74)	37.3 (2.93)	25.0 (3.08)	22.0 (1.97)	19.4 (0.63)	21.0 (0.51)
North Dakota	8.9 (1.62)	68.2 (2.27)	28.1 (2.38)	2.8 (1.21)	‡ (†)	12.0 (1.64)	23.3 (1.80)	30.0 (2.53)	34.7 (2.25)	16.4 (0.40)	18.0 (1.67)
Ohio	134.3 (12.04)	31.9 (2.84)	62.3 (2.78)	3.7 (0.93)	0.7 (0.50)	12.1 (2.33)	29.9 (2.69)	31.6 (2.88)	26.3 (2.47)	21.2 (0.97)	23.4 (0.68)
Oklahoma	46.5 (1.44)	66.5 (1.82)	28.9 (2.15)	2.9 (1.12)	0.7 (0.35)	10.9 (1.12)	31.4 (1.79)	30.7 (1.65)	27.0 (1.63)	19.7 (0.37)	20.7 (0.54)
Oregon	31.7 (1.57)	37.0 (3.13)	52.3 (3.14)	9.0 (1.33)	1.2 (0.68)	18.0 (2.00)	31.5 (2.76)	29.5 (2.18)	21.0 (1.99)	23.3 (0.74)	25.2 (0.63)
Pennsylvania	136.9 (8.48)	45.3 (2.27)	45.2 (2.19)	8.0 (1.15)	‡ (†)	12.5 (1.32)	33.6 (3.02)	26.7 (2.18)	27.2 (3.01)	20.8 (0.63)	22.4 (0.79)
Rhode Island	13.2 (0.69)	44.7 (4.09)	48.7 (4.66)	5.7 (1.54)	‡ (†)	7.7 (2.09)	37.0 (3.30)	32.2 (3.31)	23.1 (3.48)	20.7 (0.59)	22.9 (1.04)
South Carolina	49.0 (1.25)	40.9 (2.53)	52.1 (2.76)	5.1 (1.17)	0.5 (0.26)	12.8 (1.39)	31.5 (2.53)	27.3 (2.18)	28.5 (2.16)	18.5 (0.60)	21.4 (0.45)
South Dakota	10.6 (1.09)	68.6 (2.39)	30.9 (2.39)	1.1 (0.47)	0.8 (0.52)	11.4 (1.47)	23.7 (2.45)	32.5 (2.16)	32.4 (2.51)	17.9 (0.68)	20.2 (0.98)
Tennessee	67.1 (3.23)	44.9 (2.96)	43.0 (2.75)	9.3 (1.61)	0.9 (0.57)	13.6 (1.86)	28.8 (2.74)	30.8 (2.83)	26.8 (2.23)	17.7 (0.45)	23.0 (0.68)
Texas	340.4 (22.28)	70.1 (2.33)	26.3 (2.29)	2.5 (0.71)	0.6 (0.22)	17.1 (1.95)	31.2 (2.18)	27.7 (2.41)	24.0 (2.74)	17.7 (0.66)	21.7 (0.85)
Utah	27.2 (0.45)	61.1 (3.34)	30.3 (3.14)	6.1 (1.42)	0.5 (0.31)	19.9 (2.38)	32.9 (2.93)	26.0 (2.54)	21.2 (2.10)	24.0 (0.39)	29.2 (0.80)
Vermont	10.2 (0.81)	42.6 (3.33)	50.0 (3.46)	5.9 (1.38)	0.5 (0.28)	11.7 (2.24)	30.5 (2.97)	30.5 (2.92)	27.3 (2.44)	16.8 (0.61)	17.9 (0.88)
Virginia	94.0 (4.10)	57.4 (2.38)	36.1 (2.12)	4.5 (1.04)	1.0 (0.50)	14.1 (2.08)	32.8 (2.39)	26.6 (2.33)	26.5 (1.88)	18.2 (0.55)	20.8 (0.99)
Washington	58.1 (3.88)	31.4 (2.45)	60.7 (2.58)	6.4 (1.27)	0.6 (0.25)	14.1 (2.48)	27.8 (2.40)	32.6 (2.40)	25.5 (2.40)	22.8 (0.63)	24.9 (0.62)
West Virginia	22.9 (0.88)	39.5 (2.23)	51.6 (1.99)	6.7 (1.14)	0.5 (0.19)	13.1 (1.56)	26.4 (2.15)	23.1 (2.11)	37.4 (1.90)	18.6 (0.53)	21.4 (0.50)
Wisconsin	70.1 (3.21)	44.8 (3.08)	49.3 (3.67)	5.5 (1.41)	0.3 (0.18)	9.8 (1.84)	32.4 (2.32)	31.4 (2.70)	26.4 (2.27)	19.6 (0.68)	23.0 (0.51)
Wyoming	7.9 (0.45)	56.0 (2.14)	37.6 (2.19)	5.3 (1.06)	0.6 (0.37)	10.3 (1.21)	27.3 (2.49)	32.5 (2.38)	29.9 (1.94)	18.7 (0.46)	18.8 (0.73)

†Not applicable.

‡Reporting standards not met (too few cases).

[1]Teachers with less than a bachelor's degree are not shown separately.

[2]Elementary teachers are those who taught self-contained classes at the elementary level, and secondary teachers are those who taught departmentalized classes (e.g., science, art, social science, or other course subjects) at the secondary level. Teachers were classified as elementary or secondary on the basis of the grades they taught, rather than on the level of the school in which they taught.

[3]Includes certificate of advanced graduate studies.

NOTE: Data are based on a head count of all teachers rather than on the number of full-time-equivalent teachers appearing in other tables. Excludes prekindergarten teachers. Standard errors appear in parentheses. Detail may not sum to totals because of rounding, cell suppression, and omitted categories (less than bachelor's).

SOURCE: U.S. Department of Education, National Center for Education Statistics, Schools and Staffing Survey (SASS), "Public Teacher Questionnaire", 2007–08. (This table was prepared September 2009.)

Teachers' perceptions about teaching and school conditions, by control and level of school: Selected years, 1993–94 through 2007–08

Percent of teachers somewhat agreeing or strongly agreeing with statement

Statement about conditions	Public — 1993‑94 total	Public — 1999‑2000 total	Public — 2003‑04 total	Public 2007‑08 Total	Public 2007‑08 Elementary schools	Public 2007‑08 Secondary schools	Public 2007‑08 Combined schools	Private — 1993‑94 total	Private — 1999‑2000 total	Private — 2003‑04 total	Private 2007‑08 Total	Private 2007‑08 Elementary schools	Private 2007‑08 Secondary schools	Private 2007‑08 Combined schools
1	2	3	4	5	6	7	8	9	10	11	12	13	14	15
The school administration's behavior toward the staff is supportive	79.2 (0.36)	78.8 (0.38)	85.2 (0.33)	87.7 (0.39)	88.1 (0.50)	87.1 (0.47)	86.3 (1.24)	88.2 (0.42)	87.3 (0.45)	91.1 (0.78)	93.1 (0.43)	92.6 (0.48)	92.3 (1.15)	93.9 (0.74)
My principal enforces school rules for student conduct and backs me up when I need it	80.8 (0.35)	82.2 (0.33)	87.2 (0.34)	88.0 (0.37)	89.2 (0.48)	85.9 (0.51)	86.1 (1.12)	88.4 (0.41)	88.3 (0.39)	92.2 (0.75)	92.2 (0.57)	91.7 (0.70)	91.8 (1.17)	92.8 (0.97)
The principal lets staff members know what is expected of them	85.6 (0.30)	87.7 (0.26)	91.9 (0.23)	—	(†)	(†)	(†)	88.2 (0.34)	89.8 (0.35)	93.8 (0.57)	—	(†)	(†)	(†)
Principal talks to me frequently about my instructional practices	44.3 (0.46)	45.6 (0.43)	—	—	(†)	(†)	(†)	54.0 (0.64)	50.4 (0.64)	—	—	(†)	(†)	(†)
In this school, staff members are recognized for a job well done	67.9 (0.39)	68.3 (0.42)	75.5 (0.38)	76.7 (0.56)	78.3 (0.77)	74.2 (0.63)	72.3 (1.42)	81.1 (0.40)	78.9 (0.50)	83.8 (1.14)	84.0 (0.66)	84.1 (0.76)	83.0 (1.71)	84.4 (1.06)
Principal knows what kind of school he/she wants and has communicated it to the staff	80.5 (0.36)	83.2 (0.28)	87.3 (0.30)	88.4 (0.33)	89.6 (0.44)	86.6 (0.51)	84.4 (1.20)	88.6 (0.38)	88.4 (0.43)	91.9 (0.68)	91.7 (0.53)	91.3 (0.65)	90.7 (1.20)	92.6 (0.81)
Most of my colleagues share my beliefs and values about what the central mission of the school should be	84.2 (0.22)	84.7 (0.26)	88.1 (0.26)	88.3 (0.35)	90.6 (0.52)	83.8 (0.53)	87.4 (0.86)	93.2 (0.37)	92.2 (0.31)	93.8 (0.49)	93.7 (0.44)	94.9 (0.47)	90.5 (1.36)	93.7 (0.78)
There is a great deal of cooperative effort among staff	77.5 (0.31)	78.4 (0.32)	83.2 (0.36)	84.3 (0.33)	86.1 (0.47)	81.0 (0.51)	81.9 (1.20)	90.5 (0.29)	89.0 (0.42)	91.2 (0.77)	91.7 (0.63)	92.1 (0.54)	88.4 (1.43)	92.6 (1.07)
I receive a great deal of support from parents for the work I do	52.5 (0.38)	57.9 (0.40)	61.1 (0.50)	64.3 (0.52)	66.4 (0.77)	60.4 (0.66)	62.6 (1.45)	84.6 (0.41)	84.0 (0.49)	86.1 (2.33)	87.7 (0.60)	89.4 (0.68)	85.1 (1.79)	86.9 (1.00)
I make a conscious effort to coordinate the content of my courses with that of other teachers	85.0 (0.25)	84.1 (0.24)	86.3 (0.31)	—	(†)	(†)	(†)	85.2 (0.44)	81.4 (0.55)	84.6 (0.90)	—	(†)	(†)	(†)
Routine duties and paperwork interfere with my job of teaching	70.8 (0.38)	71.1 (0.30)	70.8 (0.44)	69.0 (0.53)	69.4 (0.80)	68.7 (0.69)	64.4 (1.33)	40.1 (0.65)	44.5 (0.57)	40.7 (2.70)	42.7 (0.97)	44.6 (1.26)	46.3 (2.28)	39.2 (1.74)
Level of student misbehavior in this school interferes with my teaching	44.1 (0.40)	40.8 (0.42)	37.2 (0.52)	36.0 (0.57)	33.7 (0.80)	40.2 (0.79)	38.9 (1.36)	22.4 (0.43)	24.1 (0.61)	20.7 (2.47)	20.6 (0.72)	20.9 (0.95)	19.4 (1.72)	20.6 (1.36)
Amount of student tardiness and class cutting in this school interferes with my teaching	27.9 (0.32)	31.5 (0.35)	33.4 (0.45)	33.4 (0.64)	26.4 (0.85)	47.2 (0.86)	32.8 (1.35)	16.9 (0.75)	15.0 (0.43)	16.9 (1.11)	17.9 (0.72)	17.3 (0.77)	20.4 (1.77)	17.5 (1.63)
Rules for student behavior are consistently enforced by teachers in this school, even for students who are not in their classes	61.8 (0.42)	62.6 (0.39)	71.1 (0.46)	70.6 (0.55)	78.8 (0.67)	55.1 (0.66)	68.2 (1.37)	77.6 (0.50)	75.9 (0.51)	81.0 (1.52)	80.1 (0.81)	85.5 (0.85)	69.9 (2.00)	78.4 (1.49)
I am satisfied with my class sizes	64.9 (0.38)	67.7 (0.36)	69.1 (0.43)	—	(†)	(†)	(†)	84.4 (0.40)	85.7 (0.45)	87.5 (0.99)	—	(†)	(†)	(†)
I am satisfied with my teaching salary	44.9 (0.45)	39.4 (0.36)	45.9 (0.46)	50.9 (0.64)	48.9 (0.90)	55.2 (0.73)	48.0 (1.26)	41.6 (0.59)	42.6 (0.73)	50.6 (1.76)	51.7 (0.86)	44.4 (1.11)	55.6 (2.60)	57.8 (2.05)
I sometimes feel it is a waste of time to try to do my best as a teacher	26.8 (0.35)	20.3 (0.29)	16.7 (0.33)	—	(†)	(†)	(†)	10.2 (0.65)	10.5 (0.38)	8.6 (0.69)	—	(†)	(†)	(†)
I plan with the librarian/media specialist for the integration of services into my teaching	66.9 (0.42)	58.6 (0.38)	—	—	(†)	(†)	(†)	60.6 (0.71)	48.7 (0.74)	—	—	(†)	(†)	(†)
Necessary materials are available as needed by staff	73.1 (0.42)	75.0 (0.32)	79.0 (0.42)	82.2 (0.55)	82.5 (0.76)	81.5 (0.51)	82.2 (1.06)	85.7 (0.44)	89.0 (0.38)	91.8 (0.74)	92.1 (0.54)	92.2 (0.59)	91.2 (1.33)	92.2 (1.01)
I worry about the security of my job because of the performance of my students on state or local tests	—	28.8 (0.37)	31.2 (0.43)	30.9 (0.58)	32.2 (0.81)	28.3 (0.54)	30.5 (1.31)	—	6.7 (0.29)	7.8 (0.68)	7.6 (0.46)	8.2 (0.56)	6.3 (1.06)	7.5 (0.81)
State or district content standards have had a positive influence on my satisfaction with teaching	—	(†)	—	49.3 (0.62)	52.1 (0.95)	44.1 (0.56)	48.5 (1.29)	—	(†)	—	41.1 (0.80)	49.1 (1.21)	34.3 (1.99)	35.3 (1.48)
I am given the support I need to teach students with special needs	—	60.9 (0.33)	64.5 (0.47)	67.2 (0.57)	66.2 (0.73)	68.3 (0.69)	72.7 (1.18)	—	67.1 (0.58)	71.8 (2.00)	68.4 (0.84)	66.4 (1.15)	69.6 (1.81)	70.2 (1.56)
I am generally satisfied with being a teacher at this school	—	89.7 (0.24)	90.9 (0.29)	92.8 (0.31)	93.0 (0.42)	92.4 (0.37)	93.1 (0.59)	—	93.3 (0.26)	95.2 (0.56)	95.7 (0.43)	95.2 (0.52)	95.5 (0.92)	96.3 (0.65)

—Not available.
†Not applicable.
NOTE: Standard errors appear in parentheses.

SOURCE: U.S. Department of Education, National Center for Education Statistics, Schools and Staffing Survey (SASS), "Public Teacher Questionnaire," selected years 1993–94 through 2007–08; "Private Teacher Questionnaire," selected years 1993–94 through 2007–08; and "Charter Teacher Questionnaire," 1999–2000. (This table was prepared September 2009.)

Estimated average annual salary of teachers in public elementary and secondary schools: Selected years, 1959–60 through 2010–11

School year	Current dollars					Average public school teachers' salary in constant 2009–10 dollars[2]		
	Average public school teachers' salary			Wage and salary accruals per full-time-equivalent (FTE) employee[1]	Ratio of average teachers' salary to accruals per FTE employee			
	All teachers	Elementary teachers	Secondary teachers			All teachers	Elementary teachers	Secondary teachers
1	2	3	4	5	6	7	8	9
1959–60	$4,995	$4,815	$5,276	$4,749	1.05	$36,844	$35,516	$38,917
1961–62	5,515	5,340	5,775	5,063	1.09	39,766	38,504	41,641
1963–64	5,995	5,805	6,266	5,478	1.09	42,128	40,793	44,033
1965–66	6,485	6,279	6,761	5,934	1.09	44,049	42,650	45,924
1967–68	7,423	7,208	7,692	6,533	1.14	47,307	45,937	49,022
1969–70	8,626	8,412	8,891	7,486	1.15	49,492	48,264	51,012
1970–71	9,268	9,021	9,568	7,998	1.16	50,565	49,218	52,202
1971–72	9,705	9,424	10,031	8,521	1.14	51,116	49,636	52,833
1972–73	10,174	9,893	10,507	9,056	1.12	51,511	50,088	53,196
1973–74	10,770	10,507	11,077	9,667	1.11	50,064	48,842	51,491
1974–75	11,641	11,334	12,000	10,411	1.12	48,714	47,430	50,217
1975–76	12,600	12,280	12,937	11,194	1.13	49,242	47,991	50,559
1976–77	13,354	12,989	13,776	11,971	1.12	49,313	47,965	50,871
1977–78	14,198	13,845	14,602	12,811	1.11	49,131	47,909	50,529
1978–79	15,032	14,681	15,450	13,807	1.09	47,561	46,451	48,884
1979–80	15,970	15,569	16,459	15,050	1.06	44,585	43,465	45,950
1980–81	17,644	17,230	18,142	16,461	1.07	44,145	43,109	45,391
1981–82	19,274	18,853	19,805	17,795	1.08	44,389	43,419	45,612
1982–83	20,695	20,227	21,291	18,873	1.10	45,699	44,665	47,015
1983–84	21,935	21,487	22,554	19,781	1.11	46,708	45,754	48,026
1984–85	23,600	23,200	24,187	20,694	1.14	48,361	47,541	49,563
1985–86	25,199	24,718	25,846	21,685	1.16	50,190	49,232	51,478
1986–87	26,569	26,057	27,244	22,700	1.17	51,769	50,771	53,084
1987–88	28,034	27,519	28,798	23,777	1.18	52,450	51,487	53,880
1988–89	29,564	29,022	30,218	24,752	1.19	52,871	51,902	54,041
1989–90	31,367	30,832	32,049	25,762	1.22	53,541	52,627	54,705
1990–91	33,084	32,490	33,896	26,935	1.23	53,544	52,583	54,858
1991–92	34,063	33,479	34,827	28,169	1.21	53,417	52,501	54,615
1992–93	35,029	34,350	35,880	29,245	1.20	53,268	52,235	54,562
1993–94	35,737	35,233	36,566	30,030	1.19	52,972	52,225	54,201
1994–95	36,675	36,088	37,523	30,857	1.19	52,848	52,002	54,070
1995–96	37,642	37,138	38,397	31,822	1.18	52,805	52,098	53,864
1996–97	38,443	38,039	39,184	33,058	1.16	52,433	51,882	53,443
1997–98	39,350	39,002	39,944	34,635	1.14	52,729	52,263	53,525
1998–99	40,544	40,165	41,203	36,306	1.12	53,405	52,905	54,273
1999–2000	41,807	41,306	42,546	38,176	1.10	53,523	52,882	54,469
2000–01	43,378	42,910	44,053	39,722	1.09	53,695	53,116	54,530
2001–02	44,655	44,177	45,310	40,579	1.10	54,314	53,733	55,111
2002–03	45,686	45,408	46,106	41,704	1.10	54,373	54,042	54,873
2003–04	46,542	46,187	46,976	43,301	1.07	54,206	53,792	54,711
2004–05	47,516	47,122	47,688	44,941	1.06	53,724	53,278	53,918
2005–06	49,086	48,573	49,496	46,755	1.05	53,463	52,904	53,909
2006–07	51,052	50,740	51,529	48,867	1.04	54,202	53,871	54,709
2007–08	52,800	52,385	53,262	50,670	1.04	54,055	53,630	54,528
2008–09	54,319	53,998	54,552	51,640	1.05	54,845	54,521	55,080
2009–10	55,202	54,918	55,595	52,651	1.05	55,202	54,918	55,595
2010–11	56,069	55,864	56,350	—	—	54,965	54,764	55,241

—Not available.

[1] The average monetary remuneration earned by FTE employees across all industries in a given year, including wages, salaries, commissions, tips, bonuses, voluntary employee contributions to certain deferred compensation plans, and receipts in kind that represent income. Calendar-year data from the U.S. Department of Commerce, Bureau of Economic Analysis, have been converted to a school-year basis by averaging the two appropriate calendar years in each case.

[2] Constant dollars based on the Consumer Price Index, prepared by the Bureau of Labor Statistics, U.S. Department of Labor, adjusted to a school-year basis.
NOTE: Some data have been revised from previously published figures. Standard errors are not available for these estimates, which are based on state reports.
SOURCE: National Education Association, *Estimates of School Statistics*, 1959–60 through 2010–11; and unpublished tabulations. U.S. Department of Commerce, Bureau of Economic Analysis, National Income and Product Accounts, tables 6.6B-D, retrieved November 2, 2011, from http://www.bea.gov/national/nipaweb/SelectTable.asp. (This table was prepared May 2011.)

Estimated average annual salary of teachers in public elementary and secondary schools, by state: Selected years, 1969–70 through 2010–11

State	Current dollars							Constant 2009–10 dollars[1]							Percent change, 1999–2000 to 2010–11
	1969–70	1979–80	1989–90	1999–2000	2004–05	2009–10	2010–11	1969–70	1979–80	1989–90	1999–2000	2004–05	2009–10	2010–11	
1	2	3	4	5	6	7	8	9	10	11	12	13	14	15	16
United States...	$8,626	$15,970	$31,367	$41,807	$47,516	$55,202	$56,069	$49,492	$44,585	$53,541	$53,523	$53,724	$55,202	$54,965	2.7
Alabama	6,818	13,060	24,828	36,689	38,186	47,571	48,282	39,118	36,461	42,379	46,971	43,175	47,571	47,332	0.8
Alaska	10,560	27,210	43,153	46,462	52,424	59,672	61,093	60,588	75,964	73,658	59,483	59,273	59,672	59,890	0.7
Arizona	8,711	15,054	29,402	36,902	42,905	46,952	47,553	49,980	42,027	50,187	47,244	48,510	46,952	46,617	-1.3
Arkansas	6,307	12,299	22,352	33,386	40,495	46,700	47,700	36,187	34,336	38,153	42,742	45,785	46,700	46,761	9.4
California	10,315	18,020	37,998	47,680	57,876	68,203	69,434	59,183	50,308	64,859	61,042	65,437	68,203	68,067	11.5
Colorado	7,761	16,205	30,758	38,163	43,949	49,202	49,938	44,529	45,241	52,501	48,858	49,691	49,202	48,955	0.2
Connecticut	9,262	16,229	40,461	51,780	57,737	64,350	65,571	53,141	45,308	69,063	66,291	65,280	64,350	64,280	-3.0
Delaware	9,015	16,148	33,377	44,435	50,595	57,080	57,934	51,724	45,082	56,972	56,888	57,205	57,080	56,794	-0.2
District of Columbia ..	10,285	22,190	38,402	47,076	58,456	64,548	66,601	59,010	61,950	65,549	60,269	66,093	64,548	65,290	8.3
Florida	8,412	14,149	28,803	36,722	41,590	46,708	46,702	48,264	39,501	49,164	47,013	47,023	46,708	45,783	-2.6
Georgia	7,276	13,853	28,006	41,023	46,526	53,112	53,906	41,746	38,675	47,804	52,520	52,604	53,112	52,845	0.6
Hawaii	9,453	19,920	32,047	40,578	46,149	55,063	55,063	54,237	55,612	54,701	51,950	52,178	55,063	53,979	3.9
Idaho	6,890	13,611	23,861	35,547	42,122	46,283	47,416	39,532	37,999	40,729	45,509	47,625	46,283	46,483	2.1
Illinois	9,569	17,601	32,794	46,486	55,421	62,077	63,005	54,902	49,138	55,976	59,514	62,661	62,077	61,765	3.8
Indiana	8,833	15,599	30,902	41,850	46,583	49,986	50,407	50,680	43,549	52,747	53,578	52,669	49,986	49,415	-7.8
Iowa	8,355	15,203	26,747	35,678	39,284	49,626	50,634	47,937	42,443	45,655	45,677	44,416	49,626	49,637	8.7
Kansas	7,612	13,690	28,744	34,981	39,345	46,657	47,080	43,674	38,219	49,063	44,784	44,485	46,657	46,153	3.1
Kentucky	6,953	14,520	26,292	36,380	40,522	49,543	50,038	39,893	40,537	44,878	46,575	45,816	49,543	49,053	5.3
Louisiana	7,028	13,760	24,300	33,109	39,022	48,903	49,634	40,323	38,415	41,478	42,388	44,120	48,903	48,657	14.8
Maine	7,572	13,071	26,881	35,561	39,610	46,106	47,182	43,445	36,491	45,883	45,527	44,785	46,106	46,253	1.6
Maryland	9,383	17,558	36,319	44,048	52,331	63,971	65,113	53,835	49,018	61,993	56,392	59,168	63,971	63,831	13.2
Massachusetts	8,764	17,253	34,712	46,580	54,679	69,273	71,017	50,284	48,167	59,250	59,634	61,822	69,273	69,619	16.7
Michigan	9,826	19,663	37,072	49,044	56,973	57,958	58,595	56,377	54,895	63,279	62,788	64,416	57,958	57,442	-8.5
Minnesota	8,658	15,912	32,190	39,802	46,906	52,431	53,215	49,676	44,423	54,945	50,956	53,034	52,431	52,167	2.4
Mississippi	5,798	11,850	24,292	31,857	36,590	45,644	46,818	33,266	33,083	41,464	40,785	41,370	45,644	45,896	12.5
Missouri	7,799	13,682	27,094	35,656	39,067	45,317	46,411	44,747	38,197	46,247	45,648	44,171	45,317	45,497	-0.3
Montana	7,606	14,537	25,081	32,121	38,485	45,759	47,132	43,640	40,584	42,811	41,123	43,513	45,759	46,204	12.4
Nebraska	7,375	13,516	25,522	33,237	39,456	46,227	47,521	42,314	37,734	43,564	42,552	44,611	46,227	46,586	9.5
Nevada	9,215	16,295	30,590	39,390	43,394	51,524	53,023	52,871	45,492	52,214	50,429	49,063	51,524	51,979	3.1
New Hampshire	7,771	13,017	28,986	37,734	43,941	51,443	52,792	44,586	36,341	49,477	48,309	49,682	51,443	51,753	7.1
New Jersey	9,130	17,161	35,676	52,015	56,682	65,130	66,985	52,384	47,910	60,896	66,592	64,087	65,130	65,666	-1.4
New Mexico	7,796	14,887	24,756	32,554	39,391	46,258	46,950	44,730	41,561	42,256	41,677	44,537	46,258	46,026	10.4
New York	10,336	19,812	38,925	51,020	56,200	71,633	72,708	59,303	55,311	66,442	65,318	63,542	71,633	71,277	9.1
North Carolina	7,494	14,117	27,883	39,404	43,348	46,850	46,850	42,997	39,412	47,594	50,447	49,011	46,850	45,928	-9.0
North Dakota	6,696	13,263	23,016	29,863	36,695	42,964	44,266	38,418	37,027	39,286	38,232	41,489	42,964	43,395	13.5
Ohio	8,300	15,269	31,218	41,436	48,692	55,958	57,291	47,621	42,628	53,286	53,048	55,053	55,958	56,163	5.9
Oklahoma	6,882	13,107	23,070	31,298	37,879	47,691	49,039	39,486	36,592	39,378	40,069	42,828	47,691	48,074	20.0
Oregon	8,818	16,266	30,840	42,336	48,330	55,224	56,387	50,594	45,411	52,641	54,201	54,644	55,224	55,277	2.0
Pennsylvania	8,858	16,515	33,338	48,321	53,258	59,156	60,536	50,823	46,106	56,905	61,863	60,216	59,156	59,344	-4.1
Rhode Island	8,776	18,002	36,057	47,041	53,473	59,686	60,923	50,353	50,258	61,546	60,224	60,459	59,686	59,724	-0.8
South Carolina	6,927	13,063	27,217	36,081	42,189	47,508	49,434	39,744	36,469	46,457	46,193	47,701	47,508	48,461	4.9
South Dakota	6,403	12,348	21,300	29,071	34,040	38,837	35,201	36,737	34,473	36,357	37,218	38,487	38,837	34,508	-7.3
Tennessee	7,050	13,972	27,052	36,328	42,076	46,290	47,043	40,450	39,007	46,175	46,509	47,573	46,290	46,117	-0.8
Texas	7,255	14,132	27,496	37,567	41,011	48,261	48,261	41,626	39,453	46,933	48,095	46,369	48,261	47,311	-1.6
Utah	7,644	14,909	23,686	34,946	39,456	45,885	46,571	43,858	41,623	40,430	44,739	44,611	45,885	45,654	2.0
Vermont	7,968	12,484	29,012	37,758	44,535	49,084	50,141	45,717	34,853	49,521	48,340	50,353	49,084	49,154	1.7
Virginia	8,070	14,060	30,938	38,744	42,768	50,015	51,559	46,302	39,252	52,808	49,602	48,355	50,015	50,544	1.9
Washington	9,225	18,820	30,457	41,043	45,718	53,003	53,796	52,929	52,541	51,987	52,545	51,691	53,003	52,737	0.4
West Virginia	7,650	13,710	22,842	35,009	38,360	45,959	47,253	43,892	38,275	38,989	44,820	43,372	45,959	46,323	3.4
Wisconsin	8,963	16,006	31,921	41,153	44,299	51,264	52,031	51,425	44,685	54,486	52,686	50,086	51,264	51,007	-3.2
Wyoming	8,232	16,012	28,141	34,127	40,497	55,861	56,978	47,231	44,702	48,034	43,691	45,788	55,861	55,856	27.8

[1]Constant dollars based on the Consumer Price Index (CPI), prepared by the Bureau of Labor Statistics, U.S. Department of Labor, adjusted to a school-year basis. The CPI does not account for differences in inflation rates from state to state.

NOTE: Some data have been revised from previously published figures. Standard errors are not available for these estimates, which are based on state reports.
SOURCE: National Education Association, *Estimates of School Statistics*, 1969–70 through 2010–11. (This table was prepared May 2011.)

Number and internet access of instructional computers and rooms in public schools, by selected school characteristics: Selected years, 1995 through 2008

Instructional computers and rooms, and access	All public schools	Instructional level[1] — Elementary	Secondary	Size of school enrollment — Less than 300	300 to 999	1,000 or more	Community type[2] — City	Suburban	Town	Rural	Percent of students eligible for free or reduced-price lunch[3] — Less than 35 percent	35 to 49 percent	50 to 74 percent	75 percent or more
1	2	3	4	5	6	7	8	9	10	11	12	13	14	15
Computers for instructional purposes														
Number (in thousands)														
1995[4]	5,621 (—)	3,453 (—)	2,021 (—)	850 (—)	3,600 (—)	1,171 (—)	1,497 (—)	1,526 (—)	1,404 (—)	1,195 (—)	2,905 (—)	806 (—)	950 (—)	882 (—)
2000	8,776 (174)	5,296 (149)	3,271 (113)	1,135 (73)	5,524 (121)	2,117 (103)	2,537 (179)	3,396 (213)	1,155 (132)	1,689 (131)	4,394 (147)	1,373 (93)	1,606 (112)	1,384 (107)
2005	12,672 (281)	7,701 (251)	4,783 (148)	1,566 (98)	7,966 (243)	3,139 (163)	3,132 (177)	4,058 (242)	1,819 (193)	3,663 (255)	5,352 (261)	2,193 (185)	2,687 (244)	2,440 (152)
2008	15,434 (193)	9,711 (159)	5,415 (125)	1,746 (68)	9,486 (144)	4,202 (130)	3,611 (155)	5,787 (255)	2,062 (159)	3,974 (180)	6,195 (174)	2,364 (155)	3,805 (190)	3,070 (175)
Average number per school														
1995[4]	72 (—)	60 (—)	112 (—)	41 (—)	72 (—)	164 (—)	84 (—)	83 (—)	72 (—)	54 (—)	78 (—)	59 (—)	74 (—)	67 (—)
2000	110 (2.0)	89 (2.4)	178 (5.3)	57 (3.1)	106 (2.3)	259 (9.0)	120 (4.9)	128 (4.3)	97 (5.6)	82 (3.6)	120 (3.4)	111 (5.9)	94 (5.7)	99 (5.5)
2005	154 (3.4)	124 (3.8)	253 (6.8)	75 (4.2)	149 (4.2)	388 (13.5)	165 (7.2)	170 (6.3)	154 (13.4)	132 (5.9)	166 (5.5)	153 (9.3)	147 (6.9)	139 (7.4)
2008	189 (2.9)	157 (2.8)	301 (6.5)	87 (3.4)	179 (2.9)	486 (10.4)	205 (7.5)	221 (6.1)	189 (8.0)	147 (4.2)	209 (5.6)	182 (7.7)	181 (6.8)	170 (8.2)
Number with internet access (in thousands)														
1995[4]	447 (—)	232 (—)	187 (—)	59 (—)	315 (—)	73 (—)	96 (—)	131 (—)	126 (—)	94 (—)	286 (—)	46 (—)	57 (—)	36 (—)
2000	6,759 (174)	3,813 (136)	2,778 (113)	882 (69)	4,191 (114)	1,686 (97)	1,782 (148)	2,688 (178)	955 (111)	1,335 (91)	3,608 (139)	1,064 (80)	1,215 (93)	858 (87)
2005	12,245 (274)	7,361 (246)	4,706 (151)	1,515 (98)	7,642 (239)	3,089 (162)	3,009 (173)	3,912 (238)	1,784 (193)	3,541 (239)	5,239 (259)	2,090 (176)	2,583 (228)	2,332 (146)
2008	15,162 (204)	9,508 (169)	5,356 (128)	1,710 (69)	9,308 (153)	4,144 (130)	3,517 (154)	5,716 (253)	2,028 (154)	3,901 (178)	6,131 (174)	2,321 (153)	3,739 (188)	2,971 (175)
Percent with internet access														
1995[4]	8 (—)	7 (—)	9 (—)	7 (—)	9 (—)	6 (—)	6 (—)	9 (—)	9 (—)	8 (—)	10 (—)	6 (—)	6 (—)	4 (—)
2000	77 (1.1)	72 (1.5)	85 (1.2)	78 (2.6)	76 (1.3)	80 (1.8)	70 (2.1)	79 (1.7)	83 (2.5)	79 (2.1)	82 (1.2)	77 (2.9)	76 (2.6)	62 (3.1)
2005	97 (0.4)	96 (0.5)	98 (0.4)	97 (0.7)	96 (0.5)	98 (0.5)	96 (0.7)	96 (1.1)	98 (0.6)	97 (0.7)	98 (0.6)	95 (1.0)	96 (1.0)	96 (0.8)
2008	98 (0.2)	98 (0.3)	99 (0.2)	98 (0.7)	98 (0.3)	99 (0.4)	97 (0.5)	99 (0.3)	98 (0.7)	98 (0.4)	99 (0.5)	98 (0.5)	98 (0.4)	97 (0.7)
Ratio of students to instructional computers with internet access														
2000	6.6 (0.10)	7.8 (0.20)	5.2 (0.20)	3.9 (0.30)	7.0 (0.20)	7.2 (0.30)	8.2 (0.40)	6.6 (0.20)	6.2 (0.30)	5.0 (0.30)	6.0 (0.20)	6.3 (0.40)	7.2 (0.40)	9.1 (0.70)
2005	3.8 (0.10)	4.1 (0.10)	3.3 (0.10)	2.4 (0.10)	3.9 (0.10)	4.0 (0.10)	4.2 (0.20)	4.1 (0.10)	3.4 (0.20)	3.0 (0.10)	3.8 (0.10)	3.4 (0.20)	3.6 (0.20)	4.0 (0.20)
2008	3.1 (0.04)	3.2 (0.05)	2.9 (0.05)	2.2 (0.07)	3.2 (0.05)	3.2 (0.06)	3.4 (0.12)	3.2 (0.08)	2.7 (0.09)	2.9 (0.07)	3.1 (0.06)	3.2 (0.08)	2.9 (0.08)	3.2 (0.14)
Instructional rooms[5]														
Number (in thousands)														
2000	2,905 (35)	1,864 (28)	972 (24)	377 (22)	1,871 (23)	657 (23)	866 (56)	1,086 (61)	413 (47)	541 (39)	1,380 (46)	465 (28)	570 (36)	482 (29)
2005	3,283 (71)	2,152 (70)	1,078 (27)	426 (23)	2,152 (70)	705 (30)	849 (62)	1,050 (61)	439 (41)	945 (67)	1,339 (50)	593 (51)	695 (56)	655 (39)
2008[5]	2,663 (21)	1,723 (20)	887 (15)	282 (9)	1,692 (20)	689 (18)	639 (26)	1,003 (35)	338 (24)	683 (28)	1,053 (27)	425 (26)	653 (27)	532 (22)
Percent with internet access[6]														
1995	8 (0.7)	8 (1.0)	8 (1.0)	9 (1.6)	8 (1.0)	4 (1.0)	6 (1.3)	8 (1.4)	8 (2.6)	8 (1.5)	10 (1.2)	6 (1.4)	6 (1.9)	3 (1.0)
2000	77 (1.1)	76 (1.5)	79 (1.6)	83 (2.8)	78 (1.5)	70 (2.2)	66 (2.2)	78 (2.0)	87 (2.6)	85 (1.7)	82 (1.5)	81 (2.9)	77 (2.8)	60 (3.3)
2005	94 (1.3)	93 (1.9)	95 (0.9)	92 (1.9)	94 (1.9)	94 (1.5)	88 (3.7)	96 (0.8)	98 (0.7)	95 (1.8)	96 (0.8)	88 (4.3)	96 (0.8)	91 (2.5)
2008	— (†)	— (†)	— (†)	— (†)	— (†)	— (†)	— (†)	— (†)	— (†)	— (†)	— (†)	— (†)	— (†)	— (†)

—Not available.

†Not applicable.

[1]Data for combined schools are included in the totals and in analyses by other school characteristics, but are not shown separately.

[2]Due to definitional changes for community type, estimates for years prior to 2005 may not be directly comparable with estimates for later years.

[3]Free or reduced-price lunch information was obtained on the questionnaire and supplemented, if necessary, with data from the Common Core of Data (CCD).

[4]Includes computers used for instructional or administrative purposes.

[5]In 2008, instructional rooms included classrooms only and excluded computer labs and library/media centers. Prior to 2008, instructional rooms included classrooms, computer labs and other labs, library/media centers, and other rooms used for instructional purposes.

[6]Some data differ slightly (e.g., by 1 percent) from previously published figures.

NOTE: Detail may not sum to totals because of rounding. Standard errors appear in parentheses.

SOURCE: U.S. Department of Education, National Center for Education Statistics, Fast Response Survey System (FRSS), *Internet Access in U.S. Public Schools and Classrooms: 1994–2005* and *Educational Technology in U.S. Public Schools: Fall 2008*; and unpublished tabulations. (This table was prepared August 2010.)

Percentage of public school districts with students enrolled in technology-based distance education courses and number of enrollments in such courses, by instructional level and district characteristics: 2002–03, 2004–05, and 2009–10

District characteristic	Percent of districts enrolling distance education students		Number of enrollments in technology-based distance education courses,[1] by instructional level									
			All instructional levels		Elementary schools		Middle or junior high schools		High schools		Combined or ungraded schools[2]	
1	2		3		4		5		6		7	
2002–03												
Total	36	(1.2)	317,070	(27,437)	2,780 !	(977)	6,390	(1,067)	214,140	(16,549)	93,760	(22,593)
District enrollment size												
Less than 2,500	37	(1.5)	116,300	(21,698)	‡	(†)	1,250 !	(450)	72,730	(6,924)	42,240 !	(20,502)
2,500 to 9,999	32	(1.8)	82,370	(6,384)	230 !	(109)	1,870 !	(642)	44,170	(5,832)	36,110	(1,210)
10,000 or more	50	(2.1)	118,390	(15,703)	2,480 !	(968)	3,270	(723)	97,240	(13,853)	‡	(†)
Region												
Northeast	21	(2.2)	41,950 !	(20,821)	100 !	(49)	‡	(†)	17,300	(3,656)	‡	(†)
Southeast	45	(2.6)	59,240	(6,251)	‡	(†)	2,530	(632)	50,640	(5,698)	4,680	(1,254)
Central	46	(2.3)	106,690	(7,726)	940 !	(441)	1,050 !	(412)	59,110	(6,455)	45,590	(2,529)
West	32	(2.2)	109,190	(16,010)	350 !	(165)	2,620	(782)	87,090	(14,825)	19,130 !	(8,619)
Poverty concentration												
Less than 10 percent	33	(2.1)	75,740	(11,177)	‡	(†)	2,020	(564)	55,670	(7,556)	17,470 !	(8,591)
10 to 19 percent	42	(2.1)	95,510	(7,962)	‡	(†)	1,830	(392)	78,680	(7,050)	13,560	(2,446)
20 percent or more	42	(2.5)	86,110	(13,518)	760 !	(249)	2,540 !	(837)	75,930	(13,532)	6,880	(1,557)
2004–05												
Total	37	(1.2)	506,950	(56,959)	12,540 !	(6,107)	15,150	(3,367)	309,630	(24,350)	169,630 !	(51,753)
District enrollment size												
Less than 2,500	37	(1.6)	210,200	(54,063)	610 !	(275)	‡	(†)	103,190	(17,659)	‡	(†)
2,500 to 9,999	35	(1.6)	102,730	(13,404)	‡	(†)	2,570	(731)	48,420	(5,136)	45,080	(9,429)
10,000 or more	50	(2.5)	193,440	(16,415)	5,280 !	(2,202)	6,520	(1,101)	157,440	(16,044)	24,210	(5,298)
Region												
Northeast	22	(2.0)	108,300 !	(49,777)	570 !	(206)	‡	(†)	16,860	(2,621)	‡	(†)
Southeast	46	(3.2)	112,830	(6,341)	‡	(†)	5,030	(732)	89,800	(5,276)	16,090	(1,913)
Central	45	(2.4)	128,650	(22,055)	‡	(†)	2,130 !	(953)	70,450	(13,024)	46,190 !	(15,067)
West	35	(2.1)	157,180	(22,608)	200 !	(161)	4,110 !	(1,732)	132,520	(21,287)	20,350 !	(7,587)
Poverty concentration												
Less than 10 percent	35	(1.9)	112,320	(16,778)	‡	(†)	4,070	(1,123)	80,150	(10,651)	‡	(†)
10 to 19 percent	42	(2.2)	151,050	(12,379)	‡	(†)	4,800	(602)	124,540	(10,283)	19,700	(5,835)
20 percent or more	43	(2.7)	106,610	(14,709)	‡	(†)	6,280 !	(3,111)	78,590	(13,367)	21,340	(2,905)
2009–10												
Total	55	(1.4)	1,816,390	(251,054)	78,040 !	(25,180)	154,970	(30,828)	1,348,920	(135,979)	234,460 !	(164,589)
District enrollment size												
Less than 2,500	51	(1.8)	509,030 !	(167,570)	‡	(†)	‡	(†)	408,030 !	(123,883)	6,570 !	2,753
2,500 to 9,999	66	(1.5)	579,250 !	(185,243)	25,320 !	(12,669)	23,960 !	(9,196)	312,130	(50,963)	‡	(†)
10,000 or more	74	(0.8)	728,110	(27,105)	11,540	(1,862)	77,750	(4,730)	628,760	(23,545)	10,060	2,756
Metropolitan status												
City	37	(4.0)	653,660 !	(201,665)	‡	(†)	40,400 !	(15,671)	405,740	(79,507)	‡	(†)
Suburban	47	(2.6)	527,250	(34,188)	22,900 !	(11,293)	62,210	(4,106)	434,260	(30,904)	7,880	2,347
Town	67	(2.7)	306,840	(145,000)	‡	(†)	‡	(†)	246,850 !	(107,079)	9,310 !	3,908
Rural	59	(2.5)	328,640	(36,233)	‡	(†)	15,360	(2,420)	262,070	(27,077)	‡	(†)
Region												
Northeast	39	(3.3)	77,670	(7,358)	‡	(†)	4,970	(989)	71,330	(6,651)	‡	(†)
Southeast	78	(3.7)	518,770	(63,187)	12,070 !	(4,154)	57,500	(9,828)	443,770	(50,079)	5,440 !	1,678
Central	62	(2.2)	697,140 !	(235,103)	37,920 !	(18,915)	‡	(†)	416,550	(122,633)	‡	(†)
West	51	(2.4)	522,810	(42,673)	‡	(†)	41,620	(3,384)	417,270	(33,400)	36,510 !	14,278
Poverty concentration												
Less than 10 percent	54	(2.5)	287,680	(34,577)	‡	(†)	12,620	(2,997)	231,890	(27,672)	‡	(†)
10 to 19 percent	56	(2.1)	1,009,290	(193,646)	23,540 !	(11,116)	97,220	(16,126)	682,380	(78,795)	‡	(†)
20 percent or more	56	(2.4)	519,420	(146,507)	‡	(†)	‡	(†)	434,640	(108,046)	5,750 !	2,484

—Not available.
†Not applicable.
#Rounds to zero.
!Interpret data with caution. The coefficient of variation (CV) for this estimate is 30 percent or greater.
‡Reporting standards not met. The coefficient of variation (CV) for this estimate is 50 percent or greater.
[1]Based on students regularly enrolled in the districts. Enrollments may include duplicated counts of students, since districts were instructed to count a student enrolled in multiple courses for each course in which he or she was enrolled.
[2]Combined or ungraded schools are those in which the grades offered in the school span both elementary and secondary grades or that are not divided into grade levels.

NOTE: Percentages are based on unrounded numbers. For the 2002–03 FRSS study sample, there were 3 cases for which district enrollment size was missing and 112 cases for which poverty concentration was missing. For the 2002–03 FRSS study sample, there were 3 cases for which district enrollment size was missing and 112 cases for which poverty concentration was missing. For the 2004–05 FRSS study sample, there were 7 cases for which district enrollment size was missing and 103 cases for which poverty concentration was missing. Detail may not sum to totals because of rounding or missing data. Some data have been revised from previously published figures. Standard errors appear in parentheses.
SOURCE: U.S. Department of Education, National Center for Education Statistics, Fast Response Survey System (FRSS), *Technology-Based Distance Education Courses for Public Elementary and Secondary Schools: 2002–03 and 2004–05.* (This table was prepared November 2011.)

Federal support and estimated federal tax expenditures for education, by category: Selected fiscal years, 1965 through 2011

[In millions of dollars]

Fiscal year	Total on-budget support, off-budget support, and nonfederal funds generated by federal legislation	On-budget support[1] Total	Elementary and secondary	Post-secondary	Other education[3]	Research at educational institutions	Off-budget support and nonfederal funds generated by federal legislation Total	Off-budget support Direct Loan Program[4]	Nonfederal funds Federal Family Education Loan Program[5]	Perkins Loans[6]	Income Contingent Loans[7]	Leveraging Educational Assistance Partnerships[8]	Supplemental Educational Opportunity Grants[9]	Work-Study Aid[10]	Estimated federal tax expenditures for education[2]
1	2	3	4	5	6	7	8	9	10	11	12	13	14	15	16
							Current dollars								
1965	$5,354.7	$5,331.0	$1,942.6	$1,197.5	$374.7	$1,816.3	$23.7	†	†	$16.1	†	†	†	$7.6	—
1970	13,359.1	12,526.5	5,830.4	3,447.7	964.7	2,283.6	832.6	†	$770.0	21.0	†	†	†	41.6	—
1975	24,691.5	23,288.1	10,617.2	7,644.0	1,608.5	3,418.4	1,403.4	†	1,233.0	35.7	†	$20.0	†	114.7	$8,605.0
1980	39,349.5	34,493.5	16,027.7	11,115.9	1,548.7	5,801.2	4,886.0	†	4,598.0	31.8	†	76.8	†	149.4	13,320.0
1985	47,753.4	39,027.9	16,901.3	11,174.4	2,107.6	8,844.6	8,725.5	†	8,467.0	21.4	†	76.0	†	161.1	19,105.0
1986	48,357.3	39,962.9	17,049.9	11,283.6	2,620.0	9,009.4	8,394.4	†	8,142.0	20.2	†	72.7	†	159.5	20,425.0
1987	50,724.6	41,194.7	17,535.7	10,300.0	2,820.4	10,538.6	9,529.8	†	9,272.0	20.9	$0.6	76.0	†	160.4	20,830.0
1988	54,078.7	43,454.4	18,564.9	10,657.5	2,981.6	11,250.5	10,624.3	†	10,380.0	20.6	0.5	72.8	†	150.4	17,025.0
1989	59,537.4	48,269.6	19,809.5	13,269.9	3,180.3	12,009.8	11,267.8	†	10,938.0	20.4	0.5	71.9	$22.0	215.0	17,755.0
1990	62,811.5	51,624.3	21,984.4	13,650.9	3,383.0	12,606.0	11,187.2	†	10,826.0	15.0	0.5	59.2	48.8	237.7	19,040.0
1991	70,375.6	57,599.5	25,418.0	14,707.4	3,698.6	13,775.4	12,776.1	†	12,372.0	17.3	0.5	63.5	87.7	235.0	18,995.0
1992	74,481.1	60,483.1	27,926.9	14,387.4	3,992.0	14,176.9	13,998.0	†	13,568.0	17.3	0.5	72.0	97.2	242.9	19,950.0
1993	84,741.5	67,740.6	30,834.3	17,844.0	4,107.2	14,955.1	17,000.8	†	16,524.0	29.3	†	72.4	184.6	190.5	21,010.0
1994	92,781.5	68,254.2	32,304.4	16,177.1	4,483.7	15,289.1	24,527.3	$813.0	23,214.0	52.7	†	72.4	184.6	190.5	22,630.0
1995	95,810.8	71,639.5	33,623.8	17,618.1	4,719.7	15,677.9	24,171.2	5,161.0	18,519.0	52.7	†	63.4	184.6	190.5	24,600.0
1996	96,833.0	71,327.4	34,391.5	15,775.5	4,828.0	16,332.3	25,505.6	8,357.0	16,711.0	31.1	†	31.4	184.6	190.5	26,340.0
1997	103,259.8	73,731.8	35,478.9	15,959.4	5,021.2	17,272.4	29,528.0	9,838.0	19,163.0	52.7	†	50.0	184.6	239.7	28,125.0
1998	107,810.5	76,909.2	37,486.2	15,799.6	5,148.5	18,475.0	30,901.3	10,400.1	20,002.5	45.0	†	25.0	194.3	234.4	29,540.0
1999	113,417.2	82,863.6	39,937.9	17,651.2	5,318.0	19,956.5	30,553.6	9,953.0	20,107.0	33.3	†	25.0	195.9	239.4	37,360.0
2000	119,541.6	85,944.2	43,790.8	15,008.7	5,484.6	21,660.1	33,597.4	10,347.0	22,711.0	33.3	†	50.0	199.7	256.4	39,475.0
2001	130,668.5	94,846.5	48,530.1	14,938.3	5,880.0	25,498.1	35,822.0	10,635.0	24,694.0	25.0	†	80.0	184.0	204.0	41,460.0
2002	150,034.5	109,211.5	52,754.1	22,964.2	6,297.7	27,195.5	40,823.0	11,689.0	28,606.0	25.0	†	104.0	192.0	207.0	—
2003	170,671.5	124,374.5	59,274.2	29,499.7	6,532.5	29,068.1	46,297.0	11,969.0	33,791.0	33.0	†	103.0	202.0	199.0	—
2004	185,176.7	132,420.7	62,653.2	32,433.0	6,576.8	30,757.7	52,756.0	12,840.0	39,266.0	33.0	†	102.0	244.0	271.0	—
2005	203,036.0	146,207.0	68,957.7	38,587.3	6,908.5	31,753.5	56,829.0	12,930.0	43,284.0	0.0	†	101.0	246.0	268.0	—
2006	226,978.7	166,495.7	70,948.2	57,757.7	7,074.5	30,715.2	60,483.0	12,677.0	47,307.0	0.0	†	100.0	205.0	194.0	—
2007	210,536.0	145,698.0	70,735.9	37,465.3	7,214.9	30,281.9	64,838.0	13,022.0	51,320.0	0.0	†	100.0	205.0	191.0	—
2008	221,001.1	145,003.1	71,927.9	36,395.2	7,882.2	28,797.8	75,998.0	18,213.0	57,296.0	0.0	†	98.0	201.0	190.0	—
2009	264,527.4	167,475.4	88,113.1	36,556.3	8,211.0	34,594.9 [11]	97,052.0	29,738.0	66,778.0	0.0	†	98.0	201.0	237.0	—
2010	284,670.4	179,860.4	87,548.8	50,166.3	9,326.7	32,818.5 [11]	104,810.0	84,703.0	19,618.0	0.0	†	98.0	201.0	190.0	—
2011[11]	—	—	78,509.2	64,310.0	9,427.3	—	116,582.0	116,098.0	0.0	0.0	†	98.0	196.0	190.0	—
							Constant fiscal year 2011 dollars[12]								
1965	$37,777.3	$37,610.0	$13,704.8	$8,448.4	$2,643.1	$12,813.7	$167.3	†	†	$113.7	†	†	†	$53.6	—
1970	76,685.5	71,906.3	33,468.7	19,790.9	5,537.8	13,108.9	4,779.3	†	$4,420.1	120.4	†	†	†	238.8	—
1975	97,680.5	92,128.7	42,002.0	30,240.1	6,363.2	13,523.4	5,551.8	†	4,877.8	141.1	†	$79.1	†	453.8	$34,041.7
1980	104,151.3	91,298.3	42,422.5	29,421.8	4,099.2	15,354.8	12,852.9	†	12,170.1	84.1	†	203.3	†	395.4	35,255.7
1985	93,008.4	76,013.9	32,918.4	21,764.1	4,104.9	17,226.4	16,994.5	†	16,491.0	41.7	†	148.0	†	313.8	37,210.5
1986	91,806.6	75,869.8	32,369.4	21,421.9	4,974.1	17,104.3	15,936.8	†	15,457.6	38.4	†	138.0	†	302.8	38,777.0
1987	93,354.4	75,815.5	32,273.0	18,956.3	5,190.7	19,395.4	17,538.9	†	17,064.4	38.4	†	139.9	†	295.2	38,335.9
1988	96,603.0	77,624.4	33,163.1	19,038.0	5,326.1	20,097.1	18,978.6	†	18,542.2	36.9	$1.0	130.0	†	268.7	30,412.4
1989	102,570.6	83,158.4	34,127.7	22,861.3	5,479.1	20,690.4	19,412.1	†	18,843.9	35.1	0.9	123.9	$37.9	370.4	30,588.2

See notes at end of table.

Federal support and estimated federal tax expenditures for education, by category: Selected fiscal years, 1965 through 2011—Continued

[In millions of dollars]

Fiscal year	Total on-budget support, off-budget support, and nonfederal funds generated by federal legislation	On-budget support[1] — Total	Elementary and secondary	Post-secondary	Other education[3]	Research at educational institutions	Off-budget support and nonfederal funds — Total	Off-budget support — Direct Loan Program[4]	Nonfederal funds — Federal Family Education Loan Program[5]	Perkins Loans[6]	Income Contingent Loans[7]	Leveraging Educational Assistance Partnerships[8]	Supplemental Educational Opportunity Grants[9]	Work-Study Aid[10]	Estimated federal tax expenditures for education[2]
1	2	3	4	5	6	7	8	9	10	11	12	13	14	15	16
1990	104,952.2	86,259.4	36,733.8	22,809.4	5,652.7	21,063.5	18,692.8	†	18,089.2	25.1	0.8	98.9	81.5	397.2	31,814.1
1991	112,304.1	91,916.3	40,561.7	23,469.8	5,902.2	21,982.6	20,387.9	†	19,743.0	27.7	0.8	101.4	140.0	375.0	30,311.9
1992	114,476.2	92,961.4	42,923.1	22,113.2	6,135.6	21,789.6	21,514.7	†	20,853.8	26.6	0.8	110.7	149.5	373.4	30,662.8
1993	126,818.2	101,375.9	46,144.5	26,704.1	6,146.5	22,380.7	25,442.3	†	24,728.7	43.8	†	108.4	276.5	285.2	31,442.1
1994	136,298.1	100,267.0	47,455.8	23,764.5	6,586.7	22,460.0	36,031.1	$1,194.3	34,101.9	77.4	†	106.4	271.2	279.9	33,244.0
1995	137,014.7	102,448.5	48,083.9	25,194.9	6,749.4	22,420.3	34,566.2	7,380.5	26,483.2	75.3	†	90.7	264.0	272.5	35,179.4
1996	135,227.8	99,609.0	48,027.9	22,030.6	6,742.4	22,808.2	35,618.7	11,670.6	23,337.0	43.4	†	43.9	257.8	266.0	36,784.0
1997	141,234.7	100,847.4	48,526.6	21,828.7	6,867.7	23,624.4	40,387.2	13,456.0	26,210.4	72.1	†	68.4	252.5	327.7	38,468.2
1998	146,060.5	104,195.8	50,785.8	21,405.1	6,975.1	25,029.7	41,864.7	14,089.9	27,099.2	61.0	†	33.9	263.2	317.6	40,020.5
1999	151,536.7	110,714.1	53,361.0	23,583.8	7,105.4	26,663.8	40,822.7	13,298.2	26,865.0	44.5	†	33.4	261.7	319.9	49,916.7
2000	155,839.1	112,040.2	57,087.4	19,565.9	7,149.9	28,237.0	43,798.9	13,488.7	29,606.9	43.4	†	65.2	260.3	334.3	51,461.1
2001	166,156.0	120,605.3	61,710.1	18,995.3	7,476.9	32,423.0	45,550.7	13,523.3	31,400.5	31.8	†	101.7	234.0	259.4	52,719.9
2002	187,711.4	136,636.9	66,001.8	28,731.0	7,879.2	34,024.9	51,074.6	14,624.4	35,789.6	31.3	†	130.1	240.2	259.0	—
2003	208,064.5	151,624.1	72,260.8	35,962.9	7,963.7	35,436.7	56,440.4	14,591.3	41,194.4	40.2	†	125.6	246.3	242.6	—
2004	219,450.9	156,930.3	74,249.7	38,436.0	7,794.1	36,450.6	62,520.6	15,216.5	46,533.7	39.1	†	120.9	289.2	321.2	—
2005	232,049.8	167,100.0	78,811.8	44,101.4	7,895.7	36,291.1	64,949.9	14,777.7	49,469.3	0.0	†	115.4	281.2	306.3	—
2006	250,496.2	183,746.5	78,299.3	63,742.1	7,807.5	33,897.7	66,749.7	13,990.5	52,208.5	0.0	†	110.4	226.2	214.1	—
2007	225,999.4	156,399.2	75,931.3	40,217.0	7,744.8	32,506.1	69,600.2	13,978.4	55,089.3	0.0	†	107.3	220.1	205.0	—
2008	228,850.3	150,153.1	74,482.5	37,687.8	8,162.2	29,820.6	78,697.2	18,859.9	59,331.0	0.0	†	101.5	208.1	196.7	—
2009	272,638.0	172,610.3	90,814.8	37,677.1	8,462.8	35,655.7 [11]	100,027.7	30,649.8	68,825.5	0.0	†	101.0	207.2	244.3	—
2010	288,666.6	182,397.9	88,784.0	50,874.1	9,458.3	33,281.6 [11]	106,288.7	85,898.0	19,894.8	0.0	†	99.4	203.8	192.7	—
2011[11]	—	—	78,509.2	64,310.0	9,427.3	—	116,582.0	116,098.0	0.0	0.0	†	98.0	196.0	190.0	—

—Not available.

†Not applicable.

[1]On-budget support includes federal funds for education programs tied to appropriations. Excludes federal support for medical education benefits under Medicare in the U.S. Department of Health and Human Services. Benefits excluded because data before fiscal year (FY) 1990 are not available. This program existed since Medicare began, but was not available as a separate budget item until FY 1990. Excluded amounts range from $4,440,000,000 in FY 1990 to an estimated $9,300,000,000 in FY 2011.

[2]Losses of tax revenue attributable to provisions of the federal income tax laws that allow a special exclusion, exemption, or deduction from gross income or provide a special credit, preferential rate of tax, or a deferral of tax liability affecting individual or corporate income tax liabilities.

[3]Other education includes libraries, museums, cultural activities, and miscellaneous research.

[4]The William D. Ford Federal Direct Loan Program (commonly referred to as the Direct Loan Program) provides students with the same benefits they were eligible to receive under the Federal Family Education Loan (FFEL) Program, but provides loans to students through federal capital rather than through private lenders.

[5]The Federal Family Education Loan (FFEL) Program, formerly known as the Guaranteed Student Loan Program, provided student loans guaranteed by the federal government and disbursed to borrowers. After June 30, 2010, no new FFEL loans have been originated; all new loans are originated through the Direct Loan Program.

[6]Student loans created from institutional matching funds (since 1993 one-third of federal capital contributions). Excludes repayments of outstanding loans.

[7]Student loans created from institutional matching funds (one-ninth of the federal contribution). This was a demonstration project that involved only 10 institutions and had unsubsidized interest rates. Program repealed in fiscal year 1992.

[8]Formerly the State Student Incentive Grant Program. Starting in fiscal year 2000, amounts under $30.0 million have required dollar-for-dollar state matching contributions, while amounts over $30.0 million have required two-to-one state matching contributions.

[9]Institutions award grants to undergraduate students, and the federal share of such grants may not exceed 75 percent of the total grant.

[10]Employer contributions to student earnings are generally one-third of federal allocation.

[11]Estimated.

[12]Data adjusted by the federal funds composite deflator reported in the U.S. Office of Management and Budget, *Budget of the U.S. Government, Historical Tables, Fiscal Year 2012.*

NOTE: To the extent possible, federal education funds data represent outlays rather than obligations. Some data have been revised from previously published figures. Detail may not sum to totals because of rounding. The increase in postsecondary expenditures in 2006 resulted primarily from an accounting adjustment.

SOURCE: U.S. Department of Education, Budget Service, unpublished tabulations. U.S. Department of Education, National Center for Education Statistics, unpublished tabulations. U.S. Office of Management and Budget, *Budget of the U.S. Government, Appendix,* fiscal years 1967 through 2012. National Science Foundation, *Federal Funds for Research and Development,* fiscal years 1967 through 2010. (This table was prepared October 2011.)

Federal on-budget funds for education, by agency: Selected fiscal years, 1970 through 2010

[In thousands of current dollars]

Agency	1970	1980	1990[1]	1995[1]	2000[1]	2005[1]	2007[1]	2008[1]	2009[1,2]	2010[1,2]
1	2	3	4	5	6	7	8	9	10	11
Total	**$12,526,499**	**$34,493,502**	**$51,624,342**	**$71,639,520**	**$85,944,203**	**$146,206,999**	**$145,697,988**	**$145,003,074**	**$167,475,371**	**$179,860,409**
Department of Education	4,625,224	13,137,785	23,198,575	31,403,000	34,106,697	72,893,301	71,808,014	72,177,819	85,224,697	91,893,199
Department of Agriculture	960,910	4,562,467	6,260,843	9,092,089	11,080,031	13,817,553	15,547,977	16,588,529	16,746,491	19,373,581
Department of Commerce	13,990	135,561	53,835	88,929	114,575	243,948	200,374	193,612	235,892	191,801
Department of Defense	821,388	1,560,301	3,605,509	3,879,002	4,525,080	6,320,454	6,322,843	6,578,416	6,910,849	7,183,444
Department of Energy	551,527	1,605,558	2,561,950	2,692,314	3,577,004	4,339,879	3,382,683	2,469,637	4,486,785	4,569,987
Department of Health and Human Services	1,796,854	5,613,930	7,956,011	12,469,563	17,670,867	26,107,860	26,350,200	26,487,590	28,905,843	28,042,141
Department of Homeland Security	†	†	†	†	†	624,860	484,118	410,580	558,386	538,499
Department of Housing and Urban Development	114,709	5,314	118	1,613	1,400	1,100	400	400	200	600
Department of the Interior	190,975	440,547	630,537	702,796	959,802	1,254,533	1,102,615	1,056,504	975,816	989,380
Department of Justice	15,728	60,721	99,775	172,350	278,927	608,148	829,010	824,050	890,458	947,063
Department of Labor	424,494	1,862,738	2,511,380	3,967,914	4,696,100	5,764,500	5,249,800	5,070,500	6,073,400	6,826,800
Department of State	59,742	25,188	51,225	54,671	388,349	533,309	587,120	638,280	655,520	729,520
Department of Transportation	27,534	54,712	76,186	135,816	117,054	126,900	127,500	143,378	155,733	178,146
Department of the Treasury	18	1,247,463	41,715	49,496	83,000	0	100	100	0	100
Department of Veterans Affairs	1,032,918	2,351,233	757,476	1,324,382	1,577,374	4,293,624	5,256,399	4,527,232	4,763,479	8,802,944
Other agencies and programs										
ACTION	†	2,833	8,472	†	†	†	†	†	†	†
Agency for International Development	88,034	176,770	249,786	290,580	332,500	602,100	657,700	635,320	641,425	573,100
Appalachian Regional Commission	37,838	19,032	93	10,623	7,243	8,542	7,463	7,176	6,106	5,070
Barry Goldwater Scholarship and Excellence in Education Foundation	†	†	1,033	3,000	3,000	3,000	3,000	3,000	3,000	4,000
Corporation for National and Community Service	†	†	†	214,600	386,000	472,000	395,000	333,000	401,000	965,000
Environmental Protection Agency	19,446	41,083	87,481	125,721	98,900	83,400	68,900	44,500	53,000	56,600
Estimated education share of federal aid to the District of Columbia	33,019	81,847	104,940	78,796	127,127	154,962	168,156	149,722	157,465	159,670
Federal Emergency Management Agency	290	1,946	215	170,400	14,894	†	†	†	†	†
General Services Administration	14,775	34,800	†	†	†	†	†	†	†	†
Harry S Truman Scholarship fund	†	-1,895	2,883	3,000	3,000	3,000	3,000	3,000	2,000	2,000
Institute of American Indian and Alaska Native Culture and Arts Development	†	†	4,305	13,000	2,000	6,000	6,000	7,000	8,000	8,000
Institute of Museum and Library Services	†	†	†	†	166,000	250,000	258,000	253,000	265,000	265,000
James Madison Memorial Fellowship Foundation	†	†	191	2,000	7,000	2,000	2,000	2,000	2,000	2,000
Japanese-United States Friendship Commission	†	2,294	2,299	2,000	3,000	3,000	2,000	2,000	2,000	2,000
Library of Congress	29,478	151,871	189,827	241,000	299,000	430,000	463,000	434,000	468,000	516,000
National Aeronautics and Space Administration	258,366	255,511	1,093,303	1,757,900	2,077,830	2,763,120	1,651,205	1,154,900	1,217,300	1,191,500
National Archives and Records Administration	†	†	77,397	105,172	121,879	276,000	273,000	279,000	329,000	339,000
National Commission on Libraries and Information Science	†	2,090	3,281	1,000	2,000	1,000	1,000	1,000	†	†
National Endowment for the Arts	340	5,220	5,577	9,421	10,048	10,976	11,767	12,808	12,918	14,413
National Endowment for the Humanities	8,459	142,586	141,048	151,727	100,014	117,825	121,086	124,162	134,533	267,583
National Science Foundation	295,628	808,392	1,588,891	2,086,195	2,955,244	3,993,216	4,262,057	4,298,290	7,057,771	5,085,561
Nuclear Regulatory Commission	†	32,590	42,328	22,188	12,200	15,100	10,100	2,200	7,800	9,900
Office of Economic Opportunity	1,092,410	†	†	†	†	†	†	†	†	†
Smithsonian Institution	2,461	5,153	5,779	9,961	25,764	45,890	46,101	64,768	61,104	63,107
United States Arms Control Agency	100	661	25	†	†	†	†	†	†	†
United States Information Agency	8,423	66,210	201,547	294,800	†	†	†	†	†	†
United States Institute of Peace	†	†	7,621	12,000	13,000	28,000	32,000	17,000	49,000	58,000
Other agencies	1,421	990	885	500	300	7,900	6,300	8,600	13,400	5,700

†Not applicable.

[1]Excludes federal support for medical education benefits under Medicare in the U.S. Department of Health and Human Services. Benefits excluded from total because data before fiscal year (FY) 1990 are not available. This program existed since Medicare began, but was not available as a separate budget item until FY 1990. Excluded amounts are as follows: $4,440,000,000 in FY 1990, $7,510,000,000 in FY 1995, $8,020,000,000 in FY 2000, $8,300,000,000 in FY 2005, $8,200,000,000 in FY 2007, $8,600,000,000 in FY 2008, $8,800,000,000 in FY 2009, and $9,000,000,000 in FY 2010.

[2]Estimated.

NOTE: To the extent possible, amounts reported represent outlays, rather than obligations. Some data have been revised from previously published figures. Detail may not sum to totals because of rounding. Negative amounts occur when program receipts exceed outlays.

SOURCE: U.S. Department of Education, National Center for Education Statistics, unpublished tabulations. U.S. Office of Management and Budget, *Budget of the U.S. Government, Appendix*, fiscal years 1972 through 2012. National Science Foundation, *Federal Funds for Research and Development*, fiscal years 1970 to 2010. (This table was prepared October 2011.)

Federal Programs for Education & Related Activities

Federal on-budget funds for education, by level/educational purpose, agency, and program: Selected fiscal years, 1970 through 2011

[In thousands of current dollars]

Level/educational purpose, agency, and program	1970	1980	1990[1]	1995[1]	2000[1]	2005[1]	2007[1]	2008[1]	2009[1,2]	2010[1,2]	2011[1,2]
1	2	3	4	5	6	7	8	9	10	11	12
Total	$12,526,499	$34,493,502	$51,624,342	$71,639,520	$85,944,203	$146,206,999	$145,597,988	$145,003,074	$167,475,371	$179,860,409	$78,509,229
Elementary/secondary education	5,830,442	16,027,686	21,984,361	33,623,809	43,790,783	68,957,711	70,735,875	71,927,854	88,113,117	87,548,802	$78,509,229
Department of Education[3]	2,719,204	6,629,095	9,681,313	14,029,000	20,039,563	37,477,594	37,562,078	38,330,372	52,468,074	49,621,475	38,693,642
Education for the disadvantaged	1,339,014	3,204,664	4,494,111	6,808,000	8,529,111	14,635,566	14,486,936	14,872,535	15,880,530	15,864,666	15,535,933
Impact aid program[4]	656,372	690,170	816,366	808,000	877,101	1,262,174	1,162,814	1,247,691	1,307,847	1,276,183	1,273,631
School improvement programs[5]	288,304	788,918	1,189,158	1,397,000	2,549,971	7,918,091	7,083,651	7,077,721	19,600,501	16,999,862	6,741,663
Indian education	†	93,365	69,451	71,000	65,285	121,911	117,992	115,780	118,241	127,282	127,027
English Language Acquisition	21,250	169,540	188,919	225,000	362,662	667,485	728,703	700,395	709,750	750,000	733,530
Special education	79,090	821,777	1,616,623	3,177,000	4,948,977	10,940,312	11,777,258	12,280,101	12,768,786	12,587,035	12,542,912
Vocational and adult education	335,174	860,661	1,306,685	1,482,000	1,462,977	1,967,086	1,955,780	1,894,706	2,034,226	2,016,447	1,738,946
Education Reform—Goals 2000[6]	†	†	†	61,000	1,243,479	-35,031	†	†	†	†	†
Hurricane Education Recovery	†	†	†	†	†	†	248,944	141,443	48,193	†	†
Department of Agriculture	760,477	4,064,497	5,528,950	8,201,294	10,051,278	12,577,265	14,245,994	15,296,812	15,273,387	17,875,561	19,978,556
Child nutrition programs[7]	299,131	3,377,056	4,977,075	7,644,789	9,554,028	11,901,943	13,081,994	13,932,120	13,714,903	16,383,421	18,489,136
McGovern-Dole International Food for Education and Child Nutrition Program[8]	†	†	†	†	†	86,000	98,000	89,000	133,000	210,000	215,000
Agricultural Marketing Service—commodities[9]	341,597	388,000	350,441	400,000	400,000	399,322	878,000	1,097,210	1,237,008	1,100,000	1,085,000
Special Milk Program	83,800	159,293	18,707	(7)	(7)	(7)	(7)	(7)	(7)	(7)	(7)
Estimated education share of Forest Service permanent appropriations	35,949	140,148	182,727	156,505	97,250	190,000	188,000	178,482	188,476	182,140	189,420
Department of Commerce	†	54,816	†	†	†	†	†	†	†	†	†
Local public works program—school facilities[10]	†	54,816	†	†	†	†	†	†	†	†	†
Department of Defense	143,100	370,846	1,097,876	1,295,547	1,485,611	1,786,253	1,772,293	1,863,835	1,887,223	1,981,321	2,051,799
Junior Reserve Officers Training Corps (JROTC)	12,100	32,000	39,300	155,600	210,432	315,122	324,917	352,821	358,256	359,689	377,526
Overseas dependents schools	131,000	338,846	864,958	855,772	904,829	1,060,920	1,062,367	1,110,108	1,110,476	1,186,560	1,224,578
Domestic schools[4]	†	†	193,618	284,175	370,350	410,211	385,009	400,906	418,491	435,072	449,695
Department of Energy	200	77,633	15,563	12,646	†	†	†	†	†	†	†
Energy conservation for school buildings[11]	†	77,240	15,213	10,746	†	†	†	†	†	†	†
Pre-engineering program	200	393	350	1,900	†	†	†	†	†	†	†
Department of Health and Human Services	167,333	1,077,000	2,396,793	5,116,559	6,011,036	8,003,348	7,901,700	8,003,300	9,738,023	8,547,000	8,539,300
Head Start[12]	†	735,000	1,447,758	3,534,000	5,267,000	6,842,348	6,888,000	6,877,000	8,499,123	7,234,000	7,235,000
Payments to states for Aid for Families with Dependent Children (AFDC) work programs[13]	†	†	459,221	953,000	15,000	—	—	—	—	—	—
Social Security student benefits[14]	167,333	342,000	489,814	629,559	729,036	1,161,000	1,013,700	1,126,300	1,238,900	1,313,000	1,304,300
Department of Homeland Security	†	†	†	†	†	500	500	2,600	2,600	1,900	2,100
Tuition assistance for educational accreditation—Coast Guard personnel[15]	†	†	†	†	†	500	500	2,600	2,600	1,900	2,100
Department of the Interior	140,705	318,170	445,267	493,124	725,423	938,506	859,720	822,106	782,543	783,075	804,196
Mineral Leasing Act and other funds											
Payments to states—estimated education share	12,294	62,636	123,811	18,750	24,610	60,290	52,030	50,913	24,610	23,000	20,700
Payments to counties—estimated education share	16,359	48,953	102,522	37,490	53,500	79,686	71,034	72,743	53,500	50,000	45,000
Indian Education											
Bureau of Indian Education schools	95,850	178,112	192,841	411,524	466,905	517,647	518,700	540,734	560,799	582,492	583,572
Johnson-O'Malley assistance[16]	16,080	28,081	25,556	24,359	17,387	16,510	12,000	13,782	13,797	13,589	13,415
Education construction	†	†	†	†	161,021	263,373	204,956	142,935	128,837	112,994	140,509
Education expenses for children of employees, Yellowstone National Park	122	388	538	1,000	2,000	1,000	1,000	1,000	1,000	1,000	1,000
Department of Justice	8,237	23,890	65,997	128,850	224,800	554,500	719,600	769,825	821,065	876,200	875,000
Vocational training expenses for prisoners in federal prisons	2,720	4,966	2,066	3,000	1,000	0	6,000	1,025	1,065	2,600	2,000
Inmate programs[17]	5,517	18,924	63,931	125,850	223,800	554,500	713,600	768,800	820,000	873,600	873,000

See notes at end of table.

Federal on-budget funds for education, by level/educational purpose, agency, and program: Selected fiscal years, 1970 through 2011—Continued

[In thousands of current dollars]

Level/educational purpose, agency, and program	1970	1980	1990[1]	1995[1]	2000[1]	2005[1]	2007[1]	2008[1]	2009[1,2]	2010[1,2]	2011[1,2]
1	2	3	4	5	6	7	8	9	10	11	12
Department of Labor	420,927	1,849,800	2,505,487	3,957,800	4,683,200	5,654,000	5,226,000	5,070,000	6,073,000	6,826,000	6,474,000
Job Corps	†	469,800	739,376	1,029,000	1,256,000	1,521,000	1,605,000	763,000	1,612,000	1,850,000	1,714,000
Training programs—estimated funds for education programs[18]	420,927	1,380,000	1,766,111	2,928,800	3,427,200	4,133,000	3,621,000	4,307,000	4,461,000	4,976,000	4,760,000
Department of Transportation	45	60	46	62	188	†	†	†	†	†	†
Tuition assistance for educational accreditation—Coast Guard personnel[15]	45	60	46	62	188	†	†	†	†	†	†
Department of the Treasury	†	935,903	†	†	†	†	†	†	†	†	†
Estimated education share of general revenue sharing[19]											
State[20]	†	525,019	†	†	†	†	†	†	†	†	†
Local	†	410,884	†	†	†	†	†	†	†	†	†
Department of Veterans Affairs	338,910	545,786	155,351	311,768	445,052	1,815,000	2,300,564	1,628,100	919,139	760,500	821,838
Noncollegiate and job training programs[21]	281,640	439,993	12,848	†	†	†	†	†	†	†	†
Vocational rehabilitation for disabled veterans[22]	41,700	87,980	136,780	298,132	438,635	1,815,000	2,300,564	1,628,100	919,139	760,500	821,838
Dependents' education[23]	15,570	17,813	5,723	5,961	6,417	†	†	†	†	†	†
Service members occupational conversion training act of 1992	†	†	†	7,675	†	†	†	†	†	†	†
Other agencies											
Appalachian Regional Commission	33,161	9,157	93	2,173	2,588	2,962	1,110	1,000	1,141	986	922
National Endowment for the Arts	†	4,989	4,641	7,117	6,002	8,470	8,825	9,606	9,916	11,530	10,876
Arts in education	†	4,989	4,641	7,117	6,002	8,470	8,825	9,606	9,916	11,530	10,876
National Endowment for the Humanities	20	330	404	997	812	603	75	0	0	125,054	120,000
Office of Economic Opportunity	1,072,375	†	†	†	†	†	†	†	†	†	†
Head Start[24]	325,700	†	†	†	†	†	†	†	†	†	†
Other elementary and secondary programs[25]	42,809	†	†	†	†	†	†	†	†	†	†
Job Corps[26]	144,000	†	†	†	†	†	†	†	†	†	†
Youth Corps and other training programs[26]	553,368	†	†	†	†	†	†	†	†	†	†
Volunteers in Service to America (VISTA)[27]	6,498	†	†	†	†	†	†	†	†	†	†
Other programs											
Estimated education share of federal aid to the District of Columbia	25,748	65,714	86,579	66,871	115,230	138,710	137,416	130,298	137,006	138,200	137,000
Postsecondary education	**$3,447,697**	**$11,115,882**	**$13,650,915**	**$17,618,137**	**$15,008,715**	**$38,587,287**	**$37,465,287**	**$36,395,182**	**$36,556,292**	**$50,166,341**	**$64,309,984**
Department of Education[6]	1,187,962	5,682,242	11,175,978	14,234,000	10,727,315	31,420,023	30,052,007	28,838,752	27,626,632	36,539,655	48,880,279
Student financial assistance	†	3,682,789	5,920,328	7,047,000	9,060,317	15,209,515	15,355,736	17,751,084	23,040,153	25,959,478	43,412,061
Direct Loan Program[28]	†	†	†	840,000	-2,862,240	3,020,992	5,391,146	5,333,920	1,406,154	3,481,859	2,781,709
Federal Family Education Loan Program[29]	2,323	1,407,977	4,372,446	5,190,000	2,707,473	10,777,470	6,033,322	3,288,531	526,894	3,932,994	-123,447
Higher education	1,029,131	399,787	659,492	871,000	1,530,779	2,053,288	2,399,892	2,029,379	2,241,074	2,740,665	2,388,946
Facilities—loans and insurance	114,199	-19,031	19,219	-6,000	-2,174	-1,464	-1,671	-1,688	-497	-8,360	-8,361
College housing loans[30]	774	14,082	-57,167	-46,000	-41,886	-33,521	-20,722	-17,529	-17,662	-16,725	-16,725
Educational activities overseas	774	3,561	82	†	150	169	†	†	†	†	†
Historically Black Colleges and Universities Capital Financing, Program Account	†	†	†	†	†	†	318,840	18,222	1,476	23,330	23,289
Gallaudet College and Howard University	38,559	176,829	230,327	292,000	291,060	339,823	351,665	343,164	353,310	357,977	357,261
National Technical Institute for the Deaf	2,976	16,248	31,251	46,000	43,836	53,751	57,836	58,308	63,682	68,437	65,546
Hurricane Katrina, aid to institutions	†	†	†	†	†	†	165,963	35,361	12,048	†	†
Department of Agriculture	†	10,453	31,273	33,373	30,676	61,957	64,357	66,709	73,150	80,697	81,658
Agriculture Extension Service, Second Morrill Act payments to agricultural and mechanical colleges and Tuskegee Institute	†	10,453	31,273	33,373	30,676	61,957	64,357	66,709	73,150	80,697	81,658
Department of Commerce	8,277	29,971	3,312	3,487	3,800	—	—	—	—	—	—
Sea Grant Program[31]	†	3,123	3,312	3,487	3,800	—	—	—	—	—	—
Merchant Marine Academy[32]	6,160	14,809	†	†	†	†	†	†	†	†	†
State marine schools[32]	2,117	12,039	†	†	†	†	†	†	†	†	†

See notes at end of table.

Federal on-budget funds for education, by level/educational purpose, agency, and program: Selected fiscal years, 1970 through 2011—Continued

[In thousands of current dollars]

Level/educational purpose, agency, and program	1970	1980	1990[1]	1995[1]	2000[1]	2005[1]	2007[1]	2008[1]	2009[1,2]	2010[1,2]	2011[1,2]
1	2	3	4	5	6	7	8	9	10	11	12
Department of Defense	322,100	545,000	635,769	729,500	1,147,759	1,858,301	1,846,850	1,975,323	2,262,772	2,550,667	2,297,234
Tuition assistance for military personnel	57,500	—	95,300	127,000	263,303	608,109	607,515	603,610	657,702	669,892	567,412
Service academies	78,700	106,100	120,613	163,300	212,678	300,760	354,528	359,127	371,156	402,640	348,836
Senior Reserve Officers Training Corps (SROTC)	108,100	—	193,056	219,400	363,461	537,525	434,687	549,633	653,591	885,500	851,910
Professional development education[33]	77,800	—	226,800	219,800	308,317	411,907	450,120	462,953	580,323	592,635	529,076
Department of Energy	3,000	57,701	25,502	28,027	†	†	†	†	†	†	†
University laboratory cooperative program	3,000	2,800	9,402	8,552	†	†	†	†	†	†	†
Teacher development projects	†	1,400	†	†	†	†	†	†	†	†	†
Energy conservation for buildings—higher education[11]	†	53,501	7,459	7,381	†	†	†	†	†	†	†
Minority honors vocational training	†	†	†	†	†	†	†	†	†	†	†
Honors research program	†	†	6,472	2,221	†	†	†	†	†	†	†
Students and teachers	†	†	2,169	9,873	†	†	†	†	†	†	†
Department of Health and Human Services	981,483	2,412,058	578,542	796,035	954,190	1,433,516	1,159,279	1,184,856	1,235,850	1,297,671	1,303,365
Health professions training programs[34]	353,029	460,736	230,600	298,302	340,361	581,661	302,081	318,225	354,322	406,000	408,000
Indian health manpower	†	7,187	9,508	27,000	16,000	27,000	32,000	29,000	36,000	46,000	41,000
National Health Service Corps scholarships	†	70,667	4,759	78,206	33,300	45,000	40,000	40,000	40,000	41,000	41,000
National Institutes of Health training grants[35]	†	176,388	241,356	380,502	550,220	756,014	761,034	770,481	776,313	775,186	780,944
National Institute of Occupational Safety and Health training grants	8,088	12,899	10,461	11,660	14,198	23,841	24,164	27,150	29,215	29,485	32,421
Alcohol, drug abuse, and mental health training programs[36]	118,366	122,103	81,353	†	†	†	†	†	†	†	†
Health teaching facilities[37]	†	3,078	505	365	110	†	†	†	†	†	†
Social Security postsecondary students' benefits[38]	502,000	1,559,000	†	†	†	†	†	†	†	†	†
Department of Homeland Security	†	†	†	†	†	36,400	48,900	52,400	52,700	57,539	61,300
Coast Guard Academy[15]	†	†	†	†	†	16,400	23,400	21,500	21,500	24,239	25,100
Postgraduate training for Coast Guard officers[39]	†	†	†	†	†	8,700	12,800	17,000	18,300	16,800	18,100
Tuition assistance to Coast Guard military personnel[15]	†	†	†	†	†	11,300	12,700	13,900	12,900	16,500	18,100
Department of Housing and Urban Development[30]	114,199	†	†	†	†	†	†	†	†	†	†
College housing loans[30]	114,199	†	†	†	†	†	†	†	†	†	†
Department of the Interior	31,749	80,202	135,480	159,054	187,179	249,227	176,695	180,497	147,873	160,805	93,027
Shared revenues, Mineral Leasing Act and other receipts—estimated education share	6,949	35,403	69,980	82,810	98,740	146,235	52,400	52,743	15,749	16,250	13,780
Indian programs											
Continuing education	9,380	16,909	34,911	43,907	57,576	76,271	98,463	101,795	106,029	113,504	48,310
Higher education scholarships	15,420	27,890	30,589	32,337	30,863	26,721	25,832	25,959	26,095	31,051	30,937
Department of State	30,850	†	2,167	3,000	319,000	424,000	473,000	522,000	537,000	609,000	643,000
Educational exchange[40]	30,850	†	†	†	319,000	424,000	473,000	522,000	537,000	609,000	643,000
Mutual educational and cultural exchange activities	30,454	†	†	†	303,000	402,000	453,000	503,000	517,000	585,000	616,000
International educational exchange activities	396	†	2,167	3,000	16,000	22,000	20,000	19,000	20,000	24,000	27,000
Russian, Eurasian, and East European Research and Training	†	†	†	†	†	†	†	†	†	†	†
Department of Transportation	11,197	12,530	46,025	59,257	60,300	73,000	74,000	72,000	69,000	95,000	99,000
Merchant Marine Academy[32]	†	†	20,926	30,850	34,000	61,000	61,000	59,000	54,000	79,000	80,000
State marine schools[32]	†	†	8,269	8,980	7,000	12,000	13,000	13,000	15,000	16,000	19,000
Coast Guard Academy[15]	9,342	10,000	12,074	13,500	15,500	†	†	†	†	†	†
Postgraduate training for Coast Guard officers[39]	1,655	2,230	4,173	5,513	2,500	†	†	†	†	†	†
Tuition assistance to Coast Guard military personnel[15]	200	300	582	414	1,300	†	†	†	†	†	†
Department of the Treasury	†	296,750	†	†	†	†	†	†	†	†	†
General revenue sharing—estimated state share to higher education[19,20]	†	296,750	†	†	†	†	†	†	†	†	†
Department of Veterans Affairs	693,490	1,803,847	599,825	1,010,114	1,132,322	2,478,624	2,955,835	2,899,132	3,844,340	8,042,444	10,131,521
Vietnam-era veterans	638,260	1,579,974	46,998	†	†	†	†	†	†	†	†
College student support	†	1,560,081	39,458	†	†	†	†	†	†	†	†
Work-study	†	19,893	7,540	†	†	†	†	†	†	†	†

See notes at end of table.

Federal on-budget funds for education, by level/educational purpose, agency, and program: Selected fiscal years, 1970 through 2011—Continued

[In thousands of current dollars]

Level/educational purpose, agency, and program	1970	1980	1990[1]	1995[1]	2000[1]	2005[1]	2007[1]	2008[1]	2009[1,2]	2010[1,2]	2011[1,2]
1	2	3	4	5	6	7	8	9	10	11	12
Service persons college support	18,900	46,617	8,911	†	†	†	†	†	†	†	†
Post-Vietnam veterans	†	922	161,475	33,596	3,958	1,136	914	891	448	894	719
All-volunteer-force educational assistance	†	†	269,947	868,394	984,068	2,070,996	2,227,531	2,296,543	3,013,559	1,854,917	1,535,900
Veterans	†	†	183,765	760,390	876,434	1,887,239	2,081,097	2,145,475	2,669,960	1,659,694	1,305,270
Reservists	†	†	86,182	108,004	107,634	183,757	146,434	151,068	343,599	195,223	230,630
Post 9-11 GI Bill[41]	†	†	†	†	†	†	†	†	162,053	5,542,843	7,939,707
Veteran dependents' education	36,330	176,334	100,494	95,124	131,296	388,719	511,793	434,733	469,360	507,294	536,378
Payments to state education agencies	†	†	12,000	13,000	13,000	17,773	—	—	—	—	—
Reserve Education Assistance Program (REAP)[42]	†	†	†	†	†	†	215,597	166,965	198,920	136,496	118,817
Other agencies											
Appalachian Regional Commission	4,105	1,751	—	2,741	2,286	4,407	3,498	3,120	2,985	2,464	2,600
National Endowment for the Humanities	3,349	56,451	50,938	56,481	28,395	29,253	40,446	36,472	40,795	47,949	47,000
National Science Foundation	42,000	64,583	161,884	211,800	389,000	490,000	527,000	531,000	629,000	646,000	631,000
Science and engineering education programs	37,000	64,583	161,884	211,800	389,000	490,000	527,000	531,000	629,000	646,000	631,000
Sea Grant Program[31]	5,000	†	†	†	†	†	†	†	†	†	†
United States Information Agency[43]	8,423	51,095	181,172	260,800	†	†	†	†	†	†	†
Educational and cultural affairs[40]	†	49,546	35,862	13,600	†	†	†	†	†	†	†
Educational and cultural exchange programs[44]	†	†	145,307	247,200	†	†	†	†	†	†	†
Educational exchange activities, international	†	1,549	3	†	†	†	†	†	†	†	†
Information center and library activities	8,423	†	†	†	†	†	†	†	†	†	†
Other programs											
Barry Goldwater Scholarship and Excellence in Education Foundation	†	†	1,033	3,000	3,000	3,000	3,000	3,000	3,000	4,000	4,000
Estimated education share of federal aid to the District of Columbia	5,513	13,143	14,637	9,468	11,493	14,578	29,418	17,920	19,195	20,450	21,000
Harry S Truman Scholarship fund	†	-1,895	2,883	3,000	3,000	3,000	3,000	3,000	2,000	2,000	3,000
Institute of American Indian and Alaska Native Culture and Arts Development	†	†	4,305	13,000	2,000	6,000	6,000	7,000	8,000	8,000	9,000
James Madison Memorial Fellowship Foundation	†	†	191	2,000	7,000	2,000	2,000	2,000	2,000	2,000	2,000
Other education	**$964,719**	**$1,548,730**	**$3,383,031**	**$4,719,655**	**$5,484,571**	**$6,908,504**	**$7,214,906**	**$7,882,220**	**$8,211,022**	**$9,326,725**	**$9,427,276**
Department of Education[3]	630,235	747,706	2,251,801	2,861,000	3,223,355	3,538,862	3,756,445	4,544,966	4,551,389	5,073,063	5,303,333
Administration	47,456	187,317	328,293	404,000	458,054	548,842	539,378	1,252,527	1,339,034	1,531,232	1,793,923
Libraries[45]	108,284	129,127	137,264	117,000	†	†	†	†	†	†	†
Rehabilitative services and disability research	473,091	426,886	1,780,360	2,333,000	2,755,468	2,973,346	3,177,031	3,242,297	3,185,719	3,506,861	3,474,718
American Printing House for the Blind	1,404	4,349	5,736	7,000	9,368	16,538	18,359	19,522	26,627	24,600	24,551
Trust funds and contributions	0	27	148	0	465	136	21,677	30,620	9	10,370	10,141
Department of Agriculture	135,637	271,112	352,511	422,878	444,477	468,631	515,026	517,208	542,754	567,423	552,030
Extension Service	131,734	263,584	337,907	405,371	424,174	445,631	491,026	494,208	519,754	543,423	530,030
National Agricultural Library	3,903	7,528	14,604	17,507	20,303	23,000	24,000	23,000	23,000	24,000	22,000
Department of Commerce	1,226	2,479	†	†	†	†	†	†	†	†	†
Maritime Administration											
Training for private sector employees[32]	1,226	2,479	†	†	†	†	†	†	†	†	†
Department of Health and Human Services	24,273	37,819	77,962	138,000	214,000	313,000	307,000	323,000	331,000	340,000	341,000
National Library of Medicine	24,273	37,819	77,962	138,000	214,000	313,000	307,000	323,000	331,000	340,000	341,000
Department of Homeland Security	†	†	†	†	†	†	†	†	†	341,100	380,480
Federal Law Enforcement Training Center[46]	†	†	†	†	†	†	†	†	†	323,000	348,000
Estimated disaster relief[47]	†	†	†	†	†	†	†	†	†	18,100	32,480
Department of Justice	5,546	27,642	26,920	36,296	34,727	26,148	28,056	28,425	28,993	33,563	33,563
Federal Bureau of Investigation National Academy	2,066	7,234	6,028	12,831	22,479	15,619	16,727	17,062	17,403	19,443	19,443
Federal Bureau of Investigation Field Police Academy	2,500	7,715	10,548	11,140	11,962	10,456	11,308	11,343	11,570	14,120	14,120
Narcotics and dangerous drug training	980	2,416	850	325	286	73	20	20	20	20	†
National Institute of Corrections	†	10,277	9,494	12,000	†	†	†	†	†	†	†

See notes at end of table.

Federal on-budget funds for education, by level/educational purpose, agency, and program: Selected fiscal years, 1970 through 2011—Continued

[In thousands of current dollars]

Level/educational purpose, agency, and program	1970	1980	1990[1]	1995[1]	2000[1]	2005[1]	2007[1]	2008[1]	2009[1,2]	2010[1,2]	2011[1,2]
1	2	3	4	5	6	7	8	9	10	11	12
Department of State	20,672	25,000	47,539	51,648	69,349	109,309	114,120	116,280	118,520	120,520	120,000
Foreign Service Institute	15,857	25,000	47,539	51,648	69,349	109,309	114,120	116,280	118,520	120,520	120,000
Center for Cultural and Technical Interchange[40]	4,815	†	†	†	†	†	†	†	†	†	†
Department of Transportation	3,964	10,212	1,507	650	700	1,100	200	178	133	146	150
Highways training and education grants	2,418	3,412	—	—	—	—	—	—	—	—	—
Maritime Administration											
Training for private sector employees[30]	†	†	†	†	†	†	†	†	†	†	†
Urban mass transportation—managerial training grants	1,546	500	1,507	650	700	1,100	200	178	133	146	150
Federal Aviation Administration											
Air traffic controllers second career program	—	6,300	—	—	—	—					
Department of the Treasury	18	14,584	41,488	48,000	83,000	†	†	†	†	†	†
Federal Law Enforcement Training Center[46]	18	14,584	41,488	48,000	83,000	†	†	†	†	†	†
Other agencies											
ACTION[48]	†	2,833	8,472	†	†	†	†	†	†	†	†
Estimated education funds	†	2,833	8,472	†	†	†	†	†	†	†	†
Agency for International Development	88,034	99,707	170,371	260,408	299,000	574,000	629,200	608,420	612,025	542,700	771,300
Education and human resources	61,570	80,518	142,801	248,408	299,000	574,000	629,200	608,420	612,025	542,700	771,300
American schools and hospitals abroad	26,464	19,189	27,570	12,000							
Appalachian Regional Commission	572	8,124	†	5,709	2,369	1,173	2,855	3,056	1,980	1,620	1,600
Corporation for National and Community Service[48]	†	†	†	214,600	386,000	472,000	395,000	333,000	401,000	965,000	565,000
Estimated education funds	†	†	†	214,600	386,000	472,000	395,000	333,000	401,000	965,000	565,000
Federal Emergency Management Agency[49]	290	281	215	170,400	14,894	†	†	†	†	†	†
Estimated architect/engineer student development program	40	31	200	—	—	†	†	†	†	†	†
Estimated other training programs[50]	250	250	15	170,400	14,894	†	†	†	†	†	†
Estimated disaster relief[47]	—	—	—								
General Services Administration											
Libraries and other archival activities[51]	14,775	34,800	†	†	†	†	†	†	†	†	†
Institute of Museum and Library Services[45]	†	†	†	†	166,000	250,000	258,000	253,000	265,000	265,000	277,000
Japanese-United States Friendship Commission	†	2,294	2,299	2,000	3,000	3,000	2,000	2,000	2,000	2,000	3,000
Library of Congress	29,478	151,871	189,827	241,000	299,000	430,000	463,000	434,000	468,000	516,000	530,000
Salaries and expenses	20,700	102,364	148,985	198,000	247,000	383,000	413,000	395,000	420,000	439,000	456,000
Books for the blind and the physically handicapped	6,195	31,436	37,473	39,000	46,000	47,000	50,000	39,000	48,000	77,000	74,000
Special foreign currency program	2,273	3,492	10	†	†	†	†	†	†	†	†
Furniture and furnishings	310	14,579	3,359	4,000	6,000						
National Aeronautics and Space Administration											
Aerospace education services project	350	882	3,300	5,923	6,800	—		—		—	—
National Archives and Records Administration											
Libraries and other archival activities[51]	†	†	77,397	105,172	121,879	276,000	273,000	279,000	329,000	339,000	335,000
National Commission on Libraries and Information Science[52]	†	2,090	3,281	1,000	2,000	1,000	1,000	1,000	†	†	†
National Endowment for the Arts	340	231	936	2,304	4,046	2,506	2,942	3,202	3,002	2,883	2,719
National Endowment for the Humanities	5,090	85,805	89,706	94,249	70,807	87,969	80,564	87,690	93,738	94,580	94,000
Smithsonian Institution	2,461	5,153	5,779	9,961	25,764	45,890	46,101	64,768	61,104	63,107	66,119
Museum programs and related research	2,261	3,254	690	3,190	18,000	32,000	37,000	55,600	51,000	52,000	54,000
National Gallery of Art extension service	200	426	474	771	764	890	101	168	104	107	119
Woodrow Wilson International Center for Scholars	†	1,473	4,615	6,000	7,000	13,000	9,000	9,000	10,000	11,000	12,000

See notes at end of table.

Federal on-budget funds for education, by level/educational purpose, agency, and program: Selected fiscal years, 1970 through 2011—Continued

[In thousands of current dollars]

Level/educational purpose, agency, and program	1970	1980	1990¹	1995¹	2000¹	2005¹	2007¹	2008¹	2009¹²	2010¹²	2011¹²
1	2	3	4	5	6	7	8	9	10	11	12
U.S. Information Agency—Center for Cultural and Technical Interchange[40]	†	15,115	20,375	34,000	†	†	†	†	†	†	†
U.S. Institute of Peace	†	†	7,621	12,000	13,000	28,000	32,000	17,000	49,000	58,000	50,000
Other programs											
Estimated education share of federal aid for the District of Columbia	1,758	2,990	3,724	2,457	404	1,674	1,321	1,504	1,264	1,020	982
Research programs at universities and related institutions[53]	$2,283,641	$5,801,204	$12,606,035	$15,677,919	$21,660,134	$31,753,498	$30,281,920	$28,797,817	$34,594,940	$32,818,541	—
Department of Education[54]	87,823	78,742	89,483	279,000	116,464	456,822	437,484	463,729	578,602	659,006	$608,786
Department of Agriculture	64,796	216,405	348,109	434,544	553,600	709,700	722,600	707,800	857,200	849,900	—
Department of Commerce	4,487	48,295	50,523	85,442	110,775	243,948	200,374	193,612	235,892	191,801	—
Department of Defense	356,188	644,455	1,871,864	1,853,955	1,891,710	2,675,900	2,703,700	2,739,258	2,760,854	2,651,456	—
Department of Energy	548,327	1,470,224	2,520,885	2,651,641	3,577,004	4,339,879	3,382,683	2,469,637	4,486,785	4,569,987	—
Department of Health and Human Services	623,765	2,087,053	4,902,714	6,418,969	10,491,641	16,357,996	16,982,221	16,976,434	17,600,970	17,857,470	—
Department of Homeland Security	†	†	†	†	†	309,717	127,642	91,057	151,966	137,960	—
Department of Housing and Urban Development	510	5,314	118	1,613	1,400	1,100	400	400	200	600	—
Department of the Interior	18,521	42,175	49,790	50,618	47,200	66,800	66,200	53,900	45,400	45,500	—
Department of Justice	1,945	9,189	6,858	7,204	19,400	27,500	81,354	25,800	40,400	37,300	—
Department of Labor	3,567	12,938	5,893	10,114	12,900	110,500	23,800	500	400	800	—
Department of State	8,220	188	1,519	23	†	†	†	†	†	†	†
Department of Transportation	12,328	31,910	28,608	75,847	55,866	52,800	53,300	71,200	86,600	83,000	—
Department of the Treasury	†	226	227	1,496	†	†	100	100	†	100	†
Department of Veterans Affairs	518	1,600	2,300	2,500	†	†	†	†	†	†	†
Agency for International Development	†	77,063	79,415	30,172	33,500	28,100	28,500	26,900	29,400	30,400	—
Environmental Protection Agency	19,446	41,083	87,481	125,721	98,900	83,400	68,900	44,500	53,000	56,600	—
Federal Emergency Management Agency	†	1,665	†	†	†	†	†	†	†	†	†
National Aeronautics and Space Administration	258,016	254,629	1,090,003	1,751,977	2,071,030	2,763,120	1,651,205	1,154,900	1,217,300	1,191,500	—
National Science Foundation	253,628	743,809	1,427,007	1,874,395	2,566,244	3,503,216	3,735,057	3,767,290	6,428,771	4,439,561	—
Nuclear Regulatory Commission	†	32,590	42,328	22,188	12,200	15,100	10,100	2,200	7,800	9,900	—
Office of Economic Opportunity	20,035	†	†	†	†	†	†	†	†	†	†
U.S. Arms Control and Disarmament Agency	100	661	25	†	†	†	†	†	†	†	†
Other agencies	1,421	990	885	500	300	7,900	6,300	8,600	13,400	5,700	—

See notes at end of table.

Federal on-budget funds for education, by level/educational purpose, agency, and program: Selected fiscal years, 1970 through 2011—Continued

—Not available.

†Not applicable.

[1]Excludes federal support for medical education benefits under Medicare in the U.S. Department of Health and Human Services. Benefits excluded from total because data before fiscal year (FY) 1990 are not available. This program existed since Medicare began, but was not available as a separate budget item until FY 1990. Excluded amounts are as follows: $4,440,000,000 in FY 1990, $7,510,000,000 in FY 1995, $8,020,000,000 in FY 2000, $8,300,000,000 in FY 2005, $8,200,000,000 in FY 2007, $8,600,000,000 in FY 2008, $8,800,000,000 in FY 2009, $9,000,000,000 in FY 2010, and an estimated $9,300,000,000 in FY 2011.

[2]Data for research programs at universities and related institutions are estimated.

[3]The U.S. Department of Education was created in May 1980. It formerly was the Office of Education in the U.S. Department of Health, Education, and Welfare.

[4]Arranges for the education of children who reside on federal property when no suitable local school district can or will provide for the education of these children.

[5]Includes many programs, such as No Child Left Behind, 21st Century Community Learning Centers, Class Size Reduction, Charter Schools, Safe and Drug-Free Schools, and Innovative programs.

[6]Included the School-To-Work Opportunities program, which initiated a national system to be administered jointly by the U.S. Departments of Education and Labor. Programs in the Education Reform program were transferred to the school improvement programs or discontinued in FY 2002. Amounts after FY 2002 reflect balances that are spending out from prior-year appropriations.

[7]Starting in FY 1994, the Special Milk Program has been included in the child nutrition programs.

[8]The Farm Security and Rural Investment Act of 2002 (Public Law 107-171) carries out preschool and school feeding programs in foreign countries to help reduce the incidence of hunger and malnutrition, and improve literacy and primary education.

[9]These commodities are purchased under Section 32 of the Act of August 24, 1935, for use in the child nutrition programs.

[10]Assisted in the construction of public facilities, such as vocational schools, through grants or loans. No funds have been appropriated for this program since FY 1977, and it was completely phased out in FY 1984.

[11]Established in 1979, with funds first appropriated in FY 1980.

[12]Formerly in the Office of Economic Opportunity. In FY 1972, funds were transferred to the U.S. Department of Health, Education, and Welfare, Office of Child Development.

[13]Created by the Family Support Act of 1988 to provide funds for the Job Opportunities and Basic Skills Training program. Later incorporated into the Temporary Assistance for Needy Families program.

[14]After age 18, benefits terminate at the end of the school term or in 3 months, whichever comes first.

[15]Transferred from the U.S. Department of Transportation to the U.S. Department of Homeland Security in March 2003.

[16]Provides funding for supplemental programs for eligible American Indian students in public schools.

[17]Finances the cost of academic, social, and occupational education courses for inmates in federal prisons.

[18]Some of the work and training programs were in the Office of Economic Opportunity and were transferred to the U.S. Department of Labor in FYs 1971 and 1972. From FY 1994 through FY 2001, included the School-to-Work Opportunities program, which was administered jointly by the U.S. Departments of Education and Labor.

[19]Established in 1972 and closed in FY 1986.

[20]The states' share of revenue-sharing funds could not be spent on education in FYs 1981 through 1986.

[21]Provided educational assistance allowances in order to restore lost educational opportunities to those individuals whose careers were interrupted or impeded by reason of active military service between January 31, 1955, and January 1, 1977.

[22]This program is in "Readjustment Benefits" program, Chapter 31, and covers the costs of subsistence, tuition, books, supplies, and equipment for disabled veterans requiring vocational rehabilitation.

[23]This program is in "Readjustment Benefits" program, Chapter 35, and provides benefits to children and spouses of veterans.

[24]Head Start program funds were transferred to the U.S. Department of Health, Education, and Welfare, Office of Child Development, in FY 1972.

[25]Most of these programs were transferred to the U.S. Department of Health, Education, and Welfare, Office of Education, in FY 1972.

[26]Transferred to the U.S. Department of Labor in FYs 1971 and 1972.

[27]Transferred to the ACTION Agency in FY 1972.

[28]Under the William D. Ford Federal Direct Loan Program (commonly referred to as the Direct Loan Program), the federal government uses Treasury funds to provide loan capital directly to schools, which then disburse loan funds to students.

[29]The Federal Family Education Loan (FFEL) Program eliminated the authorization to originate new FFEL loans after June 30, 2010; all new loans are originated through the Direct Loan Program. The FFEL Program made loan capital available to students and their families through private lenders. State and private nonprofit guaranty agencies administer the federal guarantee protecting FFEL lenders against losses related to borrower default. These agencies also collect on defaulted loans and provide other services to lenders.

[30]Transferred from the U.S. Department of Housing and Urban Development to the U.S. Department of Health, Education, and Welfare, Office of Education, in FY 1979.

[31]Transferred from the National Science Foundation to the U.S. Department of Commerce in October 1970.

[32]Transferred from the U.S. Department of Commerce to the U.S. Department of Transportation in FY 1981.

[33]Includes special education programs (military and civilian); legal education program; flight training; advanced degree program; college degree program (officers); and "Armed Forces Health Professions Scholarship" program.

[34]Does not include higher education assistance loans.

[35]Alcohol, drug abuse, and mental health training programs are included starting in FY 1992.

[36]Beginning in FY 1992, data were included in the National Institutes of Health training grants program.

[37]This program closed in FY 2004.

[38]Postsecondary student benefits were ended by the Omnibus Budget Reconciliation Act of 1981 (Public Law 97-35) and were completely phased out by August 1985.

[39]Includes flight training. Transferred to the U.S. Department of Homeland Security in March 2003.

[40]Transferred from the U.S. Department of State to the United States Information Agency in 1977, then transferred back to the U.S. Department of State in FY 1998.

[41]Chapter 33 was enacted in the "Post 9-11 Veterans Educational Assistance Act of 2008" (Public Law 110-252).

[42]Part of the Ronald W. Reagan National Defense Authorization Act for FY 2005 (Public Law 108-375), enacted October 28, 2004. The Reserve Education Assistance Program (REAP) provides educational assistance to members of the National Guard and Reserves who serve on active duty in support of a contingency operation under federal authority on or after September 11, 2001.

[43]Abolished in FY 1998, with functions transferred to the U.S. Department of State and the newly created Broadcasting Board of Governors.

[44]Included in the "Educational and Cultural Affairs" program in FYs 1980 through 1983, and became an independent program in FY 1984.

[45]Transferred from U.S. Department of Education to the Institute of Museum and Library Services in FY 1997.

[46]Transferred to the U.S. Department of Homeland Security in FY 2003.

[47]The disaster relief program repairs and replaces damaged and destroyed school buildings. This program was transferred from the Federal Emergency Management Agency to the U.S. Department of Homeland Security in FY 2003.

[48]The National Service Trust Act of 1993 established the Corporation for National and Community Service. In 1993, ACTION became part of this agency.

[49]The Federal Emergency Management Agency was created in 1979, representing a combination of five existing agencies. The funds for the Federal Emergency Management Agency in FY 1970 to FY 1975 were in other agencies. This agency was transferred to the U.S. Department of Homeland Security in March 2003.

[50]These programs include the Fall-Out Shelter Analysis, Blast Protection Design through FY 1992. Starting in FY 1993, earthquake training and safety for teachers and administrators for grades 1 through 12 are included.

[51]Transferred from the General Services Administration to the National Archives and Records Administration in April 1985.

[52]Public Law 110-161 transferred the National Commission on Libraries and Information Science to the Institute of Museum and Library Services starting in FY 2008.

[53]Includes federal obligations for research and development centers and R & D plant administered by colleges and universities. FY 2009 and FY 2010 data are estimated, except the U.S Department of Education data, which are actual numbers.

[54]FY 1970 includes outlays for the "Research and Training" program. FY 1975 includes the "National Institute of Education" program. FYs 1990 through 2009 include outlays for the Office of Educational Research and Improvement and the Institute of Education Sciences.

NOTE: Some data have been revised from previously published figures. To the extent possible, amounts reported represent outlays rather than obligations. Detail may not sum to totals because of rounding. Negative amounts occur when program receipts exceed outlays.

SOURCE: U.S. Department of Education, Budget Service, unpublished tabulations. U.S. Office of Management and Budget, *Budget of the U.S. Government, Appendix*, fiscal years 1972 through 2012. National Science Foundation, *Federal Funds for Research and Development*, fiscal years 1970 through 2010. (This table was prepared October 2011.)

U.S. Department of Education outlays, by type of recipient and level of education: Selected fiscal years, 1980 through 2011
[In millions of current dollars]

Year and level of education	Total	Local education agencies	State education agencies	Postsecondary students	Postsecondary institutions	Federal institutions	Other education organizations[1]	Other recipients[2]
1	2	3	4	5	6	7	8	9
1980 total	**$13,137.8**	**$5,313.7**	**$1,103.2**	**$2,137.4**	**$2,267.2**	**$249.8**	**$693.8**	**$1,372.7**
Elementary/secondary	6,629.1	5,309.4	662.2	34.2	22.0	62.5	513.4	25.5
Postsecondary	5,682.2	†	99.5	2,103.2	2,166.5	†	†	1,313.0
Other programs	747.7	4.3	341.5	†	†	187.3	180.4	34.2
Education research and statistics	78.7	†	†	†	78.7	†	†	†
1985 total	**16,701.1**	**6,225.0**	**1,502.9**	**2,434.7**	**2,362.3**	**287.3**	**503.9**	**3,385.0**
Elementary/secondary	7,296.7	6,220.8	636.0	58.0	25.2	2.4	322.4	31.9
Postsecondary	8,202.5	†	228.3	2,376.7	2,308.3	†	†	3,289.2
Other programs	1,173.1	4.2	638.6	†	†	284.9	181.5	63.9
Education research and statistics	28.8	†	†	†	28.8	†	†	†
1990 total	**23,198.6**	**8,000.7**	**2,490.3**	**3,859.6**	**3,649.8**	**441.4**	**912.2**	**3,844.4**
Elementary/secondary	9,681.3	7,995.0	700.3	80.5	85.4	113.1	650.7	56.3
Postsecondary	11,176.0	†	261.6	3,779.1	3,475.0	†	†	3,660.4
Other programs	2,251.8	5.7	1,528.5	†	†	328.3	261.5	127.8
Education research and statistics	89.5	†	†	†	89.5	†	†	†
1995 total	**31,403.0**	**11,210.7**	**3,584.0**	**4,964.7**	**5,016.1**	**485.4**	**1,349.2**	**4,792.9**
Elementary/secondary	14,029.0	11,203.3	1,410.0	190.5	170.1	70.3	946.9	37.9
Postsecondary	14,234.0	†	250.8	4,774.2	4,567.0	†	†	4,642.0
Other programs	2,861.0	7.4	1,923.2	†	†	415.1	402.3	113.0
Education research and statistics	279.0	†	†	†	279.0	†	†	†
2000 total	**34,106.7**	**16,016.0**	**4,316.5**	**4,711.7**	**5,005.7**	**506.6**	**1,820.2**	**1,730.1**
Elementary/secondary	20,039.6	16,003.5	1,989.6	260.5	198.9	48.5	1,461.8	76.8
Postsecondary	10,727.3	†	55.2	4,451.2	4,690.3	†	†	1,530.6
Other programs	3,223.4	12.5	2,271.7	†	†	458.1	358.4	122.7
Education research and statistics	116.5	†	†	†	116.5	†	†	†
2002 total	**46,324.4**	**19,742.1**	**4,967.8**	**8,306.0**	**8,668.2**	**608.9**	**2,200.3**	**1,831.3**
Elementary/secondary	25,246.2	19,729.2	2,429.8	490.0	454.9	77.6	1,829.5	235.3
Postsecondary	17,056.2	†	199.2	7,816.0	7,588.1	†	†	1,452.9
Other programs	3,396.8	12.9	2,338.8	†	†	531.3	370.8	143.1
Education research and statistics	625.2	†	†	†	625.2	†	†	†
2003 total	**57,442.9**	**23,837.7**	**6,164.6**	**11,032.5**	**10,731.8**	**657.8**	**2,478.9**	**2,539.6**
Elementary/secondary	30,749.3	23,882.8	3,141.1	594.3	637.4	109.5	2,105.6	338.6
Postsecondary	22,706.4	†	668.6	10,438.2	9,542.5	†	†	2,057.2
Other programs	3,435.2	14.9	2,354.9	†	†	548.3	373.3	143.8
Education research and statistics	551.9	†	†	†	551.9	†	†	†
2004 total	**62,903.4**	**26,012.4**	**6,334.5**	**12,005.0**	**10,977.0**	**648.9**	**2,730.1**	**4,195.4**
Elementary/secondary	33,689.4	25,990.0	3,611.7	606.2	642.5	126.4	2,300.0	412.6
Postsecondary	25,341.0	†	420.9	11,398.8	9,899.3	†	†	3,621.9
Other programs	3,437.8	22.4	2,301.9	†	†	522.5	430.1	160.9
Education research and statistics	435.2	†	†	†	435.2	†	†	†
2005 total	**72,893.3**	**28,900.2**	**7,126.3**	**14,708.2**	**13,362.4**	**669.8**	**3,023.0**	**5,103.4**
Elementary/secondary	37,477.6	28,878.6	3,971.6	698.1	790.0	145.9	2,578.4	415.0
Postsecondary	31,420.0	†	777.1	14,010.1	12,115.6	†	†	4,517.2
Other programs	3,538.9	21.6	2,377.6	†	†	523.9	444.6	171.2
Education research and statistics	456.8	†	†	†	456.8	†	†	†
2006 total	**93,571.5**	**30,236.6**	**8,331.3**	**22,955.1**	**21,376.1**	**693.2**	**2,902.3**	**7,076.8**
Elementary/secondary	38,863.4	30,214.8	4,098.7	741.5	775.1	168.6	2,455.5	409.2
Postsecondary	50,624.6	†	1,702.4	22,213.6	20,210.5	†	†	6,498.1
Other programs	3,692.9	21.8	2,530.2	†	†	524.6	446.8	169.5
Education research and statistics	390.5	†	†	†	390.5	†	†	†
2007 total	**71,808.0**	**29,008.8**	**7,429.4**	**14,269.9**	**13,877.6**	**613.2**	**2,931.5**	**3,677.7**
Elementary/secondary	37,562.1	28,990.4	4,018.7	824.4	781.5	73.8	2,460.7	412.6
Postsecondary	30,052.0	†	805.5	13,445.5	12,658.6	†	†	3,084.6
Other programs	3,756.4	18.4	2,605.2	†	†	539.4	413.0	180.5
Education research and statistics	437.5	†	†	†	437.5	†	†	†
2008 total	**72,177.8**	**29,553.0**	**7,377.7**	**14,371.2**	**13,585.9**	**1,348.8**	**2,997.9**	**2,943.3**
Elementary/secondary	38,330.4	29,533.5	4,100.2	859.6	800.2	96.3	2,518.1	422.5
Postsecondary	28,838.8	†	618.8	13,511.6	12,322.0	†	†	2,328.1
Other programs	4,545.0	19.5	2,658.7	†	†	1,252.5	421.5	192.7
Education research and statistics	463.7	†	†	†	463.7	†	†	†
2009 total	**85,224.7**	**40,300.0**	**8,402.8**	**14,828.8**	**14,782.5**	**1,415.3**	**4,068.7**	**1,426.6**
Elementary/secondary	52,468.1	40,273.4	5,562.4	893.8	1,325.9	76.3	3,590.7	745.4
Postsecondary	27,626.6	†	228.0	13,935.0	12,878.0	†	†	521.9
Other programs	4,551.4	26.6	2,612.3	†	†	1,339.0	414.1	159.3
Education research and statistics	578.6	†	†	†	578.6	†	†	†
2010 total	**91,893.2**	**38,137.0**	**8,744.6**	**18,616.4**	**18,027.3**	**2,677.1**	**3,888.2**	**1,802.5**
Elementary/secondary	49,621.5	38,112.4	5,287.1	881.1	1,216.3	84.0	3,363.9	676.7
Postsecondary	36,539.7	†	581.9	17,735.3	16,152.0	1,061.9	68.4	940.1
Other programs	5,073.1	24.6	2,875.6	†	†	1,531.2	455.9	185.7
Education research and statistics	659.0	†	†	†	659.0	†	†	†
2011 total	**93,486.0**	**29,914.9**	**7,145.2**	**26,120.2**	**24,641.3**	**2,107.0**	**2,963.9**	**593.4**
Elementary/secondary	38,693.6	29,890.3	4,175.2	878.0	801.3	82.6	2,446.7	419.4
Postsecondary	48,880.3	†	120.7	25,242.2	23,231.2	230.5	65.5	-9.9
Other programs	5,303.3	24.6	2,849.3	†	†	1,793.9	451.7	183.9
Education research and statistics	608.8	†	†	†	608.8	†	†	†

†Not applicable.

[1]Includes funds for vocational education and for federal programs at libraries and museums.

[2]Other recipients include American Indian tribes, private nonprofit agencies, and banks.

NOTE: Outlays by type of recipient are estimated based on obligation data. Negative amounts occur when program receipts exceed outlays. The increase in postsecondary expenditures in 2006 resulted primarily from an accounting adjustment. Some data have been revised from previously published figures. Detail may not sum to totals because of rounding.

SOURCE: U.S. Office of Management and Budget, *Budget of the U.S. Government*, fiscal years 1982 through 2012. U.S. Department of Education, Budget Service, unpublished tabulations. (This table was prepared November 2011.)

U.S. Department of Education appropriations for major programs, by state or jurisdiction: Fiscal year 2010
[In thousands of current dollars]

State or jurisdiction	Total	Grants for the disadvantaged[1]	Block grants to states for school improvement[2]	School assistance in federally affected areas[3]	Career/ technical and adult education[4]	Special education[5]	Language assistance[6]	American Indian education	Degree-granting institutions[7]	Student financial assistance[8]	Rehabilitation services[9]
1	2	3	4	5	6	7	8	9	10	11	12
Total, 50 states and D.C.[10]	$91,662,814	$14,810,243	$14,561,583	$1,132,631	$1,839,462	$12,032,103	$689,038	$104,331	$2,398,719	$40,916,472	$3,178,230
Total, 50 states, D.C., other activities, and other jurisdictions	94,907,411	15,559,686	15,045,434	1,204,111	1,909,241	12,318,737	750,000	104,331	2,455,431	42,248,347	3,312,093
Alabama	1,642,683	232,673	231,102	2,753	33,647	192,188	3,776	1,680	82,647	799,389	62,828
Alaska	341,726	46,845	48,699	120,999	5,566	39,590	1,162	11,422	17,098	36,719	13,627
Arizona	3,523,568	325,711	303,243	170,413	40,611	199,607	24,081	11,217	36,098	2,343,949	68,639
Arkansas	985,324	170,160	146,878	298	20,396	120,669	3,302	307	39,753	436,918	46,643
California	10,460,614	1,941,074	1,741,844	63,826	232,417	1,309,657	173,295	6,522	251,868	4,429,125	310,986
Colorado	1,318,026	170,448	218,411	16,129	24,633	165,393	11,172	764	31,581	636,388	43,107
Connecticut	812,409	121,746	154,619	4,682	16,347	140,977	5,681	0	16,497	318,135	33,726
Delaware	232,007	44,072	52,525	52	6,808	37,126	1,171	0	7,884	69,108	13,261
District of Columbia	616,230	50,226	42,750	1,081	6,055	19,357	740	0	251,781	228,483	15,757
Florida	5,277,428	775,083	778,927	7,720	109,265	668,442	44,368	67	68,913	2,654,320	170,323
Georgia	3,006,465	545,230	472,555	22,017	62,579	347,855	16,360	0	76,266	1,381,318	82,285
Hawaii	331,891	45,659	64,515	38,057	8,249	42,777	2,934	0	25,590	88,391	15,719
Idaho	451,986	55,990	78,433	6,017	9,388	59,485	2,237	419	13,044	208,697	18,277
Illinois	3,982,067	641,402	614,558	18,577	71,393	537,844	30,536	145	70,690	1,871,343	125,580
Indiana	1,833,211	268,336	293,291	124	38,409	273,618	7,108	0	19,673	866,128	66,522
Iowa	1,290,250	82,957	137,046	304	17,018	129,178	3,159	194	24,986	865,478	29,930
Kansas	813,672	118,663	134,570	25,241	15,466	114,421	3,791	1,232	30,768	337,820	31,700
Kentucky	1,396,901	244,979	215,669	682	31,406	172,672	3,594	0	50,571	627,270	50,059
Louisiana	1,537,833	332,952	249,620	8,075	33,944	200,402	3,147	897	61,405	612,941	34,450
Maine	376,362	56,215	67,373	2,650	8,134	58,970	802	153	9,431	153,444	19,190
Maryland	1,298,137	193,202	245,944	5,419	27,854	212,689	9,602	79	41,795	510,951	50,602
Massachusetts	1,647,917	236,930	287,423	662	30,835	299,176	12,777	80	34,421	674,427	71,186
Michigan	3,155,430	566,140	501,176	4,187	59,484	422,328	10,883	2,680	44,082	1,435,793	108,677
Minnesota	1,403,506	137,931	229,845	18,274	25,513	202,881	8,745	3,513	30,693	695,531	50,579
Mississippi	1,220,991	212,893	172,658	1,829	22,813	127,907	1,756	457	46,385	587,273	47,020
Missouri	1,745,750	250,766	279,507	22,136	34,716	239,395	4,984	88	29,338	818,479	66,342
Montana	361,547	48,537	61,124	42,961	7,142	40,262	551	3,174	27,878	115,347	14,570
Nebraska	498,430	69,811	89,489	17,270	9,859	78,983	2,721	822	13,382	193,727	22,365
Nevada	481,340	94,928	113,847	3,612	14,750	75,385	8,402	752	16,977	132,841	19,848
New Hampshire	302,384	42,126	68,623	8	7,819	50,817	828	0	3,383	114,660	14,118
New Jersey	2,064,377	315,910	372,913	13,173	42,128	381,005	20,018	60	28,882	825,620	64,668
New Mexico	802,540	120,273	106,094	99,226	13,428	96,567	4,927	8,398	39,861	287,297	26,468
New York	6,572,351	1,305,933	978,717	22,069	113,252	810,888	54,757	1,823	74,870	3,021,712	188,330
North Carolina	2,512,417	401,228	421,934	15,903	61,012	348,449	15,134	3,477	86,501	1,046,257	112,522
North Dakota	278,166	37,680	46,803	30,729	5,566	30,342	506	1,870	16,006	96,097	12,567
Ohio	3,385,071	560,380	540,087	1,842	65,949	461,609	8,708	0	43,000	1,598,025	105,471
Oklahoma	1,178,773	170,103	187,485	36,471	23,088	155,775	3,939	26,789	49,973	481,421	43,728
Oregon	1,055,985	163,899	169,409	2,721	21,181	136,708	8,058	2,166	18,644	491,445	41,755
Pennsylvania	3,386,021	611,368	574,039	779	68,484	452,351	13,096	0	48,469	1,481,026	136,410
Rhode Island	362,402	53,497	58,113	1,513	8,764	47,228	1,973	0	6,545	169,354	15,416
South Carolina	1,357,287	227,061	213,364	2,023	31,340	188,902	4,605	16	54,776	576,748	58,452
South Dakota	352,397	46,726	52,295	51,502	5,992	36,229	542	3,719	14,492	128,283	12,616
Tennessee	1,819,286	285,793	288,453	3,735	40,882	250,202	5,884	0	46,668	821,276	76,394
Texas	7,413,532	1,460,416	1,257,452	98,774	158,845	1,037,884	101,629	391	196,714	2,851,822	249,604
Utah	833,532	74,471	134,516	8,360	17,323	117,773	5,303	1,583	16,262	417,776	40,165
Vermont	219,164	36,247	44,004	5	5,376	29,412	500	235	10,229	77,462	15,694
Virginia	1,924,340	262,958	338,613	39,110	41,372	299,232	11,589	15	47,789	807,438	76,223
Washington	1,553,852	215,993	287,213	51,455	32,514	236,392	16,120	3,963	56,629	597,372	56,202
West Virginia	641,866	96,120	94,512	11	14,410	81,006	784	0	19,377	278,556	57,090
Wisconsin	1,401,049	205,575	257,058	12,731	30,731	223,197	6,800	2,432	40,794	562,504	59,228
Wyoming	202,318	34,930	42,243	14,444	5,309	30,902	500	728	7,361	54,587	11,314
Other activities/jurisdictions											
Indian Tribe (Set-Aside)	342,426	105,350	76,925	0	14,511	97,635	5,000	0	0	0	43,004
Other	269,050	24,248	46,957	71,392	13,185	25,000	48,750	0	0	35,064	4,454
American Samoa	46,867	10,541	14,144	0	587	6,879	1,327	0	1,585	10,164	1,641
Guam	82,153	12,446	28,371	0	1,071	15,387	1,118	0	1,941	19,263	2,555
Marshall Islands	300	0	0	0	0	0	0	0	300	0	0
Federated States of Micronesia	34,706	0	0	0	187	6,579	0	0	472	27,467	0
Northern Marianas	28,852	3,829	11,495	0	782	5,232	1,242	0	1,668	3,224	1,381
Palau	1,091	0	0	0	0	0	0	0	1,091	0	0
Puerto Rico	2,379,978	578,865	285,492	0	38,198	120,288	3,463	0	46,492	1,229,105	78,075
U.S. Virgin Islands	59,173	14,164	20,467	88	1,257	9,634	63	0	3,161	7,587	2,753

[1]Title I includes Grants to Local Education Agencies (Basic, Concentration, Targeted, and Education Finance Incentive Grants); School Turnaround Grants; Even Start; Migrant Education Grants; Striving Readers Formula Grants; and Neglected and Delinquent Children Grants.

[2]Title VI includes Improving Teacher Quality State Grants; Mathematics and Science Partnerships; Educational Technology State Grants; 21st Century Community Learning Centers; Assessing Achievement, including No Child Left Behind; Education for the Homeless Children and Youth; Rural and Low-Income Schools Program; Education Jobs Fund; and Small, Rural School Achievement Program.

[3]Includes Impact Aid—Basic Support Payments; Impact Aid—Payments for Children with Disabilities; and Impact Aid—Construction.

[4]Includes Career and Technical Education State Grants; English Literacy and Civics Education State Grants; Tech-Prep Education; State Grants for Incarcerated Youth Offenders; State Grants for Workplace and Community Transition Training for Incarcerated Individuals; and Adult Basic and Literacy Education State Grants.

[5]Includes Special Education—Grants to States; Preschool Grants; and Grants for Infants and Families.

[6]Includes English Learner Education.

[7]Includes Institutional Aid to Strengthen Higher Education Institutions serving significant numbers of low-income students; Other Special Programs for the Disadvantaged; Cooperative Education; Fund for the Improvement of Postsecondary Education; Fellowships and Scholarships; and College Access Challenge Funds.

[8]Includes Pell Grants; Leveraging Educational Assistance Partnership; Federal Supplemental Educational Opportunity Grants; Federal Work-Study; Special Allowances; and Federal Family Education Loan Program interest subsidies.

[9]Includes Vocational Rehabilitation State Grants; Supported Employment State Grants; Client Assistance State Grants; Independent Living State Grants; Services for Older Blind Individuals; Centers for Independent Living; Protection and Advocacy for Assistive Technology; Assistive Technology State Grant Program; and Protection and Advocacy of Individual Rights.

[10]Total excludes other activities and other jurisdictions.

NOTE: Data reflect revisions to figures in the *Budget of the United States Government, Fiscal Year 2012*. Detail may not sum to totals because of rounding.

SOURCE: U.S. Department of Education, Budget Service, unpublished tabulations. (This table was prepared September 2011.)

Appropriations for Title I and selected other programs under the No Child Left Behind Act of 2001, by program and state or jurisdiction: Fiscal years 2010 and 2011

[In thousands of current dollars]

State or jurisdiction	Title I total, 2010	Title I, 2011 Total	Grants to local education agencies[1]	State agency programs Neglected and Delinquent	State agency programs Migrant	Turn-around Grants	Assessing Achievement, 2011	Improving Teacher Quality State Grants, 2011
1	2	3	4	5	6	7	8	9
Total, 50 states and D.C.[2]	$14,810,243	$14,738,332	$13,794,455	$48,528	$383,981	$511,368	$370,438	$2,330,578
Total, 50 states, D.C., other activities, and other jurisdictions	15,559,686	15,442,286	14,463,416	50,326	393,981	534,562	389,951	2,468,054
Alabama	232,673	237,082	225,736	939	2,139	8,268	6,333	38,744
Alaska	46,845	44,889	35,864	234	7,236	1,556	3,537	11,563
Arizona	325,711	334,833	314,894	1,477	6,828	11,634	7,726	38,878
Arkansas	170,160	168,360	156,582	508	5,476	5,794	5,070	23,659
California	1,941,074	1,826,499	1,626,853	1,621	135,023	63,002	30,245	270,981
Colorado	170,448	167,089	153,343	664	7,310	5,772	6,551	27,353
Connecticut	121,746	113,921	107,016	2,006	1,033	3,867	5,477	22,673
Delaware	44,072	44,607	42,390	371	303	1,542	3,604	11,563
District of Columbia	50,226	52,024	49,000	1,177	0	1,847	3,275	11,563
Florida	775,083	793,886	740,529	1,657	23,607	28,093	14,797	110,257
Georgia	545,230	554,539	526,094	1,023	8,195	19,227	10,270	64,699
Hawaii	45,659	50,530	47,568	355	834	1,773	3,872	11,563
Idaho	55,990	60,489	54,120	542	3,706	2,121	4,238	11,563
Illinois	641,402	669,727	642,998	1,093	1,980	23,656	12,239	99,685
Indiana	268,336	272,045	256,459	533	5,706	9,348	7,730	41,706
Iowa	82,957	81,636	76,708	396	1,669	2,862	5,118	18,899
Kansas	118,663	127,545	110,731	347	11,977	4,491	5,100	19,349
Kentucky	244,979	243,164	226,125	934	7,672	8,434	5,985	38,137
Louisiana	332,952	313,447	298,919	1,771	2,564	10,193	6,238	54,419
Maine	56,215	55,799	52,443	193	1,213	1,950	3,826	11,563
Maryland	193,202	191,438	182,671	1,489	524	6,754	6,982	34,924
Massachusetts	236,930	231,202	219,019	2,637	1,670	7,876	7,237	43,964
Michigan	566,140	564,676	535,794	346	8,878	19,658	10,040	96,339
Minnesota	137,931	167,061	158,756	249	2,147	5,909	6,740	33,144
Mississippi	212,893	202,627	193,877	845	1,074	6,830	5,194	36,009
Missouri	250,766	256,317	244,238	1,507	1,573	8,999	7,170	42,200
Montana	48,537	47,399	44,589	121	1,044	1,645	3,649	11,563
Nebraska	69,811	69,770	61,732	318	5,281	2,439	4,318	11,840
Nevada	94,928	101,476	97,381	251	245	3,599	4,924	12,360
New Hampshire	42,126	42,599	40,527	445	152	1,476	3,876	11,563
New Jersey	315,910	315,013	299,989	2,160	2,034	10,830	9,140	55,221
New Mexico	120,273	119,195	113,838	272	955	4,131	4,505	19,135
New York	1,305,933	1,222,881	1,168,409	2,835	10,247	41,390	15,766	196,797
North Carolina	401,228	412,443	390,840	1,279	5,842	14,482	9,645	54,029
North Dakota	37,680	35,650	34,097	74	242	1,236	3,424	11,563
Ohio	560,380	595,603	570,012	1,811	2,751	21,029	11,096	91,323
Oklahoma	170,103	162,269	154,673	378	1,590	5,628	5,681	28,019
Oregon	163,899	163,987	146,454	1,121	10,622	5,790	5,533	23,655
Pennsylvania	611,368	575,819	546,045	755	9,389	19,629	11,308	98,302
Rhode Island	53,497	51,960	49,542	567	69	1,782	3,671	11,563
South Carolina	227,061	230,734	220,624	1,412	582	8,116	6,135	30,730
South Dakota	46,726	46,316	43,702	141	867	1,605	3,577	11,563
Tennessee	285,793	285,669	274,585	531	596	9,957	7,383	41,832
Texas	1,460,416	1,463,538	1,348,969	2,293	61,098	51,178	22,888	201,175
Utah	74,471	86,030	80,212	861	1,913	3,045	5,445	16,018
Vermont	36,247	35,775	33,281	597	657	1,240	3,392	11,563
Virginia	262,958	257,555	245,997	1,820	823	8,915	8,414	43,456
Washington	215,993	236,184	211,175	1,015	15,659	8,335	7,599	39,890
West Virginia	96,120	97,625	93,227	886	84	3,429	4,141	20,546
Wisconsin	205,575	222,847	213,279	1,099	658	7,811	6,952	39,917
Wyoming	34,930	34,564	32,552	573	242	1,198	3,383	11,563
Other activities/jurisdictions								
Indian Tribe Set-Aside	105,350	105,488	101,824	0	0	3,664	1,900	12,279
Other nonstate allocations	24,248	20,250	8,992	1,258	10,000	0	9,980	37,021
American Samoa	10,541	9,922	9,582	0	0	340	360	2,847
Guam	12,446	12,011	11,593	0	0	417	774	4,376
Northern Marianas	3,829	3,853	3,719	0	0	134	243	1,361
Puerto Rico	578,865	539,097	520,375	540	0	18,181	5,733	75,898
U.S. Virgin Islands	14,164	13,333	12,876	0	0	457	523	3,694

[1]Includes Basic, Concentration, Targeted, and Education Finance Incentive Grants.
[2]Total excludes other activities and other jurisdictions.
NOTE: Detail may not sum to totals because of rounding. These are preliminary estimates for fiscal year 2011.

SOURCE: U.S. Department of Education, Budget Service, Elementary, Secondary, and Vocational Education Analysis Division, unpublished tabulations. (This table was prepared September 2011.)

Selected population and enrollment statistics for countries with populations over 10 million in 2009, by continent: Selected years, 1990 through 2009

Country[1]	Midyear population (in millions)			Persons per square kilometer	First level[2]					Second level[3]					Third level[4]				
					Enrollment (in thousands)		Gross enrollment ratio[5]			Enrollment (in thousands)		Gross enrollment ratio[5]			Enrollment (in thousands)		Gross enrollment ratio[5]		
	1991	2000	2009	2009	1999–2000	2008–09	1990–91	1999–2000	2008–09	1999–2000	2008–09	1990–91	1999–2000	2008–09	1999–2000	2008–09	1990–91	1999–2000	2008–09
1	2	3	4	5	6	7	8	9	10	11	12	13	14	15	16	17	18	19	20
World total[6]	5,374	6,095	6,793	52	650,860	701,646	99	99	107	450,736	531,248[7]	52	60	68[7]	99,485	164,582[7]	14	19	27[7]
Africa																			
Algeria[8]	26	30	34	14	4,843	3,253	100	108	108	—	4,585	61	—	96	—	1,150	11	—	31
Angola	10	13	17	13	—	—	92	—	—	355	—	12	14	—	—	—	1	—	—
Burkina Faso	9	12	16	58	852	1,906	33	45	78	190	468	7	10	20	11[7]	48	1	1[7]	3
Cameroon	12	15	19	40	2,237[9]	3,351	101	86[9]	114	700	1,269	28	27	41	66[7]	174	3	4[7]	9
Chad	6	8	10	8	914	1,671	54	66	90	137	422	8[10]	11	24	6	20	1[11,12]	1	2
Cote d'Ivoire	13	17	21	65	1,944	2,383	67	73	74	620[7]	—	22	23[7]	—	104[7]	—	—	6[7]	—
Democratic Rep. of the Congo	41	52	68	30	—	10,244	70	—	90	—	3,399	21[13]	—	37	—	380	2	—	6
Egypt[8]	56	65	79	79	7,947[7]	10,407	94	93[7]	101	8,028[7]	6,696	76	76[7]	67	—	—	16[14,15]	—	—
Ethiopia	50	64	85	85	5,847	13,571	33	55	102	1,195	3,926	14	14	34	68	203	1	1	—
Ghana[8]	16	20	24	105	2,561	3,659	75	83	105	1,057	1,812	36	40	57	89	—	1[11]	1	9
Guinea	7	8	10	41	790	1,390	37	60	90	199[7]	560[7]	10	16[7]	37[7]	—	168	1	1	4
Kenya[8]	24	31	40	70	5,035	7,150	95	95	113	1,909	3,204	24[10]	39	59	—	168	2[11]	3	4
Madagascar	12	16	21	36	2,208	4,324	103	104	160	487	1,022[7]	18[10]	31	32[7]	32	68	3	2	—
Malawi	10	12	15	160	2,695	3,250	68	135	119	258[7]	667	8	18[7]	30	4	77	1	#	—
Mali	9	11	13	11	1,017	1,926	26	59	95	—	686	7	—	38	20	—	1	2	6
Morocco[8]	24	28	31	70	3,670	3,851	67	92	107	1,541	—	35	38	—	276	419	11	9	13
Mozambique[8]	13	18	22	28	2,544	5,072	67	75	114	124	598	8	6	23	12	16	#[12]	1	1
Niger	8	11	15	12	579	1,554	29	32	62	106[7]	257	7	7[7]	12	9	—	1	1	1
Nigeria[8]	99	124	157	173	19,151	21,714	91	95	89	4,290[7]	—	25	25[7]	—	204[7]	55	4[11,16]	—	5
Rwanda	7	8	11	436	1,432	2,265	70	105	151	130	347	8	11	27	—	—	#[17]	1	8
Senegal	8	9	12	62	1,108	1,653	59	68	84	250	—	16	16	—	—	94	3	—	—
South Africa	39	45	49	40	7,445	7,129	122	106	101	4,142	4,688	74	86	94	—	360	13[18]	6[7]	—
Sudan[8]	27	34	43	18	2,567	4,744	53	47	74	980	1,837	24	25	38	204[7]	—	3[11]	—	34
Tunisia	8	9	10	67	1,414	1,025	113	115	108	1,104[7]	1,202	45	76[7]	90	180	360	9	19	4
Uganda	18	24	32	164	6,559	8,298	74[19,20]	127	122	547	1,278[7]	13[10,20]	16	27[7]	56	124	1	3	—
United Republic of Tanzania	26	34	41	46	4,382	8,442	70	68	105	287[7]	1,551[7]	5	6[7]	—	—	—	#[13]	—	—
Zambia	8	10	13	18	1,590	2,841	99	82	113	—	—	24	—	—	25[7]	95	2	2[7]	4
Zimbabwe	10	12	11	29	—	—	116	—	—	—	—	50	—	—	—	1,295	5	—	8
Asia																			
Afghanistan[8]	14	22	28	44	749	4,946	27	22	104	—	1,716	9	—	44	—	95	2	—	4
Bangladesh	114	132	154	1,181	—	16,539[21]	72	—	95[21]	10,329	—	19	44	—	727	1,295	4	5	8
Cambodia	10	12	14	81	2,248	2,290	121	102	116	351	—	32	18	—	22	—	1	2	—
China	1,164	1,264	1,324	138	113,613	103,617	125	—	113	81,488	100,392	49	61	78	7,364	29,296	3	8	25
India	854	1,006	1,157	389	—	—	97	94	—	71,031	—	44[10]	46	—	9,404	—	6	10	—
Indonesia	185	214	240	133	28,202[7]	29,901	115	113[7]	121	14,264[7]	19,521	44	56[7]	79	—	4,859	9[13]	18	24
Iran, Islamic Republic of..	60	69	76	50	8,288	5,655	112	109	103	9,955	7,929	55	82	83	1,405	3,350	10[14]	18	36
Iraq	17	23	29	66	3,639	—	111	94	—	1,224	—	47[10]	37	—	289	—	12[17]	12	—
Japan	124	127	128	350	7,529	7,156	100	100	102	8,782	7,300	97	101	101	3,982	3,874	30[13]	48	59
Kazakhstan	17	16	17	6	1,208	951	87	97	109	2,003	1,741	98	93	95	370	635	40	28	41
Korea, North (DPR)	21	23	24	201	—	—	—	—	—	—	—	90	—	—	—	—	—	—	—
Korea, South (Republic of)..	43	47	49	501	4,030	3,482	105	101	104	3,959	3,986	90	97	97	3,003	3,219	39	78	100

See notes at end of table.

Selected population and enrollment statistics for countries with populations over 10 million in 2009, by continent: Selected years, 1990 through 2009—Continued

Column groupings: Columns 2–4 = Midyear population (in millions); Column 5 = Persons per square kilometer, 2009; Columns 6–10 = First level[2] (6–7 Enrollment in thousands; 8–10 Gross enrollment ratio[5]); Columns 11–15 = Second level[3] (11–12 Enrollment in thousands; 13–15 Gross enrollment ratio[5]); Columns 16–20 = Third level[4] (16–17 Enrollment in thousands; 18–20 Gross enrollment ratio[5]).

Country[1]	Pop 1991	Pop 2000	Pop 2009	Pers/km² 2009	L1 Enr 1999–2000	L1 Enr 2008–09	L1 GER 1990–91	L1 GER 1999–2000	L1 GER 2008–09	L2 Enr 1999–2000	L2 Enr 2008–09	L2 GER 1990–91	L2 GER 1999–2000	L2 GER 2008–09	L3 Enr 1999–2000	L3 Enr 2008–09	L3 GER 1990–91	L3 GER 1999–2000	L3 GER 2008–09
(col no.) 1	2	3	4	5	6	7	8	9	10	11	12	13	14	15	16	17	18	19	20
Malaysia	18	23	28	85	3,026	—	94	97	—	2,205	—	56	65	—	549	—	7	26	—
Myanmar[8]	41	47	53	81	4,858	5,095	106	103	116	2,268	2,813	23	38	53	—	—	4[13]	4	—
Nepal[8]	19	25	29	199	3,780[9]	4,782	108	118[9]	85	1,348	—	33	35	—	94	289	5	—	—
Pakistan	122	152	181	235	13,987[21]	18,468	61[22]	69[21]	—	—	9,433	23	—	33	—	—	3	—	—
Philippines	67	81	98	329	—	—	111	—	—	—	—	73	—	—	—	758	28	22	33
Saudi Arabia	16	21	25	12	—	3,255	73	—	99	—	2,990[7]	44	—	97[7]	404	—	12	—	—
Sri Lanka[8]	17	19	21	323	—	1,619	106	—	97	—	—	74	—	75	—	—	5[13,23]	—	—
Syrian Arab Republic	13	16	22	119	2,775	2,383	108	104	122	1,069	2,664	52	41	76	—	—	18	—	—
Taiwan	20	22	23	712	—	—	—	—	—	—	—	—	—	—	—	—	—	—	—
Thailand	56	62	66	129	6,101	5,371	99	94	91	5,658	4,769	30	70	—	1,900	2,417	19[12]	37	45
Turkey	58	67	77	100	6,562	—	99	98	—	3,566	4,506	47	88	—	1,588[7]	—	13	23[7]	—
Uzbekistan	21	25	28	65	2,602	1,996	81	99	92	—	—	99	—	104	305	301	30	13	10
Vietnam	69	79	89	286	10,063	6,745	103	106[7]	—	7,926	—	32	65	—	732	1,774	2	10	—
Yemen	13	17	23	43	2,464[7]	—	79[16]	74[7]	—	1,151[7]	—	23[16]	43[7]	—	173[7]	—	4[13]	10[7]	—
Europe																			
Belgium	10	10	10	344	774	732	101	106	103	1,058	810	103	146	108	356	425	40	58	66
Czech Republic	10	10	10	132	645	460	96	103	103	958	868	91	88	95	254	417	16[24]	29	61
France	59	61	64	101	3,885	4,153	108	105	109	5,929	5,862	99	109	113	2,015	2,173	40	53	55
Germany[25]	80	82	82	235	3,656	3,151	101	106	104	8,307	7,741	98	99	102	—	—	34	—	—
Greece	10	11	11	82	645	—	98	96	100	739	—	93	89	—	422	—	36	51	62
Hungary	10	10	10	112	501	390	95	102	100	1,002	913	79	95	99	307	398	14	37	—
Italy[8]	57	58	60	206	2,836	—	103	103	107	4,404	—	83	93	—	1,770	—	32	49	62
Netherlands[8]	15	16	16	487	1,279	1,290	102	108	97	1,379	1,462	120	123	121	488	619	40	52	71
Poland[8]	38	39	38	127	3,319	2,294	98	99	112	3,988	2,958	81	100	99	1,580	2,150	22	50	61
Portugal[8]	10	10	11	117	811	744	123	124	99	831	710	67	107	107	374	373	23	48	67
Romania[8]	23	22	22	96	1,189	856	91	103	—	2,226	1,862	92	81	94	453	1,098	10	24	—
Russian Federation	148	147	140	9	6,138	—	109	106	—	—	—	93	—	—	6,331	—	52	55	73
Spain[8]	39	41	46	93	2,540	2,684	109	105	107	3,246	3,065	104	111	121	1,829	1,801	37	59	81
Ukraine[8]	52	49	46	79	2,079	1,532	89	109	—	5,204	3,289	93	99	94	1,812	2,799	47	49	59
United Kingdom[8]	58	59	62	256	4,632	—	104	101	98	5,315	—	85	102	—	2,024	2,415	30	58	—
North America																			
Canada	28	31	33	4	2,456	—	103	99	—	2,519	—	101	103	—	1,212	—	95	59	—
Cuba	11	11	11	101	1,046	868	98	111	104	790	826	89	79	90	159	971	21	22	118
Guatemala	9	11	13	124	1,909	—	78	104	—	504	—	23[13]	38	—	—	—	8[12]	—	—
Mexico	86	100	111	57	14,766	14,861	114	111	117	9,094	11,475	53	73	90	1,963	2,705	15	20	28
United States	253	282	307	34	24,973	24,586	102	100	98	22,594	24,525	93	93	94	13,203	19,103	75	68	86
South America																			
Argentina	34	37	41	15	4,728	—	106	115	—	3,428	—	71	88	—	1,767[7]	—	38[13]	53[7]	—
Brazil	154	176	199	24	20,212	17,452	106	151	—	26,097	23,617	38	104	—	2,781	6,115	11[26]	16	—
Chile	13	15	17	22	1,799	—	100	100	—	1,391	—	73	83	—	452	—	21[13]	37	—
Colombia	34	39	44	42	5,221	5,299	102	119	120	3,569	4,992	50[13]	72	95	934	1,570	13	24	37

See notes at end of table.

Selected population and enrollment statistics for countries with populations over 10 million in 2009, by continent: Selected years, 1990 through 2009—Continued

Country[1]	Midyear population (in millions)			Persons per square kilometer, 2009	First level[2]					Second level[3]					Third level[4]				
					Enrollment (in thousands)		Gross enrollment ratio[5]			Enrollment (in thousands)		Gross enrollment ratio[5]			Enrollment (in thousands)		Gross enrollment ratio[5]		
	1991	2000	2009	2009	1999–2000	2008–09	1990–91	1999–2000	2008–09	1999–2000	2008–09	1990–91	1999–2000	2008–09	1999–2000	2008–09	1990–91	1999–2000	2008–09
1	2	3	4	5	6	7	8	9	10	11	12	13	14	15	16	17	18	19	20
Ecuador	10	12	15	53	1,925	—	116	115	—	917	—	55 [27]	57	—	—	—	20	—	—
Peru	22	26	29	22	4,338	—	118	122	—	2,374	—	67	85	—	—	—	30	—	—
Venezuela	20	23	27	30	3,328	3,462	96	102	103	1,543	2,252	35	59	82	668	2,123	29	28	78
Oceania																			
Australia[6]	17	19	21	3	1,906	1,992	108	101	106	2,589	2,255	82	162	133	845	1,200	35 [28]	65	82

—Not available.
#Rounds to zero.
[1]Selection based on total population for midyear 2009.
[2]First-level enrollment consists of elementary school, typically corresponding to grades 1–6 in the United States.
[3]Second-level enrollment includes general education, teacher training (at the second level), and technical and vocational education. This level generally corresponds to secondary education in the United States, grades 7–12.
[4]Third-level enrollment includes college and university enrollment, and technical and vocational education beyond the secondary school level.
[5]Data represent the total enrollment of all ages in the school level divided by the population of the specific age groups that correspond to the school level. Adjustments have been made for the varying lengths of first and second level programs. Ratios may exceed 100 because some countries have many students from outside the normal age range.
[6]Enrollment totals and ratios exclude Democratic People's Republic of Korea.
[7]Estimated by the UNESCO Institute for Statistics.
[8]Classification or data coverage of levels has been revised. Data by level may not be comparable over time.
[9]Policy change in 1999–2000: introduction of free universal primary education.
[10]General education enrollment only. Excludes teacher training and vocational education enrollments.
[11]Excludes nonuniversity institutions (such as teacher training colleges and technical colleges) and excludes distance-learning universities.
[12]Data for 1992–93.
[13]Data for 1991–92.
[14]Excludes private institutions.

[15]Data refer to universities and exclude Al Azhar.
[16]Data for 1993–94.
[17]Data for 1985–86.
[18]Not including the former Independent States of Transkei, Bophuthatswana, Venda, and Ciskei.
[19]Estimated.
[20]Data refer to government aided and maintained schools only.
[21]National estimation.
[22]Includes preprimary education.
[23]Excludes some nonuniversity institutions.
[24]Includes full-time students only.
[25]Data include both former East and West Germany.
[26]Excludes enrollments in programs formerly classified as doctoral.
[27]Including vocational education.
[28]Data do not include Vocational Education and Training Institutes (VETS).
NOTE: Data do not include adult education or special education provided outside regular schools. Some data have been revised from previously published figures.
SOURCE: United Nations Educational, Scientific, and Cultural Organization (UNESCO), Statistical Yearbook, 1999; unpublished tabulations; and tables 3B, 5, and 14, retrieved July 12, 2011, from http://stats.uis.unesco.org/unesco/ReportFolders/ReportFolders.aspx; U.S. Department of Commerce, Census Bureau, International Data Base, retrieved July 12, 2011, from http://www.census.gov/ipc/www/idb/region.php. (This table was prepared July 2011.)

Pupils per teacher in public and private elementary and secondary schools, by level of education and country: Selected years, 1985 through 2009

Country	Elementary								Junior high school (lower secondary)								Senior high school (upper secondary)							
	1985	1990	2000	2005	2006	2007	2008	2009	1985	1990	2000	2005	2006	2007	2008	2009	1985	1990	2000	2005	2006	2007	2008	2009
1	2	3	4	5	6	7	8	9	10	11	12	13	14	15	16	17	18	19	20	21	22	23	24	25
OECD average[1]	—	—	17.7	17.0	16.4	16.2	16.1	16.0	—	—	—	14.0	13.6	13.4	13.5	13.4	—	—	13.7	13.5	13.1	13.1	13.1	13.3
Australia	13.8[2]	—	17.3	16.2	16.0	15.9	15.8	15.8	—	—	—	—	—	—	—	—	—	—	—	12.1[3,4]	12.2[3,4]	12.1[3,4]	12.0[3,4]	12.0[3,4]
Austria	11.3	11.6	—	—	—	14.1	—	12.6	9.2	7.7	—	10.6	10.4	10.3	9.9	9.6	3.2	12.4	—	11.3	11.3	11.0	10.5	10.2
Belgium	—	—	15.0[5]	12.8	12.6	12.6[6]	12.6[6]	12.5[6]	—	—	—	9.4	9.4	9.2[6]	8.1[6]	8.1[6]	—	—	9.7[4,7]	9.9[7]	10.2[7]	10.2[2,4,5,8]	10.8[6,7]	10.2[6,7]
Canada	18.1	17.1	18.1	—	—	—	—	—	16.0	15.5	18.1	—	—	—	—	—	16.0	15.3	19.5	—	—	—	—	—
Chile	—	—	—	25.9	25.5	24.7	24.1	22.4	—	—	—	25.9	25.5	24.7	24.1	22.4	—	—	—	26.6	26.3	25.7	25.2	24.7
Czech Republic	(9)	(9)	19.7	17.5	17.3	18.7	18.1	18.4	(9)	(9)	14.7	13.5	12.3	12.3	11.8	11.5	(9)	(9)	11.5	12.8	11.9	12.3	12.2	12.2
Denmark	12.7	11.2	10.4	—	—	—	—	—	10.2	9.3	11.4	11.9[8]	11.8[8]	11.2[8]	10.1[8]	9.9[8]	14.8[8]	13.3	14.4	12.8	13.3	12.2	12.4[7]	12.2[7]
Estonia	(9)	(9)	—	—	14.1	14.4	16.4	16.2	(9)	(9)	10.7	10.0	12.3	11.4	16.0	13.6	(9)	(9)	—	18.0[7,10]	15.8[7,10]	15.9[7]	15.9[7]	16.8[7]
Finland	—	—	16.9	15.9	15.0	15.0	14.4	13.6	—	—	10.7	10.0	9.7	9.9	10.6	9.9	—	—	17.0[7,10]	18.0[7,10]	15.8[7,10]	15.9[7]	16.0[7]	16.6[7]
France	—	—	19.8	19.4	19.3[6]	19.7[6]	19.9[6]	19.7[6]	—	—	14.7	14.2	14.1[6]	14.3[6]	14.6[6]	14.9[6]	—	8.3	10.4	10.3	9.7[6]	9.6[6]	9.4[6]	9.6[6]
Germany[11]	20.7	20.3	19.8	18.8	18.7	18.3	18.0	17.4	16.9	14.6	15.7	15.5	15.0	15.2	15.0	15.1	—	21.0	13.9	14.0	14.3	14.3	14.0	13.9
Greece	—	—	13.4	11.1	10.6	10.1	10.1[12]	10.7	—	—	10.8	7.9	8.0	7.7	7.7[12]	—	—	—	10.5	8.8	8.3	7.3	7.3[12]	—
Hungary	—	—	10.9	10.6	10.4	10.2	10.6	—	—	—	10.9	10.4	10.2	10.2	10.9	10.8	—	—	11.4[7]	12.2	12.3	12.1	12.3	12.8
Iceland	—	—	—	—	—	—	—	15.9	—	—	12.7[3]	11.3[3]	10.6[8]	10.4	10.0[8]	10.7	—	—	9.7	10.8[7]	10.8[7]	10.2[7]	10.6[7]	10.9[7]
Ireland	—	—	21.5	17.9	19.4	17.9	17.8	15.9	—	—	12.7[2]	11.3[2]	10.6[2]	10.4[2]	12.1[2]	15.9	7.2	8.3	15.9[4,7]	15.5[4,7]	14.6[4,7]	13.2[2,4,7]	12.8[2,4,7]	12.6[2,4,7]
Israel	12.8	10.7	11.0	17.3	17.2	16.4	16.3	17.0	9.6	8.5	10.4	10.1	10.3	9.4	9.7[2]	10.0[2]	10.8	10.7	10.2	13.4	13.2	11.8	10.9	10.8
Italy	—	20.8[2]	20.9	10.6	10.7	10.5	10.6[2]	10.7[2]	—	18.6	16.8	15.1	14.9	14.8	14.7	14.5	10.8	10.7	14.0	13.0	12.7	12.5	12.3	12.2[7]
Japan	—	—	32.1	19.4	19.2	19.0	18.8	18.6	—	—	21.5	20.8	20.8	20.5	20.2	19.9	—	16.2	20.9	13.0	12.7	12.5	14.7	16.7
Korea, Republic of	—	—	—	28.0	26.7	25.6	24.1	22.5	—	—	—	20.8	20.8	20.5	20.2	19.9	—	—	—	16.0	15.9	16.2	16.5	16.7
Luxembourg	—	—	15.9[2]	—	11.3[2]	11.2[2]	12.1[2]	11.6	—	—	12.7[2]	11.3[2]	11.2[2]	11.0[2]	12.1[2]	11.6	—	7.2	9.2[2,4]	9.0[2,4]	9.0[2,4,7]	9.0[2,4]	9.1[2,4]	9.1[4]
Mexico	20.2	19.2	27.2	28.3	28.0	28.0	28.0	28.1	12.7	12.4	34.8	33.7	33.4	33.3	33.9	33.0	—	—	26.5	25.8	25.4	25.7	25.8	25.6
Netherlands	20.1	19.1	16.8[5]	15.9[5]	15.3[5]	15.6[5]	15.8[2,5]	15.8[2,5]	—	—	19.9	16.8	16.6	16.2	16.2	16.3	17.1[4]	—	17.1[4]	16.2[4]	12.7	13.3	12.8	16.1[2,4,7]
New Zealand	—	—	20.6	18.1	17.7	17.5	17.1	16.3	—	—	19.9	16.8	16.6	16.2	16.2	16.3	—	14.8[4]	13.1	12.9	12.7	13.3	12.8	12.8
Norway	—	—	12.4	11.7	11.5	11.0	10.8[2]	10.7[2]	—	—	9.9	12.7	12.6	12.4	12.9	12.9	—	11.9[4]	9.7	9.0[2,4]	9.7[2,7]	9.8[2,7]	9.9[2,7]	9.4[2,7]
Poland	—	—	12.7	11.7	11.5	11.0	10.5	10.2	—	—	11.5	12.7	12.6	12.4	12.9	12.9	—	—	16.9	12.9	12.8	12.2	12.2	12.0
Portugal	(9)	(9)	12.1	10.8	10.6	11.8	11.3	11.3	(9)	(9)	10.4	8.2	8.3	7.9	8.1	7.6	(9)	(9)	7.9	8.0	7.5	8.4[7]	7.3[7]	7.7[7]
Slovak Republic	(9)	(9)	18.3	18.9	18.6	17.9	18.6	17.7	(9)	(9)	13.5	14.1	13.7	13.9	14.5	14.0	(9)	(9)	12.8	14.3	14.2	14.1	15.1	15.1
Slovenia	—	21.2	14.9	15.0	14.9	15.2	15.8	16.7	21.4	18.8	16.8	11.1	10.2	9.5	8.9	7.9	15.3	14.8	11.9[4]	14.6	14.0	13.9	13.7	14.3[7]
Spain	26.8	21.2	14.9	14.3	14.2	13.6	13.1	13.3	10.8	10.2	12.8	12.5	12.5	11.7	11.4	11.3	—	15.9	11.9[4]	8.1	7.8	7.7	8.7	9.3
Sweden	11.6	10.6	12.8	12.2	12.1	12.3	12.2	12.1	13.1	—	11.5	12.0	12.5	11.5	11.4	11.3	16.2	15.8	14.1	14.0	13.8	13.6	14.7	13.2
Switzerland	—	—	—	14.6[2]	15.1[2]	14.8[2]	15.4[2]	15.4[2]	—	—	—	11.7[2]	12.3[2]	12.3[2]	12.1[2]	12.0[2]	—	—	—	10.5[2,3]	10.5[2,3]	10.6[2,3]	10.4[2,3]	10.4[2,3]
Turkey	31.1	30.6	30.5	25.8	26.7	26.2	24.4	22.9	—	—	17.6[3]	17.0	16.7	16.7	15.0	16.1	—	12.1	14.0	16.0	11.6[3,7]	11.3[3,7]	12.4[7]	16.9
United Kingdom	19.7	22.0	21.2	20.7	19.8	19.4	20.2	19.9	16.5	15.9	16.3	17.0	14.7	14.7	14.8	14.3	11.0	12.1	12.5[3]	11.8[3,7]	11.6[3,7]	11.3[3,7]	12.4[7]	12.3[7]
United States	17.0	15.6	15.8	14.9	14.6	14.6	14.3	14.8	(9)	(9)	16.3	15.1	14.7	14.7	14.8	14.3	16.2	15.8	14.1	16.0	15.7	15.6	15.6	15.1
Other reporting countries																								
Brazil	(9)	—	—	22.9	22.5	25.8	24.5	24.0	(9)	—	—	18.1	17.6	22.3	24.5	24.0	(9)	—	—	17.6	17.0	20.2	18.4	18.1
Russian Federation	(9)	(9)	—	—	—	17.0[2]	17.3[2]	17.9[2]	(9)	(9)	—	—	—	—	21.2	21.0	(9)	(9)	—	11.2[7,13]	9.9[4,7,13]	8.8[4,7,14]	8.7[4,7,14]	8.7[4,7,14]

—Not available.

†Not applicable. This level of education does not exist within the national education structure; students in the age group normally associated with this education level are reported in other levels.

[1]Refers to the mean of the data values for all reporting OECD countries, to which each country reporting data contributes equally. The average includes all current OECD countries for which a given year's data are available, even if they were not members of OECD in that year. However, if data were reported for less than 75 percent of the countries that were members of OECD in a given year, the average for that year is omitted.

[2]Public schools only.

[3]Includes only general programs.

[4]Includes junior high school data.

[5]Includes preprimary data.

[6]Excludes independent private institutions.

[7]Includes postsecondary non-higher-education.

[8]Includes elementary school data.

[9]Country did not exist in its current form in the given year.

[10]Includes tertiary type B education (i.e., occupation-specific education corresponding to that offered at the associate's degree level in the United States).

[11]Data for 1985 are for the former West Germany.

[12]Data included for Greece for 2008 are from 2007.

[13]Excludes general programs.

[14]Excludes part-time personnel in public institutions.

NOTE: For the U.S. data in this table, elementary school corresponds to grades 1 through 6, junior high school corresponds to grades 7 through 9, and senior high school corresponds to grades 10 through 12.

SOURCE: Organization for Economic Cooperation and Development (OECD), Online Education Database; and Education at a Glance, 2002 through 2011. U.S. Department of Education, National Center for Education Statistics, International Education Indicators: A Time Series Perspective, 1985–1995 (NCES 2000-021). (This table was prepared June 2011).

Average fourth-grade scores, class size, and instructional time in mathematics and science, by country or other jurisdiction: 2007

Country or other jurisdiction	Mathematics											Science								
	Average score[1]		Average class size		Instructional time in mathematics						Average score[1]		Average class size		Instructional time in science					
					Hours per year		As a percent of total instructional time								Hours per year		As a percent of total instructional time			
1	2		3		4		5				6		7		8		9			
International average.....	500	(†)	26	(0.1)	144	(0.5)	16	(0.1)			500	(†)	26	(0.1)	67	(0.4)	8	(#)		
Algeria	378	(5.2)	28 [2]	(0.8)	177 [3]	(4.7)	17 [2]	(0.3)			354	(6.0)	30 [2]	(0.7)	67 [3]	(4.7)	6 [2]	(0.4)		
Armenia	500	(4.3)	31 [3]	(1.6)	133	(3.4)	15	(0.4)			484	(5.7)	27	(0.7)	81	(4.0)	9	(0.4)		
Australia......................	516	(3.5)	24	(0.4)	174 [2]	(5.4)	18 [2]	(0.5)			527	(3.3)	24	(0.4)	46 [3]	(2.2)	5 [3]	(0.2)		
Austria	505	(2.0)	20	(0.3)	126	(1.1)	17	(0.2)			526	(2.5)	20	(0.3)	92	(1.0)	12	(0.1)		
Chinese Taipei	576	(1.7)	31	(0.3)	112 [3]	(2.6)	13	(0.3)			557	(2.0)	31	(0.3)	79 [3]	(1.5)	9 [2]	(0.2)		
Colombia	355	(5.0)	32	(1.0)	175 [2]	(4.7)	17	(0.5)			400	(5.4)	32	(1.1)	139 [2]	(3.9)	13 [2]	(0.4)		
Czech Republic..............	486	(2.8)	22	(0.4)	144	(1.1)	19	(0.1)			515	(3.1)	22	(0.4)	41 [2]	(1.3)	5	(0.2)		
Denmark[4]	523	(2.4)	21	(0.3)	125 [2]	(1.2)	15 [2]	(0.2)			517	(2.9)	21 [2]	(0.3)	59 [2]	(0.9)	7 [3]	(0.1)		
El Salvador	330	(4.1)	30	(0.7)	147	(2.6)	17	(0.4)			390	(3.4)	30	(0.7)	135	(3.5)	15	(0.5)		
England	541	(2.9)	28 [2]	(0.5)	183 [2]	(2.1)	19	(0.4)			542	(2.9)	27 [2]	(0.5)	70 [2]	(1.7)	7	(0.2)		
Georgia[5]	438	(4.2)	22	(0.6)	130	(1.5)	19 [3]	(0.4)			418	(4.6)	23	(0.6)	35 [2]	(2.8)	5 [3]	(0.5)		
Germany	525	(2.3)	22	(0.2)	145 [2]	(1.5)	17 [2]	(0.2)			528	(2.4)	22	(0.2)	106 [2]	(2.1)	13 [2]	(0.2)		
Hong Kong SAR[6]	607	(3.6)	35	(0.4)	150 [3]	(3.4)	15 [3]	(0.4)			554	(3.5)	35 [2]	(0.3)	72 [3]	(5.2)	7 [3]	(0.5)		
Hungary	510	(3.5)	22	(0.4)	110 [3]	(1.3)	16 [3]	(0.3)			536	(3.3)	22	(0.4)	54 [3]	(1.5)	8 [3]	(0.2)		
Iran, Islamic Republic of	402	(4.1)	24 [3]	(0.5)	105	(2.6)	15	(0.4)			436	(4.3)	24 [3]	(0.5)	83	(2.4)	12	(0.4)		
Italy	507	(3.1)	20	(0.2)	201 [2]	(2.8)	19 [2]	(0.3)			535	(3.2)	20	(0.2)	68 [2]	(1.4)	6 [2]	(0.1)		
Japan..........................	568	(2.1)	31	(0.4)	136	(1.2)	16	(0.2)			548	(2.1)	31	(0.3)	82	(1.2)	9	(0.1)		
Kazakhstan[5]................	549	(7.1)	22	(0.5)	133	(1.7)	18	(0.3)			533	(5.6)	22	(0.5)	52	(1.3)	7	(0.2)		
Kuwait[7]......................	316	(3.6)	25 [3]	(0.5)	‡	(†)	4 [3]	(0.4)			348	(4.4)	27 [3]	(1.5)	‡	(†)	‡	(†)		
Latvia[5].......................	537	(2.3)	22	(0.8)	121 [2]	(3.1)	18 [2]	(0.4)			542	(2.3)	23	(0.9)	48 [2]	(1.2)	7 [2]	(0.2)		
Lithuania[5]...................	530	(2.4)	20	(0.3)	118 [2]	(1.7)	18 [2]	(0.3)			514	(2.4)	20	(0.3)	51 [2]	(0.6)	8	(0.1)		
Morocco.......................	341	(4.7)	29 [2]	(0.8)	162 [3]	(2.5)	17 [3]	(0.3)			297	(5.9)	29 [2]	(0.8)	54 [3]	(4.2)	5 [3]	(0.3)		
Netherlands[8]................	535	(2.1)	22	(0.4)	179 [3]	(4.6)	16 [3]	(0.4)			523	(2.6)	22	(0.4)	33 [3]	(1.5)	3 [3]	(0.1)		
New Zealand..................	492	(2.3)	26 [3]	(0.4)	148	(1.8)	16	(0.2)			504	(2.6)	26 [3]	(0.4)	45 [3]	(2.5)	5 [3]	(0.3)		
Norway.........................	473	(2.5)	21	(0.5)	115	(2.5)	13	(0.3)			477	(3.5)	21	(0.5)	44 [2]	(1.9)	5 [2]	(0.2)		
Qatar..........................	296	(1.0)	28 [2]	(#)	‡	(†)	12 [3]	(#)			294	(2.6)	27 [3]	(#)	‡	(†)	‡	(†)		
Russian Federation.............	544	(4.9)	21	(0.4)	110 [3]	(1.3)	17 [3]	(0.2)			546	(4.8)	21	(0.4)	40 [3]	(1.1)	6 [3]	(0.2)		
Scotland[4]	494	(2.2)	25 [3]	(0.4)	181 [3]	(2.7)	19 [3]	(0.3)			500	(2.3)	26 [3]	(0.6)	51 [3]	(3.1)	5 [2]	(0.3)		
Singapore	599	(3.7)	38	(0.2)	201	(0.8)	21	(0.1)			587	(4.1)	38	(0.2)	82	(0.9)	9	(0.1)		
Slovak Republic	496	(4.5)	21	(0.3)	143 [2]	(0.6)	18	(0.2)			526	(4.8)	21	(0.3)	59 [2]	(0.7)	7	(0.1)		
Slovenia.......................	502	(1.8)	19	(0.3)	141 [2]	(1.0)	20 [2]	(0.2)			518	(1.9)	19	(0.3)	84 [2]	(0.8)	12 [2]	(0.1)		
Sweden........................	503	(2.5)	22	(0.5)	104 [2]	(2.3)	12 [2]	(0.3)			525	(2.9)	22	(0.6)	56 [2]	(2.5)	6 [2]	(0.3)		
Tunisia........................	327	(4.5)	25 [2]	(0.4)	166 [3]	(1.6)	18 [2]	(0.4)			318	(5.9)	25 [2]	(0.5)	71 [3]	(2.7)	8 [3]	(0.3)		
Ukraine........................	469	(2.9)	23	(0.4)	104	(1.4)	17	(0.3)			474	(3.1)	23	(0.4)	33	(1.1)	5	(0.2)		
United States[4,9]............	529	(2.4)	23 [2]	(0.4)	171 [3]	(3.7)	16 [3]	(0.3)			539	(2.7)	26 [2]	(0.7)	89 [2]	(2.5)	8 [2]	(0.2)		
Yemen.........................	224	(6.0)	46 [2]	(1.7)	134 [3]	(7.1)	15	(0.5)			197	(7.2)	45 [2]	(1.4)	83 [3]	(5.7)	10 [2]	(0.5)		

†Not applicable.
#Rounds to zero.
‡Reporting standards not met because data are available for less than 50 percent of the students.
[1]TIMSS scores are reported on a scale from 0 to 1,000, with the scale average set at 500 and the standard deviation set at 100.
[2]Data are available for at least 70 percent but less than 85 percent of students.
[3]Data are available for at least 50 percent but less than 70 percent of students.
[4]Met guidelines for sample participation rates only after substitute schools were included.
[5]National Target Population does not include all of the International Target Population defined by the Trends in International Mathematics and Science Study (TIMSS).
[6]Hong Kong is a Special Administrative Region (SAR) of the People's Republic of China.
[7]Kuwait tested the same cohort of students as other countries, but later in 2007, at the beginning of the next school year.
[8]Nearly satisfied guidelines for sample participation rates only after substitute schools were included.

[9]National Defined Population covers 90 to 95 percent of National Target Population.
NOTE: Countries were required to sample students in the grade that corresponded to the end of 4 years of formal schooling, providing that the mean age at the time of testing was at least 9.5 years. Instructional times shown in this table are actual or implemented times (as opposed to intended times prescribed by the curriculum). Teachers provided class size and instructional time in mathematics and science. Instructional time was reported as hours per week; the hours per year shown in this table were computed by multiplying the hours per week by the number of instructional weeks per year. Schools provided the total instructional time used to calculate the percentage of time devoted to mathematics and science. Standard errors appear in parentheses.
SOURCE: International Association for the Evaluation of Educational Achievement (IEA), Trends in International Mathematics and Science Study (TIMSS), 2007, *TIMSS 2007 International Mathematics Report*, by Ina V.S. Mullis et al., and *TIMSS 2007 International Science Report*, by Michael O. Martin et al. (This table was prepared June 2011.)

Average eighth-grade scores, class size, and instructional time in mathematics and science, by country or other jurisdiction: 2007

Country or other jurisdiction	Mathematics				Science			
	Average score[1]	Average class size	Instructional time in mathematics		Average score[1]	Average class size	Instructional time in science[2]	
			Hours per year	As a percent of total instructional time			Hours per year	As a percent of total instructional time
1	2	3	4	5	6	7	8	9
International average	**500** (†)	**29** (0.1)	**120** (0.4)	**12** (#)	**500** (†)	**30** (0.1)	**110** (0.7)	**11** (0.1)
Algeria	387 (2.1)	37 [3] (0.7)	‡ (†)	13 [4] (0.4)	408 (1.7)	37 [3] (0.6)	— (†)	— (†)
Armenia	499 (3.5)	25 [3] (0.4)	110 (3.9)	11 (0.4)	488 (5.8)	25 [4] (0.4)	— (†)	— (†)
Australia	496 (3.9)	26 [3] (0.3)	131 [3] (2.0)	13 [3] (0.2)	515 (3.6)	25 [4] (0.4)	123 [4] (1.8)	12 [4] (0.1)
Bahrain	398 (1.6)	31 (0.1)	96 [4] (2.8)	9 [3] (0.3)	467 (1.7)	31 (0.2)	80 [4] (3.5)	8 [3] (0.3)
Bosnia and Herzegovina	456 (2.7)	24 (0.4)	102 [3] (0.9)	11 [3] (0.3)	466 (2.8)	24 (0.4)	— (†)	— (†)
Botswana	364 (2.3)	38 (0.4)	138 [3] (1.5)	13 [3] (0.3)	355 (3.1)	37 (0.3)	138 [3] (2.1)	13 [3] (0.3)
Bulgaria[5]	464 (5.0)	22 (0.3)	93 [3] (2.0)	12 [3] (0.3)	470 (5.9)	20 (0.5)	— (†)	— (†)
Chinese Taipei	598 (4.5)	35 (0.5)	158 (3.5)	14 (0.2)	561 (3.7)	35 (0.4)	145 (3.1)	12 (0.3)
Colombia	380 (3.6)	35 [4] (0.6)	151 [3] (4.7)	12 [3] (0.7)	417 (3.5)	36 [4] (0.9)	123 [3] (5.6)	10 [3] (0.6)
Cyprus	465 (1.6)	24 [3] (0.2)	72 [4] (0.3)	8 [4] (#)	452 (2.0)	24 [4] (0.1)	— (†)	— (†)
Czech Republic	504 (2.4)	24 [3] (0.3)	128 (2.1)	14 [3] (0.2)	539 (1.9)	24 [3] (0.3)	— (†)	— (†)
Egypt	391 (3.6)	39 (0.6)	93 [3] (4.3)	8 (0.4)	408 (3.6)	39 (0.6)	86 [3] (4.1)	7 (0.4)
El Salvador	340 (2.8)	29 (0.8)	142 (2.6)	17 (0.5)	387 (2.9)	30 (0.8)	135 (2.7)	16 (0.4)
England[6]	513 (4.8)	26 [4] (0.6)	113 (1.7)	12 (0.2)	542 (4.5)	26 [4] (0.6)	137 [3] (6.6)	14 (0.7)
Georgia[7]	410 (5.9)	23 (0.6)	110 (0.8)	13 (0.2)	421 (4.8)	24 (0.5)	— (†)	— (†)
Ghana	309 (4.4)	46 [3] (1.9)	146 [3] (5.0)	13 (0.5)	303 (5.4)	44 [3] (1.9)	117 [3] (6.3)	11 (0.6)
Hong Kong SAR[6,8]	572 (5.8)	37 (0.5)	148 [3] (3.8)	14 [4] (0.4)	530 (4.9)	39 (0.3)	100 [4] (2.9)	10 [4] (0.3)
Hungary	517 (3.5)	21 (0.5)	99 [4] (1.3)	13 [4] (0.2)	539 (2.9)	23 [3] (0.4)	— (†)	— (†)
Indonesia	397 (3.8)	38 (0.9)	136 [4] (4.7)	11 [4] (0.3)	427 (3.4)	36 [3] (0.9)	— (†)	— (†)
Iran, Islamic Republic of	403 (4.1)	26 [3] (0.5)	99 [4] (2.3)	11 [4] (0.3)	459 (3.6)	26 [3] (0.5)	98 [4] (1.9)	11 [4] (0.2)
Israel[5]	463 (3.9)	33 [4] (0.4)	‡ (†)	12 [4] (0.3)	468 (4.3)	33 [3] (0.4)	111 [4] (5.0)	10 [3] (0.4)
Italy	480 (3.0)	22 (0.2)	136 [3] (1.5)	13 [3] (0.2)	495 (2.8)	22 (0.2)	69 [4] (0.8)	6 [4] (0.1)
Japan	570 (2.4)	34 (0.5)	105 (1.6)	10 (0.1)	554 (1.9)	35 (0.3)	103 [3] (1.8)	10 [3] (0.2)
Jordan	427 (4.1)	35 (0.7)	141 (1.1)	14 (0.2)	482 (4.0)	35 (0.7)	141 (1.1)	13 (0.2)
Korea, Republic of	597 (2.7)	37 [4] (0.4)	104 [4] (0.7)	11 [4] (0.2)	553 (2.0)	37 [4] (0.3)	104 [4] (0.7)	11 [4] (0.2)
Kuwait[9]	354 (2.3)	30 [4] (0.5)	‡ (†)	6 [4] (0.6)	418 (2.8)	31 [4] (0.8)	‡ (†)	6 [4] (0.5)
Lebanon	449 (4.0)	26 (0.6)	‡ (†)	‡ (†)	414 (5.9)	27 (0.7)	— (†)	— (†)
Lithuania[7]	506 (2.3)	25 [3] (0.3)	116 [3] (0.9)	13 [3] (0.2)	519 (2.5)	25 [3] (0.3)	— (†)	— (†)
Malaysia	474 (5.0)	36 (0.4)	123 (1.0)	11 (0.1)	471 (6.0)	36 (0.4)	122 (1.3)	11 (0.2)
Malta	488 (1.2)	22 (#)	128 (0.1)	13 (#)	457 (1.4)	20 (#)	— (†)	— (†)
Norway	469 (2.0)	25 [3] (0.4)	113 (1.6)	13 (0.2)	487 (2.2)	25 [4] (0.5)	85 (1.1)	10 (0.1)
Oman	372 (3.4)	32 (0.4)	150 [4] (4.5)	15 (0.5)	423 (3.0)	31 (0.5)	130 [3] (5.7)	13 (0.5)
Palestinian National Authority	367 (3.5)	38 (0.5)	100 [4] (4.0)	11 [4] (0.4)	404 (3.5)	38 (0.5)	87 [4] (3.5)	10 [4] (0.4)
Qatar	307 (1.4)	27 (#)	138 [4] (0.1)	13 [4] (#)	319 (1.7)	26 [3] (#)	‡ (†)	‡ (†)
Romania	461 (4.1)	21 (0.3)	122 [3] (1.9)	14 [3] (0.3)	462 (3.9)	21 (0.3)	— (†)	— (†)
Russian Federation	512 (4.1)	21 (0.3)	131 [3] (1.4)	15 [3] (0.2)	530 (3.9)	21 (0.3)	— (†)	— (†)
Saudi Arabia	329 (2.9)	30 (0.8)	107 [4] (3.2)	11 [3] (0.3)	403 (2.4)	30 [3] (1.1)	‡ (†)	‡ (†)
Scotland[6]	487 (3.7)	25 [3] (0.5)	135 [4] (2.2)	13 [4] (0.2)	496 (3.4)	20 [4] (0.6)	108 [4] (3.1)	10 [3] (0.3)
Serbia[7,10]	486 (3.3)	24 (0.4)	103 [4] (0.8)	13 [4] (0.2)	470 (3.2)	24 (0.4)	— (†)	— (†)
Singapore	593 (3.8)	38 (0.2)	124 (1.0)	13 (0.1)	567 (4.4)	38 (0.2)	140 (1.8)	14 (0.2)
Slovenia	501 (2.1)	16 [3] (0.2)	113 (0.4)	13 (0.1)	538 (2.2)	22 [3] (0.3)	— (†)	— (†)
Sweden	491 (2.3)	23 [4] (0.5)	93 [3] (1.4)	10 [3] (0.2)	511 (2.6)	24 [3] (0.6)	— (†)	— (†)
Syrian Arab Republic	395 (3.8)	31 (0.6)	76 [3] (3.4)	10 (0.4)	452 (2.9)	32 (0.5)	— (†)	— (†)
Thailand	441 (5.0)	38 [3] (0.6)	124 (2.3)	10 (0.2)	471 (4.3)	38 (0.6)	119 (2.2)	10 (0.2)
Tunisia	420 (2.4)	32 (0.4)	126 [4] (2.1)	10 [3] (0.2)	445 (2.1)	32 (0.4)	58 [3] (1.4)	5 [3] (0.1)
Turkey	432 (4.8)	33 (0.7)	95 (0.4)	11 (0.3)	454 (3.7)	33 (0.6)	72 (0.5)	8 (0.2)
Ukraine	462 (3.6)	25 (0.4)	130 (2.0)	15 (0.2)	485 (3.5)	25 (0.4)	— (†)	— (†)
United States[6,10]	508 (2.8)	24 [4] (0.4)	148 [4] (2.3)	13 [4] (0.2)	520 (2.9)	28 [3] (0.9)	139 [4] (2.4)	13 [4] (0.2)

—Not available.

†Not applicable.

#Rounds to zero.

‡Reporting standards not met because data are available for less than 50 percent of the students.

[1]TIMSS scores are reported on a scale from 0 to 1,000, with the scale average set at 500 and the standard deviation set at 100.

[2]Includes only general/integrated science. Does not include the 19 participating countries that teach the sciences as separate subjects (biology, chemistry, etc.) at eighth grade.

[3]Data are available for at least 70 percent but less than 85 percent of students.

[4]Data are available for at least 50 percent but less than 70 percent of students.

[5]National Defined Population covers less than 90 percent of National Target Population (but at least 77 percent). (For Bulgaria, this note applies only to science data).

[6]Met guidelines for sample participation rates only after substitute schools were included.

[7]National Target Population does not include all of the International Target Population defined by the Trends in International Mathematics and Science Study (TIMSS).

[8]Hong Kong is a Special Administrative Region (SAR) of the People's Republic of China.

[9]Kuwait tested the same cohort of students as other countries, but later in 2007, at the beginning of the next school year.

[10]National Defined Population covers 90 to 95 percent of National Target Population.

NOTE: Countries were required to sample students in the grade that corresponded to the end of 8 years of formal schooling, providing that the mean age at the time of testing was at least 13.5 years. Instructional times shown in this table are actual or implemented times (as opposed to intended times prescribed by the curriculum). Teachers provided class size and instructional time in mathematics and science. Instructional time was reported as hours per week; the hours per year shown in this table were computed by multiplying the hours per week by the number of instructional weeks per year. Schools provided the total instructional time used to calculate the percentage of time devoted to mathematics and science. Standard errors appear in parentheses.

SOURCE: International Association for the Evaluation of Educational Achievement (IEA), Trends in International Mathematics and Science Study (TIMSS), 2007, *TIMSS 2007 International Mathematics Report*, by Ina V.S. Mullis et al., and *TIMSS 2007 International Science Report*, by Michael O. Martin et al. (This table was prepared June 2011.)

Average reading literacy, mathematics literacy, and science literacy scores of 15-year-old students, by sex and country: 2009

Country or other jurisdiction	Reading literacy			Mathematics literacy			Science literacy		
	Total	Male	Female	Total	Male	Female	Total	Male	Female
1	2	3	4	5	6	7	8	9	10
OECD total[1]	492 (1.2)	475 (1.4)	508 (1.2)	488 (1.2)	496 (1.3)	481 (1.3)	496 (1.2)	498 (1.5)	494 (1.3)
OECD average[2]	493 (0.5)	474 (0.6)	513 (0.5)	496 (0.5)	501 (0.6)	490 (0.6)	501 (0.5)	501 (0.6)	501 (0.6)
Australia	515 (2.3)	496 (2.9)	533 (2.6)	514 (2.5)	519 (3.0)	509 (2.8)	527 (2.5)	527 (3.1)	528 (2.8)
Austria	470 (2.9)	449 (3.8)	490 (4.0)	496 (2.7)	506 (3.4)	486 (4.0)	494 (3.2)	498 (4.2)	490 (4.4)
Belgium	506 (2.3)	493 (3.4)	520 (2.9)	515 (2.3)	526 (3.3)	504 (3.0)	507 (2.5)	510 (3.6)	503 (3.2)
Canada	524 (1.5)	507 (1.8)	542 (1.7)	527 (1.6)	533 (2.0)	521 (1.7)	529 (1.6)	531 (1.9)	526 (1.9)
Chile	449 (3.1)	439 (3.9)	461 (3.6)	421 (3.1)	431 (3.7)	410 (3.6)	447 (2.9)	452 (3.5)	443 (3.5)
Czech Republic	478 (2.9)	456 (3.7)	504 (3.0)	493 (2.8)	495 (3.9)	490 (3.0)	500 (3.0)	498 (4.0)	503 (3.2)
Denmark	495 (2.1)	480 (2.5)	509 (2.5)	503 (2.6)	511 (3.0)	495 (2.9)	499 (2.5)	505 (3.0)	494 (2.9)
Estonia	501 (2.6)	480 (2.9)	524 (2.8)	512 (2.6)	516 (2.9)	508 (2.9)	528 (2.7)	527 (3.1)	528 (3.1)
Finland	536 (2.3)	508 (2.6)	563 (2.4)	541 (2.2)	542 (2.5)	539 (2.5)	554 (2.3)	546 (2.7)	562 (2.6)
France	496 (3.4)	475 (4.3)	515 (3.4)	497 (3.1)	505 (3.8)	489 (3.4)	498 (3.6)	500 (4.6)	497 (3.5)
Germany	497 (2.7)	478 (3.6)	518 (2.9)	513 (2.9)	520 (3.6)	505 (3.3)	520 (2.8)	523 (3.7)	518 (3.3)
Greece	483 (4.3)	459 (5.5)	506 (3.5)	466 (3.9)	473 (5.4)	459 (3.3)	470 (4.0)	465 (5.1)	475 (3.7)
Hungary	494 (3.2)	475 (3.9)	513 (3.6)	490 (3.5)	496 (4.2)	484 (3.9)	503 (3.1)	503 (3.8)	503 (3.5)
Iceland	500 (1.4)	478 (2.1)	522 (1.9)	507 (1.4)	508 (2.0)	505 (1.9)	496 (1.4)	496 (2.1)	495 (2.0)
Ireland	496 (3.0)	476 (4.2)	515 (3.1)	487 (2.5)	491 (3.4)	483 (3.0)	508 (3.3)	507 (4.3)	509 (3.8)
Israel	474 (3.6)	452 (5.2)	495 (3.4)	447 (3.3)	451 (4.7)	443 (3.3)	455 (3.1)	453 (4.4)	456 (3.2)
Italy	486 (1.6)	464 (2.3)	510 (1.9)	483 (1.9)	490 (2.3)	475 (2.2)	489 (1.8)	488 (2.5)	490 (2.0)
Japan	520 (3.5)	501 (5.6)	540 (3.7)	529 (3.3)	534 (5.3)	524 (3.9)	539 (3.4)	534 (5.5)	545 (3.9)
Korea, Republic of	539 (3.5)	523 (4.9)	558 (3.8)	546 (4.0)	548 (6.2)	544 (4.5)	538 (3.4)	537 (5.0)	539 (4.2)
Luxembourg	472 (1.3)	453 (1.9)	492 (1.5)	489 (1.2)	499 (2.0)	479 (1.3)	484 (1.2)	487 (2.0)	480 (1.6)
Mexico	425 (2.0)	413 (2.1)	438 (2.1)	419 (1.8)	425 (2.1)	412 (1.9)	416 (1.8)	419 (2.0)	413 (1.9)
Netherlands	508 (5.1)	496 (5.1)	521 (5.3)	526 (4.7)	534 (4.8)	517 (5.1)	522 (5.4)	524 (5.3)	520 (5.9)
New Zealand	521 (2.4)	499 (3.6)	544 (2.6)	519 (2.3)	523 (3.2)	515 (2.9)	532 (2.6)	529 (4.0)	535 (2.9)
Norway	503 (2.6)	480 (3.0)	527 (2.9)	498 (2.4)	500 (2.7)	495 (2.8)	500 (2.6)	498 (3.0)	502 (2.8)
Poland	500 (2.6)	476 (2.8)	525 (2.9)	495 (2.8)	497 (3.0)	493 (3.2)	508 (2.4)	505 (2.7)	511 (2.8)
Portugal	489 (3.1)	470 (3.5)	508 (2.9)	487 (2.9)	493 (3.3)	481 (3.1)	493 (2.9)	491 (3.4)	495 (3.0)
Slovak Republic	477 (2.5)	452 (3.5)	503 (2.8)	497 (3.1)	498 (3.7)	495 (3.4)	490 (3.0)	490 (4.0)	491 (3.4)
Slovenia	483 (1.0)	456 (1.6)	511 (1.4)	501 (1.2)	502 (1.8)	501 (1.7)	512 (1.1)	505 (1.7)	519 (1.6)
Spain	481 (2.0)	467 (2.2)	496 (2.2)	483 (2.1)	493 (2.3)	474 (2.5)	488 (2.1)	492 (2.5)	485 (2.3)
Sweden	497 (2.9)	475 (3.2)	521 (3.1)	494 (2.9)	493 (3.1)	495 (3.3)	495 (2.7)	493 (3.0)	497 (3.2)
Switzerland	501 (2.4)	481 (2.9)	520 (2.7)	534 (3.3)	544 (3.7)	524 (3.4)	517 (2.8)	520 (3.2)	512 (3.0)
Turkey	464 (3.5)	443 (3.7)	486 (4.1)	445 (4.4)	451 (4.6)	440 (5.6)	454 (3.6)	448 (3.8)	460 (4.5)
United Kingdom	494 (2.3)	481 (3.5)	507 (2.9)	492 (2.4)	503 (3.2)	482 (3.3)	514 (2.5)	519 (3.6)	509 (3.2)
United States	500 (3.7)	488 (4.2)	513 (3.8)	487 (3.6)	497 (4.0)	477 (3.8)	502 (3.6)	509 (4.2)	495 (3.7)
Reporting partner countries									
Albania	385 (4.0)	355 (5.1)	417 (3.9)	377 (4.0)	372 (4.7)	383 (4.2)	391 (3.9)	377 (4.8)	406 (4.0)
Argentina	398 (4.6)	379 (5.1)	415 (4.9)	388 (4.1)	394 (4.5)	383 (4.4)	401 (4.6)	397 (5.1)	404 (4.8)
Azerbaijan	362 (3.3)	350 (3.7)	374 (3.3)	431 (2.8)	435 (3.1)	427 (3.0)	373 (3.1)	370 (3.4)	377 (3.2)
Brazil	412 (2.7)	397 (2.9)	425 (2.8)	386 (2.4)	394 (2.4)	379 (2.6)	405 (2.4)	407 (2.6)	404 (2.6)
Bulgaria	429 (6.7)	400 (7.3)	461 (5.8)	428 (5.9)	426 (6.2)	430 (6.0)	439 (5.9)	430 (6.8)	450 (5.3)
Colombia	413 (3.7)	408 (4.5)	418 (4.0)	381 (3.2)	398 (4.0)	366 (3.3)	402 (3.6)	413 (4.3)	392 (3.7)
Croatia	476 (2.9)	452 (3.4)	503 (3.7)	460 (3.1)	465 (3.6)	454 (3.9)	486 (2.8)	482 (3.5)	491 (3.9)
Dubai (United Arab Emirates)	459 (1.1)	435 (1.7)	485 (1.5)	453 (1.1)	454 (1.5)	451 (1.6)	466 (1.2)	453 (1.8)	480 (1.6)
Hong Kong-China	533 (2.1)	518 (3.3)	550 (2.8)	555 (2.7)	561 (4.2)	547 (3.4)	549 (2.8)	550 (3.8)	548 (3.4)
Indonesia	402 (3.7)	383 (3.8)	420 (3.9)	371 (3.7)	371 (4.1)	372 (4.0)	383 (3.8)	378 (4.2)	387 (4.0)
Jordan	405 (3.3)	377 (4.7)	434 (4.1)	387 (3.7)	386 (5.1)	387 (5.2)	415 (3.5)	398 (5.5)	433 (4.2)
Kazakhstan	390 (3.1)	369 (3.2)	412 (3.4)	405 (3.0)	405 (3.1)	405 (3.3)	400 (3.1)	396 (3.4)	405 (3.5)
Kyrgyzstan	314 (3.2)	287 (3.8)	340 (3.2)	331 (2.9)	328 (3.4)	334 (2.8)	330 (2.9)	318 (3.7)	340 (2.9)
Latvia	484 (3.0)	460 (3.4)	507 (3.1)	482 (3.1)	483 (3.5)	481 (3.4)	494 (3.1)	490 (3.7)	497 (3.2)
Liechtenstein	499 (2.8)	484 (4.5)	516 (4.5)	536 (4.1)	547 (5.2)	523 (5.9)	520 (3.4)	527 (5.0)	511 (5.1)
Lithuania	468 (2.4)	439 (2.8)	498 (2.6)	477 (2.6)	474 (3.1)	480 (3.0)	491 (2.9)	483 (3.5)	500 (2.9)
Macao-China	487 (0.9)	470 (1.3)	504 (1.2)	525 (0.9)	531 (1.3)	520 (1.4)	511 (1.0)	510 (1.3)	512 (1.2)
Montenegro	408 (1.7)	382 (2.1)	434 (2.1)	403 (2.0)	408 (2.2)	396 (2.4)	401 (2.0)	395 (2.4)	408 (2.6)
Panama	371 (6.5)	354 (7.0)	387 (7.3)	360 (5.2)	362 (5.6)	357 (6.1)	376 (5.7)	375 (6.4)	377 (6.6)
Peru	370 (4.0)	359 (4.2)	381 (4.9)	365 (4.0)	374 (4.6)	356 (4.4)	369 (3.5)	372 (3.7)	367 (4.4)
Qatar	372 (0.8)	347 (1.3)	397 (1.0)	368 (0.7)	366 (1.2)	371 (1.0)	379 (0.9)	366 (1.4)	393 (1.0)
Romania	424 (4.1)	403 (4.6)	445 (4.3)	427 (3.4)	429 (3.9)	425 (3.8)	428 (3.4)	423 (3.9)	433 (3.7)
Russian Federation	459 (3.3)	437 (3.6)	482 (3.4)	468 (3.3)	469 (3.7)	467 (3.5)	478 (3.3)	477 (3.7)	480 (3.5)
Serbia	442 (2.4)	422 (3.3)	462 (2.5)	442 (2.9)	448 (3.8)	437 (3.2)	443 (2.4)	442 (3.1)	443 (2.8)
Shanghai-China	556 (2.4)	536 (3.0)	576 (2.3)	600 (2.8)	599 (3.7)	601 (3.1)	575 (2.3)	574 (3.1)	575 (2.3)
Singapore	526 (1.1)	511 (1.7)	542 (1.5)	562 (1.4)	565 (1.9)	559 (2.0)	542 (1.4)	541 (1.8)	542 (1.8)
Chinese Taipei	495 (2.6)	477 (3.7)	514 (3.6)	543 (3.4)	546 (4.8)	541 (4.8)	520 (2.6)	520 (3.7)	521 (4.0)
Thailand	421 (2.6)	400 (3.3)	438 (3.1)	419 (3.2)	421 (3.9)	417 (3.8)	425 (3.0)	418 (3.5)	431 (3.4)
Trinidad and Tobago	416 (1.2)	387 (1.9)	445 (1.6)	414 (1.3)	410 (2.3)	418 (1.5)	410 (1.2)	401 (2.1)	419 (1.4)
Tunisia	404 (2.9)	387 (3.2)	418 (3.0)	371 (3.0)	378 (3.3)	366 (3.2)	401 (2.7)	401 (2.9)	400 (2.8)
Uruguay	426 (2.6)	404 (3.2)	445 (2.8)	427 (2.6)	433 (3.0)	421 (2.9)	427 (2.6)	427 (3.2)	428 (2.6)

[1]Illustrates how a country compares with the OECD area as a whole. Computed taking the OECD countries as a single entity, to which each country contributes in proportion to the number of 15-year-olds enrolled in its schools.
[2]Refers to the mean of the data values for all OECD countries, to which each country contributes equally, regardless of the absolute size of the student population of each country.

NOTE: PISA scores are reported on a scale from 0 to 1,000. Standard errors appear in parentheses.
SOURCE: Organization for Economic Cooperation and Development (OECD), Program for International Student Assessment (PISA), 2009, *PISA 2009 Results: What Students Know and Can Do—Student Performance in Reading, Mathematics and Science (Volume I)*. (This table was prepared December 2010.)

Average reading scores and percentage distribution of 15-year-old students scoring at each reading literacy proficiency level, by country: 2009

Country or other jurisdiction	Average reading score	Percentage distribution at levels of reading proficiency[1]							
		Below level 1b	Level 1b	Level 1a	Level 2	Level 3	Level 4	Level 5	Level 6
1	2	3	4	5	6	7	8	9	10
OECD total[2]	**492** (1.2)	**1.1** (0.07)	**4.8** (0.15)	**13.8** (0.26)	**24.4** (0.30)	**27.9** (0.32)	**19.9** (0.31)	**7.0** (0.24)	**1.0** (0.13)
OECD average[3]	**493** (0.5)	**1.1** (0.05)	**4.6** (0.08)	**13.1** (0.13)	**24.0** (0.16)	**28.9** (0.16)	**20.7** (0.16)	**6.8** (0.10)	**0.8** (0.03)
Australia	515 (2.3)	1.0 (0.12)	3.3 (0.27)	10.0 (0.39)	20.4 (0.57)	28.5 (0.73)	24.1 (0.65)	10.7 (0.54)	2.1 (0.31)
Austria	470 (2.9)	1.9 (0.42)	8.1 (0.81)	17.5 (0.99)	24.1 (0.96)	26.0 (0.92)	17.4 (0.85)	4.5 (0.45)	0.4 (0.13)
Belgium	506 (2.3)	1.1 (0.25)	4.7 (0.46)	11.9 (0.64)	20.3 (0.67)	25.8 (0.85)	24.9 (0.75)	10.1 (0.51)	1.1 (0.19)
Canada	524 (1.5)	0.4 (0.06)	2.0 (0.19)	7.9 (0.34)	20.2 (0.61)	30.0 (0.69)	26.8 (0.58)	11.0 (0.41)	1.8 (0.17)
Chile	449 (3.1)	1.3 (0.24)	7.4 (0.77)	21.9 (0.95)	33.2 (1.11)	25.6 (1.15)	9.3 (0.71)	1.3 (0.25)	# (†)
Czech Republic	478 (2.9)	0.8 (0.29)	5.5 (0.60)	16.8 (1.06)	27.4 (0.99)	27.0 (1.00)	17.4 (0.97)	4.7 (0.45)	0.4 (0.12)
Denmark	495 (2.1)	0.4 (0.11)	3.1 (0.30)	11.7 (0.72)	26.0 (0.94)	33.1 (1.21)	20.9 (1.11)	4.4 (0.45)	0.3 (0.12)
Estonia	501 (2.6)	0.3 (0.13)	2.4 (0.38)	10.6 (0.86)	25.6 (1.26)	33.8 (1.00)	21.2 (0.81)	5.4 (0.52)	0.6 (0.20)
Finland	536 (2.3)	0.2 (0.07)	1.5 (0.20)	6.4 (0.44)	16.7 (0.62)	30.1 (0.85)	30.6 (0.88)	12.9 (0.74)	1.6 (0.24)
France	496 (3.4)	2.3 (0.52)	5.6 (0.53)	11.8 (0.84)	21.1 (1.03)	27.2 (1.04)	22.4 (1.07)	8.5 (0.83)	1.1 (0.25)
Germany	497 (2.7)	0.8 (0.23)	4.4 (0.46)	13.3 (0.79)	22.2 (0.87)	28.8 (1.09)	22.8 (0.88)	7.0 (0.57)	0.6 (0.15)
Greece	483 (4.3)	1.4 (0.38)	5.6 (0.86)	14.3 (1.07)	25.6 (1.06)	29.3 (1.20)	18.2 (0.98)	5.0 (0.54)	0.6 (0.17)
Hungary	494 (3.2)	0.6 (0.23)	4.7 (0.82)	12.3 (0.95)	23.8 (1.24)	31.0 (1.25)	21.6 (1.11)	5.8 (0.67)	0.3 (0.13)
Iceland	500 (1.4)	1.1 (0.18)	4.2 (0.43)	11.5 (0.71)	22.2 (0.80)	30.6 (0.94)	21.9 (0.84)	7.5 (0.62)	1.0 (0.19)
Ireland	496 (3.0)	1.5 (0.36)	3.9 (0.47)	11.8 (0.71)	23.3 (1.00)	30.6 (0.91)	21.9 (0.91)	6.3 (0.50)	0.7 (0.22)
Israel	474 (3.6)	3.9 (0.66)	8.0 (0.66)	14.7 (0.63)	22.5 (0.96)	25.5 (0.95)	18.1 (0.73)	6.4 (0.54)	1.0 (0.16)
Italy	486 (1.6)	1.4 (0.23)	5.2 (0.32)	14.4 (0.45)	24.0 (0.54)	28.9 (0.55)	20.2 (0.48)	5.4 (0.30)	0.4 (0.10)
Japan	520 (3.5)	1.3 (0.36)	3.4 (0.49)	8.9 (0.66)	18.0 (0.84)	28.0 (0.88)	27.0 (0.95)	11.5 (0.71)	1.9 (0.36)
Korea, Republic of	539 (3.5)	0.2 (0.15)	0.9 (0.30)	4.7 (0.63)	15.4 (1.01)	33.0 (1.23)	32.9 (1.42)	11.9 (0.96)	1.0 (0.20)
Luxembourg	472 (1.3)	3.1 (0.27)	7.3 (0.45)	15.7 (0.59)	24.0 (0.70)	27.0 (0.65)	17.3 (0.61)	5.2 (0.43)	0.5 (0.15)
Mexico	425 (2.0)	3.2 (0.34)	11.4 (0.48)	25.5 (0.56)	33.0 (0.57)	21.2 (0.59)	5.3 (0.39)	0.4 (0.07)	# (†)
Netherlands	508 (5.1)	0.1 (0.05)	1.8 (0.31)	12.5 (1.36)	24.7 (1.53)	27.6 (1.24)	23.5 (1.66)	9.1 (1.00)	0.7 (0.22)
New Zealand	521 (2.4)	0.9 (0.22)	3.2 (0.45)	10.2 (0.58)	19.3 (0.75)	25.8 (0.76)	24.8 (0.81)	12.9 (0.76)	2.9 (0.38)
Norway	503 (2.6)	0.5 (0.14)	3.4 (0.39)	11.0 (0.66)	23.6 (0.84)	30.9 (0.86)	22.1 (1.16)	7.6 (0.87)	0.8 (0.20)
Poland	500 (2.6)	0.6 (0.15)	3.1 (0.35)	11.3 (0.66)	24.5 (1.08)	31.0 (0.98)	22.3 (0.99)	6.5 (0.55)	0.7 (0.15)
Portugal	489 (3.1)	0.6 (0.14)	4.0 (0.41)	13.0 (0.97)	26.4 (1.09)	31.6 (1.09)	19.6 (0.92)	4.6 (0.48)	0.2 (0.10)
Slovak Republic	477 (2.5)	0.8 (0.28)	5.6 (0.62)	15.9 (0.83)	28.1 (1.04)	28.5 (1.14)	16.7 (0.79)	4.2 (0.48)	0.3 (0.11)
Slovenia	483 (1.0)	0.8 (0.09)	5.2 (0.34)	15.2 (0.49)	25.6 (0.71)	29.2 (0.86)	19.3 (0.80)	4.3 (0.54)	0.3 (0.12)
Spain	481 (2.0)	1.2 (0.18)	4.7 (0.39)	13.6 (0.64)	26.8 (0.84)	32.6 (0.95)	17.7 (0.68)	3.2 (0.29)	0.2 (0.08)
Sweden	497 (2.9)	1.5 (0.25)	4.3 (0.38)	11.7 (0.71)	23.5 (0.99)	29.8 (0.98)	20.3 (0.92)	7.7 (0.59)	1.3 (0.25)
Switzerland	501 (2.4)	0.7 (0.15)	4.1 (0.38)	12.1 (0.62)	22.7 (0.70)	29.7 (0.78)	22.6 (0.82)	7.4 (0.68)	0.7 (0.22)
Turkey	464 (3.5)	0.8 (0.19)	5.6 (0.63)	18.1 (0.98)	32.2 (1.16)	29.1 (1.07)	12.4 (1.11)	1.8 (0.38)	# (†)
United Kingdom	494 (2.3)	1.0 (0.20)	4.1 (0.35)	13.4 (0.64)	24.9 (0.72)	28.8 (0.84)	19.8 (0.79)	7.0 (0.47)	1.0 (0.19)
United States	500 (3.7)	0.6 (0.13)	4.0 (0.45)	13.1 (0.84)	24.4 (0.86)	27.6 (0.83)	20.6 (0.90)	8.4 (0.75)	1.5 (0.42)

See notes at end of table.

Average reading scores and percentage distribution of 15-year-old students scoring at each reading literacy proficiency level, by country: 2009—Continued

Country or other jurisdiction	Average reading score	Percentage distribution at levels of reading proficiency[1]							
		Below level 1b	Level 1b	Level 1a	Level 2	Level 3	Level 4	Level 5	Level 6
1	2	3	4	5	6	7	8	9	10
Reporting partner countries									
Albania	385 (4.0)	11.3 (0.92)	18.7 (1.32)	26.6 (1.18)	25.6 (1.33)	14.4 (1.18)	3.1 (0.48)	0.2 (0.11)	‡ (†)
Argentina	398 (4.6)	10.8 (1.10)	15.8 (1.25)	25.0 (1.30)	25.4 (1.22)	16.0 (1.04)	6.0 (0.83)	0.9 (0.23)	0.1 (0.05)
Azerbaijan	362 (3.3)	9.7 (1.05)	26.1 (1.14)	36.9 (1.21)	21.5 (1.17)	5.3 (0.77)	0.5 (0.15)	# (†)	‡ (†)
Brazil	412 (2.7)	5.0 (0.38)	16.0 (0.67)	28.6 (0.81)	27.1 (0.78)	15.9 (0.86)	6.1 (0.53)	1.2 (0.21)	0.1 (0.05)
Bulgaria	429 (6.7)	8.0 (1.09)	12.9 (1.36)	20.1 (1.35)	23.4 (1.15)	21.8 (1.43)	11.0 (1.14)	2.6 (0.50)	0.2 (0.08)
Colombia	413 (3.7)	4.2 (0.71)	13.9 (0.99)	29.0 (1.22)	30.6 (1.11)	17.1 (1.03)	4.6 (0.48)	0.5 (0.16)	# (†)
Croatia	476 (2.9)	1.0 (0.21)	5.0 (0.45)	16.5 (0.97)	27.4 (1.02)	30.6 (1.21)	16.4 (0.97)	3.1 (0.40)	0.1 (0.10)
Dubai (United Arab Emirates)	459 (1.1)	3.7 (0.23)	9.4 (0.45)	17.9 (0.50)	25.4 (0.71)	23.5 (0.77)	14.8 (0.71)	4.8 (0.49)	0.5 (0.18)
Hong Kong-China	533 (2.1)	0.2 (0.08)	1.5 (0.30)	6.6 (0.59)	16.1 (0.75)	31.4 (0.90)	31.8 (0.89)	11.2 (0.70)	1.2 (0.26)
Indonesia	402 (3.7)	1.7 (0.38)	14.1 (1.31)	37.6 (1.64)	34.3 (1.38)	11.2 (1.35)	1.0 (0.34)	‡ (†)	‡ (†)
Jordan	405 (3.3)	6.9 (0.62)	13.6 (0.78)	27.6 (0.96)	31.8 (0.98)	16.5 (0.99)	3.4 (0.44)	0.2 (0.09)	‡ (†)
Kazakhstan	390 (3.1)	7.5 (0.65)	20.4 (0.99)	30.7 (0.88)	24.1 (0.93)	13.1 (0.87)	3.7 (0.49)	0.4 (0.12)	‡ (†)
Kyrgyzstan	314 (3.2)	29.8 (1.25)	29.7 (0.91)	23.8 (0.94)	11.5 (0.83)	4.2 (0.57)	1.0 (0.28)	0.1 (0.06)	‡ (†)
Latvia	484 (3.0)	0.4 (0.15)	3.3 (0.57)	13.9 (1.00)	28.8 (1.45)	33.5 (1.21)	17.2 (1.01)	2.9 (0.44)	‡ (†)
Liechtenstein	499 (†)	‡ (†)	2.8 (1.15)	12.8 (1.83)	24.0 (2.85)	31.1 (2.76)	24.6 (2.34)	4.2 (1.39)	‡ (†)
Lithuania	468 (2.4)	0.9 (0.26)	5.5 (0.56)	17.9 (0.87)	30.0 (1.03)	28.6 (0.94)	14.1 (0.80)	2.8 (0.38)	0.1 (0.06)
Macao-China	487 (0.9)	0.3 (0.09)	2.6 (0.25)	12.0 (0.43)	30.6 (0.63)	34.8 (0.67)	16.9 (0.50)	2.8 (0.25)	0.1 (0.05)
Montenegro	408 (1.7)	5.9 (0.53)	15.8 (0.80)	27.8 (0.81)	28.0 (0.88)	16.8 (0.85)	5.0 (0.46)	0.6 (0.17)	‡ (†)
Panama	371 (6.5)	13.3 (1.83)	23.1 (1.78)	28.9 (1.79)	20.7 (1.43)	10.1 (1.36)	3.4 (0.68)	0.5 (0.23)	‡ (†)
Peru	370 (4.0)	14.1 (0.93)	22.0 (1.01)	28.7 (1.10)	22.1 (0.94)	10.1 (0.86)	2.6 (0.51)	0.4 (0.21)	# (†)
Qatar	372 (0.8)	17.8 (0.33)	22.4 (0.48)	23.2 (0.63)	18.3 (0.44)	11.1 (0.48)	5.4 (0.27)	1.5 (0.16)	0.2 (0.07)
Romania	424 (4.1)	4.1 (0.69)	12.7 (1.08)	23.6 (1.25)	31.6 (1.31)	21.2 (1.31)	6.1 (0.71)	0.7 (0.17)	‡ (†)
Russian Federation	459 (3.3)	1.6 (0.35)	6.8 (0.58)	19.0 (0.79)	31.6 (0.97)	26.8 (0.88)	11.1 (0.66)	2.8 (0.43)	0.3 (0.11)
Serbia	442 (2.4)	2.0 (0.36)	8.8 (0.67)	22.1 (0.87)	33.2 (1.02)	25.3 (0.96)	7.9 (0.56)	0.8 (0.16)	# (†)
Shanghai-China	556 (2.4)	0.1 (0.04)	0.6 (0.14)	3.4 (0.47)	13.3 (0.86)	28.5 (1.16)	34.7 (1.04)	17.0 (0.99)	2.4 (0.45)
Singapore	526 (1.1)	0.4 (0.11)	2.7 (0.26)	9.3 (0.50)	18.5 (0.60)	27.6 (0.81)	25.7 (0.73)	13.1 (0.54)	2.6 (0.34)
Chinese Taipei	495 (2.6)	0.7 (0.18)	3.5 (0.35)	11.4 (0.63)	24.6 (0.80)	33.5 (1.09)	21.0 (0.97)	4.8 (0.76)	0.4 (0.20)
Thailand	421 (2.6)	1.2 (0.29)	9.9 (0.82)	31.7 (1.12)	36.8 (1.15)	16.7 (0.82)	3.3 (0.52)	0.3 (0.15)	‡ (†)
Trinidad and Tobago	416 (1.2)	9.6 (0.51)	14.2 (0.61)	21.0 (0.81)	25.0 (0.94)	19.0 (0.86)	8.9 (0.51)	2.1 (0.27)	0.2 (0.07)
Tunisia	404 (2.9)	5.5 (0.52)	15.0 (0.78)	29.6 (1.10)	31.5 (1.22)	15.1 (1.04)	3.1 (0.52)	0.2 (0.12)	‡ (†)
Uruguay	426 (2.6)	5.5 (0.58)	12.5 (0.68)	23.9 (0.70)	28.0 (0.73)	20.3 (0.73)	8.1 (0.51)	1.7 (0.26)	0.1 (0.06)

†Not applicable.

#Rounds to zero.

‡Reporting standards not met.

[1]Level 1b: Able to locate a single piece of explicitly stated information in a prominent position in a short, syntactically simple text and make simple connections between adjacent pieces of information. Level 1a: Able to locate explicitly stated information, recognize the main theme in a text about a familiar topic, and make a simple connection between information in the text and common, everyday knowledge. Level 2: Able to locate information which may need to be inferred and may need to meet several conditions, recognize the main idea in a text, understand relationships, construe meaning within part of the text when the information is not prominent, and make comparisons or connections between the text and outside knowledge by drawing on personal experience and attitudes. Level 3: Able to recognize the relationship between several pieces of information that must meet multiple conditions; integrate parts of a text in order to identify a main idea, understand a relationship, or construe the meaning of a word or phrase; compare, contrast or categorize where the required information is not prominent or there is much competing information or other obstacles in the text; make connections, comparisons, and explanations; evaluate a feature of the text; and demonstrate an understanding of the text by relating it to everyday knowledge or by drawing on less common knowledge. Level 4: Able to locate and organize embedded information, interpret the meaning of language by taking into account the text as a whole, understand and apply categories in an unfamiliar context, use formal knowledge to hypothesize about or critically evaluate a text, and demonstrate an understanding of long or complex texts with unfamiliar form or content. Level 5: Able to locate and organize deeply embedded information, infer relevant information in the text, perform critical evaluation or form a hypothesis by drawing on specialized knowledge, and fully understand texts with unfamiliar form or context. Level 6: Able to make multiple inferences, comparisons, and contrasts that are both detailed and precise; demonstrate full understanding of texts and integrate information from more than one text; deal with unfamiliar ideas in the presence of prominent competing information; generate abstract categories for interpretation; hypothesize about or critically evaluate a complex text on an unfamiliar topic, taking into account multiple criteria or perspectives; and apply sophisticated understandings from beyond the text.

[2]Illustrates how a country compares with the OECD area as a whole. Computed by taking the OECD countries as a single entity to which each country contributes in proportion to the number of 15-year-olds enrolled in its schools.

[3]Refers to the mean of the data values for all OECD countries, to which each country contributes equally, regardless of the absolute size of the student population of each country.

NOTE: PISA scores are reported on a scale from 0 to 1,000. Detail may not sum to totals because of rounding. Standard errors appear in parentheses.

SOURCE: Organization for Economic Cooperation and Development (OECD), Program for International Student Assessment (PISA), 2009, PISA 2009 Results: What Students Know and Can Do—Student Performance in Reading, Mathematics, and Science (Volume I). (This table was prepared December 2010.)

Average mathematics scores and percentage distribution of 15-year-old students scoring at each mathematics literacy proficiency level, by country: 2009

Country or other jurisdiction	Average mathematics score	Percentage distribution at levels of mathematics proficiency[1]						
		Below level 1	Level 1	Level 2	Level 3	Level 4	Level 5	Level 6
1	2	3	4	5	6	7	8	9
OECD total[2]	**488** (1.2)	**9.3** (0.25)	**15.5** (0.33)	**22.7** (0.31)	**23.5** (0.24)	**17.3** (0.30)	**8.9** (0.24)	**2.8** (0.16)
OECD average[3]	**496** (0.5)	**8.0** (0.12)	**14.0** (0.13)	**22.0** (0.15)	**24.3** (0.17)	**18.9** (0.15)	**9.6** (0.12)	**3.1** (0.08)
Australia	514 (2.5)	5.1 (0.33)	10.8 (0.53)	20.3 (0.61)	25.8 (0.54)	21.7 (0.56)	11.9 (0.54)	4.5 (0.56)
Austria	496 (2.7)	7.8 (0.75)	15.4 (0.90)	21.2 (0.88)	23.0 (0.89)	19.6 (0.93)	9.9 (0.70)	3.0 (0.35)
Belgium	515 (2.3)	7.7 (0.63)	11.3 (0.54)	17.5 (0.69)	21.8 (0.73)	21.3 (0.76)	14.6 (0.56)	5.8 (0.44)
Canada	527 (1.6)	3.1 (0.25)	8.3 (0.42)	18.8 (0.48)	26.5 (0.86)	25.0 (0.68)	13.9 (0.45)	4.4 (0.27)
Chile	421 (3.1)	21.7 (1.19)	29.4 (1.09)	27.3 (0.98)	14.8 (0.96)	5.6 (0.59)	1.2 (0.29)	0.1 (0.09)
Czech Republic	493 (2.8)	7.0 (0.83)	15.3 (0.82)	24.2 (1.00)	24.4 (1.09)	17.4 (0.81)	8.5 (0.64)	3.2 (0.39)
Denmark	503 (2.6)	4.9 (0.49)	12.1 (0.80)	23.0 (0.91)	27.4 (1.06)	21.0 (0.89)	9.1 (0.83)	2.5 (0.47)
Estonia	512 (2.6)	3.0 (0.42)	9.6 (0.68)	22.7 (0.86)	29.9 (0.94)	22.7 (0.81)	9.8 (0.79)	2.2 (0.43)
Finland	541 (2.2)	1.7 (0.25)	6.1 (0.45)	15.6 (0.83)	27.1 (0.95)	27.8 (0.87)	16.7 (0.79)	4.9 (0.53)
France	497 (3.1)	9.5 (0.88)	13.1 (1.07)	19.9 (0.94)	23.8 (1.12)	20.1 (1.01)	10.4 (0.72)	3.3 (0.48)
Germany	513 (2.9)	6.4 (0.63)	12.2 (0.72)	18.8 (0.88)	23.1 (0.87)	21.7 (0.92)	13.2 (0.87)	4.6 (0.46)
Greece	466 (3.9)	11.3 (1.22)	19.1 (1.01)	26.4 (1.25)	24.0 (1.05)	13.6 (0.78)	4.9 (0.56)	0.8 (0.16)
Hungary	490 (3.5)	8.1 (0.99)	14.2 (0.95)	23.2 (1.18)	26.0 (1.24)	18.4 (1.02)	8.1 (0.79)	2.0 (0.45)
Iceland	507 (1.4)	5.7 (0.43)	11.3 (0.52)	21.3 (0.88)	27.3 (0.90)	20.9 (0.90)	10.5 (0.67)	3.1 (0.40)
Ireland	487 (2.5)	7.3 (0.63)	13.6 (0.74)	24.5 (1.09)	28.6 (1.20)	19.4 (0.92)	5.8 (0.59)	0.9 (0.20)
Israel	447 (3.3)	20.5 (1.17)	18.9 (0.90)	22.5 (0.92)	20.1 (0.87)	12.0 (0.71)	4.7 (0.51)	1.2 (0.28)
Italy	483 (1.9)	9.1 (0.44)	15.9 (0.48)	24.2 (0.59)	24.6 (0.48)	17.3 (0.57)	7.4 (0.40)	1.6 (0.15)
Japan	529 (3.3)	4.0 (0.57)	8.5 (0.65)	17.4 (0.90)	25.7 (1.08)	23.5 (1.04)	14.7 (0.88)	6.2 (0.78)
Korea, Republic of	546 (4.0)	1.9 (0.49)	6.2 (0.72)	15.6 (0.99)	24.4 (1.21)	26.3 (1.30)	17.7 (0.97)	7.8 (0.96)
Luxembourg	489 (1.2)	9.6 (0.53)	14.4 (0.57)	22.7 (0.72)	23.1 (0.98)	19.0 (0.82)	9.0 (0.61)	2.3 (0.36)
Mexico	419 (1.8)	21.9 (0.79)	28.9 (0.59)	28.3 (0.61)	15.6 (0.56)	4.7 (0.36)	0.7 (0.11)	# (†)
Netherlands	526 (4.7)	2.8 (0.59)	10.6 (1.33)	19.0 (1.37)	23.9 (0.98)	23.9 (1.25)	15.4 (1.18)	4.4 (0.52)
New Zealand	519 (2.3)	5.3 (0.53)	10.2 (0.54)	19.1 (0.84)	24.4 (0.88)	22.2 (0.98)	13.6 (0.74)	5.3 (0.45)
Norway	498 (2.4)	5.5 (0.50)	12.7 (0.83)	24.3 (0.93)	27.5 (1.02)	19.7 (0.86)	8.4 (0.58)	1.8 (0.34)
Poland	495 (2.8)	6.1 (0.54)	14.4 (0.75)	24.0 (0.88)	26.1 (0.77)	19.0 (0.85)	8.2 (0.61)	2.2 (0.41)
Portugal	487 (2.9)	8.4 (0.62)	15.3 (0.83)	23.9 (0.93)	25.0 (1.03)	17.7 (0.79)	7.7 (0.63)	1.9 (0.35)
Slovak Republic	497 (3.1)	7.0 (0.68)	14.0 (0.79)	23.2 (1.08)	25.0 (1.54)	18.1 (1.24)	9.1 (0.69)	3.6 (0.63)
Slovenia	501 (1.2)	6.5 (0.40)	13.8 (0.60)	22.5 (0.67)	23.9 (0.69)	19.0 (0.79)	10.3 (0.57)	3.9 (0.36)
Spain	483 (2.1)	9.1 (0.48)	14.6 (0.58)	23.9 (0.58)	26.6 (0.63)	17.7 (0.62)	6.7 (0.39)	1.3 (0.16)
Sweden	494 (2.9)	7.5 (0.65)	13.6 (0.72)	23.4 (0.81)	25.2 (0.75)	19.0 (0.88)	8.9 (0.64)	2.5 (0.35)
Switzerland	534 (3.3)	4.5 (0.40)	9.0 (0.65)	15.9 (0.63)	23.0 (0.92)	23.5 (0.80)	16.3 (0.78)	7.8 (0.75)
Turkey	445 (4.4)	17.7 (1.35)	24.5 (1.11)	25.2 (1.18)	17.4 (1.07)	9.6 (0.90)	4.4 (0.91)	1.3 (0.46)
United Kingdom	492 (2.4)	6.2 (0.46)	14.0 (0.71)	24.9 (0.88)	27.2 (1.10)	17.9 (0.96)	8.1 (0.63)	1.8 (0.27)
United States	487 (3.6)	8.1 (0.72)	15.3 (0.98)	24.4 (0.97)	25.2 (0.95)	17.1 (0.93)	8.0 (0.85)	1.9 (0.46)

See notes at end of table.

Average mathematics scores and percentage distribution of 15-year-old students scoring at each mathematics literacy proficiency level, by country: 2009—Continued

Country or other jurisdiction	Average mathematics score		Percentage distribution at levels of mathematics proficiency[1]												
			Below level 1		Level 1		Level 2		Level 3		Level 4		Level 5		Level 6	
1	2		3		4		5		6		7		8		9	
Reporting partner countries																
Albania	377	(4.0)	40.5	(1.76)	27.2	(1.22)	20.2	(1.25)	9.1	(0.85)	2.6	(0.58)	0.4	(0.16)	#	(†)
Argentina	388	(4.1)	37.2	(1.75)	26.4	(1.11)	20.8	(1.09)	10.9	(0.95)	3.9	(0.66)	0.8	(0.26)	0.1	(0.07)
Azerbaijan	431	(2.8)	11.5	(0.96)	33.8	(1.24)	35.3	(1.29)	14.8	(1.04)	3.6	(0.51)	0.9	(0.34)	0.2	(0.12)
Brazil	386	(2.4)	38.1	(1.25)	31.0	(0.91)	19.0	(0.75)	8.1	(0.64)	3.0	(0.32)	0.7	(0.19)	0.1	(0.05)
Bulgaria	428	(5.9)	24.5	(1.91)	22.7	(1.08)	23.4	(1.11)	17.5	(1.36)	8.2	(0.90)	3.0	(0.70)	0.8	(0.36)
Colombia	381	(3.2)	38.8	(2.02)	31.6	(1.30)	20.3	(1.28)	7.5	(0.66)	1.6	(0.33)	0.1	(0.06)	#	(†)
Croatia	460	(3.1)	12.4	(0.85)	20.8	(0.94)	26.7	(0.83)	22.7	(0.97)	12.5	(0.84)	4.3	(0.51)	0.6	(0.22)
Dubai (United Arab Emirates)	453	(1.1)	17.6	(0.49)	21.2	(0.59)	23.0	(0.79)	19.6	(0.63)	12.1	(0.55)	5.3	(0.39)	1.2	(0.19)
Hong Kong-China	555	(2.7)	2.6	(0.40)	6.2	(0.53)	13.2	(0.67)	21.9	(0.84)	25.4	(0.91)	19.9	(0.82)	10.8	(0.78)
Indonesia	371	(3.7)	43.5	(2.21)	33.1	(1.54)	16.9	(1.14)	5.4	(0.91)	0.9	(0.32)	0.1	(0.05)	‡	(†)
Jordan	387	(3.7)	35.4	(1.67)	29.9	(1.20)	22.9	(1.03)	9.5	(0.94)	2.1	(0.44)	0.3	(0.17)	#	(†)
Kazakhstan	405	(3.0)	29.6	(1.31)	29.6	(0.94)	23.5	(0.88)	12.0	(0.80)	4.2	(0.48)	0.9	(0.29)	0.3	(0.19)
Kyrgyzstan	331	(2.9)	64.8	(1.43)	21.8	(0.98)	9.3	(0.76)	3.3	(0.51)	0.7	(0.24)	#	(†)	‡	(†)
Latvia	482	(3.1)	5.8	(0.69)	16.7	(1.15)	27.2	(1.04)	28.2	(1.08)	16.4	(1.01)	5.1	(0.50)	0.6	(0.15)
Liechtenstein	536	(4.1)	3.0	(0.99)	6.5	(1.61)	15.0	(2.18)	26.2	(2.26)	31.2	(3.25)	13.0	(2.45)	5.0	(1.42)
Lithuania	477	(2.6)	9.0	(0.79)	17.3	(0.85)	26.1	(1.10)	25.3	(0.98)	15.4	(0.77)	5.7	(0.56)	1.3	(0.26)
Macao-China	525	(0.9)	2.8	(0.25)	8.2	(0.46)	19.6	(0.58)	27.8	(0.90)	24.5	(0.78)	12.8	(0.43)	4.3	(0.28)
Montenegro	403	(2.0)	29.6	(1.07)	28.8	(1.00)	24.6	(1.04)	12.2	(0.68)	3.8	(0.35)	0.9	(0.20)	0.1	(0.05)
Panama	360	(5.2)	51.5	(2.90)	27.3	(1.72)	13.9	(1.51)	5.6	(0.92)	1.4	(0.36)	0.4	(0.22)	#	(†)
Peru	365	(4.0)	47.6	(1.81)	25.9	(1.16)	16.9	(1.26)	6.8	(0.70)	2.1	(0.43)	0.5	(0.18)	0.1	(0.06)
Qatar	368	(0.7)	51.1	(0.56)	22.7	(0.64)	13.1	(0.48)	7.2	(0.35)	4.2	(0.25)	1.5	(0.17)	0.3	(0.08)
Romania	427	(3.4)	19.5	(1.42)	27.5	(1.15)	28.6	(1.39)	17.3	(1.02)	5.9	(0.77)	1.2	(0.33)	0.1	(0.08)
Russian Federation	468	(3.3)	9.5	(0.92)	19.0	(1.16)	28.5	(1.03)	25.0	(1.00)	12.7	(0.87)	4.3	(0.57)	1.0	(0.27)
Serbia	442	(2.9)	17.6	(1.04)	22.9	(0.84)	26.5	(1.07)	19.9	(0.97)	9.5	(0.62)	2.9	(0.41)	0.6	(0.18)
Shanghai-China	600	(2.8)	1.4	(0.26)	3.4	(0.38)	8.7	(0.63)	15.2	(0.79)	20.8	(0.79)	23.8	(0.80)	26.6	(1.19)
Singapore	562	(1.4)	3.0	(0.26)	6.8	(0.57)	13.1	(0.56)	18.7	(0.80)	22.8	(0.62)	20.0	(0.87)	15.6	(0.63)
Chinese Taipei	543	(3.4)	4.2	(0.48)	8.6	(0.65)	15.5	(0.68)	20.9	(0.88)	22.2	(0.86)	17.2	(0.92)	11.3	(1.16)
Thailand	419	(3.2)	22.1	(1.37)	30.4	(0.92)	27.3	(1.09)	14.0	(0.85)	4.9	(0.57)	1.0	(0.27)	0.3	(0.22)
Trinidad and Tobago	414	(1.3)	30.1	(0.79)	23.1	(0.97)	21.2	(0.89)	15.4	(0.63)	7.7	(0.44)	2.1	(0.25)	0.3	(0.15)
Tunisia	371	(3.0)	43.4	(1.66)	30.2	(1.46)	18.7	(0.90)	6.1	(0.69)	1.3	(0.44)	0.2	(0.16)	#	(†)
Uruguay	427	(2.6)	22.9	(1.16)	24.6	(1.08)	25.1	(0.99)	17.0	(0.73)	7.9	(0.55)	2.1	(0.34)	0.3	(0.12)

†Not applicable.
#Rounds to zero.
‡Reporting standards not met.
[1]Level 1: Able to answer questions involving familiar contexts where all relevant information is present and the questions are clearly defined. Level 2: Able to interpret and recognize situations in contexts that require no more than direct inference; extract relevant information from a single source; employ basic algorithms, formulae, procedures, or conventions; and employ direct reasoning for literal interpretations of results. Level 3: Able to execute clearly described procedures; select and apply simple problem-solving strategies; interpret and use representations based on different information sources; and develop short communications reporting one's interpretations, results, and reasoning. Level 4: Able to work effectively with explicit models for complex concrete situations that may involve constraints or call for making assumptions, select and integrate different representations, reason with some insight, and construct and communicate explanations and arguments based on one's interpretations and actions. Level 5: Able to develop and work with models for complex situations; select and evaluate appropriate problem-solving strategies; work strategically using broad, well-developed thinking and reasoning skills; and communicate one's interpretations and reasoning. Level 6: Able to concep-

tualize, generalize, and utilize information; link different information sources and representations; perform advanced mathematical thinking and reasoning; develop new approaches and strategies for attacking novel situations; and formulate and precisely communicate actions and reflections regarding findings and interpretations.
[2]Illustrates how a country compares with the OECD area as a whole. Computed by taking the OECD countries as a single entity to which each country contributes in proportion to the number of 15-year-olds enrolled in its schools.
[3]Refers to the mean of the data values for all OECD countries, to which each country contributes equally, regardless of the absolute size of the student population of each country.
NOTE: PISA scores are reported on a scale from 0 to 1,000. Detail may not sum to totals because of rounding. Standard errors appear in parentheses.
SOURCE: Organization for Economic Cooperation and Development (OECD), Program for International Student Assessment (PISA), 2009, PISA 2009 Results: What Students Know and Can Do—Student Performance in Reading, Mathematics and Science (Volume I). (This table was prepared December 2010.)

Average science scores and percentage distribution of 15-year-old students scoring at each science literacy proficiency level, by country: 2009

Country or other jurisdiction	Average science score	Percentage distribution at levels of science proficiency[1]						
		Below Level 1	Level 1	Level 2	Level 3	Level 4	Level 5	Level 6
1	2	3	4	5	6	7	8	9
OECD total[2]	496 (1.2)	5.4 (0.19)	14.6 (0.32)	24.8 (0.28)	27.1 (0.25)	19.6 (0.32)	7.3 (0.25)	1.1 (0.10)
OECD average[3]	501 (0.5)	5.0 (0.10)	13.0 (0.14)	24.4 (0.16)	28.6 (0.17)	20.6 (0.16)	7.4 (0.10)	1.1 (0.04)
Australia	527 (2.5)	3.4 (0.27)	9.2 (0.48)	20.0 (0.59)	28.4 (0.65)	24.5 (0.66)	11.5 (0.58)	3.1 (0.50)
Austria	494 (3.2)	6.7 (0.83)	14.3 (0.99)	23.8 (1.00)	26.6 (1.04)	20.6 (1.03)	7.1 (0.61)	1.0 (0.19)
Belgium	507 (2.5)	6.4 (0.57)	11.7 (0.61)	20.7 (0.65)	27.2 (0.76)	24.0 (0.82)	9.0 (0.59)	1.1 (0.19)
Canada	529 (1.6)	2.0 (0.21)	7.5 (0.37)	20.9 (0.49)	31.2 (0.62)	26.2 (0.65)	10.5 (0.45)	1.6 (0.15)
Chile	447 (2.9)	8.4 (0.83)	23.9 (1.07)	35.2 (0.94)	23.6 (1.07)	7.9 (0.69)	1.1 (0.22)	# (†)
Czech Republic	500 (3.0)	4.7 (0.57)	12.6 (0.90)	25.6 (0.97)	28.8 (1.25)	19.9 (0.87)	7.2 (0.58)	1.2 (0.22)
Denmark	499 (2.5)	4.1 (0.42)	12.5 (0.65)	26.0 (0.77)	30.6 (1.07)	20.1 (0.85)	5.9 (0.55)	0.9 (0.23)
Estonia	528 (2.7)	1.3 (0.31)	7.0 (0.72)	21.3 (1.07)	34.3 (1.10)	25.7 (1.07)	9.0 (0.63)	1.4 (0.26)
Finland	554 (2.3)	1.1 (0.19)	4.9 (0.41)	15.3 (0.73)	28.8 (0.95)	31.2 (1.08)	15.4 (0.74)	3.3 (0.34)
France	498 (3.6)	7.1 (0.82)	12.2 (0.83)	22.1 (1.25)	28.8 (1.32)	21.7 (1.02)	7.3 (0.70)	0.8 (0.22)
Germany	520 (2.8)	4.1 (0.51)	10.7 (0.81)	20.1 (0.86)	27.3 (1.08)	25.0 (1.18)	10.9 (0.68)	1.9 (0.29)
Greece	470 (4.0)	7.2 (1.07)	18.1 (1.04)	29.8 (0.96)	27.9 (1.20)	14.0 (0.95)	2.8 (0.31)	0.3 (0.11)
Hungary	503 (3.1)	3.8 (0.93)	10.4 (0.86)	25.5 (1.13)	33.2 (1.32)	21.8 (1.19)	5.1 (0.55)	0.3 (0.13)
Iceland	496 (1.4)	5.5 (0.48)	12.5 (0.63)	25.8 (0.75)	30.4 (0.94)	18.8 (0.84)	6.1 (0.43)	0.8 (0.19)
Ireland	508 (3.3)	4.4 (0.69)	10.7 (1.01)	23.3 (1.17)	29.9 (0.99)	22.9 (0.95)	7.5 (0.68)	1.2 (0.23)
Israel	455 (3.1)	13.9 (1.06)	19.2 (0.72)	26.0 (1.04)	24.1 (0.76)	12.8 (0.72)	3.5 (0.36)	0.5 (0.13)
Italy	489 (1.8)	6.1 (0.39)	14.5 (0.50)	25.5 (0.63)	29.5 (0.54)	18.6 (0.53)	5.3 (0.29)	0.5 (0.07)
Japan	539 (3.4)	3.2 (0.52)	7.5 (0.68)	16.3 (0.87)	26.6 (0.83)	29.5 (0.98)	14.4 (0.73)	2.6 (0.39)
Korea, Republic of	538 (3.4)	1.1 (0.32)	5.2 (0.68)	18.5 (1.15)	33.1 (1.13)	30.4 (1.14)	10.5 (0.90)	1.1 (0.31)
Luxembourg	484 (1.2)	8.4 (0.52)	15.3 (0.88)	24.3 (0.69)	27.1 (0.87)	18.2 (0.91)	6.0 (0.49)	0.7 (0.12)
Mexico	416 (1.8)	14.5 (0.60)	32.8 (0.64)	33.6 (0.60)	15.8 (0.61)	3.1 (0.27)	0.2 (0.05)	# (†)
Netherlands	522 (5.4)	2.6 (0.53)	10.6 (1.33)	21.8 (1.53)	26.9 (1.07)	25.3 (1.69)	11.2 (1.10)	1.5 (0.30)
New Zealand	532 (2.6)	4.0 (0.53)	9.4 (0.52)	18.1 (1.01)	25.8 (0.88)	25.1 (0.74)	14.0 (0.72)	3.6 (0.36)
Norway	500 (2.6)	3.8 (0.48)	11.9 (0.92)	26.6 (0.95)	31.1 (0.71)	20.1 (0.82)	5.9 (0.65)	0.5 (0.16)
Poland	508 (2.4)	2.3 (0.33)	10.9 (0.69)	26.1 (0.80)	32.1 (0.81)	21.2 (0.97)	6.8 (0.49)	0.8 (0.19)
Portugal	493 (2.9)	3.0 (0.35)	13.5 (0.92)	28.9 (1.08)	32.3 (1.08)	18.1 (1.00)	3.9 (0.51)	0.3 (0.13)
Slovak Republic	490 (3.0)	5.0 (0.58)	14.2 (0.89)	27.6 (1.03)	29.2 (0.95)	17.7 (0.85)	5.6 (0.53)	0.7 (0.20)
Slovenia	512 (1.1)	3.1 (0.22)	11.7 (0.45)	23.7 (0.66)	28.7 (1.05)	23.0 (0.72)	8.7 (0.61)	1.2 (0.27)
Spain	488 (2.1)	4.6 (0.37)	13.6 (0.75)	27.9 (0.67)	32.3 (0.69)	17.6 (0.57)	3.7 (0.26)	0.2 (0.05)
Sweden	495 (2.7)	5.8 (0.51)	13.4 (0.75)	25.6 (0.80)	28.4 (0.84)	18.7 (0.86)	7.1 (0.56)	1.0 (0.22)
Switzerland	517 (2.8)	3.5 (0.31)	10.6 (0.58)	21.3 (1.09)	29.8 (1.02)	24.1 (1.03)	9.2 (0.73)	1.5 (0.23)
Turkey	454 (3.6)	6.9 (0.81)	23.0 (1.13)	34.5 (1.16)	25.2 (1.24)	9.1 (1.13)	1.1 (0.29)	# (†)
United Kingdom	514 (2.5)	3.8 (0.34)	11.2 (0.68)	22.7 (0.73)	28.8 (0.97)	22.2 (0.83)	9.5 (0.61)	1.9 (0.25)
United States	502 (3.6)	4.2 (0.54)	13.9 (0.93)	25.0 (0.87)	27.5 (0.80)	20.1 (0.94)	7.9 (0.78)	1.3 (0.28)

See notes at end of table.

Average science scores and percentage distribution of 15-year-old students scoring at each science literacy proficiency level, by country: 2009—Continued

Country or other jurisdiction	Average science score	Percentage distribution at levels of science proficiency[1]						
		Below Level 1	Level 1	Level 2	Level 3	Level 4	Level 5	Level 6
1	2	3	4	5	6	7	8	9
Reporting partner countries								
Albania	391 (3.9)	26.3 (1.55)	31.0 (1.28)	27.7 (1.24)	12.9 (1.34)	2.0 (0.38)	0.1 (0.06)	‡ (†)
Argentina	401 (4.6)	25.2 (1.70)	27.2 (1.37)	26.7 (1.20)	15.4 (1.12)	4.8 (0.69)	0.6 (0.18)	# (†)
Azerbaijan	373 (3.1)	31.5 (1.68)	38.5 (1.13)	22.4 (1.07)	6.7 (0.76)	0.8 (0.22)	# (†)	‡ (†)
Brazil	405 (2.4)	19.7 (0.90)	34.5 (0.99)	28.8 (0.90)	12.6 (0.81)	3.9 (0.38)	0.6 (0.11)	# (†)
Bulgaria	439 (5.9)	16.5 (1.63)	22.3 (1.55)	26.6 (1.31)	21.0 (1.36)	10.9 (1.01)	2.4 (0.48)	0.2 (0.12)
Colombia	402 (3.6)	20.4 (1.81)	33.7 (1.23)	30.2 (1.40)	13.1 (1.04)	2.5 (0.34)	0.1 (0.05)	# (†)
Croatia	486 (2.8)	3.6 (0.47)	14.9 (0.99)	30.0 (1.07)	31.1 (1.03)	16.7 (0.98)	3.5 (0.57)	0.2 (0.10)
Dubai (United Arab Emirates)	466 (1.2)	11.0 (0.47)	19.5 (0.57)	26.0 (0.78)	22.9 (0.73)	14.9 (0.59)	4.8 (0.35)	0.8 (0.21)
Hong Kong-China	549 (2.8)	1.4 (0.31)	5.2 (0.61)	15.1 (0.73)	29.4 (0.99)	32.7 (0.99)	14.2 (0.94)	2.0 (0.30)
Indonesia	383 (3.8)	24.6 (1.77)	41.0 (1.54)	27.0 (1.55)	6.9 (1.01)	0.5 (0.22)	# (†)	‡ (†)
Jordan	415 (3.5)	18.0 (1.20)	27.6 (1.13)	32.2 (1.21)	17.6 (1.12)	4.1 (0.51)	0.5 (0.18)	# (†)
Kazakhstan	400 (3.1)	22.4 (1.31)	33.0 (1.08)	27.9 (1.14)	12.8 (0.82)	3.6 (0.62)	0.3 (0.16)	# (†)
Kyrgyzstan	330 (2.9)	52.9 (1.32)	29.0 (0.94)	13.3 (0.76)	4.0 (0.54)	0.7 (0.20)	# (†)	‡ (†)
Latvia	494 (3.1)	2.3 (0.56)	12.5 (1.00)	29.1 (1.07)	35.5 (1.16)	17.6 (1.06)	3.0 (0.47)	0.1 (0.08)
Liechtenstein	520 (3.4)	1.4 (0.74)	9.9 (1.94)	23.8 (3.07)	29.8 (3.67)	25.4 (2.67)	9.0 (1.74)	0.7 (0.67)
Lithuania	491 (2.9)	3.5 (0.65)	13.5 (0.77)	28.9 (1.02)	32.4 (1.18)	17.0 (0.84)	4.3 (0.41)	0.4 (0.13)
Macao-China	511 (1.0)	1.5 (0.21)	8.1 (0.36)	25.2 (0.77)	37.8 (0.74)	22.7 (0.98)	4.5 (0.47)	0.2 (0.08)
Montenegro	401 (2.0)	22.2 (1.01)	31.4 (0.98)	29.4 (1.04)	13.6 (0.79)	3.1 (0.39)	0.2 (0.15)	‡ (†)
Panama	376 (5.7)	32.8 (2.74)	32.4 (1.96)	23.2 (1.93)	9.3 (1.19)	2.2 (0.46)	0.2 (0.12)	‡ (†)
Peru	369 (3.5)	35.3 (1.50)	33.0 (1.29)	21.7 (1.21)	8.0 (0.79)	1.8 (0.37)	0.2 (0.12)	# (†)
Qatar	379 (0.9)	36.4 (0.58)	28.8 (0.54)	18.8 (0.56)	9.8 (0.30)	4.8 (0.23)	1.3 (0.14)	0.1 (0.05)
Romania	428 (3.4)	11.9 (1.13)	29.5 (1.57)	34.1 (1.73)	19.7 (1.18)	4.4 (0.59)	0.4 (0.12)	# (†)
Russian Federation	478 (3.3)	5.5 (0.67)	16.5 (1.06)	30.7 (1.14)	29.0 (1.15)	13.9 (0.91)	3.9 (0.50)	0.4 (0.17)
Serbia	443 (2.4)	10.1 (0.82)	24.3 (0.96)	33.9 (1.17)	23.6 (0.75)	7.1 (0.57)	1.0 (0.18)	# (†)
Shanghai-China	575 (2.3)	0.4 (0.11)	2.8 (0.36)	10.5 (0.66)	26.0 (0.99)	36.1 (1.12)	20.4 (0.96)	3.9 (0.45)
Singapore	542 (1.4)	2.8 (0.24)	8.7 (0.52)	17.5 (0.58)	25.4 (0.83)	25.7 (0.70)	15.3 (0.67)	4.6 (0.50)
Chinese Taipei	520 (2.6)	2.2 (0.34)	8.9 (0.60)	21.1 (0.91)	33.3 (1.04)	25.8 (1.10)	8.0 (0.74)	0.8 (0.22)
Thailand	425 (3.0)	12.2 (1.10)	30.6 (1.01)	34.7 (1.34)	17.5 (0.95)	4.4 (0.51)	0.6 (0.27)	# (†)
Trinidad and Tobago	410 (1.2)	25.1 (0.87)	24.9 (0.92)	25.2 (0.88)	16.0 (0.79)	7.1 (0.40)	1.8 (0.23)	0.1 (0.07)
Tunisia	401 (2.7)	21.3 (1.17)	32.4 (1.08)	30.9 (1.00)	13.0 (0.85)	2.2 (0.43)	0.2 (0.12)	# (†)
Uruguay	427 (2.6)	17.0 (0.94)	25.6 (0.86)	29.3 (1.01)	19.5 (1.02)	7.1 (0.51)	1.4 (0.22)	0.1 (0.04)

†Not applicable.
#Rounds to zero.
‡Reporting standards not met.
[1] Level 1: Able to present scientific explanations that are obvious and that follow explicitly from given evidence. Level 2: Able to provide possible explanations in familiar contexts, draw conclusions based on simple investigations, and make literal interpretations of the results of scientific inquiry or technological problem solving. Level 3: Able to select facts to explain phenomena and apply simple models or inquiry strategies, develop short statements using facts, and make decisions based on scientific knowledge. Level 4: Able to select and integrate explanations from different disciplines of science or technology, link those explanations directly to aspects of life situations, and communicate decisions using scientific knowledge and evidence. Level 5: Able to apply scientific concepts and knowledge to many complex life situations, select and evaluate appropriate scientific evidence, bring critical insights to situations, and construct explanations based on evidence and arguments based on critical analysis. Level 6: Able to consistently explain and apply scientific knowledge in a variety of complex life situations; use evidence from different sources to justify decisions; clearly and consis-

tently demonstrate advanced scientific thinking and reasoning; and develop arguments in support of recommendations and decisions that center on personal, social, or global situations.
[2] Illustrates how a country compares with the OECD area as a whole. Computed by taking the OECD countries as a single entity to which each country contributes in proportion to the number of 15-year-olds enrolled in its schools.
[3] Refers to the mean of the data values for all OECD countries, to which each country contributes equally, regardless of the absolute size of the student population of each country.
NOTE: PISA scores are reported on a scale from 0 to 1,000. Detail may not sum to totals because of rounding. Standard errors appear in parentheses.
SOURCE: Organization for Economic Cooperation and Development (OECD), Program for International Student Assessment (PISA), 2009, PISA 2009 Results: What Students Know and Can Do—Student Performance in Reading, Mathematics and Science (Volume I). (This table was prepared December 2010.)

Percentage of the population 25 to 64 years old who completed high school, by age group and country: 2001, 2005, and 2009

Country	2001 Total, 25 to 64 years old	2001 25 to 34 years old	2001 35 to 44 years old	2001 45 to 54 years old	2001 55 to 64 years old	2005 Total, 25 to 64 years old	2005 25 to 34 years old	2009 Total, 25 to 64 years old		2009 25 to 34 years old		2009 35 to 44 years old		2009 45 to 54 years old		2009 55 to 64 years old	
1	2	3	4	5	6	7	8	9		10		11		12		13	
OECD average[1]	**64.2**	**74.0**	**68.4**	**60.2**	**48.6**	**72.8**	**82.6**	**73.3**	**(0.03)**	**81.5**	**(0.06)**	**77.0**	**(0.06)**	**70.5**	**(0.07)**	**61.3**	**(0.08)**
Australia	58.9	70.7	60.2	54.6	43.8	65.0	78.6	71.0	(0.29)	82.9	(0.49)	73.3	(0.55)	66.8	(0.59)	58.0	(0.70)
Austria[2,3]	75.7	83.3	80.4	71.9	62.5	80.6	87.5	81.9	(0.12)	88.4	(0.22)	85.1	(0.21)	80.4	(0.23)	71.7	(0.30)
Belgium[2]	58.5	75.3	62.6	51.3	38.4	66.1	80.9	70.6	(0.19)	83.1	(0.33)	77.7	(0.33)	66.6	(0.37)	53.7	(0.42)
Canada[4]	81.9	89.3	84.9	81.0	66.6	85.2	90.8	87.6	(0.12)	92.0	(0.20)	90.8	(0.21)	86.6	(0.23)	80.4	(0.31)
Chile[4]	—	—	—	—	—	50.0	64.3	69.0	(0.19)	85.6	(0.24)	74.7	(0.28)	66.3	(0.32)	42.7	(0.40)
Czech Republic	86.2	92.5	89.8	84.0	76.3	89.9	93.9	91.4	(0.08)	94.2	(0.14)	94.4	(0.13)	90.5	(0.17)	85.9	(0.18)
Denmark	80.2	86.3	80.4	80.4	71.9	81.0	87.4	76.3	(0.17)	85.7	(0.43)	81.3	(0.40)	70.7	(0.34)	68.0	(0.29)
Estonia	—	—	—	—	—	89.1	87.4	88.9	(0.31)	86.3	(0.73)	92.4	(0.49)	92.9	(0.46)	83.3	(0.77)
Finland	73.8	86.8	84.3	70.0	50.9	78.8	89.4	82.0	(0.12)	90.4	(0.21)	88.4	(0.21)	83.6	(0.23)	67.5	(0.29)
France[5]	63.9	78.4	67.4	58.3	46.2	66.3	81.1	70.0	(0.10)	83.9	(0.17)	76.9	(0.18)	64.1	(0.20)	54.7	(0.21)
Germany	82.6	85.5	85.5	82.9	75.8	83.1	84.1	85.5	(0.06)	86.0	(0.13)	86.8	(0.11)	85.9	(0.11)	82.7	(0.13)
Greece	51.4	72.6	60.3	43.1	27.6	57.1	73.6	61.2	(0.12)	74.9	(0.23)	69.3	(0.23)	56.8	(0.24)	39.5	(0.25)
Hungary	70.2	80.9	78.5	71.8	44.1	76.4	85.0	80.6	(0.10)	86.0	(0.18)	82.9	(0.20)	79.8	(0.20)	72.5	(0.22)
Iceland	56.9	61.2	60.2	55.5	45.6	62.9	69.0	65.9	(0.50)	70.0	(0.93)	70.6	(0.98)	63.8	(0.97)	56.7	(1.14)
Ireland	57.6	73.4	62.4	48.2	35.3	64.5	81.1	71.5	(0.12)	85.8	(0.18)	77.2	(0.21)	64.6	(0.26)	47.6	(0.30)
Israel	—	—	—	—	—	79.2	85.7	81.8	(0.15)	87.4	(0.25)	83.9	(0.29)	77.9	(0p.34)	74.3	(0.37)
Italy	43.3	57.5	49.3	38.5	21.8	50.1	65.9	54.3	(0.08)	70.3	(0.17)	57.9	(0.16)	50.4	(0.16)	36.7	(0.16)
Japan	83.1	93.6	94.0	81.1	62.8	—	—	—	(†)	—	(†)	—	(†)	—	(†)	—	(†)
Korea, Republic of	68.0	94.6	76.8	49.1	29.9	75.5	97.3	79.9	(0.20)	97.5	(0.15)	94.1	(0.22)	71.0	(0.44)	42.6	(0.63)
Luxembourg	52.7	59.4	56.7	47.1	42.1	65.9	76.5	77.3	(0.41)	83.8	(0.80)	78.8	(0.70)	74.4	(0.80)	70.5	(0.99)
Mexico	21.6	25.4	24.7	17.5	11.1	21.3	24.0	35.2	(0.06)	41.9	(0.12)	37.2	(0.12)	32.4	(0.13)	21.3	(0.14)
Netherlands[2,5]	65.0	74.0	69.0	60.0	51.0	71.8	81.3	73.4	(0.09)	82.4	(0.17)	77.6	(0.16)	71.4	(0.17)	62.5	(0.20)
New Zealand	75.7	81.8	79.5	75.1	60.1	78.7	85.2	72.2	(0.43)	79.3	(0.84)	75.5	(0.79)	70.5	(0.84)	61.5	(0.97)
Norway[2]	85.2	93.4	90.3	81.9	69.9	77.2	83.5	80.7	(0.16)	83.6	(0.33)	83.1	(0.29)	77.3	(0.34)	78.7	(0.34)
Poland	45.9	51.7	47.5	44.5	36.4	51.4	62.5	88.0	(0.10)	93.5	(0.15)	91.5	(0.17)	88.0	(0.18)	77.5	(0.25)
Portugal	19.9	32.5	19.9	13.6	8.5	26.5	42.8	29.9	(0.16)	48.2	(0.38)	31.4	(0.32)	21.9	(0.26)	14.1	(0.23)
Slovak Republic	85.1	93.7	89.9	82.9	66.0	85.7	93.0	90.9	(0.12)	94.8	(0.19)	94.2	(0.20)	89.8	(0.25)	82.8	(0.30)
Slovenia	—	—	—	—	—	80.3	91.2	83.3	(0.19)	93.5	(0.27)	85.0	(0.39)	79.6	(0.37)	73.8	(0.46)
Spain	40.0	57.1	44.7	29.0	17.1	48.8	63.9	51.8	(0.08)	64.1	(0.16)	58.0	(0.15)	46.5	(0.16)	30.3	(0.16)
Sweden	80.6	90.7	86.3	78.4	65.1	83.6	90.6	85.8	(0.09)	91.2	(0.16)	90.8	(0.14)	85.4	(0.18)	75.7	(0.21)
Switzerland	87.4	91.8	90.0	85.1	80.6	83.0	87.9	86.9	(0.19)	90.0	(0.36)	88.4	(0.32)	86.1	(0.38)	82.5	(0.45)
Turkey	24.3	30.2	23.5	19.2	13.3	27.2	35.7	31.1	(0.09)	41.6	(0.18)	27.7	(0.17)	24.7	(0.18)	19.3	(0.20)
United Kingdom[3,5]	63.0	68.0	65.0	61.2	55.1	66.7	72.9	73.7	(0.09)	81.6	(0.17)	76.5	(0.17)	71.7	(0.18)	64.0	(0.20)
United States	87.7	88.1	88.7	89.2	82.6	87.8	86.7	88.6	(0.12)	88.3	(0.19)	88.3	(0.18)	89.1	(0.21)	88.9	(0.20)
Other reporting countries																	
Brazil[4]	—	—	—	—	—	29.5	38.0	40.7	(0.11)	52.5	(0.19)	42.0	(0.21)	33.5	(0.22)	24.5	(0.24)
Russian Federation[6]	88.0	91.0	93.7	89.4	71.2	—	—	—	(†)	—	(†)	—	(†)	—	(†)	—	(†)

—Not available.
†Not applicable.
[1]Refers to the mean of the data values for all reporting OECD countries, to which each country reporting data contributes equally. The average includes all current OECD countries for which a given year's data are available, even if they were not members of OECD in that year.
[2]Data from 2000 reported for 2001.
[3]Data in 2005 columns include some ISCED 3C short programs.
[4]Data from 2004 reported for 2005.
[5]Data in 2001 columns include some ISCED 3C short programs.

[6]Data from 2002 reported for 2001.
NOTE: Data in this table refer to degrees classified by the Organization for Economic Cooperation and Development (OECD) as International Standard Classification of Education (ISCED) level 3. ISCED level 3 corresponds to high school completion in the United States. ISCED 3C short programs do not correspond to high school completion; these short programs are excluded from this table except where otherwise noted. Standard errors appear in parentheses.
SOURCE: Organization for Economic Cooperation and Development (OECD), *Education at a Glance*, 2002, 2007, and 2011. (This table was prepared June 2011.)

Percentage of the population 25 to 64 years old who attained selected levels of postsecondary education, by age group and country: 2001 and 2009

Country	Total, any postsecondary degree — 2001 — Total, 25 to 64 years old	2001 — 25 to 34 years	2009 — Total, 25 to 64 years old	2009 — 25 to 34 years old	Vocational degree[1] (2009) — Total, 25 to 64 years old	25 to 34 years old	35 to 44 years old	45 to 54 years old	55 to 64 years old	Bachelor's or higher degree[2] (2009) — Total, 25 to 64 years old	25 to 34 years old	35 to 44 years old	45 to 54 years old	55 to 64 years old
	2	3	4	5	6	7	8	9	10	11	12	13	14	15
OECD average[3]	22.6	27.3	30.0 (0.04)	37.1 (0.08)	10.4 (0.03)	11.0 (0.07)	11.3 (0.06)	10.2 (0.06)	8.2 (0.06)	21.4 (0.03)	27.7 (0.08)	22.8 (0.07)	18.6 (0.06)	15.6 (0.06)
Australia	29.0	33.5	36.9 (0.31)	44.8 (0.65)	10.1 (0.20)	10.2 (0.39)	10.8 (0.38)	9.8 (0.37)	9.4 (0.41)	26.8 (0.29)	34.6 (0.62)	27.2 (0.55)	23.8 (0.54)	19.9 (0.57)
Austria	14.1	14.3	19.0 (0.12)	21.1 (0.28)	7.6 (0.08)	5.8 (0.16)	8.0 (0.16)	8.7 (0.16)	7.7 (0.18)	11.4 (0.10)	15.3 (0.25)	12.3 (0.19)	9.6 (0.17)	8.2 (0.18)
Belgium	27.6	37.5	33.4 (0.19)	42.5 (0.44)	15.9 (0.15)	18.3 (0.34)	17.6 (0.31)	15.4 (0.28)	12.0 (0.27)	17.5 (0.16)	24.2 (0.38)	19.3 (0.32)	14.9 (0.28)	11.4 (0.27)
Canada[4]	41.6	50.5	49.5 (0.18)	56.1 (0.36)	24.1 (0.16)	26.0 (0.32)	26.6 (0.31)	23.8 (0.29)	19.6 (0.31)	25.4 (0.16)	30.1 (0.34)	29.1 (0.32)	21.4 (0.28)	21.1 (0.32)
Chile[4]	10.1	12.3	24.4 (0.18)	34.9 (0.33)	8.0 (0.11)	11.0 (0.22)	10.0 (0.20)	6.7 (0.17)	3.1 (0.14)	16.4 (0.15)	24.0 (0.30)	14.2 (0.23)	13.6 (0.23)	13.5 (0.28)
Czech Republic[5]	11.1	11.3	15.5 (0.10)	20.2 (0.23)	[5]	[5]	[5]	[5]	[5]	15.5 (0.10)	20.2 (0.23)	14.8 (0.20)	15.6 (0.20)	10.8 (0.16)
Denmark[5]	26.8	27.5	34.3 (0.19)	44.7 (0.62)	7.2 (0.11)	8.5 (0.35)	7.9 (0.28)	6.8 (0.19)	5.7 (0.15)	27.1 (0.18)	36.2 (0.60)	31.0 (0.47)	21.5 (0.30)	20.1 (0.25)
Estonia	—	38.2	36.0 (0.47)	36.6 (1.02)	13.2 (0.33)	14.8 (0.75)	11.0 (0.58)	15.2 (0.65)	11.5 (0.66)	22.7 (0.41)	21.7 (0.87)	25.3 (0.80)	22.5 (0.75)	21.3 (0.85)
Finland	32.3	38.2	37.3 (0.16)	39.4 (0.34)	14.7 (0.11)	3.4 (0.13)	19.3 (0.26)	20.1 (0.25)	15.3 (0.22)	22.6 (0.13)	36.0 (0.87)	25.2 (0.29)	17.4 (0.23)	13.7 (0.21)
France	23.0	34.2	28.9 (0.10)	43.2 (0.23)	11.6 (0.07)	17.5 (0.18)	13.5 (0.15)	9.5 (0.12)	6.0 (0.10)	17.3 (0.08)	25.7 (0.20)	18.8 (0.17)	12.7 (0.14)	12.0 (0.14)
Germany	23.2	21.8	26.4 (0.07)	29.4 (0.16)	9.3 (0.05)	6.8 (0.09)	9.8 (0.09)	10.5 (0.09)	9.7 (0.10)	17.1 (0.06)	18.9 (0.14)	18.0 (0.12)	15.9 (0.11)	15.6 (0.12)
Greece	17.8	24.0	23.5 (0.11)	29.4 (0.24)	6.7 (0.06)	10.1 (0.16)	7.7 (0.13)	5.3 (0.09)	2.7 (0.08)	16.9 (0.09)	19.3 (0.21)	18.6 (0.19)	16.3 (0.18)	12.3 (0.16)
Hungary	14.1	14.7	19.9 (0.10)	25.1 (0.23)	#	1.0	#	#	#	19.4 (0.10)	24.1 (0.23)	18.6 (0.20)	18.1 (0.19)	16.2 (0.18)
Iceland	24.8	26.6	32.8 (0.50)	35.8 (0.98)	3.9 (0.21)	2.5 (0.31)	5.6 (0.50)	4.3 (0.41)	3.2 (0.41)	28.8 (0.48)	33.4 (0.96)	32.5 (1.01)	27.4 (0.90)	19.5 (0.91)
Ireland	35.6	47.8	35.9 (0.10)	47.6 (0.26)	14.9 (0.10)	18.7 (0.20)	16.9 (0.19)	12.2 (0.18)	8.9 (0.17)	20.9 (0.11)	28.8 (0.23)	22.5 (0.21)	16.0 (0.20)	11.4 (0.19)
Israel	—	—	44.9 (0.20)	42.9 (0.37)	15.5 (0.14)	13.4 (0.26)	16.3 (0.29)	16.4 (0.30)	16.7 (0.32)	29.4 (0.18)	29.5 (0.35)	30.8 (0.36)	28.5 (0.37)	28.4 (0.39)
Italy	10.0	11.8	14.5 (0.06)	20.2 (0.15)	#	#	#	#	#	14.1 (0.06)	19.9 (0.15)	15.0 (0.12)	11.4 (0.10)	10.0 (0.10)
Japan	33.8	47.7	43.8 (0.13)	55.7 (0.29)	19.1 (0.11)	23.9 (0.25)	23.4 (0.22)	18.6 (0.21)	11.0 (0.15)	24.6 (0.11)	31.8 (0.27)	25.3 (0.23)	26.1 (0.24)	16.4 (0.18)
Korea, Republic of	24.2	39.5	38.8 (0.25)	63.1 (0.47)	11.6 (0.16)	25.5 (0.42)	11.5 (0.30)	5.2 (0.30)	1.4 (0.15)	27.1 (0.23)	37.6 (0.47)	32.8 (0.44)	20.5 (0.39)	11.9 (0.41)
Luxembourg	18.1	23.4	34.8 (0.46)	44.5 (1.08)	14.6 (0.34)	20.4 (0.87)	14.8 (0.60)	11.3 (0.58)	11.3 (0.69)	20.2 (0.39)	24.1 (0.93)	23.1 (0.72)	17.7 (0.70)	13.6 (0.75)
Mexico[5]	15.0	17.9	15.9 (0.05)	20.2 (0.10)	1.1 (0.01)	1.2 (0.03)	1.1 (0.03)	1.2 (0.03)	0.7 (0.03)	15.9 (0.05)	20.2 (0.22)	14.9 (0.09)	15.1 (0.10)	9.8 (0.10)
Netherlands	23.2	26.5	32.8 (0.09)	40.1 (0.22)	2.8 (0.03)	2.5 (0.07)	3.3 (0.07)	2.8 (0.06)	2.3 (0.06)	30.0 (0.09)	37.6 (0.22)	30.3 (0.18)	28.0 (0.17)	25.1 (0.18)
New Zealand	29.2	28.5	40.1 (0.47)	46.7 (1.04)	16.9 (0.36)	15.9 (0.76)	15.7 (0.67)	18.3 (0.71)	17.9 (0.77)	23.2 (0.41)	30.8 (0.96)	25.5 (0.81)	19.5 (0.73)	15.8 (0.73)
Norway	30.2	37.9	36.7 (0.20)	46.8 (0.45)	2.2 (0.06)	1.4 (0.11)	1.9 (0.11)	2.7 (0.13)	2.8 (0.14)	34.5 (0.20)	45.5 (0.45)	37.8 (0.38)	30.1 (0.37)	24.4 (0.35)
Poland[5]	11.9	15.2	21.2 (0.12)	35.4 (0.27)	[5]	[5]	[5]	[5]	[5]	21.2 (0.12)	35.4 (0.29)	20.9 (0.25)	13.1 (0.19)	12.6 (0.19)
Portugal[5]	9.0	13.7	14.7 (0.12)	23.3 (0.32)	[5]	[5]	[5]	[5]	[5]	14.7 (0.12)	23.3 (0.32)	15.1 (0.24)	11.0 (0.20)	7.4 (0.17)
Slovak Republic	10.9	11.9	15.8 (0.15)	20.6 (0.35)	0.8 (0.04)	0.9 (0.08)	0.6 (0.07)	0.8 (0.07)	1.0 (0.08)	15.0 (0.15)	19.7 (0.34)	14.0 (0.30)	13.3 (0.28)	11.2 (0.25)
Slovenia	—	—	23.3 (0.22)	30.4 (0.50)	10.8 (0.16)	11.7 (0.35)	11.8 (0.35)	10.0 (0.28)	9.4 (0.31)	12.6 (0.17)	18.7 (0.42)	14.2 (0.38)	9.4 (0.27)	7.3 (0.27)
Spain	23.6	35.5	29.7 (0.07)	38.2 (0.16)	9.5 (0.05)	13.2 (0.11)	11.4 (0.10)	7.2 (0.08)	4.1 (0.07)	20.1 (0.07)	25.0 (0.15)	22.2 (0.13)	18.0 (0.12)	12.5 (0.11)
Sweden	31.6	36.9	33.0 (0.12)	42.3 (0.27)	8.7 (0.07)	8.5 (0.15)	8.3 (0.14)	9.4 (0.15)	8.9 (0.14)	24.3 (0.11)	33.9 (0.26)	26.3 (0.22)	19.3 (0.20)	18.0 (0.19)
Switzerland	25.4	25.6	35.0 (0.27)	40.0 (0.60)	10.3 (0.17)	9.4 (0.36)	11.6 (0.32)	10.6 (0.34)	9.2 (0.34)	24.7 (0.24)	30.5 (0.56)	26.3 (0.44)	22.4 (0.46)	19.1 (0.46)
Turkey[5]	8.9	10.2	12.7 (0.07)	16.6 (0.13)	[5]	[5]	[5]	[5]	[5]	12.7 (0.07)	16.6 (0.13)	11.3 (0.12)	9.7 (0.12)	9.9 (0.15)
United Kingdom	26.0	30.0	36.9 (0.10)	44.9 (0.22)	10.0 (0.06)	8.5 (0.12)	11.0 (0.12)	10.8 (0.13)	9.5 (0.12)	26.9 (0.09)	36.3 (0.21)	28.0 (0.18)	23.3 (0.17)	19.2 (0.16)
United States	37.3	39.1	41.2 (0.19)	41.1 (0.33)	9.8 (0.08)	8.9 (0.15)	10.2 (0.15)	10.8 (0.16)	9.2 (0.17)	31.4 (0.16)	32.1 (0.32)	32.9 (0.26)	29.1 (0.29)	31.7 (0.33)
Other reporting countries														
Brazil[4,5]	7.7	6.7	10.9 (0.07)	11.6 (0.12)	[5]	[5]	[5]	[5]	[5]	10.9 (0.07)	11.6 (0.12)	11.3 (0.13)	10.7 (0.14)	8.9 (0.16)
China[4]	4.6	6.1	—	—	(†)	(†)	(†)	(†)	(†)	—	(†)	—	(†)	(†)
Russian Federation[6]	54.0	55.5	—	—	(†)	(†)	(†)	(†)	(†)	—	(†)	—	(†)	(†)

—Not available.
†Not applicable.
#Rounds to zero.

[1] International Standard Classification of Education (ISCED) level 5B corresponds to the associate's degree in the United States in this table.
[2] ISCED 5A, first award, corresponds to the bachelor's degree in the United States; ISCED 5A, second award, corresponds to master's and first-professional degrees in the United States; and ISCED 6 corresponds to doctor's degrees.
[3] Refers to the mean of the data values for all reporting OECD countries, to which each country reporting data contributes equally. The average includes all current OECD countries for which a given year's data are available, even if they were not members of OECD in that year.
[4] Data from 2000 reported for 2001.
[5] Columns for bachelor's or higher degree include vocational degree data.
[6] Data from 2002 shown for 2001.
NOTE: Standard errors appear in parentheses.
SOURCE: Organization for Economic Cooperation and Development (OECD), Education at a Glance, 2002 and 2011. (This table was prepared June 2011.)

Percentage of the population 25 to 64 years old who attained a bachelor's or higher level degree, by age group and country: Selected years, 1999 through 2009

Country	1999 Total 25–64	1999 25–34	2001 Total 25–64	2001 25–34	2002 Total 25–64	2002 25–34	2003 Total 25–64	2003 25–34	2004 Total 25–64	2004 25–34	2005 Total 25–64	2005 25–34	2006 Total 25–64	2006 25–34	2007 Total 25–64	2007 25–34	2008 Total 25–64	2008 25–34	2009 Total 25–64	2009 25–34
1	2	3	4	5	6	7	8	9	10	11	12	13	14	15	16	17	18	19	20	21
OECD average[1]	**14.0**	**16.5**	**15.1**	**18.2**	**16.1**	**19.6**	**16.9**	**21.0**	**17.9**	**22.2**	**18.8**	**23.9**	**19.5**	**24.6**	**20.0**	**25.4**	**20.8**	**26.6**	**21.4 (0.03)**	**27.7 (0.08)**
Australia	17.7	20.1	19.2	23.9	20.0	24.7	20.5	24.9	21.9	27.0	22.7	29.2	23.8	29.2	24.1	30.6	25.5	31.9	26.8 (0.29)	34.6 (0.62)
Austria[2]	6.1	6.8	6.8	6.9	7.0	7.3	7.3	8.4	9.2	11.1	9.1	11.6	10.1	12.9	10.4	13.3	10.7	13.5	11.4 (0.10)	15.3 (0.25)
Belgium	12.0	16.0	12.7	17.8	12.8	17.8	13.0	18.2	13.6	19.1	13.8	19.4	14.1	19.1	14.0	18.2	16.4	22.8	17.5 (0.16)	24.2 (0.38)
Canada	19.1	23.1	20.4	25.1	21.0	26.1	22.0	27.5	22.2	27.5	23.3	29.3	24.0	—	24.6	29.5	25.2	29.8	25.4 (0.16)	30.1 (0.34)
Chile[2,3]	8.2	9.6	9.0	10.7	11.3	14.5	11.9	15.5	10.3	14.2	—	—	—	—	—	—	15.7	22.3	16.4 (0.15)	24.0 (0.30)
Czech Republic[4]	10.8	10.9	11.1	11.3	11.9	12.3	11.7	11.7	12.3	13.0	13.1	14.2	13.5	15.2	13.7	15.5	14.5	17.7	15.5 (0.10)	20.2 (0.23)
Denmark	—	—	21.5	21.7	22.8	23.4	25.0	27.2	25.2	27.2	26.0	30.7	27.1	—	25.5	32.0	27.5	34.9	27.1 (0.18)	36.2 (0.60)
Estonia	—	—	—	—	—	—	—	—	—	—	22.2	24.1	22.2	24.1	22.2	25.2	22.3	23.5	22.7 (0.41)	21.7 (0.87)
Finland[5]	13.9	15.6	14.8	18.0	15.6	20.5	16.4	23.1	17.1	23.8	18.1	26.6	19.2	29.4	20.9	31.8	21.5	32.9	22.6 (0.13)	36.0 (0.34)
France	11.0	15.3	11.9	17.5	12.4	18.6	14.2	21.9	14.3	22.0	14.8	23.7	15.6	23.7	15.9	23.8	16.4	23.7	17.3 (0.08)	25.7 (0.20)
Germany	13.0	12.9	13.5	13.5	13.4	13.5	14.1	14.0	14.7	14.8	14.8	15.1	15.1	15.1	15.6	16.1	16.4	17.5	17.1 (0.06)	18.9 (0.14)
Greece	12.2	16.6	12.4	16.6	12.7	16.9	12.6	16.9	14.6	17.2	14.5	17.7	15.1	15.1	15.4	18.7	16.8	18.6	16.9 (0.09)	19.3 (0.21)
Hungary[5]	13.5	13.7	14.1	14.7	14.2	14.8	15.3	15.3	16.7	18.9	16.9	19.1	17.4	20.1	17.7	21.1	18.7	22.9	19.4 (0.10)	24.1 (0.23)
Iceland[2]	17.8	22.3	18.8	21.1	19.9	22.9	—	—	23.5	28.2	25.9	32.5	25.6	28.5	26.1	27.9	27.9	30.6	28.8 (0.48)	33.4 (0.96)
Ireland[2]	10.6	16.1	14.0	19.8	15.9	22.8	16.3	23.0	17.8	25.8	18.4	26.2	19.9	28.3	21.1	29.9	22.2	30.6	20.9 (0.11)	28.8 (0.23)
Israel[5]	—	—	—	—	25.9	25.4	27.0	27.2	29.4	34.2	29.8	34.8	29.8	29.8	28.3	28.1	28.8	28.9	29.4 (0.18)	29.5 (0.35)
Italy[5]	9.3	10.0	10.0	11.8	10.4	12.5	—	—	11.4	14.6	11.7	15.5	12.4	16.7	13.0	18.3	14.0	19.6	14.1 (0.06)	19.9 (0.15)
Japan	18.3	23.0	19.2	24.3	20.1	25.0	20.9	26.4	—	—	22.3	27.9	23.0	29.7	23.1	29.0	24.3	30.9	24.6 (0.11)	31.8 (0.27)
Korea, Republic of	16.9	23.2	17.5	25.0	18.5	25.8	—	—	22.0	30.8	22.7	31.7	23.5	32.9	24.4	33.9	25.6	34.5	27.1 (0.23)	37.6 (0.47)
Luxembourg	11.7	13.1	11.4	15.1	11.6	14.0	—	—	13.5	17.5	17.0	23.8	16.4	—	17.7	23.8	20.0	27.9	20.2 (0.39)	24.1 (0.93)
Mexico	11.9	14.1	13.3	15.3	—	—	13.6	16.0	14.4	16.3	13.8	17.0	14.4	17.5	14.9	18.4	14.9	18.5	15.9 (0.05)	20.2 (0.10)
Netherlands	20.1	22.7	20.9	24.1	21.9	25.3	—	—	26.9	31.8	28.3	33.8	28.4	34.3	29.1	35.1	29.8	37.5	30.0 (0.09)	37.6 (0.22)
New Zealand[2]	13.1	15.6	13.9	16.9	14.8	17.6	16.1	20.7	17.6	22.8	19.7	26.2	23.0	29.3	25.3	33.0	25.1	33.6	23.2 (0.41)	30.8 (0.96)
Norway[2]	25.3	30.6	27.6	35.4	28.4	37.4	28.5	37.4	29.4	37.0	30.3	38.9	30.5	39.8	31.9	40.8	33.6	43.8	34.5 (0.20)	45.5 (0.45)
Poland[2,4]	11.3	12.3	11.9	15.2	12.1	15.6	14.2	20.4	15.7	23.2	16.9	25.5	17.9	29.5	18.7	30.0	19.6	32.1	21.2 (0.12)	35.4 (0.29)
Portugal[6]	7.1	9.3	6.6	10.3	7.1	10.4	8.4	11.2	12.5	18.6	12.8	19.1	13.5	20.1	13.7	21.4	14.3	23.2	14.7 (0.12)	23.3 (0.32)
Slovak Republic	—	—	10.3	11.2	10.4	11.4	11.2	12.6	11.8	13.6	12.8	15.4	13.3	15.2	13.3	16.8	14.0	17.8	15.0 (0.15)	19.7 (0.34)
Slovenia	—	—	—	—	—	—	—	—	—	—	—	—	10.6	—	11.7	17.6	11.8	18.4	12.6 (0.17)	18.7 (0.42)
Spain	14.8	22.1	16.9	19.7	17.3	24.7	17.9	24.7	18.9	26.6	19.9	27.0	19.8	26.0	20.0	26.0	20.0	25.7	20.1 (0.07)	25.0 (0.15)
Sweden	13.1	11.1	16.9	19.7	17.7	22.0	18.5	22.0	19.3	25.9	20.6	28.4	21.7	30.6	22.6	31.5	23.4	32.4	24.3 (0.11)	33.9 (0.26)
Switzerland	14.5	16.6	15.8	15.9	16.2	16.9	16.9	18.6	18.1	20.2	19.0	21.9	19.9	23.1	21.3	25.6	23.3	28.8	24.7 (0.24)	30.5 (0.56)
Turkey[4]	7.1	7.6	8.9	10.2	9.3	9.7	9.7	10.6	9.1	10.8	9.7	11.8	10.4	11.8	10.8	13.6	12.0	15.5	12.7 (0.07)	16.6 (0.13)
United Kingdom	16.6	18.8	18.0	18.0	18.6	23.1	19.3	23.1	20.2	25.9	20.8	26.9	21.7	28.3	22.7	29.4	23.6	30.7	26.9 (0.09)	36.3 (0.21)
United States	27.5	28.7	28.3	29.9	29.0	30.6	29.4	30.6	29.7	30.2	29.6	30.3	29.9	29.9	30.9	31.0	31.5	32.3	31.4 (0.16)	32.1 (0.32)
Other reporting countries																				
Brazil[2,4]	7.5	6.5	7.6	—	8.2	7.2	—	—	7.8	7.9	—	—	—	—	9.6	—	10.0	—	10.9 (0.07)	11.6 (0.12)
Russian Federation	—	—	—	—	20.8	21.3	—	—	—	—	—	—	—	—	—	—	—	—	— (†)	— (†)

—Not available.
†Not applicable.
[1]Refers to the mean of the data values for all reporting OECD countries, to which each country reporting data contributes equally. The average includes all current OECD members for which a given year's data are available, even if they were not members of OECD in that year.
[2]Data from 1998 reported for 1999.
[3]Data from 2000 reported for 2001.
[4]Data include vocational degrees.
[5]Data for 1999 to 2004 include vocational degrees.
[6]Data for 2004 to 2009 include vocational degrees.
NOTE: Data in this table refer to degrees classified by OECD as International Standard Classification of Education (ISCED) level 5A (first and second award) and as level 6. ISCED 5A, first award, corresponds to the bachelor's degree in the United States; ISCED 5A, second award, corresponds to master's and first-professional degrees in the United States; and ISCED 6 corresponds to doctor's degrees. Standard errors appear in parentheses.
SOURCE: Organization for Economic Cooperation and Development (OECD), *Education at a Glance*, 2001 through 2011. (This table was prepared July 2011.)

Percentage of the population 25 to 64 years old who attained a postsecondary vocational degree, by age group and country: Selected years, 1999 through 2009

Country	1999 Total, 25 to 64	1999 25 to 34	2001 Total, 25 to 64	2001 25 to 34	2002 Total, 25 to 64	2002 25 to 34	2003 Total, 25 to 64	2003 25 to 34	2004 Total, 25 to 64	2004 25 to 34	2005 Total, 25 to 64	2005 25 to 34	2006 Total, 25 to 64	2006 25 to 34	2007 Total, 25 to 64	2007 25 to 34	2008 Total, 25 to 64	2008 25 to 34	2009 Total, 25 to 64	2009 25 to 34
1	2	3	4	5	6	7	8	9	10	11	12	13	14	15	16	17	18	19	20	21
OECD average[1]	**8.4**	**10.5**	**8.9**	**10.8**	**9.0**	**10.7**	**9.5**	**11.2**	**9.0**	**10.3**	**8.8**	**9.8**	**9.0**	**10.0**	**9.4**	**10.1**	**9.7**	**10.4**	**10.4 (0.03)**	**11.0 (0.07)**
Australia	9.0	8.8	9.7	9.7	10.7	11.1	10.8	11.4	8.9	9.2	9.0	9.6	9.2	9.6	9.6	10.2	10.1	9.8	10.1 (0.20)	10.2 (0.39)
Austria[2]	4.7	5.8	7.3	7.4	7.5	7.5	7.2	7.0	9.2	9.1	8.7	8.1	7.5	6.3	7.2	5.6	7.4	5.9	7.6 (0.08)	5.8 (0.16)
Belgium	13.9	17.9	14.9	19.7	15.3	19.9	16.0	20.7	16.8	22.1	17.3	22.5	17.7	22.5	18.1	23.1	15.9	19.5	15.9 (0.15)	18.3 (0.34)
Canada	20.2	23.7	21.2	25.4	21.6	25.1	22.0	25.3	22.4	25.6	22.8	25.5	22.9	25.5	23.7	26.3	23.6	26.1	24.1 (0.16)	26.0 (0.32)
Chile[2,3]	0.9	1.4	1.0	1.6	1.5	2.3	1.2	1.7	2.8	4.1	—	—	—	—	—	—	8.5	11.5	8.0 (0.11)	11.0 (0.22)
Denmark	—	—	5.3	5.8	5.1	5.8	6.9	7.8	7.2	7.7	7.6	9.1	7.6	9.1	6.7	8.1	7.0	8.2	7.2 (0.11)	8.5 (0.35)
Estonia	—	—	—	—	—	—	—	—	—	—	11.1	8.7	11.1	8.7	11.1	9.4	12.0	12.3	13.2 (0.33)	14.8 (0.75)
Finland	17.4	21.8	17.5	20.2	17.0	18.7	16.9	16.7	16.9	14.2	16.6	11.0	15.9	9.0	15.4	7.5	15.0	5.4	14.7 (0.11)	3.4 (0.13)
France	10.5	15.6	11.2	16.7	11.6	17.4	9.2	15.5	9.6	16.0	10.0	17.7	10.6	17.0	10.9	17.7	11.1	16.9	11.6 (0.07)	17.5 (0.18)
Germany	9.9	8.6	9.7	8.2	10.0	8.3	9.9	7.8	10.3	8.1	9.7	6.8	8.9	6.8	8.7	6.5	9.0	6.5	9.3 (0.05)	6.8 (0.09)
Greece	5.5	8.6	5.4	7.4	5.7	7.1	5.7	7.1	6.0	7.4	6.7	8.4	7.0	9.0	7.4	9.4	6.6	9.6	6.7 (0.06)	10.1 (0.16)
Hungary	—	—	—	—	—	—	—	—	—	—	0.2	0.5	0.3	0.6	#	0.9	#	1.0	# (†)	1.0 (#)
Iceland	4.6	5.3	6.0	5.5	6.3	6.1	—	—	4.3	3.1	4.7	3.3	3.9	3.0	3.7	3.2	3.4	2.2	3.9 (0.21)	2.5 (0.31)
Ireland[2]	10.5	13.4	21.6	28.1	9.5	13.5	10.0	14.1	10.5	14.5	10.6	14.4	10.9	14.0	11.1	14.0	11.7	14.5	14.9 (0.10)	18.7 (0.20)
Israel	—	—	—	—	16.2	15.3	15.9	14.8	15.9	15.1	16.0	15.1	16.0	15.1	15.2	13.4	15.1	13.4	15.5 (0.14)	13.4 (0.26)
Italy	13.4	—	—	—	—	—	—	—	—	—	0.5	0.6	0.5	0.6	0.5	0.6	#	#	# (†)	# (†)
Japan	—	22.1	—	23.4	16.2	25.3	16.5	25.2	—	18.3	17.7	25.3	17.5	24.4	17.9	24.6	18.5	24.1	19.1 (0.10)	23.9 (0.25)
Korea, Republic of	5.8	11.9	6.7	14.5	7.6	15.5	7.8	16.7	8.4	18.3	8.9	19.3	9.5	20.1	10.2	21.6	10.9	23.3	11.6 (0.16)	25.5 (0.42)
Luxembourg	6.6	8.1	6.7	8.3	7.1	8.6	8.9	12.1	9.4	13.5	9.6	13.2	7.6	10.8	8.8	11.9	7.7	10.8	14.6 (0.34)	20.4 (0.87)
Mexico	1.3	2.2	1.7	2.7	3.3	6.0	1.8	2.7	2.0	3.0	1.1	1.2	1.0	1.1	1.0	1.1	1.1	1.2	1.1 (0.01)	1.2 (0.03)
Netherlands	2.5	2.4	2.3	2.4	2.5	2.4	—	—	2.4	2.4	1.8	1.6	1.8	1.7	1.7	1.6	2.4	2.2	2.8 (0.03)	2.5 (0.07)
New Zealand	13.9	10.4	15.3	11.6	15.1	11.8	14.8	11.7	7.7	5.2	7.4	4.6	15.3	13.8	15.7	14.3	14.9	13.9	16.9 (0.36)	15.9 (0.76)
Norway[2]	2.0	2.2	2.6	2.6	2.5	2.4	2.5	2.4	2.4	2.2	2.4	1.9	2.4	1.7	2.4	1.9	2.4	1.8	2.2 (0.06)	1.4 (0.11)
Portugal	2.7	3.0	2.4	3.1	2.2	2.9	2.4	3.1	—	—	0.8	0.9	0.9	0.9	0.7	0.9	0.8	0.6	— (†)	— (†)
Slovak Republic	—	—	0.6	0.6	0.6	0.5	0.6	0.6	0.6	0.7	0.8	0.9	0.9	0.9	0.7	0.7	0.8	0.6	0.8 (0.04)	0.9 (0.08)
Slovenia	—	—	—	—	—	—	—	—	—	—	9.6	9.5	9.6	9.5	10.6	12.4	10.8	11.7	10.8 (0.16)	11.7 (0.35)
Spain	6.2	11.4	6.7	11.6	7.0	12.0	7.2	11.7	7.5	11.6	8.3	12.8	8.7	13.2	9.0	13.0	9.2	13.0	9.5 (0.05)	13.2 (0.11)
Sweden	15.6	20.7	14.7	17.1	14.8	17.1	14.9	16.7	15.2	16.4	9.1	8.9	8.8	8.5	8.7	8.5	8.6	8.4	8.7 (0.07)	8.5 (0.15)
Switzerland	9.1	9.3	9.6	9.7	9.0	9.6	9.4	8.9	10.1	10.2	9.7	9.0	9.9	9.0	10.0	9.5	10.4	9.7	10.3 (0.17)	9.4 (0.36)
United Kingdom	8.2	8.4	8.0	9.0	8.3	8.1	8.7	8.9	8.8	8.7	8.8	8.1	8.7	8.2	9.1	7.7	9.0	7.7	10.0 (0.06)	8.5 (0.12)
United States	8.3	8.7	9.0	9.2	9.1	8.7	9.0	8.6	9.3	8.8	9.4	9.3	9.6	9.6	9.4	9.3	9.6	9.3	9.8 (0.08)	8.9 (0.15)
Other reporting countries																				
Russian Federation	—	—	—	—	33.5	34.2	—	—	—	—	—	—	—	—	—	—	—	—	— (†)	— (†)

—Not available.
†Not applicable.
#Rounds to zero.
[1]Refers to the mean of the data values for all reporting OECD countries, to which each country reporting data contributes equally. The average includes all current OECD countries for which a given year's data are available, even if they were not members of OECD in that year.
[2]Data from 1998 reported for 1999.
[3]Data from 2000 reported for 2001.

NOTE: Data in this table refer to degrees classified by OECD as International Standard Classification of Education (ISCED) level 5B. ISCED level 5B corresponds to the associate's degree in the United States in this table. Standard errors appear in parentheses.
SOURCE: Organization for Economic Cooperation and Development (OECD), Education at a Glance, 2001 through 2011. (This table was prepared July 2011.)

Number of bachelor's degree recipients per 100 persons at the typical age of graduation, by sex and country: 2003 through 2008

Country	Typical age of graduation, 2008	Total						Male						Female					
		2003	2004	2005	2006	2007	2008	2003	2004	2005	2006	2007	2008	2003	2004	2005	2006	2007	2008
1	2	3	4	5	6	7	8	9	10	11	12	13	14	15	16	17	18	19	20
OECD average[1]	—	—	33.9	34.7	36.2	37.5	39.1	—	27.6	27.5	28.7	30.0	31.0	—	40.5	42.3	44.0	45.3	47.5
Australia	21–23	54.8	46.9	59.9	59.6	60.7	58.9	46.7	37.4	47.9	47.4	48.6	47.0	63.4	57.0	72.5	72.5	73.4	71.4
Austria	22–26	19.0	19.6	20.4	21.7	22.4	25.8	18.7	19.0	19.0	20.4	20.8	22.7	19.4	20.3	21.8	22.9	24.0	29.1
Belgium (Flemish)	22–24	—	18.3	18.4	19.0	35.4	27.0	—	17.5	17.0	17.9	32.6	24.4	—	19.0	19.8	20.2	38.2	29.6
Canada	22–24	—	31.5	33.6	39.3	35.2	39.5	—	24.3	25.2	29.5	26.5	29.1	—	39.1	42.2	49.7	44.3	50.6
Chile	23–26	—	25.1	11.5	15.0	14.5	14.7	—	22.9	9.7	13.0	11.9	11.7	—	27.5	13.4	17.0	17.3	17.8
Czech Republic	22–24	17.3	21.0	26.0	30.7	36.4	39.2	15.9	18.8	22.6	26.5	31.0	32.2	18.8	23.4	29.5	35.2	42.1	46.6
Denmark	24–26	38.6	49.9	52.9	50.3	50.9	50.3	25.1	35.6	37.2	37.0	38.3	38.3	52.3	64.4	69.2	63.7	63.9	62.6
Estonia	22–24	—	—	28.5	26.4	27.3	23.8	—	—	17.6	15.4	17.6	14.9	—	—	39.5	37.8	37.3	32.8
Finland[2]	24–26	55.8	54.7	53.8	57.3	58.8	79.8	40.4	39.5	38.8	40.6	41.3	55.3	72.2	70.5	69.7	74.5	77.4	105.6
France	20–25	41.5	40.0	—	34.2	33.8	33.9	34.9	33.4	—	30.6	30.2	30.3	48.4	46.9	—	37.9	37.5	37.6
Germany	24–27	19.5	20.6	20.5	21.0	23.2	25.5	19.3	20.3	20.0	20.0	22.0	24.0	19.7	20.9	21.1	22.0	24.4	27.0
Greece	22–27	—	19.1	23.9	23.5	21.7	26.6	—	13.3	16.3	16.1	14.7	18.3	—	25.4	32.2	31.7	29.4	35.5
Hungary	23–24	33.6	37.3	41.5	38.2	38.8	37.6	24.6	26.6	29.0	26.1	26.2	25.2	43.2	48.4	54.5	51.0	51.8	50.4
Iceland	24–26	44.2	50.5	56.3	62.8	62.8	55.9	29.4	31.4	33.6	37.7	38.0	34.1	59.1	70.3	80.5	89.6	88.0	78.9
Ireland	21–23	36.8	38.6	40.7	42.8	44.8	46.0	29.7	31.9	33.3	33.4	36.4	36.9	44.0	45.3	48.0	52.5	53.4	55.2
Israel	26–29	—	32.3	32.9	33.4	36.1	36.3	—	25.3	25.7	26.8	29.1	29.6	—	39.6	40.2	40.3	43.1	43.1
Italy	23–25	27.8	40.1	44.8	42.7	38.7	35.8	24.0	33.3	37.3	35.1	31.6	29.5	31.6	47.2	52.7	50.6	46.1	42.3
Japan	21–23	34.4	36.3	36.9	38.7	38.8	40.6	40.1	41.4	41.3	42.8	42.9	44.9	28.5	31.0	32.2	34.3	34.4	36.0
Korea, Republic of	22–24	31.7	32.3	35.5	41.0	42.9	48.7	32.1	31.5	34.8	40.2	42.7	49.0	31.2	33.2	36.2	41.7	43.2	48.5
Mexico	23–26	14.3	13.8	15.2	18.1	18.2	17.8	13.3	13.1	14.5	16.7	16.8	16.2	15.3	14.4	15.9	19.5	19.7	19.3
Netherlands	23	42.5	42.9	47.2	49.2	47.8	46.0	36.4	37.2	40.2	42.9	41.7	39.8	48.7	48.6	54.3	55.7	54.1	52.3
New Zealand	21–23	39.0	47.6	49.0	53.5	53.8	50.0	29.1	34.9	36.6	40.6	41.6	37.6	49.1	61.0	62.0	67.0	66.0	63.0
Norway	22–25	42.0	43.3	42.1	45.1	45.0	46.1	30.0	31.5	28.8	31.9	31.8	33.9	54.2	55.3	55.8	58.8	58.7	58.8
Poland	23–25	—	44.4	45.0	44.8	46.6	48.2	—	32.6	32.8	32.9	34.4	35.0	—	56.6	57.6	57.1	59.2	61.9
Portugal	22–24	—	32.9	33.7	34.9	46.0	50.4	—	20.4	21.7	22.7	35.0	40.3	—	45.6	46.0	47.4	57.4	60.9
Slovak Republic	21–24	—	28.3	30.1	33.7	37.9	57.6	—	24.4	25.6	26.0	26.8	38.7	—	32.4	34.8	41.8	49.6	77.3
Slovenia	25–26	—	—	21.6	21.6	21.1	22.6	—	—	14.3	14.2	13.9	14.4	—	—	29.4	29.3	29.0	31.7
Spain	20–22	32.0	35.2	35.0	35.3	34.7	35.5	25.5	27.5	27.1	27.1	26.6	27.3	38.9	43.2	43.3	43.8	43.3	44.2
Sweden	25	38.4	39.9	44.0	43.3	42.2	40.9	28.6	29.7	30.8	29.8	29.1	27.9	48.5	50.5	57.6	57.2	55.8	54.7
Switzerland	24–27	20.9	22.4	25.0	27.0	28.9	30.6	23.5	24.0	26.1	26.8	28.7	29.2	18.4	20.9	23.9	27.1	29.2	32.0
Turkey	23	—	14.0	11.3	15.4	17.0	19.5	—	15.2	11.8	16.3	17.9	20.6	—	12.7	10.7	14.5	15.9	18.4
United Kingdom	20–24	—	39.2	39.8	39.0	39.0	40.2	—	34.2	34.1	33.0	32.9	33.5	—	44.3	45.7	45.2	45.4	47.2
United States	21–23	33.4	33.2	34.2	35.5	36.5	37.3	27.6	27.5	28.1	29.1	30.1	31.0	39.4	39.2	40.7	42.4	43.4	43.9
Other reporting countries																			
Brazil	22	—	15.6	17.5	21.3	22.7	25.6	—	11.8	13.3	16.2	18.4	19.9	—	19.4	21.6	26.4	27.0	31.3
Russian Federation	21–22	—	—	45.9	43.7	48.6	52.7	—	—	—	—	—	—	—	—	—	—	—	—

—Not available.

[1]Refers to the mean of the data values for all reporting OECD countries, to which each country reporting data contributes equally. The average includes all current OECD countries for which a given year's data are available, even if they were not members of OECD in that year. However, if data were reported for less than 75 percent of the countries that were members of OECD in a given year, the average for that year is omitted.

[2]Much of the increase in Finnish degree recipients between 2007 and 2008 occurred because students had a strong incentive to complete their degrees in 2008. Structural changes in the Finnish higher education system went into effect in 2009. Students who did not complete their degrees in 2008 may have had to spend extra time or take additional courses in order to meet new requirements.

NOTE: Data in this table refer to degrees classified by the Organization for Economic Cooperation and Development (OECD) as International Standard Classification of Education (ISCED) level 5A, first award. This level corresponds to the bachelor's degree in the United States. The recipients-per-100-persons ratio relates the number of people of all ages earning bachelor's degrees in a particular year to the number of people in the population at the typical age of graduation. The typical age is based on full-time attendance and normal progression through the education system (without repeating coursework, taking time off, etc.); this age varies across countries because of differences in their education systems and differences in program duration. This age is presented for the most recent year of data and may differ from previous years; please see previously published volumes of the *Digest of Education Statistics* for the typical age of graduation in previous years. Data for Luxembourg are not shown because tertiary students study for only 1 year in Luxembourg. Some data have been revised from previously published figures.

SOURCE: Organization for Economic Cooperation and Development (OECD), *Education at a Glance*, 2005 through 2011; and Online Education Database, retrieved June 21, 2011, from http://stats.oecd.org/Index.aspx. (This table was prepared June 2011.)

Percentage of bachelor's and higher level degrees awarded to women, by field of study and country: 2009

Country	All fields[1]	Education	Humanities and arts	Health and welfare	Social sciences, business and law	Services	Engineering, manufacturing, and construction	Sciences, mathematics, and computer science					Agriculture
								Total	Life sciences	Physical sciences	Mathematics and statistics	Computer science	
1	2	3	4	5	6	7	8	9	10	11	12	13	14
OECD average[2]	**58.0**	**76.8**	**65.8**	**74.8**	**57.5**	**54.0**	**26.3**	**40.6**	**63.4**	**43.8**	**45.8**	**19.2**	**52.2**
Australia[3]	56.2	74.0	64.1	75.6	53.4	54.0	24.8	37.1	55.2	49.5	37.7	19.6	57.2
Austria	54.2	80.3	65.6	67.1	57.6	38.7	25.5	33.3	68.5	31.4	37.7	17.5	62.2
Belgium	54.8	75.8	64.2	64.1	57.8	40.7	27.2	38.3	56.9	33.4	43.1	6.8	49.2
Canada[3]	59.8	76.8	64.6	83.2	57.9	60.4	23.5	49.3	62.7	45.0	42.4	17.8	57.7
Chile	57.5	74.3	61.3	70.4	52.6	45.5	27.5	35.8	58.4	40.6	47.3	22.1	46.4
Czech Republic	59.0	78.5	69.7	81.1	66.0	42.4	25.6	39.0	70.5	49.1	51.9	13.3	57.6
Denmark	60.2	72.5	64.9	80.1	52.4	24.2	31.8	37.2	62.5	38.2	42.6	20.2	73.6
Estonia	68.7	92.1	79.6	84.0	71.4	68.8	37.6	50.4	74.8	47.6	72.9	28.8	53.4
Finland	62.7	83.6	74.0	85.6	68.0	77.6	22.8	46.0	76.4	48.4	47.8	27.0	59.1
France	54.0	74.6	72.2	59.3	59.5	42.3	28.8	38.4	62.8	38.8	38.6	16.5	54.4
Germany	55.1	72.5	73.3	68.4	52.1	55.9	22.3	43.8	66.6	42.8	62.7	15.6	53.4
Hungary	65.0	78.7	74.7	80.4	70.4	59.9	24.2	35.0	66.2	44.8	45.6	19.5	50.3
Iceland	66.2	84.5	63.6	85.4	62.1	84.6	35.3	40.2	67.6	35.8	11.1	21.1	26.7
Ireland	59.5	74.2	65.5	83.1	55.1	54.3	21.2	44.1	57.6	41.5	46.7	23.4	51.3
Israel	57.4	83.3	60.2	77.8	55.1	76.1	24.2	46.8	63.0	45.1	44.1	24.6	56.4
Japan	41.1	59.3	68.1	56.6	34.4	90.6	10.8	25.2	—	—	—	—	38.7
Korea, Republic of	46.4	71.6	66.3	63.0	42.1	33.6	22.5	38.6	47.9	45.9	56.5	20.1	38.1
Mexico	54.8	72.0	58.9	64.1	58.8	59.7	28.3	42.8	58.5	55.6	42.8	36.4	34.8
Netherlands	56.5	81.1	56.7	75.2	52.4	53.4	18.7	21.1	58.0	25.3	31.1	10.2	51.7
New Zealand	61.0	81.2	65.0	79.5	57.5	52.2	29.8	44.4	60.0	43.2	48.7	23.0	47.8
Norway	61.3	74.5	58.7	82.4	55.8	41.9	24.5	36.5	70.5	42.2	33.6	13.1	59.5
Poland	65.0	77.8	76.1	72.8	68.2	54.9	33.6	44.0	72.4	64.3	67.5	16.3	56.3
Portugal	59.1	85.3	60.9	78.5	63.4	46.3	29.4	55.9	70.4	52.8	69.7	26.9	55.1
Slovak Republic	64.2	78.2	66.7	85.9	68.6	45.0	31.1	42.1	68.4	50.7	56.0	10.6	42.8
Slovenia	65.3	84.2	75.6	72.9	68.3	57.7	31.0	45.5	71.2	45.6	51.1	10.4	59.8
Spain	59.9	78.7	64.5	75.9	60.7	58.2	33.9	41.5	67.3	53.4	53.1	19.7	50.2
Sweden	64.0	79.3	61.3	82.3	62.0	59.0	28.4	46.4	65.8	49.1	34.7	24.1	61.3
Switzerland	49.7	74.3	62.1	68.3	46.8	47.5	19.1	32.8	50.5	31.2	27.5	8.9	63.5
Turkey	46.0	54.6	60.1	62.6	42.4	32.6	26.7	44.3	61.9	41.7	46.4	23.3	34.9
United Kingdom	55.7	76.3	62.2	74.1	54.8	60.3	22.5	38.2	51.7	42.6	40.7	19.0	63.9
United States	57.6	77.7	58.9	79.3	54.2	55.3	21.4	43.5	58.6	39.3	41.9	20.8	49.7
Other reporting countries													
Brazil	62.9	79.7	58.2	75.2	55.7	70.7	28.8	40.4	70.7	44.6	44.0	17.9	39.6
China[3]	46.7	—	—	—	—	—	—	—	—	—	—	—	—
Indonesia[3]	47.2	49.6	47.0	47.1	47.9	#	44.9	47.1	#	47.1	47.0	47.1	47.1

—Not available.

#Rounds to zero.

[1]May contain fields not shown in this table.

[2]Refers to the mean of the data values for all reporting OECD countries, to which each country reporting data contributes equally.

[3]Data are for 2008 instead of 2009.

NOTE: Data in this table refer to degrees classified by the Organization for Economic Cooperation and Development (OECD) as International Standard Classification of Education (ISCED) level 5A (first and second award) or level 6. ISCED 5A, first award, corresponds to the bachelor's degree in the United States; ISCED 5A, second award, corresponds to master's and first-professional degrees in the United States; and ISCED 6 corresponds to doctor's degrees. Data for Greece, Italy, and Luxembourg are not available. SOURCE: Organization for Economic Cooperation and Development (OECD), *Education at a Glance, 2011*. (This table was prepared July 2011.)

Percentage of bachelor's degrees awarded in mathematics and science, by field of study and country: Selected years, 1990 through 2008

Country	All mathematics and science degrees[1]						Natural sciences[2]						Mathematics and computer science[3]						Engineering					
	1990	1995	2000	2005	2007	2008	1990	1995	2000	2005	2007	2008	1990	1995	2000	2005	2007	2008	1990	1995	2000	2005	2007	2008
	2	3	4	5	6	7	8	9	10	11	12	13	14	15	16	17	18	19	20	21	22	23	24	25
OECD average[4]	—	—	22.7	22.7	22.2	21.9	—	—	5.7	4.8	4.6	4.7	—	—	4.1	5.3	5.0	4.8	—	—	13.6	12.8	12.6	12.4
Australia	—	19.3	21.1	21.1	20.3	19.2	—	9.9	7.6	5.9	6.5	6.4	—	3.8	5.1	8.2	6.6	5.7	—	5.6	8.5	7.0	7.2	7.0
Austria	19.6	21.1	25.7	26.8	28.6	25.6	5.3	6.0	5.0	5.4	4.7	4.7	5.2	5.3	3.4	7.2	8.7	6.9	9.0	9.9	17.3	14.2	15.2	13.9
Belgium	—	—	23.6	24.7	24.2	21.3	—	—	6.4	5.7	5.4	3.8	—	—	2.3	5.2	3.7	2.5	—	—	14.9	13.8	15.1	15.0
Canada	16.4	16.7	20.0	20.7	21.1	20.5	6.0	6.5	8.1	6.5	8.9	9.4	4.2	3.8	4.3	5.9	4.6	3.6	6.2	6.4	7.6	8.2	7.7	7.5
Chile	—	—	22.9	22.9	19.9	20.0	—	—	—	3.2	1.8	2.0	—	—	—	2.6	2.1	2.3	—	—	—	17.2	16.0	15.6
Czech Republic	(5)	—	29.5	26.7	27.5	29.1	(5)	2.5	4.2	3.9	3.4	4.6	(5)	—	8.4	3.8	4.9	5.5	(5)	—	16.9	19.0	19.2	18.9
Denmark	—	—	10.5	16.3	19.0	18.7	4.4	—	6.8	2.4	2.7	2.7	—	—	3.1	3.1	2.3	2.7	21.7	—	10.8	10.8	13.9	13.3
Estonia	(5)	—	—	23.8	21.9	21.8	(5)	—	—	6.3	5.4	5.6	(5)	—	—	6.2	6.2	6.0	(5)	—	—	11.3	10.3	10.2
Finland	33.5	37.2	32.2	30.0	28.4	26.6	4.1	4.0	3.9	2.7	2.9	5.0	5.9	6.9	3.3	5.6	5.2	6.4	23.4	26.3	24.9	21.7	20.2	15.1
France	—	—	30.1	26.0	26.3	26.1	—	—	12.2	6.5	6.6	6.3	5.9	4.7	5.5	5.5	5.6	5.5	—	—	12.5	14.0	14.1	14.3
Germany	31.3	31.6	31.7	31.3	27.4	28.2	7.2	6.7	6.4	6.3	6.7	7.6	3.5	5.2	4.9	8.1	8.3	8.2	20.5	19.7	20.3	16.9	12.4	11.2
Greece	—	—	—	25.9	22.1	23.8	—	—	—	8.3	4.8	5.3	—	—	—	8.4	6.7	7.4	—	—	—	9.2	10.6	11.2
Hungary	—	—	12.6	11.0	15.3	15.1	—	—	1.1	1.2	1.3	1.4	—	—	1.2	2.4	5.9	5.3	—	—	10.4	7.4	8.1	8.4
Iceland	—	—	16.5	14.1	13.5	14.9	—	—	6.0	5.0	3.9	3.2	—	—	4.0	3.5	2.9	3.2	—	—	6.5	5.5	6.7	8.5
Ireland	34.1	32.3	29.3	17.7	22.7	22.8	14.1	16.9	11.5	3.5	—	—	6.3	4.7	7.2	4.4	—	—	13.7	10.7	10.6	9.9	6.9	9.5
Israel	—	—	19.0	26.7	21.7	21.0	—	—	3.1	5.1	5.5	5.2	3.9	—	6.8	7.5	4.1	4.1	—	—	9.1	14.1	12.1	11.7
Italy	19.7	19.5	27.5	23.9	22.3	22.0	7.6	6.8	5.9	4.8	4.6	4.8	—	3.8	3.2	2.2	2.1	2.1	12.1	8.9	18.4	16.9	15.6	15.1
Japan	—	—	22.3	20.8	20.1	20.0	2.4	3.4	—	—	—	—	—	—	—	—	—	—	21.0	19.3	18.9	17.4	16.7	16.6
Korea, Republic of	—	—	36.9	37.0	35.6	35.1	—	—	6.3	5.2	5.2	4.8	—	—	4.3	5.4	5.9	5.9	—	—	26.3	26.3	24.5	24.5
Mexico	—	—	23.0	27.3	26.5	26.8	—	—	2.2	2.6	2.7	2.8	—	—	6.7	9.3	8.5	8.3	—	—	14.1	15.3	15.4	15.7
Netherlands	21.1	—	16.2	14.9	14.0	13.7	7.1	—	3.2	2.5	1.3	1.2	1.6	1.6	1.9	4.6	4.9	4.8	12.4	—	11.1	7.7	7.7	7.7
New Zealand	19.5	—	17.8	19.9	17.6	20.7	8.2	—	11.2	6.7	6.2	7.7	5.5	—	1.9	7.6	5.5	5.7	4.7	—	4.7	5.6	5.9	7.3
Norway	12.9	16.8	11.6	13.7	12.8	13.4	2.1	3.1	0.7	0.8	1.6	1.7	0.6	0.5	3.4	4.7	3.0	3.2	10.2	13.2	7.5	8.2	8.2	8.5
Poland	—	15.0	16.7	17.7	21.4	19.9	—	—	2.7	2.3	3.9	3.8	—	—	2.0	5.3	5.6	5.0	—	13.2	12.0	10.1	12.0	11.1
Portugal	—	—	17.5	25.6	32.7	34.2	6.7	2.2	1.7	6.0	4.9	5.5	2.8	2.8	3.6	6.2	7.6	8.0	10.5	9.9	12.2	13.4	20.3	20.7
Slovak Republic	(5)	—	21.9	24.6	21.1	19.0	(5)	—	2.0	3.7	3.4	3.3	(5)	—	4.6	4.4	5.1	4.0	(5)	—	15.3	16.5	12.7	11.7
Slovenia	(5)	—	—	17.7	17.4	16.9	(5)	—	—	4.1	3.8	3.0	(5)	—	—	2.0	2.2	2.5	(5)	—	—	11.7	11.4	11.4
Spain	15.0	18.2	22.7	24.1	24.8	24.1	5.7	4.3	5.3	4.2	3.8	3.5	2.6	4.5	4.3	5.2	5.6	5.5	6.7	9.4	13.1	14.7	15.3	15.0
Sweden	24.0	26.4	27.7	24.1	24.4	22.9	4.1	3.9	3.7	3.6	3.5	3.5	4.7	5.5	3.7	4.0	3.3	2.6	15.2	17.0	20.3	19.2	17.6	16.9
Switzerland	23.0	22.3	25.1	24.2	23.0	20.8	11.2	10.4	6.0	6.9	6.3	6.2	3.7	3.7	1.8	4.7	4.2	3.9	8.1	8.3	17.3	12.7	12.5	10.7
Turkey	20.6	20.9	24.1	22.3	17.4	18.0	4.6	5.1	7.4	6.1	5.2	5.3	2.1	2.7	3.6	4.1	3.3	3.5	13.8	13.1	13.1	12.0	8.9	9.2
United Kingdom	—	—	28.5	26.0	24.6	24.0	—	—	12.5	9.2	9.1	9.2	—	—	5.8	8.3	6.9	6.2	—	—	10.2	8.4	8.5	8.6
United States	16.9	—	17.1	16.7	16.1	15.8	5.1	—	6.6	5.8	6.3	6.4	4.0	3.3	3.9	4.8	3.7	3.4	7.8	6.7	6.6	6.2	6.0	6.0
Other reporting countries																								
Brazil	(5)	—	—	11.4	11.6	11.1	(5)	—	—	3.2	3.2	3.3	—	—	—	3.5	3.1	2.9	—	—	—	4.8	5.3	4.9
Russian Federation	—	—	—	—	—	—	(5)	—	—	—	—	—	—	—	—	—	—	—	(5)	—	—	—	—	—

—Not available.

[1]Includes life sciences, physical sciences, mathematics/statistics, computer science, and engineering.
[2]Includes life sciences and physical sciences.
[3]Includes mathematics/statistics and computer science.
[4]Refers to the mean of the data values for all reporting OECD countries, to which each country reporting data contributes equally. The average includes all current OECD countries for which a given year's data are available, even if they were not members of OECD in that year. However, if data were reported for less than 75 percent of the countries that were members of OECD in a given year, the average for that year is omitted.
[5]Country did not exist in its current form in the given year.
NOTE: Data in this table refer to degrees classified by the Organization for Economic Cooperation and Development (OECD) as International Standard Classification of Education (ISCED) level 5A, first award. This level corresponds to the bachelor's degree in the United States. Data for Luxembourg are not shown because tertiary students study for only 1 year in Luxembourg. Some data have been revised from previously published figures. Detail may not sum to totals because of rounding.
SOURCE: Organization for Economic Cooperation and Development (OECD), Online Education Database, retrieved May 10, 2011, from http://stats.oecd.org/Index.aspx; and unpublished tabulations. (This table was prepared May 2011.)

Percentage of graduate degrees awarded in mathematics and science, by field of study and country: Selected years, 1990 through 2008

Country	All mathematics and science degrees[1]						Natural sciences[2]						Mathematics and computer science[3]						Engineering					
	1990	1996	2000	2005	2007	2008	1990	1996	2000	2005	2007	2008	1990	1996	2000	2005	2007	2008	1990	1996	2000	2005	2007	2008
OECD average[4]	—	—	28.5	24.7	23.4	23.3	—	—	11.1	8.9	8.0	7.4	—	—	5.4	4.9	5.0	5.0	—	—	12.7	11.4	10.8	11.2
Australia	—	14.0	15.2	20.0	21.0	18.8	—	5.4	4.0	3.1	2.9	3.1	—	3.8	4.9	8.7	10.8	8.3	—	4.7	6.3	8.1	7.3	7.5
Austria	37.7	38.8	39.2	38.6	47.2	31.8	12.3	17.5	16.7	15.0	12.3	7.5	4.6	4.7	4.7	6.6	15.4	11.3	20.8	16.6	17.7	16.9	19.5	13.0
Belgium	—	—	19.7	18.7	18.9	18.0	—	—	—	9.3	8.9	5.4	—	—	—	3.3	4.0	3.7	—	—	7.0	6.2	6.0	8.9
Canada	20.0	22.3	22.4	18.8	27.4	26.3	7.8	7.7	7.4	5.0	10.1	9.9	3.4	3.5	4.1	4.0	4.6	4.3	8.8	11.2	10.9	9.8	12.7	12.1
Chile	—	—	—	8.5	11.2	11.4	—	—	—	2.2	3.4	2.8	—	—	—	1.6	2.6	2.3	—	—	—	4.6	5.2	6.3
Czech Republic	[5]	—	21.0	26.1	17.9	22.2	[5]	—	5.3	8.3	4.0	5.7	[5]	—	7.9	5.6	3.0	3.8	[5]	—	7.7	12.3	10.9	12.7
Denmark	22.2	12.3	27.8	23.4	21.8	21.3	5.8	3.1	9.8	7.5	7.0	5.9	4.8	1.5	2.5	9.2	7.8	7.6	11.6	7.8	15.4	6.7	7.0	7.8
Estonia	[5]	28.3	28.7	23.9	27.4	28.6	[5]	—	11.3	10.0	10.8	8.2	[5]	4.0	2.4	5.0	6.0	7.7	[5]	12.7	14.9	8.9	10.6	12.6
Finland	30.6	—	26.4	30.5	34.7	31.7	14.7	11.6	13.5	11.6	14.1	12.5	5.4	4.0	2.4	4.1	4.7	4.0	10.5	12.7	10.5	14.8	15.9	15.2
France	—	—	—	28.4	29.6	28.8	—	—	—	12.5	11.0	10.8	—	—	5.6	7.0	7.0	6.8	—	—	7.3	8.9	11.6	11.2
Germany	33.2	38.6	38.1	30.9	32.4	33.7	23.5	25.5	24.9	14.8	14.3	15.1	2.3	3.5	3.7	4.8	6.0	6.3	7.4	9.5	9.5	11.3	12.1	12.3
Greece	—	—	—	42.8	26.9	33.0	—	—	—	22.3	8.2	6.2	—	—	—	5.3	8.3	11.0	—	—	—	15.2	10.4	15.7
Hungary	—	—	9.9	6.4	7.7	8.3	—	—	1.7	1.8	2.5	2.6	—	—	0.7	1.7	2.0	1.4	—	—	7.5	2.9	3.3	4.4
Iceland	—	—	35.9	23.0	10.6	10.6	—	—	19.4	9.5	5.3	5.8	—	—	#	3.0	2.0	1.1	—	—	16.5	10.5	3.9	3.7
Ireland	34.5	23.1	28.1	16.8	17.9	19.0	19.5	10.9	6.9	4.1	—	—	5.8	3.0	15.2	6.3	—	—	9.3	9.2	6.0	6.4	5.1	6.1
Israel	—	—	18.1	17.9	18.6	18.6	—	—	9.2	8.9	9.3	9.2	—	—	2.8	3.2	3.6	3.3	—	—	6.1	5.9	5.7	6.0
Italy	—	—	11.7	15.9	18.6	—	—	—	0.3	3.5	4.7	—	—	—	5.8	3.5	2.7	—	—	—	5.7	8.9	11.3	—
Japan	—	—	54.4	50.9	47.6	47.1	—	—	8.5	9.5	8.1	8.0	—	—	4.0	3.4	4.2	4.4	45.1	44.4	41.9	38.0	35.3	34.7
Korea, Republic of	—	—	48.4	43.9	38.7	24.1	—	—	8.5	9.5	8.1	4.4	—	—	5.7	2.0	1.6	1.2	—	—	34.3	32.4	29.0	18.4
Mexico	—	—	31.4	14.7	12.9	12.1	—	—	18.9[6]	3.3	3.2	2.9	—	—	4.1[6]	3.2	2.5	3.3	—	—	8.4[6]	8.2	7.1	5.9
Netherlands	28.9	18.6	—	21.3	14.8	14.6	17.7	4.4	—	7.2	8.4	9.1	1.5	3.7	—	5.2	4.0	4.1	9.7	10.6	—	11.9	7.5	7.6
New Zealand	22.6	16.7	20.5	16.6	16.3	18.5	13.8	12.7	14.9	7.8	6.7	6.1	4.7	1.1	1.4	4.2	5.1	4.3	4.0	3.0	2.5	4.2	3.9	5.3
Norway	33.4	38.3	22.0	25.8	22.1	22.2	8.0	8.7	14.9	10.4	6.7	6.1	2.1	1.9	4.6	11.9	10.3	10.8	23.3	27.7	2.5	3.5	5.1	5.3
Poland	—	—	—	9.1	10.6	11.1	—	—	—	3.5	4.0	3.5	—	—	—	2.1	2.3	2.6	—	—	—	3.5	4.3	5.0
Portugal	—	—	39.3[6]	33.8	39.4	49.2	—	—	11.7	12.0	13.6	12.2	—	—	9.4[6]	10.0	9.4	11.2	—	—	18.2[6]	11.9	16.4	25.8
Slovak Republic	[5]	—	38.1	36.8	31.7	28.0	[5]	—	13.0	13.0	8.0	5.7	[5]	—	4.2	2.0	2.1	2.7	[5]	—	20.9	21.8	21.6	19.6
Slovenia	[5]	—	—	24.2	21.2	19.9	[5]	—	—	6.4	7.1	7.2	[5]	—	—	4.2	4.3	2.7	[5]	—	—	13.6	9.9	10.1
Spain	26.9	36.0	—	37.5[6]	19.3[6]	26.6	19.7	24.8	23.9[6]	23.8[6]	12.6[6]	14.0	1.4	4.1	5.4[6]	4.6[6]	2.3[6]	3.9	5.7	7.1	6.8[6]	9.1[6]	4.5[6]	8.7
Sweden	48.5	32.3	40.5	23.7	26.3	28.1	7.6	9.2	14.3	8.0	8.1	8.5	3.3	5.9	4.0	2.8	4.0	4.0	19.9	17.1	22.2	12.9	14.2	15.6
Switzerland	30.2	40.1	42.7	32.0	30.8	28.9	19.5	22.8	27.7	11.9	12.4	12.4	3.4	3.4	3.4	3.2	3.3	3.2	6.5	10.1	11.6	16.9	15.1	13.3
Turkey	24.0	—	25.7	21.4	18.7	18.8	7.6	—	7.6	6.7	5.2	5.6	3.3	—	3.0	3.4	3.2	3.1	13.2	—	15.2	11.2	10.3	10.4
United Kingdom	—	—	21.7	20.3	19.9	20.3	—	—	7.4	5.5	5.6	5.5	—	—	5.0	5.7	5.1	5.2	—	—	9.2	9.0	9.3	9.7
United States	14.5	13.8	13.0	13.5	12.7	13.0	4.2	4.0	3.4	3.3	3.4	3.5	3.4	3.2	3.4	3.5	3.2	3.2	6.9	6.7	6.2	6.7	6.1	6.3

—Not available.

#Rounds to zero.

[1]Includes life sciences, physical sciences, mathematics/statistics, computer science, and engineering.

[2]Includes life sciences and physical sciences.

[3]Includes mathematics/statistics and computer science.

[4]Refers to the mean of the data values for all reporting OECD countries, to which each country reporting data contributes equally. The average includes all current OECD countries for which a given year's data are available, even if they were not members of OECD in that year. However, if data were reported for less than 75 percent of the countries that were members of OECD in a given year, the average for that year is omitted.

[5]Country did not exist in its current form in the given year.

[6]Only includes doctor's (Ph.D.) degrees.

NOTE: Data in this table refer to degrees classified by the Organization for Economic Cooperation and Development (OECD) as International Standard Classification of Education (ISCED) level 5A, second award, and as ISCED 6. ISCED 5A, second award, corresponds to master's and first-professional degrees in the United States, and ISCED 6 corresponds to doctor's degrees. Data for Luxembourg are not shown because tertiary students study for only 1 year in Luxembourg. Some data have been revised from previously published figures. Detail may not sum to totals because of rounding.

SOURCE: Organization for Economic Cooperation and Development (OECD), Online Education Database, retrieved May 26, 2011, from http://stats.oecd.org/Index.aspx; and unpublished tabulations. (This table was prepared May 2011.)

Employment rates of 25- to 64-year-olds, by sex, highest level of educational attainment, and country: 2009

Country	Total population, 25 to 64 years old				Male				Female			
	All levels of education	Less than high school completion	High school completion	Associate's or higher degree	All levels of education	Less than high school completion	High school completion	Associate's or higher degree	All levels of education	Less than high school completion	High school completion	Associate's or higher degree
1	2	3	4	5	6	7	8	9	10	11	12	13
OECD average[1]	**72.7**	**56.0**	**74.2**	**83.6**	**80.5**	**67.1**	**81.5**	**88.1**	**65.0**	**46.0**	**66.2**	**79.1**
Australia	77.6	66.1	80.2	84.3	85.0	76.5	87.2	89.1	70.4	57.7	70.7	80.2
Austria	75.3	55.6	77.6	86.7	81.1	65.0	81.5	89.3	69.6	50.7	73.2	83.4
Belgium	69.8	48.0	74.0	84.2	76.2	58.7	80.5	87.2	63.3	37.0	66.8	81.6
Canada	75.4	55.1	73.7	81.7	78.9	63.1	78.0	84.5	71.9	45.4	68.7	79.4
Chile	68.4	58.3	69.2	78.0	85.7	82.3	87.6	85.3	51.6	36.2	51.7	70.6
Czech Republic	73.8	43.9	75.1	84.3	83.4	53.6	84.0	91.0	64.1	39.1	65.5	76.9
Denmark	78.8	64.6	79.7	87.4	81.9	71.0	82.3	89.1	75.6	59.0	76.4	86.0
Estonia	72.9	47.4	71.6	82.8	73.8	51.7	72.9	87.4	72.2	41.4	70.1	80.4
Finland	75.1	56.8	74.8	84.4	76.4	60.0	76.6	86.9	73.8	52.5	72.7	82.6
France	72.5	56.2	76.5	83.5	78.3	63.8	82.6	86.8	67.0	49.4	70.1	80.8
Germany	75.4	54.9	75.5	86.4	81.3	64.9	80.3	89.7	69.5	48.0	70.7	82.2
Greece	68.3	59.7	68.4	82.2	82.0	78.0	83.3	86.6	54.6	40.0	54.8	77.7
Hungary	63.6	37.4	67.0	78.8	70.5	45.5	73.1	83.7	57.0	31.9	60.0	75.1
Iceland	82.6	77.1	82.6	88.3	85.9	81.2	86.9	89.9	79.1	73.0	76.5	86.9
Ireland	68.3	50.0	69.1	82.0	74.3	59.9	76.3	86.0	62.3	37.7	62.0	78.5
Israel	70.5	44.3	69.0	82.4	77.0	59.6	75.6	87.0	64.3	26.5	62.1	78.7
Italy	64.0	51.2	73.1	79.2	76.6	69.2	82.5	84.9	51.6	32.9	63.6	74.7
Japan	76.0	—	73.1	79.7	88.7	—	85.8	92.3	63.3	—	60.8	66.6
Korea, Republic of	71.2	65.3	69.6	76.1	84.9	77.2	84.1	88.3	57.6	57.6	55.6	60.1
Luxembourg	73.4	61.6	70.2	85.1	82.5	74.9	79.2	90.6	64.1	51.2	60.9	78.6
Mexico	66.8	61.7	71.9	81.7	87.9	87.2	89.8	88.7	48.4	40.7	57.7	73.0
Netherlands	79.0	63.6	81.7	88.1	85.7	77.7	86.8	90.2	72.2	51.2	76.6	85.7
New Zealand	79.3	69.0	82.4	84.0	86.0	77.1	88.4	90.1	72.9	62.1	74.4	79.3
Norway	82.3	65.4	83.1	90.2	84.8	69.6	86.0	91.8	79.7	61.2	79.4	88.9
Poland	67.4	41.6	66.3	85.3	75.2	53.4	75.1	89.9	59.8	31.0	56.9	82.1
Portugal	73.3	69.0	80.1	86.7	79.0	76.5	83.8	87.6	67.8	61.1	76.5	86.1
Slovak Republic	70.0	30.3	72.0	83.2	78.6	39.0	80.0	89.4	61.5	25.2	63.5	77.7
Slovenia	74.3	53.7	74.6	88.4	78.0	62.5	78.0	90.3	70.5	46.4	70.3	87.1
Spain	65.7	54.0	70.6	81.1	73.6	65.7	77.0	84.6	57.6	41.6	64.0	77.8
Sweden	81.1	64.2	81.3	88.1	83.7	71.9	84.3	89.2	78.4	54.4	77.7	87.2
Switzerland	82.6	67.5	81.7	89.6	89.3	77.6	88.4	92.9	75.8	61.6	75.9	84.4
Turkey	52.0	46.3	58.3	73.6	73.5	70.5	77.9	80.6	27.2	21.8	27.2	63.1
United Kingdom	75.0	56.9	78.3	84.5	81.0	66.7	82.7	88.1	69.0	49.4	73.1	81.0
United States	71.9	52.5	68.9	80.8	76.4	61.6	72.9	85.4	67.6	41.9	64.8	76.7
Other reporting countries												
Brazil	73.2	68.7	77.4	85.6	86.3	84.4	88.8	91.3	61.2	53.5	67.7	81.5

—Not available.
[1]Refers to the mean of the data values for all reporting OECD countries, to which each country reporting data contributes equally.
NOTE: The "high school completion" columns include International Standard Classification of Education (ISCED) levels 3 and 4, with the exception of ISCED level 3C short programs. (ISCED 3C short programs do not correspond to high school completion in the United States and are included in the "less than high school completion" columns in this table.)

ISCED level 5B corresponds to the associate's degree in the United States in this table. Also included in the "associate's or higher degree" columns are the following higher level degrees: ISCED 5A, first award, which corresponds to the bachelor's degree in the United States; ISCED 5A, second award, which corresponds to master's and first-professional degrees in the United States; and ISCED 6, which corresponds to doctor's degrees.
SOURCE: Organization for Economic Cooperation and Development (OECD), *Education at a Glance, 2011.* (This table was prepared July 2011.)

Public and private education expenditures per student, by level of education and country: Selected years, 2000 through 2008

Country	Elementary education				Secondary education				Higher education			
	2000	2005	2007	2008	2000	2005	2007	2008	2000	2005	2007	2008
1	2	3	4	5	6	7	8	9	10	11	12	13
	Current dollars											
OECD average[1]	$4,304	$5,976	$6,624	$7,122	$5,779	$7,418	$8,057	$8,980	$9,509	$11,387	$12,495	$13,214
Australia	4,967	5,992	6,498	6,723	6,894	8,408	8,840	9,052	12,854	14,579	14,726	15,043
Austria	6,560	8,259	8,664	9,542	8,578	9,751	10,641	11,741	10,851	14,775	15,039	15,043
Belgium	4,310	6,648	7,363	8,528	6,889[2]	7,731[2]	8,992[2]	10,511[2]	10,771	11,960	13,482	15,020
Canada	—	—	7,648[3,4]	—	5,947[5]	7,774[3,5]	8,388	—	14,983[2]	23,329[6,7]	20,903[6]	—
Chile	1,940	2,120	2,088	2,268	2,016	2,077	2,090	2,222	7,483	6,873	6,292	6,626
Czech Republic	1,827	2,812	3,359	3,799	3,239	4,847	5,527	6,174	5,431	6,649	8,209	8,318
Denmark	7,074	8,513	9,176	10,080	7,726[8]	9,407[8]	9,675[8]	10,720[8]	11,981[8]	14,959[8]	16,466[8]	17,634[8]
Estonia	—	3,384[6]	4,058	5,579	—	3,918[6]	4,869	6,371	—	3,869	5,653[7]	6,022[7]
Finland	4,317	5,557	6,234	7,092	6,094[2]	7,324[2]	7,829[2]	8,659[2]	8,244	12,285	13,566	15,402
France	4,486	5,365	6,044	6,267	7,636	8,927	9,532	10,231	8,373	10,995	12,773	14,079
Germany	4,198	5,014	5,548	5,929	6,826	7,636	7,841	8,606	10,898	12,446	13,823	15,390
Greece	3,318[3,6]	5,146[3]	—	—	3,859[6]	8,423	—	—	3,402[6]	6,130	—	—
Hungary[6]	2,245	4,438	4,656	4,495	2,446	3,806	4,225	4,658	7,024	6,244	6,721	7,327
Iceland	5,854[6]	9,254	9,629	10,599	6,518[6]	8,411[8]	8,349[2]	9,007[2]	7,994[6]	9,474[8]	9,309	10,429
Ireland	3,385	5,732	6,901	7,795[6]	4,638	7,500	9,375	10,868[6]	11,083	10,468	12,631	16,284[6]
Israel	4,351	4,699	5,060	5,314	5,518	5,495	5,741	6,429	11,550	10,919	11,435	12,568
Italy	5,973[6]	6,835[6]	7,383[6]	8,671[6]	7,218[6]	7,648[6]	8,004[6]	9,315[6]	8,065[6]	8,026[6]	8,673	9,553
Japan	5,507	6,744	7,247	7,491	6,266[8]	7,908[8]	8,760[8]	9,092[8]	10,914[8]	12,326[8]	14,201[8]	14,890[8]
Korea, Republic of	3,155	4,691	5,437	5,420	4,069	6,645	7,860	7,931	6,118	7,606	8,920	9,081
Luxembourg[6]	—	14,079[3]	13,985[3]	13,648	—	18,845	17,928	19,898	—	—	—	—
Mexico	1,291	1,913	2,111	2,246	1,615	2,180	2,236	2,333	4,688	6,402	6,971	7,504
Netherlands	4,325	6,266	6,552	7,208	5,912	7,741	10,248	10,950	11,934	13,883	15,969	17,245
New Zealand	—	4,780	4,675	5,582	—	6,278	5,933	6,994	—	10,262	9,905	10,526
Norway	6,550[6]	9,001	9,922	11,077	8,476[2,6]	10,995[2]	11,997[2]	13,070[2]	13,353[6]	15,552	17,140	18,942
Poland[6]	2,105	3,312	4,063	4,855	—	3,055	3,590	4,525	3,222	5,593	5,576	7,063
Portugal	3,672	4,871[6]	5,011[6]	5,234[6]	5,349	6,473[6]	6,833[6]	7,357[6]	4,766	8,787[6]	10,398[6]	10,373[6]
Slovak Republic	1,308	2,806	3,499	4,137	1,927[2,9]	2,716[2,9]	3,219[2,9]	3,956[2,9]	4,949[7,9]	5,783[7,9]	5,736[7,9]	6,560[7,9]
Slovenia	—	—	—	—	—	7,065[2,5]	7,267[2,5]	8,555[2,5]	—	8,573	8,559	9,263
Spain	3,941	5,502	6,533	7,184	5,185[2]	7,211	8,730	9,792	6,666	10,089	12,548	13,366
Sweden	6,336	7,533	8,338	9,080	6,339	8,198	9,143	9,940	15,097	15,946	18,361	20,014
Switzerland[6]	6,631	8,469	9,211	9,063	9,780	12,861	13,982	17,825[2]	18,450	21,734	20,883	21,648
Turkey[6]	—	—	—	—	—	—	—	—	4,121	—	—	—
United Kingdom	3,877	6,361	8,222	8,758	5,991[2]	7,167[2]	8,892[2]	9,487[2]	9,657	13,506	15,463	15,310
United States	6,995	9,156	10,229	9,982	8,855	10,390	11,301	12,097	20,358[2]	24,370	27,010	29,910
	Constant 2010 dollars											
OECD average[1]	$5,444	$6,665	$6,959	$7,205	$7,310	$8,274	$8,465	$9,084	$12,028	$12,701	$13,126	$13,369
Australia	6,283	6,683	6,826	6,802	8,720	9,378	9,287	9,157	16,259	16,261	15,470	15,219
Austria	8,298	9,211	9,102	9,654	10,850	10,876	11,179	11,878	13,726	16,479	15,799	15,219
Belgium	5,452	7,415	7,735	8,628	8,714[2]	8,623[2]	9,446[2]	10,634[2]	13,624	13,340	14,163	15,196
Canada	—	—	8,035[3,4]	—	7,522[5]	8,671[3,5]	8,812	—	18,952[2]	26,020[6,7]	21,959[6]	—
Chile	2,454	2,365	2,193	2,294	2,550	2,317	2,196	2,248	9,465	7,665	6,610	6,704
Czech Republic	2,311	3,136	3,528	3,844	4,097	5,406	5,806	6,246	6,870	7,415	8,624	8,415
Denmark	8,948	9,495	9,639	10,198	9,773[8]	10,493[8]	10,164[8]	10,845[8]	15,155[8]	16,684[8]	17,298[8]	17,840[8]
Estonia	—	3,774[6]	4,263	5,644	—	4,370[6]	5,115	6,445	—	4,315	5,939[7]	6,092[7]
Finland	5,461	6,198	6,549	7,175	7,708[2]	8,168[2]	8,224[2]	8,760[2]	10,428	13,702	14,252	15,582
France	5,674	5,984	6,350	6,340	9,659	9,956	10,013	10,351	10,591	12,264	13,418	14,243
Germany	5,310	5,592	5,828	5,998	8,634	8,517	8,238	8,707	13,785	13,882	14,521	15,569
Greece	4,197[3,6]	5,739[3]	—	—	4,881[6]	9,394	—	—	4,303[6]	6,838	—	—
Hungary[6]	2,840	4,950	4,891	4,547	3,094	4,245	4,439	4,712	8,885	6,965	7,060	7,413
Iceland	7,405[6]	10,321	10,116	10,723	8,245[6]	9,381[8]	8,771[2]	9,112[2]	10,112[6]	10,567[8]	9,780	10,551
Ireland	4,282	6,394	7,249	7,886[6]	5,867	8,365	9,849	10,995[6]	14,019	11,675	13,269	16,474[6]
Israel	5,504	5,241	5,315	5,376	6,980	6,129	6,031	6,504	14,610	12,179	12,013	12,715
Italy	7,555[6]	7,623[6]	7,756[6]	8,772[6]	9,130[6]	8,530[6]	8,408[6]	9,424[6]	10,202[6]	8,952[6]	9,112	9,665
Japan	6,966	7,522	7,613	7,578	7,926[8]	8,820[8]	9,202[8]	9,198[8]	13,805[8]	13,748[8]	14,919[8]	15,064[8]
Korea, Republic of	3,991	5,232	5,712	5,484	5,147	7,412	8,258	8,023	7,739	8,483	9,371	9,187
Luxembourg[6]	—	15,703[3]	14,692[3]	13,807	—	21,019	18,834	20,130	—	—	—	—

See notes at end of table.

Public and private education expenditures per student, by level of education and country: Selected years, 2000 through 2008—Continued

Country	Elementary education				Secondary education				Higher education			
	2000	2005	2007	2008	2000	2005	2007	2008	2000	2005	2007	2008
1	2	3	4	5	6	7	8	9	10	11	12	13
Mexico	1,633	2,133	2,217	2,273	2,043	2,431	2,349	2,360	5,930	7,141	7,324	7,591
Netherlands	5,471	6,989	6,883	7,292	7,478	8,634	10,766	11,078	15,095	15,484	16,775	17,446
New Zealand	—	5,332	4,911	5,647	—	7,002	6,233	7,076	—	11,445	10,405	10,649
Norway	8,285 [6]	10,039	10,423	11,206	10,721 [2,6]	12,263 [2]	12,603 [2]	13,223 [2]	16,890 [6]	17,346	18,006	19,163
Poland[6]	2,663	3,694	4,268	4,911	—	3,408	3,772	4,578	4,076	6,238	5,857	7,146
Portugal	4,645	5,433 [6]	5,264 [6]	5,295 [6]	6,766	7,220 [6]	7,179 [6]	7,443 [6]	6,029	9,801 [6]	10,923 [6]	10,494 [6]
Slovak Republic	1,655	3,130	3,676	4,185	2,437 [2,9]	3,029 [2,9]	3,382 [2,9]	4,002 [2,9]	6,260 [7,9]	6,451 [7,9]	6,026 [7,9]	6,637 [7,9]
Slovenia	—	—	—	—	—	7,880 [2,5]	7,634 [2,5]	8,655 [2,5]	—	9,562	8,991	9,371
Spain	4,985	6,137	6,863	7,268	6,559 [2]	8,043	9,171	9,906	8,432	11,253	13,182	13,522
Sweden	8,014	8,402	8,759	9,186	8,018	9,144	9,605	10,056	19,096	17,786	19,289	20,248
Switzerland[6]	8,388	9,446	9,677	9,169	12,371	14,344	14,688	18,034 [2]	23,338	24,241	21,938	21,901
Turkey[6]	—	—	—	—	—	—	—	—	5,213	—	—	—
United Kingdom	4,904	7,095	8,638	8,861	7,578 [2]	7,994 [2]	9,341 [2]	9,598 [2]	12,215	15,064	16,245	15,488
United States	8,848	10,212	10,746	10,099	11,201	11,588	11,872	12,238	25,751 [2]	27,181	28,374	30,260

—Not available.

[1]Refers to the mean of the data values for all reporting OECD countries, to which each country reporting data contributes equally. The average includes all current OECD countries for which a given year's data are available, even if they were not members of OECD in that year.

[2]Includes postsecondary non-higher-education.

[3]Includes preprimary education.

[4]Includes lower secondary education.

[5]Includes elementary education.

[6]Public institutions only.

[7]Excludes occupation-specific education corresponding to that offered at the associate's degree level in the United States.

[8]Postsecondary non-higher-education included in both secondary and higher education.

[9]Occupation-specific education corresponding to that offered at the associate's degree level in the United States is included in secondary education.

NOTE: Includes all expenditures by public and private education institutions, such as administration, instruction, ancillary services for students and families, and research and development. Data adjusted to U.S. dollars using the purchasing-power-parity (PPP) index. Constant dollars based on the Consumer Price Index, prepared by the Bureau of Labor Statistics, U.S. Department of Labor.

SOURCE: Organization for Economic Cooperation and Development (OECD), *Education at a Glance*, 2002 through 2011. (This table was prepared June 2011.)

International Comparisons of Education

Public and private direct expenditures on education as a percentage of gross domestic product, by level of education and country: Selected years, 1995 through 2008

Country	All institutions (including preprimary education and subsidies to households, not separately shown)								Elementary and secondary institutions								Higher education institutions							
	Public direct expenditures					Direct expenditures, 2008			Public direct expenditures					Direct expenditures, 2008			Public direct expenditures					Direct expenditures, 2008		
	1995	2000[1]	2005[1]	2006[1]	2007[1]	Public[1]	Private	Total	1995	2000[1]	2005[1]	2006[1]	2007[1]	Public[1]	Private	Total	1995	2000[1]	2005[1]	2006[1]	2007[1]	Public[1]	Private	Total
1	2	3	4	5	6	7	8	9	10	11	12	13	14	15	16	17	18	19	20	21	22	23	24	25
OECD average[2]	**4.9**	**4.9**	**5.0**	**4.9**	**4.8**	**5.1**	**0.9**	**5.9**	**3.5**	**3.4**	**3.5**	**3.4**	**3.3**	**3.5**	**0.3**	**3.7**	**0.9**	**1.0**	**1.0**	**1.0**	**1.0**	**1.0**	**0.5**	**1.5**
Australia	4.5	4.6	4.3	4.1	3.7	3.7	1.4	5.2	3.2	3.7	3.4	3.3	2.9	3.0	0.6	3.6	1.2	0.8	0.8	0.8	0.7	0.7	0.8	1.5
Austria	5.3	5.4[3]	5.2	5.2	5.1	5.2	0.2	5.4	3.8	3.7[3]	3.5	3.5	3.5	3.5	0.1	3.6	0.9	1.2[3]	1.2	1.2	1.3	1.2	0.1	1.3
Belgium	5.0	5.1	5.8	5.9	5.9	6.3	0.3	6.6	3.4	3.4[4]	3.9	3.9	3.9	4.3	0.2	4.4	0.9	1.2[4]	1.2	1.2	1.2	1.3	0.1	1.4
Canada	5.8	5.2	4.8	4.8	—	3.7	2.7	6.4	4.0	3.3[5]	3.3[5,6]	3.2[5,6]	3.1[6]	3.0	0.9	3.9	1.5	0.6	1.5[5]	1.6[5]	1.5	0.3	1.7	2.0
Chile	—	4.2	3.3	3.0	2.5	—	—	—	—	3.2	2.7	2.4	2.5	3.0	0.9	—	—	0.6	0.3	0.3	0.3	0.3	1.7	—
Czech Republic	4.8	4.2	4.1	4.2	4.1	3.9	0.6	4.5	3.4	2.8[4]	2.7	2.7	2.5	2.5	0.3	2.8	0.7	0.8[4]	0.8	1.0	1.0	0.9	0.2	1.2
Denmark	6.5	6.4[3]	6.8	6.7	6.6	6.5	0.6	7.1	4.2	4.1[3,7]	4.4[7]	4.3[7]	4.2[7]	4.2[7]	0.1[7]	4.3[7]	1.3	1.5[3,7]	1.6[7]	1.6[7]	1.6[7]	1.6[7]	0.1[7]	1.7[7]
Estonia	—	—	4.7	4.6	4.7	5.5	0.2	5.8	—	—	3.5	3.4	3.3	3.8	#	3.9	—	—	0.9	1.6	1.6	1.6	0.2	1.3
Finland	6.6	5.5	5.9	5.7	5.7	5.7	0.1	5.9	4.2	3.5	3.8	3.7	3.6	3.8	#	3.8	1.7	1.7	1.7	1.7	1.6	1.6	0.1	1.7
France	5.8	5.7	5.6	5.5	5.5	5.5	0.5	6.0	4.1	4.0	3.8	3.7	3.7	3.7	0.2	3.9	1.0	1.0	1.1	1.1	1.2	1.2	0.2	1.4
Germany	4.5	4.3	4.2	4.1	4.0	4.1	0.7	4.8	2.9	2.9	2.8	2.7	2.6	2.6	0.4	3.0	1.0	1.0	0.9	0.9	0.9	1.0	0.2	1.2
Greece	3.7	3.7[3]	4.0	5.1?	4.9	4.8	—	—	2.8	2.7[3,6]	2.5[6]	3.2	3.2	3.0	—	—	0.8	0.9[3]	1.4	0.9	0.9	0.9	—	—
Hungary	4.9	4.4	5.1	5.1	4.9	4.8	0.7	7.9	3.3	2.8	3.3	3.2	3.2	3.0	0.2	5.1	0.8	0.9	0.9	0.9	0.9	0.9	0.7	—
Iceland	4.5	5.7[3]	7.2	7.2	7.0	7.2	0.7	7.9	3.4	4.6[3]	5.2[7]	5.1	4.9	4.9	0.2	5.1	0.7	0.8[3]	1.1[7]	1.0	1.1	1.2	0.1	1.3
Ireland	4.7	4.1	4.3	4.4	4.4	5.2	0.3	5.6	3.3	2.9[4]	3.3	3.4	3.4	4.0	0.1	4.1	0.9	1.2[4]	1.0	1.0	1.0	1.2	0.2	1.4
Israel	—	6.6	6.2	6.2	5.9	5.9	1.4	7.3	—	4.5	4.2	4.1	3.9	4.0	0.2	4.2	—	1.1	0.6	0.7	0.6	0.7	0.7	1.6
Italy	4.5	4.5	4.3	4.6	4.5	4.5	0.3	4.8	3.2	3.2	2.6[7]	3.4	3.0	3.2	0.1	3.3	0.7	0.7	0.6	0.7	0.6	0.8	0.3	1.0
Japan	3.6	3.5	3.4	3.3	3.3	3.3	1.7	4.9	2.8	2.7	2.6[7]	2.6[7]	2.5[7]	2.5[7]	0.3	2.8[7]	0.4	0.5[7]	0.5[7]	0.7	0.5[7]	0.5[7]	1.0[7]	1.5[7]
Korea, Republic of	3.6	4.3	3.4	3.3	3.3	4.7	2.8	7.6	3.0	3.3	3.4	3.4	3.1	3.4	0.8	4.2	0.3	0.6	0.6	0.6	0.6	0.6	1.9	2.6
Luxembourg	4.3	—	4.3	4.5	4.2	—	0.7	5.7	4.2	—	3.7[6]	3.3[6]	3.1[6]	2.8	0.1	2.9	—	—	0.6	0.6	0.6	0.6	—	—
Mexico	4.6	4.7	5.3	4.6	4.7	4.7	1.1	5.8	3.4	3.3	3.7	3.2	3.1	3.1	0.6	3.7	0.8	0.8	0.9	1.0	0.9	0.9	0.4	1.2
Netherlands	4.6	4.3	4.6	4.8	4.7	4.8	0.8	5.6	3.0	3.0	3.3	3.3	3.3	3.3	0.4	3.7	1.1	1.0	1.0	1.1	1.1	1.1	0.4	1.5
New Zealand	5.3	5.8	5.2	5.0	4.8	5.4	1.2	6.6	3.8	4.6	4.0	3.8	3.5	3.8	0.6	4.5	1.1	0.9	0.9	0.9	1.0	1.1	0.5	1.6
Norway	6.8	5.8	5.7	5.4	5.4	7.3	—	—	4.1	3.6	3.4	3.7	3.7	5.0	—	—	1.5	1.2	1.3	1.2	1.2	1.6	0.1	1.7
Poland	5.2	5.2[3]	5.4	5.2	4.8	5.0	0.7	5.7	3.3	3.7[3]	3.7[6]	3.3[6]	3.1[6]	3.4	0.2	3.6	0.8	0.8[3]	1.2	0.9	0.9	0.6	0.2	1.5
Portugal	5.4	5.6[3]	5.3	5.1	5.1	4.7	0.5	5.2	4.1	4.1[3]	3.8	3.6	3.5	3.4	#	3.4	1.0	1.0[3,4,8]	0.9	0.9	1.1	0.9	0.4[8]	1.3
Slovak Republic	4.6	4.0[3]	3.7	3.6	3.4	3.5	0.6	4.0	—	2.7[3,4,8]	2.5[8]	2.4[8]	2.3[8]	2.2[8]	0.4[8]	2.6[8]	1.0	0.7[3,4,8]	0.7[8]	0.9	0.7[8]	0.7[8]	0.2[8]	0.9[8]
Slovenia	4.8	4.3	5.3	5.3	4.8	4.8	0.6	5.4	3.5	3.1	3.9	3.8	3.3	3.4	0.3	3.7	0.8	0.9	1.0	1.0	1.0	1.0	0.2	1.1
Spain	4.8	4.3	4.1	4.2	4.2	4.5	0.6	5.1	3.5	3.1	2.7	2.7	2.7	2.9	0.3	3.1	0.8	0.9	0.9	0.9	0.9	1.0	0.2	1.2
Sweden	6.6	6.3	6.2	6.2	6.1	6.1	0.2	6.3	4.4	4.4[4]	4.2	4.2	4.1	4.0	#	4.1	1.6	1.5[4]	1.5	1.4	1.4	1.4	0.2	1.6
Switzerland	5.5	5.3	5.6	5.4	5.1	5.3	—	—	4.1	3.8	3.9	3.7	3.5	3.8	0.5	4.3	1.1	1.2[3]	1.4	1.4	1.3	1.3	—	—
Turkey	2.2	3.4[3]	2.7	2.7	—	—	—	—	1.4	2.4[3]	1.9	1.9	—	—	—	—	0.8	1.0[3]	0.9	0.8	—	—	—	—
United Kingdom	4.6	4.5	5.0	5.2	5.2	5.1	0.6	5.7	3.8	3.4	3.8	3.9	4.1	4.2	#	4.2	0.7	0.7	0.9	0.9	0.7	0.6	0.6	1.2
United States	5.0	4.8	4.8	5.0	5.0	5.1	2.1	7.2	3.5	3.5[5]	3.7[6]	3.7	3.7	3.8	0.3	4.1	1.1	0.9[5]	1.0	1.0	1.0	1.0	1.7	2.7
Other reporting countries																								
Brazil	—	—[3]	4.4	4.9	5.2	5.3	—	—	—	1.7	3.3	3.8	4.0	4.1	0.1	—	—	0.5	0.8	0.8	0.8	0.8	—	—
Russian Federation	3.4	3.0[3]	3.8	3.9	3.4	4.1	0.7	4.7	1.9	1.7	1.9	2.0	3.4	2.0	0.1	2.1	0.7	0.5	0.8	0.8	1.0	0.9	0.5	1.5

—Not available.
#Rounds to zero.
[1]Includes public subsidies to households attributable for education institutions and direct expenditures on education institutions from international sources, except where noted.
[2]Refers to the mean of the data values for all reporting OECD countries, to which each country reporting data contributes equally. The average includes all current OECD countries for which a given year's data are available, even if they were not members of OECD in that year.
[3]Public subsidies to households not included in public expenditures.
[4]Direct expenditures on education institutions from international sources exceed 1.5 percent of all public expenditures.
[5]Postsecondary non-higher-education included in higher education.
[6]Preprimary education (for children ages 3 and older) is included in elementary and secondary education.
[7]Postsecondary non-higher-education included in both secondary and higher education.
[8]Occupation-specific education corresponding to that offered at the associate's degree in the United States is included in secondary education.

NOTE: Public direct expenditures on education include both amounts spent directly by governments to hire educational personnel and to procure other resources, and amounts provided by governments to public or private institutions, or households. Private direct expenditures include the net of public subsidies to households for education institutions. Postsecondary non-higher-education is included in elementary and secondary education unless otherwise noted. All institutions total includes expenditures that could not be reported by level of education. Some data have been revised from previously published figures.
SOURCE: Organization for Economic Cooperation and Development (OECD), Online Education Database; and *Education at a Glance,* 2007 through 2011. U.S. Department of Education, National Center for Education Statistics, *International Education Indicators: A Time Series Perspective, 1985–1995* (NCES 2000-021). (This table was prepared June 2011.)

Selected statistics on public school libraries/media centers, by level of school: 1999–2000, 2003–04, and 2007–08

Selected statistic	1999–2000	2003–04				2007–08			
		Total	Elementary	Secondary	Combined elementary/ secondary	Total	Elementary	Secondary	Combined elementary/ secondary
1	2	3	4	5	6	7	8	9	10
Number of schools with libraries/media centers	77,300 (421)	78,300 (548)	57,400 (440)	16,300 (313)	4,600 (201)	81,900 (634)	59,700 (492)	17,800 (414)	4,400 (239)
Average number of staff per library/media center	1.89 (0.018)	1.76 (0.014)	1.66 (0.018)	2.09 (0.025)	1.74 (0.116)	1.72 (0.017)	1.65 (0.019)	2.04 (0.039)	1.42 (0.057)
Certified library/media specialists	0.81 (0.007)	0.79 (0.009)	0.73 (0.012)	1.03 (0.018)	0.73 (0.023)	0.78 (0.011)	0.73 (0.013)	0.98 (0.019)	0.66 (0.033)
Full-time	0.65 (0.007)	0.65 (0.009)	0.58 (0.010)	0.92 (0.018)	0.55 (0.027)	0.66 (0.010)	0.61 (0.012)	0.88 (0.018)	0.49 (0.032)
Part-time	0.16 (0.006)	0.14 (0.007)	0.15 (0.009)	0.11 (0.009)	0.18 (0.020)	0.13 (0.007)	0.13 (0.013)	0.10 (0.009)	0.18 (0.020)
Other professional staff	0.17 (0.007)	0.19 (0.008)	0.19 (0.011)	0.14 (0.010)	0.28 (0.036)	0.22 (0.010)	0.22 (0.013)	0.21 (0.021)	0.24 (0.027)
Full-time	0.12 (0.005)	0.13 (0.007)	0.14 (0.009)	0.11 (0.009)	0.16 (0.022)	0.13 (0.008)	0.13 (0.010)	0.14 (0.017)	0.15 (0.022)
Part-time	0.06 (0.004)	0.05 (0.005)	0.05 (0.006)	0.03 (0.004)	0.11 (0.031)	0.08 (0.007)	0.08 (0.009)	0.07 (0.013)	0.08 (0.017)
Other paid employees	0.91 (0.014)	0.78 (0.011)	0.75 (0.013)	0.93 (0.017)	0.73 (0.085)	0.72 (0.013)	0.70 (0.016)	0.86 (0.027)	0.51 (0.036)
Full-time	0.49 (0.008)	0.46 (0.009)	0.41 (0.011)	0.65 (0.017)	0.35 (0.028)	0.43 (0.013)	0.39 (0.016)	0.60 (0.022)	0.27 (0.028)
Part-time	0.41 (0.014)	0.33 (0.012)	0.34 (0.014)	0.28 (0.014)	0.38 (0.085)	0.29 (0.011)	0.31 (0.014)	0.26 (0.018)	0.24 (0.028)
Percent of libraries/media centers with certain media equipment									
Automated catalog	72.8 (0.69)	82.7 (0.66)	81.9 (0.89)	90.6 (0.76)	63.7 (2.59)	87.2 (0.71)	87.5 (0.94)	90.6 (1.08)	69.8 (2.88)
Automated circulation system	74.4 (0.65)	86.9 (0.61)	86.7 (0.82)	92.8 (0.80)	68.8 (2.45)	89.5 (0.68)	89.9 (0.87)	92.6 (0.98)	72.4 (3.15)
Media retrieval system[1]	— (†)	— (†)	— (†)	— (†)	— (†)	34.9 (1.05)	35.9 (1.33)	35.1 (1.66)	20.6 (2.32)
Connection to Internet	90.1 (0.57)	95.1 (0.35)	94.1 (0.48)	99.2 (0.22)	92.6 (1.40)	96.7 (0.40)	96.5 (0.51)	98.6 (0.51)	91.6 (1.90)
Digital video disc (DVD) player/video cassette recorder (VCR)	— (†)	87.8 (0.60)	87.0 (0.70)	90.4 (1.19)	89.1 (1.53)	87.2 (0.77)	86.7 (1.02)	89.6 (1.00)	84.5 (2.20)
Disability assistance technologies, such as TDD	— (†)	11.9 (0.50)	10.2 (0.61)	18.0 (0.79)	11.7 (1.34)	23.9 (1.05)	23.0 (1.33)	26.4 (1.34)	25.9 (2.76)
Percent of libraries/media centers with certain services									
Students permitted to check out laptops	— (†)	— (†)	— (†)	— (†)	— (†)	27.5 (1.02)	26.9 (1.27)	29.8 (1.34)	26.1 (2.57)
Staff permitted to check out laptops	— (†)	— (†)	— (†)	— (†)	— (†)	45.9 (1.07)	45.2 (1.35)	50.1 (1.50)	38.5 (2.85)
Number of library computer workstations per 100 students	— (†)	2.3 (0.04)	2.2 (0.05)	2.5 (0.05)	2.7 (0.17)	2.6 (0.05)	2.5 (0.07)	2.9 (0.06)	3.0 (0.17)
Average holdings per 100 students at the end of the school year[2]									
Books (number of volumes)	1,803 (19.7)	1,891 (45.1)	2,127 (70.2)	1,376 (20.0)	2,407 (117.7)	2,015 (30.5)	2,316 (40.2)	1,432 (36.6)	2,439 (132.3)
Audio and video materials	59 (0.9)	80 (3.7)	86 (5.7)	65 (2.2)	97 (13.6)	90 (3.8)	93 (5.6)	81 (5.2)	107 (13.3)
Average additions per 100 students during the school year[2]									
Books (number of volumes)	— (†)	99.3 (2.08)	118.4 (3.13)	61.2 (1.75)	109.2 (8.40)	95.3 (2.21)	113.3 (3.26)	62.1 (2.67)	103.4 (7.41)
Audio and video materials	— (†)	5.1 (0.19)	5.3 (0.28)	4.4 (0.20)	6.9 (0.83)	5.4 (0.49)	5.9 (0.77)	4.5 (0.41)	5.7 (0.84)
Total expenditures for library/media materials per pupil[2,3]	$23.37 (0.438)	$16.24 (0.322)	$16.00 (0.469)	$16.11 (0.320)	$21.24 (2.498)	$16.11 (0.461)	$16.18 (0.591)	$15.90 (0.647)	$17.00 (1.216)
Books	9.97 (0.153)	10.99 (0.299)	11.72 (0.452)	9.68 (0.275)	10.19 (0.631)	11.40 (0.291)	11.99 (0.389)	10.26 (0.504)	12.10 (1.094)
Audio and video materials	1.66 (0.032)	1.14 (0.045)	1.11 (0.053)	1.11 (0.062)	1.96 (0.619)	1.08 (0.055)	1.06 (0.088)	1.11 (0.054)	1.16 (0.152)
Current serial subscriptions	1.26 (0.016)	1.38 (0.025)	1.06 (0.031)	1.87 (0.049)	2.50 (0.148)	— (†)	— (†)	— (†)	— (†)
Electronic subscriptions	0.81 (0.018)	0.88 (0.033)	0.39 (0.042)	1.79 (0.061)	1.25 (0.249)	— (†)	— (†)	— (†)	— (†)

—Not available.
†Not applicable.
[1]Centralized video distribution equipment with a scheduling and control server that telecasts video to classrooms.
[2]Average holdings, acquisitions, and expenditures are from the prior school year, while enrollment counts are from the current school year.
[3]Includes other expenditures not separately shown.
NOTE: Detail may not sum to totals because of rounding. Standard errors appear in parentheses.
SOURCE: U.S. Department of Education, National Center for Education Statistics, Schools and Staffing Survey (SASS). "Public School Library Media Center Questionnaire," 1999–2000, 2003–04, and 2007–08; and "Charter School Questionnaire," 1999–2000. (This table was prepared November 2009.)

Collections, staff, and operating expenditures of the 60 largest college and university libraries: Fiscal year 2008

Institution	Rank order, by number of volumes	Number of volumes at end of year (in thousands)	Number of e-books at end of year	Number of serials at end of year	Full-time-equivalent staff		Operating expenditures (in thousands)		Public service hours per typical week	Gate count per typical week[1]	Reference transactions per typical week
					Total	Librarians	Total	Salaries and wages			
1	2	3	4	5	6	7	8	9	10	11	12
Harvard University (MA)	1	16,250	1,167	110,628	1,229	418	$117,884	$62,798	168	39,748	5,468
Yale University (CT)	2	12,284	840,000	295,557	735	175	92,248	35,781	111	14,900	1,970
University of California, Berkeley	3	11,020	610,920	87,876	487	92	48,020	24,305	77	27,502	2,100
University of Illinois at Urbana-Champaign	4	10,933	319,533	109,803	473	113	40,571	20,988	144	85,632	6,214
Columbia University in the City of New York	5	9,596	703,121	132,740	616	161	56,089	27,240	108	81,862	3,557
University of Texas at Austin	6	9,447	593,450	56,847	528	130	43,850	20,773	120	87,115	20,693
University of Michigan, Ann Arbor	7	9,175	701,019	69,457	570	169	52,395	25,853	168	73,543	2,884
Stanford University (CA)	8	8,558	419,515	33,903	680	151	78,377	41,382	105	20,100	3,074
University of California, Los Angeles	9	8,467	495,238	175,207	596	125	53,154	28,197	97	64,072	1,843
University of Wisconsin, Madison	10	7,934	766,032	54,164	553	229	43,282	23,459	148	110,368	2,640
Cornell University (NY)	11	7,750	391,897	89,000	549	118	46,798	22,667	146	98,000	1,497
University of Chicago (IL)	12	7,745	851,880	76,607	323	68	34,680	12,638	146	33,881	779
Indiana University, Bloomington	13	7,618	631,617	103,228	445	94	36,282	16,061	168	90,061	2,446
University of Minnesota, Twin Cities	14	6,878	307,082	85,075	394	93	40,734	18,118	100	36,527	2,300
University of Washington, Seattle Campus	15	6,844	387,281	61,847	458	135	36,814	19,345	138	116,000	2,128
Princeton University (NJ)	16	6,779	763,158	51,746	410	97	48,970	18,789	116	13,492	671
University of North Carolina at Chapel Hill	17	6,017	510,110	60,713	452	143	41,124	18,944	146	60,214	2,543
Ohio State University, Main Campus	18	6,016	269,097	78,903	396	62	35,833	16,642	168	39,030	1,476
Duke University (NC)	19	5,829	144,939	61,964	369	117	37,331	16,444	161	9,250	2,638
University of Pennsylvania	20	5,756	340,446	61,676	370	111	37,599	16,991	111	38,589	5,000
University of Pittsburgh, Main Campus (PA)	21	5,657	591,468	59,141	382	120	32,907	12,539	118	84,789	2,587
Pennsylvania State University, Main Campus	22	5,355	42,083	88,668	608	134	47,686	24,437	168	46,247	3,549
University of Arizona	23	5,266	645,463	24,466	239	54	24,676	9,471	142	42,916	531
University of Virginia, Main Campus	24	5,158	374,731	163,032	379	101	35,930	16,921	149	76,424	2,886
Rutgers University, New Brunswick/Piscataway	25	5,081	195,296	74,031	305	66	23,918	13,651	108	53,419	1,216
New York University	26	5,073	545,025	67,960	458	58	44,603	20,703	119	51,500	2,156
Northwestern University (IL)	27	4,843	264,066	82,822	344	97	29,147	12,518	126	28,218	1,427
Michigan State University	28	4,839	66,350	83,460	265	71	23,482	10,714	148	42,367	850
University of Kansas	29	4,799	321,320	60,838	228	54	19,543	9,105	140	42,000	2,350
University of Iowa	30	4,791	486,769	59,442	281	98	27,620	12,335	113	36,273	1,610
University of Oklahoma, Norman Campus	31	4,702	649,929	52,522	158	37	16,253	4,396	117	21,930	523
University of Georgia	32	4,637	128,694	80,748	315	81	24,451	10,106	137	17,700	1,910
Arizona State University at the Tempe Campus	33	4,422	302,266	87,566	332	93	28,571	12,266	149	75,265	2,053
University of Florida	34	4,288	280,238	71,336	402	85	29,731	13,905	111	56,209	1,587
University of Southern California	35	4,084	267,657	70,066	374	75	38,393	17,149	159	53,534	1,173
Louisiana State University and Agricultural & Mechanical College	36	4,067	346,389	101,738	192	52	15,874	—	113	32,228	712
Texas A & M University	37	3,934	461,225	86,737	359	85	34,150	12,329	146	49,683	880
University of Colorado at Boulder	38	3,928	175,377	55,519	216	58	21,454	8,693	104	40,532	1,374
University of South Carolina, Columbia	39	3,885	91,940	21,505	275	71	19,743	7,975	140	31,415	2,969
Johns Hopkins University (MD)	40	3,878	2,003,184	74,701	338	80	32,881	13,282	120	19,373	1,593
Washington University in St. Louis (MO)	41	3,841	382,891	69,400	266	93	32,366	10,219	120	30,000	1,409
Brown University (RI)	42	3,825	284,749	60,499	208	55	19,862	9,162	112	20,064	510
Brigham Young University (UT)	43	3,743	337,546	69,361	383	85	27,167	12,126	105	82,238	3,070
SUNY at Buffalo (NY)	44	3,720	369,721	80,431	242	60	19,972	10,339	168	26,000	562
University of Kentucky	45	3,720	406,014	73,251	287	79	21,414	8,257	135	57,316	1,734
Miami University (OH)	46	3,718	511,114	91,229	146	41	9,488	4,652	168	28,862	1,529
University of Maryland, College Park	47	3,717	88,393	42,393	258	119	32,156	12,600	162	47,982	5,186
University of Rochester (NY)	48	3,701	51,134	28,561	207	89	24,850	8,949	119	4,478	1,004
University of Cincinnati, Main Campus (OH)	49	3,632	459,542	86,363	185	49	21,466	7,729	95	26,700	1,600
University of Hawaii at Manoa	50	3,559	193,133	55,276	237	64	17,860	9,108	135	31,380	1,791
University of Nebraska, Lincoln	51	3,554	321,180	46,865	187	49	12,633	6,465	96	15,004	1,000
University of Missouri, Columbia	52	3,494	25,434	38,364	198	55	17,025	6,386	114	36,426	1,374
Florida State University	53	3,484	477,476	62,093	250	67	18,563	7,090	142	37,531	1,219
North Carolina State University at Raleigh	54	3,477	401,497	67,995	268	98	23,296	10,960	146	37,649	718
Wayne State University (MI)	55	3,454	206,736	20,384	247	53	20,802	9,349	142	38,599	916
University of Notre Dame (IN)	56	3,393	2,295	82,866	260	60	24,077	10,306	126	19,191	497
University of Utah	57	3,373	132,859	48,777	370	69	26,290	12,877	123	39,724	3,680
University of California, San Diego	58	3,373	231,216	34,800	367	63	30,748	16,330	114	51,347	880
University of Connecticut	59	3,368	338,682	71,371	152	61	16,262	—	114	51,539	303
University of California, Davis	60	3,354	504,736	50,442	231	53	18,652	9,568	95	33,978	1,129

—Not available.

[1]The number of entries into the library in an average week. A single person can be counted more than once.

SOURCE: U.S. Department of Education, National Center for Education Statistics, Academic Libraries Survey (ALS), fiscal year 2008. (This table was prepared July 2010.)

Public libraries, books and serial volumes, library visits, circulation, and reference transactions, by state: Fiscal years 2008 and 2009

State	Number of public libraries		Number of books and serial volumes				Library visits per capita[1]		Circulation per capita[2]		Reference transactions per capita[3]	
			In thousands		Per capita							
	2008	2009	2008	2009	2008	2009	2008	2009	2008	2009	2008	2009
1	2	3	4	5	6	7	8	9	10	11	12	13
United States	9,221 [4]	9,225 [4]	816,099	815,909	2.8	2.7	5.1	5.4	7.7	8.1	1.0	1.0
Alabama	210	210	9,615	9,546	2.2	2.1	3.5	3.7	4.4	4.6	0.8	0.9
Alaska	86	87	2,491	2,532	3.7	3.7	5.1	5.1	6.3	6.4	0.6	0.7
Arizona	86	89	8,619	8,807	1.3	1.3	4.0	4.4	7.3	7.4	0.7	0.7
Arkansas	51	52	6,450	6,578	2.4	2.5	3.7	4.0	4.9	5.3	0.7	0.7
California	181	181	74,197	75,299	2.0	2.0	4.5	4.8	5.8	6.2	0.9	0.9
Colorado	115	114	12,039	11,916	2.5	2.4	6.3	6.7	12.0	13.0	1.2	1.2
Connecticut	195	195	15,609	15,646	4.4	4.5	6.8	7.0	9.4	9.7	1.4	1.3
Delaware	21	21	1,991	1,701	2.5	2.2	5.5	5.6	10.4	10.5	0.6	0.6
District of Columbia	1	1	2,063	2,130	3.5	3.6	4.6	4.9	3.0	3.9	1.4	1.4
Florida	80	80	32,736	32,643	1.7	1.7	4.5	4.8	6.2	6.8	1.6	1.6
Georgia	59	61	16,087	16,341	1.7	1.7	4.0	4.3	4.7	5.1	1.0	0.9
Hawaii	1	1	3,399	3,383	2.6	2.6	4.6	4.7	5.5	5.6	0.7	0.7
Idaho	104	104	4,192	4,275	3.1	3.2	6.4	6.8	9.4	10.3	0.8	0.9
Illinois	634	634	45,263	45,250	3.9	3.8	6.6	7.0	9.0	9.7	1.2	1.2
Indiana	238	238	25,873	25,672	4.5	4.5	7.2	7.4	13.7	14.1	1.0	1.0
Iowa	539	541	12,235	12,143	4.1	4.1	6.3	6.5	9.6	9.7	0.6	0.6
Kansas	327	328	10,381	10,314	4.4	4.3	6.2	6.6	11.4	11.8	1.1	1.1
Kentucky	116	117	8,674	8,849	2.1	2.1	4.4	4.5	6.7	6.9	0.9	0.7
Louisiana	68	68	11,641	11,651	2.6	2.6	3.3	3.5	4.0	4.2	1.2	1.4
Maine	272	269	6,505	6,536	5.4	5.4	5.9	5.9	7.7	7.9	0.6	0.6
Maryland	24	24	14,378	13,892	2.6	2.5	5.9	6.1	9.9	10.7	1.1	1.3
Massachusetts	370	370	32,713	32,969	5.1	5.1	6.5	6.5	8.4	8.9	0.9	0.8
Michigan	384	384	34,556	35,539	3.5	3.6	5.5	6.0	8.0	8.6	0.9	1.0
Minnesota	138	138	14,762	15,535	2.8	2.9	5.5	5.6	10.7	11.2	0.8	0.7
Mississippi	50	50	5,530	5,556	1.9	1.9	3.0	3.2	2.9	3.0	0.6	0.6
Missouri	152	150	18,034	17,592	3.5	3.4	5.5	5.9	9.4	10.1	1.1	1.1
Montana	80	80	2,732	2,731	3.0	3.0	4.5	4.9	6.5	6.9	0.5	0.5
Nebraska	270	269	6,643	6,345	5.1	4.7	6.9	6.8	10.5	10.4	0.9	0.8
Nevada	22	22	5,405	4,782	2.0	1.8	4.0	4.3	6.5	7.2	0.7	0.6
New Hampshire	231	230	6,210	6,217	4.7	4.7	5.6	5.9	8.4	8.9	0.6	0.6
New Jersey	303	301	30,342	30,230	3.6	3.6	5.9	6.1	7.3	7.8	1.0	1.0
New Mexico	91	91	4,578	4,615	2.9	2.9	4.8	5.0	6.3	6.5	0.9	0.8
New York	755	756	74,635	75,760	3.9	4.0	6.2	6.3	8.2	8.4	1.5	1.5
North Carolina	77	77	16,833	16,907	1.9	1.8	4.1	4.8	5.8	6.0	1.3	1.4
North Dakota	81	85	2,453	2,575	4.3	4.5	4.3	4.4	7.2	7.8	0.7	0.8
Ohio	251	251	46,893	45,818	4.1	4.0	8.0	8.0	16.7	17.0	1.8	1.8
Oklahoma	115	115	7,249	7,278	2.4	2.4	4.9	7.0	7.0	7.1	0.7	0.7
Oregon	126	127	9,407	9,927	2.8	2.7	6.6	6.8	15.4	15.4	0.8	0.8
Pennsylvania	457	458	29,837	28,180	2.5	2.4	4.0	4.1	5.8	6.0	0.7	0.7
Rhode Island	48	48	4,420	4,334	4.2	4.1	6.0	6.4	7.0	7.3	0.8	0.8
South Carolina	42	42	9,421	9,430	2.1	2.2	3.8	4.2	5.4	6.1	1.1	1.2
South Dakota	114	112	3,134	3,096	4.5	4.2	5.6	5.4	8.4	8.4	0.9	0.9
Tennessee	187	186	11,595	11,754	1.9	1.9	3.4	3.5	4.1	4.0	0.7	0.6
Texas	561	559	41,797	41,749	1.9	1.8	3.3	3.5	4.9	5.1	0.7	0.7
Utah	69	71	6,556	6,744	2.5	2.5	6.7	7.0	13.0	13.4	1.7	1.9
Vermont	183	184	2,900	2,964	4.8	4.9	6.4	6.5	7.7	7.8	0.8	0.8
Virginia	91	91	19,181	19,151	2.5	2.5	5.2	5.5	9.2	9.8	1.0	1.0
Washington	64	63	16,433	15,377	2.5	2.3	6.5	6.7	12.1	12.9	1.0	0.9
West Virginia	97	97	5,119	5,213	2.8	2.9	3.3	3.4	4.2	4.3	0.5	0.5
Wisconsin	381	380	19,843	19,956	3.5	3.5	6.3	6.4	10.9	11.5	0.9	0.9
Wyoming	23	23	2,447	2,484	4.7	4.7	6.8	7.1	9.0	9.5	1.1	1.2

[1]The number of visits (entering the library for any purpose) per person during the year.
[2]The number of library materials lent per person during the year.
[3]A reference transaction is an information contact that involves the knowledge, use, recommendations, interpretation, or instructions in the use of one or more information sources by a member of the library staff.
[4]In 2008, of the 9,221 public libraries in the 50 states and the District of Columbia, 7,469 were single-outlet libraries and 1,752 were multiple-outlet libraries. In 2009, of the 9,225 public libraries in the 50 states and the District of Columbia, 7,466 were single-outlet libraries and 1,759 were multiple-outlet libraries. Single-outlet libraries consist of a central library, bookmobile, or books-by-mail-only outlet. Multiple-outlet libraries have two or more direct service outlets, including some combination of one central library, branch(es), bookmobile(s), and/or books-by-mail-only outlets.

NOTE: Data include imputations for nonresponse. Detail may not sum to totals because of rounding. Per capita figures are based on unduplicated populations of the areas served by public libraries.

SOURCE: Institute of Museum and Library Services, *Public Libraries Survey*, fiscal years 2008 and 2009, retrieved October 28, 2011, from https://harvester.census.gov/imls/pubs/pls/index.asp. (This table was prepared October 2011.)

Labor force participation, employment, and unemployment of persons 25 to 64 years old, by sex, race/ethnicity, and educational attainment: 2008, 2009, and 2010

Sex, race/ethnicity, and educational attainment	Labor force participation rate[1] 2008	2009	2010	Number of participants (in thousands) 2010	Employment to population ratio[2] 2008	2009	2010	Number employed (in thousands) 2010	Unemployment rate[3] 2008	2009	2010	Number unemployed (in thousands) 2010
1	2	3	4	5	6	7	8	9	10	11	12	13
All persons, all education levels	79.0 (0.04)	78.6 (0.04)	77.9 (0.04)	127,203 (81.5)	75.0 (0.04)	72.1 (0.04)	70.7 (0.04)	115,462 (89.0)	5.0 (0.03)	8.4 (0.03)	9.2 (0.03)	11,741 (42.2)
Less than high school completion	63.0 (0.11)	62.6 (0.15)	61.3 (0.14)	12,554 (52.2)	56.8 (0.13)	53.1 (0.16)	51.1 (0.14)	10,469 (45.7)	9.8 (0.12)	15.2 (0.14)	16.6 (0.13)	2,085 (18.8)
High school completion[4]	75.7 (0.08)	75.1 (0.08)	74.1 (0.08)	32,800 (70.1)	70.8 (0.09)	67.1 (0.09)	65.4 (0.09)	28,946 (65.4)	6.4 (0.05)	10.6 (0.06)	11.7 (0.08)	3,853 (27.2)
Some college, no degree	80.6 (0.09)	79.9 (0.08)	78.9 (0.08)	28,383 (61.8)	76.5 (0.10)	72.7 (0.10)	71.0 (0.09)	25,531 (56.8)	5.2 (0.06)	9.0 (0.06)	10.0 (0.07)	2,851 (22.1)
Associate's degree	84.3 (0.09)	83.9 (0.11)	83.1 (0.13)	11,427 (36.7)	81.1 (0.10)	78.3 (0.12)	76.9 (0.14)	10,566 (35.8)	3.8 (0.07)	6.6 (0.09)	7.5 (0.08)	861 (9.8)
Bachelor's or higher degree	86.4 (0.05)	86.4 (0.05)	86.1 (0.06)	42,040 (106.2)	84.1 (0.05)	82.5 (0.06)	81.8 (0.07)	39,948 (102.6)	2.6 (0.03)	4.5 (0.03)	5.0 (0.04)	2,091 (19.0)
Male, all education levels	84.9 (0.05)	84.1 (0.05)	83.2 (0.04)	66,857 (50.3)	80.6 (0.05)	76.5 (0.06)	75.1 (0.06)	60,312 (54.5)	5.1 (0.03)	9.0 (0.05)	9.8 (0.05)	6,544 (31.0)
Less than high school completion	72.7 (0.16)	71.8 (0.16)	70.5 (0.16)	7,893 (35.7)	66.2 (0.17)	61.1 (0.20)	59.2 (0.17)	6,623 (32.1)	8.9 (0.13)	14.9 (0.18)	16.1 (0.16)	1,270 (14.1)
High school completion[4]	81.9 (0.10)	81.0 (0.09)	80.0 (0.11)	18,435 (49.9)	76.5 (0.11)	71.7 (0.11)	69.8 (0.11)	16,090 (45.5)	6.6 (0.08)	11.5 (0.09)	12.7 (0.10)	2,344 (19.5)
Some college, no degree	86.1 (0.12)	84.8 (0.09)	83.7 (0.10)	14,311 (43.1)	81.8 (0.13)	76.8 (0.12)	75.1 (0.12)	12,844 (42.0)	5.0 (0.08)	9.4 (0.10)	10.2 (0.11)	1,467 (16.6)
Associate's degree	88.9 (0.14)	88.2 (0.16)	87.2 (0.16)	5,122 (23.8)	85.4 (0.16)	81.8 (0.20)	80.3 (0.20)	4,714 (22.4)	3.9 (0.08)	7.3 (0.13)	8.0 (0.13)	408 (7.3)
Bachelor's or higher degree	91.9 (0.05)	91.7 (0.07)	91.4 (0.07)	21,096 (56.8)	89.6 (0.06)	87.4 (0.08)	86.8 (0.08)	20,040 (54.8)	2.5 (0.04)	4.7 (0.05)	5.0 (0.05)	1,056 (11.8)
Female, all education levels	73.3 (0.05)	73.3 (0.06)	72.8 (0.06)	60,346 (54.2)	69.6 (0.05)	67.7 (0.07)	66.5 (0.06)	55,149 (57.8)	5.0 (0.04)	7.6 (0.04)	8.6 (0.05)	5,197 (27.6)
Less than high school completion	51.0 (0.18)	51.3 (0.22)	50.2 (0.18)	4,660 (25.0)	45.2 (0.19)	43.2 (0.23)	41.4 (0.19)	3,846 (21.8)	11.5 (0.21)	15.7 (0.21)	17.5 (0.21)	815 (11.3)
High school completion[4]	69.0 (0.11)	68.6 (0.14)	67.8 (0.11)	14,365 (40.1)	64.8 (0.12)	62.1 (0.15)	60.7 (0.12)	12,856 (36.9)	6.1 (0.09)	9.4 (0.10)	10.5 (0.10)	1,509 (15.5)
Some college, no degree	75.6 (0.13)	75.4 (0.12)	74.6 (0.11)	14,072 (41.3)	71.6 (0.14)	68.9 (0.13)	67.3 (0.11)	12,687 (39.4)	5.3 (0.08)	8.6 (0.09)	9.8 (0.09)	1,385 (12.7)
Associate's degree	80.8 (0.13)	80.6 (0.15)	80.1 (0.16)	6,305 (26.8)	77.8 (0.14)	75.8 (0.17)	74.4 (0.19)	5,852 (26.3)	3.7 (0.10)	6.0 (0.11)	7.2 (0.13)	453 (8.3)
Bachelor's or higher degree	81.2 (0.08)	81.5 (0.08)	81.4 (0.08)	20,944 (60.0)	78.9 (0.07)	77.9 (0.09)	77.4 (0.09)	19,908 (59.1)	2.7 (0.04)	4.4 (0.05)	4.9 (0.06)	1,036 (11.9)
White, all education levels	79.9 (0.04)	79.6 (0.05)	78.9 (0.05)	84,427 (54.9)	76.5 (0.05)	73.9 (0.05)	72.7 (0.05)	77,736 (59.4)	4.2 (0.03)	7.2 (0.04)	7.9 (0.04)	6,690 (30.3)
Less than high school completion	58.2 (0.23)	57.3 (0.25)	55.3 (0.22)	4,110 (27.1)	52.3 (0.23)	47.8 (0.25)	45.1 (0.23)	3,356 (23.1)	10.2 (0.18)	16.6 (0.23)	18.3 (0.22)	753 (10.7)
High school completion[4]	75.9 (0.10)	75.4 (0.10)	74.6 (0.10)	21,690 (55.3)	71.6 (0.10)	68.3 (0.11)	66.7 (0.10)	19,400 (51.4)	5.6 (0.06)	9.4 (0.08)	10.6 (0.08)	2,291 (15.0)
Some college, no degree	80.4 (0.10)	79.8 (0.10)	78.7 (0.09)	19,055 (47.4)	76.8 (0.11)	73.3 (0.11)	71.7 (0.11)	17,351 (45.6)	4.4 (0.06)	8.1 (0.07)	8.9 (0.08)	1,703 (15.0)
Associate's degree	84.5 (0.10)	84.1 (0.12)	83.5 (0.15)	8,240 (30.5)	81.7 (0.11)	79.0 (0.15)	78.0 (0.17)	7,698 (30.3)	3.3 (0.07)	6.0 (0.09)	6.6 (0.10)	543 (7.9)
Bachelor's or higher degree	86.3 (0.05)	86.3 (0.06)	86.2 (0.06)	31,332 (71.0)	84.3 (0.06)	82.8 (0.06)	82.3 (0.06)	29,931 (69.1)	2.3 (0.04)	4.1 (0.04)	4.5 (0.04)	1,401 (14.3)
Black, all education levels	75.1 (0.13)	74.3 (0.14)	73.5 (0.12)	14,393 (27.4)	68.4 (0.15)	64.4 (0.16)	62.6 (0.12)	12,257 (27.1)	9.0 (0.11)	13.3 (0.13)	14.8 (0.12)	2,136 (18.2)
Less than high school completion	50.5 (0.41)	49.5 (0.40)	48.7 (0.39)	1,385 (15.5)	41.1 (0.40)	37.4 (0.37)	35.2 (0.36)	1,001 (12.7)	18.7 (0.47)	24.4 (0.55)	27.7 (0.47)	383 (8.0)
High school completion[4]	71.9 (0.22)	70.8 (0.23)	69.6 (0.25)	4,367 (23.3)	64.3 (0.25)	59.7 (0.26)	57.2 (0.23)	3,589 (20.4)	10.6 (0.20)	15.8 (0.25)	17.8 (0.25)	778 (12.3)
Some college, no degree	80.4 (0.19)	79.0 (0.23)	78.2 (0.25)	4,067 (24.8)	73.6 (0.22)	68.7 (0.27)	66.9 (0.28)	3,479 (22.0)	8.4 (0.19)	13.1 (0.21)	14.5 (0.23)	588 (10.5)
Associate's degree	84.9 (0.38)	83.9 (0.38)	82.1 (0.36)	1,290 (13.7)	79.8 (0.45)	76.0 (0.49)	73.0 (0.42)	1,147 (12.7)	6.0 (0.33)	9.4 (0.36)	11.1 (0.35)	143 (4.9)
Bachelor's or higher degree	89.6 (0.20)	89.2 (0.21)	88.9 (0.18)	3,285 (20.8)	86.0 (0.24)	83.4 (0.24)	82.2 (0.20)	3,040 (20.1)	4.1 (0.15)	6.6 (0.15)	7.4 (0.15)	244 (5.2)
Hispanic, all education levels	78.5 (0.10)	78.3 (0.10)	77.3 (0.11)	18,906 (30.0)	73.9 (0.11)	70.4 (0.13)	68.9 (0.12)	16,846 (32.3)	5.9 (0.07)	10.1 (0.10)	10.9 (0.09)	2,060 (16.5)
Less than high school completion	71.8 (0.22)	71.7 (0.21)	70.6 (0.19)	6,169 (36.7)	66.4 (0.20)	62.9 (0.24)	61.2 (0.21)	5,351 (34.6)	7.6 (0.14)	12.3 (0.19)	13.3 (0.17)	818 (11.1)
High school completion[4]	78.6 (0.22)	78.3 (0.24)	77.1 (0.20)	5,082 (26.7)	73.9 (0.25)	69.8 (0.24)	68.4 (0.24)	4,507 (26.6)	6.0 (0.15)	10.8 (0.18)	11.3 (0.19)	575 (9.9)
Some college, no degree	83.6 (0.24)	82.7 (0.25)	81.8 (0.20)	3,607 (24.9)	79.1 (0.28)	75.2 (0.28)	73.3 (0.25)	3,235 (21.8)	5.4 (0.16)	9.2 (0.19)	10.3 (0.22)	372 (9.0)
Associate's degree	85.3 (0.36)	84.7 (0.39)	84.2 (0.36)	1,172 (14.4)	81.4 (0.39)	78.4 (0.48)	76.3 (0.47)	1,062 (14.7)	4.6 (0.25)	7.4 (0.32)	9.4 (0.36)	110 (4.1)
Bachelor's or higher degree	87.7 (0.18)	87.9 (0.23)	86.8 (0.26)	2,876 (27.5)	84.7 (0.21)	82.7 (0.26)	81.2 (0.31)	2,691 (27.0)	3.4 (0.13)	5.9 (0.18)	6.4 (0.20)	185 (5.8)
Asian, all education levels	79.8 (0.15)	79.4 (0.14)	79.0 (0.15)	6,691 (14.8)	76.5 (0.15)	74.0 (0.17)	73.1 (0.17)	6,190 (17.4)	4.1 (0.10)	6.8 (0.11)	7.5 (0.13)	501 (8.8)
Less than high school completion	66.3 (0.58)	66.4 (0.62)	65.7 (0.48)	645 (10.0)	61.4 (0.58)	59.6 (0.70)	58.0 (0.57)	569 (10.0)	7.4 (0.42)	10.2 (0.56)	11.8 (0.54)	76 (3.5)
High school completion[4]	76.6 (0.51)	75.2 (0.46)	74.6 (0.48)	956 (13.3)	72.4 (0.52)	68.6 (0.51)	67.3 (0.49)	863 (11.9)	5.5 (0.32)	8.8 (0.35)	9.8 (0.38)	94 (4.1)
Some college, no degree	79.6 (0.50)	78.4 (0.45)	78.0 (0.52)	893 (12.2)	75.8 (0.52)	71.7 (0.54)	71.1 (0.47)	812 (11.1)	4.8 (0.26)	8.5 (0.38)	9.1 (0.34)	82 (3.4)
Associate's degree	80.7 (0.59)	79.8 (0.68)	80.5 (0.64)	459 (8.4)	77.7 (0.66)	74.6 (0.69)	74.4 (0.70)	424 (7.8)	3.8 (0.36)	6.5 (0.41)	7.7 (0.44)	35 (2.2)
Bachelor's or higher degree	83.6 (0.23)	83.6 (0.24)	83.0 (0.21)	3,736 (20.1)	81.0 (0.23)	79.2 (0.27)	78.3 (0.23)	3,522 (19.9)	3.1 (0.10)	5.3 (0.13)	5.7 (0.14)	215 (5.4)
American Indian/Alaska Native, all education levels	68.5 (0.53)	68.8 (0.52)	67.0 (0.63)	724 (10.4)	62.5 (0.54)	60.0 (0.60)	56.8 (0.61)	614 (9.4)	8.7 (0.35)	12.7 (0.43)	15.2 (0.46)	110 (3.7)
Less than high school completion	46.7 (1.60)	47.3 (1.62)	46.9 (1.54)	86 (3.1)	38.7 (1.61)	36.4 (1.61)	35.1 (1.36)	64 (2.6)	17.2 (1.68)	23.1 (2.11)	25.3 (1.74)	22 (1.7)
High school completion[4]	66.8 (0.92)	67.2 (0.93)	64.4 (1.06)	225 (5.3)	60.8 (0.99)	57.0 (1.03)	52.4 (1.08)	183 (5.1)	9.0 (0.68)	15.2 (0.84)	18.7 (0.92)	42 (2.1)
Some college, no degree	73.7 (0.87)	72.6 (0.85)	71.0 (0.88)	213 (5.4)	68.4 (0.99)	63.6 (1.02)	61.0 (0.84)	183 (4.8)	7.2 (0.64)	12.4 (0.84)	14.1 (0.87)	30 (2.1)
Associate's degree	74.8 (1.77)	80.3 (1.54)	75.5 (1.78)	71 (2.9)	71.0 (1.72)	73.4 (1.78)	66.3 (1.87)	62 (2.9)	6.2 (1.02)	8.5 (1.07)	12.1 (1.46)	9 (1.0)
Bachelor's or higher degree	85.7 (0.95)	82.6 (1.24)	83.5 (1.19)	129 (4.8)	80.4 (1.11)	79.1 (1.21)	78.5 (1.36)	121 (4.6)	6.2 (0.96)	4.1 (0.52)	6.0 (0.73)	8 (1.0)

[1] Percentage of the civilian population who are employed or seeking employment.
[2] Number of persons employed as a percentage of the civilian population.
[3] The percentage of persons in the civilian labor force who are not working and who made specific efforts to find employment sometime during the prior 4 weeks.
[4] Includes equivalency credentials, such as the General Educational Development (GED) credential.

NOTE: Race categories exclude persons of Hispanic ethnicity. Totals include racial/ethnic groups not separately shown. Standard errors appear in parentheses and were computed using replicate weights. SOURCE: U.S. Department of Commerce, Census Bureau, American Community Survey, 2008, 2009, and 2010, unpublished tabulations. (This table was prepared October 2011.)

Labor force participation, employment, and unemployment of persons 16 to 24 years old who are not enrolled in school, by age group, sex, race/ethnicity, and educational attainment: 2008, 2009, and 2010

Age group, sex, race/ethnicity, and educational attainment	Labor force participation rate[1] 2008	2009	2010	Number of participants (in thousands) 2010	Employment to population ratio[2] 2008	2009	2010	Number employed (in thousands) 2010	Unemployment rate[3] 2008	2009	2010	Number unemployed (in thousands) 2010
1	2	3	4	5	6	7	8	9	10	11	12	13
16 to 19 years old												
All persons, all education levels	**66.9 (0.36)**	**63.9 (0.43)**	**62.7 (0.36)**	**1,676 (18.7)**	**50.2 (0.39)**	**43.2 (0.34)**	**41.7 (0.34)**	**1,116 (15.3)**	**25.0 (0.37)**	**32.4 (0.47)**	**33.4 (0.49)**	**560 (10.1)**
Less than high school completion	53.2 (0.64)	50.3 (0.64)	48.6 (0.62)	481 (10.0)	35.3 (0.64)	29.3 (0.56)	29.1 (0.51)	288 (7.1)	33.6 (0.87)	41.8 (0.87)	40.2 (0.79)	193 (5.5)
High school completion[4]	75.0 (0.43)	71.9 (0.52)	70.2 (0.49)	995 (13.7)	58.1 (0.49)	50.3 (0.53)	47.5 (0.53)	673 (11.1)	22.4 (0.45)	30.1 (0.56)	32.4 (0.69)	322 (8.5)
At least some college	80.9 (0.91)	75.1 (1.02)	75.1 (0.99)	200 (5.5)	69.2 (1.01)	60.2 (1.08)	58.1 (1.12)	155 (5.1)	14.5 (0.97)	19.9 (1.04)	22.6 (1.08)	45 (2.3)
Male, all education levels	**69.9 (0.44)**	**66.1 (0.52)**	**65.2 (0.49)**	**982 (12.6)**	**52.1 (0.48)**	**44.2 (0.47)**	**42.5 (0.48)**	**640 (10.1)**	**25.5 (0.44)**	**33.2 (0.60)**	**34.8 (0.62)**	**342 (7.6)**
Less than high school completion	57.8 (0.82)	54.6 (0.80)	53.0 (0.86)	318 (8.1)	38.9 (0.91)	32.5 (0.83)	32.3 (0.82)	194 (6.1)	32.7 (1.10)	40.5 (1.18)	39.0 (1.12)	124 (4.7)
High school completion[4]	78.0 (0.57)	74.1 (0.67)	73.1 (0.65)	572 (9.7)	60.1 (0.73)	51.0 (0.70)	48.1 (0.61)	376 (7.2)	23.0 (0.69)	31.2 (0.81)	34.2 (0.80)	195 (6.0)
At least some college	81.6 (1.48)	73.0 (1.54)	74.3 (1.51)	92 (3.6)	70.2 (1.68)	59.0 (1.79)	55.9 (1.59)	70 (3.3)	14.0 (1.46)	19.1 (1.68)	24.8 (1.51)	23 (1.5)
Female, all education levels	**63.0 (0.53)**	**61.1 (0.64)**	**59.5 (0.52)**	**694 (11.4)**	**47.7 (0.60)**	**41.9 (0.54)**	**40.8 (0.56)**	**476 (10.0)**	**24.4 (0.70)**	**31.5 (0.70)**	**31.4 (0.72)**	**218 (5.7)**
Less than high school completion	46.7 (1.00)	44.3 (1.04)	41.8 (0.91)	163 (5.1)	30.4 (0.94)	24.7 (0.79)	24.0 (0.84)	94 (3.8)	35.0 (1.36)	44.2 (1.59)	42.4 (1.46)	69 (3.2)
High school completion[4]	71.1 (0.72)	69.2 (0.78)	66.7 (0.69)	424 (8.8)	55.7 (0.75)	49.5 (0.83)	46.7 (0.83)	297 (8.0)	21.7 (0.75)	28.5 (0.77)	29.9 (0.99)	127 (4.6)
At least some college	80.3 (1.37)	77.1 (1.41)	75.7 (1.25)	108 (4.2)	68.3 (1.57)	61.3 (1.52)	60.1 (1.52)	86 (3.9)	14.9 (1.37)	20.5 (1.48)	20.7 (1.56)	22 (1.8)
White, all education levels	**72.0 (0.47)**	**69.3 (0.51)**	**67.5 (0.45)**	**866 (11.6)**	**55.4 (0.53)**	**48.6 (0.45)**	**46.2 (0.51)**	**594 (10.3)**	**23.0 (0.51)**	**29.8 (0.55)**	**31.5 (0.62)**	**272 (6.0)**
Less than high school completion	56.3 (0.87)	53.0 (0.73)	49.4 (0.88)	201 (6.0)	37.2 (0.87)	30.2 (0.81)	29.1 (0.72)	119 (4.2)	33.9 (1.25)	43.0 (1.42)	41.0 (1.16)	82 (3.4)
High school completion[4]	79.8 (0.56)	76.8 (0.58)	74.8 (0.52)	549 (8.8)	63.5 (0.69)	56.1 (0.59)	52.2 (0.73)	383 (7.9)	20.4 (0.55)	27.0 (0.64)	30.3 (0.86)	166 (5.3)
At least some college	82.4 (1.25)	79.9 (1.25)	81.2 (1.06)	116 (4.4)	72.1 (1.35)	66.0 (1.32)	64.7 (1.56)	92 (4.0)	12.5 (1.21)	17.4 (1.18)	20.4 (1.51)	24 (2.0)
Black, all education levels	**57.0 (0.95)**	**52.7 (1.02)**	**52.6 (0.97)**	**247 (6.7)**	**34.9 (1.04)**	**28.6 (0.88)**	**26.6 (0.88)**	**125 (5.0)**	**38.7 (1.44)**	**45.8 (1.32)**	**49.5 (1.32)**	**122 (4.3)**
Less than high school completion	41.0 (1.46)	38.4 (1.47)	37.1 (1.48)	70 (3.8)	18.9 (1.22)	16.1 (1.21)	14.1 (1.04)	26 (2.2)	53.8 (2.52)	58.1 (2.74)	62.1 (2.27)	43 (2.7)
High school completion[4]	66.6 (1.29)	61.2 (1.38)	62.6 (1.39)	149 (5.0)	44.2 (1.28)	35.1 (1.18)	33.3 (1.23)	79 (3.8)	33.6 (1.44)	42.7 (1.63)	46.7 (1.68)	70 (3.3)
At least some college	80.5 (2.63)	68.2 (2.81)	65.9 (2.86)	28 (2.1)	60.7 (3.64)	47.2 (2.93)	44.0 (2.99)	19 (1.8)	24.7 (3.69)	30.8 (3.58)	33.2 (3.64)	9 (1.2)
Hispanic, all education levels	**65.1 (0.64)**	**63.2 (0.79)**	**61.8 (0.76)**	**461 (8.9)**	**51.9 (0.79)**	**44.1 (0.68)**	**44.2 (0.80)**	**329 (7.4)**	**20.2 (0.74)**	**30.1 (0.88)**	**28.6 (0.97)**	**132 (5.3)**
Less than high school completion	58.1 (0.99)	55.8 (1.32)	55.2 (1.19)	188 (5.7)	45.0 (1.04)	37.1 (1.09)	38.3 (1.12)	130 (4.7)	22.6 (1.10)	33.5 (1.39)	30.7 (1.48)	58 (3.3)
High school completion[4]	70.8 (1.06)	69.7 (1.06)	66.9 (1.21)	231 (6.7)	57.3 (1.25)	49.2 (1.20)	48.0 (1.13)	166 (5.0)	19.0 (1.11)	29.4 (1.34)	28.2 (1.27)	65 (3.9)
At least some college	77.3 (2.04)	70.8 (2.37)	70.2 (2.49)	42 (2.6)	65.7 (2.35)	58.6 (2.75)	55.6 (2.79)	33 (2.5)	15.1 (2.09)	17.2 (2.41)	20.7 (2.56)	9 (1.1)
Asian, all education levels	**58.8 (2.86)**	**50.8 (2.61)**	**55.3 (2.92)**	**30 (2.5)**	**47.3 (2.62)**	**35.5 (2.65)**	**39.5 (2.70)**	**21 (2.0)**	**19.6 (2.80)**	**30.1 (3.49)**	**28.5 (3.03)**	**8 (1.1)**
Less than high school completion	43.1 (5.22)	38.9 (3.88)	38.5 (5.13)	5 (1.0)	32.0 (4.44)	26.3 (3.74)	26.2 (4.81)	4 (0.8)	25.7 (5.97)	32.4 (6.77)	31.8 (7.67)	2 (0.5)
High school completion[4]	68.0 (4.05)	57.3 (4.36)	60.2 (3.81)	17 (2.0)	53.7 (3.75)	39.2 (4.28)	40.6 (3.52)	11 (1.5)	20.9 (3.94)	31.6 (4.47)	32.5 (4.35)	5 (1.0)
At least some college	65.8 (7.26)	61.7 (6.28)	64.5 (5.61)	7 (1.1)	60.3 (7.14)	48.1 (6.72)	53.9 (6.16)	6 (1.0)	8.5 (3.96)	22.0 (7.08)	16.5 (5.23)	1 (0.4)
American Indian/Alaska Native, all education levels	**48.4 (3.38)**	**56.5 (3.17)**	**44.0 (3.34)**	**17 (1.5)**	**36.2 (3.58)**	**33.6 (2.79)**	**28.5 (2.87)**	**11 (1.2)**	**25.2 (3.95)**	**40.5 (4.04)**	**35.3 (4.18)**	**6 (0.9)**
Less than high school completion	29.8 (3.93)	45.2 (4.78)	30.4 (4.50)	5 (0.8)	16.4 (3.11)	21.5 (3.68)	15.7 (3.21)	3 (0.6)	45.0 (8.06)	52.4 (7.26)	48.3 (7.43)	3 (0.6)
High school completion[4]	68.0 (4.33)	66.9 (4.43)	55.6 (4.89)	10 (1.2)	53.9 (4.97)	47.1 (4.70)	38.4 (4.64)	7 (0.9)	17.5 (3.90)	29.6 (4.29)	30.9 (5.48)	3 (0.7)
At least some college	‡ (†)	67.7 (10.57)	‡ (†)	‡ (†)	64.2 (13.48)	30.8 (9.73)	44.8 (10.11)	1 (0.4)	11.9 (7.16)	54.5 (12.25)	‡ (†)	# (†)
20 to 24 years old												
All persons, all education levels	**81.9 (0.14)**	**81.0 (0.15)**	**80.2 (0.14)**	**9,806 (35.0)**	**71.7 (0.16)**	**66.6 (0.17)**	**65.3 (0.18)**	**7,983 (34.4)**	**12.4 (0.13)**	**17.8 (0.15)**	**18.6 (0.17)**	**1,823 (17.4)**
Less than high school completion	67.2 (0.36)	65.9 (0.34)	65.5 (0.38)	1,507 (19.8)	53.1 (0.38)	47.3 (0.39)	46.3 (0.41)	1,066 (16.6)	21.0 (0.42)	20.8 (0.48)	29.3 (0.53)	442 (9.4)
High school completion[4]	80.9 (0.22)	79.7 (0.26)	78.8 (0.20)	3,916 (23.7)	69.4 (0.26)	63.1 (0.28)	61.6 (0.28)	3,061 (22.1)	14.2 (0.21)	20.8 (0.26)	21.8 (0.30)	855 (12.6)
Some college, no degree	86.9 (0.25)	86.3 (0.30)	85.0 (0.30)	2,391 (21.3)	78.5 (0.31)	73.8 (0.41)	72.1 (0.39)	2,029 (20.7)	9.7 (0.25)	14.5 (0.31)	15.2 (0.31)	363 (7.6)
Associate's degree	92.6 (0.43)	92.1 (0.43)	90.6 (0.47)	497 (8.5)	87.1 (0.61)	83.5 (0.56)	82.3 (0.60)	451 (8.0)	5.9 (0.47)	9.3 (0.46)	9.2 (0.55)	46 (2.9)
Bachelor's or higher degree	94.0 (0.22)	93.5 (0.26)	93.3 (0.26)	1,495 (16.3)	89.2 (0.27)	86.5 (0.34)	86.0 (0.34)	1,377 (15.4)	5.1 (0.23)	7.5 (0.23)	7.9 (0.28)	118 (4.4)

See notes at end of table.

Labor force participation, employment, and unemployment of persons 16 to 24 years old who are not enrolled in school, by age group, sex, race/ethnicity, and educational attainment: 2008, 2009, and 2010—Continued

Age group, sex, race/ethnicity, and educational attainment	Labor force participation rate[1] 2008	2009	2010	Number of participants (in thousands) 2010	Employment to population ratio[2] 2008	2009	2010	Number employed (in thousands) 2010	Unemployment rate[3] 2008	2009	2010	Number unemployed (in thousands) 2010
1	2	3	4	5	6	7	8	9	10	11	12	13
Male, all education levels	85.3 (0.17)	84.2 (0.21)	83.0 (0.19)	5,463 (24.5)	74.2 (0.21)	67.7 (0.29)	66.3 (0.23)	4,366 (23.9)	13.0 (0.19)	19.6 (0.23)	20.1 (0.22)	1,097 (12.9)
Less than high school completion	74.6 (0.40)	73.5 (0.43)	71.8 (0.47)	1,017 (15.1)	59.7 (0.57)	53.3 (0.51)	51.8 (0.55)	733 (13.4)	20.0 (0.56)	27.5 (0.57)	27.8 (0.63)	283 (7.1)
High school completion[4]	84.9 (0.30)	83.9 (0.31)	82.6 (0.30)	2,361 (17.4)	72.9 (0.36)	65.4 (0.44)	63.9 (0.36)	1,826 (15.2)	14.2 (0.29)	22.0 (0.39)	22.7 (0.35)	535 (9.5)
Some college, no degree	90.7 (0.54)	89.1 (0.45)	87.4 (0.41)	1,221 (16.2)	81.6 (0.47)	75.3 (0.60)	73.4 (0.54)	1,024 (14.7)	10.0 (0.37)	15.5 (0.44)	16.1 (0.43)	196 (5.7)
Associate's degree	95.1 (0.54)	94.8 (0.61)	92.9 (0.66)	236 (6.0)	89.3 (0.93)	84.8 (0.92)	83.4 (0.83)	212 (5.9)	6.1 (0.75)	10.6 (0.74)	10.3 (0.83)	24 (2.0)
Bachelor's or higher degree	95.2 (0.33)	94.3 (0.36)	95.3 (0.34)	629 (9.6)	89.7 (0.46)	85.9 (0.51)	86.5 (0.56)	570 (8.9)	5.8 (0.38)	8.9 (0.38)	9.3 (0.50)	58 (3.4)
Female, all education levels	77.9 (0.23)	77.1 (0.22)	76.9 (0.23)	4,343 (22.8)	68.8 (0.27)	65.2 (0.23)	64.0 (0.29)	3,617 (23.2)	11.6 (0.20)	15.5 (0.24)	16.7 (0.25)	726 (11.0)
Less than high school completion	55.9 (0.63)	54.1 (0.56)	55.5 (0.73)	491 (10.1)	43.0 (0.65)	38.0 (0.59)	37.6 (0.79)	332 (9.2)	23.0 (0.75)	29.7 (0.89)	32.3 (0.96)	159 (5.0)
High school completion[4]	75.4 (0.42)	73.9 (0.40)	73.6 (0.33)	1,555 (15.8)	64.7 (0.48)	60.0 (0.43)	58.5 (0.43)	1,235 (13.7)	14.2 (0.36)	18.8 (0.44)	20.6 (0.50)	320 (8.8)
Some college, no degree	83.3 (0.43)	83.6 (0.43)	82.7 (0.44)	1,171 (15.6)	75.4 (0.47)	72.4 (0.53)	70.9 (0.52)	1,004 (14.5)	9.5 (0.33)	13.4 (0.41)	14.2 (0.39)	166 (4.9)
Associate's degree	90.5 (0.68)	89.5 (0.65)	88.6 (0.73)	260 (6.1)	85.3 (0.75)	82.3 (0.84)	81.3 (0.92)	239 (6.0)	5.7 (0.55)	8.1 (0.73)	8.3 (0.72)	22 (1.9)
Bachelor's or higher degree	93.2 (0.31)	93.0 (0.38)	92.0 (0.35)	866 (12.2)	88.8 (0.39)	86.9 (0.43)	85.6 (0.44)	806 (12.2)	4.7 (0.28)	6.6 (0.30)	6.9 (0.32)	60 (2.7)
White, all education levels	85.7 (0.19)	84.9 (0.18)	84.0 (0.19)	5,577 (23.9)	76.9 (0.22)	71.9 (0.24)	70.9 (0.22)	4,706 (23.0)	10.3 (0.17)	15.2 (0.19)	15.6 (0.17)	870 (9.7)
Less than high school completion	68.9 (0.56)	67.1 (0.59)	65.2 (0.67)	510 (9.2)	53.3 (0.64)	46.8 (0.69)	44.9 (0.70)	351 (7.8)	22.7 (0.77)	30.2 (0.80)	31.1 (0.88)	159 (5.3)
High school completion[4]	83.8 (0.33)	82.6 (0.34)	81.5 (0.27)	2,155 (17.2)	73.4 (0.37)	66.9 (0.42)	65.3 (0.38)	1,727 (16.7)	12.5 (0.38)	19.0 (0.36)	19.8 (0.38)	428 (8.4)
Some college, no degree	88.3 (0.31)	88.1 (0.35)	86.8 (0.36)	1,427 (15.8)	81.5 (0.39)	77.3 (0.46)	75.5 (0.48)	1,242 (15.3)	7.7 (0.31)	12.2 (0.34)	13.0 (0.37)	185 (5.5)
Associate's degree	94.4 (0.41)	93.6 (0.45)	92.5 (0.49)	357 (6.3)	89.8 (0.62)	86.7 (0.57)	86.2 (0.59)	333 (6.2)	4.9 (0.46)	7.4 (0.48)	6.9 (0.52)	25 (1.9)
Bachelor's or higher degree	95.5 (0.22)	95.0 (0.29)	95.4 (0.23)	1,127 (12.4)	91.2 (0.28)	88.5 (0.37)	89.1 (0.33)	1,053 (12.0)	4.5 (0.24)	6.8 (0.26)	6.6 (0.26)	74 (3.0)
Black, all education levels	73.0 (0.44)	72.3 (0.46)	71.4 (0.44)	1,321 (13.6)	55.9 (0.48)	50.7 (0.47)	48.5 (0.48)	896 (11.6)	23.5 (0.48)	29.9 (0.47)	32.2 (0.57)	425 (8.8)
Less than high school completion	53.1 (0.98)	52.5 (1.07)	50.2 (1.14)	202 (6.6)	32.1 (1.04)	26.9 (0.83)	24.0 (0.82)	97 (4.1)	39.5 (1.57)	48.7 (1.28)	52.1 (1.24)	105 (4.2)
High school completion[4]	73.8 (0.67)	71.8 (0.67)	71.8 (0.63)	601 (10.0)	56.0 (0.78)	48.9 (0.78)	47.1 (0.75)	394 (8.2)	24.1 (0.71)	31.9 (0.87)	34.5 (0.86)	207 (6.3)
Some college, no degree	84.4 (0.76)	84.3 (0.87)	83.4 (0.71)	380 (8.5)	69.3 (0.89)	64.6 (1.05)	63.7 (0.90)	290 (7.1)	17.9 (0.84)	23.4 (0.87)	23.6 (0.94)	90 (4.3)
Associate's degree	87.4 (1.55)	88.2 (2.37)	85.5 (2.18)	41 (2.7)	75.8 (2.14)	73.3 (3.32)	68.9 (2.68)	33 (2.4)	13.3 (2.29)	16.9 (2.69)	19.3 (2.66)	8 (1.2)
Bachelor's or higher degree	91.6 (1.28)	92.1 (1.23)	91.1 (1.30)	98 (4.0)	83.7 (1.43)	83.7 (1.56)	77.1 (1.72)	83 (3.8)	8.6 (1.10)	9.1 (1.18)	15.4 (1.43)	15 (1.5)
Hispanic, all education levels	78.3 (0.30)	78.1 (0.29)	77.8 (0.28)	2,309 (17.6)	69.6 (0.33)	65.0 (0.33)	64.1 (0.34)	1,903 (16.8)	11.1 (0.24)	16.7 (0.33)	17.6 (0.38)	406 (9.4)
Less than high school completion	71.8 (0.54)	71.3 (0.50)	72.2 (0.53)	720 (15.1)	62.2 (0.61)	57.7 (0.58)	57.1 (0.60)	569 (13.4)	13.3 (0.59)	19.0 (0.64)	20.9 (0.71)	151 (5.8)
High school completion[4]	79.2 (0.49)	79.2 (0.50)	78.4 (0.46)	954 (11.4)	70.3 (0.51)	65.3 (0.56)	64.4 (0.53)	784 (10.1)	11.2 (0.44)	17.5 (0.54)	17.8 (0.53)	170 (5.7)
Some college, no degree	85.2 (0.62)	84.4 (0.76)	82.7 (0.77)	438 (9.4)	77.5 (0.77)	72.7 (0.99)	70.6 (0.82)	374 (8.3)	9.0 (0.63)	13.9 (0.76)	14.6 (0.59)	64 (3.0)
Associate's degree	87.7 (1.77)	88.7 (1.18)	87.7 (1.44)	72 (3.5)	83.6 (2.09)	77.6 (1.82)	76.0 (1.81)	62 (3.4)	4.8 (1.21)	12.5 (1.99)	13.4 (1.63)	10 (1.2)
Bachelor's or higher degree	90.0 (1.09)	89.4 (1.23)	87.7 (1.03)	125 (3.9)	83.9 (1.37)	81.2 (1.58)	79.8 (1.34)	114 (3.4)	6.8 (0.98)	9.1 (1.10)	9.0 (0.98)	11 (1.4)
Asian, all education levels	82.2 (0.87)	78.2 (0.94)	79.1 (1.00)	279 (7.5)	74.0 (0.98)	67.2 (1.07)	67.4 (1.06)	238 (6.9)	10.0 (0.76)	14.1 (0.88)	14.8 (0.80)	41 (2.4)
Less than high school completion	74.7 (2.79)	64.8 (2.83)	66.5 (3.14)	25 (2.2)	65.5 (3.18)	50.3 (3.45)	48.8 (3.41)	19 (1.8)	12.3 (2.73)	22.4 (4.02)	26.6 (3.69)	7 (1.2)
High school completion[4]	79.7 (1.72)	76.3 (2.20)	78.2 (1.93)	71 (3.5)	68.2 (2.18)	63.6 (2.37)	64.6 (2.19)	59 (3.3)	14.4 (1.74)	16.7 (1.63)	17.4 (2.01)	12 (1.5)
Some college, no degree	82.7 (1.61)	77.7 (2.16)	79.2 (1.87)	61 (3.5)	74.6 (1.66)	67.7 (2.13)	67.4 (2.03)	54 (3.3)	9.7 (1.37)	12.9 (2.06)	11.2 (1.20)	7 (0.8)
Associate's degree	83.3 (3.93)	83.2 (3.41)	84.7 (3.31)	15 (1.7)	75.5 (4.50)	72.4 (4.34)	70.4 (3.70)	13 (1.4)	9.4 (3.31)	12.9 (3.90)	11.8 (3.26)	3 (0.6)
Bachelor's or higher degree	85.4 (1.35)	83.5 (1.28)	82.6 (1.28)	107 (3.8)	79.4 (1.62)	74.1 (1.67)	72.7 (1.49)	94 (3.4)	7.1 (0.91)	11.2 (1.08)	12.0 (0.99)	13 (1.4)
American Indian/Alaska Native, all education levels	71.0 (1.77)	66.8 (1.90)	67.7 (1.96)	79 (3.2)	56.3 (1.89)	48.1 (1.83)	45.1 (1.71)	52 (2.5)	20.7 (2.03)	27.9 (2.11)	33.4 (2.12)	26 (2.1)
Less than high school completion	58.3 (3.77)	48.5 (4.12)	54.0 (4.60)	17 (1.8)	40.6 (3.98)	26.1 (3.70)	24.0 (3.00)	7 (1.1)	30.4 (4.94)	46.2 (5.02)	55.7 (5.32)	9 (1.4)
High school completion[4]	70.5 (2.48)	71.9 (2.61)	69.6 (2.20)	37 (2.2)	59.4 (2.51)	52.2 (2.75)	47.4 (2.57)	25 (2.0)	15.7 (2.28)	27.4 (2.94)	32.0 (3.00)	12 (1.3)
Some college, no degree	79.3 (3.41)	69.0 (3.80)	74.4 (4.82)	19 (1.9)	62.5 (4.05)	55.0 (4.08)	55.6 (3.63)	15 (1.5)	21.2 (3.98)	20.2 (2.94)	24.7 (4.22)	5 (1.0)
Associate's degree	85.8 (6.34)	86.8 (5.30)	80.3! (8.90)	2 (0.5)	50.9 (11.21)	68.6 (8.53)	70.4 (9.36)	2 (0.5)	40.7 (12.12)	20.9 (8.39)	‡ (†)	‡ (†)
Bachelor's or higher degree	98.0 (1.53)	90.7 (4.95)	99.5 (0.53)	3 (0.7)	89.8 (6.72)	83.1 (6.26)	96.2 (3.64)	3 (0.7)	‡ (†)	‡ (†)	‡ (†)	‡ (†)

†Not applicable.
#Rounds to zero.
‡Interpret data with caution. The coefficient of variation (CV) for this estimate is 30 percent or greater.
‡Reporting standards not met. Either there are too few cases or the coefficient of variation (CV) is 50 percent or greater.
[1]Percentage of the civilian population who are employed or seeking employment.
[2]Number of persons employed as a percentage of the civilian population.

[3]The percentage of persons in the civilian labor force who are not working and who made specific efforts to find employment sometime during the prior 4 weeks.
[4]Includes equivalency credentials, such as the General Educational Development (GED) credential.
NOTE: Table excludes persons enrolled in school. Race categories exclude persons of Hispanic ethnicity. Totals include racial/ethnic groups not separately shown. Standard errors appear in parentheses and were computed using replicate weights.
SOURCE: U.S. Department of Commerce, Census Bureau, American Community Survey, 2008, 2009, and 2010, unpublished tabulations. (This table was prepared October 2011.)

Occupation of employed persons 25 years old and over, by educational attainment and sex: 2010

Occupation and sex	Total employed (in thousands)	Total	High school — Less than 1 year of high school	High school — 1–4 years of high school, no completion	High school — High school completion (includes equivalency)	College — Some college, no degree	College — Associate's degree	College — Bachelor's degree	College — Master's or higher degree
1	2	3	4	5	6	7	8	9	10
All persons	**121,987 (234.0)**	**100.0**	**3.1 (0.06)**	**5.1 (0.07)**	**28.1 (0.15)**	**17.1 (0.12)**	**10.6 (0.10)**	**22.9 (0.14)**	**13.0 (0.11)**
Management, professional, and related	48,913 (219.0)	100.0	0.4 (0.03)	1.0 (0.05)	11.5 (0.17)	12.1 (0.17)	10.7 (0.16)	36.1 (0.25)	28.3 (0.24)
Management, business, and financial operations	20,206 (155.0)	100.0	0.6 (0.06)	1.7 (0.11)	17.0 (0.31)	15.8 (0.30)	8.7 (0.23)	37.2 (0.39)	18.9 (0.32)
Professional and related	28,707 (179.9)	100.0	0.1 (0.03)	0.5 (0.05)	7.7 (0.18)	9.5 (0.20)	12.0 (0.22)	35.2 (0.33)	34.9 (0.33)
Education, training, and library	7,929 (100.7)	100.0	0.1! (0.05)	0.4 (0.08)	7.1 (0.33)	7.5 (0.34)	5.2 (0.29)	34.9 (0.62)	44.9 (0.65)
Preschool and kindergarten teachers	627 (28.9)	100.0	‡ (†)	‡ (†)	14.4 (1.62)	16.5 (1.71)	13.4 (1.57)	35.9 (2.22)	18.7 (1.80)
Elementary and middle school teachers	2,688 (59.5)	100.0	‡ (†)	‡ (†)	2.4 (0.34)	2.9 (0.38)	1.7 (0.29)	45.2 (1.11)	47.6 (1.11)
Secondary school teachers	1,163 (39.3)	100.0	# (†)	— (†)	0.9! (0.31)	1.6 (0.43)	1.2! (0.37)	43.1 (1.68)	53.2 (1.69)
Special education teachers	365 (22.1)	100.0	— (†)	# (†)	2.5! (0.94)	2.5! (0.94)	4.4 (1.24)	35.3 (2.89)	55.3 (3.01)
Postsecondary teachers	1,193 (39.8)	100.0	# (†)	‡ (†)	1.2! (0.36)	2.3 (0.50)	2.0 (0.47)	13.7 (1.15)	80.8 (1.32)
Other education, training, and library workers	1,892 (50.0)	100.0	‡ (†)	1.0 (0.26)	19.8 (1.06)	18.6 (1.04)	12.0 (0.87)	28.1 (1.19)	20.2 (1.07)
Service occupations	19,226 (151.7)	100.0	7.2 (0.22)	9.9 (0.25)	38.1 (0.40)	19.9 (0.33)	10.7 (0.26)	11.8 (0.27)	2.3 (0.12)
Sales and office occupations	27,833 (177.6)	100.0	1.1 (0.07)	3.5 (0.13)	33.2 (0.33)	23.8 (0.30)	11.6 (0.22)	22.4 (0.29)	4.4 (0.14)
Natural resources, construction, and maintenance	11,675 (120.9)	100.0	8.5 (0.30)	11.3 (0.34)	44.1 (0.53)	17.1 (0.40)	10.7 (0.33)	7.0 (0.27)	1.3 (0.12)
Production, transportation, and material moving	14,339 (132.9)	100.0	6.9 (0.24)	11.1 (0.30)	48.4 (0.48)	17.1 (0.36)	8.1 (0.26)	7.2 (0.25)	1.3 (0.11)
Males	**64,765 (158.6)**	**100.0**	**3.9 (0.09)**	**6.0 (0.11)**	**29.6 (0.20)**	**16.6 (0.17)**	**9.0 (0.13)**	**22.2 (0.19)**	**12.7 (0.15)**
Management, professional, and related	23,866 (151.4)	100.0	0.5 (0.05)	1.2 (0.08)	11.7 (0.24)	12.3 (0.24)	8.0 (0.20)	36.4 (0.35)	29.8 (0.34)
Management, business, and financial operations	11,606 (114.6)	100.0	0.8 (0.10)	2.0 (0.15)	17.0 (0.40)	15.3 (0.38)	7.6 (0.28)	37.8 (0.51)	19.4 (0.42)
Professional and related	12,260 (117.3)	100.0	0.2 (0.04)	0.5 (0.07)	6.7 (0.26)	9.5 (0.30)	8.4 (0.29)	35.1 (0.49)	39.6 (0.50)
Education, training, and library	2,064 (51.1)	100.0	# (†)	‡ (†)	3.5 (0.46)	4.5 (0.52)	2.9 (0.42)	30.8 (1.16)	58.0 (1.24)
Service occupations	8,253 (98.6)	100.0	7.9 (0.34)	8.8 (0.35)	36.3 (0.60)	20.5 (0.51)	9.7 (0.37)	14.0 (0.44)	2.7 (0.20)
Sales and office occupations	10,247 (108.6)	100.0	1.5 (0.14)	3.7 (0.21)	28.6 (0.51)	21.8 (0.46)	9.8 (0.33)	28.4 (0.51)	6.1 (0.27)
Natural resources, construction, and maintenance	11,152 (112.7)	100.0	8.4 (0.30)	11.4 (0.34)	44.5 (0.54)	17.0 (0.40)	10.7 (0.33)	6.8 (0.27)	1.3 (0.12)
Production, transportation, and material moving	11,247 (113.1)	100.0	6.2 (0.26)	10.7 (0.33)	48.6 (0.54)	17.5 (0.41)	8.2 (0.29)	7.5 (0.28)	1.3 (0.12)
Females	**57,222 (161.2)**	**100.0**	**2.2 (0.07)**	**4.2 (0.09)**	**26.4 (0.20)**	**17.7 (0.18)**	**12.4 (0.15)**	**23.8 (0.20)**	**13.3 (0.16)**
Management, professional, and related	25,047 (148.5)	100.0	0.2 (0.03)	0.7 (0.06)	11.4 (0.22)	11.9 (0.23)	13.2 (0.24)	35.7 (0.33)	26.9 (0.31)
Management, business, and financial operations	8,600 (97.2)	100.0	0.4 (0.07)	1.3 (0.14)	17.0 (0.45)	16.5 (0.44)	10.3 (0.36)	36.4 (0.57)	18.1 (0.46)
Professional and related	16,447 (127.9)	100.0	0.1 (0.03)	0.4 (0.06)	8.4 (0.24)	9.6 (0.25)	14.7 (0.30)	35.4 (0.41)	31.4 (0.40)
Education, training, and library	5,864 (81.6)	100.0	0.2! (0.06)	0.4 (0.09)	8.4 (0.40)	8.5 (0.40)	6.0 (0.34)	36.3 (0.69)	40.3 (0.71)
Service occupations	10,974 (108.2)	100.0	6.7 (0.26)	10.7 (0.33)	39.5 (0.51)	19.5 (0.42)	11.5 (0.34)	10.1 (0.32)	2.0 (0.15)
Sales and office occupations	17,587 (131.2)	100.0	0.8 (0.07)	3.4 (0.15)	35.8 (0.40)	25.0 (0.36)	12.7 (0.28)	18.8 (0.32)	3.4 (0.15)
Natural resources, construction, and maintenance	523 (25.1)	100.0	12.2 (1.58)	7.6 (1.28)	36.3 (2.32)	19.1 (1.89)	10.7 (1.49)	11.9 (1.56)	2.1! (0.69)
Production, transportation, and material moving	3,092 (60.2)	100.0	9.3 (0.58)	12.6 (0.66)	47.4 (0.99)	15.3 (0.71)	7.7 (0.53)	6.3 (0.48)	1.4 (0.23)

—Not available.
†Not applicable.
#Rounds to zero.
!Interpret data with caution. The coefficient of variation (CV) for this estimate is 30 percent or greater.

‡Reporting standards not met. The coefficient of variation (CV) for this estimate is 50 percent or greater.
NOTE: Detail may not sum to totals because of rounding and missing data. Standard errors appear in parentheses.
SOURCE: U.S. Department of Labor, Bureau of Labor Statistics, Office of Employment and Unemployment Statistics, unpublished 2010 annual average data from the Current Population Survey (CPS). (This table was prepared September 2011.)

Outcomes of Education

Median annual earnings of year-round, full-time workers 25 years old and over, by highest level of educational attainment and sex: 1990 through 2010

(Current dollars; standard errors shown in parentheses)

Sex and year	Total	Elementary/secondary			College						
		Less than 9th grade	Some high school, no completion[1]	High school completion (includes equivalency)[2]	Some college, no degree[3]	Associate's degree	Bachelor's or higher degree[4]				
							Total	Bachelor's degree[5]	Master's degree	Professional degree	Doctor's degree
1	2	3	4	5	6	7	8	9	10	11	12
Males											
1990	$30,730 (—)	$17,390 (—)	$20,900 (—)	$26,650 (—)	$31,730 (—)	$33,820[e] (†)	$42,670 (—)	$39,240 (—)	$49,730[e] (†)	$74,000[e] (†)	$57,190[e] (†)
1991	31,610 (—)	17,620 (—)	21,400 (—)	26,780 (—)	31,660 (—)	33,430 (—)	45,140 (—)	40,910 (—)	49,970 (—)	76,220 (—)	57,420 (—)
1992	32,060 (120)	17,290 (—)	21,270 (—)	27,280 (175)	32,080 (—)	33,690 (—)	45,800 (—)	41,360 (304)	51,870 (—)	80,550 (—)	63,150 (—)
1993	32,360 (124)	16,860 (—)	21,750 (—)	27,370 (204)	32,080 (—)	33,690 (—)	47,740 (—)	42,760 (536)	53,500 (854)	75,010 (3,040)	61,920 (1,619)
1994	33,440 (246)	17,530 (453)	22,050 (319)	28,040 (322)	32,280 (300)	35,790 (430)	49,230 (707)	43,660 (633)	—	—	—
1995	34,550 (275)	18,350 (545)	22,190 (342)	29,510 (358)	33,880 (517)	35,200 (535)	50,480 (312)	45,270 (510)	55,220 (973)	79,670 (2,582)	65,340 (2,188)
1996	35,620 (150)	17,960 (594)	22,720 (414)	30,710 (184)	34,850 (456)	37,130 (435)	51,440 (303)	45,850 (458)	60,510 (945)	85,960 (3,317)	71,230 (3,362)
1997	36,680 (149)	19,290 (629)	24,730 (466)	31,220 (171)	35,950 (293)	38,020 (774)	53,450 (755)	48,620 (851)	61,690 (771)	85,010 (4,253)	76,230 (3,611)
1998	37,910 (291)	19,380 (600)	23,960 (547)	31,480 (169)	36,930 (291)	40,270 (539)	56,520 (421)	51,410 (349)	62,240 (847)	94,740 (12,105)	75,080 (2,507)
1999	40,330 (144)	20,430 (444)	25,040 (535)	33,180 (388)	39,220 (581)	41,640 (459)	60,200 (439)	52,990 (722)	66,240 (690)	100,000 (37,836)	81,690 (3,953)
2000	41,060 (156)	20,790 (376)	25,100 (436)	34,300 (457)	40,340 (312)	41,950 (460)	61,870 (303)	56,330 (573)	68,320 (1,506)	99,410 (20,832)	80,250 (2,446)
2001	41,620 (104)	21,360 (235)	26,210 (251)	34,720 (299)	41,050 (214)	42,780 (561)	62,220 (279)	55,930 (335)	70,900 (687)	100,000 (—)	86,970 (3,013)
2002	41,150 (100)	20,920 (213)	25,900 (207)	33,210 (311)	40,850 (195)	42,860 (673)	61,700 (201)	56,080 (385)	67,280 (1,294)	100,000 (—)	83,310 (2,076)
2003	41,940 (90)	21,220 (227)	26,470 (280)	35,410 (168)	41,350 (182)	42,870 (719)	62,080 (187)	56,500 (365)	70,640 (562)	100,000 (—)	87,130 (2,528)
2004	42,090 (89)	21,660 (191)	26,280 (234)	35,730 (148)	41,900 (175)	44,400 (931)	62,800 (798)	57,220 (393)	71,530 (490)	100,000 (—)	82,400 (2,423)
2005	43,320 (367)	22,330 (220)	27,190 (237)	36,300 (141)	42,420 (323)	47,180 (367)	66,170 (356)	60,020 (653)	75,030 (1,229)	100,000 (—)	85,860 (3,061)
2006	45,760 (134)	22,710 (398)	27,650 (573)	37,030 (164)	43,830 (812)	47,070 (390)	66,930 (346)	60,910 (235)	75,430 (859)	100,000 (—)	100,000 (—)
2007	47,000 (130)	23,380 (544)	29,320 (590)	37,860 (406)	44,900 (585)	49,040 (801)	70,400 (241)	62,090 (236)	76,280 (416)	100,000 (—)	92,090 (1,894)
2008	49,000 (309)	24,260 (631)	29,680 (458)	39,010 (399)	45,820 (276)	50,150 (344)	72,220 (236)	65,800 (388)	80,960 (468)	100,000 (—)	100,000 (—)
2009	49,990 (201)	23,950 (394)	28,020 (542)	39,480 (379)	47,100 (347)	50,300 (238)	71,470 (239)	62,440 (707)	79,340 (1,568)	123,240 (2,539)	100,740 (519)
2010	50,360 (93)	24,450 (597)	29,440 (684)	40,060 (237)	46,430 (348)	50,280 (245)	71,780 (267)	63,740 (1,115)	80,960 (453)	115,300 (4,891)	101,220 (653)
Females											
1990	21,370 (—)	12,250 (—)	14,430 (—)	18,320 (—)	22,230 (—)	25,000[e] (†)	30,380 (—)	28,020 (—)	34,950[e] (†)	46,740[e] (†)	43,300[e] (†)
1991	22,040 (—)	12,070 (—)	14,460 (—)	18,840 (—)	22,140 (—)	25,620 (—)	31,310 (—)	29,080 (—)	36,040 (—)	46,260 (—)	45,790 (—)
1992	23,140 (159)	12,960 (—)	14,560 (—)	19,430 (176)	23,160 (—)	25,880 (—)	32,300 (—)	30,330 (294)	38,610 (—)	50,210 (—)	47,250 (—)
1993	23,630 (166)	12,420 (—)	15,390 (—)	19,960 (173)	23,060 (—)	25,940 (295)	34,310 (—)	31,200 (310)	39,460 (606)	50,620 (2,154)	51,120 (2,888)
1994	24,040 (165)	12,430 (427)	15,130 (328)	20,370 (158)	23,510 (327)	—	35,380 (280)	31,740 (314)	—	—	—
1995	24,880 (160)	13,580 (490)	15,830 (293)	20,460 (162)	24,000 (274)	27,310 (428)	35,260 (313)	32,050 (273)	40,260 (556)	50,000 (2,532)	48,140 (2,373)
1996	25,810 (131)	14,410 (559)	16,950 (333)	21,180 (143)	25,170 (267)	28,080 (526)	36,460 (296)	33,530 (437)	41,900 (564)	57,620 (3,635)	56,270 (3,300)
1997	26,970 (134)	14,160 (492)	16,700 (335)	22,070 (148)	26,340 (291)	28,810 (660)	38,040 (481)	35,380 (295)	44,950 (837)	61,050 (4,737)	53,040 (3,626)
1998	27,960 (199)	14,470 (429)	16,480 (322)	22,780 (254)	27,420 (271)	29,920 (513)	39,790 (408)	36,560 (305)	45,280 (760)	57,570 (1,705)	57,800 (1,881)
1999	28,840 (216)	15,100 (492)	17,020 (298)	23,060 (279)	27,760 (369)	30,920 (318)	41,750 (275)	37,990 (614)	48,100 (862)	59,900 (4,479)	60,080 (3,130)
2000	30,330 (138)	15,800 (327)	17,920 (434)	24,970 (236)	28,700 (364)	31,070 (307)	42,710 (439)	40,420 (284)	50,140 (735)	58,960 (3,552)	57,080 (2,999)
2001	31,360 (91)	16,690 (255)	19,160 (359)	25,300 (132)	30,420 (186)	32,150 (231)	44,780 (367)	40,990 (231)	50,670 (328)	61,750 (3,976)	62,120 (2,228)
2002	31,010 (83)	16,510 (297)	19,310 (360)	25,180 (121)	29,400 (299)	31,630 (211)	43,250 (568)	40,850 (173)	48,890 (595)	57,020 (2,421)	65,720 (2,268)
2003	31,570 (85)	16,910 (256)	18,940 (327)	26,070 (118)	30,140 (176)	32,250 (241)	45,120 (291)	41,330 (204)	50,160 (454)	66,490 (3,469)	67,210 (2,462)
2004	31,990 (80)	17,020 (241)	19,160 (319)	26,030 (116)	30,820 (135)	33,480 (489)	45,910 (229)	41,680 (172)	51,320 (263)	75,040 (2,436)	68,880 (2,450)
2005	33,080 (242)	16,140 (250)	20,130 (274)	26,290 (134)	31,400 (165)	33,940 (497)	46,950 (232)	42,170 (179)	51,410 (283)	70,460 (2,774)	66,850 (2,490)
2006	35,100 (113)	18,130 (408)	20,130 (270)	26,740 (136)	31,950 (165)	35,160 (376)	49,570 (441)	45,410 (259)	52,440 (561)	76,240 (2,488)	70,520 (1,779)
2007	36,090 (105)	18,260 (461)	20,400 (292)	27,240 (133)	32,840 (415)	36,330 (283)	50,400 (158)	45,770 (262)	55,430 (412)	71,100 (910)	68,990 (2,155)
2008	36,700 (109)	18,630 (494)	20,410 (295)	28,380 (283)	32,630 (355)	36,760 (243)	51,410 (145)	47,030 (237)	57,510 (745)	71,300 (2,859)	74,030 (2,144)
2009	37,260 (107)	18,480 (451)	21,230 (301)	29,150 (273)	34,090 (483)	37,270 (310)	51,880 (169)	46,830 (260)	61,070 (304)	83,910 (3,210)	76,580 (912)
2010	38,290 (272)	18,240 (592)	20,880 (334)	29,860 (260)	33,400 (410)	37,770 (588)	51,940 (159)	47,440 (336)	59,100 (1,021)	76,740 (2,723)	77,390 (2,174)

See notes at end of table.

Median annual earnings of year-round, full-time workers 25 years old and over, by highest level of educational attainment and sex: 1990 through 2010—Continued

Constant 2010 dollars[7]

Sex and year	Elementary/secondary						College		Bachelor's or higher degree[4]		
	Total	Less than 9th grade	Some high school, no completion[1]	High school completion (includes equivalency)[2]	Some college, no degree[3]	Associate's degree	Total	Bachelor's degree[5]	Master's degree	Professional degree[4]	Doctor's degree
1	2	3	4	5	6	7	8	9	10	11	12
Males											
1990	$51,270 (—)	$29,020 (—)	$34,870 (—)	$44,470 (—)	$52,940 (—)	$54,140 (†)	$71,190 (—)	$65,460 (—)	$79,620 (†)	$118,470 (—)	$91,560 (†)
1991	50,610 (—)	28,210 (—)	34,260 (—)	42,870 (—)	50,690 (—)	51,960 (—)	72,270 (—)	65,490 (—)	77,670 (—)	118,460 (—)	89,240 (—)
1992	49,820 (187)	26,880 (—)	33,060 (—)	42,400 (272)	49,890 (—)	50,840 (—)	71,190 (—)	64,270 (472)	78,270 (—)	121,550 (—)	95,290 (—)
1993	48,830 (187)	25,450 (—)	32,820 (—)	41,300 (308)	48,410 (—)	—	72,040 (—)	64,520 (809)	—	—	—
1994	49,200 (362)	25,800 (667)	32,440 (469)	41,250 (474)	47,490 (441)	52,670 (633)	72,430 (1,040)	64,240 (931)	78,720 (1,257)	110,370 (4,473)	91,110 (2,382)
1995	49,440 (393)	26,260 (780)	31,740 (489)	42,220 (512)	48,480 (740)	50,370 (765)	72,230 (446)	64,770 (730)	79,000 (1,392)	113,990 (3,694)	93,480 (3,131)
1996	49,510 (208)	24,960 (826)	31,570 (575)	42,680 (256)	48,430 (634)	51,600 (605)	71,480 (421)	63,720 (637)	84,090 (1,313)	119,470 (4,610)	98,990 (4,672)
1997	49,830 (202)	26,210 (855)	33,590 (633)	42,410 (232)	48,830 (398)	51,660 (1,052)	72,620 (1,026)	66,050 (1,156)	83,810 (1,047)	115,500 (5,778)	103,570 (4,906)
1998	50,710 (389)	25,930 (803)	32,050 (732)	42,110 (226)	49,410 (389)	53,880 (721)	75,620 (563)	68,770 (467)	83,270 (1,133)	126,740 (16,194)	100,440 (3,354)
1999	52,790 (188)	26,740 (581)	32,770 (700)	43,430 (508)	51,330 (760)	54,500 (601)	78,790 (575)	69,350 (945)	86,700 (903)	130,890 (49,522)	106,920 (5,174)
2000	51,990 (198)	26,320 (476)	31,780 (552)	43,440 (579)	51,080 (395)	53,120 (582)	78,340 (384)	71,340 (726)	86,520 (1,907)	125,880 (26,379)	101,620 (3,097)
2001	51,240 (128)	26,300 (289)	32,270 (309)	42,750 (368)	50,540 (263)	52,670 (691)	76,610 (344)	68,860 (412)	87,290 (846)	123,130 (—)	107,080 (3,710)
2002	49,880 (121)	25,360 (258)	31,400 (251)	40,250 (377)	49,520 (236)	51,950 (816)	74,790 (244)	67,970 (467)	81,550 (1,568)	121,210 (—)	100,970 (2,516)
2003	49,700 (107)	25,140 (269)	31,370 (332)	41,970 (199)	49,000 (216)	50,810 (852)	73,560 (222)	66,960 (433)	83,710 (666)	118,510 (—)	103,260 (2,996)
2004	48,580 (103)	25,000 (220)	30,330 (270)	41,240 (171)	48,360 (202)	51,260 (1,075)	72,490 (921)	66,050 (454)	82,570 (566)	115,430 (—)	95,120 (2,797)
2005	48,360 (410)	24,930 (246)	30,360 (265)	40,530 (157)	47,360 (361)	52,680 (410)	73,880 (397)	67,010 (729)	83,770 (1,372)	111,650 (—)	95,870 (3,418)
2006	49,490 (145)	24,560 (430)	29,910 (620)	40,050 (177)	47,410 (878)	50,910 (422)	72,400 (374)	65,880 (254)	81,590 (929)	108,160 (—)	108,160 (—)
2007	49,430 (137)	24,580 (572)	30,830 (620)	39,810 (427)	47,220 (615)	51,580 (842)	74,040 (253)	65,290 (248)	80,230 (437)	105,170 (—)	96,850 (1,992)
2008	49,630 (343)	24,570 (639)	30,060 (464)	39,510 (404)	46,410 (280)	50,790 (348)	73,140 (239)	66,640 (393)	82,000 (474)	101,280 (—)	101,280 (—)
2009	50,810 (204)	24,340 (400)	28,480 (551)	40,130 (385)	47,870 (353)	51,130 (242)	72,640 (243)	63,470 (719)	80,640 (1,594)	125,260 (2,581)	102,390 (528)
2010	50,360 (93)	24,450 (597)	29,440 (684)	40,060 (237)	46,430 (348)	50,280 (245)	71,780 (267)	63,740 (1,115)	80,960 (453)	115,300 (4,891)	101,220 (653)
Females											
1990	$35,660 (—)	$20,440 (—)	$24,070 (—)	$30,560 (—)	$37,080 (—)	$40,020 (†)	$50,680 (—)	$46,740 (—)	$55,950 (†)	$74,830 (†)	$69,330 (†)
1991	35,290 (—)	19,320 (—)	23,140 (—)	30,160 (—)	35,450 (—)	39,830 (—)	50,130 (—)	46,560 (—)	56,010 (—)	71,890 (—)	71,170 (—)
1992	35,960 (247)	20,140 (—)	22,630 (—)	30,190 (274)	35,990 (—)	39,060 (—)	50,210 (—)	47,130 (457)	58,270 (—)	75,770 (—)	71,300 (—)
1993	35,660 (250)	18,730 (—)	23,220 (—)	30,120 (261)	34,790 (—)	—	51,770 (—)	47,080 (468)	—	—	—
1994	35,900 (243)	18,290 (628)	22,270 (483)	29,980 (232)	34,600 (481)	38,170 (434)	52,050 (412)	46,700 (462)	58,060 (892)	74,470 (3,169)	75,210 (4,249)
1995	35,590 (229)	19,430 (701)	22,640 (419)	29,280 (232)	34,340 (392)	39,080 (612)	50,450 (448)	45,860 (391)	57,610 (796)	71,540 (3,623)	68,880 (3,395)
1996	35,870 (182)	20,030 (777)	23,560 (463)	29,430 (199)	34,980 (371)	39,030 (731)	50,670 (411)	46,590 (607)	58,230 (784)	80,080 (5,052)	78,200 (4,586)
1997	36,650 (182)	19,240 (668)	22,680 (455)	29,980 (201)	35,780 (395)	39,140 (897)	51,680 (653)	48,070 (401)	61,070 (1,137)	82,940 (6,436)	72,060 (4,926)
1998	37,400 (266)	19,350 (574)	22,050 (431)	30,470 (340)	36,680 (363)	40,030 (686)	53,220 (546)	48,910 (408)	60,580 (1,017)	77,010 (2,281)	77,320 (2,516)
1999	37,750 (283)	19,760 (644)	22,270 (390)	30,180 (365)	36,330 (483)	40,470 (416)	54,640 (360)	49,730 (804)	62,950 (1,128)	78,410 (5,862)	78,630 (4,097)
2000	38,400 (175)	20,000 (414)	22,690 (550)	31,620 (299)	36,340 (461)	39,340 (389)	54,080 (556)	51,180 (360)	63,490 (931)	74,660 (4,498)	72,280 (3,798)
2001	38,610 (112)	20,550 (314)	23,590 (442)	31,150 (163)	37,450 (229)	39,590 (284)	55,130 (452)	50,470 (284)	62,390 (404)	76,030 (4,895)	76,490 (2,743)
2002	37,590 (101)	20,010 (360)	23,400 (436)	30,520 (147)	35,640 (362)	38,330 (256)	52,420 (688)	49,520 (210)	59,260 (721)	69,110 (2,934)	79,650 (2,749)
2003	37,410 (101)	20,040 (303)	22,440 (388)	30,900 (140)	35,720 (209)	38,220 (286)	53,470 (345)	48,980 (242)	59,450 (538)	78,800 (4,111)	79,650 (2,918)
2004	36,930 (92)	19,650 (278)	22,120 (368)	30,050 (134)	35,570 (156)	38,650 (564)	53,000 (264)	48,110 (199)	59,240 (304)	86,620 (2,812)	79,510 (2,828)
2005	36,930 (270)	18,020 (279)	22,470 (306)	29,350 (150)	35,060 (184)	37,880 (555)	52,420 (259)	47,090 (200)	57,400 (316)	89,830 (3,097)	74,640 (2,780)
2006	37,960 (122)	19,610 (441)	21,770 (292)	28,920 (147)	34,560 (178)	38,030 (407)	53,620 (477)	49,110 (280)	56,720 (607)	82,470 (2,691)	76,280 (1,924)
2007	37,950 (110)	19,200 (485)	21,450 (307)	28,650 (140)	34,530 (436)	38,210 (298)	53,000 (166)	48,140 (276)	58,290 (433)	74,770 (957)	72,550 (2,266)
2008	37,170 (110)	18,870 (500)	20,670 (299)	28,740 (287)	33,040 (360)	37,230 (246)	52,070 (147)	47,630 (240)	58,250 (755)	72,210 (2,896)	74,970 (2,171)
2009	37,880 (109)	18,780 (458)	21,570 (306)	29,630 (277)	34,650 (491)	37,880 (315)	52,730 (172)	47,600 (264)	62,070 (309)	85,280 (3,263)	77,840 (927)
2010	38,290 (272)	18,240 (592)	20,880 (334)	29,860 (260)	33,400 (410)	37,770 (588)	51,940 (159)	47,440 (336)	59,100 (1,021)	76,740 (2,723)	77,390 (2,174)

See notes at end of table.

Outcomes of Education

Median annual earnings of year-round, full-time workers 25 years old and over, by highest level of educational attainment and sex: 1990 through 2010—Continued

Number of persons with earnings who worked full-time year-round (in thousands)

Sex and year	Total	Elementary/secondary — Less than 9th grade	Some high school, no completion[1]	High school completion (includes equivalency)[2]	Some college, no degree[3]	Associate's degree	College — Total	Bachelor's or higher degree[4] — Bachelor's degree[5]	Master's degree	Professional degree	Doctor's degree
1	2	3	4	5	6	7	8	9	10	11	12
Males											
1990	44,406 (268.6)	2,250 (73.9)	3,315 (89.3)	16,394 (188.0)	9,113 (144.6)	[6] (†)	13,334 (171.8)	7,569 (132.6)	[6] (†)	[6] (†)	[6] (†)
1991	44,199 (268.3)	1,807 (66.3)	3,083 (86.2)	15,025 (181.1)	8,034 (136.4)	2,899 (83.6)	13,350 (171.9)	8,456 (139.7)	3,073 (86.1)	1,147 (53.0)	674 (40.7)
1992	44,752 (269.1)	1,815 (66.5)	3,009 (85.2)	14,722 (179.5)	8,067 (136.6)	3,203 (87.8)	13,937 (175.2)	8,719 (141.7)	3,178 (87.5)	1,295 (56.3)	745 (42.8)
1993	45,873 (270.6)	1,790 (66.0)	3,083 (86.2)	14,604 (177.8)	8,493 (140.0)	3,557 (92.4)	14,346 (177.5)	9,178 (145.1)	3,131 (86.8)	1,231 (54.9)	808 (44.5)
1994	47,566 (303.0)	1,895 (69.2)	3,057 (87.6)	15,109 (188.5)	8,783 (146.2)	3,735 (96.6)	14,987 (187.8)	9,636 (152.8)	3,225 (89.9)	1,258 (56.4)	868 (46.9)
1995	48,500 (306.1)	1,946 (72.8)	3,335 (94.9)	15,331 (195.6)	8,908 (152.3)	3,926 (102.8)	15,054 (194.0)	9,597 (157.8)	3,395 (95.7)	1,208 (57.5)	853 (48.4)
1996	49,764 (301.1)	2,041 (69.2)	3,441 (89.6)	15,840 (186.5)	9,173 (144.2)	3,931 (95.6)	15,339 (183.7)	9,898 (149.6)	3,272 (87.4)	1,277 (54.8)	893 (45.9)
1997	50,807 (299.0)	1,914 (67.0)	3,548 (90.9)	16,225 (187.8)	9,170 (143.9)	4,086 (97.4)	15,864 (185.9)	10,349 (152.4)	3,228 (86.7)	1,321 (55.8)	966 (47.7)
1998	52,381 (306.4)	1,870 (66.3)	3,613 (91.7)	16,442 (189.7)	9,375 (145.7)	4,347 (100.4)	16,733 (191.2)	11,058 (157.6)	3,414 (89.2)	1,264 (54.6)	998 (48.5)
1999	53,062 (307.8)	1,993 (68.4)	3,295 (87.7)	16,589 (190.5)	9,684 (148.0)	4,359 (100.6)	17,142 (193.3)	11,142 (158.2)	3,725 (93.1)	1,267 (54.6)	1,008 (48.8)
2000	54,065 (309.7)	1,968 (68.0)	3,354 (88.4)	16,834 (191.7)	9,792 (148.8)	4,729 (104.7)	17,387 (194.6)	11,395 (159.9)	3,680 (92.6)	1,274 (54.8)	1,038 (49.5)
2001	54,013 (224.8)	2,207 (51.4)	3,503 (64.5)	16,314 (135.4)	9,494 (104.9)	4,714 (74.7)	17,780 (140.9)	11,479 (114.8)	3,961 (68.5)	1,298 (39.5)	1,041 (35.4)
2002	54,108 (225.0)	2,154 (50.7)	3,680 (66.1)	16,005 (134.2)	9,603 (105.5)	4,399 (72.2)	18,267 (142.7)	11,829 (116.5)	4,065 (69.4)	1,308 (39.6)	1,065 (35.8)
2003	54,253 (225.2)	2,209 (51.4)	3,369 (63.3)	16,285 (135.3)	9,340 (104.1)	4,696 (74.5)	18,354 (143.0)	11,846 (116.6)	4,124 (69.9)	1,348 (40.2)	1,037 (35.3)
2004	55,469 (227.0)	2,427 (53.8)	3,468 (64.2)	17,067 (138.3)	9,257 (103.6)	4,913 (76.2)	18,338 (142.9)	11,701 (115.9)	4,243 (70.9)	1,305 (39.6)	1,088 (36.1)
2005	56,717 (228.7)	2,425 (53.8)	3,652 (65.9)	17,266 (139.0)	9,532 (105.1)	5,022 (77.0)	18,820 (144.7)	12,032 (117.4)	4,275 (71.2)	1,369 (40.5)	1,144 (37.1)
2006	58,109 (230.6)	2,361 (53.1)	3,872 (67.8)	17,369 (139.4)	9,493 (104.9)	5,110 (77.7)	19,903 (148.4)	12,764 (120.7)	4,542 (73.3)	1,425 (41.3)	1,172 (37.5)
2007	58,147 (230.7)	2,142 (50.6)	3,451 (64.0)	17,224 (138.9)	9,867 (106.8)	5,244 (78.7)	20,218 (149.5)	12,962 (121.6)	4,800 (75.3)	1,332 (40.0)	1,125 (36.7)
2008	55,655 (227.2)	1,982 (48.7)	3,118 (60.9)	16,195 (135.0)	9,515 (105.0)	5,020 (77.0)	19,825 (148.1)	12,609 (120.0)	4,709 (74.6)	1,388 (40.8)	1,119 (36.7)
2009	52,445 (222.5)	1,561 (43.2)	2,795 (57.7)	15,258 (131.3)	8,609 (100.1)	4,828 (75.5)	19,395 (146.7)	12,290 (118.6)	4,575 (73.6)	1,319 (39.8)	1,212 (38.1)
2010	52,890 (223.2)	1,600 (43.8)	2,615 (55.9)	15,104 (130.7)	8,541 (99.7)	5,042 (77.2)	19,990 (148.7)	12,836 (121.1)	4,670 (74.3)	1,237 (38.5)	1,246 (38.7)
Females											
1990	28,636 (234.7)	847 (45.6)	1,861 (67.3)	11,810 (162.8)	6,462 (123.1)	[6] (†)	7,655 (133.3)	4,704 (105.8)	[6] (†)	[6] (†)	[6] (†)
1991	29,474 (237.1)	733 (42.4)	1,819 (66.5)	10,959 (157.4)	5,633 (115.3)	2,523 (78.1)	7,807 (134.6)	5,263 (111.6)	2,025 (70.1)	312 (27.7)	206 (22.5)
1992	30,346 (239.6)	734 (42.4)	1,659 (63.6)	11,039 (157.9)	5,904 (117.9)	2,655 (80.1)	8,355 (138.8)	5,604 (115.0)	2,192 (72.9)	334 (28.7)	225 (23.5)
1993	30,683 (240.5)	765 (43.3)	1,576 (62.0)	10,513 (154.4)	6,279 (121.4)	3,067 (86.0)	8,483 (139.9)	5,735 (116.3)	2,166 (72.5)	323 (28.2)	260 (25.3)
1994	31,379 (259.2)	696 (42.0)	1,675 (65.1)	10,785 (161.2)	6,256 (124.2)	3,210 (89.7)	8,756 (146.0)	5,901 (120.8)	2,174 (74.0)	398 (31.8)	283 (26.8)
1995	32,673 (268.2)	774 (46.1)	1,763 (69.3)	11,064 (168.6)	6,329 (129.5)	3,336 (94.9)	9,406 (156.3)	6,434 (130.5)	2,268 (78.5)	421 (34.0)	283 (27.9)
1996	33,549 (259.0)	750 (42.1)	1,751 (64.1)	11,363 (159.7)	6,582 (122.9)	3,468 (89.9)	9,636 (147.7)	6,689 (123.9)	2,213 (72.0)	413 (31.2)	322 (27.6)
1997	34,624 (260.1)	791 (43.2)	1,765 (64.4)	11,475 (160.0)	6,628 (123.2)	3,538 (90.7)	10,427 (153.0)	7,173 (128.0)	2,448 (75.7)	488 (34.0)	318 (27.4)
1998	35,628 (265.4)	814 (43.8)	1,878 (66.4)	11,613 (161.3)	7,070 (127.3)	3,527 (90.7)	10,725 (155.4)	7,288 (129.2)	2,639 (78.6)	468 (33.3)	329 (27.9)
1999	37,091 (269.7)	886 (45.7)	1,883 (66.5)	11,824 (162.7)	7,453 (130.6)	3,804 (94.1)	11,242 (158.9)	7,607 (131.9)	2,818 (81.2)	470 (33.3)	346 (28.6)
2000	37,762 (271.6)	930 (46.8)	1,950 (67.7)	11,789 (162.5)	7,391 (130.0)	4,118 (97.8)	11,584 (161.1)	7,899 (134.3)	2,823 (81.2)	509 (34.7)	353 (28.9)
2001	38,228 (197.0)	927 (33.4)	1,869 (47.3)	11,690 (115.8)	7,283 (92.3)	4,190 (70.5)	12,269 (118.5)	8,257 (98.1)	3,089 (60.6)	531 (25.3)	392 (21.7)
2002	38,510 (197.6)	858 (32.1)	1,841 (46.9)	11,687 (115.8)	7,354 (92.7)	4,285 (71.2)	12,484 (119.5)	8,229 (97.9)	3,281 (62.5)	572 (26.2)	402 (22.0)
2003	38,681 (197.9)	882 (32.6)	1,739 (45.6)	11,587 (115.3)	7,341 (92.6)	4,397 (72.2)	12,735 (120.6)	8,330 (98.5)	3,376 (63.4)	567 (26.1)	462 (23.6)
2004	39,072 (198.7)	917 (33.2)	1,797 (46.4)	11,392 (114.4)	7,330 (92.6)	4,505 (73.0)	13,131 (122.4)	8,664 (100.4)	3,451 (64.0)	564 (26.0)	452 (23.3)
2005	40,021 (200.6)	902 (32.9)	1,740 (45.6)	11,419 (114.5)	7,452 (93.3)	4,751 (74.9)	13,758 (125.1)	9,074 (102.6)	3,591 (65.3)	657 (28.1)	437 (22.9)
2006	41,311 (203.2)	934 (33.5)	1,802 (46.4)	11,652 (115.6)	7,613 (94.3)	4,760 (75.0)	14,549 (128.4)	9,645 (105.7)	3,746 (66.7)	662 (28.2)	497 (24.5)
2007	42,196 (204.9)	823 (31.5)	1,649 (44.4)	11,447 (114.7)	7,916 (96.1)	4,891 (76.0)	15,469 (132.1)	9,931 (107.2)	4,389 (72.1)	666 (28.3)	484 (24.1)
2008	40,979 (202.5)	814 (31.3)	1,568 (43.3)	10,851 (111.8)	7,456 (93.3)	4,955 (76.5)	15,335 (131.6)	9,856 (106.8)	4,176 (70.3)	753 (30.1)	550 (25.7)
2009	40,376 (201.4)	776 (30.5)	1,519 (42.7)	10,467 (109.9)	7,164 (91.6)	4,924 (76.3)	15,526 (132.4)	10,066 (107.9)	4,261 (71.0)	606 (27.0)	592 (26.7)
2010	40,196 (201.0)	732 (29.7)	1,371 (40.5)	10,117 (108.1)	7,150 (91.5)	4,999 (76.8)	15,826 (133.5)	9,903 (107.0)	4,576 (73.6)	622 (27.4)	725 (29.5)

See notes at end of table.

Median annual earnings of year-round, full-time workers 25 years old and over, by highest level of educational attainment and sex: 1990 through 2010—Continued

Percent of workers with earnings who worked full-time year-round

Sex and year	Total	Elementary/secondary — Less than 9th grade	Some high school, no completion[1]	High school completion (includes equivalency)[2]	Some college, no degree[3]	College — Associate's degree	Total	Bachelor's degree[5]	Master's degree	Professional degree	Doctor's degree
1	2	3	4	5	6	7	8	9	10	11	12
Males											
1990	(†)	—	—	—	—	—	(†)	—	(†)	(†)	(†)
1991	(†)	—	—	—	—	—	(†)	—	(†)	(†)	(†)
1992	(†)	—	—	—	—	—	(†)	—	(†)	(†)	(†)
1993	(†)	—	—	—	—	—	(†)	—	(†)	(†)	(†)
1994	(†)	—	—	—	—	—	(†)	—	(†)	(†)	(†)
1995	78.2 (†)	64.5 (†)	66.9 (†)	77.2 (†)	78.8 (†)	83.8 (†)	82.9 (†)	83.2 (†)	80.6 (†)	85.4 (†)	85.1 (†)
1996	81.6 (0.25)	63.9 (1.31)	69.5 (1.01)	78.7 (0.45)	79.5 (0.58)	81.7 (0.83)	83.3 (0.43)	83.9 (0.53)	80.8 (0.95)	85.4 (1.40)	83.4 (1.69)
1997	81.0 (0.24)	66.8 (1.35)	73.5 (0.99)	80.3 (0.44)	81.0 (0.58)	85.3 (0.84)	84.6 (0.42)	85.9 (0.51)	81.6 (0.96)	86.0 (1.38)	80.0 (1.68)
1998	81.0 (0.24)	66.8 (1.37)	73.5 (0.97)	80.3 (0.43)	81.0 (0.56)	85.3 (0.76)	84.6 (0.39)	85.9 (0.47)	81.6 (0.92)	86.0 (1.39)	80.0 (1.74)
1999	81.1 (0.24)	70.3 (1.32)	71.5 (1.02)	80.3 (0.43)	81.3 (0.55)	84.2 (0.78)	84.7 (0.39)	85.3 (0.48)	83.5 (0.86)	85.6 (1.40)	81.8 (1.69)
2000	81.7 (0.23)	69.2 (1.33)	71.8 (1.01)	80.9 (0.42)	82.2 (0.54)	86.6 (0.71)	84.8 (0.39)	85.6 (0.47)	82.8 (0.87)	85.8 (1.39)	82.5 (1.65)
2001	80.1 (0.17)	69.7 (0.90)	70.9 (0.71)	79.4 (0.31)	80.2 (0.40)	84.1 (0.54)	83.9 (0.28)	83.6 (0.35)	82.4 (0.60)	84.6 (1.01)	82.2 (1.18)
2002	79.4 (0.17)	70.1 (0.91)	71.3 (0.69)	77.8 (0.32)	78.8 (0.41)	81.4 (0.58)	83.9 (0.27)	84.4 (0.34)	82.2 (0.60)	85.7 (0.99)	82.8 (1.16)
2003	79.5 (0.17)	71.5 (0.89)	70.1 (0.73)	78.7 (0.31)	78.8 (0.41)	82.1 (0.56)	83.1 (0.28)	84.0 (0.34)	81.1 (0.60)	84.4 (1.00)	80.3 (1.22)
2004	80.0 (0.17)	74.7 (0.84)	71.2 (0.71)	79.1 (0.30)	79.3 (0.41)	83.6 (0.53)	83.0 (0.28)	83.1 (0.35)	83.1 (0.58)	83.3 (1.03)	81.7 (1.16)
2005	80.3 (0.16)	74.0 (0.84)	73.8 (0.69)	79.5 (0.30)	80.0 (0.40)	82.5 (0.54)	82.9 (0.27)	83.0 (0.34)	82.7 (0.58)	83.7 (1.00)	82.4 (1.12)
2006	81.1 (0.16)	73.6 (0.85)	72.9 (0.67)	79.6 (0.30)	80.1 (0.40)	85.3 (0.50)	84.7 (0.26)	85.2 (0.32)	83.5 (0.55)	85.9 (0.94)	83.4 (1.09)
2007	80.5 (0.16)	71.1 (0.91)	70.8 (0.72)	79.4 (0.30)	79.5 (0.40)	83.3 (0.52)	84.5 (0.26)	85.1 (0.32)	83.5 (0.54)	83.1 (1.03)	83.5 (1.11)
2008	77.0 (0.17)	66.3 (0.95)	64.6 (0.76)	74.6 (0.32)	76.5 (0.42)	79.4 (0.56)	82.6 (0.27)	83.2 (0.33)	80.9 (0.57)	82.4 (1.02)	83.1 (1.12)
2009	73.9 (0.18)	56.2 (1.03)	61.8 (0.79)	70.1 (0.34)	73.4 (0.45)	77.9 (0.58)	80.8 (0.28)	79.9 (0.35)	82.0 (0.56)	85.1 (0.99)	81.2 (1.11)
2010	74.8 (0.18)	58.8 (1.04)	61.6 (0.82)	71.9 (0.34)	72.9 (0.45)	78.2 (0.56)	81.4 (0.27)	81.8 (0.34)	80.0 (0.58)	81.4 (1.10)	82.2 (1.08)
Females											
1990	(†)	—	—	—	—	—	(†)	—	(†)	(†)	(†)
1991	(†)	—	—	—	—	—	(†)	—	(†)	(†)	(†)
1992	(†)	—	—	—	—	—	(†)	—	(†)	(†)	(†)
1993	(†)	—	—	—	—	—	(†)	—	(†)	(†)	(†)
1994	(†)	—	—	—	—	—	(†)	—	(†)	(†)	(†)
1995	60.7 (†)	47.9 (†)	49.4 (†)	60.0 (†)	62.0 (†)	63.7 (†)	63.5 (†)	63.4 (†)	62.4 (†)	68.4 (†)	70.0 (†)
1996	61.7 (0.32)	48.7 (1.94)	49.3 (1.29)	61.0 (0.55)	61.9 (0.73)	64.3 (1.00)	65.4 (0.60)	64.6 (0.72)	65.7 (1.25)	73.6 (2.91)	72.1 (3.29)
1997	61.7 (0.32)	48.7 (1.91)	49.3 (1.29)	61.0 (0.55)	61.9 (0.72)	64.3 (0.99)	65.4 (0.58)	64.6 (0.70)	65.7 (1.20)	73.6 (2.63)	72.1 (3.29)
1998	62.5 (0.31)	51.8 (1.94)	53.1 (1.29)	61.9 (0.55)	63.3 (0.70)	64.9 (1.00)	65.0 (0.57)	64.0 (0.69)	66.2 (1.15)	71.9 (2.71)	68.5 (3.26)
1999	63.7 (0.31)	53.0 (1.88)	54.0 (1.30)	63.0 (0.54)	64.8 (0.69)	65.1 (0.96)	66.2 (0.56)	65.9 (0.68)	66.5 (1.12)	68.4 (2.73)	68.2 (3.18)
2000	64.6 (0.30)	53.5 (1.84)	56.5 (1.30)	64.1 (0.54)	65.3 (0.69)	66.6 (0.92)	66.5 (0.55)	66.7 (0.67)	64.9 (1.11)	70.6 (2.61)	71.5 (3.13)
2001	64.3 (0.22)	54.0 (1.32)	55.5 (0.94)	63.5 (0.39)	65.1 (0.49)	65.8 (0.65)	66.6 (0.38)	66.6 (0.47)	65.6 (0.76)	70.3 (1.83)	70.9 (2.12)
2002	64.1 (0.22)	52.6 (1.36)	55.5 (0.95)	63.2 (0.39)	65.0 (0.49)	65.6 (0.65)	66.5 (0.38)	65.9 (0.47)	66.1 (0.74)	74.3 (1.73)	73.8 (2.07)
2003	64.4 (0.21)	56.5 (1.38)	53.8 (0.96)	64.4 (0.39)	64.2 (0.49)	65.6 (0.64)	66.4 (0.37)	65.8 (0.46)	66.3 (0.73)	72.3 (1.75)	71.9 (1.95)
2004	64.5 (0.21)	56.3 (1.35)	56.1 (0.96)	64.5 (0.40)	64.2 (0.49)	64.6 (0.63)	66.7 (0.37)	66.3 (0.45)	66.3 (0.72)	71.5 (1.77)	71.2 (1.97)
2005	65.3 (0.21)	56.5 (1.36)	54.5 (0.97)	65.1 (0.40)	63.5 (0.49)	67.2 (0.61)	68.2 (0.36)	68.0 (0.44)	68.3 (0.70)	71.2 (1.64)	67.3 (2.02)
2006	66.2 (0.21)	58.5 (1.35)	56.0 (0.96)	65.6 (0.39)	65.9 (0.48)	67.3 (0.61)	68.6 (0.35)	68.4 (0.43)	67.5 (0.69)	73.6 (1.61)	74.0 (1.86)
2007	66.7 (0.21)	56.8 (1.43)	55.3 (1.00)	65.7 (0.39)	66.7 (0.48)	67.3 (0.60)	69.3 (0.34)	67.8 (0.42)	70.6 (0.63)	74.1 (1.60)	71.2 (1.91)
2008	64.4 (0.21)	51.6 (1.38)	52.8 (1.01)	62.4 (0.40)	64.7 (0.49)	65.5 (0.60)	67.9 (0.34)	67.8 (0.43)	66.9 (0.65)	74.0 (1.51)	71.2 (1.80)
2009	64.3 (0.21)	52.0 (1.42)	54.5 (1.04)	62.4 (0.41)	63.9 (0.50)	64.5 (0.60)	68.0 (0.34)	68.3 (0.42)	67.5 (0.65)	66.4 (1.72)	68.3 (1.74)
2010	64.4 (0.21)	51.7 (1.46)	52.4 (1.07)	62.6 (0.42)	63.3 (0.50)	64.3 (0.60)	68.5 (0.34)	67.7 (0.42)	68.5 (0.62)	73.9 (1.66)	76.3 (1.51)

—Not available.

†Not applicable.

[1]Includes 1 to 3 years of high school for 1990.

[2]Includes 4 years of high school for 1990.

[3]Includes 1 to 3 years of college and associate's degrees for 1990.

[4]Includes 4 or more years of college for 1990.

[5]Includes 4 years of college for 1990.

[6]Not reported separately for 1990.

[7]Constant dollars based on the Consumer Price Index, prepared by the Bureau of Labor Statistics, U.S. Department of Labor.

NOTE: Detail may not sum to totals because of rounding. Standard errors appear in parentheses.

SOURCE: U.S. Department of Commerce, Census Bureau, Current Population Reports, Series P-60, *Money Income of Households, Families, and Persons in the United States,* and *Income, Poverty, and Valuation of Noncash Benefits,* 1990 through 1994; Series P-60, *Money Income in the United States,* 1995 through 2002; and Detailed Income Tabulations from the CPS, 2003 through 2010. Retrieved September 13, 2011, from http://www.census.gov/hhes/www/cpstables/032011/perinc/new03_136.htm and http://www.census.gov/hhes/www/cpstables/032011/perinc/new03_262.htm. (This table was prepared September 2011.)

Distribution of earnings and median earnings of persons 25 years old and over, by highest level of educational attainment and sex: 2010

Sex and earnings	Total	Elementary/secondary					College					
		Less than 9th grade	Some high school (no completion)	High school completion (includes equivalency)	Some college, no degree	Associate's degree	Bachelor's or higher degree					
							Total	Bachelor's degree	Master's degree	Professional degree	Doctor's degree	
1	2	3	4	5	6	7	8	9	10	11	12
Total males and females											
(in thousands)	**201,543** (220.5)	**10,277** (110.9)	**14,763** (131.7)	**61,911** (241.2)	**34,203** (192.0)	**19,047** (148.2)	**61,343** (240.4)	**39,286** (203.4)	**16,015** (136.8)	**2,980** (60.6)	**3,062** (61.5)
With earnings	133,074 (278.7)	4,136 (71.3)	6,857 (91.3)	37,182 (198.8)	23,016 (161.5)	14,225 (129.4)	47,659 (219.5)	30,316 (182.4)	12,517 (121.9)	2,361 (54.0)	2,464 (55.2)
Distribution of total persons with earnings, by total annual earnings	100.0 (†)	100.0 (†)	100.0 (†)	100.0 (†)	100.0 (†)	100.0 (†)	100.0 (†)	100.0 (†)	100.0 (†)	100.0 (†)	100.0 (†)
$1 to $4,999 or loss	5.9 (0.07)	8.8 (0.49)	11.1 (0.42)	6.7 (0.14)	6.8 (0.19)	5.3 (0.21)	4.0 (0.10)	4.3 (0.13)	3.8 (0.19)	2.9 (0.38)	1.8 (0.30)
$5,000 to $9,999	5.5 (0.07)	12.4 (0.57)	10.5 (0.41)	6.4 (0.14)	6.0 (0.17)	4.7 (0.20)	3.4 (0.09)	3.9 (0.12)	2.9 (0.17)	1.6 (0.29)	1.4 (0.26)
$10,000 to $14,999	7.0 (0.08)	19.3 (0.69)	14.5 (0.48)	8.8 (0.16)	7.1 (0.19)	6.1 (0.22)	3.7 (0.10)	4.1 (0.13)	3.1 (0.17)	1.6 (0.29)	2.6 (0.36)
$15,000 to $19,999	7.2 (0.08)	17.9 (0.67)	15.3 (0.49)	9.3 (0.17)	7.9 (0.20)	6.3 (0.23)	3.5 (0.09)	3.9 (0.12)	2.8 (0.17)	3.0 (0.39)	1.6 (0.28)
$20,000 to $24,999	8.0 (0.08)	13.5 (0.59)	12.4 (0.44)	11.7 (0.19)	8.9 (0.21)	7.3 (0.24)	3.8 (0.10)	4.4 (0.13)	3.2 (0.18)	1.8 (0.31)	1.4 (0.27)
$25,000 to $29,999	7.2 (0.08)	8.2 (0.48)	8.5 (0.38)	9.6 (0.17)	8.8 (0.21)	7.7 (0.25)	4.2 (0.10)	5.1 (0.14)	3.0 (0.17)	1.4 (0.27)	2.6 (0.36)
$30,000 to $34,999	7.8 (0.08)	5.6 (0.40)	7.4 (0.35)	9.6 (0.17)	9.1 (0.21)	9.5 (0.28)	5.6 (0.12)	6.6 (0.16)	4.5 (0.21)	2.2 (0.34)	2.2 (0.33)
$35,000 to $39,999	6.6 (0.08)	4.4 (0.36)	4.8 (0.29)	7.4 (0.15)	7.4 (0.19)	7.8 (0.25)	5.7 (0.12)	6.5 (0.16)	4.9 (0.22)	3.1 (0.40)	1.7 (0.29)
$40,000 to $49,999	11.4 (0.10)	4.4 (0.36)	6.4 (0.33)	11.5 (0.19)	12.4 (0.24)	13.8 (0.32)	11.5 (0.16)	12.6 (0.21)	10.7 (0.31)	6.6 (0.57)	6.8 (0.57)
$50,000 to $74,999	17.4 (0.12)	3.9 (0.34)	6.4 (0.33)	13.2 (0.20)	16.0 (0.27)	20.7 (0.38)	23.3 (0.22)	23.2 (0.27)	25.4 (0.43)	16.6 (0.86)	20.7 (0.91)
$75,000 to $99,999	7.1 (0.08)	0.9 (0.16)	1.3 (0.15)	3.4 (0.11)	5.6 (0.17)	6.8 (0.24)	12.3 (0.17)	11.1 (0.20)	14.6 (0.35)	12.5 (0.76)	15.4 (0.81)
$100,000 or more	8.7 (0.09)	0.7 (0.15)	1.2 (0.15)	2.5 (0.09)	4.0 (0.14)	4.0 (0.18)	19.1 (0.20)	14.4 (0.23)	21.0 (0.41)	46.6 (1.15)	41.9 (1.11)
Median earnings	$35,720 (82)	$17,040 (186)	$19,370 (292)	$28,070 (227)	$31,640 (136)	$36,390 (211)	$52,110 (114)	$47,970 (474)	$58,190 (913)	$91,200 (1,366)	$82,200 (2,192)
Number of males											
(in thousands)	**97,220** (132.1)	**5,117** (78.1)	**7,443** (93.2)	**30,370** (166.7)	**16,137** (131.5)	**8,182** (97.4)	**29,971** (166.0)	**19,017** (140.6)	**7,181** (91.7)	**1,862** (47.8)	**1,911** (48.4)
With earnings	70,706 (182.5)	2,719 (57.6)	4,242 (71.4)	21,016 (146.3)	11,715 (114.6)	6,451 (87.2)	24,563 (155.1)	15,690 (130.0)	5,839 (83.2)	1,519 (43.3)	1,515 (43.2)
Distribution of males with earnings, by total annual earnings	100.0 (†)	100.0 (†)	100.0 (†)	100.0 (†)	100.0 (†)	100.0 (†)	100.0 (†)	100.0 (†)	100.0 (†)	100.0 (†)	100.0 (†)
$1 to $4,999 or loss	4.5 (0.09)	6.5 (0.53)	8.3 (0.47)	5.0 (0.17)	5.4 (0.23)	4.0 (0.27)	3.0 (0.12)	3.3 (0.16)	2.6 (0.23)	2.1 (0.41)	2.1 (0.41)
$5,000 to $9,999	4.3 (0.09)	9.5 (0.63)	9.1 (0.49)	5.0 (0.17)	4.4 (0.21)	3.3 (0.25)	2.5 (0.11)	2.7 (0.15)	2.4 (0.22)	2.0 (0.41)	1.2 (0.31)
$10,000 to $14,999	5.6 (0.10)	17.1 (0.81)	12.1 (0.56)	6.6 (0.19)	5.6 (0.24)	4.8 (0.30)	2.6 (0.11)	2.8 (0.15)	2.5 (0.23)	1.3 (0.32)	2.3 (0.43)
$15,000 to $19,999	5.8 (0.10)	17.9 (0.82)	13.2 (0.58)	7.1 (0.20)	5.7 (0.24)	4.1 (0.28)	2.6 (0.11)	2.7 (0.14)	2.7 (0.24)	2.6 (0.45)	1.7 (0.37)
$20,000 to $24,999	7.1 (0.11)	13.9 (0.74)	12.7 (0.57)	9.9 (0.23)	7.3 (0.27)	5.3 (0.31)	3.3 (0.13)	3.9 (0.17)	2.9 (0.25)	1.4 (0.34)	0.8 (0.25)
$25,000 to $29,999	6.4 (0.10)	9.2 (0.62)	9.4 (0.50)	8.9 (0.22)	6.9 (0.26)	6.6 (0.35)	3.3 (0.13)	3.9 (0.17)	2.4 (0.22)	0.8 (0.25)	2.3 (0.43)
$30,000 to $34,999	7.1 (0.11)	6.9 (0.54)	8.5 (0.48)	9.6 (0.23)	7.8 (0.28)	7.8 (0.37)	4.3 (0.14)	5.2 (0.20)	3.1 (0.25)	2.0 (0.40)	1.9 (0.39)
$35,000 to $39,999	6.2 (0.10)	5.7 (0.50)	5.8 (0.40)	7.9 (0.21)	7.2 (0.27)	7.3 (0.36)	4.2 (0.14)	5.1 (0.20)	3.0 (0.25)	2.6 (0.45)	1.1 (0.30)
$40,000 to $49,999	11.5 (0.13)	6.0 (0.51)	8.4 (0.48)	13.4 (0.26)	13.7 (0.35)	14.5 (0.49)	9.2 (0.21)	10.3 (0.27)	8.3 (0.40)	5.4 (0.65)	5.0 (0.62)
$50,000 to $74,999	19.8 (0.17)	5.1 (0.47)	9.0 (0.49)	17.9 (0.30)	21.3 (0.42)	25.2 (0.60)	22.8 (0.30)	24.6 (0.38)	21.6 (0.60)	12.0 (0.93)	18.8 (1.12)
$75,000 to $99,999	9.0 (0.12)	1.3 (0.24)	1.8 (0.23)	5.0 (0.17)	8.3 (0.28)	10.2 (0.42)	14.7 (0.25)	14.1 (0.31)	16.3 (0.54)	13.7 (0.99)	15.4 (1.04)
$100,000 or more	12.5 (0.14)	1.0 (0.21)	1.6 (0.22)	3.8 (0.15)	6.5 (0.25)	7.0 (0.35)	27.5 (0.32)	21.3 (0.37)	32.2 (0.68)	54.1 (1.43)	47.3 (1.43)
Median earnings	$41,320 (97)	$19,630 (411)	$21,950 (231)	$32,500 (299)	$39,740 (454)	$42,350 (433)	$63,270 (908)	$57,130 (356)	$71,900 (607)	$101,470 (517)	$92,420 (3,011)

See notes at end of table.

Distribution of earnings and median earnings of persons 25 years old and over, by highest level of educational attainment and sex: 2010—Continued

Sex and earnings	Total	Elementary/secondary			College		Bachelor's or higher degree				
		Less than 9th grade	Some high school (no completion)	High school completion (includes equivalency)	Some college, no degree	Associate's degree	Total	Bachelor's degree	Master's degree	Professional degree	Doctor's degree
1	2	3	4	5	6	7	8	9	10	11	12
Number of females (in thousands)......	104,323 (146.5)	5,160 (78.6)	7,320 (92.8)	31,541 (171.6)	18,065 (138.9)	10,865 (111.3)	31,372 (171.3)	20,269 (145.6)	8,834 (101.3)	1,118 (37.2)	1,151 (37.7)
With earnings......	62,368 (197.5)	1,417 (41.8)	2,615 (56.5)	16,165 (132.6)	11,301 (113.3)	7,774 (95.4)	23,096 (153.3)	14,626 (127.0)	6,678 (88.9)	842 (32.3)	950 (34.3)
Distribution of females with earnings, by total annual earnings......	100.0 (†)	100.0 (†)	100.0 (†)	100.0 (†)	100.0 (†)	100.0 (†)	100.0 (†)	100.0 (†)	100.0 (†)	100.0 (†)	100.0 (†)
$1 to $4,999 or loss......	7.4 (0.12)	13.2 (1.00)	15.7 (0.80)	8.9 (0.25)	8.2 (0.29)	6.3 (0.31)	5.0 (0.16)	5.4 (0.21)	4.9 (0.29)	4.3 (0.78)	1.4 (0.42)
$5,000 to $9,999......	6.8 (0.11)	18.0 (1.14)	12.8 (0.73)	8.2 (0.24)	7.6 (0.28)	5.8 (0.30)	4.3 (0.15)	5.1 (0.20)	3.3 (0.25)	0.8 (0.35)	1.7 (0.47)
$10,000 to $14,999......	8.6 (0.13)	23.5 (1.26)	18.5 (0.85)	11.6 (0.28)	8.7 (0.30)	7.2 (0.33)	4.8 (0.16)	5.6 (0.21)	3.7 (0.26)	2.4 (0.59)	3.1 (0.62)
$15,000 to $19,999......	8.9 (0.13)	18.0 (1.14)	18.6 (0.85)	12.3 (0.29)	10.3 (0.32)	8.1 (0.35)	4.4 (0.15)	5.3 (0.21)	2.9 (0.23)	3.7 (0.73)	1.5 (0.44)
$20,000 to $24,999......	9.1 (0.13)	12.6 (0.99)	11.9 (0.71)	14.0 (0.30)	10.6 (0.33)	8.9 (0.36)	4.3 (0.15)	5.0 (0.20)	3.4 (0.25)	2.5 (0.60)	2.5 (0.57)
$25,000 to $29,999......	8.1 (0.12)	6.4 (0.72)	7.2 (0.57)	10.4 (0.27)	10.8 (0.33)	8.6 (0.36)	5.2 (0.16)	6.3 (0.22)	3.6 (0.25)	2.4 (0.59)	3.2 (0.63)
$30,000 to $34,999......	8.6 (0.13)	3.0 (0.51)	5.7 (0.51)	9.6 (0.26)	10.4 (0.32)	11.0 (0.40)	6.9 (0.19)	8.0 (0.25)	5.7 (0.32)	2.6 (0.61)	2.5 (0.57)
$35,000 to $39,999......	7.0 (0.11)	2.0 (0.42)	3.1 (0.38)	6.7 (0.22)	7.6 (0.28)	8.2 (0.35)	7.2 (0.19)	8.0 (0.25)	6.6 (0.34)	3.9 (0.75)	2.7 (0.59)
$40,000 to $49,999......	11.4 (0.14)	1.4 (0.35)	3.2 (0.39)	9.1 (0.25)	11.1 (0.33)	13.3 (0.43)	13.9 (0.25)	15.0 (0.33)	12.9 (0.46)	9.0 (1.10)	9.8 (1.08)
$50,000 to $74,999......	14.8 (0.16)	1.6 (0.37)	2.3 (0.32)	7.0 (0.22)	10.4 (0.32)	16.9 (0.48)	23.8 (0.31)	21.6 (0.38)	28.6 (0.62)	24.9 (1.67)	23.3 (1.53)
$75,000 to $99,999......	5.0 (0.10)	0.1 (0.11)	0.5 (0.15)	1.4 (0.10)	2.8 (0.17)	3.9 (0.25)	9.8 (0.22)	7.8 (0.25)	13.2 (0.46)	10.8 (1.20)	15.2 (1.30)
$100,000 or more[1]......	4.5 (0.09)	0.1 (0.11)	0.5 (0.16)	0.8 (0.08)	1.4 (0.12)	1.6 (0.16)	10.3 (0.22)	7.0 (0.24)	11.2 (0.43)	33.0 (1.81)	33.2 (1.71)
Median earnings[1]......	$30,460 (85)	$13,510 (472)	$15,650 (235)	$22,450 (152)	$26,620 (188)	$31,540 (196)	$45,230 (207)	$40,570 (185)	$51,100 (248)	$65,790 (2,097)	$72,060 (2,206)

†Not applicable.

[1] Excludes persons without earnings.

NOTE: Detail may not sum to totals because of rounding. Standard errors appear in parentheses.

SOURCE: U.S. Department of Commerce, Census Bureau, Current Population Survey, March 2011. Retrieved September 19, 2011, from http://www.census.gov/hhes/www/cpstables/032011/perinc/new03_000.htm. (This table was prepared September 2011.)

Number, percentage distribution, unemployment rates, and median salaries of 25- to 29-year-old bachelor's degree holders and percentage of degree holders among all 25- to 29-year-olds, by field of study: 2009

Field of study	25- to 29-year-old bachelor's degree holders								Percent of all 25- to 29-year-olds with degree in specific field	
	Number, in thousands		Percentage distribution		Unemployment rate		Median annual salary			
1	2		3		4		5		6	
Total, all bachelor's degrees	6,418	(30.8)	100.0	(†)	5.2	(0.12)	$44,900	(547)	29.9	(0.14)
Agriculture	59	(2.9)	0.9	(0.04)	2.2 !	(0.85)	38,990	(996)	0.3	(0.01)
Architecture	45	(2.3)	0.7	(0.04)	9.6	(1.58)	45,980	(1,187)	0.2	(0.01)
Area, ethnic, and civilization studies	27	(2.1)	0.4	(0.03)	7.3	(2.10)	39,950	(1,495)	0.1	(0.01)
Arts, fine and commercial										
Fine arts	250	(6.5)	3.9	(0.10)	8.8	(0.79)	35,890	(889)	1.2	(0.03)
Commercial art and graphic design	96	(4.9)	1.5	(0.08)	9.2	(1.22)	39,960	(535)	0.4	(0.02)
Business										
Business, general	224	(6.6)	3.5	(0.10)	5.2	(0.63)	45,940	(1,111)	1.0	(0.03)
Accounting	184	(5.9)	2.9	(0.09)	4.4	(0.63)	52,870	(1,429)	0.9	(0.03)
Business management and administration	372	(8.7)	5.8	(0.13)	5.9	(0.46)	43,920	(1,238)	1.7	(0.04)
Marketing and marketing research	196	(6.3)	3.0	(0.10)	5.7	(0.67)	44,770	(134)	0.9	(0.03)
Finance	168	(5.2)	2.6	(0.08)	4.8	(0.74)	51,420	(891)	0.8	(0.02)
Management information systems and statistics	27	(2.0)	0.4	(0.03)	5.8	(1.66)	55,380	(2,571)	0.1	(0.01)
Business, other and medical administration	121	(5.2)	1.9	(0.08)	4.9	(0.88)	45,070	(1,434)	0.6	(0.02)
Communications and communications technologies	384	(8.8)	6.0	(0.13)	5.4	(0.51)	39,920	(62)	1.8	(0.04)
Computer and information systems	259	(6.2)	4.0	(0.09)	5.2	(0.64)	59,060	(948)	1.2	(0.03)
Construction/electrical/transportation technologies	34	(2.2)	0.5	(0.03)	4.1	(1.19)	49,970	(2,249)	0.2	(0.01)
Criminal justice and fire protection	133	(4.5)	2.1	(0.07)	4.2	(0.72)	39,920	(453)	0.6	(0.02)
Education										
General education	143	(4.8)	2.2	(0.08)	3.3	(0.63)	39,200	(538)	0.7	(0.02)
Early childhood education	41	(2.5)	0.6	(0.04)	2.8 !	(1.00)	35,250	(889)	0.2	(0.01)
Elementary education	192	(5.2)	3.0	(0.08)	3.2	(0.49)	36,000	(896)	0.9	(0.02)
Secondary teacher education	21	(1.5)	0.3	(0.02)	3.8 !	(1.86)	38,500	(959)	0.1	(0.01)
Education, other	180	(5.0)	2.8	(0.08)	3.2	(0.59)	37,990	(825)	0.8	(0.02)
Engineering and engineering-related fields										
General engineering	55	(3.2)	0.9	(0.05)	6.0	(1.25)	59,810	(1,395)	0.3	(0.01)
Chemical engineering	30	(2.1)	0.5	(0.03)	3.6 !	(1.65)	64,960	(3,708)	0.1	(0.01)
Civil engineering	42	(2.3)	0.7	(0.03)	4.2	(1.13)	57,870	(1,794)	0.2	(0.01)
Computer engineering	55	(2.5)	0.9	(0.04)	4.9	(1.19)	59,930	(1,525)	0.3	(0.01)
Electrical engineering	95	(3.3)	1.5	(0.05)	4.3	(0.90)	63,610	(1,523)	0.4	(0.02)
Mechanical engineering	84	(3.7)	1.3	(0.06)	5.0	(0.92)	61,620	(1,700)	0.4	(0.02)
Engineering, other	74	(3.7)	1.2	(0.06)	4.3	(0.93)	58,900	(931)	0.3	(0.02)
Engineering technologies	38	(2.8)	0.6	(0.04)	7.0	(1.59)	54,270	(1,872)	0.2	(0.01)
English language and literature	200	(5.3)	3.1	(0.08)	5.7	(0.77)	37,980	(1,050)	0.9	(0.02)
Family and consumer sciences	62	(2.8)	1.0	(0.05)	2.4	(0.65)	35,940	(2,416)	0.3	(0.01)
Health professions										
General medical and health services	183	(5.2)	2.9	(0.08)	3.3	(0.60)	49,910	(1,305)	0.9	(0.02)
Nursing	164	(5.2)	2.6	(0.08)	1.5	(0.34)	52,920	(1,754)	0.8	(0.02)
History	133	(4.3)	2.1	(0.07)	7.4	(0.90)	39,660	(737)	0.6	(0.02)
Liberal arts and humanities	117	(4.4)	1.8	(0.07)	7.1	(0.88)	38,910	(1,375)	0.5	(0.02)
Linguistics and comparative language and literature	68	(3.3)	1.1	(0.05)	5.6	(1.18)	39,930	(795)	0.3	(0.02)
Mathematics	70	(3.2)	1.1	(0.05)	4.7	(1.33)	49,570	(909)	0.3	(0.01)
Multi/interdisciplinary studies	121	(4.3)	1.9	(0.07)	5.8	(0.92)	43,010	(1,947)	0.6	(0.02)
Natural sciences										
Biology	354	(6.8)	5.5	(0.10)	4.5	(0.52)	42,320	(879)	1.6	(0.03)
Environmental science	42	(2.5)	0.7	(0.04)	3.0 !	(1.15)	39,240	(603)	0.2	(0.01)
Physical sciences	104	(4.2)	1.6	(0.06)	4.2	(0.81)	44,190	(434)	0.5	(0.02)
Physical fitness, parks, recreation and leisure	96	(3.9)	1.5	(0.06)	5.9	(0.93)	39,400	(350)	0.4	(0.02)
Philosophy and religious studies	57	(3.0)	0.9	(0.05)	8.1	(1.51)	40,990	(1,388)	0.3	(0.01)
Psychology	371	(7.6)	5.8	(0.12)	5.0	(0.50)	39,910	(765)	1.7	(0.04)
Public administration and public policy	14	(1.7)	0.2	(0.03)	4.8 !	(2.69)	52,180	(4,292)	0.1	(0.01)
Social sciences										
Anthropology and archeology	33	(2.1)	0.5	(0.03)	5.6 !	(1.91)	33,280	(2,557)	0.2	(0.01)
Economics	126	(4.5)	2.0	(0.07)	5.1	(0.80)	59,010	(3,145)	0.6	(0.02)
Geography	21	(1.7)	0.3	(0.03)	5.8 !	(2.11)	40,190	(1,216)	0.1	(0.01)
International relations	20	(1.6)	0.3	(0.02)	7.4	(2.18)	45,340	(2,966)	0.1	(0.01)
Political science and government	167	(5.2)	2.6	(0.08)	6.6	(0.85)	47,510	(1,034)	0.8	(0.02)
Sociology	113	(3.9)	1.8	(0.06)	5.3	(0.94)	38,640	(1,586)	0.5	(0.02)
Miscellaneous social sciences	32	(2.4)	0.5	(0.04)	6.6 !	(2.21)	39,920	(526)	0.2	(0.01)
Social work and human services	67	(3.9)	1.0	(0.06)	4.0	(0.92)	34,970	(1,082)	0.3	(0.02)
Theology and religious vocations	32	(2.4)	0.5	(0.04)	3.7 !	(1.20)	35,320	(963)	0.1	(0.01)
Other fields	22	(2.2)	0.3	(0.03)	7.2 !	(2.59)	42,780	(3,819)	0.1	(0.01)

†Not applicable.
!Interpret data with caution. The coefficient of variation (CV) for this estimate is 30 percent or greater.
NOTE: Standard errors appear in parentheses. Detail may not sum to totals because of rounding.

SOURCE: U.S. Department of Commerce, Census Bureau, 2009 American Community Survey (ACS) Public Use Microdata Sample (PUMS) data. (This table was prepared April 2012.)

Labor force status of 2008, 2009, and 2010 high school completers, by sex, race/ethnicity, and college enrollment status: October 2008, 2009, and 2010

Selected characteristic	Total number of high school completers (in thousands)	Percent of high school completers		Percentage distribution of all high school completers			Labor force participation rate of all high school completers[1]	High school completers in civilian labor force[2] — Number (in thousands)			Unemployment rate	High school completers not in labor force (in thousands)
		Separately for those enrolled in college vs. those not enrolled	For all high school completers	Employed	Unemployed (seeking employment)	Not in labor force		Total, all completers in labor force[1]	Employed	Unemployed (seeking employment)		
1	2	3	4	5	6	7	8	9	10	11	12	13
2008 high school completers[3]												
Total	3,151 (116.3)	† (†)	100.0 (†)	41.6 (1.54)	10.6 (0.96)	47.8 (1.20)	52.2 (1.56)	1,644 (70.7)	1,310 (63.2)	334 (32.1)	20.3 (1.75)	1,507 (52.4)
Male	1,640 (83.8)	† (†)	52.1 (1.93)	39.1 (2.08)	11.3 (1.35)	49.6 (2.13)	50.4 (2.13)	827 (49.3)	641 (43.5)	186 (23.5)	22.5 (2.50)	813 (48.9)
Female	1,511 (80.6)	† (†)	47.9 (1.93)	44.2 (2.13)	9.8 (1.28)	45.9 (2.14)	54.1 (2.14)	817 (47.4)	668 (43.0)	148 (20.3)	18.2 (2.25)	694 (43.8)
White	2,091 (94.4)	† (†)	66.3 (1.82)	44.7 (1.90)	9.9 (1.15)	45.4 (1.47)	54.6 (1.91)	1,141 (59.0)	934 (53.4)	207 (25.3)	18.2 (2.01)	949 (41.6)
Black	416 (50.8)	† (†)	13.2 (1.56)	34.8 (4.34)	12.7 (3.03)	52.5 (4.55)	47.5 (4.55)	198 (26.0)	145 (22.3)	53 (13.5)	26.7 (5.85)	218 (27.3)
Hispanic	458 (69.5)	† (†)	14.5 (2.11)	40.4 (4.26)	13.3 (2.95)	46.3 (4.33)	53.7 (4.33)	246 (28.9)	185 (25.1)	61 (14.5)	24.8 (5.12)	212 (26.9)
Enrolled in college, 2008	2,161 (65.9)	100.0	68.6 (1.21)	35.0 (1.80)	6.1 (0.91)	58.9 (1.43)	41.1 (1.85)	888 (52.1)	756 (48.1)	132 (20.2)	14.9 (2.10)	1,274 (48.2)
Male	1,080 (46.6)	50.0 (1.57)	34.3 (1.23)	30.3 (2.41)	5.7 (1.22)	64.0 (2.52)	36.0 (2.52)	389 (33.9)	327 (31.1)	62 (13.6)	15.9 (3.20)	691 (45.1)
Female	1,081 (46.6)	50.0 (1.57)	34.3 (1.23)	39.6 (2.48)	6.5 (1.25)	53.9 (2.53)	46.1 (2.53)	499 (37.1)	428 (34.4)	70 (14.0)	14.1 (2.60)	583 (40.1)
2-year	871 (42.6)	40.3 (1.54)	27.7 (1.16)	48.1 (2.96)	7.9 (1.60)	44.1 (2.28)	55.9 (2.95)	488 (38.6)	419 (35.8)	69 (14.6)	14.1 (2.77)	384 (26.5)
4-year	1,290 (51.5)	59.7 (1.54)	40.9 (1.28)	26.1 (2.14)	4.9 (1.06)	69.0 (1.74)	31.0 (2.26)	400 (35.0)	337 (32.1)	64 (14.0)	15.9 (3.22)	890 (40.3)
Full-time students	2,013 (63.7)	93.1 (0.79)	63.9 (1.25)	32.9 (1.83)	5.6 (0.90)	61.5 (1.47)	38.5 (1.90)	775 (48.7)	662 (45.0)	113 (18.7)	14.5 (2.23)	1,238 (47.5)
Part-time students	149 (17.8)	6.9 (0.79)	4.7 (0.55)	62.8 (6.94)	13.2 ! (4.88)	24.1 (4.75)	75.9 (6.14)	113 (18.6)	93 (16.9)	20 ! (7.8)	17.3 ! (6.27)	36 (8.1)
Not enrolled in college, 2008	989 (45.3)	100.0	31.4 (1.21)	56.0 (2.76)	20.4 (2.25)	23.6 (1.83)	76.4 (2.37)	756 (48.1)	554 (41.2)	202 (25.0)	26.7 (2.83)	234 (20.7)
Male	560 (34.0)	56.6 (2.30)	17.8 (0.99)	56.1 (3.62)	22.1 (3.02)	21.9 (3.01)	78.1 (3.01)	438 (36.0)	314 (30.5)	124 (19.1)	28.2 (3.71)	122 (19.1)
Female	430 (29.9)	43.4 (2.30)	13.6 (0.89)	55.9 (4.00)	18.2 (3.11)	25.9 (3.53)	74.1 (3.53)	318 (29.7)	240 (25.8)	78 (14.7)	24.6 (4.03)	111 (17.6)
White	592 (35.1)	59.8 (2.28)	18.8 (1.02)	62.7 (3.48)	20.5 (2.92)	16.9 (2.08)	83.1 (2.70)	492 (38.8)	371 (33.7)	121 (19.4)	24.6 (3.42)	100 (13.5)
Black	184 (20.7)	18.6 (1.92)	5.9 (0.65)	44.2 (6.80)	21.4 (5.61)	34.4 (6.50)	65.6 (6.50)	121 (20.4)	81 (16.7)	39 (11.7)	32.6 (7.92)	63 (14.8)
Hispanic	165 (21.0)	16.7 (1.96)	5.2 (0.66)	50.5 (7.23)	19.4 (5.72)	30.1 (5.40)	69.9 (6.63)	115 (19.9)	83 (16.9)	32 ! (10.5)	27.7 (7.74)	50 (13.1)
2009 high school completers[3]												
Total	2,937 (112.6)	† (†)	100.0	36.1 (1.55)	14.3 (1.14)	49.5 (1.25)	50.5 (1.62)	1,482 (67.2)	1,062 (56.9)	421 (36.0)	28.4 (2.06)	1,455 (51.5)
Male	1,407 (78.1)	† (†)	47.9 (2.00)	36.5 (2.21)	15.0 (1.64)	48.5 (2.30)	51.5 (2.30)	724 (46.2)	513 (38.9)	211 (25.0)	29.1 (2.91)	683 (44.9)
Female	1,531 (81.1)	† (†)	52.1 (2.00)	35.8 (2.04)	13.7 (1.47)	50.5 (2.13)	49.5 (2.13)	758 (45.7)	549 (38.9)	210 (24.1)	27.7 (2.71)	772 (46.2)
White	1,863 (89.6)	† (†)	63.4 (1.92)	40.6 (1.99)	13.5 (1.39)	45.9 (1.56)	54.1 (2.02)	1,009 (55.5)	757 (48.1)	252 (27.9)	24.9 (2.40)	854 (39.5)
Black	415 (50.8)	† (†)	14.1 (1.67)	24.3 (3.91)	16.9 (3.42)	58.8 (4.49)	41.2 (4.49)	171 (24.2)	101 (18.6)	70 (15.5)	41.0 (6.99)	244 (28.9)
Hispanic	459 (69.6)	† (†)	15.6 (2.26)	31.9 (4.05)	15.0 (3.10)	53.1 (4.33)	46.9 (4.33)	215 (27.1)	146 (22.4)	69 (15.4)	31.9 (5.91)	243 (28.8)
Enrolled in college, 2009	2,058 (64.4)	100.0	70.1 (1.23)	32.1 (1.80)	10.0 (1.16)	57.9 (1.47)	42.1 (1.91)	867 (51.4)	662 (45.0)	205 (25.2)	23.7 (2.54)	1,192 (46.6)
Male	928 (43.4)	45.1 (1.60)	31.6 (1.25)	31.7 (2.63)	9.1 (1.62)	59.2 (2.78)	40.8 (2.78)	379 (33.5)	294 (29.5)	84 (15.8)	22.2 (3.68)	550 (40.3)
Female	1,130 (47.6)	54.9 (1.60)	38.5 (1.31)	32.5 (2.32)	10.7 (1.53)	56.8 (2.46)	43.2 (2.46)	488 (36.8)	367 (31.9)	121 (18.3)	24.8 (3.26)	642 (42.1)
2-year	813 (41.2)	39.5 (1.57)	27.7 (1.21)	43.9 (3.05)	15.4 (2.22)	40.8 (2.33)	59.2 (3.02)	482 (38.4)	357 (33.0)	125 (19.7)	25.9 (3.51)	332 (24.6)
4-year	1,245 (50.6)	60.5 (1.57)	42.4 (1.33)	24.5 (2.13)	6.4 (1.22)	69.1 (1.77)	30.9 (2.29)	385 (34.3)	305 (30.6)	80 (15.7)	20.8 (3.64)	860 (39.6)
Full-time students	1,885 (61.8)	91.6 (0.89)	64.2 (1.29)	29.6 (1.84)	9.1 (1.17)	61.3 (1.52)	38.7 (1.96)	729 (47.2)	558 (41.3)	172 (23.0)	23.5 (2.76)	1,156 (45.9)
Part-time students	173 (19.2)	8.4 (0.89)	5.9 (0.63)	60.1 (6.52)	19.2 (5.27)	20.7 (4.17)	79.3 (5.39)	137 (20.5)	104 (17.9)	33 ! (10.2)	24.2 (6.43)	36 (8.1)

See notes at end of table.

Labor force status of 2008, 2009, and 2010 high school completers, by sex, race/ethnicity, and college enrollment status: October 2008, 2009, and 2010—Continued

Selected characteristic	Total number of high school completers (in thousands)	Percent of high school completers — Separately for those enrolled in college vs. those not enrolled	Percent of high school completers — For all high school completers	Percentage distribution of all high school completers — Employed	Percentage distribution — Unemployed (seeking employment)	Percentage distribution — Not in labor force	Labor force participation rate of all high school completers[1]	Number (in thousands) — Total, all completers in labor force	High school completers in civilian labor force — Employed	High school completers in civilian labor force — Unemployed (seeking employment)	Unemployment rate[2]	High school completers not in labor force (in thousands)
	2	3	4	5	6	7	8	9	10	11	12	13
White	1,329 (51.7)	64.6 (1.54)	45.2 (1.34)	34.8 (2.29)	9.6 (1.42)	55.6 (1.85)	44.4 (2.39)	591 (42.5)	463 (37.6)	128 (19.9)	21.6 (2.98)	739 (36.7)
Black	289 (25.7)	14.0 (1.19)	9.8 (0.85)	23.4 (4.63)	10.6! (3.37)	66.0 (5.18)	34.0 (5.18)	98 (18.4)	68 (15.3)	31! (10.3)	31.2 (8.69)	190 (25.5)
Hispanic	272 (26.8)	13.2 (1.24)	9.3 (0.89)	29.9 (5.16)	9.0! (3.23)	61.0 (5.49)	39.0 (5.49)	106 (19.1)	81 (16.7)	25! (9.2)	23.2! (7.62)	166 (23.9)
Not enrolled in college, 2009	879 (42.8)	100.0 (†)	29.9 (1.23)	45.5 (2.94)	24.5 (2.55)	30.0 (2.09)	70.0 (2.71)	616 (43.4)	400 (35.0)	216 (25.8)	35.0 (3.38)	263 (22.0)
Male	478 (31.5)	54.4 (2.45)	16.3 (0.99)	45.7 (3.93)	26.5 (3.48)	27.8 (3.53)	72.2 (3.53)	345 (32.0)	219 (25.5)	127 (19.4)	36.7 (4.47)	133 (19.8)
Female	401 (28.9)	45.6 (2.45)	13.6 (0.92)	45.2 (4.15)	22.2 (3.46)	32.6 (3.90)	67.4 (3.90)	270 (27.4)	181 (22.4)	89 (15.7)	32.9 (4.77)	130 (19.0)
White	534 (33.3)	60.8 (2.40)	18.2 (1.04)	55.1 (3.77)	23.2 (3.21)	21.7 (2.41)	78.3 (3.12)	418 (35.8)	294 (30.0)	124 (19.6)	29.6 (3.93)	116 (14.6)
Black	126 (17.2)	14.4 (1.84)	4.3 (0.58)	26.4 (7.29)	31.3 (7.66)	42.3 (8.17)	57.7 (8.17)	73 (15.8)	33! (10.7)	39 (11.7)	54.2 (10.8)	54 (13.6)
Hispanic	186 (22.3)	21.2 (2.28)	6.3 (0.75)	34.9 (6.49)	23.6 (5.78)	41.5 (6.71)	58.5 (6.71)	109 (19.4)	65 (15.0)	44 (12.3)	40.4 (8.73)	77 (16.3)
2010 high school completers[3],[4]												
Total	3,160 (91.8)	† (†)	100.0 (†)	37.3 (1.73)	14.4 (1.18)	48.3 (1.77)	51.7 (1.77)	1,633 (70.7)	1,179 (64.9)	454 (38.1)	27.8 (2.14)	1,528 (74.0)
Male	1,679 (64.6)	† (†)	53.1 (1.30)	39.3 (2.31)	15.9 (1.71)	44.8 (2.26)	55.2 (2.26)	926 (51.5)	659 (49.2)	267 (28.2)	28.9 (2.91)	752 (48.0)
Female	1,482 (58.4)	† (†)	46.9 (1.30)	35.1 (2.32)	12.6 (1.50)	52.3 (2.52)	47.7 (2.52)	706 (45.2)	520 (38.0)	187 (23.9)	26.4 (2.85)	775 (49.5)
White	1,937 (68.7)	† (†)	61.3 (1.41)	40.9 (2.18)	12.9 (1.34)	46.2 (2.10)	53.8 (2.10)	1,041 (55.1)	792 (52.1)	249 (26.7)	23.9 (2.43)	896 (51.7)
Black	461 (36.9)	† (†)	14.6 (1.11)	24.5 (3.74)	23.3 (4.22)	52.2 (4.50)	47.8 (4.50)	220 (27.2)	113 (19.8)	107 (20.9)	48.7 (6.96)	241 (28.3)
Hispanic	507 (37.3)	† (†)	16.0 (1.05)	42.5 (4.60)	12.3 (2.68)	45.1 (4.60)	54.9 (4.60)	278 (30.6)	215 (27.9)	63 (14.3)	22.5 (4.71)	229 (29.1)
Enrolled in college, 2010	2,152 (78.8)	100.0 (†)	68.1 (1.49)	30.9 (1.94)	9.1 (1.22)	60.0 (2.13)	40.0 (2.13)	860 (51.9)	664 (46.9)	196 (26.4)	22.8 (2.77)	1,292 (70.3)
Male	1,055 (50.5)	49.0 (1.64)	33.4 (1.24)	30.1 (2.67)	11.0 (1.81)	58.9 (3.05)	41.1 (3.05)	433 (37.4)	317 (31.7)	116 (19.6)	26.8 (3.87)	621 (44.8)
Female	1,097 (55.2)	51.0 (1.64)	34.7 (1.44)	31.6 (2.68)	7.3 (1.52)	61.1 (2.84)	38.9 (2.84)	427 (37.4)	347 (34.0)	80 (17.1)	18.7 (3.66)	670 (46.3)
2-year	842 (55.9)	39.2 (2.02)	39.2 (2.02)	42.6 (3.21)	9.8 (1.93)	47.6 (3.43)	52.4 (3.43)	441 (39.3)	359 (36.1)	82 (16.2)	18.7 (3.39)	401 (41.0)
4-year	1,309 (61.1)	60.9 (2.02)	60.9 (2.02)	23.3 (2.14)	8.7 (1.50)	68.0 (2.33)	32.0 (2.33)	419 (35.5)	305 (30.9)	114 (20.4)	27.1 (4.25)	890 (52.5)
Full-time students	1,946 (76.2)	90.4 (1.11)	90.4 (1.11)	27.6 (1.91)	9.1 (1.24)	63.3 (2.16)	36.7 (2.16)	714 (48.1)	537 (41.6)	176 (24.7)	24.7 (3.01)	1,233 (67.2)
Part-time students	206 (24.7)	9.6 (1.11)	9.6 (1.11)	61.7 (5.96)	9.5! (3.27)	28.7 (5.55)	71.3 (5.55)	147 (21.0)	127 (19.9)	20! (7.0)	13.4! (4.54)	59 (13.3)
Not enrolled in college, 2010	1,009 (54.9)	100.0 (†)	31.9 (1.49)	51.0 (2.98)	25.6 (2.38)	23.4 (2.29)	76.6 (2.29)	773 (49.7)	515 (42.9)	258 (27.4)	33.4 (3.07)	236 (25.4)
Male	624 (40.4)	61.9 (2.77)	19.7 (1.15)	54.8 (3.66)	24.2 (2.99)	21.0 (2.67)	79.0 (2.67)	493 (38.9)	342 (35.6)	151 (19.9)	30.7 (3.75)	131 (17.0)
Female	385 (37.4)	38.1 (2.77)	12.2 (1.13)	45.0 (4.64)	27.8 (3.95)	27.3 (4.11)	72.7 (4.11)	280 (30.8)	173 (24.6)	107 (17.8)	38.2 (5.13)	105 (19.2)
White	571 (39.3)	56.7 (2.72)	18.1 (1.13)	56.8 (3.94)	21.9 (3.02)	21.4 (3.15)	78.6 (3.15)	449 (36.0)	324 (33.6)	125 (18.1)	27.8 (3.79)	122 (19.7)
Black	175 (24.9)	17.3 (2.11)	5.5 (0.80)	27.8 (6.61)	39.6 (6.95)	32.6 (6.23)	67.4 (6.23)	118 (21.7)	49 (13.8)	69 (16.3)	58.7 (9.00)	57 (12.3)
Hispanic	204 (25.4)	20.3 (2.34)	6.5 (0.76)	59.9 (5.86)	20.5 (5.10)	19.6 (5.11)	80.4 (5.11)	164 (23.9)	122 (19.9)	42 (11.7)	25.5 (6.01)	40 (11.0)

†Not applicable.
!Interpret data with caution. The coefficient of variation (CV) for this estimate is 30 percent or greater.
[1]The labor force participation rate is the percentage of persons who are either employed or seeking employment.
[2]The labor force includes all employed persons plus those seeking employment. The unemployment rate is the percentage of persons in the labor force who are not working and who made specific efforts to find employment sometime during the prior 4 weeks.
[3]Includes 16- to 24-year-olds who completed high school between October of the previous year and October of the given year.
[4]Includes recipients of equivalency credentials as well as diploma recipients.

[4]Beginning in 2010, standard errors were computed using replicate weights, which produced more precise values than the methodology used in prior years. For more information, see Appendix A: Guide to Sources.
NOTE: Data are for October of given year. Data are based on sample surveys of the civilian noninstitutional population. Percentages are only shown when the base is 75,000 or greater. Totals include race categories not separately shown. Race categories exclude persons of Hispanic ethnicity. Detail may not sum to totals because of rounding. Standard errors appear in parentheses.
SOURCE: U.S. Department of Commerce, Census Bureau, Current Population Survey (CPS), October 2008, 2009, and 2010. (This table was prepared August 2011.)

Labor force status of high school dropouts, by sex and race/ethnicity: October, selected years, 1980 through 2010

Year, sex, and race/ethnicity	Number of dropouts (in thousands)		Percent of all dropouts		Percentage distribution of dropouts — Employed		Unemployed (seeking employment)		Not in labor force		Labor force participation rate of dropouts[1]		Dropouts in civilian labor force[2] — Number (in thousands) — Total		Unemployed (seeking employment)		Unemployment rate		Dropouts not in labor force (in thousands)	
1	2		3		4		5		6		7		8		9		10		11	
All dropouts																				
1980	738	(44.0)	100.0	(†)	43.8	(2.97)	20.0	(2.37)	36.2	(2.87)	63.8	(2.87)	471	(35.2)	148	(19.5)	31.4	(3.44)	267	(26.5)
1985	610	(42.3)	100.0	(†)	43.5	(3.45)	24.0	(2.94)	32.5	(3.25)	67.5	(3.25)	412	(34.8)	147	(20.6)	35.6	(4.01)	198	(24.1)
1990	412	(36.0)	100.0	(†)	46.3	(4.37)	21.6	(3.57)	32.2	(4.09)	67.8	(4.09)	279	(29.7)	89	(16.6)	31.8	(4.90)	132	(20.4)
1995	604	(43.6)	100.0	(†)	47.7	(3.61)	20.0	(2.86)	32.3	(3.38)	67.7	(3.38)	409	(35.9)	121	(19.3)	29.6	(3.97)	195	(24.8)
2000	515	(28.5)	100.0	(†)	48.7	(2.77)	19.2	(3.01)	32.0	(2.59)	68.0	(2.59)	350	(23.5)	99	(17.2)	28.1	(4.16)	165	(16.2)
2005	407	(35.3)	100.0	(†)	38.3	(4.22)	18.9	(3.42)	42.8	(3.32)	57.2	(4.30)	233	(26.7)	77	(15.4)	32.9	(5.42)	174	(17.9)
2008	400	(35.0)	100.0	(†)	29.3	(3.98)	19.1	(3.46)	51.6	(3.38)	48.4	(4.38)	194	(24.4)	77	(15.4)	39.5	(6.18)	206	(19.4)
2009	383	(34.3)	100.0	(†)	21.8	(3.69)	26.7	(3.98)	51.5	(3.46)	48.5	(4.47)	186	(23.9)	103	(17.8)	55.1	(6.42)	198	(19.0)
2010[3]	340	(29.0)	100.0	(†)	30.9	(4.24)	23.0	(4.29)	46.1	(4.78)	53.9	(4.78)	183	(21.5)	78	(16.0)	42.7	(6.67)	157	(21.9)
Male																				
1980	422	(32.5)	57.2	(2.89)	50.3	(3.86)	22.0	(3.20)	27.7	(3.45)	72.3	(3.45)	305	(27.7)	93	(15.3)	30.5	(4.18)	117	(17.1)
1985	319	(29.9)	52.3	(3.39)	50.8	(4.69)	30.6	(4.32)	18.6	(3.65)	81.4	(3.65)	260	(27.0)	98	(16.6)	37.6	(5.04)	59	(12.9)
1990	217	(25.6)	52.8	(4.27)	51.3	(5.89)	28.0	(5.29)	20.7	(4.77)	79.3	(4.77)	172	(22.8)	61	(13.5)	35.3	(6.32)	45	(11.6)
1995	339	(31.5)	56.2	(3.45)	52.8	(4.64)	21.3	(3.80)	26.0	(4.07)	74.0	(4.07)	251	(27.1)	72	(14.5)	28.7	(4.88)	88	(16.1)
2000	295	(29.3)	57.3	(3.73)	56.3	(4.94)	18.3	(3.85)	25.6	(4.35)	74.4	(4.35)	220	(25.3)	54	(12.6)	24.5	(4.96)	76	(14.9)
2005	227	(25.9)	55.8	(4.24)	38.3	(5.56)	21.6	(4.71)	40.3	(5.61)	59.7	(5.61)	136	(20.1)	49	(12.1)	35.9	(7.09)	91	(16.1)
2008	191	(23.8)	47.6	(4.30)	29.3	(5.69)	24.6	(5.38)	46.1	(6.22)	53.9	(6.22)	103	(17.5)	47	(11.8)	45.6	(8.47)	88	(16.1)
2009	205	(24.6)	53.4	(4.39)	27.5	(5.37)	33.5	(5.68)	39.1	(5.88)	60.9	(5.88)	125	(19.2)	69	(14.3)	54.9	(7.68)	80	(15.4)
2010[3]	179	(21.3)	52.7	(4.17)	25.9	(4.96)	17.2	(4.40)	56.9	(5.70)	43.1	(5.70)	77	(12.4)	31	(8.5)	39.8	(8.62)	102	(17.2)
Female																				
1980	316	(27.0)	42.8	(2.77)	35.0	(4.08)	17.4	(3.24)	47.6	(4.28)	52.4	(4.28)	165	(19.6)	55	(11.3)	33.2	(5.57)	150	(18.7)
1985	291	(27.4)	47.7	(3.25)	35.5	(4.51)	16.8	(3.52)	47.8	(4.71)	52.2	(4.71)	152	(19.8)	49	(11.2)	32.1	(6.09)	139	(18.9)
1990	194	(23.2)	47.2	(4.10)	40.6	(5.87)	14.4	(4.19)	45.0	(5.94)	55.0	(5.94)	107	(17.2)	28 !	(8.8)	26.1	(7.08)	87	(15.6)
1995	265	(26.6)	43.8	(3.31)	41.1	(4.96)	18.4	(3.91)	40.5	(4.95)	59.5	(4.95)	157	(20.6)	49	(11.5)	30.9	(6.05)	107	(17.0)
2000	220	(24.3)	42.7	(3.58)	39.1	(5.40)	20.5	(4.46)	40.6	(5.43)	59.4	(5.43)	131	(18.8)	45	(11.0)	34.2	(6.80)	90	(15.6)
2005	180	(22.4)	44.2	(4.11)	38.3	(6.04)	15.6	(4.51)	46.0	(6.20)	54.0	(6.20)	97	(16.4)	28 !	(8.8)	28.8	(7.67)	83	(15.2)
2008	210	(24.1)	52.4	(4.16)	29.2	(5.24)	14.2	(4.02)	56.6	(5.71)	43.4	(5.71)	91	(15.9)	30 !	(9.1)	32.7	(8.20)	119	(18.2)
2009	179	(22.3)	46.6	(4.25)	15.2	(4.48)	19.0	(4.90)	65.8	(5.92)	34.2	(5.92)	61	(13.0)	34	(9.7)	‡	(†)	117	(18.1)
2010[3]	161	(19.3)	47.3	(4.17)	36.4	(6.46)	29.6	(7.15)	34.0	(6.82)	66.0	(6.82)	106	(17.0)	48	(13.0)	44.8	(9.14)	55	(12.5)
White																				
1980	489	(35.9)	66.2	(2.83)	50.3	(3.67)	18.0	(2.79)	31.7	(3.42)	68.3	(3.42)	334	(29.7)	88	(15.1)	26.3	(3.87)	155	(20.2)
1985	354	(32.3)	58.1	(3.43)	49.2	(4.56)	23.3	(3.82)	27.5	(4.07)	72.5	(4.07)	257	(27.5)	83	(15.4)	32.2	(4.95)	98	(16.9)
1990	242	(27.6)	58.8	(4.31)	56.3	(5.67)	18.7	(4.41)	25.0	(4.95)	75.0	(4.95)	181	(23.9)	45	(11.8)	25.0	(5.65)	60	(13.8)
1995	316	(31.6)	52.3	(3.61)	51.6	(5.00)	18.3	(3.83)	30.1	(4.59)	69.9	(4.59)	221	(26.4)	58	(13.4)	26.2	(5.21)	95	(17.3)
2000	288	(21.4)	55.9	(2.76)	60.2	(3.63)	16.5	(3.79)	23.4	(3.14)	76.6	(3.14)	221	(18.7)	47	(11.9)	21.5	(4.79)	67	(10.3)
2005	194	(24.4)	47.6	(4.34)	40.3	(6.17)	20.0	(5.05)	39.7	(6.16)	60.3	(6.16)	117	(18.9)	39	(10.9)	33.2	(7.67)	77	(15.4)
2008	152	(21.6)	38.1	(4.25)	38.6	(6.90)	20.6	(5.76)	40.9	(6.97)	59.1	(6.97)	90	(16.6)	31 !	(9.8)	34.8	(8.83)	62	(13.8)
2009	164	(22.5)	42.9	(4.43)	33.9	(6.47)	24.1	(5.87)	42.0	(6.74)	58.0	(6.74)	95	(17.1)	40	(11.1)	41.5	(8.88)	69	(14.6)
2010[3]	148	(18.9)	43.5	(4.57)	31.4	(6.58)	20.4	(5.46)	48.3	(6.82)	51.7	(6.82)	77	(13.6)	30	(8.9)	39.4	(9.52)	71	(14.1)
Black																				
1980	141	(19.9)	19.1	(2.43)	20.9	(5.77)	28.4	(6.40)	50.7	(7.09)	49.3	(7.09)	69	(14.0)	40	(10.6)	‡	(†)	71	(14.2)
1985	130	(20.2)	21.4	(2.95)	29.9	(7.13)	22.7	(6.52)	47.5	(7.78)	52.5	(7.78)	68	(14.7)	30 !	(9.7)	‡	(†)	62	(14.0)
1990	82	(16.6)	19.9	(3.62)	30.9 !	(9.42)	35.2	(9.74)	33.9	(9.64)	66.1	(9.64)	54	(13.5)	29 !	(9.9)	‡	(†)	28 !	(9.7)
1995	104	(18.5)	17.2	(2.79)	33.5	(8.40)	25.8 !	(7.78)	40.8	(8.75)	59.2	(8.75)	62	(14.2)	27 !	(9.4)	‡	(†)	42	(11.8)
2000	106	(18.7)	20.6	(3.24)	26.7	(7.79)	25.5 !	(7.68)	47.8	(8.80)	52.2	(8.80)	55	(13.5)	27 !	(9.4)	‡	(†)	51	(12.9)
2005	108	(19.3)	26.5	(4.07)	26.5	(7.89)	16.0 !	(6.56)	57.5	(8.84)	42.5	(8.84)	46	(12.6)	17 !	(7.7)	‡	(†)	62	(14.6)
2008	109	(19.4)	27.3	(4.14)	18.1 !	(6.84)	15.0 !	(6.34)	67.0	(8.36)	33.0	(8.36)	36 !	(11.2)	16 !	(7.5)	‡	(†)	73	(15.9)
2009	77	(16.2)	20.0	(3.80)	5.1 !	(4.66)	38.6	(10.33)	56.4	(10.53)	43.6	(10.53)	33 !	(10.7)	30 !	(10.1)	‡	(†)	43	(12.2)
2010[3]	64	(15.4)	18.7	(3.94)	‡	(†)	‡	(†)	‡	(†)	‡	(†)	29 !	(9.8)	17 !	(7.9)	‡	(†)	35 !	(11.6)
Hispanic																				
1980	91	(18.9)	12.3	(2.41)	47.2	(10.42)	17.9 !	(8.00)	34.8	(9.94)	65.2	(9.94)	59	(15.3)	16 !	(8.0)	‡	(†)	32 !	(11.2)
1985	105	(18.2)	17.3	(2.72)	37.9	(8.41)	32.0	(8.09)	30.1	(7.95)	69.9	(7.95)	74	(15.2)	34 !	(10.3)	‡	(†)	32 !	(10.0)
1990	72	(15.6)	17.4	(3.44)	‡	(†)	‡	(†)	‡	(†)	‡	(†)	32 !	(10.5)	10 !	(5.9)	‡	(†)	39	(11.5)
1995	174	(23.8)	28.8	(3.34)	48.5	(6.88)	20.1	(5.52)	31.4	(6.40)	68.6	(6.40)	119	(19.7)	35 !	(10.7)	29.3	(7.57)	55	(13.4)
2000	101	(18.2)	19.6	(3.18)	39.0	(8.83)	22.2 !	(7.52)	38.9	(8.82)	61.1	(8.82)	62	(14.2)	22 !	(8.6)	‡	(†)	39	(11.3)
2005	86	(17.2)	21.1	(3.76)	45.1	(9.96)	19.2 !	(7.89)	35.7	(9.59)	64.3	(9.59)	55	(13.8)	17 !	(7.6)	‡	(†)	31 !	(10.3)
2008	111	(19.6)	27.8	(4.16)	31.9	(8.21)	24.5 !	(7.58)	43.7	(8.74)	56.3	(8.74)	63	(14.7)	27 !	(9.7)	‡	(†)	49	(12.9)
2009	115	(19.9)	30.1	(4.35)	17.2 !	(6.53)	27.9	(7.77)	54.9	(8.61)	45.1	(8.61)	52	(13.4)	32 !	(10.5)	‡	(†)	63	(14.8)
2010[3]	93	(15.8)	27.3	(3.95)	33.9	(8.72)	24.1	(6.83)	42.0	(8.87)	58.0	(8.87)	54	(12.0)	22 !	(7.0)	41.6	(11.01)	39	(10.8)

†Not applicable.
!Interpret data with caution. The coefficient of variation (CV) for this estimate is 30 percent or greater.
‡Reporting standards not met (too few cases).
[1]The labor force participation rate is the percentage of persons who are either employed or seeking employment.
[2]The labor force includes all employed persons plus those seeking employment. The unemployment rate is the percentage of persons in the labor force who are not working and who made specific efforts to find employment sometime during the prior 4 weeks.
[3]Beginning in 2010, standard errors were computed using replicate weights, which produced more precise values than the methodology used in prior years. For more information, see Appendix A: Guide to Sources.

NOTE: Data are based on sample surveys of the civilian noninstitutional population. Dropouts are considered persons 16 to 24 years old who dropped out of school in the 12-month period ending in October of years shown. Includes dropouts from any grade, including a small number from elementary and middle schools. Percentages are shown only when the base is 75,000 or greater. Totals include race categories not separately shown. Race categories exclude persons of Hispanic ethnicity. Detail may not sum to totals because of rounding. Standard errors appear in parentheses.
SOURCE: U.S. Department of Commerce, Census Bureau, Current Population Survey (CPS), October, selected years, 1980 through 2010. (This table was prepared August 2011.)

Participants in state-administered adult basic education, secondary education, and English as a second language programs, by type of program and state or jurisdiction: Selected fiscal years, 2000 through 2009

State or jurisdiction	Total			2008				2009			
	2000	2005	2007	Total	Adult basic education	Adult secondary education	English as a second language	Total	Adult basic education	Adult secondary education	English as a second language
1	2	3	4	5	6	7	8	9	10	11	12
United States	2,629,643	2,543,953	2,302,827	2,364,051	1,004,660	307,825	1,051,566	2,157,155	979,604	256,323	921,228
Alabama	23,666	19,827	19,809	23,815	17,006	4,648	2,161	25,153	17,967	4,952	2,234
Alaska	5,312	3,791	2,877	3,179	2,044	460	675	3,326	2,129	476	721
Arizona	31,136	26,881	18,704	21,760	12,763	1,506	7,491	19,789	11,791	1,506	6,492
Arkansas	38,867	37,102	31,010	32,610	21,180	6,416	5,014	31,551	20,515	6,105	4,931
California	473,050	591,893	602,837	618,767	134,422	77,501	406,844	434,428	97,976	37,192	299,260
Colorado	13,818	15,011	14,683	14,203	3,775	1,264	9,164	14,298	3,929	1,331	9,038
Connecticut	30,844	31,958	27,549	27,859	7,503	7,568	12,788	28,255	7,472	7,502	13,281
Delaware	4,342	6,329	4,399	5,155	3,210	644	1,301	5,059	3,151	588	1,320
District of Columbia	3,667	3,646	3,694	3,956	2,184	218	1,554	4,247	2,362	223	1,662
Florida	404,912	348,119	264,670	260,931	112,229	31,608	117,094	256,498	113,430	30,288	112,780
Georgia	108,004	95,434	72,390	75,487	47,580	6,560	21,347	72,657	48,584	6,135	17,938
Hawaii	10,525	7,461	8,135	8,944	3,901	1,912	3,131	9,196	3,867	2,149	3,180
Idaho	10,506	7,744	6,953	7,535	4,160	581	2,794	7,429	4,541	546	2,342
Illinois	122,043	118,296	107,120	108,024	28,702	15,379	63,943	108,383	29,922	15,835	62,626
Indiana	42,135	43,498	38,468	40,226	24,927	8,121	7,178	35,995	22,939	6,791	6,265
Iowa	20,161	11,989	9,271	9,918	3,993	2,222	3,703	10,752	5,095	2,061	3,596
Kansas	11,248	9,475	8,611	8,916	4,305	1,026	3,585	9,024	4,381	902	3,741
Kentucky	31,050	30,931	31,456	40,235	27,941	8,276	4,018	39,218	26,972	8,207	4,039
Louisiana	30,929	29,367	23,642	26,633	21,255	3,486	1,892	30,559	24,588	3,696	2,275
Maine	12,430	8,151	7,878	9,270	4,754	2,958	1,558	8,604	4,448	2,400	1,756
Maryland	22,702	27,055	30,882	33,673	15,321	4,110	14,242	33,942	15,865	3,667	14,410
Massachusetts	24,053	21,448	21,706	21,491	4,864	3,526	13,101	20,372	4,813	3,295	12,264
Michigan	56,096	34,768	30,571	28,243	15,485	3,482	9,276	31,106	18,391	3,786	8,929
Minnesota	42,039	47,174	45,805	46,109	16,481	5,271	24,357	47,612	17,658	5,948	24,006
Mississippi	37,947	25,675	20,372	20,480	17,309	2,801	370	17,782	14,410	3,067	305
Missouri	41,089	37,052	33,497	36,161	24,720	4,584	6,857	35,542	24,217	4,244	7,081
Montana	4,892	3,291	2,930	3,151	2,298	639	214	3,735	2,753	772	210
Nebraska	7,917	10,226	8,503	8,435	4,022	1,024	3,389	8,588	4,213	906	3,469
Nevada	22,992	9,981	9,526	8,571	1,067	443	7,061	9,193	1,195	502	7,496
New Hampshire	5,962	5,804	5,592	5,806	1,805	1,995	2,006	5,589	1,770	1,671	2,148
New Jersey	44,317	40,889	34,198	32,823	11,660	1,747	19,416	33,901	11,626	1,400	20,875
New Mexico	23,243	24,132	20,063	22,920	12,444	2,195	8,281	23,248	12,941	2,069	8,238
New York	176,239	157,486	133,852	133,255	52,844	8,887	71,524	129,636	50,261	7,868	71,507
North Carolina	107,504	109,047	110,126	121,708	67,917	22,261	31,530	123,030	69,472	24,396	29,162
North Dakota	2,124	2,063	1,693	1,822	968	452	402	1,783	973	409	401
Ohio	65,579	50,869	48,209	50,537	34,834	8,434	7,269	46,042	32,588	6,729	6,725
Oklahoma	20,101	20,447	17,672	18,411	13,028	1,916	3,467	19,711	13,634	2,164	3,913
Oregon	25,228	21,668	21,690	23,600	10,901	2,046	10,653	22,976	10,310	2,924	9,742
Pennsylvania	49,369	54,274	50,996	52,795	27,958	10,672	14,165	34,975	21,407	5,257	8,311
Rhode Island	5,592	6,697	6,697	6,580	3,024	748	2,808	6,497	2,748	685	3,064
South Carolina	94,452	65,901	59,077	54,538	40,149	8,307	6,082	53,645	40,310	8,019	5,316
South Dakota	5,637	3,517	2,629	3,025	1,906	725	394	2,773	1,730	566	477
Tennessee	40,615	48,924	41,439	37,048	27,207	4,904	4,937	32,177	23,959	4,055	4,163
Texas	111,585	119,867	93,242	84,514	32,947	3,524	48,043	98,063	46,427	3,591	48,045
Utah	30,714	29,320	21,764	25,978	14,192	3,004	8,782	26,337	15,383	2,809	8,145
Vermont	1,146	2,015	1,756	2,505	1,890	437	178	2,461	1,841	379	241
Virginia	35,261	29,222	30,940	31,106	12,341	4,570	14,195	29,802	12,512	4,632	12,658
Washington	53,460	50,386	57,474	64,982	26,231	4,393	34,358	65,606	27,120	4,546	33,940
West Virginia	13,072	9,444	9,083	9,628	7,499	1,909	220	9,780	7,609	1,912	259
Wisconsin	27,304	26,029	24,302	23,856	12,057	5,668	6,131	23,694	13,791	4,324	5,579
Wyoming	2,767	2,379	2,385	2,877	1,457	797	623	3,136	1,618	846	672
Other jurisdictions ...	44,785	37,328	34,079	36,071	6,709	28,696	666	24,098	4,044	19,437	617
American Samoa	662	838	226	264	118	35	111	169	123	24	22
Federated States of Micronesia	0	0	0	0	0	0	0	0	0	0	0
Guam	1,092	1,062	1,079	1,154	724	306	124	633	382	166	85
Marshall Islands	335	0	0	0	0	0	0	0	0	0	0
Northern Marianas	680	740	613	583	270	121	192	607	387	77	143
Palau	132	206	55	51	0	51	0	63	0	63	0
Puerto Rico	41,043	33,463	31,924	34,019	5,597	28,183	239	22,626	3,152	19,107	367
U.S. Virgin Islands	841	1,019	182	0	0	0	0	0	0	0	0

NOTE: Adult basic education provides instruction in basic skills for adults 16 and over functioning at literacy levels below the secondary level. Adult secondary education provides instruction at the high school level for adults who are seeking to pass the GED or obtain an adult high school credential. English as a second language instruction is for adults who lack proficiency in English and who seek to improve their literacy and competence in English. Some data have been revised from previously published figures.

SOURCE: U.S. Department of Education, Office of Vocational and Adult Education (OVAE), OVAE National Reporting System, retrieved June 12, 2011, from http://wdcrobcolp01.ed.gov/CFAPPS/OVAE/NRS/. (This table was prepared June 2011.)

Participation of employed persons, 17 years old and over, in career-related adult education during the previous 12 months, by selected characteristics of participants: 1995, 1999, and 2005

Characteristic of employed person	1995		1999		2005						
	Percent of adults participating in career- or job-related courses	Number of career- or job-related courses taken, per employed adult	Percent of adults participating in career- or job-related courses	Number of career- or job-related courses taken, per employed adult	Employed persons, in thousands	In career- or job-related courses[1]	In apprenticeship programs	In personal interest courses	In informal learning activities for personal interest	Number of career- or job-related courses taken[1] — In thousands	Per employed adult
1	2	3	4	5	6	7	8	9	10	11	12
Total	**31.1** (0.54)	**0.8** (0.02)	**30.5** (1.14)	**0.7** (0.03)	**133,386** (1,508.1)	**38.8** (0.83)	**1.4** (0.24)	**21.8** (0.94)	**73.5** (1.01)	**108,443**	**0.8** (0.03)
Sex											
Male	29.0 (0.72)	0.7 (0.02)	28.3 (1.15)	0.6 (0.03)	71,754 (934.7)	31.7 (1.22)	2.0 (0.37)	18.5 (1.30)	73.4 (1.52)	44,512	0.6 (0.03)
Female	33.4 (0.83)	0.9 (0.03)	32.9 (1.14)	0.8 (0.03)	61,632 (1,219.3)	47.1 (1.43)	0.8 (0.23)	25.8 (1.23)	73.6 (1.37)	63,931	1.0 (0.05)
Age											
17 through 24 years old	18.6 (1.01)	0.4 (0.02)	19.1 (1.91)	0.4 (0.06)	15,027 (1,030.4)	26.4 (3.01)	3.0 ! (1.03)	25.2 (3.37)	71.4 (3.15)	8,024	0.5 (0.09)
25 through 29 years old	31.2 (1.46)	0.8 (0.05)	34.3 (2.44)	0.8 (0.08)	14,555 (918.4)	36.1 (2.94)	3.1 ! (1.12)	24.5 (3.66)	70.9 (4.49)	9,493	0.7 (0.06)
30 through 34 years old	31.6 (1.30)	0.8 (0.04)	34.4 (2.50)	0.8 (0.08)	15,250 (977.2)	41.0 (3.06)	2.7 ! (1.10)	23.7 (2.63)	74.0 (2.54)	12,681	0.8 (0.07)
35 through 39 years old	35.1 (1.02)	0.9 (0.03)	29.2 (2.15)	0.7 (0.07)	15,286 (922.4)	41.7 (4.16)	1.0 ! (0.46)	21.6 (3.15)	77.7 (3.00)	13,807	0.9 (0.14)
40 through 44 years old	36.6 (1.29)	0.9 (0.04)	36.4 (2.44)	0.8 (0.07)	18,141 (946.3)	39.8 (2.73)	‡ (†)	23.3 (2.60)	71.2 (3.15)	15,586	0.9 (0.07)
45 through 49 years old	39.6 (1.94)	1.0 (0.06)	30.4 (2.42)	0.7 (0.06)	18,149 (842.5)	45.0 (2.15)	0.7 ! (0.29)	19.0 (2.09)	73.5 (2.68)	16,809	0.9 (0.06)
50 through 54 years old	34.4 (1.69)	0.9 (0.04)	34.7 (2.57)	0.8 (0.07)	14,624 (732.1)	42.6 (2.49)	0.7 ! (0.32)	19.5 (1.92)	76.3 (2.27)	14,881	1.0 (0.10)
55 through 59 years old	26.7 (1.86)	0.7 (0.06)	30.3 (2.83)	0.6 (0.08)	10,522 (676.0)	44.7 (2.98)	‡ (†)	18.3 (1.93)	73.0 (2.95)	9,901	0.9 (0.09)
60 through 64 years old	21.1 (2.41)	0.5 (0.06)	27.2 (3.80)	0.7 (0.15)	6,021 (498.8)	38.9 (3.97)	‡ (†)	23.4 (3.52)	73.0 (4.22)	4,919	0.8 (0.10)
65 years old and over	13.7 (1.86)	0.4 (0.06)	20.3 (4.21)	0.4 (0.08)	5,812 (493.3)	21.6 (3.48)	# (†)	17.4 (3.13)	74.2 (3.75)	2,343	0.4 (0.07)
65 through 69	13.1 (2.28)	0.4 (0.08)	— (†)	— (†)	3,385 (415.5)	19.1 (4.05)	# (†)	20.9 (4.88)	75.4 (5.18)	1,102	0.3 (0.08)
70 and over	14.6 (2.85)	0.4 (0.09)	— (†)	— (†)	2,427 (282.3)	25.1 (5.81)	# (†)	12.6 (2.93)	72.6 (6.11)	1,241	0.5 (0.14)
Race/ethnicity											
White	33.2 (0.61)	0.8 (0.03)	32.8 (0.98)	0.6 (0.03)	94,881 (1,538.6)	41.3 (0.93)	1.2 (0.25)	22.2 (1.11)	75.3 (1.17)	82,511	0.9 (0.03)
Black	26.2 (1.46)	0.7 (0.04)	28.1 (2.34)	1.0 (0.07)	13,773 (533.2)	39.2 (3.82)	1.7 ! (0.83)	23.5 (3.04)	66.9 (3.02)	10,311	0.7 (0.11)
Hispanic	18.1 (1.00)	0.4 (0.02)	16.4 (1.83)	0.5 (0.05)	15,741 (681.1)	25.0 (2.66)	2.9 (0.85)	16.2 (2.31)	65.8 (3.39)	8,786	0.6 (0.11)
Asian	— (†)	— (†)	— (†)	— (†)	3,770 (520.7)	36.9 (7.00)	‡ (†)	32.3 (7.26)	81.1 (5.88)	2,207	0.6 (0.12)
Pacific Islander	— (†)	— (†)	— (†)	— (†)	‡ (†)	‡ (†)	‡ (†)	‡ (†)	‡ (†)	‡	‡ (†)
Asian/Pacific Islander	25.5 (2.69)	0.6 (0.07)	32.8 (4.84)	0.4 (0.15)	— (†)	— (†)	— (†)	— (†)	— (†)	—	— (†)
American Indian/Alaska Native	34.0 (6.32)	0.9 (0.20)	29.5 (11.52)	0.7 (0.52)	‡ (†)	‡ (†)	‡ (†)	‡ (†)	‡ (†)	‡	‡ (†)
Two or more races	— (†)	— (†)	— (†)	— (†)	3,786 (562.7)	39.1 (6.85)	‡ (†)	22.6 (6.34)	77.6 (8.40)	3,083	0.8 (0.15)
Other races	25.3 (2.99)	0.7 (0.09)	— (†)	— (†)	‡ (†)	‡ (†)	‡ (†)	‡ (†)	‡ (†)	‡	‡ (†)
Highest level of education completed											
Less than high school completion	8.8 (1.05)	0.1 (0.02)	7.9 (2.29)	0.4 (0.05)	16,627 (838.2)	10.4 (2.11)	2.4 ! (0.90)	8.8 (1.54)	57.0 (3.76)	2,592	0.2 (0.03)
8th grade or less	6.1 ! (2.00)	0.1 ! (0.04)	— (†)	— (†)	5,016 (599.7)	2.7 (1.12)	‡ (†)	3.8 ! (1.71)	46.7 (7.11)	197	# (†)
9th through 12th grade, no completion	10.0 (1.27)	0.2 (0.02)	— (†)	— (†)	11,610 (792.8)	13.7 (2.99)	‡ (†)	11.0 (2.06)	61.5 (4.05)	2,396	0.2 (0.04)
High school completion	20.9 (0.79)	0.4 (0.02)	21.4 (1.45)	0.8 (0.03)	34,121 (1,147.2)	24.7 (1.76)	1.3 ! (0.46)	17.1 (1.89)	63.4 (2.55)	16,640	0.5 (0.05)
Some vocational/technical	32.3 (2.50)	0.8 (0.07)	28.7 (5.76)	0.9 (0.17)	3,744 (393.1)	48.2 (5.92)	‡ (†)	25.5 (4.61)	74.0 (5.54)	3,802	1.0 (0.17)
Some college	29.9 (0.91)	0.7 (0.03)	29.0 (1.78)	0.7 (0.06)	24,479 (1,067.7)	39.9 (2.36)	1.9 ! (0.69)	25.2 (2.50)	79.8 (2.04)	18,437	0.8 (0.05)
Associate's degree	39.2 (1.58)	1.0 (0.05)	39.7 (3.07)	0.9 (0.09)	9,943 (730.7)	50.4 (3.71)	2.3 ! (0.84)	19.1 (2.86)	78.4 (3.88)	14,224	1.4 (0.21)
Bachelor's degree	44.6 (1.33)	1.2 (0.04)	43.8 (2.01)	1.0 (0.06)	26,475 (902.7)	53.1 (1.88)	‡ (†)	29.0 (1.77)	78.7 (1.94)	28,099	1.1 (0.06)
Some graduate work (or study)	50.2 (1.63)	1.4 (0.05)	46.8 (4.17)	1.2 (0.14)	17,998 (735.4)	61.1 (2.16)	‡ (†)	28.6 (2.01)	88.8 (1.16)	24,649	1.4 (0.07)
No degree	44.3 (3.18)	1.2 (0.10)	54.2 (4.94)	1.2 (0.14)	2,125 (227.9)	53.8 (5.79)	‡ (†)	39.3 (6.05)	75.0 (5.64)	2,412	1.1 (0.16)
Master's	50.5 (1.99)	1.4 (0.06)	45.3 (2.97)	1.1 (0.11)	11,330 (614.7)	62.7 (2.98)	‡ (†)	28.2 (2.27)	90.5 (1.40)	15,394	1.4 (0.09)
Doctor's	40.4 (6.42)	1.0 (0.16)	34.4 (4.79)	0.7 (0.12)	1,600 (227.2)	49.0 (5.80)	‡ (†)	28.8 (4.76)	87.8 (4.35)	2,204	1.4 (0.36)
Professional	67.6 (3.89)	2.0 (0.15)	67.6 (6.98)	1.9 (0.31)	2,943 (382.7)	66.5 (6.39)	‡ (†)	22.1 (5.05)	92.9 (2.21)	4,639	1.6 (0.21)

See notes at end of table.

Participation of employed persons, 17 years old and over, in career-related adult education during the previous 12 months, by selected characteristics of participants: 1995, 1999, and 2005—Continued

Characteristic of employed person	1995 Percent of adults participating in career- or job-related courses	1995 Number of career- or job-related courses taken, per employed adult	1999 Percent of adults participating in career- or job-related courses	1999 Number of career- or job-related courses taken, per employed adult	2005 Employed persons, in thousands	2005 Percent In career- or job-related courses[1]	2005 Percent In apprenticeship programs	2005 Percent In personal interest courses	2005 Percent In informal learning activities for personal interest	2005 Number of career- or job-related courses taken[1] In thousands	2005 Per employed adult
1	2	3	4	5	6	7	8	9	10	11	12
Locale[2]											
City	—	(†)	—	(†)	39,283 (1,391.3)	39.6 (1.67)	2.2 (0.60)	23.1 (1.43)	74.0 (1.77)	34,327	0.9 (0.05)
Suburban	—	(†)	—	(†)	48,452 (1,555.0)	41.1 (1.87)	1.2 (0.32)	23.3 (1.38)	74.2 (1.49)	39,802	0.8 (0.04)
Town	—	(†)	—	(†)	17,616 (1,060.7)	36.0 (2.64)	‡ (†)	19.6 (2.83)	71.7 (3.02)	12,947	0.7 (0.07)
Rural	—	(†)	—	(†)	27,847 (885.2)	35.4 (2.14)	1.4! (0.58)	19.0 (2.19)	72.7 (2.22)	21,135	0.8 (0.06)
Occupation											
Executive, administrative, or managerial occupations	42.9 (1.49)	1.2 (0.05)	40.6 (2.06)	1.0 (0.07)	14,596 (707.6)	53.6 (2.79)	‡ (†)	29.5 (2.89)	77.7 (2.87)	16,567	1.1 (0.09)
Engineers, surveyors, and architects	44.2 (4.46)	1.1 (0.12)	52.1 (6.96)	1.0 (0.16)	1,987 (244.9)	56.3 (5.68)	‡ (†)	30.5 (6.36)	81.0 (4.73)	2,323	1.2 (0.16)
Natural scientists and mathematicians	59.7 (3.97)	1.7 (0.15)	46.0 (6.61)	0.8 (0.14)	4,130 (445.4)	51.5 (5.64)	‡ (†)	31.2 (4.83)	85.3 (5.44)	3,693	0.9 (0.11)
Social scientists and workers, religious workers, and lawyers	59.5 (2.61)	1.8 (0.11)	56.9 (5.66)	1.7 (0.24)	4,697 (480.9)	66.8 (4.48)	‡ (†)	28.3 (3.81)	88.6 (2.95)	7,822	1.7 (0.29)
Teachers, elementary/secondary	53.9 (2.23)	1.5 (0.08)	52.1 (3.53)	1.2 (0.11)	7,085 (568.5)	67.7 (4.16)	‡ (†)	31.5 (3.93)	83.0 (2.79)	12,233	1.7 (0.13)
Teachers, postsecondary and counselors, librarians, and archivists	41.6 (4.57)	1.0 (0.15)	35.6 (5.85)	0.7 (0.14)	2,393 (420.9)	53.1 (8.63)	‡ (†)	17.7 (4.91)	90.9 (3.97)	2,122	0.9 (0.09)
Health diagnosing and treating practitioners	68.6 (5.85)	2.0 (0.23)	65.2 (11.99)	1.5! (0.50)	978 (208.8)	78.9 (7.10)	‡ (†)	27.4! (9.60)	86.6 (5.37)	1,951	2.0 (0.25)
Registered nurses, pharmacists, dieticians, therapists, and physician's assistants	72.8 (3.02)	2.2 (0.14)	72.2 (5.04)	1.8 (0.21)	2,794 (238.8)	79.7 (4.60)	‡ (†)	29.4 (4.17)	84.3 (3.70)	4,984	1.8 (0.15)
Writers, artists, entertainers, and athletes	23.4 (2.89)	0.5 (0.07)	30.6 (6.21)	0.6 (0.18)	2,969 (405.2)	29.9 (5.69)	‡ (†)	31.8 (6.15)	88.9 (4.39)	1,865	0.6 (0.15)
Health technologists and technicians	50.0 (4.08)	1.4 (0.12)	41.8 (6.00)	1.0 (0.19)	3,060 (436.7)	70.6 (7.31)	2.0 (1.50)	27.8 (6.48)	77.5 (6.40)	4,473	1.5 (0.18)
Technologists and technicians, except health	43.8 (2.67)	1.1 (0.10)	37.6 (4.87)	1.0 (0.15)	1,774 (336.5)	29.4 (8.10)	‡ (†)	5.3! (2.02)	75.2 (8.98)	1,015	0.6 (0.17)
Marketing and sales occupations	25.2 (1.26)	0.6 (0.03)	21.1 (2.27)	0.4 (0.06)	14,845 (971.9)	32.3 (3.17)	‡ (†)	20.8 (2.64)	70.5 (3.53)	7,724	0.5 (0.05)
Administrative support occupations, including clerical	30.8 (1.15)	0.7 (0.03)	27.4 (2.02)	0.6 (0.05)	21,167 (1,179.4)	36.1 (2.95)	0.8! (0.40)	28.2 (2.28)	72.9 (2.37)	15,443	0.7 (0.10)
Service occupations	22.6 (1.25)	0.6 (0.04)	21.0 (2.15)	0.5 (0.07)	17,180 (1,033.7)	33.7 (3.13)	1.1! (0.36)	16.2 (2.31)	69.0 (2.74)	13,029	0.8 (0.10)
Agriculture, forestry, and fishing occupations	12.4 (2.47)	0.2! (0.07)	12.2! (4.09)	0.2! (0.07)	2,522 (423.8)	22.4! (7.61)	‡ (†)	23.0! (11.03)	62.9 (11.04)	960	0.4! (0.12)
Mechanics and repairers	29.1 (2.62)	0.7 (0.08)	15.0 (3.40)	0.3 (0.09)	5,241 (521.6)	28.3 (4.47)	4.0! (1.44)	12.6 (3.24)	69.3 (4.36)	2,669	0.5 (0.09)
Construction and extractive occupations	18.6 (2.33)	0.3 (0.04)	13.2 (3.16)	0.2 (0.06)	6,827 (647.1)	12.4 (3.04)	5.3! (2.26)	7.8! (1.88)	69.0 (5.25)	2,323	0.3! (0.13)
Precision production[3]	25.6 (4.04)	0.6 (0.12)	18.3! (6.52)	0.4! (0.12)	10,483 (839.3)	23.5 (3.79)	‡ (†)	14.0 (3.34)	64.9 (3.74)	4,904	0.5 (0.07)
Production workers	14.8 (1.13)	0.3 (0.02)	23.0 (3.17)	0.5 (0.08)	— (†)	— (†)	— (†)	— (†)	— (†)	—	— (†)

See notes at end of table.

Participation of employed persons, 17 years old and over, in career-related adult education during the previous 12 months, by selected characteristics of participants: 1995, 1999, and 2005—Continued

Characteristic of employed person	1995		1999		2005						Number of career- or job-related courses taken[1]	
	Percent of adults participating in career- or job-related courses	Number of career- or job-related courses taken, per employed adult	Percent of adults participating in career- or job-related courses	Number of career- or job-related courses taken, per employed adult	Employed persons, in thousands	Percent of adults participating					In thousands	Per employed adult
						In career- or job-related courses[1]	In apprenticeship programs	In personal interest courses	In informal learning activities for personal interest			
1	2	3	4	5	6	7	8	9	10		11	12
Transportation and material moving	15.8 (1.83)	0.3 (0.04)	18.4 (3.62)	0.3 (0.06)	7,858 (742.5)	15.2 (2.81)	3.4 (1.77)	10.5 (3.10)	62.5 (5.32)		1,935	0.2 (0.05)
Handlers, equipment cleaners, helpers, and laborers	11.7 (2.77)	0.2 (0.06)	‡ (†)	‡ (†)	— (†)	— (†)	‡ (†)	— (†)	— (†)		—	— (†)
Miscellaneous occupations	38.8 (3.50)	1.0 (0.11)	14.2! (4.62)	0.3! (0.08)	801 (189.4)	17.2! (6.87)	‡ (†)	8.7! (4.31)	48.3 (13.96)		409	‡ (†)
Annual household income												
$10,000 or less	12.6 (1.31)	0.2 (0.03)	9.5! (3.09)	0.2! (0.05)	4,425 (444.8)	16.7 (4.35)	‡ (†)	26.2! (7.96)	69.7 (5.72)		1,556	0.4! (0.12)
$5,000 or less	8.7 (1.91)	0.1 (0.03)	— (†)	— (†)	1,635 (252.7)	19.1 (6.52)	‡ (†)	22.9! (7.91)	60.9 (8.84)		850	‡ (†)
$5,001 to $10,000	15.1 (1.62)	0.3 (0.04)	— (†)	— (†)	2,791 (454.1)	15.3 (5.68)	‡ (†)	28.1! (12.27)	74.8 (6.88)		706	0.3! (0.10)
$10,001 to $15,000	15.1 (1.71)	0.4 (0.04)	8.3 (1.88)	0.1 (0.03)	4,814 (633.4)	22.2 (5.77)	‡ (†)	17.3! (5.25)	64.5 (7.57)		2,189	0.5 (0.12)
$15,001 to $20,000	20.1 (1.36)	0.4 (0.03)	16.3 (2.75)	0.3 (0.05)	4,515 (398.8)	18.2 (3.09)	5.7! (2.71)	11.5 (1.96)	60.4 (5.11)		1,322	0.3 (0.05)
$20,001 to $25,000	20.4 (1.52)	0.5 (0.05)	18.8 (2.79)	0.4 (0.08)	5,593 (490.2)	23.8 (4.02)	1.1! (0.51)	13.3 (3.21)	71.5 (4.11)		2,817	0.5 (0.10)
$25,001 to $30,000	24.7 (1.34)	0.5 (0.03)	22.2 (2.73)	0.5 (0.07)	7,444 (680.4)	31.4 (4.88)	‡ (†)	16.7 (3.77)	73.5 (3.91)		4,322	0.6 (0.11)
$30,001 to $40,000	30.2 (1.13)	0.8 (0.03)	26.6 (2.82)	0.6 (0.07)	13,123 (928.5)	35.1 (3.45)	1.5! (0.65)	21.7 (3.71)	69.1 (3.55)		8,224	0.6 (0.06)
$40,001 to $50,000	34.7 (1.30)	0.8 (0.04)	32.3 (2.34)	0.7 (0.07)	13,647 (1,058.4)	31.5 (3.01)	1.8! (0.72)	20.1 (3.32)	73.5 (2.78)		10,072	0.7 (0.10)
$50,001 to $75,000	40.0 (1.18)	1.0 (0.04)	36.6 (1.86)	0.9 (0.06)	33,665 (1,430.4)	42.7 (1.80)	1.2! (0.51)	20.9 (2.10)	71.3 (2.55)		28,991	0.9 (0.06)
More than $75,000	45.2 (1.40)	1.3 (0.04)	42.5 (1.79)	1.0 (0.06)	46,160 (1,263.3)	48.1 (1.57)	1.3! (0.39)	26.0 (1.37)	79.2 (1.55)		48,951	1.1 (0.05)

—Not available.
†Not applicable.
#Rounds to zero.
!Interpret data with caution. The coefficient of variation (CV) for this estimate is 30 percent or greater.
‡Reporting standards not met. The coefficient of variation (CV) for this estimate is 50 percent or greater.
[1]The 2005 estimates on participation in career- or job-related courses were based on responses to multiple questions. Specifically, respondents were first asked what courses they had taken, and then whether each course was career- or job-related. In contrast, 1995 and 1999 respondents were asked a single, general question about whether they had participated in any career- or job-related courses. Therefore, 2005 results may not be comparable to results from the earlier years.

[2]Detail may not sum to totals due to missing locale information.
[3]For 2005, figures include "Production workers" occupations data.
NOTE: Data do not include persons enrolled in high school or below. Race categories exclude persons of Hispanic ethnicity. Detail may not sum to totals because of rounding. Standard errors appear in parentheses.
SOURCE: U.S. Department of Education, National Center for Education Statistics, Adult Education Survey (AE-NHES:1995, AE-NHES:1999, and AE-NHES:2005) of the National Household Education Surveys Program. (This table was prepared October 2010.)

Participation rate of persons, 17 years old and over, in adult education during the previous 12 months, by selected characteristics of participants: Selected years, 1991 through 2005

Characteristic of participant	Percent taking any program, class, or course — 1991	1995	1999	2001	2005	Basic skills/General Educational Development (GED) classes	English as a second language (ESL) classes	Part-time postsecondary education[1]	Career- or job-related courses	Apprenticeship programs	Personal-interest courses	Percent doing informal learning activities for personal interest, 2005
	2	3	4	5	6	7	8	9	10	11	12	13
Total	33.0 (0.68)	40.2 (0.48)	44.5 (0.77)	46.4 (0.55)	44.4 (0.74)	1.3 (0.22)	0.9 (0.17)	5.0 (0.29)	27.0 (0.63)	1.2 (0.18)	21.4 (0.71)	70.5 (0.79)
Sex												
Male	32.6 (1.09)	38.2 (0.65)	41.7 (1.15)	43.1 (0.83)	41.0 (1.20)	1.4 (0.41)	0.9 (0.29)	5.0 (0.44)	24.5 (0.99)	1.7 (0.31)	18.3 (1.08)	70.8 (1.10)
Female	33.2 (0.97)	42.1 (0.59)	47.1 (1.02)	49.5 (0.78)	47.5 (1.01)	1.2 (0.19)	0.9 (0.15)	5.1 (0.37)	29.2 (0.95)	0.7 (0.15)	24.2 (0.88)	70.2 (1.03)
Age												
17 to 24 years old	37.8 (1.46)	47.0 (1.12)	49.9 (2.34)	52.8 (2.04)	52.8 (2.79)	6.0 (1.48)	1.7 ! (0.61)	11.5 (1.34)	21.3 (2.22)	2.7 (0.76)	26.3 (2.60)	69.2 (2.54)
25 to 29 years old	40.0 (2.33)	49.6 (1.31)	56.5 (2.53)	52.9 (2.60)	51.6 (3.82)	1.8 (0.48)	3.3 ! (1.48)	9.1 (1.50)	29.5 (2.48)	3.2 ! (1.06)	20.9 (2.78)	66.8 (3.75)
30 to 34 years old	37.6 (2.88)	47.3 (1.41)	56.2 (2.57)	53.7 (2.18)	52.7 (2.52)	1.9 ! (0.66)	1.6 ! (0.64)	8.4 (1.28)	33.8 (2.71)	2.5 ! (0.89)	23.2 (2.23)	73.8 (2.22)
35 to 39 years old	42.1 (2.71)	47.7 (1.15)	50.1 (2.43)	54.0 (1.71)	48.6 (3.21)	0.4 ! (0.16)	0.7 ! (0.26)	6.1 (0.90)	32.6 (3.29)	0.9 ! (0.36)	20.7 (2.67)	75.5 (2.69)
40 to 44 years old	49.2 (3.28)	50.9 (1.15)	50.5 (2.43)	53.5 (1.88)	48.9 (2.43)	0.8 ! (0.31)	0.6 ! (0.23)	4.7 (0.77)	34.8 (2.30)	0.9 ! (0.42)	23.4 (2.29)	71.5 (2.62)
45 to 49 years old	40.0 (2.43)	48.7 (1.66)	49.8 (2.69)	55.4 (2.02)	49.0 (2.09)	‡ (†)	0.6 ! (0.25)	3.2 (0.48)	37.7 (1.83)	0.5 ! (0.23)	19.3 (1.88)	71.6 (2.52)
50 to 54 years old	26.8 (3.31)	42.5 (1.38)	47.2 (2.51)	51.1 (2.22)	46.6 (2.36)	‡ (†)	0.3 ! (0.15)	4.5 (0.75)	35.2 (2.25)	0.6 ! (0.28)	20.3 (1.64)	75.6 (1.89)
55 to 59 years old	29.0 (3.74)	32.2 (1.66)	38.0 (2.60)	44.1 (1.98)	42.2 (2.78)	‡ (†)	‡ (†)	1.9 (0.43)	31.9 (2.39)	‡ (†)	18.0 (1.63)	69.5 (2.56)
60 to 64 years old	17.4 (1.90)	23.7 (1.89)	31.4 (2.83)	30.8 (2.18)	37.9 (3.00)	‡ (†)	‡ (†)	0.9 ! (0.36)	20.9 (2.07)	‡ (†)	24.1 (2.40)	71.4 (3.04)
65 to 69 years old	14.2 (2.97)	18.1 (1.46)	25.4 (2.54)	20.5 (1.74)	26.2 (2.67)	‡ (†)	‡ (†)	0.5 ! (0.22)	8.1 (1.36)	‡ (†)	20.9 (2.41)	67.6 (2.52)
70 years old and over	8.6 (1.25)	13.8 (1.09)	15.0 (1.38)	21.7 (1.37)	21.5 (1.44)	‡ (†)	‡ (†)	‡ (†)	4.0 (0.78)	‡ (†)	17.9 (1.33)	62.9 (1.82)
Racial/ethnic group												
White	34.1 (0.82)	41.5 (0.54)	44.4 (0.89)	47.4 (0.59)	45.6 (0.84)	0.9 (0.23)	0.2 ! (0.08)	4.9 (0.35)	29.1 (0.70)	0.9 (0.17)	22.1 (0.87)	73.0 (0.92)
Black	25.9 (2.23)	37.0 (1.45)	46.3 (2.30)	43.3 (1.50)	46.4 (2.81)	1.9 (0.49)	‡ (†)	5.4 (0.97)	27.0 (2.53)	1.5 ! (0.73)	23.7 (2.11)	65.3 (2.02)
Hispanic	31.4 (2.63)	33.7 (1.18)	41.3 (2.51)	41.7 (2.28)	37.8 (2.43)	2.6 (0.72)	5.6 (1.22)	5.7 (1.55)	16.9 (1.72)	2.2 (0.63)	15.4 (1.75)	57.5 (2.86)
Asian	— (†)	— (†)	— (†)	— (†)	48.3 (5.39)	‡ (†)	2.6 ! (1.03)	7.6 ! (2.62)	27.2 (4.70)	‡ (†)	26.5 (5.06)	81.1 (4.10)
Pacific Islander	— (†)	— (†)	— (†)	— (†)	‡ (†)	‡ (†)	‡ (†)	‡ (†)	‡ (†)	‡ (†)	‡ (†)	‡ (†)
Asian/Pacific Islander	35.9 (5.55)	39.7 (2.92)	51.1 (4.63)	49.5 (3.81)	— (†)							
American Indian/Alaska Native	29.3 ! (11.55)	38.8 (4.85)	36.3 (9.16)	50.2 (8.28)	36.3 (10.17)	‡ (†)	‡ (†)	4.4 ! (1.82)	23.0 ! (8.51)	‡ (†)	13.0 ! (6.16)	70.6 (9.18)
Two or more races	— (†)	— (†)	— (†)	—	39.4 (4.94)	5.1 ! (2.17)	‡ (†)	3.2 ! (1.07)	23.8 (4.06)	1.3 ! (0.59)	21.0 (4.13)	77.6 (5.28)
Highest level of education completed												
8th grade or less	7.7 (1.44)	10.0 (1.10)	14.7 (2.92)	19.7 (2.84)	15.5 (2.47)	1.9 (0.57)	4.3 ! (1.70)	‡ (†)	1.7 ! (0.55)	‡ (†)	7.3 (1.24)	38.1 (3.27)
9th through 12th grade, no completion	15.8 (2.25)	20.2 (1.38)	25.6 (2.55)	25.5 (1.53)	27.2 (2.40)	7.9 (1.69)	1.1 ! (0.41)	2.1 (0.57)	7.6 (1.44)	1.5 ! (0.61)	12.5 (1.53)	55.7 (2.52)
High school completion	24.1 (1.10)	30.7 (0.84)	34.8 (1.37)	33.9 (1.07)	33.0 (1.62)	0.5 ! (0.24)	0.7 ! (0.24)	2.5 (0.36)	17.2 (1.18)	1.1 ! (0.35)	16.8 (1.27)	63.6 (1.93)
Some vocational/technical	34.2 (3.80)	41.9 (2.16)	41.1 (3.97)	50.7 (3.51)	43.3 (4.30)	‡ (†)	‡ (†)	4.5 ! (1.42)	28.3 (3.71)	1.1 ! (0.47)	23.2 (3.09)	77.6 (3.98)
Some college	41.4 (1.67)	49.3 (0.92)	51.1 (1.76)	57.4 (1.29)	51.1 (1.79)	‡ (†)	1.1 ! (0.51)	8.6 (1.06)	28.8 (1.54)	1.4 ! (0.47)	26.8 (1.80)	79.8 (1.52)
Associate's degree	49.2 (5.82)	56.1 (1.85)	56.6 (2.93)	62.5 (2.15)	56.5 (3.64)	‡ (†)	‡ (†)	6.6 (1.42)	40.8 (3.27)	1.9 ! (0.66)	20.1 (2.48)	75.9 (3.70)
Bachelor's degree	51.1 (2.46)	56.9 (1.20)	60.3 (1.84)	64.5 (1.39)	59.8 (1.56)	‡ (†)	0.4 ! (0.17)	6.3 (0.82)	44.1 (1.61)	0.4 ! (0.17)	28.6 (1.55)	79.3 (1.72)
Some graduate work (or study)	55.1 (2.90)	59.9 (1.55)	63.6 (1.96)	68.9 (1.64)	66.3 (1.99)	‡ (†)	‡ (†)	8.7 (0.86)	49.3 (2.15)	‡ (†)	30.7 (1.77)	88.0 (1.06)
No degree	— (†)	62.2 (2.67)	64.7 (4.39)	64.2 (3.54)	65.3 (4.84)	‡ (†)	‡ (†)	14.5 (2.55)	40.5 (4.68)	‡ (†)	38.7 (4.81)	78.2 (4.34)
Master's	— (†)	59.1 (1.88)	65.7 (2.64)	70.7 (2.10)	67.5 (2.59)	‡ (†)	‡ (†)	8.9 (1.31)	51.4 (2.81)	‡ (†)	30.6 (2.81)	88.8 (1.33)
Doctor's	— (†)	54.0 (6.99)	53.1 (4.73)	63.7 (3.98)	58.0 (4.94)	‡ (†)	‡ (†)	10.1 ! (3.14)	34.0 (4.53)	‡ (†)	31.4 (3.95)	90.3 (3.26)
Professional	— (†)	65.9 (3.91)	72.5 (5.75)	72.8 (3.79)	68.2 (5.77)	‡ (†)	‡ (†)	‡ (†)	59.0 (6.35)	‡ (†)	23.9 (4.35)	91.6 (2.15)
Urbanicity												
City	—	—	—	—	45.8 (1.46)	1.4 (0.31)	1.6 (0.38)	5.7 (0.59)	26.3 (1.24)	1.8 (0.43)	22.5 (1.10)	69.2 (1.39)
Suburban	—	—	—	—	46.9 (1.33)	0.9 (0.23)	0.9 ! (0.36)	5.8 (0.55)	29.7 (1.26)	0.9 (0.22)	23.4 (1.16)	73.4 (1.28)
Town	—	—	—	—	41.8 (2.33)	2.7 ! (1.16)	0.4 ! (0.14)	4.2 (0.87)	25.6 (1.74)	0.5 ! (0.21)	18.5 (1.96)	70.5 (2.43)
Rural	—	—	—	—	39.5 (2.04)	0.8 (0.22)	‡ (†)	3.3 (0.59)	24.2 (1.38)	1.2 ! (0.40)	18.3 (1.76)	67.6 (1.76)
Labor force status												
In labor force	40.7 (0.96)	49.8 (0.69)	52.1 (0.94)	52.3 (0.93)	52.3 (0.93)	1.4 (0.32)	0.8 (0.19)	6.4 (0.39)	37.1 (0.83)	1.5 (0.24)	21.9 (0.91)	73.0 (0.94)
Employed	42.0 (1.00)	50.7 (0.53)	52.5 (0.96)	53.4 (0.94)	53.4 (0.94)	1.1 (0.31)	0.7 (0.20)	6.5 (0.39)	38.8 (0.83)	1.4 (0.24)	21.8 (0.94)	73.5 (1.01)
Unemployed	26.0 (3.24)	36.6 (1.91)	44.9 (4.60)	37.8 (4.26)	37.8 (4.26)	5.8 (1.60)	1.9 ! (0.79)	5.2 (1.37)	13.5 (2.16)	‡ (†)	22.1 (3.99)	66.7 (3.80)
Not in labor force	15.7 (0.91)	21.3 (0.69)	24.9 (1.17)	27.6 (1.18)	27.6 (1.18)	1.1 (0.24)	1.3 (0.36)	2.3 (0.45)	5.7 (0.55)	0.6 ! (0.22)	20.5 (0.97)	65.2 (1.27)

See notes at end of table.

Participation rate of persons, 17 years old and over, in adult education during the previous 12 months, by selected characteristics of participants: Selected years, 1991 through 2005—Continued

Characteristic of participant	Percent taking any program, class, or course					Percent taking specific programs, classes, or courses, 2005						Percent doing informal learning activities for personal interest, 2005
	1991	1995	1999	2001	2005	Basic skills/General Educational Development (GED) classes	English as a second language (ESL) classes	Part-time postsecondary education[1]	Career- or job-related courses	Apprenticeship programs	Personal-interest courses	
1	2	3	4	5	6	7	8	9	10	11	12	13
Occupation												
Executive, administrative, or managerial occupations	49.3 (3.45)	55.8 (1.92)	57.0 (2.11)	66.2 (1.61)	64.1 (2.73)	‡ (†)	‡ (†)	6.0 (1.10)	51.8 (2.82)	‡ (†)	28.8 (2.89)	78.6 (2.71)
Engineers, surveyors, and architects	62.6 (7.85)	65.5 (4.18)	79.8 (6.01)	68.1 (4.46)	71.2 (5.68)	‡ (†)	‡ (†)	9.3 ! (3.21)	55.6 (5.60)	‡ (†)	31.4 (6.19)	81.1 (4.63)
Natural scientists and mathematicians	48.2 (9.86)	72.3 (3.52)	60.5 (6.74)	74.0 (4.46)	69.1 (4.63)	‡ (†)	‡ (†)	9.2 (2.49)	49.6 (5.27)	‡ (†)	30.2 (4.53)	85.5 (5.16)
Social scientists and workers, religious workers, and lawyers	55.6 (6.01)	76.6 (2.61)	79.3 (4.35)	83.5 (3.05)	77.7 (4.11)	‡ (†)	‡ (†)	12.8 (3.16)	64.3 (4.42)	‡ (†)	29.2 (3.52)	89.4 (2.78)
Teachers: elementary/secondary	56.0 (4.20)	54.8 (4.64)	66.5 (5.61)	79.9 (2.95)	79.7 (2.59)	‡ (†)	‡ (†)	8.3 ! (3.16)	65.0 (3.99)	‡ (†)	31.7 (3.78)	83.8 (2.62)
Teachers: college, university, postsecondary institutions	45.5 (8.31)	76.7 (1.98)	78.4 (3.11)	69.4 (4.60)	61.3 (6.96)	‡ (†)	‡ (†)	‡ (†)	49.0 (8.50)	‡ (†)	19.5 (4.98)	91.7 (3.58)
Health diagnosing and treating practitioners	67.1 (13.73)	71.1 (5.78)	79.8 (9.02)	78.5 (6.38)	88.8 (5.59)	‡ (†)	‡ (†)	15.4 (2.47)	79.5 (6.59)	‡ (†)	31.9 (9.15)	84.5 (5.63)
Registered nurses, pharmacists, dieticians, therapists, and physician's assistants	59.6 (6.69)	86.7 (2.47)	85.4 (4.10)	82.7 (3.83)	85.4 (4.05)	‡ (†)	‡ (†)	7.9 (2.17)	78.2 (4.89)	‡ (†)	27.4 (3.73)	83.1 (3.92)
Writers, artists, entertainers, and athletes	42.9 (6.63)	49.9 (4.37)	50.0 (6.93)	46.8 (6.03)	52.5 (6.59)	‡ (†)	‡ (†)	5.4 ! (2.16)	27.8 (5.02)	‡ (†)	35.3 (6.42)	88.2 (3.89)
Health technologists and technicians	68.6 (10.03)	74.8 (3.64)	66.9 (6.16)	85.6 (3.25)	72.1 (8.37)	‡ (†)	‡ (†)	6.0 ! (2.11)	63.2 (8.67)	‡ (†)	24.6 (5.91)	75.6 (7.26)
Technologists and technicians, except health and engineering	53.0 (6.49)	64.3 (2.84)	59.6 (5.07)	70.2 (3.32)	33.8 (8.53)	1.7 ! (0.59)	‡ (†)	7.1 ! (3.19)	29.1 (7.68)	‡ (†)	6.2 ! (2.14)	76.0 (8.80)
Marketing and sales occupations	34.4 (2.38)	44.2 (1.34)	44.4 (2.73)	51.1 (2.10)	45.7 (3.00)	‡ (†)	‡ (†)	4.5 (0.88)	30.2 (2.77)	‡ (†)	21.5 (2.43)	68.9 (3.37)
Administrative support occupations, including clerical	29.9 (1.74)	51.7 (1.25)	50.1 (2.29)	58.7 (1.72)	54.6 (2.70)	1.1 ! (0.53)	‡ (†)	6.6 (0.98)	33.5 (2.70)	‡ (†)	27.7 (2.18)	73.8 (2.33)
Service occupations	25.2 (1.82)	46.5 (1.38)	50.9 (2.74)	49.3 (2.24)	44.7 (2.47)	1.6 (0.39)	1.9 ! (0.88)	6.8 (1.42)	28.5 (2.64)	‡ (†)	17.5 (2.10)	65.4 (2.71)
Agriculture, forestry, and fishing occupations	14.3 ! (5.19)	26.4 (3.55)	34.3 (7.16)	46.4 (6.80)	44.4 (9.02)	‡ (†)	‡ (†)	‡ (†)	20.3 (6.92)	‡ (1.38)	21.6 ! (10.05)	64.0 (10.03)
Mechanics and repairers	32.1 (4.72)	47.6 (2.70)	42.2 (5.44)	35.1 (3.40)	40.1 (5.10)	‡ (†)	‡ (†)	6.0 ! (1.89)	27.4 (4.26)	3.8 ! (1.38)	12.7 (3.18)	69.3 (4.27)
Construction and extractive occupations	21.9 (3.38)	38.0 (2.45)	34.5 (4.78)	32.3 (3.19)	27.6 (3.73)	‡ (†)	1.1 ! (0.49)	3.2 ! (1.08)	12.3 (2.54)	5.2 ! (1.89)	11.4 (2.72)	72.3 (4.48)
Precision production[2]	31.2 (6.09)	38.3 (4.32)	38.3 (8.48)	35.1 (6.19)	33.0 (3.98)	‡ (†)	0.4 ! (0.16)	4.2 ! (1.42)	22.2 (3.41)	‡ (†)	13.3 (2.99)	63.9 (3.46)
Production workers	21.1 (2.31)	30.7 (1.29)	38.0 (3.47)	39.4 (2.82)	— (†)	‡ (†)	‡ (†)	‡ (†)	— (†)	‡ (†)	— (†)	— (†)
Transportation, material moving, Handler, equipment, cleaners, helpers, and laborers	20.7 (4.69)	28.4 (2.32)	33.3 (4.25)	30.4 (3.29)	34.6 (5.27)	‡ (†)	‡ (†)	‡ (†)	14.7 (2.63)	3.2 ! (1.57)	11.2 (2.85)	60.8 (4.98)
Miscellaneous occupations	20.8 (3.49)	25.1 (2.70)	43.0 (7.98)	64.9 (7.07)	39.2 (11.25)	‡ (†)	‡ (†)	‡ (†)	15.7 (5.81)	‡ (†)	7.8 ! (3.63)	52.2 (12.32)
Annual household income												
$5,000 or less	13.6 (1.70)	21.3 (1.59)	21.0 (3.22)	25.1 (2.92)	35.9 (4.83)	‡ (†)	‡ (†)	3.6 ! (1.52)	13.7 (4.00)	‡ (†)	17.2 (3.59)	52.9 (4.97)
$5,001 to $10,000	17.5 (2.14)	23.9 (1.37)	24.5 (3.39)	28.0 (2.74)	29.6 (4.49)	2.4 ! (0.92)	1.5 ! (0.71)	1.7 ! (0.81)	8.4 (2.11)	‡ (†)	21.8 (4.75)	61.0 (3.75)
$10,001 to $15,000	22.8 (2.60)	26.7 (1.61)	22.8 (2.45)	28.6 (2.30)	25.0 (3.41)	2.4 (0.69)	0.8 ! (0.33)	3.3 ! (1.17)	11.3 (2.52)	‡ (†)	15.5 (3.14)	58.6 (4.43)
$15,001 to $20,000	21.9 (2.35)	31.8 (1.55)	31.4 (2.75)	24.3 (2.48)	24.3 (2.54)	1.0 ! (0.38)	1.9 ! (0.62)	3.3 ! (1.19)	10.1 (1.37)	2.6 ! (1.20)	12.9 (2.00)	61.1 (3.11)
$20,001 to $25,000	26.7 (3.20)	31.4 (1.27)	35.8 (2.81)	35.2 (2.27)	28.2 (2.51)	1.7 ! (0.78)	1.3 ! (0.61)	4.4 (1.26)	12.8 (2.04)	1.1 ! (0.50)	13.6 (1.88)	63.2 (3.17)
$25,001 to $30,000	32.1 (2.51)	37.9 (1.47)	36.7 (2.61)	38.3 (2.43)	38.6 (3.63)	1.9 ! (0.65)	1.0 ! (0.49)	6.8 ! (2.09)	20.2 (3.37)	‡ (0.39)	18.4 (2.52)	71.0 (3.38)
$30,001 to $40,000	35.6 (1.84)	42.7 (0.86)	45.2 (2.05)	44.6 (1.54)	42.7 (2.65)	1.6 ! (0.53)	‡ (†)	3.7 (0.68)	22.8 (2.27)	1.1 (0.39)	23.0 (2.49)	68.7 (2.36)
$40,001 to $50,000	44.8 (1.84)	46.8 (1.39)	47.9 (2.31)	49.1 (1.93)	41.4 (2.92)	0.4 ! (0.19)	‡ (†)	2.9 (0.55)	22.4 (2.00)	1.5 ! (0.56)	20.5 (2.47)	71.9 (2.62)
$50,001 to $75,000	46.6 (2.03)	52.0 (0.94)	55.1 (1.80)	55.7 (1.48)	47.7 (1.74)	‡ (†)	‡ (†)	5.8 (0.69)	33.0 (1.37)	0.9 ! (0.36)	20.5 (1.67)	70.6 (2.15)
More than $75,000	48.7 (3.15)	58.0 (1.27)	56.9 (1.66)	— (†)	— (†)	‡ (†)	‡ (†)	— (†)	— (†)	‡ (†)	— (†)	— (†)
$75,001 to $100,000	—	— (†)	— (†)	59.7 (1.91)	56.4 (2.28)	‡ (†)	‡ (†)	7.5 (0.89)	38.6 (2.26)	1.8 ! (0.64)	25.3 (1.51)	75.0 (1.97)
More than $100,000	—	— (†)	— (†)	59.3 (1.82)	58.4 (2.11)	‡ (†)	‡ (†)	6.1 (0.70)	39.4 (1.80)	‡ (†)	28.2 (1.62)	81.2 (1.68)

—Not available.
†Not applicable.
! Interpret data with caution. The coefficient of variation (CV) for this estimate is 30 percent or greater.
‡Reporting standards not met. The coefficient of variation (CV) for this estimate is 50 percent or greater.
[1] Includes college and university degree programs, post-degree certificate programs, and vocational certificate programs.
[2] For 2005, figures include "Production workers" occupations data.

NOTE: Adult education is defined as all education activities, except full-time enrollment in higher education credential programs. Data do not include persons enrolled in high school or below. Race categories exclude persons of Hispanic ethnicity. Standard errors appear in parentheses.
SOURCE: U.S. Department of Education, National Center for Education Statistics, Adult Education Survey (AE-NHES:1991, AE-NHES:1995, AE-NHES:1999, and AE-NHES:2005) and Adult Education and Lifelong Learning Survey (AELL-NHES:2001) of the National Household Education Surveys Program. (This table was prepared November 2010.)

Degrees conferred by degree-granting institutions, by level of degree and sex of student: Selected years, 1869–70 through 2020–21

Year	Associate's degrees				Bachelor's degrees				Master's degrees				Doctor's degrees[1]			
	Total	Males	Females	Percent female	Total	Males	Females	Percent female	Total	Males	Females	Percent female	Total	Males	Females	Percent female
1	2	3	4	5	6	7	8	9	10	11	12	13	14	15	16	17
1869–70	—	—	—	—	9,371[2]	7,993[2]	1,378[2]	14.7	0	0	0	—	1	1	0	0.0
1879–80	—	—	—	—	12,896[2]	10,411[2]	2,485[2]	19.3	879	868	11	1.3	54	51	3	5.6
1889–90	—	—	—	—	15,539[2]	12,857[2]	2,682[2]	17.3	1,015	821	194	19.1	149	147	2	1.3
1899–1900	—	—	—	—	27,410[2]	22,173[2]	5,237[2]	19.1	1,583	1,280	303	19.1	382	359	23	6.0
1909–10	—	—	—	—	37,199[2]	28,762[2]	8,437[2]	22.7	2,113	1,555	558	26.4	443	399	44	9.9
1919–20	—	—	—	—	48,622[2]	31,980[2]	16,642[2]	34.2	4,279	2,985	1,294	30.2	615	522	93	15.1
1929–30	—	—	—	—	122,484[2]	73,615[2]	48,869[2]	39.9	14,969	8,925	6,044	40.4	2,299	1,946	353	15.4
1939–40	—	—	—	—	186,500[2]	109,546[2]	76,954[2]	41.3	26,731	16,508	10,223	38.2	3,290	2,861	429	13.0
1949–50	—	—	—	—	432,058[2]	328,841[2]	103,217[2]	23.9	58,183	41,220	16,963	29.2	6,420	5,804	616	9.6
1959–60	—	—	—	—	392,440[2]	254,063[2]	138,377[2]	35.3	74,435	50,898	23,537	31.6	9,829	8,801	1,028	10.5
1969–70	206,023	117,432	88,591	43.0	792,316	451,097	341,219	43.1	213,589	130,799	82,790	38.8	59,486	53,792	5,694	9.6
1970–71	252,311	144,144	108,167	42.9	839,730	475,594	364,136	43.4	235,564	143,083	92,481	39.3	64,998	58,137	6,861	10.6
1971–72	292,014	166,227	125,787	43.1	887,273	500,590	386,683	43.6	257,201	155,010	102,191	39.7	71,206	63,353	7,853	11.0
1972–73	316,174	175,413	140,761	44.5	922,362	518,191	404,171	43.8	268,654	159,569	109,085	40.6	79,512	69,959	9,553	12.0
1973–74	343,924	188,591	155,333	45.2	945,776	527,313	418,463	44.2	282,074	162,606	119,468	42.4	82,591	71,131	11,460	13.9
1974–75	360,171	191,017	169,154	47.0	922,933	504,841	418,092	45.3	297,545	166,318	131,227	44.1	84,904	71,025	13,879	16.3
1975–76	391,454	209,996	181,458	46.4	925,746	504,925	420,821	45.5	317,477	172,519	144,958	45.7	91,007	73,888	17,119	18.8
1976–77	406,377	210,842	195,535	48.1	919,549	495,545	424,004	46.1	323,025	173,090	149,935	46.4	91,730	72,209	19,521	21.3
1977–78	412,246	204,718	207,528	50.3	921,204	487,347	433,857	47.1	317,987	166,857	151,130	47.5	92,345	70,283	22,062	23.9
1978–79	402,702	192,091	210,611	52.3	921,390	477,344	444,046	48.2	307,686	159,111	148,575	48.3	94,971	70,452	24,519	25.8
1979–80	400,910	183,737	217,173	54.2	929,417	473,611	455,806	49.0	305,196	156,882	148,314	48.6	95,631	69,526	26,105	27.3
1980–81	416,377	188,638	227,739	54.7	935,140	469,883	465,257	49.8	302,637	152,979	149,658	49.5	98,016	69,567	28,449	29.0
1981–82	434,526	196,944	237,582	54.7	952,998	473,364	479,634	50.3	302,447	151,349	151,098	50.0	97,838	68,630	29,208	29.9
1982–83	449,620	203,991	245,629	54.6	969,510	479,140	490,370	50.6	296,415	150,092	146,323	49.4	99,335	67,757	31,578	31.8
1983–84	452,240	202,704	249,536	55.2	974,309	482,319	491,990	50.5	291,141	149,268	141,873	48.7	100,799	67,769	33,030	32.8
1984–85	454,712	202,932	251,780	55.4	979,477	482,528	496,949	50.7	293,472	149,276	144,196	49.1	100,785	66,269	34,516	34.2
1985–86	446,047	196,166	249,881	56.0	987,823	485,923	501,900	50.8	295,850	149,373	146,477	49.5	100,280	65,215	35,065	35.0
1986–87	436,304	190,839	245,465	56.3	991,264	480,782	510,482	51.5	296,530	147,063	149,467	50.4	98,477	62,790	35,687	36.2
1987–88	435,085	190,047	245,038	56.3	994,829	477,203	517,626	52.0	305,783	150,243	155,540	50.9	99,139	63,019	36,120	36.4
1988–89	436,764	186,316	250,448	57.3	1,018,755	483,346	535,409	52.6	316,626	153,993	162,633	51.4	100,571	63,055	37,516	37.3
1989–90	455,102	191,195	263,907	58.0	1,051,344	491,696	559,648	53.2	330,152	158,052	172,100	52.1	103,508	63,963	39,545	38.2
1990–91	481,720	198,634	283,086	58.8	1,094,538	504,045	590,493	53.9	342,863	160,842	182,021	53.1	105,547	64,242	41,305	39.1
1991–92	504,231	207,481	296,750	58.9	1,136,553	520,811	615,742	54.2	358,089	165,867	192,222	53.7	109,554	66,603	42,951	39.2
1992–93	514,756	211,964	302,792	58.8	1,165,178	532,881	632,297	54.3	375,032	173,354	201,678	53.8	112,072	67,130	44,942	40.1
1993–94	530,632	215,261	315,371	59.4	1,169,275	532,422	636,853	54.5	393,037	180,571	212,466	54.1	112,636	66,773	45,863	40.7
1994–95	539,691	218,352	321,339	59.5	1,160,134	526,131	634,003	54.6	403,609	183,043	220,566	54.6	114,266	67,324	46,942	41.1
1995–96	555,216	219,514	335,702	60.5	1,164,792	522,454	642,338	55.1	412,180	183,481	228,699	55.5	115,507	67,189	48,318	41.8
1996–97	571,226	223,948	347,278	60.8	1,172,879	520,515	652,364	55.6	425,260	185,270	239,990	56.4	118,747	68,387	50,360	42.4
1997–98	558,555	217,613	340,942	61.0	1,184,406	519,956	664,450	56.1	436,037	188,718	247,319	56.7	118,735	67,232	51,503	43.4
1998–99[3]	564,984	220,508	344,476	61.0	1,202,239	519,961	682,278	56.8	446,038	190,230	255,808	57.4	116,700	65,340	51,360	44.0
1999–2000	564,933	224,721	340,212	60.2	1,237,875	530,367	707,508	57.2	463,185	196,129	267,056	57.7	118,736	64,930	53,806	45.3
2000–01	578,865	231,645	347,220	60.0	1,244,171	531,840	712,331	57.3	473,502	197,770	275,732	58.2	119,585	64,171	55,414	46.3
2001–02	595,133	238,109	357,024	60.0	1,291,900	549,816	742,084	57.4	487,313	202,604	284,709	58.4	119,663	62,731	56,932	47.6
2002–03	634,016	253,451	380,565	60.0	1,348,811	573,258	775,553	57.5	518,699	215,172	303,527	58.5	121,579	62,730	58,849	48.4
2003–04	665,301	260,033	405,268	60.9	1,399,542	595,425	804,117	57.5	564,272	233,056	331,216	58.7	126,087	63,981	62,106	49.3
2004–05	696,660	267,536	429,124	61.6	1,439,264	613,000	826,264	57.4	580,151	237,155	342,996	59.1	134,387	67,257	67,130	50.0
2005–06	713,066	270,095	442,971	62.1	1,485,242	630,600	854,642	57.5	599,731	241,656	358,075	59.7	138,056	68,912	69,144	50.1
2006–07	728,114	275,187	452,927	62.2	1,524,092	649,570	874,522	57.4	610,597	242,189	368,408	60.3	144,690	71,308	73,382	50.7
2007–08	750,164	282,521	467,643	62.3	1,563,069	667,928	895,141	57.3	630,666	250,169	380,497	60.3	149,378	73,453	75,925	50.8
2008–09	787,325	298,141	489,184	62.1	1,601,368	685,382	915,986	57.2	662,079	263,538	398,541	60.2	154,425	75,639	78,786	51.0
2009–10	849,452	322,916	526,536	62.0	1,650,014	706,633	943,381	57.2	693,025	275,197	417,828	60.3	158,558	76,605	81,953	51.7
2010–11[4]	863,000	324,000	539,000	62.5	1,715,000	735,000	980,000	57.1	718,000	295,000	423,000	58.9	168,200	81,600	86,600	51.5
2011–12[4]	895,000	337,000	558,000	62.3	1,725,000	749,000	976,000	56.6	735,000	303,000	432,000	58.8	174,700	84,600	90,100	51.6
2012–13[4]	899,000	338,000	561,000	62.4	1,744,000	755,000	989,000	56.7	747,000	306,000	441,000	59.0	178,700	86,600	92,100	51.5
2013–14[4]	906,000	341,000	565,000	62.4	1,762,000	759,000	1,003,000	56.9	762,000	310,000	452,000	59.3	183,100	88,300	94,800	51.8
2014–15[4]	915,000	343,000	571,000	62.4	1,786,000	765,000	1,021,000	57.2	781,000	316,000	465,000	59.5	188,000	90,100	97,900	52.1
2015–16[4]	927,000	347,000	580,000	62.6	1,812,000	773,000	1,039,000	57.3	801,000	323,000	478,000	59.7	193,600	92,100	101,500	52.4
2016–17[4]	940,000	350,000	590,000	62.8	1,844,000	784,000	1,060,000	57.5	819,000	329,000	490,000	59.8	199,600	94,300	105,300	52.8
2017–18[4]	953,000	354,000	599,000	62.9	1,871,000	792,000	1,079,000	57.7	835,000	334,000	501,000	60.0	205,300	96,400	108,900	53.0
2018–19[4]	967,000	358,000	609,000	63.0	1,899,000	800,000	1,099,000	57.9	851,000	339,000	512,000	60.2	210,500	98,200	112,300	53.3
2019–20[4]	981,000	362,000	619,000	63.1	1,926,000	809,000	1,117,000	58.0	862,000	341,000	521,000	60.4	215,400	100,000	115,400	53.6
2020–21[4]	994,000	366,000	628,000	63.2	1,926,000	809,000	1,117,000	58.0	871,000	342,000	529,000	60.7	219,900	101,600	118,300	53.8

—Not available.

[1]Includes Ph.D., Ed.D., and comparable degrees at the doctoral level. Includes most degrees formerly classified as first-professional, such as M.D., D.D.S., and law degrees.

[2]Includes some degrees classified as master's or doctor's degrees in later years.

[3]Revised from previously published figures.

[4]Projected.

NOTE: Data through 1994–95 are for institutions of higher education, while later data are for degree-granting institutions. Degree-granting institutions grant associate's or higher degrees and participate in Title IV federal financial aid programs. The degree-granting classification is very similar to the earlier higher education classification, but it includes more 2-year colleges and excludes a few higher education institutions that did not grant degrees. (See Appendix A: Guide to Sources for details.) Some data have been revised from previously published figures. Detail may not sum to totals because of rounding.

SOURCE: U.S. Department of Education, National Center for Education Statistics, *Earned Degrees Conferred*, 1869–70 through 1964–65; *Projections of Education Statistics to 2020*; Higher Education General Information Survey (HEGIS), "Degrees and Other Formal Awards Conferred" surveys, 1965–66 through 1985–86; Integrated Postsecondary Education Data System (IPEDS), "Completions Survey" (IPEDS-C:87–99); and IPEDS Fall 2000 through Fall 2010, Completions component. (This table was prepared May 2011.)

Degrees conferred by degree-granting institutions, by control of institution, level of degree, and field of study: 2009–10

Field of study	All institutions				Public institutions				Private not-for-profit institutions				Private for-profit institutions			
	Associate's degrees	Bachelor's degrees	Master's degrees	Doctor's degrees[1]	Associate's degrees	Bachelor's degrees	Master's degrees	Doctor's degrees[1]	Associate's degrees	Bachelor's degrees	Master's degrees	Doctor's degrees[1]	Associate's degrees	Bachelor's degrees	Master's degrees	Doctor's degrees[1]
1	2	3	4	5	6	7	8	9	10	11	12	13	14	15	16	17
All fields, total	849,452	1,650,014	693,025	158,558	640,113	1,049,057	322,243	78,779	46,673	503,164	299,911	75,166	162,666	97,793	70,871	4,613
Agriculture and natural resources	5,894	26,336	5,211	1,147	5,667	22,499	4,237	1,062	224	3,711	956	85	3	126	18	0
Architecture and related services	552	10,051	7,280	210	548	7,144	4,320	151	4	2,856	2,875	59	0	51	85	0
Area, ethnic, cultural, gender, and group studies	199	8,621	1,775	253	169	5,561	1,045	147	30	3,027	730	106	0	33	0	0
Biological and biomedical sciences	2,664	86,400	10,725	7,666	2,573	58,836	6,527	5,150	45	27,483	4,198	2,498	46	81	0	18
Business	133,371	358,293	177,684	2,245	73,779	196,954	62,289	852	11,931	115,877	81,980	588	47,661	45,462	33,415	805
Communications, journalism, and related programs	2,839	81,266	7,636	570	2,505	56,944	3,736	476	108	23,496	3,896	94	226	826	4	0
Communications technologies	4,419	4,782	463	3	2,714	1,188	80	0	204	1,316	268	3	1,501	2,278	115	0
Computer and information sciences	32,466	39,589	17,953	1,599	14,787	18,555	8,803	1,086	1,267	9,977	7,667	485	16,412	11,057	1,483	28
Construction trades	4,617	273			3,848	271			211				558	2		
Education	17,048	101,265	182,139	9,233	14,361	71,874	86,238	5,042	631	28,595	77,720	3,032	2,056	796	18,181	1,159
Engineering	2,508	72,654	35,088	7,704	2,339	55,400	23,002	5,628	55	16,919	11,550	2,076	114	335	536	0
Engineering technologies and engineering-related fields[2]	31,850	15,596	4,258	67	21,049	12,537	2,315	24	1,397	1,721	1,760	43	9,404	1,338	183	0
English language and literature/letters	1,658	53,231	9,201	1,332	1,227	37,072	6,069	998	11	16,080	3,118	334	420	79	14	0
Family and consumer sciences	9,573	21,818	2,580	296	7,880	18,283	1,691	246	316	3,457	738	48	1,377	78	151	2
Foreign languages, literatures, and linguistics	1,683	21,516	3,755	1,091	1,340	14,840	2,695	716	343	6,672	1,060	375	0	4	0	0
Health professions and related programs	177,686	129,634	69,084	57,746	117,204	77,444	32,080	29,379	14,550	42,545	28,376	27,790	45,932	9,645	8,628	577
Homeland security, law enforcement, and firefighting	37,260	43,667	6,714	106	23,306	26,166	2,844	95	729	9,752	1,917	3	13,225	7,749	1,953	11
Legal professions and studies	10,003	3,886	5,734	44,626	5,107	1,950	1,530	15,137	438	1,150	4,185	28,354	4,458	786	19	1,135
Liberal arts and sciences, general studies, and humanities	284,775	46,953	3,804	96	272,804	31,961	1,427	44	9,437	14,859	2,341	22	2,534	133	36	30
Library science	112	85	7,448	64	112	85	6,086	63	0	0	1,362	1	0	0	0	0
Mathematics and statistics	1,051	16,030	5,634	1,592	1,044	10,556	3,898	1,180	6	5,472	1,736	412	1	2	1	0
Mechanic and repair technologies	16,305	206			10,221	158		0	1,622	47		0	4,462	1	0	0
Military technologies and applied sciences	668	56	0	0	668	41	0	0	0	0	0	0	0	15	0	0
Multi/interdisciplinary studies	17,671	37,648	5,973	631	16,804	28,408	3,452	397	148	8,925	2,141	234	719	315	380	0
Parks, recreation, leisure and fitness studies	2,016	33,318	5,617	266	1,389	24,935	4,247	243	163	8,243	1,275	23	464	140	95	0
Philosophy and religious studies	256	12,504	2,043	667	124	5,771	699	248	132	6,709	1,343	419	0	24	1	0
Physical sciences and science technologies	4,140	23,379	6,063	5,063	4,056	16,080	4,434	3,588	77	7,295	1,629	1,475	7	4	0	0
Precision production	2,787	29	10	0	2,494	11	0	0	89	18	10	0	204	0	0	0
Psychology	6,582	97,216	23,752	5,540	2,807	64,570	7,993	2,344	151	29,071	12,810	2,439	3,624	3,575	2,949	757
Public administration and social service professions	4,526	25,414	35,729	838	4,141	15,758	21,983	507	286	7,359	12,687	248	99	2,297	1,059	83
Social sciences and history	10,649	172,780	20,222	4,238	10,546	116,370	10,944	2,844	95	54,452	8,441	1,394	8	1,958	837	0
Social sciences	10,108	137,582	16,368	3,350	10,025	92,678	8,295	2,262	78	43,084	7,476	1,088	5	1,820	597	0
History	541	35,198	3,854	888	521	23,692	2,649	582	17	11,368	965	306	3	138	240	0
Theology and religious vocations	613	8,718	12,824	2,070	0	0	0	0	605	8,587	12,775	2,062	8	130	49	8
Transportation and materials moving	1,444	4,998	1,074	0	999	2,081	82	0	395	2,811	936	0	50	106	56	0
Visual and performing arts	19,567	91,802	15,552	1,599	11,501	48,753	7,497	1,132	973	34,680	7,431	467	7,093	8,369	624	0

[1]Includes Ph.D., Ed.D., and comparable degrees at the doctoral level, as well as such degrees as M.D., D.D.S., and law degrees that were formerly classified as first-professional degrees.

[2]Excludes "Construction trades" and "Mechanic and repair technologies," which are listed separately.

NOTE: Degree-granting institutions grant associate's or higher degrees and participate in Title IV federal financial aid programs. To facilitate trend comparisons, certain aggregations have been made of the degree fields as reported in the IPEDS Fall survey: "Agriculture and natural resources" includes Agriculture, agriculture operations, and related sciences and Natural resources and conservation; and "Business" includes Business management, marketing, and related support services and Personal and culinary services.

SOURCE: U.S. Department of Education, National Center for Education Statistics, Integrated Postsecondary Education Data System (IPEDS), Fall 2010, Completions component. (This table was prepared May 2011.)

Degrees conferred by degree-granting institutions in selected professional fields, by sex of student, control of institution, and field of study: Selected years, 1985–86 through 2009–10

Control of institution and field of study	1985-86	1990-91	1995-96	2000-01	2001-02	2002-03	2003-04	2004-05	2005-06	2006-07	2007-08			2008-09			2009-10		
											Total	Males	Females	Total	Males	Females	Total	Males	Females
1	2	3	4	5	6	7	8	9	10	11	12	13	14	15	16	17	18	19	20
Total, all institutions	73,910	71,948	76,734	79,707	80,698	80,897	83,041	87,289	87,655	90,064	91,309	45,916	45,393	92,004	46,900	45,104	94,103	47,538	46,565
Dentistry (D.D.S. or D.M.D.)	5,046	3,699	3,697	4,391	4,239	4,345	4,335	4,454	4,389	4,596	4,795	2,661	2,134	4,918	2,637	2,281	5,062	2,745	2,317
Medicine (M.D.)	15,938	15,043	15,341	15,403	15,237	15,034	15,442	15,461	15,455	15,730	15,646	7,935	7,711	15,987	8,164	7,823	16,356	8,468	7,888
Optometry (O.D.)	1,029	1,115	1,231	1,289	1,280	1,281	1,275	1,252	1,198	1,311	1,304	445	859	1,338	466	872	1,335	457	878
Osteopathic medicine (D.O.)	1,547	1,459	1,895	2,450	2,416	2,596	2,722	2,762	2,718	2,992	3,232	1,581	1,651	3,665	1,798	1,867	3,890	1,979	1,911
Pharmacy (Pharm.D.)	903	1,244	2,555	6,324	7,076	7,474	8,221	8,885	9,292	10,439	10,932	3,716	7,216	11,291	4,011	7,280	11,873	4,297	7,576
Podiatry (Pod.D. or D.P.) or podiatric medicine (D.P.M.)	612	589	650	528	474	439	382	343	347	331	555	305	250	431	250	181	491	276	215
Veterinary medicine (D.V.M.)	2,270	2,032	2,109	2,248	2,289	2,354	2,228	2,354	2,370	2,443	2,504	580	1,924	2,377	526	1,851	2,478	555	1,923
Chiropractic (D.C. or D.C.M.)	3,395	2,640	3,379	3,796	3,284	2,718	2,730	2,560	2,564	2,525	2,639	1,683	956	2,512	1,584	928	2,601	1,610	991
Law (LL.B. or J.D.)	35,844	37,945	39,828	37,904	38,981	39,067	40,209	43,423	43,440	43,486	43,769	23,197	20,572	44,045	23,860	20,185	44,345	23,394	20,951
Theology (M. Div, M.H.L., B.D., or Ord. and M.H.L./Rav.)	7,283	5,695	5,879	5,026	5,195	5,360	5,332	5,533	5,666	5,990	5,751	3,777	1,974	5,362	3,586	1,776	5,672	3,757	1,915
Other[1]	43	487	170	348	227	229	165	262	216	221	182	36	146	78	18	60	0	0	0
Total, public institutions	29,568	29,554	29,882	32,633	33,439	33,549	34,499	35,768	36,269	36,855	37,278	17,912	19,366	37,357	18,046	19,311	38,132	18,432	19,700
Dentistry (D.D.S. or D.M.D.)	2,827	2,308	2,198	2,477	2,525	2,493	2,498	2,577	2,669	2,769	2,760	1,577	1,183	2,870	1,551	1,319	2,984	1,694	1,290
Medicine (M.D.)	9,991	9,364	9,370	9,408	9,390	9,276	9,418	9,536	9,650	9,733	9,646	4,976	4,670	9,795	5,042	4,753	10,043	5,208	4,835
Optometry (O.D.)	441	477	499	497	503	481	476	477	462	518	492	147	345	517	176	341	507	158	349
Osteopathic medicine (D.O.)	486	493	528	562	538	571	586	568	585	637	634	306	328	679	320	359	817	384	433
Pharmacy (Pharm.D.)	473	808	1,557	3,876	4,382	4,558	4,930	5,352	5,523	5,903	6,218	2,129	4,089	6,395	2,301	4,094	6,587	2,416	4,171
Podiatry (Pod.D. or D.P.) or podiatric medicine (D.P.M.)	0	0	0	84	75	81	64	64	65	66	73	36	37	68	35	33	85	45	40
Veterinary medicine (D.V.M.)	1,931	1,814	1,889	2,017	2,052	2,023	1,912	2,033	2,048	2,116	2,123	507	1,616	1,968	443	1,525	2,048	465	1,583
Chiropractic (D.C. or D.C.M.)	0	0	0	0	0	0	0	0	0	0	0	0	0	0	0	0	0	0	0
Law (LL.B. or J.D.)	13,419	14,290	13,841	13,712	13,974	14,066	14,615	15,161	15,267	15,113	15,332	8,234	7,098	15,065	8,178	6,887	15,061	8,062	6,999
Theology (M. Div, M.H.L., B.D., or Ord. and M.H.L./Rav.)	0	0	0	0	0	0	0	0	0	0	0	0	0	0	0	0	0	0	0
Other[1]	0	0	0	0	0	0	0	0	0	0	0	0	0	0	0	0	0	0	0
Total, private institutions	44,342	42,394	46,852	47,074	47,259	47,348	48,542	51,521	51,386	53,209	54,031	28,004	26,027	54,647	28,854	25,793	55,971	29,106	26,865
Dentistry (D.D.S. or D.M.D.)	2,219	1,391	1,499	1,914	1,714	1,852	1,837	1,877	1,720	1,827	2,035	1,084	951	2,048	1,086	962	2,078	1,051	1,027
Medicine (M.D.)	5,947	5,679	5,971	5,995	5,847	5,758	6,024	5,925	5,805	5,997	6,000	2,959	3,041	6,192	3,122	3,070	6,313	3,260	3,053
Optometry (O.D.)	588	638	732	792	777	800	799	775	736	793	812	298	514	821	290	531	828	299	529
Osteopathic medicine (D.O.)	1,061	966	1,367	1,888	1,878	2,025	2,136	2,194	2,133	2,355	2,598	1,275	1,323	2,986	1,478	1,508	3,073	1,595	1,478
Pharmacy (Pharm.D.)	430	436	998	2,448	2,694	2,916	3,291	3,533	3,769	4,536	4,714	1,587	3,127	4,896	1,710	3,186	5,286	1,881	3,405
Podiatry (Pod.D. or D.P.) or podiatric medicine (D.P.M.)	612	589	650	444	399	358	318	279	282	265	482	269	213	363	215	148	406	231	175
Veterinary medicine (D.V.M.)	339	218	220	231	237	331	316	321	322	327	381	73	308	409	83	326	430	90	340
Chiropractic (D.C. or D.C.M.)	3,395	2,640	3,379	3,796	3,284	2,718	2,730	2,560	2,564	2,525	2,639	1,683	956	2,512	1,584	928	2,601	1,610	991
Law (LL.B. or J.D.)	22,425	23,655	25,987	24,192	25,007	25,001	25,594	28,262	28,173	28,373	28,437	14,963	13,474	28,980	15,682	13,298	29,284	15,332	13,952
Theology (M. Div, M.H.L., B.D., or Ord. and M.H.L./Rav.)	7,283	5,695	5,879	5,026	5,195	5,360	5,332	5,533	5,666	5,990	5,751	3,777	1,974	5,362	3,586	1,776	5,672	3,757	1,915
Other[1]	43	487	170	348	227	229	165	262	216	221	182	36	146	78	18	60	0	0	0

[1]Includes naturopathic medicine and degrees that were not classified by field by the reporting institution.

NOTE: degree-granting institutions grant associate's or higher degrees and participate in Title IV federal financial aid programs. Includes degrees that require at least 6 years of college work for completion (including at least 2 years of preprofessional training).

SOURCE: U.S. Department of Education, National Center for Education Statistics, Higher Education General Information Survey (HEGIS), "Degrees and Other Formal Awards Conferred," 1985–86; Integrated Postsecondary Education Data System (IPEDS), "Completions Survey" (IPEDS-C:91–99); and IPEDS Fall 2000 through Fall 2010, Completions component. (This table was prepared May 2011.)

Associate's degrees conferred by degree-granting institutions, by race/ethnicity and sex of student: Selected years, 1976–77 through 2009–10

Year and sex	Number of degrees conferred							Percentage distribution of degrees conferred						
	Total	White	Black	Hispanic	Asian/ Pacific Islander	American Indian/ Alaska Native	Non-resident alien	Total	White	Black	Hispanic	Asian/ Pacific Islander	American Indian/ Alaska Native	Non-resident alien
1	2	3	4	5	6	7	8	9	10	11	12	13	14	15
Total														
1976–77[1]	404,956	342,290	33,159	16,636	7,044	2,498	3,329	100.0	84.5	8.2	4.1	1.7	0.6	0.8
1980–81[2]	410,174	339,167	35,330	17,800	8,650	2,584	6,643	100.0	82.7	8.6	4.3	2.1	0.6	1.6
1989–90	455,102	376,816	34,326	21,504	13,066	3,430	5,960	100.0	82.8	7.5	4.7	2.9	0.8	1.3
1990–91	481,720	391,264	38,835	25,540	15,257	3,871	6,953	100.0	81.2	8.1	5.3	3.2	0.8	1.4
1994–95	539,691	420,656	47,067	35,962	20,677	5,482	9,847	100.0	77.9	8.7	6.7	3.8	1.0	1.8
1995–96	555,216	426,106	52,014	38,254	23,138	5,573	10,131	100.0	76.7	9.4	6.9	4.2	1.0	1.8
1996–97	571,226	429,464	56,306	43,549	25,159	5,984	10,764	100.0	75.2	9.9	7.6	4.4	1.0	1.9
1997–98	558,555	413,561	55,314	45,876	25,196	6,246	12,362	100.0	74.0	9.9	8.2	4.5	1.1	2.2
1998–99[3]	564,984	412,985	58,417	48,845	27,628	6,395	10,714	100.0	73.1	10.3	8.6	4.9	1.1	1.9
1999–2000[3]	564,933	408,822	60,208	51,563	27,778	6,474	10,088	100.0	72.4	10.7	9.1	4.9	1.1	1.8
2000–01	578,865	411,075	63,855	57,288	28,463	6,623	11,561	100.0	71.0	11.0	9.9	4.9	1.1	2.0
2001–02	595,133	417,733	67,343	60,003	30,945	6,832	12,277	100.0	70.2	11.3	10.1	5.2	1.1	2.1
2002–03	634,016	438,261	75,609	66,673	32,629	7,461	13,383	100.0	69.1	11.9	10.5	5.1	1.2	2.1
2003–04	665,301	456,047	81,183	72,270	33,149	8,119	14,533	100.0	68.5	12.2	10.9	5.0	1.2	2.2
2004–05	696,660	475,513	86,402	78,557	33,669	8,435	14,084	100.0	68.3	12.4	11.3	4.8	1.2	2.0
2005–06	713,066	485,297	89,784	80,854	35,201	8,552	13,378	100.0	68.1	12.6	11.3	4.9	1.2	1.9
2006–07	728,114	491,572	91,529	85,410	37,266	8,583	13,754	100.0	67.5	12.6	11.7	5.1	1.2	1.9
2007–08	750,164	501,079	95,702	91,274	38,843	8,849	14,417	100.0	66.8	12.8	12.2	5.2	1.2	1.9
2008–09	787,325	522,985	101,487	97,921	40,914	8,834	15,184	100.0	66.4	12.9	12.4	5.2	1.1	1.9
2009–10	849,452	552,863	113,905	112,211	44,021	10,337	16,115	100.0	65.1	13.4	13.2	5.2	1.2	1.9
Males														
1976–77[1]	209,672	178,236	15,330	9,105	3,630	1,216	2,155	100.0	85.0	7.3	4.3	1.7	0.6	1.0
1980–81[2]	183,819	151,242	14,290	8,327	4,557	1,108	4,295	100.0	82.3	7.8	4.5	2.5	0.6	2.3
1989–90	191,195	158,954	12,502	9,370	6,170	1,364	2,835	100.0	83.1	6.5	4.9	3.2	0.7	1.5
1990–91	198,634	161,858	14,143	10,738	7,164	1,439	3,292	100.0	81.5	7.1	5.4	3.6	0.7	1.7
1994–95	218,352	170,251	16,727	15,670	9,252	2,098	4,354	100.0	78.0	7.7	7.2	4.2	1.0	2.0
1995–96	219,514	169,230	17,941	15,740	10,229	1,993	4,381	100.0	77.1	8.2	7.2	4.7	0.9	2.0
1996–97	223,948	168,882	19,394	17,990	10,937	2,068	4,677	100.0	75.4	8.7	8.0	4.9	0.9	2.1
1997–98	217,613	161,212	18,686	19,108	10,953	2,252	5,402	100.0	74.1	8.6	8.8	5.0	1.0	2.5
1998–99[3]	220,508	162,339	19,844	19,484	11,688	2,234	4,919	100.0	73.6	9.0	8.8	5.3	1.0	2.2
1999–2000[3]	224,721	164,317	20,968	20,947	12,009	2,222	4,258	100.0	73.1	9.3	9.3	5.3	1.0	1.9
2000–01	231,645	166,322	22,147	23,350	12,339	2,294	5,193	100.0	71.8	9.6	10.1	5.3	1.0	2.2
2001–02	238,109	170,622	22,806	23,963	13,256	2,308	5,154	100.0	71.7	9.6	10.1	5.6	1.0	2.2
2002–03	253,451	179,163	25,591	26,461	14,057	2,618	5,561	100.0	70.7	10.1	10.4	5.5	1.0	2.2
2003–04	260,033	183,819	25,961	27,828	13,907	2,740	5,778	100.0	70.7	10.0	10.7	5.3	1.1	2.2
2004–05	267,536	188,569	27,151	29,658	13,802	2,774	5,582	100.0	70.5	10.1	11.1	5.2	1.0	2.1
2005–06	270,095	190,139	27,619	30,040	14,224	2,774	5,299	100.0	70.4	10.2	11.1	5.3	1.0	2.0
2006–07	275,187	191,565	28,273	31,646	15,510	2,873	5,320	100.0	69.6	10.3	11.5	5.6	1.0	1.9
2007–08	282,521	194,099	30,016	33,817	15,936	3,003	5,650	100.0	68.7	10.6	12.0	5.6	1.1	2.0
2008–09	298,141	203,086	31,994	36,739	17,156	3,074	6,092	100.0	68.1	10.7	12.3	5.8	1.0	2.0
2009–10	322,916	216,072	36,136	42,232	18,264	3,624	6,588	100.0	66.9	11.2	13.1	5.7	1.1	2.0
Females														
1976–77[1]	195,284	164,054	17,829	7,531	3,414	1,282	1,174	100.0	84.0	9.1	3.9	1.7	0.7	0.6
1980–81[2]	226,355	187,925	21,040	9,473	4,093	1,476	2,348	100.0	83.0	9.3	4.2	1.8	0.7	1.0
1989–90	263,907	217,862	21,824	12,134	6,896	2,066	3,125	100.0	82.6	8.3	4.6	2.6	0.8	1.2
1990–91	283,086	229,406	24,692	14,802	8,093	2,432	3,661	100.0	81.0	8.7	5.2	2.9	0.9	1.3
1994–95	321,339	250,405	30,340	20,292	11,425	3,384	5,493	100.0	77.9	9.4	6.3	3.6	1.1	1.7
1995–96	335,702	256,876	34,073	22,514	12,909	3,580	5,750	100.0	76.5	10.1	6.7	3.8	1.1	1.7
1996–97	347,278	260,582	36,912	25,559	14,222	3,916	6,087	100.0	75.0	10.6	7.4	4.1	1.1	1.8
1997–98	340,942	252,349	36,628	26,768	14,243	3,994	6,960	100.0	74.0	10.7	7.9	4.2	1.2	2.0
1998–99[3]	344,476	250,646	38,573	29,361	15,940	4,161	5,795	100.0	72.8	11.2	8.5	4.6	1.2	1.7
1999–2000[3]	340,212	244,505	39,240	30,616	15,769	4,252	5,830	100.0	71.9	11.5	9.0	4.6	1.2	1.7
2000–01	347,220	244,753	41,708	33,938	16,124	4,329	6,368	100.0	70.5	12.0	9.8	4.6	1.2	1.8
2001–02	357,024	247,111	44,537	36,040	17,689	4,524	7,123	100.0	69.2	12.5	10.1	5.0	1.3	2.0
2002–03	380,565	259,098	50,018	40,212	18,572	4,843	7,822	100.0	68.1	13.1	10.6	4.9	1.3	2.1
2003–04	405,268	272,228	55,222	44,442	19,242	5,379	8,755	100.0	67.2	13.6	11.0	4.7	1.3	2.2
2004–05	429,124	286,944	59,251	48,899	19,867	5,661	8,502	100.0	66.9	13.8	11.4	4.6	1.3	2.0
2005–06	442,971	295,158	62,165	50,814	20,977	5,778	8,079	100.0	66.6	14.0	11.5	4.7	1.3	1.8
2006–07	452,927	300,007	63,256	53,764	21,756	5,710	8,434	100.0	66.2	14.0	11.9	4.8	1.3	1.9
2007–08	467,643	306,980	65,686	57,457	22,907	5,846	8,767	100.0	65.6	14.0	12.3	4.9	1.3	1.9
2008–09	489,184	319,899	69,493	61,182	23,758	5,760	9,092	100.0	65.4	14.2	12.5	4.9	1.2	1.9
2009–10	526,536	336,791	77,769	69,979	25,757	6,713	9,527	100.0	64.0	14.8	13.3	4.9	1.3	1.8

[1]Excludes 1,170 males and 251 females whose racial/ethnic group was not available.
[2]Excludes 4,819 males and 1,384 females whose racial/ethnic group was not available.
[3]Revised from previously published figures.
NOTE: Degree-granting institutions grant associate's or higher degrees and participate in Title IV federal financial aid programs. Race categories exclude persons of Hispanic ethnicity. For 1989–90 and later years, reported racial/ethnic distributions of students by level of degree, field of degree, and sex were used to estimate race/ethnicity for students whose race/ethnicity was not reported. Detail may not sum to totals because of rounding.
SOURCE: U.S. Department of Education, National Center for Education Statistics, Higher Education General Information Survey (HEGIS), "Degrees and Other Formal Awards Conferred" surveys, 1976–77 and 1980–81; Integrated Postsecondary Education Data System (IPEDS), "Completions Survey" (IPEDS-C:90–99); and IPEDS Fall 2000 through Fall 2010, Completions component. (This table was prepared November 2011.)

Associate's degrees conferred by degree-granting institutions, by sex, race/ethnicity, and field of study: 2009-10

Field of study	Total							Males							Females						
	Total	White	Black	Hispanic	Asian/Pacific Islander	American Indian/Alaska Native	Non-resident alien	Total	White	Black	Hispanic	Asian/Pacific Islander	American Indian/Alaska Native	Non-resident alien	Total	White	Black	Hispanic	Asian/Pacific Islander	American Indian/Alaska Native	Non-resident alien
1	2	3	4	5	6	7	8	9	10	11	12	13	14	15	16	17	18	19	20	21	22
All fields, total	**849,452**	**552,863**	**113,905**	**112,211**	**44,021**	**10,337**	**16,115**	**322,916**	**216,072**	**36,136**	**42,232**	**18,264**	**3,624**	**6,588**	**526,536**	**336,791**	**77,769**	**69,979**	**25,757**	**6,713**	**9,527**
Agriculture and natural resources	5,894	5,350	68	252	43	155	26	3,783	3,467	43	164	20	75	14	2,111	1,883	25	88	23	80	12
Architecture and related services	552	318	25	138	52	2	17	266	126	15	85	29	2	9	286	192	10	53	23	0	8
Area, ethnic, cultural, gender, and group studies	199	41	38	31	5	79	5	75	10	27	10	4	23	1	124	31	11	21	1	56	4
Biological and biomedical sciences	2,664	1,407	246	499	352	55	105	851	448	76	149	109	17	52	1,813	959	170	350	243	38	53
Business	133,371	81,899	22,195	15,904	7,677	1,692	4,004	48,168	30,563	6,663	5,889	3,004	497	1,552	85,203	51,336	15,532	10,015	4,673	1,195	2,452
Communications, journalism, and related programs	2,839	1,887	278	412	138	26	98	1,327	928	120	172	67	11	29	1,512	959	158	240	71	15	69
Communications technologies	4,419	3,171	525	397	177	47	102	3,038	2,170	380	288	105	26	69	1,381	1,001	145	109	72	21	33
Computer and information sciences	32,466	21,309	5,253	3,443	1,618	342	501	24,682	16,655	3,493	2,677	1,284	237	336	7,784	4,654	1,760	766	334	105	165
Construction trades	4,617	3,749	412	285	86	72	13	4,350	3,564	373	257	75	70	11	267	185	39	28	11	2	2
Education	17,048	11,346	2,392	2,297	328	496	189	2,352	1,646	303	244	45	84	30	14,696	9,700	2,089	2,053	283	412	159
Engineering	2,508	1,637	172	305	222	20	152	2,176	1,456	147	252	184	14	123	332	181	25	53	38	6	29
Engineering technologies and engineering-related fields[1]	31,850	22,306	3,814	3,809	1,309	318	294	27,562	19,536	3,125	3,300	1,121	251	229	4,288	2,770	689	509	188	67	65
English language and literature/letters	1,658	908	165	402	122	23	38	561	307	50	152	36	7	9	1,097	601	115	250	86	16	29
Family and consumer sciences/human sciences	9,573	5,179	2,127	1,652	375	123	117	495	238	110	90	39	10	8	9,078	4,941	2,017	1,562	336	113	109
Foreign languages, literatures, and linguistics	1,683	1,141	85	357	52	7	41	318	193	10	87	16	1	11	1,365	948	75	270	36	6	30
Health professions and related programs	177,686	124,009	24,138	16,655	9,266	1,797	1,821	25,904	16,692	3,066	2,957	2,466	280	443	151,782	107,317	21,072	13,698	6,800	1,517	1,378
Homeland security, law enforcement, firefighting, and related protective services	37,260	23,559	6,137	6,213	763	437	151	19,876	14,251	1,928	2,939	482	198	78	17,384	9,308	4,209	3,274	281	239	73
Legal professions and studies	10,003	6,340	1,804	1,426	255	119	59	1,203	698	224	197	52	25	7	8,800	5,642	1,580	1,229	203	94	52
Liberal arts and sciences, general studies, and humanities	284,775	181,450	34,785	44,147	14,753	3,406	6,234	110,701	72,694	11,868	16,071	6,236	1,206	2,626	174,074	108,756	22,917	28,076	8,517	2,200	3,608
Library science	112	89	5	9				20	16	0	1	3	0	0	92	73	5	8	4	2	0
Mathematics and statistics	1,051	511	53	267	151	8	61	725	355	46	179	96	7	42	326	156	7	88	55	1	19
Mechanic and repair technologies/technicians	16,305	11,785	1,524	1,977	628	279	112	15,479	11,227	1,407	1,878	594	263	110	826	558	117	99	34	16	2
Military technologies and applied sciences	668	493	68	70	27	10	0	531	405	44	56	19	7	0	137	88	24	14	8	3	0
Multi/interdisciplinary studies	17,671	10,163	1,271	3,226	2,412	120	479	6,960	4,216	458	1,106	925	42	213	10,711	5,947	813	2,120	1,487	78	266
Parks, recreation, leisure and fitness studies	2,016	1,321	292	268	77	26	32	1,223	802	199	145	49	14	14	793	519	93	123	28	12	18
Philosophy and religious studies	256	151	48	37	9	5	6	163	101	23	27	6	4	2	93	50	25	10	3	1	4
Physical sciences and science technologies	4,140	2,603	363	526	394	44	210	2,549	1,642	197	331	214	24	141	1,591	961	166	195	180	20	69
Precision production	2,787	2,388	116	145	71	52	15	2,609	2,235	109	138	71	45	11	178	153	7	7	0	7	4
Psychology	6,582	4,138	865	1,116	269	113	81	1,271	775	147	236	73	24	16	5,311	3,363	718	880	196	89	65
Public administration and social service professions	4,526	2,329	1,341	641	100	89	26	662	331	189	103	16	17	6	3,864	1,998	1,152	538	84	72	20
Social sciences and history	10,649	5,426	1,277	2,599	974	172	201	3,809	2,077	393	826	382	52	79	6,840	3,349	884	1,773	592	120	122
Social sciences	10,108	5,047	1,250	2,494	952	167	198	3,499	1,868	376	760	368	48	79	6,609	3,179	874	1,734	584	119	119
History	541	379	27	105	22	5	3	310	209	17	66	14	4	3	231	170	10	39	8	1	0
Theology and religious vocations	613	424	130	34	7	20	11	306	206	67	20	5	4	4	307	218	63	14	2	4	7
Transportation and materials moving	1,444	1,091	84	151	65	20	33	1,235	958	69	123	50	19	16	209	133	15	28	15	1	17
Visual and performing arts	19,567	12,945	1,809	2,521	1,237	174	881	7,686	5,084	767	1,083	387	68	297	11,881	7,861	1,042	1,438	850	106	584
Other and not classified	0	0	0	0	0	0	0	0	0	0	0	0	0	0	0	0	0	0	0	0	0

[1]Excludes "Construction trades" and "Mechanic and repair technologies/technicians," which are listed separately.
NOTE: Degree-granting institutions grant associate's or higher degrees and participate in Title IV federal financial aid programs. Race categories exclude persons of Hispanic ethnicity. Reported racial/ethnic distributions of students by level of degree, field of degree, and sex were used to estimate race/ethnicity for students whose race/ethnicity was not reported. To facilitate trend comparisons, certain aggregations have been made of the degree fields as reported in the IPEDS Fall survey: "Agriculture and natural resources" includes Agriculture, agriculture operations, and related sciences and Natural resources and conservation; and "Business" includes Business management, marketing, and related support services and Personal and culinary services.
SOURCE: U.S. Department of Education, National Center for Education Statistics, Integrated Postsecondary Education Data System (IPEDS), Fall 2010, Completions component. (This table was prepared November 2011.)

Bachelor's degrees conferred by degree-granting institutions, by race/ethnicity and sex of student: Selected years, 1976–77 through 2009–10

Year and sex	Number of degrees conferred							Percentage distribution of degrees conferred						
	Total	White	Black	Hispanic	Asian/ Pacific Islander	American Indian/ Alaska Native	Non-resident alien	Total	White	Black	Hispanic	Asian/ Pacific Islander	American Indian/ Alaska Native	Non-resident alien
1	2	3	4	5	6	7	8	9	10	11	12	13	14	15
Total														
1976–77[1]	917,900	807,688	58,636	18,743	13,793	3,326	15,714	100.0	88.0	6.4	2.0	1.5	0.4	1.7
1980–81[2]	934,800	807,319	60,673	21,832	18,794	3,593	22,589	100.0	86.4	6.5	2.3	2.0	0.4	2.4
1989–90	1,051,344	887,151	61,046	32,829	39,230	4,390	26,698	100.0	84.4	5.8	3.1	3.7	0.4	2.5
1990–91	1,094,538	914,093	66,375	37,342	42,529	4,583	29,616	100.0	83.5	6.1	3.4	3.9	0.4	2.7
1994–95	1,160,134	914,610	87,236	54,230	60,502	6,610	36,946	100.0	78.8	7.5	4.7	5.2	0.6	3.2
1995–96	1,164,792	905,846	91,496	58,351	64,433	6,976	37,690	100.0	77.8	7.9	5.0	5.5	0.6	3.2
1996–97	1,172,879	900,809	94,349	62,509	68,859	7,425	38,928	100.0	76.8	8.0	5.3	5.9	0.6	3.3
1997–98	1,184,406	901,344	98,251	66,005	71,678	7,903	39,225	100.0	76.1	8.3	5.6	6.1	0.7	3.3
1998–99[3]	1,202,239	909,562	101,910	69,735	74,126	8,658	38,248	100.0	75.7	8.5	5.8	6.2	0.7	3.2
1999–2000[3]	1,237,875	929,102	108,018	75,063	77,909	8,717	39,066	100.0	75.1	8.7	6.1	6.3	0.7	3.2
2000–01	1,244,171	927,357	111,307	77,745	78,902	9,049	39,811	100.0	74.5	8.9	6.2	6.3	0.7	3.2
2001–02	1,291,900	958,597	116,623	82,966	83,093	9,165	41,456	100.0	74.2	9.0	6.4	6.4	0.7	3.2
2002–03	1,348,811	994,616	124,253	89,029	87,964	9,875	43,074	100.0	73.7	9.2	6.6	6.5	0.7	3.2
2003–04	1,399,542	1,026,114	131,241	94,644	92,073	10,638	44,832	100.0	73.3	9.4	6.8	6.6	0.8	3.2
2004–05	1,439,264	1,049,141	136,122	101,124	97,209	10,307	45,361	100.0	72.9	9.5	7.0	6.8	0.7	3.2
2005–06	1,485,242	1,075,561	142,420	107,588	102,376	10,940	46,357	100.0	72.4	9.6	7.2	6.9	0.7	3.1
2006–07	1,524,092	1,099,850	146,653	114,936	105,297	11,455	45,901	100.0	72.2	9.6	7.5	6.9	0.8	3.0
2007–08	1,563,069	1,122,675	152,457	123,048	109,058	11,509	44,322	100.0	71.8	9.8	7.9	7.0	0.7	2.8
2008–09[3]	1,601,368	1,144,614	156,615	129,527	112,508	12,221	45,883	100.0	71.5	9.8	8.1	7.0	0.8	2.9
2009–10	1,650,014	1,167,499	164,844	140,316	117,422	12,399	47,534	100.0	70.8	10.0	8.5	7.1	0.8	2.9
Males														
1976–77[1]	494,424	438,161	25,147	10,318	7,638	1,804	11,356	100.0	88.6	5.1	2.1	1.5	0.4	2.3
1980–81[2]	469,625	406,173	24,511	10,810	10,107	1,700	16,324	100.0	86.5	5.2	2.3	2.2	0.4	3.5
1989–90	491,696	414,982	23,257	14,932	19,711	1,860	16,954	100.0	84.4	4.7	3.0	4.0	0.4	3.4
1990–91	504,045	421,290	24,800	16,598	21,203	1,938	18,216	100.0	83.6	4.9	3.3	4.2	0.4	3.6
1994–95	526,131	417,878	31,793	23,626	28,992	2,739	21,103	100.0	79.4	6.0	4.5	5.5	0.5	4.0
1995–96	522,454	409,565	32,974	25,029	30,669	2,885	21,332	100.0	78.4	6.3	4.8	5.9	0.6	4.1
1996–97	520,515	403,366	33,616	26,318	32,521	2,996	21,698	100.0	77.5	6.5	5.1	6.2	0.6	4.2
1997–98	519,956	399,553	34,510	27,677	33,445	3,151	21,620	100.0	76.8	6.6	5.3	6.4	0.6	4.2
1998–99[3]	519,961	398,310	34,856	28,477	34,179	3,407	20,732	100.0	76.6	6.7	5.5	6.6	0.7	4.0
1999–2000[3]	530,367	402,954	37,029	30,304	35,853	3,463	20,764	100.0	76.0	7.0	5.7	6.8	0.7	3.9
2000–01	531,840	401,780	38,103	31,368	35,865	3,700	21,024	100.0	75.5	7.2	5.9	6.7	0.7	4.0
2001–02	549,816	414,892	39,196	32,951	37,660	3,624	21,493	100.0	75.5	7.1	6.0	6.8	0.7	3.9
2002–03	573,258	430,248	41,494	35,101	40,230	3,870	22,315	100.0	75.1	7.2	6.1	7.0	0.7	3.9
2003–04	595,425	445,483	43,851	37,288	41,360	4,244	23,199	100.0	74.8	7.4	6.3	6.9	0.7	3.9
2004–05	613,000	456,592	45,810	39,490	43,711	4,143	23,254	100.0	74.5	7.5	6.4	7.1	0.7	3.8
2005–06	630,600	467,467	48,079	41,814	45,809	4,203	23,228	100.0	74.1	7.6	6.6	7.3	0.7	3.7
2006–07	649,570	480,558	49,685	44,750	47,582	4,505	22,490	100.0	74.0	7.6	6.9	7.3	0.7	3.5
2007–08	667,928	492,137	52,247	47,884	49,485	4,523	21,652	100.0	73.7	7.8	7.2	7.4	0.7	3.2
2008–09[3]	685,382	503,357	53,473	50,629	50,741	4,849	22,333	100.0	73.4	7.8	7.4	7.4	0.7	3.3
2009–10	706,633	513,717	56,171	55,092	53,377	4,875	23,401	100.0	72.7	7.9	7.8	7.6	0.7	3.3
Females														
1976–77[1]	423,476	369,527	33,489	8,425	6,155	1,522	4,358	100.0	87.3	7.9	2.0	1.5	0.4	1.0
1980–81[2]	465,175	401,146	36,162	11,022	8,687	1,893	6,265	100.0	86.2	7.8	2.4	1.9	0.4	1.3
1989–90	559,648	472,169	37,789	17,897	19,519	2,530	9,744	100.0	84.4	6.8	3.2	3.5	0.5	1.7
1990–91	590,493	492,803	41,575	20,744	21,326	2,645	11,400	100.0	83.5	7.0	3.5	3.6	0.4	1.9
1994–95	634,003	496,732	55,443	30,604	31,510	3,871	15,843	100.0	78.3	8.7	4.8	5.0	0.6	2.5
1995–96	642,338	496,281	58,522	33,322	33,764	4,091	16,358	100.0	77.3	9.1	5.2	5.3	0.6	2.5
1996–97	652,364	497,443	60,733	36,191	36,338	4,429	17,230	100.0	76.3	9.3	5.5	5.6	0.7	2.6
1997–98	664,450	501,791	63,741	38,328	38,233	4,752	17,605	100.0	75.5	9.6	5.8	5.8	0.7	2.6
1998–99[3]	682,278	511,252	67,054	41,258	39,947	5,251	17,516	100.0	74.9	9.8	6.0	5.9	0.8	2.6
1999–2000[3]	707,508	526,148	70,989	44,759	42,056	5,254	18,302	100.0	74.4	10.0	6.3	5.9	0.7	2.6
2000–01	712,331	525,577	73,204	46,377	43,037	5,349	18,787	100.0	73.8	10.3	6.5	6.0	0.8	2.6
2001–02	742,084	543,705	77,427	50,015	45,433	5,541	19,963	100.0	73.3	10.4	6.7	6.1	0.7	2.7
2002–03	775,553	564,368	82,759	53,928	47,734	6,005	20,759	100.0	72.8	10.7	7.0	6.2	0.8	2.7
2003–04	804,117	580,631	87,390	57,356	50,713	6,394	21,633	100.0	72.2	10.9	7.1	6.3	0.8	2.7
2004–05	826,264	592,549	90,312	61,634	53,498	6,164	22,107	100.0	71.7	10.9	7.5	6.5	0.7	2.7
2005–06	854,642	608,094	94,341	65,774	56,567	6,737	23,129	100.0	71.2	11.0	7.7	6.6	0.8	2.7
2006–07	874,522	619,292	96,968	70,186	57,715	6,950	23,411	100.0	70.8	11.1	8.0	6.6	0.8	2.7
2007–08	895,141	630,538	100,210	75,164	59,573	6,986	22,670	100.0	70.4	11.2	8.4	6.7	0.8	2.5
2008–09[3]	915,986	641,257	103,142	78,898	61,767	7,372	23,550	100.0	70.0	11.3	8.6	6.7	0.8	2.6
2009–10	943,381	653,782	108,673	85,224	64,045	7,524	24,133	100.0	69.3	11.5	9.0	6.8	0.8	2.6

[1]Excludes 1,121 males and 528 females whose racial/ethnic group was not available.
[2]Excludes 258 males and 82 females whose racial/ethnic group was not available.
[3]Revised from previously published figures.
NOTE: Degree-granting institutions grant associate's or higher degrees and participate in Title IV federal financial aid programs. Race categories exclude persons of Hispanic ethnicity. For 1989–90 and later years, reported racial/ethnic distributions of students by level of degree, field of degree, and sex were used to estimate race/ethnicity for students whose race/ethnicity was not reported. Detail may not sum to totals because of rounding.
SOURCE: U.S. Department of Education, National Center for Education Statistics, Higher Education General Information Survey (HEGIS), "Degrees and Other Formal Awards Conferred" surveys, 1976–77 and 1980–81; Integrated Postsecondary Education Data System (IPEDS), "Completions Survey" (IPEDS-C:90–99); and IPEDS Fall 2000 through Fall 2010, Completions component. (This table was prepared November 2011.)

Bachelor's degrees conferred by degree-granting institutions, by sex, race/ethnicity, and field of study: 2009–10

Field of study	Total							Males							Females						
	Total	White	Black	Hispanic	Asian/Pacific Islander	American Indian/Alaska Native	Non-resident alien	Total	White	Black	Hispanic	Asian/Pacific Islander	American Indian/Alaska Native	Non-resident alien	Total	White	Black	Hispanic	Asian/Pacific Islander	American Indian/Alaska Native	Non-resident alien
1	2	3	4	5	6	7	8	9	10	11	12	13	14	15	16	17	18	19	20	21	22
All fields, total	1,650,014	1,167,499	164,844	140,316	117,422	12,399	47,534	706,633	513,717	56,171	55,092	53,377	4,875	23,401	943,381	653,782	108,673	85,224	64,045	7,524	24,133
Agriculture and natural resources	26,336	22,430	829	1,249	1,180	243	405	13,519	11,743	374	580	487	133	202	12,817	10,687	455	669	693	110	203
Architecture and related services	10,051	6,983	500	1,175	911	61	421	5,694	4,047	295	684	444	32	192	4,357	2,936	205	491	467	29	229
Area, ethnic, cultural, gender, and group studies	8,621	4,757	1,173	1,266	1,053	178	194	2,694	1,504	355	393	320	58	64	5,927	3,253	818	873	733	120	130
Biological and biomedical sciences	86,400	55,235	6,714	6,363	15,027	573	2,488	35,865	23,695	2,022	2,557	6,347	241	1,003	50,535	31,540	4,692	3,806	8,680	332	1,485
Business	358,293	241,716	41,874	30,176	26,316	2,293	15,918	183,301	130,944	15,818	13,856	13,351	1,063	8,269	174,992	110,772	26,056	16,320	12,965	1,230	7,649
Communications, journalism, and related programs	81,266	60,678	8,410	6,433	3,640	492	1,613	28,595	21,710	2,924	2,099	1,164	193	505	52,671	38,968	5,486	4,334	2,476	299	1,108
Communications technologies	4,782	3,391	478	455	304	33	121	3,445	2,508	293	348	192	26	78	1,337	883	185	107	112	7	43
Computer and information sciences	39,589	26,565	4,565	2,942	3,372	279	1,866	32,410	22,585	3,091	2,408	2,654	207	1,465	7,179	3,980	1,474	534	718	72	401
Construction trades	273	258	0	5	6	2	2	261	247	2	4	6	2	0	12	11	0	1	0	0	0
Education	101,265	84,474	6,808	6,109	1,990	898	986	20,726	17,200	1,634	1,049	418	177	248	80,539	67,274	5,174	5,060	1,572	721	738
Engineering	72,654	50,456	3,236	5,043	9,011	388	4,520	59,360	42,173	2,390	3,966	6,942	304	3,585	13,294	8,283	846	1,077	2,069	84	935
Engineering technologies and engineering-related fields[1]	15,596	11,858	1,452	1,062	656	137	431	14,014	10,861	1,160	936	568	121	368	1,582	997	292	126	88	16	63
English language and literature/letters	53,231	41,617	4,028	4,090	2,614	361	521	17,050	13,656	1,048	1,296	779	106	165	36,181	27,961	2,980	2,794	1,835	255	356
Family and consumer sciences/human sciences	21,818	16,065	2,457	1,633	1,155	219	289	2,686	1,896	363	165	186	16	60	19,132	14,169	2,094	1,468	969	203	229
Foreign languages, literatures, and linguistics	21,516	15,227	880	3,545	1,344	125	395	6,610	4,833	225	992	415	38	107	14,906	10,394	655	2,553	929	87	288
Health professions and related programs	129,634	93,675	15,046	8,826	9,048	976	2,063	19,306	12,987	2,107	1,600	2,029	142	441	110,328	80,688	12,939	7,226	7,019	834	1,622
Homeland security, law enforcement, and firefighting	43,667	26,452	8,720	6,388	1,386	406	315	22,265	15,202	3,085	2,828	811	191	148	21,402	11,250	5,635	3,560	575	215	167
Legal professions and studies	3,886	2,493	687	408	228	37	33	1,096	739	134	126	77	9	11	2,790	1,754	553	282	151	28	22
Liberal arts and sciences, general studies, and humanities	46,953	31,707	6,815	4,514	1,765	531	1,621	16,619	11,878	2,150	1,230	586	172	603	30,334	19,829	4,665	3,284	1,179	359	1,018
Library science	85	79	2	3	1	0	0	11	10	1	0	0	0	0	74	69	1	3	1	0	0
Mathematics and statistics	16,030	11,510	854	1,027	1,671	81	887	9,087	6,488	417	609	998	43	532	6,943	5,022	437	418	673	38	355
Mechanic and repair technologies/technicians	206	167	9	11	12	0	7	198	162	8	11	12	0	5	8	5	1	0	0	0	2
Military technologies and applied sciences	56	47	3	5	0	1	0	54	46	3	4	1	1	0	2	1	0	1	0	0	0
Multi/interdisciplinary studies	37,648	25,817	3,687	4,648	2,467	341	688	12,129	8,720	1,090	1,084	864	97	274	25,519	17,097	2,597	3,564	1,603	244	414
Parks, recreation, leisure, and fitness studies	33,318	25,678	3,257	2,371	1,260	279	473	17,621	13,332	1,913	1,317	665	138	256	15,697	12,346	1,344	1,054	595	141	217
Philosophy and religious studies	12,504	9,740	849	910	742	88	175	7,910	6,276	456	582	426	60	110	4,594	3,464	393	328	316	28	65
Physical sciences and science technologies	23,379	17,245	1,290	1,279	2,464	168	933	13,862	10,695	566	688	1,293	102	518	9,517	6,550	724	591	1,171	66	415
Precision production	29	20	0	1	6	0	2	19	16	0	3	3	0	0	10	4	0	1	0	0	2
Psychology	97,216	65,521	11,981	10,517	6,701	806	1,690	22,275	15,373	2,219	2,263	1,849	206	365	74,941	50,148	9,762	8,254	4,852	600	1,325
Public administration and social services	25,414	15,053	5,745	3,045	912	327	332	4,578	2,862	863	488	232	66	67	20,836	12,191	4,882	2,557	680	261	265
Social sciences and history	172,780	119,767	15,976	16,823	13,860	1,356	4,998	87,406	64,114	6,042	7,370	6,708	618	2,554	85,374	55,653	9,934	9,453	7,152	738	2,444
Social sciences	137,582	90,860	14,313	14,035	12,533	1,086	4,755	66,527	46,639	5,218	5,790	6,003	461	2,416	71,055	44,221	9,095	8,245	6,530	625	2,339
History	35,198	28,907	1,663	2,788	1,327	270	243	20,879	17,475	824	1,580	705	157	138	14,319	11,432	839	1,208	622	113	105
Theology and religious vocations	8,718	7,366	560	361	209	53	169	5,756	4,946	315	224	121	33	117	2,962	2,420	245	137	88	20	52
Transportation and materials moving	4,998	3,954	358	362	195	39	90	4,443	3,531	319	320	162	33	78	555	423	39	42	33	6	12
Visual and performing arts	91,802	69,498	5,599	7,271	5,916	628	2,890	35,768	26,738	2,489	3,015	2,268	247	1,011	56,034	42,760	3,110	4,256	3,648	381	1,879
Other and not classified	0	0	0	0	0	0	0	0	0	0	0	0	0	0	0	0	0	0	0	0	0

[1]Excludes "Construction trades" and "Mechanic and repair technologies/technicians," which are listed separately.

NOTE: Degree-granting institutions grant associate's or higher degrees and participate in Title IV federal financial aid programs. Race categories exclude persons of Hispanic ethnicity. Reported racial/ethnic distributions of students by level of degree, field of degree, and sex were used to estimate race/ethnicity for students whose race/ethnicity was not reported. To facilitate trend comparisons, certain aggregations have been made of the degree fields as reported in the IPEDS Fall survey. "Agriculture and natural resources" includes Agriculture, agriculture operations, and related sciences and Natural resources and conservation; and "Business" includes Business management, marketing, and related support services and Personal and culinary services.

SOURCE: U.S. Department of Education, National Center for Education Statistics, Integrated Postsecondary Education Data System (IPEDS), Fall 2010, Completions component. (This table was prepared November 2011.)

Master's degrees conferred by degree-granting institutions, by race/ethnicity and sex of student: Selected years, 1976–77 through 2009–10

Year and sex	Number of degrees conferred							Percentage distribution of degrees conferred						
	Total	White	Black	Hispanic	Asian/ Pacific Islander	American Indian/ Alaska Native	Non-resident alien	Total	White	Black	Hispanic	Asian/ Pacific Islander	American Indian/ Alaska Native	Non-resident alien
1	2	3	4	5	6	7	8	9	10	11	12	13	14	15
Total														
1976–77[1]	322,463	271,402	21,252	6,136	5,127	1,018	17,528	100.0	84.2	6.6	1.9	1.6	0.3	5.4
1980–81[2]	301,081	247,475	17,436	6,534	6,348	1,044	22,244	100.0	82.2	5.8	2.2	2.1	0.3	7.4
1989–90	330,152	259,196	15,752	8,001	10,608	1,105	35,490	100.0	78.5	4.8	2.4	3.2	0.3	10.7
1990–91	342,863	265,927	17,023	8,981	11,869	1,189	37,874	100.0	77.6	5.0	2.6	3.5	0.3	11.0
1994–95	403,609	297,988	24,662	13,037	17,164	1,636	49,122	100.0	73.8	6.1	3.2	4.3	0.4	12.2
1995–96	412,180	302,790	26,323	14,553	18,505	1,793	48,216	100.0	73.5	6.4	3.5	4.5	0.4	11.7
1996–97	425,260	309,637	28,875	15,560	19,372	1,954	49,862	100.0	72.8	6.8	3.7	4.6	0.5	11.7
1997–98	436,037	312,752	30,703	16,370	21,415	2,068	52,729	100.0	71.7	7.0	3.8	4.9	0.5	12.1
1998–99	446,038	318,555	33,010	17,781	22,262	2,075	52,355	100.0	71.4	7.4	4.0	5.0	0.5	11.7
1999–2000	463,185	324,990	36,606	19,379	23,523	2,263	56,424	100.0	70.2	7.9	4.2	5.1	0.5	12.2
2000–01	473,502	324,211	38,853	21,661	24,544	2,496	61,737	100.0	68.5	8.2	4.6	5.2	0.5	13.0
2001–02	487,313	331,427	41,006	22,517	25,681	2,632	64,050	100.0	68.0	8.4	4.6	5.3	0.5	13.1
2002–03	518,699	346,003	45,150	25,200	27,492	2,886	71,968	100.0	66.7	8.7	4.9	5.3	0.6	13.9
2003–04	564,272	373,448	51,402	29,806	31,202	3,206	75,208	100.0	66.2	9.1	5.3	5.5	0.6	13.3
2004–05	580,151	383,246	55,330	31,639	33,042	3,310	73,584	100.0	66.1	9.5	5.5	5.7	0.6	12.7
2005–06	599,731	397,439	59,806	32,567	34,289	3,519	72,111	100.0	66.3	10.0	5.4	5.7	0.6	12.0
2006–07	610,597	403,562	63,412	34,967	36,491	3,589	68,576	100.0	66.1	10.4	5.7	6.0	0.6	11.2
2007–08	630,666	413,179	65,914	36,972	37,722	3,777	73,102	100.0	65.5	10.5	5.9	6.0	0.6	11.6
2008–09	662,079	427,891	70,839	39,582	40,257	3,777	79,733	100.0	64.6	10.7	6.0	6.1	0.6	12.0
2009–10	693,025	445,038	76,458	43,535	42,702	3,960	81,332	100.0	64.2	11.0	6.3	6.2	0.6	11.7
Males														
1976–77[1]	172,703	144,042	7,970	3,328	3,128	565	13,670	100.0	83.4	4.6	1.9	1.8	0.3	7.9
1980–81[2]	151,602	120,927	6,418	3,155	3,830	507	16,765	100.0	79.8	4.2	2.1	2.5	0.3	11.1
1989–90	158,052	117,856	5,748	3,641	6,050	466	24,291	100.0	74.6	3.6	2.3	3.8	0.3	15.4
1990–91	160,842	117,993	6,201	4,017	6,765	495	25,371	100.0	73.4	3.9	2.5	4.2	0.3	15.8
1994–95	183,043	127,722	8,395	5,593	9,195	670	31,468	100.0	69.8	4.6	3.1	5.0	0.4	17.2
1995–96	183,481	128,325	8,758	5,940	9,644	713	30,101	100.0	69.9	4.8	3.2	5.3	0.4	16.4
1996–97	185,270	128,946	9,252	6,335	9,488	743	30,506	100.0	69.6	5.0	3.4	5.1	0.4	16.5
1997–98	188,718	128,987	9,978	6,612	10,500	792	31,849	100.0	68.3	5.3	3.5	5.6	0.4	16.9
1998–99	190,230	129,912	10,346	7,044	10,638	794	31,496	100.0	68.3	5.4	3.7	5.6	0.4	16.6
1999–2000	196,129	131,221	11,642	7,738	11,299	845	33,384	100.0	66.9	5.9	3.9	5.8	0.4	17.0
2000–01	197,770	128,516	11,878	8,371	11,561	925	36,519	100.0	65.0	6.0	4.2	5.8	0.5	18.5
2001–02	202,604	131,316	12,119	8,539	11,956	995	37,679	100.0	64.8	6.0	4.2	5.9	0.5	18.6
2002–03	215,172	135,938	13,224	9,389	12,704	1,043	42,874	100.0	63.2	6.1	4.4	5.9	0.5	19.9
2003–04	233,056	146,369	15,027	10,929	14,551	1,137	45,043	100.0	62.8	6.4	4.7	6.2	0.5	19.3
2004–05	237,155	150,076	16,136	11,501	15,238	1,167	43,037	100.0	63.3	6.8	4.8	6.4	0.5	18.1
2005–06	241,656	153,666	17,384	11,739	16,031	1,252	41,584	100.0	63.6	7.2	4.9	6.6	0.5	17.2
2006–07	242,189	154,241	18,333	12,473	16,728	1,275	39,139	100.0	63.7	7.6	5.2	6.9	0.5	16.2
2007–08	250,169	157,596	18,761	13,189	17,476	1,293	41,854	100.0	63.0	7.5	5.3	7.0	0.5	16.7
2008–09	263,538	162,994	20,174	14,324	18,724	1,350	45,972	100.0	61.8	7.7	5.4	7.1	0.5	17.4
2009–10	275,197	170,203	22,120	15,525	19,535	1,415	46,399	100.0	61.8	8.0	5.6	7.1	0.5	16.9
Females														
1976–77[1]	149,760	127,360	13,282	2,808	1,999	453	3,858	100.0	85.0	8.9	1.9	1.3	0.3	2.6
1980–81[2]	149,479	126,548	11,018	3,379	2,518	537	5,479	100.0	84.7	7.4	2.3	1.7	0.4	3.7
1989–90	172,100	141,340	10,004	4,360	4,558	639	11,199	100.0	82.1	5.8	2.5	2.6	0.4	6.5
1990–91	182,021	147,934	10,822	4,964	5,104	694	12,503	100.0	81.3	5.9	2.7	2.8	0.4	6.9
1994–95	220,566	170,266	16,267	7,444	7,969	966	17,654	100.0	77.2	7.4	3.4	3.6	0.4	8.0
1995–96	228,699	174,465	17,565	8,613	8,861	1,080	18,115	100.0	76.3	7.7	3.8	3.9	0.5	7.9
1996–97	239,990	180,691	19,623	9,225	9,884	1,211	19,356	100.0	75.3	8.2	3.8	4.1	0.5	8.1
1997–98	247,319	183,765	20,725	9,758	10,915	1,276	20,880	100.0	74.3	8.4	3.9	4.4	0.5	8.4
1998–99	255,808	188,643	22,664	10,737	11,624	1,281	20,859	100.0	73.7	8.9	4.2	4.5	0.5	8.2
1999–2000	267,056	193,769	24,964	11,641	12,224	1,418	23,040	100.0	72.6	9.3	4.4	4.6	0.5	8.6
2000–01	275,732	195,695	26,975	13,290	12,983	1,571	25,218	100.0	71.0	9.8	4.8	4.7	0.6	9.1
2001–02	284,709	200,111	28,887	13,978	13,725	1,637	26,371	100.0	70.3	10.1	4.9	4.8	0.6	9.3
2002–03	303,527	210,065	31,926	15,811	14,788	1,843	29,094	100.0	69.2	10.5	5.2	4.9	0.6	9.6
2003–04	331,216	227,079	36,375	18,877	16,651	2,069	30,165	100.0	68.6	11.0	5.7	5.0	0.6	9.1
2004–05	342,996	233,170	39,194	20,138	17,804	2,143	30,547	100.0	68.0	11.4	5.9	5.2	0.6	8.9
2005–06	358,075	243,773	42,422	20,828	18,258	2,267	30,527	100.0	68.1	11.8	5.8	5.1	0.6	8.5
2006–07	368,408	249,321	45,079	22,494	19,763	2,314	29,437	100.0	67.7	12.2	6.1	5.4	0.6	8.0
2007–08	380,497	255,583	47,153	23,783	20,246	2,484	31,248	100.0	67.2	12.4	6.3	5.3	0.7	8.2
2008–09	398,541	264,897	50,665	25,258	21,533	2,427	33,761	100.0	66.5	12.7	6.3	5.4	0.6	8.5
2009–10	417,828	274,835	54,338	28,010	23,167	2,545	34,933	100.0	65.8	13.0	6.7	5.5	0.6	8.4

[1]Excludes 387 males and 175 females whose racial/ethnic group was not available.
[2]Excludes 1,377 males and 179 females whose racial/ethnic group was not available.
NOTE: Degree-granting institutions grant associate's or higher degrees and participate in Title IV federal financial aid programs. Race categories exclude persons of Hispanic ethnicity. For 1989–90 and later years, reported racial/ethnic distributions of students by level of degree, field of degree, and sex were used to estimate race/ethnicity for students whose race/ethnicity was not reported. Data have been revised from previously published figures. Detail may not sum to totals because of rounding.
SOURCE: U.S. Department of Education, National Center for Education Statistics, Higher Education General Information Survey (HEGIS), "Degrees and Other Formal Awards Conferred" surveys, 1976–77 and 1980–81; Integrated Postsecondary Education Data System (IPEDS), "Completions Survey" (IPEDS-C:90–99); and IPEDS Fall 2000 through Fall 2010, Completions component. (This table was prepared November 2011.)

Master's degrees conferred by degree-granting institutions, by sex, race/ethnicity, and field of study: 2009–10

	Total							Males							Females						
Field of study	Total	White	Black	Hispanic	Asian/ Pacific Islander	American Indian/ Alaska Native	Non-resident alien	Total	White	Black	Hispanic	Asian/ Pacific Islander	American Indian/ Alaska Native	Non-resident alien	Total	White	Black	Hispanic	Asian/ Pacific Islander	American Indian/ Alaska Native	Non-resident alien
1	2	3	4	5	6	7	8	9	10	11	12	13	14	15	16	17	18	19	20	21	22
All fields, total	693,025	445,038	76,458	43,535	42,702	3,960	81,332	275,197	170,203	22,120	15,525	19,535	1,415	46,399	417,828	274,835	54,338	28,010	23,167	2,545	34,933
Agriculture and natural resources	5,211	3,849	176	199	195	46	746	2,509	1,901	75	86	79	22	346	2,702	1,948	101	113	116	24	400
Architecture and related services	7,280	4,826	348	439	509	28	1,130	4,012	2,789	176	259	216	12	560	3,268	2,037	172	180	293	16	570
Area, ethnic, cultural, gender, and group studies	1,775	955	176	198	146	32	268	654	361	60	86	45	7	95	1,121	594	116	112	101	25	173
Biological and biomedical sciences	10,725	6,273	608	523	1,441	54	1,826	4,611	2,750	193	210	656	27	775	6,114	3,523	415	313	785	27	1,051
Business	177,684	101,058	25,237	10,747	15,403	955	24,284	96,709	58,801	8,964	5,495	8,682	474	14,293	80,975	42,257	16,273	5,252	6,721	481	9,991
Communications, journalism, and related programs	7,636	4,779	821	491	375	41	1,129	2,410	1,641	189	145	98	14	323	5,226	3,138	632	346	277	27	806
Communications technologies	463	211	37	31	22	2	160	249	134	10	13	8	1	83	214	77	27	18	14	1	77
Computer and information sciences	17,953	6,174	1,324	694	1,752	54	7,955	13,017	4,828	772	537	1,193	42	5,645	4,936	1,346	552	157	559	12	2,310
Construction trades	0	0	0	0	0	0	0	0	0	0	0	0	0	0	0	0	0	0	0	0	0
Education	182,139	138,974	19,258	12,985	5,054	1,060	4,808	41,296	31,858	4,069	2,833	1,050	275	1,211	140,843	107,116	15,189	10,152	4,004	785	3,597
Engineering	35,088	13,427	1,063	1,298	4,006	87	15,207	27,281	10,952	743	982	2,934	61	11,609	7,807	2,475	320	316	1,072	26	3,598
Engineering technologies and engineering-related fields[1]	4,258	1,997	322	275	295	27	1,342	3,240	1,587	215	211	212	24	991	1,018	410	107	64	83	3	351
English language and literature/letters	9,201	7,474	478	504	312	63	370	3,006	2,486	112	188	85	25	110	6,195	4,988	366	316	227	38	260
Family and consumer sciences/human sciences	2,580	1,808	333	135	98	21	185	362	256	44	15	10	1	36	2,218	1,552	289	120	88	20	149
Foreign languages, literatures, and linguistics	3,755	2,099	84	567	213	36	756	1,254	754	27	183	59	10	221	2,501	1,345	57	384	154	26	535
Health professions and related programs	69,084	48,256	7,872	3,935	5,324	454	3,243	12,871	8,217	1,249	800	1,348	77	1,180	56,213	40,039	6,623	3,135	3,976	377	2,063
Homeland security, law enforcement, and firefighting	6,714	4,215	1,497	612	199	63	128	3,140	2,205	489	255	89	27	75	3,574	2,010	1,008	357	110	36	53
Legal professions and studies	5,734	1,861	320	222	289	28	3,014	2,803	978	101	98	125	14	1,487	2,931	883	219	124	164	14	1,527
Liberal arts and sciences, general studies, and humanities	3,804	2,797	366	232	143	27	239	1,522	1,129	112	84	66	7	124	2,282	1,668	254	148	77	20	115
Library science	7,448	6,217	369	449	279	42	92	1,394	1,156	61	87	61	6	23	6,054	5,061	308	362	218	36	69
Mathematics and statistics	5,634	2,532	166	167	472	12	2,285	3,376	1,564	113	113	253	4	1,329	2,258	968	53	54	219	8	956
Mechanic and repair technologies/technicians	0	0	0	0	0	0	0	0	0	0	0	0	0	0	0	0	0	0	0	0	0
Military technologies and applied sciences	0	0	0	0	0	0	0	0	0	0	0	0	0	0	0	0	0	0	0	0	0
Multi/interdisciplinary studies	5,973	4,039	462	426	368	51	627	2,118	1,479	131	127	115	10	256	3,855	2,560	331	299	253	41	371
Parks, recreation, leisure, and fitness studies	5,617	4,296	546	232	146	27	370	3,032	2,307	301	121	86	12	205	2,585	1,989	245	111	60	15	165
Philosophy and religious studies	2,043	1,512	157	84	113	18	159	1,298	982	86	51	80	12	87	745	530	71	33	33	6	72
Physical sciences and science technologies	6,063	3,621	162	213	389	19	1,659	3,652	2,200	78	120	216	11	1,027	2,411	1,421	84	93	173	8	632
Precision production	10	10	1	0	0	0	1	5	5	0	0	0	0	0	3	3	0	0	0	0	1
Psychology	23,752	16,500	3,248	2,018	995	151	840	4,797	3,520	493	369	183	37	195	18,955	12,980	2,755	1,649	812	114	645
Public administration and social services	35,729	21,810	6,869	3,395	1,588	292	1,775	8,865	5,334	1,446	797	385	69	834	26,864	16,476	5,423	2,598	1,203	223	941
Social sciences and history	20,222	12,941	1,638	1,158	1,025	130	3,330	9,963	6,653	604	500	439	60	1,707	10,259	6,288	1,034	658	586	70	1,623
Social sciences	16,368	9,664	1,508	958	933	104	3,201	7,860	4,838	542	396	393	45	1,646	8,508	4,826	966	562	540	59	1,555
History	3,854	3,277	130	200	92	26	129	2,103	1,815	62	104	46	15	61	1,751	1,462	68	96	46	11	68
Theology and religious vocations	12,824	9,048	1,733	426	645	50	922	8,302	6,003	825	284	466	35	689	4,522	3,045	908	142	179	15	233
Transportation and materials moving	1,074	863	74	69	35	10	23	924	747	66	59	22	9	21	150	116	8	10	13	1	2
Visual and performing arts	15,552	10,618	713	811	871	80	2,459	6,525	4,626	316	417	274	30	862	9,027	5,992	397	394	597	50	1,597
Other and not classified	0	0	0	0	0	0	0	0	0	0	0	0	0	0	0	0	0	0	0	0	0

[1] Excludes "Construction trades" and "Mechanic and repair technologies/technicians," which are listed separately.

NOTE: Degree-granting institutions grant associate's or higher degrees and participate in Title IV federal financial aid programs. Reported racial/ethnic distributions of students by level of degree, field of degree, and sex were used to estimate race/ethnicity for students whose race/ethnicity was not reported. To facilitate trend comparisons, certain aggregations have been made of the degree fields as reported in the IPEDS Fall survey. "Agriculture and natural resources" includes Agriculture, agriculture operations, and related sciences, and Natural resources and conservation; and "Business" includes Business management, marketing, and related support services and Personal and culinary services.

SOURCE: U.S. Department of Education, National Center for Education Statistics, Integrated Postsecondary Education Data System (IPEDS), Fall 2010, Completions component. (This table was prepared November 2011.)

Doctor's degrees conferred by degree-granting institutions, by race/ethnicity and sex of student: Selected years, 1976–77 through 2009–10

Year and sex	Number of degrees conferred[1]							Percentage distribution of degrees conferred[1]						
	Total	White	Black	Hispanic	Asian/ Pacific Islander	American Indian/ Alaska Native	Non-resident alien	Total	White	Black	Hispanic	Asian/ Pacific Islander	American Indian/ Alaska Native	Non-resident alien
1	2	3	4	5	6	7	8	9	10	11	12	13	14	15
Total														
1976–77[2]	91,218	79,932	3,575	1,533	1,674	240	4,264	100.0	87.6	3.9	1.7	1.8	0.3	4.7
1980–81[3]	97,281	84,200	3,893	1,924	2,267	312	4,685	100.0	86.6	4.0	2.0	2.3	0.3	4.8
1989–90	103,508	81,811	4,142	3,096	4,418	340	9,701	100.0	79.0	4.0	3.0	4.3	0.3	9.4
1990–91	105,547	81,791	4,429	3,210	5,120	356	10,641	100.0	77.5	4.2	3.0	4.9	0.3	10.1
1994–95	114,266	82,605	5,918	4,083	8,768	528	12,364	100.0	72.3	5.2	3.6	7.7	0.5	10.8
1995–96	115,507	82,641	6,153	4,361	8,979	607	12,766	100.0	71.5	5.3	3.8	7.8	0.5	11.1
1996–97	118,747	84,244	6,694	4,615	9,730	675	12,789	100.0	70.9	5.6	3.9	8.2	0.6	10.8
1997–98	118,735	83,690	7,018	4,705	9,814	732	12,776	100.0	70.5	5.9	4.0	8.3	0.6	10.8
1998–99	116,700	82,066	7,004	4,959	10,025	774	11,872	100.0	70.3	6.0	4.2	8.6	0.7	10.2
1999–2000	118,736	82,984	7,078	5,042	10,682	708	12,242	100.0	69.9	6.0	4.2	9.0	0.6	10.3
2000–01	119,585	82,321	7,035	5,204	11,587	705	12,733	100.0	68.8	5.9	4.4	9.7	0.6	10.6
2001–02	119,663	81,995	7,570	5,267	11,633	753	12,445	100.0	68.5	6.3	4.4	9.7	0.6	10.4
2002–03	121,579	82,549	7,537	5,503	12,008	759	13,223	100.0	67.9	6.2	4.5	9.9	0.6	10.9
2003–04	126,087	84,695	8,089	5,795	12,371	771	14,366	100.0	67.2	6.4	4.6	9.8	0.6	11.4
2004–05	134,387	89,763	8,527	6,115	13,176	788	16,018	100.0	66.8	6.3	4.6	9.8	0.6	11.9
2005–06	138,056	91,050	8,523	6,202	13,686	929	17,666	100.0	66.0	6.2	4.5	9.9	0.7	12.8
2006–07	144,690	94,248	9,377	6,593	14,924	918	18,630	100.0	65.1	6.5	4.6	10.3	0.6	12.9
2007–08	149,378	97,839	9,463	6,949	15,203	932	18,992	100.0	65.5	6.3	4.7	10.2	0.6	12.7
2008–09	154,425	101,303	10,183	7,490	15,809	978	18,662	100.0	65.6	6.6	4.9	10.2	0.6	12.1
2009–10	158,558	104,426	10,417	8,085	16,625	952	18,053	100.0	65.9	6.6	5.1	10.5	0.6	11.4
Males														
1976–77[2]	71,709	62,977	2,338	1,216	1,311	182	3,685	100.0	87.8	3.3	1.7	1.8	0.3	5.1
1980–81[3]	68,853	59,574	2,206	1,338	1,589	223	3,923	100.0	86.5	3.2	1.9	2.3	0.3	5.7
1989–90	63,963	49,697	1,928	1,775	2,673	173	7,717	100.0	77.7	3.0	2.8	4.2	0.3	12.1
1990–91	64,242	48,812	1,991	1,835	3,038	196	8,370	100.0	76.0	3.1	2.9	4.7	0.3	13.0
1994–95	67,324	48,077	2,509	2,217	4,974	270	9,277	100.0	71.4	3.7	3.3	7.4	0.4	13.8
1995–96	67,189	47,420	2,526	2,364	4,987	328	9,564	100.0	70.6	3.8	3.5	7.4	0.5	14.2
1996–97	68,387	48,113	2,704	2,481	5,334	368	9,387	100.0	70.4	4.0	3.6	7.8	0.5	13.7
1997–98	67,232	47,189	2,808	2,525	5,171	364	9,175	100.0	70.2	4.2	3.8	7.7	0.5	13.6
1998–99	65,340	45,802	2,793	2,533	5,382	402	8,428	100.0	70.1	4.3	3.9	8.2	0.6	12.9
1999–2000	64,930	45,308	2,762	2,602	5,467	333	8,458	100.0	69.8	4.3	4.0	8.4	0.5	13.0
2000–01	64,171	44,131	2,655	2,564	5,759	346	8,716	100.0	68.8	4.1	4.0	9.0	0.5	13.6
2001–02	62,731	43,014	2,821	2,586	5,645	357	8,308	100.0	68.6	4.5	4.1	9.0	0.6	13.2
2002–03	62,730	42,569	2,735	2,671	5,683	358	8,714	100.0	67.9	4.4	4.3	9.1	0.6	13.9
2003–04	63,981	43,014	2,888	2,731	5,620	357	9,371	100.0	67.2	4.5	4.3	8.8	0.6	14.6
2004–05	67,257	44,749	2,904	2,863	5,913	370	10,458	100.0	66.5	4.3	4.3	8.8	0.6	15.5
2005–06	68,912	45,476	2,949	2,850	5,977	429	11,231	100.0	66.0	4.3	4.1	8.7	0.6	16.3
2006–07	71,308	46,228	3,225	3,049	6,597	421	11,788	100.0	64.8	4.5	4.3	9.3	0.6	16.5
2007–08	73,453	48,203	3,296	3,146	6,535	447	11,826	100.0	65.6	4.5	4.3	8.9	0.6	16.1
2008–09	75,639	49,861	3,528	3,385	6,904	460	11,501	100.0	65.9	4.7	4.5	9.1	0.6	15.2
2009–10	76,605	50,705	3,622	3,641	7,230	430	10,977	100.0	66.2	4.7	4.8	9.4	0.6	14.3
Females														
1976–77[2]	19,509	16,955	1,237	317	363	58	579	100.0	86.9	6.3	1.6	1.9	0.3	3.0
1980–81[3]	28,428	24,626	1,687	586	678	89	762	100.0	86.6	5.9	2.1	2.4	0.3	2.7
1989–90	39,545	32,114	2,214	1,321	1,745	167	1,984	100.0	81.2	5.6	3.3	4.4	0.4	5.0
1990–91	41,305	32,979	2,438	1,375	2,082	160	2,271	100.0	79.8	5.9	3.3	5.0	0.4	5.5
1994–95	46,942	34,528	3,409	1,866	3,794	258	3,087	100.0	73.6	7.3	4.0	8.1	0.5	6.6
1995–96	48,318	35,221	3,627	1,997	3,992	279	3,202	100.0	72.9	7.5	4.1	8.3	0.6	6.6
1996–97	50,360	36,131	3,990	2,134	4,396	307	3,402	100.0	71.7	7.9	4.2	8.7	0.6	6.8
1997–98	51,503	36,501	4,210	2,180	4,643	368	3,601	100.0	70.9	8.2	4.2	9.0	0.7	7.0
1998–99	51,360	36,264	4,211	2,426	4,643	372	3,444	100.0	70.6	8.2	4.7	9.0	0.7	6.7
1999–2000	53,806	37,676	4,316	2,440	5,215	375	3,784	100.0	70.0	8.0	4.5	9.7	0.7	7.0
2000–01	55,414	38,190	4,380	2,640	5,828	359	4,017	100.0	68.9	7.9	4.8	10.5	0.6	7.2
2001–02	56,932	38,981	4,749	2,681	5,988	396	4,137	100.0	68.5	8.3	4.7	10.5	0.7	7.3
2002–03	58,849	39,980	4,802	2,832	6,325	401	4,509	100.0	67.9	8.2	4.8	10.7	0.7	7.7
2003–04	62,106	41,681	5,201	3,064	6,751	414	4,995	100.0	67.1	8.4	4.9	10.9	0.7	8.0
2004–05	67,130	45,014	5,623	3,252	7,263	418	5,560	100.0	67.1	8.4	4.8	10.8	0.6	8.3
2005–06	69,144	45,574	5,574	3,352	7,709	500	6,435	100.0	65.9	8.1	4.8	11.1	0.7	9.3
2006–07	73,382	48,020	6,152	3,544	8,327	497	6,842	100.0	65.4	8.4	4.8	11.3	0.7	9.3
2007–08	75,925	49,636	6,167	3,803	8,668	485	7,166	100.0	65.4	8.1	5.0	11.4	0.6	9.4
2008–09	78,786	51,442	6,655	4,105	8,905	518	7,161	100.0	65.3	8.4	5.2	11.3	0.7	9.1
2009–10	81,953	53,721	6,795	4,444	9,395	522	7,076	100.0	65.6	8.3	5.4	11.5	0.6	8.6

[1]Includes Ph.D., E.D., and comparable degrees at the doctoral level, as well as such degrees as M.D., D.D.S., and law degrees that were formerly classified as first-professional degrees.
[2]Excludes 500 males and 12 females whose racial/ethnic group was not available.
[3]Excludes 714 males and 21 females whose racial/ethnic group was not available.
NOTE: Degree-granting institutions grant associate's or higher degrees and participate in Title IV federal financial aid programs. Race categories exclude persons of Hispanic ethnicity. For 1989–90 and later years, reported racial/ethnic distributions of students by level of degree, field of degree, and sex were used to estimate race/ethnicity for students whose race/ethnicity was not reported. Data have been revised from previously published figures. Detail may not sum to totals because of rounding.
SOURCE: U.S. Department of Education, National Center for Education Statistics, Higher Education General Information Survey (HEGIS), "Degrees and Other Formal Awards Conferred" surveys, 1976–77 and 1980–81; Integrated Postsecondary Education Data System (IPEDS), "Completions Survey" (IPEDS-C:90–99); and IPEDS Fall 2000 through Fall 2010, Completions component. (This table was prepared November 2011.)

Doctor's degrees conferred by degree-granting institutions, by sex, race/ethnicity, and field of study: 2009–10

Field of study	Total							Males							Females						
	Total	White	Black	Hispanic	Asian/Pacific Islander	American Indian/Alaska Native	Non-resident alien	Total	White	Black	Hispanic	Asian/Pacific Islander	American Indian/Alaska Native	Non-resident alien	Total	White	Black	Hispanic	Asian/Pacific Islander	American Indian/Alaska Native	Non-resident alien
1	2	3	4	5	6	7	8	9	10	11	12	13	14	15	16	17	18	19	20	21	22
All fields, total	158,558	104,426	10,417	8,085	16,625	952	18,053	76,605	50,705	3,622	3,641	7,230	430	10,977	81,953	53,721	6,795	4,444	9,395	522	7,076
Agriculture and natural resources	1,147	569	51	38	41	6	442	625	299	18	14	19	3	272	522	270	33	24	22	3	170
Architecture and related services	210	84	8	7	23	1	87	116	50	3	4	10	0	49	94	34	5	3	13	1	38
Area, ethnic, cultural, gender, and group studies	253	116	35	18	29	8	47	107	56	16	9	5	2	19	146	60	19	9	24	6	28
Biological and biomedical sciences	7,666	4,198	236	335	738	24	2,135	3,600	2,011	66	156	301	8	1,058	4,066	2,187	170	179	437	16	1,077
Business	2,245	1,141	288	79	132	15	590	1,335	708	131	39	76	6	375	910	433	157	40	56	9	215
Communications, journalism, and related programs	570	369	25	17	30	0	129	224	151	8	4	14	0	47	346	218	17	13	16	0	82
Communications technologies	3	2	0	0	0	0	1	1	0	0	0	0	0	1	2	2	0	0	0	0	0
Computer and information sciences	1,599	607	48	17	146	3	778	1,250	481	31	9	108	3	618	349	126	17	8	38	0	160
Construction trades	0	0	0	0	0	0	0	0	0	0	0	0	0	0	0	0	0	0	0	0	0
Education	9,233	6,122	1,595	489	351	45	631	3,023	2,059	447	168	108	12	229	6,210	4,063	1,148	321	243	33	402
Engineering	7,704	2,471	162	209	564	9	4,289	5,934	1,917	107	139	373	8	3,390	1,770	554	55	70	191	1	899
Engineering technologies and engineering-related fields[1]	67	34	1	1	5	1	25	50	25	1	1	2	0	21	17	9	0	0	3	0	4
English language and literature/letters	1,332	1,041	61	43	56	9	122	522	422	21	16	18	3	42	810	619	40	27	38	6	80
Family and consumer sciences/human sciences	296	163	30	13	14	4	72	64	35	6	2	1	1	19	232	128	24	11	13	3	53
Foreign languages, literatures, and linguistics	1,091	562	20	97	44	4	364	446	233	5	35	10	2	161	645	329	15	62	34	2	203
Health professions and related programs	57,746	40,134	3,426	2,652	9,405	337	1,792	23,946	16,904	1,097	1,113	3,921	139	772	33,800	23,230	2,329	1,539	5,484	198	1,020
Homeland security, law enforcement, and firefighting	106	71	7	2	5	1	20	57	35	3	2	4	1	12	49	36	4	0	1	0	8
Legal professions and studies	44,626	33,106	3,216	3,190	3,764	369	981	23,552	18,415	1,216	1,553	1,704	179	485	21,074	14,691	2,000	1,637	2,060	190	496
Liberal arts and sciences, general studies, and humanities	96	71	9	5	1	0	10	40	32	4	1	0	0	3	56	39	5	4	1	0	7
Library science	64	38	4	3	2	0	17	20	10	2	2	0	0	6	44	28	2	1	2	0	11
Mathematics and statistics	1,592	706	27	34	92	2	731	1,116	523	17	25	49	2	500	476	183	10	9	43	0	231
Mechanics and repair technologies/technicians	0	0	0	0	0	0	0	0	0	0	0	0	0	0	0	0	0	0	0	0	0
Military technologies and applied sciences	0	0	0	0	0	0	0	0	0	0	0	0	0	0	0	0	0	0	0	0	0
Multi/interdisciplinary studies	631	393	48	25	31	6	128	265	159	14	13	10	3	66	366	234	34	12	21	3	62
Parks, recreation, leisure, and fitness studies	266	178	16	6	12	2	52	140	89	8	4	3	1	35	126	89	8	2	9	1	17
Philosophy and religious studies	667	481	33	24	31	1	97	450	333	19	15	18	1	64	217	148	14	9	13	0	33
Physical sciences and science technologies	5,063	2,481	102	126	256	15	2,083	3,404	1,679	57	67	157	11	1,433	1,659	802	45	59	99	4	650
Precision production	0	0	0	0	0	0	0	0	0	0	0	0	0	0	0	0	0	0	0	0	0
Psychology	5,540	4,116	376	321	326	31	370	1,478	1,152	60	75	63	11	117	4,062	2,964	316	246	263	20	253
Public administration and social services	838	454	110	36	51	4	183	323	170	31	12	15	2	93	515	284	79	24	36	2	90
Social sciences and history	4,238	2,406	196	194	204	32	1,206	2,292	1,295	79	106	84	17	711	1,946	1,111	117	88	120	15	495
Social sciences	3,350	1,762	144	146	173	20	1,105	1,805	931	56	77	71	11	659	1,545	831	88	69	102	9	446
History	888	644	52	48	31	12	101	487	364	23	29	13	6	52	401	280	29	19	18	6	49
Theology and religious vocations	2,070	1,293	246	43	148	14	326	1,525	948	139	25	124	11	278	545	345	107	18	24	3	48
Transportation and materials moving	0	0	0	0	0	0	0	0	0	0	0	0	0	0	0	0	0	0	0	0	0
Visual and performing arts	1,599	1,019	41	61	124	9	345	700	514	16	32	33	4	101	899	505	25	29	91	5	244
Other and not classified	0	0	0	0	0	0	0	0	0	0	0	0	0	0	0	0	0	0	0	0	0

[1]Excludes "Construction trades" and "Mechanic and repair technologies/technicians," which are listed separately.

NOTE: Degree-granting institutions grant associate's or higher degrees and participate in Title IV federal financial aid programs. Race categories exclude persons of Hispanic ethnicity. Reported racial/ethnic distributions of students by level of degree, field of degree, and sex were used to estimate race/ethnicity for students whose race/ethnicity was not reported. To facilitate trend comparisons, certain aggregations have been made of the degree fields as reported in the IPEDS Fall survey: "Agriculture and natural resources" includes Agriculture, agriculture operations, and related sciences and Natural resources and conservation; and "Business" includes Business management, marketing, and related support services and Personal and culinary services. Includes Ph.D., Ed.D., and comparable degrees at the doctoral level, as well as such degrees as M.D., D.D.S., and law degrees that were formerly classified as first-professional degrees.

SOURCE: U.S. Department of Education, National Center for Education Statistics, Integrated Postsecondary Education Data System (IPEDS), Fall 2010, Completions component. (This table was prepared November 2011.)

Degrees conferred by degree-granting institutions in selected professional fields, by sex, race/ethnicity, and field of study: 2009–10

Field of study	Total							Males							Females						
	Total	White	Black	Hispanic	Asian/ Pacific Islander	American Indian/ Alaska Native	Non-resident alien	Total	White	Black	Hispanic	Asian/ Pacific Islander	American Indian/ Alaska Native	Non-resident alien	Total	White	Black	Hispanic	Asian/ Pacific Islander	American Indian/ Alaska Native	Non-resident alien
1	2	3	4	5	6	7	8	9	10	11	12	13	14	15	16	17	18	19	20	21	22
All fields, total	94,103	66,172	6,850	5,430	12,691	665	2,295	47,538	35,187	2,595	2,625	5,646	322	1,163	46,565	30,985	4,255	2,805	7,045	343	1,132
Dentistry (D.D.S. or D.M.D.)	5,062	3,037	278	296	1,013	39	399	2,745	1,850	115	139	452	19	170	2,317	1,187	163	157	561	20	229
Medicine (M.D.)	16,356	10,570	1,174	852	3,421	121	218	8,468	5,719	414	435	1,726	63	111	7,888	4,851	760	417	1,695	58	107
Optometry (O.D.)	1,335	789	48	41	358	5	94	457	336	9	5	67	1	39	878	453	39	36	291	4	55
Osteopathic medicine (D.O.)	3,890	2,918	115	133	687	17	20	1,979	1,538	36	82	304	7	12	1,911	1,380	79	51	383	10	8
Pharmacy (Pharm.D.)	11,873	7,485	788	521	2,736	57	286	4,297	2,816	271	180	920	21	89	7,576	4,669	517	341	1,816	36	197
Podiatry (Pod.D. or D.P.) or podiatric medicine (D.P.M.)	491	343	43	26	58	9	12	276	207	12	14	29	7	12	215	136	31	12	29	2	5
Veterinary medicine (D.V.M.)	2,478	2,187	67	95	107	15	7	555	493	12	18	27	3	2	1,923	1,694	55	77	80	12	5
Chiropractic medicine (D.C. or D.C.M.)	2,601	2,116	125	107	175	11	67	1,610	1,331	53	72	110	6	38	991	785	72	35	65	5	29
Law (LL.B. or J.D.)	44,345	33,015	3,206	3,182	3,754	368	820	23,394	18,362	1,211	1,550	1,701	179	391	20,951	14,653	1,995	1,632	2,053	189	429
Theology (M.Div, M.H.L., B.D., or Ord.)	5,672	3,712	1,006	177	382	23	372	3,757	2,535	462	130	310	16	304	1,915	1,177	544	47	72	7	68

NOTE: Degree-granting institutions grant associate's or higher degrees and participate in Title IV federal financial aid programs. Includes degrees that require at least 6 years of college work for completion (including at least 2 years of preprofessional training). Race categories exclude persons of Hispanic ethnicity. Reported racial/ethnic distributions of students by level of degree, field of degree, and sex were used to estimate race/ethnicity for students whose race/ethnicity was not reported.

SOURCE: U.S. Department of Education, National Center for Education Statistics, Integrated Postsecondary Education Data System (IPEDS), Fall 2010, Completions component. (This table was prepared November 2011.)

Historical summary of faculty, enrollment, degrees, and finances in degree-granting institutions: Selected years, 1869–70 through 2009–10

Selected characteristic	1869–70	1879–80	1889–90	1899–1900	1909–10	1919–20	1929–30	1939–40	1949–50	1959–60	1969–70	1979–80	1989–90	1999–2000	2005–06	2008–09	2009–10
1	2	3	4	5	6	7	8	9	10	11	12	13	14	15	16	17	18
Total institutions[1]	563	811	998	977	951	1,041	1,409	1,708	1,851	2,004	2,525	3,152	3,535	4,084	4,276	4,409	4,495
Total faculty[2]	5,553[3]	11,522[3]	15,809	23,868	36,480	48,615	82,386	146,929	246,722	380,554	450,000[4]	675,000[4]	824,220[5]	1,027,830[5]	1,290,426[5]	—	1,439,144[5]
Males	4,887[3]	7,328[3]	12,704[3]	19,151	29,132	35,807	60,017	106,328	186,189	296,773	346,000[4]	479,000[4]	534,254[5]	602,469[5]	714,453[5]	—	761,035[5]
Females	666[3]	4,194[3]	3,105[3]	4,717	7,348	12,808	22,369	40,601	60,533	83,781	104,000[4]	196,000[4]	289,966[5]	425,361[5]	575,973[5]	—	678,109[5]
Total fall enrollment[6]	52,286	115,817	156,756	237,592	355,213	597,880	1,100,737	1,494,203	2,444,900	3,639,847	8,004,660	11,569,899	13,538,560	14,849,691	17,487,475	19,102,814	20,427,711
Males	41,160[3]	77,972[3]	100,453[3]	152,254	214,648[3]	314,938	619,935	893,250	1,721,572	2,332,617	4,746,201	5,682,877	6,190,015	6,515,164	7,455,925	8,188,895	8,769,504
Females	11,126[3]	37,845[3]	56,303[3]	85,338	140,565[3]	282,942	480,802	600,953	723,328	1,307,230	3,258,459	5,887,022	7,348,545	8,334,527	10,031,550	10,913,919	11,658,207
Degrees conferred																	
Associate's, total	—	—	—	—	—	—	—	—	—	—	206,023	400,910	455,102	564,933	713,066	787,325	849,452
Males	—	—	—	—	—	—	—	—	—	—	117,432	183,737	191,195	224,721	270,095	298,141	322,916
Females	—	—	—	—	—	—	—	—	—	—	88,591	217,173	263,907	340,212	442,971	489,184	526,536
Bachelor's, total[7]	9,371	12,896	15,539	27,410	37,199	48,622	122,484	186,500	432,058	392,440	792,316	929,417	1,051,344	1,237,875	1,485,242	1,601,368	1,650,014
Males	7,993	10,411	12,857	22,173	28,762	31,980	73,615	109,546	328,841	254,063	451,097	473,611	491,696	530,367	630,600	685,382	706,633
Females	1,378	2,485	2,682	5,237	8,437	16,642	48,869	76,954	103,217	138,377	341,219	455,806	559,648	707,508	854,642	915,986	943,381
Master's, total[8]	0	879	1,015	1,583	2,113	4,279	14,969	26,731	58,183	74,435	213,589	305,196	330,152	463,185	599,731	662,079	693,025
Males	0	868	821	1,280	1,555	2,985	8,925	16,508	41,220	50,898	130,799	156,882	158,052	196,129	241,656	263,538	275,197
Females	0	11	194	303	558	1,294	6,044	10,223	16,963	23,537	82,790	148,314	172,100	267,056	358,075	398,541	417,828
Doctor's, total[9]	1	54	149	382	443	615	2,299	3,290	6,420	9,829	59,486	95,631	103,508	118,736	138,056	154,425	158,558
Males	1	51	147	359	399	522	1,946	2,861	5,804	8,801	53,792	69,526	63,963	64,930	68,912	75,639	76,605
Females	0	3	2	23	44	93	353	429	616	1,028	5,694	26,105	39,545	53,806	69,144	78,786	81,953
Finances (In thousands of current dollars)																	
Current-fund revenue	—	—	—	—	$76,883	$199,922	$554,511	$715,211	$2,374,645	$5,785,537	$21,515,242	$58,519,982	$139,635,477	—	—	—	—
Educational and general income	—	—	$21,464	$35,084	67,917	172,929	483,065	571,288	1,833,845	4,688,352	16,486,177	—	—	—	—	—	—
Current-fund expenditures	—	—	—	—	—	—	507,142	674,688	2,245,661	5,601,376	21,043,113	56,913,588	134,655,571	—	—	—	—
Educational and general expenditures	—	—	95,426	253,599	457,594	747,333	377,903	521,990[10]	1,706,444	4,685,258	16,845,212	44,542,843	105,585,076	—	—	—	—
Value of physical property	—	—	—	—	—	—	2,066,049	2,753,780[10]	4,799,964	13,548,548	42,093,580	83,733,387	164,635,000	—	—	—	—
Market value of endowment funds	—	—	78,788[11]	194,998[11]	323,661[11]	569,071[11]	1,372,068[11]	1,686,283[11]	2,601,223[11]	5,322,080[11]	11,206,632	20,743,045	67,978,726	—	—	—	—

—Not available.

[1] Prior to 1979–80, excludes branch campuses.
[2] Total number of different individuals (not reduced to full-time equivalent). Beginning in 1959–60, data are for the first term of the academic year.
[3] Estimated.
[4] Estimated number of senior instructional staff based on actual enrollment data for the designated year and enrollment/staff ratios for the prior staff survey. Excludes graduate assistants.
[5] Because of revised survey procedures, data may not be directly comparable with figures prior to 1989–90. Estimated number of senior instructional staff based on actual enrollment data for the designated year and enrollment/staff ratios for the prior staff survey. Excludes graduate assistants.
[6] Data for 1869–70 to 1939–40 are for resident degree-credit students who enrolled at any time during the academic year.
[7] From 1869–70 to 1959–60, bachelor's degrees include degrees formerly classified as first-professional, such as M.D., D.D.S., and law degrees.
[8] Figures for years prior to 1969–70 are not precisely comparable with later data.
[9] Includes Ph.D., Ed.D, and comparable degrees at the doctoral level. Includes most degrees formerly classified as first-professional, such as M.D, D.D.S., and law degrees.
[10] Includes unexpended plant funds.
[11] Book value. Includes other nonexpendable funds.

NOTE: Data through 1989–90 are for institutions of higher education, while later data are for degree-granting institutions. Degree-granting institutions grant associate's or higher degrees and participate in Title IV federal financial aid programs. The degree-granting classification is very similar to the earlier higher education classification, but it includes more 2-year colleges and excludes a few higher education institutions that did not grant degrees. (See Appendix A: Guide to Sources for details.) Detail may not sum to totals because of rounding.

SOURCE: U.S. Department of Education, National Center for Education Statistics, Biennial Survey of Education in the United States; Education Directory, Colleges and Universities; Faculty and Other Professional Staff in Institutions of Higher Education; Fall Enrollment in Colleges and Universities; Earned Degrees Conferred; Financial Statistics of Institutions of Higher Education; Higher Education General Information Survey (HEGIS), "Fall Enrollment in Institutions of Higher Education," "Degrees and Other Formal Awards Conferred," and "Financial Statistics of Institutions of Higher Education" surveys; Integrated Postsecondary Education Data System (IPEDS), "Fall Enrollment Survey" (IPEDS-EF-89-99), "Fall Staff Survey" (IPEDS-S-89-99), "Finance Survey" (IPEDS-F:FY90-00), "Completions Survey" (IPEDS-C-90-00), and "Institutional Characteristics Survey" (IPEDS-IC-89-99); IPEDS Winter 2005–06 and Winter 2009–10, Human Resources component, Fall Staff section; IPEDS Spring 2006, Spring 2009, and Spring 2010, Enrollment component; and IPEDS Fall 2006, Fall 2009, and Fall 2010, Completions component. (This table was prepared November 2011.)

Total fall enrollment in degree-granting institutions, by attendance status, sex of student, and control of institution: Selected years, 1947 through 2010

Year	Total enrollment	Attendance status			Sex of student			Control of institution			
		Full-time	Part-time	Percent part-time	Male	Female	Percent female	Public	Private		
									Total	Not-for-profit	For-profit
1	2	3	4	5	6	7	8	9	10	11	12
1947[1]	2,338,226	—	—	—	1,659,249	678,977	29.0	1,152,377	1,185,849	—	—
1948[1]	2,403,396	—	—	—	1,709,367	694,029	28.9	1,185,588	1,217,808	—	—
1949[1]	2,444,900	—	—	—	1,721,572	723,328	29.6	1,207,151	1,237,749	—	—
1950[1]	2,281,298	—	—	—	1,560,392	720,906	31.6	1,139,699	1,141,599	—	—
1951[1]	2,101,962	—	—	—	1,390,740	711,222	33.8	1,037,938	1,064,024	—	—
1952[1]	2,134,242	—	—	—	1,380,357	753,885	35.3	1,101,240	1,033,002	—	—
1953[1]	2,231,054	—	—	—	1,422,598	808,456	36.2	1,185,876	1,045,178	—	—
1954[1]	2,446,693	—	—	—	1,563,382	883,311	36.1	1,353,531	1,093,162	—	—
1955[1]	2,653,034	—	—	—	1,733,184	919,850	34.7	1,476,282	1,176,752	—	—
1956[1]	2,918,212	—	—	—	1,911,458	1,006,754	34.5	1,656,402	1,261,810	—	—
1957	3,323,783	—	—	—	2,170,765	1,153,018	34.7	1,972,673	1,351,110	—	—
1959	3,639,847	2,421,016	1,218,831 [2]	33.5	2,332,617	1,307,230	35.9	2,180,982	1,458,865	—	—
1961	4,145,065	2,785,133	1,359,932 [2]	32.8	2,585,821	1,559,244	37.6	2,561,447	1,583,618	—	—
1963	4,779,609	3,183,833	1,595,776 [2]	33.4	2,961,540	1,818,069	38.0	3,081,279	1,698,330	—	—
1964	5,280,020	3,573,238	1,706,782 [2]	32.3	3,248,713	2,031,307	38.5	3,467,708	1,812,312	—	—
1965	5,920,864	4,095,728	1,825,136 [2]	30.8	3,630,020	2,290,844	38.7	3,969,596	1,951,268	—	—
1966	6,389,872	4,438,606	1,951,266 [2]	30.5	3,856,216	2,533,656	39.7	4,348,917	2,040,955	—	—
1967	6,911,748	4,793,128	2,118,620 [2]	30.7	4,132,800	2,778,948	40.2	4,816,028	2,095,720	2,074,041	21,679
1968	7,513,091	5,210,155	2,302,936	30.7	4,477,649	3,035,442	40.4	5,430,652	2,082,439	2,061,211	21,228
1969	8,004,660	5,498,883	2,505,777	31.3	4,746,201	3,258,459	40.7	5,896,868	2,107,792	2,087,653	20,139
1970	8,580,887	5,816,290	2,764,597	32.2	5,043,642	3,537,245	41.2	6,428,134	2,152,753	2,134,420	18,333
1971	8,948,644	6,077,232	2,871,412	32.1	5,207,004	3,741,640	41.8	6,804,309	2,144,335	2,121,913	22,422
1972	9,214,860	6,072,389	3,142,471	34.1	5,238,757	3,976,103	43.1	7,070,635	2,144,225	2,123,245	20,980
1973	9,602,123	6,189,493	3,412,630	35.5	5,371,052	4,231,071	44.1	7,419,516	2,182,607	2,148,784	33,823
1974	10,223,729	6,370,273	3,853,456	37.7	5,622,429	4,601,300	45.0	7,988,500	2,235,229	2,200,963	34,266
1975	11,184,859	6,841,334	4,343,525	38.8	6,148,997	5,035,862	45.0	8,834,508	2,350,351	2,311,448	38,903
1976	11,012,137	6,717,058	4,295,079	39.0	5,810,828	5,201,309	47.2	8,653,477	2,358,660	2,314,298	44,362
1977	11,285,787	6,792,925	4,492,862	39.8	5,789,016	5,496,771	48.7	8,846,993	2,438,794	2,386,652	52,142
1978	11,260,092	6,667,657	4,592,435	40.8	5,640,998	5,619,094	49.9	8,785,893	2,474,199	2,408,331	65,868
1979	11,569,899	6,794,039	4,775,860	41.3	5,682,877	5,887,022	50.9	9,036,822	2,533,077	2,461,773	71,304
1980	12,096,895	7,097,958	4,998,937	41.3	5,874,374	6,222,521	51.4	9,457,394	2,639,501	2,527,787	111,714 [3]
1981	12,371,672	7,181,250	5,190,422	42.0	5,975,056	6,396,616	51.7	9,647,032	2,724,640	2,572,405	152,235 [3]
1982	12,425,780	7,220,618	5,205,162	41.9	6,031,384	6,394,396	51.5	9,696,087	2,729,693	2,552,739	176,954 [3]
1983	12,464,661	7,261,050	5,203,611	41.7	6,023,725	6,440,936	51.7	9,682,734	2,781,927	2,589,187	192,740
1984	12,241,940	7,098,388	5,143,552	42.0	5,863,574	6,378,366	52.1	9,477,370	2,764,570	2,574,419	190,151
1985	12,247,055	7,075,221	5,171,834	42.2	5,818,450	6,428,605	52.5	9,479,273	2,767,782	2,571,791	195,991
1986	12,503,511	7,119,550	5,383,961	43.1	5,884,515	6,618,996	52.9	9,713,893	2,789,618	2,572,479	217,139 [4]
1987	12,766,642	7,231,085	5,535,557	43.4	5,932,056	6,834,586	53.5	9,973,254	2,793,388	2,602,350	191,038 [4]
1988	13,055,337	7,436,768	5,618,569	43.0	6,001,896	7,053,441	54.0	10,161,388	2,893,949	2,673,567	220,382
1989	13,538,560	7,660,950	5,877,610	43.4	6,190,015	7,348,545	54.3	10,577,963	2,960,597	2,731,174	229,423
1990	13,818,637	7,820,985	5,997,652	43.4	6,283,909	7,534,728	54.5	10,844,717	2,973,920	2,760,227	213,693
1991	14,358,953	8,115,329	6,243,624	43.5	6,501,844	7,857,109	54.7	11,309,563	3,049,390	2,819,041	230,349
1992	14,487,359	8,162,118	6,325,241	43.7	6,523,989	7,963,370	55.0	11,384,567	3,102,792	2,872,523	230,269
1993	14,304,803	8,127,618	6,177,185	43.2	6,427,450	7,877,353	55.1	11,189,088	3,115,715	2,888,897	226,818
1994	14,278,790	8,137,776	6,141,014	43.0	6,371,898	7,906,892	55.4	11,133,680	3,145,110	2,910,107	235,003
1995	14,261,781	8,128,802	6,132,979	43.0	6,342,539	7,919,242	55.5	11,092,374	3,169,407	2,929,044	240,363
1996	14,367,520	8,302,953	6,064,567	42.2	6,352,825	8,014,695	55.8	11,120,499	3,247,021	2,942,556	304,465
1997	14,502,334	8,438,062	6,064,272	41.8	6,396,028	8,106,306	55.9	11,196,119	3,306,215	2,977,614	328,601
1998	14,506,967	8,563,338	5,943,629	41.0	6,369,265	8,137,702	56.1	11,137,769	3,369,198	3,004,925	364,273
1999	14,849,691	8,803,139	6,046,552	40.7	6,515,164	8,334,527	56.1	11,375,739	3,473,952	3,055,029	418,923
2000	15,312,289	9,009,600	6,302,689	41.2	6,721,769	8,590,520	56.1	11,752,786	3,559,503	3,109,419	450,084
2001	15,927,987	9,447,502	6,480,485	40.7	6,960,815	8,967,172	56.3	12,233,156	3,694,831	3,167,330	527,501
2002	16,611,711	9,946,359	6,665,352	40.1	7,202,116	9,409,595	56.6	12,751,993	3,859,718	3,265,476	594,242
2003	16,911,481	10,326,133	6,585,348	38.9	7,260,264	9,651,217	57.1	12,858,698	4,052,783	3,341,048	711,735
2004	17,272,044	10,610,177	6,661,867	38.6	7,387,262	9,884,782	57.2	12,980,112	4,291,932	3,411,685	880,247
2005	17,487,475	10,797,011	6,690,464	38.3	7,455,925	10,031,550	57.4	13,021,834	4,465,641	3,454,692	1,010,949
2006	17,758,870	10,957,305	6,801,565	38.3	7,574,815	10,184,055	57.3	13,180,133	4,578,737	3,512,866	1,065,871
2007	18,248,128	11,269,892	6,978,236	38.2	7,815,914	10,432,214	57.2	13,490,780	4,757,348	3,571,150	1,186,198
2008	19,102,814	11,747,743	7,355,071	38.5	8,188,895	10,913,919	57.1	13,972,153	5,130,661	3,661,519	1,469,142
2009	20,427,711	12,722,782	7,704,929	37.7	8,769,504	11,658,207	57.1	14,810,642	5,617,069	3,765,083	1,851,986
2010	21,016,126	13,082,267	7,933,859	37.8	9,044,811	11,971,315	57.0	15,142,809	5,873,317	3,854,920	2,018,397

—Not available.

[1] Degree-credit enrollment only.

[2] Includes part-time resident students and all extension students (students attending courses at sites separate from the primary reporting campus). In later years, part-time student enrollment was collected as a distinct category.

[3] Large increases are due to the addition of schools accredited by the Accrediting Commission of Career Schools and Colleges of Technology.

[4] Because of imputation techniques, data are not consistent with figures for other years.

NOTE: Data through 1995 are for institutions of higher education, while later data are for degree-granting institutions. Degree-granting institutions grant associate's or higher degrees and participate in Title IV federal financial aid programs. The degree-granting classification is very similar to the earlier higher education classification, but it includes more 2-year colleges and excludes a few higher education institutions that did not grant degrees. (See Appendix A: Guide to Sources for details.) Some data have been revised from previously published figures. SOURCE: U.S. Department of Education, National Center for Education Statistics, *Biennial Survey of Education in the United States*; *Opening Fall Enrollment in Higher Education*, 1963 through 1965; Higher Education General Information Survey (HEGIS), "Fall Enrollment in Colleges and Universities" surveys, 1966 through 1985; and Integrated Postsecondary Education Data System (IPEDS), "Fall Enrollment Survey" (IPEDS-EF:86-99); and IPEDS Spring 2001 through Spring 2011, Enrollment component. (This table was prepared September 2011.)

Total fall enrollment in degree-granting institutions, by control and level of institution: 1963 through 2010

Year	All institutions					Public institutions					Private institutions				
	Total	4-year			2-year	Total	4-year			2-year	Total	4-year			2-year
		Total	University	Other 4-year			Total	University	Other 4-year			Total	University	Other 4-year	
1	2	3	4	5	6	7	8	9	10	11	12	13	14	15	16
1963[1]	4,779,609	3,929,248	—	—	850,361	3,081,279	2,341,468	—	—	739,811	1,698,330	1,587,780	—	—	110,550
1964[1]	5,280,020	4,291,094	—	—	988,926	3,467,708	2,592,929	—	—	874,779	1,812,312	1,698,165	—	—	114,147
1965[1]	5,920,864	4,747,912	—	—	1,172,952	3,969,596	2,928,332	—	—	1,041,264	1,951,268	1,819,580	—	—	131,688
1966[1]	6,389,872	5,063,902	—	—	1,325,970	4,348,917	3,159,748	—	—	1,189,169	2,040,955	1,904,154	—	—	136,801
1967	6,911,748	5,398,986	2,186,235	3,212,751	1,512,762	4,816,028	3,443,975	1,510,333	1,933,642	1,372,053	2,095,720	1,955,011	675,902	1,279,109	140,709
1968	7,513,091	5,720,269	2,266,120	3,454,149	1,792,822	5,430,652	3,783,652	1,592,707	2,190,945	1,647,000	2,082,439	1,936,617	673,413	1,263,204	145,822
1969	8,004,660	5,937,127	2,420,429	3,516,698	2,067,533	5,896,868	3,962,522	1,738,493	2,224,029	1,934,346	2,107,792	1,974,605	681,936	1,292,669	133,187
1970	8,580,887	6,261,502	2,534,336	3,727,166	2,319,385	6,428,134	4,232,722	1,832,694	2,400,028	2,195,412	2,152,753	2,028,780	701,642	1,327,138	123,973
1971	8,948,644	6,369,355	2,594,470	3,774,885	2,579,289	6,804,309	4,346,990	1,913,626	2,433,364	2,457,319	2,144,335	2,022,365	680,844	1,341,521	121,970
1972	9,214,860	6,458,674	2,620,749	3,837,925	2,756,186	7,070,635	4,429,696	1,941,040	2,488,656	2,640,939	2,144,225	2,028,978	679,709	1,349,269	115,247
1973	9,602,123	6,590,023	2,629,796	3,960,227	3,012,100	7,419,516	4,529,895	1,950,653	2,579,242	2,889,621	2,182,607	2,060,128	679,143	1,380,985	122,479
1974	10,223,729	6,819,735	2,702,306	4,117,429	3,403,994	7,988,500	4,703,018	2,006,723	2,696,295	3,285,482	2,235,229	2,116,717	695,583	1,421,134	118,512
1975	11,184,859	7,214,740	2,838,266	4,376,474	3,970,119	8,834,508	4,998,142	2,124,221	2,873,921	3,836,366	2,350,351	2,216,598	714,045	1,502,553	133,753
1976	11,012,137	7,128,816	2,780,289	4,348,527	3,883,321	8,653,477	4,901,691	2,079,929	2,821,762	3,751,786	2,358,660	2,227,125	700,360	1,526,765	131,535
1977	11,285,787	7,242,845	2,793,418	4,449,427	4,042,942	8,846,993	4,945,224	2,070,032	2,875,192	3,901,769	2,438,794	2,297,621	723,386	1,574,235	141,173
1978	11,260,092	7,231,625	2,780,729	4,451,222	4,028,467	8,785,893	4,912,203	2,062,295	2,849,908	3,873,690	2,474,199	2,319,422	718,434	1,601,314	154,777
1979	11,569,899	7,353,233	2,839,582	4,513,651	4,216,666	9,036,822	4,980,012	2,099,525	2,880,487	4,056,810	2,533,077	2,373,221	740,057	1,633,164	159,856
1980	12,096,895	7,570,608	2,902,014	4,668,594	4,526,287	9,457,394	5,128,612	2,154,283	2,974,329	4,328,782	2,639,501	2,441,996	747,731	1,694,265	197,505 [2]
1981	12,371,672	7,655,461	2,901,344	4,754,117	4,716,211	9,647,032	5,166,324	2,152,474	3,013,850	4,480,708	2,724,640	2,489,137	748,870	1,740,267	235,503 [2]
1982	12,425,780	7,654,074	2,883,735	4,770,339	4,771,706	9,696,087	5,176,434	2,152,547	3,023,887	4,519,653	2,729,693	2,477,640	731,188	1,746,452	252,053 [2]
1983	12,464,661	7,741,195	2,888,813	4,852,382	4,723,466	9,682,734	5,223,404	2,154,790	3,068,614	4,459,330	2,781,927	2,517,791	734,023	1,783,768	264,136
1984	12,241,940	7,711,167	2,870,329	4,840,838	4,530,773	9,477,370	5,198,273	2,138,621	3,059,652	4,279,097	2,764,570	2,512,894	731,708	1,781,186	251,676
1985	12,247,055	7,715,978	2,870,692	4,845,286	4,531,077	9,479,273	5,209,540	2,141,112	3,068,428	4,269,733	2,767,782	2,506,438	729,580	1,776,858	261,344
1986	12,503,511	7,823,963	2,897,207	4,926,756	4,679,548	9,713,893	5,300,202	2,160,646	3,139,556	4,413,691	2,789,618	2,523,761	736,561	1,787,200	265,857 [3]
1987	12,766,642	7,990,420	2,929,327	5,061,093	4,776,222	9,973,254	5,432,200	2,188,008	3,244,192	4,541,054	2,793,388	2,558,220	741,319	1,816,901	235,168 [3]
1988	13,055,337	8,180,182	2,978,593	5,201,589	4,875,155	10,161,388	5,545,901	2,229,868	3,316,033	4,615,487	2,893,949	2,634,281	748,725	1,885,556	259,668
1989	13,538,560	8,387,671	3,019,115	5,368,556	5,150,889	10,577,963	5,694,303	2,266,056	3,428,247	4,883,660	2,960,597	2,693,368	753,059	1,940,309	267,229
1990	13,818,637	8,578,554	3,044,670	5,533,884	5,240,083	10,844,717	5,848,242	2,290,464	3,557,778	4,996,475	2,973,920	2,730,312	754,206	1,976,106	243,608
1991	14,358,953	8,707,053	3,065,429	5,641,624	5,651,900	11,309,563	5,904,748	2,301,222	3,603,526	5,404,815	3,049,390	2,802,305	764,207	2,038,098	247,085
1992	14,487,359	8,764,969	3,050,345	5,714,624	5,722,390	11,384,567	5,900,012	2,283,834	3,616,178	5,484,555	3,102,792	2,864,957	766,511	2,098,446	237,835
1993	14,304,803	8,738,936	3,022,728	5,716,208	5,565,867	11,189,088	5,851,760	2,259,692	3,592,068	5,337,328	3,115,715	2,887,176	763,036	2,124,140	228,539
1994	14,278,790	8,749,080	3,009,072	5,740,008	5,529,710	11,133,680	5,825,213	2,244,636	3,580,577	5,308,467	3,145,110	2,923,867	764,436	2,159,431	221,243
1995	14,261,781	8,769,252	2,999,641	5,769,611	5,492,529	11,092,374	5,814,545	2,235,939	3,578,606	5,277,829	3,169,407	2,954,707	763,702	2,191,005	214,700
1996	14,367,520	8,804,193	2,984,965	5,819,228	5,563,327	11,120,499	5,806,036	2,226,529	3,579,507	5,314,463	3,247,021	2,998,157	758,436	2,239,721	248,864
1997	14,502,334	8,896,765	2,995,886	5,900,879	5,605,569	11,196,119	5,835,433	2,231,273	3,604,160	5,360,686	3,306,215	3,061,332	764,613	2,296,719	244,883
1998	14,506,967	9,017,653	3,021,136	5,996,517	5,489,314	11,137,769	5,891,806	2,249,825	3,641,981	5,245,963	3,369,198	3,125,847	771,311	2,354,536	243,351
1999	14,849,691	9,196,160	3,044,369	6,151,791	5,653,531	11,375,739	5,977,678	2,266,494	3,711,184	5,398,061	3,473,952	3,218,482	777,875	2,440,607	255,470
2000	15,312,289	9,363,858	3,061,812	6,302,046	5,948,431	11,752,786	6,055,398	2,280,122	3,775,276	5,697,388	3,559,503	3,308,460	781,690	2,526,770	251,043
2001	15,927,987	9,677,408	3,126,907	6,550,501	6,250,579	12,233,156	6,236,455	2,336,922	3,899,533	5,996,701	3,694,831	3,440,953	789,985	2,650,968	253,878
2002	16,611,711	10,082,332	3,210,271	6,872,061	6,529,379	12,751,993	6,481,613	2,403,149	4,078,464	6,270,380	3,859,718	3,600,719	807,122	2,793,597	258,999
2003	16,911,481	10,417,247	3,242,639	7,174,608	6,494,234	12,858,698	6,649,441	2,419,631	4,229,810	6,209,257	4,052,783	3,767,806	823,008	2,944,798	284,977
2004	17,272,044	10,726,181	3,258,982	7,467,199	6,545,863	12,980,112	6,736,536	2,426,495	4,310,041	6,243,576	4,291,932	3,989,645	832,487	3,157,158	302,287
2005	17,487,475	10,999,420	3,271,620	7,727,800	6,488,055	13,021,834	6,837,605	2,443,682	4,393,923	6,184,229	4,465,641	4,161,815	827,938	3,333,877	303,826
2006	17,758,870	11,240,330	3,306,973	7,933,357	6,518,540	13,180,133	6,955,013	2,459,874	4,495,139	6,225,120	4,578,737	4,285,317	847,099	3,438,218	293,420
2007	18,248,128	11,630,198	3,349,214	8,280,984	6,617,930	13,490,780	7,166,661	2,490,615	4,676,046	6,324,119	4,757,348	4,463,537	858,599	3,604,938	293,811
2008	19,102,814	12,131,436	3,412,435	8,719,001	6,971,378	13,972,153	7,331,809	2,544,529	4,787,280	6,640,344	5,130,661	4,799,627	867,906	3,931,721	331,034
2009	20,427,711	12,906,305	3,493,246	9,413,059	7,521,406	14,810,642	7,709,197	2,603,381	5,105,816	7,101,445	5,617,069	5,197,108	889,865	4,307,243	419,961
2010	21,016,126	13,335,251	3,558,175	9,777,076	7,680,875	15,142,809	7,924,771	2,649,378	5,275,393	7,218,038	5,873,317	5,410,480	908,797	4,501,683	462,837

—Not available.

[1] Data for 2-year branch campuses of 4-year institutions are included with the 4-year institutions.

[2] Large increases are due to the addition of schools accredited by the Accrediting Commission of Career Schools and Colleges of Technology.

[3] Because of imputation techniques, data are not consistent with figures for other years.

NOTE: Data through 1995 are for institutions of higher education, while later data are for degree-granting institutions. Degree-granting institutions grant associate's or higher degrees and participate in Title IV federal financial aid programs. The degree-granting classification is very similar to the earlier higher education classification, but it includes more 2-year colleges and excludes a few higher education institutions that did not grant degrees. (See Appendix A: Guide to Sources for details.) A university is an institution of higher education consisting of a liberal arts college, a diverse graduate program, and usually two or more professional school or faculties and empowered to confer degrees in various fields of study; for purposes of maintaining trend data in this publication, the selection of university institutions has not been revised since 1982. Some data have been revised from previously published figures.

SOURCE: U.S. Department of Education, National Center for Education Statistics, Opening Fall Enrollment in Higher Education, 1965; Higher Education General Information Survey (HEGIS), "Fall Enrollment in Institutions of Higher Education" surveys, 1966 through 1985; Integrated Postsecondary Education Data System (IPEDS), "Fall Enrollment Survey" (IPEDS-EF:86-99); and IPEDS Spring 2001 through Spring 2011, Enrollment component. (This table was prepared September 2011.)

Total fall enrollment in degree-granting institutions, by attendance status, sex, and age: Selected years, 1970 through 2020

[In thousands]

Attendance status, sex, and age	1970	1980	1990	2000	2002	2003	2004	2005	2006	2007	2008	2009	2010	Projected 2011	Projected 2015	Projected 2020
1	2	3	4	5	6	7	8	9	10	11	12	13	14	15	16	17
All students	8,581	12,097	13,819	15,312	16,612	16,911	17,272	17,487	17,759	18,248	19,103	20,428	21,016	21,575	22,612	24,075
14 to 17 years old	263	257	153	131	152	169	166	187	184	200	195	217	211	204	211	237
18 and 19 years old	2,579	2,852	2,777	3,258	3,363	3,355	3,367	3,444	3,561	3,690	3,813	4,041	4,119	4,295	4,282	4,648
20 and 21 years old	1,885	2,395	2,593	3,005	3,331	3,391	3,516	3,563	3,573	3,570	3,649	3,945	4,052	4,308	4,278	4,399
22 to 24 years old	1,469	1,947	2,202	2,600	2,988	3,086	3,166	3,114	3,185	3,280	3,443	3,594	3,674	3,771	4,083	4,093
25 to 29 years old	1,091	1,843	2,083	2,044	2,196	2,311	2,418	2,469	2,506	2,651	2,840	3,096	3,196	3,203	3,510	3,770
30 to 34 years old	527	1,227	1,384	1,333	1,438	1,418	1,440	1,438	1,472	1,519	1,609	1,741	1,823	1,876	2,083	2,296
35 years old and over	767	1,577	2,627	2,942	3,144	3,181	3,199	3,272	3,277	3,339	3,554	3,794	3,941	3,919	4,165	4,643
Males	5,044	5,874	6,284	6,722	7,202	7,260	7,387	7,456	7,575	7,816	8,189	8,770	9,045	9,243	9,465	9,842
14 to 17 years old	125	106	66	58	62	67	62	68	69	88	93	103	92	97	97	107
18 and 19 years old	1,355	1,368	1,298	1,464	1,507	1,474	1,475	1,523	1,604	1,669	1,704	1,806	1,842	1,887	1,861	2,002
20 and 21 years old	1,064	1,219	1,259	1,411	1,514	1,541	1,608	1,658	1,628	1,634	1,695	1,876	1,931	2,014	1,974	2,006
22 to 24 years old	1,004	1,075	1,129	1,222	1,394	1,411	1,437	1,410	1,445	1,480	1,555	1,606	1,666	1,724	1,831	1,798
25 to 29 years old	796	983	1,024	908	962	1,007	1,039	1,057	1,040	1,148	1,222	1,382	1,414	1,414	1,502	1,571
30 to 34 years old	333	564	605	581	617	602	619	591	628	638	691	709	745	764	822	876
35 years old and over	366	559	902	1,077	1,146	1,158	1,147	1,149	1,160	1,159	1,228	1,287	1,354	1,343	1,377	1,484
Females	3,537	6,223	7,535	8,591	9,410	9,651	9,885	10,032	10,184	10,432	10,914	11,658	11,971	12,332	13,147	14,233
14 to 17 years old	137	151	87	73	90	102	104	119	115	112	102	114	119	107	113	130
18 and 19 years old	1,224	1,484	1,479	1,794	1,856	1,880	1,892	1,920	1,956	2,021	2,109	2,236	2,276	2,408	2,421	2,647
20 and 21 years old	821	1,177	1,334	1,593	1,816	1,851	1,908	1,905	1,945	1,936	1,954	2,069	2,120	2,294	2,304	2,394
22 to 24 years old	464	871	1,073	1,378	1,595	1,675	1,729	1,704	1,740	1,800	1,888	1,987	2,008	2,047	2,251	2,285
25 to 29 years old	296	859	1,059	1,136	1,234	1,304	1,379	1,413	1,466	1,502	1,618	1,713	1,783	1,789	2,008	2,199
30 to 34 years old	194	663	779	752	821	816	821	847	844	881	918	1,032	1,078	1,112	1,261	1,420
35 years old and over	401	1,018	1,725	1,865	1,998	2,023	2,052	2,123	2,117	2,180	2,326	2,507	2,587	2,575	2,788	3,159
Full-time	5,816	7,098	7,821	9,010	9,946	10,326	10,610	10,797	10,957	11,270	11,748	12,723	13,082	13,361	13,881	14,697
14 to 17 years old	246	231	134	121	131	146	138	152	148	169	168	181	171	167	174	196
18 and 19 years old	2,374	2,544	2,471	2,823	2,904	2,934	2,960	3,026	3,120	3,244	3,359	3,513	3,543	3,667	3,663	3,984
20 and 21 years old	1,649	2,007	2,137	2,452	2,752	2,841	2,926	2,976	2,972	2,985	3,043	3,271	3,319	3,470	3,454	3,560
22 to 24 years old	904	1,181	1,405	1,714	1,975	2,083	2,143	2,122	2,127	2,205	2,347	2,535	2,596	2,584	2,797	2,803
25 to 29 years old	426	641	791	886	1,011	1,086	1,132	1,174	1,225	1,299	1,369	1,520	1,584	1,588	1,745	1,879
30 to 34 years old	113	272	383	418	494	489	517	547	571	556	571	663	749	771	860	949
35 years old and over	104	221	500	596	680	747	795	800	794	812	890	1,041	1,121	1,115	1,188	1,326
Males	3,504	3,689	3,808	4,111	4,501	4,638	4,739	4,803	4,879	5,029	5,234	5,671	5,837	5,932	6,071	6,341
14 to 17 years old	121	95	55	51	52	58	49	53	52	74	73	78	63	72	74	81
18 and 19 years old	1,261	1,219	1,171	1,252	1,304	1,291	1,297	1,339	1,404	1,465	1,516	1,580	1,594	1,626	1,610	1,739
20 and 21 years old	955	1,046	1,035	1,156	1,261	1,305	1,360	1,398	1,372	1,366	1,407	1,547	1,583	1,594	1,571	1,605
22 to 24 years old	686	717	768	834	958	995	1,001	982	992	1,043	1,105	1,177	1,200	1,237	1,320	1,307
25 to 29 years old	346	391	433	410	466	503	498	506	533	578	597	665	708	708	760	805
30 to 34 years old	77	142	171	186	215	209	231	225	235	231	249	281	307	314	342	370
35 years old and over	58	80	174	222	244	277	302	300	291	273	287	343	383	379	394	433
Females	2,312	3,409	4,013	4,899	5,445	5,688	5,871	5,994	6,078	6,240	6,513	7,052	7,245	7,429	7,810	8,356
14 to 17 years old	125	136	78	70	79	88	89	98	95	95	95	103	108	94	100	115
18 and 19 years old	1,113	1,325	1,300	1,571	1,599	1,643	1,662	1,687	1,716	1,779	1,843	1,933	1,949	2,040	2,053	2,244
20 and 21 years old	693	961	1,101	1,296	1,491	1,536	1,566	1,578	1,601	1,619	1,636	1,724	1,736	1,875	1,884	1,955
22 to 24 years old	218	464	638	880	1,017	1,088	1,142	1,140	1,135	1,163	1,242	1,358	1,396	1,346	1,477	1,496
25 to 29 years old	80	250	358	476	545	583	634	668	692	721	772	855	875	880	985	1,074
30 to 34 years old	37	130	212	232	279	280	286	322	336	324	322	382	442	457	517	579
35 years old and over	46	141	326	374	435	471	493	500	503	539	603	697	738	735	794	893
Part-time	2,765	4,999	5,998	6,303	6,665	6,585	6,662	6,690	6,802	6,978	7,355	7,705	7,934	8,214	8,731	9,378
14 to 17 years old	16	26	19	10	21	23	28	36	36	31	27	36	41	37	37	41
18 and 19 years old	205	308	306	435	460	421	407	417	440	446	453	528	576	629	619	665
20 and 21 years old	236	388	456	553	579	551	590	586	601	585	606	674	733	838	824	839
22 to 24 years old	564	765	796	886	1,013	1,003	1,023	992	1,058	1,074	1,096	1,059	1,078	1,187	1,285	1,280
25 to 29 years old	665	1,202	1,291	1,158	1,185	1,224	1,286	1,296	1,282	1,352	1,471	1,576	1,613	1,615	1,765	1,891
30 to 34 years old	414	954	1,001	915	944	929	923	891	901	963	1,037	1,078	1,074	1,104	1,224	1,347
35 years old and over	663	1,356	2,127	2,345	2,464	2,434	2,404	2,472	2,483	2,527	2,664	2,753	2,820	2,804	2,976	3,316
Males	1,540	2,185	2,476	2,611	2,701	2,622	2,648	2,653	2,696	2,786	2,955	3,099	3,208	3,311	3,394	3,501
14 to 17 years old	4	12	11	7	10	9	13	15	17	14	20	25	29	24	24	26
18 and 19 years old	94	149	127	212	203	183	178	184	200	204	188	226	249	261	251	262
20 and 21 years old	108	172	224	255	253	236	248	260	257	269	289	329	349	420	404	401
22 to 24 years old	318	359	361	388	436	416	436	428	452	438	450	430	467	486	511	491
25 to 29 years old	450	592	591	498	496	504	540	551	507	570	625	717	706	706	742	766
30 to 34 years old	257	422	435	395	402	392	388	365	393	406	442	428	438	450	480	506
35 years old and over	309	479	728	855	901	882	845	850	869	886	941	944	971	964	982	1,051
Females	1,225	2,814	3,521	3,692	3,964	3,963	4,014	4,038	4,106	4,192	4,401	4,606	4,726	4,903	5,337	5,877
14 to 17 years old	12	14	9	3	11	14	15	21	20	17	7	11	11	13	13	15
18 and 19 years old	112	159	179	223	256	238	230	233	240	242	265	303	327	368	368	403
20 and 21 years old	128	216	233	298	326	315	342	327	344	317	318	345	384	418	420	439
22 to 24 years old	246	407	435	497	578	587	588	564	605	637	646	629	611	701	774	789
25 to 29 years old	216	609	700	660	689	721	746	745	774	781	846	858	907	909	1,023	1,125
30 to 34 years old	158	532	567	520	542	537	535	526	508	557	595	651	636	655	744	841
35 years old and over	354	876	1,399	1,491	1,563	1,552	1,560	1,623	1,614	1,640	1,723	1,810	1,850	1,840	1,994	2,266

NOTE: Distributions by age are estimates based on samples of the civilian noninstitutional population from the U.S. Census Bureau's Current Population Survey. Data through 1995 are for institutions of higher education, while later data are for degree-granting institutions. Degree-granting institutions grant associate's or higher degrees and participate in Title IV federal financial aid programs. The degree-granting classification is very similar to the earlier higher education classification, but it includes more 2-year colleges and excludes a few higher education institutions that did not grant degrees. (See Appendix A: Guide to Sources for details.) Some data have been revised from previously published figures. Detail may not sum to totals because of rounding.

SOURCE: U.S. Department of Education, National Center for Education Statistics, Higher Education General Information Survey (HEGIS), "Fall Enrollment in Colleges and Universities" surveys, 1970 and 1980; Integrated Postsecondary Education Data System (IPEDS), "Fall Enrollment Survey" (IPEDS-EF:90-99); IPEDS Spring 2001 through Spring 2011, Enrollment component; and *Projections of Education Statistics to 2020*. U.S. Department of Commerce, Census Bureau, Current Population Survey (CPS), October, selected years, 1970 through 2010. (This table was prepared September 2011.)

Recent high school completers and their enrollment in 2-year and 4-year colleges, by sex: 1960 through 2010

[Numbers in thousands]

Year	Number of high school completers[1]			Enrolled in college[2]					
	Total	Males	Females	Total		Males		Females	
				Number	Percent	Number	Percent	Number	Percent
1	2	3	4	5	6	7	8	9	10
1960	1,679 (43.8)	756 (31.8)	923 (29.6)	758 (40.9)	45.1 (2.13)	408 (29.5)	54.0 (3.18)	350 (28.2)	37.9 (2.80)
1961	1,763 (46.0)	790 (33.2)	973 (31.3)	847 (42.9)	48.0 (2.09)	445 (30.8)	56.3 (3.10)	402 (29.9)	41.3 (2.77)
1962	1,838 (43.6)	872 (31.5)	966 (30.0)	900 (43.2)	49.0 (2.05)	480 (31.1)	55.0 (2.96)	420 (30.0)	43.5 (2.80)
1963	1,741 (44.2)	794 (32.1)	947 (30.0)	784 (41.5)	45.0 (2.09)	415 (29.8)	52.3 (3.11)	369 (28.8)	39.0 (2.78)
1964	2,145 (43.0)	997 (31.9)	1,148 (28.5)	1,037 (45.6)	48.3 (1.89)	570 (32.9)	57.2 (2.75)	467 (31.4)	40.7 (2.54)
1965	2,659 (47.7)	1,254 (35.1)	1,405 (32.0)	1,354 (51.4)	50.9 (1.70)	718 (36.7)	57.3 (2.45)	636 (35.8)	45.3 (2.33)
1966	2,612 (45.0)	1,207 (33.8)	1,405 (29.0)	1,309 (50.2)	50.1 (1.72)	709 (36.0)	58.7 (2.49)	600 (34.8)	42.7 (2.32)
1967	2,525 (37.9)	1,142 (28.4)	1,383 (24.3)	1,311 (40.9)	51.9 (1.42)	658 (28.9)	57.6 (2.09)	653 (28.9)	47.2 (1.92)
1968	2,606 (37.3)	1,184 (28.2)	1,422 (23.8)	1,444 (41.7)	55.4 (1.39)	748 (29.6)	63.2 (2.00)	696 (29.3)	48.9 (1.89)
1969	2,842 (36.0)	1,352 (26.8)	1,490 (23.7)	1,516 (42.5)	53.3 (1.34)	812 (30.3)	60.1 (1.90)	704 (29.7)	47.2 (1.85)
1970	2,758 (37.4)	1,343 (26.1)	1,415 (26.8)	1,427 (42.2)	51.7 (1.36)	741 (29.7)	55.2 (1.94)	686 (29.8)	48.5 (1.90)
1971	2,875 (37.8)	1,371 (26.6)	1,504 (27.1)	1,538 (43.2)	53.5 (1.33)	790 (30.3)	57.6 (1.90)	749 (30.8)	49.8 (1.84)
1972	2,964 (37.8)	1,423 (27.0)	1,542 (26.4)	1,459 (43.1)	49.2 (1.31)	750 (30.4)	52.7 (1.89)	709 (30.5)	46.0 (1.81)
1973	3,058 (37.1)	1,460 (27.6)	1,599 (24.6)	1,424 (43.0)	46.6 (1.29)	730 (30.6)	50.0 (1.87)	694 (30.2)	43.4 (1.77)
1974	3,101 (38.6)	1,491 (27.8)	1,611 (26.8)	1,475 (43.7)	47.6 (1.28)	736 (30.8)	49.4 (1.85)	740 (31.1)	45.9 (1.77)
1975	3,185 (38.6)	1,513 (27.3)	1,672 (27.2)	1,615 (44.8)	50.7 (1.26)	796 (31.2)	52.6 (1.83)	818 (32.1)	49.0 (1.75)
1976	2,986 (39.8)	1,451 (28.9)	1,535 (27.3)	1,458 (43.6)	48.8 (1.31)	685 (30.4)	47.2 (1.87)	773 (31.2)	50.3 (1.82)
1977	3,141 (40.7)	1,483 (29.7)	1,659 (27.7)	1,590 (45.4)	50.6 (1.29)	773 (31.8)	52.1 (1.87)	817 (32.4)	49.3 (1.77)
1978	3,163 (39.7)	1,485 (29.3)	1,677 (26.7)	1,585 (45.2)	50.1 (1.28)	759 (31.6)	51.1 (1.87)	827 (32.4)	49.3 (1.76)
1979	3,160 (40.0)	1,475 (29.2)	1,685 (27.2)	1,559 (45.1)	49.3 (1.28)	744 (31.4)	50.4 (1.88)	815 (32.4)	48.4 (1.76)
1980	3,088 (39.4)	1,498 (28.4)	1,589 (27.3)	1,523 (44.6)	49.3 (1.30)	700 (30.9)	46.7 (1.86)	823 (32.0)	51.8 (1.81)
1981	3,056 (42.2)	1,491 (30.4)	1,565 (29.1)	1,648 (45.8)	53.9 (1.30)	817 (32.4)	54.8 (1.86)	831 (32.4)	53.1 (1.82)
1982	3,100 (40.4)	1,509 (29.0)	1,592 (28.2)	1,569 (46.9)	50.6 (1.36)	741 (32.7)	49.1 (1.95)	828 (33.6)	52.0 (1.90)
1983	2,963 (41.6)	1,389 (30.4)	1,573 (28.2)	1,562 (46.7)	52.7 (1.39)	721 (32.3)	51.9 (2.03)	841 (33.6)	53.4 (1.91)
1984	3,012 (36.5)	1,429 (28.7)	1,584 (21.9)	1,663 (46.0)	55.2 (1.37)	801 (32.7)	56.0 (1.99)	862 (32.3)	54.5 (1.90)
1985	2,668 (40.1)	1,287 (28.7)	1,381 (27.9)	1,540 (45.1)	57.7 (1.45)	755 (31.6)	58.6 (2.08)	785 (32.1)	56.8 (2.02)
1986	2,786 (38.6)	1,332 (28.5)	1,454 (26.0)	1,498 (45.0)	53.8 (1.43)	743 (31.7)	55.8 (2.06)	755 (31.9)	51.9 (1.99)
1987	2,647 (40.9)	1,278 (29.8)	1,369 (28.0)	1,503 (45.1)	56.8 (1.46)	746 (31.9)	58.3 (2.09)	757 (31.9)	55.3 (2.04)
1988	2,673 (47.0)	1,334 (34.1)	1,339 (32.3)	1,575 (50.3)	58.9 (1.57)	761 (35.6)	57.1 (2.24)	814 (35.4)	60.7 (2.20)
1989	2,450 (46.5)	1,204 (32.9)	1,246 (32.8)	1,460 (48.7)	59.6 (1.64)	693 (34.0)	57.6 (2.35)	767 (34.8)	61.6 (2.27)
1990	2,362 (43.0)	1,173 (30.6)	1,189 (30.2)	1,420 (45.9)	60.1 (1.60)	680 (32.2)	58.0 (2.29)	740 (32.6)	62.2 (2.24)
1991	2,276 (41.0)	1,140 (29.0)	1,136 (29.0)	1,423 (44.8)	62.5 (1.62)	660 (31.4)	57.9 (2.33)	763 (31.9)	67.1 (2.22)
1992	2,397 (40.4)	1,216 (29.1)	1,180 (28.1)	1,483 (45.4)	61.9 (1.58)	729 (32.3)	60.0 (2.24)	754 (31.8)	63.8 (2.23)
1993	2,342 (41.4)	1,120 (30.6)	1,223 (27.7)	1,467 (45.4)	62.6 (1.59)	670 (31.9)	59.9 (2.33)	797 (32.1)	65.2 (2.17)
1994	2,517 (38.1)	1,244 (27.9)	1,273 (25.9)	1,559 (43.0)	61.9 (1.43)	754 (30.6)	60.6 (2.05)	805 (30.2)	63.2 (1.99)
1995	2,599 (40.9)	1,238 (29.9)	1,361 (27.7)	1,610 (44.5)	61.9 (1.41)	775 (31.3)	62.6 (2.03)	835 (31.5)	61.3 (1.95)
1996	2,660 (40.5)	1,297 (29.5)	1,363 (27.7)	1,729 (46.1)	65.0 (1.42)	779 (32.4)	60.1 (2.09)	950 (32.5)	69.7 (1.92)
1997	2,769 (41.8)	1,354 (31.0)	1,415 (27.9)	1,856 (47.3)	67.0 (1.38)	860 (33.6)	63.6 (2.01)	995 (32.9)	70.3 (1.87)
1998	2,810 (43.9)	1,452 (31.0)	1,358 (31.0)	1,844 (48.3)	65.6 (1.38)	906 (34.4)	62.4 (1.96)	938 (33.9)	69.1 (1.93)
1999	2,897 (41.5)	1,474 (29.9)	1,423 (28.8)	1,822 (47.8)	62.9 (1.38)	905 (34.1)	61.4 (1.95)	917 (33.4)	64.4 (1.95)
2000	2,756 (45.3)	1,251 (33.6)	1,505 (29.7)	1,745 (48.4)	63.3 (1.41)	749 (33.4)	59.9 (2.13)	996 (34.4)	66.2 (1.88)
2001	2,549 (46.5)	1,277 (33.7)	1,273 (32.0)	1,574 (47.5)	61.8 (1.48)	767 (33.7)	60.1 (2.11)	808 (33.3)	63.5 (2.08)
2002	2,796 (42.7)	1,412 (31.3)	1,384 (29.0)	1,824 (46.1)	65.2 (1.31)	877 (33.0)	62.1 (1.88)	947 (32.1)	68.4 (1.82)
2003	2,677 (42.2)	1,306 (29.9)	1,372 (29.7)	1,711 (45.2)	63.9 (1.35)	799 (31.5)	61.2 (1.97)	913 (32.3)	66.5 (1.86)
2004	2,752 (40.0)	1,327 (29.1)	1,425 (27.3)	1,835 (44.9)	66.7 (1.31)	815 (31.5)	61.4 (1.95)	1,020 (31.6)	71.5 (1.74)
2005	2,675 (40.8)	1,262 (31.5)	1,414 (24.9)	1,834 (44.8)	68.6 (1.31)	839 (32.2)	66.5 (1.94)	995 (30.6)	70.4 (1.77)
2006	2,692 (44.6)	1,328 (32.7)	1,363 (30.1)	1,776 (46.4)	66.0 (1.33)	875 (33.2)	65.8 (1.90)	901 (32.4)	66.1 (1.87)
2007	2,955 (42.6)	1,511 (30.0)	1,444 (30.3)	1,986 (47.0)	67.2 (1.26)	999 (33.4)	66.1 (1.78)	986 (33.1)	68.3 (1.79)
2008	3,151 (42.8)	1,640 (29.6)	1,511 (30.9)	2,161 (48.0)	68.6 (1.21)	1,080 (34.1)	65.9 (1.71)	1,081 (33.8)	71.6 (1.69)
2009	2,937 (45.0)	1,407 (32.8)	1,531 (30.6)	2,058 (48.0)	70.1 (1.23)	928 (33.8)	66.0 (1.84)	1,130 (33.8)	73.8 (1.64)
2010[3]	3,160 (91.8)	1,679 (64.6)	1,482 (58.4)	2,152 (78.8)	68.1 (1.49)	1,055 (50.5)	62.8 (1.88)	1,097 (55.2)	74.0 (2.31)

[1]Individuals ages 16 to 24 who graduated from high school or completed a GED during the preceding 12 months.
[2]Enrollment in college as of October of each year for individuals ages 16 to 24 who completed high school during the preceding 12 months.
[3]Beginning in 2010, standard errors were computed using replicate weights, which produced more precise values than the methodology used in prior years. For more information, see Appendix A: Guide to Sources.

NOTE: Data are based on sample surveys of the civilian population. High school completion data in this table differ from figures appearing in other tables because of varying survey procedures and coverage. High school completers include GED recipients. Standard errors appear in parentheses. Detail may not sum to totals because of rounding.
SOURCE: American College Testing Program, unpublished tabulations, derived from statistics collected by the Census Bureau, 1960 through 1969. U.S. Department of Commerce, Census Bureau, Current Population Survey (CPS), October, 1970 through 2010. (This table was prepared July 2011.)

Recent high school completers and their enrollment in 2-year and 4-year colleges, by race/ethnicity: 1960 through 2010
[Numbers in thousands]

Year	Number of high school completers[1]				Enrolled in college[2]									
					Total		White		Black[3]			Hispanic[3]		
	Total	White	Black[3]	Hispanic[3]	Number	Percent	Number	Percent	Number	Annual	3-year moving average[4]	Number	Annual	3-year moving average[4]
1	2	3	4	5	6	7	8	9	10	11	12	13	14	15
1960	1,679 (43.8)	1,565 (44.7)	— (†)	— (†)	758 (40.9)	45.1 (2.13)	717 (40.2)	45.8 (2.21)	— (†)	— (†)	— (†)	— (†)	— (†)	— (†)
1961	1,763 (46.0)	1,612 (46.9)	— (†)	— (†)	847 (42.9)	48.0 (2.09)	798 (42.2)	49.5 (2.19)	— (†)	— (†)	— (†)	— (†)	— (†)	— (†)
1962	1,838 (43.6)	1,660 (45.2)	— (†)	— (†)	900 (43.2)	49.0 (2.05)	840 (42.4)	50.6 (2.15)	— (†)	— (†)	— (†)	— (†)	— (†)	— (†)
1963	1,741 (44.2)	1,615 (45.2)	— (†)	— (†)	784 (41.5)	45.0 (2.09)	736 (40.7)	45.6 (2.17)	— (†)	— (†)	— (†)	— (†)	— (†)	— (†)
1964	2,145 (43.0)	1,964 (45.4)	— (†)	— (†)	1,037 (45.6)	48.3 (1.89)	967 (44.8)	49.2 (1.98)	— (†)	— (†)	— (†)	— (†)	— (†)	— (†)
1965	2,659 (47.7)	2,417 (50.6)	— (†)	— (†)	1,354 (51.4)	50.9 (1.70)	1,249 (50.4)	51.7 (1.78)	— (†)	— (†)	— (†)	— (†)	— (†)	— (†)
1966	2,612 (45.0)	2,403 (48.0)	— (†)	— (†)	1,309 (50.2)	50.1 (1.72)	1,243 (49.6)	51.7 (1.79)	— (†)	— (†)	— (†)	— (†)	— (†)	— (†)
1967	2,525 (37.9)	2,267 (40.3)	— (†)	— (†)	1,311 (40.9)	51.9 (1.42)	1,202 (40.1)	53.0 (1.50)	— (†)	— (†)	— (†)	— (†)	— (†)	— (†)
1968	2,606 (37.3)	2,303 (40.4)	— (†)	— (†)	1,444 (41.7)	55.4 (1.39)	1,304 (40.9)	56.6 (1.47)	— (†)	— (†)	— (†)	— (†)	— (†)	— (†)
1969	2,842 (36.0)	2,538 (39.8)	— (†)	— (†)	1,516 (42.5)	53.3 (1.34)	1,402 (42.0)	55.2 (1.41)	— (†)	— (†)	— (†)	— (†)	— (†)	— (†)
1970	2,758 (37.4)	2,461 (40.7)	— (†)	— (†)	1,427 (42.2)	51.7 (1.36)	1,280 (41.2)	52.0 (1.44)	— (†)	— (†)	— (†)	— (†)	— (†)	— (†)
1971	2,875 (38.0)	2,596 (41.1)	— (†)	— (†)	1,538 (43.2)	53.5 (1.33)	1,402 (42.5)	54.0 (1.40)	— (†)	— (†)	— (†)	— (†)	— (†)	— (†)
1972	2,964 (37.8)	2,520 (31.2)	316 (18.3)	101 (14.2)	1,459 (43.1)	49.2 (1.31)	1,252 (39.0)	49.7 (1.42)	141 (16.7)	44.6 (4.62)	38.4 (3.18)	46 (11.7)	45.0 (9.74)	(6.64)
1973	3,058 (37.1)	2,590 (30.8)	324 (18.5)	119 (13.7)	1,424 (43.0)	46.6 (1.29)	1,238 (39.2)	47.8 (1.40)	105 (15.2)	32.5 (4.30)	41.4 (2.62)	64 (13.0)	54.1 (9.01)	48.8 (5.33)
1974	3,101 (38.6)	2,620 (31.4)	325 (19.0)	121 (15.2)	1,475 (43.7)	47.6 (1.28)	1,236 (39.4)	47.2 (1.39)	154 (17.4)	47.2 (4.58)	40.5 (2.63)	57 (12.9)	46.9 (8.94)	53.1 (5.09)
1975	3,185 (38.6)	2,701 (31.9)	302 (15.4)	132 (15.8)	1,615 (44.8)	50.7 (1.26)	1,381 (40.5)	51.1 (1.37)	126 (13.6)	41.7 (3.97)	44.5 (2.29)	77 (14.5)	58.0 (8.44)	52.7 (4.88)
1976	2,986 (39.8)	2,492 (33.1)	290 (15.8)	152 (16.2)	1,458 (43.6)	48.8 (1.31)	1,217 (39.1)	48.8 (1.43)	129 (13.8)	44.4 (4.08)	45.3 (2.30)	80 (14.8)	52.7 (7.97)	53.6 (4.68)
1977	3,141 (40.7)	2,618 (34.0)	325 (19.3)	155 (16.0)	1,590 (45.4)	50.6 (1.29)	1,331 (40.8)	50.8 (1.41)	161 (17.9)	49.5 (4.65)	46.8 (2.70)	79 (14.8)	50.8 (7.96)	48.8 (4.72)
1978	3,163 (39.7)	2,615 (33.7)	345 (18.4)	135 (15.3)	1,585 (45.2)	50.1 (1.28)	1,321 (40.6)	50.5 (1.41)	160 (17.7)	46.4 (4.51)	47.5 (2.67)	56 (13.0)	42.0 (8.44)	46.1 (4.69)
1979	3,160 (40.0)	2,629 (32.7)	319 (19.7)	155 (16.1)	1,559 (45.1)	49.3 (1.28)	1,313 (40.5)	49.9 (1.41)	149 (17.5)	46.7 (4.69)	45.2 (2.62)	70 (14.3)	45.0 (7.92)	46.3 (4.83)
1980	3,088 (39.4)	2,554 (30.9)	350 (19.7)	130 (17.1)	1,523 (44.6)	49.3 (1.30)	1,273 (39.6)	49.8 (1.43)	149 (17.7)	42.7 (4.44)	44.0 (2.61)	68 (14.4)	52.3 (8.70)	49.6 (4.78)
1981	3,056 (42.2)	2,490 (34.1)	349 (20.5)	146 (17.6)	1,648 (45.8)	53.9 (1.30)	1,367 (40.5)	54.9 (1.44)	149 (17.8)	42.7 (4.44)	40.3 (2.50)	76 (15.1)	52.1 (8.19)	48.7 (4.68)
1982	3,100 (40.4)	2,474 (32.9)	382 (19.6)	173 (18.2)	1,569 (46.9)	50.6 (1.36)	1,303 (41.5)	52.7 (1.52)	137 (17.9)	35.8 (4.33)	38.8 (2.57)	75 (15.8)	43.2 (7.96)	49.4 (4.94)
1983	2,963 (41.6)	2,363 (33.1)	390 (21.1)	138 (17.8)	1,562 (46.7)	52.7 (1.39)	1,301 (40.9)	55.0 (1.55)	149 (18.7)	38.2 (4.34)	38.0 (2.47)	75 (15.7)	54.2 (8.96)	46.7 (4.72)
1984	3,012 (36.5)	2,331 (29.1)	433 (18.5)	187 (17.0)	1,663 (46.0)	55.2 (1.37)	1,375 (39.9)	59.0 (1.54)	172 (19.4)	39.8 (4.15)	39.9 (2.54)	83 (16.2)	44.3 (7.67)	49.3 (4.89)
1985	2,668 (40.1)	2,104 (32.3)	332 (19.3)	141 (19.7)	1,540 (45.1)	57.7 (1.45)	1,264 (39.2)	60.1 (1.62)	140 (17.8)	42.2 (4.78)	42.2 (2.55)	72 (17.0)	51.0 (9.76)	46.1 (5.18)
1986	2,786 (38.6)	2,146 (30.3)	378 (18.4)	169 (21.7)	1,498 (45.0)	53.8 (1.43)	1,219 (38.8)	56.8 (1.62)	140 (17.9)	36.9 (4.38)	43.5 (2.71)	74 (17.7)	44.0 (8.85)	42.3 (5.20)
1987	2,647 (40.9)	2,040 (32.4)	333 (20.6)	176 (20.9)	1,503 (45.1)	56.8 (1.46)	1,195 (38.7)	58.6 (1.65)	174 (19.3)	52.2 (4.82)	44.2 (2.65)	59 (16.1)	33.5 (8.25)	45.0 (5.04)
1988	2,673 (47.0)	2,013 (37.9)	378 (22.3)	179 (26.6)	1,575 (50.3)	58.9 (1.57)	1,230 (42.9)	61.1 (1.79)	168 (21.1)	44.4 (4.91)	49.7 (2.98)	102 (23.6)	57.1 (10.14)	48.5 (5.99)
1989	2,450 (46.5)	1,889 (37.3)	332 (21.3)	168 (26.5)	1,460 (48.7)	59.6 (1.64)	1,147 (41.7)	60.7 (1.85)	177 (20.9)	53.4 (5.27)	48.0 (2.98)	93 (22.9)	55.1 (10.51)	52.7 (6.33)
1990	2,362 (43.0)	1,819 (32.2)	331 (21.9)	121 (21.8)	1,420 (45.9)	60.1 (1.60)	1,147 (38.5)	63.0 (1.80)	155 (19.7)	46.8 (5.08)	48.9 (2.97)	52 (16.0)	42.7 (10.82)	52.5 (5.70)
1991	2,276 (41.0)	1,727 (30.3)	310 (20.2)	154 (23.5)	1,423 (44.8)	62.5 (1.62)	1,129 (37.2)	65.4 (1.82)	144 (18.8)	46.4 (5.25)	47.2 (2.93)	88 (19.9)	57.2 (9.58)	52.6 (5.52)
1992	2,397 (40.4)	1,724 (30.9)	354 (21.4)	198 (23.0)	1,483 (45.4)	61.9 (1.58)	1,109 (37.4)	64.3 (1.84)	171 (20.2)	48.2 (4.92)	50.0 (2.98)	109 (21.0)	55.0 (8.50)	58.2 (5.04)
1993	2,342 (41.4)	1,719 (32.6)	304 (20.4)	201 (23.1)	1,467 (45.4)	62.6 (1.59)	1,082 (37.9)	62.9 (1.85)	169 (19.6)	55.6 (5.28)	51.3 (2.97)	125 (21.9)	62.2 (8.22)	55.7 (4.97)
1994	2,517 (38.1)	1,915 (27.0)	316 (17.9)	178 (17.3)	1,559 (43.0)	61.9 (1.43)	1,236 (35.5)	64.5 (1.61)	161 (16.7)	50.8 (4.42)	52.4 (2.52)	87 (14.0)	49.1 (6.28)	55.0 (3.23)

See notes at end of table.

Recent high school completers and their enrollment in 2-year and 4-year colleges, by race/ethnicity: 1960 through 2010—Continued

[Numbers in thousands]

Year	Number of high school completers[1]				Enrolled in college[2]									
					Total		White		Black[3]			Hispanic[3] Percent		
	Total	White	Black[3]	Hispanic[3]	Number	Percent	Number	Percent	Number	Annual	3-year moving average[4]	Number	Annual	3-year moving average[4]
1	2	3	4	5	6	7	8	9	10	11	12	13	14	15
1995	2,599 (40.9)	1,861 (30.1)	349 (19.2)	288 (19.4)	1,610 (44.5)	61.9 (1.41)	1,197 (36.1)	64.3 (1.64)	179 (17.6)	51.2 (4.20)	52.9 (2.40)	155 (17.6)	53.7 (4.92)	51.6 (3.18)
1996	2,660 (40.5)	1,875 (30.8)	406 (17.3)	227 (18.9)	1,729 (46.1)	65.0 (1.42)	1,264 (37.5)	67.4 (1.67)	227 (19.0)	56.0 (4.03)	55.4 (2.41)	115 (16.3)	50.8 (5.79)	57.6 (2.96)
1997	2,769 (41.8)	1,909 (31.8)	384 (19.2)	336 (19.0)	1,856 (47.3)	67.0 (1.38)	1,301 (38.1)	68.2 (1.64)	225 (19.4)	58.5 (4.12)	58.8 (2.35)	220 (19.7)	65.6 (4.53)	55.3 (2.93)
1998	2,810 (43.9)	1,980 (33.0)	386 (20.2)	314 (20.8)	1,844 (48.3)	65.6 (1.38)	1,357 (39.0)	68.5 (1.61)	239 (20.0)	61.9 (4.05)	59.8 (2.31)	149 (18.3)	47.4 (4.92)	51.9 (2.79)
1999	2,897 (41.5)	1,978 (31.8)	436 (15.2)	329 (20.9)	1,822 (47.8)	62.9 (1.38)	1,311 (38.6)	66.3 (1.64)	257 (19.1)	58.9 (3.86)	58.6 (2.31)	139 (18.0)	42.3 (4.76)	47.4 (2.84)
2000	2,756 (45.3)	1,938 (32.9)	393 (20.0)	300 (22.4)	1,745 (48.4)	63.3 (1.41)	1,272 (38.8)	65.7 (1.66)	216 (19.5)	54.9 (4.11)	56.4 (2.33)	159 (19.2)	52.9 (5.03)	48.6 (2.96)
2001	2,549 (46.5)	1,834 (34.8)	381 (20.3)	241 (21.1)	1,574 (47.5)	61.8 (1.48)	1,178 (38.7)	64.3 (1.72)	210 (19.4)	55.0 (4.17)	56.4 (2.39)	124 (17.4)	51.7 (5.63)	52.8 (2.80)
2002	2,796 (42.7)	1,903 (31.3)	382 (19.1)	344 (21.6)	1,824 (46.1)	65.2 (1.31)	1,314 (36.5)	69.1 (1.55)	227 (18.7)	59.4 (3.90)	57.3 (2.33)	184 (19.2)	53.6 (4.46)	54.8 (2.77)
2003[5]	2,677 (42.2)	1,832 (30.8)	327 (18.4)	314 (20.9)	1,711 (45.2)	63.9 (1.35)	1,213 (35.9)	66.2 (1.61)	188 (17.4)	57.5 (4.25)	59.9 (2.29)	184 (18.9)	58.6 (4.61)	57.7 (2.68)
2004[5]	2,752 (40.0)	1,854 (30.9)	398 (15.5)	286 (19.9)	1,835 (44.9)	66.7 (1.31)	1,276 (36.1)	68.8 (1.57)	249 (17.9)	62.5 (3.77)	58.8 (2.34)	177 (18.4)	61.8 (4.76)	57.7 (2.60)
2005[5]	2,675 (40.8)	1,799 (30.5)	345 (16.6)	390 (20.6)	1,834 (44.8)	68.6 (1.31)	1,317 (35.4)	73.2 (1.52)	192 (17.1)	55.7 (4.15)	58.2 (2.35)	211 (19.7)	54.0 (4.18)	57.5 (2.52)
2006[5]	2,692 (44.6)	1,805 (33.2)	318 (19.0)	382 (22.1)	1,776 (46.4)	66.0 (1.33)	1,237 (36.7)	68.5 (1.60)	177 (17.3)	55.5 (4.33)	55.6 (2.35)	222 (20.5)	57.9 (4.18)	58.5 (2.43)
2007[5]	2,955 (42.6)	2,043 (29.9)	416 (17.6)	355 (22.3)	1,986 (47.0)	67.2 (1.26)	1,421 (36.8)	69.5 (1.49)	232 (18.5)	55.7 (3.78)	55.7 (2.27)	227 (20.7)	64.0 (4.22)	62.0 (2.33)
2008[5]	3,151 (42.8)	2,091 (31.3)	416 (19.7)	458 (21.9)	2,161 (48.0)	68.6 (1.21)	1,499 (37.5)	71.7 (1.44)	232 (19.2)	55.7 (3.78)	60.3 (2.15)	292 (22.0)	63.9 (3.72)	62.3 (2.25)
2009[5]	2,937 (45.0)	1,863 (31.6)	415 (19.1)	459 (24.4)	2,058 (48.0)	70.1 (1.23)	1,329 (36.3)	71.3 (1.53)	289 (19.7)	69.5 (3.51)	62.4 (2.09)	272 (22.6)	59.3 (3.80)	60.9 (2.14)
2010[5,6]	3,160 (91.8)	1,937 (68.7)	461 (36.9)	507 (37.3)	2,152 (78.8)	68.1 (1.49)	1,365 (56.9)	70.5 (1.68)	286 (33.4)	62.0 (4.81)	65.6 (2.49)	302 (31.5)	59.7 (4.18)	59.5 (2.62)

—Not available.

†Not applicable.

[1]Individuals ages 16 to 24 who graduated from high school or completed a GED during the preceding 12 months.

[2]Enrollment in college as of October of each year for individuals ages 16 to 24 who completed high school during the preceding 12 months.

[3]Due to the small sample size, data are subject to relatively large sampling errors.

[4]A 3-year moving average is an arithmetic average of the year immediately preceding, the year indicated, and the year immediately following. For 1972 and 2010, a 2-year moving average is used: The moving average for 1972 reflects an average of 1972 and 1973 and the moving average for 2010 reflects an average of 2009 and 2010. Moving averages are used to produce more stable estimates.

[5]White and Black data exclude persons identifying themselves as two or more races.

[6]Beginning in 2010, standard errors were computed using replicate weights, which produced more precise values than the methodology used in prior years. For more information, see Appendix A: Guide to Sources.

NOTE: High school completion data in this table differ from figures appearing in other tables because of varying survey procedures and coverage. High school completers include GED recipients. Race categories exclude persons of Hispanic ethnicity. Total includes persons of other racial/ethnic groups not separately shown. Standard errors appear in parentheses.

SOURCE: American College Testing Program, unpublished tabulations, derived from statistics collected by the Census Bureau, 1960 through 1969. U.S. Department of Commerce, Census Bureau, Current Population Survey (CPS), October, 1970 through 2010. (This table was prepared September 2011.)

Graduation rates of previous year's 12th-graders and college attendance rates of those who graduated, by selected high school characteristics: 1999–2000, 2003–04, and 2007–08

Selected high school characteristic	For 1998–99 school year		College attendance rate of 1998–99 graduates in 1999–2000			For 2002–03 school year		College attendance rate of 2002–03 graduates in 2003–04			For 2006–07 school year		College attendance rate of 2006–07 graduates in 2007–08 at 4-year institutions
	Number of high schools with 12th-graders	Graduation rate of 12th-graders[1]	Total	4-year institutions	2-year institutions	Number of high schools with 12th-graders	Graduation rate of 12th-graders[1]	Total	4-year institutions	2-year institutions	Number of high schools with 12th-graders	Graduation rate of 12th-graders[1]	
1	2	3	4	5	6	7	8	9	10	11	12	13	14
Public high schools	20,000 (230)	87.7 (0.67)	57.4 (0.50)	35.4 (0.43)	22.0 (0.34)	22,500 (400)	85.5 (0.77)	61.8 (0.94)	35.0 (0.61)	26.7 (0.58)	24,100 (540)	81.2 (1.34)	39.5 (0.91)
Percent of students who are Black, Hispanic, Asian, Pacific Islander, American Indian/Alaska Native, or two or more races													
Less than 5 percent	6,400 (170)	94.2 (0.79)	63.2 (0.73)	41.3 (0.67)	21.9 (0.59)	6,100 (220)	95.4 (0.41)	68.8 (0.87)	42.6 (0.96)	26.3 (0.64)	5,200 (270)	90.7 (1.23)	46.8 (1.54)
5 to 19 percent	4,800 (180)	89.1 (1.13)	58.7 (1.11)	36.6 (0.88)	22.1 (0.69)	5,200 (270)	87.8 (1.81)	63.9 (2.41)	38.0 (1.77)	26.0 (1.10)	5,400 (320)	89.9 (1.53)	48.4 (2.06)
20 to 49 percent	4,000 (170)	81.7 (2.02)	54.0 (1.16)	32.5 (0.92)	21.5 (0.70)	4,700 (180)	84.8 (1.68)	61.4 (1.44)	34.1 (1.27)	27.3 (0.94)	6,200 (440)	77.2 (2.85)	35.0 (1.89)
50 percent or more	4,800 (150)	82.5 (1.26)	51.1 (0.96)	28.7 (0.89)	22.3 (0.69)	6,500 (280)	74.8 (2.34)	53.2 (2.52)	25.8 (1.43)	27.4 (1.54)	7,300 (430)	71.4 (2.76)	30.8 (2.00)
Percent of students approved for free or reduced-price lunch													
School does not participate	2,400 (130)	80.1 (2.15)	49.7 (2.32)	30.0 (1.75)	19.7 (1.49)	2,400 (230)	71.2 (2.41)	51.4 (2.83)	23.2 (2.26)	28.1 (1.81)	2,800 (320)	66.7 (3.78)	25.4 (4.12)
0 to 25 percent	8,600 (180)	92.2 (0.55)	65.1 (0.74)	42.6 (0.67)	22.5 (0.44)	6,800 (230)	92.9 (0.59)	73.6 (0.59)	46.9 (0.78)	26.7 (0.65)	6,700 (360)	91.1 (1.24)	52.1 (1.63)
26 to 50 percent	4,800 (160)	87.3 (1.49)	57.5 (0.92)	33.4 (0.81)	24.1 (0.63)	6,700 (220)	89.4 (1.19)	64.2 (0.96)	36.7 (1.08)	27.5 (0.74)	7,300 (350)	86.7 (1.54)	41.5 (1.44)
51 to 75 percent	2,300 (140)	85.9 (2.81)	48.0 (2.18)	29.1 (1.57)	18.9 (0.92)	4,000 (270)	83.8 (2.25)	55.3 (2.76)	27.3 (1.58)	28.1 (1.58)	4,100 (290)	79.0 (3.56)	33.2 (1.91)
76 to 100 percent	2,000 (100)	79.4 (2.35)	43.0 (1.91)	22.2 (1.35)	20.7 (1.61)	2,600 (260)	72.0 (4.90)	42.3 (4.49)	20.7 (2.79)	21.6 (2.22)	3,300 (360)	63.7 (5.55)	26.0 (2.93)
School locale													
City	—	—	(†)	(†)	(†)	4,500 (240)	77.1 (1.80)	59.5 (2.00)	32.5 (1.61)	27.0 (1.28)	4,800 (300)	71.6 (2.81)	36.1 (2.73)
Suburb	—	—	(†)	(†)	(†)	4,800 (200)	83.6 (1.40)	67.4 (1.39)	40.3 (1.11)	27.1 (1.01)	5,400 (360)	80.8 (3.25)	41.2 (2.35)
Town	—	—	(†)	(†)	(†)	3,700 (200)	82.6 (3.24)	57.7 (1.94)	31.1 (1.65)	26.6 (0.97)	3,900 (310)	80.2 (2.61)	35.2 (2.28)
Rural	—	—	(†)	(†)	(†)	9,500 (390)	91.6 (0.97)	61.6 (1.92)	35.2 (1.28)	26.5 (0.99)	10,000 (460)	86.4 (1.70)	41.9 (1.47)
Private high schools	7,600 (240)	97.4 (0.55)	71.6 (1.90)	55.6 (1.74)	16.1 (1.00)	8,200 (260)	94.2 (0.86)	76.6 (1.58)	56.2 (1.77)	20.3 (1.30)	8,900 (280)	93.8 (0.91)	66.5 (1.57)
Percent of students who are Black, Hispanic, Asian, Pacific Islander, American Indian/Alaska Native, or two or more races													
Less than 5 percent	2,700 (150)	95.5 (1.53)	67.9 (3.17)	53.3 (2.85)	14.7 (1.61)	2,500 (180)	95.6 (1.59)	73.2 (3.03)	54.4 (3.31)	18.7 (2.14)	2,100 (160)	96.4 (1.19)	68.2 (3.81)
5 to 19 percent	2,500 (130)	99.1 (0.44)	82.3 (1.68)	63.6 (2.37)	18.7 (2.01)	2,900 (170)	95.2 (1.40)	84.7 (1.82)	64.2 (2.71)	20.5 (2.10)	3,500 (200)	95.6 (1.60)	70.3 (2.24)
20 to 49 percent	1,400 (100)	98.5 (0.59)	70.5 (3.90)	55.3 (3.29)	15.2 (2.24)	1,700 (140)	90.8 (2.36)	75.8 (4.16)	56.7 (3.70)	19.1 (2.52)	2,000 (190)	91.5 (2.13)	58.7 (3.39)
50 percent or more	1,000 (110)	97.0 (1.53)	55.9 (6.56)	41.6 (5.34)	14.3 (2.28)	1,100 (140)	93.6 (1.97)	63.7 (6.03)	38.3 (4.52)	25.4 (4.47)	1,400 (130)	88.6 (2.71)	65.3 (3.37)
Percent of students approved for free or reduced-price lunch													
School does not participate	6,700 (230)	97.9 (0.47)	73.8 (1.73)	57.0 (1.74)	16.8 (1.03)	7,100 (250)	95.3 (0.86)	76.7 (1.76)	56.2 (2.00)	20.5 (1.51)	7,300 (280)	95.7 (0.66)	68.3 (1.77)
0 to 25 percent	700 (70)	98.8 (0.74)	64.9 (6.49)	53.8 (5.69)	11.0 (1.40)	600 (80)	95.0 (3.62)	84.7 (4.28)	66.2 (4.35)	18.5 (2.39)	700 (100)	91.4 (7.18)	73.2 (4.64)
26 to 100 percent	‡	‡ (†)	‡	‡	‡	400 (80)	75.1 (7.62)	59.1 (8.13)	38.9 (6.70)	20.2 (4.34)	1,000 (130)	80.8 (4.70)	46.7 (6.86)
School locale													
City	—	—	(†)	(†)	(†)	—	(†)	(†)	(†)	(†)	(†)	(†)	(†)
Suburb	—	—	(†)	(†)	(†)	—	(†)	(†)	(†)	(†)	(†)	(†)	(†)
Town	—	—	(†)	(†)	(†)	—	(†)	(†)	(†)	(†)	(†)	(†)	(†)
Rural	—	—	(†)	(†)	(†)	—	(†)	(†)	(†)	(†)	(†)	(†)	(†)

—Not available.
†Not applicable.
‡Reporting standards not met. Either there are too few cases or the coefficient of variation (CV) is 50 percent or more.
[1]Includes only students who were enrolled in 12th grade in fall of the school year and graduated with a diploma by the end of the following summer.

NOTE: Data are based on a sample survey and may not be strictly comparable with data reported elsewhere. Includes all schools, including combined schools, with students enrolled in the 12th grade. Some data have been revised from previously published figures. Detail may not sum to totals because of rounding. Standard errors appear in parentheses.
SOURCE: U.S. Department of Education, National Center for Education Statistics, Schools and Staffing Survey (SASS), "Public School Questionnaire," 1999–2000, 2003–04, and 2007–08, "Private School Questionnaire," 1999–2000, 2003–04, and 2007–08, and "Charter School Questionnaire," 1999–2000. (This table was prepared October 2009.)

Total undergraduate fall enrollment in degree-granting institutions, by attendance status, sex of student, and control of institution: 1967 through 2010

Year	Total	Full-time	Part-time	Males	Females	Males Full-time	Males Part-time	Females Full-time	Females Part-time	Males Public	Males Private	Females Public	Females Private
1	2	3	4	5	6	7	8	9	10	11	12	13	14
1967[1]	6,015,683	4,344,890	1,670,793	3,502,099	2,513,584	2,569,411	932,688	1,775,479	738,105	2,491,831	1,010,268	1,801,574	712,010
1968	6,475,714	4,740,408	1,735,306	3,781,000	2,694,714	2,810,135	970,865	1,930,273	764,441	2,787,269	993,731	1,994,726	699,988
1969	6,884,485	4,992,050	1,892,435	4,007,528	2,876,957	2,952,197	1,055,331	2,039,853	837,104	2,996,025	1,011,503	2,162,292	714,665
1970	7,368,644	5,280,064	2,088,580	4,249,702	3,118,942	3,096,371	1,153,331	2,183,693	935,249	3,236,128	1,013,574	2,384,127	734,815
1971	7,744,254	5,512,996	2,231,258	4,417,873	3,326,381	3,201,118	1,216,755	2,311,878	1,014,503	3,427,012	990,861	2,580,781	745,600
1972	7,942,439	5,489,090	2,453,349	4,428,593	3,513,846	3,120,817	1,307,776	2,368,273	1,145,573	3,465,701	962,892	2,756,903	756,943
1973	8,259,671	5,578,558	2,681,113	4,537,599	3,722,072	3,134,418	1,403,181	2,444,140	1,277,932	3,579,696	957,903	2,942,716	779,356
1974	8,798,728	5,726,346	3,072,382	4,765,582	4,033,146	3,191,770	1,573,812	2,534,576	1,498,570	3,800,052	965,530	3,231,678	801,468
1975	9,679,455	6,168,396	3,511,059	5,257,005	4,422,450	3,459,328	1,797,677	2,709,068	1,713,382	4,244,632	1,012,373	3,581,400	841,050
1976	9,434,591	6,033,233	3,401,358	4,906,277	4,528,314	3,244,339	1,661,938	2,788,894	1,739,420	3,950,985	955,292	3,669,377	858,937
1977	9,716,703	6,094,023	3,622,680	4,897,197	4,819,506	3,188,262	1,708,935	2,905,761	1,913,745	3,937,407	959,790	3,905,573	913,933
1978	9,684,399	5,962,826	3,721,573	4,761,067	4,923,332	3,068,641	1,692,426	2,894,185	2,029,147	3,812,299	948,768	3,974,986	948,346
1979	9,997,977	6,079,415	3,918,562	4,820,123	5,177,854	3,086,696	1,733,427	2,992,719	2,185,135	3,865,030	955,093	4,181,801	996,053
1980	10,475,055	6,361,744	4,113,311	5,000,177	5,474,878	3,226,857	1,773,320	3,134,887	2,339,991	4,015,000	985,177	4,426,955	1,047,923
1981	10,754,522	6,449,068	4,305,454	5,108,271	5,646,251	3,260,473	1,847,798	3,188,595	2,457,656	4,089,975	1,018,296	4,558,388	1,087,863
1982	10,825,062	6,483,805	4,341,257	5,170,494	5,654,568	3,299,436	1,871,058	3,184,369	2,470,199	4,139,766	1,030,728	4,573,307	1,081,261
1983	10,845,995	6,514,034	4,331,961	5,158,300	5,687,695	3,304,247	1,854,053	3,209,787	2,477,908	4,116,682	1,041,618	4,580,436	1,107,259
1984	10,618,071	6,347,653	4,270,418	5,006,813	5,611,258	3,194,930	1,811,883	3,152,723	2,458,535	3,989,549	1,017,264	4,503,942	1,107,316
1985	10,596,674	6,319,592	4,277,082	4,962,080	5,634,594	3,156,446	1,805,634	3,163,146	2,471,448	3,952,548	1,009,532	4,524,577	1,110,017
1986	10,797,975	6,352,073	4,445,902	5,017,505	5,780,470	3,146,330	1,871,175	3,205,743	2,574,727	4,002,471	1,015,034	4,658,245	1,122,225
1987	11,046,235	6,462,549	4,583,686	5,068,457	5,977,778	3,163,676	1,904,781	3,298,873	2,678,905	4,076,349	992,108	4,842,240	1,135,538
1988	11,316,548	6,642,428	4,674,120	5,137,644	6,178,904	3,206,442	1,931,202	3,435,986	2,742,918	4,113,497	1,024,147	4,989,649	1,189,255
1989	11,742,531	6,840,696	4,901,835	5,310,990	6,431,541	3,278,647	2,032,343	3,562,049	2,869,492	4,271,822	1,039,168	5,215,920	1,215,621
1990	11,959,106	6,976,030	4,983,076	5,379,759	6,579,347	3,336,535	2,043,224	3,639,495	2,939,852	4,352,875	1,026,884	5,356,721	1,222,626
1991	12,439,287	7,221,412	5,217,875	5,571,003	6,868,284	3,435,526	2,135,477	3,785,886	3,082,398	4,530,934	1,040,069	5,617,023	1,251,261
1992	12,537,700	7,244,442	5,293,258	5,582,936	6,954,764	3,424,739	2,158,197	3,819,703	3,135,061	4,536,925	1,046,011	5,679,372	1,275,392
1993	12,323,959	7,179,482	5,144,477	5,483,682	6,840,277	3,381,997	2,101,685	3,797,485	3,042,792	4,447,266	1,036,416	5,564,521	1,275,756
1994	12,262,608	7,168,706	5,093,902	5,422,113	6,840,495	3,341,591	2,080,522	3,827,115	3,013,380	4,394,309	1,027,804	5,550,819	1,289,676
1995	12,231,719	7,145,268	5,086,451	5,401,130	6,830,589	3,296,610	2,104,520	3,848,658	2,981,931	4,380,030	1,021,100	5,523,596	1,306,993
1996	12,326,948	7,298,839	5,028,109	5,420,672	6,906,276	3,339,108	2,081,564	3,959,731	2,946,545	4,382,751	1,037,921	5,552,532	1,353,744
1997	12,450,587	7,418,598	5,031,989	5,468,532	6,982,055	3,379,597	2,088,935	4,039,001	2,943,054	4,408,364	1,060,168	5,599,115	1,382,940
1998	12,436,937	7,538,711	4,898,226	5,446,133	6,990,804	3,428,161	2,017,972	4,110,550	2,880,254	4,360,935	1,085,198	5,589,277	1,401,527
1999	12,739,445	7,753,548	4,985,897	5,584,234	7,155,211	3,524,586	2,059,648	4,228,962	2,926,249	4,458,484	1,125,750	5,715,744	1,439,467
2000	13,155,393	7,922,926	5,232,467	5,778,268	7,377,125	3,588,246	2,190,022	4,334,680	3,042,445	4,622,098	1,156,170	5,917,224	1,459,901
2001	13,715,610	8,327,640	5,387,970	6,004,431	7,711,179	3,768,630	2,235,801	4,559,010	3,152,169	4,804,014	1,200,417	6,181,857	1,529,322
2002	14,257,077	8,734,252	5,522,825	6,192,390	8,064,687	3,934,168	2,258,222	4,800,084	3,264,603	4,960,291	1,232,099	6,472,564	1,592,123
2003	14,480,364	9,045,253	5,435,111	6,227,372	8,252,992	4,048,682	2,178,690	4,996,571	3,256,421	4,956,392	1,270,980	6,566,711	1,686,281
2004	14,780,630	9,284,336	5,496,294	6,340,048	8,440,582	4,140,628	2,199,420	5,143,708	3,296,874	5,009,240	1,330,808	6,641,340	1,799,242
2005	14,963,964	9,446,430	5,517,534	6,408,871	8,555,093	4,200,863	2,208,008	5,245,567	3,309,526	5,046,002	1,362,869	6,651,728	1,903,365
2006	15,184,302	9,571,079	5,613,223	6,513,756	8,670,546	4,264,606	2,249,150	5,306,473	3,364,073	5,133,850	1,379,906	6,713,576	1,956,970
2007	15,603,771	9,840,978	5,762,793	6,727,600	8,876,171	4,396,868	2,330,732	5,444,110	3,432,061	5,300,572	1,427,028	6,837,011	2,039,160
2008	16,365,738	10,254,930	6,110,808	7,066,623	9,299,115	4,577,431	2,489,192	5,677,499	3,621,616	5,531,965	1,534,658	7,059,252	2,239,863
2009	17,565,320	11,143,499	6,421,821	7,595,481	9,969,839	4,976,727	2,618,754	6,166,772	3,803,067	5,917,296	1,678,185	7,469,297	2,500,542
2010	18,078,672	11,451,568	6,627,104	7,835,163	10,243,509	5,117,497	2,717,666	6,334,071	3,909,438	6,076,131	1,759,032	7,628,159	2,615,350

[1]Data for part-time students are for part-time resident students and all extension students (students attending courses at sites separate from the primary reporting campus). In later years, part-time student enrollment was collected as a distinct category.
NOTE: Data include unclassified undergraduate students. Data through 1995 are for institutions of higher education, while later data are for degree-granting institutions. Degree-granting institutions grant associate's or higher degrees and participate in Title IV federal financial aid programs. The degree-granting classification is very similar to the earlier higher education classification, but it includes more 2-year colleges and excludes a few higher education institutions that did not grant degrees. (See Appendix A: Guide to Sources for details.) Some data have been revised from previously published figures. Detail may not sum to totals because of rounding.
SOURCE: U.S. Department of Education, National Center for Education Statistics, Higher Education General Information Survey (HEGIS), "Fall Enrollment in Colleges and Universities" surveys, 1967 through 1985; Integrated Postsecondary Education Data System (IPEDS), "Fall Enrollment Survey" (IPEDS-EF:86–99); and IPEDS Spring 2001 through Spring 2010, Enrollment component. (This table was prepared September 2011.)

Total postbaccalaureate fall enrollment in degree-granting institutions, by attendance status, sex of student, and control of institution: 1967 through 2010

						Males		Females		Males		Females	
Year	Total	Full-time	Part-time	Males	Females	Full-time	Part-time	Full-time	Part-time	Public	Private	Public	Private
1	2	3	4	5	6	7	8	9	10	11	12	13	14
1967	896,065	448,238	447,827	630,701	265,364	354,628	276,073	93,610	171,754	351,947	278,754	170,676	94,688
1968	1,037,377	469,747	567,630	696,649	340,728	358,686	337,963	111,061	229,667	410,609	286,040	238,048	102,680
1969	1,120,175	506,833	613,342	738,673	381,502	383,630	355,043	123,203	258,299	457,126	281,547	281,425	100,077
1970	1,212,243	536,226	676,017	793,940	418,303	407,724	386,216	128,502	289,801	496,757	297,183	311,122	107,181
1971	1,204,390	564,236	640,154	789,131	415,259	428,167	360,964	136,069	279,190	513,570	275,561	305,604	109,655
1972	1,272,421	583,299	689,122	810,164	462,257	436,533	373,631	146,766	315,491	506,950	303,214	341,081	121,176
1973	1,342,452	610,935	731,517	833,453	508,999	444,219	389,234	166,716	342,283	523,274	310,179	373,830	135,169
1974	1,425,001	643,927	781,074	856,847	568,154	454,706	402,141	189,221	378,933	538,573	318,274	418,197	149,957
1975	1,505,404	672,938	832,466	891,992	613,412	467,425	424,567	205,513	407,899	560,041	331,951	448,435	164,977
1976	1,577,546	683,825	893,721	904,551	672,995	459,286	445,265	224,539	448,456	555,912	348,639	477,203	195,792
1977	1,569,084	698,902	870,182	891,819	677,265	462,038	429,781	236,864	440,401	535,748	356,071	468,265	209,000
1978	1,575,693	704,831	870,862	879,931	695,762	458,865	421,066	245,966	449,796	519,150	360,781	479,458	216,304
1979	1,571,922	714,624	857,298	862,754	709,168	456,197	406,557	258,427	450,741	503,949	358,805	486,042	223,126
1980	1,621,840	736,214	885,626	874,197	747,643	462,387	411,810	273,827	473,816	507,587	366,610	507,852	239,791
1981	1,617,150	732,182	884,968	866,785	750,365	452,364	414,421	279,818	470,547	496,825	369,960	501,844	248,521
1982	1,600,718	736,813	863,905	860,890	739,828	453,519	407,371	283,294	456,534	493,122	367,768	489,892	249,936
1983	1,618,666	747,016	871,650	865,425	753,241	455,540	409,885	291,476	461,765	493,356	372,069	492,260	260,981
1984	1,623,869	750,735	873,134	856,761	767,108	452,579	404,182	298,156	468,952	484,963	371,798	498,916	268,192
1985	1,650,381	755,629	894,752	856,370	794,011	451,274	405,096	304,355	489,656	484,940	371,430	517,208	276,803
1986	1,705,536	767,477	938,059	867,010	838,526	452,717	414,293	314,760	523,766	503,107	363,903	550,070	288,456
1987	1,720,407	768,536	951,871	863,599	856,808	447,212	416,387	321,324	535,484	497,117	366,482	557,548	299,260
1988	1,738,789	794,340	944,449	864,252	874,537	455,337	408,915	339,003	535,534	495,461	368,791	562,781	311,756
1989	1,796,029	820,254	975,775	879,025	917,004	461,596	417,429	358,658	558,346	504,528	374,497	585,693	331,311
1990	1,859,531	844,955	1,014,576	904,150	955,381	471,217	432,933	373,738	581,643	522,136	382,014	612,985	342,396
1991	1,919,666	893,917	1,025,749	930,841	988,825	493,849	436,992	400,068	588,757	535,422	395,419	626,184	362,641
1992	1,949,659	917,676	1,031,983	941,053	1,008,606	502,166	438,887	415,510	593,096	537,471	403,582	630,799	377,807
1993	1,980,844	948,136	1,032,708	943,768	1,037,076	508,574	435,194	439,562	597,514	537,245	406,523	640,056	397,020
1994	2,016,182	969,070	1,047,112	949,785	1,066,397	513,592	436,193	455,478	610,919	535,759	414,026	652,793	413,604
1995	2,030,062	983,534	1,046,528	941,409	1,088,653	510,782	430,627	472,752	615,901	527,605	413,804	661,143	427,510
1996	2,040,572	1,004,114	1,036,458	932,153	1,108,419	512,100	420,053	492,014	616,405	519,702	412,451	665,514	442,905
1997	2,051,747	1,019,464	1,032,283	927,496	1,124,251	510,845	416,651	508,619	615,632	515,823	411,673	672,817	451,434
1998	2,070,030	1,024,627	1,045,403	923,132	1,146,898	505,492	417,640	519,135	627,763	507,763	415,369	679,794	467,104
1999	2,110,246	1,049,591	1,060,655	930,930	1,179,316	508,930	422,000	540,661	638,655	510,779	420,151	690,732	488,584
2000	2,156,896	1,086,674	1,070,222	943,501	1,213,395	522,847	420,654	563,827	649,568	510,309	433,192	703,155	510,240
2001	2,212,377	1,119,862	1,092,515	956,384	1,255,993	531,260	425,124	588,602	667,391	523,597	432,787	723,688	532,305
2002	2,354,634	1,212,107	1,142,527	1,009,726	1,344,908	566,930	442,796	645,177	699,731	551,729	457,997	767,409	577,499
2003	2,431,117	1,280,880	1,150,237	1,032,892	1,398,225	589,190	443,702	691,690	706,535	555,903	476,989	779,692	618,533
2004	2,491,414	1,325,841	1,165,573	1,047,214	1,444,200	598,727	448,487	727,114	717,086	550,236	496,978	779,296	664,904
2005	2,523,511	1,350,581	1,172,930	1,047,054	1,476,457	602,525	444,529	748,056	728,401	543,221	503,833	780,883	695,574
2006	2,574,568	1,386,226	1,188,342	1,061,059	1,513,509	614,709	446,350	771,517	741,992	545,554	515,505	787,153	726,356
2007	2,644,357	1,428,914	1,215,443	1,088,314	1,556,043	632,576	455,738	796,338	759,705	556,727	531,587	796,470	759,573
2008	2,737,076	1,492,813	1,244,263	1,122,272	1,614,804	656,926	465,346	835,887	778,917	568,550	553,722	812,386	802,418
2009	2,862,391	1,579,283	1,283,108	1,174,023	1,688,368	693,917	480,106	885,366	803,002	592,273	581,750	831,776	856,592
2010	2,937,454	1,630,699	1,306,755	1,209,648	1,727,806	719,560	490,088	911,139	816,667	603,406	606,242	835,113	892,693

NOTE: Data include unclassified graduate students. Data include first-professional and gradu-ate-level students. Data through 1995 are for institutions of higher education, while later data are for degree-granting institutions. Degree-granting institutions grant associate's or higher degrees and participate in Title IV federal financial aid programs. The degree-granting classifi-cation is very similar to the earlier higher education classification, but it includes more 2-year colleges and excludes a few higher education institutions that did not grant degrees. (See Appendix A: Guide to Sources for details.) Some data have been revised from previously pub-lished figures.

SOURCE: U.S. Department of Education, National Center for Education Statistics, Higher Edu-cation General Information Survey (HEGIS), "Fall Enrollment in Colleges and Universities" sur-veys, 1967 through 1985; Integrated Postsecondary Education Data System (IPEDS), "Fall Enrollment Survey" (IPEDS-EF:86-99); and IPEDS Spring 2001 through Spring 2011, Enroll-ment component. (This table was prepared September 2011.)

Total fall enrollment in degree-granting institutions, by state or jurisdiction: Selected years, 1970 through 2010

State or jurisdiction	Fall 1970	Fall 1980	Fall 1990	Fall 2000	Fall 2005	Fall 2006	Fall 2007	Fall 2008	Fall 2009	Fall 2010	Percent change, 2005 to 2010
1	2	3	4	5	6	7	8	9	10	11	12
United States	**8,580,887**	**12,096,895**	**13,818,637**	**15,312,289**	**17,487,475**	**17,758,870**	**18,248,128**	**19,102,814**	**20,427,711**	**21,016,126**	**20.2**
Alabama	103,936	164,306	218,589	233,962	256,389	258,408	268,183	310,941	311,740	327,327	27.7
Alaska	9,471	21,296	29,833	27,953	30,231	29,853	30,616	30,717	32,406	33,653	11.3
Arizona	109,619	202,716	264,148	342,490	545,597	567,192	624,147	704,245	828,631	795,388	45.8
Arkansas	52,039	77,607	90,425	115,172	143,272	147,391	152,168	158,374	168,352	175,895	22.8
California	1,257,245	1,790,993	1,808,740	2,256,708	2,399,833	2,434,774	2,529,522	2,652,241	2,735,579	2,714,172	13.1
Colorado	123,395	162,916	227,131	263,872	302,672	308,383	310,637	325,232	352,034	372,025	22.9
Connecticut	124,700	159,632	168,604	161,243	174,675	176,716	179,005	184,178	191,806	199,384	14.1
Delaware	25,260	32,939	42,004	43,897	51,612	51,238	52,343	53,088	55,174	55,731	8.0
District of Columbia	77,158	86,675	79,551	72,689	104,897	109,505	115,153	126,110	136,851	91,992	-12.3
Florida	235,525	411,891	588,086	707,684	872,662	885,651	913,793	972,699	1,053,221	1,125,469	29.0
Georgia	126,511	184,159	251,786	346,204	426,650	435,403	453,711	476,581	532,493	568,723	33.3
Hawaii	36,562	47,181	56,436	60,182	67,083	66,893	66,601	70,104	74,809	78,073	16.4
Idaho	34,567	43,018	51,881	65,594	77,708	77,872	78,846	80,456	84,450	85,201	9.6
Illinois	452,146	644,245	729,246	743,918	832,967	830,676	837,018	859,242	900,824	906,889	8.9
Indiana	192,668	247,253	284,832	314,334	361,253	368,013	380,477	401,956	441,294	459,423	27.2
Iowa	108,902	140,449	170,515	188,974	227,722	238,634	256,259	286,891	350,631	381,842	67.7
Kansas	102,485	136,605	163,733	179,968	191,752	193,146	194,102	198,991	210,843	214,859	12.1
Kentucky	98,591	143,066	177,852	188,341	244,969	248,914	258,213	257,583	277,907	291,102	18.8
Louisiana	120,728	160,058	186,840	223,800	197,713	224,147	224,754	236,375	251,853	263,638	33.3
Maine	34,134	43,264	57,186	58,473	65,551	66,149	67,173	67,796	70,170	72,985	11.3
Maryland	149,607	225,526	259,700	273,745	314,151	319,460	327,597	338,914	358,941	377,967	20.3
Massachusetts	303,809	418,415	417,833	421,142	443,316	451,526	463,366	477,056	497,290	508,302	14.7
Michigan	392,726	520,131	569,803	567,631	626,751	634,489	643,279	652,799	686,049	698,125	11.4
Minnesota	160,788	206,691	253,789	293,445	361,701	375,899	392,393	411,055	442,281	465,336	28.7
Mississippi	73,967	102,364	122,883	137,389	150,457	151,137	155,232	160,441	173,136	178,197	18.4
Missouri	183,930	234,421	289,899	321,348	374,445	377,098	384,366	396,409	424,944	444,695	18.8
Montana	30,062	35,177	35,876	42,240	47,850	47,501	47,371	47,840	51,588	53,312	11.4
Nebraska	66,915	89,488	112,831	112,117	121,236	124,500	127,378	130,458	138,645	144,682	19.3
Nevada	13,669	40,455	61,728	87,893	110,705	112,270	116,276	120,490	125,320	129,360	16.9
New Hampshire	29,400	46,794	59,510	61,718	69,893	70,669	70,724	71,739	74,234	75,594	8.2
New Jersey	216,121	321,610	324,286	335,945	379,758	385,656	398,136	410,160	432,127	444,091	16.9
New Mexico	44,461	58,283	85,500	110,739	131,337	131,828	134,375	142,413	152,752	162,652	23.8
New York	806,479	992,237	1,048,286	1,043,395	1,152,081	1,160,364	1,172,811	1,234,858	1,289,604	1,305,595	13.3
North Carolina	171,925	287,537	352,138	404,652	484,392	495,633	502,330	528,977	568,865	586,042	21.0
North Dakota	31,495	34,069	37,878	40,248	49,389	49,519	49,945	51,327	54,433	56,903	15.2
Ohio	376,267	489,145	557,690	549,553	616,350	619,942	630,497	653,585	711,095	744,947	20.9
Oklahoma	110,155	160,295	173,221	178,016	208,053	206,236	206,382	206,757	220,650	230,573	10.8
Oregon	122,177	157,458	165,741	183,065	200,033	197,594	202,928	220,474	243,412	250,331	25.1
Pennsylvania	411,044	507,716	604,060	609,521	692,340	707,132	725,397	740,288	778,123	803,593	16.1
Rhode Island	45,898	66,869	78,273	75,450	81,382	81,734	82,900	83,893	84,673	85,110	4.6
South Carolina	69,518	132,476	159,302	185,931	210,444	212,422	217,755	230,695	246,667	257,293	22.3
South Dakota	30,639	32,761	34,208	43,221	48,768	48,931	49,747	50,444	53,342	58,370	19.7
Tennessee	135,103	204,581	226,238	263,910	283,070	290,530	297,785	307,610	332,918	351,988	24.3
Texas	442,225	701,391	901,437	1,033,973	1,240,707	1,252,709	1,269,098	1,327,148	1,447,868	1,536,858	23.9
Utah	81,687	93,987	121,303	163,776	200,691	202,151	203,679	217,224	236,590	252,107	25.6
Vermont	22,209	30,628	36,398	35,489	39,915	41,095	42,191	42,946	44,975	45,572	14.2
Virginia	151,915	280,504	353,442	381,893	439,166	456,172	478,268	500,796	545,036	576,010	31.2
Washington	183,544	303,603	263,384	320,840	348,482	348,154	352,075	362,535	382,532	388,110	11.4
West Virginia	63,153	81,973	84,790	87,888	99,547	100,519	116,848	125,333	142,484	152,431	53.1
Wisconsin	202,058	269,086	299,774	307,179	335,258	340,158	343,747	352,875	373,228	383,986	14.5
Wyoming	15,220	21,147	31,326	30,004	35,334	34,693	35,246	35,936	37,093	38,298	8.4
U.S. Service Academies[1]	17,079	49,808	48,692	13,475	15,265	12,191	15,285	15,539	15,748	15,925	4.3
Other jurisdictions	**67,237**	**137,749**	**164,618**	**194,633**	**223,165**	**226,175**	**226,849**	**236,167**	**243,792**	**264,237**	**18.4**
American Samoa	0	976	1,219	297	1,579	1,607	1,767	1,806	2,189	2,193	38.9
Federated States of Micronesia	0	224	975	1,576	2,283	2,539	2,379	2,457	3,401	2,699	18.2
Guam	2,719	3,217	4,741	5,215	6,064	5,789	5,244	5,351	5,755	6,188	2.0
Marshall Islands	0	0	0	328	604	647	557	689	847	869	43.9
Northern Marianas	0	0	661	1,078	967	968	901	791	989	1,137	17.6
Palau	0	0	491	581	651	679	668	502	651	694	6.6
Puerto Rico	63,073	131,184	154,065	183,290	208,625	211,458	212,949	222,178	227,358	247,724	18.7
U.S. Virgin Islands	1,445	2,148	2,466	2,268	2,392	2,488	2,384	2,393	2,602	2,733	14.3

[1]Data for 2000 and later years reflect a substantial reduction in the number of Department of Defense institutions included in the IPEDS survey.
NOTE: Data through 1990 are for institutions of higher education, while later data are for degree-granting institutions. Degree-granting institutions grant associate's or higher degrees and participate in Title IV federal financial aid programs. The degree-granting classification is very similar to the earlier higher education classification, but it includes more 2-year colleges and excludes a few higher education institutions that did not grant degrees. (See Appendix A: Guide to Sources for details.)
SOURCE: U.S. Department of Education, National Center for Education Statistics, Higher Education General Information Survey (HEGIS), "Fall Enrollment in Colleges and Universities" surveys, 1970 and 1980; Integrated Postsecondary Education Data System (IPEDS), "Fall Enrollment Survey" (IPEDS-EF:90); and IPEDS Spring 2001 through Spring 2011, Enrollment component. (This table was prepared November 2011.)

Total fall enrollment in public degree-granting institutions, by state or jurisdiction: Selected years, 1970 through 2010

State or jurisdiction	Fall 1970	Fall 1980	Fall 1990	Fall 2000	Fall 2005	Fall 2006	Fall 2007	Fall 2008	Fall 2009	Fall 2010	Percent change, 2005 to 2010
1	2	3	4	5	6	7	8	9	10	11	12
United States	6,428,134	9,457,394	10,844,717	11,752,786	13,021,834	13,180,133	13,490,780	13,972,153	14,810,642	15,142,809	16.3
Alabama	87,884	143,674	195,939	207,435	228,153	230,668	237,632	245,040	260,277	267,083	17.1
Alaska	8,563	20,561	27,792	26,559	28,866	28,595	29,381	29,167	30,493	32,303	11.9
Arizona	107,315	194,034	248,213	284,522	320,865	331,441	332,154	331,310	350,435	366,976	14.4
Arkansas	43,599	66,068	78,645	101,775	128,117	131,407	135,525	140,706	149,474	155,780	21.6
California	1,123,529	1,599,838	1,594,710	1,927,771	2,008,155	2,047,565	2,136,087	2,239,487	2,289,470	2,223,648	10.7
Colorado	108,562	145,598	200,653	217,897	234,509	231,901	227,984	235,265	255,438	269,407	14.9
Connecticut	73,391	97,788	109,556	101,027	111,705	112,476	114,072	118,694	123,211	127,194	13.9
Delaware	21,151	28,325	34,252	34,194	38,682	38,118	39,092	38,952	40,428	40,408	4.5
District of Columbia	12,194	13,900	11,990	5,499	5,595	5,769	5,608	5,584	5,253	5,840	4.4
Florida	189,450	334,349	489,081	556,912	648,999	651,908	683,328	709,593	759,479	790,027	21.7
Georgia	101,900	140,158	196,413	271,755	342,012	346,138	359,883	376,468	418,037	436,109	27.5
Hawaii	32,963	43,269	45,728	44,579	50,157	49,990	50,454	53,526	57,945	60,090	19.8
Idaho	27,072	34,491	41,315	53,751	60,303	59,211	60,526	61,190	63,261	64,204	6.5
Illinois	315,634	491,274	551,333	534,155	555,149	552,777	550,940	560,411	588,741	585,515	5.5
Indiana	136,739	189,224	223,953	240,023	267,298	271,704	278,951	296,950	325,072	337,705	26.3
Iowa	68,390	97,454	117,834	135,008	148,907	151,052	154,644	157,019	170,870	177,781	19.4
Kansas	88,215	121,987	149,117	159,976	170,319	170,531	170,054	172,640	182,736	185,623	9.0
Kentucky	77,240	114,884	147,095	151,973	201,579	204,198	211,234	208,970	221,508	229,725	14.0
Louisiana	101,127	136,703	158,290	189,213	181,043	192,554	193,316	203,098	215,511	224,811	24.2
Maine	25,405	31,878	41,500	40,662	47,519	47,770	48,357	48,191	49,668	51,482	8.3
Maryland	118,988	195,051	220,783	223,797	256,073	260,921	269,719	280,603	298,185	309,779	21.0
Massachusetts	116,127	183,765	186,035	183,248	188,295	192,164	198,700	205,820	218,999	224,493	19.2
Michigan	339,625	454,147	487,359	467,861	505,586	511,776	519,449	528,040	553,022	562,444	11.2
Minnesota	130,567	162,379	199,211	218,617	240,853	244,106	250,397	256,633	270,336	276,176	14.7
Mississippi	64,968	90,661	109,038	125,355	135,896	136,626	139,931	144,224	155,517	159,695	17.5
Missouri	132,540	165,179	200,093	201,509	217,722	218,475	223,155	228,737	245,568	256,119	17.6
Montana	27,287	31,178	31,865	37,387	42,997	42,995	42,857	43,565	46,653	48,261	12.2
Nebraska	51,454	73,509	94,614	88,531	93,181	94,486	96,680	99,593	104,149	107,980	15.9
Nevada	13,576	40,280	61,242	83,120	100,043	101,856	104,797	108,559	112,397	113,103	13.1
New Hampshire	15,979	24,119	32,163	35,870	41,007	41,530	41,982	42,192	43,507	44,072	7.5
New Jersey	145,373	247,028	261,601	266,921	304,315	308,374	318,296	328,838	348,934	358,256	17.7
New Mexico	40,795	55,077	83,403	101,450	120,976	121,668	124,773	132,983	143,101	150,856	24.7
New York	449,437	563,251	616,884	583,417	626,222	635,785	652,428	675,892	712,466	723,500	15.5
North Carolina	123,761	228,154	285,405	329,422	396,755	406,068	410,746	434,976	470,239	475,598	19.9
North Dakota	30,192	31,709	34,690	36,014	42,808	42,949	43,016	44,268	46,727	48,904	14.2
Ohio	281,099	381,765	427,613	411,161	453,001	452,962	460,240	475,521	522,002	547,551	20.9
Oklahoma	91,438	137,188	151,073	153,699	179,225	178,015	177,643	178,253	189,953	197,642	10.3
Oregon	108,483	140,102	144,427	154,756	163,752	160,059	165,260	181,515	201,246	208,002	27.0
Pennsylvania	232,982	292,499	343,478	339,229	380,271	388,251	396,774	404,976	425,979	432,889	13.8
Rhode Island	25,527	35,052	42,350	38,458	40,008	40,374	41,503	42,601	43,409	43,224	8.0
South Carolina	47,101	107,683	131,134	155,519	174,686	176,415	180,479	187,253	200,204	205,080	17.4
South Dakota	23,936	24,328	26,596	34,857	37,548	38,028	38,917	39,743	41,674	44,569	18.7
Tennessee	98,897	156,835	175,049	202,530	200,394	205,056	208,524	214,140	231,741	242,486	21.0
Texas	365,522	613,552	802,314	896,534	1,081,335	1,094,139	1,109,666	1,163,132	1,258,841	1,334,885	23.4
Utah	49,588	59,598	86,108	123,046	148,960	148,228	147,982	158,037	170,921	178,599	19.9
Vermont	12,536	17,984	20,910	20,021	24,090	24,385	24,829	25,552	27,028	27,524	14.3
Virginia	123,279	246,500	291,286	313,780	349,195	357,823	370,486	383,121	401,093	409,004	17.1
Washington	162,718	276,028	227,632	273,928	296,756	297,048	301,793	312,071	328,391	330,874	11.5
West Virginia	51,363	71,228	74,108	76,136	85,148	86,501	87,838	88,695	94,533	96,104	12.9
Wisconsin	170,374	235,179	253,529	249,737	268,928	272,246	273,708	280,394	295,090	301,212	12.0
Wyoming	15,220	21,121	30,623	28,715	32.611	32,860	33,705	34,426	35,682	36,292	11.3
U.S. Service Academies[1]	17,079	49,808	48,692	13,475	15,265	12,191	15,285	15,539	15,748	15,925	4.3
Other jurisdictions	46,680	60,692	66,244	84,464	82,341	80,685	80,958	82,424	87,030	83,719	1.7
American Samoa	0	976	1,219	297	1,579	1,607	1,767	1,806	2,189	2,193	38.9
Federated States of Micronesia	0	224	975	1,576	2,283	2,539	2,379	2,457	3,401	2,699	18.2
Guam	2,719	3,217	4,741	5,215	5,875	5,603	5,077	5,202	5,661	6,103	3.9
Marshall Islands	0	0	0	328	604	647	557	689	847	869	43.9
Northern Marianas	0	0	661	1,078	967	968	901	791	989	1,137	17.6
Palau	0	0	491	581	651	679	668	502	651	694	6.6
Puerto Rico	42,516	54,127	55,691	73,121	67,990	66,154	67,225	68,584	70,690	67,291	-1.0
U.S. Virgin Islands	1,445	2,148	2,466	2,268	2,392	2,488	2,384	2,393	2,602	2,733	14.3

[1]Data for 2000 and later years reflect a substantial reduction in the number of Department of Defense institutions included in the IPEDS survey.
NOTE: Data through 1990 are for institutions of higher education, while later data are for degree-granting institutions. Degree-granting institutions grant associate's or higher degrees and participate in Title IV federal financial aid programs. The degree-granting classification is very similar to the earlier higher education classification, but it includes more 2-year colleges and excludes a few higher education institutions that did not grant degrees. (See Appendix A: Guide to Sources for details.)
SOURCE: U.S. Department of Education, National Center for Education Statistics, Higher Education General Information Survey (HEGIS), "Fall Enrollment in Colleges and Universities" surveys, 1970 and 1980; Integrated Postsecondary Education Data System (IPEDS), "Fall Enrollment Survey" (IPEDS-EF:90); and IPEDS Spring 2001 through Spring 2011, Enrollment component. (This table was prepared November 2011.)

Total fall enrollment in private degree-granting institutions, by state or jurisdiction: Selected years, 1970 through 2010

State or jurisdiction	Fall 1970	Fall 1980	Fall 1990	Fall 2000	Fall 2005	Fall 2006	Fall 2007	Fall 2008	Fall 2009	Fall 2010	Percent change, 2005 to 2010
1	2	3	4	5	6	7	8	9	10	11	12
United States	2,152,753	2,639,501	2,973,920	3,559,503	4,465,641	4,578,737	4,757,348	5,130,661	5,617,069	5,873,317	31.5
Alabama	16,052	20,632	22,650	26,527	28,236	27,740	30,551	65,901	51,463	60,244	113.4
Alaska	908	735	2,041	1,394	1,365	1,258	1,235	1,550	1,913	1,350	-1.1
Arizona	2,304	8,682	15,935	57,968	224,732	235,751	291,993	372,935	478,196	428,412	90.6
Arkansas	8,440	11,539	11,780	13,397	15,155	15,984	16,643	17,668	18,878	20,115	32.7
California	133,716	191,155	214,030	328,937	391,678	387,209	393,435	412,754	446,109	490,524	25.2
Colorado	14,833	17,318	26,478	45,975	68,163	76,482	82,653	89,967	96,596	102,618	50.5
Connecticut	51,309	61,844	59,048	60,216	62,970	64,240	64,933	65,484	68,595	72,190	14.6
Delaware	4,109	4,614	7,752	9,703	12,930	13,120	13,251	14,136	14,746	15,323	18.5
District of Columbia	64,964	72,775	67,561	67,190	99,302	103,736	109,545	120,526	131,598	86,152	-13.2
Florida	46,075	77,542	99,005	150,772	223,663	233,743	230,465	263,106	293,742	335,442	50.0
Georgia	24,611	44,001	55,373	74,449	84,638	89,265	93,828	100,113	114,456	132,614	56.7
Hawaii	3,599	3,912	10,708	15,603	16,926	16,903	16,147	16,578	16,864	17,983	6.2
Idaho	7,495	8,527	10,566	11,843	17,405	18,661	18,320	19,266	21,189	20,997	20.6
Illinois	136,512	152,971	177,913	209,763	277,818	277,899	286,078	298,831	312,083	321,374	15.7
Indiana	55,929	58,029	60,879	74,311	93,955	96,309	101,526	105,006	116,222	121,718	29.5
Iowa	40,512	42,995	52,681	53,966	78,815	87,582	101,615	129,872	179,761	204,061	158.9
Kansas	14,270	14,618	14,616	19,992	21,433	22,615	24,048	26,351	28,107	29,236	36.4
Kentucky	21,351	28,182	30,757	36,368	43,390	44,716	46,979	48,613	56,399	61,377	41.5
Louisiana	19,601	23,355	28,550	34,587	16,670	31,593	31,438	33,277	36,342	38,827	132.9
Maine	8,729	11,386	15,686	17,811	18,032	18,379	18,816	19,605	20,502	21,503	19.2
Maryland	30,619	30,475	38,917	49,948	58,078	58,539	57,878	58,311	60,756	68,188	17.4
Massachusetts	187,682	234,650	231,798	237,894	255,021	259,362	264,666	271,236	278,291	283,809	11.3
Michigan	53,101	65,984	82,444	99,770	121,165	122,713	123,830	124,759	133,027	135,681	12.0
Minnesota	30,221	44,312	54,578	74,828	120,848	131,793	141,946	154,422	171,945	189,160	56.5
Mississippi	8,999	11,703	13,845	12,034	14,561	14,511	15,301	16,217	17,619	18,502	27.1
Missouri	51,390	69,242	89,806	119,839	156,723	158,623	161,211	167,672	179,376	188,576	20.3
Montana	2,775	3,999	4,011	4,853	4,853	4,506	4,514	4,275	4,935	5,051	4.1
Nebraska	15,461	15,979	18,217	23,586	28,055	30,014	30,698	30,865	34,496	36,702	30.8
Nevada	93	175	486	4,773	10,662	10,414	11,479	11,931	12,923	16,257	52.5
New Hampshire	13,421	22,675	27,347	25,848	28,886	29,139	28,742	29,547	30,727	31,522	9.1
New Jersey	70,748	74,582	62,685	69,024	75,443	77,282	79,840	81,322	83,193	85,835	13.8
New Mexico	3,666	3,206	2,097	9,289	10,361	10,160	9,602	9,430	9,651	11,796	13.9
New York	357,042	428,986	431,402	459,978	525,859	524,579	520,383	558,966	577,138	582,095	10.7
North Carolina	48,164	59,383	66,733	75,230	87,637	89,565	91,584	94,001	98,626	110,444	26.0
North Dakota	1,303	2,360	3,188	4,234	6,581	6,570	6,929	7,059	7,706	7,999	21.5
Ohio	95,168	107,380	130,077	138,392	163,349	166,980	170,257	178,064	189,093	197,396	20.8
Oklahoma	18,717	23,107	22,148	24,317	28,828	28,221	28,739	28,504	30,697	32,931	14.2
Oregon	13,694	17,356	21,314	28,309	36,281	37,535	37,668	38,959	42,166	42,329	16.7
Pennsylvania	178,062	215,217	260,582	270,292	312,069	318,881	328,623	335,312	352,144	370,704	18.8
Rhode Island	20,371	31,817	35,923	36,992	41,374	41,360	41,397	41,292	41,264	41,886	1.2
South Carolina	22,417	24,793	28,168	30,412	35,758	36,007	37,276	43,442	46,463	52,213	46.0
South Dakota	6,703	8,433	7,612	8,364	11,220	10,903	10,830	10,701	11,668	13,801	23.0
Tennessee	36,206	47,746	51,189	61,380	82,676	85,474	89,261	93,470	101,177	109,502	32.4
Texas	76,703	87,839	99,123	137,439	159,372	158,570	159,432	164,016	189,027	201,973	26.7
Utah	32,099	34,389	35,195	40,730	51,731	53,923	55,697	59,187	65,669	73,508	42.1
Vermont	9,673	12,644	15,488	15,468	15,825	16,710	17,362	17,394	17,947	18,048	14.0
Virginia	28,636	34,004	62,156	68,113	89,971	98,349	107,782	117,675	143,943	167,006	85.6
Washington	20,826	27,575	35,752	46,912	51,726	51,106	50,282	50,464	54,141	57,236	10.7
West Virginia	11,790	10,745	10,682	11,752	14,399	14,018	29,010	36,638	47,951	56,327	291.2
Wisconsin	31,684	33,907	46,245	57,442	66,330	67,912	70,039	72,481	78,138	82,774	24.8
Wyoming	0	26	703	1,289	2,723	1,833	1,541	1,510	1,411	2,006	-26.3
Other jurisdictions	20,557	77,057	98,374	110,169	140,824	145,490	145,891	153,743	156,762	180,518	28.2
American Samoa	0	0	0	0	0	0	0	0	0	0	†
Federated States of Micronesia	0	0	0	0	0	0	0	0	0	0	†
Guam	0	0	0	0	189	186	167	149	94	85	-55.0
Marshall Islands	0	0	0	0	0	0	0	0	0	0	†
Northern Marianas	0	0	0	0	0	0	0	0	0	0	†
Palau	0	0	0	0	0	0	0	0	0	0	†
Puerto Rico	20,557	77,057	98,374	110,169	140,635	145,304	145,724	153,594	156,668	180,433	28.3
U.S. Virgin Islands	0	0	0	0	0	0	0	0	0	0	†

†Not applicable.
NOTE: Data through 1990 are for institutions of higher education, while later data are for degree-granting institutions. Degree-granting institutions grant associate's or higher degrees and participate in Title IV federal financial aid programs. The degree-granting classification is very similar to the earlier higher education classification, but it includes more 2-year colleges and excludes a few higher education institutions that did not grant degrees. (See Appendix A: Guide to Sources for details.)

SOURCE: U.S. Department of Education, National Center for Education Statistics, Higher Education General Information Survey (HEGIS), "Fall Enrollment in Colleges and Universities" surveys, 1970 and 1980; Integrated Postsecondary Education Data System (IPEDS), "Fall Enrollment Survey" (IPEDS-EF:90); and IPEDS Spring 2001 through Spring 2011, Enrollment component. (This table was prepared November 2011.)

Total fall enrollment in degree-granting institutions, by attendance status, sex, and state or jurisdiction: 2009 and 2010

State or jurisdiction	Total	Fall 2009 Full-time Males	Fall 2009 Full-time Females	Fall 2009 Part-time Males	Fall 2009 Part-time Females	Total	Fall 2010 Full-time Males	Fall 2010 Full-time Females	Fall 2010 Part-time Males	Fall 2010 Part-time Females	Percent change in total, 2009 to 2010
1	2	3	4	5	6	7	8	9	10	11	12
United States	20,427,711	5,670,644	7,052,138	3,098,860	4,606,069	21,016,126	5,837,057	7,245,210	3,207,754	4,726,105	2.9
Alabama	311,740	90,276	116,575	40,790	64,099	327,327	94,444	123,752	42,572	66,559	5.0
Alaska	32,406	6,342	7,881	6,419	11,764	33,653	6,562	7,965	6,841	12,285	3.8
Arizona	828,631	221,433	390,969	84,349	131,880	795,388	200,443	348,954	95,427	150,564	-4.0
Arkansas	168,352	47,179	61,676	21,764	37,733	175,895	49,076	64,799	22,970	39,050	4.5
California	2,735,579	626,099	770,722	605,093	733,665	2,714,172	641,019	782,955	592,654	697,544	-0.8
Colorado	352,034	99,631	122,392	53,536	76,475	372,025	102,160	127,496	60,396	81,973	5.7
Connecticut	191,806	56,593	68,059	24,821	42,333	199,384	58,168	69,860	26,249	45,107	4.0
Delaware	55,174	15,817	20,998	6,442	11,917	55,731	16,297	21,291	6,491	11,652	1.0
District of Columbia	136,851	28,246	39,602	23,874	45,129	91,992	25,956	35,871	11,749	18,416	-32.8
Florida	1,053,221	262,001	346,533	174,349	270,338	1,125,469	282,158	369,808	184,371	289,132	6.9
Georgia	532,493	154,353	210,917	59,561	107,662	568,723	161,938	224,443	64,484	117,858	6.8
Hawaii	74,809	18,318	24,239	13,041	19,211	78,073	19,109	24,864	13,837	20,263	4.4
Idaho	84,450	27,003	31,566	10,249	15,632	85,201	28,188	32,776	9,516	14,721	0.9
Illinois	900,824	243,008	291,172	146,800	219,844	906,889	243,407	289,050	151,092	223,340	0.7
Indiana	441,294	140,835	164,255	55,083	81,121	459,423	144,157	171,143	58,975	85,148	4.1
Iowa	350,631	91,227	122,784	46,582	90,038	381,842	99,848	142,173	48,623	91,198	8.9
Kansas	210,843	60,461	65,507	33,358	51,517	214,859	62,076	68,148	33,588	51,047	1.9
Kentucky	277,907	74,044	101,309	44,832	57,722	291,102	77,179	105,569	47,495	60,859	4.7
Louisiana	251,853	73,245	100,796	29,354	48,458	263,638	75,624	104,892	30,645	52,477	4.7
Maine	70,170	20,434	24,406	8,542	16,788	72,985	20,938	25,130	9,341	17,576	4.0
Maryland	358,941	87,591	106,717	63,193	101,440	377,967	90,456	109,375	68,690	109,446	5.3
Massachusetts	497,290	155,861	186,652	57,864	96,913	508,302	160,196	191,255	59,403	97,448	2.2
Michigan	686,049	190,135	216,454	109,579	169,881	698,125	191,779	220,153	114,262	171,931	1.8
Minnesota	442,281	116,188	147,968	65,273	112,852	465,336	117,728	151,136	70,312	126,160	5.2
Mississippi	173,136	53,725	80,249	13,157	26,005	178,197	56,020	83,297	13,386	25,494	2.9
Missouri	424,944	115,442	144,692	62,749	102,061	444,695	121,867	152,787	64,558	105,483	4.6
Montana	51,588	18,597	19,005	5,499	8,487	53,312	19,519	20,031	5,278	8,484	3.3
Nebraska	138,645	41,658	47,038	20,594	29,355	144,682	43,591	50,166	21,496	29,429	4.4
Nevada	125,320	26,231	33,963	30,204	34,922	129,360	28,159	35,957	30,105	35,139	3.2
New Hampshire	74,234	23,963	28,747	7,452	14,072	75,594	24,786	29,333	7,750	13,725	1.8
New Jersey	432,127	129,304	144,558	64,820	93,445	444,091	133,717	148,922	66,449	95,003	2.8
New Mexico	152,752	35,368	44,203	30,517	42,664	162,652	37,515	48,372	31,861	44,904	6.5
New York	1,289,604	406,878	498,241	145,015	239,470	1,305,595	415,185	506,739	146,435	237,236	1.2
North Carolina	568,865	156,183	205,825	76,354	130,503	586,042	162,416	215,233	77,059	131,334	3.0
North Dakota	54,433	19,587	19,294	6,688	8,864	56,903	20,188	20,056	7,264	9,395	4.5
Ohio	711,095	221,178	265,304	88,902	135,711	744,947	229,754	274,365	92,960	147,868	4.8
Oklahoma	220,650	65,016	75,937	32,508	47,189	230,573	67,295	79,900	34,139	49,239	4.5
Oregon	243,412	69,405	80,798	39,727	53,482	250,331	72,648	82,748	41,282	53,653	2.8
Pennsylvania	778,123	262,130	299,399	77,012	139,582	803,593	269,181	308,381	81,247	144,784	3.3
Rhode Island	84,673	29,138	33,928	8,193	13,414	85,110	28,990	33,931	8,588	13,601	0.5
South Carolina	246,667	73,647	98,305	25,378	49,337	257,293	76,338	102,396	26,866	51,693	4.3
South Dakota	53,342	16,623	17,911	6,410	12,398	58,370	17,495	19,242	7,336	14,297	9.4
Tennessee	332,918	105,295	136,691	33,175	57,757	351,988	110,181	140,035	36,887	64,885	5.7
Texas	1,447,868	364,586	435,641	266,551	381,090	1,536,858	381,556	459,398	286,856	409,048	6.1
Utah	236,590	73,820	72,649	43,742	46,379	252,107	79,986	80,106	44,522	47,493	6.6
Vermont	44,975	16,766	17,056	3,651	7,502	45,572	17,039	17,246	3,657	7,630	1.3
Virginia	545,036	148,922	189,779	83,324	123,011	576,010	157,198	193,976	91,608	133,228	5.7
Washington	382,532	113,851	133,479	56,215	78,987	388,110	116,689	136,930	56,868	77,623	1.5
West Virginia	142,484	41,113	46,288	28,962	26,121	152,431	41,519	47,944	34,205	28,763	7.0
Wisconsin	373,228	112,744	129,611	50,151	80,722	383,986	115,135	130,916	52,063	85,872	2.9
Wyoming	37,093	10,333	10,489	7,147	9,124	38,298	11,325	10,899	7,029	9,045	3.2
U.S. Service Academies	15,748	12,821	2,909	15	3	15,925	12,859	3,046	17	3	1.1
Other jurisdictions	243,792	78,420	114,490	20,281	30,601	264,237	87,487	124,467	21,017	31,266	8.4
American Samoa	2,189	398	594	457	740	2,193	286	525	565	817	0.2
Federated States of Micronesia	3,401	912	1,096	667	726	2,699	902	1,110	347	340	-20.6
Guam	5,755	1,303	2,006	1,085	1,361	6,188	1,454	2,214	1,103	1,417	7.5
Marshall Islands	847	275	279	145	148	869	319	355	106	89	2.6
Northern Marianas	989	305	466	94	124	1,137	371	589	73	104	15.0
Palau	651	202	190	93	166	694	210	253	83	148	6.6
Puerto Rico	227,358	74,558	108,746	17,527	26,527	247,724	83,463	118,248	18,476	27,537	9.0
U.S. Virgin Islands	2,602	467	1,113	213	809	2,733	482	1,173	264	814	5.0

NOTE: Degree-granting institutions grant associate's or higher degrees and participate in Title IV federal financial aid programs.

SOURCE: U.S. Department of Education, National Center for Education Statistics, Integrated Postsecondary Education Data System (IPEDS), Spring 2010 and Spring 2011, Enrollment component. (This table was prepared November 2011.)

Total fall enrollment in public degree-granting institutions, by attendance status, sex, and state or jurisdiction: 2009 and 2010

State or jurisdiction	Total	Fall 2009				Total	Fall 2010				Percent change in total, 2009 to 2010
		Full-time		Part-time			Full-time		Part-time		
		Males	Females	Males	Females		Males	Females	Males	Females	
1	2	3	4	5	6	7	8	9	10	11	12
United States	14,810,642	3,943,800	4,586,544	2,565,769	3,714,529	15,142,809	4,049,593	4,714,257	2,629,944	3,749,015	2.2
Alabama	260,277	74,214	94,912	34,103	57,048	267,083	76,518	99,248	34,567	56,750	2.6
Alaska	30,493	6,006	7,053	6,202	11,232	32,303	6,272	7,237	6,747	12,047	5.9
Arizona	350,435	79,927	88,518	74,910	107,080	366,976	84,723	93,440	78,505	110,308	4.7
Arkansas	149,474	40,371	53,168	20,448	35,487	155,780	41,813	55,833	21,617	36,517	4.2
California	2,289,470	478,250	566,714	563,577	680,929	2,223,648	477,606	560,254	546,522	639,266	-2.9
Colorado	255,438	70,497	75,117	45,029	64,795	269,407	73,510	78,143	49,925	67,829	5.5
Connecticut	123,211	33,603	38,518	19,121	31,969	127,194	34,685	38,937	20,334	33,238	3.2
Delaware	40,428	12,466	16,395	4,081	7,486	40,408	12,768	16,596	3,889	7,155	#
District of Columbia	5,253	1,034	1,511	951	1,757	5,840	1,123	1,582	1,080	2,055	11.2
Florida	759,479	177,025	224,528	140,057	217,869	790,027	184,839	233,477	147,161	224,550	4.0
Georgia	418,037	120,549	155,414	51,266	90,808	436,109	125,722	164,711	52,949	92,727	4.3
Hawaii	57,945	14,103	16,968	10,652	16,222	60,090	14,426	17,497	11,125	17,042	3.7
Idaho	63,261	19,509	20,962	9,011	13,779	64,204	20,531	22,113	8,544	13,016	1.5
Illinois	588,741	147,893	163,017	113,074	164,757	585,515	148,736	164,668	111,855	160,256	-0.5
Indiana	325,072	100,534	110,707	46,637	67,194	337,705	102,713	114,539	49,735	70,718	3.9
Iowa	170,870	54,470	55,697	25,949	34,754	177,781	55,470	58,314	27,875	36,122	4.0
Kansas	182,736	52,745	55,212	29,742	45,037	185,623	53,791	57,366	29,790	44,676	1.6
Kentucky	221,508	58,537	75,115	39,638	48,218	229,725	60,664	77,840	41,541	49,680	3.7
Louisiana	215,511	62,541	81,967	27,172	43,831	224,811	64,304	85,262	28,158	47,087	4.3
Maine	49,668	14,023	15,291	7,246	13,108	51,482	14,320	15,285	7,997	13,880	3.7
Maryland	298,185	69,728	84,613	55,220	88,624	309,779	71,250	85,928	59,248	93,353	3.9
Massachusetts	218,999	59,071	66,491	34,452	58,985	224,493	60,625	67,998	36,152	59,718	2.5
Michigan	553,022	155,357	172,634	89,772	135,259	562,444	157,252	175,004	93,547	136,641	1.7
Minnesota	270,336	79,943	83,651	44,448	62,294	276,176	80,962	84,795	45,912	64,507	2.2
Mississippi	155,517	48,716	70,862	12,247	23,692	159,695	50,819	73,496	12,415	22,965	2.7
Missouri	245,568	69,866	82,694	35,136	57,872	256,119	73,561	88,030	36,218	58,310	4.3
Montana	46,653	16,911	16,746	5,084	7,912	48,261	17,727	17,656	4,990	7,888	3.4
Nebraska	104,149	31,973	33,181	16,160	22,835	107,980	32,187	33,796	18,006	23,991	3.7
Nevada	112,397	21,779	27,156	29,474	33,988	113,103	22,371	27,519	29,197	34,016	0.6
New Hampshire	43,507	13,857	16,029	4,824	8,797	44,072	14,237	16,328	5,121	8,386	1.3
New Jersey	348,934	100,281	114,106	55,119	79,428	358,256	103,688	117,338	56,624	80,606	2.7
New Mexico	143,101	32,046	38,902	30,209	41,944	150,856	33,814	41,626	31,441	43,975	5.4
New York	712,466	218,965	257,405	90,789	145,307	723,500	223,601	261,313	93,042	145,544	1.5
North Carolina	470,239	119,998	157,598	71,708	120,935	475,598	123,736	163,838	70,717	117,307	1.1
North Dakota	46,727	17,590	15,915	5,912	7,310	48,904	18,089	16,537	6,474	7,804	4.7
Ohio	522,002	159,492	181,633	71,940	108,937	547,551	165,589	189,221	75,642	117,099	4.9
Oklahoma	189,953	51,961	62,184	30,773	45,035	197,642	54,004	64,736	32,134	46,768	4.0
Oregon	201,246	56,446	60,587	36,100	48,113	208,002	59,321	62,975	37,509	48,197	3.4
Pennsylvania	425,979	145,781	156,232	44,300	79,666	432,889	147,532	158,010	46,340	81,007	1.6
Rhode Island	43,409	11,087	15,125	6,102	11,095	43,224	11,018	14,590	6,417	11,199	-0.4
South Carolina	200,204	57,904	74,846	22,819	44,635	205,080	59,516	77,086	23,595	44,883	2.4
South Dakota	41,674	14,125	13,738	4,708	9,103	44,569	14,655	14,253	5,398	10,263	6.9
Tennessee	231,741	69,498	86,680	27,458	48,105	242,486	71,804	89,036	29,674	51,972	4.6
Texas	1,258,841	300,579	349,605	249,329	359,328	1,334,885	313,381	367,958	268,060	385,486	6.0
Utah	170,921	46,239	41,810	40,256	42,616	178,599	49,417	45,156	40,757	43,269	4.5
Vermont	27,028	8,448	9,725	2,766	6,089	27,524	8,472	9,783	2,922	6,347	1.8
Virginia	401,093	106,400	126,512	67,872	100,309	409,004	109,290	130,008	69,590	100,116	2.0
Washington	328,391	96,579	108,324	51,327	72,161	330,874	98,417	109,883	51,872	70,702	0.8
West Virginia	94,533	32,491	35,287	9,970	16,785	96,104	33,820	37,296	9,413	15,575	1.7
Wisconsin	295,090	90,487	96,253	43,467	64,883	301,212	92,566	96,937	44,555	67,154	2.1
Wyoming	35,682	9,084	10,327	7,147	9,124	36,292	9,479	10,739	7,029	9,045	1.7
U.S. Service Academies	15,748	12,821	2,909	15	3	15,925	12,859	3,046	17	3	1.1
Other jurisdictions	87,030	28,747	42,211	6,534	9,538	83,719	28,399	40,667	6,064	8,589	-3.8
American Samoa	2,189	398	594	457	740	2,193	286	525	565	817	0.2
Federated States of Micronesia	3,401	912	1,096	667	726	2,699	902	1,110	347	340	-20.6
Guam	5,661	1,271	1,978	1,074	1,338	6,103	1,419	2,184	1,092	1,408	7.8
Marshall Islands	847	275	279	145	148	869	319	355	106	89	2.6
Northern Marianas	989	305	466	94	124	1,137	371	589	73	104	15.0
Palau	651	202	190	93	166	694	210	253	83	148	6.6
Puerto Rico	70,690	24,917	36,495	3,791	5,487	67,291	24,410	34,478	3,534	4,869	-4.8
U.S. Virgin Islands	2,602	467	1,113	213	809	2,733	482	1,173	264	814	5.0

#Rounds to zero.
NOTE: Degree-granting institutions grant associate's or higher degrees and participate in Title IV federal financial aid programs.

SOURCE: U.S. Department of Education, National Center for Education Statistics, Integrated Postsecondary Education Data System (IPEDS), Spring 2010 and Spring 2011, Enrollment component. (This table was prepared November 2011.)

Total fall enrollment in private degree-granting institutions, by attendance status, sex, and state or jurisdiction: 2009 and 2010

State or jurisdiction	Total	Fall 2009 Full-time Males	Full-time Females	Part-time Males	Part-time Females	Total	Fall 2010 Full-time Males	Full-time Females	Part-time Males	Part-time Females	Percent change in total, 2009 to 2010
1	2	3	4	5	6	7	8	9	10	11	12
United States	5,617,069	1,726,844	2,465,594	533,091	891,540	5,873,317	1,787,464	2,530,953	577,810	977,090	4.6
Alabama	51,463	16,062	21,663	6,687	7,051	60,244	17,926	24,504	8,005	9,809	17.1
Alaska	1,913	336	828	217	532	1,350	290	728	94	238	-29.4
Arizona	478,196	141,506	302,451	9,439	24,800	428,412	115,720	255,514	16,922	40,256	-10.4
Arkansas	18,878	6,808	8,508	1,316	2,246	20,115	7,263	8,966	1,353	2,533	6.6
California	446,109	147,849	204,008	41,516	52,736	490,524	163,413	222,701	46,132	58,278	10.0
Colorado	96,596	29,134	47,275	8,507	11,680	102,618	28,650	49,353	10,471	14,144	6.2
Connecticut	68,595	22,990	29,541	5,700	10,364	72,190	23,483	30,923	5,915	11,869	5.2
Delaware	14,746	3,351	4,603	2,361	4,431	15,323	3,529	4,695	2,602	4,497	3.9
District of Columbia	131,598	27,212	38,091	22,923	43,372	86,152	24,833	34,289	10,669	16,361	-34.5
Florida	293,742	84,976	122,005	34,292	52,469	335,442	97,319	136,331	37,210	64,582	14.2
Georgia	114,456	33,804	55,503	8,295	16,854	132,614	36,216	59,732	11,535	25,131	15.9
Hawaii	16,864	4,215	7,271	2,389	2,989	17,983	4,683	7,367	2,712	3,221	6.6
Idaho	21,189	7,494	10,604	1,238	1,853	20,997	7,657	10,663	972	1,705	-0.9
Illinois	312,083	95,115	128,155	33,726	55,087	321,374	94,671	124,382	39,237	63,084	3.0
Indiana	116,222	40,301	53,548	8,446	13,927	121,718	41,444	56,604	9,240	14,430	4.7
Iowa	179,761	36,757	67,087	20,633	55,284	204,061	44,378	83,859	20,748	55,076	13.5
Kansas	28,107	7,716	10,295	3,616	6,480	29,236	8,285	10,782	3,798	6,371	4.0
Kentucky	56,399	15,507	26,194	5,194	9,504	61,377	16,515	27,729	5,954	11,179	8.8
Louisiana	36,342	10,704	18,829	2,182	4,627	38,827	11,320	19,630	2,487	5,390	6.8
Maine	20,502	6,411	9,115	1,296	3,680	21,503	6,618	9,845	1,344	3,696	4.9
Maryland	60,756	17,863	22,104	7,973	12,816	68,188	19,206	23,447	9,442	16,093	12.2
Massachusetts	278,291	96,790	120,161	23,412	37,928	283,809	99,571	123,257	23,251	37,730	2.0
Michigan	133,027	34,778	43,820	19,807	34,622	135,681	34,527	45,149	20,715	35,290	2.0
Minnesota	171,945	36,245	64,317	20,825	50,558	189,160	36,766	66,341	24,400	61,653	10.0
Mississippi	17,619	5,009	9,387	910	2,313	18,502	5,201	9,801	971	2,529	5.0
Missouri	179,376	45,576	61,998	27,613	44,189	188,576	48,306	64,757	28,340	47,173	5.1
Montana	4,935	1,686	2,259	415	575	5,051	1,792	2,375	288	596	2.4
Nebraska	34,496	9,685	13,857	4,434	6,520	36,702	11,404	16,370	3,490	5,438	6.4
Nevada	12,923	4,452	6,807	730	934	16,257	5,788	8,438	908	1,123	25.8
New Hampshire	30,727	10,106	12,718	2,628	5,275	31,522	10,549	13,005	2,629	5,339	2.6
New Jersey	83,193	29,023	30,452	9,701	14,017	85,835	30,029	31,584	9,825	14,397	3.2
New Mexico	9,651	3,322	5,301	308	720	11,796	3,701	6,746	420	929	22.2
New York	577,138	187,913	240,836	54,226	94,163	582,095	191,584	245,426	53,393	91,692	0.9
North Carolina	98,626	36,185	48,227	4,646	9,568	110,444	38,680	51,395	6,342	14,027	12.0
North Dakota	7,706	1,997	3,379	776	1,554	7,999	2,099	3,519	790	1,591	3.8
Ohio	189,093	61,686	83,671	16,962	26,774	197,396	64,165	85,144	17,318	30,769	4.4
Oklahoma	30,697	13,055	13,753	1,735	2,154	32,931	13,291	15,164	2,005	2,471	7.3
Oregon	42,166	12,959	20,211	3,627	5,369	42,329	13,327	19,773	3,773	5,456	0.4
Pennsylvania	352,144	116,349	143,167	32,712	59,916	370,704	121,649	150,371	34,907	63,777	5.3
Rhode Island	41,264	18,051	18,803	2,091	2,319	41,886	17,972	19,341	2,171	2,402	1.5
South Carolina	46,463	15,743	23,459	2,559	4,702	52,213	16,822	25,310	3,271	6,810	12.4
South Dakota	11,668	2,498	4,173	1,702	3,295	13,801	2,840	4,989	1,938	4,034	18.3
Tennessee	101,177	35,797	50,011	5,717	9,652	109,502	38,377	50,999	7,213	12,913	8.2
Texas	189,027	64,007	86,036	17,222	21,762	201,973	68,175	91,440	18,796	23,562	6.8
Utah	65,669	27,581	30,839	3,486	3,763	73,508	30,569	34,950	3,765	4,224	11.9
Vermont	17,947	8,318	7,331	885	1,413	18,048	8,567	7,463	735	1,283	0.6
Virginia	143,943	42,522	63,267	15,452	22,702	167,006	47,908	63,968	22,018	33,112	16.0
Washington	54,141	17,272	25,155	4,888	6,826	57,236	18,272	27,047	4,996	6,921	5.7
West Virginia	47,951	8,622	11,001	18,992	9,336	56,327	7,699	10,648	24,792	13,188	17.5
Wisconsin	78,138	22,257	33,358	6,684	15,839	82,774	22,569	33,979	7,508	18,718	5.9
Wyoming	1,411	1,249	162	0	0	2,006	1,846	160	0	0	42.2
Other jurisdictions	156,762	49,673	72,279	13,747	21,063	180,518	59,088	83,800	14,953	22,677	15.2
American Samoa	0	0	0	0	0	0	0	0	0	0	†
Federated States of Micronesia	0	0	0	0	0	0	0	0	0	0	†
Guam	94	32	28	11	23	85	35	30	11	9	-9.6
Marshall Islands	0	0	0	0	0	0	0	0	0	0	†
Northern Marianas	0	0	0	0	0	0	0	0	0	0	†
Palau	0	0	0	0	0	0	0	0	0	0	†
Puerto Rico	156,668	49,641	72,251	13,736	21,040	180,433	59,053	83,770	14,942	22,668	15.2
U.S. Virgin Islands	0	0	0	0	0	0	0	0	0	0	†

†Not applicable.
NOTE: Degree-granting institutions grant associate's or higher degrees and participate in Title IV federal financial aid programs.

SOURCE: U.S. Department of Education, National Center for Education Statistics, Integrated Postsecondary Education Data System (IPEDS), Spring 2010 and Spring 2011, Enrollment component. (This table was prepared November 2011.)

Total fall enrollment in private not-for-profit degree-granting institutions, by attendance status, sex, and state or jurisdiction: 2009 and 2010

State or jurisdiction	Total	Full-time Males	Full-time Females	Part-time Males	Part-time Females	Total	Full-time Males	Full-time Females	Part-time Males	Part-time Females	Percent change in total, 2009 to 2010
		Fall 2009					Fall 2010				
1	2	3	4	5	6	7	8	9	10	11	12
United States	3,765,083	1,230,953	1,575,692	367,153	591,285	3,854,920	1,269,837	1,618,681	369,231	597,171	2.4
Alabama	24,736	9,028	11,990	1,511	2,207	25,136	9,267	12,342	1,446	2,081	1.6
Alaska	781	138	268	113	262	732	153	247	94	238	-6.3
Arizona	8,414	3,554	2,691	1,037	1,132	8,817	3,864	2,785	1,032	1,136	4.8
Arkansas	15,621	5,655	6,523	1,234	2,209	16,701	6,180	7,096	1,165	2,260	6.9
California	271,618	90,494	119,379	26,053	35,692	285,839	95,158	126,784	27,074	36,823	5.2
Colorado	32,224	8,656	11,961	4,613	6,994	32,938	8,545	12,378	4,778	7,237	2.2
Connecticut	64,727	22,238	28,173	5,050	9,266	66,750	22,406	28,902	5,041	10,401	3.1
Delaware	14,746	3,351	4,603	2,361	4,431	14,833	3,513	4,667	2,452	4,201	0.6
District of Columbia	76,808	23,832	32,870	8,504	11,602	78,215	24,365	33,630	8,509	11,711	1.8
Florida	163,229	49,845	61,732	23,913	27,739	162,285	51,796	61,693	22,223	26,573	-0.6
Georgia	69,007	22,737	35,136	3,811	7,323	71,144	23,348	35,888	4,201	7,707	3.1
Hawaii	13,395	3,355	5,312	2,179	2,549	14,273	3,615	5,688	2,390	2,580	6.6
Idaho	18,081	6,515	8,601	1,138	1,827	18,185	6,749	8,897	876	1,663	0.6
Illinois	225,076	71,993	93,760	21,725	37,598	227,482	73,803	94,402	21,350	37,927	1.1
Indiana	87,208	32,297	39,979	5,479	9,453	88,928	32,851	40,845	5,599	9,633	2.0
Iowa	57,863	20,233	25,733	4,109	7,788	57,373	20,250	25,377	4,047	7,699	-0.8
Kansas	24,927	6,876	8,723	3,458	5,870	25,212	7,220	8,832	3,566	5,594	1.1
Kentucky	35,007	10,850	15,635	2,991	5,531	37,608	11,561	16,756	3,202	6,089	7.4
Louisiana	26,390	8,383	12,168	1,893	3,946	27,667	8,422	12,447	2,194	4,604	4.8
Maine	18,452	6,235	8,573	1,055	2,589	19,578	6,412	9,158	1,147	2,861	6.1
Maryland	53,459	14,303	19,735	7,305	12,116	54,894	15,002	20,514	7,377	12,001	2.7
Massachusetts	271,472	94,202	117,734	22,734	36,802	276,163	96,802	120,618	22,451	36,292	1.7
Michigan	123,384	30,446	40,140	18,850	33,948	124,298	30,065	40,102	19,615	34,516	0.7
Minnesota	73,025	23,360	31,422	6,532	11,711	73,508	23,342	31,833	6,557	11,776	0.7
Mississippi	14,898	4,546	7,494	839	2,019	15,398	4,734	7,735	848	2,081	3.4
Missouri	150,209	37,109	48,176	25,794	39,130	153,824	39,201	49,995	26,023	38,605	2.4
Montana	4,935	1,686	2,259	415	575	5,051	1,792	2,375	288	596	2.4
Nebraska	31,062	8,727	12,085	4,217	6,033	32,940	10,393	14,582	3,213	4,752	6.0
Nevada	1,736	624	815	96	201	3,370	1,238	1,578	156	398	94.1
New Hampshire	25,337	8,578	10,549	2,130	4,080	26,626	9,185	11,117	2,137	4,187	5.1
New Jersey	75,967	27,030	26,961	8,992	12,984	75,979	27,649	27,358	8,454	12,518	0.0
New Mexico	1,158	494	460	56	148	1,120	443	502	48	127	-3.3
New York	526,543	171,987	214,538	51,469	88,549	526,292	174,085	217,095	49,892	85,220	0.0
North Carolina	89,075	33,261	43,873	3,946	7,995	92,027	34,585	45,286	4,043	8,113	3.3
North Dakota	5,877	1,795	2,778	500	804	6,234	1,887	2,972	502	873	6.1
Ohio	140,779	49,453	58,863	11,904	20,559	146,386	50,841	60,031	12,948	22,566	4.0
Oklahoma	22,084	8,933	9,570	1,552	2,029	22,657	8,940	9,717	1,737	2,263	2.6
Oregon	31,324	9,802	14,806	2,744	3,972	32,811	10,344	15,598	2,812	4,057	4.7
Pennsylvania	292,162	97,594	122,752	24,846	46,970	299,011	100,773	126,169	24,812	47,257	2.3
Rhode Island	41,237	18,051	18,803	2,087	2,296	41,886	17,972	19,341	2,171	2,402	1.6
South Carolina	39,017	13,634	19,687	2,153	3,543	35,089	12,153	17,866	1,901	3,169	-10.1
South Dakota	7,416	2,003	3,197	757	1,459	9,044	2,321	3,910	999	1,814	22.0
Tennessee	74,704	26,508	35,815	4,571	7,810	77,764	27,964	36,211	5,152	8,437	4.1
Texas	128,533	44,211	53,091	13,530	17,701	131,481	45,336	54,362	13,749	18,034	2.3
Utah	54,626	23,502	26,146	2,693	2,285	61,310	26,308	30,114	2,626	2,262	12.2
Vermont	17,230	7,910	7,022	885	1,413	17,433	8,192	7,223	735	1,283	1.2
Virginia	98,560	28,465	38,164	13,345	18,586	110,720	32,239	41,249	15,230	22,002	12.3
Washington	42,761	13,245	19,955	3,779	5,782	43,675	13,625	20,453	3,738	5,859	2.1
West Virginia	13,176	4,399	6,532	714	1,531	12,952	4,319	6,226	748	1,659	-1.7
Wisconsin	65,027	18,830	28,460	5,491	12,246	65,281	18,629	27,735	5,883	13,034	0.4
Wyoming	0	0	0	0	0	0	0	0	0	0	†
Other jurisdictions	133,545	41,262	62,223	11,854	18,206	137,372	42,238	62,893	12,663	19,578	2.9
American Samoa	0	0	0	0	0	0	0	0	0	0	†
Federated States of Micronesia	0	0	0	0	0	0	0	0	0	0	†
Guam	94	32	28	11	23	85	35	30	11	9	-9.6
Marshall Islands	0	0	0	0	0	0	0	0	0	0	†
Northern Marianas	0	0	0	0	0	0	0	0	0	0	†
Palau	0	0	0	0	0	0	0	0	0	0	†
Puerto Rico	133,451	41,230	62,195	11,843	18,183	137,287	42,203	62,863	12,652	19,569	2.9
U.S. Virgin Islands	0	0	0	0	0	0	0	0	0	0	†

†Not applicable.
NOTE: Degree-granting institutions grant associate's or higher degrees and participate in Title IV federal financial aid programs.

SOURCE: U.S. Department of Education, National Center for Education Statistics, Integrated Postsecondary Education Data System (IPEDS), Spring 2010 and Spring 2011, Enrollment component. (This table was prepared November 2011.)

Total fall enrollment in private for-profit degree-granting institutions, by attendance status, sex, and state or jurisdiction: 2009 and 2010

State or jurisdiction	Fall 2009					Fall 2010					Percent change in total, 2009 to 2010
	Total	Full-time		Part-time		Total	Full-time		Part-time		
		Males	Females	Males	Females		Males	Females	Males	Females	
1	2	3	4	5	6	7	8	9	10	11	12
United States	1,851,986	495,891	889,902	165,938	300,255	2,018,397	517,627	912,272	208,579	379,919	9.0
Alabama	26,727	7,034	9,673	5,176	4,844	35,108	8,659	12,162	6,559	7,728	31.4
Alaska	1,132	198	560	104	270	618	137	481	0	0	-45.4
Arizona	469,782	137,952	299,760	8,402	23,668	419,595	111,856	252,729	15,890	39,120	-10.7
Arkansas	3,257	1,153	1,985	82	37	3,414	1,083	1,870	188	273	4.8
California	174,491	57,355	84,629	15,463	17,044	204,685	68,255	95,917	19,058	21,455	17.3
Colorado	64,372	20,478	35,314	3,894	4,686	69,680	20,105	36,975	5,693	6,907	8.2
Connecticut	3,868	752	1,368	650	1,098	5,440	1,077	2,021	874	1,468	40.6
Delaware	0	0	0	0	0	490	16	28	150	296	†
District of Columbia	54,790	3,380	5,221	14,419	31,770	7,937	468	659	2,160	4,650	-85.5
Florida	130,513	35,131	60,273	10,379	24,730	173,157	45,523	74,638	14,987	38,009	32.7
Georgia	45,449	11,067	20,367	4,484	9,531	61,470	12,868	23,844	7,334	17,424	35.3
Hawaii	3,469	860	1,959	210	440	3,710	1,068	1,679	322	641	6.9
Idaho	3,108	979	2,003	100	26	2,812	908	1,766	96	42	-9.5
Illinois	87,007	23,122	34,395	12,001	17,489	93,892	20,868	29,980	17,887	25,157	7.9
Indiana	29,014	8,004	13,569	2,967	4,474	32,790	8,593	15,759	3,641	4,797	13.0
Iowa	121,898	16,524	41,354	16,524	47,496	146,688	24,128	58,482	16,701	47,377	20.3
Kansas	3,180	840	1,572	158	610	4,024	1,065	1,950	232	777	26.5
Kentucky	21,392	4,657	10,559	2,203	3,973	23,769	4,954	10,973	2,752	5,090	11.1
Louisiana	9,952	2,321	6,661	289	681	11,160	2,898	7,183	293	786	12.1
Maine	2,050	176	542	241	1,091	1,925	206	687	197	835	-6.1
Maryland	7,297	3,560	2,369	668	700	13,294	4,204	2,933	2,065	4,092	82.2
Massachusetts	6,819	2,588	2,427	678	1,126	7,646	2,769	2,639	800	1,438	12.1
Michigan	9,643	4,332	3,680	957	674	11,383	4,462	5,047	1,100	774	18.0
Minnesota	98,920	12,885	32,895	14,293	38,847	115,652	13,424	34,508	17,843	49,877	16.9
Mississippi	2,721	463	1,893	71	294	3,104	467	2,066	123	448	14.1
Missouri	29,167	8,467	13,822	1,819	5,059	34,752	9,105	14,762	2,317	8,568	19.1
Montana	0	0	0	0	0	0	0	0	0	0	†
Nebraska	3,434	958	1,772	217	487	3,762	1,011	1,788	277	686	9.6
Nevada	11,187	3,828	5,992	634	733	12,887	4,550	6,860	752	725	15.2
New Hampshire	5,390	1,528	2,169	498	1,195	4,896	1,364	1,888	492	1,152	-9.2
New Jersey	7,226	1,993	3,491	709	1,033	9,856	2,380	4,226	1,371	1,879	36.4
New Mexico	8,493	2,828	4,841	252	572	10,676	3,258	6,244	372	802	25.7
New York	50,595	15,926	26,298	2,757	5,614	55,803	17,499	28,331	3,501	6,472	10.3
North Carolina	9,551	2,924	4,354	700	1,573	18,417	4,095	6,109	2,299	5,914	92.8
North Dakota	1,829	202	601	276	750	1,765	212	547	288	718	-3.5
Ohio	48,314	12,233	24,808	5,058	6,215	51,010	13,324	25,113	4,370	8,203	5.6
Oklahoma	8,613	4,122	4,183	183	125	10,274	4,351	5,447	268	208	19.3
Oregon	10,842	3,157	5,405	883	1,397	9,518	2,983	4,175	961	1,399	-12.2
Pennsylvania	59,982	18,755	20,415	7,866	12,946	71,693	20,876	24,202	10,095	16,520	19.5
Rhode Island	27	0	0	4	23	0	0	0	0	0	-100.0
South Carolina	7,446	2,109	3,772	406	1,159	17,124	4,669	7,444	1,370	3,641	130.0
South Dakota	4,252	495	976	945	1,836	4,757	519	1,079	939	2,220	11.9
Tennessee	26,473	9,289	14,196	1,146	1,842	31,738	10,413	14,788	2,061	4,476	19.9
Texas	60,494	19,796	32,945	3,692	4,061	70,492	22,839	37,078	5,047	5,528	16.5
Utah	11,043	4,079	4,693	793	1,478	12,198	4,261	4,836	1,139	1,962	10.5
Vermont	717	408	309	0	0	615	375	240	0	0	-14.2
Virginia	45,383	14,057	25,103	2,107	4,116	56,286	15,669	22,719	6,788	11,110	24.0
Washington	11,380	4,027	5,200	1,109	1,044	13,561	4,647	6,594	1,258	1,062	19.2
West Virginia	34,775	4,223	4,469	18,278	7,805	43,375	3,380	4,422	24,044	11,529	24.7
Wisconsin	13,111	3,427	4,898	1,193	3,593	17,493	3,940	6,244	1,625	5,684	33.4
Wyoming	1,411	1,249	162	0	0	2,006	1,846	160	0	0	42.2
Other jurisdictions	23,217	8,411	10,056	1,893	2,857	43,146	16,850	20,907	2,290	3,099	85.8
American Samoa	0	0	0	0	0	0	0	0	0	0	†
Federated States of Micronesia	0	0	0	0	0	0	0	0	0	0	†
Guam	0	0	0	0	0	0	0	0	0	0	†
Marshall Islands	0	0	0	0	0	0	0	0	0	0	†
Northern Marianas	0	0	0	0	0	0	0	0	0	0	†
Palau	0	0	0	0	0	0	0	0	0	0	†
Puerto Rico	23,217	8,411	10,056	1,893	2,857	43,146	16,850	20,907	2,290	3,099	85.8
U.S. Virgin Islands	0	0	0	0	0	0	0	0	0	0	†

†Not applicable.
NOTE: Degree-granting institutions grant associate's or higher degrees and participate in Title IV federal financial aid programs.

SOURCE: U.S. Department of Education, National Center for Education Statistics, Integrated Postsecondary Education Data System (IPEDS), Spring 2010 and Spring 2011, Enrollment component. (This table was prepared November 2011.)

Fall enrollment in degree-granting institutions, by race/ethnicity of student and state or jurisdiction: 2010

State or jurisdiction	Number									Percentage distribution								
	Total	White	Black	Hispanic	Asian	Pacific Islander	American Indian/ Alaska Native	Two or more races	Non-resident alien	Total	White	Black	Hispanic	Asian	Pacific Islander	American Indian/ Alaska Native	Two or more races	Non-resident alien
1	2	3	4	5	6	7	8	9	10	11	12	13	14	15	16	17	18	19
United States	**21,016,126**	**12,722,549**	**3,038,751**	**2,741,448**	**1,218,118**	**64,046**	**196,374**	**325,275**	**709,565**	**100.0**	**60.5**	**14.5**	**13.0**	**5.8**	**0.3**	**0.9**	**1.5**	**3.4**
Alabama	327,327	201,686	101,659	7,569	4,983	252	2,630	2,238	6,310	100.0	61.6	31.1	2.3	1.5	0.1	0.8	0.7	1.9
Alaska	33,653	22,263	1,054	2,018	1,399	266	3,968	1,906	779	100.0	66.2	3.1	6.0	4.2	0.8	11.8	5.7	2.3
Arizona	795,388	463,078	124,336	130,984	22,192	4,221	21,588	10,885	18,104	100.0	58.2	15.6	16.5	2.8	0.5	2.7	1.4	2.3
Arkansas	175,895	124,345	33,786	6,186	2,682	182	1,675	2,625	4,414	100.0	70.7	19.2	3.5	1.5	0.1	1.0	1.5	2.5
California	2,714,172	1,021,262	210,445	847,507	440,641	18,523	17,964	66,889	90,941	100.0	37.6	7.8	31.2	16.2	0.7	0.7	2.5	3.4
Colorado	372,025	257,881	30,953	50,043	12,906	1,060	4,557	6,993	7,622	100.0	69.3	8.3	13.5	3.5	0.3	1.2	1.9	2.0
Connecticut	199,384	132,283	23,302	22,397	9,117	176	575	3,671	7,863	100.0	66.3	11.7	11.2	4.6	0.1	0.3	1.8	3.9
Delaware	55,731	35,752	12,168	2,837	1,980	69	188	700	2,037	100.0	64.2	21.8	5.1	3.6	0.1	0.3	1.3	3.7
District of Columbia	91,992	45,558	26,298	5,659	6,214	132	349	1,054	6,728	100.0	49.5	28.6	6.2	6.8	0.1	0.4	1.1	7.3
Florida	1,125,469	570,295	225,760	243,216	36,470	1,792	4,735	12,728	30,473	100.0	50.7	20.1	21.6	3.2	0.2	0.4	1.1	2.7
Georgia	568,723	296,125	201,192	22,894	22,013	830	1,986	9,224	14,459	100.0	52.1	35.4	4.0	3.9	0.1	0.3	1.6	2.5
Hawaii	78,073	16,836	1,986	6,113	24,246	8,046	344	15,618	4,884	100.0	21.6	2.5	7.8	31.1	10.3	0.4	20.0	6.3
Idaho	85,201	72,699	1,113	5,686	1,561	513	1,101	738	1,790	100.0	85.3	1.3	6.7	1.8	0.6	1.3	0.9	2.1
Illinois	906,889	549,135	142,143	119,125	49,648	2,031	2,892	11,732	30,183	100.0	60.6	15.7	13.1	5.5	0.2	0.3	1.3	3.3
Indiana	459,423	355,310	49,677	18,689	9,784	293	1,707	5,411	18,552	100.0	77.3	10.8	4.1	2.1	0.1	0.4	1.2	4.0
Iowa	381,842	281,426	46,699	23,362	9,958	859	2,776	4,780	11,982	100.0	73.7	12.2	6.1	2.6	0.2	0.7	1.3	3.1
Kansas	214,859	161,265	15,878	13,533	5,143	243	3,230	3,226	12,341	100.0	75.1	7.4	6.3	2.4	0.1	1.5	1.5	5.7
Kentucky	291,102	242,717	30,282	5,479	3,503	248	939	3,531	4,403	100.0	83.4	10.4	1.9	1.2	0.1	0.3	1.2	1.5
Louisiana	263,638	155,553	82,690	8,396	5,915	140	1,672	2,457	6,815	100.0	59.0	31.4	3.2	2.2	0.1	0.6	0.9	2.6
Maine	72,985	64,986	1,951	1,549	1,371	73	961	811	1,283	100.0	89.0	2.7	2.1	1.9	0.1	1.3	1.1	1.8
Maryland	377,967	196,590	112,474	21,549	24,399	587	1,381	5,779	15,208	100.0	52.0	29.8	5.7	6.5	0.2	0.4	1.5	4.0
Massachusetts	508,302	340,502	43,539	42,115	36,511	483	1,797	7,629	35,726	100.0	67.0	8.6	8.3	7.2	0.1	0.4	1.5	7.0
Michigan	698,125	509,649	103,410	22,463	22,062	885	5,226	9,230	25,190	100.0	73.0	14.8	3.2	3.2	0.1	0.7	1.3	3.6
Minnesota	465,336	339,204	60,448	16,862	19,139	511	4,179	11,067	13,926	100.0	72.9	13.0	3.6	4.1	0.1	0.9	2.4	3.0
Mississippi	178,197	97,918	71,865	2,416	1,770	184	753	846	2,445	100.0	54.9	40.3	1.4	1.0	0.1	0.4	0.5	1.4
Missouri	444,695	331,901	63,346	15,586	11,225	607	2,737	5,521	13,772	100.0	74.6	14.2	3.5	2.5	0.1	0.6	1.2	3.1
Montana	53,312	44,073	409	1,483	553	87	4,642	891	1,174	100.0	82.7	0.8	2.8	1.0	0.2	8.7	1.7	2.2
Nebraska	144,682	118,511	8,496	7,397	3,406	219	1,243	1,222	4,188	100.0	81.9	5.9	5.1	2.4	0.2	0.9	0.8	2.9
Nevada	129,360	70,654	11,025	25,290	12,135	2,263	1,430	4,033	2,530	100.0	54.6	8.5	19.6	9.4	1.7	1.1	3.1	2.0
New Hampshire	75,594	64,753	2,189	3,040	2,089	71	445	775	2,232	100.0	85.7	2.9	4.0	2.8	0.1	0.6	1.0	3.0
New Jersey	444,091	243,978	65,148	74,628	35,416	1,635	1,648	3,639	17,999	100.0	54.9	14.7	16.8	8.0	0.4	0.4	0.8	4.1
New Mexico	162,652	63,058	5,274	71,260	2,837	287	14,220	2,008	3,708	100.0	38.8	3.2	43.8	1.7	0.2	8.7	1.2	2.3
New York	1,305,595	737,122	182,707	174,360	108,164	2,496	5,230	13,792	81,724	100.0	56.5	14.0	13.4	8.3	0.2	0.4	1.1	6.3
North Carolina	586,042	367,956	152,022	24,331	13,595	839	7,149	5,444	14,706	100.0	62.8	25.9	4.2	2.3	0.1	1.2	0.9	2.5
North Dakota	56,903	47,140	1,291	833	606	74	3,381	373	3,205	100.0	82.8	2.3	1.5	1.1	0.1	5.9	0.7	5.6
Ohio	744,947	570,852	106,136	19,673	15,375	431	3,063	7,091	22,326	100.0	76.6	14.2	2.6	2.1	0.1	0.4	1.0	3.0
Oklahoma	230,573	151,870	23,514	10,720	5,959	382	22,532	6,799	8,797	100.0	65.9	10.2	4.6	2.6	0.2	9.8	2.9	3.8
Oregon	250,331	189,352	7,247	21,029	13,581	1,683	4,101	5,214	8,124	100.0	75.6	2.9	8.4	5.4	0.7	1.6	2.1	3.2
Pennsylvania	803,593	596,016	94,269	38,527	33,925	751	2,474	8,139	29,492	100.0	74.2	11.7	4.8	4.2	0.1	0.3	1.0	3.7
Rhode Island	85,110	62,538	5,660	7,589	4,010	52	398	817	4,046	100.0	73.5	6.7	8.9	4.7	0.1	0.5	1.0	4.8

See notes at end of table.

Fall enrollment in degree-granting institutions, by race/ethnicity of student and state or jurisdiction: 2010—Continued

State or jurisdiction	Number									Percentage distribution								
	Total	White	Black	Hispanic	Asian	Pacific Islander	American Indian/ Alaska Native	Two or more races	Non-resident alien	Total	White	Black	Hispanic	Asian	Pacific Islander	American Indian/ Alaska Native	Two or more races	Non-resident alien
1	2	3	4	5	6	7	8	9	10	11	12	13	14	15	16	17	18	19
South Carolina	257,293	164,081	74,582	6,598	3,758	274	1,084	3,028	3,888	100.0	63.8	29.0	2.6	1.5	0.1	0.4	1.2	1.5
South Dakota	58,370	48,307	1,246	1,115	483	106	5,096	812	1,205	100.0	82.8	2.1	1.9	0.8	0.2	8.7	1.4	2.1
Tennessee	351,988	248,301	74,647	9,448	6,776	336	1,255	4,766	6,459	100.0	70.5	21.2	2.7	1.9	0.1	0.4	1.4	1.8
Texas	1,536,858	693,401	209,393	472,438	79,805	2,321	8,165	15,794	55,541	100.0	45.1	13.6	30.7	5.2	0.2	0.5	1.0	3.6
Utah	252,107	208,929	5,808	17,084	5,987	2,019	2,743	2,760	6,777	100.0	82.9	2.3	6.8	2.4	0.8	1.1	1.1	2.7
Vermont	45,572	39,970	1,034	1,426	1,053	25	281	772	1,011	100.0	87.7	2.3	3.1	2.3	0.1	0.6	1.7	2.2
Virginia	576,010	354,478	129,731	32,390	31,858	1,744	2,552	8,383	14,874	100.0	61.5	22.5	5.6	5.5	0.3	0.4	1.5	2.6
Washington	388,110	268,919	18,324	30,591	34,496	1,842	6,024	13,789	14,125	100.0	69.3	4.7	7.9	8.9	0.5	1.6	3.6	3.6
West Virginia	152,431	124,021	13,925	6,086	2,101	413	743	2,246	2,896	100.0	81.4	9.1	4.0	1.4	0.3	0.5	1.5	1.9
Wisconsin	383,986	313,397	24,778	16,042	12,119	331	3,770	4,526	9,023	100.0	81.6	6.5	4.2	3.2	0.1	1.0	1.2	2.3
Wyoming	38,298	32,916	542	2,314	328	69	692	358	1,079	100.0	85.9	1.4	6.0	0.9	0.2	1.8	0.9	2.8
U.S. Service Academies	15,925	11,727	900	1,523	871	80	103	515	206	100.0	73.6	5.7	9.6	5.5	0.5	0.6	3.2	1.3
Other jurisdictions	**264,237**	**875**	**2,377**	**246,110**	**2,784**	**10,370**	**73**	**905**	**743**	**100.0**	**0.3**	**0.9**	**93.1**	**1.1**	**3.9**	**#**	**0.3**	**0.3**
American Samoa	2,193	9	0	0	9	2,008	1	0	166	100.0	0.4	0.0	0.0	0.4	91.6	#	0.0	7.6
Federated States of Micronesia	2,699	2	0	0	3	2,694	0	0	0	100.0	0.1	0.0	0.0	0.1	99.8	0.0	0.0	0.0
Guam	6,188	224	38	37	2,442	3,388	17	0	42	100.0	3.6	0.6	0.6	39.5	54.8	0.3	0.0	0.7
Marshall Islands	869	0	0	0	0	867	0	0	2	100.0	0.0	0.0	0.0	0.0	99.8	0.0	0.0	0.2
Northern Marianas	1,137	23	2	3	215	703	1	27	163	100.0	2.0	0.2	0.3	18.9	61.8	0.1	2.4	14.3
Palau	694	0	0	0	9	685	0	0	0	100.0	0.0	0.0	0.0	1.3	98.7	0.0	0.0	0.0
Puerto Rico	247,724	460	145	245,883	102	25	53	878	178	100.0	0.2	0.1	99.3	0.0	#	#	0.4	0.1
U.S. Virgin Islands	2,733	157	2,192	187	4	0	1	0	192	100.0	5.7	80.2	6.8	0.1	0.0	#	0.0	7.0

#Rounds to zero.
NOTE: Race categories exclude persons of Hispanic ethnicity. Degree-granting institutions grant associate's or higher degrees and participate in Title IV federal financial aid programs. Detail may not sum to totals because of rounding.

SOURCE: U.S. Department of Education, National Center for Education Statistics, Integrated Postsecondary Education Data System (IPEDS), Spring 2011, Enrollment component. (This table was prepared November 2011.)

Enrollment and degrees conferred in degree-granting women's colleges, by selected characteristics and institution: Fall 2010 and 2009–10

Institution[1]	State	Level and control[2]	Enrollment, fall 2010							Degrees awarded to females, 2009–10			
			Total	Females	Percent female	Males, full-time	Females, full-time	Males, part-time	Females, part-time	Associate's	Bachelor's	Master's	Doctor's
1	2	3	4	5	6	7	8	9	10	11	12	13	14
Total	†	†	85,769	80,352	93.7	2,211	58,667	3,206	21,685	744	12,622	4,893	288
Judson College	AL	3	322	309	96.0	6	260	7	49	†	45	†	†
Mills College	CA	3	1,589	1,473	92.7	106	1,355	10	118	†	226	121	5
Mount Saint Mary's College...	CA	3	2,862	2,564	89.6	178	2,002	120	562	146	336	100	21
Scripps College	CA	3	965	960	99.5	3	946	2	14	†	231	†	†
Saint Joseph College	CT	3	2,326	2,160	92.9	25	1,040	141	1,120	†	189	211	0
Trinity Washington University....	DC	3	2,305	2,106	91.4	47	1,149	152	957	9	105	148	†
Agnes Scott College	GA	3	917	899	98.0	16	878	2	21	†	173	14	†
Brenau University	GA	3	2,770	2,425	87.5	120	1,361	225	1,064	6	425	250	†
Spelman College	GA	3	2,177	2,177	100.0	0	2,080	0	97	†	471	†	†
Wesleyan College	GA	3	690	666	96.5	5	414	19	252	†	101	33	†
Lexington College	IL	3	55	55	100.0	0	52	0	3	2	15	†	†
Saint Mary-of-the-Woods College	IN	3	1,595	1,493	93.6	30	629	72	864	6	145	58	†
Saint Mary's College	IN	3	1,555	1,552	99.8	2	1,540	1	12	†	376	†	†
Midway College	KY	3	1,606	1,337	83.3	137	917	132	420	93	155	12	†
College of Notre Dame of Maryland	MD	3	2,982	2,581	86.6	73	694	328	1,887	†	311	302	3
Bay Path College	MA	3	2,116	2,050	96.9	21	1,359	45	691	66	283	162	†
Mount Holyoke College	MA	3	2,344	2,340	99.8	0	2,291	4	49	†	598	0	†
Pine Manor College	MA	3	485	479	98.8	6	470	0	9	4	68	10	†
Simmons College	MA	3	4,983	4,564	91.6	86	2,503	333	2,061	†	487	859	68
Smith College	MA	3	3,113	3,040	97.7	63	2,957	10	83	†	729	148	6
Wellesley College	MA	3	2,546	2,487	97.7	2	2,427	57	60	†	555	†	†
College of Saint Benedict	MN	3	2,082	2,082	100.0	0	2,038	0	44	†	486	†	†
St. Catherine University	MN	3	5,328	5,096	95.6	111	3,447	121	1,649	192	523	376	35
Cottey College	MO	4	307	307	100.0	0	303	0	4	129	†	†	†
Stephens College	MO	3	1,123	1,061	94.5	44	857	18	204	0	209	64	†
College of Saint Mary	NE	3	1,070	1,044	97.6	14	829	12	215	74	120	98	20
College of Saint Elizabeth	NJ	3	2,112	1,858	88.0	39	718	215	1,140	†	193	184	7
Barnard College	NY	3	2,390	2,390	100.0	0	2,335	0	55	†	617	†	†
College of New Rochelle	NY	3	4,812	4,368	90.8	289	3,184	155	1,184	†	800	296	†
Bennett College for Women...	NC	3	780	780	100.0	0	714	0	66	†	79	†	†
Meredith College	NC	3	2,132	2,090	98.0	4	1,760	38	330	†	397	45	†
Salem College	NC	3	1,063	1,002	94.3	26	690	35	312	†	154	36	†
Ursuline College	OH	3	1,485	1,335	89.9	65	711	85	624	†	221	97	†
Bryn Mawr College	PA	3	1,751	1,664	95.0	72	1,536	15	128	†	319	92	13
Carlow College	PA	3	2,768	2,369	85.6	141	1,556	258	813	†	321	210	0
Cedar Crest College	PA	3	1,666	1,578	94.7	20	843	68	735	†	341	33	†
Chatham University	PA	3	2,266	1,914	84.5	186	1,328	166	586	†	193	289	110
Moore College of Art and Design	PA	3	556	552	99.3	2	477	2	75	†	117	6	†
Wilson College	PA	3	790	676	85.6	24	368	90	308	12	62	9	†
Columbia College	SC	3	1,367	1,316	96.3	25	1,073	26	243	†	215	140	†
Converse College	SC	3	1,269	1,171	92.3	38	792	60	379	†	131	124	†
Hollins University	VA	3	1,024	966	94.3	25	810	33	156	†	162	66	†
Mary Baldwin College	VA	3	1,849	1,691	91.5	67	1,110	91	581	†	259	46	†
Sweet Briar College	VA	3	760	734	96.6	25	707	1	27	†	137	6	†
Alverno College	WI	3	2,759	2,708	98.2	35	1,871	16	837	5	342	109	†
Mount Mary College	WI	3	1,957	1,883	96.2	33	1,286	41	597	†	200	139	†

†Not applicable.

[1]Data are for colleges and universities identified by the Women's College Coalition as women's colleges in 2011. Excludes women's colleges whose IPEDS data are reported together with a coed institution or coordinate men's college. The following institutions were excluded for this reason: The Women's College of the University of Denver; Newcomb College Institute of Tulane University; Douglass Residential College of Rutgers University; Georgian Court University; and Russell Sage College of the Sage Colleges.

[2]1 = public, 4-year; 3 = private not-for-profit, 4-year; and 4 = private not-for-profit, 2-year.
NOTE: Degree-granting institutions grant associate's or higher degrees and participate in Title IV federal financial aid programs.
SOURCE: U.S. Department of Education, National Center for Education Statistics, Integrated Postsecondary Education Data System (IPEDS), Spring 2011, Enrollment component; and Fall 2010, Completions component. (This table was prepared December 2011.)

Enrollment and degrees conferred in degree-granting institutions that serve large proportions of Hispanic undergraduate students, by selected characteristics and institution: Fall 2010 and 2009–10

Institution	Level and control[1]	Enrollment, fall 2010					Degrees awarded to Hispanics, 2009–10			
		Total	Hispanic	Percent Hispanic[2]	Hispanic undergraduate	Hispanic postbacca-laureate	Associate's	Bachelor's	Master's	Doctor's[3]
1	2	3	4	5	6	7	8	9	10	12
Total, 50 states and District of Columbia	†	3,455,024	1,456,522	42.2	1,400,894	55,628	64,743	46,120	11,567	1,172
Total, 50 states, District of Columbia, and Puerto Rico	†	3,700,055	1,699,850	45.9	1,617,863	81,987	70,842	63,539	16,483	2,024
Alaska										
Charter College	5	618	183	29.6	183	†	8	1	†	†
Arizona										
Arizona College of Allied Health	6	832	222	26.7	222	†	13	†	†	†
Arizona Western College	2	8,545	5,064	59.3	5,064	†	290	†	†	†
Art Center Design College, Tucson	5	261	92	35.2	92	†	0	15	†	†
Art Institute of Phoenix	5	1,291	464	35.9	464	†	4	24	†	†
Art Institute of Tucson	5	477	169	35.4	169	†	0	0	†	†
Brookline College, Phoenix	5	1,636	605	37.0	605	†	19	10	†	†
Brookline College, Tempe	6	579	171	29.5	171	†	2	†	†	†
Brookline College, Tucson	6	984	575	58.4	575	†	34	†	†	†
Bryman School of Arizona	6	804	308	38.3	308	†	6	†	†	†
Carrington College, Mesa	6	1,099	349	31.8	349	†	13	†	†	†
Carrington College, Phoenix	6	977	487	49.8	487	†	2	†	†	†
Carrington College, Tucson	6	867	496	57.2	496	†	2	†	†	†
Carrington College, Westside	6	694	211	30.4	211	†	30	†	†	†
Central Arizona College	2	7,117	2,069	29.1	2,069	†	86	†	†	†
Cochise College	2	5,585	2,285	40.9	2,285	†	202	†	†	†
DeVry University, Arizona	5	2,592	785	30.3	700	85	5	30	12	†
Estrella Mountain Community College	2	8,122	3,332	41.0	3,332	†	175	†	†	†
Everest College, Mesa	5	527	162	30.7	162	†	27	†	†	†
Fortis College	6	267	104	39.0	104	†	0	†	†	†
Frank Lloyd Wright School of Architecture	3	29	3	10.3	3	0	†	0	1	†
GateWay Community College	2	7,346	2,171	29.6	2,171	†	123	†	†	†
Glendale Community College	2	21,373	6,020	28.2	6,020	†	242	†	†	†
ITT Technical Institute, Tucson	5	521	219	42.0	219	†	28	12	†	†
ITT Technical Institute, Phoenix	5	568	163	28.7	163	†	4	0	†	†
Lamson College	6	258	97	37.6	97	†	6	†	†	†
Phoenix College	2	13,000	5,367	41.3	5,367	†	249	†	†	†
Pima Community College	2	36,823	13,538	36.8	13,538	†	636	†	†	†
Pima Medical Institute, Mesa	6	1,536	463	30.1	463	†	12	†	†	†
Pima Medical Institute, Tucson	5	1,398	672	48.1	672	†	15	†	†	†
Refrigeration School Inc.	6	504	142	28.2	142	†	7	†	†	†
Sanford-Brown College, Phoenix	6	518	231	44.6	231	†	0	†	†	†
South Mountain Community College	2	6,354	2,633	41.4	2,633	†	161	†	†	†
University of Phoenix, Southern Arizona Campus	5	2,275	968	42.5	844	124	†	115	71	†
California										
Advanced College	6	225	161	71.6	161	†	0	†	†	†
Advanced Training Associates	6	48	13	27.1	13	†	†	†	†	†
Allan Hancock College	2	12,108	3,597	29.7	3,597	†	329	†	†	†
Alliant International University	3	4,065	701	17.2	47	654	†	9	63	44
American Career College, Anaheim	6	1,652	832	50.4	832	†	18	†	†	†
American Career College, Los Angeles	6	1,693	1,018	60.1	1,018	†	17	†	†	†
American Career College, Ontario	6	1,416	864	61.0	864	†	11	†	†	†
Antelope Valley College	2	14,408	5,276	36.6	5,276	†	207	†	†	†
Antioch University, Santa Barbara	3	369	97	26.3	43	54	†	8	18	1
Argosy University, Inland Empire	5	710	274	38.6	146	128	†	2	11	0
Argosy University, Los Angeles	5	555	157	28.3	61	96	†	5	13	0
Argosy University, Orange County	5	925	226	24.4	71	155	†	5	14	2
Argosy University, San Diego	5	353	90	25.5	35	55	†	1	3	0
Art Institute of California, Hollywood	5	1,775	1,065	60.0	1,065	†	12	17	†	†
Art Institute of California, Inland Empire	5	1,938	1,040	53.7	1,040	†	21	14	†	†
Art Institute of California, Los Angeles	5	2,275	1,135	49.9	1,135	†	13	55	†	†
Art Institute of California, Orange County	5	2,135	926	43.4	926	†	1	20	†	†
Art Institute of California, Sacramento	5	1,063	368	34.6	368	†	0	0	†	†
Art Institute of California, San Diego	5	2,184	851	39.0	851	†	40	69	†	†
Art Institute of California, San Francisco	5	1,651	600	36.3	599	1	1	27	0	†
Art Institute of California, Sunnyvale	5	564	177	31.4	177	†	1	0	†	†
Bakersfield College	2	19,569	10,213	52.2	10,213	†	372	†	†	†
Barstow Community College	2	2,757	788	28.6	788	†	68	†	†	†
Bethany University	3	443	144	32.5	132	12	0	9	6	†
Brandman University, part of the Chapman University System	3	6,849	1,663	24.3	900	763	7	208	149	†
Bryan College	6	946	278	29.4	278	†	6	†	†	†
Cabrillo College	2	15,387	4,811	31.3	4,811	†	250	†	†	†
California Christian College	3	20	8	40.0	8	†	0	2	†	†
California College, San Diego	5	485	152	31.3	152	†	27	11	†	†
California State Polytechnic University, Pomona	1	20,747	7,089	34.2	6,535	554	†	825	59	†
California State University, Bakersfield	1	7,906	3,817	48.3	3,310	507	†	446	92	†

See notes at end of table.

Enrollment and degrees conferred in degree-granting institutions that serve large proportions of Hispanic undergraduate students, by selected characteristics and institution: Fall 2010 and 2009–10—Continued

Institution	Level and control[1]	Enrollment, fall 2010					Degrees awarded to Hispanics, 2009–10			
		Total	Hispanic	Percent Hispanic[2]	Hispanic under-graduate	Hispanic postbacca-laureate	Associate's	Bachelor's	Master's	Doctor's[3]
1	2	3	4	5	6	7	8	9	10	12
California State University, Channel Islands	1	3,828	1,412	36.9	1,359	53	†	146	17	†
California State University, Dominguez Hills	1	13,854	6,092	44.0	5,180	912	†	493	188	†
California State University, Fresno	1	20,932	7,889	37.7	6,928	961	†	973	186	3
California State University, Fullerton	1	35,590	11,568	32.5	10,456	1,112	†	1,680	203	0
California State University, Long Beach	1	33,416	10,571	31.6	9,103	1,468	†	1,356	343	1
California State University, Los Angeles	1	20,142	10,586	52.6	9,079	1,507	†	1,059	374	†
California State University, Monterey Bay	1	4,790	1,698	35.4	1,591	107	†	124	8	†
California State University, Northridge	1	35,272	12,411	35.2	11,267	1,144	†	1,348	306	†
California State University, San Bernardino	1	16,400	7,615	46.4	6,771	844	†	903	190	†
California State University, San Marcos	1	9,722	2,946	30.3	2,778	168	†	333	11	†
California State University, Stanislaus	1	8,305	3,208	38.6	2,785	423	†	384	37	†
Cambridge Junior College, Woodland	6	46	27	58.7	27	†	†	†	†	†
Cambridge Junior College, Yuba City	6	201	86	42.8	86	†	2	†	†	†
Canada College	2	6,768	3,038	44.9	3,038	†	53	†	†	†
Career Networks Institute	6	836	263	31.5	263	†	0	†	†	†
Carrington College California, Antioch	6	520	145	27.9	145	†	7	†	†	†
Carrington College California, San Jose	6	1,006	443	44.0	443	†	45	†	†	†
Carrington College California, San Leandro	6	908	320	35.2	320	†	17	†	†	†
Carrington College California, Stockton	6	665	230	34.6	230	†	29	†	†	†
Casa Loma College, Van Nuys	4	587	217	37.0	217	†	†	†	†	†
Cerritos College	2	22,142	13,684	61.8	13,684	†	460	†	†	†
Chabot College	2	15,084	4,624	30.7	4,624	†	159	†	†	†
Chaffey College	2	19,469	10,048	51.6	10,048	†	576	†	†	†
Citrus College	2	12,386	6,770	54.7	6,770	†	375	†	†	†
College of San Mateo	2	10,288	2,736	26.6	2,736	†	100	†	†	†
College of the Canyons	2	23,332	8,521	36.5	8,521	†	248	†	†	†
College of the Desert	2	9,993	5,612	56.2	5,612	†	250	†	†	†
College of the Sequoias	2	13,470	7,196	53.4	7,196	†	377	†	†	†
Community Christian College	4	94	58	61.7	58	†	1	†	†	†
Concorde Career College, Garden Grove	6	695	296	42.6	296	†	22	†	†	†
Concorde Career College, North Hollywood	6	643	344	53.5	344	†	32	†	†	†
Concorde Career College, San Bernardino	6	729	343	47.1	343	†	24	†	†	†
Concorde Career College, San Diego	6	621	232	37.4	232	†	7	†	†	†
Contra Costa College	2	7,975	2,454	30.8	2,454	†	134	†	†	†
Crafton Hills College	2	6,108	2,054	33.6	2,054	†	87	†	†	†
Cuyamaca College	2	9,907	2,611	26.4	2,611	†	84	†	†	†
Cypress College	2	16,153	5,804	35.9	5,804	†	198	†	†	†
DeVry University, California	5	13,259	5,794	43.7	5,355	439	65	269	77	†
East Los Angeles College	2	35,100	25,161	71.7	25,161	†	668	†	†	†
El Camino College, Compton Center	2	8,729	3,285	37.6	3,285	†	52	†	†	†
El Camino Community College District	2	24,756	9,821	39.7	9,821	†	402	†	†	†
Empire College School of Business	6	609	171	28.1	171	†	24	†	†	†
Everest College, Anaheim	6	772	508	65.8	508	†	†	†	†	†
Everest College, Gardena	6	758	325	42.9	325	†	†	†	†	†
Everest College, Los Angeles, Wilshire	6	341	205	60.1	205	†	†	†	†	†
Everest College, Ontario	6	826	504	61.0	504	†	†	†	†	†
Everest College, Ontario Metro	5	1,162	757	65.1	757	†	151	23	†	†
Everest College, Reseda	6	864	575	66.6	575	†	†	†	†	†
Everest College, San Bernardino	6	847	476	56.2	476	†	4	†	†	†
Everest College, West Los Angeles	6	529	260	49.1	260	†	13	†	†	†
Evergreen Valley College	2	10,551	4,227	40.1	4,227	†	121	†	†	†
Fashion Careers College	6	83	31	37.3	31	†	11	†	†	†
FIDM/Fashion Institute of Design & Merchandising, Orange Co.	6	372	127	34.1	127	†	†	†	†	†
FIDM/Fashion Institute of Design & Merchandising, San Diego	6	292	95	32.5	95	†	12	†	†	†
Fremont College	5	390	172	44.1	172	†	37	†	†	†
Fresno City College	2	23,902	10,717	44.8	10,717	†	437	†	†	†
Fresno Pacific University	3	3,356	1,185	35.3	925	260	0	165	36	†
Fullerton College	2	22,562	9,985	44.3	9,985	†	184	†	†	†
Gavilan College	2	7,611	3,587	47.1	3,587	†	130	†	†	†
Hartnell College	2	9,812	6,413	65.4	6,413	†	274	†	†	†
Heald College, Fresno	6	2,077	612	29.5	612	†	171	†	†	†
Heald College, Modesto	6	287	158	55.1	158	†	0	†	†	†
Heald College, Salinas	6	1,479	465	31.4	465	†	202	†	†	†
Heald College, San Francisco	6	1,541	523	33.9	523	†	61	†	†	†
Heald College, San Jose	6	1,680	792	47.1	792	†	162	†	†	†
Holy Names University	3	1,164	237	20.4	172	65	†	22	5	†
Humphreys College, Stockton and Modesto Campuses	3	900	310	34.4	259	51	16	23	0	3
ICDC College	6	3,194	2,017	63.1	2,017	†	0	†	†	†
Imperial Valley College	2	8,991	8,348	92.8	8,348	†	491	†	†	†
Institute of Technology Inc.	6	1,314	516	39.3	516	†	53	†	†	†
ITT Technical Institute, Clovis	5	598	327	54.7	327	†	50	6	†	†

See notes at end of table.

Enrollment and degrees conferred in degree-granting institutions that serve large proportions of Hispanic undergraduate students, by selected characteristics and institution: Fall 2010 and 2009–10—Continued

Institution	Level and control[1]	Enrollment, fall 2010					Degrees awarded to Hispanics, 2009–10			
		Total	Hispanic	Percent Hispanic[2]	Hispanic undergraduate	Hispanic postbacca-laureate	Associate's	Bachelor's	Master's	Doctor's[3]
1	2	3	4	5	6	7	8	9	10	12
ITT Technical Institute, Concord	5	445	131	29.4	131	†	0	0	†	†
ITT Technical Institute, Corona	5	204	73	35.8	73	†	0	0	†	†
ITT Technical Institute, Culver City	5	229	125	54.6	125	†	0	0	†	†
ITT Technical Institute, Lathrop	5	723	297	41.1	297	†	74	32	†	†
ITT Technical Institute, Orange	5	994	519	52.2	519	†	110	26	†	†
ITT Technical Institute, Oxnard	5	474	248	52.3	248	†	64	32	†	†
ITT Technical Institute, San Bernardino	5	1,513	813	53.7	813	†	166	59	†	†
ITT Technical Institute, San Diego	5	1,654	671	40.6	671	†	86	32	†	†
ITT Technical Institute, San Dimas	5	907	537	59.2	537	†	113	65	†	†
ITT Technical Institute, Sylmar	5	1,046	636	60.8	636	†	110	45	†	†
ITT Technical Institute, Torrance	5	905	526	58.1	526	†	119	26	†	†
ITT Technical Institute, West Covina	5	343	279	81.3	279	†	0	0	†	†
Kaplan College, Panorama City	6	237	161	67.9	161	†	3	†	†	†
Kaplan College, Bakersfield	6	846	589	69.6	589	†	21	†	†	†
Kaplan College, Fresno	6	622	393	63.2	393	†	37	†	†	†
Kaplan College, Modesto Campus	6	1,091	589	54.0	589	†	4	†	†	†
Kaplan College, Palm Springs	6	652	289	44.3	289	†	3	†	†	†
Kaplan College, Stockton	6	521	228	43.8	228	†	14	†	†	†
Kaplan College, Vista	6	1,215	560	46.1	560	†	15	†	†	†
La Sierra University	3	2,096	638	30.4	588	50	†	46	10	1
Le Cordon Bleu College of Culinary Arts	6	2,756	1,170	42.5	1,170	†	144	†	†	†
Long Beach City College	2	26,517	10,775	40.6	10,775	†	279	†	†	†
Los Angeles City College	2	20,430	9,430	46.2	9,430	†	198	†	†	†
Los Angeles County College of Nursing and Allied Health	2	274	107	39.1	107	†	42	†	†	†
Los Angeles Film School	6	2,083	669	32.1	669	†	44	†	†	†
Los Angeles Harbor College	2	11,149	5,596	50.2	5,596	†	291	†	†	†
Los Angeles Mission College	2	11,357	8,532	75.1	8,532	†	231	†	†	†
Los Angeles ORT College, Los Angeles	4	220	75	34.1	75	†	6	†	†	†
Los Angeles ORT College, Van Nuys	4	69	23	33.3	23	†	7	†	†	†
Los Angeles Pierce College	2	21,368	8,478	39.7	8,478	†	216	†	†	†
Los Angeles Southwest College	2	7,591	2,095	27.6	2,095	†	32	†	†	†
Los Angeles Trade Technical College	2	15,734	8,770	55.7	8,770	†	175	†	†	†
Los Angeles Valley College	2	20,667	9,714	47.0	9,714	†	316	†	†	†
Los Medanos College	2	9,738	3,104	31.9	3,104	†	87	†	†	†
Merced College	2	11,086	5,598	50.5	5,598	†	220	†	†	†
MiraCosta College	2	14,529	3,837	26.4	3,837	†	128	†	†	†
Modesto Junior College	2	18,492	6,943	37.5	6,943	†	293	†	†	†
Monterey Peninsula College	2	9,674	2,399	24.8	2,399	†	71	†	†	†
Mount Saint Mary's College	3	2,862	1,457	50.9	1,224	233	70	157	35	2
Mount San Antonio College	2	29,064	15,187	52.3	15,187	†	735	†	†	†
Mount San Jacinto Community College District	2	16,108	5,552	34.5	5,552	†	349	†	†	†
Mount Sierra College	5	535	235	43.9	235	†	†	21	†	†
Napa Valley College	2	6,350	1,940	30.6	1,940	†	169	†	†	†
National Hispanic University	5	609	491	80.6	400	91	2	17	†	†
Newschool of Architecture and Design	5	644	172	26.7	132	40	†	11	10	†
Notre Dame de Namur University	3	1,790	402	22.5	288	114	†	42	25	†
Oxnard College	2	7,961	5,387	67.7	5,387	†	351	†	†	†
Pacific College	6	244	121	49.6	121	†	0	†	†	†
Pacific College of Oriental Medicine	5	588	68	11.6	24	44	0	0	10	1
Pacific Oaks College	3	462	173	37.4	71	102	†	15	38	†
Palo Verde College	2	3,898	1,231	31.6	1,231	†	54	†	†	†
Palomar College	2	26,231	8,515	32.5	8,515	†	506	†	†	†
Pasadena City College	2	27,023	10,688	39.6	10,688	†	453	†	†	†
Pima Medical Institute	6	1,000	523	52.3	523	†	18	†	†	†
Pinnacle College	6	200	77	38.5	77	†	0	†	†	†
Platt College, Los Angeles	5	358	298	83.2	298	†	64	27	†	†
Platt College, Ontario	5	672	409	60.9	409	†	66	17	†	†
Platt College, San Diego	5	360	96	26.7	96	†	30	7	†	†
Porterville College	2	4,320	2,642	61.2	2,642	†	155	†	†	†
Reedley College	2	14,919	7,949	53.3	7,949	†	300	†	†	†
Rio Hondo College	2	22,457	11,237	50.0	11,237	†	469	†	†	†
Riverside Community College	2	20,585	9,602	46.6	9,602	†	1,029	†	†	†
Sacramento City College	2	25,039	6,317	25.2	6,317	†	216	†	†	†
Sage College	6	587	177	30.2	177	†	0	†	†	†
San Bernardino Valley College	2	13,822	7,531	54.5	7,531	†	273	†	†	†
San Diego City College	2	18,549	7,629	41.1	7,629	†	209	†	†	†
San Diego Mesa College	2	25,972	6,793	26.2	6,793	†	145	†	†	†
San Diego State University	1	29,187	7,577	26.0	6,593	984	†	1,464	224	11
San Diego State University, Imperial Valley Campus	1	872	794	91.1	663	131	†	153	17	†
San Joaquin Delta College	2	18,610	6,425	34.5	6,425	†	890	†	†	†
San Joaquin Valley College, Bakersfield	6	984	485	49.3	485	†	179	†	†	†
San Joaquin Valley College, Fresno	6	943	498	52.8	498	†	181	†	†	†

See notes at end of table.

Enrollment and degrees conferred in degree-granting institutions that serve large proportions of Hispanic undergraduate students, by selected characteristics and institution: Fall 2010 and 2009–10—Continued

Institution	Level and control[1]	Enrollment, fall 2010					Degrees awarded to Hispanics, 2009–10			
		Total	Hispanic	Percent Hispanic[2]	Hispanic under-graduate	Hispanic postbacca-laureate	Associate's	Bachelor's	Master's	Doctor's[3]
1	2	3	4	5	6	7	8	9	10	12
San Joaquin Valley College, Fresno Aviation Campus	6	102	38	37.3	38	†	12	†	†	†
San Joaquin Valley College, Hesperia....................	6	694	358	51.6	358	†	0	†	†	†
San Joaquin Valley College, Modesto Campus..............	6	590	309	52.4	309	†	53	†	†	†
San Joaquin Valley College, Rancho Cucamonga	6	971	603	62.1	603	†	270	†	†	†
San Joaquin Valley College, Visalia	6	1,242	645	51.9	645	†	240	†	†	†
San Jose City College	2	11,120	4,710	42.4	4,710	†	121	†	†	†
Santa Ana College	2	31,377	15,398	49.1	15,398	†	641	†	†	†
Santa Barbara Business College, Bakersfield............	6	972	640	65.8	640	†	90	†	†	†
Santa Barbara Business College, Santa Maria	6	328	206	62.8	206	†	26	†	†	†
Santa Barbara Business College, Ventura................	6	492	283	57.5	283	†	43	†	†	†
Santa Barbara City College	2	18,827	6,256	33.2	6,256	†	240	†	†	†
Santa Monica College	2	31,118	10,280	33.0	10,280	†	346	†	†	†
Santiago Canyon College	2	13,123	5,911	45.0	5,911	†	157	†	†	†
Skyline College	2	9,912	2,484	25.1	2,484	†	100	†	†	†
South Coast College......................................	6	423	140	33.1	140	†	14	†	†	†
Southern California Institute of Technology	5	695	265	38.1	265	†	2	25	†	†
Southwestern College	2	19,476	12,414	63.7	12,414	†	707	†	†	†
Stanbridge College	5	336	88	26.2	88	†	0	†	†	†
Taft College...	2	7,920	3,858	48.7	3,858	†	68	†	†	†
United Education Institute, Huntington Park Campus......	6	4,370	3,271	74.9	3,271	†	13	†	†	†
United States University	5	317	128	40.4	112	16	†	20	0	†
University of Antelope Valley	5	967	407	42.1	407	0	14	†	†	†
University of California, Merced.........................	1	4,381	1,549	35.4	1,517	32	†	87	4	0
University of California, Riverside......................	1	20,692	6,130	29.6	5,883	247	†	795	48	16
University of La Verne	3	8,032	3,103	38.6	1,957	1,146	†	338	264	23
University of Phoenix, Central Valley Campus.............	5	2,554	1,150	45.0	1,025	125	†	112	27	†
University of Phoenix, San Diego Campus.................	5	5,491	2,132	38.8	1,920	212	†	147	46	†
University of Phoenix, Southern California Campus........	5	10,701	4,327	40.4	3,755	572	†	576	152	†
Ventura College	2	13,711	6,663	48.6	6,663	†	430	†	†	†
Victor Valley College	2	12,892	5,090	39.5	5,090	†	290	†	†	†
West Hills College, Coalinga	2	2,856	1,695	59.3	1,695	†	93	†	†	†
West Hills College, Lemoore	2	3,927	1,904	48.5	1,904	†	135	†	†	†
West Los Angeles College................................	2	11,915	3,966	33.3	3,966	†	89	†	†	†
Westwood College, Anaheim	5	1,159	608	52.5	608	†	3	86	†	†
Westwood College, Inland Empire........................	5	1,337	921	68.9	921	†	8	109	†	†
Westwood College, South Bay	5	780	384	49.2	384	†	4	71	†	†
Whittier College	3	2,288	696	30.4	549	147	†	74	17	16
Woodbury University......................................	3	1,628	483	29.7	426	57	†	61	41	†
Woodland Community College	2	2,972	1,331	44.8	1,331	†	44	†	†	†
Wyotech, Fremont...	6	2,015	726	36.0	726	†	18	†	†	†
Wyotech, Long Beach......................................	6	2,051	1,359	66.3	1,359	†	†	†	†	†
Wyotech, West Sacramento	6	1,594	451	28.3	451	†	19	†	†	†
Colorado										
Adams State College......................................	1	3,237	1,008	31.1	853	155	6	61	24	†
Aims Community College	2	5,340	1,378	25.8	1,378	†	64	†	†	†
College America, Denver.................................	5	792	219	27.7	219	†	13	7	†	†
Colorado Heights University..............................	3	144	37	25.7	37	0	†	0	0	†
Colorado State University, Pueblo.......................	1	7,379	1,662	22.5	1,470	192	†	161	13	†
Community College of Denver.............................	2	12,901	3,672	28.5	3,672	†	105	†	†	†
Concorde Career Colleges	6	651	188	28.9	188	†	10	†	†	†
Everest College, Aurora.................................	6	747	223	29.9	223	†	12	†	†	†
Everest College, Thornton...............................	6	752	373	49.6	373	†	44	†	†	†
Heritage College, Denver	6	781	219	28.0	219	†	83	†	†	†
Institute of Business and Medical Careers	6	321	85	26.5	85	†	41	†	†	†
Intellitec College, Grand Junction	6	834	262	31.4	262	†	61	†	†	†
ITT Technical Institute, Thornton	5	568	146	25.7	146	†	28	17	†	†
Lincoln College of Technology	6	1,233	350	28.4	350	†	35	†	†	†
Otero Junior College....................................	2	1,823	634	34.8	634	†	38	†	†	†
Pima Medical Institute..................................	6	1,144	416	36.4	416	†	9	†	†	†
Pueblo Community College	2	7,943	2,617	32.9	2,617	†	146	†	†	†
Trinidad State Junior College...........................	2	1,916	877	45.8	877	†	54	†	†	†
Westwood College, Denver South	5	427	121	28.3	121	†	8	10	†	†
Connecticut										
Capital Community College	2	4,518	1,432	31.7	1,432	†	94	†	†	†
Housatonic Community College	2	6,197	1,591	25.7	1,591	†	81	†	†	†
Norwalk Community College	2	6,740	1,821	27.0	1,821	†	96	†	†	†
Sanford-Brown College, Farmington.......................	6	148	46	31.1	46	†	28	†	†	†
Florida										
Acupuncture and Massage College.........................	5	158	91	57.6	29	62	†	10	10	†
AI Miami International University of Art and Design	5	4,029	1,855	46.0	1,814	41	36	100	1	†
American InterContinental University	5	849	346	40.8	314	32	36	44	12	†
Angley College...	5	401	101	25.2	101	†	9	0	†	†

See notes at end of table.

Enrollment and degrees conferred in degree-granting institutions that serve large proportions of Hispanic undergraduate students, by selected characteristics and institution: Fall 2010 and 2009–10—Continued

Institution	Level and control[1]	Enrollment, fall 2010					Degrees awarded to Hispanics, 2009–10			
		Total	Hispanic	Percent Hispanic[2]	Hispanic under-graduate	Hispanic postbacca-laureate	Associate's	Bachelor's	Master's	Doctor's[3]
1	2	3	4	5	6	7	8	9	10	12
Anthem College, Orlando	6	541	190	35.1	190	†	2	†	†	†
Argosy University, Tampa	5	684	114	16.7	27	87	†	2	10	2
Art Institute of Fort Lauderdale	5	2,953	1,141	38.6	1,141	†	97	116	†	†
Atlantic Institute of Oriental Medicine	3	129	32	24.8	7	25	†	7	7	†
Barry University	3	8,995	2,716	30.2	1,761	955	†	404	221	41
Broward College	1	40,375	13,139	32.5	13,139	†	1,409	0	†	†
Carlos Albizu University, Miami Campus	3	1,078	882	81.8	307	575	†	114	116	12
City College, Casselberry	4	278	94	33.8	94	†	20	†	†	†
City College, Miami	3	382	242	63.4	242	†	53	13	†	†
College of Business and Technology, Cutler Bay	6	216	108	50.0	108	†	0	†	†	†
College of Business and Technology, Flagler Campus	6	102	102	100.0	102	†	157	†	†	†
College of Business and Technology, Hialeah Campus	6	203	203	100.0	203	†	0	†	†	†
College of Business and Technology, Miami	6	144	135	93.8	135	†	11	†	†	†
Concorde Career Institute, Miramar	6	403	121	30.0	121	†	0	†	†	†
Concorde Career Institute, Orlando	6	178	79	44.4	79	†	0	†	†	†
Concorde Career Institute, Tampa	6	422	133	31.5	133	†	0	†	†	†
Dade Medical College, Hialeah	6	100	80	80.0	80	†	3	†	†	†
Dade Medical College, Homestead	6	62	33	53.2	33	†	0	†	†	†
Dade Medical College, Miami	6	160	120	75.0	120	†	12	†	†	†
DeVry University, Florida	5	5,821	2,175	37.4	1,757	418	21	150	74	†
Everest Institute, Hialeah	6	894	654	73.2	654	†	22	†	†	†
Everest Institute, Kendall	6	897	606	67.6	606	†	31	†	†	†
Everest University, Tampa	5	1,789	663	37.1	659	4	51	9	2	†
Florida Career College, Miami	5	4,362	1,510	34.6	1,510	†	148	22	†	†
Florida College of Natural Health, Miami	6	342	256	74.9	256	†	23	†	†	†
Florida College of Natural Health, Pompano Beach	6	433	119	27.5	119	†	10	†	†	†
Florida International University	1	42,197	25,955	61.5	22,333	3,622	38	3,918	1,014	109
Florida National College, Main Campus	5	2,819	2,504	88.8	2,504	†	283	25	†	†
Florida Technical College	6	2,088	631	30.2	631	†	63	†	†	†
Fortis College, Miami	6	894	820	91.7	820	†	91	†	†	†
Fortis College, Winter Park	6	267	82	30.7	82	†	3	†	†	†
Heritage Institute, Fort Myers	6	1,128	325	28.8	325	†	91	†	†	†
Hodges University	3	2,580	784	30.4	747	37	48	62	13	†
International Academy of Design and Technology	5	998	372	37.3	372	†	5	38	†	†
ITT Technical Institute, Fort Lauderdale	5	830	269	32.4	269	†	53	15	†	†
ITT Technical Institute, Fort Myers	5	288	89	30.9	89	†	0	0	†	†
ITT Technical Institute, Miami	5	853	696	81.6	696	†	128	40	†	†
Johnson & Wales University, Florida Campus	3	2,098	712	33.9	712	†	61	37	†	†
Kaplan College, Pembroke Pines	6	118	59	50.0	59	†	0	†	†	†
Keiser Career College, Greenacres	6	1,790	584	32.6	584	†	62	†	†	†
Keiser University, Fort Lauderdale	5	16,968	4,424	26.1	4,344	80	723	73	22	†
Le Cordon Bleu College of Culinary Arts, Miramar	6	1,434	966	67.4	966	†	363	†	†	†
Le Cordon Bleu College of Culinary Arts, Orlando	6	1,508	549	36.4	549	†	87	†	†	†
Medvance Institute, Miami	6	535	381	71.2	381	†	18	†	†	†
Medvance Institute, West Palm	6	847	233	27.5	233	†	11	†	†	†
Miami Ad School	6	187	89	47.6	89	†	0	†	0	†
Miami Dade College	1	61,674	43,840	71.1	43,840	†	5,893	132	†	†
Nova Southeastern University	3	28,741	6,603	23.0	2,068	4,535	1	358	798	266
Polytechnic University of Puerto Rico, Miami Campus	3	170	122	71.8	89	33	†	24	6	†
Professional Training Centers	6	712	687	96.5	687	†	†	†	†	†
Saint John Vianney College Seminary	3	65	24	36.9	16	8	†	6	†	†
Saint Thomas University	3	2,469	1,044	42.3	544	500	†	146	94	70
Sanford-Brown Institute, Fort Lauderdale	6	1,069	398	37.2	398	†	0	†	†	†
Sanford-Brown Institute, Orlando	6	562	231	41.1	231	†	0	†	†	†
Trinity International University	3	362	132	36.5	91	41	†	38	6	†
Universidad Politecnica de Puerto Rico, Orlando Campus	3	217	215	99.1	165	50	†	14	8	†
University of Miami	3	15,657	3,816	24.4	2,768	1,048	†	670	225	110
University of Phoenix, Central Florida Campus	5	1,567	470	30.0	417	53	†	66	24	†
University of Phoenix, South Florida Campus	5	2,208	628	28.4	493	135	†	74	34	†
Valencia Community College	2	41,583	13,254	31.9	13,254	†	1,470	†	†	†
Illinois										
City Colleges of Chicago, Harold Washington College	2	8,721	2,578	29.6	2,578	†	119	†	†	†
City Colleges of Chicago, Harry S Truman College	2	12,947	5,107	39.4	5,107	†	78	†	†	†
City Colleges of Chicago, Malcolm X College	2	8,366	2,695	32.2	2,695	†	44	†	†	†
City Colleges of Chicago, Richard J. Daley College	2	8,965	6,082	67.8	6,082	†	164	†	†	†
City Colleges of Chicago, Wilbur Wright College	2	12,660	6,445	50.9	6,445	†	227	†	†	†
Coyne College	6	929	257	27.7	257	†	32	†	†	†
Dominican University	3	3,748	744	19.9	566	178	†	86	45	0
Elgin Community College	2	12,214	4,012	32.8	4,012	†	139	†	†	†
Fox College Inc.	6	417	135	32.4	135	†	48	†	†	†
ITT Technical Institute, Mount Prospect	5	513	146	28.5	146	†	20	9	†	†
ITT Technical Institute, Oak Brook	5	470	138	29.4	138	†	26	6	†	†

See notes at end of table.

Enrollment and degrees conferred in degree-granting institutions that serve large proportions of Hispanic undergraduate students, by selected characteristics and institution: Fall 2010 and 2009–10—Continued

Institution	Level and control[1]	Enrollment, fall 2010					Degrees awarded to Hispanics, 2009–10			
		Total	Hispanic	Percent Hispanic[2]	Hispanic under-graduate	Hispanic postbacca-laureate	Associate's	Bachelor's	Master's	Doctor's[3]
1	2	3	4	5	6	7	8	9	10	12
Lexington College	3	55	14	25.5	14	†	1	3	†	†
Lincoln College of Technology	6	1,705	778	45.6	778	†	91	†	†	†
Morton College	2	5,459	4,341	79.5	4,341	†	232	†	†	†
Northeastern Illinois University	1	11,746	3,414	29.1	3,103	311	†	386	54	†
Northwestern College, Chicago	6	842	246	29.2	246	†	37	†	†	†
Northwestern College, Southwestern Campus	6	1,244	347	27.9	347	†	51	†	†	†
Saint Augustine College	3	1,568	1,371	87.4	1,371	†	133	11	†	†
Triton College	2	15,253	5,137	33.7	5,137	†	156	†	†	†
Waubonsee Community College	2	10,428	3,059	29.3	3,059	†	100	†	†	†
Westwood College, Dupage	5	610	150	24.6	150	†	3	14	†	†
Westwood College, O'Hare Airport	5	811	329	40.6	329	†	6	35	†	†
Indiana										
Calumet College of Saint Joseph	3	1,262	331	26.2	302	29	1	56	9	†
Kansas										
Dodge City Community College	2	1,807	595	32.9	595	†	39	†	†	†
Donnelly College	3	652	200	30.7	200	†	16	0	†	†
Garden City Community College	2	2,009	616	30.7	616	†	67	†	†	†
Seward County Community College and Area Technical	2	1,870	504	27.0	504	†	62	†	†	†
Massachusetts										
Cambridge College	3	4,425	644	14.6	330	314	†	37	136	0
Marian Court College	4	231	69	29.9	69	†	7	†	†	†
Northern Essex Community College	2	7,439	2,177	29.3	2,177	†	101	†	†	†
Salter College, West Boylston	6	1,120	300	26.8	300	†	36	†	†	†
Urban College of Boston	4	602	286	47.5	286	†	28	†	†	†
Nevada										
Art Institute of Las Vegas	5	1,386	464	33.5	464	†	12	18	†	†
College of Southern Nevada	1	42,747	11,256	26.3	11,256	†	339	0	†	†
DeVry University, Nevada	5	550	180	32.7	158	22	4	4	2	†
Everest College, Henderson	6	1,263	469	37.1	469	†	23	†	†	†
Pima Medical Institute	6	1,144	302	26.4	302	†	14	†	†	†
New Jersey										
Bergen Community College	2	17,197	5,116	29.7	5,116	†	413	†	†	†
Berkeley College	5	3,772	1,495	39.6	1,495	†	89	126	†	†
DeVry University, New Jersey	5	2,405	815	33.9	784	31	52	38	†	†
Eastern International College, Belleville	6	193	86	44.6	86	†	0	†	†	†
Eastern International College, Jersey City	6	258	140	54.3	140	†	0	†	†	†
Fairleigh Dickinson University, Metropolitan Campus	3	9,105	1,851	20.3	1,617	234	22	134	71	1
Felician College	3	2,195	519	23.6	472	47	2	50	3	†
Hudson County Community College	2	9,331	5,675	60.8	5,675	†	301	†	†	†
New Jersey City University	1	8,517	3,084	36.2	2,617	467	†	350	67	†
Passaic County Community College	2	9,548	4,957	51.9	4,957	†	154	†	†	†
Saint Peter's College	3	3,010	775	25.7	666	109	2	118	56	†
Union County College	2	12,878	4,202	32.6	4,202	†	198	†	†	†
University of Phoenix, Jersey City Campus	5	585	200	34.2	200	†	†	5	†	†
New Mexico										
Anamarc College	6	158	144	91.1	144	†	6	†	†	†
Art Center Design College, Albuquerque	5	292	105	36.0	105	†	0	7	†	†
Brookline College	6	599	417	69.6	417	†	21	†	†	†
Brown Mackie College, Albuquerque	6	289	92	31.8	92	†	0	0	†	†
Carrington College, Albuquerque	6	1,116	619	55.5	619	†	32	†	†	†
Central New Mexico Community College	2	29,948	13,229	44.2	13,229	†	654	†	†	†
Clovis Community College	2	4,175	1,222	29.3	1,222	†	0	†	†	†
Eastern New Mexico University, Main Campus	1	5,075	1,667	32.8	1,408	259	0	145	24	†
Eastern New Mexico University, Roswell Campus	2	4,374	1,964	44.9	1,964	†	102	†	†	†
Eastern New Mexico University, Ruidoso	2	1,002	340	33.9	340	†	1	†	†	†
ITT Technical Institute, Albuquerque	5	934	390	41.8	390	†	57	32	†	†
Luna Community College	2	2,064	1,667	80.8	1,667	†	66	†	†	†
Mesalands Community College	2	1,089	414	38.0	414	†	18	†	†	†
National American University, Albuquerque	5	652	268	41.1	268	†	5	18	†	†
National American University, Rio Rancho	5	287	117	40.8	117	†	5	11	†	†
New Mexico Highlands University	1	3,750	1,946	51.9	1,265	681	1	191	173	†
New Mexico Institute of Mining and Technology	1	1,775	409	23.0	366	43	0	50	8	0
New Mexico Junior College	2	3,535	1,494	42.3	1,494	†	59	†	†	†
New Mexico State University, Alamogordo	2	3,944	1,644	41.7	1,644	†	49	†	†	†
New Mexico State University, Carlsbad	2	1,890	938	49.6	938	†	40	†	†	†
New Mexico State University, Dona Ana	2	9,923	6,987	70.4	6,987	†	454	†	†	†
New Mexico State University, Grants	2	1,590	765	48.1	765	†	12	†	†	†
New Mexico State University, Main Campus	1	18,600	8,899	47.8	7,594	1,305	24	911	215	5
Northern New Mexico College	1	2,179	1,560	71.6	1,560	†	78	31	†	†
Pima Medical Institute	6	1,154	552	47.8	552	†	35	†	†	†
Santa Fe Community College	2	4,864	2,265	46.6	2,265	†	106	†	†	†

See notes at end of table.

Enrollment and degrees conferred in degree-granting institutions that serve large proportions of Hispanic undergraduate students, by selected characteristics and institution: Fall 2010 and 2009–10—Continued

Institution	Level and control[1]	Enrollment, fall 2010					Degrees awarded to Hispanics, 2009–10			
		Total	Hispanic	Percent Hispanic[2]	Hispanic under-graduate	Hispanic postbacca-laureate	Associate's	Bachelor's	Master's	Doctor's[3]
1	2	3	4	5	6	7	8	9	10	12
University of New Mexico, Los Alamos Campus.............	2	736	309	42.0	309	†	11	†	†	†
University of New Mexico, Main Campus.......................	1	28,688	10,604	37.0	9,043	1,561	†	1,109	225	100
University of New Mexico, Taos Branch........................	2	1,542	960	62.3	960	†	12	†	†	†
University of New Mexico, Valencia County Branch........	2	2,267	1,390	61.3	1,390	†	53	†	†	†
University of Phoenix, Albuquerque Campus	5	4,760	3,758	78.9	3,352	406	†	360	177	†
University of the Southwest	3	500	181	36.2	116	65	†	33	16	†
Western New Mexico University	1	3,506	1,970	56.2	1,797	173	30	78	28	†
New York										
Art Institute of New York City	6	1,491	653	43.8	653	†	61	†	†	†
ASA Institute of Business and Computer Technology	6	5,804	2,326	40.1	2,326	†	394	†	†	†
Berkeley College	5	5,202	1,687	32.4	1,687	†	30	117	†	†
Boricua College	3	1,309	1,098	83.9	1,018	80	107	117	23	†
Bramson ORT College..	4	851	212	24.9	212	†	29	†	†	†
College of Mount Saint Vincent	3	1,887	626	33.2	550	76	0	88	13	†
College of Westchester	5	1,219	478	39.2	478	†	117	22	†	†
CUNY, Borough of Manhattan Community College	2	22,534	8,592	38.1	8,592	†	683	†	†	†
CUNY, Bronx Community College	2	10,740	6,486	60.4	6,486	†	468	†	†	†
CUNY, City College	1	15,416	4,778	31.0	4,050	728	†	468	150	†
CUNY, Hostos Community College................................	2	6,499	3,821	58.8	3,821	†	331	†	†	†
CUNY, John Jay College of Criminal Justice	1	15,206	5,964	39.2	5,550	414	95	594	93	†
CUNY, LaGuardia Community College	2	17,569	6,752	38.4	6,752	†	513	†	†	†
CUNY, Lehman College..	1	12,115	5,833	48.1	5,116	717	†	742	188	†
CUNY, New York City College of Technology................	1	15,366	4,141	26.9	4,141	†	211	193	†	†
CUNY, Queensborough Community College...................	2	15,316	4,013	26.2	4,013	†	324	†	†	†
DeVry College of New York	5	2,798	1,048	37.5	886	162	5	32	3	†
Island Drafting and Technical Institute	6	122	32	26.2	32	†	10	†	†	†
Long Island University, Brentwood...............................	3	439	39	8.9	10	29	†	0	9	†
Long Island University, Riverhead	3	266	23	8.6	9	14	†	0	2	†
Mandl, The College of Allied Health	6	718	286	39.8	286	†	58	†	†	†
Mercy College...	3	10,851	3,181	29.3	2,333	848	39	260	205	5
Monroe College, Main Campus	5	4,595	2,413	52.5	2,316	97	516	294	30	†
Monroe College, New Rochelle	5	2,174	564	25.9	548	16	91	59	3	†
Pacific College of Oriental Medicine	5	606	70	11.6	41	29	1	1	3	†
Plaza College	5	793	253	31.9	253	†	57	11	†	†
Professional Business College	4	744	200	26.9	200	†	45	†	†	†
SBI Campus, an Affiliate of Sanford-Brown	6	587	147	25.0	147	†	7	†	†	†
SUNY, Westchester Community College	2	13,893	3,413	24.6	3,413	†	241	†	†	†
Technical Career Institutes	6	4,491	1,870	41.6	1,870	†	287	†	†	†
Vaughn College of Aeronautics and Technology	3	1,553	647	41.7	642	5	43	24	0	†
Wood Tobe-Coburn School..	6	483	232	48.0	232	†	112	†	†	†
Oregon										
Chemeketa Community College	2	12,535	3,829	30.5	3,829	†	111	†	†	†
Mount Angel Seminary	3	199	73	36.7	38	35	†	4	2	†
Pennsylvania										
Berks Technical Institute..	6	1,039	323	31.1	323	†	41	†	†	†
Lincoln Technical Institute..	6	866	237	27.4	237	†	19	†	†	†
Pace Institute	6	259	140	54.1	140	†	28	†	†	†
Pennsylvania School of Business	6	296	147	49.7	147	†	12	†	†	†
Texas										
Academy of Health Care Professions...........................	6	383	203	53.0	203	†	11	†	†	†
Allied Health Careers...	6	295	163	55.3	163	†	9	†	†	†
Alvin Community College	2	5,794	1,489	25.7	1,489	†	87	†	†	†
Amarillo College	2	11,878	3,698	31.1	3,698	†	181	†	†	†
American InterContinental University	5	557	144	25.9	136	8	9	15	3	†
Anamarc College	6	710	594	83.7	594	†	0	†	†	†
Angelo State University	1	6,856	1,719	25.1	1,592	127	21	143	20	0
Art Institute of Austin	5	1,362	492	36.1	492	†	0	0	†	†
Art Institute of Houston..	5	2,545	803	31.6	803	†	23	31	†	†
Art Institute of San Antonio..	5	196	110	56.1	110	†	0	0	†	†
Austin Community College District	2	44,100	11,767	26.7	11,767	†	310	†	†	†
Baptist Health System School of Health Professions	6	532	227	42.7	227	†	65	†	†	†
Baptist University of the Americas...............................	3	205	143	69.8	143	†	11	26	†	†
Brazosport College	1	4,196	1,200	28.6	1,200	†	47	10	†	†
Brookhaven College	2	12,784	3,790	29.6	3,790	†	147	†	†	†
Brown Mackie College, San Antonio	6	86	32	37.2	32	†	0	0	†	†
Career Point College	6	1,844	1,238	67.1	1,238	†	53	†	†	†
Clarendon College	2	1,583	466	29.4	466	†	22	†	†	†
Coastal Bend College...	2	4,348	2,883	66.3	2,883	†	152	†	†	†
College of Biblical Studies, Houston............................	3	432	130	30.1	130	†	11	5	†	†
Computer Career Center, a Division of Vista College	6	1,329	1,055	79.4	1,055	†	30	†	†	†
Concorde Career Institute	6	185	132	71.4	132	†	†	†	†	†
Culinary Institute Inc..	6	370	125	33.8	125	†	14	†	†	†

See notes at end of table.

Enrollment and degrees conferred in degree-granting institutions that serve large proportions of Hispanic undergraduate students, by selected characteristics and institution: Fall 2010 and 2009–10—Continued

Institution	Level and control[1]	Enrollment, fall 2010					Degrees awarded to Hispanics, 2009–10			
		Total	Hispanic	Percent Hispanic[2]	Hispanic under-graduate	Hispanic postbacca-laureate	Associate's	Bachelor's	Master's	Doctor's[3]
1	2	3	4	5	6	7	8	9	10	12
Del Mar College	2	12,236	7,939	64.9	7,939	†	626	†	†	†
DeVry University, Texas	5	6,635	2,215	33.4	2,015	200	21	114	22	†
Eastfield College	2	12,919	4,494	34.8	4,494	†	150	†	†	†
El Centro College	2	9,761	3,385	34.7	3,385	†	116	†	†	†
El Paso Community College	2	29,909	25,492	85.2	25,492	†	2,666	†	†	†
Everest College, Arlington	6	819	302	36.9	302	†	18	†	†	†
Everest College, Dallas	6	1,453	404	27.8	404	†	52	†	†	†
Everest College, Fort Worth	6	779	271	34.8	271	†	15	†	†	†
Everest College, Forth Worth South	6	398	166	41.7	166	†	0	†	†	†
Galen College of Nursing, San Antonio	6	763	366	48.0	366	†	29	†	†	†
Galveston College	2	2,319	678	29.2	678	†	46	†	†	†
Hallmark College of Technology/Hallmark College of Aeronautics	5	857	466	54.4	466	†	149	0	†	†
High-Tech Institute, Dallas	6	582	198	34.0	198	†	†	†	†	†
Houston Baptist University	3	2,597	659	25.4	592	67	1	66	22	†
Houston Community College	2	60,303	18,872	31.3	18,872	†	790	†	†	†
Howard College	2	4,623	1,309	28.3	1,309	†	95	†	†	†
International Academy of Design and Technology	5	725	432	59.6	432	†	1	†	†	†
International Business College, Cromo St., El Paso	6	251	223	88.8	223	†	11	†	†	†
International Business College, N. Zaragosa Rd., El Paso	6	268	254	94.8	254	†	14	†	†	†
ITT Technical Institute, Arlington	5	855	244	28.5	244	†	46	0	†	†
ITT Technical Institute, Austin	5	798	289	36.2	289	†	59	0	†	†
ITT Technical Institute, Houston North	5	1,007	344	34.2	344	†	91	0	†	†
ITT Technical Institute, Houston West	5	688	259	37.6	259	†	97	0	†	†
ITT Technical Institute, Richardson	5	706	182	25.8	182	†	65	0	†	†
ITT Technical Institute, San Antonio	5	767	441	57.5	441	†	98	0	†	†
ITT Technical Institute, Webster	5	469	176	37.5	176	†	45	0	†	†
Kaplan Career Institute, McAllen	6	1,075	1,003	93.3	1,003	†	†	†	†	†
Kaplan College, Corpus Christi	6	791	498	63.0	498	†	†	†	†	†
Kaplan College, Dallas	6	360	116	32.2	116	†	†	†	†	†
Kaplan College, El Paso	6	892	640	71.7	640	†	†	†	†	†
Kaplan College, Fort Worth	6	541	215	39.7	215	†	†	†	†	†
Kaplan College, Laredo	6	381	351	92.1	351	†	†	†	†	†
Kaplan College, Lubbock	6	570	252	44.2	252	†	†	†	†	†
Kaplan College, San Antonio	6	1,012	639	63.1	639	†	†	†	†	†
Kaplan College, San Antonio, San Pedro Campus	6	1,175	586	49.9	586	†	†	†	†	†
Laredo Community College	2	10,029	9,718	96.9	9,718	†	589	†	†	†
Le Cordon Bleu College of Culinary Arts, Austin	6	1,183	342	28.9	342	†	62	†	†	†
Le Cordon Bleu College of Culinary Arts, Dallas	6	1,046	279	26.7	279	†	81	†	†	†
Lee College	2	6,719	1,909	28.4	1,909	†	201	†	†	†
Lincoln College of Technology	6	1,839	615	33.4	615	†	4	†	†	†
Lone Star College System	2	54,412	15,467	28.4	15,467	†	675	†	†	†
Midland College	1	6,347	1,967	31.0	1,967	†	131	2	†	†
Mountain View College	2	8,460	4,349	51.4	4,349	†	210	†	†	†
North Lake College	2	12,018	3,469	28.9	3,469	†	121	†	†	†
Northwest Vista College	2	15,921	8,163	51.3	8,163	†	415	†	†	†
Northwood University	3	805	205	25.5	197	8	22	37	†	†
Odessa College	2	5,213	2,008	38.5	2,008	†	158	†	†	†
Our Lady of the Lake University, San Antonio	3	2,751	1,615	58.7	1,075	540	†	201	158	5
Palo Alto College	2	8,965	6,177	68.9	6,177	†	489	†	†	†
Pima Medical Institute	6	52	13	25.0	13	†	0	†	†	†
Remington College, Dallas Campus	6	1,324	478	36.1	478	†	66	†	†	†
Remington College, Fort Worth Campus	6	754	207	27.5	207	†	10	†	†	†
Remington College, Houston Campus	6	526	198	37.6	198	†	26	†	†	†
Remington College, Houston Southeast	6	414	147	35.5	147	†	1	†	†	†
Remington College, North Houston Campus	6	722	328	45.4	328	†	16	†	†	†
Saint Edward's University	3	5,454	1,672	30.7	1,443	229	†	295	40	†
Saint Marys University	3	4,105	2,246	54.7	1,742	504	†	310	61	58
Saint Philip's College	2	10,828	5,323	49.2	5,323	†	310	†	†	†
San Antonio College	2	25,269	12,791	50.6	12,791	†	545	†	†	†
San Jacinto Community College	2	28,549	11,869	41.6	11,869	†	690	†	†	†
Sanford-Brown College, Dallas	6	1,262	345	27.3	345	†	†	†	†	†
Sanford-Brown College, Houston, Richmond Avenue Campus	6	1,809	710	39.2	710	†	8	†	†	†
Sanford-Brown College, San Antonio	6	639	380	59.5	380	†	0	†	†	†
South Plains College	2	9,900	3,332	33.7	3,332	†	152	†	†	†
South Texas College	1	27,692	26,517	95.8	26,517	†	1,703	91	†	†
Southwest Career College	6	616	516	83.8	516	†	0	†	†	†
Southwest Institute of Technology	6	36	20	55.6	20	†	4	†	†	†
Southwest Texas Junior College	2	6,235	5,188	83.2	5,188	†	356	†	†	†
Southwestern Adventist University	3	801	232	29.0	228	4	0	15	0	†
Sul Ross State University	1	3,129	2,050	65.5	1,525	525	1	226	111	†
Texas A & M International University	1	6,853	6,321	92.2	5,474	847	†	756	194	3

See notes at end of table.

Enrollment and degrees conferred in degree-granting institutions that serve large proportions of Hispanic undergraduate students, by selected characteristics and institution: Fall 2010 and 2009–10—Continued

		Enrollment, fall 2010					Degrees awarded to Hispanics, 2009–10			
Institution	Level and control[1]	Total	Hispanic	Percent Hispanic[2]	Hispanic under-graduate	Hispanic postbacca-laureate	Associate's	Bachelor's	Master's	Doctor's[3]
1	2	3	4	5	6	7	8	9	10	12
Texas A & M University, Corpus Christi	1	10,033	3,979	39.7	3,361	618	†	538	122	12
Texas A & M University, Kingsville	1	9,673	6,250	64.6	5,192	1,058	†	791	186	12
Texas School of Business Inc.	6	585	231	39.5	231	†	†	†	†	†
Texas School of Business, Friendswood Inc.	6	390	104	26.7	104	†	†	†	†	†
Texas School of Business, Southwest Inc.	6	378	149	39.4	149	†	†	†	†	†
Texas State Technical College Harlingen	2	5,779	5,127	88.7	5,127	†	259	†	†	†
Texas State University, San Marcos	1	32,572	8,329	25.6	7,281	1,048	†	1,098	210	4
Texas Wesleyan University	3	3,378	632	18.7	483	149	†	59	20	28
University of Houston	1	38,752	8,717	22.5	7,923	794	†	1,076	151	67
University of Houston, Clear Lake	1	8,099	1,787	22.1	1,340	447	†	253	130	0
University of Houston, Downtown	1	12,900	4,771	37.0	4,734	37	†	745	7	†
University of Houston, Victoria	1	4,095	838	20.5	575	263	†	115	31	†
University of Phoenix, Austin Campus	5	470	126	26.8	115	11	†	10	7	†
University of Phoenix, San Antonio Campus	5	993	497	50.1	415	82	†	30	17	†
University of Saint Thomas	3	3,437	1,084	31.5	590	494	†	78	66	0
University of Texas at Brownsville	1	15,230	13,553	89.0	12,883	670	927	963	151	†
University of Texas at El Paso	1	22,106	17,027	77.0	14,624	2,403	†	2,382	506	16
University of Texas at San Antonio	1	30,258	13,812	45.6	12,202	1,610	†	1,779	332	8
University of Texas Health Science Center at San Antonio	1	3,310	880	26.6	332	548	†	169	57	81
University of Texas of the Permian Basin	1	4,063	1,525	37.5	1,280	245	†	195	40	†
University of Texas, Pan American	1	18,744	17,081	91.1	15,017	2,064	†	2,360	511	6
University of the Incarnate Word	3	7,214	4,137	57.3	3,389	748	2	561	139	27
Vet Tech Institute of Houston	6	348	94	27.0	94	†	25	†	†	†
Victoria College	2	4,360	1,518	34.8	1,518	†	85	†	†	†
Virginia College, Austin	6	861	350	40.7	350	†	41	†	†	†
Western Technical College, Diana Drive, El Paso	6	594	498	83.8	498	†	60	†	†	†
Western Technical College, Plaza Circle, El Paso	6	1,030	943	91.6	943	†	161	†	†	†
Western Texas College	2	3,164	967	30.6	967	†	38	†	†	†
Westwood College, Dallas	5	532	158	29.7	158	†	27	0	†	†
Westwood College, Fort Worth	5	397	107	27.0	107	†	24	0	†	†
Westwood College, Houston South	5	450	219	48.7	219	†	38	0	†	†
Wharton County Junior College	2	6,922	2,117	30.6	2,117	†	128	†	†	†
Utah										
Everest College, West Valley City	5	528	151	28.6	151	†	4	1	†	†
Virginia										
ITT Technical Institute, Chantilly	5	715	189	26.4	189	†	25	5	†	†
Sanz School	6	954	576	60.4	576	†	0	†	†	†
Washington										
Big Bend Community College	2	2,184	739	33.8	739	†	64	†	†	†
Heritage University	3	1,254	573	45.7	511	62	4	56	25	†
Wenatchee Valley College	2	3,816	952	24.9	952	†	74	†	†	†
Yakima Valley Community College	2	4,479	1,711	38.2	1,711	†	0	†	†	†
Puerto Rico										
American University of Puerto Rico, Bayamón	3	1,453	1,453	100.0	1,347	106	26	137	44	†
American University of Puerto Rico, Manati	3	1,229	1,229	100.0	1,162	67	14	157	40	†
Atenas College	3	1,395	1,395	100.0	1,395	†	120	1	†	†
Atlantic College	3	1,318	1,318	100.0	1,251	67	19	155	33	†
Bayamon Central University	3	2,479	2,479	100.0	2,084	395	9	240	117	†
Caribbean University, Bayamón	3	2,310	2,310	100.0	2,074	236	†	234	†	†
Caribbean University, Carolina	3	873	873	100.0	769	104	†	130	†	†
Caribbean University, Ponce	3	1,678	1,678	100.0	1,354	324	†	172	†	†
Caribbean University, Vega Baja	3	750	750	100.0	599	151	†	145	†	†
Carlos Albizu University	3	909	903	99.3	147	756	†	68	121	75
Centro de Estudios Multidisciplinarios, Bayamón	4	850	850	100.0	850	†	69	†	†	†
Centro de Estudios Multidisciplinarios, Humacao	4	812	812	100.0	812	†	135	†	†	†
Centro de Estudios Multidisciplinarios, San Juan	4	1,367	1,367	100.0	1,367	†	216	†	†	†
Colegio de Cinematografía, Artes y Television	6	649	649	100.0	649	†	10	†	†	†
Colegio Pentecostal Mizpa	3	299	299	100.0	299	†	16	17	†	†
Colegio Universitario de San Juan	1	1,720	1,720	100.0	1,720	†	178	90	†	†
Columbia Centro Universitario, Caguas	5	1,551	1,551	100.0	1,486	65	142	119	62	†
Columbia Centro Universitario, Yauco	5	566	566	100.0	566	†	102	31	†	†
EDIC College	6	972	972	100.0	972	†	105	†	†	†
EDP College of Puerto Rico Inc., San Juan	3	1,225	1,225	100.0	1,151	74	37	55	8	†
EDP College of Puerto Rico Inc., San Sebastian	3	1,012	1,012	100.0	1,012	†	77	70	†	†
Escuela de Artes Plasticas de Puerto Rico	1	522	521	99.8	521	†	†	66	†	†
Huertas Junior College	6	1,805	1,805	100.0	1,805	†	396	†	†	†
Humacao Community College	3	610	610	100.0	610	†	222	†	†	†
ICPR Junior College, Arecibo	6	346	346	100.0	346	†	39	†	†	†
ICPR Junior College, General Institutional	6	682	682	100.0	682	†	41	†	†	†
ICPR Junior College, Mayaguez	6	502	502	100.0	502	†	74	†	†	†
Instituto de Banca y Comercio Inc.	6	18,168	18,142	99.9	18,142	†	3	†	†	†
Instituto Tecnologico de Puerto Rico, Manati	2	802	802	100.0	802	†	252	†	†	†

See notes at end of table.

Enrollment and degrees conferred in degree-granting institutions that serve large proportions of Hispanic undergraduate students, by selected characteristics and institution: Fall 2010 and 2009–10—Continued

Institution	Level and control[1]	Enrollment, fall 2010					Degrees awarded to Hispanics, 2009–10			
		Total	Hispanic	Percent Hispanic[2]	Hispanic undergraduate	Hispanic postbaccalaureate	Associate's	Bachelor's	Master's	Doctor's[3]
1	2	3	4	5	6	7	8	9	10	12
Instituto Tecnologico de Puerto Rico, Recinto de Guayama	2	656	656	100.0	656	†	185	†	†	†
Instituto Tecnologico de Puerto Rico, Recinto de Ponce .	2	711	711	100.0	711	†	201	†	†	†
Instituto Tecnologico de Puerto Rico, Recinto de Ponce .	2	711	711	100.0	711	†	201	†	†	†
Instituto Tecnologico de Puerto Rico, Recinto de San Juan	2	717	717	100.0	717	†	173	†	†	†
Inter American University of Puerto Rico, Aguadilla........	3	4,722	4,700	99.5	4,402	298	102	194	25	†
Inter American University of Puerto Rico, Arecibo..........	3	5,340	5,039	94.4	4,614	425	76	374	61	†
Inter American University of Puerto Rico, Barranqui	3	2,422	2,407	99.4	2,302	105	60	212	48	†
Inter American University of Puerto Rico, Bayamón........	3	5,148	5,047	98.0	4,934	113	46	487	10	†
Inter American University of Puerto Rico, Fajardo...........	3	2,357	2,337	99.2	2,279	58	21	178	11	†
Inter American University of Puerto Rico, Guayama	3	2,393	2,384	99.6	2,306	78	96	216	8	†
Inter American University of Puerto Rico, Metro.............	3	10,681	10,367	97.1	7,090	3,277	56	782	567	29
Inter American University of Puerto Rico, Ponce............	3	6,460	6,391	98.9	6,029	362	99	344	42	†
Inter American University of Puerto Rico, San German ..	3	5,408	5,360	99.1	4,558	802	54	534	149	16
John Dewey College, University Division......................	3	1,443	1,443	100.0	1,443	†	145	86	†	†
Mech-Tech College LLC	6	3,659	3,659	100.0	3,659	†	146	†	†	†
National University College, Arecibo	5	1,787	1,787	100.0	1,787	†	246	105	†	†
National University College, Bayamón.......................	5	3,000	3,000	100.0	3,000	†	314	82	†	†
National University College, Ponce...........................	5	677	677	100.0	677	†	61	29	†	†
National University College, Rio Grande....................	5	1,552	1,552	100.0	1,552	†	152	82	†	†
Ponce Paramedical College Inc.	6	3,514	3,514	100.0	3,514	†	249	†	†	†
Pontifical Catholic University of Puerto Rico, Arecibo......	3	698	692	99.1	480	212	10	47	55	†
Pontifical Catholic University of Puerto Rico, Mayaguez .	3	1,507	1,505	99.9	1,384	121	16	139	52	†
Pontifical Catholic University of Puerto Rico, Ponce.......	3	8,203	8,156	99.4	5,708	2,448	16	608	150	217
Puerto Rico Conservatory of Music............................	1	441	438	99.3	405	33	†	60	3	†
Universal Career Community College Inc....................	6	1,335	1,335	100.0	1,335	†	†	†	†	†
Universal Technology College of Puerto Rico..............	4	1,549	1,549	100.0	1,549	†	182	†	†	†
Universidad Adventista de las Antillas......................	3	1,174	1,085	92.4	1,039	46	12	123	20	†
Universidad Central Del Caribe	3	485	470	96.9	177	293	23	15	4	56
Universidad Del Este	3	13,783	13,783	100.0	12,630	1,153	262	843	313	†
Universidad Del Turabo...	3	16,036	16,036	100.0	13,175	2,861	95	1,145	950	35
Universidad Metropolitana	3	12,693	12,693	100.0	10,523	2,170	82	925	735	1
Universidad Politecnica de Puerto Rico......................	3	5,167	5,167	100.0	4,465	702	†	507	212	†
Universidad Teologica del Caribe	3	261	261	100.0	261	†	†	27	†	†
University of Phoenix, Puerto Rico Campus.................	5	2,381	2,237	94.0	982	1,255	†	111	334	†
University of Puerto Rico at Cayey	1	3,631	3,631	100.0	3,631	†	0	435	†	†
University of Puerto Rico in Ponce	1	3,233	3,233	100.0	3,233	†	76	323	†	†
University of Puerto Rico, Aguadilla..........................	1	2,932	2,904	99.0	2,904	†	10	307	†	†
University of Puerto Rico, Arecibo............................	1	3,957	3,957	100.0	3,957	†	40	531	†	†
University of Puerto Rico, Bayamón..........................	1	4,992	4,992	100.0	4,992	†	49	405	†	†
University of Puerto Rico, Carolina...........................	1	4,004	3,945	98.5	3,945	†	93	506	†	†
University of Puerto Rico, Humacao..........................	1	4,314	4,314	100.0	4,314	†	110	455	†	†
University of Puerto Rico, Mayaguez.........................	1	13,221	13,221	100.0	12,165	1,056	†	1,537	135	16
University of Puerto Rico, Medical Sciences Campus.....	1	2,371	2,331	98.3	525	1,806	47	143	218	160
University of Puerto Rico, Rio Piedras Campus	1	17,539	17,208	98.1	13,880	3,328	†	2,042	282	247
University of Puerto Rico, Utuado.............................	1	1,528	1,521	99.5	1,521	†	61	63	†	†
University of Sacred Heart.......................................	3	6,095	6,095	100.0	5,083	1,012	131	530	107	†

†Not applicable.

[1] 1 = public, 4-year; 2 = public, 2-year; 3 = private not-for-profit, 4-year; 4 = private not-for-profit, 2-year; 5 = private for-profit, 4-year; and 6 = private for-profit, 2-year.

[2] Hispanic headcount enrollment (U.S. citizens and permanent residents only) as a percentage of total headcount enrollment, including both resident and nonresident students. Hispanic and total headcount enrollment include graduate as well as undergraduate students.

[2] Includes Ph.D., Ed.D., and comparable degrees at the doctoral level, as well as such degrees as M.D., D.D.S., and law degrees that were formerly classified as first-professional degrees.

NOTE: Degree-granting institutions grant associate's or higher degrees and participate in Title IV federal financial aid programs. This table includes institutions that serve large proportions of Hispanic undergraduate students, defined as institutions with a full-time-equivalent undergraduate enrollment of Hispanic students at 25 percent or more of full-time-equivalent undergraduate enrollment of U.S. citizens. Data for Hispanics include only persons who were U.S. citizens or permanent residents.
SOURCE: U.S. Department of Education, National Center for Education Statistics, Integrated Postsecondary Education Data System (IPEDS), Spring 2011, Enrollment component; and Fall 2009, Completions component. (This table was prepared December 2011.)

Fall enrollment and degrees conferred in degree-granting tribally controlled institutions, by institution: Selected years, fall 2000 through fall 2010, and 2008–09 and 2009–10

Institution	Level and control[1]	Total fall enrollment 2000	2004	2005	2006	2007	2008	2009	2010 Total	Total American Indian/ Alaska Native	Percent American Indian/ Alaska Native	Undergraduate American Indian/ Alaska Native	Degrees to American Indians/ Alaska Natives Associate's 2008–09	Associate's 2009–10	Bachelor's 2008–09	Bachelor's 2009–10
1	2	3	4	5	6	7	8	9	10	11	12	13	14	15	16	17
Tribally controlled institutions[2]	†	13,680	17,605	17,167	17,255	17,418	17,014	19,686	21,225	16,640	78.4	16,492	1,153	1,158	160	177
Alaska																
Ilisagvik College	2	322	214	278	203	439	251	226	288	155	53.8	155	4	4	†	†
Arizona																
Diné College	1	1,712	1,935	1,825	1,669	1,657	1,527	1,935	2,033	2,018	99.3	2,018	169	117	0	0
Tohono O'odham Community College	2	—	169	270	198	154	163	254	207	193	93.2	193	4	2	†	†
Kansas																
Haskell Indian Nations University	1	918	928	918	889	894	997	1,059	958	958	100.0	958	69	91	37	60
Michigan																
Bay Mills Community College	2	360	401	406	550	427	501	608	607	346	57.0	346	11	11	†	†
Saginaw Chippewa Tribal College	2	—	109	123	125	127	133	134	153	125	81.7	125	6	16	†	†
Minnesota																
Fond du Lac Tribal and Community College	2	999	1,775	1,981	2,181	2,197	2,206	2,305	2,339	242	10.3	242	33	31	†	†
Leech Lake Tribal College	2	240	195	189	198	243	228	233	235	196	83.4	196	26	26	†	†
White Earth Tribal and Community College	4	—	67	61	106	99	106	113	121	101	83.5	101	3	8	†	†
Montana																
Blackfeet Community College	4	299	561	485	467	471	492	533	473	459	97.0	459	57	54	†	†
Chief Dull Knife College	2	461	356	554	359	437	443	472	433	390	90.1	390	19	17	†	†
Fort Belknap College	2	295	257	175	161	244	168	236	214	186	86.9	186	22	18	†	†
Fort Peck Community College	2	400	504	408	441	422	436	427	452	371	82.1	371	31	23	†	†
Little Big Horn College	2	320	291	259	312	272	337	415	410	390	95.1	390	23	54	†	†
Salish Kootenai College	3	1,042	1,130	1,142	1,092	1,040	993	1,204	1,158	878	75.8	878	34	38	24	26
Stone Child College	2	38	347	344	397	305	236	303	332	310	93.4	310	23	13	†	†
Nebraska																
Little Priest Tribal College	4	141	154	109	95	120	116	141	148	140	94.6	140	11	8	†	†
Nebraska Indian Community College	2	170	190	107	115	89	92	129	177	172	97.2	172	2	5	†	†
New Mexico																
Institute of American Indian and Alaska Native Culture	1	139	176	113	192	231	249	350	325	285	87.7	285	7	3	21	19
Navajo Technical College	2	841	306	333	392	367	571	751	1,019	1,008	98.9	1,008	36	45	†	†
Southwestern Indian Polytechnic Institute	2	304	772	614	561	600	470	635	531	531	100.0	531	68	71	†	†
North Dakota																
Candeska Cikana Community College	2	9	197	198	233	223	201	250	220	207	94.1	207	33	24	†	†
Fort Berthold Community College	2	50	285	241	196	201	162	323	215	176	81.9	176	29	20	†	†
Sitting Bull College	1	22	289	287	286	290	296	335	314	286	91.1	286	34	27	9	10
Turtle Mountain Community College	3	686	787	615	788	928	951	1,058	969	886	91.4	886	75	98	8	8
United Tribes Technical College	4	204	536	885	606	604	375	476	600	537	89.5	537	69	68	†	†
South Dakota																
Oglala Lakota College[2]	1	1,174	1,501	1,302	1,485	1,456	1,531	1,804	1,830	1,708	93.3	1,639	68	92	33	41
Sinte Gleska University[2]	3	900	1,400	1,123	969	971	1,012	936	2,473	1,866	75.5	1,787	50	2	28	11
Sisseton-Wahpeton College	2	250	287	290	279	245	227	237	261	201	77.0	201	18	10	†	†
Washington																
Northwest Indian College	1	524	519	495	623	584	554	609	626	538	85.9	538	43	86	0	2
Wisconsin																
College of the Menominee Nation	3	371	507	532	513	505	512	634	615	422	68.6	422	29	33	0	†
Lac Courte Oreilles Ojibwa Community College	2	489	460	505	574	576	478	561	489	359	73.4	359	47	43	†	†

—Not available.
†Not applicable.
[1]1 = public, 4-year; 2 = public, 2-year; 3 = private not-for-profit, 4-year; and 4 = private not-for-profit, 2-year.
[2]"Total American Indian/Alaska Native" enrollment (column 11) includes graduate students and therefore does not equal "Undergraduate American Indian/Alaska Native" enrollment (column 13).
NOTE: This table only includes institutions that were in operation during the 2010–11 academic year. They are all members of the American Indian Higher Education Consortium and, with few

exceptions, are tribally controlled and located on reservations. Degree-granting institutions grant associate's or higher degrees and participate in Title IV federal financial aid programs. Totals include persons of other racial/ethnic groups not separately identified.
SOURCE: U.S. Department of Education, National Center for Education Statistics, Integrated Postsecondary Education Data System (IPEDS), Spring 2001 through Spring 2011, Enrollment component; and Fall 2009 and Fall 2010, Completions component. (This table was prepared November 2011.)

Fall enrollment, degrees conferred, and expenditures in degree-granting historically Black colleges and universities, by institution: 2009, 2010, and 2009–10

Institution	State	Level and control[1]	Total enrollment, fall 2009	Enrollment, fall 2010 Total	Black enrollment	Full-time-equivalent enrollment, fall 2010	Degrees conferred, 2009–10 Associate's	Bachelor's	Master's	Doctor's[2]	Total expenditures, 2009–10 (in thousands)
1	2	3	4	5	6	7	8	9	10	11	12
Total	†	†	322,789	326,614	265,911	284,929	3,596	31,419	7,419	2,079	$7,478,926
Alabama A&M University[3]	AL	1	5,327	5,814	5,401	5,325	†	533	219	17	138,956
Alabama State University	AL	1	5,564	5,705	5,464	5,164	†	529	245	54	135,105
Bishop State Community College	AL	2	3,598	3,725	2,219	2,436	201	†	†	†	45,137
Concordia College, Selma	AL	3	568	652	611	614	12	36	†	†	8,595
Gadsden State Community College	AL	2	6,917	7,031	1,480	5,192	544	†	†	†	61,633
H. Councill Trenholm State Technical College	AL	2	1,733	1,758	1,083	1,265	134	†	†	†	23,812
J. F. Drake Technical College	AL	2	1,258	1,557	1,157	1,019	51	†	†	†	13,882
Lawson State Community College, Birmingham Campus	AL	2	4,353	4,863	4,046	3,476	215	†	†	†	42,633
Miles College	AL	3	1,791	1,668	1,612	1,602	†	171	†	†	25,168
Oakwood College	AL	3	1,916	1,915	1,726	1,843	2	247	10	†	42,307
Selma University	AL	3	35	472	457	408	3	5	13	†	2,575
Shelton State Community College, C. A. Fredd campus	AL	2	5,808	6,075	2,155	4,432	291	†	†	†	44,814
Stillman College	AL	3	1,041	1,056	1,017	1,032	†	96	†	†	21,514
Talladega College	AL	3	700	706	640	671	†	106	†	†	13,371
Tuskegee University[3]	AL	3	2,931	2,946	2,762	2,890	†	431	51	64	119,607
Arkansas Baptist College	AR	3	640	1,119	1,046	1,021	22	28	†	†	8,835
Philander Smith College	AR	3	668	696	635	669	†	98	†	†	14,191
University of Arkansas at Pine Bluff[3]	AR	1	3,792	3,428	3,232	3,196	0	375	34	†	73,753
Delaware State University[3]	DE	1	3,609	3,757	2,810	3,512	†	436	116	7	99,109
Howard University	DC	3	10,573	10,379	9,516	9,805	†	1,163	395	373	903,500
University of the District of Columbia[3]	DC	1	4,960	5,521	3,901	3,681	109	431	62	†	109,469
Bethune-Cookman College	FL	3	3,637	3,577	3,312	3,490	†	476	17	†	60,939
Edward Waters College	FL	3	831	769	729	764	†	89	†	†	20,576
Florida A&M University[3]	FL	1	12,274	13,284	12,172	12,529	47	1,242	341	312	284,306
Florida Memorial College	FL	3	1,923	1,891	1,638	1,796	†	185	38	†	40,444
Albany State College	GA	1	4,473	4,653	4,319	4,100	†	508	136	†	66,187
Clark Atlanta University	GA	3	3,873	3,941	3,848	3,612	†	531	172	27	88,850
Fort Valley State University[3]	GA	1	3,553	3,728	3,526	3,382	8	244	53	†	76,559
Interdenominational Theological Center	GA	3	421	411	395	307	†	†	97	0	7,952
Morehouse College	GA	3	2,689	2,586	2,496	2,482	†	462	†	†	83,137
Morehouse School of Medicine	GA	3	326	329	264	314	†	†	27	51	125,210
Paine College	GA	3	907	925	902	894	†	82	†	†	18,392
Savannah State University	GA	1	3,820	4,080	3,762	3,738	†	389	51	†	69,838
Spelman College	GA	3	2,229	2,177	2,097	2,118	†	471	†	†	86,709
Kentucky State University[3]	KY	1	2,834	2,851	1,953	2,491	37	213	54	†	67,638
Dillard University	LA	3	1,011	1,187	1,153	1,135	†	107	†	†	60,304
Grambling State University	LA	1	4,992	4,994	4,344	4,669	35	713	133	4	101,296
Southern University and A&M College[3]	LA	1	7,619	6,897	6,553	6,171	†	870	283	20	176,291
Southern University at New Orleans	LA	1	3,141	3,165	3,054	2,692	14	228	132	†	41,042
Southern University at Shreveport	LA	2	3,014	2,834	2,385	2,110	215	†	†	†	31,323
Xavier University of Louisiana	LA	3	3,338	3,391	2,574	3,263	†	280	51	173	95,493
Bowie State University	MD	1	5,617	5,578	5,053	4,675	†	606	273	6	83,352
Coppin State College	MD	1	3,801	3,800	3,565	3,148	†	378	69	†	76,588
Morgan State University	MD	1	7,226	7,805	6,676	7,018	†	772	166	31	179,529
University of Maryland, Eastern Shore[3]	MD	1	4,433	4,540	3,443	4,183	†	463	49	30	96,892
Alcorn State University[3]	MS	1	3,334	3,682	3,368	3,247	29	351	138	†	80,838
Coahoma Community College	MS	2	2,565	2,741	2,685	2,501	188	†	†	†	30,340
Hinds Community College, Utica Campus	MS	2	1,220	927	888	669	138	†	†	†	0
Jackson State University	MS	1	8,783	8,687	8,002	7,368	†	982	395	70	177,531
Mississippi Valley State University	MS	1	2,850	2,636	2,512	2,307	†	319	83	†	64,508
Rust College	MS	3	1,072	960	883	860	5	127	†	†	16,905
Tougaloo College	MS	3	939	918	897	902	3	166	†	†	22,617

See notes at end of table.

Fall enrollment, degrees conferred, and expenditures in degree-granting historically Black colleges and universities, by institution: 2009, 2010, and 2009–10—Continued

Institution	State	Level and control[1]	Total enroll-ment, fall 2009	Enrollment, fall 2010 Total	Enrollment, fall 2010 Black enrollment	Full-time-equivalent enrollment, fall 2010	Degrees conferred, 2009–10 Associate's	Degrees conferred, 2009–10 Bachelor's	Degrees conferred, 2009–10 Master's	Degrees conferred, 2009–10 Doctor's[2]	Total expenditures, 2009–10 (in thousands)
1	2	3	4	5	6	7	8	9	10	11	12
Harris-Stowe State College	MO	1	1,886	1,716	1,445	1,428	†	142	†	†	26,327
Lincoln University[3]	MO	1	3,314	3,349	1,265	2,660	75	273	45	†	54,431
Bennett College for Women	NC	3	766	780	731	740	†	79	†	†	22,599
Elizabeth City State University	NC	1	3,264	3,307	2,746	3,070	†	430	14	†	76,956
Fayetteville State University	NC	1	6,283	5,781	4,313	4,785	†	876	152	11	109,633
Johnson C. Smith University	NC	3	1,466	1,331	1,284	1,311	†	218	†	†	41,574
Livingstone College	NC	3	1,082	1,156	1,138	1,150	†	111	†	†	22,931
North Carolina A&T State University[3]	NC	1	10,614	10,795	9,429	9,728	†	1,349	356	21	257,302
North Carolina Central University	NC	1	8,587	8,645	7,154	7,406	†	791	456	183	184,347
Saint Augustine's College	NC	3	1,529	1,508	1,453	1,494	†	178	†	†	36,155
Shaw University	NC	3	2,538	2,722	2,625	2,541	8	344	40	†	46,370
Winston-Salem State University	NC	1	6,427	6,333	4,892	5,846	†	1,144	181	0	137,864
Central State University	OH	1	2,436	2,288	2,217	2,139	†	212	2	†	63,560
Wilberforce University	OH	3	710	689	669	682	†	173	6	†	14,732
Langston University[3]	OK	1	2,749	2,794	2,169	2,376	13	339	89	15	60,282
Cheyney University of Pennsylvania	PA	1	1,488	1,586	1,549	1,457	†	155	41	†	44,746
Lincoln University of Pennsylvania	PA	1	2,649	2,361	2,263	2,250	†	277	220	†	60,133
Allen University	SC	3	827	848	846	830	†	52	†	†	18,051
Benedict College	SC	3	2,983	3,137	3,118	3,107	†	285	†	†	58,647
Claflin College	SC	3	1,860	1,920	1,777	1,863	†	280	31	†	40,924
Clinton Junior College	SC	4	148	143	143	138	33	†	†	†	2,466
Denmark Technical College	SC	2	1,105	1,033	997	856	74	†	†	†	15,685
Morris College	SC	3	966	1,048	1,042	1,039	†	129	†	†	19,649
South Carolina State University[3]	SC	1	4,538	4,362	4,134	3,990	†	565	123	21	119,569
Voorhees College	SC	3	701	752	706	740	†	110	†	†	17,605
Fisk University	TN	3	650	580	510	536	†	163	7	†	24,340
Lane College	TN	3	2,146	2,222	2,212	2,215	†	262	†	†	30,531
Le Moyne-Owen College	TN	3	890	987	979	927	†	65	†	†	14,939
Meharry Medical College	TN	3	786	781	678	781	†	†	18	141	131,214
Tennessee State University[3]	TN	1	8,824	8,930	6,420	7,305	114	977	381	79	171,089
Huston-Tillotson College	TX	3	882	901	645	860	†	93	†	†	16,784
Jarvis Christian College	TX	3	628	522	506	521	†	72	†	†	14,150
Paul Quinn College	TX	3	171	226	217	209	†	56	†	†	8,046
Prairie View A&M University[3]	TX	1	8,608	8,781	7,671	7,663	†	898	559	13	186,491
Saint Philip's College	TX	2	11,008	10,828	1,510	6,102	695	†	†	†	81,431
Southwestern Christian College	TX	3	201	224	199	222	30	3	†	†	6,389
Texas College	TX	3	964	927	794	894	3	93	†	†	12,307
Texas Southern University	TX	1	9,394	9,557	8,020	8,268	†	797	158	259	211,810
Wiley College	TX	3	1,237	1,351	1,240	1,308	0	159	†	†	17,588
Hampton University	VA	3	5,402	5,254	4,619	5,057	2	794	121	66	141,874
Norfolk State University	VA	1	6,993	6,964	6,111	6,081	56	712	212	8	136,881
Saint Paul's College	VA	3	584	566	549	560	†	105	†	†	20,556
Virginia State University[3]	VA	1	5,366	5,634	5,329	5,247	9	680	102	6	125,376
Virginia Union University	VA	3	1,691	1,667	1,629	1,629	†	139	124	8	29,410
Virginia University of Lynchburg	VA	3	327	555	549	309	20	18	12	9	1,845
Bluefield State College	WV	1	1,989	2,063	237	1,778	87	245	†	†	23,848
West Virginia State College	WV	1	4,003	3,190	572	2,559	†	385	11	†	54,411
University of the Virgin Islands[3]	VI	1	2,602	2,733	2,192	2,084	74	252	55	†	85,525

†Not applicable.

[1]1 = public, 4-year; 2 = public, 2-year; 3 = private not-for-profit, 4-year; and 4 = private not-for-profit, 2-year.

[2]Includes Ph.D., Ed.D., and comparable degrees at the doctoral level, as well as such degrees as M.D., D.D.S., and law degrees that were formerly classified as first-professional degrees.

[3]Land-grant institution.

NOTE: Degree-granting institutions grant associate's or higher degrees and participate in Title IV federal financial aid programs. Excludes historically Black colleges and universities that are not participating in Title IV programs. Historically Black colleges and universities are degree-granting institutions established prior to 1964 with the principal mission of educating Black Americans. Federal regulations, 20 U.S. Code, Section 1061 (2), allow for certain exceptions to the founding date. Totals include persons of other racial/ethnic groups not separately identified. Detail may not sum to totals because of rounding.

SOURCE: U.S. Department of Education, National Center for Education Statistics, Integrated Postsecondary Education Data System (IPEDS), Fall 2010, Completions component; and Spring 2010, Enrollment and Finance components. (This table was prepared December 2011.)

Fall enrollment in degree-granting historically Black colleges and universities, by sex of student and level and control of institution: Selected years, 1976 through 2010

Year	Total enrollment	Males	Females	4-year	2-year	Public Total	Public 4-year	Public 2-year	Private Total	Private 4-year	Private 2-year
1	2	3	4	5	6	7	8	9	10	11	12
All students											
1976	222,613	104,669	117,944	206,676	15,937	156,836	143,528	13,308	65,777	63,148	2,629
1980	233,557	106,387	127,170	218,009	15,548	168,217	155,085	13,132	65,340	62,924	2,416
1981	232,460	106,033	126,427	217,152	15,308	166,991	154,269	12,722	65,469	62,883	2,586
1982	228,371	104,897	123,474	212,017	16,354	165,871	151,472	14,399	62,500	60,545	1,955
1983	234,446	106,884	127,562	217,909	16,537	170,051	155,665	14,386	64,395	62,244	2,151
1984	227,519	102,823	124,696	212,844	14,675	164,116	151,289	12,827	63,403	61,555	1,848
1985	225,801	100,698	125,103	210,648	15,153	163,677	150,002	13,675	62,124	60,646	1,478
1986	223,275	97,523	125,752	207,231	16,044	162,048	147,631	14,417	61,227	59,600	1,627
1987	227,994	97,085	130,909	211,654	16,340	165,486	150,560	14,926	62,508	61,094	1,414
1988	239,755	100,561	139,194	223,250	16,505	173,672	158,606	15,066	66,083	64,644	1,439
1989	249,096	102,484	146,612	232,890	16,206	181,151	166,481	14,670	67,945	66,409	1,536
1990	257,152	105,157	151,995	240,497	16,655	187,046	171,969	15,077	70,106	68,528	1,578
1991	269,335	110,442	158,893	252,093	17,242	197,847	182,204	15,643	71,488	69,889	1,599
1992	279,541	114,622	164,919	261,089	18,452	204,966	188,143	16,823	74,575	72,946	1,629
1993	282,856	116,397	166,459	262,430	20,426	208,197	189,032	19,165	74,659	73,398	1,261
1994	280,071	114,006	166,065	259,997	20,074	206,520	187,735	18,785	73,551	72,262	1,289
1995	278,725	112,637	166,088	259,409	19,316	204,726	186,278	18,448	73,999	73,131	868
1996	273,018	109,498	163,520	253,654	19,364	200,569	182,063	18,506	72,449	71,591	858
1997	269,167	106,865	162,302	248,860	20,307	194,674	175,297	19,377	74,493	73,563	930
1998	273,472	108,752	164,720	248,931	24,541	198,603	174,776	23,827	74,869	74,155	714
1999[1]	274,321	108,301	166,020	249,156	25,165	199,826	175,364	24,462	74,495	73,792	703
2000	275,680	108,164	167,516	250,710	24,970	199,725	175,404	24,321	75,955	75,306	649
2001	289,985	112,874	177,111	260,547	29,438	210,083	181,346	28,737	79,902	79,201	701
2002	299,041	115,466	183,575	269,020	30,021	218,433	189,183	29,250	80,608	79,837	771
2003	306,727	117,795	188,932	274,326	32,401	228,096	196,077	32,019	78,631	78,249	382
2004	308,939	118,129	190,810	276,136	32,803	231,179	198,810	32,369	77,760	77,326	434
2005	311,768	120,023	191,745	272,666	39,102	235,875	197,200	38,675	75,893	75,466	427
2006	308,774	118,865	189,909	272,770	36,004	234,505	198,676	35,829	74,269	74,094	175
2007	306,515	118,640	187,875	270,915	35,600	233,807	198,300	35,507	72,708	72,615	93
2008	313,491	121,873	191,618	274,568	38,923	235,824	197,025	38,799	77,667	77,543	124
2009	322,789	125,666	197,123	280,062	42,727	246,595	204,016	42,579	76,194	76,046	148
2010	326,614	127,437	199,177	283,099	43,515	249,146	205,774	43,372	77,468	77,325	143
Black students											
1976	190,305	84,492	105,813	179,848	10,457	129,770	121,851	7,919	60,535	57,997	2,538
1980	190,989	81,818	109,171	181,237	9,752	131,661	124,236	7,425	59,328	57,001	2,327
1982	182,639	78,874	103,765	171,942	10,697	126,368	117,562	8,806	56,271	54,380	1,891
1984	180,803	76,819	103,984	171,401	9,402	124,445	116,845	7,600	56,358	54,556	1,802
1986	178,628	74,276	104,352	167,971	10,657	123,555	114,502	9,053	55,073	53,469	1,604
1988	194,151	78,268	115,883	183,402	10,749	133,786	124,438	9,348	60,365	58,964	1,401
1990	208,682	82,897	125,785	198,237	10,445	144,204	134,924	9,280	64,478	63,313	1,165
1991	218,366	87,380	130,986	207,449	10,917	152,864	143,411	9,453	65,502	64,038	1,464
1992	228,963	91,949	137,014	217,614	11,349	159,585	149,754	9,831	69,378	67,860	1,518
1993	231,198	93,110	138,088	219,431	11,767	161,444	150,867	10,577	69,754	68,564	1,190
1994	230,162	91,908	138,254	218,565	11,597	161,098	150,682	10,416	69,064	67,883	1,181
1995	229,418	91,132	138,286	218,379	11,039	159,925	149,661	10,264	69,493	68,718	775
1996	224,201	88,306	135,895	213,309	10,892	156,851	146,753	10,098	67,350	66,556	794
1997	222,331	86,641	135,690	210,741	11,590	153,039	142,326	10,713	69,292	68,415	877
1998	223,745	87,163	136,582	211,822	11,923	154,244	142,985	11,259	69,501	68,837	664
1999[1]	226,592	87,987	138,605	213,779	12,813	156,292	144,166	12,126	70,300	69,613	687
2000	227,239	87,319	139,920	215,172	12,067	156,706	145,277	11,429	70,533	69,895	638
2001	238,638	90,718	147,920	224,417	14,221	164,354	150,831	13,523	74,284	73,586	698
2002	247,292	93,538	153,754	231,834	15,458	172,203	157,507	14,696	75,089	74,327	762
2003	253,257	95,703	157,554	236,753	16,504	180,104	163,977	16,127	73,153	72,776	377
2004	257,545	96,750	160,795	241,030	16,515	184,708	168,619	16,089	72,837	72,411	426
2005	256,584	96,891	159,693	238,030	18,554	186,047	167,916	18,131	70,537	70,114	423
2006	255,150	96,508	158,642	238,446	16,704	185,894	169,365	16,529	69,256	69,081	175
2007	253,415	96,313	157,102	236,885	16,530	185,344	168,906	16,438	68,071	67,979	92
2008	258,403	98,634	159,769	240,133	18,270	186,446	168,299	18,147	71,957	71,834	123
2009	264,090	100,550	163,540	243,954	20,136	194,088	174,099	19,989	70,002	69,855	147
2010	265,911	101,644	164,267	245,163	20,748	193,843	173,238	20,605	72,068	71,925	143

NOTE: Historically Black colleges and universities are degree-granting institutions established prior to 1964 with the principal mission of educating Black Americans. Federal regulations, 20 U.S. Code, Section 1061 (2), allow for certain exceptions to the founding date. Data through 1995 are for institutions of higher education, while later data are for degree-granting institutions. Degree-granting institutions grant associate's or higher degrees and participate in Title IV federal financial aid programs. The degree-granting classification is very similar to the earlier higher education classification, but it includes more 2-year colleges and excludes a few higher education institutions that did not grant degrees. (See Appendix A: Guide to Sources for details.)

SOURCE: U.S. Department of Education, National Center for Education Statistics, Higher Education General Information Survey (HEGIS), "Fall Enrollment in Colleges and Universities," 1976 through 1985 surveys; Integrated Postsecondary Education Data System (IPEDS), "Fall Enrollment Survey" (IPEDS-EF:86-99); and IPEDS Spring 2001 through Spring 2011, Enrollment component. (This table was prepared December 2011.)

Degree-granting institutions, by control and level of institution: Selected years, 1949–50 through 2010–11

Year	All institutions			Public			Private								
										Not-for-profit			For-profit		
	Total	4-year	2-year	Total	4-year	2-year	Total	4-year, total	2-year, total	Total	4-year	2-year	Total	4-year	2-year
1	2	3	4	5	6	7	8	9	10	11	12	13	14	15	16
Excluding branch campuses															
1949–50	1,851	1,327	524	641	344	297	1,210	983	227	—	—	—	—	—	—
1959–60	2,004	1,422	582	695	367	328	1,309	1,055	254	—	—	—	—	—	—
1969–70	2,525	1,639	886	1,060	426	634	1,465	1,213	252	—	—	—	—	—	—
1970–71	2,556	1,665	891	1,089	435	654	1,467	1,230	237	—	—	—	—	—	—
1971–72	2,606	1,675	931	1,137	440	697	1,469	1,235	234	—	—	—	—	—	—
1972–73	2,665	1,701	964	1,182	449	733	1,483	1,252	231	—	—	—	—	—	—
1973–74	2,720	1,717	1,003	1,200	440	760	1,520	1,277	243	—	—	—	—	—	—
1974–75	2,747	1,744	1,003	1,214	447	767	1,533	1,297	236	—	—	—	—	—	—
1975–76	2,765	1,767	998	1,219	447	772	1,546	1,320	226	—	—	—	—	—	—
1976–77	2,785	1,783	1,002	1,231	452	779	1,554	1,331	223	—	—	—	—	—	—
1977–78	2,826	1,808	1,018	1,241	454	787	1,585	1,354	231	—	—	—	—	—	—
1978–79	2,954	1,843	1,111	1,308	463	845	1,646	1,380	266	—	—	—	—	—	—
1979–80	2,975	1,863	1,112	1,310	464	846	1,665	1,399	266	—	—	—	—	—	—
1980–81	3,056	1,861	1,195	1,334	465	869	1,722	1,396	326 [1]	—	—	—	—	—	—
1981–82	3,083	1,883	1,200	1,340	471	869	1,743	1,412	331 [1]	—	—	—	—	—	—
1982–83	3,111	1,887	1,224	1,336	472	864	1,775	1,415	360 [1]	—	—	—	—	—	—
1983–84	3,117	1,914	1,203	1,325	474	851	1,792	1,440	352	—	—	—	—	—	—
1984–85	3,146	1,911	1,235	1,329	461	868	1,817	1,450	367	—	—	—	—	—	—
1985–86	3,155	1,915	1,240	1,326	461	865	1,829	1,454	375	—	—	—	—	—	—
Including branch campuses															
1974–75	3,004	1,866	1,138	1,433	537	896	1,571	1,329	242	—	—	—	—	—	—
1975–76	3,026	1,898	1,128	1,442	545	897	1,584	1,353	231	—	—	—	—	—	—
1976–77	3,046	1,913	1,133	1,455	550	905	1,591	1,363	228	1,536	1,348	188	55	15	40
1977–78	3,095	1,938	1,157	1,473	552	921	1,622	1,386	236	—	—	—	—	—	—
1978–79	3,134	1,941	1,193	1,474	550	924	1,660	1,391	269	1,564	1,376	188	96	15	81
1979–80	3,152	1,957	1,195	1,475	549	926	1,677	1,408	269	—	—	—	—	—	—
1980–81	3,231	1,957	1,274	1,497	552	945	1,734	1,405	329 [1]	1,569	1,387	182	165	18	147
1981–82	3,253	1,979	1,274	1,498	558	940	1,755	1,421	334 [1]	—	—	—	—	—	—
1982–83	3,280	1,984	1,296	1,493	560	933	1,787	1,424	363 [1]	—	—	—	—	—	—
1983–84	3,284	2,013	1,271	1,481	565	916	1,803	1,448	355	—	—	—	—	—	—
1984–85	3,331	2,025	1,306	1,501	566	935	1,830	1,459	371	1,616	1,430	186	214	29	185
1985–86	3,340	2,029	1,311	1,498	566	932	1,842	1,463	379	—	—	—	—	—	—
1986–87	3,406	2,070	1,336	1,533	573	960	1,873	1,497	376	1,635	1,462	173	238	35	203
1987–88	3,587	2,135	1,452	1,591	599	992	1,996	1,536	460	1,673	1,487	186	323	49	274
1988–89	3,565	2,129	1,436	1,582	598	984	1,983	1,531	452	1,658	1,478	180	325	53	272
1989–90	3,535	2,127	1,408	1,563	595	968	1,972	1,532	440	1,656	1,479	177	316	53	263
1990–91	3,559	2,141	1,418	1,567	595	972	1,992	1,546	446	1,649	1,482	167	343	64	279
1991–92	3,601	2,157	1,444	1,598	599	999	2,003	1,558	445	1,662	1,486	176	341	72	269
1992–93	3,638	2,169	1,469	1,624	600	1,024	2,014	1,569	445	1,672	1,493	179	342	76	266
1993–94	3,632	2,190	1,442	1,625	604	1,021	2,007	1,586	421	1,687	1,506	181	320	80	240
1994–95	3,688	2,215	1,473	1,641	605	1,036	2,047	1,610	437	1,702	1,510	192	345	100	245
1995–96	3,706	2,244	1,462	1,655	608	1,047	2,051	1,636	415	1,706	1,519	187	345	117	228
1996–97	4,009	2,267	1,742	1,702	614	1,088	2,307	1,653	654	1,693	1,509	184	614	144	470
1997–98	4,064	2,309	1,755	1,707	615	1,092	2,357	1,694	663	1,707	1,528	179	650	166	484
1998–99	4,048	2,335	1,713	1,681	612	1,069	2,367	1,723	644	1,695	1,531	164	672	192	480
1999–2000	4,084	2,363	1,721	1,682	614	1,068	2,402	1,749	653	1,681	1,531	150	721	218	503
2000–01	4,182	2,450	1,732	1,698	622	1,076	2,484	1,828	656	1,695	1,551	144	789	277	512
2001–02	4,197	2,487	1,710	1,713	628	1,085	2,484	1,859	625	1,676	1,541	135	808	318	490
2002–03	4,168	2,466	1,702	1,712	631	1,081	2,456	1,835	621	1,665	1,538	127	791	297	494
2003–04	4,236	2,530	1,706	1,720	634	1,086	2,516	1,896	620	1,664	1,546	118	852	350	502
2004–05	4,216	2,533	1,683	1,700	639	1,061	2,516	1,894	622	1,637	1,525	112	879	369	510
2005–06	4,276	2,582	1,694	1,693	640	1,053	2,583	1,942	641	1,647	1,534	113	936	408	528
2006–07	4,314	2,629	1,685	1,688	643	1,045	2,626	1,986	640	1,640	1,533	107	986	453	533
2007–08	4,352	2,675	1,677	1,685	653	1,032	2,667	2,022	645	1,624	1,532	92	1,043	490	553
2008–09	4,409	2,719	1,690	1,676	652	1,024	2,733	2,067	666	1,629	1,537	92	1,104	530	574
2009–10	4,495	2,774	1,721	1,672	672	1,000	2,823	2,102	721	1,624	1,539	85	1,199	563	636
2010–11	4,599	2,870	1,729	1,656	678	978	2,943	2,192	751	1,630	1,543	87	1,313	649	664

—Not available.

[1]Large increases are due to the addition of schools accredited by the Accrediting Commission of Career Schools and Colleges of Technology.
NOTE: Data through 1995–96 are for institutions of higher education, while later data are for degree-granting institutions. Degree-granting institutions grant associate's or higher degrees and participate in Title IV federal financial aid programs. The degree-granting classification is very similar to the earlier higher education classification, but it includes more 2-year colleges and excludes a few higher education institutions that did not grant degrees. (See Appendix A: Guide to Sources for details.) Changes in counts of institutions over time are partly affected by increasing or decreasing numbers of institutions submitting separate data for branch campuses.
SOURCE: U.S. Department of Education, National Center for Education Statistics, *Education Directory, Colleges and Universities*, 1949–50 through 1965–66; Higher Education General Information Survey (HEGIS), "Institutional Characteristics of Colleges and Universities" surveys, 1966–67 through 1985–86; Integrated Postsecondary Education Data System (IPEDS), "Institutional Characteristics Survey" (IPEDS-IC:86–99); and IPEDS Fall 2000 through Fall 2010, Institutional Characteristics component. (This table was prepared October 2011.)

Degree-granting institutions and branches, by control and level of institution and state or jurisdiction: 2010–11

State or jurisdiction	Total institutions	All public institutions	Public 4-year: Total	Research university very high[1]	Research university high[2]	Doctoral/research university[3]	Master's[4]	Baccalaureate[5]	Special focus[6]	Public 2-year institutions	All not-for-profit institutions	Not-for-profit 4-year: Total	Research university very high[1]	Research university high[2]	Doctoral/research university[3]	Master's[4]	Baccalaureate[5]	Special focus[6]	Not-for-profit 2-year	For-profit: Total	For-profit 4-year	For-profit 2-year
1	2	3	4	5	6	7	8	9	10	11	12	13	14	15	16	17	18	19	20	21	22	23
United States	4,599	1,656	678	66	75	27	261	203	46	978	1,630	1,543	33	27	45	337	528	573	87	1,313	649	664
Alabama	75	39	14	1	3	0	9	1	0	25	19	19	0	0	1	2	10	6	0	17	10	7
Alaska	7	5	3	1	0	0	2	0	0	2	1	1	0	0	0	1	0	0	0	1	1	0
Arizona	84	24	4	2	1	0	0	0	1	20	11	11	0	0	0	2	2	7	0	49	31	18
Arkansas	51	33	11	1	1	0	5	3	1	22	12	12	0	0	0	1	9	2	0	6	4	2
California	454	148	35	8	1	0	19	5	2	113	146	141	3	1	11	26	21	79	5	160	73	87
Colorado	85	27	12	3	1	1	2	5	0	15	12	11	0	1	0	3	3	4	1	46	26	20
Connecticut	46	21	9	1	0	0	4	4	0	12	19	18	1	0	2	6	6	3	1	6	4	2
Delaware	11	5	2	1	0	0	1	0	0	3	5	4	1	0	1	1	1	1	1	1	1	0
District of Columbia	20	2	2	0	0	0	1	0	1	0	14	14	1	3	1	2	0	7	0	4	4	0
Florida	223	43	33	6	3	2	2	19	1	10	57	56	1	1	2	11	21	20	1	123	55	68
Georgia	132	67	27	2	1	1	13	9	1	40	34	32	1	1	0	4	18	8	2	31	18	13
Hawaii	20	10	4	1	0	1	0	3	0	6	6	6	0	0	0	2	1	3	0	4	3	1
Idaho	15	7	4	0	1	1	1	0	0	3	4	4	0	0	0	0	2	0	0	4	3	1
Illinois	181	60	12	2	2	1	7	0	0	48	84	80	2	2	2	16	22	36	4	37	23	14
Indiana	109	29	15	2	1	2	6	4	0	14	41	40	1	0	0	9	20	10	1	39	20	19
Iowa	66	19	3	2	0	0	1	0	0	16	34	33	0	0	0	5	19	9	1	13	12	1
Kansas	67	33	8	2	1	0	4	0	1	25	24	22	0	0	1	6	13	3	2	10	5	5
Kentucky	76	24	8	1	1	0	5	1	0	16	26	26	0	0	0	3	14	8	0	26	16	10
Louisiana	76	39	17	1	2	1	9	1	3	22	10	10	1	0	0	2	4	3	0	25	5	20
Maine	32	15	8	0	1	0	1	6	0	7	15	12	0	0	0	3	6	3	3	2	0	2
Maryland	61	29	13	1	1	1	8	1	1	16	22	22	1	0	0	4	7	10	0	10	5	5
Massachusetts	124	30	14	1	2	2	7	2	0	16	83	80	5	3	1	14	25	32	3	11	7	4
Michigan	107	45	15	3	2	2	7	1	0	30	50	50	0	0	1	9	23	17	1	12	10	2
Minnesota	113	43	12	1	0	0	8	3	0	31	36	35	0	0	3	6	11	15	1	34	29	5
Mississippi	40	24	9	0	1	0	1	6	0	15	9	9	0	0	0	3	4	2	0	7	2	5
Missouri	138	34	13	1	3	0	6	3	0	21	58	54	1	1	0	12	12	28	4	46	22	24
Montana	23	18	6	1	0	0	1	2	2	12	5	4	0	0	0	1	2	1	1	0	0	0
Nebraska	43	15	7	1	0	0	3	2	1	8	19	16	0	0	0	1	8	5	3	9	5	4
Nevada	25	7	6	0	2	0	0	4	0	1	3	3	0	0	0	0	1	2	0	15	8	7
New Hampshire	29	12	5	0	1	0	2	2	0	7	15	13	1	0	1	2	6	3	2	2	2	0
New Jersey	66	33	14	1	2	0	9	1	1	19	25	25	1	1	1	9	3	10	0	8	4	4
New Mexico	44	28	8	1	0	0	4	1	2	20	3	3	0	0	0	1	5	4	0	13	8	5
New York	302	78	43	3	3	2	20	13	4	35	180	164	6	5	6	36	31	80	16	44	18	26
North Carolina	139	75	16	3	2	2	6	3	0	59	45	44	1	0	0	5	28	9	1	19	14	5
North Dakota	21	14	8	1	1	0	1	4	1	6	6	5	0	1	0	1	1	3	1	1	1	0
Ohio	215	60	36	2	7	1	9	3	3	24	75	68	1	1	1	18	24	23	7	80	22	58
Oklahoma	60	29	17	0	2	1	4	7	2	12	14	14	0	1	1	3	5	4	0	17	9	8
Oregon	60	26	9	1	1	0	3	2	2	17	24	24	0	0	2	3	8	11	0	10	5	5
Pennsylvania	262	61	44	2	1	1	16	22	2	17	118	105	2	2	3	30	36	32	13	83	11	72
Rhode Island	13	3	2	1	1	0	0	0	0	1	10	10	0	0	0	4	1	4	1	0	0	0
South Carolina	75	33	13	1	1	1	4	5	1	20	24	22	0	0	0	4	14	4	2	18	11	7
South Dakota	25	12	7	0	1	1	0	2	2	5	8	7	0	0	0	3	3	3	1	5	5	0
Tennessee	109	22	9	1	1	2	5	0	0	13	47	45	1	0	1	10	17	16	2	40	22	18
Texas	252	108	45	7	3	3	21	5	6	63	57	53	1	1	2	16	17	16	4	87	30	57
Utah	41	12	7	1	1	0	2	3	0	5	4	3	0	0	0	1	1	0	1	25	19	6

See notes at end of table.

Degree-granting institutions and branches, by control and level of institution and state or jurisdiction: 2010–11—Continued

State or jurisdiction	Total institutions	All public institutions	Public 4-year: Total	Public 4-year: Research university very high[1]	Public 4-year: Research university high[2]	Public 4-year: Doctoral/research university[3]	Public 4-year: Master's[4]	Public 4-year: Baccalaureate[5]	Public 4-year: Special focus[6]	Public 2-year	All not-for-profit institutions	NFP 4-year: Total	NFP 4-year: Research university very high[1]	NFP 4-year: Research university high[2]	NFP 4-year: Doctoral/research university[3]	NFP 4-year: Master's[4]	NFP 4-year: Baccalaureate[5]	NFP 4-year: Special focus[6]	Not-for-profit 2-year	For-profit: Total	For-profit: 4-year	For-profit: 2-year
1	2	3	4	5	6	7	8	9	10	11	12	13	14	15	16	17	18	19	20	21	22	23
Vermont	24	6	5	0	1	0	2	2	0	1	17	16	0	0	0	5	8	3	1	1	1	0
Virginia	129	39	15	2	4	0	6	3	0	24	38	38	0	0	1	7	20	10	0	52	28	24
Washington	85	43	16	2	0	0	6	6	2	27	23	22	0	0	0	10	3	9	1	19	11	8
West Virginia	46	23	13	0	1	0	1	10	1	10	9	9	0	0	0	2	6	1	0	14	3	11
Wisconsin	84	31	14	1	1	0	9	3	0	17	29	28	0	1	0	10	10	7	1	24	21	3
Wyoming	11	8	1	0	1	0	0	0	0	7	0	0	0	0	0	0	0	0	0	3	2	1
U.S. Service Academies	5	5	5	0	0	0	0	5	0	0	†	†	†	†	†	†	†	†	†	†	†	†
Other jurisdictions	**89**	**26**	**17**	**0**	**1**	**0**	**2**	**11**	**3**	**9**	**46**	**42**	**0**	**0**	**2**	**5**	**22**	**13**	**4**	**17**	**7**	**10**
American Samoa	1	1	0	0	0	0	0	0	0	1	0	0	0	0	0	0	0	0	0	0	0	0
Federated States of Micronesia	1	1	0	0	0	0	0	0	0	1	0	0	0	0	0	0	0	0	0	0	0	0
Guam	3	2	1	0	0	0	1	0	0	1	1	1	0	0	0	0	0	1	0	0	0	0
Marshall Islands	1	1	0	0	0	0	0	0	0	1	1	0	0	0	0	0	0	0	0	0	0	0
Northern Marianas	1	1	1	0	0	0	0	1	0	0	0	0	0	0	0	0	0	0	0	0	0	0
Palau	1	1	0	0	0	0	0	0	0	1	0	0	0	0	0	0	0	0	0	0	0	0
Puerto Rico	80	18	14	0	1	0	1	9	3	4	45	41	0	0	2	5	22	12	4	17	7	10
U.S. Virgin Islands	1	1	1	0	0	0	0	1	0	0	0	0	0	0	0	0	0	0	0	0	0	0

†Not applicable.

[1]Research universities with a very high level of research activity.

[2]Research universities with a high level of research activity.

[3]Institutions that award at least 20 doctor's degrees per year, but did not have a high level of research activity.

[4]Institutions that award at least 50 master's degrees per year.

[5]Institutions that primarily emphasize undergraduate education.

[6]Four-year institutions that award degrees primarily in single fields of study, such as medicine, business, fine arts, theology, and engineering. Includes some institutions that have 4-year programs, but have not reported sufficient data to identify program category. Also includes institutions classified as 4-year under the IPEDS system, which had been classified as 2-year in the Carnegie classification system because they primarily award associate's degrees.

NOTE: Relative levels of research activity for research universities were determined by an analysis of research and development expenditures, science and engineering research staffing, and doctoral degrees conferred, by field. Further information on the research index ranking may be obtained from http://www.carnegiefoundation.org/classifications/index.asp?key=798#related.

Degree-granting institutions grant associate's or higher degrees and participate in Title IV federal financial aid programs.

SOURCE: U.S. Department of Education, National Center for Education Statistics, Integrated Postsecondary Education Data System (IPEDS), Fall 2010, Institutional Characteristics component. (This table was prepared October 2011.)

Number and percentage of degree-granting institutions with first-year undergraduates using various selection criteria for admission, by control and level of institution: Selected years, 2000–01 through 2010–11

Selection criteria	All institutions			Public institutions			Private institutions								
							Total	4-year	2-year	Not-for-profit			For-profit		
	Total	4-year	2-year	Total	4-year	2-year				Total	4-year	2-year	Total	4-year	2-year
1	2	3	4	5	6	7	8	9	10	11	12	13	14	15	16
Number of institutions with first-year undergraduates															
2000–01	3,717	2,034	1,683	1,647	580	1,067	2,070	1,454	616	1,383	1,247	136	687	207	480
2005–06	3,880	2,198	1,682	1,638	588	1,050	2,242	1,610	632	1,351	1,240	111	891	370	521
2009–10	4,112	2,404	1,708	1,628	629	999	2,484	1,775	709	1,330	1,247	83	1,154	528	626
2010–11	4,209	2,487	1,722	1,614	637	977	2,595	1,850	745	1,321	1,238	83	1,274	612	662
Percent of institutions															
Open admissions															
2000–01	40.2	12.9	73.2	63.8	12.1	91.9	21.4	13.3	40.7	14.0	11.7	34.6	36.5	22.7	42.5
2005–06	44.7	18.3	79.3	66.1	13.6	95.4	29.2	20.1	52.4	15.3	13.1	40.5	50.2	43.5	54.9
2009–10	46.6	21.9	81.3	65.7	17.2	96.3	34.0	23.5	60.2	15.3	13.2	45.8	55.6	47.9	62.1
2010–11	47.2	22.5	82.9	65.7	17.7	96.9	35.8	24.2	64.6	15.4	13.0	51.8	56.8	46.7	66.2
Some admission requirements[1]															
2000–01	58.4	85.8	25.1	35.4	87.4	7.1	76.6	85.2	56.3	84.5	86.8	63.2	60.7	75.4	54.4
2005–06	53.4	80.5	18.0	33.6	86.1	4.3	67.9	78.5	40.8	84.2	86.5	57.7	43.2	51.6	37.2
2009–10	50.7	76.6	14.3	34.2	82.7	3.6	61.6	74.4	29.5	84.2	86.4	51.8	35.5	46.2	26.5
2010–11	50.1	75.6	13.3	34.3	82.3	3.1	59.9	73.3	26.7	84.3	86.7	48.2	34.7	46.2	24.0
Secondary grades															
2000–01	34.6	58.7	5.5	23.9	63.4	2.4	43.0	56.7	10.7	60.1	64.1	23.5	8.7	12.6	7.1
2005–06	34.1	57.1	4.2	25.9	68.4	2.2	40.1	53.0	7.4	62.8	66.2	25.2	5.7	8.6	3.6
2008–09	33.9	55.7	3.2	27.5	68.4	1.7	38.1	51.2	5.4	65.8	68.2	28.9	6.2	11.0	2.2
2009–10	33.3	54.2	3.2	27.8	67.8	1.7	36.7	49.5	5.1	66.0	68.7	26.5	6.4	10.6	2.4
Secondary class rank															
2000–01	13.7	24.3	1.0	10.9	30.3	0.3	16.0	21.9	2.3	23.2	25.1	5.9	1.6	2.4	1.3
2005–06	11.3	19.4	0.7	10.4	28.7	0.2	11.9	16.0	1.6	19.3	20.5	6.3	0.7	0.8	0.6
2008–09	9.1	15.2	0.5	9.3	23.5	0.4	8.9	12.2	0.7	16.3	17.1	4.8	0.4	0.8	0.2
2009–10	8.4	13.9	0.4	9.2	22.9	0.3	7.8	10.8	0.5	15.0	15.8	3.6	0.4	0.7	0.2
Secondary school record															
2000–01	45.8	70.3	16.2	29.4	72.9	5.8	58.7	69.2	34.1	73.2	75.5	52.2	29.5	30.9	29.0
2005–06	48.5	73.3	15.9	30.8	78.2	4.2	61.4	71.6	35.4	77.6	79.7	55.0	36.7	44.3	31.3
2009–10	46.4	70.5	12.5	32.7	79.2	3.4	55.4	67.4	25.4	77.0	79.0	47.0	30.6	40.2	22.5
2010–11	45.8	70.1	10.8	33.0	78.8	3.1	53.8	67.1	20.9	77.1	79.4	42.2	29.7	42.2	18.3
College preparatory program															
2000–01	15.5	27.3	1.2	16.2	44.0	1.1	14.9	20.7	1.3	22.1	24.1	4.4	0.4	0.5	0.4
2005–06	15.2	26.4	0.6	17.4	47.1	0.8	13.6	18.8	0.3	22.4	24.3	1.8	0.2	0.5	0.0
2009–10	15.0	25.3	0.4	18.1	45.9	0.6	12.9	18.0	0.1	23.9	25.4	1.2	0.3	0.6	0.0
2010–11	14.7	24.4	0.6	18.3	45.4	0.7	12.4	17.1	0.5	24.0	25.4	2.4	0.3	0.3	0.3
Recommendations															
2000–01	20.4	34.4	3.5	2.7	7.4	0.2	34.4	45.1	9.3	46.6	49.2	22.8	10.0	20.8	5.4
2005–06	19.2	31.9	2.5	2.9	7.7	0.2	31.1	40.8	6.3	49.1	51.5	23.4	3.7	5.1	2.7
2009–10	17.8	29.0	2.0	3.0	7.6	0.1	27.5	36.6	4.8	49.5	51.2	25.3	2.2	2.3	2.1
2010–11	18.1	29.2	2.1	3.3	8.3	0.1	27.2	36.3	4.7	51.6	53.3	25.3	2.0	2.0	2.1
Demonstration of competencies[2]															
2000–01	8.0	12.1	3.0	2.2	5.0	0.7	12.7	15.0	7.1	12.1	12.7	7.4	13.7	29.0	7.1
2005–06	7.0	9.8	3.3	2.3	6.1	0.2	10.3	11.1	8.4	10.2	10.3	9.0	10.5	13.8	8.3
2009–10	6.3	8.5	3.1	2.0	4.9	0.2	9.0	9.7	7.2	9.3	9.2	10.8	8.7	11.0	6.7
2010–11	5.8	8.0	2.5	1.8	4.6	0.0	8.2	9.2	5.8	8.9	8.8	9.6	7.6	10.1	5.3
Test scores[3]															
2000–01	47.2	72.5	16.7	33.2	83.4	5.8	58.5	68.2	35.6	70.3	73.4	41.9	34.6	36.7	33.8
2005–06	36.5	62.5	2.6	31.1	82.3	2.4	40.5	55.2	3.0	65.7	70.5	12.6	2.2	4.1	1.0
2009–10	32.4	54.1	1.9	30.2	74.9	2.0	33.9	46.8	1.8	62.6	65.8	13.3	1.0	1.7	0.3
2010–11	31.3	51.6	1.9	30.4	73.9	1.9	31.8	43.9	1.7	61.6	64.9	13.3	0.9	1.6	0.3
TOEFL[4]															
2000–01	43.4	71.2	9.9	30.2	77.4	4.6	54.0	68.7	19.2	66.2	70.1	30.9	29.3	60.4	15.8
2005–06	41.5	67.9	7.1	31.0	79.3	3.9	49.3	63.8	12.3	67.0	70.6	27.0	22.4	41.1	9.2
2009–10	39.3	62.9	6.0	29.6	71.7	3.1	45.6	59.8	10.0	66.6	69.3	26.5	21.4	37.5	7.8
2010–11	38.7	61.9	5.1	29.8	71.4	2.7	44.2	58.6	8.3	66.3	69.1	25.3	21.3	37.6	6.2
No admission requirements, only recommendations for admission															
2000–01	1.4	1.2	1.7	0.8	0.5	0.9	1.9	1.5	2.9	1.5	1.4	2.2	2.8	1.9	3.1
2005–06	1.8	1.1	2.7	0.3	0.3	0.3	2.9	1.4	6.8	0.5	0.4	1.8	6.6	4.9	7.9
2009–10	2.7	1.5	4.3	0.1	0.2	0.1	4.4	2.0	10.3	0.5	0.4	2.4	8.8	5.9	11.3
2010–11	2.7	1.9	3.8	0.0	0.0	0.0	4.3	2.5	8.7	0.3	0.3	0.0	8.5	7.0	9.8

[1]Many institutions have more than one admission requirement.
[2]Formal demonstration of competencies (e.g., portfolios, certificates of mastery, assessment instruments).
[3]Includes SAT, ACT, or other admission tests.
[4]Test of English as a Foreign Language.

NOTE: Degree-granting institutions grant associate's or higher degrees and participate in Title IV federal financial aid programs. Detail may not sum to totals because of rounding. SOURCE: U.S. Department of Education, National Center for Education Statistics, Integrated Postsecondary Education Data System (IPEDS), Fall 2000 through Fall 2010, Institutional Characteristics component. (This table was prepared August 2011.)

Number of applications, admissions, and enrollees; their distribution across institutions accepting various percentages of applications; and SAT and ACT scores of enrollees, by control and level of institution: 2010–11

Application, admission, enrollment, and SAT and ACT score	All inst. Total [2]	All 4-year [3]	All 2-year [4]	Public Total [5]	Public 4-year [6]	Public 2-year [7]	Private Total [8]	Private 4-year [9]	Private 2-year [10]	Not-for-profit Total [11]	Not-for-profit 4-year [12]	Not-for-profit 2-year [13]	For-profit Total [14]	For-profit 4-year [15]	For-profit 2-year [16]
Number of undergraduate institutions reporting application data[1]	4,049	2,421	1,628	1,614	637	977	2,435	1,784	651	1,296	1,216	80	1,139	568	571
Percentage distribution of institutions by their acceptance of applications	100.0	100.0	100.0	100.0	100.0	100.0	100.0	100.0	100.0	100.0	100.0	100.0	100.0	100.0	100.0
No application criteria	49.1	23.1	87.7	65.7	17.7	96.9	38.1	25.1	73.9	15.7	13.2	53.8	63.6	50.4	76.7
90 percent or more accepted	6.6	8.1	4.4	4.0	8.8	0.9	8.4	7.9	9.7	8.7	8.7	8.8	8.0	6.2	9.8
75.0 to 89.9 percent accepted	10.6	16.1	2.4	8.6	21.0	0.4	12.0	14.3	5.4	17.0	17.8	5.0	6.2	6.2	5.4
50.0 to 74.9 percent accepted	20.9	32.8	3.3	15.8	38.1	1.2	24.3	30.8	6.5	39.5	41.0	16.3	7.0	9.0	5.1
25.0 to 49.9 percent accepted	11.1	17.4	1.7	5.3	12.7	0.4	14.9	19.1	3.7	15.1	15.4	11.3	14.7	26.9	2.6
10.0 to 24.9 percent accepted	1.3	2.0	0.3	0.6	1.4	0.1	1.8	2.2	0.6	3.1	3.0	3.8	0.4	0.5	0.2
Less than 10 percent accepted	0.3	0.5	0.1	0.1	0.2	0.0	0.5	0.6	0.3	0.8	0.8	1.3	0.1	0.0	0.2
Number of applications (in thousands)	8,174	8,057	117	4,473	4,405	68	3,701	3,652	49	3,479	3,467	12	222	185	37
Percentage distribution of applications by institutions' acceptance of applications	100.0	100.0	100.0	100.0	100.0	100.0	100.0	100.0	100.0	100.0	100.0	100.0	100.0	100.0	100.0
No application criteria	†	†	†	†	†	†	†	†	†	†	†	†	†	†	†
90 percent or more accepted	4.0	3.5	35.3	5.6	5.2	35.0	2.0	1.6	35.7	1.4	1.3	22.1	11.6	5.9	39.9
75.0 to 89.9 percent accepted	14.7	14.8	10.3	17.1	17.3	2.9	11.8	11.7	20.5	11.2	11.3	2.2	21.3	20.3	26.2
50.0 to 74.9 percent accepted	45.7	45.8	39.3	48.4	48.4	48.1	42.5	42.7	27.1	43.3	43.3	52.7	29.0	31.0	19.1
25.0 to 49.9 percent accepted	26.1	26.4	9.7	24.3	24.5	6.2	28.4	28.6	14.5	27.8	27.8	19.5	37.4	42.3	13.0
10.0 to 24.9 percent accepted	7.1	7.1	5.0	4.2	4.2	7.8	10.5	10.6	1.1	11.1	11.1	3.5	0.4	0.4	0.3
Less than 10 percent accepted	2.4	2.4	0.5	0.4	0.4	0.0	4.8	4.9	1.1	5.1	5.1	#	0.2	0.4	1.5
Number of admissions (in thousands)	4,612	4,527	85	2,706	2,658	48	1,906	1,869	37	1,769	1,762	8	136	107	29
Percentage distribution of admissions by institutions acceptance of applications	100.0	100.0	100.0	100.0	100.0	100.0	100.0	100.0	100.0	100.0	100.0	100.0	100.0	100.0	100.0
No application criteria	†	†	†	†	†	†	†	†	†	†	†	†	†	†	†
90 percent or more accepted	6.6	5.8	47.5	8.6	7.9	48.5	3.8	2.9	46.2	2.6	2.5	33.0	18.4	10.0	49.6
75.0 to 89.9 percent accepted	21.2	21.4	11.8	23.1	23.5	3.3	18.5	18.4	23.0	17.7	17.8	2.9	28.2	28.2	28.2
50.0 to 74.9 percent accepted	51.2	51.5	34.1	50.7	50.8	42.4	51.9	52.5	23.2	53.6	53.6	51.7	30.2	34.1	15.8
25.0 to 49.9 percent accepted	18.2	18.5	5.0	16.1	16.3	3.3	21.3	21.5	7.3	21.1	21.2	11.4	23.0	27.5	6.2
10.0 to 24.9 percent accepted	2.4	2.4	1.6	1.5	1.5	2.6	3.8	3.9	0.1	4.1	4.1	1.1	0.1	0.1	0.1
Less than 10 percent accepted	0.4	0.4	0.1	0.1	0.1	0.0	0.8	0.8	0.1	0.8	0.8	0.0	#	#	0.2
Number of enrollees (in thousands)	1,582	1,517	64	994	958	36	588	560	28	479	475	4	109	85	24
Percentage distribution of enrollees by institutions' acceptance of applications	100.0	100.0	100.0	100.0	100.0	100.0	100.0	100.0	100.0	100.0	100.0	100.0	100.0	100.0	100.0
No application criteria	†	†	†	†	†	†	†	†	†	†	†	†	†	†	†
90 percent or more accepted	8.4	6.9	35.4	8.2	7.1	35.5	8.8	6.6	35.4	5.7	5.6	17.6	18.5	13.1	37.7
75.0 to 89.9 percent accepted	22.0	22.3	18.1	24.7	25.0	17.9	17.6	17.5	18.3	18.0	18.2	1.7	15.1	13.6	20.4
50.0 to 74.9 percent accepted	48.5	49.2	36.1	51.3	51.6	43.3	43.8	44.9	30.2	47.5	47.6	45.8	28.7	28.8	28.2
25.0 to 49.9 percent accepted	17.8	18.3	9.8	14.1	14.6	3.3	24.0	24.7	15.2	21.6	21.5	26.0	37.6	44.3	13.7
10.0 to 24.9 percent accepted	2.8	2.9	0.6	1.7	1.7	#	4.7	5.0	1.0	5.8	5.8	8.8	0.2	0.2	#
Less than 10 percent accepted	0.4	0.4	#	#	#	0.0	1.1	1.1	#	1.3	1.3	0.0	#	0.0	#
SAT scores of enrollees															
Critical reading, 25th percentile[2]	471	472	405	458	459	403	479	480	406	479	481	406	419	419	†
Critical reading, 75th percentile[2]	583	584	512	567	568	518	591	592	507	591	593	507	556	556	†
Mathematics, 25th percentile[2]	478	479	394	471	473	388	482	483	400	483	484	400	431	431	†
Mathematics, 75th percentile[2]	588	590	514	580	582	505	593	594	523	594	595	523	539	539	†
ACT scores of enrollees															
Composite, 25th percentile[2]	20.2	20.3	16.1	19.5	19.7	16.2	20.6	20.7	16.1	20.7	20.7	17.5	17.5	18.8	†
Composite, 75th percentile[2]	25.3	25.4	21.3	24.4	24.5	20.7	25.8	25.8	22.2	25.8	25.9	21.7	24.0	23.8	†
English, 25th percentile[2]	19.2	19.4	14.4	18.5	18.7	15.1	19.7	19.8	13.2	19.8	19.8	14.6	16.0	17.7	†
English, 75th percentile[2]	25.6	25.7	21.5	24.6	24.7	21.3	26.2	26.3	22.0	26.3	26.3	21.3	24.8	24.4	†
Mathematics, 25th percentile[2]	19.1	19.2	15.6	18.6	18.8	15.9	19.4	19.5	15.1	19.5	19.5	16.0	17.4	18.6	†
Mathematics, 75th percentile[2]	25.0	25.1	20.8	24.4	24.5	20.4	25.4	25.4	21.5	25.4	25.5	21.6	22.4	22.6	†

†Not applicable.

#Rounds to zero.

‡Reporting standards not met (too few cases).

[1]Excludes institutions not enrolling first-time degree/certificate-seeking undergraduates. The total on this table differs slightly from other counts of undergraduate institutions because approximately 3.8 percent of undergraduate institutions did not report application information.

[2]Data are only for institutions that require test scores for admission. Relatively few 2-year institutions require test scores for admission. The SAT Critical reading and Mathematics scales range from 200 to 800. The ACT Composite, English, and Mathematics scales range from 1 to 36.

NOTE: Detail may not sum to totals because of rounding.

SOURCE: U.S. Department of Education, National Center for Education Statistics, Integrated Postsecondary Education Data System (IPEDS), Fall 2010, Institutional Characteristics component. (This table was prepared August 2011.)

Retention of first-time degree-seeking undergraduates at degree-granting institutions, by attendance status, control and level of institution, and percentage of applications accepted: 2006 to 2010

Control, level, and percent of applications accepted	First-time degree-seekers (adjusted entry cohort),[1] by entry year				Students from adjusted cohort returning in the following year				Percent of first-time undergraduates retained			
	2006	2007	2008	2009	2007	2008	2009	2010	2006 to 2007	2007 to 2008	2008 to 2009	2009 to 2010
1	2	3	4	5	6	7	8	9	10	11	12	13
Full-time student retention												
All institutions	2,171,714	2,269,712	2,296,305	2,386,597	1,542,175	1,619,269	1,647,198	1,714,013	71.0	71.3	71.7	71.8
Public institutions	1,524,044	1,603,819	1,654,779	1,743,668	1,072,644	1,132,790	1,167,180	1,229,276	70.4	70.6	70.5	70.5
Not-for-profit institutions	466,139	477,369	476,153	478,708	369,084	375,721	378,111	381,423	79.2	78.7	79.4	79.7
For-profit institutions	181,531	188,524	165,373	164,221	100,447	110,758	101,907	103,314	55.3	58.8	61.6	62.9
4-year institutions	1,458,731	1,505,161	1,511,976	1,465,669	1,115,529	1,152,921	1,176,973	1,153,975	76.5	76.6	77.8	78.7
Public institutions	912,401	936,000	973,089	945,951	711,490	732,384	765,163	751,623	78.0	78.2	78.6	79.5
Open admissions	62,724	60,815	81,559	47,943	38,839	38,724	52,988	30,079	61.9	63.7	65.0	62.7
90 percent or more accepted	68,835	66,114	58,002	60,147	49,274	46,731	39,851	43,654	71.6	70.7	68.7	72.6
75.0 to 89.9 percent accepted	244,177	237,913	213,388	213,441	185,457	180,287	164,559	164,061	76.0	75.8	77.1	76.9
50.0 to 74.9 percent accepted	417,093	439,824	473,007	468,817	336,199	356,969	382,451	380,473	80.6	81.2	80.9	81.2
25.0 to 49.9 percent accepted	103,118	107,824	127,960	134,042	88,908	90,123	108,601	114,477	86.2	83.6	84.9	85.4
Less than 25.0 percent accepted	7,716	10,223	13,479	14,326	7,048	9,479	12,785	13,649	91.3	92.7	94.9	95.3
Information not available	8,738	13,287	5,694	7,235	5,765	10,071	3,928	5,230	66.0	75.8	69.0	72.3
Not-for-profit institutions	457,566	468,955	468,220	470,748	363,760	370,740	373,352	376,726	79.5	79.1	79.7	80.0
Open admissions	26,679	26,571	24,220	22,613	16,116	15,227	16,499	14,349	60.4	57.3	68.1	63.5
90 percent or more accepted	13,684	16,008	16,738	15,066	9,549	11,249	11,899	10,898	69.8	70.3	71.1	72.3
75.0 to 89.9 percent accepted	102,218	93,360	81,056	80,332	78,495	71,066	61,725	62,246	76.8	76.1	76.2	77.5
50.0 to 74.9 percent accepted	190,079	196,121	210,894	218,136	148,781	152,948	164,566	170,310	78.3	78.0	78.0	78.1
25.0 to 49.9 percent accepted	93,560	100,121	98,546	98,239	81,880	86,755	84,760	84,926	87.5	86.7	86.0	86.4
Less than 25.0 percent accepted	26,696	28,631	32,190	32,980	25,639	27,621	30,570	31,790	96.0	96.5	95.0	96.4
Information not available	4,650	8,143	4,576	3,382	3,300	5,874	3,333	2,207	71.0	72.1	72.8	65.3
For-profit institutions	88,764	100,206	70,667	48,970	40,279	49,797	38,458	25,626	45.4	49.7	54.4	52.3
Open admissions	45,273	46,801	20,894	16,997	18,735	22,723	12,459	9,329	41.4	48.6	59.6	54.9
90 percent or more accepted	6,285	5,347	4,632	3,713	3,454	2,764	2,465	1,301	55.0	51.7	53.2	35.0
75.0 to 89.9 percent accepted	3,703	6,157	6,384	3,224	2,081	3,129	3,085	1,549	56.2	50.8	48.3	48.0
50.0 to 74.9 percent accepted	12,845	19,724	8,874	15,929	6,536	10,249	5,602	8,243	50.9	52.0	63.1	51.7
25.0 to 49.9 percent accepted	18,142	18,118	28,288	6,098	8,036	8,672	14,094	3,423	44.3	47.9	49.8	56.1
Less than 25.0 percent accepted	0	0	0	0	0	0	0	0	†	†	†	†
Information not available	2,516	4,059	1,595	3,009	1,437	2,260	753	1,781	57.1	55.7	47.2	59.2
2-year institutions	712,983	764,551	784,329	920,928	426,646	466,348	470,225	560,038	59.8	61.0	60.0	60.8
Public institutions	611,643	667,819	681,690	797,717	361,154	400,406	402,017	477,653	59.0	60.0	59.0	59.9
Not-for-profit institutions	8,573	8,414	7,933	7,960	5,324	4,981	4,759	4,697	62.1	59.2	60.0	59.0
For-profit institutions	92,767	88,318	94,706	115,251	60,168	60,961	63,449	77,688	64.9	69.0	67.0	67.4
Part-time student retention												
All institutions	463,234	532,827	519,619	551,181	191,586	219,857	210,836	231,593	41.4	41.3	40.6	42.0
Public institutions	419,006	475,209	477,242	502,825	171,746	194,321	192,225	211,093	41.0	40.9	40.3	42.0
Not-for-profit institutions	14,585	14,414	11,213	10,369	7,018	6,523	5,477	4,899	48.1	45.3	48.8	47.2
For-profit institutions	29,643	43,204	31,164	37,987	12,822	19,013	13,134	15,601	43.3	44.0	42.1	41.1
4-year institutions	82,367	95,410	97,051	73,376	38,257	43,441	45,678	32,720	46.4	45.5	47.1	44.6
Public institutions	48,353	48,190	63,932	34,504	23,631	23,006	31,910	17,240	48.9	47.7	49.9	50.0
Open admissions	20,223	20,645	38,295	9,470	8,298	9,122	17,982	3,852	41.0	44.2	47.0	40.7
90 percent or more accepted	3,745	3,450	2,707	3,735	1,909	1,667	1,205	1,861	51.0	48.3	44.5	49.8
75.0 to 89.9 percent accepted	8,969	8,145	7,476	6,504	4,196	3,818	3,872	3,277	46.8	46.9	51.8	50.4
50.0 to 74.9 percent accepted	11,599	12,236	11,969	11,496	6,766	6,245	6,649	6,131	58.3	51.0	55.6	53.3
25.0 to 49.9 percent accepted	3,373	3,023	3,084	3,125	2,223	1,866	1,992	2,023	65.9	61.7	64.6	64.7
Less than 25.0 percent accepted	65	44	42	44	50	34	34	35	76.9	77.3	81.0	79.5
Information not available	379	647	359	130	189	176	254	61	49.9	39.3	49.0	46.9

See notes at end of table.

Retention of first-time degree-seeking undergraduates at degree-granting institutions, by attendance status, control and level of institution, and percentage of applications accepted: 2006 to 2010—Continued

Control, level, and percent of applications accepted	First-time degree-seekers (adjusted entry cohort),[1] by entry year				Students from adjusted cohort returning in the following year				Percent of first-time undergraduates retained			
	2006	2007	2008	2009	2007	2008	2009	2010	2006 to 2007	2007 to 2008	2008 to 2009	2009 to 2010
1	2	3	4	5	6	7	8	9	10	11	12	13
Not-for-profit institutions	12,828	12,886	9,883	9,609	6,045	5,614	4,772	4,499	47.1	43.6	48.3	46.8
Open admissions	5,446	5,330	3,369	3,821	2,579	2,306	1,504	1,693	47.4	43.3	44.6	44.3
90 percent or more accepted	523	1,272	971	393	237	434	421	199	45.3	34.1	43.4	50.6
75.0 to 89.9 percent accepted	2,459	2,132	1,307	1,177	1,047	895	633	558	42.6	42.0	48.4	47.4
50.0 to 74.9 percent accepted	3,131	2,899	2,016	3,256	1,406	1,307	1,029	1,531	44.9	45.1	51.0	47.0
25.0 to 49.9 percent accepted	853	917	1,963	712	452	478	1,016	366	53.0	52.1	51.8	51.4
Less than 25.0 percent accepted	112	94	78	93	86	84	70	78	76.8	89.4	89.7	83.9
Information not available	304	242	179	157	238	110	99	74	78.3	45.5	55.3	47.1
For-profit institutions	21,186	34,334	23,236	29,263	8,581	14,821	8,996	10,981	40.5	43.2	38.7	37.5
Open admissions	10,515	20,602	10,933	10,996	4,105	9,896	4,296	4,333	39.0	48.0	39.3	39.4
90 percent or more accepted	2,212	1,616	3,518	1,375	639	735	1,037	379	28.9	45.5	29.5	27.6
75.0 to 89.9 percent accepted	2,838	2,702	2,057	3,151	1,342	959	697	1,093	47.3	35.5	33.9	34.7
50.0 to 74.9 percent accepted	2,774	4,360	3,686	4,661	1,134	1,399	1,707	2,283	40.9	32.1	46.3	49.0
25.0 to 49.9 percent accepted	2,033	3,185	2,584	1,099	627	951	1,116	342	30.8	29.9	43.2	31.1
Less than 25.0 percent accepted	0	170	48	0	0	67	22	0	?	39.4	45.8	†
Information not available	814	1,699	410	7,981	734	814	121	2,551	90.2	47.9	29.5	32.0
2-year institutions	380,867	437,417	422,568	477,805	153,329	176,416	165,158	198,873	40.3	40.3	39.1	41.6
Public institutions	370,653	427,019	413,310	468,321	148,115	171,315	160,315	193,853	40.0	40.1	38.8	41.4
Not-for-profit institutions	1,757	1,528	1,330	760	973	909	705	400	55.4	59.5	53.0	52.6
For-profit institutions	8,457	8,870	7,928	8,724	4,241	4,192	4,138	4,620	50.1	47.3	52.2	53.0

†Not applicable.

[1]Adjusted student counts exclude students who died or were totally and permanently disabled, served in the armed forces (including those called to active duty), served with a foreign aid service of the federal government (e.g., Peace Corps), or served on official church missions.

SOURCE: U.S. Department of Education, National Center for Education Statistics, Integrated Postsecondary Education Data System (IPEDS), Spring 2008 and Spring 2010, Enrollment component. (This table was prepared November 2011.)

Revenues of public degree-granting institutions, by source of revenue and level of institution: Selected years, 2005–06 through 2009–10

Level of institution and year	Total revenues	Tuition and fees[1]	Grants and contracts Total	Federal (excludes Federal Direct Student Loans)	State	Local	Sales and services of auxiliary enterprises[2]	Sales and services of hospitals	Independent operations	Other operating revenues
1	2	3	4	5	6	7	8	9	10	11
				In thousands of current dollars						
All institutions										
2005–06	$246,164,836	$41,770,600	$45,147,837	$30,333,948	$7,207,813	$7,606,076	$18,786,806	$22,100,555	$635,607	$14,483,979
2007–08	273,109,306	48,070,012	42,053,774	25,522,915	7,831,530	8,699,329	20,488,319	25,183,379	1,174,836	14,108,986
2008–09	267,385,180	51,840,367	43,095,658	26,092,100	7,403,141	9,600,416	21,358,319	27,301,883	1,036,660	14,165,654
2009–10	303,329,538	55,930,482	44,922,021	28,397,667	6,904,221	9,620,133	22,173,700	29,236,931	1,343,230	14,814,344
4-year										
2005–06	202,511,496	34,506,560	37,991,199	25,583,341	5,383,780	7,024,078	16,945,544	22,100,555	635,607	13,753,422
2007–08	223,566,529	40,083,063	37,341,007	23,518,933	5,715,188	8,106,887	18,507,934	25,183,379	1,174,836	13,135,633
2008–09	216,432,317	43,478,018	38,736,492	24,178,064	5,526,583	9,031,844	19,391,219	27,301,883	1,036,660	13,291,611
2009–10	248,104,870	46,943,248	40,635,416	26,272,013	5,301,243	9,062,160	20,099,137	29,236,931	1,343,230	13,894,006
2-year										
2005–06	43,653,340	7,264,040	7,156,638	4,750,607	1,824,034	581,998	1,841,262	0	0	730,557
2007–08	49,542,777	7,986,949	4,712,766	2,003,982	2,116,343	592,442	1,980,385	0	0	973,353
2008–09	50,952,862	8,362,349	4,359,166	1,914,036	1,876,558	568,572	1,967,100	0	0	874,043
2009–10	55,224,668	8,987,234	4,286,605	2,125,654	1,602,978	557,973	2,074,563	0	0	920,338
				Percentage distribution						
All institutions										
2005–06	100.00	16.97	18.34	12.32	2.93	3.09	7.63	8.98	0.26	5.88
2007–08	100.00	17.60	15.40	9.35	2.87	3.19	7.50	9.22	0.43	5.17
2008–09	100.00	19.39	16.12	9.76	2.77	3.59	7.99	10.21	0.39	5.30
2009–10	100.00	18.44	14.81	9.36	2.28	3.17	7.31	9.64	0.44	4.88
4-year										
2005–06	100.00	17.04	18.76	12.63	2.66	3.47	8.37	10.91	0.31	6.79
2007–08	100.00	17.93	16.70	10.52	2.56	3.63	8.28	11.26	0.53	5.88
2008–09	100.00	20.09	17.90	11.17	2.55	4.17	8.96	12.61	0.48	6.14
2009–10	100.00	18.92	16.38	10.59	2.14	3.65	8.10	11.78	0.54	5.60
2-year										
2005–06	100.00	16.64	16.39	10.88	4.18	1.33	4.22	0.00	0.00	1.67
2007–08	100.00	16.12	9.51	4.04	4.27	1.20	4.00	0.00	0.00	1.96
2008–09	100.00	16.41	8.56	3.76	3.68	1.12	3.86	0.00	0.00	1.72
2009–10	100.00	16.27	7.76	3.85	2.90	1.01	3.76	0.00	0.00	1.67
				Revenue per full-time-equivalent student in current dollars						
All institutions										
2005–06	$26,215	$4,448	$4,808	$3,230	$768	$810	$2,001	$2,354	$68	$1,542
2007–08	28,041	4,935	4,318	2,621	804	893	2,104	2,586	121	1,449
2008–09	26,574	5,152	4,283	2,593	736	954	2,123	2,713	103	1,408
2009–10	28,216	5,203	4,179	2,642	642	895	2,063	2,720	125	1,378
4-year										
2005–06	35,353	6,024	6,632	4,466	940	1,226	2,958	3,858	111	2,401
2007–08	37,297	6,687	6,229	3,924	953	1,352	3,088	4,201	196	2,191
2008–09	35,252	7,082	6,309	3,938	900	1,471	3,158	4,447	169	2,165
2009–10	38,452	7,275	6,298	4,072	822	1,404	3,115	4,531	208	2,153
2-year										
2005–06	11,921	1,984	1,954	1,297	498	159	503	0	0	200
2007–08	13,227	2,132	1,258	535	565	158	529	0	0	260
2008–09	12,991	2,132	1,111	488	478	145	502	0	0	223
2009–10	12,850	2,091	997	495	373	130	483	0	0	214
				Revenue per full-time-equivalent student in constant 2009–10 dollars[3]						
All institutions										
2005–06	$28,552	$4,845	$5,237	$3,518	$836	$882	$2,179	$2,563	$74	$1,680
2007–08	28,707	5,053	4,420	2,683	823	914	2,154	2,647	123	1,483
2008–09	26,831	5,202	4,325	2,618	743	963	2,143	2,740	104	1,421
2009–10	28,216	5,203	4,179	2,642	642	895	2,063	2,720	125	1,378
4-year										
2005–06	38,505	6,561	7,224	4,864	1,024	1,336	3,222	4,202	121	2,615
2007–08	38,184	6,846	6,378	4,017	976	1,385	3,161	4,301	201	2,243
2008–09	35,593	7,150	6,370	3,976	909	1,485	3,189	4,490	170	2,186
2009–10	38,452	7,275	6,298	4,072	822	1,404	3,115	4,531	208	2,153
2-year										
2005–06	12,984	2,161	2,129	1,413	543	173	548	0	0	217
2007–08	13,542	2,183	1,288	548	578	162	541	0	0	266
2008–09	13,116	2,153	1,122	493	483	146	506	0	0	225
2009–10	12,850	2,091	997	495	373	130	483	0	0	214

See notes at end of table.

Revenues of public degree-granting institutions, by source of revenue and level of institution: Selected years, 2005–06 through 2009–10—Continued

Level of institution and year	Nonoperating revenues									Other revenues and additions			
	Appropriations			Nonoperating grants									
	Federal	State	Local	Federal	State	Local	Gifts	Investment income	Other	Capital appropriations	Capital grants and gifts	Additions to permanent endowments	Other
1	12	13	14	15	16	17	18	19	20	21	22	23	24
In thousands of current dollars													
All institutions													
2005–06	$1,858,625	$58,720,088	$8,249,690	$2,811,434	$1,177,322	$102,497	$4,975,616	$9,597,624	$2,705,351	$5,421,660	$2,568,688	$1,004,691	$4,046,166
2007–08	1,849,775	68,375,062	9,319,219	10,022,315	1,909,570	177,555	6,070,499	5,278,643	2,251,324	7,578,049	3,090,589	1,133,783	4,973,618
2008–09	2,010,843	65,486,232	9,787,019	12,760,716	2,720,449	265,789	5,893,912	-9,487,915	3,011,240	7,038,658	2,938,605	843,528	5,317,562
2009–10	2,152,228	62,456,235	9,954,504	20,740,102	3,123,358	231,104	5,876,450	10,046,610	5,210,022	6,041,010	3,780,012	869,950	4,427,245
4-year													
2005–06	1,720,108	45,591,539	336,424	1,546,322	613,928	33,269	4,713,701	8,927,767	2,330,293	3,680,390	2,250,167	986,771	3,847,930
2007–08	1,776,452	53,268,648	453,280	5,177,569	1,201,394	103,824	5,798,732	4,430,479	1,770,108	5,637,968	2,762,277	1,120,806	4,639,141
2008–09	1,934,958	50,863,465	484,689	6,425,434	1,729,985	131,427	5,635,304	-9,958,068	2,601,770	4,987,773	2,554,107	830,264	4,975,326
2009–10	2,006,623	48,721,670	431,615	10,318,977	2,088,155	134,608	5,646,279	9,666,292	4,595,894	4,003,617	3,312,753	853,705	4,172,713
2-year													
2005–06	138,517	13,128,549	7,913,266	1,265,113	563,394	69,228	261,914	669,858	375,058	1,741,270	318,521	17,920	198,236
2007–08	73,324	15,106,414	8,865,938	4,844,746	708,176	73,731	271,766	848,164	481,216	1,940,082	328,312	12,978	334,477
2008–09	75,885	14,622,766	9,302,330	6,335,282	990,464	134,362	258,608	470,153	409,470	2,050,885	384,498	13,263	342,236
2009–10	145,606	13,734,565	9,522,890	10,421,125	1,035,203	96,496	230,170	380,318	614,128	2,037,393	467,258	16,245	254,532
Percentage distribution													
All institutions													
2005–06	0.76	23.85	3.35	1.14	0.48	0.04	2.02	3.90	1.10	2.20	1.04	0.41	1.64
2007–08	0.68	25.04	3.41	3.67	0.70	0.07	2.22	1.93	0.82	2.77	1.13	0.42	1.82
2008–09	0.75	24.49	3.66	4.77	1.02	0.10	2.20	-3.55	1.13	2.63	1.10	0.32	1.99
2009–10	0.71	20.59	3.28	6.84	1.03	0.08	1.94	3.31	1.72	1.99	1.25	0.29	1.46
4-year													
2005–06	0.85	22.51	0.17	0.76	0.30	0.02	2.33	4.41	1.15	1.82	1.11	0.49	1.90
2007–08	0.79	23.83	0.20	2.32	0.54	0.05	2.59	1.98	0.79	2.52	1.24	0.50	2.08
2008–09	0.89	23.50	0.22	2.97	0.80	0.06	2.60	-4.60	1.20	2.30	1.18	0.38	2.30
2009–10	0.81	19.64	0.17	4.16	0.84	0.05	2.28	3.90	1.85	1.61	1.34	0.34	1.68
2-year													
2005–06	0.32	30.07	18.13	2.90	1.29	0.16	0.60	1.53	0.86	3.99	0.73	0.04	0.45
2007–08	0.15	30.49	17.90	9.78	1.43	0.15	0.55	1.71	0.97	3.92	0.66	0.03	0.68
2008–09	0.15	28.70	18.26	12.43	1.94	0.26	0.51	0.92	0.80	4.03	0.75	0.03	0.67
2009–10	0.26	24.87	17.24	18.87	1.87	0.17	0.42	0.69	1.11	3.69	0.85	0.03	0.46
Revenue per full-time-equivalent student in current dollars													
All institutions													
2005–06	$198	$6,253	$879	$299	$125	$11	$530	$1,022	$288	$577	$274	$107	$431
2007–08	190	7,020	957	1,029	196	18	623	542	231	778	317	116	511
2008–09	200	6,508	973	1,268	270	26	586	-943	299	700	292	84	528
2009–10	200	5,810	926	1,929	291	21	547	935	485	562	352	81	412
4-year													
2005–06	300	7,959	59	270	107	6	823	1,559	407	642	393	172	672
2007–08	296	8,887	76	864	200	17	967	739	295	941	461	187	774
2008–09	315	8,285	79	1,047	282	21	918	-1,622	424	812	416	135	810
2009–10	311	7,551	67	1,599	324	21	875	1,498	712	620	513	132	647
2-year													
2005–06	38	3,585	2,161	345	154	19	72	183	102	476	87	5	54
2007–08	20	4,033	2,367	1,293	189	20	73	226	128	518	88	3	89
2008–09	19	3,728	2,372	1,615	253	34	66	120	104	523	98	3	87
2009–10	34	3,196	2,216	2,425	241	22	54	88	143	474	109	4	59
Revenue per full-time-equivalent student in constant 2009–10 dollars[3]													
All institutions													
2005–06	$216	$6,811	$957	$326	$137	$12	$577	$1,113	$314	$629	$298	$117	$469
2007–08	194	7,187	980	1,053	201	19	638	555	237	797	325	119	523
2008–09	202	6,571	982	1,281	273	27	591	-952	302	706	295	85	534
2009–10	200	5,810	926	1,929	291	21	547	935	485	562	352	81	412
4-year													
2005–06	327	8,669	64	294	117	6	896	1,697	443	700	428	188	732
2007–08	303	9,098	77	884	205	18	990	757	302	963	472	191	792
2008–09	318	8,365	80	1,057	285	22	927	-1,638	428	820	420	137	818
2009–10	311	7,551	67	1,599	324	21	875	1,498	712	620	513	132	647
2-year													
2005–06	41	3,905	2,354	376	168	21	78	199	112	518	95	5	59
2007–08	20	4,129	2,423	1,324	194	20	74	232	132	530	90	4	91
2008–09	20	3,764	2,395	1,631	255	35	67	121	105	528	99	3	88
2009–10	34	3,196	2,216	2,425	241	22	54	88	143	474	109	4	59

[1]Net of allowances and discounts.
[2]After deducting discounts and allowances.
[3]Constant dollars based on the Consumer Price Index, prepared by the Bureau of Labor Statistics, U.S. Department of Labor, adjusted to a school-year basis.
NOTE: Degree-granting institutions grant associate's or higher degrees and participate in Title IV federal financial aid programs. Includes data for public institutions reporting data according to either the Governmental Accounting Standards Board (GASB) or the Financial Accounting Standards Board (FASB) questionnaire. Detail may not sum to totals because of rounding.
SOURCE: U.S. Department of Education, National Center for Education Statistics, Integrated Postsecondary Education Data System (IPEDS), Spring 2006 through Spring 2011, Finance and Enrollment components. (This table was prepared November 2011.)

Revenues of public degree-granting institutions, by source of revenue and state or jurisdiction: 2009–10
[In thousands of current dollars]

State or jurisdiction	Total revenues	Operating revenue							Nonoperating revenue[1]			Other revenues and additions
		Total	Tuition and fees[2]	Federal grants and contracts	State and local grants and contracts	Sales and services of auxiliary enterprises[3]	Sales and services of hospitals	Independent operations and other	Total	State appropriations	Local appropriations	
1	2	3	4	5	6	7	8	9	10	11	12	13
United States	$303,329,538	$168,420,707	$55,930,482	$28,397,667	$16,524,354	$22,173,700	$29,236,931	$16,157,574	$119,790,614	$62,456,235	$9,954,504	$15,118,217
Alabama	6,934,719	4,451,647	1,226,737	736,601	263,018	336,523	1,228,813	659,955	2,267,669	1,289,317	1,124	215,403
Alaska.....................	818,312	362,641	106,824	127,332	70,151	39,799	0	18,535	395,617	334,826	8,993	60,054
Arizona...................	5,117,042	2,393,601	1,252,017	507,129	162,600	364,114	0	107,741	2,662,330	1,011,599	734,888	61,111
Arkansas.................	3,457,956	2,103,967	407,190	235,187	167,676	230,953	834,153	228,809	1,257,748	753,337	30,776	96,241
California	39,822,628	21,840,952	4,799,602	3,649,014	2,448,579	1,782,844	5,882,111	3,278,802	16,331,226	8,849,101	2,447,042	1,650,450
Colorado	5,038,154	3,808,206	1,373,687	870,273	425,054	442,898	375,345	320,948	1,052,576	31,950	96,324	177,372
Connecticut............	3,073,384	1,588,636	552,618	175,930	101,008	246,931	247,226	264,924	1,166,113	992,343	0	318,635
Delaware................	1,102,276	673,779	355,928	138,663	49,004	111,603	0	18,580	418,966	219,409	0	9,531
District of Columbia ...	134,971	61,381	26,696	17,418	11,661	910	0	4,696	72,118	62,070	0	1,473
Florida....................	10,345,096	4,584,040	1,712,699	1,053,872	940,012	732,924	0	144,533	5,225,242	3,075,209	0	535,813
Georgia	6,952,343	3,613,145	1,439,381	628,951	448,080	706,634	201,302	188,797	3,028,759	1,770,643	0	310,439
Hawaii	1,541,672	739,792	210,701	347,963	75,678	83,730	0	21,731	582,906	366,836	0	218,974
Idaho......................	1,177,453	539,171	232,922	113,040	48,944	107,442	0	36,824	543,837	324,563	12,900	94,444
Illinois....................	10,777,586	5,513,738	2,132,121	797,439	398,152	904,229	617,642	664,153	5,132,637	1,779,108	967,455	131,211
Indiana...................	6,412,313	3,806,613	1,924,620	576,401	269,052	688,432	0	348,108	2,500,534	1,435,079	6,932	105,166
Iowa.......................	4,532,185	3,145,524	701,366	617,268	149,538	430,821	965,672	280,859	1,324,929	781,895	99,099	61,732
Kansas...................	3,068,349	1,694,889	683,065	328,769	175,200	284,970	0	222,885	1,299,341	731,725	229,963	74,119
Kentucky................	5,109,467	3,117,415	838,262	456,040	221,480	263,142	976,869	361,622	1,724,677	967,970	16,437	267,374
Louisiana................	4,177,297	2,349,228	626,213	362,566	469,867	322,969	339,625	227,988	1,629,945	1,030,152	0	198,123
Maine.....................	878,118	496,093	209,560	70,165	63,188	97,361	0	55,820	359,223	245,705	0	22,802
Maryland.................	5,922,713	3,446,759	1,396,362	759,571	392,687	572,537	0	325,601	2,125,291	1,276,246	328,704	350,664
Massachusetts.........	4,280,525	2,686,203	1,008,631	426,569	231,325	367,090	0	652,587	1,443,776	899,748	0	150,546
Michigan.................	13,617,003	8,811,529	3,168,919	1,369,427	447,378	988,068	2,372,017	465,721	4,587,058	1,786,389	596,436	218,415
Minnesota...............	5,135,056	2,619,417	1,137,773	450,236	298,562	504,876	0	227,970	2,161,249	1,242,407	0	354,390
Mississippi	3,879,327	2,104,030	446,609	445,917	163,307	252,459	677,217	118,521	1,607,882	895,859	57,730	167,416
Missouri..................	4,723,802	2,769,484	902,564	255,837	194,118	683,566	600,238	133,162	1,815,614	992,722	146,283	138,704
Montana..................	996,292	626,615	252,111	173,606	37,702	79,349	0	83,847	315,814	174,784	8,105	53,863
Nebraska................	2,294,745	1,155,984	332,446	224,396	180,463	253,030	25,827	139,822	1,029,221	629,652	122,263	109,540
Nevada...................	1,567,739	695,419	302,887	152,749	88,969	92,384	1,152	57,278	788,321	388,082	0	83,998
New Hampshire	920,784	644,681	310,005	63,411	50,544	191,784	0	28,938	195,947	130,868	0	80,157
New Jersey	7,040,625	4,333,381	1,783,369	448,449	490,306	507,277	885,584	218,396	2,545,074	1,549,086	211,947	162,170
New Mexico	3,347,033	1,803,757	232,645	428,839	198,060	115,356	568,478	260,377	1,375,796	773,235	119,340	167,480
New York	14,281,306	6,939,637	2,244,500	828,904	969,998	867,366	1,876,918	151,951	6,736,764	4,350,324	757,504	604,905
North Carolina	9,782,673	3,789,967	1,255,177	782,588	300,561	1,297,928	0	153,713	5,402,627	3,375,984	194,949	590,079
North Dakota	1,051,135	629,441	248,473	167,076	48,545	99,267	0	66,081	360,402	267,744	185	61,292
Ohio.......................	12,101,646	7,890,623	2,984,442	776,602	530,293	930,665	2,253,927	414,695	3,851,978	1,884,232	145,807	359,045
Oklahoma................	3,933,207	2,083,108	674,335	251,643	281,080	406,543	62,229	407,276	1,531,155	928,324	48,197	318,944
Oregon...................	5,518,943	3,702,490	934,531	678,341	200,721	408,274	1,274,466	206,158	1,622,696	666,799	203,681	193,757
Pennsylvania...........	11,983,919	8,645,682	3,402,627	1,229,630	421,982	924,537	2,111,772	555,135	3,250,155	1,420,760	118,747	88,082
Rhode Island	700,705	482,080	252,267	72,260	30,837	97,192	0	29,525	186,491	137,159	0	32,133
South Carolina.........	3,955,305	2,427,029	1,101,061	398,682	331,129	350,639	0	245,518	1,349,605	604,283	61,419	178,672
South Dakota	802,946	462,689	179,463	136,307	36,950	53,919	0	56,051	256,809	163,817	0	83,448
Tennessee	4,219,730	1,887,572	812,733	350,507	210,057	277,466	0	236,809	2,099,195	1,089,782	5,184	232,962
Texas	29,111,456	12,202,024	3,950,738	2,213,193	1,813,943	1,116,490	1,587,643	1,520,018	12,895,120	5,445,771	1,384,512	4,014,311
Utah.......................	4,378,097	3,052,556	555,723	375,247	127,579	184,505	1,092,663	716,840	1,166,209	658,038	0	159,332
Vermont..................	786,823	604,201	320,259	128,881	32,984	99,276	0	22,801	161,741	76,575	0	20,881
Virginia...................	8,470,275	5,092,324	1,886,662	793,865	199,273	1,044,065	1,031,626	136,833	2,679,725	1,433,589	2,289	698,227
Washington.............	7,719,841	4,937,740	1,307,996	1,177,320	605,707	504,856	1,029,057	312,804	2,388,154	1,367,777	0	393,946
West Virginia...........	1,690,820	1,046,188	466,775	153,156	172,516	98,126	0	155,615	586,282	393,821	451	58,349
Wisconsin...............	6,159,391	3,344,058	1,192,301	677,335	426,668	477,898	0	569,857	2,470,796	1,099,243	739,123	344,537
Wyoming.................	719,082	271,356	72,563	62,284	51,593	53,550	0	31,366	426,446	300,301	49,716	21,279
U.S. Service Academies..........	1,765,275	348,225	1,324	134,828	577	94,137	117,360	0	1,400,825	0	0	16,224
Other jurisdictions	1,783,574	410,795	79,678	186,419	54,638	15,624	51,404	23,032	1,351,344	901,837	50,593	21,435
American Samoa......	19,642	8,985	2,854	5,340	0	791	0	0	10,657	0	0	0
Federated States of Micronesia	25,176	6,570	568	2,993	1,080	1,513	0	415	18,606	0	0	0
Guam......................	124,572	53,285	14,124	27,475	2,249	2,989	0	6,448	68,987	33,072	16,516	2,299
Marshall Islands.......	15,043	1,498	591	0	0	636	0	272	8,545	2,000	0	5,000
Northern Marianas	17,183	10,455	1,386	7,839	0	1,204	0	26	6,728	5,323	0	0
Palau......................	12,785	5,705	1,580	3,272	300	284	0	269	6,811	2,310	0	269
Puerto Rico.............	1,479,889	277,071	46,115	113,888	46,866	3,768	51,404	15,030	1,192,143	859,133	2,651	10,675
U.S. Virgin Islands	89,285	47,226	12,460	25,611	4,144	4,438	0	573	38,867	0	31,427	3,192

[1]Includes other categories not separately shown.
[2]Net of allowances and discounts.
[3]After deducting discounts and allowances.
NOTE: Degree-granting institutions grant associate's or higher degrees and participate in Title IV federal financial aid programs. Includes data for public institutions reporting data according to either the Governmental Accounting Standards Board (GASB) or the Financial Accounting Standards Board (FASB) questionnaire. Detail may not sum to totals because of rounding.
SOURCE: U.S. Department of Education, National Center for Education Statistics, Integrated Postsecondary Education Data System (IPEDS), Spring 2011, Finance component. (This table was prepared November 2011.)

Endowment funds of the 120 colleges and universities with the largest endowments, by rank order: 2009 and 2010

Institution	2010 rank order[1]	Market value of endowment, as of June 30 (in thousands)		Percent change, 2009 to 2010[2]	Institution	2010 rank order[1]	Market value of endowment, as of June 30 (in thousands)		Percent change, 2009 to 2010[2]
		2009	2010				2009	2010	
1	2	3	4	5	1	2	3	4	5
United States (all institutions)	†	$325,565,998	$355,790,614	9.3					
120 institutions with the largest amounts	†	243,109,149	263,961,330	8.6					
Harvard University (MA)	1	26,035,389	27,557,404	5.8	Lehigh University (PA)	61	886,234	940,430	6.1
Yale University (CT)	2	16,103,497	16,504,168	2.5	University of Iowa	62	810,368	928,388	14.6
Princeton University (NJ)	3	13,386,280	14,760,707	10.3	Yeshiva University (NY)	63	882,063	922,031	4.5
Stanford University (CA)	4	12,619,094	13,851,115	9.8	Wake Forest University (NC)	64	866,212	921,338	6.4
University of Texas System Office	5	11,083,357	12,912,209	16.5	University of Cincinnati, Main Campus (OH)	65	831,664	900,125	8.2
Massachusetts Institute of Technology	6	7,982,021	8,317,321	4.2	Tulane University of Louisiana	66	815,473	873,048	7.1
Columbia University in the City of New York (NY)	7	5,892,798	6,516,512	10.6	Baylor University (TX)	67	880,255	871,966	-0.9
University of Michigan, Ann Arbor	8	5,914,285	6,471,770	9.4	Trinity University (TX)	68	850,739	862,124	1.3
University of Pennsylvania	9	5,170,539	5,668,937	9.6	Berea College (KT)	69	791,210	846,776	7.0
University of California System Admin. Central Office	10	4,977,483	5,441,225	9.3	University of Illinois at Urbana-Champaign	70	729,373	829,810	13.8
University of Notre Dame (IN)	11	4,920,742	5,340,685	8.5	Princeton Theological Seminary (NJ)	71	749,241	815,012	8.8
University of Chicago (IL)	12	4,535,633	4,904,717	8.1	Carnegie Mellon University (PA)	72	749,640	811,733	8.3
Emory University (GA)	13	4,601,488	4,841,490	5.2	Brigham Young University (UT)	73	608,861	808,486	32.8
Duke University (NC)	14	4,440,745	4,823,572	8.6	University of Kentucky	74	701,762	793,505	13.1
Northwestern University (IL)	15	4,398,200	4,726,940	7.5	Middlebury College (VT)	75	699,684	783,225	11.9
Washington University in St. Louis (MO)	16	4,147,461	4,560,043	9.9	Baylor College of Medicine (TX)	76	696,887	767,912	10.2
University of Virginia, Main Campus	17	3,531,688	3,861,913	9.4	University of Texas Southwestern Medical Center at Dallas	77	684,691	760,725	11.1
Rice University (TX)	18	3,665,267	3,835,723	4.7	Bowdoin College (ME)	78	688,384	753,525	9.5
Cornell University (NY)	19	3,071,987	3,413,151	11.1	Indiana University, Bloomington	79	643,520	722,778	12.3
Dartmouth College (NH)	20	2,999,497	3,137,422	4.6	Vassar College (NY)	80	680,154	713,063	4.8
Vanderbilt University (TN)	21	2,833,614	3,007,607	6.1	Saint Louis University, Main Campus (MO)	81	645,800	708,345	9.7
University of Southern California	22	2,671,426	2,947,978	10.4	University of Tulsa (OK)	82	646,672	691,917	7.0
University of Texas at Austin	23	2,383,866	2,589,413	8.6	Syracuse University (NY)	83	621,951	688,791	10.7
New York University	24	2,194,839	2,409,929	9.8	University of Oklahoma, Norman Campus	84	597,911	680,505	13.8
Johns Hopkins University (MD)	25	1,983,341	2,226,665	12.3	University of Arkansas	85	623,686	673,120	7.9
University of Minnesota, Twin Cities	26	2,070,002	2,183,732	5.5	University of Louisville (KT)	86	599,712	669,043	11.6
Brown University (RI)	27	2,039,135	2,178,837	6.9	Washington State University	87	619,766	668,824	7.9
University of Pittsburgh, Pittsburgh Campus (PA)	28	1,842,796	2,020,101	9.6	Juilliard School (NY)	88	613,526	658,901	7.4
University of North Carolina at Chapel Hill	29	1,903,575	1,963,345	3.1	Oberlin College (OH)	89	604,965	645,175	6.6
University of Washington, Seattle Campus	30	1,770,281	1,929,865	9.0	University of Alabama	90	508,934	631,947	24.2
Ohio State University, Main Campus	31	1,646,908	1,871,328	13.6	Rensselaer Polytechnic Institute (NY)	91	602,636	629,728	4.5
University of Wisconsin, Madison	32	1,613,069	1,807,126	12.0	Brandeis University (MA)	92	558,517	620,204	11.0
Boston College (MA)	33	1,491,159	1,647,652	10.5	Colgate University (NY)	93	560,537	619,216	10.5
California Institute of Technology	34	1,507,703	1,631,076	8.2	University of Miami (FL)	94	538,606	618,236	14.8
University of Richmond (VA)	35	1,428,391	1,616,549	13.2	Hamilton College (NY)	95	540,154	607,490	12.5
Purdue University, Main Campus (IN)	36	1,423,009	1,587,000	11.5	Santa Clara University (CA)	96	528,892	603,618	14.1
Williams College (MA)	37	1,368,031	1,468,493	7.3	University of Tennessee	97	537,873	602,595	12.0
Case Western Reserve University (OH)	38	1,401,799	1,462,027	4.3	Berry College (GA)	98	566,087	600,523	6.1
Pomona College (CA)	39	1,345,000	1,458,974	8.5	Bryn Mawr College (PA)	99	527,194	587,527	11.4
George Washington University (DC)	40	1,261,893	1,394,281	10.5	Lafayette College (PA)	100	567,919	580,740	2.3
Amherst College (MA)	41	1,305,944	1,385,745	6.1	Cooper Union for the Advancement of Science and Art (NY)	101	530,983	579,152	9.1
University of Rochester (NY)	42	1,282,924	1,367,870	6.6	Denison University (OH)	102	533,179	573,077	7.5
Michigan State University	43	1,359,659	1,367,525	0.6	Macalester College (MN)	103	544,541	569,131	4.5
Pennsylvania State University, Main Campus	44	1,173,540	1,350,316	15.1	Pepperdine University (CA)	104	528,943	564,832	6.8
Wellesley College (MA)	45	1,287,284	1,330,244	3.3	Carleton College (MN)	105	517,310	563,439	8.9
Grinnell College (IA)	46	1,076,249	1,264,834	17.5	Rochester Institute of Technology (NY)	106	530,412	559,539	5.5
Swarthmore College (PA)	47	1,128,675	1,249,254	10.7	Rutgers University, New Brunswick (NJ)	107	508,766	556,786	9.4
Smith College (MA)	48	1,096,322	1,243,561	13.4	Mount Sinai School of Medicine (NY)	108	443,156	534,631	20.6
Tufts University (MA)	49	1,103,440	1,213,585	10.0	Mount Holyoke College (MA)	109	503,168	533,583	6.0
University of California, Los Angeles	50	997,111	1,110,981	11.4	College of William and Mary (VA)	110	489,251	533,180	9.0
University of Kansas	51	967,171	1,070,813	10.7	College of the Holy Cross (MA)	111	492,680	522,493	6.1
Southern Methodist University (TX)	52	1,032,262	1,069,399	3.6	Northeastern University (MA)	112	501,019	521,186	4.0
Texas Christian University	53	945,329	1,038,161	9.8	Indiana University, Purdue University, Indianapolis	113	470,947	520,478	10.5
University of Florida	54	1,008,921	1,037,922	2.9	Wesleyan University (CT)	114	476,481	512,875	7.6
Boston University (MA)	55	919,441	1,022,401	11.2	University of Missouri, Columbia	115	469,885	510,555	8.7
Washington and Lee University (VA)	56	897,141	1,008,161	12.4	North Carolina State University at Raleigh	116	129,619	503,110	288.1
Georgetown University (DC)	57	895,107	1,007,299	12.5	Colby College (ME)	117	452,990	502,076	10.8
University of Delaware	58	929,116	1,000,425	7.7	Furman University (SC)	118	444,223	498,282	12.2
Weill Cornell Medical College (NY)	59	894,055	965,437	8.0	Virginia Polytechnic Institute and State University	119	446,300	497,100	11.4
University of California, Berkeley	60	827,808	945,318	14.2	University of Houston (TX)	120	452,755	495,128	9.4

†Not applicable.

[1]Institutions ranked by size of endowment in 2010.

[2]Change in market value of endowment. Includes growth from gifts and returns on investments, as well as reductions from expenditures and withdrawals.

NOTE: Degree-granting institutions grant associate's or higher degrees and participate in Title IV federal financial aid programs.

SOURCE: U.S. Department of Education, National Center for Education Statistics, Integrated Postsecondary Education Data System (IPEDS), Spring 2010 and Spring 2011, Finance component. (This table was prepared November 2011.)

Expenditures of public degree-granting institutions, by level of institution, purpose of expenditure, and state or jurisdiction: 2006–07 through 2009–10

[In thousands of current dollars]

State or jurisdiction	Total expenditures, 2006–07	Total expenditures, 2007–08	Total expenditures, 2008–09			2009–10					
			All institutions	4-year institutions	2-year institutions	All institutions		4-year institutions		2-year institutions	
						Total[1]	Instruction	Total[1]	Instruction	Total[1]	Instruction
1	2	3	4	5	6	7	8	9	10	11	12
United States	$238,828,801	$261,045,829	$273,030,301	$225,363,128	$47,667,173	$281,368,314	$76,292,102	$230,216,045	$58,268,076	$51,152,269	$18,024,027
Alabama	5,120,941	5,839,899	5,964,685	5,242,474	722,211	6,324,853	1,369,418	5,523,332	1,091,201	801,521	278,217
Alaska	692,853	736,890	750,308	732,107	18,202	780,028	208,481	760,959	202,470	19,069	6,011
Arizona	4,098,686	4,421,229	4,523,629	3,314,844	1,208,785	4,721,129	1,392,360	3,396,250	961,431	1,324,879	430,928
Arkansas	2,711,428	2,923,204	3,109,431	2,701,907	407,524	3,268,738	685,427	2,807,806	530,964	460,932	154,463
California	33,939,568	37,559,728	39,706,162	29,458,744	10,247,418	39,702,048	9,906,999	29,252,715	6,593,076	10,449,333	3,313,923
Colorado	3,766,780	4,049,015	4,424,140	3,920,136	504,004	4,516,268	1,300,471	3,967,914	1,098,975	548,354	201,496
Connecticut	2,482,496	2,713,513	2,833,427	2,412,114	421,314	2,814,866	753,280	2,383,913	590,493	430,953	162,787
Delaware	853,410	905,359	937,997	809,752	128,245	967,381	369,267	837,131	312,331	130,250	56,936
District of Columbia	125,484	117,014	138,348	138,348	0	109,469	32,093	109,469	32,093	0	0
Florida	8,307,928	8,678,611	9,220,508	8,166,913	1,053,595	9,721,394	2,868,379	8,959,689	2,649,240	761,705	219,139
Georgia	5,318,459	5,798,067	6,063,773	5,110,437	953,336	6,426,195	1,729,564	5,295,181	1,345,462	1,131,014	384,102
Hawaii	1,266,174	1,576,768	1,531,975	1,300,841	231,134	1,406,821	397,620	1,185,560	303,177	221,261	94,442
Idaho	917,108	991,494	1,024,541	885,139	139,401	1,070,934	299,224	891,616	259,777	179,318	39,447
Illinois	8,317,879	8,955,961	9,350,383	6,930,267	2,420,116	9,954,173	2,807,182	7,241,944	1,974,439	2,712,229	832,743
Indiana	4,929,528	5,237,143	5,487,959	5,027,865	460,093	5,739,211	2,011,049	5,163,984	1,825,280	575,227	185,769
Iowa	3,632,046	3,896,227	4,193,485	3,382,457	811,028	4,169,366	906,691	3,343,510	592,601	825,856	314,090
Kansas	2,607,366	2,654,178	2,821,376	2,188,173	633,203	2,916,446	878,735	2,242,776	650,429	673,670	228,306
Kentucky	3,976,747	4,256,949	4,513,299	3,900,018	613,281	4,723,961	1,087,976	4,043,904	850,407	680,056	237,569
Louisiana	3,519,436	4,162,047	4,303,137	3,829,679	473,458	4,143,613	1,148,413	3,668,373	968,495	475,239	179,918
Maine	746,481	786,047	809,983	701,470	108,513	807,827	233,930	697,460	186,554	110,367	47,376
Maryland	4,643,844	4,995,230	5,282,745	4,095,732	1,187,014	5,489,313	1,508,751	4,254,907	1,048,881	1,234,407	459,870
Massachusetts	3,515,544	3,662,053	3,731,294	3,046,133	685,161	3,941,641	1,055,224	3,212,739	786,299	728,902	268,925
Michigan	10,563,666	12,675,466	11,928,733	10,184,054	1,744,680	12,411,095	3,199,085	10,516,182	2,559,497	1,894,913	639,588
Minnesota	4,112,919	4,541,298	4,679,338	3,735,577	943,761	4,782,817	1,376,650	3,794,416	960,886	988,401	415,764
Mississippi	3,111,365	3,303,199	3,445,846	2,658,956	786,891	3,591,772	838,025	2,724,671	543,269	867,101	294,756
Missouri	3,648,634	3,933,741	4,067,585	3,387,674	679,911	4,220,808	1,144,698	3,460,621	871,715	760,187	272,983
Montana	819,680	883,825	936,000	830,716	105,284	933,785	229,201	814,871	200,081	118,913	29,120
Nebraska	1,722,136	1,816,761	1,893,340	1,591,629	301,711	2,005,277	595,274	1,666,195	463,435	339,081	131,839
Nevada	1,315,804	1,374,553	1,417,355	1,352,474	64,881	1,423,657	497,226	1,356,436	469,145	67,221	28,081
New Hampshire	725,778	767,736	803,946	703,227	100,719	837,543	242,973	715,472	209,753	122,071	33,220
New Jersey	5,695,452	6,049,637	6,487,776	5,372,186	1,115,590	6,679,185	1,818,617	5,400,370	1,393,662	1,278,815	424,956
New Mexico	2,565,733	2,798,416	3,033,621	2,487,846	545,775	3,094,887	592,307	2,513,419	401,319	581,468	190,988
New York	12,607,530	13,153,312	14,393,529	11,703,776	2,689,753	14,564,719	4,317,732	11,589,967	3,108,013	2,974,753	1,209,719
North Carolina	7,649,176	8,260,453	8,648,614	6,840,438	1,808,176	9,061,392	2,975,024	7,056,268	2,150,340	2,005,124	824,684
North Dakota	787,853	840,092	900,709	823,965	76,744	960,204	307,292	881,328	278,605	78,877	28,687
Ohio	9,638,217	10,197,635	10,690,988	9,329,865	1,361,123	11,191,776	3,048,329	9,669,790	2,525,367	1,521,987	522,962
Oklahoma	2,982,655	3,229,565	3,424,475	2,987,792	436,683	3,565,946	992,330	3,091,111	834,438	474,836	157,892
Oregon	3,961,130	4,211,743	4,705,101	3,619,116	1,085,985	4,989,706	1,024,216	3,869,289	666,871	1,120,417	357,345
Pennsylvania	9,093,770	9,813,416	10,424,097	9,390,625	1,033,472	10,880,853	2,748,287	9,753,259	2,337,824	1,127,594	410,463
Rhode Island	587,678	633,263	639,371	532,054	107,317	663,552	185,353	555,414	138,259	108,138	47,094
South Carolina	3,123,388	3,420,357	3,415,654	2,731,646	684,008	3,537,943	1,156,039	2,772,919	889,406	765,024	266,633
South Dakota	546,221	590,375	626,176	562,122	64,054	686,412	194,612	613,042	170,188	73,370	24,424
Tennessee	3,289,781	3,531,341	3,607,113	3,062,117	544,996	3,781,861	1,254,507	3,156,572	1,031,795	625,289	222,712
Texas	20,016,371	23,442,222	24,222,080	20,271,928	3,950,152	25,080,639	6,628,389	20,573,456	5,079,518	4,507,183	1,548,871
Utah	3,291,002	3,554,103	3,797,090	3,520,100	276,989	3,940,464	667,772	3,653,326	560,682	287,138	107,089
Vermont	647,066	714,575	718,762	694,488	24,274	761,182	197,416	728,690	187,882	32,492	9,534
Virginia	6,311,272	6,924,955	7,183,108	6,326,116	856,992	7,329,410	1,992,818	6,374,781	1,591,236	954,629	401,582
Washington	5,980,733	6,477,202	6,714,962	5,427,477	1,287,485	6,874,560	2,104,364	5,524,094	1,533,905	1,350,466	570,458
West Virginia	1,324,271	1,426,853	1,518,943	1,417,983	100,961	1,672,009	497,712	1,524,769	449,051	147,240	48,660
Wisconsin	4,904,966	5,203,602	5,499,072	4,271,587	1,227,485	5,757,793	1,801,661	4,494,128	1,178,299	1,263,665	623,362
Wyoming	522,738	592,850	639,509	405,223	234,286	671,896	211,012	430,562	126,911	241,334	84,100
U.S. Service Academies	1,791,631	1,766,655	1,844,822	1,844,822	0	1,699,493	502,648	1,699,493	502,648	0	0
Other jurisdictions	1,549,127	1,632,804	1,721,830	1,632,194	89,636	1,776,740	522,045	1,677,523	489,344	99,217	32,701
American Samoa	11,419	12,489	12,910	0	12,910	13,243	4,183	0	0	13,243	4,183
Federated States of Micronesia	19,306	20,606	22,380	0	22,380	23,128	7,478	0	0	23,128	7,478
Guam	96,492	102,571	106,784	80,030	26,754	115,262	26,642	85,813	16,857	29,449	9,785
Marshall Islands	7,833	8,383	8,503	0	8,503	12,681	2,276	0	0	12,681	2,276
Northern Marianas	13,132	13,812	13,945	13,945	0	14,619	8,158	14,619	8,158	0	0
Palau	8,359	5,653	5,858	0	5,858	5,416	2,258	0	0	5,416	2,258
Puerto Rico	1,318,439	1,402,526	1,477,913	1,464,682	13,231	1,506,865	458,053	1,491,566	451,334	15,299	6,720
U.S. Virgin Islands	74,146	66,764	73,536	73,536	0	85,525	12,996	85,525	12,996	0	0

[1]Includes other categories not separately shown.

NOTE: Degree-granting institutions grant associate's or higher degrees and participate in Title IV federal financial aid programs. Includes data for public institutions reporting data according to either the Governmental Accounting Standards Board (GASB) or the Financial Accounting Standards Board (FASB) questionnaire. All expenditures reported by institutions for operation and maintenance of plant have been aggregated in the operation and maintenance of plant category, even in cases where they originally were reported by purpose. Similarly, all expenditures reported by institutions for depreciation have been aggregated in the depreciation category, even in cases where they originally were reported by purpose. In addition, all expenditures reported by institutions for interest have been aggregated in the interest category, even in cases where they originally were reported by purpose. Detail may not sum to totals because of rounding.

SOURCE: U.S. Department of Education, National Center for Education Statistics, Integrated Postsecondary Education Data System (IPEDS), Spring 2008 through Spring 2011, Finance component. (This table was prepared November 2011.)

Total expenditures of private not-for-profit degree-granting institutions, by purpose and level of institution: 1999–2000 through 2009–10

Level of institution and year	Total	Instruction	Research	Public service	Academic support	Student services	Institutional support	Auxiliary enterprises[1]	Net grant aid to students[2]	Hospitals	Independent operations	Other
1	2	3	4	5	6	7	8	9	10	11	12	13
					In thousands of current dollars							
All levels												
1999–2000	$80,613,037	$26,012,599	$8,381,926	$1,446,958	$6,510,951	$5,688,499	$10,585,850	$8,300,021	$1,180,882	$7,355,110	$2,753,679	$2,396,563
2000–01	85,625,016	27,607,324	9,025,739	1,473,292	7,368,263	6,117,195	11,434,074	9,010,853	1,176,160	7,255,376	3,134,609	2,022,132
2001–02	92,192,297	29,689,041	10,035,480	1,665,884	7,802,637	6,573,185	12,068,120	9,515,829	1,188,690	7,633,043	3,397,979	2,622,409
2002–03	99,748,076	32,062,218	11,079,532	1,878,380	8,156,688	7,096,223	13,157,744	9,936,478	1,173,845	7,586,208	3,879,736	3,741,024
2003–04	104,317,870	33,909,179	12,039,531	1,972,351	8,759,743	7,544,021	13,951,408	10,508,719	1,101,738	8,374,128	4,222,980	1,934,070
2004–05	110,394,127	36,258,473	12,812,857	2,000,437	9,342,064	8,191,737	14,690,328	10,944,342	1,069,591	9,180,775	4,223,779	1,679,741
2005–06	116,817,913	38,465,058	13,242,343	1,941,519	10,217,274	8,965,704	15,667,101	11,741,258	708,158	9,645,428	4,203,523	2,020,548
2006–07	124,557,725	41,223,483	13,704,450	2,036,588	10,882,028	9,591,334	16,831,353	12,451,087	728,139	10,400,055	4,680,393	2,028,816
2007–08	133,503,539	44,226,329	14,474,367	2,182,676	11,884,345	10,363,476	18,364,513	13,319,602	721,487	10,754,966	4,887,609	2,324,170
2008–09	141,349,229	46,452,942	15,262,667	2,298,526	12,579,759	11,012,204	19,400,981	13,707,921	757,852	11,930,840	5,158,480	2,787,056
2009–10	145,141,785	47,486,299	16,155,474	2,089,745	12,939,489	11,416,177	19,433,113	13,887,042	832,078	13,174,405	5,154,851	2,573,113
4-year												
1999–2000	79,699,659	25,744,199	8,376,568	1,438,544	6,476,338	5,590,978	10,398,914	8,228,409	1,162,570	7,355,110	2,752,019	2,176,011
2000–01	85,048,123	27,413,897	9,019,966	1,467,325	7,333,851	6,036,478	11,292,310	8,957,973	1,160,660	7,253,479	3,133,099	1,979,086
2001–02	91,612,337	29,492,583	10,035,394	1,658,781	7,768,870	6,497,127	11,914,149	9,470,557	1,173,725	7,632,942	3,396,831	2,571,376
2002–03	99,137,236	31,866,310	11,079,332	1,871,274	8,122,181	7,014,149	12,996,836	9,876,937	1,161,441	7,586,208	3,854,471	3,708,098
2003–04	103,733,257	33,712,542	12,039,080	1,964,898	8,726,505	7,466,472	13,774,084	10,464,984	1,084,880	8,374,128	4,221,611	1,904,075
2004–05	109,789,731	36,051,084	12,812,326	1,993,767	9,307,600	8,101,214	14,516,197	10,899,456	1,051,216	9,180,775	4,223,779	1,652,317
2005–06	116,247,359	38,249,125	13,241,769	1,931,804	10,177,381	8,894,330	15,524,004	11,696,510	699,462	9,645,428	4,203,523	1,984,024
2006–07	124,061,478	41,056,590	13,703,502	2,028,364	10,850,270	9,522,535	16,693,987	12,414,609	714,398	10,400,055	4,680,393	1,996,775
2007–08	132,967,352	44,041,162	14,473,394	2,176,695	11,847,922	10,286,780	18,216,170	13,281,694	711,903	10,754,966	4,887,609	2,289,058
2008–09	140,852,609	46,286,662	15,262,322	2,294,914	12,538,248	10,943,745	19,258,651	13,670,550	750,687	11,930,840	5,158,480	2,757,510
2009–10	144,651,140	47,320,761	16,154,889	2,084,704	12,896,579	11,347,049	19,297,756	13,852,640	824,895	13,174,405	5,154,851	2,542,611
2-year												
1999–2000	913,378	268,400	5,358	8,415	34,612	97,521	186,936	71,612	18,311	0	1,660	220,553
2000–01	576,893	193,428	5,772	5,967	34,412	80,717	141,764	52,880	15,500	1,896	1,510	43,046
2001–02	579,960	196,459	86	7,102	33,767	76,058	153,971	45,271	14,965	100	1,147	51,033
2002–03	610,840	195,909	200	7,106	34,506	82,074	160,908	59,541	12,404	0	25,265	32,926
2003–04	584,612	196,637	451	7,453	33,238	77,549	177,324	43,735	16,859	0	1,369	29,995
2004–05	604,395	207,389	532	6,670	34,464	90,523	174,131	44,886	18,375	0	0	27,425
2005–06	570,554	215,934	574	9,715	39,893	71,374	143,096	44,748	8,696	0	0	36,524
2006–07	496,247	166,893	947	8,224	31,758	68,799	137,366	36,478	13,741	0	0	32,041
2007–08	536,187	185,167	973	5,982	36,423	76,696	148,343	37,908	9,584	0	0	35,112
2008–09	496,620	166,280	345	3,612	41,511	68,459	142,330	37,372	7,165	0	0	29,546
2009–10	490,645	165,538	585	5,041	42,909	69,129	135,357	34,402	7,183	0	0	30,502
					Percentage distribution							
All levels												
1999–2000	100.00	32.27	10.40	1.79	8.08	7.06	13.13	10.30	1.46	9.12	3.42	2.97
2000–01	100.00	32.24	10.54	1.72	8.61	7.14	13.35	10.52	1.37	8.47	3.66	2.36
2001–02	100.00	32.20	10.89	1.81	8.46	7.13	13.09	10.32	1.29	8.28	3.69	2.84
2002–03	100.00	32.14	11.11	1.88	8.18	7.11	13.19	9.96	1.18	7.61	3.89	3.75
2003–04	100.00	32.51	11.54	1.89	8.40	7.23	13.37	10.07	1.06	8.03	4.05	1.85
2004–05	100.00	32.84	11.61	1.81	8.46	7.42	13.31	9.91	0.97	8.32	3.83	1.52
2005–06	100.00	32.93	11.34	1.66	8.75	7.67	13.41	10.05	0.61	8.26	3.60	1.73
2006–07	100.00	33.10	11.00	1.64	8.74	7.70	13.51	10.00	0.58	8.35	3.76	1.63
2007–08	100.00	33.13	10.84	1.63	8.90	7.76	13.76	9.98	0.54	8.06	3.66	1.74
2008–09	100.00	32.86	10.80	1.63	8.90	7.79	13.73	9.70	0.54	8.44	3.65	1.97
2009–10	100.00	32.72	11.13	1.44	8.92	7.87	13.39	9.57	0.57	9.08	3.55	1.77
4-year												
1999–2000	100.00	32.30	10.51	1.80	8.13	7.02	13.05	10.32	1.46	9.23	3.45	2.73
2000–01	100.00	32.23	10.61	1.73	8.62	7.10	13.28	10.53	1.36	8.53	3.68	2.33
2001–02	100.00	32.19	10.95	1.81	8.48	7.09	13.00	10.34	1.28	8.33	3.71	2.81
2002–03	100.00	32.14	11.18	1.89	8.19	7.08	13.11	9.96	1.17	7.65	3.89	3.74
2003–04	100.00	32.50	11.61	1.89	8.41	7.20	13.28	10.09	1.05	8.07	4.07	1.84
2004–05	100.00	32.84	11.67	1.82	8.48	7.38	13.22	9.93	0.96	8.36	3.85	1.50
2005–06	100.00	32.90	11.39	1.66	8.75	7.65	13.35	10.06	0.60	8.30	3.62	1.71
2006–07	100.00	33.09	11.05	1.63	8.75	7.68	13.46	10.01	0.58	8.38	3.77	1.61
2007–08	100.00	33.12	10.88	1.64	8.91	7.74	13.70	9.99	0.54	8.09	3.68	1.72
2008–09	100.00	32.86	10.84	1.63	8.90	7.77	13.67	9.71	0.53	8.47	3.66	1.96
2009–10	100.00	32.71	11.17	1.44	8.92	7.84	13.34	9.58	0.57	9.11	3.56	1.76
2-year												
1999–2000	100.00	29.39	0.59	0.92	3.79	10.68	20.47	7.84	2.00	0.00	0.18	24.15
2000–01	100.00	33.53	1.00	1.03	5.96	13.99	24.57	9.17	2.69	0.33	0.26	7.46
2001–02	100.00	33.87	0.01	1.22	5.82	13.11	26.55	7.81	2.58	0.02	0.20	8.80
2002–03	100.00	32.07	0.03	1.16	5.65	13.44	26.34	9.75	2.03	0.00	4.14	5.39
2003–04	100.00	33.64	0.08	1.27	5.69	13.27	30.33	7.48	2.88	0.00	0.23	5.13
2004–05	100.00	34.31	0.09	1.10	5.70	14.98	28.81	7.43	3.04	0.00	0.00	4.54
2005–06	100.00	37.85	0.10	1.70	6.99	12.51	25.08	7.84	1.52	0.00	0.00	6.40
2006–07	100.00	33.63	0.19	1.66	6.40	13.86	27.68	7.35	2.77	0.00	0.00	6.46
2007–08	100.00	34.53	0.18	1.12	6.79	14.30	27.67	7.07	1.79	0.00	0.00	6.55
2008–09	100.00	33.48	0.07	0.73	8.36	13.78	28.66	7.53	1.44	0.00	0.00	5.95
2009–10	100.00	33.74	0.12	1.03	8.75	14.09	27.59	7.01	1.46	0.00	0.00	6.22

See notes at end of table.

Total expenditures of private not-for-profit degree-granting institutions, by purpose and level of institution: 1999–2000 through 2009–10—Continued

Level of institution and year	Total	Instruction	Research	Public service	Academic support	Student services	Institutional support	Auxiliary enterprises[1]	Net grant aid to students[2]	Hospitals	Independent operations	Other
1	2	3	4	5	6	7	8	9	10	11	12	13
Expenditure per full-time-equivalent student in current dollars												
All levels												
1999–2000	$31,751	$10,246	$3,301	$570	$2,564	$2,241	$4,169	$3,269	$465	$2,897	$1,085	$944
2000–01	33,069	10,662	3,486	569	2,846	2,363	4,416	3,480	454	2,802	1,211	781
2001–02	34,841	11,220	3,793	630	2,949	2,484	4,561	3,596	449	2,885	1,284	991
2002–03	36,479	11,725	4,052	687	2,983	2,595	4,812	3,634	429	2,774	1,419	1,368
2003–04	37,240	12,105	4,298	704	3,127	2,693	4,980	3,751	393	2,989	1,508	690
2004–05	38,472	12,636	4,465	697	3,256	2,855	5,120	3,814	373	3,199	1,472	585
2005–06	40,156	13,222	4,552	667	3,512	3,082	5,386	4,036	243	3,316	1,445	695
2006–07	42,060	13,920	4,628	688	3,675	3,239	5,684	4,204	246	3,512	1,580	685
2007–08	43,978	14,569	4,768	719	3,915	3,414	6,049	4,388	238	3,543	1,610	766
2008–09	45,853	15,069	4,951	746	4,081	3,572	6,294	4,447	246	3,870	1,673	904
2009–10	45,909	15,020	5,110	661	4,093	3,611	6,147	4,393	263	4,167	1,631	814
4-year												
1999–2000	32,064	10,357	3,370	579	2,605	2,249	4,184	3,310	468	2,959	1,107	875
2000–01	33,359	10,753	3,538	576	2,877	2,368	4,429	3,514	455	2,845	1,229	776
2001–02	35,139	11,312	3,849	636	2,980	2,492	4,570	3,633	450	2,928	1,303	986
2002–03	36,742	11,810	4,106	694	3,010	2,600	4,817	3,661	430	2,812	1,429	1,374
2003–04	37,504	12,188	4,353	710	3,155	2,699	4,980	3,784	392	3,028	1,526	688
2004–05	38,726	12,716	4,519	703	3,283	2,858	5,120	3,845	371	3,238	1,490	583
2005–06	40,394	13,291	4,601	671	3,536	3,091	5,394	4,064	243	3,352	1,461	689
2006–07	42,256	13,984	4,667	691	3,696	3,243	5,686	4,228	243	3,542	1,594	680
2007–08	44,194	14,638	4,810	723	3,938	3,419	6,054	4,414	237	3,575	1,624	761
2008–09	46,080	15,143	4,993	751	4,102	3,580	6,300	4,472	246	3,903	1,688	902
2009–10	46,130	15,091	5,152	665	4,113	3,619	6,154	4,418	263	4,201	1,644	811
2-year												
1999–2000	17,148	5,039	101	158	650	1,831	3,510	1,345	344	0	31	4,141
2000–01	14,494	4,860	145	150	865	2,028	3,562	1,329	389	48	38	1,081
2001–02	14,890	5,044	2	182	867	1,953	3,953	1,162	384	3	29	1,310
2002–03	16,846	5,403	6	196	952	2,263	4,438	1,642	342	0	697	908
2003–04	16,561	5,570	13	211	942	2,197	5,023	1,239	478	0	39	850
2004–05	17,552	6,023	15	194	1,001	2,629	5,057	1,304	534	0	0	796
2005–06	18,240	6,903	18	311	1,275	2,282	4,575	1,431	278	0	0	1,168
2006–07	19,498	6,557	37	323	1,248	2,703	5,397	1,433	540	0	0	1,259
2007–08	19,867	6,861	36	222	1,350	2,842	5,496	1,405	355	0	0	1,301
2008–09	19,129	6,405	13	139	1,599	2,637	5,482	1,439	276	0	0	1,138
2009–10	19,031	6,421	23	196	1,664	2,681	5,250	1,334	279	0	0	1,183
Expenditure per full-time-equivalent student in constant 2009–10 dollars[3]												
All levels												
1999–2000	$40,649	$13,117	$4,227	$730	$3,283	$2,868	$5,338	$4,185	$595	$3,709	$1,389	$1,208
2000–01	40,934	13,198	4,315	704	3,523	2,924	5,466	4,308	562	3,469	1,499	967
2001–02	42,377	13,647	4,613	766	3,587	3,021	5,547	4,374	546	3,509	1,562	1,205
2002–03	43,415	13,955	4,822	818	3,550	3,089	5,727	4,325	511	3,302	1,689	1,628
2003–04	43,372	14,098	5,006	820	3,642	3,137	5,801	4,369	458	3,482	1,756	804
2004–05	43,498	14,287	5,049	788	3,681	3,228	5,788	4,312	421	3,617	1,664	662
2005–06	43,736	14,401	4,958	727	3,825	3,357	5,866	4,396	265	3,611	1,574	756
2006–07	44,656	14,779	4,913	730	3,901	3,439	6,034	4,464	261	3,729	1,678	727
2007–08	45,023	14,915	4,881	736	4,008	3,495	6,193	4,492	243	3,627	1,648	784
2008–09	46,296	15,215	4,999	753	4,120	3,607	6,354	4,490	248	3,908	1,690	913
2009–10	45,909	15,020	5,110	661	4,093	3,611	6,147	4,393	263	4,167	1,631	814
4-year												
1999–2000	41,050	13,260	4,314	741	3,336	2,880	5,356	4,238	599	3,788	1,417	1,121
2000–01	41,293	13,310	4,379	712	3,561	2,931	5,483	4,349	564	3,522	1,521	961
2001–02	42,740	13,759	4,682	774	3,624	3,031	5,558	4,418	548	3,561	1,585	1,200
2002–03	43,729	14,056	4,887	825	3,583	3,094	5,733	4,357	512	3,346	1,700	1,636
2003–04	43,680	14,196	5,069	827	3,675	3,144	5,800	4,407	457	3,526	1,778	802
2004–05	43,785	14,378	5,110	795	3,712	3,231	5,789	4,347	419	3,661	1,684	659
2005–06	43,996	14,476	5,012	731	3,852	3,366	5,875	4,427	265	3,650	1,591	751
2006–07	44,863	14,847	4,955	734	3,924	3,444	6,037	4,489	258	3,761	1,693	722
2007–08	45,245	14,986	4,925	741	4,031	3,500	6,198	4,519	242	3,660	1,663	779
2008–09	46,525	15,289	5,041	758	4,142	3,615	6,361	4,516	248	3,941	1,704	911
2009–10	46,130	15,091	5,152	665	4,113	3,619	6,154	4,418	263	4,201	1,644	811
2-year												
1999–2000	21,954	6,451	129	202	832	2,344	4,493	1,721	440	0	40	5,301
2000–01	17,941	6,015	180	186	1,070	2,510	4,409	1,645	482	59	47	1,339
2001–02	18,111	6,135	3	222	1,054	2,375	4,808	1,414	467	3	36	1,594
2002–03	20,049	6,430	7	233	1,133	2,694	5,281	1,954	407	0	829	1,081
2003–04	19,288	6,488	15	246	1,097	2,559	5,850	1,443	556	0	45	990
2004–05	19,845	6,810	17	219	1,132	2,972	5,718	1,474	603	0	0	900
2005–06	19,866	7,519	20	338	1,389	2,485	4,982	1,558	303	0	0	1,272
2006–07	20,701	6,962	40	343	1,325	2,870	5,730	1,522	573	0	0	1,337
2007–08	20,339	7,024	37	227	1,382	2,909	5,627	1,438	364	0	0	1,332
2008–09	19,314	6,467	13	140	1,614	2,662	5,535	1,453	279	0	0	1,149
2009–10	19,031	6,421	23	196	1,664	2,681	5,250	1,334	279	0	0	1,183

[1]Essentially self-supporting operations of institutions that furnish a service to students, faculty, or staff, such as residence halls and food services.
[2]Excludes tuition and fee allowances and agency transactions, such as student awards made from contributed funds or grant funds. These exclusions account for the majority of total student grants.
[3]Constant dollars based on the Consumer Price Index, prepared by the Bureau of Labor Statistics, U.S. Department of Labor, adjusted to a school-year basis.

NOTE: Degree-granting institutions grant associate's or higher degrees and participate in Title IV federal financial aid programs. Detail may not sum to totals because of rounding.
SOURCE: U.S. Department of Education, National Center for Education Statistics, Integrated Postsecondary Education Data System (IPEDS), Spring 2001 through Spring 2010, Enrollment component; and Spring 2002 through Spring 2011, Finance component. (This table was prepared October 2011.)

Total expenditures of private not-for-profit degree-granting institutions, by purpose and classification of institution: 2009–10

Classification of institution	Total	Instruction	Research	Public service	Academic support	Student services	Institutional support	Auxiliary enterprises[1]	Net grant aid to students[2]	Hospitals	Independent operations	Other
1	2	3	4	5	6	7	8	9	10	11	12	13
In thousands of current dollars												
Total	$145,141,785	$47,486,299	$16,155,474	$2,089,745	$12,939,489	$11,416,177	$19,433,113	$13,887,042	$832,078	$13,174,405	$5,154,851	$2,573,113
4-year	144,651,140	47,320,761	16,154,889	2,084,704	12,896,579	11,347,049	19,297,756	13,852,640	824,895	13,174,405	5,154,851	2,542,611
Research university, very high[3]	66,737,064	20,070,200	12,774,388	809,105	4,730,320	2,399,181	5,720,554	4,328,498	395,429	10,178,093	4,134,887	1,196,411
Research university, high[4]	11,429,125	4,030,437	1,147,377	138,471	1,657,228	830,300	1,528,833	1,417,077	46,476	462,684	97,337	72,906
Doctoral/research[5]	7,642,489	3,211,885	194,211	124,051	884,524	823,008	1,381,162	935,505	11,569	0	46,066	30,509
Master's[6]	22,952,137	8,900,699	280,147	257,136	2,282,482	3,288,979	4,379,995	3,051,075	157,904	107,207	80,913	165,598
Baccalaureate[7]	20,744,027	7,409,896	223,350	186,038	1,855,366	3,187,392	4,002,248	3,392,015	143,670	0	67,539	276,514
Specialized institutions[8]	15,146,299	3,697,645	1,535,417	569,902	1,486,660	818,188	2,284,965	728,471	69,847	2,426,421	728,109	800,673
Art, music, or design	1,858,594	747,297	879	17,404	211,456	183,948	406,724	202,243	6,155	0	26,774	55,713
Business and management	573,341	198,281	5,844	22	66,437	85,151	135,269	78,365	347	0	0	3,624
Engineering or technology	363,293	150,581	12,127	121	21,468	50,284	78,458	36,604	7,757	0	42	5,850
Law	576,476	250,938	4,889	8,094	87,792	70,804	127,799	15,829	1,629	0	1,592	7,110
Medical or other health	9,737,077	1,692,672	1,501,833	505,467	905,702	241,603	964,104	193,977	14,791	2,426,421	677,162	613,345
Theological	1,631,413	513,041	4,400	17,861	156,742	145,136	464,258	172,460	34,299	0	21,076	102,140
Tribal[9]	57,087	16,131	275	3,396	2,483	7,716	16,400	1,955	3,816	0	0	4,914
Other specialized	349,018	128,703	5,170	17,536	34,580	33,546	91,951	27,037	1,055	0	1,463	7,975
2-year	490,645	165,538	585	5,041	42,909	69,129	135,357	34,402	7,183	0	0	30,502
Associate's of arts	445,779	152,958	91	2,525	38,709	63,594	124,846	32,966	4,423	0	0	25,667
Tribal[9]	44,866	12,580	494	2,517	4,200	5,534	10,511	1,436	2,760	0	0	4,834
Percentage distribution												
Total	100.00	32.72	11.13	1.44	8.92	7.87	13.39	9.57	0.57	9.08	3.55	1.77
4-year	100.00	32.71	11.17	1.44	8.92	7.84	13.34	9.58	0.57	9.11	3.56	1.76
Research university, very high[3]	100.00	30.07	19.14	1.21	7.09	3.59	8.57	6.49	0.59	15.25	6.20	1.79
Research university, high[4]	100.00	35.26	10.04	1.21	14.50	7.26	13.38	12.40	0.41	4.05	0.85	0.64
Doctoral/research[5]	100.00	42.03	2.54	1.62	11.57	10.77	18.07	12.24	0.15	0.00	0.60	0.40
Master's[6]	100.00	38.78	1.22	1.12	9.94	14.33	19.08	13.29	0.69	0.47	0.35	0.72
Baccalaureate[7]	100.00	35.72	1.08	0.90	8.94	15.37	19.29	16.35	0.69	0.00	0.33	1.33
Specialized institutions[8]	100.00	24.41	10.14	3.76	9.82	5.40	15.09	4.81	0.46	16.02	4.81	5.29
Art, music, or design	100.00	40.21	0.05	0.94	11.38	9.90	21.88	10.88	0.33	0.00	1.44	3.00
Business and management	100.00	34.58	1.02	#	11.59	14.85	23.59	13.67	0.06	0.00	0.00	0.63
Engineering or technology	100.00	41.45	3.34	0.03	5.91	13.84	21.60	10.08	2.14	0.00	0.01	1.61
Law	100.00	43.53	0.85	1.40	15.23	12.28	22.17	2.75	0.28	0.00	0.28	1.23
Medical or other health	100.00	17.38	15.42	5.19	9.30	2.48	9.90	1.99	0.15	24.92	6.95	6.30
Theological	100.00	31.45	0.27	1.09	9.61	8.90	28.46	10.57	2.10	0.00	1.29	6.26
Tribal[9]	100.00	28.26	0.48	5.95	4.35	13.52	28.73	3.42	6.68	0.00	0.00	8.61
Other specialized	100.00	36.88	1.48	5.02	9.91	9.61	26.35	7.75	0.30	0.00	0.42	2.29
2-year	100.00	33.74	0.12	1.03	8.75	14.09	27.59	7.01	1.46	0.00	0.00	6.22
Associate's of arts	100.00	34.31	0.02	0.57	8.68	14.27	28.01	7.40	0.99	0.00	0.00	5.76
Tribal[9]	100.00	28.04	1.10	5.61	9.36	12.34	23.43	3.20	6.15	0.00	0.00	10.78
Expenditure per full-time-equivalent student in current dollars												
Total	$45,909	$15,020	$5,110	$661	$4,093	$3,611	$6,147	$4,393	$263	$4,167	$1,631	$814
4-year	46,130	15,091	5,152	665	4,113	3,619	6,154	4,418	263	4,201	1,644	811
Research university, very high[3]	146,335	44,008	28,010	1,774	10,372	5,261	12,543	9,491	867	22,318	9,067	2,623
Research university, high[4]	41,385	14,594	4,155	501	6,001	3,007	5,536	5,131	168	1,675	352	264
Doctoral/research[5]	27,954	11,748	710	454	3,235	3,010	5,052	3,422	42	0	168	112
Master's[6]	21,305	8,262	260	239	2,119	3,053	4,066	2,832	147	100	75	154
Baccalaureate[7]	27,096	9,679	292	243	2,423	4,163	5,228	4,431	188	0	88	361
Specialized institutions[8]	52,741	12,875	5,346	1,984	5,177	2,849	7,956	2,537	243	8,449	2,535	2,788
Art, music, or design	33,152	13,330	16	310	3,772	3,281	7,255	3,607	110	0	478	994
Business and management	18,017	6,231	184	1	2,088	2,676	4,251	2,463	11	0	0	114
Engineering or technology	25,248	10,465	843	8	1,492	3,495	5,453	2,544	539	0	3	407
Law	34,961	15,219	296	491	5,324	4,294	7,751	960	99	0	97	431
Medical or other health	109,591	19,051	16,903	5,689	10,194	2,719	10,851	2,183	166	27,309	7,621	6,903
Theological	24,271	7,633	65	266	2,332	2,159	6,907	2,566	510	0	314	1,520
Tribal[9]	22,230	6,282	107	1,323	967	3,005	6,386	761	1,486	0	0	1,914
Other specialized	35,658	13,149	528	1,792	3,533	3,427	9,394	2,762	108	0	150	815
2-year	19,031	6,421	23	196	1,664	2,681	5,250	1,334	279	0	0	1,183
Associate's of arts	18,447	6,329	4	104	1,602	2,632	5,166	1,364	183	0	0	1,062
Tribal[9]	27,764	7,785	306	1,557	2,599	3,425	6,504	888	1,708	0	0	2,992

#Rounds to zero.

[1]Essentially self-supporting operations of institutions that furnish a service to students, faculty, or staff, such as residence halls and food services.

[2]Excludes tuition and fee allowances and agency transactions, such as student awards made from contributed funds or grant funds. These exclusions account for the majority of total student grants.

[3]Research universities with a very high level of research activity.

[4]Research universities with a high level of research activity.

[5]Includes institutions that award at least 20 doctor's degrees per year, but did not have high levels of research activity.

[6]Master's institutions award at least 50 master's degrees per year.

[7]Baccalaureate institutions primarily emphasize undergraduate education. Also includes institutions classified as 4-year under the IPEDS system, which had been classified as 2-year in the Carnegie classification system because they primarily award associate's degrees.

[8]Special-focus 4-year institutions award degrees primarily in single fields of study, such as medicine, business, fine arts, theology, and engineering.

[9]Tribally controlled colleges are located on reservations and are members of the American Indian Higher Education Consortium.

NOTE: Relative levels of research activity for research universities were determined by an analysis of research and development expenditures, science and engineering research staffing, and doctoral degrees conferred, by field. Further information on the Carnegie 2005 classification system may be obtained from http://classifications.carnegiefoundation.org/resources/. Degree-granting institutions grant associate's or higher degrees and participate in Title IV federal financial aid programs. Detail may not sum to totals because of rounding. SOURCE: U.S. Department of Education, National Center for Education Statistics, Integrated Postsecondary Education Data System (IPEDS), Spring 2010, Enrollment component; and Spring 2011, Finance component. (This table was prepared October 2011.)

Total expenditures of private for-profit degree-granting institutions, by purpose and level of institution: 1999–2000 through 2009–10

Year and level of institution	Total	Instruction	Research and public service	Student services, academic and institutional support	Auxiliary enterprises[1]	Net grant aid to students[2]	Other
1	2	3	4	5	6	7	8
			In thousands of current dollars				
All institutions							
1999–2000	$3,846,246	$1,171,732	$24,738	$2,041,594	$144,305	$26,278	$437,599
2000–01	4,235,781	1,310,054	22,896	2,337,151	181,243	43,788	340,649
2001–02	5,087,292	1,517,389	16,632	2,977,225	213,195	23,283	339,567
2002–03	6,110,378	1,747,725	17,987	3,670,218	240,380	36,031	398,037
2003–04	7,364,012	1,883,733	8,606	4,592,730	249,472	56,467	573,004
2004–05	8,830,792	2,313,895	7,583	5,693,200	269,883	54,819	491,411
2005–06	10,208,845	2,586,870	8,445	6,569,329	276,587	66,569	701,044
2006–07	12,152,366	2,884,481	6,087	7,760,044	332,887	68,300	1,100,568
2007–08	13,940,442	3,238,406	9,547	9,322,781	421,714	82,072	865,922
2008–09	16,364,360	3,871,127	9,939	11,004,500	396,704	44,440	1,037,650
2009–10	19,973,659	4,750,829	13,257	13,086,981	466,042	120,215	1,536,334
4–year							
1999–2000	2,022,622	595,976	4,393	1,104,001	92,071	11,805	214,377
2000–01	2,414,655	726,328	4,878	1,385,095	113,371	18,519	166,465
2001–02	3,046,929	883,899	3,192	1,842,373	134,740	8,229	174,495
2002–03	3,754,727	1,030,470	5,339	2,337,388	153,528	14,813	213,190
2003–04	4,821,864	1,143,050	3,705	3,108,697	168,069	32,603	365,740
2004–05	5,989,792	1,430,196	3,513	4,110,514	180,036	38,639	226,894
2005–06	7,218,830	1,680,603	4,065	4,985,531	179,064	54,291	315,276
2006–07	8,837,598	1,857,765	4,303	5,909,914	228,624	56,930	780,063
2007–08	10,424,536	2,149,651	7,534	7,335,592	312,834	71,324	547,602
2008–09	12,399,217	2,580,208	7,629	8,832,095	276,200	33,417	669,669
2009–10	15,286,549	3,259,657	10,726	10,587,709	337,501	72,265	1,018,691
2–year							
1999–2000	1,823,624	575,756	20,345	937,593	52,234	14,473	223,223
2000–01	1,821,126	583,727	18,019	952,056	67,872	25,269	174,184
2001–02	2,040,363	633,490	13,440	1,134,853	78,455	15,054	165,071
2002–03	2,355,650	717,255	12,648	1,332,830	86,853	21,218	184,846
2003–04	2,542,148	740,683	4,901	1,484,033	81,403	23,864	207,264
2004–05	2,840,999	883,699	4,070	1,582,687	89,846	16,181	264,517
2005–06	2,990,015	906,267	4,381	1,583,798	97,523	12,278	385,768
2006–07	3,314,768	1,026,716	1,784	1,850,129	104,264	11,370	320,505
2007–08	3,515,906	1,088,755	2,014	1,987,189	108,880	10,747	318,320
2008–09	3,965,143	1,290,919	2,310	2,172,405	120,504	11,023	367,981
2009–10	4,687,110	1,491,172	2,531	2,499,272	128,542	47,950	517,643
			Percentage distribution				
All institutions							
1999–2000	100.00	30.46	0.64	53.08	3.75	0.68	11.38
2000–01	100.00	30.93	0.54	55.18	4.28	1.03	8.04
2001–02	100.00	29.83	0.33	58.52	4.19	0.46	6.67
2002–03	100.00	28.60	0.29	60.07	3.93	0.59	6.51
2003–04	100.00	25.58	0.12	62.37	3.39	0.77	7.78
2004–05	100.00	26.20	0.09	64.47	3.06	0.62	5.56
2005–06	100.00	25.34	0.08	64.35	2.71	0.65	6.87
2006–07	100.00	23.74	0.05	63.86	2.74	0.56	9.06
2007–08	100.00	23.23	0.07	66.88	3.03	0.59	6.21
2008–09	100.00	23.66	0.06	67.25	2.42	0.27	6.34
2009–10	100.00	23.79	0.07	65.52	2.33	0.60	7.69
4–year							
1999–2000	100.00	29.47	0.22	54.58	4.55	0.58	10.60
2000–01	100.00	30.08	0.20	57.36	4.70	0.77	6.89
2001–02	100.00	29.01	0.10	60.47	4.42	0.27	5.73
2002–03	100.00	27.44	0.14	62.25	4.09	0.39	5.68
2003–04	100.00	23.71	0.08	64.47	3.49	0.68	7.59
2004–05	100.00	23.88	0.06	68.63	3.01	0.65	3.79
2005–06	100.00	23.28	0.06	69.06	2.48	0.75	4.37
2006–07	100.00	21.02	0.05	66.87	2.59	0.64	8.83
2007–08	100.00	20.62	0.07	70.37	3.00	0.68	5.25
2008–09	100.00	20.81	0.06	71.23	2.23	0.27	5.40
2009–10	100.00	21.32	0.07	69.26	2.21	0.47	6.66
2–year							
1999–2000	100.00	31.57	1.12	51.41	2.86	0.79	12.24
2000–01	100.00	32.05	0.99	52.28	3.73	1.39	9.56
2001–02	100.00	31.05	0.66	55.62	3.85	0.74	8.09
2002–03	100.00	30.45	0.54	56.58	3.69	0.90	7.85
2003–04	100.00	29.14	0.19	58.38	3.20	0.94	8.15
2004–05	100.00	31.11	0.14	55.71	3.16	0.57	9.31
2005–06	100.00	30.31	0.15	52.97	3.26	0.41	12.90
2006–07	100.00	30.97	0.05	55.81	3.15	0.34	9.67
2007–08	100.00	30.97	0.06	56.52	3.10	0.31	9.05
2008–09	100.00	32.56	0.06	54.79	3.04	0.28	9.28
2009–10	100.00	31.81	0.05	53.32	2.74	1.02	11.04

See notes at end of table.

Total expenditures of private for-profit degree-granting institutions, by purpose and level of institution: 1999–2000 through 2009–10—Continued

Year and level of institution	Total	Instruction	Research and public service	Student services, academic and institutional support	Auxiliary enterprises[1]	Net grant aid to students[2]	Other
1	2	3	4	5	6	7	8
	Total expenditures per full-time-equivalent student in current dollars						
All institutions							
1999–2000	$10,000	$3,046	$64	$5,308	$375	$68	$1,138
2000–01	10,781	3,334	58	5,949	461	111	867
2001–02	11,144	3,324	36	6,522	467	51	744
2002–03	11,301	3,232	33	6,788	445	67	736
2003–04	11,381	2,911	13	7,098	386	87	886
2004–05	11,205	2,936	10	7,224	342	70	624
2005–06	11,336	2,873	9	7,295	307	74	778
2006–07	12,880	3,057	6	8,225	353	72	1,166
2007–08	13,527	3,142	9	9,046	409	80	840
2008–09	12,848	3,039	8	8,640	311	35	815
2009–10	12,434	2,958	8	8,147	290	75	956
4–year							
1999–2000	9,688	2,855	21	5,288	441	57	1,027
2000–01	10,588	3,185	21	6,074	497	81	730
2001–02	11,021	3,197	12	6,664	487	30	631
2002–03	10,862	2,981	15	6,762	444	43	617
2003–04	11,291	2,677	9	7,279	394	76	856
2004–05	10,818	2,583	6	7,424	325	70	410
2005–06	10,897	2,537	6	7,526	270	82	476
2006–07	12,551	2,638	6	8,393	325	81	1,108
2007–08	13,212	2,725	10	9,297	396	90	694
2008–09	12,654	2,633	8	9,013	282	34	683
2009–10	12,378	2,640	9	8,574	273	59	825
2–year							
1999–2000	10,370	3,274	116	5,332	297	82	1,269
2000–01	11,048	3,541	109	5,776	412	153	1,057
2001–02	11,333	3,519	75	6,303	436	84	917
2002–03	12,081	3,678	65	6,835	445	109	948
2003–04	11,557	3,367	22	6,747	370	108	942
2004–05	12,120	3,770	17	6,752	383	69	1,128
2005–06	12,558	3,806	18	6,652	410	52	1,620
2006–07	13,848	4,289	7	7,729	436	47	1,339
2007–08	14,555	4,507	8	8,226	451	44	1,318
2008–09	13,498	4,394	8	7,395	410	38	1,253
2009–10	12,620	4,015	7	6,729	346	129	1,394
	Total expenditures per full-time-equivalent student in constant 2009–10 dollars[3]						
All institutions							
1999–2000	$12,803	$3,900	$82	$6,796	$480	$87	$1,457
2000–01	11,485	3,552	62	6,337	491	119	924
2001–02	13,554	4,043	44	7,932	568	62	905
2002–03	13,450	3,847	40	8,079	529	79	876
2003–04	13,255	3,391	15	8,267	449	102	1,031
2004–05	12,669	3,320	11	8,168	387	79	705
2005–06	12,347	3,129	10	7,945	335	81	848
2006–07	13,675	3,246	7	8,732	375	77	1,238
2007–08	13,849	3,217	9	9,261	419	82	860
2008–09	12,973	3,069	8	8,724	314	35	823
2009–10	12,434	2,958	8	8,147	290	75	956
4–year							
1999–2000	12,404	3,655	27	6,770	565	72	1,315
2000–01	13,107	3,942	26	7,518	615	101	904
2001–02	13,404	3,889	14	8,105	593	36	768
2002–03	12,927	3,548	18	8,047	529	51	734
2003–04	13,150	3,117	10	8,478	458	89	997
2004–05	12,231	2,920	7	8,394	368	79	463
2005–06	11,869	2,763	7	8,197	294	89	518
2006–07	13,326	2,801	6	8,911	345	86	1,176
2007–08	13,526	2,789	10	9,518	406	93	711
2008–09	12,776	2,659	8	9,100	285	34	690
2009–10	12,378	2,640	9	8,574	273	59	825
2–year							
1999–2000	13,277	4,192	148	6,826	380	105	1,625
2000–01	13,676	4,384	135	7,150	510	190	1,308
2001–02	13,784	4,280	91	7,667	530	102	1,115
2002–03	14,378	4,378	77	8,135	530	130	1,128
2003–04	13,460	3,922	26	7,858	431	126	1,097
2004–05	13,704	4,263	20	7,634	433	78	1,276
2005–06	13,678	4,146	20	7,245	446	56	1,765
2006–07	14,702	4,554	8	8,206	462	50	1,422
2007–08	14,901	4,614	9	8,422	461	46	1,349
2008–09	13,628	4,437	8	7,467	414	38	1,265
2009–10	12,620	4,015	7	6,729	346	129	1,394

[1]Essentially self-supporting operations of institutions that furnish a service to students, faculty, or staff, such as residence halls and food services.
[2]Excludes tuition and fee allowances and agency transactions, such as student awards made from contributed funds or grant funds.
[3]Constant dollars based on the Consumer Price Index, prepared by the Bureau of Labor Statistics, U.S. Department of Labor, adjusted to a school-year basis.

NOTE: Degree-granting institutions grant associate's or higher degrees and participate in Title IV federal financial aid programs. Detail may not sum to totals because of rounding.
SOURCE: U.S. Department of Education, National Center for Education Statistics, Integrated Postsecondary Education Data System (IPEDS), "Fall Enrollment Survey" (IPEDS-EF:99), and Spring 2001 through Spring 2011, Enrollment and Finance components. (This table was prepared October 2011.)

Total expenditures of private for-profit degree-granting institutions, by purpose and classification of institution: 2009–10

Classification of institution	Total	Instruction	Research and public service	Student services, academic and institutional support	Auxiliary enterprises[1]	Net grant aid to students[2]	Other
1	2	3	4	5	6	7	8
			In thousands of current dollars				
Total	$19,973,659	$4,750,829	$13,257	$13,086,981	$466,042	$120,215	$1,536,334
4–year	15,286,549	3,259,657	10,726	10,587,709	337,501	72,265	1,018,691
Doctoral/research[3]	3,199,779	559,229	1,572	2,629,318	2,746	0	6,915
Master's[4]	2,302,639	418,950	1,607	1,579,561	63,351	27,248	211,922
Baccalaureate[5]	3,584,250	914,489	1,086	2,260,858	60,837	16,808	330,172
Specialized institutions[6]	6,199,881	1,366,990	6,462	4,117,971	210,567	28,210	469,682
Art, music, or design	2,196,106	553,702	3,983	1,405,523	139,582	140	93,175
Business and management	2,051,857	356,897	270	1,355,411	55,961	18,987	264,333
Engineering or technology	1,396,652	325,060	197	1,019,934	10,939	2,384	38,137
Law	107,675	26,789	1,098	54,210	49	5,383	20,147
Medical or other health	328,517	64,079	914	216,308	1,598	1,316	44,302
Other specialized	119,074	40,463	0	66,586	2,438	0	9,587
2–year	4,687,110	1,491,172	2,531	2,499,272	128,542	47,950	517,643
			Percentage distribution				
Total	100.00	23.79	0.07	65.52	2.33	0.60	7.69
4–year	100.00	21.32	0.07	69.26	2.21	0.47	6.66
Doctoral/research[3]	100.00	17.48	0.05	82.17	0.09	0.00	0.22
Master's[4]	100.00	18.19	0.07	68.60	2.75	1.18	9.20
Baccalaureate[5]	100.00	25.51	0.03	63.08	1.70	0.47	9.21
Specialized institutions[6]	100.00	22.05	0.10	66.42	3.40	0.46	7.58
Art, music, or design	100.00	25.21	0.18	64.00	6.36	0.01	4.24
Business and management	100.00	17.39	0.01	66.06	2.73	0.93	12.88
Engineering or technology	100.00	23.27	0.01	73.03	0.78	0.17	2.73
Law	100.00	24.88	1.02	50.35	0.05	5.00	18.71
Medical or other health	100.00	19.51	0.28	65.84	0.49	0.40	13.49
Other specialized	100.00	33.98	0.00	55.92	2.05	0.00	8.05
2–year	100.00	31.81	0.05	53.32	2.74	1.02	11.04
			Expenditure per full-time-equivalent student in current dollars				
Total	$12,434	$2,958	$8	$8,147	$290	$75	$956
4–year	12,378	2,640	9	8,574	273	59	825
Doctoral/research[3]	7,250	1,267	4	5,957	6	0	16
Master's[4]	11,425	2,079	8	7,837	314	135	1,052
Baccalaureate[5]	14,373	3,667	4	9,066	244	67	1,324
Specialized institutions[6]	18,093	3,989	19	12,018	615	82	1,371
Art, music, or design	22,214	5,601	40	14,217	1,412	1	942
Business and management	15,572	2,709	2	10,287	425	144	2,006
Engineering or technology	16,575	3,858	2	12,104	130	28	453
Law	27,007	6,719	275	13,597	12	1,350	5,053
Medical or other health	20,101	3,921	56	13,235	98	81	2,711
Other specialized	15,996	5,436	0	8,945	328	0	1,288
2–year	12,620	4,015	7	6,729	346	129	1,394

[1]Essentially self-supporting operations of institutions that furnish a service to students, faculty, or staff, such as residence halls and food services.

[2]Excludes tuition and fee allowances and agency transactions, such as student awards made from contributed funds or grant funds.

[3]Includes institutions that award at least 20 doctor's degrees per year, but did not have high levels of research activity.

[4]Master's institutions award at least 50 master's degrees per year.

[5]Baccalaureate institutions primarily emphasize undergraduate education. Also includes institutions classified as 4-year under the IPEDS system, which had been classified as 2-year in the Carnegie classification system because they primarily award associate's degrees.

[6]Special focus 4-year institutions award degrees primarily in single fields of study, such as medicine, business, fine arts, theology, and engineering.

NOTE: Degree-granting institutions grant associate's or higher degrees and participate in Title IV federal financial aid programs. Further information on the Carnegie 2005 classification system used in this table may be obtained from http://classifications.carnegiefoundation.org/resources/. Detail may not sum to totals because of rounding.

SOURCE: U.S. Department of Education, National Center for Education Statistics, Integrated Postsecondary Education Data System (IPEDS), Spring 2010, Enrollment component; and Spring 2011, Finance component. (This table was prepared October 2011.)

Total expenditures of private not-for-profit and for-profit degree-granting institutions, by state or jurisdiction: Selected years, 1999–2000 through 2009–10

[In thousands of current dollars]

State or jurisdiction	Not-for-profit institutions						For-profit institutions					
	1999–2000	2004–05	2006–07	2007–08	2008–09	2009–10	1999–2000	2004–05	2006–07	2007–08	2008–09	2009–10
1	2	3	4	5	6	7	8	9	10	11	12	13
United States ...	$80,613,037	$110,394,127	$124,557,725	$133,503,539	$141,349,229	$145,141,785	$3,846,246	$8,830,792	$12,152,366	$13,940,442	$16,364,360	$19,973,659
Alabama	393,465	459,250	505,523	525,506	546,535	561,968	88,190	60,629	75,727	75,320	98,444	139,366
Alaska	19,042	21,076	14,740	15,338	17,211	16,249	3,559	3,986	4,885	6,275	9,109	19,302
Arizona	143,698	147,825	136,677	156,501	165,960	176,443	278,286	1,095,783	1,942,229	2,246,491	2,722,216	3,412,261
Arkansas	230,860	239,357	251,234	275,135	287,259	289,868	5,828	11,574	17,443	20,364	26,615	31,263
California	7,871,651	10,728,872	12,121,864	12,868,260	13,421,736	13,925,287	666,020	1,243,346	1,514,687	1,742,128	2,047,729	2,552,449
Colorado	376,887	524,349	585,013	617,099	632,322	627,123	154,801	320,550	525,249	576,748	611,882	661,384
Connecticut	2,094,981	2,882,963	3,279,174	3,599,071	3,858,956	3,975,262	18,110	41,931	50,793	47,948	52,340	59,726
Delaware	52,533	87,617	105,469	114,940	124,757	132,851	†	†	†	†	†	4,042
District of Columbia ..	2,267,409	2,824,081	3,134,498	3,382,416	3,715,850	3,687,042	59,375	127,859	215,804	258,686	328,919	66,677
Florida	2,031,623	3,067,443	3,598,947	4,053,067	4,523,485	4,592,898	315,721	781,280	1,007,789	1,194,823	1,379,974	1,825,704
Georgia	2,635,438	3,442,374	3,863,137	4,070,825	4,340,833	4,497,299	106,794	261,219	339,673	395,565	509,600	675,496
Hawaii	209,135	195,152	199,856	204,318	214,383	210,680	9,422	24,996	32,583	28,731	37,439	34,299
Idaho	118,150	164,694	188,165	199,378	219,607	228,589	5,932	13,073	15,517	17,119	23,649	32,602
Illinois	5,668,566	7,113,842	8,003,782	8,659,351	9,088,501	9,512,165	166,956	620,678	797,643	939,766	988,986	1,100,032
Indiana	1,343,315	1,796,767	1,996,634	2,099,562	2,185,735	2,251,554	89,932	211,310	283,192	360,238	433,600	591,600
Iowa	740,760	921,320	1,025,119	1,096,403	1,143,991	1,156,393	34,311	146,688	346,343	502,716	758,054	1,002,405
Kansas	208,729	265,476	306,622	339,399	357,557	364,286	9,156	11,213	20,212	26,927	35,743	47,645
Kentucky	400,513	470,392	517,782	555,967	589,525	597,495	55,010	114,564	143,861	159,716	187,046	242,672
Louisiana	746,629	940,075	902,642	893,334	1,032,490	1,089,736	31,675	70,241	67,261	79,405	89,353	111,844
Maine	316,114	422,938	479,171	511,073	530,015	552,463	7,137	5,648	10,375	11,578	11,192	12,409
Maryland	2,205,880	3,497,182	3,965,788	4,182,593	4,547,357	4,792,089	5,354	41,717	58,081	58,370	70,854	115,071
Massachusetts	7,591,344	10,799,206	12,192,561	13,093,562	13,916,336	13,862,598	34,893	64,126	68,934	88,955	103,384	118,526
Michigan	995,384	1,327,051	1,433,884	1,532,229	1,563,761	1,638,367	25,340	55,391	72,457	84,783	100,224	120,070
Minnesota	1,004,427	1,297,457	1,446,858	1,542,479	1,626,949	1,622,869	123,571	325,758	547,492	685,848	784,964	928,396
Mississippi	150,123	178,142	195,996	205,197	221,582	225,484	†	8,369	19,908	24,669	16,466	21,061
Missouri	2,144,299	3,128,635	3,486,983	3,671,592	3,864,444	3,958,548	100,307	196,447	336,966	344,635	277,715	331,391
Montana	69,426	91,446	97,769	102,845	104,336	116,161	†	†	†	†	†	†
Nebraska	387,569	557,724	637,536	687,153	699,561	709,182	12,051	25,524	36,084	36,176	34,999	42,559
Nevada	7,006	9,637	30,311	37,411	43,433	73,701	29,278	104,949	119,143	123,251	118,434	143,358
New Hampshire	589,823	883,914	992,159	1,071,230	1,073,128	1,085,570	21,831	41,599	50,844	48,467	47,523	36,737
New Jersey	1,362,090	1,873,156	2,143,312	2,300,613	2,472,048	2,591,234	61,109	85,429	89,642	91,612	115,467	126,833
New Mexico	54,280	54,076	59,510	60,922	31,149	30,447	25,806	35,073	40,065	45,591	111,888	83,708
New York	12,519,671	17,680,790	20,111,046	21,721,660	22,892,724	23,511,385	326,329	624,764	685,646	667,775	718,608	762,214
North Carolina	3,530,337	4,808,306	5,540,302	5,904,228	6,272,149	6,452,783	4,041	38,078	62,947	76,722	116,192	186,514
North Dakota	56,000	88,860	95,061	97,781	94,477	87,938	1,145	7,885	6,135	12,014	14,835	20,198
Ohio	2,211,035	3,017,764	3,334,147	3,431,802	3,551,098	3,582,655	122,531	232,685	316,518	367,147	437,588	564,498
Oklahoma	338,276	392,427	463,629	479,382	515,934	523,630	32,527	72,537	76,520	85,333	103,780	110,336
Oregon	456,683	550,322	620,302	671,348	706,683	734,883	23,175	86,156	98,436	101,677	118,604	120,490
Pennsylvania	7,590,629	9,960,675	11,252,008	12,039,799	12,681,659	13,154,197	306,135	530,515	640,768	677,975	706,505	842,052
Rhode Island	828,715	1,237,106	1,367,600	1,468,749	1,554,627	1,564,624	4,519	10,073	10,278	9,076	7,084	†
South Carolina	408,127	563,952	605,736	763,573	786,592	680,369	6,627	18,374	31,925	53,667	69,377	226,848
South Dakota	69,555	99,575	111,659	117,465	117,711	119,974	18,061	23,477	31,541	30,502	30,354	41,594
Tennessee	1,971,564	3,140,336	3,717,946	3,970,594	4,262,494	4,500,016	50,921	142,256	186,957	211,102	245,140	331,287
Texas	2,490,597	3,379,710	3,718,549	4,002,023	4,283,965	4,376,280	172,327	343,221	413,618	481,695	677,625	803,401
Utah	648,035	867,956	935,899	971,056	962,042	1,012,997	36,348	62,880	78,794	103,675	115,801	144,226
Vermont	347,293	510,623	620,608	670,263	762,710	717,199	24,841	24,914	24,088	23,478	24,079	17,126
Virginia	944,905	1,311,743	1,503,421	1,587,241	1,686,972	1,841,075	65,804	258,642	350,179	380,405	443,621	614,287
Washington	600,315	778,678	847,942	921,089	964,938	988,571	51,134	104,107	117,630	123,645	140,546	161,645
West Virginia	170,653	181,181	184,220	201,405	201,699	211,877	17,926	28,634	64,316	90,811	121,720	165,043
Wisconsin	999,502	1,410,625	1,628,880	1,759,315	1,889,964	1,929,430	16,333	36,044	67,990	81,610	102,556	131,140
Wyoming	†	†	†	†	†	†	19,766	34,596	37,195	39,235	36,535	39,869
Other jurisdictions..	431,216	615,990	661,324	726,558	727,264	742,820	56,116	70,535	86,526	105,094	116,452	116,452
Guam	†	1,535	2,797	2,091	3,680	2,551	†	†	†	†	†	†
Puerto Rico	431,216	614,455	658,526	724,467	723,583	740,269	56,116	70,535	86,526	105,094	116,452	116,452

†Not applicable.
NOTE: Degree-granting institutions grant associate's or higher degrees and participate in Title IV federal financial aid programs. Detail may not sum to totals because of rounding.

SOURCE: U.S. Department of Education, National Center for Education Statistics, Integrated Postsecondary Education Data System (IPEDS), Spring 2001 through Spring 2011, Finance component. (This table was prepared February 2012.)

623

Employees in degree-granting institutions, by sex, employment status, control and level of institution, and primary occupation: Selected years, fall 1989 through fall 2009

Sex, employment status, control and level of institution, and primary occupation	1989	1991	1993	1995	1997	1999	2001	2003	2005	2007	2009	Percent change, 1999 to 2009
1	2	3	4	5	6	7	8	9	10	11	12	13
All institutions	2,473,116	2,545,235	2,602,612	2,662,075	2,752,504	2,883,175	3,083,353	3,187,907	3,379,087	3,561,428	3,723,419	29.1
Professional staff	1,531,071	1,595,460	1,687,287	1,744,867	1,835,916	1,950,861	2,132,150	2,268,268	2,459,885	2,629,401	2,782,149	42.6
Executive/administrative/managerial	144,670	144,755	143,675	147,445	151,363	159,888	152,038	184,913	196,324	217,518	230,579	44.2
Faculty (instruction/research/public service)	824,220	826,252	915,474	931,706	989,813	1,027,830	1,113,183	1,173,593	1,290,426	1,371,390	1,439,144	40.0
Graduate assistants	163,298	197,751	202,819	215,909	222,724	239,738	261,136	292,061	317,141	328,979	342,393	42.8
Other professional	398,883	426,702	425,319	449,807	472,016	523,405	605,793	617,701	655,994	711,514	770,033	47.1
Nonprofessional staff	942,045	949,775	915,325	917,208	916,588	932,314	951,203	919,639	919,202	932,027	941,270	1.0
Males	1,212,924	1,227,591	1,256,037	1,274,676	1,315,311	1,365,812	1,451,773	1,496,867	1,581,498	1,650,350	1,709,636	25.2
Professional staff	880,766	895,591	930,933	946,134	982,870	1,026,882	1,105,053	1,160,417	1,240,030	1,302,131	1,353,915	31.8
Executive/administrative/managerial	87,951	85,423	82,748	82,127	81,931	83,883	79,348	91,604	95,223	102,258	106,892	27.4
Faculty (instruction/research/public service)	534,254	525,599	561,123	562,893	587,420	602,469	644,514	663,723	714,453	743,812	761,035	26.3
Graduate assistants	98,887	119,125	120,384	123,962	125,873	132,607	142,120	156,881	167,529	173,121	180,941	36.4
Other professional	159,674	165,444	166,678	177,152	187,646	207,923	239,071	248,209	262,825	282,940	305,047	46.7
Nonprofessional staff	332,158	332,000	325,104	328,542	332,441	338,930	346,720	336,450	341,468	348,219	355,721	5.0
Females	1,260,192	1,317,644	1,346,575	1,387,399	1,437,193	1,517,363	1,631,580	1,691,040	1,797,589	1,911,078	2,013,783	32.7
Professional staff	650,305	699,869	756,354	798,733	853,046	923,979	1,027,097	1,107,851	1,219,855	1,327,270	1,428,234	54.6
Executive/administrative/managerial	56,719	59,332	60,927	65,318	69,432	76,005	72,690	93,309	101,101	115,260	123,687	62.7
Faculty (instruction/research/public service)	289,966	300,653	354,351	368,813	402,393	425,361	468,669	509,870	575,973	627,578	678,109	59.4
Graduate assistants	64,411	78,626	82,435	91,947	96,851	107,131	119,016	135,180	149,612	155,858	161,452	50.7
Other professional	239,209	261,258	258,641	272,655	284,370	315,482	366,722	369,492	393,169	428,574	464,986	47.4
Nonprofessional staff	609,887	617,775	590,221	588,666	584,147	593,384	604,483	583,189	577,734	583,808	585,549	-1.3
Full-time	1,779,044	1,812,912	1,783,510	1,801,371	1,828,507	1,918,676	2,043,208	2,083,142	2,179,864	2,281,223	2,381,702	24.1
Professional staff	1,000,396	1,031,797	1,039,094	1,066,510	1,104,834	1,180,173	1,283,684	1,337,568	1,432,107	1,526,823	1,619,517	37.2
Executive/administrative/managerial	138,454	139,116	137,834	140,990	144,529	153,722	146,523	178,691	190,078	210,257	222,282	44.6
Faculty (instruction/research/public service)	524,426	535,623	545,706	550,822	568,719	590,937	617,868	630,092	675,624	703,463	728,977	23.4
Other professional	337,516	357,058	355,554	374,698	391,586	435,514	519,293	528,785	566,405	613,103	668,258	53.4
Nonprofessional staff	778,648	781,115	744,416	734,861	723,673	738,503	759,524	745,574	747,757	754,400	762,185	3.2
Part-time	694,072	732,323	819,102	860,704	923,997	964,499	1,040,145	1,104,765	1,199,223	1,280,205	1,341,717	39.1
Professional staff	530,675	563,663	648,193	678,357	731,082	770,688	848,466	930,700	1,027,778	1,102,578	1,162,632	50.9
Executive/administrative/managerial	6,216	5,639	5,841	6,455	6,834	6,166	5,515	6,222	6,246	7,261	8,297	34.6
Faculty (instruction/research/public service)	299,794	290,629	369,768	380,884	421,094	436,893	495,315	543,501	614,802	667,927	710,167	62.5
Graduate assistants	163,298	197,751	202,819	215,909	222,724	239,738	261,136	292,061	317,141	328,979	342,393	42.8
Other professional	61,367	69,644	69,765	75,109	80,430	87,891	86,500	88,916	89,589	98,411	101,775	15.8
Nonprofessional staff	163,397	168,660	170,909	182,347	192,915	193,811	191,679	174,065	171,445	177,627	179,085	-7.6
Public 4-year	1,307,524	1,341,914	1,333,533	1,383,476	1,418,661	1,470,842	1,558,576	1,569,870	1,656,709	1,741,699	1,803,724	22.6
Professional staff	791,319	826,633	855,913	893,345	932,972	987,622	1,069,161	1,115,312	1,200,168	1,278,894	1,336,958	35.4
Executive/administrative/managerial	64,343	63,674	59,678	60,590	61,984	64,336	60,245	70,397	74,241	81,364	84,355	31.1
Faculty (instruction/research/public service)	350,720	358,376	374,021	384,399	404,109	417,086	438,459	450,123	486,691	518,221	539,901	29.4
Graduate assistants	131,970	144,344	170,916	178,342	182,481	196,393	218,260	239,600	257,578	266,429	275,872	40.5
Other professional	244,286	260,239	251,298	270,014	284,398	309,807	352,197	355,192	381,658	412,880	436,830	41.0
Nonprofessional staff	516,205	515,281	477,620	490,131	485,689	483,220	489,415	454,558	456,541	462,805	466,766	-3.4
Private 4-year	722,841	734,509	762,034	770,004	786,634	857,820	912,924	988,895	1,073,764	1,157,226	1,229,784	43.4
Professional staff	431,403	442,524	473,372	495,383	517,485	569,579	627,364	701,244	789,179	867,234	934,298	64.0
Executive/administrative/managerial	57,861	57,148	59,230	62,314	62,580	69,626	65,739	84,306	90,415	103,183	111,616	60.3
Faculty (instruction/research/public service)	232,980	232,893	251,948	262,660	278,541	296,737	325,713	364,166	430,305	472,628	498,582	68.0
Graduate assistants	22,231	23,989	28,880	33,853	36,064	38,597	41,611	52,101	59,147	62,550	66,521	72.3
Other professional	118,331	128,494	133,314	136,556	140,300	164,619	194,301	200,671	209,312	228,873	257,579	56.5
Nonprofessional staff	291,438	291,985	288,662	274,621	269,149	288,241	285,560	287,651	284,585	289,992	295,486	2.5
Public 2-year	413,245	441,414	478,980	482,454	512,086	517,967	578,394	593,466	610,978	620,784	638,352	23.2
Professional staff	287,418	306,631	337,371	336,661	358,367	364,703	408,792	422,756	440,536	449,372	467,760	28.3
Executive/administrative/managerial	19,289	20,772	21,531	21,806	22,822	21,459	22,566	25,872	26,770	27,363	27,827	29.7
Faculty (instruction/research/public service)	226,578	222,532	276,413	272,434	290,451	296,239	332,665	341,643	354,497	358,925	373,778	26.2
Graduate assistants	8,928	29,216	2,762	3,401	3,561	4,170	1,215	323	374	0	0	-100.0
Other professional	32,623	34,111	36,665	39,020	41,533	42,835	52,346	54,918	58,895	63,084	66,155	54.4
Nonprofessional staff	125,827	134,783	141,609	145,793	153,719	153,264	169,602	170,710	170,442	171,412	170,592	11.3
Private 2-year	29,506	27,398	28,065	26,141	35,123	36,546	33,459	35,676	37,636	41,719	51,559	41.1
Professional staff	20,931	19,672	20,631	19,478	27,092	28,957	26,833	28,956	30,002	33,901	43,133	49.0
Executive/administrative/managerial	3,177	3,161	3,236	2,735	3,977	4,467	3,488	4,338	4,898	5,608	6,781	51.8
Faculty (instruction/research/public service)	13,942	12,451	13,092	12,213	16,712	17,768	16,346	17,661	18,933	21,616	26,883	51.3
Graduate assistants	169	202	261	313	618	578	50	37	42	0	0	-100.0
Other professional	3,643	3,858	4,042	4,217	5,785	6,144	6,949	6,920	6,129	6,677	9,469	54.1
Nonprofessional staff	8,575	7,726	7,434	6,663	8,031	7,589	6,626	6,720	7,634	7,818	8,426	11.0

NOTE: Data through 1995 are for institutions of higher education, while later data are for degree-granting institutions. Degree-granting institutions grant associate's or higher degrees and participate in Title IV federal financial aid programs. The degree-granting classification is very similar to the earlier higher education classification, but it includes more 2-year colleges and excludes a few higher education institutions that did not grant degrees. (See Appendix A: Guide to Sources for details.) Beginning in 2007, includes institutions with fewer than 15 full-time employees; these institutions did not report staff data prior to 2007. By definition, all graduate assistants are part time.
SOURCE: U.S. Department of Education, National Center for Education Statistics, Integrated Postsecondary Education Data System (IPEDS), "Fall Staff Survey" (IPEDS-S:89–99); and IPEDS Winter 2001–02 through Winter 2009–10, Human Resources component, Fall Staff section. (This table was prepared August 2010.)

Full-time instructional faculty in degree-granting institutions, by race/ethnicity, sex, and academic rank: Fall 2005, fall 2007, and fall 2009

| Sex and academic rank | Total | White | Selected racial/ethnic groups | | | | | | Race/ethnicity unknown | Nonresident alien[3] |
			Number[1]	Percent[2]	Black	Hispanic	Asian/Pacific Islander	American Indian/Alaska Native		
1	2	3	4	5	6	7	8	9	10	11
2005										
Total...........................	675,624	527,900	109,964	16.5	35,458	22,818	48,457	3,231	9,703	28,057
Professors...........................	169,192	145,936	20,856	12.4	5,484	3,793	11,060	519	1,014	1,386
Associate professors..................	138,444	112,507	22,429	16.4	7,402	4,319	10,144	564	1,296	2,212
Assistant professors..................	159,689	114,470	31,253	19.9	9,897	5,728	14,922	706	2,809	11,157
Instructors...........................	98,555	76,359	18,368	19.0	7,462	5,261	4,740	905	1,853	1,975
Lecturers............................	27,215	20,982	4,342	16.2	1,286	1,233	1,714	109	480	1,411
Other faculty........................	82,529	57,646	12,716	15.8	3,927	2,484	5,877	428	2,251	9,916
2007										
Total...........................	703,463	540,460	119,906	17.3	37,930	24,975	53,661	3,340	11,875	31,222
Professors...........................	173,395	147,867	22,734	13.2	5,839	4,128	12,239	528	1,309	1,485
Associate professors..................	143,692	115,274	24,255	17.1	7,855	4,714	11,082	604	1,628	2,535
Assistant professors..................	168,508	117,618	34,940	21.2	10,642	6,329	17,290	679	3,593	12,357
Instructors...........................	101,429	77,609	19,470	19.7	7,480	5,800	5,225	965	2,350	2,000
Lecturers............................	31,264	23,470	5,326	17.4	1,602	1,492	2,081	151	661	1,807
Other faculty........................	85,175	58,622	13,181	15.9	4,512	2,512	5,744	413	2,334	11,038
Males...........................	409,115	314,375	67,147	16.7	17,782	13,468	34,178	1,719	6,660	20,933
Professors...........................	127,488	108,404	16,882	13.3	3,646	2,874	10,018	344	973	1,229
Associate professors..................	86,660	68,982	14,760	17.2	4,110	2,768	7,570	312	1,038	1,880
Assistant professors..................	88,741	60,407	18,207	21.0	4,607	3,265	10,037	298	1,945	8,182
Instructors...........................	46,599	35,795	8,665	19.0	2,928	2,782	2,463	492	1,066	1,073
Lecturers............................	14,784	11,045	2,367	16.4	721	613	956	77	347	1,025
Other faculty........................	44,843	29,742	6,266	14.4	1,770	1,166	3,134	196	1,291	7,544
Females...........................	294,348	226,085	52,759	18.2	20,148	11,507	19,483	1,621	5,215	10,289
Professors...........................	45,907	39,463	5,852	12.8	2,193	1,254	2,221	184	336	256
Associate professors..................	57,032	46,292	9,495	16.8	3,745	1,946	3,512	292	590	655
Assistant professors..................	79,767	57,211	16,733	21.4	6,035	3,064	7,253	381	1,648	4,175
Instructors...........................	54,830	41,814	10,805	20.2	4,552	3,018	2,762	473	1,284	927
Lecturers............................	16,480	12,425	2,959	18.3	881	879	1,125	74	314	782
Other faculty........................	40,332	28,880	6,915	17.6	2,742	1,346	2,610	217	1,043	3,494
2009										
Total...........................	728,977	551,271	130,903	18.4	39,715	28,040	59,691	3,457	16,058	30,745
Professors...........................	177,581	149,568	24,633	14.0	6,086	4,683	13,284	580	1,923	1,457
Associate professors..................	148,981	117,270	26,779	18.3	8,163	5,383	12,632	601	2,387	2,545
Assistant professors..................	171,639	117,892	37,199	22.3	10,979	6,789	18,712	719	4,617	11,931
Instructors...........................	104,521	78,329	20,951	20.7	7,806	6,577	5,566	1,002	3,396	1,845
Lecturers............................	33,332	24,895	5,851	18.0	1,812	1,583	2,318	138	882	1,704
Other faculty........................	92,923	63,317	15,490	17.2	4,869	3,025	7,179	417	2,853	11,263
Males...........................	415,821	314,712	71,889	17.7	18,026	14,865	37,261	1,737	8,973	20,247
Professors...........................	127,931	107,315	18,013	14.2	3,755	3,209	10,684	365	1,405	1,198
Associate professors..................	87,965	68,747	15,935	18.4	4,180	3,096	8,338	321	1,497	1,786
Assistant professors..................	88,665	59,607	18,954	22.0	4,568	3,422	10,658	306	2,477	7,627
Instructors...........................	46,762	35,137	9,003	19.9	2,880	3,078	2,568	477	1,583	1,039
Lecturers............................	15,724	11,702	2,620	17.2	822	650	1,084	64	466	936
Other faculty........................	48,774	32,204	7,364	15.6	1,821	1,410	3,929	204	1,545	7,661
Females...........................	313,156	236,559	59,014	19.3	21,689	13,175	22,430	1,720	7,085	10,498
Professors...........................	49,650	42,253	6,620	13.5	2,331	1,474	2,600	215	518	259
Associate professors..................	61,016	48,523	10,844	18.0	3,983	2,287	4,294	280	890	759
Assistant professors..................	82,974	58,285	18,245	22.6	6,411	3,367	8,054	413	2,140	4,304
Instructors...........................	57,759	43,192	11,948	21.4	4,926	3,499	2,998	525	1,813	806
Lecturers............................	17,608	13,193	3,231	18.8	990	933	1,234	74	416	768
Other faculty........................	44,149	31,113	8,126	19.0	3,048	1,615	3,250	213	1,308	3,602

[1]Combined number of Black, Hispanic, Asian/Pacific Islander, and American Indian/Alaska Native faculty.
[2]Combined Black, Hispanic, Asian/Pacific Islander, and American Indian/Alaska Native faculty as a percentage of total faculty, excluding race/ethnicity unknown.
[3]Race/ethnicity not collected.
NOTE: Degree-granting institutions grant associate's or higher degrees and participate in Title IV federal financial aid programs. Beginning in 2007, includes institutions with fewer than 15 full-time employees; these institutions did not report staff data prior to 2007. Race categories exclude persons of Hispanic ethnicity. Totals may differ from figures reported in other tables because of varying survey methodologies.
SOURCE: U.S. Department of Education, National Center for Education Statistics, Integrated Postsecondary Education Data System (IPEDS), Winter 2005–06, Winter 2007–08, and Winter 2009–10, Human Resources component, Fall Staff section. (This table was prepared August 2010.)

Average salary of full-time instructional faculty on 9-month contracts in degree-granting institutions, by sex, academic rank, and control and level of institution: Selected years, 1999–2000 through 2010–11

Academic year, control and level of institution	Constant 2009–10 dollars[1] All faculty, total	Current dollars — All faculty Total	Males	Females	Academic rank — Professor Total	Males	Females	Associate professor Total	Males	Females	Assistant professor	Instructor	Lecturer	No academic rank
1	2	3	4	5	6	7	8	9	10	11	12	13	14	15
1999–2000														
All institutions	$71,550	$55,888	$60,084	$48,997	$74,410	$76,478	$67,079	$54,524	$55,939	$52,091	$44,978	$34,918	$38,194	$47,389
Public	70,428	55,011	58,984	48,714	72,475	74,501	65,568	54,641	55,992	52,305	45,285	35,007	37,403	47,990
4-year	74,190	57,950	62,030	50,168	75,204	76,530	69,619	55,681	56,776	53,599	45,822	33,528	37,261	40,579
Doctoral[2]	79,698	62,253	66,882	52,287	81,182	82,445	74,653	57,744	58,999	55,156	48,190	33,345	38,883	39,350
Master's[3]	67,562	52,773	55,565	48,235	66,588	67,128	64,863	53,048	53,686	51,977	43,396	33,214	34,448	43,052
Other 4-year	61,282	47,867	49,829	44,577	60,360	60,748	59,052	49,567	50,133	48,548	42,306	35,754	36,088	38,330
2-year	61,759	48,240	50,033	46,340	57,806	59,441	55,501	48,056	49,425	46,711	41,984	37,634	40,061	48,233
Not-for-profit	74,474	58,172	62,788	49,881	78,512	80,557	70,609	54,300	55,836	51,687	44,423	34,670	40,761	41,415
4-year	74,798	58,425	63,028	50,117	78,604	80,622	70,774	54,388	55,898	51,809	44,502	34,813	40,783	41,761
Doctoral[2]	92,015	71,873	77,214	59,586	95,182	96,768	87,342	62,503	63,951	59,536	52,134	39,721	42,693	45,887
Master's[3]	63,848	49,871	52,642	45,718	62,539	63,603	59,353	50,176	51,470	48,165	41,447	33,991	37,923	44,153
Other 4-year	59,885	46,776	48,847	43,544	60,200	60,757	58,364	46,822	47,135	46,365	38,775	31,574	33,058	35,120
2-year	48,116	37,583	39,933	34,733	39,454	38,431	40,571	36,349	37,342	35,608	31,818	27,696	25,965	40,373
For-profit	37,823	29,543	30,023	28,942	45,505	44,248	49,693	48,469	53,548	43,389	33,043	29,894	—	27,958
2005–06														
All institutions	72,072	66,172	71,569	58,665	91,208	94,733	81,514	65,714	67,654	62,860	55,106	50,883	45,896	50,425
Public	69,879	64,158	69,191	57,462	87,599	91,080	78,412	65,107	67,077	62,231	55,029	52,297	44,628	50,096
4-year	74,010	67,951	73,353	59,437	91,600	93,976	83,946	66,745	68,475	64,013	56,181	40,044	44,598	47,107
Doctoral[2]	80,048	73,495	79,688	62,509	99,872	101,856	91,960	70,008	71,991	66,659	59,471	39,863	45,222	46,201
Master's[3]	65,833	60,444	63,659	56,157	77,752	78,677	75,547	62,029	62,967	60,706	52,419	39,542	43,502	45,640
Other 4-year	60,672	55,705	58,157	52,490	71,469	73,188	68,141	58,817	59,957	57,061	49,749	42,185	43,951	51,863
2-year	60,345	55,405	56,858	54,082	65,740	67,782	63,544	54,970	55,825	54,004	48,425	57,224	45,427	50,513
Not-for-profit	77,552	71,203	77,136	61,985	98,253	101,638	88,144	66,877	68,753	64,074	55,278	41,302	49,777	53,231
4-year	77,787	71,419	77,314	62,212	98,378	101,713	88,379	66,981	68,818	64,226	55,367	41,494	49,786	53,907
Doctoral[2]	94,041	86,342	93,646	72,638	119,187	121,728	109,444	76,945	79,224	73,038	65,038	45,862	51,110	55,289
Master's[3]	64,313	59,048	61,984	55,245	74,334	75,769	71,081	59,962	61,026	58,545	49,804	40,446	45,173	57,505
Other 4-year	62,532	57,413	59,743	54,149	74,655	75,548	72,485	57,536	57,613	57,430	47,629	38,145	45,957	44,713
2-year	42,588	39,101	38,817	39,307	47,174	48,786	45,945	42,433	43,628	41,753	35,437	36,264	38,908	39,399
For-profit	46,267	42,480	42,878	42,027	60,111	59,423	61,417	56,621	55,546	58,393	47,598	35,661	—	41,579
2009–10														
All institutions	74,625	74,625	80,885	66,653	103,684	108,227	92,835	74,126	76,401	71,019	62,246	57,797	52,177	56,807
Public	72,183	72,183	77,951	65,144	99,208	103,747	88,813	73,378	75,686	70,256	62,159	59,319	50,214	55,868
4-year	76,153	76,153	82,428	67,283	103,947	107,192	95,045	75,250	77,281	72,297	63,441	46,029	50,089	54,024
Doctoral[2]	81,853	81,853	89,189	70,310	113,060	115,828	103,784	78,536	80,826	74,960	66,898	44,406	50,283	53,166
Master's[3]	68,255	68,255	71,584	64,252	87,921	88,934	85,885	70,333	71,342	69,036	59,396	44,417	49,760	55,765
Other 4-year	61,202	61,202	63,678	58,349	76,448	79,143	72,073	65,000	66,297	63,338	55,003	54,050	49,432	54,487
2-year	62,265	62,265	63,698	61,047	72,377	74,425	70,429	60,633	61,565	59,853	54,162	65,505	53,548	56,239
Not-for-profit	80,593	80,593	87,603	70,686	112,155	116,406	101,138	75,570	77,768	72,509	62,401	47,843	57,508	62,242
4-year	80,744	80,744	87,724	70,843	112,261	116,477	101,308	75,670	77,831	72,649	62,472	47,885	57,520	62,542
Doctoral[2]	95,483	95,483	104,515	80,892	134,778	138,356	123,283	85,865	88,699	81,500	71,974	53,824	58,932	66,634
Master's[3]	65,777	65,777	68,776	62,133	82,520	84,065	79,455	66,528	67,507	65,320	55,470	45,312	53,637	60,591
Other 4-year	64,644	64,644	67,199	61,367	84,913	85,555	83,562	64,772	64,972	64,505	53,161	42,148	52,422	52,775
2-year	45,731	45,731	44,417	46,529	53,063	55,046	51,310	45,768	45,863	45,717	42,706	46,010	32,393	43,562
For-profit	54,842	54,842	56,689	52,925	79,574	81,765	75,817	71,376	72,429	70,199	66,027	41,742	—	53,705
2010–11														
All institutions	73,987	75,472	81,868	67,461	104,957	109,656	94,032	75,103	77,423	72,001	63,140	57,943	52,549	56,549
Public	71,273	72,704	78,603	65,615	100,228	104,924	89,731	74,054	76,442	70,877	62,847	59,391	50,377	55,364
4-year	75,348	76,861	83,288	67,937	105,067	108,473	95,978	75,947	78,069	72,920	64,211	46,441	50,291	54,372
Doctoral[2]	80,040	81,647	88,992	70,580	112,647	115,688	103,191	78,804	81,142	75,298	67,236	44,612	50,403	53,321
Master's[3]	66,836	68,178	71,414	64,322	87,677	88,613	85,849	70,215	71,267	68,866	59,511	44,640	50,029	55,807
Other 4-year	59,838	61,039	63,288	58,574	74,604	77,286	70,511	65,254	66,728	63,415	54,965	55,810	49,671	55,607
2-year	61,074	62,301	63,683	61,138	72,905	74,865	71,060	61,235	62,206	60,424	54,542	65,688	52,539	55,570
Not-for-profit	80,573	82,191	89,343	72,307	114,182	118,587	103,115	77,103	79,282	74,161	63,680	48,572	58,619	64,167
4-year	80,730	82,351	89,472	72,473	114,254	118,646	103,208	77,187	79,337	74,274	63,741	48,697	58,632	64,464
Doctoral[2]	93,158	95,028	104,049	81,199	133,973	137,938	122,085	86,108	88,927	82,039	72,242	53,916	59,923	67,857
Master's[3]	64,441	65,735	68,582	62,304	82,002	83,317	79,454	66,466	67,362	65,354	55,352	45,229	53,165	62,908
Other 4-year	64,404	65,697	68,117	62,685	86,543	87,256	85,114	65,751	65,815	65,669	53,803	42,233	54,894	53,293
2-year	45,435	46,347	45,419	46,923	50,623	51,107	50,013	49,984	49,009	50,483	45,786	44,653	28,967	45,095
For-profit	52,678	53,736	54,399	52,932	64,033	64,547	63,072	71,050	72,956	69,405	63,776	40,994	—	41,262

—Not available.

[1]Constant dollars based on the Consumer Price Index, prepared by the Bureau of Labor Statistics, U.S. Department of Labor, adjusted to an academic-year basis.
[2]Institutions that awarded 20 or more doctor's degrees during the previous academic year.
[3]Institutions that awarded 20 or more master's degrees, but less than 20 doctor's degrees, during the previous academic year.

NOTE: Degree-granting institutions grant associate's or higher degrees and participate in Title IV federal financial aid programs. Some data have been revised from previously published figures.
SOURCE: U.S. Department of Education, National Center for Education Statistics, Integrated Postsecondary Education Data System (IPEDS), "Salaries, Tenure, and Fringe Benefits of Full-Time Instructional Faculty Survey" (IPEDS-SA:99); and Winter 2005–06 through Winter 2010–11, Human Resources component, Salaries section. (This table was prepared February 2012.)

Average salary of full-time instructional faculty on 9-month contracts in degree-granting institutions, by control and level of institution and state or jurisdiction: 2010–11

[In current dollars]

State or jurisdiction	All institu-tions	Public institutions						Not-for-profit institutions						For-profit institutions
		Total	4-year institutions				2-year	Total	4-year institutions				2-year	
			Total	Doctoral[1]	Master's[2]	Other			Total	Doctoral[1]	Master's[2]	Other		
1	2	3	4	5	6	7	8	9	10	11	12	13	14	15
United States	$75,472	$72,704	$76,861	$81,647	$68,178	$61,039	$62,301	$82,191	$82,351	$95,028	$65,735	$65,697	$46,347	$53,736
Alabama	64,000	65,575	70,330	74,336	59,433	68,219	53,267	55,309	55,309	63,158	47,495	47,364	†	58,566
Alaska	72,433	73,092	73,040	74,712	71,888	†	79,053	56,908	56,908	†	56,908	†	†	†
Arizona	76,991	77,494	82,298	82,687	†	50,130	68,401	56,586	56,586	†	58,367	19,191	†	68,038
Arkansas	55,004	55,144	59,852	63,943	50,637	55,087	43,792	54,186	54,186	†	59,017	47,900	†	65,000
California	90,657	88,592	92,769	100,670	78,584	74,126	83,814	98,387	98,387	105,544	75,829	91,688	†	75,705
Colorado	68,957	67,790	72,336	77,240	55,243	58,584	47,721	76,910	76,910	78,550	77,380	54,998	†	43,530
Connecticut	91,881	84,513	90,198	95,055	75,910	†	68,272	99,820	99,952	107,770	82,711	78,295	59,400	45,595
Delaware	89,538	89,721	95,700	95,700	†	†	63,816	88,420	88,420	90,519	73,833	†	†	59,931
District of Columbia	94,498	83,359	83,359	110,002	79,981	†	†	95,625	95,625	96,574	56,313	†	†	63,314
Florida	70,085	68,986	70,826	78,233	66,607	57,557	54,235	73,308	73,308	83,360	64,517	56,975	†	78,233
Georgia	68,200	66,666	68,821	78,584	58,067	52,438	46,291	72,689	72,700	90,740	62,272	55,606	35,000	58,831
Hawaii	74,136	75,018	80,357	84,946	66,803	64,348	63,412	69,856	69,856	†	67,969	82,178	†	†
Idaho	58,426	59,081	61,089	62,400	†	48,164	48,862	51,407	51,407	†	50,817	51,912	†	†
Illinois	78,399	72,905	75,701	80,110	62,656	†	67,902	86,329	86,505	99,783	65,777	58,681	39,497	37,475
Indiana	71,651	71,020	75,515	81,335	60,819	54,575	44,145	73,003	73,141	84,112	59,231	62,450	44,351	41,910
Iowa	68,813	73,707	84,294	84,294	†	†	53,442	61,012	61,012	68,282	54,715	61,629	†	45,796
Kansas	62,787	65,173	71,980	77,171	55,780	56,907	50,093	47,688	47,997	52,454	49,753	43,497	40,318	69,288
Kentucky	60,471	61,689	66,877	75,544	58,594	†	48,439	55,563	55,563	61,482	50,675	59,017	†	59,204
Louisiana	64,072	61,835	65,144	70,415	56,215	47,669	48,099	74,272	74,272	80,765	53,055	56,012	†	40,667
Maine	71,239	68,071	72,078	77,773	†	57,587	53,825	76,120	76,466	60,240	51,016	87,563	61,382	†
Maryland	74,828	72,438	75,706	79,289	65,249	†	66,105	83,053	83,053	99,551	65,908	†	†	61,437
Massachusetts	93,549	74,880	80,902	90,610	71,029	†	59,353	101,803	101,825	111,567	83,212	83,773	45,863	64,196
Michigan	80,122	82,814	84,314	85,996	68,707	†	76,016	64,785	64,785	77,955	61,197	63,003	†	†
Minnesota	70,472	71,111	77,909	93,136	69,839	60,505	60,806	69,497	69,548	72,716	61,746	70,866	43,314	45,529
Mississippi	54,986	55,054	60,154	62,255	51,086	†	48,341	54,495	54,495	65,158	53,630	39,831	†	50,785
Missouri	67,031	63,838	66,855	73,549	58,533	55,376	54,583	73,064	73,319	88,532	55,868	51,584	53,621	55,970
Montana	56,769	58,274	60,933	63,952	54,189	47,850	42,613	47,077	48,048	†	45,993	49,462	37,444	†
Nebraska	67,292	69,688	75,297	80,505	62,298	†	51,763	60,059	60,096	71,194	51,575	54,407	49,762	†
Nevada	79,873	80,045	81,384	89,937	†	65,278	64,965	62,953	62,953	†	62,953	†	†	†
New Hampshire	80,817	78,870	85,926	94,649	72,768	81,906	54,149	84,593	84,593	97,448	58,203	62,903	†	44,704
New Jersey	93,506	92,160	99,988	102,568	93,802	†	72,532	97,109	97,109	111,043	75,489	66,295	†	58,205
New Mexico	62,456	62,129	68,549	73,452	52,612	48,596	47,492	79,473	79,473	†	79,473	†	†	†
New York	87,077	81,185	86,191	101,353	82,512	72,712	70,870	92,729	92,777	100,590	72,779	76,695	67,467	40,808
North Carolina	67,827	64,899	77,821	79,927	67,864	67,939	47,505	77,573	77,573	97,255	56,031	55,894	38,508	71,008
North Dakota	60,027	62,630	64,593	70,658	55,832	49,609	48,886	44,154	47,745	50,660	†	45,447	30,124	†
Ohio	71,407	73,515	76,943	79,623	56,555	59,442	60,275	67,040	67,091	74,786	61,121	63,906	58,219	46,490
Oklahoma	61,324	61,426	64,957	69,700	57,533	48,147	47,511	60,878	60,878	68,012	49,766	37,859	†	†
Oregon	67,897	67,199	69,479	73,344	55,909	58,912	63,906	70,115	70,115	73,527	67,178	63,268	†	†
Pennsylvania	80,874	79,050	82,470	88,521	79,949	65,110	60,709	82,983	83,283	93,361	65,487	75,142	44,154	49,558
Rhode Island	85,486	73,029	76,738	76,738	†	†	61,819	93,420	93,420	98,478	87,495	†	†	†
South Carolina	60,212	61,906	69,836	77,869	61,731	54,392	46,180	56,174	56,460	54,614	58,747	53,691	43,397	43,626
South Dakota	56,196	57,677	59,758	61,166	57,938	†	46,623	49,917	49,917	†	50,701	43,508	†	47,783
Tennessee	63,852	60,811	65,394	66,797	54,878	†	46,166	70,229	70,229	95,198	54,784	45,652	†	51,184
Texas	70,722	69,230	75,824	78,825	62,858	51,552	54,285	77,974	78,297	87,267	65,990	51,671	33,654	66,575
Utah	72,914	65,605	68,868	78,971	59,138	57,710	49,211	93,414	93,792	97,016	70,424	†	56,967	68,000
Vermont	73,040	74,519	74,519	82,053	58,802	56,624	†	71,656	74,008	†	76,400	49,394	49,879	†
Virginia	72,425	74,165	78,942	82,456	64,233	66,039	57,159	67,280	67,280	75,403	57,699	58,938	†	60,312
Washington	68,462	67,858	74,234	82,335	68,034	56,167	55,489	70,860	70,860	75,939	59,512	68,568	†	†
West Virginia	57,994	59,652	62,058	68,502	55,767	51,112	45,776	47,203	47,203	48,963	47,155	45,309	†	58,000
Wisconsin	70,645	72,463	71,904	81,873	58,821	99,657	73,574	63,738	63,897	71,998	57,115	58,553	49,920	†
Wyoming	69,880	69,880	80,026	80,026	†	†	57,937	†	†	†	†	†	†	†
U.S. Service Academies	105,651	105,651	105,651	†	†	105,651	†	†	†	†	†	†	†	†
Other jurisdictions	60,213	60,632	65,108	71,285	64,051	59,622	35,069	28,141	28,141	36,720	24,348	13,126	†	†
American Samoa	30,129	30,129	†	†	†	†	30,129	†	†	†	†	†	†	†
Federated States of Micronesia	22,045	22,045	†	†	†	†	22,045	†	†	†	†	†	†	†
Guam	59,493	59,493	64,862	†	64,862	†	51,515	†	†	†	†	†	†	†
Marshall Islands	31,924	31,924	†	†	†	†	31,924	†	†	†	†	†	†	†
Northern Marianas	42,165	42,165	42,165	†	†	42,165	†	†	†	†	†	†	†	†
Palau	†	†	†	†	†	†	†	†	†	†	†	†	†	†
Puerto Rico	65,114	65,803	65,803	71,285	†	60,366	†	28,141	28,141	36,720	24,348	13,126	†	†
U.S. Virgin Islands	63,031	63,031	63,031	†	63,031	†	†	†	†	†	†	†	†	†

†Not applicable.
[1]Institutions that awarded 20 or more doctor's degrees during the previous academic year.
[2]Institutions that awarded 20 or more master's degrees, but less than 20 doctor's degrees, during the previous academic year.

NOTE: Degree-granting institutions grant associate's or higher degrees and participate in Title IV federal financial aid programs. Data include imputations for nonrespondent institutions.
SOURCE: U.S. Department of Education, National Center for Education Statistics, Integrated Postsecondary Education Data System (IPEDS), Winter 2010–11, Human Resources component, Salaries section. (This table was prepared February 2012.)

Average salary of full-time instructional faculty on 9-month contracts in 4-year degree-granting institutions, by control and level of institution, academic rank of faculty, and state or jurisdiction: 2010–11
[In current dollars]

State or jurisdiction	Public doctoral[1]			Public master's[2]			Not-for-profit doctoral[1]			Not-for-profit master's[2]		
	Professor	Associate professor	Assistant professor	Professor	Associate professor	Assistant professor	Professor	Associate professor	Assistant professor	Professor	Associate professor	Assistant professor
1	2	3	4	5	6	7	8	9	10	11	12	13
United States	$112,647	$78,804	$67,236	$87,677	$70,215	$59,511	$133,973	$86,108	$72,242	$82,002	$66,466	$55,352
Alabama	106,204	75,837	60,725	75,454	63,379	53,060	82,866	67,500	54,512	56,749	50,049	43,350
Alaska	100,107	76,323	64,247	95,949	75,221	64,476	†	†	†	72,243	58,845	51,373
Arizona	113,769	80,422	68,620	†	†	†	†	†	†	81,866	73,700	62,597
Arkansas	90,884	66,061	59,576	63,615	56,709	48,054	†	†	†	72,241	59,213	51,823
California	128,650	84,807	75,478	94,349	75,224	65,805	139,503	93,594	78,579	92,556	74,841	64,893
Colorado	106,155	80,453	66,985	70,907	58,414	51,772	114,349	75,615	66,770	103,444	66,421	56,704
Connecticut	122,151	88,200	69,375	91,244	73,373	59,184	155,259	85,718	74,387	108,158	83,699	67,672
Delaware	132,536	88,023	75,801	†	†	†	128,149	92,732	69,413	80,971	74,876	60,952
District of Columbia	145,545	108,679	91,916	97,384	76,455	61,399	135,471	92,910	75,181	65,385	57,525	48,743
Florida	108,825	75,841	67,164	95,085	75,189	59,946	117,940	76,960	67,705	85,419	68,868	55,571
Georgia	109,200	77,220	67,852	76,152	62,391	53,565	129,410	82,333	69,045	68,099	59,950	50,741
Hawaii	107,232	81,808	69,302	82,159	70,445	61,298	†	†	†	87,389	72,807	62,992
Idaho	81,885	63,618	55,308	†	†	†	†	†	†	61,376	51,413	42,108
Illinois	113,523	76,519	69,443	85,475	68,240	60,729	145,436	86,633	76,270	77,640	66,515	56,418
Indiana	113,533	77,607	67,847	81,798	64,267	57,507	117,352	77,119	65,591	73,398	61,157	51,286
Iowa	113,966	79,277	69,273	†	†	†	90,143	65,925	56,123	66,840	56,090	48,962
Kansas	106,419	74,699	61,254	73,097	57,958	52,853	61,876	49,368	48,305	56,739	50,921	46,441
Kentucky	103,492	73,445	64,563	80,188	62,897	53,585	76,119	57,032	53,767	59,519	51,392	44,877
Louisiana	97,985	71,924	60,982	73,399	61,331	52,813	117,925	81,636	65,644	64,948	54,230	48,908
Maine	96,898	74,437	62,298	†	†	†	79,432	65,809	57,494	64,561	53,125	46,609
Maryland	110,698	82,422	70,008	85,181	67,810	60,595	142,660	92,862	84,569	75,949	66,360	55,806
Massachusetts	117,458	88,657	71,695	84,467	68,458	59,386	154,016	96,578	83,417	113,069	80,745	64,795
Michigan	115,789	81,020	68,591	84,539	71,505	58,883	103,608	76,811	64,491	72,699	58,786	52,050
Minnesota	125,935	84,041	78,713	85,016	68,346	59,246	95,038	71,980	60,457	73,661	62,257	53,474
Mississippi	89,626	67,849	58,905	63,285	54,599	49,801	82,021	61,929	58,152	68,871	52,944	48,189
Missouri	98,340	71,009	60,835	74,080	60,137	51,373	127,438	77,590	67,573	68,912	58,747	49,387
Montana	80,669	62,958	56,570	66,665	58,382	50,476	†	†	†	53,465	46,929	41,779
Nebraska	107,068	76,889	67,121	76,792	63,384	52,066	99,033	68,365	58,936	61,489	52,455	46,392
Nevada	120,344	87,006	70,423	†	†	†	†	†	†	75,352	56,770	55,854
New Hampshire	115,189	88,429	73,457	87,179	71,350	59,521	128,234	82,670	65,821	67,711	60,756	53,681
New Jersey	138,071	95,731	77,716	116,282	91,600	75,028	153,173	90,131	75,835	95,608	81,943	61,954
New Mexico	94,635	69,948	61,162	62,267	55,033	47,025	†	†	†	†	†	†
New York	132,245	92,938	75,625	106,454	81,744	68,632	141,597	92,427	76,693	92,069	73,265	60,607
North Carolina	114,564	79,431	68,643	88,809	71,968	61,670	142,299	86,922	70,471	67,926	57,967	51,218
North Dakota	93,229	75,435	64,901	76,323	58,922	52,944	58,303	54,795	48,061	†	†	†
Ohio	109,821	77,519	65,246	70,168	59,307	52,511	102,623	73,543	61,432	74,796	61,876	50,544
Oklahoma	99,188	70,341	59,900	72,234	59,920	53,756	87,457	68,796	55,629	58,434	52,825	43,840
Oregon	98,404	75,140	66,453	69,237	55,782	45,296	96,323	69,599	59,957	86,529	63,501	56,394
Pennsylvania	124,269	87,733	70,475	104,323	83,299	67,009	130,892	87,562	73,753	82,570	68,058	57,795
Rhode Island	95,728	73,310	60,576	†	†	†	139,676	81,728	73,101	106,666	88,583	70,635
South Carolina	106,617	77,235	68,288	79,125	64,349	55,759	65,095	50,629	44,648	76,463	58,475	50,395
South Dakota	82,285	64,845	56,467	78,649	62,551	53,227	†	†	†	63,376	52,522	47,169
Tennessee	89,136	67,556	56,724	69,719	55,688	48,071	130,594	85,829	69,230	65,027	57,523	48,856
Texas	113,745	78,610	67,872	82,310	66,883	59,197	118,239	82,877	71,221	85,836	65,764	53,761
Utah	102,537	73,684	67,278	71,850	61,069	53,851	122,338	90,647	80,729	84,552	69,072	61,618
Vermont	113,433	84,598	70,846	70,003	55,793	44,437	†	†	†	102,350	70,183	61,591
Virginia	115,077	80,355	65,926	80,741	65,613	56,860	105,350	76,103	58,479	69,779	58,000	50,634
Washington	106,800	79,300	71,704	83,418	68,502	64,013	101,557	74,921	64,363	75,050	60,109	54,762
West Virginia	88,525	68,798	57,265	68,255	58,726	49,488	64,906	52,317	44,718	55,282	49,043	43,541
Wisconsin	105,837	74,918	68,274	71,877	60,345	55,080	96,749	73,152	60,111	70,740	60,106	51,533
Wyoming	109,303	76,943	67,101	†	†	†	†	†	†	†	†	†
U.S. Service Academies	†	†	†	†	†	†	†	†	†	†	†	†
Other jurisdictions	79,697	66,119	60,726	84,242	66,417	55,448	‡	†	‡	†	†	42,120
American Samoa	†	†	†	†	†	†	†	†	†	†	†	†
Federated States of Micronesia	†	†	†	†	†	†	†	†	†	†	†	†
Guam	†	†	†	89,262	69,148	56,820	†	†	†	†	†	†
Marshall Islands	†	†	†	†	†	†	†	†	†	†	†	†
Northern Marianas	†	†	†	†	†	†	†	†	†	†	†	†
Palau	†	†	†	†	†	†	‡	†	‡	†	†	†
Puerto Rico	79,697	66,119	60,726	†	†	†	‡	†	‡	†	†	42,120
U.S. Virgin Islands	†	†	†	78,063	63,402	54,107	†	†	†	†	†	†

†Not applicable.
‡Reporting standards not met (too few cases).
[1]Institutions that awarded 20 or more doctor's degrees during the previous academic year.
[2]Institutions that awarded 20 or more master's degrees, but less than 20 doctor's degrees, during the previous academic year.

NOTE: Degree-granting institutions grant associate's or higher degrees and participate in Title IV federal financial aid programs. Data include imputations for nonrespondent institutions.
SOURCE: U.S. Department of Education, National Center for Education Statistics, Integrated Postsecondary Education Data System (IPEDS), Winter 2010–11, Human Resources component, Salaries section. (This table was prepared February 2012.)

Percentage of full-time instructional faculty with tenure for degree-granting institutions with a tenure system, by academic rank, sex, and control and level of institution: Selected years, 1993–94 through 2009–10

Academic year, control and level of institution	Percent of institutions with tenure systems	Percent of full-time instructional faculty with tenure												Instructor	Lecturer	No academic rank
		Total			Professor			Associate professor			Assistant professor					
		Total	Male	Female	Total	Male	Female	Total	Male	Female	Total	Male	Female			
1	2	3	4	5	6	7	8	9	10	11	12	13	14	15	16	17
1993–94																
All institutions..............	62.6	56.2	62.6	42.7	91.9	92.8	87.7	76.8	77.5	75.1	14.4	13.6	15.5	38.3	10.8	26.0
Public institutions	73.6	58.9	65.4	45.6	92.6	93.6	87.5	80.8	81.6	78.9	17.1	16.1	18.5	45.5	7.2	28.6
4-year......................	92.6	56.3	63.5	39.3	94.3	94.7	92.0	80.4	81.2	78.4	13.8	13.0	14.8	4.4	5.4	6.1
Doctoral[1]...............	100.0	54.5	62.1	35.0	94.2	94.7	90.1	81.3	82.1	79.2	7.3	6.7	8.3	2.8	2.1	5.4
Master's[2]...............	98.3	60.5	67.7	46.1	95.4	95.5	95.0	79.3	80.0	77.7	23.0	23.0	22.9	6.4	11.7	11.0
Other	76.4	51.1	56.3	40.0	88.4	88.8	86.4	76.5	77.3	74.8	22.7	22.8	22.6	4.6	15.0	6.4
2-year......................	62.1	69.9	75.4	63.0	80.7	83.7	75.5	84.2	86.4	81.5	47.7	51.1	44.6	68.9	39.9	65.7
Not-for-profit institutions.	62.0	49.5	56.0	35.5	90.3	90.8	88.1	67.6	68.1	66.5	9.0	8.7	9.4	6.1	21.9	18.9
4-year......................	66.3	49.5	56.0	35.4	90.3	90.8	88.0	67.6	68.1	66.5	9.0	8.7	9.4	5.5	21.6	15.7
Doctoral[1]...............	90.5	47.6	53.5	31.9	90.5	90.8	88.5	62.5	63.4	60.0	3.7	3.7	3.7	8.9	29.2	15.4
Master's[2]...............	76.5	51.8	59.2	38.2	90.8	91.1	89.8	71.3	72.2	69.6	13.4	13.6	13.1	2.6	0.7	10.5
Other	58.3	50.4	57.4	37.2	89.4	90.4	85.1	70.6	70.9	70.2	11.9	11.9	11.9	3.9	3.4	20.0
2-year......................	26.1	47.9	54.5	38.5	88.0	84.3	94.3	63.8	65.1	62.7	12.0	12.3	11.9	20.0	86.7	68.6
For-profit institutions	7.8	33.8	39.0	27.8	95.2	94.1	100.0	—	—	—	‡	‡	‡	32.9	—	—
1999–2000																
All institutions..............	55.0	53.7	59.6	43.2	92.8	93.1	91.2	76.8	76.9	76.7	11.8	11.0	12.9	34.1	3.4	18.3
Public institutions	72.8	55.9	62.0	45.6	93.9	94.4	91.9	81.0	81.2	80.7	14.1	13.1	15.4	39.8	4.1	21.2
4-year......................	94.6	53.2	60.3	39.3	94.2	94.6	92.5	80.8	81.0	80.3	10.0	9.5	10.6	3.9	3.0	4.0
Doctoral[1]...............	100.0	50.4	58.0	34.5	92.9	93.6	89.3	79.9	80.2	79.4	4.7	4.4	5.2	2.1	1.5	1.4
Master's[2]...............	95.5	59.1	66.0	48.0	96.9	96.9	96.8	82.7	83.0	82.1	18.1	17.8	18.5	6.4	5.9	25.3
Other	86.3	54.7	61.2	43.2	94.9	95.1	94.0	80.7	81.3	79.7	21.8	24.1	18.8	5.8	7.2	49.3
2-year......................	60.3	67.7	70.6	64.5	91.2	92.2	89.7	83.3	83.6	83.1	53.8	56.0	52.0	60.4	21.2	64.4
Not-for-profit institutions.	59.0	48.2	54.2	36.8	90.3	90.5	89.7	68.0	67.8	68.4	7.5	6.8	8.2	1.8	1.2	7.4
4-year......................	63.4	48.1	54.1	36.7	90.3	90.5	89.7	68.0	67.8	68.5	7.4	6.8	8.1	1.6	1.2	4.1
Doctoral[1]...............	81.2	43.4	49.6	29.6	88.6	88.7	87.6	62.6	62.8	62.2	3.0	2.8	3.2	1.0	1.3	0.5
Master's[2]...............	72.6	52.3	59.4	41.4	91.2	91.6	90.0	72.0	73.0	70.3	12.1	11.9	12.3	0.9	0.8	22.3
Other	54.9	53.5	59.3	44.0	93.5	93.8	92.8	73.1	71.2	76.0	9.9	9.4	10.5	3.6	1.6	23.5
2-year......................	14.0	59.7	63.3	53.6	96.0	96.0	96.0	57.1	61.3	54.3	31.6	36.7	28.3	30.2	—	65.8
For-profit institutions	4.0	77.4	77.2	77.6	47.4	50.0	33.3	—	—	—	—	—	—	86.1	—	71.9
2007–08																
All institutions..............	49.5	48.8	54.5	40.4	90.6	90.9	89.6	74.0	73.7	74.6	7.8	7.4	8.2	27.8	1.4	25.2
Public institutions	70.7	50.5	56.2	42.6	92.1	92.4	91.2	77.7	77.5	78.0	9.4	8.7	10.2	33.2	1.8	29.8
4-year......................	91.0	47.8	54.5	37.4	92.3	92.5	91.8	77.7	77.5	78.1	5.8	5.4	6.2	2.0	1.2	4.8
Doctoral[1]...............	100.0	46.1	53.2	33.9	90.6	91.0	89.2	75.0	74.8	75.3	2.2	2.0	2.5	1.1	0.7	1.1
Master's[2]...............	98.6	51.9	58.5	43.7	97.1	97.1	97.0	83.8	83.9	83.6	12.1	11.9	12.3	3.0	1.9	6.1
Other	71.6	49.1	53.5	43.2	92.2	93.5	89.8	81.3	81.8	80.5	16.3	17.1	15.4	5.1	3.1	41.6
2-year......................	57.4	63.6	66.7	60.7	89.7	91.1	88.3	77.6	77.9	77.4	45.3	48.7	42.6	56.2	21.8	68.1
Not-for-profit institutions.	57.5	44.7	50.9	35.2	87.5	87.9	86.4	66.8	66.2	67.9	4.7	4.8	4.6	0.6	0.3	8.5
4-year......................	60.2	44.7	50.9	35.2	87.5	87.9	86.4	66.8	66.2	67.9	4.7	4.7	4.6	0.4	0.3	8.2
Doctoral[1]...............	87.8	40.1	46.9	28.5	84.9	85.6	82.2	59.4	59.4	59.2	2.8	2.8	2.7	0.2	0.2	1.9
Master's[2]...............	66.0	49.8	56.1	41.7	89.9	90.5	88.4	73.7	73.9	73.4	8.3	8.9	7.8	0.7	0.6	18.0
Other	49.0	52.7	58.2	44.9	93.2	93.0	93.8	77.2	75.2	80.0	5.0	5.2	4.9	1.0	1.4	41.5
2-year......................	13.0	41.3	46.4	37.4	92.5	96.2	85.7	60.0	61.5	59.5	17.9	14.3	20.4	17.8	‡	51.6
For-profit institutions	1.4	51.3	58.0	42.1	77.4	77.8	76.5	23.7	35.3	8.0	16.0	23.8	10.3	77.9	‡	‡
2009–10																
All institutions..............	47.8	48.7	54.5	40.6	90.3	90.7	89.3	74.6	74.5	74.6	7.2	6.9	7.6	28.2	1.4	24.7
Public institutions	71.2	50.6	56.3	42.9	91.6	92.0	90.6	78.3	78.4	78.2	9.1	8.4	9.8	33.7	1.8	30.2
4-year......................	90.9	47.9	54.6	38.0	92.0	92.2	91.4	78.7	78.6	78.8	5.7	5.4	6.0	2.5	1.2	7.5
Doctoral[1]...............	99.5	45.7	52.9	34.1	90.2	90.6	88.6	75.6	75.7	75.4	2.4	2.2	2.6	0.9	0.7	1.6
Master's[2]...............	98.6	53.5	60.0	45.6	97.5	97.5	97.4	86.0	86.2	85.8	11.3	11.5	11.2	3.2	1.8	8.7
Other	72.4	51.2	55.5	46.1	92.2	93.3	90.2	84.6	85.0	84.0	20.5	21.4	19.6	11.8	3.0	58.7
2-year......................	57.7	64.1	67.2	61.4	88.2	89.6	86.9	74.1	75.2	73.3	45.2	48.3	42.9	58.4	22.6	67.6
Not-for-profit institutions.	57.1	44.3	50.6	35.2	87.8	88.2	86.6	67.2	67.0	67.6	3.8	3.8	3.7	0.6	0.3	7.1
4-year......................	59.5	44.3	50.6	35.2	87.8	88.2	86.7	67.2	67.0	67.6	3.8	3.8	3.7	0.5	0.3	7.0
Doctoral[1]...............	83.8	39.7	46.6	28.4	85.6	86.4	82.7	59.7	60.2	59.0	1.8	1.9	1.7	0.2	0.2	1.0
Master's[2]...............	65.8	49.8	55.7	42.4	89.7	90.1	88.8	74.0	74.1	73.8	7.2	7.6	6.8	0.7	0.2	20.4
Other	47.4	53.4	59.1	45.8	93.2	92.9	93.8	79.4	78.6	80.5	4.8	5.0	4.5	1.6	1.6	45.7
2-year......................	12.9	38.5	49.5	31.7	86.7	‡	70.0	59.3	64.7	56.8	20.5	18.5	21.4	8.2	‡	30.0
For-profit institutions	1.5	51.0	58.6	42.1	75.5	74.7	77.8	8.5	3.2	12.5	‡	‡	‡	87.3	‡	‡

—Not available.
‡Reporting standards not met (too few cases).
[1]Institutions that awarded 20 or more doctor's degrees during the previous academic year.
[2]Institutions that awarded 20 or more master's degrees, but less than 20 doctor's degrees, during the previous academic year.
NOTE: The coverage of this table differs from similar tables published in editions of the *Digest* prior to 2003. Previous tenure tabulations included only instructional staff classified as full-time faculty; this table includes all staff with full-time instructional duties, including faculty and other instructional staff. Data for 1993–94 are for institutions of higher education, while later data are for degree-granting institutions. Degree-granting institutions grant associate's or higher degrees

and participate in Title IV federal financial aid programs. The degree-granting classification is very similar to the earlier higher education classification, but it includes more 2-year colleges and excludes a few higher education institutions that did not grant degrees. (See Appendix A: Guide to Sources for details.) Beginning in 2007–08, includes institutions with fewer than 15 full-time employees; institutions with fewer than 15 employees did not report staff data prior to 2007–08. Some data have been revised from previously published figures.
SOURCE: U.S. Department of Education, National Center for Education Statistics, Integrated Postsecondary Education Data System (IPEDS), "Fall Staff Survey" (IPEDS-S:93–99); and Winter 2007–08 and Winter 2009–10, Human Resources component, Fall Staff section. (This table was prepared September 2010.)

629

Average undergraduate tuition and fees and room and board rates charged for full-time students in degree-granting institutions, by level and control of institution: 1964–65 through 2010–11

Year and control of institution	Constant 2009–10 dollars[1]			Current dollars																			
	Total tuition, fees, room, and board			Total tuition, fees, room, and board					Tuition and required fees (in-state for public institutions)					Dormitory rooms					Board (7-day basis)[2]				
	All insti-tutions	All 4-year	2-year	All insti-tutions	4-year institutions			2-year	All insti-tutions	4-year institutions			2-year	All insti-tutions	4-year institutions			2-year	All insti-tutions	4-year institutions			2-year
					All 4-year	Univer-sities	Other 4-year			All 4-year	Univer-sities	Other 4-year			All 4-year	Univer-sities	Other 4-year			All 4-year	Univer-sities	Other 4-year	
1	2	3	4	5	6	7	8	9	10	11	12	13	14	15	16	17	18	19	20	21	22	23	24
All institutions																							
1976–77	$8,402	$9,516	$5,900	$2,275	$2,577	$2,647	$2,527	$1,598	$924	$1,218	$1,210	$1,223	$346	$603	$611	$649	$584	$503	$748	$748	$788	$719	$750
1977–78	8,342	9,430	5,895	2,411	2,725	2,777	2,685	1,703	984	1,291	1,269	1,305	378	645	654	691	628	525	781	780	818	752	801
1978–79	8,184	9,230	5,784	2,587	2,917	2,967	2,879	1,828	1,073	1,397	1,370	1,413	411	688	696	737	667	575	826	825	860	800	842
1979–80	7,842	8,842	5,526	2,809	3,167	3,223	3,124	1,979	1,163	1,513	1,484	1,530	451	751	759	803	729	628	895	895	936	865	900
1980–81	7,759	8,756	5,580	3,101	3,499	3,535	3,469	2,230	1,289	1,679	1,634	1,705	526	836	846	881	821	705	976	975	1,020	943	1,000
1981–82	8,036	9,099	5,702	3,489	3,951	4,005	3,908	2,476	1,457	1,907	1,860	1,935	590	950	961	1,023	919	793	1,083	1,082	1,121	1,055	1,094
1982–83	8,561	9,729	5,992	3,877	4,406	4,466	4,356	2,713	1,626	2,139	2,081	2,173	675	1,064	1,078	1,150	1,028	873	1,187	1,189	1,235	1,155	1,165
1983–84	8,874	10,108	6,078	4,167	4,747	4,793	4,712	2,854	1,783	2,344	2,300	2,368	730	1,145	1,162	1,211	1,130	916	1,239	1,242	1,282	1,214	1,208
1984–85	9,350	10,575	6,515	4,563	5,160	5,236	5,107	3,179	1,985	2,567	2,539	2,583	821	1,267	1,282	1,343	1,242	1,058	1,310	1,311	1,353	1,282	1,301
1985–86[3]	9,729	10,963	6,706	4,885	5,504	5,597	5,441	3,367	2,181	2,784	2,770	2,793	888	1,338	1,355	1,424	1,309	1,107	1,365	1,365	1,403	1,339	1,372
1986–87	10,143	11,621	6,421	5,206	5,964	6,124	5,857	3,295	2,312	3,042	3,042	3,042	897	1,405	1,427	1,501	1,376	1,034	1,489	1,495	1,581	1,439	1,364
1987–88	10,280	11,735	6,105	5,494	6,272	6,339	6,226	3,263	2,458	3,201	3,168	3,220	809	1,488	1,516	1,576	1,478	1,017	1,549	1,555	1,596	1,529	1,437
1988–89	10,495	12,027	6,390	5,869	6,725	6,801	6,673	3,573	2,658	3,472	3,422	3,499	979	1,575	1,609	1,665	1,573	1,085	1,636	1,644	1,715	1,601	1,509
1989–90	10,595	12,309	6,324	6,207	7,212	7,347	7,120	3,705	2,839	3,800	3,765	3,819	978	1,638	1,675	1,732	1,638	1,105	1,730	1,737	1,850	1,663	1,622
1990–91	10,620	12,303	6,361	6,562	7,602	7,709	7,528	3,930	3,016	4,009	3,958	4,036	1,087	1,743	1,782	1,848	1,740	1,182	1,802	1,811	1,903	1,751	1,660
1991–92	11,098	12,918	6,417	7,077	8,238	8,390	8,142	4,092	3,286	4,385	4,368	4,394	1,189	1,874	1,921	1,996	1,875	1,210	1,918	1,931	2,026	1,872	1,692
1992–93	11,333	13,317	6,398	7,452	8,758	8,934	8,648	4,207	3,517	4,752	4,665	4,795	1,276	1,939	1,991	2,104	1,926	1,240	1,996	2,015	2,165	1,927	1,692
1993–94	11,756	13,780	6,594	7,931	9,296	9,495	9,186	4,449	3,827	5,119	5,104	5,127	1,399	2,057	2,111	2,190	2,068	1,332	2,047	2,067	2,201	1,992	1,718
1994–95	11,968	14,018	6,676	8,306	9,728	9,863	9,646	4,633	4,044	5,391	5,287	5,441	1,488	2,145	2,200	2,281	2,155	1,396	2,116	2,138	2,295	2,049	1,750
1995–96	12,345	14,491	6,628	8,800	10,330	10,560	10,195	4,725	4,338	5,786	5,733	5,812	1,522	2,264	2,318	2,423	2,260	1,473	2,199	2,226	2,404	2,123	1,730
1996–97	12,556	14,786	6,677	9,206	10,841	11,033	10,726	4,895	4,564	6,118	6,055	6,150	1,543	2,365	2,422	2,518	2,368	1,522	2,276	2,301	2,460	2,208	1,830
1997–98	12,847	15,111	6,957	9,588	11,277	11,382	11,205	5,192	4,755	6,351	6,232	6,408	1,695	2,444	2,507	2,575	2,469	1,598	2,389	2,419	2,576	2,327	1,900
1998–99	13,272	15,659	6,969	10,076	11,888	12,123	11,752	5,291	5,013	6,723	6,713	6,728	1,725	2,557	2,626	2,710	2,578	1,616	2,506	2,540	2,700	2,446	1,950
1999–2000	13,353	15,810	6,938	10,430	12,349	12,613	12,194	5,420	5,222	7,040	7,026	7,047	1,728	2,686	2,751	2,845	2,697	1,771	2,523	2,558	2,741	2,450	1,920
2000–01	13,393	15,996	6,766	10,820	12,922	13,177	12,775	5,466	5,377	7,372	7,360	7,377	1,698	2,821	2,893	2,999	2,833	1,781	2,621	2,658	2,818	2,565	1,987
2001–02	13,842	16,589	6,955	11,380	13,639	13,942	13,468	5,718	5,646	7,786	7,788	7,785	1,800	2,981	3,060	3,184	2,992	1,848	2,753	2,793	2,970	2,692	2,070
2002–03	14,298	17,185	7,441	12,014	14,439	14,827	14,233	6,252	6,002	8,309	8,406	8,264	1,903	3,179	3,263	3,377	3,201	2,077	2,832	2,867	3,044	2,767	2,272
2003–04	15,086	18,059	7,809	12,953	15,505	16,096	15,205	6,705	6,608	9,029	9,268	8,924	2,174	3,359	3,448	3,599	3,368	2,208	2,986	3,028	3,230	2,914	2,322
2004–05	15,595	18,666	8,022	13,793	16,510	17,219	16,165	7,095	7,122	9,706	10,051	9,559	2,338	3,572	3,662	3,813	3,583	2,354	3,100	3,142	3,355	3,023	2,404
2005–06	15,939	19,007	7,881	14,634	17,451	18,229	17,082	7,236	7,601	10,279	10,666	10,119	2,417	3,810	3,905	4,050	3,830	2,411	3,222	3,268	3,513	3,133	2,408
2006–07	16,438	19,611	7,926	15,483	18,471	19,304	18,085	7,466	8,092	10,931	11,404	10,738	2,496	4,019	4,116	4,261	4,041	2,527	3,372	3,424	3,640	3,306	2,443
2007–08	16,617	19,823	7,819	16,231	19,363	20,302	18,938	7,637	8,483	11,454	11,997	11,238	2,519	4,214	4,317	4,487	4,229	2,635	3,534	3,592	3,818	3,470	2,483
2008–09	17,257	20,606	8,318	17,092	20,409	21,471	19,934	8,238	8,893	12,045	12,667	11,804	2,618	4,446	4,557	4,744	4,462	2,780	3,754	3,807	4,060	3,669	2,839
2009–10	17,649	21,093	8,533	17,649	21,093	22,450	20,534	8,533	9,136	12,370	13,298	12,032	2,923	4,657	4,785	4,979	4,689	2,985	3,856	3,937	4,173	3,813	2,626
2010–11	18,133	21,657	8,734	18,497	22,092	23,634	21,479	8,909	9,598	12,967	14,090	12,565	3,095	4,874	5,015	5,197	4,927	3,077	4,025	4,111	4,348	3,988	2,737

See notes at end of table.

Average undergraduate tuition and fees and room and board rates charged for full-time students in degree-granting institutions, by level and control of institution: 1964–65 through 2010–11—Continued

	Constant 2009–10 dollars[1]			Current dollars																			
	Total tuition, fees, room, and board			Total tuition, fees, room, and board					Tuition and required fees (in-state for public institutions)					Dormitory rooms					Board (7-day basis)[2]				
					4-year institutions					4-year institutions					4-year institutions					4-year institutions			
Year and control of institution	All institutions	All 4-year	2-year	All institutions	All 4-year	Universities	Other 4-year	2-year	All institutions	All 4-year	Universities	Other 4-year	2-year	All institutions	All 4-year	Universities	Other 4-year	2-year	All institutions	All 4-year	Universities	Other 4-year	2-year
1	2	3	4	5	6	7	8	9	10	11	12	13	14	15	16	17	18	19	20	21	22	23	24
Public institutions																							
1964–65	6,592	—	4,427	950	—	1,051	867	638	243	—	298	224	99	271	—	291	241	178	436	—	462	402	361
1965–66	6,677	—	4,551	983	—	1,105	904	670	257	—	327	241	109	281	—	304	255	194	445	—	474	408	367
1966–67	6,755	—	4,675	1,026	—	1,171	947	710	275	—	360	259	121	294	—	321	271	213	457	—	490	417	376
1967–68	6,781	—	5,028	1,064	—	1,199	997	789	283	—	366	268	144	313	—	337	292	243	468	—	496	437	402
1968–69	6,788	—	5,366	1,117	—	1,245	1,063	883	295	—	377	281	170	337	—	359	318	278	485	—	509	464	435
1969–70	6,902	—	5,456	1,203	—	1,362	1,135	951	323	—	427	306	178	369	—	395	346	308	511	—	540	483	465
1970–71	7,022	—	5,445	1,287	—	1,477	1,206	998	351	—	478	332	187	401	—	431	375	338	535	—	568	499	473
1971–72	7,147	—	5,651	1,357	—	1,579	1,263	1,073	376	—	526	354	192	430	—	463	400	366	551	—	590	509	515
1972–73	7,382	—	6,060	1,458	—	1,668	1,460	1,197	407	—	566	455	233	476	—	500	455	398	575	—	602	550	566
1973–74	7,052	—	5,922	1,517	—	1,707	1,506	1,274	438	—	581	463	274	480	—	505	464	409	599	—	621	579	591
1974–75	6,541	—	5,603	1,563	—	1,760	1,558	1,339	432	—	599	448	277	506	—	527	497	424	625	—	634	613	638
1975–76	6,511	—	5,417	1,666	—	1,935	1,657	1,386	433	—	642	469	245	544	—	573	533	442	689	—	720	655	699
1976–77	6,606	7,146	5,504	1,789	1,935	2,067	1,827	1,491	479	617	689	564	283	582	592	614	572	465	728	727	763	692	742
1977–78	6,532	7,051	5,501	1,888	2,038	2,170	1,931	1,590	512	655	736	596	306	621	631	649	616	486	755	752	785	720	797
1978–79	6,308	6,786	5,350	1,994	2,145	2,289	2,027	1,691	543	688	777	622	327	655	664	689	641	527	796	793	823	764	837
1979–80	6,044	6,498	5,085	2,165	2,327	2,487	2,198	1,822	583	738	840	662	355	715	725	750	703	574	867	865	898	833	893
1980–81	5,938	6,381	5,072	2,373	2,550	2,712	2,421	2,027	635	804	915	722	391	799	811	827	796	642	940	936	969	904	994
1981–82	6,132	6,612	5,122	2,663	2,871	3,079	2,705	2,224	714	909	1,042	813	434	909	925	970	885	703	1,039	1,036	1,067	1,006	1,086
1982–83	6,502	7,058	5,277	2,945	3,196	3,403	3,032	2,390	798	1,031	1,164	936	473	1,010	1,030	1,072	993	755	1,136	1,134	1,167	1,103	1,162
1983–84	6,720	7,310	5,396	3,156	3,433	3,628	3,285	2,534	891	1,148	1,284	1,052	528	1,087	1,110	1,131	1,092	801	1,178	1,175	1,213	1,141	1,205
1984–85	6,984	7,544	5,752	3,408	3,682	3,899	3,518	2,807	971	1,228	1,386	1,117	584	1,196	1,217	1,237	1,200	921	1,241	1,237	1,276	1,201	1,302
1985–86[3]	7,113	7,685	5,937	3,571	3,859	4,146	3,637	2,981	1,045	1,318	1,536	1,157	641	1,242	1,263	1,290	1,240	960	1,285	1,278	1,320	1,240	1,380
1986–87	7,414	8,062	5,824	3,805	4,138	4,469	3,891	2,989	1,106	1,414	1,651	1,248	660	1,301	1,323	1,355	1,295	979	1,398	1,401	1,464	1,348	1,349
1987–88	7,577	8,238	5,736	4,050	4,403	4,619	4,250	3,066	1,218	1,537	1,726	1,407	706	1,378	1,410	1,410	1,409	943	1,454	1,456	1,482	1,434	1,417
1988–89	7,644	8,366	5,692	4,274	4,678	4,905	4,526	3,183	1,285	1,646	1,846	1,515	730	1,457	1,496	1,483	1,506	965	1,533	1,536	1,576	1,504	1,488
1989–90	7,688	8,492	5,631	4,504	4,975	5,324	4,723	3,299	1,356	1,780	2,035	1,608	756	1,513	1,557	1,561	1,554	962	1,635	1,638	1,728	1,561	1,581
1990–91	7,699	8,485	5,612	4,757	5,243	5,585	5,004	3,467	1,454	1,888	2,159	1,707	824	1,612	1,658	1,658	1,655	1,050	1,691	1,698	1,767	1,641	1,594
1991–92	8,058	8,928	5,681	5,138	5,693	6,050	5,458	3,623	1,628	2,117	2,409	1,931	936	1,731	1,785	1,789	1,782	1,074	1,780	1,792	1,852	1,745	1,612
1992–93	8,179	9,154	5,777	5,379	6,020	6,442	5,740	3,799	1,782	2,349	2,604	2,192	1,025	1,756	1,816	1,856	1,787	1,106	1,841	1,854	1,982	1,761	1,668
1993–94	8,441	9,435	5,923	5,694	6,365	6,710	6,146	3,996	1,942	2,537	2,820	2,360	1,125	1,873	1,934	1,897	1,958	1,190	1,880	1,895	1,993	1,828	1,681
1994–95	8,595	9,612	5,961	5,965	6,670	7,077	6,409	4,137	2,057	2,681	2,977	2,499	1,192	1,959	2,023	1,992	2,044	1,232	1,949	1,967	2,108	1,866	1,712
1995–96	8,776	9,839	5,915	6,256	7,014	7,448	6,730	4,217	2,179	2,848	3,151	2,660	1,239	2,057	2,121	2,104	2,133	1,297	2,020	2,045	2,192	1,937	1,681
1996–97	8,906	10,003	6,006	6,530	7,334	7,792	7,035	4,404	2,271	2,987	3,323	2,778	1,276	2,148	2,214	2,187	2,232	1,339	2,111	2,133	2,282	2,025	1,789
1997–98	9,130	10,282	6,043	6,813	7,673	8,210	7,318	4,509	2,360	3,110	3,486	2,877	1,314	2,225	2,301	2,285	2,312	1,401	2,228	2,263	2,438	2,130	1,795
1998–99	9,361	10,573	6,065	7,107	8,027	8,625	7,631	4,604	2,430	3,229	3,640	2,974	1,327	2,330	2,409	2,408	2,410	1,450	2,347	2,389	2,576	2,247	1,828
1999–2000	9,356	10,593	6,056	7,308	8,274	8,912	7,851	4,730	2,504	3,349	3,768	3,091	1,348	2,440	2,519	2,516	2,521	1,549	2,364	2,406	2,628	2,239	1,834
2000–01	9,390	10,711	5,990	7,586	8,653	9,321	8,218	4,839	2,562	3,501	3,979	3,208	1,333	2,569	2,654	2,657	2,652	1,600	2,455	2,499	2,686	2,358	1,906
2001–02	9,757	11,185	6,249	8,022	9,196	9,948	8,715	5,137	2,700	3,735	4,273	3,409	1,380	2,723	2,816	2,838	2,801	1,722	2,598	2,645	2,837	2,504	2,036
2002–03	10,118	11,648	6,666	8,502	9,787	10,604	9,280	5,601	2,903	4,046	4,686	3,668	1,483	2,930	3,029	3,023	3,032	1,954	2,669	2,712	2,895	2,580	2,164
2003–04	10,769	12,432	7,002	9,247	10,674	11,679	10,064	6,012	3,319	4,587	5,363	4,141	1,702	3,106	3,212	3,232	3,199	2,089	2,822	2,876	3,085	2,725	2,221
2004–05	11,153	12,918	7,208	9,864	11,426	12,588	10,734	6,375	3,629	5,027	5,939	4,512	1,849	3,304	3,418	3,427	3,413	2,174	2,931	2,981	3,222	2,809	2,353
2005–06	11,386	13,188	7,071	10,454	12,108	13,424	11,335	6,492	3,874	5,351	6,399	4,765	1,935	3,545	3,664	3,654	3,672	2,251	3,035	3,093	3,372	2,899	2,306
2006–07	11,731	13,587	7,235	11,049	12,797	14,215	11,983	6,815	4,102	5,666	6,842	5,020	2,018	3,757	3,878	3,875	3,881	2,407	3,191	3,253	3,498	3,083	2,390
2007–08	11,848	13,748	7,141	11,573	13,429	14,921	12,590	6,975	4,291	5,943	7,173	5,285	2,061	3,952	4,082	4,079	4,083	2,506	3,331	3,404	3,668	3,221	2,409
2008–09	12,375	14,400	7,641	12,256	14,262	15,878	13,349	7,568	4,512	6,312	7,624	5,610	2,136	4,190	4,331	4,344	4,322	2,664	3,554	3,619	3,911	3,417	2,769
2009–10	12,804	15,014	7,703	12,804	15,014	16,712	14,104	7,703	4,751	6,695	8,123	5,964	2,285	4,399	4,565	4,571	4,561	2,845	3,653	3,754	4,018	3,578	2,574
2010–11	13,297	15,605	7,925	13,564	15,918	17,722	14,979	8,085	5,076	7,136	8,751	6,325	2,439	4,640	4,824	4,771	4,857	2,960	3,848	3,958	4,200	3,798	2,685

See notes at end of table.

Average undergraduate tuition and fees and room and board rates charged for full-time students in degree-granting institutions, by level and control of institution: 1964–65 through 2010–11—Continued

	Constant 2009–10 dollars[1]			Current dollars																			
	Total tuition, fees, room, and board			Total tuition, fees, room, and board					Tuition and required fees (in-state for public institutions)					Dormitory rooms					Board (7-day basis)[2]				
					4-year institutions					4-year institutions					4-year institutions					4-year institutions		
Year and control of institution	All insti-tutions	All 4-year	2-year	All insti-tutions	All 4-year	Univer-sities	Other 4-year	2-year	All insti-tutions	All 4-year	Univer-sities	Other 4-year	2-year	All insti-tutions	All 4-year	Univer-sities	Other 4-year	2-year	All insti-tutions	All 4-year	Univer-sities	Other 4-year	2-year
	2	3	4	5	6	7	8	9	10	11	12	13	14	15	16	17	18	19	20	21	22	23	24
Private not-for-profit and for-profit institutions																							
1964–65	13,233	—	10,097	1,907	—	2,202	1,810	1,455	1,088	—	1,297	1,023	702	331	—	390	308	289	488	—	515	479	464
1965–66	13,619	—	10,576	2,005	—	2,316	1,899	1,557	1,154	—	1,369	1,086	768	356	—	418	330	316	495	—	529	483	473
1966–67	13,985	—	11,055	2,124	—	2,456	2,007	1,679	1,233	—	1,456	1,162	845	385	—	452	355	347	506	—	548	490	487
1967–68	14,053	—	11,229	2,205	—	2,545	2,104	1,762	1,297	—	1,534	1,237	892	392	—	455	366	366	516	—	556	501	504
1968–69	14,104	—	11,400	2,321	—	2,673	2,237	1,876	1,383	—	1,638	1,335	956	404	—	463	382	391	534	—	572	520	529
1969–70	14,516	—	11,435	2,530	—	2,920	2,420	1,993	1,533	—	1,809	1,468	1,034	436	—	503	409	413	561	—	608	543	546
1970–71	14,938	—	11,474	2,738	—	3,163	2,599	2,103	1,684	—	1,980	1,603	1,109	468	—	542	434	434	586	—	641	562	560
1971–72	15,364	—	11,514	2,917	—	3,375	2,748	2,186	1,820	—	2,133	1,721	1,172	494	—	576	454	449	603	—	666	573	565
1972–73	15,381	—	11,508	3,038	—	3,512	2,934	2,273	1,898	—	2,226	1,846	1,221	524	—	622	490	457	616	—	664	598	595
1973–74	14,708	—	11,203	3,164	—	3,717	3,040	2,410	1,989	—	2,375	1,925	1,303	533	—	622	502	483	642	—	720	613	624
1974–75	14,241	—	10,843	3,403	—	4,076	3,156	2,591	2,117	—	2,614	1,954	1,367	586	—	691	536	564	700	—	771	666	660
1975–76	14,315	—	10,595	3,663	—	4,467	3,385	2,711	2,272	—	2,881	2,084	1,427	636	—	753	583	572	755	—	833	718	712
1976–77	14,424	14,686	10,971	3,906	3,977	4,715	3,714	2,971	2,467	2,534	3,051	2,351	1,592	649	651	783	604	607	790	791	882	759	772
1977–78	14,389	14,672	10,893	4,158	4,240	5,033	3,967	3,148	2,624	2,700	3,240	2,520	1,706	698	702	850	648	631	836	838	943	800	811
1978–79	14,283	14,584	10,724	4,514	4,609	5,403	4,327	3,389	2,867	2,958	3,487	2,771	1,831	758	761	916	704	700	889	890	1,000	851	858
1979–80	13,715	13,994	10,473	4,912	5,013	5,891	4,700	3,751	3,130	3,225	3,811	3,020	2,062	827	831	1,001	768	766	955	957	1,078	912	923
1980–81	13,686	13,995	10,766	5,470	5,594	6,569	5,249	4,303	3,498	3,617	4,275	3,390	2,413	918	921	1,086	859	871	1,054	1,056	1,209	1,000	1,019
1981–82	14,199	14,199	10,931	6,166	6,330	7,443	5,947	4,746	3,953	4,113	4,887	3,853	2,605	1,038	1,039	1,229	970	1,022	1,175	1,178	1,327	1,124	1,119
1982–83	15,281	15,736	11,845	6,920	7,126	8,536	6,646	5,364	4,439	4,639	5,583	4,329	3,008	1,181	1,181	1,453	1,083	1,177	1,300	1,306	1,501	1,234	1,179
1983–84	15,988	16,523	11,863	7,508	7,759	9,308	7,244	5,571	4,851	5,093	6,217	4,726	3,099	1,278	1,279	1,531	1,191	1,253	1,380	1,387	1,559	1,327	1,219
1984–85	16,808	17,317	12,712	8,202	8,451	10,243	7,849	6,203	5,315	5,556	6,843	5,135	3,485	1,426	1,426	1,753	1,309	1,424	1,462	1,469	1,647	1,405	1,294
1985–86[3]	17,696	18,380	12,970	8,885	9,228	11,034	8,551	6,512	5,789	6,121	7,374	5,641	3,672	1,553	1,557	1,940	1,420	1,500	1,542	1,551	1,720	1,490	1,340
1986–87	18,854	19,562	12,439	9,676	10,039	12,278	9,276	6,384	6,316	6,658	8,118	6,171	3,684	1,658	1,673	2,097	1,518	1,266	1,702	1,708	2,063	1,587	1,434
1987–88	19,667	19,943	13,242	10,512	10,659	13,075	9,854	7,078	6,988	7,116	8,771	6,574	4,161	1,748	1,760	2,244	1,593	1,380	1,775	1,783	2,060	1,687	1,537
1988–89	20,011	20,520	14,248	11,189	11,474	13,874	10,620	7,967	7,461	7,722	9,451	7,172	4,817	1,849	1,863	2,353	1,686	1,540	1,880	1,889	2,269	1,762	1,609
1989–90	20,514	20,968	14,799	12,018	12,284	15,098	11,374	8,670	8,147	8,396	10,348	7,778	5,196	1,923	1,935	2,411	1,774	1,663	1,948	1,953	2,339	1,823	1,811
1990–91	20,894	21,423	15,055	12,910	13,237	16,503	12,220	9,302	8,772	9,083	11,379	8,389	5,570	2,063	2,077	2,654	1,889	1,744	2,074	2,077	2,470	1,943	1,989
1991–92	21,786	22,358	15,105	13,892	14,258	17,572	13,201	9,632	9,419	9,759	12,037	9,060	5,754	2,221	2,241	2,825	2,042	1,788	2,252	2,257	2,709	2,098	2,090
1992–93	22,253	22,825	15,600	14,634	15,009	18,898	13,882	9,903	9,942	10,294	13,055	9,533	6,059	2,348	2,362	3,018	2,151	1,970	2,344	2,354	2,825	2,197	1,875
1993–94	22,969	23,574	15,425	15,496	15,904	20,097	14,640	10,406	10,572	10,952	13,874	10,100	6,370	2,490	2,506	3,277	2,261	2,067	2,434	2,445	2,946	2,278	1,970
1994–95	23,354	23,923	16,096	16,207	16,602	21,041	15,363	11,170	11,111	11,481	14,537	10,653	6,914	2,587	2,601	3,469	2,347	2,233	2,509	2,520	3,035	2,362	2,023
1995–96	24,140	24,706	16,221	17,208	17,612	22,502	16,198	11,563	11,864	12,243	15,605	11,297	7,094	2,738	2,751	3,680	2,473	2,371	2,606	2,617	3,218	2,429	2,098
1996–97	24,603	25,153	16,305	18,039	18,442	23,520	16,994	11,954	12,498	12,881	16,552	11,871	7,236	2,878	2,889	3,826	2,602	2,537	2,663	2,672	3,142	2,520	2,181
1997–98	24,812	25,554	17,315	18,516	19,070	24,116	17,717	12,921	12,801	13,344	17,229	12,338	7,464	2,954	2,964	3,756	2,731	2,672	2,762	2,761	3,132	2,648	2,785
1998–99	25,512	26,250	17,544	19,368	19,929	25,443	18,430	13,319	13,428	13,973	18,340	12,815	7,854	3,075	3,091	3,914	2,850	2,581	2,865	2,865	3,188	2,765	2,884
1999–2000	25,878	26,548	17,981	20,213	20,737	26,534	19,160	14,045	14,100	14,616	19,307	13,390	8,225	3,236	3,292	4,070	2,982	3,067	2,877	2,879	3,157	2,788	2,753
2000–01	26,456	27,054	18,453	21,373	21,856	27,676	20,248	14,907	15,000	15,470	20,106	14,233	9,067	3,382	3,390	4,270	3,122	3,006	2,991	2,993	3,300	2,893	2,834
2001–02	27,261	27,848	19,248	22,413	22,896	29,115	21,220	15,825	15,742	16,211	21,176	14,923	10,076	3,567	3,576	4,478	3,301	3,116	3,104	3,109	3,462	2,996	2,633
2002–03	27,778	28,310	21,129	23,340	23,787	31,043	21,965	17,753	16,383	16,826	22,716	15,416	10,651	3,752	3,784	4,724	3,478	3,232	3,206	3,197	3,602	3,071	3,870
2003–04	28,679	29,198	22,779	24,624	25,070	32,886	23,153	19,558	17,315	17,763	24,128	16,284	11,545	3,945	3,952	4,979	3,647	3,581	3,364	3,354	3,779	3,222	3,432
2004–05	29,189	29,690	22,949	25,817	26,260	34,761	24,278	20,297	18,154	18,604	25,643	17,050	12,122	4,178	4,173	5,263	3,858	4,475	3,485	3,483	3,855	3,370	3,700
2005–06	29,307	29,770	23,312	26,908	27,333	36,510	25,302	21,404	18,862	19,292	26,954	17,702	12,450	4,400	4,404	5,517	4,085	4,173	3,645	3,637	4,039	3,515	4,781
2006–07	30,194	30,703	21,535	28,439	28,919	38,437	26,823	20,284	20,048	20,517	28,580	18,848	12,708	4,606	4,613	5,691	4,302	4,147	3,785	3,788	4,166	3,672	3,429
2007–08	30,475	30,945	22,200	29,767	30,226	40,634	28,004	21,685	20,972	21,427	30,251	19,663	13,126	4,804	4,808	6,006	4,466	4,484	3,992	3,991	4,376	3,875	4,074
2008–09	31,102	31,576	22,946	30,804	31,273	42,844	28,931	22,726	21,570	22,036	31,968	20,162	13,562	5,025	5,032	6,254	4,688	4,537	4,209	4,206	4,622	4,080	4,627
2009–10	31,023	31,488	24,483	31,023	31,488	44,619	29,043	24,483	21,444	21,908	33,315	19,941	14,876	5,249	5,249	6,539	4,897	5,217	4,331	4,331	4,765	4,205	4,390
2010–11	31,395	31,975	23,401	32,026	32,617	46,519	30,071	23,871	22,186	22,771	34,805	20,732	14,467	5,406	5,413	6,802	5,041	4,928	4,434	4,433	4,912	4,298	4,475

See notes at end of table.

Average undergraduate tuition and fees and room and board rates charged for full-time students in degree-granting institutions, by level and control of institution: 1964–65 through 2010–11—Continued

	Constant 2009–10 dollars[1]			Current dollars																			
	Total tuition, fees, room, and board			Total tuition, fees, room, and board					Tuition and required fees (in-state for public institutions)					Dormitory rooms					Board (7-day basis)[2]				
					4-year institutions					4-year institutions					4-year institutions					4-year institutions			
Year and control of institution	All institutions	4-year	2-year	All institutions	All 4-year	Universities	Other 4-year	2-year	All institutions	All 4-year	Universities	Other 4-year	2-year	All institutions	All 4-year	Universities	Other 4-year	2-year	All institutions	All 4-year	Universities	Other 4-year	2-year
1	2	3	4	5	6	7	8	9	10	11	12	13	14	15	16	17	18	19	20	21	22	23	24
Not-for-profit																							
1999–2000	26,871	27,181	14,963	20,989	21,231	26,534	19,652	11,688	14,911	15,131	19,307	13,918	6,893	3,204	3,221	4,070	2,949	2,115	2,875	2,879	3,157	2,785	2,680
2000–01	27,151	27,443	14,503	21,934	22,170	27,676	20,539	11,717	15,596	15,811	20,106	14,565	6,968	3,347	3,365	4,270	3,080	2,008	2,991	2,993	3,300	2,894	2,740
2001–02	28,072	28,288	15,775	23,080	23,262	29,115	21,547	12,970	16,446	16,604	21,176	15,301	8,126	3,536	3,544	4,478	3,253	2,304	3,104	3,109	3,462	2,993	2,540
2002–03	28,893	29,094	17,188	24,276	24,446	31,043	22,566	14,442	17,359	17,517	22,716	16,070	8,907	3,723	3,731	4,724	3,427	2,646	3,195	3,197	3,602	3,068	2,889
2003–04	29,914	30,110	18,133	25,685	25,853	32,886	23,849	15,569	18,429	18,584	24,128	17,044	9,587	3,907	3,915	4,979	3,589	2,853	3,349	3,354	3,779	3,215	3,129
2004–05	30,622	30,815	17,984	27,083	27,255	34,761	25,134	15,906	19,498	19,652	25,643	18,003	9,910	4,113	4,119	5,263	3,776	2,929	3,472	3,483	3,855	3,356	3,067
2005–06	31,063	31,251	17,785	28,520	28,692	36,510	26,526	16,329	20,568	20,732	26,954	19,046	10,318	4,315	4,323	5,517	3,964	3,017	3,637	3,637	4,039	3,516	2,994
2006–07	32,026	32,191	18,772	30,165	30,320	38,437	28,065	17,681	21,841	21,994	28,580	20,199	10,936	4,532	4,537	5,691	4,189	3,576	3,791	3,788	4,166	3,677	3,169
2007–08	32,680	32,812	19,305	31,921	32,050	40,634	29,679	18,857	23,201	23,328	30,251	21,451	11,789	4,725	4,730	6,006	4,347	3,796	3,994	3,991	4,376	3,880	3,272
2008–09	34,005	34,131	20,467	33,679	33,804	42,844	31,327	20,271	24,502	24,636	31,968	22,653	12,603	4,957	4,962	6,254	4,575	3,889	4,221	4,206	4,622	4,098	3,779
2009–10	34,939	35,061	20,776	34,939	35,061	44,619	32,489	20,776	25,413	25,552	33,315	23,485	12,656	5,174	5,178	6,539	4,776	4,116	4,353	4,331	4,765	4,228	4,004
2010–11	35,539	35,648	19,699	36,252	36,364	46,519	33,685	20,094	26,383	26,523	34,805	24,348	12,669	5,401	5,408	6,802	4,997	3,981	4,468	4,433	4,912	4,340	3,444
For-profit																							
1999–2000	20,643	21,185	20,143	16,124	16,547	†	16,547	15,734	8,707	8,661	†	8,661	8,766	4,247	4,631	†	4,631	3,912	3,171	3,255	†	3,255	3,056
2000–01	21,894	22,554	21,119	17,688	18,220	†	18,220	17,061	10,192	10,411	†	10,411	9,945	4,507	4,960	†	4,960	3,955	2,988	2,849	†	2,849	3,161
2001–02	22,594	24,049	20,624	18,576	19,772	†	19,772	16,956	10,860	11,069	†	11,069	10,629	4,629	5,396	†	5,396	3,579	3,087	3,307	†	3,307	2,748
2002–03	23,439	23,849	23,094	19,694	20,039	†	20,039	19,404	11,310	11,407	†	11,407	11,129	4,578	5,384	†	5,384	3,530	3,806	3,249	†	3,249	4,746
2003–04	25,415	25,486	26,055	21,822	21,883	†	21,883	22,371	12,278	12,398	†	12,398	12,024	5,092	5,754	†	5,754	3,992	4,451	3,730	†	3,730	6,355
2004–05	26,116	26,474	25,273	23,098	23,415	†	23,415	22,353	13,036	13,197	†	13,197	12,607	5,655	5,863	†	5,863	5,149	4,407	4,355	†	4,355	4,596
2005–06	25,658	25,296	27,959	23,557	23,225	†	23,225	25,670	13,237	13,315	†	13,315	12,959	6,085	6,485	†	6,485	4,776	4,235	3,426	†	3,426	7,935
2006–07	25,487	26,234	22,562	24,005	24,710	†	24,710	23,085	14,277	14,593	†	14,593	13,085	6,205	6,638	†	6,638	4,466	3,523	3,479	†	3,479	3,700
2007–08	25,334	25,680	24,081	24,745	25,083	†	25,083	23,522	14,409	14,644	†	14,644	13,363	6,445	6,781	†	6,781	4,901	3,892	3,658	†	3,658	5,258
2008–09	24,558	24,684	24,907	24,322	24,447	†	24,447	24,669	14,309	14,423	†	14,423	13,725	6,212	6,441	†	6,441	4,899	3,802	3,583	†	3,583	6,044
2009–10	23,826	23,556	25,993	23,826	23,556	†	23,556	25,993	13,733	13,437	†	13,437	15,146	6,248	6,338	†	6,338	5,689	3,845	3,781	†	3,781	5,158
2010–11	23,032	22,851	26,113	23,495	23,310	†	23,310	26,637	14,253	14,162	†	14,162	14,654	5,459	5,479	†	5,479	5,316	3,783	3,669	†	3,669	6,667

—Not available.

†Not applicable.

[1]Constant dollars based on the Consumer Price Index, prepared by the Bureau of Labor Statistics, U.S. Department of Labor, adjusted to a school-year basis.

[2]Data for 1986–87 and later years reflect a basis of 20 meals per week rather than meals 7 days per week. Because of this revision in data collection and tabulation procedures, data are not entirely comparable with figures for previous years. In particular, data on board rates are somewhat higher than in earlier years because they reflect the basis of 20 meals per week rather than meals served 7 days per week. Since many institutions serve fewer than 3 meals each day, the 1986–87 and later data reflect a more accurate accounting of total board costs.

[3]Room and board data are estimated.

NOTE: Data are for the entire academic year and are average total charges for full-time attendance. Tuition and fees were weighted by the number of full-time-equivalent undergraduates, but were not adjusted to reflect student residency. Room and board were based on full-time students. Data through 1995–96 are for institutions of higher education, while later data are for degree-granting institutions. Degree-granting institutions grant associate's or higher degrees and participate in Title IV federal financial aid programs. The degree-granting classification is very similar to the earlier higher education classification, but it includes more 2-year colleges and excludes a few higher education institutions that did not grant degrees. (See Appendix A: Guide to Sources for details.) Because of their low response rate, data for private 2-year colleges must be interpreted with caution. Some data have been revised from previously published figures. Detail may not sum to totals because of rounding.

SOURCE: U.S. Department of Education, National Center for Education Statistics, Higher Education General Information Survey (HEGIS), "Institutional Characteristics of Colleges and Universities" surveys, 1965–66 through 1985–86; "Fall Enrollment in Institutions of Higher Education" surveys, 1965 through 1985; Integrated Postsecondary Education Data System (IPEDS), "Fall Enrollment Survey" (IPEDS-EF-86-99) and "Institutional Characteristics Survey" (IPEDS-IC-86-99); IPEDS Spring 2001 through Spring 2011, Enrollment component; and IPEDS Fall 2000 through Fall 2010, Institutional Characteristics component. (This table was prepared November 2011.)

Average undergraduate tuition and fees and room and board rates charged for full-time students in degree-granting institutions, by control and level of institution and state or jurisdiction: 2009–10 and 2010–11

[In current dollars]

State or jurisdiction	Public 4-year							Private 4-year						Public 2-year, tuition and required fees		
	In-state, 2009–10		In-state, 2010–11				Out-of-state tuition and required fees, 2010–11	2009–10		2010–11						
	Total	Tuition and required fees	Total	Tuition and required fees	Room	Board		Total	Tuition and required fees	Total	Tuition and required fees	Room	Board	In-state, 2009–10	In-state, 2010–11	Out-of-state, 2010–11
1	2	3	4	5	6	7	8	9	10	11	12	13	14	15	16	17
United States	$15,014	$6,695	$15,918	$7,136	$4,824	$3,958	$19,622	$31,488	$21,908	$32,617	$22,771	$5,413	$4,433	$2,285	$2,439	$6,183
Alabama..................	13,052	6,061	14,416	6,808	3,934	3,674	17,427	23,234	15,896	24,318	16,649	3,819	3,850	2,834	3,422	6,738
Alaska....................	13,281	5,246	14,053	5,578	4,912	3,563	16,179	29,412	19,765	30,628	21,070	4,400	5,158	3,900	3,894	4,168
Arizona..................	15,710	6,720	17,083	7,685	5,559	3,840	20,210	22,607	10,613	20,979	12,261	4,884	3,835	1,652	1,671	7,425
Arkansas................	11,841	5,846	12,580	6,117	3,569	2,893	13,582	22,147	15,516	22,934	16,103	3,448	3,384	2,188	2,311	4,020
California...............	17,652	6,240	18,933	7,357	6,000	5,576	26,509	37,832	26,397	38,047	26,519	6,520	5,008	719	723	5,521
Colorado................	15,056	6,188	16,208	6,670	5,012	4,526	24,255	28,765	18,808	29,153	19,116	5,508	4,529	2,446	2,727	8,569
Connecticut............	18,331	8,375	19,400	8,854	5,665	4,881	24,981	43,780	31,878	44,699	32,581	6,741	5,377	3,199	3,401	10,175
Delaware................	18,383	9,026	19,541	9,646	5,907	3,988	23,047	21,852	12,951	22,928	12,989	4,811	5,127	2,816	2,942	6,840
District of Columbia	†	5,370	†	7,000	†	†	14,000	37,357	25,713	44,190	32,191	7,955	4,044	†	†	†
Florida...................	11,659	3,452	12,774	3,720	5,420	3,634	16,327	28,352	19,116	28,533	19,242	5,133	4,157	2,480	2,497	9,560
Georgia..................	12,552	4,839	14,019	5,435	5,055	3,530	18,883	30,323	20,717	30,488	20,783	5,357	4,348	2,324	2,480	7,660
Hawaii...................	14,182	5,943	15,133	6,635	4,286	4,211	19,368	22,948	12,405	23,718	12,807	4,716	6,195	1,955	2,172	6,808
Idaho....................	10,895	4,883	11,773	5,325	3,103	3,345	15,653	12,670	6,650	13,122	6,866	3,288	2,968	2,420	2,557	6,976
Illinois..................	19,355	10,443	20,054	10,562	5,218	4,274	25,148	33,272	23,166	34,411	24,070	5,714	4,628	2,670	2,947	8,595
Indiana.................	15,590	7,306	16,912	7,614	4,513	4,785	23,365	31,722	23,468	32,718	24,032	4,428	4,258	3,090	3,256	6,761
Iowa	14,174	6,712	14,855	7,157	3,839	3,860	21,265	23,019	16,392	22,749	16,041	2,986	3,723	3,549	3,769	4,833
Kansas..................	12,578	6,052	13,229	6,471	3,284	3,474	16,334	25,067	18,414	26,156	19,128	3,298	3,730	2,212	2,463	3,803
Kentucky...............	14,228	7,165	15,002	7,561	3,895	3,546	16,853	23,779	16,984	25,074	17,867	3,484	3,724	3,026	3,148	10,711
Louisiana...............	10,873	4,282	11,856	4,702	3,964	3,190	14,047	32,781	24,043	34,616	25,531	5,056	4,028	1,849	2,132	5,131
Maine....................	17,020	8,504	17,767	8,876	4,379	4,511	22,058	34,871	25,090	36,525	26,092	5,536	4,897	3,303	3,334	5,833
Maryland................	16,407	7,321	16,963	7,579	5,335	4,049	19,591	39,750	29,361	40,338	29,516	6,414	4,409	3,099	3,237	7,777
Massachusetts........	17,819	9,221	19,164	9,444	5,821	3,899	21,778	45,087	33,160	46,632	34,315	6,980	5,337	3,522	3,759	8,430
Michigan	17,852	9,638	18,333	9,839	4,323	4,170	28,558	23,170	15,524	23,945	16,184	3,831	3,930	2,312	2,486	5,167
Minnesota..............	15,730	8,728	16,385	9,285	3,846	3,254	13,945	31,927	23,814	32,261	23,838	4,489	3,933	4,791	4,965	5,589
Mississippi.............	11,583	5,046	12,051	5,301	3,934	2,817	13,500	19,666	13,563	20,029	14,098	3,025	2,905	1,837	2,141	3,908
Missouri.................	14,368	7,047	15,110	7,120	4,603	3,387	16,103	27,106	18,766	26,754	18,286	4,400	4,067	2,406	2,440	4,381
Montana................	12,399	5,612	12,891	5,753	3,277	3,861	18,458	23,438	16,471	24,314	17,356	3,265	3,694	3,121	3,173	8,519
Nebraska...............	13,265	6,229	14,081	6,602	3,708	3,771	15,525	24,895	17,778	24,863	17,633	3,811	3,418	2,248	2,391	3,306
Nevada..................	13,682	3,559	14,172	4,005	5,666	4,502	16,767	25,768	15,651	25,913	15,217	5,622	5,073	2,010	2,243	8,590
New Hampshire	20,492	10,958	21,481	11,807	5,676	3,998	23,113	37,766	27,344	38,881	27,958	6,144	4,778	6,296	6,687	14,620
New Jersey.............	21,591	10,680	22,592	11,197	7,331	4,063	22,304	38,071	26,933	39,707	28,226	6,277	5,204	3,388	3,553	6,108
New Mexico	11,809	4,655	12,520	5,021	4,132	3,367	14,996	22,210	13,413	24,480	14,996	4,447	5,037	1,338	1,462	4,045
New York................	16,147	5,720	16,606	5,764	6,732	4,110	13,792	40,115	28,646	41,626	29,742	7,135	4,750	3,724	3,848	6,890
North Carolina.........	11,874	4,559	12,874	5,270	4,261	3,343	17,950	32,252	23,788	33,290	24,313	4,623	4,354	1,639	1,832	7,843
North Dakota...........	11,891	5,968	12,503	6,162	2,717	3,624	15,202	16,419	11,227	17,342	11,869	2,450	3,023	3,873	3,929	7,302
Ohio......................	17,133	8,058	17,964	8,501	5,308	4,154	20,139	32,751	24,115	33,450	24,558	4,532	4,360	3,014	3,227	7,605
Oklahoma...............	11,444	4,955	11,938	5,244	3,499	3,194	14,816	25,811	18,105	27,059	18,921	4,148	3,989	2,423	2,578	6,436
Oregon..................	15,629	6,941	16,402	7,413	4,288	4,701	22,729	35,090	26,260	36,589	27,350	4,882	4,357	3,220	3,314	6,721
Pennsylvania...........	19,017	10,550	19,916	11,085	5,162	3,669	21,298	39,574	29,317	40,548	29,929	5,818	4,801	3,454	3,577	10,282
Rhode Island	18,509	8,435	19,815	9,250	6,417	4,149	25,594	40,295	29,420	42,610	31,400	6,222	4,988	3,376	3,652	9,792
South Carolina.........	16,788	9,439	17,641	10,147	4,778	2,715	23,774	26,156	19,000	27,049	19,560	3,754	3,735	3,477	3,643	7,543
South Dakota...........	12,022	6,128	12,603	6,414	2,744	3,445	8,464	22,207	16,024	21,871	15,129	2,946	3,795	4,357	4,700	4,622
Tennessee..............	12,748	6,048	13,759	6,407	3,948	3,403	19,694	27,925	19,965	28,745	20,461	4,566	3,718	2,941	3,128	12,262
Texas....................	13,764	6,350	14,585	6,742	4,189	3,654	18,280	30,636	22,178	31,674	22,832	4,816	4,025	1,512	1,585	4,275
Utah	10,109	4,532	10,768	4,793	2,723	3,252	14,587	14,098	6,992	14,769	7,313	3,770	3,686	2,734	2,860	8,029
Vermont.................	20,735	12,008	21,530	12,459	5,729	3,341	29,932	37,677	28,046	39,328	29,265	5,397	4,666	4,876	5,020	9,940
Virginia..................	15,616	7,795	18,110	8,658	4,458	4,994	24,254	27,247	19,365	28,317	20,178	4,205	3,934	2,853	3,384	8,130
Washington.............	15,189	6,032	16,253	6,678	5,001	4,574	21,636	35,132	26,184	36,117	27,030	4,901	4,187	3,025	3,266	5,997
West Virginia...........	12,426	4,899	12,799	4,944	4,149	3,705	15,113	17,761	10,490	18,256	10,609	3,662	3,985	2,847	2,871	7,640
Wisconsin...............	13,190	6,963	13,819	7,391	3,817	2,611	18,610	30,805	22,879	31,442	23,287	4,303	3,852	3,543	3,695	6,015
Wyoming................	10,952	3,162	11,467	3,333	3,612	4,522	9,981	†	†	†	†	†	†	2,120	2,164	5,436

†Not applicable.

NOTE: Data are for the entire academic year and are average charges. In-state tuition and fees were weighted by the number of full-time-equivalent undergraduates, but were not adjusted to reflect student residency. Out-of-state tuition and fees were weighted by the number of first-time freshmen attending the institution in fall 2010 from out of state. Room and board are based on full-time students. (See Appendix A: Guide to Sources for details.) Degree-granting institutions grant associate's or higher degrees and participate in Title IV fed-

eral financial aid programs. Some data have been revised from previously published figures. Detail may not sum to totals because of rounding.
SOURCE: U.S. Department of Education, National Center for Education Statistics, Integrated Postsecondary Education Data System (IPEDS), Fall 2009 and Fall 2010, Institutional Characteristics component; and Spring 2010 and Spring 2011, Enrollment component. (This table was prepared November 2011.)

Undergraduate tuition and fees and room and board rates for full-time students in degree-granting institutions, by percentile of charges and control and level of institution: Selected years, 2000–01 through 2010–11

[In current dollars]

Control and level of institution, and year	Tuition, fees, room, and board					Tuition and required fees				
	10th percentile	25th percentile	Median (50th percentile)	75th percentile	90th percentile	10th percentile	25th percentile	Median (50th percentile)	75th percentile	90th percentile
1	2	3	4	5	6	7	8	9	10	11
All public institutions[1]										
2000–01	$5,741	$6,880	$8,279	$9,617	$11,384	$612	$1,480	$2,403	$3,444	$4,583
2005–06	7,700	9,623	11,348	13,543	16,264	990	2,070	3,329	5,322	6,972
2007–08	8,827	10,890	12,690	15,446	17,979	1,144	2,245	3,666	5,988	7,969
2008–09	9,370	11,518	13,616	16,283	18,866	1,144	2,348	3,948	6,360	8,467
2009–10	9,433	12,069	14,446	17,146	19,898	1,200	2,492	4,370	6,726	8,726
2010–11	9,889	12,856	15,234	17,860	21,593	1,230	2,628	4,632	7,127	9,420
Public 4-year[1]										
2000–01	6,503	7,347	8,468	9,816	11,611	2,118	2,520	3,314	4,094	5,085
2005–06	8,863	10,219	11,596	13,830	16,443	3,094	3,822	5,084	6,458	8,097
2007–08	10,012	11,471	13,035	15,819	18,384	3,355	4,262	5,689	7,272	8,907
2008–09	10,638	12,169	13,983	16,614	19,291	3,687	4,399	6,056	7,819	9,399
2009–10	11,158	12,793	15,040	17,661	20,253	4,044	4,900	6,458	8,266	9,886
2010–11	11,952	13,604	15,788	18,419	22,191	4,336	5,105	6,780	8,689	11,029
Public 2-year[1]										
2000–01	3,321	3,804	4,627	5,750	6,871	310	724	1,387	1,799	2,460
2005–06	4,380	4,822	6,234	7,567	8,993	691	1,109	1,920	2,589	3,100
2007–08	4,637	5,361	6,777	8,138	10,471	590	1,200	2,091	2,819	3,384
2008–09	4,860	5,612	6,935	8,823	11,183	590	1,200	2,215	2,930	3,456
2009–10	5,114	6,008	7,048	8,981	10,977	704	1,316	2,380	3,090	3,650
2010–11	5,347	6,327	7,340	9,370	11,312	700	1,412	2,537	3,315	3,840
Private not-for-profit institutions										
2000–01	13,514	17,552	22,493	27,430	32,659	7,800	11,730	15,540	19,600	24,532
2005–06	18,243	23,258	29,497	35,918	41,707	9,981	15,375	21,070	26,265	31,690
2007–08	20,033	25,984	32,902	41,000	46,204	11,530	17,579	23,730	29,945	35,290
2008–09	21,649	27,438	34,805	43,246	48,524	12,020	18,415	24,930	31,540	37,125
2009–10	22,334	28,699	36,550	44,895	50,297	11,696	18,970	25,890	32,816	38,690
2010–11	23,125	29,865	38,063	46,737	52,229	11,794	19,610	26,920	34,250	40,082
Not-for-profit 4-year										
2000–01	13,972	17,714	22,554	27,476	32,659	8,450	11,920	15,746	19,730	24,532
2005–06	18,350	23,322	29,598	36,028	41,774	10,300	15,560	21,190	26,500	31,690
2007–08	20,278	26,160	32,925	41,000	46,242	11,754	17,640	23,842	30,158	35,290
2008–09	21,668	27,752	34,849	43,246	48,524	12,242	18,554	25,120	31,620	37,125
2009–10	22,356	28,840	36,665	44,895	50,298	12,240	19,200	26,180	32,910	38,690
2010–11	23,548	29,884	38,129	46,737	52,229	12,220	19,854	27,100	34,417	40,082
Not-for-profit 2-year										
2000–01	6,850	6,850	9,995	14,209	20,240	2,430	4,825	7,250	8,266	11,100
2005–06	8,030	15,680	16,830	20,829	28,643	4,218	8,640	9,940	12,270	14,472
2007–08	13,210	16,829	18,104	23,281	36,659	3,740	8,535	11,145	14,325	17,930
2008–09	16,085	17,568	21,595	24,390	39,463	3,740	8,900	11,800	16,250	18,000
2009–10	13,105	18,316	20,369	26,455	40,733	3,530	8,950	12,292	15,177	19,000
2010–11	10,393	19,718	21,186	27,386	30,758	3,840	9,730	12,000	14,640	18,965
Private for-profit institutions										
2000–01	13,396	15,778	19,403	21,400	21,845	6,900	8,202	9,644	12,090	14,600
2005–06	17,278	19,098	25,589	26,499	31,903	7,632	10,011	12,450	14,335	17,740
2007–08	17,040	19,113	24,540	27,369	32,724	10,669	11,850	13,200	15,600	19,769
2008–09	17,150	17,150	20,813	29,959	30,400	11,176	12,396	12,840	15,930	19,050
2009–10	17,789	17,789	21,321	31,433	32,000	9,792	9,792	12,392	15,450	19,950
2010–11	16,097	16,097	17,484	26,175	31,639	10,200	11,520	13,700	16,440	18,209
For-profit 4-year										
2000–01	13,396	15,818	20,417	21,400	21,400	7,206	8,305	9,675	12,800	15,090
2005–06	17,383	19,098	25,589	26,499	31,903	7,632	10,418	12,900	14,450	17,735
2007–08	17,040	17,636	24,540	27,369	31,512	11,066	13,119	13,200	15,600	19,769
2008–09	17,150	17,150	20,813	29,959	30,400	11,288	12,840	12,840	15,930	19,080
2009–10	17,789	17,789	21,321	31,433	32,000	9,792	9,792	11,920	15,071	19,080
2010–11	16,097	16,097	17,484	26,175	31,639	10,200	11,520	14,085	16,500	18,050
For-profit 2-year										
2000–01	15,778	15,778	19,403	21,845	21,845	6,025	7,365	9,644	12,000	14,255
2005–06	13,010	18,281	43,425	43,425	43,425	7,870	9,285	11,550	14,196	19,425
2007–08	20,272	23,327	26,727	40,232	40,232	8,665	10,170	12,170	15,070	18,850
2008–09	21,442	23,327	26,863	43,382	43,382	9,000	10,910	12,600	16,356	18,175
2009–10	22,857	22,857	26,696	26,696	26,696	10,116	11,735	13,548	17,148	21,245
2010–11	23,687	23,687	25,161	25,161	25,161	9,940	12,094	13,599	15,960	20,533

[1]Average undergraduate tuition and fees are based on in-state students only.
NOTE: Data are for the entire academic year and are average rates for full-time students. Student charges were weighted by the number of full-time-equivalent undergraduates, but were not adjusted to reflect student residency. The data have not been adjusted for changes in the purchasing power of the dollar. Degree-granting institutions grant associate's or higher degrees and participate in Title IV federal financial aid programs. Some data have been revised from previously published figures.
SOURCE: U.S. Department of Education, National Center for Education Statistics, Integrated Postsecondary Education Data System (IPEDS), Fall 2000 through Fall 2010, Institutional Characteristics component; and Spring 2001 through Spring 2011, Enrollment component. (This table was prepared November 2011.)

Average graduate and first-professional tuition and required fees in degree-granting institutions, by first-professional field of study and control of institution: 1989–90 through 2010–11

Year and control	Average full-time graduate tuition and required fees		Average full-time first-professional tuition and required fees in current dollars									
	Current dollars	Constant 2009–10 dollars	Chiropractic	Dentistry	Medicine	Optometry	Osteopathic medicine	Pharmacy	Podiatry	Veterinary medicine	Law	Theology
1	2	3	4	5	6	7	8	9	10	11	12	13
All institutions												
1989–90	$4,135	$7,058	$8,315	$10,515	$10,597	$9,469	$11,888	$5,890	$14,611	$5,470	$8,059	$4,079
1990–91	4,488	7,264	9,108	10,270	10,571	9,512	12,830	5,889	15,143	5,396	8,708	4,569
1991–92	5,116	8,023	10,226	12,049	11,646	9,610	13,004	6,731	16,257	6,367	9,469	4,876
1992–93	5,475	8,326	11,117	12,710	12,265	10,858	14,297	6,635	17,426	6,771	10,463	5,331
1993–94	5,973	8,854	11,503	14,403	13,074	10,385	15,038	7,960	17,621	7,159	11,552	5,253
1994–95	6,247	9,002	12,324	15,164	13,834	11,053	15,913	8,315	18,138	7,741	12,374	5,648
1995–96	6,741	9,456	12,507	15,647	14,860	11,544	16,785	8,602	18,434	8,208	13,278	5,991
1996–97	7,111	9,699	12,721	16,585	15,481	12,250	17,888	9,207	19,056	8,668	14,081	6,558
1997–98	7,246	9,710	13,144	17,695	16,310	12,679	18,668	9,744	19,355	9,013	14,992	6,832
1998–99	7,685	10,122	13,582	19,051	17,107	14,066	20,000	9,735	19,547	9,392	15,601	7,171
1999–2000	8,069	10,330	14,256	19,576	17,818	14,354	20,903	10,740	20,158	9,867	16,491	7,725
2000–01	8,429	10,434	15,093	22,097	19,151	15,448	21,784	11,273	20,455	10,365	17,795	7,868
2001–02	8,857	10,773	15,632	22,597	19,795	16,148	22,970	12,259	20,886	11,070	18,707	8,737
2002–03	9,226	10,980	16,758	24,517	21,206	16,439	24,379	13,597	21,633	12,142	19,810	9,485
2003–04	10,312	12,010	17,264	26,124	22,892	17,439	26,059	14,987	22,645	13,420	21,305	9,850
2004–05	11,004	12,442	18,535	28,455	24,293	18,048	27,900	15,951	23,631	14,535	22,935	10,412
2005–06	11,621	12,657	19,445	29,729	25,699	18,717	29,320	17,224	24,347	15,526	24,474	10,811
2006–07	12,312	13,071	21,473	32,004	27,086	19,886	30,604	18,634	25,594	16,551	26,042	11,628
2007–08	13,002	13,311	22,815	34,699	28,040	21,046	32,163	19,542	26,112	17,012	27,670	11,346
2008–09[1]	13,647	13,779	23,979	37,543	29,890	22,125	33,607	20,842	27,118	18,223	29,585	11,983
2009–10	14,534	14,534	—	—	—	—	—	—	—	—	—	—
2010–11	14,993	14,698	—	—	—	—	—	—	—	—	—	—
Public[2]												
1989–90	1,999	3,412	†	5,728	6,259	3,569	6,521	2,816	†	4,505	3,196	†
1990–91	2,206	3,570	†	5,927	6,437	3,821	7,188	2,697	†	4,840	3,430	†
1991–92	2,524	3,958	†	6,595	7,106	4,161	7,699	2,871	†	5,231	3,933	†
1992–93	2,791	4,244	†	7,006	7,867	5,106	8,404	2,987	†	5,553	4,261	†
1993–94	3,050	4,521	†	7,525	8,329	5,325	8,640	3,567	†	6,107	4,835	†
1994–95	3,250	4,684	†	8,125	8,812	5,643	8,954	3,793	†	6,571	5,307	†
1995–96	3,449	4,838	†	8,806	9,585	6,130	9,448	4,100	†	6,907	5,821	†
1996–97	3,607	4,919	†	9,434	10,057	6,561	9,932	4,884	†	7,343	6,565	†
1997–98	3,744	5,017	†	9,762	10,555	7,366	10,358	5,046	19,541	7,472	7,125	†
1998–99	3,897	5,133	†	10,259	11,141	7,890	10,858	5,476	19,818	7,707	7,510	†
1999–2000	4,042	5,175	†	10,795	11,610	7,922	11,377	5,997	19,578	8,271	7,824	†
2000–01	4,243	5,253	†	11,946	12,188	8,452	11,866	6,476	20,228	8,720	8,414	†
2001–02	4,496	5,468	†	13,092	13,186	9,619	12,708	7,187	21,254	9,375	9,115	†
2002–03	4,842	5,762	†	13,992	14,591	10,187	13,497	8,304	21,992	10,396	10,172	†
2003–04	5,544	6,456	†	15,613	16,500	11,537	14,994	9,424	22,638	11,763	11,838	†
2004–05	6,080	6,874	†	17,690	18,078	12,387	16,467	10,332	24,788	12,878	13,155	†
2005–06	6,493	7,072	†	19,177	19,473	13,229	17,653	11,444	24,808	13,849	14,544	†
2006–07	6,894	7,320	†	20,701	20,627	14,392	18,102	12,523	26,242	14,915	15,658	†
2007–08	7,415	7,592	†	22,037	21,206	15,489	19,310	13,490	27,322	15,838	16,962	†
2008–09[1]	7,999	8,076	†	24,787	22,959	16,285	20,898	14,476	28,942	17,070	18,461	†
2009–10	8,763	8,763	—	—	—	—	—	—	—	—	—	—
2010–11	9,247	9,065	—	—	—	—	—	—	—	—	—	—
Private												
1989–90	7,881	13,452	8,315	16,800	16,826	13,640	14,117	10,656	14,611	14,184	10,901	4,079
1990–91	8,507	13,768	9,108	18,270	17,899	13,767	15,009	11,546	15,143	14,159	12,247	4,569
1991–92	9,592	15,042	10,226	20,318	19,225	14,366	16,098	12,937	16,257	15,816	12,946	4,876
1992–93	10,008	15,219	11,117	21,309	19,585	14,459	17,098	13,373	17,426	17,103	13,975	5,331
1993–94	10,790	15,994	11,503	23,824	20,769	14,156	17,720	14,838	17,621	17,433	15,193	5,253
1994–95	11,338	16,338	12,324	24,641	21,819	14,497	18,422	14,894	18,138	17,940	16,201	5,648
1995–96	12,083	16,950	12,507	25,678	23,001	15,235	19,619	15,618	18,434	19,380	17,251	5,991
1996–97	12,537	17,099	12,721	26,618	24,242	15,949	20,714	15,934	19,056	19,526	18,276	6,558
1997–98	12,774	17,117	13,144	29,985	25,249	16,550	21,707	16,575	19,316	18,624	19,311	6,832
1998–99	13,299	17,517	13,582	31,917	26,495	17,848	22,867	16,874	19,492	19,617	20,253	7,171
1999–2000	13,821	17,694	14,256	32,268	27,702	18,317	23,791	18,220	20,259	20,128	21,393	7,725
2000–01	14,420	17,849	15,093	35,234	30,077	19,838	24,719	19,022	20,498	20,883	23,063	7,868
2001–02	15,165	18,445	15,632	36,184	30,438	20,374	25,909	20,325	20,825	21,772	24,019	8,737
2002–03	14,983	17,832	16,758	39,085	31,895	20,197	27,552	21,561	21,551	22,813	25,243	9,485
2003–04	16,209	18,878	17,264	40,414	32,913	20,955	29,095	23,022	22,647	23,941	26,746	9,850
2004–05	16,751	18,940	18,535	43,228	34,296	21,532	30,707	24,152	23,365	25,027	28,175	10,412
2005–06	17,244	18,781	19,445	45,633	35,895	22,162	32,349	25,439	24,240	26,191	29,782	10,811
2006–07	18,108	19,225	21,473	49,135	37,569	23,474	33,986	26,681	25,432	27,135	31,561	11,628
2007–08	18,878	19,327	22,815	51,803	39,280	24,503	35,299	27,884	25,928	23,558	33,481	11,346
2008–09[1]	19,230	19,416	23,979	54,774	41,289	25,757	36,708	29,618	26,842	24,646	35,622	11,983
2009–10	19,993	19,993	—	—	—	—	—	—	—	—	—	—
2010–11	20,335	19,934	—	—	—	—	—	—	—	—	—	—

—Not available.
†Not applicable.
[1]Preliminary first-professional tuition average based on 2007–08 degrees.
[2]Data are based on in-state tuition only.
NOTE: Average graduate student tuition weighted by fall full-time-equivalent graduate enrollment. Average first-professional student tuition weighted by number of degrees conferred during the academic year. Some year-to-year fluctuations in tuition data may reflect nonreporting by individual institutions. Excludes institutions not reporting degrees conferred and institutions not reporting tuition. Data through 1995–96 are for institutions of higher education, while later data are for degree-granting institutions. Degree-granting institutions grant associate's or higher degrees and participate in Title IV federal financial aid programs. The degree-granting classification is very similar to the earlier higher education classification, but it includes more 2-year colleges and excludes a few higher education institutions that did not grant degrees. (See Appendix A: Guide to Sources for details.) Some data have been revised from previously published figures.
SOURCE: U.S. Department of Education, National Center for Education Statistics, Integrated Postsecondary Education Data System (IPEDS), "Fall Enrollment Survey" (IPEDS-EF:89–99); "Completions Survey" (IPEDS-C:90–99); "Institutional Characteristics Survey" (IPEDS-IC:89–99); Fall 2000 through Fall 2009, Institutional Characteristics component; and Spring 2001 through Spring 2011, Enrollment component. (This table was prepared November 2011.)

Percentage of undergraduates receiving aid, by type and source of aid and selected student characteristics: 2007–08

Selected student characteristic	Number of undergraduates[1] (in thousands)	Any aid Total[2]	Any aid Federal[3]	Any aid Nonfederal	Grants Total	Grants Federal	Grants Nonfederal	Loans Total[4]	Loans Federal[4]	Loans Nonfederal	Work study Total[5]
	2	3	4	5	6	7	8	9	10	11	12
All undergraduates	20,928 (0.4)	65.6 (1.20)	48.2 (0.85)	48.0 (0.77)	51.7 (0.96)	27.6 (0.47)	38.5 (0.72)	38.7 (0.24)	34.9 (0.18)	14.8 (0.21)	7.4 (0.20)
Sex											
Male	9,013 (126.0)	61.4 (1.38)	43.1 (0.98)	45.7 (1.01)	46.7 (1.16)	21.7 (0.59)	37.0 (0.95)	35.0 (0.45)	31.1 (0.38)	13.8 (0.26)	7.2 (0.31)
Female	11,915 (125.7)	68.8 (1.04)	52.0 (0.74)	49.7 (0.62)	55.5 (0.78)	32.0 (0.37)	39.5 (0.61)	41.5 (0.26)	37.8 (0.24)	15.5 (0.28)	7.6 (0.18)
Race/ethnicity											
White	12,924 (109.7)	63.5 (1.32)	44.4 (0.99)	47.8 (0.83)	48.2 (0.95)	20.7 (0.39)	38.5 (0.79)	38.5 (0.54)	34.6 (0.52)	15.0 (0.28)	7.3 (0.25)
Black	2,925 (59.1)	76.2 (1.56)	63.5 (1.57)	50.5 (0.93)	63.5 (1.31)	46.4 (1.19)	38.4 (0.84)	49.6 (1.05)	46.1 (1.02)	17.7 (0.62)	7.2 (0.35)
Hispanic	2,960 (93.0)	69.0 (0.76)	53.4 (0.72)	48.8 (0.85)	58.1 (0.99)	39.5 (0.63)	39.2 (0.93)	34.4 (1.09)	30.3 (1.15)	14.1 (0.44)	7.2 (0.33)
Asian	1,236 (38.0)	53.4 (1.96)	36.7 (1.21)	42.1 (1.71)	43.1 (1.54)	22.7 (0.96)	36.0 (1.37)	25.6 (0.89)	22.4 (0.90)	9.3 (0.57)	8.7 (0.56)
American Indian/Alaska Native	176 (18.7)	70.8 (2.92)	54.3 (3.17)	48.4 (3.06)	60.4 (3.10)	39.3 (3.51)	36.3 (2.74)	35.5 (3.34)	31.9 (3.49)	12.0 (2.09)	5.3 (1.12)
Native Hawaiian/Pacific Islander	151 (11.6)	61.5 (3.28)	42.4 (3.32)	44.5 (2.97)	49.3 (3.96)	26.6 (3.02)	33.1 (3.88)	32.1 (3.01)	27.9 (2.83)	12.3 (1.57)	7.7 (1.46)
Other	61 (5.2)	64.1 (4.03)	49.2 (3.84)	41.1 (4.13)	51.1 (3.96)	33.2 (3.10)	—	35.5 (4.02)	32.8 (3.88)	12.7 (2.37)	6.1 (1.60)
Two or more races	495 (25.9)	68.1 (1.51)	53.2 (1.46)	49.7 (1.58)	53.8 (1.43)	31.2 (1.31)	40.7 (1.31)	41.6 (1.55)	38.6 (1.60)	14.0 (0.98)	11.4 (1.02)
Age											
15 to 23 years old	12,490 (60.2)	66.9 (1.02)	49.3 (0.67)	51.4 (0.72)	52.5 (0.94)	25.0 (0.40)	42.7 (0.76)	40.4 (0.25)	36.3 (0.24)	15.6 (0.21)	10.4 (0.26)
24 to 29 years old	3,621 (37.1)	66.3 (1.60)	52.5 (1.10)	43.0 (1.12)	52.0 (1.10)	36.5 (0.72)	30.6 (0.93)	41.6 (0.61)	37.4 (0.49)	16.3 (0.53)	3.8 (0.23)
30 years old or over	4,817 (52.5)	61.8 (1.55)	42.1 (1.35)	42.7 (0.95)	49.4 (1.16)	27.4 (0.77)	33.4 (0.84)	32.3 (0.55)	29.5 (0.50)	11.7 (0.42)	2.3 (0.18)
Marital status											
Not married[6]	16,761 (59.2)	66.4 (1.28)	49.6 (0.89)	49.2 (0.84)	52.7 (1.05)	28.1 (0.51)	39.8 (0.77)	40.2 (0.32)	36.2 (0.26)	15.4 (0.25)	8.6 (0.23)
Married	3,763 (58.7)	60.8 (1.01)	40.4 (0.96)	42.3 (0.71)	45.7 (0.80)	22.0 (0.54)	33.1 (0.78)	31.0 (0.50)	28.2 (0.51)	11.7 (0.39)	2.6 (0.20)
Separated	404 (13.1)	77.1 (2.32)	64.8 (1.94)	47.8 (2.75)	67.9 (2.69)	55.3 (1.97)	32.9 (2.69)	48.9 (1.66)	45.3 (1.62)	18.0 (1.49)	3.2 (0.53)
Attendance status[7]											
Full-time, full-year	8,220 (59.4)	79.5 (0.37)	63.0 (0.32)	62.9 (0.43)	64.4 (0.38)	33.0 (0.38)	52.8 (0.52)	53.3 (0.42)	49.6 (0.42)	20.1 (0.29)	13.5 (0.29)
Part-time or part-year	12,708 (59.2)	56.6 (1.86)	38.6 (1.48)	38.3 (1.13)	43.5 (1.50)	24.0 (0.97)	29.2 (0.99)	29.3 (0.63)	25.5 (0.55)	11.4 (0.34)	3.5 (0.23)
Dependency status and family income											
Dependent	11,081 (65.7)	66.5 (1.06)	48.2 (0.71)	52.5 (0.78)	51.4 (0.94)	22.1 (0.37)	43.9 (0.81)	40.6 (0.33)	36.5 (0.31)	15.9 (0.23)	11.0 (0.29)
Less than $20,000	1,263 (22.5)	80.7 (1.13)	71.4 (0.82)	57.5 (1.13)	76.7 (1.25)	68.2 (0.84)	50.4 (1.23)	40.0 (1.01)	36.7 (0.98)	12.5 (0.55)	12.1 (0.59)
$20,000–$39,999	1,853 (23.2)	78.5 (1.07)	68.5 (0.78)	59.7 (0.88)	71.8 (1.10)	59.3 (0.76)	52.2 (0.98)	44.6 (0.81)	41.7 (0.71)	15.1 (0.46)	14.6 (0.51)
$40,000–$59,999	1,852 (26.1)	66.8 (1.69)	49.3 (1.31)	54.9 (1.29)	53.1 (1.41)	23.7 (0.94)	46.5 (1.21)	43.2 (0.81)	39.0 (0.89)	17.3 (0.58)	12.5 (0.53)
$60,000–$79,999	1,646 (28.8)	63.3 (1.27)	41.6 (0.99)	51.4 (1.15)	41.7 (1.02)	1.7 (0.18)	41.2 (1.19)	42.7 (0.91)	38.5 (0.92)	18.1 (0.61)	11.0 (0.71)
$80,000–$99,999	1,398 (23.8)	63.1 (0.98)	40.0 (0.78)	51.1 (1.01)	41.7 (1.06)	0.5 (0.14)	41.6 (1.02)	43.2 (0.76)	37.7 (0.76)	18.4 (0.62)	10.2 (0.60)
$100,000 or more	3,070 (42.8)	56.4 (1.06)	32.9 (1.08)	45.9 (0.81)	37.4 (1.08)	0.6 (0.08)	37.3 (0.80)	36.6 (0.71)	30.2 (0.77)	14.5 (0.36)	8.0 (0.31)
Independent	9,847 (65.6)	64.6 (1.42)	48.2 (1.08)	42.9 (0.87)	52.0 (1.06)	33.7 (0.63)	32.3 (0.76)	45.0 (0.35)	40.6 (0.28)	13.6 (0.34)	3.3 (0.16)
Less than $10,000	2,268 (31.4)	74.0 (1.25)	63.3 (0.70)	45.9 (1.04)	67.4 (1.08)	58.3 (0.59)	33.4 (0.97)	45.6 (0.80)	42.0 (0.93)	16.0 (0.59)	6.8 (0.33)
$10,000–$19,999	1,714 (30.2)	71.5 (1.74)	62.4 (1.24)	42.9 (1.28)	62.3 (1.50)	52.3 (1.09)	30.7 (1.04)	42.0 (0.78)	38.5 (0.77)	15.8 (0.66)	3.7 (0.30)
$20,000–$29,999	1,502 (27.4)	68.6 (2.17)	54.8 (1.85)	42.9 (1.60)	51.5 (1.89)	34.9 (1.31)	30.8 (1.22)	40.6 (0.89)	36.9 (0.93)	15.4 (0.76)	3.0 (0.37)
$30,000–$49,999	2,001 (34.5)	62.9 (1.74)	44.6 (1.63)	43.9 (1.17)	49.3 (1.27)	28.4 (1.08)	33.6 (1.10)	34.9 (0.89)	31.8 (0.80)	13.1 (0.65)	1.8 (0.22)
$50,000 or more	2,362 (40.8)	49.7 (1.07)	22.4 (1.02)	39.1 (0.76)	32.4 (0.79)	0.3 (0.09)	32.3 (0.79)	20.9 (0.75)	18.4 (0.75)	9.0 (0.44)	1.2 (0.18)
Housing status[8]											
School-owned	2,964 (111.5)	80.1 (1.21)	70.1 (1.00)	60.7 (1.14)	66.6 (1.14)	23.5 (0.57)	62.3 (1.11)	57.9 (0.84)	53.7 (0.75)	22.0 (0.57)	22.5 (0.85)
Off-campus, not with parents	11,296 (219.5)	65.5 (1.53)	45.5 (1.31)	48.4 (0.91)	51.3 (1.19)	29.9 (0.77)	35.0 (0.78)	38.4 (0.51)	34.8 (0.47)	14.5 (0.33)	4.5 (0.21)
With parents	5,002 (143.6)	56.1 (1.66)	40.4 (1.14)	38.7 (1.19)	43.9 (1.67)	24.5 (0.95)	32.5 (1.26)	25.8 (0.45)	22.1 (0.40)	10.6 (0.30)	4.9 (0.26)

[1] Numbers of undergraduates may not equal figures reported in other tables, since these data are based on a sample survey of students who enrolled at any time during the school year. Includes all postsecondary institutions.
[2] Includes students who reported they were awarded aid, but did not specify the source or type of aid.
[3] Includes Department of Veterans Affairs and Department of Defense benefits.
[4] Includes Parent Loans for Undergraduate Students (PLUS).
[5] Details on federal and nonfederal work-study participants are not available.
[6] Includes students who were single, divorced, or widowed.
[7] Full-time, full-year includes students enrolled full time for 9 or more months. Part-time or part-year includes students enrolled part time for 9 or more months and students enrolled less than 9 months either part time or full time.
[8] Excludes students attending more than one institution.

NOTE: Excludes students whose attendance status was not reported. Detail may not sum to totals because of rounding and because some students receive multiple types of aid and aid from different sources. Data include undergraduates in degree-granting and non-degree-granting institutions. Data include Puerto Rico. Race categories exclude persons of Hispanic ethnicity. Standard errors appear in parentheses.
SOURCE: U.S. Department of Education, National Center for Education Statistics, 2007–08 National Postsecondary Student Aid Study (NPSAS:08). (This table was prepared August 2009.)

Weighted average tuition fee for full-time Canadian undergraduate students, by field of study
annual (dollars)

Field of study grouping	2008/2009	2009/2010	2010/2011	2011/2012	2012/2013
Education	3,652	3,739	3,850	3,804	4,006
Visual and performing arts, and communications technologies	4,377	4,592	4,748	4,591	4,793
Humanities	4,364	4,525	4,638	4,769	4,942
Social and behavioural sciences	4,251	4,431	4,586	4,656	4,862
Law, legal professions and studies	8,030	8,229	8,657	9,335	9,949
Business management and public administration	4,978	5,191	5,386	5,673	6,060
Physical and life sciences and technologies	4,679	4,885	5,049	5,247	5,478
Mathematics, computer and information sciences	4,987	5,299	5,526	5,781	6,111
Engineering	5,319	5,577	5,992	6,155	6,552
Architecture and related technologies	4,503	4,826	5,179	4,788	5,077
Agriculture, natural resources and conservation	4,366	4,697	4,803	4,961	5,095
Dentistry	13,290	13,917	15,062	16,037	16,910
Medicine	9,821	9,815	10,867	11,313	11,891
Nursing	4,422	4,558	4,662	4,731	4,909
Pharmacy	8,366	8,783	9,014	9,719	10,297
Veterinary medicine	4,959	5,609	5,612	5,889	6,224
Other health, parks, recreation and fitness	4,539	4,477	4,698	4,873	5,092

Footnotes:
1. Data for 2012/2013 are preliminary.
2. The national and provincial tuition fee averages are weighted with the latest related enrolments available. If the number of enrolments is unknown for a given program, the program is excluded from the averages. The same student enrolment figures are used for the weighting of both years (2011/2012 and 2012/2013), thereby permitting comparison of changes in the tuition fees only.
3. As the distribution of enrolment across the various programs varies from period to period, caution must be exercised when making long-term historical comparisons.
4. For Quebec, since 1998/1999, and for Nova Scotia, since 2007/2008, the weighted averages take into account the different fees paid by "in province" and "out of province" students.
5. It is important to note that tuition fee increases are generally regulated by provincial policies. However, some programs may be exempted from these policies resulting in possible increases that exceed provincial limits.
6. Data in this release do not take into account financial assistance or tax rebates provided to students. Tuition fees and additional compulsory fees represent only a portion of all costs incurred for attending university.

Source: Statistics Canada. *Table 477-0021 - Weighted average tuition fee for full-time Canadian undergraduate students, by field of study, annual (dollars),* CANSIM (database).

(accessed: 2013-02-07)

Weighted average tuition fee for full-time Canadian graduate students, by field of study
annual (dollars)

Field of study grouping	2008/2009	2009/2010	2010/2011	2011/2012	2012/2013
Education	4,697	4,410	4,981	5,089	5,283
Visual and performing arts, and communications technologies	4,255	4,562	4,834	4,409	4,625
Humanities	3,767	3,979	4,239	4,336	4,554
Social and behavioural sciences	3,990	4,109	4,605	4,556	4,790
Law, legal professions and studies	3,773	4,477	4,487	5,302	5,614
Business management and public administration	5,760	6,175	8,132	7,932	8,105
Executive MBA	29,893	27,963	37,032	36,971	38,508
Regular MBA	19,376	19,727	20,336	22,823	23,757
Physical and life sciences and technologies	4,437	5,239	5,477	5,632	5,898
Mathematics, computer and information sciences	4,277	5,488	5,735	5,716	5,964
Engineering	4,593	5,312	5,522	5,175	5,444
Architecture and related technologies	4,293	4,672	4,834	4,950	5,199
Agriculture, natural resources and conservation	3,921	4,636	4,821	4,769	4,982
Dentistry	3,171	3,218	4,337	4,365	4,559
Medicine	..	..	..	..	..
Nursing	4,892	4,925	5,090	5,117	5,360
Pharmacy	6,195	5,247	5,411	5,466	5,710
Veterinary medicine	3,304	3,675	3,435	3,173	3,321
Other health, parks, recreation and fitness	5,092	5,430	7,017	7,577	7,921

Symbol legend:
   .. Not available

Footnotes:
   1. Data for 2012/2013 are preliminary.
   2. The national and provincial tuition fee averages are weighted with the latest related enrolments available. If the number of enrolments is unknown for a given program, the program is excluded from the averages. The same student enrolment figures are used for the weighting of both years (2011/2012 and 2012/2013), thereby permitting comparison of changes in the tuition fees only.
   3. As the distribution of enrolment across the various programs varies from period to period, caution must be exercised when making long-term historical comparisons.
   4. For Quebec, since 1998/1999, and for Nova Scotia, since 2007/2008, the weighted averages take into account the different fees paid by "in province" and "out of province" students.
   5. It is important to note that tuition fee increases are generally regulated by provincial policies. However, some programs may be exempted from these policies resulting in possible increases that exceed provincial limits.
   6. Data in this release do not take into account financial assistance or tax rebates provided to students. Tuition fees and additional compulsory fees represent only a portion of all costs incurred for attending university.
   7. Starting in 2010/2011, the master of business administration programs have been excluded from the national and provincial weighted averages to eliminate the effect of the high cost of these programs on the overall tuition fee average. Dental, medical and veterinary residency programs offered in teaching hospitals and similar locations that may lead to advanced professional certification have also been excluded.

Source: Statistics Canada. *Table 477-0022 - Weighted average tuition fee for full-time Canadian graduate students, by field of study, annual (dollars),* CANSIM (database).

(accessed: 2013-02-07)

Weighted average tuition fee for full-time foreign undergraduate students, by field of study
annual (dollars)

Field of study grouping	2008/2009	2009/2010	2010/2011	2011/2012	2012/2013
Education	12,668	12,779	13,219	13,550	13,921
Visual and performing arts, and communications technologies	32,738	14,847	15,587	15,098	15,703
Humanities	14,182	15,071	15,900	16,537	17,297
Social and behavioural sciences	15,469	15,014	15,750	16,296	17,007
Law, legal professions and studies	16,924	18,924	20,487	22,909	24,203
Business management and public administration	14,296	15,522	16,349	17,637	18,577
Physical and life sciences and technologies	14,020	16,594	17,546	18,746	19,952
Mathematics, computer and information sciences	15,190	16,781	18,459	18,854	20,631
Engineering	15,587	17,470	18,526	19,526	20,742
Architecture and related technologies	15,574	16,165	17,247	17,780	18,258
Agriculture, natural resources and conservation	14,299	15,611	16,286	16,439	17,518
Dentistry	14,323	40,225	40,964	42,057	43,014
Medicine	13,974	34,198	35,422	35,502	36,067
Nursing	37,826	13,747	14,283	14,651	15,345
Pharmacy	13,472	21,936	20,795	27,300	30,098
Veterinary medicine	46,377	47,307	48,262	49,538	50,674
Other health, parks, recreation and fitness	47,850	14,950	15,683	16,069	16,738

Footnotes:
1. Data for 2012/2013 are preliminary.
2. The national and provincial tuition fee averages are weighted with the latest related enrolments available. If the number of enrolments is unknown for a given program, the program is excluded from the averages. The same student enrolment figures are used for the weighting of both years (2011/2012 and 2012/2013), thereby permitting comparison of changes in the tuition fees only.
3. As the distribution of enrolment across the various programs varies from period to period, caution must be exercised when making long-term historical comparisons.
4. It is important to note that tuition fee increases are generally regulated by provincial policies. However, some programs may be exempted from these policies resulting in possible increases that exceed provincial limits.
5. Data in this release do not take into account financial assistance or tax rebates provided to students. Tuition fees and additional compulsory fees represent only a portion of all costs incurred for attending university.

Source: Statistics Canada. *Table 477-0023 - Weighted average tuition fee for full-time foreign undergraduate students, by field of study, annual (dollars),* CANSIM (database).

(accessed: 2013-02-07)

Weighted average tuition fee for full-time foreign graduate students, by field of study
annual (dollars)

Field of study grouping	2008/2009	2009/2010	2010/2011	2011/2012	2012/2013
Education	9,107	9,241	10,467	10,661	10,898
Visual and performing arts, and communications technologies	11,024	11,552	12,449	11,980	12,265
Humanities	10,646	11,192	11,952	12,309	12,729
Social and behavioural sciences	9,929	10,391	11,716	11,853	12,159
Law, legal professions and studies	13,288	13,212	13,872	14,789	15,141
Business management and public administration	14,360	15,173	17,665	17,220	16,798
Executive MBA	31,203	29,389	34,567	34,445	31,039
Regular MBA	26,239	26,314	25,725	28,876	30,831
Physical and life sciences and technologies.	10,207	11,177	11,985	12,152	12,524
Mathematics, computer and information sciences	9,680	10,922	11,749	12,079	12,550
Engineering	10,630	12,375	13,141	13,297	13,729
Architecture and related technologies	12,050	12,473	13,127	13,453	14,060
Agriculture, natural resources and conservation	10,833	10,868	11,215	11,515	11,776
Dentistry	9,568	10,066	12,104	12,370	12,614
Medicine	..	..	..	..	..
Nursing	11,592	11,666	12,314	12,504	12,913
Pharmacy	12,504	11,491	12,003	12,216	12,517
Veterinary medicine	8,385	9,174	10,969	10,824	11,058
Other health, parks, recreation and fitness	10,803	11,045	12,679	14,069	14,521

Symbol legend:
.. Not available

Footnotes:
1. Data for 2012/2013 are preliminary.
2. The national and provincial tuition fee averages are weighted with the latest related enrolments available. If the number of enrolments is unknown for a given program, the program is excluded from the averages. The same student enrolment figures are used for the weighting of both years (2011/2012 and 2012/2013), thereby permitting comparison of changes in the tuition fees only.
3. As the distribution of enrolment across the various programs varies from period to period, caution must be exercised when making long-term historical comparisons.
4. It is important to note that tuition fee increases are generally regulated by provincial policies. However, some programs may be exempted from these policies resulting in possible increases that exceed provincial limits.
5. Data in this release do not take into account financial assistance or tax rebates provided to students. Tuition fees and additional compulsory fees represent only a portion of all costs incurred for attending university.
6. Starting in 2010/2011, the master of business administration programs have been excluded from the national and provincial weighted averages to eliminate the effect of the high cost of these programs on the overall tuition fee average. Dental, medical and veterinary residency programs offered in teaching hospitals and similar locations that may lead to advanced professional certification have also been excluded.

Source: Statistics Canada. *Table 477-0024 - Weighted average tuition fee for full-time foreign graduate students, by field of study, annual (dollars),* CANSIM (database).
Back to search

(accessed: 2013-02-07)

School board revenues, by direct source of funds
annual (dollars x 1,000)

School board revenues by direct source of funds	2006	2007	2008	2009	2010
Total revenues	43,414,001	45,802,579	47,872,221	49,724,674[r]	51,644,180
Local taxation sources	12,170,486	12,472,739	12,695,401	12,899,480	13,062,175
Provincial government sources	27,775,474	29,396,202	31,488,794	33,235,682[r]	34,936,172
Federal government sources	278,908	276,717	289,013	308,786	314,175
Student and other school fees	212,506	229,408	225,802	237,677	243,953
Other private sector sources	2,976,627	3,427,513	3,173,211	3,043,049	3,087,705

Symbol legend:
r Revised

Footnotes:
1. Source: Statistics Canada, Culture, Tourism and the Centre for Education Statistics.
2. Data are or have been converted to a calendar basis, January 1 to December 31.
3. School boards represent schools which are a part of the elementary and secondary public school system. The revenues and/or expenditures in this table exclude those of other types of publicly run elementary and secondary schools such as federal schools and special needs education schools as well as the elementary and secondary schools which are in the private school system.
4. For Nova Scotia, student and other school fees were included in other private sector sources from 1974 to 1979.
5. From 1900 to 1904, Saskatchewan and Alberta were reported under Northwest Territories.
6. Before 1969, provincial grants to reduce local taxation of property owners were included in local taxation.
8. For Quebec, student and other school fees are included within other private sector sources for 1977 to 1980.
9. Northwest Territories (including Nunavut) figures for the new territory of Nunavut (as of 1999) are still not available separately.
10. Please note that effective in 2004, Ontario financial figures are higher compared to prior years due to changes in the way the province is reporting its school board finances to Statistics Canada.
11. The 2009 data for Canada and Prince Edward Island have revised figures.

Source: Statistics Canada. *Table 478-0010 - School board revenues, by direct source of funds, annual (dollars),* CANSIM (database).
Back to search

(accessed: 2013-02-07)

School board expenditures, by function and economic classification
annual (dollars x 1,000)

Functions	2006	2007	2008	2009	2010
Total expenditures by function	43,643,973	45,708,027	47,896,142	50,151,830[r]	51,904,934
Business administration expenditures	1,380,309	1,426,163	1,476,255	1,518,013[r]	1,544,840
Instruction and educational services expenditures[3]	30,808,880	32,245,201	33,629,437	35,120,489[r]	36,435,142
Adult education expenditures	673,446	702,751	725,413	774,273	786,036
Food services expenditures	1,047,021	1,034,886	1,081,034	1,371,845[r]	1,861,807
School facilities service expenditures	4,000,429	4,161,645	4,339,294	4,431,037[r]	4,505,790
Transportation expenditures	1,970,829	2,046,268	2,130,253	2,164,196[r]	2,191,732
Capital outlay expenditures (non-allocable)	2,777,110	3,049,063	3,651,237	3,916,655[r]	3,685,778
Debt charges on capital expenditures (non-allocable)	985,949	1,042,050	863,219	855,322	893,809

Symbol legend:
r Revised

Footnotes:
1. Source: Statistics Canada, Culture, Tourism and the Centre for Education Statistics.
2. Data are or have been converted to a calendar basis, January 1 to December 31.
3. Instruction and education services expenditures include instructional administration expenditures.
4. Please note that effective in 2004, Ontario financial figures are higher compared to prior years due to changes in the way the province is reporting its school board finances to Statistics Canada.
5. The 2009 data for Canada, Prince Edward Island and Ontario have revised figures.

Source: Statistics Canada. *Table 478-0011 - School board expenditures, by function and economic classification, annual (dollars),* CANSIM (database).
Back to search

(accessed: 2013-02-07)

School board expenditures, by function and economic classification
annual (dollars x 1,000)

Economic classification	2006	2007	2008	2009	2010
Total expenditures by economic classification	43,643,973	45,708,027	47,896,142	50,151,830[r]	51,904,934
Salary and wages expenditures	28,825,691	30,197,995	31,477,180	32,911,465[r]	34,226,301
Fringe benefits expenditures	3,734,484	3,919,807	4,089,749	4,250,886[r]	4,420,034
Supply and services expenditures	3,737,000	3,792,319	3,932,497	4,213,534[r]	4,529,877
Fees and contractual services expenditures	2,957,213	3,113,186	3,274,489	3,328,525[r]	3,034,824
Other operating expenditures	626,526	593,607	607,771	675,443[r]	1,114,311
Capital expenditures (non-allocable, outlay and debt charges)	3,763,059	4,091,113	4,514,456	4,771,977[r]	4,579,587

Symbol legend:
r Revised

Footnotes:
1. Source: Statistics Canada, Culture, Tourism and the Centre for Education Statistics.
2. Data are or have been converted to a calendar basis, January 1 to December 31.
3. Instruction and education services expenditures include instructional administration expenditures.
4. Please note that effective in 2004, Ontario financial figures are higher compared to prior years due to changes in the way the province is reporting its school board finances to Statistics Canada.
5. The 2009 data for Canada, Prince Edward Island and Ontario have revised figures.

Source: Statistics Canada. *Table 478-0011 - School board expenditures, by function and economic classification, annual (dollars),* CANSIM (database).
Back to search

(accessed: 2013-02-07)

Public and private elementary and secondary education expenditures
annual (dollars x 1,000)

Type of expenditures	2005/2006	2006/2007	2007/2008	2008/2009	2009/2010
Public and private elementary and secondary education expenditures	50,582,878	53,421,944	55,728,261	58,836,775	61,925,701
Public elementary and secondary education expenditures	47,432,820	50,105,473	52,244,764	55,198,663	58,131,160
Public school board and direct government expenditures	46,265,673	48,712,957	50,895,684	53,862,326	56,459,590
Public school board expenditures	41,577,439	43,643,972	45,728,027	47,896,142	50,149,942
Public school board expenditures, net	41,537,838	43,601,833	45,682,353	47,848,425	50,100,553
Public school board expenditures transferred to private schools	-39,601	-42,139	-45,674	-47,717	-49,389
Direct government expenditures on public education	4,727,835	5,111,124	5,213,331	6,013,901	6,359,037
Direct government expenditures on services to public school boards[3]	1,062,279	1,805,414	1,564,891	1,697,780	1,825,238
Direct government expenditures on contributions to public school board teachers' pension funds[3]	2,412,397	2,569,049	2,443,977	3,103,877	3,342,671
Direct government expenditures on public education by the Department of National Defence[4]	83	117	177	105	121
Other direct government expenditures on public education[4]	1,253,076	736,544	1,204,286	1,212,139	1,191,007
Federal school expenditures	832,791	1,014,876	950,622	928,598	1,235,097
Federal school operating expenditures					
Federal school capital expenditures					
Special education expenditures on public education	156,114	208,328	214,264	211,937	233,708
Special education expenditures, handicapped outside regular public schools	108,395	153,292	166,657	163,498	172,789
Special education expenditures on provincially licensed correspondence courses	23,410	30,456	32,741	34,135	36,189
Special education expenditures, reform and correctional institutions	4,290	4,325	4,275	4,330	4,375
Special education expenditures on federal penitentiaries	20,019	20,255	10,591	9,974	20,355
Direct provincial government expenditures on administration of public education	178,243	169,312	184,194	195,802	202,766
Private elementary and secondary school expenditures	3,150,058	3,316,471	3,483,497	3,638,112	3,794,541

Symbol legend:
▓▓▓ Series is Terminated

Footnotes:
1. Source: Statistics Canada, Tourism and the Centre for Education Statistics.
2. Data are estimates for 2009-2010.
3. From 1950 to 1959 there was no separate breakdown available between direct government expenditures on services to public school boards and direct government expenditures on contributions to public school board teachers' pension funds. These were both reported under direct government expenditures on contributions to public school board teachers' pension funds.
4. From 1950 to 1959, any direct government expenditures on public education by Department of National Defence were reported under other direct government expenditures on public education.
5. Foreign and undistributed expenditures by the federal government which cannot be attributed to a particular province or territory.

Source: Statistics Canada. *Table 478-0014 - Public and private elementary and secondary education expenditures, annual (dollars),* CANSIM (database).
Back to search

(accessed: 2013-02-07)

Public and private elementary and secondary education expenditures, by direct source of funds
annual (dollars x 1,000)

Public and private elementary and secondary education expenditures by direct source of funds	2005/2006	2006/2007	2007/2008	2008/2009	2009/2010
Public and private elementary and secondary education expenditures by direct source of funds, all sources	50,582,878	53,421,944	55,728,261	58,836,775	61,925,701
Public and private elementary and secondary education expenditures by direct source of funds, all governments' sources	45,038,927	47,167,546	49,510,198	52,649,183	55,330,207
Public and private elementary and secondary education expenditures by direct source of funds, federal government sources	1,292,587	1,184,922	1,448,904	1,443,214	1,692,258
Public and private elementary and secondary education expenditures by direct source of funds, provincial government sources	31,785,490	33,807,423	35,583,659	38,505,438	40,733,162
Public and private elementary and secondary education expenditures by direct source of funds, local government sources	11,960,850	12,175,201	12,477,635	12,700,531	12,904,787
Public and private elementary and secondary education expenditures by direct source of funds, student and other school fees	1,982,169	2,086,183	2,186,739	2,262,021	2,365,624
Public and private elementary and secondary education expenditures by direct source of funds, other private sector sources	3,561,782	4,168,215	4,031,324	3,925,571	4,229,870

Footnotes:

1. Source: Statistics Canada, Tourism and the Centre for Education Statistics.
2. Data are estimates for 2009-2010.
3. Foreign and undistributed expenditures by the federal government which cannot be attributed to a particular province or territory.

Source: Statistics Canada. *Table 478-0015 - Public and private elementary and secondary education expenditures, by direct source of funds, annual (dollars),* CANSIM (database).
Back to search

(accessed: 2013-02-07)

Labour force survey estimates (LFS), by educational attainment, sex and age group
annual

Educational attainment[11]	2008	2009	2010	2011	2012
Total, all education levels	63.5	61.6	61.6	61.8	61.8
0 to 8 years[12]	20.7	20.0	19.8	19.6	20.0
Some high school[13]	45.7	41.2	40.3	40.2	39.5
High school graduate[14]	64.7	61.7	61.7	61.8	61.1
Some postsecondary[15]	64.6	60.9	60.7	60.3	60.6
Postsecondary certificate or diploma[16]	72.8	71.2	70.8	71.0	70.6
University degree[17]	76.3	75.9	75.4	74.8	75.0
Bachelor's degree	76.3	75.7	75.3	74.5	74.8
Above bachelor's degree	76.3	76.3	75.4	75.4	75.4

Footnotes:
1. Number of persons of working age. Estimates in thousands, rounded to the nearest hundred.
2. Number of civilian, non-institutionalized persons 15 years of age and over who, during the reference week, were employed or unemployed. Estimates in thousands, rounded to the nearest hundred.
3. Number of persons who, during the reference week, worked for pay or profit, or performed unpaid family work or had a job but were not at work due to own illness or disability, personal or family responsibilities, labour dispute, vacation, or other reason. Those persons on layoff and persons without work but who had a job to start at a definite date in the future are not considered employed. Estimates in thousands, rounded to the nearest hundred.
4. Full-time employment consists of persons who usually work 30 hours or more per week at their main or only job. Estimates in thousands, rounded to the nearest hundred.
5. Part-time employment consists of persons who usually work less than 30 hours per week at their main or only job. Estimates in thousands, rounded to the nearest hundred.
6. Number of persons who, during the reference week, were without work, had actively looked for work in the past four weeks, and were available for work. Those persons on layoff or who had a new job to start in four weeks or less are considered unemployed. Estimates in thousands, rounded to the nearest hundred.
7. Persons in the civilian non-institutional population 15 years of age and over who, during the reference week, were neither employed nor unemployed. Estimates in thousands, rounded to the nearest hundred.
8. The unemployment rate is the number of unemployed persons expressed as a percentage of the labour force. The unemployment rate for a particular group (age, sex, marital status) is the number of unemployed in that group expressed as a percentage of the labour force for that group. Estimates are percentages, rounded to the nearest tenth.
9. The participation rate is the number of labour force participants expressed as a percentage of the population 15 years of age and over. The participation rate for a particular group (age, sex, marital

status) is the number of labour force participants in that group expressed as a percentage of the population for that group. Estimates are percentages, rounded to the nearest tenth.

10. The employment rate (formerly the employment and population ratio) is the number of persons employed expressed as a percentage of the population 15 years of age and over. The employment rate for a particular group (age, sex, marital status) is the number employed in that group expressed as a percentage of the population for that group. Estimates are percentages, rounded to the nearest tenth.

11. The following categories refer to the highest level of schooling completed. Questions relating to educational attainment were changed in 1990, to better capture the relationship between educational attainment and labour market outcomes. Because this introduced a break in the education series, this table only contains data from 1990 onwards. Beginning January 1990, data on primary and secondary education reflects the highest grade completed. This provides a more consistent measure for those who accelerate or fail a grade than did years of school. A question on high school graduation has also been added since it is generally believed that persons who have never completed their secondary education have greater difficulty competing in the labour market. With the new questions, any education that could be counted towards a degree, certificate or diploma from an educational institution is taken as postsecondary education. The change allows more persons into the postsecondary education category. For example, trades programs offered through apprenticeship, vocational schools or private trade schools do not always require high school graduation. Such education is now considered as postsecondary while only primary or secondary would have been recognized prior to 1990. Finally, more information is collected on the type of postsecondary education: 1) some postsecondary; 2) trades certificate or diploma from a vocational or apprenticeship training; 3) Non-university certificate or diploma from a community college, CEGEP or school of nursing; 4) University certificate below bachelors degree; 5) Bachelors degree; and 6) University degree or certificate above bachelors degree.

12. Primary education, grade 8 or lower. In Quebec, secondary II or lower.

13. Attended but did not complete secondary school. In Quebec, attended at least Secondary III but did not complete Secondary V. In Newfoundland and Labrador, attended at least the first year of secondary but did not complete the fourth year.

14. Received a high school diploma. In Quebec, completed Secondary V. In Newfoundland and Labrador, completed fourth year of secondary.

15. Worked toward, but did not complete, a degree, certificate (including a trade certificate) or diploma from an educational institution, including a university, beyond the secondary level. This includes vocational schools, apprenticeship training, community college, Collège d'Enseignement Général et Professionnel (CEGEP), and school of nursing.

16. Completed a certificate (including a trade certificate) or diploma from an educational institution beyond the secondary level. This includes certificates from vocational schools, apprenticeship training, community college, Collège d'Enseignement Général et Professionnel (CEGEP), and school of nursing. Also included are certificates below a Bachelor's degree obtained at a university.

17. Attained at least a university bachelor's degree.

18. The Labour force survey collection of tables, starting with number 282-, is large with many possible cross-tabulations for the 10 provinces and other geographic regions. To ensure respondent's confidentiality, detailed data are suppressed. Data for Canada, Quebec, Ontario, Alberta and British Columbia are suppressed if the estimate is below 1,500, for Newfoundland and Labrador, Nova Scotia, New Brunswick, Manitoba and Saskatchewan, if the estimate is below 500, and for Prince Edward Island, under 200. For suppression levels within census metropolitan areas (CMAs) and economic regions (ERs), use the respective provincial suppression levels above. While suppressing to protect respondent confidentiality has the added effect of blocking-out the lowest-quality LFS data, some remaining non-suppressed data in these very large LFS CANSIM tables may be of insufficient quality to allow for accurate interpretation. Please be warned that the more detailed your LFS CANSIM download, the smaller the sample size upon which your LFS estimates will be based, and the greater the risk of downloading poorer quality data.

19. Estimates prior to 1996 are based on 2001 census population counts, while estimates from 1996 onwards are based on 2006 census population counts.

Source: Statistics Canada. *Table 282-0004 - Labour force survey estimates (LFS), by educational attainment, sex and age group, annual (persons unless otherwise noted),* CANSIM (database). Back to search

(accessed: 2013-02-07)

Number and median age of full-time teaching staff at Canadian universities
annual

Rank	Number and median	2006/2007	2007/2008	2008/2009	2009/2010	2010/2011
Total rank	Number of full time teaching staff	40,567	41,306	41,954	44,423	44,934
	Median age of full-time teaching staff	49	49	49	50	50
Full professor	Number of full time teaching staff	14,039	14,187	14,382	14,718	14,946
	Median age of full-time teaching staff	56	56	56	57	57
Associate professor	Number of full time teaching staff	13,195	13,618	14,208	14,941	15,473
	Median age of full-time teaching staff	48	48	48	48	48
Assistant professor	Number of full time teaching staff	10,910	10,986	10,824	10,591	10,161
	Median age of full-time teaching staff	39	39	39	39	39
Rank or level below assistant professor[5]	Number of full time teaching staff	2,181	2,203	2,196	3,402	3,487
	Median age of full-time teaching staff	47	46	47	49	49
Other ranks (not elsewhere classified)[6]	Number of full time teaching staff	242	312	344	771	867
	Median age of full-time teaching staff	48	50	50	49	51

Footnotes:
1. All counts with 3 or less observation are suppressed.
2. Includes M.D. (Doctor of Medicine), D.D.S. (Doctor of Dental Surgery), D.V.M. (Doctor of Veterinary Medicine).
3. Includes undergraduate and graduate diplomas and professional designations other than a degree such as C.A., C.G.A., R.I.A.
4. Includes deans, vice-deans, associate deans, directors equivalent to a dean, directors, department heads, co-ordinators or chairperson.
5. Includes lecturers and instructors.
6. Includes ungraded staff.
7. Due to a revision of the institutions in the survey, the following institutions are not included in the 2009/2010 data: in Ontario: Tyndale University College and Tyndale Seminary; in Alberta: Newman Theological College and in British Columbia: Vancouver School of Theology and Seminary of Christ the King. Thompson Rivers University was included as of 2009/2010.
8. The following institutions, previously colleges, have been granted degree granting status and are included in the 2009/2010 data: Mount Royal University, Grant MacEwan University, Vancouver Island University, Kwantlan Polytechnic University and University of the Fraser Valley.
9. The following institutions were included in the full-time University and College Academic Staff System (UCASS) survey for the first time in 2010/2011: Emily Carr University of Art and Design and Capilano University in British Columbia. Formerly, these institutions were colleges but became universities (received degree granting status) in 2009/2010

Source: Statistics Canada. *Table 477-0018 - Number and median age of full-time teaching staff at Canadian universities, by highest earned degree, staff functions, rank, sex, Canada and Provinces, annual,* CANSIM (database).
Back to search

(accessed: 2013-02-07)

Number of full-time teaching staff at Canadian universities, by rank, sex
annual (number)

Rank	Sex	2006/2007	2007/2008	2008/2009	2009/2010	2010/2011
Total rank	Both sexes	40,567	41,306	41,954	44,423	44,934
	Males	27,008	27,186	27,341	28,353	28,486
	Females	13,559	14,120	14,613	16,070	16,448
Full professor	Both sexes	14,039	14,187	14,382	14,718	14,946
	Males	11,183	11,172	11,195	11,364	11,447
	Females	2,856	3,015	3,187	3,354	3,499
Associate professor	Both sexes	13,195	13,618	14,208	14,941	15,473
	Males	8,450	8,634	8,958	9,320	9,550
	Females	4,745	4,984	5,250	5,621	5,923
Assistant professor	Both sexes	10,910	10,986	10,824	10,591	10,161
	Males	6,233	6,178	5,995	5,733	5,446
	Females	4,677	4,808	4,829	4,858	4,715
Rank or level below assistant professor[2]	Both sexes	2,181	2,203	2,196	3,402	3,487
	Males	1,026	1,064	1,032	1,566	1,612
	Females	1,155	1,139	1,164	1,836	1,875
Other ranks (not elsewhere classified)[3]	Both sexes	242	312	344	771	867
	Males	116	138	161	370	431
	Females	126	174	183	401	436

Footnotes:
1. All counts with 3 or less observation are suppressed.
2. Rank or level below assistant professor includes lecturers, instructors and other teaching staff.
3. Other ranks include staff that do not fit in the above categories.
4. Due to a revision of the institutions in the survey, the following institutions are not included in the 2009/2010 data: in Ontario: Tyndale University College and Tyndale Seminary; in Alberta: Newman Theological College and in British Columbia: Vancouver School of Theology and Seminary of Christ the King. Thompson Rivers University was included as of 2009/2010.
5. The following institutions, previously colleges, have been granted degree granting status and are included in the 2009/2010 data: Mount Royal University, Grant MacEwan University, Vancouver Island University, Kwantlan Polytechnic University and University of the Fraser Valley.
6. The following institutions were included in the full-time University and College Academic Staff System (UCASS) survey for the first time in 2010/2011: Emily Carr University of Art and Design and Capilano University in British Columbia. Formerly, these institutions were colleges but became universities (received degree granting status) in 2009/2010.

Source: Statistics Canada. *Table 477-0017 - Number of full-time teaching staff at Canadian universities, by rank, sex, Canada and Provinces, annual (number)*, CANSIM (database).
Back to search

(accessed: 2013-02-07)

Glossary of Education Terms

Accountability
measurable proof, usually in the form of student results on various tests, that teachers, schools, divisions and states are teaching students efficiently and well, usually in the form of student success rates on various tests; Virginia's accountability programs is known as the Standards of Learning which includes curriculum standards approved by the Board of Education and required state tests based on the standards.

Accreditation
a process used by the Virginia Department of Education to evaluate the educational performance of public schools in accordance regulations.

Achievement gap
the difference between the performance of subgroups of students, especially those defined by gender, race/ethnicity, disability and socioeconomic status.

ACT
one of the two commonly used tests designed to assess high school students' general educational development and their ability to complete college-level work in four skill areas: English, mathematics, reading, and science reasoning.

Adequate yearly progress (AYP)
a measurement indicating whether a school, division or the state met federally approved academic goals required by the federal Elementary and Secondary Education Act/No Child Left Behind Act (ESEA/NCLB).

Adult/Continuing education
a program of instruction provided by an adult/continuing education instructional organization for adults and youth beyond the age of compulsory school attendance including basic education and English literacy, English for speakers of other languages, civics education, GED testing services, adult secondary education and Individualized Student Alternative Education Plan (ISAEP) programs.

Advanced Placement (AP)
college-level courses available to high school students which may allow a student to earn college credit provided through the College Board.

Alignment
effort to ensure that what teachers teach is in accord with what the curriculum says will be taught and what is assessed on official tests.

Alternative assessment
a method to measure student educational attainment other than the typical multiple-choice test which may include portfolios, constructed response items and other performance-measurement tools.

Alternative education
a school or center organized for alternative programs of instruction.

Assessment
method of measuring the learning and performance of students; examples include achievement tests, minimum competency tests, developmental screening tests, aptitude tests, observation instruments, performance tasks, etc.

At-risk students
students who have a higher than average probability of dropping out or failing school.

Average daily membership (ADM)
the K-12 enrollment figure used to distribute state per pupil funding that includes students with disabilities ages 5-21, and students for whom English is a second language who entered school for the first time after reaching their 12th birthday, and who have not reached their 22nd birthday; preschool and post-graduate students are not included in ADM.

Benchmark
a standard for judging performance.

Block scheduling
a way of organizing the school day into blocks of time longer than the typical 50 minute class period; with the 4X4 block students take four 90-minute classes each day allowing for completion of an entire course in one semester instead of a full year; with an A/B or rotating block students take six to eight classes for an entire year but classes in each subject meet on alternate days for 90 minutes.

Charter school
a school controlled by a local school board that provides free public elementary and/or secondary education to eligible students under a specific charter granted by the state legislature or other appropriate authority, and designated by such authority to be a charter school.

Class period
a segment of time in the school day that is approximately 1/6 of the instructional day.

Cohort
a particular group of people with something in common.

College Board
the organization that administers SAT, AP and other standardized tests to high school students planning on continuing their educations at a post-secondary level.

Combined school
a public school that contains any combination of or all K-12 grade levels that are not considered an elementary, middle or secondary school .

Composite index of local ability to pay
a formula to determine the state and local government shares of K-12 education program costs, which is expressed as a ratio, indicating the local percentage share of the cost of education programs; for example, a locality with a composite

index of 0.3000 would pay 30 percent and the state would pay 70 percent of the costs.

Confined

due to physical, medical or emotional impairments based on certification of need, a student is restricted or limited from attendance at a regular public school during the regular school hours; this does not apply to situations where a student is restricted for discipline or non-medically based situations.

Core curriculum

the body of knowledge that all students are expected to learn in the subjects of English, mathematics, history/social science and science.

Curriculum

a plan or document that a school or school division uses to define what will be taught and the methods that will be used to educate and assess students.

Curriculum alignment

occurs when what is taught includes or exceeds the content defined by the Standards of Learning (SOL).

Data-based decision making (also referred to as "research-based decision making")

organizing, analyzing and interpreting existing sources of information and other data to make decisions.

Direct aid to public education

funding appropriated for the operation of public schools including funding for school employee benefits, Standards of Quality, incentive-based programs, allotment of sales tax and lottery revenues and specific appropriations for programs such as Governor's Schools and adult literacy initiatives.

Disaggregated data

presentation of data broken into subgroups of students instead of the entire student body which allows parents and teachers to measure how each student group is performing; typical subgroups include students who are economically disadvantaged, from different racial or ethnic groups, those who have disabilities or have limited English fluency.

Distance learning

method of instruction in locations other than the classroom or places where teachers present the lessons, which uses various forms of technology to provide educational materials and experiences to students.

Dropouts

students who leave high school before receiving a diploma.

Early childhood education

the education of young children, especially under the age of 5.

Economically disadvantaged

a student who is a member of a household that meets the income eligibility guidelines for free or reduced-price school meals (less than or equal to 185% of Federal Poverty Guidelines).

Elementary & Secondary Education Act (ESEA)

the primary federal law affecting K-12 education; the most recent reauthorization of the law is also known as the No Child Left Behind Act of 2001 (NCLB).

Elementary school

a public school with grades kindergarten through five.

Eligible students

the total number of students of school age enrolled in the school at a grade or course with a Standards of Learning test; does not include students who are allowed an exclusion such as limited English proficient (LEP) students or some students with disabilities.

English as a second language (ESL)

a program of instruction and services for non-English-speaking or limited-English-proficient students to help them learn and succeed in schools.

English-language learners (ELL)

a student whose first language is other than English and who is in a special program for learning English.

Enrollment

the act of complying with state and local requirements for registration or admission of a child for attendance in a school within a local school division; also refers to registration for courses within the student's home school or within related schools or programs.

Even Start

a federally funded program that provides family-centered education projects to help parents become full partners in the education of their children.

First time

the student has not been enrolled in the school at any time during the current school year.

Four core subject/academic areas

English, mathematics, science and history/social science for purposes of SOL testing.

Free and appropriate public education (FAPE)

requirement through the federal Individuals with Disabilities Education Act (IDEA) that education of students with disabilities (between the ages of 3 and 22) must be provided at public expense, under public supervision, at no charge to the parents and based on the child's unique needs and not on the child's disability.

General education

K-12 instruction that meets the commonwealth's Standards of Learning and prepares children for elementary, secondary and postsecondary success.

Gifted

programs that provide advanced educational opportunities including accelerated promotion through grades and classes and an enriched curriculum for students who are endowed with a high degree of mental ability.

Governor's school
a school serving gifted high school students who meet specific admissions criteria for advanced educational opportunities in areas including the arts, government and international studies, mathematics, science, and technology; both academic-year and summer governor's schools are offered.

Graduate
a student who has earned a Board of Education recognized diploma: advanced studies, advanced technical, standard, standard technical, modified standard, special or general achievement.

Head Start
a federally funded child-development program that provides health, educational, nutritional, social and other services to pre-school children from economically disadvantaged families.

Home-based instruction
non-reimbursable educational services provided in the home setting (or other agreed upon setting) in accordance with the student's individual education program who were removed from school for disciplinary or other reasons, but not the result of a medical referral.

Homebound instruction
academic instruction provided to students who are confined at home or in a health-care facility for periods that would prevent normal school attendance based upon certification of need by a licensed physician or licensed clinical psychologist. For a student with a disability, the Individual Education Program (IEP) team must determine the delivery of services, including the number of hours of services.

Home instruction (also referred to as "home schooling")
instruction of a student or students by a parent or parents, guardian or other person having control or charge of such student or students as an alternative to attendance in a public or private school in accordance with the provisions of the Code of Virginia provisions (§22.1-254.1).

Home tutoring
instruction by a tutor or teacher with qualifications prescribed by the Virginia Board of Education, as an alternative to attendance in a public or private school and approved by the division superintendent in accordance with the provisions of the Code of Virginia §22.1-254; often used as an alternative form of home schooling.

Individuals with Disabilities Education Act (IDEA)
federal law guiding the delivery of special education services for students with disabilities which includes the guarantee of "free and appropriate public education" for every school-age child with a disability and allows parental involvement in the educational planning process, encourages access to the general curriculum and delineates how school disciplinary rules and the obligation to provide a free appropriate public education for disabled children mesh.

Individualized education program (IEP)
a written plan created for a student with disabilities by the student's teachers, parents or guardians, the school administrator, and other interested parties. The plan is tailored to the student's specific needs and abilities, and outlines attainable goals.

Individualized education program team (IEP Team)
team charged with developing, reviewing and revising a student's IEP and consisting of the parent(s), the child (if appropriate), a regular education teacher, a special education teacher, an administrator qualified to supervise the provision of services and an individual who can interpret the instructional implications of evaluation results.

Individualized family service plan (IFSP)
a written plan outlining the procedure necessary to transition a child with disabilities to preschool or other appropriate services.

International Baccalaureate (IB)
a program established to provide an internationally recognized; interdisciplinary; pre-collegiate course of study offered through the International Baccalaureate Organization, headquartered in Switzerland, and examination results are accepted by more than 100 countries for university admission.

Licensed clinical psychologist
a psychologist licensed by the Virginia Board of Psychology who must either be in a treatment relationship or establishing a treatment relationship with the student to meet eligibility requirements for requesting homebound services.

Licensed physician
an individual who has been licensed by the Virginia Board of Medicine to practice medicine who can certify medical conditions for requesting homebound services.

Licensed teacher
an individual who has met all the current requirements for a teacher in the Virginia and holds a license from the Virginia State Board of Education, or, if teaching on-line, a license from Virginia or another state.

Limited-English proficient (LEP) -see English-language learners Linear weighted average
a calculation, approximating what most school divisions spend to operate their schools, used to establish the funded cost of many components of the Standards of Quality (SOQ), such as instructional salaries.

Literary fund
established in the Constitution of Virginia (Article VIII, § 8) as a permanent and perpetual school fund that provides low-interest loans to school divisions for capital expenditures, such as construction of new buildings or remodeling of existing buildings.

Locally awarded verified credit
a verified unit of credit awarded by a local school board in accordance with the SOA.

Magnet school/center (also referred to as "specialty school/center")
a public school that focuses on a particular area of study, such as performing arts or science and technology but also offer regular school subjects.

Middle school
a public school with grades 6 through 8.

Migrant Education
a program of instruction and services for children who move periodically with their families from one school to another in a different geographical area to secure seasonal employment.

National Assessment of Educational Progress (NAEP) (also referred to as "the Nation's Report Card")
the only nationally representative and continuing assessment of what America's students know and can do in various subject areas including mathematics, reading, science, writing, U.S. history, geography, civics and the arts; the federally funded program (currently contracted to Educational Testing Service in Princeton, N.J.) tests a representative sample of students in grades 4, 8 and 12 and provides information about the achievement of students nationally and state-by-state.

National Blue Ribbon Award
honors public and private K-12 schools that are either academically superior in their states or that demonstrate dramatic gains in student achievement; awarded annually by the U.S. Department of Education through the Blue Ribbon Schools Program.

Nation's Report Card
see "National Assessment of Educational Progress (NAEP)".

No Child Left behind Act of 2001 (NCLB)
see "Elementary & Secondary Education Act".

Norm-referenced tests
standardized tests designed to measure how a student's performance compares with that of other students.

Phonological Awareness Literacy Screening (PALS)
state-provided K-3 screening tool to help reduce the number of children with reading problems by detecting those problems early and providing research-based, small-group intervention.

Pedagogy
the art of teaching.

Planning period
one class period per day (or the equivalent) unencumbered of any teaching or supervisory duties.

Portfolio
a collection of student work chosen to exemplify and document a student's learning progress over time.

Pre-school child care
a school-operated program that provides custodial care of pre-school students enrolled in a school or system before school day starts and/or after a school day ends.

Proficient
test results indicating that the student demonstrated the skills and knowledge outlined in the Standards of Learning (SOL).

Professional/staff development
training for teachers, principals, superintendents, administrative staff, local school board members and Board of Education members designed to enhance student achievement and is required by the Standards of Quality (SOQ).

Psychiatrist
an medical doctor who has been licensed by the Virginia Board of Medicine and trained to practice in the science of treating mental diseases.

Reading First
federal program focuses on putting proven methods of early reading instruction into classrooms to ensure all children learn to read well by the end of third grade.

Recess
a segment of free time during the standard school day in which students are given a break from instruction.

Reconstitution
for a school rated accreditation denied, it is a process to initiate a range of accountability actions to improve pupil performance and to address deficiencies in curriculum and instruction; may include, but is not limited to, restructuring a school's governance, instructional program staff or student population.

Regular school year
the period of time between the opening day of school in the fall and the closing day of school for that school term that is at minimum 180 teaching days or 990 teaching hours.

Remedial program
a program designed to remedy, strengthen and improve the academic achievement of students who demonstrate substandard performance.

Research-based decision making
see "data-based decision making".

Response to intervention (RTI)
a method designed to identify and provide early, effective assistance to children who are having difficulty learning: Tier 1 students need extra help understanding the core curriculum, Tier 2 students consistently showing a discrepancy between their current level of performance and the expected level of performance, and Tier 3 students need even more support.

Restructuring
the implementation of a new organizational pattern or style of leadership and management to bring about renewed, more effective schools. It can mean reorganizing the school day or year and changing conventional practices, such as grouping students by age for an entire school year or giving competitive grades. Or it may refer to changing the roles of teachers and administrators, allocating more decision-making power to teachers, and involving parents in decisions.

Sampling
a way of estimating how a whole group would perform on a test by testing representative members of the group or giving different portions of the test to various subgroups.

SAT
one of the two commonly used tests designed to assess high school students' general educational development and required

for college entrance by many institutions of higher education; administered by The College Board.

School
a publicly funded institution where students are enrolled for all or a majority of the instructional day; those students are reported in fall membership at the institution and the institution, at minimum, meets requirements adopted by the Board of Education.

School age
a child who is age 5 on or before September 30 and has not reached age 20; compulsory attendance school age is 5-18.

Secondary school
a public school with any grades 9 through 12.

Special education (SPED)
a service especially designed and at no cost to the parent/guardian that adapts the curriculum, materials or instruction for students identified as having educational or physical disabilities and tailored to each student's needs and learning style and provided in a general education or special education classroom, home, hospital, separate school or other setting.

Specialty school
see "magnet school/center".

Standardized testing
tests administered and scored under uniform (standardized) conditions. Because most machine-scored, multiple-choice tests are standardized, the term is sometimes used to refer to such tests, but other tests may also be standardized.

Standard school day
a calendar day that averages at least five and one-half instructional hours for students in grades 1-12, excluding breaks for meals and recess, and a minimum of three instructional hours for students in kindergarten.

Standard school year
a school year of at least 180 teaching days or a total of at least 990 teaching hours per year.

Standard unit of credit
earned credit based on a minimum of 140-clock hours of instruction and successful completion of the requirements of the course.

Standards of Accreditation (SOA)
the Board of Education's regulations establishing criteria for approving public schools in Virginia as authorized in the Standards of Quality (SOQ).

Standards of Learning (SOL)
the minimum grade level and subject matter educational objectives, described as the knowledge and skills "necessary for success in school and for preparation for life," that students are expected to meet in Virginia public schools and specified by the Standards of Quality (SOQ).

SOL curriculum frameworks
teacher resource guides for mathematics, science, English and history/social sciences delineating essential knowledge, skills and processes required by the Standards of Learning (SOL).

Standards of Quality (SOQ)
the minimum program that every public school division in Virginia must meet; a major portion of state funding for direct air to public education is based on the SOQ; the standards are established in the Constitution of Virginia, defined in the Code of Virginia and prescribed by the Board of Education, subject to revision only by the General Assembly.

Student
a child age 5 on or before September 30 up to age 18; a child with disabilities age 2-21; a child of limited English proficiency who entered a Virginia school after age 12 but not age 22.

Student periods
means the number of students a teacher instructs per class period multiplied by the number of class periods taught.

Substitute tests
tests approved by the Board of Education as substitutes for SOL end-of-course tests for awarding verified credit for high school; examples include Advanced Placement (AP), International Baccalaureate (IB), SAT II, as well as a number of certifications and licensing examinations in career and technical fields.

Title I
federal funding program authorized by Title I of ESEA/NCLB to support instructional needs of students from low-income families to ensure that all children have a fair and equal opportunity to obtain a high-quality education and reach (at a minimum) proficiency on state academic achievement standards and assessments.

Title 1 school
a school with a high rate of disadvantaged students making it eligible for participation in federal Title I programs.

Title 1 school-wide assistance
Title 1 schools with 40 percent or greater high-poverty, student population may use federal funding to meet the needs of all students at the school.

Title 1 targeted assistance
federal funding is used to meet the needs of the educationally disadvantaged students only and the poverty percentages must be at least 35% or above the district wide average.

Transition plan
plan provided by the licensed physician or licensed clinical psychologist to explain the need for extended homebound instruction which includes the name of the student, justification for the extension of homebound instruction, additional time homebound instruction is anticipated and specific steps planned to return the student to classroom instruction.

Verified unit of credit

earned credit based on a standard unit of credit, plus a passing score on the end-of-course SOL test or substitute test approved by the Board of Education.

Vocational

a school or center organized for a program that offers a sequence of courses that are directly related to the preparation of individuals for paid or unpaid employment in current or emerging occupations requiring other than a baccalaureate or advanced diploma

Source: Virginia Department of Education

A

American Forest Foundation, 4984
American Foundation Corporation, 2778
American Foundation for Negro Affairs, 3309
American Friends Service Committee, 207
American Guidance Service, 4748
American Historical Association, 4007
American Home Economics Association, 5130
American Honda Foundation, 2908
American Indian Science & Engineering Society Annual Confe, 784
American Institute for Foreign Study, 3761
American Institute of Physics, 4749
American International School, 1551
American International School of Nouakchott, 2060
American International School of Zagreb, 232
American International School-Abu Dhabi, 1552
American International School-Abuja, 2061
American International School-Bamako, 2062
American International School-Bolivia, 1386
American International School-Bucharest, 1511
American International School-Budapest, 1512
American International School-Carinthia, 1644
American International School-Chennai, 2063
American International School-Costa Rica, 2064
American International School-Cyprus, 1513
American International School-Dhaka, 1122, 1184
American International School-Florence, 1645
American International School-Freetown, 2065
American International School-Genoa, 1646
American International School-Guangzhou, 1185
American International School-Israel, 1553
American International School-Johannesburg, 1123
American International School-Kingston, 2066
American International School-Krakow, 1514
American International School-Kuwait, 1554
American International School-Lesotho, 2067
American International School-Libreville, 2068
American International School-Lincoln Buenos Aires, 1387
American International School-Lisbon, 1647
American International School-Lome, 2069
American International School-Lusaka, 2070
American International School-Mozambique, 2071
American International School-Muscat, 1555
American International School-N'Djamena, 2072
American International School-Nouakchott, 2073
American International School-Riyadh, 1556
American International School-Rotterdam, 1648
American International School-Salzburg, 1649
American International School-Vienna, 1515, 1650
American International School-Zambia, 1124
American International Schools, 932
American Journal of Education, 4131

The American Legion, 4020
American Libraries, 4542
American Library Association, 777, 785, 4542, 4543, 4561
American Library Association (ALA) Annual Conference, 294, 785
American Locker Security Systems, 5562
American Mathematical Society, 786, 4576
American Montessori Society, 12, 4422
American Montessori Society Conference, 787
American Musicological Society, 306, 311
American Nicaraguan School, 2074
American Nuclear Society, 4750
American Overseas School-Rome, 1651
American Physiological Society, 4751
American Plastics Council, 5240
American Playground Corporation, 5736
American Psychological Association Annual Conference, 788
American Public Health Association, 789
American Public Health Association Annual Meeting, 789
American Public Human Services Association, 4277
American Samoa Department of Education, 2075
American Scholar, 4132
American School, 1388
American School & University - Who's Who Directory & Buyer, 3893
American School & University Magazine, 4333
American School Board Journal, 4334, 3330
American School Counselor Association, 198
American School Directory, 3765
American School Foundation AC, 1389
The American School Foundation of Monterrey, 1506
American School Foundation-Guadalajara, 1390
American School Foundation-Monterrey, 1391
American School Health Association, 13, 4196, 4226
American School Health Association's National School Confe, 790
American School Honduras, 2076
American School of Bucharest, 1516
American School of Kinshasa, 1125
American School of the Hague, 1652
American School-Algiers, 2077
American School-Antananarivo, 2078
American School-Asuncion, 2079
American School-Barcelona, 1653
American School-Belo Horizonte, 1392
American School-Bilbao, 1654
American School-Bombay, 1186
American School-Brasilia, 1393
American School-Campinas, 1394
American School-Doha, 1557
American School-Dschang, 2080
American School-Durango, 1395
American School-Guangzhou (China), 1187
American School-Guatemala, 1396, 2081
American School-Guayaquil, 1397
American School-Japan, 1188
American School-Kuwait, 1558
American School-Laguna Verde, 1398
American School-Las Palmas, 1655
American School-Lima, 1399
American School-London, 1656
American School-Madrid, 1657

American School-Milan, 1658
American School-Niamey, 2082
American School-Pachuca, 1400
American School-Paris, 1659
American School-Port Gentil, 2083
American School-Puebla, 1401
American School-Puerto Vallarta, 1402
American School-Recife, 1403
American School-Santo Domingo, 2030
American School-Tampico, 1404
American School-Tangier, 1126
American School-Tegucigalpa, 2084
American School-Torreon, 1405
American School-Valencia, 1660
American School-Warsaw, 2085
American School-Yaounde, 1127, 2086
American School-the Hague, 1661
American Schools Association of Central America, Columbia-, 208
American Secondary Education, 4641
American Society for Training/Development-Training Video, 3456
American Society for Engineering Education, 14
American Society for Training & Development, 3342, 3456
American Society for Training and Development Information, 3310
American Society of Civil Engineers, 6047
American Society of Educators, 4556
American Sociological Review, 4673
American Speech-Language-Hearing Association Annual Conven, 281, 791
American Students & Teachers Abroad, 4133
American Swing Products, 5737
American Technical Education Association, 792, 3522
American Technical Publishers, 4752
American Textbook Council, 361
American Time & Signal Company, 5422
American Trade Schools Directory, 4104
American Water Works Association, 4753
American for the Art, 4015, 4016, 4068
American-British Academy, 1559
American-Nicaraguan School, 2087
American-Scandinavian Foundation, 2951, 4443
American-Scandinavian Foundation Magazine, 4443
Ameritech Foundation, 2520
Amherst Regional High School, 533
Amman Baccalaureate School, 1560
Amoco Galeota School, 2088
Ampersand Press, 4754
Amsco School Publications, 4755
Amusing and Unorthodox Definitions, 3766
An Overview of the World Wide Web, 3583
Analog & Digital Peripherals, 3571
Anatolia College, 1662
Anatomical Chart Company, 5241
Anchor Audio, 5165, 6083
Anchor Pad, 5953
Anchor Pad Products, 5790, 5953
Andersen Corporation, 2635
Andersen Elementary & Middle School, 2089
Andersen Foundation, 2635
Anderson's Bookshops, 4756
Andrew W Mellon Foundation, 2700
Angeles Group, 5484
Angels School Supply, 5242
Anglican International School-Jerusalem, 1561

B

E

J

K

M

Miller, Cook & Associates, 1056
Millersville University, 3712
Millfield School, 1903
Mills Bee Lane Memorial Foundation, 2502
Milton Roy Company, 4937
Mimosa Publications, 4938
MindTwister Math, 6125
Mindplay, 6012
Mineral Area College, 571
Minneapolis Foundation, 2646
Minneapolis Public Library, 2647
Minnesota Business Educators, 549
Minnesota Congress of Parents, Teachers & Students/Minneso, 550
Minnesota Department of Children, Families & Learning, 3122
Minnesota Department of Education, 3123
Minnesota Education Update, 4242
Minnesota Leadership Annual Conference, 3385
Minnesota Library Association, 551
Minnesota School Administrators Association, 3386
Minnesota School Boards Association, 552, 3385
Minnesota School Boards Association Annual Meeting, 3387
Minority Student Guide to American Colleges, 3853
Minsk International School, 1287
Miracle Recreation Equipment Company, 5757
Miranda Lux Foundation, 2409
Miss Jackie Music Company, 4600
Mississippi Advocate for Education, 556
Mississippi Arts Commission, 557
Mississippi Business Education Association, 558
Mississippi Department of Education, 3129, 3125, 3126, 3127, 3128, 3131, 3132
Mississippi Employment Security Commission, 3130
Mississippi Institutions of Higher Learning, 559
Mississippi Library Association, 560
Mississippi Library Commission, 561
Mississippi Power Foundation, 2653
Missouri Arts Council, 563
Missouri Association of Elementary School Principals, 564
Missouri Association of Secondary School Principals, 565
Missouri Congress of Parents & Teachers/Missouri PTA, 566
Missouri Department of Education, 3135, 3133, 3134, 3137, 3138, 3139, 3140, 4243
Missouri Department of Higher Education, 567
Missouri LINC, 5110
Missouri Library Association, 568
Missouri Library Association Conference, 916
Missouri National Education Association, 569, 3377
Missouri School Boards Association, 3378
Missouri Schools, 4243
Missouri State Teachers Association, 570
Missouri State Teachers Association Conference, 3388
Misty City Software, 5845
Mitchell Foundation, 2343
Mitinet/Marc Software, 6104
Mitsubishi Professional Electronics, 5454
Mobility International USA, 3819
Model Classroom, 1057

Model Technologies, 4939
Modern American School, 1480
Modern Educational Systems, 1058
Modern Language Association Annual Conference, 827
Modern Language Journal, 4525
Modern Red Schoolhouse Institute, 1059
Modern School Supplies, 5697
ModuForm, 5532
ModuForm, Inc., 5532
Modular Hardware, 5603
Mohammed Ali Othman School, 1603
Mohon International, 5698
Mombasa Academy, 1162
Momentum, 4244
Mondo Publishing, 4940
Money for Film & Video Artists, 4015, 4068
Money for International Exchange in the Arts, 4016
Money for Visual Artists, 4017, 4069
Monkton Combe School, 1904
Monograph 1-Using a Logic Model to Review and Analyze an E, 3854
Monograph 2-Preparing Effective Environmental Educators, 3855
Monsanto Company, 5356
Monsanto Fund, 2664
Montana Arts Council, 573
Montana Association of County School Superintendents, 574
Montana Association of Elementary School Principals Confer, 3389
Montana Association of School Librarians (MASL), 575
Montana Department of Education, 3143, 3141, 3142, 3144
Montana Education Association, 4239
Montana High School Association Conference, 909
Montana Library Association, 576
Montana Office of Public Instruction, 4245
Montana School Boards Association, 1060
Montana Schools, 4245
Montana State Library, 2666
Montessori House of Children, 2241
Montessori LIFE, 4422
Montessori Observer, 4246
Montgomery Intermediate Unit 23, 1061
Monti Parioli English School, 1905
Moody Foundation, 2872
Moore Express, 1062
Moore Foundation, 2555
Moravian School, 2242
Moreguina International Primary School, 1288
Morehead State University, 3713
Morgan Buildings, Pools, Spas, RV's, 5533
Morning Glory Press, 4941
Morris & Gwendolyn Cafritz Foundation, 2469
Morrison Christian Academy, 1289
Morrison School Supplies, 5357
Morrocoy International, 2243
Mosaica Education, 1063
Motivating Students in the Classroom Video Series, 3629
Mougins School, 1906
Mount Carmel Elementary School, 2244
Mount Hagen International School, 1290
Mount Saint Agnes Academy, 2042
Mountain Pacific Association of Colleges and Employers, 191
Mountain Plains Business Education Association (M-PBEA), 602

Mountain Plains Library Association (MPLA), 661
Mountain-Plains Business Education Association (M-PBEA), 514
Mountainside Publishing Company, 4552
Mountainview School, 1907
Mrs. Glosser's Math Goodies, 6129
Mt Zaagham International School, 1291
Multi-Video, 5455
MultiMedia Schools, 4720
Multicorp, 1064
Multicultural Education: Teaching to Diversity, 3630
Multicultural Educations: Valuing Diversity, 5206
Multimedia - The Human Body, 6126
Multnomah County Library, 2808
Munich International School, 1908
Murray International School, 1292
Murree Christian School, 1293
Museum Products Company, 5699
Museum Stamps, 6227
Music Ace 2, 6228
Music Education Research Council, 3335
Music Educators Journal, 4590
Music Educators Journal and Teaching Music, 4591
Music Teacher Find, 6135
Music Teachers Association National Conference, 828
Music Teachers Guide to Music Instructional Software, 4070
Music Teachers National Association, 153, 5111, 828, 4066, 4070, 4071
Music and Guitar, 6136
Music for Little People, 4942
Music, Art, Sociology & Humanities, 2647
Musikgarten, 3714
Mussoorie International School, 1294
Myra Foundation, 2775

N

N&N Publishing Company, 4943
NAAEE Annual Conference, 829, 3390
NABE Marketplace, 287
NABE News, 4526
NACAC Bulletin, 4487
NACDA, 4604
NAEA News, 4592
NAEIR Advantage, 4247
NAEN Bulletin, 4248
NAFSA Newsletter, 4249
NAFSA's Guide to Education Abroad for Advisers & Administr, 3856
NAFSA: Association of International Educators, 3856, 3993, 4249
NAFSA: National Association of International Educators, 830
NAME National Office, 842
NAPNSC Accrediting Commission for Higher Education, 4331
NAPSEC News, 4250
NASA Educational Workshop, 3715
NASA Headquarters, 4948
NASDSE National Conference, 831
NASDTEC Knowledge Base, 3488
NASFAA Newsletter, 4449
NASILP Journal, 4527
NASP Publications, 4944
NASPA - Student Affairs Administrators in Higher Education, 160

O

S

U

X

Y

Z

Canada

Colorado

Connecticut

Delaware

Assessments & Accountability Branch Delaware Department of Education, 3034
Attention Deficit Disorder Association, 29
Crystal Trust, 2460
Delaware Business Education Association, 439
Delaware Department of Education, 3035
Delaware Department of Education: Administrative Services, 3036
Delaware Division of Libraries, 440
Delaware Division of the Arts, 441
Delaware Higher Education Commission, 442
Delaware Library Association, 443
Delaware State Education Association, 444
Delaware State Education for Homeless Children and Youth, 445
Educational Publishing Summit, 816
HW Buckner Charitable Residuary Trust, 2461
Improvement & Assistance Branch Delaware Department of Education, 3037
International Reading Association, 329
International Reading Association Annual Convention, 764
JCB/Early Childhood Education Consultant Service, 1023
Longwood Foundation, 2462
Pyramid Educational Consultants, 1087
Teachers in Touch, 3563

District of Columbia

AACTE Briefs, 3521
AAUW National Convention, 768
ACE Fellows Program, 3338, 3649
AFL-CIO Guide to Union Sponsored Scholarships, Awards & Student Aid, 2950
AFT Convention, 3339
ASPIRA Association, 1
Abe Wouk Foundation, 2463
Academic Travel Abroad, 204
Accounting & Financial Management Services, 2962
American Association for Higher Education & Accreditation, 3305
American Association of Colleges for Teacher Education-Directory, 773, 3306, 3455, 3455
American Association of Collegiate Registrars & Admissions Officers, 154, 3341
American Association of Sex Educators, Counselors & Therapists (AASECT), 196
American Association of Sexuality Educators, Counselors & Therapists Conference, 778
American Council of Trustees and Alumni, 7
American Council on Education (ACE), 8
American Council on Education Annual Meeting, 780
American Council on Education Library & Information Service, 446
American Educational Research Association, 783, 3307
American Educator, 3525
American Federation of Teachers, 11
American Psychological Association Annual Conference, 788
American Public Health Association Annual Meeting, 789
American Society for Engineering Education, 14
Appropriate Inclusion and Paraprofessionals, 3457
Arts Education Partnership, 307
Assistance to States Division, 2963
Associates for Renewal in Education (ARE), 447
Association For Childhood Education Internatio nal, 15
Association Of American Geographers, 360
Association for Canadian Studies in the US, 214
Association for Childhood Education International Bi-Annual Conference, 747
Association for Community-Based Education, 17

Association for Persons with Severe Handicaps Annual Conference, 799
Association of American Colleges & Universities Annual Meeting, 805
Association of Community College Trustees Conference, 806
Association of International Educators (NAFSA), 221
Association of Science-Technology Centers Incorporated Conference, 344, 807
Building Life Options: School-Community Collaborations, 3465
Cable in the Classroom, 33
Center for Applied Linguistics (CAL), 283
Center for Lifelong Learning, 35
Center on Education Policy, 36
Character Education: Making a Difference, 3598
Clearinghouse on Reading, English & Communication, 328
Coming Up Short? Practices of Teacher Educators Committed to Character, 3467
Compensatory Education Program, 2965
Consortium for School Networking, 376
Contracting Out: Strategies for Fighting Back, 3469
Council for Advancement & Support of Education, 41
Council for Advancement and Support of Education, 751
Council for Christian Colleges and Universitie s, 42
Council for Educational Development and Research, 5092
Council for the Accreditation of Educator Preparation, 44
Council of Chief State School Officers, 158
Council of Graduate Schools, 45
Council of Independent Colleges, 46
Council on Hemispheric Affairs, 241
Council on Postsecondary Accreditation, 47
DC Office of Special Education, 3038
Distance Education & Training Council, 3316
District Of Columbia Commission on the Arts an d Humanities, 448
District of Columbia Department of Education, 3039
District of Columbia Library Association, 449
District of Columbia Office of the State Super intendent of Education, 450
ERIC - Education Resources Information Center, 52
ERIC Clearinghouse on Languages and Linguistics, 284
ERIC Clearinghouse on Teaching and Teacher Education, 3317
ERIC/CASS Virtual Libraries: Online Resources for Parents, Teachers, and Counselors, 201
Educational Leadership Institute, 3318
Elementary Secondary Bilingual & Research Branch, 2966
Elementary, Secondary & Vocational Analysis, 2967
Eleven Principles of Effective Character Education, 3615
English Language Fellow Program, 187
Eugene & Agnes E Meyer Foundation, 2464
Excelencia in Education, 63
Foundation Center-District of Columbia, 2465
Foundation for Educational Innovation, 1005
Foundation for the National Capitol Region, 2466
Gilbert & Jaylee Mead Family Foundation, 2467
Grants and Contracts Service, 2916
HEATH Resource Center at the National Youth Transitions Center, 72
Higher Education Center, 5099
Hitachi Foundation, 2468
Infocus: A Newsletter of the University Continuing Education Association, 3536
Institute for Educational Leadership, 74
Intel Science Talent Search Scolarship, 2957
InterAction - American Council for Voluntary International Action, 75
International Research and Exchanges Board (IREX), 257
International Society For Technology In Educat ion, 259

International Society for Technology in Education, 77, 379
Journal of Economic Education, 3541
Kaludis Consulting Group, 1031
Mathematical Association of America (MAA), 302
McKenzie Group, 1050
Middle Grades Education in an Era of Reform, 3486
Morris & Gwendolyn Cafritz Foundation, 2469
NAAEE Annual Conference, 829, 3390
NAFSA: National Association of International Educators, 830
NASDTEC Knowledge Base, 3488
NASPA - Student Affairs Administrators in Higher Education, 160
NASPA Annual Conference, 832
NEA Foundatrion for the Improvement of Education, 5112
National Academy of Education, 85, 2919
National Alliance of Black School Educators Conference, 837
National Association For Gifted Children, 87
National Association for Multicultural Education, 842
National Association for the Education of Young Children, 184
National Association of Federally Impacted Schools, 93
National Association of Independent Schools Conference, 845
National Association of Private Schools for Exceptional Children Conference, 164, 846
National Association of Special Education Teac hers, 95
National Association of Student Financial Aid Administrators, 167
National Association of Student Financial Aid Administrators, 849, 900
National Black Child Development Institute, 850, 5113
National Center for ESL Literacy Education, 330
National Center for Education Statistics, 2969
National Center for Improving Science Education, 5114
National Center on Education & the Economy, 1065, 5120
National Clearinghouse for Bilingual Education, 5124
National Coalition for Parent Involvement in Education (NCPIE), 103
National Coalition of ESEA Title 1 Parents, 852
National Council for Geographic Education Annual Meeting, 364, 3403
National Council for Science and the Environment, 109
National Council of Higher Education, 110, 855
National Council of State Directors of Adult Education, 168
National Council of Urban Education Associations, 111
National Council on Disability, 2970
National Dissemination Center for Children with Disabilities, 115
National Education Association, 116
National Education Association Annual Meeting, 3407
National Education Association Student Program, 117
National Education Association-Retired, 118, 858
National Education Policy Institute, 119
National Educational Computing Conference, 3408
National Endowment For The Arts, 317
National Institute on Disability and Rehabilitation Research, 382
National Library of Education, 2972
National Occupational Information Coordinating Committee Conference, 3409
National Science Resources Center, 5133
National Trust for Historic Preservation: Office of Education Initiatives, 2973
National Women's Student Coalition (NWSC), 129
No Child Left Behind, 2974
North American Association for Environmental Education, 133, 367
Office for Civil Rights, 2975

Florida

Georgia

Hawaii

Idaho

Illinois

American Academy of Pediatrics, 4
American Association of French Teachers Conference, 774
American Association of School Librarians National Conference, 777
American Association of Teachers of French, 278
American Library Association (ALA) Annual Conference, 294, 785
Ameritech Foundation, 2520
Arts Scholarships, 2952
Association for Library & Information Science Education Annual Conference, 296, 3347
Awards and Recognition Association, 30
Career Evaluation Systems, 944
Carus Corporate Contributions Program, 2521
Center for the Study of Reading, 5088
Chauncey & Marion Deering McCormick Foundation, 2522
Chicago Community Trust, 2523
Chicago Principals Association Education Conference, 3356
Clearinghouse on Early Education and Parenting (CEEP), 183
Coleman Foundation, 2524
Community Foundation for Jewish Education, 959
Creative Learning Consultants, 968
Curriculum Center - Office of Educational Services, 3666
Danforth Foundation, 2657
DeVry University, 3668
Dellora A & Lester J Norris Foundation, 2525
Directory of Curriculum Materials Centers, 3470
Dr. Scholl Foundation, 2527
Easter Seals Communications, 55
Eastern Illinois University School of Technology, 3671
Educational Specialties, 991
Educator & School Development, 3050
Educator Certification, 3051
Energy Concepts, 3678
Evanston Public Library, 2528
Farny R Wurlitzer Foundation, 2529
Finance & Support Services, 3052
Grover Hermann Foundation, 2530
How to Raise Test Scores, 3477
IASB Joint Annual Conference, 3363
Illinois Affiliation of Private Schools for Exceptional Children, 478
Illinois Art Council, 479
Illinois Assistant Principals Conference, 3366
Illinois Association of School Administrators, 480
Illinois Association of School Business Officials, 481
Illinois Business Education Association (IBEA), 482
Illinois Citizens' Education Council, 483
Illinois Department of Education, 3053
Illinois Education Association, 484
Illinois Homeless Education Program, 485
Illinois Library Association, 486
Illinois Library Association Conference, 898
Illinois Resource Center Conference of Teachers of Linguistically Diverse Students, 3367
Illinois School Library Media Association, 487
Illinois Student Assistance Commission, 488
Illinois Vocational Association Conference, 899
Independent Schools Association of the Central States, 73, 159
Innovative Learning Group, 1013
Institute of Cultural Affairs, 247
International Association of School Librarianship, 298
International Awards Market, 757
International Council on Education for Teaching, 3319
Janice Borla Vocal Jazz Camp, 3695
Joyce Foundation, 2531
Kodaly Teaching Certification Program, 3702
Lloyd A Fry Foundation, 2532
Lutheran Education Association, 83

Lutheran Education Association National Administrators Conference, 825
Management Simulations, 1044
Midwestern Regional Educational Laboratory, 5109
National Council of English Teachers Conference, 3406
National Council of Teachers of English, 288
National Lekotek Center, 120
North American Students of Cooperation, 135
North Central Business Education Association (NCBEA), 571
North Central Regional Educational Laboratory, 5134
Northern Trust Company Charitable Trust, 2533
Orff-Schulwerk Teacher Certification Program, 3721
Philip H Corboy Foundation, 2535
Polk Brothers Foundation, 2536
Prince Charitable Trust, 2537
Regenstein Foundation, 2538
Requirements for Certification of Teachers & Counselors, 3497
Richard H Driehaus Foundation, 2539
Robert E Nelson Associates, 1096
Robert R McCormick Tribune Foundation, 2540
Rockford Systems, 3734
School Improvement & Assessment Services, 3055
Sears-Roebuck Foundation, 2541
Sigma Tau Delta, 292
Spencer Foundation, 2542
Sulzer Family Foundation, 2543
Teaching for Intelligence Conference, 887
Top Quality School Process (TQSP), 3514
Wavelength, 3647, 3756
Workforce Education and Development, 3758

Indiana

Agency for Instructional Technology, 370, 3304
Allen County Public Library, 2546
American Camp Association National Conference, 779
Art to Remember, 2931
Arvin Foundation, 2547
Association for Educational Communications & Technology Annual Convention, 373, 3346
Ball State University, 3653
Before the School Bell Rings, 3461
Beyond Tracking: Finding Success in Inclusive Schools, 3462
C/S Newsletter, 3529
Center for Professional Development & Services, 949
Center for School Assessment & Research, 3057
Clowes Fund, 2548
Community Relations & Special Populations, 3058
Dekko Foundation, 2549
ERIC Clearinghouse for Social Studies Education, 363
East Central Educational Service Center, 978
Educational Services Company, 990
Eli Lilly & Company Corporate Contribution Program, 2550
External Affairs, 3059
Foellinger Foundation, 2551
History of Science Society, 348
Hoosier Science Teachers Association Annual Meeting, 897
ISBA/IAPSS Annual Conference, 3365
Indiana Arts Commission, 489
Indiana Association of School Business Officials, 490
Indiana Business Education Association, 491
Indiana Commission for Higher Education, 492
Indiana Department of Education, 3060
Indiana Library Federation, 493
Indiana State Teachers Association, 494
Indiana University-Purdue University of Indianapolis, IUPUI, 3688
Indianapolis Foundation, 2552

International Curriculum Management Audit Center, 3691
John W Anderson Foundation, 2553
July in Rensselaer, 3697
Law of Teacher Evaluation: A Self-Assessment Handbook, 3479
Lilly Endowment, 2554
National Student Exchange, 127
Office of Legal Affairs, 3061
Office of School Financial Management, 3062
Office of the Deputy Superintendent, 3063
PDK International Conference, 3427
Phi Delta Kappa International, 270
Piano Workshop, 3727
Priority Computer Services, 1082
Professional Computer Systems, 1084
Revolution Revisited: Effective Schools and Systemic Reform, 3501
School Improvement & Performance Center, 3064
Solution Tree, 146
Teachers Association in Instruction Conference, 3441
Teachers as Leaders, 3506
Voices in the Hall: High School Principals at Work, 3646
W Brooks Fortune Foundation, 2556

Iowa

Book of Metaphors, Volume II, 3463
Cedar Rapids Public Library, 2557
Community Colleges Division, 3065
Division of Library Services, 3066
Educational Services for Children & Families, 3067
Elementary & Secondary Education, 3068
Ethical Issues in Experiential Education, 3474
Financial & Information Services, 3069
Gershowitz Grant and Evaluation Services, 2915
IASB Convention, 3362
Iowa Arts Council, 495
Iowa Business Education Association, 496
Iowa College Student Aid Commission, 497
Iowa Council Teachers of Math Conference, 3368
Iowa Department of Education, 3070
Iowa Library Association, 498
Iowa Public Television, 3071
Iowa Reading Association Conference, 3369
Iowa State Education Association, 499
Iowa State Education for Homeless Children and Youth, 500
Janet Hart Heinicke, 1026
National Association of Media and Technology Centers, 381
Noel/Levitz Centers, 1070
Profiles, 1086
RJ McElroy Trust, 2558
SAI Annual Conference, 3434
Theory of Experiential Education, 3512
UNI Overseas Recruiting Fair, 907
Vocational Rehabilitation Services, 3072

Kansas

American Council on Education in Journalism and Mass Communication (ACEJMC), 279
Character Education: Restoring Respect & Responsibility in our Schools, 3599
Classroom Teacher's Guide for Working with Paraeducators Video Set, 3601
Closing the Achievement Gap, 3466
Conferencing with Students & Parents Video Series, 3603
Council for Learning Disabilities, 752, 3314
Creating Schools of Character Video Series, 3607
Critical Thinking Video Set, 3609
Depco, 3670
Discipline Techniques you can Master in a Minute Video Series, 3612

Educating Homeless Children and Youth, 501
Education Data, 982
Educational Resources, 989
Eleven Principals of Effective Character Education, 3614
Finishing Strong: Your Personal Mentoring & Planning Guide for the Last 60 Days of Teaching, 3475
Four State Regional Technology Conference, 3682
Great Classroom Management Series DVD, 3617
Great Classroom Management Video Series VHS, 3618
Handling Chronically Disruptive Students at Risk Video Series, 3619
Hearlihy & Company, 3620
Inclusion: The Next Step DVD, 3478
Inclusion: The Next Step the Video Series, 3623
Institute for Research in Learning Disabilities, 5102
Integrating Technology into the Curriculum Video Series, 3624
Journalism Education Association, 286, 824, 3544, 3544
Kansas Arts Commission, 502
Kansas Association of School Librarians, 503
Kansas Board of Regents, 504
Kansas Business Education Association, 505
Kansas Department of Education, 3073
Kansas Education Association, 506
Kansas Library Association, 507
Kansas School Boards Association Conference, 3371
Lesson Plans and Modifications for Inclusion and Collaborative Classrooms, 3626
Lesson Plans for the Substitue Teacher: Elementary Edition, 3481
Mentoring Teachers to Mastery Video Series, 3628
Motivating Students in the Classroom Video Series, 3629
National Teachers Hall of Fame, 3333
Office of the Commissioner, 3074
On The Go! for the Educational Office Professional, 3547
On-The-Go For Educational Office Professionals, 3548
Paraeducator's Guide to Instructional & Curricular Modifications, 3549
Personal Planner and Training Guide for the Paraprofessional, 3491
Pittsburg State University, 3728
Retaining Great Teachers, 3555
School-Wide Strategies for Retaining Great Teachers Video Series, 3635
Special Education Services Department, 3075
Sprint Foundation, 2560
Students-at-Risk Video Series, 3639
Teacher Education & Licensure, 3076
Teaching for Results, 3510
Technology Integration for Teachers, 3566
The Board, 3567
The Master Teacher, 3644
The Professor In The Classroom, 3568
Training Video Series for the Substitute Teacher, 3645
USA Kansas Annual Convention, 3447
Understanding and Relating To Parents Professionally, 3516
Welcome to Teaching and our Schools, 3517
Wichita Public Library, 2561
You Can Handle Them All, 3519
You Can Handle Them All Discipline Video Series, 3648
Your Personal Mentoring & Planning Guide for the First 60 Days of Teaching, 3520

Kentucky

Ashland Incorporated Foundation, 2562
Bluegrass Regional Recycling Corporation, 941
Curriculum, Assessment & Accountability Council, 3078
EDUCAUSE Annual Convention, 815

EPPA Consulting, 976
Education Technology Office, 3079
Gheens Foundation, 2563
James Graham Brown Foundation, 2564
KSBA Annual Conference, 3370
Kentucky Arts Council, 508
Kentucky Association of School Administrators, 1032
Kentucky Department for Libraries and Archives, 509
Kentucky Department of Education, 3080
Kentucky Education for Homeless Children and Youth, 510
Kentucky Higher Education Assistance Authority, 511
Kentucky Library Association, 512
Kentucky School Media Association, 513
Kentucky School Superintendents Association Meeting, 3372
Kentucky State University, 3701
Louisville Free Public Library, 2565
Morehead State University, 3713
Performance Learning Systems, 3726
Regional Services Centers, 3081
Southeast Regional Center for Drug-Free Schools & Communities, 5151
VV Cooke Foundation Corporation, 2567

Louisiana

Academic Programs Office, 3084
Advance Program for Young Scholars, 2
Association for Addicted Professionals, 199
Basics Plus, 938
Baton Rouge Area Foundation, 2568
Booth-Bricker Fund, 2569
East Baton Rouge Parish Library, 2570
Fred B & Ruth B Zigler Foundation, 2571
LSBA Convention, 3373
Louisiana Association of Business Educators, 515
Louisiana Association of Educators, 516
Louisiana Association of School Business Officials (LASBO), 517
Louisiana Children's Research Center for Development & Learning, 1039
Louisiana Department of Education, 3085
Louisiana Division of the Arts, 518
Louisiana Education for Homeless Children and Youth, 519
Louisiana Library Association, 520
Louisiana Office of Student Financial Assistance, 521
Management & Finance Office, 3086
Mid-South Educational Research Association Annual Meeting, 3383
New Orleans Public Library, 2572
Office of Educator Support, 3087
Shreve Memorial Library, 2573
Special Education Services, 3001, 3082, 3088, 3088
Standards, Assessments & Accountability, 3089

Maine

Administrator and Teacher Certification, 3090
Adult Education, 3091
American Musicological Society, 306
CIEE Annual Conference, 749
Clarence E Mulford Trust, 2574
Council on International Educational Exchange (CIEE), 242
Edward E Ford Foundation, 2582
Harold Alfond Trust, 2575
Information Exchange, 5101
Institute for Global Ethics, 1018
Maine Arts Commission, 523
Maine Association of School Libraries, 524
Maine Department of Education, 3092
Maine Library Association, 525

Maine Principals Association Conference, 3379

Maryland

Abell Foundation, 2576
Aegon USA, 2577
Aid for Education, 2929
American Association of Physics Teachers National Meeting, 341, 775
American Dance Therapy Association, 305
American School Health Association, 13
American School Health Association's National School Conference, 790
American Speech-Language-Hearing Association Annual Convention, 281, 791
BBX Teacher Clearinghouse, 3460
Beverly Celotta, 940
CHADD: Children & Adults with Attention Deficit/Hyperactivity Disorder, 32, 808
Career & Technology Education, 3093
Center for Organization of Schools, 5084
Center for Social Organization of Schools, 5086
Center for Technology in Education, 5087
Certification & Accreditation, 3094
Childrens Youth Funding Report, 2932
Clarence Manger & Audrey Cordero Plitt Trust, 2578
Clark-Winchcole Foundation, 2579
Commonwealth Foundation, 2580
Division of Library Development and Services, 526
Dr. Anthony A Cacossa, 974
Dresher Foundation, 2581
ERIC Clearinghouse on Assessment & Evaluation, 53
Educational Productions Inc, 3613
Educational Systems for the Future, 992
Enoch Pratt Free Library, 2583
France-Merrick Foundation, 2584
Grayce B Kerr Fund, 2585
Henry & Ruth Blaustein Rosenberg Foundation, 2586
Hummel Sweets, 2938
Instruction Division, 3095
International Baccalaureate American Global Centre, 253
International Clearinghouse for the Advancement of Science Teaching, 3625
International Dyslexia Association (IDA), 285
International Dyslexia Association Annual Conference, 760
International Performance Improvement Conference, 822
James M Johnston Trust for Charitable and Educational Purposes, 2587
John W Kluge Foundation, 2588
Kentland Foundation, 2889
Library Development & Services, 3096
Margaret Hall Foundation, 2566
Marion I & Henry J Knott Foundation, 2589
Maryland Center for Career and Technology Education, 3710
Maryland Department of Education, 3097
Maryland Educational Media Organization, 527
Maryland Educational Opportunity Center, 1046
Maryland Elco Incorporated Educational Funding Company, 1047
Maryland Library Association, 529
Maryland State Arts Council, 530
Maryland State Teachers Association, 531
NCSS Summer Workshops, 3716
National Association for Bilingual Education, 287, 839
National Association of School Psychologists Annual Convention, 203, 847
National Clearinghouse for Alcohol & Drug Information, 5123
National Council for History Education Conference, 3404
National Council for Social Studies Annual Conference, 3405
National Council for the Social Studies, 365

Massachusetts

Michigan

Minnesota

Mississippi

Missouri

Montana

Nebraska

Nevada

New Hampshire

New Jersey

New Mexico

New York

Scholarships in the Health Professions, 2961
Seth Sprague Educational and Charitable
  Foundation, 2754
Sexuality Information & Education Council of the
  US, 144
Sidney Kreppel, 1103
Special Programs, 2352
Starr Foundation, 2755
Stewart Howe Alumni Service of New York, 1107
Superintendents Work Conference, 3439
Teachers & Writers Collaborative, 293
Teachers College: Columbia University, 3749
Tiger Foundation, 2756
Tisch Foundation, 2757
Travelers Group, 2758
Tribeca Learning Center-PS 150, 185
U.S. Conference on Adult Literacy (USCAL), 893
Union Pen Company, 2948
United Nations Development Program, 274
United States-Japan Foundation, 2924
Vocational & Educational Services for Disabled,
  3174
White Plains Public Library, 2759
William Randolph Hearst Foundation, 2760
William T Grant Foundation, 2761
World Trade Centers Association, 152
www.nprinc.com, 3586

North Carolina

AE Finley Foundation, 2762
Association Of International Education Adminis
  trators, 211
Association of Boarding Schools, 26
Auxiliary Services, 3175
Cannon Foundation, 2763
Dickson Foundation, 2764
Duke Endowment, 2765
FHI 360, 64
Financial & Personnel Services, 3176
First Union University, 2766
Foundation for the Carolinas, 2767
Kathleen Price and Joseph M Bryan Family
  Foundation, 2768
Mary Reynolds Babcock Foundation, 2769
Measurement, 1051
Musikgarten, 3714
NCASA Annual Conference, 3391
National Association of Academic Advisors for
  Athletics, 323
National Early Childhood Technical Assistance
  System, 178, 5127
National Society for Experiential Education
  Conference, 125, 870
Non-Profit Resource Center/Pack Memorial
  Library, 2770
North Carolina Arts Council, 614
North Carolina Association of Educators (NCAE),
  616
North Carolina Business Education Association
  (NCBEA), 617
North Carolina Department of Education, 3177
North Carolina Department of Instructional
  Services, 3178
North Carolina Department of Public Instruction
  (DPI), 618
North Carolina Library Association (NCLA), 619
North Carolina State Education Assistance Auth
  ority, 620
Poetry Alive!, 1078
SERVE, 5145
SERVE Conference, 880
Staff Development & Technical Assistance, 3179
State Library of North Carolina, 2771
William R Kenan Jr Charitable Trust, 2772
Winston-Salem Foundation, 2773
Z Smith Reynolds Foundation, 2774

North Dakota

Myra Foundation, 2775
North Dakota Council on the Arts, 622
North Dakota Department of Education, 3180
North Dakota Department of Public Instruction
  Division, 3181
North Dakota Education Association (NDEA), 623
North Dakota Library Association, 624
North Dakota State Board for Vocational &
  Technical Education, 3182
North Dakota Vocational Educational Planning
  Conference, 911
Study & State Film Library, 3183
Tom & Frances Leach Foundation, 2776

Ohio

Akron Community Foundation, 2777
American Association for Employment in Education
  Annual Conference, 772
American Foundation Corporation, 2778
Analog & Digital Peripherals, 3571
Association for Integrative Studies, 21
Association for Middle Level Education, 22, 336
Balance Sheet, 3527
Blind School, 3184
Brief Legal Guide for the Independent Teacher,
  3464
Burton D Morgan Foundation, 2779
Curriculum, Instruction & Professional
  Development, 3185
Dayton Foundation, 2780
Direct Instructional Support Systems, 973
E-Z Grader Software, 3572
Early Childhood Education, 3186
Edison Welding Institute, 3672
Education Concepts, 981
Educational Theatre Association Conference, 817
Eisenhower National Clearinghouse for
  Mathematics and Science Education, 301
Emco Maier Corporation, 3677
Eva L & Joseph M Bruening Foundation, 2781
Fastech, 3679
Federal Assistance, 3187
GAR Foundation, 2782
George Gund Foundation, 2783
Gold Medal Products, 2936
Hobart Institute of Welding Technology, 3687
Hoover Foundation, 2784
Industrial Training Institute, 3689
Institute for Development of Educational Activities,
  1017
International Thespian Society, 310
Journal on Excellence in College Teaching, 3543
Kent State University, 3700
Kettering Fund, 2785
Kulas Foundation, 2786
Lilly Conference on College Teaching, 3374
Louise H & David S Ingalls Foundation, 2787
Louise Taft Semple Foundation, 2788
Marketing Education Resource Center, 1045
Martha Holden Jennings Foundation, 2789
Mead Corporation Foundation, 2790
Music Teachers Association National Conference,
  828
Music Teachers National Association, 153, 5111
NMSA Annual Education Conference & Exhibit,
  3394
National Center for Science Teaching & Learning,
  5118
National Council for Black Studies, 108
National Middle School Association, 3322
National School Safety and Security Services, 1069
National Staff Development Council, 3323
Nord Family Foundation, 2791
North American Montessori Teachers' Association,
  877
Ohio Arts Council, 626

Ohio Association of School Business Officials, 627
Ohio Association of Secondary School
  Administrators, 628
Ohio Bell Telephone Contribution Program, 2792
Ohio Business Teachers Association, 3422
Ohio Department of Education, 3188
Ohio Library Council, 629
Ohio Library Council Trade Show, 904
Ohio Public School Employees Association
  Convention, 3423
Ohio School Boards Association Capital Conference
  & Trade Show, 905
Ohio Secondary School Administrators Association
  Conference, 3424
Ohio State Library Foundation Center, 2793
Ohio Technology Education Association (OTEA),
  630
Ome Resa, 1071
Owens Community College, 3722
Owens-Corning Foundation, 2794
Personnel Services, 3189
Procter & Gamble Fund, 2795
Public Library of Cincinnati, 2796
Reading Recovery Council of North America, 333
Root Learning, 1098
School Finance, 3054, 3190
School Food Service, 3191
School for the Deaf, 3192
Student Development, 3194
Summit Vision, 148
Teacher Education & Certification, 3083, 3195
Thomas J Emery Memorial, 2797
Timken Foundation of Canton, 2798
Today's Catholic Teacher, 3569
Tooling University, 3751
Vocational & Career Education, 3196
Wolfe Associates, 2799

Oklahoma

Accreditation & Standards Division, 3197
Action in Teacher Education, 3523
Association for Continuing Higher Education
  Directory, 914, 3459
Association for Disabled Students, 18
At-Risk Students: Identification and Assistance
  Strategies, 3597
Center for the Study of Small/Rural Schools, 5089
Conflict Resolution Strategies in Schools, 3604
Cooperative Learning Strategies, 3606
Crisis Management in Schools, 3608
Curriculum Alignment: Improving Student
  Learning, 3610
Education Extension, 58
Federal/Special/Collaboration Services, 3198
Grace & Franklin Bernsen Foundation, 2800
Improving Parent/Educator Relationships, 3621
Improving Student Thinking in the Content Area,
  3622
Managing Students Without Coercion, 3627
Mervin Bovaird Foundation, 2801
Multicultural Education: Teaching to Diversity,
  3630
National Association of Trade & Industrial
  Instructors, 98
National Career Development Association
  Conference, 3400
National Network for Early Language Learning
  (NELL), 290
National Rural Education Association Annual
  Convention, 122, 866
Oklahoma Arts Council, 632
Oklahoma City University, 2802
Oklahoma Department of Career and Technology
  Education, 3199
Oklahoma Department of Education, 3200
Oklahoma Department of Education; Financial
  Services, 3201
Oklahoma Department of Libraries, 633
Oklahoma Education Association (OEA), 634
Oklahoma Library Association (OLA), 635

Oregon

Pennsylvania

Rhode Island

South Carolina

Teaching Education, 3564

South Dakota

Finance & Management, 3242
John McLaughlin Company, 1028
Services for Education, 3243
South Dakota Arts Council, 662
South Dakota Community Foundation, 2839
South Dakota Department of Education & Cultural
    Affairs, 3244
South Dakota Education Association (SDEA), 663
South Dakota Library Association, 664
South Dakota State Historical Society, 3245
South Dakota State Library, 2840
Special Education Office, 3246

Tennessee

Alliance for Technology Access Conference, 371
Benwood Foundation, 2841
Christy-Houston Foundation, 2842
Frist Foundation, 2843
Institute of Higher Education, 3690
JR Hyde Foundation, 2844
Lyndhurst Foundation, 2845
Mental Edge, 3575
Modern Red Schoolhouse Institute, 1059
Nashville Public Library, 2846
Oosting & Associates, 1072
Plough Foundation, 2847
RJ Maclellan Charitable Trust, 2848
School Memories Collection, 2943
Special Education, 3056, 3113, 3193, 3193, 3214,
    3247
Teaching and Learning, 3248
Tennessee Arts Commission, 666
Tennessee Association of Secondary School
    Principals (TASSP), 667
Tennessee Department of Education, 3249
Tennessee Higher Education Commission, 668
Tennessee Library Association, 669
Tennessee School Boards Association, 670
Tennessee School Boards Association Conference,
    3442
Vocational Education, 3004, 3167, 3250, 3250

Texas

Accountability Reporting and Research, 3251
Albert & Ethel Herzstein Charitable Foundation,
    2849
American Schools Association of Central America,
    Columbia-Caribbean and Mexico, 208
Annual State Convention of Association of Texas
    Professional Educators, 3345
Burlington Northern Foundation, 2850
Burnett Foundation, 2851
Center for Educational Leadership Trinity
    University, 3655
Center for Occupational Research & Development,
    3659
Center for Play Therapy, 182, 3660
Center for Play Therapy Fall Conference, 3354
Center for Play Therapy Summer Institute, 915
Chief Counsel, 3217, 3252
Children's Literature Festival, 920
Choristers Guild's National Festival & Directors'
    Conference, 811
Clinical Play Therapy Videos: Child-Centered
    Developmental & Relationship Play Therapy,
    3602
Conference for Advancement of Mathematics
    Teaching, 813
Continuing Education, 3253

Cooper Industries Foundation, 2852
Corpus Christi State University, 2853
Cullen Foundation, 2854
Curriculum Development & Textbooks, 3254
Curriculum, Assessment & Professional
    Development, 3255
Curriculum, Assessment and Technology, 3256
Dallas Public Library, 2855
Drug Information & Strategy Clearinghouse, 50
Education of Special Populations & Adults, 3257
Educational Technology Design Consultants, 993
El Paso Community Foundation, 2856
Ellwood Foundation, 2857
Eugene McDermott Foundation, 2858
Ewing Halsell Foundation, 2859
Exxon Education Foundation, 2860
Field Services, 3258
Fondren Foundation, 2861
GTE Foundation, 2913
George Foundation, 2862
Gordon & Mary Cain Foundation, 2863
Haggar Foundation, 2864
Health Occupations Students of America, 190
Hobby Foundation, 2865
Houston Endowment, 2866
Houston Public Library, 2867
Internal Operations, 3259
International Exhibit, 761
International Trombone Festival, 766
Intervention in School and Clinic, 3539
James R Dougherty Jr Foundation, 2868
Journal of Classroom Interaction, 3540
Learning for Life, 3480
Leland Fikes Foundation, 2869
MD Anderson Foundation, 2870
Mary Jo Williams Charitable Trust, 2559
Meadows Foundation, 2871
Moody Foundation, 2872
Multicorp, 1064
National Athletic Trainers' Association, 325
National Board for Professional Teaching Stand
    ards, 99
National Educational Systems (NES), 179
Operations & School Support, 3260
Paul & Mary Haas Foundation, 2873
Permanent School Fund, 3261
Perot Foundation, 2874
Psychological Corporation, 172
RW Fair Foundation, 2875
Records Consultants, 1091
Region 6: Education Department, 3262
Royal Barney Hogan Foundation, 2417
Sid W Richardson Foundation, 2876
Southwest Association College and University
    Housing Officers, 923
Southwestern Educational Development Laboratory,
    5154
Special Interest Group for Computer Science
    Education, 5155
Storytelling for Educational Enrichment The Magic
    of Storytelling, 3742
Strake Foundation, 2877
TASA/TASB Convention, 3440
Texas Association of Secondary School Principals
    (TASSP), 671
Texas Classroom Teachers Association Conference,
    924
Texas Commission on the Arts, 672
Texas Department of Education, 3263
Texas Higher Education Coordinating Board, 673
Texas Homeless Education Office, 674
Texas Library Association (TLA), 675
Texas Library Association Conference, 925
Texas Middle School Association Conference, 3443
Texas State Teachers Association, 3444
Texas Vocational Home Economics Teachers
    Association Conference, 926
Trull Foundation, 2878
Voyager Expanded Learning, 186
www.mmhschool.com, 3585

Utah

Applied Technology Education Services, 3264
Marriner S Eccles Foundation, 2879
Ruth Eleanor Bamberger and John Ernest
    Bamberger Memorial Foundation, 2880
Salt Lake City Public Library, 2881
School Management Study Group, 1099
Schools for the Deaf & Blind, 3266
Utah Arts Council, 677
Utah Education Association (UEA), 678
Utah Library Association (ULA), 150
Utah Office of Education, 3267
Utah Office of Education; Agency Services
    Division, 3268
Utah State Library Division, 679
Utah System of Higher Education, 680

Vermont

Building Blocks For Literacy, 173
Career & Lifelong Learning, 3269
Center for Rural Studies, 3312
Connect, 3663
Core Services, 3270
Family & School Support, 3271
Financial Management Team, 3272
Learning Materials Workshop, 3706
School Development & Information, 3273
Teaching & Learning, 3274
Vermont Arts Council, 682
Vermont Community Foundation, 2882
Vermont Department of Education, 3275
Vermont Department of Libraries, 683, 2883
Vermont Library Association, 684
Vermont National Education Association (VTNEA),
    685
Vermont Special Education, 3276
Vermont Student Assistance Corporation, 686
Volunteers for Peace, 687
William T & Marie J Henderson Foundation, 2884
World Learning, 277

Virginia

AASA National Conference on Education, 3337
ASCD Annual Conference & Exhibit Show, 769
Action Alliance for Virginia's Children and Youth,
    688
Administrative Services, 3277
American Alliance for Health, Physical Education,
    Recreation and Dance(AAHPERD), 320
American Art Therapy Association, Inc., 304
American Association of School Administrators
    National Conference on Education, 155, 776
American Council on the Teaching of Foreign
    Languages Annual Conference, 280, 781
American Counseling Association, 197
American Counseling Association Annual
    Conference & Expo, 782
American International Schools, 932
American School Counselor Association, 198
American Society for
    Training/Development-Training Video, 3456
American Society for Training & Development
    International Conference & Exposition, 3342
American Society for Training and Development
    Information Center, 3310
Annual NCEA Convention & Exposition, 794
Association for Advancement of Computing in
    Education (AACE), 342
Association for Business Communication (ABC),
    16
Association for Career and Technical Education,
    372

Washington

West Virginia

Wisconsin

Wyoming

Arts

Civics & Government

Economics

English

Foundation for Critical Thinking Regional Workshop & Conference, 818
Frank Schaffer Publications, 4857
Frog Publications, 4860
Games2Learn, 5822
Gareth Stevens, 4861
Greenwillow Books, 4866
Henry Holt Books for Young Readers, 4875
Holiday House, 4878
International Reading Association Annual Convention, 764
Journalism Education Association, 824
Kane/Miller Book Publishers, 4899
Lake Education, 4905
Learning Connection, 4909
Learning Links, 4911
Lee & Low Books, 4912
Lerner Publishing Group, 4914
Linden Tree Children's Records & Books, 4915
Lodestar Books, 4918
Lothrop, Lee & Shepard Books, 4919
MacMillan Children's Books, 4922
Macmillan/McGraw-Hill School Division, 4924
Margaret K McElderry Books, 4928
Mari, 4929
Media and American Democracy, 3711
Millbrook Press, 4936
Mondo Publishing, 4940
Narrative Press, 4947
National Center for ESL Literacy Education, 330
National Council of Teachers of English, 4951
National Writing Project, 4958
New Canaan Publishing Company, 4959
North South Books, 4962
PF Collier, 4967
Perfection Learning Corporation, 4971
Phoenix Learning Resources Conference, 922
Picture Book Learning Volume-1, 4055
Pocket Books/Paramount Publishing, 4979
Random House/Bullseye/Alfred A Knopf/Crown Books for Young Readers, 4991
Rhythms Productions, 4995
Riverside Publishing Company, 4997
Scholastic, 5006
School Book Fairs, 5007
Scott Foresman Company, 5010
Signet Classics, 5012
Silver Moon Press, 5013
Simon & Schuster Children's Publishing, 5014
Stack the Deck Writing Program, 5020
Sundance Publishing, 5025
TMC/Soundprints, 5029
Theme Connections, 5034
Tor Books/Forge/SMP, 5040
Tricycle Press, 5041
Troll Associates, 5042
Trumpet Club, 5043
Turn-the-Page Press, 5044
U.S. Conference on Adult Literacy (USCAL), 893
Upstart Books, 5046
Useful Learning, 5047
Viking Children's Books, 5049
Warren Publishing House, 5054
Winston Derek Publishers, 5061
Writing Lab Newsletter, 4540
Zaner-Bloser K-8 Catalog, 5075

Foreign Language

AATF National Bulletin, 4499
ACTFL Newsletters, 4500
Alaska Department of Education Bilingual& Bicultural Education Conference, 3340
American Association of French Teachers Conference, 774
American Association of Teachers of French, 278
American Council on the Teaching of Foreign Languages, 280
American Council on the Teaching of Foreign Languages Annual Conference, 781
Asian American Curriculum Project (AACP), 295

Barron's Educational Series, 4768
Bilingual Research Journal, 4503
Bilingual Review Press, 4504
CEA Forum, 4505
CIEE Annual Conference, 749
Center for Applied Linguistics (CAL), 283
Central States Conference on the Teaching of Foreign Languages, 3355
Directory of Central America Classroom Resources, 4101
DynEd International, 4826
ERIC Clearinghouse on Languages and Linguistics, 284
Edumate-Educational Materials, 4841
Elementary Secondary Bilingual & Research Branch, 2966
Ellis, 4842
Foreign Language Annals, 4516
Frog Publications, 4860
Illinois Resource Center Conference of Teachers of Linguistically Diverse Students, 3367
International Association of Teachers of English as a Foreign Language, 756
Kane/Miller Book Publishers, 4899
Learning Connection, 4909
Lee & Low Books, 4912
Modern Language Association Annual Conference, 827
Mondo Publishing, 4940
National Association for Bilingual Education, 287
National Association for Bilingual Education, 839
National Center for ESL Literacy Education, 330
National Clearinghouse for Bilingual Education Newsletter, 4528
National Federation of Modern Language Teachers Association (NFMLTA), 289
National Network for Early Language Learning (NELL), 290
Northeast Conference on the Teaching of Foreign Languages, 3418
Northeast Teachers Foreign Language Conference, 3419
Office of Bilingual Education and Minority Languages Affairs, 2976
Pacific Northwest Council on Languages Annual Conference, 3429
SLEP Program Office, 6214
Santillana Publishing, 5005
Studies in Second Language Acquisition, 4537
TESOL Journal: A Journal of Teaching and Classroom Research, 4538
TESOL Quarterly, 4539
TOEFL Test and Score Manual, 6264
Teachers of English to Speakers of Other Languages Convention and Exhibit, 886

Geography

African-American Institute, 359
American Association for State & Local History, 4746
Art Visuals, 4759
Asian American Curriculum Project, 4760
Association for Refining Cross-Cultured International, 935
Association for the Advancement of International Education, 802
Center for Appalachian Studies Annual Conference, 809
Choices Education Project, 4797
Colloquoy on Teaching World Affairs, 4681
Council for Indian Education, 362
Dinah-Might Activities, 4819
Directory of Central America Classroom Resources, 4101
Ethnic Arts & Facts, 4846
Geography: A Resource Guide for Secondary Schools, 4103
Goethe House New York, 4863
Hands-On Prints, 4870
High Touch Learning, 4876

Ingenuity Works, 5828
International Schools Association, 1021
Jacaranda Designs, 4892
Kane/Miller Book Publishers, 4899
Keep America Beautiful, 4900
Langenseheidt Publishing, 4906
Lerner Publishing Group, 4914
NYSTROM, 4946
National Council for Geographic Education Annual Meeting, 3403
National Geographic School Publishing, 4953
National Geographic Society, 4954
New England History Teachers Association, 366
North South Books, 4962
Population Connection, 4980
Rand McNally, 4989
Roots & Wings Educational Catalog-Australiafor Kids, 4998
Routledge/Europa Library Reference, 5000
Sharpe Reference, 5011
Social Science Education Consortium, 5016
VIDYA Books, 5048
Western History Association, 369
World & I, 5064
World Bank, 5066
World Book Educational Products, 5067
World Eagle, 5068
World Resources Institute, 5069

History

Alarion Press, 4742
Alumni Newsletter, 4672
American Association for State & Local History, 4746
American Sociological Review, 4673
AnthroNotes, 4651
AnthroNotes, 4674
AppleSeeds, 4675
Art Visuals, 4759
Asian American Curriculum Project, 4760
Bluestocking Press Catalog, 4773
Boletin, 4676
California Weekly Explorer, 4677
Calliope, 4678
Center for Education Studies, 361
Center for Learning, 5083
Choices Education Project, 4797
Cobblestone, 4680
Colloquoy on Teaching World Affairs, 4681
Council for Indian Education, 362
Dinocardz Company, 4820
Editorial Projects in Education, 4832
Educators Guide to FREE Social Studies Materials, 4102
Ethnic Arts & Facts, 4846
Faces, 4682
Facts on File, 4852
Goethe House New York, 4863
History Matters Newsletter, 4685
History of Science Society, 348
Jacaranda Designs, 4892
Lerner Publishing Group, 4914
Middle States Council for the Social Studies Annual Regional Conference, 3384
NYSTROM, 4946
National Council for History Education Conference, 3404
National Council on Economic Education, 4952
National Women's History Project, 4957
National Women's History Project Annual Conference, 872
New England History Teachers Association, 366
New Press, 4960
Organization of American Historians, 4965
Pennsylvania Council for the Social Studies Conference, 3430
Personalizing the Past, 4973
Perspectives on History Series, 4974
Pleasant Company Publications, 4978
Routledge/Europa Library Reference, 5000

Mathematics

Reading & Language Arts

NCLB Reform Listings

Science

Special Education

Technology